LISSAUER'S ENCYCLOPEDIA OF POPULAR MUSIC IN AMERICA

1888 to the Present

LISSAUER'S ENCYCLOPEDIA OF POPULAR MUSIC IN AMERICA

1888 to the Present

Researched and Written by

ROBERT LISSAUER

PARAGON HOUSE
New York

First edition, 1991

Published in the United States by

Paragon House
90 Fifth Avenue
New York, NY 10011

LIBRARY OF CONGRESS CATALOGING-IN-PUBLICATION DATA

Lissauer, Robert
Lissauer's encyclopedia of popular music in America : 1888 to the
present / Robert Lissauer.—1st U.S. ed.
p.   cm.
Includes bibliographical references.
ISBN 1-55778-015-3 : $135.00
1. Popular music—United States—Bibliography.   2. Popular music—
—United States—Chronology.   I. Title.   II. Title: Encyclopedia of
popular music in America.
ML128.P63L57 1991
781.64'0973—dc20   90-33935
                                                        CIP
                                                        MN

Manufactured in the United States of America

Book design by Kathryn Parise

The paper used in this publication meets the minimum
requirements of American National Standard for Information Sciences—Permanence of Paper for Printed
Library Materials, ANSI Z39.48-1984.

To The Players, where it all began.

Table of Contents

Acknowledgments

Over the five years that have transpired in the development of this work, from concept to completion, there have been so many who have helped me. With great fear of omitting someone, I want to express my gratitude to:

Ken Stuart, Editor-in-Chief at Paragon House for believing in the project and in me; Perry Browne, my agent, for his help, contractual advice, and friendship; the late John Hammond who saw the need for this book and expressed his thoughts in a wonderful letter to the publisher; Joe Soll who not only advised me on the purchase of my computer and allied hardware and software, but programmed the original data base and became my computer guru; Frankie McCormick for introducing me to Joe Soll; Connie Heintz, Tom Shay, Doug Wheeler, and the anonymous other technical support people at askSam Systems for their patience with my layman's queries regarding software problems; Tejas Edwards of Plus Development Corporation for telephonically leading me through the installation of a hardcard in my computer; Michael Kerker of The American Society of Composers, Authors, and Publishers (ASCAP) for his interest in this project; Nancy Rosenthal and Eileen Duffy of the Index Department of ASCAP for furnishing me with title and writer information; Dan Singer of Broadcast Music, Inc. (BMI) for the same; Louis Rachow, the former librarian of The Hampden-Booth Library of The Players for his unstinting assistance with locating reference sources; Bob Dadarria, a computer genius for helping immeasurably in the latter stages of the book by unraveling the mystery of how to alphabetize the more than 19,000 entries in Section I. To the talented, considerate, and thoughtful Senior Editor at Paragon, PJ Dempsey, thanks for always being there to answer questions, give advice and caring. Thanks also to her assistant, Chris O'Connell. Additional gratitude to Production Editor Ed Paige, his assistant Bennett Paris, and Production Manager Felecia Monroe for their untiring efforts in their all-important roles. I cannot express enough thanks to Mary Dorian who came aboard late in the game to diligently proofread and assemble the listings in Section III. Appreciation also to Parke Peterbaugh for his interest in and suggestions pertaining to the material in the Rock Era.

For advice and/or information freely given during the course of the writing of this book I want to thank: Lee Adams, Kim Burrafato, Jeri Cummins, Alfred Drake, John Eaton, Leonard Feist, Marvin Fisher, Milt Gabler, Stanley Green, John Hundley, David A. Jasen, Ellen Donaldson Kaiser, Robert Kimball, Mark Korrin, Helmy Kresa, Miles Krueger, Sid Lippman, James T. Maher, Gerald Marks, the late Joseph Meyer, Duke Niles, Troy Seals, Hilda Schneider, Alfred Simon, Bill Simon, George T. Simon, Charles Strouse, Jack Sturgell, Kay Swift, Bill Thomas, Tony Triolo, Walter Wager, Larry Wagner, and Billy Edd Wheeler.

And to eight close friends of mine who are no longer with us but with whom I shared a fervent interest in popular songs, their creators and interpreters, Don Burr, Myron "Pappy" Earnhart, Del Hughes, Johnny Lowman, Tom Mack, Leonard Patrick, Alan Tigner, and Shel Toomer, "wish you were here."

And to Belle, whose understanding and emotional support came at the right time.

Special thanks to my children, Geoffrey, John, and Lianne, for having to listen to their father talk about "the book," possibly to extremes, during these years.

Introduction

In the mid-1980s, I often would have lunch in the Grill Room of The Players, a club on Gramercy Park in New York City, of which I have been a member for 25 years. In this Victorian room there are two oversized rectangular tables with banquettes on one side and large Windsor chairs on the other, where members may dine informally, insult each other, discuss world events, especially if they pertain to the theater, music, literary happenings, or argue for the sake of arguing.

On numerous occasions, a member, upon seeing me and knowing that I had more than a passing interest in popular music, would pull from his pocket or wallet a piece of paper on which he had written a question regarding the original performance of a show or movie song, or the authorship, or year of initial prominence of a pop or nonproduction song, or the name of a singer with a big band who introduced the song, or a current hit record. If I knew the answer, I would furnish it. If I didn't, I would inform the questioner that I would look it up in my book, sheet music, or record collection and get him the requested information. One member in particular, John Hundley, who as a leading man in the musical theater in the twenties introduced Rodgers and Hart's "With a Song in My Heart" in *Spring Is Here*, and after a successful career as a performer became an executive at CBS, was one who almost always had a question ready, not necessarily to stump

me, but usually to refresh his memory or to settle a friendly argument he may have had earlier.

One day while leaving the Club, the thought occurred to me that there should be a single volume reference source containing all of this information. I carefully went through my own books, checked the publications in the Music Division of the New York Public Library at Lincoln Center, the Music Division of the Library of Congress in Washington, D.C., and the shelves of many bookstores. I found no single publication containing all of the information that I felt should be included. There were books on theater songs, movie songs, jazz, swing, rhythm and blues, country and western, rock and roll, folk music, ragtime, etc., some of which I owned and many of which would later be of help to me in the research for my book. There were numerous overviews of the field and a few volumes attempting to be encyclopedic in their approach. I found the former, in most cases, to be incomplete and too often filled with blatant errors; many of the latter, unfortunately, perpetuated these errors. In the bibliography of this work, I credit those books that I found most helpful in my research.

Now I was into it! I realized, with some apprehension for the enormity of the task ahead of me, that if I could interest a publisher in taking on an encyclopedia based on the most popular art form in America, I faced an assignment that would occupy all of my time for a period of years. I wrote a nine-page proposal in which I said that this could be done on a computer. I didn't say that I had never touched a computer and hadn't the foggiest idea of how one worked. I foresaw, however, that if I were to use index cards on which to register the information garnered through my research, it might take 25 years to complete the task. I originally planned to cover the years of this century, starting with 1900, but I soon realized that, if I were going to have the term "popular music" in the title, I could not omit the bounteous output of the last decade of the 19th century, the "Gay Nineties." I chose, then, 1888 as the first year and, under the optimistic impression that I would finish the work in three years, thought that "1888 to 1988" would look good on the jacket. It took me a year longer than estimated (four years since my first entry), and, therefore, I was able to include songs of 1989. In retrospect, 1888 was a logical starting year, as that was the genesis of the soon-to-burgeon popular song industry, when 28th Street between Broadway and Sixth Avenue in New York City would become known as "Tin Pan Alley."

A friend suggested that I submit my proposal to Ken Stuart, Editor-in-Chief of Paragon House. Ken immediately became excited about the project and never lost his enthusiasm for it. His encouragement and availability kept me stimulated during the writing.

After signing a contract to write the book, I sought out a computer counselor to advise me as to the purchase of computer hardware and software and to instruct me in the use of the various components. He and I set up a data base program so that I could file and retrieve information as needed. He taught me how to use templates for adding and extracting material, and guided me in other maneuvers that sometimes threatened to overwhelm me. This was a new language I was learning! I practiced on the computer, studied the manuals, and had in-person as well as telephone sessions with my adviser. I frequently called various manufacturers whose products were involved

in my struggles for technical support. In January, 1986, two months after first laying hands on the keyboard, I started the actual writing.

I have had a continuing love affair with popular music from the age of nine, when I not only received my first music lessons, but realized that the man who lived in the same New York apartment building and who drove a jazzy Auburn Phaeton was Richard Rodgers. The same Richard Rodgers who with Lorenz Hart was turning out at least one Broadway hit a year, each with a sterling score. My tastes in music were catholic, embracing almost every form. My interest in classical or "serious" music (a phrase I detest as I feel all composition is "serious") is of no concern here as this is a book about *popular* music.

What *is* popular music? It is the most familiar, renowned, and popular art form in America. I do not say "arguably" because in my mind the question is not debatable. No matter in which part of the country we have been raised, songs have been a part of our lives. We have sung them, hummed them, whistled and played them. We have heard them in the mountains, on the levees, on the rivers, and on the streets; we have heard them on the radio and on records, in music stores, on the stage and on the screen, in elevators and in supermarkets, on television, and in discotheques. Songs have seen us off to war, helped us elect presidents, made us laugh and made us cry, pervaded our sleep, and perhaps most importantly, have given us memories.

Popular music is a generic term for music accepted by the general public in almost every form or style excepting concert and ecclesiastical music, although many popular songs were developed from melodies written by classical composers such as "Our Love," "Concerto for Two," "Moon Love" (Tchaikowsky), "My Reverie" (Debussy), and "Till the End of Time" (Chopin). Hymns have gained popular acceptance such as "Amazing Grace" and "In the Garden," as have numerous spirituals.

The songs discussed in this book range from ballads of the late 1880s through ragtime instrumentals, minstrel songs, ethnic songs, war songs, comedy songs, operetta numbers and jazz songs, instrumentals, blues, show songs, movie songs, nonproduction pop songs, boogie-woogie, be bop, gospel songs, country and western songs, rhythm and blues songs, rock and roll, and many other forms. The entries reflect many changes in our social mores and political points of view. There are songs of chauvinism, jingoism, and militarism that are embarrassing today but reflect the thinking and feelings of a former period. Today, one would never consider performing some of the dialect songs of the past, or stuttering songs, or especially those that, in the 1890s were called "coon songs." These last were not deemed offensive then; in fact some of the more popular were written by black writers, such as Ernest Hogan who penned "All Coons Look Alike to Me," or Gussie L. Davis who wrote many hits including "The Baggage Coach Ahead." The titles of the songs, as repugnant as they are today, are part of the history of popular music and for that reason are included.

It was not until the early 1940s that charts, as we know them today, were printed in the music business trade papers. Hence, I researched issues of *Variety* and *Billboard* for information, as well as newspaper and magazine articles and many books. I have culled my information from archival and library sources as well as from my own reference books and sheet music and record collection. I sought information from willing colleagues in music and theater who never hesitated to clarify a point when asked.

The methods of popularizing songs have gone through many changes over a century, from the music halls through vaudeville, theater, sheet music counter demonstrations, silent films with live accompaniment, soundtracks of motion pictures (talkies), orchestras in hotel ballrooms and dancehalls, and radio and television shows. Songs have become popular due to reproduced cylinders, piano rolls, phonograph records of RPM speeds of 78, 45, 33⅓ and in sizes of 7″ to 12″ in diameter, and by compact discs and audio tapes. In the late 1930s when disc jockeys started playing records on radio, a new form of promotion and exploitation of popular music was initiated.

That outlet is today as big as ever and has been augmented by discotheques and MTV, the latter using videotapes of singers or bands performing their numbers.

In discussing this book during its writing, I have been asked frequently what were my criteria for song selection. I have striven to be objective in my choices, basing my reasons for inclusion on the information uncovered in my research regarding the impact a song or instrumental made on the public at a given time. This impact may have been caused by its introduction, authorship, effect on future compositions, or what I deemed general significance in the overall picture of a century of popular music. I have not let personal taste enter into my choice for inclusion or exclusion.

The hits were easy to choose. Some songs, however, were not popular "the first time around," but caught on and became familiar over a period of time. Others, such as Stephen Sondheim's "Send in the Clowns," or Burke and Van Heusen's "Here's That Rainy Day," never were #1 sheet music or record bestsellers, but as favorites of singers and musicians, became what is known as standards. Some have been included because of the prominence of the performers who introduced them, or because the songs marked important steps in the careers of their writers; some because they had historical or social pertinence.

Over 19,000 songs are included in this volume. I would like to remind the reader that this is a book about *songs*. The criteria mentioned earlier precludes covering every song recorded by an individual, group, or band be they Glenn Miller, Frank Sinatra, The Beatles, or Michael Jackson. They all had recordings that were "ships that passed in the night," or "B" sides of single records, or album cuts that, in the vernacular of the music business, "never caught fire." Similarly, I have selected songs from shows and films that have had a life independent of the original production. Some were included because of their places in theatrical or musical history, their connection with particular performers or other reasons explained in the accompanying text.

In the event of inadvertent omissions of deserving songs, I invite the readers to write to me in care of the publisher with information about such songs. In researching, writing, and editing a work of this size, it is possible that an occasional error will have been made, be it typographical, clerical, or factual. While great care has been taken to avert mistakes, a note to the writer pointing one out would be gratefully received.

New York City, N.Y.

How To Use This Book

The book is divided into three parts:

SECTION I (The Songs)

in which over 19,000 entries are listed alphabetically *letter–by–letter*. This is standard procedure for reference works, but a word of explanation and an example may be helpful. Letter-by-letter alphabetization requires that all entries are sequenced alphabetically until the first punctuation mark (period, comma, exclamation mark, etc.) and not merely word by word. For example, "A"-You're Adorable (a y o etc.) appears at the end of the A entries, not at the beginning. Accordingly, Weep No More, My Baby appears before We Must Be Vigilant.

Of course, the English articles "a," "an," or "the" will not precede the title, which will be listed alphabetically by the first word following said article; example: Man That Got Away, The. As the plural articles "these" and "those" are used as essential parts of a title, they will appear first in the alphabetical listing; example: These Foolish Things, and Those Were the Days. In foreign songs, the article will appear first, also; example: El Rancho Grande, and La Vie en Rose.

The format is to show the title, followed by the name(s) of the writer(s), the date of the song's introduction or initial popularity, sometimes followed by another date or dates if the revival is of hit status. Then follows the text giving information regarding the introduction of the work, if known, productions in which it was used, major recordings and/or recordings of interest, and other pertinent facts.

SECTION II (The Chronology)

enables the reader to look at any year from 1888 to the present and find in alphabetical order every title in Section I attributed to that particular year.

SECTION III (The Writers)

alphabetically includes each composer and/or lyricist mentioned in Section I with the list of every title credited to that writer in that section.

To summarize, the reader may find a song by looking it up alphabetically in Section I, or may find which songs were popular in a certain year by turning to Section II, or may find a listing of the selected works of a given writer by turning to Section III.

YEAR

The Choice of year for each entry is either the year of introduction of a song, such as in a show or movie, or if its popularity resulted from a recording, the year of its reaching the "charts." If a song or record debuted on the charts in December of a given year and its popularity peaked in the succeeding year, the latter date is used. In some instances, such as a Christmas song, the seasonal date will prevail.

COPYRIGHT

We do not concern ourselves with the date of copyright in this volume. Frequently, a song was copyrighted years before it was published, or published and/or recorded well before it came into prominence. References are often made to those situations, as in the cases of "I Left My Heart in San Francisco" and "That's My Desire." If you are interested in a song's copyright history it is suggested that you check with the Copyright Office of The Library of Congress in Washington, D.C.

PUBLISHERS

The information contained herein is limited to the song, its creators, its performance history, and other points of salience. You will note that I have not included publishers' names in the credits. This is because of copyright renewals where it is common for each writer or the estate or appointee of said writer to become the controller of a share of said copyright, or because of the sale or merger of publishing catalogs or companies.

To find the publisher or administrator of a song, I suggest that you telephone or write to the Index Departments of the following performing rights organizations: The American Society of Composers, Authors and Publishers (ASCAP), Broadcast Music, Inc. (BMI), or The Society of European Stage Authors and Composers, Inc. (SESAC).

ARTISTS

Artists occasionally changed the spelling of their names, or in the cases of some groups, their complete names during the courses of their careers. I have attempted to credit them in the entries in this book as they credited themselves at specific times. For example, you will find Connie Boswell changed her name to Connee Boswell; Janie Fricke to Frickie; The

Nitty Gritty Dirt Band had a few releases as The Dirt Band; the Young Rascals became The Rascals, etc.

CHARTS

While lists of best-selling sheet music and records were run in trade papers as far back as 1905, it was not until the 1940s when charts, as we know them today, began to play an important role in the rating and ranking of the popular song, especially with the advent of airplay and sales of phonograph records. It was in the post-World War II period that recordings replaced the live performance of singers and big bands on radio as the primary means of popularizing songs. You will find references to "Your Hit Parade" during the years 1935 to 1958. This radio show (a television show in its last eight years) was the public's authority on national popularity of songs. Its survey, conducted by the advertising agency of Batten, Barton, Durstine, and Osborn for the sponsor, Lucky Strike cigarettes, was predominantly based on record and sheet music sales and radio performances. The radio information was furnished by two daily services provided for the music and advertising industries, The Accurate Report and The Peatman Report. When disc jockeys started featuring their own Top 10, 20, or 40 ratings, the influence of "Your Hit Parade" was doomed, although it should be noted that, during the year 1959, the TV show had a brief revival playing the top songs based on ratings by *Billboard* magazine.

The charts referred to in the entries in Section I are usually specified as Pop, Country, or R&B. The Pop chart represents *all* songs and recordings into the early 1940s, when trade publications such as *Billboard* and *Variety* started breaking down their charts into categories such as Pop, Country and Western (C&W), and Rhythm and Blues (R&B). Country and Western records, referred to as "Country" or "C&W" in the text have retained the same definition. Today some trade papers break down their charts into "Adult," "Adult Contemporary," "Album Rock Tracks," "Modern Rock Tracks," "Black Singles," etc. Music stores in the early 1940s used the term "Race Records," which was wisely discontinued and succeeded by "R&B," "Soul," and "Black." For reasons of clarity and simplicity, I use the term "R&B" to embrace all of those genres. It serves no purpose to break down recordings connoted by color, especially when there are so many Pop records by black artists such as Nat "King" Cole, Duke Ellington, Fats Waller, Ella Fitzgerald, Johnny Mathis, Louis Armstrong, The Supremes, Dionne Warwick, The 5th Dimension, and Michael Jackson, to name just a few.

Many records that started in the R&B field crossed over to the Pop market and vice versa, as did crossovers in the C&W and Pop markets. In some cases, R&B and C&W charts show the same record or song highly ranked. When a record is referred to as an "R&B" or "C&W Crossover," it may be assumed that the record crossed over to the pop charts.

As this is an encyclopedia of the *songs* themselves, which through its text shows the evolution of popular music since the 1880s, it does not purport to be an annotated history of the field.

Rock 'n' Roll, which came into its own in the mid-fifties, is included, of course, in the Pop category. Although its style has undergone many changes in its thirty-five-year life, it comprises about a third of the period covered in this book and roughly a fifth of the entries.

When the term "chart version" or "chart record" is used, it means that said record was in the Top 100 on the national charts. (I could not include every song that may have had a brief appearance on the charts.) Most of the songs alluded to were high up on the charts and are indicated by "Top 40," "Top 20," "Top 10," or "#1." As mentioned in the introduction, there are many cases of songs that never were chart entries but were performed and recorded so often over a period of time that they became standards. All chart positions, unless otherwise specified, refer to the U.S. charts.

There is a disparity in the #1 songs in the Country listings as opposed to the other charts. One may conjecture why the majority of songs

that reach the top position on the Country charts remain there for just one week. In the last decade, there have been as many as forty-eight #1 Country songs in a year!

AWARDS

The two major awards for Best Song of the Year are the Academy Award, or Oscar, presented by The American Academy of Motion Picture Arts and Sciences, and the Grammy (Award) presented by The National Academy of Recording Arts and Sciences, referred to acronymically as NARAS. As only five songs are nominated for the Academy Award each year, I have tried to include each nominee as well as the winner. In the case of the Grammy Award, there are so many categories and nominees (NARAS being an organization concerned with recordings in every field) that in most cases I have limited the noting of awards to the Pop, Country, and R&B Songs of the Year.

RANDOM NOTES

When a country or nationality is mentioned in referring to a recording, such as "by the Canadian quintet, The Bells," it usually, but not necessarily, pertains to the origin of the song and the recording itself.

From the mid-1940s to the mid-1980s, independent or nonproduction songs were for the most part popularized via disc jockey airplays of single records. Those singles, if hits, would usually be incorporated in albums, very often as the title song. Conversely, in the mid-to-late 1980s, with the decrease in the manufacture of singles, standout tracks from albums that were receiving major airplay would be made into singles.

When referring to orchestras, the entry "Recorded by Tommy Dorsey and his Orchestra," should be self-explanatory. If it reads ". . .Tommy Dorsey, vocal by Frank Sinatra," it is understood that Sinatra was the vocalist with Dorsey's orchestra. If it reads ". . .Vaughn Monroe, with his Orchestra," it means that Monroe was the vocalist with his own orchestra.

When the term "gold record" is used, it refers to a single that has sold a million copies or an LP (album) that has sold five hundred thousand copies. The gold record is awarded by The Record Industry Association of America (RIAA) to the manufacturer (record company) and artist after a certification of the sales. The first award was given in 1958. In 1961, due to the issuance of multi-LP collections, the criterion was revised and the gold LP was awarded for factory billings of over a million dollars. In 1976, the term "platinum record" was used for singles selling over two million copies and LPs selling over a million units.

In this book, for reasons of brevity, you will find terms such as "gold record by. . ." instead of "awarded to," etc. This does not imply that an artist recorded a gold record. The record industry often refers to a record as having "gone gold" or "gone platinum."

There are many cases of a musical composition taking up both sides of a single, and listed as Part I and II. Again, as we deal with songs, this book will note the work, the artist, and the label, but will not differentiate which side or part was the more popular.

When no text follows the title, writer, and date, it usually means that there was no one artist or band associated with the song. It was not unusual in the days before recordings generated hits for a song to be promoted or plugged by its publisher until it gained popularity. There are many cases where a song had gained popularity, had large sheet music sales or later, airplay, but no information could be found pertaining to performers who were associated with it.

Many older songs have more space allotted to them than contemporary songs for the obvious reason that, because of their age, many have become standards, have been revived, and have been performed in numerous subsequent stage and screen productions. As opposed to today when it is the exception for a song to have a cover record, it was the norm in the period before the mid-1950s for many singers and bands to record a new song, be it an independent song or one emanating from a production. It was not unusual to find three or four versions of a hit on the best-seller lists.

Glossary

Album Collection of recordings, formerly 10″ or 12″ 78rpm records, each in its own sleeve in an album. With the advent of long-playing records, they were found on a two-sided 12″ 33⅓rpm record (occasionally 10″) and called LPs. Albums are now on compact discs (CDs) of various sizes.

Coupled With Song on the reverse or flip side of a single.

Crossover Record that originated in one market such as R&B or C&W and also became popular in another, such as Pop.

Flip Side Reverse side of a single.

Independent Song Nonproduction song.

Interpolation Song added to, but not written for, the original score of a stage or screen production.

Medley Two or more songs played successively.

Production Song Song written specifically for a stage or screen production.

Single Two-sided disc, a 10″ 78rpm or later a 7″ 45rpm, as opposed to an album or LP.

Soundtrack Reference in this text is to the performance of a song in a motion picture that is heard but not seen, such as under the credits or in the background.

Standard A song that over a period of years has remained popular, taken its place in artists' repertoires, and is generally recognizable.

Abbreviations

w.	Words
m.	Music
w/m	Words and Music
(TM)	Theater musical
(TP)	Theater play (nonmusical)
(MM)	Motion picture musical
(MP)	Motion picture (nonmusical)
(TVM)	TV musical
(TVP)	TV play (nonmusical), or game show
(TVMP)	Made-for-television motion picture
R&R	Rock 'n' roll
R&B	Rhythm and blues
C&W	Country and Western (interchangeable with "Country")
Pop	As opposed to C&W and R&B; mostly used to denote market or charts
DJ	Disc jockey
EP	Extended play record, i.e., two songs (or cuts) per side on a 7″ 45rpm disc
LP	Long-playing record (or album) usually 12″ 33⅓rpm
ASCAP	American Society of Composers, Authors, and Publishers
BMI	Broadcast Music, Inc.
NARAS	National Academy of Recording Arts and Sciences
RIAA	Record Industry Association of America
adapt.	Adaptation or adapted from
a.k.a.	Also known as
arr.	Arrangement or arranged by
q.v.	Quod vide/Which see
bio	Film biography
biopic	Film biography
demo	Demonstration record made for singers, publishers, or record companies
rpm	Revolutions per minute
pseud.	pseudonym
Engl.	English
Fr.	French
Ger.	German
Gr.	Greek
It.	Italian
Port.	Portuguese
Sp.	Spanish

Section I

THE SONGS

(Alphabetically)

A

Aaron Loves Angela. w/m José Feliciano and Janna Feliciano, 1975. Sung by José Feliciano on the soundtrack of (MP) *Aaron Loves Angela*.

Aba Daba Honeymoon, The. w/m Arthur Fields and Walter Donovan, 1914, 1951. Introduced by Ruth Roye at the Palace Theatre in New York. #1 record by Arthur Collins and Byron Harlan (Victor). Revived in (MM) *Two Weeks With Love* by Debbie Reynolds and Carleton Carpenter, 1950. Their recording sold over a million records (MGM), 1951. The song was then on "Your Hit Parade" for nine weeks.

A Banda (Parade). w. Bob Russell (Engl.), w/m Chico Buarque de Hollanda (Port.), 1967. Instrumental recorded by Herb Alpert and the Tijuana Brass (A&M).

ABC. w/m Berry Gordy, Jr., Fonce Mizell, Freddie Perren, and Deke Richards, 1970. #1 record by The Jackson 5 (Motown).

A.B.C.'S of Love, The. w/m George Goldner and Richard Barrett, 1956. Best selling record by Frankie Lymon and The Teenagers (Gee).

Abdul Abulbul Amir. w/m Frank Crumit, 1927. Adapted from a nineteenth century English song credited to William Percy French. Frank Crumit popularized it in vaudeville and on radio.

Abergavenny. w/m Ronnie Scott and Marty Wilde, 1969. Recorded by British rock singer Marty Wilde under pseudonym of Shannon (Heritage).

Abilene. w/adapt. m. John D. Loudermilk, Lester Brown, Bob Gibson, and Albert Stanton, 1963. Based on traditional song. Leading record by George Hamilton IV (RCA).

About a Quarter to Nine. w. Al Dubin, m. Harry Warren, 1935. Sung by Al Jolson in (MM) *Go Into Your Dance*. Jolson's singing voice was used for title role acted by Larry Parks, in a duet with Evelyn Keyes in (MM) *The Jolson Story*, 1946. In the sequel (MM) *Jolson Sings Again*, 1949, the number was repeated in a montage from the earlier film. Tammy Grimes and Wanda Richert revived it in David Merrick's (TM) "42nd Street," 1980.

Above and Beyond (The Call of Love). w/m Harlan Howard, 1960, 1989. Country hit by Buck Owens (Capitol). Revived by Rodney Crowell (Columbia) 1989.

Above the Stars. w/m Bob Merrill, 1962. From (MM) *The Wonderful World of the Brothers Grimm*. Leading recording by the British clarinetist Acker Bilk and his Orchestra (Atco).

Abracadabra. w/m Steve Miller, 1982. The title track from The Steve Miller Band album became a #1 gold record single (Capitol).

Abraham, Martin, and John. w/m Dick Holler, 1968. Title refers to the first names of Lincoln, King, and Kennedy, all assassinated. Leading records: Dion (Laurie); Smokey Robinson and The Miracles (Tamla); Moms Mabley (Mercury); Tom Clay, in medley with "What The World Needs Now" (Mowest).

Absence Makes the Heart Grow Fonder. w. Arthur Gillespie, m. Herbert Dillea, 1900. Best-selling recording by the tenor Harry MacDonough (Victor) (Edison).

Absence Makes the Heart Grow Fonder (for Somebody Else). w. Sam M. Lewis and Joe Young, m. Harry Warren, 1930. Popular song originally recorded by Gene Austin (Victor); Bernie Cummins's Orchestra (Victor); Tom Gerun (Brunswick); Art Gillham (Columbia), and others. Orrin Tucker had a 1941 release (Columbia).

Absent. w. Catherine Young Glen, m. John W. Metcalf, 1899.

Absent Minded Me. w. Bob Merrill, m. Jule Styne, 1964. Introduced and recorded by Barbra Streisand, coupled with "Funny Girl," which was written for but not used in the stage production of the same name (Columbia).

Absinthe Frappe. w. Glen MacDonough, m. Victor Herbert, 1904. Sung by Harry Davenport in the operetta (TM) *It Happened in Nordland*. It was interpolated in the film biography of the composer, (MM) *The Great Victor Herbert*, featuring Walter Connolly in the title role, 1934.

Absolute Beginners. w/m David Bowie, 1986. Introduced by David Bowie in (MM) *Absolute Beginners* and on records (EMI-America).

Accent on Youth. w. Tot Seymour, m. Vee Lawnhurst, 1935. Title song for (MP) *Accent on Youth*, starring Sylvia Sidney and Herbert Marshall. Leading recording by Duke Ellington, featuring alto saxophone solo by Johnny Hodges (Brunswick).

Ac-Cent-Tchu-Ate the Positive. w. Johnny Mercer, m. Harold Arlen, 1944. Introduced by Bing Crosby and Sonny Tufts in (MM) *Here Come the Waves*. Nominated for Academy Award. Best-selling records by Bing Crosby and The Andrews Sisters (Decca), and Johnny Mercer (Capitol). Artie Shaw, vocal by Imogene Lynn (Victor), and Kay Kyser, vocal by Dorothy Mitchell (Columbia), also had popular recordings. The song was on "Your Hit Parade" for thirteen weeks, four times as #1.

Accident'ly on Purpose. w/m Don McCray and Ernest Gold, 1940.

Accidents Will Happen. w. Johnny Burke, m. James Van Heusen, 1950. Introduced by Bing Crosby and Dorothy Kirsten in (MM) *Mr. Music*.

According to My Heart. w/m Gary Walker, 1957. C&W hit by Jim Reeves (RCA).

According to the Moonlight. w. Jack Yellen and Herb Magidson, m. Joseph Meyer, 1935. Introduced by Alice Faye in (MM) *George White's 1935 Scandals*. She also recorded it (Melotone), as did Harry Richman (Columbia), and Victor Young's Orchestra, vocal by Jimmy Ray (Decca).

Ace in the Hole. w/m Cole Porter, 1941. Sung by Mary Jane Walsh, Sunny O'Dea, Nanette Fabray, and ensemble in (TM) *Let's Face It*, starring Danny Kaye. This song not to be confused with the standard of the same title by George Mitchell and James Dempsey.

Ace in the Hole. w/m George D. Mitchell and James E. Dempsey, 1926. Standard "saloon" and sing-a-long song. Featured in speakeasys and night clubs by Tommy Lyman. Among many recordings: The University Six (Harmony), Chick Bullock's Orchestra (A.R.C.), Red McKenzie (National), Clancy Hayes with Bob Scobey's Orchestra (GTJ), Anita O'Day (Signature), Lu Watters (Mercury).

Aching, Breaking Heart. w/m Roe E. Hall, 1962. Recorded by George Jones (Mercury).

Acorn in the Meadow. w/m Richard Adler and Jerry Ross, 1953. Introduced by Harry Belafonte in (TM) *John Murray Anderson's Almanac.*

Across 110th Street. w/m Bobby Womack, 1972. Introduced by Bobby Womack on the soundtrack of (MP) *Across 110th Street*, starring and co-produced by Anthony Quinn.

Across the Alley from the Alamo. w/m Joe Green, 1947. Top records by The Mills Brothers (Decca); Stan Kenton, vocal by June Christy (Capitol); Woody Herman, with his Orchestra (Columbia).

Across the Breakfast Table (Looking at You). w/m Irving Berlin, 1930. Introduced by Al Jolson in (MM) *Mammy*. Revived in the album, "Michael Feinstein Sings Irving Berlin" (Columbia), 1987.

Across the Track Blues. m. Edward Kennedy "Duke" Ellington, 1943. Jazz instrumental introduced and recorded by Duke Ellington and his Orchestra (Victor).

Action. w/m Brian Connolly, Steve Priest, Andy Scott, and Mick Turner, 1976. Recorded by the English band, Sweet (Capitol).

Action. w/m Steve Venet and Tommy Boyce, 1965. Introduced in (TVP) "Where the Action Is." Leading record by Freddy Cannon (Warner Bros.). Revived by Evelyn "Champagne" King (RCA), 1984.

Action Jackson. w/m Bernadette Cooper, 1988. Introduced by the female trio, Madame X, headed by the writer, as title song on the soundtrack of (MP) *Action Jackson*, and on the album and single (Lorimar).

Actions Speak Louder than Words. w. George Horncastle, m. Felix McGlennon, 1891.

Act Naturally. w. Vonie Morrison, m. Johnny Russell, 1963. Country hit by Buck Owens (Capitol). The Beatles recorded it, cou-

pled with their #1 hit "Yesterday" (Capitol) (q.v.), 1965.

Adam and Eve. w/m Paul Anka, 1960. Recorded by Paul Anka (ABC-Paramount).

Adam and Evil. w/m Fred Wise and Randy Starr, 1966. Introduced by Elvis Presley in (MM) *Spinout.*

Addicted. w/m Cheryl Wheeler, 1988. #1 Country chart single by Dan Seals (Capitol).

Addicted to Love. w/m Robert Palmer, 1986. #1 Pop chart song by the British songwriter/singer, Robert Palmer (Island).

Address Unknown. w/m Carmen Lombardo, Johnny Marks, and Dedette Lee Hill, 1939. Title suggested by the best-selling book. Introduced and recorded by Guy Lombardo and his Royal Canadians (Decca). Best-seller: the Ink Spots (Decca).

Add Some Music to Your Day. w. Brian Wilson, m. Mike Love, and Joe Knott, 1970. Recorded by The Beach Boys (Brother).

Adelaide. w/m Frank Loesser, 1955. Written for (MM) *Guys and Dolls*, and sung in the film by Frank Sinatra.

Adelaide's Lament. w/m Frank Loesser, 1950. Introduced by Vivian Blaine in (TM) *Guys and Dolls*. She also sang it in the movie version (MM) *Guys and Dolls*, 1955.

Adios. w. Eddie Woods, m. Enric Madriguera, 1931, 1941. The theme song of the Madriguera band, recorded in 1931 (Columbia). Glenn Miller revived it with a hit record, arranged by Jerry Gray (Bluebird), 1941. Among other recordings over the years are: Xavier Cugat (Victor), Tony Pastor (Bluebird), Carol Bruce (Decca), Giselle McKenzie (Capitol), Laurindo Almeida (Coral), Claude Thornhill (Trend).

Adios Amigo. w. Ralph Freed, m. Jerry Livingston, 1962. Popular record by Jim Reeves (RCA).

Adorable. w. George Marion, Jr., m. Richard A. Whiting, 1933. Sung by French actor

Henri Garat about Janet Gaynor in (MM) *Adorable*. Featured and recorded by Wayne King, with his Orchestra (Brunswick); pianist Lee Sims (Brunswick); Little Jack Little (Bluebird); Freddy Martin and the Hotel Bossert Orchestra (Melotone).

Adoring You. w. Joseph McCarthy, m. Harry Tierney, 1924. From (TM) *Ziegfeld Follies of 1924*. Recorded as instrumental by Paul Whiteman (Victor).

Adult Education. w/m Daryl Hall, John Oates, and Sara Allen, 1984. Top 10 single by Hall and Oates (RCA).

Adventures in Paradise. w/m Minnie Riperton, Richard Rudolph, and Joe Sample, 1976. R&B chart record by Minnie Riperton (Epic).

Adventures in Paradise. See **Theme from "Adventures in Paradise."**

Affair of the Heart. w/m Rick Springfield, Blaise Tosti, and Danny Tate, 1983. Top 10 record by Rick Springfield (RCA).

Affair to Remember, An. w. Harold Adamson and Leo McCarey, m. Harry Warren, 1957. Introduced by Vic Damone on the soundtrack, under the titles, of (MP) *An Affair to Remember*. Nominated for Academy Award, 1957. Damone had a hit record (Columbia).

Afraid to Dream. w. Mack Gordon, m. Harry Revel, 1937. Introduced by Don Ameche, then reprised by Alice Faye and Tony Martin in (MM) *You Can't Have Everything*. Benny Goodman had a popular record (Victor).

Africa. w/m David Paich and Jeff Porcaro, 1982. #1 record by the group, Toto (Columbia).

African Waltz. m. Galt McDermot, 1961. Jazz instrumental recorded by Cannonball Adderley (Riverside). Winner Grammy Award (NARAS) for Best Instrumental Theme and Best Original Jazz Composition, 1961.

Afrikaan Beat. m. Bert Kaempfert, 1962. Popular instrumental by Bert Kaempfert and his Orchestra (Decca).

After All. w/m Tom Snow and Dean Pitchford, 1989. Hit Country record by Rodney Crowell (Columbia).

After All. w. Bud Green, m. Guy Wood, 1939. Recorded by Dick Todd (Bluebird) and the bands of Bob Chester, vocal by Dolores O'Neill (Bluebird); Tommy Dorsey, vocal by Jack Leonard (Victor); Gene Krupa, vocal by Irene Daye (Columbia); Jan Savitt, vocal by Bon Bon (Decca).

After All, You're All I'm After. w. Edward Heyman, m. Arthur Schwartz, 1933. Sung by John Beal in (TP) *She Loves Me Not*. Bing Crosby sang it in the musical film version (MM) *She Loves Me Not*, 1934.

After All That I've Been to You. w. Jack Drislane, m. Chris Smith, 1912. Popular waltz.

After All the Good Is Gone. w/m Conway Twitty, 1976. #1 Country chart record by Conway Twitty (MCA).

After All These Years. w. Fred Ebb, m. John Kander, 1984. Introduced by The Men in (TM) *The Rink*.

After All This Time. 1989. Hit Country record by Rodney Crowell (Columbia).

Afterbeat, The. w/m Johnny Mercer and Fred Astaire, 1988. Posthumous song of both writers sung and danced by Tommy Tune and The Manhattan Rhythm Kings on the special (TVM) "An Evening at The Pops: A Tribute to Fred Astaire," accompanied by The Boston Pops Orchestra conducted by John Williams.

Afterglow. w. Al Stillman and Buck Ram, m. Oscar Levant, 1936. Leading record by Leo Reisman and his Orchestra (Brunswick).

After Graduation Day. w. Sylvia Dee, m. Sidney Lippman, 1947. Introduced by the chorus in (TM) *Barefoot Boy with Cheek*. Leading records by Eddy Duchin, vocal by Buddy Clark (Columbia); Kate Smith (Columbia); Sammy Kaye, vocal by Johnnie Ryan and The Glee Club (RCA Victor).

After Hours. w. Robert Bruce and Buddy Feyne, m. Avery Parrish, 1940. Introduced as an instrumental by Erskine Hawkins and his Orchestra, with Parrish on piano (Bluebird); also recorded by Eddie Barefield and his Band (Sonora). Lyrics were added for publication. Among later recordings, Randy Brooks and his Orchestra (Decca); organist Ethel Smith (Decca).

After I Say I'm Sorry (What Can I Say?). w/m Walter Donaldson and Abe Lyman, 1926. Popular standard with many recordings. Introduced and recorded by Abe Lyman and his Orchestra (Brunswick). It was played in the background of (MM) *Love Me or Leave Me*, 1955. In the same year it was performed by the band in (MM) *Pete Kelly's Blues*.

After Loving You. w/m Eddie Miller and Milton Schafer, 1962. Recorded by Eddy Arnold (RCA), 1962 and Della Reese (RCA), 1965.

After Midnight. w/m J. J. Cale, 1970. Top 20 record by British singer, Eric Clapton (Atlantic). Writer/singer J. J. Cale recorded his version (Shelter), 1972, followed by Scottish singer, Maggie Bell (Atlantic), 1974.

After My Laughter Came Tears. w/m Charles Tobias and Roy Turk, 1928. Featured and recorded by Cliff "Ukulele Ike" Edwards (Columbia).

Afternoon Delight. w/m Bill Danoff, 1977. #1 gold record by the quartet, Starland Vocal Band (Windsong). The title, while suggesting other pleasures, was taken from the heading on a lunch menu in a Washington, D. C., restaurant.

After School. w/m Dick Wolf and Warren Nadel, 1957. Introduced and Top 40 record by Randy Starr (Dale).

After Sundown. w. Arthur Freed, m. Nacio Herb Brown, 1933. Introduced by Bing Crosby in (MM) *Going Hollywood*. Crosby recorded it (Brunswick).

After That I Want a Little More. w. Alfred Bryan, m. Fred Fisher, 1911.

After the Ball. w/m Charles K. Harris, 1892. Introduced in Milwaukee by J. Aldrich Libby in (TM) *A Trip to Chinatown*, followed by May Irwin at Tony Pastor's in New York, and John Philip Sousa who featured it at the Chicago World's Fair. During its first surge of popularity, it sold five million copies of sheet music. Recordings by whistler John Yorke Atlee (Columbia) and Irish tenor George J. Gaskin also sold well. It was sung by Norma Terris in (TM) *Show Boat*, 1927, and by her successor, Irene Dunne, who then sang it in the film version (MM) *Show Boat*, 1936. In other films, it was sung by Alice Faye in (MM) *Lillian Russell*, 1940; Scotty Beckett in (MM) *The Jolson Story*, 1946; Gloria Jean in (MM) *There's a Girl in My Heart*, 1950; Kathryn Grayson in (MM) *Show Boat*, 1951.

After the Fall. w/m Steve Perry and John Friga, 1983. Recorded by the group, Journey (Columbia).

After the Fire. w/m Peter Townshend, 1985. Recorded by British singer, Roger Daltrey (Atlantic).

After the Fire Is Gone. w/m L. E. White, 1971. C&W and Pop chart success by Conway Twitty and Loretta Lynn (Decca).

After the Goldrush. w/m Neil Young, 1974. Best-selling record by the English folk trio, Prelude (Island).

After the Lights Go Down Low. w/m Alan White and Leroy Lovett, 1956. Hit record by Al Hibbler, arranged and conducted by Jack Pleis (Decca).

After the Love Has Gone. w/m David Foster, Jay Graydon, and Bill Champlin, 1979. Gold record hit by the group, Earth, Wind and

Fire (Arc). Winner Grammy Award (NARAS) for "Rhythm and Blues Song" of the Year.

After the Lovin'. w/m Richie Adams and Alan Bernstein, 1977. Gold record by the English recording star, Engelbert Humperdinck (Epic).

After the Roses Have Faded Away. w. Bessie Buchanan, m. Ernest R. Ball, 1914.

After Twelve O'Clock. w. Johnny Mercer, m. Hoagy Carmichael, 1932. Mercer wrote the lyrics under the pseudonym of "Joe Moore." Recorded by Hoagy Carmichael and his Orchestra, with vocal aid from Dick Robertson (Victor).

After You. w/m Sam Coslow and Al Siegel, 1937. Introduced by Harry Barris, Bing Crosby, Frances Faye, and Martha Raye in (MM) *Double or Nothing*.

After You, Who? w/m Cole Porter, 1932. Introduced by Fred Astaire in (TM) *Gay Divorce*. Recorded by Fred Astaire (Columbia) and Eddy Duchin, coupled with "Night and Day" (Brunswick).

After You Get What You Want, You Don't Want It. w/m Irving Berlin, 1920. Featured and recorded (Columbia) by Van and Schenck. Revived by Marilyn Monroe in (MM) *There's No Business Like Show Business*, 1954.

After You've Gone. w. Henry Creamer, m. Turner Layton, 1918. Featured and popularized by Al Jolson at the Winter Garden and by Sophie Tucker in vaudeville. It was one of the first recordings by the Benny Goodman Trio (Victor) and featured by his quartet in (MM) *Make Mine Music*, 1946. Judy Garland sang it in (MM) *For Me and My Gal*, 1942; Jolson dubbed his voice on the soundtrack for Larry Parks in (MM) *Jolson Sings Again*, 1949; Louis Armstrong performed it in (MM) *The Five Pennies*, 1959. It was sung by Leland Palmer in the Bob Fosse film (MM) *All That Jazz*, 1979.

Again. w. Dorcas Cochran, m. Lionel Newman, 1949. Introduced by Ida Lupino in (MP) *Roadhouse*. Most popular recordings: Vic Damone (Mercury); Doris Day (Columbia); Mel Tormé (Capitol); Gordon Jenkins, vocal by Joel Graydon (Decca); Art Mooney, vocal by Johnny Martin and Madely Russell (MGM); Tommy Dorsey and his Orchestra, as an instrumental (RCA Victor). Song heard in (MP) *Island in the Sun*, 1957; (MP) *Best of Everything*, 1959.

Against All Odds (Take a Look at Me Now). w/m Phil Collins, 1984. Title song of (MP) *Against All Odds*, sung on the soundtrack by Phil Collins. Nominated for Academy Award. The single release by Collins became a #1 gold record (Atlantic).

Against the Wind. w/m Bob Seger, 1980. Top 10 record by Bob Seger (Capitol).

Agent Double-O-Soul. w. Bill Sharpley and Charles Hatcher, m. Charles Hatcher, 1965. Popular recording by Edwin Starr, pseudonym for Hatcher (Ric-Tic).

Age of Not Believing. w/m Robert B. Sherman and Richard M. Sherman, 1971. Introduced by Angela Lansbury in (MM) *Bedknobs and Broomsticks*. Nominated for Academy Award.

Aggravatin' Papa (Don't You Try to Two-time Me). w/m Roy Turk, J. Russel Robinson, and Addy Britt, 1923. Featured and recorded by Marion Harris (Brunswick), Sophie Tucker (Okeh), Bessie Smith (Columbia).

Agony. w/m Stephen Sondheim, 1987. Introduced by Chuck Wagner and Robert Westenberg in (TM) *Into The Woods*.

Ah, But Is It Love? w. E. Y. Harburg, m. Jay Gorney, 1933. Introduced by Roger Pryor and Lillian Miles in (MM) *Moonlight and Pretzels*.

Ah, But It Happens. w. "By" Dunham, m. Walter Kent, 1948. Featured and recorded by Frankie Laine (Mercury).

Ah! Sweet Mystery of Life. w. Rida Johnson Young, m. Victor Herbert, 1910. Introduced by Emma Trentini and Orville Harrold in (TM) *Naughty Marietta*. Nelson Eddy and Jeanette MacDonald sang it in the film version

(MM) *Naughty Marietta*, 1935 and Allan Jones sang it in (MM) *The Great Victor Herbert*, 1939.

Ah, The Apple Trees. See **When the World Was Young**.

Ah, The Moon Is Here. w. Irving Kahal, m. Sammy Fain, 1933. Sung by Dick Powell and Frank McHugh in (MM) *Footlight Parade*.

Ahab the Arab. w/m Ray Stevens, 1962. Novelty, Top 10 record by Ray Stevens (Mercury).

Ah Still Suits Me. w. Oscar Hammerstein II. m. Jerome Kern, 1936. Written specially for this version of (MM) *Show Boat*, it was sung by Paul Robeson and Hattie McDaniel.

A–Huggin' and A–Chalkin'. See **Huggin' and Chalkin**.

Ai No Corrida. w/m Chaz Jankel and Kenny Young, 1981. Top 10 R&B, chart Pop record by Quincy Jones, vocal by Dune (A&M).

Ain'tcha? w/m Mack Gordon and Max Rich, 1930. Sung by Helen Kane in (MM) *Pointed Heels* and on records (Victor).

Ain'tcha Glad? w. Andy Razaf, m. Thomas "Fats" Waller, 1933. Introduced and featured by Waller. Benny Goodman led an all-star studio band in an early recording (Columbia).

Ain't Dat a Shame? w. John Queen, m. Walter Wilson, 1901. Comedy record by Dan Quinn (Victor).

Ain't Even Done with the Night. w/m John Cougar Mellencamp, 1981. Recorded by John Cougar Mellencamp (Riva).

Ain't Gonna Bump No More (with No Big Fat Woman). w/m Bennie Lee McGinty and William Killen, 1977. R&B and Pop chart gold record by Joe Tex (Epic).

Ain't Gonna Lie. w. Tony Powers, m. George Fischoff, 1966. Recorded by Keith (Mercury).

Ain't Got a Dime to My Name. w. Johnny Burke, m. James Van Heusen, 1942. Introduced by Bing Crosby in (MM) *Road to Morocco*.

Ain't Got No. w. Gerome Ragni and James Rado, m. Galt MacDermot, 1967. Introduced in the off-Broadway production of (TM) *Hair* by Walker Daniels, Gerome Ragni, Steve Dean, Arnold Wilkerson, and company. The show was re-produced on Broadway, 1968, and the number was sung by Steve Curry, Lamont Washington, Melba Moore, and company. Recorded in medley with "I Got Life," from the same show, by Nina Simone (RCA), 1969.

Ain't Got No Home. w/m Clarence Henry, 1956. Novelty hit on R&B and Pop charts by Clarence "Frogman" Henry, who got his nickname from this record (Argo). Revived by The Band (Capitol), 1973.

Ain't Got Time for Nothin'. w/m Harlan Howard, 1963. Country chart record by Bob Gallion (Hickory).

Ain't Had No Lovin'. w/m Dallas Frazier, 1966. Country hit by Connie Smith (RCA).

Ain't It a Shame. w/m W. A. Hann, Joseph Simms, and Al W. Brown, 1922.

Ain't It a Shame. See **Ain't That a Shame**.

Ain't It De Truth? w. E. Y. Harburg, m. Harold Arlen, 1957. Written for, filmed, and deleted from the movie version of *Cabin in the Sky*, 1943. Introduced on the stage by Lena Horne in (TM) *Jamaica*.

Ain't It Funky Now. m. James Brown, 1969. R&B and Pop instrumental hit by James Brown (King).

Ain't It Funny What a Difference Just a Few Hours Make? w. Henry M. Blossom, Jr., m. Alfred G. Bobyn, 1903. Introduced by Raymond Hitchock in (TM) *The Yankee Consul*. Leading record by Billy Murray (Victor).

Ain't It True? w/m Mike Lewis and Joe Sauter, 1965. Featured and recorded by Andy Williams (Columbia).

Ain't Love a Bitch. w/m Gary Grainger and Rod Stewart, 1979. Recorded by the English singer, Rod Stewart (Warner Bros.).

Ain't Love Grand. w/m Melvin Van Peebles, 1972. Introduced by the orchestra and reprised by Rhetta Hughes and the company in (TM) *Don't Play Us Cheap*.

Ain't Misbehavin'. w. Andy Razaf, m. Thomas "Fats" Waller and Harry Brooks, 1929. Introduced by Margaret Simms, Paul Bass, and Russell Wooding's Hallelujah Singers in (TM) *Hot Chocolates*, an all-Negro revue. Shortly after the opening, Louis Armstrong joined the company and played the song on solo trumpet during the intermission. Leading records by Leo Reisman, vocal by Lew Conrad (Victor); Ruth Etting (Columbia); Fats Waller (Victor). In films, Waller performed it in (MM) *Stormy Weather*, 1943; Mary Beth Hughes in (MM) *Follow the Band*, 1943; Louis Armstrong and his band in (MM) *Atlantic City*, 1944; Dan Dailey in (MM) *You Were Meant for Me*, 1948; Mickey Rooney and Armstrong in (MM) *The Strip*, 1951; Jane Russell, Alan Young, and Anita Ellis, dubbing for Jeanne Crain, in (MM) *Gentlemen Marry Brunettes*, 1955. It served as the title song for (MM) *Ain't Misbehavin'* featuring Piper Laurie and Rory Calhoun, 1955. It was sung by the company as the title song of the Waller musical (TM) *Ain't Misbehavin'*, 1978. Hank Williams, Jr. had a #1 Country chart record (Warner Bros.), 1986.

Ain't Nobody. w/m David Wolinski, 1983. Recorded by Rufus and Chaka Khan (Warner Bros.).

Ain't Nobody Here But Us Chickens. w/m Alex Kramer and Joan Whitney, 1947. Featured and recorded by Louis Jordan and his Tympany Five (Decca).

Ain't Nobody Home. w/m Jerry Ragavoy, 1966. Leading records by Howard Tate (Verve), and B. B. King (ABC), 1972.

Ain't No Cure for Love. w/m Leonard Cohen, 1987. Country chart single from the album "Famous Blue Raincoat" by Jennifer Warnes (Cypress).

Ain't No Mountain High Enough. w/m Nicholas Ashford and Valerie Simpson, 1967. First hit record by the newly formed team of Marvin Gaye and Tammi Terrell (Tamla). In 1970, it became the first #1 record for Diana Ross (Motown).

Ain't No Road Too Long. w/m Waylon Jennings, 1985. Introduced by Waylon Jennings and Big Bird in (MM) *Sesame Street Presents Follow That Bird*.

Ain't No Stoppin' Us Now. w/m Jerry Cohen, Gene McFadden, and John Whitehead, 1979. Platinum record by the duo, McFadden and Whitehead (Philadelphia International).

Ain't No Sunshine. w/m Bill Withers, 1971. R&B/Pop gold record by Bill Withers (Sussex). Winner Grammy Award (NARAS) Best Rhythm and Blues Song.

Ain't Nothing But a Man. w/m Merle Kilgore, 1962. Introduced and recorded by Merle Kilgore (Mercury).

Ain't Nothing like the Real Thing. w/m Nicholas Ashford and Valerie Simpson, 1968. Top 10 record by Marvin Gaye and Tammi Terrell (Tamla). Revived by Aretha Franklin (Atlantic), 1974, and Donny and Marie Osmond (Polydor), 1977.

Ain't Nothing' Goin' on But the Rent. w/m Gwen Guthrie, 1986. #1 R&B crossover record by Gwen Guthrie (Polydor).

Ain't Nothing You Can Do. w/m Deadric Malone and Joseph W. Scott, 1964. Hit record by Bobby Bland (Duke).

Ain't No Way. w/m Carolyn Franklin, 1968. Top 20 record by Aretha Franklin (Atlantic).

Ain't No Way To Treat a Lady. w/m Harriet Schock, 1975. Top 10 record by Helen Reddy (Capitol).

Ain't No Woman Like the One I Got. w/m Dennis Lambert and Brian Potter, 1973. #1 gold record by The Four Tops (Dunhill).

Ain't She Somethin' Else. w/m Bill Rice and Jerry Foster, 1985. #1 Country chart single by Conway Twitty (Warner Bros.).

Ain't She Sweet? W. Jack Yellen, m. Milton Ager, 1927. A top hit of its day, featured and recorded by Ben Bernie (Brunswick); Paul Whiteman's Rhythm Boys [Bing Crosby, Harry Barris, and Al Rinker] (Victor); Gene Austin (Victor); Harry Richman (Brunswick); The Dixie Stompers [Fletcher Henderson] (Harmony). Jimmie Lunceford and his band recorded Sy Oliver's arrangement (Vocalion), 1939. It was heard in (MM) *Margie*, 1946, and sung by Dan Dailey, Jeanne Crain, and Barbara Lawrence in (MM) *You Were Meant for Me*, 1948. Pianist Carmen Cavallaro dubbed it on the soundtrack for Tyrone Power in the title role of (MM) *The Eddy Duchin Story*, 1956. Top 20 record by The Beatles (Atco), 1964.

Ain't That a Grand and Glorious Feeling? w. Jack Yellen, m. Milton Ager, 1927.

Ain't That a Groove. w/m James Brown and Nat Jones, 1966. R&B/Pop chart hit by James Brown (King, Part 1).

Ain't That a Shame (a.k.a. **Ain't It a Shame**). w/m Antoine "Fats" Domino and Dave Bartholomew, 1955. Label of Fats Domino's first recording read "Ain't It a Shame." He had a #1 R&B hit that crossed over to the pop charts (Imperial). Pat Boone had his first hit record with the song (Dot). Revived in 1963 by The Four Seasons (Vee-Jay) and in 1979 by Cheap Trick (Epic).

Ain't That Just like a Man? w/m Don Raye and Gene De Paul, 1943. Introduced by Ann Miller in (MM) *What's Buzzin', Cousin?* Popular record by Margaret Whiting, with Freddie Slack's Orchestra (Capitol).

Ain't That Just like a Woman. w/m Fleecie Moore and Claude Demetrius, 1947. Featured and recorded by Louis Jordan and his Tympany Five (Decca).

Ain't That Just like Me. w/m Earl Carroll and Billy Guy, 1964. Recorded by the British rock group, The Searchers (Kapp).

Ain't That Love. w/m Fred Smith, 1965. Leading record by the R&B group, The Four Tops (Columbia).

Ain't That Love. w/m Ray Charles, 1957. Top 10 R&B chart record by Ray Charles (Atlantic).

Ain't That Loving You. w/m Deadric Malone, 1962. Recorded by Bobby Bland (Duke).

Ain't That Lovin' You, Baby. w/m Jimmy Reed, 1955. R&B hit, introduced and recorded by Jimmy Reed (Vee-Jay). Elvis Presley recorded it in 1958 (RCA). Released in 1964, it made the Top 20 in the pop charts.

Ain't That Peculiar? w/m William Robinson, Warren Moore, Marv Taplin, and Robert Rogers, 1965. Top 10 record by Marvin Gaye (Tamla). Revived by the female rock quartet, Fanny (Reprise), 1972, and the group Diamond Reo (Big Tree), 1975.

Ain't Too Proud to Beg. w/m Eddie Holland and Norman Whitfield, 1966. Hit records by The Temptations (Gordy), and The Rolling Stones (Rolling Stones), 1974.

Ain't Understanding Mellow. w. Herscholt Polk, m. Homer Talbert, 1972. Crossover (R&B/Pop) hit by Jerry Butler and Brenda Lee Eager (Mercury).

Ain't Wastin' Time No More. w/m Greg Allman, 1972. Recorded by The Allman Brothers Band (Capricorn).

Ain't We Got Fun? w/m Richard A. Whiting, Raymond B. Egan, and Gus Kahn, 1921. Recorded by Van and Schenck (Columbia) and featured in vaudeville by Ruth Roye. It was interpolated in (MM) *On Moonlight Bay*, 1951 and sung by Doris Day and Gordon MacRae in (MM) *By the Light of the Silvery Moon*, 1952.

Ain't You Ashamed? w. Sidney D. Mitchell and Lew Brown, m. Seymour Simons, 1923. Early recordings by The Carolina Club

Orchestra, directed by Hal Kemp (Columbia), and The Arcadia Peacock Orchestra of St. Louis (Okeh).

Ain't You Comin' Back, Mary Ann, to Maryland? w. Noble Sissle, m. Eubie Blake, 1919. Popularized by Sissle and Blake in vaudeville, and interpolated during run of (TM) *Shuffle Along*, 1923. Leading record by Nina Reeves (Gennett).

Ain't You Coming Back to Old New Hampshire, Molly? w. Robert F. Roden, m. J. Fred Helf, 1906. Ballad, with leading recording by Harry MacDonough (Victor).

Air. w. Gerome Ragni and James Rado, m. Galt MacDermot, 1967. Introduced by Sally Eaton, Shelley Plimpton, and Jonelle Allen in the off-Broadway production of (TM) *Hair*. In the Broadway version, 1968, it was sung by Eaton, Plimpton, and Melba Moore.

Airegin. m. Sonny Rollins, 1954. Jazz number first recorded by Rollins, with an all-star group (Prestige). Title is the reverse spelling of "Nigeria."

Air Mail Special. m. Benny Goodman, Jimmy Mundy, and Charlie Christian, 1941. Hit instrumental introduced by Benny Goodman and his Orchestra (Columbia) after an earlier version by the Goodman Sextet titled "Good Enough to Keep" (Okeh).

Air Mail to Heaven. w/m Kent Westberry, 1961. C&W chart record by Carl Smith (Columbia).

Airplane Song (My Airplane). w/m Owens Castleman and Mike Murphy. 1967. Recorded by The Royal Guardsmen (Laurie).

"Airport" Love Theme. m. Alfred Newman, 1970. From (MP) *Airport*. Top 40 instrumental by guitarist Vincent Bell (Decca).

Air That I Breathe, The. w/m Albert Hazlewood and Mike Hazlewood, 1974. Gold record by the British group, The Hollies (Epic).

Airy, Fairy Lillian. w. Tony Raymond, m. Maurice Levi, 1894. Featured by Lillian Russell in (TM) *Princess Nicotine*.

Alabam. w/m Lloyd T. Copas, 1960. Introduced by the writer/singer, known as Cowboy Copas (Starday). Covered, and best-selling version by Pat Boone (Dot).

Alabama Barbecue. w. Benny Davis, m. J. Fred Coots, 1936. Introduced in a Cotton Club revue.

Alabama Jubilee. w. Jack Yellen, m. George L. Cobb, 1915. Featured and recorded by the team of Arthur Collins and Byron Harlan (Columbia). Revived by Red Foley (Decca), 1951.

Alabama Song. w. Bertolt Brecht, m. Kurt Weill, 1928. Introduced by Lotte Lenya in Leipzig, Germany, in the opera, *Aufstieg und Fall der Stadt Mahagonny*, known in English as (TM) *The Rise and Fall of the City of Mahagonny*. It was sung by Estelle Parsons in a New York production at the off-Broadway Phyllis Anderson Theatre, 1970.

Alabama Stomp. w. Henry Creamer, m. Jimmy Johnson, 1926. From (TM) *Earl Carroll Vanities of 1926*. Red Nichols, the well known cornetist and bandleader, obviously liked this tune as he recorded it three times: under his own name (Brunswick), the Red Heads (Perfect), and Red and Miff's [Mole] Stompers (Edison).

Alabamy Bound. w. B. G. DeSylva and Bud Green, m. Ray Henderson, 1925. A popular railroad song featured by Al Jolson, Eddie Cantor, and Blossom Seeley. It was sung by The Ink Spots and danced by The Nicholas Brothers in (MM) *The Great American Broadcast*, 1941; heard on the soundtrack in (MM) *Broadway*, 1942, and in (MM) *Is Everybody Happy?* 1943; sung by Eddie Cantor in (MM) *Show Business*, 1944; sung by the chorus in (MM) *With a Song in My Heart*, 1952.

Aladdin. w. Basil Hurdon, m. Dyer Hurdon, 1962. Recorded by Bobby Curtola (Del-Fi).

Alaiyo. w. Robert Brittan, m. Judd Woldin, 1973. Introduced by Robert Jackson and Deborah Allen in (TM) *Raisin*.

Album of My Dreams, The. w. Lou Davis, m. Harold Arlen, 1929. Arlen's first published song. Introduced by Rudy Vallee and his Connecticut Yankees.

Alcoholic Blues, The. w. Edward Laska, m. Albert Von Tilzer, 1919. Recorded by Billy Murray (Victor) and the Louisiana Five (Columbia).

Al Di La. w. Ervin Drake (Engl.), Mogo (It.), m. C. Donida, 1962. Winner of the San Remo Song Festival, 1961. Sung by Emilio Pericoli in the Italian film (MP) *Rome Adventure*, 1962. Pericoli's recording was released in the U.S. and became a Top 10 hit (Warner Brothers). Other chart versions by Connie Francis (MGM), 1963, and The Ray Charles Singers (Command), 1964.

Alexander, Don't You Love Your Baby No More? w. Andrew B. Sterling, m. Harry Von Tilzer, 1904. Popular in vaudeville and minstrel shows.

Alexander and His Clarinet. w. Irving Berlin, m. Ted Snyder, 1910. Recorded by Arthur Collins and Byron G. Harlan (Columbia).

Alexander's Bag-Pipe Band. w/m Irving Berlin, E. Ray Goetz, and A. Baldwin Sloane, 1912. Introduced in (TM) *Hokey Pokey*.

Alexander's Ragtime Band. w/m Irving Berlin, 1911. Introduced by Emma Carus. Within a year of its publication, this song was being performed by dozens of vaudeville headliners and became one of the fastest bestsellers of sheet music in popular music history. While the song refers to a ragtime band, it, in itself, is not a ragtime tune, but more of a syncopated march. Alice Faye sang it in (MM) *Alexander's Ragtime Band*, 1938; Ethel Merman, Dan Dailey, Donald O'Connor, Mitzi Gaynor, and Johnny Ray sang it in (MM) *There's No Business Like Show Business*, 1954.

Alexander the Swoose (Half Swan—Half Goose). w. Ben Forrest and Glenn Burrs, m. Frank Furlett and Leonard Keller, 1941. Novelty, featured by the bands of Kay Kyser (Columbia); Art Kassel (Bluebird); Johnny Messner (Decca).

Alfie. w. Hal David, m. Burt Bacharach, 1966. Introduced by Cher on the soundtrack of (MP) *Alfie*. Nominated for Academy Award. Cher's recording (Imperial) was a hit as was Dionne Warwick's (Scepter), 1967. Stevie Wonder recorded it instrumentally under the name of Eivets Rednow (his name backwards) (Gordy), 1968.

Al Fresco. w. Glen MacDonough, m. Victor Herbert,1904. Written as an intermezzo for the piano, it became the opening chorus for Act II of (TM) *It Happened in Nordland*. It also was heard in (MM) *The Great Victor Herbert*, 1939.

Algy, The Piccadilly Johnny with the Little Glass Eye. w/m Harry B. Morris, 1895.

Alibi Baby. w. Edward Heyman and Tot Seymour, m. Vee Lawnhurst, 1937. Featured and recorded by Dolly Dawn (Variety) and Mal Hallett and his Orchestra, vocal by Teddy Grace (Decca).

Alibi Baby. w. Howard Dietz, m. Arthur Samuels, 1923. Howard Dietz's first published and professionally performed song. Introduced by Luella Gear in (TM) *Poppy*.

Alice Blue Gown. w. Joseph McCarthy, m. Harry Tierney, 1919. Introduced by Edith Day in (TM) *Irene*. The reference was to the color, light blue, which was the favorite of Alice Roosevelt Longworth, the daughter of Theodore Roosevelt. The song became one of the most popular of all American waltzes. Anna Neagle sang it in (MM) *Irene*, 1940. Debbie Reynolds sang it in the Broadway revival (TM) *Irene*, 1973.

Alice in Wonderland. w/m Howard Greenfield and Neil Sedaka, 1963. Leading record by Neil Sedaka (RCA).

Alice in Wonderland. w. Bob Hilliard, m. Sammy Fain, 1951. Title song of Disney's animated feature film (MM) *Alice in Wonderland.*

Alice in Wonderland. w/m Murray Mencher, Charles Tobias, and Jack Scholl, 1934. Recorded by Isham Jones and his Orchestra (Victor).

Alice Long (You're Still My Favorite Girlfriend). w/m Tommy Boyce and Bobby Hart, 1968. Top 40 record by Tommy Boyce and Bobby Hart (A&M).

Alice's Restaurant. w/m Arlo Guthrie, 1967. Introduced by Arlo Guthrie in his album "Alice's Restaurant Massacree" (Reprise). A shorter version was released as a single. Guthrie sang it in (MM) *Alice's Restaurant*, 1969.

Alive Again. w/m James Pankow, 1978. Written by the trombonist for the jazz-oriented rock group, Chicago, which recorded the song (Columbia).

Alive and Kicking. w/m Jim Kerr, Michael McNeil, Charles Burchill, Mel Gaynor, and John Gibbin, 1985. Recorded by the Scottish quintet, Simple Minds (A&M).

All. w. Raymond Jessel and Marian Grudeff (Engl.), m. Nino Oliviero, 1966. Original Italian title, "Una Moglie Americana," words by Nico Fidenco, heard in (MP) *Run for Your Life.* English vocal recorded by James Darren (Warner Bros.), 1967.

All Aboard for Blanket Bay. w. Andrew B. Sterling, m. Harry Von Tilzer, 1910. Featured and recorded by Ada Jones (Columbia).

All Aboard for Dixieland. w. Jack Yellen, m. George L. Cobb, 1913. Popular recordings by Ada Jones and The Peerless Quartet (Columbia) and The American Quartet (Victor).

All Aboard for Dreamland. w. Andrew B. Sterling, m. Harry Von Tilzer, 1904. Popularized via vaudeville performances and the hit recording by Byron G. Harlan (Edison).

Allah's Holiday. w. Otto Harbach, m. Rudolf Friml, 1916. From (TM) *Katinka*, sung by Edith Day.

All Alone. w/m Irving Berlin, 1924. Already popular as an independent song, it was interpolated by Grace Moore and Oscar Shaw in (TM) *Music Box Revue of 1924.* That exposure was followed by successful recordings by Al Jolson (Brunswick), Paul Whiteman (Victor), John McCormack (Victor), and many others. Alice Faye sang it in (MM) *Alexander's Ragtime Band*, 1938.

All Alone. w. Will Dillon, m. Harry Von Tilzer, 1911. Popular recording by Ada Jones and Billy Murray (Victor).

All Alone Am I. w. Arthur Altman (Engl.), Jean Ioannides (Gr.), m. Manos Hadjidakis, 1962. Originally a Greek popular song. Top 10 record by Brenda Lee (Decca).

All Alone in This World Without You. w/m Owen Bradley, Vernice McAlpin, and Betty Wade, 1946. Hit C&W record by Eddy Arnold (RCA).

All Alone Monday. w. Bert Kalmar, m. Harry Ruby, 1926. The hit song from (TM) *The Ramblers*, starring Clark & McCullough, and introduced by Jack Whiting and Marie Saxon. Sung by June Clyde and Hugh Trevor in the film version, retitled (MM) *The Cuckoos*, which starred Bert Wheeler and Robert Woolsey, 1930. Sung by Gale Robbins in the Kalmar and Ruby story (MM) *Three Little Words*, 1950.

All Along the Watchtower. w/m Bob Dylan, 1968. Introduced by Bob Dylan in his album "John Wesley Harding" (Columbia). Top 20 record by The Jimi Hendrix Experience (Reprise).

All-American Boy, The. w/m Bill Parsons and Orville Lunsford, 1959. Hit record by Bobby Bare (Fraternity). A printing error on the label credited Bill Parsons as the singer, and as Bare was in the Army when the record was released, Parsons toured with the record, lip synching to it on TV, in theaters, at record hops, etc.

All-American Girl. w/m Al Lewis, 1932. Popularized by George Olsen's Orchestra, vocal by Fran Frey (Victor).

All American Girls. w/m Joni Sledge, Narada Walden, Lisa Walden, and Allee Willis, 1981. Recorded by Sister Sledge (Cotillion).

Alla My Love. w/m Jimmy Gately and Harold Donny, 1962. Country hit by Webb Pierce (Decca).

All Ashore. w/m Billy Hill, 1938. Leading records: Sammy Kaye, vocal by Tommy Ryan (Victor); Paul Whiteman, vocal by the Modernaires (Decca).

All at Once. w. Ira Gershwin, m. Kurt Weill, 1945. Introduced by Fred MacMurray and ensemble in (MM) *Where Do We Go from Here?* Popular records by Kay Armen, with Guy Lombardo and his Orchestra (Decca); Don Cornell (Coral); Cab Calloway with his Orchestra (Columbia).

All at Once You Love Her. w. Oscar Hammerstein II, m. Richard Rodgers, 1955. Introduced by William Johnson, Judy Tyler, and Jerry La Zarre, and reprised by Helen Traubel in (TM) *Pipe Dream.* Recorded by Perry Como (RCA Victor).

All by Myself. w/m Eric Carmen, 1976. Top 10 gold record by Eric Carmen (Arista).

All by Myself. w/m Antoine "Fats" Domino and Dave Bartholomew, 1955. R&B hit by Fats Domino (Imperial).

All by Myself. w/m Irving Berlin, 1921. Introduced by Charles King at The Palace Theatre in New York. First recorded and featured by Ted Lewis (Columbia) and Frank Crumit (Columbia). It had sales of sheet music and records in the millions, plus over 150,000 piano rolls! It was revived by Bing Crosby in (MM) *Blue Skies*, 1946.

All by Yourself in the Moonlight. w/m Jay Wallis, 1929. An English song recorded by Irving Aaronson and His Commanders (Victor).

All Coons Look Alike to Me. w/m Ernest Hogan, 1896. Introduced by the composer in vaudeville. Hogan, black himself, later regretted writing the song because of the objectionable noun "coon." In the song, a woman, after being jilted by her lover, shows her "sour grapes" attitude by saying all the men she knows look alike to her.

All Cried Out. w/m Full Force, 1986. Top 10 single by Lisa Lisa and Cult Jam with Full Force (Columbia).

All Cried Out. w. Buddy Kaye, m. Philip Springer, 1964. Leading recording by Dusty Springfield.

All Day and All of the Night. w/m Ray Davies, 1965. Recorded by the British rock group, The Kinks. Top 10 record in the U.S. (Reprise).

All Dressed Up With a Broken Heart. w/m Fred Patrick, Claude Reese, and Jack Val, 1947. Leading records by Peggy Lee (Capitol); Buddy Clark (Columbia); Alan Dale (Signature).

Allegheny Al. w. Oscar Hammerstein II, m. Jerome Kern, 1937. Sung by Irene Dunne and Dorothy Lamour in (MM) *High, Wide and Handsome.*

Allegheny Moon. w/m Al Hoffman and Dick Manning, 1956. Popularized by best-selling record by Patti Page (Mercury).

Allentown. w/m Billy Joel, 1983. Recorded by Billy Joel (Columbia).

Allergies. w/m Paul Simon, 1983. Recorded by Paul Simon (Warner Bros.).

All er Nothin'. w. Oscar Hammerstein II, m. Richard Rodgers, 1943. Introduced by Celeste Holm and Lee Dixon in (TM) *Oklahoma!* In the film version (MM) *Oklahoma!*,

1955, it was sung by Gloria Grahame and Gene Nelson.

Alley Cat. m. Frank Bjorn, 1962. Danish instrumental, "Omkring et Flygel." Recorded in Denmark and released in the U.S. by Bent Fabric and His Piano (Atco). Played on the soundtrack of (MM) *Rock 'n' Roll High School*, 1979.

Alley Oop. w/m Dallas Frazier, 1960. #1 novelty record by Gary Paxton who, because of a contractual conflict, recorded under the name of The Hollywood Argyles (Lute). Chart record also by Dante and The Evergreens (Madison).

Allez-Vous-En (Go Away). w/m Cole Porter, 1953. Introduced by Lilo in (TM) *Can-Can*. It was played in the background during an Apache dance in (MM) *Can-Can*, 1960. Kay Starr had a popular recording, with Harold Mooney's Orchestra (Capitol).

All for Love of You. w. Dave Reed, m. Ernest R. Ball, 1908.

All for the Love of a Girl. w/m Johnny Horton, 1969. Top 10 Country chart record by Claude King (Columbia).

All for the Love of Sunshine. w. Mike Curb, m. Lalo Schifrin and Harley Hatcher, 1970. Sung on the soundtrack of (MP) *Kelly's Heroes* by Hank Williams, Jr.

All for You. w. Henry Blossom, m. Victor Herbert, 1915. From (TM) *The Princess Pat.*

All God's Chillun Got Rhythm. w. Gus Kahn, m. Bronislaw Kaper and Walter Jurmann, 1937. Introduced by Ivy Anderson and chorus in (MM) *A Day At The Races*, starring the Marx Brothers. Anderson recorded it (Variety) and was followed by some of the biggest names in music, such as Judy Garland, who sang it on her record debut (Decca); Bunny Berigan (Victor); Fletcher Henderson (Vocalion); Artie Shaw (Brunswick); Duke Ellington (Brunswick); Bud Powell (Mercury); Maynard Ferguson (EmArcy); Sonny Stitt (Prestige).

All Grown Up. w/m Howard Hausey, 1958. Top 10 C&W chart record by Johnny Horton (Columbia).

All His Children. w. Alan Bergman and Marilyn Bergman, m. Henry Mancini, 1971. Sung on the soundtrack of (MP) *Sometimes a Great Notion* by Charlie Pride. Nominated for an Academy Award, 1971.

All I Ask of You. w. Charles Hart and Richard Stilgoe, m. Andrew Lloyd Webber, 1988. Introduced in the U.S. by Steven Barton and Sarah Brightman, and reprised by Michael Crawford in the Broadway production of the British musical (TM) *The Phantom of the Opera*. Recorded by Barbra Streisand in her album "Till I Loved You" (Columbia).

All I Can Do. w/m Dolly Parton, 1976. Hit Country record by Dolly Parton (RCA).

All I Could Do Was Cry. w/m Berry Gordy, Jr., Gwen Gordy, and Raquel Davis, 1960. Recorded by Etta James (Argo).

All I Do Is Dream of You. w. Arthur Freed, m. Nacio Herb Brown, 1934. Introduced by Gene Raymond in (MP) *Sadie McKee*. In 1934, Chico Marx played the song in his unique pianistic style in (MM) *A Night at the Opera*. Debbie Reynolds sang it in (MM) *Singin' In The Rain*, 1952 and then with Bobby Van in (MM) *The Affairs of Dobie Gillis*, 1953. It was interpolated in (MM) *The Boyfriend*, 1971.

All I Ever Need Is You. w/m Jimmy Holiday and Eddie Reeves, 1971. Top 10 record by Sonny and Cher (Kapp). Hit revival by Country singers Dottie West and Kenny Rogers (United Artists), 1979.

Alligator Crawl. w. Andy Razaf and Joe Davis, m. Thomas "Fats" Waller, 1927. Introduced on records by Louis Armstrong (Okeh) and Fess Williams (Vocalion). Also recorded by Doc Cook (Columbia), 1928 and Fats Waller (Victor), 1934.

All I Have to Do Is Dream. w/m Boudleaux Bryant, 1958. #1 record and one of the biggest hits of the year by The Everly Brothers (Cadence). Top 40 revivals by Richard Chamberlain (MGM), 1963; Glen Campbell and Bobbie Gentry (Capitol), 1970. Others: The Nitty Gritty Dirt Band (United Artists), 1975; Andy Gibb and Victoria Principal (RSO), 1981.

All I Have to Offer You Is Me. w/m Dallas Frazier and A. L. "Doodle" Owens, 1969. Country hit record and first Pop chart entry by Charley Pride (RCA).

All I Know. w/m Jim Webb, 1973. Top 10 record by [Art] Garfunkel (Columbia).

All In Down and Out (Sorry, I Ain't Got It, You Could Have It, Etc.). w. Cecil Mack, m. Chris Smith, Billy B. Johnson, and Elmer Bowman, 1906. Featured by Bert Williams in vaudeville. Recorded by him as "Sorry I Ain't Got It, You Could Have It If I Had It Blues" (Columbia). Leading recording by Arthur Collins (Victor). In 1938, Uncle Dave Mason, of Grand Ole Opry fame, recorded his version (Bluebird).

All I Need. w/m Mike Rutherford and Christopher Neil, 1986. Top 10 record by the group, Mike + The Mechanics (Atlantic).

All I Need. w/m Glen Ballard, Cliff Magness, and David Pack, 1985. Top 10 record by Jack Wagner (Qwest).

All I Need. w/m Eddie Holland, R. Dean Taylor, and Frank Wilson, 1967. Top 10 record by The Temptations (Gordy).

All I Need Is the Girl. w. Stephen Sondheim, m. Jule Styne, 1959. Introduced by Paul Wallace with Sandra Church in (TM) *Gypsy.* In (MM) *Gypsy,* 1962, Wallace repeated his role, this time with Natalie Wood.

All I Need Is Time. See **Lo Mucho Que Te Quiero.**

All I Need Is You. w/m Mitchell Parish, Benny Davis, and Peter De Rose, 1942. Leading records by Dinah Shore (Victor); Vaughn Monroe, singing with his Orchestra (Victor); Claude Thornhill and his Orchestra (Okeh).

All I Need to Know. w. Cynthia Weil and Tom Snow, m. Tom Snow and Barry Mann, 1983. Introduced by Bill Medley (Liberty), 1981. Chart record by Bette Midler (Atlantic).

All in Fun. w. Oscar Hammerstein II, m. Jerome Kern, 1939. Introduced by Frances Mercer and Jack Whiting in (TM) *Very Warm for May.* George Murphy sang it in the film version (MM) *Broadway Rhythm,* 1944.

All in Love Is Fair. w/m Stevie Wonder, 1974. Recorded by Barbra Streisand (Columbia).

All in My Mind. w/m Leroy Kirkland, Maxine Brown, and Fred Johnson, 1961. Crossover (R&B/Pop) hit by Maxine Brown (Nomar).

All I Really Want to Do. w/m Bob Dylan, 1965. Introduced and recorded by Bob Dylan (Columbia), 1964. Hit records by Cher (Imperial) and The Byrds (Columbia), 1965.

All I Remember Is You. w. Eddie DeLange, m. James Van Heusen, 1939. Recorded by Artie Shaw, vocal by Helen Forrest (Bluebird); Jimmy Dorsey, vocal by Helen O'Connell (Decca); Tommy Dorsey, vocal by Jack Leonard (Victor); Dick Jurgens, vocal by Eddy Howard (Decca).

All I See Is You. w. Clive Westlake, m. Ben Weisman, 1966. Top 20 record by the British singer, Dusty Springfield (Philips).

All I Wanted. w/m Steve Walsh and Steve Morse, 1986. Recorded by the group, Kansas, featuring guitarist Steve Morse (MCA).

All I Wanted Was the Dream. w/m Peter Allen, 1988. Introduced by Peter Allen in (TM) *Legs Diamond.*

All I Want for Christmas (Is My Two Front Teeth). w/m Don Gardner, 1946. #1 record and a million seller for Spike Jones and his City Slickers (RCA Victor).

All I Want Is Forever. w/m Diane Warren, 1989. From (MM) *Tap.* Hit R&B chart single by James "J. T." Taylor and Regina B. (Epic).

All I Want Is You. w/m John Boylan, 1987. Recorded by Carly Simon (Arista).

All My Ex's Live in Texas. w/m Sanger D. Shafer and Lyndia J. Shafer, 1987. #1 Country chart song by George Strait (MCA).

All My Life. w. Sidney Mitchell, m. Sam H. Stept, 1936. Introduced by Phil Regan in (MM) *Laughing Irish Eyes* and recorded by him (Brunswick). Teddy Wilson played piano on three recordings of the song that year: 1) his band, with vocal by Ella Fitzgerald (Brunswick); 2) for Putney Dandridge's vocal (Vocalion); 3) with the Benny Goodman Trio, vocal by Helen Ward (Victor). The song was heard in (MM) *Johnny Doughboy*, 1943.

All My Love. w. Mitchell Parish (Engl.), Henri Contet (Fr.), m. Paul Durand, 1950. French song titled "Bolero," introduced by Jacqueline François. Patti Page had a #1 million-seller (Mercury). Other Top 20 records by Bing Crosby (Decca) and the orchestras of Percy Faith (Columbia) and Guy Lombardo (Decca).

All My Love. See **You Were Made For (All My Love).**

All My Love Belongs to You. w/m Henry Glover and Sally Nix, 1948. R&B chart hit record by Bull Moose Jackson and His Buffalo Bearcats (King).

All My Loving. w/m John Lennon and Paul McCartney, 1964. Introduced and recorded by The Beatles (Capitol) and sung by them in (MM) *A Hard Day's Night*.

All My Rowdy Friends (Have Settled Down). w/m Hank Williams, Jr., 1981. #1 Country chart record by Hank Williams, Jr. (Elektra).

All My Rowdy Friends Are Coming Over Tonight. w/m Hank Williams, Jr., 1984. Top 10 Country chart song by Hank Williams, Jr. (Warner Bros.).

All My Tomorrows. w. Sammy Cahn, m. James Van Heusen, 1959. Introduced by

Frank Sinatra in (MP) *Hole in the Head* and on records (Reprise).

All Night Long. w/m Joe Walsh, 1980. First heard on the soundtrack of (MP) *Urban Cowboy*. Popular record by Joe Walsh (Full Moon).

All Night Long. w/m Johnny Otis, 1951. Popular R&B record by Johnny Otis and Mel Walker (Savoy).

All Night Long. w/m Shelton Brooks, 1913. Introduced by Belle Baker in vaudeville. Leading record by Ada Jones and Billy Murray (Victor).

All Night Long (All Night). w/m Lionel Richie, 1983. #1 gold record from the platinum album "Can't Slow Down" by Lionel Richie (Motown). The song, containing Jamaican-style chants, referred to a Caribbean celebration. Richie sang it in a spectacular production, with 200 break-dancers and the international athletes, at the televised closing ceremonies of the 1984 Olympic Games at Los Angeles.

All of a Sudden. w/m Harry Woods, 1932. Featured and recorded by Glen Gray and the Casa Loma Orchestra (Brunswick) and Cliff "Ukulele Ike" Edwards (Brunswick).

All of a Sudden My Heart Sings. w. Harold Rome (Engl.), Jean Marie Blanvillain (Fr.), m. Henri Herpin, 1945. Rome's English version of this French song was introduced by Kathryn Grayson in (MM) *Anchors Aweigh*, and recorded by her (MGM). Other popular versions by Hildegarde (Decca); Guy Lombardo and his Orchestra (Decca); Martha Stewart (Bluebird); Johnny Johnston (Capitol). Revived with Top 40 records by Paul Anka (ABC-Paramount), 1959, and Mel Carter (Imperial), 1965.

All of Me. w/m Seymour Simons and Gerald Marks, 1931. Introduced in vaudeville and on radio by Belle Baker. Heard in (MM) *Careless Lady*, starring John Boles and Joan Bennett, 1932; sung by Frank Sinatra in (MM) *Meet*

Danny Wilson, 1952; by Gloria De Haven in (MM) *Down Among the Sheltering Palms*, 1953; by Diana Ross, as Billie Holiday, in (MM) *Lady Sings the Blues*, 1972. It was the title of the film starring Steve Martin and Lily Tomlin in 1984. Among the myriad of recordings are those by: Paul Whiteman, vocal by Mildred Bailey (Victor); Bailey (Majestic) and on LP "All of Me" (Monmouth-Evergreen); Kate Smith (Velvetone); Billie Holiday (Okeh); Russ Columbo (Victor); Nick Lucas (Hit of the Week); Frank Sinatra (Capitol); Helen O'Connell with Jimmy Dorsey (Decca); Illinois Jacquet (Mercury); Louis Jordan (Decca); Benny Carter (Bluebird); Willie Nelson (Columbia).

All of My Life. w/m Irving Berlin, 1945. Leading records by Sammy Kaye, vocal by Billy Williams (Victor); The Three Suns (Hit); Bing Crosby, with John Scott Trotter's Orchestra (Decca).

All of These and More. w. Sheldon Harnick, m. Jerry Bock, 1958. Introduced by Barbara McNair and Lonnie Sattin in (TM) *Body Beautiful*.

All of You. w. Cynthia Weil, m. Tony Renis and Julio Iglesias, 1984. Duet recorded by Spanish singer, Julio Iglesias, and Diana Ross (Columbia).

All of You. w/m Cole Porter, 1955. Introduced by Don Ameche in (TM) *Silk Stockings*. In the film version, (MM) *Silk Stockings*, 1956, it was sung by Fred Astaire and Carole Richards, the latter dubbing on the soundtrack for Cyd Charisse, and danced by Charisse and Astaire.

All or Nothing At All. w. Jack Lawrence, m. Arthur Altman, 1943. Frank Sinatra's vocal with Harry James and his Orchestra was recorded and released four years earlier (Columbia). It was reissued, with Sinatra given top billing, and sold over a million copies.

All Out of Love. w/m Graham Russell, 1980. Gold record by the Australian duo, Air Supply, comprised of Graham Russell and Russ Hitchcock (Arista).

All Over Again. w/m Johnny Cash, 1958. Featured and recorded by Johnny Cash (Columbia).

All Over Nothing At All. w. J. Keirn Brennan and Paul Cunningham, m. James Rule, 1922. Featured and recorded by Nora Bayes (Columbia). Revived by Ella Fitzgerald (Decca), 1937.

All Over the World. w/m Jeff Lynne, 1980. Recorded by the British group, Electric Light Orchestra (MCA).

All Over the World. w. Charles Tobias, m. Al Frisch, 1963. Featured and recorded by Nat "King" Cole (Capitol).

All Right. w/m Christopher Cross, 1983. Recorded by Christopher Cross (Warner Bros.).

All Right. w/m Faron Young, 1955. Country hit by Faron Young (Capitol).

All Right, Louie, Drop the Gun. w/m Ray Carter and Lucille Johnson, 1949. Introduced, featured, and recorded by the comedy team of Dick and Gene Wesson (National).

All Right Now. w/m Paul Rodgers and Andy Fraser 1970. Top 10 U.S. release of the recording by the British band, Free, of which the writers were members (A&M). Chart versions by Lea Roberts (United Artists), 1975, and Rod Stewart (Warner Bros.), 1985.

All's Fair in Love and War. w. Al Dubin, m. Harry Warren, 1937. Introduced by Dick Powell and Joan Blondell in a Busby Berkley production number in (MM) *Gold Diggers of 1937* in which Blondell led seventy goose-stepping girls in uniform across a highly polished stage. Powell recorded it (Decca).

All She'd Say Was "Umh Hum." w/m King Zany, Mac Emery, Gus Van, and Joe Schenck, 1920. Performed by Van and Schenck in (TM) *Ziegfeld Follies of 1920*.

All She Wants to Do Is Dance. w/m Danny Kortchmar, 1985. Top 10 single by Don Henley (Geffen).

All She Wants To Do Is Rock. w/m Teddy McRae and Wynonie Harris, 1949. The second #1 R&B song with "rock" in the title, before the acknowledged R&R period, by Wynonie Harris (King). See also *Good Rockin' Tonight.*

All Shook Up. w/m Otis Blackwell and Elvis Presley, 1957. #1 hit by Elvis Presley (RCA).

All Strung Out. w/m Nino Tempo and Jerry Riopell, 1966. Hit record by Nino Tempo and April Stevens (White Whale). Revived by John Travolta (Midland International), 1977.

All That Glitters Is Not Gold. w. Lee Kuhn, m. Alice Cornett and Eddie Asherman, 1946. Featured and recorded by Dinah Shore, with Sonny Burke's Orchestra (Columbia), and by Mildred Bailey, with Eddie Sauter's Orchestra (Majestic).

All That Glitters Is Not Gold. w. George A. Norton, m. James W. Casey, 1901. Featured by Blanche Ring.

All That I Am. w/m Sid Tepper and Roy C. Bennett, 1966. Introduced by Elvis Presley in (MM) *Spinout* and on records (RCA).

All That I Ask of You Is Love. w. Edgar Selden, m. Herbert Ingraham, 1910. Popular ballad. Leading record by Henry Burr (Columbia).

All That I'm Asking Is Sympathy. w. Benny Davis, m. Joe Burke, 1929. Recorded by Ted Weems, vocal by Art Jarrett (Victor).

All That I Want Is You. w. Joe Goodwin, m. James V. Monaco, 1920.

All That Jazz. w. Fred Ebb, m. John Kander, 1975. Introduced by Chita Rivera and company in (TM) *Chicago.* Recorded by Liza Minnelli (Columbia).

All That Love Went to Waste. w. Sammy Cahn, m. George Barrie, 1973. Introduced on the soundtrack of (MP) *A Touch of Class* by Madeline Bell. Nominated for an Academy Award.

All That Meat and No Potatoes. w/m Thomas "Fats" Waller and Ed Kirkeby, 1941. Introduced and recorded by Fats Waller (Bluebird). Also recorded by Bon Bon (Decca) and Les Brown and his band, vocal by Betty Bonney (Okeh).

All the Children in a Row. w. Fred Ebb, m. John Kander, 1984. Introduced by Liza Minnelli and Scott Ellis in (TM) *The Rink.*

All the Gold in California. w/m Larry Gatlin, 1979. Country chart record by Larry Gatlin and The Gatlin Brothers (Columbia).

All the King's Horses. w/m Alec Wilder, Edward Brandt, and Howard Dietz, 1930. Introduced by Margaret Lee in (TM) *Three's A Crowd.*

All the Love in the World. w/m John Spinks, 1986. Recorded by the British trio, The Outfield (Columbia).

All the Quakers Are Shoulder Shakers Down in Quaker Town. w. Bert Kalmar and Edgar Leslie, m. Pete Wendling, 1919. The song referred to the shimmy, a popular dance of the day.

All the Right Moves. w/m Tom Snow and Barry Alfonso, 1983. From (MP) *All the Right Moves.* Recorded by Jennifer Warnes and Chris Thompson (Casablanca).

All These Things. w/m Allan Toussaint, 1976. #1 Country chart record by Joe Stampley (ABC/Dot).

All the Things You Are. w. Oscar Hammerstein II, m. Jerome Kern, 1939. Introduced by Hiram Sherman, Frances Mercer, Ralph Magelssen (pseud. Ralph Stuart), and Hollace Shaw in (TM) *Very Warm for May.* An all-time standard, its first popular recording was by Tommy Dorsey, vocal by Jack Leonard (Victor). While the show was not a success, running less than eight weeks on Broadway, the song was on "Your Hit Parade" for eleven weeks, twice in the #1 position. It was sung by Ginny Simms in (MM) *Broadway Rhythm,* loosely based on *Very Warm for May* in 1944;

by Tony Martin in the Kern biography (MM) *Till the Clouds Roll By*, 1946; by Mario Lanza in (MM) *Because You're Mine*, 1952.

All the Time. w/m Wayne P. Walker and Mel Tillis, 1967. Hit Country record by Jack Greene (Decca).

All the Time. w/m Jay Livingston and Ray Evans, 1958. Introduced by Tony Randall and Jacquelyn McKeever in (TM) *Oh Captain!*

All the Time. w. Ralph Freed, m. Sammy Fain, 1946. Introduced by the English star, Pat Kirkwood, in her only U.S. film, with Guy Lombardo's Orchestra in (MM) *No Leave, No Love*. Recorded by Guy Lombardo and his Royal Canadians (Decca) and Kay Kyser, vocal by Mike Douglas (Columbia).

All the Way. w. Sammy Cahn, m. James Van Heusen, 1957. Introduced by Frank Sinatra, as the lead, in the Joe E. Lewis story, (MM) *The Joker is Wild*, and on the best-selling recording (Capitol). The song won the Academy Award for Best Song, 1957.

All the World Loves a Lover. w. Robert B. Smith, m. Jean Gilbert, 1912. Sung by Sallie Fisher in (TM) *Modest Suzanne*.

All the World Will Be Jealous of Me. w. Al Dubin, m. Ernest R. Ball, 1917. This was Al Dubin's first published song.

All the Young Dudes. w/m David Bowie, 1972. Recorded by the English group, Mott the Hoople, produced by Bowie (Epic).

All This and Heaven Too. w. Eddie De-Lange, m. James Van Heusen, 1940. Written to help promote the Bette Davis film of the same title. Leading recordings by Jimmy Dorsey, vocal by Bob Eberly (Decca); Tommy Dorsey, vocal by Frank Sinatra (Victor); Charlie Barnet, vocal by Larry Taylor (Bluebird).

All This Love. w/m Eldra DeBarge, 1983. Recorded by the family group, DeBarge. Written by the keyboardist (Gordy).

All Those Years Ago. w/m George Harrison, 1981. Written as a tribute to the late John Lennon, Harrison's record attained the #2 spot on the charts (Dark Horse).

All Through the Day. w. Oscar Hammerstein II, m. Jerome Kern, 1946. Kern's last score, composed shortly before his death. Song introduced by Louanne Hogan, dubbing on the soundtrack for Jeanne Crain, in (MM) *Centennial Summer*. Nominated for Academy Award, 1946. Leading records by Frank Sinatra, with Axel Stordahl's Orchestra (Columbia); Perry Como, with Andre Kostalanetz's Orchestra (RCA Victor); Margaret Whiting, with Carl Kress's Orchestra (Capitol).

All Through the Night. w/m Jules Shear, 1984. Top 10 record by Cyndi Lauper (Portrait).

All Through the Night. w/m Cole Porter, 1934. Introduced by Bettina Hall and William Gaxton in (TM) *Anything Goes*. It was heard on the soundtrack of the first film version in 1936 and in the 1956 remake (MM) *Anything Goes*, sung by Bing Crosby and danced by Zizi Jeanmaire.

All Time High. w. Tim Rice, m. John Barry, 1983. Introduced on the soundtrack of the James Bond film (MP) *Octopussy*, by Rita Coolidge. Chart record by Coolidge (A&M).

All Together Now. w/m John Lennon and Paul McCartney, 1968. Introduced by The Beatles in their animated film (MM) *Yellow Submarine*.

All Too Soon. w. Carl Sigman, m. Edward Kennedy "Duke" Ellington, 1940. Introduced and recorded by Duke Ellington and his Orchestra (Victor). Other records of note by Mildred Bailey (Decca), Billy Taylor (Prestige), Tony Scott and Sarah Vaughan (Gotham).

Ally Ally Oxen Free. w/m Rod McKuen, Tom Drake, and Steven Yates, 1963. Featured by The Kingston Trio (Capitol).

All You Need Is a Quarter. w. Betty Comden and Adolph Green, m. Jule Styne, 1960. Introduced by the chorus in (TM) *Do Re Mi*. Song refers to a jukebox.

All You Need Is Love. w/m John Lennon and Paul McCartney, 1967. Gold record by The Beatles (Capitol). The group sang it on the soundtrack of their animated film (MM) *Yellow Submarine*, 1968.

All You Want to Do Is Dance. w. Johnny Burke, m. Arthur Johnston, 1937. Sung in (MM) *Double or Nothing* and on records (Decca) by Bing Crosby.

All You Zombies. w/m Rob Hyman and Eric Bazilian, 1985. Recorded by the quintet, The Hooters (Columbia).

Alma, Where Do You Live? w. George V. Hobart, m. Adolph Philipp, 1910. Introduced by Kitty Gordon in (TM) *Alma, Where Do You Live?*

Almost. w/m Vic McAlpin and Jack Toombs, 1952. C&W song with leading record by George Morgan (Columbia).

Almost Always. w/m Kathleen Lichty, Lew Douglas, and Frank Lavere, 1953. Recorded by Joni James, with Lew Douglas's Orchestra (MGM).

Almost Grown. w/m Chuck Berry, 1959. Recorded by Chuck Berry (Chess).

Almost in Love. w. Randy Starr, m. Luiz Bonfa, 1968. Introduced by Elvis Presley in (MM) *Live a Little, Love a Little*, and on a chart single (RCA). It became the title song of a subsequent Presley LP (RCA).

Almost in Your Arms (a.k.a. **Love Song From "Houseboat"**). w/m Jay Livingston and Ray Evans, 1958. Introduced by Sophia Loren in (MP) *Houseboat*. Nominated for Academy Award. Leading record by Johnny Nash (ABC-Paramount).

Almost Like Being in Love. w. Alan Jay Lerner, m. Frederick Loewe, 1947. Introduced by David Brooks and Marion Bell in (TM) *Brigadoon*. Gene Kelly sang it in the film version (MM) *Brigadoon*, 1954.

Almost Paradise. m. Norman Petty, 1957. Instrumental for piano soloist introduced by The Norman Petty Trio (ABC-Paramount). Leading record by Roger Williams (Kapp), followed by Lou Stein, with Bill Fontaine's Orchestra (RKO Unique).

Almost Paradise . . . Love Theme from "Footloose." w. Dean Pitchford, m. Eric Carmen, 1984. From the film with songs, *Footloose*. Top 10 record by Mike Reno and Ann Wilson (Columbia).

Almost Persuaded. w/m Billy Sherrill and Glenn Sutton, 1966. Crossover (C&W/Pop) hit by David Houston (Epic). Winner of Grammy Award (NARAS) for Best Country and Western Song, 1966. Comedy version, "Almost Persuaded No. 2," was recorded by Ben Colder, pseudonym for Sheb Wooley (MGM).

Almost Saturday Night. w/m John Fogerty, 1975. Introduced on records by John Fogerty (Asylum). Revived by Dave Edmunds (Swan Song), 1981.

Almost Summer. w/m Brian Wilson, Alan Jardine, and Mike Love, 1978. Introduced by Celebration, featuring Mike Love, in (MP) *Almost Summer*, and on records (MCA). The writers were all members of the group The Beach Boys.

Almost There. w/m Jack Keller and Gloria Shayne, 1964. From (MP) *I'd Rather Be Rich*. Recorded by Andy Williams (Columbia).

Aloha Oe (Farewell to Thee). w/m Queen Liliuokalani, 1908. Written in Hawaii in 1878, but popularized in the U.S. thirty years later. In films, it was sung by: Bobby Breen in (MM) *Hawaii Calls*, 1938; Jeanette MacDonald in (MM) *I Married an Angel*, 1942; Elvis Presley in (MM) *Blue Hawaii*, 1962. Among recordings: Presley (RCA), Harry Owens (Decca), Don Ho (Reprise), Andy Williams (Columbia), Joe "Fingers" Carr (Capitol), Dorothy Lamour (Coast).

Alone. w/m Billy Steinberg and Tom Kelly, 1987. #1 record by the band, Heart, from the album "Bad Animals" (Capitol).

Alone. w. Arthur Freed, m. Nacio Herb Brown, 1935. Introduced by Allan Jones and

Kitty Carlisle, and reprised as a harp solo by Harpo Marx in (MM) *A Night At the Opera*, starring the Marx Brothers. Judy Garland sang it in (MM) *Andy Hardy Meets Debutante*, 1940. It was also heard in (MM) *Born to Sing*, 1942.

Alone (Why Must I Be Alone). w. Selma Craft, m. Morton Craft, 1957. Top 20 record by The Shepherd Sisters (Lance).

Alone Again (Naturally). w/m Raymond (Gilbert) O'Sullivan, 1972. Gold recording from England by the Irish-born Gilbert O'Sullivan (Epic).

Alone at a Table for Two. w/m Billy Hill, Daniel Richman, and Ted Fio Rito, 1935. Introduced and recorded by Ted Fio Rito and his Orchestra (Decca). Best-selling record by Guy Lombardo and His Royal Canadians (Victor).

Alone at Last. w. and adaptation of music by Johnny Lehmann, 1960. Another lyric set to first theme, first movement, from Tchaikowsky's *Concerto No. 1 in B-Flat Minor, for Piano and Orchestra*. (See *Tonight We Love* and *Concerto for Two*.) This adaptation was recorded by Jackie Wilson (Brunswick).

Alone at Last. w. Bob Hilliard, m. Victor Young, 1952. From (MP) *Something to Live For*.

Alone at Last. w. Gus Kahn, m. Ted Fio Rito, 1925. Featured and recorded by Carl Fenton (Walter Haenschen) and his Orchestra (Brunswick); Lewis James (Columbia); Henry Burr (Victor).

Alone Together. w. Howard Dietz, m. Arthur Schwartz, 1932. Introduced by Jean Sargent and danced by Clifton Webb and Tamara Geva in (TM) *Flying Colors*. Artie Shaw had a big selling record (Bluebird), 1939.

Alone Too Long. w. Dorothy Fields, m. Arthur Schwartz, 1954. Introduced by Wilbur Evans and Shirley Booth in (TM) *By the Beautiful Sea*. Popular record by Nat "King" Cole (Capitol).

Alone with You. w/m Lester Vanadore and Roy Drusky, 1958. Hit C&W and Pop record by Faron Young (Capitol).

Along Came Jones. w/m Jerry Leiber and Mike Stoller, 1959. Novelty hit by The Coasters (Atco). Revived by Ray Stevens (Monument), 1969.

Along Came Ruth. w/m Irving Berlin, 1915. Title suggested by the play of the same name. Leading recording by Arthur Fields (Victor).

Along Comes a Woman. w/m Peter Cetera and Mark Goldenberg, 1985. Recorded by the group, Chicago (Full Moon).

Along Comes Mary. w/m Tandyn Almer, 1966. Hit record by The Association (Valiant).

Along the Navajo Trail. w/m Dick Charles, Eddie DeLange, and Larry Markes, 1945. Hit records by Bing Crosby and The Andrews Sisters (Decca); Gene Krupa, vocal by Buddy Stewart (Columbia); Dinah Shore (Victor).

Along the Rocky Road to Dublin. w. Joe Young, m. Bert Grant, 1915. Popular recording by the American Quartette (Victor).

Along the Santa Fe Trail. w. Al Dubin and Edwina Coolidge, m. Will Grosz, 1940. Heard in (MP) *Santa Fe Trail*. Top recording: Glenn Miller, vocal by Ray Eberle (Bluebird).

Along with Me. w/m Harold Rome, 1946. Introduced by Danny Scholl and Paula Bane in (TM) *Call Me Mister*. Among recordings: Margaret Whiting (Capitol), Artie Shaw and his Orchestra (Musicraft), Jan Savitt and his Orchestra (ARA).

Alphabet Street. w/m Prince Rogers Nelson, 1988. Written and recorded by Prince (Paisley Park).

Alphagenesis. w. Kenn Long, m. Long and Jim Crozier, 1970. Sung by the company in the off-Broadway musical (TM) *Touch*.

Already Gone. w/m Bob Strandlund and Jack Tempchin, 1974. Recorded by The Eagles (Asylum).

Already It's Heaven. w/m Billy Sherrill and Glenn Sutton, 1968. #1 Country chart record by David Houston (Epic).

Alright, Okay, You Win. w/m Sid Wyche, 1955. Count Basie, vocal by Joe Williams, had the first hit record (Crest), followed by Peggy Lee, with Jack Marshall's Orchestra (Capitol), 1959.

Alvin's Harmonica. w/m Ross Bagdasarian, 1959. Novelty hit by David Seville and The Chipmunks (Liberty). Seville was pseudonym for Bagdasarian.

Alvin's Orchestra. w/m Ross Bagdasarian, 1960. Novelty by David Seville [Bagdasarian] and the Chipmunks (Liberty).

Always. w/m Jonathan Lewis, David Lewis, and Wayne Lewis, 1987. #1 single from the album "All In the Name of Love" by the group, Atlantic Starr (Warner Bros.). Not to be confused with the 1925 standard.

Always. w/m Irving Berlin, 1925, 1944. Written for, but dropped from the score of the Marx Brothers' stage musical, *The Cocoanuts*. Upon being published, it became an instant hit in ballrooms, clubs, vaudeville, and on radio and records, resulting in huge sheet music sales. Among early popular records: the bands of Vincent Lopez (Okeh) and George Olsen (Victor); singers Henry Burr (Victor) and Nick Lucas (Brunswick). It was played by Ray Noble and his Orchestra, and sung by an uncredited singer in the Lou Gehrig story (MP) *The Pride of the Yankees*, 1942. Deanna Durbin revived it in (MM) *Christmas Holiday*, 1944, landing the song on "Your Hit Parade" for nine weeks. It was sung by the chorus in (MM) *Blue Skies*, 1946.

Always. w. Charles Horwitz, m. Frederick V. Bowers, 1899.

Always Alone. w/m Ted Daffan, 1941. Introduced and recorded by Ted Daffan and His Texans (Okeh). Also recorded by Louise Massey and The Westerners, vocal by Curt Massey (Okeh).

Always and Always. w. Bob Wright and Chet Forrest, m. Edward Ward, 1937. Introduced by Joan Crawford in (MP) *Mannequin*. Recorded by Larry Clinton and his Orchestra (Victor), 1938.

Always and Forever. w/m Rod Temperton, 1976. Recorded by the group, Heatwave (Epic).

Always Have Always Will. w/m Johnny Mears, 1986. #1 Country chart record by Janie Frickie (Columbia).

Always in All Ways. w. Leo Robin, m. Richard A. Whiting and W. Franke Harling, 1930. Introduced by Jeanette MacDonald and Jack Buchanan in (MM) *Monte Carlo*.

Always in My Heart. w. Kim Gannon, m. Ernesto Lecuona, 1942. Introduced by Gloria Warren in (MM) *Always in My Heart*. Nominated for Academy Award. Popularized and recorded by Glenn Miller, vocal by Ray Eberle (Bluebird); Kenny Baker, accompanied by Harry Sosnik's Orchestra (Decca); Jimmy Dorsey, vocal by Bob Eberly (Decca).

Always in the Way. w/m Charles K. Harris, 1903. Harris's last hit. Recorded by Byron G. Harlan (Edison, Columbia).

Always Late (With Your Kisses). w/m Lefty Frizzell and Blackie Crawford, 1951. Country hit, recorded by Lefty Frizzell (Columbia).

Always Leave Them Laughing When You Say Good-bye. w/m George M. Cohan, 1903. From (TM) *Mother Goose*. Popular recording by Billy Murray (Columbia).

Always on My Mind. w/m Johnny Christopher, Mark James, and Wayne Thompson, 1982. Country and Pop hit record by Willie Nelson (Columbia). Winner Grammy Award (NARAS) Song of the Year and Country Song of the Year. Revived by the British duo, The Pet Shop Boys, from their album "Introspective" (EMI), 1988.

(There's) Always Something There to Remind Me. w. Hal David, m. Burt Bacharach, 1964. First chart record by Lou Johnson (Big Hill), 1964, followed by Sandie Shaw (Reprise), 1965; Dionne Warwick (Scepter), 1968; R. B. Greaves (Atco), 1970; the English duo, Naked Eyes, Top 10 (EMI America), 1983.

Always Together. w/m Bobby Miller, 1968. Top 20 record by The Dells (Cadet).

Always True to You in My Fashion. w/m Cole Porter, 1949. Introduced by Lisa Kirk in (TM) *Kiss Me Kate*. Popular recordings by Jo Stafford (Capitol) and Jane Harvey (MGM). In the film version (MM) *Kiss Me Kate*, 1953, it was sung by Ann Miller and Tommy Rall.

Always Wanting You. w/m Merle Haggard, 1975. Hit Country record by Merle Haggard (Capitol).

Amanda. w/m Tom Scholz, 1986. #1 record by the group Boston (MCA).

Amanda. w/m Bob McDill, 1979. Country and Pop chart hit by Waylon Jennings (RCA).

Amapola (Pretty Little Poppy). w. Joseph M. Lacalle (Sp.), Albert Gamse (Engl.), m. Joseph M. Lacalle, 1941. Originally a popular Spanish song, first published in the U.S. in 1924. The Castillians had a popular record (Columbia), 1934. Deanna Durbin sang it in (MM) *First Love*, 1939. The recording by Jimmy Dorsey and his Orchestra, vocals by Bob Eberly and Helen O'Connor, was one of the top sellers of the year (Decca), 1941. It was on "Your Hit Parade" for nineteen weeks, six times in the #1 position.

Amazing Grace. w/m Rev. John Newton, 1971. This hymn, written in 1799, had a popular version by Judy Collins, recorded in St. Paul's Chapel, Columbia University, New York (Elektra). An instrumental by The Royal Scots Dragoon Guards, bagpipes solo by Major Tony Crease, reached the U.S. Top 20 (RCA), 1972.

Amazing Love. w/m John Schweers, 1973. Country chart hit record by Charley Pride (RCA).

Amber Tresses Tied with Blue. w/m A. P. Carter, 1932. First sung by The Carter Family.

Ame Caline (a.k.a. Soul Coaxing). m. Michel Polnareff, 1968. Top 40 U.S. instrumental, recorded in France by pianist/flutist/conductor Raymond Lefevre (Four Corners).

Amen. w/m Otis Redding, 1968. Top 40 record by Otis Redding (Atco).

Amen. w/m Jerry Goldsmith, 1963. Introduced by Sidney Poitier and the nuns in (MP) *Lilies of the Field*. First popular record, The Impressions (ABC-Paramount), 1964.

Amen (Yea-Man). w/m Roger Segure, Bill Hardy, and Vic Schoen, 1942. Introduced by Woody Herman and his Orchestra in (MM) *What's Cookin'?* Recorded by Woody Herman, vocal by Herman (Decca), and Abe Lyman, vocal by Rose Blaine (Bluebird).

America. w/m Neil Diamond, 1980. Introduced by Neil Diamond in the third screen version of (MM) *The Jazz Singer*. Diamond's recording made the Top 10 (Columbia).

America. w/m Paul Simon, 1972. Introduced by Simon and Garfunkel in their album "Bookends" (Columbia), 1968. Chart U.S. single by the British group Yes (Atlantic).

America. w. Stephen Sondheim, m. Leonard Bernstein, 1957. Introduced by Chita Rivera, Marilyn Cooper, and members of "The Sharks" in (TM) *West Side Story*. In the film version (MM) *West Side Story*, 1961, it was performed by George Chakiris, Rita Moreno, and "The Sharks."

America, Here's My Boy. w. Andrew B. Sterling, m. Arthur Lange, 1917. Patriotic World War 1 song. Leading record by The Peerless Quartet (Victor).

America, I Love You. w. Edgar Leslie, m. Archie Gottler, 1915. One of the more popular patriotic songs to be written before the entry of the United States into World War I. It was performed in (MM) *Tin Pan Alley*, 1940, by Alice Faye, John Payne, and the Brian Sisters.

America Is. w. Hal David, m. Joe Raposo, 1985. Written for the centennial of The Statue of Liberty in New York Harbor.

America Is My Home. w/m James Brown and Hayward E. Moore, 1968. Recorded by James Brown (King).

American Beauty Rose. w/m Hal David, Redd Evans, and Arthur Altman, 1950. Popularized and recorded by Frank Sinatra, with Mitch Miller's Dixieland Orchestra (Columbia), and Eddy Howard, with his orchestra (Mercury).

American City Suite. w/m Terry Cashman and Tommy West, 1972. Recorded by Cashman and West (Dunhill). Suite comprised of "Sweet City Song," "All Around the Town," and "A Friend Is Dying."

American Dream. w/m Neil Young, 1988. Single by Crosby, Stills and Nash from their album of the same name (Atlantic).

American Dream, An. w/m Rodney Crowell, 1980. Top 20 record by The Dirt Band, with vocal harmony sung by Linda Ronstadt (United Artists).

American Heartbeat. w/m Frankie Sullivan and Jim Peterik, 1982. Recorded by the quintet Survivor (Scotti Brothers).

American Made. w/m Robert Dipiero and Patrick McManus. 1983. Recorded by The Oak Ridge Boys (MCA).

American Me. w/m Thom Schuyler, J. Fred Knobloch, and Paul Overstreet, 1987. Country chart single by S-K-O [the writers] (MTM).

American Music. w/m Parker McGee, 1982. Recorded by The Pointer Sisters (Planet).

American Patrol. m. E. H. Meacham, 1901, 1917, 1942. The march was written in the 1880s and was made popular by the "March King," John Philip Sousa, whose band

featured it in concerts and first recorded it in 1901 (Gram-o-phone), re-recorded it during World War I (Victor). Prince's Orchestra, led by Charles Adams Prince, also had a popular record (Columbia), 1917. For World War II there was the famous march/swing arrangement by Glenn Miller and his Orchestra (Victor), 1942. It was performed by the band in (MM) *The Glenn Miller Story*, 1954. See also *We Must Be Vigilant*.

American Pie. w/m Don McLean, 1972. #1 gold record, Parts I & II, by Don McLean (United Artists). It was the top record of the year in sales and performances.

American Storm. w/m Bob Seger, 1986. Recorded by Bob Seger and The Silver Bullet Band (Capitol).

American Trilogy, An. w/m Mickey Newbury, 1971. Hit C&W/Pop record consisting of "Dixie," "Battle Hymn of the Republic," and "All My Trials," by Mickey Newbury (Elektra). Elvis Presley had a chart version of his "live" Las Vegas performance of the trilogy (RCA).

American Tune. w/m Paul Simon, 1974. Recorded by Paul Simon (Columbia).

American Tune. w. B. G. De Sylva and Lew Brown, m. Ray Henderson, 1928. Introduced by Harry Richman and the ensemble in (TM) *George White's Scandals of 1928.*

Am I Blue? w. Grant Clarke, m. Harry Akst, 1929. Introduced by Ethel Waters in the first all-color, all-talking, all-singing musical film (MM) *On With The Show*, and on records (Columbia). It was also heard in (MM) *So Long Letty*, 1930; (MM) *Is Everybody Happy?* 1943; (MP) *To Have and Have Not* sung by Hoagy Carmichael and Andy Williams (the latter dubbing for Lauren Bacall!), 1944; (MM) *Funny Lady* sung by Barbra Streisand, 1975. #1 Country chart revival by George Strait (MCA), 1987.

Amie. w/m Craig Fuller, 1975. Hit record by the Country-rock group, Pure Prairie League (RCA).

Am I Gonna Have Trouble with You? w. Charles Tobias, m. Sammy Fain, 1936.

Amigo's Guitar. w/m John D. Loudermilk, Muriel D. Wright and Roy Botkin, 1960. C&W hit by Kitty Wells (Decca).

Am I in Love? w. Ted Varnick, m. Nick Aquaviva, 1954. Popular record by Joni James, with Lew Douglas's Orchestra (MGM).

Am I in Love? w/m Jack Brooks, 1952. Introduced by Bob Hope and Jane Russell in (MM) *Son of Paleface*. Nominated for Academy Award, 1952.

Am I in Love. w. Al Dubin, m. Harry Warren, 1937. Introduced by Kenny Baker in (MP) *Mr. Dodds Takes the Air*. Recorded by the bands of Hal Kemp (Victor); George Hall (Vocalion); Jolly Coburn (Bluebird).

Am I Losing You? w/m Jim Reeves, 1960. Crossover (C&W/Pop) chart song by Jim Reeves (RCA). The Partridge Family had a popular version (Bell), 1972.

Am I Proud? w/m Teddy Powell and Leonard Whitcup, 1940. Featured and recorded by Tommy Dorsey, vocal by Anita Boyer (Victor), and Freddy Martin, vocal by Eddie Stone (Bluebird).

Am I That Easy to Forget? w/m Carl Belew, W. S. Stevenson, and Shelby Singleton, 1959. Hit C&W record by Carl Belew (Decca). Successful Pop versions by Debbie Reynolds (Dot), 1960 and Engelbert Humperdinck (Parrot), 1968.

Am I the Same Girl. See **Soulful Strut**.

Am I Wasting My Time? w. Jack Manus, m. Sanford Green, 1932. Featured by Nell Roy and recorded by Ruby Newman's Orchestra (Victor).

Am I Wasting My Time on You? w/m Howard Johnson and Irving Bibo, 1926. Leading records by Lewis James (Columbia) and Ben Selvin, vocal by Franklyn Baur (Columbia).

Among My Souvenirs. w. Edgar Leslie, m. Horatio Nicholls, 1927. This standard was a collaboration of an English composer (pseudonym for Lawrence Wright, the London-based publisher) and an American lyricist. Introduced with a hit record by Paul Whiteman, vocal by Jack Fulton, Charles Gaylord, and Austin Young (Victor). Hoagy Carmichael sang it in (MP) *The Best Years of Our Lives*, 1946. Connie Francis revived it with a Top 10 hit (MGM), 1959. Marty Robbins had a chart Country version (Columbia), 1976.

Amor. w. Sunny Skylar (Engl.), Ricardo Lopez Mendez (Sp.), m. Gabriel Ruiz, 1944. Mexican song, introduced in the U.S. by Ginny Simms in (MM) *Broadway Rhythm*. Bestselling record by Bing Crosby (Decca). Others: Andy Russell (Capitol); Xavier Cugat (Columbia). It was heard in (MM) *Swing in the Saddle*, 1946. Song revived by The Four Aces, with Jack Pleis's Orchestra (Decca), 1954.

Amore, Scusami. See **My Love, Forgive Me**.

Amos Moses. w/m Jerry Reed, 1971. Gold record novelty Country and Pop record by Jerry Reed (RCA).

Amorous Goldfish, The. w. Harry Greenbank, m. Sidney Jones, 1896. Introduced in (TM) *The Geisha* in London in April and then in the New York production in September.

Amsterdam. w. Mort Shuman and Eric Blau (Engl.), Jacques Brel (Fr.), m. Jacques Brel, 1968. Introduced in France by Jacques Brel. Mort Shuman introduced the English version in the off-Broadway musical (TM) *Jacques Brel is Alive and Well and Living in Paris*, 1968.

Amy. w/m Cynthia Weil and Barry Mann, 1963. Recorded by Paul Petersen (Colpix).

Anaheim, Azusa and Cucamonga Sewing Circle, Book Review and Timing Association. w/m Jan Berry, Roger Christian, and Don Altfeld, 1964. Introduced and recorded by Jan and Dean (Liberty).

Anastasia. w. Paul Francis Webster, m. Alfred Newman, 1957. Theme from (MP) *Anastasia*. Top recording by Pat Boone (Dot).

Anatole (of Paris). w/m Sylvia Fine, 1939. Introduced by Danny Kaye in (TM) *Straw Hat Revue*. Kaye performed it in (MP) *The Secret Life of Walter Mitty*, 1947.

Anchors Aweigh. w. Alfred H. Miles and Royal Lovell, m. Charles Zimmerman, 1906. Originally written as a football song for the midshipmen at the Naval Academy at Annapolis, Md., it has become the song of the U.S. Navy. Popular recordings by The U.S. Naval Academy Band (Columbia), 1921, and Paul Tremaine and his Orchestra (Columbia), 1930. It was played by the orchestra directed by José Iturbi in (MM) *Anchors Aweigh*, 1945.

And a Little Bit More. w. Alfred Bryan, m. Fred Fisher, 1907. Comedy song. Leading record by Arthur Collins and Byron Harlan (Columbia).

Andalucia. m. Ernesto Lecuona, 1930. From "Andalucia Suite, Española" for solo piano. See *Malagueña* and *Breeze and I, The*.

Andalucia. See **Malagueña.**

And Get Away. w/m Gilbert Moorer and William E. Sheppard, 1967. Recorded by The Esquires (Bunky).

And He'd Say "Oo-La-La! Wee-Wee." w. George Jessel, m. Harry Ruby, 1919. Ruby's first song hit. Introduced by George Jessel at the Palace in New York. Six recordings by Billy Murray (Columbia, Gennett, Emerson, Path, Empire, Victor).

And Her Golden Hair Was Hanging Down Her Back. w. Monroe H. Rosenfeld, m. Felix McGlennon, 1894. Recorded on numerous labels by Dan Quinn.

And Her Mother Came Too. w. Peter Dion Titheradge, m. Ivor Novello, 1914. English comedy song. Interpolated in (TM) *A Musical Jubilee* by Cyril Ritchard, 1975.

And Her Tears Flowed Like Wine. w. Joe Greene, m. Stan Kenton and Charles Lawrence, 1944. Introduced, featured, and best-selling record by Stan Kenton, vocal by Anita O'Day (Capitol). Others: Ella Fitzgerald, with the Song Spinners, and Johnny Long's Orchestra (Decca); Phil Moore (Victor).

Andiamo. w. Dorothy Fields, m. Harold Arlen, 1951. Introduced by Ezio Pinza in (MM) *Mr. Imperium*. Pinza recorded it with John Green's Orchestra (RCA Victor).

And I Am Telling You I'm Not Going. w. Tom Eyen, m. Henry Krieger, 1982. Introduced by Jennifer Holliday in (TM) *Dream Girls*. Her single from the original cast album was on the charts for three months (Geffen).

And I Love Her. w/m John Lennon and Paul McCartney, 1964. Introduced by The Beatles in (MM) *A Hard Day's Night*, and recorded by them (Capitol). See *And I Love Him*.

And I Love Him. w/m John Lennon and Paul McCartney, 1965. Esther Phillips recorded this version of The Beatles hit "And I Love Her" (Atlantic).

And I Love You So. w/m Don McLean, 1973. Introduced by Bobby Goldsboro (United Artists), 1971. Hit record by Perry Como (RCA).

And I Still Do. w. Edgar Leslie, m. Fred E. Ahlert, 1934. Recorded by Ina Ray Hutton and her Melodears (Victor).

And Love Was Born. w. Oscar Hammerstein II, m. Jerome Kern, 1932. Introduced by Reinald Werrenrath in (TM) *Music in the Air*. Recorded by Lawrence Tibbett (Victor) and Leo Reisman, vocal by Howard Phillips (Victor).

And Mimi. w/m Jimmy Kennedy and Nat Simon, 1947. Most popular recordings by Art Lund (MGM) and Dick Haymes (Decca).

Andrea. w/m Samuel Marvin Chazen, 1966. Recorded by The Sunrays (Tower).

And Roses and Roses. w/m Ray Gilbert and Dorival Caymmi, 1965. Popularized by Andy Williams (Columbia).

And She Was. w/m David Byrne, m. Chris Frantz, Tina Weymouth, and Jerry Harrison, 1985. Written and recorded by the quartet, Talking Heads (Sire).

And So Do I. w. Eddie De Lange, m. Paul Mann, and Stephan Weiss, 1940. Top records by Jimmy Dorsey, vocal by Helen O'Connell (Decca); Tommy Dorsey, vocal by Connie Haines (Victor); Raymond Scott, vocal by Nan Wynn (Columbia); Francis Langford, conducted by Victor Young (Decca).

And So Goodbye. w/m Allie Wrubel, 1933. Featured and recorded by the bands of Ray Noble (HMV-Victor); Jan Garber (Victor); Barney Rapp (Bluebird).

And So Little Time. w. Nick Kenny, m. Abner Silver, 1943. Featured and recorded by Jerry Wald and his Orchestra (Decca) and The Three Suns (Hit).

And So to Bed. w. Mack Gordon, m. Harry Revel, 1932. Popularized by George Olsen and his Orchestra, vocal by Ethel Shutta (Victor). Later recordings of note: Artie Shaw's Orchestra, vocal by Mel Tormé and his Mel-Tones (Musicraft); Hildegarde (Decca); Skitch Henderson (Capitol).

And So to Sleep Again. w/m Joe Marsala and Sunny Skylar, 1951. Patti Page, through overdubbing, was a one-person quartet on the hit record (Mercury). Other popular versions by April Stevens (RCA Victor); Dick Haymes (Decca); Paul Weston, vocal by The Norman Luboff Choir (Columbia).

And Suddenly. w/m Mike Brown and Bert Sommer, 1968. Recorded by The Cherry People (Heritage).

And That Reminds Me (a.k.a. **My Heart Reminds Me.** w. Al Stillman, m. Camillo Bargoni, 1957. Adapted from the Italian composer Bargoni's "Concerto Autunno." Under title "My Heart Reminds Me," Kay Starr had a hit record (Mercury). With alternate title preferred by lyricist Stillman, "And That Reminds Me," Della Reese had a hit version

(Jubilee). Revived by The Four Seasons (Crewe), 1969.

And the Angels Sing. w. Johnny Mercer, m. Ziggy Elman, 1939. Originally written as an instrumental, "Fralich in Swing," and recorded by Ziggy Elman and his Orchestra (Bluebird). Mercer wrote the lyric, and Benny Goodman recorded it (Victor) featuring Elman on trumpet and vocal by Martha Tilton. The record was a hit and was followed by Glenn Miller (Bluebird); Jan Savitt, vocal by Bon Bon (Decca); Count Basie, vocal by Helen Humes (Vocalion); Alec Templeton (Victor). It was on Your Hit Parade twelve times, four in the #1 spot.

And the Beat Goes On. w/m William Shelby, Stephen Shockley, and Leon Sylvers, 1980. #1 R&B and Pop chart gold record by the soul group, Whispers (Solar).

And the Cradle Will Rock. w/m Eddie Van Halen, Alex Van Halen, Michael Anthony, and David Lee, 1980. Recorded by the group Van Halen (Warner Bros.).

And the Green Grass Grew All Around. w. William Jerome, m. Harry Von Tilzer, 1912. Popular recordings by The American Quartette (Victor) and Walter Van Brunt (Columbia).

And Then It's Heaven. w/m Edward Seiler, Sol Marcus, and Al Kaufman, 1946. Introduced by Phil Brito in (MM) *Sweetheart of Sigma Chi.* Brito's recording was arranged and conducted by Walter Gross (Musicraft). Harry James, vocal by Buddy De Vito (Columbia), also had a popular version.

And Then Some. w. Tot Seymour, m. Vee Lawnhurst, 1935. Hit record by Ozzie Nelson and his Orchestra (Brunswick). Other popular versions by the bands of Bob Crosby (Decca) and Joe Reichman (Melotone).

And Then You Kissed Me. w. Sammy Cahn, m. Jule Styne, 1944. Introduced by Frank Sinatra in (MM) *Step Lively*, a musical remake of *Room Service*.

And Then Your Lips Met Mine. w/m Matty Malneck, Frank Signorelli, and Ozzie

Nelson, 1930. A collaborative effort by three musicians and/or band leaders. Nelson recorded it (Brunswick) as did Bert Lown and his Orchestra (Victor).

And There You Are. w. Ted Koehler, m. Sammy Fain, 1945. Introduced by Xavier Cugat and his Orchestra in (MP) *Week-End at the Waldorf.* Featured and recorded by Kate Smith (Columbia).

And They Called It Dixieland (They Made It Twice As Nice As Paradise). w. Raymond Egan, m. Richard A. Whiting, 1916.

And This Is My Beloved. w/m Robert Wright and George Forrest, 1953. Adapted from the first theme (Nocturne) of the third movement of Alexander Borodin's *String Quartet No. 2 in D*, this was introduced by Doretta Morrow, Richard Kiley, Alfred Drake, and Henry Calvin in (TM) *Kismet.* In (MM) *Kismet,* 1955, it was sung by Howard Keel, Ann Blyth, and Vic Damone.

And We Danced. w/m Rob Hyman and Eric Bazilian, 1985. Recorded by the quintet, The Hooters (Columbia).

And When I Die. w/m Laura Nyro, 1969. Introduced by Laura Nyro in her first album "More Than a New Discovery" (Verve), 1966. Gold record by Blood, Sweat & Tears (Columbia, 1969).

And You And I. w/m Jon Anderson, Bill Bruford, Steve Howe, and Chris Squire, 1972. Recorded by the British group, Yes, and written by members (Atlantic).

And You'll Be Home. w. Johnny Burke, m. James Van Heusen, 1950. Introduced by Bing Crosby in (MM) *Mr. Music.*

Anema e Core (With All My Heart and Soul). w. Mann Curtis and Harry Akst (Engl.), Tito Manlio (It.), m. Salve d'Esposito, 1954. First sung by Ferrucio Tagliavini in the Italian film of the same name. Eddie Fisher had a hit record with English lyrics (RCA Victor).

Angel. w. Stephen Tyler, w/m Desmond Child, 1988. Hit single by the group Aerosmith (Geffen).

Angel. w/m Angela Winbush, 1987. #1 R&B chart single by Angela Winbush (Mercury).

Angel. w/m Madonna and Steve Bray, 1985. Top 10 record by Madonna (Sire).

Angel. w/m Rory Bourke and Gayle Barnhill, 1973. Top 20 record by Aretha Franklin (Atlantic).

Angel. w. Jay Livingston and Ray Evans, m. Max Steiner, 1965. Theme from (MP) *Those Calloways.* Recorded by Johnny Tillotson (MGM).

Angel. w. Arthur Freed, m. Harry Warren, 1945. Introduced by Lucille Bremer in (MM) *Yolanda and the Thief.* Leading recording by Kay Kyser, vocal by Mike Douglas (Columbia).

Angel. w. Mitchell Parish, m. Peter DeRose, 1940. Introduced in (TM) *Earl Carroll Vanities (12th Edition).* Leading record by Tommy Dorsey, vocal by Allan DeWitt (Victor). DeWitt was the interim singer between Jack Leonard, who was drafted, and Frank Sinatra.

Angela Mia (My Angel). w. Lew Pollack, m. Erno Rapee, 1928. Theme song of (MP) *Street Angel,* starring Janet Gaynor and Charles Farrell. Top records by Paul Whiteman, vocal by Jack Fulton, Charles Gaylord, and Al Rinker (Victor); Vincent Lopez, vocal by James Lewis (Brunswick). Revived by Jimmy Dorsey, vocal by Bob Carroll (MGM), 1940s; Don, Dick, N' Jimmy (Crown), 1954.

Angel Baby. w/m Rose Hamlin, 1960. Introduced and recorded by Rosie and The Originals (Highland).

Angel Baby. w/m Joe Penny, 1958. Featured and recorded by Dean Martin (Capitol).

Angel Child. w. Georgie Price and Benny Davis, m. Abner Silver, 1922. Performed by

Georgie Price in (TM) *Spice of 1922* and recorded by Al Jolson (Columbia).

Angel Eyes. w. Earl Brent, m. Matt Dennis, 1953. Matt Dennis introduced the song in (MP) *Jennifer.*

Angel Eyes. w. Alfred Bryan, m. James Kendis and Herman Paley, 1910. Popular recording by Billy Murray and Elida Morris (Victor).

Angel Face. w. Robert B. Smith, m. Victor Herbert, 1920. From (TM) *Angel Face.*

Angel Flying Too Close to the Ground. w/m Willie Nelson, 1981. Introduced in (MM) *Honeysuckle Rose* and #1 Country chart record by Willie Nelson (Columbia). The film based on *Intermezzo* was retitled *On the Road Again.*

Angelina. w/m Tommie Connor and Edward Lisbona, 1953. Recorded by Lou Monte (RCA Victor)

Angelina (the Waitress at the Pizzeria). w/m Allan Roberts and Doris Fisher, 1944. Featured and recorded by Louis Prima, with his Orchestra (Hit).

Angel in Blue. w/m Seth Justman, 1982. Recorded by The J. Geils Band (EMI America).

Angel in Disguise. w. Kim Gannon, m. Paul Mann and Stephan Weiss, 1940. Bestseller: Dick Todd (Bluebird). Others: Bob Crosby, vocal by Marion Mann (Decca); the bands of Ozzie Nelson (Bluebird) and Lou Breese (Varsity).

Angel in Your Arms. w/m Thomas Brasfield, Herbert Ivey, and Terry Woodford, 1977. Top 10 gold record by the female trio, Hot (Big Tree).

Angelito. w/m René Herrera and René Ornellos, 1964. Recorded in English and Spanish by the writers, René and René (Columbia).

Angel of the Morning. w/m Chip Taylor, 1967. Top 10 record by Merilee Rush and The Turnabouts (Bell). Revived with a Top 10 gold record by Juice Newton (Capitol), 1981.

Angels Came Thru, The. w. Al Dubin, m. Ernesto Lecuona, 1941. Leading record by Glenn Miller, vocal by Ray Eberle (Bluebird). Others: Charlie Spivak, vocal by Garry Stevens (Okeh); Bob Crosby's Orchestra (Decca).

Angels in the Sky. w/m Dick Glasser, 1956. Hit record by The Crew Cuts (Mercury).

Angels Listened In, The. w/m Billy Dawn Smith and Sid Faust, 1959. Recorded by The Crests (Co-ed).

Angel Smile. w/m Luther Dixon, Billy Dawn, and Bert Keyes, 1958. Top 40 record by Nat "King" Cole (Capitol).

Angels with Dirty Faces. w. Maurice Spitalny, m. Fred Fisher, 1938. Title derived from, but not written for, film of same name. Leading records by Cab Calloway, vocal by June Richmond (Vocalion); Tommy Dorsey, vocal by Edythe Wright (Victor); Blue Barron and his Orchestra (Bluebird).

Angelus, The. w. Robert B. Smith, m. Victor Herbert, 1913. Sung by Christie MacDonald in (TM) *Sweethearts.* In the film version (MM) *Sweethearts*, 1938, it was sung by Jeanette MacDonald.

Angie. w/m Mick Jagger and Keith Richards, 1973. #1 gold record by the British group The Rolling Stones (Rolling Stones).

Angie Baby. w/m Alan O'Day, 1974. #1 gold record by Helen Reddy (Capitol).

Angry. w. Dudley Mecum, m. Henry Brunies and Jules Cassard, 1925. First recorded by The New Orleans Rhythm Kings, Jelly Roll Morton on piano (Gennett), 1923. Popularized and recorded by Ted Lewis and his Orchestra (Columbia) and pianist Art Gillham (Columbia). Revived by Tiny Hill and his Orchestra, who recorded it and used it as his theme song (Vocalion), 1939. Kay Starr, with Dave Cavanaugh's Orchestra, had a popular recording (Capitol), 1951.

Animal. w/m Steve Clark, Phil Collen, Mutt Lange, and Rick Savage, 1987. Recorded by the English group, Def Leppard (Mercury).

Animal Crackers in My Soup. w. Ted Koehler and Irving Caesar, m. Ray Henderson, 1935. Introduced by Shirley Temple in (MM) *Curly Top.* In (MM) *Rebecca of Sunnybrook Farm*, 1938, at the age of ten, Temple sang the song in a medley of her "past hits." It was in the repertoire of Tiny Tim who recorded it in 1968 (Reprise).

Animal House. w/m Stephen Bishop, 1978. Introduced by Stephen Bishop on the soundtrack of (MP) *National Lampoon's Animal House*, and on records (ABC).

Anita, You're Dreaming. w/m Waylon Jennings and Don Bowman, 1966. Country chart record by Waylon Jennings (RCA).

Anna. w. William Engvick (Engl.), m. R. Vatro, 1953. Original Italian lyrics by F. Giordano. Title song of Italian film (MP) *Anna*, sung by Silvano Mangano, whose recording (MGM) became a million-seller.

Anna (Go to Him). w/m Arthur Alexander, 1962. Introduced and recorded by Arthur Alexander (Dot).

Annabelle. w. Lew Brown, m. Ray Henderson, 1923. Non-production song.

Annabel Lee. w. Irving Caesar and John Murray Anderson, m. Louis A. Hirsch, 1923. From (TM) *Greenwich Follies of 1923*.

Anna Marie. w/m Cindy Walker, 1958. Leading C&W and Pop record by Jim Reeves (Columbia).

Annie Doesn't Live Here Anymore. w. Joe Young and Johnny Burke, m. Harold Spina, 1933. The first hit for writers Burke and Spina. Introduced on radio, popularized, and recorded by Guy Lombardo and the Royal Canadians, vocal by Carmen Lombardo (Melotone). Other recordings by Art Kahn (Perfect) and Ramona, with Roy Bargy's Orchestra (Victor).

Annie Fanny. w/m Lynn Easton, 1965. Written by the drummer of The Kingsmen, the rock band that recorded it (Wand).

Annie Get Your Yo-Yo. w/m Deadric Malone and Joseph Scott, 1962. Recorded by Little Junior Parker (Duke).

Annie Had a Baby. w/m Henry Glover and Lois Mann, 1954. Top R&B record by The Midnighters (Federal).

Annie's Song. w/m John Denver, 1974. A #1 gold record by John Denver (RCA) who wrote the song for his wife, Ann Martell, although her name is not mentioned in the lyric. It was used as the wedding song for many couples during the 1970s.

Anniversary Song. w/m Al Jolson and Saul Chaplin, 1946. Based on the 1880 waltz "Donauwellen" (Danube Waves) by J. Ivanovici. Sung on the soundtrack of (MM) *The Jolson Story* by Al Jolson, dubbing for Larry Parks. Jolson's recording, taken from the soundtrack, was a million-seller (Decca). Dinah Shore's recording, accompanied by Morris Stoloff's Orchestra, was a #1 hit (Columbia). Other Top 10 versions by Guy Lombardo, vocal by Kenny Gardner (Decca); Tex Beneke, vocal by Garry Stevens and The Mello Larks (RCA Victor); Andy Russell, accompanied by Paul Weston's Orchestra (Capitol). The song was on "Your Hit Parade" for seventeen weeks, six times in the #1 position.

Anniversary Waltz, The. w. Al Dubin, m. Dave Franklin, 1941. Introduced and bestseller recorded by Bing Crosby (Decca). Not to be confused with "Anniversary Song."

Another. w. Vic McAlpin, m. Roy Drusky, 1960. Top 10 Country record by Roy Drusky (Decca).

Another Autumn. w. Alan Jay Lerner, m. Frederick Loewe, 1951. Introduced by Tony Bavaar in (TM) *Paint Your Wagon*. Not used in film.

Another Brick in the Wall. w/m Roger Waters, 1980. #1 gold record, from the platinum LP "The Wall," by the English rock band Pink Floyd (Columbia).

Another Bridge to Burn. w/m Harlan Howard, 1963. Chart Country song by "Little" Jimmy Dickens (Columbia).

Another Cup of Coffee. w. Earl Shuman, m. Leon Carr, 1964. Introduced and recorded by Brook Benton (Mercury).

Another Day. w/m Paul McCartney and Linda McCartney, 1971. Top 10 record by Paul McCartney (Apple).

Another Day, Another Heartache. w/m P. F. Sloan and Steve Barri, 1967. Recorded by The 5th Dimension (Soul City).

Another Girl. w/m John Lennon and Paul McCartney, 1965. Introduced by The Beatles in (MM) *Help!*

Another Honky Tonk Night on Broadway. w/m Milton L. Brown, Stephen H. Dorff, and Snuff Garrett, 1982. Top 10 Country chart record by David Frizzell and Shelly West (Warner Bros.)

Another Hundred People. w/m Stephen Sondheim, 1970. Sung by Pamela Myers and company in (TM) *Company*.

Another Lonely Song. w/m Tammy Wynette, Billy Sherrill, and Norro Wilson, 1974. Country chart hit record by Tammy Wynette (Epic).

Another Night. w. Hal David, m. Burt Bacharach, 1966. Recorded by Dionne Warwick (Scepter).

Another Night Like This. w. Harry Ruby (Engl.), Ernesto Lecuona (Sp.), m. Ernesto Lecuona, 1947. Lecuona's original Cuban song was titled "En Una Noche Asi." English lyric written for and introduced by Dick Haymes in (MM) *Carnival in Costa Rica*. Recorded by Haymes (Decca) and Desi Arnaz and his Orchestra (Victor).

Another One Bites the Dust. w/m John Deacon, 1980. #1 platinum single from the platinum album by the English group Queen (Elektra).

Another Op'nin', Another Show. w/m Cole Porter, 1949. Introduced by Annabelle Hill and ensemble in (TM) *Kiss Me Kate*. Song not used in film version.

Another Place, Another Time. w/m Jerry Chesnut, 1968. C&W hit and Pop chart record by Jerry Lee Lewis (Smash).

Another Rag. m. Theodore F. Morse, 1911.

Another Saturday Night. w/m Sam Cooke, 1963. Introduced and hit record by Sam Cooke (RCA). Revived with Top 10 record by Cat Stevens (A&M), 1974.

Another Sleepless Night. w/m Rory Bourke and Charlie Black, 1982. Recorded by Anne Murray (Capitol).

Another Sleepless Night. w. Howard Greenfield, m. Neil Sedaka, 1960. Recorded by Jimmy Clanton (Ace).

Another Somebody Done Somebody Wrong Song. See **Hey, Won't You Play Another Somebody Done Somebody Wrong Song.**

Another Time, Another Place. w/m Mike Leander and Edward Seago, 1971. Written in England and recorded by Engelbert Humperdinck (Parrot).

Another Time, Another Place. w/m Jay Livingston and Ray Evans, 1958. Title song of (MP) *Another Time, Another Place*. Leading record by Patti Page (Mercury).

Another World. w/m John Leffler and Ralph Schuckett, 1987. Theme of the daytime soap opera (TVP) "Another World." Top 10 Country chart record by Crystal Gayle and Gary Morris (Warner Bros.).

Answer Me, My Love. w. Carl Sigman (Engl.), w. (Ger.) and m. Gerhard Winkler and Fred Rauch, 1954. Top 10 record by Nat "King" Cole (Capitol).

Answer to Rainbow at Midnight. w/m Lost John Miller, 1946. Sequel to "Rainbow at

Midnight," both recorded by Ernest Tubb (Decca).

Anticipation. w/m Carly Simon, 1972. Top 20 single by Carly Simon (Elektra).

Anticipation Blues. w/m Ernie Ford and Cliffie Stone, 1950. Introduced and recorded by Tennessee Ernie Ford (Capitol).

Anybody But Me. w/m Ronnie Self and Dub Allbritten, 1960. Coupled with hit record, "Fool #1" by Brenda Lee (Decca).

Any Bonds Today? w/m Irving Berlin, 1941. The official song of the U.S. Defense Bond program. Introduced and featured by Barry Wood. Recorded by The Andrews Sisters with Jimmy Dorsey and his Orchestra (Decca).

Any Day Now. w/m Bob Hilliard and Burt Bacharach, 1963. Popularized by Chuck Jackson (Wand). Revived by Ronnie Milsap (RCA), 1982.

Any Little Girl That's a Nice Little Girl Is the Right Little Girl for Me. w. Thomas J. Gray, m. Fred Fisher, 1910. Popular record by Billy Murray and the American Quartette (Victor).

Any Love. w/m Luther Vandross and Marcus Miller, 1988. Recorded by Luther Vandross (Epic).

Any Moment Now. w. E. Y. Harburg, m. Jerome Kern, 1944. Introduced by Deanna Durbin in (MM) *Can't Help Singing*, and recorded by her, coupled with "More and More" from the same film (Decca).

Anymore. w/m Roy Drusky, Vic McAlpin, and Marie Wilson, 1960. Introduced and hit C&W record by Roy Drusky (Decca). Pop cover by Teresa Brewer (Coral).

Any Old Place I Hang My Hat Is Home Sweet Home to Me. w. William Jerome, m. Jean Schwartz, 1901. Popular recording by Will Denny (Gram-o-Phone).

Any Old Place with You. w. Lorenz Hart, m. Richard Rodgers, 1919. This was the first published Rodgers and Hart song and their first to be performed on Broadway. It was sung by Eve Lynn and Alan Hale in (TM) *A Lonely Romeo*. While the song was not a hit, it caused attention because of its lyrical and musical originality and, to quote Rodgers, its "ending with the sure-fire laugh getter, 'I'd go to hell for ya, / Or Philadelphia!' "

Any Old Port in a Storm. w. Arthur J. Lamb, m. Kerry Mills, 1908. A nautical number introduced in *Cohan and Harris's Minstrel Show*. Leading recording by Frank Stanley (Victor).

Any Old Time. w/m Artie Shaw, 1938. Recorded by Artie Shaw, vocal by Billie Holliday (Bluebird).

Any Old Time. w/m Jimmie Rodgers, 1930. Introduced by Rodgers (Victor). Webb Pierce revived it with a hit Country record (Decca), 1956.

Anyone Can Whistle. w/m Stephen Sondheim, 1964. Introduced by Lee Remick in (TM) *Anyone Can Whistle*.

Anyone Who Had a Heart. w. Hal David, m. Burt Bacharach, 1964. Hit record by Dionne Warwick (Scepter).

Anyone Who Isn't Me Tonight. w/m Casey Kelly and Julie Didier, 1978. Top 10 Country record by Kenny Rogers and Dottie West (United Artists).

Anyone Would Love You. w/m Harold Rome, 1959. Introduced by Andy Griffith and Dolores Gray in (TM) *Destry Rides Again*.

Any Other Way. w. Ben Tarver and John Clifton, m. John Clifton, 1966. Introduced by Lesslie Nicole and Tom Noel in (TM) *Man With a Load of Mischief*. Recorded by Annette Sanders (Monmouth-Evergreen).

Any Place I Hang My Hat Is Home. w. Johnny Mercer, m. Harold Arlen, 1946. Introduced by Robert Pope and Ruby Hill in (TM) *St. Louis Woman*.

Any Place the Old Flag Flies. w/m George M. Cohan, 1911. Sung by Cohan in (TM) *The Little Millionaire.*

Any Rags? w/m Thomas S. Allen, 1902. Novelty hit about a rag picker. Popular in vaudeville. Leading record by Arthur Collins (Victor).

Anything Can Happen Mambo. w. Sid Wayne, m. Joe Sherman, 1954. Featured and recorded by Dolores Hawkins (Epic).

Anything for You. w/m Gloria Estefan, 1988. #1 single by Gloria Estefan and Miami Sound Machine, from the album "Let It Loose" (Epic).

(I Would Do) Anything for You. w/m Alex Hill, Bob Williams, and Claude Hopkins, 1932. Recorded by and the theme song of Claude Hopkins and his Band (Columbia). This standard has enjoyed many recordings. Among them: Benny Goodman (Victor); Jimmie Noone (Vocalion); Red Norvo (Brunswick); Frankie Laine (Mercury); the Page Cavanaugh Trio (Victor).

Anything Goes. w/m Cole Porter, 1934. Introduced by Ethel Merman, with The Foursome in (TM) *Anything Goes.* She sang it in the first film version (MM) *Anything Goes,* 1936. It was heard orchestrally in the Porter biography (MM) *Night and Day,* 1946, and was sung by Mitzi Gaynor in the 1956 remake (MM) *Anything Goes.* Revived by the quintet Harpers Bizarre (Warner Bros.), 1967.

Anything That's Part of You. w/m Don Robertson, 1962. Recorded by Elvis Presley (RCA).

Anything You Can Do. w/m Irving Berlin, 1946. Introduced by Ethel Merman and Ray Middleton in (TM) *Annie Get Your Gun.* In the film version (MM) *Annie Get Your Gun,* 1950, it was sung by Betty Hutton and Howard Keel.

Anything Your Heart Desires. w/m Billy Walker, 1967. Top 10 Country chart record by Billy Walker (Monument).

Anything You Say. w/m Walter Donaldson, 1928. Recorded by Cliff "Ukulele Ike" Edwards (Columbia).

Any Time (a.k.a. **Anytime**). w/m Herbert Happy Lawson, 1921, 1948, 1950. This song had a moderate success when first published. In 1948, Eddie Arnold revived it and had a million-selling country record (Victor). In 1951, Eddie Fisher had his first million-seller and the song was on "Your Hit Parade" for seventeen weeks.

Anytime. See **Any Time**.

Anytime (I'll Be There). w/m Paul Anka, 1975. First chart record by Frank Sinatra (Reprise), followed by Paul Anka (United Artists), 1976.

Any Time, Any Place, Anywhere. w/m Johnny Morris and Laurie Tate, 1950. #1 R&B record by Johnny Morris and Laurie Tate (Atlantic).

Anytime At All. w/m Baker Knight, 1965. Leading record by Frank Sinatra (Reprise).

Any Time's Kissing Time. w. Oscar Asche, m. Frederic Norton, 1917. From the American production of (TM) *Chu Chin Chow,* which was a London hit in 1916.

Any Way the Wind Blows. w/m William Dunham, Joseph Hooven, and Marilyn Hooven, 1960. Introduced by Doris Day in (MP) *Please Don't Eat the Daisies,* and recorded by her, with Frank DeVol's Orchestra (Columbia).

Any Way You Want It. w/m Steve Perry and Neil Schon, 1980. Recorded by the group Journey (Columbia).

Any Way You Want It. w/m Dave Clark, 1964. Hit record by The Dave Clark Five (Epic).

Any Way You Want Me (That's How I Will Be). w/m Aaron Schroeder and Cliff Owens, 1956. Recorded by Elvis Presley (RCA).

Anywhere. w. Sammy Cahn, m. Jule Styne, 1945. Introduced by Janet Blair in (MM) *To-*

night and Every Night. Nominated for an Academy Award. Also heard in (MM) *Glamour Girl*, 1947.

Anywhere I Wander. w/m Frank Loesser, 1952. Introduced by Danny Kaye in (MM) *Hans Christian Andersen*. Mel Tormé had an early chart record (Capitol), but Julius LaRosa, who featured it on the Arthur Godfrey TV and radio shows and recorded it with Archie Bleyer's Orchestra, had the best-seller (Cadence).

Apache. m. Jerry Lordan, 1961. Introduced in England by The Shadows (Br. Columbia). Hit instrumental in the U.S. by Jordan Ingmann and His Guitar (Atco).

Apache '65. m. Jerry Lordan and Albert Carmen, 1965. Instrumental recorded by The Arrows (Tower).

Apalachicola, Fla. w. Johnny Burke, m. James Van Heusen, 1947. Introduced by Bing Crosby and Bob Hope in (MM) *Road to Rio*.

Apartment, The. See **Theme from the Apartment.**

Apeman. w/m Ray Davies, 1971. Recorded by the British group The Kinks (Reprise).

Apollo Jump. m. Ernest Puree, Prince Robinson, and Lucius "Lucky" Millinder, 1943. Introduced and recorded by Lucky Millinder and his Orchestra (Decca).

Apple Blossoms and Chapel Bells. w/m Al Hoffman, Walter Kent, and Mann Curtis, 1940. Leading record by Orrin Tucker, singing with his Orchestra (Columbia).

Apple Blossom Wedding, An. w. Jimmy Kennedy, m. Nat Simon, 1947. Most popular records by Sammy Kaye, vocal by Don Cornell (RCA Victor); Eddy Howard, with his Orchestra (Majestic); Buddy Clark, with Mitchell Ayres's Orchestra (Columbia).

Apple Doesn't Fall, The. w. Fred Ebb, m. John Kander, 1984. Introduced by Chita Rivera and Liza Minnelli in (TM) *The Rink*.

Apple Dumpling Gang, The. w. Byron Berline, m. Bruce Langhorne, 1975. Title song, sung on the soundtrack of (MP) *The Apple Dumpling Gang*.

Apple for the Teacher, An. w. Johnny Burke, m. James V. Monaco, 1939. Introduced by Bing Crosby and Linda Ware in (MM) *The Star Maker*. Crosby and Connie Boswell then recorded it (Decca).

Apple Green. w/m Charles Singleton, 1960. Featured and recorded by June Valli (Mercury).

Apple Honey. m. Woody Herman, 1945. Instrumental, introduced by Woody Herman and his Orchestra (Columbia). The Herman band played it in (MM) *Earl Carroll Vanities*, 1945.

Apple of My Eye. w/m Roy Head, 1965. Recorded by Roy Head (Back Beat).

Apples, Peaches, Pumpkin Pie. w/m Maurice Irby, Jr., 1967. Top 10 record by Jay and The Techniques (Smash).

Apricot Brandy. m. Michael Fonfara and Danny Weis, 1969. Chart instrumental by the rock group Rhinoceros (Elektra).

April Fools, The. w. Hal David, m. Burt Bacharach, 1969. The song was written for (MP) *April Fools*, but used only in the soundtrack album, performed by Percy Faith, his Orchestra and Chorus (Columbia). Dionne Warwick had a Top 40 single (Scepter).

April in Fairbanks. w/m Murray Grand, 1956. Introduced by Jane Connell in (TM) *New Faces of 1956*.

April in My Heart. w/m Helen Meinard and Hoagy Carmichael, 1938. From (MP) *Say It in French*. Recorded by Cab Calloway (Vocalion); Billie Holiday, with Teddy Wilson's combo (Brunswick); Francis Langford (Decca).

April in Paris. w. E. Y. Harburg, m. Vernon Duke, 1932. Introduced by Evelyn Hoey in (TM) *Walk a Little Faster*. Hoey died during the run of the show and the song was then sung by another leading member of the company, John Hundley. Doris Day sang it with Claude Dauphin in (MM) *April in Paris*, 1953. Among the many recordings: Doris Day (Columbia), Buster Bailey (Varsity), Vic Damone (Mercury), Will Bradley (Columbia), Freddy Martin (Brunswick), the Sauter-Finegan Orchestra (Victor), Thelonious Monk (Blue Note), Coleman Hawkins (Victor). The band most associated with the song is that of Count Basie's, which recorded it three times (Verve) (Crest) (Dot). The Dot recording was with the Mills Brothers, produced by Tom Mack.

April in Portugal. w. Jimmy Kennedy (Engl.), m. Raul Ferrao, 1953. Original Portuguese words and title "Coimbra" by José Galhardo. Instrumental hit record by Les Baxter and his Orchestra (Capitol). Other chart recordings by Vic Damone (Mercury); Richard Hayman and his Orchestra (Mercury); Freddy Martin and his Orchestra (RCA Victor); Tony Martin, with Lennie Hayton's Orchestra (RCA Victor).

April Love. w. Paul Francis Webster, m. Sammy Fain, 1957. Introduced by Pat Boone in (MM) *April Love* and nominated for Academy Award, 1957. Boone's recording was a #1 hit (Dot).

April Played the Fiddle. w. Johnny Burke, m. James V. Monaco, 1940. Introduced in (MM) *If I Had My Way* and on records (Decca) by Bing Crosby.

April Showers. w. B. G. DeSylva, m. Louis Silvers, 1921. Interpolated by Al Jolson in (TM) *Bombo* at the Winter Garden in New York and recorded by him (Columbia). He sang it on the soundtracks of (MM) *The Jolson Story*, 1946 and (MM) *Jolson Sings Again*, 1949. His new recording (Decca), 1946, sold over a million copies. It was the title song of (MM) *April Showers*, 1948, sung by Ann Sothern and Jack Carson.

Apurksody. m. Gene Krupa, 1938. Theme song of, and recorded by, Gene Krupa and his Orchestra (Okeh). The title combines Krupa,

in reverse, with the last two syllables of "rhapsody."

Aqua Boogie (A Psychoalphadiscobeta-bioaquadoloop). w/m George Clinton, William Collins, and Bernie Worrell, 1978. Recorded by Parliament, "A Parliafunka-delicament Thang," which the group claims stands for a musical entity recording under various names (Casablanca).

Aquarius. w. Gerome Ragni and James Rado, m. Galt MacDermot, 1967. Introduced by the company in the off-Broadway production of (TM) *Hair*. In the Broadway production, 1968, it was sung by Ronald Dyson and company. The 5th Dimension had a #1 gold record of the song in medley with "Let the Sunshine In" (Soul City), 1969.

Araby. w/m Irving Berlin, 1915. Featured by Eddie Cantor in vaudeville. Leading record by Harry MacDonough (Victor).

Arc of a Diver. w/m Steve Winwood and Vivian Stanshall, 1981. Recorded by the English singer, Steve Winwood (Island).

Aren't You Glad You're You? w. Johnny Burke, m. James Van Heusen, 1945. Introduced by Bing Crosby in (MM) *The Bells of St. Mary's*. Crosby had the leading recording (Decca). Song nominated for Academy Award.

Aren't You Kind of Glad We Did? w. Ira Gershwin, m. George Gershwin, 1947. A 30s melody by George, added posthumously with a new lyric by Ira to the score of (MM) *The Shocking Miss Pilgrim*, in which it was introduced by Dick Haymes and Betty Grable.

Are the Good Times Really Over (I Wish a Buck Was Still Silver). w/m Merle Haggard, 1982. Top 10 Country chart record by Merle Haggard (Epic).

Are These Really Mine? w/m Sunny Skylar, David Saxon, and Robert Cook, 1945. Featured and recorded by Vaughn Monroe, with his Orchestra (Victor).

Are We Ourselves? w/m Cy Curnin, Jamie West-Oram, Dan K. Brown, and Adam

Brown, 1984. Recorded by the British group, The Fixx (MCA).

Are You Ever Gonna Love Me. w/m Tom Shapiro and Chris Waters, 1989. Hit Country single by Holly Dunn (Warner Bros.).

Are You From Dixie? ('Cause I'm From Dixie, Too). w. Jack Yellen, m. George L. Cobb, 1915. Yellen's first hit, given a big push by the popular recording by Billy Murray and Irving Kaufman (Victor). Revived by Freddie "Schnicklefritz" Fisher and his Band (Decca) 1951.

Are You Happy? w/m Theresa Bell, Jerry Butler, and Kenny Gamble, 1969. Top 40 record by Jerry Butler (Mercury).

Are You Happy, Baby. w/m Bob Stone, 1981. #1 Country chart record by Dottie West (Liberty).

Are You Havin' Any Fun? w. Jack Yellen, m. Sammy Fain, 1939. Introduced by Ella Logan, the Kim Loo Sisters, and the Three Stooges in (TM) *George White's Scandals* (1939 Edition). Logan had a popular record (Columbia), as did Tommy Dorsey, vocal by Edythe Wright (Victor).

Are You in the Mood for Mischief? w. Mack Gordon, m. Harry Revel, 1938. Introduced by Alice Faye in (MP) *Tailspin*.

Are You Lonely for Me? w/m Bert Berns, 1967. Recorded by Freddie Scott (Shout).

Are You Lonesome Tonight? w. Roy Turk, m. Lou Handman, 1927, 1960. First hit recordings by Vaughn DeLeath (Edison), Henry Burr (Victor), and Little Jack Little (Columbia). Revived by Elvis Presley with a #1 record (Victor), 1960. Donny Osmond had a popular version (MGM), 1973. Song was in (MM) *Elvis*, 1979, dubbed on the soundtrack by Ronnie McDowell for Kurt Russell in the title role.

Are You Makin' Any Money? w/m Herman Hupfeld, 1933. Sung by Lillian Miles in (MM) *Moonlight and Pretzels*. Recorded by

Paul Whiteman and his Orchestra, vocal by Ramona (Victor).

Are You Man Enough? w/m Dennis Lambert and Brian Potter, 1973. Sung by The Four Tops on the soundtrack of (MP) *Shaft in Africa*, and on records (Dunhill).

Are You Mine? w. Don Grashey, m. Jim Amadeo and Myrna Petrunka, 1955. Introduced and recorded and Top 10 C&W chart record by Myrna Lorrie and Buddy DeVal (Abbott). Lorrie was pseudonym for thirteen-year-old co-composer Petrunka. Cover record and #2 C&W chart hit by Ginny Wright and Tom Tall (Fabor); chart record also by Red Sovine and Goldie Hill (Decca).

Are You on the Road to Lovin' Me Again? w/m Deborah Kay Hupp and Robert Morrison, 1980. #1 Country chart record by Debby Boone (Warner Brothers).

Are You Ready? w/m Charlie Allen and John Hill, 1970. Top 20 record by the quintet, Pacific Gas and Electric (Columbia).

Are You Ready for the Country? w/m Neil Young, 1976. Hit Country record by Waylon Jennings (RCA).

Are You Really Mine? w/m Al Hoffman, Dick Manning, and Mark Markwell, 1958. Top 10 record by Jimmie Rodgers (Roulette).

Are You Satisfied? w/m Sheb Wooley and Escamilla Homer, 1956. Featured and recorded by Rusty Draper (Mercury).

Are You Sincere? w/m Wayne Walker, 1958. Popularized by Andy Williams (Cadence).

Are You Sincere? w. Alfred Bryan, m. Albert Gumble, 1908.

Are You Single? w/m Steve Washington, Curt Jones, Starleanna Young, Philip Fields, and J. Ivory, 1981. R&B chart record by the group Aurra (Salsoul).

Are You Sorry? w. Benny Davis, m. Milton Ager, 1925.

Are You Sure Hank Done It This Way? w/m Waylon Jennings, 1975. Country hit and Pop chart record by Waylon Jennings (RCA).

Are You Teasing Me? w/m Ira Louvin and Charles Louvin, 1952. Featured and recorded by Carl Smith (Columbia).

Are You There (with Another Girl)? w. Hal David, m. Burt Bacharach, 1966. Recorded by Dionne Warwick (Scepter).

Are You Willing, Willie? w/m Marion Worth, 1960. Country chart record by Marion Worth (Columbia).

Are You With It? w. Arnold Horwitt, m. Harry Revel, 1945. Introduced by Dolores Gray in (TM) *Are You With It?* Recorded by June Richmond (Mercury).

Ariel. w/m Dean Friedman, 1977. Recorded by Dean Friedman (Lifesong).

Arizona. w/m Kenny Young, 1970. Top 10 gold record by Mark Lindsay (Columbia).

Arkansas Blues. w/m Anton Lada and Spencer Williams, 1921. Featured and recorded by blues singer Lucille Hegamin and her Blue Flame Syncopators (Banner). Among other versions: Little Ramblers (Columbia); The Goofus Five (Okeh).

Armen's Theme (a.k.a. **Yesterday and You).** w/m Ross Bagdasarian, 1956. Leading instrumental records by the orchestras of David Seville, pseudonym for Bagdasarian (Liberty) and Joe Reisman (RCA). Titled for the composer's wife, Armen. Bobby Vee had a chart record in 1963, when lyrics were added with new title, "Yesterday and You" (Liberty).

Arm in Arm. w/m Meredith Willson, 1963. Introduced by Janis Paige and Valerie Lee in (TM) *Here's Love.*

Arms for the Love of America (The Army Ordnance Song). w/m Irving Berlin, 1941. The subtitle explains the substance of the march.

Arms of Mary. w/m Iain Sutherland, 1976. Recorded by the English duo and group The Sutherland Brothers and Quiver (Columbia). The Canadian group, Chilliwack, had a chart version (Mushroom), 1978.

Army Air Corps, The. w/m Robert M. Crawford, 1939, 1943. The official song of the Air Corps during World War II. After the Corps became a service of its own, the song was retitled "The U.S. Air Force," Among recordings, mostly in 1943, were those by: Dick Powell (Decca); Alvino Rey and his Orchestra (Bluebird); John Charles Thomas (Victor); Skitch Henderson and his Orchestra (Capitol); Major Glenn Miller and the AAF Orchestra (12″ V–disc). It was featured prominently in (TM) *Winged Victory*, the Air Force production, 1943 and (MM) *Ice-Capade Revue* and (MM) *Follow the Band*, 1943.

Around The Corner. w. Gus Kahn, m. Art Kassel, 1930. Featured by Art Kassel and Rudy Vallee.

A–Round the Corner (Beneath the Berry Tree). w/m Josef Marais, 1952. Adaptation of the South African folk song. Top recordings by Jo Stafford (Capitol); the Weavers with Gordon Jenkins's Orchestra (Decca).

Around the World. w. Harold Adamson, m. Victor Young, 1957. Theme from Michael Todd's (MP) *Around the World in 80 Days.* Best-selling records, instrumental: the orchestras of Victor Young (Decca) and Mantovani (London); vocal: Bing Crosby (Decca) and The McGuire Sisters (Coral).

Arrah Go On, I'm Gonna Go Back to Oregon. w. Sam M. Lewis and Joe Young, m. Bert Grant, 1916. Introduced by Maggie Cline. Top record by The Peerless Quartet (Victor).

Arrah Wanna. w. Jack Drislane, m. Theodore F. Morse, 1906. Song referred to marriage plans discussed by an Irish man and an American woman. Recorded by Billy Murray (Victor) and Arthur Collins (Columbia).

Arrested for Driving While Blind. w/m Frank Beard, Billy Gibbons, and Joe

37

Hill, 1977. Written and recorded by the trio ZZ Top (London).

Arrivederci, Roma (Goodbye to Rome). w. Carl Sigman (Engl.), m. Renato Ranucci, 1955. First popular recording by Georgia Gibbs (Mercury). In 1958, Mario Lanza sang it in (MM) *Seven Hills of Rome*. His performance was released on records (RCA). Pianist Roger Williams also had a chart version (Kapp), 1958.

Arrow Through Me. w/m Paul McCartney, 1979. Recorded by McCartney's group Wings (Columbia).

Art for Art's Sake. w/m Graham Gouldman and Eric Stewart, 1975. Written by two members of the English group 10cc (Mercury).

Arthur Murray Taught Me Dancing in a Hurry. w. Johnny Mercer, m. Victor Schertzinger, 1942. Introduced by Betty Hutton in (MM) *The Fleet's In*, Schertzinger's last score. He died in October of the previous year after composing the songs and directing the film. Best-selling records by Jimmy Dorsey, vocal by Helen O'Connell (Decca), and the King Sisters (Bluebird).

Arthur's Theme (the Best That You Can Do). w. Carole Bayer Sager, w/m Christopher Cross, Peter Allen, m. Burt Bacharach, 1981. Introduced on the soundtrack of (MP) *Arthur* by Christopher Cross. Winner Academy Award. #1 gold record single by Christopher Cross (Warner Bros.).

Artificial Flowers. w. Sheldon Harnick, m. Jerry Bock, 1960. Introduced by Ron Husmann and chorus in (TM) *Tenderloin*. Popular recording by Bobby Darin (Atco).

Artificial Rose. w/m Tom T. Hall, 1965. Country hit recorded by Jimmy Newman (Decca).

Artistry in Rhythm. m. Stan Kenton, 1944. Instrumental theme song of Stan Kenton and his Orchestra. His recording was a million-seller (Capitol).

As Deep as the Deep Blue Sea. w. René Bronner, m. H. W. Petrie, 1910.

As Far as I'm Concerned. w/m Dale Parker, 1954. Country hit by Red Foley (Decca).

Ashby de la Zooch. w/m Milton Drake, Al Hoffman, and Jerry Livingston, 1966. Featured and recorded by The Merry Macs (Decca).

Asia. w. E. Ray Goetz, m. John Lindsay, 1913. From the Lew Fields musical (TM) *All Aboard*.

Asia Minor. m. Roger King Mozian, 1961. Instrumental introduced in 1951 by Machito and his Orchestra (Mercury). Popularized by Kokomo (Felsted) in 1961.

As If I Didn't Know. w/m Jerry Samuels and Larry Kusik, 1961. Leading record by Adam Wade (Coed).

Ask Anyone In Love. w/m Susan Shapiro and Ted Shapiro, 1960. Featured and recorded by Tony Bennett (Columbia).

Ask Anyone Who Knows. w/m Eddie Seiler, Sol Marcus, and Al Kaufman, 1947. Popular recordings by The Ink Spots (Decca); Margaret Whiting (Capitol); Anita Ellis (Mercury).

Ask Her While the Band is Playing. w. Glen MacDonough, m. Victor Herbert, 1908. From (TM) *Algeria*, which was revised and retitled *The Rose of Algeria* the following year.

Asking for You. w. Betty Comden and Adolph Green, m. Jule Styne, 1960. Introduced by John Reardon in (TM) *Do Re Mi*.

Ask Me. w. Bill Giant, Florence Kaye, Bernie Baum (Engl.), m. Domenico Modugno, 1964. Modugno originally wrote the song in Italy (with his Italian words) in 1958. Elvis Presley's English version was released in 1964 (RCA).

Ask Me. w. Sunny Skylar (Engl.), Carl Niessen (Ger.), m. Heino Gaze, 1956. Featured and recorded by Nat "King" Cole (Capitol).

Ask Me Nice. w/m Mose Allison, 1961. Recorded by Mose Allison (Columbia).

Ask Me No Questions. w/m Riley B. "B. B." King, 1971. Recorded by B. B. King (ABC).

Ask the Lonely. w/m William Stevenson and Ivy Hunter, 1965. R&B and Pop hit by The Four Tops (Motown).

Ask the Man in the Moon. w. J. Cheever Goodwin, m. Woolson Morse, 1891. Introduced by De Wolf Hopper in (TM) *Wang*.

Ask the Stars. w. Frank Stammers, m. Harold Orlob, 1919. From (TM) *Nothing But Love*.

A—Sleepin' at the Foot of the Bed. w/m Teddy McRae and Wynonie Harris, 1949. Leading recording by Wynonie Harris (King).

Asleep in the Deep. w. Arthur J. Lamb, m. H. W. Petrie, 1897. A bass singer's delight, with its downward scale ending on the lowest note of the song and the last syllable of the word "beware."

As Long As He Needs Me. w/m Lionel Bart, 1963. Introduced by Georgia Brown in the London production, and then in New York in (TM) *Oliver!* Shani Wallace sang it in (MM) *Oliver!* 1968.

As Long As He Takes Care of Home. w/m Philip Mitchell, 1975. Recorded by Candi Staton (Warner Bros.).

As Long As I Have You. w. Neville Fleeson, m. Albert Von Tilzer, 1922. From (TM) *The Gingham Girl*.

As Long As I Know He's Mine. w/m William Robinson, Jr., 1963. Crossover (R&B/Pop) record by The Marvelettes (Tamla).

As Long As I Live. w/m Alex Zanetis, 1968. Top 10 Country record by George Jones (Musicor).

As Long As I Live. w/m Roy Acuff, 1955. Top 10 Country hit by Kitty Wells and Red Foley (Decca). Acuff wrote and introduced the song ten years earlier.

As Long As I Live. w. Ted Koehler, m. Harold Arlen, 1934. Introduced by Lena Horne (at age sixteen) and Avon Long in the revue, *The Cotton Club Parade*, at the Cotton Club in Harlem, New York. Arlen recorded it, coupled with "Ill Wind," from the same revue (Victor).

As Long As I'm Dreaming. w. Johnny Burke, m. James Van Heusen, 1947. Introduced by Bing Crosby in (MM) *Welcome Stranger*. Leading records by Crosby (Decca); Tex Beneke and the Glenn Miller Orchestra, vocal by Garry Stevens (RCA Victor).

As Long As the Shamrock Grows Green. w. James Brickman, m. Nat Osborne, 1912. Recorded by Walter Van Brunt (Victor).

As Long As There's Music. w. Sammy Cahn, m. Jule Styne, 1944. Introduced by Frank Sinatra in (MM) *Step Lively*, musical version of *Room Service*.

As Long As the World Rolls On. w. George Graff, Jr., m. Ernest R. Ball, 1907. Popular records by Alan Turner (Victor); Reinald Werrenrath (Edison); Henry Burr (Columbia); The Peerless Quartet (Zon-o-Phone).

As Long As We Got Each Other. w. John Bettis, m. Steven Dorff, 1985. Sung by B. J. Thomas as theme of series (TVP) "Growing Pains."

As Simple As That. w/m Jerry Herman, 1961. Introduced by Mimi Benzell and Robert Weede in (TM) *Milk and Honey*.

As Tears Go By. w/m Mick Jagger and Keith Richards, 1964. English song first released in the U.S. by Marianne Faithfull (London). In 1966, the British group, The Rolling Stones (of which the writers were members), had a Top 10 U.S. release (London).

As the Girls Go. w. Harold Adamson, m. Jimmy McHugh, 1948. Introduced by Bobby Clark in (TM) *As the Girls Go*.

As Time Goes By. w/m Herman Hupfeld, 1931, 1942. Introduced by Frances Williams in (TM) *Everybody's Welcome*, based on the play *Up Pops the Devil*. Although it received some popularity through Rudy Vallee's recording and radio broadcasts, it was not until 1942, when Dooley Wilson sang it at the piano at Rick's Place in (MP) *Casablanca*, that it attained its standing as one of the all-time favorites. In its revival, the song was on "Your Hit Parade" for twenty-one weeks.

As Usual. w/m Alex Zanetis, 1963. Featured and recorded by Brenda Lee (Decca).

As We Walk into the Sunset. w/m Charlie Abbott, 1941. Featured and recorded by the bands of Tommy Dorsey (Victor); Sonny Dunham (Bluebird); Jan Savitt (Victor).

As You Desire Me. w/m Allie Wrubel, 1932. Wrubel's first big hit. Popularized on radio and records by Russ Columbo (Victor); also by Donald Novis (Victor), and Arthur Tracy, "The Street Singer." (Brunswick). Sarah Vaughan, later, had a notable recording (Columbia).

At a Georgia Camp Meeting. w/m Kerry Mills, 1897. Originally an instrumental two-step. The song and dance team of Genaro and Bailey extended it into a routine that became one of the first major cakewalk hits.

At a Perfume Counter. w. Edgar Leslie, m. Joe Burke, 1938. Introduced by Morton Downey and Wini Shaw at Billy Rose's Casa Mañana, a New York nightclub. Recorded by Jimmy Dorsey, vocal by Bob Eberly (Decca); Blue Barron, vocal by Russ Carlyle (Bluebird); Dave Brubeck (Fantasy).

At a Sidewalk Penny Arcade. w/m Martin Kalmanoff, Jimmy MacDonald, Aaron Schroeder, and Eddie White, 1948. Featured and recorded by Sammy Kaye and his Orchestra (RCA Victor).

At Dawning. w. Nelle Richmond Eberhart, m. Charles Wakefield Cadman, 1906. A concert song that attained great popularity. It has had numerous recordings by such artists as: Jesse Crawford, the organist (Victor); The Victor Herbert Orchestra (Victor); John McCor-

mack (Victor); Paul Robeson (Victor); John Charles Thomas (Brunswick).

"A" Team, The. w/m Leonard Whitcup, Barry Sadler, and Phyllis G. Landsberg, 1966. Recorded by S/Sgt. Barry Sadler (RCA).

At Ease, Heart. w/m Jimmy Jay, 1966. Country chart record by Ernie Ashworth (Hickory).

Athena. w/m Peter Townshend, 1982. Recorded by the British group The Who (Warner Bros.).

A-Tisket A-Tasket. w/m Al Feldman (Van Alexander) and Ella Fitzgerald, 1938. Based on nursery rhyme. Popularized by Ella Fitzgerald with Chick Webb's Orchestra (Decca). Fitzgerald sang it in (MM) *Ride Em Cowboy*, 1942, and June Allyson and Gloria De Haven sang it in (MM) *Two Girls and a Sailor*, 1944.

Atlanta, G. A. w. Sunny Skylar, m. Arthur Shaftel, 1946. Leading recordings by Sammy Kaye, vocal by Billy Williams (Victor), and Woody Herman, with his Orchestra (Columbia).

Atlanta Blues. w/m W. C. Handy, 1924. Recorded by Sara Martin, with Clarence Williams (Okeh), and later by Eddie Condon (Decca), 1939.

Atlantis. w/m Donoval Leitch, 1969. Top 10 U.S. release by the Scottish singer/writer, Donovan (Epic).

At Last. w. Mack Gordon, m. Harry Warren, 1942. Introduced in (MM) *Orchestra Wives* by Glenn Miller and his Orchestra, Lynn Bari (voice dubbed on sound track by Pat Friday) and Ray Eberle. Miller had a hit record, vocal by Eberle (Bluebird). In 1952, Ray Anthony, vocal by Tommy Mercer, had a Top 10 record (Capitol). Revived by Etta James (Argo), 1961.

At Least You Could Say Hello. w/m Sammy Mysels, Dick Robertson, and Charles McCarthy, 1939. Featured and recorded by Larry

Clinton, vocal by Terry Allen (Victor), and Jack Teagarden, vocal by Kitty Kallen (Columbia).

At Long Last Love. w/m Cole Porter, 1938. Introduced by Clifton Webb in (TM) *You Never Know*. The song served as the title of the all-Cole Porter film (MM) *At Long Last Love*, sung by Burt Reynolds, Cybill Shepherd, Madeline Kahn, and Duilio Del Prete, in 1975.

At Mail Call Today. w/m Gene Autry and Fred Rose, 1945. #1 Best-selling C&W record by Gene Autry (Okeh), followed by Red Foley, with Lawrence Welk's Orchestra (Decca).

At Midnight (My Love Will Lift You Up). w/m Tony Maiden and Lalomie Washburn, 1977. Recorded by Rufus featuring Chaka Khan (ABC).

At My Front Door (Crazy Little Mama Song). w/m John C. Moore and Ewart G. Abner, Jr., 1955. R&B hit for The El Dorados (Vee-Jay) and Top 10 Pop hit for Pat Boone (Dot). Revived with a chart record by Dee Clark in 1960 (Abner).

Atomic. w/m Deborah Harry and James Mollica III, 1980. Single from the album "Eat to the Beat" by the group Blondie (Chrysalis).

At Peace with the World. w/m Irving Berlin, 1926. Introduced and recorded by Al Jolson (Brunswick). Instrumental record by Isham Jones and his Orchestra (Brunswick) and vocal record by Lewis James and Franklyn Baur (Victor).

At Seventeen. w/m Janis Ian, 1975. Top 10 record by Janis Ian (Columbia).

At Sundown. w/m Walter Donaldson, 1927. Over two million records by various artists were sold in its first year. It was a great favorite with radio and vaudeville performers, which in turn resulted in huge sheet music sales. The song has been featured in seven motion pictures: (MM) *Glorifying the American Girl*, 1929; (MM) *This Is the Life*, 1944, sung by the Bobby Brooks Quartet; (MM) *Music for Millions*, 1944, sung by Marsha Hunt; (MM) *Margie*, 1946; (MM) *The Fabulous Dorseys*, in which it was played by the Dorsey Band and Paul Whiteman, 1947; (MM) *Love Me or Leave Me*, sung by Doris Day, portraying Ruth Etting, who had featured the song during her career, 1955; (MM) *The Joker Is Wild* in which Frank Sinatra portrayed Joe E. Lewis, 1957.

Attack. w/m Sandy Linzer and Denny Randall, 1966. Introduced in (MP) *The Girl in Daddy's Bikini*, and on records by The Toys (Dyno Voice).

At the Balalaika. w. Eric Maschwitz, Robert Wright, and George Forrest, m. George Posford, 1939. Sung by Ilona Massey, Nelson Eddy, and the Russian Cossack Choir in (MM) *Balalaika*, the only song retained from the English stage musical of 1936, on which the film was based. Maschwitz wrote the original lyrics, and Wright and Forrest wrote the new version for the film. Recorded by Nelson Eddy (Columbia).

At the Ballet. w. Edward Kleban, m. Marvin Hamlisch, 1975. Introduced by Carole Bishop, Nancy Lane, and Kay Cole in (TM) *A Chorus Line*. In the film version, (MM) *A Chorus Line*, 1985, it was sung by Vicki Frederick, Michelle Johnston, and Pam Klinger.

At the Cafe Rendevous. w. Sammy Cahn, m. Jule Styne, 1949. Introduced by Doris Day in (MM) *It's a Great Feeling*.

At the Candlelight Cafe. w/m Mack David, 1947. From (MP) *Tisa*. Leading records: Gordon MacRae (Capitol); Dinah Shore (Columbia); Jack Fina, vocal by Harry Prime (MGM).

At the Close of a Long, Long Day. w. Billy Moll, m. Johnny Marvin, 1932.

At the Club. w/m Gerry Goffin and Carole King, 1965. Recorded by The Drifters (Atlantic).

At the Codfish Ball. w. Sidney D. Mitchell, m. Lew Pollack, 1936. Introduced by Shirley Temple and Buddy Ebsen in (MM) *Captain January*. This and most of Shirley Temple's vocals can be heard on soundtrack albums of hers released by 20th-Fox records.

At the Crossroads. w. Bob Russell, m. Ernesto Lecuona, 1942. Adapted from "Malagueña" from *Andalucia—Suite Espagñole*, by Lecuona. Original Spanish lyrics by Tomas Rios. Best-selling record: Jimmy Dorsey, vocal by Bob Eberly (Decca).

At the Devil's Ball. w/m Irving Berlin, 1912. Minstrel and dance song. Leading record by The Peerless Quartet (Victor).

At the End of a Beautiful Day. w/m William H. Perkins, 1916. Recorded by Jane Kenyon (Victor).

At the End of the Rainbow. See **End, The.**

At the End of the Road. w. Ballard MacDonald, m. James F. Hanley, 1925. Popular recordings by Fred Waring's Pennsylvanians (Victor) and Lewis James (Columbia).

At the Flying "W". w/m Allie Wrubel, 1948. Among recordings: Elliot Lawrence, vocal by Rosalind Patton (Columbia); Hal Derwin (Capitol).

At the Hop. w/m Artie Singer, David White, and John Medora, 1958. #1 hit by Danny and The Juniors (ABC-Paramount).

At the Jazz Band Ball. w/m Edwin B. Edwards, Nick LaRocca, Tony Spargo, and Larry Shields, 1918. The writers were all members of the Original Dixieland Jazz Band that first recorded this jazz favorite (Victor), 1918. Among others to follow were Bix Beiderbecke (Okeh); Bob Crosby (Decca); Sidney Bechet (Brunswick); Bud Freeman (Columbia).

At the Levee on Revival Day. w. Charles R. McCarron and Fred E. Mierisch, m. Chris Smith, 1912. Recorded by Arthur Collins and Byron G. Harlan (Victor).

At the Mississippi Cabaret. w. A. Seymour Brown, m. Albert Gumble, 1914.

At the Moving Picture Ball. w. Howard Johnson, m. Joseph H. Santly, 1920. Revived by Freddie "Schnicklefritz" Fisher (Decca), 1939. Interpolated by the ensemble in (TM) *A Musical Jubilee*, 1975.

At the Scene. w/m Dave Clark and Lenny Davidson, 1966. Top 20 record by the British group The Dave Clark Five (Epic).

At the Zoo. w/m Paul Simon, 1967. Top 20 record by Simon and Garfunkel (Columbia).

At This Moment. w/m Billy Vera, 1986. #1 record by Billy Vera and The Beaters (Rhino). The song was first recorded "live" in an L.A. night club by Vera's group, then named Billy and The Beaters, for a Japanese-owned label (Alfa), 1981. The original master was re-released on the new label after it was played on two episodes of the series (TVP) "Family Ties," and caused a rush of orders to distributors from retail record stores.

Attitude Dancing. w/m Jacob Brackman and Carly Simon, 1975. Recorded by Carly Simon (Elektra).

At Your Beck and Call. w/m Eddie DeLange and Buck Ram, 1938. Recorded by singer Mildred Bailey (Vocalion); the bands of Jimmy Dorsey (Decca), Hot Lips Page (Bluebird), Artie Shaw (Bluebird).

At Your Command. w/m Harry Barris, Bing Crosby, and Harry Tobias, 1931. This song, written by three Harrys (Crosby was named Harry Lillis Crosby), had hit records by Crosby (Brunswick) and his former employer, Gus Arnheim and his Orchestra (Victor). Also recorded by Fred Rich (Columbia), Sleepy Hall (Melotone), and later, Gordon MacRae (Capitol).

Aubrey. w/m David Gates, 1973. Top 20 record by the group Bread (Elektra). Arranged and produced by Gates, who also was lead singer, guitarist, and keyboardist of the combo.

Auf Wiedersehen. w. Herbert Reynolds, m. Sigmund Romberg, 1915. This was Romberg's first successful song, introduced by Vivienne Segal and Cecil Lean in (TM) *The Blue Paradise*. Helen Traubel sang it in the Romberg film biography (MM) *Deep In My Heart*, 1954.

Auf Wiedersehen, My Dear. w/m Al Hoffman, Ed G. Nelson, Al Goodhart, and Milton Ager, 1932. Popularized by Russ Columbo (Victor).

Auf Wiederseh'n, Sweetheart. w. John Sexton and John Turner, m. Eberhard Storch, 1952. German song, popularized and recorded by Vera Lynn in England and the U.S. with a million-selling record (London).

Aunt Hagar's Blues. w/m W. C. Handy, 1920. King Oliver (Vocalion) and W. C. Handy's band (Okeh) had early recordings. Among others were Ted Lewis (Columbia), Paul Whiteman with Jack Teagarden featured (Decca), Eddie Condon (Decca), Bob Chester (Bluebird). It was heard in the Handy film bio, starring Nat Cole as Handy, (MM) *St. Louis Blues*, 1958.

Au Reet. w/m Fud Livingston, Arthur Russell, and Bob Mosely, 1941. Recorded by the Jimmy Dorsey (Decca) and Sam Donahue (Okeh) bands.

Au Revoir, but Not Goodbye, Soldier Boy. w. Lew Brown, m. Albert Von Tilzer, 1917.

Au Revoir, Pleasant Dreams. w. Jack Meskill, m. Jean Schwartz, 1930. Closing theme song of Ben Bernie, who would recite the lyrics while his band played the melody in the background. He recorded it (Brunswick), coupled with his opening theme, "It's A Lonesome Old Town, (q. v.)."

Aurora. w. Harold Adamson (Engl.), m. Mario Lago and Roberto Roberti, 1941. Brazilian song, with original Portuguese words by the composers. Introduced in the U.S. in (MM) *Hold That Ghost*, starring Abbott and Costello, and on records by the Andrews Sisters (Decca).

Authority Song, The. w/m John Cougar Mellencamp, 1984. Recorded by John Cougar Mellencamp (Riva).

Autobahn. m. Ralf Hutter and Florian Schneider, 1975. Instrumental, composed and played by the German duo, Kraftwerk (Vertigo).

Automatic. w/m Mark Goldenberg and Brock Walsh, 1984. Top 10 record by The Pointer Sisters (Planet).

Autumn in New York. w/m Vernon Duke, 1935. Introduced in the revue (TM) *Thumbs Up!* by J. Harold Murray. A major standard, and unique in that Duke also wrote the words. A cross section of records: Richard Himber, vocal by Joey Nash (Victor); Billie Holiday (Clef); Buddy DeFranco (Clef); Page Cavanaugh Trio (Mastertone); Modern Jazz Quartet (Prestige); Jo Stafford (Capitol).

Autumn Leaves. w. Johnny Mercer (Engl.), Jacques Prevert (Fr.), m. Joseph Kosma, 1955. Roger Williams's instrumental version was a #1 record and million-seller (Kapp). Steve Allen, with George Cates's Orchestra, had his first chart record (Coral). Among many recordings were those by Jo Stafford (Capitol); Monica Lewis, with Nelson Riddle (Capitol); Stan Getz (Roost); Buddy Morrow, vocal by Tommy Mercer (RCA Victor).

Autumn Nocturne. w. Kim Gannon, m. Josef Myrow, 1942. Associated, as an instrumental, with Claude Thornhill and his Orchestra, featuring Thornhill at the piano (Columbia).

Autumn of My Life. w/m Bobby Goldsboro, 1968. Hit C&W/Pop record by Bobby Goldsboro (United Artists).

Autumn Serenade. w. Sammy Gallop, m. Peter De Rose, 1945. Harry James and his Orchestra had the leading record of this instrumental (Columbia). The lyric was added later.

Autumn Waltz, The. w. Bob Hilliard, m. Cy Coleman, 1956. Featured and recorded by Tony Bennett (Columbia).

Avalon. w/m B. G. DeSylva, Al Jolson, and Vincent Rose, 1920. Introduced by Al Jolson at the Winter Garden. An infringement suit claiming that the melody was plagiarized from Puccini's aria, "E lucevan le stelle" from the opera *La Tosca*, was won by Puccini and his publisher. They were awarded $25,000 and all future royalties. In 1937, the Benny Goodman Quartet had a hit single (Victor). The performance was repeated in (MM) *The Benny Goodman Story*, 1956, in which Goodman played clarinet on the soundtrack for Steve Allen who portrayed him. It was sung by Jeanette MacDonald with Robert Young in (MM) *Cairo*, 1942. Al Jolson dubbed his voice for Larry Parks in (MM) *The Jolson Story*, 1946. The song was also heard on the soundtrack of (MM) *Margie*, 1946. Gogi Grant, dubbing for Ann Blyth in the title role, sang it with The De Castro Sisters in (MM) *The Helen Morgan Story*, 1957.

Avalon Town. w. Grant Clarke, m. Nacio Herb Brown, 1928. Featured and recorded by Gus Arnheim's Orchestra (Okeh) and the Cliquot Club Eskimos (Columbia).

Avenging Annie. w/m Andy Pratt, 1973. Introduced and recorded by Andy Pratt (Columbia). Revived by English singer Roger Daltrey (MCA), 1977.

Ave Satani. m. Jerry Goldsmith, 1976. Introduced on the soundtrack of (MP) *The Omen*. Nominated for an Academy Award.

Awake in a Dream. w. Leo Robin, m. Frederick Hollander, 1936. Introduced by Marlene Dietrich, singing to Gary Cooper, in (MP) *Desire*.

Away All Boats. w. Leonard Adelson, m. Frank Skinner and Albert Skinner, 1956. From the theme of (MP) *Away All Boats*. Recorded by Al Hibbler, with Jack Pleis's Orchestra (Decca).

Away Down South in Heaven. w. Bud Green, m. Harry Warren, 1927.

Away from You. w. Sheldon Harnick, m. Richard Rodgers, 1975. Introduced by Nicol Williamson and Penny Fuller in (TM) *Rex*.

Awful Sad. m. Edward Kennedy "Duke" Ellington, 1929. A jazz instrumental (Brunswick).

Axel F. m. Harold Faltermeyer, 1985. Title refers to Axel Foley, played by Eddie Murphy in (MP) *Beverly Hills Cop*, in which the music was played on the soundtrack. German composer/keyboardist Harold Faltmeyer had a Top 10 instrumental (MCA).

Ay, Ay, Ay. w/m Osman Perez Freire, 1927. Not to be confused with "Cielito Lindo (Ay, Ay, Ay, Ay)." Among recordings of this are Jan August (Diamond) and Jan Peerce (Royale).

"A"—You're Adorable (The Alphabet Song). w/m Buddy Kaye, Fred Wise, and Sidney Lippman, 1949. Written in 1941, but not recorded until eight years later when Perry Como and the Fontane Sisters had their #1 hit (RCA Victor).

Azure. w. Irving Mills, m. Edward Kennedy "Duke" Ellington, 1937. Introduced and recorded (Master) by Duke Ellington and his Orchestra. Among other recordings: Cab Calloway (Vocalion), Bunny Berigan (Victor), J. C. Heard (Continental), Les Brown (Coral), and Sammy Davis, Jr. (Capitol).

B

Babalu. w. Bob Russell (Engl.), Margarita Lecuona (Sp.), m. Margarita Lecuona, 1939. Cuban song introduced by Xavier Cugat and his Orchestra. Russell's lyrics were written in 1942. The Cugat orchestra played it in (MM) *Two Girls and a Sailor*, 1944. Miguelito Valdes, with whom the song is most identified, sang it in (MM) *Pan-Americana*, 1945.

Babbitt and the Bromide, The. w. Ira Gershwin, m. George Gershwin, 1927. Introduced by Fred and Adele Astaire in (TM) *Funny Face*. Astaire and Gene Kelly teamed up for their only joint screen appearance, doing the number in (MM) *Ziegfeld Follies*, 1946.

Babe. w/m Dennis De Young, 1979. #1 gold record by the quintet Styx (A&M). De-Young, vocalist and keyboardist for the group, wrote the song for his wife as an expression of his regrets for having to be away from her so much of the time.

Babes in Arms. w. Lorenz Hart, m. Richard Rodgers, 1937. Introduced by Mitzi Green, Ray Heatherton, Alfred Drake, and chorus in (TM) *Babes in Arms*. In the film version (MM) *Babes in Arms*, 1939, it was sung by Judy Garland, Mickey Rooney, Douglas McPhail, Betty Jaynes, and chorus.

Babes in the Wood. w. Schuyler Greene, m. Jerome Kern, 1916. Introduced by Ernest Truex in the hit Princess Theatre show (TM) *Very Good Eddie.*

Baby. w. Raymond Peck, m. Percy Wenrich, 1926. From (TM) *Baby*, starring Bernice Clare and J. Harold Murray. Records by Adelaide Hall with Lew Leslie's Blackbirds Orchestra (Brunswick) and Roger Wolfe Kahn's Orchestra (Victor).

Baby. w. Gus Kahn, m. Egbert Van Alstyne, 1919. From (TM) *Ziegfeld's Midnight Frolic* at the New Amsterdam Roof.

Baby! w. Dorothy Fields, m. Jimmy McHugh, 1928. Written for but dropped from (TM) *Blackbirds of 1928* prior to the Broadway opening.

Baby! w, B. G. DeSylva and Ira Gershwin, m. George Gershwin, 1925. Introduced by Emma Haig and Andrew Tombes in (TM) *Tell Me More*, which opened pre-Broadway as *My Fair Lady*.

B-A-B-Y. w/m David Porter and Isaac Hayes, 1966. Hit record by Carla Thomas (Stax).

Baby (You've Got What It Takes). w/m Murray Stein and Clyde Otis, 1960. Hit record by Dinah Washington and Brook Benton (Mercury).

Baby, Baby (I Know You're a Lady). w/m Norro Wilson and Alex Harvey, 1970. Hit Country record by David Houston (Epic).

Baby, Baby, All the Time. w/m Bobby Troup, 1948. Featured and recorded by Tommy Dorsey, vocal by Lucy Ann Polk (Victor). Revived by Julie London (Liberty), 1956.

Baby, Baby, Baby. w. Mack David, m. Jerry Livingston, 1953. Introduced by Teresa Brewer in (MM) *Those Redheads from Seattle*. Brewer (Coral) and Tommy Edwards (MGM) each had popular recordings.

Baby, Baby, Don't Cry. w/m Alfred Cleveland, Terry Johnson, and William Robinson, 1969. Top 10 hit by Smokey Robinson and The Miracles (Tamla).

Baby, Come Back. w/m Eddy Grant, 1968. Recorded by the English/Jamaican quintet The Equals (RCA).

Baby, Come to Me. w/m Rod Temperton, 1983. Recorded by Patti Austin and James Ingram (Qwest), 1982. After the record had a short life on the charts, it was played on the daytime show (TVP) "General Hospital." The audience reaction was so strong that the record company re-released the single and it became a #1 gold record.

Baby, Don't Do It. w/m Lowman Pauling, 1953. #1 R&B record by The Five Royales (Apollo).

Baby, Don't Go. w/m Sonny Bono, 1965. Top 10 hit featured and recorded by Sonny and Cher (Reprise).

Baby, Don't Tell on Me. w/m James Rushing, William "Count" Basie, and Lester Young, 1939. Introduced and recorded (Vocalion) by Count Basie, vocal by Jimmy Rushing.

Baby, Hold On. w/m James Lyon and Eddie Money. 1978. Recorded by Eddie Money (Columbia).

Baby, I Done Got Wise. w/m Big Bill Broonzy, 1940. Introduced and recorded by blues singer Big Bill [Broonzy] (Vocalion).

(You're So Square) Baby, I Don't Care. w/m Jerry Leiber and Mike Stoller, 1982. Introduced by Elvis Presley in (MM) *Jailhouse Rock*, 1957. Revived with chart record by Joni Mitchell (Geffen).

Baby, I Love You. w/m Jeff Barry, Ellie Greenwich, and Phil Spector, 1964, 1969. Introduced by The Ronettes (Philles). Million-selling record by Andy Kim (Steed), 1969.

Baby, I Love Your Way. w/m Ron Vanzant and Allen Collins, 1989. Hit single by Will To Power (Epic).

Baby, I Love Your Way. w/m Peter Frampton, 1976. Top 20 record by the British singer/composer Peter Frampton (A&M).

Baby, I'm A-Want You. w/m David Gates, 1971. Gold record by the group Bread, of which Gates was leader (Elektra).

Baby, I'm for Real. w/m Marvin Gaye and Anna Gaye, 1969. Top 20 record by The Originals (Soul).

Baby, I'm Hooked (Right into Your Love). w/m Cedric Martin and Van Ross Redding, 1984. Recorded by the soul band Con Funk Shun (Mercury).

Baby, I'm Yours. w/m Van McCoy, 1965. Crossover (R&B/Pop) hit record by Barbara Lewis (Atlantic). Revived by Jody Miller (Epic), 1971 and Debbie Boone (Dot), 1978.

Baby, I Need Your Loving. w/m Brian Holland, Eddie Holland, and Lamont Dozier, 1964. Crossover (R&B/Pop) hit by The Four Tops (Motown). Top 10 hit by Johnny Rivers (Imperial), 1967, and chart record by O. C. Smith (Columbia), 1970.

Baby, It's Cold Outside. w/m Frank Loesser, 1949. Introduced by Esther Williams, Ricardo Montalban, Betty Garrett, and Red Skelton in (MM) *Neptune's Daughter*. Academy Award winning song. Hit records by Johnny Mercer and Margaret Whiting (Capitol); Dinah Shore and Buddy Clark (Columbia); Ella Fitzgerald and Louis Jordan (Decca). Revived in 1962 by Ray Charles and Betty Carter (ABC-Paramount).

Baby, It's You. w/m Mack David, Burt Bacharach, and Barney Williams, 1962. Hit record by The Shirelles (Scepter). Revived with a Top 10 record by the rock quintet Smith (Dolton), 1969.

Baby, Let Me Hold Your Hand. w/m Ray Charles, 1951. R&B song, first chart record by Ray Charles (Swing Time).

Baby, Let's Wait. w/m Pam Sawyer and Lori Burton, 1968. Top 40 record by The Royal Guardsmen (Laurie).

Baby, Make Your Own Sweet Music. w/m Sandy Linzer and Denny Randell, 1968. Recorded by Jay and The Techniques (Smash).

Baby, Now That I've Found You. w/m John Macleod and Tony Macaulay, 1968. Top 20 U.S. release by the English/West Indian group The Foundations (Uni).

Baby, Please Come Back Home. w/m Donald Davis and Jimmy Barnes, 1967. Recorded by J. J. Barnes (Groovesville).

Baby, Scratch My Back. w/m James Moore, 1966. Instrumental popularized by harmonicist Slim Harpo, pseudonym for Moore, who was also known as Harmonica Slim (Excello).

Baby, Take a Bow. w. Lew Brown, m. Jay Gorney, 1934. This was sung and danced as a specialty number by six-year-old Shirley Temple in (MM) *Stand Up and Cheer* and made her an overnight star.

Baby, Take Me in Your Arms. w/m Tony Macaulay and John Macleod, 1970. Top 40 U.S. release by the English singer, Jefferson (Janus).

Baby, Talk to Me. w. Lee Adams, m. Charles Strouse, 1960. Introduced by Dick Van Dyke and quartet in (TM) *Bye Bye Birdie*. Song not used in film version.

Baby, the Rain Must Fall. w. Ernie Sheldon, m. Elmer Bernstein, 1965. Sung by We Three in (MP) *Baby, The Rain Must Fall*. Hit record by Glenn Yarborough (RCA).

Baby, We're Really in Love. w/m Hank Williams, 1952. Country hit by Hank Williams (MGM).

Baby, What a Big Surprise. w/m Peter Cetera, 1977. Top 10 record by the group Chicago (Columbia).

Baby, What Else Can I Do? w. Walter Hirsch, m. Gerald Marks, 1939. Leading records by Ethel Waters (Bluebird); Ella Fitzgerald (Decca); Tommy Dorsey, vocal by Anita Boyer, arranged by Sy Oliver (Victor).

Baby, When You Ain't There. w. Mitchell Parish, m. Edward Kennedy "Duke" Ellington, 1932. Recorded by Ellington's Band (Brunswick).

Baby, Won't You Please Come Home. w/m Charles Warfied and Clarence Williams, 1922. A jazz standard with many recordings, among which are Clarence Williams (Perfect); Bessie Smith (Columbia); The Mills Brothers (Brunswick); McKinney's Cotton Pickers (Victor); Jimmie Lunceford (Vocalion); Fletcher Henderson (Vocalion); Sidney Bechet (Victor). Sung by Jo Stafford and Nat "King" Cole in (MM) *That's the Spirit*, 1945.

Baby, Won't You Say You Love Me? w. Mack Gordon, m. Josef Myrow, 1950. Introduced by Betty Grable in (MM) *Wabash Avenue*. Leading records by Ella Fitzgerald (Decca); Herb Jeffries (Columbia); Ray Robbins (Capitol).

Baby, You Come Rollin 'Cross My Mind. w/m Jesse Lee Kincaid, 1968. Recorded by The Peppermint Trolley Company (Acta).

Baby, You're a Rich Man. w/m John Lennon and Paul McCartney, 1967. Top 40 record by The Beatles, coupled with the #1 gold record recipient "All You Need Is Love" (Capitol).

Baby, You're Right. w/m James Brown and Joe Tex, 1961. Crossover (R&B and pop) hit by James Brown (King).

Baby, You've Got It. w/m Joseph Hooven, Alfred Smith, and Jerry Winn, 1967. Top 40 record by Brenton Wood (Double Shot).

Baby Blue. w/m Aaron Barker, 1988. #1 Country single from the album "If You Ain't Lovin', You Ain't Livin' " (MCA).

Baby Blue. w/m Pete Ham, 1972. Top 20 record by the British quartet Badfinger (Apple).

Baby Blue Eyes. w/m Jesse Greer, Walter Hirsch, and George Jessel, 1922. Introduced by George Jessel in the revue (TM) *Troubles of 1922.*

Baby Boy. w/m Mary Kay Place, 1976. Introduced by Mary Kay Place, as Loretta Haggers, the would-be Country music star in the series (TVP) "Mary Hartman, Mary Hartman." Place's recording was on the charts for thirteen weeks (Columbia).

Baby Bye Bye. w/m Gary Morris and James Brantley, 1984. #1 Country chart song by Gary Morris (Warner Bros.).

Baby Come Back. w/m Peter Beckett and John Charles Crowley, 1978. # 1 gold record by the group Player (RSO).

Baby Come Close. w/m Pamela Moffett, William "Smokey" Robinson, and Marvin Tarplin, 1974. Recorded by Smokey Robinson (Tamla).

Baby Come to Me. w/m Jeffrey Cohen and Narada Michael Walden, 1989. Hit R&B chart record by Regina Belle (Columbia).

Baby Doll. w. Bernard Hanighen, m. Kenyon Hopkins, 1956. Music adapted from the theme of (MP) *Baby Doll.* Leading record by Andy Williams, with Archie Bleyer's Orchestra (Cadence).

Baby Don't Get Hooked on Me. w/m Mac Davis, 1972. #1 gold record by Mac Davis (Columbia).

Baby Elephant Walk (a.k.a. Theme from "Hatari"). m. Henry Mancini, 1962. From (MP) *Hatari.* Recorded under "Theme, etc." title by Henry Mancini and his Orchestra (RCA). As "Baby Elephant Walk," leading instrumentals by Lawrence Welk and his Orchestra (Dot), and The Miniature Men (Dolton).

Baby Face. w. Benny Davis, m. Harry Akst, 1926, 1948. Introduced by Jan Garber, vocal by Benny Davis (Victor). Among other top recordings: "Whispering" Jack Smith (Victor); Ben Selvin and his Orchestra (Brunswick); The Ipana Troubadours, led by Sam Lanin, vocal by Lewis James (Columbia). In 1948, it was on "Your Hit Parade" for nine weeks due to the million-seller by Art Mooney and his band (MGM) and the popular recording by another Jack Smith, "The Voice with a Smile" (Capitol). Other chart versions by Little Richard (Specialty), 1958; Bobby Darin (Atco), 1962; The Wing and a Prayer Fife and Drum Corps (Wing and a Prayer), 1976. In films, it was sung by Mary Eaton in (MM) *Glorifying the American Girl*, 1930; by Al Jolson, dubbing for Larry Parks, in (MM) *Jolson Sings Again*, 1949; by Julie Andrews in (MM) *Thoroughly Modern Millie*, 1967.

Baby Grand. w/m Billy Joel, 1987. Popular single by Billy Joel featuring Ray Charles (Columbia).

Baby I Lied. w/m Deborah Allen, Rory Bourke, and Rafe Van Hoy, 1983. Country/Pop chart hit record by Deborah Allen (RCA).

Baby I Love You. w/m Ronny Shannon, 1967. Gold record by Aretha Franklin (Atlantic).

Baby I'm Burnin'. w/m Dolly Parton, 1979. Country and Pop chart hit by Dolly Parton (RCA).

Baby I'm Yours. w/m Steve Wariner and Guy Clark, 1988. Top 10 chart record by Steve Wariner (MCA).

Baby Jane. w/m Rod Stewart and Jay Davis, 1983. Recorded by the English singer Rod Stewart (Warner Bros.).

Baby Let Me Take You in My Arms. w/m Abrim Tillman, 1972. Recorded by the soul group Detroit Emeralds (Westbound).

Baby Love. w/m Stephen Bray, Mary Kessler, and Regina Richards, 1986. Top 10 record by Regina [Richards] (Atlantic).

Baby Love. w/m Brian Holland, Eddie Holland, and Lamont Dozier, 1964. #1 hit by The Supremes (Motown).

Baby Me. w/m Archie Gottler, Lou Handman, and Harry Harris, 1939. Featured and recorded by Glenn Miller, vocal by Kay Starr (Bluebird).

Baby Mine. w. Ned Washington, m. Frank Churchill, 1941. From the Walt Disney cartoon feature (MM) *Dumbo*. Nominated for an Academy Award. Recordings by Les Brown, vocal by Betty Bonney (Okeh), and Jane Froman (Columbia).

Baby Rose. w. Louis Weslyn, m. George Christie, 1911. Introduced by Maude Lambert.

Baby's Awake Now. w. Lorenz Hart, m. Richard Rodgers, 1929. Sung by Inez Courtney and Thelma White in (TM) *Spring Is Here*.

Baby's Back Again. w/m Betty Robinson, 1968. Top 10 Country chart record by Connie Smith (RCA).

Baby's Best Friend, A. w. Lorenz Hart, m. Richard Rodgers, 1928. Show-stopping number introduced by Beatrice Lillie in the unsuccessful (TM) *She's My Baby*. Lillie repeated the song, retitled "Lullaby," in the London production *Charlot's Masquerade*, 1930.

Baby's Birthday Party. w/m Ann Ronell, 1930.

Baby's Got a Hold on Me. w/m Josh Leo, Jeff Hanna, and Bob Carpenter, 1987. Top 10 Country chart single from the album "Hold On" by The Nitty Gritty Dirt Band (Warner Bros.).

Baby's Got Her Blue Jeans On. w/m Bob McDill, 1985. Country chart song recorded by Mel McDaniel (Capitol).

Baby's Gotten Good at Goodbye. w/m Troy Martin and Tony Martin, 1989. Hit Country record by George Strait (MCA).

Baby Shoes. w. Joe Goodwin and Ed Rose, m. Al Piantadosi, 1916. A sentimental ballad recorded by Edna Brown (Victor) and Henry Burr (Columbia).

Baby Sittin' Boogie. w/m Jonathan Parker, 1960. Novelty hit by Buzz Clifford (Columbia).

Baby's Prayer. w. R. A. Mullen, m. R. L. Halle, 1898.

Baby's Prayer Will Soon Be Answered. w/m Billy Baskette, Gus Van, and Joe Schenck, 1919. The answer song to "Just a Baby's Prayer at Twilight (For Her Daddy Over There)" was recorded by the singer of the first hit, Henry Burr (Columbia), and featured in vaudeville by the duet, the co-writers, Van and Schenck.

Baby Talk. w/m Melvin H. Schwartz, 1959. Popular record by Jan and Dean (Dore).

Baby Tell Me, Can You Dance. w/m Bryan Loren, 1987. Top 10 R&B chart crossover record by Shanice Wilson (A&M).

Baby That's Backatcha. w/m William "Smokey" Robinson, 1975. Recorded by Smokey Robinson (Tamla).

Baby Workout. w/m Alonzo Tucker and Jackie Wilson, 1963. Top 10 record by Jackie Wilson (Brunswick).

Bachelor Boy. w/m Bruce Welch and Cliff Richard, 1962. Hit record from England by Cliff Richard and The Shadows (Epic).

Bachelor in Paradise. w. Mack David, m. Henry Mancini, 1961. Academy Award nominee from (MP) *Bachelor in Paradise*.

Bach Goes to Town. m. Alec Templeton, 1938. A Bach Prelude and Fugue rewritten as a swing instrumental that became a hit record for Benny Goodman and his Orchestra (Victor).

Back, Back, Back to Baltimore. w. Harry H. Williams, m. Egbert Van Alstyne, 1904. Novelty song.

Back and Forth. w/m Kevin Kendricks, Tomi Jenkins, Nathan Leftenant, and Larry Blackmon, 1987. Top 10 R&B chart record by the group Cameo (Atlanta Artists).

Back Bay Polka. w. Ira Gershwin, m. George Gershwin, 1947. An unpublished melody of George's with new lyrics by Ira, introduced in (MM) *The Shocking Miss Pilgrim* by Allyn Joslyn, Charles Kemper, Elizabeth Patterson, Lillian Bronson, Arthur Shields, and Betty Grable.

Back Bay Shuffle. m. Artie Shaw and Teddy McRae, 1938. Introduced and recorded by Artie Shaw and his Orchestra (Bluebird).

Back Beat Boogie. m. Harry James, 1940. Instrumental, recorded by Harry James and his Orchestra (Columbia).

Backfield in Motion. w/m Mel Hardin and Tim McPherson, 1969. Gold record by the cousin-writer team, Mel and Tim (Bamboo).

Back Home Again. w/m John Denver, 1974. Top 10 record by John Denver (RCA).

(Back Home Again in) Indiana. See **Indiana (Back Home Again in).**

Back Home in Tennessee. w. William Jerome, m. Walter Donaldson, 1915. This Tennessee song was Brooklyn-born Donaldson's first hit. Introduced by Al Jolson. Popular instrumental recording by Prince's Orchestra (Columbia).

Back in Baby's Arms. w/m Bob Montgomery, 1987. Introduced by Emmylou Harris on the soundtrack of (MP) *Planes, Trains, and Automobiles*, and on her Country chart single (Hughes).

Back in Black. w/m Angus Young, Malcolm Young, and Brian Johnson, 1981. Recorded by the Australian rock band AC/DC (Atlantic).

Back in Love Again. See **(Every Time I Turn Around) Back in Love Again.**

Back in My Arms Again. w/m Brian Holland, Eddie Holland, and Lamont Dozier, 1965. This song marked the fifth consecutive #1 hit by The Supremes (Motown).

Back in Stride. w/m Frankie Beverly, 1985. #1 R&B chart record by Maze featuring Frankie Beverly (Capitol).

Back in the High Life Again. w. Will Jennings, m. Steve Winwood, 1987. Popular recording by English recording artist Steve Winwood (Island).

Back in the Saddle Again. w/m Gene Autry and Ray Whitley, 1940. Recorded by and theme song of Gene Autry (Okeh).

Back in the U.S.A. w/m Chuck Berry, 1959. Chart record by Chuck Berry (Chess). Revived with Top 20 version by Linda Ronstadt (Asylum), 1978.

Back in the U.S.S.R. w/m John Lennon and Paul McCartney, 1969. Introduced in The Beatles' "White Album" (Apple). Chart single by Chubby Checker (Buddah).

Back in Your Own Back Yard. w/m Dave Dreyer, Al Jolson, and Billy Rose, 1928. Featured by Al Jolson, and then sung by him in (MM) *Say It With Songs*, 1929. Leading records by the orchestras of Gus Arnheim (Okeh), Paul Whiteman (Victor), Jan Garber (Columbia), and singer Ruth Etting (Columbia). Jolson later sang it on the soundtrack of (MM) *Jolson Sings Again*, 1949, dubbing for Larry Parks, and on records (Decca).

Back Off Boogaloo. w/m Richard Starkey (Ringo Starr), 1972. Top 10 record by former Beatle, Ringo Starr (Apple).

Back on the Chain Gang. w/m Chrissie Hynde, 1983. Written by the American member and lead singer of the English quartet, The Pretenders, who had a Top 10 record (Sire).

The song was first heard in the film (MP) *The King of Comedy.*

Back on the Street Again. w/m Stephen Gillette, 1967. Leading recording by The Sunshine Company (Imperial).

Back o' Town Blues. w/m Louis Armstrong and Luis Russell, 1924. First known recording by the Original Indiana Five (Perfect). Armstrong featured it with his All-stars in the late 1940s. It is probable that he and Russell "adapted" the blues.

Back Pocket Money. w/m Tom T. Hall, 1966. Top 10 Country record by Jimmy Newman (Decca).

Back Stabbers. w/m Leon Huff, Gene McFadden, and John Whitehead, 1972. Gold record by The O'Jays (Philadelphia International).

Backstage. w/m Fred Anisfield and Willie Denson, 1966. Top 40 record by Gene Pitney (Musicor).

Back Street Affair. w/m Billy Wallace, 1952. Hit C&W record by Webb Pierce (Decca).

Back to Back. w/m Irving Berlin, 1939. Introduced by Mary Healy in (MM) *Second Fiddle.* Best-selling record by Jimmy Dorsey, vocal by Helen O'Connell (Decca).

Back to Life. w/m Paul Hooper, Beresford Romeo, and Simon Law, 1989. Hit R&B chart single by Soul II Soul, featuring Caron Wheeler (Virgin).

Back to My Old Home Town. w/m Nora Bayes and Jack Norworth, 1910. Featured and recorded by Jack Norworth (Victor).

Back to Paradise. w/m Giraldo, Jim Vallance, and Bryan Adams, 1987. Recorded by the group, 38 Special, on the soundtrack of (MP) *Revenge of the Nerds II* and on a chart record (A&M).

Back to the Carolina You Love. w. Grant Clarke, m. Jean Schwartz, 1914. Recorded by Al Jolson (Victor).

Back to the Island. w/m Leon Russell, 1976. Chart record by Leon Russell (Shelter).

Backtrack. w/m Faron Young and Alex Zanetis, 1962. C&W hit by Faron Young.

Back Up, Buddy. w/m Boudleaux Bryant, 1954. Featured and recorded by Carl Smith (Columbia).

Back Up Train. w/m Palmer E. James, 1966. Chart record by Al Green and The Soul Mates (Hot Line).

Backward, Turn Backward. w/m Dave Coleman, 1954. Leading recordings by Jane Froman (Capitol), Pee Wee King (RCA Victor), Jane Russell and Johnny Desmond (Coral).

Back When My Hair Was Short. w/m Glenn Leopolo, 1973. Recorded by the trio Gunhill Road (Kama Sutra).

Back Where You Belong. w/m Gary O'Connor, 1982. Recorded by the sextet 38 Special (A&M).

Bad. w/m Michael Jackson, 1987. Title song from the platinum album by Michael Jackson. This was one of four #1 singles ("I Just Can't Stop Loving You," "The Way You Make Me Feel," "Man in the Mirror") from said album (Epic).

Bad, Bad Leroy Brown. w/m Jim Croce, 1973. #1 gold record by Jim Croce (ABC). Popular version by Frank Sinatra (Reprise), 1974.

Bad, Bad Whiskey. w/m Thomas Maxwell Davis, 1950. Leading record by Amos Milburn (Aladdin).

Bad and the Beautiful, The (a.k.a. **Love Is for the Very Young**). w. Dory Langdon Previn, m. David Raskin, 1953. Theme from (MP) *The Bad and the Beautiful.* Recorded in concert version by Percy Faith (Columbia). Lyric added later.

Bad Blood. w. Phil Cody, m. Neil Sedaka, 1975. #1 gold record by Neil Sedaka, with back-up vocal by Elton John (Rocket).

Bad Boy. w/m Larry Dermer, Joe Galdo, and Rafael Vigil, 1986. Top 10 single by the group Miami Sound Machine (Epic).

Bad Case of Loving You (Doctor, Doctor). w/m John Martin, 1979. Recorded by English singer Robert Palmer (Island).

Badge. w/m Eric Clapton and George Harrison, 1969. Recorded by the English group Cream (Atco).

Bad Girl. w/m Howard Greenfield and Neil Sedaka, 1963. Introduced and recorded by Neil Sedaka (RCA).

Bad Girls. w/m Joe Esposito, Eddie Hokenson, Bruce Sudano, and Donna Summer, 1979. #1 platinum record by Donna Summer (Casablanca).

Bad Humor Man, The. w. Johnny Mercer, m. Jimmy McHugh, 1940. Introduced in (MM) *You'll Find Out* and on records by Kay Kyser and his Kollege of Musical Knowledge, vocal by Ish Kabibble (Columbia). Also recorded by Jimmy Dorsey, vocal by Helen O'Connell (Decca).

Badinage. m. Victor Herbert, 1897. Instrumental.

Bad in Everyman, The. w. Lorenz Hart, m. Richard Rodgers, 1934. Sung by Shirley Ross in (MP) *Manhattan Melodrama*. See **Blue Moon**.

Bad Is for Other People. w. Robert Wells, m. Cy Coleman, 1966. Introduced in night clubs by Buddy Barnes. Recorded by Mabel Mercer and Bobby Short (Atlantic).

Badlands. w/m Bruce Springsteen, 1978. Recorded by Bruce Springsteen (Columbia).

Bad Luck. w/m Victor Carstarphen, Gene McFadden, and John Whitehead, 1975. Top 20 record by Harold Melvin and The Blue Notes (Philadelphia International, Part 1). The Atlanta Disco Band had a chart instrumental version (Ariola), 1976.

Bad Luck. w/m Jules Taub and Sam Ling, 1956.

Bad Man Blunder. w/m Lee Hays and Cisco Houston, 1960. Novelty featured and recorded by The Kingston Trio (Capitol).

Bad Medicine. w/m Jon Bon Jovi, Richie Sambora, and Desmond Child, 1988. Hit record by the group Bon Jovi (Mercury).

Bad Moon Rising. w/m John Fogerty, 1969. Gold record by Creedence Clearwater Revival (Fantasy).

Bad News. w/m John D. Loudermilk, 1964. Country chart hit by Johnny Cash (Columbia).

Bad Seed. w/m Bill Anderson, 1966. Hit Country record by Jan Howard (Decca).

Bad Time. w/m Mark Farner, 1975. Written by the guitarist of the group, Grand Funk, which had a Top 10 recording (Capitol).

Bad to Me. w/m John Lennon and Paul McCartney, 1964. Recorded in England by Billy J. Kramer, with The Dakotas, coupled with "Little Children" (Imperial).

Bagdad. w. Jack Yellen, m. Milton Ager, 1924. Introduced in vaudeville by Fred Waring's Pennsylvanians. Best-selling record (instrumental) by Paul Specht and his Orchestra (Columbia).

Bagdad. w. Harold Atteridge, m. Al Jolson, 1918. Jolson introduced this in (TM) *Sinbad* at the Winter Garden.

Bagdad. w. Anne Caldwell, m. Victor Herbert, 1912. Introduced by David C. Montgomery in (TM) *The Lady of the Slipper*.

Bags' Groove. m. Milt Jackson, 1954. Introduced and recorded by Milt Jackson's combo (Blue Note). Title from Jackson's nickname, "Bags."

Bake Dat Chicken Pie. w/m Frank Dumont, 1906.

Baker Street. w/m Gerry Rafferty, 1979. Gold record from England by Gerry Rafferty (United Artists).

Balboa. w. Sidney D. Mitchell, m. Lew Pollack, 1936. One of three songs Judy Garland sang in her first feature film (MM) *Pigskin Parade*, in which her name was in the ninth billing position. The other songs were "It's Love I'm After" and "The Texas Tornado (q.v.)."

Bali Ha'i. w. Oscar Hammerstein II, m. Richard Rodgers, 1949. Introduced by Juanita Hall, as "Bloody Mary," Myron McCormick, and William Tabbert in (TM) *South Pacific*. In (MM) *South Pacific*, 1958, Juanita Hall portrayed her stage role, but her vocal was dubbed on the soundtrack by Muriel Smith. Among the many popular recordings: Perry Como (RCA Victor), Paul Weston and his Orchestra (Capitol), Bing Crosby (Decca), Peggy Lee (Capitol), Frank Sinatra (Columbia).

Ballad for Americans. w. John Latouche, m. Earl Robinson, 1940. Originally titled "Ballad for Uncle Sam," this cantata was introduced by Gordon Clarke in the WPA Federal Theatre production of (TM) *Sing for Your Supper* at the Adelphi Theatre in New York 1939. Paul Robeson (Victor) and Bing Crosby (Decca) each had big-selling albums (four sides, 78 RPM) of the patriotic work. Busby Berkeley staged it as the finale for (MM) *Born to Sing*, 1942.

Ballad of a Teenage Queen. w/m Jack Clement, 1958. C&W and pop chart record by Johnny Cash (Sun).

Ballad of Black Gold, The. (See **Blowing Wild**).

Ballad of Bonnie and Clyde, The. w/m Mitch Murray and Peter Callander, 1968. Written and recorded in England. Top 10 U.S. chart release by Georgie Fame (Epic). Inspired by, but not from, the film of the same title.

Ballad of Cat Ballou, The. w. Mack David, m. Jerry Livingston, 1965. Introduced by Nat "King" Cole in (MP) *Cat Ballou*. Song nominated for Academy Award, 1965.

Ballad of Davy Crockett, The. w. Tom Blackburn, m. George Bruns, 1955. Introduced by Fess Parker in (MP) *Davy Crockett—King of the Wild Frontier*. Parker had a popu-

lar recording (Columbia), but the #1 record was by Bill Hayes (Cadence) followed by Tennessee Ernie Ford (Capitol).

Ballad of Easy Rider. w/m Roger McGuinn, 1969. Introduced by The Byrds on the soundtrack of (MP) *Easy Rider* and recorded by them (Columbia).

Ballad of Forty Dollars. w/m Tom T. Hall, 1968. Top 10 Country chart record by Tom T. Hall (Mercury).

Ballad of Gator McClusky. w/m Jerry Reed, 1976. Sung by Jerry Reed in (MP) *Gator*, starring Burt Reynolds and Jack Weston.

Ballard of Ira Hayes, The. w/m Peter La Farge, 1964. Written about the American Indian Marine hero who participated in raising the American flag at Iwo Jima in World War II. Leading record by Johnny Cash (Columbia).

Ballad of Irving, The. w/m John Aylesworth, Frank Peppiatt, and Dick Williams, 1966. Comedy record by deep-voiced radio and TV announcer Frank Gallop (Kapp).

Ballad of Jed Clampett. w/m Paul Henning, 1962. Theme of the series (TVP) "The Beverly Hillbillies." Recorded by Flatt and Scruggs (Columbia).

Ballad of John and Yoko, The. w/m John Lennon and Paul McCartney, 1969. Gold record by The Beatles (Apple).

Ballad of Paladin, The. w/m Johnny Western, Richard Boone, and Sam Rolfe, 1958, 1962. Introduced by Johnny Western on the series (TVP) "Have Gun, Will Travel." Leading record, instrumental by Duane Eddy (RCA), 1962.

Ballad of the Alamo. w. Paul Francis Webster, m. Dimitri Tiomkin, 1960. From (MP) *The Alamo*. Popular record by Marty Robbins (Columbia).

Ballad of the Christmas Donkey, The. w/m Carol Hall, 1967. Featured and recorded by Ed Ames (RCA).

Ballad of the Green Berets, The. w/m Barry Sadler and Robin Moore, 1966. #1 hit and gold record by S/Sgt. Barry Sadler (RCA).

Ballad of the Sad Young Men, The. w. Fran Landesman, m. Tommy Wolf, 1959. Introduced by Tani Seitz in (TM) *The Nervous Set*.

Ballad of Two Brothers. w/m Curly Putman, Buddy Killen, and Bobby Braddock, 1968. Country and Pop chart hit by Autry Inman (Epic).

Ballad of Wild River, The. w/m Marshall T. Pack, 1960. Top 10 C&W chart record by Gene Woods (Hap).

Ballad of You and Me and Pooneil. w/m Paul Kantner, 1967. Recorded by Jefferson Airplane, the group of which Kantner was co-founder/guitarist/vocalist (RCA).

Ball and Chain. w/m Willie Mae Thornton, 1968. First popularized by Big Brother and The Holding Company, with Janis Joplin, in their album "Cheap Thrills" (Columbia). Chart single by Tommy James (Roulette), 1970.

Ballerina. w/m Bob Russell and Carl Sigman, 1947. Seventeen weeks on "Your Hit Parade," five times in the #1 position. Vaughn Monroe, with his Orchestra (RCA Victor), had the best-selling recording, followed by Buddy Clark, accompanied by Dick Jones's Orchestra (Columbia); Bing Crosby, John Scott Trotter conducting (Decca); Jimmy Dorsey, vocal by Bob Carroll (MGM); Nat Cole revived it, Nelson Riddle conducting (Capitol), 1957.

Ballerina Girl. w/m Lionel Richie, 1987. Top 10 R&B and Pop chart record by Lionel Richie (Motown).

Ballin' the Jack. w. Jim Burris, m. Chris Smith, 1913. Introduced in vaudeville by the song and dance team of Billy Kent and Jeanette Warner. Prince's Orchestra had a best-selling instrumental record (Columbia). It was interpolated in the touring company of (TM) *The Girl from Utah*, 1914. In films, it was performed by Judy Garland and Gene Kelly in

(MM) *For Me and My Gal*, 1942; Danny Kaye in (MM) *On The Riviera*, 1951; Dean Martin in (MM) *That's My Boy*, 1942.

Ball of Confusion (That's What the World Is Today). w/m Norman Whitfield and Barrett Strong, 1970. Top 10 hit record by The Temptations (Gordy).

Ball of Fire. w/m Tommy James, Bruce Sudano, Mike Vale, Woody Wilson, and Paul Nauman, 1969. Top 20 record by Tommy James and The Shondells (Roulette).

Ballroom Blitz. w/m Mike Chapman and Nicky Chinn, 1975. Top 10 record by the British rock group Sweet (Capitol).

Baltimore. w/m Boudleaux Bryant and Felice Bryant, 1964. Hit country record by Sonny James (Capitol).

Baltimore Oriole. w. Paul Francis Webster, m. Hoagy Carmichael, 1945. Performed by Hoagy Carmichael in (MP) *To Have and Have Not*.

Bam, Bam, Bamy Shore. w. Mort Dixon, m. Ray Henderson, 1925. Featured and recorded by the bands of Paul Ash (Brunswick) and Ted Lewis (Columbia).

Bambalina. w. Otto Harbach, Oscar Hammerstein, m. Vincent Youmans, Herbert Stothart, 1923. Edith Day and a female chorus introduced this song in the hit (TM) *Wildflower*. Paul Whiteman and his Orchestra had one of the biggest-selling records of the year (Victor). While Youmans and Stothart are listed as co-composers on all of the songs in the score, the manuscripts indicate that this and the title song were composed by Youmans.

Bamboo. w. Buddy Bernier, m. Nat Simon, 1950. Leading record by Vaughn Monroe, with his Orchestra (RCA Victor).

Bamboo Cage. See **Smellin' of Vanilla.**

Banana Boat Song, The (a.k.a. **Day-O**). w/m Alan Arkin, Bob Carey, and Erik Darling, 1957. Introduced and hit record by The Tarriers (Glory). Harry Belafonte's version (RCA) became a best-seller and the song has remained identified with him. Stan Freberg's parody, with "interruptions" by Peter Leeds, became popular later in the year (Capitol). Three other recordings made the Top 40: The Fontane Sisters (Dot), Steve Lawrence (Coral), Sarah Vaughan (Mercury). Belafonte sang it on the soundtrack of (MP) *Beetlejuice* and its album (Geffen), 1988.

Bandana Days. w/m Noble Sissle and Eubie Blake, 1921. From the hit show (TM) *Shuffle Along.* Eubie Blake recorded it in 1921 (Victor) and Noble Sissle (Variety), 1937.

Bandanna Land. w. Glen MacDonough, m. Victor Herbert, 1905. From (TM) *It Happened in Nordland.*

Bandit, The. w/m Dick Feller, 1977. Introduced by Jerry Reed in (MP) *Smokey and the Bandit.*

Bandit, The. w. John Turner and Michael Carr (Engl.), m. Alfredo Ricardo de Nascime, 1954. A.k.a. "O Cangaceiro," from the Mexican film of the same name. Leading record by Percy Faith and his Orchestra (Columbia).

Band of Gold. w/m Ronald Dunbar and Edythe Wayne, 1970. Gold record by Freda Payne (Invictus).

Band of Gold. w. Bob Musel, m. Jack Taylor, 1955. Introduced, recorded, and first popularized by Kit Carson [well-known previously as Liza Morrow] (Capitol). Don Cherry followed with a chart record (Columbia). Revived in 1966 by Mel Carter (Imperial).

Band on the Run. w/m Paul McCartney and Linda McCartney, 1974. #1 gold record single from the album of the same name by Paul McCartney and Wings (Apple).

Band Played On, The. w. John E. Palmer, m. Charles B. Ward, 1895. Introduced by Ward, a vaudevillian, at Hammerstein's Harlem Opera House. Popular recording by Dan Quinn (Columbia). Interpolated in (MM) *The Strawberry Blonde,* 1941, by James Cagney and Rita Hayworth, and sung by Dennis Morgan in (MP) *CattleTown,* 1951. Hit record by Guy Lombardo's Orchestra (Decca), 1941.

Bang, Bang (My Baby Shot Me Down). w/m Sonny Bono, 1966. Top 10 hit by Cher (Imperial).

Bang A Gong (Get It On). w/m Marc Bolan, 1972. Top 10 record by the British group, T. Rex, led by the writer (Reprise). Revived by the studio group, Witch Queen (Roadshow), 1979, and Top 10 record by the quartet, The Power Station, under the title "Get It On" (Capitol), 1985.

Bangla-Desh. w/m George Harrison, 1971. Performed by George Harrison at Madison Square Garden in New York City at the benefit concert for the Bangladesh refugees, which was filmed as (MM) *The Concert for Bangladesh.* Harrison's rendition was released as a single (Apple).

Bang-Shang-A-Lang. w/m Jerry Barry, 1968. Top 40 hit by the studio group formed by Don Kirshner, The Archies (Calendar).

Banjo Boy. w. Buddy Kaye (Engl.), Charly Niessen (Ger.), m. Charly Niessen, 1960. From the German film *Kein Mann zum Heiraten.* Leading record, from Denmark, by the twelve- and fourteen-year-old brothers, Jan and Kjeld (Kapp). American versions by Dorothy Collins (Top Rank) and Art Mooney, vocal by The Ivys (MGM).

Banjo's Back in Town, The. w/m Earl Shuman, Alden Shuman, and Marshall Brown, 1955. Popularized by Teresa Brewer, with Dick Jacobs's Orchestra (Coral).

Banjo Song, A. w. Howard Weeden, m. Sidney Homer, 1910.

Barbara. w. Billy Rose, m. Abner Silver, 1927.

Barbara Ann. w/m Fred Fassert, 1961, 1966. Recorded as a demo in 1958, and written by a member of the vocal group The Regents, it was released and became a hit record after they had disbanded (Gee). Revived with a Top 10 version by The Beach Boys, featuring Dean Torrence of Jan and Dean, as lead vocalist (Capitol), 1966.

Barcelona. w/m Stephen Sondheim, 1970.

Introduced by Dean Jones and Susan Browning in (TM) *Company*.

Barcelona. w. Gus Kahn, m. Tolchard Evans, 1926.

Barefootin'. m. Robert Parker, 1966. Instrumental by saxophonist-bandleader Robert Parker (Nola).

Bare Necessities, The. w/m Terry Gilkyson, 1967. Sung by Phil Harris and Bruce Reitherman on the sound track of the animated film (MP) *The Jungle Book*. Nominated for Academy Award, 1967.

Baretta's Theme. See **Keep Your Eye on the Sparrow**.

Bargain Store, The. w/m Dolly Parton, 1975. Hit Country record by Dolly Parton (RCA).

Barnacle Bill the Sailor. w/m Carson Robison and Frank Luther, 1929. Famous recording by Hoagy Carmichael, featuring Bix Beiderbecke, Benny Goodman, Tommy Dorsey, Gene Krupa, Joe Venuti, and others. Vocal by Carmichael, Venuti, and Carson Robison (Victor). Frank Luther also recorded it (Brunswick). The song had origins in folk, sea chanty, and bawdy versions.

Barney Google. w/m Billy Rose and Con Conrad, 1923. Introduced by Eddie Cantor in vaudeville. This novelty song, based on the popular cartoon character with the "goo-goo-googly eyes," later became a staple of Olsen and Johnson's act. It was recorded by Jones and Hare for two different labels in 1923 (Columbia, Brunswick) and by Georgie Price (Victor).

Barnum Had the Right Idea. w/m George M. Cohan, 1911. From (TM) *The Little Millionaire*.

Barnyard Blue. w/m Edwin B. Edwards, Nick LaRocca, Tony Spargo, and Larry Shields, 1919. The writers were all members of the Original Dixieland Jazz Band who were the first to record this (Victor).

Barracuda. w/m Michael Derosier, Roger Fisher, Ann Wilson, and Nancy Wilson, 1977. Top 20 record by the rock band Heart (Portrait).

Barrelhouse Bessie from Basin Street. w. Herb Magidson, m. Jule Styne, 1942. Featured and recorded by Bob Crosby, vocal by Eddie Miller (Decca).

Barrelhouse Music. w/m Willard Robison, 1935. Featured and recorded by Mildred Bailey (Vocalion) and Ramona (Victor).

Bar Room Buddies. w/m Milton Brown, Clifton Crofford, Stephen Dorff, and Snuff Garrett, 1980. Introduced by Clint Eastwood and Merle Haggard in (MM) *Honky Tonk Man*, and recorded by them (Elektra).

Bar Room Polka. w/m Vaughn Horton, 1949. Top 20 record by Russ Morgan and his Orchestra (Decca).

Barry's Boys. w/m June Reizner, 1964. Satire on the campaign of presidential nominee Barry Goldwater, introduced by Gerry Matthews, Jamie Ross, and Nagle Jackson in the cabaret revue "Baker's Dozen." Recorded by The Chad Mitchell Trio (Mercury).

Baseball Game. See **(Love Is Like A) Baseball Game**.

Basin Street Blues. w/m Spencer Williams, 1928. Introduced and recorded by Louis Armstrong (Vocalion), re-released, 1938, then again ten years later (Okeh). In the late 40s, he re-recorded it (Decca 1 & 2). In 1931, a hit version was recorded by a band calling themselves The Charleston Chasers (Columbia). Among the personnel: conductor and clarinet, Benny Goodman; arranger and trombone, Glenn Miller; drums, Gene Krupa; vocal and trombone, Jack Teagarden. The biggest hit, of the many recordings, was by Bing Crosby and Connie Boswell, with John Scott Trotter's Orchestra (Decca), 1937. Louis Armstrong performed the song in three films: (MM) *New Orleans*, 1947; with Jack Teagarden in (MM) *The Strip*, 1951; with Gene Krupa in (MM) *The Glenn Miller Story*, 1954.

Basketball Jones Featuring Tyrone Shoelaces. w/m Tommy Chong and Richard "Cheech" Marin, 1973. Hit novelty satirizing "Love Jones," q. v. by Cheech and Chong (Ode).

Batdance. w/m Prince Rogers Nelson, 1989. From (MP) *Batman*. Hit record by Prince (Warner Bros.).

Batman Theme. m. Neal Hefti, 1966. Theme from series (TVP) "Batman." Top 40 instrumental records by Neal Hefti (RCA) and The Marketts (Warner Bros.). Winner Grammy Award (NARAS) for Best Instrumental Theme, 1966.

Battle of Kookamonga, The. w. J. J. Reynolds and Jimmy Driftwood, m. Jimmy Driftwood, 1959. A parody of the hit "The Battle of New Orleans," recorded by Homer and Jethro, produced by Chet Atkins (RCA).

Battle of New Orleans, The. w/m Jimmy Driftwood, 1959. Based on an early nineteenth century folk tune celebrating the event in the title, Johnny Horton had a #1 hit with the new version (Columbia). Grammy Award Winner (NARAS) for Song of the Year, 1959. Among later popular recordings were those by Harpers Bizarre (Warner Bros), 1968, and The Nitty Gritty Dirt Band (United Artists), 1974.

Battleship Chains. w/m Terry Anderson, 1987. Recorded by the group Georgia Satellites (Elektra).

Battleship Kate. w. Ada Rives, m. Wilbur Sweatman, 1924. Recorded by Sweatman's Band (Radiex).

Baubles, Bangles, and Beads. w/m Robert Wright and George Forrest, 1953. Based on music of Alexander Borodin, as was the entire score of (TM) *Kismet*, in which this was introduced by Doretta Morrow. Peggy Lee had a chart record (Decca). Ann Blyth sang it in (MM) *Kismet*, 1955. The Kirby Stone Four had a popular record (Columbia), 1958.

Bayou Boys. w/m Troy Seals, 1989. Hit Country record by Eddy Raven (Universal).

Bazoom. See **I Need Your Lovin'.**

Be. w/m Neil Diamond, 1973. Sung on the soundtrack of (MP) *Jonathan Livingston Seagull* and on records (Columbia) by Neil Diamond.

Beach Baby. w/m Gil Shakespeare and John Carter, 1974. Written in England and Top 10 recording by the British studio group First Class (UK).

Beach Girl. w/m Terry Melcher and Bruce Johnson 1964. Featured and recorded by Pat Boone (Dot).

Be a Clown. w/m Cole Porter, 1948. Introduced by Gene Kelly and The Nicholas Brothers, and reprised by Kelly and Judy Garland in (MM) *The Pirate*. Kelly and Garland recorded it (MGM).

Beale Street Blues. w/m W. C. Handy, 1917. A favorite Handy blues, recorded by many, including Jelly Roll Morton (Victor), Joe Venuti and Eddie Lang (Mercury), Bob Crosby (Decca), and Wingy Manone (Bluebird).

Beale Street Mama. w. Roy Turk, m. J. Russel Robinson, 1923. First recorded by Lucille Hegamin (Cameo). Other popular versions by Fletcher Henderson and his Orchestra (Paramount); Ted Lewis and his Orchestra (Columbia); and in 1932 Cab Calloway and his Orchestra (Banner).

Beans! Beans!! Beans!!! w. Elmer Bowman, m. Chris Smith, 1912. Novelty song recorded by Gus Van (Columbia).

Beans and Corn Bread. w/m Freddie Clark and Fleecie Moore, 1949. #1 R&B chart record by Louis Jordan and His Tympany Five (Decca).

Beans in My Ears. w/m Len H. Chandler, Jr., 1964. Novelty hit by The Serendipity Singers (Philips).

Be Anything (But Be Mine). w/m Irving Gordon, 1952. Leading record by Eddy Howard (Mercury). Other popular versions by Peggy Lee (Decca); Champ Butler (Columbia); Helen O'Connell (Capitol).

Be a Performer. w. Carolyn Leigh, m. Cy Coleman, 1962. Introduced by Joey Faye, Mort Marshall, and Virginia Martin in (TM) *Little Me.*

Bear Mash Blues. w/m Sammy Lowe, 1941. Introduced and recorded by Erskine Hawkins and his Orchestra (Bluebird).

Bear with Me a Little Longer. w/m Darrell Glenn, 1966. Top 10 Country chart record by Billy Walker (Monument).

Beast of Burden. w/m Mick Jagger and Keith Richards, 1978. Hit record by The Rolling Stones (Rolling Stones). Revived by Bette Midler (Atlantic), 1984.

Beat Goes On, The. w/m Sonny Bono, 1967. Hit record by Sonny and Cher (Atco). The pair used it as the theme song of their variety show (TVM), 1971-1974.

Beat It. w/m Michael Jackson, 1983. #1 gold record, one of five Top 10 singles from the platinum album "Thriller" by Michael Jackson, produced by Quincy Jones (Epic). See also **Eat It.**

Beat Me Daddy, Eight to the Bar. w/m Don Raye, Hugie Prince, and Eleanore Sheehy, 1940. Introduced and recorded by Will Bradley, vocal by Ray McKinley (Columbia, Parts 1 & 2). The Andrew Sisters (Decca) also had a hit record.

Beatnik Fly. w/m Ira Mack and Tom King, 1960. Instrumental rock version of folk song "Blue Tail Fly," by the band, Johnny and The Hurricanes (Warwick).

Beat of a Heart. w/m Patty Smyth, Zack Smith, and Keith Mack, 1985. Recorded by the band, Scandal, featuring Patty Smyth (Columbia).

Beat of My Heart, The. w. Johnny Burke, m. Harold Spina, 1934. Following the introduction by Ramona, with Paul Whiteman's Orchestra, this hit was recorded by Ray Noble

(HMV-Victor); Leo Reisman (Brunswick); Smith Ballew (Melotone); Ben Pollack (Columbia); the Pickens Sisters (Victor).

Beatrice Fairfax, Tell Me What to Do! w. Grant Clarke and Joseph McCarthy, m. James V. Monaco, 1916. Popular song, referring to the early advice-columnist. Leading record by Ada Jones (Victor).

Beat's So Lonely. w/m Charlie Sexton and Keith Forsey, 1986. Chart single by Charlie Sexton (MCA).

Beat Street Breakdown. w/m Melvin Glover and Reggie Griffin, 1984. Chart single by Grandmaster Melle Mel and The Furious Five (Atlantic) from (MP) *Beat Street.*

Beau Night in Hotchkiss Corners. w. Herb Magidson, m. Ben Oakland, 1941. Introduced in the revue in the New York nightclub, George White's Gay White Way. Most popular record: Artie Shaw, vocal by Anita Boyer (Victor).

Beautiful. w/m Stephen Sondheim, 1983. Introduced by Barbara Bryne and Mandy Patinkin in (TM) *Sunday in the Park with George.*

Beautiful. w. James Goldman, John Kander, and William Goldman, m. John Kander, 1962. Introduced by Shelley Berman in (TM) *A Family Affair.*

Beautiful. w. Haven Gillespie, m. Larry Shay, 1927. This was Dick Powell's first single (Vocalion).

Beautiful Brown Eyes. w/m traditional, 1952. Country song in the public domain. Therefore various writers are credited on different recordings and sheet music. Among artists who had well-received recordings were Rosemary Clooney (Columbia); Jimmy Wakely and Les Baxter (Capitol); Art Mooney and his Orchestra (MGM).

Beautiful Candy. w/m Bob Merrill, 1961. Introduced by Anna Maria Alberghetti, puppets, and chorus in (TM) *Carnival.*

Beautiful Eyes. w/m Frankie Adams, Leonard Rosen, and Neal Madaglia, 1948. Chart record by Art Mooney and his Orchestra (MGM).

Beautiful Eyes. w. George Whiting and Carter De Haven, m. Ted Snyder, 1909. Interpolated by Laura Gerite in (TM) *Mr. Hamlet of Broadway*, starring Eddie Foy. Leading record by Ada Jones (Victor).

Beautiful Faces Need Beautiful Clothes. w/m Irving Berlin, 1920. From (TM) *Ziegfeld Follies of 1920*. Recorded by Paul Whiteman's Orchestra (Victor).

Beautiful Girl w. Arthur Freed, m. Nacio Herb Brown, 1933. Sung by Bing Crosby in (MM) *Going Hollywood* and recorded by him with Jimmie Grier's Orchestra (Brunswick); also by the orchestras of Bernie Cummins (Columbia) and Freddy Martin, with vocal by Terry Shand (Brunswick).

Beautiful Girls. w. Bert Kalmar, m. Harry Ruby, 1922. From (TM) *Greenwich Village Follies of 1922*.

Beautiful Isle of Somewhere. w Mrs. Jessie Brown Pounds, m. John S. Ferris, 1901. First published in 1897, it was sung at the funeral of President McKinley in Buffalo, N.Y. The song grew in popularity. Leading records by Harry Anthony and James Harrison (Edison), 1908, and John McCormack (Victor), 1916.

Beautiful Lady in Blue, A. w. Sam M. Lewis, m. J. Fred Coots, 1936. Introduced on radio and records (Brunswick) by Jan Peerce. Also featured and recorded by Jan Garber's (Decca) and Johnny Johnson's (Melotone) bands.

Beautiful Lies. w/m Jack Rhodes, 1956. Recorded by Jean Shepard (Capitol).

Beautiful Love. w. Haven Gillespie, m. Victor Young, Wayne King, and Egbert Van Alstyne, 1931. Van Alstyne's last song success and Young's second of a great career (his first was "Sweet Sue," three years earlier). Introduced by Wayne King and recorded by James Melton (Columbia) and Lewis James (Victor). Later versions by Donald Novis, with

the Victor Young Orchestra (Decca) and Art Tatum (Decca), 1934.

Beautiful Morning, A. w/m Felix Cavaliere and Edward Brigati, 1968. Gold record by The Rascals (Atlantic).

Beautiful Ohio. w. Ballard MacDonald, m. Robert A. King, 1918. King wrote the lyrics under the pseudonym of Mary Earl because of a "for hire" contract he had with his publisher. The dispute was settled and King received full royalties, which were considerable, as the song sold millions of copies of sheet music. This waltz was often used as background music for acrobatic acts in vaudeville and circuses.

Beautiful People. w/m Kenny O'Dell, 1967. Introduced and recorded by Kenny O'Dell (Vegas). Simultaneous Top 40 record by Bobby Vinton (Liberty).

Beautiful Sunday. w/m David Balfe and Peter Green, 1972. Top 20 record by English singer Daniel Boone (Mercury).

Beautiful You. w/m Dave Hanner, 1981. Top 10 Country chart record by The Oak Ridge Boys (MCA).

Beauty Is Only Skin Deep. w/m Eddie Holland and Norman Whitfield, 1966. Top 10 record by The Temptations (Gordy).

Beauty School Dropout. w/m Jim Jacobs and Warren Casey, 1972. Introduced by Alan Paul, Marya Small, and chorus in (TM) *Grease*. It was also included in the film version (MM) *Grease*, 1978.

Be-Baba-Leba (or Be-Baba-Luba). w/m Helen Humes, 1945. Numerous songs were based on, or referred to, phrases associated with a developing form of jazz called "be-bop," "re-bop," or just plain "bop." Humes featured and recorded her version (Philo). See also **Hey! Ba-Ba-Re-Bop.**

Be-Baba-Luba. See **Be-Baba-Leba.**

Bebe. w. Sam Coslow, m. Abner Silver, 1923. Dedicated to film star Bebe Daniels. Recorded by Billy Jones (Columbia).

Be-Bop-a-Lula. w/m Gene Vincent and Tex Davis, 1956. Introduced and hit record by Gene Vincent (Capitol). Vincent sang it in (MM) *The Girl Can't Help It,* 1957.

Be-Bop Baby. w/m Pearl Lenghurst, 1957. Hit record by Ricky Nelson (Imperial).

Be Careful, It's My Heart. w/m Irving Berlin, 1942. Introduced by Bing Crosby, Fred Astaire, and Marjorie Reynolds in (MM) *Holiday Inn.* Crosby had a hit record (Decca), as did Tommy Dorsey, vocal by Frank Sinatra (Victor). Song appeared on "Your Hit Parade" at the same time as Berlin's "I Left My Heart at the Stage Door Canteen." Coincidentally, both songs had the identical penultimate melodic line.

Because. w/m Dave Clark, 1964. Hit record by the British rock group The Dave Clark Five (Epic).

Because. w. Edward Teschemacher, m. Guy d'Hardelot (Mrs. W. I. Rhodes, née Helen Guy), 1902. Concert song that also has had popular appeal. Sung by Deanna Durbin in (MM) *Three Smart Girls Grow Up,* 1939, and Mario Lanza in (MM) *The Great Caruso,* 1951. Perry Como had a million seller (Victor), 1951.

Because. w. Charles Horwitz, m. Frederick V. Bowers, 1898. Introduced in (TM) *The French Maid.* Popular recordings by tenor Albert Campbell (Edison), 1899, and the Haydn Quartet (Gram-o-Phone), 1900.

Because I Love You. w/m Irving Berlin, 1926. Recorded by Henry Burr (Victor).

Because I'm Married Now. w/m Herbert Ingraham, 1907. Comedy song interpolated in numerous musicals and revues. Leading record by Billy Murray (Victor.)

Because My Baby Don't Mean "Maybe" Now. w/m Walter Donaldson, 1928. Featured and recorded by Ruth Etting (Columbia), and Paul Whiteman, vocal by Bing Crosby, Jack Fulton, Charles Gaylord, and Austin Young (Columbia).

Because of Once Upon a Time. w/m Bernard Maltin, Harry Stride, and Joe Young, 1935. Featured and recorded by Fats Waller (Victor) and the Johnny Green Orchestra (Columbia).

Because of You. w. Arthur Hammerstein, m. Dudley Wilkinson, 1940, 1951. Achieved some popularity via recordings by Larry Clinton, vocal by Peggy Mann (Bluebird), and the orchestras of Horace Heidt (Columbia), and Tommy Tucker (Okeh). Song was revived in (MP) *I Was An American Spy,* 1951, recorded by Tony Bennett, and became his first million-seller (Columbia). It was on "Your Hit Parade" for twenty-three weeks, eleven times in the #1 spot, the second most of any song in the survey's history. ("Too Young" was first with twelve appearances.)

Because the Night. w/m Patti Smith and Bruce Springsteen, 1978. Recorded by The Patti Smith Group (Arista). Included in the album "Bruce Springsteen and The E Street Band Live" (Columbia), 1986.

Because They're Young. w. Aaron Schroeder and Wally Gold, m. Don Costa, 1960. Introduced, instrumentally, by Duane Eddy in (MM) *Because They're Young,* and on a Top 10 record (Jamie).

Because You're Mine. w. Sammy Cahn, m. Nicholas Brodsky, 1952. Introduced by Mario Lanza in (MM) *Because You're Mine.* Nominated for Academy Award, 1952. Leading records by Mario Lanza, a million-seller (RCA Victor), and Nat "King" Cole (Capitol).

Because You're You. w. Henry Blossom, m. Victor Herbert, 1906. Sung by Allene Crater and Neal McCay in (TM) *The Red Mill.*

Bedelia. w. William Jerome, m. Jean Schwartz, 1903. Introduced and popularized by Blanche Ring in (TM) *The Jersey Lily.* Leading recordings by The Haydn Quartet (Victor), Billy Murray (Edison), George J. Gaskin (Columbia), Arthur Pryor's Band (Victor).

Bed of Rose's. w/m Harold Reid, 1971. Crossover (C&W/Pop) hit by The Statler Brothers (Mercury).

Beechwood 4-5789. w/m William Stevenson, George Gordy, and Marvin Gaye, 1962. Top 20 record by The Marvelettes (Tamla). Revived by The Carpenters (A&M), 1982.

Been to Canaan. w/m Carole King, 1972. Recorded by Carole King (Ode).

Beep Beep. w/m Donald Clapps and Carl Cicchetti, 1958. Novelty hit by The Playmates (Roulette).

Beer Barrel Polka. w. Lew Brown (Engl.), m. Jaromir Vejvoda, 1939. Based on the Czech song "Skoda Lasky," with words by Vasek Zeman and Wladimir A. Timm. Introduced in the United States by Will Glahe and his Musette Orchestra (Victor), the bestselling record was by the Andrews Sisters (Decca). Its many recordings made it one of the top sheet music sellers and juke box favorites of the year.

Beer That Made Milwaukee Famous, The. w/m Dan McAvoy, 1903. Comedy song introduced by Dan McAvoy in (TM) *Mr. Bluebeard*. Popular recording by Dan Quinn (Victor). The title emanated from the slogan, still in use, for Schlitz Beer.

Bee's Knees. w. Leo Wood, m. Ray Lopez and Ted Lewis, 1922. Introduced instrumentally by Ted Lewis and his Orchestra (Columbia).

Before and After. w/m Van McCoy, 1965. Popular record by the British folk-rock duo, Chad and Jeremy (Columbia).

Before I Kiss the World Goodbye. w. Howard Dietz, m. Arthur Schwartz, 1963. Introduced by Mary Martin in (TM) *Jennie*, based on the life of actress Laurette Taylor.

Before I'm Over You. w/m Betty Sue Perry, 1964. Country hit by Loretta Lynn (Decca).

Before My Heart Finds Out. w/m Randy Goodrum, 1978. Recorded by Gene Cotton (Ariola).

Before the Next Teardrop Falls. w/m Ben Peters and Vivian Keith, 1975. #1 gold record by Freddy Fender (ABC/Dot).

Before the Parade Passes By. w/m Lee Adams, Charles Strouse, and Jerry Herman, 1964. Introduced by Carol Channing in (TM) *Hello, Dolly!*; and sung by Barbra Streisand in the film version (MM) *Hello, Dolly!*, 1969. While the show was in Detroit, prior to its Broadway opening, director Gower Champion called in Strouse and Adams for an additional song. Their title and concept were accepted and rewritten by Herman.

Before This Day Ends. w/m Roy Drusky, Vic McAlpin, and Marie Wilson, 1961. C&W chart hit by George Hamilton IV (ABC-Paramount).

Before You Call. w/m Fred Rose, 1949. Hit Country record by Dave Landers (MGM).

Before You Go. w/m Buck Owens and Don Rich, 1965. Hit Country song by Buck Owens (Capitol).

Beg, Borrow, and Steal. w/m Lou Zerato and Joey Day, 1967. Top 40 record by the group Ohio Express (Cameo).

Begat, The. w. E. Y. Harburg, m. Burton Lane, 1947. Introduced by Lorenzo Fuller, Robert Pitkin, Louis Sharp, and Jerry Laws in (TM) *Finian's Rainbow*. Keenan Wynn, Avon Long, Jester Hairston, and Roy Glenn performed it in the screen adaptation (MM) *Finian's Rainbow*, 1968.

Beggar to a King. w/m J. P. Richardson, 1961. Country hit by Hank Snow (RCA Victor); recorded and released a year-and-a-half after the death of the writer, who was also known as The Big Bopper.

Beggin'. w/m Peggy Farina and Bob Gaudio, 1967. Top 20 recored by The Four Seasons (Philips).

Begging for Love. w/m Irving Berlin, 1931. Introduced and recorded by Rudy Vallee (Victor).

Begging to You. w/m Marty Robbins, 1963. Crossover (C&W/Pop) hit by Marty Robbins (Columbia).

(I've Got) Beginner's Luck. w. Ira Gershwin, m. George Gershwin, 1937. Introduced by Fred Astaire in (MM) *Shall We Dance*. Leading records by Astaire, with Johnny Green's Orchestra (Brunswick); Tommy Dorsey, vocal by Edythe Wright (Victor).

Beginning of My End, The. w/m Guy Draper, 1969. Top 40 record by the Howard University soul group, The Unifics (Kapp).

Beginnings. w/m Robert Lamm, 1971. Top 10 single from the 1969 album by the group, Chicago, of which Lamm was keyboardist (Columbia).

Begin the Beguine. w/m Cole Porter, 1935. First sung by June Knight, who then danced to it with Charles Walters in (TM) *Jubilee*. The number did not catch on with the public until Artie Shaw and his Band recorded Jerry Gray's arrangement (Bluebird), 1938. The record sold over two million copies, establishing the song and making Shaw the #1 band of the year. Fred Astaire and Eleanor Powell danced to it in (MM) *Broadway Melody of '40* and Deanna Durbin sang it in (MM) *Hers to Hold*, 1943. In the Cole Porter story (MM) *Night and Day*, 1946, it was sung by Carlos Ramirez and danced by George Zoritch and Milada Mladova. Richard Maltby and his Orchestra recorded the unique "Begin the Beguine March" ("X"), 1955.

Be Glad. w/m Ken Westberry and Justin Tubb, 1969. Top 10 Country record by Del Reeves (United Artists).

Be Good to Yourself. w/m Steve Perry, Jonathan Cain, and Neal Schon, 1986. Top 10 single, written and recorded by the trio Journey (Columbia).

Beg Your Pardon. w/m Francis Craig and Beasley Smith, 1947. Best-selling record by Francis Craig, vocal by Bob Lamb (Bullet). Others of note: Frankie Carle, vocal by Marjorie Hughes (Columbia); Larry Green, vocal by Don Grady (RCA Victor); The Dinning Sisters (Capitol).

Behind Blue Eyes. w/m Peter Townshend, 1971. Top 40 U.S. record by the British group The Who (Decca).

Behind Closed Doors. w/m Kenny O'Dell, 1973. Country/Pop chart hit by Charlie Rich (Epic). Winner Grammy Award (NARAS) Country Song of the Year.

Behind the Tears. w/m Ned Miller and Sue Miller, 1965. Country hit by Sonny James (Capitol).

Be Honest with Me. w/m Fred Rose and Gene Autry, 1941. Introduced by Autry in (MM) *Ridin' On a Rainbow* and on records (Okeh). Nominated for Academy Award. Interpolated in (MM) *Strictly in the Groove*, same year by Jimmy Wakely and later recorded by him (Coral). Records also by Bing Crosby (Decca); Freddy Martin, vocal by Clyde Rodgers and Eddie Stone (Bluebird).

Bei Mir Bist Du Schoen (Means That You're Grand). w. Sammy Cahn, Saul Chaplin (Engl.), Jacob Jacobs (Yid.), m. Sholem Secunda, 1937. Originally in a Yiddish musical *I Would If I Could*, performed by Ivan Lebedeff, 1933, and titled *Bei Mir Bistu Shein*. The new version was introduced with the hit recording of the Andrews Sisters (Decca). The song was one of the top sheet music sellers of the year and was on "Your Hit Parade" for nine weeks, two in the #1 position. The Andrews Sisters sang it in (MM) *Take it Big*, 1944. Revived by Louis Prima and Keely Smith (Dot), 1959.

Being Alive. w/m Stephen Sondheim, 1970. Introduced by Dean Jones and cast in (TM) *Company*.

Being in Love. w/m Meredith Wilson, 1962. Introduced in the film version (MM) *The Music Man* by Shirley Jones.

Bein' Green. w/m Joe Raposo, 1971. Introduced by Jim Henson, as the voice of the Muppet, Kermit the Frog, on the childrens' series (TVM) "Sesame Street." Recorded by Frank Sinatra (Reprise).

Being with You. w/m William "Smokey" Robinson, 1981. #1 R&B/Pop gold record by Smokey Robinson (Tamla).

Be Italian (Ti Voglio Bene). w/m Maury Yeston, 1982. Introduced by Kathi Moss and company in (TM) *Nine*.

Be Kind to Your Parents. w/m Harold Rome, 1954. Introduced by Florence Henderson and Lloyd Reese in (TM) *Fanny*.

Believe in Humanity. w/m Carole King, 1973. Recorded by Carole King (Ode).

Believe It, Beloved. w. George Whiting and Nat Schwartz, m. J. C. Johnson, 1934. One of Fats Waller's major successes (Victor). Also recorded by Isham Jones, vocal by Eddie Stone (Decca); Red Allen (Perfect). In the early 50s, Al Hibbler, with Johnny Hodges's Orchestra, had a popular version (Mercury).

Believe It or Not. See **Theme from "The Greatest American Hero."**

Believe Me, Beloved. w. Joseph Herbert, m. Efrem Zimbalist, 1920. From (TM) *Honeydew*.

Believe What You Say. w/m Johnny Burnette and Dorsey Burnette, 1958. Top 10 record by Ricky Nelson (Imperial).

Bella Bella Marie. w. Don Pelosi and Leo Towers (Engl.), m. Gerhard Winkler, 1947. Original German title "Capri Fischer," words by Ralph Maria Siegel. Popular U.S. recordings by The Andrew Sisters (Decca); Jack Smith, with Jan Garber's Orchestra (Capitol); Eddy Howard (Mercury); Johnny Desmond (Columbia).

Bella Linda. w. Steve Barri and Larry Gross (Engl.), I. Mogol (It.), m. L. Battisti, 1969. Italian song. Top 40 English version by The Grass Roots (Dunhill).

Bell Bottom Blues. w/m Eric Clapton, 1971. Written and recorded in England by Derek [Eric Clapton] and the Dominos (Atco). Clapton re-recorded it under his own name (Polydor), 1973.

Bell Bottom Blues. w. Hal David, m. Leon Carr, 1954. Leading record by Teresa Brewer, with Jack Pleis's Orchestra (Coral).

Bell Bottom Trousers. w/m Moe Jaffe, 1945. Adapted from a traditional sea chantey and in its new guise, applied to sailors in the U.S. Navy. Top 10 records by Guy Lombardo, vocal by Jimmy Brown (Decca); Tony Pastor, vocal by Ruth McCullogh (Victor); Kay Kyser, vocal by Ferdy and Slim (Columbia); Louis Prima, vocal by Lily Ann Carol (Majestic); Jerry Colonna (Capitol).

Belle. w/m Al Green, Reuben Fairfax, and Fred Jordan, 1977. Top 10 R&B and Pop chart record by Al Green (Hi).

Belle, Belle, My Liberty Belle. w/m Bob Merrill, 1951. Leading record by Guy Mitchell, with Mitch Miller's Orchestra (Columbia).

Belle of Avenoo A, The. w/m Safford Waters, 1895.

Belle of the Ball. w. Mitchell Parish, m. Leroy Anderson, 1954. Recorded instrumentally by Leroy Anderson's Orchestra (Decca) and vocally by Marian Marlowe (Columbia).

Belle of the Ball, The. w/m Charles K. Harris, 1906. Thirteen years after Harris's monumental hit, "After the Ball," he wrote another "story" song about a ball. Recorded by the bass, Frank Stanley (Victor).

Belles of Southern Bell. w/m Don Wayne, 1965. Country chart hit by Del Reeves (United Artists).

Bells, The. w/m Anna Gaye, Marvin Gaye, Berry Gordy, Jr., and Elgie Stover, 1979. First recorded by James Brown (King), 1960. Top 10 hit by The Originals (Soul), 1970.

Bells, The. w/m Billy Ward, 1953. Hit R&B record by Billy Ward and his Dominoes (Federal).

Bells Are Ringing. w. Betty Comden and Adolph Green, 1956. Introduced by the chorus in (TM) *Bells Are Ringing*, and in the film version (MM) *Bells Are Ringing*, 1960.

Bells of Saint Mary's, The. w. Douglas Furber, m. A. Emmett Adams, 1917. An English song that attained popularity in the U.S. with glee clubs and concert bands. The New Zealand-born soprano, Frances Alda, recorded a popular solo version (Victor), 1920. Bing Crosby and Ingrid Bergman starred in the film (MM) *The Bells of Saint Mary's*, 1945, which revived the song.

Bells of San Raquel, The. w. Fred Wise and Milton Leeds (Engl.), w. (Sp.)/m Lorenzo Barcelata, 1941. The original Mexican title was "Por Ti Aprendi a Querer." Most popular recordings by Dick Jurgens, vocal by Harry Cool (Okeh); Glen Gray and the Casa Loma Orchestra, vocal by Kenny Sargent (Decca); Art Jarrett (Victor); Claude Thornhill and his Orchestra (Columbia).

Bell Waltz, The. See **Music of Love.**

Belly Up to the Bar, Boys. w/m Meredith Wilson, 1960. Introduced by Tammy Grimes, Joseph Sirola, and men in (TM) *The Unsinkable Molly Brown*. In the film version (MM) *The Unsinkable Molly Brown*, 1964, it was sung and danced by Debbie Reynolds and company.

Beloved. w. Paul Francis Webster, m. Nicholas Brodsky, 1954. Introduced by Mario Lanza, singing on the soundtrack for Edmund Purdom, in (MM) *The Student Prince*.

Beloved. w. Gus Kahn, m. Joe Sanders, 1928. Popular recordings by Ruth Etting (Columbia); the orchestras of Coon-Sanders (Victor); Guy Lombardo (Columbia); Don Bestor (Victor).

Beloved, Be Faithful. w/m Erwin Drake and Jimmy Shirl, 1950. Most popular recording by Russ Morgan and his Orchestra (Decca).

Beloved, It Is Morn. w. Emily Hickey, m. Florence Aylward, 1896. First published and introduced in London, England.

Be Mine. w. Jack Elliot, m. Harold Spina, 1950. Leading records by Mindy Carson (Victor), and June Hutton, with Vic Schoen's Orchestra (Decca).

Be Mine! w. Desmond O'Connor, m. Harold Fields (adapt.), 1948. Adapted from the traditional Spanish song "La Paloma." Most popular recordings by the British singer, Ann Shelton (London), and Jo Stafford and Gordon MacRae (Capitol).

Be Mine Tonight. w. Sunny Skylar (Engl.), w. (Sp.) and m. Maria Teresa Lara, 1952. Original title in Mexico "Noche de Ronda." Leading recordings by Les Baxter and his Orchestra (Capitol); Bill Farrell (MGM).

Bemsha Swing. m. Thelonious Monk and Denzil Best, 1952. Introduced by Thelonious Monk (Blue Note).

Be My Baby. w/m Jeff Barry, Ellie Greenwich, and Phil Spector, 1963. Introduced and hit record by The Ronettes, produced by Phil Spector (Philles). Later popular records by Andy Kim (Steed) and Cissy Houston (Janus).

Be My Guest. w/m Antoine "Fats" Domino, John Marascalco, and Tommy Boyce, 1959. Featured and recorded by Fats Domino (Imperial).

Be My Life's Companion. w/m Bob Hilliard and Milton De Lugg, 1952. The Mills Brothers, with Sy Oliver's Orchestra (Decca), had the biggest hit recording followed by Rosemary Clooney (Columbia).

Be My Little Baby Bumble Bee. w. Stanley Murphy, m. Henry I. Marshall, 1912. Introduced by the Dolly Sisters in (TM) *Ziegfeld Follies of 1912*. Ada Jones and Billy Murray had a hit record (Victor). It was sung by June Haver in (MM) *Irish Eyes Are Smiling*, 1944; Doris Day and Russell Arms in (MM) *By the Light of the Silvery Moon*, 1953; Eddie Cantor, dubbing for Keefe Brasselle in (MM) *The Eddie Cantor Story*, 1953.

Be My Little Teddy Bear. w. Vincent Bryan, m. Max Hoffman, 1907. Introduced by Anna Held in (TM) *A Parisian Model*. Popular record by Ada Jones and Billy Murray (Edison).

Be My Love. w. Sammy Cahn, m. Nicholas Brodsky, 1950. Introduced by Mario Lanza and Kathryn Grayson in (MM) *The Toast of New Orleans*. Nominated for Academy Award. Lanza's recording, with Ray Sinatra's Orchestra and The Jeff Alexander Choir (RCA Victor), sold over two million copies. It was sung by Doretta Morrow (auditioning over the telephone) in the Lanza film (MM) *Because You're Mine*, 1952, and by Connie Francis in (MM) *Looking for Love*, 1964.

Ben. w/m Don Black and Walter Scharf, 1972. Performed on the soundtrack of (MP) *Ben*, and on his first #1 record by Michael Jackson (Motown). Song nominated for an Academy Award.

Bench in the Park, A. w. Jack Yellen, m. Milton Ager, 1930. Introduced by the Brox Sisters, the Rhythm Boys (Bing Crosby, Harry Barris, Al Rinker), George Chiles, and Paul Whiteman and his Orchestra in (MM) *King of Jazz*. Recorded by Whiteman and the Rhythm Boys (Columbia).

Bend Down, Sister. w. Ballard MacDonald and David Silverstein, m. Con Conrad, 1931. Performed by Charlotte Greenwood in (MM) *Palmy Days*, starring Eddie Cantor.

Bend Me, Shape Me. w. Scott English, m. Laurence Weiss, 1968. Gold record by The American Breed (Acta).

Be Near Me. w/m Martin Fry and Mark White, 1985. Top 10 record by the English group, ABC (Mercury).

Beneath Still Waters. w/m Dallas Frazier, 1970, 1980. Country chart record by Diana Trask (Dot), 1970. #1 record by Emmylou Harris (Warner Bros), 1980.

Ben Hur Chariot Race. m. E. T. Paull, 1899. A march.

Be Nice to Me. w/m Todd Rundgren, 1971. Recorded by Runt [Todd Rundgren] (Bearsville).

Benji's Theme. See **I Feel Love**.

Bennie and the Jets. w/m Elton John and Bernie Taupin, 1974. #1 gold record by the English singer/writer Elton John (MCA).

Be Quiet, Mind. w/m Liz Anderson, 1961. Top 10 C&W chart record by Del Reeves (Decca). Ott Stephens also had a chart version (Reprise), 1964.

Berlin Melody, The. m. Heino Gaze, 1961. German instrumental recorded in the U.S. by Billy Vaughn and his Orchestra (Dot).

Bermuda. w/m Cynthia Strother and Eugene R. Strother, 1952. Hit record by The Bell Sisters, Cynthia and Kay, sixteen and eleven, respectively, accompanied by Henri René and his Orchestra (RCA Victor). Popular record by Ray Anthony, vocal by Tommy Mercer and Marcie Miller (Capitol).

Bernadette. w/m Brian Holland, Lamont Dozier, and Eddie Holland, 1967. Top 10 record by The Four Tops (Motown).

Bernadine. w/m Johnny Mercer, 1957. Title song sung by Pat Boone in his first film (MP) *Bernadine*. Boone also had the best-selling recording (Dot).

Bernie's Tune. w/m Bernie Miller, Mike Stoller, and Jerry Leiber, 1953. Introduced as instrumental by the Gerry Mulligan Quartet (Pacific Jazz). Recorded by the vocal group The Cheers (Capitol).

Bertha Butt Boogie, The. w/m Jimmy Castor and John Pruitt, 1975. Top 20 novelty by The Jimmy Castor Bunch (Atlantic).

Besame Mucho. w. Sunny Skylar, m. Consuelo Velazquez, 1943. Mexican song, with original Spanish words by Velazquez. #1 record by Jimmy Dorsey, vocal by Kitty Kallen and Bob Eberly (Decca). Andy Russell (Capitol) and Abe Lyman and his Orchestra (Hit) also had popular recordings. Song heard in (MM) *Follow the Boys*, 1944.

Beside a Babbling Brook. w. Gus Kahn, m. Walter Donaldson, 1923. Featured and recorded by Marion Harris (Brunswick).

Beside a Moonlit Stream. w. Sam Coslow, m. Frederick Hollander, 1938. Recordings: Buddy Clark (Vocalion); the bands of Al Donahue (Vocalion); Horace Heidt (Brunswick); Sammy Kaye (Victor); Freddy Martin (Bluebird).

Beside an Open Fireplace. w/m Paul Denniker and Will Osborne, 1929. Introduced and used as a theme song by Will Osborne and his Band. Also recorded by the bands of Jack Denny (Brunswick) and The Dorsey Brothers (Regal).

Beside You. w/m Jay Livingston and Ray Evans, 1947. Introduced by Bob Hope and Dorothy Lamour in (MP) *My Favorite Brunette*, and recorded by them (Capitol).

Bess, Oh Where's My Bess? w. Du Bose Heyward and Ira Gershwin, m. George Gershwin, 1935. Introduced by Todd Duncan, with Ruby Elzy and Helen Dowdy in (TM) *Porgy and Bess*. Sung by Robert McFerrin, dubbing for Sidney Poitier, in (MM) *Porgy and Bess*, 1959.

Bess, You Is My Woman Now. w. DuBose Heyward and Ira Gershwin, m. George Gershwin, 1935. Introduced by Todd Duncan and Anne Brown in (TM) *Porgy and Bess*. In (MM) *Porgy and Bess*, 1959, the vocals were dubbed by Robert McFerrin for Sidney Poitier and by Adele Addison for Dorothy Dandridge in the title roles.

Best Disco in Town, The. w. Henri Belodo (Fr.) and Phil Hurtt, m. Jacques Morali and Ritchie Rome, 1976. French/English medley by the studio group The Ritchie Family (Marlin).

Best Dressed Beggar (in Town), The. w/m Houston Turner, 1962. Country chart record by Carl Smith (Columbia).

Best I Get Is Much Obliged to You, The. w/m Benjamin Hapgood Burt, 1907.

Be Still, My Heart. w/m Allan Flynn and Jack Egan, 1934. Popular recordings by the Freddy Martin (Brunswick) and Russ Morgan (Melotone) orchestras; Gertrude Niesen (Columbia); and the Pickens Sisters (Victor).

Be Still My Beating Heart. w/m Sting, 1988. Popular record by the British singer/songwriter Sting (A&M).

Best Is Yet to Come, The. w. Carolyn Leigh, m. Cy Coleman, 1959. Introduced and recorded by Tony Bennett (Columbia). The song is a favorite with jazz musicians and singers.

Best Man, The. w/m Roy Alfred and Fred Wise, 1946. Best-selling record by The King [Nat] Cole Trio (Capitol). Also featured and recorded by Les Brown, vocal by Butch Stone (Columbia).

Best Man in the World, The. w/m John Barry, Sue Ennis, Anne Wilson, and Nancy Wilson, 1986. Introduced by Ann Wilson in (MP) *The Golden Child* and on records (Capitol).

Best of Both Worlds. w/m Mark London and Don Black, 1968. Top 40 U.S. release by the Scottish star Lulu (Epic).

Best of Everything, The. w. Sammy Cahn, m. Alfred Newman, 1959. Introduced by Johnny Mathis in (MP) *The Best of Everything*, and on records (Columbia). Nominated for Academy Award, 1959.

Best of Everything, The. w. B. G. DeSylva and Arthur Jackson, m. George Gershwin, 1919. Introduced by Jack Hazzard and ensemble in (TM) *La, La, Lucille*.

Best of Me, The. w/m David Foster, Jeremy Lubbock, and Richard Mars, 1986. Chart single by David Foster and Olivia Newton-John (Atlantic).

Best of My Love. w/m Maurice White and Al McKay, 1977. #1 R&B and Pop chart record by the trio The Emotions (Columbia).

Best of My Love. w/m Glenn Frey, Don Henley, and J. D. Souther, 1975. #1 record by The Eagles (Asylum).

Best of Times, The. w/m Jerry Herman, 1983. Introduced by Elizabeth Parrish, George Hearn, and company in (TM) *La Cage Aux Folles.*

Best of Times, The. w/m Dennis De-Young, 1981. Gold record by the quintet Styx (A&M).

Best That You Can Do, The. See **Arthur's Theme.**

Best Thing for You, The. w/m Irving Berlin, 1950. Introduced by Ethel Merman and Paul Lukas in (TM) *Call Me Madam.* Merman and George Sanders sang it in (MM) *Call Me Madam,* 1953.

Best Things Happen While You're Dancing, The. w/m Irving Berlin, 1954. Introduced by Danny Kaye and Vera-Ellen in (MM) *White Christmas.*

Best Things in Life Are Free, The. w. B. G. DeSylva and Lew Brown, m. Ray Henderson, 1927. Sung by John Price Jones and Mary Lawlor in (TM) *Good News.* George Olsen and his Orchestra appeared in the production and had a hit recording (Victor). In the 1930 film, (MM) *Good News,* Mary Lawlor sang it with Stanley Smith. In the 1947 version, it was sung by June Allyson, reprised by Mel Tormé, then in French by Peter Lawford. In the De-Sylva, Brown and Henderson story (MM) *The Best Things in Life Are Free,* 1956, the song was performed by Gordon MacRae, Dan Dailey, Ernest Borgnine, and Sheree North. Larry Kert and the ensemble sang it in (TM) *A Musical Jubilee,* 1975.

Best Thing That Ever Happened to Me. w/m Jim Weatherly, 1974. First recorded by Ray Price (Columbia), 1973, as "You're the Best Thing That Ever Happened to Me." Gladys Knight and the Pips had a gold record version (Buddah).

Best Wishes. w/m Roy Milton, 1952. Recorded by Roy Milton (Specialty).

Best Wishes. w. Ted Koehler, m. Edward Kennedy "Duke" Ellington, 1932. Introduced and recorded by Duke Ellington and his Orchestra (Brunswick).

Be Sure to Wear Some Flowers in Your Hair. See **San Francisco (Be Sure to Wear Some Flowers in Your Hair).**

Betcha By Golly, Wow. w/m Thom Bell and Linda Creed, 1972. Gold record by The Stylistics (Avco).

Beth. w/m Peter Criss, Bob Ezrin, and Paul Stanley, 1976. Top 10 gold record by the hard rock band Kiss (Casablanca).

Be Thankful for What You've Got. w/m William De Vaughn, 1974. Top 10 record by William De Vaughn (Roxbury).

Be There. w/m Allee Willis and Franne Golde, 1987. Introduced by The Pointer Sisters on the soundtrack of (MP) *Beverly Hills Cop II* and on a chart single (MCA).

Be True to Your School. w/m Brian Wilson, 1963. Hit record by The Beach Boys, with cheerleading by The Honeys. Record included the college marching song, "On Wisconsin" (Capitol).

Bette Davis Eyes. w. Donna Weiss, m. Jackie De Shannon, 1981. First recorded in an album "New Arrangement" (Capitol), 1975, by Jackie De Shannon. Kim Carne's version (EMI America) became one of the biggest hits of 1981, being #1 for nine weeks and, of course, earning a gold record. It was #1 in twenty-one countries and was a double Grammy Award (NARAS) winner, Song of the Year, and Record of the Year.

Better Days. w/m Melissa Manchester and Carole Bayer Sager, 1976. Recorded by Melissa Manchester (Arista).

Better Love Next Time, A. w/m Bobby Wood and John Christopher, 1989. Hit Country record by Merle Haggard (Epic).

Better Love Next Time. w/m Larry Keith, Steve Pippin, and Johnny Slate, 1979. Recorded by the group Dr. Hook (Capitol).

Better Luck Next Time. w/m Irving Berlin, 1948. Introduced by Judy Garland in (MM) *Easter Parade*.

Better Man. w/m Clint Patrick Black and James Hayden Nicholas, 1989. Country chart hit by Clint Black (RCA).

Better Move It on Home. w/m Ray Griff, 1971. Top 10 Country record by Porter Wagoner and Dolly Parton (RCA).

Better Place to Be. w/m Harry Chapin, 1976. Recorded by Harry Chapin (Elektra, Parts 1 & 2).

Better Than Ever. w. Carole Bayer Sager, m. Marvin Hamlisch, 1979. Introduced by Candice Bergen in (MP) *Starting Over*.

Betty Co-Ed. w/m J. Paul Fogarty and Rudy Vallee, 1930. A popular song in the rhythm of a football marching song, introduced by Rudy Vallee on his radio show and on records (Victor). Also recorded by Bob Haring (Brunswick). It was the title song of (MP) *Betty Co-ed* in 1947.

Betty My Angel. w/m Jerry Fuller, 1959. Introduced and recorded by Jerry Fuller (Challenge).

Between a Kiss and a Sigh. w. Johnny Burke, m. Arthur Johnston, 1938. Recorded and popularized by Tommy Dorsey, vocal by Edythe Wright (Victor), and Al Donahue, vocal by Paula Kelly (Vocalion).

Between Blue Eyes and Jeans. w/m Kenneth McDuffie, 1985. Top 10 Country chart single by Conway Twitty (Warner Bros.).

Between 18th and 19th on Chestnut Street. w/m Will Osborne and Dick Rodgers, 1940. A Philadelphia-inspired song with popular recordings by Bing Crosby and Connie Boswell (Decca) and the bands of Bob Crosby (Decca), Will Osborne (Varsity), Bob Zurke (Victor), Charlie Barnet (Victor), Freddie Slack (Mercury).

Between the Devil and the Deep Blue Sea. w. Ted Koehler, m. Harold Arlen, 1930. Introduced by Aida Ward in the revue *Rhythmania* at the Cotton Club in Harlem, New York.

Between the Sheets. w/m Ernest Isley, Marvin Isley, Ronald Isley, Rudolph Isley, O'Kelly Isley, and Christopher Jasper, 1983. Top 10 R&B record by The Isley Brothers (T-Neck).

Between Trains. w/m Robbie Robertson, 1983. Introduced by Robbie Robertson in (MP) *The King of Comedy*.

Beware (Brother, Beware). w/m Morry Lasco, Dick Adams, and Fleecie Moore, 1946. Top 40 record by Louis Jordan and his Tympany Five (Decca).

Beware My Heart. w/m Sam Coslow, 1947. Introduced by Vaughn Monroe in (MM) *Carnegie Hall*. Leading record by Margaret Whiting (Capitol).

Beware of It. w/m Cy Coben, 1954. Top 10 C&W chart record by Johnnie and Jack (RCA).

Bewildered. w/m Leonard Whitcup and Teddy Powell, 1938. Recorded by Tommy Dorsey and his Orchestra (Victor). Revived 1949, by Billy Eckstine (MGM) and Herb Jeffries (Columbia).

Bewitched, Bothered, and Bewildered. w. Lorenz Hart, m. Richard Rodgers, 1941, 1950. Introduced by Vivienne Segal in (TM) *Pal Joey*. In the film version (MM) *Pal Joey*, 1957, it was sung by Frank Sinatra and, dubbing for Rita Hayworth on the soundtrack, Jo Ann Greer. It was revived in 1950, and was on "Your Hit Parade" for sixteen weeks, five times as #1. Best-selling record by Bill Snyder and his Orchestra (Tower). Others: Gordon Jenkins, vocal by Mary Lou Williams (Decca); Jan August and Jerry Murad's Harmonicats (Mercury); Mel Tormé (Capitol); Doris Day (Columbia).

Beyond the Blue Horizon. w. Leo Robin, m. Richard A. Whiting and W. Franke Harling, 1930. Introduced by Jeanette MacDonald in (MM) *Monte Carlo* and reprised by her in (MM) *Follow the Boys*, 1944. She also recorded it (Victor). Her singing this from a train window, punctuated by the rhythmic pattern of blasts of steam emanating from the area of the revolving wheels, has placed this song atop the list of "railroad songs."

Beyond the Reef. w/m Jack Pitman, 1950. Leading records by Bing Crosby (Decca); Margaret Whiting and Jimmy Wakely (Capitol); Blue Barron and his Orchestra (MGM); Eddie Grant (Capitol).

Beyond the Sea. w. Jack Lawrence (Engl.), m. Charles Trenet, 1947, 1960. Original French title "La Mer," lyrics by Charles Trenet who introduced it in France and in the United States. Popular instrumental recordings by Harry James (Columbia), Benny Goodman (Capitol), Montovani (London). Tex Beneke and his Band recorded it, vocal by Garry Stevens (RCA Victor). Singer Bobby Darin revived it with a Top 10 record (Atco), 1960.

Beyond the Valley of the Dolls. w/m Stu Phillips and Bob Stone, 1970. Sung on the soundtrack of (MP) *Beyond the Valley of the Dolls* by The Sandpipers.

Be Your Man. w/m Jesse Johnson, 1985. Recorded by Jesse Johnson's Revue (A&M).

Bianca. w/m Cole Porter, 1949. Introduced by Harold Lang in (TM) *Kiss Me Kate*. Not used in film.

Bibbidi-Bobbidi-Boo. w/m Mack David, Al Hoffman, and Jerry Livingston, 1950. Introduced by the voice of Ilene Woods, as Cinderella, in the animated film (MM) *Cinderella*.

Nominated for Academy Award. Among recordings: Ilene Woods (Bluebird), Jo Stafford and Gordon MacRae (Capitol), Perry Como (RCA Victor), Dinah Shore (Columbia).

Bible Tells Me So, The. w/m Dale Evans, 1955. Introduced by Roy Rogers and Dale Evans. Most popular records by Don Cornell (Coral) and Nick Noble (Wing).

Bicycle Race. w/m Freddy Mercury, 1978. Recorded in England by the group Queen (Elektra).

Bicyclettes de Belsize. See **Les Bicyclettes de Belsize.**

Bidin' My Time. w. Ira Gershwin, m. George Gershwin, 1930. Introduced by the male quartet, The Foursome, in (TM) *Girl Crazy*. In the second film version (MM) *Girl Crazy*, 1943 (the song was not used in the 1932 adaptation), it was sung by Judy Garland and a male quartet. In a loosely adapted script based on the same story (MM) *When the Boys Meet the Girls*, 1966, it was sung by Herman's Hermits. It was also heard in (MM) *Rhapsody in Blue*, the George Gershwin biography, 1945, and in (MM) *The Glenn Miller Story*, 1954.

Biff'ly Blue. m. Henry "Red" Allen, Jr., 1929. Jazz instrumental recorded by Red Allen (Victor).

Big, Bright Green Pleasure Machine, The. w/m Paul Simon, 1966. Sung by Simon and Garfunkel in their album "Parsley, Sage, Rosemary, and Thyme." They then performed it on the soundtrack of (MP) *The Graduate*, 1967.

Big Apple, The. w. Buddy Bernier, m. Bob Emmerich, 1937. A song about a dance called "The Big Apple," introduced and recorded by Tommy Dorsey and his Orchestra (Victor). Among other recordings: Clyde Lucas and his Orchestra (Variety), and Frank Froeba, vocal by the Al Rinker Trio (Decca).

Big Bad John. w/m Jimmy Dean, 1961. Hit record by Jimmy Dean (Columbia). Winner of Grammy Award (NARAS) for Best Country and Western Recording, 1961.

Big Bad Wolf Was Dead, The. w/m Val Burton and Will Jason, 1934. From the Wheeler and Woolsey film (MM) *Cock-eyed Cavaliers*. Recorded by Ted Fio Rito and his Orchestra (Brunswick).

Big Bass Viol, The. w/m M. T. Bohannon, 1910.

Big Boss Man. w/m Luther Dixon and Al Smith, 1961. Chart record by Jimmy Reed (Vee-Jay). Elvis Presley had a Top 40 version (RCA), 1967.

Big Boy. m. Milton Ager, 1924. Recorded by The Wolverines (Gennett), Bud Freeman (Decca), and Ray McKinley (Capitol).

Big Boy Blue. w/m Peter Tinturin, Jack Lawrence, and Dan Howell, 1937.

Big Boy Pete. See **Jolly Green Giant.**

Big Brass Band from Brazil, The. w/m Bob Hilliard and Carl Sigman, 1947. Introduced by the company in the revue (TM) *Angel in the Wings*. Most played version by Jack Smith, with Frank De Vol's Orchestra (Capitol). Biggest seller by Art Mooney, as it was coupled with his #1 hit, "I'm Looking Over a Four Leaf Clover" (MGM).

Big Butter and Egg Man, The. w/m Sidney Clare, Cliff Friend, and Joseph H. Santly, 1926. A phrase that Texas Guinan used in referring to her wealthier customers allegedly inspired this title. The song was recorded by Louis Armstrong (Okeh), Phil Baker (Columbia), Wild Bill Davison (CMS), and Muggsy Spanier (Bluebird).

Big Chief De Sota. w/m Andy Razaf and Fernando Arbello, 1936. Swing number introduced and recorded by Fletcher Henderson and his Orchestra (Vocalion). Popularized by Fats Waller (Victor) and Ray Noble, with a Glenn Miller arrangement (Victor).

Big City. w/m Dean Holloway and Merle Haggard, 1982. #1 Country chart record by Merle Haggard (Epic).

Big City Blues. w. Sidney D. Mitchell, m. Archie Gottler and Con Conrad, 1929. Intro-

duced by Lola Lane in (MM) *Fox Movietone Follies of 1929*. Many records were released concurrently with the film, among which were those by Annette Hanshaw (Okeh); the bands of Bert Lown (Harmony); George Olsen (Victor); Lou Gold, vocal by Irving Kaufman (Perfect); Arnold Johnson, vocal by Scrappy Lambert (Brunswick).

Big City Miss Ruth Ann. w/m Thomas Lazaros, 1973. Top 40 record by the sextet Galley (Sussex).

Big Cold Wind. w/m Robert Mosely and Bob Elgin, 1961. Featured and recorded by Pat Boone (Dot).

Big D. w/m Frank Loesser, 1956. Introduced by Shorty Long and Susan Johnson in (TM) *The Most Happy Fella*.

Big Daddy. w/ Peter Udell, m. Lee Pockriss, 1958. Introduced by Jill Corey in (MM) *Senior Prom*, and recorded by her with Mitch Miller's Orchestra (Columbia).

Big Foot Ham. m. Ferdinand "Jelly Roll" Morton, 1923. Jelly Roll Morton's first recording (Paramount).

Big Fun. w/m Kool and The Gang (10 writers), 1982. Recorded by Kool and The Gang (De-Lite).

Bigger and Better Than Ever. w. Irving Caesar, m. Cliff Friend, 1929. Introduced and recorded (Brunswick) by Frances Williams in (TM) *George White's Scandals of 1929*.

Biggest Aspidastra in the World, The. w/m Thomas Connor, W. G. Haines, and James S. Hancock, 1938. English song introduced in the U.S. and recorded by Gracie Fields (Decca).

Biggest Part of Me. w/m David Pack, 1980. Top 10 record by the trio Ambrosia (Warner Bros.).

Big Girls Don't Cry. w/m Bob Crewe and Bob Gaudio, 1962. #1 record by The Four Seasons (Vee-Jay).

Big Guitar, The. m. Francis De Rosa, Robert Genovese, and Larry Coleman, 1958. Instrumental, introduced by Frank De Rosa and his D Men (Dot). Best-selling record by The Owen Bradley Quintet (Decca).

Big Hunk O' Love, A. w/m Aaron Schroeder and Sid Wyche, 1959. #1 hit by Elvis Presley (RCA). One of four recordings made by him during his term of military service (RCA).

Big Hurt, The. w/m Wayne Shanklin, 1959. Hit record by Miss Toni Fisher (Signet).

Big Iron. w/m Marty Robbins, 1960. Crossover (C&W/Pop) hit by Marty Robbins (Columbia).

Big John. w/m John Patton and Amiel Summers, 1961. Recorded by The Shirelles (Scepter).

Big John's Special. m. Horace Henderson, 1934. Introduced and recorded by Fletcher Henderson's Orchestra (Decca); also recorded by the Mills Blue Rhythm Band (Columbia). The best-seller, however, was Benny Goodman's 1938 hit (Victor).

Big Log. w/m Robert Plant, Robbie Blunt, and Jezz Woodruffe, 1982. Recorded by Robert Plant (Atlantic).

Big Love. w/m Lindsay Buckingham, 1987. Top 10 single by the British band, Fleetwood Mac, from their album "Tango in the Night" (Warner Bros.)

Big Mamou. w/m Link Davis, 1953. Louisiana Cajun song, sung in French and English. Leading records by Pete Hanley (Okeh) and Dolores Gray (Decca).

Big Man. w/m Glen Larson and Bruce Belland, 1958. Hit record by The Four Preps (Capitol).

Big Man in Town. w/m Bob Gaudio, 1964. Recorded by The Four Seasons (Philips).

Big Midnight Special. w/m Wilma Lee Cooper, 1959. C&W hit by Wilma Lee and Stoney Cooper (Hickory).

Big Movie Show in the Sky. w. Johnny Mercer, m. Robert Emmet Dolan, 1949. Intro-

duced by Danny Scholl in (TM) *Texas Li'l Darlin'.*

Big Noise from Winnetka. w/m Ray Bauduc, Bob Crosby, Bob Haggart, and Gil Rodin, 1940. Ray Bauduc on drums and Bob Haggart on bass and whistling the melody line through his teeth were featured with Bob Crosby's Band in introducing and recording the number (Decca). They performed it in (MM) *Let's Make Music,* 1941, and in (MM) *Reveille With Beverly,* 1943.

Big Ole Brew. w/m Russell Smith, 1982. Top 10 Country chart record by Mel McDaniel (Capitol).

Big River, Big Man. w/m Mike Phillips and George Watson, 1961. Recorded by Claude King (Columbia).

Big Shot. w/m Billy Joel, 1979. Recorded by Billy Joel (Columbia).

Big Spender. w. Dorothy Fields, m. Cy Coleman, 1966. Introduced by Helen Gallagher, Thelma Oliver, and The Girls in (TM) *Sweet Charity.* Chita Rivera, Paula Kelly, and The Girls sang it in the film version (MM) *Sweet Charity,* 1969. Popular record by Peggy Lee (Capitol).

Big Time. w/m Peter Gabriel, 1987. Top 10 single by the British singer Peter Gabriel (Geffen).

Big Train (From Memphis). w/m John Fogerty, 1985. Country chart record by John Fogerty, on flip side of Pop chart hit "The Old Man Down the Road" (Warner Bros.).

Big Wheels in the Moonlight. w/m Bob McDill, 1989. Hit Country single by Dan Seals (Capitol).

Big Wide World. w/m Teddy Randazzo, Bobby Weinstein, and Billy Barberis, 1963. Introduced and recorded by Teddy Randazzo (Colpix).

Big Wind. w/m Alex Zanetis, Wayne P. Walker, and George McCormick, 1969. Top 10 Country record by Porter Wagoner (RCA).

Big Yellow Taxi. w/m Joni Mitchell, 1970.

Top 40 record by The Neighborhood (Big Tree). Joni Mitchell had a chart version that same year (Reprise), but a new version, recorded "live" at one of her concerts, was released in 1975 and attained a Top 40 position on the charts.

Bi-I-Bi. w/m Bob Russell, Judy Freeland, and Beverly Freeland, 1941. Recorded by Horace Heidt, vocal by Donna Wood and The Don Juans (Columbia).

Bijou. w. Jon Hendricks, m. Ralph Burns, 1945. Introduced as an instrumental by Woody Herman and his Orchestra, arranged by Ralph Burns (Columbia). Revived with lyric version by Lambert, Hendricks, and Ross (Columbia), 1960.

Bilbao Song, The. w. Johnny Mercer (Engl.), Bertolt Brecht (Ger.), m. Kurt Weill, 1961. Introduced in Berlin, Germany, 1929, in what later became (TM) *The Happy End*, in the U.S., 1977. Mercer wrote the English lyrics in 1961, and it was popularized by Andy Williams on television and records (Cadence).

Bill. w. P. G. Wodehouse and Oscar Hammerstein II, m. Jerome Kern, 1928. Wodehouse had written an earlier version for the musical *Oh, Lady! Lady!!* 1918, but it was dropped from the show. Marilyn Miller, who later rejected "Time On My Hands" (q.v.), rejected this in "Sally." It was finally introduced in (TM) *Show Boat* by Helen Morgan, who then made a hit record (Victor). Helen Morgan sang it in the movie version (MM) *Show Boat*, 1929, and its remake, 1936. Annette Warren sang it on the soundtrack for Ava Gardner in the third version, 1951. In (MM) *The Helen Morgan Story*, 1957, Gogi Grant dubbed it on the soundtrack for Ann Blyth in the title role.

Bill Bailey, Won't You Please Come Home. w/m Hughie Cannon, 1902. An instant hit after being introduced by John Queen, a minstrel. It has been recorded often by such stars as Kid Ory (Columbia), Jimmy Durante and Eddie Jackson (MGM), and Bobby Darin, who had a million-seller (Atco),

1960. Danny Kaye and Louis Armstrong performed it in (MM) *The Five Pennies*, 1959.

Billboard, The. m. John N. Klohr, 1901. Popular march, especially favored by circus bands. Also recorded by Ralph Flanagan's Orchestra (Victor) 1950.

Billie Jean. w/m Michael Jackson, 1983. One of four hit singles from Michael Jackson's platinum album "Thriller" (Epic). This #1 gold record won a Grammy Award (NARAS) for Rhythm and Blues Song of the Year, 1983.

Billie's Bounce. m. Charlie Parker, 1945. An early record (Savoy) by the great alto saxist Charlie Parker and his group, featuring Dizzy Gillespie (trumpet), Miles Davis (trumpet), Max Roach (drums), and Curly Russell (bass).

Billion Dollar Babies. w/m Alice Cooper and Michael Bruce, 1973. Recorded by Alice Cooper (Warner Bros.).

Billy. 1959. Hit record by Kathy Linden (Felsted).

Billy (For When I Walk). w/m Joe Goodwin, James Kendis, Herman Paley, 1911. Revived in 1939 by Orrin Tucker, vocal by Bonnie Baker (Vocalion).

Billy, Don't Be a Hero. w/m Peter Callendar and Mitch Murray, 1974. Written in England and introduced by the British group, Paper Lace, whose record went to #1 in that country. Before their recording was released in the U.S., it was covered by the American septet, Bo Donaldson and The Heywoods, and became a #1 gold record (ABC). The Paper Lace release (Mercury) only reached #96 on the U.S. charts.

Billy and Sue. w/m Mark Charron, 1966. Recorded by B. J. Thomas and The Triumphs (Hickory).

Billy Bayou. w/m Roger Miller, 1958. Featured and recorded by Jim Reeves (RCA).

Bim Bam Baby. w/m Sammy Mysels, 1952. Featured and recorded by Frank Sinatra (Columbia).

Bimbo. w/m Rod Morris, 1954. Country hit by Jim Reeves (Abbott).

Bimbombey. w/m Mack David, Hugo Peretti, and Luigi Creatore, 1958. Popularized by Jimmy Rodgers (Roulette).

Bimini Bay. w. Gus Kahn and Raymond B. Egan, m. Richard Whiting, 1921. Leading records by The Benson Orchestra of Chicago (Victor), Ted Lewis (Columbia), and Paul Whiteman (Victor).

Bing! Bang! Bong! w/m Jay Livingston and Ray Evans, 1958. Introduced in (MP) *Houseboat* by Sophia Loren.

Bird Dog. w/m Boudleaux Bryant, 1958. Popularized by The Everly Brothers (Cadence).

Bird in a Gilded Cage, A. w. Arthur J. Lamb, m. Harry Von Tilzer, 1900. One of the most successful turn-of-the-century ballads. Its sheet music sale was over two million copies. The song was interpolated in the Ann Sothern film (MP) *Ringside Maisie*, 1941, and in (MM) *Coney Island*, 1943. Among recordings, Beatrice Kay (Columbia) and Virginia O'Brien (Decca).

Bird Man, The. w. Mack David, m. Elmer Bernstein, 1962. From (MP) *The Bird Man of Alcatraz*. Recorded by The Highwaymen, narration by Burt Lancaster (United Artists).

Bird on Nellie's Hat, The. w. Arthur J. Lamb, m. Alfred Solman, 1906. Lamb's third "bird" song (see: Section III, Writers, Lamb). This comedy song was featured in vaudeville and recorded by Helen Trix (Victor). Revived by Joan Morris in her album "Vaudeville" (Nonesuch).

Bird on the Wire. w/m Leonard Cohen, 1968. Recorded in albums by Judy Collins (Elektra) and Leonard Cohen (Columbia).

Birds and the Bees, The. w/m Herb Newman, 1965. Hit record by Jewel Akens (Era).

Bird's the Word, The. w/m Al Frazier, John E. Harris, Carl White, and Turner Wilson, 1963. Surfing record by The Rivingtons (Liberty).

Bird That Never Sings, The. w. Arthur J. Lamb, m. Monroe H. Rosenfeld, 1902. Sequel to Lamb's "A Bird in a Gilded Cage." Recorded by the counter-tenor Richard José (Victor).

Birmingham Bertha. w. Grant Clarke, m. Harry Akst, 1929. Introduced and recorded (Columbia) by Ethel Waters in (MM) *On With The Show*. The record was coupled with "Am I Blue?" from the same film. Other recordings were the bands of Jimmie Noone (Vocalion), B. A. Rolfe (Edison), Don Voorhees (Domino), Miff Mole (Okeh), and Walter Barnes (Brunswick).

Birmingham Bounce. w/m Sid "Hardrock" Gunter, 1950. Featured and recorded by Red Foley (Decca).

Birmin'ham. w/m Hugh Martin and Ralph Blane, 1955. Introduced by Rosalind Russell and Eddie Albert in (MM) *The Girl Rush*.

Birthday. w/m John Lennon and Paul McCartney, 1969. Introduced in The Beatles' "White Album" (Apple). Top 40 record by The Underground Sunshine (Intrepid), 1969.

Birth of Passion, The. w. Otto Harbach, m. Karl Hoschna, 1910. Introduced by Lina Abarbanell and Jack Gardner in (TM) *Madame Sherry*.

Birth of the Blues, The. w. B. G. DeSylva and Lew Brown, m. Ray Henderson, 1926. Introduced by Harry Richman in (TM) *George White's Scandals*. He (Vocalion) and Paul Whiteman and his Orchestra (Victor) had the first hit records. In motion pictures, it was sung by Bing Crosby in (MM) *The Birth of the Blues*, 1941; played by the band in (MM) *When My Baby Smiles at Me*, 1948; played on the soundtrack of (MM) *Painting the Clouds with Sunshine*, 1951; played on the soundtrack of (MM) *The Jazz Singer*, starring Danny Thomas, 1953; sung by Gordon MacRae and danced by Sheree North and Jacques D'Amboise in the screen biography of DeSylva, Brown and Henderson (MM) *The Best Things in Life Are Free*, 1956. Frank Sinatra had a hit record (Capitol), 1952.

Bit by Bit. w. Frannie Golde, m. Harold Faltermeyer, 1985. Lyrics to theme from (MP) *Fletch*, starring Chevy Chase. Recorded by Stephanie Mills (MCA).

Bitch Is Back, The. w/m Elton John and Bernie Taupin, 1974. Top 10 record by Elton John (MCA).

Bits and Pieces. w/m Dave Clark and Mike Smith, 1964. Top 10 hit, produced in England by The Dave Clark Five (Epic).

Bitter Bad. w/m Melanie Safka, 1973. Recorded by Melanie (Neighborhood).

B. J. the D. J. w/m Hugh X. Lewis, 1964. #1 Country chart hit by Stonewall Jackson (Columbia).

Black and Blue. w. Andy Razaf, m. Thomas "Fats" Waller and Harry Brooks, 1929. Introduced by Edith Wilson in (TM) *Hot Chocolates*. Recordings of note include those by Louis Armstrong (Okeh); Jack Teagarden (Decca); Gene Krupa (Victor); the DeParis Brothers Orchestra (Commodore); Frankie Laine (Mercury), his first record for that label. It was performed by the Company in the Fats Waller musical (TM) *Ain't Misbehavin'*, 1978. It became the title song of (TM) *Black and Blue*, 1989.

Black and Tan Fantasy. m. Edward Kennedy "Duke" Ellington, 1927. Instrumental, first recorded by Duke Ellington and his Washingtonians (Brunswick) (Okeh) (Columbia). Re-recorded as "New Black and Tan Fantasy" (Brunswick), 1938.

Black and White. w. David Arkin, m. Earl Robinson, 1972. #1 gold record by Three Dog Night (Dunhill).

Blackberry Boogie. w/m Ernie Ford, 1952. Recorded by Tennessee Ernie Ford (Capitol).

Black Betty. w/m Kaye Dunham, 1977. Top 20 record by the quartet Ram Jam (Epic).

Blackboard of My Heart. w/m Lyle Gaston and Hank Thompson, 1956. Top 10 C&W chart by Hank Thompson (Capitol).

Black Bottom, w. B. G. DeSylva and Lew Brown, m. Ray Henderson, 1926. Introduced by Anne Pennington in (TM) *George White's Scandals of 1926*. The dance, on which this was based, has been attributed to Alberta Hunter and described as dragging one's feet through the muddy flats of a Southern river. Judy Garland sang it in (MM) *A Star is Born*, 1954. In the biography of DeSylva, Brown and Henderson, (MM) *The Best Things in Life Are Free*, 1956, it was performed by Sheree North, Jacques D'Amboise, and chorus.

Black Bottom Stomp. m. Ferdinand "Jelly Roll" Morton, 1926. Introduced and recorded by Jelly Roll Morton's Red Hot Peppers (Victor).

Black Butterfly. w. Irving Mills, m. Edward Kennedy "Duke" Ellington, 1937. Introduced and recorded by Duke Ellington and his Orchestra (Brunswick). Recorded by Cootie Williams's big band (Okeh), 1940, and by Joe Thomas (Key), 1946.

Black Coffee. w/m Paul Francis Webster and Sonny Burke, 1948. Featured and recorded by Sarah Vaughan (Columbia), Peggy Lee (Decca), Ella Fitzgerald (Decca).

Black Denim Trousers and Motorcycle Boots. w/m Jerry Leiber and Mike Stoller, 1955. Leading record by The Cheers, with Les Baxter's Orchestra (Capitol). Vaughn Monroe, with his Orchestra, also had a chart record (RCA).

Black Dog. w/m John Paul Jones, Jimmy Page, and Robert Plant, 1972. Top 20 record by the British group Led Zeppelin (Atlantic). The writers comprised three-fourths of the heavy metal combo.

Black Eyed Susan Brown. w. Herb Magidson, m. Al Hoffman and Al Goodhart, 1933. Recorded by Glen Gray and the Casa Loma Orchestra, vocal by Pee Wee Hunt (Victor), and Clarence Williams, vocal by Floyd Casey (Vocalion).

Black Friday. w/m Walter Becker and Donald Fagen, 1974. Recorded by the group Steely Dan (ABC).

Black is Black. w/m Tony Hayes, M. Grainger, and Steve Wadey, 1966. English song recorded by the quintet Los Bravos (Press).

Black Jazz. m. Gene Gifford, 1932. Introduced and recorded by Glen Gray and the Casa Loma Orchestra, for which Gifford was chief arranger and founder of their style (Brunswick).

Black Lace. w. Maria Shelton, m. Carl Fischer, 1949. Introduced by Frankie Laine, with Carl Fischer's Orchestra (Mercury).

Blackland Farmer. w/m Frankie Miller, 1961. Introduced and recorded by Frankie Miller (Starday). Wink Martindale also had a popular version (Dot).

Black Magic Woman. w/m Peter Green, 1970. Top 10 record by the group Santana (Columbia).

Black Market. w/m Frederick Hollander, 1948. Introduced by Marlene Dietrich in (MP) *A Foreign Affair* and on records (Decca).

Black Moonlight. w/m Arthur Johnston and Sam Coslow, 1933. Introduced by Bing Crosby in (MM) *Too Much Harmony* and recorded by him with Jimmie Grier's Orchestra (Brunswick).

Black Night. w/m Jessie Mae Robinson, 1951. Hit R&B recording by Charles Brown (Aladdin).

Black Pearl. w/m Phil Spector, Toni Wise, and Irwin Levine, 1969. Top 20 record by Sonny Charles and The Checkmates, Ltd. (A&M).

Black Sheep. w/m Daniel Darst and Robert Altman, 1983. #1 Country record by John Anderson (Warner Bros.)

Black Slacks. w/m Joe Bennett and Jimmy Denton, 1957. Hit record by Joe Bennett and The Sparkletones (ABC-Paramount).

Blacksmith Blues, The. w/m Jack Holmes, 1952. Ella Mae Morse had a million-seller with Nelson Riddle's Orchestra (Capitol).

Black Superman—"Muhammad Ali." w/m Johnny Wakelin, 1975. Novelty record by the British group Johnny Wakelin and The Kinshasa Band (Pye).

Black Velvet. m. Jimmy Mundy and Illinois Jacquet, 1949. Jazz instrumental introduced and recorded by Illinois Jacquet and his Orchestra (RCA Victor). Also recorded by Will Hudson and his Orchestra (Decca). See also "Don'cha Go 'Way Mad."

Black Water. w/m Pat Simmons, 1975. Written about the Mississippi River, the recording by The Doobie Brothers became a #1 gold record, produced by Ted Templeman (Warner Bros.).

Blah, Blah, Blah. w. Ira Gershwin, m. George Gershwin, 1931. Originally titled "Lady of the Moon," written for the unproduced musical "Ming Toy." It was then retitled "I Just Looked at You," lyric co-authored by Gus Kahn, but dropped from the musical *Show Girl*, before production, The final version was introduced by El Brendel and Manya Roberti in (MM) *Delicious*. Revived by Tommy Tune and Twiggy in (TM) *My One and Only*, 1983.

Blame It on My Last Affair. w/m Henry Nemo and Irving Mills, 1939. Featured and recorded by Mildred Bailey (Vocalion); the bands of Count Basie, vocal by Helen Humes (Decca); Harry James (Brunswick); Spud Murphy (Bluebird); Mitchell Ayres (Vocalion).

Blame It on My Youth. w. Edward Heyman, m. Oscar Levant, 1934. First popular records: the Dorsey Brothers, vocal by Bob Crosby (Decca), and Jan Garber, vocal by Lee Bennett (Victor). Gordon MacRae had a later recording, arranged and conducted by Van Alexander (Capitol).

Blame It on the Bossa Nova. w/m Cynthia Weil and Barry Mann, 1963. Top 10 record by Eydie Gorme (Columbia).

Blame It on the Rain. w/m Dianne Warren, 1989. Hit record by Milli Vanilli (Arista).

Blame It on the Rhumba. w. Harold Adamson, m. Jimmy McHugh, 1937. Introduced in (MM) *Top of the Town* and recorded (Brunswick) by Gertrude Niesen.

Blame It on the Samba. w. Ray Gilbert (Engl.), m. Ernesto Nazareth, 1948. Originally a Brazilian song "Cavaquinho." Introduced in the U.S. by The Dinning Sisters in the animated film (MM) *Melody Time*.

Blame My Absent-Minded Heart. w. Sammy Cahn, m. Jule Styne, 1949. Introduced by Doris Day in (MM) *It's a Great Feeling*. Leading record by Mindy Carson, with Henri René's Orchestra (RCA Victor).

Blanket on the Ground. w/m Roger Bowling, 1975. Hit Country record by Billie Jo Spears (United Artists).

Blaze Away! m. Abe Holzmann, 1901. A march.

Blazing Saddles. w. Mel Brooks, m. John Morris, 1974. Sung by Frankie Laine on the soundtrack of (MP) *Blazing Saddles*. Nominated for an Academy Award.

Blessed Are the Believers. w/m Charlie Black, Rory Bourke, and Sandy Pinkard, 1981. Recorded by Anne Murray (Capitol).

Blessed Is the Rain. w/m Tony Romeo, 1969. Recorded by The Brooklyn Bridge (Buddah).

Bless 'Em All. w/m Jimmie Hughes and Frank Lake, additional lyrics by Al Stillman, 1941. English song, popular in World War II. Leading records by The Jesters (Decca) and Barry Wood and The King Sisters (Victor). The song was sung in (MP) *Marine Raiders*, 1941, and (MP) *Captains of the Clouds*, 1942.

Bless the Beasts and Children. w/m Barry DeVorzon and Perry Botkin, Jr., 1971. Performed on the soundtrack of (MP) *Bless the Beasts and Children* and on records by The Carpenters (A&M). Song nominated for Academy Award, 1971.

Bless This House. w/m May H. Morgan and Helen Taylor, 1927. This spiritual song from England has had popular recordings by Risë Stevens (Columbia), Eileen Farrell (Decca), Gracie Fields (London), and Mahalia Jackson (Apollo).

Bless Yore Beautiful Hide. w. Johnny Mercer, m. Gene De Paul, 1954. Introduced by Howard Keel in (MM) *Seven Brides for Seven Brothers*.

Bless You. w/m Barry Mann and Cynthia Weil, 1961. Recorded by Tony Orlando (Epic).

Bless You. w/m Don Baker and Eddie Lane, 1939. Among recordings: Fats Waller (Bluebird); Barry Wood (Vocalion); Gray Gordon, vocal by Cliff Grass (Victor); Griff William's Orchestra (Sonora).

Bless Your Heart. w/m Freddie Hart and Jack Lebsock, 1972. Hit Country record by Freddie Hart (Capitol).

Bless Your Heart. w/m Duke Enston, Harry Stride, and Milton Drake, 1933. Featured and recorded by George Olsen and his Orchestra (Columbia).

Blinded by the Light. w/m Bruce Springsteen, 1977. First recorded by Bruce Springsteen and included in his album "Greetings from Asbury Park" (Columbia), 1972. #1 gold record by the English group, Manfred Mann's Earth Band (Warner Bros.).

Blind Man. w/m Deadric Malone and Joseph Scott, 1965. Recorded by Bobby Bland (Duke) and Little Milton (Checker).

Blistered. w/m Billy Edd Wheeler, 1969. Top 10 Country chart and Pop chart crossover record by Johnny Cash (Columbia).

Blizzard, The. w/m Harlan Howard, 1961. Introduced and recorded by Jim Reeves (RCA).

Blob, The. w. Mack David, m. Burt Bacharach, 1958. Title song of (MP) *The Blob*. Recorded by The Five Blobs (Columbia), in reality, singer Bernie Knee multi-tracking five vocals (Columbia).

Blond Sailor, The. w. Mitchell Parish and Bell Leib (Engl.), m. Jacob Pfeil, 1945. Original German song, "Fahr Mich in die Ferne, Mein Blonder Matrose," with lyrics by the composer, Pfeil. Popular record by The Andrews Sisters (Decca).

Blondy. w. Arthur Freed, m. Nacio Herb Brown, 1929. From (MM) *Marianne* starring Marion Davies and Lawrence Gray. Recorded by the orchestras of Smith Ballew (Okeh), and Jack Denny (Brunswick).

Blood Red and Goin' Down. w/m Curly Putman, 1973. Crossover (C&W/Pop) hit by Tanya Tucker (Columbia).

Bloodshot Eyes. w/m Hank Penny and Ruth Hall, 1950. Top 10 R&B record by Hank Penny (King).

Bloody Mary. w. Oscar Hammerstein II, m. Richard Rodgers, 1949. Introduced by the "Sailors, Seabees, and Marines" in (TM) *South Pacific*. In the film version, 1958, it was sung by The Ken Darby Singers.

Bloody Well Right. w/m Richard Davies and Roger Hodgson, 1975. Recorded by the British quintet Supertramp (A&M).

Bloop, Bleep! w/m Frank Loesser, 1947. Novelty about leaky faucet, introduced and recorded by Danny Kaye (Decca). Best-selling version by Alvino Rey, vocal by Rocky Coluccio (Capitol).

Blossom Fell, A. w/m Howard Barnes, Harold Cornelius, and Dominic John, 1955. English song. Best-seller by Nat "King" Cole (Capitol).

Blossoms on Broadway. w. Leo Robin, m. Ralph Rainger, 1937. Introduced by Shirley Ross in (MM) *Blossoms on Broadway*. Featured on radio and recorded by Jan Garber and his Orchestra (Brunswick).

Blossoms on the Bough, The. w. Sammy Gallop, m. Carl Sigman, 1949. Featured and recorded by The Andrews Sisters (Decca).

Blow, Gabriel, Blow. w/m Cole Porter, 1934. Introduced by Ethel Merman in (TM) *Anything Goes*. It was heard on the soundtrack in the Porter biography (MM) *Night and Day*, 1946, and performed by Bing Crosby, Donald O'Connor, Mitzi Gaynor, and Zizi Jeanmaire in the second film version, (MM) *Anything Goes*, 1956.

Blow Away. w/m George Harrison, 1979. Recorded in England by former Beatle, George Harrison (Dark Horse).

Blowing Away. w/m Laura Nyro, 1970. Introduced by Laura Nyro in her debut album "More Than a New Discovery" (Verve-Forecast), 1967. Top 40 record by The 5th Dimension (Soul City), 1970.

Blowing Wild (a.k.a. **Ballad of Black Gold, The**). w. Paul Francis Webster, m. Dimitri Tiomkin, 1953. From (MP) *Blowing Wild*. Popular record by Frankie Laine (Columbia).

Blowin' in the Wind. w/m Bob Dylan, 1963. Introduced by Bob Dylan. Hit record by Peter, Paul, and Mary (Warner Bros.). Stevie Wonder had a Top 10 version (Tamla), 1966.

Blowin' the Blues Away. w. Ira Gershwin, m. Phil Charig, 1926. Introduced by Lew Brice, Betty Compton, Helen Morgan, Evelyn Bennett, Gay Nell, and Elizabeth Morgan in (TM) *Americana*.

Blow Out the Candle. w/m Phil Moore, 1952. Featured and recorded by Jane Wyman (Decca).

Blow the Smoke Away. w. Will M. Hough and Frank R. Adams, m. Joseph E. Howard, 1906. Introduced by James Norval in (TM) *The Time, The Place and The Girl*, which played in Chicago, 1906, and in New York, 1907. Composer Joe Howard recorded it (Brunswick).

Blue, Blue Day. w/m Don Gibson, 1958. Introduced and recorded by Don Gibson (RCA).

Blue, Turning Grey over You. w. Andy Razaf, m. Thomas "Fats" Waller, 1930. First recorded by Louis Armstrong (Okeh) and Lee Morse (Columbia). Waller later recorded it on a 12″ 78 RPM disc (Victor). Other notable cuttings by Gene Krupa (Victor) and Frankie Laine (Mercury).

Blue (and Broken Hearted). w. Grant Clarke and Edgar Leslie, m. Lou Handman, 1922. Introduced and recorded by Marion Harris (Brunswick).

Blue Again. w. Dorothy Fields, m. Jimmy McHugh, 1930. Featured on radio and recorded (Columbia) by the Ipana Troubadors. Also recorded by Louis Armstrong (Okeh); Red Nichols (Brunswick); Duke Ellington, vocal by Sid Gary (Victor); Marion Harris (Brunswick); Lee Morse (Columbia); the Revelers (Victor).

Blue and Lonesome. w/m Peter Chatman, Jr., 1949. Top 10 R&B chart record by Memphis Slim, performing name of the writer (Miracle).

Blue and Sentimental. w/m William "Count" Basie, Mack David, Jerry Livingston, 1938. Introduced as an instrumental by Count Basie and his Orchestra (Decca).

Blue and the Gray (or, **Mother's Gift to Her Country, A).** w/m Paul Dresser, 1900. A Civil War-inspired ballad.

Blue Angel. w/m Roy Orbison and Joe Melson, 1960. Top 10 record by Roy Orbison (Monument).

Blue Autumn. w/m Bobby Goldsboro, 1966. Recorded by Bobby Goldsboro (United Artists).

Blue Bayou. w/m Roy Orbison and Joe Melson, 1963, 1977. Introduced and recorded by Roy Orbison (Monument). Revived with a gold record hit by Linda Ronstadt (Asylum), 1977.

Blue Bell. w. Edward Madden and Theodora (Dolly) Morse, m. Theodore Morse, 1904. Popular song of the day with recordings by The Haydn Quartet (Victor), Frank Stanley and Byron Harlan (Edison), Henry Burr (Columbia). As "Goodbye My Bluebell," it was performed by Scotty Beckett in (MM) *The Jolson Story*, 1946. Co-lyricist Morse became charter and first woman member of ASCAP, 1914.

Bluebell. w. Paul Francis Webster, m. Jerry Livingston, 1958. Recorded by Mitch Miller's Orchestra and Chorus (Columbia).

Blueberry Hill. w/m Al Lewis, Larry Stock, and Vincent Rose, 1940, 1956. Glenn Miller, vocal by Ray Eberle (Bluebird), had a hit recording along with Connie Boswell (Decca), and Sammy Kaye (Victor). The song was on "Your Hit Parade" for fourteen weeks, and in the Top 10 on all record and sheet music charts. Gene Autry interpolated it in (MM) *The Singing Hill*, 1941. Fats Domino had a million-seller record (Imperial), 1956, and the song again reached the Top 10, an even bigger hit this time. Louis Armstrong's 1949 version, with Gordon Jenkin's Orchestra, was re-released and became a Top 40 record (Decca), 1956.

Bluebird. w/m Leon Russell, 1975. Recorded by Helen Reddy (Capitol).

Bluebird. w/m Stephen Sills, 1967. Recorded by The Buffalo Springfield, a group of which Sills was then a member (Atco).

Bluebird Island. w/m Hank Snow, 1951. Featured and recorded by Hank Snow (RCA Victor).

Bluebird of Happiness. w. Edward Heyman and Harry Parr, m. Sandor Hamati, 1934, 1948. Introduced at the Radio City Music Hall in New York by Jan Peerce, who featured it in his concert and radio appearances. He recorded it in 1948 (Victor), as did Art Mooney, vocal by Bud Brees and the Galli Sisters and recitation by Mooney (MGM). Mooney's record was his third consecutive million-seller.

Bluebird on Your Windowsill (There's A). w/m Elizabeth Clarke and Robert Mellin, 1949. Recorded by Doris Day, with George Siravo's Orchestra (Columbia).

Bluebirds in My Belfry. w. Johnny Burke, m. James Van Heusen, 1944. Introduced by Betty Hutton in (MM) *And the Angels Sing.*

Bluebirds in the Moonlight. w. Leo Robin, m. Ralph Rainger, 1940. Sung by the voices of Lanny Ross and Jessica Dragonette on the soundtrack of the feature-length cartoon (MM) *Gulliver's Travels.* Popular recordings by Glenn Miller, vocal by Marion Hutton (Bluebird); Dick Jurgens, vocal by Eddie Stone (Vocalion), Benny Goodman, vocal by Mildred Bailey (Columbia).

Blue Canary. w/m Vincent Fiorino, 1953. Featured and recorded by Dinah Shore (RCA Victor).

Blue Champagne. w/m Jimmy Eaton, Grady Watts, and Frank Ryerson, 1941. #1 record by Jimmy Dorsey, vocal by Bob Eberly (Decca). Revived by Manhattan Transfer (Atlantic) in 1975.

Blue Christmas. w/m Billy Hayes and Jay Johnson, 1948. Top recordings by Russ Morgan, with his Orchestra (Decca); Hugo Winterhalter and his Orchestra (RCA Victor); Ernest Tubb (Decca). The family group, The Browns, had a popular version (RCA Victor), 1960.

Blue Collar Man (Long Nights). w/m Tommy Shaw, 1978. Recorded by the quintet Styx (A&M).

Blue Danube Blues. w. Anne Caldwell, m. Jerome Kern, 1921. Introduced by Louise Groody and Oscar Shaw in (TM) *Good Morning, Dearie.* The music was intentionally "borrowed" from Johann Strauss.

Blue Devils of France, The. w/m Irving Berlin, 1918. A salute to the French soldiers in W.W.I, introduced by Lillian Lorraine in *Ziegfeld Follies—1918.*

Blue Evening. w/m Gordon Jenkins and Joe Bishop, 1939. Introduced and recorded by Woody Herman and his Orchestra (Decca). Also recorded by Frances Langford (Decca) and Glenn Miller, vocal by Ray Eberle (Bluebird).

Blue Eyes. w. Gary Osborne, m. Elton John, 1982. Recorded by the English singer Elton John (Geffen).

Blue Eyes Crying in the Rain. w/m Fred Rose, 1975. Written thirty years earlier, Willie Nelson revived it with a Country and Pop hit record (Columbia).

Blue Feeling. m. Edward Kennedy "Duke" Ellington, 1934. Recorded by Duke Ellington and his Orchestra (Victor).

Blue Flame. m. James Noble, 1942. Woody Herman and his Orchestra, who used this instrumental as their theme and recorded it a year earlier (Decca), performed it in (MM) *What's Cookin'?*

Blue Hawaii. w. Leo Robin, m. Ralph Rainger, 1937, 1962. Introduced by Bing Crosby in (MM) *Waikiki Wedding.* Academy Award Winner, Best Song. Crosby's recording was coupled with the hit song "Sweet Leilani," from the same film. Elvis Presley sang it in (MM) *Blue Hawaii,* 1962, and on records (RCA). Billy Vaughn and his Orchestra had a Top 40 record (Dot).

Blue Hours. w. Roy Turk, m. Wayne King and Jerry Castillo, 1933. Introduced and recorded by Wayne King and his Orchestra (Brunswick).

Blue Interlude. w. Manny Kurtz and Irving Mills, m. Benny Carter, 1934. Featured by Benny Carter's Band. Recorded by Chuck Richards (Vocalion), 1935, Benny Goodman (Victor), The Chocolate Dandies (Decca), the recording band for which Carter played alto sax and arranged, 1938.

Blue Is the Night. w/m Fred Fisher, 1930. Theme song of (MP) *Their Own Desire,* which starred Norma Shearer.

Blue Jean. w/m David Bowie, 1984. Top 10 record by English singer David Bowie (EMI America).

Blue Kentucky Girl. w/m Johnny Mullins, 1965. Hit Country record by Loretta Lynn (Decca). Revived by Emmylou Harris (Reprise), 1979.

Blue Kentucky Moon. w/m Walter Donaldson, 1931. Popular records by Gene Austin (Perfect), Guy Lombardo (Columbia), Johnny "Scat" Davis (Crown).

Blue Lament. w. Dave Franklin, m. Joe Bishop, 1934. Introduced and recorded by Isham Jones, vocal by Eddie Stone. Bishop, along with Jones, was the arranger for the band at that time.

Blue Light Boogie. w/m Jessie Mae Robinson and Louis Jordan, 1950. Hit record by Louis Jordan and his Tympany Five (Decca).

Blue Lou. w/m Edgar Sampson and Irving Mills, 1933. Jazz standard first recorded by Benny Carter (Okeh). Among other standout records through the years: Chick Webb (Decca); Bunny Berigan (Brunswick); Fletcher Henderson (Vocalion); Metronome All-star Band (Victor), 1939; Benny Goodman Sextet (Capitol) and big band, arrangement by Neal Hefti (Capitol); Eddie Heywood (Commodore); George Barnes (Key); Ray Brown (Mercury).

Blue Lovebird. w. Gus Kahn, m. Bronislaw Kaper, 1940. Introduced by Alice Faye and Don Ameche in (MM) *Lillian Russell*. Recordings by the bands of Kay Kyser, vocal by Ginny Simms (Columbia); Mitchell Ayres (Bluebird); Larry Clinton (Victor); Frankie Masters (Vocalion).

Blue Mirage (Don't Go). w. Sam Coslow, m. Lotar Olias, 1955. German composition. Ralph Marterie and his Orchestra had a popular instrumental (Mercury).

Blue Monday. w/m Antoine "Fats" Domino and Dave Bartholomew, 1957. Introduced by Fats Domino in (MM) *The Girl Can't Help It*, and on a hit record (Imperial).

Blue Money. w/m Van Morrison, 1971. Top 40 record by Van Morrison (Warner Bros.).

Blue Monk. m. Thelonious Monk, 1954. Jazz instrumental introduced by Thelonious Monk (Prestige).

Blue Moon. w. Lorenz Hart, m. Richard Rodgers, 1934, 1961. Written originally with a different lyric, titled "Prayer" for Jean Harlow in (MM) *Hollywood Revue*, cut from film before release. Hart wrote new lyric, "The Bad in Every Man," sung by Shirley Ross in (MP) *Manhattan Melodrama*, 1934. With another new lyric, and titled "Blue Moon," the song was published in 1934 and became the only successful Rodgers and Hart song not associated with a production. It has been interpolated extensively in films. Harpo Marx played it as his harp solo in (MM) *At The Circus*, 1939; Mel Tormé sang it in the Rodgers and Hart biography (MM) *Words and Music*, 1948; Jane Froman dubbed for Susan Hayward on the soundtrack of the Froman story (MM) *With a Song in My Heart*, 1952; India Adams dubbed for Joan Crawford in (MM) *Torch Song*, 1954; prominently featured on the soundtracks of (MM) *This Could Be the Night*, 1957, and (MM) *New York, New York*, 1977. The Marcels had a #1 record hit (Colpix), 1961.

Blue Moon of Kentucky. w/m Bill Monroe, 1947. Featured and recorded by Bill Monroe and The Blue Grass Boys (Decca).

Blue Morning, Blue Day. w/m Lou Gramm and Mick Jones, 1979. Recorded by the group Foreigner (Atlantic).

Blue on Blue. w. Hal David, m. Burt Bacharach, 1963. Hit record by Bobby Vinton (Epic).

Blue Orchids. w/m Hoagy Carmichael, 1939. Glenn Miller, with vocal by Ray Eberle (Bluebird), had the best-seller, followed closely by the bands of Tommy Dorsey (Victor); Benny Goodman (Columbia); Bob Crosby (Decca); singer Dick Todd (Bluebird). The song became #1 in popularity and was on "Your Hit Parade" for ten weeks.

Blue Prairie. w/m Bob Nolan and Tim Spencer, 1936. Introduced by the Sons of the Pioneers. In addition to the two writers, Roy Rogers, then known as Dick Weston, was also in the group.

Blue Prelude. w/m Joe Bishop and Gordon Jenkins, 1933. Introduced by Isham Jones and his Orchestra, arranged by Bishop (Victor). Glen Gray and the Casa Loma Orchestra (Brunswick) and George Hall's Orchestra, vocal by Loretta Lee (Bluebird), also had popular records. Among many other recordings over the years: Woody Herman, who used it as his first theme (Decca), 1940; Clyde McCoy (Decca); Jan August and the Harmonicats (Mercury); Lena Horne (Black & White); Gordon Jenkins (Decca); Adrian Rollini, vocal by Howard Phillips (Columbia); Boyd Raeburn (Guild).

Blue Rain. w. Johnny Mercer, m. James Van Heusen, 1939. Featured and recorded by Mildred Bailey (Vocalion); Glenn Miller, vocal by Ray Eberle (Bluebird); Tommy Dorsey, vocal by Jack Leonard (Victor).

Blue Rhythm Fantasy. m. Teddy Hill and Chappie Willet, 1936. Instrumental associated with Teddy Hill and his Orchestra who recorded it (Vocalion) and again, a year later (Bluebird). It was not, however, his theme, which was "Uptown Rhapsody." Gene Krupa had a two-sided version (Okeh), 1940.

Blue River. w. Alfred Bryan, m. Joseph Meyer, 1927. Leading records by Frankie Trumbauer, vocal by Seger Ellis (Okeh); Jean Goldkette, vocal by Lewis James (Victor); The California Ramblers, vocal by Ed Kirkeby (Edison).

Blue Rondo a la Turk. w. Dave Brubeck, 1960. Introduced and recorded by The Dave Brubeck Quartet (Columbia).

Blue Room, The. w. Lorenz Hart, m. Richard Rodgers, 1926. Introduced by Eva Puck and Sammy White in (TM) *The Girl Friend.* Perry Como sang it in the Rodgers and Hart biography (MM) *Words and Music,* 1948. It was also heard on the soundtrack of (MM) *Young Man with a Horn,* 1950, and (MM) *The Eddy Duchin Story,* 1956.

Bluer Than Blue. w/m Randy Goodrum, 1978. Recorded by Michael Johnson (EMI America).

Blues, Stay Away from Me. w/m Alton Delmore, Rabon Delmore, Wayne Raney, and Henry Glover, 1949. Introduced and recorded by The Delmore Brothers (King). Best-seller: Owen Bradley and his Quintet, vocal by Jack Shook and Dottie Dillard (Coral).

Blues, The. w/m Randy Newman, 1983. Recorded by Randy Newman and Paul Simon (Warner Bros).

Bluesette. w. Norman Gimbel, m. Jean Thielemans, 1963. Introduced as instrumental by jazz harmonicist-guitarist-whistler Jean "Toots" Thielemans (ABC-Paramount). First vocal by Sarah Vaughan (Mercury), 1964.

Blues from "Kiss Me Deadly" (a.k.a. **I'd Rather Have the Blues**). w/m Frank De-Vol, 1955. Introduced by Nat "King" Cole in (MP) *Kiss Me Deadly.*

Blue Shadows. w/m Lloyd C. Glenn, 1950. Hit R&B record by Lowell Fulson (Swingtime).

Blue Shadows. w. Raymond Klages, m. Louis Alter, 1928. Introduced by Joey Ray in (TM) *Earl Carroll Vanities of 1928.* Popular recording by Johnny Hamp, vocal by Frank Munn (Victor).

Blue Shadows on the Trail. w. Johnny Lange, m. Elliot Daniel, 1948. Introduced by Roy Rogers and The Sons of the Pioneers in the animated cartoon film (MM) *Melody Time,* and recorded by them (RCA Victor). Top selling records: Bing Crosby (Decca); Vaughn Monroe, with his Orchestra (RCA Victor).

Blue Side of Lonesome. w/m Leon Payne, 1966. Posthumous #1 Country, Pop crossover hit by Jim Reeves (RCA).

Blues in Advance. w/m Neil Drummond, 1952. Featured and recorded by Dinah Shore (RCA Victor).

Blues in My Heart. w. Irving Mills, m. Benny Carter, 1931. Introduced by Fletcher Henderson and his Orchestra (Columbia). This "bluesy ballad" has also been recorded by Ethel Waters, with Herman Chittison (Victor); Cab Calloway (Perfect); Bert Lown (Victor);

Lee Sims (Brunswick); Chick Webb (Brunswick); Eddie "Lockjaw" Davis (Roost); and others.

Blues in My Mind. w/m Fred Rose, 1944. Featured and recorded by Roy Acuff (Okeh).

Blues in the Night. w. Johnny Mercer, m. Harold Arlen, 1941. Introduced by William Gillespie, with Jimmie Lunceford's Orchestra in (MM) *Blues in the Night.* Nominated for Academy Award. Best-selling record by Jimmie Lunceford and his Orchestra, vocal by Willie Smith (Decca 1 & 2). Among other top recordings: Dinah Shore (Bluebird); Judy Garland (Decca); the Benny Goodman Sextet (Okeh); the bands of Artie Shaw (Victor); Woody Herman (Decca); Cab Calloway (Okeh). It was interpolated in (MM) *Thank Your Lucky Stars,* by John Garfield, 1943.

Blue Skies. w/m Irving Berlin, 1927. Specially written for Belle Baker who introduced it in (TM) *Betsy,* the score of which was otherwise written by Rodgers and Hart. It became the hit song of the show and one of the sheet music best-sellers of the year. Al Jolson sang it in (MM) *The Jazz Singer,* 1927, and again in (MM) *The Jolson Story,* 1946, dubbing for Larry Parks. In other films, it was sung by Eddie Cantor in (MM) *Glorifying the American Girl,* 1929; Ethel Merman and Alice Faye in (MM) *Alexander's Ragtime Band,* 1938; Bing Crosby in (MM) *Blue Skies,* 1946, and (MM) *White Christmas,* 1954. Revived by Willie Nelson (Columbia), 1978.

Blue Skirt Waltz, The. w. Mitchell Parish, m. Vaclav Blaha, 1948. Original instrumental published in Prague, Czechoslovakia. Frankie Yankovic and his Yanks, vocal by The Marlin Sisters, had a million-selling record (Columbia).

Blue Sky Avenue. w. Herb Magidson, m. Con Conrad, 1934. Introduced by Gene Austin in (MM) *Gift of Gab.* Austin recorded it (Victor) as did the bands of Jan Garber (Victor) and Ted Weems (Columbia).

Blues My Naughty Sweetie Gives to Me, The. w/m Charles McCarron, Carey Morgan, and Arthur Swanstrom, 1919. Featured and recorded by Ted Lewis and his Orchestra (Columbia).

Blues on Parade. m. Woody Herman and Toby Tyler, 1940. Instrumental by Woody Herman and his Orchestra (Decca).

Blues Plus Booze (Means I Lose). w/m Elkin Brown, 1966. Country chart record by Stonewall Jackson (Columbia).

Blues Power. w/m Eric Clapton and Leon Russell, 1980. Recorded by the British singer Eric Clapton.

Blues Serenade, A. w/m Frank Signorelli, Jimmy Lytell, Vincent Grande, and Mitchell Parish, 1935. Glenn Miller, vocal by Smith Ballew, had an early record (Columbia). In 1937, Henry King and his Orchestra made the song their theme and recorded it (Decca). Bing Crosby, backed by Matty Malneck's Orchestra (Decca), Johnny Hodges (Vocalion), and Duke Ellington (Brunswick) all recorded it in 1938.

Blue Star (the Medic Theme). w. Edward Heyman, m. Victor Young, 1955. Theme from the series (TVP) "Medic." Most played recording by Felicia Sanders (Columbia). Les Baxter and his Orchestra's version was coupled with his big selling instrumental "Unchained Melody" (q. v.) (Capitol).

Bluest Eyes in Texas. w/m Dave Robbins, Vern Stephenson, and Tim Dubois, 1988. #1 Country chart record by the group Restless Heart (RCA).

Blue's Theme. m. Mike Curb, 1966. Performed by guitarist Davie Allan in (MP) *The Wild Angels.* Recorded by Davie Allan and The Arrows (Tower).

Blue Suede Shoes. w/m Carl Lee Perkins, 1956. Introduced and Top 5 record by Carl Perkins (Sun), followed by Elvis Presley (RCA) and in the film (MM) *G. I. Blues* in 1960. Revived by Johnny Rivers with a Top 40 record (United Artists) in 1973. In the biographical film (MM) *Elvis* in 1979, it was performed by Kurt Russell in the title role, with the vocal dubbed by Ronnie McDowell.

Blue Tango. m. Leroy Anderson, 1952. Leroy Anderson and his Orchestra's #1 recording sold over two million copies. Other popular records by the orchestras of Hugo Winterhalter (RCA Victor), Guy Lombardo (Decca), Les Baxter (Capitol).

Blue Velvet. w/m Bernie Wayne and Lee Morris, 1951, 1963. Tony Bennett had first popular recording (Columbia). Revived by Bobby Vinton, with a #1 hit in 1963 (Epic). Title song of 1986 film (MP).

Blue Venetian Waters. w. Gus Kahn, m. Bronislaw Kaper and Walter Jurmann, 1937. Written for the ballet sequence in (MM) *A Day At The Races*, starring the Marx Brothers.

Blue Violins. m. Ray Martin, 1951. Top 20 instrumental by Hugo Winterhalter and his Orchestra (RCA Victor).

Blue Winter. w/m Ben Raleigh and John Gluck, Jr., 1963. Featured and recorded by Connie Francis (MGM).

Blue Yodel. w/m Jimmie Rodgers, 1928. Rodgers, the famous country writer/singer recorded twelve versions of this (Victor). His first was his initial recording on this label. His ninth version had a jazz backing by Louis and Lil Hardin Armstrong (Victor).

Blue Yodel #8 (a.k.a. New Mule Skinner Blues). w/m Jimmie Rodgers and George Vaughn, 1931. Recorded by Jimmie Rodgers (Victor) and Roy Acuff (Okeh). Top 10 Pop chart hit by The Fenderman ("Mule Skinner Blues") (Soma), 1960.

Blushing Moon. See **Luna Rossa.**

Boa Constrictor. w/m Shel Silverstein, 1966. Recorded by Johnny Cash (Columbia), 1966.

Boats Against the Current. w/m Eric Carmen, 1978. Recorded by Eric Carmen (Arista).

Bobbie Sue. w/m Wood Newton, Adele Tyler, and Daniel Tyler, 1982. Recorded by The Oak Ridge Boys (MCA).

Bobbin' Up and Down. m. Theodore F. Morse, 1913. Instrumental recorded by the Victor Military Band (Victor).

Bobby's Girl. w/m Henry Hoffman and Gary Klein, 1962. Top 10 record by Marcie Blane (Seville).

Bobby Sox to Stockings. w/m Richard di Cicco, Russell Faith, and Clarence Kehner, 1959. Recorded by Frankie Avalon (Chancellor).

Bobo's. w. Fred Ebb, m. John Kander, 1977. Introduced by Liza Minnelli in (TM) *The Act*.

Bob White (Whatcha Gonna Swing Tonight?). w. Johnny Mercer, m. Bernard Hanighen, 1937. Hit record by Bing Crosby and Connie Boswell, coupled with "Basin Street Blues" (Decca). Other popular versions by Johnny Mercer (Brunswick); Benny Goodman, vocal by Martha Tilton (Victor); Gene Kardos, vocal by Bea Wain (Melotone).

Bob Wills Boogie. m. Bob Wills, L. R. Bernard, and M. Kelso, 1947. Hit instrumental by Bob Wills and His Texas Playboys (Columbia).

Bo Diddley. w/m Ellas McDaniel (Bo Diddley), 1955. Hit record by Bo Diddley, R&B and R&R guitarist/singer (Checker).

Body and Soul. w. Edward Heyman, Robert Sour, and Frank Eyton, m. John Green, 1930. Introduced by Gertrude Lawrence on a British Broadcasting Company radio show. Bert Ambrose, the popular English bandleader, heard the song, recorded it, and made it a hit. Max Gordon, the American theatrical producer, obtained the rights to the song for his revue (TM) *Three's A Crowd*, and the performances of torch singer Libby Holman and dancers Clifton Webb and Tamara Geva helped make the song a classic. Holman had a hit record (Brunswick), but the #1 recorded version was by Paul Whiteman, vocal by Jack Fulton (Columbia). Ida Lupino sang it in (MP) *The Man I Love*, 1946; it was heard in (MM) *The Eddy Duchin Story*, 1956; Gogi Grant, dubbing for Ann Blyth in the title role, sang it in (MM) *The Helen Morgan Story*, 1957. It was the first number recorded by the Benny Goodman Trio (Victor), 1935. Of the many versions, Coleman Hawkins, the great tenor saxophonist, had one of the major jazz records of all time (Bluebird), 1939.

Body Language. w/m Freddie Mercury, 1982. Recorded by the British group Queen (Elektra).

Bohemian Rhapsody. w/m Freddie Mercury, 1976. Top 10 gold record by the British group, Queen, of which Mercury was vocalist (Elektra).

Bojangles of Harlem. w. Dorothy Fields, m. Jerome Kern, 1936. Introduced by Fred Astaire in (MM) *Swing Time*, which was choreographed by Hermes Pan and the only number Astaire ever performed in blackface. Initial records of the song by Astaire (Brunswick), Bob Howard (Decca), and Tempo King's combo (Bluebird).

Bolero at the Savoy. w/m Charles Carpenter, Gene Krupa, and James Mundy, 1939. Introduced and recorded by Gene Krupa, vocal by Anita O'Day (Columbia).

Boll Weevil Song, The. w/m Clyde Otis and Brook Benton, 1961. Novelty hit by Brook Benton (Mercury).

Bonanza! w/m Jay Livingston and Ray Evans, 1961. Theme from the series (TVP) "Bonanza!" Popular instrumental version by guitarist Al Caiola (United Artists).

Bonaparte's Retreat. w/m Pee Wee King, 1950. Introduced by Pee Wee King (RCA Victor). Top 10 records by Kay Starr, with Lou Busch's Orchestra (Capitol); Gene Krupa and his Orchestra (RCA Victor).

Bon Bon Buddy. w. Alex Rogers, m. Will Marion Cook, 1907. Featured in vaudeville by Williams and Walker.

Bon Bon Vie (Gimme the Good Life). w/m Lawrence Russell Brown and Sandy Linzer, 1981. Recorded by T. S. Monk, a group com-posed of the son and daughter of jazz pianist Thelonious Monk, Thelonious, Jr. and Boo Boo, and Yvonne Fletcher (Mirage).

Boneyard Shuffle. m. Hoagy Carmichael and Irving Mills, 1925. Carmichael backed this with "Washboard Blues" when he recorded it as pianist with Hitch's Happy Harmonists (Gennett). Lyrics were later added by Fred Callahan and Mitchell Parish.

Bongo Rock. m. Preston Epps and Arthur Egnoian, 1959. Hit instrumental by Preston Epps (Original Sound). Revived by The Incredible Bongo Band (MGM), 1973.

Bonne Nuit—Goodnight. w/m Jay Livingston and Ray Evans, 1951. Introduced by Bing Crosby in (MM) *Here Comes the Groom*.

Bonnie Blue Gal. w. William Engvick, m. Jessie Cavanaugh, 1955. Adapted from the Civil War song "Bonnie Blue Flag." Leading records by Lawrence Welk (Coral) and Mitch Miller (Columbia), with their orchestras and choruses.

Bonnie Came Back. m. Lee Hazlewood and Duane Eddy, 1960. Adapted from the traditional "My Bonnie Lies Over the Ocean." Chart instrumental by guitarist Duane Eddy (Jamie).

Bonnie Jean (Little Sister). w/m David Lynn Jones, 1987. Top 10 Country chart record by David Lynn Jones (Mercury). Included in his album "Hard Times on Easy Street."

Bon Voyage. w/m O. O. Merritt and Vin Roddie, 1957. Popularized via recording by Janice Harper (Prep).

Bony Moronie. w/m Larry Williams, 1957. Introduced and recorded by Larry Williams (Specialty).

Boo-Ga-Loo. w/m Billy Gordon and Sylvester Potts, 1965. Recorded by Tom and Jerrio (ABC-Paramount).

Boogaloo Down Broadway. w/m Jesse James, 1967. Top 10 record by The Fantastic Johnny C (Phil-L.A.).

Boogie Bands and One Night Stands. w/m Greg Dempsey, 1974. Recorded by Kathy Dalton (DiscReet).

Boogie Blues. w/m Gene Krupa and Ray Biondi, 1946. Featured and recorded by Gene Krupa, vocal by Anita O'Day (Columbia).

Boogie Child. w/m Barry Gibb, Maurice Gibb, and Robin Gibb, 1977. Sung by the British brother-trio, The Bee Gees, on the soundtrack of (MM) *Saturday Night Fever*, and on records (RSO).

Boogie Chillen'. w/m John Lee Hooker, 1949. #1 record on the R&B charts by John Lee Hooker (Modern).

Boogie Down. w/m Leonard Caston, Anita Poree, and Frank Wilson, 1974. Top 10 chart record by Eddie Kendricks (Tamla).

Boogie Fever. w/m Freddie Perren and Keni St. Lewis, 1976. #1 gold record by the family group The Sylvers (Capitol).

Boogie Nights. w/m Rod Temperton, 1977. Platinum record by the group Heatwave (Epic).

Boogie on Reggae Woman. w/m Stevie Wonder, 1974. Top 10 record by Stevie Wonder (Tamla).

Boogie Oogie Oogie. w/m Janice Marie Johnson and Perry Kibble, 1978. #1 platinum single by the group A Taste of Honey (Capitol).

Boogie Shoes. w/m Harry Wayne Casey and Richard Finch, 1977. Performed by K. C. and The Sunshine Band in (MM) *Saturday Night Fever* and on records (T.K.).

Boogie Wonderland. w. Alec Willis, m. Jonathan Lind, 1979. Gold record by Earth, Wind & Fire with The Emotions (ARC).

Boogie Woogie. m. Clarence "Pinetop" Smith, 1929, 1943. Recorded and released as "Pinetop's Boogie" by the twenty-four-year-old pianist-composer a few months before, as an innocent bystander, he was killed in a Chicago night club fight. Tommy Dorsey and his Orchestra recorded it (Victor), 1938. It became

their biggest instrumental hit when it was reissued during the musicians' record strike, 1943.

Boogie Woogie. See **Pine Top's Boogie Woogie.**

Boogie Woogie Blue Plate. w. John De Vries, m. Joe Bushkin, 1947. Featured and recorded by Louis Jordan and his Tympany Five (Decca).

Boogie Woogie Bugle Boy (of Company B). w/m Don Raye and Hughie Prince, 1941, 1973. Introduced by the Andrews Sisters in (MM) *Buck Privates* and recorded (Top 10) by them (Decca). Song nominated for an Academy Award. Andrews Sisters sang it again in (MM) *Swingtime Johnny*, 1943. Bette Midler revived it (Atlantic), 1973.

Boogie Woogie Maxixe. w. Sammy Gallop, m. Gil Rodin and Bob Crosby, 1939. Recorded as instrumental by Bob Crosby and his Orchestra (Decca). In 1953, lyrics were added and The Ames Brothers had a popular record (RCA Victor).

Boogie Woogie Prayer. m. Meade Lux Lewis, Pete Johnson, and Albert Ammons, 1941. Introduced by the composer-pianists at "Spirituals to Swing" concert at Carnegie Hall, New York and recorded by them (Vocalion, Parts 1 & 2).

Boog-It. w/m Cab Calloway, Buck Ram, and Jack Palmer, 1940. Top records by Glenn Miller, vocal by Marion Hutton (Bluebird); Gene Krupa (Okeh); Cab Calloway (Vocalion); Jimmy Dorsey, vocal by Helen O'Connell (Decca).

Booglie Wooglie Piggy. w/m Roy Jordan, 1941. Introduced and recorded by Glenn Miller, vocal by Ray Eberle and the Modernaires (Bluebird). Other records by Will Bradley, vocal by Ray McKinley (Columbia); Les Brown, vocal by Doris Day (Okeh); Una Mae Carlisle (Bluebird).

Boo-Hoo. w. Edward Heyman, m. John Jacob Loeb and Carmen Lombardo, 1937. Introduced, featured, and recorded by Guy Lombardo, vocal by brother Carmen (Victor). One of the year's biggest hits (eleven weeks on "Your Hit Parade," six times in the #1 position), there also was a popular recording by Fats Waller (Victor).

Book of Love. w/m Warren Davis, George Malone, and Charles Patrick, 1958. Introduced and recorded by The Monotones (Argo).

Boom Boom Boomerang. w/m Lonnie Coleman, 1955. Popularized by The De Castro Sisters (Abbott).

Boomps-A-Daisy. w/m Annette Mills, 1938. English song interpolated during run of the American revue (TM) *Hellzapoppin'* and performed by the chorus.

Booted. w/m Roscoe Gordon, 1952. #1 R&B record by Roscoe Gordon (Chess).

Boots and Saddle. See **Take Me Back to My Boots and Saddle.**

Booze and Blues. w/m J. Guy Suddoth, 1924. Recorded by Ma Rainey (Paramount).

Boozers and Losers. w. Murray Grand, m. Cy Coleman, 1970. Introduced as title song of album by Claire Hogan (Columbia).

Bop. w/m Jennifer Kimball and Paul Davis, 1986. #1 Country and crossover Pop chart record by Dan Seals (EMI America).

Boplicity. m. Miles Davis, 1949. Featured and recorded by Miles Davis and his Orchestra (Capitol).

Boppin' the Blues. w/m Carl Lee Perkins and Howard Griffin, 1956. C&W and Pop chart hit by Carl Perkins (Sun).

Bop 'Til You Drop. w/m Rick Springfield, 1984. Sung in (MP) *Hard to Hold* and on records by Rick Springfield (RCA).

Bop-Ting-A-Ling. w/m Winfield Scott, 1955. R&B hit by LaVern Baker (Atlantic).

Border, The. w/m Russ Ballard and Dewey Bunnell, 1983. Recorded by the group America (Capitol).

Borderline. w/m Reginald Lucas, 1984. First Top 10 record by Madonna (Sire).

Border Song. w/m Elton John and Bernie Taupin, 1970. Introduced by Elton John on records in his self-named album and a single (MCA). The hit version was by Aretha Franklin (Atlantic).

Born Again. w/m Isaac Hayes and David Porter, 1969. Introduced and recorded by Sam and Dave (Atlantic).

Born A Woman. w/m Martha Sharp, 1966. Recorded by Sandy Posey (MGM).

Born Free. w. Don Black, m. John Barry, 1966. Introduced on the soundtrack of (MP) *Born Free* by Matt Monro and recorded by him (Capitol). Academy Award Winner, 1966. Hit records by Roger Williams (Kapp) and The Hesitations (Kapp), 1968.

Borning Day, The. w/m Fred Hellerman and Fran Minkoff, 1963. Introduced and recorded by Harry Belafonte (RCA).

Born in the U.S.A. w/m Bruce Springsteen, 1984. Hit single from Bruce Springsteen's platinum album of the same name (Columbia).

Born to Be Alive. w/m Patrick Hernandez, 1979. Recorded by Patrick Hernandez (Columbia).

Born to Be Blue. w/m Robert Wells and Mel Tormé, 1947. Introduced and recorded by Mel Tormé and his Mel-Tones (Musicraft).

Born to Be in Love with You. w/m Hank Hunter and Van Trevor, 1966. Country chart record by Van Trevor (Band Box).

Born to Be Kissed. w. Howard Dietz, m. Arthur Schwartz, 1934. From the film (MP) *The Girl from Missouri*. Recorded by Paul Whiteman and his Orchestra, with vocal by Ramona (Victor), and by Ben Selvin's studio orchestra, vocal by Howard Phillips (Columbia).

Born to Be My Baby. w/m Richie Sambora and Desmond Child, 1989. Hit record by the band Bon Jovi (Mercury).

Born to Be Wild. w/m Mars Bonfire, 1968. Gold record by the quintet Steppenwolf (Dunhill). The writer, Bonfire (pseudonym for Dennis Edmonton), was the guitarist of the group. Wilson Pickett had a chart record (Atlantic), 1969.

Born to Be with You. w/m Don Robertson, 1956. Hit record by The Chordettes, with Archie Bleyer's Orchestra (Cadence). In 1968, Sonny James had a #1 C&W chart version (Capitol).

Born to Boogie. w/m Hank Williams, Jr., 1987. #1 Country chart record by Hank Williams, Jr. (Warner Bros.).

Born to Lose. w/m Frankie Brown, 1943. C&W hit recording by Ted Daffan and His Texans (Okeh).

Born Too Late. w. Fred Tobias, m. Charles Strouse, 1958. Hit record by The Poni-Tails (ABC-Paramount).

Born to Run. w/m Paul Kennerley, 1982. Country chart hit by Emmylou Harris (Warner Bros.).

Born to Run. w/m Bruce Springsteen, 1975. First chart record by Bruce Springsteen (Columbia).

Born to Sing the Blues. w. Leonard Adelson, m. Imogene Carpenter, 1955. Introduced by Imogene Carpenter. Leading record by Vic Damone (Mercury).

Born to Wander. w/m Tom Baird, 1971. Top 20 record by Rare Earth (Rare Earth).

Born to Wander. w/m Al Peterson, 1964. Introduced by The Four Seasons (Philips).

Born Yesterday. w/m Don Everly, 1986. Country chart record by The Everly Brothers (Mercury).

Boss, The. w/m Nick Ashford and Valerie Simpson, 1979. Recorded by Diana Ross (Motown).

Bossa Nova Baby. w/m Jerry Leiber and Mike Stoller, 1963. Introduced by Elvis Presley in (MM) *Fun in Acapulco* and on records (RCA).

Bossa Nova U.S.A. m. Dave Brubeck, 1963. Introduced and recorded by The Dave Brubeck Quartet (Columbia).

Boss Guitar. m. Duane Eddy and Lee Hazelwood, 1963. Recorded by Duane Eddy (RCA).

Boston Beguine. w/m Sheldon Harnick, 1952. The song that brought fame to both Alice Ghostley, who sang it in the revue (TM) *New Faces of 1952*, and writer Sheldon Harnick.

Botch-A-Me (Ba-Ba-Baciami Piccina). w. (Engl. and m. adapt.) Eddie Y. Stanley, w/m (It.) R. Morbelli, L. Astore 1952. Introduced in the Italian film "Una Famiglia Impossible." Hit record by Rosemary Clooney (Columbia).

Both Sides Now (a.k.a. From Both Sides Now). w/m Joni Mitchell, 1968. Top 10 single by folksinger Judy Collins (Elektra). Joni Mitchell included it in her album "Clouds" (Reprise), 1969.

Bottle Let Me Down, The. w/m Merle Haggard, 1966. Top 10 Country chart record by Merle Haggard (Capitol).

Bottle of Wine. w/m Tom Paxton, 1968. Introduced in concert by Tom Paxton, 1963. Top 10 record by The Fireballs (Atco), 1968.

Boulevard. w/m Jackson Browne, 1980. Recorded by singer/composer Jackson Browne (Asylum).

Boulevard of Broken Dreams, The. w. Al Dubin, m. Harry Warren, 1934, 1950. Introduced by Constance Bennett, Tullio Carminati, Russ Columbo, and The Boswell Sisters in (MM) *Moulin Rouge*. Many recordings including those by the orchestras of Hal Kemp (Brunswick); Jan Garber, vocal by Lee Bennett (Victor); Ted Weems, vocal by Elmo Tanner (Bluebird). Frances Langford recorded it, conducted by Harry Sosnik (Decca), 1939. In 1950, Tony Bennett revived it with his first hit record (Columbia).

Bounce Me Brother with a Solid Four. w/m Don Raye and Hughie Prince, 1941. Introduced by the Andrews Sisters in (MM) *Buck Privates* and recorded by them (Decca).

Bouquet of Roses. w/m Steve Nelson and Bob Hilliard, 1948. Popular records by Eddy Arnold (RCA Victor) and Dick Haymes (Decca).

Bourbon Street Parade. m. Paul Barbarin, 1952. Popularized by The Dukes of Dixieland (Okeh).

Boutonniere. w. Bob Hilliard, m. David Mann, 1950. Recorded by Mindy Carson (Columbia).

Bo-Weavil Blues. w/m Gertrude "Ma" Rainey, 1924. Recorded by Ma Rainey, accompanied by Lovie Austin and Her Blues Serenaders (Paramount) and Bessie Smith (Columbia).

Bo Weevil. w/m Antoine "Fats" Domino and Dave Bartholomew, 1956. Introduced by Fats Domino (Imperial). Both he and Teresa Brewer (Coral) had hit records.

Bowery, The. w. Charles H. Hoyt, m. Percy Gaunt, 1892. Interpolated by Harry Conor in (TM) *A Trip to Chinatown*. Its entry into the score turned the show into a success. It was sung by Gale Storm in (MM) *Sunbonnet Sue*, 1945, and was the basis of a ballet sequence in the John Philip Sousa biographical film (MM) *Stars and Stripes Forever*, 1952.

Bowling Green. w/m Jay Ertel and Terry Slater, 1967. Chart record by The Everly Brothers (Warner Bros.).

Bowl of Roses, A. w. W. E. Henley, m. Robert Coningby Clarke, 1905. An English import.

Boxer, The. w/m Paul Simon, 1968. Top 10 record by Simon and Garfunkel (Columbia).

Boy! What Love Has Done to Me! w. Ira Gershwin, m. George Gershwin, 1930. Introduced by Ethel Merman in (TM) *Girl Crazy*.

Boy and a Girl Were Dancing, A. w. Mack Gordon, m. Harry Revel, 1932. Featured and recorded by Morton Downey (Perfect).

Boy from New York City, The. w/m John Taylor, 1965. Top 10 record by The Ad Libs (Blue Cat). Revived with a Top 10 hit by The Manhattan Transfer (Atlantic), 1981.

Boy from Texas, A Girl from Tennessee, A. w/m Joseph Allan McCarthy, Jack Segal, and John Benson Brooks, 1948. Leading records by Nat "King" Cole (Capitol); Phil Brito, with Richard Maltby's Orchestra (Musicraft); Johnny Johnston (MGM).

Boy Guessed Right, The. w/m Lionel Monckton, 1898. From (TM) *A Runaway Girl*.

Boy in Khaki, a Girl in Lace, A. w. Charles Newman, m. Allie Wrubel, 1942. World War II song.

Boy Meets Horn. m. Edward Kennedy "Duke" Ellington and Rex Stewart, 1939. Introduced and recorded by Duke Ellington, featuring trumpeter Rex Stewart (Brunswick). Also recorded by Benny Goodman's Orchestra (Columbia).

Boy Named Sue, A. w/m Shel Silverstein, 1969. Gold record by Johnny Cash (Columbia). Grammy Award (NARAS) winner Best Country and Western Song. The song was inspired by a man named Sue K. Hicks, a Tennessee attorney, named for his mother who died during his birth.

Boy Next Door, The. w/m Hugh Martin and Ralph Blane, 1944. Introduced by Judy Garland in (MM) *Meet Me in St. Louis*. Revived by Donna Kane in the stage version (TM) *Meet Me in St. Louis*, 1989.

Boy on a Dolphin. w. Paul Francis Webster (Engl.), m. Takis Morakis, 1957. Original Greek song "Tinafto," lyrics by Jean Fermanoglou. Adapted by Hugo W. Friedhofer for introduction by Julie London on soundtrack of (MP) *Boy on a Dolphin*.

Boys Are Back in Town, The. w/m Phil Lynott, 1976. Top 20 record by the Irish quartet, Thin Lizzy, led by Lynott (Mercury).

Boys Are Coming Home Today, The. w/m Paul Dresser, 1903.

Boys in the Back Room, The. w. Frank Loesser, m. Frederick Hollander, 1939. Introduced by Marlene Dietrich in (MP) *Destry Rides Again.*

Boys Night Out. w/m Timothy B. Schmit, Will Jennings, and Bruce Gaitsch, 1987. Chart record by Timothy B. Schmit from his album "Timothy B." (MCA).

Boys' Night Out, The. w. Sammy Cahn, m. James Van Heusen, 1962. From (MP) *The Boys' Night Out.* Recorded by Patti Page (Mercury).

Boys of Summer, The. w/m Don Henley and Mike Campbell, 1984. Top 10 single from the gold album "Building the Perfect Beast" by Don Henley (Warner Bros.).

Boy Ten Feet Tall, A. w. Ned Washington, m. Les Baxter, 1964. Theme from (MP) *A Boy Ten Feet Tall.*

Boy Without a Girl, A. w/m Sid Jacobson and Ruth Sexter, 1959. Top 10 record by Frankie Avalon (Chancellor).

Branded Man. w/m Merle Haggard, 1967. Hit Country record by Merle Haggard (Capitol).

Branded Wherever I Go. w/m Roy Acuff, 1943. Introduced and recorded by the Country star, Roy Acuff (Okeh).

Brand New Key. w/m Melanie Safka, 1971. #1 gold record by Melanie (Neighborhood).

Brand New Lover. w/m Peter Burns, Michael Percy, Timothy Lever, and Steven Coy, 1986. Chart single by the English quartet Dead or Alive (Epic).

Brand New Me, A. w/m Kenny Gamble, Jerry Butler, and Theresa Bell, 1969. Top 40 record by Dusty Springfield (Atlantic). Also recorded by Aretha Franklin (Atlantic), 1971, flip side of "Bridge Over Troubled Water."

Brand New World. w. Stephen Schwartz, m. Charles Strouse, 1986. Introduced by opera star Teresa Stratas in (TM) *Rags.*

Brandy (You're a Fine Girl). w/m Elliot Lurie, 1972. #1 gold record by the quartet Looking Glass, which originated at Rutgers University (Epic).

Brandy. See **Mandy** a.k.a. **Brandy.**

Brass in Pocket (I'm Special). w/m Chrissie Hynde and James Honeyman-Scott, 1980. Anglo-American written song that became the first chart record for the English quartet, The Pretenders, featuring American Chrissie Hynde as lead singer (Sire).

Brazil. w. Bob Russell (Engl.), m. Ary Barroso, 1943. Samba, with original Portuguese title ("Aquarela do Brasil") and lyrics by Barroso. First heard in feature cartoon film (MM) *Saludos Amigos,* and by Eddy Duchin's Orchestra. Best-selling records by Xavier Cugat, vocal by the band (Columbia), and Jimmy Dorsey, vocal by Bob Eberly and Helen O'Connell (Decca). It was sung by Carmen Miranda in (MM) *The Gang's All Here,* 1943; Nan Wynn in (MM) *Jam Session,* 1944; the title song of (MM) *Brazil,* 1944; played by the band in (MM) *The Road to Rio,* 1948, and (MM) *The Eddy Duchin Story,* 1956. Les Paul coupled it with "Lover" for his first hit record utilizing the technique of multi-guitar tracks (overdubbing), in this case, six (Capitol), 1948. Revived with Top 20 record by the disco group The Ritchie Family (20th Century), 1975.

Bread and Butter. w/m Larry Parks and Jay Turnbow, 1964. Hit record by The Newbeats (Hickory).

Break Away. w/m Benny Gallagher and Graham Lyle, 1976. English song recorded by Art Garfunkel (Columbia).

Breakaway, The. w. Sidney D. Mitchell, m. Archie Gottler and Con Conrad, 1929. Introduced by Sue Carol and David Rollins in (MM) *Fox Movietone Follies of 1929.* Leading record by Arnold Johnson and his Orchestra, with Harold Arlen as band pianist (Brunswick).

Break Away (From That Boy). w/m Boudleaux Bryant and Felice Bryant, 1965. Top 40 C&W/Pop record by The Newbeats (Hickory).

Breakdance. w. Irene Cara and Bunny Hall, m. Giorgio Moroder, 1984. Top 10 record by Irene Cara (Geffen).

Breakdown. w/m Tom Petty, 1977. Recorded by Tom Petty and The Heartbreakers (Shelter).

Breakdown. w/m Jimmy Cliff, 1971. Jamaican song. Top 40 record by Rufus Thomas (Stax).

Breakdown Dead Ahead. w/m Boz Scaggs and David Foster, 1980. Recorded by Boz Scaggs (Columbia).

Breakfast Ball. w. Ted Koehler, m. Harold Arlen, 1934. Introduced by Jimmie Lunceford and his Orchestra in the Cotton Club revue, *Cotton Club Parade*, in Harlem, New York. Lunceford recorded it, with Sy Oliver's arrangement (Victor). Also recorded by Benny Goodman (Columbia).

Breakfast for Two. w/m Joe McDonald, 1975. Recorded by Country Joe McDonald (Fantasy).

Breakfast with the Blues. w. David Martin, m. Vic McAlpin, 1964. Country chart record by Hank Snow (RCA).

Breakin' Away. w/m Al Jarreau, Thomas Canning, and Jay Graydon, 1982. Recorded by Al Jarreau (Warner Bros.).

Breakin' in a Brand New Broken Heart. w/m Howard Greenfield and Jack Keller, 1961. Hit record by Connie Francis (MGM).

Breakin' in a Pair of Shoes. w/m Ned Washington, Dave Franklin, and Sam H. Stept, 1936. Introduced and recorded by Benny Goodman and his Orchestra (Victor). Other recordings by: Gene Kardos, vocal by Bea Wain (Melotone); Frankie Trumbauer (Brunswick); Cleo Brown (Decca).

Breakin' . . . There's No Stopping Us. w/m Ollie Brown and Jerry Knight, 1984. From (MM) *Breakin'*. Top 10 record by Ollie and Jerry (Polydor).

Breakin' the Rules. w/m Hank Thompson, Billy Gray, and Al Blasingame, 1954. Introduced and recorded by Hank Thompson (Capitol).

Breaking Up Is Hard to Do. w/m Neil Sedaka and Howard Greenfield, 1962. #1 hit by Neil Sedaka (RCA). Sedaka recorded a new version in 1975 that reached the Top 10 (Rocket).

Breaking Us in Two. w/m Joe Jackson, 1983. Written and recorded by English-born Joe Jackson (A&M).

Break It to Me Gently. w. Carole Bayer Sager, m. Marvin Hamlisch, 1977. #1 R&B chart record by Aretha Franklin (Atlantic).

Break It to Me Gently. w/m Diane Lampert and Joe Seneca, 1962. Introduced by Brenda Lee (Decca). Revived by Juice Newton (Capitol), 1982.

Break My Mind. w/m John D. Loudermilk, 1967. Country chart hit by George Hamilton IV (RCA).

Break My Stride. w/m Matthew Wilder and Greg Prestopino, 1983. Top 10 record by Matthew Wilder (Private).

Breakout. w/m Corinne Drewery, Andy Connell, and Martin Jackson, 1987. Chart single by the British trio, Swing Out Sister, from their album "It's Better to Travel" (Mercury).

Breaks, The. w/m Robert Ford, James Moore, Russell Simmons, Lawrence Smith, Kurt Walker, 1980. Gold record 12″ single by Kurtis Blow, Pseudonym for disco DJ, Kurt Walker (Mercury).

Break the News to Mother. w/m Charles K. Harris, 1897. A big favorite of the American soldiers in the Spanish-American war.

Breakup Song, The (They Don't Write 'Em). w/m Greg Kihn, Steve Wright, and Gary Philips, 1981. Recorded by The Greg Kihn Band (Beserkley).

Break Up to Make Up. w/m Thom Bell, Kenny Gamble, and Linda Creed, 1973. Gold record by The Stylistics (Avco).

Break Your Promise. w/m Thomas Bell and William Hart, 1968. Top 40 record by The Delfonics (Philly Groove).

Breath Away from Heaven. w/m George Harrison, 1987. Sung by former Beatle George Harrison (who co-produced the film) on the soundtrack of (MP) *Shanghai Surprise*, starring Madonna and Sean Penn. Harrison included the song in his album "Cloud Nine" (Dark Horse).

Breathless. w/m Otis Blackwell, 1958. Top 10 record by Jerry Lee Lewis (Sun). Featured in (MP) *Breathless*, a remake of the 1959 Jean-Luc Godard film, 1983.

Breeze (Blow My Baby Back to Me). w/m Ballard MacDonald, Joe Goodwin, and James F. Hanley, 1919. First popular recording by The American Quartet (Victor). Favorite with jazz musicians.

Breeze, The (That's Bringin' My Honey Back to Me). w/m Tony Sacco, Richard B. Smith, and Al Lewis, 1934. Popularized by the Dorsey Brothers Orchestra, vocal by Kay Weber (Decca); Anson Weeks, vocal by Kay St. Germaine (Brunswick); Henry King (Victor).

Breeze and I, The. w. Al Stillman, m. Ernesto Lecuona, 1940. Adapted from Lecuona's *Andalucia, Suite Española* for solo piano, by Tutti Camerata, who arranged the hit recording by Jimmy Dorsey, vocal by Bob Eberly (Decca). The song was on "Your Hit Parade" for thirteen weeks. Ethel Smith played an organ solo of the number in (MM) *Cuban Pete*, starring Desi Arnaz, 1946. See **Malagueña.**

Breezin' m. Bobby Womack, 1976. Instrumental by guitarist George Benson (Warner Bros.).

Breezin' Along with the Breeze. w/m Haven Gillespie, Seymour Simons, and Richard Whiting, 1926. Among the popular recordings

were those by The Revelers (Victor); the Hoosier Hot Shots (Vocalion); Red Nichols (Okeh); the Smoothies (Bluebird); and Lou Breese and his Orchestra (Decca), who used it as his theme song for obvious reasons. In films, Danny Thomas sang it in (MM) *The Jazz Singer*, 1952; it was played by the band in (MM) *Pete Kelly's Blues*, 1955; Gogi Grant sang it, dubbing for Ann Blyth, in the title role of (MM) *The Helen Morgan Story*, 1957.

Brian's Song. m. Michel Legrand, 1972. Introduced as title theme of (TVP) "Brian's Song." Leading record by Michel Legrand (Bell).

Brick House. w/m William King, Ronald LaPread, Thomas McClary, Walter Orange, Lionel Richie, Milan Williams, 1977. Top 10 R&B/Pop chart record by The Commodores (Motown).

Bridge of Sighs. w/m James Thornton, 1900.

Bridge over Troubled Water. w/m Paul Simon, 1970. Best-selling record of the year as single and title number of album by Simon and Garfunkel (Columbia). Winner of Grammy Awards (NARAS) for Song of the Year and Record of the Year. Aretha Franklin had a gold record version (Atlantic), 1971.

Bridge Washed Out, The. w. Sandra Smith and Mart Melshee, m. Jimmy Louis, 1965. #1 Country chart record by Warner Mack (Decca).

Brigadoon. w. Alan Jay Lerner, m. Frederick Loewe, 1947. Sung by the company in (TM) *Brigadoon*, and the chorus in (MM) *Brigadoon*, 1954.

Brighten the Corner Where You Are. w. Ina Duley Ogdon, m. Charles H. Gabriel, 1913. A hymn, recorded and popularized by Homer Rodeheaver (Victor).

Bright Eyes. w. Harry B. Smith, m. Otto Motzan, and M. K. Jerome, 1921. Popular instrumental versions by the bands of Paul Whiteman (Victor), and Leo Reisman (Columbia).

Bright Lights, Big City. w/m Jimmy Reed, 1961. Introduced and recorded by blues singer Jimmy Reed (Vee-Jay). In 1971, Sonny James's version became #1 on the country charts (Capitol).

Brighton Hill. w/m Jackie DeShannon, Jimmy Holiday, and Randy Myers, 1970. Recorded by Jackie DeShannon (Imperial).

Brilliant Disguise. w/m Bruce Springsteen, 1987. Top 10 single from Bruce Springsteen's album "Tunnel of Love" (Columbia).

Bring Back My Daddy to Me. w. William Tracey and Howard Johnson, m. George W. Meyer, 1917.

Bring Back My Golden Dreams. w. Alfred Bryan, m. George W. Meyer, 1911.

Bring Back the Thrill. w. Ruth Poll, m. Pete Rugolo, 1951. Top recording by Eddie Fisher (RCA Victor). Others of note: Billy Eckstine, arranged and conducted by Pete Rugolo (MGM); Don Cherry (Decca).

Bring Back Those Minstrel Days. w. Ballard MacDonald, m. Martin Broones, 1926. Introduced in the revue (TM) *Rufus Lemaire's Affairs*, which was the first presentation at the new Majestic Theatre in New York.

Bring Back Those Wonderful Days. w. Darl MacBoyle, m. Nat Vincent, 1919. Featured by Bert Williams in (TM) *Ziegfeld Follies—1919* and recorded by him (Victor), and by Arthur Fields (Columbia).

Bringin' on the Heartbreak. w/m Steve Clark, Joe Elliott, and Pete Willis, 1984. Recorded by the British quintet Def Leppard (Mercury).

Bring It on Home to Me. w/m Sam Cooke, 1962. Introduced and hit record by Sam Cooke (RCA). The British group, The Animals, had a Top 40 version (MGM), 1965, followed by Eddie Floyd (Stax), 1968. Carla Thomas had an answer record to Cooke's, "I'll Bring It Home to You," Atlantic, 1962. Hit Country version by Mickey Gilley (Playboy), 1976.

Bring It Up. w/m James Brown and Nat Jones, 1967. R&B/Pop hit by James Brown (King).

Bring Me a Rose. w. Arthur Wimperis, m. Lionel Monckton, 1910. Introduced in (TM) *The Arcadians* by Phyllis Dare in London, and by Julia Sanderson in New York. In 1939, Sanderson and her husband, Frank Crumit, recorded the song (Decca).

Bring the Boys Home. w/m Angelo Bond, General Johnson, and Greg S. Perry, 1971. Hit R&B/Pop record by Freda Payne (Invictus).

Bristol Stomp. w. Kal Mann, m. Dave Appell, 1961. Hit record by The Dovells (Parkway).

Broadway. w. B. G. DeSylva and Lew Brown, m. Ray Henderson, 1927. Introduced by Lou Holtz and The Embassy Boys in (TM) *Manhattan Mary*. It was heard in the film version (MM) *Follow the Leader*, 1930, which marked the talking-screen debuts of Ed Wynn, Ginger Rogers, and Ethel Merman.

Broadway Baby. w/m Stephen Sondheim, 1971. Introduced by Ethel Shutta in (TM) *Follies*.

Broadway Melody. w. Arthur Freed, m. Nacio Herb Brown, 1929. Introduced by Charles King in (MM) *The Broadway Melody*, which won the Academy Award as Best Picture of 1929. Performed by Gene Kelly and Cyd Charisse in (MM) *Singin' in the Rain*, 1952.

Broadway Rhythm. w. Arthur Freed, m. Nacio Herb Brown, 1935. Introduced (dancing) by Eleanor Powell and (singing) by Frances Langford in (MM) *Broadway Melody of '36*. Powell again performed it in (MM) *Broadway Melody of '38*. Judy Garland sang it in (MM) *Babes in Arms*, 1939, and it was heard in (MM) *Presenting Lily Mars*, 1943. Gene Kelly and Cyd Charisse performed it in a major production number in (MM) *Singin' in the Rain*, 1952.

Broadway Rose. w. Eugene West, m. Martin Fried, and Otis Spencer, 1920. Popular record by The Peerless Quartet (Victor).

Broadway's Gone Hillbilly. w. Lew Brown, m. Jay Gorney, 1934. Introduced by Sylvia Froos in (MM) *Stand Up and Cheer.*

Broken Down in Tiny Pieces. w/m John Adrian, 1976. Hit Country record by Billy "Crash" Craddock (ABC/Dot).

Broken Down Merry-Go-Round. w/m Arthur Herbert and Fred Stryker, 1950. Top 20 record by Margaret Whiting and Jimmy Wakely (Capitol).

Broken Heart and a Pillow Filled with Tears. w/m Paul Anka, 1961. Recorded by Patti Page (Mercury).

(Here Am I) Broken Hearted. w. B. G. DeSylva, Lew Brown, m. Ray Henderson, 1927. Featured by Belle Baker and Ruth Etting and recorded by Nick Lucas (Brunswick) and Paul Whiteman (Victor). In the screen biography of the writers (MM) *The Best Things in Life Are Free*, it was sung by Gordon MacRae, Dan Dailey, and Ernest Borgnine. Johnny Ray recorded a hit single (Columbia), 1951.

Broken Hearted Me. w/m Randy Goodrum, 1979. Recorded by Canadian singer Anne Murray (Capitol).

Broken-Hearted Melody. w. Hal David, m. Sherman Edwards, 1959. Featured and hit record by Sarah Vaughan (Mercury).

Broken Hearted Melody. w. Gus Kahn, m. Isham Jones, 1922. Introduced and recorded by Isham Jones and his Orchestra (Brunswick).

Broken Lady. w/m Larry Gatlin, 1975. Hit Country record by Larry Gatlin (Monument). Grammy Award Winner (NARAS) Country Song of the Year, 1976.

Broken Record, The. w/m Cliff Friend, Charlie Tobias, and Boyd Bunch, 1936. Best-selling record by Guy Lombardo and the Royal Canadians (Victor). Bunch was arranger for the band. Among other records of the novelty: Wingy Manone (Vocalion); Ted Fio Rito (Decca); the Mound City Blowers (Champion).

Broken Wings. w/m Steven George, John Lang, and Richard Page, 1985. #1 single by the quartet Mr. Mister (RCA).

Brooklyn. w/m Lefty Pedroski, 1977. Recorded by Cody Jameson (Atco).

Brooklyn Bridge. w. Sammy Cahn, m. Jule Styne, 1947. Introduced by Frank Sinatra in (MM) *It Happened in Brooklyn.*

Brooklyn Roads. w/m Neil Diamond, 1968. Recorded by Neil Diamond (Uni).

Brother, Can You Spare a Dime? w. E. Y. Harburg, m. Jay Gorney, 1932. Probably the most representative song of the depression years, it was introduced by Rex Weber in (TM) *Americana.* The three recordings of note, at that time, were by Bing Crosby (Brunswick), Leo Reisman (Victor), and Rudy Vallee (Columbia).

Brotherhood of Man. w/m Frank Loesser, 1961. Introduced by Robert Morse, Sammy Smith, and Ruth Kobart in (TM) *How to Succeed in Business without Really Trying.* In (MM) *How to Succeed in Business without Really Trying*, 1967, it was sung by Morse, Rudy Vallee, and Kobart.

Brother Louie. w/m Errol Brown and Anthony Wilson, 1973. #1 gold record by the rock group Stories (Kama Sutra).

Brother Love's Travelling Salvation Show. w/m Neil Diamond, 1969. Top 40 record by Neil Diamond (Uni).

Brother Rapp. w/m James Brown, 1970. Top 10 R&B, Top 40 Pop chart record by James Brown (King).

Brother Sun, Sister Moon. w/m Donovan Leitch, 1973. Sung on the soundtrack of the Zefferelli film *Brother Sun, Sister Moon* by Donovan.

Brother Trucker. w/m James Taylor, 1978. Introduced by Joe Mantegna and company in (TM) *Working.*

Brown Baby. w/m Oscar Brown, Jr. 1962. Introduced and recorded by Oscar Brown, Jr. (Columbia). Interpolated in off-Broadway (TM) *Joy* by Jean Pace, 1970.

Brown Bird Singing, A. w. Rodney Richard Bennett, m. Haydn Wood, 1922. Bennett used the pseudonym of Royden Barrie.

Brown Eyed Girl. w/m Van Morrison, 1967. Recorded in New York, this became the first solo hit single for Irish-born Van Morrison (Bang).

Brown Eyed Woman. w/m Barry Mann and Cynthia Weil, 1968. Recorded by Bill Medley (MGM).

Brown Eyes, Why Are You Blue? w. Alfred Bryan, m. George W. Meyer, 1925. Popular song in vaudeville and on radio and records. Leading record by Nick Lucas (Brunswick).

Brown October Ale. w. Harry B. Smith, m. Reginald De Koven, 1891. From (TM) *Robin Hood.*

Brown Sugar. w/m Mick Jagger and Keith Richards, 1971. #1 U.S. record by the British group The Rolling Stones (Rolling Stones).

Bruce. w/m Rick Springfield, 1984. Novelty song written and sung by the Australian, Rick Springfield, about his being mistaken for Bruce Springsteen (Mercury).

Brush Those Tears from Your Eyes. w/m Oakley Haldeman, Al Trace, and Jimmy Lee, 1948. C&W song, with best-selling records by Barry Green (Rainbow), Evelyn Knight and The Starlighters (Decca), Al Trace and his Orchestra (Regent), Buddy Clark and The Modernaires (Columbia), Billy Vaughn and his Orchestra (Dot).

Brush Up Your Shakespeare. w/m Cole Porter, 1949. Introduced by Harry Clark and Jack Diamond in (TM) *Kiss Me Kate.* In (MM) *Kiss Me Kate,* 1953, it was sung by Keenan Wynn and James Whitmore.

Bubble, The. w. Otto Harbach, m. Rudolf Friml, 1913. Sung in (TM) *High Jinks* by Emile Lea, Burrell Barbaretto, and Mana Zucca.

Bubble Loo, Bubble Loo. w. Paul Francis Webster, m. Hoagy Carmichael, 1948. Leading record by Peggy Lee (Capitol).

Bubbles in My Beer. w/m Tommy Duncan, Cindy Walker, and Bob Wills, 1948. Introduced and hit record by Bob Wills and His Texas Playboys (Columbia). Revived by Ray Pennington (Monument), 1971.

Buckaroo. m. Bob Morris, 1965. Crossover (C&W/Pop) instrumental hit by Buck Owens (Capitol).

Bucket "T". w/m Don Altfeld, Roger Christian, and Dean Torrence, 1965. Recorded by Ronnie and The Daytonas (Mala).

Buckle Down, Winsocki. w/m Hugh Martin and Ralph Blane, 1941. Rousing football song, introduced by Tommy Dix, Stuart Langley, and chorus in (TM) *Best Foot Forward.* Dix, with chorus, sang it in the film version (MM) *Best Foot Forward,* 1943. First recordings by Benny Goodman and his Orchestra, vocal by Tommy Dix (Columbia), Art Jarrett (Victor), and Fred Waring and the Pennsylvanians (Decca).

Buddha. w. Ed Rose, m. Lew Pollack, 1919.

Buds Won't Bud. w. E. Y. Harburg, m. Harold Arlen, 1940. Introduced by Hannah Williams in the pre-Broadway tryout of the musical *Hooray for What!,* 1937, but dropped from the show. Judy Canova sang it in (MM) *Andy Hardy Meets Debutante* and recorded it (Decca), 1940. That year it was also recorded by Tommy Dorsey, vocal by Connie Haines (Victor); Benny Goodman, vocal by Helen Forrest (Columbia); Phil Harris (Decca). It was heard in (MM) *Cairo,* starring Jeanette MacDonald, 1942.

Budweiser's a Friend of Mine. w. Vincent P. Bryan, m. Seymour Furth, 1907.

Buenos Aires. w. Tim Rice, m. Andrew Lloyd Webber, 1979. Introduced on Broadway in the American production of the British musical (TM) *Evita,* by Patti LuPone and Mandy Patinkin.

Buffalo Soldier. w/m David Barnes, Margaret Lewis, and Myra Smith, 1970. Recorded by The Flamingos (Polydor).

Buffalo Stance. w/m Cameron McVey, Jamie Morgan, and Phil Ramikin, 1989. Hit single by Neneh Cherry (Virgin).

Bugle Call Rag. m. Jack Pettis, Billy Meyers, and Elmer Schoebel, 1923. Another version of one of the all-time jazz standards, played and/or recorded by a multitude of bands. Schoebel, as pianist with the Friars Society Orchestra, recorded it as "Bugle Call Blues" (Gennett). Benny Goodman's band played it in (MM) *The Big Broadcast of '37,* and Glenn Miller's in (MM) *Orchestra Wives,* 1942. It was also heard in (MM) *Stage Door Canteen,* 1943, and (MM) *The Benny Goodman Story,* 1955.

Bugle Call Rag. w/m Eubie Blake and Carey Morgan, 1916. First recorded by The Victor Military Band (Victor). Another version of a ragtime treatment of the same bugle call is credited to Jack Pettis, Billy Meyers, and Elmer Schoebel, 1923. Schoebel, as pianist with The Friars Society Orchestra, called the tune "Bugle Call Blues" when he recorded it with the band (Gennett), 1923.

Build a Little Home. w. Al Dubin, m. Harry Warren, 1933. Sung by Eddie Cantor in (MM) *Roman Scandals.* Records: Eddy Duchin (Victor); Ruth Etting (Brunswick); Barney Rapp (Bluebird); Joe Venuti's Orchestra, vocal by Howard Phillips (Melotone).

Building a Home for You. w. Gus Kahn, m. Joseph H. Santly, 1931. Introduced and recorded by Guy Lombardo (Columbia).

Building a Nest for Mary. w. Billy Rose, m. Jesse Greer, 1929. Recorded by Herman Kenin (Victor), the bandleader who was to succeed James C. Petrillo as president of the American Federation of Musicians.

Build Me Up, Buttercup. w/m Tony McCaulay and Michael D'Abo, 1969. U.S. gold record by the British group The Foundations (Uni).

Bumble Bee. w/m Leroy Fullylove, 1965. First recorded by LaVern Baker (Atlantic), 1960. Top 40 record by The Searchers (Kapp).

Bumble Boogie. m. Jack Fina, 1946. Instrumental, adapted from Rimsky-Korsakov's "Flight of the Bumble Bee." Recorded by Freddy Martin, featuring Jack Fina on piano (Victor).

Bummin' Around. w/m Pete Graves, 1953. Leading records by Jimmy Dean (4 Star) and T. Texas Tyler (Decca).

Bundle of Old Love Letters, A. w. Arthur Freed, m. Nacio Herb Brown, 1929. Sung by Charles Kaley in (MM) *Lord Byron of Broadway.*

Bundle of Southern Sunshine, A. w/m Sunny Clapp, 1952. Featured and recorded by Eddy Arnold (RCA Victor).

Bungle in the Jungle. w/m Ian Anderson, 1974. Top 20 record by the British group Jethro Tull (Chrysalis).

Bunny Hop, The. w/m Ray Anthony and Leonard Auletti, 1952. Popular song and dance number introduced by Ray Anthony, vocal by Tommy Mercer (Capitol).

Burnin' for You. w/m Donald Roeser and Richard Meltzer, 1981. Recorded by The Blue Oyster Cult (Columbia).

Burning Bridges. w/m Melvin Miller, 1960. Hit record by Jack Scott (Top Rank).

Burning Down the House. w/m David Byrne, Chris Frantz, Jerry Harrison, and Tina Weymouth, 1983. Written and recorded by the quartet Talking Heads (Sire).

Burning Heart. w/m Frankie Sullivan and Jim Peterik, 1985. From (MP) *Rocky IV.* Top 10 record by the quintet Survivor (Scotti Brothers).

Burning Love. w/m Dennis Linde, 1972. Gold record by Elvis Presley (RCA). Title song of album by Doctor and The Medics (I.R.S.), 1987.

Burning Memories. w/m Mel Tillis and Wayne P. Walker, 1964. C&W hit by Ray Price (Columbia).

Burning of Atlanta, The. w/m Chuck Taylor, 1962. Recorded by Claude King (Columbia).

Burning of Rome, The. m. E. T. Paull, 1903. A march.

Burnin' Old Memories. w/m Larry Boone, Paul Nelson, and Gene Nelson, 1989. Hit Country single by Kathy Mattea (Mercury).

Burn Rubber (Why You Wanna Hurt Me). w/m Lonnie Simmons, Rudolph Taylor, and Charley Wilson, 1981. Recorded by The Gap Band (Mercury).

Burn That Candle. w/m Winfield Scott, 1955. Recorded by The Cues, R&B group including composer Scott (Capitol). High Pop chart record by Bill Haley and His Comets (Decca).

Bushel and a Peck, A. w/m Frank Loesser, 1950. Introduced by Vivian Blaine in (TM) *Guys and Dolls*. Best-selling records by Betty Hutton and Perry Como (RCA Victor); Margaret Whiting and Jimmy Wakely (Capitol); Doris Day (Columbia). Song not used in film version.

Business in F. m. Archie Bleyer, 1931. Recorded by bands of Fletcher Henderson (Columbia) and Gene Kardos (Victor).

Bus Stop. w/m Graham Gouldman, 1966. Recorded in England by The Hollies (Imperial).

Bus Stop Song, The (a.k.a. **Paper of Pins, A**). w/m Ken Darby, 1956. The Four Lads introduced this on the soundtrack of (MP) *Bus Stop*, and had the leading record (Columbia).

Bust a Move. w/m M. Ross, M. Young, and M. Dike, 1989. Hit record by Young M. C. (Delicious Vinyl).

Busted. w/m Harlan Howard, 1963. Introduced and recorded by Johnny Cash (Columbia), 1962. Ray Charles had a hit recording that won a Grammy Award (NARAS) for Best Rhythm and Blues Recording, 1963 (ABC-Paramount). Country chart hit by John Conlee (MCA), 1982.

Bustin' Loose. w/m Chuck Brown, 1979. #1 R&B and Pop chart record by Chuck Brown and The Soul Searchers (Source).

Bustin' Out. w/m James Johnson, Jr., 1979. Recorded by Rick James (Gordy).

Busy Doing Nothing. w. Johnny Burke, m. James Van Heusen, 1949. Introduced by Bing Crosby, Cedric Hardwicke, and William Bendix in (MM) *A Connecticut Yankee in King Arthur's Court*. Recorded by Jack Smith (Capitol).

But as They Say That's Life. See **That's Life (But as They Say).**

But Beautiful. w. Johnny Burke, m. James Van Heusen, 1948. Introduced by Bing Crosby in (MM) *Road to Rio*, and recorded by him (Decca). Other top versions by Frank Sinatra (Columbia), Margaret Whiting (Capitol), Art Lund (MGM).

But Definitely. w. Mack Gordon, m. Harry Revel, 1936. Sung by Shirley Temple in (MM) *Poor Little Rich Girl*. She can be heard singing it on one of the series of soundtrack albums released by 20th Fox records. Popular singles by Ray Noble, vocal by Al Bowlly (Victor); Joe Reichman, vocal by Buddy Clark (Melotone); Bunny Berigan and his Orchestra (Vocalion).

But I Did. w. Al Jacobs, m. Joseph Meyer, 1945. Dinah Shore, with Russ Case's Orchestra, had a popular recording (Victor).

But I Do. w/m Robert Guidry, 1961. Originally titled "I Don't Know Why," but changed because of conflict with standard of same name. Recorded by Clarence "Frogman" Henry (Argo). Revived in 1973 by Bobby Vinton (Epic).

But I Do, You Know I Do. w. Gus Kahn, m. Walter Donaldson, 1926. Recorded by Ruth Etting (Columbia).

But in the Morning, No! w/m Cole Porter, 1939. Sung by Ethel Merman and Bert Lahr in (TM) *Dubarry Was a Lady.*

But It's Alright. w/m J. J. Jackson and Pierre Tubbs, 1966. Top 40 record by J. J. Jackson (Calla). Upon re-release, it again made the charts (Warner Bros.), 1969.

But Not for Me. w. Ira Gershwin, m. George Gershwin, 1930. Introduced by Ginger Rogers and reprised by Willie Howard in (TM) *Girl Crazy.* The song was heard in the first film version (MM) *Girl Crazy,* 1932, and then outstandingly performed by Judy Garland in the 1943 remake (MM) *Girl Crazy.* In another version, titled (MM) *When the Boys Meet the Girls,* 1966, it was sung by Connie Francis and Harve Presnell. Ella Fitzgerald sang it on the soundtrack of (MP) *But Not for Me,* 1959, starring Clark Gable. Among leading records: Judy Garland (Decca); Harry James, vocal by Helen Forrest (Columbia); Teddy Wilson (Columbia); Lee Wiley (Liberty Music Shops); André Previn (Victor); Jackie Gleason's Orchestra (Capitol).

Butterfingers. w/m Irving Berlin, 1934. Among recordings: Don Bestor (Victor); Connie Boswell (Brunswick); Vincent Lopez (Bluebird); Adrian Rollini (Vocalion).

Butterflies. w/m Bob Merrill, 1953. Popular record by Patti Page (Mercury).

Butterfly. w/m Bernie Lowe and Kal Mann, 1957. Popularized via the hit records by Charlie Gracie (Cameo) and Andy Williams (Cadence).

Buttons and Bows. w/m Jay Livingston and Ray Evans, 1948. Introduced by Bob Hope in (MM) *Paleface.* Academy Award winning song, 1948. Dinah Shore, with The Happy Valley Boys, had a million-seller (Columbia). Other Top 10 records by The Dinning Sisters (Capitol) and Betty Garrett (MGM).

Button Up Your Heart. w. Dorothy Fields, m. Jimmy McHugh, 1930. Sung by Evelyn Hoey and Charles Barnes in the short-lived (TM) *The Vanderbilt Revue.* It was featured on radio and recorded by the Ipana Troubadors (Columbia).

Button Up Your Overcoat. w. B. G. DeSylva and Lew Brown, m. Ray Henderson, 1929. Introduced by Zelma O'Neal and Jack Haley in (TM) *Follow Thru.* Hit records by Helen Kane (Victor); Paul Whiteman, vocal by Vaughn DeLeath (Victor); Ruth Etting (Columbia). Sung by Nancy Carroll in the film version (MM) *Follow Thru,* 1930. In the DeSylva, Brown and Henderson screen biography (MM) *The Best Things in Life Are Free,* 1956, it was sung by Gordon MacRae, Ernest Borgnine and Dan Dailey as the writers, respectively, with Sheree North.

But Where Are You? w/m Irving Berlin, 1936. Introduced by Harriet Hilliard in (MM) *Follow the Fleet.* She recorded it with husband Ozzie Nelson and his Orchestra (Brunswick), coupled with "Get Thee Behind Me Satan," which she sang in the same film. Also recorded by Jane Froman (Decca).

But You Know I Love You. w/m Mike Settle, 1969. Top 20 record by The First Edition (Reprise). Revived by Dolly Parton (RCA), 1981.

But You're Mine. w/m Sonny Bono, 1965. Featured and recorded by Sonny and Cher (Atco).

Buying a Book. w/m Joe Tex, 1969. Recorded by Joe Tex (Dial).

Buy Me for the Rain. w. Greg Copeland, m. Steve Noonan, 1967. Chart record by The Nitty Gritty Dirt Band (Liberty).

Buzz Buzz A-Diddle It. w/m Frank C. Slay, Jr. and Bob Crewe, 1961. Popular record by Freddy Cannon (Swan).

Buzz-Buzz-Buzz. w/m J. Gray and R. Byrd, 1957. Top 20 record by The Hollywood Flames (Ebb).

Buzz Me. w/m Danny Baxter and Fleecie Moore, 1945. Leading records by Louis Jordan and his Tympany Five (Decca) and Ella Mae Morse, with Billy May's Orchestra (Capitol).

By and By. w. Brian Hooker, m. George Gershwin, 1922. Introduced by Thomas Conkey and Eva Clark in (TM) *Our Nell*, originally titled *Hayseed*.

By a Rippling Stream. w/m Bernice Petkere, 1932.

By a Waterfall. w. Irving Kahal, m. Sammy Fain, 1933. Introduced by Dick Powell, Ruby Keeler, and hundreds of girls in a Busby Berkeley-directed fifteen-minute production number in (MM) *Footlight Parade*. Powell recorded it (Brunswick) as did Guy Lombardo, vocal by Carmen Lombardo (Brunswick), Ozzie Nelson (Vocalion), and Adrian Rollini (Melotone).

Bye, Bye, Baby (Baby Goodbye). w/m Bob Crewe and Bob Gaudio, 1965. Recorded by The Four Seasons (Philips).

Bye and Bye. w. Lorenz Hart, m. Richard Rodgers, 1925. Introduced by Helen Ford and Charles Purcell in (TM) *Dearest Enemy*.

Bye Bye Baby. w. Leo Robin, m. Jule Styne, 1949. Introduced by Carol Channing and Jack McCauley in (TM) *Gentlemen Prefer Blondes*. Sung by Marilyn Monroe in (MM) *Gentlemen Prefer Blondes*, 1953, and on records (MGM). Channing and Peter Palmer revived it in the Broadway sequel (TM) *Lorelei*, 1974.

Bye Bye Baby. w. Walter Hirsch, m. Lou Handman, 1936. Featured and recorded by Charlie Barnet and his Orchestra (Bluebird), vocal by the Modernaires and coupled with "Make Believe Ballroom," which record became the theme of Martin Block's radio show of the same name. Other popular versions by Fats Waller (Victor); Ted Weems, vocal by Parker Gibbs (Decca); Nat Brandwynne (Brunswick).

Bye Bye Birdie. w. Lee Adams, m. Charles Strouse, 1963. Introduced in (MM) *Bye Bye Birdie* by Ann-Margaret. The song was written especially for the film version of the stage musical.

Bye Bye Blackbird. w. Mort Dixon, m. Ray Henderson, 1926. Hit records by Gene Austin (Victor) and George Olsen's Orchestra (Victor) launched this standard. Georgie Price used it as his theme song in vaudeville. Frankie Laine sang it in (MM) *Rainbow 'Round My Shoulder*, 1952. Eddie Cantor, who earlier featured it in his vaudeville act, sang it on the soundtrack, dubbing for Keefe Brasselle in (MM) *The Eddie Cantor Story*, 1953. It was played by the band in (MM) *Pete Kelly's Blues*, 1955.

Bye Bye Blues. w/m Bert Lown, Chauncey Gray, Fred Hamm, and Dave Bennett, 1930. Introduced, used as a theme song, and recorded (Columbia) by bandleader Bert Lown. Revived in the early fifties by Les Paul and Mary Ford (Capitol). The number has long been a favorite with tap and soft shoe dancers.

Bye Bye Dearie. w. Andrew B. Sterling, m. Harry Von Tilzer, 1907. Popular song in vaudeville, featured by Willie and Eugene Howard and others. Leading recording by Frank Stanley and Henry Burr (Columbia).

Bye Bye Love. w/m Felice Bryant and Boudleaux Bryant, 1957. The first hit record by The Everly Brothers (Cadence).

By Heck. w. L. Wolfe Gilbert, m. S. R. Henry, 1915. An instrumental written in 1914 with words added a year later. Recorded by the Dorsey Brothers Orchestra (Decca), 1934.

By Myself. w. Howard Dietz, m. Arthur Schwartz, 1938. Introduced by Jack Buchanan in (TM) *Between the Devil*, which opened late December, 1937. Fred Astaire sang it in (MM) *The Band Wagon*, 1953, and Judy Garland sang it in her last musical film (MM) *I Could Go On Singing*, 1965.

By My Side. w/m Bert Lown, Chauncey Gray, Harry Link, and Dorothy Dick, 1931. Introduced and recorded by Bert Lown and his Orchestra (Victor).

By Now. w/m Donald Pfrimmer, Charles Quillen, and Dean Dillon, 1981. Top 10 Country chart record by Steve Wariner (RCA).

By Special Permission of the Copyright

Owners, I Love You. w. Owen Murphy and Robert A. Simon, m. Lewis Gensler, 1931. From (TM) *The Gang's All Here.* Recorded by the orchestras of Hal Kemp (Brunswick) and Nat Shilkret (Victor).

By Strauss. w. Ira Gershwin, m. George Gershwin, 1937. Introduced by Gracie Barrie and Robert Shafer, and danced by Mitzi Mayfair in (TM) *The Show Is On,* which opened Christmas night, 1936. It was revived in (MM) *An American in Paris,* 1951, by Gene Kelly, Oscar Levant, and Georges Guetary.

By the Beautiful Sea. w. Harold R. Atteridge, m. Harry Carroll, 1914. Introduced in vaudeville by the Stanford Brothers. Performed by Fred Astaire and Ginger Rogers in (MM) *The Story of Vernon and Irene Castle,* 1939. Constance Moore sang it in (MM) *Atlantic City,* 1944, and a girls' chorus performed it in (MM) *Some Like It Hot,* 1959.

By the Bend of the River. w. Bernhardt Haig, m. Clara Edwards, 1927.

By the Fireside (In the Gloaming). w/m Ray Noble, Jimmy Campbell, and Reg Connelly, 1932. English song introduced in the United States on radio by Rudy Vallee. In addition to imported recordings by Ray Noble and his band (HMV-Victor) and Jessie Matthews (Columbia). Prominent waxings were made by Eddy Duchin (Columbia); Donald Novis (Victor); George Olsen's Orchestra, vocal by Ethel Shutta (Victor); and Kate Smith (Columbia).

By the Light of the Silvery Moon. w. Edward Madden, m. Gus Edwards, 1909. Introduced by Georgie Price in one of Gus Edwards's vaudeville revues, featuring child performers. Later that same year, Lillian Lorraine sang it in (TM) *Ziegfeld Follies of 1909.* Doris Day and Gordon MacRae sang it as the title song in (MM) *By the Light of the Silvery Moon,* 1952. Other films in which it was used were: (MM) *The Story of Vernon and Irene Castle,* 1939; (MM) *Birth of the Blues,* played by Guy Lombardo and the Royal Canadians, 1941; (MM) *Babes on Broadway,* 1942; (MM) *Hello,*

Frisco, Hello, sung by Alice Faye, 1943; (MM) *The Jolson Story,* 1946; (MM) *Always Leave Them Laughing,* 1949; (MM) *Two Weeks With Love,* sung by Jane Powell, 1950. It has always been a staple of barbershop quartets, glee clubs, and sing-alongs.

By the Mississinewah. w/m Cole Porter, 1943. Introduced by Ethel Merman and Paula Laurence in (TM) *Something for the Boys.*

By the River of the Roses. w. Marty Symes, m. Joe Burke, 1943. Popular record by Woody Herman, with his Orchestra (Decca).

By the River Sainte Marie. w. Edgar Leslie, m. Harry Warren, 1931. A favorite of big bands. Among the recordings: Henry Busse (Victor), Jimmie Lunceford (Decca), Tommy Dorsey (Victor), Guy Lombardo (Columbia), Will Osborne (Melotone), Gene Krupa (Columbia). Frankie Laine revived it in the coupling with his million-seller "That's My Desire" q. v. (Mercury), 1947.

By the Sad Sea Waves. w. Lester Barrett, m. Lester Thomas, 1895.

By the Saskatchewan. w. C. M. S. McLellan, m. Ivan Caryll, 1911. Introduced by John E. Young and Ida M. Adams in (TM) *The Pink Lady.* Leading recording by Reinald Werrenrath and The Haydn Quartet (Victor).

By the Sycamore Tree. w. Haven Gillespie, m. Pete Wendling, 1931. Featured and recorded by Rudy Vallee (Hit of the Week); Paul Whiteman, with Jack Fulton vocal (Victor); Dorsey Brothers' Orchestra (Columbia); Art Kahn (Melotone); later, Stan Getz (Norgran).

By the Sycamore Tree. w. George V. Hobart, m. Max Hoffmann, 1903. Popular song from (TM) *The Rogers Brothers in London,* one of a series of "Rogers Brothers" shows. Leading recordings by Bob Roberts (Columbia) and Harry MacDonough (Edison).

By the Time I Get to Phoenix. w/m Jim Webb, 1967. Hit record by Glen Campbell (Capitol). Chart versions by Isaac Hayes (Enterprise), 1969; The Mad Lads (Volt), 1969;

Glen Campbell and Anne Murray singing it in medley with "I Say a Little Prayer" (Capitol), 1971; Isaac Hayes and Dionne Warwick, in medley with "I Say a Little Prayer" (ABC), 1977. Wanda Jackson had a Country chart version: "By the Time You Get to Phoenix" (Capitol), 1968.

By the Watermelon Vine, Lindy Lou.   w/m Thomas S. Allen, 1914.

By the Waters of Minnetonka.   w. J. M. Cavanass, m. Thurlow Lieurance, 1921. Though published seven years earlier, it became popular this year. Revived by Glenn Miller and his Orchestra, with a two-sided recording (Bluebird), 1938. This was one of his early records for that label.

By the Way.   w. Mack Gordon, m. Josef Myrow, 1948. Introduced in the Betty Grable/ Dan Dailey film (MM) *When My Baby Smiles at Me.* Leading record by Perry Como (RCA Victor).

By-U, By-O (The Lou'siana Lullaby).   w/m Jack Owens, Ted McMichael, Leo V. Killion, and Mack Fenton, 1941. Top 10 record by Woody Herman, vocal by Muriel Lane (Decca).

C

Cabaret. w. Fred Ebb, m. John Kander, 1966. Introduced by Jill Haworth in (TM) *Cabaret*. Chart record by Herb Alpert and The Tijuana Brass (A&M), 1968. Sung by Liza Minelli in (MM) *Cabaret*, 1972.

Cabaret. w/m Al Russell and Joel Cowan, 1949. Leading records by Eve Young, later known as Karen Chandler (RCA Victor), and Patti Page (Mercury).

Cab Driver. w/m Carson Parks, 1968. Last Top 40 hit by The Mills Brothers (Dot).

Cabin in the Cotton. w. Mitchell Parish, m. Frank Perkins, 1932. Interpolated by Bert Lahr in (TM) *George White's Music Hall Follies*. Featured by Bing Crosby and recorded by him with Lennie Hayton's Orchestra (Brunswick) and also by Cab Calloway (Brunswick). Other popular versions by Johnny Hamp (Victor), Barron Lee and the Blue Rhythm Band (Perfect), and Singin' Sam [Harry Frankel] (Perfect). Later, Neal Hefti, with vocal by Frances Wayne, had a well-received record (Coral).

Cabin in the Sky. w. John Latouche, m. Vernon Duke, 1940. Introduced by Ethel Waters in (TM) *Cabin in the Sky*. She sang it with Eddie "Rochester" Anderson in the film version (MM) *Cabin in the Sky* in 1943 and recorded it twice (Continental and Liberty Music Shops). Other top recordings by Ella Fitzgerald (Decca) and Benny Goodman, vocal by Helen Forrest (Columbia).

Ça C'est L'Amour. w/m Cole Porter, 1957. Introduced by Taina Elg in (MM) *Les Girls*. Popular record by Tony Bennett (Columbia).

Ça C'est Paris! See **Paree!**

Cadillac Car. w. Tom Eyen, m. Henry Krieger, 1981. Introduced by the company in (TM) *Dreamgirls*.

Cae Cae. w. Lohn La Touche (Engl.), Pedro Barrios (Sp.), m. Roberto Martina, 1941. Martina also wrote the original Portuguese lyrics for this Brazilian song that was introduced in the United States in (MM) *That Night in Rio* by Carmen Miranda. It was again heard in (MM) *She's for Me*, 1943.

Caissons Go Rolling Along, The (Over Hill, Over Dale.) w/m Edmund L. Gruber, 1918. Written by a lieutenant in the Artillery Corps of the U.S. Army, while stationed in the Philippines in 1908. John Philip Sousa wrote a band arrangement in 1918 and called it the "U.S. Field Artillery March" and was erroneously credited as composer.

Cajun Baby. w. Hank Williams, m. Hank Williams, Jr., 1969. Hit country recording by Hank Williams, Jr. of his father's lyric, which he set to music (MGM).

Cajun Moon. w/m Jimmy Rushing, 1986. #1 Country chart single by Ricky Skaggs (Epic).

Cajun Queen, The. w/m Wayne P. Walker, 1962. Record narrated by Jimmy Dean (Columbia).

Cajun Stripper, The. w/m Doug Kershaw and Rusty Kershaw, 1968. Introduced and recorded by Doug Kershaw (RCA). C&W chart record by Jim Ed Brown (RCA), 1968.

Cake Walking Babies from Home. w/m Chris Smith, Henry Troy, and Clarence Williams, 1924. Recorded by Mutt Carey and his New Yorkers (Century) and Lu Watters (JM).

Cakewalk Your Lady. w. Johnny Mercer, m. Harold Arlen, 1946. Performed by the chorus in (TM) *St. Louis Woman.*

Calcutta. w. Lee Pockriss and Paul Vance (Engl.), m. Heino Gaze, 1961. Originally a German song with numerous lyrics and titles. Introduced in the U.S. with the #1 record, an instrumental version, by Lawrence Welk and his Orchestra (Dot). The Four Preps had a vocal version (Capitol).

Caldonia (a.k.a. **Caldonia Boogie**). w/m Fleecie Moore, 1945. Louis Jordan and his Tympany Five had a million-seller called "Caldonia Boogie" (Decca), and performed it in (MM) *Swing Parade of 1946.* Woody Herman, with his Orchestra, had a hit record (Columbia). Erskine Hawkins, vocal by Ace Harris (Victor), also had a popular version.

Calendar Girl. w/m Howard Greenfield and Neil Sedaka, 1961. Top 10 record by Neil Sedaka (RCA).

Calico Rag. w/m Al Dexter and James B. Paris, 1945. Featured and recorded by Al Dexter (Columbia).

California, Here I Come. w. Al Jolson, B. G. Desylva, m. Joseph Meyer, 1924. Interpolated by Al Jolson in the road tour of (TM) *Bombo.* He later sang it in (TM) *Big Boy.* He recorded it (Brunswick), as did Georgie Price (Victor). George Jessel sang it in (MM) *Lucky Boy,* 1929; Benny Goodman and his Orchestra played it in (MM) *Hollywood Hotel,* 1937. Jolson sang in it (MM) *Rose of Washington Square,* 1939; with Evelyn Keyes in (MM) *The*

Jolson Story, 1946; and dubbed for Larry Parks in (MM) *Jolson Sings Again,* 1949. It was sung by the chorus in a medley in (MM) *With a Song in My Heart,* 1952. It was the theme song of Abe Lyman and His Californians.

California and You. w. Edgar Leslie, m. Harry Puck, 1914. Recorded by Irving Kaufman (Victor), and Henry Burr and Albert Campbell (Columbia).

California Dreamin'. w/m John E. A. Phillips and Michelle G. Phillips, 1966. Gold record by The Mamas and The Papas (Dunhill). Chart records by Bobby Womack (Minit), 1969; the trio, America (American International), 1979; The Beach Boys (Capitol), 1986.

California Girl and the Tennessee Square. w/m Jack Clement, 1969. Crossover (C&W/Pop) hit by Tompall and The Glaser Brothers (MGM).

California Girls. w/m Brian Wilson, 1965, 1985. Top 10 hit by The Beach Boys (Capitol). Revived by David Lee Roth with a success of equal standing (Warner Bros.), 1985.

California Melodies. m. David Rose, 1942. Theme song for "California Melodies Hour," featuring David Rose and his Orchestra. Recorded by Pete Rugolo and his Orchestra (Columbia).

California Nights. w. Howard Liebling, m. Marvin Hamlisch, 1967. Top 20 record by Leslie Gore (Mercury).

California Polka. w/m Dale Fitzsimmons, 1946. C&W hit record by Tex Williams (Capitol).

California Saga (On My Way to Sunny Californ-i-a). w/m Mike Love, 1973. Recorded by The Beach Boys (Brother).

California Soul. w/m Nicholas Ashford and Valerie Simpson, 1969. Top 40 record by The 5th Dimension (Soul City). Also recorded by Marvin Gaye and Tammi Terrell (Tamla), 1970.

California Sun. w/m Henry Glover and Morris Levy, 1961. Introduced by Joe Jones (Roulette). Top 10 record by The Rivieras (Riviera), 1964.

Californ-i-ay. w. E. Y. Harburg, m. Jerome Kern, 1944. Introduced by Deanna Durbin and Robert Paige in (MM) *Can't Help Singing.*

Calinda, The (Boo-Joom, Boo-Joom, Boo!). w/m Herman Hupfeld, 1927. Sung by the company in the revue (TM) *A La Carte.* Popular record by Paul Whiteman, vocal by Bing Crosby, Jack Fulton, Charles Gaylord, and Austin Young (Victor). This was Hupfeld's first song success.

Calla Calla. w. Lenny Adelson and Margarite Almeda, m. Eddie Samuels, 1951. Leading record by Vic Damone, with George Bassman's Orchestra (Mercury).

Calling America. w/m Jeff Lynne, 1986. Recorded by The Electric Light Orchestra (CBS Associated).

Calling Dr. Love. w/m Gene Simmons, 1977. Top 20 record by the group, Kiss, written by their bassist (Casablanca).

Calling Occupants of Interplanetary Craft. w/m Terry Draper and John Woloschuk, 1977. Recorded first by the Canadian group, Klaatu (Capitol), followed by The Carpenters (A&M).

Calling to Her Boy Just Once Again. w/m Paul Dresser, 1900. Ballad hit, featured in vaudeville by the tenor Richard José.

Calling You. w/m Bob Telson, 1988. Sung by Javetta Steele on the sound track of (MP) *Baghdad Cafe* and its album (Island). Nominated for an Academy Award.

Call Me. w/m Peter Cox and Richard Drummie, 1985. Written and recorded by the British duo Go West (Chrysalis).

Call Me. w/m Randy Muller, 1982. #1 R&B record, and Pop chart record by the octet Skyy (Salsoul).

Call Me. w/m Giorgio Moroder and Deborah Harry, 1980. Introduced by the group, Blondie, in (MP) *American Gigolo.* #1 gold record by Blondie (Chrysalis).

Call Me. w/m Aretha Franklin, 1970. Top 20 record by Aretha Franklin (Atlantic).

Call Me. w/m Tony Hatch, 1966. English song. Leading hit by California Chris Montez (A&M).

Call Me. w/m Clyde Otis and Belford C. Hendricks, 1958. Introduced and most popular record by Johnny Mathis (Columbia).

Call Me (Come Back Home). w/m Al Green, Al Jackson, and Willie Mitchell, 1973. Top 10 record by Al Green (Hi).

Call Me Darling. w. Dorothy Dick (Engl.), w/m Bert Reisfeld, Mart Fryberg, Rolf Marbet, 1931. Original title in German: "Sag' Mir Darling." Popularized and recorded by Russ Columbo (Victor) and Arthur Tracy, "The Street Singer" (Brunswick).

Call Me Irresponsible. w. Sammy Cahn, m. James Van Heusen, 1963. The song was written in 1955 for Fred Astaire to sing in a proposed, but abandoned, motion picture. Eight years later, the film (MP) *Papa's Delicate Condition* was produced, this time starring Jackie Gleason, who introduced the song. It won the Academy Award for Best Song of 1963. The leading records were by Frank Sinatra (Reprise) and Jack Jones (Kapp).

Call Me Lightning. w/m Peter Townshend, 1968. Recorded by the British group The Who (Decca).

Call Me Mister. w/m Harold Rome, 1946. Introduced by Bill Callahan in (TM) *Call Me Mister,* and performed by Dan Dailey and Betty Grable in the movie version (MM) *Call Me Mister,* 1951.

Call Me Mr. In-between. w/m Harlan Howard, 1962. Hit record by Burl Ives (Decca).

Call Me Up in Dreamland. w/m Van Morrison, 1971. Recorded by Van Morrison (Warner Bros.).

Call Me Up Some Rainy Afternoon. w/m Irving Berlin, 1910. Ada Jones and the American Quartet had a best-selling record (Victor).

Call of the Canyon. w/m Billy Hill, 1940. Popular records by the orchestras of Glenn Miller (Bluebird); Guy Lombardo (Decca); Kay Kyser (Columbia); vocal groups, The Charioteers (Columbia) and The King Sisters (Bluebird).

Call of the Far-away Hills, The. See **Shane.**

Call of the South, The. w/m Irving Berlin, 1924. From (TM) *Music Box Revue of 1924.* Al Jolson sang it in (MM) *Mammy.* 1930.

Call on Me. w/m Lee Loughrane, 1974. Top 10 record by Chicago (Columbia).

Call on Me. w/m Deadric Malone, 1963. Leading recording by Bobby Bland (Duke).

Call Operator 210. w/m Floyd Dixon, 1952. Introduced and recorded by Floyd Dixon (Aladdin).

Call to the Heart. w/m Gregg Giuffria, 1985. Recorded by the quintet, Giuffria, led by the keyboardist/composer (MCA).

Calypso. w/m John Denver, 1975. John Denver dedicated the song to Jacques Cousteau and the personnel of his ship, *The Calypso.* The recording was released on the flip side of Denver's hit "I'm Sorry" (RCA).

Calypso Blues. w. Don George, m. Nat "King" Cole, 1950. Introduced and recorded by Nat "King" Cole (Capitol).

Calypso Melody. m. Larry Clinton, 1957. Instrumental, recorded by David Rose and his Orchestra (MGM).

Camel Hop. m. Mary Lou Williams, 1938. Instrumental recorded by Benny Goodman, arranged by Mary Lou Williams.

Camelot. w. Alan Jay Lerner, m. Frederick Loewe, 1960. Introduced by Richard Burton in (TM) *Camelot.* In the film version (MM) *Camelot,* 1967, it was sung by Richard Harris.

Came So Far for Beauty. w/m Leonard Cohen and John Lissauer, 1979. Introduced by Leonard Cohen in his album "Recent Songs" (Columbia), 1988. Revived by Jennifer Warnes in her album "Famous Blue Raincoat" (Cypress).

Canadian Capers. w. Earl Burtnett, m. Gus Chandler, Bert White, and Henry Cohen, 1915. Popularity came mostly as an instrumental. Among its better known records were those by Paul Whiteman (Victor) in 1921 and Claude Hopkins (Columbia) in 1933. It was performed by Frankie Carle and his Orchestra in (MM) *My Dream Is Yours* in 1949.

Canadian Sunset. w. Norman Gimbel, m. Eddie Heywood, 1956. Pianist Eddie Heywood, with Hugo Winterhalter and his Orchestra, had the top instrumental recording (RCA); Andy Williams had the top vocal (Cadence).

Canal Street Blues. m. Joseph "King" Oliver, 1924. Jazz standard, composed, introduced, and recorded by cornetist King Oliver, and his Band (Gennett). Among the many recorded versions to follow were those by the bands of Richard M. Jones (Session), Red Allen (Decca), Turk Murphy (Good Time Jazz), Lu Watters (West Coast).

Can Anyone Explain? (No! No! No!). w/m Bennie Benjamin and George David Weiss, 1950. Seven Top 40 records! The Ames Brothers (Coral); Ray Anthony, vocal by Ronnie Deauville (Capitol); Louis Armstrong and Ella Fitzgerald, with Sy Oliver's Orchestra (Decca); Vic Damone, with Ralph Marterie's Orchestra (Mercury); Larry Green, with the Honeydreamers (RCA Victor); Dick Haymes, with Four Hits and a Miss (Decca); Dinah Shore, with Harry Zimmerman's Orchestra (Columbia).

(I Can Do Without Broadway, But) Can Broadway Do Without Me? w/m Jimmy Durante, 1929. Introduced by Clayton, Jackson, and Durante in (TM) *Show Girl* and recorded by them (Columbia). Sung by Jimmy Durante with Xavier Cugat's Orchestra in (MM) *On an Island with You*," starring Esther Williams, 1948.

Can-Can. w/m Cole Porter, 1953. Introduced by Lilo, Gwen Verdon, and the ensemble in (TM) *Can-Can*. In the film version (MM) *Can-Can*, 1960, it was performed by Shirley MacLaine, Juliet Prowse, and the ensemble.

Cancel the Flowers. w/m Eddie Seiler, Sol Marcus, and Bennie Benjamin, 1941.

Candida. w/m Tony Wine and Irving Levine, 1970. Gold record by the vocal trio Dawn (Bell).

Candle in the Wind. w. Bernie Taupin, m. Elton John, 1987. First recorded by Elton John in his album "Goodbye Yellow Brick Road" (MCA), as a tribute to the late Marilyn Monroe, 1973. Re-recorded on an album and Top 10 single with The Melbourne Symphony Orchestra (MCA), 1987.

Candle on the Water. w/m Al Kasha and Joel Hirschhorn, 1977. Introduced by Helen Reddy in the live action/animated Disney feature (MM) *Pete's Dragon*. Nominated for an Academy Award.

Candy. w/m Larry Blackmon and Tomi Jenkins, 1987. Chart single by the group Cameo (Atlanta Artists).

Candy. w/m Mack David, Joan Whitney, and Alex Kramer, 1944. No. 1 record by Johnny Mercer, Jo Stafford, and The Pied Pipers (Capitol). Other big sellers by Dinah Shore (Victor); Johnny Long, vocal by Dick Robertson (Decca); The Four King Sisters, with Buddy Cole's Orchestra (Victor).

Candy and Cake. w/m Bob Merrill, 1950. Introduced, featured, and recorded by Arthur Godfrey, with Archie Bleyer's Orchestra (Columbia).

Candy Girl. w/m Maurice Starr and Michael Jonzun, 1983. Recorded by the group New Edition (Streetwise).

Candy Girl. w/m Larry Santos, 1963. Top 10 record by The Four Seasons (Vee-Jay).

Candy Kisses. w/m George Morgan, 1948. C&W song introduced by George Morgan (Columbia). Best-seller: Eddy Howard, with his Orchestra (Mercury). Others: Danny Kaye (Decca); Elton Britt (Victor).

Candy Man. w/m Fred Neil and Beverly Ross, 1961. Recorded by Roy Orbison, coupled with hit record "Crying" (Monument). Song not to be confused with 1971 success of the same name.

Candy Man, The. w/m Leslie Bricusse and Anthony Newley, 1971. Introduced on the soundtrack of (MM) *Willy Wonka and the Chocolate Factory* by Aubrey Wood. #1 gold record by Sammy Davis, Jr. (MGM), 1972.

Candy Store Blues. w/m Nick Castle, Herb Jeffries, and Eddie Beal, 1949. Sung by eleven-year-old Toni Harper in (MM) *Manhattan Angel*, and recorded by her (Columbia).

Can I Change My Mind? w/m Barry Despenza and Carl Wolfolk, 1969. Gold record by Tyrone Davis (Dakar).

Can I Forget You? w. Oscar Hammerstein, II, m. Jerome Kern, 1937. Introduced by Irene Dunne in (MM) *High, Wide and Handsome*.

Can I Get a Witness. w/m Eddie Holland, Lamont Dozier, and Brian Holland, 1963. Top 20 record by Marvin Gaye (Tamla). Revived by Lee Michaels (A&M), 1971.

Can I Help It? w. Eddie DeLange, m. James Van Heusen, 1939. Featured and recorded by the orchestras of Larry Clinton (Victor), Bob Crosby (Decca), Horace Heidt (Columbia), Ramona and Her Men of Music (Varsity).

Can I Steal a Little Love? w/m Phil Tuminello, 1956. Introduced by John Saxon in

(MM) *Rock, Pretty Baby.* Leading record by Frank Sinatra (Capitol).

Can I Trust You? w. Paul Vance and Eddie Snyder (Engl.), A. Testa (It.), m. M. Remigi, 1966. Italian song "Io Ti Daro Di Piu?" sung in English by the Irish trio The Bachelors (London).

Cannonball. m. Duane Eddy and Lee Hazlewood, 1958. Popular instrumental recording by guitarist Duane Eddy (Jamie).

Can't Buy Me Love. w/m John Lennon and Paul McCartney, 1964. Introduced by The Beatles in (MM) "A Hard Day's Night," and on their #1 hit gold record (Capitol).

Can'tcha Say (You Believe in Me). w/m J. Green, Tom Scholz, and Brad Delp, 1987. Performed in medley with "Still in Love" by the group Boston (MCA).

Can't Even Get the Blues. w/m Rich Carnes and Thomas William Damphier, 1982. Country hit by Reba McEntire (Mercury).

Can't Fight This Feeling. w/m Kevin Cronin, 1985. #1 chart record by the quintet REO Speedwagon (Epic).

Can't Find the Time. w/m Bruce Arnold, 1969. Introduced and recorded by the group Orpheus (MGM). Revived by Rose Colored Glass (Bang), 1971.

Can't Get Enough. w/m Mick Ralphs, 1974. Written by the guitarist of the British group, Bad Company, which had a Top 10 U.S. release (Swan Song).

Can't Get Enough of Your Love, Babe. w/m Barry White, 1974. #1 gold record by Barry White (20th Century).

Can't Get Indiana off My Mind. w. Robert De Leon, m. Hoagy Carmichael, 1940. Among top records: Bing Crosby (Decca) and Hal Kemp's Orchestra (Victor).

Can't Get It Out of My Head. w/m Jeff Lynne, 1975. Written by the leader of the British group, Electric Light Orchestra, which had a Top 20 U.S. release (United Artists).

Can't Get Out of This Mood. w. Frank Loesser, m. Jimmy McHugh, 1942. Introduced by Ginny Simms in (MM) *Seven Days Leave.* Top records by Kay Kyser, vocal Harry Babbitt (Columbia); Johnny Long, vocal Four Teens (Decca).

Can't Get Over (the Bossa Nova). w/m Steve Lawrence, Eydie Gormé, and Marilyn Gins, 1964. Introduced and recorded by Eydie Gormé (Columbia).

Can't Get Over You. w/m Frankie Beverly, 1989. Hit R&B chart record by Maze, featuring Frankie Beverly (Warner Bros.).

Can't Get Used to Losing You. w/m Doc Pomus and Mort Shuman, 1963. Hit record by Andy Williams (Columbia).

Can't Help Falling in Love. w/m George David Weiss, Hugo Peretti, and Luigi Creatore, 1962. Introduced by Elvis Presley in (MM) *Blue Hawaii.* Presley's recording was a million-seller (RCA). Revived with chart records by Al Martino (Capitol) and Andy Williams (Columbia), 1970. Top 40 version by Corey Hart (EMI America), 1987.

Can't Help Lovin' Dat Man. w. Oscar Hammerstein, II, m. Jerome Kern, 1928. Sung by Helen Morgan, Tess Gardella, Norma Terris, Jules Bledsoe, and Allan Campbell in (TM) *Show Boat.* Helen Morgan sang it in (MM) *Show Boat,* 1929, and (MM) *Show Boat,* 1936. In the latter, she was joined by Hattie McDaniel, Paul Robeson, and Irene Dunne. In the 1951 version (MM) *Show Boat,* Annette Warren sang it on the soundtrack, dubbing for Ava Gardner. Lena Horne sang it in the Kern biography (MM) *Till the Clouds Roll By,* 1946. Gogi Grant dubbed it for Ann Blyth in the title role of (MM) *The Helen Morgan Story,* 1957.

Can't Help Singing. w. E. Y. Harbug, m. Jerome Kern, 1944. Introduced by Deanna Durbin and Robert Paige in (MM) *Can't Help Singing.*

Can This Be Love? w. Paul James, m. Kay Swift, 1930. Sung by Alice Boulden in (TM) *Fine and Dandy,* which starred Joe Cook.

Among the recordings were those by the Arden-Ohman Orchestra (Victor), Frank Luther (Victor), Jacques Renard (Brunswick), Fred Rich (Perfect), and in 1940, Woody Herman (Decca).

Can This Be the End of the Rainbow? w. Sammy Cahn, m. Saul Chaplin, 1941. Introduced by Judy Garland and recorded by her with Bobby Sherwood's Orchestra (Decca), coupled with the version by Woody Herman and his Orchestra.

Can't I? w/m Leroy Lovett, 1953. Leading records by Nat "King" Cole, with Billy May's Orchestra (Capitol), and The Ames Brothers, with Hugo Winterhalter's Orchestra (RCA Victor).

Can't Seem to Make You Mine. w/m Sky Saxon, 1967. Recorded by The Seeds (GNP Crescendo).

Can't Smile Without You. w/m Chris Arnold, David Martin, and Geoff Morrow, 1975. English song with gold record by Barry Manilow (Arista).

Can't Stay Away from You. w/m Gloria Estefan, 1988. Recorded by Gloria Estefan and Miami Sound Machine (Epic).

Can't Stop Dancin'. w/m John Pritchard, Jr. and Ray Stevens, 1977. Top 20 record by The Captain and Tennille (A&M).

Can't Stop Loving You. w/m Wayne Bickerton and Tony Waddington, 1970. Top 40 U.S. release of the British recording by Tom Jones (Parrot).

Can't Stop My Heart from Loving You. w/m Jamie O'Hara and Kieran Kane, 1987. #1 Country chart single from the self-titled album, written and recorded by The O'Kanes (Columbia).

Can't Take My Eyes off You. w/m Bob Crewe and Bob Gaudio, 1967. Gold record by Frankie Valli (Philips). Hit record by The Lettermen, who sang it in medley with "Goin' Out of My Head" (Capitol), 1968. Nancy Wilson had a chart version (Capitol), 1969.

Can't Wait Another Minute. 1986. Chart record by the British brother-sister quintet Five Star (RCA).

Can't We Be Friends? w. Paul James (pseudonym for James Warburg), m. Kay Swift, 1929. Introduced by Libby Holman in the first edition of (TM) *The Little Show*. In (MM) *Young Man With a Horn*, 1952, Harry James played the trumpet on the soundtrack for Kirk Douglas who performed the role loosely based on the life of Bix Beiderbecke.

Can't We Be Sweethearts? w/m Herbert Cox and George Goldner, 1956. Recorded by The Cleftones (Gee).

Can't We Talk It Over? w. Ned Washington, m. Victor Young, 1932. Featured and recorded by Ruth Etting (Banner) and by the bands of Eddy Duchin (Columbia), Ben Bernie (Brunswick), Jack Teagarden (Varsity), Vincent Rose (Perfect), Ruby Newman (Victor).

Can't We Try. w/m Dan Hill and B. Hill, 1987. Canadian song and Top 10 hit by Dan Hill with Vonda Sheppard (Columbia).

Can't You Do a Friend a Favor. w. Lorenz Hart, m. Richard Rodgers, 1943. Introduced in the Broadway revival of the musical (TM) *A Connecticut Yankee* by Vivienne Segal and Dick Foran.

Can't You Hear Me Callin', Caroline? w. William H. Gardner, m. Caro Roma, 1914. Featured and recorded by George MacFarlane (Victor).

Can't You Hear My Heartbeat? w/m Carter-Lewis, 1965. Top 10 record by the British group Herman's Hermits (MGM). Carter-Lewis was pseudonym for John Shakespeare and Kenneth Hawker.

Can't You Read between the Lines? w. Sammy Cahn, m. Jule Styne, 1945. Leading records by Jimmy Dorsey, vocal by Jean Cromwell (Decca) and Kay Kyser and his Orchestra (Columbia).

Can't You See? w. Roy Turk, m. Fred E. Ahlert, 1931. Recorded by Mildred Bailey with Paul Whiteman's Orchestra (Victor) and Phil Spitalny and his Band (Perfect).

Can't You See It? w. Lee Adams, m. Charles Strouse, 1964. Introduced by Sammy Davis, Jr. in (TM) *Golden Boy.*

Can't You See That She's Mine? w/m Dave Clark and Mike Smith, 1964. Hit record, produced in England by The Dave Clark Five (Epic).

Can't You Take It Back and Change It? w/m Thurland Chattaway, 1911.

Can't You Understand? w. Jack Osterman, m. Victor Young, 1929. Introduced by vaudeville star Jackie Osterman.

Can U Read My Lips. w/m Michael Carpenter, Eric Strickland, and Arthur Zamora, 1989. R&B chart single hit by Z'Looke (Orpheus).

Can We Still Be Friends. w/m Todd Rundgren, 1978. Recorded by Todd Rundgren (Bearsville). Covered by the English singer Robert Palmer (Island), 1980.

Can You Dance (Baby Tell Me). See **Baby Tell Me, Can You Dance?**

Can You Find It in Your Heart. w. Al Stillman, m. Robert Allen, 1956. Popularized by Tony Bennett (Columbia).

Can You Jerk Like Me. w/m William Stevenson and Ivy Hunter, 1965. Chart record by The Contours (Gordy).

Can You Please Crawl Out Your Window? w/m Bob Dylan, 1966. Introduced and recorded by Bob Dylan (Columbia).

Can You Read My Mind (Love Theme from "Superman"). w. Leslie Bricusse, m. John Williams, 1979. Based on the love theme from (MP) *Superman.* Leading recording by Maureen McGovern (Warner Bros.).

Can You Stand the Rain. w/m James Harris III and Terry Lewis, 1989. Hit single by New Edition (MCA).

Can You Tame Wild Wimmen? w. Andrew B. Sterling, m. Harry Von Tilzer, 1918. Novelty song directed to a lion tamer. Leading records by Billy Murray (Victor) and Arthur Fields (Edison).

Caprice Viennois. m. Fritz Kreisler, 1910. A composition originally written for violin and piano.

Captain Kidd. w/m Roy Alfred and Marvin Fisher, 1945. Featured and recorded by Ella Mae Morse (Capitol).

Captain of Her Heart, The. w/m Kurt Maloo and Felix Haugh, 1986. Recorded by the German quartet, Double, of which the writers were half (A&M).

Captains of the Clouds. w. Johnny Mercer, m. Harold Arlen, 1942. From (MP) *Captains of the Clouds.* Official song of the Royal Canadian Air Force in World War II.

Cara-Lin. w/m Bob Feldman, Jerry Goldstein, and Richard Gottehrer, 1965. Top 40 record by The Strangeloves, trio comprised of the writers (Bang).

Caramba! It's the Samba! w/m Irving Taylor, George Wyle, and Edward Pola, 1948. Recorded by Peggy Lee, with Dave Barbour and The Brazilians (Capitol).

Cara Mia. w/m Tulio Trapani and Lee Lange, 1954, 1965. Hit record, made in England, by David Whitfield, with Mantovani's Orchestra (London). Revived by the Top 10 record by Jay and The Americans (United Artists), 1965.

Caravan. w. Irving Mills, m. Juan Tizol and Edward Kennedy "Duke" Ellington, 1937. Introduced and recorded by Duke Ellington and his Orchestra (Master). Billy Eckstine had a hit record (MGM), 1949, as did Ralph Marterie and his Orchestra (Mercury), 1953.

Caravan of Love. w/m Ernie Isley, Christopher Jasper, and Marvin Isley, 1985. Chart single by Isley, Jasper, Isley (CBS Associated).

Carefree Highway. w/m Gordon Lightfoot, 1974. Top 10 record by the Canadian singer/writer Gordon Lightfoot (Reprise).

Careless. w/m Lew Quadling, Eddy Howard, and Dick Jurgens, 1939. Song was submitted to the Irving Berlin publishing company by the writers who, respectively, were the arranger, vocalist, and leader of the popular band. Berlin heard Dave Dreyer, his company manager, going over the melody at the piano. Liking the tune, but not the lyric or title, they foresaw a problem. If they rejected the song, they felt that Jurgens, who had a lot of air time with his band, would not play any future songs published by the Berlin company. Berlin took the song home and, overnight, wrote a new lyric with the tile of "Careless." His company published the song, though Berlin received neither credit nor royalty as a writer. The financial returns were huge as it became a #1 song, thanks to the performance and recordings by Jurgens (Vocalion); Glenn Miller, vocal by Ray Eberle, (Bluebird); Tommy Dorsey (Victor); Phil Harris (Varsity); Tony Martin (Decca); and many others.

Careless Hands. w. Bob Hilliard, m. Carl Sigman, 1949. Hit record by Mel Tormé, accompanied by Sonny Burke's Orchestra (Capitol). Other chart records by Sammy Kaye, vocal by Don Cornell (RCA Victor); Bing Crosby (Decca); Bob and Jeanne (Decca).

Careless Kisses. w/m Tim Spencer, 1950. Top recordings by the bands of Russ Morgan (Decca); Eddy Howard (Mercury).

Careless Love. See **Loveless Love.**

Careless Whisper. w/m George Michael and Andrew Ridgeley, 1985. Single first released in England as a solo by George Michael. He and guitarist Ridgeley were listed as Wham! on the #1 gold record in the U.S. (Columbia).

Carelessly. w. Charles and Nick Kenny, m. Norman Ellis, 1937. Featured and recorded by Teddy Wilson, vocal by Billie Holiday (Brunswick) and Kay Thompson (Victor).

Caresses. w/m James V. Monaco, 1920. Alice Delysia interpolated the song in the English/French import (TM) *Afgar.* Paul Whiteman recorded a popular instrumental version (Victor).

Carey. w/m Joni Mitchell, 1971. Recorded by Joni Mitchell (Reprise).

Caribbean. w/m Mitchell Torok, 1953. Recorded by Mitchell Torok and the Louisiana Hayride Band (Abbott).

Caribbean Cocktail. m. Larry Wagner and Frank Shuman, 1957. Instrumental recorded by Larry Wagner and his Orchestra (Forest).

Caribbean Queen (No More Love on the Run). w/m Keith Diamond and Billy Ocean, 1984. #1 gold record by Billy Ocean (Jive/Arista)]

Carioca. w. Edward Eliscu and Gus Kahn, m. Vincent Youmans, 1933. Sung by Etta Moten and danced by Fred Astaire and Ginger Rogers (their first film together) in (MM) *Flying Down to Rio.* Nominated for Academy Award, 1934. Among hundreds of recordings are those by: Xavier Cugat (Victor), Andre Kostalanetz (Columbia), Artie Shaw (Victor), Jack Jones (Kapp), Boston Pops (Victor), Gerry Mulligan (Fantasy), Mel Tormé (Bethlehem), Joe Harnell (Columbia), Oscar Peterson (Verve), Art Lund (Coral), Buddy De Franco (MGM).

Carissima. w/m Arthur Penn, 1903. Introduced in (TM) *The Red Feather*, 1903.

Carnegie Blues. m. Edward Kennedy "Duke" Ellington, 1945. Ellington's Orchestra played his compositon "Black, Brown and Beige" at his 1943 Carnegie Hall concert. A blues theme from that work was the basis of this instrumental, featured and recorded by the Ellington band (Victor).

Carny Town. w/m Randy Starr and Fred Wise, 1964. Introduced by Elvis Presley in (MM) *Roustabout* and on records (RCA).

C. C. Rider. See **See See Rider Blues.**

Carol. w/m Chuck Berry, 1958. Introduced and recorded by Chuck Berry (Chess). Revived by Tommy Roe (ABC-Paramount), 1964.

Carolina, I'm Coming Back to You. w. Jack Caddigan, m. Jimmy McHugh, 1916. McHugh's first published song.

Carolina Day. w/m Livingston Taylor, 1971. Recorded by Livingston Taylor (Capricorn).

Carolina in the Morning. w. Gus Kahn, m. Walter Donaldson, 1922. Introduced by Willie and Eugene Howard in (TM) *The Passing Show of 1922*. Betty Grable and June Haver sang it in *The Dolly Sisters*, 1945; Robert Alda and Ann Southern sang it in (MM) *April Showers*, 1948; Al Jolson, dubbing for Larry Parks, sang it in (MM) *Jolson Sings Again*, 1949; Patrice Wymore sang it in the Kahn film bio (MM) *I'll See You In My Dreams*, 1951.

Carolina in the Pines. w/m Michael Murphey, 1975. Hit Country/Pop record by Michael Murphey (Epic).

Carolina Moon. w. Benny Davis, m. Joe Burke, 1929. Best remembered as the theme song of Morton Downey, who used it on his radio shows and in public appearances. Popular recordings by Smith Ballew (Okeh), Jesse Crawford (Victor), Gene Austin (Victor), jazz organist Ernie Felice (Capitol).

Carolina Rolling Stone. w. Mitchell Parish, m. Harry D. Squires, 1924. Parish's first published song. Recorded by Al Bernard (Brunswick).

Carolina Shout. m. James P. Johnson, 1922. Instrumental, featured, and recorded by jazz pianist James P. Johnson (Okeh).

Carolina Sunshine. w. Walter Hirsch, m. Erwin R. Schmidt, 1919.

Caroline, No. w. Tony Asher and Brian Wilson, m. Brian Wilson, 1966. Recorded by Brian Wilson (Capitol).

Carolyn. w/m Tommy Collins, 1971. C&W/Pop hit by Merle Haggard (Capitol).

Carousel. w. Eric Blau, Mort Shuman (Engl.), Jacques Brel (Fr.), m. Jacques Brel, 1968. Original French title "La Valse Mille Temps," introduced and recorded in France by Jacques Brel (Philips), 1959. English version sung in the off-Broadway hit (TM) *Jacques Brel Is Alive and Well and Living in Paris* by Elly Stone, 1968. See also **Days of the Waltz, The**.

Carousel Waltz, The. m. Richard Rodgers, 1945. Played by the orchestra in the Amusement Park opening of (TM) *Carousel*, and in the film version (MM) *Carousel*, 1956.

Carpet Man. w/m Jim Webb, 1968. Top 40 record by The 5th Dimension (Soul City).

Carrie. w/m Joey Tempest and M. Michael, 1987. Top 10 single by the Swedish quintet Europe (Epic).

Carrie (Marry Harry). w. Junie McCree, m. Albert Von Tilzer, 1909. Introduced by Sophie Tucker.

Carrie-Anne. w/m Allan Clarke, Tony Hicks, and Graham Nash, 1967. The writers were members of the British group, The Hollies, which had a Top 10 record (Epic).

Carroll County Accident. w/m Bob Ferguson, 1969. Crossover (C&W/Pop) chart hit by Porter Wagoner (RCA).

Carry Me Back. w/m Felix Cavaliere, 1969. Top 40 record by The Rascals, of which the writer was a member (Atlantic).

Carry Me Back to the Lone Prairie. w/m Carson J. Robison, 1934. Based on the 1850 folk song "The Ocean Burial," from the poem by E. H. Chapin. Later known as "Bury Me Not on the Lone Prairie" and/or "The Dying Cowboy," this version was sung by James Melton in (MM) *Stars Over Broadway* in 1935, after being introduced by Robison on radio the year before. Melton recorded it twice (Victor), once with the "Carry" and once with the "Bury" lyric.

Carry On, Wayward Son. w/m Kerry Livgren, 1977. Top 20 record by the group Kansas (Kirshner).

Cars. w/m Gary Numan, 1980. Recorded in England by Gary Numan (Atco).

Car Wash. w/m Norman Whitfield, 1977. Introduced as the theme of the film with songs, (MP) *Car Wash.* It was played instrumentally, and sung by the group Rose Royce. They were awarded a platinum record (MCA).

Casa Loma Stomp. m. Eugene Gifford, 1930. Recorded three times by Glen Gray and the Casa Loma Orchestra, 1930 (Okeh), 1933 (Victor), 1937 (Decca). Also by Connie's Inn Orchestra (Melotone). Gifford, as chief arranger, set the style for the Casa Loma band, which is considered by many to have been the first swing band to gain popular public acceptance. This was their initial hit instrumental.

Casanova. w/m Reggie Calloway, 1987. #1 R&B, Top 10 Pop chart record by the trio Levert (Atlantic).

Casey Jones. w. T. Lawrence Seibert, m. Eddie Newton, 1909. One of the most famous American railroad songs. Three popular recordings by The American Quartet (Victor), Billy Murray (Edison), and Arthur Collins and Buron Harlan (Columbia). It was sung by Gene Autry in (MM) *Sunset in Wyoming*, 1941, and interpolated in (TM) *Sing Out, Sweet Land*, 1944.

Casino Royale. w. Hal David, m. Burt Bacharach, 1967. Instrumental, introduced by Herb Alpert and the Tijuana Brass in (MP) *Casino Royale* and on records (A&M).

Castle of Dreams. w. Joseph McCarthy, m. Harry Tierney, 1919. Introduced by Bernice McCabe and ensemble in (TM) *Irene*. It was also played under the title and as background music in the film version (MM) *Irene*, 1940. The melody is an adaptation of a theme in Chopin's "Minute Waltz."

Castle Rock. w. Ervin Drake and Jimmy Shirl, m. Al Sears, 1951. Leading record by Frank Sinatra, with Harry James's Orchestra (Columbia). Popular versions by The Fontane Sisters, with Norman Leyden's Orchestra (RCA Victor) and, as an instrumental, by Johnny Hodges and his Orchestra (Mercury).

Castles in the Air. w/m Don McLean, 1972. Introduced and recorded by Don McLean (United Artists), 1972. His re-recording reached the Top 40 (Millennium), 1981.

Cast Your Fate to the Wind. w. Carel Werber, m. Vincent Guaraldi, 1962. Jazz instrumental hit by the piano-led Vince Guaraldi Trio (Fantasy). Popular instrumental record by the British group Sounds Orchestral (Parkway), 1965. Leading chart vocal versions by Tony Alaimo (ABC-Paramount), 1965, and Shelby Flint (Valiant), 1966.

Casual Look, A. w/m Ed Wells, 1956. Introduced and recorded by The Six Teens, of which the writer was lead singer (Flip).

Cat, The. m. Lalo Schifrin, 1964. Introduced on soundtrack of (MP) *Joy House.* Introduced on records by Lalo Schifrin and his Orchestra (Verve). Leading recording by jazz organist Jimmy Smith (Verve). Song, winner Grammy Award (NARAS) for Best Original Jazz Composition, 1964.

Cat and the Canary, The. w. Ray Evans, m. Jay Livingston, 1945. From (MP) *Why Girls Leave Home.* Nominated for Academy Award.

Cat Came Back, The. w/m Henry S. Miller, 1893. Introduced by Billy Rice of Haverly's Minstrels and featured by Tony Pastor. A novelty, still performed, especially in schools.

Catch a Falling Star. w/m Paul Vance and Lee Pockriss, 1958. Perry Como's recording (RCA) was the first gold record certified by the RIAA, indicating sales of over a million copies. It was coupled with a second hit, "Magic Moments" (q.v.) and was one of the Top 10 songs of the year.

Catch a Little Raindrop. w/m Dorsey Burnette and Joe Osborn, 1966. Country chart record by Claude King (Columbia).

Catch Me (I'm Falling). w/m Jade Starling and Whey Cooler, 1987. From (MP) *Hiding Out.* Top 10 record by the writer-led quintet Pretty Poison (Virgin).

Catch the Wind. w/m Donovan Phillip Leitch, 1965. First U.S. hit by the Scottish-born singer/songwriter Donovan (Hickory).

Catch Us If You Can. w/m Dave Clark and Lenny Davidson, 1965. Introduced by The Dave Clark Five in the British film (MM) *Having a Wild Weekend* (Br. title: *Catch Us If You Can*).

Caterina. w/m Earl Shuman and Maurice "Bugs" Bower, 1961. Popular record by Perry Como, with Mitchell Ayre's Orchestra (RCA).

Cathedral in the Pines. w/m Charles Kenny and Nick Kenny, 1938. First recorded by Orrin Tucker and his Orchestra. Revived in 1957 by Pat Boone (Dot).

Cathy's Clown. w/m Don Everly and Phil Everly, 1960. #1 hit by The Everly Brothers (Cadence). Revived with Country chart hit by Reba McEntire (MCA), 1989.

Cat in the Window (The Bird in the Sky), The. w/m Garry Bonner and Alan Gordon, 1967. Top 40 record by Petula Clark (Warner Bros.).

Cat People (Putting Out Fire). w/m David Bowie and Giorgio Moroder, 1982. Introduced on the soundtrack of (MP) *Cat People* and on records (Backstreet) by David Bowie.

Cat Scratch Fever. w/m Ted Nugent, 1977. Recorded by Ted Nugent (Epic).

Cat's in the Cradle. w/m Harry Chapin and Sandra Chapin, 1974. Singer/writer Harry Chapin was on tour when his son was born. The story of the song was suggested by his wife, and tells of a father and son who can't find time to be with each other. #1 gold record (Elektra). Song included in the multi-media

Broadway production (TM) *The Night That Made America Famous*, 1975.

Cattle Call, The. w/m Tex Owens, 1934. Revived in 1955 by Eddy Arnold (Victor).

Caught Up in the Rapture. w/m Garry Glen and Diane Quander, 1986. Top 10 R&B chart crossover record by Anita Baker (Elektra).

Caught Up in You. w/m Jeff Carlisi, Jim Peterik, Richard Barnes, and Frankie Sullivan, 1982. Top 10 record by the sextet, 38 Special (A&M).

Cause I Love You, That's A-Why. w/m Bob Merrill, 1952. Popular recording by Guy Mitchell and Mindy Carson, with Mitch Miller's Orchestra (Columbia).

Cause My Baby Says It's So. w. Al Dubin, m. Harry Warren, 1937. Introduced by Dick Powell in (MM) *The Singing Marine* and recorded by him (Decca) and the bands of Kay Kyser (Brunswick) and Mal Hallett (Decca).

Causing a Commotion. w/m Madonna and Steve Bray, 1987. From (MP) *Who's That Girl?*, starring Madonna, who had a Top 10 single (Sire).

Cavernism. m. James Mundy and Earl Hines, 1933. Mundy arranged this instrumental for Earl "Fatha" Hines's Band who recorded this twice, 1933 (Brunswick) and 1934 (Decca). It became Hines's theme.

Cecilia. w/m Paul Simon, 1970. Gold record single from the album "Bridge Over Troubled Water" by Simon and Garfunkel (Columbia). Not to be confused with the standard "Cecilia."

Cecilia. w. Herman Ruby, m. Dave Dreyer, 1925. Featured by Whispering Jack Smith on radio and records (Victor). The song had a big sheet music and piano roll sale. Revived by Dick Jurgens, vocal by Ronnie Kemper (Vocalion), 1940.

Celebrate. w/m Gary Bonner and Alan Gordon, 1970. Top 20 record by Three Dog Night (Dunhill).

Celebration. w/m Ronald Bell, Kool and The Gang, 1980. Platinum single by Kool and The Gang (De-Lite). The song was the theme song of the 1981 Superbowl, and was played at the Democratic National Convention upon the nomination of presidential candidate Walter Mondale, 1984.

Celery Stalks at Midnight. m. Will Bradley and George Harris, 1941. Instrumental, featured and recorded by Will Bradley and his Orchestra (Columbia) and a No. 2 version (Signature), 1947.

Cement Mixer (Put-Ti, Put-Ti). w/m Slim Gaillard and Lee Ricks, 1946. Novelty hit, with leading records by Alvino Rey, vocal by Rocky Coluccio (Capitol); Charlie Barnet, vocal by Art Robey (Decca); Jimmie Lunceford, vocal by Joe Thomas (Majestic); The Slim Gaillard Trio (Cadet).

Centerfield. w/m John Fogerty, 1985. Chart single from the platinum album of the same name by John Fogerty (Warner Bros.).

Centerfold. w/m Seth Justman, 1981. #1 gold record by the J. Geils Band (EMI America).

Centipede. w/m Michael Jackson, 1984. Recorded by the eldest member of the Jackson family, Rebbie Jackson, written and produced by Michael Jackson (Columbia).

Century's End. w/m Donald Fagen and T. Meher, 1988. Introduced by Donald Fagen on soundtrack of (MP) *Bright Lights, Big City*, and its album (Warner Bros.).

Certain. w/m Bill Anderson, 1965. Country chart record by Bill Anderson (Decca).

Certain Girl, A. w/m Naomi Neville, 1961. Chart record by Ernie K-Doe (Minit). Revived by Warren Zevon (Asylum), 1980.

Certain Smile, A. w. Paul Francis Webster, m. Sammy Fain, 1958. Introduced by Johnny Mathis in (MP) *A Certain Smile* and on records (Columbia). Song nominated for Academy Award.

Cerveza. m. Boots Brown, 1958. Popular instrumental by Boots Brown and His Blockbusters (RCA). Brown was a pseudonym for top trumpeter Milton "Shorty" Rogers.

C'Est La Vie. w/m Robbie Nevil, 1987. Recorded by Robbie Nevil (Manhattan).

C'Est La Vie. w/m Edward R. White and Mack Wolfson, 1955. Top 20 record by Sara Vaughan (Mercury).

C'Est La Vie. w. Stella Unger, m. Victor Young, 1955. Introduced by Robert Clary, Beatrice Arthur, and Kurt Kasznar in (TM) *Seventh Heaven*, based on the play by Austin Strong and two film versions.

C'Est Magnifique. w/m Cole Porter, 1953. Introduced by Lilo and Peter Cookson in (TM) *Can-Can*. In (MM) *Can-Can*, 1960, it was sung by Shirley MacLaine and Frank Sinatra.

C'Est Si Bon. w. Jerry Seelen (Engl.), Andrez Hornez (Fr.), m. Henri Betti, 1950, 1953. French song. First popular records in the U.S. by Johnny Desmond (MGM) and Danny Kaye (Decca). Eartha Kitt's hit record (RCA Victor) in 1953 established the song in the standard category.

C'Est Vous (It's You). w/m Abner Silver, Harry Richman, and Abner Greenberg, 1927.

Cha Cha Cha, The. w/m Kal Mann and Dave Appell, 1962. Top 10 record by Bobby Rydell (Cameo).

Cha-Hua-Hua. m. Joe Lubin and I. J. Roth, 1958. Top 40 instrumental by The Pets (Arwin).

Chained. w/m Frank Wilson, 1968. Hit record by Marvin Gaye (Tamla).

Chained to a Memory. w/m Jenny Lou Carson, 1946. Featured and recorded by Eddy Arnold (Victor).

Chain Gang. w/m Sam Cooke, 1960. Hit record by Sam Cooke (RCA). Jackie Wilson and Count Basie and his Orchestra had a popular version (Brunswick), 1968. It was released posthumously as the title song of

"Chain Gang Medley" by Jim Croce (ABC), 1976.

Chain Gang. w/m Sol Quasha and Herb Yakus, 1956. Top 20 record by Bobby Scott (ABC-Paramount).

Chain of Fools, w/m Don Covay, 1968. Gold record by Aretha Franklin (Atlantic).

Chains. w/m Gerry Goffin and Carole King, 1962. First recorded by The Cookies (Dimension).

Chains of Love. w. Ahmet Ertegun, m. Van Walls, 1951. Million-selling R&B hit by Joe Turner with Van "Piano Man" Walls (Atlantic). Popular singles by Pat Boone (Dot), 1956; The Drifters (Atlantic), 1965; Bobby Bland (Duke), 1969.

Chair, The. w/m Hank Cochran and Dean Dillon, 1985. #1 Country chart single by George Strait (MCA).

Champagne. w/m Peter Townshend, 1975. Written especially for the film verson of the rock-opera (MM) *Tommy* and introduced by Ann-Margaret.

Champagne Jam. w/m Buddy Buie, Robert Nix, and J. R. Cobb, 1978. Recorded by the group Atlanta Rhythm Section (Polydor).

Champagne Waltz, The. w/m Con Conrad, Ben Oakland, and Milton Drake, 1934. Popular waltz featured by ballroom orchestras. The team of Veloz and Yolanda danced to it as the title song of (MM) *Champagne Waltz*, 1937.

Chances Are. w. Al Stillman, m. Robert Allen, 1957. Popularized by Johnny Mathis (Columbia).

Change Is Gonna Come, A. w/m Sam Cooke, 1965. Hit record by Sam Cooke (RCA).

Change of Heart. w/m Essra Mohawk and Cyndi Lauper, 1987. Top 10 single by Cyndi Lauper (Portrait).

Change of Heart. w/m Eric Carmen, 1978. Recorded by Eric Carmen (Arista).

Change of Heart. w/m Buddy Buie and James B. Cobb, 1969. Recorded by Dennis Yost and The Classics IV (Imperial).

Change of Heart, A. w. Harold Adamson, m. Jule Styne, 1943. Introduced in (MM) *Hit Parade of 1953*. Nominated for Academy Award. When film was released for television, it was retitled *Change of Heart*.

Change Partners. w/m Stephen Stills, 1971. Recorded by Stephen Stills (Atlantic).

Change Partners. w/m Irving Berlin, 1938. This Academy Award nominee was introduced by Fred Astaire and Ginger Rogers in (MM) *Carefree*. Leading recordings by Astaire (Brunswick); Jimmy Dorsey, vocal by Bob Eberly (Decca); Larry Clinton, vocal by Dick Todd (Victor); Lawrence Welk and his Orchestra (Vocalion).

Changes. w/m David Bowie, 1972. Recorded in England by David Bowie (RCA). Chart re-release, 1975.

Changes. w/m Walter Donaldson, 1927. Made popular via the classic recording of Bill Challis's arrangement for Paul Whiteman's Orchestra featuring the Rhythm Boys [Bing Crosby, Al Rinker, and Harry Barris] and Bix Beiderbecke (Victor). Among other recordings of note: Benny Goodman and his Orchestra (Victor), 1937; Bobby Short, in his album, "The Mad 20's" (Atlantic), 1974.

Changes in Latitudes, Changes in Attitudes. w/m Jimmy Buffett, 1977. Recorded by Jimmy Buffett (ABC).

Change Your Mind. w/m Ray Noble, 1935. Introduced by Carl Brisson in (MM) *Ship Cafe*.

Changing My Tune. w. Ira Gershwin, m. George Gershwin, 1947. Betty Grable introduced this heretofore unpublished song in (MM) *The Shocking Miss Pilgrim*. Leading records: Judy Garland (Decca) and Mel Tormé and the Mel-Tones, with Artie Shaw and his Orchestra (Musicraft).

Changing Partners. w. Joe Darion, m. Larry Coleman, 1953. Patti Page had a million-seller (Mercury). Other chart records by Kay Starr (Capitol); Dinah Shore (RCA Victor); Bing Crosby (Decca).

Chanson D'Amour (Song of Love). w/m Wayne Shanklin, 1958. First recording and best-seller by Art and Dotty Todd (Era). Popular cover by The Fontane Sisters (Dot).

Chansonette. w. Dailey Paskman, Sigmund Spaeth, and Irving Caesar, m. Rudolf Friml, 1927. Originally published as a piano instrumental, "Chanson." See also "Donkey Serenade."

Chantez, Chantez. w. Albert Gamse, m. Irving Fields, 1957. Introduced, featured, and recorded by Dinah Shore (RCA).

Chanticleer Rag, The. w. Edward Madden, m. Albert Gumble, 1910. Following the success of Rostand's play *Chanticleer* (Rooster), the writers, aware that chorus ladies were referred to as "chickens," wrote this revue song. Popular recording by Arthur Collins and Byron G. Harlan (Columbia).

Chantilly Lace. w/m J. P. Richardson, 1958. Hit record by The Big Bopper [disc jockey Richardson's recording pseudonym] (Mercury). It was heard in (MM) *The Buddy Holly Story*, 1978, and in the Ritchie Valens story (MM) *La Bamba*, 1987. Richardson, Holly, and Valens were all killed in a plane crash in 1958. Revived by Mitch Ryder in medley with "You've Got Personality" (DynoVoice), 1968; Jerry Lee Lewis (Mercury), 1972.

Chant of the Jungle. w. Arthur Freed, m. Nacio Herb Brown, 1929. Introduced by Joan Crawford in (MP) *Untamed*.

Chant of the Weed. w/m Don Redman, 1932. Introduced and recorded by Redman and his Band (Brunswick) and again in 1940 (Bluebird). It was used as his theme. Also recorded by Harlan Lattimore (Columbia), and later by André Kostalanetz and his Orchestra (Victor).

Chapel by the Sea. w. Mary Margaret Hadler Gilbert, m. Vivian Gilbert, 1962. Popular instrumental version by Billy Vaughn and his Orchestra (Dot).

Chapel in the Moonlight. See **In the Chapel in the Moonlight.**

Chapel of Love. w/m Phil Spector, Ellie Greenwich, and Jeff Barry, 1964. #1 chart record by The Dixie Cups (Red Bird). Revived by Bette Midler (Atlantic), 1973.

Charade. w. Johnny Mercer, m. Henry Mancini, 1963. Title song of (MP) *Charade*. Leading recordings by Henry Mancini and his Orchestra (RCA), Sammy Kaye and his Orchestra (Decca), vocal recording by Andy Williams (Columbia).

Chariot. See **I Will Follow Him.**

Chariots of Fire (Race to the End). w. Jon Anderson, m. Vangelis, 1981. From the Academy Award-winning score of (MP) *Chariots of Fire*. #1 instrumental record by keyboardist/composer Vangelis [pseudonym for Greek-born Evangelos Papathanassiou] (Polydor).

Charity Ball. w/m Jean Millington, June Millington, and Alice DeBuhr, 1971. Written by three members of the female quartet, Fanny, whose record made the Top 40 (Reprise).

Charleston. w/m Cecil Mack and James P. Johnson, 1923. Introduced by Elizabeth Welch in the all-black revue (TM) *Runnin' Wild*. This became the dance sensation that is most representative of the period. Hit record by Arthur Gibbs and His Gang (Victor). It was interpolated in a production number in (MM) *Tea For Two*, 1950, by Virginia Gibson and Billy De Wolfe, and also used in (MM) *Has Anybody Seen My Gal*, 1952.

Charleston Alley. w/m Robert Bruce, 1941. Introduced and recorded by Charlie Barnet and his Orchestra (Bluebird). Revived by Lambert, Hendricks, and Ross (Columbia), 1960.

Charleston Crazy. w/m Porter Grainger and Bob Ricketts, 1924. Introduced on records by Fletcher Henderson and his Orchestra (Vocalion).

Charley, My Boy. w/m Gus Kahn and Ted Fio Rito, 1924. Eddie Cantor had a popular record (Columbia).

Charlie Brown. w/m Jerry Leiber and Mike Stoller, 1959. Novelty hit by The Coasters (Atco).

Charlie's Angels. See **Theme from "Charlie's Angels."**

Charlie's Shoes. w/m Roy Baham, 1962. Country hit by Billy Walker (Columbia).

Charmaine. w/m Erno Rapee and Lew Pollack, 1927, 1951. Music composed by Rapee in Hungary fourteen years earlier. It was used as the theme song of the silent (MP) *What Price Glory?*, 1926, and played by orchestra or piano to accompany film. Guy Lombardo's Orchestra had their first hit recording (Columbia) with this song. Interestingly, this sentimental ballad has been a favorite of jazz musicians with recordings by Jimmie Lunceford (Decca), Gene Ammons (Prestige), Arnett Cobb (Okeh), Neal Hefti (Coral), Billy May (Capitol). In 1951, Montovani and his Orchestra had a lush arrangement (London) that became a million-seller and was responsible for many new recordings. It was used as a recurrent theme in the background of the remake of (MP) *What Price Glory*, 1952. Harry James and his Orchestra played it in (MM) *Two Girls and a Sailor*, 1944. It was heard in the background of (MM) *Thoroughly Modern Millie*, 1967.

Charmer. w/m Tim Moore, 1975. Recorded by Tim Moore (Asylum).

Charming. w. Clifford Grey, m. Herbert Stothart, 1930. Introduced by Ramon Navarro in (MM) *Devil May Care*. Recorded by Smith Ballew (Okeh), Frank Munn (Brunswick), Leo Reisman and his Orchestra (Victor).

Charming Little Faker. w. Johnny Burke, m. Frankie Masters and Kahn Keene, 1940.

Introduced and popularized by Frankie Masters and his Orchestra via daily broadcasts from the Taft Hotel in New York City, and recorded by them (Vocalion).

Charm of You, The. w. Sammy Cahn, m. Jule Styne, 1945. Introduced in (MM) *Anchors Aweigh* and on records (Columbia) by Frank Sinatra.

Charms. w/m Howard Greenfield and Helen Miller, 1963. Recorded by Bobby Vee (Liberty).

Chase, The. m. Giorgio Moroder, 1978. From the Academy Award-winning score of (MP) *Midnight Express*, played and recorded by Giorgio Moroder (Casablanca).

Chasing Shadows. w. Benny Davis, m. Abner Silver, 1935. Featured and recorded by the Dorsey Brothers, vocal by Bob Eberly (Decca). Other records of note: Henry King (Columbia), Putney Dandridge (Vocalion), Enric Madriguera (Victor), Louis Prima (Brunswick), Jack Shilkret (Bluebird).

Chattanooga Choo Choo. w. Mack Gordon, m. Harry Warren, 1941. Introduced by Glenn Miller and his Orchestra, sung by Paula Kelly, Tex Beneke, and the Modernaires, and danced by the Nicholas Brothers and Dorothy Dandridge in (MM) *Sun Valley Serenade*. Miller's recording with the same singers (Bluebird) became a million-seller. His record was #1 for nine weeks and the song, an Academy Award nominee, was on "Your Hit Parade" for thirteen weeks, twice in the #1 position. Carmen Miranda sang it in (MM) *Springtime in the Rockies*, 1942; Dan Dailey sang it in (MM) *You're My Everything*, 1949. In (MM) *The Glenn Miller Story*, 1954, it was played by the band, with James Stewart (as Miller) leading, and sung by Frances Langford and the Modernaires. Later Top 40 records by pianist Floyd Cramer (RCA), 1962, and the studio disco group, Tuxedo Junction (Butterfly), 1978.

Chattanoogie Shoe Shine Boy. w/m Harry Stone and Jack Stapp, 1950. #1 record by

Red Foley (Decca), with Top 10 pop records by Bing Crosby (Decca); Phil Harris (RCA Victor); Frank Sinatra (Columbia).

Cheaper to Keep Her. w/m Mack Rice, 1973. Top 20 record by Johnnie Tayor (Stax).

Cheatin' on Me. w. Jack Yellen, m. Lew Pollack, 1925. Introduced by Sophie Tucker. First best-selling record by Ben Bernie and his Orchestra (Vocalion). Popular record by Jimmie Lunceford, vocal by Trummy Young (Okeh), 1939.

Check It Out. w/m John Cougar Mellencamp, 1988. Recorded by John Cougar Mellencamp from his album "The Lonesome Jubilee" (Mercury).

Chee Chee-oo Chee (Sang the Little Bird). w. John Turner and Geoffrey Parsons (Engl.), m. Severio Seracini, 1955. Italian song, winner at San Remo Song Festival. Popular record by Perry Como and Jaye P. Morgan (RCA).

Cheek to Cheek. w/m Irving Berlin, 1935. Sung by Fred Astaire and danced by Astaire and Ginger Rogers in (MM) *Top Hat.* Also recorded by Astaire (Brunswick). Nominated for Academy Award. It was heard on the soundtrack of (MM) *Alexander's Ragtime Band*, 1938.

Cheerful Little Earful. w. Ira Gershwin and Billy Rose, m. Harry Warren, 1930. Introduced by Hannah Williams in (TM) *Sweet and Low.* Recorded by Ben Selvin (Columbia) heading a studio band featuring Benny Goodman.

Cheer Up. w. Raymond Klages, m. Jesse Greer, 1930. Featured and recorded by Belle Baker (Brunswick).

Cheeseburger in Paradise. w/m Jimmy Buffett, 1978. Novelty by Jimmy Buffett (ABC).

Chelsea Bridge. m. Billy Strayhorn, 1941. Instrumental introduced by Duke Ellington and his Orchestra (Victor).

Chelsea Morning. w/m Joni Mitchell, 1969. Introduced by Joni Mitchell and recorded in her album "Clouds" (Reprise). Popular single by Judy Collins (Elektra).

Cherie. w. Kal Mann, m. Bernie Lowe and Dave Appell, 1961. Recorded by Bobby Rydell (Cameo).

Cherie. w. Leo Wood, m. Irving Bibo, 1921. Featured and recorded by Paul Whiteman and his Orchestra (Victor).

Cherie, I Love You. w/m Lillian Rosedale Goodman, 1926. Leading recordings by Ben Bernie, vocal by Paul Hagan and Jack Pettis (Brunswick); clarinetist Ross Gorman and his Orchestra (Columbia); Fred Waring's Pennsylvanians (Victor).

Cherish. w/m Kool and The Gang, 1985. Top 10 single from the gold album "Emergency" by Kool & The Gang (De-Lite).

Cherish. w/m Terry Kirkman, 1966, 1971. Gold records by The Association (Valiant), 1966, and David Cassidy (Bell), 1971.

Cherokee. m. Ray Noble, 1938. Introduced and recorded by Ray Noble and his Orchestra, arrangement by Will Hudson (Brunswick). In 1939, Charlie Barnet and his Orchestra (Bluebird) made the best-selling record of this future instrumental standard. Others of interest by the Benny Goodman Sextet (Capitol), George Shearing Trio (Discovery), Herbie Fields (Victor), Earl Bostic (King), Don Byas (Savoy). Charlie Barnet and his Band played it in (MM) *Jam Session*, 1944, and the Krupa Band played it in (MM) *The Gene Krupa Story*, 1959.

Cherokee Boogie (Eh-Oh-Aleena). w/m William Chief Redbird and Moon Mullican, 1951. Top 10 record on the C&W charts by Moon Mullican (King).

Cherokee Maiden. w/m Cindy Walker, 1976. #1 Country chart record by Merle Haggard (Capitol).

Cherry. w/m Don Redman, 1928. First recorded by McKinney's Cotton Pickers, vocal by Jean Napier, arranged by Don Redman (Victor). Among the leading bands who recorded the song are: Erskine Hawkins, vocal by Jimmy Mitchelle (Bluebird); Bob Crosby, vocal by Nappy Lamare (Decca); Louis Armstrong, vocal by Armstrong (Decca); Benny Goodman, vocal by Jimmy Mundy (Harmony); Harry James (Columbia).

Cherry, Cherry. w/m Neil Diamond, 1966. First Top 10 record by Neil Diamond (Bang). Diamond's live version, from the LP "Hot August Night," became a Top 40 single (MCA), 1973.

Cherry Blossoms on Capitol Hill. w. Carl Sigman, m. Joseph Meyer, 1941. Featured and recorded by Vaughn Monroe and his Orchestra (Bluebird).

Cherry Bomb. w/m John Cougar Mellencamp, 1987. Top 10 single from the platinum album "The Lonesome Jubilee" by John Cougar Mellencamp (Mercury).

Cherry Hill Park. w/m Robert Nix and Billy Gilmore, 1969. Top 20 record by Billy Joe Royal (Columbia).

Cherry Pie. w/m Joe Josea and Marvin Phillips, 1960. Top 20 record by Skip and Flip (Brent).

Cherry Pink and Apple Blossom White. w. Mack David (Engl.), Jacques Larue (Fr.), m. Louiguy, 1955. Theme of (MP) *Underwater.* #1 instrumental hit by Perez Prado and his Orchestra (RCA Victor) and popular vocal by Alan Dale, with Dick Jacob's Orchestra (Coral). Revived by Jerry Murad's Harmonicats (Columbia), 1961.

Cherry Red. w/m Pete Johnson and Joe Turner, 1941. First recorded by Joe Turner, singing with pianist Pete Johnson (Vocalion), 1939. Cootie Williams (Majestic) and blues singer Eddie Vinson (Mercury) and their bands also had well-received versions.

Chevy Van. w/m Sammy Johns, 1975. Top 10 hit by Sammy John (GRC).

Chew, Chew, Chew, Chew Your Bubble Gum. w/m Buck Ram and Ella Fitzgerald, 1939. Introduced and recorded by Chick Webb, vocal by Ella Fitzgerald (Decca).

Chewy Chewy. w/m Kris Resnick and Joey Levine, 1968. Gold record by the group Ohio Express (Buddah).

Cheyenne. w. Stan Jones, m. William Lava, 1955. Theme of TV series "Cheyenne."

Cheyenne (Shy Ann). w. Harry H. Williams, m. Egbert Van Alstyne, 1906. By the writers of another song about American Indians "Navajo." Popular record by Billy Murray (Victor).

Chi-Baba, Chi-Baba (My Bambina Go to Sleep). w/m Mack David, Jerry Livingston, and Al Hoffman, 1947. Perry Como had a million-selller (RCA Victor). Other top recordings: Blue Barron's Orchestra (MGM), The Charioteers (Columbia), Peggy Lee (Capitol).

Chica Boo. w/m Lloyd Glenn, 1951. Recorded by Lloyd Glenn (Swing Time).

Chica Chica Boom Chic. w. Mack Gordon, m. Harry Warren, 1941. Introduced by Carmen Miranda, Alice Faye, and Don Ameche in (MM) *That Night in Rio.* Miranda then recorded it (Decca).

Chicago. w/m Graham Nash, 1971. Top 40 record by Graham Nash (Atlantic).

Chicago. w/m Fred Fisher, 1922. A million seller in sheet music due to its many vaudeville performances and the recording by Paul Whiteman (Victor). Fred Astaire and Ginger Rogers danced to it in a medley in (MM) *The Story of Vernon and Irene Castle*, 1939. It was also in the Fisher film bio (MM) *Oh, You Beautiful Doll*, 1949; sung by Jane Froman, dubbing for Susan Hayward in the Froman story (MM) *With a Song in My Heart*, 1952; sung by Frank Sinatra in (MM) *The Joker Is Wild*, 1957. It was played under the titles and in the closing scene of (MP) *Roxie Hart*, 1957, starring Ginger Rogers, which was based on the stage play *Chicago.* A Broadway musical version was produced in 1975 that reverted to the original title. The song, however, was not included as a new score was written for the production.

Chicago, Illinois. w. Leslie Bricusse, m. Henry Mancini, 1982. Introduced by Leslie Ann Warren in (MP) *Victor/Victoria.*

Chicago Style. w. Johnny Burke, m. James Van Heusen, 1953. Introduced by Bing Crosby and Bob Hope in (MM) *Road to Bali.*

Chick-a-Boom (Don't Ya Jes' Love It). w/m Janis Lee Guinn and Linda Martin, 1971. Top 10 novelty record by Daddy Dewdrop (Sunflower).

Chicken Reel. m. Joseph M. Daly, 1910. A two-step, first recorded by Billy Murray and Arthur Collins (Victor).

Chicken Song, The (I Ain't Gonna Take It Settin' Down). w/m Terry Shand and Bob Merrill, 1951. Novelty, recorded by Guy Lombardo, vocal Cliff Grass (Decca); Red Foley and Ernest Tubb (Decca); Dottie O'Brien and Joe "Fingers" Carr (Capitol); Billy Cotton (London).

Chicken Soup with Rice. w. Maurice Sendak, m. Carole King, 1975. From the soundtrack of the animated television show (TVM) "Really Rosie." Recorded on her album "Really Rosie" by Carole King (Ode).

Chicken Walk, The. w/m Irving Berlin, 1916. Dance hit, introduced by Elsie Janis and The Fairbanks Twins in (TM) *The Century Girl.* Sometimes called "Broadway Chicken Walk."

Chickery Chick. w. Sylvia Dee, m. Sidney Lippman, 1945. Novelty hit, with #1 record by Sammy Kaye, vocal by Nancy Norman and Billy Williams (Victor). Other top recordings by Gene Krupa, vocal by Anita O'Day (Columbia); George Olsen, with his first chart record in eleven years, and vocal by Judith Blair and Ray Adams (Majestic); Evelyn Knight, with Bob Haggart's Orchestra (Decca). The song was on "Your Hit Parade" for thirteen weeks.

Chico and the Man (Main Theme). w/m José Feliciano, 1974. Main theme from the series (TVP) "Chico and the Man." José Feliciano recorded the song (RCA).

Child of Clay. w/m Jimmy Curtiss and Ernie Maresca, 1967. Top 40 record by Jimmie Rodgers (A&M).

Child of the Universe. w. Roger McGuinn, m. Dave Grusin, 1968. Sung by The Byrds on the soundtrack of (MP) *Candy.*

Children and Art. w/m Stephen Sondheim, 1983. Introduced by Bernadette Peters and Mandy Patinkin in (TM) *Sunday in the Park with George.*

Children's Marching Song, The (a.k.a. This Old Man). w/m adapted by Malcolm Arnold, 1958. Based on an English children's song. This version was performed by Ingrid Bergman and the Orphans' Chorus in (MP) *The Inn of the Sixth Happiness.* Cyril Stapleton, his Orchestra and Children's Chorus (London), and Mitch Miller and his Orchestra and Chorus (Columbia) had the leading records.

Chili Bean. w. Lew Brown, m. Albert Von Tilzer, 1920. Introduced by Aileen Stanley in the short-lived revue (TM) *Silks and Satins.* Recorded by Frank Crumit with The Paul Biese Trio (Columbia).

Chim Chim Cheree. w/m Richard M. Sherman and Robert B. Sherman, 1964. Introduced by Dick Van Dyke, Julie Andrews, Karen Dotrice, and Matthew Garber in (MM) *Mary Poppins.* Academy Award Winner, Best Song, 1964. Popular record by The New Christy Minstrels (Columbia), 1965.

Chime Bells. w/m Bob Miller and Elton Britt, 1934. Britt, who had featured this song, had a hit record in 1948 (Victor).

Chimes Blues. m. Joseph "King" Oliver, 1923. Jazz instrumental written and recorded by King Oliver with the Creole Jazz Band (Gennett). Among other versions: pianist Charlie Davenport (Gennett), 1929; Joe Marsala's Chicagoans (Epic), 1937; Turk Murphy (Good Time Jazz), 1949.

Chimes of Freedom. w/m Bob Dylan, 1964. Introduced and recorded by Bob Dylan (Columbia). Revived by Bruce Springsteen on the album of the same name (Columbia), 1988.

Chimes of Spring. w. L. Wolfe Gilbert, m. Paul Lincke, 1930. Written originally in Germany (1903) as an instrumental waltz titled "Spring, Beautiful Spring" ("O Fruhling, Wie Bist Du So Schon"). The lyrics with the new title were written in 1930 and a popular record was made by Bob Haring (Brunswick).

China Boy. w/m Dick Winfree and Phil Boutelje, 1922. First hit record by Paul Whiteman and his Orchestra (Victor), 1929. Revived in 1936 by the Benny Goodman Trio (Victor). It was that unit's first recording. They then played it on the soundtrack on (MM) *The Benny Goodman Story*, 1956.

China Doll. w/m Cindy Walker, 1960. Recorded by The Ames Brothers (RCA).

China Girl. w/m Iggy Pop and David Bowie, 1983. Top 10 single from the album by the English singer David Bowie, "Let's Dance" (EMI America).

China Grove. w/m Tom Johnston, 1973. Written by the lead vocalist of The Doobie Brothers, the group that had the Top 10 record (Warner Bros.).

Chinatown, My Chinatown. w. William Jerome, m. Jean Schwartz, 1910. Written and published in 1906, it became the hit of the revue (TM) *Up and Down Broadway*. Among films in which it has been heard are: (MM) *Bright Lights*, 1931; (MM) *Is Everybody Happy?*, 1943; (MM) *Jolson Sings Again*, 1949; (MM) *The Seven Little Foys*, 1955; (MP) *Young Man With A Horn*, 1950. Some standout recordings are: Mills Brothers (Decca), Louis Prima (Brunswick), Slim and Slam (Vocalion), Fletcher Henderson (Columbia), Tommy Dorsey and The Clambake Seven (Victor).

Chincherinchee. w/m John Jerome, 1956. British song, popularized in the U.S. by Perry Como (RCA).

Chin-Chin-Chinaman. w. Harry Greenbank, m. Sidney Jones, 1896. Introduced in London, in (TM) *The Geisha* in April and then in the New York production in September.

Chinese Lullaby. w/m Robin Hood Bowers, 1919. Originally written for the play *East Is West*. Used as the theme song for the film (MP) *East Is West*, 1930. The song was revived in the Deanna Durbin film (MM) *The Amazing Mrs. Holiday*, 1943.

Ching-Ching and a Ding Ding Ding. w/m Richard M. Sherman and Robert B. Sherman, 1960. Recorded by Hayley Mills (Vista).

Chin Up, Cheerio, Carry On! w. E. Y. Harburg, m. Burton Lane, 1941. Introduced by Judy Garland in (MM) *Babes on Broadway*.

Chip Chip. w/m Jeff Barry, Cliff Crawford, and Arthur Resnick, 1962. Top 10 record by Gene McDaniels (Liberty).

Chipmunk Song, The (Christmas Don't Be Late). w/m Ross Bagdasarian, 1958. #1 hit Christmas record by David Seville and the Chipmunks (Liberty). Seville was the pseudonym for Bagdasarian, who named the Chipmunks Alvin, Simon, and Theodore, after three executives of his record company: Bennett, Waronker, and Keep, respectively.

Chiquita. w. L. Wolfe Gilbert, m. Mabel Wayne, 1928. Recorded by Paul Whiteman, vocal by Jack Fulton (Victor).

Chiquita Banana. w/m Leonard MacKenzie, Garth Montgomery, and William Wirges, 1946. Originally written as a singing commercial for the banana industry instructing consumers "Don't ever put a banana . . . in the refrigerator." Xavier Cugat and his Orchestra played it in (MM) *This Time for Keeps*, 1947.

Chiquitita. w/m Benny Anderson, Buddy McCluskey, and Bjorn Ulvaeus, 1979. Recorded by the Swedish quartet Abba (Atlantic).

Chirpy Chirpy Cheep Cheep. w/m Harold Stott, 1971. Introduced and recorded in England by Lally Stott (Phillips). Hit record, also recorded in England, by the Trinidadian brother and sister duo, Mac and Katie Kissoon (ABC).

Chiseled in Stone. w/m Vern Gosdin and Max D. Barnes, 1988. Top 10 Country chart record by Vern Gosdin (Columbia).

Chitty Chitty Bang Bang. w/m Richard M. Sherman and Robert B. Sherman, 1968. Introduced by Dick Van Dyke, Sally Ann Howes, Adrian Hill, and Heather Ripley in (MM) *Chitty Chitty Bang Bang*. Nominated for Academy Award. Leading record, instrumental version by Paul Mauriat and his Orchestra (Philips).

Chiu, Chiu. w. Alan Surgal (Engl.), m. Nicanor Molinare (and Sp. words), 1942. Interpolated in (MM) *You Were Never Lovelier* by Xavier Cugat, vocal by Lina Romay.

Chlo-E. w. Gus Kahn, m. Neil Moret, 1927. A popular song when published, but its biggest seller was Spike Jones's novelty version (Victor), 1944. The Jones aggregation performed the song in (MM) *Bring On The Girls*, 1945.

Chocolate Shake. w. Paul Francis Webster, m. Edward Kennedy "Duke" Ellington, 1941. Introduced by Ivy Anderson in the West Coast revue *Jump for Joy*. Duke Ellington's Band, vocal by Ivy Anderson, recorded it (Victor) coupled with "I Got It Bad (and That Ain't Good)."

Choice of Colors. w/m Curtis Mayfield, 1969. Top 40 record by The Impressions (Curtom).

Chokin' Kind, The. w/m Harlan Howard, 1967. Introduced and Country chart record by Waylon Jennings (RCA). Hit R&B and Pop chart record by Joe Simon (Sound Stage), 1969.

Chon Kina. w. Harry Greenbank, m. Sidney Jones, 1896. Introduced in (TM) *The Geisha* in London in April and in the New York production in September.

Choo Choo Ch'Boogie. w/m Denver Darling, Vaughn Horton, and Milton Gabler, 1946. Million-seller by Louis Jordan and his Tympany Five (Decca).

Choo Choo Train. w/m Donnie Fritts and Eddie Hinton, 1968. Top 40 record by The Box Tops (Mala).

Choo Choo Train (Ch-Ch-Foo). w. Jack Lawrence (Engl.); Fr. w/m Marc Fontenoy, 1953. Original French title "Le Petit Train." Novelty record by Doris Day with Paul Weston's Orchestra (Columbia).

Choo'n Gum. w. Mann Curtis, m. Vic Mizzy, 1950. Popularized by Teresa Brewer, with Jimmy Lytell's Orchestra (London).

Christine Sixteen. w/m Gene Simmons, 1977. Recorded by the group Kiss (Casablanca).

C-H-R-I-S-T-M-A-S. w. Jenny Lou Carson, m. Eddie Arnold, 1949. Introduced by Eddy Arnold (RCA Victor).

Christmas Dream. w. Tim Rice (Engl.), André Heller (Ger.), m. Andrew Lloyd Webber, 1974. Main title theme, sung on the soundtrack of (MP) *The Odessa File*, by Perry Como and The London Boy Singers. Recorded by Como (RCA).

Christmas Dreaming. w/m Irving Gordon and Lester Lee, 1947. Recorded by Frank Sinatra (Columbia).

Christmas in Killarney. w/m John Redmond, James Cavanaugh, and Frank Weldon, 1950. Leading records by Percy Faith and his Orchestra and Chorus (Columbia) and Dennis Day (RCA Victor).

Christmas Island. w/m Lyle L. Moraine, 1947. Recorded by The Andrews Sisters with Guy Lombardo's Orchestra (Decca). While never a top record on the charts, it became a million-seller because of its annual Christmas popularity.

Christmas Night in Harlem. w. Mitchell Parish, m. Raymond Scott, 1934. Interpolated in the 1933-1934 edition of Lew Leslie's (TM) *Blackbirds*. Top record by Paul Whiteman and his Orchestra, vocal by Jack Teagarden (Victor).

Christmas Song, The. w. Robert Wells, m. Mel Tormé, 1946. Sometimes referred to by its opening line, "Chestnuts roasting on an open fire . . .," this seasonal classic was introduced by Mel Tormé. Its prominence, however, evolved from the first recording by The King Cole Trio (Capitol), which has sold millions of copies. Les Brown, with vocal by Doris Day, had a popular version (Columbia). Nat Cole re-recorded the song, this time with Nelson Riddle's Orchestra (Capitol), 1954.

Christopher Columbus. w. Andy Razaf, m. Leon Berry, 1936. Introduced and recorded (Vocalion) by, and the theme song of, Fletcher Henderson and his Orchestra. The arrangement was written by his brother, Horace. Fletcher, on the other hand, wrote the arrangement for Benny Goodman and his Orchestra, which turned out to be the big seller on records (Victor). In the same year, Teddy Wilson (Brunswick), Andy Kirk (Decca), and Louis "King" Garcia (Bluebird) and their bands all recorded the number.

Chrysanthemum Tea. w/m Stephen Sondheim, 1976. Introduced by members of the company in (TM) *Pacific Overtures*.

Chuck E.'s in Love. w/m Rickie Lee Jones, 1979. Hit record by Rickie Lee Jones (Warner Bros.).

Chug-A-Lug. w/m Roger Miller, 1964. Hit crossover (C&W/Pop) novelty record by Roger Miller (Smash).

Church Bells May Ring. w/m Morty Craft and The Willows, 1956. First recording by The Willows (Melba). Best-seller by The Diamonds, who had a Top 20 in all categories (Mercury).

Church on Cumberland Road, The. w/m John Sherrell, Dennis Robbins, Robbins Scott, Robert Di Piero, 1989. Hit Country record by Shenandoah (Columbia).

Church of the Poison Mind. w/m Mikey Craig, Roy Hay, John Moss, and George O'Dowd, 1983. Top 10 single from the platinum album "Colour by Numbers" written and recorded by the British group, Culture Club, led by Boy George [O'Dowd] (Epic/Virgin).

Ciao, Ciao, Bambina. w. Mitchell Parish (Engl.), m. Domenico Modugno, 1959. Original Italian title "Piove," with lyrics by Edoardo Verde and Domenica Modugno. Winner first prize at San Remo Song Festival. Chart records included French instrumental version by Jacky Noguez (Jamie) and Modugno's Italian recording "Piove" (Decca).

Cielito Lindo (Ay, Ay, Ay, Ay). w. Neil Wilson, m. C. Fernandez and S. Yradier, 1923. This was one of the more popular arrangements and translations of the public domain Mexican song.

Cigarettes, Whusky and Wild, Wild Women. w/m Tim Spence, 1947. Introduced and recorded (Decca) by The Sons of the Pioneers, of which Spencer was an original member. Red Ingle and The Natural Seven, vocal by The Main St. Choral Society, also had a popular version (Capitol).

Cimarron (Roll on). w/m Johnny Bond, 1942. Introduced and recorded by Johnny Bond (Columbia). Sung by Gene Autry in (MP) *Heart of the Rio Grande*.

Cincinnati, Ohio. w/m Bill Anderson, 1967. Hit Country record by Connie Smith (RCA).

Cincinnati Dancing Pig. w. Al Lewis, m. Guy Wood, 1950. Hit record by Red Foley (Decca).

Cincinnati Kid, The. w. Dorcas Cochran, m. Lalo Schifrin, 1965. Introduced on the soundtrack of (MP) *The Cincinnati Kid* and on records (ABC-Paramount) by Ray Charles.

Cincinnati Lou. w/m Merle Travis and Shug Fisher, 1946. Introduced and recorded by Merle Travis (Capitol).

Cinco Robles (a.k.a. Five Oaks). w. Larry Sullivan, m. Dorothy Wright, 1957. Introduced and chart record by Russell Arms (Era). Followed by Les Paul and Mary Ford (Capitol).

Cinderella. 1987. Top 10 Country chart record by Vince Gill (RCA).

Cinderella, Stay in My Arms. w. Jimmy Kennedy, m. Michael Call, 1939. Featured and recorded by Kenny Baker (Victor).

Cinderella's Fella. w. Arthur Freed, m. Nacio Herb Brown, 1933. Sung by Fifi D'Orsay, then reprised by Marion Davies in (MM) *Going Hollywood*. Ferde Grofé's Orchestra recorded it (Columbia).

Cindy, Oh Cindy. w/m Bob Barron and Burt Long, 1956. Based on a Georgia sea chantey. Introduced and first hit record by Vince Martin, with The Tarriers (Glory), followed by Eddie Fisher, who also had a hit recording of the song (RCA).

Cindy's Birthday. w/m Jeff Hooven and Hal Winn, 1962. Hit record by Johnny Crawford (Del-Fi).

Cinnamon. w/m Johnny Cymbal and George Tobin, 1968. Top 20 record by Derek, who was Scottish singer/writer Cymbal (Bang).

Cinnamon Cinder, The (It's a Very Nice Dance). w/m Russ Regan, 1963. Introduced at the Cinnamon Cinder Club in Hollywood, California by The Pastel Six, and recorded by them (Zen).

Cinnamon Girl. w/m Neil Young, 1970. First and biggest seller by The Gentrys (Sun), followed by Neil Young (Reprise).

Cinnamon Sinner. w/m Lincoln Chase, 1954. First hit by Lincoln Chase. Featured and recorded by Tony Bennett (Columbia).

Circle Game, The. w/m Joni Mitchell, 1970. Introduced by Joni Mitchell and recorded by her in an LP "Ladies of the Canyon"

(Reprise). Buffy Sainte-Marie also recorded it in an album "Fire and Fleet," from which a single was released (Vanguard).

Circles. w/m Wayne Lewis and David Lewis, 1982. Recorded by the band, Atlantic Starr (A&M).

Circumstances. w/m Ronnie Self, 1964. Top 10 Country chart record by Billy Walker (Columbia).

Circus. w. Bob Russell, m. Louis Alter, 1949. Most popular records: Tony Martin (RCA Victor), Bill Farrell (MGM).

Circus Is on Parade, The. w. Lorenz Hart, m. Richard Rodgers, 1935. Introduced by Henderson's Singing Razorbacks, a male chorus of thirty-two, in Billy Rose's (TM) *Jumbo*. In the film version (MM) *Billy Rose's Jumbo*, 1962, it was sung by Doris Day, Stephen Boyd, Jimmy Durante, and Martha Raye.

Ciribiribin. w. Tell Taylor (Engl.), Rudolf Thaler (It.), m. A. Pestalozza, 1911. A popular Italian song that was popularized in the U.S. via the instrumental recordings by Prince's Orchestra (Columbia) and Sodero's Band (Edison). Grace Moore sang it in (MM) *One Night of Love*, 1934, and on records (Brunswick). It was interpolated in (MM) *Hit the Deck*, 1955, by Jane Powell, Russ Tamblyn, Kay Armen, Vic Damone, Debbie Reynolds, and Ann Miller. Harry James and his Orchestra's recording sold over a million copies (Columbia), 1940. It became James's theme song.

Cisco Kid, The. w/m Lonnie Jordan, Howard Scott, Charles Miller, B. B. Dickerson, Harold Brown, Dee Allen, 1972. Written and gold record by the band, War (United Artists).

Cissy Strut. m. Arthur Neville, Leo Nocentelli, George Porter, Jr., Joseph Modeliste, Jr., 1969. Top 40 instrumental by The Meters (Josie).

C-I-T-Y. w/m John Cafferty, 1985. Recorded by John Cafferty and The Beaver Brown Band (Scotti Brothers).

City Called Heaven. w/m Bob Warren, 1941. Featured and recorded by Glen Gray and the Casa Loma Orchestra, vocal by Kenny Sargent (Decca); Les Brown, vocal by Ralph Young (Okeh); Shep Fields, vocal by Pat Fry (Bluebird); Will Bradley and his Orchestra (Columbia).

City Lights. w/m Bill Anderson, 1958. C&W and Pop success by Ray Price (Columbia). Ivory Joe Hunter (Dot), 1959, and Debbie Reynolds (Dot), 1960 also had chart versions.

City of Angels. w/m Nick Jovan and Bev Dunham, 1956. Popular recording by The Highlights (Bally).

City of New Orleans, The. w/m Steve Goodman, 1972, 1984. Top 20 record by Arlo Guthrie (Reprise). Willie Nelson's hit version (Columbia), 1984, won the song a Grammy Award (NARAS) for Country Song of the Year, 1984.

Civilization (Bongo, Bongo, Bongo). w/m Bob Hilliard and Carl Sigman, 1947. Novelty introduced by Elaine Stritch in the revue (TM) *Angel in the Wings.* Best-selling record: Danny Kaye and The Andrews Sisters (Decca). Others: Ray McKinley, with his Orchestra (Majestic); Louis Prima, with his Orchestra (RCA Victor); Jack Smith, with Frank DeVol's Orchestra (Capitol); Woody Herman, with his Orchestra (Columbia).

C-Jam Blues (or "C" Jam Blues). m. Edward Kennedy "Duke" Ellington and Leon Albany "Barney" Bigard, 1942. Introduced and recorded by Duke Ellington and his Orchestra (Victor) and performed by them in (MM) *Jam Session,* 1944. Also recorded by the bands of Tiny Grimes (Blue Note) and Billy Strayhorn (Mercer).

Clair. w/m Raymond (Gilbert) O'Sullivan, 1972. Gold record, produced in England by Gordon Mills, by Gilbert O'Sullivan (MAM).

Clap for the Wolfman. w/m Burton Cummings, Bill Wallace, and Kurt Winter, 1974. Written by members of the Canadian group Guess Who (RCA). The recording included excerpts from broadcasts of disc jockey Wolfman Jack.

Clap Hands! Here Comes Charley! w. Billy Rose and Ballard MacDonald, m. Joseph Meyer, 1925. Introduced by Johnny Marvin (Okeh). Among later records are Fletcher Henderson's Dixie Stompers (Harmony), Eddie Peabody (Banner), Chick Webb (Decca), Red Norvo (Brunswick), Count Basie (Vocalion). It was revived by Jimmy Dorsey (Columbia), 1950.

Clapping Song, The (Clap Pat Clap Slap). w/m Lincoln Chase, 1965. Top 10 record by Shirley Ellis (Congress).

Clap Yo' Hands. w. Ira Gershwin, m. George Gershwin, 1926. Introduced by Harland Dixon, Betty Compton, Paulette Winston, Constance Carpenter, Janette Gilmore, and the ensemble in (TM) *Oh, Kay!* It was heard in the background in the George Gershwin biography (MM) *Rhapsody in Blue,* 1946. Fred Astaire and Kay Thompson performed it in (MM) *Funny Face,* 1956.

Clara's Dancing School. w/m Brian Gari, 1988. Introduced by Teresa Tracy in the off-Broadway musical (TM) *Late Nite Comic.*

Clarinet Lament. m. Edward Kennedy "Duke" Ellington and Albany "Barney" Bigard, 1936. Instrumental written for clarinetist Bigard with Ellington's band (Brunswick).

Clarinet Marmalade. m. Edwin B. Edwards, Nick LaRocca, Tony Spargo, and Larry Shields, 1918. The writers were all members of the Original Dixieland Jazz Band who first recorded the instrumental (Victor).

Classical Gas. m. Mason Williams, 1968. Hit instrumental by guitarist Mason Williams (Warner Bros.). Winner Grammy Award (NARAS) for Best Instrumental Theme, 1968.

Cleanin' Women. w/m Micki Grant, 1978. Introduced by Lynne Thigpen in (TM) *Working.*

Clean Up Woman. w/m Clarence Reid and Willie Clarke, 1971. Hit R&B/Pop record by Betty Wright (Alston).

Clean Up Your Own Back Yard. w/m Scott Davis and Billy Strange, 1969. From the Elvis Presley film (MM) *The Trouble with Girls*. Top 40 record by Presley (RCA).

Clear Out of This World. w. Al Dubin, m. Jimmy McHugh, 1940. Introduced by Jane Froman, Robert Shackleton, and Virginia O'Brien in (TM) *Keep Off the Grass*, and recorded by O'Brien (Columbia).

Clementine. Adapted by Woody Harris, 1960. Based on Percy Montrose's 1884 song, originally titled "Oh, My Darling Clementine." Bobby Darin had a popular recording of the updated version (Atco).

Cleo's Back. m. William Woods and Autry DeWalt, 1965. Popular R&B instrumental by Jr. Walker (Autry DeWalt) and The All Stars (Soul).

Cleo's Mood. m. William Woods and Autry DeWalt, 1966. Popular R&B instrumental follow-up to "Cleo's Back" by Jr. Walker (Autry DeWalt) and The All Stars (Soul).

Cleopatterer. w. P. G. Wodehouse, m. Jerome Kern, 1917. Georgia O'Ramey introduced this comedy song in (TM) *Leave It to Jane*. June Allyson sang it in the Kern film biography (MM) *Till the Clouds Roll By* in 1946.

Climb Ev'ry Mountain. w. Oscar Hammerstein II, m. Richard Rodgers, 1959. Introduced by Patricia Neway in (TM) *The Sound of Music*. In the film version (MM) *The Sound of Music*, 1965, it was dubbed on the soundtrack by Margery McKay for Peggy Wood.

Climbing Up the Ladder of Love. w. Raymond Klages, m. Jesse Greer, 1926. From (TM) *Earl Carroll Vanities of 1926*.

Clinging Vine. w/m Earl Shuman, Leon Carr, and Grace Lane, 1964. Featured and recorded by Bobby Vinton (Epic).

Cling to Me. w. Edgar Leslie, m. Joe Burke, 1936. Originally recorded by the bands of Richard Himber (Victor), Ted Fio Rito (Decca), Nat Brandwynne (Melotone), and others. Revived in the 1950s by Eileen Barton, Johnny Desmond, and the McGuire Sisters (Coral).

Clock, The. w/m David J. Mattis, 1953. Hit R&B record by Johnny Ace (Duke).

Close As Pages in a Book. w. Dorothy Fields, m. Sigmund Romberg, 1945. Introduced by Maureen Cannon and Wilbur Evans in (TM) *Up in Central Park*. Leading recording by Benny Goodman, vocal by Jane Harvey (Columbia); Frances Langford (ARA). In the film version (MM) *Up in Central Park*, 1948, it was sung by Deanna Durbin and Dick Haymes.

Close Encounters of the Third Kind. See **Theme from Close Encounters of the Third Kind.**

Close Harmony. w. Betty Comden and Adolph Green, m. Jule Styne, 1964. Introduced by Jack Cassidy, Lou Jacobi, Tina Louise, and men in (TM) *Fade Out—Fade In*.

Closer I Get to You, The. w/m Reggie Lucas and James Mtume, 1978. Gold R&B/Pop record by Roberta Flack and Donny Hathaway (Atlantic).

Closer Than Friends. w/m Bernard Leon Jackson, Jr. and Edward David Townsend, 1989. Hit R&B chart single by Surface (Columbia).

Closest Thing to Heaven, The. w/m Howard Greenfield and Neil Sedaka, 1964. Recorded by Neil Sedaka (RCA).

(Closest Thing To) Perfect. w/m Michael Omartian, Bruce Sudano, and Jermaine Jackson, 1985. From the soundtrack of (MP) *Perfect*, Jermaine Jackson had a chart record (Arista).

Close the Door. w/m Kenny Gamble and Leon Huff, 1978. #1 R&B and crossover Pop chart gold record by Teddy Pendergrass (Philadelphia International).

Close to Cathy. w. Earl Shuman, m. Bob Goodman, 1962. Recorded by Mike Clifford (United Artists).

Close to Me. w. Sam M. Lewis, m. Peter De Rose, 1936.

Close to My Heart. w. Andrew B. Sterling, m. Harry Von Tilzer, 1915.

Close to You. w/m Al Hoffman, Jerry Livingston, and Carl Lampl, 1943. Featured and recorded by Frank Sinatra (Columbia).

Close Your Eyes. w/m Chuck Willis, 1955. Popular R&B record by The Five Keys (Capitol). Revived with hit version by Peaches and Herb (Date), 1967.

Close Your Eyes. w/m Bernice Petkere, 1932. The best-selling records in the U.S. were recorded by the British bands: Jack Hylton (Brunswick); Ambrose (Columbia); Lew Stone, vocal by Al Bowlly (Br. Decca).

Cloud Nine. w/m Barrett Strong and Norman Whitfield, 1968. Top 10 record by The Temptations (Gordy). Chart instrumental by Mongo Santamaria and his Orchestra (Columbia), 1969.

Clouds. w. Gus Kahn, m. Walter Donaldson, 1935. Featured and recorded by Gladys Swarthout (Victor); Ray Noble, vocal by Al Bowlly (Victor); Benny Goodman (Columbia); Emil Coleman (Decca). Later, Les Brown (Coral); Andy Kirk and his "Clouds of Joy" [song not to be confused with his theme "Cloudy"] (Decca).

Clouds Will Soon Roll By, The. w/m Billy Hill and Harry Woods, 1932. Recorded by Anson Weeks and his Orchestra (Brunswick).

Cloudy Summer Afternoon (Raindrops). w/m Travis Edmunson, 1966. Chart record by Barry McGuire (Dunhill).

Clown, The. w/m Brenda Barnett, Charles Chalmers, Sandra Rhodes, and Conway Twitty, 1982. Hit record by Country singer Conway Twitty (Elektra).

Clowns, The. w. Ray Errol Fox (Engl.), m. Nino Rota, 1971. Theme from Fellini's film, originally made for Italian TV, (MP) *The Clowns.*

Club Paradise. w/m Jimmy Cliff, 1986. Introduced by Jimmy Cliff and Elvis Costello in (MP) *Club Paradise.*

C'mon and Swim w. Thomas Coman, m. Sly Stewart, 1964. Crossover (R&B/Pop) hit record by Bobby Freeman (Autumn).

C'mon Everybody. w/m Eddie Cochran and Jerry Capehart, 1958. Introduced and recorded by Eddie Cochran (Liberty).

C'mon Marianne. w/m L. Russell Brown and Raymond Bloodworth, 1967. Top 10 record by The Four Seasons (Philips).

Coal Black Mammy. w. Laddie Cliff, m. Ivy St. Helier, 1922. English song featured and recorded by Al Jolson (Columbia) and Paul Whiteman and his Orchestra (Victor).

Coal Miner's Daughter. w/m Loretta Lynn, 1971. Crossover (C&W/Pop) hit by Loretta Lynn (Decca). Sung by Sissy Spacek in (MP) *Coal Miner's Daughter*, 1980.

Coat of Many Colors. w/m Dolly Parton, 1971. Top 10 Country chart record by Dolly Parton (RCA).

Coax Me a Little Bit. w. Charles Tobias, m. Nat Simon, 1946. Popularized by The Andrews Sisters (Decca).

Cobbler's Song, The. w. Oscar Asche, m. Frederic Norton, 1917. From (TM) *Chu Chin Chow.*

Coca Cola Cowboy. w/m Irving Dain, Stephen Dorff, James S. Pinkard, and Sam Atchley, 1979. Sung by Mel Tillis on the soundtrack of (MP) *Every Which Way But Loose,* and on his hit Country chart record (MCA).

Cockeyed Mayor of Kaunakakai. w. R. Alex Anderson and Al Stillman, m. R. Alex Anderson, 1935. Introduced by Hilo Hattie (Clara Inter) in (MM) *Song of the Islands.*

Cock-Eyed Optimist, A. w. Oscar Hammerstein II, m. Richard Rodgers, 1949. Introduced by Marty Martin in (TM) *South Pacific*. Sung by Mitzi Gaynor in (MM) *South Pacific*, 1958.

Cocktails for Two. w/m Arthur Johnston and Sam Coslow, 1934. Introduced by Carl Brisson in (MM) *Murder at the Vanities*. It was interpolated by Miriam Hopkins in (MM) *She Loves Me Not* later in 1934. In 1944, Spike Jones and his City Slickers had a hit novelty record (Victor), played at a fast tempo with hiccups, shattering cocktail glasses, horn honks, and other effects, contrary to the original ballad feel of the song. Jones and his Band then performed their version in (MM) *Ladies' Man*, 1947.

Coco. w. Alan Jay Lerner, m. André Previn, 1969. Introduced by Katharine Hepburn in (TM) *Coco*.

Cocoanut Grove. w/m Harry Owens, 1938. Introduced by Harry Owens and his Royal Hawaiian Orchestra in (MM) *Cocoanut Grove*. Owens recorded it (Decca). Other versions: Benny Goodman (Columbia), Teddy Wilson (Columbia), Johnny Long (Decca).

Cocoanut Sweet. w. E. Y. Harburg, m. Harold Arlen, 1957. Introduced by Lena Horne and Adelaide Hall in (TM) *Jamaica*.

Cocoanut Woman. w/m Harry Belafonte, 1957. Calypso song, featured and recorded by Harry Belafonte (RCA).

Coconut. w/m Harry Nilsson, 1972. Top 10 record by Nilsson (RCA).

Coffee in the Morning, Kisses in the Night. w. Al Dubin, m. Harry Warren, 1934. Introduced by the Boswell Sisters in (MM) *Moulin Rouge*. The Boswells had the most popular recording (Brunswick). Eddy Duchin (Victor) and Gus Arnheim (Brunswick) also had well-received releases.

Coffee Song, The (They've Got an Awful Lot of Coffee in Brazil). w/m Bob Hilliard and Dick Miles, 1946. Introduced in a revue production number at Copacabana, a New York night club. The song was featured and recorded by Frank Sinatra (Columbia) and has since been associated with him.

Coffee Time. w. Arthur Freed, m. Harry Warren, 1945. Introduced by Fred Astaire, Lucille Bremer, and chorus in (MM) *Yolanda and the Thief*. Recorded by Kay Kyser, vocal by Mike Douglas (Columbia). Also published as an instrumental, "Java Junction."

Cohen Owes Me Ninety-Seven Dollars. w/m Irving Berlin, 1915. Comedy song about the plaint of a dying man, who recovers when his son collects the debt.

Cold, Cold Heart. w/m Hank Williams, 1951. Introduced by Hank Williams (MGM). Tony Bennett had a #1 record and million-seller, accompanied by Mitchell Ayres's Orchestra (Columbia). In (MM) *Your Cheatin' Heart*, 1965, the Hank Williams biography, it was sung on the soundtrack by Hank Williams, Jr., dubbing for George Hamilton.

Cold and Lonely (Is the Forecast for Tonight). w/m Roy Botkin, 1963. Country chart record by Kitty Wells (Decca).

Cold as Ice. w/m Lou Gramm and Mike Jones, 1977. Top 10 record by the group Foreigner (Atlantic).

Cold Blooded. w/m Rick James, 1983. Recorded by Rick James (Gordy).

Cold Dark Waters. w/m Don Owens, 1962. Top 10 Country record by Porter Wagoner (RCA).

Cold Hard Facts of Life. w/m Bill Anderson, 1967. Hit Country record by Porter Wagoner (RCA).

Cold Hearted. w/m Elliot Wolff, 1989. Hit record by Paula Abdul (Virgin).

Cold Hearts/Closed Minds. w/m Nanci Griffith, 1987. Country chart record by Nanci Griffith (MCA).

Cold Sweat. w/m James Brown and Alfred Ellis, 1967. Top 10 record by James Brown and The Famous Flames (King, Part I).

Cold Turkey. w/m John Lennon, 1969. Top 40 record by The Plastic Ono Band, founded by Lennon (Apple).

Cole Slaw. w/m Jesse Stone, 1949. Lyric version of "Sorghum Switch" (q.v.). First recording under this title by Frank Culley (Atlantic). R&B chart hit by Louis Jordan and his Tympany Five (Decca).

College Life. w. Porter Emerson Browne, m. Henry Frantzen, 1906.

College Rhythm. w. Mack Gordon, m. Harry Revel, 1934. Introduced by Lyda Roberti and Jack Oakie in (MM) *College Rhythm*. They recorded the song separately, (Columbia) and (Perfect) respectively. Johnny "Scat" Davis (Decca), Jolly Coburn (Victor), Jimmie Grier (Brunswick), and their bands also had recorded versions.

College Swing. w. Frank Loesser, m. Hoagy Carmichael, 1938. Title song of (MM) *College Swing* sung by Betty Grable, Martha Raye, and Skinnay Ennis.

Collegiana. w. Dorothy Fields, m. Jimmy McHugh, 1928. Popular recording by Fred Waring's Pennsylvanians (Victor).

Collegiate. w/m Moe Jaffe and Nat Bonx, 1925. Introduced in vaudeville and on records by Fred Waring's Pennsylvanians (Victor). It was later heard in two Marx Brothers films, (MM) *Animal Crackers*, 1930, and (MM) *Horse Feathers*, 1932. It also was interpolated in (MM) *The Time, the Place and the Girl*, 1929.

Colonel Bogey. m. Kenneth J. Alford (pseud. of Major F. J. Ricketts), 1916, 1958. A popular march written by the bandmaster of the British 2nd Battalion, Argyll and Sutherland Highlanders. It was revived in 1958 in (MP) *The Bridge on the River Kwai* and had a hit record by Mitch Miller and his Orchestra (Columbia). See also "River Kwai March."

Colorado. w/m Rick Roberts, 1972. Leading record by Danny Holien (Tumbleweed).

Colored Lights. w. Fred Ebb, m. John Kander, 1984. Introduced by Liza Minnelli in (TM) *The Rink*.

Color Him Father. w/m Richard Spencer, 1969. Gold record by the septet The Winstons. The composer was lead singer (Metromedia). Winner Grammy Award (NARAS) for Best Rhythm and Blues Song.

Color My World. w/m Tony Hatch and Jackie Trent, 1967. Top 20 record by the English star Petula Clark (Warner Bros.)

Colors of My Life, The. w. Michael Stewart, m. Cy Coleman, 1980. Introduced by Jim Dale and Glenn Close in (TM) *Barnum*.

Colour of Love, The. w/m Wayne Braithwaite, Barry Eastmond, Jolyon Skinner, and Billy Ocean, 1988. Top 10 R&B and Pop chart crossover by Billy Ocean (Jive).

Columbus Stockade Blues. w. Jimmie Davis and Eva Sargent, 1943. Introduced and recorded by Jimmie Davis (Decca). Revived by Vaughn Monroe and the Sons of the Pioneers (Victor), 1948.

Comancheros, The. w/m Tillman Franks, 1961. Inspired by the John Wayne film of the same name. Recorded by Claude King (Columbia).

Come, Josephine, in My Flying Machine. w. Alfred Bryan, m. Fred Fisher, 1910. Introduced in vaudeville and recorded (Victor) by Blanche Ring. Fred Astaire performed it in (MM) *The Story of Vernon and Irene Castle* in 1939. It was also heard in the film biography of Fisher (MM) *Oh, You Beautiful Doll*, 1949.

Come, Take a Trip in My Airship. w. Ren Shields, m. George Evans, 1904. The song was inspired by the Wright Brother's Kitty Hawk flight in 1903.

Come After Breakfast, Bring 'Long Your Lunch and Leave 'Fore Supper Time. w/m J. Tim Brymn, Chris Smith, and James

Henry Burris, 1909. Introduced by S. H. Dudley in the touring production (TP) *His Honor The Barber*. Recorded by Arthur Collins (Columbia).

Come a Little Bit Closer. w/m Tommy Boyce, Bobby Hart, and Wes Farrell, 1964. Hit record by Jay and The Americans (United Artists).

Come Along, My Mandy. w/m Tom Mellor, Alfred J. Lawrance, Harry Gifford, Nora Baynes, Jack Norworth, 1910. An English song that, with new lyrics by Nora Bayes and Jack Norworth, was introduced and interpolated by them in (TM) *The Jolly Bachelors*, and then recorded (Victor).

Come and Dance with Me. w. Harold Atteridge, m. Melville Gideon and Louis A. Hirsch, 1911. Introduced by Gaby Beslys and male chorus in (TM) *Vera Violetta*.

Come and Get It. w/m Paul McCartney, 1970. From the British film (MP) *The Magic Christian*. Top 10 record in the U.S. by the quartet Badfinger (Apple).

Come and Get These Memories. w/m Brian Holland, Lamont Dozier, and Eddie Holland, 1963. Popularized by Martha and The Vandellas (Gordy).

Come and Get Your Love. w/m Lolly Vegas, 1974. Top 10 record by the group Redbone (Epic).

Come and Have a Swing with Me. w. Anne Caldwell, m. Ivan Caryll, 1917. From (TM) *Jack 'O Lantern* starring Fred Stone.

Come and Stay with Me. w/m Jackie De Shannon, 1965. Popular record by English singer Marianne Faithfull (London).

Come As You Are. w/m Peter Wolf and Tim Mayer, 1987. Album title song and chart single by Peter Wolf (EMI America).

Come Away Melinda. w/m Fred Hellerman and Fran Minkoff, 1962, Introduced, featured, and recorded by Harry Belafonte (RCA).

Come Back. w/m Seth Justman and Peter Wolf, 1980. Recorded by the rock group, The J. Geils Band (EMI America).

Come Back. w/m Ray Charles, 1955. Popular R&B record by Ray Charles (Atlantic).

Come Back, Charleston Blue. w. Al Cleveland and Quincy Jones, m. Donny Hathaway, 1972. Sung on the soundtrack of (MP) *Come Back, Charleston Blue* by Donny Hathaway and Valerie Simpson.

Come Back, My Honey Boy, to Me. w. Edgar Smith, m. John Stromberg, 1900. From Weber and Fields's (TM) *Fiddle Dee Dee*.

Comeback, The. w/m Danny Dill, 1962. C&W hit by Faron Young (Capitol).

Come Back to Arizona. w. Alfred Bryan, m. Herman Paley, 1916.

Come Back to Me. w. Alan Jay Lerner, m. Burton Lane, 1965. Introduced by John Cullum in (TM) *On a Clear Day You Can See Forever*. In (MM) *On a Clear Day You Can See Forever*, 1970, it was sung by Yves Montand.

Come Back to Sorrento. w. G. Battista de Curtis, m. Ernesto de Curtis, 1904. Original title: "Torna a Surriento." Song interpolated in (MM) *Luxury Liner*, 1947, (MM) *The Sunny Side of the Street*, 1951, and (MM) *Serenade*, 1955. Among the many recordings were those by Toni Arden (Columbia); Gracie Fields, coupled with her biggest hit, "Now Is the Hour" (London); Stan Kenton and Band (Capitol); and Dean Martin (Capitol).

Come Back When You Grow Up. w/m Martha Sharp, 1967. #1 gold record by Bobby Vee and The Strangers (Liberty).

Come Back with the Same Look in Your Eyes. w. Don Black, m. Andrew Lloyd Webber, 1986. Introduced by Bernadette Peters in (TM) *Song and Dance*.

Come By Sunday. w/m Murray Grand, 1955. Introduced and featured by Eartha Kitt. Leading record by Jeri Southern (Decca).

Come Closer to Me. w. Al Stewart (Engl.), m. Osvaldo Farres, 1945. Mexican song, known as "Acertate Mas," with Spanish words by Farres. This version was sung by Carlos Ramirez in (MM) *Easy to Wed*. Most popular record by Bob Eberly, with Carmen Cavallaro's Orchestra (Decca).

Come Dance with Me. w. George Blake, m. Richard Liebert, 1950. Records: the orchestras of Wayne King (RCA Victor), Ray Noble (Columbia), Fred Waring (Decca). Sung by Mario Lanza in (MM) *The Seven Hills of Rome*, 1958.

Come Dancing. w/m Ray Davies, 1983. Top 10 record by the English group, The Kinks, of which Davies was lead singer/guitarist (Arista).

Come Down Ma' Evenin' Star. w. Robert B. Smith, m. John Stromberg, 1902. Introduced by Lillian Russell in Weber and Fields's (TM) *Twirly Whirly*, shortly after the manuscript was found in the pocket of the composer who had committed suicide in his New York apartment. The song was later used in (MM) *Broadway to Hollywood*, 1933; sung by Alice Faye in the title role of (MM) *Lillian Russell*, 1940; (MM) *My Wild Irish Rose*, 1947. Revived by Joan Morris in her album "After the Ball" (Nonesuch).

Comedy Tonight. w/m Stephen Sondheim, 1962. Introduced by Zero Mostel in (TM) *A Funny Thing Happened on the Way to the Forum*, 1966. Mostel also sang it in (MM) *A Funny Thing Happened on the Way to the Forum*, 1966.

Come Follow, Follow Me. w. Fred Karlin, m. Marsha Karlin, 1972. From the children's film (MM) *The Little Ark*. Nominated for Academy Award.

Come from the Heart. w/m R. Leigh and S. Clark, 1989. Hit Country record by Kathy Mattea (Mercury).

Come Get to This. w/m Marvin Gaye, 1973. Recorded by Marvin Gaye (Tamla).

Come Go with Me. w/m Lewis Martine, 1987. One of four Top 10 singles ("Point of No Return," "Let Me Be the One," "Seasons Change") (q.v.) from the debut album "Exposure" by the female disco trio Exposé (Epic).

Come Go with Me. w/m Clarence E. Quick, 1957. Introduced and hit record by the Dell-Vikings, of which Quick was one of the singers (Dot). Chart records by Dion (Laurie) in 1963 and The Beach Boys (Caribou) in 1982.

Come Home. w/m Dave Clark and Mike Smith, 1964. Hit record by the English rock group The Dave Clark Five (Epic).

Come Home, Dewey, We Won't Do a Thing to You. w/m Paul Dresser, 1899.

Come In from the Rain. w/m Melissa Manchester and Carole Bayer Sager, 1977. Recorded by The Captain and Tennille (A&M).

Come into My Heart. w/m Lloyd Price and Harold Logan, 1959. Top 10 R&B and Top 40 Pop chart record by Lloyd Price (ABC-Paramount).

Come Live with Me. w/m Boudleaux Bryant and Felice Bryant, 1973. Hit Country and Pop chart record by Roy Clark (Dot), covered by Ray Charles (Crossover).

Come Monday. w/m Jimmy Buffett, 1974. Recorded by Jimmy Buffett (Dunhill).

Come Next Spring. w. Lenny Adelson, m. Max Steiner, 1955. Sung on the soundtrack of (MP) *Come Next Spring* by Tony Bennett.

Come On, Do the Jerk. w/m Donald Whited, Warren Moore, Robert Rogers, and William Robinson, 1964. Hit record by The Miracles (Tamla).

Come On, Let's Go. w/m Richard Valenzuela, 1958, 1966. First chart record by Ritchie Valens [né Valenzuela] (Del-Fi). Revived by The McCoys (Bang). 1966.

Come On, Papa. w. Edgar Leslie, m. Harry Ruby, 1918. Comedy song of World War I in which French girls would offer their favors to American soldiers. The Avon Comedy Four, consisting of Irving Kaufman, Harry Goodwin, and the team of Smith and Dale had a popular record (Columbia). Fred Astaire and Vera-Ellen performed it in the Kalmar-Ruby film biography (MM) *Three Little Words*, 1950.

Come On, Spark Plug! w/m Billy Rose and Con Conrad, 1923. A follow-up to the authors' hit "Barney Google." This did not enjoy the success of its predecessor.

Come On-a My House. w/m Ross Bagdasarian and William Saroyan, 1951. The cousins, playwright Saroyan and Bagdasarian, conceived the basic idea for the song while traveling by car in the Southwest in the late 1930s. It was interpolated in (TP) *Son*, an off-Broadway play by Saroyan. Kay Armen was the first to record it (Federal), and was followed by Rosemary Clooney (Columbia), whose version was the #1 record for two months, and one of the biggest sellers of the year. Clooney sang it in (MM) *The Stars Are Singing*, 1953.

Come On and Pet Me. See **Sometimes I'm Happy.**

Come On and Play Ball with Me. w. Edward Madden m. Gus Edwards, 1909. From (TM) *Ziegfeld Follies of 1909*.

Come On Down to My Boat. w/m Wes Farrell and Jerry Goldstein, 1967. Hit record by the quintet Every Mother's Son (MGM).

Come On Down Town. w/m George M. Cohan, 1908. From (TM) *The Yankee Prince*.

Come On Eileen. w/m Kevin Rowland, Jimmy Patterson, and Kevin Adams, 1983. #1 record by the British group Dexys Midnight Runners (Mercury).

Come On in (You Did the Best You Could Do). w/m Rick Corles and George Green, 1986. Top 10 Country chart record by The Oak Ridge Boys (MCA).

Come On Over. w/m Barry Gibb and Robin Gibb, 1976. Recorded by Olivia Newton-John (MCA).

Come On Over to My Place. w/m Barry Mann and Cynthia Weil, 1965. Recorded by The Drifters (Atlantic).

Come On (Shout). w/m Marti Sharron and Gary Skardina, 1985. Introduced on soundtrack of *Girls Just Want to Have Fun*, and records (Mercury) by Alex Brown.

Come On Up. w/m Felix Cavaliere, 1966. Recorded by The Young Rascals, of which Cavaliere was a member (Atlantic).

Come Out, Come Out, Wherever You Are. w. Sammy Cahn, m. Jule Styne, 1944. Introduced by Frank Sinatra in (MM) *Step Lively*. Featured and recorded by Charlie Barnet, vocal by Kay Starr (Decca).

Come Out of the Kitchen, Mary Ann. w/m James Kendis and Charles Bayha, 1930.

Come Prima (For the First Time). w. Buck Ram (Engl.), M. Panzeri (Ital.), m. V. di Paola and S. Taccani, 1958. Italian song. Leading records by Polly Bergen, in English (Columbia); and Tony Dallara, released in U.S. under name of Tony Dalardo (Mercury), in Italian.

Come Rain or Come Shine. w. Johnny Mercer, m. Harold Arlen, 1946. Introduced by Ruby Hill and Harold Nicholas in (TM) *St. Louis Woman*. First popular recordings by Margaret Whiting, accompanied by Paul Weston's Orchestra (Capitol), and Helen Forrest and Dick Haymes, accompanied by Earle Hagen's Orchestra (Decca).

(Come 'Round Here) I'm the One You Need. w/m Eddie Holland, Lamont Dozier, and Brian Holland, 1966. Hit record by The Miracles (Tamla).

Come Runnin' Back. w/m Dick Glasser, 1966. Recorded by Dean Martin (Reprise).

Come Running. w/m Van Morrison, 1970. Top 40 record by Van Morrison (Warner Bros.).

Come Sail Away. w/m Dennis De Young, 1977. Top 10 record by the group Styx (A&M).

Comes A-long A-love. w/m Al Sherman, 1952. Recorded by Kay Starr, with Harold Mooney's Orchestra (Capitol).

Come Saturday Morning. w. Dory Previn, m. Fred Carlin, 1969. Introduced on the soundtrack of (MM) *The Sterile Cuckoo* by The Sandpipers and recorded by them (A&M). Song nominated for Academy Award.

Come See. w/m Curtis Mayfield, 1965. R&B/Pop chart hit by Major Lance (Okeh).

Come See about Me. w/m Brian Holland, Lamont Dozier, and Eddie Holland, 1964. Hit R&B/Pop record by The Supremes (Motown). Also recorded by Nella Dodds (Wand), 1964, and Jr. Walker and The All Stars (Soul), 1968.

Comes Love. w/m Sam H. Stept, Charles Tobias, and Lew Brown, 1939. Sung by Judy Canova and danced by Dixie Dunbar in (TM) *Yokel Boy*. Among recordings: Dorothy Lamour (Bluebird); Benny Goodman (Columbia): Artie Shaw (Bluebird); Harry James, vocal by Connie Haines (Brunswick); Larry Clinton, vocal by Ford Leary (Victor.)

Come Softly to Me. w/m Gary Troxel, Gretchen Christopher, and Barbara Ellis, 1959. The writers, known as the Fleetwoods, had a #1 hit record (Dolphin).

Comes Once in a Lifetime. w. Betty Comden and Adolph Green, m. Jule Styne, 1961. Introduced by Sydney Chaplin and Carol Lawrence in (TM) *Subways Are for Sleeping*.

Come Tell Me What's Your Answer, Yes or No. w/m Paul Dresser, 1898.

Come to Baby, Do. w/m Inez James and Sidney Miller, 1945. Leading records by Les Brown, vocal by Doris Day (Columbia) and Duke Ellington, vocal by Joya Sherrill (Victor).

Come Together. w/m John Lennon and Paul McCartney, 1969. #1 gold record by The Beatles (Apple). Other versions: Ike and Tina Turner (Minit), 1970; Top 40 record by the group Aerosmith (Columbia), 1978.

Come to Me. w/m Tony Green, 1979. Recorded by the sixteen-year-old Canadian singer France Joli (Prelude).

Come to Me. w. Don Black, m. Henry Mancini, 1976. Sung on the soundtrack of (MP) *The Pink Panther Strikes Again* by Tom Jones.

Come to Me. w/m Marvin Johnson and Berry Gordy, Jr., 1959. Introduced and recorded by Marv Johnson (United Artists). Revived by Otis Redding (Volt), 1964, and Aretha Franklin (Arista), 1981.

Come to Me. w. Peter Lind Hayes, m. Robert Allen, 1958. From (TVP) "Come to Me." Leading record by Johnny Mathis (Columbia).

Come to Me. w. B. G. DeSylva and Lew Brown, m. Ray Henderson, 1931. In their last collaboration for a production, the writing trio created this for the Gloria Swanson film (MP) *Indiscreet*. Featured and recorded by Frank Parker (Columbia); Scrappy Lambert (Hit of the Week); Jacques Renard (Brunswick); Adrian Schubert (Crown).

Come to Me, Bend to Me. w. Alan Jay Lerner, m. Frederick Loewe, 1947. Introduced by Lee Sullivan in (TM) *Brigadoon*. In the film version (MM) *Brigadoon*, 1954, it was sung by John Gustafson, dubbing on the soundtrack for Jimmy Thompson, but deleted from the final print much to the outrage of the writers who considered it one of their favorite songs.

Come Tomorrow. w/m Bob Elgin, Frank Augustus, and Dolores Phillips, 1965. Recorded by the British group Manfred Mann (Ascot).

Come to the Fair. w/m Easthope Martin and Helen Taylor, 1917.

Come to the Land of Bohemia. w/m Ren Shields and George Evans, 1907.

Come to the Mardi Gras. w. Ervin Drake and Jimmy Shirl (Engl.), m. Max Bulhoes and Milton DeOliviera, 1947. Original Brazilian title "Nao Tenho Lagrimas," Portuguese words by the composers. Leading record by Freddy Martin and his Orchestra (RCA Victor).

Come to the Masquerade. w. Ben Tarver and John Clifton, m. John Clifton, 1966. Introduced by Reid Shelton in (TM) *Man with a Load of Mischief.*

Come to the Moon w. Ned Wayburn and Lou Paley, m. George Gershwin, 1919. Introduced by Paul Frawley and Lucille Chalfant in the revue "Demi-Tasse" for the opening of the Capitol Theatre in New York. Recorded by Gene Roderich's Orchestra (Brunswick). The number was included in the PBS special (TVM) "Celebrating Gershwin," 1987.

Come to the Sunshine. w/m Van Dyke Parks, 1967. Recorded by Harper's Bizarre (Warner Bros.)

Come Up and See Me Sometime. w. Arthur Swanstrom, m. Louis Alter, 1933. Sung by Lillian Roth in (MM) *Take a Chance.*

Come Walk with Me. w/m Burkett Graves, 1959. C&W success by Stoney Cooper and Wilma Lee (Hickory).

Come What May. w. Allen Schiller, m. Al Sanchez, 1952, Leading record by Patti Page (Mercury).

Come with Me. w/m Chuck Howard, 1979. #1 Country chart record by Waylon Jennings (RCA).

Coming Around Again. w/m Carly Simon, 1986. Introduced by Carly Simon on the soundtrack of (MP) *Heartburn* and on records (Arista).

Coming On Strong. w/m David Wilkins, 1966. Pop chart hit by Brenda Lee (Decca).

Coming to America. w/m Nile Rodgers and Nancy Huang, 1988. Performed by The System on the soundtrack of (MP) *Coming to America*, and its album (Atco).

Coming Up (Live at Glasgow). w/m Paul McCartney, 1980. #1 gold record by Paul McCartney and Wings (Columbia). Released as the "B" side of a coupling with a studio version of the same song, this hit version was recorded "live" at the Glasgow Apollo in Scotland.

Comin' Home Baby. w. Bob Dorough, m. Ben Tucker, 1962. Featured and recorded by Mel Tormé (Atlantic).

Comin' Home Soldier. w/m Gene Allan and Bobby Vinton, 1966. Popular record by Bobby Vinton (Epic).

Comin' In and Out of Your Life. w/m Richard Parker and Bobby Whiteshide, 1981. Recorded by Barbra Streisand (Columbia).

Comin' In on a Wing and a Prayer. w. Harold Adamson, m. Jimmy McHugh, 1943. The title came from a statement by an Air Force pilot telling of an emergency landing during World War II. Introduced by Eddie Cantor at an Air Force base. Song sold over a million copies of sheet music and was on "Your Hit Parade" for eighteen weeks, three times as #1. Leading recordings by The Song Spinners (Decca); Willie Kelly's Orchestra (Hit); Four Vagabonds (Bluebird).

Comme Çi, Comme Ça. w. Joan Whitney and Alex Kramer (Engl.); m. Bruno Coquatrix, 1949. Original French words by Pierre Dudan. Among many recordings: Frank Sinatra (Columbia), Vic Damone (Mercury), Margaret Whiting (Capitol), Tony Martin (RCA Victor), Johnny Desmond (MGM).

Comment Allez-Vous? w. (Engl.)/m. Murray Grand, 1957. Introduced in the French musical (TM) *Triple Galop.* Leading record by Blossom Dearie and The Blue Stars (Verve). Interpolated in the off-Broadway revue (TM) *Night Club Confidential.*

Comment Allez-Vous? (How Are Things with You?). w. Ralph Blane and Robert Wells, m. Josef Myrow, 1953. Introduced by Gilbert Roland in (MM) *The French Line.*

Common Man. w/m Sammy Johns, 1983. Song's first appearance on Country chart was recording by the writer Sammy Johns (Elektra), 1981. John Conlee's version became a #1 hit (MCA), 1983.

Commotion. w/m John Fogerty, 1969. Recorded by Creedence Clearwater Revival (Fantasy).

Communication Breakdown. w/m Roy Orbison and Bill Dees, 1967. Recorded by Roy Orbison (MGM).

Company Way, The. w/m Frank Loesser, 1961. Introduced by Robert Morse, Sammy Smith, and Charles Nelson Reilly in (TM) *How to Succeed in Business Without Really Trying.* In (MM) *How to Succeed in Business Without Really Trying,* 1966, it was sung by Morse, Smith, and Anthony Teague.

Company You Keep, The. w/m Dolly Parton and Bill Owens, 1966. Top 10 Country record by Bill Phillips (Decca).

Compared to What. w/m Gene McDaniels, 1970. Recorded by Les McCann and Eddie Harris (Atlantic).

Composer, The. w/m William Robinson, 1969. Top 40 record by Diana Ross and The Supremes (Motown).

Comrades. w/m Felilx McGlennon, 1894. Popular in England before its success of this year in the United States.

Concentratin' (on You). w. Andy Razaf, m. Thomas "Fats" Waller, 1931. Introduced and featured by Fats Waller. Leading records by Mildred Bailey (Victor); The California Ramblers (Columbia); Blanche Calloway (Victor).

Concert in the Park. w/m Dave Franklin and Cliff Friend, 1939. Featured and recorded by Vincent Lopez, vocal by Betty Hutton (Bluebird).

Concerto for Clarinet. m. Artie Shaw, 1941. Instrumental recorded by Artie Shaw and his Orchestra (Victor 12″, Parts 1 & 2) and featured by them in (MM) *Second Chorus.*

Concerto for Cootie. See **Do Nothin' Till You Hear From Me.**

Concerto for Two. w. Jack Lawrence, m. Peter I. Tchaikowsky, 1941. Based on the 1st theme of the 1st movement of Tchaikowsky's *Piano Concerto No. 1 in B♭ Minor,* arranged by Robert C. Haring. Best-selling record by Claude Thornhill and his Orchestra, vocal by Dick Harding (Columbia). See "Piano Concerto in B♭", "Tonight We Love", and "Alone at Last".

Conchita, Marquita, Lolita, Pepita, Rosita, Juanita Lopez. w. Herb Magidson, m. Jule Styne, 1942. Introduced by Johnnie Johnston in (MM) *Priorities on Parade.*

Concrete and Clay. w/m Tommy Moeller and Brian Parker, 1965. English song. Top 40 records by the British sextet Unit Four Plus Two (London) and American singer Eddie Rambeau (DynoVoice).

Condition Red. w/m Fred Briggs and Donald Davis, 1968. Recorded by the Goodees (Hip).

Confess. w/m Bennie Benjamin and George David Weiss, 1948. Best-selling records by Patti Page (Mercury), Doris Day and Buddy Clark (Columbia), Tony Martin (RCA Victor).

Confessin'. See **I'm Confessin' That I Love You.**

Confessin' the Blues. w/m Jay McShann and Walter Brown, 1941. Introduced and recorded by Jay McShann and his Orchestra, vocal by Walter Brown, featuring Charlie Parker on alto saxophone (Decca).

Confidentially. w. Al Dubin and Johnny Mercer, m. Harry Warren, 1938. Introduced by John Payne in (MM) *Garden of the Moon.*

Confirmation. m. Charlie Parker, 1953. Introduced and recorded by Charlie Parker (Clef) and the Tempo Jazzmen (Dial).

Confucius Say. w/m Carmen Lombardo and Cliff Friend, 1940. Title suggested by the renewed interest in the maxims of the sixth century Chinese philosopher. Recorded and featured by Guy Lombardo, vocal by the Lombardo Trio (Decca); and Hal Kemp, vocal by the Smoothies (Victor).

Conga. w/m Enrique Garcia, 1985. Top 10 record by the group Miami Sound Machine (Epic).

Congo Love Song. w. Bob Cole, m. J. Rosamond Johnson, 1903. Interpolated by Marie Cahill in (TM) *Nancy Brown.* Leading record by Mina Hickman (Victor).

Congratulations. w/m Gary Prim, Tena R. Clark, and Mary Vesta Williams-White, 1989. Hit R&B single by Vesta (A&M).

Congratulations. w/m Sid Robin and Paul Weston, 1949. Most popular recording by Jo Stafford (Capitol).

Congratulations. w/m Maceo Pinkard, Coleman Goetz, Bud Green, and Sam H. Stept, 1930. Recorded by the Dorsey Brothers Orchestra (Regal), Smith Ballew (Okeh), Nat Shilkret (Victor), Jack Denny (Brunswick), Paul Small (Velvetone).

Congratulations to Someone. w. Roy Alfred, m. Al Frisch, 1953. Featured and recorded by Tony Bennett (Columbia) and Gordon MacRae (Capitol).

Connecticut. w. Ralph Blane, m. Hugh Martin, 1947. Recorded by Bing Crosby and Judy Garland (Decca); The Modernaires with Paula Kelly (Columbia); Herbie Fields, vocal by the Romanticists (RCA Victor).

Conquistador. w/m Gary Booker and Keith Reid, 1972. Top 20 record by the British group Procol Harum (A&M).

Conscience. w/m Barry Mann and Cynthia Weil, 1962. Recorded by James Darren (Colpix).

Conscience, I'm Guilty. w/m Jack Rhodes, 1956. Hit C&W record by Hank Snow (RCA).

Consider Yourself. w/m Lionel Bart, 1963. From the British musical (TM) *Oliver!* Introduced in the U.S. by Michael Goodman, Bruce Prochnik, and the boys. In (MM) *Ol-*

iver!, 1968, it was sung by Mark Lester, Jack Wild, and the boys.

Consolation. w. Edward Madden, m. Theodore F. Morse, 1908.

C-O-N-S-T-A-N-T-I-N-O-P-L-E. w/m Harry Carlton, 1928. A "spelling" song that was a novelty hit. Paul Whiteman (Victor) had the most popular recording of this English import.

Constantly. w. Johnny Burke, m. James Van Heusen, 1942. Introduced by Bing Crosby in (MM) *Road to Morocco,* and on records (Decca).

Constantly. w. Chris Smith and James Henry Burris, m. Bert Williams, 1910. Introduced by Bert Williams in (TM) *Ziegfeld Follies of 1910* and recorded by him (Columbia).

Contented. w. Roy Turk, m. Don Bestor, 1932. Featured and recorded by Don Bestor and his Orchestra (Victor). The song was the theme of the long-running Carnation Milk radio show.

Continental, The. w. Herb Magidson, m. Con Conrad, 1934. Introduced in a seventeen-minute production number in (MM) *The Gay Divorcée* by Fred Astaire, Ginger Rogers, Erik Rhodes, and Lillian Miles. It was the first Academy Award winning song.

Contrasts. m. Jimmy Dorsey, 1941. Theme song of Jimmy Dorsey's Orchestra (Decca), taken from his saxophone solo in prior recording, "Oodles of Noodles" (q.v.).

Control. w/m James Harris III, Terry Lewis, and Janet Jackson, 1987. #1 R&B chart and Top 10 Pop chart record by Janet Jackson (A&M).

Controversy. w/m Prince Rogers Nelson, 1982. Written and recorded by Prince (Warner Bros.).

Convict and the Bird, The. w/m Paul Dresser, 1888.

Convoy. w. Bill Fries, m. Louis "Chip" Davies, 1976. A novelty #1 gold record about CB radios, performed by C. W. McCall, who in reality was co-writer Bill Fries, an advertising agency executive (MGM). The song became the basis of the film of the same name, 1978.

Cooking Breakfast for the One I Love. w. Billy Rose, m. Henry Tobias, 1930. Introduced by Fanny Brice in (MM) *Be Yourself.* Records by Brice (Victor) in addition to those by Annette Hanshaw (Okeh) and Libby Holman, backed by Roger Wolfe Kahn's Orchestra (Brunswick).

Cook with Honey. w/m Valerie Carter, 1973. Recorded by Judy Collins (Elektra).

Cool. w. Dez Dickerson, m. Prince Rogers Nelson, 1982. Recorded by The Time (Warner Bros.).

Cool. w. Stephen Sondheim, m. Leonard Bernstein, 1957. Introduced by Mickey Calin and "The Jets" in (TM) *West Side Story.* In the film version (MM) *West Side Story,* 1961, it was performed by Tucker Smith and "The Jets."

Cool Change. w/m Glenn Shorrock, 1979. Top 10 record by The Little River Band, with Shorrock as lead singer (Capitol).

Cool It Now. w/m Vincent Brantley and Rick Timas, 1984. #1 R&B and Top 10 Pop chart gold record by the teenage group New Edition (MCA).

Cool Jerk. w/m Donald Storball, 1966. Top 10 record by the vocal trio The Capitols (Karen).

Cool Love. w/m David Jenkins, Cory Lerios, and John Pierce, 1981. Written by three-fourths of the recording quartet Pablo Cruise (A&M).

Cool Night. w/m Paul Davis, 1981. Recorded by Paul Davis (Arista).

Cool Places. w/m Ron Mael and Russell Mael, 1983. Recorded by Sparks [the Mael brothers] and Jane Wiedlin (Atlantic).

Cool Water. w/m Bob Nolan, 1936, 1948. Introduced by The Sons of the Pioneers, of

whom Nolan was a founding member, along with Roy Rogers, then known as Dick Weston. In 1948, the group had another hit version, this time supporting Vaughn Monroe (Victor).

Coon! Coon! Coon! w/m Leo Friedman, 1901. Advertised as a "coon-comique." Popular in vaudeville and minstrel shows.

Copacabana (At the Copa). w. Jack Feldman and Bruce Sussman, m. Barry Manilow, 1978. Gold record by Barry Manilow (Arista).

Copenhagen. w. Walter Melrose, m. Charlie Davis, 1924. An instrumental favorite. Among the many recordings are those by the Wolverines (Gennett); Artie Shaw (twice on Brunswick); Glen Gray and the Casa Loma Orchestra (Decca); Fletcher Henderson (Vocalion); Tommy Dorsey (Victor); Earl Hines (Decca); Teresa Brewer, one of the few vocal renditions (London).

Copper Canyon. w/m Jay Livingston and Ray Evans, 1949. Title song of (MP) *Copper Canyon.*

Copper-Colored Gal. w. Benny Davis, m. J. Fred Coots, 1936. Bob Howard (Decca) had a popular recording.

Coquette. w. Gus Kahn, m. Carmen Lombardo and John Green, 1928. The first published song for Green, written while he was a student at Harvard. It was inspired by the Broadway play of the same name. Introduced and recorded (Columbia) by Guy Lombardo and the Royal Canadians. Revived in 1953 by Tony Martin in (MM) *Easy to Love.* Featured and recorded by Fats Domino (Imperial) in 1958, coupled with his hit, "Whole Lotta Loving."

Corazon. w/m Carole King, 1973. Instrumental by writer/singer/pianist Carole King (Ode).

Corcovado. See **Quiet Nights of Quiet Stars.**

Corner of the Sky. w/m Stephen Schwartz, 1972. Introduced by John Rubinstein in (TM)

Pippin. Top 20 record by The Jackson 5 (Motown).

Cornet Man. w. Bob Merrill, m. Jule Styne, 1964. Introduced by Barbra Streisand in (TM) *Funny Girl.* Not used in film.

Corns for My Country. w/m Jean Barry, Dick Charles, and Leah Worth, 1944. Introduced in (MM) *Hollywood Canteen,* and on records by The Andrews Sisters (Decca).

Corn Silk. w. Irving Kahal, m. Wayne King and Hal Bellis, 1940. Featured and recorded by the bands of Wayne King (Victor), Guy Lombardo (Decca), Benny Goodman (Columbia).

Corrine, Corrina (Corinna, Corinna). w/m J. Mayo Williams and Bo Chatman. New words: Mitchell Parish, 1929, 1960. Adapted from traditional blues with various spellings of title. Under "Corinna Blues" recorded by Blind Lemon Jefferson (Paramount) in 1927 or 1928. Frankie "Half-Pint" Jaxon recorded "Corrine Blues" in 1929. Cab Calloway had a big-selling record (Perfect) of the above title in 1932; followed by Art Tatum, with vocal by Big Joe Turner (Decca); Bob Howard (Decca); and Sharkey Bonano (Capitol). In 1960-1961, Ray Peterson (Dunes) had a best-seller under the title of "Corinna, Corinna" using the new lyric of Mitchell Parish.

Corvette Song, The. See **One I Loved Back Then, The.**

Cosi Cosa. w. Ned Washington, m. Bronislaw Kaper and Walter Jurmann, 1935. Introduced by Allan Jones in (MM) *A Night at the Opera,* starring the Marx Brothers. Jones recorded it (Victor) and sang it again in (MM) *Everybody Sing,* 1938.

Cossack Love Song (Don't Forget Me). w. Otto Harbach and Oscar Hammerstein II, m. George Gershwin and Herbert Stothart, 1926. Sung by Tessa Kosta and Guy Robertson in (TM) *Song of the Flame.*

Cottage for Sale, A. w. Larry Conley, m. Willard Robison, 1930. First popular record-

ings by Ruth Etting (Columbia), Guy Lombardo (Columbia), Frank Munn with Bernie Cummins's Orchestra, Paul Small (Okeh), the Revelers (Victor). Among later releases: Phil Brito (Musicraft), Harry Cool (Fredlo), Billy Eckstine (National), Errol Garner (National).

Cotton. w. Ted Koehler, m. Rube Bloom, 1935. Featured and recorded by Duke Ellington, with vocal by Ivy Anderson (Brunswick).

Cotton Candy. m. Russ Damon, 1964. Instrumental hit recorded by trumpeter Al Hirt, with his Orchestra (RCA).

Cottonfields. w/m Traditional; adapted by Huddie Ledbetter, 1962. Written in the mid-nineteenth century, this version was introduced by Huddie "Leadbelly" Ledbetter in the forties. It was popularized by The Highwaymen (United Artists), 1962. Saxophonist Ace Cannon recorded it instrumentally (Hi), 1963.

Cotton Jenny. w/m Gordon Lightfoot, 1972. Recorded by Canadian singer Anne Murray (Capitol).

Cotton Mill Man. w/m Joe Langston, 1964. C&W chart record by Jim and Jesse (Epic).

Cotton Tail. m. Edward Kennedy "Duke" Ellington, 1940. Instrumental introduced and recorded by Duke Ellington and his Orchestra (Victor). Other versions: Bobby Sherwood (Capitol) and Flip Phillips (Mercury).

Could Be. w. Johnny Mercer, m. Walter Donaldson, 1939. Among records: Bob Haymes (King); Glen Gray and The Casa Loma Orchestra, vocal by Pee Wee Hunt (Decca); Barry Wood (Brunswick); Sammy Kaye and his Orchestra (Victor); Johnny Messner and his Orchestra (Bluebird).

Could I Fall in Love? w/m Randy Starr, 1967. Introduced by Elvis Presley in (MM) *Double Trouble.*

Could I Have This Dance. w/m Wayland Holyfield and Bob House, 1980. From (MP) *Urban Cowboy.* Leading record by Anne Murray (Capitol).

Could It Be I'm Falling in Love? w/m Melvin Steals and Mervin Steals, 1972. R&B/Pop gold record by The Spinners (Atlantic).

Could It Be Magic. w/m Barry Manilow and Adrienne Anderson, 1975. Top 10 record by Barry Manilow (Arista). Chart version by Donna Summer (Oasis), 1976.

Could It Be You. w/m Cole Porter, 1943. Introduced by Bill Johnson in (TM) *Something for the Boys*.

Couldn't Get It Right. w/m Colin Cooper, Peter Haycock, John Cuffley, Derek Holt, Frederick Jones, 1977. Written and Top 10 record by the British quintet Climax Blues Band (Sire).

Could This Be Magic. w/m Hiram Johnson and Richard Blandon, 1957. Popularized by The Dubs (Gone).

Could've Been. w/m Lois Blaisch, 1988. Million-selling #1 record by seventeen-year-old Tiffany (MCA). Included in her platinum album "Tiffany."

Count Every Star. w. Sammy Gallop, m. Bruno Coquatrix, 1950. Leading records by Ray Anthony, vocal by Dick Noel (Capitol); Dick Haymes, with Artie Shaw and his Orchestra (Decca); instrumental version by Hugo Winterhalter and his Orchestra (RCA Victor).

Counting The Blues. w/m Gertrude "Ma" Rainey, 1924. Introduced and recorded by Ma Rainey (Paramount).

Count Me In. w/m Glen D. Hardin, 1965. Top 10 record by Gary Lewis and The Playboys (Liberty).

Count Me Out. w/m Vincent Brantley and Rick Timas, 1985. Recorded by the teenage group New Edition (MCA).

Count on Me. w/m Jesse Barish, 1978. Top 10 record by Jefferson Starship (Grunt).

Country Boy. w/m Tony Colton, Albert Lee, and Ray Smith, 1985. #1 Country chart record by Ricky Skaggs (Epic).

Country Boy. w/m Felice Bryant and Boudleaux Bryant, 1949. C&W chart hit by "Little" Jimmy Dickens (Columbia).

Country Boy (You Got Your Feet in L.A.). w/m Dennis Lambert and Brian Potter, 1975. Top 20 record by Glen Campbell (Capitol).

Country Boy Can Survive, A. w/m Hank Williams, Jr., 1982. Recorded by Hank Williams, Jr. (Elektra/Curb).

Country Cousin, The. w. Alfred Bryan, m. Vincent Youmans, 1920. This was Youmans's first published song and the only one he would write not associated with a production. It was dedicated to Elaine Hammerstein, who was starring in a popular silent film of the same name.

Country Girl. w/m Roy Drusky, 1959. Hit C&W record by Faron Young (Capitol).

Country Girl—City Man. w/m Ted Daryll and Chip Taylor, 1968. Top 40 record by Billy Vera and Judy Clay (Atlantic).

Country Girls. w/m Troy Seals and Eddie Setser, 1985. #1 Country chart record by John Schneider (MCA).

Country Music Is Here to Stay. w/m Ferlin Husky, 1959. C&W hit by Simon Crum (Capitol).

Country Road. w/m James Taylor, 1971. Top 40 record by James Taylor (Warner Bros.).

Country Style. w. Johnny Burke, m. James Van Heusen, 1947. Introduced in (MM) *Welcome Stranger* and recorded (Decca) by Bing Crosby.

Country Sunshine. w/m Dottie West and Bill Davis, 1973. Crossover (Country/Pop) chart hit by Dottie West (RCA).

Count the Days (1—2—3—4—5—6—7). w/m Charlie Foxx, Brooks O'Dell, and Yvonne Williams, 1968. Chart record by Inez and Charlie Foxx (Dynamo).

County Fair. w/m Mel Tormé and Robert Wells, 1948. Introduced and recorded by Mel

Tormé (Musicraft). Sung in the live-action/animated Disney film (MM) *So Dear to My Heart*, 1948.

Count Your Blessings. w/m Nicholas Ashford and Valerie Simpson, 1986. Chart single by Ashford and Simpson (Capitol).

Count Your Blessings. w/Irving Caesar and Edgar Guest, m. Ferde Grofé, 1933. Recorded by Ferde Grofé's Orchestra (Columbia); Freddy Martin, vocal by Elmer Feldkamp (Brunswick); Harry Sosnik, vocal by Bob Hannon (Victor).

Count Your Blessings (Instead of Sheep). w/m Irving Berlin, 1954. Introduced by Bing Crosby and Rosemary Clooney in (MM) *White Christmas*. Nominated for Academy Award. Crosby, with Joseph Lilley's Orchestra (Decca), and Clooney, with Buddy Cole's Orchestra (Columbia), recorded it separately as they were signed to different labels. Eddie Fisher, accompanied by Hugo Winterhalter, had the best-seller (RCA Victor).

Couple of Song and Dance Men, A. w/m Irving Berlin, 1946. Introduced by Fred Astaire and Bing Crosby, with Cliff Nazarro at the piano in (MM) *Blue Skies*. Astaire and Crosby recorded the number (Decca).

Couple of Swells, A. w/m Irving Berlin, 1948. Introduced by Fred Astaire and Judy Garland in (MM) *Easter Parade*.

Courtin' in the Rain. w/m T. Texas Tyler, 1954. Hit record by T. Texas Tyler (4 Star).

Court of Love. w/m Guy Draper, 1968. Top 40 record by The Unifics (Kapp).

Court of the Crimson King. w/m Ian McDonald and Peter Sinfield, 1970. Recorded by the British group King Crimson (Atlantic, Part 1).

Covered Wagon Days. w/m Will Morrisey and Joe Burrows, 1923. This was written to be played by piano or orchestra accompanying the silent-screen film classic, (MP) *The Covered Wagon*. It was interpolated in the short lived musical (TM) *The Newcomers* in 1923.

Cover Me. w/m Bruce Springsteen, 1984. Top 10 record by Bruce Springsteen (Columbia).

Cover Me. w/m Marlin Green and Eddie Hilton, 1967. Recorded by Percy Sledge (Atlantic).

Cover Me Up with Sunshine. w. Mort Dixon, m. Ray Henderson, 1927. Recorded by Jean Goldkette's Orchestra (Victor).

Cover Me Up with the Sunshine of Virginia. w. Sam M. Lewis and Joe Young, m. George W. Meyer, 1924.

Cover of "Rolling Stone," The. w/m Shel Silverstein, 1973. Gold record by the group Dr. Hook and the Medicine Show (Columbia).

Coward of the County. w/m Roger Bowling and Billy Edd Wheeler, 1979. #1 Country and Top 10 Pop chart gold record by Kenny Rogers (United Artists).

Cowboy and the Lady, The. w/m Bobby Goldsboro, 1977. Country chart records by Patsy Sledd (Mega), 1976; Tommy Cash (Monument), 1977; Bobby Goldsboro (Epic), 1977; John Denver, C&W and Pop (RCA), 1981. Answer song, "The Cowgirl and the Dandy," recorded by Brenda Lee (MCA), 1980.

Cowboy and the Lady, The. w. Arthur Quenzer, m. Lionel Newman, 1938. Title song of (MP) *The Cowboy and the Lady*. Song nominated for Academy Award.

Cowboy Boots. w/m Baker Knight, 1963. Crossover (C&W/Pop) chart record by Dave Dudley (Golden Wing).

Cowboy from Brooklyn. w. Johnny Mercer, m. Harry Warren, 1938. Introduced by Dick Powell in (MM) *Cowboys from Brooklyn*. Records by the bands of Tommy Dorsey (Victor), Jimmy Dorsey (Decca), Johnny Messner (Vocalion.)

Cowboy in the Continental Suit, The. w/m Marty Robbins, 1964. Country hit by Marty Robbins (Columbia).

Cowboy Rides Away, The. w/m Sonny

Throckmorton and Casey Kelly, 1985. Top 10 Country chart single by George Strait from his album "Does Fort Worth Ever Cross Your Mind?" (MCA).

Cowboys and Clowns. w/m Stephen Dorff, Snuff Garrett, Larry Herbstritt, and Gary Harju, 1980. #1 Country chart hit by Ronnie Milsap (RCA).

Cowboy Serenade, The. w/m Rich Hall, 1941. Most popular records by Kay Kyser, vocal by Harry Babbitt (Columbia); and Glenn Miller, vocal by Ray Eberle (Bluebird). Others of note: Gene Krupa, vocal by Howard Dulany (Okeh); The Charioteers (Okeh); Art Jarrett (Victor). It was sung as the title song by Gene Autry in (MP) *Cowboy Serenade*, 1942.

Cowboys to Girls. w/m Kenny Gamble and Leon Huff, 1968. Gold record by the Intruders (Gamble).

Cowboy's Work Is Never Done, A. w/m Sonny Bono, 1972. Top 10 record by Sonny and Cher (Atco).

Cow Cow Blues. m. Charles "Cow Cow" Davenport, 1928. Introduced and recorded by ragtime pianist Davenport (Vocalion) and as "New Cow Cow Blues" (Paramount). Later successful records by Bob Crosby and his Orchestra (Decca), jazz pianist Sam Price (Decca), Bob Zurke (Victor). When "Cow-Cow Boogie" was released, 1941, controversy arose and the writers of the derivative work bought out Davenport's sheet music and record royalty rights. See also "Cow-Cow Boogie."

Cow-Cow Boogie. w/m Don Raye, Gene DePaul, and Benny Carter, 1942. Originally sung in the film (MM) *Rise 'Em Cowboy* by Ella Fitzgerald, but deleted from the film before release. Ella Mae Morse, with Freddie Slack's Orchestra, recorded a hit version (Capitol), which was then done by them in (MM) *Reveille with Beverly*, 1943. Song derived from "Cow Cow Blues" (q.v.) by ragtime pianist Charles Davenport who, by agreement, sold his sheet music and record royalty rights to the writers of this number.

Cowgirl and the Dandy, The. See **Cowboy and the Lady, The.**

Cow Town. w/m Jack Padgett, 1962. Top 10 Country record by Webb Pierce (Decca).

Crackerbox Palace. w/m George Harrison, 1977. Top 20 record by George Harrison (Dark Horse).

Crack Killed Applejack. w/m Mitch "General Kane" McDowell and Cray Owen, 1986. R&B chart record by the rap group General Kane (Motown). The song was written after the drug-caused death of the college basketball star Len Bias.

Cracklin' Rosie. w/m Neil Diamond, 1970. #1 gold record by Neil Diamond (Uni).

Cradle of Love. w/m Jack Fautheree and Wayne Gray, 1960. Hit record by Johnny Preston (Mercury).

Crawlin'. w/m Rudolph Toombs, 1953. Hit R&B record by The Clovers (Atlantic).

Crazay. w/m Jesse Johnson, 1986. Recorded by Jesse Johnson featuring Sly Stone (A&M).

Craze-ology. m. Lawrence "Bud" Freeman, 1929. Jazz instrumental recorded by Bud Freeman (Okeh).

Crazy. w/m A. Qunta, I. Davies, R. Kretschmer, 1987. Chart record by the Australian quartet Icehouse (Chrysalis).

Crazy. w/m Kenny Rogers and Richard Marx, 1985. Recorded by Kenny Rogers in his album "What About Me?" (RCA).

Crazy. w/m Willie Nelson, 1961. Crossover (C&W and Pop) hit by Patsy Cline (Decca).

Crazy, He Calls Me. w. Bob Russell, m. Carl Sigman, 1949. Leading record by Billie Holiday (Decca).

Crazy, Man, Crazy. w/m Bill Haley, 1953. First chart record by Bill Haley and His Comets (Essex). This is considered by many researchers and authorities in the field to be the first rock song to appear on the Pop charts.

Crazy, She Calls Me. See **Crazy He Calls Me.**

Crazy Arms. w/m Chuck Seals and Ralph Mooney, 1956. Popularized by Ray Price (Columbia). Revived by Bob Beckham (Decca), 1960.

Crazy Blues. w/m Perry Bradford, 1921. Mamie Smith and Her Jazz Hounds (Okeh) followed by the Original Dixieland Jazz Band (Victor) had big-selling records. Smith was the first blues singer to be commercially recorded.

Crazy 'Bout Ya, Baby. w. Pat Barrett, m. Rudi Maugeri, 1954. Written by two of the Crew-Cuts for their first success (Mercury).

Crazy Downtown. See **Downtown**.

Crazy for You. w. John Bettis, m. Jon Lind, 1985. Introduced by Madonna in (MP) *Vision Quest*. Her recording became a #1 gold record (Geffen).

Crazy from the Heart. w/m David Bellamy and Don Schlitz, 1987. Top 10 Country chart single by The Bellamy Brothers (MCA). Its popularity made it the title song of their ensuing album.

Crazy Heart. w/m Fred Rose and Maurice Murray, 1951. Top record by Guy Lombardo, vocal by Kenny Gardner (Decca). Also recorded by Hank Williams (MGM), who is sometimes listed as one of the writers, and Helen O'Connell (Capitol).

Crazy Horses. w/m Alan Osmond, Merrill Osmond, Wayne Osmond, 1972. Top 20 record by The Osmonds (MGM).

Crazy in the Night (Barking at Airplanes). w/m Kim Carnes, 1985. Recorded by Kim Carnes (EMI America).

Crazy Little Thing Called Love. w/m Freddie Mercury, 1980. #1 gold record by the British rock group Queen (Elektra).

Crazy Love. w/m Rusty Young, 1979. Recorded by the country-rock band Poco (ABC).

Crazy Love. w/m Van Morrison, 1971. Recorded by Helen Reddy (Capitol).

Crazy Love. w/m Paul Anka, 1958. Top 20 record by Paul Anka (ABC-Paramount).

Crazy Mama. w/m Mick Jagger and Keith Richards, 1972. Top 40 record by J. J. Cale (Shelter).

Crazy on You. w/m Ann Wilson, Nancy Wilson, and Mike Fisher, 1976. Recorded by the group, Heart, of which the Wilson sisters were members, and Fisher was manager (Mushroom).

Crazy Otto Rag, The. w/m Edward R. White, Mack Wolfson, Hugo Peretti, and Luigi Creatore. 1955. Top records by Honky Tonk piano players, Crazy Otto (Decca), and Johnny Maddox (Dot).

Crazy Over You. w/m Radney Foster and Bill Lloyd, 1987. Top 10 Country chart song by Foster and Lloyd (RCA).

Crazy People. w. Edgar Leslie, m. James V. Monaco, 1932. Introduced by the Boswell Sisters in (MM) *The Big Broadcast*. Recorded by Cliff "Ukulele Ike" Edwards (Brunswick), and the band of Gene Kardos (Victor) and Benny Krueger (Brunswick).

Crazy Rhythm. w. Irving Caesar, m. Joseph Meyer and Roger Wolfe Kahn, 1928. Introduced and recorded by Ben Bernie (Brunswick). It was then interpolated in (TM) *Here's Howe*, by Ben Bernie, Peggy Chamberlain, and June O'Dea. Dan Dailey sang it in (MM) *You Were Meant for Me*, 1948, and Gene Nelson and Patrice Wymore performed it in (MM) *Tea for Two*, 1950. Among the many recordings were those by Johnny Marvin (Victor); Roger Wolfe Kahn's Orchestra (Victor); Benny Goodman (Columbia); Jazz at the Philharmonic [two sides] (Disc); Doris Day, Gene Nelson, and the Page Cavanaugh Trio (Columbia); Skitch Henderson (Capitol).

Crazy Wild Desire. w/m Mel Tillis and Webb Pierce, 1962. Hit C&W record by Webb Pierce.

Crazy with Love. w/m Al Goodhart, Al Hoffman, and Maurice Sigler. 1936. From the English musical (TM) *This'll Make You Whis-*

tle. American release by the English band Ambrose and his Orchestra (Decca).

Crazy Words, Crazy Tune (Vo-Do-De-O-Do). w. Jack Yellen, m. Milton Ager, 1927. Novelty song with popular recordings by Jones and Hare (Columbia), Frank Crumit (Victor), Vaughn DeLeath (Brunswick), Irving Aaronson and His Commanders (Victor). Jerry Lewis revived it in the late 1950s (Capitol).

Crazy World. w. Leslie Bricusse, m. Henry Mancini, 1981. Introduced by Julie Andrews in (MP) *Victor/Victoria*.

Creep, The. w. Carl Sigman, m. Andy Barton, 1954. Melody was written in England. First U.S. release by British orchestra leader Ted Heath (London). Popular American records by The Three Suns (RCA Victor); the orchestras of Ralph Marterie (Mercury) and Stan Kenton (Capitol).

Creeque Alley. w/m John Phillips and Michelle Gilliam Phillips, 1967. Top 10 hit by The Mamas and The Papas (Dunhill).

Creole Belle. w. George Sidney, m. J. Bodewalt Lampe, 1900.

Creole Love Call. w/m Edward Kennedy "Duke" Ellington, 1927. Introduced by Adelaide Hall, with Duke Ellington and his Orchestra, at The Cotton Club in Harlem, New York City, and on records (Victor).

Creole Rhapsody. m. Edward Kennedy "Duke" Ellington, 1931. Parts I and II recorded by Ellington (Victor 12″ 78 rpm).

Crescendo in Blue. m. Edward Kennedy "Duke" Ellington, 1937. Recorded by Duke Ellington and his Orchestra, coupled with "Diminuendo in Blue" (Brunswick).

Cricket on the Hearth, The. w. Robert B. Smith, m. Victor Herbert, 1913. From (TM) *Sweethearts*.

Cried Like a Baby. w. Paul Williams, m. Craig Doerge, 1971. Top 20 record by Bobby Sherman (Metromedia).

Crimson and Clover. w/m Peter Lucia and Tommy James, 1969. #1 chart record by Tommy James and The Shondells (Roulette). Revived with a Top 10 hit by Joan Jett and The Blackhearts (Boardwalk), 1982.

Crinoline Days. w/m Irving Berlin, 1922. Introduced by Grace LaRue in (TM) *The Music Box Revue of 1922*. Best-selling record by Paul Whiteman and his Orchestra (Victor).

Criss-Cross. m. Thelonious Monk, 1962. Jazz instrumental, introduced and recorded by Thelonious Monk (Columbia).

Cristofo Columbo. w/m Francis J. Bryant, 1895. Source of many off-color parodies.

Croce di Oro (Cross of Gold). w. Bob Haring, m. Kim Gannon, 1955. Top 20 record by Patti Page, with Jack Rael's Orchestra (Mercury). Joan Regan, the British singer, also had a chart version (London).

Crocodile Rock. w/m Elton John and Bernie Taupin, 1973. Gold record by the British singer/writer Elton John (MCA).

Crosby, Columbo, and Vallee. w. Al Dubin, m. Joe Burke, 1931. A novelty referring to the three famous "crooners," Bing, Russ, and Rudy, respectively.

Cross-Eyed Kelly (From Penn-Syl-Van-Eye-Ay). w/m Al Lewis, Al Sherman, and Abner Silver, 1934. Popularized by Joe Haymes and his Orchestra (Melotone).

Crossfire. m. T. J. Fowler and Tom King, 1959. Instrumental by Johnny and The Hurricanes (Warwick).

Cross My Broken Heart. w/m Stephen Bray and Tony Pierce, 1987. Top 10 record by The Jets, introduced on the soundtrack of (MP) "Beverly Hills Cop II"(MCA).

Cross over the Bridge. w/m Bennie Benjamin and George David Weiss, 1954. Million-seller by Patti Page, with Jack Rael's Orchestra (Mercury).

Cross Patch. w. Tot Seymour, m. Vee Lawnhurst, 1936. Featured and recorded by the bands of Louis Prima and Willie Bryant, both on the same label (Brunswick).

Crossroads. w/m Robert Johnson, 1969. Top 40 U.S. record by the British group Cream (Atco).

Cross the Brazos at Waco. w/m Kay Arnold, 1964. Country hit by Billy Walker (Columbia).

'Cross the Great Divide (I'll Wait for You). w. Sam M. Lewis, m. George W. Meyer, 1914. Popular record by The Haydn Quartet (Victor).

Crosstown. w/m James Cavanaugh, John Redmond, and Nat Simon, 1940. Recorded by Glenn Miller, vocal by Jack Lathrop (Bluebird).

Crosstown Traffic. w/m Jimi Hendrix, 1968. Recorded by The Jimi Hendrix Experience (Reprise).

Cross Your Fingers. w. Arthur Swanstrom and Benny Davis, m. J. Fred Coots, 1929. Introduced by Shirley Vernon and Milton Watson in (TM) *Sons o' Guns*, which starred Jack Donahue and Lili Damita.

Cross Your Heart. w. B. G. DeSylva, m. Lewis E. Gensler, 1926. Introduced by Mary Lawlor and Clarence Nordstrom in (TM) *Queen High*. Leading records by Roger Wolfe Kahn, vocal by Henry Burr (Victor); and Vaughn DeLeath and Ed Smalle (Columbia).

Crowd, The. w/m Roy Orbison and Joe Melson, 1962. Top 40 record by Roy Orbison (Monument).

Crude Oil Blues, The. w/m Jerry Reed, 1974. Hit novelty Country record by Jerry Reed (RCA).

Cruel Love. w/m Arthur Smiley, 1960. Top 10 Country record by Lou Smith (KRCO).

Cruel Shoes. w/m Steve Martin, 1979. Comedy record by Steve Martin (Warner Bros.).

Cruel Summer. w/m Tony Swain and Steve Jolley, 1984. Top 10 record by the British female trio Bananarama (London).

Cruel to Be Kind. w/m Robert Ian Gomm and Nick Lowe, 1979. Recorded by the English singer Nick Lowe (Columbia).

Cruisin'. w/m William "Smokey" Robinson and Marvin Tarplin, 1979. Top 10 record by Smokey Robinson (Tamla).

Cruising Down the River (on a Sunday Afternoon). w/m Eily Beadell and Nell Tollerton, 1949. English song, which four years earlier had won an amateur songwriting contest, became one of the biggest hits of the year in the U.S., as evidenced by its being on "Your Hit Parade" for nineteen weeks, eight times as #1. The bands of Blue Barron (MGM) and Russ Morgan (Decca) each had million-sellers, and Jack Smith (Capitol) and Frankie Carle with vocal by Marjorie Hughes (Columbia) had Top 10 records.

Crumblin' Down. w/m John Cougar Mellencamp, 1983. Top 10 record by John Cougar Mellencamp (Riva).

Crumbs Off the Table. w. Scherrie Payne, Ronald Dunbar, and Edith Wayne, m. Dunbar and Wayne, 1969. Recorded by The Glass House (Invictus).

Crush on You. w/m Jerry Knight and Aaron Zigman, 1986. Top 10 R&B and Pop chart record by the eight-brother-and-sister group The Jets (MCA).

Cry. w/m Kevin Godley and Lol Creme, 1985. Recorded by the British duo Godley and Creme (Polydor).

Cry. w/m Churchill Kohlman, 1951. Johnnie Ray's first hit record was #1 on the charts for almost three months and sold over two-million records (Okeh), coupled with another hit, "The Little White Cloud That Cried." Revivals include: instrumental by The Knightsbridge Strings (Top Rank), 1959; Ray Charles (ABC-Paramount), 1965; Ronnie Dove (Diamond), 1966; Country singers Lynn Anderson (Columbia), 1972, and Crystal Gayle (Warner Bros.), 1986.

Cry, Baby, Cry. w/m Jimmy Eaton, Terry Shand, Remus Harris, and Irving Melsher,

1938. Best-selling records: the orchestras of Kay Kyser (Brunswick) and Larry Clinton (Victor).

Cry, Cry Baby. w/m Robert Ellen and Mack Ellen, 1950. Hit record by Ed Wiley (Sittin' In).

Cry, Cry, Cry. w/m John Scott Sherrill and Don Devaney, 1988. #1 Country chart song by the group, Highway 101, from the album of their name (Warner Bros.).

Cry, Cry, Darling. w/m Jimmy Newman and J. D. Miller, 1954. Introduced and recorded by Jimmy Newman (Dot).

Cry Baby. w/m Norman Meade and Bert Russell, 1963. Top 10 record by Garnett Mimms and the Enchanters (United Artists). Revived by Janis Joplin (Columbia), 1971.

Cry-Baby Heart. w/m Leon Payne, 1949. C&W chart hit by George Morgan (Columbia).

Cry Freedom. w/m George Fenton and Jonas Gwangwa, 1987. Introduced by the writers in (MP) *Cry Freedom*. Nominated for an Academy Award.

Cryin' for the Carolines. w. Sam M. Lewis and Joe Young, m. Harry Warren, 1930. Introduced by Lawrence Gray in (MM) *Spring Is Here*. Popular recordings by Belle Baker (Brunswick), Guy Lombardo (Columbia), Arthur Schutt (Okeh), Sid Garry (Harmony).

Cryin', Prayin', Wishin', Waitin'. w/m C. Stewart, J. Smith, and Charlie Gore, 1955. Country record by Hank Snow (RCA).

Crying. w/m Roy Orbison and Joe Melson, 1961. Top 10 hit by Roy Orbison (Monument). Jay and The Americans had a Top 40 version in 1966 (United Artists) and Don McLean revived it with a Top 10 record in 1981 (Millennium).

Crying for Joy. w. Billy Rose, m. James V. Monaco, 1948. Among recordings: Dinah Shore (Columbia); Russ Case, vocal by Peggy Mann (RCA Victor).

Crying Heart Blues (a.k.a. **Cryin' Heart Blues**). w/m J. Brown, 1951. Top 10 C&W chart record by Johnnie and Jack (RCA).

Crying in the Chapel. w/m Artie Glenn, 1953. Introduced and recorded by the composer's son, Darrell Glenn (Valley). Top recording by June Valli (RCA Victor). Other chart versions by Rex Allen (Decca), The Orioles (Jubilee), Ella Fitzgerald (Decca), Art Lund (Coral). Adam Wade revived the song (Epic), 1965, with a chart record, but Elvis Presley followed with a release that reached the Top 10 (RCA).

Crying in the Rain. w/m Carole King and Howard Greenfield, 1962. Hit record by The Everly Brothers (Warner Brothers).

Crying My Heart Out over You. w/m Carl Butler, Louise Certain, Jerry Organ, and Gladys Stacey, 1982. First recorded by the Bluegrass duo. Lester Flatt and Earl Scruggs (Columbia), 1960. Country music singer Ricky Skaggs had a #1 hit (Epic), 1982.

Crying Myself to Sleep. w/m Bob Atcher, 1942. Atcher had a popular record (Okeh).

Crying Myself to Sleep. w. John Klenner, m. Peter Wendling, 1930. Popularized by the bands of Bert Lown (Victor) and Ben Bernie (Brunswick).

Crying Shame. w/m Brent Maher, 1987. Top 10 Country chart record by Michael Johnson (RCA).

Crying Time. w/m Buck Owens, 1966. Top 10 record by Ray Charles (ABC-Paramount). Winner Grammy Award (NARAS) Rhythm and Blues Song of the Year.

Cry Like a Baby. w/m Dan Pennington and Dewey Lindon Oldham, 1968. Top 10 record by The Box Tops (Mala). Revived by Kim Carnes (EMI America), 1980.

Cry Like the Wind. w. Betty Comden and Adolph Green, m. Jule Styne, 1960. Introduced by Nancy Dussault in (TM) *Do Re Mi*.

Cry Me a River. w/m Arthur Hamilton, 1955. Popularized by the hit recording of Julie

London (Liberty). London sang it in (MM) *The Girl Can't Help It*, 1957. Revived in 1970 by Joe Cocker, recorded while performing at Fillmore East in New York (A&M).

Cry Myself to Sleep. w/m Paul Kennerly, 1986. #1 Country chart hit by the mother/daughter duo The Judds (RCA).

Cry of the Wild Goose, The. w/m Terry Gilkyson, 1950. #1 million-seller for Frankie Laine (Mercury) and Top 20 record for Tennessee Ernie Ford (Capitol).

Crystal Blue Persuasion. w/m Tommy James, Mike Vale, and Ed Gray, 1969. Top 10 record by Tommy James and The Shondells (Roulette).

Crystal Chandelier. w/m Ted Harris, 1965. Recorded by Vic Dana (Dolton).

Cry to Me. w/m Bert Russell, 1962. First popular record by Solomon Burke (Atlantic). Later chart versions by Betty Harris (Jubilee), 1963, and Freddie Scott (Shout), 1967.

Cuando Caliente El Sol. See **Love Me with All Your Heart.**

Cuanto Le Gusta (La Parranda). w. Ray Gilbert, m. Gabriel Ruiz, 1948. Introduced by Carmen Miranda in (MM) *A Date with Judy*. Best-selling record by Carmen Miranda and The Andrews Sisters (Decca). Other top versions by Jack Smith (Capitol); Eve Young, later to be known as Karen Chandler (RCA Victor); as an instrumental, Xavier Cugat and his Orchestra (Columbia).

Cuban Love Song. w/m Dorothy Fields, Jimmy McHugh, and Herbert Stothart, 1931. Introduced by Lawrence Tibbett, who sang it in (MM) *Cuban Love Song* and on records (Victor). Other recordings by Guy Lombardo (Columbia); Paul Whiteman, with vocal by Jack Fulton (Victor); Art Jarrett (Brunswick). Gordon MacRae had a later release (Capitol).

Cubanola Glide, The. w. Vincent P. Bryan, m. Harry Von Tilzer, 1909. One of the early songs about a specific ballroom or social dance. It was popularized by Sophie Tucker in vaudeville. Leading recordings by Arthur Collins and Byron Harlan (Columbia), Billy Murray (Victor), instrumental by Prince's Orchestra (Columbia).

Cuban Pete. w/m Norman Henderson (pseud.: José Norman), 1937. An English song that received good airplay here and was revived in 1946 when it became the title song of (MM) *Cuban Pete*, starring Desi Arnaz, who recorded it with his Orchestra (Victor).

Cuckoo in the Clock. w. Johnny Mercer, m. Walter Donaldson, 1939. Leading records by Benny Goodman, vocal by Johnny Mercer (Victor); Glenn Miller, vocal by Marion Hutton (Bluebird).

Cuddle Buggin' Baby. w/m Red Rowe, 1950. Featured and recorded by Eddy Arnold (RCA Victor).

Cuddle Me. w/m Ronnie Gaylord, 1954. Introduced and recorded by Ronnie Gaylord (Mercury).

Cuddle Up a Little Closer, Lovey Mine. w. Otto Harbach, m. Karl Hoschna, 1908. This was Harbach's first hit song, written before he changed his name from Hauerbach. It was introduced in (TM) *The Three Twins*. Ada Jones and Billy Murray had a hit recording (Victor). Song has had many film performances such as Mary Martin in (MM) *Birth of the Blues*, 1941; Betty Grable in (MM) *Coney Island*, 1943; Bob Haymes in the Ted Lewis bio (MM) *Is Everybody Happy?*, 1943; Fred Astaire and Ginger Rogers in (MM) *The Story of Vernon and Irene Castle*, 1939; and Gordon MacRae in (MM) *On Moonlight Bay*, 1951.

Cum On Feel the Noize. w/m Noddy Holder and Jim Lea, 1983. Introduced by the British quartet, Slade, of which the writers were members (Polydor), 1973. Top 10 gold record by the American quartet Quiet Riot (Pasha), 1983.

Cupid. w/m Sam Cooke, 1961. Introduced and Top 20 record by Sam Cooke (RCA). Later Top 40 versions by Johnny Nash (JAD), 1970, and Tony Orlando and Dawn (Elektra), 1976.

Top 10 record in medley with "I've Loved You for a Long Time," by The Spinners (Atlantic), 1980.

Cupid and I. w. Harry B. Smith, m. Victor Herbert, 1897. Hit waltz from the operetta (TM) *The Serenade.* Performed by Alice Nielsen.

Cupid's Boogie. w/m Johnny Otis, 1950. Hit R&B record by Little Esther, Mel Walker, and Johnny Otis (Savoy).

Cup of Coffee, a Sandwich and You, A. w. Billy Rose and Al Dubin, m. Joseph Meyer, 1926. Introduced by Gertrude Lawrence and Jack Buchanan in *Charlot's Revue of 1926,* and recorded by them (Columbia). It was sung by Barbara Lawrence and reprised by Jean Crain in (MM) *Margie,* 1946.

Curly Shuffle, The. w/m Peter Quinn, 1983. Hit novelty, based on the movements of The Three Stooges, by the band Jump 'n the Saddle, of which Quinn was lead singer (Atlantic). The music was added to footage by the Three Stooges and the resulting videotape became the rallying song for the New York Mets baseball team at Shea Stadium during the late eighties.

Curly Top. w. Ted Koehler, m. Ray Henderson, 1935. Sung by John Boles to Shirley Temple in (MM) *Curly Top.*

Curse of an Aching Heart, The (or, You Made Me What I Am Today). w. Henry Fink, m. Al Piantadosi, 1913. An 1890s type sentimental ballad that found favor in a later period. It was sung by Eddie Cantor in (MM) *Show Business* in 1944

Curse of the Dreamer, The. w/m Paul Dresser, 1899.

Curtain in the Window. w/m Lee Ross, 1958. C&W hit by Ray Price (Columbia).

Cutie Pie. w/m Al Hudson, G. Hudson, D. Robertson, T. Dudley, G. Green, J. Meadows, T. Morgan, 1982. Top 10 R&B record by the group One Way (MCA).

Cut the Cake. w/m Roger Ball, Malcolm Duncan, Alan Gorrie, Robbie McIntosh, Onnie McIntyre, Hamish Stuart, 1975. Top 10 record written by the members of the Scottish group Average White Band (Atlantic).

Cuttin' In. w/m John Watson, 1962. Introduced and recorded by Johnny "Guitar" Watson (King).

Cu-Tu-Gu-Ru. See **Jack, Jack, Jack.**

Cuzz You're So Sweet. w/m John Kane, 1954. Novelty C&W by Simon Crum, pseudonym for Ferlin Husky (Capitol).

Cycles. w/m Gayle Caldwell, 1968. Top 40 record by Frank Sinatra (Reprise).

Cynthia's in Love. w. Jack Owens, m. Earl White and Billy Gish, 1946. Recorded by Tex Beneke, vocal by Artie Malvin, Lillian Lane and The Crew Chiefs (RCA Victor); Bob Eberly (Decca); Skitch Henderson and his Orchestra (Capitol); Frankie Carle, vocal by Marjorie Hughes (Columbia).

D

Da'Butt. w/m Marcus Miller and Mark Stevens, 1988. Introduced on the soundtrack of (MP) *School Daze* by the group E.U. (Experience Unlimited). Their single became a #1 R&B and crossover Pop chart entry (EMI-Manhattan).

Daddies Need to Grow Up Too. 1987. Top 10 Country chart hit by the duo The O'Kanes (Columbia).

Daddy. w/m Bobby Troup, 1941. One of the biggest hits of the year, fifteen weeks on "Your Hit Parade," six times as #1, this was introduced in a minor film (MP) *Two Latins from Manhattan*, by Joan Davis and Jinx Falkenburg. Sammy Kaye, with his band singing the chorus in unison, recorded it and had a #1 record (Victor).

Daddy, Daddy. w/m Rudolph Toombs, 1952. Chart R&B recording by Ruth Brown (Atlantic).

Daddy, Don't You Walk So Fast. w/m Peter Callander and Geoff Stephens, 1972. Introduced in England by Daniel Boone. Gold record in the U.S. by Wayne Newton (Chelsea).

Daddy, What If. w/m Shel Silverstein, 1974. Country record by Bobby Bare, with his five-year-old son, Bobby Jr. (RCA).

Daddy, You've Been a Mother to Me. w/m Fred Fisher, 1920. Popularized in vaudeville. Recorded by the tenors Henry Burr (Victor, Vocalion, Path) and Lewis James (Columbia).

Daddy Could Swear, I Declare. w/m Johnny Bristol, Gladys Knight, and Merrald (Bubba) Knight, 1973. Top 20 record by Gladys Knight and The Pips (Soul).

Daddy Frank (the Guitar Man). w/m Merle Haggard, 1971. Hit Country record by Merle Haggard (Capitol).

Daddy Has a Sweetheart (and Mother Is Her Name). w. Gene Buck, m. Dave Stamper, 1912. Introduced by Lillian Lorraine at Hammerstein's Victoria Theatre in New York and then interpolated by her in (TM) *Ziegfeld Follies of 1912*. It was recorded by Edna Brown, pseudonym for contralto Elsie Baker (Victor).

Daddy Long Legs. w. Sam M. Lewis and Joe Young, m. Harry Ruby, 1919. The song was inspired by the popular film of the same name, starring Mary Pickford.

Daddy O. w/m Louis Innis, Buford Abner, and Charlie Gore, 1955. Chart records by The Fontane Sisters (Dot) and Bonnie Lou (King).

Daddy-O (I'm Gonna Teach You Some Blues). w/m Don Raye and Gene De Paul, 1948. Introduced by Virginia Mayo, voice dubbed on the soundtrack by Jerri Sullivan, with The Page Cavanaugh Trio in (MM) *A Song*

Is Born, starring Danny Kaye. Dinah Shore's recording was coupled with the million-seller "Buttons and Bows" (Columbia).

Daddy Sang Bass. w/m Carl Lee Perkins, 1969. C&W and Pop hit record by Johnny Cash (Columbia).

Daddy's Gone a-Hunting. w. Dory Previn, m. John Williams, 1971. Sung on the soundtrack of (MP) *Daddy's Gone a-Hunting* by Lyn Roman.

Daddy's Hands. w/m Holly Dunn, 1986. Top 10 Country chart record by Holly Dunn (MTM).

Daddy's Home. w/m James Sheppard and William Miller, 1961. As an answer to The Heartbeat's "A Thousand Miles Away" (q. v.), this hit was written and recorded by the lead singer of both groups, the second being Shep and The Limelites (Atlantic). Later chart versions by Jermaine Jackson (Motown), 1973, and Cliff Richard (EMI American), 1982.

Daddy's Little Girl. w/m Bobby Burke and Horace Gerlach, 1950. Hit records by Dick Todd (Rainbow) and The Mills Brothers (Decca). Revived by Al Martino (Capitol), 1967.

Daddy's Little Girl. w. Edward Madden, m. Theodore F. Morse, 1906. Popular recordings by Byron G. Harlan (Victor, Edison).

Daddy's Little Man. w/m Mac Davis, 1969. Top 40 record by O. C. Smith (Columbia).

Daddy Was an Old Time Preacher Man. w/m Dolly Parton and Dorothy Jo Hope, 1970. Hit Country record by Dolly Parton and Porter Wagoner (RCA).

Daddy Wouldn't Buy Me a Bow-Wow. w/m Joseph Tabrar, 1892. Featured by Vesta Victoria.

Dad Gave My Dog Away. w/m T. Texas Tyler, Mary Jean Shurtz, and Jake Taylor, 1948. Hit C&W record by T. Texas Tyler (Four Star).

Da Doo Ron Ron (When He Walked Me Home). w/m Jeff Barry, Ellie Greenwich, and Phil Spector, 1963, 1977. Introduced and recorded by The Crystals, produced by Phil Spector (Phillies). #1 million-seller by Shaun Cassidy (Warner Bros.), 1977.

Daisies Won't Tell. w/m Anita Owen, 1908.

Daisy a Day. w/m Jud Strunk, 1973. Top 20 record by Jud Strunk (MGM).

Daisy Bell (or, Bicycle Built for Two). w/m Harry Dacre, 1892. Written in the U.S. by the English composer, the song had its first success in London performed by Kate Lawrence. Tony Pastor introduced it in the U.S. at his Music Hall.

Daisy Jane. w/m Gerry Beckley, 1975. Top 20 record by the group America (Warner Bros.).

Dallas. w/m Jerrold Immel, 1978. Theme of series (TVP) "Dallas." Recorded by Floyd Cramer (RCA), 1980.

Dallas Blues. w. Hart A. Wand, m. Lloyd Garrett, 1918. A blues standard with many recordings by such performers as Ted Lewis (Columbia), Glen Gray and the Casa Loma Orchestra (Brunswick), Wingy Manone (Bluebird), and Woody Herman (Decca).

Daly's Reel. m. Joseph M. Daly, 1911. Two step.

Dames. w. Al Dubin, m. Harry Warren, 1934. Sung by Dick Powell in a Busby Berkeley production number in (MM) *Dames.* Performed by Lee Roy Reams and ensemble in (TM) *42nd Street,* 1980.

Damned If I Do. w/m Eric Woolfson, 1979. Recorded by the English duo, The Alan Parsons Project, consisting of the writer and Parsons (Arista).

Dance, Dance, Dance. w/m Brian Wilson and Carl Wilson, 1964. Top 10 record by The Beach Boys (Capitol).

Dance, Dance, Dance (Yowsah, Yowsah, Yowsah). w/m Nile Rodgers, Bernard Edwards, and Kenny Lehman, 1977. Gold record by the disco group Chic (Atlantic).

Dance, Everyone, Dance. w. and musical adaptation by Sidney Danoff, 1958. Based on the Israeli song "Hava Nagila." Top 40 record by Betty Madigan (Coral).

Dance, Little Lady. w/m Noël Coward, 1928. Sung by Noël Coward and danced by Florence Desmond and dancers in (TM) *This Year of Grace!*, which was the American production of the hit English revue.

Dance, My Darlings. w. Oscar Hammerstein II, m. Sigmund Romberg, 1935. Introduced by Nancy McCord and ensemble in (TM) *May Wine*.

Dance (Disco Heat). w/m Victor Orsborn and Eric Robinson, 1978. Recorded by Sylvester (Fantasy).

Dance Away. w/m Bryan Ferry, 1979. Recorded by the English group Roxy Music (Atco).

Dance Away the Night. w. Harlan Thompson, m. Dave Stamper, 1929. Sung by J. Harold Murray and Norma Terris in (MM) *Married in Hollywood.*

Dance Floor. w/m Roger "Zapp" Troutman and Larry Troutman, 1982. #1 R&B chart record by the funk band Zapp (Warner Bros.).

Dance Hall Days. w/m Jack Hues, 1984. Recorded by the British group, Wang Chung, of which Hues was lead singer/keyboardist/guitarist (Geffen).

Dance Me Loose. w. Mel Howard, m. Lee Erwin, 1952. Featured and recorded by Arthur Godfrey, with The Chordettes and Archie Bleyer's Orchestra (Columbia). Also recorded by Russ Morgan and Band (Decca).

Dance of the Paper Dolls. w/m Johnny Tucker, Joe Schuster, and Ira Schuster, 1928. The piano team of Ohman and Arden had a popular record (Victor).

Dance of the Spanish Onion. m. David Rose, 1942. Instrumental recorded by David Rose and his Orchestra (Victor).

Dance On, Little Girl. w/m Paul Anka, 1961. Hit record by Paul Anka (ABC-Paramount).

Dance: Ten; Looks: Three. w. Edward Kleban, m. Marvin Hamlisch, 1975. Introduced by Pamela Blair in (TM) *A Chorus Line.* In (MM) *A Chorus Line*, 1985, it was sung by Audrey Landers.

Dance the Night Away. w/m Michael Anthony, David Lee Roth, Alex Van Halen, and Eddie Van Halen, 1979. Written and recorded by the group Van Halen (Warner Bros.).

Dance to the Music. w/m Sylvester Stewart, 1968. First hit record by Sly (Stewart) and The Family Stone (Epic).

Dance with a Dolly (With a Hole in Her Stocking). w/m Terry Shand, Jimmy Eaton, and David Kapp, 1944. Adaptation of public domain melody known as "Lubly Fan," "Buffalo Gals (Won't You Come Out Tonight?)," and other titles. Featured by Russ Morgan, vocal by Al Jennings (Decca); Evelyn Knight (Decca); Tony Pastor, with his Orchestra (Bluebird). Song on "Your Hit Parade" for fifteen weeks. It was sung by The Andrews Sisters in (MM) *Her Lucky Night*, 1945, and was also in (MM) *On Stage Everybody*, 1945.

Dance with Me. w/m Peter Brown and Robert Rans, 1978. Top 10 record by Peter Brown, background vocal by Betty Wright (Drive).

Dance with Me. w/m John Hall and Johanna Hall, 1975. Top 10 record by the group Orleans (Asylum).

Dance with Me. w/m Louis Lebish, George Treadwell, Irv Nahan, and Elmo Glick, 1959. Glick was pseudonym for Jerry Leiber and Mike Stoller. Recorded by The Drifters (Atlantic).

Dance with Me Henry. w/m Johnny Otis, Hank Ballard, and Etta James, 1955. A new version of the 1954 R&B hit "Work With Me Annie," (q.v.), revised and recorded by Etta James under the title "Wallflower" (Modern). Further confusing the listings and credits, Georgia Gibbs had a hit cover record with the title changed to "Dance With Me Henry (Wallflower)" (Mercury).

Dance Wit' Me. w/m Rick James, 1982. Recorded by Rick James (Gordy).

Dancin' Cowboys. w/m David Bellamy, 1980. Country chart hit by The Bellamy Brothers (Warner Bros.).

Dancin' Fool. w/m Frank Zappa, 1974. Recorded by the Canadian group The Guess Who (RCA). Chart version by Frank Zappa (Zappa), 1979.

Dancing Bear. w/m John Phillips, 1968. Recorded by The Mamas and The Papas (Dunhill).

Dancing Fool. w. Harry B. Smith and Francis Wheeler, m. Ted Snyder, 1922. Popular instrumental record by The Club Royal Orchestra (Victor).

Dancing in the Dark. w/m Bruce Springsteen, 1984. Top 10 record by Bruce Springsteen (Columbia). Not to be confused with standard of the same title.

Dancing in the Dark. w. Howard Dietz, m. Arthur Schwartz, 1931. Sung by John Barker and danced by Tilly Losch in (TM) *The Band Wagon*. It was the title song of and danced by Betsy Drake in (MM) *Dancing in the Dark* in 1949. Fred Astaire and Cyd Charisse danced to it in (MM) *The Band Wagon* in 1953. Artie Shaw and his Orchestra had a million-seller (Victor) in 1941. There is a lyric line: "We're waltzing in the wonder of why we're here," but the song is not a waltz. For a similar case see "Till I Waltz Again With You."

Dancing in the Moonlight. w/m Sherman Kelly, 1972. Top 20 record by the sextet King Harvest (Perception).

Dancing in the Moonlight. w. Gus Kahn, m. Walter Donaldson, 1934. Featured and recorded by Ruth Etting (Brunswick).

Dancing in the Sheets. w. Dean Pitchford, m. Bill Wolfer, 1984. From (MM) *Footloose*. Recorded by the vocal trio Shalamar (Columbia).

Dancing in the Street. w/m William Stevenson and Marvin Gaye, 1964. Hit record by Martha and The Vandellas (Gordy). Later versions by The Mamas and The Papas (Dunhill), 1967; pianist Ramsey Lewis (Cadet), 1967; Top 40 record by Van Halen (Warner Bros.), 1982; Top 10 record, from the Live-Aid Concert, by Mick Jagger and David Bowie (EMI America), 1985.

Dancing Machine. w/m Hal Davis, Donald Fletcher, and Weldon Parks, 1974. Top 10 record by The Jacksons (Motown).

Dancing on a Dime. w. Frank Loesser, m. Burton Lane, 1940. Performed by Grace MacDonald and Robert Paige in (MM) *Dancing on a Dime*.

Dancing on the Ceiling. w/m Lionel Richie and Carlos Rios, 1986. Top 10 record by Lionel Richie (Motown). Not to be confused with the 1930 standard of the same title.

Dancing on the Ceiling. w. Lorenz Hart, m. Richard Rodgers, 1930. Written for the Ed Wynn musical *Simple Simon*, but dropped before the opening. Introduced by Jessie Matthews and Sonnie Hale in London in (TM) *Ever Green*. Matthews sang it in the slightly retitled British film version (MM) *Evergreen*, 1934. Jack Hylton, the British bandleader, had the first popular recording (Victor). The song was heard in the background of the Rodgers and Hart biography (MM) *Words and Music*, 1948.

Dancing Queen. w/m Benny Anderson, Bjorn Ulvaeus, and Stig Anderson, 1977. #1 gold record by the Swedish quartet Abba (Atlantic).

Dancing Tambourine. w. W. C. Polla, 1927. A piano instrumental to which words were added by Phil Ponce. Recorded by Radiolites (Columbia) and Paul Whiteman and his Orchestra (Victor).

Dancing the Devil Away. w. Bert Kalmar and Otto Harbach, m. Harry Ruby, 1927. Introduced by Mary Eaton in (TM) *Lucky*. It was used as a production number in (MM) *The Cuckoos*, starring Wheeler and Woolsey, 1930.

Dancing Time. w. George Grossmith (England), Howard Dietz (U.S.), m. Jerome Kern, 1924. Grossmith wrote the lyrics for the 1922 London musical (TM) *The Cabaret Girl* and Dietz wrote his for the short-lived New York musical (TM) *Dear Sir*.

Dancing under the Stars. w/m Harry Owens, 1936. Introduced and recorded by Harry Owens and his Royal Hawaiian Orchestra (Decca). Also recorded by Nye Mayhew (Vocalion) and Jesse Crawford (Bluebird) and their orchestras.

Dancing with My Shadow. w/m Harry Woods, 1935. Recordings by the bands of the Dorsey Brothers, vocal by Kay Weber (Decca), Henry King (Columbia), Joe Reichman (Melotone).

Dancing with Tears in My Eyes. w. Al Dubin, m. Joe Burke, 1930. Written for the musical motion picture *Dancing Sweeties*. The song was filmed and recorded on the sound track but removed before the final print was made as being "not good enough." It was introduced on radio by Rudy Vallee and recorded by Ruth Etting (Columbia), Nick Lucas (Brunswick), Joe Venuti (Okeh), organist Lew White (Brunswick), and others. It became one of the big hits of the year and a standard.

Dancing Your Memory Away. w/m Eddie Burton and Thomas Grant, 1982. Top 10 Country chart by Charlie McClain (Epic).

Dancin' Man. w/m Vinnie Barrett and Yvonne Gray, 1977. Recorded by Q (Epic).

Dancin' Party. w. Kal Mann, m. Dave Appell, 1962. Hit record in the Twist era by Chubby Checker (Parkway).

Dancin' Shoes. w/m Carl Storie, 1979. Introduced by the Indianapolis quintet, The Faith Band, of which Storie was lead singer (Mercury). Best-selling cover record by Nigel Olsson (Bang).

Dancin' with Someone (Longin' for You). w/m Bennie Benjamin, George David Weiss, and Alex Alstone, 1953. Popular record by Teresa Brewer, with Jack Pleis's Orchestra (Coral).

Dandelion. w/m Mick Jagger and Keith Richards, 1967. Top 20 hit by the British group The Rolling Stones (London).

Dandy. w/m Ray Davies, 1966. Top 10 record by the British group Herman's Hermits (MGM).

Danger! Heartbreak Ahead. w/m Carl Stutz and Nathan C. Barefoot, Jr., 1955. Hit record by Jaye P. Morgan, with Hugo Winterhalter's Orchestra (RCA Victor).

Danger Heartbreak Dead Ahead. w/m Ivy Hunter, Clarence Paul, William Stevenson, 1965. Recorded by The Marvelettes (Tamla).

Danger—Love at Work. w. Mack Gordon, m. Harry Revel, 1937. Introduced by Alice Faye and Louis Prima and his Band in (MM) *You Can't Have Everything*. Later in the same year, it was the title song of (MP) *Danger—Love at Work*, starring Ann Sothern and Jack Haley.

Danger Zone. w/m Giorgio Moroder and Tom Whitlock, 1986. Introduced by Kenny Loggins on the soundtrack of (MP) *Top Gun* and his Top 10 single (Columbia).

Dangling Conversation, The. w/m Paul Simon, 1966. Featured and recorded by Simon and Garfunkel (Columbia).

Dangling on a String (You've Got Me). w/m Ronald Dunbar and Edythe Wayne, 1970. Top 40 record by the vocal group Chairmen of the Board (Invictus).

Dang Me. w/m Roger Miller, 1964. Novelty hit, introduced and recorded by Roger Miller

(Smash). Winner Grammy Award (NARAS) for Best Country and Western Song.

Daniel. w/m Elton John and Bernie Taupin, 1973. Top 10 U.S. record by the British singer Elton John (MCA).

Danke Schoen. w. Milt Gabler (Engl.), Kurt Schwabach (Ger.), m. Bert Kaempfert, 1963. German song. Popularized in the U.S. by Wayne Newton (Capitol).

Danny Boy. w/m Frederick Edward Weatherly, 1913. Adapted from the traditional Irish "Londonderry Air," *c.* 1855. Featured in concerts and recorded by the operatic contralto Ernestine Schumann-Heink (Victor). Among hit recordings: instrumental by Glenn Miller and his Orchestra (Bluebird), 1940; Conway Twitty (MGM), 1959; Andy Williams (Columbia), 1961; Patti LaBelle and The Blue Belles (Parkway), 1965; Ray Price (Columbia), 1967.

Danny Deever. w. Rudyard Kipling, m. Walter Damrosch, 1897. A concert song. Damrosch's music was set to the popular poem of Kipling.

Danny's Song. w/m Kenny Loggins, 1973. Written by Loggins for his young nephew, the song was a Top 10 record for the Canadian singer Anne Murray (Capitol).

Dansero. w. Sol Parker, m. Richard Hayman and Elliot Daniels, 1953. Leading instrumental recordings by Richard Hayman (Mercury) and Urbie Green (Blue Note).

Dapper Dan (the Sheik of Alabam'). w. Lew Brown, m. Albert Von Tilzer, 1921. Featured and recorded by Frank Crumit (Columbia).

Dardanella. w. Fred Fisher, m. Felix Bernard and Johnny S. Black, 1919. Originally a piano rag entitled "Turkish Tom Tom" by Black. Fisher, as publisher, wrote a lyric with a new title, after which Bernard claimed that it was his melody. A settlement was made and both composers received title credit. Ben Selvin's Novelty Orchestra recorded it (Victor) and sold over a million copies, while the sheet music sales were even more. The song was

heard in (MM) *Two Girls and a Sailor*, 1944, and then in the Fisher screen bio (MM) *Oh, You Beautiful Doll*, 1949.

Dare Me. w/m Sam Lorber and Dave Innis, 1985. Recorded by The Pointer Sisters (RCA).

Dark as a Dungeon. w/m Merle Travis, 1947. Introduced and recorded by Merle Travis (Capitol).

Darkest Street in Town. w/m Howard Greenfield and Kenny Karen, 1963. Recorded by Jimmy Clanton (Ace).

Dark Hollow. w/m Bill Browning, 1959. C&W chart record by Luke Gordon (Island). Cover and Top 10 version by Jimmie Skinner (Mercury).

Dark Horse. w/m George Harrison, 1974. Top 10 hit, written and recorded in England by George Harrison (Apple).

Dark Is the Night. w. Sammy Cahn, m. Nicholas Brodsky, 1951. Introduced by Jane Powell in (MM) *Rich, Young and Pretty*.

Dark Lady. w/m John Durrill, 1974. #1 gold record by Cher (MCA).

Dark Moon. w/m Ned Miller, 1957. Leading recordings by Bonnie Guitar (Dot) and Gale Storm (Dot).

Darkness, Darkness. w/m Jesse Colin Young, 1970. Recorded by The Youngbloods (RCA).

(When It's) Darkness on the Delta. w. Marty Symes and Al Neiburg, m. Jerry Livingston, 1933. Livingston's first hit. Introduced by Mildred Bailey. Among recordings: Isham Jones (Victor), Ted Fio Rito (Brunswick), Del Lampe (Crown), Chick Bullock (Melotone), Dukes of Dixieland (Okeh).

Darktown Strutters' Ball, The. w/m Shelton Brooks, 1917. A classic in the ragtime idiom, popularized by Sophie Tucker in vaudeville. Fred Astaire and Ginger Rogers performed it in (MM) *The Story of Vernon and Irene Castle*, 1937. It was also interpolated in

(MM) *Broadway*, 1942; the Texas Guinan film bio (MM) *Incendiary Blonde*, 1944; (MM) *The Dolly Sisters*, 1946; and (MM) *Little Boy Lost*, 1953.

Darlene. w/m Mike Geiger, Woody Mullis, and Ricky Rector, 1988. #1 Country record by T. Graham Brown (Capitol).

Darlin'. w/m Brian Wilson and Mike Love, 1968. Top 20 record by The Beach Boys (Capitol). Revived by Paul Davis, featuring Susan Collins (Bang), 1978, and the group Yipes!! (Millennium), 1980.

Darlin' Darlin' Baby (Sweet, Tender Love). w/m Kenny Gamble and Leon Huff, 1977. #1 R&B chart record by The O'Jays (Philadelphia International).

Darling, Je Vous Aime, Beaucoup. w/m Anna Sosenko, 1935. Introduced, recorded (Columbia), and used as a theme song by Hildegarde, the singer-pianist. Simone Simone sang it in (MM) *Love and Hisses*, 1938. Nat Cole had a hit single (Capitol), 1955.

Darling, Not Without You. w. Edward Heyman and Al Sherman, m. Abner Silver, 1936. Featured and recorded by Dolly Dawn (Bluebird) and the bands of Ted Weems, vocal by Perry Como (Decca); Artie Shaw, vocal by Peg La Centra (Brunswick); Red Allen (Vocalion); Ruby Newman (Victor).

Darling, You Know I Wouldn't Lie. w/m Wayne Kemp and Red Lane, 1969. Top 10 Country chart record by Conway Twitty (Decca).

Darling Baby. w/m Brian Holland, Eddie Holland, and Lamont Dozier, 1966. Recorded by The Elgins (V.I.P.).

Darling Be Home Soon. w/m John Sebastian, 1967. Sung on the soundtrack of (MP) *You're A Big Boy Now*, 1966, by The Lovin' Spoonful and on their 1967 Top 20 hit (Kama Sutra).

Darling Sue. w. Andrew B. Sterling, m. Harry Von Tilzer, 1907.

Darn It Baby, That's Love. w/m Joan Edwards and Lynn Duddy, 1950. Introduced by

Bill Norvas and Phyllis Cameron in (TM) *Tickets Please*. Recordings: Arthur Godfrey and Janette Davis (Columbia), Tony Martin and Fran Warren (RCA Victor).

Darn That Dream. w. Eddie DeLange, m. James Van Heusen, 1939. A successful song from an unsuccessful musical (TM) *Swingin' the Dream*, based on *A Midsummer Night's Dream*. It was introduced by Maxine Sullivan, Louis Armstrong, Bill Bailey, the Dandridge Sisters (including Dorothy), the Rhythmettes, and the Deep River Boys. Among recordings: Benny Goodman, vocal by Mildred Bailey (Columbia); Tommy Dorsey, vocal by Anita Boyer (Victor); Paul Whiteman, vocal by Joan Edwards and the Modernaires (Decca); Miles Davis (Capitol); Erskine Butterfield (Decca); Don Elliot (Savoy).

Das Sweet Dreamer. w/m Des Parton, 1975. Top 20 record from England by the octet Sweet Sensation (PYE).

Datin'. w/m Fred Wise and Randy Starr, 1966. Introduced by Elvis Presley and Donna Butterworth in (MM) *Paradise, Hawaiian Style*. Recorded by Presley in two albums (RCA).

Daughter of Darkness. w/m Les Reed and Geoff Stephens, 1970. Recorded in England, Top 20 on the U.S. charts by Tom Jones (Parrot).

Daughter of Rosie O'Grady, The. w. Monty C. Brice, m. Walter Donaldson, 1918. Introduced at the Palace Theatre by Pat Rooney. The son of the famed vaudevillian of an earlier period was associated with the song for half a century. He accompanied his singing of it with a waltz clog. Gordon MacRae sang it in (MM) *The Daughter of Rosie O'Grady*, 1950.

Davenport Blues. m. Leon "Bix" Beiderbecke, 1925. A favorite band blues recorded first by Bix and His Rhythm Jugglers (Gennett) and subsequently by such as Red Nichols's Charleston Chasers (Columbia); Jimmy McPartland, with Marian McPartland on piano (Prestige); Adrian Rollini (Decca); Bunny Berigan (Victor); Tommy Dorsey (Victor).

Davey Jones' Locker. w/m H. W. Petrie, 1901.

Dawn. w. Robert Stolz, m. Herbert Stothart, 1927. Introduced by Louise Hunter and Paul Gregory in (TM) *Golden Dawn.* Featured and recorded by James Melton (Columbia).

Dawn (Go Away). w/m Bob Gaudio and Sandy Linzer, 1964. Top 10 record by The Four Seasons (Philips).

Dawn of Correction. w/m Raymond Gilmore, John Madara, and David White, 1965. Answer to "Eve of Destruction." Recorded by The Spokesman, the trio who wrote the song (Decca).

Day After Day. w/m William Peter Ham, 1972. Gold record by the British quartet Badfinger (Apple).

Day After Day. w. Bud Green, m. Richard Himber, 1938. Introduced and recorded by Richard Himber and his Orchestra (Victor). Also featured and recorded by Barry Wood (Brunswick).

Day After Day (It's Slippin' Away). w/m Stuart Margolin, Thomas Reynolds, and Jerry Riopelle, 1969. Recorded by Shango (A&M).

Day After Forever, The. w. Johnny Burke, m. James Van Heusen, 1944. Introduced by Bing Crosby and Jean Heather in (MM) *Going My Way.* Crosby had a popular record (Decca) as did Andy Russell (Capitol).

Day Before Spring, The. w. Alan Jay Lerner, m. Frederick Loewe, 1945. Introduced by Irene Manning in (TM) *The Day Before Spring.*

Daybreak. w/m Barry Manilow and Adrienne Anderson, 1977. Recorded by Barry Manilow (Arista).

Daybreak. w. Harold Adamson, m. Ferde Grofé, 1942. Based on the "Mardi Gras" theme from Grofé's *Mississippi Suite.* Kathryn Grayson sang it in (MM) *Thousands Cheer,* 1943. Most popular records by Tommy Dorsey, vocal by Frank Sinatra (Victor); Harry James, vocal by Johnny McAfee (Columbia); Jimmy Dorsey, vocal by Bob Eberly (Decca). Revived 1955, by Al Hibbler, arranged and conducted by Jack Pleis (Decca).

Daybreak. See **Storybook Children.**

Daybreak Express. m. Edward Kennedy "Duke" Ellington, 1934. Featured by Ellington's Orchestra.

Day by Day. w/m Rob Hyman, Eric Bazilian, and Rick Chertoff, 1986. Recorded by the quintet The Hooters (Columbia).

Day by Day. w. John-Michael Tebelak, m. Stephen Schwartz, 1971. Introduced by Robin Lamont and company in the off-Broadway hit that moved to Broadway (TM) *Godspell.* Their single, taken from the cast album, made the Top 20 (Bell). Lamont and company also performed it in (MM) *Godspell,* 1974.

Day by Day. w. Sammy Cahn, m. Paul Weston and Axel Stordahl, 1946. Recorded by Frank Sinatra, with Axel Stordahl's Orchestra (Columbia); Jo Stafford, with Paul Weston's Orchestra; Les Brown, vocal by Doris Day (Day by Day by Day!) (Columbia); Bing Crosby and Mel Tormé, with the Mel-Tones (Decca).

Daydream. w/m John B. Sebastian, 1966. Hit record by The Lovin' Spoonful, of which Sebastian was lead singer, guitarist, and harmonicist (Kama Sutra).

Daydream Believer. w/m John Stewart, 1967. #1 gold record by The Monkees (Colgems). Revived by Anne Murray (Capitol), 1980.

Day Dreaming. w/m Aretha Franklin, 1972. Top 10 record by Aretha Franklin (Atlantic).

Day Dreaming. w. Gus Kahn, m. Jerome Kern, 1941. Gus Kahn's last published song, and a rare case of a non-production song by Kern. It received great exposure by being coupled with Glenn Miller's million-selling instrumental, "A String of Pearls" (Bluebird).

Day Dreaming All Night Long. w. Johnny Mercer, m. Harry Warren, 1938. Sung by

Rudy Vallee and Rosemary Lane in (MM) *Gold Diggers in Paris.*

Day Dreams. w. Robert B. Smith, m. Heinrich Reinhardt, 1910. From (TM) *The Spring Maid.*

Day Dreams Come True at Night. w/m Dick Jurgens 1940. Theme song of Dick Jurgens and his Orchestra. Recorded by Jurgens (Vocalion) and Shep Fields and his Orchestra (Bluebird).

Day for Decision. w/m Allen N. Peltier, 1966. Spoken by Johnny Sea (Warner Bros.).

Day I Let You Get Away, The. w/m Tot Seymour, Vee Lawnhurst, and Boyd Bunch, 1936. Recorded by Isham Jones, vocal by Woody Herman (Decca); Tommy Dorsey's Clambake Seven, vocal by Edythe Wright (Victor); Jack Shilkret (Brunswick).

Day-In Day-Out. w/m David Bowie, 1987. Chart record by David Bowie (EMI America).

Day In—Day Out. w. Johnny Mercer, m. Rube Bloom, 1939. #1 hit, ten weeks on "Your Hit Parade" and a favorite with the big bands. Among recordings: Bob Crosby (Decca), Tommy Dorsey (Victor), Artie Shaw (Bluebird), Al Donahue (Vocalion). Tony Martin had a well-received vocal version (Decca).

Day in the Life of a Fool, A. w. Carl Sigman (Engl.), Antonio Mariz (Port.), m. Luiz Bonfa, 1966. English version of "Manha de Carnaval" from (MM) *Black Orpheus,* 1959. This version was popularized by Jack Jones (Kapp).

Day into Night. w/m Don Gibson, 1962. Top 10 C&W chart record by Kitty Wells (Decca).

Day Is Done. w/m Peter Yarrow, 1969. Top 40 record by Peter, Paul, and Mary (Warner Bros.).

Day-O. See **Banana Boat Song, The.**

Day of Jubilo. w/m Terry Gilkyson, 1952. Recorded by Guy Mitchell, with Mitch Miller's Orchestra (Columbia).

Days Gone By. w. Sheldon Harnick, m. Jerry Bock, 1963. Introduced by Ludwig Donath and Daniel Massey in (TM) *She Loves Me.*

Days Gone Down (Still Got the Light in Your Eyes). w/m Gerry Rafferty, 1979. Recorded by the Scottish-born Gerry Rafferty (United Artists).

Days of Sand and Shovels, The. w/m Doyle Marsh and George Reneau, 1969. Top 40 record by Bobby Vinton (Epic).

Days of the Waltz, The. w. Will Holt (Engl.), m. Jacques Brel, 1964. An English version of a Brel song, introduced and featured by Felicia Sanders. See also "Carousel."

Days of Wine and Roses. w. Johnny Mercer, m. Henry Mancini, 1962. Sung under the titles in (MP) *Days of Wine and Roses.* Academy Award winner, 1962. Leading recordings by Andy Williams (Columbia) and Henry Mancini and his Orchestra (RCA). Grammy Award (NARAS) winner Song of the Year, 1963.

Day That You Grew Colder, The. w/m Paul Dresser, 1905.

Day the Rains Came, The. w. Carl Sigman (Engl.), Pierre Delanoe (Fr.), m. Gilbert Becaud, 1958. Introduced in France by Gilbert Becaud as "Le Jour ou la Pluie Viendra." Popular U.S. releases by Jane Morgan (Kapp) and, instrumentally, Raymond Lefevre and his Orchestra (Kapp).

Day the World Stood Still, The. w/m Jerry Foster and Bill Rice, 1968. Top 10 C&W chart record by Charley Pride (RCA).

Daytime Friends. w/m Ben Peters, 1977. Recorded by Kenny Rogers (United Artists).

Day Tripper. w/m John Lennon and Paul McCartney, 1965. Hit record by The Beatles (Capitol). Other chart versions by pianist Ramsey Lewis (Cadet), 1967, and Anne Murray (Capitol), 1975.

Day You Came Along, The. w/m Arthur Johnston and Sam Coslow, 1933. Sung by Bing Crosby in (MM) *Too Much Harmony.* His record was a best-seller. Other recordings by Irving Aaronson and his Commanders (Vocalion); Meyer Davis (Columbia); Victor Young, vocal by Scrappy Lambert (Brunswick); Will Osborne (Melotone); Conrad Thibault (Victor).

Dazz. w/m Reggie Hargis, Eddie Irons, and Ray Ransom, 1976. #1 R&B and #3 Pop chart record by the disco group Brick (Bang). Title is combination of "dance" and "jazz."

Deacon Blues. w/m Walter Becker and Donald Fagen, 1978. Recorded by the group Steely Dan (ABC).

Deacon Jones. w/m Johnny Lange, Hy Heath, and Richard Loring, 1943. Recorded by the Pied Pipers (Capitol) and Louis Jordan and his Band (Decca). Featured in (MM) *Hi Good Lookin'*, 1944, and by Jordan in (MM) *Meet Miss Bobby Socks*, 1944.

Deacon's Hop. m. Cecil J. McNeely, 1949. Instrumental hit by the saxophonist/composer Big Jay McNeely and Band (Savoy).

Dead End Street. w. Ben Raleigh, m. David Axelrod, 1967. Top 40 record by Lou Rawls (Capitol).

Dead Giveaway. w/m Joey Gallo, Marquis Dair, and Leon Sylvers, 1983. Recorded by the trio Shalamar (Solar).

Dead Man's Curve. w/m Jan Berry, Roger Christian, Artie Kornfeld, and Brian Wilson, 1964. Top 10 record by Jan and Dean (Liberty).

Dead Skunk. w/m Loudon Wainwright III, 1973. Top 20 record by Loudon Wainwright III (Columbia).

Dear, On a Night Like This. w. Irving Caesar, m. Con Conrad, 1928.

Dear Eloise. w/m Allan Clarke, Tony Hicks, and Graham Nash, 1967. Written by three members of the British group, the Hollies, which had a chart record (Epic).

Dearest (You're the Nearest to My Heart). w. Benny Davis, m. Harry Akst, 1923. Featured and recorded by Nora Bayes (Columbia) and Paul Whiteman and his Orchestra (Victor).

Dearest, Darest I?. w. Johnny Burke, m. James Van Heusen, 1940. Introduced by Eddie "Rochester" Anderson in (MM) *Love Thy Neighbor*, starring Jack Benny and Fred Allen. Recorded by Ray McKinley, with Will Bradley's Orchestra (Columbia).

Dear Eyes That Haunt Me. w. Harry B. Smith, m. Emmerich Kallman, 1927. From (TM) *The Circus Princess*.

Dear Friend. w. Sheldon Harnick, m. Jerry Bock, 1963. Introduced by Barbara Cook in (TM) *She Loves Me*.

Dear God. w/m Andy Partridge, 1987. Popularity achieved via track being added to later pressings of the album "Skylarking" by the British group XTC (Geffen).

Dear Heart. w. Jay Livingston and Ray Evans, m. Henry Mancini, 1964. Title song from (MP) *Dear Heart*. Popular recordings by Andy Williams (Columbia), Jack Jones (Kapp), Henry Mancini, with chorus and Orchestra (RCA).

Dear Hearts and Gentle People. w. Bob Hilliard, m. Sammy Fain, 1950. The title derived from a note in Stephen Foster's handwriting, found in his pocket after his death. Bing Crosby had a million-seller (Decca) and Dinah Shore (Columbia) and Gordon MacRae (Capitol) also had popular versions. The song was on "Your Hit Parade" for fifteen weeks.

Dearie. w/m Bob Hilliard and David Mann, 1950. Popularized by the recording of Ray Bolger and Ethel Merman, accompanied by Sy Oliver's Orchestra (Decca). Other chart versions by Guy Lombardo and his Orchestra (Decca); Jo Stafford and Gordon MacRae (Capitol).

Dearie. w/m Clare Kummer. 1905. Introduced by Sallie Fisher in (TM) *Sergeant Brue*.

Dear Ivan. w/m Jimmy Dean, 1962. Spoken by Jimmy Dean (Columbia).

Dear John. w/m Aubrey Gass and Tex Ritter, 1951. Recorded by Hank Williams, coupled with "Cold, Cold Heart" (MGM).

Dear John Letter, A. w/m Billy Barton, Fuzzy Owen, and Lewis Talley, 1953. Leading records by Jean Shepard (Capitol) and Pat O'Day and the Four Horseman (MGM).

Dear Lady Twist. w/m Frank J. Guida, 1962. Top 10 record by Gary U.S. Bonds (Legrand).

Dear Little Boy. See **Dear Little Girl**.

Dear Little Boy of Mine. J. Keirn Brennan, m. Ernest R. Ball, 1918.

Dear Little Cafe. w/m Noël Coward, 1929. Evelyn Laye and Gerald Nodin sang this in the New York production of (TM) *Bitter Sweet*, after Peggy Wood and Georges Metaxa had introduced it in the London production. In the 1933 British film version (MM) *Bitter Sweet*, it was sung by Anna Neagle and Fernand Gravet; in the 1940 U.S. version, by Jeanette MacDonald and Nelson Eddy.

Dear Little Girl. w. Ira Gershwin, m. George Gershwin, 1926. Introduced by Oscar Shaw and Gertrude Lawrence in (TM) *Oh, Kay!* Julie Andrews and Daniel Massey sang it as "Dear Little Boy" in (MM) *Star!*, 1968.

Dear Lonely Hearts. w/m Bob Halley and Emil Anton, 1962. Featured and recorded by Nat "King" Cole (Capitol).

Dear Lover. w/m Carl Davis and Gerald Sims, 1965. Recorded by Mary Wells (Atco).

Dearly Beloved. w. Johnny Mercer, m. Jerome Kern, 1942. Fred Astaire and Rita Hayworth sang (Nan Wynn dubbed voice on soundtrack for Hayworth) and danced this, backed by Xavier Cugat's Orchestra in (MM) *You Were Never Lovelier*. Nominated for Academy Award. Leading recordings by Dinah Shore (Victor); Glenn Miller, vocal by Skip Nelson (Victor); Alvino Rey, vocal by Bill Schallen (Bluebird).

Dear Mom. w/m Maury Coleman Harris, 1941 A serviceman's letter home in the early days of World War II. Introduced and recorded by Sammy Kaye, vocal by Allan Foster (Victor).

Dear Mr. Jesus. w/m R. Klender, 1986. Recorded by the evangelical youth chorus, PowerSource, featuring the solo voice of six-year-old Sharon Batts (PowerSource).

Dear Okie. w/m Doye O'Dell and Rudy Scooter, 1948. Introduced and recorded by Doye O'Dell (Exclusive) and covered by Jack Rivers (Capitol).

Dear Old Broadway. w. Jesse L. Lasky, m. Charles Berton, 1909.

Dear Old Girl. w. Richard Henry Buck, m. Theodore F. Morse, 1903. Huge sheet music scale in first two years of publication, and popular recordings by J.W. Myers (Columbia), the Haydn Quartet (Victor), Harry MacDonough (Edison). Revived by Arthur Godfrey (Columbia) in the fifties.

Dear Old Pal of Mine. w. Harold Robe, m. Lt. Gitz Rice, 1918. Recorded by John McCormack (Victor).

Dear Old Rose. w. Jack Drislane, m. George W. Meyer, 1912.

Dear Old Southland. w. Henry Creamer, m. Turner Layton, 1921. Adaptation of the Negro spiritual "Deep River." Recorded by Paul Whiteman (Victor) and Vernon Dalhart (Edison Amberol).

Dear Old Stockholm. m. Stan Getz, 1951. Jazz instrumental recorded by Stan Getz (Roost); Miles Davis (Blue Note).

Dear One. w/m John Lawrence Finneran and Vincent Finneran, 1962. Popular record by Larry Finnegan (a.k.a. Finneran) (Old Town).

Dear Prudence. w/m John Lennon and Paul McCartney, 1968. Introduced by The Beatles in their "White Album" (Apple). Recorded by the Five Stairsteps (Buddah), 1970, and Katfish (Big Tree), 1975.

Dear Uncle Sam. w/m Loretta Lynn, 1966. Hit country record by Loretta Lynn (Decca).

Dear World. w/m Jerry Herman, 1969. Introduced by Angela Lansbury and company in (TM) *Dear World*.

Death of Floyd Collins, The. w. Andrew Jenkins, m. Irene Spain, 1925. Ballad of the young cave explorer who was trapped in a Kentucky cave. Recorded by Vernon Dalhart (Victor) (Columbia) (Edison Amberol).

Death of Hank Williams, The. w/m Jack Cardwell, 1953. Top 10 C&W record by Jack Cardwell (King).

Death of Little Kathy Fiscus, The. w/m Jimmy Osborne, 1949. C&W chart song by Jimmy Osborne (King).

Deceivin' Blues. w/m Johnny Otis, 1950. R&B hit by Little Esther, Mel Walker, and Johnny Otis (Savoy).

December and May (or, Mollie Newell Don't Be Cruel). w. Edward B. Marks, m. William Lorraine, 1893. Introduced by Lydia Yeamans at Tony Pastor's in New York City.

December 1963 (Oh, What a Night). w/m Bob Gaudio and Judy Parker, 1976. #1 gold record by the Four Seasons, lead vocal by Gerri Polci (Warner Bros.).

Deck of Cards, The. w/m T. Texas Tyler, 1948, 1959. Introduced and recorded by T. Texas Tyler (4 Star). Best-selling record by Phil Harris (RCA Victor). Revived with hit recording, recited by Wink Martindale (Dot).

Declaration. w. Kenn Long, m. Long and Jim Crozier, 1970. Sung by the company in the off-Broadway musical (TM) *Touch*.

Decoration Day. See **I Was Looking for My Boy, She Said.**

Dede Dinah. w. Bob Marcucci, m. Peter De Angelis, 1958. First hit record by Frankie Avalon (Chancellor).

Dedicated Follower of Fashion. w/m Ray Davies, 1966. Recorded by the British group The Kinks (Reprise).

Dedicated to the One I Love. w/m Lowman Pauling and Ralph Bass, 1961, 1967. First recorded by The Shirelles (Scepter), 1959. Their record was re-released in 1961 and became a Top 10 hit. #2 hit by The Mamas and The Papas in 1967 (Dunhill). Bernadette Peters had a chart version (MCA), 1981.

Dedicated to You. w/m Sammy Cahn, Saul Chaplin, and Hy Zaret, 1937. Zaret's first song success. Featured and recorded by Andy Kirk, vocal by Pha Terrell (Decca).

Dedication Song, The. w/m Russ Reagan, 1966. Recorded by Freddy Cannon (Swan).

De Do Do Do, De Da Da Da. w/m Gordon "Sting" Sumner, 1980. Top 10 record by the English-formed trio Police (A&M).

'Deed I Do. w. Walter Hirsch, m. Fred Rose, 1926. Johnny Marvin (Victor) had the first record of this standard. Among those who followed were: Jack Teagarden (Capitol); Bunny Berigan (Victor); Ruth Etting (Columbia); Lena Horne (MGM); Ben Pollack (Victor); Charlie Barnet, vocal by Mary Ann McCall (Bluebird); Tommy Dorsey, vocal by Edythe Wright (Victor).

Deep Blue. w/m George Harrison, 1971. Recorded by George Harrison (Apple).

Deep Down Inside. w. Carolyn Leigh, m. Cy Coleman, 1962. Introduced in (TM) *Little Me* by Sid Caesar, Virginia Martin, Mickey Deems, and chorus.

Deeper Love. w/m Diane Warren, 1987. Introduced by Meli'sa Morgan on the soundtrack of (MP) *The Golden Child*, the soundtrack album, and single record (Capitol).

Deeper Than the Night. w/m Tom Snow and John Vastano, 1979. Recorded by Olivia Newton-John (MCA).

Deep Forest. w. Andy Razaf, m. Reginald Forsythe and Earl Hines, 1933. Introduced and used as theme by Earl Hines and his Orchestra (Bluebird). Also featured on radio and recorded by Paul Whiteman and his Orchestra, with solo by harpist Caspar Reardon (Victor).

Deep in a Dream. w. Eddie DeLange, m. James Van Heusen, 1938. Steady air play plus recordings by Connie Boswell, with Woody Herman's Orchestra (Decca); Cab Calloway (Vocalion); Bob Crosby, vocal by Marion Mann (Decca); Skinnay Ennis (Victor); and others helped make this a "Hit Parader" for fourteen weeks.

Deep in My Heart. w. Zelda Sears, m. Vincent Youmans, 1924. Introduced by Leonard Ceeley and Irene Dunne in (TM) *Lollipop*.

Deep in My Heart, Dear. w. Dorothy Donnelly, m. Sigmund Romberg, 1924. Introduced by Howard Marsh and Ilse Marvenga in (TM) *The Student Prince*. In the 1954 film version of the operetta (MM) *The Student Prince*, Mario Lanza, dubbing for Edmund Purdom, sang and recorded it (Victor). It was also featured throughout the screen biography of Romberg (MM) *Deep in My Heart*, 1954.

Deep Inside My Heart. w/m Randy Meisner and Eric Kaz, 1980. Recorded by Randy Meisner, vocal background by Kim Carnes (Epic).

Deep in the Heart of Texas w. June Hershey, m. Don Swander, 1941. An audience participation song, with four handclaps coming every eighth bar, starting with the fourth bar, it was on "Your Hit Parade," commencing early 1942, for twelve weeks, five times in the # 1 position. Best-selling recordings by Alvino Rey, vocal by Skeets Hurfurt and Bill Schallen (Bluebird); and Horace Heidt and his Orchestra (Columbia). The song has been heard in many films. Among them: (MM) *I'll Get By*, sung by Dennis Day, 1950; (MM) *Rich, Young and Pretty*, sung by Wendell Corey in French, 1951; (MM) *With a Song in My Heart*, dubbed by Jane Froman for Susan Hayward portraying Froman, 1952; (MP) *The Teahouse of the August Moon*, sung by Glenn Ford, Eddie Albert, and Marlon Brando, 1957; (MM) *Texas Carnival*, 1959.

Deep in Your Eyes. w. William LeBaron, m. Victor Jacobi, 1920. Introduced by Joseph Santley and Ivy Sawyer in (TM) *The Half Moon*. Recorded by Prince's Orchestra (Columbia) and Lucy Isabelle Marsh (Victor).

Deep Night. w. Rudy Vallee, m. Charlie Henderson, 1929. One of Vallee's earliest hits (Victor) as a singing (crooning) bandleader. Gogi Grant, dubbing for Ann Blyth in the title role, sang it in (MM) *The Helen Morgan Story*, 1957.

Deep Purple. w/m Ritchie Blackmore, Roger Glover, and Ian Gillan, 1985. Written by members of the British band Deep Purple (Mercury).

Deep Purple. w. Mitchell Parish, m. Peter DeRose, 1934, 1939, 1963. Written and first published as a piano composition and introduced orchestrally by Paul Whiteman and his Orchestra, a year later. Parish added the lyrics in 1939 and the song reached the #1 position on "Your Hit Parade," with top records by Larry Clinton, vocal by Bea Wain (Victor); and Bing Crosby (Decca). Doris Rhodes, who had her own radio show emanating from New York, used it as her theme song and billed herself as "The Deep Purple Girl." Billy Ward had a Top 40 record (Liberty), 1957; Nino Tempo and April Stevens had a #1 version (Atco), 1963; Donny and Marie Osmond had a hit (MGM), 1976. Andre De Shields and company sang it in the Mitchell Parish musical (TM) *Stardust*, 1987.

Deep River. w/m Henry Thacker Burleigh, 1917. This was really an arrangement based on a traditional Negro spiritual from the second half of the nineteenth century. Among the major recordings were those by Paul Robeson (Victor); Sy Oliver's arrangement for Tommy Dorsey's band on a 12″ 78 rpm (Victor); Morton Gould's orchestra (Decca); Ezio Pinza (Columbia).

Deep Song. w. Douglas Cross, m. George Cory, 1947. Featured and recorded by Billie Holiday (Decca).

Déjà Vu. w. Adrienne Anderson, m. Isaac Hayes, 1979. Recorded by Dionne Warwick (Arista).

Delaware. w/m Irving Gordon, 1960. Featured and recorded by Perry Como (RCA).

Delicado. w. Jack Lawrence, m. Waldyr Azevedo, 1952. Percy Faith and his Orchestra's instrumental version was a #1 hit (Columbia). Stan Kenton (Capitol), Ralph Flanagan (RCA Victor), and their bands also had chart records. Leading vocal release by Dinah Shore (RCA Victor).

Delilah. w/m Les Reed and Barry Mason, 1968. Hit record, recorded in England by Tom Jones (Parrot).

Delilah. w. Jimmy Shirl, m. Henry Manners, 1941. Introduced and recorded by Glenn Miller, vocal by Tex Beneke and the Modernaires with Paula Kelly (Bluebird).

Delilah Jones. w. Sylvia Fine, m. Elmer Bernstein, 1956. Based on a musical theme from (MP) *The Man with the Golden Arm.* Leading record by The McGuire Sisters (Coral). See also **Man with the Golden Arm, The.**

Delirious. w/m Prince Rogers Nelson, 1983. Top 10 record by Prince (Warner Bros.).

Delishious. w. Ira Gershwin, m. George Gershwin, 1931. Sung by Raul Roulien in (MM) *Delicious.* This was the first Gershwin score written directly for a movie musical.

Delta Dawn. w/m Alex Harvey and Larry Collins, 1972. First recording by Tanya Tucker (Columbia). Helen Reddy had a #1 gold record version (Capitol), 1973.

Delta Lady. w/m Leon Russell, 1969. Recorded by Joe Cocker (A&M).

Denise. w/m Neil Levenson, 1963. Recorded by Randy and The Rainbows (Rust).

Dennis the Menace. w/ Dick Manning, m. Al Hoffman, 1952. Based on the comic strip character. Recorded by Rosemary Clooney and Jimmy Boyd (Columbia).

Den of Iniquity. w. Lorenz Hart, m. Richard Rodgers, 1940. Introduced by Vivienne Segal and Gene Kelly in (TM) *Pal Joey.*

Dependin' on You. w/m Michael McDonald and Pat Simmons, 1979. Recorded by The Doobie Brothers, the group of which the writers were members (Warner Bros.).

De Rainbow Road. w. Edward Harrigan, m. David Braham, 1891.

Der Fuehrer's Face. w/m Oliver Wallace, 1942. From the cartoon film (MM) *Donald Duck in Nutsy Land.* Novelty hit by Spike Jones and his City Slickers, vocal by Carl Grayson and Willie Spicer (Bluebird). A lampoon of Hitler, the record featured a Bronx cheer, or raspberry, at each mention of the dictator.

Der Kommissar. w. Falco (Ger.), Andrew Piercy (Engl.), m. Robert Ponger, 1983. Top 10 record by the Piercy-led English band After the Fire (Epic).

Dern Ya. w/m Roger Miller and Justin Tubb, 1964. Answer song to "Dang Me" (q.v.). C&W chart record by Ruby Wright (Rik).

Desert Moon. w/m Dennis De Young, 1984. Top 10 record by Dennis De Young (A&M).

Desert Song, The. w. Otto Harbach and Oscar Hammerstein II, m. Sigmund Romberg, 1926. Sung by Robert Halliday and Vivienne Segal in (TM) *The Desert Song.* It was sung in the three movie versions of (MM) *The Desert Song*: in 1929 by John Boles and Carlotta King; in 1943 by Dennis Morgan and Irene Manning; and in 1953 by Gordon MacRae and Kathryn Grayson.

Desifinado. w. Newton Mendonça, m. Antonio Carlos Jobim, 1962. Brazilian instrumental popularized in the U.S. by tenor saxophonist Stan Getz and guitarist Charlie Byrd (Verve). See "Slightly Out of Tune."

Desire. w. Paul "Bono" Hewson, m. U2, 1988. Introduced by the Irish group, U2, on the soundtrack of (MP) *Rattle and Hum*, the album and single (Island).

Desire. w/m Barry Gibb, Maurice Gibb, and Robin Gibb, 1980. Top 10 record by Andy Gibb (RSO).

Desiree. w/m Neil Diamond, 1978. Top 20 record by Neil Diamond (Columbia).

Desperado. w/m Don Henley and Glenn Frey, 1973. Title song of the album by the Eagles (Asylum). Top 10 Country chart record by Johnny Rodriguez (Mercury), 1977.

Desperadoes Waiting for a Train. w/m Guy Clark, 1973. Introduced by Tom Rush in his album "Ladies Love Outlaws" (Columbia). Revived by Waylon Jennings, Willie Nelson, Johnny Cash, and Kris Kristofferson in the album "Highwayman," from which a Country chart single emerged (Columbia).

Desperado Love. w/m Michael Garvin and Sammy Johns, 1986. #1 Country chart record by Conway Twitty (Warner Bros.).

Destination Moon. w. Roy Alfred, m. Marvin Fisher, 1951. Featured and recorded by Nat "King" Cole (Capitol).

Detour. w/m Paul Westmoreland, 1945. Popular C&W song, with many recordings, revived by Patti Page, 1951 (Mercury).

Detour Ahead. w/m Herb Ellis, Lou Carter, and John Frigo, 1949. Featured and recorded by Billie Holiday (Aladdin); Woody Herman, vocal by Mary Ann McCall (Capitol).

Detroit City. w/m Mel Tillis and Danny Dill, 1963. C&W hit introduced by Bobby Bare (RCA). Grammy Award winner (NARAS) Country Song of the Year. Welsh singer Tom Jones had a London-recorded hit version (Parrot), 1967.

Detroit Rock City. w/m Paul Stanley and Bob Ezrin, 1976. Recorded by the group Kiss (Casablanca).

Devil in Disguise. See **You're the Devil in Disguise.**

Devil Inside. w/m Andrew Farriss and Michael Hutchence, 1988. Recorded by the Australian group INXS (Atlantic).

Devil in the Bottle. w/m Bobby David, 1975. Recorded by T. G. Sheppard (Melodyland).

Devil May Care. w. Johnny Burke, m. Harry Warren, 1940. Best-selling records by Tommy Dorsey, vocal by Frank Sinatra (Victor); and Benny Goodman, vocal by Helen Forrest (Columbia).

Devil or Angel. w/m Blanche Carter, 1955, 1960. R&B chart record by The Clovers (Atlantic). Revived in 1960 by Bobby Vee, who had a Top 10 hit recording (Liberty).

Devil's Gun. w/m Stanley Rogers, 1977. Recorded by the disco band, C.J. and Co. (Westbound).

Devil Went Down to Georgia, The. w/m Tommy Crain, Charlie Daniels, Taz Di Gregorio, Fred Edwards, Charles Hayward, and Jim Marshall, 1979. Gold record by The Charlie Daniels Band (Epic).

Devil with the Blue Dress On. w/m Frederick Long and William Stevenson, 1966. Hit record by Mitch Ryder and The Detroit Wheels, in medley titled "Devil with the Blue Dress On and Good Golly Miss Molly" (New Voice). Revived by Pratt and McClain (Reprise), 1976.

Devil Woman. w/m Christine Authors and Terry Britten, 1976. Top 10 record by the British actor/singer Cliff Richard (Rocket).

Devil Woman. w/m Marty Robbins, 1962. Crossover hit (C&W/pop) by Marty Robbins (Columbia).

Devoted to You. w/m Boudleaux Bryant, 1958. Introduced and recorded by The Everly Brothers (Cadence).

(What Do We Do on A) Dew-Dew-Dewy Day. w/m Al Sherman, Charles Tobias, and Howard Johnson, 1927. Featured and recorded by Ruth Etting (Columbia).

Dial My Heart. w/m Antonio Reid, Daryl Simmons, and Kenneth Edmonds, 1989. Hit R&B chart single by the group Boys (Motown).

Diamond Girl. w/m Jimmy Seals and Dash Crofts, 1973. Top 10 record by Seals and Crofts (Warner Bros.).

Diamonds. w/m James Harris III and Terry Lewis, 1987. #1 R&B chart and Top 10 Pop chart record by Herb Alpert, lead and background vocals by Janet Jackson and Lisa Keith, respectively (A&M).

Diamonds and Rust. w/m Joan Baez, 1975. Recorded by Joan Baez (A&M).

Diamonds Are a Girl's Best Friend. w. Leo Robin, m. Jule Styne, 1949. Introduced by Carol Channing in (TM) *Gentlemen Prefer Blondes*. It was sung by Marilyn Monroe in (MM) *Gentlemen Prefer Blondes*, 1953.

Diamonds Are Forever. w/m John Barry and Don Black, 1971. Sung by Shirley Bassey on the soundtrack of the James Bond film (MP) *Diamonds Are Forever*, and on records (United Artists).

Diamonds on the Soles of Her Shoes. w/m Paul Simon and Joseph Shabalala, 1986. Recorded by Paul Simon in his album "Graceland."

Diana. w/m Paul Anka, 1957. First hit for sixteen-year-old Canadian singer-songwriter Paul Anka (ABC-Paramount).

Diane (I'm in Heaven When I See You Smile). w/m Erno Rapee and Lew Pollack, 1927. Theme song of (MP) *Seventh Heav-*

en starring Janet Gaynor and Charles Farrell. Best-selling record by Nat Shilkret and his Orchestra, vocal by Franklyn Baur, Lewis James, and Elliot Shaw (Victor). Revived with a Top 10 record by the Irish trio The Bachelors (London), 1964.

Diary. w/m David Gates, 1972. Top 20 record by the group Bread (Elektra).

Diary, The. w. Howard Greenfield, m. Neil Sedaka, 1959. First record success by Neil Sedaka (RCA).

Dickey-Bird Song, The. w. Howard Dietz, m. Sammy Fain, 1948. Introduced by Jeanette MacDonald, Ann E. Todd, Jane Powell, and Mary Eleanor Donahue, and reprised by José Iturbi in (MM) *Three Daring Daughters*. Leading records by Freddy Martin, vocal by Glen Hughes (RCA Victor); Larry Clinton, vocal by Helen Lee and the Dipsy Doodlers (Decca).

Dicty Glide, The. m. Edward Kennedy "Duke" Ellington, 1929. Introduced and recorded by Duke Ellington (Victor).

Did I Remember? w. Harold Adamson, m. Walter Donaldson, 1936. Jean Harlow's lips moved but the voice was Virginia Verrill's, dubbing for the star in (MP) *Suzy*. Cary Grant, in a rare vocal performance, reprised it. The song was an Academy Award nominee, and on "Your Hit Parade" for sixteen weeks, six of them in the #1 spot. Leading records: Dick Powell (Decca) and Billie Holiday (Vocalion). Grant's sequence (above) was included in (MM) *That's Entertainment*, 1974.

Did It in a Minute. w/m Janna Allen, Sara Allen, and Daryl Hall, 1982. Top 10 record by Daryl Hall and John Oates (RCA).

Didja Ever? w. Mann Curtis, m. Vic Mizzy, 1951. Introduced by Tony Martin in (MM) *Easy to Love*.

Didn't I (Blow Your Mind This Time). w. Thom Bell and William Hart, m. Thom

Bell, 1970. Gold record R&B/Pop hit by The Delfonics (Philly Groove).

Didn't We. w/m Jim Webb, 1969. Recorded by Richard Harris (Dunhill). Revived by Barbra Streisand (Columbia), 1973.

Didn't We Almost Have It All. w. Will Jennings, m. Michael Masser, 1987. #1 record by Whitney Houston, from her album "Whitney" (Arista).

Did You Close Your Eyes? (When We Kissed). w/m Bob Merrill, 1957. Introduced by Gwen Verdon and George Wallace in (TM) *New Girl in Town.*

Did You Ever Get That Feeling in the Moonlight? w/m James Cavanaugh, Larry Stock, and Ira Schuster, 1945. Leading recordings by Perry Como (Victor) and Russ Morgan, with his Orchestra (Decca).

Did You Ever Have to Make Up Your Mind? w/m John Sebastian, 1966. Top 10 record by The Lovin' Spoonful (Kama Sutra).

Did You Ever See a Dream Walking? w. Mack Gordon, m. Harry Revel, 1933. Introduced by Jack Haley in (MM) *Sitting Pretty.* Eddy Duchin, vocal by Lew Sherwood, had a #1 record (Victor). Among other top versions: Guy Lombardo, vocal by Carmen Lombardo (Brunswick); Bing Crosby (Brunswick); Meyer Davis and his Orchestra (Columbia); The Pickens Sisters (Victor).

Did You Have a Happy Birthday? w/m Paul Anka and Howard Greenfield, 1963. Introduced and recorded by Paul Anka (ABC-Paramount).

Did You Mean It? w. Abe Lyman and Sid Silvers, m. Phil Baker, 1927. Recorded by Jay C. Flippen and His Gang (Perfect), Segar Ellis's Band (Okeh), Marion Harris (Victor). It was revived by Benny Goodman's Orchestra with a vocal by Ella Fitzgerald (Victor), 1936.

Did Your Mother Come from Ireland? w/m Jimmy Kennedy and Michael Carr, 1936. English song that attained great popularity in the United States.

Did You See Her Eyes? w/m Jeff Barry, 1969. Top 40 record by The Illusion (Steed).

Did You See Jackie Robinson Hit That Ball? w/m Buddy Johnson, 1949. Introduced and recorded by Buddy Johnson, vocal by Ella Johnson (Decca).

Died in Your Arms (I Just). See **I Just Died in Your Arms.**

Different Drum. w/m Mike Nesmith, 1967. Recorded by The Stone Poneys, featuring Linda Ronstadt (Capitol).

Different Worlds. w. Norman Gimbel, m. Charles Fox, 1979. Theme from the series (TVP) *Angie,* sung by Maureen McGovern, who also recorded it (Warner Bros.).

Diga Diga Doo. w. Dorothy Fields, m. Jimmy McHugh, 1928. Introduced by Adelaide Hall in (TM) *Blackbirds of 1928.* This show marked the Broadway debut of the Fields-McHugh team and the start of Field's lengthy career. This was one of five notable songs in the revue. The others: "I Can't Give You Anything But Love," "I Must Have That Man," "Doin' the New Low Down," and "Porgy." Lena Horne sang it in (MM) *Stormy Weather,* 1943. Duke Ellington recorded the song for two different labels (Okeh) (Victor).

Digging Your Scene. w/m Robert Howard, 1986. Recorded by the British quartet The Blow Monkeys (RCA).

Diggin' Up Bones. w/m Paul Overstreet and Al Gore, 1986. #1 Country chart record by Randy Travis (Warner Bros.).

Dig You Later (A Hubba-Hubba-Hubba). w. Harold Adamson, m. Jimmy McHugh, 1945. Introduced in (MM) *Doll Face* and on records by Perry Como (Victor).

Dim, Dim, the Lights (I Want Some Atmosphere). w/m Beverly Ross and Julius Dixon, 1954. Featured by Bill Haley and His Comets (Decca).

163

Dim All the Lights. w/m Donna Summer, 1979. Gold record by Donna Summer (Casablanca).

Dime a Dozen. w/m Cindy Walker, 1949. Popularized by Margaret Whiting (Capitol) and Sammy Kaye, vocal by the Three Kaydets (RCA Victor).

Diminuendo in Blue. m. Edward Kennedy "Duke" Ellington, 1937. Introduced and recorded (Brunswick) by Duke Ellington and his Orchestra, coupled with "Crescendo in Blue."

Dinah. w. Sam M. Lewis and Joe Young, m. Harry Akst, 1925. Ethel Waters introduced this at the Plantation Club in New York and later recorded it (Columbia). Eddie Cantor interpolated it in the long-running (TM) *Kid Boots*, which helped it become a big hit and eventually, a major standard. Bing Crosby sang it in (MM) *The Big Broadcast*, 1932. Jeanette MacDonald interpolated it in (MM) *Rose Marie*, 1936. It was heard in (MM) *Broadway*, starring George Raft in 1942. George Murphy, Constance Moore, Eddie Cantor, and Joan Davis sang it in (MM) *Show Business*, 1944.

Ding-a-Ling. w/m Dave Appell, Bernie Lowe, and Kal Mann, 1960. Recorded by Bobby Rydell (Cameo).

Ding-Dong! The Witch Is Dead. w. E.Y. Harburg, m. Harold Arlen, 1939. Introduced by Judy Garland, Lorraine Bridges, dubbing on the soundtrack for Billie Burke, and the Munchkins in (MM) *The Wizard of Oz*. Revived with a Top 20 record by the studio group The Fifth Estate (Jubilee), 1967.

Dinner at Eight. w. Dorothy Fields, m. Jimmy McHugh, 1933. Written to promote (MP) *Dinner at Eight*. The song, however, was not used in the film. It was introduced on network radio by Frances Langford, singing from Grauman's Chinese Theatre in Hollywood. Records by Connie Boswell (Brunswick), Art Jarrett (Victor), Jacques Renard (Vocalion).

Dinner for One, Please James. w/m Michael Carr, 1936. Popularized by the performances and recordings of the bands of Hal Kemp, vocal by Skinnay Ennis (Brunswick), and Ray Noble (Victor).

Dinner Music for a Pack of Hungry Cannibals. m. Raymond Scott, 1938. Instrumental recorded by the Raymond Scott Quintette (Master).

Dinner with Gershwin. w/m Brenda Russell, 1987. Chart single by Donna Summer (Geffen).

Dipsy Doodle, The. w/m Larry Clinton, 1937. Featured by Larry Clinton and his Orchestra. Among top recordings: Chick Webb, vocal by Ella Fitzgerald (Decca); Tommy Dorsey's Clambake Seven (Victor); Sammy Kaye and his Orchestra (Vocalion); Milt Herth Trio (Decca).

Dirty Diana. w/m Michael Jackson, 1988. #1 record by Michael Jackson (Epic).

Dirty Hands, Dirty Face. w. Edgar Leslie, m. James V. Monaco, 1923. Featured by Al Jolson who also sang it in (MM) *The Jazz Singer*, 1927.

Dirty Laundry. w/m Don Henley and Danny Kortchmar, 1982. Top 10 gold record by Don Henley (Asylum).

Dirty Man. 1967. R&B/Pop chart record by soul singer Laura Lee (Chess).

Dirty Water. w/m Ed Cobb, 1966. Top 20 record by The Standells (Tower). Revived by the British group The Inmates (Polydor), 1980.

Dirty White Boy. w/m Lou Gramm and Mick Jones, 1979. Recorded by the Anglo-American group Foreigner (Atlantic).

Dis-Advantages of You, The. w/m Mitch Leigh, 1967. Instrumental based on a cigarette commercial, recorded by The Brass Ring, a studio band headed by leading reed player/arranger Phil Bodner (Dunhill).

Disco Duck. w/m Rick Dees, 1976. #1 novelty hit by the disc jockey Rick Dees and His Cast of Idiots (RSO).

Disco Inferno. w/m Leo Green and Ron Kersey, 1977. Introduced by The Trammps in (MM) *Saturday Night Fever*, and Top 20 record by them (Atlantic).

Disco Lady. w/m Don Davis, Harvey Scales, and L. Vance, 1976. The first single qualified to be awarded a platinum record, indicating certification by the RIAA to have sold over two million copies. Johnnie Taylor's recording (Columbia) was #1 for four weeks and on the charts for nineteen. Oddly, the song was not a dance record but was about disco.

Disco Lucy. See **I Love Lucy Theme.**

Disco Nights (Rock-Freak). w/m Keith Crier, Herb Lane, Emmanuel LeBlanc, and Paul Service, 1979. R&B/Pop gold record written and recorded by the Bronx, N.Y. soul quartet, GQ (Arista).

Disco Queen. w/m Errol Brown and Anthony Wilson, 1975. Recorded by the English group Hot Chocolate (Big Tree).

Dis-Donc, Dis-Donc. w. Julian Moore, David Heneker, Monty Norman (Engl.), m. Marguerite Monnot, 1960. Original French lyrics by Alexandre Breffort. Introduced in (TM) *Irma La Douce* by Colette Renard in Paris, 1956, and by Elizabeth Seal in the London production, 1958, and in the New York presentation two years later.

Dissertation on the State of Bliss (a.k.a. **Love and Learn**). w. Ira Gershwin, m. Harold Arlen, 1954. Introduced by Bing Crosby and Jacqueline Fontaine in (MP) *The Country Girl.*

Distant Drums. w/m Cindy Walker, 1966. Crossover (C&W/Pop) hit by Jim Reeves (RCA).

Distant Melody. w. Betty Comden and Adolph Green, m. Jule Styne, 1954. Introduced by Mary Martin and Kathy Nolan in (TM) *Peter Pan.*

Distant Shores. w/m James Guercio, 1966. Recorded by the British duo Chad and Jeremy (Columbia).

Dites-Moi. w. Oscar Hammerstein II, m. Richard Rodgers, 1949. Introduced by Barbara Luna and Michael De Leon in (TM) *South Pacific.* In (MM) *South Pacific,* 1958, it was sung by Giorgio Tozzi (dubbing for Rossano Brazzi), Mitzi Gaynor, and the children.

D-I-V-O-R-C-E. w/m Curly Putman and Bobby Braddock, 1968. C&W/Pop hit by Tammy Wynette (Epic).

Divorce Me C.O.D. w/m Merle Travis and Cliffie Stone, 1946. Best-selling record by Merle Travis (Capitol). Later recording by Cootie Williams (Derby).

Dixie Highway. w. Gus Kahn, m. Walter Donaldson, 1922. Recorded and popularized by Aileen Stanley (Victor).

Dixie Land, I Love You. w. A. Seymour Brown, m. Nat D. Ayer, 1909. Recorded the same year by Billy Murray (Victor).

Dixieland Band. w. Johnny Mercer, m. Bernard Hanighen, 1935. Introduced and recorded by Benny Goodman, vocal by Helen Ward (Columbia). Other recordings of note: Bob Crosby, vocal by Joe Harris (Decca); Kay Starr (Crystalette); Johnny Mercer (Capitol).

Dixieland Delight. w/m Ronnie Rogers, 1983. One of twenty-one consecutive #1 Country chart records by the group Alabama (RCA).

Dixie Vagabond. w. Gus Kahn, m. Walter Donaldson, 1927.

Dizzy. w/m Tommy Roe and Freddy Weller, 1969. #1 gold record by Tommy Roe (ABC).

Dizzy Atmosphere. m. John Birks "Dizzy" Gillespie, 1944. Instrumental recorded by Dizzy Gillespie and his Combo (Musicraft).

Dizzy Fingers. m. Zez Confrey, 1923. A popular piano solo. Introduced by Zez Confrey who later made a hit recording (Victor), 1927.

It was played by Carmen Cavallaro on the soundtrack, dubbing for Tyrone Power in the title role in (MM) *The Eddy Duchin Story*, 1956.

D. J. Cried, The. w/m Joyce Ann Allsup, 1965. Top 10 Country chart record by Ernest Ashworth (Hickory).

D. J. for a Day. w/m Tom T. Hall, 1963. Recorded by Jimmy Newman (Decca).

Do, Do, My Huckleberry Do. w. Harry Dillon, m. John Dillon, 1893. A novelty featured in vaudeville by the Dillon Brothers.

Doan Ye Cry, Mah Honey. w/m Albert W. Noll, 1899.

Doatsy Mae. w/m Carol Hall, 1978. Introduced by Susan Mansur in (TM) *Best Little Whorehouse in Texas*.

Dock of the Bay, The (Sittin' On). See **Sittin' on the Dock of the Bay.**

Doctor! Doctor! w/m Thomas Bailey, Alanah Currie, and Joe Leeway, 1984. Written and recorded by the British-based trio, calling themselves The Thompson Twins (Arista).

Doctor Detroit. See **Theme from "Doctor Detroit."**

Doctor Jazz. w. Walter Melrose, m. Joe "King" Oliver, 1927. First recorded by Jelly Roll Morton's Red Hot Peppers (Victor). Pianist Art Hodes and his group had a popular jazz record (Blue Note), 1944.

Doctor, Lawyer, Indian Chief. w. Paul Francis Webster, m. Hoagy Carmichael, 1945. Introduced by Betty Hutton in (MM) *The Stork Club* and recorded by her (Capitol). Other chart recordings by Les Brown, vocal by Butch Stone (Columbia) and Hoagy Carmichael (ARA).

Doctor My Eyes. w/m Jackson Browne, 1972. Top 10 record by Jackson Browne (Asylum).

Doctor's Orders. w/m Roger Cook, Roger Greenaway, and Geoff Stephens, 1975. English song recorded by the American singer Carol Douglas (Midland International).

Do, Do, Do. w. Ira Gershwin, m. George Gershwin, 1926. Sung by Oscar Shaw and Gertrude Lawrence in (TM) *Oh, Kay!* George Olsen and his Orchestra and Gertrude Lawrence had popular records (Victor). Doris Day and Gordon MacRae interpolated the song in (MM) *Tea For Two*, 1950; Gogi Grant sang it on the soundtrack for Ann Blyth in the title role of (MM) *The Helen Morgan Story*, 1957; Julie Andrews sang it in the film, loosely based on the life of Gertrude Lawrence, (MM) "Star!" 1968.

Dodging a Divorcée. m. Reginald Foresythe, 1935. Novelty instrumental, originally written and published as a piano solo. Its popularity was spawned by the recordings of the bands of Reginald Foresythe (Columbia), Hal Kemp (Brunswick), Paul Whiteman (Victor), and the English band of (Bert) Ambrose (Decca).

Dodo, The. w/m Milton Addington, Dickey Lee, and Allen Reynolds, 1964, Recorded by Gene Simmons (Hi).

Does Anybody Know I'm Here? w/m Bobby Miller, 1969. Top 40 record by The Dells (Cadet).

Does Anybody Really Know What Time It Is? w/m Robert Lamm, 1970. Top 10 single by the group Chicago (Columbia).

Does He Mean That Much to You? w/m Jack Rollins and Don Robertson, 1962. Featured and recorded by Eddy Arnold (RCA).

Does My Ring Hurt Your Finger? w/m Doris Clement, John Crutchfield, and Don Robertson, 1967. Top 10 Country chart record by Charley Pride (RCA).

Doesn't Somebody Want to Be Wanted. w/m Mike Appel, Jimmy Cretecos, and Wes Farrell, 1971. Gold record by The Partridge Family (Bell).

Does the Spearmint Lose Its Flavor on the Bedpost over Night? w. Billy Rose and

Marty Bloom, m. Ernest Breuer, 1924. Comedy song, introduced by Harry Richman and featured and recorded by Ernest Hare and Billy Jones (Cameo). Revived via a hit release by the British Lonnie Donegan and his Skiffle Group (Dot), 1961. The title was changed to "Does Your Chewing Gum Lose Its Flavor, etc.," to avoid conflicts with competing chewing gum sponsors on radio and T.V.

Does Your Chewing Gum Lose Its Flavor on the Bedpost Overnight? See **Does the Spearmint Lose Its Flavor, etc.**

Does Your Heart Beat for Me? w. Mitchell Parish, m. Russ Morgan and Arnold Johnson, 1936. Introduced by and theme song of Russ Morgan and his Orchestra (Brunswick), 1936, (Decca), 1939. It was sung by Jason Graae in the Mitchell Parish musical (TM) *Stardust*, 1987.

Does Your Mama Know about Me? w/m Tom Baird and Tommy Chong, 1968. Top 40 record by Bobby Taylor and The Vancouvers (Gordy).

Does Your Mother Know? w/m Benny Anderson and Bjorn Alvaeus, 1979. Recorded by the Swedish group Abba (Atlantic).

Dogface Soldier. w/m Bert Gold and Ken Woodrow Hart, 1955. Written during WW II by two GIs. Revived in (MP) *To Hell and Back*, 1955. Recorded, with additional lyrics by John Dolph, by Russ Morgan and his Orchestra (Decca).

Doggie in the Window, The. w/m Bob Merrill, 1953. Patti Page had a #1 best-seller (Mercury) and was responsible for the song reaching the top position on "Your Hit Parade."

Doggin' Around. w/m Lena Agree, 1960. First recorded by Jackie Wilson (Brunswick). Revived in 1983 with a Top 10 R&B chart crossover record by the trio, Klique, under title of "Stop Doggin' Me Around" (MCA).

Doggone It, Baby, I'm in Love. w/m Arnett Keefer and Jack Amway, 1953. Leading

records by Carl Smith (Columbia), Giselle MacKenzie (Capitol).

Doggone Right. w/m William Robinson, Al Cleveland, and Marv Tarplin, 1969. Top 40 record by Smokey Robinson and The Miracles (Tamla).

Doghouse Boogie. w/m Hawkshaw Hawkins and Booth Woodall, 1948. Top 10 C&W chart record by Hawkshaw Hawkins (King).

Do I Do. w/m Stevie Wonder, 1981. R&B/Pop chart hit by Stevie Wonder (Tamla).

Do I Hear a Waltz? w. Stephen Sondheim, m. Richard Rodgers, 1965. Introduced by Elizabeth Allen in (TM) *Do I Hear a Waltz?*

Do I Hear You Saying, "I Love You?" w. Lorenz Hart, m. Richard Rodgers, 1928. Introduced by Flora Le Breton and Charles King in (TM) *Present Arms.*

Do I Love You? w/m Cole Porter, 1939. Introduced by Ronald Graham and Ethel Merman in (TM) *DuBarry Was a Lady.* Gene Kelly sang it in the film version (MM) *DuBarry Was a Lady*, 1943; Ginny Simms sang it in the Porter story (MM) *Night and Day*, 1945.

Do I Love You Because You're Beautiful? w. Oscar Hammerstein II, m. Richard Rodgers, 1957. Introduced in (TVM) "Cinderella" by Jon Cypher and Julie Andrews. Popular recordings by Vic Damone (Columbia) and Tony Martin (RCA).

Doing It All for My Baby. w/m Phil Cody and M. Duke, 1987. Top 10 single for Huey Lewis and The News (Chrysalis).

Doin' Our Thing. w/m Clarence Carter, Allyn Lee, and Clemmie McCants, 1969. Recorded by Clarence Carter (Atlantic).

Doin' the New Low-Down. w. Dorothy Fields, m. Jimmy McHugh, 1928. Introduced by Bill Robinson in (TM) *Blackbirds of 1928*, which marked his ascent to stardom. Recorded by Robinson (Columbia); and Duke Ellington, vocal by publisher Irving Mills (Okeh).

Doin' the Raccoon. w. Raymond Klages, m. J. Fred Coots, 1928. George Olsen and his Orchestra had the popular record of this song that stated that "highbrow, lowbrow, intermejiate, make believe they're all collegiate. . ." It was featured in (MM) *The Time, The Place, And The Girl*, starring Betty Compson and Grant Withers, 1929.

Doin' The Susi-Q. w. Benny Davis, m. J. Fred Coots, 1936. A popular song and dance, introduced in the revue *Cotton Club Parade* at the famed Harlem night club. Lil Armstrong's Orchestra recorded it (Decca).

Doin' the Uptown Lowdown. w. Mack Gordon, m. Harry Revel, 1933. Introduced by Frances Williams in (MM) *Broadway Thru a Keyhole*. Among recordings: Mildred Bailey (Brunswick); Richard Himber, vocal by Johnny Mercer (Vocalion); Ted Weems, vocal by Parker Gibbs (Victor); Isham Jones (Victor); Abe Lyman, vocal by Ella Logan (Brunswick); Joe Venuti (Dccca).

Doin' the Voom Voom. m. Edward Kennedy "Duke" Ellington, 1929. Instrumental recorded by Ellington (Victor) (Columbia).

Doin' What Comes Natur'lly. w/m Irving Berlin, 1946. Introduced by Ethel Merman in (TM) *Annie Get Your Gun*. Best-selling records by Dinah Shore, with Spade Cooley's Orchestra (Columbia); Freddy Martin and his Orchestra (RCA Victor); Jimmy Dorsey, vocal by Dee Parker (Decca). In the 1950 film version (MM) *Annie Get Your Gun*, it was sung by Betty Hutton.

Do It ('Till You're Satisfied). w/m Billy Nichols, 1974. Gold record by the disco septet B. T. Express (Roadshow).

Do It Again. w/m Walter Becker and Donald Fagen, 1972. Popularized by the group Steely Dan (Columbia). Recorded in medley with "Billie Jean" by Club House (Atlantic), 1983.

Do It Again. w/m Brian Wilson and Mike Love, 1968. Hit record by The Beach Boys (Capitol).

Do It Again! w. B. G. DeSylva, m. George Gershwin, 1922. Introduced by Irene Bordoni in (TP) *The French Doll*. Paul Whiteman and his Orchestra had an instrumental hit record (Victor). Later that year it was sung as "Please Do It Again" by Alice Delysia in (TM) *Mayfair and Montmartre* in London. Because of its double-entendre lyric, the song was banned from radio for a long period of time. It was heard in the background in the Gershwin film bio (MM) *Rhapsody in Blue*, 1945, and sung by Carol Channing in (MM) *Thoroughly Modern Millie*, 1967.

Do It Again. w/m Irving Berlin, 1912.

Do It Again, a Little Bit Slower. w/m Wayne Thompson, 1967. Top 20 hit by Jon and Robin and The In Crowd (Abnak).

Do It Any Way You Wanna. w/m Leon Huff, 1975. #1 R&B Top 20 Pop chart instrumental by People's Choice (TSOP).

Do It Baby. w/m Freddie Perren and Christine Yarian, 1974. Top 20 record by The Miracles (Tamla).

Do It or Die. w/m Buddy Buie, J. R. Cobb, and Ronnie Hammond, 1979. Recorded by Atlanta Rhythm Section (Polydor).

Do It Right. w/m Randy Clark, 1964. Recorded by Brook Benton (Mercury).

Do It to It. w/m Quincy Jones, 1972. Sung on the soundtrack by Little Richard in (MP) *$* (*Dollars*).

Do It to My Mind. w/m Johnny Bristol, 1976. Recorded by Johnny Bristol (Atlantic).

Do I Worry? w/m Stanley Cowan and Bobby Worth, 1941. Introduced and best-selling record by The Ink Spots (Decca). Tommy Dorsey with vocal by Frank Sinatra (Victor) also had a popular version, as did Bea Wain (Victor). The Ink Spots interpolated it in (MM) *Pardon My Sarong*, 1942.

Dolce Far Niente. w/m Meredith Willson, 1960. Introduced by Mitchell Gregg in

(TM) *The Unsinkable Molly Brown*. Song not used in the film version.

Dolimite. w. Buddy Feyne, m. William Johnson, 1940. Leading recordings by the bands of Erskine Hawkins (Bluebird) and Jimmy Dorsey (Decca).

Dollar Down, A. w/m Cisco Houston, 1960. Novelty featured and recorded by The Limeliters (RCA).

Doll Dance, The. m. Nacio Herb Brown, 1927. Piano solo. Recorded by the bands of Nat Shilkret (Victor) and Earl Burtnett (Columbia).

Dolly. w. Ira Gershwin and Schuyler Greene, m. Vincent Youmans, 1921. Sung by Oscar Shaw and Fred Santley in (TM) *Two Little Girls in Blue*. Gershwin wrote it pseudonymously as Arthur Francis.

Dolly Dagger. w/m Jimi Hendrix, 1971. Recorded by Jimi Hendrix for his concert film, *Rainbow Bridge*, and released posthumously (Reprise).

Dolores. w. Frank Loesser, m. Louis Alter, 1941. Introduced by Frank Sinatra, in his screen debut, with Tommy Dorsey's Orchestra in (MM) *Las Vegas Nights*. They recorded a best-seller (Victor) as did Bing Crosby (Decca). Nominated for an Academy Award, 1941.

Domani (Tomorrow). w. Tony Velona, m. Ulpio Minucci, 1955. Popularized and recorded by Julius La Rosa (Cadence).

Do Me Baby. w/m Prince Rogers Nelson, 1986. #1 R&B chart and Pop chart entry by Meli'sa Morgan (Capitol).

Domestic Life. w/m John Conlee, 1987. Top 10 Country chart record by John Conlee (Columbia).

Dominique. w. Noel Regney (Engl.), w (Fr.)/m Soeur Sourire, O. P., 1963. Belgian song, recorded in French. Introduced by "The Singing Nun," Sister Luc-Gabrielle, under pseudonym of Soeur Sourire ("Sister Smile") (Philips).

Domino. w. Don Raye (Engl.), Jacques Plante (Fr.), m. Louis Ferrari, 1951. Originally a French popular song. Leading records in U.S. by Tony Martin (RCA Victor), Bing Crosby (Decca), Doris Day (Columbia).

Dominoes. w/m Robbie Nevil, Barry Eastman, and Bobby Hart, 1986. Chart record by Robbie Nevil (Manhattan).

Dommage, Dommage (Too Bad, Too Bad). w/m Paul Vance and Lee Pockriss, 1966. Leading records by Paul Vance (Scepter) and Jerry Vale (Columbia).

Don'cha Go 'Way Mad. w. Al Stillman, m. Jimmy Mundy and Illinois Jacquet, 1950. Song based on the Jacquet jazz composition "Black Velvet." Popularized by Harry James and his Orchestra (Columbia) and Ella Fitzgerald (Decca).

Doncha' Think It's Time. w/m Clyde Otis and Willie Dixon, 1958. Recorded by Elvis Presley (RCA).

Donde Esta Santa Claus? (Where Is Santa Claus?) w/m Rod Parker, Al Greiner, and George Scheck, 1958. Christmas novelty by Augie Rios (Metro).

Dondi. w. Earl Shuman, m. Mort Garson, 1960. Introduced on the soundtrack of (MP) *Dondi*, based on the comic-strip character, by Patti Page.

Donkey Serenade. w. Robert Wright and George Forrest, m. Rudolf Friml and Herbert Stothart, 1937. Originally a piano solo, titled "Chanson." Words were added, 1927, by Dailey Paskman, Sigmund Spaeth, and Irving Caesar and retitled "Chansonette." The final version, with new title, lyrics, and some music changes, was introduced by Allan Jones in (MM) *The Firefly*, 1937. Jones, with whom the song is associated, recorded it (Victor) as did singers Frank Parker (Victor); Lanny Ross (Silvertone 12″); organist Eddie Dunstedter (Decca); and bands, headed by Artie Shaw (Bluebird) and Horace Heidt (Columbia). It was heard in the Olsen and Johnson film (MM)

Crazy House, 1943, and was played by pianist José Iturbi in (MM) *Anchors Aweigh*, 1945.

Donna. w/m Ritchie Valens, 1958. Hit record by Ritchie Valens (Del-Fi). It was featured in the Valens story (MM) *La Bamba*, 1987.

Donna Lee. m. Charlie Parker, 1947. First recorded by Charlie Parker and a combo that included Miles Davis, Bud Powell, and other instrumental stars (Savoy).

Donna the Prima Donna. w/m Dion Di Mucci and Ernie Maresca, 1963. Hit record by Dion (Columbia).

Do Not Forsake Me. See **High Noon**.

Do Nothin' Till You Hear from Me. w. Bob Russell, m. Edward Kennedy "Duke" Ellington, 1943. Adapted from the Ellington band's instrumental "Concerto for Cootie," 1940, featuring trumpet player Cootie Williams. When new version became popular, Ellington's original recording was re-issued and retitled (Victor). Best-selling records: Stan Kenton, vocal by Red Dorris (Capitol), his first chart record; Woody Herman, with his Orchestra (Decca).

Don't. w/m Jerry Leiber and Mike Stoller, 1957. #1 million-seller by Elvis Presley (RCA).

Don't Ask Me to Be Friends. w/m Gerry Goffin and Jack Keller, 1962. Recorded by The Everly Brothers (Warner Bros.)

Don't Ask Me Why. w/m Billy Joel, 1980. Written and recorded by Billy Joel (Columbia).

Don't Ask Me Why. w. Fred Wise, m. Ben Weisman, 1958. Introduced by Elvis Presley in (MM) *King Creole*, and recorded by him, coupled with #1 record "Hard Headed Woman" (RCA).

Don't Ask to Stay Until Tomorrow. w. Carol Connors, m. Artie Kane, 1977. Sung on the soundtrack of (MP) *Looking for Mr. Goodbar* by Marlena Shaw.

Don't Be a Baby, Baby. w. Buddy Kaye, m. Howard Steiner, 1946. Introduced and recorded by The Mills Brothers (Decca). Also

recorded by the Benny Goodman Sextet, vocal by Art Lund (Columbia).

Don't Be a Drop-Out. w/m James Brown and Nat Jones, 1966. Recorded by James Brown (King).

Don't Be Afraid, Little Darlin'. w/m Barry Mann and Cynthia Weil, 1963. Top 40 record by Steve Lawrence (Columbia).

Don't Be Afraid to Tell Your Mother. w/m Pinky Tomlin, Coy Poe, and Jimmie Grier, 1935. Introduced and recorded by Pinky Tomlin, with Jimmie Grier's Orchestra. Other popular records by the Mills Brothers (Decca), Little Jack Little (Columbia), Charlie Barnet and his Orchestra (Bluebird).

Don't Be Angry. w/m Nappy Brown, Rose Marie McCoy, and Fred Mendelsohn, 1955. Introduced and hit R&B record by Nappy Brown (Savoy). Covered and Top 20 Pop record by The Crew Cuts (Mercury).

Don't Be Angry with Me. w/m Walter Donaldson, 1926. Recorded by the orchestras of Jean Goldkette (Victor) and Frank Signorelli (Perfect).

Don't Be a Woman If You Can. w. Ira Gershwin, m. Arthur Schwartz, 1946. Introduced by Mary Wickes, Marthe Errolle, and Ruth Matteson in (TM) *Park Avenue*.

Don't Be Cruel. w/m Babyface, L. A. Reid and Daryl Simmons, 1988. #1 R&B and Top 10 Pop chart recorded by Bobby Brown (MCA). Not to be confused with the Elvis Presley hit of the same title (q.v.).

Don't Be Cruel. w/m Otis Blackwell and Elvis Presley, 1956. A rare circumstance when both sides of a single became #1 hits in every category. This was the case with Elvis Presley's recording. Blackwell wrote the song and Presley, after making some changes to fit his style, recorded it at the same session with "Hound Dog," with which it was coupled (RCA). Revived with a Top 10 Country chart version by The Judds (RCA), 1987. Hit single by the group Cheap Trick (Epic), 1988.

Don't Believe Everything You Dream.

w. Harold Adamson, m. Jimmy McHugh, 1943. From (MM) *Around the World*. Recorded by The Ink Spots (Decca).

Don't Be Like That. w/m Archie Gottler, Maceo Pinkard, and Charles Tobias, 1928. Introduced and recorded by Helen Kane (Victor). Other records by Lee Morse (Columbia), Harry Richman (Brunswick), the bands of Jean Goldkette (Victor) and Abe Lyman (Brunswick).

Don't Be So Mean to Baby ('Cause Baby's So Good to You). w/m Peggy Lee and Dave Barbour, 1947. Introduced and recorded by Peggy Lee (Capitol).

Don't Be That Way. w. Mitchell Paris, m. Edgar Sampson and Benny Goodman, 1938. Introduced as an instrumental in 1934 by Chick Webb and his Orchestra, Sampson was listed as sole composer and arranger. Lyrics were added in 1938 and Benny Goodman had a hit record, also arranged by Sampson (Victor). Among other recordings: Mildred Bailey, with Red Norvo's Band (Vocalion); Teddy Wilson (Brunswick); Bing Crosby (Decca); Lionel Hampton (Victor); Roy Eldridge (Key).

Don't Bet Money, Honey. w/m Linda Scott, 1961. Introduced and Top 10 record by Linda Scott (Canadian-American).

Don't Bite the Hand That's Feeding You. w. Thomas Hoier, m. James Morgan, 1915.

Don't Blame It All on Broadway. w. Joe Young and Harry Williams, m. Bert Grant, 1913.

Don't Blame Me. w. Dorothy Fields, m. Jimmy McHugh, 1933. One of the biggest hits of the year in sheet music, record sales, and radio performances. Among recordings: Ethel Waters (Brunswick), Leo Reisman (Brunswick), Rudy Vallee (Victor), Irene Taylor (Vocalion). Later recordings included Erroll Garner (Mercury); Charlie Parker, with Miles Davis (Dial); Andy Russell (Capitol); The Everly Brothers (Warner Bros.). It was sung by Freddie Stewart in (MM) *Freddie Steps Out*, 1946; Betty Garrett in (MM) *Big City*, 1948;

Vic Damone in (MM) *The Strip*, 1951; Constance Towers in (MM) *Bring Your Smile Along*, 1955. Ann Miller and Eddie Pruett sang it in (TM) *Sugar Babies*, 1980.

Don't Blame the Children. w. Ivan Reeve, m. H. B. Barnum, 1967. Spoken by Sammy Davis, Jr. (Reprise).

Don't Bother Me. w/m George Harrison, 1964. Sung by the Beatles in (MM) *A Hard Day's Night*, and recorded by them (Capitol).

Don't Bother Me, I Can't Cope. w/m Micki Grant, 1972. Introduced by the company in (TM) *Don't Bother Me, I Can't Cope*.

Don't Break the Heart That Loves You. w/m Benny Davis and Murray Mencher, 1962. Hit record by Connie Francis (MGM).

Don't Bring Lulu. w. Billy Rose and Lew Brown, m. Ray Henderson, 1925. Featured and recorded by Ernest Hare and Billy Jones (Okeh) and Billy Murray (Victor).

Don't Bring Me Down. w/m Jeff Lynne 1979. Gold record by the British group, Electric Light Orchestra (Jet).

Don't Bring Me Down. w/m Gerry Goffin and Carole King, 1966. Recorded by the British group The Animals (MGM).

Don't Burn the Candle at Both Ends. w/m Benny Carter, Irving Gordon, and Louis Jordan, 1948. Top 10 R&B records by Louis Jordan and his Tympany Five (Decca) and pianist/singer Martha Davis (Decca).

Don't Call Him a Cowboy. w/m Deborah Kay Hupp, Johnny McRae, and Brian Morrison, 1985. Album title song and #1 Country chart single by Conway Twitty (Warner Bros.).

Don't Call It Love. w. Dean Pitchford, m. Tom Snow, 1985. Top 10 Country chart single by Dolly Parton (RCA).

Don't Call It Love. w. Ned Washington, m. Allie Wrubel, 1947. From (MP) *I Walk Alone*. Leading records by Freddy Martin, vocal by Stuart Wade (RCA Victor); Monica

Lewis, with Guy Lombardo's Orchestra (Decca).

Don't Call Me from a Honky Tonk. w/m Harlan Howard, 1963. C&W hit by Johnny and Jonie Mosby (Columbia).

Don't Call My Name. w/m Bennie Benjamin and George David Weiss, 1953. Leading record by Helene Dixon, with George Siravo's Orchestra (Okeh).

Don't Call Us, We'll Call You. w/m John Canter and Jerry Corbetta, 1975. Top 10 record by the quartet Sugarloaf (Claridge).

Don't Change On Me. w/m Eddie Reeves and Jimmy Holiday, 1971. Top 40 record by Ray Charles (ABC).

Don't Close Your Eyes. w/m Bob McDill, 1988. #1 Country chart song by Keith Whitley (RCA).

Don't Come Around Here No More. w/m Tom Petty and Dave Stewart, 1985. Recorded by Tom Petty and The Heartbreakers (MCA).

Don't Come Home A-Drinkin' (With Lovin' on Your Mind). w/m Loretta Lynn and Peggy Sue Wells, 1967. Hit Country record by Loretta Lynn (Decca).

Don't Come Knockin'. w/m Antoine "Fats" Domino, 1960. Recorded by Fats Domino (Imperial).

Don't Come Running Back to Me. w/m Sid Tepper and Roy C. Bennett, 1965. Introduced and recorded by Nancy Wilson (Capitol).

Don't Cross Your Fingers, Cross Your Heart. w/m Johnny Marks, Al Donahue, and Larry Shay, 1938.

Don't Cry. w/m Geoff Downes and John Wetton, 1983. Top 10 record by the English group Asia (Geffen).

Don't Cry. w/m Frank Loesser, 1956. Introduced by Art Lund in (TM) *The Most Happy Fella.*

Don't Cry, Baby. w/m Stella Unger, Saul

Bernie and James P. Johnson, 1943, 1961. First leading recordings by the orchestras of Erskine Hawkins (Bluebird) and Lucky Millinder (Decca). Revived by Etta James (Argo), 1961, and Aretha Franklin (Atlantic), 1962.

Don't Cry, Cherie. w. Lew Brown, m. Ray Henderson, 1941. Featured and recorded by the bands of Sammy Kaye (Victor) and Gene Krupa (Okeh).

Don't Cry, Frenchy, Don't Cry. w. Sam M. Lewis and Joe Young, m. Walter Donaldson, 1919. Post World War I song.

Don't Cry, Joe (Let Her Go, Let Her Go, Let Her Go). w/m Joe Marsala, 1949. Leading records: Gordon Jenkins, vocal by Betty Brewer (Decca); Frank Sinatra (Columbia); Ralph Flanagan, vocal by Harry Prime (Bluebird).

Don't Cry Daddy. w/m Scott Davis, 1969. From Elvis Presley's last film (MM) *Change of Habit.* Presley's recording was a Top 10 gold record (RCA).

Don't Cry for Me, Argentina. w. Tim Rice, m. Andrew Lloyd Webber, 1979. Sung on Broadway by Patti LuPone in (TM) *Evita.* Introduced in the original London production by Julie Covington, 1976. Chart record by Festival (RSO), 1980.

Don't Cry No More. w/m Deadric Malone, 1960. Recorded by Bobby Bland (Duke).

Don't Cry Out Loud. w. Carole Bayer Sager and Peter Allen, m. Allen, 1979. Recorded by Melissa Manchester (Arista).

Don't Deceive Me. w/m Chuck Willis, 1953. Top 10 R&B chart record by Chuck Willis (Okeh). Revived by Ruth Brown with a crossover (R&B/Pop) hit (Atlantic), 1960.

Don't Disturb This Groove. w/m Mic Murphy and David Frank, 1987. # 1 R&B chart, Top 10 Pop chart record, written and performed by the duo The System (Atlantic).

Don't Do Me Like That. w/m Tom Petty, 1979. Top 10 record by Tom Petty and The Heartbreakers (Backstreet).

Don't Dream It's Over. w/m Neil Finn, 1987. Top 10 record by the Australian/New Zealand trio Crowded House (Capitol).

Don't Drop It. w/m Terry Fell, 1954. Featured and recorded by Carl Smith (Columbia).

Don't Eat the Yellow Snow. w/m Frank Zappa, 1974. Novelty record by Frank Zappa (DiscReet).

Don't Ever Be Lonely (a Poor Little Fool Like Me). w/m Eddie Cornelius, 1972. Recorded by The Cornelius Brothers and Sister Rose (United Artists).

Don't Ever Change. w. Walter Hirsch, m. Lou Handman, 1937. Among recordings: Blue Barron, vocal by Russ Carlyle (Variety); Will Osborne and his Orchestra (Decca); later, Helene Dixon (Epic).

Don't Ever Leave Me. w. Oscar Hammerstein II, m. Jerome Kern, 1929. Introduced by Helen Morgan and Robert Chisholm in (MM) *Sweet Adeline*. Irene Dunne sang it in (MM) *Sweet Adeline*, 1935, and Gogi Grant, dubbing for Ann Blyth in the title role, sang it in (MM) *The Helen Morgan Story*, 1957.

Don't Expect Me to Be Your Friend. w/m Kent Lavoie, 1973. Top 10 record by Lobo [Lavoie's pseudonym] (Big Tree).

Don't Explain. w. Arthur Herzog, Jr., m. Billie Holiday, 1946. Introduced and recorded by Billie Holiday (Decca).

Don't Fall in Love with a Dreamer. w/m Kim Carnes and Dave Ellingson, 1980. Top 10 record by Kenny Rogers with Kim Carnes (United Artists).

Don't Fall in Love with Me. w/m Ivory Joe Hunter, 1948. Recorded by Ivory Joe Hunter (King).

Don't Fear the Reaper. w/m Donald Roeser, 1976. Top 20 record by the quintet Blue Oyster Cult (Columbia).

Don't Fence Me In. w/m Cole Porter, 1944. Based on a poem by Robert Fletcher, Porter wrote this ten years earlier for an unproduced film. Roy Rogers and The Sons of the Pioneers introduced it, and The Andrews Sisters reprised it in (MM) *Hollywood Canteen*. One of the year's biggest hits, sixteen weeks on "Your Hit Parade," eight times as #1. Bing Crosby and The Andrews Sisters' record (Decca) was also #1 for eight weeks. Sammy Kaye and his Orchestra (Victor), Gene Autry (Columbia), and Kate Smith, with Four Chicks and Chuck (Columbia), also had popular records.

Don't Fight It. w. Steve Pitchford, Kenny Loggins, and Steve Perry, m. Loggins and Perry, 1982. Recorded by Kenny Loggins with Steve Perry (Columbia).

Don't Fight the Feelings of Love. w/m John Schweers, 1973. Hit Country record by Charley Pride (RCA).

Don't Forbid Me. w/m Charles Singleton, 1957. #1 record hit by Pat Boone (Dot).

Don't Forget. See **Non Dimenticar.**

Don't Forget I Still Love You. w/m Guy Louis, 1964. Top 20 record by Bobbi Martin (Coral).

Don't Forget 127th Street. w. Lee Adams, m. Charles Strouse, 1964. Introduced by Sammy Davis, Jr., Johnny Brown, and company in (TM) *Golden Boy*.

Don't Forget Tonight, Tomorrow. w/m Jay Milton and Ukie Sherin, 1945. Leading record by Frank Sinatra, with the Charioteers (Columbia).

Don't Get Around Much Anymore. w. Bob Russell, m. Edward Kennedy "Duke" Ellington, 1942. Russell's words to the Ellington instrumental "Never No Lament" were introduced and recorded by the Ellington band, vocal by Al Hibbler (Columbia). Successful records were also made by The Ink Spots (Decca) and Glen Gray and the Casa Loma Orchestra, vocal by Kenny Sargent and the LeBrun Sisters (Decca).

Don't Get Me Wrong. w/m Chrissie Hynde, 1986. Top 10 single by the quartet, The Pretenders, of which Hynde was lead singer (Sire).

Don't Give In to Him. w/m Gary Usher, 1969. Hit record by Gary Puckett and The Union Gap (Columbia).

Don't Give Up. w/m Peter Gabriel, 1987. Recorded by the English singers Peter Gabriel and Kate Bush (Geffen).

Don't Give Up. w/m Tony Hatch and Jackie Trent, 1968. Top 40 record by the English singer Petula Clark (Warner Bros.).

Don't Give Up on Us. w/m Tony Macaulay, 1977. Written by the British songwriter Tony Macaulay; the American singer/TV actor David Soul ["Starsky & Hutch"] recorded the song (Private Stock). It became a hit first in England, then in the U.S., where it achieved #1 gold record status.

Don't Give Up the Old Love for New. w/m James Thornton, 1895.

Don't Give Up the Ship (Shipmates All Forever). w. Al Dubin, m. Harry Warren, 1935. Introduced by Dick Powell in (MM) *Shipmates Forever*, one of six films Powell made this year. Recorded by Powell (Decca) and Tommy Dorsey (Victor).

Don't Go. w/m Marlon Jackson, 1987. Top 10 R&B chart record by Marlon Jackson (Capitol).

Don't Go Breaking My Heart. w/m Elton John and Bernie Taupin, 1976. Written under the pseudonyms of Ann Orson and Carte Blanche, this #1 gold record was made by the British artists Elton John and Kiki Dee (Rocket).

Don't Go in the Lion's Cage Tonight. w. John Gilroy, m. E. Ray Goetz, 1906.

Don't Go Near the Indians. w/m Lorene Mann, 1962. Recorded by Rex Allen (Mercury).

Don't Go Out into the Rain (You're Gon- na Melt). w/m Kenny Young, 1967. Top 20 record by the British group Herman's Hermits (MGM).

Don't Go Out Tonight, Boy. w. George Cooper, m. Charles E. Pratt, 1894.

Don't Go to Strangers. w/m J. D. Martin and Russell Smith, 1987. #1 Country chart single from the album "I Tell It Like It Used to Be" by T. Graham Brown (Capitol).

Don't Go to Strangers. w. Redd Evans, m. Arthur Kent and Dave Mann, 1956. Popularized by Vaughn Monroe, with his Orchestra (RCA Victor). Etta Jones had a popular version in 1960 (Prestige).

Don't Hang Up. w. Kal Mann, m. Dave Appell, 1962. Hit record by the Orlons (Cameo).

Don't Hang Your Dreams on a Rainbow. w. Irving Kahal, m. Arnold Johnson, 1929. From *Earl Carroll's Sketch Book*. Recorded by Arnold Johnson's Orchestra (Brunswick) and Fred Rich's Orchestra (Columbia).

Don't Hold Back. w/m James Jamerson, Jr. and David Williams, 1978. Recorded by the studio disco band, Chanson, vocal by the writers (Ariola).

Don't Hold Everything. w. B. G. DeSylva and Lew Brown, m. Ray Henderson, 1928. Introduced by Alice Boulden in (TM) *Hold Everything*. Sheree North sang it in the film biography of the writers (MM) *The Best Things in Life Are Free*, 1956.

Don't It Make My Brown Eyes Blue. w/m Richard Leigh, 1977. Gold record hit by Crystal Gayle (United Artists). Grammy Award (NARAS) winner Country and Western Song of the Year.

Don't It Make You Wanna Dance? w/m Rusty Wier, 1975. Introduced and recorded by Rusty Wier (20th Century). Bonnie Raitt sang it in (MP) *Urban Cowboy*, 1980.

Don't It Make You Want to Go Home? w/m Joe South, 1969. First recorded by Joe South and The Believers (Capitol), followed by Brook Benton and The Dixie Flyers (Cotillion), 1971.

Don't Just Stand There. w/m Lor Crane and Bernice Ross, 1965. Hit record by Patty Duke (United Artists).

Don't Just Stand There (When You Feel Like You're in Love). w/m Cherokee Jack Henley and Ernest Tubb, 1952. C&W hit, with leading recording by Carl Smith (Columbia).

Don't Keep Me Hanging On. w/m Sonny James and Carole Smith, 1971. Country hit by Sonny James (Capitol).

Don't Knock My Love. w. Wilson Pickett, m. Brad Shapiro, 1971. Top 20 record by Wilson Pickett (Atlantic). Later recorded by Marvin Gaye and Diana Ross (Motown), 1974.

Don't Laugh. w/m Rebe Gosdin, 1957. C&W chart record by The Louvin Brothers (Capitol).

Don't Leave Me Dolly. w. William H. Gardner, m. Harry Weill, 1898.

Don't Leave Me This Way. w/m Kenny Gamble, Leon Huff, and Cary Gilbert, 1977. From the album "Any Way You Like It" by Thelma Houston (Tamla), 1976, it was released as a single and became a #1 R&B and Pop chart record.

Don't Let Go. w/m Ian Hunter Patterson, 1984. Chart record by the English group Wang Chung (Geffen).

Don't Let Go. w/m Jesse Stone, 1957. Popularized by Roy Hamilton (Epic). Revivals by Commander Cody and His Lost Planet Airmen (Warner Bros.), 1975, and Isaac Hayes (Polydor), 1979.

Don't Let Go the Coat. w/m Peter Townshend, 1981. Recorded by the English rock group The Who (Warner Bros.).

Don't Let Her Go. w. Aaron Schroeder, m. Abner Silver, 1955. Recorded by Frank Sinatra (Capitol).

Don't Let Him Shop Around. w/m Berry Gordy, Jr. and William "Smokey" Robinson, 1961. Answer song to The Miracle's hit, "Shop Around," recorded by Debbie Dean (Motown).

Don't Let Him Take Your Love from Me. w/m Barrett Strong and Norman Whitfield, 1969. Recorded by The Four Tops (Motown).

Don't Let It Bother You. w. Mack Gordon, m. Harry Revel, 1934. Introduced by Fred Astaire in (MM) *The Gay Divorcée.*

Don't Let It End. w/m Dennis DeYoung, 1983. Top 10 record by the rock quintet Styx (A&M).

Don't Let Julia Fool Ya. w/m Burke Bivens, Jerome Brainin, and Art Kassel, 1941. Best-selling record by Skinnay Ennis and his Orchestra (Victor).

Don't Let Love Hang You Up. w/m Kenny Gamble, Leon Huff, and Jerry Butler, 1969. Recorded by Jerry Butler (Mercury).

Don't Let Me Be Lonely Tonight. w/m James Taylor, 1973. Top 20 record by James Taylor (Warner Bros.).

Don't Let Me Be Misunderstood. w/m Bennie Benjamin, Sol Marcus, and Gloria Caldwell, 1965. Hit record by the English group The Animals (MGM). Also recorded by Nina Simone (Philips). Revived by the studio-conceived disco group, Santa Esmeralda, vocal by Leroy Gomez (Casablanca), 1978.

Don't Let Me Cross Over. w/m Penny Jay, 1963. A crossover hit (C&W/Pop) by Carl Butler (Columbia).

Don't Let Me Down. w/m John Lennon and Paul McCartney, 1969. Recorded by The Beatles, with organist Billy Preston (Apple).

Don't Let Me Dream. w/m Leonard Joy, Richard Loring, and Ned Washington, 1945. Featured and recorded by Phil Brito (Musicraft); the bands of Randy Brooks (Decca) and Stan Kenton (Capitol).

Don't Let That Moon Get Away. w. John-ny Burke, m. James V. Monaco, 1938. Intro-duced in (MM) *Sing You Sinners* and on records (Decca) by Bing Crosby. Also recorded by the Hal Kemp (Victor) and Shep Fields (Bluebird) bands.

Don't Let the Green Grass Fool You. w/m Jerry Akines, Johnnie Bellmon, Victor Drayton, and Reginald Turner, 1971. Top 20 record by Wilson Pickett (Atlantic).

Don't Let the Joneses Get You Down. w/m Norman Whitfield and Barrett Strong, 1969. Top 20 record by The Temptations (Gor-dy).

Don't Let the Rain Come Down (Crooked Little Man). w/m Ersel Hickey and Ed E. Miller, 1964. Top 10 record by The Seren-dipity Singers (Philips).

Don't Let the Rain Fall Down on Me. w/m Jim Ryan, 1967. Chart hit by The Critters (Kapp).

Don't Let the Stars Get in Your Eyes. w/m Slim Willet, 1952. Introduced and #1 C&W record by Slim Willet (4 Star), followed by Skeets McDonald (Capitol) and Ray Price (Columbia), whose records also reached the C&W Top 10. Perry Como's Pop version, with Mitchell Ayre's Orchestra, was #1 on the charts for five weeks and sold over a million copies (RCA Victor). Red Foley then had an-other C&W Top 10 version (Decca), 1953. Other Pop chart records by Giselle Mac-Kenzie, with Buddy Cole's Orchestra (Capitol) and Eileen Barton, with Jack Pleis's Orchestra (Coral). See also "I Let the Stars Gets in My Eyes."

Don't Let the Sun Catch You Cryin'. w/m Joe Greene, 1946. Featured and recorded by Louis Jordan and his Tympany Five (Dec-ca).

Don't Let the Sun Catch You Crying. w/m Gerry Marsden, 1964. Hit record by the Liverpudlian group Gerry and The Pacemakers (Laurie).

Don't Let the Sun Go Down on Me. w/m Elton John and Bernie Taupin, 1974. U.S. gold record by the British singer Elton John (MCA).

Don't Let Your Love Go Wrong. w. George Whiting and Nat Schwartz, m. J. C. Johnson, 1934. Early recordings by Red Allen (Perfect); Isham Jones, vocal by Eddie Stone (Victor); the Boswell Sisters (Brunswick); and Gene Kardos's band (Vocalion).

Don't Live a Lie. w/m Gene Autry and Johnny Bond, 1945. Introduced and recorded by C&W artist Gene Autry (Columbia).

Don't Look Any Further. w/m Franne Golde, Duane Hitchings, and Dennis Lam-bert, 1984. Recorded by Dennis Edwards, with added vocal by Siedah Garrett (Gordy).

Don't Look at Me That Way. w/m Cole Porter, 1928. Introduced by Irene Bordoni in (TM) *Paris* and recorded by her (Victor).

Don't Look Back. w/m Tom Scholz, 1978. Top 10 record by the group Boston (Epic).

Don't Look Now (But Your Broken Heart Is Showin'). w/m Ernest Tubb, 1947. Intro-duced and recorded by Ernest Tubb (Decca).

Don't Lose My Number. w/m Phil Col-lins, 1985. Top 10 single from the platinum album "No Jacket Required" by the English singer Phil Collins (Atlantic).

Don't Make It Easy for Me. w/m Earl Thomas Conley and Randy Scruggs, 1984. #1 Country chart record by Earl Thomas Conley (RCA).

Don't Make Me Over. 1989. Hit R&B chart single by Sybil (Next Plateau).

Don't Make Me Over. w. Hal David, m. Burt Bacharach, 1963. Introduced by Dionne Warwick (Scepter), and her first chart record, which marked the beginning of a long string of successes written and produced for her by the team of Bacharach and David. Revived by Sybil (Next Plateau), 1989.

Don't Make Me Wait for Love. w/m Preston Glass, Narada Michael Walden, and W. Afanasieff, 1987. R&B and Pop chart record by saxophonist Kenny G, with vocal by Lenny Williams (Arista).

Don't Make My Baby Blue. w/m Cynthia Weil and Barry Mann, 1963. Chart record by Frankie Laine (Columbia).

Don't Mean Nothing. w/m Richard Marx and Bruce Gaitsch, 1987. Top 10 single by jingle singer/songwriter Richard Marx from his self-named album (Manhattan).

Don't Mention Love to Me. w. Dorothy Fields, m. Oscar Levant, 1935. Sung in (MM) *In Person* and on records (Decca) by Ginger Rogers. Isham Jones's Orchestra (Victor) and Kay Thompson (Brunswick) also recorded it.

Don't Mess Up a Good Thing. w/m Oliver Sain, 1965. Crossover (R&B/Pop) record by Fontella Bass and Bobby McClure (Tamla).

Don't Mess with Bill. w/m William Robinson, 1966. Crossover (R&B/Pop) hit by The Marvelettes (Tamla).

Don't Mind the Rain. w. Ned Miller, m. Chester Conn, 1924. Featured and recorded by Blossom Seeley (Columbia) and Ace Brigode (Okeh).

Don't Pay the Ferryman. w/m Chris De Burgh, 1983. Recorded by the Irish singer/writer Chris De Burgh (A&M).

Don't Pity Me. w. Sid Jacobson, m. Lou Stallman, 1959. Popular record by Dion and The Belmonts (Laurie).

Don't Play That Song (You Lied). w/m Ahmet M. Ertegun and Betty Nelson, 1962. Hit crossover record (R&B/Pop) by Ben E. King (Atlantic). Aretha Franklin also had a hit version (Atlantic), 1970.

Don't Pull Your Love. w/m Dennis Lambert and Brian Potter, 1971. Gold record by Hamilton, Joe Frank, and Reynolds (Dunhill). Revived by Glen Campbell in medley with

"Then You Can Tell Me Goodbye" (Capitol), 1976.

Don't Push It, Don't Force It. w/m Leon Haywood, 1980. Top 10 on the R&B chart, and Pop chart entry by Leon Haywood (20th Century).

Don't Put It Down. w. Gerome Ragni and James Rado, m. Galt MacDermot, 1968. Introduced by Gerome Ragni and Steve Curry in (TM) *Hair*.

Don't Put Me Down. w/m Jimmy Liggins, 1949. R&B chart record by Jimmy Liggins (Specialty).

Don't Put Me Off at Buffalo Any More. w. William Jerome, m. Jean Schwartz, 1901.

Don't Rain on My Parade. w/m Bob Merrill, m. Jule Styne, 1964. Introduced by Barbra Streisand in (TM) *Funny Girl*, and sung by her in the film version, (MM) *Funny Girl*, 1968.

Don't Read the Letter. w. Howard Greenfield, m. Jack Keller, 1961. Recorded by Patti Page (Mercury).

Don't Rob Another Man's Castle. w/m Jenny Lou Carson, 1949. Leading record by Eddy Arnold (RCA Victor). Also recorded by Ernest Tubb and The Andrews Sisters (Decca).

Don't Rock the Boat, Dear. w. Ralph Blane and Harold Arlen, m. Harold Arlen, 1950. Introduced by Betty Grable and Dan Dailey in (MM) *My Blue Heaven.*

Don't Rush Me. w/m Jeffrey Franzel and Alexandra Forbes, 1989. Hit record by Taylor Dayne (Arista).

Don't Say Goodnight. w. Al Dubin, m. Harry Warren, 1934. Introduced by Dick Powell in a Busby Berkeley production number in (MM) *Wonder Bar*. Powell recorded it (Brunswick), as did Gus Arnheim (Brunswick) and Tal Henry (Bluebird) and their orchestras.

Don't Say Goodnight (It's Time for Love). w/m Ernest Isley, Ronald Isley, Marvin Isley, Rudolph Isley, O'Kelly Isley, Chris

Jasper, 1980. #1 R&B, Top 40 Pop chart two-sided single by The Isley Brothers (T-Neck).

Don't Say Nothin' Bad (About My Baby). w/m Gerry Goffin and Carole King, 1963. Top 10 record by the vocal trio The Cookies (Dimension).

Don't Say No Tonight. w/m Ron Broomfield and McKinley Horton, 1986. Recorded by Eugene Wilde [pseudonym for Broomfield] (Philly World).

Don't Say You Don't Remember. w/m Estelle Levitt and Helen Miller, 1972. Top 20 record by Beverly Bremers (Scepter).

Don't Shed a Tear. w/m Eddie Schwartz and Rob Friedman, 1988. Recorded by Paul Carrack from his album "One Good Reason" (Chrysalis).

Don't Sit Under the Apple Tree (with Anyone Else But Me). w. Lew Brown and Charles Tobias, m. Sam H. Stept, 1942. Popular with the servicemen and women in World War II, and the general public as evidenced by the sales of records and sheet music. Best-selling records by Glenn Miller, vocal by Marion Hutton, Tex Beneke, and the Modernaires (Bluebird) and the Andrews Sisters (Decca) who sang it in (MM) *Private Buckaroo*, 1943.

Don't Sleep in the Subway. w/m Tony Hatch and Jackie Trent, 1967. Top 10 hit by British singer Petula Clark (Warner Bros.).

Don't Smoke in Bed. w/m Willard Robison, 1948. Featured and recorded by Peggy Lee (Capitol).

Don't Squeeze My Sharmon. w/m Carl Belew and Van Givens, 1967. Top 10 Country chart record by Charlie Walker (Epic). Title derived from the bathroom tissue slogan "Don't squeeze the Charmin."

Don't Stand So Close to Me. w/m Sting (pseud. for Gordon Sumner), 1981. Top 10 record by the English trio Police (A&M). New chart version, but not Top 10, released in 1986 (A&M).

Don't Stay Away. w/m Lefty Frizzell and Loys Southerland, 1952. C&W hit by Lefty Frizzell (Columbia).

Don't Stay Away Too Long. w/m Al Hoffman and Dick Manning, 1955. Recorded by Eddie Fisher (RCA).

Don't Stop. w/m Christine McVie, 1977. Top 10 record by the British blues band Fleetwood Mac (Warner Bros.).

Don't Stop Believin'. w/m Steve Perry, Neal Schon, and Jonathan Cain, 1981. Top 10 record written by members of the group Journey (Columbia).

Don't Stop Believin'. w/m John Farrar, 1976. Recorded by Olivia Newton-John (MCA).

Don't Stop the Music. w/m Jonah Ellis, Lonnie Simmons, and Alisa Peoples, 1981. Gold Record by the duo of Yarbrough and Peoples (Mercury).

Don't Stop 'Til You Get Enough. w/m Michael Jackson, 1979. #1 platinum single from Michael Jackson's album "Off the Wall," produced by Quincy Jones (Epic).

Don't Sweetheart Me. w. Charles Tobias, m. Cliff Friend, 1943. Best-selling record by Lawrence Welk, vocal by Wayne Marsh (Decca).

Don't Take It Away. w/m Max D. Barnes and Troy Seals, 1979. First recorded by Jody Miller (Epic), 1975. #1 Country chart record by Conway Twitty (MCA), 1979.

Don't Take It Out on Me. w/m Hank Thompson, 1955. Introduced and recorded by Hank Thompson (Capitol).

Don't Take It So Hard. w/m Mark Lindsay, 1968. Top 40 record by Paul Revere and The Raiders (Columbia).

Don't Take Me Home. w. Vincent Bryan, m. Harry Von Tilzer, 1908.

Don't Take Our Charlie for the Army. w/m Noël Coward, 1963. Introduced by Tessie O'Shea and ensemble in (TM) *The Girl Who Came to Supper.*

Don't Take Your Guns to Town. w/m Johnny Cash, 1959. Hit C&W and Pop record by Johnny Cash (Columbia).

Don't Take Your Love from Me. w/m Henry Nemo, 1941. Introduced and featured by Mildred Bailey. Best-selling recordings upon release: Artie Shaw, vocal by Lena Horne (Victor) and Alvino Rey, vocal by Yvonne King (Bluebird). Popular version by Glen Gray and the Casa Loma Orchestra, vocal by Eugenie Baird (Decca), 1944.

Don't Talk to Strangers. w/m Rick Springfield, 1982. #2 chart hit by the Australian singer/writer Rick Springfield (RCA).

Don't Talk to Strangers. w. Bob Durand, m. Ron Elliott, 1965, 1982. Recorded by The Beau Brummels (Autumn).

Don't Telephone, Don't Telegraph, Tell a Woman. w/m Al Stewart and Tex Williams, 1948. Crossover C&W/Pop chart record by Tex Williams and The Western Caravan (Capitol).

Don't Tell Her That You Love Her. w/m Paul Dresser, 1896.

Don't Tell Her What Happened to Me. w. B. G. DeSylva and Lew Brown, m. Ray Henderson, 1930. Non-production song with many recordings. Among them: Isham Jones, vocal by Eddie Stone (Brunswick); Ted Wallace (Columbia); the Boswell Sisters (Okeh); Eddy Howard (Majestic); Nick Lucas (Brunswick); Nat Shilkret (Victor).

Don't Tell Me. w/m Buddy Pepper, 1947. Introduced by Ava Gardner, with the dubbed-in voice of Eileen Wilson in (MP) *The Hucksters.* Recorded by Helen Forrest (MGM); Margaret Whiting (Capitol); Les Brown and his Orchestra (Columbia).

Don't Tell Me Goodnight. w/m Kent Lavoie, 1975. Recorded by Lobo, a.k.a. Lavoie (Big Tree).

Don't Tell Me Your Troubles. w/m Don Gibson, 1959. C&W and Pop chart record by Don Gibson (RCA).

Don't the Girls All Get Prettier at Closing Time? w/m Baker Knight, 1976. Country chart hit by Mickey Gilley (Playboy).

Don't Think Twice, It's All Right. w/m Bob Dylan, 1963. Introduced and recorded by Peter, Paul, and Mary (Warner Bros.). Chart record by The Wonder Who? (Philips), 1965.

Don't Throw It All Away. See **Our Love (Don't Throw It All Away).**

Don't Throw Your Love Away. w/m Billy Jackson and Jimmy Wisner, 1964. Top 20 record by the British rock quartet The Searchers (Kapp).

Don't Touch Me. w/m Hank Cochran, 1966. Crossover hit (C&W/Pop) by Jeannie Seely (Monument). Revived by Bettye Swann (Capitol), 1969.

Don't Touch Me There. w/m Jane Dornackle and Ron Nagle, 1976. Recorded by The Tubes (A&M).

Don't Try to Fight It, Baby. w/m Gerry Goffin and Jack Keller, 1963. Chart record by Eydie Gormé (Columbia).

Don't Try to Lay No Boogie Woogie on the King of Rock and Roll. w/m Jeff Thomas, 1970. Recorded by Crow (Amaret) and followed by John Baldry (Warner Bros.), 1971.

Don't Underestimate My Love for You. w/m Steve Diamond, Steve Dorff, and Dave Loggins, 1986. #1 Country chart record by Lee Greenwood (MCA).

Don't Wait on Me. w/m Harold Reid and Don Reid, 1981. Written by two members of the group, The Statler Brothers, whose recording reached the Top 10 on the Country charts (Mercury).

Don't Wait Too Long. w/m Sunny Skylar, 1963. Featured and recorded by Tony Bennett (Columbia).

Don't Wake Me Up, I'm Dreaming. w. Beth Slater Whitson, m. Herbert Ingraham, 1910.

Don't Wake Me Up, Let Me Dream. w. L. Wolfe Gilbert, m. Mabel Wayne and Abel Baer, 1925. Featured and recorded by the orchestras of Vincent Lopez (Okeh) and Howard Lanin (Victor).

Don't Wake Me Up in the Morning, Michael. w/m Al Kasha, 1969. Recorded by The Peppermint Rainbow (Decca).

Don't Wake Up My Heart. w. Sam M. Lewis, m. George W. Meyer and Pete Wendling, 1938. Featured and recorded by the bands of Benny Goodman (Victor) and Woody Herman (Decca).

Don't Walk Away. w/m Rick Springfield, 1984. Sung by Rick Springfield in (MP) *Hard to Hold* and on records (RCA).

Don't Wanna Lose You. w/m Gloria Estefan, 1989. Hit single by Gloria Estefan (Epic).

Don't Want to Live Inside Myself. w/m Barry Gibb, 1971. Recorded by the British brother trio The Bee Gees (Atco).

Don't Want to Live Without It. w/m Dave Jenkins and Cory Lerios, 1978. Recorded by the quartet Pablo Cruise (A&M).

Don't Waste Your Time. w/m Jonah Ellis, 1984. Recorded by the duo Yarbrough and Peoples (Total Experience).

Don't We All Have the Right. w/m Roger Miller, 1988. #1 Country chart single by Ricky Van Shelton (Columbia).

Don't Worry. w/m Marty Robbins, 1961. Marty Robbins not only wrote and published the song but his record was a C&W and Pop chart hit (Columbia).

Don't Worry, Be Happy. w/m Bobby McFerrin, 1988. From (MP) *Cocktail*. #1 record by Bobby McFerrin (EMI). Winner Grammy Award (NARAS) Song and Record of the Year.

Don't Worry Baby. w/m Brian Wilson and Roger Christian, 1964. Introduced and hit record by The Beach Boys (Capitol). The Tokens had a chart record in 1970 (Buddah), and B. J. Thomas revived it with a hit version in 1977 (MCA). Sung on the soundtrack of (MP) *Tequila Sunrise* by The Beach Boys and The Everly Brothers and the soundtrack album (Capitol), 1988.

Don't Worry 'Bout Me. w. Ted Koehler, m. Rube Bloom, 1939. A Top 10 song with many recordings, among which were the bands of Les Brown, vocal by Miriam Shaw (Bluebird); Horace Heidt (Brunswick); Count Basie, vocal by Helen Humes (Vocalion); Bob Crosby, vocal by Marion Mann (Decca); and singer Ginny Simms (Vocalion). Later records by Savannah Churchill (Victor); Teddy Wilson, vocal by Sarah Vaughan (Musicraft); Zoot Sims (Discovery); Stan Getz (Savoy).

Don't Worry 'Bout Me Baby. w/m Deborah Allen, Bruce Channel, and Kieran Kane, 1982. #1 Country chart record by Janie Fricke (Columbia).

Don't You (Forget About Me). w/m Keith Forsey and Steve Schiff, 1985. Introduced on the soundtrack of (MP) *The Breakfast Club* and on a #1 chart record by the Scottish rock group Simple Minds (A&M).

Don't You Believe It. w. Bob Hilliard, m. Burt Bacharach, 1962. Popularized by Andy Williams (Columbia).

Don't You Care. w/m Gary Beisbier and Jim Holvay, 1967. Top 10 record by The Buckinghams (Columbia).

Don't You Ever Get Tired of Hurting Me? w/m Hank Cochran, 1966. First Country chart record by Ray Price (Columbia). Price, paired with Willie Nelson, recorded a chart version (Columbia), 1981. Ronnie Milsap had a #1 hit record (RCA), 1989.

Don't You Forget It. w. Al Stillman, m. Henry Mancini, 1963. Adapted from Mancini's instrumental "Tinpanola." Top 40 record by Perry Como (RCA).

Don't You Get So Mad. w/m Jeffrey Osborne, Michael Sembello, and Donald Freeman, 1983. R&B hit and Pop chart record by Jeffrey Osborne (A&M).

Don't You Know. w/m Bobby Worth, 1959. Based on "Musetta's Waltz" from the opera *La Boheme* by Puccini. Hit record by Della Reese (RCA).

Don't You Know. w/m Ray Charles, 1954. R&B hit by Ray Charles (Atlantic).

Don't You Know I Care (Or, Don't You Care to Know?). w. Mack David, m. Edward Kennedy "Duke" Ellington, 1944. Introduced and recorded by Duke Ellington, vocal by Al Hibbler (Victor). Also recorded by June Hutton, with Paul Weston's Orchestra (Capitol).

Don't You Know I Love You? w/m Ahmet Ertegun, 1951. The Clovers (Atlantic) had their first million-seller.

Don't You Know What the Night Can Do? w. Will Jennings, m. Steve Winwood, 1988. A U.K. beer commercial turned into a Pop chart hit by Steve Winwood (Virgin).

Don't You Love Me Anymore? w/m Mack David, Al Hoffman, and Jerry Livingston, 1947. Leading records by Buddy Clark, with Mitchell Ayres's Orchestra (Columbia); Freddy Martin, vocal by Clyde Rogers (RCA Victor); José Mellis, vocal by Jeannie Williams (Mercury).

Don't You Miss Your Baby? w/m Eddie Durham, William "Count" Basie, and Jimmy Rushing, 1939. Introduced and recorded by Count Basie, vocal by Jimmy Rushing (Decca).

Don't You Want Me. w/m Franne Golde, D. Bryant, and Jody Watley, 1987. Top 10 single from the platinum debut album of her name by Jody Watley (MCA).

Don't You Want Me. w/m Jo Calis, Phil Oakey, and Philip Adrian Wright, 1982. #1 gold record by the British sextet The Human League (A&M).

Don't You Worry 'Bout a Thing. w/m Stevie Wonder, 1974. Top 20 record by Stevie Wonder (Tamla).

Doo De Doo on an Old Kazoo. w/m Irving Taylor, George Wyle, and Edward Pola, 1948. Featured and recorded by Art Mooney and his Orchestra (MGM).

Doodle Doo Doo. w/m Art Kassel and Mel Stitzel, 1924. This became the theme song of the composer-band leader whose aggregation was known as Art Kassel and his Kassels in the Air. He recorded it twice (Brunswick) (Vogue). Other releases by Joe "Fingers" Carr (Capitol), Tiny Hill (Vocalion), Clyde McCoy (Decca).

Doo Doo Doo Doo Doo (Heartbreaker). w/m Mick Jagger and Keith Richards, 1974. Recorded by the British group The Rolling Stones (Rolling Stones).

Door Is Still Open to My Heart, The. w/m Chuck Willis, 1955, 1964. R&B hit by The Cardinals (Atlantic). Revived in 1964 with a Top 10 record by Dean Martin (Reprise).

Door of My Dreams, The. w. Otto Harbach and Oscar Hammerstein II, m. Rudolf Friml, 1924. Introduced by Mary Ellis in (TM) *Rose-Marie*. The song was not included in either of the film versions.

Door's Always Open, The. w/m Dickey Lee and Bob McDill, 1976. Country chart hit by Dave and Sugar (RCA).

Door Will Open, A. w. Don George, m. John Benson Brooks, 1946. Featured and recorded by Tommy Dorsey, vocal by Stuart Foster (Victor).

Doo Wacka Doo. w. Clarence Gaskill and Will Donaldson, m. George Horther, 1924. Recorded by Isham Jones (Brunswick) and Paul Whiteman (Victor).

Do-Re-Mi. w. Oscar Hammerstein II, m. Richard Rodgers, 1959. Introduced by Mary Martin and the children in (TM) *The Sound of Music*. In the film version (MM) *The Sound of Music*, 1965, it was sung by Julie Andrews and the children.

Do Right. w/m Paul Davis, 1980. Recorded by Paul Davis (Bang).

Dormi, Dormi. w/m Don Marcotte, 1949. Recorded by Axel Stordahl and his Orchestra (Columbia).

Dormi, Dormi, Dormi. w. Sammy Cahn, m. Harry Warren, 1958. Introduced by Salvatore Baccaloni and Jerry Lewis, singing the lullaby to infant triplets in (MM) *Rock-a-Bye-Baby*.

Do Something. w. Bud Green, m. Sam H. Stept, 1929. From (MM) *Syncopation*. Popularized by the recordings of Helen Kane (Victor); McKinney's Cotton Pickers (Victor); The Sunshine Boys, Joe Mooney and his brother, Danny (Columbia); and Zelma O'Neal (Brunswick).

Do Something for Me. w/m William E. Ward and Rose Marks, 1950. The record that brought attention to the R&B group. The Dominoes, with Clyde McPhatter as lead singer and Billy Ward on piano (Federal).

Do Something to Me. w/m Jimmy Calvert, Norman Marzano, and Paul Naumann, 1968. Recorded by Tommy James and The Shondells (Roulette).

Do That to Me One More Time. w/m Toni Tennille, 1979. #1 gold record by The Captain and Tennille (Casablanca).

Do the Bird. w. Kal Mann, m. Dave Appell, 1963. Hit record by Dee Dee Sharp (Cameo).

Do the Boomerang. w/m Henry Cosby, Autry DeWalt, and Willie Woods, 1965. Crossover (R&B/Pop) hit by Jr. Walker and the All Stars (Soul).

Do the Choo Choo. w/m Kenny Gamble and Leon Huff, 1968. Recorded by Archie Bell and The Drells (Atlantic).

Do the Clam. w/m Dolores Fuller, Sid Wayne, and Ben Weisman, 1965. Sung by Elvis Presley, with support from Gary Crosby, Joby Baker, and Jimmy Hawkins in (MM) *Girl Happy*. Presley recorded it (RCA).

Do the Freddie. w/m Lou Courtney and Dennis Lambert, 1965. Top 20 hit by Freddie and the Dreamers (Mercury).

Do the Funky Penguin. w/m Jo Bridges, Tom Nixon, Mack Rice, and Rufus Thomas, 1972. Recorded by Rufus Thomas (Stax).

Do the New York. w/m J. P. Murray, Barry Trivers, and Ben Oakland, 1931. Sung by Harry Richman in (TM) *Ziegfeld Follies of 1931*. Glen Gray and the Casa Loma Orchestra recorded it (Brunswick).

Do They Know It's Christmas? w/m Bob Geldof and Midge Ure, 1984. Co-written and produced by Irishman Bob Geldof who organized the recording stars for the purpose of assisting famine relief in Ethiopia. The assembled group was called Band Aid and was comprised of: Paul Young, Boy George and Jon Moss of Culture Club, Wham!, Sting, Phil Collins, Duran Duran, Bananarama, Spandau Ballet, Style Council, Boomtown Rats, and members of Kool and The Gang, U2, Ultravox, Status Quo, and Heaven 17 (Columbia).

Double Check Stomp. m. Barney Bigard and Irving Mills, 1930. Instrumental, recorded by Duke Ellington (Victor). The title was undoubtedly inspired by the band's appearance in the Amos 'n' Andy film (MM) *Check and Double Check* shortly before this recording session.

Double Crossing Blues. w/m Johnny Otis, 1950. In the Top 10 on the R&B charts for five months, the recording by Little Esther, Mel Walker, and Johnny Otis (Savoy) was the #2 R&B Song of the Year.

Double Dutch Bus. w/m Frankie Smith and William Bloom, 1981. Gold record by Frankie Smith (WMOT). The title comes from the childrens' jump rope game.

Double Lovin'. w/m George Jackson and Mickey Buckins, 1971. Top 20 record by The Osmonds (MGM).

Double Shot (of My Baby's Love). w/m Don M. Smith and Cyril E. Vetter, 1966. Hit record by The Swingin' Medallions (Smash).

Double Trouble. w. Leo Robin, m. Ralph Rainger and Richard A. Whiting, 1935. Introduced by Lyda Roberti, Jack Oakie, and Henry Wadsworth in (MM) *The Big Broadcast of 1936*. Recorded by the bands of Ray Noble, arranged by Glenn Miller (Victor); Red McKenzie (Decca); Frank Dailey (Bluebird); the vocal group Babs and her Brothers (Decca).

Double Vision. w/m Lou Gramm and Mick Jones, 1978. Gold record by the group Foreigner (Atlantic).

Do-Wacka-Do. w/m Roger Miller, 1964. Top 40 novelty record by Roger Miller (Smash). Not to be confused with the 1924 song "Doo Wacka Doo."

Do Wah Diddy Diddy. w/m Jeff Barry and Ellie Greenwich, 1964. #1 chart record by the British rock group Manfred Mann (Ascot).

Do What You Do. w/m Ralph Dino and Larry DiTomaso, 1984. Recorded by Jermaine Jackson, formerly of the Jacksons (Arista).

Do What You Do. w. Ira Gershwin and Gus Kahn, m. George Gershwin, 1929. Introduced by Ruby Keeler and Frank McHugh in (TM) *Show Girl*. Recorded by Zelma O'Neal (Brunswick) and B. A. Rolfe's Orchestra (Edison).

Do What You Do, Do Well. w/m Ned Miller and Sue Miller, 1965. Crossover (C&W/Pop) chart song by Ned Miller (Fabor).

Down a Carolina Lane. w. Mitchell Parish, m. Frank Perkins, 1933. Popularized and recorded by the bands of Isham Jones (Victor) and George Hall, vocal by Loretta Lee (Bluebird).

Down Among the Sheltering Palms. w. James Brockman, m. Abe Olman, 1915. The song was sung by Keenan Wynn and a quartet in (MM) *That Midnight Kiss*, 1949. It was heard as the title song in the film starring Mitzi Gaynor, Gloria De Haven, and William Lundigan, (MM) *Down Among The Sheltering Palms*, 1952, and was performed by a chorus in (MM) *Some Like It Hot*, 1959.

Down Among the Sugar Cane. w. Avery and Hart, m. Cecil Mack and Chris Smith, 1908.

Down Argentina Way. w. Mack Gordon, m. Harry Warren, 1940. Introduced in Spanish by the voice of Carlos Albert, dubbing for Don Ameche, in (MM) *Down Argentine Way*. Reprised in a song-and-dance number (sung in English) by Betty Grable. Top recording by Dinah Shore (Bluebird). Nominated for Academy Award.

Down at Lulu's. w/m Joey Levine and Kris Resnick, 1968. Top 40 record by the group Ohio Express (Buddah).

Down at the Huskin' Bee. w. Monroe H. Rosenfeld, m. Henry R. Stern, 1909. Originally published in 1908 as an instrumental titled "S. R. Henry's Barn Dance" that contained a pseudonym for the composer.

Down at the Roadside Inn. w/m Al Dexter, 1947. Recorded by Al Dexter (Okeh).

Down by the Lazy River. w/m Alan Osmond and Merrill Osmond, 1972. Gold record by The Osmonds (MGM).

Down by the O-Hi-O. w. Jack Yellen, m. Abe Olman, 1920. Popularized by Van and Schenk in vaudeville and via their interpolation in (TM) *Ziegfeld Follies*. Leading recording by Billy Murray and Billy Jones, the latter under the pseudonym of "Victor Roberts" (Victor). Revived by The Andrews Sisters (Decca), and the Smoothies (Bluebird), 1940.

Down by the Old Mill Stream. w/m Tell Taylor, 1910. An all-time sing-along favorite.

Down by the River. w/m Neil Young, 1970. Leading record by Buddy Miles (Mercury). Also recorded by Brooklyn Bridge (Buddah).

Down by the River. w/m Jan Crutchfield and Teddy Wilburn, 1963. C&W hit by Faron Young (Capitol).

Down by the River. w. Lorenz Hart, m. Richard Rodgers, 1935. Introduced in (MM) *Mississippi* and recorded (Decca) by Bing Crosby.

Down by the River. w. Henry Creamer, m. Turner Layton, 1923.

Down by the Riverside. w/m Paul Barnes, 1900. Popular development of Negro spiritual from the Civil War period. Became a favorite with glee clubs and jazz bands. Among recordings: Turk Murphy (Good Time Jazz), Bunk Johnson (Jazzman), Conrad Janis (Circle), and Jim Robinson (Columbia).

Down by the Silvery Rio Grande. w. Dave Weisberg and Robert F. Roden, m. Charles Spiedel, 1913.

Down by the Station. w/m Lee Ricks and Slim Gaillard, 1948. Based on popular children's song. Introduced and recorded by Slim Gaillard with his combo (MGM). Top records by Tommy Dorsey, vocal by Denny Dennis, Lucy Ann Polk and The Sentimentalists (Victor); Guy Lombardo and his Orchestra (Decca).

Down by the Station. See **Early in the Morning.**

Down by the Winegar Woiks. w/m Don Bestor, Roger Lewis, and Walter Donovan, 1925. Featured and recorded by the Troubadors (Victor).

Downhearted. w. Bob Hilliard, m. Dave Mann, 1953. Popular recording by Eddie Fisher (RCA Victor).

Down Hearted Blues. w/m Alberta Hunter, 1923. The many recordings include Alberta Hunter (Paramount) (Decca); Bessie Smith (Columbia); Fletcher Henderson (Vocalion); Sissle and Blake (Perfect); Mildred Bailey (Decca).

Down Home Blues. w/m Tom Delaney, 1921. First recorded by Ethel Waters (Black Swan).

Down in Bom-Bombay. w. Ballard MacDonald, m. Harry Carroll, 1915.

Down in Dear Old New Orleans. w. Joe Young, m. Con Conrad and Jay Whidden, 1912. Sung by Rae Samuels in (TM) *Ziegfeld Follies of 1912*.

Down in Honky Tonky Town. w. Charles McCarron, m. Chris Smith, 1916. Revived in 1947 by Ray Bauduc and Band (Capitol).

Down in Jungle Town. w. Edward Madden, m. Theodore F. Morse, 1908.

Down in Mexico. w/m Jerry Leiber and Mike Stoller, 1956. Top 10 R&B chart record by The Coasters (Atco).

Down in Poverty Row. w. Gussie L. Davis, m. Arthur Trevelyan, 1895. Featured by Bonnie Thornton.

Down in the Boondocks. w/m Joe South, 1965. Hit record by Billy Joe Royal (Columbia).

Down in the Depths (On the Ninetieth Floor). w/m Cole Porter, 1936. Introduced by Ethel Merman in (TM) *Red, Hot and Blue!* Merman recorded it, coupled with "It's De-Lovely" from the same show (Liberty Music Shops).

Down in the Mouth Blues. m. Bubber Miley and Arthur Ray, 1924. Recorded by the Texas Blues Destroyers (Perfect).

Down on Love. w/m Mick Jones and Lou Gramm, 1985. Chart record by the Anglo-American group Foreigner (Atlantic).

Down on Me. w/m Janis Joplin, 1968. Introduced and recorded by Big Brother and The Holding Company, Janis Joplin lead singer

(Mainstream). A chart single from a "live" Joplin concert was released posthumously (Columbia), 1972.

Down on the Brandywine. w. Vincent P. Bryan, m. J. B. Mullen, 1904.

Down on the Corner. w/m John Fogerty, 1969. Gold record hit, coupled with equally rated "Fortunate Son," by Creedence Clearwater Revival (Fantasy).

Down on the Farm. w/m John Greenebaum, Troy Seals, and Eddie Setser, 1985. Song written to help publicize the current plight of the American farmer. Introduced and recorded by Charley Pride (RCA).

Down on the Farm (They All Ask for You). w. Raymond A. Browne, m. Harry Von Tilzer, 1902.

Down on the Farm in Harvest Time. w. Andrew K. Allison, m. Dick Richards, 1913.

Down South Camp Meetin'. w. Irving Mills, m. Fletcher Henderson, 1935. Introduced and recorded by Fletcher Henderson and his Band (Decca), followed by the California Ramblers, led by Charlie Barnet (Variety). Benny Goodman had the biggest selling record (Columbia).

Down the Aisle of Love. w/m The Quin-Tones, 1958. Recorded by the Quin-Tones (Hunt).

Down the Field. w. C. W. O'Connor, m. Stanleigh P. Friedman, 1911. A Yale University marching song.

Down the Old Church Aisle. w/m Ray Perkins, 1921. From (TM) *Greenwich Village Follies of 1921*. Recorded by Ted Lewis (Columbia).

Down the Old Ox Road. w. Sam Coslow, m. Arthur Johnston, 1933. Introduced by Bing Crosby in (MM) *College Humor* and recorded by him (Brunswick). Paul Whiteman (Victor) had a popular record. Among later releases: Maxine Sullivan (Victor), Elliot Lawrence (Decca).

Down the River of Golden Dreams. w. John Klenner, m. Nathaniel Shilkret, 1930.

Down the Road a Piece. w/m Don Raye, 1941. Introduced and recorded by Will Bradley and his Orchestra, featuring Ray McKinley [vocal and drums] and Freddie Slack [piano] (Columbia).

Down the Trail of Achin' Hearts. w/m Jimmy Kennedy and Nat Simon, 1951. Most popular recording by Patti Page (Mercury).

Down the Winding Road of Dreams. w. Margaret Cantrell, m. Ernest R. Ball, 1922.

Down to My Last Broken Heart. w/m Chick Rains, 1981. Top 10 Country record by Janie Fricke (Columbia).

Downtown. w/m Tony Hatch, 1965. #1 record and million-seller by the English singer Petula Clark (Warner Bros.). Allan Sherman recorded a parody version, "Crazy Downtown" (Warner Bros.). Mrs. Miller, the popular counterpart of Florence Foster Jenkins, and contemporary of the inimitable Sam Sacks, made the charts with her polytonal interpretation of the song (RCA).

Downtown Train. w/m Tom Waits, 1986. Introduced on the soundtrack of (MP) *Down by Law* by Tom Waits. Chart record by Patty Smyth (Columbia), 1987.

Down T'Uncle Bill's. w/m Johnny Mercer and Hoagy Carmichael, 1935. Recorded by Frankie Trumbauer and his Orchestra (Victor).

Down Under. w/m Colin Hay and Roy Strykert, 1982. #1 gold record by the Australian quintet Men At Work (Columbia).

Down Went McGinty. w/m Joseph Flynn, 1889.

Down Where the Cotton Blossoms Grow. w. Andrew B. Sterling, m. Harry Von Tilzer, 1901.

Down Where the Silv'ry Mohawk Flows. w. Monroe H. Rosenfeld, m. John and Otto Heinzman, 1905.

Down Where the Sun Goes Down. w. Verne Buck, m. Isham Jones, 1928. Recorded by the Coon-Sanders Orchestra (Victor), Abe Lyman's Orchestra (Brunswick), and later, the Firehouse Five Plus Two (Good Time Jazz).

Down Where the Swanee River Flows. w. Charles McCarron, m. Charles S. Alberte, 1916. The Peerless Quartette (Victor) had a popular recording.

Down Where the Trade Winds Blow. w/m Harry Owens, 1938. Introduced by Bobby Breen in (MM) *Hawaii Calls*.

Down Where the Wurzburger Flows. w. Vincent P. Bryan, m. Harry Von Tilzer, 1902. Introduced by Nora Bayes at the Orpheum Theatre in N.Y.C. The song was such a success that Miss Bayes was often referred to as "The Wurzburger Girl." It was used as a promotional song for Wurzburger beer. In 1903 Von Tilzer wrote a popular sequel called "Under The Anheuser Bush" (q.v.), with lyrics by Andrew B. Sterling.

Down with Love. w. E. Y. Harburg, m. Harold Arlen, 1937. Introduced by Jack Whiting, June Clyde, and Vivian Vance in (MM) *Horray for What*. Lee Wiley had a well-received recording (Schirmer).

Down Yonder. w/m L. Wolfe Gilbert, 1921, 1951. This song, while performed by some leading entertainers when it first came out, remained in obscurity until 1951 when it was recorded by pianist Del Wood in Nashville (Tennessee). Her million-seller was responsible for many other recordings and for the song's fourteen weeks on "Your Hit Parade."

Do Ya. w/m Jeff Lynne, 1977. First recorded by the British group The Move (United Artists), 1972. The Ensemble, with personnel changes, and renamed Electric Light Orchestra, recut the song and had a Top 40 record (United Artists), 1977.

Do Ya'. w/m K. T. Oslin, 1987. #1 Country chart record by K. T. Oslin (RCA).

Do Ya Love Me? w. Haven Gillespie, m. Mabel Wayne, 1930.

Do Ya Think I'm Sexy? w/m Carmen Appice and Rod Stewart, 1979. #1 platinum record by Londoner Rod Stewart (Warner Bros.).

Do Ya Wanna Get Funky with Me. w/m Peter Brown and Robert Rans, 1977. Top 20 record by Peter Brown, background vocal by Betty Wright (Drive).

Do You Believe in Love. w/m Robert John Lange, 1982. Top 10 record by Huey Lewis and The News (Chrysalis).

Do You Believe in Magic? w/m John Sebastian, 1965. Top 10 record by The Lovin' Spoonful (Kama Sutra). Revived by Shaun Cassidy (Warner Bros.), 1977.

Do You Believe Me Now? w/m Max Barnes and Vern Gosdin, 1987. Top 10 Country chart record by Vern Gosdin (Columbia).

Do You Call That a Buddy? w/m Don Raye and Wesley Wilson, 1940. Featured and recorded by Louis Jordan and his Tympany Five (Decca) and Larry Clinton, vocal by Butch Stone (Bluebird).

Do You Care? w. Jack Elliott, m. Lew Quadling, 1941. Leading records by Sam Donahue, vocal by Irene Daye (Bluebird); Dinah Shore (Bluebird); Bob Crosby's Orchestra (Decca); Frances Wayne, with Neal Hefti's Orchestra (Coral) in the fifties.

Do You Ever Think of Me? w. John Cooper and Harry D. Kerr, m. Earl Burtnett, 1920. Recorded by Paul Whiteman (Victor). Revived in (MM) *That's the Spirit*, 1945.

Do You Feel Like We Do. w/m Peter Frampton, Michael Gallagher, John Sidmos, and Rick Wills, 1976. Top 10 record by the British singer/guitarist Peter Frampton (A&M).

Do You Get Enough Love. w/m Bunny Sigler and Kenny Gamble, 1986. #1 R&B chart record by Shirley Jones [not the actress/singer] (Philadelphia International).

Do You Hear What I Hear? w/m Noel Regney and Gloria Shayne, 1962. Christmas song popularized by Bing Crosby (Decca).

Do You Know the Way to San Jose? w. Hal David, m. Burt Bacharach, 1968. Top 10 hit record by Dionne Warwick (Scepter).

Do You Know What I Mean. w/m Lee Michaels, 1971. Top 10 record by Lee Michaels (A&M).

Do You Know What It Means to Miss New Orleans? w. Eddie De Lange, m. Louis Alter, 1947. Introduced in (MM) *New Orleans* by Louis Armstrong and His All-Stars, Billie Holiday, Woody Herman, and Dorothy Patrick. Recorded by Louis Armstrong (Victor). Bob Scobey and his Band had a later record (Good Time Jazz).

Do You Know Where You're Going To? See **Theme from "Mahogany."**

Do You Know Why? w. Johnny Burke, m. James Van Heusen, 1940. Introduced by Mary Martin and The Merry Macs in (MM) *Love Thy Neighbor*. Leading records by Tommy Dorsey, vocal by Frank Sinatra (Victor); Glenn Miller (Bluebird); Bob Crosby (Decca); Dick Todd (Bluebird).

Do You Know You Are My Sunshine. w/m Don Reid and Harold Reid, 1978. Country hit by The Statler Brothers (Mercury).

Do You Love Me? w. Sheldon Harnick, m. Jerry Bock, 1964. Introduced by Zero Mostel and Maria Karnilova in (TM) *Fiddler on the Roof*. In the film version, (MM) *Fiddler on the Roof*, 1971, it was sung by Topol and Norma Crane.

Do You Love Me? w/m Berry Gordy, Jr., 1962. Introduced and Top 10 record by The Contours (Gordy). The England-based Dave Clark Five had a U.S. hit version (Epic), 1964. The Contours' version was heard in (MP) *Dirty Dancing*, 1988.

Do You Love Me? w/m Harry Ruby, 1946. Introduced by Dick Haymes, with Harry James and his Orchestra in (MM) *Do You Love Me?*

James recorded it, with vocal by Ginnie Powell (Columbia), as did Phil Brito (Musicraft) and Johnny Desmond (Victor).

Do You Love What You Feel? w/m David Wolinski, 1979. Recorded by Rufus and Chaka Khan (MCA).

Do You Mind? w/m Lionel Bart, 1960. From the British film (MP) *Let's Get Married*. Leading records by Andy Williams (Cadence) and Anthony Newley (London).

Do Your Duty. w/m Wesley Wilson, 1933. Recorded by Bessie Smith (Okeh).

Do You Really Want to Hurt Me. w/m Roy Hay, John Moss, Mikey Craig, and George "Boy George" O'Dowd, 1983. Top 10 hit by the British quartet Culture Club (Epic/Virgin).

Do You Remember? w. Will Holt, m. Gary William Friedman, 1983. Introduced by Ted Thurston and company in (TM) *Taking My Turn*.

Do Your Thing. w/m Charles Wright, 1969. Top 20 record by The Watts 103rd Street Rhythm Band, of which Wright was the leader (Warner Bros.).

Do You Think I'm Disco? w. Steve Dahl, Carmine Appice, and Rod Stewart, m. Appice and Stewart, 1979. A parody of Rod Stewart's big hit "Do Ya Think I'm Sexy," recorded by disc jockey Steve Dahl and Teenage Radiation (Ovation).

Do You Wanna Dance? See **Do You Want to Dance?**

Do You Wanna Go to Heaven. w/m Curly Putman and Bucky Jones, 1980. #1 Country chart record by T. G. Sheppard (Warner Bros.).

Do You Wanna Jump, Children? w/m James Van Heusen, Willie Bryant, and Victor Selsman, 1938. Top recordings by Cab Calloway, vocal by Calloway (Vocalion); and Count Basie, vocal by Jimmy Rushing (Decca).

Do You Wanna Make Love. w/m Peter McCann, 1977. Hit record by Peter McCann (20th Century).

Do You Wanna Touch Me (Oh Yeah). w/m Gary Glitter and Mike Leander, 1982. English song, recorded by Joan Jett and The Blackhearts (Boardwalk).

Do You Want to Dance? (a.k.a. **Do You Wanna Dance?**). w/m Bobby Freeman, 1958. Introduced and Top 10 record by Bobby Freeman (Josie). Later chart records by Del Shannon (Amy), 1964; The Beach Boys (Capitol), 1965; The Mamas and The Papas (Dunhill), 1968; Bette Midler (Atlantic), 1973.

Do You Want to Know a Secret? w/m John Lennon and Paul McCartney, 1964. Hit record by The Beatles (Vee-Jay).

Drag City. w/m Roger Christian, Jan Berry, and Brian Wilson, 1964. Top 10 record by Jan and Dean (Liberty).

Draggin' the Line. w/m Robert L. King and Tommy James, 1979. Top 10 record by Tommy James (Roulette).

Dragnet. m. Walter Schumann, 1953. The theme from the series (TVP) "Dragnet." Popular instrumental recording by Ray Anthony and his Orchestra (Capitol). The music was used on the soundtrack of (TVMP) "Dragnet," 1954, and the parody (MP) *Dragnet*, 1987.

Dreadlock Holiday. w/m Eric Stewart and Graham Gouldman, 1978. Recorded by the British group 10cc (Polydor).

Dream. w/m Johnny Mercer, 1944. Mercer introduced this as the closing theme for his network radio show. The Pied Pipers had a million-seller (Capitol), followed by a hit record by Frank Sinatra (Columbia). The Four Aces, arranged and accompanied by Jack Pelvis, revived it with their recording (Decca), 1954.

Dream, A. w. Charles B. Cory, m. J. C. Bartlett, 1895.

Dream, Dream, Dream. w. Mitchell Parish, m. Jimmy McHugh, 1954. Recorded by Percy Faith and his Orchestra (Columbia).

Dream, Dream, Dream. w/m John Redmond and Lou Ricca, 1946. Introduced and recorded by The Mills Brothers (Decca).

Dream a Little Dream of Me. w. Gus Kahn, m. Fabian André and Wilbur Schwandt, 1931, 1968. Introduced and recorded by Wayne King and his Orchestra (Victor). Popular records by Frankie Laine (Mercury) and Jack Owens (Decca), 1950. Mama Cass (Elliot), with The Mamas and The Papas, had a hit record (Dunhill), 1968.

Dream a Little Longer. w/m Grace LeBoy Kahn, 1950. Recorded by Tex Beneke and The Glenn Miller Orchestra (RCA Victor).

Dream Along with Me (I'm on My Way to a Star). w/m Carl Sigman, 1956. Sung by Perry Como as the opening theme for his TV show, and recorded by him (RCA).

Dream Babies. w. Will Holt, m. Gary William Friedman, 1970. Introduced by Gerri Dean in the off-Broadway musical that moved to Broadway (TM) *The Me Nobody Knows*.

Dream Baby (How Long Must I Dream). w/m Cindy Walker, 1962. Top 10 on C&W and Pop charts by Roy Orbison (Monument). Revived by Glen Campbell (Capitol), 1971.

(He's My) Dreamboat. w/m John D. Loudermilk, 1961. Recorded by Connie Francis (MGM).

Dreamboat Annie. w/m Ann Wilson and Nancy Wilson, 1977. Recorded by the rock band Heart (Mushroom).

Dream Daddy. w. Louis Herscher, m. George Keefer, 1923. Leading record by Carl Fenton, vocal by Billy Jones and Ernest Hare (Brunswick).

Dream Dancing. w/m Cole Porter, 1941. Danced by Fred Astaire and Rita Hayworth in (MM) *You'll Never Get Rich*. It was heard in (MM) *This Could Be the Night*, 1957.

Dreamer. w/m Rick Davies and Roger Hodgson, 1980. Chart single from the 1974 album "Crime of the Century" by the British quintet Supertramp (A&M).

Dreamer, The. w. Frank Loesser, m. Arthur Schwartz, 1943. Introduced by Dinah Shore in (MM) *Thank Your Lucky Stars*. Most popular record: Kay Armen (Decca).

Dreamer's Holiday, A. w. Kim Gannon, m. Mabel Wayne, 1949. Most popular recordings by Perry Como (RCA Victor), Buddy Clark (Columbia), Gordon Jenkins and his Orchestra (Decca), Ray Anthony and his Orchestra (Capitol).

Dreamer with a Penny. w/m Allan Roberts and Lester Lee, 1949. Introduced in (TM) *All for Love* by Jack Smart. Recorded by Herb Jeffries (Columbia).

Dream Girl. w/m Marvin Phillips and Jesse Belvin, 1953. Popular R&B single by Jesse and Marvin (Specialty).

Dream House. w. Earl Foxe, m. Lynn Cowan, 1928.

Dreamin'. w/m L. Montgomery and G. Paschal, 1989. Hit R&B chart single by Vanessa Williams (Wing).

Dreamin'. w/m Ted Ellis and Barry De Vorzon, 1960. Recorded by Johnny Burnette (Liberty).

Dreaming. w/m Alan Tarney and Leo Sayer, 1980. Top 10 record by the British singer/actor Cliff Richard (EMI America).

Dreaming. w/m Deborah Harry and Chris Stein, 1979. Recorded by the group Blondie (Chrysalis).

Dreaming. w. J. P. McAvoy, m. Henry Souvaine, 1926. From (TM) *Americana*.

Dreaming. w. L. W. Heiser, m. J. Anton Dailey, 1906.

Dreaming Out Loud. w/m Sam Coslow, 1940. Sung by Frances Langford in (MM) *Dreaming Out Loud* and recorded by her (Dec-

ca). Also recorded by Benny Goodman, vocal by Helen Forrest (Columbia); and Artie Shaw, vocal by Martha Tilton (Victor).

Dream Is a Wish Your Heart Makes, A. w/m Mack David, Al Hoffman, and Jerry Livingston, 1949. Introduced by the voice of Ilene Woods on the soundtrack of the animated film (MM) *Cinderella*.

Dream Lover. w/m Bobby Darin, 1959. Hit record by Bobby Darin (Atco).

Dream Lover. w. Clifford Grey, m. Victor Schertzinger, 1929. Sung by Jeanette MacDonald in (MM) *The Love Parade*.

Dream Merchant. See **Mr. Dream Merchant.**

Dream Never Dies, The. w/m Richard Cooper, 1978. Recorded by The Cooper Brothers (Capricorn).

Dream of My Boyhood Days, A. w/m Paul Dresser, 1896.

Dream of Olwen, The. w. Winifred May, m. Charles Williams, 1947. Theme of the British film (MP) *While I Live.*

Dream of You. w/m Sy Oliver, Jimmie Lunceford, and Edward P. Moran, 1934. Introduced and recorded by Jimmie Lunceford and his Orchestra (Decca). Revived in 1949 by Tommy Dorsey's Band (Victor) and the Mills Brothers (Decca).

Dream On. w/m Steve Tallarico, 1976. First released by the group Aerosmith (Columbia), 1973. Upon its re-release, 1976, it was on the charts for twenty weeks, reaching the #6 position.

Dream On. w/m Dennis Lambert and Brian Potter, 1974. Pop chart recording by The Righteous Brothers (Haven). Top 10 Country chart record by The Oak Ridge Boys (MCA), 1979.

Dream on Little Dreamer. w/m Jan Crutchfield and Fred Burch, 1965. Popularized by Perry Como (RCA).

Dreams. w/m Eddie Van Halen, Alex Van Halen, Michael Anthony, and Sammy Hagar, 1989. Chart single by the band Van Halen (Warner Bros.).

Dreams. w/m Stevie Nicks, 1977. #1 gold record by the group Fleetwood Mac (Warner Bros.).

Dreams Are a Dime a Dozen. w/m Pat McCarthy, James Cavanaugh, and Sammy Mysels, 1947. Best-selling record by Vaughn Monroe, with his Orchestra (Victor).

Dreams of the Everyday Housewife. w/m Chris Gantry, 1968. Popular records by Glen Campbell (Capitol) and Wayne Newton (MGM).

Dreamstreet. m. Errol Garner, 1961. Instrumental introduced and recorded by Erroll Garner (ABC-Paramount).

Dreamsville, Ohio. w/m Judy Freedland, Craig Lee, and Al Rinker, 1941. Featured and recorded by the orchestras of Glenn Miller (Bluebird) and Charlie Spivak (Okeh).

Dreamtime. w/m Daryl Hall and John Beeby, 1986. Top 10 record by Daryl Hall, his first solo chart record without his partner, John Oates (RCA).

Dream Train. w. Charles Newman, m. Billy Baskette, 1929. Featured and recorded by Abe Lyman and his Californians (Brunswick); Ford and Glenn (Columbia); Nat Shilkret's Orchestra (Victor).

Dream Valley. w. Charles Kenny and Nick Kenny, m. Joe Burke, 1940. Featured and recorded by Eddy Duchin, vocal by Johnny Drake (Columbia); and Sammy Kaye, vocal by Tommy Ryan (Victor).

Dream Warriors. w/m George Lynch and Jeff Pilson, 1987. Introduced by the group, Dokken, on the soundtrack of (MP) *A Nightmare on Elm Street 3* and on their album *Back for the Attack* (Elektra).

Dream Weaver. w/m Gary Wright, 1976. Top 10 gold record by Gary Wright (Warner Bros.).

Dreamy. w. Sydney Shaw, m. Erroll Garner, 1960. Instrumental introduced by Erroll Garner, 1956. First vocal recording by Adam Wade (Epic).

Dreamy Alabama. w/m Mary Earl (pseud. of Robert A. King), 1919.

Dreamy Hawaiian Moon. w/m Harry Owens, 1938. Harry Owens and his Royal Hawaiian Orchestra performed this in (MM) *Cocoanut Grove* and recorded it (Decca).

Dreamy Melody. w/m Ted Koehler, Frank Magine, and C. Naset, 1922. This was Koehler's first published song. Million-selling instrumental record by Art Landry and his Orchestra (Gennett).

Dreidel. w/m Don McLean, 1973. Recorded by Don McLean (United Artists).

Dress You Up. w/m Peggy Stanziale and Andrea LaRusso, 1985. Top 10 single by Madonna (Sire).

Drift Away. w/m Mentor Williams, 1973. Gold record by Dobie Gray (Decca).

Drifter. w/m Don Pfrimmer and Archie Jordan, 1981. #1 Country chart record by Sylvia (RCA).

Drifting and Dreaming. w. Haven Gillespie, m. Egbert Van Alstyne, Erwin R. Schmidt, Loyal Curtis, 1925. This was Gillespie's first hit and Van Alstyne's last. George Olsen and his Orchestra (Victor) had a hit record, and twenty-five years later Les Brown (Columbia) and his band had a big seller. In between there were records by such as Carson Robison and Bud Billings (MW) [Montgomery Ward] and Orrin Tucker (Columbia) who used it as his theme song.

Drifting Apart. w/m Hal Gurnee, 1967. Top 10 Country record by Warner Mack (Decca).

Drill, Ye Tarriers, Drill. w/m Anonymous, 1888. Introduced by Thomas F. Casey, who often claimed authorship, at Tony Pastor's. Featured in Charles H. Hoyt's (TM) *A Brass Monkey*. Recorded by George J. Gaskin,

"The Silver Voiced Irish Tenor" (North American).

Drinking Song (Drink! Drink! Drink!). w. Dorothy Donnelly, m. Sigmund Romberg, 1924. Introduced by Raymond Marlowe and the Student chorus in (TM) *The Student Prince.* In the film version (MM) *The Student Prince,* 1954, Mario Lanza sang it, dubbing for Edmond Purdom. Lanza's recording (Victor) was backed with *Deep in My Heart, Dear* from the same operetta.

Drinkin' Thing. w/m Wayne Carson, 1974. Hit country record by Gary Stewart (RCA).

Drinkin' Wine, Spo-Dee-O-Dee. w/m Granville "Stick" McGhee and J. Mayo Williams, 1949. An R&B hit, introduced and recorded by Stick McGhee and his Buddies (Atlantic). Revived by Jerry Lee Lewis (Mercury), 1973.

Drink with Me to Days Gone By. w. Herbert Kretzmer (Engl.), w/m (Fr.) A. Boubil, m. Claude-Michel Schonberg, 1987. Introduced in the U.S. by Anthony Crivello in (TM) *Les Miserables.*

Drip Drop. w/m Jerry Leiber and Mike Stoller, 1958, 1963. Introduced by The Drifters (Atlantic). Revived with a Top 10 record by Dion (Columbia), 1963.

Drive. w/m Ric Ocasek, 1984. Top 10 record by the group, The Cars, vocal by bassist Ben Orr (Elektra).

Drive My Car. w/m John Lennon and Paul McCartney, 1965. Introduced in an LP by The Beatles (Capitol). Chart singles by Bob Kuban (Musicland), 1966 and the disco band Gary Toms Empire (Pickwick Int'l), 1975.

Driver's Seat. w/m Paul Roberts, 1979. Recorded by the British group Rock 'n' The Tears (Atlantic).

Driving Wheel. w/m Roosevelt Sykes, 1961. Recorded by Little Junior Parker (Duke).

Drivin' My Life Away. w/m Eddie Rabbitt, Even Stevens, and David Malloy, 1980. Introduced on the soundtrack of (MP) *Roadie.* Hit C&W and Pop record by Eddie Rabbitt (Elektra).

Drivin' Nails in My Coffin'. w/m Jerry Irby, 1946. Hit C&W records by Floyd Tillman (Columbia) and Ernest Tubb (Decca).

Dropkick Me, Jesus. w/m Paul Craft, 1976. Country chart song recorded by Bobby Bare (RCA).

Drop Me Off in Harlem. w. Nick Kenny, m. Edward "Duke" Ellington, 1933. Sometimes known as "Drop Me Off At Harlem." Two Ellington releases (Brunswick, Columbia).

Drowning in the Sea of Love. w/m Kenny Gamble and Leon Huff, 1971. R&B/Pop gold record by Joe Simon (Spring).

Drown in My Own Tears. w/m Henry Glover, 1956. Introduced and recorded by Ray Charles (Atlantic).

Drownin' My Sorrows. w/m Hunter Vincent and Bill Justis, 1963. Chart record by Connie Francis (MGM).

Drumboogie. w/m Gene Krupa, 1941. Introduced and recorded by Gene Krupa, vocal by Irene Daye (Okeh).

Drummin' Man. w/m Tiny Parham and Gene Krupa, 1939. Introduced and recorded by Gene Krupa. Vocal by Irene Daye (Columbia).

Drums in My Heart. w. Edward Heyman, m. Vincent Youmans, 1932. Introduced by Gregory Gaye in (TM) *Through the Years.* Recorded by André Kostalanetz (Columbia), Jack Pleis (Columbia), Tutti Camarata (Everest).

Dry Your Eyes. w/m Maurice Coates, 1967. Hit record by Brenda and The Tabulations, written by a member of the R&B group (Dionn).

Duck, The. w/m Earl Nelson and Fred Sledge Smith, 1965. Top 20 record by Jackie Lee [pseud. for Earl Nelson] (Mirwood).

Dude (Looks Like a Lady). w/m Steve Tyler, Joe Perry, and Desmond Child, 1987. Recorded by Aerosmith, from their album "Permanent Vacation" (Geffen).

Dueling Banjos. m. Arthur Smith, 1972. The tune was written in 1955, but achieved public acceptance via the performance by banjoists Eric Weissberg and Steve Mandell in (MP) *Deliverance.* Their recording was awarded a gold record (Warner Bros.), 1973.

Duel in the Sun. w. Stanley Adams, m. Dmitri Tiomkin, 1948. Adapted from a theme from (MP) *Duel in the Sun.*

Duke of Earl. w/m Earl Edwards, Eugene Dixon, and Bernie Williams, 1962. Gene Chandler, pseudonym for Eugene Dixon, had a #1 record (Vee-Jay).

Dukes of Hazzard. See **Theme from "Dukes of Hazzard."**

Duke Steps Out, The. m. Edward Kennedy "Duke" Ellington, 1929. Instrumental recorded by Ellington (Victor).

Dum-De-Da. See **She Understands Me.**

Dum-Dot Song. w/m Julian Kay, 1947. A popular treatment of the childrens' nonsense song "Dye Dut da Denny in da Dum Dot (I Put the Penny in the Gum Slot)." Popularized by Frank Sinatra (Columbia).

Dum Dum. w/m Jackie De Shannon and Sharon Sheeley, 1961. Top 10 record by Brenda Lee (Decca).

Duncan. w/m Paul Simon, 1972. Recorded by Paul Simon (Columbia).

Dungaree Doll. w. Ben Raleigh, m. Sherman Edwards, 1955. Hit record by Eddie Fisher (RCA Victor).

Dusic. w/m Jimmy Brown, Reggie Harris, and Ray Ransom, 1977. Recorded by the group, Brick, as a follow-up to their disco hit "Dazz," (Bang), (q.v.). This title combines "dance" and "music."

Dusk in Upper Sandusky. m. Larry Clinton and Jimmy Dorsey, 1937. Introduced and recorded by Jimmy Dorsey and his Orchestra, arranged by Larry Clinton (Decca).

Dusk on the Desert. w. Irving Mills, m. Edward Kennedy "Duke" Ellington, 1937. Introduced and recorded (Brunswick) by Duke Ellington and his Orchestra.

Dusky Stevedore. w. Andy Razaf, m. J. C. Johnson, 1928. Recorded by Thelma Terry and Her Play-boys (Columbia); Mary Dixon (Vocalion); Nat Shilkret [theme song] (Victor); Frankie Trumbauer, featuring Bix Beiderbecke (Okeh); The Revelers (Victor); Louis Armstrong (Okeh).

Dust. w/m Johnny Marvin, 1938. Introduced by Roy Rogers in (MM) *Under Western Stars.* Nominated for Academy Award.

Dust. w. Andy Rice, m. Fred Fisher, 1930. Introduced by May Boley in (MM) *Children of Pleasure*, based on the play by Crane Wilbur, *The Songwriter.*

Dust in the Wind. w/m Kerry Livgren, 1978. Top 10 record by the group Kansas (Kirshner).

Dust Off That Old Pianna (Oh, Suzanna). w/m Irving Caesar, Sammy Lerner, and Gerald Marks, 1935. Recorded by the New Orleans Rhythm Kings (Decca); Fats Waller (Victor); Harriet Hilliard with Ozzie Nelson's Orchestra (Brunswick); Bob Hannon (Decca); George Hall's Orchestra, vocal by Loretta Lee and Sonny Schuyler (Bluebird).

Dusty Rag. m. May Aufderheide, 1908. The ragtime composition was published when the composer was nineteen. It sold so well that her father purchased the rights and started a publishing firm. It was issued by six piano roll companies and published in sheet music and orchestrations. It was recorded in 1942 by Bunk Johnson's Jazz Band (Jazz Information); the Crane River Jazz Band (CRJ) in 1951; Turk Murphy's Band (Good Time Jazz) in the 1950s.

Dusty Road. w/m Leon René and Otis René, 1935. Recorded by Nelson Eddy (Victor) and interpolated by him in (MM) *Let Freedom Ring*, 1938.

D. W. Washburn. w/m Jerry Leiber and Mike Stoller, 1968. Top 20 record by The Monkees (Colgems).

D'Ye Love Me? w. Otto Harbach and Oscar Hammerstein II, m. Jerome Kern, 1925. Sung by Marilyn Miller and danced by Jack Donahue in (TM) *Sunny*. In the film version (MM) *Sunny*, 1930, it was performed by the same combination. It was also in the 1941 remake, starring Anna Neagle.

D'Yer Maker. w/m John Baldwin, John Bonham, and Robert Plant, 1973. Recorded by the group Led Zeppelin (Atlantic), 1973.

Dying Gambler Blues. w/m Jack Gee, 1924. Recorded by Bessie Smith (Columbia).

Dynamite. w/m Andy Goldmark and Bruce Roberts, 1984. Recorded by Jermaine Jackson, one of the Jackson brothers (Arista).

Dynasty. See **Theme from "Dynasty."**

Dynomite. m. Tony Camillo, 1975. Top 10 instrumental by Tony Camillo's studio group Bazuka (A&M).

E

Each Minute Seems a Million Years. w/m Cook Watson, 1944. Hit Country record by Eddy Arnold (Bluebird).

Each Moment (Spent with You). w/m Billy Worth and Billy Hogan, 1960. C&W hit by Ernest Ashworth (Decca).

Each Night at Nine. w/m Floyd Tillman, 1944. World War II C&W song introduced and recorded by Floyd Tillman (Decca).

Eadie Was a Lady. w. B. G. DeSylva, m. Richard Whiting and Nacio Herb Brown, 1932. Introduced by Ethel Merman in (TM) *Take a Chance* and recorded by her as a two-sided song (Brunswick). Cab Calloway had a popular version (Brunswick). Lillian Roth sang it in the movie version (MM) *Take a Chance*, 1933. She recorded it, coupled with the title song of her film biography (MP) *I'll Cry Tomorrow* (Coral), 1955.

Eagle and Me, The. w. E. Y. Harburg, m. Harold Arlen, 1944. Introduced by Dooley Wilson and chorus in (TM) *Bloomer Girl*.

Earache My Eye Featuring Alice Bowie. w/m Tommy Chong, Richard "Cheech" Marin, and Gaye DeLorme, 1974. Top 10 comedy record by Cheech and Chong (Ode).

Earful of Music, An. w. Gus Kahn, m. Walter Donaldson, 1934. Introduced by Ethel Merman in the opening number of (MM) *Kid Millions*, starring Eddie Cantor. Records:

Merman, with Johnny Green's Orchestra (Brunswick); Cantor (Melotone); George Hall, vocal by Loretta Lee (Bluebird); Emil Coleman (Columbia); Mal Hallett (Melotone); Anson Weeks, vocal by Kay St. Germaine (Brunswick).

Early Autumn. w. Johnny Mercer, m. Ralph Burns and Woody Herman, 1949. Adapted from Burns's "Summer Sequence," which he arranged earlier for Woody Herman's band. First recording was instrumental version, featuring Stan Getz on tenor saxophone (Capitol). Mercer wrote his lyric in 1952, and Herman recorded it with his band (Mars), as did Jo Stafford (Columbia).

Early Bird. w. Sidney D. Mitchell, m. Lew Pollack, 1936. Shirley Temple introduced this in (MM) *Captain January*.

Early in the Morning. w/m Lonnie Simmons, Rudolph Taylor, and Charles Wilson, 1982. Recorded by The Gap Band (Total Experience). Robert Palmer included it in his album "Heavy Nova" (EMI), 1988.

Early in the Morning. w. Meg Karlin, m. Fred Karlin, 1977. Introduced in (MP) *Minstrel Man*, a turn-of-the-century story about black minstrelsy and ragtime.

Early in the Morning. w/m Mike Leander and Eddie Seago, 1969. Top 20 U.S. release by the British quintet Vanity Fare (Page One).

Early in the Morning. w/m Bobby Darin and Woody Harris, 1958. Top 40 record by Bobby Darin and The Rinky-Dinks (Atco).

Early in the Morning (Down by the Station). w/m adapted by Bruce Belland and Glen Larson, 1960. Adapted from the traditional song "Down by the Station" by two of The Four Preps, and recorded by the group (Capitol).

Early Morning Blues. w. Joseph Allan McCarthy, m. Cy Coleman, 1956. Written for, featured, and recorded by Mabel Mercer (Atlantic).

Early Mornin' Rain. w/m Gordon Lightfoot, 1965. Featured and recorded by Peter, Paul and Mary (Warner Bros.). Revived by Oliver (United Artists), 1971.

Earth Angel (Will You Be Mine). w/m Jesse Belvin, 1955. Introduced and recorded by The Penguins, who had a crossover (R&B/Pop) hit (Dootone). It was successfully covered by The Crew-Cuts (Mercury). Among successful recordings to follow: Gloria Mann (Sound), Johnny Tillotson (Cadence), 1960, The Vogues (Reprise), 1969. Revived by teenage group, The New Edition, with a hit record (MCA), 1986. It was on the soundtrack of (MP) The Karate Kid Part II, 1986.

Earthbound. w/m Jack Taylor, Clive Richardson, and Bob Musel, 1956. Leading records by Sammy Davis, Jr. (Decca) and Mario Lanza (RCA).

Ease On Down the Road. w/m Charlie Smalls, 1974. Introduced in (TM) The Wiz, the musical version of L. Frank Baum's book "The Wonderful Wizard of Oz" by Stephanie Mills, Hinton Battle, Tiger Haynes, and Ted Ross. Leading reocrd by the Detroit studio group Consumer Rapport (Wing and Prayer). The song was sung in the film version (MM) The Wiz and on records (MCA) by Diana Ross and Michael Jackson, 1978.

Easier Said Than Done. w/m William Linton and Larry Huff, 1963. #1 chart record by The Essex (Roulette).

Easier to Love. w. Richard Maltby, Jr., m. David Shire, 1983. Introduced by James Congdon in (TM) Baby.

East Bound and Down. w/m Jerry Reed and Dick Feller, 1977. Introduced by Jerry Reed in (MP) Smokey and the Bandit.

Easter Parade. w/m Irving Berlin, 1933. Melody was based on an earlier Berlin tune (1917) "Smile and Show Your Dimple." The new version was introduced by Marilyn Miller, Clifton Webb, and company in the first act finale of (TM) As Thousands Cheer. Don Ameche sang it in (MM) Alexander's Ragtime Band, 1938; Bing Crosby in (MM) Holiday Inn, 1942; Judy Garland and Fred Astaire in Easter Parade, 1948. The best-selling records were made by Harry James (Columbia), 1942 and Guy Lombardo (Decca), 1947. Among others: Clifton Webb, with Leo Reisman's Orchestra (Victor); Freddy Martin (Vocalion); Jimmie Lunceford (Brunswick); Henry King (Columbia); Roy Rogers and Dale Evans (Victor).

East of Eden. See **Theme from East of Eden**.

East of the Sun (and West of the Moon). w/m Brooks Bowman, 1935. From the Princeton University Triangle Club show Stags at Bay. One of three songs ("Love and a Dime" and "Will Love Find a Way?" [q.v.]) to emerge commercially from the undergraduate show. Bowman, a senior and writer or co-writer of all three, was offered a contract to compose songs for the movies after graduation. En route to California, he was killed in an automobile accident. The song was featured and recorded by Hal Kemp, vocal by Bob Allen (Brunswick); Bob Crosby (Decca); Arthur Tracy, "The Street Singer" (Decca). Tommy Dorsey, with vocal by Frank Sinatra (Bluebird), 1941, helped establish the song as a standard. Among later recordings of note: Sarah Vaughan (Continental), George Shearing (MGM), Dick Hyman (MGM), Paul Weston (Capitol).

East St. Louis Toodle-oo. m. Bubber Miley and Edward Kennedy "Duke" Ellington, 1926. The original theme song of Duke Ellington's Orchestra. First recorded by his band named "Duke Ellington and his Washingtonians" (Vocalion) (Path) (Cameo). His first big-selling recording was of the same song (Columbia), 1927.

East Side of Heaven. w. Johnny Burke, m. James V. Monaco, 1939. Sung in (MM) *East Side of Heaven* and on records (Decca) by Bing Crosby.

Easy. w/m Lionel Richie, 1978. Introduced by The Commodores in (MP) *Thank God It's Friday*, and on records (Motown).

Easy, Easy Baby. w/m Rudolph Toombs, 1952. R&B record by Varetta Dillard (Savoy).

Easy Come, Easy Go. w/m Diane Hilderbrand and Jack Keller, 1970. Hit record by Bobby Sherman (Metromedia).

Easy Come, Easy Go. w. Edward Heyman, m. John Green, 1934. Outstanding recording by Lee Wiley, with Johnny Green and his Orchestra (Brunswick). Eddy Duchin, vocal by The De Marco Sisters, had a popular version (Victor).

Easy Come—Easy Go. w/m Bill Anderson, 1963. Country chart record by Bill Anderson (Decca).

Easy Does It. w. Sy Oliver, m. Sy Oliver and James "Trummy" Young, 1940. Introduced and recorded by Tommy Dorsey, playing a Sy Oliver arrangement (Victor). Among other early versions: Sonny Burke (Vocalion), Bobby Byrne (Decca), Count Basie (Columbia), The Smoothies (Bluebird).

Easy Living. w. Leo Robin, m. Ralph Rainger, 1937. Jazz standard associated with Billie Holiday who recorded it twice, first with Teddy Wilson's combo (Brunswick) and later on her own session (Decca).

Easy Lover. w/m Philip Bailey, Phil Collins, and Nathan East, 1984. Top 10 record by Philip Bailey with Phil Collins (Columbia).

Easy Loving. w/m Freddie Hart, 1971. #1 Country and Top 20 Pop chart gold record by Freddie Hart (Capitol).

Easy on the Eyes. w/m Cy Coben and Eddy Arnold, 1952. Featured and recorded by Eddy Arnold (RCA Victor).

Easy Part's Over, The. w/m Jerry Foster and Bill Rice, 1968. Country hit by Charley Pride (RCA).

Easy Question. See **Such an Easy Question.**

Easy Street. w. Martin Charnin, m. Charles Strouse, 1977. Introduced by Dorothy Loudon, Bob Fitch, and Barbara Erwin in (TM) *Annie*. In the film version (MM) *Annie*, 1982, it was sung by Carol Burnett, Tim Curry, and Bernadette Peters.

Easy Street. w/m Alan Rankin Jones, 1941. Featured and recorded by the bands of Jimmie Lunceford (Decca); Sonny Dunham (Bluebird); Guy Lombardo (Decca); vocalist Martha Tilton (Decca).

Easy to Be Hard. w/m Gerome Ragni and James Rado, m. Galt MacDermot, 1967. Introduced by Suzannah Evans, Linda Compton, Paul Jabara, and company in the off-Broadway production of (TM) *Hair*. In the Broadway production (TM) *Hair*, 1968, it was sung by Lynn Kellogg. Top 10 record by Three Dog Night (Dunhill), 1969. In the film version (MM) *Hair*, 1979, it was sung by Cheryl Barnes, and the soundtrack version was released as a single (RCA).

Easy to Love. w/m Cole Porter, 1936. Originally written for William Gaxton in the Broadway musical *Anything Goes*, but dropped from the score as Gaxton did not have the vocal range required. Porter reworked the lyric and it became the hit song of (MM) *Born to Dance*, in which it was sung by James Stewart, danced by Eleanor Powell, mimed by Reginald Gardiner, and reprised by Frances Langford who recorded it (Decca). Among other popular recordings: Hal Kemp, vocal by Bob Allen (Brunswick); Shep Fields, vocal by Dick Robertson (Bluebird); Dick Jurgens, vocal by Eddy Howard (Melotone); Maxine Sullivan (Vocalion); Teddy Wilson (Brunswick); later, George Shearing (MGM); Dinah Shore and Buddy Clark (Columbia); Errol Garner (Columbia). It was heard in the background of the Porter story (MM) *Night and Day*, 1945, and was sung by the operatic tenor, Lauritz Melchior, in (MM) *This Time for Keeps*, 1947.

Eat, Drink and Be Merry. w/m Celia Ferguson and Sandra Ferguson, 1956. C&W record by Porter Wagoner (RCA).

Eat It. w/m Al Yankovic, 1984. Parody of Michael Jackson's hit "Beat It" by "Weird Al" Yankovic (Rock 'n' Roll).

Ebb Tide. w. Carl Sigman, m. Robert Maxwell, 1953. Composed as an instrumental by the harpist Robert Maxwell, its first hit recording was by the British band leader Frank Chacksfield (London). Lyrics were added and sung on chart records by Vic Damone (Mercury) and Roy Hamilton (Epic). The Platters had a popular version (Mercury), 1960, after which it was heard in (MP) *Sweet Bird of Youth*, 1962. Lenny Welch had a hit recording (Cadence), 1964, and The Righteous Brothers had a Top 10 version (Philles), 1966.

Ebb Tide. w. Leo Robin, m. Ralph Rainger, 1937. Written for (MP) *Ebb Tide*, this song, not to be confused with the 1953 hit of the same title, was recorded by many bands and singers including Bunny Berigan (Victor), Ozzie Nelson (Bluebird), Tommy Tucker (Vocalion), Claude Thornhill (Vocalion), Chuck Berry (Variety), Dick Robertson (Decca).

Ebony and Ivory. w/m Paul McCartney, 1982. Seven weeks at the #1 chart position for this gold record by Paul McCartney and Stevie Wonder (Columbia).

Ebony Eyes. w/m Bob Welch, 1978. Recorded by Bob Welch (Capitol).

Ebony Eyes. w/m John Loudermilk, 1961. Hit record by The Everly Brothers, coupled with another Top 10 side, "Walk Right Back" (Warner Brothers).

Ebony Rhapsody. w/m Arthur Johnston and Sam Coslow, 1934. Introduced by Duke Ellington and his Orchestra in (MM) *Murder at the Vanities*.

Echoes. w/m Bennie Benjamin and George David Weiss, 1950. Leading records by Jo Stafford and Gordon MacRae (Capitol) and The Ink Spots (Decca).

Echoes of Harlem. m. Edward Kennedy "Duke" Ellington, 1936. This instrumental "belonged" to the outstanding trumpet player Cootie Williams. Ellington wrote, introduced, and recorded it featuring Williams as soloist (Brunswick). Two years later, Williams recorded it with his own band (Vocalion).

Echoes of Love. w/m Earl Randle, Pat Simmons, and Willie Mitchell, 1977. Recorded by the group The Doobie Brothers (Warner Bros.).

Echo of Spring. w/m Clarence Williams and William H. Smith, 1935. Recorded by the co-writer Willie "The Lion" Smith (Decca) and later as "Echoes of Spring" (Commodore).

Echo of Your Footsteps, The. w/m Jenny Lou Carson, 1949. Featured and recorded by Eddy Arnold (RCA Victor).

Echo Park. w/m Buzz Clifford, 1969. Top 40 record by Keith Barbour (Epic).

Echo Said "No," The. w/m Art Kassel, 1947. Best-selling record by Mary Martin with Guy Lombardo's Orchestra (Decca).

Ecstasy Tango. m. José Belmonte, 1952. Instrumental, first published in England. Leading recording by Geraldo and his Orchestra (Columbia). Also recorded by The Three Suns (RCA Victor).

Eddie, My Love. w/m Aaron Collins, Maxwell Davis, and Sam Ling, 1956. Introduced by the R&B duo, The Teen Queens, sisters of co-writer Collins (RPM). Their chart record was covered by The Fontane Sisters (Dot) and The Chordettes (Cadence), both groups having Pop chart hits.

Eddy's Song. w/m Charles R. Grean and Cy Coben, 1953. Featured and recorded by Eddy Arnold (RCA Victor).

Edge of Heaven, The. w/m George Michael, 1986. Top 10 record by the group Wham! (Columbia).

Edge of Seventeen (Just Like the White Winged Dove). w/m Stevie Nicks, 1982. Recorded by Stevie Nicks (Modern).

Eel, The. m. Bud Freeman, 1933. Freeman, the tenor saxist, recorded this jazz instrumental twice with Eddie Condon (Brunswick, Columbia), and in 1939 with his own group (Bluebird).

Eeny, Meeny, Meiny, Mo. w/m Johnny Mercer and Matt Malneck, 1935. Introduced by Johnny Mercer in (MM) *To Beat the Band.* Bob Crosby (Decca) had the first recording, followed by Ginger Rogers and Johnny Mercer (Decca) and Benny Goodman (Victor). A year later, Billie Holiday recorded it with Teddy Wilson's all-star group (Brunswick).

Egg and I, The. w/m Herman Ruby, Harry Akst, Bert Kalmar, and Al Jolson, 1947. Title song of (MP) *The Egg and I.* Leading recordings by Sammy Kaye, vocal by Mary Marlowe (RCA Victor), and Dinah Shore (Columbia).

Eggplant That Ate Chicago, The. w/m Norman Greenbaum, 1966. Recorded by the jug band, Dr. West's Medicine Show and Junk Band, founded by the writer (Go Go).

Egyptian Ella. w/m Walter Doyle, 1931. The recording by Ted Lewis and his Orchestra (Brunswick) featured Benny Goodman and Fats Waller.

Eh, Cumpari! w/m Julius La Rosa and Archie Bleyer, 1953. Adapted from the Italian folk song, this was introduced and recorded by Julius La Rosa (Cadence). His recording sold over a million copies.

8 × 10. w. Bill Anderson, m. Walter Haynes, 1963. Crossover (C&W/Pop) chart record by Bill Anderson (Decca).

Eight Days a Week. w/m John Lennon and Paul McCartney, 1965. #1 gold record by The Beatles (Capitol).

Eight Is Enough. w. Molly Ann Leiken, m. Lee Holdridge, 1978. Sung as theme of (TVP) "Eight Is Enough" by Grant Goodeve.

Eight Men, Four Women. w/m Deadric Malone, 1967. R&B/Pop chart record by O. V. Wright (Back Beat).

Eight Miles High. w/m Gene Clark, David Crosby, and James McGuinn, 1966. Top 20 record by The Byrds (Columbia). The writers were members of the group. The Byrds recorded another version of the song in their album "Never Before" (Columbia), 1987.

Eighteen. w/m Alice Cooper, Michael Bruce, Glen Buxton, Dennis Dunaway, Neal Smith, 1971. Top 40 record by Alice Cooper (Warner Bros.).

Eighteen Wheels and a Dozen Roses. w/m Paul Nelson and Gene Nelson, 1988. #1 Country chart single from the album "Untasted Honey" by Kathy Mattea (Mercury).

Eighteen with a Bullet. w/m Barry Hammond and Pete Wingfield, 1975. Top 20 record by the British keyboard player Pete Wingfield (Island). The number in the title derives from a chart position in a trade publication, and the bullet indicates the entry is moving up rapidly.

Eighteen Yellow Roses. w/m Bobby Darin, 1963. Top 10 record by Bobby Darin (Capitol).

Eighth Veil, The. m. Edward Kennedy "Duke" Ellington and Billy Strayhorn, 1953. Instrumental, recorded by Duke Ellington, featuring trumpeter Cat Anderson (Columbia).

80's Ladies. w/m K. T. Oslin, 1987. Top 10 Country chart record from the album of the same name by K. T. Oslin (RCA).

867-5309/Jenny. w/m Alex Call and Jim Keller, 1982. Top 10 record by the rock band Tommy Tutone (Columbia).

Eileen Alana Asthore. w. Henry Blossom, m. Victor Herbert, 1917. Introduced by Walter Scanlon in (TM) *Eileen.*

Either It's Love or It Isn't. w/m Allan Roberts and Doris Fisher, 1947. From (MP) *Dead Reckoning.* Recordings: The Pied Pipers and June Hutton, conducted by Paul Weston (Capitol); Frankie Carle, vocal by Marjorie Hughes (Columbia); Charlie Ventura and his Band (National); Harry Cool (Signature).

El Capitan. m. John Philip Sousa, 1896. A march, comprised of melodies from Sousa's comic opera (TM) *El Capitan.* It was featured in the Sousa film biography (MM) *Stars and Stripes Forever*, 1952.

El Choclo. m. A. G. Villoldo, 1912. An Argentine tango that had a popular recording by the Victor Orchestra. See also "Kiss of Fire."

El Condor Pasa. w/m Paul Simon and Daniel Robles, 1970. Top 20 record by Simon and Garfunkel (Columbia).

El Cumbanchero. w/m Rafael Hernandez, 1943. Mexican song popularized by Enric Madriguera and his Orchestra (Decca).

Eleanor Rigby. w/m John Lennon and Paul McCartney, 1966. Recorded by The Beatles, coupled with *Yellow Submarine* (Capitol). Both songs were included in their animated film (MM) *Yellow Submarine*, 1968. Hit records by Ray Charles (ABC/TRC), 1969, and Aretha Franklin (Atlantic), 1969.

Election Day. w/m Nick Rhodes, Roger Taylor, and Simon LeBon, 1985. Top 10 single by the English group Arcadia (Capitol). The writers, featured with the group, were also members of Duran Duran.

Electric Avenue. w/m Eddy Grant, 1983. Top 10 gold record, produced in Barbados, by Eddy Grant (Portrait).

Electric Blue. w/m Ian Davies and John Oates, 1988. Hit single by the Australian group Icehouse (Chrysalis).

Elena. w/m Robert Wright and George Forrest, 1961. Introduced by Alfred Drake, Arthur Rubin, and ensemble in (TM) *Kean.*

Elenore. w/m Howard Kaylan, Mark Volman, Jim Pons, Al Nichol, and John Barbata, 1968. Top 10 record by The Turtles (White Whale).

Eleven More Months and Ten More Days. w/m Arthur Fields and Fred Hall, 1930. Featured by Fields and Hall and recorded by Vernon Dalhart under pseudonym of Mack Allen (Harmony).

Eleven Roses. w/m Lamar Morris and Dorrell McCall, 1972. Hit Country record by Hank Williams, Jr. (MGM).

11th Hour Melody. w. Carl Sigman, m. Winfred Palmer, 1956. Leading records by Al Hibbler (Decca) and Lou Busch (Capitol).

Eli Green's Cakewalk. w/m David Reed and Sadie Koninsky, 1896.

Eli's Coming. w/m Laura Nyro, 1968. Introduced by Laura Nyro in her album "Eli and the Thirteenth Confession." Top 10 record by the group Three Dog Night (Dunhill), 1969.

Elizabeth. w/m Jimmy Fortune, 1984. #1 Country chart record by the group, The Statler Brothers, of which the writer was a member (Mercury).

Elizabeth. w. Irving Caesar, m. Robert Katscher, 1931. The original German words were written by G. Herczeg and Katscher. The English version was introduced by Al Jolson in (TM) *Wonder Bar.*

Elmer's Tune. w/m Elmer Albrecht, Sammy Gallop, and Dick Jurgens, 1941. Introduced and recorded as an instrumental by Dick Jurgens and his Orchestra, arranged by Lew Quadling (Okeh). Glenn Miller then recorded it with a vocal by Ray Eberle and The Modernaires (Bluebird) and the song became #1 in the country, fifteen weeks on "Your Hit Parade." It was revived by the country pianist, Del Wood, who had a hit record (Republic), 1953.

Eloise. w/m Kay Thompson and Robert Wells, 1956. Song based on the character of the same name from the book series by Kay Thompson. Recorded by Thompson (Cadence).

El Paso. w/m Marty Robbins, 1959. #1 Country and Pop chart hit by Marty Robbins (Columbia). Winner Grammy Award (NARAS) for Country Song of the Year.

El Paso City. w/m Marty Robbins, 1976. Country chart hit by Marty Robbins (Columbia).

El Rancho Grande. w. Silvano R. Ramos (Sp.), Bartley Costello (Engl.), m. Silvano R. Ramos, 1934, 1939. Bing Crosby's hit record (Decca), 1939, gave the song its major acceptance and place on "Your Hit Parade." Gene Autry sang it in (MM) "Rancho Grande," 1940, and Roy Rogers in (MM) *My Pal Trigger*, 1946, with Dale Evans and Gabby Hayes. Among recordings: Autry (Conqueror), Tito Guizar, (Victor and Mercury), Louise Massey and the Westerners (Vocalion), Bob Chester (Bluebird), Ethel Smith (Decca), Jan Savitt (Decca). In 1958 The Champs had a Top 40 version titled "El Rancho Rock" (Challenge). See also "El Rancho Rock."

El Rancho Rock. w. Ben Raleigh, m. Silvano Ramos, 1958. Top 40 instrumental, based on the Mexican song "El Rancho Grande," recorded by The Champs (Challenge). See also "El Rancho Grande."

Elsie from Chelsea. w/m Harry Dacre, 1896.

Elusive Butterfly. w/m Bob Lind, 1966. Top 10 record by Bob Lind (World Pacific).

Elvira. w/m Dallas Frazier, 1966, 1981. Introduced and recorded by Dallas Frazier (Capitol). Revived with a platinum record by The Oak Ridge Boys (MCA), 1981.

El Watusi. m. Ray Barretto, 1963. Instrumental by the combo of percussionist Ray Barretto (Tico).

Emaline. w. Mitchell Parish, m. Frank Perkins, 1934. An instant favorite with jazz musicians as evidenced by some of the recordings in its first year: Cab Calloway (Victor); Mildred Bailey, with band led by Benny Goodman (Columbia); Frankie Trumbauer (Brunswick); Charlie Barnet (Melotone); and the nonpareil performance by the great pianist Art Tatum (Decca).

Emanon. m. John Birks "Dizzy" Gillespie and Milton Shaw, 1946. Title is "no name" backwards. Introduced by Dizzy Gillespie, arranged by Tadd Dameron (Musicraft).

Embraceable You. w. Ira Gershwin, m. George Gershwin, 1930. Originally written for the unproduced musical *Ming Toy*, it was introduced by Allen Kearns and Ginger Rogers in (TM) *Girl Crazy*. Red Nichols's pit band included Benny Goodman, Glenn Miller, Jimmy Dorsey, Jack Teagarden, and Gene Krupa. It was sung by Eddie Quillan and Dorothy Lee in the first film adaptation (MM) *Girl Crazy* and by Judy Garland in the 1943 version. A 1966 film, loosely based on *Girl Crazy*, (MM) *When the Boys Meet the Girls*, featured Harve Presnell singing the ballad. It was performed by Joan Leslie in the George Gershwin biography (MM) *Rhapsody in Blue* in 1945; heard in (MM) *Always Leave Them Laughing*, starring Milton Berle in 1949; danced to by Leslie Caron in (MM) *An American in Paris* in 1951; sung by Jane Froman on the soundtrack for Susan Hayward in the Froman story (MM) *With a Song in My Heart* in 1952; played by Liberace in (MM) *Sincerely Yours* in 1955.

Emergency. w/m Kool and The Gang, 1985. Title song, released from the album by Kool and The Gang (De-Lite).

Emily. w. Johnny Mercer, m. Johnny Mandel, 1964. Based on a theme from (MP) *The Americanization of Emily*. First popular recording by Andy Williams (Columbia).

Emma. w/m Errol Brown and Tony Wilson, 1975. Top 10 record by the English group Hot Chocolate (Big Tree).

Emotion. w/m Barry Gibb and Robin Gibb, 1978. Platinum record by the Australian singer Samantha Sang (Private Stock).

Emotion (Amoreuse). w. Patti Dahlstrom (Engl.), Veronique Marie Sanson, (Fr.), M. Sanson, 1975. English version of French song popularized by Helen Reddy (Capitol).

Emotional Rescue. w/m Mick Jagger and Keith Richards, 1980. Top 10 record by The Rolling Stones (Rolling Stones).

Emotion in Motion. w/m Ric Ocasek, 1986. Recorded by Ric Ocasek (Geffen).

Emotions. w/m Mel Tillis and Ramsey Kearney, 1961. Hit record by Brenda Lee (Decca).

Emperor Jones. w/m Allie Wrubel, 1933. Another song by Wrubel using the title of a play or book. Ex.: "As You Desire Me"; "Farewell to Arms"; "Gone With the Wind," (q.v.). Connie Boswell recorded this (Brunswick).

Empire Strikes Back, The. m. John Williams, 1980. Darth Vader and Yoda's themes from (MP) *The Empire Strikes Back*, recorded instrumentally by Meco (RSO).

Empty Arms. w/m Ivory Joe Hunter, 1957, 1971. Introduced and recorded by Ivory Joe Hunter (Atlantic). Best-seller by Teresa Brewer (Coral). Revived by Sonny James with a #1 country record in 1971 (Capitol).

Empty Bed Blues. w/m J. C. Johnson, 1928. Bessie Smith made a two-sided recording that has become a classic (Columbia).

Empty Garden (Hey Hey Johnny). w. Bernie Taupin, m. Elton John, 1982. Recorded by the British singer Elton John (Geffen).

Empty Pages. w/m Steve Winwood and Jim Capaldi, 1970. Recorded by the British rock group, Traffic, of which the writers were members (United Artists).

Empty Pockets Filled with Love. w/m Irving Berlin, 1961. Introduced by Anita Gillette and Jack Haskell in (TM) *Mr. President*.

Empty Saddles. w. J. Keirn Brennan, m. Billy Hill, 1936. This was based on a poem written by Brennan and sung by Bing Crosby in (MM) *Rhythm on the Range* and on records (Decca). Roy Rogers, under the name of Dick Weston, appeared with the Sons of the Pioneers in the film with Crosby, and he and the group later recorded the song (Decca).

Empty Tables. w. Johnny Mercer, m. James Van Heusen, 1976. Recorded by Frank Sinatra (Reprise).

Enchanted. w/m Buck Ram, 1959. Featured and recorded by The Platters (Mercury).

Enchanted Island. w. Al Stillman, m. Robert Allen, 1958. Leading record by The Four Lads (Columbia).

Enchanted Sea, The. w/m Frank Metis and Randy Starr, 1959. Hit instrumental first recorded by the writers under name of The Islanders (Mayflower). Other Top 40 record by Martin Denny and his Orchestra (Liberty).

Enclosed, One Broken Heart. w/m Sadie Nordin Sallis and Eddy Arnold, 1950. Introduced and recorded by Eddy Arnold (RCA Victor).

Encore. w/m Terry Lewis and James Harris III, 1984. #1 on the R&B charts by soul singer Cheryl Lynn (Columbia).

Encore, Cherie. w. Alice D. Simms, m. J. Fred Coots, 1948. Art Mooney and his Orchestra (MGM) had a million-seller, coupled with the hit "Baby Face." Also recorded by Tex Beneke's Orchestra (RCA Victor).

End, The (a.k.a. **At the End of the Rainbow**). w. Sid Jacobson, m. Jimmy Krondes, 1958. Featured and recorded by Earl Grant (Decca).

Ending with a Kiss. w. Harlan Thompson, m. Lewis E. Gensler, 1934. Introduced by Lanny Ross in (MM) *Melody in Spring*.

Endless Love. w/m Lionel Richie, 1981. Introduced on the soundtrack of (MP) *Endless Love* by Diana Ross and Lionel Richie. Their single release became one of the most successful duets of all time. #1 on the charts for nine consecutive weeks, it sold over two million discs (Motown). Nominated for Academy Award. Double Grammy Award (NARAS) winner Song of the Year and Record of the Year.

Endlessly. w/m Clyde Otis and Brook Benton, 1959. Recorded by Brook Benton (Mercury).

Endlessly. w. Kim Gannon, m. Walter Kent, 1945. Introduced by Constance Moore in (MM) *Earl Carroll Vanities.* Nominated for Academy Award.

Endless Sleep. w/m Jody Reynolds and Dolores Nance, 1958. Rockabilly hit by Jody Reynolds (Demon). Revived by Hank Williams, Jr. (MGM) 1964.

Endless Summer Nights. w/m Richard Marx, 1988. Popular single by Richard Marx, from the album of his name (EMI).

End of a Love Affair, The. w/m Edward C. Redding, 1950. Introduced and later recorded by Mabel Mercer (Atlantic). First recorded by Dinah Shore (RCA Victor). Among others who performed their versions on discs: Frank Sinatra (Capitol), Margaret Whiting (Capitol), Helen Merrill (Mercury), Herb Jeffries (Bethlehem).

End of Our Road, The. w/m Roger Penzabene, Barrett Strong, and Norman Whitfield, 1968. Top 20 record by Gladys Knight and The Pips (Soul). Chart record by Marvin Gaye (Tamla).

End of the World, The. w. Sylvia Dee, m. Arthur Kent, 1963. Top 10 record by Skeeter Davis (RCA).

End of the World, The. w/m Fred Rose, 1942. Country and Western song recorded by Jimmie Davis (Decca); the Sons of the Pioneers (RCA Victor); Slim Whitman (Imperial); Bob Crosby and the Bobcats, vocal by Mary Lee (Decca).

Engine, Engine Number Nine. w/m Roger Miller, 1965. Top 10 record by Roger Miller (Smash).

Engine Number 9 (Get Me Back on Time). w/m Kenny Gamble and Leon Huff, 1970. Top 20 record by Wilson Pickett (Atlantic).

England Swings. w/m Roger Miller, 1965. Top 10 record by Roger Miller (Smash).

English Muffins and Irish Stew. w. Bob Hilliard, m. Moose Charlap, 1956. Introduced and recorded by Sylvia Syms (Decca).

Enjoy Yourself. w/m Kenny Gamble and Leon Huff, 1976. Top 10 gold record by The Jacksons (Epic).

Enjoy Yourself (It's Later Than You Think). w. Herb Magidson, m. Carl Sigman, 1950. Most popular recordings by Guy Lombardo, vocal by Kenny Gardner (Decca) and Doris Day (Columbia).

Entertainer, The. w/m Billy Joel, 1974. Popular single by Billy Joel from his album "Streetlife Serenade" (Columbia).

Entertainer, The. w/m Tony Clarke, 1965. R&B and Pop chart hit by Tony Clarke (Chess).

Entertainer, The. m. Scott Joplin, 1902, 1974. A popular piano ragtime and big sheet music seller when first published. Among recordings: Mutt Carey's New Yorkers (Century), 1947, and Ken Colyer's Jazzmen (British Decca), 1955. The composition was given new popularity by its use on the soundtrack of (MP) *The Sting,* 1974, played by Marvin Hamlisch, whose recording became a gold record awardee (MCA).

Envy. w. Eve London, m. David Gussin, 1949. Introduced and recorded by Fran Warren (Columbia).

Epistle to Dippy. w/m Donovan Leitch, 1967. Popular U.S. release by Scottish singer/writer Donovan (Epic).

Epistrophy. m. Thelonious Monk, Kenny Clarke, and Cootie Williams, 1942. Introduced by Cootie Williams and his Orchestra at the Savoy Ballroom in New York City. Recorded by Kenny Clarke's bop band in late forties (Victor).

Ephraham Played upon the Piano. w. Vincent Bryan, m. Irving Berlin, 1911. From (TM) *Ziegfeld Follies of 1911*.

Erbie Fitch's Twitch. w. Dorothy Fields, m. Albert Hague, 1959. Show-stopping number performed by Gwen Verdon in (TM) *Redhead*.

Eres Tu (Touch the Wind). w. (Sp.)/m. Joan Calderon Lopez, w. (Engl.) Jay Livingstone and Ray Evans, 1974. Top 10 record by the Spanish sextet, Mocedades, featuring the Amezaga Sisters (Tara).

Escape (the Piña Colada Song). w/m Rupert Holmes, 1979. The song had two distinctions: (1) It was the last #1 gold record of the seventies; (2) it was unusual for the period, in that it was a "story" song, with a beginning, a middle, and an ending. It was recorded by its writer, Rupert Holmes (Infinity).

Eso Beso (That Kiss). w/m Joe Sherman and Noel Sherman, 1962. Leading record by Paul Anka (RCA).

Especially for You. w/m Orrin Tucker and Phil Grogan, 1939. Popular records by Jimmy Dorsey, vocal by Helen O'Connell (Decca); Orrin Tucker, vocal by "Wee" Bonnie Baker (Vocalion); Jack Teagarden, vocal by Linda Keene (Brunswick); Vincent Lopez, vocal by Sonny Schuyler (Bluebird).

Estrellita. w/m Manual M. Ponce, 1914. Spanish composition, introduced in the U.S. by McKee's Orchestra (Victor). Among other popular recordings over the years: Lanny Ross (Victor); Jessica Dragonette (Victor); Lily Pons, with André Kostelanetz's Orchestra (Co-lumbia); whistler Fred Lowery (Columbia); the bands of Benny Goodman (Victor), Harry James (Columbia), Larry Clinton (Bluebird), Sonny Dunham (Varsity).

Eternal Flame. w/m Susanna Hoffs, Tom Kelly, and Bill Steinberg, 1989. Hit record by the group Bangles (Columbia).

Eternally (a.k.a. **Limelight** or **The Terry Theme**). w. Geoffrey Parsons, m. Charles Chaplin, 1953. Theme from Charlie Chaplin's (MP) *Limelight*. Leading instrumental version by Frank Chacksfield and his Orchestra (London). Leading vocal by Vic Damone with Richard Hayman's Orchestra (Mercury).

Et Maintenant. See **What Now My Love.**

Et Pourtant. See **Yet . . . I Know.**

Evangeline. w. Billy Rose, m. Al Jolson, 1929. Featured by Jolson and recorded by Scrappy Lambert (Brunswick) and Andy Sannella's Orchestra (Columbia).

Evelina. w. E. Y. Harburg, m. Harold Arlen, 1944. Introduced by David Brooks and Celeste Holm in (TM) *Bloomer Girl*.

Even Cowgirls Get the Blues. w/m Rodney Crowell, 1978. First Country chart record by La Costa [Tucker] (Capitol). Others: Lynn Anderson (Columbia), 1980; Johnny Cash and Waylon Jennings (Columbia), 1986.

Evenin'. w. Mitchell Parish, m. Harry White, 1934. Introduced and recorded by Cab Calloway (Victor). Recorded by Count Basie's combo, Jones-Smith Incorporated, vocal by Jimmy Rushing (Vocalion), 1937; and by his big band (Okeh), 1940. Michele Bautier revived it in the Parish musical (TM) *Stardust*, 1987.

Evening Star. w. Roy Turk, m. Fred E. Ahlert, 1928. Recorded by the bands of Paul Whiteman and Irving Aaronson (both Victor).

Even It Up. w/m Sue Ennis, Ann Wilson, and Nancy Wilson, 1980. Recorded by the rock band Heart (Epic).

Even Now. w/m Bob Seger, 1983. Recorded by Bob Seger and The Silver Bullet Band (Capitol).

Even Now. w. Marty Panzer, m. Barry Manilow, 1978. Recorded by Barry Manilow (Arista).

Even Now. w/m Richard Adler, Jerry Ross, and David Kapp, 1953. Popular recording by Eddie Fisher (RCA Victor).

Even the Bad Times Are Good. w. Peter Callander, m. Mitch Murray, 1967. Recorded by The British group The Tremeloes (Epic).

Even the Nights Are Better. w/m J. L. Wallace, Kenneth Bell, and Terry Skinner, 1982. Top 10 record by the Australian duo Air Supply (Arista).

Even Tho'. w/m Willie Jones, Curt Peeples, and Webb Pierce, 1954. Introduced and recorded by Webb Pierce (Decca).

Eventually. w/m Ronnie Self and Dub Allbritten, 1961. Recorded by Brenda Lee (Decca).

Eve of Destruction. w/m Phil Sloan and Steve Barri, 1965. #1 record by Barry McGuire (Dunhill).

Ever After. w/m Stephen Sondheim, 1988. Introduced by Tom Aldredge and company in (TM) *Into the Woods.*

Everchanging Times. w/m Burt Bacharach, Carole Bayer Sager, and Bill Conti, 1987. Theme from (MP) *Baby Boom*, recorded by Siedah Garrett (Qwest).

Evergreen (Love Theme from "A Star Is Born"). w. Paul Williams, m. Barbra Streisand, 1976. Introduced by Barbra Streisand in (MM) *A Star Is Born.* Academy Award winner for Best Song. Streisand's recording was a #1 gold record and Grammy Award (NARAS) winner Song of the Year, 1977.

Everlasting Love. w/m James Cason and Mac Gayden, 1967. Hit records by Robert Knight (Rising Sons), 1967; Carl Carlton (Back Beat), 1974; Rex Smith and Rachel Sweet (Columbia), 1981.

Everlasting Love, An. w/m Barry Gibb, 1978. Gold record by the British singer Andy Gibb (RSO).

Everlovin'. w/m Dave Burgess, 1961. Introduced and recorded by Dave Burgess (Challenge).

Every Beat of My Heart. w/m Johnny Otis, 1961. Top 10 record by The Pips (Vee-Jay).

Everybody. w/m Tommy Roe, 1963. Introduced and recorded by Tommy Roe (ABC-Paramount).

Everybody But Me. w/m Dave Burgess, 1962. Country chart hit by Ernest Ashworth (Hickory).

Everybody Dance. w/m Jesse Johnson and Ta Mara, 1985. Recorded by the quintet Ta Mara and The Seen (A&M).

Everybody Has a Laughing Place. w. Ray Gilbert, m. Allie Wrubel, 1946. From (MM) *Song of the South.* Recorded by Burl Ives (Decca).

Everybody Have Fun Tonight. w/m Wang Chung and Peter Wolf, 1986. Top 10 record by the British group Wang Chung (Geffen).

Everybody Is a Star. w/m Sylvester (Sly) Stewart, 1970. Recorded by Sly and the Family Stone (Epic).

Everybody Knew But Me. w/m Irving Berlin, 1945. Leading recordings by the orchestras of Woody Herman (Columbia) and Louis Prima (Majestic).

Everybody Knows. w/m Jimmy Duncan and Les Reed, 1964. Featured and recorded by Steve Lawrence (Columbia).

Everybody Knows (I Still Love You). w/m Dave Clark and Lenny Davidson, 1964. Introduced and Top 20 record by The Dave Clark Five (Epic). Reissued 1968.

Everybody Likes to Cha Cha Cha. w/m Barbara Campbell, 1959. Recorded by Sam Cooke (Keen).

Everybody Loves a Clown. w/m Gary Lewis, Leslie Thomas, and Leon Russell, 1965. Top 10 record by Gary Lewis and The Playboys (Liberty).

Everybody Loves a Lover. w. Richard Adler, m. Robert Allen, 1958. Popular record by Doris Day, orchestra conducted by Frank DeVol (Columbia). Revived by The Shirelles in 1963 (Scepter).

Everybody Loves an Irish Song. w/m William J. McKenna, 1916. Popular recording by the American Quartette (Victor).

Everybody Loves Me But You. w/m Ronnie Self, 1962. Hit record by Brenda Lee (Decca).

Everybody Loves My Baby (But My Baby Don't Love Nobody But Me). w/m Jack Palmer and Spencer Williams, 1924. Among the recordings in its first year: Aileen Stanley (Victor); Gene Rodemich (Brunswick); the Goofus Five (Okeh); Clarence Williams' Blue Five, featuring Louis Armstrong (Okeh). Later recordings by Earl Hines (Victor) and Ruth Etting (Columbia) who featured it in her act. It was sung in her screen bio (MM) *Love Me or Leave Me* by Doris Day in the role of Etting.

Everybody Loves Somebody. w. Irving Taylor, m. Ken Lane, 1948, 1964. When first published, Frank Sinatra recorded it with Nelson Riddle's Orchestra (Columbia). The song was a modest success. In 1964, Dean Martin's version (Reprise) was a #1 million-seller and established the song as a standard.

Everybody Needs Love. w/m Eddie Holland and Norman Whitfield, 1967. Top 40 record by Gladys Knight and The Pips (Soul).

Everybody Needs Somebody to Love. w/m Bert Berns, Solomon Burke, and Jerry Wexler, 1967. Introduced and recorded by Solomon Burke (Atlantic). Top 40 record by Wilson Pickett (Atlantic), 1967.

Everybody Ought to Be in Love. w/m Paul Anka, 1977. Introduced and recorded by Paul Anka (United Artists).

Everybody Ought to Have a Maid. w/m Stephen Sondheim, 1962. Introduced by David Burns, Zero Mostel, Jack Gilford, and John Carradine in (TM) *A Funny Thing Happened on the Way to the Forum*. In the 1966 film version (MM) *A Funny Thing Happened on the Way to the Forum* it was sung by Zero Mostel, Phil Silvers, Jack Gilford, and Michael Hordern.

Everybody Plays the Fool. w/m Jim Bailey, Rudy Clark, and Kenneth Williams, 1972. Gold record by The Main Ingredient (RCA).

Everybody Rag with Me. w. Gus Kahn, m. Grace LeBoy, 1914.

Everybody Says Don't. w/m Stephen Sondheim, 1964. Introduced by Harry Guardino in (TM) *Anyone Can Whistle*.

Everybody's Doin' It Now. w/m Irving Berlin, 1911. Doin' what? The turkey trot! Early recordings by Collins and Harlan (Victor) and the Columbia Quartette (Columbia). Revived by Alice Faye, Dixie Dunbar, and Wally Vernon in (MM) *Alexander's Ragtime Band*, 1938. It was interpolated by the chorus in (MM) *Easter Parade*, 1948.

Everybody's Everything. w/m Carlos Santana, Milton Brown, and Tyrone Moss, 1971. Top 20 record by the Latin-rock group Santana (Columbia).

Everybody's Gone Crazy 'Bout the Doggone Blues. w. Henry Creamer, m. Turner Layton, 1917. Marion Harris had a popular recording (Victor).

Everybody's Got a Home But Me. w. Oscar Hammerstein II, m. Richard Rodgers, 1955. Introduced by Judy Tyler in (TM) *Pipe Dream*. Leading records by Eddie Fisher (RCA) and Roy Hamilton (Epic).

Everybody's Got the Right to Love. w/m Lou Stallman, 1970. Top 40 record by The Supremes (Motown).

Everybody's Got to Learn Sometime. w/m James Warren, 1980. Recorded by the British duo known as The Korgis (Asylum).

Everybody's Had the Blues. w/m Merle Haggard, 1973. #1 Country and chart Pop song by Merle Haggard (Capitol).

Everybody Sing. w. Arthur Freed, m. Nacio Herb Brown, 1937. Introduced by Judy Garland in (MM) *Broadway Melody of '38*. It was coupled with "All God's Chillun Got Rhythm" on her record debut (Decca).

Everybody's Making Money But Tschaikovsky. w/m Krippens, Roe, and Broad, 1942. Novelty referring to the spate of hits to which words were written to melodies by Tschaikovsky, whose music was in the public domain. Introduced and recorded by Les Brown and his Orchestra, vocal by Betty Bonney (Okeh).

Everybody's Out of Town. w. Hal David, m. Burt Bacharach, 1970. Top 40 record by B. J. Thomas (Scepter).

Everybody's Somebody's Fool. w. Howard Greenfield, m. Jack Keller, 1960. #1 hit record by Connie Francis (MGM).

Everybody's Talking. w/m Fred Neil, 1969. Sung on the soundtrack of (MP) *Midnight Cowboy* by (Harry) Nilsson. He had a Top 10 single (RCA).

Everybody Step. w/m Irving Berlin, 1921. Introduced by the Brox Sisters in (TM) *The Music Box Revue*. Ethel Merman sang it in (MM) *Alexander's Ragtime Band*, 1938, and Bing Crosby sang it in (MM) *Blue Skies*, 1946. It was first recorded by Paul Whiteman (Victor) and Ted Lewis (Columbia).

Everybody Two-Step. w. Earle C. Jones, m. Wallie Herzer, 1912. Popular recording by the American Quartette (Victor).

Everybody Wants to Rule the World. w/m Roy Orzabal, Ian Stanley, and Chris Hughes, 1985. #1 record by the British duo comprised of Orzabel and Curt Smith, Tears for Fears (Mercury).

Everybody Wants You. w/m Billy Squier, 1982. Recorded by Billy Squier (Capitol).

Everybody Works But Father. w/m Jean Havez, 1905.

Every Breath I Take. w/m Gerry Goffin and Carole King, 1961. Chart record by Gene Pitney (Musicor).

Every Breath You Take. w/m Sting (pseud. for Gordon Sumner), 1983. #1 gold record from the platinum album "Synchronicity" by the British group The Police. Grammy Award (NARAS) winner Song of the Year, 1983.

Every Day. w. Arthur Jackson, m. William Daly, 1922. Popular instrumental records for the same company by the bands of Ted Lewis and Ted Weems (Columbia).

Every Day. See **Every Day I Have the Blues**.

Every Day I Have the Blues (a.k.a. **Every Day**). w/m Peter Chatman, 1950. Introduced by Lowell Fulson (Swing Time). Count Basie, vocal by Joe Williams (Clef), and B. B. King (RPM) had chart records, 1955. Billy Stewart revived it (Chess), 1967.

Every Day Is Ladies' Day with Me. w. Henry Blossom, m. Victor Herbert, 1906. Introduced by Neal McCay in (TM) *The Red Mill*.

Every Day I Write the Book. w/m Elvis Costello, 1983. Recorded by the English singer Elvis Costello (Columbia).

Every Day of My Life. w/m Jimmie Crane and Al Jacobs, 1956. Introduced and popular record by The McGuire Sisters (Coral). Revived with Top 40 record by Bobby Vinton (Epic), 1972.

Every Day of My Life. w/m Morty Berk, Billy Hays, and Harry James, 1942. Recorded

1939, released 1940 and again in 1944 by Harry James, vocal by Frank Sinatra (Columbia). It was the latter release that became popular along with the version by Helen Forrest with Victor Young's Orchestra (Decca).

Everyday People. w/m Sylvester Stewart, 1969. Gold record hit by Sly and The Family Stone (Epic). Revived by Joan Jett and The Blackhearts (Blackheart), 1983.

Every Day's a Holiday. w. Barry Trivers, m. Sam Coslow, 1938. Introduced by Mae West in (MM) *Every Day's a Holiday*. Among recordings: Al Bowlly (Bluebird); Cab Calloway (Vocalion); Bob Crosby (Decca); Glenn Miller, vocal by Kathleen Lane (Brunswick); Fats Waller (Victor). It was featured in a movie short starring George Hall and his Orchestra by The Landt Trio and White.

Everyday with You Girl. w/m Buddy Buie and James B. Cobb, 1969. Top 20 record by The Classic IV featuring Dennis Yost (Imperial).

Every Girlie Loves Me But the Girlie I Love. w. Otto Harbach, m. Karl Hoschna, 1911. From (TM) *The Girl of My Dreams*.

Every Kinda People. w/m Andy Fraser, 1978. Top 20 record by the English singer Robert Palmer (Island).

Every Little Bit Added to What You've Got Makes Just a Little Bit More. w/m William A. Dillon and Lawrence Dillon, 1907.

Every Little Kiss. w/m Bruce Hornsby, 1987. Chart record, a remix of the 1986 release by Bruce Hornsby and The Range (RCA).

Every Little Movement (Has a Meaning All Its Own). w. Otto Harbach, m. Karl Hoschna, 1910. Introduced by Frances Demarest and Carl Martens in (TM) *Madame Sherry*. Marta Eggerth sang it in (MM) *Presenting Lily Mars* in 1943, Robert Alda in (MM) *April Showers* in 1948, Jack Smith in (MM) *On Moonlight Bay* in 1951, and it was played orchestrally in (MM) *The Jolson Story* in 1946.

Every Little Step. w/m Antonio Reid and Kenneth Edmonds, 1989. Hit record by Bobby Brown (MCA).

Every Little Thing She Does Is Magic. w/m Sting (pseud. for Gordon Sumner), 1981. Top 10 record by the British group The Police (A&M).

Every Minute of the Hour. w/m Charles Kenny and Nick Kenny, 1936. Recordings by Ted Fio Rito and his Orchestra (Decca); George Hall, vocal by Dolly Dawn (Bluebird); Leo Reisman, vocal by Larry Stewart (Brunswick).

Every Night There's a Light. w/m Paul Dresser, 1898. A "mother ballad" introduced by Dick José.

Every Now and Then. w/m Al Sherman, Abner Silver, and Al Lewis, 1935. Recorded by the orchestras of George Hall (Bluebird), Wingy Manone (Vocalion), Ramona (Victor).

Every 1's a Winner. w/m Errol Brown, 1978. Top 10 R&B/Pop gold record by the English group Hot Chocolate (Infinity).

Everyone Says "I Love You." w. Bert Kalmar, m. Harry Ruby, 1932. From the Marx Brothers' (MM) *Horse Feathers*. Top recordings by the bands of Isham Jones, vocal by Eddie Stone (Victor), and Anson Weeks (Brunswick).

Everyone's Gone to the Moon. w/m Kenneth King, 1965. Recorded in England by Jonathan (Kenneth) King (Parrot).

Everyone's Laughing. w/m Calvin Carter, 1957. Recorded by The Spaniels (Vee-Jay).

Every Race Has a Flag But the Coon. w/m Will A. Heelan and J. Fred Helf, 1900.

Every Rose Has Its Thorn. w/m Dall and Daville, 1989. Hit record by Poison (Enigma).

Every So Often. w. Johnny Mercer, m. Harry Warren, 1947. Recorded by Martha Tilton (Capitol).

Every Step of the Way. w. Al Stillman, m. Robert Allen, 1963. Top 40 record by Johnny Mathis (Columbia).

Everything Beautiful. w/m Jay Livingston and Ray Evans, 1961. Introduced by George Gobel and the girls in (TM) *Let It Ride!*

Everything Beautiful Happens at Night. w. Tom Jones, m. Harvey Schmidt, 1963. Introduced by George Church, Scooter Teague, Lesley Warren, and ensemble in (TM) *110 In The Shade.*

Everything But You. w. Don George, m. Edward Kennedy "Duke" Ellington and Harry James, 1945. Featured and recorded by Duke Ellington, vocal by Joya Sherrill (Victor).

Everything Happens to Me. w. Tom Adair, m. Matt Dennis, 1941. The first hit song for each of the writers. Introduced and recorded by Tommy Dorsey, vocal by Frank Sinatra (Victor).

Everything I Have Is Yours. w. Harold Adamson, m. Burton Lane, 1933. Introduced by Joan Crawford and Art Jarrettt in (MM) *Dancing Lady.* In 1952, Monica Lewis sang it in (MM) *Everything I Have Is Yours*, starring Marge and Gower Champion. Early recordings include those by George Olsen and his Orchestra (Columbia), Rudy Vallee (Victor), Freddy Martin (Brunswick), Ruth Etting (Brunswick), Irene Taylor (Vocalion). Billy Eckstine revived it with his gold record (MGM) in the early fifties.

Everything I Miss at Home. w/m James Harris III and Terry Lewis, 1989. Hit R&B chart single by Cherrelle (Tabu).

Everything I Need. w/m Colin Hay, 1985. Recorded by the Australian quintet Men At Work (Columbia).

Everything Is Beautiful. w/m Ray Stevens, 1970. #1 C&W/Pop gold record by Ray Stevens (Barnaby).

Everything Is Hotsy Totsy Now. w. Irving Mills, m. Jimmy McHugh, 1925. Popular records by Gene Austin (Victor), the Coon-Sanders Orchestra (Victor), Van and Schenck (Columbia), and later Freddie "Schnicklefritz" Fisher (Columbia).

Everything Is Peaches Down in Georgia. w. Grant Clarke, m. Milton Ager and George W. Meyer, 1918. Ager's first hit.

Everything Makes Music When You're in Love. w. Sammy Cahn, m. James Van Heusen, 1965. Introduced by Ann-Margaret in (MP) *The Pleasure Seekers.*

Everything's Alright. w. Tim Rice, m. Andrew Lloyd Weber, 1971. Introduced by Yvonne Elliman, Jeff Fenholt, Ben Vereen, and chorus in (TM) *Jesus Christ Superstar.* In the film version (MM) *Jesus Christ Superstar*, 1973, it was sung by Yvonne Elliman.

Everything's Been Done Before. w/m Harold Adamson, Jack King, and Edwin H. Knopf, 1935. From (MP) *Reckless*, in which Jean Harlow's songs were dubbed by Virginia Verrill. Art Jarrett featured, recorded (Victor), and made it his theme song.

Everything's Coming Up Roses. w. Stephen Sondheim, m. Jule Styne, 1959. Introduced by Ethel Merman in (TM) *Gypsy.* In the film version (MM) *Gypsy*, 1962, it was performed by Rosalind Russell, partially dubbed by Lisa Kirk. The music, with a different set of lyrics by Sammy Cahn and titled "Betwixt and Between," was first written for and deleted from the musical *High Button Shoes* in 1947.

Everything's Gonna Be All Right. w. Benny Davis, m. Harry Akst, 1926. Introduced in vaudeville by Benny Davis. Featured on radio and recorded by The Ipana Troubadors, directed by Sam Lanin, vocalist Irving Kaufman (Columbia).

Everything She Wants. w/m George Michael, 1985. One of three #1 singles from the platinum album "Make It Big" by the English duo Wham! (Columbia).

Everything's in Rhythm with My Heart. w/m Al Goodhart, Al Hoffman, and Maurice Sigler, 1936. Introduced by Jessie Matthews in (MM) *First a Girl*, a British film. Featured and recorded by Rudy Vallee and his Orchestra (Victor).

Everything's Made for Love. w/m Al Sherman, Charles Tobias, and Howard Johnson, 1927.

Everything's Up to Date in (Kansas City). w. Oscar Hammerstein II, m. Richard Rodgers, 1943. Introduced by Lee Dixon with Betty Garde and male ensemble in (TM) *Oklahoma!* In the film version (MM) *Oklahoma!*, it was sung by Gene Nelson, Charlotte Greenwood, and chorus, 1955.

Everything That Glitters (Is Not Gold). w/m Dan Seals and Bob McDill, 1986. #1 Country chart record by Dan Seals (EMI America).

Everything That Touches You. w/m Terry Kirkman, 1968. Top 10 record by The Association (Warner Bros.).

Everything Works If You Let It. w/m Rick Nielsen, 1980. Introduced in (MP) *Roadie*, and recorded by the quartet Cheap Trick (Epic).

Everything Your Heart Desires. w/m Daryl Hall, 1988. Chart single by Daryl Hall and John Oates from their album "Ooh Yeah" (Arista).

Everything You Said Came True. w/m Dave Franklin and Cliff Friend, 1937. Featured and recorded by Frances Langford, with Phil Ohman's Orchestra (Decca); the bands of Bernie Cummins (Vocalion); Frank Dailey (Vocalion); Jimmie Grier (Decca).

Every Time I Think of You. w/m Jack Conrad and Ray Kennedy, 1979. Recorded by the British quartet The Babys (Chrysalis).

Every Time I Turn Around (Back in Love Again). w/m Len Hanks and Zane Grey, 1977. Hit record by the R&B/funk band L.T.D. (A&M).

Everytime Two Fools Collide. w/m Jeffrey Tweel and Jan Dyer, 1978. Hit Country record by Kenny Rogers and Dottie West (United Artists).

Everytime You Go Away. w/m Daryl Hall, 1985. #1 record by British singer Paul Young (Columbia).

Every Time You Touch Me (I Get High). w/m Charlie Rich and Billy Sherrill, 1975. Hit Country/Pop chart record by Charlie Rich (Epic).

Every Tub. w. Jon Hendricks, m. Eddie Durham and William "Count" Basie, 1938. First recording by King Oliver (Vocalion) in 1927, arranged by Eddie Durham. The Basie band's swing version (Decca) was released eleven years later, at which time his name was added to the credits. A lyric was added by Jon Hendricks, for the vocal group of Lambert, Hendricks, and Ross, and was included in their album based on tunes popularized by Basie, "Sing Along with Basie" (Roulette).

Everywhere. w/m Christine McVie, 1987. Recorded by the British band Fleetwood Mac (Warner Bros.).

Everywhere You Go. w/m Larry Shay, Joe Goodwin, and Mark Fisher, 1927. First published and performed by singers and orchestras on radio, 1927. Revived by Guy Lombardo, vocal by Don Rodney (Decca), and by Doris Day (Columbia), 1949.

Every Which Way But Loose. w/m Milton Brown, Stephen Dorff, and Snuff Garrett, 1978. Sung by country singer, Eddie Rabbitt, on the soundtrack of (MP) *Every Which Way But Loose*, and on records (Elektra).

Every Woman in the World. w/m Dominic Bugatti and Frank Musker, 1980. Top 10 record by the Australian duo Air Supply (Arista).

Evil Gal Blues. w/m Leonard Feather and Lionel Hampton, 1944. Introduced and recorded by Dinah Washington, with Lionel Hampton's Sextet (Keynote); also by Etta Jones (Black and White); Albinia Jones (National).

Evil on Your Mind. w/m Harlan Howard, 1966. Country hit by Jan Howard (Decca).

Evil Ways. w/m Clarence Henry, 1970. Top 10 record by the Latin group Santana (Columbia).

Evil Woman. w/m Jeff Lynne, 1976. Top 10 record by the British group Electric Light Orchestra (United Artists).

Evil Woman (a.k.a. **Evil Man**). w/m Larry Wiegand, Richard Wiegand, and David Waggoner, 1969. Top 20 record by the quintet Crow (Amaret).

Ev'rybody Loves You. w. Al Dubin, m. Jack Little, 1929. Popular recordings by Little Jack Little (Columbia), Frank Crumit with the Jacques Renard Orchestra (Victor), Johnny Marvin and Aileen Stanley (Victor), and Arnold Johnson's Orchestra (Brunswick).

Ev'ry Day. w. Irving Kahal, m. Sammy Fain, 1935. Introduced by Rudy Vallee in (MM) *Sweet Music*, featured on his radio show, and recorded by him (Victor).

Ev'ry Day Away from You. w. Charles Tobias, m. Jay Mills, 1929.

Ev'ry Day I Love You (Just a Little Bit More). w. Sammy Cahn, m. Jule Styne, 1948. Introduced by Dennis Morgan in (MM) *Two Guys from Texas*. Recordings: Vaughn Monroe (RCA Victor), Dick Haymes (Decca), Jo Stafford (Capitol).

Ev'ry Little Bit Helps. w. George Whiting, m. Fred Fisher, 1904. Fisher's first popular song.

Ev'ry Night about This Time. w. Ted Koehler, m. James V. Monaco, 1942. Featured and recorded by The Ink Spots (Decca); Kay Kyser and his Orchestra (Columbia); Jimmy Dorsey, vocal by Bob Eberly (Decca).

Ev'ry Street's a Boulevard in Old New York. w. Bob Hilliard, m. Jule Styne, 1953. Jack Whiting introduced it in (TM) *Hazel Flagg*, which was a musical version of the

1937 film *Nothing Sacred*. The song was performed by Dean Martin and Jerry Lewis in (MM) *Living It Up*, 1954, which was a film version of *Hazel Flagg* (and/or a remake of *Nothing Sacred*), and retained some of the musical numbers from the stage show.

Ev'ry Sunday Afternoon. w. Lorenz Hart, m. Richard Rodgers, 1940. Introduced by Marta Eggert and Leif Erickson in (TM) *Higher and Higher*. Recordings include: Benny Goodman, vocal by Helen Forrest (Columbia); Charlie Barnett, vocal by Mary Ann McCall (Bluebird); Shirley Ross, who appeared in the musical but did not sing this song (Decca).

Ev'rything I Love. w/m Cole Porter, 1941. Introduced by Danny Kaye and Mary Jane Walsh in (TM) *Let's Face It*. Top recordings by Glenn Miller, vocal by Ray Eberle (Bluebird); Benny Goodman, vocal by Peggy Lee (Okeh); Jimmy Dorsey, vocal by Bob Eberly (Decca).

Ev'rything I've Got. w. Lorenz Hart, m. Richard Rodgers, 1942. Introduced by Ray Bolger and Benay Venuta in (TM) *By Jupiter*. Early recordings by Cy Walter (Liberty Music Shops) and Freddy Martin's Band (Victor).

Ev'ry Time. w/m Ralph Blane and Hugh Martin, 1941. Introduced by Maureen Cannon and reprised by Rosemary Lane in (TM) *Best Foot Forward*. Virginia Weidler sang it in the film version (MM) *Best Foot Forward*, 1943. Nancy Walker, who appeared in both productions, recorded it, coupled with "Shady Lady Bird" from the same show (Bluebird).

Ev'rytime We Say Goodbye. w/m Cole Porter, 1944. Introduced by Nan Wynn in (TM) *Seven Lively Arts*. Featured and recorded by The Benny Goodman Quintet, vocal by Peggy Mann (Columbia); Stan Kenton, vocal by Anita O'Day (Capitol); Hildegarde (Decca); Charlie Spivak, vocal by Irene Daye (Victor); George Paxton, vocal by Alan Dale (Hit).

Exactly Like You. w. Dorothy Fields, m. Jimmy McHugh, 1930. Introduced by Gertrude Lawrence and Harry Richman in Lew Leslie's (TM) *International Revue*. It was interpolated by Anita Morris in (TM) *Sugar Babies*, 1980. In films, Carmen Cavallaro played it on the soundtrack for Tyrone Power in the title role of (MM) *The Eddy Duchin Story*, 1956.

Excuse Me (I Think I've Got a Heartache). w/m Harlan Howard and Buck Owens, 1961. Hit C&W record by Buck Owens (Capitol).

Exodus. w. Charles E. (Pat) Boone, m. Ernest Gold, 1961. The music was the main theme from (MP) *Exodus*. Leading instrumental recordings by Ferrante and Teicher (United Artists); Mantovani (London); Eddie Harris, jazz version (Vee Jay). Pat Boone added lyrics and had a popular record titled "The Exodus Song (This Land Is Mine)" (Dot).

Exodus Song, The. See **Exodus**.

Experience. w. Johnny Burke, m. James Van Heusen, 1948. Introduced by Dorothy Lamour in (MM) *Road to Rio*.

Experience Unnecessary. w/m Gladys Shelley, Hugo Peretti, and Luigi Creatore, 1955. Featured and recorded by Sarah Vaughan (Mercury).

Explosion in My Soul. w/m Kenneth Gamble and Leon A. Huff, 1967. Top 40 record by The Soul Survivors (Crimson).

Express. w/m Lomas, Risbrook, Risbrook, Rowe, Thompson, Ward, and Woods, 1975. Instrumental written and recorded by the disco group B. T. Express (Roadshow).

Expressway to Your Heart. w/m Kenneth Gamble and Leon A. Huff, 1967. Top 10 record by The Soul Survivors (Crimson).

Express Yourself. w/m Charles Wright, 1970. Top 20 record by Charles Wright and The Watts 103rd Street Rhythm Band (Warner Bros.).

Eye in the Sky. w/m Eric Woolfson and Alan Parsons, 1982. Recorded by the writers and their production, The Alan Parsons Project (Arista).

Eye of the Tiger. w/m Frank Sullivan and Jim Peterik, 1982. From the film (MP) *Rocky III*. Nominated for an Academy Award. #1 platinum record by the quintet Survivor (Scotti Brothers). Winner Grammy Award (NARAS) Song of the Year.

Eyes of a New York Woman, The. w/m Mark James, 1968. Top 40 record by B. J. Thomas (Scepter).

Eyes of Blue, Eyes of Brown. w/m Costen and Andrew B. Sterling, 1901.

Eyes of Love, The (Carol's Theme). w. Bob Russell, m. Quincy Jones, 1967. From (MP) *Banning*. Nominated for Academy Award.

Eyes Without a Face. w/m Billy Idol and Steve Stevens, 1984. Top 10 record by the British singer Billy Idol (Chrysalis).

F

Fable of the Rose. w. Bickley Reichner, m. Josef Myrow, 1940. Most popular recordings by Benny Goodman, vocal by Helen Forrest (Columbia); Glen Gray and the Casa Loma Orchestra, vocal by Kenny Sargent (Decca); Tommy Dorsey, vocal by Frank Sinatra (Victor); Charlie Barnet, vocal by Mary Ann McCall (Bluebird); Buster Bailey (Varsity).

Fabulous. w. Jon Sheldon, m. Harry Land, 1957. Leading record by Charlie Gracie (Cameo). Popular version by Steve Lawrence (Coral).

Fabulous Character. w/m Bennie Benjamin and Sol Marcus, 1956. Leading record by Sarah Vaughan (Mercury).

Face in the Crowd, A. 1987. Top 10 Country chart record by Michael Martin Murphey and Holly Dunn (Warner Bros.).

Face It Girl, It's Over. w. Frank H. Stanton, m. Andy Badale, 1968. Top 40 record by Nancy Wilson, produced by Dave Cavanaugh (Capitol).

Face on the Dime, The. w/m Harold Rome, 1946. The song, referring to the late president, Franklin D. Roosevelt, whose likeness was on the newly minted dimes, was introduced by Lawrence Winters in (TM) *Call Me Mister.*

Face the Face. w/m Pete Townshend, 1985. Recorded by the English singer/guitarist, Pete Townshend (Atco).

Face to Face. w/m Randy Owen, 1988. #1 Country chart record by the group Alabama (RCA).

Face to Face. w. Sammy Cahn, m. Sammy Fain, 1953. Introduced by Gordon MacRae and Jane Powell in (MM) *Three Sailors and a Girl.* MacRae recorded it (Capitol).

Face to Face. w/m Grant Colfax Tuller, 1899.

Face to Face. w/m Herbert Johnson, 1897.

Face to Face with the Girl of My Dreams. w/m Richard Howard, 1914.

Face to the Wall. w/m Bill Anderson and Faron Young, 1960. C&W hit recorded by Faron Young (Capitol).

Facts of Life, The. w/m Johnny Mercer, 1960. Introduced by Steve Lawrence and Eydie Gormé as title song on the soundtrack of (MP) *The Facts of Life.* Nominated for Academy Award, 1960.

Fade Away. w/m Bruce Springsteen, 1981. Recorded by Bruce Springsteen (Columbia).

Faded Love. w/m John Wills and Bob Wills, 1963. Recorded by Jackie De Shannon (Liberty) and Patsy Cline (Decca).

Faded Summer Love, A. w/m Phil Baxter, 1931. Leading recordings by Bing Crosby (Brunswick), and Paul Whiteman and his Orchestra, vocal by Jack Fulton (Victor). Revived by Kitty Kallen and Georgie Shaw with The Dave Lambert Singers (Decca), 1956.

Fade Out—Fade In. w. Betty Comden and Adolph Green, m. Jule Styne, 1964. Introduced by Carol Burnett and Dick Patterson in (TM) *Fade Out—Fade In.*

Fa-Fa-Fa-Fa-Fa (Sad Song). w/m Otis Redding and Steve Cropper, 1966. Recorded by Otis Redding (Volt).

Fair and Warmer. w. Al Dubin, m. Harry Warren, 1934. Introduced by Dick Powell and Ted Fio Rito's Orchestra in (MM) *Twenty Million Sweethearts* and then recorded (Brunswick).

Fair Warning. w/m Harold Rome, 1959. Introduced by Dolores Gray in (TM) *Destry Rides Again.*

Fairytale. w/m Anita Pointer and Bonnie Pointer, 1974. Top 20 record by The Pointer Sisters (Blue Thumb).

Fairy Tales. w/m William J. Reitz, 1950. Paul Weston and his Orchestra had a popular instrumental (Capitol), as did Owen Bradley and his Orchestra (Coral).

Faith. w/m George Michael, 1987. Title track from the album and #1 single by British singer/songwriter George Michael (Columbia).

Faith. w/m Jack Lawrence and Stan Freeman, 1964. Introduced by Richard Kiley and company in (TM) *I Had a Ball.*

Faith Can Move Mountains. w. Ben Raleigh, m. Guy Wood, 1952. Leading records by Nat "King" Cole (Capitol) and Frankie Laine (Columbia).

Faithful Forever. w. Leo Robin, m. Ralph Rainger, 1939. Sung on the soundtrack for the animated feature-length film (MM) *Gulliver's Travels* by Jessica Dragonette and Lanny Ross. Song nominated for an Academy Award. Ross recorded it (Schirmer), as did many others including: Kenny Baker (Victor); Glenn Miller and his Orchestra (Bluebird); Phil Harris (Varsity); Arthur Tracy, "The Street Singer" (Decca); Ginny Simms (Vocalion).

Faithfully. w/m Jonathan Cain, 1983. Written by the keyboardist of the group Journey (Columbia).

Faithless Love. w/m J. D. Souther, 1984. Country chart hit by Glen Campbell (Atlantic America).

Fake. w/m James Harris III and Terry Lewis, 1987. #1 R&B chart record by Alexander O'Neal (Tabu).

Faking Love. w/m Bobby Braddock and Matraca Berg, 1982. #1 Country chart record by T. G. Sheppard and Karen Brooks (Warner Bros.).

Fakin' It. w/m Paul Simon, 1967. Recorded by Simon and Garfunkel (Columbia).

Falcon and the Dove, The. See **Love Theme from "El Cid."**

Fallen Angel. w/m Webb Pierce, Wayne Walker, and Marijohn Wilkin, 1961. Recorded by Webb Pierce (Decca).

Fallen Star, A. w/m James Joiner, 1957. Leading recordings by Jimmy Newman (Dot), Nick Noble (Mercury), Ferlin Husky (Capitol), The Hilltoppers (Dot).

Fallin'. w. Howard Greenfield, m. Neil Sedaka, 1958. Featured and recorded by Connie Francis (MGM).

Fallin' Again. w/m Greg Fowler, Teddy Gentry, and Randy Owen, 1988. #1 Country chart record by Alabama (RCA).

Fallin' for You for Years. w/m Troy Seals and Mike Reed, 1987. Top 10 Country chart record and included in the album "Borderline" by Conway Twitty (MCA).

Falling. w/m Gene McFadden and Franne Golde, 1986. #1 R&B chart record by Melba Moore (Capitol).

Falling. w/m Lenny LeBlanc and Edward Struzick, 1977. Top 20 record by the duo LeBlanc and Carr (Big Tree).

Falling. w/m Roy Orbison, 1963. Introduced and recorded by Roy Orbison (Monument).

Falling Again. w/m Bob McDill, 1981. Top 10 Country chart record by Don Williams (MCA).

Falling Back to You. w/m Billy Phillips and Webb Pierce, 1958. Top 10 C&W record by Webb Pierce (Decca).

Falling in Love Again (Can't Help It). w. Sammy Lerner (Engl.), m. Frederick Hollander, 1931. Introduced by Marlene Dietrich in (MP) *The Blue Angel*. The English-born, German-educated composer scored the film in Berlin for director Josef Von Sternberg and wrote the song that was to be forever associated with the star. Dietrich recorded it (Victor) (Decca, twice) and included it in several albums.

Falling in Love with Love. w. Lorenz Hart, m. Richard Rodgers, 1938. Introduced by Muriel Angelus and female chorus in (TM) *The Boys from Syracuse*. In the film version (MM) *The Boys from Syracuse*, 1940, it was sung by Allan Jones and Rosemary Lane, and was interpolated by Binnie Hale in the London revue *Up and Doing* the same year.

Falling Leaves. w. Mack David, m. Frankie Carle, 1940. Introduced and recorded by Horace Heidt, featuring Frankie Carle at the piano (Columbia). Best-selling record by Glenn Miller, vocal by Ray Eberle. Others: Jimmy Dorsey, vocal by Bob Eberly (Decca); Wayne King (Victor). After World War II, the Glenn Miller Band, headed by Tex Beneke, recorded it (Victor).

Fallin' in Love. w/m Dan Hamilton and Ann Hamilton, 1975. #1 gold record by Hamilton, Joe Frank, and Reynolds (Playboy).

Fall in Love with Me. w/m Maurice White, Wayne Vaughn, and D. Vaughn, 1983. Top 10 R&B chart record by the group Earth, Wind & Fire (Columbia).

Fall on Me. w/m Bill Berry, Peter Buck, Mike Mills, and Michael Stipe, 1986. Written and recorded by the quartet R.E.M. (I.R.S.).

Fame. w. Dean Pitchford, m. Michael Gore, 1980. Introduced in (MM) *Fame* by Irene Cara and cast members. Top 10 single by Cara (RSO). Grammy Award winner (NARAS) Song of the Year.

Fame. w/m John Lennon, David Bowie, and Carlos Alomar, 1975. Introduced by David Bowie in his album "Young Americans" (RCA). A single was released and became a #1 gold record.

Fame and Fortune. w. Fred Wise, m. Ben Weisman, 1960. Coupled with #1 hit "Stuck on You," these were the first recordings by Elvis Presley after his discharge from the Army (RCA).

Family Affair. w/m Sylvester Stewart, 1971. #1 chart record by Sly and The Family Stone (Epic).

Family Bible. w/m Walt Breeland, Claude Gray, and Paul Buskirk, 1960. Introduced and Top 10 C&W chart record by Claude Gray (Decca). Later versions by George Jones (Mercury), 1961, and Willie Nelson (Songbird), 1980.

Family Man. w/m T. Cross, R. Fenn, M. Frye, M. Oldfield, M. Pert, and M. Reilly, 1983. Top 10 record by Daryl Hall and John Oates (RCA).

Family Man. w/m J. A. Balthrop, 1960. C&W hit by Frankie Miller (Starday).

Family of Man, The. w. Jack Conrad, m. Paul Williams, 1972. Top 20 record by Three Dog Night (Dunhill).

Family Tradition. w/m Hank Williams, Jr., 1979. Recorded by Country singer Hank Williams, Jr. (Elektra).

Famous Last Words of a Fool. w/m Dean Dillon and Rex Huston, 1988. #1 Country chart record by George Strait (MCA).

Fancy. w/m Bobbie Gentry, 1969. Top 40 record by Bobbie Gentry (Capitol).

Fancy Meeting You. w. E. Y. Harburg, m. Harold Arlen, 1936. Sung by Dick Powell in (MM) *Stage Struck* and recorded by him (Decca).

Fancy Our Meeting. w. Douglas Furber, m. Joseph Meyer and Philip Charig, 1929. Introduced by Jack Buchanan and Elsie Randolph in London in (TM) *That's a Good Girl*, 1928. Introduced in the U.S. in the revue (TM) *Wake Up and Dream*, by Jack Buchanan and Jessie Matthews.

Fancy Pants. m. Floyd Cramer, 1965. Instrumental by Al Hirt and his Orchestra (RCA).

Fandango. w. Johnny Bradford, m. Frank Perkins, 1952. Hugo Winterhalter and his Orchestra had a popular instrumental record (RCA Victor).

Fan It. w/m Frankie Jaxon and Dan Howell, 1941. Original recording by Frankie "Half Pint" Jaxon (Vocalion), 1929, credited to above writers. Red Nichols, vocal by Ray McKinley, recorded it (Brunswick), 1931, followed by Isham Jones (Decca) and Bob Wills (Vocalion) 1936. In 1941 (Decca) and 1946 (Columbia), Woody Herman's Woodchoppers recorded it with writers' credits going to Herman and Joe Bishop, his arranger.

Fannie Mae. w/m Waymon Glasco, 1960. Recorded by Buster Brown (Fire).

Fanny. w/m Harold Rome, 1954. Introduced by William Tabbert in (TM) *Fanny*. Popular records by Eddie Fisher (RCA Victor) and Fred Waring's Pennsylvanians (Decca). It was played under the credits in the film version (MP) *Fanny*, 1961.

Fanny (Be Tender with My Love). w/m Barry Gibb, Maurice Gibb, and Robin Gibb, 1976. Top 20 record by the British brother-trio The Bee Gees (RSO).

Fantastic Voyage. w/m Lakeside, 1981. Written and recorded by the nine-member group Lakeside (Solar).

Fantasy. w/m Aldo Nova, 1982. Recorded by Canadian singer Aldo Nova (Portrait).

Fantasy. w/m Maurice White, Verdine White, and Eddie de Barrio, 1978. Recorded by the group Earth, Wind & Fire (Columbia).

Faraway Part of Town, The. w. Dory Langdon Previn, m. André Previn, 1960. Sung by Judy Garland on the soundtrack of (MP) *Pepe*. Nominated for Academy Award, 1960.

Far Away Places. w/m Joan Whitney and Alex Kramer, 1949. Nineteen weeks on "Your Hit Parade," three times in the #1 position, this had Top 10 records by Bing Crosby (Decca), Margaret Whiting (Capitol), Perry Como (RCA Victor), Dinah Shore (Columbia).

Fare Thee Honey, Fare Thee Well. w/m John Akers and J. Mayo Williams, 1938. First recorded by Connie Boswell, with Ben Pollack's Orchestra (Decca), followed by Count Basie's Quartet (Decca), Eddie Durham (Decca), Andy Kirk with vocal by June Richmond (Decca), and Marie Cahill (Victor).

Fare Thee Well, Annabelle. w. Mort Dixon, m. Allie Wrubel, 1935. Sung by Rudy Vallee in (MM) *Sweet Music* and recorded by him (Victor).

Fare-Thee-Well to Harlem. w. Johnny Mercer, m. Bernard Hanighen, 1934. Introduced and recorded by Paul Whiteman and his Orchestra, with vocal by Johnny Mercer (Bluebird). Jack Teagarden, who was featured on the Whiteman disk, also recorded it with his Band (Brunswick) as did Benny Morton (Columbia).

Farewell. w/m Willie Littlefield, 1949. R&B chart record by Little Willie Littlefield (Modern). Revived by The Ethics (Vent), 1969.

Farewell, My Lovely. w. Howard Dietz, m. Arthur Schwartz, 1935. Sung by Woods Miller and danced by Paul Haakon and Nina Whitney in (TM) *At Home Abroad*.

Farewell Amanda. w/m Cole Porter, 1949. Introduced by David Wayne in (MP) *Adam's Rib*, starring Spencer Tracy and Katherine Hepburn.

Farewell Blues. w/m Paul Joseph Mares and Elmer Schoebel, 1922. A much recorded blues standard. Among the many releases are the jazz band, The Friars' Society Orchestra (Gennett), who later became The New Orleans Rhythm Kings; Ted Lewis (Columbia); Paul Whiteman (Victor); Cab Calloway (Brunswick); Woody Herman (Decca).

Farewell to Arms. w. Allie Wrubel, m. Abner Silver, 1933. Featured and recorded by Morton Downey (Melotone); Arthur Tracy, "The Street Singer" (Brunswick); Anson Weeks's Orchestra, vocal by Donald Novis. Later recordings by Vera Lynn (London); Bill Farrell (MGM); Harry Belafonte, when he was starting his career as a pop-jazz singer (Capitol).

Farewell to Dreams. w. Gus Kahn, m. Sigmund Romberg, 1937. Written for (MM) *Maytime*, but deleted from the final print. Nelson Eddy and Jeanette MacDonald had their duet released on records (Victor).

Far from Over. w/m Frank Stallone and Vince DiCola, 1983. Sung by Frank Stallone on the soundtrack of (MP) *Staying Alive*, and on the Top 10 single release (RSO).

Far from the Home I Love. w. Sheldon Harnick, m. Jerry Bock, 1964. Introduced by Julia Migenes and Zero Mostel in (TM) *Fiddler on the Roof*. It was sung by Michele Marsh in (MM) *Fiddler on the Roof*, 1971.

Farther Up the Road. w/m Don Robey and J. Veasey, 1957. First hit record by Bobby Bland (Duke).

Fascinating Rhythm. w. Ira Gershwin, m. George Gershwin, 1924. Introduced by Fred and Adele Astaire and Cliff "Ukulele Ike" Edwards in (TM) *Lady, Be Good*. Hit records by Edwards (Pathé) (Perfect). In the 1941 screen version (MM) *Lady Be Good*, Eleanor Powell danced while Connie Russell sang it. Tommy Dorsey and his Band played it in (MM) *Girl Crazy*, 1943. Hazel Scott, the jazz pianist and singer, performed it in the George Gershwin story (MM) *Rhapsody in Blue*, 1945.

Fascination. w. Harold Atteridge, m. Sigmund Romberg, 1915. From (TM) *A World of Pleasure*.

Fascination. w. Dick Manning, m. F. D. Marchetti, 1904, 1957. Marchetti composed his "Valse Tzigane" for cafe orchestra in France. It became the recurrent theme in the Gary Cooper-Audrey Hepburn-Maurice Chevalier (MP) film *Love in the Afternoon*, 1957. Jane Morgan, singing Manning's lyric, had a million-selling record the same year (Kapp), and the song attained the #1 spot on "Your Hit Parade."

Fascination (Keep Feeling). See **(Keep Feeling) Fascination**.

Fast Car. w/m Tracy Chapman, 1988. Hit single by Tracy Chapman from her debut album of her name (Elektra).

Faster Horses. w/m Tom T. Hall, 1976. Hit Country record by Tom T. Hall (Mercury).

Fatal Fascination. w. Harlan Thompson, m. Lewis E. Gensler, 1935. Introduced by Eddie Davis and reprised by Carl Brisson in (MM) *Ship Cafe*. Davis was co-owner and M.C. of the popular New York nightclub that was once a speakeasy, Leon and Eddie's.

Fatal Rose of Red, The. w/m J. Fred Helf and Ed Gardenier, 1900.

Fatal Wedding, The. w. H. H. Windom, m. Gussie L. Davis, 1893. Introduced by Windom, a popular singer-songwriter.

Fate. w/m Dick Wolf and Randy Starr, 1958. Recorded by Country star Red Foley (Decca).

Fate. w/m Robert Wright and George Forrest, 1953. Based on a theme from Borodin's

Symphony No. 2 in B Minor, it was introduced by Alfred Drake and Doretta Morrow in (TM) *Kismet*.

Fat Gal. w/m Merle Travis, 1948. Introduced and recorded by Merle Travis (Capitol).

Father Figure. w/m George Michael. 1988. #1 single from the album "Faith" by the British singer/songwriter George Michael (Columbia).

Fatherhood Blues. w. Richard Maltby, Jr., m. David Shire, 1983. Introduced by James Congdon, Martin Vidnovic, and Todd Graff in (TM) *Baby*.

Fat Man, The. w/ Antoine "Fats" Domino, m. Dave Bartholomew, 1950. Featured and recorded by Fats Domino (Imperial).

Fat Meat Is Good Meat. w/m Irene Higginbotham, 1942. Chart record by Jimmy Lytell and his All-star Seven, vocal by Savannah Churchill (Beacon). Later recorded by Churchill (Celebrity).

Favorite Waste of Time. w/m Marshall Crenshaw, 1983. Recorded by Bette Midler (Atlantic).

F.D.R. Jones. w/m Harold Rome, 1938. Introduced by Rex Ingram in (TM) *Sing Out The News*. Standout recordings: Ella Fitzgerald, with Chick Webb's Orchestra (Decca); Cab Calloway (Vocalion).

Feather Your Nest. w/m James Kendis, James Brockman, and Howard Johnson, 1920. Interpolated by The Duncan Sisters in (TM) *Tip Top*.

Feed Me: Git It. w. Howard Ashman, m. Alan Mencken, 1982. Introduced by Lee Wilkof and Ron Taylor in the off-Broadway musical (TM) *Little Shop of Horrors*.

Feed the Birds. w/m Richard M. Sherman and Robert B. Sherman, 1964. Introduced by Julie Andrews in (MM) *Mary Poppins*.

Feelin' Alright. w/m David Mason, 1969. Written by the guitarist of the English group, Traffic, and introduced by them in their album

of the same name (United Artists). Chart single by Joe Cocker (A&M), revived in 1972. Instrumental version by Mongo Santamaria and his Orchestra (Atlantic). Grand Funk Railroad recorded it (Capitol), 1971.

Feeling Drowsy. m. Henry "Red" Allen, Jr., 1929. Recorded by Allen with the Luis Russell Band (Victor).

Feeling Good. w/m Leslie Bricusse and Anthony Newley, 1965. Introduced by Gilbert Price in (TM) *The Roar of the Greasepaint— The Smell of the Crowd*.

Feeling I'm Falling. w. Ira Gershwin, m. George Gershwin, 1928. Introduced by Gertrude Lawrence and Paul Frawley in (TM) *Treasure Girl*.

Feelin' Groovy. See **59th Street Bridge Song, The**.

Feelings. w. (Engl)/m. Morris Albert and Mauricio Kaiserman, 1975. Brazilian song with Portuguese words by Thomas Fundera. Gold record by Morris Albert (RCA). Many cover records and one of the most performed songs of the year.

Feelin' High. w. Howard Dietz, m. Walter Donaldson, 1934. Introduced by Shirley Ross and Harry Barris in (MM) *Hollywood Party*. This was one of two collaborations by these top writers. See also "Jungle Fever."

Feelin' High and Happy. w. Ted Koehler, m. Rube Bloom, 1938. Featured and recorded by Benny Goodman, vocal by Martha Tilton (Vocalion); Gene Krupa, vocal by Helen Ward (Brunswick); Hot Lips Page (Bluebird).

Feelin's. w/m Troy Seals, Don Goodman, and Will Jennings, 1975. Hit Country record by Conway Twitty and Loretta Lynn (MCA).

Feelin' Stronger Every Day. w/m Peter Cetera and James Pankow, 1973. Written by two members of the group Chicago, which had a Top 10 record (Columbia).

Feelin' the Feelin'. w/m David Bellamy, 1989. Top 10 Country chart record by The Bellamy Brothers (Curb).

Feel It Again. w/m Ray Coburn, 1986. Recorded by the Canadian quintet Honeymoon Suite (Warner Bros.).

Feel Like Makin' Love. w/m Mick Ralphs and Paul Rodgers, 1975. Top 10 record by the British group Bad Company (Swan Song).

Feel Like Makin' Love. w/m Gene McDaniels, 1974. #1 gold record by Roberta Flack (Atlantic). Bob James, keyboardist, had an instrumental chart version (CTI), 1974.

Feels Like the First Time. w/m Mick Jones, 1977. Top 10 record by the Anglo-American rock group Foreigner (Atlantic).

Feel So Bad. w/m Sam "Lightnin' " Hopkins, 1967. Top 10 on the R&B charts by Little Milton (Checker).

Feel So Fine. w/m Leonard Lee, 1960. Leading record by Johnny Preston (Mercury).

Feel So Good. w/m Calvin White, 1967. Top 40 record sung in medley listed as "Let the Good Times Roll" and "Feel So Good," by Bunny Sigler (Parkway).

Feel So Good. w/m Leonard Lee, 1955. R&B chart maker by Shirley and Lee (Aladdin).

Feels So Good. m. Chuck Mangione, 1978. Instrumental hit by flugelhornist Chuck Mangione and his Orchestra (A&M).

Feels So Real (Won't Let Go). w/m Patrice Rushen and Fred Washington, 1984. Recorded by Patrice Rushen (Elektra).

Feels So Right. w/m Randy Owen, 1981. Recorded by the quartet Alabama (RCA).

Feet Up (Pat Him on the Po-Po). w/m Bob Merrill, 1952. Top 20 record by Guy Mitchell, with Mitch Miller's Orchestra (Columbia).

Fella with an Umbrella, A. w/m Irving Berlin, 1948. Introduced by Judy Garland and Peter Lawford in (MM) *Easter Parade.* Most popular record by Bing Crosby (Decca).

Fellow Needs a Girl, A. w. Oscar Hammerstein II, m. Richard Rodgers, 1947. Introduced by William Ching and Annamary Dickey in (TM) *Allegro.* Recorded by Frank Sinatra (Columbia) and Perry Como (RCA Victor).

Fellow on a Furlough, A. w/m Bobby Worth, 1943. Leading records by Al Sack and his Orchestra (AS); Phil Hanna, with Leonard Joy's studio orchestra (Decca); Louis Prima and his Band (Hit). Bob Crosby sang it in (MM) *Meet Miss Bobby Socks,* 1944.

Femininity. w/m Jay Livingston and Ray Evans, 1958. Introduced by Abbe Lane in (TM) *Oh Captain!* and recorded by her (RCA). Because of contractual problems, Lane's songs were sung on the cast album by Eileen Rodgers (Columbia).

Ferdinand the Bull. w. Larry Morey, m. Albert Hay Malotte, 1938. Theme song of Walt Disney's animated cartoon (MP) *Ferdinand the Bull.* It was sung on the soundtrack by Sterling Holloway.

Fernando. w/m Benny Anderson, Stig Anderson, and Bjorn Ulvaeus, 1976. Top 20 record by the Swedish quartet Abba (Atlantic).

Ferry Across the Mersey. w/m Gerry Marsden, 1965. Introduced by Gerry and the Pacemakers in the British film (MM) *Ferry Across the Mersey.* The group had a Top 10 U.S. record (Laurie).

Ferryboat Serenade, The. w. Harold Adamson (Engl.), Mario Panzeri (It.), m. Eldo di Lazzaro, 1940. Original Italian title "La Piccinina." Introduced in the United States by Gray Gordon and his Orchestra (Bluebird). The Andrews Sisters had the biggest seller (Decca). Others: Alvino Rey, vocal by The King Sisters (Bluebird); Kay Kyser and his Band (Columbia). The song was a #1 hit.

Feudin' and Fightin'. w. Al Dubin and Burton Lane, m. Burton Lane, 1947. Introduced in revue (TM) *Laffing Room Only,* 1944, by Pat Brewster. Song became popular this year via performances and recordings by Dorothy Shay, "The Park Avenue Hillbilly"

(Columbia); Jo Stafford (Capitol); Bing Crosby (Decca).

Fever. w/m John Davenport and Eddie Cooley, 1956, 1958. Top 10 R&B record by Little Willie John (King). Featured and recorded by Peggy Lee in 1958 (Capitol), she has remained associated with the song. The rock band, The McCoys, had a hit in 1965 (Bang).

Fez, The. w/m Walter Becker, Donald Fagen, and Paul Griffin, 1976. Recorded by the group Steely Dan (ABC).

Ffun. w/m Mike Cooper, 1978. #1 R&B and chart Pop record by the Soul group Con Funk Shun (Mercury).

Fiddle Dee Dee. w. Sammy Cahn, m. Jule Styne, 1949. From (MM) *It's a Great Feeling*. Leading records by Johnny Desmond (MGM); the bands of Lionel Hampton (RCA Victor), Guy Lombardo (Decca), Jimmy Dorsey (Columbia).

Fiddle Faddle. m. Leroy Anderson, 1948. Anderson's first big hit. Recorded by Ethel Smith (Decca) and later by Anderson's Orchestra (Decca).

Fiddler on the Roof. m. Sheldon Harnick and Jerry Bock, 1964. Theme played by "the fiddler" in (TM) *Fiddler on the Roof*. Popular recording by The Village Stompers (Epic). In the film version (MM) *Fiddler on the Roof*, Isaac Stern played the violin on the soundtrack, dubbing for Tutte Lemkow.

Fidgety Feet. w. Ira Gershwin, m. George Gershwin, 1926. Introduced by Harlan Dixon, Marian Fairbanks, and the ensemble in (TM) *Oh, Kay!* Instrumental record by Fletcher Henderson and his Orchestra (Brunswick).

Fidgety Feet. m. Edwin B. Edwards, Nick LaRocca, Tony Spargo, Larry Shields, 1924. This instrumental was written and introduced by members of the Original Dixieland Jazz Band (Victor).

Fidgety Joe. w. Frank Loesser, m. Matty Malneck, 1939. Sung by Betty Grable and danced by Eddie "Rochester" Anderson in (MM) *Man About Town*.

Fido Is a Hot Dog Now. w. Charles McCarron, m. Raymond Walker, 1914.

Fields of Fire. w/m Big Country, 1984. Written and recorded by the Scottish rock quartet Big Country (Mercury).

Fiesta. m. Heino Gaze, 1962. German instrumental. Leading recording by Dave "Baby" Cortez (Emit). Also recorded by Lawrence Welk (Dot), 1963.

Fiesta. w/m Walter G. Samuels and Leonard Whitcup, 1931. Henry Busse and his Orchestra (Victor) helped to popularize this song.

Fifi. w/m Sam Coslow, 1937. Mae West, as Mme. Fifi, performed it in (MM) *Every Day's a Holiday*.

Fifteen Cents. w/m Chris Smith, 1913.

Fifteen Minute Intermission. w/m Sunny Skylar and Bette Cannon, 1940. Popular records by Cab Calloway (Okeh); The King Sisters (Bluebird); Andy Kirk, vocal by June Richmond (Decca).

Fifteen Years Ago. w/m Ray Smith, 1970. Recorded by Conway Twitty (Decca).

Fifth of Beethoven, A. m. Walter Murphy, 1976. Based on Beethoven's *Fifth Symphony*, Walter Murphy and The Big Apple Band recorded a #1 gold record disco instrumental (Private Stock).

Fifty Million Frenchmen (Can't Be Wrong). w. Willie Raskin and Billy Rose, m. Fred Fisher, 1927. Introduced, featured, and recorded by Sophie Tucker (Okeh).

59th Street Bridge Song, The (a.k.a. **Feelin' Groovy**). w/m Paul Simon, 1967. Introduced by Simon and Garfunkel in LP "Parsley, Sage, Rosemary, and Thyme" (Columbia), 1966. Hit record by Harpers Bizarre (Warner Bros.).

Fifty Percent. w. Alan Bergman and Marilyn Bergman, m. Billy Goldenberg, 1978. Introduced by Dorothy Loudon in (TM) *Ballroom*.

50 Ways to Leave Your Lover.   w/m Paul Simon, 1976. A #1 gold record single from Paul Simon's album "Still Crazy After All These Years" (Columbia).

Fight.   w/m Paul Jabara, Bob Esty, and Bruce Roberts, 1979. Introduced by Barbra Streisand in (MP) *The Main Event*, and recorded by her in medley as "The Main Event/ Fight" (Columbia).

(You Gotta) Fight for Your Right (to Party).   w/m Adam Horovitz, Adam Yauch, Michael Diamond, and Rick Rubin, 1987. Written and recorded by (the first three writers) the white rap band The Beastie Boys (Def Jam).

Fightin' Side of Me, The.   w/m Merle Haggard, 1970. Country hit and Pop chart record by Merle Haggard (Capitol).

Fight the Power.   w/m Ernest Isley, Marvin Isley, O'Kelly Isley, Ronald Isley, Rudolph Isley, 1975. Gold record by The Isley Brothers (T-Neck, Part 1).

Final Countdown, The.   w/m Joey Tempest, 1987. Top 10 single and album title song by the Swedish quintet Europe (Epic).

Finally Got Myself Together (I'm a Changed Man).   w/m Edward Townshend, 1974. Top 20 record by The Impressions (Curtom).

Find Another Fool.   w/m Marv Ross, 1982. Recorded by the group Quarterflash, headed by Ross and his wife, Rindy (Geffen).

Find Another Girl.   w/m Jerry Butler and Curtis Mayfield, 1961. Top 40 record by Jerry Butler (Vee-Jay).

Find Me a Primitive Man.   w/m Cole Porter, 1929. Introduced by Evelyn Hoey, Billy Reed, Lou Duthers, and ensemble in (TM) *Fifty Million Frenchmen*. It was sung by Madeline Kahn in (MM) *At Long Last Love*, 1975. Patrice Munsel and Tammy Grimes sang it in (TM) *A Musical Jubilee*, 1975.

Find Your Way Back.   w/m Craig Chaquico and Thomas Borsdorf, 1981. Recorded by the group Jefferson Starship (Grunt).

Fine, Fine Boy, A.   w/m Jeff Barry, Ellie Greenwich, and Phil Spector, 1963. Recorded by Darlene Love (Philles).

Fine and Dandy.   w. Paul James, m. Kay Swift, 1930. Introduced by Joe Cook and Alice Boulden in (TM) *Fine and Dandy*.

Fine and Mellow.   w/m Billie Holiday, 1940. Introduced and recorded by Billie Holiday (Commodore), followed by Andy Kirk, vocal by June Richmond (Decca).

Fine Brown Frame.   w/m Guadalupe Cartiero and J. Mayo Williams, 1948. Introduced 1944, by Buddy Johnson, vocal by Arthur Prysock (Decca). Revived in 1948 by singer-pianist Nellie Lutcher and her Rhythm (Capitol).

Fine Fine Day, A.   w/m Tony Carey, 1984. Recorded by Tony Carey (MCA).

Fine Mess, A.   w. Dennis Lambert, m. Henry Mancini, 1986. Introduced by The Temptations on the soundtrack of (MP) *A Fine Mess* and on records (Motown).

Fine Romance, A.   w. Dorothy Fields, m. Jerome Kern, 1936. Introduced by Ginger Rogers and Fred Astaire in (MM) *Swing Time*. Virginia O'Brien sang it in the Kern biography (MM) *Till the Clouds Roll By* in 1946. It was included in the four-LP set, "The Fred Astaire Story" (Mercury). Bing Crosby and his wife, Dixie Lee, had a popular record (Decca).

Finer Things, The.   w. Will Jennings, m. Steve Winwood, 1987. Top 10 record by British singer/musician Steve Winwood (Island).

Finest, The.   w/m James Harris III and Terry Lewis, 1986. Recorded by The S.O.S. Band, meaning "Sounds of Success" (Tabu).

Finger of Suspicion Points at You, The.   w/m Paul Mann and Al Lewis, 1954. Written by American songwriters, but first published and recorded in England. British record by Dicky Valentine (London) popular in U.S.

Finger Poppin' Time. w/m Hank Ballard, 1960. Introduced and recorded by Hank Ballard and The Midnighters (King).

Fingertips. w/m Henry Cosby and Clarence Paul, 1963. Two-sided hit by Little Stevie Wonder (Tamla).

Fings Ain't Wot They Used T'Be. w/m Lionel Bart, 1960. From the British (TM) *Fings Ain't Wot They Used T'Be.*

Fini. w/m Richard Adler and Jerry Ross, 1953. Introduced by Polly Bergen in (TM) *John Murray Anderson's Almanac.* Popular record by Eydie Gormé, with Neal Hefti's Orchestra (Coral).

Fins. w/m Jimmy Buffett, Barry Chance, Tom Corcoran, and Deborah McCall, 1979. Recorded by Jimmy Buffett (MCA).

Fire. w/m Bruce Springsteen, 1978. Top 10 gold record by The Pointer Sisters (Planet).

Fire. w/m Jimmy Williams, Clarence Satchell, Leroy Bonner, Marshall Jones, William Beck, Ralph Middlebrook, and Marvin Pierce, 1975. Written by the members of the group Ohio Players. Their collaboration resulted in a #1 gold single taken from their album of the same title (Mercury).

Fire! w/m Arthur Brown, Vincent Crane, Peter Kerr, and Finesilver, 1968. English song and recording. Gold U.S. record by The Crazy World of Arthur Brown (Atlantic).

Fire. w/m Jimi Hendrix, 1967. Introduced by The Jimi Hendrix Experience in their debut album (Reprise). Chart record by Five by Five (Paula), 1968.

Fire and Ice. w/m Tom Kelly, Scott Sheets, and Pat Benatar, 1981. Recorded by Pat Benatar (Chrysalis).

Fire and Rain. w/m James Taylor, 1970. Top 10 record by James Taylor, his first hit (Warner Bros.).

Fire and Smoke. w/m Earl Thomas Conley, 1981. #1 Country record by Earl Thomas Conley (Sunbird).

Firefly. w. Carolyn Leigh, m. Cy Coleman, 1958. Popularized by Tony Bennett (Columbia).

Fire I Can't Put Out, A. w/m Darrell Staedtler, 1983. #1 C&W chart record by George Strait (MCA).

Fire Lake. w/m Bob Seger, 1980. Recorded by Bob Seger (Capitol).

Fire With Fire. w/m Chas Sandford, 1986. Introduced by the quintet Wild Blue on the soundtrack of (MP) *Fire With Fire* and on records (Chrysalis).

Fireworks. w. Betty Comden and Adolph Green, m. Jule Styne, 1960. Introduced by John Reardon and Nancy Dussault in (TM) *Do Re Mi.*

First, Last and Always. w. Benny Davis, m. Harry Akst, 1923.

First Anniversary. w/m Aaron Schroeder and Sid Wayne, 1959. Leading record by Cathy Carr (Roulette).

First Born. w/m John Lehman, 1956. Popularized by Tennessee Ernie Ford (Capitol).

First Class Private Mary Brown. w/m Frank Loesser, 1944. Written for the Army Special Service show *About Face!* at Camp Shanks, New York. It became a popular song and the basis of the WAC revue *PFC Mary Brown*, 1944.

First Cut Is the Deepest, The. w/m Cat Stevens, 1977. English song with first U.S. release by Keith Hampshire (A&M), 1973. Leading record by Rod Stewart (Warner Bros.).

First Date, First Kiss, First Love. w. Mary Stovall and Dan Welch, m. Dan Welch, 1957. Hit record by Sonny James (Capitol).

First I Look at the Purse. w/m William "Smokey" Robinson and Robert Rogers, 1965. Recorded by The Contours (Gordy).

First Lady Waltz. w. Ned Washington, m. Jimmy McHugh, 1961. Dedicated to Mrs. John F. Kennedy, upon the inauguration of President John F. Kennedy.

First Name Initial. w/m Aaron Schroeder and Martin Kalmanoff, 1959. Featured and recorded by Annette [Funicello] (Vista).

First of May. w/m Barry Gibb, Maurice Gibb, and Robin Gibb, 1969. Recorded in England by the brother trio The Bee Gees (Atco).

First Thing Every Morning (and the Last Thing Every Night), The. w/m Jimmy Dean and Ruth Roberts, 1965. Recorded by Jimmy Dean (Columbia).

First Time Ever I Saw Your Face, The. w/m Ewan MacColl, 1971. English song, first recorded by Kitty White (Horizon), 1962. Roberta Flack sang it on the soundtrack of (MP) *Play Misty for Me.* Her recording became a #1 gold record (Atlantic), 1972, winning Grammy (NARAS) awards for Song of the Year and Record of the Year.

First Time I Saw You, The. w. Allie Wrubel, m. Nathaniel Shilkret, 1937. Introduced in (MP) *The Toast of New York* by Frances Farmer. The song was popularized via the airplay and recordings of the bands of Charlie Barnet (Bluebird); Bunny Berigan, vocal by Ford Leary (Victor); Emery Deutsch (Brunswick); Jimmie Lunceford, vocal by Dan Grissom (Decca).

First Time It Happens, The. w/m Joe Raposo, 1981. From (MP) *The Great Muppet Caper.* Nominated for Academy Award.

First Warm Day in May, The. w/m Bart Howard, 1956. Introduced by Mabel Mercer and recorded in her first album (Atlantic). Popular version by Rosemary Clooney (Columbia).

First We Take Manhattan. w/m Leonard Cohen, 1987. Popular track from album by Jennifer Warnes "Famous Blue Raincoat," a collection of Canadian poet/singer Leonard Cohen songs (Cypress). Cohen included it in his album "I'm Your Man" (Columbia), 1988.

First You Have Me High (Then You Have Me Low). w. Lew Brown, m. Harold Arlen, 1935. Introduced by Ethel Merman in (MM) *Strike Me Pink.* No songs from the stage production of the same title were used.

Fish, The. w. Kal Mann, m. Bernie Lowe and Dave Appell, 1961. Top 40 song introduced and recorded by Bobby Rydell (Cameo).

Fishin' for the Moon. w/m Eddie Seiler, Sol Marcus, and Guy Wood, 1945. Leading records by Vaughn Monroe, with his Orchestra (Victor) and Dick Robertson, with Johnny Long's Orchestra (Decca).

Fishin' in the Dark. w/m Wendy Waldman and Jim Photoglo, 1987. #1 Country chart record by The Nitty Gritty Dirt Band (Warner Bros.).

Fishnet. w/m Morris Day, James Harris III, and Terry Lewis, 1988. #1 R&B chart record by Morris Day (Warner Bros.).

Fist City. w/m Loretta Lynn, 1968. Country hit by Loretta Lynn (Decca).

Fit as a Fiddle. w/m Arthur Freed, Al Hoffman, and Al Goodhart, 1932. This popular song attained additional identification with the last lyric lines of the release (bridge), the catch-phrase "with a hey-nonny-nonny and a hot-cha-cha." Featured by many radio singers and bands. Best-selling record: Fred Waring and the Pennsylvanians (Victor). Revived by Fred Astaire and Donald O'Connor in (MM) *Singing in the Rain,* 1952.

5 D (Fifth Dimension). w/m James McGuinn, 1966. Recorded by The Byrds (Columbia).

Five Feet High and Rising. w/m Johnny Cash, 1959. Featured and recorded by Johnny Cash (Columbia).

5:15. w/m Peter Townshend, 1979. From the British film (MM) *Quadrophenia.* Leading record by the London group The Who (Polydor).

Five Foot Two, Eyes of Blue (Has Anybody Seen My Girl). w. Sam M. Lewis and Joe Young, m. Ray Henderson, 1925. This song typifies the flapper age with its lyric and melody and is often used as an identification of that period in the background for motion pictures and TV shows. Gene Austin helped popularize it with his hit record (Victor). Art Mooney and his Band had a popular record (MGM), 1948. Song was on the soundtrack of (MM) *Has Anybody Seen My Girl?*, 1952, and (MM) *Love Me Or Leave Me*, 1955.

Five Guys Named Moe. w. Larry Wynn, m. Jerry Bresler, 1941. Novelty recorded by Louis Jordan and his Tympany Five (Decca).

Five Hundred Miles Away from Home. w. Bobby Bare and Hedy West, m. Charlie Williams and Hedy West, 1963. Top 10 record by Bobby Bare (RCA).

Five Little Fingers. w/m Bill Anderson, 1964. Hit Country record by Bill Anderson (Decca).

Five Long Years. w/m Eddie Boyd, 1952. Eddie Boyd had a #1 R&B hit (J.O.B.).

Five Minutes More. w. Sammy Cahn, m. Jule Styne, 1946. Introduced by Phil Brito in (MM) *Sweetheart of Sigma Chi.* #1 record by Frank Sinatra (Columbia). Other popular versions by Tex Beneke, with his Orchestra (RCA Victor); The Three Suns (Majestic); Skitch Henderson, vocal by Ray Kellogg (Capitol). Song was on "Your Hit Parade" for sixteen weeks, five times as #1.

Five O'Clock Whistle, The. w/m Josef Myrow, Kim Gannon, and Gene Irwin, 1940. Of the many recordings, Glenn Miller, vocal by Marion Hutton, had the best-seller (Bluebird), followed (not necessarily in order of sales) by Ella Fitzgerald (Decca); Erskine Hawkins's Band (Bluebird); Duke Ellington, vocal by Ivy Anderson (Victor); Woody Herman's Band (Decca); Ray McKinley, with Will Bradley's Band (Columbia); George Shearing (MGM).

Five O'Clock World. w/m Allen Reynolds, 1965. Recorded by The Vogues (Co & Ce).

Five Pennies, The. w/m Sylvia Fine, 1959. Introduced by Danny Kaye and Louis Armstrong in (MM) *The Five Pennies*. Nominated for Academy Award, 1959.

Five Salted Peanuts. w/m Charlie Abbott, 1945. Featured and recorded by Tony Pastor, with his Orchestra (Victor).

5-10-15 Hours. w/m Rudolph Toombs, 1952. Hit record by Ruth Brown (Atlantic).

5-10-15-20 (25-30 Years of Love). w/m Tony Boyd and Archie Powell, 1970. Top 20 record by The Presidents (Sussex).

Flame, The. w/m Robert Mitchell and Dick Graham, 1988. Hit single by the band, Cheap Trick, from the album "Lap of Luxury" (Epic).

Flames of Paradise. w/m Bruce Roberts and Andy Goldmark, 1987. Chart single by Jennifer Rush with Elton John from the album "Heart Over Mind" (Epic).

Flamingo. w. Edmund Anderson, m. Ted Grouya, 1941. Introduced and recorded by Duke Ellington, vocal by Herb Jeffries (Victor). Song associated with and featured by Jeffries who also recorded it as a single (Exclusive) and with Les Brown's Orchestra (Coral). Earl Bostic and his Band had an R&B hit in 1951 (King). Herb Alpert and The Tijuana Brass had a Top 40 version (A&M), 1966. Recorded by many bands, singers, and jazz soloists.

Flamin' Mamie. w/m Fred Rose and Paul Whiteman, 1926. Introduced by Paul Whiteman and his Orchestra. Best-seller: Coon-Sanders' Original Nighthawk Orchestra (Victor).

Flannel Petticoat Gal. w. Oscar Hammerstein II and W. C. Duncan, m. Vincent Youmans and Herbert Stothart, 1924. Performed by Hal Skelly and Kitty Kelly in (TM) *Mary Jane McKane.*

Flapperette. m. Jesse Greer, 1926. A banjo instrumental recorded by Harry Reser (Brunswick) and Eddie Dunstetter (Decca). Orchestra instrumental by Nat Shilkret (Victor).

Flashdance . . . What a Feeling. w. Keith Forsey and Irene Cara, m. Giorgio Moroder, 1983. Introduced by Irene Cara on the soundtrack of (MM) *Flashdance*. Winner Academy Award, 1983. Cara's recording became a #1 gold record (Casablanca).

Flash Light. w/m George Clinton, William Collins, and Bernie Worrell, 1978. Top 20 record by the group Parliament (Casablanca).

Flat Foot Floogie, The. w/m Slim Gaillard, Slam Stewart, and Bud Green, 1938. Novelty hit introduced by Slim and Slam (Gaillard and Stewart) and recorded by them (Vocalion). Other popular records: Wingy Manone (Bluebird), Milt Herth Trio (Decca), Woody Herman (Decca), Benny Goodman (Victor), Will Hudson (Brunswick).

Flat Top. w/m Cowboy Copas and Tommy Hill, 1961. Top 10 C&W chart record by Cowboy Copas (Starday).

Fleet's In, The. w. Johnny Mercer, m. Victor Schertzinger, 1942. Introduced by Betty Jane Rhodes in (MM) *The Fleet's In*.

Flesh Failures, The. See **Let the Sunshine In**.

Fletch, Theme From. See **Bit by Bit**.

Flim Flam Man. w/m Laura Nyro, 1967. Introduced by Laura Nyro in her album "More Than a New Discovery" (Verve). Chart single by Barbra Streisand (Columbia), 1971.

Flings. w/m Bob Merrill, 1957. Showstopping number performed by Thelma Ritter, Lulu Bates, and Mara Landi in (TM) *New Girl in Town*.

Flip Flop and Fly. w/m Charles Calhoun and Lou Willie Turner, 1955. Leading record by Joe Turner (Atlantic).

Flirtation Walk. w. Mort Dixon, m. Allie Wrubel, 1934. Introduced by Dick Powell and Ruby Keeler in (MM) *Flirtation Walk*. Powell recorded it (Brunswick) as did many others including Irving Aaronson and his Commanders (Columbia); Eddy Duchin, vocal by Lew Sherwood (Victor); Hal Kemp, vocal by Skinnay Ennis (Brunswick); George Hall, vocal by Sonny Schuyler (Bluebird); and Victor Young's Orchestra (Decca). Elliot Lawrence and his Orchestra recorded it in the early fifties (Decca).

Flirtin' with Disaster. w/m Danny Joe Brown, David Hludeck, and Harvey Thomas, 1980. Recorded by the sextet, Molly Hatchet (Epic).

Floatin' Down to Cotton Town. w/m F. Henri Klickmann and Jack Frost, 1919. Revived in 1936 by Wingy Manone (Bluebird).

Float On. w/m Arnold Ingram, James Mitchell, and Marvin Willis, 1977. Top 10 record by The Floaters (ABC). Cheech and Chong recorded a comedy version titled "Bloat On Featuring the Bloaters" (Ode).

Florida, the Moon and You. w. Gene Buck, m. Rudolf Friml, 1926. Introduced by Peggy Fears and Irving Fisher in (TM) *No Foolin'*. The show opened on Broadway as *Ziegfeld's American Revue*, but changed its title to that of its song hit.

Flower of Dawn. w/m Russ Morgan, Eddie DeLange, and Carl Lamagna, 1940. Featured and recorded (twice) by Russ Morgan and his Music in the Morgan Manner (Decca) and Eddy Duchin, vocal by Patricia Norman (Vocalion).

Flower of Love. w/m Leon Ashley and Margie Singleton, 1968. Top 10 Country chart record by Leon Ashley (Ashley).

Flowers for Madame. w/m Charles Tobias, Charles Newman, and Murray Mencher, 1935. Leading records by the orchestras of Ray Noble, vocal by Al Bowlly (Victor); Bob Crosby (Decca); Jack Shilkret (Bluebird).

Flowers Mean Forgiveness. w/m Al Frisch, Edward R. White, and Mack Wolfson, 1956. Featured and recorded by Frank Sinatra (Capitol).

Flowers on the Wall. w/m Lewis De Witt, 1965. Top 10 record by The Statler Brothers (Columbia).

Floy Joy. w/m William "Smokey" Robinson, 1972. Top 20 record by The Supremes (Motown).

Fluffy Ruffles. m. Cecil Duane Crabb, 1907. The first ragtime success of the Indiana composer. This enjoyed a big sheet music sale.

Fly, Robin, Fly. w/m Silvester Levay and Stephan Prager, 1975. #1 gold record from Germany by the studio disco group Silver Convention (Midland International).

Fly, The. w/m John Madara and Dave White, 1961. Top 10 record by Chubby Checker (Parkway).

Fly Away. w/m John Denver, 1976. Top 20 record by John Denver, vocal backing by Olivia Newton-John (RCA).

Fly by Night. w/m Ritchie Adams and Neval Nader, 1961. Featured and recorded by Andy Williams (Columbia).

Flying Down to Rio. w. Edward Eliscu and Gus Kahn, m. Vincent Youmans, 1933. The title song of (MM) *Flying Down to Rio* was introduced by Fred Astaire and chorus. This, probably the first American samba (the tempo markings did not identify that rhythm), was one of four popular songs (q. v.) to emerge from Youman's last published score. Astaire recorded it (Columbia) coupled with "Music Makes Me" from the same film. Rudy Vallee had a successful record coupled with "Orchids in the Moonlight" from the same score (Victor). The fourth song was "Carioca."

Flyin' Home. w. Sid Robin, m. Lionel Hampton and Benny Goodman, 1939. Standard swing instrumental for which lyrics were added later. Introduced by the Benny Good-man Sextet, featuring Lionel Hampton (Columbia). Hampton recorded it twice (Victor) (Decca). Among many other recordings: Illinois Jacquet, 1 & 2 (Aladdin); Johnny Guarnieri (Majestic); Art Tatum, (Comet 12″); Will Bradley (Columbia); Charlie Barnet (Bluebird); Tiny Grimes, 1 & 2 (Blue Note); vocally, Ella Fitzgerald (Decca).

Fly Like an Eagle. w/m Steve Miller, 1977. Top 10 gold record by Steve Miller (Capitol).

Fly Me to the Moon (In Other Words). w/m Bart Howard, 1954. Introduced in cabaret by Mabel Mercer. First recording by Felicia Sanders (Columbia) under original title "In Other Words." Through popularity via many ensuing recordings, airplay, and TV and radio performances, the song became known by its opening line, "Fly Me to the Moon," and the sheet music was reprinted with the new title. Joe Harnell and Orchestra had a hit record in 1962 as "Fly Me to the Moon Bossa Nova" (Kapp). Song is now a standard.

FM (No Static At All). w/m Walter Becker and Donald Fagen, 1978. Sung on the soundtrack of (MP) *FM* by the group, Steely Dan, which also had a popular record (MCA).

Foggy Day, A (in London Town). w. Ira Gershwin, m. George Gershwin, 1937. Introduced by Fred Astaire in (MM) *Swingtime* and recorded by him (Brunswick). Popular records by Hal Kemp, vocal by Skinnay Ennis (Victor); Bob Crosby, vocal by Kay Weber (Decca); and in 1950, Les Brown (Columbia).

Foggy Mountain Breakdown. m. Earl Scruggs, 1968. Originally recorded by Lester Flatt and Earl Scruggs (Mercury), 1949. Performed on the soundtrack of (MP) *Bonnie and Clyde*, 1967, by Flatt and Scruggs and released as a record (Columbia), 1968.

Foggy River. w/m Fred Rose, 1946. Among recordings were those by Hugo Winterhalter and his Orchestra (Victor) and Jane Harvey with The Page Cavanaugh Trio (Victor).

Folies Bergere. w/m Maury Yeston, 1982. Introduced by Liliane Montevecchi, Stephanie Cotsirilos, and company in (TM) *Nine.*

Folks Who Live on the Hill, The. w. Oscar Hammerstein II, m. Jerome Kern, 1937. Introduced by Irene Dunne in (MM) *High, Wide, and Handsome.* Hit records by Bing Crosby (Decca) and Ozzie Nelson, vocal by Harriet Hilliard (Bluebird).

Followed Closely by Teardrops. w. Fred Tobias, m. Paul Evans, 1962. Recorded by Hank Locklin (RCA).

Following the Sun Around. w. Joseph McCarthy, m. Harry Tierney, 1927. Sung by J. Harold Murray in (TM) *Rio Rita.* John Boles sang it in the first film adaptation (MM) *Rio Rita,* 1929. The song was excluded from the 1942 version. Carl Fenton's Band recorded the song, coupled with the title song, "Rio Rita" (Brunswick).

Follow Me. w/m John Denver, 1971. Popular single by Mary Travers (Warner Bros.). It was heard in (MP) *The Gospel Road,* 1973.

Follow Me. w. Alan Jay Lerner, m. Frederick Loewe, 1960. Introduced by Mary Sue Berry in (TM) *Camelot.* In (MM) *Camelot,* 1967, it was sung by Vanessa Redgrave.

Follow the Boys. w/m Benny Davis and Murray Mencher, 1962. Introduced by Connie Francis in (MM) *Follow the Boys* and on records (MGM).

Follow the Fold. w/m Frank Loesser, 1950. Introduced by Isabel Bigley, Pat Rooney, Sr., and chorus in (TM) *Guys and Dolls.* In the film version (MM) *Guys and Dolls,* 1955, it was sung by Jean Simmons, Kay Kuter, and chorus.

Follow the Swallow. w. Billy Rose and Mort Dixon, m. Ray Henderson, 1924. Introduced, featured, and recorded by Al Jolson (Brunswick).

Follow You Follow Me. w/m Anthony Banks, Phil Collins, and Mike Rutherford, 1978. Recorded by the English group Genesis (Atlantic).

Follow Your Heart. w. Sidney D. Mitchell, m. Victor Schertzinger, 1936. Sung by Marion Talley and Michael Bartlett in (MM) *Follow Your Heart.*

Folsom Prison Blues. w/m Johnny Cash, 1956, 1968. Johnny Cash first recorded this country standard in 1956 (Sun). Its popularity remained and he re-recorded it in 1968 when, in addition to being #1 on the C&W charts, it was high up in the Pop surveys.

Food, Glorious Food. w/m Lionel Bart, 1963. Introduced by Bruce Prochnik and the boys in the U.S. (Broadway) production of (TM) *Oliver!* In (MM) *Oliver!,* 1968, it was sung by Mark Lester and the boys.

Fool, Fool, Fool. w/m Max Powell and Wayne P. Walker, 1967. Top 10 Country record by Webb Pierce (Decca).

Fool, Fool, Fool. w/m Ahmet Ertegun, 1951. Hit R&B record by The Clovers (Atlantic) and Pop version by Kay Starr with The Lancers (Capitol).

Fool (If You Think It's Over). w/m Chris Rea, 1978. Top 20 record by the English singer Chris Rea (United Artists).

Fool, The. w/m Naomi Ford, 1956. Top 10 record by Sanford Clark (Dot).

Fooled. w. Mann Curtis, m. Doris Tauber, 1955. Featured and recorded by Perry Como (RCA).

Fooled Around and Fell in Love. w/m Elvin Bishop, 1976. Top 10 gold record by guitarist Elvin Bishop, assisted by Jefferson Starship vocalist Mickey Thomas (Capricorn).

Fool for You. w/m Curtis Mayfield, 1968. Top 40 record by The Impressions (Curtom).

Fool for You, A. w/m Ray Charles, 1955. Introduced and popular recording by Ray Charles (Atlantic). Revived in 1968 by The Impressions (Curtom).

Fool for Your Love. w/m Don Singleton, 1983. Country chart record by Mickey Gilley (Epic).

Fool Hearted Memory. w/m Alan R. Mevis and Byron Hill, 1982. #1 Country chart record by George Strait (MCA).

Foolin'. w/m Steve Clark, Joe Elliott, and Robert John Lange, 1983. Recorded by the British quintet Def Leppard (Mercury).

Foolin' Around. w/m Harlan Howard and Buck Owens, 1961. Introduced and hit C&W record by Buck Owens (Capitol). Pop chart record by Kay Starr (Capitol).

Fool in Love, A. w/m Ike Turner, 1960. Chart record by Ike and Tina Turner (Sue).

Fool in Love, A. w. George McQueen, m. Sid Lippman, 1933. Featured and recorded by Tommy Tucker and his Band (Crown). Note: This Lippman is not to be confused with the composer who has written numerous songs under the shortened first name, but is referred to as Sidney in this volume.

Foolin' Myself. w. Jack Lawrence, m. Peter Tinturin, 1937. Best-selling record by Teddy Wilson, vocal by Billie Holiday (Brunswick).

Fool in the Rain. w/m John Paul Jones, Jimmy Page, and Robert Plant, 1980. Last chart song by the British group, Led Zeppelin, of which the writers were members (Swan Song).

Foolish Beat. w/m Debbie Gibson, 1988. Chart single by Debbie Gibson (Atlantic).

Foolish Heart. w/m Steve Perry and Randy Goodrum, 1985. Single from the platinum album "Street Talk" by Steve Perry (Columbia).

Foolish Heart. w. Ogden Nash, m. Kurt Weill, 1943. Introduced by Mary Martin in (TM) *One Touch of Venus*, and recorded by her, coupled with "That's Him" from the same show (Decca). For the film version, a new lyric was written for the same melody. See also "My Heart Is Showing."

Foolish Little Girl. w/m Howard Greenfield and Helen Miller, 1963. Top 10 record by The Shirelles (Scepter).

Foolish Tears. w/m Jenny Lou Carson, 1948. Most popular recordings by Al Morgan (London), Spade Cooley (RCA Victor), Axel Stordahl and his Orchestra (Columbia).

Fool Never Learns, A. w/m Sonny Curtis, 1964. Featured and recorded by Andy Williams (Columbia).

Fool #1. w/m Kathryn R. Fulton, 1961. Hit record by Brenda Lee (Decca).

Fool on the Hill, The. w/m John Lennon and Paul McCartney, 1968. Introduced by The Beatles in their album "Magical Mystery Tour" (Capitol). Top 10 single by Sergio Mendes and Brasil '66 (A&M), 1968.

Fools' Hall of Fame. w/m Aaron Schroeder and Wally Gold, 1959. Featured and recorded by Pat Boone (Dot).

Fool's Paradise. w/m Bob Merrill, 1949. Featured and recorded by Billy Eckstine (MGM).

Fools Rush In. w. Johnny Mercer, m. Rube Bloom, 1940. Based on a composition of Bloom's titled "Shangri-La," it became a #1 hit with many recordings by top artists, among them: Glenn Miller, vocal by Ray Eberle (Bluebird); Mildred Bailey (Columbia); Harry James, vocal by Dick Haymes (Varsity); Kay Kyser, vocal by Ginny Simms (Columbia); Tommy Dorsey, vocal by Frank Sinatra (Victor). Top 40 records by Brook Benton, 1960 (Mercury); Ricky Nelson, 1963 (Decca).

Fool Such as I, A (Now and Then There's). w/m Bill Trader, 1953, 1959. Hit Country record by Hank Snow (RCA Victor). Pop versions by Jo Stafford (Capitol) and Tommy Edwards (MGM). Revived with a #2 chart record by Elvis Presley (RCA Victor), 1959, and by Bob Dylan (Columbia), 1974.

Fool to Cry. w/m Mick Jagger and Keith Richards, 1976. Top 10 record by The Rolling Stones (Rolling Stones).

Fool Was I, A. w. Roy Alfred, m. Kurt Adams, 1953. Leading recording by Nat "King" Cole (Capitol).

Footloose. w. Dean Pitchford, m. Kenny Loggins, 1984. Main title theme from (MM) *Footloose*, sung on the soundtrack by Kenny Loggins. His recording became a #1 gold record (Columbia) and Academy Award nominee.

Footloose and Fancy Free. w. Gus Kahn, m. Carmen Lombardo, 1935.

Footloose Love Theme. See **Almost Paradise . . . Love Theme From**.

Footprints in the Snow. w/m Boyd Lane, 1947. Hit record by Bill Monroe, The Father of Bluegrass (Columbia).

Footsteps. w/m Barry Mann and Hank Hunter, 1960. Popularized by Steve Lawrence (ABC-Paramount).

Footsteps of a Fool. w/m Danny Harrison and Don Carter, 1962. Top 10 Country chart record by Judy Lynn (United Artists).

For a Dancer. w/m Jackson Browne, 1974. Introduced by Jackson Browne in his album "Late for the Sky." Leading record by the English trio Prelude (Pye), 1976.

For All the Wrong Reasons. w/m David Bellamy, 1982. #1 Country chart record by The Bellamy Brothers (Elektra).

For All We Know. w. Arthur James and Robb Wilson, m. Fred Karlin, 1970. Sung on the soundtrack of (MP) *Lovers and Other Strangers* by Larry Meredith. Winner Academy Award. Gold record by The Carpenters (A&M), 1971.

For All We Know. w. Sam M. Lewis, m. J. Fred Coots, 1934. Introduced by Morton Downey on his radio show. Featured and recorded by Isham Jones and his Orchestra, vocal by Joe Martin (Victor); Hal Kemp, vocal by Bob Allen (Brunswick); Nick Lucas (Banner); Kay Kyser (Columbia). The Andrews Sisters had a popular record in 1942 (Decca).

For a Penny. w/m Charles Singleton, 1959. Recorded by Pat Boone (Dot).

For a Rocker. w/m Jackson Browne, 1984. Recorded by Jackson Browne (Asylum).

For Baby (a.k.a. For Bobbie). w/m John Denver, 1966. Popularized via album cuts by Peter, Paul, and Mary (Warner Bros.) and John Denver (RCA).

For Bobbie. See **For Baby**.

For Dancers Only. w. Don Raye and Vic Schoen, m. Sy Oliver, 1937. Introduced and recorded by Jimmie Lunceford and his Orchestra, arrangement by Sy Oliver (Decca). Lyric was added later.

For Dixie and Uncle Sam. w. J. Keirn Brennan, m. Ernest R. Ball, 1916. Recorded by Nora Bayes (Victor).

For Emily, Whenever I May Find Her. w/m Paul Simon, 1972. First recorded by Simon and Garfunkel in their album "Parsley, Sage, Rosemary, and Thyme" (Columbia), 1966. Chart single (Columbia), 1972.

Forever. w/m Buddy Killen, 1960. Country hit by The Little Dippers (University). Other popular records by Billy Walker (Columbia), and guitarist Pete Drake (Smash), 1964.

Forever Amber. w. Johnny Mercer, m. David Raksin, 1947. Based on theme from (MP) *Forever Amber*. Recorded by Bobby Sherwood and his Orchestra (Capitol).

Forever and a Day. w/m Hugh Martin and Timothy Gray, 1964. Introduced by Tammy Grimes and Edward Woodward in (TM) *High Spirits*.

Forever and Always. w/m Lefty Frizzell and Lessie Lyle, 1952. Introduced and recorded by Lefty Frizzell (Columbia).

Forever and Ever. w. Malia Rosa (Engl.), m. Franz Winkler, 1949. From Zurich, Switzerland, the original German title, "Fliege mit Mir in Die Hermat," had words by Winkler. English version introduced and recorded by Gracie Fields (London). Popular recordings by Russ Morgan and his Orchestra (Decca); Perry Como (Victor); Margaret Whiting (Capitol); Dinah Shore (Columbia).

Forever and Ever, Amen. w/m Paul Overstreet and Don Schlitz, 1987. #1 Country chart record by Randy Travis. Winner Grammy Award (NARAS) Country Song of the Year.

Forever Came Today. w/m Eddie Holland, Lamont Dozier, and Brian Holland, 1968. Top 40 record by Diana Ross and The Supremes (Motown). Chart record by The Jackson 5 (Motown), 1975.

Forever Darling. w. Sammy Cahn, m. Bronislau Kaper, 1956. Introduced by Desi Arnaz in (MP) *Forever Darling*. Leading record by The Ames Brothers (RCA).

Forever in Blue Jeans. w/m Richard Bennett and Neil Diamond, 1979. Recorded by Neil Diamond (Columbia).

"Forever" Is a Long, Long Time. w. Darl MacBoyle, m. Albert Von Tilzer, 1916.

Forever Is Ending Today. w/m Ernest Tubb, Johnny Bond, and Ike Cargill, 1948. C&W hit record by Ernest Tubb (Decca).

Forever Man. w/m Jerry Lynn Williams, 1985. Recorded by English singer Eric Clapton (Duck).

For Every Man There's a Woman. w. Leo Robin, m. Harold Arlen, 1948. Introduced by Tony Martin in (MM) *Casbah*. Nominated for Academy Award. Recorded by Martin (RCA Victor) and, in a reunion, Peggy Lee with Benny Goodman and his Orchestra (Capitol).

Forever Your Girl. w/m O. Leiber, 1989. Hit single by Paula Abdul (Virgin).

Forget Domani. w/m Normal Newell and Riz Ortolani, 1965. From the British film (MP) *The Yellow Rolls Royce*. Leading U.S. records by Frank Sinatra (Reprise) and Connie Francis (MGM).

Forget Him. w/m Tony Hatch, 1963. English song. U.S. hit by Bobby Rydell (Cameo).

Forget Me Not. w/m Larry Kolber, m. Larry Martin, 1958. Introduced and recorded by The Kalin Twins (Decca).

Forget Me Nots. w/m Patrice Rushen, Fred Washington, and Tony McFadden, 1982. Recorded by Patrice Rushen (Elektra).

Forgive Me. w. Jack Yellen, m. Milton Ager, 1927. Gene Austin (Victor) and Ruth Etting (Columbia) had best-selling records. Revived by Eddie Fisher with a Top 10 record (RCA Victor), 1952.

Forgive My Heart. w. Sammy Gallop, m. Chester Conn, 1955. Popularized by Nat "King" Cole (Capitol).

Forgive This Fool. w/m Bill Cook, 1955. Recorded by Roy Hamilton (Epic).

Forgiving You Was Easy. w/m Willie Nelson, 1985. #1 Country chart single from the album "Me and Paul," by Willie Nelson (Columbia). The "Paul" in the album title was Nelson's drummer, Paul English. The phrase originated when Dizzy Dean, the great St. Louis Cardinal baseball pitcher, would refer to himself and his pitching teammate brother, Paul Dean.

Forgotten. w. Flora Wulschner, m. Eugene Cowles, 1894.

Forgotten Dreams. m. Leroy Anderson, 1957. Instrumental recorded by Leroy Anderson and his Orchestra (Decca).

For Heaven's Sake. w/m Don Meyer, Elise Bretton, and Sherman Edwards, 1946. Introduced and recorded by Claude Thornhill, vocal by Fran Warren (Columbia). Among other versions: Helen Forrest (MGM), George Shearing (Capitol), Billie Holiday (Columbia), Billy Vaughn (Dot).

For Love of Ivy. w/m Bob Russell, m. Quincy Jones, 1968. Introduced on the soundtrack of (MP) *For Love of Ivy* by Shirley Horn. Nominated for Academy Award.

For Lovin' Me. w/m Gordon Lightfoot, 1965. Featured and recorded by Peter, Paul and Mary (Warner Bros.). Waylon Jennings had a Country hit version (RCA), 1966.

For Mama. w. Don Black (Engl.), Robert Gall (Fr.), m. Charles Aznavour, 1965. Introduced in France as "La Mamma" by Charles Aznavour. Chart records in the U.S. by Connie Francis (MGM) and Jerry Vale (Columbia).

For Me and My Gal. w. Edgar Leslie and E. Ray Goetz, m. George W. Meyer, 1917, 1943. Recorded by the popular vaudeville team of Van and Schenck (Victor) and performed by such stars of vaudeville as Eddie Cantor, George Jessel, Sophie Tucker, Belle Baker, and Al Jolson. It was one of the biggest sheet music sellers of the year. In 1942, Judy Garland and Gene Kelly sang it in (MM) *For Me and My Gal.* Their record (Decca) became a hit in 1943 and the song was on "Your Hit Parade" for seven weeks.

For My Baby. w/m Clyde Otis and Brook Benton, 1961. Top 40 record by Brook Benton (Mercury).

For My Good Fortune. w/m Otis Blackwell and Bobby Stevenson, 1958. Featured and recorded by Pat Boone (Dot).

For My Sweetheart. w. Gus Kahn, m. Walter Donaldson, 1926.

For No Rhyme or Reason. w/m Cole Porter, 1938. Introduced by Toby Wing, Charles Kemper, the Debonairs, and danced by the Hartmans in (TM) *You Never Know.*

For Old Times' Sake. w/m B. G. DeSylva, Lew Brown, and Ray Henderson, 1928. Independent song. Popular record by Annette Hanshaw (Harmony).

For Old Time's Sake. w/m Charles K. Harris, 1900.

For Once in My Life. w. Ronald Miller, m. Orlando Murden, 1967. Popularized by Tony Bennett (Columbia). Hit record by Stevie Wonder (Tamla), 1968.

For Once in Your Life. w. Jack Segal, m. Marvin Fisher, 1947. Featured and recorded by Frankie Carle and his Orchestra (Columbia).

For Rent. w/m James Loden and Jack Morrow, 1956. Featured and recorded by Sonny James (Capitol).

Forsaking All Others. w/m Allie Wrubel and Don George, 1947. Among popular recordings: Louis Prima and his Orchestra (RCA Victor).

For Sentimental Reasons (I Love You). w. Deek Watson, m. William Best, 1946. #1 record by The King Cole Trio (Capitol). Other hit records by Eddy Howard, with his Orchestra (Majestic); Dinah Shore (Columbia); Charlie Spivak, vocal by Jimmy Saunders (RCA Victor); Ella Fitzgerald, with the Delta Rhythm Boys (Decca). The following year, Red Ingle, with Jo Stafford as "Cinderella G. Stump," had a #1 hit novelty version titled "For Seventy Mental Reasons," coupled with "Temptation" titled "Tim-Tayshun" (Capitol). Sam Cooke had a chart version in 1958 (Keen).

For the First Hundred Years. w. Johnny Burke, m. James Van Heusen, 1944. Introduced by Betty Hutton, Dorothy Lamour, Diana Lynn, and Mimi Chandler as a sisters quartet in (TM) *And the Angels Sing.*

For the First Time. See **Come Prima.**

For the First Time (I've Fallen in Love). w. Charles Tobias, m. David Kapp, 1943. Featured and recorded by Dick Haymes with The Song Spinners (Decca). Sung by Donald O'Connor in (MM) *Patrick the Great*, 1945.

For the Good Times. w/m Kris Kristofferson, 1971. #1 Country and Top 20 Pop chart record by Ray Price (Columbia).

For the Love of Him. w/m Bobbi Martin and Al Mortimer, 1970. Top 20 record by Bobbi Martin (United Artists).

For the Love of Money. w/m Kenny Gamble, Leon Huff, and Anthony Jackson, 1974. Top 10 record by The O'Jays (Philadelphia International).

For the Love of You. w/m Ernest Isley, Marvin Isley, O'Kelly Isley, Ronald Isley, and Rudolph Isley, 1975. Popular record by The Isley Brothers (T-Neck, Parts 1 & 2).

For the Roses. w/m Joni Mitchell, 1972. Title song of the album by Joni Mitchell (Asylum).

For the Very First Time. w/m Irving Berlin, 1952. Featured and recorded by Tony Martin (RCA Victor).

Fortress Around Your Heart. w/m Sting, 1985. Top 10 single by English singer/guitarist Sting (A&M).

Fortunate Son. w/m John Fogerty, 1969. Back-to-back hit with "Down on the Corner" by Creedence Clearwater Revival (Fantasy).

Fortuneteller. w/m Basil Hurdon and Dyer Hurdon, 1962. Canadian authorship. Recorded by Bobby Curtola (Del-Fi).

Forty Cups of Coffee. w/m Danny Overbea, 1953. Top record: Ella Mae Morse, with Dave Cavanaugh's Orchestra (Capitol).

Forty Days and Forty Nights. w/m Bernie Roth, 1956. Top 10 R&B chart record by Muddy Waters (Chess).

Forty-Five Minutes from Broadway. w/m George M. Cohan, 1906. Introduced as that title song in (TM) *Forty-five Minutes from Broadway* by Victor Moore. It was performed by James Cagney in Cohan's film biography (MM) *Yankee Doodle Dandy* in 1942. It was sung by Joel Grey and Loni Ackerman in (TM) *George M!* at the Palace Theatre in New York, 1968.

40 Hour Week (for a Livin'). w/m Dave Loggins, Lisa Silver, and Don Schlitz, 1985. #1 Country chart single from the album "40 Weeks" by the group Alabama (RCA).

Forty Miles of Bad Road. m. Duane Eddy and Al Casey, 1959. Top 10 instrumental by Duane Eddy (Jamie).

Forty-Second Street. w. Al Dubin, m. Harry Warren, 1933. Introduced by Dick Powell, Ruby Keeler, and chorus in (MM) *Forty-Second Street*. It was featured as the title song in David Merrick's (TM) *42nd Street*, 1980, by Wanda Richert and Lee Roy Reams.

For What It's Worth (Stop, Hey What's That Sound). w/m Stephen Stills, 1967. Top 10 record by The Buffalo Springfield (Atco). Chart records by The Staple Singers (Epic) and a King Curtis instrumental (Atco).

For Yasgur's Farm. w/m G. Collins, G. Gardes, L. Laing, F. Pappalardi, D. Rea, G. Ship, 1970. Written and recorded by the group, Mountain (Windfall), as a tribute to Max Yasgur, on whose farm the Woodstock Festival was held in August, 1969.

For You. w. Al Dubin, m. Joe Burke, 1931, 1964. One of the best-selling records of the year by Glen Gray and the Casa Loma Orchestra with outstanding vocal by Kenny Sargent (Brunswick). It established the song and enhanced the popularity of the band. They twice re-recorded the song (Decca, Capitol). Interpolated in (MP) *Holy Terror*, 1931. Revived by Nat Cole (Capitol) and Rosemary Clooney (Columbia), 1956. Ricky Nelson had a Top Ten hit (Decca), 1964.

For You, for Me, Forever More. w. Ira Gershwin, m. George Gershwin, 1947. Posthumous George Gershwin melody, to which Ira wrote lyrics for Dick Haymes and Betty Grable to introduce as a duet in (MM) *The Shocking Miss Pilgrim*. Leading records by Dick Haymes and Judy Garland (Decca); Benny Goodman, vocal by Eve Young, later to be known as Karen Chandler (Columbia); Jane Froman (Majestic); Mel Tormé, with Artie Shaw's Orchestra (Musicraft).

For You Alone. w. P. J. O'Reilly, m. Henry E. Geehl, 1909.

For You a Rose. w. Will D. Cobb, m. Gus Edwards, 1917. Recorded by Edna Brown (Victor).

For You Blue. w/m George Harrison, 1970. Performed by The Beatles in the documentary (MM) *Let It Be*, and on records (Apple).

For Your Eyes Only. w/m Bill Conti and M. Leeson, 1981. Title song of the James Bond film (MP) *For Your Eyes Only*, sung on the soundtrack by Sheena Easton. Nominated for an Academy Award. Easton's recording became a Top 10 hit (Liberty).

For Your Love. w/m Graham Gouldman, 1965. Top 10 record by the English group The Yardbirds (Epic).

For Your Love. w/m Ed Townsend, 1958. Top 20 record by Ed Townsend (Capitol). Popular record by Peaches and Herb (Date), 1967.

For Your Precious Love. w/m Arthur Brooks, Richard Brooks, and Jerry Butler, 1958. Introduced and Top 40 record by Jerry Butler and The Impressions (Abner/ Falcon). Later chart records by Garnett Mimms (United Artists), new version by Jerry Butler (Vee-Jay), 1966, Jackie Wilson and Count Basie and his Orchestra (Brunswick), 1968.

Fountain Fay. w. Robert B. Smith, m. Heinrich Reinhardt, 1910. From (TM) *The Spring Maid*.

Four Brothers. w. Jon Hendricks, m. Jimmy Guiffre, 1948. Instrumental arranged by Guiffre for Woody Herman's "Second Herd" (Columbia). It featured four saxophonists, Zoot Sims, Serge Chaloff, Stan Getz, and Herbie Steward. The Dave Lambert Singers (Avalon 1 & 2) and Marian McPartland (Federal) also recorded it.

Four in the Morning (I Can't Take It Anymore). w/m Jack Blades, 1985. Recorded by the quintet Night Ranger (MCA/ Camel).

Four or Five Times. w/m Byron Gay, 1927. A favorite of jazz musicians. First hit record by King Oliver and his Jazz Band, vocal by Andy Pendleton and Willie Jackson (Brunswick). Among other top records to follow were by Jimmie Lunceford (Decca); Jimmy

Noone (Vocalion); Isham Jones (Decca); Woody Herman (Decca); Sy Oliver (Decca); The Benny Goodman Sextet, vocal by Goodman (Columbia).

Four-O-Thirty-Three. w/m Earl Montgomery and George Jones, 1966. Hit country record by George Jones (Musicor).

Four Strong Winds. w/m Ian Tyson, 1963. First chart record by The Brothers Four (Columbia). Others: Bobby Bare (RCA), 1964, and Neil Young harmonizing with Nicolette Larson (Reprise), 1979.

Fourteen Carat Mind. w/m Dallas Frazier and Larry Lee, 1981. Hit Country record by Gene Watson (MCA).

1432 Franklin Pike Circle Hero. w/m Bobby Russell, 1968. Top 40 record by Bobby Russell (Elf).

Four Walls. w/m George Campbell and Marvin Moore, 1957. Top record by Jim Reeves (RCA). Chart record by Jim Lowe (Dot) and, in 1962, by Kay Starr (Capitol).

Four Walls. w/m Dave Dreyer, Al Jolson, and Billy Rose, 1928. Featured and recorded by Al Jolson (Brunswick).

Four Winds and the Seven Seas. w. Hal David, m. Don Rodney, 1949. David's first hit song. Top 20 records by Sammy Kaye, vocal by Tony Alamo (RCA Victor); Mel Tormé, with Frank DeVol's Orchestra (Capitol); Vic Damone, with Glenn Osser's Orchestra (Mercury); Herb Jeffries, with Hugo Winterhalter's Orchestra (Columbia); Guy Lombardo, vocal by composer Don Rodney (Decca).

Fou the Noo (or Something in the Bottle for the Morning). w. Harry Lauder and Gerald Grafton, m. Harry Lauder, 1904. Published in England, Lauder popularized it in the U.S.

Foxey Lady. w/m Jimi Hendrix, 1968. Chart record by Jimi Hendrix (Reprise).

Fox on the Run. w/m Brian Connolly, Steve Priest, Andy Scott, and Mike Tucker, 1975. Written and gold record by the British group Sweet (Capitol).

Frankenstein. w/m Edgar Winter, 1973. #1 gold record (instrumental) by The Edgar Winter Group (Epic).

Frankie. w/m Joy Denny, 1985. Recorded by the Sledge sister quartet known as Sister Sledge (Atlantic).

Frankie. w. Howard Greenfield, m. Neil Sedaka, 1959. Popularized by Connie Francis (MGM).

Frankie and Johnny. w/m Traditional. Folk song going back to the mid-nineteenth century. First known recording by Palmer Jones, recorded in Kansas City, Mo. Among recordings: Ted Lewis (Columbia) and Frank Crumit (Victor), 1927; Guy Lombardo (Decca), 1942; Brook Fenton (Mercury), 1961; Sam Cooke (RCA), 1963. In films, Mae West sang it in (MM) *She Done Him Wrong*, 1933; title song of (MM) *Frankie and Johnny*, starring Helen Morgan, 1936; danced by Cyd Charisse, John Brascia, and Liliane Montevecchi and sung off-camera by Sammy Davis, Jr. with special lyrics by Sammy Cahn in (MM) *Meet Me in Las Vegas*, 1956. Elvis Presley sang it as title song of (MM) *Frank and Johnny* and on records (RCA), 1966.

Frank Mills. w. Gerome Ragni and James Rado, m. Galt MacDermot, 1967. Sung by Shelley Plimpton in the off-Broadway production (TM) *Hair*, and in the Broadway version (TM) *Hair*, 1968.

Frasquita Serenade. See **My Little Nest of Heavenly Blue.**

Fraulein. w/m Lawton Williams, 1957. Bobby Helms had a C&W/Pop crossover hit (Decca). Steve Lawrence had a modest Pop success (Coral).

Freak-a-Zoid. w/m Reginald Calloway, Vincent Calloway, and William Simmons, 1983. Recorded by the R&B/funk band Midnight Star (Solar).

Freakshow on the Dance Floor. w/m The Bar-Kays, 1984. Introduced by The Bar-Kays in the breakdance film (MM) *Breakin'* and on records (Mercury).

Freaky Dancin'. w/m Larry Blackmon and Tomi Jenkins, 1981. Top 10 R&B chart record by the group Cameo (Chocolate City).

Freckles. w. Howard Johnson, m. Cliff Hess and Milton Ager, 1919. Featured and recorded (Columbia) by Nora Bayes.

Freddie's Dead. w/m Curtis Mayfield, 1972. Sung on the soundtrack of (MP) *Superfly* by Curtis Mayfield. His recording was awarded a gold record (Curtom).

Frederick. w/m Patti Smith, 1979. Recorded by The Patti Smith Group (Arista).

Free. w/m Henry J. Redd and Nathan L. Watts, 1977. Top 10 R&B hit by Deniece Williams (Columbia).

Free. w/m Robert Lamm, 1971. Top 20 record by the jazz/rock group Chicago (Columbia). The writer played the keyboard instruments with the septet.

Free. w. Sammy Gallop, m. David Saxon, 1947. Featured and recorded by Billy Eckstine (MGM).

Free Again. w. Robert Colby (Engl.), M. Jourdan (Fr.), m. Armand Canfora and Joss Baselli, 1969. Original French title: "Non, C'est Rien." Recorded in French and English by Barbra Streisand (Columbia).

Free and Easy, The. w. Roy Turk, m. Fred E. Ahlert, 1930. Introduced by Buster Keaton in (MM) *Free and Easy*.

Free As a Bird. w/m Shel Silverstein, 1971. Introduced by Dustin Hoffman, as a rock composer-singer in (MP) *Who Is Harry Kellerman and Why Is He Saying Those Terrible Things About Me?*

Free Bird. w/m Allen Collins and Ronnie Van Zant, 1974. Popular record by the band Lynyrd Skynyrd (MCA). Their "live" concert version was also released as a single and made the charts (MCA), 1977.

Freebootin'. w/m Richard M. Sherman and Robert B. Sherman, 1973. Introduced in (MM) *Tom Sawyer* by Johnny Whitaker as Tom, and Jeff East as Huck Finn.

Freedom. w/m George Michael, 1985. Top 10 record by the British duo Wham! (Columbia).

Freedom. w/m Jimi Hendrix, 1971. Recorded by Jimi Hendrix (Reprise).

Freedom Overspill. w/m Steve Winwood, George Fleming, and Jake Hooker, 1986. Pop chart single by the British singer/musician Steve Winwood (Island).

Freedom Train, The. w/m Irving Berlin, 1947. Written to publicize The Freedom Train that traversed the United States exhibiting the Declaration of Independence, The Bill of Rights, and other documents of Americana. Hit record by Bing Crosby and The Andrews Sisters (Decca).

Free Home Demonstration. w/m Charles R. Grean and Cy Coben, 1953. Featured and recorded by Eddy Arnold (RCA Victor).

Free Man in Paris. w/m Joni Mitchell, 1974. Popular single by Joni Mitchell (Asylum).

Free Ride. w/m Dan Hartman, 1973. Top 20 record by The Edgar Winter Group (Epic). The family R&B quintet, Tavares, had a chart version (Capitol), 1976.

Free the People. w/m Barbara Keith, 1970. Recorded by Delaney and Bonnie and Friends (Atco). They sang it in the documentary (MM) *Medicine Ball Caravan*, 1971.

Freeway of Love. w/m Narada Michael Walden and Jeffrey Cohen, 1985. #1 R&B chart, #3 Pop chart hit by Aretha Franklin (Arista). Grammy Award (NARAS) winner Rhythm and Blues Song of the Year.

Freeze-Frame. w/m Seth Justman and Peter Wolf, 1982. Top 10 gold record by The J. Geils Band (EMI America).

Freight Train. w/m Paul James and Fred Williams, 1957. Original song allegedly written, but not copyrighted, by British amateur Elizabeth Cotten. Song sung regionally in England. Commercially recorded by The Charles McDevitt Skiffle Group, vocal by Nancy Wiskey and released in the U.S. (Chic). Bestselling record by Rusty Draper (Mercury).

French Foreign Legion. w. Aaron Schroeder, m. Guy Wood, 1959. Popular recording by Frank Sinatra (Capitol).

French Kissin'. w/m Chuck Lorrie, 1986. Recorded by Debbie Harry (Geffen).

French Lesson, The. w/m Betty Comden, Adolph Green, and Roger Edens, 1947. Introduced by June Allyson and Peter Lawford in (MM) *Good News*, and on records (MGM).

French Military Marching Song. w. Otto Harbach and Oscar Hammerstein II, m. Sigmund Romberg, 1926. Introduced by Vivienne Segal in (TM) *The Desert Song*. Sung by Carlotta King in (MM) *The Desert Song*, 1929, and by Irene Manning in the remake, 1943.

Frenesi. w. Ray Charles and Bob Russell (Engl.), m. Alberto Dominguez, 1940. A Mexican song with original Spanish lyrics by Dominguez. Artie Shaw and his Orchestra (Victor) had a tremendous instrumental hit. His recording was #1 for thirteen weeks, and in the Top 10 for thirty weeks. The song was on "Your Hit Parade" for nineteen weeks, three times as #1. Other popular instrumental versions by Woody Herman (Decca), Glenn Miller (Bluebird), and Xavier Cugat (Victor). In the fifties, the Dave Brubeck Quartet had a well-received version (Fantasy).

Fresh. w/m Kool and The Gang, 1985. Top 10 record by Kool and The Gang (De-Lite).

Fresh as a Daisy. w/m Emmitt Rhodes, 1971. Recorded by Emmitt Rhodes (Dunhill).

Freshie. w. Harold Berg, m. Jesse Greer, 1925. Suggested by the Harold Lloyd film (MP) *The Freshman*. Recorded by Fred Waring's Pennsylvanians as a follow-up to "Collegiate" (q.v.) (Victor).

Friday Night Blues. w/m Sonny Throckmorton and Rafe Van Hoy, 1980. Introduced and Country chart record by Sonny Throckmorton (Mercury). Top 10 version by John Conlee (MCA).

Friday on My Mind. w/m Harry Wanda and George Young, 1967. Recorded in England by the Australian quintet, The Easybeats, two members of whom were the writers (United Artists).

Friday's Child. w/m Lee Hazlewood, 1966. Top 40 record by Nancy Sinatra (Reprise).

Friend, Lover, Woman, Wife. w/m Mac Davis, 1969. Recorded by O. C. Smith (Columbia).

Friendliest Thing, The. w/m Ervin Drake, 1964. Introduced by Bernice Massi in (TM) *What Makes Sammy Run?* Recorded by Eydie Gormé (Columbia).

Friendly Persuasion (a.k.a. Thee I Love). w. Paul Francis Webster, m. Dmitri Tiomkin, 1956. Title song of (MP) *Friendly Persuasion*. Nominated for Academy Award. Hit record by Pat Boone (Dot).

Friendly Star. w. Mack Gordon, m. Harry Warren, 1950. Introduced in (MM) *Summer Stock*, and on records (MGM) by Judy Garland.

Friendly Tavern Polka. w/m Jerry Bowne and Frank DeVol, 1941. Featured and recorded by Horace Heidt and his Orchestra (Columbia) and again popular three years later upon its re-release.

Friend of Mine Is Going Blind, A. w/m John Dawson Read, 1975. Recorded by John Dawson Read (Chrysalis).

Friend of Yours, A. w. Johnny Burke, m. James Van Heusen, 1945. Featured and recorded by Tommy Dorsey, vocal by Stuart Fos-ter (Victor); Bing Crosby (Decca); Jerry Wald and his Orchestra (Majestic).

Friends. w/m Johnny Slate and Dan Morrison, 1981. #1 Country chart record by Razzy Bailey (RCA).

Friends. w/m Mark Klingman and Buzzy Linhart, 1973. Top 40 single by Bette Midler (Atlantic).

Friends. w/m Elton John and Bernie Taupin, 1971. Sung by Elton John on the soundtrack of the British film, (MP) *Friends*, and on records (Uni).

Friends. w/m Brian Wilson, Carl Wilson, Dennis Wilson, and Al Jardine, 1968. Written and recorded by the Beach Boys (Capitol).

Friends and Lovers. w/m Paul Gordon and Jay Gruska, 1986. Introduced on the soap opera (TVP) "Days of Our Lives," featuring Gloria Loring, who had a Top 10 record with Carl Anderson (USA Carrere).

Friendship. w/m Cole Porter, 1939. Introduced by Ethel Merman and Bert Lahr in (TM) *Du Barry Was a Lady*. Kay Kyser, vocal by Ish Kabibble (Columbia), had a popular record. In the 1943 film version (MM) *Du Barry Was a Lady*, it was performed by Gene Kelly, Lucille Ball, Red Skelton, Margaret O'Brien, Zero Mostel, Rags Ragland, and Tommy Dorsey and his Orchestra. Dorsey, with a vocal by Jo Stafford and the Pied Pipers, had a popular recording. The song was heard in (MM) *At Long Last Love* in 1975.

Friendship Train. w/m Norman Whitfield and Barrett Strong, 1969. Top 20 record by Gladys Knight and The Pips (Soul).

Friends with You. w/m Bill Danoff and Taffy Nivert, 1971. Recorded by John Denver (RCA).

Fright Night. w/m J. Lamont, 1985. Introduced by the J. Geils Band in (MP) *Fright Night* and on records (Private I).

Frim Fram Sauce, The. w/m Joe Ricardel and Redd Evans, 1946. Novelty hit for The

King Cole Trio (Capitol). Also recorded by Ella Fitzgerald and Louis Armstrong (Decca).

Frog and the Grog, The. w/m Robert Wright and George Forrest, 1961. Introduced by Christopher Hewett, Robert Penn, Arthur Rubin, and Alfred Drake in (TM) *Kean.*

Froggy Bottom. w/m John Williams, 1930. Recorded twice by Andy Kirk and his Orchestra (Brunswick) (Decca). The composer was a saxophonist in the band and the pianist and arranger was his wife, the famous Mary Lou Williams. It was also recorded by Josh White (Asch) and Jessie Price (Capitol).

From a Jack to a King. w/m Ned Miller, 1963. Crossover (C&W/Pop) hit by Ned Miller (Fabor).

(Here They Come) From All Over the World. w/m Phil Sloan and Steve Barri, 1965. Theme of the (TVM) "T.A.M.I." [Teen-Age Music International] Show. Recorded by Jan and Dean (Liberty).

From Another World. w. Lorenz Hart, m. Richard Rodgers, 1940. Introduced by Shirley Ross, Marta Eggert, Jack Haley, Eva Condon, Robert Chisholm, and company in (TM) *Higher and Higher.* Records by Ross (Decca); Mildred Bailey (Columbia); Buddy Clark (Varsity); the bands of Larry Clinton (Victor), Dick Jurgens (Vocalion), Bob Crosby (Decca), Charlie Barnett (Bluebird).

From a Window. w/m John Lennon and Paul McCartney, 1964. Introduced and recorded in England by Billy J. Kramer with The Dakotas (Imperial).

From Both Sides Now. See **Both Sides Now.**

From Broadway to Main Street. w. Harlan Thompson, m. Harry Archer, 1923. From (TM) *Little Jessie James.*

From Graceland to the Promised Land. w/m Merle Haggard, 1977. Tribute to Elvis Presley by Country music singer Merle Haggard, backed by The Jordanaires (MCA).

From Here to Eternity. w. Robert Wells, m. Fred Karger, 1953. Song inspired by but not written for the film. Recorded by Frank Sinatra, with Nelson Riddle's Orchestra (Capitol).

From Me to You. w/m John Lennon and Paul McCartney, 1963. English song introduced in the U.S. by Del Shannon (Big Top). The Beatles' record was released in the U.S. (Vee-Jay), 1964.

From Monday On. w. Bing Crosby, m. Harry Barris, 1928. Made popular via the classic recording by Paul Whiteman and his Orchestra, featuring the Rhythm Boys [Bing Crosby, Harry Barris, and Al Rinker] and a cornet solo by Bix Beiderbecke (Victor). Also recorded by Red McKenzie, vocal by Leo Watson (Decca), 1934.

From Now On. w/m Cole Porter, 1938. Introduced by William Gaxton and Tamara in (TM) *Leave It to Me!* Recorded by Frances Langford (Decca) and the bands of Eddy Duchin (Brunswick), Les Brown (Bluebird), Ruby Newman (Decca), Sammy Kaye (Victor), Lawrence Welk (Vocalion).

From One Love to Another. w. Albert Gamse (Engl.), m. Ernesto Lecuona, 1941. Cuban song, originally titled "Danza Lucumi." Recordings by the orchestras of Glenn Miller (Bluebird), Bob Crosby (Decca), Benny Goodman (Columbia).

From Russia with Love. w/m Lionel Bart, 1964. English song introduced on soundtrack by Matt Munro in (MP) *From Russia With Love.* Leading instrumental records by The Village Stompers (Epic) and Al Caiola (United Artists).

From the Bottom of My Heart (Dammi, Dammi, Dammi). w/m Danny Di Minno and George Cardini, 1962. Featured and recorded by Dean Martin (Reprise).

From the Candy Store on the Corner to the Chapel on the Hill. w/m Bob Hilliard, 1956. Recorded by Tony Bennett, with singer Lois Winter (Columbia).

From the First Hello to the Last Good-bye. w/m Johnny Burke, 1956. Recorded by Jane Morgan (Kapp).

From the Land of the Sky-Blue Water. w. Nelle Richmond Eberhart, m. Charles Wakefield Cadman, 1908. From "Four American Indian Songs" written for concert singers.

From the Top of Your Head to the Tip of Your Toes. w. Mack Gordon, m. Harry Revel, 1935. Introduced by Bing Crosby in (MM) *Two for Tonight* and recorded (Decca).

From the Vine Came the Grape. w. Paul Cunningham, m. Leonard Whitcup, 1954. Hit records by The Gaylords (Mercury); The Hilltoppers (Dot).

From the Word Go. w/m Michael Garvin and Christopher Dunn, 1989. Hit Country record by Michael Martin Murphey (Warner Bros.).

From This Moment On. w/m Cole Porter, 1953. Written three years earlier for the Broadway musical *Out of This World*, but not used. It was added to the score of (MM) *Kiss Me Kate*, and sung by Ann Miller, Tommy Rall, Bobby Van, Bob Fosse, and Carol Haney.

Frosty the Snowman. w/m Steve Nelson and Jack Rollins, 1950. A million-seller follow-up to "Rudolph the Red-Nosed Reindeer" (q. v.) etc. for Gene Autry (Columbia). Other Top 40 versions by Nat "King" Cole (Capitol), Guy Lombardo and his Royal Canadians (Decca).

Fuddy Duddy Watchmaker, The. w. Frank Loesser, m. Jimmy McHugh, 1943. Introduced by Betty Hutton in (MM) *Happy Go Lucky*. Featured and recorded by Kay Kyser, vocal by Julie Conway (Columbia).

Fugitive, The (a.k.a. **I'm a Lonesome Fugitive**). w/m Liz Anderson and Casey Anderson, 1967. #1 Country chart record by Merle Haggard (Capitol). The title was later changed to "I'm a Lonesome Fugitive."

Fugue for Tinhorns. w/m Frank Loesser, 1950. Introduced by Stubby Kaye, Johnny Silver, and Douglas Deane in (TM) *Guys and Dolls*. In the screen version (MM) *Guys and Dolls*, 1955, it was sung by Frank Sinatra, Johnny Silver, and Dan Dayton. The song was originally written with different lyrics and titled "Three Cornered Tune." Blossom Dearie, in the album "Frank Loesser Revisited" (Painted Smiles) and Sara Brightman in "Songs That Got Away" (Polydor) have recorded it, each employing the multi-track technique to sing the three parts.

Full Moon (Noche de Luna). w. Bob Russell (Engl.), m. Gonzalo Curiel and Marcelene Odette, 1942. Mexican song, original Spanish words by Curiel. Best-selling records by Jimmy Dorsey, vocal by Bob Eberly (Decca); Benny Goodman, vocal by Peggy Lee (Okeh); Orrin Tucker, vocal by Bob Haymes (Columbia).

Full Moon and Empty Arms. w/m Buddy Kaye and Ted Mossman, 1946. Adapted from the second theme of the third movement of Rachmaninoff's *Piano Concerto No. 2 in C Minor*, Opus 18. Leading records by Frank Sinatra (Columbia); Ray Noble, vocal by Snooky Lanson (Columbia).

Full Time Job. w/m Gerry Teifer, 1952. Leading records by Eddy Arnold (RCA Victor) and Doris Day and Johnny Ray (Columbia).

Fun. See **Ffun**.

Fun, Fun, Fun. w/m Brian Wilson, 1964. Hit record by The Beach Boys (Capitol).

Fun and Fancy Free. w/m Bennie Benjamin and George Weiss, 1947. From the Disney cartoon film (MM) *Fun and Fancy Free*. Recorded by Phil Harris (RCA Victor), Buddy Weed (MGM), Gene Krupa and his Orchestra (Columbia).

Funkin' for Jamaica (N.Y.). w/m Tom Browne, 1980. #1 R&B chart record by jazz trumpeter Tom Browne (GRP).

Funky Broadway. w/m Arlester Christian, 1967. Chart record introduced by the group (led by the writer) Dyke and The Blazers (Original Sound). Wilson Pickett's hit cover record reached the top 10 (Atlantic).

Funky Judge. w. André Williams, m. Leo Hutton, 1968. Recorded by Bull and The Matadors (Toddlin' Town).

Funky Nassau. w/m Tyrone Fitzgerald and Ralph Munnings, 1971. Jamaican Song recorded by the quartet The Beginning of the End (Alston).

Funky Street. w. Earl Simms and Arthur Conley, m. Arthur Conley, 1968. Top 20 record by Arthur Conley (Atco).

Funkytown. w/m Steven Greenberg, 1980. #1 platinum record by Lipps, Inc., vocal by Cynthia Johnson, from the LP "Mouth to Mouth" (Casablanca). Top 10 record by the Australian quartet PseudoEcho (RCA), 1987.

Funky Worm. w/m Leroy Bonner, Marshall Jones, Ralph Middlebrook, W. Morrison, and A. Noland, 1973. Novelty written and recorded by The Ohio Players (Westbound).

Funny. See **Funny How Time Slips Away**.

Funny (Not Much). w/m Hughie Prince, Bob Merrill, Philip Broughton, and Marcia Neil, 1952. Featured and recorded by Nat "King" Cole (Capitol).

Funny, Dear, What Love Can Do. w/m Charlie Straight, Joe Bennett, George Little, 1930. Featured and recorded by Ruth Etting (Columbia), Wayne King's Orchestra (Victor), Marion Harris (Brunswick), Ray Miller's Band (Brunswick).

Funny, Familiar, Forgotten Feelings. w/m Mickey Newbury, 1967. Introduced by Country singer Don Gibson (RCA). Pop cover record by Tom Jones (Parrot).

Funny Face. w/m Donna Fargo, 1973. Gold record C&W/Pop hit by Donna Fargo (Dot).

Funny Face. w. Ira Gershwin, m. George Gershwin, 1927. Introduced by Fred and Adele Astaire in (TM) *Funny Face*. Fred Astaire performed it in (MM) *Funny Face*, 1956. Revived by Denny Dillon and Bruce McGillin (TM) *My One and Only*, 1983.

Funny Girl. w. Bob Merrill, m. Jule Styne, 1964. Written for but dropped from the score of the musical of the same name that starred Barbra Streisand who recorded it (Columbia). Streisand then sang it in the film version (MM) *Funny Girl*, 1968. Nominated for Academy Award, 1968.

Funny How Time Slips Away (a.k.a. Funny). w/m Willie Nelson, 1962. Top 40 record by Joe Elledge, produced by Chet Atkins (RCA). Other chart records by Johnny Tillotson (Cadence), 1963; Joe Hinton, record titled "funny" (Back Beat), 1964; Dorothy Moore (Malaco), 1976; The Spinners (Atlantic), 1983.

Funny Old Hills, The. w. Leo Robin, m. Ralph Rainger, 1938. Introduced by Bing Crosby in (MM) *Paris Honeymoon* and on records (Decca).

Funny Thing. w. Carl Sigman, m. Arthur Williams, 1954. Top record by Tony Bennett (Columbia).

Funny Way of Laughin'. w/m Hank Cochran, 1962. Top 10 C&W and Pop chart hit record by Burl Ives (Decca). Winner Grammy Award (NARAS) for Country and Western Song of the Year.

Fun to Be Fooled. w. Ira Gershwin and E. Y. Harburg, m. Harold Arlen, 1934. Sung by Frances Williams and Bartlett Simmons and danced by Esther Junger in (TM) *Life Begins at 8:40*. Recorded by Richard Himber and his Orchestra, vocal by Joey Nash (Victor).

Future's So Bright, I Gotta Wear Shades. w/m Pat MacDonald, 1986. Recorded by the husband and wife duo MacDonald Timbuk 3 (I.R.S.).

Futuristic Rhythm. w. Dorothy Fields, m. Jimmy McHugh, 1929. Introduced by Wanda Goll in (TM) *Hello, Daddy*. Recorded by Louisiana Rhythm Kings (Vocalion); Irving Mills and His Hotsy Totsy Gang, vocal by Smith Ballew (Brunswick).

Fuzzy Wuzzy. w/m Milton Drake, Al Hoffman, and Jerry Livingston, 1944. Introduced and recorded by Al Trace and his Silly Symphonists (National). Also featured and recorded by The Jesters (Decca).

G

Gabrielle. w. Alan Jay Lerner, m. André Previn, 1969. Introduced by Jon Cypher in (TM) *Coco*.

Gaby Glide, The. w. Harry Pilcer, m. Louis A. Hirsch, 1911. Written for the American debut of the French star, Gaby Deslys, who introduced it with Harry Pilcer in (TM) *Vera Violetta*.

Gal in Calico, A. w. Leo Robin, m. Arthur Schwartz, 1946. Introduced by Dennis Morgan, Jack Carson, and Martha Vickers in (MM) *The Time, The Place and The Girl*. Nominated for Academy Award, 1947. Popular records by Johnny Mercer (Capitol); Tex Beneke with The Crew Chiefs and his Orchestra (RCA Victor); Benny Goodman, vocal by Eve Young, later known as Karen Chandler (Columbia); Bing Crosby (Decca).

Galveston. w/m Jim Webb, 1969. Gold record by Glen Campbell (Capitol). Chart instrumental by Roger Williams (Kapp).

Galway Bay. w/m Dr. Arthur Colahan, 1949. Irish song, published in England. Top records in the United States: million seller by Bing Crosby, with Victor Young's Orchestra (Decca); Clark Dennis, with Buddy Cole's Orchestra (Capitol); Ann Shelton, with the Wardour Singers and Roy Robertson's Orchestra (London); Fran Allison (Rondo) (Mercury); Carmel Quinn (Columbia).

Gal Who Invented Kissin', The. w/m Charles Orr and Earl Griswold, 1952. Popular C&W record by Hank Snow (RCA Victor).

Gambler, The. w/m Don Schlitz, 1978. Country/Pop hit record by Kenny Rogers (United Artists). Winner Grammy Award (NARAS) for Country Song of the Year.

Gambler's Guitar. w/m Jim Lowe, 1953. Top 10 record by Rusty Draper (Mercury). Songwriter/DJ Lowe also recorded it (Mercury).

Gamblin' Polka Dot Blues. w/m Jimmie Rodgers, 1932. Introduced by Rodgers. Bob Wills (Vocalion) had a big-selling record (Vocalion). Revived in 1949 by Tommy Duncan (Capitol).

Game of Love, The. w/m Clint Ballard, Jr., 1965. #1 record from England by Wayne Fontana and The Mindbenders (Fontana).

Game of Love, The. w. Matt Dubey, m. Harold Carr, 1956. Introduced by Ethel Merman in (TM) *Happy Hunting*.

Game of Triangles, The. w/m Cy Coben, 1967. Country record by Liz Anderson, Bobby Bare, and Norma Jean (RCA).

Games People Play. w/m Eric Woolfson and Alan Parsons, 1981. Written and recorded by the leaders of the British production The Alan Parsons Project (Arista).

Games People Play. w/m Joe South, 1969. Hit C&W and Pop record by Joe South (Capitol). Winner Grammy Award (NARAS) Song of the Year.

Games That Daddies Play, The. w/m Conway Twitty, 1976. Country chart hit by Conway Twitty (MCA).

Games That Lovers Play. w. Larry Kusick and Eddie Snyder (Engl.), m. James Last, 1966. Original German title, "Eine Ganze Nacht," lyrics by Gunter Loose. Leading U.S. versions by Eddie Fisher (RCA) and Wayne Newton (Capitol).

Games Without Frontiers. w/m Peter Gabriel, 1980. Chart single from the album "Peter Gabriel" by the English singer (Mercury).

Gandy Dancers' Ball, The. w/m Paul Weston and Paul Mason Howard, 1952. Featured and recorded by Frankie Laine (Columbia).

Gang That Sang Heart of My Heart, The (a.k.a. **Heart of My Heart**). w/m Ben Ryan, 1926. Title refers to the 1899 song "Heart of My Heart, I Love You." This song has become a standard "saloon" number and sing-a-long favorite. Featured by the night club singer, Tommy Lyman, and recorded by such artists as Les Elgart's Band (Columbia); Frankie Laine (Mercury); Merv Griffin, with Freddy Martin's Orchestra (Victor); Roberta Sherwood (Decca). Don Cornell, Alan Dale, and Johnny Desmond, with Jack Pleis's Orchestra (Decca) had a Top 10 record called "Heart of My Heart," 1953–1954.

Garden in the Rain, A. w. James Dyrenforth, m. Carroll Gibbons, 1929. An English import, with many recordings over the years. Among them: Earl Burtnett's Orchestra (Brunswick), George Olsen's Band with a Fran Frey vocal, Willard Robison (Columbia), Jane Froman (Majestic), Rubinoff (Brunswick), and Jerry Gray (Decca).

Garden of Eden, The. w/m Dennise Haas Norwood, 1956. Popularized by Joe Valino (Vik).

Garden of My Dreams. w. Gene Buck, m. Dave Stamper, 1918. From (TM) *Ziegfeld's 9 O'clock Frolic* at the New Amsterdam Roof.

Garden of Roses, The. w. J. E. Dempsey, m. Johann C. Schmid, 1909.

Garden of the Moon. w. Al Dubin and Johnny Mercer, m. Harry Warren, 1938. Title song of (MM) *Garden of the Moon.* Recorded by Jimmy Dorsey, vocal by Bob Eberly (Decca); bands of Red Norvo (Brunswick), Skinnay Ennis (Victor).

Garden of Your Heart, The. w. Edward Teschemacher, m. Francis Dorel, 1914.

Garden Party. w/m Rick Nelson, 1972. An autobiographical song written and recorded by Rick Nelson after he, with his band, was booed at a concert at Madison Square Garden in New York for having changed to a long-hair look. His recording went gold (Decca).

Gather Lip Rouge While You May. w/m B. G. DeSylva, Leo Robin, and Richard A. Whiting, 1933. Sung by Lillian Harvey in (MM) *My Weakness.*

Gaucho Serenade, The. w/m James Cavanaugh, John Redmond, and Nat Simon, 1940. Most popular recording by Dick Todd (Bluebird). Others: Glenn Miller, vocal by Ray Eberle (Bluebird); Eddy Duchin, vocal by June Robbins (Columbia).

Gay Caballero, A. w/m Frank Crumit and Lou Klein, 1928. Featured and recorded by Crumit (Victor) and Frank Luther (Brunswick).

Gay Ranchero, A (Las Altenitas). w. Abe Tuvim and Francia Luban (Engl.), J. J. Espinosa (Sp.), m. J. J. Espinosa, 1936. Roy Rogers sang this in (MM) *King of the Cowboys,* 1943 and in (MM) *The Gay Ranchero,* 1948.

G'bye Now. w/m Ole Olsen, Chic Johnson, Ray Evans, and Jay Livingston, 1941. The first song success for Livingston and Evans, written for (MM) *Hellzapoppin',* starring Olsen and Johnson. Best-selling records by Woody Herman's Woodchoppers, vocal by Bing Crosby (Decca); Horace Heidt, vocal by Ronnie Kemper (Columbia); Martha Tilton (Decca); Vaughn Monroe, vocal by Monroe (Bluebird).

Gee! w/m Viola Watkins, Daniel Norton, and William Davis, 1953. R&B hit by The Crows (Rama).

Gee, Baby. w/m Johnny Otis, 1951. Recorded by Johnny Otis and Mel Walker (Savoy).

Gee, But I Hate to Go Home Alone. w. Joe Goodwin, m. James F. Hanley, 1922. Popular record by Billy Jones (Victor).

Gee, But It's Great to Meet a Friend from Your Home Town. w. William Tracey, m. James McGavisk, 1910.

Gee, But It's Lonely. w/m Phil Everly, 1958. Leading record by Pat Boone (Dot).

Gee, But You're Swell. w. Charles Tobias, m. Abel Baer, 1937. Leading record by Benny Goodman, vocal by Helen Ward (Victor). Chick Webb (Decca) and Russ Morgan (Brunswick) and their bands also recorded the song.

Gee, I'd Like to Make You Happy. w/m Larry Shay, Ward and Montgomery, 1930. Recorded by The Boswell Sisters (Okeh) and Fred Waring and his Pennsylvanians (Victor).

Gee, Officer Krupke. w. Stephen Sondheim, m. Leonard Bernstein, 1957. Introduced by Eddie Roll, Grover Dale, and "The Jets" in (TM) *West Side Story*. In (MM) *West Side Story*, 1961, it was performed by Russ Tamblyn and "The Jets."

Gee Baby, Ain't I Good to You? w. Don Redman and Andy Razaf, m. Don Redman, 1929. Introduced by McKinney's Cotton Pickers when Redman was playing alto saxophone with the band (Victor). Chuck Berry made a 12″ record (Commodore), 1941, followed by the Nat "King" Cole Trio (Capitol), 1944.

Gee Whiz! (Look at His Eyes). w/m Carla Thomas, 1961. Introduced and recorded by Carla Thomas (Atlantic). Revived by Bernadette Peters (MCA), 1980.

Geisha Girl. w/m Lawton Williams, 1958. Leading record by country singer Hank Locklin (RCA).

General Hospi-Tale. w/m Harry King and L. Tedesco, 1981. Novelty, satirizing the TV show "General Hospital" by the female quartet The Afternoon Delights (MCA).

Genius of Love. Tom Tom Club, 1982. Recorded by Tom Tom Club, a studio project (Sire).

Gentleman Is a Dope, The. w. Oscar Hammerstein II, m. Richard Rodgers, 1947. Introduced by Lisa Kirk in (TM) *Allegro*. Popular record by Jo Stafford (Capitol).

Gentleman Jimmy. w. Sheldon Harnick, m. Jerry Bock, 1959. Introduced by Eileen Rodgers and girls in (TM) *Fiorello!*

Gentleman Obviously Doesn't Believe, The. w/m Michael Carr and Edward Pola, 1935. Featured and recorded by Hal Kemp and his Orchestra, vocal by Skinnay Ennis (Brunswick). Recorded by the Dorsey Brothers, vocal by Kay Weber (Decca); and Joe Haymes, vocal by Cliff Weston (Perfect).

Gentlemen Prefer Blondes. w. B. G. DeSylva, m. Lewis E. Gensler, 1926. Introduced by Luella Gear in (TM) *Queen High*. Featured and recorded by Billy Jones and Ernie Hare (Edison).

Gentle on My Mind. w/m John Hartford, 1967. C&W hit by Glen Campbell (Capitol), 1967. Winner Grammy Award (NARAS) for Best Country and Western Song. Record reissued in 1968 and became Pop chart hit. Other successful versions by Patti Page (Mercury), 1968; Aretha Franklin (Atlantic), 1969.

George Jackson. w/m Bob Dylan, 1971. Top 40 record by Bob Dylan (Columbia).

Georgette. w. Lew Brown, m. Ray Henderson, 1922. Introduced by Ted Lewis in (TM) *Greenwich Village Follies of 1922*. This marked the first collaboration of two-thirds of what was to become the great songwriting team of DeSylva, Brown and Henderson.

Georgia. w. Howard Johnson, m. Walter Donaldson, 1922. Popular instrumental recording by the orchestras of Paul Whiteman (Victor) and Carl Fenton (Brunswick), and vocal recording by The Peerless Quartet (Victor).

Georgia Blues. w. Billy Higgins, m. Benton Overstreet, 1923. First recording by Ethel Waters (Black Swan).

Georgia Grind. m. Spencer Williams, 1915. Many recordings of this jazz standard, among them Louis Armstrong (Okeh), Eddie Condon (Commodore), and the Memphis Night Hawks (Perfect).

Georgia Jubilee. m. Benny Goodman, Arthur Schutt, 1934. Instrumental introduced and recorded by Benny Goodman and his Band (Columbia). Also recorded by Isham Jones and his Orchestra (Victor).

Georgianna. w/m Red MacKenzie, Frankie Carle, and Austen Croom-Johnson, 1937. Leading recordings by McKenzie (Vocalion) and Count Basie's Band (Decca).

Georgia on My Mind. w. Stuart Gorrell, m. Hoagy Carmichael, 1930, 1960. First recorded by Hoagy Carmichael (Victor) and Mildred Bailey (Victor). The latter featured it throughout her career, along with another Carmichael standard "Rockin' Chair" (q.v.) In 1960, Ray Charles's recording (ABC-Paramount) sold over a million copies and won the Grammy Award (NARAS) for Best Male Vocal Recording and Best Popular Single Performance of the Year. In 1978, another revival was brought about by Willie Nelson's recording (Columbia), which won the Grammy Award (NARAS) for Best Male Country Vocal Performance.

Georgia Porcupine. w/m George Fischoff, 1974. Instrumental by pianist/composer George Fischoff (United Artists).

Georgia Rose. w. Jimmy Flynn and Alex Sullivan, m. Harry Rosenthal, 1921. Introduced by Emmett Anthony in revue (TM) *Put and Take.* Leading record by The Sterling Trio (Victor). Revived by Tony Bennett (Columbia), 1966.

Georgy Girl. w. Jim Dale, m. Tom Springfield, 1966. Introduced by The Seekers, on the soundtrack of the British film (MP) *Georgy Girl.* Released as a single and earned a gold record (Capitol).

Geronimo's Cadillac. w/m Michael Murphey and Charles Quarto, 1972. Recorded by Michael Murphey (A&M).

Gertie from Bizerte. w/m James Cavanaugh, Walter Kent, and Bob Cutter (a.k.a. Robert C. Haring), 1943. Cleaned-up version of bawdy song sung by Allied soldiers in North Africa in World War II.

Get a Job. w/m Earl T. Beal, Raymond W. Edwards, William F. Horton, Richard A. Lewis, 1958. The writers comprised The Silhouettes, who had a hit record (Ember).

Get a Little Dirt on Your Hands. w/m Bill Anderson, 1962. Hit country record by Bill Anderson (Decca).

Getaway. w/m Peter Cor and Beloyd Taylor, 1976. #1 R&B chart hit by the group Earth, Wind & Fire (Columbia).

Get Back. w/m John Lennon and Paul McCartney, 1969. Gold record by The Beatles, with Billy Preston on organ (Apple). Preston revived it in (MM) *Sgt. Pepper's Lonely Hearts Club Band* and on records (A&M), 1978.

Getcha Back. w/m Mike Love and Terry Melcher, 1985. Recorded by The Beach Boys (Caribou).

Get Closer. w/m Jonathan Carroll, 1982. Recorded by Linda Ronstadt (Asylum).

Get Closer. w/m Jim Seals and Dash Crofts, 1976. Top 10 record by Seals and Crofts, featuring Carolyn Wills, Bob B. Soxx, and The Blue Jeans (Warner Bros.).

Get Dancin'. w/m Bob Crewe and Kenny Nolan, 1974. Top 10 record by Bob Crewe's studio group Disco Tex and The Sex-o-lettes (Chelsea).

Get Down. w/m Raymond (Gilbert) O'Sullivan, 1973. Hit record by Gilbert O'Sullivan (MAM).

Get Down, Get Down (Get on the Floor). w/m Raeford Gerald and Joe Simon, 1975. Top 10 record by Joe Simon (Spring).

Get Down on It. w/m Kool and The Gang, 1982. Top 10 record, written and recorded by Kool and The Gang (De-Lite).

Get Down Tonight. w/m Harry Wayne Casey and Richard Finch, 1975. #1 record by the group, KC and The Sunshine Band, produced by "KC" Casey and Finch (T.K.).

Get Happy. w. Ted Koehler, m. Harold Arlen, 1930. Arlen's first hit came about while, as one of the orchestrators for Vincent Youmans's musical, "Great Day!," he was substituting as rehearsal pianist and had grown bored with repeating the standard two-bar vamp that was used to set the tempo for a musical number. He began to vary and improvise the pick-up strain and the tune of "Get Happy" evolved. It was brought to the attention of Koehler, who wrote a lyric and succeeded in getting it into (TM) *Nine-fifteen Revue*. While the show flopped, Ruth Etting's rendition established the song. Judy Garland sang it in (MM) *Summer Stock* in 1950; Jane Froman, in her life story, (MM) *With a Song in My Heart*, dubbed her voice on the soundtrack for Susan Hayward in 1952. It was also heard in (MM) *Young Man With a Horn* in 1950 and, in 1956, in (MM) *Cha-Cha-Cha-Boom*.

Get It On. See **Bang a Gong (Get It On)**.

Get It Right. w/m Luther Vandross and Marcus Miller, 1983. #1 on the R&B charts, and Pop chart entry by Aretha Franklin (Arista).

Get It Right Next Time. w/m Gerry Rafferty, 1979. Recorded by the Scotland-born Gerry Rafferty (United Artists).

Get It Together. w/m James Brown, Alfred Ellis, and Buddy Hobgood, 1967. Chart record by James Brown and The Famous Flames (King, Part I).

Get It While You Can. w/m Jerry Ragavoy and Mort Shuman, 1971. Recorded by Janis Joplin (Columbia).

Get Me to the Church on Time. w. Alan Jay Lerner, m. Frederick Loewe, 1956. Introduced by Stanley Holloway in (TM) *My Fair Lady*, and sung by him in the film version (MM) *My Fair Lady*, 1964.

Get Me to the World on Time. w/m Annette Tucker and Jill Jones, 1967. Top 40 record by The Electric Prunes (Reprise).

Get Off. w/m Carlos Driggs and Ishmael Ledesma, 1978. Top 10 record by the Latin band Foxy (Dash).

Get off My Cloud. w/m Mick Jagger and Keith Richards, 1965. #1 record by the British rock group The Rolling Stones (London).

Get on the Good Foot. w/m James Brown, Joe Mims, and Fred Wesley, 1972. #1 R&B and Pop chart million-seller by James Brown (Polydor, Part 1).

Get On Up. w/m Gilbert Moorer, Johnny Taylor, and Bill Sheppard, 1967. Hit record by The Esquires (Bunky).

Get Out and Get Under the Moon. w. Charles Tobias and William Jerome, m. Larry Shay, 1928. Featured and recorded by Paul Whiteman and his Orchestra (Victor) and Helen Kane, with Nat Shilkret's Orchestra (Victor).

Get Out Now. w/m Ritchie Cordell and Bo Gentry, 1968. Recorded by Tommy James and The Shondells (Roulette).

Get Out of Denver. w/m Bob Seger, 1974. Recorded by Bob Seger (Palladium).

Get Out of My Life, Woman. w/m Allen Toussaint, 1966. Recorded by Lee Dorsey (Amy).

Get Out of Town. w/m Cole Porter, 1938. Introduced by Tamara in (TM) *Leave It to Me!* Among recordings: Frances Langford (Decca); the bands of Eddy Duchin (Brunswick), Les Brown (Bluebird), Ruby Newman (Decca), Lawrence Welk (Vocalion).

Get Outta My Dreams, Get Into My Car. w/m Robert John "Mutt" Lange and Billy

Ocean, 1988. #1 single by the British singer/writer Billy Ocean (Jive).

Get Out Those Old Records. w/m Carmen Lombardo and John Jacob Loeb, 1951. Introduced and recorded by Guy Lombardo, vocal by Carmen Lombardo and Kenny Gardner (Decca). Also recorded by Georgia Gibbs (Coral); Mary Martin with son Larry [Hagman] (Columbia).

Get Ready. w/m William Robinson, 1966, 1970. Produced by writer "Smokey" Robinson, song was introduced by The Temptations, whose record reached the Top 40 (Gordy). The version by Rare Earth, another Detroit group, became a Top 10 hit (Rare Earth), 1970.

Get Rhythm in Your Feet. w. Bill Livingston, m. J. Russel Robinson, 1935. Recorded by the bands of Henry "Red" Allen (Vocalion) and Jack Shilkret (Bluebird).

Get Thee Behind Me Satan. w/m Irving Berlin, 1936. Introduced by Harriet Hilliard in (MM) *Follow the Fleet.* The song, originally written for Ginger Rogers in *Top Hat*, was deleted from the film before its release. Hilliard recorded it with husband Ozzie Nelson's Orchestra (Brunswick).

Getting Closer. w/m Paul McCartney, 1979. Recorded by McCartney's group Wings (Columbia).

Getting Some Fun Out of Life. w. Edgar Leslie, m. Joe Burke, 1937. Recorded by Billie Holiday (Vocalion) and by Bernie Cummins's Band (Vocalion).

Getting to Know You. w. Oscar Hammerstein II, m. Richard Rodgers, 1951. Introduced by Gertrude Lawrence and members of the company in (TM) *The King and I.* In (MM) *The King and I*, 1956, it was sung by Marni Nixon, dubbing on the soundtrack for Deborah Kerr, and the children.

Gettin' Together. w/m Ritchie Cordell, 1967. Top 20 record by Tommy James and The Shondells (Roulette).

Get Together (a.k.a. **Let's Get Together**). w/m Chester Powers, 1965, 1969. Top 40 record by We Five (A&M). Chart version by The Youngbloods (RCA), 1967. In 1969, the song and their recording were selected as the theme for The National Conference of Christians and Jews, resulting in the award of a gold record, indicative of sales of over a million discs for the re-release.

Get Up (I Feel Like Being a Sex Machine). w/m James Brown, 1970. R&B/Pop chart hit by James Brown (King, Part 1).

Get Up and Boogie (That's Right). w/m Silvester Levay and Stephen Prager, 1976. Top 10 gold record by the German studio disco group The Silver Convention (Midland International).

Get Used to It. w/m Roger Voudouris and Michael Omartian, 1979. Recorded by Roger Voudouris (Warner Bros.).

Get While the Gettin's Good. w/m Bill Anderson, 1967. Top 10 Country record by Bill Anderson (Decca).

Get Your Kicks On Route 66. w/m Robert Troup, 1946. Big hit for The King Cole Trio (Capitol). Bing Crosby and The Andrews Sisters also had a popular version (Decca).

Ghetto Woman. w/m Riley B. "B. B." King and Dave Clark, 1971. Recorded by "B. B." King (ABC).

Ghostbusters. w/m Ray Parker, Jr., 1984. Introduced on the soundtrack of (MP) *Ghostbusters*, and on the ensuing #1 gold record by Ray Parker, Jr. (Arista). Nominated for an Academy Award.

Ghost of the Blues. w/m J. Tim Brymn and Sidney Bechet, 1924. Recorded by Piron's New Orleans Band (Columbia).

Ghost of the Violin, The. w. Bert Kalmar, m. Ted Snyder, 1912.

Ghost Riders in the Sky. See **Riders in the Sky.**

Ghost That Never Walked, The. w. William Jerome, m. Jean Schwartz, 1904. From (TM) *Piff! Paff!! Pouf!!!* that featured Eddie Foy.

Ghost Town. w. Ted Varnick, m. Nick Aquaviva, 1956. Popular record by Don Cherry (Columbia).

Giannina Mia. w. Otto Harbach, m. Rudolf Friml, 1912. Introduced by Emma Trentini in (TM) *The Firefly.* Allan Jones sang it in the film version (MM) *The Firefly,* 1937.

Giant. w. Paul Francis Webster, m. Dimitri Tiomkin, 1956. Based on music from (MP) *Giant.* Leading records by the orchestras of Les Baxter (Capitol); Art Mooney (MGM); Jack Pleis, vocal by Ralph Young (Decca).

G.I. Blues. w/m Floyd Tillman, 1944. Introduced and recorded by Floyd Tillman (Decca).

Gid-ap Garibaldi. w. Howard Johnson and Billy Moll, m. Harry Warren, 1927.

Giddyup Go. w/m Tommy Hill and Red Sovine, 1966. C&W/Pop record, spoken by Red Sovine (Starday).

Gidget. w. Patti Washington, m. Fred Karger, 1959. Introduced by James Darren in (MP) *Gidget* and on records (Colpix).

Gift Today, A (the Bar Mitzvah Song). w/m Harold Rome, 1962. Sung by Elliot Gould, Lillian Roth, Ken Le Roy, Marilyn Cooper, and chorus in (TM) *I Can Get It for You Wholesale.*

Gigi. w. Alan Jay Lerner, m. Frederick Loewe, 1958. Introduced by Louis Jourdan in (MM) *Gigi.* Academy Award winner, 1958. Best-selling record by Vic Damone (Columbia). In the stage version (TM) *Gigi,* 1973, it was sung by Daniel Massey.

Gigi. w. Harold Adamson, m. Florence Veran, 1953. French melody to which Adamson added English lyrics. Popular recording by Les Baxter and his Orchestra (Capitol). (Not to be confused with the movie song).

Gigolette. w. Irving Caesar, m. Franz Lehar, 1925. Sung by Jack Buchanan in (TM) *Charlot's Revue* and recorded by him (Columbia).

Gigolo, The. w/m O'Bryan Burnette II and Don Cornelius, 1982. Chart record by the singer billed as O'Bryan (Capitol).

G.I. Jive. w/m Johnny Mercer, 1944. Best-selling records by Johnny Mercer (Capitol) and Louis Jordan and his Tympany Five (Decca).

Gilly, Gilly, Ossenfeffer, Katsenellen Bogen by the Sea. w/m Al Hoffman and Dick Manning, 1954. Recorded by The Four Lads, with Norman Leyden's Orchestra (Columbia).

Gimme, Gimme Good Lovin'. w/m Joey Levine and Ritchie Cordell, 1969. Recorded by a studio group named Crazy Elephant (Bell).

Gimme a Little Kiss, Will Ya, Huh? w. Roy Turk and Jack Smith, m. Maceo Pinkard, 1926. Popularized by "Whispering" Jack Smith (Victor). Also recorded by Jean Goldkette (Victor); Billy Jones (Banner); Gene Krupa, vocal by Buddy Stewart (Columbia); Jerry and Patti Lewis (Capitol); April Stevens (RCA Victor). Sung by Deanna Durbin in (MP) *Lady on a Train,* 1945.

Gimme All Your Lovin'. w/m Frank Beard, Billy Gibbons, and Dusty Hill, 1983. Written and recorded by the trio ZZ Top (Warner Bros.).

Gimme a Pigfoot. w/m Wesley Wilson, 1933. Featured and recorded by Bessie Smith (Okeh).

Gimme Dat Ding. w/m Albert Hammond and Mike Hazelwood, 1970. Novelty, recorded by the British studio group The Pipkins (Capitol). Often used as background music on "The Benny Hill Show" on television.

Gimme Little Sign. w/m Joseph Hooven, Alfred Smith, and Jerry Winn, 1967. Top 10 record by Brenton Wood (pseud. for Alfred Smith) (Double Shot).

Gimme Mick. w/m Gilda Radner and Paul Shaffer, 1979. Introduced by Gilda Radner in her revue (TM) *Gilda Live*, and in the subsequent filming (MM) *Gilda Live*, 1980.

Gimme Shelter. w/m Mick Jagger and Keith Richards, 1969. Introduced by The Rolling Stones in their album "Let It Bleed" (London). First chart single by Merry Clayton, who sang on the above version (Ode). Sung by the Rolling Stones in the filmed documentary of their 1969 American tour (MM) *Gimme Shelter*, 1970. Chart record by Grand Funk Railroad (Capitol), 1971.

Gimme Some Lovin'. w/m Steve Winwood, Muff Winwood, and Spencer Davis, 1967, 1980. Written and recorded in England by The Spencer Davis Group (United Artists). Revived by The Blues Brothers in their film (MM) *The Blues Brothers* and hit record (Atlantic), 1980.

Gimme That Wine. w/m Jon Hendricks, 1960. Introduced and recorded by Lambert, Hendricks and Ross (Columbia).

Gina. w/m Paul Vance and Leon Carr, 1962. Top 10 record by Johnny Mathis (Columbia).

Ginger Bread. w/m Clint Ballard, Jr. and Hank Hunter, 1958. Popularized by Frankie Avalon (Chancellor).

Gin House Blues, The. w. Henry Troy, m. Fletcher Henderson, 1926. Featured and recorded by Bessie Smith (Columbia).

Gin Mill Blues. m. Joe Sullivan, 1938. Introduced and recorded by famed jazz pianist, Joe Sullivan (Columbia), 1934. Bob Crosby and his Orchestra cut their popular record (Decca), 1937, and the Light Crust Doughboys, theirs (Vocalion), 1938.

Ginny Come Lately. w. Peter Udell, m. Gary Geld, 1962. Recorded by Brian Hyland (ABC-Paramount).

Girl!, A Girl!, A (Zoom-Ba Di Alli Nella). w/m Bennie Benjamin and George David Weiss, 1954. Popular record by Eddie Fisher (RCA Victor).

Girl, Don't Let It Get You Down. w/m Kenny Gamble and Leon Huff, 1980. Top 10 R&B record by The O'Jays (TSOP).

Girl, You Know It's True. w/m William Pettaway, Rodney Holloman, Kayode Aderjemo, Kevin Liles, Sean Spencer, 1989. Hit Pop/R&B chart record by Milli Vanilli (Arista).

Girl, You'll Be a Woman Soon. w/m Neil Diamond, 1967. Top 10 record by Neil Diamond (Bang).

Girl at the Ironing Board, The. w. Al Dubin, m. Harry Warren, 1934. Introduced by Joan Blondell in (MM) *Dames*.

Girl Can't Help It, The. w/m Richard Penniman, 1957. Title song from the Jayne Mansfield-Tom Ewell film, (MM) *The Girl Can't Help It*, sung by Little Richard. His recording became a Top 10 R&B chart entry (Specialty).

Girl Come Running. w/m Bob Crewe and Bob Gaudio, 1965. Top 40 record by The Four Seasons (Philips).

Girl Don't Come. w/m Chris Andrews, 1965. Recorded in England by Sandie Shaw (Reprise).

Girlfriend. w/m Babyface and L. A. Reid, 1987. #1 R&B chart and Top 10 Pop crossover record by Pebbles, pseudonym for Perri McKissack (MCA).

Girl Friend, The. w. Lorenz Hart, m. Richard Rodgers, 1926. Introduced by Eva Puck and Sammy White in (TM) *The Girl Friend*. Danced by Cyd Charisse in the Rodgers and Hart story (MM) *Words and Music*, 1948. Hit record by George Olsen, vocal by the trio of Bob Borger, Fran Frey, and Larry Murphy (Victor).

Girl Friend of the Whirling Dervish, The. w. Al Dubin and Johnny Mercer, m. Harry Warren, 1938. Introduced by John Payne, Jerry Colonna, Johnny "Scat" Davis, Joe Venuti, and other cast members in (MM) *Garden of the Moon*. Records by Van Alexander, vocal by Butch Stone (Bluebird); Skinnay Ennis (Victor); Guy Lombardo (Decca).

Girl from Ipanema. w. Norman Gimbel (Engl.), m. Antonio Carlos Jobim, 1964. Brazilian song, original Portuguese title, "Garota de Ipanema," words by Vinicus De Moraes. Hit record by saxophonist Stan Getz, vocals by Astrud Gilberto (Engl.) and Joao Gilberto (Port.) (Verve).

Girl from Spanish Town, The. w/m Marty Robbins, 1963. Country chart record by Marty Robbins (Columbia).

Girl from the North Country. w/m Bob Dylan, 1969. Recorded by Bob Dylan and Johnny Cash in the Dylan LP "Nashville Skyline" (Columbia).

Girlie Was Just Made to Love, A. w. Joe Goodwin, m. George W. Meyer, 1911.

Girl I Knew Somewhere, The. w/m Michael Nesmith, 1967. Recorded by The Monkees (Colgems).

Girl I'm Gonna Miss You. w/m Dietmar Kawohl, Frank Farian, Peter Bischof Fallenstein, 1989. Hit record by Milli Vanilli (Arista).

Girl I Never Loved, The. w/m Randy Starr, 1967. Introduced by Elvis Presley in (MM) *Clambake*.

Girl in Love. w. Chet Kelley, m. Tom King, 1966. Recorded by The Outsiders (Capitol).

Girl in the Wood. w/m Terry Gilkyson, Neal Gilkyson, and Stuart Gilkyson, 1952. Introduced by Frankie Laine in (MM) *Rainbow 'Round My Shoulder*, and recorded by him with Paul Weston's Orchestra (Columbia).

Girl in Trouble, A. (Is a Temporary Thing). w/m Debora Iyall, David Kahne, Peter Woods, and Frank Zincavage, 1984. Recorded by the quintet Romeo Void (Columbia).

Girl Is Mine, The. w/m Michael Jackson, 1982. Top 10 gold record by Michael Jackson and Paul McCartney (Epic).

Girl Is You and the Boy Is Me, The. w. B. G. DeSylva and Lew Brown, m. Ray Henderson, 1926. Introduced by Harry Richman and Frances Williams in (TM) *George White's Scandals of 1926*.

Girl I Used to Know, A. w/m Jack Clement, 1962. Popularized by George Jones and The Jones Boys (United Artists). Revived by Bobby Vee (Liberty), 1966.

Girl Like You, A. w/m Eddie Brigati and Felix Cavaliere, 1967. Top 10 record by The Young Rascals (Atlantic).

Girl Most Likely, The. w/m Margaret Lewis and Mira Smith, 1969. C&W/Pop crossover hit by Jeannie C. Riley (Plantation).

Girl of My Dreams. w/m Ronald Thomas, 1979. English song recorded by Bram Tchaikowsky [né Peter Bramall] (Polydor).

Girl of My Dreams. w/m Sunny Clapp, 1927. Standard, first recorded by Seger Ellis (Columbia), Blue Steele (Victor), Willard Robison (Perfect). Hit record by Gene Austin, whistling by Bob McGimsey (Victor), 1928.

Girl on a Swing. w/m Bob Miranda, 1966. Top 40 U.S. release by the British group Gerry and The Pacemakers (Lurie).

Girl on Page 44, The. w. Richard Adler, m. Robert Allen, 1958. Recorded by The Four Lads (Columbia).

Girl on the Billboard. w/m Walter Haynes and Hank Mills, 1965. Recorded by Del Reeves (United Artists).

Girl on the Magazine Cover, The. w/m Irving Berlin, 1915. Introduced by Joseph Santley in (TM) *Stop! Look! Listen!* It was sung by Dick Beavers in (MM) *Easter Parade* in 1948.

Girl on the Police Gazette, The. w/m Irving Berlin, 1937. Introduced by Dick Powell,

Alice Faye, and chorus in (MM) *On the Avenue*. Powell recorded it (Decca) as did the bands of Shep Fields (Bluebird); Wayne King (Victor); Abe Lyman, vocal by Sonny Schuyler (Decca).

Girls. w/m Dwight Twilley, 1984. Recorded by Dwight Twilley (EMI America).

Girls, Girls, Girls. w/m Tommy Lee, Mick Mars, and Nikki Sixx, 1987. Chart single by the heavy metal band, Motley Crue, from their album of the same name (Elektra).

Girls Can't Do What the Guys Do. w/m Clarence H. Reid and Willie J. Clark, 1968. Top 40 record by Betty Wright (Alston).

Girls I Never Kissed, The. w/m Mike Leiber and Jerry Stoller, 1987. Recorded by Frank Sinatra and Paul Anka (Reprise).

Girls in Love. w/m Garry Bonner and Alan Gordon, 1967. Popular recording by Gary Lewis and The Playboys (Liberty).

Girls Just Want to Have Fun. w/m Robert Hazard, 1984. Gold record single from the platinum album "She's So Unusual," by Cyndi Lauper (Portrait). Song inspired 1985 film of same name.

Girl's Night Out, A. w/m Jeff Bullock and Brent Maher, 1985. #1 Country chart record by the mother/daughter duo The Judds (RCA).

Girls of My Dreams, The. w/m Irving Berlin, 1920. Introduced by the tenor, John Steel, in (TM) *Ziegfeld Follies of 1920*, and recorded by him (Victor).

Girls of Summer, The. w/m Stephen Sondheim, 1981. Introduced by Suzanne Henry in the off-Broadway (TM) *Marry Me A Little*.

Girls' School. w/m Denny Laine and Paul McCartney, 1977. Recorded by McCartney's group Wings (Capitol).

Girls Talk. w/m Elvis Costello, 1979. Recorded by the Welsh singer Dave Edmunds (Swan Song).

Girls Were Made to Take Care of Boys. w/m Ralph Blane, 1949. From (MM) *One Sunday Afternoon*. Recorded by Rose Murphy (RCA Victor) and Herb Jeffries (Columbia).

Girl That I Marry, The. w/m Irving Berlin, 1946. Introduced by Ray Middleton in (TM) *Annie Get Your Gun*. Howard Keel sang it in the film version (MM) *Annie Get Your Gun*, 1950. Leading records by Frank Sinatra (Columbia); Eddy Howard, with his Orchestra (Majestic).

Girl Trouble. w/m Andy Rice and Fred Fisher, 1930. Introduced by Lawrence Gray in (MM) *Children of Pleasure*. Recorded by Jack Denny (Brunswick).

Girl Watcher. w/m Buck Trail, 1968. Gold record by the sextet The O'Kaysions (ABC).

Girl Who Used to Be Me, The. w/m Alan Bergman and Marilynn Bergman, m. Marvin Hamlisch, 1989. Sung on the soundtrack of (MP) *Shirley Valentine*. Nominated for an Academy Award.

Girl with a Brogue, The. w. Arthur Wimperis, m. Lionel Monckton, 1909. From (TM) *The Arcadians*. It was sung by Phyllis Dare in London and Julia Sanderson in New York.

Girl with the Golden Braids, The. w. Stanley Kahan, m. Eddie Snyder, 1957. Featured and recorded by Perry Como (RCA).

Girl with the Heather Green Eyes, The. w. Mack Discant, m. Guy Wood, 1957. Among recordings: Ralph Young (Everest), The Arbors (Mercury), Frank Fields and his Orchestra (Dot).

Gitarzan. w/m Ray Stevens and Bill Everette, 1969. Gold record novelty hit by Ray Stevens (Monument).

Give a Broken Heart a Break. w. Dave Franklin, m. Isham Jones, 1935. Featured and recorded by Freddy Martin, vocal by Elmer Feldkamp (Brunswick); Richard Himber, vocal by Stuart Allen (Victor).

Give a Damn. w/m Stuart Scharf, 1968. Written as the theme song for The New York Urban Coalition campaign, and recorded by Spanky and Our Gang (Mercury).

Give a Little Bit. w/m Rick Davies and Roger Hodgson, 1977. Recorded by the British quartet, Supertramp, and written by two of its members (A&M).

Give a Little Love. w/m Paul Kennerly, 1988. Top 10 Country single by the mother/daughter duo The Judds (RCA).

Give a Little Whistle. w. Carolyn Leigh, m. Cy Coleman, 1960. Introduced by Lucille Ball, Keith Andes, and chorus in (TM) *Wildcat*.

Give a Little Whistle. w. Ned Washington, m. Leigh Harline, 1940. Sung by the voices of Cliff Edwards as "Jiminy Cricket" and Dickie Jones as "Pinocchio" in the feature-length cartoon (MM) *Pinocchio*. Recorded by Edwards (Decca).

Give a Man a Horse He Can Ride. w. James Thomson, m. Geoffrey O'Hara, 1917.

Give Him a Great Big Kiss. w/m George Morton, 1965. Recorded by The Shangri-Las (Red Bird).

Give Ireland Back to the Irish. w/m Paul McCartney and Linda McCartney, 1972. Recorded by the McCartney group Wings (Apple).

Give It All You Got. m. Chuck Mangione, 1980. The number was featured on the ABC-TV network during the 1980 Olympics. Chart instrumental by flugelhornist/bandleader Chuck Mangione (A&M).

Give It All You've Got. w/m Jay Livingston and Ray Evans, 1958. Introduced by Susan Johnson in (TM) *Oh Captain!*

Give It Back to the Indians. w. Lorenz Hart, m. Richard Rodgers, 1939. Sung by Mary Jane Walsh and danced by Hal LeRoy and students (including Van Johnson) in (TM) *Too Many Girls*. The song humorously reversed the praise of the city referred to in Rodgers and Hart's earlier "Manhattan."

Give It to Me. w/m Peter Wolf and Seth Justman, 1973. Written by the vocalist and keyboardist of The J. Geils Band that recorded it (Atlantic).

Give It to Me Baby. w/m Rick James, 1981. #1 R&B chart record by Rick James (Gordy).

Give It to the People. w/m Dennis Lambert and Brian Potter, 1974. Top 20 record by The Righteous Brothers (Haven).

Give It Up. w/m Harry Wayne Casey and Deborah Carter, 1984. Chart record by KC, pseudonym for the co-writer (Meca).

Give It Up or Turnit A Loose. w/m C. Bobbitt, 1969. #1 R&B and Top 20 Pop chart hit by James Brown (King).

Give Me a Band and My Baby. w. Leo Robin, m. Jule Styne, 1955. Standout number from (MM) *My Sister Eileen*, performed by Betty Garrett, Janet Leigh, Bob Fosse, and Tommy Rall.

Give Me a Heart to Sing To. w. Ned Washington, m. Victor Young, 1936. Introduced by Helen Morgan in (MM) *Frankie and Johnny*, which was filmed two years earlier but held up because of censorship problems. Morgan recorded it (Victor) as did Guy Lombardo, with vocal by brother Carmen (Decca).

Give Me a Moment Please. w. Leo Robin, m. Richard A. Whiting and W. Franke Harling, 1930. Jeanette MacDonald and Jack Buchanan sang this as a love duet over the telephone in (MM) *Monte Carlo*. The violinist, Dave Rubinoff, used it as his radio theme.

Give Me a Night in June. w/m Cliff Friend, 1927. Leading records by The Ipana Troubadors (Columbia) and Johnny Marvin (Victor).

Give Me 40 Acres. w/m Earl Greene and John Greene, 1964. Country hit by The Willis Brothers (Starday).

Give Me His Last Chance. w/m Lionel Cartwright, 1989. Hit Country record by Lionel Cartwright (MCA).

Give Me Just a Little More Time. w/m Brian Holland and Edythe Wayne, 1970. Gold record by The Chairmen of the Board (Invictus).

Give Me Liberty or Give Me Love. w. Leo Robin, m. Ralph Rainger, 1933. Sung by Claudette Colbert in (MM) *Torch Singer*. Recorded by Mildred Bailey (Brunswick), Annette Hanshaw (Perfect), Irene Taylor (Vocalion).

Give Me Love. w/m Cindy Walker, 1955. Recorded by The McGuire Sisters (Coral).

Give Me Love (Give Me Peace on Earth). w/m George Harrison, 1973. #1 record from England by George Harrison (Apple).

Give Me More, More, More of Your Kisses. w/m Lefty Frizzell and Ray Price, 1952. Featured and recorded by Lefty Frizzell (Columbia).

Give Me My Mammy. w. B. G. DeSylva, m. Walter Donaldson, 1921. Interpolated by Al Jolson in (TM) *Bombo* during the New York run.

Give Me One Hour. w. Brian Hooker, m. Rudolf Friml, 1928. From (TM) *The White Eagle*. Later recorded by Gladys Swarthout (Victor).

Give Me One More Chance. w/m J. P. Pennington and Sonny Lemaire, 1984. #1 Country chart record by the group, Exile, of which the writers were members (Epic).

Give Me the Moonlight, Give Me the Girl. w. Lew Brown, m. Albert Von Tilzer, 1917. Revived by Betty Grable and John Payne in (MM) *The Dolly Sisters*, 1945.

Give Me the Moon Over Brooklyn. w/m Jason Matthews and Terry Shand, 1946. Bestselling record by Hildegarde with Guy Lombardo and his Royal Canadians (Decca).

Give Me the Night. w/m Rod Temperton, 1980. #1 R&B, #4 Pop chart record by George Benson (Warner Bros.).

Give Me the Reason. w/m Luther Vandross and Nat Adderley, Jr., 1986. From (MP) *Ruthless People*, Luther Vandross had a Top 10 R&B crossover record (Epic).

Give Me the Simple Life. w. Harry Ruby, m. Rube Bloom, 1945. Sung by John Payne and June Haver in (MM) *Wake Up and Dream*. Popular recordings by Benny Goodman, vocal by Liza Morrow (Columbia) and Bing Crosby, with Jimmy Dorsey's Orchestra (Decca). Revived in (MM) *Let's Make Love*, 1960.

Give Me Wings. 1986. #1 Country chart song by Michael Johnson (RCA).

Give Me Your Affection, Honey. w. Alfred Bryan, m. Pete Wendling and Carmen Lombardo, 1931.

Give Me Your Hand. w/m Dorothy Stewart, 1949. Featured and recorded by Perry Como (RCA Victor).

Give Me Your Tired, Your Poor. w. Emma Lazarus, m. Irving Berlin, 1949. The words are from the poem inscribed on the base of The Statue of Liberty in New York harbor. Introduced by Allyn McLerie in (TM) *Miss Liberty*.

Give My Regards to Broadway. w/m George M. Cohan, 1904. Introduced by Cohan in the title role of (TM) *Little Johnny Jones*. Eddie Buzzell sang it in the 1929 film version (MM) *Little Johnny Jones*. It was done subsequently by James Cagney in the Cohan biography (MM) *Yankee Doodle Dandy*, 1942; by Al Jolson, dubbing his voice on the soundtrack for Keefe Brasselle, in (MM) *Jolson Sings Again*, 1949; by a chorus in (MM) *With a Song in My Heart*, 1952; as the title song by Dan Dailey and Charles Winninger in (MM) *Give My Regards to Broadway*, 1948. Joel Grey, playing Cohan, sang it in (TM) *George M.!* at the Palace Theatre in New York, 1968.

Give Myself a Party. w/m Don Gibson, 1958. Introduced and recorded by Don Gibson (RCA).

Give Peace a Chance. w/m John Lennon and Paul McCartney, 1969. Top 20 U.S. chart record by The Plastic Ono Band (Apple).

Give the People What They Want. w/m Kenny Gamble and Leon Huff, 1975. Recorded by The O'Jays (Philadelphia International).

Give to Live. w/m Sammy Hagar, 1987. Single from the self-titled album "Sammy Hagar" (Geffen).

Give Us This Day. w. Buddy Kaye, m. Bobby Day, 1956. Popularized by Joni James (MGM).

Give Us Your Blessing. w/m Jeff Barry and Ellie Greenwich, 1963. Introduced by Ray Peterson (Dunes). Popular recording by The Shangri-Las (Red Bird), 1965.

Giving It All Away. w/m David Courtney and Leo Sayer, 1973. Recorded in England by Roger Daltrey (Track).

Giving It Up for Your Love. w/m Jerry Williams, 1980. Top 10 record by Delbert McClinton (Capitol).

Giving Up. w/m Van McCoy, 1964. Top 40 record by Gladys Knight and The Pips (Maxx). Donny Hathaway had a chart version (Atco), 1972.

Giving Up Easy. w/m Jerry Foster and Bill Rice, 1981. Country chart record by Leon Everette (Orlando), 1979. When reissued (RCA), 1980, the record reached the Top 10 on the Country charts.

Giving You the Best That I Got. w/m Anita Baker, Randy Holland, and Skip Scarborough, 1988. Recorded by Anita Baker and title song of her album (Elektra). Winner Grammy Award (NARAS) Rhythm and Blues Song of the Year.

Glad All Over. w/m Dave Clark and Mike Smith, 1964. U.S. hit release of the English recording by The Dave Clark Five (Epic).

Glad Rag Doll. w. Jack Yellen, m. Milton Ager and Dan Dougherty, 1929. From (MP) *Glad Rag Doll*. Recorded by "Whispering" Jack Smith (Victor).

Glad to Be Home. w/m Irving Berlin, 1962. Introduced by Nanette Fabray in (TM) *Mr. President*.

Glad to Be Unhappy. w. Lorenz Hart, m. Richard Rodgers, 1936. Introduced by Doris Carson and David Morris in (TM) *On Your Toes*. Among standout recordings: Lena Horne (Black and White) and Lee Wiley (Gala). The Mamas and The Papas quartet had a Top 40 version (Dunhill), 1967.

Glamorous Life, The. w/m Prince Rogers Nelson, 1984. Top 10 R&B and Pop chart record by Sheila E. [Escovedo] (Warner Bros.).

Glendora. w/m Ray Stanley, 1956. Featured and recorded by Perry Como (RCA).

Gloomy Sunday. w. Sam M. Lewis (Engl.), m. Rezso Seress, 1936. Original Hungarian title was "Szomoru Vasarnap," words by Laszlo Javor, and publicized as the "suicide song." The story was circulated, possibly by the publisher, that numerous disappointed lovers in Hungary took their own lives by jumping off bridges after hearing the song. Some radio stations in the U.S. banned the song, fearing the same results. Recorded in England by Paul Robeson (HMV), then in the U.S. by the orchestras of Paul Whiteman (Victor), Henry King (Decca), Vincent Lopez (Melotone). The best-seller, however, was by Billie Holiday in 1941 (Okeh). Ironically, the composer committed suicide in 1968.

Gloria. w. Trevor Veitch (Engl.), (It.) w/m Giancarlo Bigazzi and Umberto Tozzi, 1982. Top 10 gold record by Laura Branigan (Atlantic).

Gloria. w/m Emanuel Johnson and Michael Stokes, 1977. Top 10 R&B hit by the group Enchantment (United Artists).

Gloria. w/m Van Morrison, 1965. First recorded by the Belfast, Ireland rock quintet, Them (Parrot). Leading seller by the Chicago band, The Shadows of Knight (Dunwich), 1966.

Gloria. w/m Leon René, 1948. Popular record by The Mills Brothers (Decca).

Gloria's Theme. w. Mack David, m. Bronislau Kaper, 1960. Based on theme from (MP) *Butterfield 8*. Recorded by Adam Wade (Coed).

Glory Days. w/m Bruce Springsteen, 1985. Top 10 record by Bruce Springsteen (Columbia).

Glory of Love. w/m Peter Cetera, David Foster, and Diane Nini, 1986. Sung on the soundtrack of (MP) *The Karate Kid II* and on a #1 chart record by Peter Cetera (Full Moon).

Glory of Love, The. w/m Billy Hill, 1936. Introduced, featured, and recorded by Rudy Vallee and his Orchestra (Melotone). Benny Goodman, with vocal by Helen Ward and arranged by Spud Murphy, had a big seller (Victor). In 1951, The Five Keys had a #1 R&B record (Aladdin). Song was heard in the Hepburn-Tracy-Poitier film (MP) *Guess Who's Coming to Dinner*, 1967. Revived by Bette Midler in (MP) *Beaches*, 1988.

Glory Road, De. w. Clement Wood, m. Jacques Wolfe, 1928. Lawrence Tibbett recorded this on a 12″ record (Victor). He sang it in (MM) *Metropolitan* in 1935.

Glow-Worm, The. w. Johnny Mercer (new lyric), m. Paul Lincke, 1907, 1952. The original English words were by Lilla Cayley Robinson. Lincke first wrote the German words under the title "Glühwürmchen," 1902. The initial U.S. performance was by May Naudain in (TM) *The Girl Behind the Counter*. Lucy Isabelle Marsh (Columbia) and The Victor Orchestra (Victor) each had hit records. In 1952 the Mills Brothers, with Hal McIntyre's Orchestra (Decca), had a #1 hit with Mercer's words, which have now become the standard U.S. version. Mercer's vocal with Alvino Rey's Orchestra (Capitol), which had been recorded and distributed three years earlier, was re-released and sold well.

Go, Boy, Go. w/m Floyd F. Wilson, 1954. Country hit by Carl Smith (Columbia).

Go, Cat, Go. w/m Harlan Howard, 1964. Top 10 C&W song by Norma Jean (RCA).

Go, Jimmy, Go. w/m Doc Pomus and Mort Shuman, 1959. Hit record by Jimmy Clanton (Ace).

Go Ahead and Cry. w/m Bill Medley, 1966. Top 40 record by The Righteous Brothers (Verve).

Go All the Way. w/m Eric Carmen, 1972. Gold record by the group Raspberries (Capitol). Carmen was lead singer.

Go Away Little Girl. w/m Gerry Goffin and Carole King, 1963, 1971. Introduced and #1 record by Steve Lawrence (Columbia). Revived by The Happenings (B. T. Puppy), 1966. Donny Osmond had a #1 million-selling version (MGM), 1971, marking the first time in the rock era that a song reached #1, with recordings by two different artists.

Go Away with Me. w/m Dan Welch, 1957. C&W hit by The Wilburn Brothers (Decca).

Go Back. w/m Mike Fennelly, 1970. Top 40 record by the quintet Crabby Appleton (Elektra).

Go Back You Fool. w/m Don Robertson and Hal Blair, 1955. Recorded by Faron Young (Capitol).

God, Love, and Rock and Roll. w/m Skip Knape and David Teegarden, 1970. Written and Top 40 record by Teegarden and Van Winkle (Westbound).

God Bless America. w/m Irving Berlin, 1939. Originally written for, but deleted from, the 1918 all-soldier show (TM) *Yip, Yip, Yaphank*. Kate Smith asked Berlin for a "patriotic" song for her radio broadcast on Armistice Day, 1938. With a few lyric changes, she introduced it to the public. Berlin turned all royalties over to a fund for the Boy and Girl Scouts of America. In a national poll in the late 1950s, the song was chosen second to "The Star Spangled Banner" as the most popular patriotic song. In films, it was sung by Kate Smith in (MM) *This Is The Army*, 1943; Deanna Durbin in (MM) *Hers to Hold*, 1943; Lotte Lehmann and Marni Nixon, the latter dubbing for Margaret O'Brien, in (MM) *Big City*, 1948.

God Bless the Child. w/m Arthur Herzog, Jr. and Billie Holiday, 1941. Introduced, recorded by, and associated with Billie Holiday (Okeh).

God Bless the U.S.A. w/m Lee Greenwood, 1984. Country chart hit by Lee Greenwood (MCA).

God Bless Us All. w. Tom Murray, m. Tony Burello, 1953. Popular record by five-year-old Brucie Weil, with Don Costa's Band (Barbour).

Godchild. m. George Wallington, 1949. Jazz instrumental first recorded by Miles Davis and his Orchestra (Capitol), then by Chubby Jackson and his Orchestra (Columbia).

Godfather, The. See **Love Theme from "The Godfather."**

God Only Knows. w. Tony Asher and Brian Wilson, m. Brian Wilson, 1966. Recorded by The Beach Boys, coupled with hit "Wouldn't It Be Nice" (Capitol). Revived by Marilynn Scott (Big Tree), 1978.

Go Down Gamblin'. w. David Clayton Thomas, m. Fred Lipsius, 1971. Top 40 single by Blood, Sweat & Tears (Columbia).

God's Country. w. Haven Gillespie, m. Beasley Smith, 1950. Leading records by Frank Sinatra (Columbia) and Vic Damone (Mercury).

God's Country. w/m E. Y. Harburg and Harold Arlen, 1937. Introduced by Jack Whiting and the 5 Reillys in (TM) *Hooray for What!* It was interpolated in (MM) *Babes in Arms* in 1939 by Judy Garland, Mickey Rooney, Betty Jaynes, Douglas McPhail, and chorus.

Gods Were Angry with Me, The. w/m Bill Mackintosh and Rona Mackintosh, 1950. Popular record by Margaret Whiting and Jimmy Wakely (Capitol).

God Will. w/m Lyle Lovett, 1987. Country chart record by Lyle Lovett (MCA).

Go Fly a Kite. w. Johnny Burke, m. James V. Monaco, 1939. Introduced by Bing Crosby in (MM) *The Star Maker* and on records (Decca). Also recorded by the bands of Artie Shaw (Bluebird) and Tommy Dorsey (Victor).

Go Home. w/m Stevie Wonder, 1986. Top 10 R&B/Pop chart record by Stevie Wonder (Tamla).

Go Home. w/m Onie Wheeler, 1961. Featured and recorded by Lester Flatt and Earl Scruggs (Columbia).

Go Home and Tell Your Mother. w. Dorothy Fields, m. Jimmy McHugh, 1930. Sung by Robert Montgomery and Dorothy Jordan in (MM) *Love in the Rough*. Popular records by Gus Arnheim and his Orchestra (Victor), Johnny Marvin (Victor), Don Voorhees's Orchestra (Hit of the Week).

Goin' Back. w/m Gerry Goffin and Carole King, 1968. Recorded by The Byrds (Columbia).

Goin' Down. w/m Greg Guidry and D. Martin, 1982. Recorded by singer/pianist Greg Guidry (Columbia).

Going, Going, Gone. w/m Phil Baxter, 1933.

Going Back to Cali. w/m Rick Rubin and J. T. Smith, 1988. Introduced on the soundtrack of (MP) *Less Than Zero*, and on a chart single by the rap artist, L. L. Cool J (Def Jam).

Going for a Pardon. w. James Thornton and Clara Hauenschild, m. James Thornton, 1896.

Going Home Train. w/m Harold Rome, 1946. Introduced in (TM) *Call Me Mister* by Lawrence Winters. Bobby Short sang it in the film version (MM) *Call Me Mister*, 1951.

Going in Circles. w. Anita Poree, m. Jerry Peters, 1969. Gold record by The Friends of Distinction (RCA).

Going My Way. w. Johnny Burke, m. James Van Heusen, 1944. Introduced by Bing Crosby and Risë Stevens in (MM) *Going My Way.* Crosby recorded it with the Williams Brothers (including Andy) and John Scott Trotter's Orchestra (Decca).

Goin' Gone. w/m Pat Alger, Bill Dale, and Fred Kohler, 1988. #1 Country chart record by Kathy Mattea (Mercury).

Going Through the Motions (of Living). w/m Jean Chapel and Bob Tubert, 1963. Country chart record by Sonny James (Capitol).

Going to a Go-Go. w/m Warren Moore, William Robinson, Robert Rogers, and Marv Taplin, 1966. R&B/Pop hit by The Miracles (Tamla). Revived by The Rolling Stones (Rolling Stones), 1982.

Going Up. m. Edward Kennedy "Duke" Ellington, 1942. Introduced by Duke Ellington and his Orchestra in (MM) *Cabin in the Sky.*

Going Up. w. Otto Harbach, m. Louis A. Hirsch, 1918. The hit show (TM) *Going Up* opened on Christmas night, 1917, and the songs became popular during the following calendar year. It featured Frank Craven, Edith Day, Ruth Donnelly, Marion Sunshine, and Donald Meek.

Going Up the Country. w/m Alan Wilson, 1969. Hit record by the blues-rock band Canned Heat (Liberty). The writer was a singer/guitarist/harmonicist with the group.

Goin' Home. w/m Antoine "Fats" Domino and Alvin E. Young, 1952. Million-selling, #1 R&B record by Fats Domino (Imperial).

Goin' Home. w/m Williams Arms Fisher, 1922. Adapted from the 2nd Movement, "Largo," of the symphony *From the New World* by Dvorak.

Goin' Out of My Head. w/m Teddy Randazzo and Bobby Weinstein, 1964, 1968. Hit record by Little Anthony and The Imperials (DCP). The Lettermen revived it with a Top 10 version in medley with "Can't Take My Eyes

off You" (q.v.) (Capitol), 1968. Frank Sinatra had a chart record (Reprise), 1969.

Goin' Steady. w/m Faron Young, 1953. C&W hit by Faron Young (Capitol).

Goin' to Chicago Blues. w/m Jimmy Rushing and William "Count" Basie, 1941. Introduced and recorded by Count Basie, vocal by Jimmy Rushing (Okeh), and later by Al Hibbler with the Count Basie Orchestra (Mercury).

Goin' to Heaven on a Mule. w. Al Dubin, m. Harry Warren, 1934. Sung by Al Jolson in (MM) *Wonder Bar.*

Goin' to the Bank. w/m Dennis Lambert, Andy Goldmark, and Franne Golde, 1986. Top 10 R&B chart crossover record by The Commodores (Polydor).

Goin' to the River. w/m Antoine "Fats" Domino and Dave Bartholomew, 1953. Featured and recorded by Fats Domino (Imperial).

Goin' to Town. m. Bubber Miley and Edward Kennedy "Duke" Ellington, 1929. Jazz instrumental with well-received recordings by Luis Russell (Victor), 1931, and Red Nichols (Brunswick), 1932.

Go into Your Dance. w. Al Dubin, m. Harry Warren, 1935. Introduced by Al Jolson in a production number in (MM) *Go into Your Dance.* Performed by Carole Cook, Wanda Richert, Karen Prunczik, Ginny King, Jeri Kansas, Lee Roy Reams, and chorus in (TM) *42nd Street.*

Gold. w/m John Stewart, 1979. Top 10 record by John Stewart (RSO).

Gold and Silver. m. Franz Lehar, 1904. A popular waltz originally published under the German title "Gold und Silber."

Gold Diggers' Song, The. See **We're in the Money**.

Golden Age of Rock 'n' Roll. w/m Ian Hunter, 1974. Recorded by the British group Mott the Hoople (Columbia).

Golden Boy. w. Lee Adams, m. Charles Strouse, 1964. Introduced by Paula Wayne in (TM) *Golden Boy.*

Golden Days. w. Dorothy Donnelly, m. Sigmund Romberg, 1924. Introduced by Howard Marsh and Greek Evans in (TM) *The Student Prince*. In (MM) *The Student Prince*, 1954, it was sung by Mario Lanza, dubbing for Edmund Purdom.

Golden Earrings. w. Jay Livingston and Ray Evans, m. Victor Young, 1947. Introduced by Marlene Dietrich in (MP) *Golden Earrings*. Peggy Lee had a #1 record (Capitol). Dinah Shore also had a popular version (Columbia).

Golden Gate. w. Billy Rose and Dave Dreyer, m. Al Jolson and Joseph Meyer, 1928. Sung by Al Jolson in (MM) *The Singing Fool*, and on records (Brunswick).

Golden Guitar. w/m Curtis Leach and Billy Gray, 1966. Country chart record by Bill Anderson (Decca).

Golden Ring. w/m Bobby Braddock and Rafe Van Hoy, 1976. Hit Country record by George Jones and Tammy Wynette (Epic).

Golden Rocket. w/m Hank Snow, 1951. Hit C&W record by Hank Snow (RCA Victor).

Golden Years. w/m David Bowie, 1976. Top 10 record by the British singer David Bowie (RCA).

Goldfinger. w. Leslie Bricusse and Anthony Newley, m. John Barry, 1965. Introduced on the soundtrack of the James Bond film (MP) *Goldfinger* by Shirley Bassey, who also had the best-selling record of the song (United Artists). Other popular versions: instrumentals by guitarist Billy Strange (GNP Crescendo), and orchestra conducted by composer John Barry (United Artists).

Gold Rush Is Over, The. w/m Cindy Walker, 1952. Hit Country recording by Hank Snow (RCA Victor).

Gold Will Buy Most Anything But a True Girl's Heart. w. Charles E. Foreman, m. Monroe H. Rosenfeld, 1898.

Golliwog's Cake Walk. m. Claude Debussy, 1908. A popular piano solo from "The Children's Corner."

Gomen Nasai (Forgive Me). w. Benedict Myers, m. Raymond Hattori, 1953. Recorded by a U.S. soldier, Richard Bowers, with the Tokyo Orchestra. It became a chart record (Columbia). Other popular versions by Eddy Howard (Mercury) and Harry Belafonte (RCA Victor).

Gone. w/m Smokey Rogers, 1957. Featured and recorded by Ferlin Husky (Capitol). Revived in 1972 by Joey Heatherton (MGM).

Gone at Last. w/m Paul Simon, 1975. Recorded by Paul Simon and Phoebe Snow (Columbia).

Gone Fishin'. w/m Nick Kenny and Charles Kenny, 1950. Introduced and recorded by Arthur Godfrey (Columbia). Best-selling record by Bing Crosby and Louis Armstrong (Decca), 1951.

Gone Too Far. w/m David Malloy, Eddie Rabbitt, and Even Stevens, 1980. Country and Pop chart record by Eddie Rabbitt (Elektra).

Gone Too Far. w/m John Ford Coley, 1977. Recorded by England Dan (Seals) and John Ford Coley (Big Tree).

Gone with the Wind. w. Herb Magidson, m. Allie Wrubel, 1937. Many songs were written using the title of the best-selling novel, but the Magidson-Wrubel collaboration became the standard. Among the top recordings: Mel Tormé (Musicraft); Dick Haymes (Decca); Claude Thornhill combo, vocal by Maxine Sullivan (Vocalion); Martha Raye (Columbia); Art Tatum (Decca); Billy May (Capitol); Stan Getz (Roost); Benny Carter (Norgran).

Gonna Build a Big Fence Around Texas. w/m Cliff Friend, Katherine Phillips, and George Olsen, 1944. Leading record by Gene Autry (Columbia) in a "fence" coupling with "Don't Fence Me In." Also cut by Dick Robertson, with Johnny Long's Orchestra (Decca).

Gonna Build a Mountain. w/m Leslie Bricusse and Anthony Newley, 1962. Introduced by Anthony Newley in (TM) *Stop the World—I Want to Get Off*.

Gonna Find Me a Bluebird. w/m Marvin Rainwater, 1957. Hit C&W record by Marvin Rainwater (MGM).

Gonna Fly Now (Theme from "Rocky"). w/m Bill Conti, Carol Connors, and Ayn Robbins, 1977. Introduced on the soundtrack of (MP) *Rocky* by DeEtta Little and Nelson Pigford. Nominated for an Academy Award. #1 gold record instrumental by the composer/conductor of the film, Bill Conti (United Artists).

Gonna Get a Girl. w. Al Lewis, m. Howard Simon, 1927. Lewis's first popular song. Later recorded by Tony Pastor (Columbia) and the Benny Goodman Sextet (Capitol).

Gonna Get Along Without Ya Now. w/m Milton Kellem, 1952, 1956. First chart record by Teresa Brewer, with Ray Bloch's Orchestra (Coral). In 1956, Patience and Prudence, the eleven- and fourteen-year-old McIntyre sisters, had a Top 10 record (Liberty). Other chart versions: Skeeter Davis (RCA Victor), 1964; Tracy Dey (Amy), 1964; Trini Lopez (Reprise), 1967.

Gonna Give Her All the Love I've Got. w/m Barrett Strong and Norman Whitfield, 1967. R&B/Pop chart hit by Jimmy Ruffin (Soul).

Gonna Send You Back to Georgia (a.k.a. **Gonna Send You Back to Walker**). w/m Johnnie Mathews and Jake Hammonds, Jr., 1964. Introduced and recorded by Timmy Shaw (Wand). The Animals, using the "Walker" title, also had a popular version (MGM), 1965.

Gonna Send You Back to Walker. See **Gonna Send You Back to Georgia**.

Gonna Take a Lot of River. w/m Jon Kurhajetz and Mark Henley, 1988. #1 Country chart record by The Oak Ridge Boys (MCA).

Go Now. w/m Larry Banks and Milton Bennett, 1965. U.S. Top 10 release of the English recording by The Moody Blues (London).

Good, Good, Good (That's You—That's You). w/m Doris Fisher and Allan Roberts, 1944. Best-selling records by Xavier Cugat, vocal by Del Campo (Columbia) and Sammy Kaye, vocal by Nancy Norman and Billy Williams (Victor).

Good, the Bad and the Ugly, The. m. Ennio Morricone, 1968. Main title theme of Italian film (MP) *The Good, the Bad and the Ugly* (*Il Buono, Il Brutto, Il Cattivo*). Top 10 instrumental record by Hugo Montenegro and his Orchestra (RCA).

Good Bait. m. Tadd Dameron and William "Count" Basie, 1944. Recorded by Dizzy Gillespie and his All-Star Quintet (Manor) and James Moody and Band, 1949 (Prestige).

Goodbye. w/m Jeff Watson and Jack Blades, 1986. Recorded by the quintet Night Ranger (MCA/Camel).

Goodbye. w/m John Lennon and Paul McCartney, 1969. Top 20 record by Mary Hopkin, produced by Paul McCartney in London (Apple).

Goodbye. w/m Gordon Jenkins, 1935. The closing theme of Benny Goodman and his Orchestra, arranged by Gordon Jenkins (Victor).

Goodbye, Boys. w. Andrew B. Sterling and William Dillon, m. Harry Von Tilzer, 1913.

Goodbye, Columbus. w/m James Yester, 1969. Popular single from the soundtrack of (MP) *Goodbye, Columbus*, sung and recorded by The Association (Warner Bros.).

Good-Bye, Dolly Gray. w. Will D. Cobb, m. Paul Barnes, 1900.

Good-Bye, Eliza Jane. w. Andrew B. Sterling, m. Harry Von Tilzer, 1903. Ragtime song, not to be confused with the traditional minstrel number "Goodbye Liza Jane."

Good-Bye, Flo. w/m George M. Cohan, 1904. Sung by Ethel Levey in (TM) *Little Johnny Jones.*

Goodbye, Girls, I'm Through. w. John Golden, m. Ivan Caryll, 1914. From (TM) *Chin-Chin.*

Goodbye, Good Luck, God Bless You. w. J. Keirn Brennan, m. Ernest R. Ball, 1916.

Goodbye, John. w. Edward Eager, m. Alec Wilder, 1949. Introduced and featured by Mabel Mercer.

Goodbye, Little Darlin', Goodbye. w/m Johnny Marvin and Gene Autry, 1940. Introduced by Gene Autry in (MP) *South of the Border* and recorded by him (Columbia), Bing Crosby (Decca), Dick Robertson (Decca), Wayne King (Victor).

Goodbye, Little Girl, Goodbye. w. Will D. Cobb, m. Gus Edwards, 1904. Recorded by Mina Hickman (Victor) and Byron G. Harlan (Columbia record and cylinder).

Goodbye, Little Girl of My Dreams. w. Richard Howard, m. Fred Phillips, 1913.

Goodbye, Ma! Goodbye, Pa! Goodbye, Mule! w. William Herschell, m. Barclay Walker, 1917.

Goodbye, Mr. Ragtime. w. William Jerome, m. Jean Schwartz, 1908. First performed in the touring show (TM) *Cohan and Harris' Minstrels.*

Goodbye, My Lady Love. w/m Joseph E. Howard, 1904.

Goodbye, My Love. w/m James Brown, 1968. Top 10 R&B and Top 40 Pop chart record by James Brown (King).

Goodbye, Rose. w. Addison Burkhart, m. Herbert Ingraham, 1910.

Goodbye, So Long. w/m Ike Turner, 1971. Introduced by Ike and Tina Turner in (MP) *Taking Off.*

Goodbye, Sweetheart, Goodbye. w. Arthur J. Lamb, m. Harry Von Tilzer, 1905.

Good Bye Again. m. Georges Auric, 1961. Theme from (MP) *Goodbye Again,* starring Ingrid Bergman. Leading recording by Ferrante and Teicher (United Artists).

Goodbye Baby. w/m Jack Scott, 1959. Popular record by Jack Scott (Carlton).

Goodbye Blues. w. Dorothy Fields and Arnold Johnson, m. Jimmy McHugh, 1932. Introduced by the four Mills Brothers on radio and records (Brunswick). It subsequently became their theme, in which they vocally simulated the instruments of a band, accompanied only by a guitar played by brother John. They performed it in (MM) *The Big Broadcast* in 1932.

Goodbye Broadway, Hello France. w. C. Francis Reisner and Benny Davis, m. Billy Baskette, 1917. The song was the rousing finale of (TM) *The Passing Show of 1917* and a major World War I hit.

Goodbye Cruel World. w/m Gloria Shayne, 1961. Top 10 hit by James Darren (Colpix).

Goodbye Dear, I'll Be Back in a Year. w/m Mack Kay, 1941. Prior to the entry of the U.S. in World War II, the servicemen's draft was for a one-year period; hence, the optimistic title. Recorded by Horace Heidt and his Musical Knights (Columbia).

Goodbye Girl. w/m David Gates, 1978. Introduced by David Gates on the soundtrack as title song of Neil Simon's (MP) *Goodbye Girl,* 1977. Gates's recording made the Top 20 (Elektra).

Goodbye Jimmy, Goodbye. w/m Jack Vaughn, 1959. Popularized by Kathy Linden (Felsted).

Good-Bye Jonah. w. Al Stillman, m. Arthur Schwartz, 1937. Introduced by Ford L. Buck and John W. Bubbles in (TM) *Virginia.* Recordings by the bands of Tommy Dorsey (Victor), Russ Morgan (Brunswick), Bernie Cummins (Vocalion), Teddy Grace (Decca).

Goodbye Mama, I'm Off to Yokohama. w/m J. Fred Coots, 1942. Written and published immediately after the Japanese attack on Pearl Harbor, 12/7/41, it reached the charts two months later with the recording by Teddy Powell, vocal by Dick Judge and Peggy Mann (Bluebird).

Goodbye My Lover, Goodbye. w/m Robert Mosley, Lamar Simington, and Leroy Swearingen, 1965. Introduced and recorded by the Liverpool quartet The Searchers (Kapp).

Goodbye Saving Grace. w/m Jon Butcher, 1987. Popular track from the album "Wishes" by Jon Butcher (Capitol).

Goodbye Stranger. w/m Rick Davies and Roger Hodgson, 1979. Recorded by the British quartet Supertramp (A&M).

Goodbye Sue. w/m Jimmy Rule, Lou Ricca, and Jules Loman, 1943. Perry Como's first chart record as a single was the best-selling version (Victor).

Goodbye to Love. w. John Bettis, m. Richard Carpenter, 1972. Top 10 record by The Carpenters (A&M).

Goodbye to Love. w/m Geoffrey Clarkson, Harry Clarkson, Carl Field, 1931. Recorded by Benny Krueger (Brunswick), Bert Lown (Victor), Freddie Martin (Columbia).

Goodbye to Rome. See **Arrivederci, Roma**.

Goodbye to You. w/m Zack Smith, 1983. Recorded by the rock band Scandal (Columbia).

Goodbye Yellow Brick Road. w/m Elton John and Bernie Taupin, 1973. Gold record and album title song by British singer Elton John (MCA).

Good Clean Fun. w. Sheldon Harnick, m. Jerry Bock, 1960. Introduced by Maurice Evans and chorus in (TM) *Tenderloin*.

Good Day Sunshine. w/m John Lennon and Paul McCartney, 1967. Introduced by The Beatles in their LP "Revolver" (Capitol), 1966. Chart single by Claudine Longet (A&M).

Good Earth, The. m. Neal Hefti, 1944. Instrumental, introduced, and recorded by Woody Herman and his Orchestra (Columbia).

Good Evening, Caroline. w. Jack Norworth, m. Albert Von Tilzer, 1908.

Good Evening, Friends. w. Irving Caesar, m. Robert Katscher, 1931. Original German words by Geza Herczeg and Karl Farkas. From (TM) *Wonder Bar*, based on the German musical *Wunderbar*. It received its first English-language production in London in 1930. This information also applies to the other two songs "Oh, Donna Clara" and "Elizabeth" (q.v.) from the same show. In London, this was sung by Carl Brisson, and on Broadway, by Al Jolson.

Good for Nothin' but Love. w. Eddie DeLange, m. James Van Heusen, 1939. Featured and recorded by Benny Goodman, vocal by Martha Tilton (Victor) and also recorded by Nan Wynn (Vocalion).

Good for You—Bad for Me. w. B. G. De Sylva and Lew Brown, m. Ray Henderson, 1930. Sung by Russ Brown and Pearl Osgood in (TM) *Flying High*. The song was not in the film version. Recorded by Fred Waring's Pennsylvanians (Victor) and the Knickerbockers (Columbia).

Good Friends. w/m Joni Mitchell, 1986. Chart single by Joni Mitchell (Geffen).

Good Friends. w/m Murray Grand, 1980. Popular with cabaret artists.

Good Girls Don't. w/m Doug Fieger, 1979. Recorded by the group The Knack (Capitol).

Good Golly Miss Molly. w/m Robert Blackwell and John Marascalco, 1958. Introduced and Top 10 record by Little Richard (Specialty). Revived by the English group The Swinging Blue Jeans (Imperial), 1964. Mitch Ryder and The Detroit Wheels had a Top 10 hit, in a recorded medley titled "Devil With the Blue Dress On and Good Golly Miss Molly" (New Voice), 1976.

Good-Hearted Woman, A. w/m Waylon Jennings and Willie Nelson, 1972. Country and Pop chart hit by the writer/singers who recorded as Waylon and Willie (RCA).

Good Life, The. w. Jack Reardon, m. Sacha Distel, 1963. Based on melodic theme from the French film (MP) *The Seven Capital Sins*. Popularized by Tony Bennett (Columbia).

Good Little, Bad Little You. w. Bud Green, m. Sam H. Stept, 1929.

Good Lovin'. w/m Rudy Clark and Arthur Resnick, 1965. Introduced by The Olympics (Loma). #1 record by The Young Rascals (Atlantic), 1966.

Good Lovin'. w/m Leroy Kirkland, Danny Taylor, Ahmet Ertegun, and Jesse Stone, 1953. Top 10 R&B record by The Clovers (Atlantic).

Good Lovin' (Makes It Right). w/m Billy Sherrill, 1971. Country hit by Tammy Wynette (Epic).

Good Lovin' Ain't Easy to Come By. w/m Nicholas Ashford and Valerie Simpson, 1969. Top 40 record by Marvin Gaye and Tammi Terrell (Tamla).

Good Luck Charm. w/m Aaron Schroeder and Wally Gold, 1962. #1 hit record by Elvis Presley (RCA).

Good Man Is Hard to Find, A. w/m Eddie Green, 1918. Introduced by Alberta Hunter, recorded by Marion Harris (Victor), and popularized by Sophie Tucker. It was featured in (MM) *Meet Danny Wilson*, 1952.

Good Mornin'. w/m Sam Coslow, 1937. Introduced by Martha Raye in (MM) *Mountain Music*.

Good Morning. w. Arthur Freed, m. Nacio Herb Brown, 1939. Introduced by Mickey Rooney and Judy Garland in (MM) *Babes in Arms*. Gene Kelly, Debbie Reynolds, and Donald O'Connor sang it in (MM) *Singin' in the Rain* in 1952. Their recorded version was released as a single (MGM).

Good Morning, Carrie. w. Cecil Mack, m. Albert Von Tilzer, 1902. Featured and recorded by Bert Williams and George Walker (Victor).

Good Morning, Dearie. w. Anne Caldwell, m. Jerome Kern, 1921. Introduced by Louise Groody in (TM) *Good Morning, Dearie*.

Good Morning, Mr. Zip-Zip-Zip! (with Your Hair Cut Just As Short As Mine. w/m Robert Lloyd, 1918.

Good Morning Blues. w/m William "Count" Basie, Eddie Durham, and Jimmy Rushing, 1938. Introduced and recorded by Count Basie and his Orchestra, vocal by Jimmy Rushing (Decca). Also recorded by Huddie "Leadbelly" Ledbetter (Asch).

Good Morning Glory. w. Mack Gordon, m. Harry Revel. 1933. From (MM) *Sitting Pretty* and sung by practically the entire cast: Jack Haley, Jack Oakie, Art Jarrett, Ginger Rogers, and the Pickens Sisters. The latter recorded it (Victor) as did George Hall, vocal by Loretta Lee (Bluebird).

Good Morning Heartache. w/m Irene Higginbotham, Ervin Drake, and Dan Fisher, 1946. Introduced, recorded by, and associated with Billie Holiday (Decca). It was sung by Diana Ross, as Holiday, in (MM) *Lady Sings the Blues*, 1972. Ross's recording rated in the Top 40 (Motown), 1973.

Good Morning Starshine. w. Gerome Ragni and James Rado, m. Galt MacDermot, 1967. Introduced by Jill O'Hara and company in the off-Broadway production (TM) *Hair*. In the Broadway version (TM) *Hair*, 1968, it was sung by Lynn Kellogg, Melba Moore, James Rado, and Gerome Ragni. Top 10 single by Oliver (Jubilee).

Good Morning to All. See **Happy Birthday to You**.

Good News. w/m Sam Cooke, 1964. Hit record by Sam Cooke (RCA).

Good News. w. B. G. DeSylva and Lew Brown, m. Ray Henderson, 1927. Introduced by Zelma O'Neal in (TM) *Good News*. In the first film version, (MM) *Good News*, 1930, the number was performed by Dorothy McNulty (later known as Penny Singleton) and the ensemble. Joan McCracken performed it in the 1947 version, and Gordon MacRae, Ernest Borgnine, and Dan Dailey, as DeSylva, Brown and Henderson, respectively, demonstrated it in their screen biography (MM) *The Best Things in Life Are Free*, 1956. George Olsen's Orchestra, which appeared in the original show, also recorded it as one of four sides (two singles) of songs from the score (Victor).

Goodnight. w/m Roy Orbison and Bill Dees, 1965. Introduced and recorded by Roy Orbison (Monument).

Goodnight, Irene. w/m Huddie "Leadbelly" Ledbetter, arr. by John Lomax and Alan Lomax, 1950. The first recording was by Leadbelly for the Library of Congress archives, while he was serving time in a Louisiana State prison in the mid-thirties. The Weavers, with Gordon Jenkins's Orchestra (Decca), brought it to the general public with a #1 hit in 1950. Other popular versions by Gordon MacRae and Jo Stafford (Capitol) and Red Foley and Ernest Tubb (Decca).

Goodnight, Ladies. w. Harry H. Williams, m. Egbert Van Alstyne, 1911.

Good Night, Little Girl, Good Night. w. Julia M. Hayes, m. J. C. Macy, 1898. Popular song of the day. Revived in 1906 via the successful recording of Henry Burr (Columbia).

Good Night, Lovely Little Lady. w. Mack Gordon, m. Harry Revel, 1934. Sung by Leon Errol in (MM) *We're Not Dressing*.

Goodnight, My Beautiful. w. Jack Yellen, m. Sammy Fain, 1939. Sung by Harry Stockwell and danced by The Knight Sisters in (TM) *George White's Scandals* (1939 edition).

Goodnight, My Love. w. Mack Gordon, m. Harry Revel, 1936. Introduced by Shirley Temple and reprised by Alice Faye in (MM) *Stowaway*. Alice Faye recorded it (Brunswick), but the biggest selling record was by Benny Goodman, vocal by Ella Fitzgerald (Victor). Hildegarde coupled it with "I Wanna Go to the Zoo" (q.v.) from the above film (Columbia). Used as closing theme of Jim Lowe's popular radio program on WNEW, New York.

Goodnight, My Own True Love. w. William Jerome, m. Jean Schwartz, 1904. From (TM) *Piff! Paff!! Pouf!!!*

Goodnight, Nurse. w. Thomas J. Gray, m. W. Raymond Walker, 1912.

Goodnight, Sweetheart, Goodnight. See **Goodnight, Well It's Time to Go.**

Goodnight, Well It's Time to Go. w/m Calvin Carter and James Hudson, 1954. Originally titled "Goodnight, Sweetheart, Goodnight." R&B hit by The Spaniels (Vee-Jay), covered by the McGuire Sisters, who had a hit record (Coral). Sunny Gale, with Joe Reisman's Orchestra, had a popular version (RCA Victor). Heard in the background of (MM) *La Bamba*, 1987; and sung by Tom Selleck, Steve Gutenberg, and Ted Danson in (MP) *Three Men and a Baby*, 1988.

Goodnight, Wherever You Are. w/m Dick Robertson, Al Hoffman, and Frank Weldon, 1944. Recorded by Russ Morgan and his Orchestra (Decca) and Mary Martin (Decca).

Goodnight Angel. w. Herb Magidson, m. Allie Wrubel, 1938. Introduced in (MM) *Radio City Revels*. Recorded by Hal Kemp, vocal by Bob Allen (Victor). Kemp and band were in the movie. Also recorded by the bands of Artie Shaw (Brunswick), Shep Fields (Bluebird), Reggie Childs (Decca).

Goodnight Little Girl of My Dreams. w. Charles Tobias, m. Joe Burke, 1933. Featured and recorded by Elton Britt (Melotone). Also recorded by Victor Young's Orchestra, vocal by Red McKenzie (Brunswick).

Goodnight Moon. w/m Walter Donaldson 1931. Popular records by Jack Denny and Orchestra (Victor); Ben Selvin, with vocal by

Dick Robertson (Columbia); the Pickens Sisters (Victor); Roy Fox, vocal by Al Bowlly (Br. Decca).

Goodnight My Love (Pleasant Dreams). w/m George Motola and John Marascalco, 1957. Top 40 record by The McGuire Sisters (Coral). Later chart records by Ray Peterson (RCA), 1959; The Fleetwoods (Dolton), 1963; Ben E. King (Atco), 1966; Paul Anka (RCA), 1969.

Goodnight My Someone. w/m Meredith Willson, 1957. Introduced by Barbara Cook in (TM) *The Music Man.* In the film version (MM) *The Music Man,* 1962, it was sung by Shirley Jones and Robert Preston.

Goodnight Saigon. w/m Billy Joel, 1983. Recorded by Billy Joel (Columbia).

Goodnight Sweetheart. w/m Ray Noble, James Campbell, and Reg Connelly, 1931. English song. "American version" by Rudy Vallee, who introduced it in the U.S. on his radio program and had a best-seller (Victor). It was interpolated in (TM) *Earl Carroll's Vanities of 1931* by Milton Watson and Woods Miller. The song had huge sheet music sales and was the #1 song of the year and became the standard closing number for dance bands. In films, it was performed by Ray Noble in (MM) *The Big Broadcast* of 1936 (in 1935!), sung by Rudy Vallee in (MP) *The Palm Beach Story* in 1942, sung by Gene Autry in (MM) *Stardust on the Sage* in 1942, sung by a chorus in (MM) *You Were Meant for Me* in 1948.

Goodnight Tonight. w/m Paul McCartney, 1979. Top 10 record by McCartney's group Wings (Columbia).

Good Ol' Boys. See **Theme from "Dukes of Hazzard."**

Good Old Fashioned Cocktail, A (with a Good Old Fashioned Girl). w. Al Dubin, m. Harry Warren, 1935. Introduced by Ruby Keeler in (MM) *Go Into Your Dance.*

Good Old U.S.A., The. w. Jack Drislane, m. Theodore F. Morse, 1906.

Good Ole Boys Like Me. w/m Bob McDill, 1980. Country hit record by Don Williams (MCA).

Good Rockin' Tonight. w/m Roy Brown, 1948. Considered by many in popular music to be the forerunner of the idiom mixing rhythm and blues with rock 'n' roll. First hit record by Wynonie "Mr. Blues" Harris (King). The writer, Roy Brown, had a Top 10 R&B chart version (DeLuxe). Revived by Pat Boone (Dot), 1959.

Good Thing. w/m David Steele and Roland Gift, 1989. Hit single by the group Fine Young Cannibals (I.R.S.).

Good Thing. w/m Mark Lindsay, Terry Melcher, and Paul Revere, 1967. Top 10 record by Paul Revere and The Raiders (Columbia).

Good Thing Going. w/m Stephen Sondheim, 1981. Introduced by Lonny Price, Jim Walton, and company in (TM) *Merrily We Roll Along.*

Good Time Baby. w. Kal Mann, m. Bernie Lowe and Dave Appell, 1961. Recorded by Bobby Rydell (Cameo).

Good-Time Charley. w. Johnny Burke, m. James Van Heusen, 1946. Introduced by Bing Crosby and Bob Hope in (MM) *Road to Utopia.*

Good Time Charlies. w/m Jerry Chesnut, 1969. Top 10 Country chart record by Del Reeves (United Artists).

Good Time Charlie's Got the Blues. w/m Danny O'Keefe, 1972. Introduced and Top 10 record by Danny O'Keefe (Signpost).

Good Times. w/m George Young and Harry Vanda, 1987. Chart single from the soundtrack of (MP) *The Lost Boys* by the Australian group INXS and Jimmy Barnes (Atlantic).

Good Times. w/m Bernard Edwards and Nile Rodgers, 1979. Written and #1 gold record by the producers of the group Chic (Atlantic).

Good Times. w. Marilyn Bergman and Alan Bergman, m. Dave Grusin, 1974. Theme of series (TVP) "Good Times."

Good Times, Bad Times. w/m John Bonham, Jimmy Page, and John Paul Jones, 1969. Written by members of, and recorded by the British group, Led Zeppelin (Atlantic).

Good Times Are Coming, The. w. Hal David, m. John Barry, 1970. Sung by Mama Cass on the soundtrack of (MP) *Monte Walsh*.

Good Times Roll. w/m Ric Ocasek, 1979. Written by the lead singer of The Cars (Elektra).

Good Timin'. w/m Clint Ballard, Jr. and Fred Tobias, 1960. Top 10 record by Jimmy Jones (Cub).

Good to Go. w/m James Avery, Tony Fischer, Robert Reed, and T. Reed, Jr., 1986. Introduced by the group Trouble Funk in (MM) *Good to Go*, and on records (Island).

Good Vibrations. w. Mike Love and Brian Wilson, m. Brian Wilson, 1966. #1 gold record by The Beach Boys (Capitol). Revived by Todd Rundgren (Bearsville), 1976.

Good Woman Blues. w/m Ken McDuffie, 1976. Country chart hit by Mel Tillis (MCA).

Good Year for the Roses, A. w/m Jerry Chesnut, 1970. Hit Country record by George Jones (Musicor).

Goody Goodbye. w. James Cavanaugh, m. Nat Simon, 1940. Featured and recorded by Dolly Dawn (Vocalion); Ted Weems, vocal by Perry Como (Decca); The Smoothies (Bluebird); Gray Gordon's Orchestra (Victor).

Goody Goody. w/m Johnny Mercer and Matty Malneck, 1936. Song made "Your Hit Parade" for twelve weeks, and the #1 spot for four. Popularized by Benny Goodman, vocal by Helen Ward (Victor), and Bob Crosby (Decca). It was revived in the fifties by Paula Kelly and the Modernaires (Coral).

Goody Goody Gumdrops. w/m Billy Carl, Jerry Kasenetz, Jeff Katz, and Reid Whitelaw, 1968. Top 40 record by The 1910 Fruitgum Company (Buddah).

Goody Two Shoes. w/m Adam Ant and Marco Pirroni, 1982. Recorded by the English singer Adam Ant (Epic).

Goofus. w. Gus Kahn, m. Wayne King and William Harold, 1932. Novelty, with a Country and Western flavor. Among many recordings: Red Nichols (Brunswick), Hoosier Hot Shots (Victor), Wayne King (Victor), Phil Harris (Victor), Freddie "Schnicklefritz" Fisher (Decca), Louise Massey and the Westerners (V-disc 12″), Johnny Mercer (Capitol).

Goo Goo Barabajagal (Love Is Hot). w/m Donovan Leitch, 1969. Top 40 U.S. release by the Scottish singer/writer Donovan (Epic).

Goona Goo, The. w/m Fred Ahlert, Harry Reser, and Joe Young, 1937. Swing novelty. Among bands who recorded it were: Tommy Dorsey (Victor); Bunny Berigan (Brunswick); Clyde McCoy (Decca); Johnny Hamp (Bluebird); Boots and His Buddies, under title of "The Goo" (Bluebird).

Goonies 'R' Good Enough, The. w/m Cyndi Lauper, Stephen Lunt, and Arthur Stead, 1985. From the film (MP) *The Goonies*, Cyndi Lauper had a Top 10 single (Portrait).

Go On with the Wedding. w/m Arthur Korb, Charlie Purvis, and Milton Yakus, 1956. Recorded by Patti Page (Mercury), Kitty Kallen and Georgie Shaw (Decca).

Go See the Doctor. w/m Mohandas DeWese, 1987. Written and recorded by rap singer Kool Moe Dee (Jive).

Got a Bran' New Suit. w. Howard Dietz, m. Arthur Schwartz, 1935. Introduced by Ethel Waters (singing) and Eleanor Powell (dancing) in (TM) *At Home Abroad*. Recorded by Eleanor Powell (Victor); Louis Armstrong (Decca); George Hall, vocal by Dolly Dawn (Bluebird).

Got a Date with an Angel. w. Clifford Grey and Sonny Miller, m. Jack Waller and Joseph Turnbridge, 1931. An English song,

first recorded by Ray Noble and the New Mayfair Orchestra (Victor). The best-selling record
was by Hal Kemp, with vocal by Skinnay Ennis (Brunswick). Ennis formed his own band
and used it as his theme. He recorded it as a
single (Signature) and title song of his LP
(MGM). Kemp recorded a new version (Victor), 1937.

Got a Hold on Me. w/m Christine McVie
and Todd Sharp, 1984. Top 10 record by the
British singer Christine McVie (Warner
Bros.).

Got a Pair of New Shoes. w. Arthur
Freed, m. Nacio Herb Brown, 1937. The song
was written for and performed by Eleanor Powell in (MM) *Broadway Melody of '38*, but was
cut from the film before release. It was then
sung by Judy Garland in (MM) *Thoroughbreds
Don't Cry.*

**Got Her Off My Hands But Can't Get Her
Off My Mind.** w. Sam Lewis and Joe
Young, m. Fred Phillips, 1951. Written in the
thirties, popularized by The Mills Brothers
(Decca).

Got Me Doin' Things. w. Mack Gordon,
m. Harry Revel, 1935. From (MM) *Love in
Bloom*. Recorded by Ted Fio Rito and his
Orchestra (Brunswick); Teddy Hill, vocal by
Bill Dillard (Melotone).

Got My Heart Set on You. w/m Dobie
Gray and Bud Reneau, 1986. Introduced on
the Country charts by the trio Mason Dixon
(Texas). Covered and #1 Country chart record
by John Conlee (Columbia).

Got My Mind on Music. w. Mack Gordon,
m. Harry Revel, 1938. Introduced by Alice
Faye, Joan Davis, Marjorie Weaver, and the
Raymond Scott Quintet in (MM) *Sally, Irene
and Mary.*

Got My Mind Set on You. w/m Rudy
Clark, 1987. #1 single by George Harrison
from his album "Cloud Nine" (Dark Horse).
Originally recorded by James Ray (Caprice),
1962.

Got My Mojo Working. w/m McKinley
Morganfield, 1966. Popular record by or-
ganist/singer Jimmy Smith (Verve).

Got No Time. w. Gus Kahn, m. Richard
Whiting, 1925. In 1925, the Little Ramblers
(formerly the Scranton Sirens), featuring a
young trombonist named Tommy Dorsey, recorded this. In 1939, Dorsey, with his own big
band, again recorded it (Victor).

Go to Sleep, Go to Sleep, Go to Sleep.
w. Sammy Cahn, m. Fred Spielman, 1950.
Popular record by Mary Martin and Arthur
Godfrey (Columbia).

Go to Sleepy, Little Baby. w. Harry Tobias and Henry Tobias, m. Judy Canova and
Zeke Canova, 1946. Theme song of Judy Canova, and recorded by her (Mercury).

Gotta Be This or That. w/m Sunny Skylar,
1945. Benny Goodman did the vocal on this
best-seller, with his Orchestra (Columbia).
Sammy Kaye, vocal by Nancy Norman and
Billy Williams (Victor); and Glen Gray and the
Casa Loma Band, vocal by Fats Daniels (Decca), also had popular versions.

Gotta Feelin' for You. w. Jo Trent, m.
Louis Alter, 1929. Introduced by Joan Crawford, Paul Gibbons, and the Baltimore Trio in
(MM) *Hollywood Revue of 1929*. A year later it
was heard in (MM) *Chasing Rainbows.*

Gotta Get Me Somebody to Love. w/m
Allie Wrubel, 1946. Introduced by Gregory
Peck in (MP) *Duel in the Sun*. Recorded by
George Paxton and his Orchestra (Majestic).

Gotta Get Some Shut-eye. w. Johnny
Mercer, m. Walter Donaldson, 1939. Records:
Glenn Miller, vocal by Marion Hutton (Blue-
bird); Benny Goodman, vocal by Martha Tilton
(Victor); Kay Kyser, vocal by Ginny Simms
(Brunswick).

Gotta Get You Home Tonight. w/m Mc-
Kinley Horton and Ronnie Broomfield, 1985.
Recorded by Eugene Wilde (pseudonym for
Broomfield) (Philly World).

Gotta Gimme Whatcha Got. w/m Julia Lee, 1947. Introduced and recorded by Julia Lee (Capitol).

Gotta Have Me Go with You. w. Ira Gershwin, m. Harold Arlen, 1954. Introduced by Judy Garland, Jack Harmon, and Don McCabe in (MM) *A Star Is Born.*

Gotta Hold On to This Feeling. w/m Johnny Bristol, Joe Hinton, and Pam Sawyer, 1970. R&B/Pop hit by Jr. Walker and The All Stars (Soul).

Gotta Move. w/m Peter Matz, 1963. Featured and recorded by Barbra Streisand (Columbia).

Gotta Serve Somebody. w/m Bob Dylan, 1987. R&B chart single by Luther Ingram (Profile). Dylan introduced the song eight years earlier (Columbia).

Gotta Travel On. w/m Paul Clayton, Larry Ehrlich, David Lazar, and Tom Six, 1959. Based on nineteenth century English song. This version recorded by Billy Grammer (Monument). Timi Yuro had a popular record in 1963 (Liberty).

Got the Bench, Got the Park (But I Haven't Got You). w/m Al Sherman, Al Lewis, and Fred Phillips, 1931. Among the recordings were the orchestras of Paul Whiteman (Victor), Fred Rich (Columbia), and Noble Sissle (Brunswick).

Got the Jitters. w. Paul Francis Webster and Billy Rose, m. John Jacob Loeb, 1934. Introduced in a production number featuring Ben Pollack's Band in a night club at the Casino de Paris, New York. Pollack recorded it (Columbia), as did Isham Jones, vocal by Eddie Stone (Victor); Don Redman (Melotone); and Adrian Rollini, heading an all-star studio band (Melotone).

Got the Moon in My Pocket. w. Johnny Burke, m. James Van Heusen, 1942. Introduced by Kay Kyser and his Orchestra in (MM) *My Favorite Spy,* and on records (Columbia).

Got the South in My Soul. w/m Ned Washington, Lee Wiley, and Victor Young, 1932. Introduced by Lee Wiley and recorded by Harlan Lattimore (Columbia) and Don Redman's Orchestra (Brunswick).

Got to Be Real. w/m David Foster, Cheryl Lynn, and David Paitch, 1979. Gold record #1 R&B, crossover Pop chart hit by Cheryl Lynn (Columbia).

Got to Be There. w/m Elliot Willensky, 1971. Top 10 record, the first solo hit by Michael Jackson (Motown). Revived by Chaka Khan (Warner Bros.), 1983.

Got to Get You into My Life. w/m John Lennon and Paul McCartney, 1975, 1978. Introduced by The Beatles in their album "Revolver" (Capitol), 1966. Hit singles by Blood, Sweat & Tears (Columbia), 1975; The Beatles (Capitol), 1976. Sung on the soundtrack of (MM) *Sgt. Pepper's Lonely Hearts Club Band,* 1978, and gold record by Earth, Wind & Fire (Columbia).

Got to Get You off My Mind. w/m Solomon Burke, Delores Burke, and J. B. Moore, 1965. Crossover (R&B/Pop) hit record by Solomon Burke (Atlantic).

Got to Give It Up. w/m Marvin Gaye, 1977. #1 single by Marvin Gaye (Tamla).

Got You on My Mind. w/m Joe Thomas and Howard Biggs, 1952. Leading record by John Greer (RCA Victor).

Go Way Back Sit Down. w. Elmer Bowman, m. Al Johns, 1901.

Go Where You Wanna Go. w/m John Philips, 1967. First chart record by The 5th Dimension (Soul City).

Go Your Own Way. w/m Lindsey Buckingham, 1977. Top 10 record by the British group Fleetwood Mac (Warner Bros.).

Graceland. w/m Paul Simon, 1986. Title song of the album by Paul Simon (Warner Bros.). Name derived from Elvis Presley's Tennessee home, now a museum.

Graduation Day. w/m Joe Sherman and Noel Sherman, 1956. Popularized by The Rover Boys (ABC-Paramount) and The Four Freshmen (Capitol). Revived in 1967 by The Arbors (Date).

Grand Knowing You. w. Sheldon Harnick, m. Jerry Bock, 1963. Introduced by Jack Cassidy in (TM) *She Loves Me.*

Grandma Got Run Over by a Reindeer. w/m Randy Brooks, 1983. Country Christmas novelty, introduced by the husband and wife duo, Elmo 'n' Patsy [Shropshire], recorded by them (Soundwaves), and heard in (MP) *The Right Stuff.*

Grandma Harp. w/m Merle Haggard, 1972. Country chart hit by Merle Haggard (Capitol).

Grandma's Hands. w/m Bill Withers, 1971. Recorded by Bill Withers (Sussex).

Grandmother's Song. w/m Steve Martin, 1978. Comedy record by film and TV star Steve Martin (Warner Bros.).

Grand Old Ivy. w/m Frank Loesser, 1961. Robert Morse and Rudy Vallee introduced it in (TM) *How to Succeed in Business Without Really Trying* and repeated it in the film version (MM) *How to Succeed in Business Without Really Trying,* 1966.

Grandpa (Tell Me 'bout the Good Old Days). w/m Jamie O'Hara, 1986. #1 Country chart song by the mother-and-daughter duo The Judds (RCA). Winner, Grammy Award (NARAS) Country Song of the Year.

Grandpa's Spells. m. Ferdinand "Jelly Roll" Morton, 1925. First record by Creath's Jazzomaniacs (Okeh). Jelly Roll Morton recorded it, featuring Kid Ory on trombone (Victor), 1927.

Grand Piano Blues. m. Earl Hines, 1929. Recorded by Hines (Victor).

Grant Avenue. w. Oscar Hammerstein II, m. Richard Rodgers, 1958. Introduced by Pat Suzuki in (TM) *Flower Drum Song.* In (MM) *Flower Drum Song,* 1961, it was dubbed on the soundtrack by B. J. Baker for Nancy Kwan.

Grass Is Always Greener, The. w. Fred Ebb, m. John Kander, 1981. Introduced by Lauren Bacall and Marilyn Cooper in (TM) *Woman of the Year.*

Grass Is Getting Greener All the Time, The. w/m Johnny Burke, Charles Newman, and Harold Spina, 1933. Popularized on radio and records by Little Jack Little (Bluebird).

Grass Is Greener, The. w/m Barry Mann and Mike Anthony, 1963. Recorded by Brenda Lee (Decca).

Graveyard Bound Blues. w/m Monette Moore and Arthur Ray, 1924. First recordings by Monette Moore (Ajax) and Ida Cox (Paramount).

Gravier Street Blues. w/m Clarence Williams, 1924. Recorded by Williams as an instrumental (Okeh), and vocally by Lonnie Johnson with Johnny Dodds' Band (Decca), 1940.

Gravy (for My Mashed Potatoes). w. Kal Mann, m. Dave Appell, 1962. Hit successor by Dee Dee Sharp (Cameo) to her "Mashed Potato Time" (q.v.).

Gravy Waltz. m. Steve Allen and Ray Brown, 1963. Instrumental record by Steve Allen (Dot). Winner Grammy Award (NARAS) as Best Original Jazz Composition.

Grazing in the Grass. w. Harry Elston, m. Philemon Hou, 1968. #1 gold record instrumental by trumpeter/bandleader Hugh Masakela (Uni). The Friends of Distinction had a gold record vocal version (RCA), 1969.

Grease. w/m Barry Gibb, 1978. Sung on the soundtrack of (MM) *Grease,* and #1 platinum record by Frankie Valli (RSO). The song was written specially for the film version of the stage musical.

Great Airplane Strike, The. w/m Mark Lindsay, Terry Melcher, and Paul Revere,

1966. Top 40 record by Paul Revere and The Raiders (Columbia).

Great Balls of Fire. w/m Jack Hammer and Otis Blackwell, 1957. Jerry Lee Lewis's recording (Sun) sold over five million copies. He has performed it in (MM) *Jamboree*, 1957, and (MM) *American Hot Wax*, 1978. Tiny Tim's version (Reprise) received some airplay in 1978.

Great Day! w. William (Billy) Rose and Edward Eliscu, m. Vincent Youmans, 1929. Introduced by baritone Lois Deppe and the Jubilee Singers in (TM) *Great Day!* Paul Whiteman's recording (Victor) coupled the song with another standout from the show, "Without A Song," (q.v.), both with solo vocals by Bing Crosby. The third standard from this short-lived production was "More Than You Know" (q.v.). Barbra Streisand sang it in a production number in (MM) *Funny Lady*, 1974. John Raitt sang it in (TM) *A Musical Jubilee*, 1975.

Greatest American Hero. See **Theme from "The Greatest American Hero."**

Greatest Love of All, The. w. Linda Creed, m. Michael Masser, 1977. Sung on the soundtrack of the Muhammad Ali biography (MP) *The Greatest*, by George Benson, who then had a chart single (Arista). Whitney Houston recorded it in her debut album (Arista), 1985. After being released as the "B" side of a single, and because of the popularity gained from airplay, it was re-released and became a #1 hit.

Greatest Show on Earth, The. w. Ned Washington, m. Victor Young, 1952. Title song of (MP) *The Greatest Show on Earth*.

Great Gosh A'mighty! (It's a Matter of Time). w/m Richard Penniman and Billy Preston, 1986. Introduced by Little Richard [Penniman] in (MP) *Down and Out in Beverly Hills*, and on records by Little Richard (MCA).

Great Indoors, The. w/m Cole Porter, 1930. Introduced by Frances Williams and ensemble in (TM) *The New Yorkers*.

Great Lie, The. m. Andy Gibson and Cab Calloway, 1944. Instrumental, featured by Harry James and his Orchestra (Columbia).

Great Pretender, The. w/m Buck Ram, 1956. #1 hit record by The Platters (Mercury) and one of the top ten songs of the year. The Platters performed it in (MM) *The Girl Can't Help It*, 1957. Stan Freberg had a popular parody recording (Capitol).

Great Speckle(d) Bird, The. w/m Rev. Guy Smith, 1937. Featured and recorded by Roy Acuff (Okeh).

Green, Green. w/m Randy Sparks and Barry McGuire, 1963. The writers, members of The New Christy Minstrels, based the number on traditional songs and recorded it with their group (Columbia).

Green, Green Grass of Home. w/m Curly Putman, 1966. Crossover (C&W/Pop) hit introduced by Porter Wagoner (RCA). At the end of the year, Tom Jones's version, recorded in England, became a hit in the U.S. and established the song in the Pop market (Parrot).

Greenback Dollar. w/m Hoyt Axton and Ken Ramsey, 1963. Based on a traditional American folk song. Recorded by The Kingston Trio (Capitol).

Greenbacks. w/m Renald Richard, 1955. Top 10 R&B chart record by Ray Charles, who recorded this at a radio station in Atlanta, Georgia (Atlantic).

Green Door, The. w. Marvin Moore, m. Bob Davis, 1956. #1 record by Jim Lowe (Dot).

Greener Pastures. w/m Marijohn Wilkin, 1961. C&W record by Stonewall Jackson (Columbia).

Green Eyed Lady. w/m Jerry Corbetta, J. C. Phillips, and David Riordan, 1970. Top 20 record by the group Sugarloaf (Liberty).

Green Eyes. w. E. Rivera and Eddie Woods (Engl.), m. Nilo Menendez, 1931, 1941. This Cuban song, originally titled "Aquellos Ojos Verdes," with Spanish lyrics by

Adolfo Utrero, was introduced by Don Azpiazu and his Havana Casino Orchestra. In 1941, Jimmy Dorsey recorded it with a vocal by Bob Eberly and Helen O'Connell (Decca). They had a #1 record and the song was high on "Your Hit Parade." Dorsey, Eberly, and O'Connell performed the song in (MM) *The Fabulous Dorseys* in 1946.

Greenfields. w/m Terry Gilkyson, Rich Dehr, and Frank Miller, 1960. Popularized by The Brothers Four (Columbia).

Green Finch and Linnet Bird. w/m Stephen Sondheim, 1978. Introduced by Sara Rice in (TM) *Sweeney Todd, The Demon Barber of Fleet Street.*

Green Grass. w/m Tommy Boyce and Susan Hudson, 1966. Top 10 record by Gary Lewis and The Playboys (Liberty).

Green Grass Starts to Grow, The. w. Hal David, m. Burt Bacharach, 1971. Recorded by Dionne Warwick (Scepter).

Green Leaves of Summer, The. w. Paul Francis Webster, m. Dimitri Tiomkin, 1960. From (MP) *The Alamo.* Nominated for Academy Award, 1960. Leading vocal record by The Brothers Four (Columbia). Popular instrumental by the British Dixieland band, Kenny Ball and his Jazzmen (Kapp), 1962.

Green Light. w/m Annette Tucker and Nancie Mantz, 1968. Recorded by The American Breed (Acta).

Green Light. w/m Hank Thompson, 1948. Introduced and recorded by Hank Thompson (Capitol).

Green Onions. m. Steve Cropper, Al Jackson, Jr., Lewis Steinberg, and Booker T., 1962. Million-selling instrumental by Booker T. and the MG's (Stax).

Green River. w/m John Fogerty, 1968. Hit record by Creedence Clearwater Revival (Fantasy).

Green Tambourine. w/m Paul Leka and Shelley Pinz, 1968. #1 gold record by The Lemon Pipers (Buddah).

Green-Up Time. w. Alan Jay Lerner, m. Kurt Weill, 1948. Introduced by Nanette Fabray in (TM) *Love Life.* Popular recording by Buddy Clark (Columbia).

Green Years. w/m Don Reid and Arthur Altman, 1954. Popular recording by Eddie Fisher (RCA Victor).

Grievin' My Heart Out for You. w/m Jimmie Davis, 1946. Leading records by The Sons of the Pioneers (Victor), Ted Daffan (Decca).

Grin and Bear It. w/m John D. Loudermilk and Marijohn Wilkin, 1959. Hit C&W record by Jimmy Newman (MGM).

Grits Ain't Groceries (All Around the World). 1969. Crossover (R&B/Pop) record by Little Milton (Checker).

Grizzly Bear. w/m Irving Berlin and George Bottsford, 1910. Introduced by Sophie Tucker. Popular records by The American Quartet (Victor) and Arthur Collins (Indestructible). Sung by Alice Faye and danced by Jack Oakie and June Havoc in (MM) *Hello, Frisco, Hello,* 1943.

Groove Line, The. w/m Rod Temperton, 1978. Gold record by the group Heatwave (Epic).

Groove Me. w/m King Floyd, 1970. #1 R&B and Pop Top 20 gold record by King Floyd (Chimneyville). Fern Kinney had a chart version (Malaco), 1979.

Groovin'. w/m Eddie Brigati and Felix Cavaliere, 1967. #1 gold record by The Young Rascals (Atlantic). Top 40 instrumental version by Booker T. and The MG's (Stax).

Groovin' High. m. John Birks "Dizzy" Gillespie, 1945. Initially recorded by Dizzy Gillespie and his Sextet (Guild); later by Gerald Wilson and his big band (Excelsior).

Groovy Grubworm. m. Harlow Wilcox and Bobby Warren, 1969. Top 40 instrumental by Harlow Wilcox and The Oakies (Plantation).

Groovy Kind of Love, A. w/m Toni Wine and Carole Bayer Sager, 1966, 1988. Top 10

U.S. release by the British group The Mind-benders (Fontana). Revived by Phil Collins in (MP) *Buster*, the soundtrack album, and a hit single (Atlantic), 1988.

Groovy Situation. w/m Herman Davis and Russell R. Lewis, 1970. Top 20 record by Gene Chandler (Mercury).

Growin' Up. w/m Bruce Springsteen, 1972. Introduced by Bruce Springsteen and included in his album "Greetings from Asbury Park" (Columbia). Chart record by Dan Hill (20th Century), 1976.

Grow Some Funk of Your Own. w/m Elton John, Bernie Taupin, and David Johnstone, 1976. Top 20 record by the British singer Elton John (MCA).

G.T.O. w/m John Wilkin, 1964. Top 10 record by Ronny and The Daytonas (Mala).

Guaglione (a.k.a. The Man Who Plays the Mandolino). w. Alan Bergman and Marilyn Bergman (Engl.), m. Guiseppe Fucilli, 1958. Introduced by Dean Martin in (MM) *10,000 Bedrooms*. Original Italian words by Nicola Salerno were heard on the recording by Renato Carasone (Capitol). Perez Prado and his Orchestra had a popular instrumental version (RCA).

Guantanamera. w. José Marti (Sp.), m. Pete Seeger and Hector Angulo, 1966. Setting of the poem by the Cuban writer. Introduced by Pete Seeger. Top 10 record by the California-based trio The Sandpipers (A&M).

Guenevere. w. Alan Jay Lerner, m. Frederick Loewe, 1960. Sung by the chorus in (TM) *Camelot*, and in (MM) *Camelot*, 1967.

Guess I'll Hang My Tears Out to Dry. w. Sammy Cahn, m. Jule Styne, 1945. From (TM) *Glad to See You*, which closed in Philadelphia during its pre-Broadway tryout. Harry James, with vocal by Kitty Kallen, popularized the song (Columbia).

Guess Things Happen That Way. w/m Jack Clement, 1958. Featured and recorded by Johnny Cash (Sun).

Guess Who. w. Ralph Freed, m. Burton Lane, 1936. Recorded by Eddy Duchin, vocal by Jerry Cooper (Victor), and Teddy Wilson (Brunswick).

Guess Who I Saw Today? w. Elisse Boyd, m. Murray Grand, 1952. Introduced in (TM) *New Faces of 1952* by June Carroll, who repeated it in the film version (MM) *New Faces*, 1954. Leading recordings by Nancy Wilson (Capitol); Eydie Gormé (ABC-Paramount); Toni Tennille (Casablanca).

Guess Who's in Town. w. Andy Razaf, m. J. C. Johnson, 1928. Featured and recorded by Ethel Waters (Columbia). Revived by Bobby Short as the title song of his album (Atlantic), 1988.

Guilty. w/m Barry Gibb, Maurice Gibb, and Robin Gibb, 1980. Written by the brother-members of the English group The Bee Gees. Barbra Streisand and Barry Gibb collaborated for a Top 10 gold record (Columbia).

Guilty. w/m Alex Zanetis, 1963. Crossover (C&W/Pop) chart record by Jim Reeves (RCA).

Guilty. w. Gus Kahn, m. Richard A. Whiting and Harry Akst, 1931, 1947. Featured, popularized, and recorded by Ruth Etting (Columbia); Russ Columbo (Victor); Gene Austin (Perfect); Ozzie Nelson (Brunswick). Revived in 1947 by Margaret Whiting [daughter of Richard] (Capitol); Ella Fitzgerald, with Eddie Heywood (Decca); Sammy Kaye (Columbia); Johnny Desmond with the Page Cavanaugh Trio (Victor).

Guilty of Loving You. w/m Jerry Fuller, 1961. Introduced and recorded by Jerry Fuller (Challenge).

Guitar Boogie. m. Arthur Smith, 1948. Instrumental, introduced, and recorded by Arthur Smith (MGM, originally released on Super-Disc).

Guitar Man. w/m David Gates, 1972. Recorded by the group Bread (Elektra).

Guitar Man. w/m Jerry Reed, 1968. Chart record by Elvis Presley (RCA). A remixed version was released posthumously and was on the Pop charts for fourteen weeks (RCA), 1981.

(Dance with the) Guitar Man. m. Duane Eddy and Lee Hazelwood, 1962. Recorded by Duane Eddy (RCA).

Guitar Polka. w. James B. Paris, m. Al Dexter, 1945. Al Dexter and his Troopers had an instrumental hit (Columbia). The lyrics were added subsequently.

Guitars, Cadillacs, Etc., Etc. w/m Dwight Yoakam, 1986. Top 10 Country chart record by Dwight Yoakam (Reprise).

Guitar Town. w/m Steve Earle, 1986. Top 10 Country chart record by Steve Earle (MCA).

Gulf Coast Blues. w/m Clarence Williams, 1923. Introduced and recorded by Bessie Smith, accompanied only by Clarence Williams on piano (Columbia). It was coupled with Smith's first hit record "Down Hearted Blues" (q.v.).

Gum Drop. w/m Rudolph Toombs, 1955. Popular recording by The Crew Cuts (Mercury).

Guns of Navarone, The. w. Paul Francis Webster, m. Dimitri Tiomkin, 1961. Based on a theme from (MP) *The Guns of Navarone.* Leading recording by Joe Reisman and his Orchestra (Landa).

Gus the Theatre Cat. w. T. S. Eliot, w/m Andrew Lloyd Webber, 1982. Introduced by Stephen Hanan in (TM) *Cats.*

Guy Is a Guy, A. w/m Oscar Brand, 1952. Adaptation of WW II G.I.'s song, "A Gob Is a Slob," which was based on an eighteenth century British song "I Went to the Alehouse (A Knave Is a Knave)." Doris Day, accompanied by Paul Weston's Orchestra (Columbia), had a #1 record.

Guys and Dolls. w/m Frank Loesser, 1950. Sung by the chorus in (TM) *Guys and Dolls* and (MM) *Guys and Dolls,* 1955.

Guy What Takes His Time, A. w/m Ralph Rainger, 1933. Written for and introduced by Mae West in (MP) *She Done Him Wrong.*

Gypsy, The. w/m Billy Reid, 1946. One of the biggest hits of the year in sheet music sales, record sales, and airplay, this British import was on "Your Hit Parade" for twenty weeks, seven times in the #1 position. Top recordings by The Ink Spots (Decca); Dinah Shore (Columbia); Sammy Kaye, vocal by Mary Marlow (RCA Victor); Hildegarde with Guy Lombardo and his Orchestra (Decca).

Gypsy Dream Rose. w. James Kendis and Frank Samuels, m. Meyer Gusman, 1929.

Gypsy Fiddler. m. Ray Martin, 1948. Introduced and recorded by the British orchestra leader Ray Martin (Columbia). Recorded in the U.S. by violinist Florian Zabach (Decca).

Gypsy in My Soul, The. w. Moe Jaffe, m. Clay Boland, 1938. From the University of Pennsylvania Mask and Wig revue *Fifty-Fifty.* Among many recordings of this standard: Mildred Bailey (Crown); Jan Savitt, vocal by Bon Bon (Bluebird); Clyde McCoy and his Orchestra (Decca); Margaret Whiting (Capitol); Marian McPartland (Savoy).

Gypsy Love Song (Slumber On, My Little Gypsy Sweetheart). w. Harry B. Smith, m. Victor Herbert, 1898. Introduced by Eugene Cowles in (TM) *The Fortune Teller.*

Gypsy Man. w/m S. Allen, H. Brown, R. Dickerson, L. Jones, C. Miller, L. Oskar, and H. Scott, 1973. Top 10 single, written and recorded by the group War (United Artists).

Gypsys. w/m Robert Stone, 1971. #1 gold record by Cher (Imperial).

Gypsy Without a Soul, A. w. Irving Gordon, m. Edward Kennedy "Duke" Ellington, Lou Singer, and Juan Tizol, 1938. Introduced and recorded by Duke Ellington and his Orchestra (Brunswick).

Gypsy Woman. w/m Curtis Mayfield, 1961, 1970. First popular recording by The Impressions (ABC-Paramount). In 1970, Brian Hyland revived it with a million-seller (Uni).

271

H

Ha-Cha-Cha. w/m Gus Kahn and Werner R. Heymann, 1934. From (MM) *Caravan*. Recorded by Rudy Vallee (Victor).

Had a Dream About You, Baby. w/m Bob Dylan, 1987. Introduced by Bob Dylan in (MP) *Hearts of Fire* and recorded on the album of the same name (Columbia).

H-A-Double R-I-G-A-N. See **Harrigan**.

Ha Ha Said the Clown. w/m Anthony Hazzard, 1967. Recorded by the English group The Yardbirds (Epic).

Hail, Hail, the Gang's All Here. w. D. A. Esrom (Morse), m. Theodore F. Morse and Arthur Sullivan, 1917. Derived from a melody from *The Pirates of Penzance*, this became a favorite with the American troops in World War I.

Hair of Gold, Eyes of Blue. w/m Sunny Skylar, 1948. Best-sellers of the song included records by Gordon MacRae (Capitol); The Harmonicats, as an instrumental (Universal); Jack Emerson (Metronome); Jack Lathrop (RCA Victor); Art Lund (MGM).

Hair on My Chinny-Chin-Chin, The. w/m Ronald Blackwell, 1966. Recorded by Sam the Sham and The Pharaohs (MGM).

Hairspray. w/m Rachel Sweet, Anthony Battaglea, and Willa Bassen, 1988. Title song of (MP) *Hairspray*, sung on the soundtrack by Rachel Sweet.

Hajji Baba (Persian Lament). w. Ned Washington, m. Dimitri Tiomkin, 1954. Introduced by Nat "King" Cole in (MP) *The Adventures of Hajji Baba*, and recorded by him with Nelson Riddle's Orchestra (Capitol).

Half a Heart Is All You Left Me (When You Broke My Heart in Two). w/m Al Morgan, William S. Walker, and Tubby Rives, 1950. Featured and recorded by Al Morgan (London) and Eddy Howard (Mercury).

Half a Mind. w/m Roger Miller, 1958. C&W hit by Ernest Tubb (Decca).

Half a Photograph. w. Bob Russell, m. Hal Stanley, 1953. Leading record by Kay Starr, with Harold Mooney's Orchestra (Capitol).

Half a Sixpence. w/m David Heneker, 1965. Introduced by Tommy Steele and Polly James in New York in (TM) *Half a Sixpence*, which had made its debut in London, 1963. Steele and and Julia Foster sang it in the film version (MM) *Half a Sixpence*, 1967.

Half as Much. w/m Hank Williams, 1952. Introduced by Hank Williams (MGM). Million-seller by Rosemary Clooney, with Percy Faith's Orchestra (Columbia).

Half-Breed. w/m Al Capps and Mary Dean, 1973. #1 gold record by Cher (MCA).

Half Caste Woman. w/m Noël Coward, 1931. Sung by Helen Morgan in (TM) *Ziegfeld*

Follies of 1931. The song was introduced by Ada May in Charles B. Cochran's (TM) *1931 Revue* in London.

Half of It, Dearie, Blues, The. w. Ira Gershwin, m. George Gershwin, 1924. Introduced by Fred Astaire and Kathlene Martyn in (TM) *Lady, Be Good!*

Half Past Forever (Till I'm Blue in the Heart). w/m Tom Brasfield, 1986. Top 10 Country chart hit by T. G. Sheppard (Columbia).

Half the Way. w/m Ralph Murphy and Bobby Wood, 1979. Recorded by Crystal Gayle (Columbia).

Half-Way to Heaven. w. Al Dubin, m. J. Russel Robinson, 1928.

Halfway to Paradise. w/m Gerry Goffin and Carole King, 1961. Top 40 records by Tony Orlando (Epic) and in revival by Bobby Vinton (Epic), 1968.

Hallelujah! w. Leo Robin and Clifford Grey, m. Vincent Youmans, 1927. Youmans wrote the music while stationed at the Great Lakes Naval Training Station in World War I. It was performed by the Navy band at the base and then by John Philip Sousa's band. When a rousing number was needed for (TM) *Hit The Deck*, words were added, Stella Mayhew and chorus sang it, and the song became a show stopper and major standard. In the 1930 film adaptation (MM) *Hit The Deck*, it was sung by Marguerite Padula, and in the 1955 remake, by Tony Martin, Russ Tamblyn, and Vic Damone. It served as the finale of (TM) *A Musical Jubilee*, 1975, sung by John Raitt and the company.

Hallelujah, I'm a Bum. w. Lorenz Hart, m. Richard Rodgers, 1933. Sung by Al Jolson in (MM) *Hallelujah, I'm a Bum.*

Hallelujah I Love Her/Him So. w/m Ray Charles, 1956. Introduced and recorded by Ray Charles (Atlantic). In 1959, Peggy Lee, in her popular version, substituted the male pronoun for the female (Capitol).

Hambone. w/m Leon Washington and Red Saunders, 1952. Adaptation of a P. D. children's song. Introduced by Red Saunders, vocal by Dolores Hawkins (Okeh), followed by Jo Stafford and Frankie Laine (Columbia), and The Bell Sisters and Phil Harris, with Henri René's Orchestra (RCA Victor).

Hamp's Boogie Woogie. m. Milt Buckner and Lionel Hampton, 1944. Instrumental recorded by Lionel Hampton and his Orchestra (Decca).

Handbag Is Not a Proper Mother, A. w. Anne Croswell, m. Lee Pockriss, 1960. Introduced by Sara Seegar and John Irving in the off-Broadway (TM) *Ernest in Love*, based on Oscar Wilde's play, *The Importance of Being Earnest.*

Handbags and Gladrags. w/m Mike D'Abo, 1970. English song, introduced on "The Rod Stewart Album" (Mercury). Leading singles by the jazz-oriented Chase (Epic), 1971, and Rod Stewart (Mercury), 1972.

Handful of Keys. w. Richard Maltby, Jr. and Murray Horwitz, m. Thomas "Fats" Waller, 1933. Originally recorded instrumentally by Fats Waller (Victor). Popular version by the Benny Goodman Quartet (MGM), 1937. With specially written lyrics, based on an idea by Marty Grosz, it was revived by the company in (TM) *Ain't Misbehavin'*, 1978.

Handful of Stars, A. w/m Jack Lawrence and Ted Shapiro, 1940. Lawrence was at the Copacabana nightclub in New York, watching headliner Sophie Tucker perform, when he became conscious of a two-bar melodic strain that accompanist Ted Shapiro was repeating as a filler between Tucker's numbers. With Shapiro's permission, he developed the thirteen notes into the popular song. Leading records: Glenn Miller, vocal by Ray Eberle (Bluebird); Jimmy Dorsey, vocal by Bob Eberly (Decca); Artie Shaw, vocal by Anita Boyer (Victor); Ina Ray Hutton's all-male Orchestra, vocal by Stuart Foster (Okeh).

Handicap, The. w. Dave Reed, Jr., m. George Rosey (George M. Rosenberg), 1895. A march, for which words were added in 1923.

Hand in Hand. w/m Jack Lawrence, 1947. Recorded by Sammy Kaye, vocal by Don Cornell and Laura Leslie (RCA Victor).

Hand Me Down World. w/m Kurt Winter, 1970. Top 20 record by The Guess Who (RCA).

Hands Across America. w/m Marc Blatte, John Carnes, and Larry Gottlieb, 1986. Theme song for the six million Americans who linked hands from New York to Los Angeles on May 25th, as a pledge to fight hunger and homelessness. Recorded by The Voices of America (EMI America).

Hands Across the Sea. m. John Philip Sousa, 1899. A march.

Hands Across the Table. w. Mitchell Parish, m. Jean Delettre, 1934. This sixteen-bar song was introduced by Lucienne Boyer in the revue (TM) *Continental Varieties*. Heavily performed by bands on remote radio broadcasts. Among top recordings: Hal Kemp, vocal by Skinnay Ennis (Brunswick); the Dorsey Brothers Orchestra, vocal by Kay Weber (Decca); Eddy Duchin (Victor); Lee Wiley (Decca); Lud Gluskin (Columbia); Joe Reichman, vocal by Paul Small (Banner). Michele Bautier sang it in the Mitchell Parish musical (TM) *Stardust*, 1987.

Hands Off. w/m Jay McShann and Priscilla Bowman, 1956. Jay McShann and Priscilla Bowman had a #1 R&B record (Vee-Jay).

Hands to Heaven. w/m David Gaspar and Marcus Lillington, 1988. Single by the British group, Breathe, from the album "All That Jazz" (A&M).

Hand That Rocks the Cradle, The. w/m Ted Harris, 1987. Top 10 Country chart hit by Glen Campbell and Steve Wariner (MCA).

Hand That Rocks the Cradle, The. w. Charles W. Berkeley, m. William H. Holmes, 1895.

Hand to Hold On To. w/m John Cougar Mellencamp, 1982. Recorded by John Cougar Mellencamp (Riva).

Handy Man. w/m Otis Blackwell and Jimmy Jones, 1960, 1977. Introduced and Top 10 record by Jimmy Jones (Cub). Del Shannon had a Top 40 record in 1964 (Amy). Top 10 record by James Taylor (Columbia), 1977.

Hang 'Em High. m. Dominic Frontiere, 1968. Main title theme of (MP) *Hang 'Em High*. Top recordings by Hugo Montenegro and his Orchestra (RCA) and Booker T. and The MG's (Stax).

Hang Fire. w/m Mick Jagger and Keith Richards, 1982. Recorded by The Rolling Stones (Rolling Stones).

Hanging Tree, The. w. Mack David, m. Jerry Livingston, 1959. Marty Robbins introduced it as the title song of (MP) *The Hanging Tree*, and recorded it with Ray Conniff and his Orchestra (Columbia). Song nominated for Academy Award.

Hangin' on a String (Contemplating). w/m Carl McIntosh, Jayne Eugene, and Steve Nichol, 1985. #1 R&B chart and crossover Pop chart single by the London trio Loose Ends (MCA).

Hangin' on the Garden Gate. w. Gus Kahn, m. Ted Fio Rito, 1930. Featured on radio and recorded by the Ipana Troubadors (Columbia). Other popular records by Ted Fio Rito's Orchestra (Victor) and those of Jack Denny (Brunswick), Sam Lanin (Harmony), and Vincent Lopez (Perfect).

Hangin' Tough. w/m Maurice Starr, 1989. Hit record by the group New Kids on the Block (Columbia).

Hang On in There Baby. w/m Johnny Bristol, 1974. Top 10 record by Johnny Bristol (MGM).

Hang On Sloopy. w/m Bert Russell and Wes Farrell, 1965. First recorded by The Vibrations as "My Girl Sloopy" (Atlantic), 1964. #1 record by The McCoys (Bang). Popular instrumental by The Ramsey Lewis Trio (Cadet).

Hang On to Me. w. Ira Gershwin, m. George Gershwin, 1924. Introduced by Fred and Adele Astaire in (TM) *Lady, Be Good!*

Hang Out the Stars in Indiana. w. Billy Moll, m. Harry Woods, 1931. Popularized via the English recording (HMV) of Ray Noble and his Orchestra with vocal by Al Bowlly; then released in the United States (Victor).

Hang Up. w. Dorothy Fields, m. Arthur Schwartz, 1954. Introduced by Mae Barnes in (TM) *By the Beautiful Sea.*

Hang Up My Rock and Roll Shoes. w/m Chuck Willis, 1958. Featured and recorded by Chuck Willis (Atlantic).

Hang Your Head in Shame (Don't Your Conscience Ever Bother You). w/m Fred Rose, Ed. G. Nelson, and Steve Nelson, 1943. Best-selling record by Red Foley (Decca). Among others: Tex Ritter (Capitol); Foley and the Andrews Sisters (Decca); Bob Wills (Columbia); Patti Page (Mercury).

Hang Your Heart on a Hickory Limb. w. Johnny Burke, m. James V. Monaco, 1939. Introduced by Bing Crosby, Jane Jones, and the Music Maids in (MM) *East Side of Heaven.* Recorded by Crosby (Decca).

Hank Williams, You Wrote My Life. w/m Paul Craft, 1975. Hit Country record by Moe Bandy (Columbia).

Hanky Panky. w/m Jeff Barry and Ellie Greenwich, 1966. Tommy James and The Shondells recorded the song (Snap) in 1963. Master was sold in 1966 and became a #1 gold record (Roulette).

Hannah! w. Joseph C. Farrell, m. Henry Frantzen, 1903.

Hannah, Won't You Open That Door? w. Andrew B. Sterling, m. Harry Von Tilzer, 1904.

Happening, The. w. Eddie Holland, Lamont Dozier, and Brian Holland, m. Frank De Vol, 1967. Introduced on the soundtrack of (MP) *The Happening* by The Supremes. Their single release became a #1 Pop chart hit (Motown). Top 40 instrumental version by Herb Alpert and The Tijuana Brass (A&M).

Happenings Ten Years Time Ago. w/m Jeff Beck, Jim McCarty, Jimmy Page, and Keith Relf, 1966. Recorded by the English rock group The Yardbirds (Epic).

Happiest Girl in the Whole U.S.A. w/m Donna Fargo, 1971. Gold record (Country and Pop) by Donna Fargo (Dot).

Happiest Moments in Life, The. w/m Harry Stride and Eddie V. Deane, 1959. Featured and recorded by Helen Curtis (Jubilee).

Happiness Ahead. w. Mort Dixon, m. Allie Wrubel, 1934. Sung by Dick Powell in (MM) *Happiness Ahead* and recorded by him (Brunswick). Ted Lewis and his Orchestra (Decca) and the Pickens Sisters (Victor) also had popular releases.

Happiness Is. w/m Paul Parnes and Paul Evans, 1965. Popular song that gained fame as a TV and radio jingle for Kent cigarettes before the FCC ban on tobacco advertising.

Happiness Is Just a Thing Called Joe. w. E. Y. Harburg, m. Harold Arlen, 1943. Written for Ethel Waters in the film version (MM) *Cabin in the Sky.* Nominated for an Academy Award for Best Song, 1943. Popular recording by Woody Herman, vocal by Frances Wayne (Decca). It was sung by Susan Hayward, as Lillian Roth, in (MP) *I'll Cry Tomorrow*, 1956.

Happiness Street (Corner Sunshine Square). w/m Mack Wolfson and Edward R. White, 1956. Leading records by Tony Bennett (Columbia) and Georgia Gibbs (Mercury).

Happy. w/m David Townsend, Bernard Jackson, and David Conley, 1987. Top 10 R&B chart and Pop crossover record by the trio Surface (Columbia).

Happy. w/m Mick Jagger and Keith Richards, 1972. Recorded by the British group The Rolling Stones (Rolling Stones).

Happy. w/m Tony Michaels and Vinny Gorman, 1967. Recorded by The Sunshine Company (Imperial).

Happy, Happy Birthday Baby. w/m Margo Sylvia and Gilbert Lopez, 1957. Top 10 record by The Tune Weavers (Checker).

Happy (Love Theme from "Lady Sings the Blues"). w. William "Smokey" Robinson, m. Michel Legrand, 1972. Lyric version of the instrumental love theme from (MM) *Lady Sings the Blues*. Recorded by Bobby Darin (Motown).

Happy Anniversary. w/m Beeb Birtles and David Briggs, 1978. Recorded by the Australian group Little River Band (Harvest).

Happy Anniversary. w. Al Stillman, m. Robert Allen, 1959. Introduced by Mitzi Gaynor in (MP) *Happy Anniversary*. Leading records by Jane Morgan (Kapp) and The Four Lads (Columbia).

Happy as the Day Is Long. w. Ted Koehler, m. Harold Arlen, 1933. Sung and danced by Henry Williams in the twenty-second edition of *Cotton Club Parade* at the Cotton Club in Harlem, New York. Recorded by the bands of: Duke Ellington, vocal by Ivy Anderson (Brunswick); Fletcher Henderson (Decca); Adrian Rollini, vocal by Howard Phillips (Columbia); Joe Haymes (Melotone).

Happy Birthday, Dear Heartache. w/m Mack David and Archie Jordan, 1984. Top 10 Country chart record by Barbara Mandrell (MCA).

Happy Birthday, Merry Christmas. w/m Ron Kitson, 1965. Country chart hit by Loretta Lynn (Decca).

Happy Birthday, Sweet Sixteen. w/m Neil Sedaka and Howard Greenfield, 1961. Top 10 record by Neil Sedaka (RCA).

Happy Birthday Darlin'. w/m Chuck Howard, 1979. #1 Country chart record by Conway Twitty (MCA).

Happy Birthday to Love. w/m Dave Franklin, 1939. Introduced by Kay Kyser and his Orchestra in (MM) *That's Right—You're Wrong* and recorded by them (Columbia) and by Bob Crosby's Orchestra (Decca).

Happy Birthday to Me. w/m Bill Anderson, 1962. C&W chart record by Hank Locklin (RCA).

Happy Birthday to You. w. Patty Smith Hill, m. Mildred J. Hill. 1893. Originally written as "Good Morning to All," published in "Song Stories for Children." The song was copyrighted under the new title much later and, contrary to what many people think, is not in the public domain. It is considered to be the most sung song in the world.

Happy Days. w. Norman Gimbel, m. Charles Fox, 1974. Introduced by Truett Pratt and Jerry McClain in the series (TVP) "Happy Days." Top 10 record by Pratt and McClain (Reprise), 1976.

Happy Days and Lonely Nights. w. Billy Rose, m. Fred Fisher, 1929. Recorded by Ruth Etting (Columbia), The Knickerbockers (Columbia), and Eva Taylor (Okeh). Revived by The Fontaine Sisters (Dot), 1954.

Happy Days Are Here Again. w. Jack Yellen, m. Milton Ager, 1929. This was written for Charles King and Bessie Love in (MM) *Chasing Rainbows*. Prior to its release a year later, it was introduced by George Olsen's orchestra in New York and then, Hollywood. The song was so well received that MGM, though the film had already been completed, restaged, rescored, and reshot the number. Franklin Delano Roosevelt used it as his campaign song, 1932. Fred Allen, Raymond Walburn, and Andrew Tombes sang it in (MM) *Thanks A Million*, 1935. Barbra Streisand's slow version was a popular record (Columbia), 1963. It was a theme song of the Lucky Strike radio program "Your Hit Parade." ASCAP selected this song as one of sixteen for its all-time Hit Parade.

Happy Days in Dixie. m. Kerry Mills, 1896. Two-step march.

Happy Ending. w. Bert Kalmar, m. Harry Ruby, 1923. From (TM) *Helen of Troy, New York*.

Happy Feet. w. Jack Yellen, m. Milton Ager, 1930. Introduced by the Sisters G. and Paul Whiteman and his Orchestra in (MM) *The King of Jazz*. Whiteman recorded it (Columbia), as did Leo Reisman (Victor), the Revelers (Victor), and Cab Calloway (Perfect).

Happy Go Lucky. w. Frank Loesser, m. Jimmy McHugh, 1943. Introduced by Mary Martin and Dick Powell in (MM) *Happy Go Lucky*.

Happy Go Lucky Lane. w. Sam M. Lewis and Joe Young, m. Joseph Meyer, 1928.

Happy-Go-Lucky Me. w/m Paul Evans, 1960. Popular record by Paul Evans (Guaranteed).

Happy-Go-Lucky You (and Broken Hearted Me). w/m Al Goodhart, Al Hoffman, and J. F. Murray, 1932. Popular records by Bing Crosby (Brunswick); Glen Gray and the Casa Loma Orchestra, vocal by Kenny Sargent (Brunswick); Charles "Buddy" Rogers and his Orchestra (Victor); Smith Ballew (Perfect); Al Bowlly (Br. Decca).

Happy Habit. w. Dorothy Fields, m. Arthur Schwartz, 1954. Introduced by Mae Barnes in (TM) *By the Beautiful Sea*.

Happy Heart. w. Jackie Rae, m. James Last, 1969. German song. English version featured and recorded by Andy Williams (Columbia) and by Petula Clark (Warner Bros.).

Happy Holiday. w/m Irving Berlin, 1942. Introduced by Bing Crosby and Marjorie Reynolds in (MM) *Holiday Inn*. Crosby recorded it with John Scott Trotter's Orchestra (Decca).

Happy Hunting Horn. w. Lorenz Hart, m. Richard Rodgers, 1940. Introduced by Gene Kelly, Jane Fraser, and chorus in (TM) *Pal Joey*.

Happy in Love. w. Jack Yellen, m. Sammy Fain, 1941. Introduced by Ella Logan in (TM) *Sons o' Fun*, the revue starring Olsen and Johnson. Leading recordings by Glenn Miller, with vocal by Marion Hutton (Bluebird) and Eddy Howard (Columbia).

Happy Jack. w/m Peter Townshend, 1967. Hit record by the British group The Who (Decca).

Happy Journey. w. Fred Jay (Engl.), Nicola Wilke (Ger.), m. Charles Nowa, 1962. Original German title, "Wenn du Heimkommst," translates to "When You Come Home," which, interestingly, is the reverse in meaning to the English title. Hank Locklin's version reached the Top 10 on the Country charts (RCA).

Happy Man. w/m Greg Kihn and Steve Wright, 1982. Recorded by The Greg Kihn Band (Beserkley).

Happy Music. w/m David Laracuente and Richard Brown, Jr., 1976. Top 10 R&B record by The Blackbyrds (Fantasy).

Happy Organ, The. w/m Ken Wood (pseud. for Walter R. Moody), David Clowney, James Kreigsmann, 1959. #1 hit instrumental by Dave "Baby" Cortez, né Clowney (Clock).

Happy People. w/m Donald Baldwin, Jeffrey Bowen, and Lionel Richie, 1975. Recorded by The Temptations (Gordy).

Happy Song (Dum, Dum), The. w/m Otis Redding and Steve Cropper, 1968. Posthumously released recording by Otis Redding that reached the Top 40 on the charts (Volt).

Happy State of Mind. w/m Bill Anderson, 1968. Country hit by Bill Anderson (Decca).

Happy Summer Days. w/m Ritchie Adams, Wes Farrell, and Larry Kusick, 1966. Recorded by Ronnie Dove (Diamond).

Happy Talk. w. Oscar Hammerstein II, m. Richards Rodgers, 1949. Introduced by Juanita Hall in (TM) *South Pacific*. In the film version (MM) *South Pacific*, 1958, Juanita Hall's voice was dubbed by Muriel Smith.

Happy Times. w/m Sylvia Fine, 1949. Written for and performed by Danny Kaye in (MM) *The Inspector General*.

Happy Times (Are Here to Stay). w/m Gerry Goffin, Cynthia Weil, and Carole King, 1961. Popularized by Tony Orlando (Epic).

Happy to Be Unhappy. w/m Bobby Bare, 1963. Country song hit by Gary Buck (Petal).

Happy to Be with You. w/m June Carter, Johnny Cash, and Merle Kilgore, 1966. Top 10 Country record by Johnny Cash (Columbia).

Happy Together. w/m Gary Bonner and Alan Gordon, 1967. #1 gold record by The Turtles (White Whale). Revived by the Canadian a capella quartet The Nylons (Open Air), 1987.

Happy to Make Your Acquaintance. w/m Frank Loesser, 1956. Introduced by Jo Sullivan, Robert Weede, and Susan Johnson in (TM) *The Most Happy Fella.*

Happy Wanderer, The (Val-De-Ri, Val-De-Ra). w. Antonia Ridge (Engl.), m. Friedrich Wilhelm Möller, 1954. German song, "Der Fröhliche Wanderer," words by F. Siegesmund and Edith Möller. Sung on tour by the Oberkirchen Children's Choir. Popular recordings by Frank Weir and his Orchestra (London); Henri René and his Orchestra (RCA Victor); Tommy Leonetti, with Nelson Riddle's Orchestra (Capitol).

Happy Whistler. m. Don Robertson, 1956. Instrumental hit by Don Robertson (Capitol).

Harbor Lights. w. Jimmy Kennedy, m. Hugh Williams (pseud. for Will Grosz), 1937, 1950. This English import was a success its first time out (ten weeks on "Your Hit Parade") and an even bigger one its second (#1!). Introduced here via the recording of the English band of Roy Fox (Victor). Being featured by Rudy Vallee, plus great air-play, and recorded by such performers as Frances Langford (Decca), Claude Thornhill (Vocalion), and Emery Deutsch (Brunswick) resulted in instant popularity. Revived in 1950 via hit records by the bands of Sammy Kaye (Columbia), Guy Lombardo (Decca), Ray Anthony (Capitol), Ralph Flanagan (RCA Victor), and a vocal by Bing Crosby (Decca). The Platters had a Top 10 record (Mercury), 1960.

Harbor of Love, The. w. Earle C. Jones, m. Charlotte Blake, 1911.

Hard Candy Christmas. w/m Carol Hall, 1978. Sung by "the girls" in (TM) *Best Little Whorehouse in Texas.* Sung by Dolly Parton and "the girls" in the film version, 1982.

Hard Day's Night, A. w/m John Lennon and Paul McCartney, 1964. Introduced by The Beatles in (MM) *A Hard Day's Night*, and on a #1 gold record (Capitol). Title came from Beatle Ringo Starr's aside, referring to an all-night recording session of some of the songs from the film. Top 40 instrumental version by The Ramsey Lewis Trio (Cadet), 1966.

Harden My Heart. w/m Marv Ross, 1981. Top 10 record by the group Quarterflash (Geffen).

Harder They Come, The. w/m Jimmy Cliff, 1973. Reggae song introduced by Jimmy Cliff in the Jamaican film (MP) *The Harder They Come.*

Hardest Part, The. w/m Deborah Harry and Chris Stein, 1980. Recorded by the group Blondie (Chrysalis).

Hard Habit to Break. w/m Steve Kipner and John Parker, 1984. Top 10 record by the group Chicago (Full Moon).

Hard Headed Woman. w/m Claude De Metrius, 1958. Introduced by Elvis Presley in (MM) *King Creole*, and on records (RCA).

Hard Hearted Hannah (The Vamp of Savannah). w. Jack Yellen, Bob Bigelow, and Charles Bates, 1924. Popular in vaudeville and on records. Among the latter are those by Belle Baker (Victor); Lucille Hegamin (Cameo); Dolly Kay (Columbia); Ray McKinley (Capitol); Peggy Lee (Capitol); Ray Charles (ABC-Paramount). Ella Fitzgerald sang it in (MM) *Pete Kelly's Blues*, 1955.

Hard Luck Blues. w/m Roy Brown, 1950. Hit R&B recording by Roy Brown (De Luxe).

Hard Luck Woman. w/m Paul Stanley, 1977. Recorded by the hard rock band Kiss (Casablanca).

Hard Rain's A-Gonna Fall. w/m Bob Dylan, 1963. Introduced by Bob Dylan (Columbia).

Hard Times. w/m James Taylor, 1981. Recorded by James Taylor (Columbia).

Hard Times for Lovers. w/m Hugh Prestwood, 1979. Recorded by Judy Collins (Elektra).

Hard to Get. w/m Jack Segal, 1955. Introduced by Gisele MacKenzie on (TVP) "Justice." Her recording, which was featured in the TV play, was arranged and conducted by Richard Maltby and became a top hit ("X").

Hard to Say I'm Sorry. w/m Peter Cetera and David Foster, 1982. Introduced on the soundtrack of (MP) *Summer Lovers* by the group, Chicago, whose recording became a #1 gold record (Full Moon).

Hard Way, The. w. Johnny Burke, m. James Van Heusen, 1945. Introduced by Betty Hutton in (MM) *Duffy's Tavern*, and recorded by her (Capitol); also by Dolores Martel (Victor).

Hare Krishna (a.k.a. Be-In). w. Gerome Ragni and James Rado, m. Galt MacDermot, 1967. Sung by the company in the off-Broadway production (TM) *Hair*. The company sang it as "Be-In" in the Broadway production (TM) *Hair*, 1968.

Harlem Air Shaft. m. Edward Kennedy "Duke" Ellington, 1940. Instrumental recorded by Duke Ellington and his Orchestra (Victor).

Harlem Nocturne. m. Earle Hagen, 1940. Introduced by Ray Noble and his Orchestra (Columbia). Recorded and featured as his band theme by Randy Brooks (Decca). Chart instrumental by Herbie Fields and his Orchestra (Parrot), 1953. The instrumental quintet, The Viscounts, had a hit version (Madison), 1960, and in its re-release (Amy), 1965.

Harlem on My Mind. w/m Irving Berlin, 1933. Introduced by Ethel Waters in (TM) *As Thousands Cheer* and recorded by her (Columbia). Also recorded by Gertrude Niesen (Victor) and Thelma Carpenter (Majestic).

Harlem Shuffle. w/m Bob Relf and Earl Nelson, 1964, 1986. Written and recorded by Bob and Earl (Marc). Chart record by The Traits (Scepter), 1966. Revived with Top 10 record by The Rolling Stones (Rolling Stones), 1986.

Harlem Speaks. m. Edward Kennedy "Duke" Ellington, 1933. Instrumental introduced by Ellington but not recorded until 1936 (Decca).

Harmonica Harry. w/m Phil Baxter, 1930. Popular records by the bands of Ted Weems, vocal by Parker Gibbs (Victor); Ted Lewis (Columbia); Jimmy Joy (Brunswick); Fred Hall's Sugar Babies (Okeh).

Harmony. w/m James Goldman, William Goldman, and John Kander, 1962. Introduced by Bibi Osterwald, Gino Conforti, Linda Lavin, and Jack De Lon in (TM) *A Family Affair*, Kander's Broadway debut as a composer.

Harmony. w. Johnny Burke, m. James Van Heusen, 1947. Introduced by William Gaxton and Victor Moore in the short-lived Broadway musical (TM) *Nellie Bly*, 1945. Interpolated in (MM) *Variety Girl* by Bob Hope and Bing Crosby, 1947. Popular record by Johnny Mercer and The King Cole Trio (Capitol).

Harmony in Harlem. w. Irving Mills, m. Edward Kennedy "Duke" Ellington, and Johnny Hodges, 1938. Recorded by Duke Ellington, featuring saxophonist Hodges (Brunswick).

Harper Valley P.T.A. w/m Tom T. Hall, 1968. #1 C&W and Pop chart gold record hit by Jeannie C. Riley (Plantation).

Harriet. w/m Abel Baer and Paul Cunningham, 1945. Featured and recorded by Gene Krupa, vocal by Anita O'Day (Columbia).

Harrigan. w/m George M. Cohan, 1908. Recognizable as "H-A-Double R-I-G-A-N Spells Harrigan," it was sung by James C. Marlowe in (TM) *Fifty Miles from Boston*. Revived by James Cagney and Joan Leslie in Cohan's film biography (MM) *Yankee Doodle Dandy*, 1942, and by Joel Grey and company in (TM) *George M!*, 1968.

Harry Lime Theme, The. See **Third Man Theme**.

Harry Truman. w/m Robert Lamm, 1975. Written by the keyboard player of the group, Chicago, which had a Top 20 record (Columbia).

Harvard Blues. w. Eddie Frazier, m. William "Count" Basie and Tab Smith, 1942. Introduced by Count Basie, vocal by Jimmy Rushing (Okeh).

Has Anybody Here Seen Kelly? w/m C. W. Murphy, Will Letters, and William J. McKenna, 1910. English song introduced in the U.S. in (TM) *The Jolly Bachelors* by Nora Bayes, and recorded by her (Victor). McKenna, an American, revised the original lyric as it contained many geographical and topical references unfamiliar to the U.S. audience.

Hatari. See **Theme from "Hatari"** and **Baby Elephant Walk**.

Hat My Father Wore On St. Patrick's Day, The. w. William Jerome, m. Jean Schwartz, 1909. Recorded by Billy Murray (Victor).

Hats Off to Larry. w/m Del Shannon, 1961. Hit record by Del Shannon (Big Top).

Hats Off to Me. w. Edward Harrigan, m. David Braham, 1891.

Haunted Heart. w. Howard Dietz, m. Arthur Schwartz, 1948. Introduced by John Tyers in (TM) *Inside U.S.A.* Leading recordings by Perry Como (RCA Victor) and Jo Stafford (Capitol).

Haunted House. w/m Robert Geddins, 1964. Popular record by Gene Simmons (Hi).

Haunted House Blues. w/m J. C. Johnson, 1924. Recorded by Bessie Smith (Columbia).

Haunted Nights. m. Edward Kennedy "Duke" Ellington, 1929. Recorded by Ellington (Victor).

Haunting Me. w. Eddie De Lange, m. Joseph Myrow, 1935.

Havana. w/m E. Ray Goetz, James Kendis, Herman Paley, 1910.

Have a Good Time. w/m Felice Bryant and Boudleaux Bryant, 1952. Featured and popularized by Tony Bennett (Columbia).

Have a Heart. w. Harold Adamson, m. Burton Lane, 1931. Introduced in (TM) *Earl Carrol Vanities* (ninth edition) by Lillian Roth and Woods Miller. This was the first song success for Lane and his first collaboration with Adamson.

Have a Heart. w. P. G. Wodehouse, m. Jerome Kern, 1917. Introduced by Thurston Hall in (TM) *Have a Heart.* Kern wrote a different song with the same title, with lyrics by Gene Buck, for (TM) *Ziegfeld Follies of 1916.*

Have a Heart. w. Gene Buck, m. Jerome Kern, 1916. From (TM) *Ziegfeld Follies of 1916.* In an unusual situation, Kern wrote another "Have a Heart," with lyrics by P. G. Wodehouse, which was the title song of a 1917 musical.

Have a Little Dream on Me. w. Billy Rose and John Murray, m. Phil Baxter, 1934.

Have a Little Faith. w/m Billy Sherrill and Glenn Sutton, 1968. Country hit and Pop chart record by David Houston (Epic).

Have a Little Faith in Me. w. Sam M. Lewis and Joe Young, m. Harry Warren, 1930. Introduced by Bernice Claire and Alexander Gray in (MM) *Spring Is Here.* Popular recordings by Guy Lombardo (Columbia), Seger Ellis (Okeh), Art Gillham (Columbia), Arthur Schutt (Okeh).

Have I Stayed Away Too Long? w/m Frank Loesser, 1943. Introduced and recorded by Perry Como (Victor). Also recorded by Tex Grande and His Range Riders (De Luxe).

Have I Stayed Too Long? w/m Sonny Bono, 1966. Recorded by Sonny and Cher (Atco).

Have I the Right? w/m Alan Blaikley and Howard Blaikley, 1964. Hit record by the English rock quintet The Honeycombs (Interphon).

Have I Told You Lately? w/m Harold Rome, 1962. Introduced by Bambi Linn and Ken Le Roy in (TM) *I Can Get It for You Wholesale.*

Have I Told You Lately That I Love You? w/m Scott Wiseman, 1945. Of the early records, Gene Autry had the best-seller (Columbia). Among the many other artists to record this standard were: Bing Crosby and the Andrews Sisters (Decca), Tony Martin and Fran Warren (RCA Victor), Elvis Presley (RCA Victor), Billy Vaughn (Dot), the Sons of the Pioneers (RCA Victor), Vera Lynn (London), Ricky Nelson (Imperial), Foy Willing (Hit) (Mercury).

Have Mercy. w/m Paul Kennerly, 1985. #1 Country chart single by the mother/daughter duo The Judds (RCA).

Have Mercy. w. Buck Ram and Chick Webb, m. Buck Ram, 1939. Introduced and recorded by Chick Webb, vocal by Ella Fitzgerald (Decca), followed by Red Norvo, vocal by Mildred Bailey (Vocalion).

Have Mercy, Baby. w/m Billy Ward, 1952. #1 R&B hit by The Dominoes (Federal).

Haven't Got Time for the Pain. w/m Jacob Brackman and Carly Simon, 1974. Top 20 record by Carly Simon (Elektra).

Haven't You Heard. w/m Patrice Rushen, 1980. Recorded by Patrice Rushen (Elektra).

Have You Ever Been Lonely? (Have You Ever Been Blue?). w. Billy Hill, m. Peter DeRose, 1933. Hill wrote this under pseudonym of George Brown.

Have You Ever Loved Somebody. w/m Barry Eastmond and Terry Skinner, 1987. Chart record by Freddie Jackson (Capitol).

Have You Ever Seen the Rain. w/m John Fogerty, 1971. Gold record by Creedence Clearwater Revival (Fantasy).

Have You Forgotten (the Thrill)? w. Leo Robin, m. Dana Suesse, 1931. Popularized by Ruth Etting (Perfect) and Henry Busse's Orchestra (Victor).

Have You Forgotten So Soon? w. Sam Coslow and Edward Heyman, m. Abner Silver, 1938. Featured and recorded by the bands of Sammy Kaye (Victor), Kay Kyser (Brunswick), Lawrence Welk (Vocalion).

Have You Got Any Castles, Baby? w. Johnny Mercer, m. Richard A. Whiting, 1937. Introduced by Priscilla Lane, making her screen debut in (MM) *Varsity Show.* Recorded by Dick Powell (Decca).

Have You Had Your Love Today. w/m Terry Stubbs and Derrick Pearson, 1989. Hit R&B chart record by The O'Jays (EMI).

Have You Heard? w/m Lew Douglas, Frank Levere, and Roy Rodde, 1952. Hit record by Joni James, with Lew Douglas's Orchestra (MGM).

Have You Looked into Your Heart? w/m Teddy Randazzo, Bobby Weinstein, and Billy Barberis, 1965. Leading record by Jerry Vale (Columbia).

Have You Met Miss Jones? w. Lorenz Hart, m. Richard Rodgers, 1937. Introduced by Joy Hodges and Austin Marshall in the musical starring George M. Cohan as President Franklin D. Roosevelt, (TM) *I'd Rather Be Right.* In 1939, it was interpolated in the London revue (TM) *All Clear* by Bobby Howes. In the 1955 film (MM) *Gentlemen Marry Brunettes*, it was sung by Jane Russell, Anita Ellis dubbing for Jeanne Crain, Alan Young, Robert Farnon dubbing for Scott Brady, and Rudy Vallee. The song is a great favorite with jazz musicians.

Have You Never Been Mellow. w/m John Farrar, 1975. #1 Country and Pop chart record by Olivia Newton-John (MCA).

Have Yourself a Merry Little Christmas. w/m Hugh Martin and Ralph Blane, 1944. Sung by Judy Garland to Margaret O'Brien in (MM) *Meet Me in St. Louis.* Leading records by Garland (Decca), Frank Sinatra (Columbia).

Have You Seen Her? w/m Barbara Acklin and Eugene Record, 1971. Top 10 R&B/Pop hit by The Chi-Lites (Brunwsick).

Have You Seen Your Mother, Baby, Standing in the Shadow? w/m Mick Jagger and Keith Richards, 1966. Top 10 U.S. release by the British group The Rolling Stones (London).

Havin' A Wonderful Wish. w/m Jay Livingston and Ray Evans, 1949. From (MP) *Sorrowful Jones*. Recorded by Benny Goodman, vocal by Buddy Greco (Capitol); Shep Fields and his Orchestra (MGM); Vera Lynn (London).

Having a Party. w/m Sam Cooke, 1962. Introduced and hit record by Sam Cooke (RCA). Revived by The Ovations, who injected some lines from other hit soul records (MGM), 1973.

(You're) Having My Baby. w/m Paul Anka, 1974. #1 Gold record by Paul Anka with Odia Coates (United Artists). After the song had attained popularity, a controversy arose regarding its title. As a concession to the National Organization of Women, Anka changed it to "(You're) Having Our Baby."

Having Myself a Fine Time. w. Richard Maltby, Jr., m. David Shire, 1971. Sung on the soundtrack of (MP) *Summertree* by Hamilton Camp.

Havin' Myself a Time. w. Leo Robin, m. Ralph Rainger, 1938. Introduced by Martha Raye in (MM) *Tropic Holiday*. Recorded by Billie Holiday (Vocalion).

Hawaiian Butterfly. w. George A. Little, m. Billy Baskette and Joseph H. Santly, 1917.

Hawaiian War Chant. w. Ralph Freed (Engl.), m. Johnny Noble and Prince Leleiohaku, 1936. Numerous radio performances upon publication, with best-selling record by Tommy Dorsey and his Orchestra (Victor), 1939. Spike Jones and his City Slickers had a hit comedy version (Victor), 1946, and Dave Lambert had a jazz-oriented vocal in the early fifties (Capitol). Harry Owens and his Royal Hawaiians played it in the Deanna Durbin film (MM) *It's a Date*, and in (MM) *Song of the Islands*, 1942. It was also heard in (MM) *Moonlight in Hawaii*, 1941, and in (MM) *Song of the Open Road*, 1944. There are over a hundred recorded versions.

Hawaiian Wedding Song, The. w. Al Hoffman and Dick Manning (Engl.), m. Charles E. King, 1959. Written in 1926 with original Hawaiian words and title "Ke Kali Nei Au" by Charles E. King. New version featured and recorded by Andy Williams (Cadence).

Hawaii Five-O. m. Mort Stevens, 1969. Theme of the series (TVP) "Hawaii Five-O." Top 10 instrumental by The Ventures (Liberty).

Hawaii Tattoo. m. Michael Thomas, 1965. Imported Belgian instrumental by The Waikikis (Kapp).

Hawk-Eye. w/m Boudleaux Bryant, 1955. Best-selling Pop record by Frankie Laine (Columbia).

Hay, Straw. w. Oscar Hammerstein II, m. Vincent Youmans, 1928. Sung and danced by Louise Brown and Harland Dixon in (TM) *Rainbow*. The number was performed by the company in the film version (MM) *Song of the West*, 1930.

Hayfoot, Strawfoot. w/m Hans Lengsfelder, Ervin Drake, and Paul McGrane, 1942. Introduced and recorded by Duke Ellington, vocal by Ivy Anderson (Victor).

Hazy Shade of Winter, A. w/m Paul Simon, 1966. Top 20 record by Simon and Garfunkel (Columbia). Sung by The Bangles on the soundtrack of (MP) *Less Than Zero*, and a Top 10 single (Columbia), 1987.

He. w. Jack Mullan, m. Jack Richards, 1955. Top 10 record in all categories by Al Hibbler, with Jack Pleis's Orchestra (Decca). Popular version, also, by The McGuire Sisters with Dick Jacobs's Orchestra (Coral). The Righteous Brothers had a chart record in 1966 (Verve).

Headache Tomorrow, A (or A Heartache Tonight). w/m Chick Rains, 1981. #1 Country chart record by Mickey Gilley (Epic).

Head Games. w/m Lou Gramm and Mick Jones, 1979. Recorded by the Anglo-American group Foreigner (Atlantic).

Headin' Down The Wrong Highway. w/m Ted Daffan, 1945. Most popular recordings by Ted Daffan (Columbia) and Ernest Tubb (Decca).

Headin' for Louisville. w. B. G. DeSylva, m. Joseph Meyer, 1925. Featured and recorded by Ben Bernie and his Orchestra (Brunswick), and Red Nichols's The Redheads (Perfect).

Heading for Harlem. w. Eddie Dowling, m. James F. Hanley, 1927. From the musical starring Eddie Dowling and Ray Dooley, (TM) *Sidewalks of New York*. It was recorded by the orchestras of Jimmy Lytell (Perfect) and Nat Shilkret (Victor).

Headin' Home. w. Ned Washington, m. Herbert Stothart, 1935. Introduced by Harry Stockwell in (MM) *Here Comes the Band*.

Headlines. w/m Midnight Star, 1986. Written and recorded by the band, Midnight Star, formed at Kentucky State University (Solar).

Head over Heels. w/m Charlotte Caffey and Kathy Valentine, 1984. Written by two members of the female group The Go-Go's (I.R.S.)

Head over Heels in Love. w. Mack Gordon, m. Harry Revel, 1937. Jessie Matthews sang this in the British film (MM) *Head over Heels* and recorded it (Decca). Tommy Dorsey (Victor) and Lud Gluskin (Brunswick) and their orchestras also recorded it.

Head to Toe. w/m Full Force, 1987. #1 R&B and Pop chart record by Lisa Lisa and Cult Jam (Columbia).

Heah Me Talkin' to Ya. w/m Louis Armstrong, 1928. Recorded by Louis Armstrong twice (Okeh), 1928, (Decca), 1939; Ma Rain-

ey (Paramount), 1928; Johnny Dodds's Orchestra (Victor), 1929.

He Ain't Got Rhythm. w/m Irving Berlin, 1937. Introduced by Alice Faye, the Ritz Brothers, and chorus in (MM) *On the Avenue*. Among recordings: Teddy Wilson, vocal by Billie Holiday (Brunswick); Benny Goodman, arranged by Jimmy Mundy, vocal by Jimmy Rushing (Victor); Jimmie Lunceford and his Orchestra (Decca).

He Ain't Heavy . . . He's My Brother. w. Bob Russell, m. Bobby Scott, 1970. Top 10 record by the British group The Hollies (Epic); Top 20 version by Neil Diamond (Uni); recorded by Olivia Newton-John (MCA), 1976.

He Ain't No Angel. w/m Jeff Barry and Ellie Greenwich, 1965. Featured and recorded by The Ad Libs (Blue Cat).

Heard It in a Love Song. w/m Toy Caldwell, 1977. Written by the lead guitarist of The Marshall Tucker Band, which had a Top 20 record (Capricorn).

Hear My Song, Violetta. w. Buddy Bernier, Bob Emmerich (Engl.), m. Rudolf Luckesch, Othmar Klose, 1940. Imported from Vienna, Austria, with original German words by Ermenegildo Carosio and Othmar Klose. First U.S. release by Will Glahe and his Musette Orchestra (Victor). Glenn Miller, vocal by Ray Eberle, had best-selling record (Bluebird).

Hearsay. w/m John Colbert and Norman West, 1972. Recorded by the group, The Soul Children, of which the writers were members (Stax).

Heart. w/m Richard Adler and Jerry Ross, 1955. Introduced by Russ Brown, Jimmie Komack, Nathaniel Frey, and Albert Linville in (TM) *Damn Yankees*. Hit records by Eddie Fisher, with Hugo Winterhalter's Orchestra (RCA Victor), and The Four Aces, with Jack Pleis's Orchestra (Decca). Brown, Komack, Frey, and Linville again performed the song in the film version (MM) *Damn Yankees*, 1958.

Heart (I Hear You Beating). w/m Barry Mann and Cynthia Weil, 1963. Leading records by Kenny Chandler (Laurie) and Wayne Newton (Capitol).

Heartache for a Keepsake. w/m Roger Miller, 1962. Recorded by Kitty Wells (Decca).

Heartaches. w. John Klenner, m. Al Hoffman, 1931, 1947. While Guy Lombardo (Columbia) introduced this, Ted Weems is the bandleader associated with the song. He recorded it with a whistling chorus by Elmo Tanner (Bluebird), 1931. Weems, with Tanner, re-recorded it (Decca), 1937. Ten years later, a Charlotte, N.C. disc jockey discovered the recording and started playing it to a huge response. Decca reissued it, and the song reached #1 on "Your Hit Parade." The Marcels had a Top 10 version (Colpix), 1961.

Heartaches by the Number. w/m Harlan Howard, 1959. C&W and Pop hit. Leading record by Guy Mitchell (Columbia). Revived in 1965 by Johnny Tillotson (MGM).

Heartache Tonight. w/m Glen Frey, Don Henley, Bob Seger, and J. D. Souther, 1979. #1 gold record by The Eagles (Asylum).

Heart and Soul. w/m Carol Decker and Ronnie Rogers, 1987. Top 10 single by the English group, T'Pau, of which Decker was lead singer (Virgin).

Heart and Soul. w/m Mike Chapman and Nicky Chinn, 1983. Top 10 record by Huey Lewis and The News (Chrysalis). Not to be confused with the Loesser-Carmichael standard of the same title.

Heart and Soul. w. Frank Loesser, m. Hoagy Carmichael, 1938. Introduced by Larry Clinton and his Orchestra in a movie short (MM) *A Song Is Born*, then recorded by him with vocal by Bea Wain (Victor). Gene Krupa and his Band performed it in (MM) *Some Like It Hot*, 1939 (not to be confused with Billy Wilder's 1959 classic film of the same name). This standard has become a great favorite of beginner pianists, because of the "We Want Cantor" chord progressions, I VI II V, which recur throughout the song. Eddy Duchin, who had one of the popular records (Brunswick), built his introduction around the sequence. Hit revivals by Johnny Maddox (Dot), 1956, The Cleftones (Gee), 1961, Jan and Dean (Challenge), 1961.

Heartbeat. w/m Eric Kaz and Wendy Waldman, 1986. Top 10 record by actor/singer Don Johnson (Epic).

Heartbeat in the Darkness. w/m Dave Loggins and Russell Smith, 1986. #1 Country chart hit by Don Williams (Capitol).

Heartbeat—It's a Lovebeat. w/m William Hudspeth and Michael Kennedy, 1973. Gold record by the Canadian quintet The DeFranco Family (20th Century).

Heart Be Careful. w/m Billy Walker and Jay Bovington, 1963. Country hit by Billy Walker (Columbia).

Heartbreak (It's Hurting Me). w/m Jon Thomas and C. Hoyles, 1960. Recorded by Little Willie John (King) and Jon Thomas (ABC-Paramount).

Heartbreak, U.S.A. w/m Harlan Howard, 1961. Country hit by Kitty Wells (Decca).

Heartbreak Beat. w/m John Ashton, Richard Butler, and Tim Butler, 1987. Written and recorded by the British trio Psychedelic Furs (Columbia).

Heartbreaker. w/m Barry Gibb, Robin Gibb, and Maurice Gibb, 1982. Top 10 record by Dionne Warwick (Arista).

Heartbreaker. w/m Geoff Gill and Cliff Wade, 1980. English song recorded by Pat Benatar (Chrysalis).

Heartbreaker. w/m Carole Bayer Sager and David Wolfert, 1978. Country/Pop hit by Dolly Parton (RCA).

Heartbreaker. w/m John Bonham, John Paul Jones, Jimmy Page, and Robert Plant, 1970. Written and introduced by Led Zeppelin in an album (Atlantic). Chart single by Grand Funk Railroad (Capitol).

Heartbreaker. w/m Morty Berk, Frank Campano, and Max C. Freedman, 1947. Introduced and recorded by the Philadelphia-based Ferko String Band (Palda), which had a popular record, along with The Andrews Sisters (Decca).

Heartbreak Hotel. w/m Michael Jackson, 1981. Recorded by The Jacksons (Epic). Not to be confused with the earlier Presley hit of the same title.

Heartbreak Hotel. w/m Mae Boren Axton, Tommy Durden, and Elvis Presley, 1956. Elvis Presley's first #1 hit record (RCA). In 1979, it was included in the Dick Clark produced and directed film biography (MM) *Elvis*, sung by Ronnie McDowell on the soundtrack, dubbing for Kurt Russell who portrayed Presley.

Heartbreak Kid, The. w/m Michael Price and Dan Walsh, 1974. Recorded by Bo Donaldson & The Heywoods (ABC).

Heart Full of Love, A (for A Handful of Kisses). w/m Eddy Arnold, Steve Nelson, and Ray Soehnel, 1948. Featured and recorded by Eddy Arnold (RCA Victor).

Heart Full of Soul. w/m Graham Gouldman, 1965. Top 10 record by the British group The Yardbirds (Epic).

Heart Heeler. w/m Tom Gmeiner and John Greenebaum, 1976. Country record hit by Mel Tillis (MCA).

Heart Hotels. w/m Dan Fogelberg, 1980. Recorded by Dan Fogelberg (Full Moon).

Heart in Hand. w/m Shari Sheeley and Jackie De Shannon, 1962. Popular record by Brenda Lee (Decca).

Heart in New York, A. w/m Benny Gallagher and Graham Lyle, 1981. Recorded by Art Garfunkel (Columbia).

Heart Is Quicker Than the Eye, The. w. Lorenz Hart, m. Richard Rodgers, 1936. Introduced by Luella Gear and Ray Bolger in (TM) *On Your Toes*. Ramona, the former Paul Whiteman singer-pianist, recorded it (Liberty Music Shops).

Heartless. w/m Ann Wilson and Nancy Wilson, 1978. The Wilson sisters were featured performers with the group, Heart, which recorded the number (Mushroom).

Heart Like a Wheel. w/m Anna McGarrigle, 1974. First recorded by Linda Ronstadt as title song of an album (Capitol). Kate and Anna McGarrigle included it on the album of their names (Warner Bros.), 1975. Top 40 version by The Steve Miller Band (Capitol), 1981.

Heart of Glass. w/m Deborah Harry and Chris Stein, 1979. #1 gold record by the group, Blondie, of which the writers were members (Chrysalis).

Heart of Gold. w/m Neil Young, 1972. #1 gold record by Neil Young, with backup vocal by Linda Ronstadt and James Taylor (Reprise).

Heart of My Heart, I Love You (the Story of the Rose). w. "Alice," m. Andrew Mack, 1899. Originally popular with barbershop quartets. See also **Gang That Sang Heart of My Heart, The.**

Heart of Rock and Roll, The. w/m Johnny Cola and Huey Lewis, 1984. Top 10 record by Huey Lewis & The News (Chrysalis).

(I Wish I Had A) Heart of Stone. w/m R. Leighan Wayland and D. Holyfield, 1989. Hit Country record by Baillie and The Boys (RCA).

Heart of Stone. w/m Mick Jagger and Keith Richards, 1965. Top 20 record by The Rolling Stones (London).

Heart of Stone, A. w/m Ord Hamilton and Bruce R. Sievier, 1937. Featured and recorded by Hal Kemp, vocal by Skinnay Ennis (Brunswick).

Heart of the Night. w/m Paul Cotton, 1979. Recorded by the band Poco (MCA).

Heart Over Mind. w/m Mel Tillis, 1961. C&W hit by Ray Price (Columbia).

Hearts. w/m Jeff Barish, 1981. Top 10 record by Marty Balin (EMI America).

Hearts and Flowers. w. Mary D. Brine, m. Theodore Moses Tobani, 1899. Entire melody appears in "Wintermärchen" (1891) by Hungarian composer Alphonse Czibulka. The music for this song became a standard background by pianists playing for silent movies in scenes where the heroine was pleading for mercy from the villain.

Hearts Aren't Made to Break (They're Made to Love). w/m Roger Murrah and Steve Dean, 1986. #1 Country chart record by Lee Greenwood (MCA).

Hearts of Stone. w. Eddy Ray, m. Rudy Jackson, 1955. Initial recording by The Charms (DeLuxe). Best-seller by The Fontane Sisters who had their biggest hit, a #1 record (Dot). Bill Black's Combo revived it with an instrumental version in 1961 (Hi); and John Fogerty, as the Blue Ridge Rangers, had a Top 40 record (Fantasy) in 1973.

Hearts on Fire. w/m Bryan Adams and Jim Vallance, 1987. Single by Canadian singer/songwriter Bryan Adams, from his album "Into the Fire" (A&M).

Hearts on Fire. w/m Randy Meisner and Eric Kaz, 1981. Recorded by Randy Meisner (Epic).

Heart Strings. w/m Merle Moore, 1951. Featured and recorded by Eddy Arnold (RCA Victor).

Heartstrings. w. Stanley Adams, m. Maria Grever, 1935.

Heart to Heart. w/m David Foster, Kenny Loggins, and Michael McDonald, 1982. Recorded by Kenny Loggins (Columbia).

Heart to Heart Talk. w/m Lee Ross, 1960. Top 10 C&W chart song by Bob Wills and Tommy Duncan (Liberty).

Heather Honey. w/m Tommy Roe, 1969. Top 40 record by Tommy Roe (ABC).

Heather on the Hill, The. w. Alan Jay Lerner, m. Frederick Loewe, 1947. Introduced by David Brooks and Marion Bell in (TM) *Briga-doon* and recorded by them (RCA Victor). In the film version, 1954, it was sung by Gene Kelly, with Carole Richards dubbing on the soundtrack for Cyd Charisse.

Heat Is On, The w. Keith Forsey, m. Harold Faltermeyer, 1985. From (MP) *Beverly Hills Cop*. Top 10 single by Glenn Frey (MCA).

Heat of the Moment. w/m Geoffrey Downes and John Wetton, 1982. Top 10 record by the English group Asia (Geffen).

Heat of the Night. w/m Bryan Adams and Jim Vallance, 1987. Top 10 single by Canadian singer/songwriter Bryan Adams from his album "Into the Fire" (A&M).

Heat Wave. w/m Eddie Holland, Brian Holland, and Lamont Dozier, 1963. Hit records by Martha and The Vandellas (Gordy), 1963, and Linda Ronstadt (Asylum), 1975. Not to be confused with Irving Berlin's similarly titled song.

Heat Wave. w/m Irving Berlin, 1933. Sung by Ethel Waters and danced by Letitia Ide and José Limon in (TM) *As Thousands Cheer*. Ethel Merman sang it in (MM) *Alexander's Ragtime Band*, 1938; Olga San Juan sang it with a chorus and danced to it with Fred Astaire in (MM) *Blue Skies*, 1946; Bing Crosby and Danny Kaye performed it in a montage in (MM) *White Christmas*, 1954; Marilyn Monroe sang it in (MM) *There's No Business Like Show Business*, 1954.

Heaven. w/m Eric Turner, Jerry Dixon, John Oswald, Joseph Cagle, and Stephen Chamberlin, 1989. Hit single by the band Warrant (Columbia).

Heaven. w/m Bryan Adams and Jim Vallance, 1985. Introduced on the soundtrack of (MP) *A Night in Heaven* by Bryan Adams, 1983. Two years later, the single, from the soundtrack LP, became a hit and reached #1 on the charts (A&M).

Heaven. w/m Felix Cavaliere, 1969. Top 40 record by The Rascals (Atlantic).

Heaven Can Wait. w. Eddie DeLange, m. James Van Heusen, 1939. Introduced and recorded by Tommy Dorsey, vocal by Jack Leonard (Victor). Other versions of this "Hit Parader" (eleven weeks, twice as #1) by bands of Glen Gray's Casa Loma (Decca); Kay Kyser, vocal by Harry Babbitt (Brunswick); Mitchell Ayres (Vocalion); Van Alexander (Bluebird).

Heaven Drops Her Curtain Down. w/m Sammy Mysels and George Mysels, 1952. Recorded by Toots Camarata, vocal by Bob Carroll (Decca); and Freddy Martin, vocal by Merv Griffin (RCA Victor).

Heaven Help This Heart of Mine. w/m Walter G. Samuels, Leonard Whitcup, and Teddy Powell, 1937. Recorded by Mildred Bailey (Vocalion), Dick Robertson (Decca), Eddy Duchin and his Orchestra (Victor).

Heaven Help Us All. w/m Ronald Miller, 1970. Top 10 record by Stevie Wonder (Tamla).

Heaven in My Arms. w. Oscar Hammerstein II, m. Jerome Kern, 1939. Introduced by Jack Whiting, Frances Mercer, and Hollace Shaw in (TM) *Very Warm for May*. Featured and recorded by Tommy Dorsey, vocal by Anita Boyer (Victor); and Paul Whiteman, vocal by Joan Edwards (Decca).

Heaven in Your Eyes. w/m Paul Dean, Johnny Dexter, Debra Mae Moore, and Mike Reno, 1986. Introduced by the quintet, Loverboy, on the soundtrack of (MP) *Top Gun* and on records (Columbia).

Heaven Is a Place on Earth. w/m Rick Nowels and Ellen Shipley, 1987. #1 single by Belinda Carlisle (MCA).

Heaven Knows. w/m Pete Bellotte, Giorgio Moroder, and Donna Summer, 1979. Top 10 gold record by Donna Summer and Brooklyn Dreams (Casablanca).

Heaven Knows. w/m Dan Walsh and Harvey Price, 1969. Top 40 record by The Grass Roots (Dunhill).

Heavenly Father. w/m Edna McGriff, 1952. Introduced and recorded by Edna McGriff (Jubilee).

Heavenly Hideaway. w. Jules Loman, m. Louis Ricca, 1942. Featured and recorded by Jimmy Dorsey, vocal by Bob Eberly (Decca); Horace Heidt, vocal by Gordon MacRae (Columbia); Sonny Dunham and his Band (Bluebird).

Heavenly Music. w/m Sam Coslow, 1950. Introduced by Gene Kelly in (MM) *Summer Stock* and on records (MGM).

Heaven Must Be Missing an Angel. w/m Kenny St. Louis and Freddy Perrin, 1976. R&B gold record by the family group Tavares (Capitol).

Heaven Must Have Sent You. w/m Eddie Holland, Lamont Dozier, and Brian Holland, 1966. Introduced and recorded by The Elgins (V.I.P.). Top 20 revival by Bonnie Pointer (Motown), 1979.

Heaven on the Seventh Floor. w/m Dominic Bugatti and Frank Musker, 1977. Top 10 gold record by the British actor/singer Paul Nicholas (RSO).

Heaven Says Hello. w/m Cindy Walker, 1968. Country hit by Sonny James (Capitol).

Heaven's Just a Sin Away. w/m Jerry Gillespie, 1977. Recorded by the father-daughter duo The Kendalls (Ovation).

Heaven Will Protect the Working Girl. w. Edgar Smith, m. A. Baldwin Sloane, 1910. Sung by Marie Dressler in (TM) *Tillie's Nightmare*.

Heavy Metal (Taking a Ride). w/m Don Felder, 1981. Introduced in the Canadian-made, animated film (MP) *Heavy Metal*. Recorded by Don Felder (Full Moon).

He Brought Home Another. w/m Paul Dresser, 1896.

He Cried. See **She Cried**.

He'd Have to Get Under—Get Out and Get Under. w. Grant Clarke and Edgar Leslie, m. Maurice Abrahams, 1913. Introduced by Bobby North in (TM) *The Pleasure Seekers*. The song referred to the problems of an early automobile owner.

He Don't Love You (Like I Love You). w/m Jerry Butler, Calvin Carter, and Curtis Mayfield, 1975. #1 record by the vocal trio Tony Orlando and Dawn (Elektra). See also "He Will Break Your Heart."

Heebie Jeebies. w/m Boyd Atkins, 1926.

He Fought for a Cause He Thought Was Right. w/m Paul Dresser, 1896. Introduced and made popular by Dick José.

He Gives Us All His Love. w/m Randy Newman, 1971. Sung on the soundtrack of (MP) *Cold Turkey* by Randy Newman.

He Goes to Church on Sunday. w. Vincent Bryan, m. E. Ray Goetz, 1907. Eddie Foy introduced this song in (TM) *The Orchid*.

He Hasn't a Thing Except Me. w. Ira Gershwin, m. Vernon Duke, 1936. Fanny Brice sang this spoof of "My Man" in (TM) *Ziegfeld Follies of 1936*.

Heidelberg Stein Song. w. Frank Pixley, m. Gustav Luders, 1902. Drinking song sung by the chorus in (TM) *The Prince of Pilsen*.

Heigh-Ho. w. Larry Morey, m. Frank Churchill, 1938. The Dwarf's marching song from Walt Disney's animated feature-length cartoon (MM) *Snow White and the Seven Dwarfs*.

Heigh-Ho, Everybody, Heigh-Ho. w/m Harry Woods, 1929. Sung by Rudy Vallee in (MM) *The Vagabond Lover* and recorded (Victor). Vallee, whose band made its name at the Heigh-Ho Club in New York City in 1928, started his broadcasts with the greeting, "Heigh Ho, Everybody!" which inspired Woods to write the song.

Heigh Ho, the Gang's All Here. w. Harold Adamson, m. Burton Lane, 1933. Performed by Fred Astaire and Joan Crawford in (MM) *Dancing Lady*.

Heiraten. See **Married**.

He Isn't You. See **She Wasn't You**.

Helen Wheels. w/m Paul McCartney and Linda McCartney, 1974. Top 10 record by Paul McCartney and Wings (Apple).

Hell and High Water. w/m T. Graham Brown and Alex Harvey, 1986. #1 Country chart song by T. Graham Brown (Capitol).

He'll Have to Go. w/m Joe Allison and Audrey Allison, 1960. Hit C&W and Pop record by Jim Reeves (RCA). See also "He'll Have to Stay."

He'll Have to Stay. w. Charles Grean, m. Charles Grean, Joe Allison, and Audrey Allison, 1960. Answer song to "He'll Have to Go," recorded by Jeanne Black (Capitol).

Hell in a Bucket. w/m Jerry Garcia and Robert Hunter, 1987. Popular airplay track from the album "In the Dark" by The Grateful Dead (Arista).

Hello. w/m Lionel Richie, 1984. #1 gold single from Lionel Richie's #1 platinum album "Can't Slow Down" (Motown).

Hello, Aloha, How Are You? w. L. Wolfe Gilbert, m. Abel Baer, 1926. Sung by Fran Frey with George Olsen's Orchestra (Victor).

Hello, Broadway! w/m George M. Cohan, 1915. From (TM) *Hello, Broadway!* starring Cohan, William Collier, and Peggy Wood.

Hello, Central, Give Me No Man's Land. w. Sam M. Lewis and Joe Young, m. Jean Schwartz, 1918. Introduced by Al Jolson in (TM) *Sinbad* at the Winter Garden, and recorded by him (Columbia).

Hello, Dolly! w/m Jerry Herman, 1964. Introduced by Carol Channing and company in (TM) *Hello, Dolly!* #1 hit record by Louis Armstrong (Kapp). Grammy Award (NARAS) winner Best Song of the Year. Infringement suit brought by copyright owners of 1949 song "Sunflower," claiming melodic similarity. An out-of-court settlement ensued. In (MM) *Hello, Dolly!*, it was sung by Barbra Streisand, Walter Matthau, Louis Armstrong, and company, 1969.

Hello, Frisco! w. Gene Buck, m. Louis A. Hirsch, 1915. A song referring to the newly opened "cross-country" telephone service. Ina Claire introduced it in (TM) *Ziegfeld Follies of 1915.* Recorded by Elida Morris and Sam Ash (Columbia). It became two-thirds of the title song of (MM) "Hello, Frisco, Hello," 1943, in which it was sung by Alice Faye, John Payne, Jack Oakie, and June Havoc. The song was also interpolated in the Eva Tanguay story (MM) *The I Don't Care Girl,* 1953.

Hello, Goodbye. w/m John Lennon and Paul McCartney, 1967. #1 gold record by The Beatles (Capitol).

Hello, Hawaii, How Are You? w. Bert Kalmar and Edgar Leslie, m. Jean Schwartz, 1915. Nora Bayes had a popular recording (Victor).

Hello, Hello. w/m Peter Kraemer and Terry MacNeil, 1967. Hit record by The Sopwith "Camel" (Kama Sutra). Also recorded by Claudine Longet (A&M).

Hello, Honey. w. George V. Hobart, m. Raymond Hubbell, 1913. Introduced by Elizabeth Brice in *Ziegfeld Follies of 1913.*

Hello, I Love You. w/m John Densmore, Robert Krieger, Raymond Manzarek, and James Morrison, 1968. #1 gold record written and recorded by The Doors (Elektra).

Hello, It's Me. w/m Todd Rundgren, 1970. Introduced and recorded by the quartet, The Nazz, featuring guitarist Todd Rundgren (SGC). The re-recording by Rundgren reached the #5 position on the Pop charts (Bearsville), 1973.

Hello, Ma Baby. w/m Joseph E. Howard and Ida Emerson, 1899. Howard's first song success.

Hello, Mary Lou. w/m Gene Pitney, 1961. Hit record by Ricky Nelson (Imperial).

Hello, Montreal. w. Mort Dixon and Billy Rose, m. Harry Warren, 1928.

Hello, My Lover, Goodbye. w. Edward Heyman, m. John Green, 1931. Frances Langford, in her only Broadway show, introduced it in the short-lived (TM) *Here Goes the Bride,* starring Clark and McCullough and produced by cartoonist Peter Arno.

Hello, Swanee, Hello! w. Addy Britt, m. Sam Coslow, 1927. Featured and recorded by Ben Bernie (Brunswick) and Fred Waring's Pennsylvanians (Victor).

Hello, Young Lovers. w. Oscar Hammerstein II, m. Richard Rodgers, 1951. Introduced by Gertrude Lawrence in (TM) *The King and I.* Best-selling record by Perry Como (RCA Victor). In (MM) *The King and I,* it was performed by Deborah Kerr, with her voice dubbed on the soundtrack by Marni Nixon, 1956.

Hello Again. w/m Neil Diamond and Alan Lindgren, 1980. Introduced by Neil Diamond in the third version of (MP) *The Jazz Singer.* His single made the Top 10 on the charts (Capitol).

Hello and Goodbye. w/m Robert Lissauer, 1951. Sung by Elton Warren and Fred Thomas and danced by Donald McKayle and Elizabeth Williamson in (TM) *Just a Little Simple,* Langston Hughes's and Alice Childress's off-Broadway musical.

Hello Beautiful. w/m Walter Donaldson, 1931. Introduced on radio and recorded by Maurice Chevalier (Victor).

Hello Bluebird. w/m Cliff Friend, 1926. Popular recordings by Vincent Lopez and Orchestra (Brunswick), Jay C. Flippen (Perfect), Nick Lucas (Brunswick), and, in 1953, Teresa Brewer (Coral).

Hello Central, Give Me Heaven. w/m Charles K. Harris, 1901. One of the first successful "telephone" songs. Popular recording by Byron G. Harlan (Edison).

Hello Darlin'. w/m Conway Twitty, 1970. C&W hit and Pop chart record by Conway Twitty (Decca).

Hello Fool. w/m James Coleman and Willie Nelson, 1961. Country hit recorded by Ralph Emery (Liberty).

Hello Heartache, Goodbye Love. w/m Hugo Peretti, Luigi Creatore, and George David Weiss, 1963. Top 40 record by Little Peggy March (RCA).

Hello—Hooray. w/m Rolf Kempf, 1973. Introduced by Judy Collins in her album "Who Knows Where the Time Goes" (Elektra), 1968. Chart record by Alice Cooper (Warner Bros.).

Hello Mudduh, Hello Fadduh! (A Letter from Camp). w. Allan Sherman, m. adapted by Lou Busch, 1963. Music based on "Dance of the Hours" from Amilcare Ponchielli's opera *La Gioconda*. Hit comedy record by Allan Sherman (Warner Bros.).

Hello Old Friend. w/m Eric Clapton, 1976. Recorded by English singer/guitarist/writer Eric Clapton (RSO).

Hello Out There. w/m Kent Westberry and Wayne P. Walker, 1963. C&W chart hit by Carl Belew (RCA).

Hello Stranger. w/m Barbara Lewis, 1963. Hit record by Barbara Lewis (Atlantic). Revived by Yvonne Elliman (RSO), 1977.

Hello Trouble. w/m Orville Couch and Eddie McDuff, 1963. Hit C&W recording by Orville Couch (Vee-Jay).

Hello 'Tucky. w. B. G. DeSylva, m. Joseph Meyer, 1925. Interpolated by Al Jolson in (TM) *Big Boy*.

Hello Twelve, Hello Thirteen, Hello Love. w. Edward Kleban, m. Marvin Hamlisch, 1975. Sung by the company in (TM) *A Chorus Line*. Song not in film version.

Hello Walls. w/m Willie Nelson, 1961. Country hit by Faron Young (Capitol).

Hell's Bells. m. Art Kassel, 1932. The early theme song of Art Kassel and his Kassels in the Air. Recorded by Kassel (Columbia, Bluebird), Jimmie Lunceford (Decca), and Clyde McCoy (Capitol).

He Loved Me Till the All-clear Came. w. Johnny Mercer, m. Harold Arlen, 1942. Introduced by Cass Daley in (MM) *Star-Spangled Rhythm*. She sang it again in (MM) *Riding High*, 1943.

He Loves and She Loves. w. Ira Gershwin, m. George Gershwin, 1927. Introduced by Adele Astaire and Allen Kearns in (TM) *Funny Face*. In the 1956 film (MM) *Funny Face* it was sung by Fred Astaire. In the 1984 all-Gershwin musical, (TM) *My One and Only*, it was performed by Tommy Tune and Twiggy.

He Loves Me All the Way. w/m Billy Sherrill, Carmol Taylor, and Norro Wilson, 1970. Country hit and Pop chart record by Tammy Wynette (Epic).

Help! w/m John Lennon and Paul McCartney, 1965. Introduced by The Beatles in (MM) *Help!*, and gold record by the group (Capitol).

Help Is on Its Way. w/m Glenn Shorrock, 1977. Top 20 record by the Australian group Little River Band (Harvest).

Help Me. w/m Joni Mitchell, 1974. Top 10 single by Joni Mitchell (Asylum).

Help Me, Girl. w. Scott English, m. Laurence Weiss, 1966. Top 40 records by The Outsiders (Capitol), and Eric Burdon and The Animals (MGM).

Help Me, Rhonda. w/m Brian Wilson, 1965. #1 record by The Beach Boys (Capitol). Revived by Johnny Rivers (Epic), 1975.

Help Me, Somebody. w/m Lowman Pauling, 1953. R&B hit by The Five Royales (Apollo).

Help Me Make It Through the Night. w/m Kris Kristofferson, 1970. Sammi Smith was awarded a gold record for her hit C&W and Pop record (Mega). Chart versions by Joe Simon (Spring), and O. C. Smith (Columbia). Grammy Award (NARAS) winner Country and Western Song of the Year. Sung on the soundtrack of (MP) *Fat City* by Sammi Smith, 1971. Top 40 record by Gladys Knight and The Pips (Soul), 1972.

Help Yourself. w. Jack Fishman (Engl.), Mogol (It.), m. C. Donida, 1968. Italian song, "Gli Occhi Miei." English version recorded by Tom Jones (Parrot).

Help Yourself to Happiness. w/m Harry Revel, Mack Gordon, and Harry Richman, 1931. Introduced by Harry Richman in (TM) *Ziegfeld Follies of 1931.* This was Revel's first significant song. Recordings by Glen Gray and the Casa Loma Orchestra (Brunswick) and Smith Ballew, with an early Benny Goodman Band (Columbia).

Helter Skelter. w/m John Lennon and Paul McCartney, 1968. Introduced in The Beatles' "White Album" (Apple).

He May Be Your Man (But He Comes to See Me Sometimes). w/m Lem Fowler, 1922. Recorded by the Cotton Pickers (Brunswick), Lucille Hegamin (Banner), and Helen Humes (Banner).

He Needs Me. w/m Arthur Hamilton, 1955. Introduced by Peggy Lee in (MM) *Pete Kelly's Blues.*

Henry's Made a Lady out of Lizzie. w/m Walter O'Keefe, 1928. Comedy song about Henry Ford's Tin Lizzie becoming a respectable family car was featured by O'Keefe in vaudeville and on radio. Recorded by Billy Jones and Ernie Hare, The Happiness Boys (Victor).

Hep Cat Baby. w/m Cy Coben, 1954. Top 10 C&W chart record by Eddy Arnold (RCA).

Her Bathing Suit Never Got Wet. w. Charles Tobias, m. Nat Simon, 1945. Popularized by The Andrews Sisters (Decca).

Here. w/m Dorcas Cochran and Harold Grant, 1954. Based on the aria, "Caro Nome," from Verdi's opera *Rigoletto.* Leading recording by Tony Martin, with Henri René's Orchestra (RCA Victor).

Here, There and Everywhere. w/m John Lennon and Paul McCartney, 1966. Introduced by The Beatles in their album "Revol-

ver." Popular single by Emmylou Harris (Reprise), 1976.

Hereafter. w. Alan Courtney, m. John Jacob Loeb, 1942. Featured and recorded by Les Brown, vocal by Ralph Young (Okeh); and Teddy Powell, vocal by Ruth Gaylor (Bluebird).

Here Am I. w. Oscar Hammerstein II, m. Jerome Kern, 1929. Introduced by Helen Morgan and Violet Carson in (TM) *Sweet Adeline.* It was sung in the film version (MM) *Sweet Adeline* by Irene Dunne, 1935.

Here Am I (Broken Hearted). See **Broken Hearted (Here Am I).**

Here and Now. w/m Noël Coward, 1963. Introduced by Florence Henderson in (TM) *The Girl Who Came to Supper.*

(Lookie, Lookie, Lookie) Here Comes Cookie. w/m Mack Gordon, 1935. Introduced by Gracie Allen in (MM) *Love in Bloom.* Best-selling record by Glen Gray and the Casa Loma Orchestra, vocal by Pee Wee Hunt (Decca). Others: Ted Fio Rito, vocal by Muzzy Marcellino (Brunswick); Jan Garber (Victor); Teddy Hill (Melotone).

Here Comes Emily Brown. w. Jack Meskill, m. Con Conrad, 1930.

Here Comes Heaven. w/m Joy Byers and Robert F. Tubert, 1968. C&W hit and Pop chart record by Eddy Arnold (RCA).

Here Comes Heaven Again. w. Harold Adamson, m. Jimmy McHugh, 1945. Introduced by Perry Como in (MM) *Doll Face* and on records (Victor).

Here Comes My Baby. w/m Cat Stevens, 1967. Hit record by the British quartet The Tremeloes (Epic).

Here Comes My Baby Back Again. w/m Bill West and Dottie West, 1964. Country hit by Dottie West (RCA).

Here Comes My Ball and Chain. w. Lou Davis, m. J. Fred Coots, 1929. Recorded by the Coon-Sanders Orchestra (Victor). Joe

Sanders, when he had his own band after the death of Carleton Coon, again recorded the song (Decca), 1936. It was also done by Bert Lown (Harmony) and Jimmy Palmer (Mercury).

Here Comes My Daddy Now (Oh Pop-Oh Pop-Oh Pop). w. L. Wolfe Gilbert, m. Lewis F. Muir, 1912.

Here Comes My Girl. w/m Tom Petty and Mike Campbell, 1980. Recorded by Tom Petty and The Heartbreakers (Backstreet).

Here Comes Santa Claus (Down Santa Claus Lane). w/m Gene Autry and Oakley Haldeman, 1947. Gene Autry's recording (Columbia) was a million-seller.

Here Comes Summer. w/m Jerry Keller, 1959. Introduced and recorded by Jerry Keller (Kapp). Chart record by Wildfire (Casablanca), 1977.

Here Comes That Heartache Again. w. Roy Alfred, m. Al Frisch, 1953. Featured and recorded by Tony Bennett (Columbia).

Here Comes That Rainy Day Feeling Again. w/m Roger Cook, Roger Greenaway, and Anthony Gordon Instone, 1971. Top 20 record by the English quintet The Fortunes (Capitol).

Here Comes the Judge. w/m Billie Jean Brown, Suzanne dePasse, and Frederick "Shorty" Long, 1968. Based on the catchphrase popularized by comedian "Pigmeat" Markham, Shorty Long recorded a Top 10 version of the novelty (Soul).

Here Comes the Judge. Dick Alen, Bob Astor, Dewey "Pigmeat" Markham, and Sarah Harvey, 1968. Novelty song based on catchphrase of comedian "Pigmeat" Markham. Top 20 record by Markham (Chess).

Here Comes the Night. w/m Bert Berns, 1965. Top 40 record by the Irish rock group Them (Parrot).

Here Comes the Rain, Baby. w/m Mickey Newbury, 1967. C&W hit and Pop chart record by Eddy Arnold (RCA).

Here Comes the Rain Again. w/m Annie Lennox and David Stewart, 1984. Top 10 single from the British album "Touch" by The Eurythmics (RCA).

Here Comes the Show Boat. w. Billy Rose, m. Maceo Pinkard, 1927. Popularized on radio and records by Vaughn De Leath (Edison). The song was interpolated in the score of (MM) *Show Boat*, 1929.

Here Comes the Sun. w/m George Harrison, 1971. Introduced by The Beatles in their album "Abbey Road" (Capitol), 1969. Top 20 record by Richie Havens (Stormy Forest), 1971.

Here Comes the Sun. w. Arthur Freed, m. Harry Woods, 1930. Introduced and recorded (Hit of the Week) by Vincent Lopez and his Orchestra. Other popular recordings by Charles King (Brunswick); the orchestras of Bert Lown (Victor) and Earl Burtnett (Brunswick).

Here Come the British. w. Johnny Mercer, m. Bernard Hanighen, 1934. Top records by Paul Whiteman's Orchestra, vocal by Johnny Mercer (Victor), and Glen Gray and the Casa Loma Orchestra, vocal by Pee Wee Hunt (Brunswick).

Here Come Those Tears Again. w/m Jackson Browne and Nancy Farnsworth, 1977. Recorded by Jackson Browne (Asylum).

Here Goes. w. Ted Koehler, m. Harold Arlen, 1934. Introduced in the nightclub revue *Cotton Club Parade* by Jimmie Lunceford and his Orchestra, who then recorded it (Victor) as did Ben Pollack and his Band, vocal by Joe Harris (Columbia).

Here I Am. w/m Craig Wasson, 1978. Introduced by Craig Wasson in (MP) *The Boys in Company C.*

Here I Am. w. Hal David, m. Burt Bacharach, 1965. From (MP) *What's New Pussycat?* Recorded by Dionne Warwick (Scepter).

Here I Am (Come and Take Me). w/m Lee Charles, Chuck Jackson, and Marvin Yancey, 1973. Gold record by Al Green (Hi).

Here I Am (Just When I Thought I Was Over You). w/m Norman Sallitt, 1981. Top 10 record by the Australian duo Air Supply (Arista).

Here I Am Again. w/m Shel Silverstein, 1972. Hit Country record by Loretta Lynn (Decca).

Here I Am Baby. w/m William Robinson, 1968. Recorded by The Marvelettes (Tamla).

Here I Go Again. w/m David Coverdale and Bernie Marsden, 1987. First released in England on the album "Saints and Sinners" by the group Whitesnake, 1982. A new version by the British group was recorded and became a #1 hit in the U.S. (Geffen), 1987.

Here I Go Again. w/m William Robinson, Al Cleveland, Terry Johnson, and Warren Moore, 1969. Recorded by Smokey Robinson and The Miracles (Tamla).

Here I'll Stay. w. Alan Jay Lerner, m. Kurt Weill, 1948. Introduced by Nanette Fabray and Ray Middleton in (TM) *Love Life*. Popular recording by Jo Stafford (Capitol).

Here in My Arms (It's Adorable). w. Lorenz Hart, m. Richard Rodgers, 1925. Introduced by Helen Ford and John Purcell in Rodgers and Hart's first successful book musical (TM) *Dearest Enemy*.

Here in My Heart. w/m Pat Genaro, Lou Levinson, and Bill Borrelli, 1952. Vic Damone introduced it on records (Mercury), but Al Martino had the big hit with his first million-seller (B.B.S.). Tony Bennett also had a popular version (Columbia).

Here Is My Heart. w. Leo Robin, m. Ralph Rainger, 1935. From (MM) *Here Is My Heart,* starring Bing Crosby and Kitty Carlisle. Bing did not record it, but his brother Bob did, as vocalist with the Dorsey Brothers Band (Decca). Also recorded by Tony Martin, with Tom Coakley's Band (Brunswick).

Here It Comes Again. w/m Les Reed and Barry Mason, 1965. English song and record by The Fortunes (Press).

Here It Is Monday and I've Still Got a Dollar. w. Maurice Sigler, m. Michael Cleary, 1932. Leading records by Rudy Vallee (Columbia) and Fred Waring (Victor).

Here Lies an Actor. w/m Paul Dresser, 1888.

Here Lies Love. w. Leo Robin, m. Ralph Rainger, 1932. Introduced by Arthur Tracy, Bing Crosby, and Vincent Lopez and his Orchestra in (MM) *The Big Broadcast.* Recordings include Crosby (Brunswick); Ray Noble and his Orchestra, vocal by Al Bowlly (Victor); Sam Coslow (Victor); Jimmie Grier and his Orchestra (Victor).

Here's Hoping. w. Harold Adamson, m. J. Fred Coots, 1932. Recorded by Paul Whiteman's Orchestra, vocal by Jack Fulton (Victor).

Here's Love. w/m Meredith Willson, 1963. Title song of (TM) *Here's Love*, introduced by Laurence Naismith and Ensemble.

Here's Love in Your Eye. w. Leo Robin, m. Ralph Rainger, 1936. Introduced by Benny Fields, Larry Adler, and Benny Goodman and his Orchestra in (MM) *The Big Broadcast of 1937.* Goodman recorded it with Helen Ward doing the vocal (Victor).

Here's Some Love. w/m Richard Mainegra and Jack Roberts, 1976. Country/Pop chart record by Tanya Tucker (MCA).

Here's That Rainy Day. w. Johnny Burke, m. James Van Heusen, 1953. Introduced by Dolores Gray in (TM) *Carnival in Flanders.* Torch song has become a standard through being in the repertoire of top singers and musicians.

Here's to Love. w. Ray Errol Fox, m. Hod David, 1969. Introduced by the cast in the nightclub revue *Weigh-In (Way Out)* at the Upstairs at the Downstairs, New York. Song was interpolated by the cast in the off-Broadway revue (TM) *Broadway Juke Box,* 1981. It has been performed in cabarets by such singers as Karen Morrow, Nancy Dussault, Andrea Marcovicci, Penny Fuller, and Marc Allen. Recorded by Jack Jones (RCA).

Here's to Love. w/m Jay Livingston and Ray Evans, 1949. Introduced by Dean Martin, making his screen debut with Jerry Lewis, in (MP) *My Friend Irma*.

Here's to My Lady. w. Johnny Mercer, m. Rube Bloom, 1951. Featured and recorded by Nat "King" Cole (Capitol).

Here's to Romance. w. Herb Magidson, m. Con Conrad, 1935. Introduced by Nino Martini in (MM) *Here's to Romance*.

Here's to Us. w. Carolyn Leigh, m. Cy Coleman, 1962. Introduced by Nancy Andrews and chorus in (TM) *Little Me*.

Here's What I'm Here For. w. Ira Gershwin, m. Harold Arlen, 1954. Sung by Judy Garland but cut from the original release of (MM) *A Star Is Born*. Recorded by Garland (Decca).

(Here They Come) From All Over the World. w/m Phil Sloan and Steve Barri, 1965. Theme of the (TVM) T.A.M.I. (Teen-Age Music International) Show. Recorded by Jan and Dean (Liberty).

Here We Are. w. Gus Kahn, m. Harry Warren, 1929. Featured and recorded by Ben Bernie (Brunswick); Ted Weems's Orchestra, with vocal by Art Jarrett; Tom Waring, this time as a single and not with brother Fred's band (Brunswick).

Here We Go Again. w/m Donnie H. Lanier and Russell Don Steagall, 1967. Top 20 record by Ray Charles (ABC-TRC). Chart version by Nancy Sinatra (Reprise), 1969.

Her Eyes Don't Shine Like Diamonds. w/m Dave Marion, 1894. Featured in vaudeville by John Russell of the Russell Brothers.

Here You Are. w. Leo Robin, m. Ralph Rainger, 1942. From (MM) *My Gal Sal*. Among recordings: Les Brown, vocal by Ralph Young (Columbia); Glen Gray and the Casa Loma Orchestra, vocal by Kenny Sargent (Decca); Sammy Kaye, vocal by Elaine Beatty (Victor); Freddy Martin, vocal by Stuart Wade (Bluebird); Chico Marx and his Orchestra (Hit).

Here You Come Again. w/m Barry Mann and Cynthia Weil, 1977. C&W/Pop gold record by Dolly Parton (RCA).

Here You Come with Love. w/m Charles N. Daniels (Neil Moret), Harry Tobias, and Jo Trent, 1933. Recorded by orchestras of Leo Reisman, vocal by Reisman (Victor); Bert Lown (Bluebird); Freddy Martin and the Hotel Bossert Orchestra (Oriole).

Her Face. w/m Bob Merrill, 1961. Introduced by Jerry Orbach in (TM) *Carnival*.

Hernando's Hideaway. w/m Richard Adler and Jerry Ross, 1954. Introduced by Carol Haney in (TM) *The Pajama Game*. Leading records by Archie Bleyer and his Orchestra (Cadence); Guy Lombardo, vocal by Kenny Gardner (Decca); Johnnie Ray, with Joe Reisman's Orchestra (Columbia). Carol Haney repeated her role and the song in (MM) *The Pajama Game*, 1957.

Heroes and Villains. w/m Brian Wilson and Van Dyke Parks, 1967. Top 20 record by The Beach Boys (Brother).

Her Royal Majesty. w/m Gerry Goffin and Carole King, 1961. Top 10 record by James Darren (Colpix).

Her Town Too. w/m James Taylor, J. D. Souther, and Waddy Wachtel, 1981. Recorded by James Taylor and J. D. Souther (Columbia).

He's a Bad Boy. w/m Gerry Goffin and Carole King, 1963. Recorded by Carole King (Dimension).

He's a Cousin of Mine. w. Cecil Mack, m. Chris Smith and Silvio Hein, 1906. Sung by Marie Cahill in (TM) *Marrying Mary*.

He's a Devil in His Own Home Town. w. Grant Clarke and Irving Berlin, m. Irving Berlin, 1914.

He's a Good Guy (Yes He Is). w/m William "Smokey" Robinson, 1964. Recorded by The Marvelettes (Tamla).

He's a Good Man to Have Around. w. Jack Yellen, m. Milton Ager, 1929. Introduced by Sophie Tucker in (MM) *Honky Tonk* and recorded by her (Victor), coupled with "The Last of the Red Hot Mammas." Among other artists who did the song in that medium were Billy Murray with the Yuban Radio Orchestra (Perfect); Libby Holman with the Cotton Pickers (Brunswick); and later, Kay Starr, arranged and conducted by Frank DeVol (Columbia).

He's a Heartache (Looking for a Place to Happen). w/m Jeff Silbar and Larry Henley, 1983. #1 Country chart record by Janie Fricke (Columbia).

He's a Rag Picker. w/m Irving Berlin, 1914.

He's a Real Gone Guy. w/m Nellie Lutcher, 1947. Introduced and recorded by Nellie Lutcher and Her Rhythm (Capitol).

He's a Rebel. w/m Gene Pitney, 1962. #1 chart record by The Crystals (Philles).

He's a Tramp. w/m Peggy Lee and Sonny Burke, 1955. Sung by Peggy Lee on the soundtrack of Walt Disney's first full-length animated cartoon in CinemaScope (MM) *The Lady and the Tramp.*

He Says the Same Things to Me. w. Peter Udell, m. Gary Geld, 1964. Country chart record by Skeeter Davis (RCA).

He's Back and I'm Blue. w/m Michael Woody and Robert Anderson, 1988. #1 Country chart hit by The Desert Rose Band, from the album of their name (MCA).

He's Good for Me. w. Dorothy Fields, m. Cy Coleman, 1973. Introduced by Michele Lee in (TM) *Seesaw,* based on the play *Two for the Seesaw.*

He's Got the Whole World in His Hands. w/m Geoff Love, 1958. Traditional gospel song adapted by Love. Thirteen-year-old Laurie London's English recording became a #1 million-seller in the U.S. (Capitol). Later that year, Mahalia Jackson had a popular version (Columbia).

He's Me Pal. w. Vincent P. Bryan, m. Gus Edwards, 1905.

He's My Friend. w/m Meredith Willson, 1964. Introduced by Harve Presnell in (MM) *The Unsinkable Molly Brown.* The song was not in the stage production.

He's My Guy. w. Don Raye, m. Gene De Paul, 1942. Among recordings: Harry James, vocal by Helen Forrest (Columbia); Dinah Shore (Victor); Tommy Dorsey, vocal by Jo Stafford (Victor); Dick Stabile, vocal by Gracie Barry (Decca); Freddie Slack, vocal by Ella Mae Morse (Capitol). It was heard in two 1943 films—(MM) *Hi Ya, Chum* and (MM) *Follow the Band.*

He's My Uncle. w. Charles Newman, m. Lew Pollack, 1940. One of the early patriotic songs of the pre-WW II period. Leading record by Dick Powell (Decca) coupled with "America, I Love You," a hit from WW I (q.v.).

He's 1-A in the Army and He's A-1 in My Heart. w/m Redd Evans, 1941. An early military draft song. Popularized and recorded by Harry James, vocal by Helen Forrest (Columbia); Les Brown, vocal by Betty Bonney (Okeh).

He's So Fine. w/m Ronnie Mack, 1963. #1 record by The Chiffons (Laurie). Chart records by Jody Miller (Epic), 1971; Kristy and Jimmy McNichol (RCA), 1978; Jane Olivor (Columbia), 1978.

He's So Heavenly. w/m Shari Sheeley and Jackie De Shannon, 1962. Popularized by Brenda Lee (Decca).

He's So Shy. w. Cynthia Weil, m. Tom Snow, 1980. Top 10 gold record by The Pointer Sisters (Planet).

He's So Unusual. w. Al Lewis and Al Sherman, m. Abner Silver, 1929. Introduced by Helen Kane in (MM) *Sweetie* and recorded by her (Victor). Other recordings of note by Annette Hanshaw (Harmony), Meyer Davis (Brunswick), and Vaughan DeLeath (Brunswick).

He's Sure the Boy I Love. w/m Barry Mann and Cynthia Weil, 1963. Recorded by The Crystals, with Darlene Love and The Blossoms (Philles).

He's the Greatest Dancer. w/m Bernard Edwards and Nile Rodgers, 1979. Top 10 record by the four Sledge sisters who performed as Sister Sledge (Cotillion).

He's the Last Word. w. Gus Kahn, m. Walter Donaldson, 1927. Popular recordings by Ben Pollack, vocal by The Williams Sisters (Victor), and Ben Bernie and his Hotel Roosevelt Orchestra, vocal by Scrappy Lambert and Billy Hillbot (Brunswick).

He Stopped Loving Her Today. w/m Bobby Braddock and Curly Putman, 1980. Hit Country record by George Jones (Epic).

He Touched Me. See **She Touched Me.**

He Treats Your Daughter Mean (Mama). w/m Charles Singleton and J. H. Wallace, 1953. Hit R&B record by Ruth Brown (Atlantic).

He Walked Right In, Turned Around, and Walked Right Out Again. w. Ed Rose, m. Maxwell Silver, 1906.

He Wears a Pair of Silver Wings. w. Eric Maschwitz, m. Michael Carr, 1942. British song popularized in the U.S. by Kay Kyser, vocal by Harry Babbitt (Columbia) and Dinah Shore (Victor).

He Will Break Your Heart (a.k.a. **He Don't Love You—Like I Love You**) w. Jerry Butler, Calvin Carter, and Curtis Mayfield, 1960. Introduced and Top 10 record by Jerry Butler (Vee Jay). #1 record under alternate title by Tony Orlando and Dawn (Elektra), 1975.

Hey! Ba-Ba-Re-Bop. w/m Lionel Hampton and Curley Hamner, 1946. Introduced and recorded by Lionel Hampton and his Orchestra (Decca). Tex Beneke, with the band of the late Glenn Miller, had the best-seller (Victor). See also **Be-Baba-Leba.**

Hey, Babe, Hey. w/m Cole Porter, 1936. Sung and danced by "the ensemble," comprised of Eleanor Powell, James Stewart, Sid Silvers, Frances Langford, Buddy Ebsen, and Una Merkel in (MM) Born to Dance.

Hey! Baby. w/m Margaret Cobb and Bruce Channel, 1962. Hit record by Bruce Channel (Smash). Revived by José Feliciano (RCA), 1969, and Ringo Starr (Atlantic), 1977.

Hey, Baby (They're Playin' Our Song). w/m Gary Beisbier and Jim Holvay, 1967. Top 20 record by The Buckinghams (Columbia).

Hey, Doll Baby. w/m Titus Turner, 1956. R&B record by The Clovers (Atlantic).

Hey, Good Lookin'. w/m Hank Williams, 1951. Introduced and million-seller recorded by Hank Williams (MGM). Pop hit version by Frankie Laine and Jo Stafford (Columbia). Song was sung by Hank Williams, Jr. on the soundtrack, dubbing for George Hamilton, who played the role of Williams (Sr.) in his life story (MM) *Your Cheatin' Heart*, 1965.

Hey, Good-Lookin'. w/m Cole Porter, 1943. Introduced by Ethel Merman and Bill Johnson, and reprised by Betty Bruce and Bill Callahan in (TM) *Something for the Boys*. This song was a forerunner, via the opening melodic line and lyric, of Hank Williams's similarly titled country hit.

Hey! Jealous Lover. w/m Sammy Cahn, Kay Twomey, and Bee Walker, 1956. Introduced and hit record by Frank Sinatra (Capitol).

Hey, Leroy, Your Mama's Callin' You. w. Johnnie Pruitt, m. Jimmy Castor, 1967. Hit instrumental by saxophonist Jimmy Castor (Smash).

Hey, Little Cobra. w/m Marshall Connors and Carol Connors, 1964. Recorded by The Rip Chords (Columbia).

Hey, Little Girl. w/m Bobby Stevenson and Otis Blackwell, 1959. Leading record by Dee Clark (Abner).

Hey, Little Lucy! (Don'tcha Put No Lipstick On). w/m Aaron Schroeder, George David Weiss, and Sharon Silbert, 1959. Featured and recorded by Conway Twitty (MGM).

Hey, Look Me Over! w. Carolyn Leigh, m. Cy Coleman, 1960. Introduced by Lucille Ball and Paula Stewart in (TM) *Wildcat*. First chart record by The Pete King Chorale (Kapp).

Hey, Loretta. w/m Shel Silverstein, 1974. Country chart hit by Loretta Lynn (MCA).

Hey, Miss Fannie. w/m Ahmet Ertegun, 1952. Featured and recorded by The Clovers (Atlantic).

Hey! Mister Cotton-Picker. w/m Dok Stanford and Robert Mitchum, 1953. Featured and recorded by Tennessee Ford (Capitol).

Hey, Mr. Banjo. w/m Freddy Morgan and Norman Malkin, 1955. Hit record by The Sunnysiders (Kapp).

Hey, Mr. Postman. w. Don Raye, m. Paul Weston, 1946. Top record by Ella Mae Morse, with Freddie Slack's Orchestra (Capitol).

Hey, Rube! w. J. Sherrie Matthews, m. Harry Bulger, 1891.

Hey, Schoolgirl. w. Arthur Garfunkel, m. Paul Simon, 1957. Popular record by Tom and Jerry (Big). The performing name of the duo was a pseudonym for the writers who, under their real names, became major recording artists in 1965.

Hey, That's No Way to Say Goodbye. w/m Leonard Cohen, 1967. Introduced by Canadian poet/novelist/songwriter/folk singer Leonard Cohen in concert and in his album "Songs of Leonard Cohen" (Columbia). Also recorded by Judy Collins in her album "Wildflower" (Elektra).

Hey, Western Union Man. w/m Kenny Gamble, Leon Huff, and Jerry Butler, 1968. Top 20 record by Jerry Butler (Mercury).

Hey, What Did the Bluebird Say? w. Ted Koehler, m. Jimmy McHugh, 1936. Sung by Shirley Temple in (MM) *Dimples*.

(Hey, Won't You Play) Another Somebody Done Somebody Wrong Song. w/m Larry Butler and Chips Moman, 1975. #1 gold record by B. J. Thomas (ABC). Grammy Award (NARAS) winner, C&W Song of the Year.

Hey, Young Fella. w. Dorothy Fields, m. Jimmy McHugh, 1933. Written for the opening show at the Radio City Music Hall in New York. As part of the production, Fields sang it, with McHugh at the piano. The song was sung by a female chorus in (MM) *Dancing Lady* in 1933.

Hey Big Brother. w/m Dino Fekaris and Nick Zesses, 1971. Top 20 record by the rock group Rare Earth (Rare Earth).

Hey Bobba Needle. w/m Kal Mann and Dave Appell, 1964. Top 40 record by Chubby Checker (Parkway).

Hey Bobby. w/m K. T. Oslin, 1989. Hit Country single by K. T. Oslin (RCA).

Hey Deanie. w/m Eric Carmen, 1978. Gold record by Shaun Cassidy (Warner/Curb).

Hey Girl. w/m Gerry Goffin and Carole King, 1963. Top 10 record by Freddie Scott (Colpix). Top 40 record, sang in medley with "My Girl" (q.v.) by Bobby Vee (Liberty), 1968. Revived with a #1 million-seller by Donny Osmond (MGM), 1972.

Hey Girl (I Like Your Style). w/m Norman Whitfield, 1973. Recorded by The Temptations (Gordy).

Hey Joe. w/m Dino Valenti, 1966. Recorded by The Leaves (Mira), then Wilson Pickett (Atlantic), 1969.

Hey Joe. w/m Boudleaux Bryant, 1953. Featured and recorded by Carl Smith (Columbia).

Hey Jude. w/m John Lennon and Paul McCartney, 1968. The #1 record of the year, it was the biggest hit by The Beatles (Capitol) in the following categories: best-selling single; most number of weeks on the Pop charts (19); most number of weeks as #1 (9); longest single in time of any 45-rpm record played on American radio (7 minutes, 11 seconds); longest fade-out of any record (approximately 3 minutes). Wilson Pickett had a Top 40 version (Atlantic), 1969.

Hey Little Girl. w/m Curtis Mayfield, 1963. Top 20 record by Major Lance (Okeh).

Hey Nineteen. w/m Walter Becker and Donald Fagen, 1980. Top 10 record by the group, Steely Dan, and written by its leaders (MCA).

Hey Paula. w/m Ray Hildebrand, 1963. #1 hit record by Paul and Paula (Philips). "Paul" was the writer, Ray Hildebrand; "Paula" was Jill Jackson. The first release of the record was by "Jill and Ray" (Le Cam).

Hey There. w/m Richard Adler and Jerry Ross, 1954. Introduced by John Raitt in (TM) *The Pajama Game*. Rosemary Clooney had a #1, million-selling recording (Columbia). Other hit records, on a lesser scale, by Sammy Davis, Jr. (Decca) and Johnnie Ray (Columbia). Raitt sang it in the 1957 film version (MM) *The Pajama Game*.

Hey There, Good Times. w. Michael Stewart, m. Cy Coleman, 1977. Introduced by John Miller, Michael Mark, Joe Saulter, and Ken Bichel in (TM) *I Love My Wife*.

Hey There Lonely Boy (a.k.a. **Hey There Lonely Girl**). w. Earl Shuman, m. Leon Carr, 1963. Top 40 record by Ruby and The Romantics (Kapp). Revived with a million-selling record by Eddie Holman (ABC), 1970, and Robert John (EMI America), 1980. The latter versions used the "girl" title.

Hey You. w/m Randy Bachman, 1975. Recorded by the Canadian group Bachman-Turner Overdrive (Mercury).

Hey You! Get Off My Mountain. w/m The Dramatics, 1973. Hit R&B and Pop chart record by The Dramatics (Volt).

Hi, Hi, Hi. w/m Paul McCartney and Linda McCartney, 1973. Top 10 record by the writers' group Wings (Apple).

Hi, Mom! w/m Eric Kaz and John Andreolli, 1970. Sung on the soundtrack of (MP) *Hi, Mom!* by Jeffrey Usser.

Hi, Neighbor! w/m Jack Owens, 1941. Introduced by The Merry Macs and Jane Frazee in (MM) *San Antonio Rose*. Recordings by the bands of Orrin Tucker (Columbia) and Sonny Dunham (Bluebird).

Hiawatha. w. James O'Dea, m. Neil Moret (Charles N. Daniels), 1903. Moret wrote the melody as an instrumental, referring to a town in Kansas (not Longfellow's poem) where his sweetheart lived. With its quasi-American Indian melody, it was introduced by John Philip Sousa's band in 1901, but it was not until O'Dea wrote the lyric in 1903 that it became a hit.

Hiawatha's Melody of Love. w. Alfred Bryan and Artie Mehlinger, m. George W. Meyer, 1920. Written as a popular song and interpolated in (TM) *The Midnight Rounders of 1920* at The Century Theatre.

Hibiscus. w. Carolyn Leigh, m. Cy Coleman, 1958. Introduced and recorded by Jo Stafford (Columbia).

Hicktown. w/m Scott Turner and Charlie Williams, 1965. Top 10 Country record by Tennessee Ernie Ford (Capitol).

Hide Away. w/m Freddy King and Sonny Thompson, 1961. Named after Mel's Hide Away Lounge, Chicago, Illinois. Recorded instrumentally by blues singer/guitarist Freddy King (Federal).

Hideaway. w/m Robert Goodman, 1958. Recorded by The Four Esquires (Paris).

Hi-De-Ho. w/m Gerry Goffin and Carole King, 1970. Top 20 record by Blood, Sweat & Tears (Columbia).

Hi-Diddle-Diddle. w/m Hal Keidel and Carleton Coon, 1926. Popular records by Ted Lewis (Columbia), Red Nichols's Red Heads (Perfect), and, later, Phil Harris and the Bell Sisters (Victor).

High, High, High Up in the Hills. w. Sam M. Lewis and Joe Young, m. Maurice Abrahams, 1927. Frank Crumit (Victor) had a popular record.

High, Wide, and Handsome. w. Oscar Hammerstein II, m. Jerome Kern, 1937. Introduced by Irene Dunne in (MM) *High, Wide, and Handsome*. In a wide spectrum of styles, typical of Kern tunes, it was recorded by Gus Arnheim's Orchestra (Brunswick); Edgar Hayes's swing band, vocal by Bill Darnell (Decca); Tempo King's swing combo (Vocalion); and western singer, Tex Ritter (Decca).

High and Low. w. Howard Dietz and Desmond Carter, m. Arthur Schwartz, 1931. Introduced by Roberta Robinson and John Barker in (TM) *The Band Wagon*. It was played by the orchestra in (MM) *The Band Wagon* in 1953.

High and the Mighty, The. w. Ned Washington, m. Dimitri Tiomkin, 1954. The theme from (MP) *The High and the Mighty*. Nominated for an Academy Award. Leading instrumental version by the orchestras of Les Baxter (Capitol); Victor Young (Decca); Leroy Holmes, whistling chorus by Fred Lowery (MGM); Dimitri Tiomkin (Coral). The leading vocal recording by Johnny Desmond, with George Cates's Orchestra (Coral).

High Cotton. w/m Scott Anders and Roger Murrah, 1989. Hit Country single by Alabama (RCA).

Higher and Higher. See **Your Love Keeps Lifting Me Higher and Higher.**

Higher Ground. w/m Stevie Wonder, 1973. #1 R&B and #4 Pop chart hit by Stevie Wonder (Tamla).

Higher Love. w. Will Jennings, m. Steve Winwood, 1986. #1 record by the English singer/musician Steve Winwood (Island). Winner Grammy Award (NARAS) Record of the Year.

High Hopes. w. Sammy Cahn, m. James Van Heusen, 1959. Introduced in (MP) *A Hole in the Head* by Frank Sinatra and Eddie Hodges, who also recorded it (Capitol). Academy Award-winning song, 1959.

High Noon (a.k.a. **Do Not Forsake Me**). w. Ned Washington, m. Dimitri Tiomkin, 1952. Introduced by the voice of Tex Ritter in (MP) *High Noon*. Winner of Academy Award for Best Song, 1952. Ritter recorded it (Capitol), but best-seller was by Frankie Laine (Columbia).

High on a Windy Hill. w/m Joan Whitney and Alex Kramer, 1940. The first hit for the songwriting team. Best-selling record by Jimmy Dorsey, vocal by Bob Eberly (Decca). Others: Lanny Ross (Victor), and the bands of Vaughn Monroe (Bluebird), Gene Krupa (Okeh), Sammy Kaye (Victor).

High on Emotion. w/m Chris DeBurgh, 1984. Written and recorded by the Irish-born Chris DeBurgh (A&M).

High on the List. w. Johnny Burke, m. James Van Heusen, 1950. Introduced by Bing Crosby in (MM) *Mr. Music*. Leading record by Bing Crosby and The Andrews Sisters, with Vic Schoen's Orchestra (Decca).

High on You. w/m Frankie Sullivan and Jim Peterik, 1985. Top 10 single by the quintet Survivor (Scotti Brothers).

High School Confidential. w/m Ron Hardgrave and Jerry Lee Lewis, 1958. Introduced and recorded by Jerry Lee Lewis (Sun).

High School Dance. w/m Edmund Sylvers, James Sylvers, Joseph Sylvers, and Leon Sylvers, 1977. Recorded by the Memphis group consisting of nine brothers and sisters, The Sylvers (Capitol).

High School Nights. w/m Dave Edmunds, Sam Gould, and John David, 1985. Introduced by Dave Edmunds in (MP) *Porky's Revenge* and on records (Columbia).

High Society. m. Porter Steele, 1901. March, now a major Dixieland standard, has been recorded by many jazz artists such as Bob Crosby (Decca), Bobby Hackett (Vocalion), Jelly Roll Morton (Bluebird), Jimmy Dorsey (Columbia), Lionel Hampton (Victor), Louis Armstrong (Decca). There have been numerous lyrics written to the music that is in the public domain.

High Society Blues. w. Joseph McCarthy, m. James F. Hanley, 1930. Sung by Charles Farrell in (MM) *High Society Blues*.

High Society Calypso. w/m Cole Porter, 1956. Introduced by Louis Armstrong and the All-Stars in (MM) *High Society*.

High Steel. w. Jack Heinz, m. Edward Thomas, 1956. Recorded by Lonnie Sattin (Capitol).

High Up on a Hill Top. w/m Abel Baer, George Whiting, and Ivan Campbell, 1928. Recorded by Sid Gary (Cameo), Hal Kemp's Orchestra (Brunswick), Guy Lombardo and His Royal Canadians (Columbia).

Highway 40 Blues. w/m Larry Cordle, 1983. #1 Country chart record by Ricky Skaggs (Epic).

Highwayman. w/m Jim Webb, 1985. Written eight years earlier, it was recorded by Waylon Jennings, Willie Nelson, Johnny Cash, and Kris Kristofferson on the album "The Highwayman." Winner Grammy Award (NARAS) for Country Song of the Year.

Highway Robbery. w/m Garvin and Jones, 1989. Hit Country single by Tanya Tucker (Capitol).

Highways Are Happy Ways. w/m Harry Harris, Tommy Malie, and Larry Shay, 1927. Leading record by Ted Weems, vocal by Parker Gibbs and Dusty Rhodes (Victor).

Highway 61 Revisited. w/m Bob Dylan, 1965. Title song from Bob Dylan's album (Columbia).

Highway to Hell. w/m Angus Young, Malcolm Young, and Bon Scott, 1979. Recorded by the Australian rock band AC/DC (Atlantic).

Hi-Heel Sneakers. w/m Robert Higgenbotham, 1964. #1 R&B and Top 20 Pop hit by Tommy Tucker (Checker). Among other chart records: Stevie Wonder (Tamla), 1965; The Ramsey Lewis Trio (Cadet, Part 1), 1966; José Feliciano (RCA), 1968. See also "Slip-in Mules (No High Heel Sneakers)."

Hijack. m. José Miro, 1975. Top 20 instrumental of Spanish number by flutist Herbie Mann (Atlantic).

Hi-Lili, Hi-Lo. w. Helen Deutsch, m. Bronislau Kaper, 1952. Introduced by Leslie Caron and Mel Ferrer in (MM) *Lili*. A popular single, with Caron and Ferrer, and Hans Som-

mer and the MGM Studio Orchestra, was released from the soundtrack album (MGM).

Hillbilly Fever. w/m Vaughn Horton, 1950. Best-selling record by Little Jimmy Dickens (Columbia).

Hillbilly Fever, No. 2. w/m Vaughn Horton, 1950. Best-selling record by Red Foley and Ernest Tubb (Decca).

Hills of Home, The. w. Floride Calhoun, m. Oscar J. Fox, 1925.

Hills of Old Wyomin', The. w. Leo Robin, m. Ralph Rainger, 1936. Introduced by Frances Langford in (MM) *Palm Springs* and recorded by her (Decca). Other popular recordings: Jan Garber, vocal by Lee Bennett (Decca); Russ Morgan, vocal by Dick Robertson (Brunswick); Tex Ritter (Decca); Sons of the Pioneers, featuring Bob Nolan and Roy Rogers, then known as Dick Weston (Decca).

Hills of Tomorrow, The. w/m Stephen Sondheim, 1981. Introduced by the company in (TM) *Merrily We Roll Along*.

Hill Street Blues. See **Theme from "Hill Street Blues."**

Hill Where the Lord Hides. m. Chuck Mangione, 1971. Instrumental by Chuck Mangione (Mercury).

Him. w/m Rupert Holmes, 1980. Top 10 record by Rupert Holmes (Columbia).

Him or Me. w/m Gene Griffin, Wesley Adams, Larry McCain, Larry Singletary, and Lee Drakeford, 1989. Hit R&B chart single by the group Today (Motown).

Him or Me, What's It Gonna Be? w/m Mark Lindsay and Terry Melcher, 1967. Top 10 record by Paul Revere and The Raiders (Columbia).

Hindustan. w/m Oliver G. Wallace and Harold Weeks, 1917. A favorite instrumental with big bands, first recorded by the Joseph C. Smith Orchestra (Victor) in 1918. Bob Crosby in 1939 (Decca) and Alvino Rey in 1941 (Bluebird) had popular recordings.

Hip, Hip, Hooray. w/m Henry Nemo and Milt Ebbins, 1942. Best-seller by Vaughn Monroe, vocal by the Four V's (Victor). It was coupled with the #1 record *When the Lights Go On Again* (q.v.). Others: Johnny "Scat" Davis (Hit); Andy Kirk, vocal by June Richmond (Decca).

Hip City—Pt. 2. w/m Autry DeWalt and Janie Bradford, 1968. Crossover (R&B/Pop) chart hit by Jr. Walker and The All Stars (Soul).

Hip Hug-Her. w/m Steve Cropper, Donald V. Dunn, Al Jackson, Jr., and Booker T. Jones, 1967. Top 40 instrumental, written by members of the band who recorded it, Booker T. and The MG's (Stax).

Hippy Hippy Shake. w/m Charles Romero, 1964. Top 40 record by the English quartet The Swinging Blue Jeans (Imperial). Revived on the soundtrack of (MP) *Cocktail* and its album (Elektra) by The Georgia Satellites, 1988.

Hip to Be Square. w/m Bill Gibson, Sean Hopper, and Huey Lewis, 1986. Top 10 record by Huey Lewis and The News (Chrysalis).

His Eyes—Her Eyes. w. Marilyn and Alan Bergman, m. Michel Legrand, 1968. Song based on a theme from (MP) *The Thomas Crown Affair*. First vocal recording by Sarah Vaughan (Mainstream), 1972.

His Feet Too Big for de Bed. w/m Dick Sanford, Hernan Braña, and Sammy Mysels, 1947. Featured and recorded by Stan Kenton, vocal by June Christy (Capitol).

His Last Thoughts Were of You. w. Edward B. Marks, m. Joseph W. Stern, 1894. Featured in vaudeville by Lottie Gilson.

His Latest Flame (Marie's the Name). w/m Doc Pomus and Mort Shuman, 1961. Top 10 hit by Elvis Presley (RCA).

His Name Was Dean. w/m Eddie Stuart, 1956. Tribute to late actor James Dean. Introduced by Nathan Russell, with Ray Ellis's Orchestra (Forest). Among other records: Jimmy Wakely, with George Cates's Orchestra (Coral).

His Rocking Horse Ran Away. w. Johnny Burke, m. James Van Heusen, 1944. Introduced by Betty Hutton in (MM) *And the Angels Sing* and on records (Capitol).

History Repeats Itself. w/m Buddy Starcher, 1966. Spoken by Buddy Starcher (Boone) and Cab Calloway (Boom).

Hit and Run. w/m The Bar-Kays, 1982. Eleven writers are credited with authorship of this Top 10 R&B chart number by The Bar-Kays (Mercury).

Hit and Run Affair. w/m Don Roseland, Ray Cormier, and Mel Van, 1954. Leading recording by Perry Como (RCA Victor).

Hitchin' a Ride. w/m Peter Callendar and Mitch Murray, 1970. Gold record by the British group Vanity Fare (Page One).

Hitch It to the Horse. w/m Jesse James, 1968. Top 40 record by The Fantastic Johnny C. (Phil-L.A.).

Hitchy-Koo. w. L. Wolfe Gilbert, m. Lewis F. Muir and Maurice Abrahams, 1912. A popular ragtime song of the day. The title, but not the song, was used between 1917 and 1920 for a series of revues presented by and starring Raymond Hitchcock.

Hittin' on Me. w/m Buddy Johnson, 1953. R&B record by Buddy Johnson (Mercury).

Hittin' the Bottle. w. Ted Koehler, m. Harold Arlen, 1930. From (TM) *Earl Carroll Vanities of 1930*. Main recordings by Frankie Trumbauer (Okeh) and Jimmie Lunceford (Decca).

Hittin' the Ceiling. w. Sidney D. Mitchell, m. Con Conrad and Archie Gottler, 1929. From (MM) *Broadway*. Recorded by Smith Ballew (Okeh) and Paul Specht (Columbia).

Hit Me with Your Best Shot. w/m Eddie Schwartz, 1980. Top 10 gold record by Pat Benatar (Chrysalis).

Hit Record. See **Overnight Sensation.**

Hit the Road, Jack. w/m Percy Mayfield, 1961. #1 hit by Ray Charles (ABC-Paramount). Winner Grammy Award (NARAS) for Best Rhythm and Blues Recording. Revived by Canadian trio, The Stampeders, whose recording included a telephone conversation with disc jockey Wolfman Jack (Quality), 1976.

Hit the Road to Dreamland. w. Johnny Mercer, m. Harold Arlen, 1942. Introduced by Mary Martin, Dick Powell, and the Golden Gate Quartet in (MM) *Star Spangled Rhythm.* Leading record by Freddie Slack, vocal by the Mellowaires (Capitol).

Hobo Flats. w/m Oliver Nelson, 1963. Popular instrumental by jazz organist Jimmy Smith (Verve).

Hobo on Park Avenue. m. Will Hudson, 1935. Introduced and recorded by the Hudson-DeLange Orchestra (Brunswick).

Hocus Pocus. m. Jan Akkerman and Thijs Van Leer, 1973. Top 10 instrumental by the Dutch quartet Focus (Sire).

Ho Ho Song, The. w/m Red Buttons, Joe Darion, and Jack Wolf, 1953. Novelty song, introduced and recorded by Red Buttons with Elliot Lawrence's Orchestra, coupled with "Strange Things Are Happening" (q.v.), (Columbia).

Ho-Hum. w. Edward Heyman, m. Dana Suesse, 1931. Introduced and recorded by Gus Arnheim's Orchestra, with vocal by Bing Crosby (Victor).

Hold Back the Night. w/m Graham Parker, 1977. Introduced in England and released in the U.S. by Graham Parker and The Rumour (Mercury). U.S. and best-selling record by The Trammps (Buddah), 1976.

Hold 'Em Joe. w/m Harry Thomas, 1954. Introduced by Harry Belafonte in (TM) *John Murray Anderson's Almanac,* and recorded by him with Hugo Winterhalter's Orchestra (RCA Victor).

Hold Everything. w/m Red Hayes and Bud-dy Dee, 1956. Top 10 C&W chart record by Red Sovine and Webb Pierce (Decca).

Hold Her Tight. w/m Alan Osmond, Wayne Osmond, and Merrill Osmond, 1972. Top 20 record by The Osmonds (MGM).

Holding Back the Years. w/m Mick Hucknall and Neil Moss, 1986. #1 record by the British sextet, Simply Red, led by singer/ writer Mick "Red" Hucknall (Elektra).

Holding on (When Love Is Gone). w/m John McGhee and Jeffrey Osborne, 1978. #1 R&B and Pop chart entry recorded by the group L.T.D. (A&M).

Holding On to Nothing. w/m Jerry Chesnut, 1968. Hit Country record by Porter Wagoner and Dolly Parton (RCA).

Holding Out for a Hero. w. Dean Pitchford, m. Jim Steinman, 1984. Introduced on the soundtrack of (MM) *Footloose* and on records by Bonnie Tyler (Columbia).

Holdin' On to Yesterday. w/m David Pack and Joseph Puerta, 1975. Top 20 record by the trio Ambrosia (20th Century).

Hold Me. w/m K. T. Oslin, 1988. #1 Country chart record by K. T. Oslin (RCA).

Hold Me. w/m Sheila Escovedo, Connie Guzman, and E. Minnifield, 1987. Top 10 R&B chart record and Pop chart entry by Sheila E. (Paisley Park).

Hold Me. w/m Christine McVie and Robbie Patton, 1982. Top 10 record by the British group Fleetwood Mac (Warner Bros.).

Hold Me. w/m Jack Little, Dave Oppenheim, and Ira Schuster, 1933. Introduced by Little Jack Little. Recorded by Eddy Duchin (Victor), Ted Fio Rito (Brunswick), Peggy Lee (Capitol).

Hold Me. w/m Art Hickman and Ben Black, 1920. Interpolated in (TM) *The Ziegfeld Follies of 1920* after its opening by Art Hickman and his Orchestra and recorded by him instrumentally (Columbia).

Hold Me, Thrill Me, Kiss Me. w/m Harry

Noble, 1952. Popularized via gold record by Karen Chandler, arranged and accompanied by Jack Pleis and his Orchestra (Coral). Revived by Mel Carter (Imperial), 1965.

Hold Me—Hold Me—Hold Me. w. Betty Comden and Adolph Green, m. Jule Styne, 1951. Introduced by Dolores Gray in (TM) *Two on the Aisle.* Popular record by Gloria De Haven, with Guy Lombardo and his Orchestra (Decca).

Hold Me in Your Arms. w/m Ray Heindorf, Charles Henderson, and Don Pippin, 1954. Introduced by Doris Day in (MM) *Young at Heart.* Interesting to note that the three writers are all composers.

Hold Me Now. w/m Thomas Bailey, Alannah Currie, and Joe Leeway, 1984. Written and Top 10 record by the England-based trio, born respectively in England, New Zealand, and South Africa, and calling themselves The Thompson Twins (Arista).

Hold Me Tight. w/m Johnny Nash, 1968. Top 10 record by Johnny Nash (JAD).

Hold My Hand. w/m Jack Lawrence and Richard Myers, 1954. From (MP) *Susan Slept Here.* Nominated for Academy Award. Don Cornell, accompanied by Jerry Carr's Orchestra (Coral), had a million-selling record.

Hold My Hand. w. Jack Yellen and Irving Caesar, m. Ray Henderson, 1934. Introduced by Rudy Vallee in (MM) *George White's Scandals.* Recorded by Vallee (Victor), Frances Langford (Melotone), and the bands of Ted Black (Bluebird) and Vincent Rose (Perfect).

Hold My Hand. w. Douglas Furber, m. Noel Gay, 1932. From the British (TM) *Me and My Girl.* Leading record by Ray Noble and his Orchestra (Victor). In the New York hit revival, 1986, it was sung by Robert Lindsay, Maryann Plunkett, and chorus.

Hold On. w/m Ian Thomas, 1982. Recorded by the group Santana (Columbia).

Hold On. w/m Ian Gomm, 1979. Recorded by the British singer/writer Ian Gomm (Stiff/Epic).

Hold On! I'm Comin'. w/m Isaac Hayes and David Porter, 1966. #1 R&B and Top 40 Pop record by Sam and Dave (Stax). Chart version by Chuck Jackson and Maxine Brown (Wand).

Hold On Tight. w/m Jeff Lynne, 1981. Top 10 record by the British group Electric Light Orchestra (Jet).

Hold On to My Love. w/m Robin Gibb and Blue Weaver, 1980. Top 10 record by Jimmy Ruffin, produced by Robin Gibb (RSO).

Hold On to the Nights. w/m Richard Marx, 1988. Top 10 single by Richard Marx from the album of his name (EMI).

Hold the Line. w/m David Paich, 1978. Top 10 record by the group Toto (Columbia).

Hold Tight—Hold Tight (Want Some Sea Food, Mama). w/m Leonard Kent, Edward Robinson, Leonard Ware, Jerry Brandow, Willie Spotswood, 1939. Recorded and popularized by the Andrews Sisters (Decca).

Hold What You've Got. w/m Joe Tex, 1965. Crossover (R&B/Pop) hit by Joe Tex (Dial).

Hold Your Head Up. w/m Rod Argent and Chris White, 1972. Top 10 record by the British quartet Argent (Epic).

Hold Your Man. w. Arthur Freed, m. Nacio Herb Brown, 1933. Written as the theme song for Jean Harlow, opposite Clark Gable in (MP) *Hold Your Man.* In the same year, Winnie Lightner sang it in another MGM film (MM) *Dancing Lady.* Records by: Morton Downey (Perfect), Gertrude Niesen (Columbia), Don Bestor and his Orchestra (Victor).

Hole in the Wall. m. Steve Cooper, Al Jackson, Booker T. Jones, and N. Nathan, 1965. Crossover instrumental (R&B/Pop) by the band The Packers (Pure Soul).

Holiday. w/m 1987. Top 10 R&B crossover record by Kool & The Gang (Mercury).

Holiday. w/m Barry Gibb, Maurice Gibb, and Robin Gibb, 1967. Top 20 record by the

British brother trio who wrote the song, The Bee Gees (Atco).

Holiday for Love. w/m Webb Pierce, Wayne P. Walker, and Mel Tillis, 1958. Leading C&W record by Webb Pierce (Decca).

Holiday for Strings. m. David Rose, 1943. #1 instrumental by David Rose and his Orchestra (Victor).

Holier Than Thou. w/m Dan Goggin, 1986. Introduced by Edwina Lewis in the off-Broadway musical (TM) *Nunsense*.

Holly, Jolly Christmas, A. w/m Johnny Marks, 1962. From the Christmas program (TVM) "Rudolph the Red-Nosed Reindeer."

Holly Holy. w/m Neil Diamond, 1969. Gold record by Neil Diamond (Uni). Chart record by Jr. Walker and The All Stars (Soul), 1971.

Hollywood. w/m Michael Omartian and Boz Scaggs, 1978. Recorded by Boz Scaggs (Columbia).

Hollywood. w/m John D. Loudermilk, 1961. Recorded by Connie Francis (MGM).

Hollywood Nights. w/m Bob Seger, 1978. Recorded by Bob Seger (Capitol).

Hollywood Swinging. w/m Rickey West, Charles Smith, George Brown, Robert Bell, Ronald Bell, Robert Mickens, Dennis Thomas, 1974. Top 10 single written and recorded by Kool and The Gang (De-Lite).

Holy Cow. w/m Allen Toussaint, 1966. Recorded by Lee Dorsey (Amy).

Homburg. w. Keith Reid, m. Gary Brooker, 1967. Top 40 record by the British group, Procol Harum, of which Brooker was lead vocalist and pianist (A&M).

Home. w/m Roger Miller, 1959. Featured and recorded by Jim Reeves (RCA).

Home. w/m Peter Van Steeden, Harry Clarkson, and Geoff Clarkson, 1931. Geoff Clarkson was sixteen years old when he and his father wrote this with the aid of bandleader Van Steeden. The publisher arranged for a multiple debut on radio, it being introduced on numerous network shows on Thanksgiving eve. It was recorded by Mildred Bailey (Victor); Van Steeden (Victor); Arthur Tracy, "The Street Singer" (Brunswick); Louis Armstrong (Okeh); Irving Kaufman (Crown), and many others. The song was heard in the Andrews Sisters film (MM) *Moonlight and Cactus* in 1944.

Home Again Blues. w/m Harry Akst and Irving Berlin, 1921. Recorded by the Gene Rodemich band (Brunswick) and the Original Dixieland Jazz Band (Victor). This was Berlin's last collaborative song.

Home Cookin'. w/m Henry Cosby, Melvin Moy, and Eddie Willis, 1969. Recorded by Jr. Walker and The All Stars (Soul).

Home Cookin'. w/m Jay Livingston and Ray Evans, 1950. Introduced by Bob Hope and Lucille Ball in (MP) *Fancy Pants*. Popular recorded versions by Bob Hope and Margaret Whiting (Capitol) and Dorothy Shay, "The Park Avenue Hillbilly" (Columbia).

Home for the Holidays. w. Al Stillman, m. Robert Allen, 1954. Hit Christmas record by Perry Como, with Mitchell Ayres's Orchestra (RCA Victor).

Home in San Antone. w/m Floyd Jenkins, 1943. Bob Wills and his Texas Playboys had the first popular record (Okeh).

Home in the Clouds, A. w/m Benny Carter and Benny Goodman, 1939. Introduced and recorded by Benny Goodman, vocal by Martha Tilton (Victor).

Homely Girl. w/m Eugene Record and Stanley McKenney, 1974. Recorded by The Chi-Lites (Brunswick).

Home of the Blues. w/m Johnny Cash, Glenn Douglas, and Vic McAlpin, 1958. Crossover (C&W & Pop) hit by Johnny Cash (Sun).

Home of the Brave. w/m Barry Mann and Cynthia Weil, 1965. Recorded by Jody Miller

(Capitol) and Bonnie and The Treasures (Phi-Dan).

Homesick. w/m Irving Berlin, 1922. Recorded and featured by Nora Bayes (Columbia) and Ted Lewis (Columbia).

Homesick—That's All. w/m Gordon Jenkins, 1945. Recorded by Frank Sinatra, with The Ken Lane Singers (Columbia).

Home Town. w/m Jimmy Kennedy and Michael Carr, 1938. English song. American recording by Pinky Tomlin (Brunswick).

Homeward Bound. w/m Paul Simon, 1966. Top 10 hit by Simon and Garfunkel (Columbia).

Homework. w/m Irving Berlin, 1949. Introduced by Mary McCarty in (TM) *Miss Liberty*. Jo Stafford (Capitol) had a popular recording.

Home You're Tearing Down, The. w/m Betty Sue Perry, 1965. Country hit recorded by Loretta Lynn (Decca).

Homing. w. Arthur L. Salmon, m. Teresa del Riego, 1917. First published in London.

Honest and Truly. w. Leo Wood, m. Fred Rose, 1924. Fred Rose, the country and western writer, co-wrote this song, which has had recordings in country, jazz, and popular fields. Among those: Fred Rose (Brunswick), Henry Burr (Victor), Jimmie Lunceford (Decca), Ralph Flanagan (Victor), Billy May (Capitol).

Honest I Do. w/m Jimmy Reed and Ewart G. Abner, Jr., 1957. R&B and Pop hit by Jimmy Reed (Vee-Jay).

Honestly. w. Bud Green, m. Jack Little, 1940. Popularized and recorded by Eddy Duchin, with vocal by Stanley Worth (Columbia).

Honestly Sincere. w. Lee Adams, m. Charles Strouse, 1960. Introduced by Dick Gautier in (TM) *Bye Bye Birdie*. Sung by Jesse Pearson in the film version (MM) *Bye Bye Birdie*, 1963.

Honesty. w/m Billy Joel, 1979. Recorded by Billy Joel (Columbia).

Honey. w/m Bobby Russell, 1968. Introduced by Bob Shane. #1 C&W/Pop gold record by Bobby Goldsboro, which sold over five million copies (United Artists). The song won the Country Music Association award for Song of the Year.

Honey. w. Seymour Simons and Haven Gillespie, m. Richard A. Whiting, 1929. Featured and recorded by Rudy Vallee (Victor), it became a million copy sheet music seller in its first year. It was featured in (MP) *Her Highness and the Bellboy*, starring Hedy Lamarr and Robert Walker, 1945.

Honey, Don't Leave L.A. w/m Danny Kortchmar, 1978. Recorded by James Taylor (Columbia).

Honey, Do You Think It's Wrong? w/m Al Dexter and Frankie Marvin, 1945. Recorded by Al Dexter (Columbia).

Honey (Open That Door). w/m Mel Tillis, 1984. #1 Country chart record by Ricky Skaggs (Epic).

Honey-Babe. w. Paul Francis Webster, m. Max Steiner, 1955. With traditional roots, this was developed into the marching song in (MP) *Battle Cry*. Art Mooney and his Orchestra had a Top 10 record (MGM).

Honey Boy. w. Jack Norworth, m. Albert Von Tilzer, 1907. The song was featured by Sophie Tucker in vaudeville and was a tribute to George "Honey Boy" Evans, the popular minstrel. Evans got the nickname after his hit of 1894. See also "I'll Be True to My Honey Boy."

Honey Bun. w. Oscar Hammerstein II, m. Richard Rodgers, 1949. Introduced by Mary Martin, Myron McCormick, and the ensemble in (TM) *South Pacific*. Mitzi Gaynor and Ray Walston sang it in (MM) *South Pacific*.

Honey-Bun. w. Zelda Sears, m. Vincent Youmans, 1924. Sung by Ada May in (TM) *Lollipop*.

Honey Chile. w/m Sylvia Moy and Richard Morris, 1967. Top 20 record by Martha and The Vandellas (Gordy).

Honeycomb. w/m Bob Merrill, 1957. #1 record by Jimmie Rodgers (Roulette).

Honey Come Back. w/m Jim Webb, 1970. Top 20 record by Glen Campbell (Capitol).

Honeydripper, The. w/m Joe Liggins, 1945. Joe Liggins, rhythm and blues singer, pianist, and bandleader, had a million-seller that was on the R&B charts for seventeen weeks (Exclusive). Jimmie Lunceford, vocal by the Delta Rhythm Boys, also had a popular record (Decca).

Honey Gal. w/m Shelton Brooks, 1909. One of Brooks's first popular songs, due in part to its introduction by Al Jolson at the Winter Garden in New York.

Honey Hush. w/m Lou Willie Turner, 1954. Leading record by Joe Turner (Atlantic).

Honey in the Honeycomb. w. John LaTouche, m. Vernon Duke, 1940. Introduced by Katherine Dunham in (TM) *Cabin in the Sky*. Sung by Lena Horne and Ethel Waters in the film version (MM) *Cabin in the Sky*, 1943.

Honey Love. w/m Clyde McPhatter and J. Gerald, 1954. Top 10 R&B record by The Drifters (Atlantic).

Honey-Love. w. Jack Drislane, m. George W. Meyer, 1911.

Honey Love (We've Got). See **We've Got Honey Love.**

Honeymoon, The. m. George Rosey (George M. Rosenberg), 1894. March instrumental.

Honeymoon Hotel. w. Al Dubin, m. Harry Warren, 1933. Sung by Dick Powell and Ruby Keeler in (MM) *Footlight Parade*. Records: Dick Powell (Brunswick); Rudy Vallee, vocal by then band singer Alice Faye (Bluebird); Freddy Martin, vocal by Terry Shand (Brunswick); Ozzie Nelson (Vocalion).

Honeymoon Is Over, The. w. Tom Jones, m. Harvey Schmidt, 1966. Introduced by Mary Martin and Robert Preston in (TM) *I Do! I Do!*

Honeymoon on a Rocket Ship. w/m Johnnie Masters, 1953. Featured and recorded by Hank Snow (RCA Victor).

Honeysuckle Rose. w. Andy Razaf, m. Thomas "Fats" Waller, 1929. Introduced in the nightclub revue *Load of Coal* at Connie's Inn, New York. Recorded by many in addition to Waller (Victor), among whom are: Frankie Trumbauer (Columbia); the Dorsey Brothers on a two-sided recording (Decca); Red Norvo (Columbia); and a popular revival by Willie Nelson in 1980 (Columbia) that was followed by its use as the title song in (MM) *Honeysuckle Rose* starring Nelson in 1981. Other films were (MM) *Walking My Baby Back Home* starring Donald O'Connor and Paula Kelly, dubbing for Janet Leigh, 1938; (MM) *Tin Pan Alley*, sung by Betty Grable and chorus, 1940; (MM) *Thousands Cheer*, sung by Lena Horne, 1943; and (MM) *New York, New York*, 1977. It was also performed by Ken Page and Nell Carter in the Fats Waller musical (TM) *Ain't Misbehavin'*, 1978.

Honeythief, The. w/m John McElhone, Bill McLeod, Graham Skinner, and Harry Travers, 1987. Chart single from the album "Hipsway," written and recorded by the Scottish quartet of the same name (Columbia).

Hong Kong Blues. w/m Hoagy Carmichael, 1939. Recorded by Carmichael (Brunswick), followed a year later by Tommy Dorsey and his Orchestra (Victor). Carmichael sang it at the piano in (MP) *To Have and Have Not*, 1944.

Honky Cat. w/m Elton John and Bernie Taupin, 1972. Top 10 record by English singer Elton John (Uni).

Honky Tonk w. Henry Glover, m. Bill Doggett, Billy Butler, Shep Shephard, Clifford Scott, 1956. Hit instrumental by Bill Doggett (King). Revived instrumentally by James Brown (Polydor).

Honky Tonk Blues. w/m Hank Williams, 1952. Country chart hit by Hank Williams (MGM), 1952. Charley Pride's version hit #1 on the Country charts (RCA), 1980.

Honky Tonk Girl. w/m Chuck Harding, 1954. Featured and recorded by Hank Thompson (Capitol).

Honky Tonkin'. w/m Hank Williams, 1948. One of Williams's first hit records (Sterling). Revived by Hank Williams, Jr. (Elektra), 1982.

Honky Tonk Man. w/m Johnny Horton, Tillman Franks, and Howard Hausey, 1956. Leading record by Johnny Horton (Columbia). Revived with Top 10 Country chart single by Dwight Yoakam (Reprise), 1986.

Honky Tonk Moon. w/m Dennis O'Rourke, 1988. #1 Country chart record by Randy Travis (Warner Bros.).

Honky Tonk Song. w/m Mel Tillis and A. R. Peddy, 1957. Hit C&W record by Webb Pierce (Decca).

Honky Tonk Train (a.k.a. **Honky Tonk Train Blues**). m. Meade Lux Lewis, 1939. Boogie Woogie pianist Lewis originally recorded it in the late twenties in Chicago. It was not until 1937, when John Hammond brought him to New York, that he re-recorded it (Victor). He was to again preserve it on discs on a 12" record (Blue Note), 1940 and (Decca), 1941. The hit version was by Bob Crosby and his Orchestra, (Decca), 1939, featuring Bob Zurke on piano. Among others: Frankie Trumbauer and his Band (Varsity), Dick Hyman (MGM), Mel Henke (Vita), Milt Herth (Decca).

Honky Tonk Women. w/m Mick Jagger and Keith Richards, 1969. #1 gold record by the English group The Rolling Stones (London).

Honolulu. w. Gus Kahn, m. Harry Warren, 1939. Introduced by Gracie Allen in (MM) *Honolulu*. Recorded by Tommy Dorsey, vocal by Edythe Wright (Victor); Glen Gray and the Casa Loma Orchestra (Decca); Van Alexander and his Orchestra (Bluebird).

Honolulu Lulu. w/m Jan Berry, Roger Christian, and Lou Adler, 1963. Hit record by Jan and Dean (Liberty).

Hoodle Addle. w/m Ray McKinley, 1947. Introduced and best-selling record by Ray McKinley, vocal by band members Lou Stein, Mundell Lowe, and Ward Erwin (Majestic). Also recorded by Ella Mae Morse (Capitol).

Hoodoo Man, The. w. Harry D. Kerr, m. Nacio Herb Brown, 1924. Recorded by Paul Whiteman (Victor).

Hooked on a Feeling. w/m Mark James, 1969, 1974. Top 10 record by B. J. Thomas (Scepter). The Swedish sextet, Blue Swede, had a #1 gold record in the U.S. (EMI), 1975.

Hooked on Music. w/m Mac Davis, 1981. Country chart hit by Mac Davis (Casablanca).

Hooked on You. w/m David Gates, 1977. Recorded by the group Bread (Elektra).

Hooked on Your Love. w/m Curtis Mayfield, 1976. Introduced by Irene Cara and Lonette McKee in (MM) *Sparkle*. Leading record by Aretha Franklin (Atlantic).

Hoo-oo, Ain't You Coming Out To-night? w/m Herbert Ingraham, 1908.

Hoop-De-Doo. w. Frank Loesser, m. Milton De Lugg, 1950. Introduced by Milton De Lugg and his Band on the late-night network TV show "Broadway Open House." Most popular records: Perry Como (RCA Victor), Kay Starr (Capitol), Russ Morgan and his Orchestra (Decca), Doris Day (Columbia).

Hooray for Captain Spaulding. w. Bert Kalmar, m. Harry Ruby, 1928. Groucho Marx and cast members introduced this in (TM) *Animal Crackers*. Marx repeated his performance in the film version (MM) *Animal Crackers*, 1930. Red Skelton and Fred Astaire sang it in the Kalmar and Ruby biography (MM) *Three Little Words*, 1950.

Hooray for Hazel. w/m Tommy Roe, 1966. Top 10 record by Tommy Roe.

Hooray for Hollywood

Hooray for Hollywood. w. Johnny Mercer, m. Richard A. Whiting, 1938. Introduced by Frances Langford, Johnny "Scat" Davis, and Benny Goodman and his Orchestra in (MM) *Hollywood Hotel*. It became the unofficial theme song of the movie capitol. Sammy Davis sang it in (MM) *Pepe* in 1960.

Hooray for Love. w. Leo Robin, m. Harold Arlen, 1948. Introduced by Tony Martin in (MM) *Casbah*. Recorded by: Tony Martin (RCA Victor), Johnny Mercer (Capitol).

Hooray for Love. w. Dorothy Fields, m. Jimmy McHugh, 1935. Introduced by Gene Raymond in (MM) *Hooray for Love*.

Hoosier Sweetheart. w/m Billy Baskette, Paul Ash, and Joe Goodwin, 1927.

Hootie Blues. w/m Jay McShann and Charles Parker, 1942. Historic recording as it was the first to feature a solo by alto saxist Charlie Parker who co-wrote the number with pianist McShann. Introduced by the band of McShann (whose nickname was "Hootie"), vocal by Walter Brown (Decca).

Hopeless. w/m Doc Pomus and Alan Jeffreys, 1963. Featured and recorded by Andy Williams (Columbia).

Hopelessly Devoted to You. w/m John Farrar, 1978. Introduced by Olivia Newton-John in (MM) *Grease* and on her gold record (RSO). Nominated for an Academy Award.

Hope That We Can Be Together Soon. w/m Kenny Gamble and Leon Huff, 1975. Recorded by Sharon Paige and Harold Melvin & The Blue Notes (20th Century).

Hope You're Feelin' Me Like I'm Feelin' You. w/m Jim Rushing and Bobby David, 1975. Hit Country record by Charley Pride (RCA).

Hoping That You're Hoping. w/m Betty E. Harrison, 1956. Recorded by The Louvin Brothers (Capitol).

Hoppy, Gene, and Me. w/m Thomas "Snuff" Garrett, Stephen Dorff, and Milton Brown, 1975. Western star Roy Rogers recorded this novelty about movie cowboys, William "Hopalong Cassidy" Boyd, Gene Autry, and himself (20th Century).

Hop-Scotch Polka (Scotch Hot). w/m William "Billy" Whitlock, Carl Sigman, and Gene Rayburn, 1949. Introduced in vaudeville in England by Billy Whitlock. Based on traditional Scottish folk song. Hit U.S. records by Art Mooney and his Orchestra (MGM) and Guy Lombardo and his Royal Canadians (Decca).

Horse, The. m. Jesse James, 1968. Cliff Nobles & Co. had a gold record instrumental (Phil-L.A.).

Horse Fever. m. Jesse James, 1968. Instrumental successor to "The Horse," (q.v.), recorded by Cliff Nobles & Co. (Phil-L.A.).

Horses. w. Byron Gay, m. Richard A. Whiting, 1926. A novelty hit recorded by George Olsen's Orchestra with vocal by Fran Frey (Victor); The Georgians, vocal by Johnny Morris (Columbia); Billy Jones (Regal); Arthur Fields with the California Ramblers (Perfect).

Horse Told Me, The. w. Johnny Burke, m. James Van Heusen, 1950. Introduced by Bing Crosby in (MM) *Riding High*.

Horse with No Name, A. w/m Lee Bunnell, 1972. #1 gold record by the trio America composed of sons of U.S. military personnel based in England (Warner Bros.).

Horse with the Dreamy Eyes, The. w. George Forrest and Robert Wright, m. Walter Donaldson, 1937. Sung in (MP) *Saratoga* by Cliff Edwards, Clark Gable, Jean Harlow (her last film), Hattie McDaniel, and Una Merkel.

Hostess with the Mostes' on the Ball, The. w/m Irving Berlin, 1950. Introduced by Ethel Merman in (TM) *Call Me Madam*, and repeated in (MM) *Call Me Madam*, 1953.

Hot and Bothered. m. Edward Kennedy "Duke" Ellington, 1928. Recorded by Ellington (Okeh).

Hot Blooded. w/m Lou Gramm, 1978. Gold record by the group Foreigner (Atlantic).

308

Hot Canary, The. m. Paul Nero, 1949. Adapted from the Belgian song "Le Canari," the first recording was by Paul Weston with Nero as solo violinist (Capitol). Violinist Florian Zabach, with Al Rickey's Orchestra, had a million-seller (Decca), 1951.

Hot Child in the City. w/m James McCulloch and Nick Gilder, 1978. #1 platinum-selling single by Nick Gilder (Chrysalis).

Hot Diggity (Dog Ziggity Boom). w/m Al Hoffman and Dick Manning, 1956. Adapted from the 1st theme of *España, Rhapsody for Orchestra*, by Alexis Chabrier. Hit record by Perry Como (RCA).

Hotel California. w/m Don Felder, Don Henley, and Glenn Frey, 1977. #1 gold record by The Eagles (Asylum).

Hotel Happiness. w. Earl Shuman, m. Leon Carr, 1963. Featured and Top 10 record by Brook Benton (Mercury).

Hot Fun in the Summertime. w/m Sylvester Stewart, 1969. Top 10 record by Sly [Stewart] and The Family Stone (Epic). Revived by the group Dayton (Liberty), 1982.

Hot Girls in Love. w/m Paul Dean and Bruce Fairbarn, 1983. Recorded by the Canadian group Loverboy (Columbia).

Hot Heels. w. Ballard MacDonald and Billy Rose, m. Lee David, 1928. From (TM) *Padlocks of 1927*.

Hot House Rag. m. Paul Pratt, 1914. Originally issued by five different piano roll companies.

Hot in the City. w/m Billy Idol, 1982. Recorded by the English singer Billy Idol (Chrysalis).

Hot Legs. w/m Rod Stewart, 1978. Recorded by British singer Rod Stewart (Mercury).

Hot Line. w/m Kenny St. Lewis and Freddie Perren, 1976. Top 10 gold record by the family group The Sylvers (Capitol).

Hot Lips. w/m Henry Busse, Henry Lange, and Lou Davis, 1922. Busse's distinctive

trumpet solo was featured in Paul Whiteman's recording (Victor). When Busse formed his own band, it became his opening theme, which he recorded (Decca), 1934.

Hot 'n' Nasty. w/m Steve Marriott, Greg Ridley, Jerry Shirley, and Clem Clempson, 1972. Written and recorded by the English group Humble Pie (A&M).

Hot Number. w/m Ishmael Ledesma, 1979. Recorded by the Latino band Foxy (Dash).

Hot Pants (She Got to Use What She Got to Get What She Wants). w/m James Brown and Fred Wesley, 1971. #1 R&B and Top 20 Pop record by James Brown (People).

Hot Pastrami. w/m Dessie Rozier, 1963. Chart record by The Dartells (Dot).

Hot Rod Hearts. w/m Stephen Geyer and Bill LaBounty, 1980. Recorded by Robbie Dupree (Elektra).

Hot Rod Lincoln. w/m Charles Ryan and W. S. Stevenson, 1960, 1972. Hit Country and Pop novelty by Johnny Bond (Republic) and Charlie Ryan and The Timberline Riders (4 Star). Revived with a Top 10 record by Commander Cody and His Lost Planet Airmen (Paramount), 1972.

Hot Rod Race. w/m George Wilson, 1951. Novelty, sung by Tiny Hill with his Orchestra (Mercury).

Hot Smoke and Sassafras. w/m Roy E. Cox, Jr. and William Rodney Prince, 1969. Top 20 record by The Bubble Puppy (International Artists).

Hot Stuff. w/m Pete Bellotte, Harold Faltermeyer, and Keith Forsey, 1979. From her album "Bad Girls," disco queen Donna Summer had a #1 platinum single (Casablanca).

Hot Stuff. w/m Mick Jagger and Keith Richards, 1976. Recorded by The Rolling Stones (Rolling Stones).

Hot Summer Nights. w/m Walter Egan, 1978. Introduced, and chart record by Walter

Egan (Columbia). The group, Night, had a Top 20 version (Planet), 1979.

Hot Tamale Alley. w/m George M. Cohan, 1895. Cohan's first hit, written at the age of seventeen. Introduced in vaudeville by Mary Irwin.

Hottentot Potentate, The. w. Howard Dietz, m. Arthur Schwartz, 1935. Introduced by Ethel Waters in (TM) *At Home Abroad.*

Hot Time in the Old Town Tonight. w. Joe Hayden, m. Theodore H. Metz, 1896. Metz was bandleader of McIntyre and Heath Minstrels who introduced the song. Theodore Roosevelt's Rough Riders adopted it during the battle of San Juan Hill. The first recording was by ragtime singer, Lew Spencer, in 1897 as the publisher's vehicle for plugging the song.

Hot Time in the Town of Berlin, A (When the Yanks Go Marching In). w. John De Vries, m. Joe Bushkin, 1944. #1 best-selling record by Bing Crosby and The Andrews Sisters (Decca).

Hot Toddy. w. Herb Hendler, m. Ralph Flanagan, 1952. Ralph Flanagan and his Orchestra had a hit instrumental version (RCA Victor).

Hot Toddy. m. Benny Carter, 1932. Jazz instrumental, featured and recorded by Cab Calloway and his Orchestra (Brunswick).

Hound Dog. w/m Jerry Leiber and Mike Stoller, 1953, 1956. Introduced and R&B hit record by Big Mama Thornton (Peacock). Three years later, Elvis Presley recorded it and had a two-sided #1 record, coupled with "Don't Be Cruel" (q.v.) (RCA). Sung by Sha-Na-Na in (MM) *Grease,* 1978.

Hound Dog Man. w/m Doc Pomus and Mort Shuman, 1959. Introduced by Fabian in (MM) *Hound Dog Man* and on records (Chancellor).

Hourglass. w. Chris Difford, m. Glenn Tilbrook, 1987. Chart single by the English quartet, Squeeze, of which the writers were members (A&M).

Hour Never Passes, An. w/m Jimmy Kennedy, 1944. Featured and recorded as an instrumental by Jimmy Dorsey and his Orchestra (Decca).

Hour of Parting, The. w. Gus Kahn, m. Mischa Spoliansky, 1931. Bert Lown (Victor) and Victor Young (Brunswick) and their bands had popular recordings. Later jazz versions by Benny Goodman, featuring Ziggy Elman (Columbia); Teddy Wilson (Brunswick); and Earl Bostic (King).

House at Pooh Corner. w/m Kenny Loggins, 1971. Recorded by The Nitty Gritty Dirt Band (United Artists).

House I Live In, The (That's America to Me). w/m Earl Robinson and Lewis Allan, 1942. Patriotic work, first recorded by Paul Robeson (Columbia); later by Conrad Thibault (Decca). The Delta Rhythm Boys sang it in (MM) *Follow the Boys,* 1944. Frank Sinatra sang it in the Academy Award-winning movie short (MM) *The House I Live In,* 1945. His version became a Top 40 record (Columbia).

House Is Haunted, The (By the Echo of Your Last Goodbye). w. Billy Rose, m. Basil G. Adlam, 1934. Introduced by Jane Froman in (TM) *Ziegfeld Follies.* It was recorded by Ramona, with Paul Whiteman's Orchestra (Victor).

House Is Not a Home, A. w. Hal David, m. Burt Bacharach, 1964. Title song of (MP) *A House Is Not a Home.* Recorded by Dionne Warwick (Scepter).

House of Bamboo. w/m William Crompton and Norman Murrells, 1960. English song. Leading U.S. recording by Earl Grant (Decca).

House of Blue Lights. w/m Don Raye and Freddie Slack, 1946. Leading recording by Freddie Slack, vocal by Ella Mae Morse (Capitol). The Andrews Sisters had a popular version (Decca). Revived with a Top 20 record by Chuck Miller (Mercury), 1955.

House of Flowers. w. Truman Capote and Harold Arlen, m. Harold Arlen, 1954. Introduced in (TM) *House of Flowers* by Diahann Carroll and Rawn Spearman.

House of the Rising Sun. w/m Alan Price (adaptation), 1964. Adaptation of American traditional song. #1 hit by the English group The Animals (MGM). Million-seller revival by Frijid Pink (Parrot), 1970.

Housequake. w/m Prince Rogers Nelson, 1987. Introduced by Prince in the concert-film (MM) *Sign O' the Times.*

House That Jack Built, The. w/m Bobby Lance and Fran Robbins, 1968. Top 10 hit by Aretha Franklin (Atlantic).

House with Love in It, A. w. Sylvia Dee, m. Sidney Lippman, 1956. Popularized by The Four Lads (Columbia).

Houston. w/m Lee Hazlewood, 1965. Top 40 record by Dean Martin (Reprise).

Houston (I'm Comin' to See You). w/m David Paich, 1974. Recorded by Glen Campbell (Capitol).

Houston Solution. w/m Paul Overstreet and Don Schlitz, 1989. Hit Country record by Ronnie Milsap (RCA).

How About Me? w/m Irving Berlin, 1928. This Berlin ballad received great exposure through the recordings of Ben Bernie, with vocal by Scrappy Lambert (Bluebird); Morton Downey (Victor); Nick Lucas (Brunswick); Fred Waring's Pennsylvanians (Victor).

How About You? w. Ralph Freed, m. Burton Lane, 1941. Introduced by Judy Garland and Mickey Rooney in (MM) *Babes on Broadway.* Nominated for Academy Award, 1941. Best-selling record: Tommy Dorsey, vocal by Frank Sinatra (Victor).

How Am I Supposed to Live Without You? w/m Mitchell Bolton and Doug James, 1983. Recorded by Laura Branigan (Atlantic).

How Am I to Know? w. Dorothy Parker, m. Jack King, 1929. Sung by Russ Columbo in (MP) *Dynamite.* Ava Gardner sang it in (MP) *Pandora and the Flying Dutchman,* 1951. Among the many recordings were those by Smith Ballew (Okeh); the Arden-Ohman Orchestra, vocal by Scrappy Lambert (Victor);

Glenn Miller, in an early (1937) session (Decca); Tommy Dorsey, vocal by Jack Leonard (Victor); Stan Kenton (Capitol).

How Are Things in Glocca Morra? w. E. Y. Harburg, m. Burton Lane, 1947. Introduced by Ella Logan in (TM) *Finian's Rainbow.* Leading recordings, other than singles from the Original Cast album (RCA), by Buddy Clark (Columbia); Martha Tilton (Capitol); Tommy Dorsey, vocal by Stuart Foster (Victor); Dick Haymes (Decca). In the 1968 film version (MM) *Finian's Rainbow,* it was sung by Petula Clark, Fred Astaire, Tommy Steele, Don Francks, Barbara Hancock, and chorus.

How Blue the Night. w. Harold Adamson, m. Jimmy McHugh, 1944. Introduced by Dick Haymes in (MM) *Four Jills in a Jeep.* Haymes had the top recording (Decca).

How 'bout Us. w/m Dana Walden, 1981. Recorded by the sextet Champaign (Columbia).

How Can I Be Sure? w/m Eddie Brigati and Felix Cavaliere, 1967. Top 10 record by The Young Rascals (Atlantic). David Cassidy had a popular version (Bell), 1972.

How Can I Ever Be Alone? w. Oscar Hammerstein II, m. Arthur Schwartz, 1940. From the New York World's Fair production (TM) *American Jubilee.* Sung by Lucy Monroe (as Jenny Lind) and Gene Marvey, and danced by Paul Haakon and the ballet corps. Featured and recorded by Abe Lyman and his Californians, vocal by Frank Parrish (Bluebird); Mildred Bailey (Columbia); Larry Clinton, vocal by Terry Allen (Victor).

How Can I Fall. w/m David Glasper, Marcus Lillington, Michael Delahunty, and Ian Spice, 1989. Hit record by the group Breathe (A&M).

How Can I Meet Her? w/m Gerry Goffin and Jack Keller, 1962. Recorded by The Everly Brothers (Warner Bros.).

How Can I Tell Her It's Over? w/m Barry Mann and Cynthia Weil, 1966. Featured and recorded by Andy Williams (Columbia).

How Can I Unlove You. w/m Joe South, 1971. Crossover (C&W/Pop) chart record by Lynn Anderson (Columbia).

(How Can I Write on Paper) What I Feel in My Heart. w/m Don Carter, Danny Harrison, George Kent, and Jim Reeves, 1961. Introduced and recorded by Jim Reeves (RCA).

How Can You Describe a Face? w. Betty Comden and Adolph Green, m. July Styne, 1961. Introduced by Sydney Chaplin in (TM) *Subways Are for Sleeping.*

How Can You Face Me? w. Andy Razaf, m. Thomas "Fats" Waller, 1934. Introduced and recorded by Fats Waller and his Orchestra (Victor).

How Can You Forget? w. Lorenz Hart, m. Richard Rodgers, 1938. Sung by Jeni LeGon in (MM) *Fools for Scandal.* Recorded by Tommy Dorsey, vocal by Edythe Wright (Victor).

How Can You Mend a Broken Heart. w/m Barry Gibb and Robin Gibb, 1971. #1 gold record by British brother trio The Bee Gees (Atco).

How Can You Say "No" (When All the World Is Saying "Yes"?). w. Al Dubin and Irving Kahal, m. Joe Burke, 1932. Introduced by Dick Powell in (MP) *Blessed Event.*

How Can You Say You Love Me? w. Roy Turk, m. Fred E. Ahlert, 1932. Recorded by Jack Denny and his Orchestra (Victor).

How Come You Do Me Like You Do? w/m Gene Austin and Roy Bergere, 1924. Early records by Gene Austin (Victor) and Marion Harris (Brunswick). It was sung by Peggy Ryan and Johnny Coy in (MM) *That's the Spirit,* 1945, and by Betty Grable and Jack Lemmon in (MM) *Three for the Show,* 1955.

How Could We Be Wrong. w/m Cole Porter, 1933. Introduced by Gertrude Lawrence in (TM) *Nymph Errant* in London. Her recorded version was released in the U.S. (Victor).

How Could You? w. Al Dubin, m. Harry Warren, 1937. Sung by Ann Sheridan in (MP) *San Quentin.* Recorded by Teddy Wilson, vocal by Billie Holiday (Brunswick); Tommy Dorsey, vocal by Edythe Wright (Victor); and Anson Weeks's Orchestra (Decca).

How Could You Believe Me When I Said I Love You When You Know I've Been a Liar All My Life. w. Alan Jay Lerner, m. Burton Lane, 1951. Introduced by Fred Astaire and Jane Powell in (MM) *Royal Wedding.* Their version was released as a single (MGM). Tied for longest title in this book (see Ozzie Nelson, Section III.)

How Deep Is the Ocean? w/m Irving Berlin, 1932. Featured and recorded by Bing Crosby (Brunswick). Among other records of the song's introductory period were those by Ethel Merman (Victor) and Paul Whiteman and his Orchestra, vocal by Joan Edwards (Victor). Later standout versions by Coleman Hawkins (Signature); Dick Haymes (Decca); Benny Goodman, with vocal by Peggy Lee (Columbia); Margaret Whiting (Capitol); and Artie Shaw (Musicraft). In 1946, Bing Crosby sang it with a male quartet in (MM) *Blue Skies,* and in 1952, Frank Sinatra sang it in (MM) *Meet Danny Wilson.*

How Deep Is Your Love. w/m Barry Gibb, Maurice Gibb, and Robin Gibb, 1977. Introduced by The Bee Gees on the soundtrack of (MM) *Saturday Night Fever,* and on their #1 gold single (RSO).

How Did He Look? w. Gladys Shelley, m. Abner Silver, 1940. Featured by many singers in the cabaret field and included in numerous albums.

How'dja Like to Love Me? w. Frank Loesser, m. Burton Lane, 1938. Introduced by Bob Hope and Martha Raye in (MM) *College Swing.* Leading records: Larry Clinton, vocal by Bea Wain (Victor); Dolly Dawn (Vocalion); the orchestras of Horace Heidt (Brunswick), and Abe Lyman (Bluebird).

How Does That Grab You, Darling? w/m Lee Hazlewood, 1966. Top 10 record by Nancy Sinatra (Reprise).

How Do I Know It's Real? w/m Dan Shapiro, Lester Lee, and Jerry Seelen, 1942. Featured and recorded by Kate Smith (Columbia); Maxine Sullivan (Decca); Tommy Tucker, vocal by Amy Arnell (Okeh); Hal McIntyre and his Orchestra (Victor); Kay Kyser and his Orchestra (Columbia).

How Do I Know It's Sunday? w. Irving Kahal, m. Sammy Fain, 1934. Introduced by Hal LeRoy in (MM) *Harold Teen.* Most popular recordings by Will Osborne and his Orchestra (Melotone); Guy Lombardo, vocal by Carmen Lombardo (Brunswick); and Harry Sosnik, vocal by Bob Hannon (Victor).

How Do I Make You. w/m Billy Steinberg, 1980. Top 10 record by Linda Ronstadt (Asylum).

How Do I Survive? w/m Paul Bliss, 1980. Recorded by Amy Holland (Capitol).

How Do I Turn You On. w/m Tom Reid and Robert Byrne, 1987. #1 Country chart record by Ronnie Milsap (RCA).

How Do You Catch a Girl? w/m Ronald Blackwell, 1967. Top 40 record by Sam the Sham and The Pharaohs (MGM).

How Do You Do? w/m Hans Christian Van Hemert and Herricas Von Hoof, 1972. Gold U.S. record by the Dutch duo who recorded under the name of Mouth and MacNeal (Philips).

How Do You Do (Everybody). w/m Phil Fleming, Charles Harrison, and Cal De Voll, 1924. Radio theme song of and recorded by Jones and Hare, sometimes called "The Happiness Boys," and later "The Interwoven Pair," (Brunswick) (Edison). Also recorded by Art Gillham (Columbia).

How Do You Do It. w/m Mitch Murray, 1964. Hit record by the English group Gerry and The Pacemakers (Laurie).

How Do You Do It? w. E. Y. Harburg, m. Lewis Gensler, 1932. Introduced by Donald Stewart in (TM) *Ballyhoo of 1932.* Abe Lyman and his Band recorded it with vocal by Harlan Lattimore (Brunswick).

How Do You Keep the Music Playing? w. Marilyn Bergman and Alan Bergman, m. Michel Legrand, 1982. Introduced on the soundtrack of (MP) *Best Friends.* Nominated for Academy Award. Recording by Patti Austin and James Ingram (Qwest).

How Do You Speak to an Angel? w. Bob Hilliard, m. Jule Styne, 1953. Introduced by John Howard in (TM) *Hazel Flagg,* the Broadway musical based on the film *Nothing Sacred.* Leading records by Eddie Fisher (RCA Victor) and Gordon MacRae (Capitol). Dean Martin sang it in the film version of *Hazel Flagg,* (MM) *Living It Up,* 1954.

How Do You Talk to a Baby? w/m Wayne P. Walker and Webb Pierce, 1962. Country hit by Webb Pierce (Decca).

How'd We Ever Get This Way? w/m Jeff Barry and Andy Kim, 1968. Top 40 hit by Andy Kim (Steed).

How D'ya Like Your Eggs in the Morning? w. Sammy Cahn, m. Nicholas Brodsky, 1951. Introduced by The Four Freshmen in (MM) *Rich, Young and Pretty.*

How D'ya Talk to a Girl. w. Sammy Cahn, m. James Van Heusen, 1966. Introduced by Norman Wisdom and Gordon Dilworth in (TM) *Walking Happy.*

How'd You Like to Spoon with Me? w. Edward Laska, m. Jerome Kern, 1905. Interpolated in (TM) *The Earl and the Girl* and sung by Georgia Caine and Victor Morley, it was Kern's first American hit. See "Mister Chamberlain." Angela Lansbury sang it in the Kern film biography (MM) *Till the Clouds Roll By* in 1946.

How Far Is Heaven? w/m Jimmie Davis and Tillman Franks, 1956. Popular country song recorded by Kitty Wells (Decca).

How High the Moon. w. Nancy Hamilton, m. Morgan Lewis, 1940, 1951. Introduced as a ballad in the revue (TM) *Two for the Money,* sung by Alfred Drake and Frances Comstock, and danced by Tommy Wonder, Eunice Healey, William Archibald, and Nadine Gae. It was introduced on records by Larry Clinton, vocal by Terry Allen (Victor). The best-seller, its first time around, was by Benny Goodman, vocal by Helen Forrest (Columbia). In 1951, Les Paul and Mary Ford had one of the top records of the year (Capitol), and the song made "Your Hit Parade" for the second time. Hit two-sided record by Ella Fitzgerald (Verve), 1960.

How I Feel. w. Will Holt, m. Gary William Friedman, 1970. Introduced in the off-Broadway musical (TM) *The Me Nobody Knows* by Beverly Ann Bremers and José Fernandez.

How Important Can It Be? w/m Bennie Benjamin and George David Weiss, 1955. Hit record by Joni James (MGM). Sarah Vaughan also had a popular version (Mercury).

How It Lies, How It Lies, How It Lies! w. Paul Francis Webster, m. Sonny Burke, 1949. Most popular recordings by Connie Haines (Coral) and Kay Starr (Capitol).

Howlin' at the Moon. w/m Hank Williams, 1951. Featured and recorded by Hank Williams (MGM).

How Little We Know. w. Johnny Mercer, m. Hoagy Carmichael, 1944. Introduced by Hoagy Carmichael in (MP) *To Have and Have Not.*

How Little We Know (How Little It Matters). w. Carolyn Leigh, m. Philip Springer, 1956. Leading record by Frank Sinatra (Capitol).

How Long. w/m Paul Carrack, 1975. Written by the lead singer of Ace, the British quartet that had a Top 10 record (Anchor).

How Long, How Long Blues. w/m Leroy Carr, 1929. Carr recorded this in numbered versions five times in two years (Vocalion). Other popular recordings by Red Nichols, arranged by Glenn Miller (Brunswick); Count Basie, vocal by Jimmy Rushing (Decca); Bertha "Chippie" Hill (Circle); Huddie "Leadbelly" Ledbetter (Asch); Barney Bigard (12" Black and White); Jimmy Yancey (12" Session); Ray Charles (ABC).

How Long (Betcha' Got a Chick on the Side). w/m Anita Pointer, Ruth Pointer, June Pointer, and Bonnie Pointer, 1975. Top 20 record by The Pointer Sisters (Blue Thumb).

How Long Did I Dream? w. Johnny Burke, m. James Van Heusen, 1942. Introduced by Ginny Simms with Kay Kyser's Orchestra in (MM) *Playmates* and recorded by them (Columbia). Other records by Frankie Masters, vocal by Lou Hurst (Okeh); Lou Breese and his Orchestra (Decca); and Art Jarrett, with his Orchestra. All were coupled with "Humpty Dumpty Heart" (q.v.) from the same film.

How Long Has It Been? w. Jim Throckmorton, m. David Snyder, 1966. Top 10 Country record by Bobby Lewis (United Snyder).

How Long Has This Been Going On? w. Ira Gershwin, m. George Gershwin, 1928. Introduced by Bobbe Arnst in (TM) *Rosalie* after having been dropped from the score of (TM) *Funny Face* a year earlier.

How Long Will It Last? w. Max Lief, m. Joseph Meyer, 1932. Introduced by Joan Crawford in (MP) *Possessed*. Recorded by Bing Crosby (Brunswick), Jacques Renard's Orchestra (Brunswick), and pianist Arthur Schutt (Crown).

How Long Will It Take. w/m Warner McPherson, 1967. Written and Top 10 Country chart record by Warner Mack (Decca).

How Long Will My Baby Be Gone? w/m Buck Owens, 1968. Country hit by Buck Owens and His Buckaroos (Capitol).

How Lovely to Be a Woman. w. Lee Adams, m. Charles Strouse, 1960. Introduced by Susan Watson in (TM) *Bye Bye Birdie*. Sung in (MM) *Bye Bye Birdie*, 1963, by Ann-Margret.

How Lucky Can You Get. w. Fred Ebb, m. John Kander, 1975. Introduced by Barbra Streisand in (MM) *Funny Lady*. Nominated for an Academy Award.

How Lucky You Are. w. Desmond O'Connor, m. Eddie Cassen, 1947. British import popularized and recorded by The Andrews Sisters (Decca); Anita Ellis (Mercury); Eliot Lawrence and his Orchestra (Columbia); Charlie Spivak, vocal by Tommy Mercer (Victor); Johnny Johnston (MGM).

How Many Hearts Have You Broken? w. Marty Symes, m. Al Kaufman, 1944. Featured and top recordings by The Three Suns (Hit); Stan Kenton, vocal by Gene Howard (Capitol); Tiny Hill, with his Orchestra (Decca).

How Many Tears. w/m Gerry Goffin and Carole King, 1961. Recorded by Bobby Vee (Liberty).

How Many Times? w/m Irving Berlin, 1926. Non-production song with many recordings. Among them: Benny Krueger and his Orchestra (Brunswick); Ernest Hare and Billy Jones (Columbia); Sam Lanin's Orchestra (Cameo); Jay C. Flippen (Perfect); Dorothy Collins (MGM); Vincent Lopez, coupled with his theme "Nola" (q.v.) (Bluebird); Bonnie Baker with Orrin Tucker's Orchestra, coupled with their biggest hit, "Oh Johnny, Oh Johnny, Oh!" (q.v.) (Columbia). It was sung by The Brox Sisters in (MM) *The Time, The Place and The Girl*, 1929, and was heard in the background of (MM) *Blue Skies*, 1946.

How Many Times Can We Say Goodbye? w/m Steve Goldman, 1983. Recorded by Dionne Warwick and Luther Vandross (Arista).

How Many Times Do I Have to Tell You? w. Harold Adamson, m. Jimmy McHugh, 1944. Introduced by Dick Haymes in (MM) *Four Jills in a Jeep*. Haymes recorded it with Emil Newman's Orchestra (Decca).

How'm I Doin'. w/m Charles Strouse, 1985. Introduced by Lenny Wolpe, as New York City Mayor Edward Koch, in the off-Broadway musical (TM) *Mayor*. The title phrase was often asked by Koch of his constituents during the early years of his administration.

How'm I Doin'? (Hey, Hey!). w/m Lem Fowler and Don Redman, 1932. Originally written by Fowler as "Twee Twa-Twa," 1923. Redman revised it, after which the new version

was introduced by the Mills Brothers, who had a best-selling record (Brunswick). Others: Fred Waring's Pennsylvanians, vocal by Johnny "Scat" Davis (Victor); the bands of Don Redman (Brunswick); Claude Hopkins (Columbia); Louis Prima (Brunswick); Sharkey Bonano (Capitol).

How Much Can a Lonely Heart Stand? w/m Sandra Rhodes, 1963. Recorded by Skeeter Davis (RCA).

How Much I Feel. w/m David Pack, 1978. Recorded by the trio Ambrosia (Warner Bros.).

How Much Is That Doggie in the Window? See **Doggie in the Window, The.**

How Much Love. w. Leo Sayer, m. Barry Mann, 1977. Top 20 record by the English singer Leo Sayer (Warner Bros.).

How Much More Can She Stand? w/m Harry Compton, 1971. #1 Country and Pop crossover record by Conway Twitty (Decca).

How's Chances? w/m Irving Berlin, 1933. Introduced by Clifton Webb and Marilyn Miller in (TM) *As Thousands Cheer*. Recorded by Leo Reisman and his Orchestra, vocal by Clifton Webb (Victor); also by the bands of Freddy Martin (Brunswick) and Meyer Davis (Victor).

How's Every Little Thing in Dixie? w. Jack Yellen, m. Albert Gumble, 1916.

How Soon (Will I Be Seeing You?). w/m Carroll Lucas and Jack Owens, 1947. Top records by Jack Owens (Tower); Vaughn Monroe, with his Orchestra (RCA Victor); Bing Crosby (Decca); Dinah Shore (Columbia).

How Soon We Forget. w/m Colonel Abrams, 1987. Top 10 R&B chart record by Colonel Abrams [real name], (MCA).

How Strange? w. Gus Kahn, m. Earl Brent, Herbert Stothart, 1939. Music adapted from "Kak Strano" by B. A. Prozorovsky. Introduced by Norma Shearer in (MP) *Idiot's Delight*.

How Sweet It Is (to Be Loved by You). w/m Brian Holland, Lamont Dozier, and Eddie Holland, 1965. Crossover (R&B/Pop) hit by Marvin Gaye (Tamla), followed by Jr. Walker and The All Stars (Soul), 1966. James Taylor had a Top 10 record (Warner Bros.), 1975.

How Sweet You Are. w. Frank Loesser, m. Arthur Schwartz, 1943. Introduced by Dinah Shore in (MM) *Thank Your Lucky Stars* and on records (Victor). Other popular versions by Kay Armen (Decca) and Jo Stafford (Capitol).

How's Your Romance? w/m Cole Porter, 1932. Introduced by Erik Rhodes and the female ensemble in (TM) *Gay Divorce.*

How the Time Flies. w/m Tommy Jarrett, 1958. Chart record by Jerry Wallace (Challenge).

How To. w/m Frank Loesser, 1961. Introduced by Robert Morse in (TM) *How to Succeed in Business Without Really Trying*, and repeated in (MM) *How to Succeed in Business Without Really Trying*, 1966.

(How to Be A) Millionaire. w/m Martin Fry and Mark White, 1986. Chart record by the English group ABC (Mercury).

How to Handle a Woman. w. Alan Jay Lerner, m. Frederick Loewe, 1960. Introduced by Richard Burton in (TM) *Camelot.* Popular recording by Johnny Mathis (Columbia). In (MM) *Camelot*, 1967, it was sung by Richard Harris.

How to Win Friends and Influence People. w. Lorenz Hart, m. Richard Rodgers, 1938. Introduced by Audrey Christie and Charles Walters in (TM) *I Married an Angel.* Leading recording by Larry Clinton, vocal by Bea Wain (Victor). Perhaps apocryphal, it was said that as so many songs of the period were "borrowing" titles of popular books or plays, Hart, on a dare, wrote a lyric using the unlikely title of Dale Carnegie's best-selling personality-improver.

How Was I to Know? w. Eddie DeLange, m. Will Hudson, 1934. Recorded by the Hudson-DeLange Orchestra (Brunswick).

How Will I Know. w/m George Merrill, Shannon Rubicam, and Narada Michael Walden, 1986. #1 single from the debut self-titled album by Whitney Houston (Arista).

How Ya Baby? w. J. C. Johnson, m. Thomas "Fats" Waller, 1937. Revived in the Waller musical (TM) *Ain't Misbehavin'*, 1978, by André de Shields and Charlaine Woodard.

How Ya Gonna Keep 'Em Down on the Farm? (After They've Seen Paree). w. Sam M. Lewis and Joe Young, m. Walter Donaldson, 1919. A big post–World War I hit. First recorded (Victor) and featured by Nora Bayes, followed by Sophie Tucker, Eddie Cantor, and others in vaudeville. Judy Garland sang it in (MM) *For Me and My Gal*, 1942. Eddie Cantor dubbed his voice on the sound track for Keefe Brasselle, who portrayed him, in (MM) *The Eddie Cantor Story*, 1953. Cantor also recorded the song with Victor Young's Orchestra (Decca).

How You Gonna See Me Now. w/m Alice Cooper, Dick Wagner, and Bernie Taupin, 1978. Recorded by Alice Cooper (Warner Bros.).

Huckleberry Duck. w. Jack Lawrence, m. Raymond Scott, 1939. Instrumental introduced and recorded by Raymond Scott and his Orchestra (Columbia). The Milt Herth Trio also recorded it (Decca). Lyrics added later.

Huckleberry Finn. w/m Cliff Hess, Sam M. Lewis, and Joe Young, 1917. Introduced in vaudeville and recorded (Victor) by Van and Schenck.

Hucklebuck, The. w. Roy Alfred, m. Andy Gibson, 1948. Influenced by Charlie Parker's "Now's the Time" (q.v.), this was popularized by Tommy Dorsey and his Orchestra (RCA Victor) and Frank Sinatra, with Axel Stordahl conducting (Columbia).

Huggin' and Chalkin' (a.k.a. **A-Huggin' and A-Chalkin'**). w/m Clancy Hayes and Kermit Goell, 1946. Novelty, with leading records by Kay Kyser, vocal by Jack Martin (Columbia); Hoagy Carmichael, with The Chalkadees and Vic Schoen's Orchestra (Decca);

Johnny Mercer, with Paul Weston's Orchestra (Capitol).

Hugs and Kisses. w. Raymond Klages, m. Louis Alter, 1926. From (TM) *Earl Carroll Vanities of 1925*. It was also included in the 1926 edition. Featured on radio and recorded by Don Voorhees's Orchestra.

Huguette Waltz. w. Brian Hooker, m. Rudolf Friml, 1925. Introduced by Jane Carroll in (TM) *The Vagabond King*. In the film version (MM) *The Vagabond King*, 1930, it was sung by Lillian Roth, and in the 1956 remake, by Rita Moreno.

Hula Hoop Song, The. w/m Donna Jeane Kohler and Carl A. Maduri, Jr., 1958. Georgia Gibbs (Roulette) and Teresa Brewer (Coral) each had chart recordings of the song referring to the current craze.

Hula Love. w/m Buddy Knox, 1957. Hit record by Buddy Knox (Roulette).

Hulla-Baloo-Balay. w. Ben Tarver and John Clifton, m. John Clifton, 1966. Introduced by Reid Shelton in (TM) *Man with a Load of Mischief*.

Human. w/m James Harris III (a.k.a. Jimmy Jam) and Terry Lewis, 1986. #1 hit by the British band The Human League (A&M).

Human Nature. w. John Bettis, m. Jeff Porcaro, 1983. Top 10 record by Michael Jackson (Epic).

Human Touch. w/m Rick Springfield, 1983. Recorded by the Australian singer/actor/composer Rick Springfield (RCA).

Humming. w. Louis Breau, m. Ray Henderson, 1920. Interpolated by The Duncan Sisters in (TM) *Tip Top*. This was Ray Henderson's first song success.

Hummingbird. w/m Jimmy Seals and Dash Crofts, 1973. Recorded by Seals and Crofts (Warner Bros.).

Hummingbird. w/m Don Robertson, 1955. Les Paul and Mary Ford had a Top 10 record (Capitol) and Frankie Laine's version was also popular (Columbia).

Hummin' to Myself (I've Got the Words— I've Got the Tune). w. Herb Magidson and Monty Siegel, m. Sammy Fain, 1932.

Humpty Dumpty Heart. w. Johnny Burke, m. James Van Heusen, 1942. Introduced by Harry Babbitt, with Kay Kyser's Orchestra, in (MM) *Playmates* and on records (Columbia). Also recorded by Glenn Miller, vocal by Ray Eberle (Bluebird), coupled with "How Long Did I Dream?" from the same film; the bands of Frankie Masters (Okeh), Lou Breese (Decca), Art Jarrett (Victor).

(I've Got a) Humpty Dumpty Heart. w/m Henry Boyce, 1948. C&W song recorded by Hank Thompson (Capitol).

Hundred Million Miracles, A. w. Oscar Hammerstein II, m. Richard Rodgers, 1958. Introduced by Miyoshi Omeki, Conrad Yama, Keye Luke, Juanita Hall, and Rose Quong in (TM) *Flower Drum Song*. In film version (MM) *Flower Drum Song*, 1961, it was sung by Miyoshi Omeki, John Dodson (dubbing for Kam Tong), and chorus.

Hundred Pounds of Clay, A. w/m Bob Elgin, Luther Dixon, and Kay Rogers, 1961. Hit record by Gene McDaniels (Liberty).

Hundred Years from Today, A. w. Ned Washington and Joe Young, m. Victor Young, 1934. Introduced by Kathryn Perry in Lew Leslie's (TM) *Blackbirds*, which opened in early December 1933. It was featured in (MP) *Girl from Missouri* in 1934. Ethel Waters, with the Benny Goodman Orchestra, established the song (Columbia), which has been recorded by many artists. Among them are: Jack Teagarden (Brunswick); Glen Gray and the Casa Loma Orchestra, vocal by Lee Wiley (Brunswick); Eddy Duchin (Victor); Sarah Vaughan, with Georgia Auld's Orchestra (Musicraft).

Hung on You. w/m Gerry Goffin, Carole King, and Phil Spector, 1965. Chart record by The Righteous Brothers (Philles).

Hungry. w/m Barry Mann and Cynthia Weil, 1966. Top 10 hit by Paul Revere and The Raiders (Columbia).

Hungry Eyes. w/m John De Nicola and Franke Previte, 1987. Top 10 single by Eric Carmen from the soundtrack of (MP) *Dirty Dancing.*

Hungry Eyes. w/m Merle Haggard, 1969. Hit Country record by Merle Haggard (Capitol).

Hungry for Love. w/m Al Hamilton, Bob Hamilton, and Joanne Jackson, 1965. Top 40 instrumental by The San Remo Golden Strings (Ric-Tic).

Hungry Heart. w/m Bruce Springsteen, 1980. Top 10 record by Bruce Springsteen (Columbia).

Hungry Like the Wolf. w/m Duran Duran, 1983. Written and Top 10 record by the English group, Duran Duran (Harvest).

Hungry Years, The. w/m Neil Sedaka and Howard Greenfield, 1976. Recorded by Wayne Newton (Chelsea).

Hunkadola. w. Cliff Friend and Jack Yellen, m. Joseph Meyer, 1935. From (MM) *George White's 1935 Scandals.* Benny Goodman and his band recorded it in their first session for Victor records.

Hunter Gets Captured by the Game, The. w/m William Robinson, 1966. Recorded by The Marvelettes (Tamla).

Hurdy Gurdy Man. w/m Donovan Leitch, 1968. Top 10 record in the U.S. by the Scottish singer/writer Donovan (Epic).

Hurrah for Baffin's Bay! w. Vincent P. Bryan, m. Theodore F. Morse, 1903. Interpolated in Fred Stone's (TM) *The Wizard of Oz* after its opening. It became the show's hit song. Bob Roberts had a popular recording (Columbia).

Hurricane. w/m Keith Stegall, Tom Schuyler, and Stewart Harris, 1981. Top 10 Country chart record by Leon Everette (RCA).

Hurricane. w/m Bob Dylan and Jacques Levy, 1976. Top 20 record by Bob Dylan (Columbia). The song was dedicated to Reuben

"Hurricane" Carter, the boxer whose conviction on murder charges was opposed and appealed. He served time, but eventually was released and pardoned.

Hurry, Hurry. w/m Richard Larkin and Benny Carter, 1944. Introduced and recorded by Benny Carter, vocal by Savannah Churchill (Capitol), followed by Lucky Millinder, with his Orchestra (Decca).

Hurry, It's Lovely Up Here. w. Alan Jay Lerner, m. Burton Lane, 1965. Introduced by Barbara Harris and John Cullum in (TM) *On a Clear Day You Can See Forever.* In (MM) *On a Clear Day You Can See Forever,* 1970, it was sung by Barbra Streisand and Yves Montand.

Hurry Home. w/m Joseph Meyer, Buddy Bernier, and Bob Emmerich, 1938. Among many recordings: Thelma Carpenter (Majestic); the bands of Bob Crosby (Decca); Kay Kyser (Brunswick); Jan Savitt, vocal by Carlotta Dale (Bluebird); Al Donahue, vocal by Paula Kelly (Vocalion); Sammy Kaye (Victor).

Hurry On Down. w/m Nellie Lutcher, 1947. The first hit record by the West Coast singer-pianist Nellie Lutcher and Her Rhythm (Capitol).

Hurt. w/m Jimmie Crane and Al Jacobs, 1961. Introduced by Roy Hamilton (Epic) in 1953. Timi Yuro had a Top 10 hit (Liberty), 1961. Elvis Presley had a chart version (RCA Victor), 1976. #1 Country chart record by Juice Newton (RCA), 1985.

Hurt Her Once for Me. w/m Johnny Russell and Vince Finneran, 1967. Top 10 Country chart record by The Wilburn Brothers (Decca).

Hurting Each Other. w/m Gary Geld and Peter Udell, 1972. Gold record by The Carpenters (A&M).

Hurtin's All Over, The. w/m Harlan Howard, 1966. Country hit by Connie Smith (RCA).

Hurts Me to My Heart. w/m Charles Singleton and Rose Marie McCoy, 1954. R&B hit by Faye Adams (Herald).

Hurt So Bad. w/m Teddy Randazzo, Bobby Hart, and Bobby Wilding, 1965. Hit records by Little Anthony and The Imperials (DCP); The Lettermen (Capitol), 1969; Linda Ronstadt (Asylum), 1980.

Hurt So Good. w/m John Cougar Mellencamp and George Michael Green, 1982. #2 gold record by John Cougar (Riva).

Hurts So Good. w/m R. Michael Donovan, 1973. Sung on the soundtrack of (MP) *Cleopatra Jones*, and recorded by Millie Jackson (Spring).

Husbands and Wives. w/m Roger Miller, 1966. Crossover (C&W/Pop) chart record by Roger Miller (Smash).

Hush, Hush, Sweet Charlotte. w. Mack David, m. Frank DeVol, 1965. Introduced by Al Martino on the soundtrack of (MP) *Hush, Hush, Sweet Charlotte*. Nominated for Academy Award. Hit record by Patti Page (Columbia).

Hushabye. w/m Doc Pomus and Mort Shuman, 1959. Top 40 record by The Mystics (Laurie). Revived by Jay and The Americans (United Artists), 1969.

Hushabye Mountain. w/m Richard M. Sherman and Robert B. Sherman, 1968. Introduced by Dick Van Dyke and Sally Ann Howes in (MM) *Chitty Chitty Bang Bang*.

Hustle, The. m. Van McCoy, 1975. #1 gold record instrumental by Van McCoy and The Soul City Symphony (Avco). It was originally a track on McCoy's album "Disco Baby" and was written for the "new" dance, which had couples dancing together again as an alternative to each partner doing his or her own thing.

Hustlin' and Bustlin' for Baby. w/m Harry Woods, 1933. Featured and recorded by Louis Armstrong (Melotone). Also recorded by Adrian Rollini, leading studio band of top musicians such as the Dorseys, Goodman, Berigan, Venuti, and Teagarden (Melotone).

Hut-Sut Song, The. w/m Leo V. Killion, Ted McMichael, and Jack Owens, 1941. A novelty double-talk song, sometimes subtitled "A Swedish Serenade." Hit records by Freddy Martin, vocal by Eddie Stone (Bluebird); Horace Heidt, vocal by Donna Wood and the Don Juans (Columbia); The King Sisters, with Alvino Rey and his Orchestra (Bluebird); The Merry Macs (Decca). The latter vocal group sang it in (MM) "San Antonio Rose," 1941. It was heard in (MP) *From Here to Eternity*, 1953.

Hymne. m. Vangelis, 1987. Country chart instrumental by Joe Kenyon, pseudonym for guitarist Jerry Kennedy, and pianist David Briggs (Mercury). The melody was originally written for a Gallo Wine commercial.

Hymn for a Sunday Evening. w. Lee Adams, m. Charles Strouse, 1960. Introduced by Paul Lynde, Marijane Maricle, Susan Watson, and Johnny Borden in (TM) *Bye Bye Birdie*. In (MM) *Bye Bye Birdie*, 1963, it was sung by Paul Lynde, Mary La Roche, Ann-Margret, and Bryan Russell.

Hyperactive. w/m Dennis Nelson, Tony Haynes, and Robert Palmer, 1986. Recorded by English singer/songwriter Robert Palmer (Island).

Hypnotized. w/m Richard Poindexter and Gloria Spolan, 1967. R&B/Pop hit by Linda Jones (Loma).

Hypnotize Me. w/m Jack Hues and Nick Feldman, 1987. From (MP) *Innerspace*. Written and recorded by the English group Wang Chung (Geffen).

Hysteria. w/m Steve Clark, Phil Collen, Joe Elliott, Robert John Lange, Rick Savage, 1988. Single and title song of the album "Hysteria" by Def Leppard (Mercury).

I

I. w/m Buddy Arnold, Milton Berle, and Riccardo Drigo, 1952. Leading record by Don Cornell, with Jack Pleis's Orchestra (Coral).

I, Yi, Yi, Yi, Yi (I Like You Very Much). w. Mack Gordon, m. Harry Warren, 1941. Introduced by Carmen Miranda in (MM) *That Night in Rio*, and recorded by her (Decca). The Andrews Sisters, though, had the best-seller (Decca).

I (Who Have Nothing). w. Jerry Leiber and Mike Stoller (Engl.), m. Carlo Donida, 1963. Original Italian song titled "Uno Dei Tanti," words by B. Mogol. Ben E. King had the first English language hit, a Top 10 entry (Arco), 1963. Terry Knight and The Pack had a chart version (Lucky Eleven), 1967; Tom Jones had a Top 20 record (Parrot), 1970; Sylvester had a Top 40 record (Fantasy), 1979.

I Adore Him. w/m Jan Berry and Artie Kornfeld, 1963. Top 40 record by The Angels (Smash).

I Ain't Down Yet. w/m Meredith Willson, 1960. Introduced by Tammy Grimes and men in (TM) *The Unsinkable Molly Brown*. In (MM) *The Unsinkable Molly Brown*, 1964, it was sung by Debbie Reynolds and Harve Presnell.

I Ain't Ever Satisfied. w/m Steve Earle, 1987. Popular track from the album "Exit O" by Steve Earle and The Dukes (MCA).

I Ain't Gonna Give Nobody None o' This Jelly Roll. w. Spencer Williams, m. Clarence Williams, 1919. Recorded by Sidney Bechet (Victor) and Wilbur Sweatman (Columbia).

I Ain't Gonna Stand for It. w/m Stevie Wonder, 1980. Top 10 R&B, Pop chart record by Stevie Wonder (Tamla).

I Ain't Got Nobody. w. Roger Graham and Dave Peyton, m. Spencer Williams, 1916. Frequently, but incorrectly, confused with the Bert Williams song "Nobody" (q.v.). Marion Harris first recorded it as "I Ain't Got Nobody Much" (Victor), 1917. She then had another hit version with the shorter title (Columbia), 1921, after which it was recorded by such artists as Bessie Smith (Columbia), Sophie Tucker (Okeh), Louis Armstrong (Okeh), Fats Waller (Victor), Wingy Manone (Bluebird), Earl "Fatha" Hines (Okeh). Revived by David Lee Roth in medley with "Just a Gigolo" (Warner Bros.), 1985.

I Ain't Got Nothin' But the Blues. w. Don George, m. Edward Kennedy "Duke" Ellington, 1944. Introduced and recorded by Duke Ellington, vocal by Al Hibbler (Victor). Also recorded by Lena Horne (Victor).

I Ain't Got to Love Nobody Else. w/m Charlie Moore, Lee Jones, and Robert Wrightsill, 1968. Recorded by the soul group The Masqueraders (Bell).

I Ain't Lazy—I'm Just Dreamin'. w/m Dave Franklin, 1934. Introduced by Isham Jones and his Orchestra. Recordings by a studio band led by Benny Goodman (Columbia) and Eddie Elkins (Melotone). Revived in the early fifties by Red Foley (Decca).

I Ain't Living Long like This. w/m Rodney Crowell, 1980. Country hit by Waylon Jennings (RCA).

I Ain't Never. w/m Mel Tillis and Webb Pierce, 1959. Hit C&W and Pop record by Webb Pierce (Decca). Pop cover record by The Four Preps (Capitol). Revived by Mel Tillis (MGM), 1972.

I Ain't Nobody's Darling. w. Elmer Hughes, m. Robert A. King, 1921. Featured and recorded by Frank Crumit (Columbia).

I Almost Lost My Mind. w/m Ivory Joe Hunter, 1950. Introduced by Ivory Joe Hunter (MGM). Popular record by Nat "King" Cole (Capitol). Revived by Pat Boone, with a #1 record (Dot), 1956.

I Always Get Lucky with You. w/m Gary Church, Freddy Powers, and Tex Whitson, 1983. Country hit by George Jones (Epic).

I Always Knew. w/m Cole Porter, 1943. Introduced by Jaye Martin and Janet Blair in (MM) *Something to Shout About*. Reprised by Blair and Don Ameche.

I Am an American. w/m Paul Cunningham, Ira Schuster, and Leonard Whitcup, 1940. Introduced and featured by Gray Gordon, vocal by Meredith Blake and Art Perry (Bluebird).

I Am a Rock. w/m Paul Simon, 1966. Hit record by Simon and Garfunkel (Columbia).

I Am by Your Side. w/m Corey Hart, 1986. Recorded by Corey Hart (EMI America).

I Am in Love. w/m Cole Porter, 1953. Introduced by Peter Cookson in (TM) *Can-Can*. Popular recording by Nat "King" Cole (Capitol). Song played in the background of (MM) *Can-Can*, 1960.

I Am . . . I Said. w/m Neil Diamond, 1971. Top 10 record by Neil Diamond (Uni).

I Am Love. w/m David Foster, Maurice White, and Alice Willis, 1983. Recorded by Jennifer Holliday (Geffen).

I Am Love. w/m Donald Fenceton, Mel Larson, Gerald Marcellino, and Roderick Rancifer, 1975. Top 20 two-part record by The Jackson 5 (Motown).

I Am Loved. w/m Cole Porter, 1950. Introduced by Priscilla Gillette in (TM) *Out of This World*.

I Am Only Human After All. w. Ira Gershwin and E. Y. Harburg, m. Vernon Duke, 1930. This was Duke's first successful American song. It was introduced in (TM) *Garrick Gaieties of 1930* by James Norris, Velma Vavra, Philip Loeb, Nan Blackstone, Imogene Coca, and Sterling Holloway.

I Am the Walrus. w/m John Lennon and Paul McCartney, 1967. Recorded by The Beatles (Capitol).

I Am What I Am. w/m Jerry Herman, 1983. Introduced by George Hearn in (TM) *La Cage Aux Folles*.

I Am Woman. w. Helen Reddy, m. Ray Burton, 1972. #1 gold record by Helen Reddy (Capitol).

I Am Woman, You Are Man. See **You Are Woman, I Am Man.**

I Apologize. w/m Al Hoffman, Al Goodhart and Ed Nelson, 1931, 1951. Introduced by Bing Crosby. Early recordings by Kate Smith, under pseudonym of Ruth Brown (Harmony); Nat Shilkret's Orchestra, vocal by Paul Small (Victor); Phil Spitalny (Hit of the Week). In 1951, Billy Eckstine revived the song with a hit recording arranged and conducted by Pete Rugolo (MGM).

I Begged Her. w. Sammy Cahn, m. Jule Styne, 1945. Introduced by Frank Sinatra and Gene Kelly in (MM) *Anchors Aweigh*.

I Beg of You. w/m Rose Marie McCoy and Kelly Owens, 1958. Popular record by Elvis Presley, coupled with #1 hit "Don't" (RCA).

I Believe. w/m Ervin Drake, Irvin Graham, Jimmy Shirl, and Al Stillman, 1952. One of the top hits of the year in sheet music and record sales, it was on "Your Hit Parade" for twenty weeks after being introduced by Jane Froman on her TV show "U.S.A. Canteen." Froman recorded it (Capitol), but the best-seller and most played version was by Frankie Laine (Columbia).

I Believe. w. Sammy Cahn, m. Jule Styne, 1947. Introduced by Frank Sinatra, Jimmy Durante, and Billy Roy in (MM) *It Happened in Brooklyn*. Recorded by Frank Sinatra (Columbia). (Not to be confused with the 1953 Frankie Laine hit of the same title.)

I Believe I'm Gonna Love You. w/m Harry Lloyd and Gloria Sklerov, 1975. Featured and recorded by Frank Sinatra (Reprise).

I Believe in Love. w. Alan Bergman and Marilyn Bergman, m. Kenny Loggins, 1976. Introduced by Barbra Streisand in (MM) *A Star Is Born*. Best-selling record by Kenny Loggins (Columbia), 1977.

I Believe in Love. w/m Charles H. Anderson, 1968. Country chart records by Bonnie Guitar (Dot) and Stonewall Jackson (Columbia).

I Believe in Miracles. w. Sam M. Lewis, m. George W. Meyer and Pete Wendling, 1935. Most popular records by Dick Powell (Brunswick), Wingy Manone (Vocalion), Dorsey Brothers (Decca), Little Jack Little (Columbia), Don Bestor (Brunswick).

I Believe in Music. w/m Mac Davis, 1972. Top 40 record by the sextet Gallery (Sussex).

I Believe in You. w/m Roger Cook and Sam Hogin, 1980. Country/Pop chart hit by Don Williams (MCA).

I Believe in You. w/m George Dunlap and Buddy Cannon, 1980. Hit Country record by Mel Tillis (MCA).

I Believe in You. w/m Frank Loesser, 1961. Introduced by Robert Morse in (TM) *How to Succeed in Business Without Really Trying*, and repeated in (MM) *How to Succeed in Business Without Really Trying*, 1966.

I Believe in You. w/m Robert Carr, Johnny Mitchell, and Sam Weiss, 1958. R&B record by Robert and Johnny (Old Town).

I Believe in You (You Believe in Me). w/m Don Davis, 1973. #1 R&B, #11 Pop chart gold record by Johnnie Taylor (Stax).

(I Believe) There's Nothing Stronger Than Our Love. w/m Paul Anka, 1975. Recorded by Paul Anka, backed vocally by Odia Coates (United Artists).

I Believe You. w/m Robert Fischer and Ricci Mareno, 1977. Recorded by Dorothy Moore (Malaco); covered by The Carpenters (A&M), 1978.

I Belong to You. w/m Barry White, 1975. Recorded by the female trio Love Unlimited (20th Century).

I Built a Dream One Day. w. Oscar Hammerstein II, m. Sigmund Romberg, 1935. Introduced by Walter Slezak, Walter Woolf King, and Robert C. Fischer in (TM) *May Wine*.

I Cain't Say No. w. Oscar Hammerstein II, m. Richard Rodgers, 1943. Introduced by Celeste Holm in (TM) *Oklahoma!* In the film version (MM) *Oklahoma!* 1955, it was sung by Gloria Grahame.

I Call Your Name. 1979. Top 10 R&B chart record by the sextet Switch (Gordy).

I Came, I Saw, I Conga'd. w/m James Cavanaugh, John Redmond, and Frank Weldon, 1941.

I Came Here to Talk for Joe. w. Charles Tobias and Lew Brown, m. Sam H. Stept, 1942. Featured and recorded by Sammy Kaye, vocal by Don Cornell (Victor); Shep Fields, vocal by Ralph Young (Bluebird); Kay Kyser and his Orchestra (Bluebird).

I Can. w/m Walter Marks, 1964. Introduced by Chita Rivera and Nancy Dussault in (TM) *Bajour*.

I Can Always Find a Little Sunshine in the Y.M.C.A. w/m Irving Berlin, 1918. An end-of-war song from (TM) *Yip, Yip, Yaphank*.

I Can Cook Too. w. Betty Comden and Adolph Green, m. Leonard Bernstein, 1944. Introduced by Nancy Walker in (TM) *On the Town*, a musical based on the ballet *Fancy Free*, which had music by Bernstein and choreography by Jerome Robbins. Walker's original cast album cut was released as a single (Decca). She also included it in another album (Dolphin).

I Can Dance. See **Long Tall Glasses.**

I Can Dance with Everyone But My Wife. w. Joseph Cawthorn and John Golden, m. John Golden, 1917. Introduced by Cawthorn in (TM) *Sybil*.

I Can Do That. w. Edward Kleban, m. Marvin Hamlisch, 1975. Introduced by Wayne Cilento in (TM) *A Chorus Line*. In (MM) *A Chorus Line*, 1985, it was performed by Wayne Cilento.

I Can Dream, Can't I? w. Irving Kahal, m. Sammy Fain, 1938, 1949. One of two future hits from a flop show that ran only fourteen performances (see "I'll Be Seeing You"). Both were introduced by Tamara in (TM) *Right This Way*. Early recordings by Glen Gray and the Casa Loma Orchestra, vocal by Kenny Sargent (Decca); Harry James, vocal by Helen Humes (Brunswick); Al Bowlly (Bluebird). The song attained some initial popularity, as indicated by its three appearances on "Your Hit Parade." This was greatly surpassed in 1949 when it was in the Top 10 for seventeen weeks, twice in the #1 position. The revival was due to the hit record by The Andrews Sisters (Decca). The Glenn Miller Orchestra led by Tex Beneke (RCA Victor) and Toni Arden (Columbia) also had popular versions.

I Can Dream About You. w/m Dan Hartman, 1984. From (MP) *Streets of Fire*. Dan Hartman had a Top 10 record (MCA).

I Can Get It for You Wholesale. w/m Charles Tobias and Jack Ellis, 1929. Introduced and featured by Eddie Cantor.

I Can Have It All. w. Garry Trudeau, m. Elizabeth Swados, 1983. Introduced by Laura Dean and ensemble in (TM) *Doonesbury*.

I Can Hear Music. w/m Jeff Barry, Ellie Greenwich, and Phil Spector, 1969. First recorded by The Ronettes (Philles), 1966. Hit record by The Beach Boys (Capitol), 1969.

I Can Help. w/m Billy Swan, 1974. #1 gold record crossover (C&W/Pop) record by Billy Swan (Monument).

I Can Make It with You. w/m Chip Taylor, 1966. Leading records by The Pozo-Seco Singers (Columbia) and Jackie De Shannon (Imperial).

I Can Mend Your Broken Heart. w/m Don Gibson, 1962. C&W hit by Don Gibson (RCA).

I Can Never Go Home Anymore. w/m Jerry Grimaldi and George Morton, 1965. Top 10 record by The Shangri-Las (Red Bird).

I Can See Clearly Now. w/m Johnny Nash, 1972. #1 gold record by Johnny Nash (Epic).

I Can See for Miles. w/m Peter Townshend, 1967. Top 10 record by the British group The Who (Decca).

I Can See It. w. Tom Jones, m. Harvey Schmidt, 1960. Introduced by Kenneth Nelson and Jerry Orbach in (TM) *The Fantasticks*.

I Can See You. w. Sammy Cahn, m. Nicholas Brodsky, 1950. Introduced by Vic Damone in (MM) *Rich, Young and Pretty*. Recorded by Damone (Mercury) and Don Cherry (Decca).

I Can't Afford to Dream. w. Lew Brown and Charles Tobias, m. Sam H. Stept, 1939. Added to the score of (TM) *Yokel Boy* after the Broadway opening. Recorded by Artie Shaw and his Orchestra (Bluebird) and Harry James, vocal by Connie Haines (Brunswick).

I Can Take or Leave Your Loving. w/m Rick Jones, 1968. Top 40 record by the British group Herman's Hermits (MGM).

I Can't Be Bothered Now. w. Ira Gershwin, m. George Gershwin, 1937. Introduced by Fred Astaire in (MM) *Damsel in Distress*.

I Can't Begin to Tell You. w. Mack Gordon, m. James V. Monaco, 1945. Introduced by John Payne and reprised by Payne and Betty Grable in (MM) *The Dolly Sisters*. Song nominated for an Academy Award, 1946. Top recordings by Bing Crosby, with Carmen Cavallaro's Orchestra (Decca) and Harry James, vocal by "Ruth Haag," a pseudonym for Betty Grable (Columbia). The song was heard in (MM) *You're My Everything*, 1949, and sung by Ginger Rogers in (MP) *Dreamboat*, 1952.

I Can't Believe I'm Losing You. w. Phil Zeller, m. Don Costa, 1968. Popularized by Frank Sinatra (Reprise).

I Can't Believe It's True. w/m Charles Newman, Ben Bernie, and Isham Jones, 1932. Popularly recorded by the bands of Isham Jones, vocal by Eddie Stone (Brunswick); Roger Wolfe Kahn (Columbia); Bert Lown (Victor); Will Osborne (Melotone); and singer Frances Langford (Columbia).

I Can't Believe She Gives It All to Me. w/m Conway Twitty, 1976. #1 Country chart hit by Conway Twitty (MCA).

I Can't Believe That You're in Love with Me. w. Clarence Gaskill, m. Jimmy McHugh, 1927. Popular song, with leading record by Roger Wolfe Kahn and his Orchestra (Victor). Revived by The Ames Brothers (RCA Victor), 1953. The following year it was used as the theme for (MP) *The Caine Mutiny*. Connie Francis sang it in (MM) *Looking for Love*, 1964. It was heard as orchestral background in (MM) *Thoroughly Modern Millie*, 1967.

I Can't Believe That You've Stopped Loving Me. w/m Dallas Frazier and A. L. "Doodle" Owens, 1970. Crossover (C&W/Pop) record by Charley Pride (RCA).

I Can't Control Myself. w/m Reg Presley, 1966. Recorded by the English quartet, the Troggs, of which the writer was lead singer. (Fontana, Atco).

I Can't Dance to That Music You're Playin'. w/m Deke Richards and Debbie Dean, 1968. Chart record by Martha and The Vandellas (Gordy).

I Can't Do This Sum. w. Glen McDonough, m. Victor Herbert, 1903. Sung by Mabel Barrison in (TM) *Babes in Toyland*. It was heard later in the film versions (MM) *Babes in Toyland*, 1934, starring Laurel and Hardy, and in the 1961 production starring Ray Bolger, Ed Wynn, and Tommy Sands.

I Can't Do Without You. w/m Irving Berlin, 1928.

I Can Tell by the Way You Dance (You're Gonna Love Me Tonight). w/m Robb Strandlund and Sandy Pinkard, 1984. #1 Country chart record by Vern Gosdin (Compleat).

I Can't Escape from You. w. Leo Robin, m. Richard A. Whiting, 1936. Introduced by Bing Crosby in (MM) *Rhythm on the Range* and recorded by him (Decca). Jimmie Lunceford's Orchestra (Decca) also had a popular recording.

I Can't Explain. w/m Peter Townshend, 1965. The first U.S. chart record by the British group The Who (Decca).

I Can't Face the Music (Without Singing the Blues). w. Ted Koehler, m. Rube Bloom, 1938. Recorded by Mildred Bailey, with Red Norvo's Orchestra (Vocalion); Teddy Wilson, vocal by Nan Wynn (Brunswick); Jimmy Dorsey, vocal by June Richmond (Decca); Larry Clinton, vocal by Bea Wain (Victor); Dinah Washington (Mercury).

I Can't Get Close Enough. w/m Sonny LeMaire and J. P. Pennington, 1987. #1 Country chart record by the quintet Exile (Epic).

I Can't Get Mississippi off My Mind. w. Joe Young, m. Harry Akst, 1931. Bert Lown (Victor) and Paul Tremaine (Columbia) had a hand in popularizing this via broadcasts and recordings.

I Can't Get Next to You. w/m Barrett Strong and Norman Whitfield, 1969. #1 record by The Temptations (Gordy). Chart version by Al Green (Hi), 1971.

I Can't Get No Satisfaction. w/m Mick Jagger and Keith Richards, 1965. #1 gold record by The Rolling Stones (London). Otis Redding had a Top 40 version (Volt), 1966.

I Can't Get Over You. w/m The Dramatics, 1977. Top 10 R&B chart record by The Dramatics (ABC).

I Can't Get Started. w. Ira Gershwin, m. Vernon Duke, 1936. Introduced by Bob Hope and Eve Arden in (TM) *Ziegfeld Follies* (1936 edition). While recorded by many, the song is indelibly associated with the great trumpeter-bandleader, Bunny Berigan, who recorded the song twice (Vocalion) (Victor 12″) and used it as his theme song. Berigan sang the vocals, in addition to his trumpet solos.

I Can't Get the One I Want. w. Herman Ruby and Billy Rose, m. Lou Handman, 1924.

I Can't Get There from Here. w/m Dallas Frazier, 1967. Top 10 Country chart record by George Jones (Musicor).

I Can't Get You out of My Heart. w/m Danny Di Minno and Jimmy Crane, 1959. Featured and recorded by Al Martino (20th Fox).

I Can't Give You Anything but Love. w. Dorothy Fields, m. Jimmy McHugh, 1928. Originally written for Patsy Kelly to perform in *Harry Delmars's Revels*, 1927, but dropped from the show. Introduced by Aida Ward in (TM) *Blackbirds of 1928.* Cliff "Ukelele Ike" Edwards had the first hit record (Columbia). In other stage shows, it was performed by André De Shields and Charlaine Woodard in (TM) *Ain't Misbehavin'*, 1978; by Mickey Rooney and Ann Miller in (TM) *Sugar Babies*, 1980. In films, Katharine Hepburn sang it in part in (MP) *Bringing Up Baby*, 1938; it was the title song of a 1940 film; Allan Jones sang it in (MM) *True to the Army*, 1942; Lena Horne and

Bill Robinson performed it in (MM) *Stormy Weather*, 1943; Louis Armstrong sang and played it in (MM) *Jam Session*, 1944; Gloria De Haven sang it in French in (MM) *So This Is Paris*, 1955; Gogi Grant, dubbing for Ann Blyth in the title role, sang it on the soundtrack of (MM) *The Helen Morgan Story*, 1957. Rose Murphy recorded it in 1948, playing piano and singing in a high-pitched voice, substituting "chee-chee" for the "baby" that followed the title. It became a million-seller (Majestic).

I Can't Go for That (No Can Do). w/m Daryl Hall, John Oates, and Sara Allen, 1982. #1 gold record by Daryl Hall and John Oates (RCA).

I Can't Go On Without You. w/m Henry Glover and Sally Nix, 1948. Top recordings by Ella Fitzgerald (Decca) and Bull Moose Jackson (King).

I Can't Grow Peaches on a Cherry Tree. w/m Estelle Levitt and C. Monte, 1966. Recorded by Just Us, a duo comprised of the producers, Chip Taylor and Al Gorgoni (Colpix).

I Can't Hear You No More. w. Gerry Goffin, m. Carole King, 1976. Recorded by Helen Reddy (Capitol).

I Can't Help It. w/m Barry Gibb, 1980. Recorded by Andy Gibb and Olivia Newton-John (RSO).

I Can't Help It (If I'm Still in Love with You). w/m Hank Williams, 1951. Introduced and recorded by Hank Williams (MGM). Best-selling record: Guy Mitchell, with Mitch Miller's Orchestra (Columbia). This country standard has had chart records by Margaret Whiting (Dot), Adam Wade (Coed), Johnny Tillotson (Cadence), B. J. Thomas and the Triumphs (Scepter), Al Martino (Capitol).

I Can't Help Myself (Sugar Pie, Honey Bunch). w/m Brian Holland, Lamont Dozier, and Eddie Holland, 1965. #1 R&B and Pop chart hit by The Four Tops (Motown). Top

40 revivals by Donnie Elbert (Avco), 1972, and Bonnie Pointer (Motown), 1980.

I Can't Help You, I'm Falling Too. See **Please Help Me, I'm Falling.**

I Can't Hold Back. w/m Frank Sullivan and Jim Peterik, 1984. Recorded by the quintet Survivor (Scotti Brothers).

I Can't Hold On. w/m Karla Bonoff, 1978. Recorded by Karla Bonoff (Columbia).

I Can't Let Go. w/m Chip Taylor and Al Gorgoni, 1966. Chart record by the English group The Hollies (Imperial). Revived by Linda Ronstadt (Asylum), 1980.

I Can't Lose That Longing for You. w. Mort Dixon, m. Jesse Greer, 1937. Featured and recorded by Guy Lombardo, vocal by Carmen Lombardo (Victor).

I Can't Love You Anymore (Any More Than I Do). w. Herb Magidson, m. Allie Wrubel, 1940. Top record by Benny Goodman, vocal by Helen Forrest (Columbia).

I Can't Love You Enough. w/m Dorian Burton, Howard Plummer, Jr., and LaVern Baker, 1956. R&B chart-maker by LaVern Baker (Atlantic).

I Can't Quit Her. w/m Al Kooper and Irv Levine, 1968. Introduced by Blood, Sweat & Tears in an album (Columbia). Leading single by the vocal group The Arbors (Date), 1969.

I Can't Remember. w/m Bill Anderson and Bette Anderson, 1965. Hit C&W record by Connie Smith (RCA).

I Can't Remember. w/m Irving Berlin, 1933. Featured and recorded by Eddy Duchin (Victor).

I Can't Remember to Forget. w. Bill Hampton, m. George Duning, 1940. Featured and recorded by Jan Garber and his Orchestra (Okeh); Hal Kemp, vocal by Bob Allen (Victor); Charlie Barnet, vocal by Bob Carroll (Bluebird).

I Can't Resist You. w. Ned Wever, m. Will Donaldson, 1940. Featured and recorded by Benny Goodman, vocal by Helen Forrest (Columbia); Hal Kemp, vocal by Maxine Gray (Victor).

I Can't See for Lookin'. w/m Nadine Robinson and Arnold Stanford, 1944. One of the earliest hit records by The King Cole Trio, coupled with "Straighten Up and Fly Right" (q.v.) (Capitol).

I Can't See Myself Leaving You. w/m Ronnie Shannon, 1969. Top 40 record by Aretha Franklin (Atlantic).

I Can't Stand It. w/m Peter Frampton, 1981. Introduced by Peter Frampton (A&M).

I Can't Stand It. w/m Eric Clapton, 1981. Top 10 record by the British Eric Clapton and his Band (RSO).

I Can't Stand Myself (When You Touch Me). w/m James Brown, 1968. R&B/Pop hit by James Brown (King).

I Can't Stand the Rain. w/m Donald Bryant, Bernard Miller, and Ann Peebles, 1973. Recorded by Ann Peebles (Hi). Top 20 version by the quintet Eruption (Ariola), 1978.

I Can't Stay Mad at You. w/m Gerry Goffin and Carole King, 1963. Top 10 record by Skeeter Davis (RCA).

I Can't Stop Dancing. w/m Kenny Gamble and Leon Huff, 1968. Top 10 record by Archie Bell and The Drells (Atlantic).

I Can't Stop Loving You. w/m Don Gibson, 1958, 1962. Country/Pop crossover chart record by Don Gibson (RCA). In 1962, Ray Charles's version became a #1 million-seller (ABC-Paramount), and caused the song to receive a Grammy Award (NARAS) as Rhythm and Blues Song of the Year. Other recordings of note: Count Basie and his Orchestra (Reprise), 1963, and Conway Twitty (Decca), 1972.

I Can't Stop Thinking of You. w/m Guy Louis and Lee Bayer, 1965. Recorded by Bobbi Martin, with Henry Jerome's Orchestra (Coral).

I Can't Take My Eyes off You. w. Rida Johnson Young, m. Paul Rubens, 1904.

I Can't Tell a Waltz from a Tango. w/m Al Hoffman and Dick Manning, 1954. Popular recording by Patti Page (Mercury).

I Can't Tell Why I Love You, But I Do. w. Will D. Cobb, m. Gus Edwards, 1900. The first hit for this team. Interpolated in (MM) *Belle of the Yukon*, 1944, (MP) *In Old Sacramento*, 1946, and (MM) *Somebody Loves Me*, 1952.

I Can't Tell You Why. w/m Glenn Frey, Don Henley, and Timothy Schmit, 1980. Top 10 record by The Eagles (Asylum).

I Can't Think ob Nuthin' Else But You. w/m Harry Dacre, 1896.

I Can't Turn You Loose. w/m Otis Redding, 1968. Recorded by The Chambers Brothers (Columbia).

I Can't Wait. w/m Stevie Nicks, Rick Nowels, and Eric Pressly, 1986. Chart song from the album "Rock a Little" by Stevie Nicks (Atlantic).

I Can't Wait. w/m John Smith, 1986. Written by John Smith, who with his wife, lead singer Valerie Day, formed the nucleus of the Portland, Oregon group, Nu Shooz (Atlantic). Top 10 record.

I Can't Win for Losing You. w/m Robert Byrne and Rick Bowles, 1987. #1 Country chart record by Earl Thomas Conley (RCA).

I Can't Work No Longer. w/m Curtis Mayfield, 1965. Crossover (R&B/Pop) record by Billy Butler and The Chanters (Okeh).

I Care. w/m Tom T. Hall, 1975. #1 Country chart record by Tom T. Hall (Mercury).

I Cheated Me Right Out of You. w/m Bobby Barker, 1979. #1 Country chart record by Moe Bandy (Columbia).

Ich Liebe Dich (I Love You). w/m Fred Fisher and Martin Broones, 1929. Introduced in (MP) *The Wonder of Women*. Recorded by Bob Haring (Brunswick) and Andy Sannella (Okeh).

I Chose to Sing the Blues. w/m Ray Charles and Jimmy Holiday, 1966. Recorded by Ray Charles (ABC/TRC).

I Concentrate on You. w/m Cole Porter, 1940. Sung by Douglas McPhail and danced by Fred Astaire and Eleanor Powell in (MM) *Broadway Melody of 1940*. Popular records by Tommy Dorsey, vocal by Anita Boyer (Victor); Eddy Duchin, vocal by Stanley Worth (Columbia); Glen Gray and the Casa Loma Orchestra, vocal by Kenny Sargent (Decca).

I Could Be Happy with You. w/m Sandy Wilson, 1953. Introduced in London in (TM) *The Boy Friend* by Anne Rogers and Anthony Hayes. Julie Andrews and John Hewer sang it in the New York production, 1954.

I Could Go On Singing. w. E. Y. Harburg, m. Harold Arlen, 1963. Introduced by Judy Garland in her last film (MM) *I Could Go On Singing*.

I Could Have Danced All Night. w. Alan Jay Lerner, m. Frederick Loewe, 1956. Introduced by Julie Andrews in (TM) *My Fair Lady*. Leading record by Sylvia Syms, with Jack Pleis's Orchestra (Decca). Sung by Marni Nixon, dubbing on the soundtrack for Audrey Hepburn, in (MM) *My Fair Lady*, 1964.

I Could Have Told You. w. Carl Sigman, m. James Van Heusen, 1954. Leading record by Frank Sinatra, with Nelson Riddle's Orchestra (Capitol).

I Could Kiss You for That. w. Johnny Mercer, m. Jimmy McHugh, 1940. Introduced by Orrin Tucker and Bonnie Baker in (MM) *You're the One*.

I Could Make You Care. w. Sammy Cahn, m. Saul Chaplin, 1940. From (MP) *Ladies Must Live*. Most popular recording: Tommy Dorsey, vocal by Frank Sinatra (Victor). Others: The Ink Spots (Decca), Bea Wain (Victor), Jack Leonard (Okeh), Gray Gordon and his Orchestra (Bluebird).

I Could Never Be President. w/m Homer Banks, Bettye Crutcher, and Raymond Jackson, 1969. Recorded by Johnnie Taylor (Stax).

I Could Never Lie to You. w/m Ronald Rice and Patrick McBride, 1969. Recorded by The New Colony Six (Mercury).

I Could Never Love Another (After Loving You). w/m Roger Penzabene, Barrett Strong, and Norman Whitfield, 1968. Hit record by The Temptations (Gordy).

I Could Never Miss You More Than I Do. w/m Neil Harrison, 1981. Recorded by the Scottish singer/actress Lulu (Alfa).

I Could Never Take the Place of Your Man. w/m Prince Rogers Nelson, 1987. Written and introduced by Prince in (MM) *Sign o' the Times*. Top 10 single by Prince (Paisley Park).

I Couldn't Believe My Eyes. w/m Walter G. Samuels, Leonard Whitcup, and Teddy Powell, 1935.

I Couldn't Be Mean to You. w. Stanley Adams, m. Jesse Greer, 1934. Most popular record: Dorsey Brothers, vocal by Bob Crosby (Decca).

I Couldn't Keep from Crying. w/m Marty Robbins, 1953. Introduced and recorded by Marty Robbins (Columbia).

I Couldn't Leave You if I Tried. w/m Rodney Crowell, 1988. #1 Country chart record by Rodney Crowell (Columbia).

I Couldn't Live Without Your Love. w/m Tony Hatch and Jackie Trent, 1966. Recorded in England. Top 10 U.S. release by Petula Clark (Warner Bros.).

I Couldn't Sleep a Wink Last Night. w. Harold Adamson, m. Jimmy McHugh, 1944. Introduced by Frank Sinatra in (MM) *Higher and Higher*. His recording, coupled with "A Lovely Way to Spend an Evening" (q.v.) from the same film, was backed by the unaccompanied (because of the musicians' strike) Bobby Tucker Singers, and was a Top 10 record.

I Couldn't Tell Them What to Do. w. Roy Turk, m. Vee Lawnhurst, 1933. Featured and recorded by Isham Jones, vocal by Eddie Stone (Victor) and Will Osborne (Melotone).

I Could Use a Dream. w. Walter Bullock, m. Harold Spina, 1938. Introduced by Tony Martin and Alice Faye in (MM) *Sally, Irene and Mary*.

I Could Write a Book. w. Lorenz Hart, m. Richard Rodgers, 1941. Introduced by Gene Kelly and Leila Ernst in (TM) *Pal Joey*. In the 1957 film version (MM) *Pal Joey*, it was sung by Frank Sinatra and Trudy Erwin (dubbing for Kim Novak). Early recordings by Eddy Duchin, vocal by Tony Leonard (Columbia); Cy Walter (Liberty Music Shops); Bob Chester, vocal by Bill Darnell (Bluebird). Later: Frank Sinatra (Columbia), Les Brown and his Orchestra (Columbia), Ted Straeter (MGM), Kai Winding (Savoy), Jerry Butler (Mercury).

I Cover the Waterfront. w. Edward Heyman, m. John Green, 1933. Written to help promote the film of the same name. After Ben Bernie and his Orchestra introduced it, the song gained such popularity that the soundtrack was re-scored to make the song the theme song of the film. Among the many recordings over the years: Annette Hanshaw (Perfect); Bert Lown (Bluebird); Eddy Duchin (Victor); Will Osborne (Perfect); Billie Holiday (V-disc 12" and Commodore); Eddie Heywood (Commodore); The Ink Spots (Decca); Artie Shaw (Victor); Joe Sullivan, vocal by Helen Ward (Vocalion); Mel Tormé (Musicraft); Sarah Vaughan (Musicraft).

I Cried. w/m Michael Elias and Billy Duke, 1954. Leading records by Patti Page (Mercury) and Tommy Leonetti (Capitol).

I Cried a Tear. w/m Al Julia and Fred Jay, 1958. Hit record by LaVern Baker (Atlantic).

I Cried for You. w. Arthur Freed, m. Gus Arnheim and Abe Lyman, 1923. This was the first big hit for each of the writers. At the time, Arnheim was playing piano in Lyman's orchestra and later would lead his own band. The song was revived in 1938 by Glen Gray and the Casa Loma Orchestra, with a vocal by Kenny Sargent (Decca). Judy Garland sang it in (MM) *Babes in Arms*, 1939. It was performed by Harry James and his Orchestra, and sung by Helen Forrest in (MM) *Bathing Beauty*, 1944; heard in the Blossom Seeley bio (MM) *Somebody Loves Me*, 1952; (MM) *Love Me or Leave Me*, 1955; (MM) *The Joker Is Wild*, 1957; (MM) *Lady Sings the Blues*, 1972.

I Cross My Fingers. w/m Walter Kent and Walter Farrar, 1950. Popular records by Bing Crosby (Decca); Percy Faith, vocal by Russ Emery (Columbia); Perry Como (RCA Victor).

Ida! Sweet as Apple Cider. w. Eddie Munson, m. Eddie Leonard, 1903. Introduced by Leonard while he was appearing with the Primrose and West company. He then interpolated it in (TM) *Roly Boly Eyes*, 1919. The song was later associated with Eddie Cantor, who performed it in vaudeville and on radio. It was sung by Cantor, dubbing the voice for Keefe Brasselle in (MM) *The Eddie Cantor Story*, 1953. It was also sung in the Texas Guinan film biography (MM) *Incendiary Blonde*, 1945.

Idaho. w/m Jesse Stone, 1942. Leading records by Alvino Rey, vocal by Yvonne King (Bluebird) and Benny Goodman, vocal by Dick Haymes (Columbia). It became the title song for (MP) *Idaho*, starring Roy Rogers.

I'd Be a Legend in My Time. See **Legend in My Time**.

I'd Be Lost Without You. w/m Sunny Skylar, 1946. Featured and recorded by Frankie Carle, vocal by Marjorie Hughes (Columbia); Guy Lombardo, vocal by Don Rodney (Decca).

I'd Climb the Highest Mountain. w. Lew Brown and Sidney Clare, 1926. Among the many recordings in its first year were those by Al Jolson (Brunswick), Art Gillham (Columbia), Roger Wolfe Kahn's Orchestra (Victor), Lee Sims (Brunswick), "Whispering" Jack Smith (Victor). The Ink Spots had a popular record (Decca), 1946.

I'd Do Anything. w/m Lionel Bart, 1963. Introduced in the U.S. in the Broadway production of the British musical (TM) *Oliver!* by Michael Goodman, Georgia Brown, Bruce Prochnik, Alice Playten, Clive Revill, and the boys. In the film version (MM) *Oliver!*, 1968, it was sung by Ron Moody, Shani Wallace, Mark Lester, Jack Wild, and the boys.

I Didn't Get to Sleep At All (Last Night). w/m Tom Macaulay, 1973. Gold record by The 5th Dimension (Bell).

I Didn't Know About You. w. Bob Russell, m. Edward Kennedy "Duke" Ellington, 1944. Adapted from Ellington's instrumental "Sentimental Lady." Recorded by the Ellington band, vocal by Joya Sherrill (Victor); Count Basie, vocal by Thelma Carpenter (Columbia); Lena Horne (Victor); Jo Stafford (Capitol); Boyd Raeburn, vocal by Don Darcy (Guild).

I Didn't Know What Time It Was. w. Lorenz Hart, m. Richard Rodgers, 1939. Introduced by Marcy Westcott and Richard Kollmar in (TM) *Too Many Girls*. Trudi Erwin dubbed it on the soundtrack for Lucille Ball in (MM) *Too Many Girls*, 1940. Interpolated by Frank Sinatra in (MM) *Pal Joey*, 1957.

I Didn't Mean to Turn You On. w/m James Harris III and Terry Lewis, 1986. Introduced by Cherelle (Tabu), 1984. Top 10 record by English singer Robert Palmer (Island), 1986.

I Didn't Raise My Boy to Be a Soldier. w. Alfred Bryan, m. Al Piantadosi, 1915. A hit anti-war song, written before the entry of the U.S. into World War I, and one that created other controversies. A plagiarism suit on the melody was won by a composer named Cohalin. As a pro-war spirit was developing, many "answer" songs were written opposing the sentiments expressed in Bryan's lyrics. Hit records by Morton Harvey (Victor) and The Peerless Quartet (Columbia). Performed on Broadway by Lillian Gish in (TM) *A Musical Jubilee*, 1975.

I Didn't Slip, I Wasn't Pushed, I Fell. w/m Edward Pola and George Wyle, 1950. Best-selling records by Doris Day (Columbia) and Bing Crosby (Decca).

I Didn't Want to Do It. w/m Adolph Smith and Harvey Gladstone, 1954. R&B success by The Spiders (Imperial).

I Dig Rock and Roll Music. w/m Dave Dixon, James Mason, and Paul Stookey, 1967. Top 10 hit by Peter, Paul, and Mary (Warner Bros.).

I'd Know You Anywhere. w. Johnny Mercer, m. Jimmy McHugh, 1940. Introduced by Ginny Simms and Harry Babbitt, with Kay Kyser's Kollege of Musical Knowledge, in (MM) *You'll Find Out*, and recorded by them (Columbia). Nominated for Academy Award.

I'd Leave My Happy Home for You. w. Will A. Heelan, m. Harry Von Tilzer, 1899. Popularized by Blanche Ring at Tony Pastor's Music Hall in New York.

I'd Like to See the Kaiser with a Lily in His Hand. w/m Henry Leslie and Howard Johnson, m. Billy Frisch, 1918. From (TM) *Doing Our Bit*. This was one of the stronger titled anti-Kaiser songs of World War I.

I'd Like to Teach the World to Sing (in Perfect Harmony). w/m William Backer, Roger Cook, Raquel Davis, and Roger Greenaway, 1972. Based on a Coca-Cola radio and TV commercial. Hit records by the British/Australian group The New Seekers (Elektra) and The Hillside Singers, directed by Al Ham (Metromedia).

I'd Love to Be a Monkey in the Zoo. w. Bert Hanlon, m. Willie White, 1917.

I'd Love to Fall Asleep and Wake Up in My Mammy's Arms. w. Sam M. Lewis and Joe Young, m. Fred E. Ahlert, 1920. Popular record by The Peerless Quartet (Victor) (Okeh).

I'd Love to Lay You Down. w/m Johnny MacRae, 1980. #1 Country chart hit by Conway Twitty (MCA).

I'd Love to Live in Loveland. w/m W. R. Williams (Will Rossiter), 1910. Recorded later by Dennis Day (Victor) and Arthur Godfrey (Decca).

I'd Love to Spend (One Hour with You). See **One Hour with You.**

I'd Love to Take Orders from You. w. Al Dubin, m. Harry Warren, 1935. From the Dick Powell and Ruby Keeler film (MM) *Shipmates Forever*. Popular recordings by Mildred Bailey (Vocalion), Phil Harris (Decca), Enric Madriguera (Columbia).

I'd Love You to Want Me. w/m Kent Lavoie (a.k.a. Lobo), 1972. Gold record by Lobo (Big Tree).

I'd Never Stand in Your Way. w/m Fred Rose and Hy Heath, 1953. Popular record by Joni James (MGM).

I Do. w/m Melvin Mason, Jesse Smith, Willie Stephenson, Frank Paden, 1965. Written and recorded by The Marvelows (ABC-Paramount). Revived with a Top 40 record by the J. Geils Band (EMI America), 1982.

I Do, I Do, I Do, I Do, I Do. w/m Benny Anderson, Stig Anderson, and Bjorn Ulvaeus, 1976. Top 20 record by the Swedish group Abba (Atlantic).

I Do Love You. w/m Billy Stewart, 1965. R&B and Pop hit by Billy Stewart (Chess). Revived by the group GQ (Arista), 1979.

I Do Not Know a Day I Did Not Love You. w. Martin Charnin, m. Richard Rodgers, 1970. Introduced by Walter Willison in (TM) *Two by Two*.

I Don't Believe I'll Fall in Love Today. w/m Harland Howard, 1961. Leading record by Warren Smith (Liberty).

I Don't Believe You've Met My Baby. w/m Autry Inman, 1956. C&W hit by The Louvin Brothers (Capitol).

I Don't Blame You At All. w/m William "Smokey" Robinson, 1971. Top 20 record by The Miracles (Tamla).

I Don't Care. w/m Webb Pierce and Cindy Walker, 1955. Country hit by Webb Pierce (Decca).

I Don't Care. w. Jean Lenox, m. Harry O. Sutton, 1905. The song was made popular by Eva Tanguay in vaudeville. It was sung by Judy Garland in (MM) *In the Good Old Summertime*, 1949, and by Mitzi Gaynor in the film biography of Tanguay, (MM) *The I Don't Care Girl*, 1953.

I Don't Care (Just As Long As You Love Me). w/m Buck Owens, 1965. Hit Country record by Buck Owens (Capitol).

I Don't Care If It Rains All Night. w. Sammy Cahn, m. Jule Styne, 1948. From (MM) *Two Guys from Texas*, starring Jack Carson and Dennis Morgan. Leading recordings by Johnny Mercer (Capitol) and Johnny Johnston (MGM).

I Don't Care If the Sun Don't Shine. w/m Mack David, 1950. Best-selling record by Patti Page, with D'Artega's Orchestra (Mercury). Revived by Elvis Presley (RCA), 1956.

I Don't Care Much. w. Fred Ebb, m. John Kander, 1963. Featured and recorded by Barbra Streisand (Columbia).

I Don't Care Who Knows It. w. Harold Adamson, m. Jimmy McHugh, 1945. Introduced by Vivian Blaine in (MM) *Nob Hill*. Leading record by Harry James, vocal by Kitty Kallen (Columbia).

I Don't Hurt Anymore. w. Jack Rollins, m. Don Robertson, 1954. Crossover hits—Country by Hank Snow (RCA Victor), R&B by Dinah Washington (Mercury).

I Don't Know. w/m Willie Mabon, 1952. R&B hit introduced and recorded by Willie Mabon (Chess). Pop version by Buddy Morrow, vocal by Frankie Lester (RCA Victor). Revived by Ruth Brown (Atlantic), 1959.

I Don't Know a Thing About Love. w/m Harlan Howard, 1984. Country chart hit by Conway Twitty (Warner Bros.).

I Don't Know Enough About You. w/m Peggy Lee and Dave Barbour, 1946. Introduced and recorded by Peggy Lee (Capitol). Hit record, also, by The Mills Brothers (Decca).

I Don't Know How to Love Him. w. Tim Rice, m. Andrew Lloyd Webber, 1970. Introduced by Yvonne Elliman in (TM) *Jesus Christ Superstar*. Helen Reddy had a Top 20 version (Capitol). Elliman's single made the Top 40 (Decca). Elliman also sang it in the film version (MM) *Jesus Christ Superstar*, 1973.

I Don't Know If It's Right. w/m J. Fitch, 1979. Gold R&B/Pop chart record by Evelyn "Champagne" King (RCA).

I Don't Know Where I'm Going But I'm on My Way. w/m George Fairman, 1917. A hit song about a draftee's philosophy in World War I. Leading record by The Peerless Quartet (Victor).

I Don't Know Where to Start. w/m Thom Schuyler, 1982. Country and Pop chart record by Eddie Rabbitt (Elektra).

I Don't Know Why. w/m Stevie Wonder, Lula Hardaway, Don Hunter, and Paul Riser, 1969. Top 10 record, coupled with the hit "My Cherie Amour," (q.v.) by Stevie Wonder (Tamla).

I Don't Know Why. w. Roy Turk, m. Fred E. Ahlert, 1931. Featured and recorded by Russ Columbo (Victor) who, despite other top recordings, was the artist associated with the genesis of this standard.

I Don't Know Why You Don't Want Me. w/m Rosanne Cash and Rodney Crowell, 1985. #1 Country chart record by Rosanne Cash (Columbia).

I Don't Like It Like That. See **I Like It Like That.**

I Don't Like Mondays. w/m Bob Geldof, 1979. Song referred to a San Diego, California girl who shot eleven people on a Monday. Recorded by the Irish sextet The Boomtown Rats (Columbia).

I Don't Like to Sleep Alone. w/m Paul Anka, 1975. Top 10 record by Paul Anka (United Artists).

I Don't Love You Anymore. w/m Bill Anderson, 1964. Country hit record by Charlie Louvin (Capitol).

I Don't Mind. w/m James Brown, 1961. Crossover hit (R&B and Pop charts) by James Brown (King).

I Don't Mind At All. w/m Lyle Workman and Brent Bourgeois, 1987. Chart single by Bourgeois Tagg from the album "Yo Yo" (Island).

I Don't Mind the Thorns (If You're the Rose). w/m Jan Buckingham and Linda Young, 1985. #1 Country chart single by Lee Greenwood (MCA).

I Don't Mind Walking in the Rain. w. Al Hoffman, m. Max Rich, 1930. Hoffman's first popular song. Recorded by Bix Beiderbecke (Victor).

I Don't Need Anything But You. w. Martin Charnin, m. Charles Strouse, 1977. Introduced by Reid Shelton, Andrea McArdle, and Sandy Faison in (TM) *Annie*. In the film version (MM) *Annie*, 1982, it was performed by Albert Finney, Aileen Quinn, and Ann Reinking.

I Don't Need No Doctor. w/m Nicholas Ashford and Valerie Simpson, 1966. Chart records by Ray Charles (ABC), 1966; the English band Humble Pie (A&M), 1971; New Riders of the Purple Sage (Columbia), 1972.

I Don't Need You. w/m Rick Christian, 1981. Top 10 record by Kenny Rogers (Liberty).

I Don't See Me in Your Eyes Anymore. w/m Bennie Benjamin and George David Weiss, 1949. Most popular recordings by Gordon Jenkins, vocal by The Stardusters (Decca) and Perry Como accompanied by Mitchell Ayres's Orchestra (RCA Victor). Revived by Charlie Rich (RCA), 1974.

I Don't Stand a Ghost of a Chance with You. w. Bing Crosby and Ned Washington, m. Victor Young, 1933. Introduced and recorded by Bing Crosby (Brunswick). Other early popular recordings by Cab Calloway (Okeh), Ted Fio Rito (Brunswick), Frankie Trumbauer (Varsity). Interpolated in (MM) *Folies Bergere*, starring Maurice Chevalier, 1935. Revived in 1939–1940 by Bea Wain (Victor); Lionel Hampton (Victor); Bobby Hackett (Vocalion); Will Bradley, vocal by Carlotta Dale (Columbia); Andy Kirk (Decca). Among later important records: Charlie Ventura (Sun); George Shearing (MGM); Slim Gaillard (MGM); Dexter Gordon (Dial); Sarah Vaughan (Musicraft); Lester Young (Savoy).

I Don't Think I'll Fall in Love Today. w. Ira Gershwin, m. George Gershwin, 1928. Introduced by Gertrude Lawrence and Paul Frawley in (TM) *Treasure Girl*.

I Don't Think I'm in Love. w. Sammy Cahn, m. James Van Heusen, 1966. Introduced by Norman Wisdom and Louise Troy in (TM) *Walking Happy*.

I Don't Think She's in Love Anymore. w/m Kent Robbins, 1982. Country chart hit by Charley Pride (RCA).

I Don't Think That Man Should Sleep Alone. 1987. Top 10 R&B chart crossover record by Ray Parker, Jr. (Geffen).

I Don't Wanna Be a Loser. w/m Ben Raleigh and Mark Barkan, 1964. Recorded by Lesley Gore (Mercury).

I Don't Wanna Go On with You Like That. w. Bernie Taupin, m. Elton John, 1988. Hit single from the album "Reg Strikes Back," by the English singer/composer, Elton John (MCA).

I Don't Wanna Live Without Your Love. w/m Diane Warren and Albert Hammond, 1988. Recorded by the group, Chicago, from the album "Chicago XIX" (Reprise).

I Don't Wanna Lose You, Baby. w/m Van McCoy, 1965. Top 40 record by the British duo Chad and Jeremy (Columbia).

I Don't Wanna Lose Your Love. w/m Joey Carbone, 1984. Top 10 Country chart record by Crystal Gayle (Warner Bros.).

I Don't Wanna Play House. w/m Billy Sherrill and Glen Sutton, 1967. Country hit by Tammy Wynette (Epic).

I Don't Want Another Sister. w. Leroi Scarlett, m. Edna Williams, 1908.

I Don't Want Nobody to Give Me Nothing (Open up the Door, I'll Get It Myself). w/m James Brown, 1969. Top 10 R&B and Top 20 Pop chart hit by James Brown (King).

I Don't Want to Be a Memory. w/m Sonny Lemaire and J. P. Pennington, 1983. #1 Country chart record by the band Exile (Epic).

I Don't Want to Be Right (If Loving You Is Wrong). w/m Horner Banks, Carl Hampton, and Raymond Jackson, 1972. Top 10 record by Luther Ingram (KoKo). Popular versions by Millie Jackson (Spring), 1975, and Barbara Mandrell (ABC), 1979.

I Don't Want to Cry. w/m Luther Dixon and Chuck Jackson, 1961. Introduced and recorded by Chuck Jackson (Wand).

I Don't Want to Do Wrong. w/m Johnny Bristol, William Guest, Walter Jones, Gladys Knight, Meradi Knight, Jr., Catherine Shaffner, 1971. Top 20 record by Gladys Knight and The Pips (Soul).

I Don't Want to Get Well (I'm in Love with a Beautiful Nurse). w. Howard Johnson and Harry Pease, m. Harry Jentes, 1917. A hospitalized soldier's lament. Featured and recorded by Van and Schenck (Victor). It was sung by George Murphy and Eddie Cantor in (MM) *Show Business*, 1944.

I Don't Want to Have to Marry You. w/m Fred Imus and Philip Sweet, 1976. Hit Country record by Jim Ed Brown and Helen Cornelius (RCA).

I Don't Want to Live Without You. w/m Mick Jones, 1988. Chart single by the Anglo-American group, Foreigner, from their album "Inside Information" (Atlantic).

I Don't Want to Lose Your Love. w/m Gene McFadden, Jimmy McKinney, Linda Vitali, and John Whitehead, 1987. Top 10 R&B chart record by Freddie Jackson (Capitol).

I Don't Want to Love You (Like I Do). w/m Henry Pritchard, 1944. Records: Phil Brito (Musicraft), Kitty Kallen and Richard Hayes (Mercury).

I Don't Want to Make History (I Just Want to Make Love). w. Leo Robin, m. Ralph Rainger, 1936. Introduced by Frances Langford in (MM) *Palm Springs* and recorded by her (Decca). Bob Crosby's Band (Decca), Stuff Smith's combo, featuring Jonah Jones (Vocalion), and Vincent Lopez and his Orchestra (Melotone) also featured it.

I Don't Want to Play in Your Yard. w. Philip Wingate, m. H. W. Petrie, 1894. A novelty, sung in a child's voice.

I Don't Want to See You Again. w/m John Lennon and Paul McCartney, 1964. Top 20 record by the British duo Peter and Gordon (Capitol).

I Don't Want to Set the World on Fire. w/m Eddie Seiler, Sol Marcus, Bennie Benjamin, and Eddie Durham, 1941. Introduced by Harlan Leonard and His Rockets (Bluebird), late 1940. Covered by Tommy Tucker, vocal by Amy Arnell (Okeh), who by recording it and featuring it on broadcasts made it into a hit. The Ink Spots (Decca) and Horace Heidt, vocal by Larry Cotton, Donna Wood, and the Don Juans (Columbia) also had best-sellers. The song was on "Your Hit Parade" for fifteen weeks, four in the #1 spot.

I Don't Want to Spoil the Party. w/m John Lennon and Paul McCartney, 1965. Coupled with the hit, "Eight Days a Week," by The Beatles (Capitol). Revived with the Country chart hit by Roseanne Cash (Columbia), 1989.

I Don't Want to Talk About It. w/m Danny Whitten, 1975. Introduced by Rod Stewart in his album "Atlantic Crossing" (Warner Bros.), 1975. Chart single, 1980.

I Don't Want to Walk Without You. w. Frank Loesser, m. Jule Styne, 1942. Introduced by Johnny Johnston in (MM) *Sweater Girl* and sung again in (MM) *You Can't Ration Love*, 1944. #1 record by Harry James, vocal by Helen Forrest (Columbia). Other chart records by Bing Crosby (Decca) and Dinah Shore (Bluebird). Phyllis McGuire had a chart record (Reprise), 1964, and Barry Manilow revived it successfully (Arista), 1980.

I Don't Want Your Kisses (If I Can't Have Your Love). w. Fred Fisher, m. Martin Broones, 1929. From (MM) *So This Is College*, starring Robert Montgomery, Elliott Nugent, and Sally Starr.

I Do the Rock. w. Tim Curry, m. Michael Kamen, 1979. Recorded by the British actor/singer Tim Curry (A&M).

I Double Dare You. w. Jimmy Eaton, m. Terry Shand, 1937. Introduced, featured, and recorded (Brunswick) by Freddy Martin and his Orchestra, with vocal by Terry Shand, who also was the pianist with the band. Louis Armstrong (Decca) had a well-received recording. The song reached #1 and was on "Your Hit Parade" for twelve weeks.

I Do What I Do. w/m Michael Des Barres, Jonathan Elias, and John Taylor, 1986. Theme from the film (MP) *9½ Weeks*, sung on the soundtrack and on records by British singer John Taylor (Capitol).

I Do You. w/m Linda Mallah and Rick Kelly, 1987. Recorded by the family group The Jets (MCA).

I'd Rather Be a Lobster Than a Wise Guy. w. Edward Madden, m. Theodore F. Morse, 1907.

I'd Rather Be an Old Man's Sweetheart (Than a Young Man's Fool). w/m Clarence Carter, George Jackson, and Raymond Moore, 1969. Recorded by Candi Staton (Fame).

I'd Rather Be Blue Over You (Than Be Happy with Somebody Else). w. Billy Rose, m. Fred Fisher, 1928. Sung by Fanny Brice in (MM) *My Man*, and on records (Victor). Barbra Streisand, as Brice, sang it in (MM) *Funny Girl*, 1968.

I'd Rather Be Gone. w/m Merle Haggard, 1969. Top 10 Country chart record by Hank Williams, Jr. (MGM).

I'd Rather Be Me. w. Johnny Mercer, m. Harold Arlen, 1945. Introduced by Bing Crosby, dubbing for Eddie Bracken as part of the plot, in (MM) *Out of This World*. Recorded by Crosby (Decca).

I'd Rather Be Right. w. Lorenz Hart, m. Richard Rodgers, 1937. The title song of (TM) *I'd Rather Be Right*, which starred George M. Cohan in the role of President Franklin D. Roosevelt. Cohan sang the number with Joy Hodges, Austin Marshall, Mary Jane Walsh, and ensemble. In 1968, it was sung by Joel Grey, playing Cohan, in (TM) *George M.*

I'd Rather Be Sorry. w/m Kris Kristofferson, 1971. Hit Country/Pop chart song by Ray Price (Columbia).

I'd Rather Be the Girl in Your Arms. w. Harlan Thompson, m. Harry Archer, 1926. Recorded by Jean Goldkette (Victor) and B. A. Rolfe (Edison).

I'd Rather Die Young. w/m Beasley Smith, Billy Vaughn, and Randy Wood, 1953. Coupled with the hit revival of "P.S. I Love You" (q.v.) by the Hilltoppers (Dot).

I'd Rather Drink Muddy Water. w/m Eddie Miller, 1936. Composer, not to be confused with tenor saxophonist of same name, introduced this blues that later had a popular recording by The Cats and the Fiddle (Bluebird), 1940.

I'd Rather Have the Blues. See **Blues from "Kiss Me Deadly."**

I'd Rather Lead a Band. w/m Irving Berlin, 1936. Fred Astaire introduced it in (MM) *Follow the Fleet* and recorded it (Brunswick), as did Bunny Berigan (Vocalion); Glen Gray and the Casa Loma Orchestra, vocal by Pee Wee Hunt (Decca); Nat Brandwynne's Orchestra (Melotone).

I'd Rather Leave While I'm in Love. w/m Peter Allen and Carole Bayer Sager, 1979. Recorded by Rita Coolidge (A&M).

I'd Rather Listen to Your Eyes. w. Al Dubin, m. Harry Warren, 1935. Introduced by Dick Powell in (MM) *Shipmates Forever*. Leading records: Mildred Bailey (Vocalion), the bands of Phil Harris (Decca), Enric Madriguera (Victor), Chick Bullock (Melotone), Jacques Renard (Brunswick).

I'd Rather Loan You Out. w/m Roy Drusky, Vic McAlpin, and Lester Vanadore, 1961. Recorded by Roy Drusky (Decca).

I'd Rather Love You. w/m Johnny Duncan, 1971. Country and Pop chart record by Charley Pride (RCA).

I'd Really Love to See You Tonight. w/m Parker McGee, 1976. Gold record by England Dan [Seals] and John Ford Coley (Big Tree).

I Dreamed. w/m Charles Green and Marvin Moore, 1956. Popularized by Betty Johnson (Bally).

I Dreamed a Dream. w. (Engl.) H. Kretzmer, (Fr.) A. Boublil, J. M. Natel, m. C.-M. Schönberg, 1987. Introduced in the U.S. by Randy Graff in (TM) *Les Miserables*. Recorded by Neil Diamond on the album "Hot August Night II" (Columbia).

I Dreamed Last Night. w/m Justin Hayward, 1975. Recorded by the British duo Justin Hayward and John Lodge (Threshold).

I Dreamed of a Hillbilly Heaven. w. Hal Sothern, m. Eddie Dean, 1955. Song commemorating and naming many country singers and writers who had passed on. Best-selling record by Eddie Dean, with The Frontiersmen (Sage & Sand). Also recorded by Arlie Duff, with The Anita Kerr Singers (Decca). Revived, with some name changes, by Tex Ritter (Capitol), 1961.

I Dream of You. w/m Marjorie Goetschius and Edna Osser, 1944. Tommy Dorsey, with vocal by Freddy Stewart, had a million-seller, coupled with the band's hit instrumental "Opus No. 1" (q.v.) (Victor). Other hit records by Frank Sinatra (Columbia), Andy Russell (Capitol), Perry Como (Victor).

I Dreamt I Dwelt in Harlem. w. Robert B. Wright, m. Jerry Gray, Ben Smith, and Leonard W. Ware, 1941. Co-composer Jerry Gray arranged Glenn Miller's popular version of the song (Bluebird), which was also recorded by The King Sisters (Bluebird).

I Dream Too Much. w. Dorothy Fields, m. Jerome Kern, 1935. Introduced by Lily Pons in (MM) *I Dream Too Much*. Pons recorded it (Victor) coupled with "I'm the Echo" (q.v.) from the same film.

I'd Still Believe You True. w/m Paul Dresser, 1900. Featured by Charles Kent.

I'd Still Stay Yes. w/m Kenny Edmonds, Gary Scelsa, and Fenderetta, 1987. Top 10 Crossover (R&B/Pop) single by the female group Klymaxx (Constellation).

I'd Trade All of My Tomorrows (for Just One Yesterday). w/m Jenny Lou Carson, 1947. Popular recording by Eddy Arnold (RCA Victor).

I Dug a Ditch (in Wichita). w. Lew Brown and Ralph Freed, m. Burton Lane, 1943. Introduced by Kathryn Grayson and Kay Kyser's Orchestra in (MM) *Thousands Cheer*. Best-selling record by Willie Kelly and his Orchestra (Hit).

I'd Wait a Million Years. w/m Gary Zekley and Mitch Bottler, 1969. Top 20 record by The Grass Roots (Dunhill).

I Enjoy Being a Girl. w. Oscar Hammerstein II, m. Richard Rodgers, 1958. Introduced by Pat Suzuki and dancers in (TM) *Flower Drum Song*. In the film version, (MM)

Flower Drum Song, 1961, it was sung by B. J. Baker, dubbing for Nancy Kwan.

If. w/m David Gates, 1971. Top 10 record by the group Bread (Elektra).

If. w. Robert Hargreaves and Stanley Damerell, m. Tolchard Evans, 1951. English song published seventeen years earlier. Perry Como's record was a #1 million-seller (RCA Victor), followed by Jo Stafford (Capitol), Billy Eckstine (MGM), Dean Martin (Capitol), Guy Lombardo and his Royal Canadians (Decca).

If a Girl Like You Loved a Boy Like Me. w/m Will D. Cobb and Gus Edwards, 1905.

I Fall in Love Too Easily. w. Sammy Cahn, m. Jule Styne, 1945. Introduced by Frank Sinatra in (MM) *Anchors Aweigh*. Nominated for Academy Award, 1945.

I Fall in Love with You Every Day. w. Frank Loesser, m. Manning Sherwin and Arthur Altman, 1938. Introduced by Florence George and John Payne in (MM) *College Swing*. Recordings: Larry Clinton, vocal by Bea Wain (Victor); Jimmy Dorsey, vocal by Bob Eberly (Decca); Dolly Dawn, with George Hall's Orchestra (Vocalion); Horace Heidt (Brunswick); Abe Lyman (Bluebird).

I Fall in Love with You Ev'ry Day. w/m Sam H. Stept, 1946. Leading recordings by Merv Griffin (Victor), Bobby Sherwood and his Orchestra (Capitol).

I Fall to Pieces. w/m Hank Cochran and Harlan Howard, 1961. Hit C&W record by Patsy Cline (Decca).

If a Man Answers. w/m Bobby Darin, 1962. Introduced by Bobby Darin in (MP) *If a Man Answers*, in which he co-starred with Sandra Dee, and on records (Capitol).

If and When. w. Sammy Cahn, m. Josef Myrow, 1963. Introduced and recorded by Patti Page (Columbia).

If Anyone Fails. w/m Sandy Stewart and Stevie Nicks, 1983. Recorded by Stevie Nicks (Modern).

I Faw Down an' Go Boom! w/m James Brockman, Leonard Stevens, and B. B. B. Donaldson, 1928. Novelty song recorded by George Olsen (Victor), Fred Hall (Okeh), Eddie Cantor (Victor).

If a Woman Answers (Hang Up the Phone). w/m Barry Mann and Cynthia Weil, 1962. Recorded by Leroy Van Dyke (Mercury).

If Dreams Come True. w. Al Stillman, m. Robert Allen, 1958. Top 10 record by Pat Boone (Dot).

If Dreams Come True. w. Irving Mills, m. Edgar Sampson and Benny Goodman, 1938. Introduced and recorded by Benny Goodman and his Orchestra (Victor). Other versions: Andy Kirk and his Clouds of Joy, arranged by Edgar Sampson (Decca); Bobby Hackett (Vocalion); Teddy Wilson (Brunswick); the Hank D'Amico Sextet (MGM).

I Feel a Song Comin' On. w. Dorothy Fields and George Oppenheimer, m. Jimmy McHugh, 1935. Introduced by Harry Barris, Frances Langford, Alice Faye, and Patsy Kelly in (MM) *Every Night at Eight* and reprised, in a melancholy manner, by Alice Faye. Among early recordings: Frances Langford (Brunswick); Paul Whiteman, vocal by Ramona (Victor); Johnny "Scat" Davis (Decca); Frank Dailey's Orchestra (Bluebird). It was heard in (MM) *Follow the Boys*, 1944. It was interpolated by Ann Miller and chorus in (TM) *Sugar Babies*, 1980. For many years, the song was a favorite of nightclub performers who used it as an "opener."

I Feel at Home with You. w. Lorenz Hart, m. Richard Rodgers, 1927. Introduced by June Cochrane and Jack Thompson in (TM) *A Connecticut Yankee*.

I Feel Fine. w/m John Lennon and Paul McCartney, 1964. #1 gold record by The Beatles (Capitol).

I Feel for You. w/m Prince Rogers Nelson, 1984. #1 R&B gold record by Chaka Khan, rap by Grandmaster Melle Mel, harmonica by Stevie Wonder (Warner Bros.). Winner Grammy Award (NARAS) Rhythm and Blues Song of the Year, 1984.

I Feel Good All Over.   w/m Annette Hardeman and Gabe Hardeman, 1987. #1 R&B chart single from the album "If I Were Your Woman" by Stephanie Mills (MCA).

I Feel Like a Bullet (in the Gun of Robert Ford).   w/m Elton John and Bernie Taupin, 1976. Top 10 record by English singer Elton John (MCA).

I Feel Like a Feather in the Breeze.   w. Mack Gordon, m. Harry Revel, 1936. Introduced by the co-eds in (MM) *Collegiate*. Among recordings: Richard Himber, vocal by Stuart Allen (Victor); Jan Garber, vocal by Lee Bennett (Decca); Johnny Johnson (Melotone); Art Karle (Vocalion).

I Feel Like Cryin'.   w/m Lewi Werly Fairburn, 1955. Top 10 C&W chart record by Carl Smith (Columbia).

I Feel–Like–I'm–Fixin'–to–Die Rag.   w/m Joe McDonald, 1967. Title song of album by Country Joe and The Fish (Vanguard).

I Feel Like I'm Gonna Live Forever.   w. Bob Hilliard, m. Jule Styne, 1953. Introduced by Helen Gallagher in (TM) *Hazel Flagg*.

I Feel Like Loving You Again.   w/m Bobby Braddock and Sonny Throckmorton, 1980. #1 Country chart record by T. G. Sheppard (Warner Bros.).

I Feel Love.   w/m Donna Summer, Giorgio Moroder, and Pete Bellotte, 1977. Hit record by Donna Summer (Casablanca).

I Feel Love (Benji's Theme).   w. Euel Box, m. Betty Box, 1974. Sung by Charlie Rich on the soundtrack of (MP) *Benji*. Nominated for an Academy Award.

I Feel Pretty.   w. Stephen Sondheim, m. Leonard Bernstein, 1957. Introduced by Carol Lawrence in (TM) *West Side Story*. In the film version (MM) *West Side Story*, 1961, it was sung by Marni Nixon on the soundtrack, dubbing for Natalie Wood.

I Feel So Bad.   w/m Chuck Willis, 1954. Top 10 R&B record by Chuck Willis (Okeh). Revived by Elvis Presley (RCA), 1961.

I Feel So Low When I'm High.   w/m Robert Lissauer, 1953. Introduced by Jayne Manners at Cafe Society, in New York City. Featured by Robert Alda in nightclubs and on TV. Sung by Constance Moore in (MM) *Spree*, 1967.

I Feel So Smoochie.   w/m Phil Moore, 1947. Featured and recorded by Lena Horne (MGM).

I Feel the Earth Move.   w/m Carole King, 1971. Recorded by Carole King (Ode).

I Fell in Love with You.   w. Arnold B. Horwitt, m. Richard Lewine, 1948. Introduced by Kyle MacDonnell and Jack Kilty in (TM) *Make Mine Manhattan*. Recorded by Ray Noble, vocal by Al Hendrickson (Columbia).

If Ever I See You Again.   w/m Joe Brooks, 1978. Introduced by Joe Brooks in (MP) *If Ever I See You Again*. Leading recording by Roberta Flack (Atlantic).

If Ever I Would Leave You.   w. Alan Jay Lerner, m. Frederick Loewe, 1960. Introduced by Robert Goulet in (TM) *Camelot*. In (MM) *Camelot*, 1967, it was sung by Franco Nero.

If Ever You're in My Arms Again.   w. Cynthia Weil and Michael Masser, m. Tom Snow and Michael Masser, 1984. Top 10 record by Peabo Bryson (Elektra).

If He Can Fight Like He Can Love, Good Night Germany.   w. Grant Clarke and Howard Johnson, m. George W. Meyer, 1918. Rae Samuels popularized this World War I comedy song in vaudeville.

If He Cared.   w. Clifford Grey, m. Herbert Stothart, 1929. Sung by Marion Harris, in (MM) *Devil May Care*.

If He Comes In, I'm Going Out.   w. Cecil Mack, m. Chris Smith, 1910.

If He Really Knew Me. w. Carole Bayer Sager, m. Marvin Hamlisch, 1978. Introduced by Lucie Arnaz and Robert Klein in (TM) *They're Playing Our Song.*

If He Walked into My Life. w/m Jerry Herman, 1966. Introduced by Angela Lansbury in (TM) *Mame.* Popular recording by Eydie Gormé (Columbia). In the film version (MM) *Mame,* 1974, it was sung by Lucille Ball.

If Hollywood Don't Need You. w/m Bob McDill, 1982. #1 Country chart record by Don Williams (MCA), 1983.

If I Can Dream. w/m W. Earl Brown, 1968. Top 20 record by Elvis Presley (RCA).

I Can Dream, Can't I? w. Irving Kahal, m. Sammy Fain, 1938, 1949. One of two future hits from a flop show that ran only fourteen performances (see *I'll Be Seeing You*). Both were introduced by Tamara in (TM) *Right This Way.* Early recordings by Glen Gray and the Casa Loma Orchestra, vocal by Kenny Sargent (Decca); Harry James, vocal by Helen Humes (Brunswick); Al Bowlly (Bluebird). The song attained some initial popularity, as indicated by its three appearances on "Your Hit Parade." This was greatly surpassed in 1949 when it was in the Top 10 for seventeen weeks, twice in the #1 position. The revival was due to the hit record by The Andrews Sisters (Decca). The Glenn Miller Orchestra led by Tex Beneke (RCA Victor) and Toni Arden (Columbia) also had popular versions.

If I Can't Have You. w/m Barry Gibb, Maurice Gibb, and Robin Gibb, 1977. Introduced in (MM) *Saturday Night Fever* by Yvonne Elliman, whose single became a #1 gold record (RSO). It marked the first time that a motion picture had four #1 singles emanate from one score, and the fourth consecutive #1 record by a writer (Barry Gibb), eclipsing the record set by Lennon and McCartney in 1964. The other film songs were: "How Deep Is Your Love," "Stayin' Alive," and "Night Fever." The other Barry Gibb song (written in collab-oration with younger brother, Andy) was "(Love is) Thicker Than Water."

If I Can't Have You. w/m Etta James and Harvey Fuqua, 1960. Introduced and recorded by Etta and Harvey (Chess).

If I Can't Have You. w. Al Bryan, m. George W. Meyer, 1929. Introduced by Colleen Moore in (MM) *Footlights and Fools.* Recorded by Gus Arnheim's Orchestra (Okeh) and by Annette Hanshaw (Okeh).

If I Cared a Little Bit Less. w/m Berkeley Graham and Carley Mills, 1942. Leading recordings by The Ink Spots (Decca) and Sammy Kaye, vocal by Don Cornell (Victor).

If I Could Be with You (One Hour Tonight). w. Henry Creamer, m. James P. Johnson, 1930. Recorded by Louis Armstrong (Okeh) and McKinney's Cotton Pickers (Victor). Danny Thomas sang it (MM) *The Jazz Singer,* 1953, and Frank Sinatra, portraying Joe E. Lewis, sang it in (MM) *The Joker's Wild,* 1957.

If I Could Build My Whole World Around You. w/m Johnny Bristol, Vernon Bullock, and Harvey Fuqua, 1967. Top 10 record by Marvin Gaye and Tammi Terrell (Tamla).

If I Could Learn to Love (As Well As I Fight). w. Herman Ruby, m. M. K. Jerome, 1929. The song was written for and performed by Georges Carpentier, the former French boxing champion, who sang it with Alice White and Patsy Ruth Miller in (MM) *Show of Shows.*

If I Could Only Win Your Love. w/m Charlie Louvin and Ira Louvin, 1975. Country/Pop hit by Emmylou Harris (Reprise).

If I Could Reach You. w/m Landy McNeil, 1972. Top 10 record by The 5th Dimension (Bell).

If I Could Turn Back Time. w/m Dianne Warren, 1989. Hit single by Cher (Geffen).

If I'd Been the One. w/m Don Barnes, Jeff Carlisi, Larry Steele, and Donnie Van Zant,

1983. Recorded by the sextet 38 Special (A&M).

If I Didn't Care. w/m Jack Lawrence, 1939. The Ink Spots (Decca) had the best-selling record and then performed the song in (MM) *The Great American Broadcast*, 1941. Other recordings: Count Basie, vocal by Helen Humes (Vocalion); Kate Smith (Victor); Van Alexander and his Band (Bluebird); Gray Gordon, vocal by Cliff Grass (Victor). Later hit records by The Hilltoppers (Dot), 1954; Connie Francis (MGM), 1958; The Platters (Mercury), 1961; The Moments (Stang), 1970.

If I Didn't Have a Dime (to Play the Jukebox). w/m Bert Russell and Phil Medley, 1962. Recorded by Gene Pitney (Musicor).

If I Didn't Have You. w. E. Y. Harburg, m. Milton Ager, 1931.

If I Didn't Love You. w/m Mark Barkan and Pam Sawyer, 1965. Recorded by Chuck Jackson (Wand).

If I Ever Lose This Heaven. w/m Pam Sawyer and Leon Ware, 1975. Recorded by the Scottish group, Average White Band, a.k.a. AWB (Atlantic).

If I Ever Love Again. w/m Russ Carlyle and Dick Reynolds, 1949. Jo Stafford (Capitol) had the best-seller.

If I Fell. w/m John Lennon and Paul Mc-Cartney, 1964. Introduced by The Beatles in (MM) *A Hard Day's Night*, and on records (Capitol).

If I Forget You. w/m Irving Caesar, 1933.

If I Gave You. w/m Hugh Martin and Timothy Gray, 1964. Introduced by Edward Woodward and Louise Troy in (TM) *High Spirits.*

If I Give My Heart to You. w/m Jimmie Crane, Al Jacobs, and Jimmy Brewster, 1954. Hit records by Doris Day (Columbia); Denise Lor (Majar); Connee Boswell, with her last chart record (Decca).

If I Had a Dozen Hearts. w. Paul Francis Webster, m. Harry Revel, 1945. Introduced as a duet by Betty Hutton and Andy Russell in (MM) *The Stork Club.*

If I Had a Girl. w/m Sid Tepper and Roy C. Bennett, 1959. Recorded by Rod Lauren (RCA).

If I Had a Girl Like You. w. Billy Rose and Mort Dixon, m. Ray Henderson, 1925. Popular song with singers and bands. Rudy Vallee made a hit out of it with his performances in theaters and on radio and records (Victor), 1930.

If I Had a Hammer. w/m Lee Hays and Pete Seeger, 1958, 1962, 1963. Introduced by The Weavers. Hit records by Peter, Paul and Mary (Warner Bros.), 1962, and Trini Lopez (Reprise), 1963.

If I Had a Million Dollars. w. Johnny Mercer, m. Matty Malneck, 1934. Introduced by the Boswell Sisters in (MM) *Transatlantic Merry-Go-Round* and recorded by them (Brunswick). Other recordings: the bands of Richard Himber (Victor), Emil Coleman (Columbia), Joe Haymes (Melotone), and singers Jack Fulton (Vocalion), Eddie Stone (Bluebird). In the late forties, revived by Tony Pastor's Band with vocal by the Clooney Sisters, Betty and Rosemary (Columbia).

If I Had a Rocket Launcher. w/m Bruce Cockburn, 1985. Recorded by the Canadian singer Bruce Cockburn (Gold Mountain).

If I Had a Talking Picture of You. w. B. G. DeSylva and Lew Brown, m. Ray Henderson, 1929. Sung by Charles Farrell, Janet Gaynor, and the kindergarteners in (MM) *Sunny Side Up*. It was later sung by Byron Palmer in the DeSylva, Brown and Henderson biography (MM) *The Best Things in Life Are Free*, 1956.

If I Had a Thousand Lives to Live. w. Sylvester Maguire, m. Alfred Solman, 1908.

If I Had a Wishing Ring. w. Marla Shelton, m. Louis Alter, 1946. Introduced by

Andy Russell in (MM) *Breakfast in Hollywood.* Russell recorded it (Capitol), as did Tommy Dorsey, vocal by Stuart Foster (Victor) and Kate Smith (Columbia).

If I Had My Druthers. w. Johnny Mercer, m. Gene De Paul, 1956. Introduced by Peter Palmer in (TM) *L'il Abner.*

If I Had My Life to Live Over. w/m Henry Tobias, Larry Vincent, and Moe Jaffe, 1939, 1947. Introduced in 1939 by bands and singers, but reached popularity eight years later through recordings by Larry Vincent and The Feilden Foursome (20th Century); Buddy Clark (Columbia); the Dinning Sisters (Columbia); Kate Smith (MGM); and others.

If I Had My Way. w. Lou Klein, m. James Kendis, 1913. Hit record by The Peerless Quartet (Victor). Revived by Bing Crosby in (MM) *If I Had My Way,* 1940. It was also heard in (MM) *Sunbonnet Sue,* 1945.

If I Had the Wings of an Angel. See **Prisoner's Song, The.**

If I Had You. w/m Ted Shapiro, Jimmy Campbell, and Reg Connelly, 1929. First published in England, it became a major standard there and in the U.S. Over the title on the American edition of the sheet music is the phrase, "The Prince of Wales' Favorite Foxtrot." Featured and recorded by Rudy Vallee and his Connecticut Yankees (Harmony). Popular record by the British singer Al Bowlly (Brunswick). Dan Dailey sang it in (MM) *You Were Meant for Me,* 1948.

If I Kiss You (Will You Go Away?). w/m Liz Anderson, 1967. Country hit by Lynn Anderson (Chart).

If I Knew. w/m Meredith Willson, 1960. Introduced by Harve Presnell in (TM) *The Unsinkable Molly Brown.* Song not used in the film version.

If I Knew Then (What I Know Now). w/m Dick Jurgens and Eddy Howard, 1939. Introduced and recorded by Dick Jurgens, vocal by Eddy Howard (Vocalion). Orrin Tucker, with

vocal by Bonnie Baker, also had a popular version (Columbia).

If I Knew You Were Comin' I'd 've Baked a Cake. w/m Al Hoffman, Bob Merrill, and Clem Watts, 1950. Eileen Barton's record was #1 and a million-seller (National).

If I Knock the "L" out of Kelly. w. Sam M. Lewis and Joe Young, m. Bert Grant, 1916. From (TM) *Step This Way.* Recorded by Marguerite Farrell (Victor).

If I Love Again. w. Jack Murray, m. Ben Oakland, 1933. Introduced by Stanley Smith and Ona Munson in (TM) *Hold Your Horses.* The song was popular with radio singers in the thirties. Barbra Streisand sang it in (MM) *Funny Lady* in 1975. Later records by Artie Shaw (Victor), Glen Gray and the Casa Loma Orchestra (Decca), and Paul Weston (Capitol).

If I Loved You. w. Oscar Hammerstein II, m. Richard Rodgers, 1945. Introduced by John Raitt and Jan Clayton in (TM) *Carousel.* It was sung by Gordon MacRae and Shirley Jones in the film version (MM) *Carousel,* 1956. Top records by Perry Como (Victor); Frank Sinatra (Columbia); Bing Crosby (Decca). Revived by Roy Hamilton (Epic), 1954, and Chad and Jeremy (World Art), 1965.

If I May. w/m Charles Singleton and Rose Marie McCoy, 1955. Top 10 record by Nat "King" Cole and The Four Knights (Capitol).

If I'm Dreaming, Don't Wake Me Too Soon. w. Al Dubin, m. Joe Burke, 1929. Sung by Marilyn Miller and Alexander Gray in (MM) *Sally.* Recorded by Wayne King and his Orchestra (Victor) on their first session. Vocal by Elmo Tanner, who would later be featured with Ted Weems.

If I'm Going to Die I'm Going to Have Some Fun. w/m George M. Cohan, 1907. From (TM) *The Honeymooners.*

If I'm Lucky. w. Eddie DeLange, m. Josef Myrow, 1946. Introduced in (MM) *If I'm Lucky,* and on records by Perry Como (RCA Victor).

If I Only Had A Brain. w. E. Y. Harburg, m. Harold Arlen, 1939. Sung by Ray Bolger as the Scarecrow in (MM) *The Wizard of Oz.*

If I Only Had a Heart. w. E. Y. Harburg, m. Harold Arlen, 1939. Sung by Jack Haley as the Tin Man in (MM) *The Wizard of Oz.*

If I Only Had a Match. w/m Lee Morris, Arthur Johnston, and George W. Meyer, 1947. Introduced and recorded by Al Jolson (Decca).

If I Only Had the Nerve. w. E. Y. Harburg, m. Harold Arlen, 1939. Sung by Bert Lahr as The Cowardly Lion in (MM) *The Wizard of Oz.*

If I Ruled the World. w. Leslie Bricusse, m. Cyril Ornadel, 1965. Introduced by Harry Secombe in London and then in New York, in (TM) *Pickwick.* Popular record by Tony Bennett (Columbia).

If I Said You Have a Beautiful Body, Would You Hold It Against Me? w/m David Bellamy, 1979. Country and Pop chart hit by The Bellamy Brothers (Warner Bros.).

If I Should Lose You. w. Leo Robin, m. Ralph Rainger, 1935. Introduced by Gladys Swarthout and John Boles in (MM) *Rose of the Rancho.* Among recordings: Isham Jones, vocal by Woody Herman (Decca); Harry Richman (Decca); Richard Himber and his Orchestra (Victor); June Christy (Capitol); Milt Hinton (Staff).

If It Ain't Love. w/m Andy Razaf, Don Redman, and Thomas "Fats" Waller, 1932. Featured by Fats Waller and recorded by the orchestras of Isham Jones (Brunswick) and Chick Webb (Vocalion).

If It Ain't One Thing . . . It's Another. w/m Richard "Dimples" Fields and Belinda Wilson, 1982. #1 R&B record by Richard "Dimples" Fields (Boardwalk).

If It Don't Come Easy. w/m Dave Gibson and Craig Karp, 1988. #1 Country chart single from the album "Love Me Like You Used To" by Tanya Tucker (Capitol).

If It Isn't Love. w/m James Harris III and Terry Lewis, 1988. Chart single from the album "Heart Break" by New Edition (MCA).

If It Pleases You. w/m Wayne P. Walker, 1965. C&W chart record by Billy Walker (Columbia).

If It's the Last Thing I Do. w. Sammy Cahn, m. Saul Chaplin, 1937. Axel Stordahl arranged this for the Tommy Dorsey Band (Victor) and fifteen years later for his wife, singer June Hutton (Capitol). Other early recordings by Frances Langford (Decca); Jimmie Greer and his Band (Decca); Ben Pollack, vocal by Peggy Mann (Decca).

If It's True. w/m Don Redman, Jule Penrose, and Gus Bently, 1933. Introduced and recorded by Don Redman, vocal by Harlan Lattimore (Brunswick). Charlie Spivak and his Orchestra recorded it in 1941 (Okeh).

If It's You. w. Milton Drake, m. Ben Oakland and Artie Shaw, 1940. Introduced and recorded by Artie Shaw, vocal by Anita Boyer (Victor). Best-seller: Vaughn Monroe with his Orchestra (Bluebird). Others: Ray Noble, vocal by Snooky Lanson (Columbia); Dinah Shore (Bluebird).

If It Wasn't for the Moon. w. Harry Tobias, m. Pinky Tomlin, 1940.

If I Was a Millionaire. w. Will D. Cobb, m. Gus Edwards, 1910. From one of Gus Edwards's vaudeville revues comprised of child performers.

If I Were a Bell. w/m Frank Loesser, 1950. Introduced by Isabel Bigley in (TM) *Guys and Dolls.* Popular recordings by Frankie Laine (Mercury), Doris Day (Columbia), Mindy Carson (RCA Victor). In the film version, (MM) *Guys and Dolls,* 1955, it was sung by Jean Simmons and Marlon Brando.

If I Were a Carpenter. w/m Tim Hardin, 1966. Introduced by Tim Hardin. Hit record by Bobby Darin (Atlantic). Top 40 records by The Four Tops (Motown), 1968; Johnny Cash and June Carter (Columbia), 1970. Other chart versions by Bob Seger (Palladium), 1972; Leon Russell (Shelter), 1974.

If I Were a Rich Man. w. Sheldon Harnick, m. Jerry Bock, 1964. Introduced by Zero Mostel in (TM) *Fiddler on the Roof*. In the film version, (MM) *Fiddler on the Roof*, 1971, it was sung by Topol.

If I Were King. w. Leo Robin, m. Newell Chase and Sam Coslow, 1930. Written for the film version (MM) *The Vagabond King* and sung by Dennis King. The title came from the play on which the Broadway musical was based.

If I Were Sure of You. w. Ted Koehler, m. Rube Bloom, 1939. Featured and recorded by Horace Heidt, vocal by Larry Cotton (Brunswick); Bob Crosby, vocal by Marion Mann (Decca); Al Kavelin's Orchestra (Vocalion).

If I Were Your Woman. w/m Gloria Jones, Pam Sawyer, and Clay McMurray, 1971. Top 10 record by Gladys Knight and The Pips (Soul).

If Love Were All. w/m Noël Coward, 1929. Introduced in the U.S. by Mireille in (TM) *Bitter Sweet*. Ivy St. Helier first sang it in the British production. It was heard in (MM) *Bitter Sweet*, starring Jeanette MacDonald and Nelson Eddy, 1940.

(If Loving You Is Wrong) I Don't Want to Be Right. w/m Homer Banks, Carl Hampton, and Raymond Jackson, 1972. Top 10 record by Luther Ingram (KoKo). Popular versions by Millie Jackson (Spring), 1975, and Barbara Mandrell (ABC), 1979.

If Money Talks, It Ain't on Speaking Terms with Me. w/m J. Fred Helf, 1902.

If My Friends Could See Me Now. w. Dorothy Fields, m. Cy Coleman, 1966. Introduced by Gwen Verdon in (TM) *Sweet Charity*. In the film version (MM) *Sweet Charity*, 1969, it was sung by Shirley MacLaine. Chart record by Linda Clifford (Curtom), 1978.

If My Heart Could Only Talk. w/m Walter G. Samuels, Teddy Powell, and Leonard Whitcup, 1937. Most popular records by Tommy Dorsey and his Orchestra (Victor) and Billie Holiday (Vocalion).

If'n. w. Matt Dubey, m. Harold Carr, 1956. Introduced by Gordon Polk and Virginia Gibson in (TM) *Happy Hunting*.

If Not for You. w/m Bob Dylan, 1971. Introduced by Dylan in his album "New Morning" (Columbia), 1970. The recording by Olivia Newton-John became her first U.S. chart hit (Uni). Country singer/actor Bobby Wright had a chart version (Decca), 1973.

If Not for You. w/m Jerry Chesnut, 1969. Top 10 Country chart record by George Jones (Musicor).

If Only You Knew. w/m Kenny Gamble, Dexter Wansel, and Cynthia Biggs, 1983. #1 R&B, Pop chart entry by Patti LaBelle (Philadelphia International).

If Only You Were Mine. w. Harry B. Smith, m. Victor Herbert, 1899. From (TM) *The Singing Girl*.

I Fooled You This Time. w/m Gene Dixon and Kenneth Lewis, 1966. Top 10 R&B and Pop chart.

I Forget, I Forget. w/m Felix McGlennon, 1888.

I Forgot More Than You'll Ever Know. w/m Cecil A. Null, 1953. Featured and recorded by The Davis Sisters (RCA Victor).

I Forgot to Be Your Lover. w/m William Bell and Booker T. Jones, 1969. Recorded by William Bell (Stax).

I Forgot to Remember to Forget. w/m Stanley A. Kesler and Charles A. L. Feathers, 1956. Recorded by Elvis Presley (RCA).

I Fought the Law. w/m Sonny Curtis, 1966. Top 10 record by The Bobby Fuller Four (Mustang). Revived in 1975 by Sam Neely (A&M).

I Found a Dream. w. Don Hartman, m. Jay Gorney, 1935. Sung by John Boles and Dixie Lee in (MM) *Redheads on Parade*.

I Found a Girl. w/m P. F. Sloan and Steve Barri, 1965. Top 40 record by Jan and Dean (Liberty).

I Found a Love. w/m Willie Schofield, Wilson Pickett, and Robert West, 1962. Recorded by The Falcons, Wilson Pickett as lead singer (Lu Pine). Pickett had a popular solo version (Atlantic), 1967.

I Found a Love, Oh What a Love. w/m Jeanie Allen, 1965. Pop chart record by Jo Ann (Campbell) and Troy (Seals) (Atlantic).

I Found a Million Dollar Baby (in a Five and Ten Cent Store). w. Billy Rose and Mort Dixon, m. Harry Warren, 1931. Introduced by Ted Healy, Fanny Brice, Phil Baker, and Lew Brice in Billy Rose's (TM) *Crazy Quilt*. Bing Crosby recorded it twice (Brunswick) (Decca). It was heard in (MP) *Million Dollar Baby*, 1941, and sung by Streisand, as Fanny Brice, in (MM) *Funny Lady*, 1975.

I Found a New Baby. w/m Jack Palmer and Spencer Williams, 1926. One of the all-time jazz standards. It is sometimes titled "I've Found . . . etc." Among the myriad of recordings are those by the Chicago Rhythm Kings (Brunswick); Frankie Trumbauer (Okeh); Isham Jones (Decca); McKinney's Cotton Pickers (Victor); The New Orleans Feetwarmers with Sidney Bechet (Bluebird); Benny Goodman's Orchestra (Victor), and his Sextet (Columbia); Lionel Hampton (Victor); Bud Freeman (Bluebird); Erskine Hawkins (Vocalion).

I Found a Rose in the Devil's Garden. w/m Fred Fisher and Willie Raskin, 1921. Recorded by The Sterling Trio (Victor) and the tenor, Sam Ash (Columbia).

I Found a True Love. w/m Bobby Womack and Reggie Young, 1968. Recorded by Wilson Pickett (Atlantic).

I Found My Girl in the U.S.A. w/m Jimmie Skinner, 1957. Top 10 C&W record by Jimmie Skinner (Mercury).

I Found Someone. w/m Michael Bolton and Mark Mangold, 1987. Top 10 single from the album "Cher" by Cher (Geffen).

I Found the End of the Rainbow. w/m John Mears, Harry Tierney, and Joseph McCarthy, 1918.

I Found You in the Rain. w/m Harold Barlow, 1941. Adapted from Chopin's *Prelude No. 7 in A*, Opus 28. Featured and recorded by Claude Thornhill, vocal by Dick Harding (Columbia), and Glen Gray and the Casa Loma Orchestra, vocal by Kenny Sargent (Decca).

If She Should Come to You (La Montaña). w. Alec Wilder (Engl.), G. Moreu (Sp.), m. Augusto Alguero, 1960. Spanish song. Leading vocal record by Anthony Newley (London). Frank DeVol and his Rainbow Strings had the top instrumental version (Columbia), followed by Roger Williams (Kapp).

If She Would Have Been Faithful. w/m Randy Goodrum and Steve Kipner, 1987. Single by the group Chicago (Warner Bros.).

If Teardrops Were Pennies. w/m Carl Butler, 1951, 1973. Leading records in Country and Pop by Carl Smith (Columbia) and Rosemary Clooney (Columbia). Revived with hit Country record by Porter Wagoner and Dolly Parton (RCA), 1973.

If Teardrops Were Silver. w/m Don Wayne, 1966. Top 10 Country record by Jean Shepard (Capitol).

If the Man in the Moon Were a Coon. w/m Fred Fisher, 1905. The first hit by the German-born composer. Tommy Dorsey and the Clambake Seven recorded it (Victor) in 1937.

If the Moon Turns Green. w. Paul Coates, m. Bernard Hanighen, 1935. Leading recordings by Billie Holiday (Clef); the bands of Paul Whiteman, vocal by Ramona (Victor); Henry Busse (Decca); Jimmie Grier (Brunswick); Art Kassel (Bluebird); Taft Jordan (Melotone); and Bob Howard (Decca).

343

If the Rain's Got to Fall. w/m David Heneker, 1965. Introduced on Broadway in the London-originated production (TM) *Half a Sixpence*, by Tommy Steele, Will Mackenzie, Norman Allen, and Grover Dale. Steele and company sang it in the film version (MM) *Half a Sixpence*, 1967.

If There Is Someone Lovelier Than You. w. Howard Dietz, m. Arthur Schwartz, 1934. Written as part of an original score for the nighttime radio series "The Gibson Family," it was introduced on the stage by Georges Metaxa in (TM) *Revenge with Music.*

If This Is Goodbye. w/m Robert Wright and George Forrest, 1965. Based on a theme from the 1st movement of *Concerto No. 2 in C Minor* by Sergei Rachmaninoff. It was introduced by Constance Towers and Michael Kermoyan in (TM) *Anya.*

If This Is It. w/m John Colla and Huey Lewis, 1984. Top 10 record by Huey Lewis and The News (Chrysalis).

If This Is Love (I'd Rather Be Lonely). w/m Cholly Bassoline, Marty Coleman, and Michael Valvano, 1967. Recorded by The Precisions (Drew).

If This Isn't Love. w. E. Y. Harburg, m. Burton Lane, 1947. Introduced by Donald Richards and Ella Logan in (TM) *Finian's Rainbow*. In the film version (MM) *Finian's Rainbow*, 1968, it was sung by Don Francks, Petula Clark, Fred Astaire, and Barbara Hancock.

If This World Were Mine. w/m Marvin Gaye, 1968. Recorded by Marvin Gaye and Tammi Terrell (Tamla).

If Washington Should Come to Life. w/m George M. Cohan, 1906. From (TM) *George Washington, Jr.*

If We Can't Be the Same Old Sweethearts (We'll Just Be The Same Old Friends). w. Joseph McCarthy, m. James V. Monaco, 1915. Leading record by Irving Kaufman (Victor). Revived by Andy Russell and The Pied Pipers (Capitol) in the mid-forties.

If We Make It Through December. w/m Merle Haggard, 1974. #1 Country and Pop chart hit record by Merle Haggard (Capitol).

If We Only Have Love. w. Mort Shuman and Eric Blau (Engl.), Jacques Brel (Fr.), m. Jacques Brel, 1968. Sung by the company in the off-Broadway musical (TM) *Jacques Brel Is Alive and Well and Living in Paris*. Chart record by Dionne Warwick (Warner Bros.), 1972.

If We're Not Back in Love by Monday. w/m Sonny Throckmorton and Glenn Martin, 1977. Country hit by Merle Haggard (MCA). Millie Jackson had a R&B/Pop chart version "If You're Not Back in Love by Monday" (Spring).

If We Try. w/m Don McLean, 1973. Recorded by Don McLean (United Artists).

If We Were in Love. w. Alan Bergman and Marilyn Bergman, m. John Williams, 1981. Introduced by Placido Domingo in (MM) *Yes, Giorgio*. Nominated for Academy Award.

If You Ain't Lovin' (You Ain't Livin'). w/m George Strait, 1988. #1 Country chart single from the album "If You Ain't Lovin', You Ain't Livin' " by George Strait (MCA).

If You Ain't Lovin' (You Ain't Livin'). w/m Tommy Collins, 1955. C&W hit by Faron Young (Capitol).

If You Are but a Dream. w/m Moe Jaffe, Jack Fulton, and Nat Bonx, 1942. Based on Anton Rubinstein's piano piece, "Romance, No. 1 in E Flat." Recorded by Jimmy Dorsey and his Orchestra (Decca). Leading version recorded by Frank Sinatra, arranged and conducted by Axel Stordahl (Columbia), 1945.

If You Believed in Me. w. L. Wolfe Gilbert, m. Abel Baer, 1929. Popularized by George Olsen and his Orchestra, vocal by Fran Frey (Victor) and Don Voorhees's Orchestra (Perfect).

If You Build a Better Mousetrap. w. Johnny Mercer, m. Victor Schertzinger, 1942. Introduced by Betty Hutton, with Jimmy Dorsey's Orchestra in (MM) *The Fleet's In*. Best-selling recording by Jimmy Dorsey, vocal by Bob Eberly and Helen O'Connell (Decca).

If You Can Do It: I Can Too!! 1987. Top 10 R&B chart record by Melissa Morgan (Capitol).

If You Can't Bite, Don't Growl. w/m Tommy Collins, 1966. Top 10 Country chart record by Tommy Collins (Columbia).

If You Can Want. w/m William Robinson, 1968. Top 20 record by Smokey Robinson and The Miracles (Tamla).

If You Cared for Me. w. Ed Rose, m. Ted Snyder, 1908.

If You Change Your Mind. w/m Roseanne Cash and Hank De Vito, 1988. #1 Country chart record by Roseanne Cash (Columbia).

If You Could Only Come with Me. w/m Noël Coward, 1929. Georges Metaxa introduced this in the London production of (TM) *Bitter Sweet* and his understudy there, Gerald Nodin, introduced it in the U.S. as the leading man of the Broadway production. Fernand Gravet sang it in the first film adaptation (British), 1933, and Nelson Eddy sang it in the U.S. version (MM) *Bitter Sweet*, 1940.

If You Could Read My Mind. w/m Gordon Lightfoot, 1971. Top 10 record by the Canadian singer/songwriter Gordon Lightfoot (Reprise).

If You Could See Her (The Gorilla Song). w. Fred Ebb, m. John Kander, 1966. Introduced by Joel Grey in (TM) *Cabaret*. In the film version (MM) *Cabaret*, 1972, Grey repeated the song, this time dancing with Louise Quick dressed as the gorilla.

If You Could See Me Now. w. Carl Sigman, m. Tadd Dameron, 1946. Featured and recorded by Sarah Vaughan (Musicraft).

If You Don't, Somebody Else Will. w/m Johnny Mathis, Jimmy Lee, and Geraldine Hamilton, 1955. Introduced by Jimmy and Johnny (Chess).

If You Don't Know, I Ain't Gonna Tell You. w/m George Hamilton IV, 1962. Top 10 C&W chart record by George Hamilton IV (RCA Victor).

If You Don't Know Me by Now. w/m Kenny Gamble and Leon Huff, 1972, 1989. Gold record by Harold Melvin and The Blue Notes (Philadelphia International). Hit record by Simply Red (Elektra), 1989.

If You Don't Want My Love. w/m Mike Gately, Bob Pedrick, and L. David, 1968. Recorded by Robert John, a.k.a Pedrick (Columbia).

If You Don't Want My Peaches (You'd Better Stop Shaking My Tree). w/m Irving Berlin, 1914.

If You Ever Change Your Mind. w/m Parker McGee and Bob Gundry, 1980. #1 Country chart record by Crystal Gayle (Columbia).

If You Ever Change Your Mind. w/m Grady Watts, Maurice Sigler, and Bud Green, 1939. Introduced by Glen Gray and the Casa Loma Orchestra. Recorded by Artie Shaw, vocal by Helen Forrest (Bluebird), and Tommy Dorsey, vocal by Edythe Wright (Victor).

If You Feel Like Singing, Sing. w. Mack Gordon, m. Harry Warren, 1950. Introduced by Judy Garland in (MM) *Summer Stock*.

If You Go. w. Geoffrey Parsons (Engl.), Michel Emer (Fr.), m. Michel Emer, 1952. Original French title: "Si Tu Partais." Leading recordings by Vera Lynn (London); Patty Andrews (Decca); Odette, in English and French (MGM); Helen Merrill (Mercury); Gordon Jenkins and his Orchestra (Decca).

If You Go Away. w. Rod McKuen (Engl.), w. (Fr.) and m. Jacques Brel, 1966. Original French title "Ne Me Quitte Pas," introduced in France by Jacques Brel. Chart records by Damita Jo (Epic), 1966, and Terry Jacks (Bell), 1974.

If You Haven't Got Love. w. B. G. De Sylva and Lew Brown, m. Ray Henderson, 1931. Written for the Gloria Swanson film (MP) *Indiscreet*. The two songs in this film were the last collaboration of the three writers. (See "Come to Me.") This was recorded by Red Nichols's Orchestra, with vocal by Paul Small (Victor).

If You Knew Susie (Like I Know Susie). w. B. G. DeSylva, m. Joseph Meyer, 1925. Al Jolson tried the song out briefly during the run of the musical (TM) *Big Boy*, but dropped it. It was presented to Eddie Cantor, with whom the song has since been associated. Cantor's recording (Columbia) and vaudeville performances made it into a standard. Buddy Doyle, impersonating Cantor, sang it in (MM) *The Great Ziegfeld*, 1936. Frank Sinatra and Gene Kelly performed it in (MM) *Anchors Aweigh*, 1945. Cantor produced, starred in, and sang the song under the credits of (MM) *If You Knew Susie*, 1948. Cantor, dubbing for Keefe Brasselle, sang it on the soundtrack of (MM) *The Eddie Cantor Story*, 1953.

If You Knew What It Meant to Be Lonesome. w/m Jimmy Wakely and Lee "Lasses" White, 1946. Recorded by Jimmy Wakely (Capitol).

If You Know What I Mean. w/m Neil Diamond, 1976. Top 20 record by Neil Diamond (Columbia).

If You Leave. w/m Paul Humphreys, Andrew McCluskey, Malcolm Holmes, and Martin Cooper, 1986. Written and Top 10 record by the British quartet Orchestral Manoeuvres in the Dark (A&M).

If You Leave Me Now. w/m Peter Cetera, 1976. #1 gold record single from the album "Chicago X" by the jazz-rock band Chicago (Columbia). Song written by group's bassist.

(If You Let Me Make Love to You Then) Why Can't I Touch You? w/m C. C. Courtney and Peter Link, 1969. Introduced by the company in the off-Broadway musical (TM) *Salvation*. Top 10 record by Ronnie Dyson (Columbia), 1970.

If You Look in Her Eyes. w. Otto Harbach, m. Louis A. Hirsch, 1917. From (TM) *Going Up*. Henry Burr had a popular recording (Victor).

If You Love Me. w/m Ray Noble, 1936. Introduced by Ray Noble and his Orchestra and recorded by Jane Froman (Decca) and Jan Garber and his Orchestra (Decca).

If You Love Me (Let Me Know). w/m John Rostill, 1974. Country and Pop hit record by Olivia Newton-John (MCA).

If You Love Me (Really Love Me). w. Geoffrey Parsons (Engl.), Edith Piaf (FR.), m. Marguerite Monnot, 1953. Introduced in France in 1949 as "Hymne a L'Amour" by Edith Piaf. Popularized in the U.S. by Kay Starr (Capitol) and Vera Lynn (London).

(If You) Love Me Just a Little. w/m La Forrest Cope a.k.a. La La, 1987. R&B chart record by La La (Arista).

If You Love Somebody Set Them Free. w/m Sting, 1985. Top 10 record by the English singer Sting [né Gordon Sumner] (A&M).

If You Need Me. w/m Wilson Pickett, Robert Bateman, and Sonny Sanders, 1963. Introduced and recorded by Solomon Burke (Atlantic). Chart record also by Wilson Pickett (Double-L).

If You Please. w. Johnny Burke, m. James Van Heusen, 1943. Introduced by Bing Crosby in (MM) *Dixie*, and recorded by him (Decca).

If You Really Love Me. w/m Stevie Wonder and Syreeta Wright, 1971. Top 10 record by Stevie Wonder (Tamla).

If You're Ever Down in Texas, Look Me Up. w. William D. Dunham, m. Terry Shand, 1947. Featured and recorded by Phil Harris, with his Orchestra (Victor).

If You're Gonna Play in Texas (You Gotta Have a Fiddle in the Band). w/m Dan Mitchell and Murry Kellum, 1984. #1 Country chart hit by the group Alabama (RCA).

If You're in Love, You'll Waltz. w. Joseph McCarthy, m. Harry Tierney, 1927. Introduced by Ethelind Terry and J. Harold Murray in (TM) *Rio Rita*.

If You Remember Me. w. Carole Bayer Sager, m. Marvin Hamlisch, 1979. Introduced on the soundtrack of (MP) *The Champ* by Chris Thompson and Night, who also recorded it (Planet).

If You're Not Back in Love by Monday. See **If We're Not Back in Love by Monday.**

If You're Not Gone Too Long. w/m Wanda Ballman, 1967. Top 10 Country chart record by Loretta Lynn (Decca).

If You're Ready (Come Go with Me). w/m Homer Banks, Carl Hampton, and Ray Jackson, 1973. Gold record by the family soul group The Staple Singers (Stax).

If You're Thinking You Want a Stranger (There's One Coming Home). w/m Blake Mevis and David Willis, 1982. Top 10 Country chart record by George Strait (MCA).

If Your Heart's in the Game. w. Joseph McCarthy, m. Harry Tierney, 1924. From (TM) *Kid Boots*, starring Eddie Cantor and Mary Eaton.

If You See My Sweetheart. w/m Paul Dresser, 1897.

If You See Sally. w. Gus Kahn and Raymond Egan, m. Walter Donaldson, 1927. Featured and recorded by Ted Lewis, with his Orchestra (Columbia).

If You Stub Your Toe on the Moon. w. Johnny Burke, m. James Van Heusen, 1949. Introduced by Bing Crosby in (MM) *A Connecticut Yankee in King Arthur's Court*, and recorded by him (Decca) and by Tony Martin (RCA Victor).

If You Talk in Your Sleep. w/m Bobby (Red) West and Johnny Christopher, 1974. C&W/Pop hit by Elvis Presley (RCA).

If You Turn Me Down. w. Carl Sigman, m. Peter De Rose, 1951. Recorded by Dinah Shore (RCA Victor) and Toni Arden (Columbia).

If You've Got a Heart. w/m Bobby Goldsboro, 1965. Introduced and recorded by Bobby Goldsboro (United Artists).

If You've Got the Money (I've Got the Time). w/m Lefty Frizzell and Jim Beck, 1950. C&W/Pop hit, introduced by Lefty Frizzell (Columbia) and followed by Jo Stafford (Capitol). Revived by Willie Nelson (Columbia), 1976.

If You Wanna Be Happy. w/m Carmela Guida, Frank J. Guida, and Joseph Royster, 1963. Hit record by Jimmy Soul (S.P.Q.R.).

If You Wanna Get to Heaven. w/m John Dillon and Steve Cash, 1974. Recorded by The Ozark Mountain Daredevils (A&M).

If You Want Me to Stay. w/m Sylvester Stewart, 1973. Gold record by Sly (Stewart) and The Family Stone (Epic).

If You Want the Rainbow (You Must Have the Rain). w. Mort Dixon and Billy Rose, m. Oscar Levant, 1928. Introduced by Fanny Brice in (MM) *My Man*. Recorded by Brice (Victor) and Eva Taylor (Okeh).

If You Want to Be a Top Banana. w/m Johnny Mercer, 1951. Introduced by Phil Silvers in (TM) *Top Banana*. Silvers sang it in (MM) *Top Banana*, 1954.

If You Were I and I Were You. w. Henry Blossom, m. Victor Herbert, 1908. From (TM) *The Prima Donna*.

If You Were in My Place. w. Henry Nemo, Irving Mills, m. Edward Kennedy "Duke" Ellington, 1938. Introduced by Duke Ellington and his Orchestra. Recorded by him (Brunswick), by Jimmy Dorsey, with vocal by June Richmond (Decca), and by Mildred Bailey (Vocalion).

If You Were Mine. w/m Jimmy Lewis, 1970. Recorded by Ray Charles (ABC/TRC).

If You Were Mine. w. Johnny Mercer, m. Matt Malneck, 1935. Introduced by Roger Pryor in (MM) *Beat the Band*. Among recordings: Billie Holiday, with Teddy Wilson's Band (Brunswick); Lanny Ross (Brunswick); Jan Garber (Victor); Jerry Cooper (Rainbow).

If You Were Only Mine. w. Charles Newman, m. Isham Jones, 1932. Featured by Isham Jones and his Orchestra. Revived in the late forties by Buddy Clark (Columbia); Don Cornell (Coral); and Dick Haymes, with Artie Shaw's Band (Decca).

If You Were the Only Girl in the World. w. Clifford Grey, m. Nat D. Ayer, 1916, 1946. Rudy Vallee revived this song in (MM) *The Vagabond Lover* in 1929. The song was on "Your Hit Parade" in 1946 and was again revived in (MM) *By the Light of the Silvery Moon* in 1952, sung by Doris Day and Gordon MacRae.

I Gave You Up Just Before You Threw Me Down. w. Bert Kalmar, m. Harry Ruby and Fred E. Ahlert, 1922. Popular record by Billy Murray and Gladys Rice who recorded under the name of Rachel Grant (Victor).

I Get a Kick Out of You. w/m Cole Porter, 1934. Introduced by Ethel Merman and William Gaxton in (TM) *Anything Goes*. Merman repeated it in (MM) *Anything Goes*, 1936; Ginny Simms sang it in the Porter biography (MM) *Night and Day*, 1946; Billy Daniels sang it in (MM) *Sunny Side of the Street*, 1951; Jeanmaire sang it and danced with an ensemble in the 1956 remake (MM) *Anything Goes*; it was featured in (MM) *At Long Last Love*, 1975.

I Get Along Without You Very Well. w/m Hoagy Carmichael, 1939. The lyrics were based on a poem Carmichael had been given on a visit to Indiana University. Carmichael, with some changes, wrote the song and forgot about it. Some years later he found it and arranged to have it published. A search was made for the unknown poet who turned out to be a Mrs. Jane Brown Thompson of Philadelphia. Dick Powell introduced it on a network radio program. Mrs. Thompson never heard the song. She died one day before the broadcast. The best-selling records were by the orchestras of Red Norvo, vocal by Terry Allen (Vocalion); and Larry Clinton, vocal by Bea Wain (Victor). Carmichael and Jane Russell sang it in (MP) *The Las Vegas Story*, 1952. Popular single by Karen Chandler (Dot), 1967.

I Get Around. w/m Brian Wilson, 1964. #1 gold record by The Beach Boys (Capitol).

I Get Carried Away. w. Betty Comden and Adolph Green, m. Leonard Bernstein, 1946. Introduced by Betty Comden and Adolph Green in (TM) *On the Town*.

I Get Ideas (When I Dance with You). w. Dorcas Cochran, m. Lenny Sanders, 1951. Based on the Argentine tango "Adios Muchachos." Tony Martin had a million-seller (RCA Victor). Other chart records by Louis Armstrong (Decca); Peggy Lee, with Billy May's Orchestra (Capitol).

I Get So Lonely. See **Oh, Baby Mine.**

I Get the Blues When It Rains. w. Marcy Klauber, m. Harry Stoddard, 1929. Recorded by such varied artists as Guy Lombardo and his Royal Canadians (Columbia), Ford and Glenn (Columbia), Tiny Hill (Vocalion), Elton Britt (Victor), The Merry Macs (Decca), Lee Castle (12" V-Disc) in World War II.

I Get the Fever. w/m Bill Anderson, 1966. Country hit, recorded by Bill Anderson (Decca).

I Get the Neck of the Chicken. w. Frank Loesser, m. Jimmy McHugh, 1942. Introduced by Mary McGuire in (MM) *Seven Days Leave*. Top recording by Freddy Martin, vocal by Eddie Stone (Victor).

I Get the Sweetest Feeling. w/m Van McCoy and Alicia Evelyn, 1968. Top 40 record by Jackie Wilson (Brunswick).

I Get Weak. w/m Diane Warren, 1988. Popular single by Belinda Carlisle (MCA).

I Give You My Word. w/m Al Kavelin and Merril Lyn, 1940. Introduced and recorded by

Al Kavelin, vocal by Bill Darnell (Okeh). Best-selling record by Eddy Duchin, vocal by June Robbins (Columbia).

I Go Ape. w. Howard Greenfield, m. Neil Sedaka, 1959. Chart record by Neil Sedaka (RCA).

I Go Crazy. w/m Rocco Barker, Nick Marsh, Kevin Mills, and James Mitchell, 1987. Introduced by the British quintet, Flesh for Lulu, on the soundtrack of (MP) *Some Kind of Wonderful.* Song included in the group's album "Long Live the New Flesh" (Capitol).

I Go Crazy. w/m Paul Davis, 1978. Top 10 hit by Paul Davis (Bang) that was on the charts for forty weeks, first appearing in the summer of 1977.

I Go for That. w. Frank Loesser, m. Matty Malneck, 1938. Introduced by Dorothy Lamour in (MM) *St. Louis Blues* and on records (Brunswick).

I Got a Code in My Dose. w/m Arthur Fields, Fred Hall, and Billy Rose, 1929. Novelty song introduced and recorded by Fred "Sugar" Hall's Sugar Babies, with vocal by Arthur Fields.

I Got a Feeling. w/m Baker Knight, 1958. Hit record by Ricky Nelson (Imperial).

I Got a Line on You. w/m Randy California, 1969. Top 40 record by the group, Spirit, of which the writer was lead guitarist (Ode).

I Got a Name. w. Norman Gimbel, m. Charles Fox, 1973. Introduced by Jim Croce on the soundtrack of (MP) *The Last American Hero* and on a Top 10 recording (ABC).

I Got a Wife. w. Erwin Wenzlaff, m. Eddie Mascari, 1959. Novelty, recorded by The Mark IV (Mercury).

I Got a Woman (I Got a Sweetie). w/m Ray Charles, 1955. R&B hit by Ray Charles (Atlantic). Other top records by jazz organist Jimmy McGriff, instrumental (Sue, Part I), 1962; Freddie Scott (Colpix), 1963; Rick Nelson (Decca), 1963; Ray Charles (ABC-Paramount Part I), 1965.

I Gotcha. w/m Joe Tex, 1972. Gold record by Joe Tex (Dial).

I Got Dreams. w/m Bill La Bounty and Steve Wariner, 1989. Hit Country single by Steve Wariner (MCA).

I Got Everything I Want. w/m Jack Lawrence and Stan Freeman, 1964. Introduced by Doretta Morrow in (TM) *I Had a Ball.*

I Got It Bad and That Ain't Good. w. Paul Francis Webster, m. Edward Kennedy "Duke" Ellington, 1941. Introduced by Ivy Anderson in a California revue (TM) *Jump for Joy.* The band recordings by Duke Ellington, vocal by Anderson and featuring an alto saxophone solo by Johnny Hodges (Victor), and Benny Goodman, vocal by Peggy Lee (Columbia), were the best sellers.

I Got Life. w. Gerome Ragni and James Rado, m. Galt MacDermot, 1967. Introduced in the off-Broadway production (TM) *Hair* by Walker Daniels and Marijane Maricle. In the Broadway production (TM) *Hair*, 1968, it was sung by James Rado and company. Nina Simone sang it on a single, in medley with "Ain't Got No" from the same show (RCA), 1969.

I Got Loaded. w/m Harrison Nelson, 1951. #1 R&B record by Peppermint Harris (Aladdin).

I Got Lost in His Arms. w/m Irving Berlin, 1946. Introduced by Ethel Merman in (TM) *Annie Get Your Gun.* Merman's version from the original cast album was released as a single (Decca). Also recorded by Jane Froman, arranged and conducted by Jerry Gray (Majestic). The song was omitted from the film version, 1950. Tony Bennett sang it as "I Got Lost in Her Arms" in his album "The Art of Excellence," (CBS), 1986.

I Got Love. w. Peter Udell, m. Gary Geld, 1970. Introduced by Melba Moore in (TM) *Purlie.*

I Got Love. w. Dorothy Fields, m. Jerome Kern, 1935. Introduced by Lily Pons in (MM) *I Dream Too Much.* The orchestra was conducted by Andre Kostalanetz, who was married to the star at the time.

I Got Lucky in the Rain. w. Harold Adamson, m. Jimmy McHugh, 1948. Introduced by Bill Callahan and Fran Warren in (TM) *As the Girls Go*. Recorded by Janette Davis and Jerry Wayne (Columbia).

I Got Mexico. w/m Eddy Raven and Frank J. Myers, 1984. #1 Country chart record by Eddy Raven (RCA).

I Got My Mind Made Up (You Can Get It Girl). w/m Raymond Earl, Kim Miller, and Scott Miller, 1979. #1 R&B, Top 20 Pop gold record by the group Instant Funk (Salsoul).

I Go to Pieces. w/m Del Shannon, 1965. Top 10 hit by Peter and Gordon (Capitol). Revived by Cotton, Lloyd and Christian (20th Century), 1975.

I Go to Rio. w/m Peter Allen and Adrienne Anderson, 1977. Introduced by Peter Allen in his album "Taught by Experts" (A&M). Chart record by the quartet Pablo Cruise (A&M), 1979.

I Got Plenty O' Nuttin'. w. Ira Gershwin and Du Bose Heyward, m. George Gershwin, 1935. Introduced by Todd Duncan and chorus in (TM) *Porgy and Bess*. It was interpolated on the soundtrack of the George Gershwin film biography (MM) *Rhapsody in Blue* in 1945. In (MM) *Porgy and Bess*, it was sung by Robert McFerrin, dubbing his voice on the soundtrack for Sidney Poitier.

I Got Rhythm. w. Ira Gershwin, m. George Gershwin, 1930. Introduced by Ethel Merman in her Broadway debut, with the Foursome and ensemble in (TM) *Girl Crazy*. Popular records by Red Nichols, whose all-star band played in the pit (Brunswick); Ethel Waters (Columbia); Louis Armstrong (Columbia, Okeh). It was heard in all three film adaptations. After the Wheeler and Woolsey version (MM) *Girl Crazy*, 1932, Judy Garland, Mickey Rooney, and Tommy Dorsey and his Orchestra performed it in the well-received 1943 remake. A further remake, under the title of (MM) *When the Boys*

Meet the Girls, 1966, was presented in which it was sung by Connie Francis, Harve Presnell, and Louis Armstrong. It was heard in the background of the Gershwin bio (MM) *Rhapsody in Blue*, 1945. In 1934, Gershwin's "Variations on 'I Got Rhythm' for Piano and Orchestra" was introduced in Boston with Charles Previn conducting, and the composer at the piano. Morton Gould scored a symphonic adaptation of "I Got Rhythm," introduced on his network radio program, 1944. The Happenings, a vocal group, had a Top 10 record (B. T. Puppy), 1967.

I Got Stoned and I Missed It. w/m Shel Silverstein, 1975. Novelty song recorded by Jim Stafford (MGM).

I Got Stripes. w/m Johnny Cash and Charlie Williams, 1959. Featured and recorded by Johnny Cash (Columbia).

I Got Stung. w/m Aaron Schroeder and David Hill, 1958. Million-selling record by Elvis Presley (RCA).

I Gotta Gal I Love (in North and South Dakota). w. Sammy Cahn, m. Jule Styne, 1947. Introduced by Eddie Bracken in (MM) *Ladies' Man*.

I Gotta Go Get My Baby. w/m Marvin Rainwater and Kay Adelman, 1955. Recorded by Teresa Brewer (Coral).

I Gotta Have My Baby Back. w/m Floyd Tillman, 1949. Hit C&W chart record by Floyd Tillman (Columbia). Other records by Red Foley (Decca) and Glen Campbell (Capitol).

I Gotta Keep Movin'. w/m Micki Grant, 1972. Introduced by Alex Bradford and company (which included Micki Grant, the writer) in the off-Broadway musical (TM) *Don't Bother Me, I Can't Cope*.

I Gotta Know. w/m Paul Evans and Matt Williams, 1960. Recorded by Elvis Presley, coupled with gold record winner "Are You Lonesome Tonight" (q.v.) (RCA).

I Gotta Right to Sing the Blues. w. Ted Koehler, m. Harold Arlen, 1932. Introduced by Lillian Shade in (TM) *Earl Carroll Vanities* (10th Edition). Constance Moore sang it in (MM) *Earl Carroll Sketchbook* in 1946. Early recordings by Louis Armstrong (Victor), Benny Goodman (Columbia), Ethel Merman (Victor), and Cab Calloway (Brunswick). Jack Teagarden recorded it (Okeh) in 1941 and subsequently used it as his theme song, featuring his trombone and his vocal. Other recordings of note include Lena Horne (Victor), Carol Bruce (Schirmer), Ellis Larkins (Decca), Fran Warren (Victor), Dorothy Lamour (Bluebird), and the big band of Gerald Wilson (Excelsior).

I Got the Feelin'. w/m James Brown, 1968. Top 10 record by James Brown and The Famous Flames (King).

I Got the Feelin' (It's Over). w/m Gregory Abbott, 1987. Top 10 R&B chart crossover record by Gregory Abbott (Columbia).

I Got the Feelin' (Oh No, No). w/m Neil Diamond, 1966. Top 20 record by Neil Diamond (Bang).

I Got the Sun in the Morning. w/m Irving Berlin, 1946. Introduced by Ethel Merman in (TM) *Annie Get Your Gun*. Sung by Betty Hutton in the film version (MM) *Annie Get Your Gun*, 1950.

I Got You. w/m Neil Finn, 1980. Chart single from the album "True Colours" by the New Zealand sextet, Split Enz, whose name came from their country (A&M).

I Got You. w/m Ricci Mareno and Gordon Gailbraith, 1968. Top 10 Country chart record by Waylon Jennings and Anita Carter (RCA).

I Got You (I Feel Good). w/m James Brown, 1966. Top 10 Pop chart hit by James Brown (King).

I Got You Babe. w/m Sonny Bono, 1965. #1 and gold record by Sonny and Cher (Atco). The team sang it in their starring vehicle (MM) *Good Times*, 1967. Revived by the British reggae octet, UB40, with Chrissie Hynde (A&M), 1985.

I Guess I'll Always Love You. w/m Eddie Holland, Lamont Dozier, and Brian Holland, 1966. Recorded by The Isley Brothers (Tamla).

I Guess I'll Get the Papers (and Go Home). w/m Hughie Prince and Hal Kanner, 1946. Leading recordings by The Mills Brothers (Decca) and Les Brown, vocal by Jack Haskell (Columbia).

I Guess I'll Have to Change My Plan (the Blue Pajama Song). w. Howard Dietz, m. Arthur Schwartz, 1929. The original lyric to this melody was titled "I Love to Lie Awake in Bed" and was written much earlier by Lorenz Hart, while he and Schwartz were counselors at a boys' summer camp. With a new lyric by Dietz, it was introduced by Clifton Webb in (TM) *The Little Show.* Fred Astaire and Jack Buchanan, in a memorable top hat and white tie number, performed it in (MM) *The Band Wagon*, 1953. The vocal from the soundtrack was released as a single (MGM). Ramona, with Paul Whiteman's Orchestra (Victor), Rudy Vallee and his Orchestra (Columbia), Johnny Mercer (Capitol), and Hazel Scott (Signature) made notable recordings. Dick Shawn interpolated it in (TM) *A Musical Jubilee*, 1975.

I Guess I'll Have to Dream the Rest. w. Mickey Stoner and Martin Block, m. Harold Green, 1941. Featured and recorded by Glenn Miller, vocal by Ray Eberle and the Modernaires (Bluebird) and Tommy Dorsey, vocal by Frank Sinatra and the Pied Pipers (Victor).

I Guess I'll Have to Telegraph My Baby. w/m George M. Cohan, 1898. An early Cohan success and the first popular song about the wireless form of communication.

I Guess I'll Never Learn. w/m John Hathcock and Weldon Allard, 1962. Top 10 Country chart song by Charlie Phillips (Columbia).

I Guess I'm Crazy (for Loving You). w/m Werly Fairburn, 1964. Crossover (C&W/Pop) hit by Jim Reeves (RCA).

I Guess It Had to Be That Way. w/m Arthur Johnston and Sam Coslow, 1933. Written for but not used in the film *Too Much Harmony*, starring Bing Crosby. Crosby, however, recorded it with Jimmie Grier's Orchestra backing him (Brunswick). Also recorded by the bands of Bernie Cummins (Columbia) and Ted Weems, vocal by Red Ingle (Bluebird).

I Guess It Never Hurts to Hurt Sometimes. w/m Randy Van Warner, 1984. #1 Country chart record by The Oak Ridge Boys (MCA).

I Guess That's Why They Call It the Blues. w. Bernie Taupin, m. Elton John, 1983. Top 10 record by the English singer Elton John (Geffen).

I Guess the Lord Must Be in New York City. w/m Harry Nilsson, 1969. Top 40 record by Nilsson (RCA).

I.G.Y. (What a Beautiful World). w/m Donald Fagen, 1982. Title refers to the International Geophysical Year (July 1957–Dec. 1958). Donald Fagen, co-founder of the group Steely Dan, had a chart record (Warner Bros.).

I Had a Ball. w/m Jack Lawrence and Stan Freeman, 1964. Introduced by Doretta Morrow and chorus in (TM) *I Had a Ball.*

I Had a Dream. w/m Mark Lindsay and Terry Melcher, 1967. Top 20 record by Paul Revere and The Raiders (Columbia).

I Had a Little Talk with the Lord. w. Mann Curtis, m. Vic Mizzy, 1944. Featured and recorded by Frankie Carle and his Orchestra (Columbia).

I Had Myself a True Love. w. Johnny Mercer, m. Harold Arlen, 1946. Introduced by June Hawkins in (TM) *St. Louis Woman.*

I Hadn't Anyone Till You. w/m Ray Noble, 1938. Introduced and recorded by Tony Martin, with Ray Noble and his Orchestra (Brunswick). Also recorded by the orchestras of Jimmy Dorsey (Decca) and Blue Barron (Bluebird). Among later recordings: Vic Damone (Mercury), Mel Tormé (Capitol), Stan Getz (Norgran).

I Had the Craziest Dream. w. Mack Gordon, m. Harry Warren, 1942. Introduced by Harry James and his Orchestra, vocal by Helen Forrest in (MM) *Springtime in the Rockies*, Betty Grable's first starring film. The recording by James and Forrest became a #1 best-seller (Columbia).

I Had Too Much to Dream (Last Night). w/m Nancie Mantz and Annette Tucker, 1967. Recorded by the "psychodelic" rock group the Electric Prunes (Reprise).

I Hang My Head and Cry. w/m Fred Rose, Ray Whitley, and Gene Autry, 1942. Introduced and recorded by Gene Autry (Okeh).

I Happen to Like New York. w/m Cole Porter, 1931. The song was added to (TM) *The New Yorkers* after the opening. It was performed by Rags Ragland. Among recordings: Frank Sinatra (Reprise), Bobby Short (Atlantic).

I Hate Men. w/m Cole Porter, 1949. Introduced by Patricia Morison in (TM) *Kiss Me Kate*. In the film version (MM) *Kiss Me Kate*, 1953, it was sung by Kathryn Grayson.

I Hate Myself (for Being So Mean to You). w. Benny Davis and Joe Young, m. Milton Ager, 1934. Top recordings by Ozzie Nelson and his Orchestra, vocal by Harriet Hilliard (Brunswick), and the Boswell Sisters (Brunswick).

I Hate Myself for Loving You. w/m Joan Jett and Desmond Child, 1988. Popular single by Joan Jett and The Blackhearts from the album "Up Your Alley" (Blackheart).

I Hate to Lose You. w. Grant Clarke, m. Archie Gottler, 1918.

I Have But One Heart. w. Marty Symes, m. Johnny Farrow, 1947. Music adapted from "O Marinariello" (Ital.). Best-selling record by Vic Damone, who sang choruses in English and Italian (Mercury). Other popular recordings: Frank Sinatra (Columbia); Carmen Cavallaro, vocal by Bob Allen (Decca); Monica Lewis (Signature).

I Have Dreamed. w. Oscar Hammerstein II, m. Richard Rodgers, 1951. Introduced by Doretta Morrow and Larry Douglas in (TM) *The King and I.* Rita Moreno and Carlos Rivas sang it in (MM) *The King and I,* 1956.

I Have Eyes. w. Leo Robin, m. Ralph Rainger, 1938. First heard in (MM) *Artists and Models* in 1937, it was reintroduced by Bing Crosby and Shirley Ross in (MM) *Paris Honeymoon* a year later. Top records by Crosby (Decca); Les Brown (Bluebird); Red Norvo (Brunswick); Artie Shaw, vocal by Helen Forrest (Bluebird).

I Have Learned to Respect the Power of Love. w/m Angela Winbush and Ren Moore, 1986. #1 R&B chart record by Stephanie Mills (MCA).

I Have Loved You, Girl (But Not Like This Before). w/m Earl Thomas Conley, 1983. First recorded by the writer, not using his middle name (GRT), 1975. Re-recorded as Earl Thomas Conley, his single reached the #2 position on the Country charts (RCA), 1983.

I Haven't Got a Worry in the World. w. Oscar Hammerstein II, m. Richard Rodgers, 1946. Introduced by Helen Hayes in (TP) *Happy Birthday.* Recorded by Frances Langford (Mercury) and Hildegarde (Decca).

I Haven't Got Time for the Pain. See Haven't Got Time for the Pain.

I Haven't Time to Be a Millionaire. w. Johnny Burke, m. James V. Monaco, 1940. Premiered by Bing Crosby in (MM) *If I Had My Way* and on records (Decca).

I Have to Have You. w. Leo Robin, m. Richard A. Whiting, 1929. Introduced by Helen Kane in (MM) *Pointed Heels.* Kane recorded it (Victor), as did Annette Hanshaw (Okeh), the Louisiana Rhythm Kings (Brunswick), The Sunshine Boys [Joe and Dan Mooney] (Columbia).

I Have to Tell You. w/m Harold Rome, 1954. Introduced by Florence Henderson in (TM) *Fanny.*

I Hear a Rhapsody. w/m George Fragos, Jack Baker, and Dick Gasparre, 1940. Featured and popularized by Jimmy Dorsey, vocal by Bob Eberly (Decca) and Dennis Day (Victor). Heard in (MM) *Casa Mañana,* 1951. Chart record by Frank Sinatra (Columbia), 1952.

I Hear a Symphony. w/m Brian Holland, Lamont Dozier, and Eddie Holland, 1965. #1 record by The Supremes (Motown).

I Heard. w/m Don Redman, 1931. The initial year saw recordings by the orchestras of Don Redman (Brunswick), Fred Waring (Victor), and Harlan Lattimore (Columbia). The Mills Brothers (Brunswick) had one of their early hits, coupled with "How'm I Doin'?" (q.v.).

I Heard a Heart Break Last Night. w/m Leon Payne, 1968. Top 10 Country chart record by Jim Reeves (RCA).

I Heard a Rumor. w/m Sarah Dallin, Siobhan Fahey, Keren Woodward, Matt Aitken, Pete Waterman, Mike Stock, 1987. Sung by the British female trio, Bananarama, on the soundtrack of (MP) *Disorderlies* and on a Top 10 single (London). The first three writers were the singing trio, and the latter three the producers.

I Heard It Through the Grapevine. w/m Norman Whitfield and Barrett Strong, 1967. Top 10 record by Gladys Knight and The Pips (Soul), followed by the #1 record by Marvin Gaye (Tamla), 1968. Other chart versions by King Curtis [instrumental] (Atco), 1968; The Creedence Clearwater Revival, from a 1970 LP "Cosmo's Factory" (Fantasy); Roger (Warner Bros.), 1981. Used in an award-winning TV commercial for California raisins, 1987.

I Heard the Bluebirds Sing. w/m Hod Pharis, 1957. Hit Country record by The Browns (RCA Victor).

I Heard You Cried Last Night. w. Jerrie Kruger, m. Ted Grouya, 1943. From (MP) *Cinderella Swings It.* Popularized by the performances and recording by Harry James, vocal by Helen Forrest (Columbia). Dick Haymes, with the Song Spinners, had a Top 20 recording (Decca).

I Hear Music. w. Frank Loesser, m. Burton Lane, 1940. Introduced in (MM) *Dancing on a Dime* by Peter Lind Hayes, Eddie Quillan, Frank Jenks, and Robert Paige. Among recordings: Billie Holiday (Okeh); Gene Krupa, vocal by Irene Day (Okeh); Larry Clinton, vocal by Peggy Mann (Victor); Russ Morgan and his Orchestra (Decca); George Shearing (MGM).

I Hear Trumpets Blow. w/m Mitchell Margo, Philip Margo, Henry Medress, and Jay Siegel, 1966. Written and recorded by The Tokens (B. T. Puppy).

I Hear You Calling Me. w. Harold Harford, m. Charles Marshall, 1908. Concert song featured and recorded by John McCormack (Victor) and Lucrezia Bori (Victor).

I Hear You Knocking. w/m Dave Bartholomew and Pearl King, 1955, 1971. R&B hit by Smiley Lewis (Imperial) and #2 Pop hit by Gale Storm (Dot). Fats Domino had a moderate success in 1961 (Imperial). Welsh singer-guitarist Dave Edmunds revived it with a hit record (MAM), 1971.

I Hit a New High. w. Harold Adamson, m. Jimmy McHugh, 1937. Introduced by Lily Pons in (MM) *Hitting a New High.*

I Honestly Love You. w/m Peter Allen and Jeff Barry, 1974. Peter Allen was originally going to record the song, but Olivia Newton-John heard it and pleaded to introduce it. It became her first #1 gold record (MCA) and winner of the Grammy Award (NARAS) for Record of the Year.

I Hope Gabriel Likes My Music. w/m Dave Franklin, 1936. Popularized and recorded by Gene Krupa and his Orchestra (Victor). Also recorded by Frankie Trumbauer (Brunswick), Stuff Smith (Vocalion), Stew Pletcher (Bluebird).

I Hope We Get to Love in Time. w/m James Dean and John Henry Glover, 1976.

R&B/Pop chart record by Marilyn McCoo and Billy Davis, Jr. (ABC).

I Hung My Head and Cried. w/m Jimmie Davis and Cliff Bruner, 1942. Introduced and recorded by Jimmie Davis (Decca) and followed by Elton Britt (Bluebird).

I Just Called to Say I Love You. w/m Stevie Wonder, 1984. Introduced on the soundtrack of (MP) *The Woman in Red* by Stevie Wonder. His single became a #1 gold record (Motown) and an international hit. Winner Academy Award, Best Song, and Grammy Award (NARAS) Song of the Year. Song used for long-distance telephone commercials on radio and television.

I Just Came to Get My Baby. w/m Wayne Kemp, 1968. Top 10 Country chart record by Faron Young (Mercury).

I Just Can't Get Her out of My Mind. w/m Larry Gatlin, 1975. #1 Country chart record by Johnny Rodriguez (Mercury).

I Just Can't Help Believing. w/m Cynthia Weil, m. Barry Mann, 1970. Top 10 record by B. J. Thomas (Scepter).

I Just Can't Make My Eyes Behave. w. Will D. Cobb, m. Gus Edwards, 1906. Interpolated in the score of (TM) *A Parisian Model* by Anna Held.

I Just Can't Stop Loving You. w/m Michael Jackson, 1987. #1 chart duet by Michael Jackson and Siedah Garrett, from the Jackson album "Bad" (Epic).

I Just Couldn't Take It, Baby. w. Mann Holiner, m. Alberta Nichols, 1934. Introduced by Gretchen Branch, Phil Scott, Kathryn Perry, and Eloise Uggams in Lew Leslie's (TM) *Blackbirds.* Ethel Waters recorded this with Benny Goodman's Orchestra (Columbia). Jack Teagarden (Brunswick), Eddy Duchin (Victor) and their bands also had popular releases. Later, outstanding recordings were made by Lionel Hampton (Victor), Hal Kemp (Victor), and Frances Wayne, backed by Neal Hefti's Band (Coral).

(I Just) Died in Your Arms. w/m Nick Van Eede, 1987. #1 record by the group Cutting Crew (Virgin).

I Just Don't Know. w. Joseph Stone, m. Robert Allen, 1957. Popularized by The Four Lads (Columbia).

I Just Don't Know What to Do with Myself. w. Hal David, m. Burt Bacharach, 1966. Recorded by Dionne Warwick (Scepter).

I Just Don't Like This Kind of Livin'. w/m Hank Williams, 1949. Introduced and recorded by Hank Williams (MGM).

I Just Don't Understand. w/m Marijohn Wilkin and Kent Westbury, 1961. Featured and recorded by Ann-Margret (RCA).

I Just Fall in Love Again. w/m Stephen Dorff, Larry Herbstritt, Harry Lloyd, and Gloria Sklerov, 1979. Recorded by Anne Murray (Capitol).

I Just Roll Along. w. Jo Trent, m. Peter DeRose, 1928.

I Just Wanna Stop. w/m Ross Vannelli, 1978. Top 10 record by the Canadian singer Gino Vannelli (A&M).

I Just Want to Be Your Everything. w/m Barry Gibb, 1977. First record, first #1, first gold record by Andy Gibb, the youngest brother of the Bee Gees (RSO).

I Just Want to Go Back and Start the Whole Thing Over. w/m Paul Dresser, 1901.

I Just Want to Love You. w/m David Malloy, Eddie Rabbitt, and Even Stevens, 1978. Country chart hit by Eddie Rabbitt (Elektra).

I Just Wish You Were Someone I Love. w/m Larry Gatlin, 1978. Hit Country record by Larry Gatlin (Monument).

I Keep Coming Back. w/m Johnny Slate, Jim Hurt, and Larry Keith, 1980. #1 Country chart record by Razzy Bailey (RCA).

I Keep Forgettin' (Every Time You're Near). w/m Jerry Leiber and Mike Stoller,

1962, 1982. Introduced by Chuck Jackson (Wand). Revived with Top 10 Pop and R&B chart record by Michael McDonald (Warner Bros.), 1982.

I Kiss Your Hand, Madame. w. Sam M. Lewis and Joe Young, m. Ralph Erwin, 1929. Original German words by Fritz Rotter. Bing Crosby recorded this for his second solo release (Columbia). Lanny Ross used it as his radio theme song in the thirties. Later recordings included those by Donald Novis (Decca), Paul Whiteman (Decca), Merv Griffin (Columbia), and Spike Jones (Victor).

I Knew Him So Well. w. Tim Rice, m. Bjorn Ulvaeus and Benny Andersson, 1986. Introduced in England in (TM) *Chess* and recorded for the cast album by Elaine Page (RCA). Included in the platinum album "Whitney" sung by Whitney Houston and her mother, Cissy Houston (Arista), 1987. The Broadway production had a short run, 1988.

I Knew It All the Time. w/m Mitch Murray, 1964. Hit by the English rock group, The Dave Clark Five, released in the U.S. (Congress).

I Knew You Were Waiting for Me. w/m Simon Climie and Dennis Morgan, 1987. #1 chart record written by the British Climie and the American Morgan and sung as a duet by the American Aretha Franklin and the British George Michael (Arista).

I Knew You When. w/m Joe South, 1965. Hit record by Billy Joe Royal (Columbia). Revived by Linda Ronstadt (Asylum), 1983.

I Knew You When. w. Herb Magidson, m. J. Fred Coots, 1934. Featured and recorded by Connie Boswell (Brunswick).

I Know (You Don't Want Me No More). w/m Barbara George, 1961. #1 R&B hit and Top 10 on pop charts, recorded by Barbara George (A.F.O.).

I Know About Love. w. Betty Comden and Adolph Green, m. Jule Styne, 1960. Introduced by John Reardon in (TM) *Do Re Mi.*

I Know a Heartache When I See One. w/m

Charlie Black, Rory Bourke, and Kerry Chater, 1979. Recorded by Jennifer Warnes (Arista).

I Know a Place. w/m Tony Hatch, 1965. Hit record by Petula Clark, produced in England by Hatch (Warner Bros.).

I Know How He Feels. w/m Rick Bowles and William Robinson, 1988. #1 Country chart record by Reba McEntire (MCA).

I Know I'm Losing You. w/m Cornelius Grant, Eddie Holland, and Norman Whitfield, 1966. Top 10 record, first by The Temptations (Gordy), and then Rare Earth (Rare Earth), 1970. Later chart versions by Rod Stewart with Faces (Mercury), 1971, and Uptown (Oak Lawn), 1987.

I Know Now. w. Al Dubin, m. Harry Warren, 1937. Introduced by Dick Powell and Doris Weston in (MM) *The Singing Marine* and recorded by Powell (Decca).

I Know One. w/m Jack Clement, 1960. Prominent C&W and Pop chart record by Jim Reeves (RCA). Revived by Charley Pride (RCA), 1967.

I Know That You Know. w. Anne Caldwell, m. Vincent Youmans, 1926. Sung by Beatrice Lillie and Charles Purcell in (TM) *Oh, Please!* It was interpolated by Polly Walker and Jack Oakie in (MM) *Hit the Deck*, 1929, and in the remake by Vic Damone, 1955. It was heard in (MM) *Powers Girl*, 1943, and performed by Doris Day, Gordon MacRae, and Gene Nelson in (MM) *Tea for Two*, 1950. Among the hundreds of recordings are those by Nat "King" Cole (Capitol), Benny Goodman (Victor), Art Tatum (Harmony) (Roost), Teddy Wilson (Verve), Roger Williams (Kapp), Joe Harnell (Columbia).

I Know the Feeling. w. Anne Croswell, m. Lee Pockriss, 1963. Introduced by Vivien Leigh in (TM) *Tovarich*.

I Know There's Something Going On. w/m Russ Ballard, 1982. Chart record by the Norwegian singer Frida, a member of Abba (Atlantic).

I Know What Boys Like. w/m Christopher Butler, 1982. Recorded by the sextet The Waitresses (Polydor).

I Know What I Like. w/m Chris Hayes and Huey Lewis, 1987. Top 10 single by Huey Lewis and The News from his album "Fore" (Chrysalis).

I Know Where I'm Goin'. w/m Randy Starr and Dick Wolf, 1958. Popularized by George Hamilton IV (ABC-Paramount).

I Know Where I'm Going. w/m Don Schlitz, Craig Bickhardt, and Brent Maher, 1987. #1 Country chart record from the album "Heartland" by the mother and daughter duo The Judds (MCA).

I Know Why (and So Do You). w. Mack Gordon, m. Harry Warren, 1941. The hit ballad from (MM) *Sun Valley Serenade*, introduced by Glenn Miller and his Orchestra, Pat Friday (dubbing for Lynn Bari), and the Modernaires. It was reprised by Sonja Henie and John Payne dancing to a phonograph record. Miller had a hit recording, vocal by Paula Kelly and the Modernaires (Bluebird). The song was again heard in (MM) *The Glenn Miller Story*, 1954.

I Know Your Heart. w/m Hugh Martin and Timothy Gray, 1964. Introduced by Edward Woodward and Tammy Grimes in (TM) *High Spirits*.

Iko Iko. w/m Joe Jones, Marilyn Jones, Sharon Jones, and Jessie Thomas, 1965. Recorded by The Dixie Cups (Red Bird). Revived by Dr. John (Atco), 1972.

I Laughed at Love. w. Bennie Davis, m. Abner Silver, 1952. Leading recording by Sunny Gale (RCA Victor).

I Learned a Lesson I'll Never Forget. w/m Joe Davis, 1944. Best-selling record by The Five Red Caps, forerunners of Steve Gibson and/or Damita Jo and The Red Caps (Beacon). Popular versions by Helen Forrest (Decca) and Lawrence Welk and his Orchestra (Decca).

I Left My Hat in Haiti. w. Alan Jay Lerner, m. Burton Lane, 1951. Introduced by Fred Astaire in (MM) *Royal Wedding*.

I Left My Heart at the Stage Door Canteen. w/m Irving Berlin, 1942. Introduced by (Corporal) Earl Oxford in the all-soldier show (TM) *This Is the Army*, produced to raise funds for Army Emergency Relief. Oxford (now Sergeant) sang it in the film version (MM) *This Is the Army*, 1943. All proceeds from the publication of the songs also went to AER. Leading records by Sammy Kaye, vocal by Don Cornell (Victor), and Charlie Spivak, vocal by Garry Stevens (Columbia). See also "Be Careful, It's My Heart."

I Left My Heart in San Francisco. w. Douglass Cross, m. George Cory, 1962. Eight years after its publication in 1954, Tony Bennett established the song with his Grammy Award (NARAS) winning Record of the Year (Columbia).

I Left My Love on One of the Thousand Islands. See **Thousand Islands Song, The**.

I Left My Sugar Standing in the Rain. w. Irving Kahal, m. Sammy Fain, 1927. Featured and recorded by Paul Whiteman's Rhythm Boys, comprised of Bing Crosby, Al Rinker, and Harry Barris (Victor).

I Let a Song Go out of My Heart. w. Henry Nemo, John Redmond, Irving Mills, m. Edward Kennedy "Duke" Ellington, 1938. Originally written as an instrumental. Mildred Bailey, with Red Norvo's Orchestra, featured and recorded it (Vocalion) and was responsible for its initial popularity.

I Let the Stars Get in My Eyes. w/m Slim Willet, 1953. #1 C&W chart record by Goldie Hill (Decca). Answer song to "Don't Let the Stars Get in Your Eyes" (q.v.).

I Lie. w/m Thomas William Damphier, 1982. Top 10 Country chart record by Loretta Lynn (MCA).

I Like. w/m Tim Gatling, Aaron Hall, Teddy Riley, and Gene Griffin, 1989. Hit R&B chart single by Guy (Uptown).

I Like Dreamin'. w/m Kenny Nolan, 1977. Top 10 gold record by Kenny Nolan (20th Century).

I Like It, I Like It. w. Mann Curtis, m. Vic Mizzy, 1951. Popular record by Jane Turzy (Decca).

I Like It Like That. w/m Chris Kenner and Alan Toussaint, 1961. Hit record by Chris Kenner (Instant). The Dave Clark Five had a Top 10 version in 1965 (Epic). In 1961, The Bobbettes had an answer record titled "I Don't Like It Like That" (Gone).

I Like Mountain Music. w. James Cavanaugh, m. Frank Weldon, 1933. Introduced and popularized by Ethel Shutta with George Olsen's Orchestra (Victor) and also recorded by Ted Weems and his Orchestra, vocal by Elmo Tanner.

I Like Myself. w. Betty Comden and Adolph Green, m. André Previn, 1955. Introduced by Gene Kelly, singing and dancing on roller skates, in (MM) *It's Always Fair Weather*.

I Like the Likes of You. w. E. Y. Harburg, m. Vernon Duke, 1934. Sung by Judith Barron and Brian Hutchins (Robert Cummings) and danced by Vilma and Buddy Ebsen in (TM) *Ziegfeld Follies*.

I Like the Way. w/m Ritchie Cordell and Bo Gentry, 1967. Top 40 record by Tommy James and The Shondells (Roulette).

I Like to Do Things for You. w. Jack Yellen, m. Milton Ager, 1930. Performed by Paul Whiteman's Orchestra and the Rhythm Boys [Bing Crosby, Al Rinker, and Harry Barris] in (MM) *The King of Jazz* and recorded by them (Columbia). Also recorded by Pletcher's Eli Prom Trotters (QRS).

I Like to Lead When I Dance. w. Sammy Cahn, m. James Van Heusen, 1964. Introduced by Frank Sinatra in (MM) *Robin and the Seven Hoods*.

I Like to Recognize the Tune. w. Lorenz Hart, m. Richard Rodgers, 1939. Introduced by Eddie Bracken, Marcy Westcott, Mary Jane Walsh, Richard Kollmar, and Hal LeRoy in (TM) *Too Many Girls*. It was interpolated in (MM) *Meet the People* in 1944 by June Allyson, Virginia O'Brien, Vaughn Monroe and his Orchestra with Ziggy Talent and chorus.

I Like What You're Doing (to Me). w/m Homer Banks, Bettye Crutcher, and Raymond Jackson, 1969. Recorded by Carla Thomas (Stax).

I Like You. w/m Harold Rome, 1954. Introduced by William Tabbert and Ezio Pinza in (TM) *Fanny*.

I Like Your Kind of Love. w/m Melvin Endsley, 1957. Featured and recorded by Andy Williams (Cadence).

I Live for Love. w. Mort Dixon, m. Allie Wrubel, 1935. The title song of (MM) *I Live for Love*, introduced by Everett Marshall.

I Live for Your Love. w/m Pam Reswick, Alan Rich, and Steve Werfel, 1988. Top 10 R&B and Pop chart entry by Natalie Cole from her album "Everlasting" (Manhattan).

I Live the Life I Love. w/m Clay Boland, 1938. Introduced and recorded by Jan Savitt, vocal by Bon Bon (Victor). Also recorded by Richard Himber, vocal by Stuart Allen (Victor).

I'll Always Be Glad to Take You Back. w/m Ernest Tubb, 1942. Introduced and recorded by Ernest Tubb (Decca).

I'll Always Be in Love with You. w. Bud Green and Herman Ruby, m. Sam H. Stept, 1929. Introduced by Morton Downey in (MM) *Syncopation* and recorded by him under the direction of Nat Shilkret (Victor). Fred Waring's Pennsylvanians, who also appeared in the film, had a popular record (Victor). Revived by Jack Pleis and his Orchestra (Decca), 1957.

I'll Always Come Back. w/m K. T. Oslin, 1988. #1 Country chart song by K. T. Oslin (MCA).

I'll Always Love You. w/m Jimmy George, 1988. Top 10 single by Taylor Dayne (MCA).

I'll Always Love You. w/m William Stevenson and Ivy Hunter, 1965. Top 40 record by The Spinners (Motown).

I'll Always Love You. w/m Jay Livingston and Ray Evans, 1950. Introduced by Dean Martin in (MP) *My Friend Irma Goes West*. Recorded by Martin, with Paul Weston's Orchestra (Capitol), and by Martha Tilton (Coral).

I'll Be Alright Without You. w/m Steve Perry, Jonathan Cain, and Neal Schon, 1987. Chart single written and recorded by the trio Journey (Columbia).

I'll Be Around. w/m Earl Randle, 1972. #1 R&B, #3 Pop chart gold record by The Spinners (Atlantic).

I'll Be Around. w/m Alec Wilder, 1943. Featured and recorded by the Mills Brothers (Decca) and coupled with "Paper Doll" (q.v.), one of the biggest sellers of the decade. Among other recordings: Cab Calloway (Okeh), George Shearing (MGM).

I'll Be Back. w. Gene Autry and Eddie Dean, m. Rex Preis and Bill Bryan, 1945. Coupled with #1 C&W record "At Mail Call Today" by Gene Autry (Okeh).

I'll Be Blue, Just Thinking of You. w. George Whiting, m. Pete Wendling, 1930. Numerous recordings were made in its first year, among them: Ruth Etting (Columbia); Aileen Stanley (Victor); Smith Ballew, under the pseudonym of Bob Blue (Okeh); Bert Lown (Columbia); Nat Shilkret (Victor).

I'll Be Coming Back for More. w/m Curly Putman and Sterling Whipple, 1979. Country chart hit by T. G. Sheppard (Warner Bros.).

I'll Be Doggone. w/m Warren Moore, William Robinson, and Marv Tarplin, 1965. #1 R&B and Top 10 Pop record by Marvin Gaye (Tamla).

I'll Be Faithful. w. Ned Washington, m. Allie Wrubel, 1933. Introduced by Art Jarrett. Popular recordings by the bands of Jan Garber (Victor); Bernie Cummins (Columbia); Anson Weeks (Brunswick); and the studio all-star band led by Adrian Rollini, vocal by Howard Phillips (Melotone). Billy Eckstine revived it in the early fifties (MGM).

I'll Be Glad When You're Dead, You Rascal You. See **You Rascal You.**

I'll Be Good to You. w. Senora Sam, w/m George Johnson and Louis Johnson, 1976. Top 10 gold record by The Brothers Johnson (A&M).

I'll Be Happy When the Preacher Makes You Mine. w. Sam M. Lewis and Joe Young, m. Walter Donaldson, 1919.

I'll Be Hard to Handle. w. Bernard Dougall, m. Jerome Kern, 1933. Introduced by Lyda Roberti in (TM) *Roberta.* These were special lyrics for Roberti, not written by Otto Harbach, who wrote the other show lyrics. Ginger Rogers sang it in (MM) *Roberta* in 1935. In the 1952 remake, (MM) *Lovely to Look At,* Ann Miller sang it with additional new lyrics by Dorothy Fields.

I'll Be Home. w/m Stan Lewis and Ferdinand Washington, 1956. R&B hit by The Flamingos (Checker) and pop hit by Pat Boone (Dot).

I'll Be Home for Christmas. w/m Kim Gannon, Walter Kent, and Buck Ram, 1943. Wartime Christmas hit. Bing Crosby's recording sold over a million copies the first year (Decca).

I'll Be Leaving Alone. w/m Dickey Lee and Wayland Holyfield, 1977. Hit Country chart record by Charley Pride (RCA).

I'll Be Loving You (Forever). w/m Maurice Starr, 1989. Hit single by the group New Kids on the Block (Columbia).

I'll Be Married to the Music of a Military Band. w. Henry Blossom, m. Victor Herbert, 1908. From (TM) *The Prima Donna.*

I'll Be Over You. w/m Steve Lukather and Randy Goodrum, 1986. Recorded by the group Toto (Columbia).

I'll Be Satisfied. w/m Berry Gordy, Jr., Gwen Gordy, and Tyran Carlo, 1959. Popularized by Jackie Wilson (Brunswick).

I'll Be Seeing You. w. Irving Kahal, m. Sammy Fain, 1938, 1944. Introduced by Tamara in the short-lived musical (TM) *Right This Way.* It became one of the biggest ballad hits of World War II and was on "Your Hit Parade" for twenty-four weeks, ten times in the #1 position. The best-selling recording was by Tommy Dorsey, vocal by Frank Sinatra (Victor), followed by Frances Langford (Decca). In the fifties, it became the closing theme song of Liberace on television and in clubs and theaters.

I'll Be There. w/m Hal Davis, Berry Gordy, Jr., Willie Hutch, and Bob West, 1970. #1 record by The Jackson 5 (Motown).

I'll Be There. w/m Ben E. King, Jerry Leiber, and Mike Stoller, 1961. Answer song to hit, "Stand by Me," recorded by Damita Jo (Mercury).

I'll Be There. w/m Bobby Darin, 1960. Introduced and recorded by Bobby Darin (Atco). Best-selling record by Gerry and The Pacemakers (Laurie), 1965.

I'll Be There for You. w/m Bon Jovi and Richie Sambora, 1989. Hit recording by the band Bon Jovi (Mercury).

I'll Be There If You Ever Want Me. w/m Rusty Gabbard and Ray Price, 1954. Introduced and recorded by Ray Price (Columbia).

I'll Be True. w/m William McLemore, 1954. Hit R&B record by Faye Adams (Herald).

I'll Be True to My Honey Boy. w/m George Evans, 1894. Featured by the author, a famous blackface minstrel, who became known as George "Honey Boy" Evans because of the popularity of the song.

I'll Be True to You. w/m Alan Rhody, 1978. Hit Country chart record by The Oak Ridge Boys (ABC).

I'll Be with You in Apple Blossom Time. w. Neville Fleason, m. Albert Von Tilzer, 1920. Featured by Nora Bayes and recorded by Charles Harrison (Victor), and Ernest Hare (Brunswick). The Andrews Sisters revived it in 1941 with their hit record (Decca) and their performance of it in (MM) *Buck Privates*. Recorded by Tab Hunter, whose version was in the Top 40 (Warner Bros.), 1959, and Wayne Newton, who had a chart record (Capitol), 1965.

I'll Be with You When the Roses Bloom Again. w. Will D. Cobb, m. Gus Edwards, 1901. One of Edwards's early hits that later became a favorite of country singers.

I'll Be Your Baby Tonight. w/m Bob Dylan, 1968, 1987. Introduced by Bob Dylan in his album "John Wesley Harding" (Columbia), 1968. Country chart records by Glen Garrison (Imperial), 1968, Claude King (Columbia), 1970, Judy Rodman [Top 10] (MTM), 1987.

I'll Be Yours (J'Attendrai). w. Anna Sosenko (Engl.), Louis Poterat (Fr.), m. Dino Olivieri, 1945. French song, originally published in Italy. Introduced in the U.S. and recorded by Hildegarde (Decca).

I'll Bring It Home to You. See **Bring It on Home to Me.**

I'll Build a Stairway to Paradise. w. B. G. DeSylva and Ira Gershwin, m. George Gershwin, 1922. Ira Gershwin wrote this under the pseudonym of Arthur Francis. Sung and danced by Winnie Lightner, Pearl Regay, and the company in (TM) *George White's Scandals of 1922*. Paul Whiteman conducted the pit orchestra. It was heard in the background of the George Gershwin film bio (MM) *Rhapsody in Blue*, 1945, and was sung by Georges Guetary in (MM) *An American in Paris*, 1951. Played in the background of (MP) *Beaches*, 1988.

I'll Buy That Dream. w. Herb Magidson, m. Allie Wrubel, 1945. Introduced by Anne Jeffreys in (MM) *Sing Your Way Home*. Best-selling records by Helen Forrest and Dick Haymes, with Victor Young's Orchestra (Decca); Harry James, vocal by Kitty Kallen (Columbia).

I'll Buy You a Star. w. Dorothy Fields, m. Arthur Schwartz, 1951. Introduced by Johnny Johnston in (TM) *A Tree Grows in Brooklyn*.

I'll Close My Eyes. w. Buddy Kaye, m. Billy Reid, 1947. Popular records by Andy Russell (Capitol); Johnny Desmond, with the Page Cavanaugh Trio (Victor); Mildred Bailey (Majestic); Hildegarde (Decca); Jack Fina and his Orchestra (Mercury); Ray Anthony and his Orchestra (Sonora).

I'll Come Back as Another Woman. w/m Bob Carpenter and Kent Robbins, 1986. Top 10 Country chart record by Tanya Tucker (Capitol).

I'll Come Running. w/m Connie Smith, 1967. C&W hit by Connie Smith (RCA).

I'll Come Running Back to You. 1958. Top 40 record by Sam Cooke (Specialty).

I'll Cry Instead. w/m John Lennon and Paul McCartney, 1964. Introduced by The Beatles in (MM) *A Hard Day's Night*, and on records (Capitol).

I'll Cry Tomorrow. w. Johnny Mercer, m. Alex North, 1956. Title song of the film biography of Lillian Roth (MM) *I'll Cry Tomorrow*, based on the book of the same name. North scored the film. Recorded by Lillian Roth (Coral).

I'll Cry Tomorrow. w/m Dave Dreyer, Gerald Marks, and Lillian Roth, 1954. Written upon publication of Lillian Roth's autobiography, which later was made into a film of the same name.

I'll Dance at Your Wedding. w. Herb Magidson, m. Ben Oakland, 1947. Popular records by Buddy Clark, with Ray Noble's

Orchestra (Columbia); Tony Martin (RCA Victor); Peggy Lee (Capitol).

I'll Dream Tonight. w. Johnny Mercer, m. Richard A. Whiting, 1938. Introduced by Dick Powell and Priscilla Lane in (MM) *Cowboy from Brooklyn*. Among recordings: the bands of Eddy Duchin (Victor); Orrin Tucker (Vocalion); Teddy Wilson, vocal by Nan Wynn (Brunswick).

I'll Drown My Tears. w/m Henry Glover, 1952. Recorded by Sonny Thompson (King).

I'll Follow My Secret Heart. w/m Noël Coward, 1934. Introduced in London, and then in the U.S., by Yvonne Printemps in (TM) *Conversation Piece*. This waltz has been recorded by Lee Wiley (Decca), Lily Pons (Columbia), Hildegarde (Decca), among many others.

I'll Follow You. w. Roy Turk, m. Fred E. Ahlert, 1932. Featured and recorded by Ben Bernie and his Orchestra (Brunswick); Paul Whiteman's Orchestra, vocal by Red McKenzie (Victor); and Ethel Merman (Victor). Later, Red Norvo and his Band recorded it (Capitol).

I'll Forget You. w. Annelu Burns, m. Ernest R. Ball, 1921. Recorded by the popular tenor John Steel (Victor). The song was revived by Dick Haymes in (MM) *Irish Eyes Are Smiling*, 1944, and by Gordon MacRae in (MM) *By the Light of the Silvery Moon*, 1952.

I'll Forgive You, But I Can't Forget. w/m J. L. Frank and Pee Wee King, 1944. Featured and recorded by Roy Acuff (Okeh).

I'll Get Along Somehow. 1950. R&B record by Larry Darnell (Regal).

I'll Get By. w. Roy Turk, m. Fred E. Ahlert, 1928, 1944. Among the first recordings that popularized this song were those by Gus Arnheim's Orchestra (Okeh), Nick Lucas (Brunswick), The Ipana Troubadors (Columbia), Aileen Stanley (Victor). It was interpolated by Harry Richman in (MM) *Puttin' On The Ritz*, 1930. It was sung by Irene Dunne in (MP) *A Guy Named Joe*, co-starring with

Spencer Tracy, 1943. Dinah Shore sang it in (MM) *Follow The Boys*, 1944. Her performance and the #1 record by Harry James, with vocal by Dick Haymes (Columbia), resulted in the song being on "Your Hit Parade" for twenty-two weeks. Dan Dailey performed it in (MM) *You Were Meant for Me*, 1948; June Haver sang it in (MM) *I'll Get By*, 1950, in which it was also used as the recurrent theme. Judy Garland sang it in (MM) *A Star Is Born*, 1954; Gogi Grant, dubbing for Ann Blyth on the soundtrack, sang it in (MM) *The Helen Morgan Story*, 1957.

I'll Get Over You. w/m Richard Leigh, 1976. Chart record by Crystal Gayle (United Artists).

I'll Get You. w. Will D. Cobb, m. Gus Edwards, 1913.

I'll Go Down Swinging. w/m Bill Anderson, 1964. C&W chart record by Porter Wagoner (RCA).

I'll Go Home with Bonnie Jean. w. Alan Jay Lerner, m. Frederick Loewe, 1947. Introduced by Lee Sullivan in (TM) *Brigadoon*. In the film version (MM) *Brigadoon*, 1954, it was performed by Van Johnson and Jimmy Thompson, with John Gustafson dubbing in the singing for Thompson.

I'll Go On Alone. w/m Marty Robbins, 1953. Popular Country record by Webb Pierce (Decca).

I'll Go to My Grave Loving You. w/m Don Reid, 1975. Country/Pop chart record by The Statler Brothers (Mercury).

I'll Hate Myself in the Morning. w/m Jack Lawrence, 1947. Leading records by Sammy Kaye, vocal by Don Cornell and Laura Leslie (RCA Victor), and Frankie Carle, vocal by Marjorie Hughes (Columbia).

I'll Just Have a Cup of Coffee (Then I'll Go). w/m Bill Brock, 1961. Popular crossover (C&W and Pop) record by Claude Gray (Mercury).

I'll Have to Say I Love You in a Song. w/m Jim Croce, 1974. Top 10 record by Jim Croce (ABC).

I'll Hold Out My Hand. w/m Chip Taylor and Al Gorgoni, 1969. Recorded by The Clique (White Whale).

I'll Hold You in My Heart (Till I Can Hold You in My Arms). w/m Eddy Arnold, Hal Harton, and Tommy Dilbeck, 1947. Million-seller for Eddy Arnold (RCA Victor).

I'll Keep Holding On. w/m William Stevenson and Ivy Hunter, 1965. Hit record by The Marvelettes (Tamla).

I'll Keep Holding On (Just to Your Love). w/m Robert F. Tubert and Sonny James, 1965. C&W hit by Sonny James (Capitol).

I'll Keep On Loving You. w/m Floyd Tillman, 1939. Introduced and recorded by Floyd Tillman (Victor).

I'll Keep You Satisfied. w/m John Lennon and Paul McCartney, 1964. Recorded in England by Billy J. Kramer with the Dakotas (Imperial).

I'll Know. w/m Frank Loesser, 1950. Introduced by Isabel Bigley and Robert Alda in (TM) *Guys and Dolls*. Leading records by Sarah Vaughan (Columbia), Billy Eckstine (MGM), Fran Warren (RCA Victor), Coleman Hawkins (Roost). In (MM) *Guys and Dolls*, 1955, it was sung by Marlon Brando and Jean Simmons. Popular record by Sammy Davis, Jr., with Jack Pleis's Orchestra (Decca), 1956.

I'll Leave This World Loving You. w/m Wayne Kemp, 1988. #1 Country chart record by Ricky Van Shelton (Columbia).

I'll Lend You Everything I've Got Except My Wife. w. Jean C. Havez, m. Harry Von Tilzer, 1910. Introduced by Bert Williams in (TM) *Ziegfeld Follies of 1910*.

I'll Love You Forever. w/m Donald Davis and Robert Earl Johnson, 1966. Recorded by the R&B trio The Holidays (Golden World).

I'll Love You in My Dreams. w/m Abel Baer, Horace Heidt, and Benee Russell, 1931. Theme song of and recorded by Horace Heidt and his Musical Knights (Brunswick).

I'll Make a Ring Around Rosie. w. William Jerome, m. Jean Schwartz, 1910.

I'll Make All Your Dreams Come True. w/m Wes Farrell and Bernice Ross, 1965. Top 40 record by Ronnie Dove (Diamond).

I'll Meet You Halfway. w/m Wes Farrell and Gerry Goffin, 1971. Top 10 record by The Partridge Family (Bell).

I'll Never Ask for More. w. Roy Turk, m. Fred E. Ahlert, 1929. Popularized by Aileen Stanley (Victor); Arnold Johnson's Orchestra (Brunswick); and the Dorsey Brothers, with vocal by Smith Ballew (Okeh).

I'll Never Be Free. w/m Bennie Benjamin and George David Weiss, 1950. Top 10 record by Kay Starr and Tennessee Ernie Ford (Capitol).

I'll Never Be in Love Again. 1987. Top 10 Country chart record by Don Williams (Capitol).

I'll Never Be the Same. w. Gus Kahn, m. Matty Malneck, and Frank Signorelli, 1932. Kahn wrote lyric to an instrumental, "Little Buttercup." The retitled song met with popular acceptance through recordings by such artists as Ruth Etting (Banner); Paul Whiteman, vocal by Mildred Bailey (Victor); Adelaide Hall (Brunswick); Guy Lombardo (Brunswick); and later Artie Shaw (Victor); Ziggy Elman (Bluebird); Phil Napoleon (Swan); Teddy Wilson and Orchestra (Brunswick).

I'll Never Dance Again. w/m Barry Mann and Mike Anthony, 1962. Featured and recorded by Bobby Rydell (Cameo).

I'll Never Fail You. w. Irving Taylor, m. Vic Mizzy, 1938. Among recordings: Teddy Wilson, vocal by Billie Holiday (Brunswick); Andy Kirk, vocal by Pha Terrell (Decca); Blue Barron and his Orchestra (Bluebird).

I'll Never Fall in Love Again. w. Hal David, m. Burt Bacharach, 1968. Introduced by Jill O'Hara and Jerry Orbach in (TM) *Promises, Promises*. First single, outside of those released from the cast album, by Burt Bacharach and his Orchestra and Chorus (A&M), 1969. Top 10 version by Dionne Warwick (Scepter), 1970.

I'll Never Fall in Love Again. w/m Lonnie Donegan and Jimmie Currie, 1967. Recorded in England by Tom Jones. Released in the U.S. (Parrot), 1967. Upon its re-release in 1969, it earned a gold record.

I'll Never Find Another You. w/m Tom Springfield, 1965. Hit record by the Australian group The Seekers (Capitol). Country singer Sonny James had a chart version (Capitol), 1967.

I'll Never Forget. w/m Leo M. Cherne, 1942. Featured by the bands of Glen Gray and the Casa Loma Orchestra (Decca), Dick Jurgens (Okeh), Hal McIntyre (Victor).

I'll Never Get out of This World Alive. w/m Hank Thompson and Fred Rose, 1953. Hank Williams had a popular C&W recording (MGM).

I'll Never Have to Dream Again. w. Charles Newman, m. Isham Jones, 1932. Introduced by Isham Jones and his Orchestra. Early recordings by Connie Boswell (Brunswick), Jack Hylton (Br. Decca), Elmer Feldkamp (Crown). Jones later recorded it with Curt Massey (Coast) (Capitol).

I'll Never Know. w. Roy Jordan, m. Ulpio Minucci, 1955. Recorded by The Four Lads (Columbia).

I'll Never Let a Day Pass By. w. Frank Loesser, m. Victor Schertzinger, 1941. From (MM) *Kiss the Boys Goodbye*. Leading recordings by the bands of Charlie Barnet (Bluebird); Harry James, vocal by Dick Haymes (Columbia); Charlie Spivak (Okeh).

I'll Never Let You Worry My Mind. w/m Earl Nunn and Red Foley, 1945. Featured and recorded by Red Foley (Decca).

I'll Never Love This Way Again. w/m Will Jennings and Richard Kerr, 1979. Top 10 gold record by Dionne Warwick (Arista).

I'll Never Say Goodbye. w. Alan Bergman and Marilyn Bergman, m. David Shire, 1979. Sung by Melissa Manchester on the soundtrack of (MP) *The Promise*.

I'll Never Say "Never Again" Again. w/m Harry Woods, 1935. Featured and recorded by the bands of: Benny Goodman, vocal by Helen Ward (Columbia); Ozzie Nelson (Brunswick); Dorsey Brothers (Decca); Henry "Red" Allen (Vocalion); Frank Dailey (Bluebird). Revived by Dinah Shore (RCA), 1957.

I'll Never Say No. w/m Meredith Willson, 1960. Introduced by Harve Presnell in (TM) *The Unsinkable Molly Brown*. In the film version, (MM) *The Unsinkable Molly Brown*, 1964, Presnell sang it with Debbie Reynolds.

I'll Never Slip Around Again. w/m Floyd Tillman, 1949. Sequel to "Slippin' Around" (q.v.). Top recordings by Margaret Whiting and Jimmy Wakely (Capitol), and Floyd Tillman (Columbia).

I'll Never Smile Again. w/m Ruth Lowe, 1940. Tommy Dorsey, with vocal by Frank Sinatra and the Pied Pipers, had one of the biggest hit records of the year (Victor). It was #1 on the charts for twelve weeks. Sinatra, in his screen debut, sang it with the Dorsey band in (MM) *Las Vegas Nights*, 1941.

I'll Never Stop Loving You. w/m Dave Loggins and J. D. Martin, 1985. #1 Country chart record by Gary Morris (Warner Bros.).

I'll Never Stop Loving You. w. Sammy Cahn, m. Nicholas Brodsky, 1955. Introduced by Doris Day as Ruth Etting in her story (MM) *Love Me or Leave Me*. Day had the best-selling record (Columbia).

I'll Never Tell You I Love You. w. Irving Mills, m. Will Hudson, 1936. Introduced and recorded by the Hudson-De Lange Orchestra, vocal by Georgia Gibbs (Brunswick). Ozzie Nelson and his Band also recorded it (Bluebird).

I'll Paint You a Song. w/m Mac Davis, 1970. Sung on the soundtrack of (MP) *Norwood* by Mac Davis.

I'll Pin a Note on Your Pillow. w/m Carol Berzas, Donald Goodman, and Nelson Larkin, 1987. Top 10 Country chart record by Billy Joe Royal (Atlantic America).

I'll Plant My Own Tree. w. Dory Previn, m. André Previn, 1967. Sung by Margaret Whiting, dubbing on the soundtrack for Susan Hayward, in (MP) *Valley of the Dolls*.

I'll Play for You. w/m Jimmy Seals and Dash Crofts, 1975. Top 20 record by Seals and Crofts (Warner Bros.).

I'll Pray for You. w. Kim Gannon, m. Arthur Altman, 1942. Best-selling records by The Andrews Sisters (Decca); Tony Pastor, vocal by Johnny McAfee (Bluebird); Jack Leonard (Okeh); Clyde Lucas's Orchestra (Elite).

I'll Pray for You. w. Roy King, m. Stanley Hill, 1940. Featured and recorded by Mildred Bailey (Columbia).

I'll Remember. w. Ralph Freed, m. Burton Lane, 1939. Featured and recorded by singers Barry Wood (Vocalion) and Phil Regan (Decca); bandleaders Artie Shaw, vocal by Helen Forrest (Bluebird), and Jack Teagarden, vocal by Kitty Kallen (Columbia).

I'll Remember. See **In the Still of the Nite.**

I'll Remember April. w. Don Raye and Patricia Johnston, m. Gene De Paul, 1942. Introduced by Dick Foran in (MM) *Ride 'em Cowboy*. Most popular record by Woody Herman and his Orchestra (Decca).

I'll Remember Her. w/m Noël Coward, 1963. Introduced by José Ferrer in (TM) *The Girl Who Came to Supper*.

I'll Remember Suzanne. w/m Jack Segal and Dick Miles, 1944. Introduced and recorded by Gene Krupa and his Orchestra (Columbia).

I'll Remember Today. w. William Engvick, m. Edith Piaf, 1957. Leading record by Patti Page (Mercury).

I'll Remember You. w. Frank Stammers, m. Harold Orlob, 1919. From (TM) *Nothing But Love*.

I'll Repossess My Heart. w/m Paul Yandell, 1965. Country hit, recorded by Kitty Wells (Decca).

I'll Sail My Ship Alone. w/m Lois Mann, Morry Burns, Henry Bernard, and Henry Thurston, 1950. One of the biggest C&W hits of the year. Moon Mullican's record (King) sold over a million copies.

I'll Save the Last Dance for You. See **Save the Last Dance for Me.**

I'll Say She Does. w/m B. G. DeSylva, Gus Kahn, and Al Jolson, 1918. Introduced by Jolson in (TM) *Sinbad*. His recording (Columbia) was released in 1919.

I'll See Him Through. w/m Norro Wilson and Billy Sherrill, 1970. Country hit by Tammy Wynette (Epic).

I'll See You Again. w/m Noël Coward, 1929. Sung by Evelyn Laye and Gerald Nodin in (TM) *Bitter Sweet* in New York and by Peggy Wood and Georges Metaxa in London later the same year. This waltz, one of Coward's most popular songs, was also sung in the 1948 film version (MM) *Bitter Sweet* by Jeanette MacDonald and Nelson Eddy.

I'll See You in C-U-B-A. w/m Irving Berlin, 1920. From (TM) *Ziegfeld Midnight Frolic*. A popular song, following the unpopular passage of the Volstead Act (Prohibition). Hit records by Billy Murray (Victor, and five other labels) and Ted Lewis and his Orchestra (Columbia). It was revived in 1946 by Bing Crosby and Olga San Juan in (MM) *Blue Skies*.

I'll See You in My Dreams. w. Gus Kahn, m. Isham Jones, 1924. Introduced by Isham Jones and his Orchestra. Hit instrumental record by Isham Jones conducting Ray Miller's Orchestra (Brunswick). In films, it was heard in the background of (MM) *Rose of Washington Square*, 1939; sung by Bob Crosby in (MM) *Pardon My Rhythm*, 1944; sung by Jeanette MacDonald in (MM) *Follow the Boys*, 1944; played on an off-screen phonograph, and hummed by Jean Crain in (MM) *Margie*, 1946. Doris Day sang it as the title song of the Kahn bio in (MM) *I'll See You in My Dreams*, 1951. Revived by Pat Boone (Dot), 1962.

I'll Share My World with You. w/m Ben Wilson, 1969. Hit Country record by George Jones (Musicor).

I'll Sing You a Thousand Love Songs. w. Al Dubin, m. Harry Warren, 1936. Introduced by Robert Paige, who was still acting under the name of David Carlyle, in (MM) *Cain and Mabel*, starring Clark Gable and Marion Davies. Interpolated into the song were: "The Shadow Waltz," "The Rose in Her Hair" (both Dubin/Warren), and "L'Amour, Toujours, L'Amour" (Cushing/Friml).

I'll Stand By. w. Benny Davis, m. J. Fred Coots, 1936. Featured and recorded by Eddy Duchin, vocal by Jerry Cooper (Victor).

I'll Step Aside. w/m Johnny Bond, 1947. Popular C&W record by Ernest Tubb (Decca).

I'll Still Be Loving You. w/m Mary Ann Kennedy, Pat Bunch, Pam Rose, and Todd Cerney, 1987. #1 Country single by the group Restless Heart (RCA).

I'll String Along with You. w. Al Dubin, m. Harry Warren, 1934. Introduced by Dick Powell and Ginger Rogers in (MM) *Twenty Million Sweethearts*. In the remake, retitled (MM) *My Dream Is Yours*, 1949, it was sung by Doris Day to Jack Carson. Danny Thomas sang it in (MM) *The Jazz Singer*, 1953. It later was used as a recurrent theme in (MP) *Battle Cry*, 1955.

I'll Take an Option on You. w. Leo Robin, m. Ralph Rainger, 1933. Introduced by Frank Fay in (TM) *Tattle Tales*. Recorded by Paul Whiteman (Victor) and Ted Fio Rito (Brunswick), and their orchestras. Dorothy

Lamour made a recording of it in 1939 (Bluebird).

I'll Take Care of You. w/m Brook Benton, 1960. Recorded by Bobby Bland (Duke).

I'll Take Care of Your Cares. w. Mort Dixon, m. James V. Monaco, 1927, 1967. Featured and recorded by Franklyn Baur (Victor). Revived forty years later by Frankie Laine (ABC-Paramount).

I'll Take Good Care of You. w/m Bert Berns and Jerry Ragovoy, 1966. Recorded by Garnet Mimms and produced by Ragovoy (United Artists).

I'll Take Romance. w. Oscar Hammerstein II, m. Ben Oakland, 1937. Introduced by Grace Moore in (MM) *I'll Take Romance*. It was interpolated by Gloria Jean in (MM) *Manhattan Angel*, 1948, and played by the orchestra on the soundtrack of (MM) *Jolson Sings Again*, 1949. It was also heard in (MM) *Holiday in Havana*, 1949, and in the (MM) *The Eddy Duchin Story*, 1956.

I'll Take Tallulah. w. E. Y. Harburg, m. Burton Lane, 1942. Introduced by Red Skelton and Bert Lahr and danced by Eleanor Powell with Tommy Dorsey and his Orchestra in (MM) *Ship Ahoy*. Recorded by Dorsey, vocal by Frank Sinatra and the Pied Pipers (Victor).

I'll Take You Home. w/m Cynthia Weil and Barry Mann, 1963. Recorded by The Drifters (Atlantic).

I'll Take You There. w/m Alvertis Isbell, 1972. #1 record by the family soul group The Staple Singers (Stax).

I'll Take You Where the Music's Playing. w/m Jeff Barry and Ellie Greenwich, 1965. Recorded by The Drifters (Atlantic).

I'll Try Anything. w/m Mark Barkan and Vic Millrose, 1967. Recorded in England by Dusty Springfield (Philips).

I'll Try Something New. w/m William "Smokey" Robinson, 1962, 1969. Top 40 record by The Miracles, of which Robinson was lead singer (Tamla). Hit record by the combined talents of Diana Ross and The Supremes, and The Temptations (Motown), 1969. Revived by A Taste of Honey (Capitol), 1982.

I'll Tumble 4 Ya. w/m Roy Hay, Jon Moss, Mikey Craig, and George "Boy George" O'Dowd, 1983. Top 10 record written and performed by the British quartet Culture Club (Epic/Virgin).

I'll Wait. w/m Alex Van Halen, Eddie Van Halen, Michael Anthony, David Lee Roth, and M. H. McDonald, 1984. Recorded by the band Van Halen (Warner Bros.).

I'll Wait. w/m Alec Wilder, 1949. Featured and recorded by Dinah Washington (Mercury).

I'll Wait for You. w. Bob Marcucci, m. Peter De Angelis, 1958. Popular record by Frankie Avalon (Chancellor).

I'll Walk Alone. w. Sammy Cahn, m. Jule Styne, 1944, 1952. Introduced by Dinah Shore in (MM) *Follow the Boys.* Nominated for Academy Award. Shore had #1 record (Victor). Top 10 records by Martha Tilton (Capitol) and Mary Martin (Decca). Revived in 1952 when, dubbing for Susan Hayward, Jane Froman sang it on the soundtrack of her biography (MM) *With a Song in My Heart,* and recorded it (Capitol). Other popular 1952 versions by Don Cornell (Coral), Richard Hayes (Mercury), Margaret Whiting (Capitol).

I'll Walk with God. w. Paul Francis Webster, m. Nicholas Brodsky, 1954. Added to the score of (MM) *The Student Prince* and sung by Mario Lanza, who also recorded it (RCA Victor).

Ill Wind. w. Ted Koehler, m. Harold Arlen, 1934. Introduced by Aida Ward in the nightclub revue *Cotton Club Parade* in Harlem, New York. Maxine Sullivan (Victor), Lena Horne (Victor), Ellis Larkins (Decca), and Frank Sinatra (Capitol) have had later popular recordings.

Ilona. w. Sheldon Harnick, m. Jerry Bock, 1963. Sung by Jack Cassidy in (TM) *She Loves Me.*

I Long to See the Girl I Left Behind. w/m John T. Kelly, 1893.

I Lost My Sugar in Salt Lake City. w/m Leon René and Johnny Lange, 1942. Introduced by Mae E. Johnson in (MM) *Stormy Weather.* Johnny Mercer had a popular record with Freddie Slack's Band (Capitol). Jan Garber and his Orchestra performed it in (MM) *Jam Session,* 1944.

I Lost the Best Pal That I Had. w/m Dick Thomas, 1920.

I Love. w/m Tom T. Hall, 1974. Crossover (C&W/Pop) hit by Tom T. Hall (Mercury).

I Love a Lassie (or, Ma Scotch Bluebell). w/m Harry Lauder and Gerald Grafton, 1906. One of Lauder's biggest hits, which he performed in vaudeville and on records (Victor).

I Love a New Yorker. w. Ralph Blane and Harold Arlen, m. Harold Arlen, 1950. Introduced by Dan Dailey and Betty Grable in (MM) *My Blue Heaven.*

I Love an Old Fashioned Song. w. Sammy Cahn, m. Jule Styne, 1946. From the Danny Kaye film (MM) *The Kid from Brooklyn.* Top recordings: Kay Kyser, vocal by Mike Douglas (Columbia); Freddy Martin's Orchestra (Victor).

I Love a Parade. w. Ted Koehler, m. Harold Arlen, 1931. Introduced by Cab Calloway in the Cotton Club revue *Rhythmania.* In 1932 Harry Richman sang it in (TM) *George White's Music Hall Varieties* and recorded it (Columbia). Winnie Lightner sang it in (MM) *Manhattan Parade* in 1932.

I Love a Piano. w/m Irving Berlin, 1916. Introduced by Harry Fox and ensemble in (TM) *Stop! Look! Listen!* It was performed by Fred Astaire and Judy Garland in a medley in (MM) *Easter Parade* in 1948.

I Love a Rainy Night. w/m Eddie Rabbitt, Even Stevens, and David Malloy, 1980. #1 gold record by Eddie Rabbitt (Elektra).

I Loved 'Em Every One. w/m Phil Sampson, 1981. Country/Pop record by T. G. Sheppard (Warner Bros.).

I Loved You, Kate, in Ireland. w/m M. F. Carey, 1890. Favorite song of heavyweight champion John L. Sullivan.

I Loved You Once in Silence. w. Alan Jay Lerner, m. Frederick Loewe, 1960. Introduced by Julie Andrews in (TM) *Camelot.* Sung by Vanessa Redgrave in the film version (MM) *Camelot,* 1967.

I Love Her, She Loves Me (I'm Her He, She's My She). w/m Irving Caesar and Eddie Cantor, 1922. Introduced and recorded by Eddie Cantor (Columbia).

I Love How You Love Me. w/m Barry Mann and Larry Kolber, 1961. Hit record by The Paris Sisters (Gregmark). Revived via the million-seller by Bobby Vinton (Epic), 1968.

I Love It. w. E. Ray Goetz, m. Harry Von Tilzer, 1910. Recorded by The American Quartette (Victor).

I Love Life. w. Irwin M. Cassel, m. Mana-Zucca, 1923. A concert song that became a popular favorite. Introduced by Charles Hackett and then featured by John Charles Thomas.

I Love Louisa. w. Howard Dietz, m. Arthur Schwartz, 1931. Sung by Fred and Adele Astaire and company in the first act finale of the revue (TM) *The Band Wagon.* Betsy Drake sang it in (MM) *Dancing in the Dark,* 1949. In the 1953 film adaptation (MM) *The Band Wagon,* Fred Astaire, Oscar Levant, Cyd Charisse, Nanette Fabray, and a chorus performed it.

I Love Love. w. Channing Pollock and Rennold Wolf, m. Charles J. Gebest, 1911. From (TM) *The Red Widow,* starring Raymond Hitchcock.

"I Love Lucy" Theme. w. Harold Adamson, m. Eliot Daniel, 1953, 1977. Theme from popular series (TVP) "I Love Lucy." Hit instrumental disco record titled "Disco Lucy" by the studio group Wilton Place Street Band (Island), 1977.

I Love Music. w/m Kenny Gamble and Leon Huff, 1976. #1 R&B, Top 10 Pop gold record by the O'Jays (Philadelphia International).

I Love My Baby (My Baby Loves Me). w. Bud Green, m. Harry Warren, 1925. Introduced and recorded by Fred Waring's Pennsylvanians (Victor). Heard in (MM) *The Joker Is Wild,* 1957.

I Love My Friend. w/m Billy Sherrill and Norro Wilson, 1974. Crossover (C&W/Pop) hit record by Charlie Rich (Epic).

I Love My Wife. w. Michael Stewart, m. Cy Coleman, 1977. Title song of (TM) *I Love My Wife,* introduced by Lenny Baker and James Naughton. Leading record by Frank Sinatra (Reprise).

I Love My Wife, But Oh, You Kid! w/m Harry Armstrong and Billy Clark, 1909.

I Love Paris. w/m Cole Porter, 1953. Introduced by Lilo in (TM) *Can-Can.* Leading recording by Les Baxter and his Orchestra (Capitol). Frank Sinatra and Maurice Chevalier sang it in the film version (MM) *Can-Can,* 1960.

I Love Rock 'n' Roll. w/m Jake Hooker and Alan Merrill, 1982. Originally recorded by the British-based band, The Arrows, and written by two of its members, it was an answer to the Rolling Stone's "It's Only Rock 'n' Roll (But I Like It)" (q.v.). The song did not attain popularity, but the writers, believing in it, re-recorded it for their group's British TV series. Joan Jett, touring England with an American band, heard the song and eventually recorded it with a new group, the Blackhearts (Boardwalk). It became the title song of the album, which was awarded a platinum record. The single was #1 for seven weeks, also earning a platinum record.

I Loves You, Porgy. w. Du Bose Heyward and Ira Gershwin, m. George Gershwin, 1935. Introduced by Anne Brown and Todd Duncan in the opera (TM) *Porgy and Bess.* Adele Addison, dubbing for Dorothy Dandridge in the role of Bess, sang it in (MM) *Porgy and Bess,* 1959, Nina Simone had a hit record (Bethlehem).

I Love the College Girls. w/m Moe Jaffe and Nat Box, 1926. Featured and recorded by Fred Waring's Pennsylvanians (Victor).

I Love the Girl. See **I Love the Guy.**

I Love the Guy. w/m Cy Coben, 1950. Best-sellers: Sarah Vaughan (Mercury) and Fran Warren (RCA Victor).

I Love the Ladies. w. Grant Clarke, m. Jean Schwartz, 1914.

I Love the Land of Old Black Joe. w. Grant Clarke, m. Walter Donaldson, 1920. Introduced by Marion Davies in (TM) *Ed Wynn's Carnival.*

I Love the Name of Mary. w. George Graff, Jr., m. Ernest R. Ball and Chauncey Olcott, 1910. From (TM) *Barry of Ballymore.*

I Love the Nightlife (Disco Round). w/m Alicia Bridges and Susan Hutcheson, 1978. Hit disco record by Alicia Bridges (Polydor).

I Love the Sunshine of Your Smile. w. Jack Hoffman, m. Jimmy MacDonald, 1951. Leading record by The Four Knights (Capitol).

I Love the Way You Love. w/m Berry Gordy, Jr. and Mikaljohn, 1960. Top 10 R&B and Pop chart record by Marv Johnson (United Artists).

I Love the Way You Say Goodnight. w/m Edward Pola and George Wyle, 1951. Introduced by Gene Nelson and Doris Day in (MM) *Lullaby of Broadway.*

I Love to Dance. w. Alan Bergman and Marilyn Bergman, m. Billy Goldenberg, 1978. Introduced by Vincent Gardenia and Dorothy Loudon in (TM) *Ballroom.* Sandy Duncan performed it in (TM) *Five, Six, Seven, Eight . . . Dance!* at the Radio City Music Hall in New York, 1983.

I Love to Dance with Annie. w/m Boudleaux Bryant and Felice Bryant, 1964. Country hit by Ernest Ashworth (Hickory).

I Love to Laugh. w/m Richard M. Sherman and Robert B. Sherman, 1963. Introduced by Julie Andrews, Dick Van Dyke, and Ed Wynn in (MM) *Mary Poppins.*

I Love to See You Smile. w/m Randy Newman, 1989. Sung on soundtrack of (MP) *Parenthood.* Academy Award nomination for Best Song.

I Love to Sing-A. w. E. Y. Harburg, m. Harold Arlen, 1936. Cab Calloway joined with Al Jolson in presenting this in (MM) *The Singing Kid.* Calloway recorded it (Brunswick).

I Love You. w/m Derek Holt, 1981. Recorded by the British quintet The Climax Blues Band (Warner Bros.).

I Love You. w/m Chris White, 1968. English song recorded by the California sextet People (Capitol).

I Love You. w/m Billy Barton, 1954. Top 10 Country chart record, vocal by Ginny Wright, narration by Jim Reeves (Fabor).

I Love You. w/m Cole Porter, 1944. Introduced by Wilbur Evans in (TM) *Mexican Hayride.* Bing Crosby's record (Decca) was #1 for five weeks. Other popular versions by Enric Madriguera and his Orchestra (Hit), Jo Stafford (Capitol), Perry Como (Victor).

I Love You. w/m Robert Wright and George Forrest, 1943. Adapted from "Ich Liebe Dich" by Edvard Grieg, this was introduced in the musical based on the life of the composer (TM) *Song of Norway,* by Helena Bliss, Walter Kingsford, Ivy Scott, and the chorus.

I Love You. w. Harlan Thompson, m. Harry Archer, 1923. Introduced by Nan Halperin and Jay Velie in (TM) *Little Jessie James.* This song was the most popular show tune of the year. Paul Whiteman, whose band was in the pit, had the leading record (Victor).

I Love You, Don't You Forget It. See **Don't You Forget It.**

I Love You, I Love You, I Love You (Sweetheart of All My Dreams). See

Sweetheart of All My Dreams (I Love You, I Love You, I Love You).

I Love You, Samantha. w/m Cole Porter, 1956. Introduced by Bing Crosby in (MM) *High Society.*

I Love You, Yes I Do. w/m Sally Nix and Henry Glover, 1947. Introduced and best-selling record by Bull Moose Jackson (King). Sammy Kaye, vocal by Don Cornell, had a chart record (RCA Victor). Jackson re-recorded it (7 Arts), 1961.

I Love You a Thousand Ways. w/m Jim Beck and Lefty Frizzell, 1951. Introduced and recorded by Lefty Frizzell (Columbia).

I Love You Babe. w/m Babyface and L. A. Reid, 1987. Top 10 R&B chart record by Babyface (Solar).

I Love You Because. w/m Leon Payne, 1950, 1963. Hit C&W records by Leon Payne (Capitol) and Ernest Tubb (Decca). Al Martino had a Top 10 Pop chart hit in 1963 (Capitol).

I-Love-You Drops. w/m Bill Anderson, 1966. Introduced and hit Country record by Bill Anderson (Decca). Also recorded by Leroy Pullins (Kapp). Top 40 Pop chart version by Bill Dana (Dolton).

I Love You for All Seasons. w/m Sheila Young, 1971. Recorded by the female trio, Fuzz, of whom Young was a member (Calla).

I Love You in the Same Old Way—Darling Sue. w. Walter H. Ford, m. John W. Bratton, 1896. Featured by the minstrel tenor Dick José.

I Love You Madly. w/m Charles Jones, 1955. Introduced by R&B team Charlie and Ray (Herald). Top 40 best-seller by The Four Coins (Epic). Revived by The Fantastic Four in 1968 (Soul).

I Love You More and More Every Day. w/m Don Robertson, 1964. Top 10 record by Al Martino (Capitol).

I Love You More Today. w/m L. E. White, 1969. Country record hit by Conway Twitty (Decca).

I Love You Much Too Much. w. Don Raye (Engl.), m. Alex Olshey and Chaim Towber, 1940. Original Yiddish lyrics by Olshey and Towber. Leading record by Bob Zurke and his Delta Rhythm Band, vocal by Evelyn Poe (Victor).

I Love You 1000 Times. w/m Luther Dixon, 1966. Recorded by The Platters (Musicor).

I Love You So (The Merry Widow Waltz). w. Adrian Ross, m. Franz Lehar, 1907. Introduced in the U.S. by Ethel Jackson and Donald Brian in (TM) *The Merry Widow,* one of the most enduring operettas of all time. Coincidentally, the two hits from the show, this and "Vilia," start with the same four notes of the scale. Jeanette MacDonald and Maurice Chevalier sang this in (MM) *The Merry Widow,* 1934. It was heard again in the 1952 version with Lana Turner (voice dubbed by Trudy Erwin) and Fernando Lamas performing.

I Love You So Much. w. Bert Kalmar, m. Harry Ruby, 1930. Sung by Bert Wheeler and Dorothy Lee in (MM) *The Cuckoos.* In the Kalmar and Ruby screen biography (MM) *Three Little Words,* 1950, it was sung by Arlene Dahl and a male chorus. In its first year, it was recorded by the Arden-Ohman Orchestra (Victor), Smith Ballew (Okeh), Bob Haring (Brunswick), Eddie Walters (Columbia). Revived by Vicki Young (Capitol), 1953.

I Love You So Much It Hurts. w/m Floyd Tillman, 1948. C&W song introduced by Floyd Tillman (Columbia), followed by hit record by Jimmy Wakely (Capitol). The song "crossed over" to the Pop market and had chart records by The Mills Brothers (Decca); Buddy Clark (Columbia); and "The British Vaughn Monroe," Reggie Goff, with Cyril Stapleton's Orchestra (London).

I Love You This Morning. w. Alan Jay Lerner, m. Frederick Loewe, 1945. Introduced by Bill Johnson and Irene Manning in (TM) *The Day Before Spring.*

I Love You Truly. w/m Carrie Jacobs-Bond, 1906. While originally published in 1901 as part of "Seven Songs," it was not until it was reprinted as a separate selection that it became a big sheet music seller. It has enjoyed lasting popularity and is frequently played at weddings as the first dance of the bride and groom. Bing Crosby's 1934 recording of the song was the initial release by the new label, Decca.

I'm a Believer. w/m Neil Diamond, 1966. Gold record by The Monkees (Colgems). Revived by Neil Diamond (Bang), 1971.

I'm a Better Man (for Having Loved You). w. Hal David, m. Burt Bacharach, 1969. Top 40 record by Engelbert Humperdinck (Parrot).

I'm a Big Girl Now. w/m Al Hoffman, Milton Drake, and Jerry Livingston, 1946. #1 record by Sammy Kaye, vocal by Betty Barclay (Victor).

I'm a Black Sheep Who's Blue. w. Leo Robin, m. Ralph Rainger, 1934. Introduced by Dorothy Dell in (MM) *Little Miss Marker*.

I Made It Through the Rain. w/m Jack Feldman, Gerald Kenny, Barry Manilow, Drey Shepperd, Bruce Sussman, 1980. Top 10 record by Barry Manilow (Arista).

I'm a Ding Dong Daddy from Dumas. w/m Phil Baxter, 1930. Early recordings by Louis Armstrong (Okeh), Ben Pollack (Perfect), and Bob Wills, the King of Western Swing (Vocalion). Played by The Benny Goodman Quartet in (MM) *Hollywood Hotel*, 1937.

I'm a Dreamer, Aren't We All? w. B. G. DeSylva and Lew Brown, m. Ray Henderson, 1929. Sung by Janet Gaynor accompanying herself on a zither in (MM) *Sunny Side Up*.

I'm a Drifter. w/m Bobby Goldsboro, 1969. C&W/Pop success by Bobby Goldsboro (United Artists).

I'm a Fool. w/m Joey Cooper and Red West, 1965. Top 20 record by Dino, Desi and Billy (Reprise).

I'm a Fool for Loving You. w. Sam M. Lewis, m. Pete Wendling, 1936. Band recordings by: Fletcher Henderson (Victor), Ted Fio Rito (Decca), Leo Reisman (Brunswick), Jack Shilkret (Melotone).

I'm a Fool to Care. w/m Ted Daffan, 1954. Introduced six years earlier by Ted Daffan. Les Paul and Mary Ford revived it and had a Top 10 record (Capitol).

I'm a Fool to Want You. w/m Jack Wolf, Joel Herron, and Frank Sinatra, 1951. Introduced and recorded by Frank Sinatra (Columbia). Also featured and recorded by Billy Eckstine (MGM).

I'm Afraid the Masquerade Is Over. See **Masquerade Is Over, The.**

I'm Afraid to Come Home in the Dark. w. Harry H. Williams, m. Egbert Van Alstyne, 1907.

Image of a Girl. w. Marvin Rosenberg, m. Richard Clasky, 1960. Top 10 record by The Safaris, two of whom wrote the song (Eldo).

Image of You, The. w. Joe Young, m. Fred E. Ahlert, 1937.

Imaginary Lover. w/m Buddy Buie, Robert Nix, and Dean Daughtry, 1978. Top 10 record by The Atlanta Rhythm Section (Polydor).

Imagination. w. Johnny Burke, m. James Van Heusen, 1940. No. 1 hit song with best-selling record by Glenn Miller, vocal by Ray Eberle (Bluebird).

Imagination. w. Irving Caesar, m. Roger Wolfe Kahn and Joseph Meyer, 1928. Introduced by Irene Delroy and Allen Kearns in (TM) *Here's Howe*. Ben Bernie, who appeared in the show, recorded it with his Orchestra (Brunswick), as did Miff Mole (Okeh), The Charleston Chasers (Columbia), the bands of Roger Wolfe Kahn (Victor), Harry Reser (Columbia), both of which coupled it with "Crazy Rhythm" (q.v.) from the same show.

Imagine. w/m John Lennon, 1971. Top 10 record by John Lennon/Plastic Ono Band (Apple).

Imagine That. w/m Justin Tubb, 1962. Introduced and recorded by Patsy Cline (Decca).

I'm a Happy Man. w/m Casey Spencer, 1965. Recorded by The Jive Five (United Artists).

I'm a Hundred Percent for You. w. Mitchell Parish and Irving Mills, m. Ben Oakland, 1935. Featured and recorded by Fats Waller (Victor), Benny Goodman (Columbia), Don Bestor (Brunswick).

I Make a Fool of Myself. w/m Bob Crewe and Bob Gaudio, 1967. Top 20 record by Frankie Valli (Philips).

I'm a Little Blackbird Looking for a Bluebird. W. Grant Clarke and Roy Turk, m. George W. Meyer and Arthur Johnston, 1924. Introduced by Florence Mills in the revue (TM) *Dixie to Broadway.* Eva Taylor with Clarence Williams's Orchestra had a popular recording (Okeh).

I'm Alive. w/m Clint Ballard, Jr., 1980. Gold record by the British group Electric Light Orchestra (MCA).

I'm All Bound 'Round with the Mason Dixon Line. w. Sam M. Lewis and Joe Young, m. Jean Schwartz, 1917. Recorded (Victor) and featured by Al Jolson; also recorded by Irving Kaufman (Columbia).

I'm All Smiles. w. Herbert Martin, m. Michael Leonard, 1965. Sung by Carmen Alvarez in (TM) *The Yearling.* Introduced and recorded by Barbra Streisand (Columbia).

I'm Alone Because I Love You. w/m Ira Schuster and Joe Young, 1930. Popular waltz. Recorded by "Bud Billings," pseudonym for Frank Luther (Victor).

I'm a Lonely Little Petunia (in an Onion Patch). w/m John N. Kamano, William E. Faber, and Maurice Merl, 1946. Canadian novelty recorded by Two-Ton Baker and his Music Makers (Mercury).

I'm a Lonesome Fugitive. See **Fugitive, The.**

I'm A Lonesome Little Raindrop (Looking for a Place to Fall). w. Joe Goodwin and Murray Roth, m. James F. Hanley, 1920. Introduced by Frank Crumit in (TM) *Greenwich Follies of 1920,* and on records (Columbia).

I'm a Long Gone Daddy. w/m Hank Williams, 1948. Hit Country chart record by Hank Williams (MGM).

I'm Alright. w/m Kenny Loggins, 1980. Theme from (MP) *Caddyshack.* Top 10 record by Kenny Loggins (Columbia).

I'm Always Chasing Rainbows. w. Joseph McCarthy, m. Harry Carroll, 1917, 1946. The hit song from (TM) *Oh, Look!* was introduced by Harry Fox. The melody is taken from Chopin's *Fantaisie Impromptu in C# Minor.* The song has been used in many films, among them (MM) *Rose of Washington Square,* 1939; (MM) *Ziegfeld Girl,* sung by Judy Garland and Charles Winninger, 1941; (MM) *Nobody's Darling,* 1943; (MM) *The Merry Monahans,* 1944; (MM) *The Dolly Sisters* in which John Payne sang it, 1946. Perry Como then had a hit record (RCA Victor), and the revived song was on "Your Hit Parade" for twelve weeks.

I'm Always Hearing Wedding Bells. w. Robert Mellin (Engl.), Fred Rauch (Ger.), m. Herbert Jaarczyk, 1955. Originally titled "Hochzeitsglocken," from the German film of the same name. Recorded by Eddie Fisher (RCA Victor).

I'm Always on a Mountain When I Fall. w/m Chuck Howard, 1978. Top 10 Country chart record by Merle Haggard (Capitol).

I'm a Man. w/m Jimmy Miller and Steve Winwood, 1967. Top 10 U.S. release from England by the Spencer Davis Group (United Artists).

I'm a Man. w/m Ellas McDaniel, 1965. Top 20 record by the English group The Yardbirds (Epic).

I'm a Man. w/m Doc Pomus and Mort Shuman, 1959. Recorded by Fabian (Chancellor).

I'm a Midnight Mover. w/m Wilson Pickett and Bobby Womack, 1968. Top 40 record by Wilson Pickett (Atlantic).

I'm an Indian. w. Blanche Merrill, m. Leo Edwards, 1920. Introduced by Fanny Brice in (TM) *Ziegfeld Follies of 1922*, and recorded by her (Victor), 1922. Brice sang it in (MM) *My Man*, 1928.

I'm an Indian Too. w/m Irving Berlin, 1946. Introduced by Ethel Merman in (TM) *Annie Get Your Gun*. Sung in the film version (MM) *Annie Get Your Gun*, 1950, by Betty Hutton.

I'm an Old, Old Man. w/m Lefty Frizzell, 1952. Introduced and recorded by Lefty Frizzell (Columbia).

I'm an Old Cow Hand (from the Rio Grande). w/m Johnny Mercer, 1936. Bing Crosby introduced it in (MM) *Rhythm on the Range* and had a hit recording (Decca). Roy Rogers sang it in (MM) *King of the Cowboys* in 1943 and recorded it with the Sons of the Pioneers (Decca).

I'm an Ordinary Man. w. Alan Jay Lerner, m. Frederick Loewe, 1956. Introduced by Rex Harrison in (TM) *My Fair Lady*, and sung by him in the film version (MM) *My Fair Lady*, 1964.

I'm a Nut. w/m Leroy Pullins, 1966. Novelty Country and Pop chart hit by Leroy Pullins (Kapp). Produced by Robert Lissauer and Billy Edd Wheeler.

I'm a One Woman Man. w/m Johnny Horton, 1957. Introduced and recorded by Johnny Horton (Columbia).

I'm a People. w/m Dallas Frazier, 1966. Top 10 Country chart song by George Jones (Musicor).

I'm a Popular Man. w/m George M. Cohan, 1907. Introduced by Cohan in his musical (TM) *The Honeymooners*.

I'm a Ramblin' Man. w/m Ray Pennington, 1974. Country hit and Pop chart entry by Waylon Jennings (RCA).

(I'm a) Road Runner. w/m Brian Holland, Lamont Dozier, and Eddie Holland, 1966. Top 20 record by Jr. Walker and The All Stars (Soul).

I Married an Angel. w. Lorenz Hart, m. Richard Rodgers, 1938. Introduced by Dennis King in (TM) *I Married an Angel*. In 1942, it was sung as the title song in (MM) *I Married an Angel*, the last film to star the team of Jeanette MacDonald and Nelson Eddy.

I'm a Shy Guy. w/m Nat Cole, 1945. Featured and recorded by The King Cole Trio (Capitol).

I'm a Stand by My Woman Man. w/m Kent Robbins, Billy Sherrill, and Tammy Wynette, 1976. Hit Country record by Ronnie Milsap (RCA).

I'm a Stranger Here Myself. w. Ogden Nash, m. Kurt Weill, 1943. Introduced by Mary Martin in (TM) *One Touch of Venus*. Not used in film.

I'm Available. w/m Dave Burgess, 1957. Popular record by Margie Rayburn (Liberty). Not to be confused with song of the same title from (TM) *Mr. Wonderful*.

I'm Available. w/m Jerry Bock, Larry Holofcener, and George David Weiss, 1956. Introduced by Chita Rivera in (TM) *Mr. Wonderful*.

I'm a Vamp from East Broadway. w/m Bert Kalmar, Harry Ruby, and Irving Berlin, 1920. Comedy song performed by Fanny Brice in (TM) *Ziegfeld Follies of 1920*.

I'm Awfully Glad I Met You. w. Jack Drislane, m. George W. Meyer, 1909.

I'm a Woman. w/m Mike Stoller and Jerry Leiber, 1963. Featured and recorded by Peggy Lee (Capitol). Revived by Maria Muldaur (Reprise), 1975.

I'm a Yankee Doodle Dandy. See **Yankee Doodle Boy, The.**

I May Be Crazy But I Ain't No Fool. w/m Alex Rogers, 1904. Featured by Williams and Walker in vaudeville.

I May Be Dancing with Somebody Else. w/m Jack Little, Dave Oppenheim, and Ira Schuster, 1933. Introduced and featured by Little Jack Little. Recorded by Will Osborne and his Orchestra (Melotone).

I May Be Gone for a Long, Long Time. w. Lew Brown, m. Albert Von Tilzer, 1917. Introduced by Grace LaRue in (TM) *Hitchy-Koo*.

I May Be Wrong (But I Think You're Wonderful). w. Harry Ruskin, m. Henry Sullivan, 1929. This standard, the only hit song by either writer, was introduced by Jimmy Savo and Trixie Friganza in the revue (TM) *John Murray Anderson's Almanac*. It was interpolated in numerous motion pictures, among them were (MM) *Swingtime Johnny* in 1943; (MM) *You're My Everything*, sung by Dan Dailey, 1949; (MM) *Young Man with a Horn*, sung by Doris Day, 1950; (MM) *Sunny Side of the Street*, 1951; and *Starlift*, sung by Jane Wyman, 1951.

I May Never Get to Heaven. w/m Buddy Killen and Bill Anderson, 1979. Introduced and recorded by Don Gibson (RCA), 1960. #1 C&W chart hit by Conway Twitty (MCA), 1979.

I'm Bad. 1987. Top 10 R&B chart record by L. L. Cool J, pseudonym for rap artist James Todd Smith (Def Jam).

I'm Beginning to See the Light. w/m Edward Kennedy "Duke" Ellington, Don George, Johnny Hodges, Harry James, 1944. #1 record by Harry James, vocal by Kitty Kallen (Columbia). Other Top 10 versions by Ella Fitzgerald and The Ink Spots (Decca) and Duke Ellington, vocal by Joya Sherrill (Victor). Song eleven weeks on "Your Hit Parade," twice as #1.

I'm Bitin' My Fingernails and Thinking of You. w/m Ernest Tubb, Roy West, Ernest Benedict, and Lenny Sanders, 1949. Popular recording by Ernest Tubb and The Andrews Sisters (Decca).

I'm Blue (The Gong-Gong Song). w/m Ike Turner, 1962. Introduced in the nightclub and theater act, "The Ike and Tina Turner Revue," by The Ikettes and recorded by them (Atco).

I'm Bringing a Red, Red Rose. w. Gus Kahn, m. Walter Donaldson, 1928. Introduced by Frances Upton and Paul Gregory in (TM) *Whoopee*. Recorded by Ruth Etting (Columbia), Paul Whiteman (Victor), Ben Bernie (Brunswick), and B. A. Rolfe (Edison).

I'm Building Up to an Awful Letdown. w. Johnny Mercer, m. Fred Astaire, 1936. Recorded by Fred Astaire (Brunswick), Red McKenzie (Decca), Little Ramblers (Bluebird).

I'm Checking Out—Go'om Bye. w/m Billy Strayhorn and Edward Kennedy "Duke" Ellington, 1939. Recorded by Duke Ellington, with vocal by Ivy Anderson and Sonny Greer (Columbia).

I'm Coming Home. w/m Linda Creed and Thom Bell, 1974. Introduced by Johnny Mathis (Columbia), 1973. Top 20 record by The Spinners (Atlantic).

I'm Coming Home. w/m Johnny Horton, 1957. Introduced and recorded by Johnny Horton (Columbia).

I'm Coming Out. w/m Bernard Edwards and Nile Rodgers, 1980. Top 10 record by Diana Ross (Motown).

I'm Coming Virginia. w. Will Marion Cook and Donald Heywood, m. Donald Heywood, 1927. Interpolated by Ethel Waters in the revue (TM) *Africana*, and recorded by her (Columbia). Paul Whiteman, with vocal by The Rhythm Boys [Bing Crosby, Harry Barris, and Chuck Rinker] had a popular record that year (Victor). It was revived in 1937 by Maxine Sullivan with Claude Thornhill's arrangement and musical direction (Vocalion), coupled with their big hit "Loch Lomond" (q.v.). Two years later, Artie Shaw had a successful record (Bluebird). Sung by Warren Beatty in (MP) *Mickey One*, 1965.

I'm Comin' Home, Cindy. w/m Trini Lopez and Phil Zeller, 1966. Introduced and recorded by Trini Lopez (Reprise).

I'm Confessin' That I Love You. w. Al J. Neiburg, m. Doc Daugherty and Ellis Reynolds, 1930. First popular record by Louis Armstrong (Okeh).

I'm Counting on You. w. Milton Drake, m. Ben Oakland, 1934. Recorded by Paul Whiteman and his Orchestra, vocal by Ramona (Victor).

I'm Crazy 'bout My Baby. w. Alex Hill, m. Thomas "Fats" Waller, 1931. Introduced by Ted Lewis and his Band with Fats Waller on piano (Columbia).

I'm Crying. w/m Eric Burdon and Alan Price, 1964. Introduced by the British group The Animals (MGM).

I'm Crying Just for You. w. Joseph McCarthy, m. James V. Monaco, 1913. Popular record (Victor) by Ada Jones and Billy Murray.

I'm Doin' Fine Now. w/m Thom Bell and Sherman Marshall, 1973. Top 20 record by the quartet New York City (Chelsea).

I'm Down in the Dumps. w/m Wesley Wilson, 1933. Recorded by Bessie Smith (Okeh).

I'm Down to My Last "I Love You." w/m Billy Sherrill and Glenn Sutton, 1969. Country hit, recorded by David Houston (Epic).

I'm Dreaming. w/m Richard Kerr and Gary Osborne, 1977. Recorded by Jennifer Warnes (Arista).

I'm Easy. w/m Keith Carradine, 1975. Introduced by Keith Carradine in (MM) *Nashville* and on a Top 20 recording by Keith Carradine. The song won an Academy Award, 1975.

I Met Her in Church. w/m Dan Pennington and Dewey Lindon Oldham, 1968. Top 40 record by The Box Tops (Mala).

I Met Her on Monday. w. Charles Newman, m. Allie Wrubel, 1942. Most popular record by Freddy Martin, vocal by Eddie Stone (Victor).

I'm Every Woman. w/m Nick Ashford and Valerie Simpson, 1978. Recorded by Chaka Khan (Warner Bros.).

I'm Falling in Love with Someone. w. Rida Johnson Young, m. Victor Herbert, 1910. Introduced by Orville Harrold in (TM) *Naughty Marietta*. In the film (MM) *Naughty Marietta*, 1935, it was sung by Nelson Eddy. Allan Jones sang it in (MM) *The Great Victor Herbert*, 1939.

I'm Fascinating. w. Lee Adams, m. Charles Strouse, 1962. Sung and soft-shoe danced by Ray Bolger in (TM) *All American*.

I'm Feeling Fine. w/m Paul Williams, 1976. Sung by Paul Williams in the British film (MM) *Bugsy Malone*.

I'm Feelin' Like a Million. w. Arthur Freed, m. Nacio Herb Brown, 1937. Introduced by Eleanor Powell and George Murphy in (MM) *Broadway Melody of 1938*.

I'm Fit to Be Tied. w/m Walter Donaldson, 1939. Introduced by Ginny Simms in (MM) *That's Right—You're Wrong* and recorded by her (Vocalion).

I'm Flying. w. Carolyn Leigh, m. Moose Charlap, 1954. Introduced by Mary Martin, Kathy Nolan, Robert Harrington, and Joseph Stafford in (TM) *Peter Pan*. Sandy Duncan performed it in her revue at The Radio City Music Hall, *Five-Six-Seven-Eight . . . Dance!* 1983.

I'm Following You. w. Ballard MacDonald, m. Dave Dreyer, 1930. Introduced by the Duncan Sisters in (MM) *It's a Great Life* and their vocal performance was preserved on wax (Victor).

I'm Forever Blowing Bubbles. w. Jean Kenbrovin, m. John W. Kellette, 1919. The song was interpolated in (TM) *The Passing Show*. The lyricist's name is a combined pseudonym for James Kendis, James Brockman, and Nat Vincent who had contractual publishing conflicts at the time. The song became one of the biggest hits of the day. The leading record was by Ben Selvin's Novelty Orchestra

(Victor). The song later was heard in (MM) *The Great American Broadcast*, 1941, and in (MM) *On Moonlight Bay*, 1951, sung by Jack Smith.

I'm for Love. w/m Hank Williams, Jr., 1985. #1 Country chart record by Hank Williams, Jr. (Warner Bros.).

I'm for Real. w/m Howard Hewett and Stanley Clark, 1986. Recorded by Howard Hewett (Elektra).

I'm for You One Hundred Percent. w. James Dyrenforth and Billy Rose, m. Carroll Gibbons, 1931. Recorded by Ted Weems and his Orchestra, vocal by Parker Gibbs (Victor); Smith Ballew (Crown); Roy Fox (Br. Decca, released in U.S.).

I'm Free. w/m Peter Townshend, 1969. Introduced in the recorded rock opera *Tommy*, by The Who (Decca). A single was released and reached the Top 40. A film version (MM) *Tommy* was made and released in 1975.

I'm Gettin' Better. w/m Jim Reeves, 1960. Featured and recorded by Jim Reeves (RCA).

I'm Getting Myself Ready for You. w/m Cole Porter, 1930. Sung by Frances Williams, Barrie Oliver, Ann Pennington, and Maurice Lapue in (TM) *The New Yorkers*. Emil Coleman and his Orchestra coupled the recording with "Where Have You Been?" (q.v.) from the same show (Brunswick).

I'm Getting Tired So I Can Sleep. w/m Irving Berlin, 1942. Introduced by Pvt. William Horne in (TM) *This Is the Army*, the all-soldier show organized to benefit the Army Emergency Relief Fund. In the film version (MM) *This Is the Army*, it was sung by Sgt. James Burell. Best-selling recording by Jimmy Dorsey, vocal by Bob Eberly (Decca).

I'm Gettin' Sentimental over You. w. Ned Washington, m. George Bassman, 1932. First recorded by the Dorsey Brothers Orchestra (Brunswick). Tommy Dorsey adopted it as his theme song and it has remained identified with him. His recording (Victor) has been a longtime best-seller. The number was heard in (MM) *Keep*

'*Em Flying* in 1941. Dorsey and his Band played it as an instrumental in (MM) *Du Barry Was a Lady* in 1943 and in (MM) *A Song Is Born* in 1948.

I'm Glad I'm Not Young Anymore. w. Alan Jay Lerner, m. Frederick Loewe, 1958. Introduced by Maurice Chevalier in (MM) *Gigi*, and sung by Alfred Drake in the stage version (TM) *Gigi*, 1973.

I'm Glad I Waited for You. w. Sammy Cahn, m. Jule Styne, 1946. Introduced by Alfred Drake in (MM) *Tars and Spars*. Best-selling recordings: Peggy Lee (Capitol), Frankie Carle and his Orchestra (Columbia), Helen Forrest (Decca), Freddy Martin, vocal by Clyde Rogers (Victor).

I'm Glad There Is You. w. Paul Medeira, m. Jimmy Dorsey, 1942. Among recordings that helped establish song were those by Jimmy Dorsey, vocal by Bob Eberly (Decca); Dennis Day (Capitol); Hazel Scott (Decca).

I'm Goin' Down. w/m Bruce Springsteen, 1985. Top 10 single by Bruce Springsteen (Columbia).

I'm Going to Wear You Off My Mind. w/m Clarence Johnson, Lloyd Smith, and Warren Smith, 1921. Recorded by Leona Williams (Columbia) and King Oliver (Gennett).

I'm Goin' Shoppin' with You. w. Al Dubin, m. Harry Warren, 1935. Introduced by Dick Powell in (MM) *The Gold Diggers of 1935* and on records (Brunswick). Winifred Shaw, who was in the motion picture, recorded it with Dick Jurgens's Orchestra (Decca). Others: Russ Morgan (Perfect) and Little Jack Little (Columbia).

I'm Goin' South. w/m Abner Silver and Harry Woods, 1921. Harry Woods's first hit. Introduced by Al Jolson during run of (TM) *Bombo*. Upon completion of the road tour, both he (Brunswick) and Georgie Price (Victor) recorded the song. Jolson's version was coupled with "California Here I Come" (q.v.). Eddie Cantor interpolated it in (TM) *Kid Boots*, 1924.

I'm Gone. w/m Lester Lee and Dave Bartholomew, 1953. Leading R&B recording by Shirley and Lee (Aladdin).

I'm Gonna Be a Country Girl Again. w/m Buffy Sainte-Marie, 1971. Chart single and title song of Buffy Sainte-Marie's album (Vanguard).

I'm Gonna Be a Wheel Someday. w/m Dave Bartholomew and Antoine "Fats" Domino, 1959. Featured and recorded by Fats Domino (Imperial).

I'm Gonna Be Strong. w/m Barry Mann and Cynthia Weil, 1963. Top 10 record by Gene Pitney (Musicor).

I'm Gonna Be Warm This Winter. w/m Hank Hunter and Mark Barkan, 1963. Popularized by Connie Francis (MGM).

I'm Gonna Change Everything. w/m Alex Zanetis, 1962. Crossover hit (C&W/Pop) by Jim Reeves (RCA).

I'm Gonna Charleston Back to Charleston. w/m Roy Turk and Lou Handman, 1925. Popular song during the Charleston dance craze.

I'm Gonna Clap My Hands. w/m Mike Riley and Eddie Farley, 1936. While introduced and recorded by the band of the writers of "The Music Goes 'Round and 'Round," Riley and Farley (Decca), the best-selling version was by Gene Krupa, vocal by Helen Ward (Victor).

I'm Gonna Get Him. w/m Irving Berlin, 1962. Introduced in Berlin's last show score (TM) *Mr. President*, by Nanette Fabray and Anita Gillette.

I'm Gonna Get Married. w/m Harold Logan and Lloyd Price, 1959. Introduced and hit record by Lloyd Price (ABC-Paramount).

I'm Gonna Get You. w/m Dennis Linde, 1988. #1 Country chart song by Eddy Raven (RCA).

I'm Gonna Get You. w/m Gus Arnheim, Harry Tobias, and Jules Lemare, 1931. Introduced and recorded by Gus Arnheim and his Orchestra, with vocal by Bing Crosby (Victor).

I'm Gonna Go Fishin'. w. Peggy Lee, m. Edward Kennedy "Duke" Ellington, 1960. Based on a theme from the background music of (MP) *Anatomy of a Murder*. Introduced and recorded by Peggy Lee (Capitol).

I'm Gonna Hire a Wino to Decorate Our Home. w/m De Wayne Blackwell, 1982. Country chart hit by David Frizzell (Warner Bros.).

I'm Gonna Knock on Your Door. w/m Aaron Schroeder and Sid Wayne, 1961. Recorded by Eddie Hodges (Cadence).

I'm Gonna Laugh You Right out of My Life. w. Joseph Allan McCarthy, m. Cy Coleman, 1956. Featured and recorded by Nat "King" Cole (Capitol).

I'm Gonna Live Till I Die. w/m Al Hoffman, Walter Kent, and Mann Curtis, 1950. Introduced on records by Danny Scholl (National). Frankie Laine had the first chart version (Mercury). The song has been a favorite "big" opening number for singers in nightclubs.

I'm Gonna Lock My Heart (and Throw Away the Key). w. Jimmy Eaton, m. Terry Shand, 1938. Kay Kyser and his Orchestra (Brunswick) and Al Donahue, vocal by Paula Kelly (Vocalion), had popular records.

I'm Gonna Love Her for the Both of Us. w/m Jim Steinman, 1981. Recorded by Meat Loaf (Epic).

I'm Gonna Love That Gal. See **I'm Gonna Love That Guy.**

I'm Gonna Love That Guy. w/m Frances Ash, 1945. An English song recorded by Marion Hutton, with Randy Brooks's Orchestra (Decca); Benny Goodman, vocal by Dottie Reid (Columbia). Perry Como recorded it as "I'm Gonna Love That Gal" (Victor).

I'm Gonna Love You Just a Little Bit More, Baby. w/m Barry White, 1973. Gold record by Barry White (20th Century).

I'm Gonna Make Hay While the Sun Shines in Virginia. w. Sam Lewis and Joe Young, m. Archie Gottler, 1916. Featured and recorded by Marion Harris (Victor).

I'm Gonna Make You Love Me. w/m Ken Gamble, Jerry Ross, and Jerry Williams, 1968. First recorded by Dee Dee Warwick (Mercury), 1966. Top 40 record by Madeline Bell (Philips), 1968, followed by a #2 chart hit by Diana Ross and The Supremes and The Temptations (Motown), 1969.

I'm Gonna Make You Mine. w/m Tony Romeo, 1969. Top 10 record by Lou Christie (Buddah).

I'm Gonna Meet My Sweetie Now. w. Benny Davis, m. Jesse Greer, 1927. Popular records by Kate Smith (Columbia) and Jean Goldkette's Orchestra (Victor).

I'm Gonna Miss You, Girl. w/m Jesse Winchester, 1988. Top 10 Country chart record by Michael Martin Murphey (Warner Bros.).

I'm Gonna Move On. w/m Warner McPherson, 1968. Written and Top 10 Country chart record by Warner Mack (Decca).

I'm Gonna Move to the Outskirts of Town. w/m William Weldon and Andy Razaf, 1942. Introduced and recorded by Louis Jordan and his Tympany Five (Decca). Some other popular recordings by Big Bill Broonzy (Okeh), then re-released (Columbia); Jimmy Lunceford, vocal by Dan Grissom (Decca 1 & 2); Count Basie, vocal by Jimmy Rushing (Columbia); Louis Jordan with his Orchestra (Decca); Ray Charles (Impulse), 1961.

I'm Gonna Pin My Medal on the Girl I Left Behind. w/m Irving Berlin, 1918.

I'm Gonna Play the Honky Tonks. w/m Marie Adams and Don D. Robey, 1952. R&B hit, recorded by Marie Adams (Peacock).

I'm Gonna See My Baby. w/m Phil Moore, 1945. Recorded by Johnny Mercer (Capitol), Jimmie Lunceford and his Orchestra (Decca), Webb Pierce (Decca).

I'm Gonna Sit Right Down and Write Myself a Letter. w. Joe Young, m. Fred E. Ahlert, 1936, 1957. Recorded by and associated with Fats Waller (Victor). Also recorded by Ted Weems's Band (Decca) and the Boswell Sisters (Decca). Connee Boswell later made a solo single (Decca) as did Johnny Mercer (Capitol). In 1957, Billy Williams revived it with a hit record (Coral). Ken Page performed the song in the Fats Waller musical (TM) *Ain't Misbehavin'*, 1978.

I'm Gonna Tear Your Playhouse Down. w/m Earl Randle, 1972. Introduced by Ann Peebles in her album "Straight from the Heart" (Hi). Top 20 record by the English singer Paul Young (Columbia), 1985.

I'm Gonna Walk and Talk with My Lord. w/m Martha Carson, 1953. Leading record by Johnnie Ray (Columbia).

I'm Gonna Wash That Man Right Outa My Hair. w. Oscar Hammerstein II, m. Richard Rodgers, 1949. Introduced by Mary Martin, and reprised by Ezio Pinza in (TM) *South Pacific*. In (MM) *South Pacific*, 1958, it was sung by Mitzi Gaynor.

I'm Growing Fonder of You. w. Joe Young, m. George W. Meyer, and Pete Wendling, 1935. Recordings: Fats Waller (Victor), Connie Boswell (Brunswick), Archie Bleyer (Vocalion).

I'm Hans Christian Andersen. w/m Frank Loesser, 1952. Introduced by Danny Kaye in (MM) *Hans Christian Andersen*.

I'm Happy Just to Dance with You. w/m John Lennon and Paul McCartney, 1964. Introduced in (MM) *A Hard Day's Night*, and on records by The Beatles (Capitol).

I'm Happy That Love Has Found You. w/m Arthur Jacobson, Joseph La Pallo, and William Haberman, 1980. Top 40 record by Jimmy Hall (Epic).

I'm Henry VIII, I Am. w/m Fred Murray and R. P. Weston, 1965. Written in 1911, and featured by the English vaudevillian Harry

Champion. #1 hit and gold record by Herman's Hermits (MGM).

I'm Hip. w/m Dave Frishberg and Bob Dorough, 1965. Featured and recorded by Blossom Dearie (Fontana), Bob Dorough (Focus), Mel Tormé (Concord Jazz), and others.

I'm Hummin'—I'm Whistlin'—I'm Singin'. w. Mack Gordon, m. Harry Revel, 1934. Sung by Bing Crosby in (MM) *She Loves Me Not*.

I'm Hurtin'. w/m Roy Orbison and Joe Melson, 1961. Recorded by Roy Orbison (Monument).

(Yes) I'm Hurting. w/m Don Gibson, 1966. Top 10 Country record by Don Gibson (RCA).

I Might Be Your Once-in-a-While. w. Robert B. Smith, m. Victor Herbert, 1919. Introduced by John E. Young and Emilie Lea in (TM) *Angel Face*. Mary Martin sang it in (MM) *The Great Victor Herbert*, 1939.

I Might Fall Back on You. w. Oscar Hammerstein II, m. Jerome Kern, 1927. Originally titled, "Cheer Up," this was added to (TM) *Show Boat* during its run and performed by Eva Puck and Sammy White. Marge and Gower Champion sang and danced the number in the third film version (MM) *Show Boat*, 1951.

I'm in a Dancing Mood. w/m Al Hoffman, Al Goodhart, and Maurice Sigler, 1936. Introduced in the British film (MM) *This'll Make You Whistle* by Jack Buchanan and Elsie Randolph whose recording (Brunswick, Br.) was released in the United States. The English bandleader, Ambrose, also had a U.S. release (Decca).

I'm in Love. w/m Paul Laurence and Timmy Allen, 1987. Top 10 R&B chart record by Lillo Thomas, from her album "Lillo" (Capitol).

I'm in Love. w/m Kashif (pseud. for Michael Jones), 1981. Recorded by Evelyn "Champagne" King (RCA).

I'm in Love. w/m Bobby Womack, 1967. Recorded by Wilson Pickett (Atlantic). Revived by Aretha Franklin (Atlantic), 1974.

I'm in Love. w. Sammy Cahn, m. Jule Styne, 1948. Introduced by Doris Day in her film debut (MM) *Romance on the High Seas*.

I'm in Love. w. William LeBaron, m. Fritz Kreisler, 1919. From (TM) *Apple Blossoms*.

I'm in Love Again. w/m Vic McAlpin and George Morgan, 1959. C&W hit.

I'm in Love Again. w/m Antoine "Fats" Domino and Dave Bartholomew, 1956. Introduced and hit record by Fats Domino (Imperial). Popular version by The Fontane Sisters (Dot). Revived by Rick Nelson in 1963 (Imperial) and Pia Zadora in 1982 (Elektra).

I'm in Love Again. w/m Cole Porter, 1924, 1951. Sung by the Dolly Sisters and danced by James Naulty and Robert Alton in (TM) *Greenwich Follies of 1924* and repeated in the subsequent edition. Jane Wyman sang it in the Porter biography (MM) *Night and Day*, 1946. Revived with hit record by April Stevens (RCA Victor), 1951.

I'm in Love with Miss Logan. w/m Ronny Graham, 1952. Introduced by Robert Clary in (TM) *New Faces of 1952*, and repeated by him in (MM) *New Faces*, 1954.

I'm in Love with the Honorable Mr. So and So. w/m Sam Coslow, 1939. Sung by Virginia Bruce in (MP) *Society Lawyer* and popularized on records by Frances Langford (Decca), and the bands of Artie Shaw, vocal by Helen Forrest (Bluebird); Gray Gordon, vocal by Betty Bradley (Victor); Del Courtney (Vocalion).

I'm in Love with You. w. Paul Titsworth, m. Lynn F. Cowan, 1929. From (MM) *The Great Gabbo*, sung by Betty Compson and Donald Douglas.

I'm in Seventh Heaven. w/m Al Jolson, B. G. DeSylva, Lew Brown, and Ray Henderson, 1929. Sung by Jolson in (MM) *Say It with Songs*.

I'm in the Market for You. w. Joseph Mc-Carthy, m. James F. Hanley, 1930. Sung by Janet Gaynor and Charles Farrell in (MM) *High Society Blues*. Recorded by Louis Armstrong (Okeh), songwriter Sammy Fain (Velvetone), Bob Haring (Brunswick), the Keynoters (Key 12″), and later, Harry James (Columbia).

I'm in the Mood. w/m John Lee Hooker and Jules Taub, 1951. R&B record by John Lee Hooker (Modern).

I'm in the Mood for Love. w. Dorothy Fields, m. Jimmy McHugh, 1935. Introduced by Frances Langford in (MM) *Every Night at Eight*. She also sang it over the credits in (MM) *Palm Springs*, 1938. It was sung by Gloria DeHaven in (MP) *Between Two Women*, 1944, and Langford, again, in (MM) *People Are Funny*, 1946. Dean Martin sang it in (MM) *That's My Boy*, 1951. The song has been recorded over 500 times and has sold sheet music copies in the millions.

I'm into Something Good. w/m Gerry Goffin and Carole King, 1964. Hit record by the English group Herman's Hermits (MGM). Chart record by Earl-Jean (Colpix).

I'm in You. w/m Peter Frampton, 1977. Hit record by the English singer Peter Frampton (A&M).

I Miss a Little Miss. w. Tot Seymour, m. J. Fred Coots, 1930. Featured and recorded by Nick Lucas (Brunswick), Ben Selvin (Columbia), Seger Ellis (Columbia), Roy Smeck (Melotone).

I Missed Me. w/m Bill Anderson, 1960. Featured and recorded by Jim Reeves (RCA).

I Miss My Swiss (My Swiss Miss Misses Me). w. L. Wolfe Gilbert, m. Abel Baer, 1925. While the song was written for (TM) *Chauve Souris*, it was never used in the U.S. production, but became a hit in Paris and then, through vaudeville performances, be-

came a hit here. Featured and recorded by Ernest Hare and Billy Jones (Victor).

I Miss You. w/m Lynn Malsby, 1985. Top 10 single from the album "Meeting in the Ladies Room," by the female sextet Klymaxx (Constellation).

I Miss You Already. w/m Marvin Rainwater and Faron Young, 1957. Recorded by Faron Young (Capitol).

I Miss You Most of All. w. Joseph McCarthy, m. James V. Monaco, 1913.

I Miss You So. w/m Jimmy Henderson, Bertha Scott, and Sid Robin, 1940. Recorded by The Cats and The Fiddle (Bluebird). Top 40 revivals by Chris Connor (Atlantic), 1957; Paul Anka (ABC-Paramount), 1959; Little Anthony and The Imperials (DCP), 1965.

I'm Just a Country Boy. w/m Fred Hellerman and Marshall Barer, 1957. Introduced and recorded by Harry Belafonte (RCA Victor). Recorded in 1963 by George McCurn, arranged and conducted by Herb Alpert (A&M). Revived by Don Williams (Dot), 1977.

I'm Just a Lucky So and So. w. Mack David, m. Edward Kennedy "Duke" Ellington, 1946. Introduced and recorded by Duke Ellington, vocal by Al Hibbler (Victor). Also recorded by Herb Jeffries (Exclusive).

I'm Just an Old Chunk of Coal (But I'm Gonna Be a Diamond Some Day). w/m Billy Jo Shaver, 1981. Top 10 Country chart record by John Anderson (Warner Bros.).

I'm Just an Ordinary Human. w. Larry Yoell, m. Al Jacobs, 1934. Among recordings, the bands of: Tom Coakley (Victor), Art Kassel (Bluebird), Ozzie Nelson (Brunswick).

I'm Just a Singer (in a Rock and Roll Band). w/m John Lodge, 1973. Top 20 U.S. record by the British group The Moody Blues (Threshold).

I'm Just a Vagabond Lover. w/m Rudy Vallee and Leon Zimmerman, 1929. Introduced and recorded (Victor) by Rudy Vallee. It was the title song of his first film (MM) *Vagabond Lover* in 1929. He and his orchestra performed it the following year in the Ziegfeld supervised film (MM) *Glorifying the American Girl*.

I'm Just Me. w/m Glenn Martin, 1970. Country hit and Pop chart record by Charley Pride (RCA).

I'm Just Wild About Animal Crackers. w/m Fred Rich, Sam Coslow, and Harry Link, 1926. Popular recording by Irving Aaronson and His Commanders (Victor).

I'm Just Wild About Harry. w/m Noble Sissle and Eubie Blake, 1921. The big hit from (TM) *Shuffle Along*, sung by the chorus. In 1939, the song was interpolated in two major films (MM) *Babes in Arms*, by Mickey Rooney and Judy Garland in a minstrel sequence, and (MM) *Rose of Washington Square*, by Alice Faye and Louis Prima and his Band. It has also been heard in (MM) *Broadway*, 1942; (MM) *Is Everybody Happy?* 1943; and (MM) *Jolson Sings Again*, 1949, in which Jolson dubbed his voice on the soundtrack for Larry Parks. Tammy Grimes interpolated it in (TM) *A Musical Jubilee*, 1975.

I'm Just Your Fool. w/m Buddy Johnson, 1954. R&B hit by Buddy Johnson (Mercury).

I'm Keeping Company. w. Lucy Bender Sokole, m. Dave Dreyer and Vee Lawnhurst, 1931.

I'm Keeping Those Keepsakes for You. w. Richard B. Smith, m. Fred E. Ahlert, 1935. Among recordings, the bands of: Paul Whiteman (Victor), Charlie Barnet (Bluebird), Jimmie Grier (Brunswick), Art Kassel (Brunswick).

I'm Knee Deep in Daisies (and Head over Heels in Love). w/m Paul Ash, Larry Shay, and Joe Goodwin, 1925. Featured and recorded by George Olsen, vocal by Fran Frey and Bob Rice (Victor).

I'm Late. w. Bob Hilliard, m. Sammy Fain, 1951. Introduced by the voice of Bill Thompson on the soundtrack of Walt Disney's full-length animated cartoon (MM) *Alice in Wonderland*.

I'm Laughin'. w. Lew Brown, m. Jay Gorney, 1934. Sung by Nick (later Dick) Foran and Tess Gardella in (MM) *Stand Up and Cheer*. Recorded by Frank Luther (Melotone).

I'm Leaving It (All) Up to You. w/m Dewey Terry and Don F. Harris, 1963. #1 record by Dale and Grace (Montel). Donny and Marie Osmond had a million-selling version, with "all" inserted in the title (MGM), 1974.

I'm Like a Fish Out of Water. w. Paul Francis Webster, m. Harry Revel, 1943. Introduced by Ginny Simms in (MM) *Hit the Ice*, co-starring Abbott and Costello.

I'm Like a New Broom. w. Dorothy Fields, m. Arthur Schwartz, 1951. Introduced by Johnny Johnston in (TM) *A Tree Grows in Brooklyn*.

I'm Like a Ship Without a Sail. w/m James Brockman, James Kendis, 1919.

I'm Livin' in a Great Big Way. w. Dorothy Fields, m. Jimmy McHugh, 1935. Introduced by Bill Robinson and Jeni Le Gon in (MM) *Hooray for Love*. Top record by Benny Goodman, with vocal by Buddy Clark (Columbia).

I'm Livin' in Shame. w/m Henry Cosby, Berry Gordy, Pam Sawyer, R. Dean Taylor, and Frank Williams, 1969. Top 10 record by Diana Ross and The Supremes (Motown).

I'm Living in Two Worlds. w/m Jan Crutchfield, 1966. Top 10 C&W/Pop crossover record by Bonnie Guitar (Dot).

I'm Looking for a Guy Who Plays Alto and Baritone and Doubles on a Clarinet and Wears a Size 37 Suit. w/m Ozzie Nelson, 1940. Novelty about the plight of a bandleader having to replace an obese musician. Recorded by Ozzie Nelson and his Orchestra (Bluebird). Tied for longest title in this book. (See Alan Jay Lerner, Section III.)

I'm Looking for a Nice Young Fellow Who Is Looking for a Nice Young Girl. w. Jeff T. Branen, m. S. R. Henry, 1910.

I'm Looking Out the Window. w/m Don Raye, 1959. Featured and recorded by Peggy Lee, arranged by Jack Marshall (Capitol).

I'm Looking over a Four Leaf Clover. w. Mort Dixon, m. Harry Woods, 1927, 1948. A popular song with recordings by Nick Lucas (Brunswick), Ben Bernie (Brunswick), Jean Goldkette (Victor), the Revelers (Victor), Paul Specht (Columbia). In 1948, Art Mooney and his Orchestra's million-plus selling record (MGM) was responsible for the song making "Your Hit Parade" for fourteen weeks, twice in the #1 position. Al Jolson, dubbing for Larry Parks, sang it on the soundtrack of (MM) *The Jolson Story*, 1949. It was also heard, in a montage, in the remake of (MM) *The Jazz Singer*, 1952.

I'm Losing My Mind over You. w/m Al Dexter and James B. Paris, 1945. Featured and recorded by Al Dexter (Columbia) and Teddy Grace (Decca).

I'm Lost. w/m Otis René, 1944. First recorded by The King Cole Trio (Excelsior) and later by The Dinning Sisters (Capitol).

I'm Mad. w/m Willie Mabon, 1953. R&B hit by Willie Mabon (Chess).

I'm Madly in Love with You. w. Benny Davis, m. J. Fred Coots, 1938. Recorded by Cab Calloway (Vocalion), Erskine Hawkins (Bluebird).

I'm Making Believe. w. Mack Gordon, m. James V. Monaco, 1944. From (MM) *Sweet and Low Down*. Nominated for Academy Award. Ella Fitzgerald and The Ink Spots combined for a hit record (Decca).

I'm Mandy, Fly Me. w/m Eric Stewart, Graham Gouldman, and Kevin Godley, 1976. Written by three members of the British group 10cc (Mercury).

Immigrant, The. w/m Neil Sedaka and Phil Cody, 1975. Recorded by Neil Sedaka (Rocket), 1975.

Immigrant Song. w/m Robert Plant and Jimmy Page, 1971. Top 20 hit by Led Zeppelin (Atlantic).

I'm Missin' Mammy's Kissin' (and I Know She's Missin' Mine). w. Sidney Clare, m. Lew Pollack, 1921.

I'm Movin' On. w/m Hank Snow, 1950. Hank Snow's recording (RCA Victor) was #1 on the Country charts for four months.

I'm My Own Grandpaw (Grandmaw). w/m Dwight Latham and Moe Jaffe, 1948. Novelty, with best-selling records by Guy Lombardo, vocal by Don Rodney (Decca); Tony Pastor, with The Clooney Sisters, Rosemary and Betty (Columbia); "Grandmaw" lyric sung by Jo Stafford, with The Starlighters and Paul Weston's Mountain Boys (Capitol).

I'm Never Satisfied. w/m Herb Perry, 1952. Leading record by Nat "King" Cole (Capitol).

I'm No Angel. w/m Tony Colton and P. Palmer, 1987. Popular track and single from the album "I'm No Angel" by The Gregg Allman Band (Epic).

I'm No Angel. w/m Gladys Du Bois, Ben Ellison, and Harvey O. Brooks, 1933. Sung by Mae West in (MM) *I'm No Angel*. Recordings: Mae West (Brunswick); Ramona, with Roy Bargy's Orchestra (Victor); Charlie Barnet's Band (Melotone).

I'm Nobody's Baby. w/m Benny Davis, Milton Ager, and Lester Santly, 1921, 1940. A favorite of female singers in vaudeville and on records. Among the many are Marion Harris (Columbia); Helen Forrest with Benny Goodman (Columbia); Connie Haines with Tommy Dorsey (Victor); Betty Hutton with Nelson Riddle (Capitol); Marian Mann with Bob Crosby (Decca); Judy Garland with Bobby Sherwood (Decca). Sung by Garland in (MM)

Andy Hardy Meets a Debutante, 1940. That performance, with some of the above recordings, revived the song and it was on "Your Hit Parade" for eleven weeks.

I'm No Stranger to the Rain. w/m Sonny Curtis and Ronald Hellard, 1989. Hit Country record by Keith Whitley (RCA).

I'm Not At All in Love. w/m Richard Adler and Jerry Ross, 1954. Introduced by Janis Paige in (TM) *The Pajama Game*. Doris Day sang it in (MM) *The Pajama Game*, 1957.

I'm Not Crazy Yet. w/m Don Rollins, 1966. Country chart record by Ray Price (Columbia).

I'm Not Gonna Let It Bother Me Tonight. w/m Buddy Buie, Robert Nix, and Dean Daughtry, 1978. Recorded by The Atlanta Rhythm Section (Polydor).

I'm Not in Love. w/m Graham Gouldman and Eric Stewart, 1975. Top 10 record by the British group 10cc (Mercury).

I'm Not Lisa. w/m Jessi Colter, 1975. Hit Country and Pop record by Jessi Colter, produced by Waylon Jennings (Capitol).

I'm Not That Lonely Yet. w/m Bill Rice and Mary S. Rice, 1982. Top 10 Country chart record by Reba McEntire (Mercury).

I'm Not Your Steppin' Stone. w/m Tommy Boyce and Bobby Hart, 1967. Top 40 hit by The Monkees (Colgems).

I'm Old Fashioned. w. Johnny Mercer, m. Jerome Kern, 1942. Introduced by Fred Astaire and Rita Hayworth (voice dubbed by Nan Wynn), singing and dancing to the music of Xavier Cugat's Orchestra in (MM) *You Were Never Lovelier*. In addition to Astaire's recording (Decca), and Cugat's (Columbia), there was a popular version by Glen Gray and the Casa Loma Band, vocal by Kenny Sargent (Decca).

I'm on a See-saw. w. Desmond Carter, m. Vivian Ellis, 1935. Fats Waller (Victor) and Anson Weeks with vocal by Kay St. Germaine (Brunswick) were among many to perform and/or record this English song.

I'm One of God's Children (Who Hasn't Got Wings). w. Oscar Hammerstein II and Harry Ruskin, m. Louis Alter, 1931. Introduced by Janet Reade with Ted Black's Band in (TM) *Ballyhoo*. Ruskin, the book writer, suggested the title. Despite the short run of the musical, there were recordings by: Nat Shilkret (Victor), the New Orleans Ramblers (Melotone), Libby Holman (Brunswick), Lee Morse (Columbia).

I'm on Fire. w/m Bruce Springsteen, 1985. Top 10 single from Bruce Springsteen's platinum album "Born in the U.S.A." (Columbia).

I'm on Fire. w/m D. English, G. Leonard, R. Street, O. Williams, B. Wright, Jr., 1975. Second chart record with same title in same year, although different songs. This by the group 5000 Volts (Philips), and Jim Gilstrap (Roxbury).

I'm on Fire. w/m Dwight Twilley, 1975. Top 20 record by The Dwight Twilley Band (Shelter).

I'm on My Way. w. Alan Jay Lerner, m. Frederick Loewe, 1951. Sung by members of the company in (TM) *Paint Your Wagon*, and in (MM) *Paint Your Wagon*, 1969.

I'm on My Way Home. w/m Irving Berlin, 1926. Popular recordings by Vincent Lopez's Orchestra (Brunswick) and "Whispering" Jack Smith (Victor).

I'm on the Crest of a Wave. w. B. G. De-Sylva and Lew Brown, m. Ray Henderson, 1928. From (TM) *George White's Scandals of 1928*, sung by Harry Richman. George Olsen and his Orchestra had a popular recording (Victor).

I'm on the Outside (Looking In). w/m Teddy Randazzo and Bobby Weinstein, 1964. Crossover (R&B/Pop) hit record by Little Anthony and The Imperials (DCP).

I'm on the Water Wagon Now. w. Paul West, m. John W. Bratton, 1903. From (TM) *The Office Boy.*

I'm Painting the Town Red. w. Charles Tobias and Charles Newman, m. Sam H. Stept, 1935. Among recordings: the bands of Richard Himber (Victor), Teddy Wilson (Brunswick), Little Ramblers (Bluebird), and singer-pianist Bob Howard (Decca).

Impatient Years, The. w. Sammy Cahn, m. James Van Heusen, 1955. Introduced in (TVM) "Our Town" based on Thornton Wilder's play.

I'm Playing with Fire. w/m Irving Berlin, 1932. Recorded by Johnny Marvin (Melotone); Jack Denny and his Orchestra, vocal by Paul Small (Victor); and later by Dorothy Collins (MGM).

I'm Popeye the Sailor Man. w/m Sammy Lerner, 1934. Theme song of the film cartoon *Popeye the Sailor.*

Impossible. w/m Steve Allen, 1956. Introduced on records by Nat "King" Cole (Capitol). Chart version by Gloria Lynne (Everest), 1961.

Impossible Dream, The (The Quest). w. Joe Darion, m. Mitch Leigh, 1965. Introduced by Richard Kiley in (TM) *Man of La Mancha.* Leading records by Jack Jones (Kapp), followed by The Hesitations (Kapp) and Roger Williams (Kapp), 1968. In the film version (MM) *Man of La Mancha,* 1972, Simon Gilbert dubbed the song on the soundtrack for Peter O'Toole.

I'm Prayin' Humble. m. Bob Haggart, 1938. Instrumental, introduced, featured, and recorded by Bob Crosby and his Orchestra, with Haggart on bass (Decca).

I'm Putting All My Eggs in One Basket. w/m Irving Berlin, 1936. Introduced by Fred Astaire, singing at the piano, and then as a challenge dance with Ginger Rogers in (MM) *Follow the Fleet.* Among the many recordings: Astaire (Brunswick), Guy Lombardo and his

Orchestra (Victor), the Boswell Sisters (Decca), Louis Armstrong (Decca), the Stuff Smith combo (Vocalion).

I'm Ready. w/m Al Lewis, Sylvester Bradford, and Antoine "Fats" Domino, 1959. Featured and recorded by Fats Domino (Imperial).

I'm Ready. w/m Willie Dixon, 1954. R&B hit by Muddy Waters (Chess).

I'm Ready for Love. w/m Eddie Holland, Lamont Dozier, and Brian Holland, 1966. Top 10 record by Martha and The Vandellas (Gordy).

I'm Real. w/m James Brown and Full Force, 1988. Top 10 R&B chart record by James Brown (Scotti Brothers).

I'm Ridin' for a Fall. w. Frank Loesser, m. Arthur Schwartz, 1943. Introduced by Joan Leslie and Dennis Morgan in (MM) *Thank Your Lucky Stars.*

I'm Satisfied. w. Mitchell Parish, m. Edward Kennedy "Duke" Ellington, 1933. Introduced and recorded by Ellington (Brunswick). Tom Coakley, with vocal by Carl Ravazza, under pseudonym of Carl Ravell, also recorded it (Victor).

I'm Saving My Love. w/m Alex Zanetis, 1963. Crossover (C&W/Pop) hit by Skeeter Davis (RCA).

I'm Sending You Red Roses. w/m Wallace Fowler, 1942. Introduced and recorded by Jimmy Wakely (Decca).

I'm Shooting High. w. Ted Koehler, m. Jimmy McHugh, 1936. Introduced by Alice Faye in (MM) *King of Burlesque,* and recorded by her (Melotone). Other top releases: Louis Armstrong (Decca); Jan Garber, vocal by Lee Bennett (Decca); Lud Gluskin, vocal by Buddy Clark (Brunswick); Little Jack Little (Columbia); Wingy Manone (Vocalion); Little Ramblers (Bluebird). It was interpolated in (TM) *Sugar Babies* in 1980 by Anne Miller and Mickey Rooney.

I'm Sitting High on a Hilltop. w. Gus Kahn, m. Arthur Johnston, 1935. Introduced by Dick Powell in (MM) *Thanks a Million.* Recorded by Powell (Decca), Paul Whiteman (Victor), the Mound City Blue Blowers (Champion), the Original Dixieland Jazz Band (Vocalion), Dolly Dawn (Bluebird), Johnny Hamp (Melotone), Paul Pendarvis (Columbia).

I'm Sitting on Top of the World. w. Sam M. Lewis and Joe Young, m. Ray Henderson, 1925. Introduced and recorded (Brunswick) by Al Jolson. He also sang it in (MM) *The Singing Fool*, 1928, and dubbed his voice on the soundtrack for Larry Parks in (MM) *The Jolson Story*, 1946. The song was also heard in (MM) *Has Anybody Seen My Gal?*, 1952; (MM) *I'll Cry Tomorrow*, 1955; (MM) *Love Me or Leave Me*, 1955; and (MM) *Thoroughly Modern Millie*, 1967. A little known recording by a future well-known name, Glenn Miller, was released in 1937 (Decca).

I'm Sitting Pretty in a Pretty Little City. w/m Lou Davis, Henry Santly, and Abel Baer, 1923.

I'm So Afraid of You. w. Bert Kalmar, m. Harry Ruby, 1931. Recorded by the bands of Isham Jones (Brunswick) and Bert Lown (Victor).

I'm So Anxious. w/m William Rush, 1979. Recorded by Southside Johnny and The Asbury Jukes (Mercury).

I'm So Excited. w/m Anita Pointer, June Pointer, Ruth Pointer, and Trevor Lawrence, 1984. First recorded by The Pointer Sisters (Planet), 1982. Their release made the R&B and Pop charts. Two years later, a remix was made and the new version became a Top 10 Pop chart record.

I'm So Glad I'm Standing Here Today. w/m Will Jennings and Joe Sample, 1981. Recorded by The Crusaders with Joe Cocker as "guest artist" (MCA).

I'm So in Love with You. w/m Sonny James and John Skye, 1956. Featured by The Wilburn Brothers (Decca).

I'm So Lonesome I Could Cry. w/m Hank Williams, 1949. Introduced with a hit record by Hank Williams (MGM). Other versions: Gordon MacRae, with Walter Gross's Orchestra (Musicraft); Clark Dennis (Capitol). Revived by Johnny Tillotson (Cadence), 1962; B. J. Thomas (Scepter), 1966; famed football player Terry Bradshaw (Mercury), 1976.

I'm So Miserable Without You. w/m Eugene Strasser and George Winters, 1965. Country chart record by Billy Walker (Columbia).

I'm So Proud. w/m Curtis Mayfield, 1964. Hit record by The Impressions (ABC-Paramount). Revived by the trio The Main Ingredient (RCA), 1971.

I'm So Right Tonight (But I've Been So Wrong for So Long), w. "By" Dunham, m. Terry Shand, 1947. Leading records by Jo Stafford (Capitol), Dinah Shore (Columbia), Phil Harris (RCA Victor).

I'm Sorry. w/m John Denver, 1975. From the album "Windsong" by John Denver (RCA). The single reached #1 on the charts and was awarded a gold record.

I'm Sorry. w/m Thomas Bell and William Hart, 1968. Recorded by The Delfonics (Philly Groove).

I'm Sorry. w/m Ronnie Self and Dub Allbritten, 1960. #1 record by Brenda Lee (Decca).

I'm Sorry, Sally. w. Gus Kahn, m. Ted Fio Rito, 1928. Recorded by Morton Downey (Victor); Al Bowlly (Br. Brunswick); Ray Miller's Orchestra with Muggsy Spanier (Brunswick); Fred Waring's Pennsylvanians (Victor).

I'm Sorry Dear. w/m Anson Weeks, Harry Tobias, and Johnnie Scott, 1931. Introduced and recorded by Anson Weeks and his Orchestra (Columbia). Bing Crosby's version was coupled with his theme "Where the Blue of the Night Meets the Gold of the Day" (q.v.) (Brunswick). Other records by the bands of: Lofner (Carol)-Harris (Phil) (Victor); Red

McKenzie (Columbia); Jacques Renard (Brunswick).

I'm Sorry for Myself. w/m Irving Berlin, 1939. Introduced by Rudy Vallee and Mary Healy in (MM) *Second Fiddle.* Among recordings: the orchestras of Glenn Miller (Bluebird); Ben Bernie (Vocalion); Hal Kemp, vocal by Nan Wynn (Victor).

I'm Sorry I Made You Cry. w/m N. J. Clesi, 1918. A hit ballad of its day, it was later sung by Alice Faye in (MM) *Rose of Washington Square* in 1939, and by Betty Hutton in (MM) *Somebody Loves Me* in 1952.

I'm Stepping Out with a Memory Tonight. w. Herb Magidson, m. Allie Wrubel, 1940. Introduced by Kate Smith on her weekly network radio show. Featured and recorded by Glenn Miller (Bluebird); Tony Martin (Decca); Kay Kyser, vocal by Ginny Simms (Columbia); Al Donahue, vocal by Phil Brito. Heard in (MM) *Footlight Serenade,* 1942.

I'm Stickin' with You. w/m Jimmy Bowen and Buddy Knox, 1957. Recorded by Jimmy Bowen with The Rhythm Orchids (Roulette). Originally released on another label (Triple-D), coupled with the big hit "Party Doll," (q.v.) by Buddy Knox on both records.

I'm Still Caring. w/m Rudy Vallee and John Klenner, 1929. Featured and recorded by Vallee (Victor).

I'm Still Crazy. w/m Buddy Cannon and Vern Gosdin, 1989. Hit Country single by Vern Gosdin (Columbia).

I'm Still Here. w/m Stephen Sondheim, 1971. Introduced by Yvonne De Carlo in (TM) *Follies.*

I'm Still in Love with You. w/m Al Green, Al Jackson, and Willie Mitchell, 1972. Gold record by Al Green (Hi).

I'm Still Loving You. w/m George Richey and Glenn Sutton, 1974. Top 10 Country chart record by Joe Stampley (Dot).

I'm Still Not over You. w/m Willie Nelson, 1967. Top 10 Country record by Ray Price (Decca).

I'm Still Standing. w. Bernie Taupin, m. Elton John, 1983. Recorded by the English singer/songwriter Elton John (Geffen).

I'm Stone in Love with You. w/m Anthony Bell, Thom Bell, and Linda Creed, 1972. R&B/Pop gold record by The Stylistics (Avco).

I'm Sure of Everything But You. w. Charles O'Flynn, m. Pete Wendling and George W. Meyer, 1932.

I'm Telling You Now. w/m Freddie Garrity and Mitch Murray, 1965. #1 recording, produced in England by Freddie and the Dreamers (Tower).

I'm Tellin' the Birds, I'm Tellin' the Bees (How I Love You). w. Lew Brown, m. Cliff Friend, 1927. Featured and recorded by Cliff "Ukulele Ike" Edwards (Perfect) (Pathé).

I'm the Echo (You're the Song). w. Dorothy Fields, m. Jerome Kern, 1935. Introduced in (MM) *I Dream Too Much* and recorded (Victor) by Lily Pons.

I'm the First Girl in the Second Row (in the Third Scene of the Fourth Number). w/m Hugh Martin, 1948. Introduced by Nancy Walker in (TM) *Look Ma, I'm Dancin'!*

(I'm the Girl on) Wolverton Mountain. w/m Merle Kilgore and Claude King, 1962. Pop and Country hit record by Jo Ann Campbell (Cameo).

I'm the Greatest Star. w. Bob Merrill, m. Jule Styne, 1964. Introduced by Barbra Streisand in (TM) *Funny Girl,* and repeated by her in the film version (MM) *Funny Girl,* 1968.

I'm the Last of the Red Hot Mammas. w. Jack Yellen, m. Milton Ager, 1929. Introduced in (MM) *Honky Tonk* and recorded (Victor) by Sophie Tucker.

I'm the Lonely One. w/m Gordon Mills, 1964. Recorded in England by Cliff Richard (Epic).

I'm the Lonesomest Gal in Town. w. Lew Brown, m. Albert von Tilzer, 1912. A hit ballad, revived by Kay Starr in the early fifties (Capitol). It was also heard in (MM) *Make Believe Ballroom*, 1949, and (MP) *South Sea Sinner*, 1950.

I'm the Medicine Man for the Blues. w. Grant Clarke, m. Harry Akst, 1929. Introduced by Ted Lewis in (MM) *Is Everybody Happy?* Recorded by Lewis (Columbia).

I'm the Only Hell (Mama Ever Raised). w/m Bobby Borchers, Wayne Kemp, and Mack Vickery, 1977. Top 10 Country record by Johnny Paycheck (Epic).

I'm Thinking Tonight of My Blue Eyes. w/m A. P. Carter, 1930, 1942. Introduced and recorded (Melotone) by the Carter Family. It was revived in 1942 by Bob Atcher who had a million-seller (Okeh) and later by Burl Ives (Decca).

I'm Thrilled. w. Sylvia Dee, m. Sidney Lippman, 1941. Introduced, featured, and recorded by Glenn Miller, vocal by Ray Eberle (Bluebird). Miller included the complete score by Jerry Gray, in his book on arranging, as an example of writing for a band and singer.

I'm Through with Love. w. Gus Kahn, m. Matt Malneck and Fud Livingston, 1931. Introduced by Mildred Bailey. Early recordings by Bing Crosby (Brunswick); Henry Busse (Victor); Don Voorhees (Hit of the Week). In 1938, Glen Gray and the Casa Loma Orchestra, with vocal by Kenny Sargent, had a popular release (Decca), as did Dinah Shore in 1941 (Bluebird). It was heard in (MM) *Honeymoon Lodge*, 1943, and on the soundtrack of the Gus Kahn story (MM) *I'll See You in My Dreams*, 1952. Bobby Van sang it in (MP) *The Affairs of Dobie Gillis*, 1953, and Marilyn Monroe sang it in (MP) *Some Like It Hot*, 1959.

I'm Throwing Rice (at the Girl I Love). w/m Steve Nelson, Ed Nelson, Jr., and Eddy Arnold, 1949. Top 20 record by Eddy Arnold (RCA Victor).

I'm Tickled Pink with a Blue-Eyed Baby. w. Charles O'Flynn, m. Pete Wendling, 1930.

I'm Tired. w/m Mel Tillis, Ray Price, and A. R. Peddy, 1957. Popular country record by Webb Pierce (Decca).

I'm Tired. w. William Jerome, m. Jean Schwartz, 1901. Popular song of its day.

I'm Tired of Everything But You. w/m Isham Jones, 1925. Popular instrumental by Isham Jones and his Orchestra (Brunswick).

I'm Too Far Gone (to Turn Around). w/m Clyde Otis and Belford Hendricks, 1966. Recorded by Bobby Bland (Duke).

I'm Trusting in You. w/m Fred Rose, 1941. Featured and recorded by Bob Crosby and his Orchestra (Decca) and Roy Rogers (Decca).

I'm Unlucky. w. William Jerome, m. Jean Schwartz, 1902. From (TM) *The Wild Rose*.

I'm Unlucky at Gambling. w/m Cole Porter, 1929. Introduced by Evelyn Hoey and Larry Ceballos's Hollywood Dancers in (TM) *Fifty Million Frenchmen*. Eve Arden sang it in the Porter biography (MM) *Night and Day*, 1946.

I Must Be Dreaming. w/m Willy DeVille, 1986. Introduced by Willy DeVille in his album "Sportin' Life" (Atlantic). Chart single by the quintet Giuffria (MCA/Camel).

I Must Be Dreaming. w/m Al Dubin and Al Sherman, 1928.

I Must Be Seeing Things. w/m Bob Brass, Al Kooper, and Irwin Levine, 1965. Top 40 record by Gene Pitney (Musicor).

I Must Have That Man. w. Dorothy Fields, m. Jimmy McHugh, 1928. Introduced by Adelaide Hall in (TM) *Blackbirds of 1928*. She also recorded it with Lew Leslie's Blackbirds Orchestra (Victor). Other recordings were made by Billie Holiday with Teddy Wilson (Brunswick), Lee Morse (Columbia), Ella Fitzgerald (Decca), Duke Ellington's Orchestra (Victor).

I Must Love You. w. Lorenz Hart, m. Richard Rodgers, 1928. Sung by Helen Ford and William Williams in (TM) *Chee-Chee*, a short-lived musical. Two years later the melody reappeared in (TM) *Simple Simon* with new lyrics, titled "Send for Me" (q.v.).

I Must See Annie Tonight. w/m Cliff Friend and Dave Franklin, 1938. Introduced and recorded by Guy Lombardo and His Royal Canadians (Decca).

I'm Waiting for Ships That Never Come In. w. Jack Yellen, m. Abe Olman, 1927.

I'm Waiting Just for You. w/m Carolyn Leigh, Henry Glover, and Lucky Millinder, 1951. Popular recordings by Lucky Millinder, vocal by Annisteen Allen (King), and Rosemary Clooney (Columbia). Revived by Pat Boone (Dot), 1957.

I'm Walking. w/m Dave Bartholomew and Antoine "Fats" Domino, 1957. Hit record by Fats Domino (Imperial). Sung by Ricky Nelson on the Ozzie and Harriet (Nelson) TV show and recorded by him (Verve), coupled with his first hit, "A Teenager's Romance."

I'm Walking Behind You. w/m Billy Reid, 1953. #1 million-seller by Eddie Fisher (RCA Victor).

I'm Walking the Dog. w/m W. C. Grimsley and E. M. Grimsley, 1953. Popular C&W record by Webb Pierce (Decca).

I'm Wastin' My Tears on You. w/m Tex Ritter and Frank Harford, 1944. C&W hit record by Tex Ritter (Capitol).

I'm Wild About Horns on Automobiles That Go "Ta-Ta-Ta-Ta." w/m Clarence Gaskill, 1928. Novelty Song.

I'm Wishing. w. Larry Morey, m. Frank Churchill, 1937. Sung by Adriana Caselotti, as the voice of Snow White in the animated cartoon feature film (MM) *Snow White and the Seven Dwarfs*.

I'm With You. w. Betty Comden and Adolph Green, m. Jule Styne, 1964. Introduced by Carol Burnett and Jack Cassidy in (TM) *Fade Out—Fade In*.

I'm Wondering. w/m Henry Cosby, Sylvia Moy, and Stevie Wonder, 1967. Hit record by Stevie Wonder (Tamla).

I'm Young and Healthy. w. Al Dubin, m. Harry Warren, 1933. Introduced by Dick Powell, Toby Wing, and chorus in (MM) *Forty-Second Street*. Popular recordings: Bing Crosby (Brunswick); Fred Waring, vocal by Tom Waring (Victor); Ben Selvin, bandleader who assembled top musicians for studio recording only (Columbia).

I'm Your Boogie Man. w/m Harry Wayne Casey and Richard Finch, 1977. #1 chart single by KC and The Sunshine Band, taken from their album "Part 3" (T.K.).

I'm Your Girl. w. Oscar Hammerstein II, m. Richard Rodgers, 1953. Introduced by Isabel Bigley and Bill Hayes in (TM) *Me and Juliet*.

I'm Your Hoochie Cooche Man. w/m Willie Dixon, 1954. Chart R&B record by Muddy Waters (Chess). Popular record by jazz organist Jimmy Smith (Verve), 1966.

I'm Your Man. w/m Leonard Cohen, 1988. Title song of the album by the Canadian singer/poet Leonard Cohen (Columbia).

I'm Your Man. w/m George Michael, 1985. Top 10 record by the British duo Wham! (Columbia). Also recorded by Barry Manilow (Columbia), 1986.

I'm Your Puppet. w/m Dewey Lindon Oldham and Dan Pennington, 1966. Top 10 record by James and Bobby Purify (Bell).

I'm Yours. w/m Don Robertson and Hal Blair, 1965. Recorded by Elvis Presley (RCA).

I'm Yours. w/m Robert Mellin, 1952. Most popular records by Don Cornell (Coral) and Eddie Fisher (RCA Victor).

I'm Yours. w. E. Y. Harburg, m. John Green, 1930. Introduced in the film short (MM) *Leave It to Lester*. Featured and recorded by the bands of Bert Lown (Victor) and Ben Bernie (Brunswick). Interpolated in (MM) *Second Chorus*, 1941, and (MM) *The Stooge*, 1953.

I'm Yours to Command. w/m Russ Columbo, 1951. Posthumous song released seventeen years after Columbo was killed in a shooting accident. First records by Sammy Kaye, vocal by Tony Alamo (Columbia); Herb Jeffries (Coral); Sonny Burke and his Orchestra (Decca).

I'm Yours to Keep. w/m Herb Fisher, 1950. R&B recording by The Herb Fisher Trio (Modern).

In a Big Country. w/m Big Country, 1983. Recorded by the Scottish quartet Big Country (Mercury).

In a Blue and Pensive Mood. w/m Al J. Neiburg, Marty Symes, and Jerry Livingston, 1935. Al Bowlly (Victor) and Richard Himber's Orchestra (Victor) had popular recordings.

In Acapulco. w. Mack Gordon, m. Harry Warren, 1945. Introduced by Betty Grable and Carmen Cavallaro in (MM) *Billy Rose's Diamond Horseshoe*. Recorded by Carmen Cavallaro and his Orchestra (Decca) and Georgia Gibbs (Victor).

In a Cosy Corner. m. John W. Bratton, 1901. Piano instrumental.

In-A-Gadda-Da-Vida. w/m Doug Ingle, 1968. Top 30 single edited down from a seventeen-minute album cut by the rock band Iron Butterfly (Atco). Performed by the group, Slayer, on the soundtrack of (MP) *Less Than Zero*, 1987.

In a Great Big Way. w. Dorothy Fields, m. Jimmy McHugh, 1928. Comedy song introduced by Billy Taylor and Betty Starbuck in (TM) *Hello, Daddy!* Recorded by Annette Hanshaw (Harmony).

In a Letter to You. w/m Eddy Raven, 1989. Hit Country single by Eddy Raven (Universal).

In a Little Bookshop. w/m Kay Twomey, Al Goodhart, and George W. Meyer, 1947. Featured and recorded by Vaughn Monroe, with his Orchestra (RCA Victor).

In a Little Dutch Kindergarten. w/ Al Bryan, m. Larry Stock, 1937. Based on a Dutch lyric by Herre De Vos. Popularized in the United States by Bobby Breen (Decca) and Blue Barron's Orchestra (Bluebird).

In a Little Gypsy Tea Room. w. Edgar Leslie, m. Joe Burke, 1935. Featured and recorded by Jan Garber (Victor) and Bob Crosby (Decca).

In a Little Hula Heaven. w. Leo Robin, m. Ralph Rainger, 1937. Introduced by Bing Crosby and Shirley Ross in (MM) *Waikiki Wedding* and recorded by Bing Crosby (Decca).

In a Little Red Barn (on a Farm Down in Indiana). w. Joe Young, m. Milton Ager and Jean Schwartz, 1934.

In a Little Spanish Town. w. Sam M. Lewis and Joe Young, m. Mable Wayne, 1926. This song was the first major hit for Mabel Wayne. It was popularized by Paul Whiteman (Victor) and the Revelers (Victor). Among other recordings to follow were Albert Ammons and the Rhythm Kings (Mercury); Bing Crosby (Decca); Glenn Miller, on an early recording (Columbia); Joe Bushkin (Commodore). Virginia O'Brien, June Allyson, and Gloria De Haven sang it in (MM) *Thousands Cheer*, 1943.

In a Mellow Tone. w. Milt Gabler, m. Edward Kennedy "Duke" Ellington, 1940. Originally an instrumental, recorded by Duke Ellington and his Orchestra (Victor). Among later vocal recordings: The Mills Brothers (Decca); Ella Fitzgerald (Verve).

In America. w/m Tom Crain, Charlie Daniels, Joel Di Gregorio, Fred Edwards, Charles Hayward, James Marshall, 1980. Recorded by The Charlie Daniels Band (Epic).

In a Mist. m. Leon Bismarck "Bix" Beiderbecke, 1927. A piano solo first recorded by Beiderbecke (Okeh). Other recordings by the bands of Frankie Trumbauer (Brunswick); Red Norvo (Brunswick); Bunny Berigan, featuring Joe Lippman as pianist-arranger (Victor); Jimmy McPartland, featuring Marion McPartland on piano (Prestige); Harry James (Columbia).

In a Moment. w/m Alfred Brown, Ronald Hamilton, James Harris, and James Lee, Jr., 1969. Recorded by The Intrigues (Yew).

In a Moment of Madness. w. Ralph Freed, m. Jimmy McHugh, 1944. Introduced by Helen Forrest, with Harry James's Orchestra in (MM) *Two Girls and a Sailor*. Forrest, having left James's band upon completion of the film, recorded it as a single (Decca).

In a Monastery Garden. m. Albert William Ketelbey, 1915. An English instrumental that met with popularity in America. Among the recordings are those by Harry Sosnik and his Orchestra (Decca) and Lew White, the renowned organist (Victor).

In an Eighteenth Century Drawing Room. m. Raymond Scott, 1939. Based on Mozart's *Sonata in C for Pianofort* (K545). Introduced and recorded by the Raymond Scott Quintette.

In and Out of Love. w/m Brian Holland, Lamont Dozier, and Eddie Holland, 1967. Hit record by the Supremes (Motown).

In a New York Minute. w/m Michael Garvin, Tom Shapiro, and Chris Waters, 1985. Top 10 Country chart record by Ronnie McDowell (Epic).

In an Old Dutch Garden (By an Old Dutch Mill). w. Mack Gordon, m. Will Grosz, 1940. Best-selling records by Glenn Miller, vocal by Ray Eberle (Bluebird); Dick Jurgens, vocal by Eddy Howard (Vocalion); Eddy Duchin and Orchestra (Columbia).

In a Persian Market. m. Albert W. Ketelbey, 1920. Larry Clinton's band revived it with a popular record in 1939 (Victor).

In Arcady. w. Schuyler Greene, m. Jerome Kern, 1915. From (TM) *Nobody Home*.

In a Sentimental Mood. w. Manny Kurtz and Irving Mills, m. Edward Kennedy "Duke" Ellington, 1936. Introduced and recorded by Duke Ellington and his Orchestra (Brunswick). Among other early recordings of this standard: Jimmy Dorsey (Decca), Ben Pollack (Variety), Benny Goodman (Victor), harpist Caspar Reardon (Liberty Music Shops).

In a Shanty in Old Shanty Town. w. Joe Young, m. Ira Schuster and Jack Little, 1932. Introduced and recorded by Little Jack Little (Columbia). Best-selling records by Ted Lewis and his orchestra (Columbia), Singin' Sam (Oriole), Ted Black (Victor), Red Allen (Apollo). It was sung by Teddy Joyce in (MM) *The Crooner*, 1932. Revived with hit record by Johnny Long and his Band (Decca), 1946.

In-Between. w/m Roger Edens, 1938. Sung by Judy Garland in (MM) *Love Finds Andy Hardy*, lamenting that she was "too old for toys, and too young for boys."

In Buddy's Eyes. w/m Stephen Sondheim, 1971. Introduced by Dorothy Collins in (TM) *Follies*.

Incense and Peppermints. w/m John Carter and Tim Gilbert, 1967. #1 gold record by Strawberry Alarm Clock (Uni).

In Chi Chi Castenango. w. Henry Myers, m. Jay Gorney, 1940. Introduced by Josephine Del Mar, Robert Davis, and Doodles Weaver in the revue (TM) *Meet The People*.

Inch Worm. w/m Frank Loesser, 1951. Introduced by Danny Kaye in (MM) *Hans Christian Andersen*.

"In" Crowd, The. w/m Billy Page, 1965. Top vocal record by Dobie Gray (Charger). Top 10 instrumental single by The Ramsey Lewis Trio (Argo).

In Dear Old Georgia. w. Harry Williams, m. Egbert Van Alstyne, 1905.

In Dear Old Illinois. w/m Paul Dresser, 1902.

Independent (On My Own). w. Betty Comden and Adolph Green, m. Jule Styne, 1957. Introduced by Sydney Chaplin in (TM) *Bells Are Ringing*. Song not used in film version.

Indescribably Blue. w/m Darrell Glenn, 1967. Recorded by Elvis Presley (RCA).

(Back Home Again in) Indiana. w. Ballard MacDonald, m. James F. Hanley, 1917. A longtime favorite with vocal and jazz groups. In (MM) *The Five Pennies*, 1939, it was played by Red Nichols's Five Pennies with Nichols dubbing the trumpet for Danny Kaye who played the role of the bandleader. In 1952, in (MM) *With a Song in My Heart*, Jane Froman, whose bio it was, dubbed the singing for Susan Hayward. The song was also played in (MM) *The Gene Krupa Story* in 1960.

Indiana Moon. w. Denny Davis, m. Isham Jones, 1923. Introduced by Isham Jones and his Orchestra.

Indiana Wants Me. w/m R. Dean Taylor, 1970. Top 10 record by the Canadian writer/ singer R. Dean Taylor (Rare Earth).

Indian Giver. w/m Bobby Bloom, Bo Gentry, and Ritchie Cordell, 1969. Top 10 record by the 1910 Fruitgum Company (Buddah).

Indian Lake. w/m Tony Romeo, 1968. Top 10 record by the family group The Cowsills (MGM).

Indian Love Call. w. Otto Harbach and Oscar Hammerstein II, m. Rudolf Friml, 1924. Introduced by Mary Ellis and Dennis King in (TM) *Rose-Marie*. Nelson Eddy and Jeanette MacDonald sang it in (MM) *Rose Marie*, 1936 [note the dropped hyphen in the movie title]. Their recording, with orchestra directed by Nat Shilkret, was a million-seller (Victor). In the remake (MM) *Rose Marie*, 1954, it was sung by Fernando Lamas and Ann Blyth. Artie Shaw had a hit recording, vocal by Tony Pastor and coupled with the all-time hit "Begin the Beguine" (q.v.) (Bluebird), 1938. Song was revived with a million-selling record by the Country singer Slim Whitman (Imperial), 1952.

Indianola. m. Henry R. Stern and Domenico Savino, 1917. A piano solo written under the pseudonyms of S. R. Henry and D. Onivas.

Indian Reservation (The Lament of the Cherokee Reservation Indian). w/m John D. Loudermilk, 1968, 1971. Top 20 record by Don Fardon (GNP Crescendo). The Raiders had the best-seller, a #1 gold record (Columbia), 1971.

Indian Summer. w. Al Dubin, m. Victor Herbert, 1919, 1939. Herbert wrote this as a piano solo. Twenty years later and fifteen years after the death of Victor Herbert, Al Dubin wrote lyrics to it and it rose to #1 on "Your Hit Parade." Tommy Dorsey, with vocal by Jack Leonard (RCA Victor), and Glenn Miller, with vocal by Ray Eberle (Bluebird), each had hit records.

Indiscretion. w/m Sammy Cahn, Paul Weston, and Alessandro Cicognini, 1954. Adapted from music of Cicognini from the score of (MP) *Indiscretion of an American Wife*. Leading recording by Jo Stafford, with Liberace at the piano (Columbia).

In Dreams. w/m Roy Orbison, 1963. Hit record by Roy Orbison (Monument). Orbison's record was played on the soundtrack of (MM) *Blue Velvet*, 1986.

I Nearly Let Love Go Slipping Through My Fingers. w/m Harry Woods, 1936. Introduced by Jessie Matthews in the British film (MM) *It's Love Again*. She recorded it (Decca), as did the Original Dixieland Jazz Band (Vocalion) and the English band led by Lew Stone (Decca) who coupled it with the title song.

I Need a Lover. w/m John Cougar Mellencamp, 1979. Recorded by John Cougar (Riva).

I Need Love. w/m J. T. Smith, B. Erving, D. Pierce, D. Simon, and S. Etts, 1987. #1 R&B chart single by the rapper, L. L. Cool J (pseudonym for James Todd Smith), from the album "Bigger and Deffer" (Def Jam).

I Need Lovin'. w. Henry Creamer, m. Jimmy Johnson, 1926. Recorded by Tiny Hill (Mercury), Art Jarrett with Jimmy Noone's Band (Brunswick), Terry Shand (Decca), Orrin Tucker (Vocalion), and Blanche Calloway twice, (Victor) 1931 and (Perfect) 1934.

I Need More of You. w/m David Bellamy, 1985. #1 Country chart single by The Bellamy Brothers (MCA).

I Need Somebody. w/m R. Balderrana, F. Lugo, R. Martinez, F. Rodriquez, E. Serrato, 1966. Top 40 record by ?(Question Mark) and The Mysterians (Cameo).

I Need to Be in Love. w. John Bettis and Albert Hammond, m. Richard Carpenter, 1976. Recorded by The Carpenters (A&M).

I Need to Know. w/m Tom Petty, 1978. Recorded by Tom Petty and The Heartbreakers (Shelter).

I Need You. w/m Gerry Beckley, 1972. Top 10 record by the trio America (Warner Bros.).

I Need You. w/m George Harrison, 1965. Introduced by The Beatles in (MM) *Help!*

I Need You Now. w/m Jimmie Crane and Al Jacobs, 1954. #1 hit record by Eddie Fisher, with Hugo Winterhalter's Orchestra (RCA Victor).

I Need Your Love Tonight. w/m Sid Wayne and Bix Reichner, 1959. One of four records, all hits, cut by Elvis Presley during his Army service (RCA).

I Need Your Lovin'. w/m Wille Jennings, Clarence Paul, and Sonny Woods, 1959. First chart record by Roy Hamilton (Epic) followed by Don Gardner and Dee Dee Ford (Fire), 1962.

I Need Your Lovin' (Bazoom). w/m Jerry Leiber and Mike Stoller, 1954. Chart record for The Cheers (Capitol).

I Need You So. w/m Ivory Joe Hunter, 1950. Introduced by Ivory Joe Hunter (MGM). Best-selling record of the song by Don Cornell,

with Hugh Winterhalter's Orchestra (RCA Victor).

In Egern on the Tegern See. w. Oscar Hammerstein II, m. Jerome Kern, 1932. Sung by Ivy Scott in (TM) *Music in the Air.*

I Never Cry. w/m Alice Cooper and Dick Wagner, 1976. Gold record by Alice Cooper (Warner Bros.).

I Never Felt More Like Falling in Love. w. Ralph Freed, m. Robert Allen, 1957. Featured and recorded by Tony Bennett (Columbia).

I Never Felt This Way Before. w. Mack Gordon, m. Josef Myrow, 1956. Introduced by Eddie Fisher and Debbie Reynolds in (MM) *Bundle of Joy.*

I Never Had a Chance. w/m Irving Berlin, 1934. Popularized and recorded by Isham Jones (Decca). Lew Stone, the English bandleader, had a popular record with vocal by Al Bowlly (Decca), as did Georgie Price (Banner).

I Never Had a Worry in the World. w/m Jim Morehead and Sandra Kent, 1950. Recorded by Dinah Shore (Columbia) and by Robert Quinlan, Jan August, and The Harmonicats (Mercury).

I Never Had the One I Wanted. w/m Jimmy Louis, Sheb Wooley, and Claude Gray, 1966. Top 10 Country chart record by Claude Gray (Decca).

I Never Has Seen Snow. w. Truman Capote and Harold Arlen, m. Harold Arlen, 1954. Introduced by Diahann Carroll in (TM) *House of Flowers.*

I Never Knew (That Roses Grew). w. Gus Kahn, m. Ted Fio Rito, 1925. Introduced by Ted Fio Rito and his Orchestra. Popular records by Gene Austin (Victor), Ross Gorman (Columbia), Vincent Lopez and his Orchestra (Okeh). Revived with hit recording by Sam Donahue, vocal by Bill Lockwood (Capitol).

I Never Knew Heaven Could Speak. w. Mack Gordon, m. Harry Revel, 1939. Introduced by Alice Faye in (MM) *Rose of Washing-*

ton Square. Among recordings: Bob Crosby, vocal by Marion Mann (Decca); Hal Kemp, vocal by Bob Allen (Victor); Red Nichols, vocal by Bill Darnell (Bluebird).

I Never Knew I Could Love Anybody (Like I'm Loving You.). w/m Tom Pitts, Raymond B. Egan, and Roy Marsh, 1920. Recorded by Paul Whiteman on one of his first sessions (Victor). The song has been heard in (MM) *The Great American Broadcast*, 1941; (MM) *Strictly in the Groove*, 1942; (MM) *Honeymoon Lodge*, 1943; (MM) *Cruisin' Down the River*, 1953; and (MM) *Pete Kelly's Blues*, 1955.

I Never Liked O'Regan. w/m Joseph Flynn, 1890.

I Never Loved a Man (the Way I Love You). w/m Ronny Shannon, 1967. Aretha Franklin's recording of the song was her first gold record (Atlantic).

I Never Mention Your Name. w. Mack Davis and Don George, m. Walter Kent, 1943. Most popular records by Jack Leonard, with Ray Bloch's Orchestra (Okeh); and Dick Haymes, with the Song Spinners (Decca).

I Never Promised You a Rose Garden. See **Rose Garden**.

I Never Said Goodbye. w/m Les Reed and Barry Mason, 1973. Recorded in England by Engelbert Humperdinck (Parrot).

I Never Saw a Better Night. w. Johnny Mercer, m. Lewis E. Gensler, 1935. From (MM) *Old Man Rhythm*. Recordings by Richard Himber, vocal by Allen Stuart (Victor); the Johnny Green Orchestra (Brunswick); Bob Howard (Decca).

I Never See Maggie Alone. w. Harry Tilsley, m. Everett Lynton, 1927, 1949. British song featured and recorded in the U.S. by Irving Aaronson and his Commanders, vocal by Phil Saxe (Victor). Revived by country singer Kenny Roberts, who had a million-seller (Coral), and Art Mooney, vocal by Tex Fletcher (MGM).

Infatuation. w/m Rod Stewart, Duane Hutchings, and Michael Omartian, 1984. Top 10 record by the English singer Rod Stewart (Warner Bros.).

Inflation. w/m Zeke Manners and Lester Lee, 1946. C&W hit by Zeke Manners (Victor).

In Florida Among the Palms. w/m Irving Berlin, 1916. From (TM) *Ziegfeld Follies of 1916*.

Information Blues. w/m Roy Milton. 1950. Recorded by Roy Milton (Specialty).

In France They Kiss on Main Street. w/m Joni Mitchell, 1976. Recorded by Joni Mitchell (Asylum).

In God's Country. w/m U2, 1987. Chart single from the album "The Joshua Tree" by the Irish group U2 (Island).

In Good Old New York Town. w/m Paul Dresser, 1899. Popularized by Lottie Gilson in vaudeville.

Inka Dinka Doo. w/m Jimmy Durante and Ben Ryan, 1934. Introduced and recorded by Durante (Brunswick, Decca). Ferde Grofé and his Orchestra recorded it in its premier year (Columbia). Durante, with whom the song will always be associated, performed it in three films: (MM) *Palooka*, 1934, (MM) *Two Girls and a Sailor*, 1944, and (MM) *This Time for Keeps*, 1947.

In Love. w/m Mike Reid and Sam Dees, 1986. #1 Country chart record by Ronnie Milsap (RCA).

In Love in Vain. w. Leo Robin, m. Jerome Kern, 1946. From Kern's last score, written shortly before his fatal heart attack. Introduced by Louanne Hogan, dubbing on the soundtrack for Jeanne Crain, in (MM) *Centennial Summer*.

In Love with Love. w. Anne Caldwell, m. Jerome Kern, 1923. Introduced by Dorothy Stone in (TM) *Stepping Stones*.

In My Arms. w. Frank Loesser, m. Ted Grouya, 1943. From (MP) *See Here, Private Hargrove.* Best-selling record by Dick Haymes (Decca), whose recording was coupled with another hit, "It Can't Be Wrong" (q.v.).

In My Darkest Hour. w/m Dave Mustaine and Dave Ellefson, 1988. Introduced by Megadeth in (MP) *The Decline and Fall of Western Civilization, Part II.*

In My Dreams. w/m Kevin Cronin and Tom Kelly, 1987. Chart single from the album "Life as We Know It" by the group REO Speedwagon (Epic).

In My Dreams. w/m Jimmy Shearer, 1948. Featured and recorded by Vaughn Monroe, with The Moon Maids and his Orchestra (RCA Victor).

In My Eyes. w/m Barbara Wyrick, 1984. #1 Country chart record by John Conlee (MCA).

In My Harem. w/m Irving Berlin, 1913.

In My House. w/m Rick James, 1985. Top 10 record by the female quartet Mary Jane Girls (Gordy).

In My Life. w/m John Lennon and Paul McCartney, 1966. Introduced by The Beatles in their album "Rubber Soul" (Capitol). Judy Collins made it the title song of an album of hers (Elektra), 1966.

In My Little Hope Chest. w/m W. Franke Harling and Sam Coslow, 1930. From (MM) *Honey,* starring Nancy Carroll.

In My Little Red Book. w/m Ray Bloch, Nat Simon, and Al Stillman, 1938. Among recordings: Dick Powell (Decca); Ted Weems, vocal by Perry Como (Decca); The Original Dixieland Jazz Band (Bluebird).

In My Loneliness. w/m Jon Mayer and Leida Snow, 1976. Recorded by Nancy Wilson (Capitol).

In My Lonely Room. w/m Brian Holland, Eddie Holland, and Lamont Dozier, 1964.

Chart record by Martha and The Vandellas (Gordy).

In My Merry Oldsmobile. w. Vincent P. Bryan, m. Gus Edwards, 1905. The song referred to an almost-trans-continental trip (Detroit, Michigan to Portland, Oregon) to publicize the car and the Lewis and Clark Exposition. It was sung by Donald O'Connor, Jack Oakie, and Peggy Ryan in (MM) *The Merry Monahans.* It was later used as a radio and television commercial theme for the automobile.

In My Own Little Corner. w. Oscar Hammerstein II, m. Richard Rodgers, 1957. Introduced by Julie Andrews in (TVM) *Cinderella.*

In My Room. w/m Brian Wilson and Gary Usher, 1963. Popular record by The Beach Boys (Capitol).

In My Sweet Little Alice Blue Gown. See **Alice Blue Gown.**

Innamorata (Sweetheart). w. Jack Brooks, m. Harry Warren, 1955. Sung by Dean Martin, and sung and danced by Shirley MacLaine in (MM) *Artists and Models.* Recorded by Martin (Capitol) and Jerry Vale (Columbia).

Inner City Blues (Make Me Wanna Holler). w/m Marvin Gaye and James Myx, Jr., 1971. Top 10 record by Marvin Gaye (Tamla).

Inner Light, The. w/m George Harrison, 1968. Chart record coupled with the gold record-awarded side "Lady Madonna" (q.v.) by The Beatles (Capitol).

Innocent Man, An. w/m Billy Joel, 1984. Top 10 single by Billy Joel (Columbia).

In Old Chicago. w. Mack Gordon, m. Harry Revel, 1938. Sung by Alice Faye and chorus in (MM) *In Old Chicago.* Dick Stabile recorded it (Bluebird).

In Old New York. See **Streets of New York, The.**

In Other Words. See **Fly Me to the Moon.**

In Our Time. w/m Lee Hazlewood, 1966. Recorded by Nancy Sinatra (Reprise).

In Paris and in Love. w. Leo Robin, m. Sigmund Romberg, 1954. Introduced by Jeanmaire and David Atkinson in (TM) *The Girl in Pink Tights.*

Inseparable. w/m Charles Jackson, Jr. and Marvin Yancy, 1976. Chart record by Natalie Cole (Capitol).

In Shadowland. w. Sam M. Lewis and Joe Young, m. Ruth Brooks and Fred E. Ahlert, 1924.

Inside—Looking Out. w. Eric Burdon and Bryan Chandler, m. Burdon, Chandler, and Alan Lomax, 1966. Recorded by the English group The Animals (MGM).

Inside Love (So Personal). w/m Kashif, 1983. Recorded by George Benson (Warner Bros.).

Instant Karma (We All Shine On). w/m John Lennon, 1970. Gold Record by John Ono Lennon (Apple).

Intermezzo. w. Robert Henning, m. Heinz Provost, 1941. Theme of the Swedish motion picture (MP) *Intermezzo*, featuring Ingrid Bergman, 1936. It was remade in the United States (1939) as (MP) *Intermezzo: A Love Story*, with Leslie Howard, co-starring Bergman in her first American film. The musical theme subtitled "Souvenir de Vienne," was an integral part of the American version. Through the success of the movie, heavy radio play, and many record releases, the song became #1 on all of the charts and "Your Hit Parade." Among the top recordings, all instrumental except for Freddy Martin, vocal by Clyde Rogers (Bluebird), were those by Guy Lombardo (#1) (Decca); Wayne King (Victor); Benny Goodman (Columbia); Charlie Spivak (Okeh).

Intermission Riff. w. Steve Graham, m. Ray Wetzel, 1946. Featured and recorded by Stan Kenton and his Orchestra (Capitol).

In the Air Tonight. w/m Phil Collins, 1981. Recorded by the English vocalist/writer Phil Collins (Atlantic).

In the Arms of Love. w. Ray Evans and Jay Livingston, m. Henry Mancini, 1966. From the soundtrack of (MP) *What Did You Do in the War, Daddy?* Leading record by Andy Williams (Columbia).

In the Baggage Coach Ahead. w/m Gussie L. Davis, 1896. This was the most famous song written by the first successful black songwriter in Tin Pan Alley. Introduced by Imogene Comer.

In the Blue of Evening. w. Tom Adair, m. Alfred A. D'Artega, 1942. Introduced by D'Artega and his Orchestra. Best-selling record by Tommy Dorsey, vocal by Frank Sinatra (Victor).

In the Bottle Blues. m. Joe "King" Oliver, Eddie Lang, and Clarence Williams, 1929. This instrumental, written by three leading jazz musicians, was first recorded by Williams and his Orchestra (Okeh).

In the Bush. w/m Patrick Adams and Sandra Cooper, 1978. Recorded by the disco trio Musique (Prelude).

In the Chapel in the Moonlight. w/m Billy Hill, 1936, 1954. Best-selling records by Shep Fields and his Orchestra (Bluebird) and Ruth Etting (Decca). The song was on "Your Hit Parade" for fourteen weeks, reaching the #1 position. Eighteen years later, via a hit record by Kitty Kallen arranged and conducted by Jack Pleis (Decca), it again made the survey, this time reaching #5. Later successful records by The Bachelors (London), 1965, and Dean Martin (Reprise), 1967.

In the Cool, Cool, Cool of the Evening. w. Johnny Mercer, m. Hoagy Carmichael, 1951. Introduced by Bing Crosby and Jane Wyman in (MM) *Here Comes the Groom*. The song was the Academy Award winner, 1951. Hit records by Crosby and Wyman (Decca) and Frankie Laine and Jo Stafford (Columbia).

In the Cool of the Evening. w. Walter Bullock, m. Jule Styne, 1940. Introduced by Frances Langford in (MM) *Hit Parade of 1941*, and on records (Decca). It was interpolated in (MM) *Is Everybody Happy*, 1943.

In the Dark. w/m Billy Squier, 1981. Recorded by Billy Squier (Capitol).

In the Dark. m. Leon "Bix" Beiderbecke, 1931. Instrumental, first recorded, arranged by, and featuring Beiderbecke at the piano with his band (Victor). Later recorded by Jess Stacy (Decca) and Bobby Sherwood (Capitol).

In the Evening. w/m Walter Donaldson, 1924.

In the Evening by the Moonlight. w. Andrew B. Sterling, m. Harry Von Tilzer, 1912.

In the Garden (He Walks with Me and He Talks with Me). w/m C. Austin Miles, 1912. One of the most popular of the Protestant hymns. Jimmy Randolph recorded a contemporary gospel version, arranged and conducted by Bob Mersey (Arliss), 1961.

In the Garden of my Heart. w. Caro Roma, m. Ernest R. Ball, 1908. Popular song of the day. Sung by Nelson Eddy in his film debut in (MM) *Broadway to Hollywood*, 1933.

In the Garden of Tomorrow. w. George Graff, Jr., m. Jessie L. Deppen, 1924.

In the Ghetto. w/m Scott Davis, 1969. Gold record by Elvis Presley (RCA). Chart record by Candi Staton (Fame), 1972.

In the Gold Fields of Nevada. w. Edgar Leslie, m. Archie Gottler, 1915.

In the Good Old Summertime. w. Ren Shields, m. George Evans, 1902. Introduced by Blanche Ring in (TM) *The Defender*. When it was initially published, the song sold over a million copies of sheet music. It was the title song of the Judy Garland-Van Johnson film (MM) *In The Good Old Summertime*.

In the Great Somewhere. w/m Paul Dresser, 1901.

In the Heat of the Night. w. Marilyn Bergman and Alan Bergman, m. Quincy Jones, 1967. Sung by Ray Charles on the soundtrack of (MP) *In the Heat of the Night*, and on his Top 40 record (ABC/TRC).

In the House of Too Much Trouble. w/m Will A. Heelan and J. Fred Helf, 1900.

In the Jailhouse Now. w/m Jimmie Rodgers, 1928. Written and recorded by the famous country singer/writer Jimmie Rodgers (Victor). Johnny Cash had a hit record (Columbia), 1962.

In the Land of Beginning Again. w. Grant Clarke, m. George W. Meyer, 1918. The song was revived by Bing Crosby in (MM) *The Bells of St. Mary's* in 1945 and recorded by him (Decca).

In the Land of Harmony. w. Bert Kalmar, m. Ted Snyder, 1911. Recorded by Arthur Collins (Columbia) and The American Quartet (Victor).

In the Land of Oo-Bla-Dee. w/m Mary Lou Williams and Milton Orent, 1949. Introduced by Mary Lou Williams and her Band (King). Best-selling record by The Benny Goodman Sextet, vocal by Buddy Greco (Capitol).

In the Little Red School House. w/m Al Wilson and James A. Brennan, 1921. Featured and recorded by Earnest Hare and Billy Jones (Edison).

In the Merry Month of May. w. Ren Shields, m. George Evans, 1903. Introduced by Ren Sheilds in vaudeville. Sequel to the writers' hit "In The Good Old Summertime" (q.v.).

In the Merry Month of Maybe. w. Ira Gershwin and Billy Rose, m. Harry Warren, 1931. Sung by Ethel Norris and Tom Monroe in Billy Roses's (TM) *Crazy Quilt*. Frankie Trumbauer and his Orchestra recorded it (Brunswick).

In the Middle of a Heartache. w/m Laurie Christenson, Pat Franzese, and Wanda Jackson, 1961. Introduced and recorded by Wanda Jackson (Capitol).

In the Middle of a Kiss. w/m Sam Coslow, 1935. Sung in (MP) *College Scandal* by Johnny Downs. Recordings: Hal Kemp, vocal by Skinnay Ennis (Brunswick); Morton Downey (Melotone); Gertrude Niesen (Columbia); Jan Garber, vocal by Lee Bennett (Victor); Smith Ballew (Melotone).

In the Middle of an Island. w/m Nick Aquaviva and Ted Varnick, 1957. Leading record by Tony Bennett (Columbia), followed by Tennessee Ernie Ford (Capitol).

In the Middle of May. w. Al Stillman, m. Fred E. Ahlert, 1945. Featured and recorded by Freddy Martin and his Orchestra (Victor) and The Pied Pipers (Capitol).

In the Middle of Nowhere. w. Harold Adamson, m. Jimmy McHugh, 1944. Introduced by Perry Como in his film debut in (MM) *Something for the Boys*, the film version of Cole Porter's stage musical. The only Porter song kept was the title song.

In the Middle of the House. w/m Bob Hilliard, 1956. Novelty. Leading records by Vaughn Monroe (RCA), Rusty Draper (Mercury).

In the Middle of the Night. w. Billy Rose, m. Walter Donaldson, 1925.

In the Midnight Hour. w/m Wilson Pickett and Steve Cropper, 1965. Introduced and recorded by Wilson Pickett (Atlantic). Revived by The Mirettes (Revue), 1968; Cross Country (Atco), 1973; Samantha Sang (U.A.), 1979.

In the Mission of St. Augustine. w/m Jack Chiarelli, 1953. Introduced and recorded by Sammy Kaye, vocal by Jeffrey Clay (Columbia).

In the Misty Moonlight. w/m Cindy Walker, 1964. Top 20 record by Jerry Wallace (Challenge). Chart record by Dean Martin (Reprise), 1967. Country chart record by George Morgan (Four Star), 1975.

In the Mood. w. Andy Razaf, m. Joe Garland, 1939. See **Tar Paper Stomp**, an instrumental by Joe Garland and Wingy Manone on which this was based. New version introduced in 1938 by Edgar Hayes and his Orchestra (Decca). Glenn Miller's recording (Bluebird) became his biggest seller to-date and remained associated with him. The Miller band played it in (MM) *Sun Valley Serenade*, 1941. It was heard again in (MM) *The Glenn Miller Story*, 1954. Top 10 instrumental by Ernie Fields and his Band (Rendezvous), 1959. Other chart versions by Bette Midler (Atlantic), 1974; Henhouse Five Plus Too (Warner Bros.), 1977.

In the Moon Mist. w. and adapt. Jack Lawrence, m. Benjamin Louis Godard, 1946. Adapted from a theme from the nineteenth century French composer's *Berceuse from Jocelyn*. Among recordings: Johnny Desmond (Victor), Randy Brooks and his Orchestra (Decca), Will Osborne and his Orchestra (Black and White).

In the Name of Love. w/m Kenny Rankin and Estelle Levitt, 1964. Introduced and recorded by Peggy Lee (Capitol).

In the Navy. w. Henri Belolo, Victor Willis, and Jacques Morali, m. Morali, 1979. Top 10 gold record by The Village People (Casablanca).

In the Park in Paree. w. Leo Robin, m. Ralph Rainger, 1933. Introduced by Maurice Chevalier in (MM) *A Bedtime Story*. In 1963, he sang it in a cameo appearance in (MP) *A New Kind of Love*. The song was recorded by the bands of: Paul Whiteman (Victor), Ted Fio Rito (Brunswick), Roy Smeck (Melotone), Paul Tremaine (Bluebird). Freddy Martin recorded it under two pseudonyms, the Hotel Bossert Orchestra (Columbia) and Ed Lloyd (Melotone).

In the Quiet Morning. w/m Mimi Farina, 1971. Written in memory of Janis Joplin; recorded by the writer's sister Joan Baez (A&M).

In the Rain. w/m Tony Hester, 1972. Top 10 record by The Dramatics (Volt).

In the Shade of the New Apple Tree. w. E. Y. Harburg, m. Harold Arlen, 1937. From (TM) *Hooray for What!* Introduced by Jack Whiting and June Clyde, backed by the vocal arranger Hugh Martin and his singing group, including his future songwriting partner Ralph Blane.

In the Shade of the Old Apple Tree. w. Harry H. Williams, m. Egbert Van Alsytne, 1905. Leading recordings by Henry Burr (Edison), Albert Campbell (Columbia), The Haydn Quartette (Victor), and Arthur Pryor's Band (Victor).

In the Shadows. w. E. Ray Goetz, m. Herman Finck, 1910. Published as an orchestral dance. Goetz's words were added in 1911.

In the Shape of a Heart. w/m Jackson Browne, 1986. Recorded by Jackson Browne (Elektra).

In the Still of the Night. w/m Cole Porter, 1937. Introduced by Nelson Eddy in (MM) *Rosalie.* Among recordings: Tommy Dorsey, vocal by Jack Leonard (Victor); Jack Marshard, vocal by Vaughn Monroe (Brunswick); Leo Reisman's Orchestra (Brunswick); Helen O'Connell (Capitol). It was heard in the Porter biography (MM) *Night and Day* in 1945.

In the Still of the Nite (a.k.a. **I'll Remember**). w/m Fred Parris, 1956. A top R&B hit by The Five Satins, recorded in a church basement in New Haven, Conn. (Ember). Their record was high on the pop charts in 1956 and again in 1960. The guitar duo of Santo and Johnny had a popular instrumental version in 1964. (Canadian-American) and Paul Anka revived it vocally in 1969 (RCA).

In the Summer of His years. w. Herbert Kretzmer, m. David Lee, 1963. Written in England as a tribute to the assassinated American President John F. Kennedy. Introduced by Millicent Martin on the BBC series (TVP) "That Was the Week That Was." Her recording was released in the U.S. (ABC-Paramount). Connie Francis also had a popular version (MGM).

In the Summertime. w/m Ray Dorset, 1970. Gold record by the British skiffle quartet, Mungo Jerry, led by Ray Dorset (Janus).

In the Sweet Bye and Bye. w. Vincent P. Bryan, m. Harry Von Tilzer, 1902. A popular song of its day, not to be confused with the hymn of the same title.

In the Town Where I Was Born. w. Dick Howard and William Tracey, m. Al Harriman, 1914. Leading record by Owen McCormack (Edison).

In the Valley of the Moon. w/m Charles Tobias and Joe Burke, 1933. Featured on radio and records by Singin' Sam, the Barbasol Man (Melotone), and George Hall and his Orchestra (Bluebird).

In the Wee Small Hours of the Morning. w. Bob Hilliard, m. David Mann, 1955. Featured and recorded by Frank Sinatra (Capitol).

In the Wildwood Where the Bluebells Grow. w/m Herbert H. Taylor, 1907.

In the Year 2525 (Exordium and Terminus). w/m Rick Evans, 1969. #1 gold record by the Nebraska duo of Zager and Evans (RCA).

Into Each Life Some Rain Must Fall. w/m Allan Roberts and Doris Fisher, 1944. #1 record by Ella Fitzgerald and The Ink Spots (Decca). Revived by Teresa Brewer, accompanied by Les Brown's Orchestra (Coral).

Into My Heart. w. Roy Turk, m. Fred E. Ahlert, 1930. Introduced by Ramon Novarro in (MM) *In Gay Madrid.*

In Too Deep. w/m Tony Banks, Phil Collins, and Mike Rutherford, 1987. Top 10 record from the album, "Invisible Touch," written and recorded by the British trio Genesis (Atlantic).

Into the Mystic. w/m Van Morrison, 1970. Recorded by Johnny Rivers (Imperial).

Into the Night. w/m Benny Mardones and Robert Tepper, 1980. Recorded by Benny Mardones (Polydor).

Invincible. w/m Holly Knight and Simon Climie, 1985. Based on a theme from (MP) *The Legend of Billie Jean.* Top 10 record by Pat Benatar (Chrysalis).

Invisible Tears. w/m Ned Miller and Sue Miller, 1964. Popular recording by The Ray Conniff Singers (Columbia). Also recorded by Ned Miller (Fabor).

Invisible Touch. w/m Phil Collins, Mike Rutherford, and Tony Banks, 1986. Written and #1 record by the British trio Genesis (Atlantic).

Invitation. w. Paul Francis Webster, m. Bronislau Kaper, 1953. Theme from (MP) *Invitation.* Webster's lyrics were added later. Leading recording by Les Brown and his Orchestra (Coral).

Invitation to a Broken Heart. w/m Phil Baker, Paul Mann, and Al Lewis, 1951. Recorded by Toni Arden, with Percy Faith's Orchestra (Columbia).

Invitation to the Blues. w/m Doris Fisher, Allan Roberts, and Arthur Gershwin, 1944. Featured and recorded by Ella Mae Morse (Capitol).

In Walked Bud. m. Thelonious Monk, 1948. Jazz instrumental recorded by Thelonious Monk (Blue Note).

In Your Eyes. w/m Peter Gabriel, 1986. Recorded by the British singer/writer Peter Gabriel (Geffen).

In Your Letter. w/m Gary Richrath, 1981. Recorded by the quintet REO Speedwagon (Epic).

In Your Own Little Way. w. Charles Newman, m. J. Fred Coots, 1937. Featured and recorded by the bands of Jimmie Grier, vocal by Joy Hodges (Brunswick) and Charlie Barnet, vocal by Kathleen Lane (Bluebird).

In Zanzibar—My Little Chimpanzee. w. Will D. Cobb, m. Gus Edwards, 1904. From (TM) *The Medal and the Maid.*

I Only Have Eyes for You. w. Al Dubin, m. Harry Warren, 1934. Introduced by Dick Powell and Ruby Keeler in (MM) *Dames.* In one of Busby Berkeley's most imaginatively staged scenes, Powell, in a subway dream sequence, sees Keeler on dozens of billboards and then on boards on the backs of a chorus of girls. The scene culminates with the pictures, jigsaw-fashion, interlocking into one giant-size photo of Keeler. The song was interpolated on the soundtrack by Al Jolson, dubbing for Larry Parks in (MM) *Jolson Sings Again,* 1949; on the soundtrack of (MM) *Young Man with a Horn,* 1950; by Gordon MacRae and Virginia Gibson in (MM) *Tea for Two,* 1950. The Flamingos revived it with a hit record in 1959 (End), as did Art Garfunkel in 1975 (Columbia).

I Only Want a Buddy, Not a Sweetheart. w/m Eddie Jones, 1939. Leading recordings by Dick Jurgens, vocal by Eddy Howard (Vocalion), and Louise Massey and the Westerners, vocal by Curt Massey (Vocalion).

I Only Want to Be with You. w/m Mike Hawker and Ivor Raymonde, 1964. English song. First chart record by Dusty Springfield (Philips). Later successful versions by The Bay City Rollers (Arista), 1976; The Tourists (Epic), 1980; Nicolette Larson (Warner Bros.), 1982.

I.O.U. w/m Kerry Chater and Austin Roberts, 1983. Country/Pop chart crossover record by Lee Greenwood (MCA).

I Overlooked an Orchid. w/m Shirley Lyn, Carl Smith, and Carl Story, 1974. #1 Country record by Mickey Gilley (Playboy).

I Pity the Fool. w/m Deadric Malone, 1961. First record by Bobby Bland (Duke), followed in 1971 by Ann Peebles (Hi).

I Played Fiddle for the Czar. w. Mack Gordon, m. Harry Revel, 1932. Novelty written for but deleted from an unsuccessful

Broadway musical (TM) *Smiling Faces*. Introduced and featured by Ben Bernie and his Orchestra.

I Pledge My Love. w/m Dino Fekaris and Freddie Perren, 1908. Recorded by Peaches and Herb (Polydor).

I Poured My Heart into a Song. w/m Irving Berlin, 1939. Sung by Tyrone Power and Rudy Vallee in (MM) *Second Fiddle*, and recorded by Vallee (Decca). Also recorded by the bands of Jimmy Dorsey (Decca), Artie Shaw (Bluebird), and Jan Garber (Vocalion). Academy Award nominee for Best Song.

I Prefer the Moonlight. w/m G. Chapman and M. Wright, 1987. Top 10 title song single from the album by Kenny Rogers (RCA).

I Promise to Remember. w/m Jimmy Castor and Jimmy Smith, 1956. Popular record by Frankie Lymon and The Teenagers (Gee).

I Promise You. w. Johnny Mercer, m. Harold Arlen, 1944. Introduced by Bing Crosby and Betty Hutton in (MM) *Here Come the Waves*.

I Put My Hand In. w/m Jerry Herman, 1963. Introduced by Carol Channing and company in (TM) *Hello, Dolly!* Song not used in film version.

I Quit My Pretty Mama. w/m Ivory Joe Hunter and Lois Mann, 1950. R&B chart hit by Ivory Joe Hunter (King).

I Raised My Hat. w/m Franz Steininger and Edward Pola, 1933. Written and first published in London. Introduced in U.S. by Rudy Vallee on his radio show and recorded by him (Victor). Other records: Enric Madriguera (Columbia), Adrian Rollini (Melotone), Guy Lombardo (Perfect).

I Ran (So Far Away). w/m Ali Score, Mike Score, Frank Maudley, and Paul Reynolds, 1982. Top 10 record by the English quartet A Flock of Seagulls (Jive).

I Ran All the Way Home. w/m Bennie Benjamin and George David Weiss, 1951. Leading recordings by Sarah Vaughn (Colum-

bia), Buddy Greco (Coral), Dean Martin (Capitol).

I Really Didn't Mean It. w/m Luther Vandross, 1987. Top 10 R&B chart record by Luther Vandross (Epic).

I Really Don't Need No Light. w/m Jeffrey Osborne and David Wolinski, 1982. Top 10 R&B, chart Pop record by Jeffrey Osborne (A&M).

I Really Don't Want to Know. w/ Howard Barnes, m. Don Robertson, 1954. Hit recording by Les Paul and Mary Ford (Capitol). Revived with chart records by Tommy Edwards (MGM), 1960; "Little Esther" Phillips (Lenox), 1963; Ronnie Dove (Diamond), 1966; Elvis Presley (RCA), 1971.

Ireland Is Ireland to Me. w. Fiske O'Hara and J. Keirn Brennan, m. Ernest R. Ball, 1915.

Ireland Must Be Heaven, for My Mother Came from There. w. Joseph McCarthy and Howard Johnson, m. Fred Fisher, 1916. Charles Harrison (Victor) had a popular recording.

I Remember It Well. w. Alan Jay Lerner, m. Frederick Loewe, 1958. Introduced by Maurice Chevalier and Hermione Gingold in (MM) *Gigi*. Sung by Alfred Drake and Maria Karnilova in the stage version (TM) *Gigi*, 1973.

I Remember the Cornfields. w/m Martin Mayne and Harry Ralton, 1950. English song first recorded by Ann Shelton (London). Evelyn Knight, with Gordon Jenkins's Orchestra had first U.S. recording (Decca) followed by Guy Lombardo and his Orchestra (Decca), Billy Vaughn and his Orchestra (Dot), Rod McKuen (Decca), and others.

I Remember You. w. Johnny Mercer, m. Victor Schertzinger, 1942. Introduced by Dorothy Lamour, Bob Eberly, and Jimmy Dorsey and his Orchestra in (MM) *The Fleet's In*. The Dorsey-Eberly combination (Decca) and Harry James, vocal by Helen Forrest (Columbia), had the most popular recordings. Revived in the early fifties by the George Shearing Trio (MGM). English singer Frank Ifield had a Top 10 record in 1962 (Columbia).

Irene. w. Joseph McCarthy, m. Harry Tierney, 1919. The title song of (TM) *Irene* was introduced by Edith Day and ensemble. In the film version (MM) *Irene*, 1940, it was sung by the chorus. Debbie Reynolds and ensemble sang it in the 1973 revival on Broadway.

Irma La Douce. w. Julian More, David Heneker, Monty Norman, m. Marguerite Monnot, 1960. Original French lyrics by Alexandre Breffort. Introduced in the U.S. in the New York production of the French musical (TM) *Irma La Douce* by Elizabeth Seal who two years earlier sang it in the London production.

Irresistible. w. Johnny Burke, m. Harold Spina, 1934. Most popular record: Glen Gray and the Casa Loma Orchestra, vocal by Kenny Sargent (Decca).

Irresistible You. w/m Don Raye and Gene DePaul, 1944. Introduced by Ginny Simms, George Murphy, and Tommy Dorsey's Orchestra in (MM) *Broadway Rhythm.* Leading records: Simms (Columbia); Woody Herman, with his Orchestra (Decca); Johnny Johnston (Capitol).

I Said My Pajamas (and Put On My Pray'rs). w/m Edward Pola and George Wyle, 1950. Best-selling record by Tony Martin and Fran Warren, with Henri René's Orchestra (RCA Victor). Other popular versions by Ethel Merman and Ray Bolger, with Sy Oliver's Orchestra (Decca); Doris Day, with composer George Wyle's Orchestra (Columbia); Margaret Whiting, with Frank DeVol's Orchestra (Capitol).

I Said No. w. Frank Loesser, m. Jule Styne, 1941. Introduced by Betty Jane Rhodes in (MM) *Sweater Girl* and on records (Decca). Top-selling and most-played records, however, were by Alvino Rey, vocal by Yvonne King (Bluebird) and Jimmy Dorsey, vocal by Helen O'Connell (Decca).

I Sang Dixie. w/m Dwight Yoakam, 1989. Hit Country record by Dwight Yoakam (Reprise).

Is Anybody Goin' to San Antone? w/m Dave Kirby and Glenn Martin, 1970. Hit C&W and Pop chart record by Charley Pride (RCA).

I Saw Her Again. w/m John Phillips and Dennis Doherty, 1966. Top 10 record by The Mamas and The Papas (Dunhill). Written by two members of the popular quartet.

I Saw Her at Eight O'Clock. w. Johnny Mercer, m. Matt Malneck, 1935. Sung by Johnny Mercer, Evelyn Poe, and Fred Keating in (MM) *To Beat the Band.*

I Saw Her Standing There. w/m John Lennon and Paul McCartney, 1964. Coupled with The Beatles' first U.S single hit "I Want To Hold Your Hand" (Capitol). Revived as "I Saw Him Standing There" by Tiffany (MCA), 1988.

I Saw Him Standing There. See **I Saw Her Standing There.**

I Saw Linda Yesterday. w/m Dickey Lee and Allen Reynolds, 1963. Introduced and recorded by Dickey Lee (Smash).

I Saw Me. w/m June Davis, 1963. Country chart record by George Jones (United Artists).

I Saw Mommy Kissing Santa Claus. w/m Tommie Connor, 1952. Thirteen-year-old Tommy Boyd had a #1 million-seller with this Christmas novelty (Columbia). Other popular versions by Molly Bee (Capitol) and Spike Jones, vocal by George Rock (RCA Victor).

I Saw Stars. w/m Maurice Sigler, Al Goodhart, and Al Hoffman, 1934. Popular song on radio and in sheet music sales. Among recordings: Paul Whiteman (Victor), Joe Haymes (Melotone), Freddy Martin (Brunswick), Morton Downey (Perfect).

I Saw the Light. w/m Todd Rundgren, 1971. Top 20 record by Todd Rundgren (Bearsville).

I Saw the Light. w/m Hank Williams, 1948. Introduced and popularized by Hank Williams. In his film story (MM) *Your Cheatin' Heart*, 1965, it was sung by Hank Williams, Jr., dubbing for George Hamilton who played the composer-singer.

I Say a Little Prayer. w. Hal David, m. Burt Bacharach, 1967. Gold records by Dionne Warwick, who introduced the song (Scepter) and Aretha Franklin (Atlantic), 1986. Glen Campbell and Anne Murray sang it in medley with "By the Time I Get to Phoenix" (q.v.) (Capitol), 1971.

I Say Hello. w/m Harold Rome, 1959. Introduced by Dolores Gray in (TM) *Destry Rides Again*.

I Say It's Spinach. w/m Irving Berlin, 1932. Sung by J. Harold Murray and Katherine Carrington in (TM) *Face the Music*. The title comes from a Peter Arno cartoon in The New Yorker showing a rich young boy rejecting a plate of broccoli that is being served to him, and saying: "I say it's spinach . . . . and the hell with it!"

I Scream, You Scream (We All Scream for Ice Cream). w/m Robert King, Howard Johnson, and Billy Moll, 1927. Featured and recorded by Fred Waring's Pennsylvanians, vocal by Waring, Poley McClintock, and singers (Victor).

I'se a Muggin'. w/m Stuff Smith, 1936. Introduced and featured by Stuff Smith and his combo, featuring trumpeter Jonah Jones, at the Onyx Club on 52nd Street, New York. The group's recording (Vocalion), the hit record, was on two sides of a 78-rpm disc as were those by Paul Whiteman's Three T's [C-melody saxophonist Frankie Trumbauer, trombonist Jack Teagarden, trumpeter Charlie Teagarden] (Victor) and Mezz Mezzrow's combo (Bluebird). This novelty swing tune went into the books of many big bands.

I Second That Emotion. w/m William Robinson and Alfred Cleveland, 1967. Top 10 record by writer Smokey Robinson and The Miracles (Tamla).

I See a Million People (But All I Can See Is You). w. Robert Sour, m. Una Mae Carlisle, 1941. Introduced by Una Mae Carlisle (Bluebird). Best-selling record: Cab Calloway, vocal by Calloway (Okeh).

I See the Light. w/m John Durrill, Norman Ezell, and Mike Rabon, 1966. Recorded by The Five Americans (HBR).

I See the Moon. w/m Meredith Willson, 1953. Introduced by The Mariners on the Arthur Godfrey television show and recorded by them (Columbia). The Voices of Walter Schumann, a choral group, also recorded it (RCA Victor).

I See the Want in Your Eyes. w/m Wayne Carson Thompson, 1974. Hit Country record by Conway Twitty (MCA).

I See Two Lovers. w. Mort Dixon, m. Allie Wrubel, 1934. Introduced by Dick Powell in (MM) *Flirtation Walk*. Helen Morgan interpolated it in (MM) *Sweet Music* in 1935 and her interpretation was released as a single (Brunswick). Eddy Duchin recorded it (Victor) and Russ Columbo's version was released posthumously (Special Edition).

I See Your Face Before Me. w. Howard Dietz, m. Arthur Schwartz, 1937. Introduced by Evelyn Laye and reprised by Adele Dixon and Jack Buchanan in (TM) *Between the Devil*.

Is Everybody Happy Now? w/m Maurice Rubens, Jack Osterman, and Ted Lewis, 1927. Introduced by Ted Lewis in (TM) *Artists and Models of 1927*. Lewis and band played it in (MM) *Is Everybody Happy?* in 1929.

I'se Your Nigger if You Wants Me, Liza Jane. w/m Paul Dresser, 1896.

I Shall Be Released. w/m Bob Dylan, 1968. Recorded in albums by Bob Dylan (Columbia) and The Band (Capitol). Leading single by The Box Tops (Mala), 1969.

I Shall Sing. w/m Van Morrison, 1974. Top 40 record by Art Garfunkel (Columbia).

I Shot the Sheriff. w/m Bob Marley, 1974. English-born Eric Clapton recorded this Jamaican reggae song in his album "461 Ocean Boulevard," the address of the Miami house in which he lived during the recording of the LP. The single release became a #1 gold record (RSO).

I Should Be So Lucky. w/m Mike Stock, Matt Aitken, and Pete Waterman, 1988. Recorded by Kylie Minogue from the album "Kylie" (Geffen).

I Should Be with You. w/m Steve Wariner, 1988. Top 10 Country chart record by Steve Wariner (MCA).

I Should Care. w/m Sammy Cahn, Axel Stordahl, and Paul Weston, 1945. Introduced by Robert Allen in (MM) *Thrill of a Romance*. Best-seller by Frank Sinatra (Columbia). Other top recordings: Martha Tilton (Capitol); Tommy Dorsey, vocal by Bonnie Lou Williams and the Sentimentalists (Victor); Jimmy Dorsey, vocal by Teddy Walters (Decca). Later chart records by Ralph Flanagan, vocal by Harry Prime (RCA Victor), 1952; Jeff Chandler (Decca), 1954.

I Should Have Known Better. w/m John Lennon and Paul McCartney, 1964. Introduced by The Beatles in (MM) *A Hard Day's Night*, and on records (Capitol).

I Should Have Known You Years Ago. w/m Hoagy Carmichael, 1940. From (MP) *Road Show*. Featured and recorded by Carol Bruce (Decca), The Charioteers (Columbia), Wayne King (Victor) and Freddy Martin (Bluebird) and their orchestras.

Is I in Love? I Is. w. Mercer Cook, m. J. Russel Robinson, 1932.

Is It Any Wonder? w/m Archie Gottler, Robert Hayes, and Leroy Rodde, 1953. Recorded by Joni James (MGM).

Is It Because I'm Black? w/m Jimmie Jones, Glenn C. Watts, and Syl Johnson, 1970. Recorded by Syl Johnson (Twilight).

Is It Love. w/m Richard Page, Steve George, Robert John Lange, and Pat Mastelotto, 1986. Top 10 single by the quartet Mr. Mister (RCA).

Is It Possible? w. Al Dubin, m. Jimmy McHugh, 1939. Introduced by Bobby Clark and Della Lind in (TM) *The Streets of Paris*. Leading record by Jimmy Dorsey, vocal by Helen O'Connell (Decca).

Is It Possible? w. Mort Dixon, m. Harry Woods, 1927.

Is It Really Me? w. Tom Jones, m. Harvey Schmidt, 1963. Introduced by Inga Swenson and Robert Horton in (TM) *110 in the Shade*.

Is It Really Over? w/m Jim Reeves, 1965. Crossover (C&W/Pop) hit by Jim Reeves (RCA).

Is It Something You've Got? w/m Barry Dispenza and Carl Wolfolk, 1969. Top 40 record by Tyrone Davis (Dakar).

Is It True What They Say About Dixie? w. Irving Caesar and Sammy Lerner, m. Gerald Marks, 1936. Al Jolson and Rudy Vallee helped make it a #1 song. In 1943, Iris Adrian and Robin Raymond sang it in (MM) *His Butler's Sister*, starring Deanna Durbin and Franchot Tone. In (MM) *Jolson Sings Again*, 1949, Jolson sang it again, dubbing for Larry Parks.

Is It Wrong (for Loving You). w/m Warner McPherson, 1957. Country/Pop hit recorded by Warner Mack [McPherson] (Decca). Other chart versions by Webb Pierce (Decca), 1960, and Sonny James (Capitol), 1974.

Is It You. w/m Lee Ritenour, Eric Tagg, and Bill Camplin, 1981 Recorded by guitarist Lee Ritenour, vocal by Eric Tagg (Elektra).

Island Girl. w/m Elton John and Bernie Taupin, 1975. #1 gold record by Elton John (MCA).

Island in the Sun. w/m Harry Belafonte and Irving L. Burgie (Lord Burgess), 1957. Introduced by Harry Belafonte in (MP) *Island in the Sun*, and on records (RCA).

Island in the West Indies. w. Ira Gershwin, m. Vernon Duke, 1936. Sung by Gertrude Niesen and ensemble and danced by

Josephine Baker in (TM) *Ziegfeld Follies of 1936*.

Islands in the Stream. w/m Barry Gibb, Robin Gibb, and Maurice Gibb, 1983. From the platinum album "Eyes That See in the Dark" came the best-selling single of the year, also earning a platinum record, by Kenny Rogers and Dolly Parton (RCA).

Isle D'Amour. w. Earl Carroll, m. Leo Edwards, 1913. Introduced by José Collins in (TM) *Ziegfeld Follies of 1913*. Ann Blyth sang it in (MM) *The Merry Monahans* in 1944.

Isle O' Dreams, The. w. George Graff, Jr. and Chauncey Olcott, m. Ernest R. Ball, 1913. Introduced by Chauncey Olcott in (TM) *The Isle O' Dreams*.

Isle of Capri. w. Jimmy Kennedy, m. Will Grosz, 1935. Published in London, shortly after a song with a similar melody, "Ich Bin ein Kleiner Armer Strassensänger" (I Am a Small, Poor Street Singer") was published and performed in a popular revue in Vienna. The Viennese song, also a tango, had words by Beda and music by Paul Reif and Bruno Uher. When "Capri" became a hit in England, Reif, a young composer, sued and won a cash settlement acknowledging his creation. After he emigrated to America, he regretted not demanding royalties and writer's credit. Featured and recorded in the U.S. by Xavier Cugat and his Orchestra (Victor) and many others, the song became a million-copy seller of sheet music. Joe "Wingy" Manone had a hit jazz recording (Vocalion).

Isle of Our Dreams, The. w. Henry Blossom, m. Victor Herbert, 1906. From (TM) *The Red Mill*.

Is My Baby Blue Tonight? w. William Tracey, m. Lou Handman, 1943. Featured and recorded by Lawrence Welk, vocal by Jayne Walton (Decca).

Isn't He Adorable? w. Joseph Allan McCarthy, m. Cy Coleman, 1956. Introduced and featured by Mabel Mercer and later recorded by her (Atlantic). The verse was recorded in-strumentally by Frank Fields and his Orchestra as the title number of his album "Fields and Dreams" (Dot), 1957.

Isn't It Always Love. w/m Karla Bonoff, 1979. Country chart hit by Lynn Anderson (Columbia).

Isn't It a Pity. w/m George Harrison, 1970. Flip side of hit record "My Sweet Lord" by George Harrison (Apple).

Isn't It a Pity? w. Ira Gershwin, m. George Gershwin, 1933. Introduced by George Givot and Josephine Huston in (TM) *Pardon My English*.

Isn't It a Shame? w. Al Sherman and Al Lewis, m. Abner Silver, 1934. Leading records by Jan Garber, vocal by Lee Bennett (Victor); Connie Boswell (Brunswick); Freddy Martin, vocal by Buddy Clark (Brunswick); Joe Reichman, vocal by Chick Bullock (Melotone).

Isn't It Great to Be Married? w. Schuyler Greene, m. Jerome Kern, 1916. From the Princess Theatre production (TM) *Very Good Eddie*.

Isn't It Heavenly? w. E. Y. Harburg, m. Joseph Meyer, 1933. Recordings by Morton Downey (Melotone); the bands of Eddy Duchin (Victor), Will Osborne (Melotone), Bert Lown (Bluebird), and Victor Young (Brunswick).

Isn't It Kinda Fun? w. Oscar Hammerstein, m. Richard Rodgers, 1945. Introduced by Dick Haymes and Vivian Blaine in (MM) *State Fair*. In the 1962 remake (MM) *State Fair*, it was sung by Ann-Margret and David Street.

Isn't It Lonely Together. w/m Rod McBrien and Estelle Levitt, 1975. Recorded by Stark and McBrien (RCA).

Isn't It Romantic? w. Lorenz Hart, m. Richard Rodgers, 1932. The opening number of (MM) *Love Me Tonight*, sung by Maurice Chevalier, Jeanette MacDonald, Bert Roach, Tyler Brook, and Rolf Sedan. In 1948, it was heard as the title song of (MM) *Isn't It Roman-*

tic? that starred Veronica Lake, Mona Free-man, Billy De Wolfe, and Pearl Bailey. It was also the title of a 1985 Broadway play.

Isn't It Time. w/m Ray Kennedy and Jack Conrad, 1977. Recorded by the British quartet The Babys (Chrysalis).

Isn't Life Strange? w/m John Lodge, 1972. Recorded by the British group The Moody Blues (Threshold).

Isn't Love the Grandest Thing? w. Jack Scholl, m. Louis Alter, 1935. Introduced by Bert Wheeler and Dorothy Lee in (MM) *The Rainmakers.*

Isn't Love the Strangest Thing? w. Benny Davis, m. J. Fred Coots, 1936. Recorded by Duke Ellington, vocal by Ivy Anderson (Brunswick).

Isn't She the Sweetest Thing? (Oh Maw, Oh Paw). w. Gus Kahn, m. Walter Donald-son, 1925. Featured in vaudeville and re-corded by Georgie Price (Victor).

Isn't That Just Like Love. w. Johnny Burke, m. James Van Heusen, 1940. Sung by Mary Martin, with the Merry Macs in (MM) *Love Thy Neighbor.* Records: Glenn Miller (Bluebird), Tommy Dorsey (Victor), Bob Crosby (Decca).

Isn't This a Lovely Day? w/m Irving Ber-lin, 1935. Introduced by Fred Astaire and danced by Astaire and Ginger Rogers in (MM) *Top Hat.* Astaire also recorded it (Brunswick).

Isn't This a Night For Love? w/m Val Bur-ton and Will Jason, 1933. From (MM) *Melody Cruise*, starring Phil Harris and Charles Rug-gles.

I Sold My Heart to the Junk Man. w/m Otis J. René and Leon René, 1935. Recorded by Etta Jones with the J. C. Heard Orchestra (Victor).

I Speak to the Stars. w. Paul Francis Webster, m. Sammy Fain, 1954. Introduced by Doris Day in (MM) *Lucky Me.*

Israelites. w/m Desmond Dacris and Leslie Kong, 1969. Top 10 reggae record by the Jamaican group headed by Dacris, under the name of Desmond Dekker and The Aces (Uni).

Is She My Girl Friend? w. Jack Yellen, m. Milton Ager, 1927.

Is She Really Going Out with Him? w/m Joe Jackson, 1979. Recorded by English singer/writer/pianist Joe Jackson (A&M).

Istanbul (Not Constantinople). w. Jimmy Kennedy, m. Nat Simon, 1953. Popularized by The Four Lads (Columbia).

I Started a Joke. w/m Barry Gibb, Robin Gibb, and Maurice Gibb, 1969. Top 10 record by the British trio of brothers, The Bee Gees (Atco).

Is That All There Is? w/m Jerry Leiber and Mike Stoller, 1969. Written earlier for an un-produced musical. Peggy Lee's recording es-tablished the song (Capitol).

Is That Religion? w/m Mitchell Parish and Maceo Pinkard, 1930.

Is That the Way to Treat a Sweetheart? w. Charles Tobias, m. Nat Simon, 1938. Pop-ularized and recorded by Tommy Tucker, vo-cal by Amy Arnell (Vocalion).

Is There Somebody Else? w/m Sammy Mysels, Nelson Cogane, and Dick Robertson, 1940. Recorded by Ella Fitzgerald (Decca) and The Delta Rhythm Boys and The Gulf Coast Five (Decca).

Is There Something I Should Know? w/m Duran Duran, 1983. Top 10 record by the English band Duran Duran (Capitol).

Is This Love. w/m David Coverdale and John Sykes, 1987. Recorded by the British group, Whitesnake, from the album of their name (Geffen).

Is This Love. w/m Jim Peterik and Frankie Sullivan, 1986. Top 10 record by the quintet Survivor (Scotti Brothers).

Is This Me? w/m Bill West and Dottie West, 1963. Country hit by Jim Reeves (RCA).

I Still Believe. w/m Antonia Armato and Bepee Cantarelli, 1988. Chart single by Brenda K. Starr from the album of her name (MCA).

I Still Believe in Love. w. Carole Bayer Sager, m. Marvin Hamlisch, 1978. Introduced by Lucie Arnaz in (TM) *They're Playing Our Song.*

I Still Believe in Waltzes. w/m Michael Hughes, Johnny MacRae, and Bob Morrison, 1981. Country chart hit by Conway Twitty and Loretta Lynn (MCA).

I Still Believe in You. w/m Steve Hill and Christopher Hillman, 1989. Hit Country record by The Desert Rose Band (MCA/Curb).

I Still Can't Get Over Loving You. w/m Ray Parker, Jr., 1983. Recorded by Ray Parker, Jr. (Arista).

I Still Feel the Same About You. w/m Dick Reid and Dick Manning, 1950. Leading records by Georgia Gibbs with The Owen Bradley Sextette (Coral); the Three Suns with The Sons of the Pioneers (RCA Victor).

I Still Get a Thrill (Thinking of You). w. Benny Davis, m. J. Fred Coots, 1930. Featured and recorded by the Guy Lombardo (Columbia) and Ted Weems (Victor) bands, the latter with vocal by Art Jarrett. Later releases by Harry Belafonte, before he turned to folk singing (Capitol); Francis Craig (Bullet); Art Lund (MGM); Dean Martin (Capitol). Dick Haymes had a hit (Decca), 1950.

I Still Get Jealous. w. Sammy Cahn, m. Jule Styne, 1947. Introduced by Nanette Fabray and Jack McCauley in (TM) *High Button Shoes.* Fabray and McCauley's cut from the cast album was released as a single (RCA Victor). Popular recordings by The Three Suns (RCA Victor); Harry James, vocal by Buddy DiVito (Columbia); Gordon MacRae (Capitol); Guy Lombardo, vocal by Kenny Gardner (Decca); Jimmy Dorsey and his Orchestra (MGM).

I Still Haven't Found What I'm Looking For. w/m U2, 1987. #1 single from the album "The Joshua Tree" by the Irish group U2 (Island).

I Still Look at You That Way. w. Howard Dietz, m. Arthur Schwartz, 1963. Introduced by Mary Martin in (TM) *Jennie.*

I Still Love to Kiss You Goodnight. w. Walter Bullock, m. Harold Spina, 1937. Introduced by Pat Paterson in (MM) *Fifty-Second Street.* Featured and recorded by Tommy Tucker, vocal by Amy Arnell (Vocalion).

I Still Love You. w. Jack Yellen, m. Milton Ager, 1928.

I Still See Elisa. w. Alan Jay Lerner, m. Frederick Lowe, 1951. Introduced by James Barton in (TM) *Paint Your Wagon*, and recorded by him (RCA Victor). In (MM) *Paint Your Wagon*, 1969, it was sung by Clint Eastwood.

I Surrender, Dear. w. Gordon Clifford, m. Harry Barris, 1931. Introduced, featured, and recorded (Victor) by Gus Arnheim and his Orchestra, featuring the Rhythm Boys, solo by Bing Crosby. Louis Armstrong also had a recording (Okeh). In 1947, it was heard as the title song of (MM) *I Surrender, Dear*, starring Gloria Jean.

Is You Is or Is You Ain't My Baby? w/m Billy Austin and Louis Jordan, 1944. Introduced by Louis Jordan in (MM) *Follow the Boys* and recorded by him (Decca), sharing the top chart spot with Bing Crosby's version for the same label (Decca). The Andrews Sisters sang it in (MM) *Her Lucky Night*, 1945, and The Delta Rhythm Boys sang it in (MM) *Easy to Look At*, 1945. Revived by Buster Brown (Fire), 1960.

Is Zat You, Myrtle? w/m Bill Carlisle, Charles Louvin, and Ira Louvin, 1953. Top 10 C&W novelty record by The Carlisles (Mercury).

It Ain't Cool to Be Crazy About You. w/m Dean Dillon and Robbie Porter, 1986. #1 Country chart record by George Strait (MCA).

It Ain't Enough. w/m Corey Hart, 1982. Recorded by Corey Hart (EMI America).

It Ain't Gonna Rain No Mo'. w/m Wendell Hall, 1923. Hall, a popular writer/singer/ukelelist, adapted this from a traditional Southern tune. His record (Victor), on which he accompanied himself on the ukelele, sold over two million copies. The sheet music sales were also in the millions. It was interpolated in (MM) *Has Anybody Seen My Gal*, 1952.

It Ain't Me, Babe. w/m Bob Dylan, 1964. Introduced by Bob Dylan and recorded by him (Columbia). Chart record by Johnny Cash (Columbia). Top 10 version by The Turtles (White Whale), 1965.

It Ain't Necessarily So. w. Ira Gershwin, m. George Gershwin, 1935. Introduced by John W. Bubbles in (TM) *Porgy and Bess*. In the film version, (MM) *Porgy and Bess*, 1959, it was performed by Sammy Davis, Jr. It was interpolated on the soundtrack of the George Gershwin film story (MM) *Rhapsody in Blue* in 1945. Among recordings are those by Paul Robeson (Columbia); Lawrence Tibbett (Columbia); Martha Raye (Columbia).

I Take It Back. w/m Perry C. Buie and James B. Cobb, 1967. Top 10 record by Sandy Posey (MGM).

I Take It on Home. w/m Kenny O'Dell, 1972. Country hit, recorded by Charlie Rich (Epic).

I Take the Chance. w/m Ira Louvin and Charles Louvin, 1956. C&W record by Jim Ed and Maxine Brown (RCA). Revived by Ernest Ashworth (Hickory), 1963.

I Take What I Want. w. David Porter and Mabon Hodges, m. Isaac Hayes, 1967. Recorded by James and Bobby Purify (Bell).

Italian Street Song. w. Rida Johnson Young, m. Victor Herbert, 1910. Introduced by Emma Trentini in (TM) *Naughty Marietta*. Sung by Jeanette MacDonald in (MM) *Naughty Marietta*, 1935, and Jane Powell in (MM) *Holiday in Mexico*, 1945.

Italian Theme, The. w. Buddy Kaye (Engl), m. Angelo Giacomazzi and Clyde Hamilton, 1956. Popular instrumental by Cyril Stapelton and his Orchestra (London).

I Talk to the Trees. w. Alan Jay Lerner, m. Frederick Loewe, 1951. Introduced by Tony Bavaar and Olga San Juan in (TM) *Paint Your Wagon*. In (MM) *Paint Your Wagon*, 1969, it was sung by Clint Eastwood.

It All Belongs to Me. w/m Irving Berlin, 1927. From (TM) *Ziegfeld Follies of 1927*.

It All Comes Back to Me Now. w/m Hy Zaret, Joan Whitney, and Alex Kramer, 1941. A Top 5 song, its best-selling records were by Hal Kemp, vocal by Bob Allen (Victor); Ted Weems, vocal by Perry Como (Decca); Gene Krupa, vocal by Howard Dulaney (Okeh); Eddy Duchin, vocal by June Robbins (Columbia).

It All Depends on You. w. B. G. DeSylva and Lew Brown, m. Ray Henderson, 1926. Al Jolson interpolated this in the touring production of (TM) *Big Boy*, which had a short run on Broadway the prior year. Jolson sang it in (MM) *The Singing Fool*, 1928. Doris Day sang it as Ruth Etting in her biography (MM) *Love Me or Leave me*, 1955. Gordon MacRae, Ernest Borgnine, Dan Dailey, and Sheree North performed it in the biography of the writers (MM) *The Best Things in Life Are Free*, 1956.

It Amazes Me. w. Carolyn Leigh, m. Cy Coleman, 1958. Introduced by Mabel Mercer. First recording by Tony Bennett (Columbia).

I Taut I Saw a Puddy Tat. w/m Alan Livingston, Billy May, and Warren Foster, 1950. Novelty. Leading records by Mel Blanc, with Billy May's Orchestra (Capitol); and, in her first recording in twenty years, Helen Kane (Columbia).

It Can't Be Wrong. w. Kim Gannon, m. Max Steiner, 1943. Lyrics to the theme from (MP) *Now, Voyager*, starring Bette Davis and Paul Henreid, were sung by Dick Haymes, with the Song Spinners (Decca), Haymes's first #1 record. The song was on "Your Hit Parade" for twenty weeks.

Itchycoo Park. w/m Ronnie Lane and Steve Marriott, 1967. Recorded in England by the quartet Small Faces, of which the writers were members (Immediate).

Itchy Twitchy Feeling. w/m James Oliver, 1958. Top 40 record by Bobby Hendricks, vocal backing by The Coasters (Sue).

It Could Happen to You. w. Johnny Burke, m. James Van Heusen, 1944. Introduced by Dorothy Lamour and Fred MacMurray in (MM) *And the Angels Sing*. Best-selling records by Jo Stafford (Capitol) and Bing Crosby (Decca).

It Couldn't Be True (Or Could It?) w. Sylvia Dee, m. Sidney Lippman, 1946. Recorded by Tex Beneke and the Glenn Miller Orchestra, vocal by Garry Stevens (RCA Victor); Judy Canova (ARA). Also the bands: Les Brown, vocal by Jack Haskell (Columbia); Guy Lombardo (Decca); Buddy Rich (Mercury); Al Donahue (4-Star); Henry Jerome (Davis).

It Couldn't Have Been Any Better. w/m Ray Griff, 1977. #1 Country chart song by Johnny Duncan, harmony vocal by Janie Fricke (Columbia).

It Didn't Take Long. w/m Holly Knight, 1981. Recorded by the quintet Spider (Dreamland).

It Doesn't Matter Anymore. w/m Paul Anka, 1959. Popular record by Buddy Holly (Coral). Revived by Linda Ronstadt (Capitol), 1975.

It Don't Come Easy. w/m Richard Starkey (Ringo Starr). 1971. Gold record by Beatle alumnus Ringo Starr (Apple).

It Don't Hurt Me Half as Bad. w/m Joe Allen, Deoin Lay, and Bucky Lindsey, 1981. Top 10 Country chart record by Ray Price (Dimension).

It Don't Mean a Thing (If It Ain't Got That Swing). w. Irving Mills, m. Edward Kennedy "Duke" Ellington, 1932. Introduced by Duke Ellington and his Orchestra, vocal by Ivy Anderson. Ellington also recorded it on a 12"

V-disc in World War II. Other important recordings: the Boswell Sisters (Brunswick); Lionel Hampton (Victor); the Mills Brothers (Decca); Paul Gonsalves (EmArcy). The song might well be the first to have used the word "swing" in the context of the form of music to become popular in the late thirties.

It Don't Seem Like the Same Old Smile. w/m James Thornton, 1896. Said to have been written in Bellevue Hospital in New York where the author was "drying out." The "smile" in the title referred to a shot of whiskey which he cadged from an attendant.

It Don't Worry Me. w/m Keith Carradine, 1975. Introduced by Keith Carradine and reprised by Barbara Harris and chorus in (MM) *Nashville*.

It Feels So Good to Be Loved So Bad. w/m Victoria Pike, Roger Joyce, and Teddy Randazzo, 1977. Recorded by The Manhattans (Columbia).

It Goes Like It Goes. w. Norman Gimbel, m. David Shire, 1979. Sung by Jennifer Warnes on the soundtrack of (MP) *Norma Rae*. Academy Award winning song, 1979.

It Goes Like This (That Funny Melody). w. Irving Caesar, m. Cliff Friend, 1928. Novelty song, recorded by Johnny Johnson's Orchestra (Victor), Cliff "Ukulele Ike" Edwards (Columbia), and Fred Hall (Okeh).

It Had to Be You. w. Gus Kahn, m. Isham Jones, 1924, 1944. This major standard had six top selling records in its first year: Marion Harris (Brunswick); Sam Lanin (Okeh); Paul Whiteman (Victor); Cliff "Ukulele Ike" Edwards (Perfect); Isham Jones (Brunswick); Billy Murray and Aileen Stanley (Victor). It has been recorded extensively since. The song has been heard in (MM) *Show Business*, 1944, sung by George Murphy and Constance Moore; (MM) *Incendiary Blonde*, the Texas Guinan story starring Betty Hutton, 1944; (MM) *Living in a Big Way*, 1946; in the Gus Kahn story, (MM) *I'll See You in My Dreams*, 1951, in which Danny Thomas sang it. From the exposure due to the two 1944 film musicals, the revived song was on "Your Hit Parade" for twelve weeks.

I Thank My Lucky Stars. w/m Wayne P. Walker, 1964. Popularized by Eddy Arnold (RCA).

I Thank You. w/m David Porter and Isaac Hayes, 1969. Top 10 record by Sam and Dave (Stax). Chart records by Donny Hathaway and Juen Conquest (Curtom), 1972, and the trio ZZ Top (Warner Bros.), 1980.

It Happened in Monterey. w. Billy Rose, m. Mabel Wayne, 1930. Introduced by John Boles and company in (MM) *The King of Jazz*. Recorded by Paul Whiteman and his Orchestra (Columbia).

It Happened in Sun Valley. w. Mack Gordon, m. Harry Warren, 1941. Introduced by Glenn Miller and his Orchestra, Ray Eberle, Tex Beneke, and The Modernaires in (MM) *Sun Valley Serenade*, and on records (Bluebird).

It Happened Just That Way. w/m Roger Miller, 1964. Introduced and recorded by Roger Miller (Smash).

It Happens Every Spring. w. Mack Gordon, m. Josef Myrow, 1949. Title song of (MP) *It Happens Every Spring*. Recorded by Frank Sinatra (Columbia) and Art Lund (MGM).

It Happens to the Best of Friends. w. Mitchell Parish, m. Rube Bloom, 1934. Featured and recorded by Benny Goodman and his Orchestra (Columbia).

I Think I Know. w/m Curly Putman, 1961. Leading record by Marion Worth (Columbia).

I Think I'll Just Stay Here and Drink. w/m Merle Haggard, 1981. Hit Country record by Merle Haggard (MCA).

I Think I Love You. w/m Tony Romeo, 1970. #1 gold record by The Partridge Family (Bell).

I Think It's Going to Rain Today. w/m Randy Newman, 1966. Introduced and featured by Judy Collins (Elektra). Randy Newman included it in his album "Randy Newman Live" (Reprise), 1971. Revived by Bette Midler in (MP) *Beaches* and its soundtrack album (Atlantic), 1988.

I Think It's Love. w/m Jermaine Jackson, Michael Omartian, and Stevie Wonder, 1986. Recorded by Jermaine Jackson (Arista).

I Think of You. w/m Jack Elliott and Don Marcotte, 1941. Based on the second Theme of the 1st Movement of Sergei Rachmaninoff's *Piano Concerto No. 2 in C Minor*. Introduced and recorded by Tommy Dorsey, vocal by Frank Sinatra (Victor). It was sung by Jane Powell, accompanied by José Iturbi, in (MM) *Holiday in Mexico*, 1946. For another theme from the same concerto, see: *Full Moon and Empty Arms*.

I Think We're Alone Now. w/m Ritchie Cordell, 1967, 1987. Hit record by Tommy James and The Shondells (Roulette). Chart record by The Rubinoos, a Berkeley, California quartet, led by John Rubin (Beserkley). Revived by the #1 hit single from the self-titled debut album of the sixteen-year-old singer Tiffany (MCA).

I Thought About You. w. Johnny Burke, m. James Van Heusen, 1939. Introduced and recorded by Benny Goodman, vocal by Mildred Bailey (Columbia). Other band records of note: Hal Kemp (Victor); Will Bradley, vocal by Carlotta Dale (Vocalion); Bob Crosby, vocal by Teddy Grace (Decca). Later, by pianist-singer Nellie Lutcher (Capitol).

I Thought I Saw a Pussy Cat. See **I Taut I Saw a Puddy Tat.**

I Threw a Bean Bag at the Moon. w. Stanley Adams, m. Milton Ager, 1935. Featured and recorded by Russ Morgan, vocal by Chick Bullock (Melotone) and Art Kassel and his Orchestra (Bluebird).

I Threw a Kiss in the Ocean. w/m Irving Berlin, 1942. Wartime song featured and recorded by Kate Smith (Columbia) and Jimmy Dorsey, vocal by Helen O'Connell (Decca).

I Threw Away the Rose. w/m Merle Haggard, 1967. Top 10 Country chart record by Merle Haggard (Capitol).

I Threw It All Away. w/m Bob Dylan, 1969. Recorded by Bob Dylan (Columbia).

It Hurts to Be in Love. w/m Howard Greenfield and Helen Miller, 1964. Hit record by Gene Pitney (Musicor). Revived by Dan Hartman (Blue Sky), 1981.

It Hurts to Be in Love. w/m Rudy Toombs and Julius Dixon, 1957. R&B recording by Annie Laurie (DeLuxe).

I Tipped My Hat (And Slowly Rode Away). w/m Larry Markes and Dick Charles, 1947. Popular records by Jack Smith (Capitol) and Harry James, vocal by Art Lund (Columbia).

It Is Better to Love. w. Dusty Negulescu, m. Marguerite Monnot, 1962. Introduced by Maurice Chevalier in (MM) *Jessica.*

It Is No Secret (What God Can Do). w/m Stuart Hamblen, 1951. Introduced by Stuart Hamblen (Columbia). Hit records by Bill Kenny, former lead singer of The Ink Spots (Decca), and Jo Stafford (Columbia).

It Isn't Fair. w. Richard Himber, m. Richard Himber, Frank Warshauer, and Sylvester Sprigato, 1933, 1950. Introduced and recorded by, and the theme song of, Richard Himber and his Orchestra (Vocalion). Other recordings of note at that time were by Hal Kemp (Brunswick), Jack Fulton (Vocalion), and Elmer Feldkamp (Crown). In 1950, Don Cornell, singing with Sammy Kaye's Orchestra, revived the song with a best-seller (Victor) that enabled it to spend twelve weeks on "Your Hit Parade." Other recordings by Les Brown (Columbia); Benny Goodman, vocal by Buddy Greco (Capitol); Bill Farrell, orchestra conducted by Russ Case (MGM).

It Isn't Right. w/m Robert Mellin, 1956. Leading record by The Platters (Mercury).

It Keeps Right on A-Hurtin' (Since I Left). w/m Johnny Tillotson and Lorene Mann, 1962. Introduced and recorded by Johnny Tillotson (Cadence).

It Keeps You Running. w/m Michael McDonald, 1976. Top records by Carly Simon (Elektra), 1976, and The Doobie Brothers, the group of which the writer was lead vocalist and keyboardist (Warner Bros.).

It'll Be Me. w/m Sonny Lemaire and James P. Pennington, 1986. First recorded by Tom Jones (Mercury), 1984. #1 Country chart record by the group Exile (Epic).

It Looks Like Rain in Cherry Blossom Lane. w. Edgar Leslie, m. Joe Burke, 1937.

It Looks to Me Like a Big Night Tonight. w. Harry Williams, m. Egbert Van Alstyne, 1908.

It Made You Happy When You Made Me Cry. w/m Walter Donaldson, 1926. Popular recordings by Gene Austin (Victor), Segar Ellis (Okeh), Waring's Pennsylvanians (Victor), Connee Boswell (Decca), and Mel Tormé (Capitol).

It Makes No Difference Now. w/m Floyd Tillman and Jimmie Davis, 1939. David introduced this country standard, which has since been recorded by such artists as Eddy Arnold (Victor); Gene Autry (Okeh); Burl Ives (Decca). It was heard in (MM) *Strictly in the Groove* in 1942.

It May Be Winter Outside (But in My Heart It's Spring). w/m Paul Politi and Barry White, 1966. Recorded by Felice Taylor (Mustang).

It May Sound Silly. w/m Ivory Joe Hunter, 1955. Introduced and recorded by Ivory Joe Hunter (Atlantic). Featured and recorded by The McGuire Sisters (Coral).

It Might As Well Be Spring. w. Oscar Hammerstein II, m. Richard Rodgers, 1945. Introduced by Louanne Hogan, dubbing for Jeanne Crain, in (MM) *State Fair.* It won the Academy Award for Best Song of the Year. In the 1962 remake, the José Ferrer-directed (MM) *State Fair*, it was sung by Anita Gordon dubbing for Pamela Tiffin. Leading recordings by Margaret Whiting, with Paul Weston's Orchestra (Capitol) and Dick Haymes (Decca).

It Might As Well Rain Until September. w/m Gerry Goffin and Carole King, 1962. Introduced and recorded by Carole King (Dimension).

It Might Be You. w. Alan Bergman and Marilyn Bergman, m. Dave Grusin, 1983. Introduced in (MP) *Tootsie*. Nominated for an Academy Award. Pop chart record by Steven Bishop (Warner Bros.).

It Might Have Been a Diff'rent Story. w. Raymond Klages and Jack Meskill, m. James V. Monaco, 1933. Featured and recorded by the bands of Hal Kemp, vocal by Skinnay Ennis (Brunswick), and Richard Himber (Vocalion).

It Must Be Him. w. Mack David (Engl.), Maurice Vidalin (Fr.), m. Gilbert Becaud, 1967. Introduced in France under original title, "Seul sur Son Etoile," by Gilbert Becaud. Vicki Carr had a hit record of the English version (Liberty).

It Must Be Jelly ('Cause Jam Don't Shake Like That). w. Sunny Skylar, m. George Williams and J. Chalmers "Chummy" Mac-Gregor, 1942. Introduced and recorded by Glenn Miller, vocal by the Modernaires in 1942 (Victor). Not released until late 1943. Williams was arranger and MacGregor pianist for the Miller Band.

It Must Be Love. w/m Bob McDill, 1979. Hit Country record by Don Williams (MCA).

It Must Be Love. w. Harlan Thompson, m. Harry Archer, 1925. From (TM) *Merry, Merry*. Recorded by Archer (Vocalion).

It Must Be True. w/m Gus Arnheim, Harry Barris, and Gordon Clifford, 1930. Introduced and recorded by Gus Arnheim and his Orchestra, with vocal by Bing Crosby. It was with this record that Crosby, having left Whiteman and the Rhythm Boys, started attracting attention as a soloist. Sleepy Hall (Melotone) and Guy Lombardo (Columbia) followed with well-received recordings.

It Must Have Been a Dream. w/m Les Hite, Charles Lawrence, and Al Stillman, 1935. Theme song of and recorded by Les Hite and his Orchestra (Varsity).

It Never Entered My Mind. w. Lorenz Hart, m. Richard Rodgers, 1940. Introduced by Shirley Ross in (TM) *Higher and Higher* and recorded by her (Decca). Band versions by Larry Clinton, vocal by Terry Allen (Victor); Benny Goodman, vocal by Helen Forrest (Columbia).

It Never Rains in Southern California. w/m Albert Hammond and Mike Hazelwood, 1972. U.S. gold record by the British singer Albert Hammond (Mums).

It Never Was You. w. Maxwell Anderson, m. Kurt Weill, 1938. Introduced by Richard Kollmar and Jeanne Madden in (TM) *Knickerbocker Holiday*. Judy Garland sang it in her last film (MM) *I Could Go On Singing* in 1963. First recordings: Eddy Duchin (Brunswick) and Ray Herbeck (Vocalion) and their orchestras.

I Told Ya I Love Ya, Now Get Out. w/m Lou Carter, Herb Ellis, and John Frigo, 1947. Featured and recorded by Woody Herman and his Orchestra (Columbia).

I Told You So. w/m Randy Travis, 1988. #1 Country chart hit by Randy Travis (Warner Bros.).

I Told You So. w. Fred Ebb, m. John Kander, 1981. Introduced by Roderick Cook and Grace Keagy in (TM) *Woman of the Year*.

It Only Happens Once. w/m Frankie Laine, 1949. Leading records by Kay Kyser, vocal by Harry Babbitt (Columbia) and The Ames Brothers (Coral).

It Only Happens When I Dance with You. w/m Irving Berlin, 1948. In (MM) *Easter Parade*, it was sung by Fred Astaire, danced by Astaire and Ann Miller, and reprised by Judy Garland. Frank Sinatra had the most popular recording (Columbia).

It Only Hurts for a Little While. w. Mack David, m. Fred Spielman, 1956. Popularized by The Ames Brothers (RCA).

It Only Takes a Minute. w/m Dennis Lambert and Brian Potter, 1975. Top 10 record by the family group Tavares (Capitol).

It Only Takes a Moment. w/m Jerry Herman, 1964. Introduced by Charles Nelson Reilly, Eileen Brennan, and company in (TM) *Hello, Dolly!* In the film version (MM) *Hello, Dolly!* 1969, it was sung by Michael Crawford, Marianne McAndrew, and chorus.

It's a Big, Wide, Wonderful World. w/m John Rox, 1940. Introduced by Wynn Murray, Walter Cassell, Bill Johnson, and Marie Nash, and danced by Rosita Moreno, Anita Alvarez, and William Archibald in (TM) *All in Fun.* Featured by Nancy Nolan at the Monkey Bar of the Hotel Elysée in New York. Buddy Clark revived it with a popular recording (Columbia), 1949. It was heard in (MM) *Rhythm Inn*, 1951, and in (MP) *Sweet Bird of Youth*, starring Geraldine Page and Paul Newman, 1962.

It's a Blue World. w/m Robert Wright and George Forrest, 1940. Introduced by Tony Martin in (MM) *Music in My Heart.* Nominated for Academy Award. Top record by Martin (Decca), followed by Glenn Miller, vocal by Ray Eberle (Bluebird).

It's a Bore. w. Alan Jay Lerner, m. Frederick Loewe, 1958. Introduced by Louis Jourdan and Maurice Chevalier in (MM) *Gigi.* In the stage version (TM) *Gigi*, 1973, it was sung by Daniel Massey and Alfred Drake.

It's About Time. w. Johnny Mercer, m. Peter Tinturin, 1932. One of Mercer's first songs. Introduced by Ray Perkins on his radio show.

It's a Chemical Reaction, That's All. w/m Cole Porter, 1955. Introduced by Hildegarde Neff in (TM) *Silk Stockings.* In the film version (MM) *Silk Stockings*, 1956, it was danced by Cyd Charisse, whose vocal was dubbed on the soundtrack by Carole Richards.

It's a Cute Little Way of My Own. w. Robert B. Smith, m. Harry Tierney, 1916. From (TM) *Follow Me*, starring Anna Held.

It's a Funky Thing. See **Memphis Underground.**

It's a Good Day. w/m Peggy Lee and Dave Barbour, 1947. Introduced and recorded by Peggy Lee (Capitol).

It's a Grand Night for Singing. w. Oscar Hammerstein II, m. Richard Rodgers, 1945. Introduced by William Marshall, Dick Haymes, and chorus, and reprised by Vivian Blaine, with Marshall and the chorus in (MM) *State Fair.* In the 1962 remake of the musical film (MM) *State Fair*, it was sung by Pat Boone, Anita Gordon (dubbing for Pamela Tiffin), Ann-Margret, Bobby Darin, and Alice Faye.

It's a Great Big World. w. Johnny Mercer, m. Harry Warren, 1946. Introduced by Virginia O'Brien, Judy Garland, and Betty Russell (dubbing for Cyd Charisse) in (MM) *The Harvey Girls.* The same trio recorded it (Decca).

It's a Great Day for the Irish. w/m Roger Edens, 1940. Sung by Judy Garland and Douglas MacPhail in (MM) *Little Nellie Kelly.*

It's a Great Feeling. w. Sammy Cahn, m. Jule Styne, 1949. Introduced by Doris Day in (MM) *It's a Great Feeling.* Song nominated for Academy Award.

It's a Great Life. w/m Joe Allison, Audrey Allison, and Faron Young, 1956. Top 10 Country chart record by Faron Young (Capitol).

It's a Great Life (if You Don't Weaken). w. Leo Robin, m. Richard A. Whiting and Newell Chase, 1930. Sung by Maurice Chevalier in (MM) *Playboy of Paris.*

It's a Hap-Hap-Happy Day. w/m Sammy Timberg, Winston Sharples, and Al J. Neiburg, 1940. From the feature-length animated cartoon (MM) *Gulliver's Travels.* Most popular recordings by Eddy Duchin, vocal by The Earbenders (Columbia); Guy Lombardo, vocal by the Lombardo Trio (Decca); Ginny Simms (Vocalion).

It's a Heartache. w/m Ronnie Scott and Steve Wolfe, 1978. A British song that became a Country/Pop hit. Top 10 gold record by Australian singer Bonnie Tyler (RCA).

It's a Helluva Way to Run a Love Affair. w. Arnold Horwitt, m. Albert Hague, 1955. Introduced by Shirl Conway in (TM) *Plain and Fancy.*

It's a Hundred to One. w/m Dick Jurgens and Ronnie Kemper, 1939. Recorded by Jack Teagarden (Brunswick); Jan Savitt, vocal by Bon Bon (Decca); Tommy Dorsey's Clambake Seven (Victor); and Dick Todd (Decca).

It's a Laugh. w/m Daryl Hall, 1978. Recorded by Daryl Hall and John Oates (RCA).

It's All Down to Goodnight Vienna. w/m John Lennon, 1975. Former Beatle Lennon wrote it. Recorded by former Beatle Ringo Starr (Apple).

It's All Forgotten Now. w/m Ray Noble, 1934. Introduced and recorded in England by Ray Noble and his Orchestra, vocal by Al Bowlly (HMV); released in U.S. (Victor). Also recorded by Hal Kemp, vocal by Bob Allen (Brunswick) and Red McKenzie with The Spirits of Rhythm (Decca).

It's All I Can Do. w/m Ric Ocasek, 1979. Recorded by The Cars, with Ocasek as lead vocalist (Elektra).

It's All in the Game. w. Carl Sigman, m. Charles Gates Dawes, 1951, 1958. Lyric written to an instrumental, "Melody," that General Dawes (later to become Vice-President of the United States under Calvin Coolidge) composed in 1912. Tommy Edwards (MGM) had the first popular recording. In 1958, he re-recorded it and the new version became a #1 song in all categories (MGM). Revived by Cliff Richard (Epic), 1964, and The Four Tops (Motown), 1970.

It's All Over. w/m Curtis Mayfield, 1964. Crossover (R&B/Pop) chart record by Walter Jackson (Okeh).

It's All Over (But the Crying). w/m Hank Williams, Jr., 1966. Recorded by Kitty Wells (Decca). Top 10 Country chart version by Hank Williams, Jr. (MGM), 1968.

It's All Over Now. w/m Jeanie Allen, 1961. Recorded by Jeanie Allen (Arliss).

It's All Over Now. w/m Sunny Skylar and Don Marcotte, 1946. Featured and recorded by Frankie Carle, vocal by Marjorie Hughes (Columbia), and Peggy Lee (Capitol).

It's All Over Now, Baby Blue. w/m Bob Dylan, 1965. Recorded in albums by Bob Dylan (Columbia) and Joan Baez (Vanguard).

It's All Right. w/m Curtis Mayfield, 1963. Top 10 record by The Impressions (ABC-Paramount).

It's All Right with Me. w/m Cole Porter, 1953. Introduced by Peter Cookson in (TM) *Can-Can.* In the film version (MM) *Can-Can,* 1960, it was sung by Frank Sinatra and Louis Jourdan.

It's All Wrong, But It's All Right. w. Pete Bellotte, m. Giorgio Moroder, 1978. Recorded by Dolly Parton (RCA).

It's All Yours. w. Dorothy Fields, m. Arthur Schwartz, 1939. Introduced by Ethel Merman and Jimmy Durante in (TM) *Stars in Your Eyes.* Among recordings: Frances Langford (Decca); Tommy Dorsey and his Orchestra (Victor); Jimmy Dorsey, vocal by Helen O'Connell (Decca).

It's Almost Tomorrow. w. Wade Buff, m. Gene Adkinson, 1955. Leading record by The Dream Weavers (Decca). Other chart versions by Jo Stafford (Columbia); Snooky Lanson (Dot); David Carroll (Mercury).

It's a Lonesome Old Town (When You're Not Around). w. Harry Tobias, m. Charles Kisco, 1931. Ben Bernie used this as his band's opening theme song for radio broadcasts and personal appearances. His recording of it was coupled with his closing theme "Au Revoir, Pleasant Dreams" (Brunswick).

It's a Long Lane That Has No Turning. w. Arthur Penn, m. Manuel Klein, 1911. From (TM) *Around the World.*

It's a Long Way to Tipperary. w/m Jack Judge and Harry H. Williams, 1912. Popular song interpolated by Montgomery and Stone in (TM) *Chin Chin,* and by Al Jolson in (TM) *Dancing Around,* 1914. Popular records by The American Quartet (Victor) and John McCormack (Victor). In films, it was heard in the background of (MM) *The Story of Vernon and Irene Castle,* 1939; sung by Judy Garland in (MM) *For Me and My Gal,* 1942; sung by Julie Andrews in (MM) *Darling Lili,* 1970.

It's a Lovely, Lovely World. w/m Boudleaux Bryant, 1952. Country record success by Carl Smith (Columbia). Revived via a Top 10 record by Gail Davies (Warner Bros.), 1981.

It's A Lovely Day Today. w/m Irving Berlin, 1950. Introduced by Russell Nype and Galina Talva in (TM) *Call Me Madam.* It was sung by Donald O'Connor and Vera-Ellen in (MM) *Call Me Madam,* 1953.

It's a Lovely Day Tomorrow. w/m Irving Berlin, 1940. Introduced by Irene Bordoni in (TM) *Louisiana Purchase.* Recorded by Gladys Swarthout (Victor). It was played over the title credits in the film version, (MM) *Louisiana Purchase,* 1942.

It's a Love Thing. w/m William Shelby and Dana Griffey, 1981. Top 10 R&B chart record by The Whispers (Solar).

It's Alright. w/m Mac Gayden and Jerry Tuttle, 1965. Top 10 Country chart record by Bobby Bare (RCA).

It's Alright. w/m Chris Andrews, 1965. Recorded in England by Adam Faith (Amy).

It's Always Fair Weather When Good Fellows Get Together. See **Stein Song, A.**

It's Always Love. w. Bob Merrill, m. Jule Styne, 1972. Introduced by Tony Roberts in

(TM) *Sugar,* the stage musical version of the film (MM) *Some Like It Hot.*

It's Always You. w. Johnny Burke, m. James Van Heusen, 1941. Introduced by Bing Crosby in (MM) *Road to Zanzibar* and on records (Decca). A recording by Tommy Dorsey, vocal by Frank Sinatra (Victor), was made in 1941, released briefly, and then re-released two years later, and attained a Top 10 spot on the charts.

It's a Mad, Mad, Mad, Mad World. w. Mack David, m. Ernest Gold, 1963 From (MP) *It's a Mad, Mad, Mad, Mad World.* Nominated for Academy Award.

It's a Man Down There. w/m George L. Crockett and Jack Daniels, 1965. Chart record by blues singer/writer G. L. Crockett (4 Brothers).

It's a Man's, Man's, Man's World. w/m Betty Jean Newsome and James Brown, 1966. #1 R&B and Top 10 Pop chart hit by James Brown (King).

It's a Million to One You're in Love. w. Benny Davis, m. Harry Akst, 1927.

It's a Miracle. w/m George "Boy George" O'Dowd, Jon Moss, Mikey Craig, and Phil Pickett, 1984. Recorded by the British group Culture Club (Epic/Virgin).

It's a Miracle. w/m Barry Manilow and Marty Panzer, 1975. Top 20 record by Barry Manilow (Arista).

It's a Mistake. w/m Colin Hay, 1983. Top 10 record by the Australian quintet, Men At Work, of which Hay was lead singer/guitarist (Columbia).

It's a Most Unusual Day. w. Harold Adamson, m. Jimmy McHugh, 1948. Introduced by Jane Powell in (MM) *A Date with Judy.* Popular record by Ray Noble, vocal by Anita Gordon (Columbia).

It's a New World. w. Ira Gershwin, m. Harold Arlen, 1954. Introduced by Judy Garland in (MM) *A Star Is Born.*

It's an Old Southern Custom. w. Jack Yellen, m. Joseph Meyer, 1935. Introduced by Alice Faye in (MM) *George White's 1935 Scandals.*

It's Another World. w/m Darrell Statler, 1965. Country chart hit by The Wilburn Brothers (Decca).

It's Anybody's Spring. w. Johnny Burke, m. James Van Heusen, 1946. Introduced by Bing Crosby in (MM) *Road to Utopia.*

It's a Pity to Say Goodnight. w/m Billy Reid, 1946. British song with leading U.S. recordings by Ella Fitzgerald and The Delta Rhythm Boys (Decca) and Stan Kenton, vocal by June Christy (Capitol). Among others: Claude Thornhill and his Orchestra (Columbia), The Four King Sisters (RCA Victor), Eydie Gormé (Am-Par).

It's a Shame. w/m Stevie Wonder, Lee Garrett, and Syreeta Wright, 1970. Top 20 record by The Spinners (V.I.P.).

It's a Sin. w/m Nick Tennant and Chris Lowe, 1987. Chart single, written and recorded by the British duo The Pet Shop Boys (EMI America).

It's a Sin. w/m Zeb Turner and Fred Rose, 1947. #1 C&W record by Eddy Arnold (Victor). Top 10 revival by Marty Robbins (Columbia), 1969.

It's a Sin to Tell a Lie. w/m Billy Mayhew, 1936, 1955. Introduced on the radio by Kate Smith. Popularized and recorded by Fats Waller (Victor); Bobby Breen (Decca); Russ Morgan, vocal by Dick Robertson (Brunswick). Somethin' Smith & The Redheads revived it with a hit record (Epic), 1955. Nell Carter and the company sang it in the Fats Waller musical (TM) *Ain't Misbehavin'*, 1978.

It's a Sin When You Love Somebody. w/m Jim Webb, 1975. Popularized via its coupling with the hit "You Are So Beautiful" (q.v.) by Joe Cocker (A&M).

It's a Woman's World. w/m Sammy Cahn, m. Cyril Mockridge, 1954. Sung by The Four Aces under the titles, on the soundtrack of (MP) *Woman's World.* The group had a popular recording, with Jack Pleis's Orchestra (Decca).

It's a Wonderful World. w. Harold Adamson, m. Leo Watson and Jan Savitt, 1940. Introduced and recorded by Jan Savitt, vocal by Bon Bon (Decca). Best-selling record: Charlie Barnet, vocal by Mary Ann McCall (Bluebird).

It's Been a Long, Long Time. w. Sammy Cahn, m. Jule Styne, 1945. A song that had great meaning to returning service personnel and their loved ones at the conclusion of World War II. Fourteen weeks on "Your Hit Parade," five times as #1, it had top-of-the-chart records by Bing Crosby, with Les Paul's Trio (Decca) and Harry James, vocal by Kitty Kallen (Columbia). It was heard in (MM) *I'll Get By*, a remake of (MM) *Tin Pan Alley*, 1950.

It's Been a Long Time. w/m James Baker and Melvin Wilson, 1974. Recorded by the group, The New Birth (RCA).

It's Been So Long. w/m Autry Inman, 1953. #1 C&W chart record by Webb Pierce (Decca).

It's Been So Long. w. Harold Adamson, m. Walter Donaldson, 1936. Hit song. Leading records by Benny Goodman, vocal by Helen Ward (Victor); Freddy Martin, vocal by Terry Shand (Brunswick); Bunny Berigan, vocal by Chick Bullock (Vocalion).

It's Been So Long, Darlin'. w/m Ernest Tubb, 1946. Recorded by Ernest Tubb (Decca) and Don Cherry (Decca).

It's Beginning to Look a Lot Like Christmas. w/m Meredith Wilson, 1951. Popularized by Perry Como, with The Fontane Sisters (RCA Victor).

It's Better in the Dark. w. Sammy Cahn, m. James Van Heusen, 1956. Popularized by Tony Martin (RCA).

It's Better with a Band. w. David Zippel, m. Wally Harper, 1983. Performed by Sandy

Duncan in her revue at the Radio City Music Hall (TM) *Five-Six-Seven-Eight . . . Dance!*

It's Bigger Than You and Me. w. Leo Robin, m. Jule Styne, 1955. Introduced by Jack Lemmon, singing to Betty Garrett in (MM) *My Sister Eileen.*

It's Dark on Observatory Hill. w. Johnny Burke, m. Harold Spina, 1934. Featured and recorded by Ozzie Nelson and his Orchestra (Brunswick). Revived in the late fifties by Bob Eberly and Helen O'Connell (Capitol).

It's Delightful Down in Chile. w. Leo Robin, m. Jule Styne, 1949. Introduced by Carol Channing in (TM) *Gentlemen Prefer Blondes.*

It's Delightful to Be Married. w. Anna Held, m. Vincent Scott, 1907. Anna Held wrote new English lyrics to the French song "La Petite Tonkinoise" and interpolated it in (TM) *A Parisian Model.* She became associated with it thereafter.

It's De-Lovely. w/m Cole Porter, 1936. Introduced by Ethel Merman and Bob Hope in (TM) *Red, Hot and Blue!* Merman recorded it (Liberty Music Shops) but the best-selling record was by Eddy Duchin and his Orchestra, vocal by Jerry Cooper (Victor). It was interpolated by Donald O'Connor and Mitzi Gaynor in (MM) *Anything Goes* in 1956 and in the all-Cole Porter score for (MM) *At Long Last Love* in 1975.

It's Dreamtime. w. Jack Brooks, m. Walter Schumann, 1947. Introduced by Deanna Durbin in (MM) *I'll Be Yours.* Among recordings: Mel Tormé, arranged and conducted by Sonny Burke (Musicraft); Harry Cool (Mercury); Andy Russell (Capitol).

It's Easy to Remember. w. Lorenz Hart, m. Richard Rodgers, 1935. Introduced in (MM) *Mississippi* and recorded (Decca) by Bing Crosby.

It's Easy to Say (a.k.a. **Song from "10."**) w. Robert Wells, m. Henry Mancini, 1979. Introduced by Dudley Moore in (MP) *10.*

It's Ecstasy When You Lay Down Next to Me. w/m Nelson Pigford and Ekundayo Paris, 1977. #1 R&B and Top 10 Pop chart and gold record by Barry White (20th Century).

It Seems Like Old Times. w. Charles Tobias, m. Sam H. Stept, 1938. Not to be confused with the standard "Seems Like Old Times" (q.v.). Mildred Bailey recorded this one (Vocalion).

It Seems to Be Spring. w. George Marion, Jr., m. Richard A. Whiting, 1930. Sung by Jeanette MacDonald and James Hall in (MM) *Let's Go Native.*

It's Eight O'Clock. w/m Sid Bass, Ken Hecht, and Russ Morgan, 1940. Based on the opening five notes of the tobacco auctioneer's chant. Introduced and recorded by Russ Morgan and his Orchestra (Decca). Also recorded by Ray Herbeck, vocal by band members (Okeh).

It's for You. w/m John Lennon and Paul McCartney, 1964. Introduced and recorded in England by Cilla Black (Capitol). Revived by Springwell (Parrot), 1971.

It's Four in the Morning. w/m Jerry Chesnut, 1971. Hit Country and Pop chart record by Faron Young (Mercury).

It's Funny to Everyone But Me. w/m Dave Franklin and Isham Jones, 1934, 1939. Introduced by Isham Jones and his Orchestra, the song became popular in 1939, via renewed airplay and recordings by the Ink Spots (Decca). Helped also by the orchestras of Harry James, vocal by Frank Sinatra (Columbia); Blue Barron (Bluebird); Gray Gordon (Victor).

It's Getting Better. w/m Barry Mann and Cynthia Weil, 1969. Top 40 record by Mama Cass (Dunhill).

It's Going to Take Some Time. w/m Carole King and Toni Stern, 1972. Top 20 record by The Carpenters (A&M).

It's Gonna Be a Beautiful Night. w/m Prince Rogers Nelson, 1987. Sung by Prince in the concert film (MM) *Sign O' the Times.*

It's Gonna Be All Right. w/m Gerry Marsden, 1965. Hit English recording by Gerry and The Pacemakers (Laurie).

It's Gonna Take a Little Bit Longer. w/m Ben Peters, 1972. Hit Country record by Charley Pride (RCA).

It's Gonna Take a Miracle. w/m Teddy Randazzo, Bobby Weinstein, and Lou Stallman, 1965. Recorded by The Royalettes (MGM). Revived with a Top 10 record by Deniece Williams (ARC), 1982.

It's Gonna Work Out Fine. w/m Rose Marie McCoy and Sylvia McKinney, 1961. Popular recording by Ike and Tina Turner (Sue).

It's Good News Week. w/m Kenneth King, 1966. Recorded in England by Hedgehoppers Anonymous (Parrot).

It's Good to Be Alive. w/m Bob Merrill, 1957. Introduced by Gwen Verdon in (TM) *New Girl in Town.*

It's Got the Whole World Shakin'. w/m Sam Cooke, 1964. Introduced and recorded by Sam Cooke (RCA).

It's Got to Be Love. w. Lorenz Hart, m. Richard Rodgers, 1936. Introduced by Doris Carson and Ray Bolger in (TM) *On Your Toes.* Popular record by Hal Kemp and his Orchestra, vocal by Skinnay Ennis (Brunswick).

It's Great to Be Alive. w. Johnny Mercer, m. Robert Emmett Dolan, 1949. Introduced by Danny Scholl in (TM) *Texas Li'l Darlin'.* Recorded by Jo Stafford and Johnny Mercer (Capitol).

It's Great to Be a Soldier Man. w. Jack Drislane, m. Theodore F. Morse, 1907.

It's Great to Be in Love Again. w. Ted Koehler, m. Jimmy McHugh, 1936. Introduced and recorded by Jane Froman (Decca).

It's Growing. w/m William Robinson and Warren Moore, 1965. Crossover (R&B/Pop) hit by The Temptations (Gordy).

It's Hard to Laugh or Smile. m. Bennie Moten, 1929. Moten also introduced and recorded this instrumental (Victor).

It Should Have Been Me. w/m Norman Whitfield and William Stevenson, 1968. Hit record by Gladys Knight and The Pips (Soul). Revived by soul singer Yvonne Fair (Motown), 1976.

It Shouldn't Happen to a Dream. w. Don George, m. Edward Kennedy "Duke" Ellington and Johnny Hodges, 1946. Featured and recorded by Duke Ellington, vocal by Al Hibbler (Musicraft).

It's Impossible. w. Sid Wayne (Engl.), m. Armando Manzanero, 1971. Mexican song, "Somos Novios," Spanish words by Manzanero. Top 10 English version record by Perry Como (RCA).

It's in His Kiss. See **Shoop Shoop Song, The.**

It's in the Book. w/m Johnny Standley and Art Thorsen, 1952. Comedy number, which was a take-off of fundamentalist preachers, became a #1 million-seller by Johnny Standley, with Horace Heidt and his Musical Knights (Capitol).

It's in the Way You Use It. w/m Eric Clapton and Robbie Robertson, 1986. From the film (MP) *The Color of Money,* and the soundtrack album (MCA).

It's Just About Time. w/m Jack Clement, 1985. Introduced and recorded by Johnny Cash (Sun).

It's Just a Little Bit Too Late. w/m Clint Ballard, Jr. and Les Ledo, 1965. Recorded in England by Wayne Fontana and The Mindbenders (Fontana).

It's Just a Matter of Time. w/m Brook Benton, Belford Hendricks, and Clyde Otis, 1959. Hit record by Brook Benton (Mercury). Sonny James had a #1 Country record (Capitol), 1970.

It's Late. w/m Dorsey Burnette, 1959. Hit record by Ricky Nelson (Imperial).

It's Like Taking Candy from a Baby. w. Bob Russell, m. Al Russell and Joel Cowan, 1948. Featured by Tony Pastor, vocal by Rosemary Clooney (Columbia).

It's Like We Never Said Goodbye. w/m Roger Greenaway and Geoff Stephens, 1980. Recorded by Crystal Gayle (Columbia).

It's Love. w. Betty Comden and Adolph Green, m. Leonard Bernstein, 1953. Introduced by Edie Adams and George Gaynes in (TM) *Wonderful Town*, based on the book and film *My Sister Eileen*.

It's Love, Baby. w/m Ted Jarrett, 1955. Popular R&B records by Louis Brooks and His Hi-Toppers (Eccello) and The Midnighters (Federal).

It's Love, Love, Love. w/m Alex Kramer, Joan Whitney, and Mack David, 1944. Introduced in (MM) *Stars on Parade*, and a #1 record by Guy Lombardo, vocal by Skip Nelson (Decca).

It's Love I'm After. w. Sidney D. Mitchell, m. Lew Pollack, 1936. Introduced by Judy Garland, as one of three songs she sang in her first feature film (MM) *Pigskin Parade*. She had ninth billing! Recorded by Mildred Bailey (Vocalion), Tony Martin (Decca), and the bands of Charlie Barnet (Bluebird) and Al Donahue (Decca).

It's Magic. w. Sammy Cahn, m. Jule Styne, 1948. Introduced by Doris Day in her first film (MM) *Romance on the High Seas*. Nominated for Academy Award. In addition to the million-seller by Day (Columbia), the song had no less than five other Top 20 chart records: Dick Haymes (Columbia), Gordon MacRae (Capitol), Tony Martin (RCA Victor), Sarah Vaughan (Musicraft), Vic Damone (Mercury). Revived by The Platters (Mercury), 1962.

It's Make Believe Ballroom Time. w. Mickey Stoner and Martin Block, m. Harold Green, 1940. Recorded by Glenn Miller and The Modernaires as the new theme song of Martin Block's popular WNEW New York radio show. It replaced the original theme "Make

Believe Ballroom" (q.v.), during the ASCAP-radio licensing dispute. Though Block has died, the Miller recording remains the opening signature of the ongoing program.

It's Midnight. w/m J. Taub and Willie Littlefield, 1949. R&B chart hit by Little Willie Littlefield (Modern).

It's Moonlight All the Time on Broadway. w. Ren Shields, m. Percy Wenrich, 1908. Popular song that referred to the lights on Broadway.

It's My Life. w/m Roger Atkins and Carl D'Errico, 1965. Top 40 record by the British group The Animals (MGM).

It's My Party. w/m John Gluck, Jr., Wally Gold, and Herb Wiener, 1963. #1 record by Lesley Gore (Mercury). Revived by the British duo, Dave Stewart [all instruments] and Barbara Gaskin [vocal] (Platinum), 1982.

It's My Turn. w. Carole Bayer Sager, m. Michael Masser, 1980. Introduced on the soundtrack of (MP) *It's My Turn*, and on a Top 10 record by Diana Ross (Motown).

It's My Turn Now. w. Sammy Cahn, m. Saul Chaplin, 1939. Recorded by the bands of Woody Herman (Decca) and Roy Eldridge (Varsity).

It's Never Too Late. w/m John Kay and Nick St. Nicholas, 1969. Recorded by Steppenwolf (Dunhill).

It's Never Too Late (to Say You're Sorry). w/m Carmen Lombardo and John Jacob Loeb, 1939. Introduced and recorded by Guy Lombardo and his Royal Canadians (Decca). Covered by Jan Garber, vocal by Lee Bennett (Vocalion); Gray Gordon, vocal by Betty Bradley (Victor); Kate Smith (Victor): Barry Wood (Brunswick).

It's Nice to Be with You. w/m Jerry Goldstein, 1968. Recorded by The Monkees (Colgem).

It's Nobody's Business But My Own. w/m Will Skidmore and Marshall Walker, 1919. Introduced by Bert Williams in (TM) *Ziegfeld*

Follies of 1919 and recorded by him that year (Columbia).

It's No Crime. w/m Antonio Reid, Kenneth Edmonds, and Daryl Simmons, 1989. Hit R&B chart single by Babyface (Solar).

It's No Fun. w/m Milton Ager, Murray Mencher, and Charles Newman, 1936. Recorded by Jimmy Dorsey, vocal by Seger Ellis (Decca); Wingy Manone (Bluebird); Gene Kardos, vocal by Bea Wain (Melotone).

It's No Sin. See **Sin.**

It's Not for Me to Say. w. Al Stillman, m. Robert Allen, 1957. From (MP) *Lizzie*. Popularized by Johnny Mathis, who recorded his first Top 10 hit (Columbia).

It's Not Love (But It's Not Bad). w/m Glenn Martin and Hank Cochran, 1972. Country hit by Merle Haggard (Capitol).

It's Not Over ('Til It's Over). w/m Robbie Nevil, John Van Torgeron, and Phil Gladston, 1987. Top 10 single from the album "No Protection" by the group Starship (Grunt). Title derived from the remark attributed to baseball's Yogi Berra.

It's Not Unusual. w/m Gordon Mills and Les Reed, 1965. Top 10 hit by Tom Jones (Parrot). This was the Welsh star's first record success. Bobby Van sang it in (MP) *Lost Flight*, 1969.

It's Not Where You Start. w. Dorothy Fields, m. Cy Coleman, 1972. Introduced by Tommy Tune and company in (TM) *Seesaw*.

It's Now or Never. w/m Aaron Schroeder and Wally Gold, 1960. Melody adapted from the Italian song "O Sole Mio," lyrics by G. Capurro, music by Edoardo di Capua. #1 million-seller by Elvis Presley (RCA). John Schneider had a chart version (Scotti Br.), 1981.

It's Now Winter's Day. Tommy Roe, 1967. Popular recording by Tommy Roe (ABC).

It's Only a Paper Moon. w. E. Y. Harburg and Billy Rose, m. Harold Arlen, 1933. Written for the play (TP) *The Great Magoo*, and originally titled "If You Believed in Me." It was sung with the new title by June Knight and Charles "Buddy" Rogers in (MM) *Take A Chance*, 1933. It was heard in (MP) *Too Young to Know*, starring Joan Leslie and Robert Hutton, 1945. It inspired the title and was heard in the background of (MP) *Paper Moon* with Ryan and Tatum O'Neal, 1973, and was sung by Barbra Streisand in (MM) *Funny Lady*, 1975. Often recorded, some of the biggest sellers were by: Ella Fitzgerald (Decca), The King Cole Trio (Capitol), The Mills Brothers (Decca).

It's Only for You. 1987. Top 10 Country record by Tanya Tucker (Capitol).

It's Only Love. w/m Bryan Adams and Jim Vallance, 1985. Recorded by Bryan Adams and Tina Turner (A&M).

It's Only Love. w/m Mark James and Steve Tyrell, 1969. Leading records by B. J. Thomas (Scepter) and Elvis Presley (RCA).

It's Only Love. w/m Hank Cochran, 1966. Multi-used title. This Country version by Jeannie Seely (Monument).

It's Only Love. w/m John Lennon and Paul McCartney, 1966. Introduced in 1965 by The Beatles in their LP "Rubber Soul," (Capitol). Top 40 hit by Tommy James and The Shondells (Roulette).

It's Only Make Believe. w/m Paul Minshall and James Buckshon, 1987. Top 10 Country chart vocal by Ronnie McDowell, guest vocal by Conway Twitty (Curb).

It's Only Make Believe. w/m Conway Twitty and Jack Nance, 1958. #1 C&W and Pop chart record by Conway Twitty (MGM). Revived by Glen Campbell (Capitol), 1970.

It's Only Rock 'N' Roll (But I Like It). w/m Mick Jagger and Keith Richards, 1974. Top 20 record by The Rolling Stones (Rolling Stones).

It's Only the Beginning. w/m Aaron Schroeder and Sid Wayne, 1959. Introduced and recorded by The Kalin Twins (Decca).

It's Over. w/m David Paitch and Boz Scaggs, 1976. Recorded by Boz Scaggs (Columbia).

It's Over. w/m Jimmie Rodgers, 1966. Introduced and C&W/Pop chart hit by Jimmie Rodgers (Dot). Eddy Arnold had a popular version in 1968 (RCA).

It's Over. w/m Roy Orbison and Bill Dees, 1964. Top 10 record by Roy Orbison (Monument).

It's Over Because We're Through. w/m Willie Bryant and Leonard Reed, 1932. Recorded by Willie Bryant (Victor) and Chick Webb (Decca).

It's Raining Again. w/m Rick Davies and Roger Hodgson, 1982. The writers were members of the British quartet, Supertramp, which had a chart record (A&M).

It's Raining Men. w/m Paul Jabarra and Paul Shaffer, 1983. Recorded by the duo The Weather Girls (Columbia).

It's Raining Sunbeams. w. Sam Coslow, m. Frederick Hollander, 1937. Introduced in (MM) *100 Men and a Girl* and recorded by Deanna Durbin (Decca).

It's Sad to Belong. w/m Randy Goodrum, 1977. Recorded by England Dan and John Ford Coley (Big Tree).

It's So Easy. w/m Linda Ronstadt, 1977. Top 10 hit by Linda Ronstadt (Asylum).

It's So Nice to Have a Man Around the House. w. Jack Elliott, m. Harold Spina, 1950. Featured and recorded by Dinah Shore (Columbia).

It's So Peaceful in the Country. w/m Alec Wilder, 1941. Most popular recordings by Mildred Bailey (Decca) and Harry James, vocal by Dick Haymes (Columbia).

It's Still Rock and Roll to Me. w/m Billy Joel, 1980. #1 gold single from the platinum LP "Glass Houses" by Billy Joel, produced by Phil Ramone (Columbia).

It's Such a Small World. w/m Rodney Crowell, 1988. #1 Country chart song by Rodney Crowell and Roseanne Cash (Columbia).

It's Swell of You. w. Mack Gordon, m. Harry Revel, 1937. Introduced by Alice Faye and Buddy Clark, dubbing for Jack Haley, in (MM) *Wake Up and Live*. Many recordings in addition to Alice Faye's (Brunswick) include: Ruth Etting (Decca); the orchestras of Duke Ellington (Master), Ozzie Nelson (Bluebird), Chick Webb (Decca), Little Jack Little (Vocalion), Teddy Wilson (Brunswick), Emery Deutsch (Brunswick).

It Started All Over Again. w/m Gerry Goffin and Jack Keller, 1962. Recorded by Brenda Lee (Decca).

It Started All Over Again. w. Bill Carey, m. Carl Fischer, 1942. Introduced and recorded by Tommy Dorsey, vocal by Frank Sinatra (Victor).

It's the Animal in Me. w. Mack Gordon, m. Harry Revel, 1935. Sung by Ethel Merman in a sequence for the 1934 musical film *We're Not Dressing*. The scene was cut and inserted into (MM) *The Big Broadcast of 1936*. Recorded by Merman (Brunswick).

It's the Darndest Thing. w. Dorothy Fields, m. Jimmy McHugh, 1931. From (TP) *Singin' the Blues*. Recorded by Fletcher Henderson (Victor).

It's the Dreamer in Me. w/m Jimmy Dorsey and James Van Heusen, 1938. Most popular records by Bing Crosby (Decca); Jimmy Dorsey and his Orchestra (Decca); Harry James, vocal by Helen Humes (Brunswick).

It's the End of the World as We Know It (and I Feel Fine). w/m Bill Berry, Pete Buck, Mike Mills, and Michael Stipe, 1987. Popular track from the album "R.E.M. No. 5: Document" by the quartet R.E.M. (I.R.S.).

It's the Girl. w. Dave Oppenheim, m. Abel Baer, 1931. Popular recordings by Lee Morse

(Columbia); Leo Reisman, with Eddy Duchin on piano (Victor); Fred Rich (Hit of the Week); Bob Haring (Perfect).

It's the Going Home Together. w. John Latouche, m. Jerome Moross, 1954. Introduced by Stephen Douglass and Priscilla Gillette in (TM) *The Golden Apple.*

It's the Hard Knock Life. w. Martin Charnin, m. Charles Strouse, 1977. Introduced by Andrea McArdle and the girls in (TM) *Annie.* In the film (MM) *Annie,* 1982, it was sung by Aileen Quinn and the girls.

It's the Irish in Your Eyes, It's the Irish in Your Smile. w. Will Dillon, m. Albert Von Tilzer, 1916.

It's the Little Things. w/m Sonny Bono, 1966. Introduced by Sonny and Cher in (MM) *Good Times* and on records (Atco).

It's the Little Things in Texas. w/m Richard Rodgers, 1962. Introduced in the third film version (second musical) (MM) *State Fair,* by Alice Faye and Tom Ewell.

It's the Little Things That Count. w. Haven Gillespie, m. Seymour Simons, 1938. Featured and recorded by Jan Savitt, vocal by Bon Bon (Bluebird); Bunny Berigan, vocal by Ruth Gaylor (Victor); Dorothy Shay (Columbia).

It's the Natural Thing to Do. w. Johnny Burke, m. Arthur Johnston, 1937. Introduced by Bing Crosby in (MM) *Double or Nothing.* Crosby's recording (Decca) and Mildred Bailey's (Vocalion) were the biggest sellers.

It's the Same Old Dream. w. Sammy Cahn, m. Jule Styne, 1947. Introduced by Frank Sinatra in (MM) *It Happened in Brooklyn.* Top records by Tommy Dorsey, vocal by Stuart Foster (Victor); The Pied Pipers, with June Hutton (Capitol).

It's the Same Old Shillelagh. w/m Pat White, 1940. Featured and recorded by Bing Crosby (Decca).

It's the Same Old Song. w/m Eddie Holland, Lamont Dozier, and Brian Holland,

1965. Hit record by The Four Tops (Motown). Revived by KC and The Sunshine Band (T.K.), 1978.

It's the Sentimental Thing to Do. w. Roy Alfred, m. Marvin Fisher, 1947. Leading recording by Vaughn Monroe, with his Orchestra (RCA Victor).

It's the Strangest Thing. w. Fred Ebb, m. John Kander, 1977. Introduced by Liza Minnelli in (TM) *The Act.*

It's The Talk of the Town. w. Marty Symes and Al J. Nieburg, m. Jerry Livingston, 1933. Featured, recorded, and popularized by Glen Gray and the Casa Loma Orchestra, vocal by Kenny Sargent (Brunswick). Fletcher Henderson (Columbia) and Red McKenzie (Vocalion) also had early popular recordings of this standard.

It's Time to Cry. w/m Paul Anka, 1959. Top 10 record by Paul Anka (ABC-Paramount).

It's Time to Pay the Fiddler. w/m Walter Haynes and Donald Choate, 1975. #1 Country chart record by Cal Smith (RCA).

It's Too Late. w. Toni Stern, m. Carole King, 1971. #1 gold record by Carole King (Ode). Winner Grammy Award (NARAS) Record of the Year.

It's Too Late. w/m Wilson Pickett, 1963. Introduced and recorded by Wilson Pickett (Double-L).

It's Too Late. w/m Chuck Willis, 1956. Introduced and recorded by Chuck Willis (Atlantic).

It's Too Late, Baby, Too Late. w/m Gayle Candis Brown and Hazel Johnson, 1965. Chart record by singer Arthur Prysock (Old Town).

It's Too Soon to Know. w/m Deborah Chessler, 1948. Top records by The Orioles (Natural); Dinah Washington (Mercury); Ella Fitzgerald (Decca); Andy Russell, with the Pied Pipers (Capitol). Revived, 1958, by Pat

Boone (Dot). Later versions by Etta James (Argo).

It's Tulip Time in Holland. w. Dave Radford, m. Richard A. Whiting, 1915. Whiting's first song hit. Later sung in a Dutch skating scene in (MM) *Hello, Frisco, Hello*, 1943, and in (MM) *April Showers*, 1948.

It's Up to You. w/m Jerry Fuller, 1963. Top 10 record by Rick Nelson (Imperial).

It's Up to You. w/m Al Dexter and James B. Paris, 1946. C&W hit record by Al Dexter (Columbia).

It's Wearin' Me Down. w/m J. C. Johnson and Fletcher Henderson, 1932. Introduced and recorded by Fletcher Henderson's Orchestra (Vocalion).

It's Whatcha Do with Whatcha Got. w/m Don Raye and Gene de Paul, 1948. From Walt Disney's live-action film (MM) *So Dear to My Heart*.

It's Winter Again. w. Arthur Freed, m. Al Goodhart and Al Hoffman, 1932. Popular record by Hal Kemp and his Orchestra (Brunswick).

It's Within Your Power. w. Mack Gordon, m. Harry Revel, 1933. Featured and recorded by Bing Crosby (Brunswick). Ray Noble's Band, with vocal by Al Bowlly, had their English recording (HMV) released in the U.S. (Victor).

It's Wonderful. w. Felix Cavaliere, m. Eddie Brigati, 1968. Top 20 record by The Young Rascals (Atlantic).

It's Wonderful. w. Mitchell Parish, m. Stuff Smith, 1938. Among the many who recorded this ballad are: Louis Armstrong (Decca); Red Norvo, vocal by Mildred Bailey (Brunswick); Benny Goodman, vocal by Martha Tilton (Victor); Bob Crosby (Decca); Maxine Sullivan (Vocalion); Shep Fields (Bluebird).

Itsy Bitsy Teenie Weenie Yellow Polka Dot Bikini. w/m Paul Vance and Lee Pockriss, 1960. #1 novelty hit by Brian Hyland (Leader).

It's You. w/m Meredith Willson, 1957. Introduced by The Buffalo Bills in (TM) *The Music Man*. Song not used in film version.

It's You I Love. w/m Antoine "Fats" Domino and Dave Bartholomew, 1957. Introduced and recorded by Fats Domino (Imperial).

It's You I Need. See **Loneliness Made Me Realize.**

It's You or No One. w. Sammy Cahn, m. Jule Styne, 1948. Introduced by Doris Day in her first film (MM) *Romance on the High Seas*.

It's Your Thing. w/m Ronald Isley, Rudolph Isley, and O'Kelly Isley, 1969. Top 10 record by The Isley Brothers (T-Neck).

It's Your World. w/m Marty Robbins, 1961. Introduced and recorded by Marty Robbins (Columbia).

It's You That I Need. w/m Verdell Lanier and Michael Stokes, 1978. Recorded by the quintet Enchantment (Roadshow).

It Takes a Little Rain (to Make Love Grow). w/m Roger Murrah and Steve Dean, 1987. #1 Country chart record by The Oak Ridge Boys (MCA).

It Takes a Little Rain with the Sunshine to Make the World Go 'Round. w. Ballard MacDonald, m. Harry Carroll, 1913.

It Takes a Long, Long Train with a Red Caboose (to Carry My Blues Away). w/m Larry Markes and Dick Charles, 1947. Leading record by Dinah Shore, with Sonny Burke's Orchestra (Columbia).

It Takes a Lot of Money. w/m Bob Morris, 1966. Hit Country record by Warner Mack (Decca).

It Takes a Woman. w/m Jerry Herman, 1964. Introduced by David Burns in (TM) *Hello, Dolly!* In the film version (MM) *Hello, Dolly!*, 1969, it was sung by Walter Matthau, Michael Crawford, Danny Lockin, and chorus, and reprised by Barbra Streisand.

It Takes Time. w/m Arthur Korb, 1947. Leading recordings: Benny Goodman, vocal by Johnny Mercer (Capitol); Guy Lombardo, vocal by Kenny Gardner (Decca).

It Takes Two. w/m Sylvia Moy and William Stevenson, 1967. Top 20 record by Marvin Gaye and Kim Weston (Tamla).

It Tears Me Up. w/m Dewey Lindon Oldham and Dan Pennington, 1966. Recorded by Percy Sledge (Atlantic).

It Tickles. w/m Tommy Collins and Wanda Collins, 1955. Top 10 C&W chart record by Tommy Collins (Capitol).

I Turned You On. w/m O'Kelly Isley, Ronald Isley, and Rudolph Isley, 1969. Top 40 record by The Isley Brothers (T-Neck).

It Was Almost like a Song. w. Hal David, m. Archie Jordan, 1977. Country/Pop hit record by Ronnie Milsap (RCA).

It Was a Night in June. w. Mack Gordon, m. Harry Revel, 1933.

It Was a Very Good Year. w/m Ervin Drake, 1966. Featured, recorded, and associated with Frank Sinatra (Reprise). His recording, which was released at the end of 1965, won the Grammy Award (NARAS) for Best Vocal Performance—Male.

It Was I. w/m Gary Paxton, 1959. Popular record by Flip and Skip (Brent). Paxton was "Flip."

It Was Meant to Be. w. Bert Kalmar, m. Harry Ruby, 1923. From (TM) *Helen of Troy, New York*.

It Wasn't God Who Made Honky Tonk Angels. w/m J. D. Miller, 1952. Country hit by Kitty Wells (Decca).

It Was Only a Sun Shower. w. Irving Kahal and Francis Wheeler, m. Ted Snyder, 1927. Recorded by the bands of Ted Weems (Victor) and Sam Lanin (Cameo).

It Was So Beautiful. w. Arthur Freed, m. Harry Barris, 1932. In a highly unusual case, this song was heard in two musical films, produced by two different studios in its premiere year: (1) (MM) *Blondie of the Follies*, starring Robert Montgomery and Marion Davies, and (2) (MM) *The Big Broadcast*, sung by Kate Smith. It was also recorded by Ruth Etting (Banner), Harry Richman (Columbia), and Ozzie Nelson and his Orchestra (Brunswick). Al Bowlly had an English recording (Br. Decca), which was released in the U.S.

It Was Sweet of You. w. Sidney Clare, m. Richard A. Whiting, 1934. Introduced by Frank Parker in (MM) *Transatlantic Merry-Go-Round* and recorded by him (Columbia).

It Was Written in the Stars. w. Leo Robin, m. Harold Arlen, 1948. Introduced by Tony Martin in (MM) *Casbah* and on records (RCA Victor).

It Won't Be Long (Till I'll Be Leaving). w/m Roy Acuff, 1942. Introduced and recorded by Roy Acuff (Columbia).

It Won't Be Long Now. w. B. G. DeSylva and Lew Brown, m. Ray Henderson, 1927. From (TM) *Manhattan Mary*. Recorded by Paul Whiteman (Victor), Jones and Hare (Victor), and the blues singers, Rosa Henderson (Vocalion), and Clara Smith (Columbia).

It Won't Be Wrong. w/m Harvey Gerst and James McGuinn, 1966. Recorded by The Byrds (Columbia).

It Would Have Been Wonderful. w/m Stephen Sondheim, 1973. Introduced by Len Cariou and Laurence Guittard in (TM) *A Little Night Music*.

I Understand. w. Kim Gannon, m. Mabel Wayne, 1940. Introduced, recorded, and popularized by Jimmy Dorsey, vocal by Bob Eberly (Decca).

I Understand Just How You Feel. w/m Pat Best, 1954, 1961. Based on the melody of "Auld Lang Syne." The Four Tunes (Jubilee) and June Valli (RCA Victor) had popular recordings. In 1961, the G-Clefs had an R&B and Pop hit (Terrace). The English group Freddie and the Dreamers revived it in 1965 (Mercury).

I Ups to Him and He Ups to Me. w/m Jimmy Durante, 1929. Introduced by Clayton, Jackson, and Durante in (TM) *Show Girl* and recorded by them (Columbia). Durante later recorded it as a solo (Decca).

I Used to Be Color Blind. w/m Irving Berlin, 1938. Introduced by Fred Astaire and Ginger Rogers in (MM) *Carefree*. Recorded by each of them, separately: Astaire (Brunswick), Rogers (Bluebird).

I Used to Love You (But It's All Over Now). w. Lew Brown, m. Albert Von Tilzer, 1920. Top records by Frank Crumit (Columbia) and The Peerless Quartet (Victor).

I've a Longing in My Heart for You, Louise. w/m Charles K. Harris, 1900.

I've Already Loved You in My Mind. w/m Conway Twitty, 1977. Hit Country chart record by Conway Twitty (MCA).

I've Always Been Crazy. w/m Waylon Jennings, 1978. Hit record by Country artist Waylon Jennings (RCA).

I've a Shooting Box in Scotland. w/m Thomas Lawrason Riggs and Cole Porter, 1916. Originally written for a one-performance show, *Paranoia*, by the Yale University Dramatic Association, 1914. The song was first professionally performed by Dorothie Bigelow and John Goldsworthy in Porter's first Broadway production (TM) *See America First*. Another "first" for Porter was the initial recording of one of his songs, this one by the Joseph C. Smith Orchestra (Victor).

I've a Strange New Rhythm in My Heart. w/m Cole Porter, 1937. Sung and tapped by Eleanor Powell in (MM) *Rosalie*. Recorded by Artie Shaw and his Orchestra, vocal by Leo Watson (Brunswick).

I've Been Around Long Enough to Know. w/m Bob McDill and Dickey Lee, 1984. First recorded by Joel Sonnier, a Louisiana accordionist known as the "Cajun Valentino" (Mercury), 1975. Revived with a #1 Country chart record by John Schneider (MCA), 1984.

I've Been Everywhere. w/m Geoffrey Mack, 1962. Australian song. First U.S. hit record by Hank Snow (RCA).

I've Been Floating Down the Old Green River. w. Bert Kalmar, m. Joe Cooper, 1915. A song interpolated into (TM) *Maid in America*. Billy Murray recorded it (Victor). The song was also heard in (MM) *Wabash Avenue*, 1950.

I've Been Here! w. Earl Shuman (Engl.), Michel Vaucaire (Fr.), m. Charles Dumont, 1966. French song, "Le Mur." Recorded in the U.S. in French and English by Barbra Streisand (Columbia).

I've Been Hurt. w/m Ray Whitley, 1969. Recorded by Bill Deal and The Rhondels (Heritage).

I've Been in Love Before. w/m Nick Ede, 1987. Pop chart single by Cutting Crew, from the album "Boardwalk" (Virgin).

I've Been Invited to a Party. w/m Noël Coward, 1963. Introduced by Florence Henderson in (TM) *The Girl Who Came to Supper*.

I've Been Lonely Too Long. w/m Eddie Brigati and Felix Cavaliere, 1967. Top 20 record by The Young Rascals (Atlantic).

I've Been Lookin'. w/m Jeff Hanna and J. Ibbotson, 1988. Top 10 Country chart record by The Nitty Gritty Dirt Band (Warner Bros.).

I've Been Loving You Too Long (to Stop Now). w/m Otis Redding and Jerry Butler, 1965. Introduced and recorded by Otis Redding (Volt). Revived by Ike and Tina Turner (Blue Thumb), 1969.

I've Been Searching. w/m Murphy Maddux, 1956. Popular record by Kitty Wells (Decca).

(I've Been) Searchin' So Long. w/m James Pankow, 1974. Top 10 record by Chicago (Columbia). Pankow was trombonist with the jazz-oriented group.

I've Been Thinking. w/m Boudleaux Bryant, 1955. Featured and recorded by Eddy Arnold (RCA Victor).

423

I've Been This Way Before. w/m Neil Diamond, 1975. Recorded by Neil Diamond (Columbia).

I've Come Here to Stay. w. Edward Harrigan, m. David Braham, 1890. From Harrigan and Hart's (TM) *Reilly and the 400*. In (TM) *Harrigan 'n' Hart*, 1985, Mark Hamill, as Tony Hart, sang the song with the title "I've Come Home to Stay."

I've Come of Age. w. Sid Jacobson, m. Lou Stallman, 1959. Recorded by Billy Storm (Columbia).

I've Come to Wive It Wealthily in Padua. w/m Cole Porter, 1949. Introduced by Alfred Drake in (TM) *Kiss Me Kate*. Sung by Howard Keel in (MM) *Kiss Me Kate*, 1953.

I've Enjoyed as Much of This as I Can Stand. w/m Bill Anderson, 1963. C&W hit by Porter Wagoner (RCA).

I've Found a New Baby. See **I Found a New Baby.**

I've Found Someone of My Own. w/m Frank K. Robinson, 1971. Top 10 record by The Free Movement (Decca).

I've Gone Romantic on You. w. E. Y. Harburg, m. Harold Arlen, 1937. Introduced by Jack Whiting and June Clyde in (TM) *Hooray For What!* Recorded by trombonist Jack Jenney and his Orchestra (Vocalion).

I've Got a Crush on You. w. Ira Gershwin, m. George Gershwin, 1930. Introduced by Mary Hay and Clifton Webb in the short-lived (TM) *Treasure Girl*, 1928. Two years later, Doris Carson and Gordon Smith performed it in (TM) *Strike Up the Band*. In both productions, it was done in a lively tempo, according to Gershwin's instructions (allegretto giocoso). It was not until Lee Wiley recorded it (Liberty Music Shop) in a slow tempo and as a sentimental ballad that the permanent change was effected. In films it was sung by: Frank Sinatra in (MM) *Meet Danny Wilson*, 1952; Betty Grable and Jack Lemmon in (MM) *Three for the Show*, 1955; Gogi Grant, dubbing on the soundtrack for Ann Blyth, in (MM) *The Helen Morgan Story*, 1958.

I've Got a Date with a Dream. w. Mack Gordon, m. Harry Revel, 1938. Introduced by Art Jarrett, Buddy Ebsen, and Joan Davis in (MM) *My Lucky Star*, starring Sonja Henie and Cesar Romero. Leading records: Benny Goodman, vocal by Martha Tilton (Victor), and Horace Heidt and his Orchestra (Brunswick).

I've Got a Feeling for You (or, **Way Down in My Heart**). w. Edward Madden, m. Theodore F. Morse, 1904.

I've Got a Feeling I'm Falling. w. Billy Rose, m. Thomas "Fats" Waller and Harry Link, 1929. Sung by Helen Morgan in (MM) *Applause*. Nell Carter sang it in the Fats Waller musical (TM) *Ain't Misbehavin'*, 1978.

I've Got a Feelin' You're Foolin'. w. Arthur Freed, m. Nacio Herb Brown, 1935. Introduced by Eleanor Powell, Robert Taylor, Frances Langford, and June Knight in (MM) *Broadway Melody of 1936*. It was performed by a chorus and orchestra in a montage in (MM) *Singin' in the Rain* in 1952, and by Jane Froman, dubbing for Susan Hayward in the Froman biography (MM) *With a Song in My Heart*, also in 1952.

I've Got a Gal in Kalamazoo. w. Mack Gordon, m. Harry Warren, 1942. Introduced by Glenn Miller and his Orchestra, Marion Hutton, Tex Beneke, The Modernaires, and The Nicholas Brothers (dancing) in (MM) *Orchestra Wives*. The Miller aggregation recorded it for a #1 hit (Victor). Song nominated for Academy Award.

I've Got a Lovely Bunch of Coconuts (Roll or Bowl a Ball, a Penny a Pitch). w/m Fred Heatherton, 1949. English song introduced in the U.S. and recorded with a million-seller by Freddy Martin, vocal by Merv Griffin (RCA Victor). Danny Kaye had a popular version (Decca).

I've Got a New Heartache. w/m Wayne P. Walker, 1957. Recorded by Ray Price (Columbia).

I've Got a New Lease on Love. w. Joe Young, m. Fred E. Ahlert, 1937. Featured and recorded by Isham Jones, vocal by Eddie Stone (Vocalion).

I've Got an Invitation to a Dance. w. Marty Symes and Al J. Neiburg, m. Jerry Livingston, 1935.

I've Got a One Track Mind. w. Johnny Mercer, m. Jimmy McHugh, 1940. Introduced by Kay Kyser and his Kollege of Musical Knowledge in (MM) *You'll Find Out*. Kyser and Band recorded it (Columbia).

I've Got a Pain in My Sawdust. w. Henry Edward Warner, m. Herman Avery Wade, 1909.

I've Got a Pocketful of Dreams. w. Johnny Burke, m. James V. Monaco, 1938. Introduced in (MM) *Sing You Sinners* by Bing Crosby, who also had a hit recording of the song (Decca).

I've Got a Pocketful of Sunshine. w. Gus Kahn, m. Arthur Johnston, 1935. Introduced in (MM) *Thanks a Million* and recorded (Decca) by Dick Powell.

I've Got a Rock and Roll Heart. w/m Troy Seals, Eddie Setser, and Steve Diamond, 1983. Recorded by the English singer/guitarist Eric Clapton (Duck).

I've Got a Tiger by the Tail. w/m Buck Owens and Harlan Howard, 1965. Crossover (C&W/Pop) hit by Buck Owens (Capitol).

I've Got a Warm Spot in My Heart for You. w. Harold Spina, m. Johnny Burke, 1934. Recorded by Isham Jones, vocal by Joe Martin (Victor), and Adrian's (Rollini) Ramblers (Brunswick).

I've Got Bonnie. w/m Gerry Goffin and Carole King, 1962. Recorded by Bobby Rydell (Cameo).

I've Got Dreams to Remember. w/m Otis Redding, Velma Redding, and Joe Rock, 1968. Recorded by Otis Redding (Atco).

I've Got Five Dollars. w. Lorenz Hart, m. Richard Rodgers, 1931. Introduced by Harriette Lake (Ann Sothern) and Jack Whiting in (TM) *America's Sweetheart*. In (MM) *Gentlemen Marry Brunettes*, 1955, it was sung by Jane Russell and Robert Farnon, dubbing for Scott Brady.

I've Got Five Dollars and It's Saturday Night. w/m Ted Daffan, 1956. Introduced by Ted Daffan (Columbia). Hit record by Faron Young (Capitol).

I've Got Just About Everything. w/m Bob Dorough, 1962. Featured and recorded by Tony Bennett (Columbia).

I've Got Love on My Mind. w/m Charles Jackson, Jr. and Marvin Yancy, 1977. #1 R&B, #5 Pop chart gold record by Natalie Cole (Capitol).

I've Got Me. w. John Latouche, m. Edward Kennedy "Duke" Ellington, 1947. Introduced by Alfred Drake in (TM) *Beggar's Holiday*.

I've Got My Captain Working for Me Now. w/m Irving Berlin, 1919. Revived in (MM) *Blue Skies* by Bing Crosby and Billy De Wolfe in 1946.

I've Got My Eyes on You. w/m Paul Winley, 1954. R&B number introduced and recorded by The Clovers (Atlantic). Not to be confused with the Cole Porter song of the same title.

I've Got My Eyes on You. w/m Cole Porter, 1940. Introduced by Fred Astaire and Eleanor Powell in (MM) *Broadway Melody of 1940*. Popular records by Tommy Dorsey, vocal by Alan De Witt (Victor), and Bob Crosby, vocal by Marion Mann (Decca).

I've Got My Fingers Crossed. w. Ted Koehler, m. Jimmy McHugh, 1936. Introduced by Alice Faye in (MM) *King of Burlesque*. Recorded by Faye (Melotone); Louis Armstrong (Decca); Fats Waller (Victor); Lud Gluskin, vocal by Buddy Clark (Brunswick); Wingy Manone (Vocalion); Mound City Blue Blowers (Champion). In the Fats Waller musical (TM) *Ain't Misbehavin'*, 1978, it was performed by Armelia McQueen, Charlaine Woodard, and Ken Page.

I've Got My Heart Set on You. w. Mack Gordon, m. Harry Revel, 1937. Sung by Tony Martin in (MM) *Ali Baba Goes to Town*, starring Eddie Cantor. Recorded by Larry Clinton, vocal by Bea Wain (Victor), and Glen Gray and the Casa Loma Orchestra (Decca).

I've Got My Love to Keep Me Warm. w/m Irving Berlin, 1937, 1949. Introduced by Dick Powell, Alice Faye, and E. E. Clive in (MM) *On the Avenue*. Both Powell (Decca) and Faye (Brunswick) made solo records. In 1949, Les Brown and his Orchestra revived the song with a best-selling instrumental version (Columbia).

I've Got News for You. w/m Fred Wise and Randy Starr, 1965. Performed by Nita Talbot, in a mock striptease, while removing newspapers in which she appeared clad, and reprised by Shelley Fabares, in (MM) *Girl Happy*, starring Elvis Presley.

I've Got News for You. w/m Roy Alfred, 1948. Featured and recorded by Woody Herman with his Orchestra (Columbia).

I've Got Rings on My Fingers (or, **Mumbo Jumbo Jijiboo J. O'Shea**). w. F. J. Barnes and R. P. Weston, m. Maurice Scott, 1909. Introduced by Blanche Ring in (TM) *The Midnight Sons*. She then sang it in (TM) *The Yankee Girl* in 1910, and also recorded it (Victor).

I've Got Sand in My Shoes. w/m Artie Resnick and Kenny Young, 1964. Recorded by The Drifters (Atlantic).

I've Got Sixpence. w/m Desmond Cox, Elton Box, and Stan Bradbury, 1943. British marching song popular with the Royal Air Force and the United States servicemen.

I've Gotta Be Me. w/m Walter Marks, 1968. Introduced by Steve Lawrence in (TM) *Golden Rainbow*. Hit record by Sammy Davis, Jr. (Reprise).

I've Gotta Crow. w. Carolyn Leigh, m. Moose Charlap, 1954. Introduced by Mary Martin and Kathy Nolan in (TM) *Peter Pan*.

I've Gotta Get a Message to You. w/m Barry Gibb, Robin Gibb, and Maurice Gibb, 1968. Top 10 record by the British brother trio The Bee Gees (Atco).

I've Gotta Get Up and Go to Work. w/m Herman Hupfeld, 1933. Introduced by Roger Pryor in (MM) *Moonlight and Pretzels*.

I've Got the Girl. w/m Walter Donaldson, 1926. Recorded by Gene Austin (Victor).

I've Got the Music in Me. w/m Bias Boshell, 1974. From England, Top 20 record by The Kiki Dee Band (Rocket).

I've Got the Time, I've Got the Place, But It's Hard to Find the Girl. w. Ballard MacDonald, m. S. R. Henry, 1910.

I've Got the World on a String. w. Ted Koehler, m. Harold Arlen, 1933. Introduced by Aida Ward in the revue *Cotton Club Parade* at the Cotton Club in Harlem, New York. June Haver and Gloria De Haven sang it in (MM) *I'll Get By*, the remake of *Tin Pan Alley*, 1950. The first records of note were by Bing Crosby (Brunswick), Cab Calloway (Brunswick), and Louis Armstrong (Victor). Among others to record this standard were: Mildred Bailey (Crown), Frank Sinatra (Capitol), Woody Herman (Columbia), Red McKenzie with the Spirits of Rhythm (Decca), Buddy Cole (Capitol), Hot Lips Page (Melrose), Bobby Hackett (Columbia), and Benny Carter (Norgran).

I've Got the Yes! We Have No Bananas Blues. w. Lew Brown, m. James F. Hanley and Robert King, 1923. Novelty featured and hit records by Eddie Cantor (Columbia) and Belle Baker (Victor).

I've Got to Be a Rug Cutter. w/m Edward Kennedy "Duke" Ellington, 1937. Introduced by Duke Ellington and his Orchestra in (MM) *The Hit Parade*.

I've Got to Be Somebody. w/m Joe South, 1966. Top 40 record by Billy Joe Royal (Columbia).

I've Got to Get Hot. w. Jack Yellen, m. Ray Henderson, 1936. Introduced by Gracie Barrie in (TM) *George White's Scandals* (12th Edition), which opened on Christmas Night, 1935.

I've Got to Have a Reason. w/m Lenny Davidson and Dave Clark, 1967. Recorded in England by The Dave Clark Five (Epic).

I've Got to Pass Your House (to Get to My House). w/m Lew Brown, 1933. Introduced by Gertrude Niesen at the Paradise, a New York nightclub.

I've Got to Sing a Torch Song. w. Al Dubin, m. Harry Warren, 1933. Sung by Dick Powell in (MM) *Golddiggers of 1933* and on records (Perfect). Others: Ray Noble (HMV); Ramona, with Roy Bargy (Victor); Hal Kemp (Brunswick); Freddy Martin, under pseudonym of Ed Lloyd (Perfect). Revived by Fletcher Henderson in 1942 (Decca).

I've Got to Use My Imagination. w/m Gerry Goffin and Barry Goldberg, 1973. Gold record by Gladys Knight and The Pips (Buddah).

I've Got You on My Mind. w/m Cole Porter, 1932. Sung by Fred Astaire and Claire Luce in (TM) *Gay Divorce*. Astaire recorded it with Leo Reisman's Orchestra, coupled with "Night and Day" (q.v.) (Victor).

I've Got Your Number. w. Carolyn Leigh, m. Cy Coleman, 1962. Introduced by Swen Swenson in (TM) *Little Me*.

I've Got You to Lean On. w/m Stephen Sondheim, 1964. Introduced by Angela Lansbury, Gabriel Dell, Arnold Soboloff, and James Frawley in (TM) *Anyone Can Whistle*.

I've Got You Under My Skin. w/m Cole Porter, 1936. Introduced by Virginia Bruce in (MM) *Born to Dance*. Academy Award nominee. Ginny Simms sang it in the Porter biography (MM) *Night and Day*, 1946; and soprano Marina Koshetz sang it in (MM) *Luxury Liner*, 1948. Among the early recordings: Hal Kemp, vocal by Skinnay Ennis (Brunswick); Ray Noble, vocal by Al Bowlly (Victor); Dick Jurgens,

vocal by Eddy Howard (Melotone); Frances Langford (Decca). Among later single records: Peggy Lee (Decca), Stan Getz (Birdland), Terry Gibbs (Savoy), novelty version by Stan Freberg (Capitol), Louis Prima and Keely Smith (Capitol). The Four Seasons had a Top 10 hit (Philips), 1966.

I've Grown Accustomed to Her Face. w. Alan Jay Lerner, m. Frederick Loewe, 1956. Introduced by Rex Harrison in (TM) *My Fair Lady*, and sung by him in (MM) *My Fair Lady*, 1964.

I've Grown So Used to You. w/m Thurland Chattaway, 1901.

I've Had Enough. w/m Paul McCartney, 1978. Recorded by McCartney's group Wings (Capitol).

I've Had It. w. Ray Ceroni and Carl Bonura, m. Ray Ceroni, 1959. Recorded by The Bell Notes (Time). Revived by the female quartet Fanny (Casablanca), 1974.

I've Had My Moments. w. Gus Kahn, m. Walter Donaldson, 1934. Sung by June Clyde, Jimmy Durante, Polly Moran, and Eddie Quillan in (MM) *Hollywood Party*. Popular recordings by the orchestras of Leo Reisman (Brunswick) and Will Osborne (Melotone) and the English band led by Lew Stone, vocal by Al Bowlly (Decca).

I've Had This Feeling Before. w/m Sam H. Stept, 1943. Featured by Johnny Long, vocal by Bob Houston and Helen Young (Decca).

(I've Had) the Time of My Life. w/m John DeNicola, Donald Markowitz and Franke Previte. 1987. Recorded on the soundtrack of (MP) *Dirty Dancing* and a #1 single by Bill Medley and Jennifer Warnes (RCA). Academy Award winner, Best Song.

I've Heard That Song Before. w. Sammy Cahn, m. Jule Styne, 1943. Introduced in (MM) *Youth on Parade* by Bob Crosby, with his orchestra. Harry James, vocal by Helen Forrest (Columbia), had a million-selling record, #1 on the charts for thirteen weeks. The song was on, "Your Hit Parade" for fifteen weeks, four times as #1. Nominated for an Academy Award.

I've Hitched My Wagon to a Star. w. Johnny Mercer, m. Richard A. Whiting, 1938. Introduced by Dick Powell and Raymond Paige's Orchestra in (MM) *Hollywood Hotel.*

I've Just Come Back to Say Good-bye. w/m Charles K. Harris, 1897.

I've Just Seen Her (as Nobody Else Has Seen Her). w. Lee Adams, m. Charles Strouse, 1962. Introduced by Ron Husmann in (TM) *All American.*

I've Lost You. w/m Ken Howard and Alan Blaikley, 1970. English song. Top 40 record by Elvis Presley (RCA).

I've Never Been in Love Before. w/m Frank Loesser, 1950. Introduced by Robert Alda and Isabel Bigley in (TM) *Guys and Dolls.* Among many recordings, in addition to the cast album, were: Billy Eckstine (MGM); Doris Day (Columbia); Bob Haymes (King); George Shearing (MGM); Margaret Whiting (Capitol); Ralph Flanagan, vocal by Harry Prime (RCA Victor). Song not used in film version.

I've Never Been to Me. w/m Ken Hirsch and Ron Miller, 1982. First released by Charlene (Prodigal), 1977. The master was re-released (Motown), 1982, and was on the Pop charts for twenty weeks, reaching the #3 position.

I've Never Forgotten. w. Sammy Cahn, m. Jule Styne, 1946. Introduced by Constance Moore in (MM) *Earl Carroll Sketchbook.*

I've Never Found a Girl (to Love Me Like You Do). w/m Booker T. Jones, Eddie Floyd, and Alvertis Isbell, 1968. Top 40 record by Eddie Floyd (Stax).

I've Only Myself to Blame. w/m Redd Evans and David Mann, 1947. Popular records by The King Cole Trio (Capitol); Arthur Prysock (Decca); Doris Day (Columbia); George Paxton and his Orchestra (MGM).

I've Passed This Way Before. w/m James Dean and William Witherspoon, 1967. R&B and Pop chart record by Jimmy Ruffin (Soul).

I've Run Out of Tomorrows. w. Lewis Compton, m. Vernon Mize and Hank Thompson, 1959. Recorded by Hank Thompson (Capitol).

I've Taken Quite a Fancy to You. w. Edward Madden, m. Theodore F. Morse, 1908.

I've Told Ev'ry Little Star. w. Oscar Hammerstein II, m. Jerome Kern, 1932. Introduced by Walter Slezak and reprised by Katherine Carrington in (TM) *Music in the Air.* Gloria Swanson sang it in the film version (MM) *Music in the Air,* 1934. Among recordings: Jack Denny, vocal by Paul Small (Victor); Eddy Duchin (Brunswick); Irene Dunne (Decca). Revived via Top 10 record by Linda Scott (Canadian-American), 1961. Sung by Dick Shawn and female ensemble in (TM) *A Musical Jubilee,* 1975.

I've Waited, Honey, Waited Long for You. w/m George A. Nichols, 1899.

Ivory Tower. w/m Jack Fulton and Lois Steele, 1956. Hit records by Cathy Carr (Fraternity), The Charms (DeLuxe), Gale Storm (Dot).

Ivy. w/m Hoagy Carmichael, 1947. The theme from (MP) *Ivy.* Leading recordings by Jo Stafford (Capitol), Dick Haymes (Decca), Vic Damone (Mercury).

Ivy, Cling to Me. w. Alex Rogers, m. James P. Johnson and Isham Jones, 1923. Featured and recorded by Isham Jones and his Orchestra (Brunswick).

Ivy Rose. w/m Al Hoffman and Dick Manning, 1957. Featured and recorded by Perry Como (RCA).

I Waited a Little Too Long. w/m Sidney Miller and Donald O'Connor, 1952. Leading recording by Kay Starr (Capitol).

I Waited Too Long. w. Howard Greenfield, m. Neil Sedaka, 1959. Featured and recorded by LaVern Baker (Atlantic).

I Wake Up Smiling. w. Edgar Leslie, m. Fred E. Ahlert, 1933. Featured and recorded by Guy Lombardo and the Royal Canadians (Brunswick) and Morton Downey (Perfect).

I Walk Alone. Herbert Wilson, 1968. Country and Pop chart record by Marty Robbins (Columbia).

I Walked In. w. Harold Adamson, m. Jimmy McHugh, 1945. From (MM) *Nob Hill.* Popular records by Glen Gray and the Casa Loma Orchestra (Decca) and Gene Krupa, vocal by Buddy Stewart (Columbia).

I Walk the Line. w/m Johnny Cash, 1956. Johnny Cash's first chart record as a singer/writer (Sun). Title song of (MP) *I Walk the Line*, 1970.

I Walk with Music. w. Johnny Mercer, m. Hoagy Carmichael, 1940. Introduced by Kitty Carlisle and Jack Whiting in (TM) *Walk with Music.* Recorded by Buddy Clark (Varsity); Bob Chester, vocal by Dolores O'Neill (Bluebird); Frankie Masters and his Orchestra (Vocalion).

I Wanna Be a Cowboy. w/m Brian Chatton, Nico Ramsden, Nick Richards, and Jeff Jeopardi, 1986. Recorded by the British quintet Boys Don't Cry (Profile).

I Wanna Be Around. w/m Johnny Mercer and Sadie Vimmerstedt, 1963. Mrs. Vimmerstedt, a housewife from Youngstown, Ohio, sent Johnny Mercer the title and idea for the song. Mercer wrote it and shared the royalties which emanated from the hit recording by Tony Bennett (Columbia).

I Wanna Be Free. w/m Loretta Lynn, 1971. Hit Country and Pop record by Loretta Lynn (Decca).

I Wanna Be in Winchell's Column. w. Mack Gordon, m. Harry Revel, 1938. Introduced in (MM) *Love and Hisses* by Dick Baldwin and recorded by Isham Jones and his Orchestra (Vocalion).

I Wanna Be Loved. w. Edward Heyman and Billy Rose, m. John Green, 1933, 1950.

Introduced in Billy Rose's nightclub revue *Casino de Paree.* The Andrews Sisters revived it with their hit record (Decca), 1950, helping the song to ten weeks on "Your Hit Parade." Coupled with "The Boulevard of Broken Dreams" (q.v.) it marked Tony Bennett's first hit record (Columbia), 1955. Ricky Nelson had a popular version (Imperial), 1959.

I Wanna Be Loved by You. w. Bert Kalmar, m. Harry Ruby and Herbert Stothart, 1928. Introduced by Helen Kane in (TM) *Good Boy.* Kane ended each eight-bar phrase with "boop-boop-a-doop," which became her trademark and gave rise to the Betty Boop character. Her recorded version was a hit (Victor). The song was revived in the late forties by Rose Murphy (Majestic) who substituted "Chee Chee" for the "boops." In the Kalmar and Ruby biography, (MM) *Three Little Words*, 1950, Kane, dubbing for Debbie Reynolds on the soundtrack, sang it with Carlton Carpenter. In (MM) *Gentlemen Marry Brunettes*, 1955, it was sung by Jane Russell, Rudy Vallee, and Anita Ellis, the latter dubbing for Jeanne Crain. Marilyn Monroe sang it in (MM) *Some Like It Hot*, 1959. It was sung in (TM) *A Musical Jubilee*, 1975, by Patrice Munsel, Tammy Grimes, and Lillian Gish.

I Wanna Be Sedated. w/m Douglas Colvin, John Cummings, and Jeffrey Hyman, 1979. Sung by The Ramones in (MM) *Rock 'n' Roll High School.*

I Wanna Be Where You Are. w/m Arthur Ross and Leonard Ware, 1972. Top 20 record by Michael Jackson (Motown).

I Wanna Be with You. w/m Eric Carmen, 1973. Top 20 record by The Raspberries, lead singer—Carmen (Capitol).

I Wanna Be Your Lover. w/m Prince Rogers Nelson, 1980. Recorded by Prince (Warner Bros.).

I Wanna Dance Wit' Choo (Doo Dat Dance). w/m Bob Crewe and Danny Randell, 1975. Recorded by Disco Tex and The Sex-o-lettes (Chelsea).

I Wanna Dance with Somebody (Who Loves Me). w/m George Merrill and Shannon Rubicam, 1987. #1 single from the platinum album "Whitney" by Whitney Houston (Arista).

I Wanna Dance with You. w/m Eddie Rabbitt and B. J. Walker, Jr., 1988. #1 Country chart record by Eddie Rabbitt (RCA).

I Wanna Do More. w/m Jerry Leiber and Mike Stoller, 1956. Top 10 R&B chart record by Ruth Brown and Her Rhythmakers (Atlantic).

I Wanna Get Married. w. Dan Shapiro and Milton Pascal, m. Phil Charig, 1944. Introduced by Gertrude Niesen in (TM) *Follow the Girls*, and recorded by her, accompanied by Harry Sosnik's Orchestra (Decca).

I Wanna Go Back. w/m Morty Byron, Danny Chauncey, and Ira Walker, 1987. Single from the album "Can't Hold Back" by Eddie Money (Columbia).

I Wanna Go Back to Bali. w. Al Dubin, m. Harry Warren, 1938. Introduced by Rudy Vallee in (MM) *Gold Diggers in Paris*. Recorded by Freddie "Schnicklefritz" Fisher (Decca) and Jimmy Grier (Decca) and their bands.

I Wanna Go Home. w/m Jack Joyce, 1949. Popular recording by Perry Como, with the Fontane Sisters (RCA Victor).

I Wanna Go to the Zoo. w. Mack Gordon, m. Harry Revel, 1936. Sung by Shirley Temple in (MM) *Stowaway*. It was recorded by Hildegarde (Columbia), coupled with "Goodnight, My Love" (q.v.) from the same film.

I Wanna Go Where You Go, Do What You Do. See **Then I'll Be Happy**.

I Wanna Live. w/m John D. Loudermilk, 1968. C&W and Pop hit by Glen Campbell (Capitol).

I Wanna Love Him So Bad. w/m Jeff Barry and Ellie Greenwich, 1964. Top 10 record by The Jelly Beans (Red Bird).

I Wanna Play House with You. w/m Cy Coben, 1951. Featured and recorded by Eddy Arnold (RCA Victor).

I Wanna Sing About You. w/m Dave Dreyer and Cliff Friend, 1931. Recorded by Bert Lown (Victor), Paul Tremaine (Columbia), and Howard Joyner, with vocal by Bob Howard (Columbia).

I Wanna Testify. w/m George Clinton and Deron Taylor, 1967. Top 20 record by The Parliaments (Revilot), followed by Johnnie Taylor (Stax), 1969.

I Wanna Wrap You Up. w. Remus A. Harris, m. Terry Shand, 1940. Featured and recorded by Patricia Norman (Vocalion), and these bands: Bob Crosby, vocal by Teddy Grace (Decca); Van Alexander (Varsity); Frankie Masters (Vocalion).

I Want a Bowlegged Woman. w/m Henry Glover and Sally Nix, 1948. Hit R&B chart record by Bull Moose Jackson and His Buffalo Bearcats (King).

I Want'a Do Something Freaky to You. w/m Leon Haywood (20th Century), 1975. Top 20 record by Leon Haywood (20th Century).

I Want a Girl (Just Like the Girl That Married Dear Old Dad). w. William Dillon, m. Harry Von Tilzer, 1911. Revived by George Murphy, Constance Moore, Eddie Cantor, and Joan Davis in (MM) *Show Business* in 1944 and by Al Jolson and minstrels in (MM) *The Jolson Story* in 1946.

I Want a Little Girl. w. Billy Moll, m. Murray Mencher, 1930. A jazz favorite recorded by McKinney's Cotton Pickers (Victor); Count Basie, with vocal by Jimmy Rushing (Okeh); the Kansas City Six (Commodore); Buck Clayton (Hot Record Society); the Commanders (Decca).

I Want a Man. w. Oscar Hammerstein II, m. Vincent Youmans, 1928. Introduced by Libby Holman in (TM) *Rainbow*.

I Want a New Drug. w/m Christopher Hayes and Huey Lewis. 1984. Top 10 record by Huey Lewis and The News (Chrysalis).

I Want Candy. w/m Bob Feldman, Jerry Goldstein, Richard Gottehrer, and Bert Berns, 1965. Hit record by The Strangeloves (Bang). Revived by the English group Bow Wow Wow (RCA), 1982.

I Want Her. w/m Keith Sweat and Teddy Riley, 1988. #1 R&B and Top 10 Pop chart record by Keith Sweat (Elektra).

I Want It All. w. Richard Maltby, Jr., m. David Shire, 1983. Introduced in (TM) *Baby* by Catherine Cox, Liz Callaway, and Beth Fowler.

I Want My Mama (a.k.a. **Mama Yo Quiero).** w. Al Stillman (Engl.), w/m Jararaca and Vincente Paiva (Portu.), 1940. Originally a Brazilian song, "Mamae Eu Quero." This version introduced in (TM) *Earl Carroll Vanities*. Song is associated with Carmen Miranda, who sang it in (MM) *Down Argentine Way*, 1940, and recorded it (Decca). Chico and Harpo Marx played it as a piano duet in (MP) *The Big Store*, 1941; Mickey Rooney impersonated Miranda singing it in (MM) *Babes on Broadway*, 1942; Harold Nicholas (of the Nicholas Brothers) sang and danced it in (MM) *Reckless Age*, 1944; it was heard in (MM) *Ladies' Man*, starring Eddie Bracken, 1947; Jerry Lewis mimed the number to a Miranda recording in the Martin and Lewis (MM) *Scared Stiff*, 1953.

I Want My Share of Love. w. Sammy Cahn, m. Saul Chaplin, 1939. Featured and recorded by the bands of Larry Clinton, vocal by Bea Wain (Victor); Jan Savitt, vocal by Carlotta Dale (Decca); Mitchell Ayres (Vocalion).

I Want to (Do Everything for You). w/m Joe Tex, 1965. Introduced and recorded by Joe Tex (Dial).

I Want to Be a Cowboy's Sweetheart. w/m Patsy Montana, 1946. Rosalie Allen had a hit Country record of this ten-year-old song (RCA).

I Want to Be a Minstrel Man. w. Harold Adamson, m. Burton Lane, 1934. Performed by Eddie Cantor and George Murphy (in blackface) in a minstrel number in (MM) *Kid Millions*. The melody was used with a new title and lyrics in "Royal Wedding," 1951. See also **You're All the World to Me**.

I Want to Be Bad. w. B. G. De Sylva and Lew Brown, m. Ray Henderson, 1928. Introduced by Zelma O'Neal in (TM) *Follow Thru*. Recorded by Helen Kane (Victor). Nancy Carroll sang it in the film version, (MM) *Follow Thru*, 1930.

I Want to Be Evil. w/m Raymond Taylor and Lester Judson, 1953. Featured and recorded by Eartha Kitt (RCA Victor).

I Want to Be Happy. w. Irving Caesar, m. Vincent Youmans, 1925. In the biggest hit of the season (TM) *No, No, Nanette*, this was sung by Charles Winninger, Louis Groody, and chorus. In the 1971 production it was performed by Jack Gilford, Susan Watson, Ruby Keeler, and a singing, tap-dancing chorus. Lena Horne performed the song as a jazz waltz in her Broadway show (TM) *Lena Horne: The Lady and Her Music*, 1981. It was sung in (MM) *No, No, Nanette*, 1930, which featured Alexander Gray and Bernice Claire; in the 1940 remake featuring Anna Neagle and Victor Moore; in (MM) *Tea For Two*, 1950, sung by Doris Day and Gordon MacRae. In 1958, the orchestras of Enoch Light (Grand Award) and Tommy Dorsey, led by Warren Covington (Decca), each had popular recordings of "I Want to Be Happy Cha Cha."

I Want to Be Happy Cha Cha. See **I Want to Be Happy**.

I Want to Be Loved (But by Only You). w/m Savannah Churchill, 1947. Introduced and recorded by Savannah Churchill (Manor). Among other versions: Benny Goodman, vocal by Lillian Lane (Capitol); Beryl Davis (Victor); Lionel Hampton (Decca); Cootie Williams and his Orchestra (Majestic).

I Want to Be Sure. w/m Gene Autry and Merle Travis, 1945. Introduced and recorded by Gene Autry (Columbia).

I Want to Be the Only One. w/m Ernie Peterson, 1948. Recorded by Jon and Sandra Steele (Damon) and The Mills Brothers (Decca).

I Want to Be Wanted. w. Kim Gannon (Engl.), A. Testa (Ital.), m. Pino Spotti, 1960. Italian song originally titled "Per Tutta la Vita." Leading record by Brenda Lee (Decca).

I Want to Be Wanted. w/m Bob Atcher, 1943. Introduced and recorded by and radio theme song of Country singer Bob Atcher (Okeh).

I Want to Be with You. w. Lee Adams, m. Charles Strouse, 1964. Introduced by Sammy Davis, Jr. and Paula Wayne in (TM) *Golden Boy*. Leading records by Nancy Wilson (Capitol), and Dee Dee Warwick (Mercury), 1966.

I Want to Be with You. w. B. G. De Sylva, m. Vincent Youmans, 1932. Written for (TM) *Take a Chance*, but cut before opening. The song was published, however, and has found its way into the repertoire of many singers and instrumentalists.

I Want to Be with You Always. w/m Lefty Frizzell and Jim Beck, 1951. A crossover hit (C&W and Pop) for Lefty Frizzell (Columbia).

I Want to Be Your Man. w/m Larry Troutman, 1987. #1 R&B chart and Top 10 Pop chart record by Roger [pseud. for Troutman] from his album "Unlimited!" (Reprise).

I Want to Get Next to You. w/m Norman Whitfield, 1976. Introduced by Rose Royce in (MP) *Car Wash* and on records (MCA).

I Want to Go Back to Michigan, Down on the Farm. w/m Irving Berlin, 1914. The song was sung by Judy Garland in (MM) *Easter Parade* in 1948. The Andrews Sisters recorded it (Decca) in 1939.

I Want to Go with You. w/m Hank Cochran, 1966. Country and Pop chart hit by Eddy Arnold (RCA).

I Want to Hold You in My Dreams Tonight. w/m Robert Dean, Jr. and Stella Parton, 1975. Top 10 Country chart record by Stella Parton (Country Soul).

I Want to Hold Your Hand. w/m John Lennon and Paul McCartney, 1964. The first U.S. hit and million-selling record by The Beatles (Capitol). It became the biggest-selling British single of all times. It was performed by four Beatles imitators in (MM) *I Wanna Hold Your Hand*, 1979.

I Want to Know. w/m Pylia Parham, Robert Geddins, and Ronald Badger, 1960. R&B Top 10 record by Sugar Pie De Santo (Veltone).

I Want to Know What Love Is. w/m Mick Jones, 1985. #1 gold record by the Anglo-American group, Foreigner, backup singing by The New Jersey Mass Choir and Jennifer Holliday (Atlantic).

I Want to Know You Before We Make Love. w/m Candy Parton and Becky Hobbs, 1987. Hit Country single from the album "Borderline" by Conway Twitty (MCA).

I Want to Make the World Turn Around. w/m Steve Miller, 1986. Recorded by The Steve Miller Band (Capitol).

I Want to Marry a Male Quartette. w. Otto Harbach, m. Rudolf Friml, 1916. From (TM) *Katinka*.

I Want to Stay Here. w/m Gerry Goffin and Carole King, 1963. Featured and recorded by Steve (Lawrence) and Eydie (Gormé) (Columbia).

I Want to Take You Higher. w/m Sylvester Stewart, 1969. Introduced and recorded by Sly and The Family Stone, and produced by Sly (Sylvester Stewart) Stone (Epic). When Ike and Tina Turner had a Top 40 version (Liberty), 1970, the Stone record was re-issued and also made the Top 40.

I Want to Thank Your Folks. w/m Bennie Benjamin and George David Weiss, 1947.

Most popular record by Perry Como (RCA Victor).

I Want to Walk to San Francisco. w. Gretchen Cryer, m. Nancy Ford, 1970. Performed by the company in the off-Broadway (TM) *The Last Sweet Days of Isaac.*

I Want to Walk You Home. w/m Antoine "Fats" Domino, 1959. Hit record by Fats Domino (Imperial).

I Want What I Want When I Want It. w. Henry Blossom, m. Victor Herbert, 1906. Introduced by William Pruette in (TM) *Mlle. Modiste*, which opened on Christmas night, 1905.

I Want You. w/m Arthur Ross and Leon Ware, 1976. #1 R&B, Top 20 Pop chart record by Marvin Gaye (Tamla).

I Want You. w/m Bob Dylan, 1966. Introduced and recorded by Bob Dylan (Columbia).

I Want You. w/m George M. Cohan, 1907. From Cohan's (TM) *The Talk of New York.*

I Want You, I Need You. w/m Ben Ellison and Harvey O. Brooks, 1933. Introduced by Mae West in (MM) *I'm No Angel.* Recorded by her (Brunswick); also by Isham Jones (Victor) and Charlie Barnet (Melotone). It was the first recording by a band under Barnet's leadership. He was twenty years old!

I Want You, I Need You, I Love You. w. George Mysels, m. Ira Kosloff, 1956. #1 hit record by Elvis Presley (RCA).

I Want You All to Myself (Just You). w/m John Koch and Roy Carroll, 1954. Popular recording by Kitty Kallen, with Jack Pleis's Orchestra (Decca).

I Want You Back. w/m Berry Gordy, Jr., Fonce Mizell, Freddie Perren, and Deke Richards, 1969. Their first hit, and #1 on the R&B and Pop charts, by The Jackson 5 (Motown).

I Want You for Christmas. w. Charles Tobias, m. Sam H. Stept and Ned Washington, 1937.

I Want Your Love. w/m Bernard Edwards and Nile Rodgers, 1979. Gold record by Chic, the disco group produced by the writers (Atlantic).

I Want Your Sex. w/m George Michael, 1987. Introduced on the soundtrack of (MP) *Beverly Hill Cop II.* Leading single by the English songwriter/singer, George Michael, from his album "Faith" (MCA).

I Want You to Be My Baby. w/m Jon Hendricks, 1955. Leading records by Georgia Gibbs (Mercury) and Lillian Briggs (Epic).

I Want You to Be My Girl. w/m George Goldner and Richard Barrett, 1956. Recorded by Frankie Lymon and The Teenagers (Gee).

I Want You to Meet My Baby. w/m Barry Mann and Cynthia Weil, 1964. Featured and recorded by Eydie Gormé (Columbia).

I Want You Tonight. w/m Dave Jenkins, Cory Lerios, and Allee Willis, 1979. Recorded by the quartet Pablo Cruise (A&M).

I Want You to Want Me. w/m Rick Nielsen, 1979. Top 10 record by the quartet Cheap Trick (Epic).

I Was Born in Virginia. w/m George M. Cohan, 1906. Introduced so successfully by Ethel Levey in (TM) *George Washington, Jr.* that the song became known as "Ethel Levey's Virginia Song."

I Was Country When Country Wasn't Cool. w/m Kye Fleming and Dennis Morgan, 1981. Country chart hit by Barbara Mandrell (MCA).

I Was Doing All Right. w. Ira Gershwin, m. George Gershwin, 1938. Introduced by Ella Logan in (MM) *The Goldwyn Follies*, the last score by George Gershwin who died after completing four songs for it. Recorded by Logan (Decca); Red Norvo's Orchestra, vocal by Mildred Bailey (Brunswick); Larry Clinton's Orchestra (Victor); Jimmy Dorsey, vocal by Bob Eberly (Decca). All coupled it with "Love Is Here to Stay" from the same film.

I Washed My Hands in Muddy Water. w/m Joe Babcock, 1966. Popular record by Johnny Rivers (Imperial).

I Was Kaiser Bill's Batman. m. Roger Greenway and Roger Cook, 1967. Instrumental, recorded in England and reaching the Top 20 on the U.S. charts, by Whistling Jack Smith (Deram).

I Was Looking for My Boy, She Said (or, Decoration Day). w/m Paul Dresser, 1895.

I Was Lucky. w. Jack Meskill, m. Jack Stern, 1935. Introduced by Maurice Chevalier and Ann Sothern in (MM) *Folies Bergere.*

I Was Made for Dancin'. w/m Michael Lloyd, 1979. Recorded by Leif Garrett (Scotti Brothers).

I Was Made for Lovin' You. w/m Desmond Child, Vini Poncia, and Paul Stanley, 1979. Gold record by the rock band Kiss (Casablanca).

I Was Made to Love Her. w/m Henry Cosby, Lulu Hardaway, Sylvia Moy, and Stevie Wonder, 1967. Hit record by Stevie Wonder (Tamla). Instrumental chart record by R&B saxophonist King Curtis (Atco), 1968.

I Wasn't Born to Follow. w/m Gerry Goffin and Carole King, 1969. Introduced by The Byrds on the soundtrack of (MP) *Easy Rider.*

I Was Only Joking. w/m Gary Grainger and Rod Stewart 1978. Recorded by English singer Rod Stewart (Warner Bros.).

I Was Saying to the Moon. w. Johnny Burke, m. Arthur Johnston, 1937. From the Mae West (MM) *Go West Young Man.* Among bands who recorded it: Reggie Childs (Decca), George Hamilton (Victor), King Tempo (Bluebird), Dick Stabile (Vocalion), Rudy Vallee (Melotone).

I Was the One. w/m Aaron Schroeder, Claude De Metrius, Hal Blair, and Bill Peppers, 1956. Flip side of Elvis Presley's "Heartbreak Hotel" (q.v.) (RCA).

I Watch the Love Parade. w. Otto Har-

bach, m. Jerome Kern, 1931. Introduced in (TM) *The Cat and the Fiddle* by George Meader and Flora Le Breton. In the film version (MM) *The Cat and the Fiddle,* 1934, it was sung by Jeanette MacDonald and Ramon Novarro.

I Went Out of My Way. w/m Helen Bliss, 1941. Best-selling record by Teddy Powell, vocal by Ruth Gaylor (Bluebird). Also recorded by bands of Tommy Dorsey (Victor), Frankie Masters (Okeh), Orrin Tucker (Columbia). Revived by Paul Weston's Orchestra (Columbia), 1954.

I Went Out of My Way (to Make You Happy). w. Vic McAlpin, m. Roy Drusky and Jean Elrod, 1961. Top Country chart song by Roy Drusky (Decca).

I Went to Your Wedding. w/m Jessie Mae Robinson, 1952. #1 record, with sales of over a million copies by Patti Page (Mercury). Other chart records by Steve Gibson and The Red Caps, featuring Damita Jo (RCA Victor), and comedy version by Spike Jones, vocal by Sir Frederic Gas (RCA Victor).

I Whistle a Happy Tune. w. Oscar Hammerstein II, m. Richard Rodgers, 1951. Introduced by Gertrude Lawrence and Sandy Kennedy in (TM) *The King and I.* In (MM) *The King and I,* 1956, it was sung by Marni Nixon, dubbing on the soundtrack for Deborah Kerr.

I Will. w/m Dick Glasser, 1965. Chart record by Vic Dana (Dolton), 1962. Top 10 record by Dean Martin (Reprise), 1965.

I Will Always Love You. w/m Dolly Parton, 1974. Crossover (Country/Pop) hit by Dolly Parton (RCA).

I Will Always Think About You. w/m Ronnie Rice and Les Kummel, 1968. Top 40 record by The New Colony Six (Mercury).

I Will Be There. w/m Tom Snow and Jennifer Kimball, 1987. #1 Country chart song by Dan Seals (EMI America).

I Will Follow. w/m Adam Clayton, Dave Evans, Paul Hewson, and Larry Mullen, Jr., 1984. Written and recorded by the Irish quartet U2 (Island).

I Will Follow Him. w. Norman Gimbel and Arthur Altman (Engl.), m. J. W. Stole and Del Roma, 1963. French song, originally titled "Chariot," words by Jacques Plante. #1 U.S. record by fifteen-year-old Little Peggy March (RCA).

I Will Follow You. w/m Jerry Herman, 1961. Introduced by Tommy Rall in (TM) *Milk and Honey*.

I Will Live My Life for You. w. Marcel Stellman, m. Henri Salvador, 1963. French song, coupled by Tony Bennett with his hit "I Wanna Be Around" (q.v.) (Columbia).

I Will Love You. w/m Shelby Flint and Barry De Vorzon, 1963. Recorded by Richard Chamberlain (MGM).

I Will Survive. w/m Dino Fekaris and Freddie Perren, 1979. Originally the "B" side of the record, the performance of Gloria Gaynor singing of a woman finding independence from her self-centered lover caught on with the public and became a platinum #1 hit (Polydor).

I Will Wait. w/m Mildred Colclough, 1951. Recorded by a group from the Frederick Douglass High School in Baltimore, Md., The Four Buddies (Savoy).

I Will Wait for You. w. Norman Gimbel (Engl.), Jacques Demy (Fr.), m. Michel Legrand, 1965. Introduced in French by Danielle Licari, dubbing on the soundtrack for Catherine Deneuve, and José Bartel, dubbing for Nino Castelnuovo in the French film (MP) *The Umbrellas of Cherbourg*. Song nominated for Academy Award. First recording in English by Steve Lawrence (Columbia).

I Wish. w/m Stevie Wonder. 1977. #1 single from the #1 album "Songs in the Key of Life" by Stevie Wonder (Tamla).

I Wish. w/m Allan Roberts and Doris Fisher, 1945. Featured and recorded by The Mills Brothers (Decca).

I Wished on the Moon. w. Dorothy Parker, m. Ralph Rainger, 1935. Introduced by Bing Crosby in (MM) *The Big Broadcast of 1936*. Besides Crosby (Decca), notable recordings were made by Billie Holiday, with Teddy Wilson's Orchestra (Brunswick); Ray Noble, Al Bowlly doing the vocal (Victor); Lanny Ross (Brunswick); Henry "Red" Allen (Vocalion); Little Jack Little (Columbia). Teddi King had a later recording (MGM). This was one of two song hits written by Dorothy Parker, the short story writer and drama critic.

I Wish I Could Fall in Love Today. w/m Harlan Howard, 1961. C&W chart hit by Ray Price (Columbia).

I Wish I Could Shimmy Like My Sister Kate. w/m Armand J. Piron, 1922. The song, written three years earlier, caught on as Gilda Gray and others were performing the dance, the shimmy, in theater, vaudeville, and nightclubs. It was used in (MM) *Wabash Avenue*, starring Betty Grable, 1950, and in (MP) *The Girl Can't Help It*, starring Jayne Mansfield, 1957. Hit record by The Mary Kaye Trio (Capitol), 1952.

I Wish I Could Tell You. w. Harry Ruby, m. Rube Bloom, 1945. Introduced by June Haver in (MM) *Wake Up and Dream*. Top records: Dick Haymes (Decca), Benny Goodman and his Orchestra (Columbia), Phil Brito (Musicraft).

I Wish I Didn't Love You So. w/m Frank Loesser, 1947. Introduced by Betty Hutton in (MM) *The Perils of Pauline*. Top recordings by Vaughn Monroe, with his Orchestra (RCA Victor); Dinah Shore (Columbia); Betty Hutton (Capitol); Dick Haymes (Decca).

I Wish I'd Never Been Born. w/m Howard Greenfield and Jack Keller, 1960. Recorded by Patti Page (Mercury).

I Wish I Had a Girl. w. Gus Kahn, m. Grace LeBoy, 1907. Popularized by Mollie Williams, this became Kahn's first song hit. It was later heard in the Kahn film biography (MM) *I'll See You in My Dreams*, sung by Danny Thomas as Kahn, and Doris Day as Grace LeBoy (Mrs. Gus Kahn), 1951.

(I Wish I Had a) Heart of Stone. See **Heart of Stone (I Wish I Had a)**.

I Wish I Had a Nickel. w/m Tommy Sutton and W. S. Barnhart, 1949. C&W chart record by Jimmy Wakely (Capitol).

I Wish I Had My Old Girl Back Again. w. Ballard MacDonald, m. Paul Wallace, 1909.

I Wish I Had Never Met Sunshine. w/m Dale Evans, Oakley Haldeman, and Gene Autry, 1945. Leading records by Gene Autry (Columbia), Roy Rogers (Victor), Wesley Tuttle (Capitol).

I Wish I Knew. w. Mack Gordon, m. Harry Warren, 1945. Introduced by Dick Haymes and Betty Grable in (MM) *Billy Rose's Diamond Horseshoe*, with best-selling record by Haymes (Decca).

I Wish It Would Rain. w/m Roger Penzabene, Barrett Strong, and Norman Whitfield, 1968. Top 10 record by The Temptations (Gordy) and chart version by Gladys Knight and The Pips (Soul).

I Wish I Was Eighteen Again. w/m Sonny Throckmorton, 1980. The octogenarian comedian, George Burns, had a chart record of the song (Mercury).

I Wish I Was the Willow. w. Frank Loesser, m. Burton Lane, 1938. From (MP) *Spawn of the North*, starring Dorothy Lamour. Recorded by Terry Shand (Decca); Dick Jurgens, vocal by Eddy Howard (Vocalion); Sammy Kaye (Victor); Frank Dailey, vocal by Howard DuLany (Vocalion).

I Wish I Were Aladdin. w. Mack Gordon, m. Harry Revel, 1935. Introduced by Bing Crosby in (MM) *Two for Tonight*. Recorded by Crosby (Decca) and the Riley-Farley Band (Decca).

I Wish I Were in Love Again. w. Lorenz Hart, m. Richard Rodgers, 1937. Introduced by Grace McDonald and Rolly Pickert in (TM) *Babes in Arms*. Judy Garland and Mickey Rooney sang it in the Rodgers and Hart story (MM) *Words and Music*, 1948, and on a single record (MGM).

I Wish I Were Twins. w. Frank Loesser and Eddie DeLange, m. Joseph Meyer, 1934.

DeLange's first successful song. Introduced by Fats Waller (Victor). Among recordings: Adrian's (Rollini) Ramblers, vocal by Ella Logan (Brunswick); Red Allen (Perfect); Coleman Hawkins (Decca); Emil Coleman (Columbia).

I Wish I Wuz. w/m Sid Kuller and Lyn Murray, 1951. From (MP) *Slaughter Trail*. Recorded by Rosemary Clooney (Columbia).

I Wish That I Could Hide Inside This Letter. w. Charles Tobias, m. Nat Simon, 1943. Featured and recorded by Lawrence Welk and his Orchestra (Decca).

I Wish That I Could Hurt That Way Again. w/m Rafe Vanhoy, Curly Putman, and Roger Cook, 1986. Top 10 Country chart record by T. Graham Brown (Capitol).

I Wish That We Were Married. w/m Marion Weiss and Edna Lewis, 1962. Hit record by the R&B quintet Ronnie and The Hi-Lites (Joy).

I Wish That You Were Here Tonight. w/m Paul Dresser, 1896.

I Wish You Love. w. Albert Beach (Engl.), m. Charles Trenet, 1955. Original French title, with lyrics by Trenet, "Que Reste-til de Nos Amours." Featured by Felicia Sanders. Gloria Lynne's 1964 recording (Everest) became a big juke box and airplay favorite.

I Woke Up in Love This Morning. w/m L. Russell Brown and Irwin Levine, 1971. Top 20 record by The Partridge Family (Bell).

I Woke Up Too Soon. w/m Dave Franklin, 1935. Featured and recorded by Glen Gray and the Casa Loma Orchestra, vocal by Kenny Sargent (Decca). Also the orchestras of Archie Bleyer (Vocalion), Richard Himber (Victor), Henry King (Columbia), Joe Reichman (Melotone).

I Wonder. w/m Cecil Gant and Raymond Leveen, 1944. Recorded by Gant (Gilt-Edge), a blues singer-pianist from Nashville. He was billed as "Private Cecil Gant, the G.I. Singsation."

I Wonder, I Wonder, I Wonder. w/m

436

Daryl Hutchins, 1947. Best-selling records by Eddy Howard, with his Orchestra (Majestic) and Guy Lombardo, vocal by Don Rodney (Decca).

I Wonder Do You Think of Me. w/m Sanger Shafer, 1989. Hit Country record by Keith Whitley (RCA).

I Wonder If I Take You Home. w/m Full Force, 1985. Top 10 R&B and Pop chart record by Lisa Lisa & Cult Jam with Full Force (Columbia). Lisa Lisa & Cult Jam was an R&B/rap trio and Full Force was a band, the members of which produced and backed the trio.

I Wonder If She'll Ever Come Back to Me. w/m Paul Dresser, 1896.

I Wonder If She's Waiting. w. Andrew B. Sterling, m. Harry Von Tilzer, 1899.

I Wonder If You Still Care for Me. w. Harry B. Smith and Francis Wheeler, 1921. Leading record by tenor Charles Hart (Columbia).

I Wonder What Became of Me. w. Johnny Mercer, m. Harold Arlen, 1946. Introduced by June Hawkins in (TM) *St. Louis Woman*. While deleted from the show after its opening, the song has become a staple in the repertoires of many cabaret singers.

I Wonder What's Become of Sally. w. Jack Yellen, m. Milton Ager, 1924. Introduced at the Palace Theatre in New York by Van and Schenck. In addition to their recording (Columbia), the same year saw records by Al Jolson (Brunswick), Bennie Krueger's Band (Brunswick), and Ted Lewis (Columbia).

I Wonder What She's Doing Tonight. w/m Tommy Boyce and Bobby Hart, 1968. Top 10 record by Tommy Boyce and Bobby Hart (A&M).

I Wonder What the King Is Doing Tonight. w. Alan Jay Lerner, m. Frederick Loewe, 1960. Introduced by Richard Burton in (TM) *Camelot*. In the 1967 film version (MM) *Camelot*, it was sung by Richard Harris.

I Wonder Where My Baby Is Tonight. w. Gus Kahn, m. Walter Donaldson, 1925.

Popular record by Henry Burr and Billy Murray, marking the only duet recorded by the two stars (Victor).

I Wonder Where My Lovin' Man Has Gone. w. Earle C. Jones, m. Richard Whiting and Charles L. Cooke, 1914. This was Whiting's first published song.

I Wonder Where She Is Tonight. w/m Paul Dresser, 1899. Featured by Dick José.

I Wonder Who's Dancing with You Tonight. w. Mort Dixon and Billy Rose, m. Ray Henderson, 1924. Leading record by Benny Krueger and his Orchestra (Brunswick).

I Wonder Who She's Seeing Now. w/m Jimmy George and Lou Pardini, 1987. Recorded by The Temptations (Motown).

I Wonder Who's Kissing Her Now. w. Will M. Hough and Frank R. Adams, m. Joseph E. Howard and Harold Orlob, 1909. Introduced by Joseph E. Howard in (TM) *The Prince of Tonight*. The song sold over three million copies of sheet music and was always associated with Howard throughout his long career as a performer on stage, in clubs, and on radio and T.V. In 1947, Orlob, who had composed the music under a "for hire" contract for Howard's company, sued and succeeded in having his name included as co-composer. Buddy Clark dubbed in the voice for Mark Stevens, as Howard in his film bio (MM) *I Wonder Who's Kissing Her Now*, 1947. It was also in (MM) *The Time, the Place and the Girl*, 1929.

I Wonder Why. w. Ricardo Weeks, m. Melvin Anderson, 1958. Top 40 record by Dion and The Belmonts (Laurie).

I Wonder Why. w. Raymond Klages, m. J. Fred Coots, 1922. From (TM) *Sally, Irene and Mary*. This was the first success for both Klages and Coots.

I Wonder Why You Said "Goodbye." w/m Ernest Tubb, 1941. Early country hit by Ernest Tubb (Decca).

I Won't Be an Actor No More. w/m George M. Cohan, 1900. One of Cohan's early successes.

I Won't Be Home No More. w/m Hank Williams, 1953. Featured and recorded by Hank Williams (MGM).

I Won't Be Home Tonight. w/m Tony Carey, 1982. Recorded by Tony Carey (Rocshire).

I Won't Believe It. w/m J. Russel Robinson, Victor Selsman, and Martin Block, 1939. Recordings: Glen Gray and the Casa Loma Orchestra (Decca); Gene Krupa, vocal by Irene Daye (Brunswick); Al Donahue, vocal by Paula Kelly (Vocalion).

I Won't Be the Fool Anymore. w/m James Sheppard and Joe Thomas, 1957. Recorded by The Heartbeats (Rama).

I Won't Come in While He's There. w/m Gene Davis, 1967. Country hit, recorded by Jim Reeves (RCA).

I Won't Cry Anymore. w. Fred Wise, m. Al Frisch, 1951. Popularized by Tony Bennett (Columbia).

I Won't Dance. w. Dorothy Fields and Jimmy McHugh, m. Jerome Kern, 1935. Introduced by Fred Astaire and Ginger Rogers in (MM) *Roberta*. An earlier version, with lyrics by Oscar Hammerstein II, was performed by Adele Dixon and Richard Dolman in the London musical *Three Sisters*, 1934. Because of the past successful collaboration with composer McHugh, Fields gave him co-lyricist credit. Van Johnson and Lucille Bremer sang it in the Kern biography (MM) *Till the Clouds Roll By*, 1946, and Marge and Gower Champion performed it in the remake of *Roberta*, (MM) *Lovely to Look At*, 1952.

I Won't Forget You. w/m Bobby Dall, C. C. Deville, Brett Michael, and Rikki Rocket, 1987. Chart single by the quartet Poison (Enigma).

I Won't Forget You. w/m Harlan Howard, 1965. Crossover (C&W/Pop) hit by Jim Reeves (RCA).

I Won't Grow Up. w. Carolyn Leigh, m. Moose Charlap, 1954. Introduced by Mary Martin, Robert Harrington, Joseph Stafford, and Kathy Nolan in (TM) *Peter Pan*.

I Won't Hold You Back. w/m Steve Lukather, 1983. Top 10 record by the group Toto; composed by the guitarist (Columbia).

I Won't Last a Day Without You. w/m Roger Nichols and Paul Williams, 1974. Introduced by Maureen McGovern (20th Century), 1973. Top 20 record by The Carpenters (A&M), 1974. Recorded in medley with "Let Me Be the One" by Al Wilson (Rocky Road), 1975.

I Won't Mention It Again. w/m Cam Mullins and Carolyn Jean Yates, 1971. Hit Country and Pop record by Ray Price (Columbia).

I Won't Need You Anymore (Always and Forever). w/m Troy Seals and Max D. Barnes, 1987. #1 Country chart single from the album "Always and Forever" by Randy Travis (Warner Bros.).

I Won't Say I Will, But I Won't Say I Won't. w. B. G. DeSylva and Ira Gershwin (pseud: Arthur Francis), m. George Gershwin, 1923. Introduced by Irene Bordoni in (TP) *Little Miss Bluebeard*.

I Won't Take Less Than Your Love. w/m Paul Overstreet and Don Schlitz, 1988. #1 Country chart record by Tanya Tucker with Paul Davis and Paul Overstreet (Capitol).

I Won't Tell a Soul. w/m Ross Parker and Hughie Charles, 1938. Recorded by Barry Wood (Brunswick) and the bands of Bunny Berigan (Victor), Andy Kirk (Decca), and Lawrence Welk (Vocalion).

I Would Be in Love (Anyway). w/m Bob Gaudio and Jake Holmes, 1970. Leading record by Frank Sinatra (Reprise).

I Would Die 4 U. w/m Prince Rogers Nelson, 1984. Introduced by Prince in (MM) *Purple Rain*. The single from the platinum soundtrack album was a Top 10 chart record (Warner Bros.).

I Would Do Anything for You. See **Anything for You (I Would Do).**

I Wouldn't Be a Man. w/m Don Williams, 1987. Top 10 Country chart record by Don Williams (Capitol).

I Wouldn't Change You for the World. w. Charles Newman, m. Isham Jones, 1931. Featured and recorded by Guy Lombardo and his Royal Canadians (Columbia).

I Wouldn't Change You If I Could. w/m Arthur Q. Smith and Paul H. Jones, 1983. #1 Country chart record by Ricky Skaggs (Epic).

I Wouldn't Have Missed It for the World. w/m Kye Fleming, Dennis Morgan, and Charles Quillen, 1982. Country and Pop hit by Ronnie Milsap (RCA).

I Wouldn't Take a Million. w. Mack Gordon, m. Harry Warren, 1940. Introduced by Shirley Temple in (MM) *Young People*. Most popular records by Glenn Miller, vocal by Ray Eberle (Bluebird); Orrin Tucker, vocal by "Wee" Baker (Columbia); Tommy Dorsey, vocal by Connie Haines (Victor).

I Wouldn't Trade You for the World. w/m Bill Smith, Curtis Kirk, and Bill Taylor, 1964. Recorded by the Irish trio The Bachelors (London).

I Wouldn't Treat a Dog (the Way You Treated Me). w/m Steve Barri, Michael Omartian, Michael Price, and Dan Walsh, 1974. Recorded by Bobby Bland (Dunhill).

I Write the Songs. w/m Bruce Johnston, 1976. First heard in an album by The Captain and Tennille (A&M), 1975. It was next recorded and released as a single in Great Britain by David Cassidy, produced by the writer, Johnston (RCA). Barry Manilow then recorded it for his album "Tryin' to Get the Feeling" (Arista). When the song was released as a single, it quickly rose to the #1 position on the charts and became one of the biggest hits of 1976. It won a Grammy Award (NARAS) as Song of the Year.

I Yust Go Nuts at Christmas. w/m Harry Stewart, 1949. Sung in a Swedish dialect and coupled with "Yingle Bells" by Yogi Yorgesson, a pseudonym for Harry Stewart (Capitol).

439

J

Jack! Jack! Jack! w. Joe Davis (Engl.), Armando Castro (Sp.), m. Armando Castro, 1947. Puerto Rican song, originally titled "Cu-Tu-Gu-Ru." Hit vocal record by Jack Smith (Capitol). Popular band record by Enric Madriguera (National).

Jack, You're Dead. w/m Richard Miles and Walter Bishop, 1947. Recorded by Louis Jordan and his Tympany Five (Decca).

Jack and Diane. w/m John Cougar Mellencamp, 1982. #1 gold record from the album "American Fool," by John Cougar (Riva).

Jack and Jill. w/m Ray Parker, Jr., 1978. Top 10 record by the band Raydio, formed by Parker (Arista).

Jackie Blue. w/m Steve Cash and Larry Lee, 1975. Top 10 record by The Ozark Mountain Daredevils (A&M).

Jack in the Box. m. Zez Confrey, 1927. Piano instrumental.

Jackson. w/m Billy Edd Wheeler and Gaby Rodgers, 1967. Top 20 Pop chart record by Nancy Sinatra and Lee Hazlewood (Reprise). Popular Country record by Johnny Cash and June Carter (Columbia).

Jack the Bear. m. Edward Kennedy "Duke" Ellington, 1940. Instrumental recorded by Duke Ellington and his Orchestra (Victor).

Jacob's Ladder. w/m Bruce Hornsby and John Hornsby, 1987. #1 record by Huey Lewis and The News (Chrysalis).

Ja-Da. w/m Bob Carleton, 1918. A popular novelty that was interpolated in the minstrel show scene in (MM) *Babes in Arms*, 1939, and was sung by Alice Faye in (MM) *Rose of Washington Square*, 1939. It was also heard in (MM) *The Great American Broadcast*, 1941.

Jailer, Bring Me Water. w/m Bobby Darin, 1962. Introduced by Bobby Darin (Atco). Popular record by Trini Lopez (Reprise), 1964.

Jail House Blues. w/m Bessie Smith and Clarence Williams, 1924. Introduced and first recorded by Bessie Smith, accompanied on piano by Clarence Williams (Columbia), followed by Virginia Liston, also accompanied by the composer (Okeh). Gene Austin had a well-received version (Banner), 1933.

Jailhouse Rock. w/m Jerry Leiber and Mike Stoller, 1957. Introduced by Elvis Presley in (MM) *Jailhouse Rock*, and sung by him on #1 record (RCA). Heard in (MM) *The Blues Brothers*, 1980.

Jalousie (Jealousy). w. Vera Bloom, m. Jacob Gade, 1925, 1951. An English import with new lyrics. Leo Reisman and his Orchestra (Victor) had a hit instrumental (Victor), 1932; The Boston Pops, under direction of Arthur Fiedler, had a million-seller titled "Tango Tzigane" (Victor), 1938; Harry James and his Orchestra had a popular instrumental version (Columbia), 1947; Kathryn Grayson sang it in (MM) *Anchors Aweigh*, 1945. It was also heard in (MM) *Paris Honeymoon*, 1939, and in (MM) *Painting the Clouds with Sunshine*, 1951. Frankie Laine had a million-selling record (Columbia), 1951.

Jamaica Fairwell. w/m Lord Burgess, 1957. Lord Burgess adapted the West Indian folk song. Harry Belafonte featured and recorded it (RCA).

Jamaica Ska. w/m Byron Lee, 1964. Recorded by the Jamaican group The Ska Kings (Atlantic).

Jambalaya (on the Bayou). w/m Hank Williams, 1952. Introduced and recorded by Hank Williams (MGM). Best-selling record by Jo Stafford (Capitol). Other popular versions by Bobby Comstock (Atlantic), 1960; Fats Domino (Imperial), 1962; The Nitty Gritty Dirt Band (United Artists), 1972; John Fogerty, billed as The Blue Ridge Rangers (Fantasy), 1973.

Jamboree. w. Harold Adamson, m. Jimmy McHugh, 1937. Introduced in (MM) *Top of the Town* and recorded (Brunswick) by Gertrude Niesen. Also recorded by the Jimmy Dorsey (Decca) and Paul Ash (Variety) bands.

Jamboree Jones. w/m Johnny Mercer, 1938. Introduced by Paul Whiteman, vocal by Johnny Mercer (Decca). Mercer again recorded it (Capitol).

James (Hold the Ladder Steady). w/m John D. Loudermilk, 1962. Hit record by Sue Thompson (Hickory).

James Bond Theme, The. m. Monty Norman, 1963. Theme from (MP) *From Russia with Love*. Popular instrumental record by guitarist Billy Strange (GNP Crescendo), 1964.

James Dean. w/m Jackson Browne, Glenn Frey, Don Henley, and J. D. Souther, 1974. Recorded by The Eagles (Asylum).

Jamie. w/m Ray Parker, Jr., 1984. Recorded by Ray Parker, Jr. (Arista).

Jamie. w/m Barrett Strong and William Stevenson, 1962. Top 40 record by Eddie Holland (Motown).

Jammin' Me. w/m Tom Petty, Mike Campbell, and Bob Dylan, 1987. Popular track and single from the album "Let Me Up (I've Had Enough)" by Tom Petty and The Heartbreakers (MCA).

Jam on It. w/m Maurice Cenac, 1984. Recorded by the rap group Newcleus (Sunnyview).

Jam Tonight. w/m Freddie Jackson and Paul Laurence, 1987. #1 R&B chart record by Freddie Jackson (Capitol).

Jam Up Jelly Tight. w/m Tommy Roe and Freddy Weller, 1969. Gold record by Tommy Roe (ABC).

Jane. w/m David Freiberg, Jim McPherson, Craig Chaquico, and Paul Kantner, 1979. Recorded by the group Jefferson Starship (Grunt).

Japanese Sandman, The. w. Raymond B. Egan, m. Richard A. Whiting, 1920. Popularized by Nora Bayes in vaudeville and on records (Columbia). Other leading recordings by Paul Whiteman (Victor) and Benny Goodman (Victor).

Japanese Sunset, A. w. Archie Bell, m. Jessie L. Deppen, 1924.

Japansy. w. Alfred Byran, m. John Klenner, 1928. Popular recordings by Guy Lombardo (Columbia), Johnny Hamp (Victor), Jimmie Noone (Decca).

J'Attendrai. See **I'll Be Yours.**

Java. m. Allen Toussaint, Alvin Tyler, Murray Sporn, and Marilyn Schack, 1964. Instrumental, first recorded by Floyd Cramer (RCA), 1962. Hit record by Al Hirt (RCA), 1964. Both produced by Chet Atkins.

Java Jive. w. Milton Drake, m. Ben Oakland, 1941. Most popular record by The Ink Spots (Decca); also recorded by the King Sisters, with Alvino Rey's Orchestra (Bluebird).

Jazz Cocktail.   m. Benny Carter, 1932. Introduced and recorded by Duke Ellington and his Band (Brunswick).

Jazzman.   w/m Carole King and Donald Palmer, 1974. Top 10 (#2) record by Carole King (Ode).

Jazz Me Blues.   m. Tom Delaney, 1921. A jazz standard with many recordings, among which are The Original Dixieland Jazz Band (Victor), the Wolverines (Gennett), Bix Beiderbecke (Okeh), Bunny Berigan (Victor), Jimmy Dorsey (Columbia), Les Paul (Capitol).

Jazznocracy.   m. Will Hudson, 1934. Hudson arranged his jazz instrumental for Jimmie Lunceford who recorded it and used it as his band theme (Victor).

Jazz Nocturne.   m. Dana Suesse, 1931. Suite for solo piano. See also "My Silent Love."

Jealous.   w. Tommy Malie and Dick Finch, m. Jack Little, 1924. Introduced by Little Jack Little. Leading records by Marion Harris (Brunswick) and Ben Selvin and his Orchestra (Vocalion). Revived by The Andrews Sisters (Decca), 1941.

Jealous Heart.   w/m Jenny Lou Carson, 1943, 1949. Introduced by Jenny Lou Carson (Decca) and also featured and recorded by Tex Ritter (Capitol). Revived in 1949, via hit records by singer-pianist Al Morgan (London); Hugo Winterhalter, vocal by Johnny Thompson (Columbia); Jack Owens (Decca); Bill Lawrence, with Henri René's Orchestra (RCA Victor). Later chart records by Tab Hunter (Warner Bros.), 1958, and Connie Francis (MGM), 1965.

Jealous Kind of Fella.   w/m Josephine Armstead, Garfield Green, Maurice Dollison, and Rudolph Browner, 1969. Top 10 record by Garland Green (Uni).

Jealous Love.   w/m Bobby Womack and "King" Curtis Ousley, 1968. Recorded by Wilson Pickett (Atlantic).

Jealous Lover. a.k.a. **Theme from "The Apartment."**   m. Charles Williams, 1960. Originally published in England, 1949. Revived as theme in (MP) *The Apartment*, 1960, with top 10 record by Ferrante and Teicher (United Artists).

Jealousy. See **Jalousie.**

Jean.   w/m Rod McKuen, 1969. Introduced by Rod McKuen on the soundtrack of (MP) *The Prime of Miss Jean Brodie*. Nominated for Academy Award. Gold record by Oliver (Crewe).

Jean.   w/m Paul Dresser, 1895.

Jeannine, I Dream of Lilac Time.   w. L. Wolfe Gilbert, m. Nathaniel Shilkret, 1928. The theme song of (MP) *Lilac Time*, which starred Colleen Moore and Gary Cooper. Leading records by Gene Austin (Victor), Nat Shilkret and The Victor Orchestra (Victor), John McCormack (Victor).

Jeans On.   w/m David Dundas and Roger Greenaway, 1977. Originally a jingle in England for Brutus Jeans. Top 20 U.S. release by David Dundas, the British singer/actor/songwriter (Chrysalis).

Jeepers Creepers.   w. Johnny Mercer, m. Harry Warren, 1938. Introduced by Louis Armstrong with an assist from Maxine Sullivan in (MM) *Going Places*. Armstrong had a hit record (Decca). This Academy Award nominee was #1 on "Your Hit Parade" for five weeks. It has been heard in (MM) *My Dream Is Yours* in 1949 and in (MP) *Cheap Detective* in 1978. Among the many recordings of this song are those by: Gene Krupa (Brunswick); Larry Clinton, vocal by Ford Leary (Victor); Paul Whiteman, vocal by the Modernaires (Decca); Ethel Waters (Bluebird); Stan Kenton, vocal by Chris Connors (Capitol); Lester Young (Prestige); Don Elliott (Savoy).

Jeep's Blues.   m. Edward Kennedy "Duke" Ellington and Johnny Hodges, 1938. Popular jazz record by Johnny Hodges and his Orchestra (Vocalion).

Jelly Jungle (of Orange Marmalade). w/m Paul Leka and Shelley Pinz, 1968. Recorded by the rock quintet The Lemon Pipers (Buddah).

Jelly Roll Blues. m. Ferdinand "Jelly Roll" Morton, 1915. This famous piano composition dates from 1905 but was not published until this year. In addition to Morton's recording (Gennett) in 1924, there have been many others, among them Bunny Berigan (Victor), Edmonia Henderson (Paramount), and the Lawson-Haggart Jazz Band (Decca).

Jennie Lee. w/m Jan Berry and Arnie Ginsburg, 1958. Based on the 1861 song "Aura Lee." Leading records by Jan and Arnie (Arwin) and Billy Ward and his Dominoes (Liberty).

Jennie Lee. w. Arthur J. Lamb, m. Harry Von Tilzer, 1902. Popular record by Harry MacDonough (Victor).

Jennifer. w/m Carole Bayer Sager and Peter Allen, 1971. Introduced by Bobby Sherman in (TVP) "Getting Together," and on records (Metromedia).

Jennifer Eccles. w/m Allan Clarke and Graham Nash, 1968. Top 40 record, written by two members of the British group The Hollies (Epic).

Jennifer Juniper. w/m Donovan Leitch, 1968. Top 40 hit in the U.S. by the Scottish-born writer/singer Donovan (Epic).

Jenny (The Saga Of). w. Ira Gershwin, m. Kurt Weill, 1941. Introduced by Gertrude Lawrence in (TM) *Lady in the Dark*, and recorded by her (Victor) as one of six sides of a 10″ 78-rpm album she made of tunes from the show. Danny Kaye, who was in the same production, also recorded it, coupled with "Tschaikowsky," (q.v.) which he sang in the show (Columbia). Mildred Bailey, with the Delta Rhythm Boys (Decca), had the first popular record. Ginger Rogers sang it in the 1944 film version (MM) *Lady in the Dark*, as did Julie Andrews in the title role of (MM) *Star!*,

loosely based on Gertrude Lawrence's career, 1968.

Jenny, Jenny. w/m Enotris Johnson and Richard Penniman, 1957. Recorded by Little Richard [Penniman] (Specialty).

Jenny, Take a Ride! w/m Enotris Johnson and Richard Penniman, 1966. Top 10 record by Mitch Ryder and The Detroit Wheels (New Voice).

Jenny Rebecca. w/m Carol Hall, 1965. Featured and recorded by Barbra Streisand (Columbia). Carol Hall included it in her album "If I Be Your Lady" (Columbia), 1971.

Jeopardy. w/m Greg Kihn and Steven Wright, 1983. Top 10 record by The Greg Kihn Band (Beserkley).

Jeremiah Peabody's Polyunsaturated Quick Dissolving Fast Acting Pleasant Tasting Green and Purple Pills. w/m Ray Stevens, 1961. Obviously a novelty. Introduced and recorded by Ray Stevens (Mercury).

Jeremy. w. Dorothea Joyce, m. Lee Holdridge, 1973. Sung on the soundtrack of (MP) *Jeremy* by Glynnis O'Connor.

Jericho. w. Leo Robin, m. Richard Myers, 1929. Introduced by Fred Waring and the Pennsylvanians in (MM) *Syncopation*. In 1943, in (MM) *I Dood It* starring Red Skelton and Eleanor Powell, it was sung by Lena Horne with Hazel Scott at the piano.

Jerk, The. w/m Don Julian, 1964. Introduced and recorded by The Larks, originally known as Don Julian and The Meadowlarks (Money).

Jersey Bounce. m. Bobby Plater, Tiny Bradshaw, Edward Johnson, and Robert B. Wright, 1941. Best-selling record by Benny Goodman and his Orchestra (Okeh). The Goodman Band played it in (MM) *Sweet and Low Down*, 1944, and in (MM) *The Benny Goodman Story*, 1955.

Jersey Walk. w. Eddie Dowling and Henry Creamer, m. James F. Hanley, 1926. From

(TM) *Honeymoon Lane*, which starred Dowling and was the vehicle for Kate Smith's Broadway musical debut. Lee Morse recorded this song (Puritan).

Jeru. m. Gerry Mulligan, 1949. Mulligan arranged the number as well as played on the recording by Miles Davis and his big band, which included pianist Al Haig, alto saxist Lee Konitz, drummer Max Roach, trombonist Kai Winding, and other jazz stars (Capitol).

Jerusalem. w. Alan Bergman and Marilyn Bergman, m. Herb Alpert, 1970. Instrumental record by Herb Alpert and The Tijuana Brass (A&M).

Jesse. w/m China Burton, 1985. Chart single from Julian Lennon's 1984 platinum album "Valotte" (Atlantic).

Jesse. w/m Carly Simon and Mike Mainieri, 1980. Carly Simon's recording did not make the Top 10, but earned a gold record for sales of over a million copies (Warner Bros.).

Jesse. w/m Janis Ian, 1973. Recorded by Roberta Flack (Atlantic).

Jessica. m. Dickey Betts, 1973. Instrumental by The Allman Brothers Band, composed by their guitarist (Capricorn).

Jessica. w. Dusty Negulesco, m. Marguerite Monnot, 1962. Introduced by Maurice Chevalier in (MM) *Jessica*.

Jessie's Girl. w/m Rick Springfield, 1981. Rick Springfield's performance of this song was one of the first to be presented on MTV when the concept was introduced. The Australian-born singer/actor had a #1 gold record (RCA).

Jesus Is a Soul Man. w/m Jack Cardwell and Lawrence Reynolds, 1969. Top 40 record by Lawrence Reynolds (Warner Bros.).

Jesus Is Just Alright. w/m Arthur Reynolds, 1970. Recorded by The Byrds (Warner Bros.). Top 40 version by The Doobie Brothers (Warner Bros.), 1973.

Jet. w/m Paul McCartney and Linda McCartney, 1974. Top 10 record by Paul McCartney and Wings (Apple).

Jet. w/m Harry Revel, Bennie Benjamin, and George David Weiss, 1950. Melody originally a theme in an instrumental album "Perfume Set to Music," composed by Harry Revel and performed by Les Baxter and his Orchestra (RCA Victor). Hit record by Nat "King" Cole, with the Ray Charles Singers and Joe Lipman's Orchestra (Capitol).

Je T'Aime . . . Moi Non Plus. w/m Serge Gainsbourg, 1969. Recorded in French by the British/French duo Jane Birkin and Serge Gainsbourg (ABC). Sylvia and Ralfi Pagan recorded it as "Soul Je T'Aime" (Vibration), 1973.

Jet Airliner. w/m Paul Pena, 1977. Recorded by Steve Miller Band (Capitol).

Je Vous Aime. w/m Sam Coslow, 1947. Introduced in (MM) *Copacabana* and recorded (Capitol) by Andy Russell.

Jewel of Asia, The. w. Harry Greenbank, m. James Philp, 1896. From (TM) *The Geisha*, produced in London in April and in New York in September. Philp was also a performer in the original London company.

Jezebel. w/m Wayne Shanklin, 1951. Million-selling record by Frankie Laine (Columbia).

Jezebel. w. Johnny Mercer, m. Harry Warren, 1938. Title song of (MP) *Jezebel*, not to be confused with the 1951 song.

Jig Walk. w. Jo Trent, m. Edward Kennedy "Duke" Ellington, 1924. This is assumed to have been Ellington's first recording, following its introduction in an all-Negro revue that toured Germany. It was later recorded by the Three Deuces (Commodore).

Jilted. w/m Robert Colby and Dick Manning, 1954. Best-selling record by Teresa Brewer, with Jack Pleis's Orchestra (Decca).

Jim. w. Nelson Shawn, m. Caesar Petrillo and Edward Ross, 1941. Introduced and recorded by Dinah Shore (Bluebird). Other best-seller by Jimmy Dorsey, vocal by Bob Eberly and Helen O'Connell (Decca).

Jim Dandy. w/m Lincoln Chase, 1957. Hit record by LaVern Baker (Atlantic). Revived in 1974 by the sextet, Black Oak Arkansas, featuring Jim "Dandy" Mangrum and Ruby Starr (Atco).

Jim Judson from the Town of Hackensack. w/m Paul Dresser, 1905.

(I'm) Jimmy, the Well-dressed Man. w/m Jimmy Durante, 1928. Interpolated by Clayton, Jackson, and Durante in (TM) *Show Girl.* Later featured by Durante on radio and television.

Jimmy Brown Song, The. See **Three Bells, The.**

Jimmy Had a Nickel. w/m Al Goodhart, Al Hoffman, and Maurice Sigler, 1934. Popular novelty song.

Jimmy Lee. w/m Jeffrey Cohen, Preston Glass, and Narada Michael Walden, 1987. Recorded by Aretha Franklin in her album "Aretha" (Arista).

Jimmy Mack. w/m Eddie Holland, Lamont Dozier, and Brian Holland, 1967. Top 10 record by Martha and The Vandellas (Gordy). Revived by Scottish singer Sheena Easton (EMI America), 1986.

Jimmy's Girl. w/m Lee Pockriss and Paul Vance, 1961. Recorded by Johnny Tillotson (Cadence).

Jimmy Valentine. w. Edward Madden, m. Gus Edwards, 1911. Based on the O. Henry story, "A Retrieved Reformation." The song was used as the background theme for (MP) *Alias Jimmy Valentine* starring William Haines, 1928. Bing Crosby sang it in the Gus Edwards story (MM) *The Star Maker,* 1939.

Jimtown Blues. w/m Fred Rose, 1924.

Jingle, Jangle, Jingle. w. Frank Loesser, m. Joseph J. Lilley, 1942. From (MP) *The Forest Rangers.* #1 in radio performances,

sheet music, and record sales and fourteen weeks on "Your Hit Parade," five times in the #1 position. Record leaders: The Merry Macs (Decca) and Kay Kyser, vocal by Julie Conway and Harry Babbitt (Columbia). Others: Gene Autry (Okeh); Freddy Martin, vocal by Clyde Rogers and Stuart Wade (Victor).

Jingle Bell Rock. w/m Joseph Beal and James Boothe, 1957. Top Christmas hit by Bobby Helms, who then had annual seasonal successes with his recording (Decca). In 1961, Bobby Rydell and Chubby Checker teamed up and had a Top 40 version (Cameo).

Jingle Jangle. w/m Jeff Barry and Andy Kim, 1969. Gold record by The Archies (Kirshner).

Jitter Bug. w/m Cab Calloway and Irving Mills, 1934. Introduced by Calloway's Orchestra and recorded by Clark Randall, a pseudonym for Gil Rodin, arranged by Deane Kincaide (Brunswick). It is the first known usage of the term "jitterbug" in a song.

Jitterbug, The. w. E. Y. Harburg, m. Harold Arlen, 1939. Sung by Judy Garland, Ray Bolger, Jack Haley, and Bert Lahr in a scene deleted from (MM) *The Wizard of Oz.* Garland recorded the song, coupled with "Over the Rainbow" (q.v.) from the same film (Decca).

Jitterbug Waltz, The. w. Richard Maltby, Jr., m. Thomas "Fats" Waller, 1942. Introduced and recorded by Fats Waller (Bluebird). Revived, with new lyric, by the company in the Waller show (TM) *Ain't Misbehavin',* 1978.

Jive Talkin'. w/m Barry Gibb, Maurice Gibb, and Robin Gibb, 1975. #1 gold record by the brother trio The Bee Gees (RSO).

Jivin' Around. w/m Ernie Freeman, J. Gray, and John Dolphin, 1956. Introduced and recorded by Ernie Freeman (Cash). The Al Casey Combo had a popular instrumental version in 1962 (Stacy).

Jo-Ann. w/m John Cunningham and James Cunningham, 1958. Popular record by The Playmates (Roulette).

Joanna. w/m Kool & The Gang, 1983. Written and Top 10 record by Kool & The Gang (De-Lite).

Joanne. w/m Michael Nesmith, 1970. Top 40 record by Michael Nesmith and The First National Band (RCA).

Joan of Arc, They Are Calling You. w. Alfred Bryan and Willie Weston, m. Jack Wells, 1917.

Jockey on the Carousel, The. w. Dorothy Fields, m. Jerome Kern, 1935. Sung by Lily Pons in (MM) *I Dream Too Much*, and on records (Columbia).

Joe Hill. w. Alfred Hayes, m. Earl Robinson, 1938. "New" folk song about a martyred union organizer.

Joe Knows How to Live. w/m Max D. Barnes, Graham Lyle, and Troy Seals, 1988. #1 Country chart single by Eddy Raven (RCA).

Joe Turner Blues. w. Walter Hirsch, m. W. C. Handy, 1916. A well-known Handy composition, but often incorrectly associated with the blues shouter, Big Joe Turner, who was five years old when this was written. Big Joe did record it, however, with Benny Carter's band in 1941.

Joey. w/m Herb Wiener, James J. Kriegsmann, and Salmirs-Bernstein, 1954. Leading recordings by Betty Madigan (MGM), Jeri Southern (Decca).

Joey, Joey, Joey. w/m Frank Loesser, 1956. Introduced by Art Lund in (TM) *The Most Happy Fella*.

Joey Baby. w/m Jane Connell, 1962. Recorded by Anita and Th' So-and-So's (RCA). The group was better known as The Anita Kerr Singers.

Joey's Song. m. Joe Reisman, 1957. Instrumental, introduced and recorded by Joe Reisman and his Orchestra (RCA). Popular record by Bill Haley and his Comets (Decca), 1959.

Joey's Theme. m. Eddy Manson, 1953. The theme of (MP) "The Little Fugitive," played on the soundtrack by harmonicist/composer Eddy Manson. Popular recording by the Sauter-Finegan Band (RCA Victor).

Johanna. w/m Stephen Sondheim, 1978. Introduced by Victor Garber, reprised by Edmund Lyndeck, Len Cariou, Merle Louis, and company in (TM) *Sweeney Todd, The Demon Barber of Fleet Street.*

John Birch Society, The. w/m Michael Brown, 1962. Novelty satirizing the extremist right-wing organization, introduced in the nightclub revue *Seven Come Eleven*. Recorded by The Chad Mitchell Trio (Kapp).

Johnny (Is the Boy for Me). w. Marcel Stellman and Paddy Roberts, m. Les Paul, 1953. Chart record by Les Paul and Mary Ford (Capitol).

Johnny Angel. w. Lyn Duddy, m. Lee Pockriss, 1962. #1 chart record by Shelley Fabares (Colpix).

Johnny B. Goode. w/m Chuck Berry, 1958. Top 10 record by Chuck Berry (Chess). Later chart records by Dion [DiMucci] (Columbia), 1964; Buck Owen and His Buckaroos (Capitol), 1969; Johnny Winter (Columbia), 1970.

Johnny Concho Theme (Wait for Me). w. Dick Stanford, m. Nelson Riddle, 1956. Introduced by Frank Sinatra in (MP) *Johnny Concho*, and on records (Capitol).

Johnny Doughboy Found a Rose in Ireland. w. Kay Twomey, m. Al Goodhart, 1942. Sixteen weeks on "Your Hit Parade," reaching the #2 position, it was played and sung frequently on the radio and had numerous recorded versions, the most popular of which were by Kay Kyser, vocal by the Glee Club (Columbia); Guy Lombardo, vocal by Kenny Gardner (Decca); Kenny Baker (Decca). It suggested the title of and was heard in (MM) *Johnny Doughboy*, 1943.

Johnny Fedora and Alice Blue Bonnet. w. Allie Wrubel and Ray Gilbert, m. Allie

Wrubel, 1946. Introduced by the Andrews Sisters on the soundtrack of the cartoon film (MM) *Make Mine Music.*

Johnny Get Angry. w. Hal David, m. Sherman Edwards, 1962. Top 10 record by Joanie Sommers (Warner Bros.).

Johnny Guitar. w. Peggy Lee, m. Victor Young, 1954. Sung by Peggy Lee on the soundtrack of (MP) *Johnny Guitar.* See also **My Restless Lover.**

Johnny Loves Me. w/m Barry Mann and Cynthia Weil, 1962. Top 40 record by Shelley Fabares (Colpix).

Johnny One Note. w. Lorenz Hart, m. Richard Rodgers, 1937. Introduced by Wynn Murray (singing) and Mitzi Green and Duke McHale (dancing) in (TM) *Babes in Arms.* It was not included in the 1939 film version (only two Rodgers and Hart songs from the show were), which starred Mickey Rooney and Judy Garland. Garland, however, sang it in the Rodgers and Hart story (MM) *Words and Music,* 1948. Her performance was released as a single (MGM).

Johnny One Time. w/m Dallas Frazier and A. L. Owens, 1969. Hit C&W and Pop song by Brenda Lee (Decca).

Johnny's Theme. m. Paul Anka and Johnny Carson, 1962. Theme song of the TV variety show "The Tonight Show," starring Johnny Carson.

Johnny Zero. w. Mack David, m. Vee Lawnhurst, 1943. Top 10 record by The Song Spinners (Decca), an unaccompanied vocal group that became popular during the musicians' strike against recording companies.

John's Idea. m. William "Count" Basie and Eddie Durham, 1937. Big band swing instrumental, recorded by Count Basie (Decca).

John Silver. m. Ray Krise and Jimmy Dorsey, 1938. Swing instrumental introduced and recorded by Jimmy Dorsey and his Orchestra (Decca). The Dorsey Band played it in (MM)

"Lost in a Harem," starring Abbott and Costello and Marilyn Maxwell, 1944.

Johnson Rag. m. Guy H. Hall and Henry Kleinhauf, 1917, 1949. An instrumental that later became a favorite of big bands. Among them: Glenn Miller (Bluebird), Jerry Gray (Decca), Pete Daily (Capitol), Larry Clinton (Victor). In 1940, lyrics were added by Jack Lawrence. Revived in 1949 with hit record by the Jack Teter Trio (London), and followed by the bands of Russ Morgan (Decca); Jimmy Dorsey (Columbia); Claude Thornhill, vocal by Joe Derisi and the Snowflakes (RCA Victor).

John Wayne. w. Paul Williams, m. Charles Fox, 1977. Sung by Seals and Crofts on the soundtrack of (MP) *One on One.*

John Wesley Harding. w/m Bob Dylan, 1968. Title song of the album by Bob Dylan (Columbia).

Joint Is Jumpin', The. w. Andy Razaf, m. Thomas "Fats" Waller and James C. Johnson, 1937. Introduced by Fats Waller and his Rhythm (Victor). Recorded by Gene Sedric and his Honey Bears (Vocalion), 1939. Sung by the cast in the Waller musical (TM) *Ain't Misbehavin',* 1978.

Joint Is Really Jumpin' at Carnegie Hall. w/m Ralph Blane, Hugh Martin, and Roger Edens, 1943. Sung by Judy Garland in (MM) *Thousands Cheer.*

Join Together. w/m Peter Townshend, 1972. Top 20 U.S. release of the English recording by The Who (Decca).

Joker, The. w/m Eddie Curtis and Steve Miller, 1973. #1 gold record by The Steve Miller Band (Capitol).

Joker, The. w/m Leslie Bricusse and Anthony Newley, 1965. Introduced by Anthony Newley in (TM) *The Roar of the Greasepaint— the Smell of the Crowd.*

Joker, The (That's What They Call Me). w/m Billy Myles, 1957. Introduced and leading record by Billy Myles (Ember). Popular cover record by The Hilltoppers (Dot).

447

Joker Went Wild, The. w/m Bobby Russell, 1966. Top 40 record by Brian Hyland (Philips).

Jolene. w/m Dolly Parton, 1974. Crossover (C&W/Pop) hit by Dolly Parton (RCA).

Jolly Green Giant. w/m Don F. Harris, Dewey Terry, Jr., and Lynn Easton, 1965. First released, before altered lyrics, as "Big Boy Pete," by The Olympics (Arvee), 1960. Top 10 record by The Kingsmen (Wand), 1965.

Jolly Holiday. w/m Richard M. Sherman and Robert B. Sherman, 1963. Introduced by Dick Van Dyke and Julie Andrews in (MM) *Mary Poppins.*

Joltin' Joe DiMaggio. w. Alan Courtney, m. Ben Homer, 1941. Tribute to the baseball star, written by a disc jockey (w.) and the arranger (m.) for Les Brown and his Orchestra, who introduced and recorded it with vocal by Betty Bonney (Okeh).

Jones Boy, The. w. Mann Curtis, m. Vic Mizzy, 1954. Popular record by The Mills Brothers (Decca).

Jonny. w. Edward Heyman, m. Frederick Hollander, 1933. Introduced by Marlene Dietrich in (MM) *Song of Songs* and recorded by her (Brunswick).

Joobalai. w. Leo Robin, m. Ralph Rainger, 1938. Sung by Bing Crosby, Franceska Gaal, and chorus in (MM) *Paris Honeymoon.* Crosby recorded it (Decca).

José Cuervo. w/m Cathy Jordan, 1981. #1 Country chart record by Shelly West (Warner Bros.).

Joseph! Joseph! w. Sammy Cahn, Saul Chaplin (Engl.), m. Nellie Casman, Samuel Steinberg, 1938. Original Yiddish lyrics by Casman and Steinberg. The new version was introduced and recorded by the Andrews Sisters (Decca) as a follow-up to their hit, "Bei Mir Bist du Schoen." Also recorded by Emery Deutsch, with vocal by Nan Wynn (Vocalion).

Josephine. w/m Cole Porter, 1955. Introduced by Gretchen Wyler and ensemble in (TM) *Silk Stockings.*

Josephine. w. Gus Kahn, m. Wayne King and Burke Bivens, 1937. Wayne King and his Orchestra had the best-selling record (Victor), which, incidentally, was to become the band's all-time #1 seller. The song was featured on radio and recorded by Frank Crumit (Decca), Tommy Dorsey and the Clambake Seven (Victor), Sammy Kaye and his Orchestra (Vocalion).

Josephine, My Jo. w. Cecil Mack, m. J. Tim Brymn, 1901.

Joshua. w/m Dolly Parton, 1970. Country hit by Dolly Parton (RCA).

Josie. w/m Walter Becker and Donald Fagen, 1978. Written by the two leaders of the studio group Steely Dan (ABC).

Journey's End. w. Joseph McCarthy, m. Harry Tierney, 1922. From (TM) *Up She Goes.*

Journey to a Star, A. w. Leo Robin, m. Harry Warren, 1943. Introduced by Alice Faye in (MM) *The Gang's All Here.* Best-selling record by Judy Garland (Decca).

Journey to the Center of the Mind. w/m Ted Nugent and Steve Farmer, 1968. Top 20 record by The Amboy Dukes (Mainstream).

Joy. w/m Reggie Calloway, Vincent Calloway, and Joel Davis, 1988. #1 R&B chart record and Pop crossover by Teddy Pendergrass (Elektra).

Joy. m. J. S. Bach, 1972. Adaptation of "Jesu, Joy of Man's Desiring." Top 10 instrumental by the English studio band Apollo 100 (Mega).

Joy. w/m Mitch Ryder, Lawrence Russell Brown, and Raymond Bloodworth, 1967. First solo record by Mitch Ryder, without The Detroit Wheels (New Voice).

Joystick. w/m Eric Fearman and Bobby Harris, 1984. Recorded by Dazz Band (Motown).

Joy to the World. w/m Hoyt Axton, 1971. Gold record by Three Dog Night (Dunhill).

Jubilation T. Cornpone. w. Johnny Mercer, m. Gene De Paul, 1956. Introduced by Stubby Kaye in (TM) *L'il Abner*.

Jubilee. w. Stanley Adams, m. Hoagy Carmichael, 1938. Introduced in (MM) *Everyday's a Holiday* and recorded by Louis Armstrong and his Orchestra (Decca). Other recordings: Cab Calloway (Vocalion); Harry James, vocal by Helen Humes (Brunswick); Kay Thompson and The Williams Brothers (Columbia).

Judaline. w. Don Raye, m. Gene De Paul, 1948. From (MM) *A Date with Judy*. Recorded by the orchestras of: Tommy Dorsey (RCA Victor), Ray Noble (Columbia), George Paxton (MGM).

Judy. w/m Hoagy Carmichael and Sammy Lerner, 1934. First recordings by Carmichael's band, with his vocal (Victor); Glen Gray and the Casa Loma Orchestra, vocal by Pee Wee Hunt (Decca); the Dorsey Brothers (Brunswick). Among later recordings: Lionel Hampton (Victor), 1937; Bob Chester (Bluebird), 1939; Lee Konitz and Lennie Tristano (New Jazz), 1949. Alan Dale cut a vocal (Signature), 1947.

Judy in Disguise (with Glasses). w/m John Fred and Andrew Bernard, 1967. #1 gold record, a parody of The Beatles' "Lucy in the Sky with Diamonds" by John Fred (Paula).

Judy's Turn to Cry. w. Edna Lewis, m. Beverly Ross, 1963. Top 10 hit by Lesley Gore (Mercury).

Jug of Wine, A. w. Alan Jay Lerner, m. Frederick Loewe, 1945. Introduced by Patricia Marshall in (TM) *The Day Before Spring* and recorded by Gordon MacRae (Musicraft).

Juicy Fruit. w/m James Mtume, 1983. #1 on the R&B charts, and gold record by the band Mtume (Epic).

Ju Ju Hand. w/m Domingo Samudio, 1965. Recorded by Sam the Sham and the Pharaohs (MGM).

Juke. w/m Walter Jacobs, 1952. #1 R&B record by Little Walter (Checker).

Juke Box Baby. w. Noel Sherman, m. Joe Sherman, 1956. Part of a two-sided hit by Perry Como (RCA). Coupled with "Hot Diggity" (q.v.).

Juke Box Hero. w/m Lou Gramm and Mick Jones, 1982. Recorded by the Anglo-American band Foreigner (Atlantic).

Juke Box Saturday Night. w. Al Stillman, m. Paul McGrane, 1942. Popular record by Glenn Miller, vocal by Marion Hutton, Tex Beneke, and the Modernaires (Victor) that included takeoffs of The Ink Spots, Harry James, and others. The Modernaires with Paula Kelly recorded "New Juke Box Saturday Night," with George Cates's Orchestra (Coral), 1953.

Julia. w/m John Jarvis and Don Cook, 1987. Top 10 Country chart record by Conway Twitty from the album "Borderline" (MCA).

Julia. w/m John Lennon and Paul McCartney, 1968. Introduced by The Beatles in their "White Album" (Capitol). Chart instrumental by Ramsey Lewis (Cadet), 1969.

Julie. w. Tom Adair, m. Leith Stevens, 1956. Introduced by Doris Day on the soundtrack of (MP) *Julie*. Nominated for Academy Award. Recorded by Doris Day (Columbia).

Julie, Do Ya Love Me. w/m Tom Bahler, 1970. Gold record by Bobby Sherman (Metromedia).

Jump. w/m Edward Van Halen, Alex Van Halen, Michael Anthony, and David Lee Roth, 1984. #1 gold record single from the platinum album "1984" by the band Van Halen (Warner Bros.).

Jump. w/m Curtis Mayfield, 1976. Introduced by Irene Cara and Lonette McKee in (MM) *Sparkle*. Leading record by Aretha Franklin (Atlantic).

Jump (for My Love). w/m Marti Sharron, Steve Mitchell, and Gary Skardina, 1984. Top 10 record by The Pointer Sisters (Planet).

Jump for Joy. w. Paul Francis Webster, m. Edward Kennedy "Duke" Ellington, 1941. Title song of West Coast revue (TM) *Jump for Joy*. Recorded by Duke Ellington and his Orchestra, vocal by Herb Jeffries (Victor).

Jumpin' at the Woodside. m. William "Count" Basie, 1939. Basie and his Band introduced it, but Benny Goodman and his Band had the best-selling record (Victor). Illinois Jacquet revived it in 1947 (Apollo).

Jumping Jack. w/m Clint Ballard, Jr. and Hank Hunter, 1958. Introduced and recorded by The Kalin Twins (Decca).

Jumpin' Jack Flash. w/m Mick Jagger and Keith Richards, 1968. Top 10 record by The Rolling Stones, the British rock group (London). Recorded by Johnny Winter (Columbia), 1971. Title song of (MP) *Jumpin' Jack Flash*, 1986. Sung on the soundtrack and on a single by Aretha Franklin (Arista), 1986. The Rolling Stones version is included in the soundtrack album (Mercury).

Jumpin' Jive, The. w/m Cab Calloway, Frank Froeba, and Jack Palmer, 1939. Introduced and recorded by Cab Calloway (Vocalion). Other prominent recordings by Jimmy Dorsey, vocal by Helen O'Connell (Decca); Lionel Hampton (Victor); Van Alexander (Bluebird).

Jump into the Fire. w/m Harry Nilsson, 1972. Recorded by Harry Nilsson (RCA).

Jump Jim Crow. w. Rida Johnson Young, m. Victor Herbert, 1917. From (TM) *Maytime*.

Jump Over. w/m Frank C. Slay, Jr., and Bob Crewe, 1960. Leading record by Freddy Cannon, arranged by Frank Slay (Swan).

Jump Start. w/m Reggie Calloway and Vincent Calloway, 1987. Top 10 R&B chart and Pop chart entry by Natalie Cole, from her album "Everlasting" (Manhattan).

Jump to It. w/m Luther Vandross and Marcus Miller, 1982. Recorded by Aretha Franklin (Arista).

Jump Town. m. Harry James and Jack Matthias, 1943. Popular instrumental recorded by Harry James and his Orchestra (Columbia).

Junco Partner. w/m Ellen Shad, 1952. Top 20 record by Richard Hayes, with Eddie Sauter's Orchestra (Mercury).

June Brought the Roses. w. Ralph Stanley, m. John Openshaw, 1924. Concert or art song. Leading recordings by Marcia Freer (Victor) and The Troubadors, under the direction of Nat Shilkret (Victor).

June Comes Around Every Year. w. Johnny Mercer, m. Harold Arlen, 1945. Introduced by the voice of Bing Crosby, dubbed on the soundtrack for Eddie Bracken, who was portraying a singing telegram delivery boy in (MM) *Out of This World*. Recorded by Crosby (Decca); Tommy Dorsey, vocal by Stuart Foster (Victor); Woody Herman, with his Orchestra (Decca).

June in January. w. Leo Robin, m. Ralph Rainger, 1935. Introduced by Bing Crosby and Kitty Carlisle in (MM) *Here Is My Heart*. Frank Sinatra sang it in (MM) *The Joker Is Wild* in 1957. Crosby had the biggest-selling record (Decca), but this major hit was recorded by many others, including: Harry Richman (Columbia); and the bands of Ted Fio Rito (Brunswick), Art Kassel (Bluebird), Richard Himber (Victor), Al Kavelin (Vocalion), Little Jack Little (Columbia), Guy Lombardo (Decca).

June Is Bustin' Out All Over. w. Oscar Hammerstein II, m. Richard Rodgers, 1945. Introduced by Christine Johnson and Jean Darling and danced by Pearl Lang and the ensemble in (TM) *Carousel*. In the 1957 film version (MM) *Carousel*, it was sung by Barbara Ruick, Claramae Turner, and chorus.

June Moon. w/m Ring Lardner and George S. Kaufman, 1929. Written for (TP) *June Moon* as a stereotypical "hack" Tin Pan Alley song.

June Night. w. Cliff Friend, m. Abel Baer, 1924. Featured, popularized, and recorded by

Ted Lewis and his Band (Columbia) and Fred Waring's Pennsylvanians (Victor).

Jungle Boogie. w/m Kool & The Gang, 1974. Eight members of Kool & The Gang collaborated to write this gold record number for their group (De-Lite).

Jungle Drums. w. Carmen Lombardo and Charles O'Flynn, m. Ernesto Lecuona, 1930. The lyrics were written to the instrumental "Canto Karabali." This version was introduced and featured by Guy Lombardo and the Royal Canadians. It was recorded in 1938 by Sidney Bechet (Vocalion); Artie Shaw (Bluebird); and Dinah Shore, with Xavier Cugat's Orchestra (Victor).

Jungle Fantasy. m. Esy Morales, 1948. Hit instrumental record by flutist Esy Morales and his Latin-American Orchestra (Rainbow).

Jungle Fever. m. Bill Ador, 1972. Gold record instrumental by the Belgian sextet The Chakachas (Polydor).

Jungle Fever. w. Howard Dietz, m. Walter Donaldson, 1934. From (MP) *Operator 13*, starring Marion Davies and Gary Cooper. Records by the Mills Brothers (Brunswick) and Red Nichols (Bluebird).

Jungle Love. w/m Jesse Johnson, Morris Day, and Prince Rogers Nelson, 1985. Introduced in (MM) *Purple Rain* and on records by The Time, featuring Morris Day (Warner Bros.).

Jungle Love. w/m Greg Douglas and Leonard Turner, 1977. Recorded by the Steve Miller Band (Capitol).

Junior. w/m Walter Donaldson, 1929. Written in honor of the birth of Donaldson's twin brother's son. Featured and recorded by Franklyn Baur (Victor) and Ben Selvin's Orchestra (Columbia).

Junior's Farm. w/m Paul McCartney and Linda McCartney, 1974. Top 10 record by Paul McCartney & Wings (Apple).

Junk Food Junkie. w/m Larry Groce, 1976. Top 10 novelty record by Larry Groce,

recorded "live" at McCabe's in Santa Monica, California.

Junk Man. w. Frank Loesser, m. Joseph Meyer, 1934. Loesser's first song success. Featured and recorded by Benny Goodman's Orchestra, vocal by Mildred Bailey (Columbia); Isham Jones, vocal by Eddie Stone (Victor); the Spirits of Rhythm (Decca); and in 1936, Jack Teagarden (Brunswick).

Just a Baby's Prayer at Twilight. w. Sam M. Lewis and Joe Young, m. M. K. Jerome, 1918. Million-selling record by Henry Burr (Victor).

Just a Bird's Eye View of My Old Kentucky Home. w. Gus Kahn, m. Walter Donaldson, 1926. Featured and recorded by Abe Lyman and his Orchestra (Brunswick).

Just a Blue Serge Suit. w/m Irving Berlin, 1945. Post-war song popularized by Vaughn Monroe with his Orchestra (Victor), and The Merry Macs (Decca).

Just a Cottage Small (By a Waterfall). w. B. G. DeSylva, m. James F. Hanley, 1925. Popular ballad with leading records by John McCormack (Victor) and Franklyn Baur (Columbia).

Just a Dream. w/m Jimmy Clanton and Cosimo Matassa, 1958. Introduced and recorded by Jimmy Clanton (Ace).

Just a Dream. w/m William Lee Conley and "Big Bill" Broonzy, 1939. Big Bill Broonzy, one of the great early blues singers, recorded this (Vocalion) and followed it with "Just a Dream (No. 2)," same year, same label.

Just a Gigolo. w. Irving Caesar (Eng.), Julius Brammer (Ger.), m. Leonello Casucci, 1930. A Viennese popular song, originally titled "Schöner Gigolo," introduced in the U.S. by Irene Bordoni. First successful recording by Vincent Lopez and his Orchestra (Hit of the Week). The label was that of a 78-rpm record, pressed on a flexible disc, with a new issue each week selling at newsstands. Other early releases: Bing Crosby (Victor),

Harry Richman (Brunswick), Roy Smeck (Melotone), Louis Armstrong (Okeh), Sid Garry (Harmony). Louis Prima and his Band had a popular recording in the sixties (Capitol). David Lee Roth revived it in medley with "I Ain't Got Nobody" (Warner Bros.), 1985.

Just a Girl That Men Forget. w. Al Dubin and Fred Rath, m. Joe Garron, 1923.

Just a Housewife. w/m Craig Carnelia, 1978. Introduced by Susan Bigelow in (TM) *Working*.

Just a Kid Named Joe. w. Mack David, m. Jerry Livingston, 1938. Featured and recorded by Jan Savitt, vocal by Bon Bon (Bluebird).

Just a Little. w/m Ron Elliott and Robert Durand, 1965. Hit record by The Beau Brummels (Autumn).

Just a Little Bit. w/m Del Gordon, 1960. Crossover (R&B/Pop) success by Roscoe Gordon (Vee-Jay). Top 40 version by Roy Head (Scepter), 1965.

Just a Little Bit Better. w/m Kenny Young, 1965. Top 10 record by the English group Herman's Hermits (MGM).

Just a Little Bit of You. w/m Eddie Holland and Brian Holland, 1975. Recorded by Michael Jackson (Motown).

Just a Little Bit South of North Carolina. w/m Sunny Skylar, Bette Cannon, and Arthur Shaftel, 1941. Best-selling record by Gene Krupa, vocal by Anita O'Day (Okeh).

Just a Little Closer. w. Howard Johnson, m. Joseph Meyer, 1930. Sung by Charles King in (MP) *Remote Control*. Recorded by Nick Lucas (Brunswick).

Just a Little Fond Affection. w/m Lewis Ilda, Elton Box, and Desmond Cox, 1946. British song interpolated in (MM) *Swing Parade of 1946* by Connee Boswell. Best-selling record by Gene Krupa, vocal by Buddy Stewart (Columbia).

Just a Little Home for the Old Folks. w. Edgar Leslie, m. Fred E. Ahlert, 1932.

Just a Little Joint with a Juke Box. w/m Hugh Martin and Ralph Blane, 1941. Introduced by Nancy Walker and Kenny Bowers in (TM) *Best Foot Forward*.

Just a Little Lovin'. w. Andrew B. Sterling, m. Harry Von Tilzer, 1912.

Just a Little Lovin' (Will Go a Long, Long Way). w/m Zeke Clements and Eddy Arnold, 1948. Eddy Arnold had a million-seller (RCA Victor). Four years later, Eddie Fisher had a popular version (RCA Victor).

Just a Little Rocking Chair and You. w. Bert Fitzgibbon and Jack Drislane, m. Theodore F. Morse, 1905.

Just a Little Too Much. w/m Johnny Burnette, 1959. Popular record by Ricky Nelson (Imperial).

Just a Memory. w. B. G. DeSylva and Lew Brown, m. Ray Henderson, 1927. A popular ballad recorded by the orchestras of Paul Whiteman (Victor) and Vincent Lopez, vocal by Frank Munn (Brunswick). It was sung by Sheree North and chorus in the biography of the writers (MM) *The Best Things in Life Are Free*. In 1957, Gogi Grant sang it on the soundtrack, dubbing for Ann Blyth in the title role of (MM) *The Helen Morgan Story*, 1957.

Just a Mood. w. Spencer Williams, m. Benny Carter, 1937. Recorded in England (Vocalion) by Benny Carter and his Band. Teddy Wilson, with vocal by Mildred Bailey, had a two-sided version (Brunswick).

Just an Echo in the Valley. w/m Harry Woods, Jimmy Campbell, and Reg Connelly, 1932. An English-published song, collaborated on by the American, Woods. Bing Crosby introduced it in the U.S. on his radio show and then interpolated it in (MM) *Going Hollywood* in 1933.

Just an Hour of Love. w. Al Bryan, m. Eddie Ward, 1929. Introduced by Irene Bordoni in (MM) *The Show of Shows*.

Just Another Day Wasted Away (Waiting for You). w/m Charles Tobias and Roy

Turk, 1927. Featured and recorded by Fred Waring's Pennsylvanians (Victor).

Just Another Love. w/m Paul Davis, 1986. #1 Country chart record by Tanya Tucker (Capitol).

Just Another Night. w/m Mick Jagger, 1985. Recorded by Mick Jagger (Columbia).

Just Another Polka. w/m Frank Loesser and Milton De Lugg, 1953. Popular records by Eddie Fisher (RCA Victor) and Jo Stafford (Columbia).

Just a Pair of Blue Eyes. w/m Dude Martin and Ted Johnson, 1948. C&W chart hit record by Tex Williams (Capitol).

Just a Prayer Away. w. Charles Tobias, m. David Kapp, 1945. Featured and recorded by Bing Crosby (Decca) and Sammy Kaye, vocal by Billy Williams (Victor).

Just a Quiet Evening. w. Johnny Mercer, m. Richard A. Whiting, 1937. Introduced by James Newill (Nevill) dubbing for Ross Alexander in (MM) *Ready, Willing and Able*. Among recordings: Eddy Duchin, vocal by Jerry Cooper (Victor); Shep Fields (Bluebird); Orlando Roberson (Variety).

Just Around the Corner. w. Dolph Singer, m. Harry Von Tilzer, 1925. Popular record by the vocal group The Revelers (Victor).

Just As I Am. w/m Dick Wagner and Robert Hegel, 1985. Recorded by the Australian duo Air Supply (Arista).

Just A-sittin' and A-rockin'. w. Lee Gaines, m. Billy Strayhorn and Edward Kennedy "Duke" Ellington, 1945. First recorded by Duke Ellington, vocal by Ivy Anderson (Victor). Best-selling record by Stan Kenton, vocal by June Christy (Capitol). Others: Delta Rhythm Boys (Decca), Thelma Carpenter (Majestic).

Just Ask Your Heart. w. Pete Damato and Joe Ricci, m. Diane De Nota, 1959. Top 10 record by Frankie Avalon (Chancellor).

Just As Much As Ever. w/m Larry Coleman and Charles Singleton, 1959. Introduced and

Top 40 record by Bob Beckham (Decca). Revived by Bobby Vinton (Epic), 1968.

Just a Song Before I Go. w/m Graham Nash, 1977. Top 10 record by Crosby, Stills & Nash (Atlantic).

Just As the Sun Went Down. w/m Lyn Udall, 1898.

Just As Though You Were Here. w. Eddie DeLange, m. John Benson Brooks, 1942. Featured and recorded by Tommy Dorsey, vocal by Frank Sinatra and the Pied Pipers (Victor).

Just A-Wearyin' for You. w. Frank Stanton, m. Carrie Jacobs-Bond, 1901. A concert song that gained popularity through vaudeville performances early in the century. It originally appeared in a Jacobs-Bond collection, "Seven Songs," and then was published independently.

Just Because. w/m Sami McKinney, Michele O'Hara, and Alexandra Louise Brown, 1989. Hit R&B chart single by Anita Baker (Elektra).

Just Because. w/m Lloyd Price, 1957. Introduced and recorded by Lloyd Price (ABC-Paramount).

Just Because She Made Them Goo-goo Eyes. w/m John Queen and Hughie Cannon, 1900.

Just Because You're You. w. Carolyn Leigh, m. Nacio Herb Brown, Jr., 1952. Featured and recorded by Jo Stafford (Columbia).

Just Because You're You. w/m Cliff Friend, 1932.

Just Be Good to Me. w/m Terry Lewis and James Harris III, 1983. Recorded by The S.O.S. Band (Tabu).

Just Between You and Me. w/m Jack H. Clement, 1966. Charley Pride's first hit record, Top 10 on the C&W charts (RCA).

Just Between You and Me. w/m Lee Cathy and Jack Keller, 1957. Featured and recorded by The Chordettes (Cadence).

Just Beyond the Rainbow. w. Arnold B. Horwitt, m. Harry Revel, 1945. Introduced by June Richmond in (TM) *Are You with It?* and recorded by her, coupled with the title song of the musical (Mercury).

Just Be Yourself. w/m Charles Singleton, Larry Blackmon, and Toni Jenkins, 1982. R&B chart record by the group Cameo (Chocolate City).

Just Born (to Be Your Baby). w/m Luther Dixon and Billy Dawn Smith, 1957. Popularized by Perry Como (RCA).

Just Call. w/m Sherrick, 1987. Written and recorded by singer/songwriter Sherrick (Warner Bros.).

Just Call Me Lonesome. w/m Rex Griffin, 1955. C&W song popularized by Eddy Arnold (RCA Victor).

Just Come Home. w. Carl Sigman (Engl.). Edith Piaf (Fr.), m. Marguerite Monnot, 1960. French song featured in Paris by Edith Piaf. Recorded in the U.S. by Hugo and Luigi (RCA).

Just Coolin'. w/m Dwight Myers and Edward Riley, 1989. Hit R&B chart single by Levert featuring Heavy D (Atlantic).

Just Don't Want to Be Lonely Tonight. w/m Vinnie Barrett, Bobby Eli, and John Freeman, 1974. First chart recording by Ronnie Dyson (Columbia), 1973. Top 10 version by The Main Ingredient (RCA).

Just Dropped in (to See What Condition My Condition Was In). w/m Mickey Newbury, 1968. Top 10 record by Kenny Rogers and The First Edition (Reprise).

Just for a Thrill. w/m Lillian Hardin Armstrong and Don Raye, 1939. Recorded by Lil Armstrong and her Band (Decca), and The Ink Spots (Decca).

Just for Now. w/m Dick Redmond, 1948. Introduced by Alexis Smith in (MP) *Whiplash.* Recorded by Frank Sinatra (Columbia); The Three Suns, vocal by Artie Dunn with the Sun Maids (RCA Victor).

Just for Old Time's Sake. w/m Hank Hunter and Jack Keller, 1961. Featured and recorded by The McGuire Sisters (Coral).

Just for Once. w. Dorothy Fields, m. Albert Hague, 1959. Introduced by Gwen Verdon, Richard Kiley, and Leonard Stone in (TM) "Redhead."

Just for the Sake of Our Daughter. w/m Monroe H. Rosenfeld, 1897.

Just for Tonight. w. Carole Bayer Sager, m. Marvin Hamlisch, 1978. Introduced by Lucie Arnaz in (TM) *They're Playing Our Song.*

Just for You. w/m Claude Putman and Larry Butler, 1968. Top 10 Country record by Ferlin Husky (Capitol).

Just Friends. w. Sam M. Lewis, m. John Klenner, 1931. Introduced by "Red" McKenzie (Columbia). Featured and recorded by Russ Columbo (Victor), Morton Downey (Perfect), Art Jarrett (Brunswick), and the orchestras of Jack Denny (Victor) and Ben Selvin (Columbia). Among many other later recordings of this standard: Glen Gray and the Casa Loma Orchestra, vocal by Kenny Sargent (Decca); the Dinning Sisters (Capitol); Andy Russell (Capitol); Charlie Parker (Mercury).

Just Get Up and Close the Door. w/m Linda Hargrove, 1975. Hit Country record by Johnny Rodriguez (Mercury).

Just Good Ol' Boys. w/m Ansley Fleetwood, 1979. #1 Country chart record by Moe Bandy and Joe Stampley (Columbia).

Just Got Paid. w/m Johnny Kemp and Gene Griffin, 1988. #1 R&B and Top 10 Pop chart record from the album "Secrets of Flying" by the Bahamian-born performer/songwriter Johnny Kemp (Columbia)

Just Hot! m. Phil Napoleon, Frank Signorelli, and Jimmy McHugh, 1923. Jazz instrumental, first recorded by The Cotton Pickers, featuring Napoleon on trumpet and Signorelli on piano (Brunswick). Other versions soon thereafter by Fletcher Henderson (Vocalion), The Original Memphis Five (Pathe), Waring's Pennsylvanians (Victor).

Just Imagine. w. B. G. DeSylva and Lew Brown, m. Ray Henderson, 1927. Introduced by Mary Lawlor, Ruth Mayon, and Shirley Vernon in (TM) *Good News*. It was not used in the first film adaptation, 1930, but June Allyson sang it in the second version (MM) *Good News*, 1947. It served as the title for the first science-fiction musical (MM) *Just Imagine*, 1930.

Just in Case. w/m James P. Pennington and Sonny Lemaire, 1986. #1 Country chart record by The Forester Sisters (Warner Bros.).

Just in Time. w. Betty Comden and Adolph Green, m. Jule Styne, 1956. Introduced by Sydney Chaplin and Judy Holliday in (TM) *Bells Are Ringing*. Leading record: Tony Bennett (Columbia). Sung by Judy Holliday and Dean Martin in (MM) *Bells Are Ringing*, 1960.

Just Keep It Up. w/m Otis Blackwell, 1959. Recorded by Dee Clark (Abner).

Just Let Me Look at You. w. Dorothy Fields, m. Jerome Kern, 1938. Sung by Irene Dunne in (MM) *Joy of Living*.

Just Like a Butterfly (That's Caught in the Rain). w. Mort Dixon, m. Harry Woods, 1927. Introduced in vaudeville by Blossom Seely. Featured on radio and recorded by The Ipana Troubadors (Columbia).

Just Like a Gypsy. w/m Seymour Simons and Nora Bayes, 1919. Introduced by Nora Bayes in the 1918 musical (TM) *Ladies First*. Ann Sheridan sang it in the Bayes film bio (MM) *Shine On, Harvest Moon* in 1944.

Just Like a Man. w. Ogden Nash, m. Vernon Duke, 1952. Introduced by Bette Davis in the revue (TM) *Two's Company*.

Just Like a Melody out of the Sky. w/m Walter Donaldson, 1928. Featured and recorded by Gene Austin (Victor); Cliff "Ukulele Ike" Edwards (Columbia); Paul Whiteman, vocal by Jack Fulton, Charles Gaylord, and Austin Young (Columbia).

Just Like a Woman. w/m Bob Dylan, 1966. Introduced and recorded by Bob Dylan (Columbia).

Just Like Me. w/m Richard Dey and Roger Hart, 1966. Popular record by Paul Revere and The Raiders (Columbia).

Just Like Paradise. w/m David Lee Roth and Brent Tuggle, 1988. Single, from the album "Skyscraper" by David Lee Roth (Warner Bros.).

Just Like Romeo and Juliet. See **Romeo and Juliet (Just Like).**

Just Like Washington Crossed the Delaware, General Pershing Will Cross the Rhine. w. Howard Johnson, m. George W. Meyer, 1918. World War I song popularized by the recordings of The Peerless Quartet (Victor) and Prince's Orchestra (Columbia).

Just Like Starting Over. w/m John Lennon, 1980. First release by John Lennon in five years (Geffen). He was assassinated while this record was on its way to becoming a #1 gold record. The single was taken from his new album with Yoko Ono, "Double Fantasy."

Just Lovin' You. w/m James O'Hara and Kieren Kane, 1987. Top 10 Country chart record by the duo The O'Kanes (Columbia).

Just My Imagination (Running Away with Me). w/m Norman Whitfield and Barrett Strong, 1971. #1 hit record by The Temptations (Gordy).

Just My Luck. w. Sheldon Harnick, m. Jerry Bock, 1957. Introduced by Mindy Carson in (TM) *The Body Beautiful*.

Just My Luck. w. Johnny Burke, m. James Van Heusen, 1945. Introduced by Joy Hodges and William Gaxton in (TM) *Nellie Bly*. Kitty Kallen recorded it (Signature).

Just Once Again. w. Paul Ash, m. Walter Donaldson, 1927. Recorded and featured by the orchestras of Paul Whiteman (Victor), Paul Ash (Columbia), and Chuck Foster (Okeh).

Just Once Around the Clock. w. Oscar Hammerstein II, m. Sigmund Romberg, 1935. Song by Vera Van, Walter Woolf King, and Leo G. Carroll in (TM) *May Wine*.

Just Once in My Life. w/m Gerry Goffin, Carole King, and Phil Spector, 1965. Top 10 record by The Righteous Brothers (Philles).

Just One Girl. w. Karl Kennett, m. Lyn Udall,.1898. Popular waltz, revived by Gordon MacRae in (MM) *By the Light of the Silvery Moon*, 1952.

Just One Look. w/m Gregory Carroll and Doris Payne, 1963. Introduced and Top 10 record by Doris Troy [Payne] (Atlantic). Later chart records by The Hollies (Imperial), 1964 and 1967; Anne Murray (Capitol), 1974; Linda Ronstadt (Asylum), 1979.

Just One More. w/m George Jones, 1957. Introduced and hit C&W record by George Jones (Starday).

Just One More Chance. w. Sam Coslow, m. Arthur Johnston, 1931. Bing Crosby (Brunswick) and Russ Columbo (Victor) vied for top sales on this song. Ruth Etting (Perfect), Abe Lyman's Orchestra (Brunswick), and Gus Arnheim's Orchestra (Victor) also had popular recordings. It later was done by the Harmonicats (Mercury), Les Paul and Mary Ford (Capitol), Dinah Washington (Mercury), and Cozy Cole (Key 12″), among others. It was sung by Dick Powell in (MM) *College Coach* in 1933 and by Dean Martin in (MM) *The Stooge* in 1953.

Just One of the Guys. w/m Marc Tanner and Jon Reede, 1985. Introduced by the trio, Shalamar, on the soundtrack of (MP) *Just One of the Guys.*

Just One of Those Things. w/m Cole Porter, 1935. Introduced by June Knight and Charles Walters in (TM) *Jubilee.* Sung by Lena Horne in (MM) *Panama Hattie*, 1942; Ginny Simms in the Porter biography (MM) *Night and Day*, 1946; Doris Day in (MM) *Lullaby of Broadway*, 1951; Peggy Lee in (MM) *The Jazz Singer*, 1953; Frank Sinatra in (MM) *Young at Heart*, 1955; Maurice Chevalier in (MM) *Can-Can*, 1960; Madeline Kahn in (MM) *At Long Last Love*, 1975.

Just One Time. w/m Don Gibson, 1960. Country and Pop hit, introduced and recorded by Don Gibson, produced by Chet Atkins (RCA). Revived by Connie Smith (RCA), 1971.

Just One Way to Say I Love You. w/m Irving Berlin, 1949. Introduced by Eddie Albert and Allyn McLerie in (TM) *Miss Liberty.* Popular records by Jo Stafford (Columbia) and Perry Como (Victor).

Just Plain Lonesome. w. Johnny Burke, m. James Van Heusen, 1942. Introduced by Kay Kyser and his Orchestra in (MM) *My Favorite Spy.* Recorded by them (Columbia) and Freddy Martin, vocal by Clyde Rogers (Bluebird).

Just Remember I Love You. w/m Rick Roberts, 1977. Popular record by the group Firefall (Atlantic).

Just Say I Love Her. w/m Martin Kalmanoff, Sam Ward, Jack Val, and Jimmy Dale, 1950. Leading record: Vic Damone (Mercury), Johnny Desmond (MGM), Eddie Fisher (RCA Victor).

(Do You Love Me) Just Say Yes. w/m Bob DiPiero, John Scott Sherrill, and Dennis Robbins, 1988. #1 Country chart record by the quartet Highway 101 (Warner Bros.).

Just Squeeze Me (But Don't Tease Me). Lee Gaines, m. Edward Kennedy "Duke" Ellington, 1946. Adapted from an Ellington instrumental, "Subtle Slough." This version first recorded by Ellington, vocal by Ray Nance (Victor); Matt Dennis, with Paul Weston and his Orchestra (Capitol); The Delta Rhythm Boys (Decca).

Just Tell Her Jim Said Hello. w/m Jerry Leiber and Mike Stoller, 1962. Recorded by Elvis Presley (RCA).

Just Tell Her That You Saw Me. w/m Paul Dresser, 1895.

Just That Type of Girl. w/m B. Cooper, 1987. Top 10 R&B chart record by the trio Madame X (Atlantic).

Just the Facts. w/m James Harris III and Terry Lewis, 1987. From the phrase used by

Sgt. Friday in the TV series "Dragnet." Sung by Patti LaBelle on the soundtrack of (MP) *Dragnet* and on a single (MCA).

Just the Other Day. w. Redd Evans, m. Austen Herbert Croom-Johnson, 1946. First recorded by Sam Donahue, vocal by Mynell Allen (Capitol); then by Gene Krupa, vocal by Carolyn Grey (Columbia); Kitty Kallen (Musicraft).

Just the Two of Us. w/m Bill Withers, William Salter, and Ralph MacDonald, 1981. Top 10 Pop and R&B chart record by saxophonist Grover Washington, Jr., and singer/guitarist Bill Withers (Elektra). Winner Grammy Award (NARAS) for Rhythm and Blues Song of the Year.

Just the Way You Are. w/m Billy Joel, 1978. Gold record by Billy Joel (Columbia). Winner of Grammy Awards (NARAS) for both Record of the Year and Song of the Year.

Just the Way You Like It. w/m Terry Lewis and James Harris III, 1984. Recorded by The S.O.S. Band (Tabu).

Just to Be Close to You. w/m Lionel Richie, 1976. Top 10 record by The Commodores, of whom Richie was a member (Motown).

Just to Ease My Worried Mind. w/m Roy Acuff, 1940. Popular C&W record by Roy Acuff (Columbia).

Just Too Many People. w/m Melissa Manchester and Vini Poncia, 1975. Recorded by Melissa Manchester (Dunhill).

Just to Satisfy You. w/m Don Bowman and Waylon Jennings, 1982. Country and Pop chart hit by Waylon [Jennings] and Willie Nelson (RCA).

Just to See Her. w/m Jimmy George and Lou Pardini, 1987. Top 10 R&B and Pop chart record by Smokey Robinson, from his album "One Heartbreak" (Motown).

Just Wait 'Til I Get You Alone. w/m Felice Bryant and Boudleaux Bryant, 1953. Country chart hit by Carl Smith (Columbia).

Just Walking in the Rain. w/m Johnny Bragg and Robert S. Riley, 1956. After it was introduced and recorded by The Prisonaires, inmates of the Tennessee State Penitentiary (Sun), 1953, Johnnie Ray, with Ray Conniff's Orchestra, had a hit record (Columbia).

Just We Two. w. Dorothy Donnelly, m. Sigmund Romberg, 1924. Introduced by Roberta Beatty and John Coast in (TM) *The Student Prince.*

Just What I Needed. w/m Ric Ocasek, 1978. Written by the leader of the group The Cars (Elektra).

Just When I Needed You the Most. w/m Randy Vanwarmer, 1979. Gold record by Randy Vanwarmer (Bearsville).

Just When We're Falling in Love. w. Bob Russell, m. Sir Charles Thompson and Illinois Jacquet, 1952. Lyric by Russell to jazz standard "Robbins Nest." Recorded by Les Brown, vocal by Lucy Ann Polk (Coral). See also **Robbins Nest**.

Just You. w/m Sonny Bono, 1965. Top 40 hit by Sonny and Cher (Atco).

Just You, Just Me. w. Raymond Klages, m. Jesse Greer, 1929. Introduced by Marion Davies and Lawrence Gray in (MM) *Marianne.* Popular record by Cliff *Ukulele Ike* Edwards (Columbia). It was also heard in (MM) *This Could Be the Night,* 1957, and (MM) *New York, New York,* 1977. The recording by Betty Carter and Ray Charles (Dunhill) has been a favorite with disc jockeys.

Just Young. w/m Lya Roberts, 1958. Introduced by Andy Rose (Aamco), followed by Paul Anka (ABC-Paramount).

Just You 'N' Me. w/m James Pankow, 1973. Top 20 record by the group Chicago (Columbia).

Just You Wait. w. Alan Jay Lerner, m. Frederick Loewe, 1956. Introduced by Julie Andrews in (TM) *My Fair Lady.* In the film version (MM) *My Fair Lady,* 1964, it was sung on the soundtrack by Marni Nixon, dubbing for Audrey Hepburn.

K

(My Heart Goes) Ka-Ding-Dong. w/m Robert Jordan and John McDermott, Jr., 1956. Chart records by The G. Clefs (Pilgrim), The Diamonds (Mercury), The Hilltoppers (Dot).

Ka-lu-a. w. Anne Caldwell, m. Jerome Kern, 1921. Introduced by Oscar Shaw in (TM) *Good Morning, Dearie.* It was played by the orchestra in the Kern biographical film (MM) *Till the Clouds Roll By.*

Kansas City. w/m Jerry Lieber and Mike Stoller, 1959. Written originally as "K. C. Lovin' " in 1952. New version a #1 hit by Wilbert Harrison (Fury). Other hit versions by Trini Lopez (Reprise), 1963, and James Brown (King), 1967.

Kansas City (Everything's Up to Date In). w. Oscar Hammerstein II, m. Richard Rodgers, 1943. Introduced by Lee Dixon, with Betty Garde and Male Ensemble in (TM) *Oklahoma!* In the film version (MM) *Oklahoma!*, it was sung by Gene Nelson, Charlotte Greenwood, and Chorus, 1955.

Kansas City Kitty. w. Edgar Leslie, m. Walter Donaldson, 1929. Introduced and recorded by Rudy Vallee (Victor). Also recorded by the Cotton Pickers (Brunswick). It was the title song of and featured in (MM) *Kansas City Kitty*, 1944.

Kansas City Shuffle. m. Bennie Moten, 1927. Instrumental, first recorded by the Bennie Moten's Kansas City Orchestra (Victor).

Kansas City Song. w/m Red Simpson and Buck Owens, 1970. Hit Country record by Buck Owens (Capitol).

Kansas City Star. w/m Roger Miller, 1965. Novelty introduced and recorded by Roger Miller (Smash).

Kansas City Stomp(s). m. Ferdinand "Jelly Roll" Morton, 1923. First recorded by Jelly Roll Morton (Gennett). He performed and recorded it numerous other times under the plural title on many labels. The Red Nichols Band, The Tennessee Tooters, recorded it (Vocalion), 1925.

"Karate Kid II" Theme, The. See **Glory of Love.**

Karma Chameleon. w/m George "Boy George" O'Dowd, Jon Moss, Mikey Craig, and Phil Pickett, 1983. #1 gold single from the platinum album "Colour by Numbers," by the British group Culture Club (Epic/Virgin).

Kashmiri Song. w. Laurence Hope, m. Amy Woodeforde-Finden, 1903. From the suite "Four Indian Love Lyrics."

Kate (Have I Come Too Early Too Late). w/m Irving Berlin, 1947. Eddy Howard, with his Orchestra, had a Top 10 record (Majestic). Ray Bloch, vocal by Alan Dale, also had a well-received version (Signature).

Kathleen. w/m Helene Mora, 1894. Introduced in vaudeville by the composer, known as the "female baritone."

Kathy O'. w/m Charles Tobias, Larry Shayne, and Jack Sher, 1958. Introduced by The Diamonds as title song of (MP) "Kathy O' " and recorded by them (Mercury).

Katie Went to Haiti. w/m Cole Porter, 1939. Introduced by Ethel Merman in (TM) *Du Barry Was a Lady*. In the film version (MM) *Du Barry Was a Lady*, 1943, it was performed by Tommy Dorsey and his Orchestra, Dick Haymes, Jo Stafford, and the Pied Pipers.

Katinka. w. Benee Russell, m. Henry Tobias, 1926. Recorded by George Olsen and his Orchestra (Victor).

Katinka. w. Otto Harbach, m. Rudolf Friml, 1916. Introduced by Sam Ash in (TM) *Katinka*.

Katmandu. w/m Bob Seger, 1975. Recorded by Bob Seger (Capitol).

Kaw-liga. w/m Hank Williams and Fred Rose, 1953. Introduced and recorded by Hank Williams (MGM). Dolores Gray also had a popular version (Decca). Revived by Charley Pride (RCA), 1969.

Kay. w/m Hank Mills, 1969. Recorded by John Wesley Ryles (Columbia).

Kayleigh. w/m Fish, 1985. Recorded by the British quartet, Marillion, led by Fish, pseudonym for Derek William Dick (Capitol).

Keem-o-sabe. m. Bernard Binnick and Bernice Borisoff, 1969. Top 20 instrumental recorded by the Philadelphia studio group The Electric Indian (United Artists).

Keep a Knockin'. w/m Richard Penniman, 1957. Introduced by Little Richard (Penniman) in (MM) *Mr. Rock 'n' Roll* and on records (Specialty).

Keep a Little Cozy Corner in Your Heart for Me. w. Jack Drislane, m. Theodore F. Morse, 1905.

Keeper of My Heart. w/m Jerry Irby and Bob Wills, 1948. Hit record by Bob Wills and His Texas Playboys (MGM).

Keeper of the Castle. w/m Dennis Lambert and Brian Potter, 1972. Top 10 record by The Four Tops (Dunhill).

Keep Feeling (Fascination). w/m Phil Oakey and Jo Callis, 1983. Top 10 record by the British group The Human League (A&M).

Keeping the Faith. w/m Billy Joel, 1985. Recorded by Billy Joel (Columbia).

Keepin' Myself for You. w. Sidney Clare, m. Vincent Youmans, 1929. Written for (MM) *Hit the Deck* and introduced by Polly Walker and Jack Oakie. In the remake, 1955, it was sung by Tony Martin. First recorded by the bands of Bert Lown (Perfect) and Paul Specht (Columbia). Artie Shaw and the Gramercy Five had a popular recording (Victor), 1940. Mel Tormé also recorded it (Bethlehem).

Keepin' Out of Mischief Now. w. Andy Razaf, m. Thomas "Fats" Waller, 1932. Introduced by Fats Waller. Among recordings: Louis Armstrong (Okeh), Isham Jones (Brunswick), James P. Johnson (Decca), Nat Jaffe (Signature), Tommy Dorsey (Victor), Buddy Greco (London), Nellie Lutcher (Capitol), Pee Wee Russell (Commodore). Sung by Charlaine Woodard in the Fats Waller musical (TM) *Ain't Misbehavin'* in 1978.

Keep It a Secret. w/m Jessie Mae Robinson, 1952. Featured and recorded by Slim Whitman (Imperial), Jo Stafford (Columbia), Bing Crosby (Decca).

Keep It Comin' Love. w/m Harry Wayne Casey and Richard Finch, 1977. Top 10 hit by KC & The Sunshine Band (T.K.).

Keep It Gay. w. Oscar Hammerstein II, m. Richard Rodgers, 1953. Introduced vocally by Mark Dawson and danced by Bob Fortier and the chorus in (TM) *Me and Juliet*.

Keep Me in Mind. w/m Glenn Sutton and George Richey, 1973. Country hit by Lynn Anderson (Columbia).

Keep My Mem'ry in Your Heart. w/m Ernest Tubb, 1945. Introduced and recorded by C&W singer, Ernest Tubb (Decca).

Keep On Dancing. w/m Willie David Young, 1965. Top 10 hit record by The Gentrys (MGM).

Keep On Doin' What You're Doin'. w. Bert Kalmar, m. Harry Ruby, 1934. Introduced by Ruth Etting in the Wheeler and Woolsey film (MM) *Hips, Hips, Horray*. Recorded by Benny Goodman's studio band (Columbia) and Adrian's (Rollini) Ramblers (Brunswick).

Keep On Loving You. w/m Kevin Cronin, 1981. #1 gold record from the platinum album "Hi Infidelity," by the quintet REO Speedwagon (Epic). The group took its name from a fire truck built sixty years earlier by the car maker Ransom Eli Olds.

Keep On Lovin' Me Honey. w/m Nicholas Ashford and Valerie Simpson, 1968. Hit record by Marvin Gaye and Tammi Terrell (Tamla).

Keep On Movin'. w/m Beresford Romeo, 1989. Hit R&B chart single by Soul II Soul, featuring Caron Wheeler (Virgin).

Keep on Pushing. w/m Curtis Mayfield, 1964. Top 10 hit record by The Impressions (ABC-Paramount).

Keep On Singing. w/m Bobby Hart and Danny Janssen, 1974. Recorded by Austin Roberts (Chelsea), 1973. Top 20 record by Helen Reddy (Capitol), 1974.

Keep On Smilin'. w/m John Anthony, Jack Hall, James Hall, Maurice Hirsch, and Lewis Ross, 1974. Top 10 record by the Alabama rock band, Wet Willie (Capricorn).

Keep on the Sunny Side. w. Jack Drislane, m. Theodore F. Morse, 1906.

Keep On Truckin'. w/m Leonard Caston, Anita Poree, and Frank Wilson, 1973. #1 R&B and Pop chart gold record by Eddie Kendricks (Tamla).

Keep Romance Alive. w. Bert Kalmar, m. Harry Ruby, 1934. Introduced by Ruth Etting in the Wheeler and Woolsey film (MM) *Hips,*

Hips, Hooray. Recorded by Etting (Brunswick).

Keep Searchin' (We'll Follow the Sun). w/m Del Shannon, 1964. Introduced and hit record by Del Shannon (Amy).

Keep Smiling at Trouble. w. Al Jolson and B. G. DeSylva, m. Lewis E. Gensler, 1925. Introduced by Al Jolson in (TM) *Big Boy*. Jolson then sang it in (MM) *The Singing Fool*, 1928.

Keep Sweeping the Cobwebs off the Moon. w. Sam M. Lewis and Joe Young, m. Oscar Levant, 1927. This was Levant's first published song. Leading record by Ruth Etting, backed by Ted Lewis and His Band (Columbia).

Keep the Ball Rollin'. w/m Sandy Linzer and Denny Randell, 1967. Hit record by Jay and The Techniques (Smash).

Keep the Fire Burnin'. w/m Kevin Cronin, 1982. Top 10 single from the platinum album "Good Trouble," by the quintet, REO Speedwagon (Epic).

Keep the Home Fires Burning. w. Lena Guilbert Ford, m. Ivor Novello, 1915. An English song that had great meaning during the ensuing war years. Popular U.S. records by James F. Harrison (Victor) and John McCormick (Victor). Julie Andrews sang it in (MM) *Darling Lili*, 1970.

Keep the One You Got. w/m Joe Tex, 1968. Recorded by Joe Tex (Dial).

Keep Young and Beautiful. w. Al Dubin, m. Harry Warren, 1933. Introduced by Eddie Cantor in (MM) *Roman Scandals*.

Keep Your Eye on Me. w/m James Harris III and Terry Lewis, 1987. Top 10 R&B/Pop chart crossover record by Herb Alpert, vocal by Lisa Keith and Terry Lewis (A&M).

Keep Your Eye on the Ball. w. Joseph McCarthy, m. Harry Tierney, 1924. From the Eddie Cantor musical (TM) *Kid Boots*.

Keep Your Eye on the Sparrow (Baretta's Theme). w/m Morgan Ames and Dave Grusin, 1975. Introduced by Sammy Davis, Jr. in the series (TVP) "Baretta." Leading records by Merry Clayton (Ode), Rhythm Heritage (ABC), Sammy Davis, Jr. (20th Century), 1976.

Keep Your Hands Off My Baby. w/m Gerry Goffin and Carole King, 1962. Introduced and recorded by Little Eva (Dimension).

Keep Your Hands to Yourself. w/m Dan Baird, 1986. Top 10 record by the quartet, Georgia Satellites (Elektra).

Keep Your Skirts Down, Mary Ann. w. Andrew B. Sterling, m. Robert A. King and Ray Henderson, 1925. Leading records by Billy Murray (Victor) and Aileen Stanley (Victor).

Keep Your Temper. m. Willie Smith, 1924. Recorded by The Gulf Coast Seven, featuring the composer, Willie "The Lion" Smith on piano (Columbia).

Keep Your Undershirt On. w. Bert Kalmar, m. Harry Ruby, 1930. From (TM) *Top Speed*, which opened on Christmas night, 1929, and the film version (MM) *Top Speed*, 1930. Recorded by Ben Pollack's Band, with vocal by Scrappy Lambert (Victor).

Kentuckian Song, The. w/m Irving Gordon, 1955. From (MP) *The Kentuckian*, starring Burt Lancaster. The Hilltoppers had a Top 20 recording (Dot).

Kentucky. w/m Henry Pritchard, 1944. Recorded by the Bands of Art Mooney (MGM) and Louis Prima (Hit).

Kentucky Babe. w. Richard Buck, m. Bessie Davis, 1896. Popularized by Bessie Davis. A staple in the repertoire of male quartets and glee clubs.

Kentucky Days. w. Jack Mahoney, m. Percy Wenrich, 1912.

Kentucky Rain. w/m Eddie Rabbitt and Dick Heard, 1970. Top 20 record by Elvis Presley.

Kentucky Sue. w. Lew Brown, m. Albert Von Tilzer, 1912.

Kentucky's Way of Saying Good Mornin'. w. Gus Kahn, m. Egbert Van Alstyne, 1925.

Kentucky Waltz. w/m Bill Monroe, 1946. Recorded by Bill Monroe (Columbia); Rosemary Clooney, with Percy Faith's Orchestra (Columbia); Tennessee Ernie Ford (Capitol); Eddy Arnold (RCA Victor).

Kentucky Woman. w/m Neil Diamond, 1967. Top 40 records by Neil Diamond (Bang), and the British rock band, Deep Purple (Tetragrammaton), 1968.

Kewpie Doll. w/m Sid Tepper and Roy C. Bennett, 1958. Popularized by Perry Como (RCA).

Key Largo. w/m Sonny Limbo and Bertie Higgins, 1982. Top 10 record by Florida singer, Bertie Higgins (Kat Family).

Key to the Highway. w/m Bill Broonzy and Charles Segar, 1941. Recorded by the blues singer, Big Bill Broonzy (Okeh).

Kickin' Our Hearts Around. w/m Wanda Jackson, 1963. C&W hit by Buck Owens (Capitol).

Kickin' the Cat. m. Joe Venuti and Eddie Lang, 1927. Jazz instrumental recorded by Joe Venuti and Eddie Lang (Okeh).

Kickin' the Clouds Away. w. B. G. DeSylva and Ira Gershwin, m. George Gershwin, 1925. Show-stopping number performed by Phyllis Cleveland, Esther Howard, Lou Holtz, and the ensemble in (TM) *Tell Me More!* (Show's original title during its pre-Broadway tryout was *My Fair Lady*, which was deemed "too uncommercial.") Performed by Roscoe Lee Browne in (TM) *My One and Only*, 1983.

Kicking the Gong Around. w. Ted Koehler, m. Harold Arlen, 1931. Introduced by Cab Calloway in the revue, *Rhythmania*, at the Cotton Club in New York. Calloway and his

Orchestra recorded it (Brunswick) and, in 1932, performed it in (MM) *The Big Broadcast*.

Kicks. w/m Barry Mann and Cynthia Weil, 1966. Top 10 record by Paul Revere and The Raiders (Columbia).

Kid Again, A. w/m Johnny Melfi and Roger Perry, 1965. Introduced by Barbra Streisand on (TVM) "My Name is Barbra," and recorded by her (Columbia).

Kid Charlemagne. w/m Walter Becker and Donald Fagen, 1976. Recorded by the group, Steely Dan (ABC).

Kid Days. w. Jesse Glick, m. Irving M. Wilson, 1919.

Kiddio. w/m Brook Benton and Clyde Otis, 1960. Top 10 record by Brook Benton (Mercury).

Kids. w. Lee Adams, m. Charles Strouse, 1960. Introduced by Paul Lynde and Marijane Maricle in (TM) *Bye Bye Birdie*. In the film version (MM) *Bye Bye Birdie*, 1963, it was sung by Lynde, Dick Van Dyke, Bryan Russell, and Maureen Stapleton.

Kid's a Dreamer, The. w/ Charles Snider, m. Martin Snider, 1949. Featured and recorded by Rosemary Clooney (Columbia).

Kids in America. w/m Ricky Wilde and Marty Wilde, 1925. Recorded by British singer, Kim Wilde, and written by her brother and father (EMI America).

Kids of the Baby Boom. w/m David Bellamy, 1987. #1 Country chart song by The Bellamy Brothers, from their album "Country Rap" (Curb).

Kids Say the Darndest Things. w/m Billy Sherrill and Glenn Sutton, 1973. Crossover (Country/Pop) hit by Tammy Wynette (Epic).

Kille Kille (Indian Love Talk). w. Irving Taylor, m. Vic Mizzy, 1942. Recorded by The King Sisters, with Alvino Rey's Orchestra (Bluebird).

Killer Queen. w/m Freddie Mercury, 1975. Top 20 record by the English rock group, Queen, of which the writer was lead vocalist.

Killing Me Softly with His Song. w. Norman Gimbel, m. Charles Fox, 1973. Introduced by Lori Lieberman (RCA). #1 gold record by Roberta Flack (Atlantic). Winner Grammy Award (NARAS) Song of the Year and Flack's version, Record of the Year.

Killing of Georgie, The. w/m Rod Stewart, 1977. Recorded by Rod Stewart (Warner Bros.).

Killin' Time. w/m Clint Patrick Black, 1989. Hit Country single by Clint Black (RCA).

Kinda Like You. w. Edward Heyman, w. Vincent Youmans, 1932. Introduced by Martha Mason and Nick Long, Jr. in (TM) *Through the Years*.

Kinda Lonesome. w/m Leo Robin, Sam Coslow, and Hoagy Carmichael, 1938. Introduced by Maxine Sullivan, backed by the Hall Johnson Choir in (MM) *St. Louis Blues*. Recorded by Sullivan (Victor) and Dorothy Lamour (Brunswick).

Kind of a Drag. w/m James Holvay, 1967. #1 chart hit by The Buckinghams (U.S.A.).

Kind of Boy You Can't Forget, The. w/m Jeff Barry and Ellie Greenwich, 1963. Top 20 record by The Raindrops, who were the writers multiple-tracking their vocals (Jubilee).

King Cotton. m. John Philip Sousa, 1895. A march, written for the Cotton States Exposition in Atlanta. It was performed in the Sousa biographical film (MM) *Stars and Stripes Forever*, 1952.

King for a Day. w/m Tom Bailey, Alannah Currie, and Joe Leeway, 1986. Written and Top 10 record by the oddly named trio, from England, New Zealand, and South Africa, respectively, and calling themselves The Thompson Twins (Arista).

King for a Day. w. Sam M. Lewis and Joe Young, m. Ted Fio Rito, 1928.

King Is Gone, The. w/m Lee Morgan and Ronnie McDowell, 1977. A tribute to the late Elvis Presley, Ronnie McDowell had a C&W/Pop gold record (Scorpion).

King Joe. w. Richard Wright, m. William "Count" Basie, 1941. The talents of a novelist and a bandleader combined to write this tribute to Joe Louis, the boxing champion. Another unlikely combination recorded it, Paul Robeson and the Count Basie Orchestra (Okeh, 1 & 2).

King of Clowns. w/m Howard Greenfield and Neil Sedaka, 1962. Introduced and recorded by Neil Sedaka (RCA).

King of Swing. w. Al Stillman, m. George Gershwin, 1936. Introduced by Ford L. Buck and John W. Bubbles ("Buck and Bubbles") at the Radio City Music Hall in New York.

King of the Road. w/m Roger Miller, 1965. Introduced and gold record by Roger Miller (Smash). Grammy Award (NARAS) Winner Best Country and Western Song, 1965. See also **Queen of the House**.

King of the Whole Wide World. w/m Ruth Bachelor and Bob Roberts, 1962. Introduced by Elvis Presley in (MM) *Kid Galahad* and on records (RCA).

King Porter Stomp. m. Ferdinand "Jelly Roll" Morton, 1924. A favorite with the big bands. First recorded by Jelly Roll Morton (Gennett). Fletcher Henderson had a major hand in its popularity, recording it twice (Columbia) (Vocalion) and writing the arrangement that was one of Benny Goodman's earliest and biggest hits (Victor). Other top recordings: Erskine Hawkins (Bluebird), Glenn Miller (Bluebird), Harry James (Brunswick), Bob Crosby (Decca). It was played in (MM) *Hollywood Canteen*, 1944, and in (MM) *The Benny Goodman Story*, 1955.

King's Horses, The (and the King's Men). w/m Noel Gay and Harry Graham, 1930. An English novelty, introduced, featured, and recorded (Brunswick) by Ben Bernie and "all the lads." Dick Robertson (Hit of the Week) and Jack Hylton's English Orchestra (Victor) also had releases.

King Size Papa. w/m Johnny Gomez and Paul Vance, 1947. Julia Lee and Her Boy Friends had an R&B hit recording (Capitol).

King Tut. w/m Steve Martin, 1978. Gold record novelty by TV and film star, Steve Martin, with The Toot Uncommons (Warner Bros.).

Kinkajou, The. w. Joseph McCarthy, m. Harry Tierney, 1927. Introduced by Ada May in (TM) *Rio Rita*. Dorothy Lee sang it in the film adaptation (MM) *Rio Rita*, 1929. The title refers to a fugitive bandit chased from Texas to Mexico.

Kiss. w/m Prince & The Revolution, 1986. #1 gold record by Prince & The Revolution (Paisley Park).

Kiss an Angel Good Mornin'. w/m Ben Peters, 1971. Gold Country and Pop record by Charley Pride (RCA). Winner of Grammy Award (NARAS) Best Country Song, 1972.

Kiss and Let's Make Up. w/m Charles K. Harris, 1891. Harris's first hit.

Kiss and Say Goodbye. w/m Winfred "Blue" Lovett, 1976. Written by the lead singer of The Manhattans whose recording reached not only the #1 position on both the R&B and Pop charts but was the second single certified platinum by RIAA for selling over two million copies (Columbia).

Kiss Away. w/m Billy Sherrill and Glenn Sutton, 1965. Recorded by Ronnie Dove (Diamond).

Kisses Don't Lie. w/m Pearl Butler and George Sherry, 1954. Featured by Carl Smith (Columbia).

Kisses Sweeter Than Wine. w. Paul Campbell, m. Joel Newman, 1951, 1957. Campbell is a pseudonym for the members of The Weavers: Pete Seeger, Lee Hays, Fred Hellerman, and Ronnie Gilbert. It is said, but disputed, that Newman was a pseudonym for Huddie "Leadbelly" Ledbetter who died a year before the first hit recording of the song by The Weavers with Leo Diamond's Orchestra (Decca). In 1957, Jimmie Rodgers, with Hugo Peretti's Orchestra (Roulette), had a record that was Top 10 in all categories.

Kiss Goodnight, A. w/m Freddie Slack, Reba Nell Herman, and Floyd Victor, 1945. Leading records: Freddie Slack, vocal by Liza Morrow (Capitol); Woody Herman, with his Orchestra (Columbia); Ella Fitzgerald, with Randy Broooks's Orchestra (Decca).

Kiss Her Now. w/m Jerry Herman, 1969. Introduced by Angela Lansbury in (TM) *Deer World.*

Kissin' Bug Boogie. w. Allan Roberts, m. Robert Allen, 1951. Leading record by Jo Stafford (Capitol).

Kissin' Cousins. w/m Fred Wise and Randy Starr, 1964. Introduced by Elvis Presley in (MM) *Kissin' Cousins.* Gold record by Presley (RCA).

Kissing a Fool. w/m George Michael, 1988. George Michael's fifth chart single from the album "Faith" (Columbia).

Kissin' on the Phone. w. Earl Wilson, m. Leonard Whitcup, 1961. Featured and recorded by Paul Anka (ABC-Paramount).

Kiss in the Dark, A. w. B. G. DeSylva, m. Victor Herbert, 1922. Introduced by Edith Day in (TM) *Orange Blossoms*, the last Victor Herbert show produced in his lifetime. Mary Martin sang the song in (MM) *The Great Victor Herbert*, 1939. Gordon MacRae sang it and June Haver danced to it in (MM) *Look for the Silver Lining*, 1949.

Kissin' Time. w/m James Frazier and Leonard Frazier, 1959. Introduced and recorded by Bobby Rydell (Cameo). Revived by the hard rock band Kiss (Casablanca), 1974.

Kiss in Your Eyes, The. w. Johnny Burke, m. Richard Heuberger, 1948. Burke wrote English lyrics for the adaptation of "Im Chambre Separee" from Heuberger's "Der Opern-

ball," which was introduced by Bing Crosby in (MM) *The Emperor Waltz.*

Kiss Me, Honey, Do. w. Edgar Smith, m. John Stromberg, 1898. Introduced by Peter F. Dailey in Weber and Fields's (TM) *Hurly Burly.*

Kiss Me, My Honey, Kiss Me. w. Irving Berlin, m. Ted Snyder, 1910.

Kiss Me, Sailor. w/m Eddie Rambeau and Bud Rehak, 1964. Recorded by Diane Renay (20th Century).

Kiss Me Again. w. Henry Blossom, m. Victor Herbert, 1906. Sung by Fritzi Scheff in (TM) *Mlle. Modiste* and associated with her throughout her career. Susanna Foster sang it in (MM) *The Great Victor Herbert* in 1939. Prior to that, in 1931, it was the title song and underscored theme of (MM) *Mlle. Modiste.* Note: *Mlle. Modiste* opened on Christmas night, 1905, and the songs from the production became popular in 1906.

Kiss Me Another. w. Fred Ebb, m. Charles Friedman, 1956. Leading record by Georgia Gibbs (Mercury).

Kiss Me Goodbye. w/m Barry Mason and Les Reed, 1968. Top 20 U.S. record by the British star Petula Clark (Warner Bros.).

Kiss Me No Kisses. w/m Ervin Drake, 1964. Introduced by Sally Ann Howes in (TM) *What Makes Sammy Run?*

Kiss Me Quick. w/m Doc Pomus and Mort Shuman, 1964. Popularized by Elvis Presley (RCA).

Kiss Me Sweet. w/m Milton Drake, 1949. Popular records by Sammy Kaye, vocal by Don Cornell and Laura Leslie (RCA Victor) and Kitty Kallen, with Mitch Miller's Orchestra (Mercury).

Kiss of Fire. w/m Lester Allen and Robert Hill, 1952. Adapted from the Argentinian A. G. Villoldo's tango, "El Choclo." Georgia Gibbs had a #1 million-selling record (Mercury). Other hit versions by Tony Martin (RCA

Victor); Toni Arden (Columbia); Billy Eckstine (MGM); Louis Armstrong (Decca).

Kiss on My List. w/m Janna Allen and Daryl Hall, 1981. #1 gold record by Daryl Hall and John Oates, from their LP "Voices" (RCA).

Kiss Polka, The. w. Mack Gordon, m. Harry Warren, 1941. Introduced by Sonja Henie with John Payne and Glenn Miller's Orchestra in (MM) *Sun Valley Serenade.* Miller recorded it with a vocal by The Modernaires (Bluebird).

Kiss the Boys Goodbye. w. Frank Loesser, m. Victor Schertzinger, 1941. Introduced by Mary Martin in (MM) *Kiss the Boys Goodbye,* and recorded by her (Decca). Best-selling records by Tommy Dorsey, vocal by Connie Haines (Victor), and Bea Wain (Victor).

Kiss the Bride. w. Bernie Taupin, m. Elton John, 1983. Recorded by Elton John (Geffen).

Kiss the Girl. w/ Howard Ashman, m. Alan Menken, 1989. Introduced on the soundtrack of the animated feature film (MM) *The Little Mermaid.* Nominated for an Academy Award.

Kiss to Build a Dream On, A. w. Bert Kalmar and Oscar Hammerstein II, m. Harry Ruby, 1951. Originally written as "Moonlight on the Meadow," 1935, by Kalmar and Ruby, then rewritten with Hammerstein with new title and lyric for the Marx Brothers film *A Night at the Opera,* but not used. Finally introduced in 1951 by Kay Brown and Louis Armstrong in (MM) *The Strip.* Armstrong recorded it (Decca), and the song and his recording have become standards.

Kiss Waltz. w. C. M. S. McLellan, m. Ivan Caryll, 1911. Introduced by Alice Dovey in (TM) *The Pink Lady.*

Kiss Waltz, The. w. Al Dubin, m. Joe Burke, 1930. Introduced by Sue Carol in (MM) *Dancing Sweeties.*

Kiss You All Over. w/m Mike Chapman and Nicky Chinn, 1978. #1 gold record by the group Exile (Warner/Curb).

Kiss Your Minstrel Boy Goodbye. w. William Jerome, m. Jean Schwartz, 1908.

Kitten on the Keys. m. Zez Confrey, 1921. Popular piano instrumental. Confrey recorded it twice in 1921 (Victor) (Columbia), and at least three other times on various labels. It has also been cut by numerous piano-led bands.

K-K-K-Katy. w/m Geoffrey O'Hara, 1918. A "stammering song," it became one of the most popular novelty hits of World War I. Jack Oakie and chorus performed it in (MM) *Tin Pan Alley,* 1940.

Klassicle Rag. m. Cecil Duane Crabb, 1911. Originally played by the composer on USMC piano rolls. In an unusual case, Crabb also designed the sheet music for this and many other songs in the catalog of J. H. Aufderheide & Co., a leading publisher of ragtime numbers.

Knee Deep. w/m Leroy Pullins, 1966. Recorded by Leroy Pullins, coupled with the hit, "I'm a Nut" (q.v.) (Kapp).

Knee Deep (Not Just). w/m George Clinton and Philippe Wynn, 1979. Recorded by Clinton's group Funkadelic (Warner Bros.).

Knee Deep in the Blues. w/m Melvin Endsley, 1956. Introduced and recorded by Marty Robbins (Columbia). Best-selling record by Guy Mitchell (Columbia).

Knick Knacks on the Mantel. w. Raymond B. Egan, m. Ted Fio Rito, 1936. Featured on radio and recorded by the orchestras of Rudy Vallee (Victor) and Ted Fio Rito (Decca).

Knight in Rusty Armour. w/m Mike Leander and Charles Mills, 1967. Popular U.S. release by the British duo Peter and Gordon (Capitol).

Knights of the Mystic Star. w. Edward Harrigan, m. David Braham, 1891. From (TM) *The Last of the Hogans.* In (TM) *Harrigan 'n' Hart,* 1885, it was sung by Armelia McQueen and Company.

Knock, Knock, Who's There? w/m Bill Tipton, Bill Davies, Johnny Morris, and Vincent Lopez, 1936. Novelty based on popular word game. Introduced, featured, and recorded by Vincent Lopez and his Orchestra (Melotone). Ted Weems, with vocal by Red Ingle, had a popular record (Decca).

Knockin' on Heaven's Door. w/m Bob Dylan, 1973. Sung by Bob Dylan on the soundtrack of (MP) *Pat Garrett and Billy the Kid*, and a Top 20 record (Columbia).

Knock Me a Kiss. w/m Mike Jackson, 1942. Most popular recordings: Louis Jordan and his Tympany Five (Decca); Gene Krupa, vocal by Roy Eldridge (Columbia); Danny Kaye (Capitol).

Knock on Wood. w/m Eddie Floyd and Steve Cropper, 1966. Introduced and Top 40 record by Eddie Floyd (Stax). Otis (Redding) and Carla (Thomas) recorded their version, which reached the same position a year later for the same company (Stax), 1967. Revived by Amii Stewart, whose #1 record sold over two million copies (Ariola), 1979.

Knock Three Times. w/m Irwin Levine and L. Russell Brown, 1970. #1 gold record by the trio Dawn (Bell).

Knock Wood. w. Andrew B. Sterling, m. Harry Von Tilzer, 1911.

Knothole. w/m Bill Carlisle and Virginia Suber, 1953. C&W chart novelty record by The Carlisles (Mercury).

Knot of Blue, A. w. Glen MacDonough, m. Victor Herbert, 1904. From (TM) *It Happened in Nordland*.

Knowing Me, Knowing You. w/m Benny Anderson, Stig Anderson, and Bjorn Ulvaeus, 1977. Top 20 record by the Swedish quartet Abba (Atlantic).

Knowing When to Leave. w. Hal David, m. Burt Bacharach, 1968. Introduced by Jill O'Hara in (TM) *Promises, Promises*.

Kodachrome. w/m Paul Simon, 1973. #2 chart record by Paul Simon (Columbia).

Kokomo. w/m Mike Love, Scott Mackenzie, Terry Melcher, and John Phillips, 1988. Sung by The Beach Boys on the soundtrack of (MP) *Cocktail*. Their rendition may be heard on the soundtrack album and hit single (Elektra).

Kokomo, Indiana. w. Mack Gordon, m. Josef Myrow, 1947. Introduced by Betty Grable and Dan Dailey in (MM) *Mother Wore Tights*. Leading recordings by Vaughn Monroe, with his Orchestra (RCA Victor), and Dinah Shore, with Sonny Burke's Orchestra (Columbia).

Ko Ko Mo (I Love You So). w/m Forest Wilson, Jake Porter, and Eunice Levy, 1955. R&B hit by Gene and Eunice (Combo). Pop hit by Perry Como (RCA Victor) and The Crew Cuts (Mercury).

Kookie, Kookie (Lend Me Your Comb). w/m Irving Taylor, 1959. Introduced on series (TVP) "77 Sunset Strip." Edd Byrnes, known on the series as "Kookie," recorded the novelty song with Connie Stevens and had a Top 10 record (Warner Brothers).

Kookie Little Paradise, A. w. Bob Hilliard, m. Lee Pockriss, 1960. Featured and recorded by Jo Ann Campbell (ABC-Paramount).

Kozmic Blues. w/m Janis Joplin and Gabriel Mekler, 1969. First solo chart record by Janis Joplin (Columbia).

K-ra-zy for You. w. Ira Gershwin, m. George Gershwin, 1928. Introduced by Clifton Webb and Mary Kay in (TM) *Treasure Girl*.

Krazy Kat. m. Chauncey Morehouse and Frank Trumbauer, 1927. Jazz instrumental. Title suggested by the comic strip and animated cartoon character. Introduced and recorded by Frankie Trumbauer and his Orchestra (Okeh).

Kum Ba Yah. w. Tommy Leonetti (Engl.), m. adapted by Otto Zucker, 1969. Based on a traditional Afro-American slave song. Sometimes referred to as "Come By Here."

Kung Fu Fighting. w/m Carl Douglas, 1974. #1 gold record, produced in England by the India-born Biddu, and recorded by the Jamaica-born Carl Douglas (20th Century). Released as the "B" side of a single, it eventually sold over nine million copies internationally.

Kyrie. w/m Richard Page, Steve George, and John Lang, 1986. #1 chart record by the group Mr. Mister (RCA).

L

La, La, La (If I Had You). w/m Danny Janssen, 1969. Gold record by Bobby Sherman (Metromedia).

La Bamba. w/m William Clauson, 1959, 1987. Based on traditional wedding song used in some Mexican states, said to go back two centuries. Chart record by Ritchie Valens, coupled with the hit side, "Donna" (Del-Fi). It became a bigger hit on its own as the title song of the Ritchie Valens story (MM) *La Bamba*, 1987, sung on the soundtrack and on the #1 single by the East Los Angeles band Los Lobos (Slash).

La Cucaracha. w. Stanley Adams (Engl.), m. Juan Y. D'Lorah, 1934. Adapted from a traditional Mexican folk song and introduced by D'Lorah in a film short (MM) *La Cucuracha*.

La Cumparsita. w. Carol Raven, m. G. H. Matos Rodriguez, 1916. The lyrics to this tango were added in 1932.

Ladder of Love, The. w/m Clint Ballard, Jr., 1957. Leading records by The Flamingos (Decca) and Johnny Nash (ABC-Paramount).

Ladder of Roses, The. w. R. H. Burnside, m. Raymond Hubbell, 1915. From (TM) *Hip-Hip-Hooray*.

La Dee Dah. w/m Frank C. Slay, Jr. and Bob Crewe, 1958. Top 10 record by Billy (Ford) and Lillie (Bryant) (Swan).

Ladies Night. w/m Robert Bell, James "J. T." Taylor, George Brown, Charles Smith, M. Muhammad, E. Toon, and Ronald Bell, 1979. R&B/Pop hit written and recorded by Kool and The Gang (De-Lite).

Ladies Who Lunch, The. w/m Stephen Sondheim, 1970. Introduced by Elaine Stritch in (TM) *Company*. Recorded by Barbra Streisand in "The Broadway Album" (Columbia), 1985.

La Dolce Vita (The Sweet Life). m. Nina Rota, 1961. Theme from the Italian film (MP) *La Dolce Vita*. Leading record: instrumental by Ray Ellis and his Orchestra (RCA).

Lady. w/m Lionel Richie, 1980. #1 gold record by Kenny Rogers, written and produced by Lionel Richie (Liberty).

Lady. w/m Graham Goble, 1979. Top 10 record by the Australian group Little River Band (Harvest).

Lady. w/m Dennis DeYoung, 1975. Top 10 record by the quintet Styx (Wooden Nickel).

Lady. w. Larry Kusik, Charles Singleton (Engl.), m. Bert Kaempfert, Herbert Rehbein, 1967. Originally a German song. Top 40 English version by Jack Jones (Kapp).

Lady (You Bring Me Up). w/m William King, Howard Hudson, and S. King, 1981. R&B/Pop crossover hit by The Commodores (Motown).

Lady, Play Your Mandolin. w. Irving Caesar, m. Oscar Levant, 1930. Popularized in vaudeville by Nick Lucas and Blossom Seeley.

Lady Bird. w/m Lee Hazlewood, 1967. Top 20 record by Nancy Sinatra and Lee Hazlewood (Reprise).

Lady Blue. w/m Howard Kaylan, 1975. Top 20 record by Leon Russell (Shelter).

Lady Came from Baltimore, The. w/m Tim Hardin, 1967. Leading record by Bobby Darin (Atlantic).

Lady Dances, The. w. Lew Brown, m. Harold Arlen, 1936. Introduced by Eddie Cantor, Rita Rio (later known as Donna Drake), and the Goldwyn Girls in (MM) *Strike Me Pink.*

Lady Down on Love. w/m Randy Owen, 1981. #1 Country and Pop chart crossover record by the quartet, Alabama, of which Owen was lead singer/guitarist (RCA).

Lady from 29 Palms, The. w/m Allie Wrubel, 1947. Popular versions by Freddy Martin and his Orchestra (RCA Victor); The Andrews Sisters (Decca); Tony Pastor, with his Orchestra (Columbia).

Lady Godiva. w/m Mike Leander and Charles Mills, 1966. Top 10 record by The British duo, Peter and Gordon (Capitol).

Lady I Love, The. w. Joe Young, M. Bernice Petkere 1932. Introduced and recorded by Russ Columbo (Victor).

Lady in Ermine, The. w. Cyrus Wood, m. Al Goodman, 1922. The title song of (TM) *The Lady in Ermine,* sung by Harry Fender, Gladys Walton, and Helen Shipman.

Lady in Red, The. w/m Chris DeBurgh, 1987. Top 10 single by the Irish-born singer Chris DeBurgh (A&M). First released in England where it was a #1 record. Not to be confused with the 1935 standard of the same title.

Lady in Red, The. w. Mort Dixon, m. Allie Wrubel, 1935. Introduced by Wini Shaw and reprised, country style, by Judy Canova in

(MM) *In Caliente.* Among recordings: Xavier Cugat (Victor), Ethel Merman (Brunswick), Louis Prima (Brunswick), Henry Busse (Decca), Stan Getz (New Jazz).

Lady Is a Tramp, The. w. Lorenz Hart, m. Richard Rodgers, 1937. Introduced by Mitzi Green in (TM) *Babes in Arms.* Sung by June Preisser in the 1939 film version (MM) *Babes in Arms,* by Lena Horne in the Rodgers and Hart story (MM) *Words and Music,* 1948, and interpolated in (MM) *Pal Joey* by Frank Sinatra, 1957.

Lady Jane. w/m Mick Jagger and Keith Richards, 1966. Recorded by the British group The Rolling Stones (London).

Lady Lay Down. w/m Rafe Van Hoy and Don Cook, 1978. #1 Country chart record by John Conlee (ABC). Revived by Tom Jones (Mercury), 1981.

Lady Love. w/m Yvonne Gray and Sherman Marshall, 1978. Recorded by Lou Rawls (Philadelphia International).

Lady Love. w/m Lester Lee and Bob Russell, 1952. From (MP) *Sound Off.* Leading recording by Vaughn Monroe, with his Orchestra (RCA Victor).

Lady Loves, A. w. Mack Gordon, m. Josef Myrow, 1953. Introduced by Debbie Reynolds in (MM) *I Love Melvin.*

Lady Luck. w/m Lloyd Price and Harold Logan, 1960. Chart record by Lloyd Price (ABC-Paramount).

Lady Luck. w/m Ray Perkins, 1929. Introduced by Ted Lewis and his Orchestra in (MM) *Show of Shows.* The entire cast, with fifteen principals, reprised it as the finale.

Lady Luck, Smile on Me. w. Joseph McCarthy, m. Harry Tierney, 1922. From (TM) *Up She Goes.*

Lady Madonna. w/m John Lennon and Paul McCartney, 1968. Gold record by The Beatles (Capitol).

Lady Marmalade. w/m Bob Crewe and Kenny Nolan, 1975. #1 gold record by the group LaBelle (Epic).

Lady of Spain. w/m Robert Hargreaves, Tolchard Evans, Stanley J. Damerell, Henry J. Tilsley, 1931, 1952. This import became popular in the U.S. via two British recordings: Ray Noble (Victor) and Roy Fox, the American bandleader who became well known in England (Br. Decca). Al Bowlly, who later gained fame with Noble, sang the vocal for Fox. It was revived in 1952, with Eddie Fisher's million-seller (Victor) and Les Paul's hit instrumental version (Capitol).

Lady of the Evening. w/m Irving Berlin, 1922. Sung by the tenor, John Steel, in (TM) *The Music Box Revue of 1922*. Steel also had a popular record (Victor), as did Paul Whiteman (Victor).

Lady's in Love with You, The. w. Frank Loesser, m. Burton Lane, 1939. Introduced by Bob Hope and Shirley Ross, with Gene Krupa's Band, in (MM) *Some Like It Hot*. Hope and Ross recorded it (Decca), and Gene Krupa, vocal by Irene Daye, preserved the band version (Brunswick). Other notable releases by Glenn Miller, vocal by Tex Beneke (Bluebird); Benny Goodman (Victor); Bob Crosby (Decca). Nellie Lutcher revived it in 1947 (Capitol).

Lady's Man. w/m Cy Coben, 1952. Featured and recorded by Hank Snow (RCA Victor).

Lady Soul. w/m Mark Holden, 1986. R&B/Pop crossover hit record by The Temptations (Gordy).

Lady Takes the Cowboy Every Time, The. w/m Larry Gatlin, 1984. Country chart hit by Larry Gatlin and The Gatlin Brothers Band (Columbia).

Lady Willpower. w/m Jerry Fuller, 1968. Top 10 record by Gary Puckett and The Union Gap (Columbia).

Lady Writer. w/m Mark Knopfler, 1979. Recorded by the English group Dire Straits; Knopfler, lead singer and producer (Warner Bros.).

L. A. Freeway. w/m Guy Clark, 1973. Recorded by Jerry Jeff Walker (MCA).

La Grange. w/m Billy Gibbons, Frank Beard, and Joe Hill, 1973. Written and recorded by the Texas trio ZZ Top (London).

La Isla Bonita. w/m Madonna, Patrick Leonard, and Bruce Gaitsch, 1987. Top 10 single by Madonna, from her album "True Blue" (Warner Bros.).

La La La. w/m Richard Rodgers, 1962. Introduced by Noelle Adam and Alvin Epstein in (TM) *No Strings*.

La La La La La. w/m Brian Holland, Eddie Holland, and Lamont Dozier, 1964. Recorded by the Latin quartet The Blendells (Reprise).

La La Means I Love You. w. William Hart, m. Thomas Bell, 1968. Top 10 record by The Delfonics (Philly Groove). Revived by Tierra (Boardwalk), 1981.

Lalena. w/m Donovan Leitch, 1968. Written and recorded in England by Donovan (Epic).

Lambeth Walk. w. Douglas Furber, L. Arthur Rose, m. Noel Gay (pseud. for R. M. Armitage), 1938, 1986. Introduced by Lupino Lane in London musical (TM) *Me and My Girl*. First recorded in the United States by Duke Ellington and his Orchestra (Brunswick). Performed by Robert Lindsay, Maryanne Plunkett, and company in hit Broadway revival, 1986.

Lament to Love. w/m Mel Tormé, 1941. Tormé's first published song, written at age fifteen. Leading instrumental records by Harry James (Columbia) and Sonny Dunham (Bluebird). Other versions: Les Brown, vocal by Betty Bonney (Okeh); Lanny Ross (Victor).

L'Amour, Toujours, L'Amour (Love Everlasting). w. Catherine Chisholm Cushing, m. Rudolf Friml, 1922. One of the few Friml songs not written for a production. Recorded and featured by a variety of artists including

Jessica Dragonette (Brunswick), Lily Pons (Columbia), Maxine Sullivan (Victor), and Meredith Willson's Orchestra (Decca). It was heard in (MM) *Cain and Mabel*, starring Marion Davies and Clark Gable, 1936, and sung by Susanna Foster in (MM) *This Is the Life*, 1944.

Lamp Is Low, The. w. Mitchell Parish, m. Peter DeRose and Bert Shefter, 1939. Adapted from Maurice Ravel's *Pavanne pour une Infante Defunte*. Best-selling record by Glenn Miller, vocal by Ray Eberle (Bluebird).

Lamplight. w/m James Shelton, 1934. Introduced by James Shelton, with Henry Fonda and Imogene Coca in (TM) Leonard Sillman's *New Faces*. Featured and recorded by Hal Kemp and his Orchestra, vocal by Skinnay Ennis, and featuring the arranger, John Scott Trotter, at the piano (Brunswick).

Lamplighter's Serenade, The. w. Paul Francis Webster, m. Hoagy Carmichael, 1942. Glenn Miller with vocal by Ray Eberle (Bluebird) had the best-seller as it was coupled with the #1 record "Don't Sit Under the Apple Tree" (q.v.) Bing Crosby's was the most popular of all versions (Decca). Frank Sinatra's was one of his first releases as a single, after his leaving the Dorsey band (Bluebird).

Lamplit Hour, The. w. Thomas Burke, m. Arthur A. Penn, 1919.

Lamp of Memory, The. w. Al Stillman (Engl.), m. Gonzalo Curiel, 1942. Original title "Incertidumbre," Spanish words by Curiel. Featured and recorded by Lanny Ross (Victor), Jack Leonard (Victor), Carol Bruce (Decca), the bands of Benny Goodman (Okeh) and Tony Pastor (Bluebird).

Lamp on the Corner, The. w/m Ned Washington and Agustin Lara, 1938. Sung by Tito Guizar in (MM) *Tropic Holiday*.

Landlord. w/m Nick Ashford and Valerie Simpson, 1980. Recorded by Gladys Knight & The Pips (Columbia).

Land of Confusion. w/m Tony Banks, Phil Collins, and Mike Rutherford, 1986. Written

and Top 10 record by the British trio Genesis (Atlantic).

Land of Dreams. w. Norman Gimbel, m. Eddie Heywood, 1954. Introduced and recorded by Hugo Winterhalter and his Orchestra, featuring Eddie Heywood at the piano (RCA Victor).

Land of Golden Dreams, The. w. C. M. Denison, m. E. F. Dusenberry, 1912.

Land of Hope and Glory, The. w. Arthur C. Benson, m. Edward Elgar, 1902. Originally published in England.

Land of Milk and Honey, The. w/m John Hurley and Ronnie Wilkins, 1966. Top 40 record by The Vogues (Co & Ce).

Land of My Best Girl, The. w. Ballard MacDonald, m. Harry Carroll, 1914.

Land of 1000 Dances. w/m Chris Kenner and Antoine "Fats" Domino, 1963. First recording by Chris Kenner (Instant), followed by Cannibal and The Headhunters (Rampart), 1965; Thee Midniters (Chattahoochee); Top 10 record by Wilson Pickett (Atlantic), 1966; instrumental by Electric Indian (United Artists), 1969; The J. Geils Band (EMI America), 1983.

Land of the Heart's Desire, The. w. Channing Pollock, m. Theodore F. Morse, 1908.

Land Where the Good Songs Go, The. w. P. G. Wodehouse, m. Jerome Kern, 1917. Introduced in (TM) *Miss 1917*, by Bessie McCoy. It was sung by Lucille Bremer in The Kern biographical film (MM) *Till the Clouds Roll By*, 1946.

Lane in Spain, A. w. Al Lewis, m. Carmen Lombardo, 1927. This was Lombardo's first song success.

Language of Love, The. w/m Dan Fogelberg, 1984. Recorded by Dan Fogelberg (Full Moon).

Lanky Yankee Boys in Blue, The. w. Edward Madden, m. Theodore F. Morse, 1908.

La Novia. See **Wedding, The.**

471

Lantern of Love. w. Raymond Peck, m. Percy Wenrich, 1926. From (TM) *Castles in the Air.* Recorded by Paul Ash (Columbia).

La Pachanga. w. Jeanne Pollack (Engl.), Eduardo Davidson (Sp.), m. Eduardo Davidson, 1961. Spanish song, introduced in the U.S. on an imported German recording by Audrey Arno and The Hazy Osterwald Sextet (Decca).

La Parranda. See **Cuanto le Gusta.**

La Plume de Ma Tante. w/m Al Hoffman and Dick Manning, 1959. Independent song, not from the stage musical of same name. Recorded by Hugo and Luigi and their Orchestra, with The Children's Chorus (RCA).

Lara's Theme. See **Somewhere My Love.**

Laroo, Laroo, Lilli Bolero. w. Sylvia Dee and Elizabeth Moore, m. Sidney Lippman, 1948. Popular recordings by Peggy Lee (Capitol) and Perry Como (RCA Victor).

La Rosita. w. Allan Stuart, m. Paul Dupont, 1923.

Las Altenitas. See **Gay Ranchero, A.**

La Seine. See **River Seine, The.**

Lasso the Moon. w/m Steven Dorff and Milton Brown, 1985. Introduced by Gary Morris in the send-up western film (MP) *Rustler's Rhapsody.* His recording made the Country charts (Warner Bros.).

Last Call for Love. w/m E. Y. Harburg, Margery Cummings, and Burton Lane, 1942. Introduced by Tommy Dorsey, vocal by Frank Sinatra, Connie Haines, and the Pied Pipers in (MM) *Ship Ahoy,* and recorded by them (Victor).

Last Chance to Turn Around. w/m Tony Bruno, Bob Elgin, and Vic Millrose, 1965. Hit record by Gene Pitney (Musicor).

Last Cheater's Waltz. w/m Sonny Throckmorton, 1979. Hit Country record by T. G. Sheppard (Warner Bros.).

Last Child. w/m Steve Tyler and Brad Whitford, 1976. Recorded by the hard-rock band Aerosmith (Columbia).

Last Dance, The. w/m Paul Jabara, 1978. Introduced by Donna Summer in (MP) *Thank God, It's Friday.* Winner Academy Award for Best Song. Gold record by Donna Summer (Casablanca). Winner Grammy Award (NARAS) Rhythm and Blues Song of the Year.

Last Date. m. Floyd Cramer, 1960. Hit instrumental by Nashville pianist Floyd Cramer (RCA). Lawrence Welk and his Orchestra also had a popular version (Dot). See also **Lost Her Love on Our Last Date.**

Last Day in the Mines. w/m Jimmy Key, 1964. Country hit by Dave Dudley (Mercury).

Last Farewell, The. w/m Roger Whittaker and R. A. Webster, 1975. Top 20 record by the British singer Roger Whittaker (RCA).

Last Game of the Season, The (A Blind Man in the Bleachers). w/m Sterling Whipple, 1975. Top 20 record by David Geddes (Big Tree). Also recorded by Kenny Starr (MCA).

Lasting Love. w/m Hunt Stevens and Jack Ackerman, 1957. Popular record by Sal Mineo (Epic).

Last Kiss. w/m Wayne Cochran, 1964. Introduced by Wayne Cochran (Gala), 1961. J. Frank Wilson and The Cavaliers established the song with a Top 10 hit (Josie), 1964. Revived by Wednesday (Sussex), 1974.

Last Love Song, The. w/m Hank Williams, Jr., 1974. Hit Country record by Hank Williams, Jr. (MGM).

Last Mile Home, The. w/m Walter Kent and Walton Farrar, 1949. Introduced and featured by Gracie Fields (London). Popular U.S. record by Jo Stafford (Columbia).

Last Night. m. Charles Axton, Jerry Lee Smith, Floyd Newman, Chips Moman, 1961. Instrumental hit by The Mar-Keys (Satellite).

Last Night. w/m Nick Kenny, Charles Kenny, and Austen Croom-Johnson, 1939. Best-selling recordings by Glenn Miller, vocal by Ray Eberle (Bluebird) and Hal Kemp and his Orchestra (Victor).

Last Night I Didn't Get to Sleep At All. w/m Tony Macaulay, 1973. Gold record by The 5th Dimension (Belk).

Last Night I Dreamed of You. w. Walter Hirsch, m. Lou Handman, 1937. Introduced by Frances Langford in (MM) *The Hit Parade*.

Last Night I Dreamed You Kissed Me. w. Gus Kahn, m. Carmen Lombardo, 1928. Popular records by Paul Whiteman (Columbia) and Dick Powell (Vocalion).

Last Night on the Back Porch (I Loved Her Best of All). w. Lew Brown, m. Carl Schraubstader, 1923. Successful records by Paul Whiteman and his Orchestra (Victor) and Ernest Hare and Billy Jones (Okeh).

Last Night Was the End of the World. w. Andrew B. Sterling, m. Harry Von Tilzer, 1912. A popular recording was made by Henry Burr (Victor).

Last Night When We Were Young. w. E. Y. Harburg, m. Harold Arlen, 1936. Lawrence Tibbett recorded the song (Victor 12″) prior to his singing it in (MM) *Metropolitan*. The record was released, but the song was deleted from the film. Judy Garland, in *In the Good Old Summertime*, 1949, and Frank Sinatra, in *Take Me Out to the Ball Game*, 1949, suffered the same fate, as the producer again deleted the song after filming it, deeming the number "too sad." Both Garland (Capitol) and Sinatra (Columbia) recorded it. Despite the ominous start, the song is a standard today.

Last One to Know, The. w/m Matraca Berg and Jane Mariash, 1987. #1 Country chart single and album title song by Reba McEntire (MCA).

La Strada. See **Love Theme from "La Strada."**

Last Ride, The. w. Robert Halcomb, m. Ted Daffan, 1959. Hit C&W record by Hank Snow (RCA).

Last Round-up, The. w/m Billy Hill, 1933. Hill gained fame from this, the first big hit for which he wrote words and music. Introduced at the Paramount Theatre in New York by Joe Morrison with George Olsen and his Orchestra whose record (Columbia) became an immediate best-seller. Bing Crosby (Brunswick), Rudy Vallee (Bluebird), Arthur Tracy (Vocalion), Richard Himber (Vocalion), and Conrad Thibault (Victor) followed with their releases. In early January of 1934, it was interpolated in (TM) *Ziegfeld Follies* by Don Ross and reprised by Willie and Eugene Howard. Gene Autry sang it in (MM) *The Singing Hills* in 1941, and Roy Rogers in (MM) *Don't Fence Me In* in 1945.

Last Song. w/m Larry Evoy, 1973. Gold record by the Canadian trio Edward Bear (Capitol). Written by the lead singer.

Last Tango in Paris. w. Dory Previn, m. Gato Barbieri, 1973. Introduced as title theme on the soundtrack of (MP) *Last Tango in Paris* by Gato Barbieri. Instrumental record by Herb Alpert and The Tijuana Brass (A&M).

Last Thing I Want Is Your Pity, The. w/m Frank Loesser, 1948. C&W song featured and recorded by Red Foley (Decca).

Last Thing on My Mind, The. w/m Tom Paxton, 1964. Introduced and recorded by Tom Paxton (Elektra). Revived by Porter Wagoner and Dolly Parton (RCA), 1968, and by Neil Diamond (MCA), 1973.

Last Time, The. w/m Mick Jagger and Keith Richards, 1965. Top 10 record by the British group The Rolling Stones (London).

Last Time I Felt Like This, The. w. Alan Bergman and Marilyn Bergman, m. Marvin Hamlisch, 1978. Sung on the soundtrack of (MP) *Same Time, Next Year* by Johnny Mathis and Jane Olivor.

Last Time I Saw Him. w/m Michael Masser and Pam Sawyer, 1974. Top 20 record by Diana Ross (Motown).

Last Time I Saw Paris, The. w. Oscar Hammerstein II, m. Jerome Kern, 1941. Dedicated to Noël Coward, it referred to the capture of Paris by the Nazis. Ann Sothern sang it in (MM) *Lady Be Good*. Winner of the Academy Award for Best Song of the Year, which award was disputed because of the song's interpolation in the film after its prior release as a nonproduction number. Dinah Shore sang it in the Kern biography (MM) *Till the Clouds Roll By*, 1946.

Last Time I Saw Richard, The. w/m Joni Mitchell, 1971. Introduced by Joni Mitchell and included in her album "Blue" (Reprise).

Last Time I Saw You, The. w/m Edna Osser and Marjorie Goetschius, 1945. Popularized by Les Brown, vocal by Doris Day (Columbia).

Last Train to Clarksville. w/m Tommy Boyce and Bobby Hart, 1966. #1 gold record by The Monkees (Colgems).

Last Two Weeks in July, The. w. Sam M. Lewis, m. Abel Baer, 1939. Popularized by Al Donahue, vocal by Phil Brito (Vocalion).

Last Waltz, The. w/m Les Reed and Barry Mason, 1967. Hit record, recorded in England by Engelbert Humperdinck (Parrot).

Last Waltz, The. w/m Webb Pierce and Myrna Freeman, 1952. Introduced and recorded by Webb Pierce (Decca).

Last Word in Lonesome Is Me, The. w/m Roger Miller, 1966. Country and Pop chart hit by Eddy Arnold (RCA).

L. A. Sunshine. w/m Dee Allen, Harold Brown, B. B. Dickerson, Gerald Goldstein, Lonnie Jordan, Lee Oskar, Charles Miller, and Howard Scott, 1977. Recorded by the band War (Blue Note).

Late, Late Show, The. w. Roy Alfred, m. Murray Berlin, 1956. Featured by Dakota Staton (Capitol).

Late in the Evening. w/m Paul Simon, 1980. Introduced in (MM) "One Trick Pony" by Paul Simon, who also had a Top 10 record (Columbia).

Lately. w/m Dave Conley, Bernard Jackson, and David Townsend, 1987. Top 10 R&B chart single written and recorded by the trio Surface (Columbia).

Lately Song, The. w. Sammy Cahn, m. Sammy Fain, 1953. Sung and danced by Gordon MacRae, Jack E. Leonard, Gene Nelson, and Jane Powell in (MM) *Three Men and a Girl*.

Late Nite Comic. w/m Brian Gari, 1988. Sung by Robert LuPone in the off-Broadway musical (TM) *Late Nite Comic*. The composer sang it on the album (Original Cast).

Late Now. w/m Tim Gayle, J. Fred Coots, and Matt Furin, 1949. Most popular records by Evelyn Knight, with Sonny Burke's Orchestra (Decca), and Mel Tormé, with Frank DeVol's Orchestra (Capitol)

Later Tonight. w. Leo Robin, m. Nacio Herb Brown, 1943. Introduced by Woody Herman with his Band in (MM) *Wintertime*, starring Sonja Henie. Leading record by Kay Armen, with the unaccompanied vocal group The Balladiers (Decca).

Latins Know How. w/m Irving Berlin, 1940. Introduced by Irene Bordoni in (TM) *Louisiana Purchase* and recorded by Joan Edwards (Liberty Music Shops).

Latin Tune, A Manhattan Moon, and You, A. w. Al Dubin, m. Jimmy McHugh, 1940. Introduced by Ray Bolger and Betty Bruce in (TM) *Keep Off the Grass*.

Laugh, Clown, Laugh. w. Sam M. Lewis and Joe Young, m. Ted Fio Rito, 1928. Featured and made popular by Harry Richman (Brunswick), Ted Lewis (Columbia), and Irving Kaufman with William F. Wirges's Orchestra (Brunswick). Alan Dale revived it (Coral) in the mid-fifties.

Laugh, I Thought I'd Die. w. Fran Landesman, m. Tommy Wolf, 1959. Introduced by Richard Hayes in (TM) *The Nervous Set.*

Laugh, Laugh. w/m Ronald C. Elliott, 1965. Top 20 record by The Beau Brummels (Autumn).

Laugh and Call It Love. w. Johnny Burke, m. James V. Monaco, 1938. Introduced by Bing Crosby in (MM) *Sing You Sinners.* Recorded by Crosby (Decca) and Russ Morgan and his Orchestra (Decca).

Laugh and the World Laughs with You. w. Ella Wheeler Wilcox, m. Louis Gottschalk, 1896.

Laugh at Me. w/m Sonny Bono, 1965. Top 10 record by Sonny [Bono] (Atco).

Laughing. w/m Randy Bachman and Burton Cummings, 1969. Gold record by the Canadian group The Guess Who (RCA).

Laughing Boy. w/m William Robinson, 1963. Crossover (R&B/Pop) hit, recorded by Mary Wells (Motown).

Laughing Boy. w/m Jack Segal, 1949. Introduced and recorded by Eve Young, later to be known as Karen Chandler (RCA Victor).

Laughing Irish Eyes. w. Sidney D. Mitchell, m. Sam H. Stept, 1936. Sung in (MM) *Laughing Irish Eyes* and recorded by Phil Regan (Brunswick).

Laughing on the Outside (Crying on the Inside). w. Ben Raleigh, m. Bernie Wayne, 1946. Best-selling records: Sammy Kaye, vocal by Billy Williams (RCA Victor); Dinah Shore (Columbia); Andy Russell (Capitol). Revived, 1953, by The Four Aces, with Jack Pleis's Orchestra (Decca).

Laughing Water. w. George Totten Smith, M. Frederick W. Hager, 1903. From (TM) *Mother Goose.*

Laughter in the Rain w/m Neil Sedaka and Phil Cody, 1975. #1 record by Neil Sedaka (Rocket).

Laura. w. Johnny Mercer, m. David Raksin, 1945. After the film opened, Mercer wrote the lyric to the recurrent theme from (MP) *Laura.* Song has become a major standard with many recordings. Among the first popular versions were those by Woody Herman, with his Orchestra (Columbia); Johnny Johnston (Capitol); Freddy Martin and his Orchestra (Victor); Jerry Wald, vocal by Dick Merrick (Majestic); Dick Haymes (Decca).

Laura (What's He Got That I Ain't Got?). w/m Leon Ashley and Margie Singleton, 1967. Introduced and Country hit record by Leon Ashley (Ashley). Pop chart versions by Frankie Laine (ABC) and Brook Benton (Reprise).

Laurie (Stange Things Happen). w/m Milton C. Addington, 1965. Country/Pop record by Dickey Lee (TCF-Hall).

La Veeda. w. Nat Vincent, m. John Alden, 1920.

Lavendar Blue (Dilly Dilly). w. Larry Morey, m. Eliot Daniel, 1949. Based on an eighteenth-century English folk song. This version was introduced by Burl Ives in Walt Disney's live-action film (MM) *So Dear to My Heart.* Academy award nominee. Ives, with "Captain Stubby and the Buccaneers," had a best-seller (Decca) as did Dinah Shore (Columbia); Sammy Kaye, vocal by The Three Kaydets (RCA Victor); Jack Smith (Capitol). Revived by Sammy Turner (Big Top), 1959.

La Vie en Rose. w. Mack David (Engl.), Edith Piaf (Fr.), m. Louiguy, 1950. First English title, "You're Too Dangerous, Cherie," 1948. This version, with original French title, was introduced in the U.S. by Edith Piaf, whose recording (Columbia) was a million-seller. Other hit versions by Tony Martin (RCA Victor); Paul Weston and his Orchestra (Capitol); Bing Crosby (Decca); Louis Armstrong (Decca).

Lawd, You Made the Night Too Long. w. Sam M. Lewis, m. Isham Jones, 1932. Originally recorded by Louis Armstrong (Okeh); the Boswell Sisters with Don Redman's Orchestra (Brunswick 12″); Paul Whiteman, vocal by

Red McKenzie (Victor); the Pickens Sisters (Victor). A parody, with words by Milton Berle and Fred Whitehouse, titled "Sam, You Made the Pants Too Long," was featured in nightclubs by Joe E. Lewis and on a popular record by Vaughn Monroe's Orchestra, sung by Ziggy Talent (Bluebird), 1940, and revived by Barbra Streisand (Columbia), 1966.

Lawdy Miss Clawdy. w/m Lloyd Price, 1952. Introduced and #1 R&B record by Lloyd Price (Specialty). Revived by Gary Stites (Carlton), 1960, and The Buckinghams (U.S.A.), 1967.

Lawyers in Love. w/m Jackson Browne, 1983. Recorded by Jackson Browne (Asylum).

Lay, Lady, Lay. w/m Bob Dylan, 1969. Top 10 single by Bob Dylan (Columbia). Other chart records by Ferrante and Teicher [instrumental] (United Artists) and The Isley Brothers (T-Neck).

Lay Down (Candles in the Wind). w/m Melanie Safka, 1970. Top 10 record by Melanie, with The Edwin Hawkins Singers (Buddah).

Lay Down Sally. w/m Eric Clapton, Marc Levy, and George Terry, 1978. Gold record by English singer/guitarist Eric Clapton (RSO).

Lay Down Your Arms. w. Paddy Roberts (Engl.), Ake Gerhard (Swed.), m. Ake Gerhard and Leon Land, 1956. Swedish song. Leading U.S. records by The Chordettes (Cadence), and Anne Shelton, who introduced the song in England (London).

Lay Down Your Weary Tune. w/m Bob Dylan, 1964. Introduced and recorded by Bob Dylan (Columbia).

Layla. w/m Eric Clapton and Jim Gordon, 1971. Written and recorded in England and titled after the nickname of Beatle George Harrison's wife, the record by Derek (a.k.a. Eric Clapton) and The Dominos was released in the U.S. (Atco) and was a chart entry. Its re-release in 1972 achieved a Top 10 rating.

Lay Your Hands on Me. w/m Tom Bailey, Alannah Currie, and Joe Leeway, 1985. Written and Top 10 record by the British-based trio known as The Thompson Twins (Arista).

Laziest Gal in Town, The. w/m Cole Porter, 1950. Written in 1927. Earliest recording by Frankie Trumbauer, vocal by Fredda Gibson, later known as Georgia Gibbs (Varsity), 1940. Popularized via performance by Marlene Dietrich in (MP) *Stage Fright*, 1950. Featured and recorded by Mae Barnes (Atlantic).

Lazy. w/m Irving Berlin, 1924. One of three big hits for Berlin this year. See "All Alone" and "What'll I Do." It was featured and recorded by Blossom Seeley (Columbia), Paul Whiteman (Victor), and Al Jolson (Brunswick). It was heard in the background of (MM) *Alexander's Ragtime Band*, 1938; (MM) *Holiday Inn*, 1942, sung by Bing Crosby; (MM) *There's No Business Like Show Business*, 1954, sung by Mitzi Gaynor, Donald O'Connor, and Marilyn Monroe.

Lazy Afternoon. w. John Latouche, m. Jerome Moross, 1954. Introduced by Kaye Ballard in (TM) *The Golden Apple*.

Lazybones. w/m Johnny Mercer and Hoagy Carmichael, 1933. Mercer's first big hit. Introduced and recorded by Mildred Bailey (Brunswick), it was popularized and recorded by Ben Bernie (Brunswick). Also, Glen Gray and the Casa Loma Orchestra, vocal by Pee Wee Hunt (Victor); Irving Aaronson and the Commanders, vocal by Dick Robertson (Vocalion). Louis Armstrong had a well-received recording (Decca) in 1939.

Lazy Countryside. w/m Bobby Worth, 1947. From the cartoon film (MM) *Fun and Fancy Free*. Recorded by Margaret Whiting (Capitol).

Lazy Day. w. Tony Powers, m. George Fischoff, 1967. Recorded by Spanky and Our Gang (Mercury).

Lazy Day. w. Earl Martin and Gus Kahn, m. George Posford and Grace Le Boy Kahn,

1932. The sheet music credits Martin and Posford with "English lyrics and English melody" and Gus and Grace Le Boy Kahn with "American lyrics and American melody." The song was featured and recorded in the U.S. by Bing Crosby (Brunswick), and the bands of Jack Denny (Victor) and Roger Wolfe Kahn (Columbia).

Lazy Lou'siana Moon. w/m Walter Donaldson, 1930. Recorded by Guy Lombardo (Columbia), Paul Small (Okeh), and Annette Hanshaw (Velvetone).

Lazy Mary. w. Lou Monte (Engl.), Paolo Citorello (Ital.), m. Paolo Citorello, 1958. Original Italian song, "Luna Mezzo Mare." Recorded by Lou Monte (RCA). See also **Oh! Ma-Ma (The Butcher Boy).**

Lazy Mood w. Johnny Mercer, m. Eddie Miller, 1947. Introduced by Matt Dennis (Capitol). Song adapted from tenor saxophonist Eddie Miller's instrumental, "Slow Mood," recorded by Bob Crosby's Bobcats, 1938.

Lazy Moon w. Bob Cole, m. J. Rosamond Johnson, 1903. Introduced by the minstrel George Primrose. Song was later used in (MM) *Here Comes Cookie*, starring Burns and Allen, 1935.

Lazy Rhapsody. w/m Howard M. Jackson, Mitchell Parish, Harry Sosnik, and Ned Washington, 1932. Theme song of Harry Sosnik and his Orchestra.

Lazy Rhapsody. m. Edward Kennedy "Duke" Ellington, 1932. Instrumental recorded by Ellington and his Orchestra (Brunswick).

Lazy River. w/m Hoagy Carmichael and Sidney Arodin, 1931. Introduced via the recording by Hoagy Carmichael, featuring Benny Goodman, Gene Krupa, Bix Beiderbecke, Jack Teagarden, and Joe Venuti (Victor). Later popular records by the Mills Brothers (Decca); Benny Goodman (Capitol); and the Merry Macs, with Glen Gray and the Casa Loma Orchestra. In 1961, hit records by Bobby Darin (Atco), and Si Zentner and his Band (Liberty). Carmichael performed it in (MP) *The Best Years of Our Lives*, 1944. It was heard in (MM) *Cowboy Canteen*, starring June Frazee, 1943. Louis Prima and Keely Smith sang it in (MM) *Hey Boy, Hey Girl*, 1959.

Lazy Summer Night. w/m Harold Spina, 1958. Introduced in (MP) *Andy Hardy Comes Home*. Leading record by The Four Preps (Capitol).

Lazy Weather. w. Jo Trent, m. Peter De Rose, 1927.

L. David Sloane. w/m Angela Martin and Wilbur Meshel, 1968. Chart record by Michelle Lee (Columbia).

Leader of the Band. w/m Dan Fogelberg, 1982. Top 10 record by Dan Fogelberg (Full Moon).

Leader of the German Band, The. w. Edward Madden, m. Theodore F. Morse, 1905.

Leader of the Laundromat. w/m Paul Vance and Lee Pockriss, 1965. Parody of the hit record "Leader of the Pack." Top 20 record by The Detergents (Roulette).

Leader of the Pack. w/m Jeff Barry, Ellie Greenwich, and George Morton, 1964. #1 chart record by The Shangri-Las (Red Bird).

Lead Me On. w. Allee Willis, m. David Lasley, 1979. Gold record by Maxine Nightingale (Windsong).

Lead Me On. w/m Leon C. Copeland, 1971. Country hit by Conway Twitty and Loretta Lynn (Decca).

Lean Baby. w. William May, m. Roy Alfred, 1951. Records: Billy May and his Orchestra (Capitol), Frank Sinatra (Capitol).

Leaning on the Lamp Post. w/m Noel Gay, 1937, 1966. Introduced in the English film (MM) "Feather Your Nest," by George Formby. In 1966, Herman's Hermits had a Top 10 record (MGM). Interpolated by Robert

Lindsay in the Broadway production of the English musical (TM) *Me and My Girl*, 1986.

Leanin' on the Ole Top Rail. w/m Nick Kenny and Charles Kenny, 1940. Sung by Gene Autry in (MP) *Ride, Tenderfoot, Ride*. Popular records by: Bob Crosby, vocal by Crosby (Decca); Ozzie Nelson, vocal by Rose Ann Stevens (Bluebird); the duet of two Horace Heidt alumni, singer Larry Cotton and whistler Fred Lowery (Columbia); Patsy Montana (Conqueror); Barry Wood (Vocalion); and, on one of her earlier singles, Patti Page (Mercury).

Lean on Me. w/m Bill Withers, 1972, 1987. #1 R&B and Pop chart gold record by Bill Withers (Sussex). The song was revived by the quintet, Club Nouveau, whose recording, as its predecessor did, reached the #1 position (Warner Bros.).

Leap Frog. w. Leo Corday, m. Joe Garland, 1941. Theme song of and recorded by Les Brown and his Orchestra (Columbia). Other version of note: Louis Armstrong (Decca) and Charlie Parker (Clef).

Learning. w. Marty Symes and Al J. Neiburg, m. Jerry Livingston, 1934. Best-selling record by Glen Gray and the Casa Loma Orchestra, vocal by Kenny Sargent (Brunswick).

Learning McFadden to Waltz. w/m M. F. Carey, 1890.

Learning to Fly. w/m David Gilmour, Bob Ezrin, Moore, and Carin, 1987. Single by the reorganized British group, Pink Floyd, from their album "A Momentary Lapse of Reason" (Columbia).

Learnin' the Blues. w/m Dolores Vicki Silvers, 1955. Introduced, popularized, and a #1 record hit by Frank Sinatra (Capitol).

Learn to Croon. w. Sam Coslow, m. Arthur Johnston, 1933. Introduced by Bing Crosby in (MM) *College Humor*. Recorded by Crosby (Brunswick) and Fran Frey (Columbia); the bands of Don Bestor (Victor), Ambrose (HMV), and Jimmie Grier (Brunswick).

Learn to Do the Strut. w/m Irving Berlin, 1923. Introduced by Joseph Santley, Ivy Sawyer, and The Brox Sisters in (TM) *Music Box Revue of 1923*. Vincent Lopez and his Orchestra had a popular instrumental recording (Okeh).

Learn to Smile. w. Otto Harbach, m. Louis A. Hirsch, 1921. Introduced by Finita De Soria, Elizabeth Hines, and Carl Hammer in (TM) *The O'Brien Girl*. Recorded by Paul Whiteman and his Orchestra (Victor) and John McCormack (Victor).

Leather and Lace. w/m Stevie Nicks, 1982. Top 10 record by Stevie Nicks and Don Henley (Modern).

Leave It to Jane. w. P. G. Wodehouse, m. Jerome Kern, 1917. Edith Hallor introduced it in (TM) *Leave It to Jane*. June Allyson sang it in the Kern film biography (MM) *Till the Clouds Roll By* in 1946.

Leave Me Alone (Ruby Red Dress). w/m Linda Laurie, 1973. Gold record by Helen Reddy (Capitol).

Leave Me Lonely. 1986. #1 Country chart record by Gary Morris (Warner Bros.).

Leave Me with a Smile. w/m Charles Koehler and Earl Burtnett, 1921.

Leave My Dream Alone. w/m Warner McPherson, 1969. Written and Top 10 Country record by Warner Mack (Decca).

Leave Us Face It. w/m Abe Burrows and Frank Loesser, 1945. From (MM) *Duffy's Tavern*, loosely based on the radio show of that name.

Leaving Louisiana in the Broad Daylight. w/m W. D. Cowart and Rodney Cowell, 1980. #1 Country chart record by The Oak Ridge Boys (MCA).

Leaving Me. w/m M. Barge and Jimmie Jiles, 1973. #1 crossover (R&B/Pop) gold record by The Independents (Wand).

Leaving on a Jet Plane. w/m John Denver, 1969. #1 gold record by Peter, Paul, and Mary (Warner Bros.).

Leavin' on Your Mind. w/m Wayne P. Walker and Webb Pierce, 1963. Crossover (C&W/Pop) chart record by Patsy Cline (Decca).

Le Freak. w/m Nile Rodgers and Bernard Edwards, 1978. #1 platinum record by the disco group, Chic, formed by the writers (Atlantic).

Left All Alone Again Blues. w. Anne Caldwell, m. Jerome Kern, 1920. Introduced by Stella Hoban in (TM) *The Night Boat.* Marion Harris recorded this before the show opened in New York (Columbia).

Left in the Dark. w/m Jim Steinman, 1984. Recorded by Barbra Streisand (Columbia).

Left Right Out of Your Heart. w. Earl Shuman, m. Mort Garson, 1958. Featured and recorded by Patti Page (Mercury).

Left to Right. w/m Lorene Mann, 1960. Country hit by Kitty Wells (Decca).

Legacy, The. w. Betty Comden and Adolph Green, m. Cy Coleman, 1978. Introduced by John Cullum in (TM) *On the Twentieth Century.*

Legalize My Name. w. Johnny Mercer, m. Harold Arlen, 1946. Introduced by Pearl Bailey in (TM) *St. Louis Woman.* First recording, other than cast album, by Gertrude Niesen (Decca).

Legend, The. w/m Jerry Reed, 1977. Introduced by Jerry Reed in (MP) *Smokey and the Bandit.*

(I'd Be) Legend in My Time, A. w/m Don Gibson, 1974. Introduced by Don Gibson (RCA), 1960. #1 C&W chart record by Ronnie Milsap (RCA), 1974.

"Legend of Billie Jean" Theme. See **Invincible.**

Legend of Bonnie and Clyde, The. w/m Merle Haggard and Bonnie Owens, 1968. Hit Country record by Merle Haggard (Capitol).

Legend of Wyatt Earp, The. w. Harold Adamson, m. Harry Warren, 1955. Theme song of the TV show "The Life and Legend of Wyatt Earp."

Legs. w/m Billy Gibbons, Dusty Hill, and Frank Beard, 1984. Top 10 hit, written and recorded by the trio ZZ Top (Warner Bros.).

Lemon Drop. m. George Wallington, 1949. Jazz instrumental introduced and recorded by Chubby Jackson and his combo (Rainbow) and also featured and recorded by Woody Herman and his Orchestra, arrangement by Shorty Rogers (Capitol).

Lemon in the Garden of Love, A. w. M. E. Rourke, m. Richard Carle, 1906. A comedy number sung by Richard Carle in (TM) *The Spring Chicken.* It was also heard in (MM) *Ma, He's Making Eyes At Me,* 1940, featuring Constance Moore and Tom Brown.

Lemon Tree. w/m Will Holt, 1962. Initial record success for Peter, Paul and Mary (Warner Bros.). Revived by Trini Lopez with a Top 20 version (Reprise), 1965.

Lenox Avenue Shuffle. m. Bubber Miley and Arthur Ray, 1924. This instrumental was recorded by the Texas Blue Destroyers, featuring Miley on trumpet (Perfect).

Leona. w/m Cindy Walker, 1962. Introduced and Top 10 Country chart record by Stonewall Jackson (Columbia). Revived by the rock band Wet Willie (Capricorn), 1975, and the Nashville group Sawyer Brown (Capitol), 1985.

Leopard-Skin Pill-Box Hat. w/m Bob Dylan, 1967. Recorded by Bob Dylan (Columbia).

Les Bicyclettes de Belsize. w/m Les Reed and Barry Mason, 1968. French title, English song, American hit by Engelbert Humperdinck (Parrot).

Less and Less. w/m Roger Miller, 1965. Country chart record by Charlie Louvin (Capitol).

Lesson, The. w/m Mack David, 1968. Top 40 record by Vikki Carr (Liberty).

Lesson in Leavin', A. w/m Randy Goodrum and L. Brent Maher, 1980. Crossover (C&W/Pop) record by Dottie West (United Artists).

Lessons in Love. w/m Wally King, Wally Badarou, and Phil Gould, 1987. Recorded by the English group Level 42 (Polydor).

Let a Smile Be Your Umbrella. w. Irving Kahal and Francis Wheeler, m. Sammy Fain, 1928. Introduced in vaudeville by Fain and (Artie) Dunn (later of the Three Suns). Popularized on radio and via recordings by the orchestras of Roger Wolfe Kahn (Victor) and Sam Lanin, vocal by Irving Kaufman (Okeh). It was interpolated in (MM) *It's a Great Life* by the Duncan Sisters, 1929, and by Dan Dailey and Charles Winninger in (MM) *Give My Regards to Broadway*, 1948.

Let a Woman Be a Woman, Let a Man Be a Man. w/m Arlester "Dyke" Christian, 1969. Top 40 record by Dyke and The Blazers (Original Sound).

Let Bygones Be Bygones. w. Charles Shackford, m. Kerry Mills, 1897.

Let 'Em In. w/m Paul McCartney and Linda McCartney, 1976. Top 10 record by McCartney's group Wings (Capitol).

Let Forgiveness In. w/m Rex Griffin and Webb Pierce, 1961. Country hit by Webb Pierce (Decca).

Let Go. w/m D. Duncan, 1989. Hit R&B chart single by Sharon Bryant (Wing).

Let Her Dance. w/m Carl Spencer, Bernie Lawrence, and Henry Glover, 1960. Top 10 record by Billy Bland (Old Town). Originally released as "Let the Little Girl Dance."

Let Her In. w/m Gary Benson, 1976. Top 10 record by John Travolta (Midland International).

Let Him Go. w/m William Wadhams, 1985. Recorded by the quintet Animotion (Mercury).

Let It Alone. w. Alex Rogers, m. Bert Williams, 1906.

Let It Be. w/m John Lennon and Paul McCartney, 1970. Title song of The Beatles' documentary (MM) *Let It Be*, and #1 gold record by the group (Apple).

Let It Be Me. w. Mann Curtis (Engl.), m. Gilbert Becaud, 1957. Original French song, "Je T'Appartiens," words by Pierre Delanoe, and introduced in France by Gilbert Becaud. Introduced in the U.S. by Jill Corey on (TVP) "Climax." She had a popular recording (Columbia), and in 1960, The Everly Brothers had a Top 10 version (Cadence). Later successful versions by Jerry Butler and Betty Everett (Vee-Jay), 1964; The Sweet Inspirations (Atlantic), 1967; Glen Campbell and Bobbie Gentry (Capitol), 1969; Willie Nelson (Columbia), 1982.

Let It Go, Let It Flow. w/m Dave Mason, 1978. Recorded by the English singer/guitarist Dave Mason (Columbia).

Let It Rain. w/m Richard Martin, 1972. Recorded in England by Eric Clapton (Polydor).

Let It Rain! Let It Pour! (I'll Be in Virginia in the Morning). w. Cliff Friend, m. Walter Donaldson, 1925. Popular song with leading records by Gene Austin (Victor); Nat Shilkret, vocal by Vernon Dalhart (Victor); Ben Selvin, vocal by Irving Kaufman (Vocalion).

Let It Ride. w/m Randy Bachman and C. Fred Turner, 1974. Recorded by the Canadian group The Bachman-Turner Overdrive (Mercury).

Let It Ring. w/m Joan Edwards and Lynn Duddy, 1955. Recorded by Doris Day (Columbia).

Let It Shine. w/m Linda Hargrove, 1976. Recorded by the group Santana (Columbia).

Let It Shine. w/m Neil Young, 1976. C&W/ Pop chart record by Olivia Newton-John (MCA).

Let It Snow! Let It Snow! Let It Snow! w. Sammy Cahn, m. Vaughn Monroe, 1946. Perennial Christmas/winter song, first popularized by the performance and hit record of Vaughn Monroe with his Orchestra (Victor), and recordings by Woody Herman with his Orchestra (Columbia), and Connee Boswell with Russ Morgan's Orchestra (Decca). The song made #1 on "Your Hit Parade" and was on the survey for thirteen weeks.

Let It Whip. w/m Reginald Andrews and Leon Chancler, 1982. #1 R&B and crossover Top 10 Pop chart record by The Dazz Band (Motown).

Let Love Come Between Us. w/m Joe Sobotka and John Wyker III, 1967. Top 40 record by James and Bobby Purify.

Let Me. w/m Mark Lindsay, 1969. Top 20 record by Paul Revere and The Raiders (Columbia).

Let Me Be. w/m P. F. Sloan, 1965. Recorded by The Turtles (White Whale).

Let Me Be Good to You. w/m Isaac Hayes, David Porter, and Carl Wells, 1966. Recorded by Carla Thomas (Stax).

Let Me Belong to You. w. Peter Udell, m. Gary Geld, 1961. Chart record by Brian Hyland (ABC-Paramount).

Let Me Be the Clock. w/m William "Smokey" Robinson, 1980. Recorded and produced by Smokey Robinson (Tamla).

Let Me Be the One. w/m Lewis Martine, 1987. Top 10 record by the female disco trio, Exposé, from their debut album "Exposure" (Arista).

Let Me Be the One. w/m David Foster, 1986. Chart single by the British brother-sister quintet Five Star (RCA).

Let Me Be the One. w/m Paul Blevins, Joe Hobson, and W. S. Stevenson, 1953. Introduced and recorded by Hank Locklin (4 Star).

Let Me Be There. w/m John Rostil, 1974. Olivia Newton-John's first gold record (MCA).

Let Me Be Your Angel. w/m Bunny Hill and Narada Michael Walden, 1980. Crossover (R&B/Pop) chart record by soul singer Stacey Lattisaw (Cotillion).

Let Me Call You Sweetheart. w/m Beth Slater Whitson and Leo Friedman, 1910. This was always a sing-along favorite. Best-selling record by The Peerless Quartet (Columbia). In films, it was sung by Betty Grable in (MM) *Coney Island*, 1943; sung and danced by Gene Kelly in (MM) *Thousands Cheer*, 1943; sung by Beatrice Kay in *Billy Rose's Diamond Horseshoe*, 1945; heard in (MM) *The Rose*, starring Bette Midler, 1979.

Let Me Do It My Way. w/m David Battaglia and Julius Dixon, 1962. Featured and recorded by Jo Ann Campbell (Cameo).

Let Me Down Easy. w/m Bryan Adams and Jim Vallance, 1986. Recorded by the British singer Roger Daltrey (Atlantic).

Let Me Entertain You. w. Stephen Sondheim, m. Jule Styne, 1959. From (TM) *Gypsy*. First sung by Jacqueline Mayro and Karen Moore, as children; then by Lane Bradbury and Sandra Church, as the grown children. In the film version (MM) *Gypsy*, 1962, it was sung by Natalie Wood.

Let Me Give My Happiness to You. w/m George Posford and Douglas Furber, 1933. An English hit made popular in the U.S. via recordings of Ray Noble's Band (HMV/Victor); Lew Stone's band, vocal by Al Bowlly (Br. Decca); Jessie Matthews (Columbia). U.S. recording by Ted Weems, vocal by Elmo Tanner (Bluebird).

Let Me Go. w/m Ray Parker, Jr., 1982. Recorded by Ray Parker, Jr. (Arista).

Let Me Go, Devil. w/m Jenny Lou Carson, 1953. Introduced and recorded by Georgie Shaw (Decca). See **Let Me Go, Lover!**

Let Me Go, Lover! w/m Jenny Lou Carson, Al Hill (pseud. for Kay Twomey, Fred Wise,

Ben Weisman), 1954. Original song (see "Let Me Go, Devil") was retitled with a new lyric to be used on a CBS-TV "Studio One" play. As the new lyric writers were members of ASCAP, but the original writer (Carson) and the publisher were with BMI, and at a time when a song could not be shared between affiliates of different performing rights organizations, the new contributors wrote under a pseudonym, choosing half the name of the publisher, Hill and Range. Joan Weber, whose record was used on the TV show, had her only hit, a #1 record (Columbia). Other Pop chart versions by Teresa Brewer, with The Lancers (Coral); Patti Page (Mercury); and a #1 C&W chart version by Hank Snow (RCA).

Let Me Go Home, Whiskey. w/m Shifte Henry, 1953. R&B record by Amos Milburn (Aladdin).

Let Me Go the Right Way. w/m Berry Gordy, Jr., 1962. Introduced and recorded by The Supremes (Motown).

Let Me Go to Him. w. Hal David, m. Burt Bacharach, 1970. Top 40 record by Dionne Warwick (Scepter).

Let Me In. w/m Yvonne Baker, 1962. Top 10 record by The Sensations (Argo).

Let Me In. w/m Bob Merrill, 1951. Leading records by The Fontane Sisters, with Texas Jim Robertson (RCA Victor); Blue Barron, vocal by Johnny Goodfellow and the Blue Notes (MGM); Bobby Wayne, with Richard Hayman's Orchestra (London).

Let Me Know. w/m Slim Willet, 1953. Introduced and recorded by Slim Willet (King).

Let Me Linger Longer in Your Arms. w. Cliff Friend, m. Abel Baer, 1924. Popular song in vaudeville and on radio. The Peerless Quartet, lead vocal by Henry Burr, had a successful record (Victor), 1926.

Let Me Love You. w/m Bart Howard, 1954. Introduced and featured by Mabel Mercer (Atlantic).

Let Me Love You Tonight. w/m Dan Greer, Jeff Wilson, and Steve Woodard, 1980. Top 10 record by the group Pure Prairie League (Casablanca).

Let Me Love You Tonight. w. Mitchell Parish, m. Rene Touzet, 1944. From a Cuban song "No Te Importe Saber." First U.S. recording by Woody Herman, vocal by Billie Rogers, 1942, but released two years later (Decca). Popular recordings by Xavier Cugat and Orchestra (Columbia), Joan Brooks (Musicraft), Frances Langford (ARA). In 1947, it was coupled by Nellie Lutcher with her hit "He's a Real Gone Guy" (q.v.) (Capitol).

Let Me Off Uptown. w/m Redd Evans and Earl Bostic, 1941. Introduced and recorded by Gene Krupa, vocal by Anita O'Day and Roy Eldridge, with a featured trumpet solo by the latter (Okeh).

Let Me Serenade You. w/m John Finley, 1973. Top 20 record by Three Dog Night (Dunhill).

Let Me Sing and I'm Happy. w/m Irving Berlin, 1930. Introduced by Al Jolson in (MM) *Mammy*, and recorded by him (Brunswick). Other popular versions by Ruth Etting (Columbia); Gene Austin (Victor); Ben Selvin's Orchestra, vocal by Smith Ballew (Columbia); Sid Gary (Velvetone). Jolson sang it on the soundtrack for Larry Parks in (MM) *The Jolson Story*, 1946. The clip was used in a montage in (MM) *Jolson Sings Again*, 1949. The performance was released as a record (Decca).

Let Me Tell You About Love. w/m Joe Souter, 1989. Hit Country single by The Judds (RCA).

Let Me Tickle Your Fancy. w/m Jermaine Jackson, Paul M. Jackson, Jr., Marilyn McLeod, Pamela Sawyer, 1982. Recorded by ex-Jackson 5 brother, Jermaine Jackson (Motown).

Let Me Touch You. w/m Kenny Gamble and Leon Huff, 1987. Top 10 R&B chart record by The O'Jays (Philadelphia International).

Let Me Try Again. w. Sammy Cahn and Paul Anka (Engl.), m. Claude André Vasoir, 1973. Original French song, "Laisse Moi le Temps," words by Michel Jourdan. English version recorded by Frank Sinatra (Reprise).

Let Me Up (I've Had Enough). w/m Tom Petty and Mike Campbell, 1987. Title song of the album by Tom Petty and The Heartbreakers (MCA).

Let My Love Open the Door. w/m Peter Townshend, 1980. Top 10 record by the British singer/writer Peter Townshend (Atco).

Let My Song Fill Your Heart. w/m Ernest Charles, 1936. Popular concert song which, in 1947, Eileen Farrell featured, recorded (Decca), and used as the theme for her radio show The Family Hour.

Let Old Mother Nature Have Her Way. w/m Loys Southerland and Louie Clark, 1951. Leading record by Carl Smith (Columbia).

Let's All Sing Like the Birdies Sing. w. Robert Hargreaves and Stanley J. Damerell, m. Tolchard Evans and H. Tilsley, 1932. This English novelty was featured and recorded in the U.S. by Ben Bernie and "all the lads" (Brunswick).

Let's Be Buddies. w/m Cole Porter, 1940. Introduced by Ethel Merman and eight-year-old Joan Carroll in (TM) *Panama Hattie*. Because of child labor laws, Carroll was not allowed to sing, but was able to speak on stage. Porter solved the problem of a duet by writing a recitation for her to do with Merman. Buddy Clark recorded it (Okeh). Ann Sothern and Virginia O'Brien sang it in (MM) *Panama Hattie*, 1942.

Let's Begin. w. Otto Harbach, m. Jerome Kern, 1933. Sung by George Murphy and reprised by Ray Middleton, Bob Hope, and Tamara in (TM) *Roberta*. Emil Coleman recorded it, coupled with *Smoke Gets in Your Eyes* (q.v.) from the same show (Columbia). Performed by Fred Astaire in the 1935 film version (MM) *Roberta*.

Let's Be Sweethearts Again. w/m Jerry Marlowe and Eddie Maxwell, 1948. Featured and recorded by Margaret Whiting (Capitol).

Let's Call a Heart a Heart. w. Johnny Burke, m. Arthur Johnston, 1936. Introduced by Bing Crosby in (MM) *Pennies from Heaven* and recorded by him (Decca). Also recorded by Billie Holiday (Vocalion) and Artie Shaw and his Orchestra, with vocal by Peg La Centra (Brunswick).

Let's Call It a Day. w. Lew Brown, m. Ray Henderson, 1933. Introduced by Carolyn Nolte and Milton Watson in (TM) *Strike Me Pink*. Featured on radio by Frank Munn and recorded by him with the Arden-Ohman Orchestra (Victor).

Let's Call the Whole Thing Off. w. Ira Gershwin, m. George Gershwin, 1937. Introduced by Fred Astaire and Ginger Rogers in (MM) *Shall We Dance*. Among records: Astaire, with Johnny Green's Orchestra (Brunswick); Eddy Duchin, vocal by Jerry Cooper (Victor); Jimmy Dorsey (Decca); Billie Holiday (Vocalion); The Ink Spots (Decca).

Let's Clean Up the Ghetto. w/m Cary Gilbert, Kenny Gamble, and Leon Huff, 1977. The song was co-written and produced by the owners of the record company, Gamble and Huff, with all profits earmarked for a charity project. It was recorded by a group comprised of singing stars Lou Rawls, Billy Paul, Teddy Pendergass, The O'Jays, Archie Bell, and Dee Dee Sharp, who called themselves, for the session, The Philadelphia International All Stars (Philadelphia International).

Let's Dance. w/m David Bowie, 1983. #1 gold single, title song of the platinum album by English star David Bowie (EMI America).

Let's Dance. w/m Chris Montez, 1962. Top 10 record by Chris Montez (Monogram).

Let's Dance w/m Fanny Baldridge, Gregory Stone, and Joseph Bonime, 1935. Based on the 4th theme of Carl Maria Von Weber's *Invitation to the Dance*, this was the opening theme song of Benny Goodman and his Orchestra, who recorded it (Columbia). The

Goodman Band played it in (MM) *Sweet and Low Down* in 1944. In (MM) *The Benny Goodman Story*, 1956 Goodman dubbed the clarinet solo for Steve Allen who portrayed him in the film.

Let's Do It (Let's Fall in Love). w/m Cole Porter, 1928. Introduced by Irene Bordoni and Arthur Margetson in (TM) *Paris*. It was sung by Ginny Simms in the Porter biography (MM) *Night and Day*, 1945. In (MM) *Anything Goes*, 1956, it was interpolated as part of a dream ballet featuring Zizi Jeanmaire. Frank Sinatra and Shirley MacLaine interpolated it in (MM) *Can Can*, 1960.

Let's Do It Again. w/m Curtis Mayfield, 1975. Title song from (MP) *Let's Do It Again*. #1 gold record by The Staple Singers (Curtom).

Let's Do It Again. w/m Desmond O'Connor and Ray Hartley, 1950. British song. Bestselling U.S. recording by Alan Dale (Columbia).

Let's Do the Freddie. w/m Doc Pomus and Dave Appell, 1965. Chart record by Chubby Checker (Parkway).

Let's Face the Music and Dance. w/m Irving Berlin, 1936. Sung by Fred Astaire and danced by him with Ginger Rogers in (MM) *Follow the Fleet*. It was heard in the background of (MM) *There's No Business Like Show Business* in 1954. Leading records: Astaire (Brunswick); Ray Noble and his Orchestra (Victor).

Let's Fall in Love. w. Ted Koehler, m. Harold Arlen, 1934. Arlen's first song written especially for a film. It was introduced by Art Jarrett and reprised by Ann Sothern in (MM) *Let's Fall in Love*. It was sung by Don Ameche and Dorothy Lamour in the remake of that film (MP) *Slightly French*, 1949; by Robert Cummings in (MP) *Tell It to the Judge*, 1949; heard in (MM) *Sunny Side of the Street*, 1951; sung by Judy Holliday and Jack Lemmon in (MP) *It Should Happen to You*, 1954; played by pianist Carmen Cavallaro, dubbing for Tyrone Power in the title role of (MM) *The Eddy Duchin Story*, 1956; sung by Jack Jones in (MM) *Juke Box Rhythm*, 1959; and an extract was sung by Bing Crosby in (MM) *Pepe*, 1960. Revived by Peaches and Herb (Date), 1967.

Let's Fall to Pieces Together. w/m Dickey Lee, Tommy Rocco, and Johnny Russell, 1984. #1 Country chart record by George Strait (MCA).

Lets Fly Away. w/m Cole Porter, 1930. Sung by Charles King and Hope Williams in (TM) *The New Yorkers*. Recorded by Lee Wiley (Liberty Music Shop).

Let's Get Away from It All. w. Tom Adair, m. Matt Dennis, 1941. Top 10 record by Tommy Dorsey, vocal by Frank Sinatra, Connie Haines, and the Pied Pipers (Victor).

Let's Get It On. w/m Marvin Gaye and Edward Townshend, 1973. #1 record by Marvin Gaye (Tamla).

Let's Get Lost. w. Frank Loesser, m. Jimmy McHugh, 1943. Introduced by Mary Martin in (MM) *Happy Go Lucky*. #1 record by Vaughn Monroe, with The Four Lee Sisters and his Orchestra (Victor). Other top records by Kay Kyser, vocal by Julie Conway, Harry Babbitt, Max Williams, and Jack Martin (Columbia); Jimmy Dorsey, vocal by Bob Eberly (Decca).

Let's Get Serious. w/m Lee Garrett and Stevie Wonder, 1980. #1 R&B and Top 10 Pop chart record by Jermaine Jackson (Motown).

Let's Get Together. w/m Richard Sherman and Robert Sherman, 1961. From the (MP) *The Parent Trap*, starring Hayley Mills, who then had a hit record (Vista).

Let's Get Together. m. Chick Webb, 1934. The theme song of and recorded by Chick Webb and his Band (Columbia). Arranged, and allegedly composed, by Edgar Sampson.

Let's Get Together. See **Get Together.**

Let's Give Love Another Chance. w. Harold Adamson, m. Jimmy McHugh, 1937.

Introduced by Lily Pons in (MM) *Hitting a New High.*

Let's Give Three Cheers for Love. w. Mack Gordon, m. Harry Revel, 1934. Introduced by Lanny Ross in (MM) *College Rhythm.* In addition to Ross's recording (Brunswick), there were releases by the bands of Little Jack Little (Columbia), Tom Coakley (Victor), and Jimmie Grier (Brunswick).

Let's Go! w/m Wang Chung, 1987. Top 10 single by the British group Wang Chung (Geffen).

Let's Go. w/m Ric Ocasek, 1979. Recorded by the group The Cars (Elektra).

Let's Go, Let's Go, Let's Go. w/m Hank Ballard, 1960. Hit record by Hank Ballard and The Midnighters (King).

Let's Go All the Way. w/m Gary Cooper, 1986. Top 10 single by the duo Sly Fox (Capitol).

Let's Go Back to the Waltz. w/m Irving Berlin, 1962. Introduced by Nanette Fabray and chorus in (TM) *Mr. President.*

Let's Go Bavarian. w. Harold Adamson, m. Burton Lane, 1933. Performed by Fred Astaire and Joan Crawford in (MM) *Dancing Lady.* George Olsen, with vocal by Ethel Shutta and Fran Frey, had a popular record (Victor).

Let's Go Crazy. w/m Prince Rogers Nelson, 1984. Introduced by Prince and The Revolution in (MM) *Purple Rain,* and on their #1 gold record (Warner Bros.).

Let's Go Eat Worms in the Garden. w. Paul James (pseud. for James Paul Warburg), m. Kay Swift, 1930. Introduced by Joe Cook in (TM) *Fine and Dandy.*

Let's Go Fly a Kite. w/m Richard M. Sherman and Robert B. Sherman, 1963. Introduced by Glynis Johns and David Tomlinson in (MM) *Mary Poppins.*

Let's Go Get Stoned. w/m Nicholas Ashford, Valerie Simpson, and Joseph Armstead,

1966. Top 40 record by Ray Charles (ABC/ TRC).

Let's Go Steady Again. w/m Howard Greenfield and Neil Sedaka, 1963. Introduced and recorded by Neil Sedaka (RCA).

Let's Go to Church (Next Sunday Morning). w/m Steve Allen, 1950. Top recording by Margaret Whiting and Jimmy Wakely (Capitol).

Let's Go West Again. w/m Irving Berlin, 1950. Originally written for *Annie Get Your Gun,* but deleted. The recordings made this year were the last by both Al Jolson (Decca) and Eddy Duchin, who recorded it with his Orchestra, vocal by Tommy Mercer (Columbia).

Let's Groove. w/m Maurice Wright and Wayne Vaughn, 1981. #1 R&B, Top 10 Pop chart record by Earth, Wind & Fire (ARC).

Let's Hang On. w/m Bob Crewe, Sandy Linzer, and Denny Randell, 1965. Top 10 record by The Four Seasons (Philips). Revived by Barry Manilow with a Top 40 record (Arista), 1982.

Let's Have Another Cigarette. w. Herb Magidson, m. Allie Wrubel, 1937. Introduced by Harriet Hilliard and Gene Raymond in (MM) *Life of the Party.* Hilliard recorded it with Ozzie Nelson's Orchestra (Bluebird). Among other disc versions, Bunny Berigan (Victor) and Jan Garber (Brunswick).

Let's Have Another Cup of Coffee. w/m Irving Berlin, 1932. Introduced by J. Harold Murray and Katherine Carrington in (TM) *Face the Music.* The song was used as the theme song of the long-running radio show, The Maxwell House Show Boat, starring Lanny Ross and Annette Hanshaw. Ethel Merman sang it in (MM) *There's No Business Like Show Business,* 1954.

Let's Have a Party. w/m Phil Baxter, Cliff Friend, and Joe Haymes, 1932. Joe Haymes's band recorded this song twice in 1932 (Victor, Columbia).

Let's Hear It for the Boy. w. Dean Pitchford, m. Tom Snow, 1984. Introduced on the soundtrack of (MP) *Footloose* by Deniece Williams. Nominated for an Academy Award. The single release became a #1 gold record (Columbia).

Let's Invite Them Over. w/m Onie Wheeler, 1963. C&W chart record by George Jones and Melba Montgomery (United Artists).

Let's Kiss and Make Up. w. Ira Gershwin, m. George Gershwin, 1927. Introduced by Fred and Adele Astaire in (TM) *Funny Face*. Fred Astaire sang it in (MM) *Funny Face*, 1957.

Let's Kiss and Make Up. w. Joseph McCarthy, m. Harry Tierney, 1922. From (TM) *Up She Goes*.

Let's K-nock K-nees. w. Mack Gordon, m. Harry Revel, 1934. Performed by Edward Everett Horton and Betty Grable in (MM) *The Gay Divorcée*.

Let's Live a Little. w/m Ruth E. Coletharp and Vic McAlpin, 1951. Featured and recorded by Carl Smith (Columbia).

Let's Live for Today. w. Michael Julien (Engl.), Mogol and D. Shapiro (Ital.), m. Mogol and D. Shapiro, 1967. Italian song. Top 10 record in English by The Grass Roots (Dunhill).

Let's Lock the Door (and Throw Away the Key). w/m Roy Alfred and Wes Farrell, 1965. Popular recording by Jay and The Americans (United Artists).

Let's Love. w/m Richie Ferraris and Norman Kaye, 1959. Featured and recorded by Johnny Mathis (Columbia).

Let's Make Memories Tonight. w. Lew Brown and Charles Tobias, m. Sam H. Stept, 1939. Introduced in (TM) *Yokel Boy* by Lois January. Featured and recorded by Kenny Baker (Victor) and Horace Heidt and his Orchestra (Brunswick).

Let's Make Up Before We Say Goodnight. w/m Lynn Duddy, Joan Edwards, and

Julius Schachter, 1953. Introduced and recorded by Julius La Rosa, with Archie Bleyer's Orchestra (Cadence).

Let's Misbehave. w/m Cole Porter, 1928. Because of the close relationship in lyric content to "Let's Do It," this was dropped from (TM) *Paris* before coming to Broadway. It also was sung by Irene Bordoni. It had previously been heard in *La Revue des Ambassadeurs* in Paris in 1927. Irving Aaronson and His Commanders who performed in both productions recorded it (Victor). It was then published as an independent song.

Let's Not Be Sensible. w. Sammy Cahn, m. James Van Heusen, 1962. Introduced in the last of the Bob Hope-Bing Crosby "road" pictures, *The Road to Hong Kong*, by Bing Crosby and Joan Collins.

Let's Not Talk About Love. w/m Cole Porter, 1941. Sung by Danny Kaye and Eve Arden in (TM) *Let's Face It* and recorded by Kaye (Columbia).

Let's Not Waste a Moment. w/m Jerry Herman, 1961. Introduced by Robert Weede in (TM) *Milk and Honey*.

Let's Put It All Together. w/m Luigi Creatore, Hugo Peretti, and George David Weiss, 1974. Top 20 record by The Stylistics (Avco).

Let's Put Our Heads Together. w. E. Y. Harburg, m. Harold Arlen, 1937. From (MM) *Gold Diggers of 1937*, it was introduced by Dick Powell and Joan Blondell, and then recorded by Powell (Decca).

Let's Put Out the Lights and Go to Sleep. w/m Herman Hupfeld, 1932. Sung by Harry Richman, Lily Damita, and Bert Lahr in (TM) *George White's Music Hall Follies*. Popular recordings by Rudy Vallee (Columbia), Bing Crosby (Brunswick), and Paul Whiteman, featuring Ramona (Victor).

Let's Say Goodbye. w/m Noël Coward, 1939. Recorded by Nöel Coward (Victor) and Gertrude Lawrence (Decca).

Let's Say Goodbye Like We Said Hello. w/m Ernest Tubb and Jimmie Skinner, 1948. Introduced and featured by Ernest Tubb (Decca).

Let's Say Goodnight 'Til It's Morning. w. Otto Harbach and Oscar Hammerstein II, m. Jerome Kern, 1925. Introduced by Mary Hay and Jack Donahue in (TM) *Sunny.*

Let's Sing Again. w. Gus Kahn, m. Jimmy McHugh, 1936. Bobby Breen, at the age of eight, introduced this in his first film (MM) *Let's Sing Again,* and on his first record (Decca). Also recorded by Fats Waller (Victor); Ted Weems, vocal by Elmo Tanner (Decca); Mal Hallett (Vocalion).

Let's Sit and Talk About You. w. Dorothy Fields, m. Jimmy McHugh, 1929. Introduced by Mary Lawlor and Allen Kearns in (TM) *Hello, Daddy.* Ben Pollack, whose band played in the musical, recorded the song twice this year, with his own band (Victor) and with The Louisiana Rhythm Kings (Okeh).

Let's Spend the Night Together. w/m Mick Jagger and Keith Richards, 1967. Recorded by The Rolling Stones (London).

Let's Start All Over Again. w/m Joel Hirschhorn and Al Kasha, 1966. Recorded by Ronnie Dove (Diamond).

Let's Start Love Over. w/m Miles Jaye, 1987. Top 10 R&B chart record by Miles Jaye (Island).

Let's Start the New Year Right. w/m Irving Berlin, 1942. Introduced by Bing Crosby in (MM) *Holiday Inn.* Crosby's recording (Decca) was coupled with "White Christmas," (q.v.) the all-time best-seller.

Let's Stay Together. w/m Al Green, Al Jackson, and Willie Mitchell, 1972. #1 gold record by Al Green (Hi). Instrumental version by Isaac Hayes (Enterprise). Revived by Tina Turner (Capitol), 1984.

Let's Stop Talkin' About It. w/m Rory Bourke, Rafe Van Hoy, and Deborah Allen, 1984. #1 Country chart record by Janie Fricke (Columbia).

Let's Stop the Clock. w. Haven Gillespie, m. J. Fred Coots, 1939. Featured and recorded by the bands of Jimmy Dorsey (Decca), Horace Heidt (Brunswick), Johnny Messner (Bluebird).

Let's Take an Old Fashioned Walk. w/m Irving Berlin, 1949. Introduced by Eddie Albert and Allyn McLerie in (TM) *Miss Liberty.* Chart records: Perry Como (RCA Victor), Frank Sinatra and Doris Day (Columbia).

Let's Take an Old-Fashioned Walk. 1907. Ada Jones and Billy Murray had a #1 best-selling record (Columbia).

Let's Take a Walk Around the Block. w. Ira Gershwin and E. Y. Harburg, m. Harold Arlen, 1934. Introduced by Earl Oxford and Dixie Dunbar in (TM) *Life Begins at 8:40.*

Let's Take the Long Way Around the World. w/m Archie Jordan and Naomi Martin, 1978. Hit Country record by Ronnie Milsap (RCA).

Let's Take the Long Way Home. w. Johnny Mercer, m. Harold Arlen, 1944. Introduced by Bing Crosby and Betty Hutton in (MM) *Here Come the Waves.* Best-selling records by Jo Stafford (Capitol) and Cab Calloway (Columbia).

Let's Talk About My Sweetie. w. Gus Kahn, m. Walter Donaldson, 1926. Nineteen-year-old Ruth Etting's first record success (Columbia). Also recorded by Paul Ash's Orchestra (Columbia) and blues singer Rosa Henderson (Columbia).

Let's Think About Living. w/m Boudleaux Bryant, 1960. Novelty hit by Bob Luman (Warner Bros.).

Let's Turkey Trot. w/m Gerry Goffin and Jack Keller, 1963. Recorded by Little Eva (Dimension).

Let's Twist Again. w/m Kal Mann and Dave Appell, 1961. Hit record by Chubby Checker.

Grammy Winner (NARAS) for Best Rock and Roll Recording, 1961.

Let's Wait Awhile. w/m James Harris III, Terry Lewis, Janet Jackson, and Reginald Andrews, 1987. #1 R&B and Top 10 Pop chart record by Janet Jackson, the youngest of the Jacksons (A&M)

Let's Work. w/m Mick Jagger and Dave Stewart, 1987. Chart single and track from the album "Primitive Cool" by Mick Jagger (Columbia).

Letter, The. w/m Wayne Thompson, 1967. #1 gold record by The Box Tops (Mala). Hit records by The Arbors (Date), 1969; and Joe Cocker, with Leon Russell and The Shelter People (A&M), 1970. A new version with additional lyrics by Dave Kolin, titled "Vanna, Pick Me a Letter," was recorded on the album "Dr. Dave" (TSR), 1987. This referred to Vanna White, the hostess of the popular TV game show "Wheel of Fortune."

Letter Full of Tears. w/m Don Covay, 1962. Recorded by Gladys Knight and The Pips (Fury).

Letters Have No Arms. w/m Archie Gibson and Ernest Tubb, 1950. Country hit, recorded by Ernest Tubb (Decca).

Letter Song. w. William Le Baron, m. Ernest R. Ball, 1919. From (TM) *Apple Blossoms.*

Letter Song, The. w. Stanislaus Stange, m. Oscar Straus, 1909. From (TM) *The Chocolate Soldier.* Also in (MM) *The Chocolate Soldier* in 1941.

Letters That Cross in the Mail. w/m Rupert Holmes, 1974. Featured and recorded by Barbra Streisand (Columbia).

Letter That Johnny Walker Read, The. w/m Ray Benson, Chris Frayn, and Leroy Preston, 1975. Top 10 Country chart record by the group Asleep at the Wheel (Capitol).

Let That Be a Lesson to You. w. Johnny Mercer, m. Richard A. Whiting, 1938. Performed by the majority of the leading players in the cast of (MM) *Hollywood Hotel,* namely: Dick Powell, Rosemary Lane, Benny Goodman and his Orchestra, Johnny "Scat" Davis, Ted Healy, and Mabel Todd. Louis Armstrong and his Band recorded it (Decca).

Let That Be a Lesson to You. w/m Isham Jones, 1932. Featured by the Jones Orchestra and recorded by the Coon-Sanders Orchestra (Victor) and Vincent Rose's Orchestra (Perfect).

Let the Bells Keep Ringing. w/m Paul Anka, 1958. Introduced and recorded by Paul Anka (ABC-Paramount).

Let the Feeling Flow. w/m Peabo Bryson, 1982. Recorded by Peabo Bryson (Capitol).

Let the Four Winds Blow. w/m Antoine "Fats" Domino and Dave Bartholomew, 1957. First chart record by Roy Brown (Imperial), followed by Fats Domino's hit record in 1961 (Imperial).

Let the Good Times In (Open Up the Door). See **Open Up the Door.**

Let the Good Times Roll. w/m Leonard Lee, 1956. #1 R&B and Top 20 Pop Chart hit record by Shirley and Lee (Aladdin). Revived by Ray Charles in 1960 (Atlantic) and Bunny Sigler, 1967, who joined it with "Feel So Good" (q.v.) (Parkway).

Let the Good Times Roll. w/m Sam Theard and Fleecie Moore, 1946. Featured and recorded by Louis Jordan and his Tympany Five (Decca).

Let the Little Girl Dance. See **Let Her Dance.**

Let the Music Lift You Up. 1987. Top 10 Country record by Reba McEntire (MCA).

Let the Music Play. w/m Chris Barbosa and Ed Chisolm, 1984. Crossover (R&B/Pop) Top 10 gold record by Shannon [née Brenda Shannon Greene] (Mirage).

Let There Be Drums. m. Sandy Nelson and Richard Podoler, 1961. Top 10 instrumental by rock 'n' roll drummer Sandy Nelson (Imperial).

Let There Be Love. w. Ian Grant, m. Lionel Rand, 1940. Most popular records by Sammy Kaye, vocal by Tommy Ryan (Victor); Kay Kyser, vocal by Harry Babbitt (Columbia); Al Donahue, vocal by Phil Brito (Vocalion). Pearl Bailey had a well-received version, 1952 (Coral).

Let the Rest of the World Go By. w. J. Keirn Brennan, m. Ernest R. Ball, 1919. First recorded by Elizabeth Spencer and Charles Hart (Victor). Morton Downey, the popular tenor, featured it on his radio shows and recorded it (Decca), 1940. Dick Haymes and a male quartet sang it in the Ball screen bio (MM) *Irish Eyes Are Smiling*, 1944.

Let the River Run. w/m Carly Simon, 1988. Sung by Carly Simon on the soundtrack of (MP) *Working Girl* and its album (Arista). Winner Academy Award, Best Song.

Let the Sunshine In (a.k.a. **The Flesh Failures**). w. Gerome Ragni and James Rado, m. Galt MacDermot, 1967. Billed as "The Flesh Failures," it was introduced in the Broadway musical (TM) *Hair*, and performed by James Rado, Lynn Kellogg, Melba Moore, and company. The 5th Dimension recorded it in medley with "Aquarius" (q.v.) from the same show, and were awarded a gold record and the Grammy Award (NARAS) for Record of the Year for their #1 hit (Soul City), 1969.

Let the World Keep on a Turnin'. w/m Buck Owens, 1968. Hit Country record by Buck Owens and Buddy Alan (Capitol).

Let Your Love Flow. w/m Larry Williams, 1976. #1 record by The Bellamy Brothers (Warner Bros.).

Let Yourself Go. w/m James Brown and Bud Hobgood, 1967. Recorded by James Brown (King).

Let Yourself Go. w/m Irving Berlin, 1936. Introduced by Fred Astaire and Ginger Rogers in (MM) *Follow the Fleet*. Among recordings: Astaire (Brunswick), Ray Noble and his Orchestra (Victor), Bunny Berigan and his Orchestra (Vocalion), the Boswell Sisters (Decca).

'Leven-Thirty Saturday Night. w/m Jess Kirkpatrick, Earl Burtnett, and Bill Grantham, 1930. Recorded by the bands of Burtnett (Brunswick), Fess Williams (Victor), Arthur Schutt (Okeh), Lou Gold (Harmony), Ambrose (HMV), and by singer Whispering Jack Smith (Victor).

Levon. w/m Elton John and Bernie Taupin, 1971. Top 40 record by Elton John (Uni).

Liar. w/m Russ Ballard, 1971. Introduced in an album by the British group, Argent, in the album of their name (Epic), 1969. Top 10 single by Three Dog Night (Dunhill), 1971.

Liar, Liar. w/m James J. Donna, 1965. Hit record by the University of Minnesota-formed quartet The Castaways (Soma). Revived by Debbie Harry on the soundtrack of (MP) *Married to the Mob*, 1988.

Liberty Bell, It's Time to Ring Again. w. Joe Goodwin, m. Halsey K. Mohr, 1917. A patriotic song from World War I.

Licking Stick—Licking Stick. w/m James Brown, Bobby Byrd, and Alfred Ellis, 1968. Top 20 record by James Brown and The Famous Flames (King, Part 1).

Lick It Up. w/m Paul Stanley and Vinnie Vincent, 1983. Title song single from the album by the group Kiss (Mercury).

Lida Rose. w/m Meredith Willson, 1957. Introduced by The Buffalo Bills in (TM) *The Music Man*, and sung by them in the film version (MM) *The Music Man*, 1962.

Lido Shuffle. w/m David Paich and Boz Scaggs, 1977. Top 20 record by Boz Scaggs (Columbia).

Liebesfreud. m. Fritz Kreisler, 1910. A popular composition for violin and piano.

Liebeslied. m. Fritz Kreisler, 1910. A composition for violin and piano.

Liechtensteiner Polka. w/m Edmund Kotscher and R. Lindt, 1957. German song, recorded by the accordionist-bandleader Will Glahe (London).

Lie Detector. w. Jack Heinz, m. Robert Lissauer, 1955. Country record by Arlie Duff with The Anita Kerr Singers, coupled with "I Dreamed of a Hillbilly Heaven" (q.v.) (Decca).

Lies. w/m Jonathan Butler, 1987. Top 10 R&B/Pop chart crossover record by Jonathan Butler (Jive).

Lies. w/m Buddy Randell and Beau Charles, 1965. Recorded by The Knickerbockers (Challenge).

Lies. w. George E. Springer, m. Harry Barris, 1930. Recorded by Gene Austin (Perfect) and Benny Kreuger (Brunswick). Later cuts by Perry Como (Victor), Snooky Lanson (London), Julia Lee (Capitol).

Lie to Me. w/m Brook Benton and Margie Singleton, 1962. Introduced and recorded by Brook Benton (Mercury).

Lie to You for Your Love. w/m Frankie Miller, Jeff Barry, David Bellamy, and Howard Bellamy, 1985. Top 10 Country chart record by The Bellamy Brothers (MCA).

Life Begins at Sweet Sixteen. w. Jack Yellen, m. Ray Henderson, 1936. Introduced by Gracie Barrie in (TM) *George White's Scandals, 12th Edition.*

Life Begins When You're in Love. w. Lew Brown and Harry Richman, m. Victor Schertzinger, 1936. Introduced in (MM) *The Music Goes 'Round* by Harry Richman who also recorded it (Decca). Other disc versions: Isham Jones, vocal by Woody Herman (Decca); Teddy Wilson (Brunswick); Richard Himber, vocal by Allen Stuart (Victor).

Life Can Be Beautiful. w. Harold Adamson, m. Jimmy McHugh, 1947. From (MP) *Smash Up.* Recorded by Harry James, vocal by Marion Morgan (Columbia).

Life During Wartime (This Ain't No Party . . . This Ain't No Disco . . . This Ain't No Foolin' Around). w/m David Byrne, 1979. Recorded by the quartet Talking Heads (Sire).

Life Gets Better. w/m Graham Parker, 1983. Single from the LP "The Real Macaw" by the English singer Graham Parker (Arista).

Life Gets Tee-Jus, Don't It. w/m Carson Robinson, 1948. Best-selling records by Carson Robinson (MGM), Tex Williams (Capitol).

Life Goes to a Party. m. Harry James and Benny Goodman, 1937. Recorded by the Goodman band (Victor) and the James band (Brunswick).

Life I Lead, The. w/m Richard M. Sherman and Robert B. Sherman, 1964. Introduced by David Tomlinson in (MM) *Mary Poppins.*

Life in a Looking Glass. w. Leslie Bricusse, m. Henry Mancini, 1986. Introduced on the soundtrack of (MP) *That's Life!* by Tony Bennett. Nominated for an Academy Award.

Life in a Northern Town. w/m Nick Laird-Clowes and Gilbert Gabriel, 1986. Top 10 record written by two-thirds of the English trio The Dream Academy (Warner Bros.).

Life in One Day. w/m Howard Jones, 1985. Recorded by the English singer/songwriter Howard Jones (Elektra).

Life in the Fast Lane. w/m Glenn Frey, Don Henley, and Joe Walsh, 1977. Written by members of The Eagles, who had a Top 10 record (Asylum).

Life Is a Beautiful Thing. w/m Jay Livingston and Ray Evans, 1951. Introduced by Dinah Shore in (MM) *Aaron Slick from Punkin Crick,* and recorded by her (RCA Victor) and Evelyn Knight (Decca).

Life Is a Carnival. w/m Rick Danko, Levon Helm, and Robbie Robertson, 1971. Recorded by The Band (Capitol).

Life Is a Rock (But the Radio Rolled Me). w/m Norman Dolph and Paul DiFranco, 1974.

Top 10 novelty recorded by the studio group Reunion (RCA).

Life Is a Song (Let's Sing It Together). w. Joe Young, m. Fred E. Ahlert, 1935. Introduced on radio by Frank Parker.

Life is Just a Bowl of Cherries. w. B. G. DeSylva and Lew Brown, m. Ray Henderson, 1931. Introduced by Ethel Merman in (MM) *George White's Scandals, 11th edition.* Rudy Vallee introduced it on radio and had a hit record (Victor). Sleepy Hall and his Collegians (Melotone), Eubie Blake's Orchestra (Crown), and Frank Parker (Columbia) also had a hand in its popularity. Joan Davis and Jack Haley performed it in (MM) *George White's Scandals of 1945.*

Life Is Only What You Make It, After All. w. Edgar Smith, m. A. Baldwin Sloane, 1910. From (TM) *Tillie's Nightmare.*

Life Is So Peculiar. w/m Johnny Burke and James Van Heusen, 1950. In (MM) *Mr. Music,* Bing Crosby, Peggy Lee, and the Merry Macs introduced the song vocally. Marge and Gower Champion reprised it as a dance, and later on in the film Groucho Marx and Crosby did it in a sketch. Popular records were made by Bing Crosby and The Andrews Sisters (Decca) and Louis Armstrong and Louis Jordan (Decca).

Life Is What You Make It. w. Johnny Mercer, m. Marvin Hamlisch, 1971. Sung on the soundtrack of (MP) *Kotch* by Johnny Mathis. Nominated for Academy Award.

Life of the Party, The. w. Fred Ebb, m. John Kander, 1968. Introduced by David Wayne in (TM) *The Happy Time.*

Life's a Funny Proposition After All. w/m George M. Cohan, 1904. Introduced by Cohan in the title role of (TM) *Little Johnny Jones.*

Life's Been Good. w/m Joe Walsh, 1978. Recorded by Joe Walsh (Asylum).

Life's Highway. w/m Richard Leigh and Roger Murrah, 1986. #1 Country chart record by Steve Wariner (MCA).

Lifetime of Loneliness, A. w. Hal David, m. Burt Bacharach, 1965. Recorded by Jackie DeShannon, produced by the writers (Imperial).

Life to Go. w/m George Jones, 1959. Leading C&W record by Stonewall Jackson (Columbia).

Life Turned Her That Way. w/m Harlan Howard, 1967. Country chart record by Mel Tillis (Kapp). #1 record by Country singer Ricky Van Shelton (Columbia), 1988.

Life Upon the Wicked Stage. w. Oscar Hammerstein II, m. Jerome Kern, 1928. Introduced by Eva Puck and the female ensemble in (TM) *Show Boat.* In the 1936 adaptation (MM) *Show Boat,* it was performed by Queenie Smith and Sammy White; in the 1951 version, by Marge and Gower Champion. Virginia O'Brien sang it in the Kern biography (MM) *Till the Clouds Roll By,* 1946.

Lift Every Voice and Sing. w. James W. Johnson, m. J. Rosamond Johnson, 1900.

Light at the End of the Tunnel. w. Richard Stilgoe, m. Richie Havens, 1987. Introduced in the U.S. by the company in (TM) *Starlight Express.*

Lighthouse. w/m Jim Lowe, 1953. Featured and recorded by Rusty Draper (Mercury).

Light My Fire. w/m John Densmore, Robert Krieger, Raymond Manzarek, and Jim Morrison, 1967. Written, introduced, and #1 gold record by The Doors (Elektra). José Feliciano had a Top 10 hit (RCA), 1968.

Lightning's Girl. w/m Lee Hazlewood, 1967. Top 40 record by Nancy Sinatra (Reprise).

Lightnin' Strikes. w. Lou Christie, m. Twyla Herbert, 1966. #1 gold record by Lou Christie (MGM).

Light of a Clear Blue Morning. w/m Dolly Parton, 1977. Hit Country and Pop chart record by Dolly Parton (RCA).

Light of Day. w/m Bruce Springsteen, 1987. Title song from (MM) *Light of Day*, starring Joan Jett and Michael J. Fox. It was introduced by a group created for the film, The Barbusters, whose version was on the soundtrack album and a chart single sans Fox (Blackheart).

Light of Love. w/m Charles Singleton, 1958. Featured and recorded by Peggy Lee (Capitol).

Lights Are Low, the Music Is Sweet, The. w/m Cliff Friend and Carmen Lombardo, 1934. Introduced and featured by Guy Lombardo and his Royal Canadians, vocal by Carmen Lombardo (Melotone).

Light Sings. w. Will Holt, m. Gary William Friedman, 1971. Introduced by Devin Lindsay and company in the off-Broadway musical (TM) *The Me Nobody Knows*. Recorded by The 5th Dimension (Bell).

Lights Out. w/m Peter Wolf and Don Covay, 1984. Recorded by Peter Wolf (EMI America).

Lights Out. w/m Billy Hill, 1935. Based on "taps," this ballad was introduced on radio by Ozzie Nelson and his Orchestra, vocal by Harriet Hilliard and broadcast by many bands. Among the recordings: Eddy Duchin (Victor), Dick Robertson (Champion), Spade Cooley (Victor), Little Jack Little (Columbia), Victor Young's Orchestra (Decca).

(Lights Went Out in) Massachusetts. w/m Barry Gibb, Maurice Gibb, and Robin Gibb, 1967. Written and recorded by the British trio of brothers, The Bee Gees (Atco).

Like a Baby. w/m John Madara, David White, and Len Barry, 1966. Top 40 record by Len Barry (Decca).

Like a Bolt from The Blue. w. Mitchell Parish and Irving Mills, m. Ben Oakland, 1935. Leading record: Benny Goodman, vocal by Buddy Clark (Columbia).

Like an Old Time Movie. w/m John Philips, 1967. Hit record by Scott McKenzie (Ode).

Like a Prayer. w/m Patrick Leonard and Madonna Ciccone, 1989. Hit recording by Madonna (Sire).

Like a Rock. w/m Bob Seger, 1986. Recorded by Bob Seger and The Silver Bullet Band (Capitol).

Like a Rolling Stone. w/m Bob Dylan, 1965. One of Bob Dylan's biggest hit singles (Columbia).

Like a Sad Song. w/m John Denver, 1976. Leading record by John Denver (RCA).

Like a Virgin. w/m Billy Steinberg and Tom Kelly, 1984. #1 gold record by Madonna, produced by Nile Rodgers (Sire).

Like a Young Man. w/m Jerry Herman, 1961. Introduced by Robert Weede in (TM) *Milk and Honey*.

Like He Loves Me w. Anne Caldwell, m. Vincent Youmans, 1926. Sung by Beatrice Lillie in (TM) *Oh, Please!*

Like Love. w. Dory Langdon Previn, m. André Previn, 1960. Sung by Jack Jones on his record debut (Kapp).

Like Me a Little Bit Less (Love Me a Little Bit More). w. Harold Adamson, m. Burton Lane, 1934. Introduced by Mary Carlisle in (MM) *Palooka*. Leading record by Gus Arnheim, vocal by Shirley Ross (Brunswick).

Like No Other Night. w/m Don Barnes, Jon Bettis, Jeff Carlisi, and Jim Vallance, 1986. Chart record by the sextet 38 Special (A&M).

Like Ordinary People Do. w. Lorenz Hart, m. Richard Rodgers, 1931. Sung by Ben Lyon, Inez Courtney, and Ona Munson in (MM) *The Hot Heiress*.

Like Someone in Love. w. Johnny Burke, m. James Van Heusen, 1944. Introduced by Dinah Shore in (MM) *Belle of the Yukon*. Shore (Victor) and Bing Crosby (Decca) had the most popular recordings.

Like to Get to Know You. w/m Stuart Scharf, 1968. Top 20 record by Spanky and Our Gang (Mercury).

Like Young. m. André Previn 1959. Instrumental recorded by André Previn, with David Rose's Orchestra (MGM).

Lilacs in the Rain. w. Mitchell Parish, m. Peter DeRose, 1939. Lyrics added to earlier piano piece. This was one of three major hits for DeRose this year ("Deep Purple," "The Lamp Is Low") which, collectively, were on "Your Hit Parade" for thirty-one weeks. Among recordings: Tony Martin (Decca); Dick Jurgens, vocal by Eddy Howard (Vocalion); Horace Heidt's Orchestra (Columbia).

Lilac Wine. w/m James Shelton, 1950. Introduced by Hope Foye in the short-lived revue (TM) *Dance Me a Song.*

Li'l Darlin'. m. Neal Hefti, 1958. Jazz standard, introduced and recorded by Count Basie and his Orchestra (Roulette).

Lili Marlene. w. Tommie Connor (Engl.), Hans Leip (Ger.), m. Norbert Schultze, 1944. From a German poem by Leip, written in World War I and set to music in 1939. Heard while being broadcast to the German Army in Africa, it was adopted by the British Eighth Army. Anne Shelton's English hit record (London) started the song's popularity with the Allied countries. Marlene Dietrich featured it in public appearances and on radio. Leading records by Perry Como (Victor), Hildegarde (Decca), Martha Tilton (Coral). Revived by Al Martino (Capitol), 1968.

L'il Liza Jane. w/m Countess Ada De Lachau, 1916. A favorite with male quartets and glee clubs. Among recordings are those by Papa Celestin (RWP) and Ray Bauduc's Band (Capitol).

Lilly Done the Zampoughi Every Time I Pulled Her Coattail. w/m Melvin Van Peebles, 1971. Introduced by Garrett Morris and Barbara Alston in *Ain't Supposed to Die a Natural Death.*

Li'l Red Riding Hood. w/m Ronald Blackwell, 1966. Hit record by Sam the Sham and The Pharaohs (MGM).

Lily Belle. w/m Dave Franklin and Irving Taylor, 1945. Featured and recorded by Freddy Martin, vocal by Gene Conklin and the Martin Men (Victor) and The Pied Pipers (Capitol).

Lily of Laguna. w. Paul Francis Webster, m. Ted Fio Rito, 1942. Bing Crosby and Mary Martin had a popular duet recording coupled with "Wait Till the Sun Shines, Nellie" (Decca).

Lily of the Valley w. L. Wolfe Gilbert, m. Anatole Friedland, 1917.

Limbo Rock. w/m Jon Sheldon and William E. Strange, 1962. Introduced and Top 40 instrumental by The Champs (Challenge), followed by a Top 10 vocal version by Chubby Checker (Parkway).

Limehouse Blues. w. Douglas Furber, m. Philip Braham, 1924. First performed in the London revue (TM) *A to Z* by Teddie Gerard, 1922. Introduced in the United States in (TM) *Charlot's Revue of 1924* by Gertrude Lawrence in her American stage debut. In (MM) *Ziegfeld Follies*, 1944, it was performed by Fred Astaire, Lucille Bremer, and Pamela Britton. In (MM) *Star!*, 1968, the film biography of Gertrude Lawrence, it was sung by Julie Andrews and Garrett Lewis.

Limelight. w. Neil Peart, m. Alex Lifeson and Geddy Lee, 1981. Written and recorded by the Canadian trio Rush (Mercury).

Limelight. See **Eternally.**

Lincoln, Grant, or Lee. w/m Paul Dresser, 1903.

Linda. w/m Jack Lawrence, 1947. #1 record by Buddy Clark, with Ray Noble's Orchestra (Columbia).

Linda. w/m Ann Ronell, 1944. From (MP) *The Story of G. I. Joe.* Nominated for Academy Award, 1945.

Linda. w. Ted Koehler, m. Harold Arlen, 1930. Introduced in the revue *Brown Sugar* at the Cotton Club in Harlem, New York. Arlen recorded it with Red Nichols's Orchestra (Brunswick). Early recording by Benny Goodman (Melotone).

Linda on My Mind. w/m Conway Twitty, 1975. Country hit and Pop chart record by Conway Twitty (MCA).

Ling, Ting, Tong. w/m Mable Godwin, 1955. Leading recordings by The Charms (De-Luxe) and The Five Keys (Capitol). Buddy Knox brought it back to the charts in 1961 (Liberty).

Linger Awhile. w. Harry Owens, m. Vincent Rose, 1923. The first hit for Owens. Paul Whiteman had a million-seller (Victor). Whiteman's band played it in (MM) *King of Jazz*, 1930. The song was heard in (MM) *The Great American Broadcast*, 1941, and in (MM) *Give My Regards to Broadway*, 1948.

Linger in My Arms a Little Longer, Baby. w/m Herb Magidson, 1946. Popular recording by Peggy Lee (Capitol).

Linger Longer Girl, The. w. Arthur J. Lamb, m. Alfred Solman, 1906.

Lion Sleeps Tonight, The w/m Hugo Peretti, Luigi Creatore, George David Weiss, and Albert Stanton, 1961, 1972. Based on the South African Zulu song, "Mbube," as was "Wimoweh." This version became a #1 million-seller by The Tokens (RCA Victor), 1961, and revived with a hit record by Robert John (Atlantic), 1972. See also "Wimoweh."

Lips of Wine. w. Shirley Wolfe, m. Sy Soloway, 1957. Recorded by Andy Williams (Cadence).

Lipstick and Candy and Rubbersole Shoes. w/m Bob Haymes, 1956. Featured and recorded by Julius La Rosa (RCA).

Lipstick on Your Collar. w. Edna Lewis, m. George Goehring, 1959. Hit record by Connie Francis (MGM).

Lipstick Traces (on a Cigarette). w/m Naomi Neville, 1962. Introduced and chart record by Benny Spellman (Minit), 1962, followed by The O'Jays (Imperial), 1965.

Lisbon Antigua (in Old Lisbon). w. Harry Dupree, m. Raul Portela, J. Galhardo, and A. Do Vale, 1956. First published in Portugal, 1937, as "Lisboa Antigua." Hit instrumental record by Nelson Riddle and his Orchestra (Capitol). Mitch Miller and his Orchestra also had a popular instrumental version (Columbia).

Listen, People. w/m Graham Gouldman, 1966. Introduced by the British group, Herman's Hermits, in (MM) *When the Boys Meet the Girls*, a remake of the Gershwins' *Girl Crazy*. Five non-Gershwin songs were interpolated in the film. Herman's Hermits had a Top 10 record (MGM).

Listen Here. m. Eddie Harris, 1968. Jazz instrumental by tenor saxophonist Eddie Harris (Atlantic).

Listening. w/m Irving Berlin, 1924. Introduced by Grace Moore in (TM) *Music Box Revue of 1924*, and recorded by her, accompanied by Rosario Bourdon's Orchestra (Victor).

Listen Like Thieves. w/m INXS, 1986. Written and recorded by the Australian sextet INXS (Atlantic).

Listen My Children and You Shall Hear. w. Ralph Freed, m. Burton Lane, 1937. Introduced by Martha Raye in (MM) *Double or Nothing* and recorded by Count Basie and his Orchestra (Decca).

Listen to Her Heart. w/m Tom Petty, 1978. Recorded by Tom Petty and The Heartbreakers (Shelter).

Listen to the German Band. w. Mack Gordon, m. Harry Revel, 1932. Introduced, featured, and recorded by George Olsen's Orchestra, vocal by Ethel Shutta (Victor).

Listen to the Music. w/m Tom Johnston, 1972. Top 20 record by the Doobie Brothers, of whom Johnston was lead vocalist (Warner Bros.).

Listen to What the Man Said. w/m Paul McCartney and Linda McCartney, 1975. #1 gold record by Wings (Capitol).

Listen to Your Heart   w/m Per Gessle and Mats Persson, 1989. Hit single by Roxette (EMI).

Little Alabama Coon.   w/m Hattie Starr, 1893. After initial popularity, interpolated in (TM) *Aladdin, Jr.* in 1895. Recorded by opera singers Mabel Garrison (Victor) and Frieda Hempel (Edison) about twenty-five years after its publication.

Little Angel with a Dirty Face.   w/m Dale Parker, 1950. Top 10 C&W chart record by Eddy Arnold (RCA).

Little Annie Rooney.   w/m Michael Nolan, 1890. Introduced in English music halls by Nolan. The popularity of the song reached America, where it was introduced by Annie Hart, known as "The Bowery Girl," at New York City's Old London Theatre. The song became a hit, but none of the vast sheet music royalties went to the writer, as international copyright law had not as yet been enacted. The song inspired the title for the film (MP) *Little Annie Rooney*, starring Mary Pickford, 1925.

Little Arrows.   w/m Albert Hammond and Mike Hazlewood, 1968. English song and record. Top 20 on the U.S. charts by Leapy Lee (Decca).

Little Birdies Learning How to Fly.   w. Hugh Morton, m. Gustav Kerker, 1898. From (TM) *The Telephone Girl.*

Little Birdie Told Me So, A.   w. Lorenz Hart, m. Richard Rodgers, 1926. Sung by Helen Ford in (TM) *Peggy-Ann.* It was recorded by Roger Wolfe Kahn's Orchestra (Victor) and Lee Wiley, with Joe Bushkin (Gala). The latter version, with other Wiley/Rodgers recordings, was put into an album (Monmouth-Evergreen).

Little Bird Told Me, A.   w/m Harvey O. Brooks, 1948. First recording by R&B singer-pianist Paula Watson (Supreme), followed by Evelyn Knight, whose version became a million-seller (Decca). Also popular were records by Blu Lu Parker (Capitol) and Jerry Wayne and Janette Davis (Columbia).

Little Biscuit.   w. E. Y. Harburg, m. Harold Arlen, 1957. Introduced by Ossie Davis and Josephine Premice in (TM) *Jamaica.*

Little Bit Independent, A.   w. Edgar Leslie, m. Joe Burke, 1935. Hit song revived in the fifties by Nat Cole (Capitol).

Little Bit in Love, A.   w/m Steve Earle, 1988. Top 10 Country chart record by Patty Loveless (MCA).

Little Bit in Love.   w. Betty Comden and Adolph Green, m. Leonard Bernstein, 1953. Introduced by Edith (Edie) Adams in (TM) *Wonderful Town.*

Little Bit Me, a Little Bit You, A.   w/m Neil Diamond, 1967. #2 record by The Monkees (Colgems).

Little Bit More, A.   w/m Gene McFadden, Jimmy McKinney, and Linda Vitali, 1986. #1 R&B record by Melba Moore with Freddie Jackson (Capitol).

Little Bit More, A.   w/m Bobby Gosh, 1976. Top 20 record by the group Dr. Hook (Capitol).

Little Bit of Heaven, A.   w/m Arthur Resnick and Kenny Young, 1965. Recorded by Ronnie Dove (Diamond).

Little Bit of Heaven, A (Shure They Called It Ireland).   w. J. Keirn Brennan, m. Ernest R. Ball, 1914. From (TM) *Heart of Paddy Whack.* First recorded by Charles Harrison (Victor), 1914. Best-selling versions by George MacFarlane (Victor) and John McCormack (Victor). Gloria Jean sang it as the title song in (MM) *A Little Bit of Heaven*, 1940. It was heard in Ball's film bio (MM) *Irish Eyes Are Smiling*, 1944. Dennis Morgan sang it in (MM) *My Wild Irish Rose*, 1947.

Little Bit of Love (Is All It Takes), A.   w/m Ric Wyatt, Jr. and Chris Perren, 1986. Recorded by the teenage group New Edition (MCA).

Little Bit of Soap, A.   w/m Bert Russell, 1961. Hit record by The Jarmels (Laurie).

Over the next two decades, three recordings on the same label (Bang) made the charts: The Exciters, 1966; Paul Davis, 1970, Nigel Olsson, 1979.

Little Bit o'Soul. w/m Carter-Lewis, 1967. Gold record by The Music Explosion (Laurie).

Little Bitty Girl. w/m Clint Ballard, Jr. and Fred Tobias, 1960. Coupled with the hit "Wild One" (q.v.) by Bobby Rydell (Cameo).

Little Bitty Pretty One. w/m Robert Byrd, 1957. First hit recording by R&B singer, Thurston Harris, backed by The Sharps (Aladdin). Clyde McPhatter had a popular version in 1962. Revived with a Top 20 record by The Jackson 5 (Motown) in 1972.

Little Bitty Tear, A. w/m Hank Cochran, 1962. Hit record by Burl Ives (Decca).

Little Black Book. w/m Jimmy Dean, 1962. Introduced and recorded by Jimmy Dean (Columbia).

Little Blue Man, The. w/m Fred Ebb and Paul Klein, 1958. Novelty recorded by Betty Johnson, with the voice of the Little Blue Man by Hugh Downs (Atlantic).

Little Boxes. w/m Malvina Reynolds, 1962. Featured and recorded by Pete Seeger (Columbia) and The Womenfolk (RCA).

Little Boy. w/m Jeff Barry, Ellie Greenwich, and Phil Spector, 1964. Recorded by The Crystals (Philles).

Little Boy, The. w. Al Stillman, m. Guy Wood, 1964. Featured and recorded by Tony Bennett (Columbia).

Little Boy and the Old Man. See **Little Child.**

Little Boy Blue. w. Eugene Field, m. Ethelbert Nevin, 1891.

Little Boy Called "Taps." w. Edward Madden, m. Theodore F. Morse, 1904.

Little Boy Sad. w/m Wayne Walker, 1961. Leading record by Johnny Burnette (Liberty).

Little Brown Gal. w/m Don McDiarmid, Johnny Noble, and Lee Wood, 1935. A Hawaiian song.

Little Bunch of Shamrocks, A. w. William Jerome and Andrew B. Sterling, m. Harry Von Tilzer, 1913.

Little Bungalow, A. w/m Irving Berlin, 1925. Introduced by Jack Barker and Mabel Withee in the Marx Brothers musical (TM) *The Cocoanuts*.

Little Butterfly. w/m Irving Berlin, 1923. The popular tenor, John Steel, sang it in (TM) *The Music Box Revue* and recorded it (Victor).

Little by Little. w/m Walter O'Keefe and Robert Emmet Dolan, 1929. Theme song of Little Jack Little, pianist-singer on radio and later bandleader. First recorded by Guy Lombardo and his Royal Canadians (Columbia). Red Nichols had a release (Capitol) in 1947.

Little Child. w/m Wayne Shanklin, 1956. Under original title of "Little Boy and the Old Man," it was sung by Frankie Laine and Jimmy Boyd (Columbia), 1953. With title and some lyric changes, it was recorded by Eddie Albert and Sondra Lee (Kapp) and the father-daughter team of Cab and Lael Calloway (ABC-Paramount).

Little Children. w/m Mort Shuman and J. Leslie McFarland, 1964. Recorded in England by Billy J. Kramer and The Dakotas (Imperial).

Little Church Around the Corner, The. w. Alexander Gerber, m. Sigmund Romberg, 1919. From (TM) *The Magic Melody*.

Little Curly Hair in a High Chair. w. Charles Tobias, m. Nat Simon, 1940. Introduced by Eddie Cantor on his network radio show and interpolated by him in (MP) *Forty Little Mothers*. Cantor also recorded it (Columbia).

Little Darlin'. w/m Maurice Williams, 1957. Originally recorded by The Gladiolas (Excello), of which Williams was the lead singer. Best-selling record by The Diamonds (Mercury). Revived by Dustin Hoffman and Warren Beatty in (MP) *Ishtar*, and on a single (Capitol), 1987.

Little Darling, I Need You. w. Eddie Holland, Lamont Dozier, and Brian Holland, 1966. First recorded by Marvin Gaye (Tamla). Revived by The Doobie Brothers (Warner Bros.), 1977.

Little Devil. w/m Howard Greenfield and Neil Sedaka, 1961. Introduced and recorded by Neil Sedaka (RCA)

Little Diane. w/m Dion Di Mucci, 1962. Top 10 record by the song's writer, Dion (Laurie).

Little Dipper. m. Robert Maxwell, 1959. Instrumental recorded by The Mickey Mozart Quintet (Roulette). The leader's name was a pseudonym for the harpist/composer Robert Maxwell.

Little Drops of Rain. w. E. Y. Harburg, m. Harold Arlen, 1962. Introduced on the soundtrack of the full-length cartoon (MM) *Gay Purr-ee* by Judy Garland, and reprised by Robert Goulet.

Little Drummer Boy, The. w/m Katherine Davis, Henry Onerati, and Harry Simeone, 1958. Christmas standard introduced and recorded by The Harry Simeone Chorale (20th Fox).

Little Dutch Mill. w. Ralph Freed, m. Harry Barris, 1934. Featured and recorded by Guy Lombardo and his Royal Canadians, vocal by Carmen Lombardo (Brunswick); Don Bestor and his Orchestra (Victor); Al Bowlly (Decca) and Arthur Tracy, "The Street Singer" (Vocalion).

Little Games. w/m Harold Spiro and Phil Wainman, 1967. Recorded by the English group The Yardbirds (Epic).

Little Girl. w/m Don Baskin and Bob Gonzalez, 1966. Top 10 record by The Syndicate of Sound, a rock group of which the writers were two-fifths (Bell).

Little Girl. w/m Madeline Hyde and Francis Henry, 1931. First popular recordings by the orchestras of Sam Lanin (Perfect); Fred Rich (Hit-of-the-Week); Joe Venuti, vocal by Harold Arlen (Columbia). Revived by Nat "King" Cole (Capitol), 1948.

Little Girl, Don't Cry. w/m Doris Davis and Lucius "Lucky" Millinder, 1949. Introduced and recorded by Lucky Millinder and his Orchestra (RCA Victor). Best-selling record by Benny Goodman, vocal by Buddy Greco (Capitol).

Little Girl Blue. w. Lorenz Hart, m. Richard Rodgers, 1935. Introduced by Gloria Grafton in Billy Rose's (TM) *Jumbo*. Sung by Doris Day in the film version (MM) *Billy Rose's Jumbo*, 1962. It was a staple in the repertoire of Mabel Mercer, who also recorded it (Atlantic).

Little Girl from Little Rock, A. w. Leo Robin, m. Jule Styne, 1949. Introduced by Carol Channing in (TM) *Gentlemen Prefer Blondes*. Single records by Ethel Merman (Decca) and Dorothy Shay, "The Park Avenue Hillbilly" (Columbia). Sung by Marilyn Monroe in (MM) *Gentlemen Prefer Blondes*, 1953.

Little Girl I Once Knew, The. w/m Brian Wilson, 1965. Top 40 record by The Beach Boys (Capitol).

Little Girl of Mine. w/m George Goldner and Herbert Cox, 1956. Recorded by The Cleftones (Gee).

Little Girls, Goodbye. w. William Le Baron, m. Victor Jacobi, 1919. Introduced by John Charles Thomas in (TM) *Apple Blossoms*.

Little Good News, A. w/m Charlie Black, Rory Bourke, and Thomas Rocco, 1983. Country/Pop crossover hit by Anne Murray (Capitol).

Little Gray House, The. w. Maxwell Anderson, m. Kurt Weill, 1949. Introduced by Todd Duncan in (TM) *Lost in the Stars*. Sung by Brock Peters in (MM) *Lost in the Stars*, 1974.

Little Green Apples. w/m Bobby Russell, 1968. The song made its first impact on the Country charts via Roger Miller's recording (Smash). O. C. Smith followed with his gold record version, which topped the Pop charts (Columbia). The song won Grammy Awards (NARAS) for Song of the Year and Best Country and Western Song.

Little Grey Home in the West. w. D. Eardley-Wilmot, m. Herman Lohr, 1911. Among numerous recordings were those by John McCormack, Buddy Morrow, and the Sons of the Pioneers (all Victor).

Little Gypsy Maid, The. w. Harry B. Smith and Cecil Mack, m. Will Marion Cook, 1902. Interpolated by Irene Bentley in (TM) *The Wild Rose.*

Little Heartache, A. w/m Wayne P. Walker, 1962. Hit C&W record by Eddy Arnold (RCA).

Little Honda. w/m Brian Wilson, 1964. Top 10 hit by The Hondells (Mercury). Also recorded by The Beach Boys, of whom the writer was a member (Capitol).

Little House That Love Built, The. w. Al Dubin, m. Harry Warren, 1936. Introduced by James Melton in (MM) *Sing Me a Love Song* and on records (Decca). Abe Lyman, vocal by Sonny Schuyler, also recorded it (Decca).

Little House upon the Hill, The. w. Ballard MacDonald and Joe Goodwin, m. Harry Puck, 1915. Popular vaudeville song. Leading record by James F. Harrison and James Reed (Columbia).

Little in Love, A. w/m Alan Tarney, 1981. Recorded by the English singer/actor Cliff Richard (EMI America).

Little Is Enough, A. w/m Peter Townshend, 1980. Recorded by the British vocalist/guitarist Pete Townshend (Atco).

Little Jack Frost Get Lost. w. Al Stillman, m. Seger Ellis, 1948. Leading recordings by Ray McKinley and his Orchestra (RCA Victor) and Frankie Carle, vocal by Marjorie Hughes (Columbia).

Little Jazz Bird. w. Ira Gershwin, m. George Gershwin, 1924. Introduced by Cliff Edwards in (TM) *Lady, Be Good!* Revived by Blossom Dearie (Verve). Interpolated by Tommy Tune and Twiggy in (TM) *My One and Only*, 1983.

Little Jeannie. w. Gary Osborne, m. Elton John, 1980. Top 10 gold record by the English singer/songwriter Elton John (MCA).

Little Joe. w. Ned Miller, m. Jule Styne, 1931. This was Styne's first song success. Recorded by Louis Armstrong (Okeh); Mildred Bailey (Vocalion); Ted Weems's Orchestra, vocal by Art Jarrett (Victor). Later, Mary Lou Williams made a 12" disc (Asch).

Little Joe from Chicago. w/m Mary Lou Williams and Henry Wells, 1938. Written for and dedicated to agent Joe Glaser, who founded Associated Booking Corporation, a leading agency in the band field. Williams was playing piano and Wells, trombone, for Andy Kirk and his Clouds of Joy when they recorded it (Decca). Wingy Manone and his Band also had a version (Bluebird).

Little Kiss at Twilight, A. w. Leo Robin, m. Ralph Rainger, 1938. Introduced by Martha Raye in (MM) *Give Me a Sailor.*

Little Kiss Each Morning, a Little Kiss Each Night, A. w/m Harry Woods, 1929. Introduced by Rudy Vallee in (MM) *The Vagabond Lover* and recorded by him (Victor). Also recorded by Seger Ellis's Orchestra (Okeh).

Little Lady Make Believe. w. Charles Tobias, m. Nat Simon, 1938. Among leading records: Dorothy Lamour, with Herbie Kay's Orchestra (Brunswick); George Olsen, vocal by Eddy Howard (Decca); Charles "Buddy" Rogers and his Orchestra (Vocalion).

Little Lamb. w. Stephen Sondheim, m. Jule Styne, 1959. Introduced by Sandra Church in (TM) *Gypsy*. In the film version (MM) *Gypsy*, 1962, it was sung by Natalie Wood.

Little Latin Lupe Lu. w/m Bill Medley, 1963. Introduced by The Righteous Brothers (Moonglow). Other popular versions by The Kingsmen (Wand), 1964; Mitch Ryder and The Detroit Wheels (New Voice), 1966.

Little Lies. w/m Christine McVie and Eddy Quintela, 1987. Single from the album "Tango in the Night" by the British group Fleetwood Mac (Warner Bros.).

Little Lonely One. w/m Bob Brass and Irvin Levine, 1965. Recorded before but released after his first hit, "It's Not Unusual," (q.v.) by Tom Jones (Tower).

Little Lost Child, The. w. Edward B. Marks, m. Joseph W. Stern, 1894. The first song to be illustrated by slides and projected on a screen in a theater. This ballad became one of the major hits of the 1890s.

Little Love, a Little Kiss, A. w. Nilson Fysher (Fr.), Adrian Ross (Engl.), m. Lao Silesu, 1912. A French song, "Un Peu d'Amour," translated into English.

Little Love Can Go a Long, Long Way, A. w. Paul Francis Webster, m. Sammy Fain, 1955. First heard in (MM) *Ain't Misbehavin'*. The Dream Weavers had a popular recording (Decca).

Little Mama. w/m Carmen Taylor, Willis Carroll, Ahmet Ertegun, and Jerry Wexler, 1954. Top 10 R&B record by The Clovers (Atlantic).

Little Man. w/m Sonny Bono, 1966. Introduced and recorded by Sonny and Cher (Atco).

Little Man, You've Had a Busy Day. w. Maurice Sigler and Al Hoffman, m. Mabel Wayne, 1934. Title from the best-selling book by Hans Fallada. Popular records by Isham Jones, vocal by Eddie Stone (Victor); the Pickens Sisters (Victor); Frank Luther (Melotone); Emil Coleman and his Orchestra (Columbia). Jerry Lewis and wife, Patti, later recorded it (Capitol).

Little Man Who Wasn't There, The. w. Harold Adamson, m. Bernard Hanighen, 1939. Featured and recorded by Mildred Bailey (Vocalion); Bob Crosby, vocal by Teddy Grace (Decca); Ray Herbeck and his Orchestra (Vocalion).

Little Man with a Candy Cigar. w. Townsend Brigham, m. Matt Dennis, 1941. Introduced and recorded by Tommy Dorsey, vocal by Jo Stafford (Victor).

Little Me. w. Carolyn Leigh, m. Cy Coleman, 1962. Title song of (TM) *Little Me*, sung by Nancy Andrews and Virginia Martin.

Little More Love, A. w/m John Farrar, 1979. Top 10 gold record by Olivia Newton-John (MCA).

Little Mother of Mine. w. Walter H. Brown, m. Harry T. Burleigh, 1917.

Little Old Clock on the Mantel, The. w. Gus Kahn, m. Ted Fio Rito, 1924. Popularized and recorded by Russo and Fio Rito's Oriole Orchestra (Brunswick).

Little Old Lady. w. Stanley Adams, m. Hoagy Carmichael, 1937. Introduced by Mitzi Mayfair and Charles Walters in (TM) *The Show Is On*. A #1 hit (eleven weeks on "Your Hit Parade"), it was recorded by, among others, Ray Noble, vocal by Al Bowlly (Victor); Abe Lyman, vocal by Sonny Schuyler (Decca); Shep Fields and his Rippling Rhythm (Bluebird); Dick Robertson (Decca).

Little Old Lady (from Pasadena), The. w/m Roger Christian and Don Altfeld, 1964. Top 5 record by Jan and Dean (Liberty).

Little Old Man. See **Uptight (Everything's Alright).**

Little Old Mill, The (Went Round and Round). w/m Don Pelosi, Lewis Ilda, and Leo Towers, 1947. English song. Top-selling U.S. record by Sammy Kaye, vocal by The Three Kaydets (RCA Victor).

Little Old New York. w. Sheldon Harnick, m. Jerry Bock, 1960. Introduced by Eileen

Rodgers, Lee Becker, and chorus in (TM) *Tenderloin*.

Little Ole Winedrinker Me. w/m Hank Mills and Dick Jennings, 1967. First recorded by Robert Mitchum (Monument). Dean Martin, who covered the release, had the best-seller (Reprise).

Little Ole You. w. Wayne P. Walker and Mel Tillis, m. Wayne P. Walker, 1963. Hit Country record by Jim Reeves (RCA).

Little on the Lonely Side, A. w/m Dick Robertson, Frank Weldon, and James Cavanaugh, 1944. Featured and recorded by Frankie Carle, vocal by Paul Allen (Columbia); Guy Lombardo, vocal by Jimmy Brown (Decca); the Phil Moore Four, vocal by Phil Moore and Billy Daniels (Victor).

Little Pal. w/m B. G. DeSylva, Lew Brown, Ray Henderson, and Al Jolson, 1929. Jolson sang this in (MM) *Say It with Songs*.

Little Peach. w. Arthur Wimperis, m. Sigmund Romberg, 1925. Introduced by Doris Patston in (TM) *Louie the 14th*.

Little Prince, The (from Who Knows Where). w. Alan Jay Lerner, m. Frederick Loewe, 1974. Sung by Richard Kiley in (MM) *The Little Prince*. Nominated for an Academy Award.

Little Red Corvette. w/m Prince Rogers Nelson, 1983. Top 10 record by Prince (Warner Bros.).

Little Red Fox, The (N'ya, N'ya, Ya Can't Catch Me). w. James V. Kern, Hy Heath, and Johnny Lange, m. Lew Porter, 1939. Introduced by Kay Kyser and his Orchestra, vocal by Harry Babbitt in (MM) *That's Right— You're Wrong*.

Little Red Rooster. w/m Willie Dixon, 1963. Top 20 record by Sam Cooke (RCA).

Little Rock. w/m Pat McManus, Bob Di Piero, and Gerry House, 1986. #1 Country chart record by Reba McEntire (MCA).

Little Rock Getaway. m. Joe Sullivan, 1937. First recorded as piano solo by Sullivan (Decca) in 1935. In 1937, Bob Crosby and his Orchestra, featuring Bob Zurke who replaced Sullivan on piano, recorded a Deane Kincaide arrangement (Decca). This established the number as a top instrumental. Among other recordings of note are those by Frankie Trumbauer (Varsity); Armand Hug and Ray Bauduc, piano and drums (Okeh); Light Crust Doughboys, featuring Knocky Parker on piano (Okeh); Les Paul (Capitol).

Little Rosa. w/m Red Sovine and Webb Pierce, 1956. Recorded by Red Sovine and Webb Pierce (Decca).

Little Rose of the Rancho. w. Leo Robin, m. Ralph Rainger, 1936. From (MM) *Rose of the Rancho* starring John Boles and Gladys Swarthout. Recorded by Xavier Cugat and his Orchestra (Victor).

Little Shoemaker, The. w. Geoffrey Parsons, John Turner (Engl.), Avril Lamarque (Fr.) m. Rudi Revil, 1954. French title: "Le Petit Cordonnier." Leading recordings by The Gaylords (Mercury); Hugo Winterhalter's "Orchestra and Chorus and a Friend" (RCA Victor). The "friend," as lead singer of the chorus, was Eddie Fisher.

Little Sir Echo. w. Laura R. Smith, m. J. S. Fearis, 1917, 1939. The twenty-two-year-old song, with a new arrangement by Joe Marsala and Adele Girard, became a "Hit Parade" number in 1939. The best-selling records were by Horace Heidt (Brunswick), Jan Savitt (Decca), and Dick Jurgens, with a vocal by Eddy Howard (Vocalion).

Little Sister. w/m Doc Pomus and Mort Shuman, 1961. Top 10 record by Elvis Presley (RCA). Revived by Dwight Yoakam (Reprise), 1987.

Little Skipper from Heaven Above, A. w/m Cole Porter, 1936. Sung by Jimmy Durante and the ensemble in (TM) *Red, Hot, and Blue!*

Little Space Girl. w/m Jesse Lee Turner, 1959. Top 40 novelty by Jesse Lee Turner (Carlton).

Little Star. w/m Vito Picone and Arthur Venosa, 1958. Hit record by The Elegants (Apt).

Little Street Where Old Friends Meet, A. w. Gus Kahn, m. Harry Woods, 1932.

Little Susie. m. Ray Bryant, 1960. Instrumental by Ray Bryant's Combo (Signature) (Columbia).

Little Things. w/m Bobby Goldsboro, 1965. Top 20 record by Bobby Goldsboro (United Artists).

Little Things in Life, The. w/m Irving Berlin, 1930. Sung on radio and recorded (Victor) by popular tenor James Lewis. Earl Burtnett and his Band also recorded it (Brunswick). Revived in the early fifties by Bob Eberly and Helen O'Connell (Capitol).

Little Things Mean a Lot. w/m Edith Lindeman and Carl Stutz, 1954. One of the biggest record hits of the year, sung by Kitty Kallen with Jack Pleis's Orchestra (Decca).

Little Things You Used to Do, The. w. Al Dubin, m. Harry Warren, 1935. Introduced by Helen Morgan in (MM) *Go into Your Dance* and recorded by her (Brunswick). Other records by the orchestras of Johnny Green (Columbia); Enric Madriguera (Brunswick), Jack Shilkret (Bluebird).

Little Too Late. w/m Alex Call, 1983. Recorded by Pat Benatar (Chrysalis).

Little Toot. w/m Allie Wrubel, 1948. Introduced by The Andrews Sisters in Walt Disney's animated olio of musical numbers, (MM) *Melody Time*. Don Wilson, the radio announcer, and sidekick Jack Benny, had a successful children's record (Capitol).

Little Town Flirt. w/m Marion McKenzie and Del Shannon, 1963. Introduced and recorded by Del Shannon (Big Top).

Little Town in the Ould County Down. w. Richard W. Pascoe, m. Monte Carlo and Alma Sanders, 1920.

Little Walter. w/m Denzil Foster, Thomas McElroy, and Tony! Toni! Tone! 1988. #1 R&B and Pop chart entry by the trio Tony! Toni! Tone! (Wing).

Little White Cloud That Cried, The. w/m Johnnie Ray, 1951. Coupled with "Cry," this first hit record for Johnnie Ray (Okeh) sold over two-million copies.

Little White Gardenia, A. w/m Sam Coslow, 1935. Introduced by Carl Brisson in (MM) *All the King's Horses*. Among the recordings: Al Bowlly (Victor), Morton Downey (Perfect), and the orchestras of Emil Coleman (Decca) and Art Kassel (Bluebird).

Little White House, The (at the End of Honeymoon Lane). w. Eddie Dowling, m. James F. Hanley, 1926. Introduced by Eddie Dowling in (TM) *Honeymoon Lane*. Dowling sang it in the film version (MP) *Honeymoon Lane*, 1931. Recorded by Frank Munn (Brunswick), Johnny Marvin (Okeh), Fred Waring's Pennsylvanians (Victor).

Little White Lies. w/m Walter Donaldson, 1930. One of the biggest hits of the year in sheet music and record sales. Fred Waring and his Pennsylvanians, vocal by Clare Hanlon (Victor), was the leading seller, followed by Ted Wallace, vocal by Elmer Feldkamp (Columbia). Dick Haymes with Four Hits and a Miss and orchestra conducted by Gordon Jenkins (Decca) had a million seller with their revival, 1948. Dinah Shore also had a chart version (Columbia). Among other notable singles: Mel Tormé (Musicraft); George Shearing (Capitol); Ella Fitzgerald, with Chick Webb's Orchestra (Decca); Lee Morse and Her Bluegrass Boys (Columbia).

Little Willy. w/m Mike Day, 1973. Gold record by the English band Sweet (Bell).

Little Woman. w/m Danny Janssen, 1969. Gold record by Bobby Sherman (Metromedia).

Little You. w/m Gordon Mills, 1965. Written and recorded in England by Freddie and The Dreamers (Mercury).

Live and Let Die. w/m Paul McCartney and Linda McCartney, 1973. Title song of the James Bond film (MP) *Live and Let Die*. Nominated for Academy Award. Gold record by the McCartneys' group, Wings (Apple).

Live and Let Live. w/m Cole Porter, 1953. Introduced by Lilo in (TM) *Can-Can*.

Live and Love Tonight. w. Sam Coslow, m. Arthur Johnston, 1934. Sung by Carl Brisson and Kitty Carlisle in (MM) *Murder at the Vanities*. Duke Ellington and his Orchestra, who were in the film, recorded it (Victor), as did the orchestras of Johnny Green (Brunswick) and Will Osborne (Melotone).

Live Fast, Love Hard, Die Young. w/m Joe Allison, 1955. Featured and recorded by Faron Young (Capitol).

Live for Life. w. Norman Gimbel (Engl.), m. Francis Lai, 1967. Lyric written to theme from French-Italian film (MP) *Live for Life*. Leading record by Jack Jones (RCA).

Live My Life. w/m Allee Willis and Danny Sembello, 1987. Sung on the soundtrack of (MP) *Hiding Out* and on the soundtrack album by Boy George (Virgin).

Livery Stable Blues. m. Marvin Lee, 1917. Recorded by the Original Dixieland Band (Victor) and W. C. Handy's Orchestra (Columbia). Revived by Bunny Berigan and his Band (Victor), 1938.

Live to Tell. w/m Madonna Ciccone and Pat Leonard, 1986. Theme of (MP) *At Close Range*, starring Sean Penn and Christopher Walken. #1 single by Madonna, married to Penn at the time (Sire).

Live Wire. w/m Brian Holland, Eddie Holland, and Lamont Dozier, 1964. Recorded by Martha and The Vandellas (Gordy).

Livin' for the Weekend. w/m Cary Gilbert, Kenny Gamble, and Leon Huff, 1976. Recorded by The O'Jays (Philadelphia International).

Livin' for You. w/m Al Green and Willie Mitchell, 1974. Top 20 record by Al Green (Hi).

Livin' for Your Love. 1984. Top 10 R&B chart record by Melba Moore (Capitol).

Living Daylights, The. w. Pal Waaktaar, m. John Barry, 1987. Sung on the soundtrack of the James Bond film (MP) *The Living Daylights* by the Norwegian trio, A-Ha, and on the soundtrack album (Warner Bros.).

Living Doll. w/m Lionel Bart, 1959. Introduced by Cliff Richards in the British film *Serious Charge*. His recording was released in the U.S. (ABC-Paramount).

Living for the City. w/m Stevie Wonder, 1973. Hit R&B/Pop record by Stevie Wonder (Tamla). Winner Grammy Award (NARAS) Rhythm and Blues Song of the Year, 1974.

Living in a Box. w/m Marcus Vere and S. Piggot, 1987. Chart record by the British trio, Living in a Box, from their self-named album (Chrysalis).

Living in a House Divided. w/m Tom Bahler, 1972. Recorded by Cher (Kapp).

Living in America. w/m Dan Hartman and Charlie Midnight, 1986. Introduced by James Brown in (MP) *Rocky IV* and on his Top 10 single (Scotti Brothers).

Living Inside Myself w/m Gino Vannelli, 1981. Top 10 record by the Canadian singer/ songwriter Gino Vannelli (Arista).

Living in the Past. w/m Ian Anderson, 1972. Written in England by the lead singer of the group, Jethro Tull, whose recording made the Top 20 in the U.S. (Chrysalis).

Living in the Promiseland. w/m David Lynn Jones, 1986. #1 Country chart song by Willie Nelson (Columbia). Jones recorded it in his album "Hard Times on Easy Street" (Mercury), 1987.

Living in the U.S.A. w/m Steve Miller, 1968. The recordings by The Steve Miller Band reached the charts twice (Capitol), 1968 and 1974.

Living Loving Maid (She's Just a Woman). w/m Jimmy Page and Robert Plant, 1970. Chart single and album cut by the British group, Led Zeppelin, and written by two of its members (Atlantic).

Living Next Door to Alice. w/m Mike Chapman and Nicky Chinn, 1977. Hit record by the British quartet Smokie (RSO).

Living Proof. w/m Johnny MacRae and S. Clarke, 1989. Hit Country record by Ricky Van Shelton (Columbia).

Livingston Saturday Night. w/m Jimmy Buffett, 1978. Introduced by Jimmy Buffett in (MP) *FM*, and on records (ABC).

Living Together, Growing Together. w. Hal David, m. Burt Bacharach, 1973. Introduced in (MM) *Lost Horizon*, a new version of the James Hilton novel and film. Recorded by The 5th Dimension (Bell).

Living Years, The. w/m Brian Robertson and Mike Rutherford, 1989. Hit record by the group Mike + The Mechanics (Atlantic).

Livin' in the Sunlight, Lovin' in the Moonlight. w. Al Lewis, m Al Sherman, 1930. Introduced by Maurice Chevalier in (MM) *The Big Pond*. In addition to his recording (Victor), the bands of Ben Bernie (Brunswick) and Paul Whiteman (Victor) also had releases.

Livin' It Up (Friday Night). w/m Leroy Bell and Casey James, 1979. Crossover (R&B/ Pop) gold record by the duo Bell and James (A&M).

Livin' on a Prayer. w/m Jon Bon Jovi, Richie Sambora, and Desmond Child, 1987. #1 single from the album "Slippery When Wet" by the band Bon Jovi (Mercury).

Livin' Thing. w/m Jeff Lynne, 1976. Recorded by the English group Electric Light Company (United Artists).

Liza (All the Clouds'll Roll Away). w. Gus Kahn and Ira Gershwin, m. George Gershwin, 1929. Sung by Nick Lucas and danced by Ruby Keeler and ensemble in (TM) *Show Girl*. During a tryout performance in Boston, Al Jolson, who had recently married Keeler, stood up in the audience and sang the song. The publicity aided the show. Ethel Smith, the organist, played it in (MM) *George White's Scandals* in 1945; Robert Alda and Oscar Levant performed it in the Gershwin biography (MM) *Rhapsody in Blue* in 1945; Jolson sang it in (MM) *The Jolson Story*, dubbing for Larry Parks in 1946; Patrice Wymore sang it in (MM) *Starlift* in 1951; Liberace played it on the piano in (MM) *Sincerely Yours* in 1955.

Lizzie and the Rainman. w/m Larry Henley and Kenny O'Dell, 1975. Popularized by Country singer Tanya Tucker (MCA).

Lizzie Borden. w/m Michael Brown, 1952. Introduced by Joseph Lautner, Bill Mullikin, Paul Lynde, Patricia Hammerlee, and company in (TM) *New Faces*, 1954. Revived by The Chad Mitchell Trio (Kapp), 1962.

Load-Out, The. w/m Jackson Browne and Bryan Garufalo, 1978. Recorded by Jackson Browne (Asylum).

Loads of Love. w/m Richard Rodgers, 1962. Introduced by Diahann Carroll in (TM) *No Strings*.

Loch Lomond. w/m traditional, 1937. Maxine Sullivan had a hit record (Vocalion) with Claude Thornhill's swing arrangement and accompaniment of this traditional song of Scotland. Thornhill arranged a big band version for Benny Goodman, with vocal by Martha Tilton [and Benny!] (Victor), 1937. Maxine Sullivan sang it in (MM) *St. Louis Blues*, 1938. Deanna Durbin sang it in (MM) *It's a Date*, 1940, and recorded it (Decca). It was heard in (MM) *Bathing Beauties* and (MM) *Babes on Swing Street*, 1944, and in (MM) *Junior Prom*, 1946.

Lock, Stock, and Teardrops. w/m Roger Miller, 1963. Country chart record by Roger

Miller (RCA). Revived by Diana Trask (Dial), 1968, and k.d. lang (Sire), 1988.

Locking Up My Heart. w/m Brian Holland, Lamont Dozier, and Eddie Holland, 1963. Recorded by The Marvelettes (Tamla).

Loco-Motion, The. w/m Gerry Goffin and Carole King, 1962, 1974, 1988. #1 Pop chart hit by Little Eva (Dimension); by the heavy metal band Grand Funk (Capitol), 1974; by Kylie Minogue (Geffen), 1988, making this the only song in the rock era to reach the #1 ranking by three different artists.

Loco Weed. w/m Mel Tillis and Jim Denny, 1960. Recorded by Mel Tillis (Columbia).

Loddy Lo. w/m Dave Appell and Kal Mann, 1963. Hit record by Chubby Checker (Parkway).

Lodi. w/m John Fogerty, 1969. Recorded by Creedence Clearwater Revival (Fantasy).

Logical Song, The. w/m Rick Davies and Roger Hodgson, 1979. Top 10 record by the British quintet Supertramp (A&M).

Lola. w/m Ray Davies, 1970. Top 10 hit by the British group, The Kinks, of which Davies was lead singer (Reprise).

Lolita Ya-Ya. m. Nelson Riddle and Bob Harris, 1962. Instrumental hit, based on a theme from (MP) *Lolita*, recorded by The Ventures (Dolton).

Lollipop. w/m Beverly Ross and Julius Dixon, 1958. Hit record by The Chordettes (Cadence). Second popular version by Ronald and Ruby (RCA).

Lollipops and Roses. w/m Tony Velona, 1962. Popularized by Jack Jones (Kapp). Paul Petersen also had a chart record (Colpix).

Lolly Pop Mama. w/m Roy Brown, 1948. Top 10 R&B chart record by Wynonie Harris (King).

Lo Mucho Te Quiero (the More I Love You). w/m Sammy Ibarra, René Ornelas, and René Herrera, 1969. Top 20 record by René and René (Columbia).

London Is a Little Bit of All Right. w/m Noël Coward, 1963. Introduced by Tessie O'Shea and ensemble in (TM) *The Girl Who Came to Supper*.

London Town. w/m Denny Laine and Paul McCartney, 1978. Recorded by McCartney's group Wings (Capitol).

Loneliness Made Me Realize (It's You I Need). w/m Eddie Holland and Norman Whitfield, 1967. Top 20 record by The Temptations (Gordy).

Loneliness of Evening. w. Oscar Hammerstein II, m. Richard Rodgers, 1965. Dropped from the Broadway musical *South Pacific* before opening, it was interpolated by Stuart Damon, as the Prince in (TVM) "Cinderella," 1965.

Lonely. w/m Ramon Novarro, Clifford Grey, and Herbert Stothart, 1930. Sung by Ramon Novarro in (MM) *Call of the Flesh*.

L-o-n-e-l-y. w/m Bobby Vinton, 1965. Introduced and recorded by Bobby Vinton (Epic).

Lonely Again. w/m Jean Chapel, 1966. Crossover (C&W/Pop) chart record by Eddy Arnold (RCA).

Lonely Alone. w/m J. D. Martin and John Jarrard, 1986. Top 10 Country chart record by The Forester Sisters (Warner Bros.).

Lonely Blue Boy. w. Fred Wise, m. Ben Weisman, 1960. Top 10 record by Conway Twitty (MGM).

Lonely Boy. w/m Andrew Gold, 1977. Top 10 record by Andrew Gold (Asylum).

Lonely Boy (I'm Just a). w/m Paul Anka, 1959. Introduced in (MM) *Girls Town*. Recorded by Paul Anka (ABC-Paramount) and later, by Donny Osmond (MGM), 1972.

Lonely Bull, The. m. Sol Lake, 1962. Top 10 instrumental hit by Herb Alpert and The Tijuana Brass (A&M).

Lonely Days. w/m Barry Gibb, Maurice Gibb, and Robin Gibb, 1971. Recorded by the

British trio of brothers The Bee Gees (Atco). Their U.S. release became a gold record awardee.

Lonely for You. w/m Gary Stites, 1959. Introduced by Gary Stites (Carlton).

Lonely Goatherd, The. w. Oscar Hammerstein II, m. Richard Rodgers, 1959. Introduced by Mary Martin and the children in (TM) *The Sound of Music*. It was sung by Julie Andrews in (MM) *The Sound of Music*, 1965.

Lonely Heart. w/m Irving Berlin, 1933. Sung by Harry Stockwell and danced by Letitia Ide and José Limon in (TM) *As Thousands Cheer*. Recorded by Meyer Davis's Orchestra (Columbia) and Everett Marshall (12″ Decca).

Lonely Island. w/m Eden Ahbez, 1958. Featured and recorded by Sam Cooke (Keen).

Lonely Is the Name. w. Carl Sigman (Engl.), m. Bert Kaempfert and Herbert Rehbein, 1967. German song. Leading English version by Sammy Davis, Jr. (Reprise).

Lonely Lane. w. Irving Kahal, m. Sammy Fain, 1933. Introduced by Dick Powell in (MM) *College Coach*. Recorded by Wendell Hall (Victor).

Lonely Little Melody. w. Gene Buck, m. Dave Stamper, 1924. Introduced by Vivienne Segal and Irving Fisher in (TM) *Ziegfeld Follies of 1924*. Recorded by Paul Whiteman (Victor).

Lonely Little Robin. w/m Cy Coben, 1951. C&W song introduced and recorded by The Pinetoppers, with The Marlin Sisters and Ray Smith (Coral). Other recordings by Mindy Carson (Columbia), Rex Allen (Mercury), Marion Morgan (MGM).

Lonely Melody. w. Benny Meroff and Sam Coslow, m. Hal Dyson, 1927. Adapted from a melody by A. Grünfeld. Popular recordings by the bands of Bernie Cummins (Brunswick), Benny Meroff (Okeh), Paul Whiteman (Victor).

Lonely Night. w/m Alec Wilder, 1949. Melody adapted from *Berceuse*, by the Finnish composer Armas Jarnefelt. First recording by Vic Damone (Mercury).

Lonely Night (Angel Face). w/m Neil Sedaka, 1976. Top 10 record by The Captain & Tennille (A&M).

Lonely Nights. w/m Harris Stewart and Keith Stegall, 1981. #1 Country chart record by Mickey Gilley (Epic).

Lonely Nights. w/m Zell Sanders, 1955. The Hearts had a popular R&B recording (Baton).

Lonely Ol' Night. w/m John Cougar Mellencamp, 1985. Top 10 record by John Cougar Mellencamp (Riva).

Lonely One, The. m. Lee Hazlewood and Duane Eddy, 1959. Instrumental featured and recorded by Duane Eddy (Jamie).

Lonely River. w/m Gene Autry and Fred Rose, 1942. Introduced and recorded by Gene Autry (Okeh).

Lonely Street. w/m Carl Belew, Kenny Sowder, and W. S. Stevenson, 1959. Hit record by Andy Williams (Cadence).

Lonely Teardrops. w/m Lee Ross, 1962. Country chart record by Rose Maddox (Capitol).

Lonely Teardrops. w/m Berry Gordy, Jr., Gwen Gordy, and Tyran Carlo, 1958. #1 R&B and Top 10 Pop chart record by Jack Wilson (Brunswick). Later chart versions by Brian Hyland (Uni), 1971; Narvel Felts, Top 10 C&W (ABC/Dot), 1976.

Lonely Teenager. w/m Salvatore Pippa, Alfred Di Paoli, and Silvio Faraci, 1961. Recorded by Dion (Belmonts).

Lonely Town. w. Betty Comden and Adolph Green, m. Leonard Bernstein, 1945. Introduced by John Battles in (TM) *On the Town*. Recorded by Mary Martin (Decca) and Maynard Ferguson, with his Orchestra (EmArcy).

Lonely Troubadour. w/m John Klenner, 1929. Introduced, featured, and recorded by

Rudy Vallee (Victor). Also recorded by Ted Lewis (Columbia), Meyer Davis (Brunswick), and Don Voorhees (Perfect). Note: This, as most of Klenner's hits, were ballads of remorse: "Heartaches," "Just Friends," "On the Street of Regret," and "Crying Myself to Sleep (q.v.)."

Lonelyville. w/m Dave Burgess, 1961. First recorded and Country chart song by Ray Sanders (Liberty). Also recorded by Dave Dudley (Mercury), 1966.

Lonely Weekends. w/m Charlie Rich, 1960. Introduced and recorded by Charlie Rich (Phillips).

Lonely Wine. w/m Roy Wells, 1950. Leading record by Les Baxter and his Orchestra (Capitol).

Lonely Woman. w. Margo Guryan, m. Ornette Coleman, 1960. Jazz instrumental recorded by Ornette Coleman (Atlantic). Recorded vocally by June Christy, with Stan Kenton's Orchestra (Capitol).

Lonesome. w. Edgar Leslie, m. George W. Meyer, 1909.

Lonesome and Sorry. w. Benny Davis, m. Con Conrad, 1926. Ruth Etting's first hit record (Columbia). Her public performance established the song. Revived by Guy Lombardo, vocal by Kenny Gardner (Decca), 1939.

Lonesome in the Moonlight. w. Benee Russell, m. Abel Baer, 1928. Popular record by Paul Whiteman (Victor).

Lonesome Loser. w/m David Briggs, 1979. Top 10 record by the Australian group Little River Band (Capitol).

Lonesome Lover. w. Alfred Bryan, m. James V. Monaco, 1930. Popularized and recorded by Isham Jones and his Orchestra (Brunswick).

Lonesome Mama Blues. w. A. W. Brown, m. Billie Brown, 1922. Featured and recorded by Mamie Smith and Her Jazz Hounds (Okeh).

Lonesome Me. w. Andy Razaf, m. Thomas "Fats" Waller and Con Conrad, 1932. Recorded by Russ Columbo (Victor); the bands of Tom Gerun, vocal by Woody Herman (Brunswick); Mal Hallett (Okeh); Paul Specht (Columbia).

Lonesome Nights. w. Irving Mills, m. Benny Carter, 1934. Introduced and recorded by Carter's band (Okeh). Also recorded by Leroy Carr (Vocalion).

Lonesome Number One. w/m Don Gibson, 1961. Crossover (C&W/Pop) hit by Don Gibson (RCA).

Lonesome Polecat. w. Johnny Mercer, m. Gene De Paul, 1954. Introduced by six of the brothers (sans Howard Keel), Marc Platt, Jeff Richards, Matt Mattox, Russ Tamblyn, Tommy Rall, and Jacques D'Amboise in (MM) *Seven Brides for Seven Brothers*.

Lonesome Road, The. w. Gene Austin, m. Nathaniel Shilkret, 1928. Based on a Negro spiritual. Jules Bledsoe, the original "Joe" in (TM) *Show Boat*, dubbed his voice for Stepin Fetchit in the first film version (MM) *Show Boat*, 1929, which was originally made as a silent film. The musical sequences were added later, making it, in effect, a part-sound, part-silent picture. The song was also heard in (MM) *Cha-Cha-Cha-Boom*, 1956. Popular records by Gene Austin (Victor); Ted Lewis, with Four Dusty Travelers and his Band (Columbia); Bing Crosby (Decca), 1939.

Lonesome 7-7203. w/m Justin Tubb, 1963. Country hit by Hawkshaw Hawkins (King).

Lonesomest Girl in Town, The. w. Al Dubin, m. Jimmy McHugh and Irving Mills, 1925. Featured and recorded by Cliff "Ukulele Ike" Edwards (Perfect), Ben Bernie and his Orchestra (Brunswick), and Morton Downey (Brunswick).

Lonesome Town. w/m Baker Knight, 1958. Top 10 record by Ricky Nelson (Imperial).

Lonesome Whistle Blues. w/m Rudy Toombs and Elson Teat, 1961. R&B hit and Pop chart record by Freddy King (Federal).

Lone Star State of Mind. w/m Patrick Alger, Gene Levine, and Fred Koller, 1987. Hit Country chart record by Nanci Griffith (MCA).

Long, Long Way from Home. w/m Lou Gramm, Mick Jones, and Ian McDonald, 1978. Written by three members of the group Foreigner (Atlantic).

'Long About Midnight. w/m Roy Brown, 1949. #1 R&B chart record by Roy Brown (DeLuxe).

Long About Midnight. w/m Alex Hill and Irivng Mills, 1934. Introduced and recorded by Cab Calloway and his Orchestra (Victor). Featured and recorded by Frankie Trumbauer (Brunswick), Mildred Bailey (Vocalion), Willie Bryant (Victor), Louis Prima (Brunswick).

Long Ago and Far Away. w. Ira Gershwin, m. Jerome Kern, 1944. Introduced by Gene Kelly and, dubbing on the soundtrack for Rita Hayworth, Nan Wynn in (MM) *Cover Girl.* Nominated for Academy Award. Popular recordings by Helen Forrest and Dick Haymes (Decca), Bing Crosby (Decca), Jo Stafford (Capitol), Perry Como (Victor), Guy Lombardo with vocal by Tony Craig (Decca).

Long Ago and Far Away. w. Leo Robin, m. Ralph Rainger, 1936. From (MM) *Three Cheers for Love.* Not to be confused with the more famous 1944 Ira Gershwin-Jerome Kern song of the same title, this was recorded by Tommy Dorsey, vocal by Jack Leonard (Victor); Charlie Barnet (Bluebird); Ben Bernie (Decca); Nat Brandwynne, vocal by Buddy Clark (Brunswick).

Long Ago in Alcala. w. F. E. Weatherley and Adrian Ross, m. Andre Meassager, 1894. From the comic opera (TM) *Mirette,* produced in London, after which it became popular in the U.S.

Long Ago Tomorrow. w. Hal David, m. Burt Bacharach, 1971. The title derived from the American release of the British film that was titled *The Raging Moon* in the U.K., but changed to (MP) *Long Ago Tomorrow* in the U.S. Recorded by B. J. Thomas (Scepter).

Long and Winding Road, The. w/m John Lennon and Paul McCartney, 1970. Introduced by The Beatles in their documentary (MM) *Let It Be Me.* Their #1 record (Apple) was the last hit they had as a group. They disbanded in April of this year.

Long As the Rose Is Red. w/m Al Byron and Paul Evans, 1962. Answer song to Bobby Vinton's hit, "Roses Are Red (My Love) (q.v.)" recorded by Florraine Darlin (Epic).

Long Before I Knew You. w. Betty Comden and Adolph Green, m. Jule Styne, 1956. Introduced by Judy Holliday and Sydney Chaplin in (TM) *Bells Are Ringing.* Song not used in film version.

Long Before You Came Along. w. E. Y. Harburg, m. Harold Arlen, 1942. Introduced by Kathryn Grayson and John Carroll in the remake (MM) *Rio Rita,* starring Abbott and Costello.

Long Black Veil. w/m Marijohn Wilkin and Danny Dill, 1959. C&W hit by Lefty Frizzell (Columbia).

Long Cool Woman (in a Black Dress). w/m Roger Cook, Allan Clarke, and Roger Greenaway, 1972. Gold U.S. record by The British group The Hollies (Epic).

Longer. w/m Dan Fogelberg, 1980. Hit single by Dan Fogelberg (Full Moon).

Longest Day, The. w/m Paul Anka, 1962. Introduced on the soundtrack of (MP) *The Longest Day* by Mitch Miller's Orchestra and Chorus.

Longest Time, The. w/m Billy Joel, 1984. Recorded by Billy Joel (Columbia).

Longest Walk, The. w. Edward Pola, m. Fred Spielman, 1955. Popularized by Jaye P. Morgan, with Hugo Winterhalter's Orchestra (RCA).

Longest Way 'Round Is the Shortest Way Home, The. w. Ren Shields, m. Kerry Mills, 1908. Popular vaudeville song about "spooning" in an automobile.

Longfellow Serenade. w/m Neil Diamond, 1974. Top 10 record by Neil Diamond (Columbia).

Long Gone. w/m Alfonso "Sonny" Thompson and Lewis Simkins, 1948. Two-sided crossover (R&B/Pop) hit by Sonny Thompson (Miracle).

Long Gone. w/m W. C. Handy and Chris Smith, 1920. Introduced and recorded by W. C. Handy (Okeh). Among later versions, The Ray McKinley Trio (Decca).

Long Gone Lonesome Blues. w/m Hank Williams, 1950. #1 C&W hit by Hank Williams (MGM). Revived by Hank Williams, Jr. with crossover (C&W/Pop) hit (MGM), 1964.

Long Haired Country Boy. w/m Charlie Daniels, 1975. Chart record by The Charlie Daniels Band (Kama Sutra).

Long Hard Road (The Sharecropper's Dream). w/m Rodney Crowell, 1984. #1 Country chart record by The Nitty Gritty Dirt Band (Warner Bros.).

Long Hot Summer, The. w. Sammy Cahn, m. Alex North, 1958. Introduced by Jimmie Rodgers on the soundtrack, under the credits of (MP) *The Long Hot Summer*. Also recorded by Rodgers (Roulette).

Long Hot Summer Nights. w/m Wendy Waldman, 1978. Chart record by Wendy Waldman (Warner Bros.).

Longing for You. w. Bernard Jansen, m. Walter Dana, 1951. Based on "A Waltz Dream" by Oscar Straus. Most popular recordings by Vic Damone (Mercury); Sammy Kaye, vocal by Tony Alamo (Columbia); Teresa Brewer, with Jack Pleis's Orchestra (London).

Longing for You. w. Jack Drislane, m. Theodore F. Morse, 1905. Popular recording by Byron G. Harlan (Columbia).

Long John. w. Arnold Sundgaard, m. Paul Campbell, 1954. Recorded by Lonnie Donegan (Mercury).

Long Legged Ladies of Labrador. w. Mack Discant, m. Charlotte Chait, 1958. Recorded by Morty Craft and his Orchestra (MGM).

Long-Legged Guitar Pickin' Man. w/m Marshall Grant, 1967. Top 10 Country chart record by Johnny Cash and June Carter (Columbia).

Long Line of Love, A. w/m Paul Overstreet and Thom Schuyler, 1987. #1 Country chart single from the album "Americana" by Michael Martin Murphey (Warner Bros.).

Long Live Our Love. w/m Sidney Barnes and J. J. Jackson, 1966. Recorded by The Shangri-Las (Red Bird).

Long Live Rock. w/m Peter Townshend, 1979. Introduced by The Who in the British film (MM) *The Kids Are Alright*, and on records (MCA).

Long Lonely Nights. w/m Lee Andrews, Bernice Davis, Douglas Henderson, and Mimi Uniman, 1957. Recorded by Lee Andrews and The Hearts (Chess) and Clyde McPhatter (Atlantic). Bobby Vinton revived it successfully in 1965 (Epic), and it again hit the charts with the recording by The Dells (Cadet) in 1970.

Long Long Time. w/m Gary White, 1970. Top 40 record by Linda Ronstadt (Capitol).

Long Night, A. w. Loonis Reeves McGlohon, m. Alec Wilder, 1981. Recorded by Frank Sinatra in his LP *She Shot Me Down* (Reprise).

Long Tall Glasses (I Can Dance). w/m David Courtney and Leo Sayer, 1975. Top 10 English import, by Leo Sayer (Warner Bros.).

Long Tall Sally. w/m Enotris Johnson, Richard Penniman, and Robert A. Blackwell, 1956. Introduced and hit R&B and Pop record by Little Richard [Penniman] (Specialty). Hit Pop record by Pat Boone (Dot).

Long Time. w/m Tom Scholz, 1977. Recorded by the group Boston (Epic).

Long Time Gone. w/m David Crosby, 1968. Popular cut from the Crosby, Stills and Nash album of their own name (Atlantic).

Long Time Gone. w. Frank Harford, m. Tex Ritter, 1946. C&W hit, first recorded by Tex Ritter (Capitol). Revived by Dave Dudley (Mercury), 1966.

Long Train Runnin'. w/m Tom Johnston, 1973. Top 10 record by The Doobie Brothers (Warner Bros.).

Look, The. w/m Per Gessle, 1989. Hit single by Roxette (EMI).

Look at 'Er. w/m Bob Merrill, 1957. Introduced by George Wallace in (TM) *New Girl in Town.*

Look at Me. w. Jack Brooks, m. Walter Scharf, 1949. Recorded by: Buddy Clark (Columbia), Art Lund (MGM), Stuff Smith (Asch).

Look at Me (I'm in Love). w/m Al Goodman, Harry Ray, and William Brown, 1975. Recorded by The Moments (Stang).

Look at That Face. w/m Leslie Bricusse and Anthony Newley, 1965. Introduced by Cyril Ritchard, Sally Smith, and chorus in (TM) *The Roar of the Greasepaint—The Smell of the Crowd.*

Look at the World and Smile. w. Anne Caldwell, m. Raymond Hubbell, 1927. From (TM) "Yours Truly," which starred Irene Dunne. The song was recorded and featured on radio by Harry Reser's Cliquot Club Eskimos (Columbia). Also recorded by Jean Goldkette and his Orchestra (Victor).

Look Away. w/m Dianne Warren, 1989. Pop chart single hit by the group Chicago (Reprise).

Look for the Silver Lining. w. B. G. DeSylva, m. Jerome Kern, 1921. Introduced by Irving Fisher and Marilyn Miller in (TM) *Sally,* which opened in late December, 1920, and

became a hit in the following year. Marilyn Miller and Alexander Grey sang it in (MM) *Sally,* 1929. In the Kern film biography (MM) *Till the Clouds Roll By,* 1946, it was sung by Judy Garland. June Haver, in the role of Miller in her screen bio, sang it with Gordon MacRae in (MM) *Look for the Silver Lining,* 1949.

Look Homeward, Angel. w/m Wally Gold, 1957. Introduced and recorded by The Four Esquires, a group formed at Boston University, of which the writer was a member (London), 1956. Johnnie Ray had a Top 40 record (Columbia), 1957. Other popular versions by The Monarchs (Sound Stage), 1964, and The Ray Conniff Singers (Columbia), 1968.

Lookin' for a Love. w/m James Alexander and Zelda Samuels, 1962, 1974. Introduced by The Valentinos, comprised of the Womack Brothers (Sar), 1962. The J. Geils Band had a Top 40 record (Atlantic), 1972. Bobby Womack of the aforementioned brothers recorded a solo version and was awarded a gold record (United Artists), 1974.

Lookin' for Love. w/m Wanda Mallette, Bob Morrison, and Patti Ryan, 1980. Introduced in (MP) *Urban Cowboy.* Johnny Lee had a Top 10 C&W/Pop chart gold record (Full Moon).

Lookin' for Love. w/m Johnny Rotella, 1966. Chart record by The Ray Conniff Singers (Columbia).

Looking at the World Through a Windshield. w/m Jerry Chesnut and Mike Hoyer, 1968. Top 10 Country chart record by Del Reeves (United Artists).

Looking at the World Through Rose Colored Glasses. w/m Tommy Malie and Jimmy Stieger, 1926. Introduced by Jackie Osterman in the second edition of the revue (TM) *A Night in Paris.* Recorded by Fred Waring (Victor) and Paul Ash (Columbia).

Looking at You. w/m Cole Porter, 1930. Introduced by Clifton Webb and Dorothy

Dickson with Noble Sissle's Orchestra at Les Ambassadeurs in Paris, 1928. The first U.S. performance was by Jessie Matthews, Sonnie Hale, and ensemble in (TM) *Wake Up and Dream.* Recorded by Lewis James (Victor) and Lee Wiley (Liberty Music Shop).

Looking at You (Across the Breakfast Table). w/m Irving Berlin, 1930. Introduced by Al Jolson in (MM) *Mammy.* Revived in the album "Michael Feinstein Sings Irving Berlin" (Columbia), 1987.

Looking Back. w. Betty Comden and Adolph Green, m. Jule Styne, 1974. Introduced by Carol Channing in (TM) *Lorelei.*

Looking Back. w/m Brook Benton, Belford Hendricks, and Clyde Otis, 1958. Top 10 record by Nat "King" Cole (Capitol).

Looking for a Boy. w. Ira Gershwin, m. George Gershwin, 1926. Introduced by Queenie Smith in (TM) *Tip-Toes.*

Looking for a New Love. w/m André Cymone and Jody Watley, 1987. #1 R&B and #2 Pop chart record by Jody Watley, from the album of her name (MCA).

Looking for Love. w/m Hank Hunter and Stan Vincent, 1964. Introduced by Connie Francis in (MM) *Looking for Love* and on records (MGM).

Looking for More in '64. w/m B. Moore, 1964. C&W novelty hit record by disc jockey Jim Nesbitt (Chart).

Looking for Space. w/m John Denver, 1976. Recorded by John Denver (RCA).

Looking Through the Eyes of Love. w. Carole Bayer Sager, m. Marvin Hamlisch, 1979. Sung on the soundtrack of (MP) *Ice Castles* by Melissa Manchester. Nominated for an Academy Award.

Looking Through the Eyes of Love. w/m Barry Mann and Cynthia Weil, 1965. Introduced and popularized by Gene Pitney (Musicor). Revived by The Partridge Family (Bell), 1973.

Look in My Eyes. w/m Richard Barrett, 1961. Recorded by The Chantels (Carlton).

Look in My Eyes Pretty Woman. w/m Dennis Lambert and Brian Potter, 1975. Top 20 record by Tony Orlando and Dawn (Bell).

Lookin' out My Back Door. w/m John Fogerty, 1970. Gold record by Creedence Clearwater Revival (Fantasy).

Lookin' Through the Windows. w/m Clifton Davis, 1972. Top 20 record by The Jackson 5 (Motown).

Look Into Your Heart. w/m Curtis Mayfield, 1976. Introduced by Irene Cara and Lonette McKee in (MM) *Sparkle.* Leading record by Aretha Franklin (Atlantic).

Look-Ka Py Py. m. Leo Nocentelli, George Porter, Arthur Neville, and Joseph Modeliste, 1969. Instrumental by The Meters (Josie).

Look No Further. w/m Richard Rodgers, 1962. Introduced by Diahann Carroll and Richard Kiley in (TM) *No Strings.*

Look of Love. w/m Jeff Barry and Ellie Greenwich, 1965. Top 40 record by Lesley Gore (Mercury).

Look of Love, The. w. Hal David, m. Burt Bacharach, 1967. Introduced by Dusty Springfield on the soundtrack of (MP) *Casino Royale.* Song nominated for Academy Award. Springfield's record made the Top 20 (Philips). Sergio Mendes and Brasil '66 had a Top 10 version (A&M), 1968.

Look of Love (Part One). w/m Martin Fry, Mark Lickley, Stephen Singleton, and David Palmer, 1982. Recorded by the British rock group ABC (Mercury).

Look Out, Broadway. w/m Fred Wise and Randy Starr, 1966. Introduced by Elvis Presley in (MM) *Frankie and Johnny* and on records (RCA).

Look Over There. w/m Jerry Herman, 1983. Introduced by Gene Barry in (TM) *La Cage Aux Folles.*

Looks Like We Made It. w/m Will Jennings and Richard Kerr, 1977. #1 gold record by Barry Manilow (Arista).

Look Through Any Window. w/m Graham Gouldman and Charles Silverman, 1966. English export of the recording by The Hollies (Imperial).

Look Through My Window. w/m John Phillips, 1966. Hit record by The Mamas and The Papas (Dunhill).

Look to the Rainbow. w. E. Y. Harburg, m. Burton Lane, 1947. Introduced by Ella Logan and Donald Richards in (TM) *Finian's Rainbow*. Recorded by Fran Warren, who played the Logan role in the road company, 1950 (Victor). Fred Astaire, Petula Clark, and Don Francks performed it in the film version (MM) *Finian's Rainbow*, 1968.

Look to Your Soul. w/m James Hendricks, 1968. Recorded by Johnny Rivers (Imperial).

Look What I've Got. w. Leo Robin, m. Ralph Rainger, 1933. Introduced by Maurice Chevalier in (MM) *A Bedtime Story*. There were recordings by the bands of: Paul Whiteman (Victor); Freddy Martin, under pseudonym of Ed Lloyd (Perfect); Ted Fio Rito (Brunswick).

Look What They've Done to My Song, Ma. w/m Melanie Safka, 1970. Introduced by Melanie. Top 20 hit by The New Seekers (Elektra). Ray Charles had a popular version (ABC/TRC), 1972.

Look What You Done for Me. w/m Al Green, Willie Mitchell, and Al Jackson, 1972. Crossover (R&B/Pop) gold record by Al Green (Hi).

Look What You Started. 1988. Top 10 R&B chart record by The Temptations (Motown).

Look What You've Done. w/m Wes Farrell and Bob Johnston, 1967. Top 40 record by The Pozo-Seco Singers (Columbia).

Look What You've Done. w. Bert Kalmar and Irving Caesar, m. Harry Ruby and Harry

Akst, 1932. Introduced by Eddie Cantor and Lyda Roberti in (MM) *The Kid from Spain*. Recorded by Cantor (Columbia) and Ozzie Nelson and his Orchestra (Brunswick).

Look What You've Done to Me. w/m Boz Scaggs and David Foster, 1980. Recorded by Boz Scaggs (Columbia).

Look Who's Dancing. w. Dorothy Fields, m. Arthur Schwartz, 1951. Introduced by Shirley Booth and Marcia Van Dyke in (TM) *A Tree Grows in Brooklyn*.

Look Who's Here. w. Harold Adamson, m. Burton Lane, 1933. Lane's first popular song. Leading recordings by Ted Weems, vocal by Parker Gibbs (Victor); Paul Ash and his Orchestra (Brunswick).

Look Who's Talkin'. w/m Ted Daffan, 1944. Introduced and recorded by Ted Daffan and The Texans (Okeh).

Loop De Loop. w/m Teddy Vann, 1963. Crossover (R&B/Pop) hit by Johnny Thunder (King).

Loose Talk. w/m Freddie Hart and Ann Lucas, 1954. Popular country record for Carl Smith (Columbia). Revived by Buck Owens and Rose Maddox (Capitol), 1961.

Loosey's Rap. w/m Rick James, 1988. #1 R&B chart record by Rick James featuring Rosanne Shante (Reprise).

Lord, I Hope This Day Is Good. w/m Dave Hanner, 1982. #1 Country chart song by Don Williams (MCA).

Lord Knows I'm Drinking, The. w/m Bill Anderson, 1973. Crossover (C&W/Pop) record by Cal Smith (Decca).

Lorna's Here. w. Lee Adams, m. Charles Strouse, 1964. Introduced by Paula Wayne in (TM) *Golden Boy*.

Lorraine, My Beautiful Alsace Lorraine. w. Alfred Bryan, m. Fred Fisher, 1917.

Lose Again. w/m Karla Bonoff, 1977. Recorded by Karla Bonoff in her self-titled album

(Columbia). Leading single by Linda Ronstadt (Asylum).

Loser (with a Broken Heart), The. w/m Leon Russell and Don Nix, 1966. Chart record by Gary Lewis and The Playboys (Liberty).

Loser's Cathedral. w/m Glenn Sutton and Billy Sherrill, 1967. Hit Country chart record by David Houston (Epic).

Lose That Long Face. w. Ira Gershwin, m. Harold Arlen, 1954. Sung by Judy Garland in (MM) *A Star Is Born*, but deleted from the initial release.

Losing My Mind. w/m Stephen Sondheim, 1971. Introduced by Dorothy Collins in (TM) *Follies*.

Losing You. w. Carl Sigman (Engl.), m. Jean Renard, 1963. French song, originally titled "Un Ange est Venu," words by Pierre Havet. Top 10 U.S. record by Brenda Lee (Decca).

Losing Your Love. w/m Bill Anderson and Buddy Killen, 1961. C&W hit and Pop chart record by Jim Reeves (RCA).

Lost. w. Johnny Mercer and Macy O. Teetor, m. Phil Ohman, 1936. Recorded by Ruth Etting (Bluebird), Hal Kemp (Brunswick), Guy Lombardo (Victor), Vincent Lopez (Melotone), Peggy Mann (Coral).

Lost and Found. w/m Pinky Tomlin and Harry Tobias, 1938. Recorded by Pinky Tomlin (Brunswick); Kay Kyser, vocal by Harry Babbitt (Brunswick); Kenny Baker (Decca); Jimmy Dorsey, vocal by Bob Eberly (Decca); Dick Stabile, vocal by Paula Kelly (Bluebird).

Lost April. w. Eddie DeLange, m. Emil Newman and Herbert Spencer, 1948. From (MP) *The Bishop's Wife*, this was DeLange's last song success. Popular record by Nat "King" Cole (Capitol).

Lost Her Love on Our Last Date. w. Conway Twitty, m. Floyd Cramer, 1971. Lyric version of Cramer's hit instrumental "Last Date" (q.v.). #1 Country chart record by Conway Twitty (Decca). Emmylou Harris had a #1

Country chart record, titled "Lost His Love on Our Last Date," (Warner Bros.), 1982.

Lost Highway. w/m Hank Williams, 1949. Introduced and recorded by Hank Williams (MGM). Revived by Don Gibson (RCA), 1967.

Lost Horizon. w. Hal David, m. Burt Bacharach, 1972. Sung on the soundtrack of (MM) *Lost Horizon* by Shawn Phillips.

Lost in a Dream. w. Edgar Leslie, m. Rube Bloom, 1949. Introduced and recorded by Billy Eckstine (MGM). This was the last popular song in the long career of Edgar Leslie.

Lost in a Fog. w. Dorothy Fields, m. Jimmy McHugh, 1934. Written specifically for and introduced by the Dorsey Brothers' Orchestra, making their debut at Ben Marden's Riviera nightclub in Fort Lee, New Jersey. McHugh sang the vocal with the band, which was comprised of such leading musicians as Glenn Miller, Paul Weston, Charlie Spivak, Axel Stordahl, Ray McKinley and, of course, Jimmy and Tommy Dorsey. They then recorded the song with their regular singer, Bob Crosby (Decca). The best-selling record was by Rudy Vallee (Victor) who featured it on his radio shows. Other recordings by Connie Boswell (Brunswick); Jane Froman (Decca); Leo Reisman and his Orchestra (Brunswick); and later, Les Brown and his Band (Coral).

Lost in Emotion. w/m Full Force, 1987. #1 record by Lisa Lisa and Cult Jam, from their album "Spanish Fly" (Columbia).

Lost in Love. w/m Graham Russell, 1980. Top 10 hit record by the Australian duo, Air Supply, comprised of the writer and Russ Hitchcock (Arista).

Lost in Loveliness. w. Leo Robin, m. Sigmund Romberg, 1954. Introduced by David Atkinson in (TM) *The Girl in Pink Tights*. Leading recordings by Billy Eckstine (MGM) and Dolores Gray (Decca).

Lost in Meditation. w. Irving Mills, m. Edward Kennedy "Duke" Ellington, Juan Tizol, Lou Singer, 1938. Introduced by Duke Ellington and his Orchestra, and recorded by Johnny Hodges and his Orchestra (Vocalion).

Lost in the Fifties Tonight (In the Still of the Night). w/m Mike Reid, Troy Seals, and Freddy Parris, 1985. #1 Country chart hit by Ronnie Milsap (RCA). The title in parentheses is that of a major fifties hit (q.v.).

Lost in the Stars. w. Maxwell Anderson, m. Kurt Weill, 1949. Introduced by Todd Duncan in (TM) *Lost in the Stars*. Brock Peters sang it in the film version (MM) *Lost in the Stars*, 1974.

Lost in Your Eyes. w/m Deborah Ann Gibson, 1989. Hit record by Debbie Gibson (Atlantic).

Lost Love. w/m Percy Mayfield, 1951. R&B hit by Percy Mayfield (Specialty).

Lost Someone. w/m James Brown, Lloyd Stallworth, and Bobby Byrd, 1962. Introduced and recorded by James Brown (King).

Lost Without Your Love. w/m David Gates, 1976. Top 10 record by the group Bread (Elektra).

Lot in Common, A. w. Johnny Mercer, m. Harold Arlen, 1943. Introduced by Fred Astaire and Joan Leslie in (MM) *The Sky's the Limit*.

Lot of Livin' to Do, A. w. Lee Adams, m. Charles Strouse, 1960. Introduced by Dick Gautier, Susan Watson, and The Teenagers in (TM) *Bye Bye Birdie*. In the film version (MM) *Bye Bye Birdie*, 1963, it was sung by Jesse Pearson, Ann-Margret, and Bobby Rydell.

Lotta Love. w/m Neil Young, 1979. Top 10 record by Nicolette Larson (Warner Bros.).

Louie, Louie. w/m Richard Berry, 1963. First hit record of the song by The Kingsmen (Wand), followed by The Sandpipers (A&M), 1966. John Belushi recorded it on the soundtrack of (MP) *National Lampoon's Animal House*, 1978. His version was then released as a single (MCA).

Louise. w. Leo Robin, m. Richard A. Whiting, 1929. Introduced by Maurice Chevalier

in his first full-length American film (MM) *Innocents of Paris*. It was his initial U.S. record release (Victor). Paul Whiteman's Rhythm Boys [Bing Crosby, Al Rinker, and Harry Barris] also recorded it (Victor). The song, always associated with Chevalier, was performed by Johnny Johnson and Betty Jane Rhodes in (MM) *You Can't Ration Love* in 1944; by Jerry Lewis in (MM) *The Stooge* in 1953; by Neil Diamond in the third version of (MM) *The Jazz Singer* in 1980.

Louisiana. w. Bob Schafer and Andy Razaf, m. J. C. Johnson, 1928. Although recorded by many jazz groups, this is most associated with Paul Whiteman's recording, which featured The Rhythm Boys [Bing Crosby, Harry Barris, and Al Rinker] and cornetist Bix Beiderbecke (Victor). A year later, Beiderbecke recorded it with his "gang" (Okeh). Among other recordings of note are those by Count Basie (Columbia); Duke Ellington (Brunswick); Toots Mondello, featuring Ziggy Elman (Varsity); Pete Dailey (Capitol); Pete Kelly's Big Seven (Capitol).

Louisiana Fairy Tale. w. Haven Gillespie and Mitchell Parish, m. J. Fred Coots, 1935.

Louisiana Hayride. w. Howard Dietz, m. Arthur Schwartz, 1932. Sung by the company in (TM) *Flying Colors*. Nanette Fabray sang it in (MM) *The Band Wagon* in 1953. Her performance was released on records (MGM). The Boswell Sisters had a popular record in the song's origin year (Brunswick).

Louisiana Man. w/m Doug Kershaw, 1961. Introduced by the Kershaw Brothers, billed as Rusty and Doug (Hickory). Other records by The Pozo-Seco Singers (Columbia), 1967, and Bobbie Gentry (Capitol), 1968.

Louisiana Purchase. w/m Irving Berlin, 1940. Introduced by Carol Bruce, the Martins [quartet, including Hugh Martin and Ralph Blane] and the Buccaneers. It was sung by the chorus in (MM) *Louisiana Purchase*, 1942. Among records: Carol Bruce (Schirmer) and Kay Thompson (Columbia).

Louisville Lady. w/m Peter DeRose and Billy Hill, 1933. Recorded by the bands of

Paul Ash (Columbia), Joe Haymes (Melotone), Anson Weeks (Brunswick), and Isham Jones, with vocal by Eddie Stone (Victor).

Louisville Lou. w. Jack Yellen, m. Milton Ager, 1923. First hit record by the pianist Arthur Gibbs and his Gang (Okeh). Ted Lewis and his Orchestra also had a popular version (Columbia).

Lounging at the Waldorf. w. Richard Maltby, Jr., m. Thomas "Fats" Waller, 1936. Recorded instrumentally by Fats Waller (Victor). Revived by Armelia McQueen, Charlaine Woodard, Ken Page, and Nell Carter in (TM) *Ain't Misbehavin'*, 1978.

Lovable. w. Gus Kahn, m. Harry Woods, 1932. Featured by Art Jarrett and recorded by Hal Kemp, vocal by Skinnay Ennis (Brunswick); Paul Whiteman (Victor); and Benny Krueger (Brunswick).

Lovable and Sweet. w. Sidney Clare, m. Oscar Levant, 1929. From (MM) *Street Girl*, which starred Betty Compson, Jack Oakie, and Gus Arnheim's Orchestra. The latter recorded the song (Victor) as did Al Goodman's Orchestra (Brunswick), the Charleston Chasers (Columbia), Annette Hanshaw (Okeh), and Sammy Fain, the songwriter (Victor).

Love. w. Floyd Huddleston, m. George Bruns, 1973. Sung on the soundtrack by Nancy Adams in the animated feature (MM) *Robin Hood*. Nominated for the Academy Award.

Love. w/m Ralph Blane and Hugh Martin, 1946. Introduced by Lena Horne in (MM) *Ziegfeld Follies*. Leading record by Judy Garland (Decca).

L-O-V-E. w/m Bert Kaempfert and Milt Gabler, 1964. Featured and recorded by Nat "King" Cole (Capitol).

L-O-V-E (LOVE). w/m Al Green, Willie Mitchell, and Mabon Hodges, 1975. Top 20 record by Al Green (Hi).

Love (Can Make You Happy). w/m Jack Sigler, 1969. Gold record by the group Mercy (Sundi).

Love, Don't Turn Away. w. Tom Jones, m. Harvey Schmidt, 1963. Introduced by Inga Swenson in (TM) *110 in the Shade*.

Love, Here Is My Heart! w. Adrian Ross, m. Lao Silesu, 1915.

Love, Honor and Obey. w. Joseph McCarthy and Joe Goodwin, m. Chris Smith, 1912.

Love, I Hear. w/m Stephen Sondheim, 1962. Introduced by Brian Davies in (TM) *A Funny Thing Happened on the Way to the Forum*. Song not used in film version.

Love, Look Away. w. Oscar Hammerstein II, m. Richard Rodgers, 1958. Introduced by Arabella Hong in (TM) *Flower Drum Song*. In the film version (MM) *Flower Drum Song*, 1961, it was performed in a dream ballet sequence by Reiko Sato.

Love, Love, Love. w/m Ted Jarrett, 1956. Leading C&W record by Webb Pierce (Decca).

Love, Love, Love. w/m Teddy McRae, Sid Wyche, and Sonny David, 1956. Popular R&B record by The Clovers (Atlantic).

Love (Makes the World Go 'Round). w/m Paul Anka, 1963. Introduced and recorded by Paul Anka (RCA).

Love, Reign o'er Me. w/m Peter Townshend, 1973. Recorded by the English group The Who (Track).

Love, You Ain't Seen the Last of Me. w/m Kendall Franceschi, 1987. Top 10 Country chart song by John Schneider (MCA).

Love, You Didn't Do Right by Me. w/m Irving Berlin, 1954. Introduced by Rosemary Clooney in (MM) *White Christmas*. Leading records by Clooney (Columbia) and Peggy Lee (Decca).

Love, You Funny Thing. w. Roy Turk, m. Fred E. Ahlert, 1932. Featured and recorded by top artists Bing Crosby (Brunswick); Ruth Etting (Banner); George Olsen, vocal by Fran Frey (Victor); Guy Lombardo (Brunswick);

Kate Smith (Columbia); Phil Spitalny (Hit of the Week).

Love, Your Magic Spell Is Everywhere. w. Elsie Janis, m. Edmund Goulding, 1929. Introduced by Gloria Swanson in (MP) *The Trespasser*. The title originally did not have the word "magic" in it, although it was in the lyric. The composer directed and wrote the screenplay. Kate Smith recorded the song for her first release, coupled with "I May Be Wrong" (q.v.) (Harmony).

Love Ain't Nothin' But the Blues. w. Joe Goodwin, m. Louis Alter, 1929. This was interpolated in (MM) *Lord Byron of Broadway*. In 1930, it was featured in (MP) *Untamed*, starring Joan Crawford and sung in (MM) *Chasing Rainbows* by Charles King, who also recorded it (Brunswick). Smith Ballew, singing with Frankie Trumbauer's Orchestra, recorded it (Okeh).

Love Among the Young. w. Norman Gimbel, m. Alec Wilder, 1955. Leading record by Rosemary Clooney (Columbia).

Love and a Dime. w/m Brooks Bowman, 1935. From the Princeton University Triangle Club production *Stags at Bay*. Featured and recorded by Hal Kemp, vocal by Skinnay Ennis (Brunswick); Glen Gray and the Casa Loma Orchestra (Decca); Jan Garber (Victor).

Love and Kisses. w. Sid Silvers, m. Phil Baker, 1927. Recorded by the orchestras of Paul Whiteman (Victor), Paul Ash (Columbia, and Chick Webb (Decca).

Love and Learn. w. Edward Heyman, m. Arthur Schwartz, 1937. Introduced by Lily Pons in (MM) *That Girl from Paris*. Among recordings: Artie Shaw, vocal by Peg LaCentra (Brunswick); Eddy Duchin (Victor); Shep Fields (Bluebird); Miff Mole (Vocalion); Abe Lyman (Decca).

Love and Learn. See Dissertation on the State of Bliss.

Love and Liberty. w/m Laura Lee, 1972. R&B/Pop chart record by soul singer, Laura Lee (Hot Wax).

Love and Marriage. w. Sammy Cahn, m. James Van Heusen, 1955. Introduced by Frank Sinatra on TV in the musical version of Thornton Wilder's play (TVP) *Our Town*. Sinatra had a hit recording (Capitol). Among other records, Dinah Shore's was the most popular (RCA).

Love and the Weather. w/m Irving Berlin, 1947. Featured and recorded by Jo Stafford (Columbia) and Kenny Baker (Decca).

Love Ballad. w/m Skip Scarborough, 1976, 1979. Top 20 record by L.T.D. (A&M). Group's initials stood for "Love, Togetherness, and Devotion." George Benson revived the song with his Top 20 version (Warner Bros.), 1979.

Love Bites. w/m Steve Clark, Phil Collen, Joe Elliott, Robert John Lange, Rick Savage, 1988. Hit single from the album "Hysteria" by the British group Def Leppard (Mercury).

Love Bizarre, A. w/m Sheila Escovedo and Prince Rogers Nelson, 1985. Introduced by Sheila E. in (MP) *Krush Grove*. Recorded by Sheila E., with backing by co-writer Prince (Paisley Park).

Love Boat. w. Arthur Freed, m. Nacio Herb Brown, 1929. Sung by James Burroughs in (MM) *The Broadway Melody*.

Love Boat, The. w. Gene Buck, m. Victor Herbert, 1920. A production number from (TM) *The Ziegfeld Follies of 1920*, sung by John Steel.

"Love Boat" Theme. w. Paul Williams, m. Charles Fox, 1976. Music introduced as theme of long-running series (TVP) "Love Boat." Added lyric sung by Jack Jones, who then had a popular record release (MGM), 1980.

Love Bones. w/m Alvertis Isbell and Don Davis, 1970. Recorded by Johnnie Taylor (Stax).

Lovebug Itch, The. w/m Jenny Lou Carson and Roy Botkin, 1950. Featured and recorded by Eddy Arnold (RCA Victor) and Joe "Fingers" Carr (Capitol).

Love Bug Leave My Heart Alone. w/m Richard Morris and Sylvia Moy, 1967. Hit record by Martha and The Vandellas (Gordy).

Love Bug Will Bite You, The (If You Don't Watch Out). w/m Pinky Tomlin, 1937. Pinky Tomlin (Brunswick) had the best-selling record. Others: the Mills Brothers (Decca); the orchestras of Jimmy Dorsey (Decca), Louis Prima (Vocalion), Guy Lombardo (Victor), George Hall with vocal by the Modernaires (Variety).

Love Came out of the Night. w. Ed G. Nelson, m. Fred Rose, 1936. Recorded by Eddy Duchin, vocal by Jerry Cooper (Victor); George Hall, vocal by Dolly Dawn (Bluebird); Jan Garber (Decca); later, Danny Davis (MGM).

Love Came to Me. w/m Dion Di Mucci and John Falbo, 1962. Top 10 hit by Dion (Laurie).

Love Changes. w/m Skip Scarborough, 1987. Top 10 R&B chart record by Kashif and Meli'sa Morgan (Arista).

Love Child. w/m Pam Sawyer, R. Dean Taylor, Frank Wilson, and Deke Richards, 1968. #1 record by Diana Ross and The Supremes (Motown).

Love Come Down. w/m Kashif, 1982. Recorded by Evelyn "Champagne" King (RCA).

Love Days. w. William Jerome, m. Jean Schwartz, 1908. Introduced by Frank Morrell in the touring vaudeville show "Cohan & Harris's Minstrels."

Love Don't Love Nobody. w/m Joseph Jefferson and Charles Simmons, 1950, 1974. Introduced and R&B hit record by Roy Brown (Deluxe). The Spinners had a Top 20 version (Atlantic), 1974. Revived by Jean Carn (TSOP), 1981.

Love Don't You Go Through No Changes on Me. w/m Patrick Grant and Gwen Guthrie, 1975. Recorded by Sister Sledge (Atco).

Love Dropped in for Tea. w. Johnny Burke, m. Harold Spina, 1935. Featured and recorded by Rudy Vallee and his Connecticut Yankees (Victor) and Freddy Martin and his Orchestra (Brunswick).

Love Eyes. w/m Lee Hazlewood, 1967. Top 20 record by Nancy Sinatra (Reprise).

Love Eyes. w. Norman Gimbel, m. Moose Charlap, 1958. Introduced by Ralph Young in (TM) *Whoop-Up*.

Love for Love. w. Ted Koehler, m. Erich Wolfgang Korngold, 1947. From (MP) *Escape Me Never*. Leading recording by Claude Thornhill, vocal by Fran Warren (Columbia). Others: Curt Massey, with Rafael Mendez's Orchestra (Coast); Anita Ellis (Mercury); Andy Russell (Capitol).

Love for Sale. w/m Cole Porter, 1930. Introduced by Kathryn Crawford and the Three Girl Friends [June Shafer, Ida Pearson, and Stella Friend] in (TM) *The New Yorkers*. The song was initially banned from radio because of its allusion to the world's oldest profession. It became a hit, however, through the sale of recordings made by Fred Waring, his Orchestra, and the Three Girl Friends, all of whom appeared in the show (Victor), and by Libby Holman (Brunswick). Among many later recordings were those by: Hal Kemp, vocal by the Smoothies (Victor); Jack Teagarden, vocal by Kitty Kallen (Varsity); Stan Kenton, arranged by Pete Rugolo (Capitol); Oscar Peterson (Mercury); Dinah Washington (EmArcy). The song was heard on the soundtrack of the Porter film biography (MM) *Night and Day*, 1945.

Love for Sale. w. Brian Hooker, m. Rudolf Friml, 1925. Introduced by Jane Carroll in (TM) *The Vagabond King*. Not to be confused with the standard from *The New Yorkers*.

Love from a Heart of Gold. w/m Frank Loesser, 1961. Introduced by Rudy Vallee and Virginia Martin in (TM) *How to Succeed in Business Without Really Trying*. Song not used in film version.

Love Grows (Where My Rosemary Goes). w/m Tony Macaulay and Barry Mason, 1970. Gold record by the British quintet Edison Lighthouse (Bell).

Love Hangover. w/m Marilyn McLeod and Pam Sawyer, 1976. #1 record by Diana Ross (Motown). Also recorded by The 5th Dimension (ABC).

Love Has Driven Me Sane. w. John Guare, m. Galt MacDermott, 1971. Sung by Raul Julia and company in (TM) *Two Gentlemen of Verona.*

Love Has Finally Come At Last. w/m Bobby Womack, 1984. Top 10 record on the R&B charts by Bobby Womack and Patti LaBelle (Beverly Glen).

Love Has Joined Us Together. w/m Billy Dawn Smith and Marguerite James, 1955. Co-writer James was pseudonym for publisher and former bandleader Teddy Powell. Top 10 R&B chart record by Ruth Brown and Clyde McPhatter (Atlantic).

Love Has Made You Beautiful. w/m Merle Kilgore, 1960. Top 10 C&W chart record by Merle Kilgore (Starday).

Love Has No Pride. w/m Eric Kaz and Libby Titus, 1973. Recorded by Linda Ronstadt (Asylum).

Love Has No Right. w/m Nelson Larkin and Randy Scruggs, 1989. Hit Country single by Billy Joe Royal (Atlantic America).

Love Has Wings. w. C. C. S. Cushing and E. P. Heath, m. Emmerich Kallman, 1913. From (TM) *Sari.*

Love Helps Those. w/m Paul Overstreet, 1989. Top 10 Country chart record by Paul Overstreet (MTM).

Love Her Madly. w/m John Densmore, Robbie Krieger, and Ray Manzarek, 1971. Top 20 record by The Doors (Elektra).

Love Hurts. w/m Boudleaux Bryant, 1976. Gold record by the Scottish group Nazareth (A&M). Chart record by the English singer/drummer Jim Capaldi (Island).

Love I Long For, The. w. Howard Dietz, m. Vernon Duke, 1944. Introduced by June Havoc and David Newill in (TM) *Sadie Thompson*, the musical version of *Rain*. Most popular records by Harry James and his Orchestra (Columbia), Vaughn Monroe, with his Orchestra (Victor), The Three Suns (Hit).

Love I Lost, The. w/m Kenny Gamble and Leon Huff, 1973. Hit record by Harold Melvin & The Blue Notes (Philadelphia International).

Love in a Home. w. Johnny Mercer, m. Gene De Paul, 1956. Introduced by Peter Palmer and Edie Adams in (TM) *L'il Abner*. Popular record by Doris Day. (Columbia).

Love in Bloom. w. Leo Robin, m. Ralph Rainger, 1934. Introduced by Bing Crosby and Kitty Carlisle in (MM) *She Loves Me Not*. Nominated for an Academy Award. Crosby's record (Brunswick) was the best seller. Among others: Paul Whiteman (Victor), Hal Kemp (Brunswick), Claude Hopkins (Decca), and George Price (Banner). Jack Benny performed the song in (MM) *College Holiday*, 1937, and it became his theme song for the rest of his long career. Lynn Overman sang it in (MP) *New York Town*, 1941. Judy Canova sang it in (MM) *True to the Army*, 1942.

Love in Every Room. w. Jack Fishman (Engl.), m. Bernard Kesslair, 1968. French song titled "Même Si Tu Revenais," words by Jacques Chaumelle and Claude François. Introduced in France by François. Popular instrumental recording by Paul Muriat and his Orchestra (Philips).

Love in the First Degree. w/m Jim Hurt and James Dubois, 1982. Hit crossover (C&W/Pop) record by the quartet Alabama (RCA).

Love in the Shadows. w/m Neil Sedaka and Phil Cody, 1976. Top 20 record by Neil Sedaka (Rocket).

Love Is a Battlefield. w/m Mike Chapman and Holly Knight, 1983. Top 10 record by Pat Benatar (Chrysalis).

Love Is a Dancing Thing. w. Howard Dietz, m. Arthur Schwartz, 1935. Sung by Woods Miller and danced by Paul Hakon and Nina Whitney in (TM) *At Home Abroad*, which starred Beatrice Lillie and Ethel Waters.

Love Is a Golden Ring. w/m Richard Dehr, Frank Miller, and Terry Gilkyson, 1957. Popularized by Frankie Laine (Columbia).

Love Is a House. w/m Martin Lascalles, Geoff Gurd, and G. Foster, 1987. #1 R&B chart record by Force M.D.'s (Tommy Boy).

Love Is a Hurtin' Thing. w. Ben Raleigh, m. Dave Linden, 1966. Top 20 record by Lou Rawls (Capitol).

Love Is Alive. w/m Kent Robbins, 1985. #1 Country chart single by The Judds (RCA).

Love Is Alive. w/m Gary Wright, 1976. Top 10 record by Gary Wright (Warner Bros.).

Love Is All. w. Harry Tobias, m. Pinky Tomlin, 1940. Introduced in (MM) *It's a Date* and on records by Deanna Durbin (Decca).

Love Is All Around. w/m Reg Presley, 1968. Top 10 record by the English group, The Troggs, of which the writer was lead singer (Fontanta).

Love Is All We Need. w/m Ben Raleigh and Don Wolf, 1958. Hit record by Tommy Edwards (MGM). Other chart versions by Vic Dana (Dolton), 1964; Mel Carter (Imperial), 1966.

Love Is Alright Tonite. w/m Rick Springfield, 1982. Recorded by the Australian singer/composer/actor Rick Springfield (RCA).

Love Is a Many-Splendored Thing. w. Paul Francis Webster, m. Sammy Fain, 1955. Title song from (MP) *Love Is a Many-Splendored Thing*. Winner, Academy Award for Best Song, 1955. #1 recording on all charts by The Four Aces, arranged and conducted by Jack Pleis (Decca).

Love Is a Merry-Go-Round. w. Johnny Mercer, m. Rube Bloom, 1937. Featured and recorded by the bands of Bunny Berigan (Victor) and Charlie Barnet, vocal by Kathleen Lane (Bluebird).

Love Is a Rose. w/m Neil Young, 1975. Recorded by Linda Ronstadt (Asylum).

Love Is a Simple Thing. w. June Carroll, m. Arthur Siegel, 1952. Introduced by Rosemary O'Reilly, Robert Clary, Eartha Kitt, and June Carroll in (TM) *New Faces of 1952*, and repeated by them in (MM) *New Faces*, 1954.

Love Is a Sometimes Thing. w/m Jan Howard, 1970. Top 10 Country chart record by Bill Anderson (Decca).

Love Is a Song. w. Larry Morey, m. Frank Churchill, 1942. Academy Award nominee from The Walt Disney feature-length cartoon (MM) *Bambi*. No vocal credits were given.

Love Is a Stranger. w/m Annie Lennox and Davis Stewart, 1983. Written and recorded by the U.K. duo The Eurythmics (RCA).

Love Is a Very Light Thing. w/m Harold Rome, 1954. Introduced by Ezio Pinza in (TM) *Fanny*.

Love I Saw in You Was Just a Mirage, The. w/m William Robinson and Marvin Taplin, 1967. Top 40 record by Smokey Robinson and The Miracles (Tamla).

Love Is Better in the A.M. w/m Don Davis, Melvin Griffin, and Harvey Scales, 1977. Recorded by Johnnie Taylor (Columbia).

Love Is Blue. w. Brian Blackburn (Engl), Pierre Cour (Fr.), m. André Popp, 1968. Original French title "L'amour est Bleu." Recorded by French conductor/arranger/harpsichordist Paul Mauriat and his Orchestra, the instrumental became an immediate U.S. hit (Philips). It was #1 for five weeks and was rated the #2 hit of the year. The recording sold over four million copies. The leading vocal versions were by Al Martino (Capitol); Claudine Longet (A&M); in medley, "I Can Sing a Rainbow/Love Is Blue" by The Dells (Cadet), 1969.

Love is Forever. w/m Billy Ocean and Barry Eastmond, 1986. Chart record by Billy Ocean from his album "Love Zone" (Jive).

Love Is for the Very Young. See **Bad and the Beautiful, The.**

Love Is Here and Now You're Gone. w/m Brian Holland, Lamont Dozier, and Eddie Holland, 1967. #1 chart record by The Supremes (Motown).

Love Is Here to Stay. w. Ira Gershwin, m. George Gershwin, 1938. The last song written by George Gershwin, who died while composing the score for (MM) *The Goldwyn Follies.* This standard was introduced in the film by Kenny Baker. Gene Kelly sang it with Leslie Caron in (MM) *An American in Paris*, 1951, and recorded it (MGM). Leading early recordings by Red Norvo, vocal by Mildred Bailey (Vocalion); Larry Clinton (Victor); Jimmy Dorsey, vocal by Bob Eberly (Decca). In the early fifties, Jackie Gleason had a popular recording with orchestra featuring trumpeter Bobby Hackett (Capitol).

Love Is in Control (Finger on the Trigger). w/m Quincy Jones, Merria Ross, and Rod Temperton, 1982. Top 10 record by Donna Summer (Mercury).

Love Is in the Air. w/m Harry Vanda and George Young, 1978. Top 10 record by John Paul Young (Scotti Brothers).

Love Is in the Air. w/m Marty Robbins, 1968. Country chart record by Marty Robbins (Columbia).

Love Is Just a Four-Letter Word. w/m Bob Dylan, 1969. Chart single by Joan Baez (Vanguard).

Love Is Just Around the Corner. w. Leo Robin, m. Lewis E. Gensler, 1935. Introduced by Bing Crosby in (MM) *Here Is My Heart* and on records (Decca). It was sung by Robert Cummings in (MM) *Millions in the Air* in 1935.

(Love Is Like a) Baseball Game. w/m Kenny Gamble and Leon Huff, 1968. Top 40 record by The Intruders (Gamble).

Love Is Like a Butterfly. w/m Dolly Parton, 1974. Country hit by Dolly Parton (RCA).

Love Is Like a Cigarette. w/m Jerome Jerome, Richard Byron, and Walter Kent, 1936. Recorded by Duke Ellington, vocal by Ivy Anderson (Brunswick).

Love Is Like A Cigarette. w. Glen MacDonough, m. Victor Herbert, 1908. Originally in (TM) *Algeria* and then in the revised and retitled *The Rose of Algeria* in 1909, sung by Frank Pollock.

Love Is Like a Firefly. w. Otto Harbach, m. Rudolf Friml, 1912. First sung by Emma Trentini in (TM) *The Firefly.* In (MM) *The Firefly*, 1937, it was sung by Jeanette MacDonald.

Love Is Like an Itching in My Heart. w/m Brian Holland, Lamont Dozier, and Eddie Holland, 1966. Top 10 record by The Supremes (Motown).

Love Is Like Oxygen. w/m Trevor Griffin and Andrew Scott, 1978. Top 10 record by the English rock band Sweet (Capitol).

Love Is Like That (What Can You Do?) w/m Benee Russell, 1931. Introduced and featured by Ruth Etting. Also recorded by Smith Ballew, with Red Nichols and his Band (Brunswick).

Love Is Love Anywhere. w. Ted Koehler, m. Harold Arlen, 1934. From (MM) *Let's Fall in Love.* Recorded by three piano-playing bandleaders: Eddy Duchin (Victor), Henry King [under the name of Don Walker] (Vocalion), and Fred Rich (Columbia).

Love Is Never Out of Season. w. Lew Brown, m. Sammy Fain, 1937. Introduced by Harriet Hilliard in (MM) *New Faces of 1937* and recorded by her with Ozzie Nelson's Orchestra (Bluebird). Among other recordings: Tommy Dorsey, vocal by Jack Leonard (Victor); George Hill, vocal by Dolly Dawn (Variety); Gene Kardos's Band (Melotone); Emery Deutsch's Band (Brunswick).

Love Is No Excuse. w/m Justin Tubb, 1964. Top 10 Country chart record by Jim Reeves and Dottie West (RCA).

Love Is on a Roll. w/m Roger Cook and John Prine, 1983. #1 Country chart record by Don Williams (MCA).

Love Is on the Air Tonight. w. Johnny Mercer, m. Richard A. Whiting, 1937. Introduced in (MM) *Varsity Show* and on records (Decca) by Dick Powell.

Love Is So Terrific. w. Artie Shaftel, m. Sunny Skylar, 1948. Most popular version by Art Lund, with Johnny Thompson's Orchestra (MGM).

Love Is Strange. w/m Ethel Smith, Mickey Baker, and Sylvia Robinson, 1957. Hit record by Mickey and Sylvia (Groove). Revived in 1967 by Peaches and Herb (Date).

Love Is Sweeping the Country. w. Ira Gershwin, m. George Gershwin, 1932. Introduced by George Murphy, June O'Dea, and the ensemble in the Pulitzer Prize winner (TM) *Of Thee I Sing*. The music for the interlude [patter] was originally composed for *Ming Toy*, an unproduced musical based on the play *East Is West*.

Love Is the Answer. w/m Todd Rundgren, 1979. Top 10 record by England Dan [Seals] and John Ford Coley (Big Tree).

Love Is the Best of All. w. Henry Blossom, m. Victor Herbert, 1915. Introduced by Eleanor Painter in (TM) *The Princess Pat.*

Love Is the Darndest Thing. w. Johnny Burke, m. James Van Heusen, 1946. Introduced by Betty Hutton in (MM) *Cross My Heart*, the remake of the Carole Lombard comedy *True Confession.*

Love Is the Drug. w/m Roger Lewis, 1976. Recorded by the British band Roxy Music (Atco).

Love Is the Foundation. w/m William C. Hall, 1973. Country chart hit record by Loretta Lynn (MCA).

Love Is the Reason. w. Dorothy Fields, m. Arthur Schwartz, 1951. Introduced by Shirley Booth in (TM) *A Tree Grows in Brooklyn.*

Love Is the Seventh Wave. w/m Sting, 1985. Recorded by the English singer, Sting, pseudonym for Gordon Sumner (A&M).

Love Is the Sweetest Thing. w/m Ray Noble, 1933. The song was first heard in the British film (MM) *Say It with Music*, played by Jack Payne's Orchestra, which also recorded it on an English label (Imperial) but not released in the U.S. Ray Noble and his band's (HMV) version, with vocal by Al Bowlly, was released in the U.S. (Victor) and the song became one of the hits of the year. Other recordings of note: Jack Fulton (Vocalion); Joe Morrison (Columbia); Conrad Thibault (Victor). It was heard in (MP) *Confidential Agent*, starring Charles Boyer and Lauren Bacall in 1945.

Love Is the Thing. w. Ned Washington, m. Victor Young, 1933. Featured by Ethel Waters and coupled with "Stormy Weather" on her record (Brunswick). It was also recorded by Morton Downey (Perfect); Glen Gray and the Casa Loma Orchestra, vocal by Kenny Sargent (Brunswick); and Richard Himber, vocal by Joey Nash (Vocalion). Later, Andy Kirk and his Clouds of Joy (Decca) and Beryl Brooks (Mercury) had well-received discs.

(Love Is) Thicker Than Water. w/m Barry Gibb and Andy Gibb, 1978. #1 record by British singer Andy Gibb (RSO).

Love Is Where You Find It. w. Earl K. Brent, m. Nacio Herb Brown, 1948. Introduced by Kathryn Grayson in (MM) *The Kissing Bandit*, and recorded by her (MGM).

Love Is Where You Find It. w. Al Dubin and Johnny Mercer, m. Harry Warren, 1938. Introduced by John Payne and Johnny "Scat" Davis in (MM) *Garden of the Moon*. Leading records by Jimmy Dorsey, vocal by Bob Eberly (Decca), and Kay Kyser, vocal by Harry Babbitt (Brunswick). Not to be confused with the 1948 song.

Love I You (You I Love). w/m Sammy Carlisi, 1954. Popular record by The Gaylords (Mercury).

Love Jones. w/m Randolph Murph, Ralph Eskridge, and Clarence Johnson, 1972. Gold record by the group The Brighter Side of Darkness (20th Century). See also "Basketball Jones Featuring Tyrone Shoelaces."

Love Land. w/m Don Trotter and Charles Wright, 1970. Top 20 record by Charles Wright and and The Watts 103rd Street Rhythm Band (Warner Bros.).

Loveless Love (or Careless Love). w/m W. C. Handy, 1921. The source of this tune is constantly questioned. "Loveless Love" is always credited to Handy, while "Careless Love" is sometimes credited to Handy and Spencer Williams, but folk song historians such as Alan Lomax in his book *The Folk Songs of North America* opine that the song originated as a blues, sung by "wandering Negro workers." As the latter title with music is in the public domain, many arrangers have copyrighted their versions. The "Loveless" title has been recorded by Handy (Varsity), Fats Waller (Victor), Noble Sissle (Decca), The Mills Brothers (Decca), and Billie Holiday (Okeh), among many others. The "Careless" title has been recorded by Papa Celestin (Okeh), Ethel Waters (Victor), Lee Wiley (Decca), Bessie Smith [as "Careless Love Blues"] (Columbia), and others.

Love Letters. w. Edward Heyman, m. Victor Young, 1945. Theme from (MP) *Love Letters*. Nominated for Academy Award. Hit recording by Dick Haymes (Decca). Revived by Ketty Lester (Era), 1962, and Elvis Presley (RCA), 1966.

Love Letters in the Sand. w. Nick Kenny and Charles Kenny, m. J. Fred Coots, 1931, 1957. Nick Kenny wrote the basis of the lyric as a poem in his column in the New York Mirror. Coots then set a completed lyric version to music. George Hall, on the air fourteen times a week, featured it in broadcasts from the Taft Hotel in New York and made the song a hit. He recorded it (Bluebird) and later used it as his theme. In 1957, Pat Boone sang it in his first film (MP) *Bernadine*. His recording was a million-seller, #1 on the charts for seven weeks and in the Top 40 for twenty-four weeks (Dot).

Lovelier Than Ever. w/m Frank Loesser, 1948. Introduced by Paul England and Jane Lawrence in (TM) *Where's Charley?*

Love Lies. w. Carl Sigman and Ralph Freed, m. Joseph Meyer, 1940. Many recordings, the most popular of which was by Tommy Dorsey, vocal by Frank Sinatra (Victor). Among others: Larry Clinton, vocal by Terry Allen (Bluebird); Gene Krupa, vocal by Howard Dulany (Okeh); The Mills Brothers (Decca); Frances Langford (Decca); Sammy Kaye, vocal by Tommy Ryan (Varsity).

Loveliest Night in the Year, The. w. Paul Francis Webster, m. adapted by Irving Aaronson, 1951. Adapted from the 1888 waltz by Juventino Rosas, "Over the Waves" ("Sobre las Olas"). Ann Blyth sang it in (MM) *The Great Caruso*, starring Mario Lanza, but Lanza recorded it and had a million-seller (RCA Victor). Other popular versions by Helen O'Connell (Capitol) and organist Ethel Smith (Decca).

Love Light in Flight. w/m Stevie Wonder, 1984. Sung on the soundtrack of the film (MP) *The Woman in Red*, and on records by Stevie Wonder (Motown).

Lovelight in the Starlight. w. Ralph Freed, m. Frederick Hollander, 1938. From (MP) *Her Jungle Love*, starring Dorothy Lamour, who recorded it with Herbie Kay's Orchestra (Brunswick). Also recorded by Jan Savitt, vocal by Carlotta Dale (Bluebird); Horace Heidt (Brunswick); Charles "Buddy" Rogers, vocal by Bob Hannon (Vocalion); Ruby Newman and his Orchestra (Decca).

Love Like Ours, A. w. Mann Holiner, m. Alberta Nichols, 1944. Sung by June Allyson and Gloria DeHaven in (MM) *Two Girls and a Sailor.*

Love Like This, A. w. Ned Washington, m. Victor Young, 1943. Adapted from Young's love theme from (MP) *For Whom the Bell Tolls.* Popular recording by Carmen Cavallaro and his Orchestra (Decca).

Loveliness of You, The. w. Mack Gordon, m. Harry Revel, 1937. Introduced by Tony Martin in (MM) *You Can't Have Everything.*

Love Lives On. w. Cynthia Weil and Will Jennings, m. Barry Mann and Bruce Broughton, 1987. Sung on the soundtrack of (MP) *Harry and the Hendersons* by Joe Cocker and on the soundtrack album (MCA)

Love Locked Out. w. Max Kester, m. Ray Noble, 1934. Introduced and featured by Ray Noble and his Orchestra (Victor). In the early fifties, baritone Bill Farrell (MGM) revived it.

Love Looks Good on You. w/m Jerry Shook, 1964. Hit C&W record by David Houston (Epic). Also recorded by Lefty Frizzell (Columbia), 1965.

Lovely. w/m Stephen Sondheim, 1962. Introduced by Brian Davies and Preshy Marker, and reprised by Zero Mostel and Jack Gilford in (TM) *A Funny Thing Happened on the Way to the Forum.* In (MM) *A Funny Thing Happened on the Way to the Forum,* 1966, it was sung by Zero Mostel, Michael Crawford, Annette André, and Jack Gilford.

Lovely. w. Edgar Leslie, m. Fred E. Ahlert, 1933.

Lovely Lady. w. Ted Koehler, m. Jimmy McHugh, 1936. Introduced by Kenny Baker in (MM) *King of Burlesque.* Recorded by Glen Gray and the Casa Loma Orchestra (Decca), Bing Crosby (Decca), Vincent Lopez and his Orchestra (Bluebird), Dick Robertson (Champion).

Lovely Night, A. w. Oscar Hammerstein II, m. Richard Rodgers, 1957. Introduced by Julie Andrews, Ilka Chase, Kay Ballard, and Alice Ghostley in (TVM) *Cinderella.*

Lovely One. w/m Michael Jackson and Randy Jackson, 1980. Recorded by The Jacksons (Epic).

Lovely One. w. Frank Loesser, m. Manning Sherwin, 1937. Loesser's first song written for a movie was featured as a production number in Walter Wanger's (MM) *Vogues of '38.*

Lovely Rita (Meter Maid). w/m John Lennon and Paul McCartney, 1967. Introduced by The Beatles in their album "Sgt. Pepper's Lonely Hearts Club Band" (Capitol).

Lovely to Look At. w. Dorothy Fields and Jimmy McHugh, m. Jerome Kern, 1935. Introduced in a fashion show scene by Irene Dunne, then reprised and danced by Fred Astaire and Ginger Rogers in (MM) *Roberta.* In a remake of *Roberta* in 1952, it became the title song of (MM) *Lovely to Look At,* and was sung by Howard Keel. The song was nominated for an Academy Award in 1935, and was #1 on "Your Hit Parade" on the second week of that radio show.

Lovely Way to Spend an Evening, A. w. Harold Adamson, m. Jimmy McHugh, 1944. Introduced by Frank Sinatra in (MM) *Higher and Higher.* Sinatra's popular recording was made during the musicians' strike and had only vocal backing by the Bobby Tucker Singers (Columbia).

Lovely Work of Art, A. w/m James Joiner, 1960. C&W chart hit by Jimmy Newman (MGM).

Love Machine. w/m Bill Griffin and Pete Moore, 1975. #1 gold record by The Miracles (Tamla). This was Part 1 of the original cut in the album "City of Angels," which was too long to be released as a single.

Love Makes a Woman. w/m Carl Davis, Eugene Record, and William Sanders, 1968. Top 20 record by Barbara Acklin (Brunswick).

Love Makes Such Fools of Us All. w. Michael Stewart, m. Cy Coleman, 1980. Introduced by Marianne Tatum in (TM) *Barnum.*

Love Makes the World Go 'Round. w/m Deon Jackson, 1966. Introduced and Top 20 record by Deon Jackson (Carla). Revived by Odds and Ends (Today) and Kiki Dee (Rare Earth), 1971.

Love Makes the World Go 'Round. w/m Bob Merrill, 1961. Song billed in program as "Theme," but more popularly known as above. It was introduced in (TM) *Carnival* by Anna Maria Alberghetti.

Love Makes the World Go 'Round. w/m Ollie Jones, 1958. Featured and recorded by Perry Como.

Love Makes the World Go 'Round. w. Clyde Fitch, m. William Furst, 1896. From (TM) *Bohemia.*

Love Me. w/m Barry Gibb, Maurice Gibb, and Robin Gibb, 1976. Top 20 record by Yvonne Elliman (RSO).

Love Me. w/m Mike Stoller and Jerry Leiber, 1956. Top 10 record by Elvis Presley (RCA Victor).

Love Me. w. Sammy Cahn, m. Jule Styne, 1945. Introduced by Andy Russell in (MM) *The Stork Club,* and on records (Capitol).

Love Me. w. Ned Washington, m. Victor Young, 1934. Among the recordings over the years: Jack Teagarden (Brunswick); Don Bestor (Victor); Woody Herman, vocal by Mary Ann McCall (Decca); Billy Eckstine (MGM); Dean Martin, with Dick Stabile's Orchestra (Capitol).

Love Me! Love Me! Love Me! w/m Frank Anderson, Rene LaMarre, and Viviane Greene, 1949. Popular records by Buddy Clark (Columbia), Eddy Howard and his Orchestra (Mercury), Jack Fina and his Orchestra (MGM).

Love Me Again. w. Alice Wills, m. David Lasley, 1978. Recorded by Rita Coolidge (A&M).

Love Me and the World Is Mine. w. Dave Reed, Jr., m. Ernest R. Ball, 1906. Introduced in vaudeville by Maude Lambert and later featured in concert by the tenor John McCormack. Sung by Jeanette MacDonald in (MM) *San Francisco,* 1936. Dick Haymes sang it in the role portraying the composer in Ball's screen biography (MM) *Irish Eyes Are Smiling,* 1944.

Love Me Do. w/m John Lennon and Paul McCartney, 1964. #1 record by The Beatles (Tollie).

Love Me for a Reason. w/m Johnny Briston, Wade Browd, Jr., and David Jones, Jr., 1974. Top 10 record by The Osmonds (MGM).

Love Me Forever. w/m Beverly Guthrie and Gary Lynes, 1957. Leading records by The Four Esquires (Paris) and Eydie Gormé (ABC-Paramount). Revived by Roger Williams (Kapp), 1967.

Love Me Forever. w. Gus Kahn, m. Victor Schertzinger, 1935. Introduced by Grace Moore in (MM) *Love Me Forever.*

Love Me Just a Little (If You). See **(If You) Love Me Just a Little.**

Love Me Like You Used To. w/m Paul Davis and Bobby Emmons, 1987. Top 10 Country chart record by Tanya Tucker (Capitol).

Love Me Little, Love Me Long. w/m Percy Gaunt, 1893.

Love Me or Leave Me. w. Gus Kahn, m. Walter Donaldson, 1928. Introduced by Ruth Etting in (TM) *Whoopee,* and on records (Columbia). Benny Goodman and his Orchestra made two different well-received instrumental versions of the song (Columbia), 1934 and 1936. In the Gus Kahn biography (MM) *I'll See You in My Dreams,* 1951, it was sung by Patrice Wymore. The song was so associated with Etting that it became the title song for her screen biography (MM) *Love Me or Leave Me,* 1955, in which Doris Day played the role of Etting. Lena Horne (RCA) and Sammy Davis, Jr. (Decca) followed with chart records. For additional sidelight, see "Lullaby of Birdland."

Love Me Over Again. w/m Don Williams, 1980. #1 Country chart record by Don Williams (MCA).

Love Me Tender. w/m Elvis Presley and Vera Matson, 1956. Melody based on the Civil War song, "Aura Lee, or the Maid with the Golden Hair," by (w.) W. W. Fosdick, (m.) George R. Poulton. Introduced by Elvis Presley in (MM) *Love Me Tender*, his first film. His recording was a #1 million-seller (RCA). In 1962, Richard Chamberlain revived the song (MGM). Percy Sledge had a popular version in 1967 (Atlantic). It was heard in (MM) *FM*, 1978.

Love Me to Pieces. w/m Melvin Endsley, 1957. Introduced by Jill Corey on (TVP) *Studio One Summer Theatre*. Her recording (Columbia) made the Top 20.

Love Me Tomorrow. w/m Peter Cetera and David Foster, 1982. Recorded by the group Chicago (Full Moon).

Love Me Tonight. w. Barry Mason (Engl.), D. Pace (It.), m. L. Pilat and M. Panzeri, 1969. Italian song, "All Fina della Strada." Top 20 record in English by Tom Jones (Parrot).

Love Me Tonight. w. Bing Crosy and Ned Washington, m. Victor Young, 1932. Recorded by Bing Crosby, with Lenny Hayton's Orchestra (Brunswick). Note: By great coincidence, this and the Rodgers and Hart song of the same title came out simultaneously, with a marked similarity in the pitches and intervals of the melodic lines. There was never any question of plagiarism, however.

Love Me Tonight. w. Lorenz Hart, m. Richard Rodgers, 1932. Introduced by Jeanette MacDonald and Maurice Chevalier in (MM) *Love Me Tonight*.

Love Me Tonight. w. Brian Hooker, m. Rudolf Friml, 1925. Introduced by Dennis King and Carolyn Thompson in (TM) *The Vag-*

abond King. Dennis King and Jeanette MacDonald sang it in (MM) *The Vagabond King*, 1930.

Love Me Two Times. w/m John Densmore, Robert Krieger, Raymond Manzarek, and James Morrison, 1968. Written by the personnel of The Doors, who had a Top 20 record (Elektra).

Love Me Warm and Tender. w/m Paul Anka, 1962. Recorded by Paul Anka (RCA).

Love Me with All Your Heart (Cuando Caliente el Sol). w. Michael Vaughn (Engl.), Mario Rigual (Sp.), m. Carlos Rigual, 1963. First U.S. recording of this Mexican song by Steve Allen, with The Copacabana Trio singing the Spanish lyrics (Dot). Under the English title, the Ray Charles Singers had a hit record (Command), 1963. The Irish trio, The Bachelors, had a Top 40 version in 1966 (London).

Love Minus Zero—No Limit. w/m Bob Dylan, 1965. Introduced by Bob Dylan and recorded by him in an LP (Columbia). Single chart version by Turley Richards (Warner Bros.), 1970.

(I Wanna) Love My Life Away. w/m Gene Pitney, 1961. Introduced and recorded by Gene Pitney (Musicor).

Love My Way. w/m John Ashton, Timothy Butler, Richard Butler, and Vincent Ely, 1983. Recorded by the British group Psychedelic Furs (Columbia).

Love Nest, The. w. Otto Harbach, m. Louis A. Hirsch, 1920. The hit song of (TM) *Mary*, introduced by Jack McGowan and Janet Velie. In (MM) *The Helen Morgan Story*, 1957, it was sung by Gogi Grant, dubbing for Ann Blyth in the title role. The melody was used as the theme song for the Burns and Allen Show on radio and T.V.

Love Never Goes Away. w/m Al Kasha and Joel Hirschhorn, 1982. Introduced by Debbie Boone in the stage version (TP) *Seven Brides for Seven Brothers*.

Love Never Went to College. w. Lorenz Hart, m. Richard Rodgers, 1939. Introduced by Marcy Westcott and Richard Kollmar in (TM) *Too Many Girls*. Frances Langford sang it in (MM) *Too Many Girls*, 1940. Leading records by Benny Goodman (Columbia); Bob Chester, vocal by Dolores O'Neill (Bluebird); Hal Kemp, vocal by The Smoothies (Victor).

Love of My Life. w/m Cole Porter, 1948. Introduced by Judy Garland in (MM) *The Pirate*. Leading records: Judy Garland (MGM) and Harry James, vocal by Marion Morgan (Columbia).

Love of My Life, The. w. Johnny Mercer, m Artie Shaw, 1940. Introduced by Fred Astaire in (MM) *Second Chorus*. Astaire recorded it (Columbia) as did Artie Shaw, vocal by Anita Boyer (Victor). Nominated for Academy Award.

Love of My Man, The. w/m Ed Townsend, 1963. Recorded by the gospel/blues singer Theola Kilgore (Serock).

Love on a Greyhound Bus. w. Ralph Blane and Kay Thompson, m. George Stoll, 1946. Introduced by Pat Kirkwood in (MM) *No Leave, No Love*. Best-selling records: Guy Lombardo and his Orchestra (Decca); Kay Kyser, vocal by Lucy Ann Polk (Columbia).

Love on a Two-Way Street. w/m Sylvia Robinson and Bert Keyes, 1970. Gold record by the Moments (Stang). Revived with a Top 40 record by fifteen-year-old singer Stacy Lattisaw (Cotillion), 1981.

Love on My Mind. w/m Ray Charles, 1962. Recorded by Ray Charles and Milt Jackson (Atlantic).

Love on the Rocks. w/m Neil Diamond (Engl.) and Gilbert Becaud (Fr.), 1980. Introduced by Neil Diamond in the third version of (MM) *The Jazz Singer*, and on records (Capitol).

Love on Your Side. w/m Tom Bailey, Alannah Currie, and Joe Leeway, 1983. Recorded by the British-based trio with the unlikely name of The Thompson Twins (Arista).

Love or Let Me Be Lonely. w. Anita Poree, m. Skip Scarborough, 1970. Top 10 record by The Friends of Distinction (RCA). Revived by Paul Davis (Arista), 1982.

Love or Something Like It. w/m Steven Glassmeyer and Kenny Rogers, 1978. Recorded by Kenny Rogers (Untied Artists).

Love Out Loud. w/m Thomas Schuyler, 1989. Hit country record by Earl Thomas Conley (RCA).

Love Over and Over Again. w/m Bobby DeBarge and Bunny DeBarge, 1980. Top 10 R&B chart hit by the sextet Switch (Gordy).

Love Overboard. w/m Reggie Calloway, 1987. #1 R&B and crossover Pop chart record by Gladys Knight and The Pips (MCA).

Love Passes By. w. Jack Scholl, m. Victor Schertzinger, 1935. Introduced in (MM) *Let's Live Tonight* and on records (Columbia) by Tullio Carminati. Also recorded by Vincent Rose and his Orchestra (Melotone).

Love Plus One. w/m Nick Heyward, 1982. Recorded by the British sextet Haircut One Hundred (Arista).

Love Potion Number Nine. w/m Jerry Leiber and Mike Stoller, 1959. Chart record by The Clovers (United Artists). In 1965, the English rock group, the Searchers, had a Top 10 record (Kapp).

Love Power. w. Carole Bayer Sager, m. Burt Bacharach, 1987. R&B and Pop chart record by Dionne Warwick and Jeffrey Osborne from the album "Reservations for Two" (Arista).

Love Power. w/m Willie Hutch, 1975. Top 10 R&B and chart Pop record by Wille Hutch (Motown).

Love Power. w/m Teddy Vann, 1967. Recorded by The Sandpebbles, produced by the writer (Calla).

Love Put a Song in My Heart. w/m Ben Peters, 1975. #1 Country chart record by Johnny Rodriguez (Mercury).

Lover. w. Lorenz Hart, m. Richard Rodgers, 1932. Introduced by Jeanette MacDonald in (MM) *Love Me Tonight.* Sung by Gloria Jean in (MM) *Moonlight in Vermont,* 1943, and heard orchestrally, under the titles in the Rodgers and Hart biography (MM) *Words and Music,* 1948. Peggy Lee, who had a million-seller (Capitol), 1952, sang it in (MM) *The Jazz Singer,* 1953. It also was one of Les Paul's early successes utilizing his multi-track recording technique (Capitol), 1948.

Lover, Come Back to Me. w. Oscar Hammerstein II, m. Sigmund Romberg, 1928. Introduced by Evelyn Herbert in (TM) *The New Moon.* Lawrence Tibbett, followed by a reprise by Grace Moore, sang it in the 1930 film adaptation (MM) *New Moon* (the article was dropped from the title). Jeanette MacDonald and Nelson Eddy sang it in the 1940 version, and Tony Martin and Joan Weldon did the duet in the Romberg biography (MM) *Deep in My Heart,* 1954.

Lover, Please. w/m Billy Swan, 1962. Top 10 record by Clyde McPhatter (Mercury).

Loverboy. w/m Billy Alessi and Bobby Alessi, 1984. Top 10 record by the English-raised Trinidadian, Billy Ocean (Jive).

Lover Come Back. w. Alan Spilton, m. Alan Spilton and Frank DeVol, 1962. Introduced by Doris Day in (MP) *Lover Come Back,* and on records, orchestra conducted by Frank DeVol (Columbia).

Love Really Hurts Without You. w/m Benjamin Findon and Les Charles, 1976. Recorded by Billy Ocean (Ariola).

Love Reunited. w/m Chris Hillman and Stephen Hill, 1987. Top 10 Country chart record by The Desert Rose Band (MCA/Curb).

Lovergirl. w/m Teena Marie (pseudonym for Mary Brockert), 1985. Top 10 single from the album "Starchild," by Teena Marie (Epic).

Lover in Me, The. w/m Kenneth Edmonds, Antonio Reid, and Daryl Summons, 1989. Hit record by Sheena Easton (MCA).

Lover Is Blue, A. w/m Charles Carpenter, James R. Mundy, and James Oliver "Trummy" Young, 1939. Featured and recorded by Tommy Dorsey, vocal by Jack Leonard (Victor).

Lover Man (Oh, Where Can You Be?) w/m Jimmy Davis, Roger "Ram" Ramirez, and Jimmy Sherman,   1942. Associated with Billie Holiday who had a best-seller with Camarata's Orchestra (Decca), 1945. Among the vast number of recordings over the years: Claude Thornhill (Columbia), Errol Garner (Apollo), Charlie Parker (JATP), Stan Kenton (Capitol), Sarah Vaughan (Musicraft) (Mercury), Duke Ellington (RCA Victor), Art Tatum (American), Steve Allen (Coral), Dick Hyman (MGM). Diana Ross sang it as Billie Holiday in her story (MM) *Lady Sings the Blues,* 1972.

Love Rollercoaster. w/m Jimmy Williams, Clarence Satchell, Leroy Bonner, Marshall Jones, Ralph Middlebrook, Marvin Pierce, and William Beck, 1976. Written and #1 gold record by The Ohio Players (Mercury).

Lover's Concerto, A. w/m Sandy Linzer and Denny Randell, 1965. Adapted from Beethoven's *Minuet in G.* #2 chart and gold record by The Toys (DynoVoice). Sarah Vaughan had a popular version (Mercury), 1966.

Lover's Gold. w. Bob Merrill, m. Morty Nevins, 1949. Introduced by The Three Suns, of which Nevins was a member. Featured and recorded by Dinah Shore (Columbia).

Lover's Holiday. w/m Bob McRee, Edward Thomas, Jr., and Clifton Thomas, 1968. Top 40 record by Peggy Scott and Jo Jo Benson (SSS International).

Lover's Lullaby, A. w. Andy Razaf, m. Frankie Carle and Larry Wagner, 1940. Top recordings by Glen Gray and the Casa Loma Orchestra (Decca), Horace Heidt and His Musical Knights (Columbia), Frankie Masters' Orchestra (Vocalion).

Lover's Quarrel, A. w/m Vic McAlpin and Newt Richardson, 1953. Popularized by Sarah Vaughan's recording (Mercury).

Lover's Question, A. w/m Brook Benton and Jimmy Williams, 1959. Leading record by Clyde McPhatter (Atlantic). Chart records by Ernestine Anderson (Mercury), 1961; Otis Redding (Atco), 1969; Loggins and Messina (Columbia), 1975.

Lovers Who Wander. w/m Dion Di Mucci and Ernest Maresca, 1962. Top 10 record by Dion (Laurie).

Love Saw It. w/m Antonio Reid, Kenneth Edmonds, and Daryl Simmons, 1989. Hit R&B chart record by Karyn White (Warner Bros.).

Love's Been a Little Bit Hard on Me. w/m Gary Burr, 1982. Top 10 record by Juice Newton (Capitol).

Love's Comin' at Ya. w/m Paul Lawrence Jones, 1982. Top 10 R&B chart record by Melba Moore (EMI America).

Love Sends a Little Gift of Roses. w. Leslie Cooke, m, John Openshaw, 1919. A popular vocal selection. Among the contrasting recordings are John McCormack (Victor) and the Andrews Sisters (Decca). The melody was remarkably similar to "Salut D'Amour" by Edward Elgar.

Love's Gonna Live Here. w/m Buck Owens, 1963. C&W hit by Buck Owens (Capitol).

Love's Got a Line on You. w/m Zack Smith and Kathe Green, 1983. Recorded by the rock band Scandal (Columbia).

Love's Grown Deep. w/m Kenny Nolan, 1977. Recorded by Kenny Nolan (20th Century).

Love Shack. w/m Cynthia Wilson, Cather Pierson, J. Strickland, and Fredrick Schneider, 1989. Hit record by B-52's (Reprise).

Love She Can Count On, A. w/m William Robinson, 1963. Top 40 record by The Miracles (Tamla).

Lovesick Blues. w. Irving Mills, m. Cliff Friend, w/m revised by Hank Williams, 1922, 1949. Original version recorded and performed by many artists over the years, such as Bertha "Chippie Hill" (Okeh), Anita O'Day (London), Bill Darnell (Coral). In 1949, Hank Williams revised the song, and his recording (MGM) sold over a million copies and was the #1 Country hit of the year.

Love's Lines, Angles, and Rhymes. w/m Dorothea Joyce, 1971. Top 20 record by The 5th Dimension (Bell).

Love's Made a Fool of You. w/m Buddy Holly and Bob Montgomery, 1966. Written in 1958, but first chart record in 1966 by The Bobby Fuller Four (Mustang). Revived by Cochise (United Artists), 1971.

Loves Me Like a Rock. w/m Paul Simon, 1973. Gold record by Paul Simon (Columbia).

Love Somebody. w/m Rick Springfield, 1984. Sung by Rick Springfield in (MP) *Hard to Hold* and on hit record (RCA).

Love Somebody. w/m Joan Whitney and Alex Kramer, 1947. #1 record hit by Doris Day and Buddy Clark (Columbia).

Love Someone Like Me. w/m Holly Dunn and Radney Foster, 1987. Hit Country chart record by Holly Dunn (MTM).

Love Song, A. w/m Dona Lynn George and Kenny Loggins, 1974. Top 20 record by Anne Murray (Capitol).

Love Song from "Houseboat." See **Almost in Your Arms.**

Love Song from "Mutiny on the Bounty." w. Paul Francis Webster, m. Bronislau Kaper, 1962. Introduced on the soundtrack of (MP) *Mutiny on the Bounty*. Nominated for Academy Award, 1962.

Love Song of Long Ago, A. w. Gus Kahn, m. Sigmund Romberg, 1937. Heard in (MP) *They Gave Him a Gun*. Featured and recorded by Xavier Cugat, vocal by Buddy Clark (Victor) and Henry "Red" Allen (Vocalion).

Love Songs of the Nile. w. Arthur Freed, m. Nacio Herb Brown, 1933. Sung by Ramon Novarro in (MP) *The Barbarian*. Records: Adrian Schubert and his Orchestra, vocal by Elmer Feldkamp (Crown); Wayne King (Brunswick); The Merry Macs (Victor); Leo Reisman, vocal by Howard Phillips (Victor).

Love So Right. w/m Barry Gibb, Maurice Gibb, and Robin Gibb, 1976. Top 10 gold record by the British brother trio The Bee Gees (RSO).

Love's Own Sweet Song. w. C. C. S. Cushing and E. P. Heath, m. Emmerich Kallman, 1914. A waltz from (TM) *Sari*.

Love's Roundelay. w. Joseph Herbert, m. Oscar Straus, 1908. From (TM) *The Waltz Dream*.

Love's Theme. w/m Barry White, 1974. #1 gold record instrumental by the writer-directed studio orchestra Love Unlimited (20th Century).

Love Stinks. w/m Seth Justman and Peter Wolf, 1980. Written by two members of the J. Geils band, the rock group that recorded it (EMI America).

Love Supreme, A. w. Phil Downing and D. Cole, m. John Coltrane, 1988. Lyricized disco version of saxophonist John Coltrane's 1964 jazz composition (Island).

Love Takes Care of Me. w/m Jimmy Peppers, 1968. Top 10 Country chart record by Jack Greene (Decca).

Love Takes Time. w/m Lance Hoppen and Marilyn Mason, 1979. Recorded by the group Orleans (Infinity).

Love Theme from "A Star Is Born." See **Evergreen**.

Love Theme from "El Cid" (The Falcon and the Dove). w. Paul Francis Webster, m. Miklos Rozsa, 1961. From (MP) *El Cid*. Nominated for Academy Award, 1961.

Love Theme from "Eyes of Laura Mars" (a.k.a. **Prisoner**). w. John Desautels, m. Karen Lawrence, 1978. Introduced on the soundtrack of (MP) *Eyes of Laura Mars* and on records by Barbra Streisand (Columbia).

Love Theme from "La Strada." w. Don Raye (Engl.), M. Galdieri and N. Rota (It.), m. Galdieri and Rota, 1954. A.k.a. "Traveling Down a Lonely Road," and "Gelsomina." Theme from (MP) *La Strada*. Among recordings: Teddi King (RCA), Richard Hayman (Mercury), David Rose (MGM).

Love Theme from "One Eyed Jacks." m. Hugh Friedhofer, 1961. From (MP) *One Eyed Jacks*, starring Marlon Brando. Popular record by the piano duo Ferrante and Teicher (United Artists).

Love Theme from "Romeo and Juliet" (A Time for Us). w. Larry Kusick and Eddie Snyder, m. Nino Rota, 1969. Based on theme from (MP) *Romeo and Juliet*. #1 instrumental by Henry Mancini and his Orchestra (RCA). Leading vocal record by Johnny Mathis (Columbia).

Love Theme from "Shogun" (Mariko's Theme). See **Shogun**.

Love Theme from "St. Elmo's Fire." m. David Foster, 1985. Instrumental by David Foster, from (MP) *St. Elmo's Fire* (Atlantic).

Love Theme from "Suzie Wong." m. George Duning, 1960. From (MP) *The World of Suzie Wong*.

Love Theme from "The Godfather" (a.k.a **Speak Softly Love**). w/ Larry Kusik, m. Nino Rota, 1972. Instrumental theme from (MP) *The Godfather*. Leading instrumental recording by Nino Rota (Paramount). Most popular vocal versions by Andy Williams (Columbia) and Al Martino (Capitol).

Love the One You're With. w/m Stephen Stills, 1971. Top 20 record by Stephen Stills (Atlantic).

Love the World Away. w/m Bob Morrison and Johnny Wilson, 1980. From (MP) *Urban Cowboy*. Recorded by Kenny Rogers (United Artists).

Love Thy Neighbor. w. Mack Gordon, m. Harry Revel, 1934. Introduced by Bing Crosby, Ethel Merman, and Leon Errol in (MM) *We're Not Dressing*. Crosby also had the hit record (Brunswick).

Love T.K.O. w/m Cecil Womack and Gib Nobel, 1980. Recorded by Teddy Pendergrass (Philadelphia International).

Love to Love You, Baby. w/m Pete Bellotte, Giorgio Moroder, and Donna Summer, 1976. Top 10 gold record, recorded in Germany by Donna Summer (Oasis).

Love Touch (Theme from "Legal Eagles"). w/m Mike Chapman, Holly Knight, and Gene Black, 1986. Introduced by Rod Stewart on soundtrack of *Legal Eagles* (MP) and on his Top 10 record (Warner Bros.).

Love Train. w/m Kenny Gamble and Leon Huff, 1973. R&B/Pop #1 gold record by The O'Jays (Philadelphia International).

Love Walked In. w. Ira Gershwin, m. George Gershwin, 1938. Introduced by Kenny Baker in (MM) *The Goldwyn Follies*, George Gershwin's last score. He completed four songs for the film, including "Our Love Is Here to Stay," (q.v.) before his untimely death at the age of thirty-nine. This classic was on "Your Hit Parade" for thirteen weeks, five times in the #1 position. The song was included in the George Gershwin biography, (MM) *Rhapsody in Blue*, 1945. The Flamingos (End), 1959, and Dinah Washington (Mercury), 1960, had chart records.

Love Walks In. w/m Eddie Van Halen, Michael Anthony, Sammy Hagar, and Alex Van Halen, 1986. Recorded by the band Van Halen (Warner Bros.).

Love Will Conquer All. w/m Lionel Richie, Cynthia Weil, and Greg Phillinganes, 1986. Top 10 R&B/Pop chart record by Lionel Richie (Motown).

Love Will Find a Way. w/m Cha Cha Shaw, 1987. Popular track from the album "Big Generator," by the group Yes (Atco).

Love Will Find a Way. w/m Dave Jenkins and Cory Lerios, 1978. Recorded by the quartet Pablo Cruise (A&M).

Love Will Find a Way. w/m Jackie De-Shannon, Jimmy Holiday, and Randy Myers, 1969. Top 40 record by Jackie DeShannon (Imperial).

Love Will Find a Way. w/m Noble Sissle and Eubie Blake, 1921. Introduced by Roger Matthews and Lottie Gee in (TM) *Shuffle Along*. This successful book show has often been erroneously referred to as a revue.

Love Will Find Its Way to You. w/m Dave Loggins and J. D. Martin, 1988. #1 Country record by Reba McEntire (MCA).

Love Will Keep Us Together. w. Howard Greenfield, m. Neil Sedaka, 1975. Originally recorded by Neil Sedaka in his album "Sedaka's Back" (Rocket), 1974. The Captain and Tennille recorded their single version that became not only their first hit but a #1 gold record (A&M). Their Spanish version, "Por Amor Viviremos" (A&M), also was popular and marked the first time that two versions of a record were on the charts, recorded by the same artist in different languages. The English version won Grammy Awards (NARAS) for Record of the Year and Song of the Year, 1975.

Love Will Save the Day. w/m Toni C., 1988. Top 10 R&B and Pop chart record by Whitney Houston from her album "Whitney" (Arista).

Love Will Turn You Around. w/m Kenny Rogers, Even Stephens, Thom Schuyler, and Dave Malloy, 1982. Introduced in (MP) *Six Pack* and on records, by Kenny Rogers (Liberty).

Love with the Proper Stranger. w. Johnny Mercer, m. Elmer Bernstein, 1964. Introduced on the soundtrack of (MP) *Love with the Proper Stranger* by Jack Jones, and on records (Kapp).

Love Won't Let Me Wait. w/m Bobby Eli and Vinnie Barrett, 1975. Gold record by Major Harris (Atlantic).

Love Ya. w. Charles Tobias, m. Peter De Rose, 1951. Introduced by Doris Day and Jack Smith in (MM) *On Moonlight Bay.*

Lovey Came Back. w. Sam M. Lewis and Joe Young, m. Lou Handman, 1923. This was the first recording made by Vincent Lopez and his Orchestra (Okeh).

Lovey Dovey. w/m Ahmet Ertegun and Memphis Curtis, 1954. R&B hit record by The Clovers (Atlantic). Other chart records by Clyde McPhatter (Atlantic), 1959; Buddy Knox (Liberty), 1961; Otis and Carla (Stax), 1968.

Love You Down. w/m Melvin Riley, 1987. Chart record by the group Ready for the World (MCA).

Love You Inside Out. w/m Barry Gibb, Maurice Gibb, and Robin Gibb, 1979. The sixth consecutive and last #1 record by the British brother trio The Bee Gees (RSO).

Love You Most of All. w/m B. Campbell, 1958. Featured and recorded by Sam Cooke (Keen).

Love You Save, The. w/m Berry Gordy, Jr., Fonce Mizell, Freddie Perren, and Deke Richards, 1970. #1 record by The Jackson 5 (Motown).

Love You Save (May Be Your Own), The. w/m Joe Tex, 1966. Recorded by Joe Tex (Dial).

Love You So. w/m Ron Holden, 1960. Top 10 record by Ron Holden, backed by The Thunderbirds (Donna).

Love Zone. w/m Barry Eastmond, Wayne Braithwaite, and Billy Ocean, 1986. Top 10 single from the album of the same title by Billy Ocean (Jive).

Lovin', Touchin', Squeezin. w/m Steve Perry, 1979. Perry was lead vocalist of the group, Journey, when they recorded this (Columbia).

Lovin' Every Minute of It (Cyclone Ride). w/m Douglas Davis and Robert Lange, 1985. Top 10 record by the Canadian group Loverboy (Columbia).

Loving Arms. w/m Tom Jans, 1973. Chart records by Dobie Gray (MCA), and Kris Kristofferson and Rita Coolidge (A&M), 1974.

Loving Her Was Easier (Than Anything I'll Ever Do Again). w/m Kris Kristofferson, 1971. C&W/Pop hit by Kris Kristofferson (Monument); Country chart record by Roger Miller (Mercury). Revived with a Top 10 record by Tompall and The Glaser Brothers (Elektra), 1981

Loving Up a Storm. w/m Dan Morrison and Johnny Slate, 1980. #1 Country chart record by Razzy Bailey (RCA).

Loving You. w/m Jerry Leiber and Mike Stoller, 1957. Recorded by Elvis Presley (RCA).

Loving You (Was Worth This Broken Heart). w/m Helen Carter, 1961. Leading records on the C&W charts by Bob Gallion (Hickory) and Porter Wagoner (RCA).

Loving You Is Sweeter Than Ever. w/m Stevie Wonder and Ivy Hunter, 1966. Recorded by The Four Tops (Motown).

Lovin' Machine, The. w/m Larry Kingston, 1966. Hit Country record by Johnny Paycheck (Little Darlin').

Lovin' Only Me. w/m Even Stevens and Hillary Kanter, 1989. Country chart hit record by Ricky Skaggs (Epic).

Lovin' on Next to Nothin'. w/m Alan Rich, Howie Rice, and Jeff Pescetto, 1988. Top 10 R&B chart record by Gladys Knight and The Pips (MCA).

Lovin' Sam, the Sheik of Alabam'. w. Jack Yellen, m. Milton Ager, 1922. Introduced by Grace Hayes in (TM) *The Bunch and Judy*. Kirk Douglas and Hoagy Carmichael performed it in (MM) *Young Man with a Horn*, 1950.

Lovin' Spree. w. Joan Springer, m. Phil Springer, 1954. Popular record by Eartha Kitt, with Henri René's Orchestra (RCA Victor).

Lovin' Things, The. w/m Jet Loring and Arthur Schroek, 1969. Recorded by the rock group The Grass Roots (Dunhill).

Lovin' You. w/m Kenny Gamble and Leon Huff, 1987. #1 R&B chart record by The O'Jays (Philadelphia International).

Lovin' You. w/m Minnie Riperton and Richard Rudolph, 1975. #1 gold single from the album "Perfect Angel" by Minnie Riperton (Epic).

Lovin' You. w/m John Sebastian, 1967. Top 40 record by Bobby Darin (Atlantic).

Lovin' You More. w/m Shel Silverstein, 1973. Introduced by Rip Torn in (MP) *Payday*.

Low and Lonely. w/m Floyd Jenkins, 1942. Most popular recording by Roy Acuff (Decca).

Lowdown. w/m David Paich and Boz Scaggs, 1976. Pop/R&B gold record by Boz Scaggs (Columbia). Grammy Award (NARAS) winner, Rhythm and Blues Song of the Year.

Low-Down Lullaby. w. Leo Robin, m. Ralph Rainger, 1934. Sung by Dorothy Dell in (MM) *Little Miss Marker*.

Lowdown Popcorn. m. James Brown, 1969. Instrumental by James Brown (King).

Low Down Rhythm. w. Raymond Klages, m. Jesse Greer, 1929. Introduced by Jane Purcell and dancers in (MM) *Hollywood Revue of 1929*.

Low Down Rhythm in a Top Hat. w/m Al Donahue, Jimmy Eaton, and Terry Shand, 1939. The title was the phrase used by Al Donahue to describe his band. Recorded by them (Vocalion) and used as their theme.

Low Rider. w/m Dee Allen, Harold Brown, B. B. Dickerson, Lonnie Jordan, Lee Oskar, Charles Miller, and Howard Scott, 1975. Top 10 record by the band War (United Artists).

Luckenbach, Texas (Back to the Basics of Love). w/m Bobby Emmons and Chips Moman, 1977. Country/Pop hit record by Waylon Jennings (RCA).

Lucifer. w/m Bob Seger, 1970. Recorded by The Bob Seger System (Capitol).

Lucille. w/m Roger Bowling and Hal Bynum, 1977. Top 10 gold record by Kenny Rogers (United Artists).

Lucille. w/m Albert Collins and Richard Penniman, 1957. Recorded by Little Richard (Specialty), and in 1960 by The Everly Brothers (Warner Bros.).

Luck Be a Lady. w/m Frank Loesser, 1950. Introduced by Robert Alda in (TM) *Guys and Dolls*. Sung in (MM) *Guys and Dolls*, 1955, by Marlon Brando.

Lucky Boy. w/m Irving Berlin, 1925. From (TM) *The Cocoanuts* starring the Marx Brothers.

Lucky Charm. w/m Gregory Paul Scelsa, Kenneth Edmonds, and Daryl Simmons, 1989. Hit R&B chart single by the group Boys (Motown).

Lucky Day (This Is My). w. B. G. DeSylva and Lew Brown, m. Ray Henderson, 1926. Introduced by Harry Richman in (TM) *George*

White's Scandals of 1926. Interpolated by Maurice Chevalier in (MM) *The Big Pond*, 1930. Dan Dailey sang it in the DeSylva, Brown and Henderson story (MM) *The Best Things in Life Are Free*, 1956. At one point, it was the theme song for "Your Hit Parade," which was sponsored by Lucky Strike cigarettes.

Lucky Fella. w. Dorothy Fields, m. Jimmy McHugh, 1933. Sung in the (MP) *The Prizefighter and the Lady*, starring the future heavyweight champion Max Baer and Myrna Loy. Recorded by Tom Coakley, with vocal by Carl Ravell [pseudonym of Carl Ravazza] (Victor).

Lucky in Love. w. B. G. DeSylva and Lew Brown, m. Ray Henderson, 1927. Another hit song from (TM) *Good News*, this was sung by Mary Lawlor and John Price Jones. George Olsen, whose band appeared in the show, had a popular record, with vocal by Fran Frey, Bob Borger, and Bob Rice (Victor). The song was cut from the 1930 film version, but was sung by Patricia Marshall, June Allyson, Peter Lawford, and other cast members in (MM) *Good News*, 1947. It was sung by Gordon MacRae, Ernest Borgnine, and Dan Dailey as DeSylva, Brown and Henderson in (MM) *The Best Things in Life Are Free*, 1957.

Lucky Jim. w. Charles Horwitz, m. Frederick V. Bowers, 1896.

Lucky Lady. w. Fred Ebb, m. John Kander, 1975. Introduced by Liza Minnelli in (MP) *Lucky Lady.*

Lucky Ladybug. w/m Frank C. Slay, Jr. and Bob Crewe, 1958. Recorded by Billy and Lillie (Swan).

Lucky Lindy. w. L. Wolfe Gilbert, m. Abel Baer, 1927. The most popular of the songs commemorating Lindbergh's solo flight across the Atlantic. This one was popularized by Vernon Dalhart who coupled it with "Lindbergh, the Eagle of the U.S.A." (Columbia).

Lucky Lips. w/m Jerry Leiber and Mike Stoller, 1957. Hit record by Ruth Brown (Atlantic) and covered by Gale Storm (Dot). Re-

vived in 1963 by British singer Cliff Richard (Epic).

Luck Man. w/m Greg Lake, 1971. Recorded by the English trio, Emerson, Lake, and Palmer (Cotillion).

Lucky Me. Lovable You. w. Jack Yellen, m. Milton Ager, 1930. Introduced by Charles King in (MM) *Chasing Rainbows* and recorded by him (Brunswick).

Lucky Seven. w. Howard Dietz, m. Arthur Schwartz, 1930. Introduced by Joey Ray in (TM) *The Second Little Show.* Recorded by Leo Reisman and his Orchestra (Victor).

Lucky Star. w/m Madonna Ciccone, 1984. Top 10 record by Madonna (Sire).

Lucky to Be Me. w. Betty Comden and Adolph Green, m. Leonard Bernstein, 1945. Introduced by John Battles in (TM) *On the Town.* Recorded by Mary Martin (Decca) and Horace Heidt and his Orchestra (Columbia).

Lucy in the Sky with Diamonds. w/m John Lennon and Paul McCartney, 1967. Introduced by The Beatles in their album, "Sgt. Pepper's Lonely Hearts Club Band" (Capitol), and sung by them in the animated film (MM) *Yellow Submarine*, 1968. Elton John had a #1 hit record, reggae guitar by Dr. Winston O'Boogie, who, for contractual reasons, could not use his real name of John Lennon (MCA), 1975.

Luka. w/m Suzanne Vega, 1987. Top 10 single by Suzanne Vega (A&M). The song contained a strong statement regarding child abuse.

Lullaby in Blue. w. Mack Gordon, m. Josef Myrow, 1956. Introduced by Eddie Fisher and Debbie Reynolds in (MM) *Bundle of Joy.*

Lullaby in Ragtime. w/m Sylvia Fine, 1959. Introduced by Danny Kaye and Eileen Wilson, the latter dubbing on the soundtrack for Barbara Bel Geddes, in (MM) *The Five Pennies.*

Lullaby in Rhythm. w. Walter Hirsch, m. Benny Goodman, Edgar Sampson, and Clarence Profit, 1938. Introduced and recorded (Victor) by Benny Goodman. Other leading versions by Nan Wynn (Vocalion), Woody Herman (Decca), Harry James (Brunswick), Dexter Gordon (Dial), Charlie Ventura (Victor).

Lullaby of Birdland. w. George David Weiss, m. George Shearing, 1952. Named after the New York jazz club at which the pianist George Shearing and his group were appearing. The music business story has it that Shearing, while playing the Walter Donaldson tune "Love Me or Leave Me," (q.v.) improvised a jazz chorus, the melody of which became a standard in its own right. Among many recordings: Shearing (MGM), Wild Bill Davis (Okeh), Erroll Garner (Columbia), Stan Getz (Roost); Johnny Smith (Roost).

Lullaby of Broadway. w. Al Dubin, m. Harry Warren, 1935. Introduced by Wini Shaw and Dick Powell in a spectacular Busby Berkeley production number in (MM) *Golddiggers of 1935*. One of the biggest hits of the year, it won the Academy Award for Best Song and was #1 on "Your Hit Parade." It was heard in a montage in (MM) *The Jolson Story*, 1946; in (MM) *Young Man with a Horn*, 1950; Doris Day sang it in (MM) *Lullaby of Broadway*, 1951. It was performed by Jerry Orbach and company in David Merrick's (TM) *42nd Street*, 1980.

Lullaby of Love. w/m Larry Butler and Billy Sherrill, 1966. Recorded by the female trio The Poppies (Epic).

Lullaby of the Leaves. w. Joe Young, m. Bernice Petkere, 1931. First recorded by Ben Selvin (Columbia), Connie Boswell (Brunswick), George Olsen (Victor), Roy Smeck (Melotone). The ballad became a favorite with jazz musicians as evidenced by later recordings by Art Tatum (Decca), Gerry Mulligan (Pacific Jazz), Cal Tjader (Galaxy), Dizzy Gil-

lespie (Discovery), and a vocal by Frances Wayne, backed by Neal Hefti (Exclusive).

Lulu's Back in Town. w. Al Dubin, m. Harry Warren, 1935. Introduced by Dick Powell and the Mills Brothers in (MM) *Broadway Gondolier*. Recordings of note: Dick Powell (Brunswick), Fats Waller (Victor), Ted Fio Rito (Brunswick), Wingy Manone (Vocalion), Mills Brothers (Decca, Dot), Mel Tormé (Musicraft), Jerry Vale (Columbia).

Lumberjack, The. w/m Hal Willis and Ginger Willis, 1964. Country hit by Hal Willis (Sims). Pop version by Brook Benton (Mercury).

Luna Rossa (a.k.a. **Blushing Moon).** w. Kermit Goell (Engl.), V. de Crescenzo (It.), m. Antonio Viscione, 1952. Leading recordings by Alan Dean (MGM) and Tony Martin (RCA Victor).

Lush Life. w/m Billy Strayhorn, 1949. Written eleven years earlier, the first and definitive recording was made by Nat "King" Cole (Capitol).

Lusty Month of May, The. w. Alan Jay Lerner, m. Frederick Loewe, 1960. Introduced by Julie Andrews and the chorus in (TM) *Camelot*. In the film version, (MM) *Camelot*, 1967, it was sung by Vanessa Redgrave.

Luther Played the Boogie. w/m Johnny Cash, 1959. C&W hit by Johnny Cash (Sun).

Lydia, The Tattooed Lady. w. E. Y. Harburg, m. Harold Arlen, 1939. Introduced by Groucho Marx in (MM) *At the Circus*.

Lyin' Eyes. w/m Glenn Frey and Don Henley, 1975. To 10 record by The Eagles, two of whom wrote it (Asylum).

Lynda. w.m Bill LaBounty and Pat McLaughlin, 1987. #1 Country chart record by Steve Wariner (MCA).

M

Ma! (He's Making Eyes at Me). w. Sidney Clare, m. Con Conrad, 1921. Written for and introduced by Eddie Cantor in (TM) *The Midnight Rounders*. It was revived as the title song for (MM) *Ma! He's Making Eyes at Me*, 1940. Judy Canova sang it in (MM) *Singin' in the Corn*, 1946. Eddie Cantor dubbed it on the soundtrack for Keefe Brasselle in (MM) *The Eddie Cantor Story*, 1953. Revived by the ten-year-old Scottish singer Lena Zavaroni (Stax), 1974.

Ma! I Miss Your Apple Pie. w/m Carmen Lombardo and John Jacob Loeb, 1941. Lament of a draftee. Introduced and best-selling record by Guy Lombardo, vocal by the Lombardo Trio [Carmen Lombardo, Mert Curtis, Fred Henry] (Decca).

Ma Belle. w. Clifford Grey, m. Rudolf Friml, 1928. Introduced by Dennis King in (TM) *The Three Musketeers*. Leading recording by Robert Merrill (Victor).

Ma Belle Amie. w/m Hans van Eijck and Peter Tetteroo, 1970. Product of The Netherlands. Top 10 U.S. release by The Tee Set (Colossus).

Ma Blushin' Rosie. w. Edgar Smith, m. John Stromberg, 1900. Introduced by Fay Templeton in Weber and Fields's (TM) *Fiddle Dee Dee*. The song later became associated with Al Jolson who featured it in his Winter Garden shows and who sang it on the soundtrack of (MM) *The Jolson Story*, 1946, and

(MM) *Jolson Sings Again*, 1949. His Decca recording sold over a million copies. The song has also been interpolated in (MM) *Broadway to Hollywood*, 1933, and the film starring June Haver and Gordon MacRae, (MM) *The Daughter of Rosie O'Grady*, 1950.

MacArthur Park. w/m Jim Webb, 1968. Originally composed as the seven-minute coda of a twenty-two minute cantata. Webb produced a hit single for Richard Harris (Dunhill). Waylon Jennings and The Kimberlys had a C&W/Pop chart version (RCA), 1969. The Four Tops had their R&B styled recording in the Top 40 (Motown), 1971. Donna Summer then revived it with a #1 gold record disco version (Casablanca), 1978.

Machine Gun. w/m Milan Williams, 1974. Crossover (R&B/Pop) chart instrumental by The Commodores (Motown).

Macho Man. w. Henri Belolo, Victor Willis, and Peter Whitehead, m. Jacques Morali, 1978. Gold record by the disco group Village People (Casablanca).

Mack the Black. w/m Cole Porter, 1948. Introduced by Judy Garland in (MM) *The Pirate*.

Mack the Knife (a.k.a. **Moritat**). w. Marc Blitzstein (Engl.), Bertolt Brecht (Ger.), m. Kurt Weill, 1956, 1959. Introduced as "Moritat" in Berlin in *Die Dreigroschenoper* (*The Threepenny Opera*), 1928. First recorded in the U.S. by Lotte Lenya. The English version of the musical was first presented in concert form at Brandeis University, 1952. Scott Merrill sang it in the hit off-Broadway production of (TM) *The Threepenny Opera* at the Theatre DeLys in Greenwich Village, New York, 1954. In 1956, the Dick Hyman Trio had an instrumental hit recording titled "Moritat (A Theme from *The Three̩ nny Opera*)" (MGM). Louis Armstrong had t' ͅ first successful vocal record under the tit' ͅ of "Mack the Knife" (Columbia), 1956. 'Ihis version inspired the Bobby Darin #1 record of 1959 (Atco), which was the Grammy Award (NARAS) winner of Record of the Year, firmly establishing the song and Darin. Ella Fitzgerald had a hit version (Verve), 1960.

MacNamara's Band. w. John J. Stamford, m. Shamus O'Connor, 1917. An Irish standard, first published in London, England. Recorded by Bing Crosby (Decca) and the McFarland Twins (Bluebird) among many others.

Ma Curly Headed Babby. w. George H. Clutsam, 1926.

Macushla. w. Josephine V. Rowe, Dermot MacMurrough, 1910.

Mad. w/m Tom T. Hall, 1964. Country hit record by Dave Dudley (Mercury).

Mad About Him, Sad About Him, How Can I Be Glad About Him Blues. w/m Larry Markes and Dick Charles, 1942. Featured and best-seller recorded by Dinah Shore (Victor). Among other recordings: Janette Davis (Columbia), Jack Carroll (RKO Unique), Dick Hyman (MGM).

Mad About the Boy. w/m Noël Coward, 1935. Originally performed in the London revue (TM) *Words and Music*. Popularized in the U.S. via recordings, then sung by Penelope Dudley Ward, Gladys Henson, Laura Duncan, and Beatrice Lillie in (TM) *Set to Music* [American version of *Words and Music*], 1939. Among recordings: Belle Baker (Gala); Lena Horne (Victor); Gertrude Lawrence (Decca); Beatrice Lillie (Liberty Music Shop, Parts 1 & 2); Dinah Washington (Mercury).

Mad About You. w/m Paula Brown, Mitchell Young Evans, and James Whelan, 1986. Top 10 solo hit by Belinda Carlisle (I.R.S.).

Mad About You. w. Walter Bishop, m. Ram Ramirez, 1944. Featured and recorded by Ike Quebec and his Band (Blue Note 12").

Mad Dogs and Englishmen. w/m Noël Coward, 1931. Introduced by Beatrice Lillie in (TM) *The Third Little Show*. Coward recorded it (Victor) in 1933 and in later albums. Danny Kaye also performed it on stage, radio, television, and records (Decca).

Made in Japan. w/m Bob Morris and Faye Morris, 1972. Hit Country record by Buck Owens and His Buckaroos (Capitol).

Madeleine. w/m Eric Blau and Mort Shuman, m. Jacques Brel, 1968. Introduced by the Company in (TM) *Jacques Brel Is Alive and Well and Living in Paris*.

Madelon. w. Louis Bousquet (Fr.) and Alfred Bryan (Engl.), m. Camille Robert, 1918. Leading record by The Victor Military Band (Victor).

Mademoiselle. w/m Max and Harry Nesbitt, 1934.

Mademoiselle de Paree. w. Mitchell Parish (Engl.), m. Paul Durand, 1948. French song, "Mademoiselle de Paris." Original lyrics by Henri Contet.

Mademoiselle from Armentieres (Hinky Dinky Parlay Voo). w/m anonymous, 1917. The origin of this song has never been proven. It was a favorite of American troops in World War 1, with many parodies. See: "What Has Become of Hinky Dinky Parlay Voo." Sung in (TM) *A Musical Jubilee* by Cyril Ritchard and Dick Shawn, 1975.

Mademoiselle in New Rochelle. w. Ira Gershwin, m. George Gershwin, 1930. Sung by (Bobby) Clark and (Paul) McCullough in (TM) *Strike Up the Band*.

Made to Love (Girls, Girls Girls). w/m Phil Everly, 1962. Popular record by fifteen-year-old Eddie Hodges (Cadence).

Madison, The. w/m Al Brown, 1960. One of two versions of a new dance. This recorded by Al Brown's Tunetoppers, instructions by Cookie Brown (Amy).

Madison Time. w. Eddie Morrison, m. Ray Bryant, 1960. A new dance, instructions spoken by Eddie Morrison and music played by The Ray Bryant Trio (Columbia, Parts 1 & 2).

Madly in Love. w. Ogden Nash, m. Vernon Duke, 1956. Introduced by Tammy Grimes in (TM) *The Littlest Revue*.

Maggie May. w/m Rod Stewart and Martin Quittenton, 1971. #1 gold record from England by Rod Stewart (Mercury).

Maggie Murphy's Home. w. Edward Harrigan, m. David Braham, 1890. Introduced by Emma Pollack in the Harrigan and Hart show (TM) *Reilly and the 400*. In (TM) *Harrigan 'n Hart*, 1985, it was sung by Tudi Roche, Harry Groener, Clent Bowers, and Company.

Magic. w/m Ric Ocasek, 1984. Recorded by The Cars (Elektra).

Magic. w/m John Farrar, 1980. Introduced in (MM) *Xanadu* by Olivia Newton-John. The platinum soundtrack album produced the #1 gold single by Newton-John (MCA).

Magic. w/m David Paton and Bill Lyall, 1975. Gold record written by two thirds of the Scottish trio Pilot (EMI).

Magical Mystery Tour, The. w/m John Lennon and Paul McCartney, 1967. Title song of the album by The Beatles (Capitol). The trio Ambrosia sang it on the soundtrack of (MM) *All This and World War II* and had a Top 40 record (20th Century).

Magic Bus, The. w/m Peter Townshend, 1968. Hit record by the English group The Who (Decca).

Magic Carpet Ride. w/m John Kay and Rushton Moreve, 1968. Top 10 gold record by the quintet Steppenwolf (Dunhill).

Magic Is the Moonlight. w. Charles Pasquale (Engl.), m. Maria Grever, 1944. Origi-

nal title: "Te Quiero Dijiste," words by Grever. Sung by Carlos Ramirez in (MM) *Bathing Beauty*. Popular records by the bands of Art Kassel (Hit) and Freddy Martin (Victor). Andy Russell sang it in (MM) *Breakfast in Hollywood*, 1946, and recorded it (Capitol). Jane Powell and Ann Sothern sang it in (MM) *Nancy Goes to Rio*, 1950, and Sothern recorded it (MGM).

Magic Man. w/m Herb Alpert, Michael Stokes, and Melvin Ragin, 1981. Instrumental by Herb Alpert (A&M).

Magic Man. w/m Ann Wilson and Nancy Wilson, 1976. Top 10 record by the group, Heart, of which Ann and Nancy Wilson were lead singer and guitarist/keyboardist, respectively (Mushroom).

Magic Melody, The. w. Schuyler Greene, m. Jerome Kern, 1915. Introduced by Adele Rowland in (TM) *Nobody Home*.

Magic Moment. w. Howard Dietz, m. Arthur Schwartz, 1961. Introduced by Barbara Cook in (TM) *The Gay Life*.

Magic Moments. w. Hal David, m. Burt Bacharach, 1958. Part of two-sided hit by Perry Como, coupled with "Catch a Falling Star" (q.v.) (RCA).

Magic of Your Eyes, The. w/m Arthur A. Penn, 1917. A popular recording was made by Charles Harrison (Victor).

Magic Tango, The. w. Jimmy Kennedy (Engl.), m. Philippe-Gerard, 1954. Label reads "Hugo Winterhalter's Orchestra and Chorus and a Friend." The "friend" was Eddie Fisher (RCA Victor).

Magic Touch, The (You've Got). w/m Buck Ram, 1956. Popularized by The Platters (Mercury). Revived via radio and television commercials for the Hyatt Hotels and Resorts chain, 1988.

Magic Town. w/m Barry Mann and Cynthia Weil, 1966. Chart record by The Vogues (Co & Ce).

Magnet and Steel. w/m Walter Egan, 1978. Top 10 hit record by Walter Egan (Columbia).

Magnificent Seven, The. m. Elmer Bernstein, 1960. Theme from (MP) *The Magnificent Seven.* Leading recording by guitarist Al Caiola (United Artists).

Magnolias in the Moonlight. w. Walter Bullock, m. Victor Schertzinger, 1936. Introduced by Michael Bartlett in (MM) *Follow Your Heart.*

Magnum P.I. See **Theme from "Magnum P.I."**

Maharajah of Magador, The. w/m Lewis Harris and John Jacob Loeb, 1947. Novelty recorded by Vaughn Monroe, vocal by Ziggy Talent (RCA Victor).

Mah Jong. w. Billy Rose, m. Con Conrad, 1924. The song referred to the Chinese game that had become a current fad.

Mah Lindy Lou. w/m Lily Strickland, 1920.

Mah-Na-Mah-Na m. Piero Umiliani, 1969. From the Italian film (MP) *Sweden—Heaven and Hell (Viva la Sauna)* Leading record, instrumental by Piero Umiliani (Ariel). Familiarly heard as the background music on (TVP) "The Benny Hill Show."

Maiden with the Dreamy Eyes. w. James Weldon Johnson, m. Bob Cole, 1901. Introduced by Anna Held in (TM) *The Little Duchess.*

Maine. w/m Richard Rodgers, 1962. Introduced by Diahann Carroll and Richard Kiley in (TM) "No Strings."

Main Event, The. w/m Bob Esty, Paul Jabara, and Bruce Roberts, 1979. Introduced by Barbra Streisand in (MP) *The Main Event,* and recorded in medley with "Fight" (q.v.) from the same film (Columbia).

Mainliner (The Hawk with Silver Wings). w/m Stuart Hamblen, 1955. Top 10 C&W chart record by Hank Snow (RCA).

Main Stem. m. Edward Kennedy "Duke" Ellington, 1944. Instrumental, introduced and recorded by Duke Ellington and his Orchestra two years earlier (Victor), but re-released and gained prominence in 1944.

Mainstreet. w/m Bob Seger, 1977. Recorded by Bob Seger (Capitol).

Mairzy Doats. w/m Milton Drake, Al Hoffman, and Jerry Livingston, 1944. Novelty adapted from the childrens' rhyme, starting with "mares eat oats, and does eat oats, etc." Introduced and recorded (Hit) by Al Trace [who sometimes is erroneously credited with writing the song] and his Silly Symphonists. Biggest selling record was by The Merry Macs (Decca). Song was a runaway hit, although short lived as is often the case with novelties.

Major Tom (Coming Home). w/m Peter Schilling and David Lodge, 1983. Recorded by Peter Schilling (Elektra).

Make a Miracle. w/m Frank Loesser, 1948. Introduced by Ray Bolger and Allyn McLerie in (TM) *Where's Charlie.* Recorded by Bolger, coupled with "Once in Love with Amy" (q.v.) (Decca).

Make a Move on Me. w/m John Farrar and Tom Snow, 1982. Top 10 record by Olivia Newton-John (MCA).

Make Believe. w/m Bo Gentry and Joey Levine, 1969. Top 40 record by the studio group, Wind, with Tony Orlando as lead singer (Life).

Make Believe. w. Oscar Hammerstein II, m. Jerome Kern, 1928. Introduced by Norma Terris and Howard Marsh in (TM) *Show Boat.* The popular duet was not used in the first film version, 1929. In (MM) *Show Boat,* 1936, it was sung by Irene Dunne and Allan Jones, and in the 1951 version by Kathryn Grayson and Howard Keel. Kathryn Grayson, this time with Tony Martin, sang it in the Kern biography (MM) *Till the Clouds Roll By,* 1946.

Make Believe. w. Benny Davis, m. Jack Shilkret, 1921. Leading records by Nora Bayes (Columbia), and instrumental versions by the orchestras of Paul Whiteman (Victor) and Isham Jones (Brunswick).

Make Believe. w. Jack Brislane, m. Theodore F. Morse, 1908. Popular waltz recorded by Ada Jones and Billy Murray (Victor).

Make Believe Ballroom. w. Andy Razaf, m. Paul Denniker, 1936. Recorded by Charlie Barnet with vocal by the Modernaires (Bluebird), and the theme song of Martin Block's popular WNEW, New York radio show, "Make Believe Ballroom," from 1936–1940. When ASCAP-licensed songs were taken off the air because of the dispute with the radio stations, it was replaced by "It's Make Believe Ballroom Time" (q.v.). Although a settlement was made, the new song remained.

Make-Believe Island. w. Charles Kenny and Nick Kenny, m. Will Grosz and Sam Coslow, 1940. Top records by Mitchell Ayres and his Orchestra (Bluebird); Jan Savitt and his Orchestra (Decca).

Make Her Mine. w. Sammy Cahn, m. Chester Conn, 1954. Recorded by Nat "King" Cole (Capitol).

Make It Another Old-Fashioned Please. w/m Cole Porter, 1940. Introduced by Ethel Merman in (TM) *Panama Hattie.*

Make It Easy on Yourself. w. Hal David, m. Burt Bacharach, 1962. Popularized by Jerry Butler (Vee-Jay). Later Top 40 records by The Walker Brothers (Smash), 1965, and Dionne Warwick (Scepter), 1970.

Make It Last Forever. w/m Keith Sweat and Teddy Riley, 1988. Top 10 R&B chart record by Keith Sweat and Jacci McGhee (Vintertainment).

Make It Real. w/m Linda Mallah, Rich Kelly, and Dan Powell, 1988. Top 10 record by The Jets (MCA).

Make It with You. w/m David Gates, 1970. #1 gold record by the group, Bread, with lead singer/guitarist David Gates (Elektra). Revived by the group, Whisper (Soul Train), 1977.

Make Love Stay. w/m Dan Fogelberg, 1983. Recorded by Dan Fogelberg (Full Moon).

Make Love to Me. w. Bill Norvas, Allan Copeland, m. Paul Mares, Leon Rappolo, Ben Pollack, George Brunies, Mel Stitzel, Walter Melrose, 1954. Lyric version of "Tin Roof Blues" (q.v.). Jo Stafford had a #1 million-selling record (Columbia).

Make Love to Me. w. Kim Gannon, m. Paul Mann and Stephan Weiss, 1941. Recordings: Artie Shaw, vocal by Paula Kelly (Victor); Anita Boyer (Okeh).

Make Me Belong to You. w/m Chip Taylor and Billy Vera, 1966. Recorded by R&B singer Barbara Lewis (Atlantic).

Make Me Lose Control. w/m Eric Carmen and Dean Pitchford, 1988. Top 10 record by Eric Carmen (Arista).

Make Me Smile. w/m James Pankow, 1970. Top 10 single by the group Chicago (Columbia).

Make Me the Woman That You Go Home To. w/m Clay McMurray, 1971. Top 40 record by Gladys Knight and The Pips (Soul).

Make Me Thrill. w. Eddie V. Deane, m. Robert Lissauer, 1955. Recorded by Karen Rich, with Larry Wagner's Orchestra (Decca).

Make Me Your Baby. w/m Roger Atkins and Helen Miller, 1965. R&B/Pop chart hit by Barbara Lewis (Atlantic).

Make Me Yours. w/m Betty Jean Champion, 1967. Recorded by Bettye Swann [Champion] (Money).

Make My Day. w/m Dewayne Blackwell, 1984. Novelty record, based on the film directed by and starring Clint Eastwood, *Sudden Impact.* Recorded by T. G. Sheppard and Clint Eastwood (Warner Bros.).

Make My Life with You. w/m Gary Burr, 1985. #1 Country chart song by The Oak Ridge Boys (MCA).

Make No Mistake He's (She's) Mine. w/m Kim Carnes, 1985, 1987. Introduced by Barbra Streisand and Kim Carnes (Columbia), 1985. With the "She's Mine" title variation, Ronnie Milsap and Kenny Rogers had a #1 Country chart version, from the album "Heart and Soul" (RCA), 1987.

Make Someone Happy. w. Betty Comden and Adolph Green, m. Jule Styne, 1960. Introduced by John Reardon in (TM) *Do Re Mi.* Leading record by Perry Como (RCA).

Make That Move. w/m William Shelby, Ricky Smith, and Steve Washington, 1981. Recorded by the trio Shalamar (Solar).

Make the Man Love Me. w. Dorothy Fields, m. Arthur Schwartz, 1951. Introduced by Marcia Van Dyke and answered by Johnny Johnston in (TM) *A Tree Grows in Brooklyn.*

Make the World Go Away. w/m Hank Cochran, 1963. Hit song in the Country and Pop fields by, respectively, Ray Price (Columbia) and Timi Yuro (Liberty). Eddy Arnold had a hit in both categories in 1965 (RCA). Revived by Donny and Marie Osmond in 1975 (MGM).

Make Up Your Mind. w/m George Jones, Starleana Young, and Steve Washington, 1982. Recorded by the group Aurra (Salsoul).

Make Way for Tomorrow. w. Ira Gershwin and E. Y. Harburg, m. Jerome Kern, 1944. Introduced by Gene Kelly, Phil Silvers, and Martha Mears, dubbing for Rita Hayworth, in (MM) *Cover Girl.*

Make with the Kisses. w. Johnny Mercer, m. James Van Heusen, 1939. Popularized by Benny Goodman, vocal by Mildred Bailey (Columbia); Will Bradley, vocal by Carlotta Dale (Vocalion); Les Brown and his Orchestra (Bluebird); Bea Wain (Victor).

Make Your Own Kind of Music. w/m Barry Mann and Cynthia Weil, 1969. Top 40 record by Mama Cass Elliot (Dunhill). Recorded in medley with "Sing a Song" (q.v.) by Barbra Streisand (Columbia), 1972.

Make Yourself Comfortable. w/m Bob Merrill, 1954. Recorded by Sarah Vaughan (Mercury).

Makin' Faces at the Man in the Moon. w/m Max Rich, Kate Smith, Al Hoffman, and Ned Washington, 1931. Kate Smith coupled this with the first recording of her theme "When the Moon Comes Over the Mountain" (q.v.) (Clarion).

Making Believe. w/m Jimmy Work, Roscoe Reid, and Joe Hobson, 1955. Country recordings by Kitty Wells (Decca) and Jimmy Work (Dot).

Making Every Minute Count. w/m John Morier, 1967. Top 40 record by Spanky and Our Gang (Mercury).

Making Eyes. w/m Harry Von Tilzer, 1905. From (TM) *Lifting the Lid.*

Making Love. w/m Carole Bayer Sager, Burt Bacharach, and Bruce Roberts, 1982. Introduced on the soundtrack of (MP) *Making Love,* and recorded by Roberta Flack (Atlantic).

Making Love in the Rain. w/m Jimmy Jam and Terry Lewis, 1987. Top 10 R&B and Pop chart record by Herb Alpert, vocal by Lisa Keith (A&M).

Making Love Out of Nothing At All. w/m Jim Steinman, 1983. Top 10 gold record by the Australian duo Air Supply (Arista).

Making Memories. w/m Larry Kusik and Eddie Snyder, 1967. Popular record by Frankie Laine (ABC).

Making Our Dreams Come True. w. Norman Gimbel, m. Charles Fox, 1976. Sung as theme of the series (TVP) "LaVerne & Shirley" and on records by Cyndi Grecco (Private Stock).

Making Plans. w/m Dolly Parton, 1980. Top 10 Country chart record by Porter Wagoner and Dolly Parton (RCA).

Makin' It. w/m Dino Fekaris and Freddie Perren, 1979. Sung by David Naughton in

(TVP) "Makin' It" and on his Top 10 gold record (RSO).

Makin' Love. w/m Floyd Robinson, 1959. Recorded by Floyd Robinson (RCA).

Makin' Love, Mountain Style. w. Jack Scholl, m. Herb Moulton, 1947. Featured and recorded by Dorothy Shay, "The Park Avenue Hillbilly" (Columbia).

Makin' Up for Lost Time (The "Dallas" Lovers' Song). w/m Gary Morris and Dave Loggins, 1986. Theme from the series (TVP) "Dallas." #1 Country chart record by Crystal Gayle and Gary Morris (Warner Bros.).

Makin' Whoopee. w. Gus Kahn, m. Walter Donaldson, 1928. Introduced by Eddie Cantor in (TM) *Whoopee*, who, after making a hit record (Victor), sang it in the film adaptation, (MM) *Whoopee*, 1930. Cantor sang it in (MM) *Show Business*, 1940, and on the soundtrack, dubbing for Keefe Brasselle, in (MM) *The Eddie Cantor Story*, 1953. In the Gus Kahn story, (MM) *I'll See You in My Dreams*, 1951, it was sung by Danny Thomas and Doris Day. Other early hit records by Paul Whiteman, vocal by The Rhythm Boys [Bing Crosby, Harry Barris, and Chuck Rinker] (Victor) and Ben Bernie, vocal by Scrappy Lambert (Brunswick).

Malagueña. m. Ernesto Lecuona, 1930. From *Andalucia, Suite Española* for solo piano. Among more popular recordings were those by Jan August (Diamond), Oscar Levant (Columbia), the Harmonicats (Mercury), Billy Butterfield (Capitol), Enoch Light (Continental).

Malinda. w/m Alfred Cleveland, Terry Johnson, and William Robinson, 1969. Recorded by Bobby Taylor and The Vancouvers (Gordy).

Malinda. w. Stanley Murphy, m. Henry I. Marshall, 1912.

Mama. w/m Mark Charron, 1966. Top 40 record by B. J. Thomas (Scepter).

Mama. w. Harold Barlow and Phil Brito (Engl.), B. Cherubini (It.), m. C. A. Bixio, 1946, 1960. Italian song, introduced on records in the U.S. by Phil Brito (Musicraft) (MGM). Connie Francis had a hit record in 1960, with new English lyrics by Geoffrey Parsons and James John Phillips (MGM)

(Mama) He Treats Your Daughter Mean. w/m Charles Singleton and J. H. Wallace, 1953. Hit R&B record by Ruth Brown (Atlantic).

Mama, Come Get Your Baby Boy. w/m Leon Merritt and Alvin Alton, 1953. Top 10 C&W record by Eddy Arnold (RCA). Revived by Johnny Darrell (United Artists), 1970.

Mama, He's Crazy. w/m Kenny O'Dell, 1983. Country chart hit by the mother and daughter duo The Judds (RCA).

Mama, Teach Me to Dance. w/m Al Hoffman and Dick Manning, 1956. Popularized by Eydie Gormé (ABC-Paramount).

Mama, That Moon Is Here Again. w. Leo Robin, m. Ralph Rainger, 1938. Introduced by Martha Raye in (MM) *The Big Broadcast of 1938*. Among recordings to follow were Shep Fields and his Rippling Rhythm (Bluebird); Glen Gray and his Casa Loma Orchestra, vocal by Pee Wee Hunt (Decca); Isham Jones, vocal by Eddie Stone (Perfect).

Mama and Daddy Broke My Heart. w/m Spade Cooley, 1949. Top 10 Country chart record by Eddy Arnold (RCA).

Mama Can't Buy You Love. w/m Leroy Bell and Casey James, 1979. Top 10 gold record by Elton John (MCA).

Mamacita. w/m Gerald Levert and Marc Gordon, 1988. Top 10 R&B record by Troop (Atlantic).

Mama Didn't Lie. w/m Curtis Mayfield, 1963. Crossover hit (R&B/Pop) by Jan Bradley (Chess).

Mama Doll Song, The. w. Charles Tobias, m. Nat Simon, 1954. Introduced and recorded by Patti Page (Mercury).

Mama Don't Allow It. w/m Charles Davenport, 1929. In addition to Davenport (Vocalion), it has been recorded by such artists as Ham Gravy (Vocalion); Frankie "Half Pint" Jaxon (Vocalion); Connee Boswell (Decca); Julia Lee (Capitol).

Mama from the Train. w/m Irving Gordon, 1956. Hit record by Patti Page (Mercury).

Mama Goes Where Papa Goes (Or Papa Don't Go Out Tonight). w. Jack Yellen, m. Milton Ager, 1923. Introduced and featured by Sophie Tucker. Recorded by Sam Lanin and his Orchestra (Okeh).

Mama Guitar. w. Budd Schulberg and Tom Glazer, m. Tom Glazer, 1957. Introduced by Andy Griffith in (MP) *A Face in the Crowd.* Leading records by Don Cornell (Coral) and Julius La Rosa (RCA).

Mama Inez. w. L. Wolfe Gilbert (Engl.), m. Eliseo Grenet, 1931. This rhumba, originally titled "Ay! Mama-Ines" in Cuba, was introduced in the U.S. by Enric Madriguera and his Orchestra, broadcasting from the Biltmore Hotel, New York, and recorded by him (Columbia).

Mama Liked the Roses. w/m Johnny Christopher, 1970. Recorded by Elvis Presley, and coupled with "The Wonder of You" (q.v.) (RCA).

Mama Look a Booboo. w/m Lord Melody (Fitzroy Alexander), 1957. Featured and recorded by Harry Belafonte (RCA).

Mama Loves Papa (Papa Loves Mama). w/m Cliff Friend and Abel Baer, 1923. Introduced and featured by Sophie Tucker. Recorded instrumentally by Isham Jones and his Orchestra (Brunswick).

Mama Said. w/m Luther Dixon and William Denson, 1961. Hit record by The Shirelles (Scepter).

Mama Sang a Song. w/m Bill Anderson, 1962. Narration with music recorded by Stan Kenton and his Orchestra (Capitol), Walter Brennan (Liberty), Bill Anderson (Decca).

Mama's Gone, Goodbye. w/m Peter Bocage and A. J. Piron, 1924. First recorded by Piron's New Orleans Orchestra, followed by Wingy Manone (Bluebird), Tiny Hill (Vocalion), Viola McCoy (Banner), Harry Cool (Mercury), Cass Daley (Decca), Griff Williams (Okeh), and others.

Mama's Never Seen Those Eyes. w/m J. L. Wallace and Terry Skinner, 1986. #1 Country chart record by The Forester Sisters (Warner Bros.).

Mama Spank. w/m Liz Anderson, 1967. Top 10 Country chart record by Liz Anderson (RCA).

Mama's Pearl. w/m Berry Gordy, Jr., Fonce Mizell, Freddie Perren, and Deke Richards, 1971. Top 10 record by the Jackson 5 (Motown).

Mama Told Me (Not to Come). w/m Randy Newman, 1970. First recorded by Randy Newman in his album "12 Songs" (Reprise). The group Three Dog Night then had a #1 single, which earned a gold record (Dunhill).

Mama Tried. w/m Merle Haggard, 1968. Hit Country record by Merle Haggard (Capitol). Sung by Haggard in (MP) *Killers Three*, 1968.

Mama Used to Say. w/m Junior Giscombe and Bob Carter, 1982. Top 10 R&B and Pop crossover record by the English singer/writer Junior (Mercury).

Mamaw. w/m John Foley, 1981. Introduced by John Foley in the off-Broadway (TM) *Pump Boys and Dinettes.*

Mama Will Bark. w/m Dick Manning, 1951. Novelty, recorded by Frank Sinatra and Dagmar (Columbia).

Mama Yo Quiero. See **I Want My Mama.**

Mambo Baby. w/m Charles Singleton and Rose Marie McCoy, 1954. R&B hit by Ruth Brown (Atlantic).

Mambo Italiano. w/m Bob Merrill, 1954. Hit record by Rosemary Clooney (Columbia).

Mambo Jambo. w. Raymond Karl and Charlie Towne, m. Perez Prado, 1950. Hit record by Sonny Burke and his Orchestra (Decca), which is regarded as the generator of the mambo popularity in the U.S.

Mambo Rock. w/m Bix Reichner, Mildred Phillips, and Jim Ayre, 1955. Introduced and recorded by Bill Haley and His Comets (Decca).

Mame. w/m Jerry Herman, 1966. Introduced by Charles Braswell and company in (TM) *Mame.* Popular recordings by Bobby Darin (Atlantic), Louis Armstrong (Mercury), Herb Alpert and The Tijuana Brass (A&M). In the film version, (MM) *Mame,* 1974, it was sung by Robert Preston and company.

Mamie. w. Will D. Cobb, m. Gus Edwards, 1901.

Mamie, Come Kiss Your Honey. w/m May Irwin, 1893. Introduced by May Irwin in (TM) *A Country Sport.*

Mamma Mia. w/m Benny Anderson, Stig Anderson, and Bjorn Alvaeus, 1976. Recorded by the Swedish quartet Abba (Atlantic).

Mammas, Don't Let Your Babies Grow Up to Be Cowboys. w/m Ed Bruce and Patsy Bruce, 1978. Introduced by Ed Bruce (United Artists). Hit C&W/Pop record by Waylon Jennings and Willie Nelson (RCA).

Mammy Blue. w. Paul Trim (Engl.), Hubert Giraud (Fr.), m. Hubert Giraud, 1971. French song, recorded in Spain by the septet Los Pop Tops (ABC). Additional chart record by New York rock quartet Stories (Kama Sutra), 1973.

Mammy Jinny's Jubilee. w. L. Wolfe Gilbert, m. Lewis F. Muir, 1913.

Mammy O' Mine. w. William Tracey, m. Maceo Pinkard, 1919. Recorded and popularized by Adele Rowland (Decca) and instrumental version by Yerkes Jazarimba Orchestra (Victor).

Mammy's Chocolate Soldier. w. Sidney Mitchell, m. Archie Gottler, 1918. Featured in vaudeville and recorded by Marion Harris (Victor).

Mammy's Little Coal Black Rose. w. Raymond Egan, m. Richard Whiting, 1916. Dialect song featured by Al Jolson. Popular recording by The Orpheus Quartet (Victor).

Mammy's Little Pumpkin Colored Coon. w/m Hillman and Perrin, 1897. From the musical farce (TM) *The Good Mr. Best.*

Mam'selle. w. Mack Gordon, m. Edmund Goulding, 1947. Theme from (MP) *The Razor's Edge,* to which lyrics were added. Art Lund with Leroy Holmes's Orchestra (MGM) and The Pied Pipers with June Hutton (Capitol) had popular records.

Managua Nicaragua. w. Albert Gamse, m. Irving Fields, 1947. #1 records by Guy Lombardo and his Royal Canadians (Decca) and Freddy Martin, vocal by Stuart Wade (RCA Victor).

Mañana. w/m Jimmy Buffett, 1978. Recorded by Jimmy Buffett (ABC).

Mañana (Is Soon Enough for Me). w/m Peggy Lee and Dave Barbour, 1948. #1 record by Peggy Lee, and her first million-seller (Capitol).

Man and a Half, A. w/m Larry Chambers, George Jackson, Melvin Leakes, and Raymond Moore, 1968. Recorded by Wilson Pickett (Atlantic).

Man and a Train, A. w. Hal David, m. Frank DeVol, 1973. Sung on the soundtrack of (MP) *Emperor of the North* by Marty Robbins.

Man and a Woman, A. w. Jerry Keller (Engl.), Pierre Barouh (Fr.), m. Francis Lai, 1966. Original French title of film from which it emanated, and song, *Un Homme et Une Femme.* U.S. release, (MP) *A Man and a Woman.* Leading records by Tamiko Jones with Herbie Mann (Atlantic); Francis Lai and his Orchestra (United Artists).

Man and His Dream, A. w. Johnny Burke, m. James V. Monaco, 1939. Introduced by Bing Crosby in (MM) *The Star Maker*, a film loosely based on the career of Gus Edwards. Crosby recorded it (Decca).

Mandalay. w/m Earl Burtnett, Abe Lyman, and Gus Arnheim, 1924. Popularized by Al Jolson, who featured it and recorded it with Abe Lyman's Orchestra (Brunswick). Also recorded by Paul Whiteman (Victor).

Mandolin Rain. w/m Bruce Hornsby and John Hornsby, 1987. Pop and Country chart hit by Bruce Hornsby and The Range (RCA).

Mandolins in the Moonlight. w/m George David Weiss and Aaron Schroeder, 1958. Featured and recorded by Perry Como (RCA).

Mandy (a.k.a. **Brandy**). w/m Scott English and Richard Kerr, 1972, 1974. Originally recorded as "Brandy" by Scott English (Janus). Barry Manilow, for his first hit—and a gold record—recorded it as "Mandy" (Bell), 1974. New title not to be confused with the Berlin standard.

Mandy. w/m Irving Berlin, 1919. The song was originally written for and performed in a minstrel-show sequence in the all-soldier show (TM) *Yip, Yip, Yaphank*, 1918. The song was then interpolated in (TM) *Ziegfeld Follies*, 1919, where it was sung again in a minstrel-show setting, this time by Van and Schenck, Marilyn Miller, and Ray Dooley. Eddie Cantor sang it in a production number in (MM) *Kid Millions*, 1934. It then was heard, again in a minstrel routine by an all-soldier cast, in Irving Berlin's World War II (TM) *This Is The Army*, 1942, and in the film version, (MM) *This Is The Army*, 1943. It was sung in (MM) *White Christmas*, 1954, by Trudy Stevens (dubbing for Vera-Ellen) and a minstrel-show ensemble.

Mandy, Make Up Your Mind. w. Grant Clarke and Roy Turk, m. George W. Meyer and Arthur Johnston, 1924. Introduced by Florence Mills in (TM) *Dixie to Broadway*.

This was Johnston's first song success. The song was recorded by Paul Whiteman (Victor); Clarence Williams, featuring Louis Armstrong and Sidney Bechet (Okeh); Fletcher Henderson (Paramount); Tommy Dorsey (Victor).

Mandy Is Two. w. Johnny Mercer, m. Fulton McGrath, 1942. Mercer wrote this in honor of his daughter Amanda's second birthday. Among records: Bing Crosby (Decca) and Guy Lombardo, vocal by Kenny Gardner (Decca).

Mandy Lee. w/m Thurland Chattaway, 1899. A favorite with barbershop quartets.

Mandy 'n' Me. w. Bert Kalmar, m. Con Conrad, 1921. Popular record by The American Quartet (Victor).

Maneater. w/m Daryl Hall, John Oates, and Sara Allen, 1982. #1 gold record from the platinum LP, "H2O," by Daryl Hall and John Oates (RCA).

Man from Laramie, The. w. Ned Washington, m. Lester Lee, 1955. Title song of (MP) *The Man from Laramie*.

Man from the South, The (with a Big Cigar in His Mouth). w/m Rube Bloom and Harry Woods, 1930. Popularized by the recordings of Ted Weems (Victor); Joe Venuti, with Bloom on piano (Okeh); Rube Bloom and His Bayou Boys (Columbia).

Mangos. w/m Sid Wayne and Dee Libbey, 1957. Introduced by Micki Marlo in (TM) *Ziegfeld Follies*. Leading record by Rosemary Clooney (Columbia).

Manha de Carnaval. w. Antonio Mariz, m. Luis Bonfa, 1960. Introduced by Breno Mello in the Academy Award-winning French film *Black Orpheus*. See also "A Day in the Life of a Fool."

Manhattan. w. Lorenz Hart, m. Richard Rodgers, 1925. Sung by June Cochrane and Sterling Holloway in the revue (TM) *Garrick Gaieties*. This was the first hit for the team of Rodgers and Hart. In their biography (MM) *Words and Music*, 1948, it was sung by Tom

Drake, Mickey Rooney, and Marshall Thompson. In 1956, Carmen Cavallaro played it on the soundtrack in (MM) *The Eddy Duchin Story*. It was also heard in the background in (MM) *Beau James*, 1957 and (MM) *With a Song in My Heart*, 1957.

Manhattan Mary. w. B. G. DeSylva and Lew Brown, m. Ray Henderson, 1927. The title song of (TM) *Manhattan Mary*.

Manhattan Merry-Go-Round. w. Pinky Herman, m. Gustave Haenschen, 1936. Theme song of the popular weekly radio show of the same name.

Manhattan Rag. m. Hoagy Carmichael, 1930. First recorded by Frankie Trumbauer and his Orchestra, with Carmichael on piano (Okeh), and then by the studio band, Irving Mills and his Hotsy Totsy Gang (Brunswick), with an arrangement by Matty Malneck.

Manhattan Serenade. w. Harold Adamson, m. Louis Alter, 1928, 1942. First published as a piano solo. In the mid-thirties, it served as the theme for the radio series "Easy Aces." Adamson's lyrics were added, 1942, and the song was recorded by, among others, Harry James, vocal by Helen Forrest (Columbia); Jimmy Dorsey, vocal by Bob Eberly (Decca); Tommy Dorsey, vocal by Jo Stafford (Victor). Eleven weeks on "Your Hit Parade" followed.

Manhattan Spiritual. m. Billy Maxted, 1959. Instrumental recorded by the British bandleader Reg Owen and his Orchestra (Palette).

Maniac. w/m Michael Sembello and Dennis Matkosky, 1983. Introduced by Jennifer Beals in (MM) *Flashdance*. Nominated for an Academy Award. #1 record by Michael Sembello (Casablanca).

Manic Monday. w/m Prince Rogers Nelson, 1986. Top 10 single by the quartet The Bangles (Columbia).

Man I Love, The. w. Ira Gershwin, m. George Gershwin, 1928. Introduced by Adele Astaire in the pre-Broadway tryout of (TM) *Lady, Be Good!* 1924. Song dropped from the show. Sung by Vivian Hart and Roger Pryor in the pre-Broadway tryout of the first version of (TM) *Strike Up the Band*, 1927. Morton Downey, in the same show, sang a version titled *The Girl I Love*. The production never made it to New York. Marilyn Miller rehearsed it for the musical, *Rosalie*, 1928, but the song was again dropped. Through performances by singers and dance bands, the song has become an all-time standard and one of the Gershwins' most performed compositions. In films, it was performed by pianist Hazel Scott in the George Gershwin biography, (TM) *Rhapsody in Blue*, 1945; sung by Doris Day, accompanied by Harry James as Bix Beiderbecke in (MM) *Young Man with a Horn*, 1950; played in a Gershwin medley by Liberace in (MM) *Sincerely Yours*, 1955; heard on the soundtrack of (MM) *The Eddy Duchin Story*, 1957; sung by Diana Ross as Billie Holiday in (MM) *Lady Sings the Blues*, 1972; performed by the band in (MM) *New York, New York*, 1977.

Man in Black. w/m Johnny Cash, 1971. Hit Country and Pop chart record by Johnny Cash (Columbia).

Man in the Mirror. w/m Siedah Garrett and Glen Ballard, 1988. The fourth #1 single from the album "Bad" by Michael Jackson (Epic).

Man in the Raincoat, The. w/m Warwick Webster, 1955. Canadian song introduced and recorded by Priscilla Wright (Unique). Also performed and recorded by Marion Marlowe (Cadence).

Man of Constant Sorrow. w/m Peter Yarrow and Paul Stookey, 1962. Introduced by Peter, Paul and Mary (Warner Bros.).

Man on the Corner. w/m Phil Collins, 1982. Recorded by the English group Genesis (Atlantic).

Man on the Flying Trapeze, The. w/m Walter O'Keefe, 1933. Based on the English music hall song, "The Flying Trapeze," written in 1868 by George Leybourne and Alfred

Lee. O'Keefe, a popular American comedian in vaudeville and radio, introduced this version. Eddie Cantor recorded it (Melotone) and later, André Kostalanetz (Brunswick) and Spike Jones (Victor) had versions. Rudy Vallee sang it in (MM) *George White's Scandals*, 1934, and (MM) *Two Many Blondes*, 1941. It was also heard in (MM) *Twenty Million Sweethearts* in 1934.

Man on Your Mind. w/m Glenn Shorrock and Kerryn Tolhurst, 1982. Recorded by the Australian group Little River Band (Capitol).

Mansion of Aching Hearts, The. w. Arthur J. Lamb, m. Harry Von Tilzer, 1902. A sentimental ballad that was a follow-up to "A Bird in a Gilded Cage." Popular recording by Byron G. Harlan (Edison).

Mansion on the Hill, A. w/m Hank Williams and Fred Rose, 1948. Recorded by Hank Williams (MGM).

Man Size Love. w/m Rod Temperton, 1986. Recorded on the soundtrack of (MP) *Running Scared* and on a chart single by the female sextet Klymaxx (MCA).

Man Smart, Woman Smarter. w/m Norman Span, 1976. Recorded by the English singer Robert Palmer (Island).

Manteca. m. John Birks "Dizzy" Gillespie and Gil Fuller, 1948. Instrumental recorded by Dizzy Gillespie and his Orchestra (Victor).

Man That Broke the Bank at Monte Carlo, The. w/m Fred Gilbert, 1892. An English song written about Arthur De Courcey Bower who worked as a shill [come-on] for the gambling casino. Introduced in America by William "Old Hoss" Hoey.

Man That Got Away, The. w. Ira Gershwin, m. Harold Arlen, 1954. Introduced by Judy Garland in (MM) *A Star Is Born*. Garland is universally associated with the song, having performed it in every medium.

Man Upstairs, The. w/m Dorinda Morgan, Hal Stanley, and Gerry Manners, 1954. Popular record by Kay Starr, with Harold Mooney's Orchestra (Capitol).

Man Who Comes Around, The. w/m Tommy Tucker, John Lair, and Bud Green, 1940. Top 10 record by Tommy Tucker, vocal by Kelly Rand (Vocalion).

Man Who Owns Broadway, The. w/m George M. Cohan, 1909. From (TM) *The Man Who Owns Broadway*.

Man Who Plays the Mandolino, The. See **Guaglione.**

Man Who Robbed the Bank at Santa Fe, The. w/m Jerry Leiber, Mike Stoller, and Billy Edd Wheeler, 1963. Hit C&W record by Hank Snow (RCA).

Man Who Shot Liberty Valance, The. w. Hal David, m. Burt Bacharach, 1962. Title suggested by the film of the same name. Hit record by Gene Pitney (Musicor).

Man with a Dream, A. w. Stella Unger, m. Victor Young, 1955. Introduced by Ricardo Montalban in (TM) *Seventh Heaven*.

Man with a Horn. w. Eddie DeLange, m. Bonnie Lake and Jack Jenney, 1946. Jazz standard and theme of trumpeter Ray Anthony and his Orchestra. This was published shortly after the death of co-composer Jack Jenney, the great trombonist.

Man with a Load of Mischief. w. Ben Tarver and John Clifton, m. John Clifton, 1966. Introduced by Virginia Vestoff in (TM) *Man with a Load of Mischief*. Popular recording by Ralph Carmichael and his Orchestra (Kapp).

Man Without Love, A. w. Barry Mason (Engl.), D. Pace, M. Panzeri, and R. Livraghi, (It.), M. Pace, Panzeri, and Livraghi, 1968. Italian song. Top 20 English version by Engelbert Humperdinck (Parrot).

Man with the Banjo, The. w. Robert Mellin (Engl.), m. Fritz Schulz Reichel, 1954. New lyrics for German song. Recorded by The Ames Brothers (RCA Victor).

Man with the Child in His Eyes, The.
w/m Kate Bush, 1979. Recorded by the British
singer Kate Bush (EMI America).

Man with the Golden Arm, The. w. Sammy Cahn, m. James Van Heusen, 1956. Titled
after the film of the same name, but not used in
the production.

Man with the Golden Arm, The (Main Title). m. Elmer Bernstein, 1956. Best-selling
records of the main title theme, by the orchestras of Morris Stoloff (Decca) and Elmer Bernstein (Decca).

Man with the Ladder and the Hose. w/m
T. Mayo Geary, 1904.

Man with the Mandolin, The. w. James
Cavanaugh and John Redmond, m. Frank
Weldon, 1939. Best-selling records by Glenn
Miller, vocal by Marion Hutton (Bluebird) and
Horace Heidt, vocal by Larry Cotton (Brunswick). Ten weeks on "Your Hit Parade," attaining the #2 position.

Many a New Day. w. Oscar Hammerstein
II, m. Richard Rodgers, 1943. Introduced by
Joan Roberts [singing] and Joan McCracken,
Kate Friedlich, and Katherine Sergava [dancing] in (TM) *Oklahoma!* In the film version
(MM) *Oklahoma!*, 1955, it was sung by Shirley Jones.

Many Dreams Ago. w. Al Stillman, m.
Fred Ahlert, 1939. Top recordings by Hal
Kemp, vocal by Nan Wynn (Victor); and Jan
Savitt, vocal by Bon Bon (Decca).

Many Happy Hangovers to You. w/m
Johnny MacRae, 1966. Country chart record
by Jean Shepard (Capitol).

Many Happy Returns of the Day. w. Al
Dubin, m. Joe Burke, 1931. Featured and
recorded by Bing Crosby (Brunswick); Frank
Parker (Columbia); and Adrian Schubert's Orchestra, with vocal by Paul Small (Crown).

Many Rivers to Cross. w/m Jimmy Cliff,
1973. Sung by Jimmy Cliff in (MP) *The Harder
They Come.*

Many Tears Ago. w/m Winfield Scott,
1960. Hit record by Connie Francis (MGM).

Many Times. w. Jessie Barnes (Engl.), m.
Felix Stahl, 1953. New lyrics for Belgian song.
First U.S. record: instrumental version by Percy Faith and his Orchestra (Columbia). Eddie
Fisher, with Hugo Winterhalter's Orchestra,
had a hit vocal record (RCA Victor).

Maple Leaf Rag. m. Scott Joplin, 1899.
One of Joplin's most popular compositions,
and the first ragtime composition to sell a
million copies of sheet music. Among the
many recordings are those by Vess Ossman,
"The King of the Banjo" (Columbia), 1907;
The U.S. Marine Band (Columbia), 1907; The
New Orleans Feetwarmers (Victor), 1932;
Tommy Dorsey (Victor), 1936; Art Hodes
(Brunswick), 1944; Eddie Condon (Decca),
1950.

Marcheta. w/m Victor Schertzinger, 1913.

Marching Along Together. w/m Edward
Pola and Franz Steininger, 1933. Written in
England, Mort Dixon added some "Americanized" lyrics to the U.S. version. Introduced
in the U.S. by Kate Smith. Featured and recorded by Ben Bernie and "all the lads" (Columbia) and Ted Weems, with vocal and whistling supplied by Elmo Tanner (Bluebird).

Marching Through Berlin. w/m Belford
Hendricks, 1942. Adapted from the German
anthem, "Deutschland Über Alles," Ethel
Merman introduced it (MM) *Stage Door Canteen*, and recorded it (Victor).

March of the Grenadiers. w. Clifford
Grey, m. Victor Schertzinger, 1929. Sung by
Jeanette MacDonald with male chorus in (MM)
The Love Parade. She also recorded it (Victor).

March of the Musketeers. w. P. G. Wodehouse and Clifford Grey, m. Rudolf Friml,
1928. Introduced by Dennis King, Douglas
Dumbrille, Detmar Poppen, Joseph Macauley,
and chorus in (TM) *The Three Musketeers.*

March of the Siamese Children. m. Richard Rodgers, 1951. Staged with the children in

(TM) *The King and I* and repeated in (MM) *The King and I*, 1956.

March of the Toys, The. w. Glen Mac-Donough, m. Victor Herbert, 1903. Introduced by Mabel Barrison and William Norris in (TM) *Babes in Toyland*. It was heard in the films (MM) *The Great Victor Herbert*, 1939, and (MM) *Babes in Toyland*, featuring Laurel and Hardy, 1934, and in the Disney re-make, 1961.

March of Time, The. w. Ted Koehler, m. Harold Arlen, 1930. Sung by Harry Stockwell and John Hale in (TM) *Earl Carroll Vanities of 1930*.

March Winds and April Showers. w/m Walter G. Samuels, Leonard Whitecup, and Teddy Powell. 1935. Featured and recorded by Ruth Etting (Columbia); Abe Lyman and his Orchestra (Brunswick); Victor Young, vocal by Jimmy Ray (Decca).

Margaritaville. w/m Jimmy Buffett, 1977. Top 10 record by Jimmy Buffett (ABC).

Margie. w. Benny Davis, m. Con Conrad and J. Russel Robinson, 1920. First performed and recorded by The Original Dixieland Jazz Band (Victor) and Gene Rodemich and his Orchestra (Columbia). The following year it was interpolated by Eddie Cantor in (TM) *The Midnight Rounders* at the Winter Garden in New York. Tom Brown sang it and Joy Hodges reprised it in (MP) *Margie*, 1940. It was sung on the soundtrack of (MM) *Margie*, 1946. Cantor sang it, dubbing for Keefe Brasselle, in (MM) *The Eddie Cantor Story*, 1953.

Margie's at the Lincoln Park Inn. w/m Tom T. Hall, 1969. Hit Country record by Bobby Bare (RCA).

Maria. w. Oscar Hammerstein II, m. Richard Rodgers, 1959. Introduced by Patricia Neway, Muriel O'Malley, Elizabeth Howell, and Karen Shepard in (TM) *The Sound of Music*. In (MM) *The Sound of Music*, 1965, it was sung by Anna Lee, Marni Nixon, Portia Nelson, and Evadne Baker.

Maria. w. Stephen Sondheim, m. Leonard Bernstein, 1957. Introduced by Larry Kert in (TM) *West Side Story*. Leading vocal record by Johnny Mathis (Columbia); leading instrumental by Roger Williams (Kapp). Jim Bryant, dubbing on the soundtrack for Richard Beymer, sang it in (MM) *West Side Story*, 1961.

Maria, My Own. w. L. Wolfe Gilbert (Engl.), m. Ernesto Lacuona, 1931. Originally titled "Maria-la-o" from the Cuban operetta of the same name.

Maria Elena. w. S. K. (Bob) Russell (Engl.), m. Lorenzo Barcelata, 1941. Original Spanish words by Barcelata written for and dedicated to the wife of Mexican President Portes Gil. The music was first heard as the background theme of (MP) *Bordertown*, starring Paul Muni, 1935. Lawrence Welk and his Orchestra introduced the English version via his recording (Okeh). Jimmy Dorsey, with vocal by Bob Eberly (Decca), followed with their #1 hit, which helped the song stay on "Your Hit Parade" for twenty-two weeks. Revived with the hit instrumental recording by the Brazilian brothers, Los Indios Tabajares (RCA), 1963.

Maria from Bahia. w. Albert Gamse, m. Paul Misraki, 1948. Argentinian song with original Spanish words by Misraki. Popular American record by The Starlighters (Capitol).

Marianne. w/m Jerry Herman, 1979. Introduced by Ron Holgate, and reprised by Joel Grey in (TM) *The Grand Tour*.

Marianne. w/m Terry Gilkyson, Frank Miller, and Rick Dehr, 1957. Adaptation of Bahamian folk song. Introduced and hit record by the three writers, performing as Terry Gilkyson and The Easy Riders (Columbia). The Hilltoppers also had a high chart record (Dot).

Marianne. w. Oscar Hammerstein II, m. Sigmund Romberg, 1928. Introduced by Robert Halliday in (TM) *The New Moon*. Lawrence Tibbett sang it in (MM) *New Moon*, 1930, and Nelson Eddy sang it in the 1940 version.

Marian the Librarian. w/m Meredith Willson, 1957. Introduced by Robert Preston in (TM) *The Music Man*. Preston also sang it in (MM) *The Music Man*, 1962.

Marie. w/m Irving Berlin, 1928. Written as a waltz and as the theme song of (MP) *The Awakening*, starring Vilma Banky. It had not much more than slight initial popularity until Tommy Dorsey and his Orchestra recorded a million-seller (Victor), 1937. Dorsey changed the time signature to ¼ and the musicians sang "filler" lyrics behind the vocal by Jack Leonard. The record, Dorsey's first big hit, featured an outstanding trumpet solo by Bunny Berigan. The song was heard in the background of (MM) *Alexander's Ragtime Band*, 1938. It was played by the Tommy Dorsey Band and sung by Janet Blair and Stuart Foster in (MM) *The Fabulous Dorseys*, 1947. Dorsey again played it in (MM) *A Song Is Born*, 1948, and an unidentified trio sang it in (MM) *There's No Business Like Show Business*, 1954. The Four Tunes had a popular record that year (Jubilee). The Irish group, The Bachelors, had a Top 20 U.S. chart hit (London), 1965.

Marie from Sunny Italy. w. Irving Berlin, m. M. Nicholson, 1907. Berlin's first published song. Introduced by him while he was a singing waiter in a downtown New York restaurant.

Marieke. w. Eric Blau (Engl.), Jacques Brel (Fr.), m. Jacques Brel and Gérard Jouannest, 1968. Introduced in France by Jacques Brel, 1961. Introduced in English by Ellie Stone and company in the off-Broadway revue (TM) *Jacques Brel Is Alive and Well and Living in Paris.*

Marie Laveau. w/m Shel Silverstein and Baxter Taylor III, 1974. Country hit by Bobby Bare (RCA).

Mariko's Theme (Love Theme from "Shogun"). See **Shogun.**

Marina. w/m Rocco Granata, 1959. A truly international song with three chart records in the U.S.: the Belgian composer/singer Rocco

Granata (Laurie); the Dutch singer Willy Alberti, who sang in Italian (London); the Parisian orchestra leader, Jacky Noguez, who recorded it instrumentally (Jamie).

Marlena. w/m Bob Gaudio, 1963. Recorded by The Four Seasons coupled with the hit "Candy Girl" (Vee-Jay).

Marmalade, Molasses, and Honey. w. Alan Bergman and Marilyn Bergman, m. Maurice Jarre, 1972. Sung by Andy Williams on the soundtrack of (MP) *The Life and Times of Judge Roy Bean*. Nominated for an Academy Award.

Marrakesh Express. w/m Graham Nash, 1969. First hit by Crosby, Stills and Nash (Atlantic).

Marriage-Go-Round, The. w/m Alan Bergman, Marilyn Bergman, and Lew Spence, 1961. Sung on the soundtrack of (MP) *The Marriage-Go-Round* by Tony Bennett.

Marriage Type Love. w. Oscar Hammerstein II, m. Richard Rodgers, 1953. Introduced by Arthur Maxwell and Helena Scott in (TM) *Me and Juliet.*

Marriage Vow. w/m Jenny Lou Carson, 1949. Featured and recorded by Hank Snow, "The Singing Ranger" (RCA Victor).

Married (Heiraten). w. Fred Ebb, m. John Kander, 1966. Introduced by Lotte Lenya and Jack Gilford in (TM) *Cabaret*. In (MM) *Cabaret*, 1972, it was sung on the soundtrack in German as "Heiraten" by Greta Keller.

Married But Not to Each Other. w/m Denise LaSalle and Francis Miller, 1977. Country chart hit record by Barbara Mandrell (ABC/Dot).

Married by the Bible, Divorced by the Law. w/m Johnny Rector, Pee Wee Truehitt, and Neva Starns, 1952. Country song popularized by Hank Snow (RCA Victor).

Married I Can Always Get. w/m Gordon Jenkins, 1956. Introduced by Gordon Jenkins's Orchestra and chorus in "Manhattan

Tower" (Capitol), a suite that was an outgrowth of the initial Decca album. It was also presented as a network TV show. This song was not in the original album. Recorded by Teddi King (RCA), Jeri Southern (Decca), Patti Page (Mercury).

Married Man, A. w/m Marian Grudeff and Raymond Jessel, 1965. Introduced by Peter Sallis in (TM) *Baker Street*. Chart single by Richard Burton (MGM).

Married Men. w/m Dominic Bugatti and Frank Musker, 1979. Recorded by Bette Midler (Atlantic).

Marrying for Love. w/m Irving Berlin, 1950. Introduced by Ethel Merman in (TM) *Call Me Madam*. Merman had a popular single (Decca), as did Rosemary Clooney and Guy Mitchell (Columbia). In (MM) *Call Me Madam*, 1953, George Sanders sang it as a solo.

Marry Me a Little. w/m Stephen Sondheim, 1981. Introduced by Suzanne Henry in the off-Broadway (TM) *Marry Me a Little*.

Mars. See **Stars in Your Eyes.**

Marshmallow Moon. w/m Jay Livingston and Ray Evans, 1951. Featured in (MM) *Aaron Slick from Punkin Crick*. The song title became the film title for the Great Britain release.

Marshmallow World, A. w. Carl Sigman, m. Peter De Rose, 1951. Christmas song, featured and recorded by Bing Crosby (Decca).

Marta. w. L. Wolfe Gilbert (Engl.), m. Moises Simons, 1931. The third hit song from Cuba this year with English lyrics by Gilbert . . . and all starting with "M." See: "Mama Inez" and "Maria, My Own." This was the theme song of Arthur Tracy, "The Street Singer," who recorded it at least three times (Brunswick, Decca, London). He sang it in (MM) *The Big Broadcast* in 1932.

Martian Hop. w/m John Spirt, Robert Rappaport, and Steve Rappaport, 1963. Novelty recording by The Ran-Dells (Chairman).

Marty. w. Paddy Chayefsky, m. Harry Warren, 1955. Written as a promotional song for the film.

Marvelous Toy, The. w/m Tom Paxton, 1963. Featured and recorded by The Chad Mitchell Trio (Mercury).

Mary. w. Otto Harbach, m. Louis A. Hirsch, 1920. The title song of (TM) *Mary*, introduced by Janet Velie and chorus.

(What Are You Waiting For) Mary. w/m Walter Donaldson, 1927. Recorded by Paul Whiteman and his Orchestra (Victor), organist Jesse Crawford (Victor), James Melton (Columbia); Al Goodman's Orchestra (Brunswick). During World War II, George Paxton and his Band recorded it on a 12″ V-disc with two other girls names' songs, "Margie" and "Louise" (q.v.).

Mary, Dear. w/m Harry DeCosta and M. K. Jerome, 1922.

Mary, You're a Little Bit Old Fashioned. w. Marion Sunshine, m. Henry I. Marshall, 1914. Recorded by Charles Harrison (Victor).

Mary Ann. w. Benny Davis, m. Abner Silver, 1928. Popular recordings by Cliff "Ukulele Ike" Edwards (Columbia) and the Dorsey Brothers Orchestra (Okeh).

Mary Had a Little Lamb. w/m Paul McCartney and Linda McCartney, 1972. Recorded by the new McCartney group Wings (Apple).

Mary Had a Little Lamb. w. Marty Symes, m. Matty Malneck, 1936. Among recordings: Willie Bryant (Bluebird), Putney Dandridge (Vocalion), André Kostalanetz (Brunswick), Teddy Wilson (Brunswick).

Mary in the Morning. w/m Johnny Cymbal and Mike Lendell, 1967. Top 40 record by Al Martino (Capitol).

Mary Lou. w/m Ronnie Hawkins and Jacqueline Magill, 1959. Introduced and recorded by Ronnie Hawkins (Roulette).

Mary Lou. w. Abe Lyman and George Waggner, m. J. Russel Robinson, 1926. Introduced and featured by Abe Lyman and his Orchestra.

Mary's a Grand Old Name. w/m George M. Cohan, 1905. First performed by Fay Templeton in Cohan's (TM) *Forty-Five Minutes from Broadway*. It was sung by James Cagney, Joan Leslie, and Irene Manning in (MM) *Yankee Doodle Dandy*, the film biography of Cohan, 1942. It was danced to by Cagney and Bob Hope in (MM) *The Seven Little Foys*, 1955. Revived in (TM) *George M!* by Jacqueline Alloway, 1968.

Mary's Idea. m. Mary Lou Williams, 1939. Instrumental recorded by Andy Kirk and his Clouds of Joy, with the composer on piano (Decca).

Mary's Little Lamb. w/m Barry Mann and Cynthia Weil, 1962. Recorded by James Darren (Colpix).

Mary's Prayer. w/m Gary Clark, 1987. Chart record by Danny Wilson, the group from The Seychelles (Virgin).

Ma Says, Pa Says. w/m Josef Marais, 1952. South African song popularized in U.S. via recording of Doris Day and Johnnie Ray (Columbia).

M*A*S*H. See **Song from M*A*S*H.**

Mashed Potato Time. w/m Jon Sheldon and Harry Land, 1962. Hit record by Dee Dee Sharp (Cameo).

Mas Que Nada. 1966. Brazilian song recorded by Sergio Mendes and Brasil '66 (A&M).

Masquerade. w. Paul Francis Webster, m. John Jacob Loeb, 1928. The first song success for each of the writers. Early recordings by the orchestras of Ted Black (Victor) and Morton Gould (Columbia); also by Jesse Crawford, the organist (Victor), and Arthur Tracy, "The Street Singer" (Brunswick).

Masquerade Is Over, The. w. Herb Magidson, m. Allie Wrubel, 1939. A Top 10 song, helped by the band recordings of Jimmy Dorsey (Decca); Larry Clinton, vocal by Bea Wain (Victor); and Horace Heidt (Brunswick).

Massachusetts. w. Andy Razaf, m. C. Luckeyth "Luckey" Roberts, 1942. Leading records by Johnny Long and his Orchestra (Decca) and Gene Krupa, vocal by Anita O'Day (Okeh).

Massachusetts (Lights Went Out In). See **Lights Went Out in Massachusetts.**

Master Blaster (Jammin'). w/m Stevie Wonder, 1980. Top 10 record by Stevie Wonder (Tamla).

Master Jack. w/m David Markantonatos, 1968. Recorded by the South African quintet Four Jacks and a Jill (RCA).

Masters of War. w/m Bob Dylan, 1963. Introduced and recorded by Bob Dylan (Columbia).

Matador, The. w/m Carl Davis, William B. Butler, and Major Lance, 1964. Crossover (R&B/Pop) hit by Major Lance (Okeh).

Matador, The. w/m Johnny Cash and June Carter, 1963. Crossover (C&W/Pop) hit by Johnny Cash (Columbia).

Matamoros. w/m Kay Arnold, 1965. Top 10 Country chart record by Billy Walker (Columbia).

Matchbox. w/m Carl Perkins, 1964. Top 20 record by The Beatles (Capitol).

Matchmaker, Matchmaker. w. Sheldon Harnick, m. Jerry Bock, 1964. Introduced by Joanna Merlin, Julia Migenes, and Tanya Everett in (TM) *Fiddler on the Roof*. In the film version (MM) *Fiddler on the Roof*, it was sung by Rosalind Harris, Michele Marsh, and Neva Small.

Material Girl. w/m Peter Brown and Robert Rans, 1985. Top 10 single from the platinum album "Like a Virgin," by Madonna (Sire).

Matilda, Matilda! w/m Harry Thomas, 1953. Calypso song, featured and recorded by Harry Belafonte (RCA Victor).

Matinee. w. Bob Russell, m. Carl Sigman, 1948. Leading records by Vaughn Monroe, with his Orchestra (RCA Victor), and Buddy Clark (Columbia).

Mating Game, The. w. Lee Adams, m. Charles Strouse, 1959. Introduced by Debbie Reynolds in (MP) *The Mating Game*.

Matter of Trust, A. w/m Billy Joel, 1986. Top 10 record by Billy Joel (Columbia).

Maverick. w. Paul Francis Webster, m. David Buttolph, 1958. Theme of series (TVP) "Maverick."

Maxim's. w. Adrian Ross, m. Franz Lehar, 1907. Sung by Donald Brian in the N.Y. production (TM) of *The Merry Widow*. In the 1934 film version (MM) *The Merry Widow* it was performed by Maurice Chevalier and Edward Everett Horton [with new lyrics by Lorenz Hart and Gus Kahn]. In the 1952 (MM) film, Fernando Lamas and Richard Hayden sang it with new lyrics, this time by Paul Francis Webster.

Maybe. w. Martin Charnin, m. Charles Strouse, 1977. Introduced by Andrea McArdle in (TM) *Annie*. Sung by Aileen Quinn in the film version (MM) *Annie*, 1982.

Maybe. w/m Richard Barrett and George Goldner, 1958. Top 40 record by The Chantels (End). Revived by The Three Degrees (Roulette), 1970.

Maybe. w/m Allan Flynn and Frank Madden, 1940, 1952. A #1 song, thirteen weeks on "Your Hit Parade" and a topper in sheet music and record sales. The best-selling record by The Ink Spots (Decca) was on the charts for seventeen weeks. Perry Como and Eddie Fisher teamed up for a successful revival of the song (Victor), 1952.

Maybe. w. Ira Gershwin, m. George Gershwin, 1926. Introduced by Gertrude Lawrence and Oscar Shaw in (TM) *Oh, Kay!* This song is not to be confused with the 1940 hit or the song from *Annie*.

Maybe I Know. w/m Jeff Barry and Ellie Greenwich, 1964. Popular record by Lesley Gore (Mercury).

Maybe I'm a Fool. w/m Lloyd Chiate, Lee Garrett, Eddie Money, and Robert Taylor, 1979. Recorded by Eddie Money (Columbia).

Maybe I'm Amazed. w/m Paul McCartney, 1977. Top 10 record by McCartney's group Wings (Capitol). This was a live concert recording of a song from McCartney's first solo album (Apple), 1970.

Maybe It's Because. w. Harry Ruby, m. Johnnie Scott, 1949. Popular recordings by Dick Haymes, with Gordon Jenkins's Orchestra (Decca); Eddy Howard, with his Orchestra (Mercury); Connie Haines, with Roy Ross's Orchestra (Coral); Bob Crosby, vocal by Marion Morgan (Columbia).

Maybe It's Because I Love You Too Much. w/m Irving Berlin, 1933. Recorded by the bands of Leo Reisman, vocal by Fred Astaire (Victor); Guy Lombardo (Brunswick); Ray Noble (HMV/Victor); Freddy Martin, under pseudonym of Bob Causer, vocal by Elmer Feldkamp (Perfect).

Maybe Just Today. w/m Martha Sharp, 1968. Recorded by Bobby Vee (Liberty).

Maybellene. w/m Chuck Berry, Russ Frato, and Alan Freed, 1955. Chuck Berry's first recording became an instant R&B and Pop hit (Chess).

Maybe Some Other Time. w/m Ervin Drake, 1964. Sung by Robert Alda and Sally Ann Howes in (TM) *What Makes Sammy Run?*

Maybe This Time. w. Fred Ebb, m. John Kander, 1972. Written for the film version of (MM) *Cabaret* and introduced in the film by Liza Minnelli.

Maybe You'll Be There. w. Sammy Gallop, m. Rube Bloom, 1948. Gordon Jenkins, vocal by Charles Levere, had a million-seller (Decca).

Maybe Your Baby's Got the Blues. w/m Troy Seals and Graham Lyle, 1987. #1 Country chart song by the mother/daughter duo The Judds (RCA).

May I. w/m Maurice Williams, 1969. Recorded by Bill Deal and The Rhondels (Heritage).

May I? w. Mack Gordon, m. Harry Revel, 1934. Introduced by Bing Crosby in (MM) *We're Not Dressing* and recorded by him (Brunswick).

May I Have the Next Romance with You? w. Mack Gordon, m. Harry Revel, 1937. Introduced by Jessie Matthews in the British film (MM) *Head Over Heels in Love*. Matthews's recording was released in the U.S. (Decca), and Ruth Etting recorded it here for the same label (Decca).

May I Never Love Again. w/m Sano Marco and Jack Erickson, 1940. Most popular recording list topped by Bob Chester, vocal by Dolores O'Neill (Bluebird); Ted Weems, vocal by Perry Como (Decca); Ginny Simms (Okeh); The Charioteers (Columbia).

May the Bird of Paradise Fly up Your Nose. w/m Neal Merritt, 1965. Novelty hit record by "Little" Jimmy Dickens (Columbia).

May the Good Lord Bless and Keep You. w/m Meredith Willson, 1950. The impetus to the song's national reception was given by Tallullah Bankhead who, at the conclusion of her weekly network radio show, would sing the song with her guests, accompanied by the orchestra of Meredith Willson. Frankie Laine had a popular recording (Mercury).

May You Always. w/m Larry Markes and Dick Charles, 1959. Featured and recorded by The McGuire Sisters (Coral).

Me. w/m Alex Zanetis, 1964. Top 10 Country chart record by Bill Anderson (Decca). Revived by Sherry Grooms (Parachute), 1978.

Me. w/m Irving Berlin, 1931. Featured and recorded by Ruth Etting (Perfect).

Me, Myself, and I. w/m Edwin Birdsong, Kelvin Mercer, David Jolicoeur, Vincent Mason, Paul Huston, George Clinton, and Phil Wynn, 1989. Hit R&B chart record by De La Soul (Tommy Boy).

Me, Myself and I (Are All in Love with You). w/m Irving Gordon, Alvin S. Kaufman, and Allan Roberts, 1937. Featured and recorded by Billie Holiday (Vocalion) and Bob Howard (Decca).

Meadowgreen. w/m Roger Miller, 1966. Country chart record by The Browns (RCA).

Meadowland (a.k.a. **Meadowlands**). m. Lev Knipper, 1943. Many U.S. arrangements of the Soviet Army song "Cavalry of the Steppes." Introduced in the United States by The Red Army Choir in concert.

Meadowlands. See **Meadowland**.

Meadows of Heaven, The. w. Joseph Allan McCarthy, m. Joseph Meyer, 1949. Featured and recorded by Perry Como (RCA Victor).

Me and Baby Brother. w/m Dee Allen, Harold Brown, B. B. Dickerson, Lonnie Jordan, Lee Oskar, Charles Miller, Howard Scott, 1973. Written and recorded by the band War (United Artists).

Me and Bobby McGee. w/m Kris Kristofferson and Fred L. Foster, 1971. #1 chart hit by Janis Joplin (Columbia). Jerry Lee Lewis had a Top 40 version (Mercury).

Me and Julio Down by the Schoolyard. w/m Paul Simon, 1972. Top 40 record by Paul Simon (Columbia).

Me and Marie. w/m Cole Porter, 1935. Introduced by Melville Cooper and Mary Boland in (TM) *Jubilee*. Recorded by Johnny Green's Orchestra (Brunswick).

Me and Mrs. Jones. w/m Kenny Gamble, Leon Huff, and Cary Gilbert, 1972. #1 gold record by Billy Paul (Philadelphia International).

Me and My Arrow. w/m Harry Nillson, 1970. Introduced by Harry Nillson on the soundtrack of the animated show (TVM) "The Point." His recording was in the Top 40 (RCA). The song was included in the score of the London stage adaptation.

Me and My Melinda. w/m Irving Berlin, 1942. Featured and recorded by the bands of Kay Kyser (Columbia); Gene Krupa, vocal by Johnny Desmond (Okeh); Vaughn Monroe (Bluebird); Bunny Berigan (Elite).

Me and My Shadow. w. Billy Rose, m. Al Jolson and Dave Dreyer, 1927. Featured by Al Jolson and Ted Lewis's band. Early recordings by "Whispering" Jack Smith (Victor), Johnny Marvin and Aileen Stanley (Columbia), Lee Sims (Brunswick). Pearl Bailey had a popular record in the early fifties (Coral). It was performed by Ted Lewis and his Band in (MM) *Hold That Ghost*, 1941; Donald O'Connor in (MM) *Feudin' Fussin' and A-fightin'*, 1948; heard in the Fanny Brice story, *Funny Lady*, 1975. In 1962, Frank Sinatra and Sammy Davis, Jr. had a popular recording, coupled with "Sam's Song" (q.v.) (Reprise).

Me and the Blues. w. Ted Koehler, m. Harry Warren, 1947. Recorded by Mildred Bailey, accompanied by Ellis Larkins (Majestic).

Me and the Boy Friend. w. Sidney Clare, m. James V. Monaco, 1924. Popularized in vaudeville and on records by Jane Green (Victor).

Me and the Man in the Moon. w. Edgar Leslie, m. James V. Monaco, 1928. Featured and recorded by Helen Kane (Victor); Ted Weems's Orchestra, vocal by Art Jarrett (Victor); Arnold Johnson's Orchestra (Brunswick); Cliff "Ukulele Ike" Edwards (Columbia).

Me and the Moon. w. Walter Hirsch, m. Lou Handman, 1936. Featured on radio and in locations, and recorded by the bands of Jimmie Lunceford (Decca), Shep Fields (Bluebird), Richard Himber (Victor).

Me and You and a Dog Named Boo. w/m Kent Lavoie, 1971. Top 10 record by Lobo, pseudonym for the writer (Big Tree).

Meanest Thing You Ever Did Was Kiss Me, The. w/m Al Lewis, Murray Mencher, and Charles Newman, 1937. Featured and recorded by Dolly Dawn (Bluebird).

Mean Green Mother from Outer Space. w. Howard Ashman, m. Alan Menken, 1986. Written for the film version, (MM) *Little Shop of Horrors*, based on the off-Broadway musical hit, which in turn was based on the 1960 film of the same name. Song recorded on the soundtrack by Levi Stubbs, as the voice of the man-eating plant, Audrey II. Nominated for an Academy Award, Best Song.

Meaning of the Blues, The. w/m Bobby Troup and Leah Worth, 1957. Introduced by Julie London in (MP) "The Great Man."

Mean to Me. w. Roy Turk, m. Fred E. Ahlert, 1929. Introduced and recorded by Ruth Etting (Columbia). It was sung by Doris Day as Etting in her biography (MM) *Love Me or Leave Me*, 1955. In 1972, Diana Ross sang it, as Billie Holiday, in (MM) *Lady Sings the Blues*. In 1978, Nell Carter sang it in (TM) *Ain't Misbehavin'*.

Mean Woman Blues. w/m Jerry West and Whispering Smith, 1963. Top 10 record by Roy Orbison (Monument).

Meatballs. w. Norman Gimbel, m. Elmer Bernstein, 1979. Sung by Rick Dees on the soundtrack of (MP) *Meatballs*.

Mecca. w/m Neval Nader and John Gluck, Jr., 1963. Hit record by Gene Pitney (Musicor).

Medicine Man. w/m Terry Cashman, Gene Pistilli, and Tommy West, 1969. Top 40 record by The Buchanan Brothers (Event, Part 1).

Medic Theme. See **Blue Star.**

Meditation (Meditacao). w. Norman Gimbel (Engl.), Newton Medonca (Port.), m. Antonio Carlos Jobim, 1963. Brazilian song. First popularized in the U.S. as an instrumental by jazz guitarist Charlie Byrd (Riverside). First English vocal by Pat Boone (Dot). Popular version by Claudine Longet (A&M), 1966.

Meek Shall Inherit, The. w. Howard Ashman, m. Alan Menken, 1982. Introduced by the company in the off-Broadway (TM) *Little Shop of Horrors*. Sung in the film version (MM)

Little Shop of Horrors, 1986, by Rick Moranis and cast members.

Meeskite. w. Fred Ebb, m. John Kander, 1966. Introduced by Jack Gilford in (TM) *Cabaret*. The song was not used in the film version as Gilford's role was deleted from the script.

Meeting Over Yonder. w/m Curtis Mayfield, 1965. Chart record by The Impressions (ABC-Paramount).

Meet Me at No Special Place (And I'll Be There at No Particular Time). w. Arthur Terker and Harry Pyle, m. J. Russel Robinson, 1947. Recorded by Nat "King" Cole (Capitol) and The Joe Mooney Quartet (Decca).

Meet Me at the Station, Dear. w. Sam M. Lewis and Joe Young, m. Ted Snyder, 1917. Introduced by Gladys Clark and Henry Bergman in (TM) *The Passing Show of 1917*.

Meet Me Down at the Corner. w. Will D. Cobb, m. Harry Hoyt, 1906. Introduced by Clara Palmer in (TM) *The Blue Moon*. Popular recording by Len Spencer and Ada Jones (Columbia).

Meet Me in Bubble Land. w. Casper Nathan and Joe Manne, m. Isham Jones, 1919. This was Isham Jones's first song success.

Meet Me in Rose-Time, Rosie. w. William Jerome, m. Jean Schwartz, 1909. Introduced by Earl Benham in the touring show (TM) *Cohan and Harris' Minstrels*. Fannie Ward sang it in the play (TP) *The New Lady Bantock*. Leading records by Frank Stanley and Byron Harlan (Columbia) and The Haydn Quartet (Victor).

Meet Me in St. Louis, Louis. w. Andrew B. Sterling, m. Kerry Mills, 1904. Popular song, written in the year of the Louisiana Purchase Exposition in St. Louis, and performed by many headliners. It was revived in 1944 by Judy Garland, Margaret O'Brien, Lucille Bremer, Henry Daniels, Jr., and producer Arthur Freed, dubbing for Leon Ames, in (MM) *Meet Me in St. Louis*. It was sung by the ensemble in the stage version, *Meet Me in St. Louis*, 1989.

Meet Me Tonight in Dreamland. w. Beth Slater Whitson, m. Leo Friedman, 1908. A tremendous hit of its day. Judy Garland sang it in the music store scene in (MM) *The Good Old Summertime*, 1949, and also recorded it (MGM).

Meet Mister Callaghan. w/m Eric Spear, 1952. British import. Top records by Les Paul (Capitol) and The Harry Grove Trio (London).

Meet the Beat of My Heart. w. Mack Gordon, m. Harry Revel, 1938. Introduced by Judy Garland in (MM) *Love Finds Andy Hardy*. Leading recordings by Hal Kemp, vocal by Bob Allen (Victor); Charles "Buddy" Rogers, vocal by Bob Hannon (Vocalion); Gene Krupa and his Orchestra (Brunswick).

Meet the Sun Half Way. w. Johnny Burke, m. James V. Monaco, 1940. Introduced by Bing Crosby in (MM) *If I Had My Way*. Best-selling record: Crosby (Decca). Others: Hal Kemp, vocal by Janet Blair (Victor); The Smoothies (Bluebird); Barry Wood (Decca).

Melancholy Lullaby. w. Edward Heyman, m. Benny Carter, 1939. Introduced and recorded by Benny Carter and his Band (Vocalion). Also recorded by Glenn Miller, vocal by Bob Eberle (Bluebird); and Ginny Simms (Vocalion).

Melancholy Me. w/m Joe Thomas and Howard Biggs, 1954. Popular recordings by Eddy Howard (Mercury); Ella Fitzgerald, with Sy Oliver's Orchestra (Decca); The Smith Brothers ("X").

Melancholy Minstrel, The. w/m Kay Twomey, Fred Wise, and Al Frisch, 1948. Featured and recorded by Vaughn Monroe and his Orchestra (RCA Victor) and Snooky Lanson (Mercury).

Melancholy Mood. w/m Vick Knight, 1939. Among recordings: Bob Crosby and his Orchestra (Decca); Kenny Baker (Victor); Jess Stacy (Varsity); Martha Raye (Brunswick); Bob

Zurke (Victor); Artie Shaw, vocal by Helen Forrest (Bluebird).

Melancholy Music Man. w/m Garry Bonner and Alan Gordon, 1967. Recorded by The Righteous Brothers (Verve).

Melancholy Rhapsody. w. Sammy Cahn, m. Ray Heindorf, 1950. Based on a theme from the soundtrack of (MM) *Young Man with a Horn*, in which it was played on the trumpet by Harry James, dubbing for Kirk Douglas.

Melancholy Serenade. m. Jackie Gleason, 1953. Theme song of The Jackie Gleason Show, a weekly television comedy revue. Recorded by Jackie Gleason and his Orchestra (Capitol).

Melba Waltz, The. w. Norman Newell, m. Mischa Spoliansky, 1953. Introduced by Patrice Munsel, playing the title role of Nellie Melba in (MM) *Melba*. Leading recording by Frank Parker and Marion Marlowe, with Percy Faith's Orchestra (Columbia).

Melinda. w. Alan Jay Lerner, m. Burton Lane, 1965. Introduced by John Cullum in (TM) *On a Clear Day You Can See Forever*. In (MM) *On a Clear Day You Can See Forever*, 1970, it was sung by Yves Montand.

Melissa. w/m Greg Allman and Stephen Alaimo, 1972. Recorded by The Allman Brothers Band (Capricorn).

Mellow Yellow. w/m Donovan Leitch, 1966. Gold record by the writer, billed as Donovan, with "whispering vocals" by Paul McCartney (Epic), followed by a comedy record by Senator Bobby and Senator McKinley, of The Hardly-Worthit Players (Epic), 1967.

Melodie d'Amour. w. Leo Johns (Engl.), m. Henri Salvador, 1957. Hit English version of French song by The Ames Brothers, with Hugo Winterhalter's Orchestra (RCA).

Melody. m. Charles G. Dawes, 1912. See also "It's All in the Game."

Melody for Two. w. Al Dubin, m. Harry Warren, 1937. Introduced in (MM) *Melody for Two* and recorded (Decca) by James Melton.

Melody from the Sky, A. w. Sidney D. Mitchell, m. Louis Alter, 1936. Introduced by Fuzzy Knight in (MP) *The Trail of the Lonesome Pine*, one of two hits (see "Twilight on the Trail") from the "nonmusical film," or "motion picture-with-songs." This song received heavy airplay, many recordings, and was nominated for an Academy Award. Among varied styles of recordings: Eddy Duchin (Victor); Bunny Berigan, vocal by Chick Bullock (Vocalion); Freddy Martin, vocal by Elmer Feldkamp (Brunswick); Jack Shilkret and his Orchestra (Melotone); Sons of the Pioneers, with Roy Rogers (Decca); Tex Ritter (Decca); Mezz Mezzrow (Bluebird); Flip Phillips (Signature).

Melody in Spring. w. Harlan Thompson, m. Lewis E. Gensler, 1934. Introduced by Lanny Ross in (MM) *Melody in Spring*.

Melody of Love. w. Tom Glazer, m. H. Engelmann, 1903, 1955. Originally written as a piano piece. Recorded by The Victor Orchestra (Victor), 1910. Kenny Baker sang it as "Whisper That You Love Me," with lyrics by John Klenner (Decca), 1942. New title and lyrics were provided in 1955, and it became a hit with top records by The Four Aces, with Jack Pleis's Orchestra (Decca); Billy Vaughn and his Orchestra (Dot); Frank Sinatra and Ray Anthony (Capitol).

Melody Time. w/m Bennie Benjamin and George David Weiss, 1948. Title song, sung on the soundtrack of animated cartoon film (MM) *Melody Time*, by Buddy Clark.

Memo from Turner. w/m Mick Jagger and Keith Richards, 1970. Performed by Mick Jagger in the British film (MP) *Performance*.

Memories. w/m Billy Strange and Scott Davis, 1969. Introduced by Elvis Presley on the special (TVM) "Elvis," and Top 40 record by him (RCA). Recorded by The Lettermen, in medley with "Traces" (Capitol), 1970.

Memories. w. Gus Kahn, m. Egbert Van Alstyne, 1915. Major sheet music seller and multi-recorded song in the year of its publication. Later heard as background music in (MM) *Tin Pan Alley*, 1940; played by the Ted Lewis Band in (MM) *Is Everybody Happy?*, 1943; sung by an unidentified tenor singing the role of John McCormack in the Gus Kahn screen biography (MM) *I'll See You in My Dreams*, 1951.

Memories Are Made of This. w/m Terry Gilkyson, Rick Dehr, and Frank Miller, 1956. Dean Martin, backed by The Easy Riders [the writers], had a #1 hit (Capitol). Gale Storm also had a high chart version (Dot).

Memories of France. w. Al Dubin, m. J. Russel Robinson, 1928. Popular recordings by singers Henry Burr (Brunswick), Gene Austin (Victor), and Arnold Johnson and his Orchestra (Brunswick).

Memories of You. w. Andy Razaf, m. Eubie Blake, 1930. Introduced by Minto Cato in Lew Leslie's (TM) *Blackbirds of 1930*. Ethel Waters had the first recording (Columbia). In 1938, Glen Gray and the Casa Loma Orchestra, with an outstanding trumpet solo by Sonny Dunham, made the now famed best-selling record (Decca). It became Dunham's theme song when he had his own bands and he recorded it three times (Bluebird, Varsity, and Embassy). Among other outstanding versions are those by Bud Freeman (Commodore); the Benny Goodman Sextet (Columbia); Illinois Jacquet (Apollo); and Eubie Blake in the double LP set "The 86 Years of Eubie Blake" (Columbia). In (MM) *The Benny Goodman Story*, 1956, the Goodman trio played it, and in (MM) *The Gene Krupa Story*, 1959, it was sung by Anita O'Day.

Memory. w. Trevor Nunn and T. S. Eliot, m. Andrew Lloyd Webber, 1982. Introduced in the U.S. by Betty Buckley in (TM) *Cats*. Leading records by Barbra Streisand (Columbia) and Barry Manilow (Arista).

Memory Lane. w. B. G. DeSylva, m. Larry Spier and Con Conrad, 1924. Leading records by Fred Waring's Pennsylvanians, vocal by Tom Waring (Victor) and Paul Specht and his Orchestra (Columbia).

Memory No. 1. w/m Wayne P. Walker and Max Powell, 1964. Hit C&W record by Webb Pierce (Decca).

Memphis. w/m Chuck Berry, 1963. Hit instrumental by guitarist Lonnie Mack (Fraternity), followed a year later by #2 chart record by Johnny Rivers (Imperial).

Memphis Blues. w. George A. Norton, m. W. C. Handy, 1913. Handy's first publication and the first published blues. Handy wrote it in 1912 as an instrumental to help elect Edward H. Crump as mayor of Memphis. It was called "Mr. Crump," and because of its popularity, Norton added lyrics in 1913. Often recorded, it was sung by Bing Crosby in (MM) *The Birth of the Blues*, 1941. It has also been heard in (MM) *Belle of the Nineties*, 1934, and in Handy's film bio (MM) *St. Louis Blues*, *1938*.

Memphis in June. w. Paul Francis Webster, m. Hoagy Carmichael, 1945. Introduced by Hoagy Carmichael in (MP) *Johnny Angel*. Carmichael recorded it (ARA), as did Betty Jane Bonney (Victor), Johnny Mercer (Capitol), Harry James and his Orchestra (Columbia).

Memphis Soul Stew. m. Curtis Ousley, 1967. Instrumental, written and recorded by R&B saxophonist King Curtis (Atco).

Memphis Underground. m. Herbie Mann, 1969. Jazz flutist Herbie Mann recorded the instrumental version and also a vocal version, featuring Little Milton, titled "It's a Funky Thing" (Atlantic).

Men, The. See **Theme from "The Men."**

Men All Pause, The. w/m Bernadette Cooper, Joyce Simmons, and D. McDaniels, 1985. Introduced on soundtrack of (MP) *The Slugger's Wife*. Recorded by the female sextet Klymaxx (Constellation).

Men Are Gettin' Scarce. w/m Joe Tex, 1968. Top 40 record by Joe Tex (Dial).

Mendocino. w/m Douglas Sahm, 1969. Top 40 record by the Sir Douglas Quintet (Smash). Written by the leader.

Men in My Little Girl's Life, The. w. Eddie V. Deane and Mary Candy, m. Gloria Shayne, 1966. Top 10 record by Mike Douglas (Epic).

Mental Cruelty. w/m Larry Davis and Dixie Davis, 1961. Top 10 C&W chart record by Buck Owens and Rose Maddox (Capitol).

Mention My Name in Sheboygan. w/m Bob Hilliard, Dick Sanford, and Sammy Mysels, 1947. Introduced, featured, and recorded by Beatrice Kay (Columbia).

Mercedes Boy. w/m Pebbles, 1988. #1 R&B and Top 10 Pop record by Pebbles, pseudonym for Perri McKissack (MCA).

Mercy. w/m Steven Feldman and Joey Levine, 1969. Top 40 record by The Ohio Express with Joey Levine as lead singer (Buddah).

Mercy, Mercy. w/m Don Covay and Ronnie Miller, 1964. Crossover (R&B/Pop) hit by Don Covay and The Goodtimers (Rosemart).

Mercy, Mercy Me (The Ecology). w/m Marvin Gaye, 1971. Top 10 record by Marvin Gaye (Tamla).

Mercy, Mercy, Mercy. w. Gail Levy, Vincent Levy, m. Joseph Zawinul, 1967. Introduced and recorded as an instrumental by saxophonist Cannonball Adderley and his group, of which the composer was pianist (Capitol). Biggest seller was by the quintet The Buckinghams (Columbia). Also recorded by Marlena Shaw (Cadet), and Larry Williams and Johnny Watson (Okeh).

Mercy, Mr. Percy. w/m Mae Moten, 1953. R&B hit by Varetta Dillard (Savoy).

Merry Christmas Baby. w/m Lou Baxter and Johnny Moore, 1947. Holiday R&B chart hit by Johnny Moore's Three Blazers (Exclusive).

Merry Christmas Polka, The. w. Paul Francis Webster, m. Sonny Burke, 1950. Leading recordings by The Andrews Sisters, with Guy Lombardo and his Orchestra (Decca); Freddy Martin, vocal by Merv Griffin (RCA Victor).

Merry-Go-Round Broke Down, The. w/m Cliff Friend and Dave Franklin, 1937.

Merry Little Minuet. w/m Sheldon Harnick, 1953. Introduced by Orson Bean in the revue (TM) *John Murray Anderson's Almanac.* Charlotte Rae then featured it in her nightclub act. In 1958, The Kingston Trio popularized it (Capitol).

Merry Widow Waltz, The. See **I Love You So.**

Message, The. w/m Melvin Glover, Sylvia Robinson, E. Fletcher, and Clifton Chase, 1982. Recorded by Grandmaster Flash and The Furious Five (Sugar Hill).

Message in a Bottle. w/m Gordon Sumner, 1979. Recorded by the English group, Police, with Gordon "Sting" Sumner as lead vocalist (A&M).

Message in Our Music. w/m Kenny Gamble and Leon Huff, 1976. Recorded by the O'Jays (Philadelphia International).

Message of the Violet, The. w. Frank Pixley, m. Gustav Luders, 1903. Introduced by Albert Parr and Anna Lichter in (TM) *The Prince of Pilsen.*

Message to Michael. w. Hal David, m. Burt Bacharach, 1966. Top 10 record by Dionne Warwick (Scepter).

Messin' Around. w/m Floyd Hunt, 1948. R&B chart hit by Memphis Slim [Peter Chapman, Jr.] (Miracle).

Mess of Blues, A. w/m Doc Pomus and Mort Shuman, 1960. Recorded by Elvis Presley (RCA).

Method of Modern Love. w/m Daryl Hall and Jana Allen, 1985. Top 10 single from the platinum album "Big Bam Boom" by Daryl Hall and John Oates (RCA), 1984.

Me Too (Ho, Ho, Ha, Ha). w. Charles Tobias and Al Sherman, m. Harry Woods, 1926. This was Tobias's first hit. Recorded by Paul Whiteman (Victor).

Metro, The. w/m John Crawford, 1983. Recorded by the trio Berlin (Geffen).

Metro Polka. w/m Willie Evans and Vaughn Horton, 1951. Popularized by Frankie Laine (Mercury).

Mewsette. w. E. Y. Harburg, m. Harold Arlen, 1961. Introduced by Robert Goulet on the soundtrack of the feature-length cartoon film (MM) *Gay Purr-ee.*

Mexicali Rose. w. Helen Stone, m. Jack B. Tenney, 1923. Popular song on radio. Revived by Bing Crosby in (MM) *Rhythm on the Range* and on records with John Scott Trotter's Orchestra (Decca), 1936. Sung by Gene Autry as title song of (MM) *Mexicali Rose*, 1939. Autry sang it again in (MM) *Barbed Wire*, 1952. Roy Rogers sang it in (MM) *Song of Texas*, 1943.

Mexican Drummer Man. m. Scott Turner, 1964. Recorded by Herb Alpert and The Tijuana Brass (A&M).

Mexican Joe. w/m Mitchell Torok, 1953. Jim Reeves and His Circle O Ranch Boys had a million-selling Country hit (Abbott).

Mexican Pearls. w/m Don Randi and Joe Mikolas, 1965. Popular instrumental by Billy Vaughn and his Orchestra (Dot).

Mexican Radio. w/m Stanard Ridgway, Charles Gray, Oliver Nanini, and Marc Moreland, 1983. Recorded by the group Wall of Voodoo (I.R.S.).

Mexican Shuffle. m. Sol Lake, 1964. Instrumental recorded by Herb Alpert and The Tijuana Brass (A&M).

Mexico. w/m James Taylor, 1975. Recorded by James Taylor (Warner Bros.).

Mexico. m. Boudleaux Bryant, 1961. Instrumental hit by Bob Moore and his Orchestra (Monument).

Mexico Joe. w. Johnny Lange, m. Leon René, 1943. Featured and recorded by Ivy Anderson (Exclusive).

Miami. w/m Con Conrad, B. G. DeSylva, and Al Jolson, 1925. Interpolated in (TM) *Big Boy* by Al Jolson. It was recorded by George Olsen and his Orchestra (Victor).

Miami Beach Rhumba. w. Albert Gamse (Engl.), Johnnie Camacho (Sp.), m. Irving Fields, 1947. Featured by The Irving Fields Trio.

Miami Vice Theme. m. Jan Hammer, 1985. Theme from the soundtrack of the series (TVP) "Miami Vice." #1 instrumental record by the composer/keyboardist Jan Hammer (MCA).

Mi Casa, Su Casa (My House Is Your House). w/m Al Hoffman and Dick Manning, 1957. Featured and recorded by Perry Como (RCA).

Michael. w/m Larry Brownlee and Charles Matthews, 1965. Chart record by The C.O.D.'s (Kellmac).

Michael (Row the Boat Ashore). w/m arr. by Dave Fisher, 1961. Based on a pre-Civil War song, originated by Southern slaves who commuted between their island quarters and the mainland. Introduced and #1 hit record by The Highwaymen (United Artists).

Michael from the Mountains. w/m Joni Mitchell, 1967. Introduced by Joni Mitchell and recorded in her album "Joni Mitchell" (Reprise). Also recorded by Judy Collins in her album "Wildflower" (Elektra).

Michelle. w/m John Lennon and Paul McCartney, 1966. Introduced by The Beatles in their album "Rubber Soul." Winner Grammy Award (NARAS) for Song of the Year. Leading single by the British duo David and Jonathan (Capitol). Other chart records by saxophonist

Bud Shank (World Pacific) and Billy Vaughn and his Orchestra (Dot).

Mickey. w/m Nicky Chinn and Mike Chapman, 1982. Originally released as part of a pre-MTV early video cassette "Word of Mouth," 1980, Toni Basil's single became #1 in Australia and #2 in Great Britain. It took two years for its U.S. release to catch on, but when it did, it rose to #1 and a platinum record was awarded to the singer/video director/choreographer (Chrysalis).

Mickey. w. Harry H. Williams, m. Neil Moret, 1918. One of the earliest songs written specifically for use as a background theme and to help exploit a silent film, (MP) *Mickey*, starring Mabel Normand.

Mickey's Monkey. w/m Lamont Dozier, Brian Holland, and Eddie Holland, 1963. Top 10 record by The Miracles (Tamla).

Middle-age Crazy. w/m Sonny Throckmorton, 1977. Country record hit by Jerry Lee Lewis (Mercury).

Middle of the Night. w/m Ahmet Ertegun, 1952. R&B hit by The Clovers (Atlantic).

Middle of the Road. w/m Chrissie Hynde, 1984. Recorded by the quartet The Pretenders (Sire).

Midnight. w/m Boudleaux Bryant and Chet Atkins, 1952. Leading recording by Red Foley (Decca).

Midnight, Me and the Blues. w/m Jerry House, 1974. Hit country record by Mel Tillis (MGM).

Midnight at the Oasis. w/m David Nichtern, 1974. Top 10 record by Maria Muldaur (Reprise).

Midnight Blue. w/m Lou Gramm and Bruce Turgeon, 1987. Top 10 single by Lou Gramm from his album "Ready or Not" (Atlantic).

Midnight Blue. w. Carole Bayer Sager and Melissa Manchester, m. Melissa Manchester. 1975. Top 10 record by Melissa Manchester (Arista).

Midnight Blue. w. Edgar Leslie, m. Joe Burke, 1936. (TM) *Ziegfeld Follies of 1936* opened on January 30 and ran until mid-May when it closed "for the summer months." The insertion of this song was among the changes in the new production.

Midnight Confessions. w/m Lou Josie, 1968. Gold record awarded to The Grass Roots (Dunhill).

Midnight Cowboy. m. John Barry, 1969. Theme from (MP) *Midnight Cowboy*. Top 10 record by the piano duo Ferrante and Teicher (United Artists). Grammy Award (NARAS) winner, Best Instrumental Theme.

Midnight Fire Alarm. m. Harry J. Lincoln, 1900. March, arranged by E. T. Paull.

Midnight Flyer. w/m Mayme Watts and Robert Mosely, 1959. Featured and recorded by Nat "King" Cole (Capitol).

Midnight in Moscow. m. arr. by Kenny Ball and Jan Burgers, 1962. Based on Russian song titled "Padmeskoveeye Vietchera." Recorded in England instrumentally by Kenny Ball and His Jazzmen (Kapp).

Midnight in Paris. w. Herb Magidson, m. Con Conrad, 1935. Introduced by Nino Martini in (MM) *Here's to Romance*.

Midnight Lace. w/m Jerome Howard and Joe Lubin, 1960. From the Doris Day film (MP) *Midnight Lace*. Recordings by the orchestras of Ray Ellis (MGM), Ray Conniff (Columbia, Parts 1 & 2), David Carroll (Mercury).

Midnight Mary. w/m Ben Raleigh and Art Wayne, 1963. Hit record by Joey Powers (Amy).

Midnight Masquerade. w/m Bernard Bierman, Arthur Bierman, and Jack Mann, 1946. Popularized by Frankie Carle, vocal by Marjorie Hughes (Columbia), and Monica Lewis, accompanied by Ray Bloch's Orchestra (Signature).

Midnight Rider. w/m Gregg Allman and Kim Payne, 1972. Introduced by The Allman

Brothers Band in the album "Idlewild South" (Capricorn), 1970. Top 40 single by Joe Cocker (A&M), 1972. Top 20 version by Gregg Allman (Capricorn), 1974.

Midnight Special. w/m Traditional, 1941. Many adaptations and recordings of this traditional American folk song. This date was chosen because of the renascence of the number by Huddie "Leadbelly" Ledbetter with the Golden Gate Quartet (Victor). Among other popular versions: The Weavers, with Gordon Jenkins's Orchestra (Decca); Harry Belafonte (RCA); Paul Evans (Guaranteed); Johnny Rivers (Imperial).

Midnight Sun. w. Johnny Mercer, m. Sonny Burke and Lionel Hampton, 1947. Introduced and recorded as an instrumental by Lionel Hampton and his Orchestra (Decca). Mercer's lyrics were added in 1954.

Midnight Train to Georgia. w/m Jim Weatherly, 1973. #1 gold record by Gladys Knight and The Pips (Buddah).

'Mid the Green Fields of Virginia. w/m Charles K. Harris, 1898.

Mighty Lak' a Rose. w. Frank Stanton, m. Ethelbert Nevin, 1901. Written in the year of Nevin's death, this concert song gained popularity through vaudeville performances. Among earlier recordings: Frances Alda (Victor); Anna Case (Edison); Lillian Nordica (Columbia); John McCormack (Gramophone); Geraldine Farrar, accompanied by violinist Fritz Kreisler (Victor). Deanna Durbin sang it in (MM) *The Amazing Mrs. Holiday*, 1943. Later recordings include the Francis Craig Orchestra (Columbia), and a jazz version by Don Elliot (Savoy).

Mighty Like the Blues. w/m Leonard Feather, 1938. Woody Herman and his Orchestra introduced it, but the records were by Joe Marsala (Vocalion) and the Sextet of the Rhythm Club of London (Bluebird).

Mighty Love, A. w/m Joseph B. Jefferson, Bruce Hawes, and Charles Simmons, 1974. Top 20 record by The Spinners (Atlantic).

Mighty Quinn (Quinn, the Eskimo). w/m Bob Dylan, 1968. Top 10 U.S. hit by the British group Manfred Mann (Mercury). Bob Dylan included it in his two-record album "Self Portrait" (Columbia), 1970.

Mile After Mile. w. Buddy Bernier, m. Kurt Weill, 1939. From the pageant *Railroads on Parade* at the New York World's Fair.

Milenberg Joys. m. Leon Rappolo, Paul Mares, and Ferdinand "Jelly Roll" Morton, 1925. This jazz instrumental has had many recordings, among which are the New Orleans Rhythm Kings [Rappolo and Mares were members] (Gennett), Glen Gray and the Casa Loma Orchestra (Brunswick), Larry Clinton (Victor), Bob Crosby (Decca), Tommy Dorsey [two sides] (Victor).

Miles and Miles of Texas. w/m Tom Camfield and Diane Johnston, 1976. Country chart record by the group Asleep at the Wheel (Capitol).

Milk and Honey. w/m Jerry Herman, 1961. Introduced by Tommy Rall, Juki Arkin, and company in (TM) *Milk and Honey*. Sung by Leslie Uggams and ensemble in (TM) *Jerry's Girls*, the all-Jerry Herman revue, 1985.

Milk Cow Blues. w/m Kokomo Arnold, 1934. Notable recordings: Josh White (Banner) and Bob Crosby (Decca).

Milkman, Keep Those Bottles Quiet. w/m Done Raye and Gene De Paul, 1944. Introduced by Nancy Walker in (MM) *Broadway Rhythm*. Most popular recorded versions by Ella Mae Morse (Capitol); Woody Herman, with his Orchestra (Decca); The King Sisters (Bluebird).

Milkman's Matinee, The. w/m Paul Denniker, Joe Davis, and Andy Razaf, 1936. Recorded by Charlie Barnet and his Orchestra, vocal by the Modernaires (Bluebird), as the theme song of the all-night radio show on WNEW, New York. Tommy Dorsey and the Clambake Seven also recorded the number (Victor). The theme has been used for over forty years.

Miller's Cave. w/m Jack Clement, 1960. Hit Country record by Hank Snow (RCA). Revived by Bobby Bare with a crossover (C&W/Pop) version (RCA), 1964.

Miller's Daughter Marianne, The. w/m Jimmy Kennedy, Will Grosz, and Billy Hill, 1937. Recorded by Horace Heidt (Brunswick) and Dick Robertson (Decca).

Millionaire (How to Be a). See **How to Be a Millionaire.**

Million and One. w/m Yvonne Devaney, 1966. C&W chart hit by Billy Walker (Monument). Pop best-sellers by Dean Martin (Reprise) and Vic Dana (Dolton).

Million Dreams, A. w. Gus Kahn, m. J. C. Lewis, Jr., 1932. Featured and recorded by Ben Bernie and his Orchestra (Brunswick).

Million Dreams Ago, A. w/m Lew Quadling, Eddy Howard, and Dick Jurgens, 1940. Dick Jurgens, vocal by Harry Cool (Okeh), had the best-selling record. Quadling was arranger for the band and Howard was former vocalist, now out on his own. Other popular version by Glenn Miller, vocal by Ray Eberle (Bluebird).

Million to One, A. w/m Phil Medley, 1960. Popularized by Jimmy Charles (Promo). Later chart records by The Five Stairsteps (Buddah), 1968; Brian Hyland (Dot), 1969; Donny Osmond (MGM), 1973.

Million Years or So, A. w/m Charlie Williams, 1963. C&W chart record by Eddy Arnold (RCA).

Mill Valley. w/m Rita Abrams, 1970. Recorded by Miss Abrams and The Strawberry Point School Third Grade Class (Reprise). The recording artists were comprised of teacher and her students from the Marin County, California town named in the title.

Millwork. w/m James Taylor, 1978. Introduced as "Millworker" by James Taylor in his album "Flag" (Columbia). With new title, sung by Robin Lamont in (TM) *Working.*

Milord. w. B. G. Lewis (Engl.), Joseph Mustacchi (Fr.), m. Marguerite Monnot, 1961.

Introduced in France by Edith Piaf. Her recording was the first released in the U.S. (Capitol). Other chart recordings by Teresa Brewer (Coral) and, in 1964, a previously recorded but unreleased version by Bobby Darin (Atco).

Mimi. w. Lorenz Hart, m. Richard Rodgers, 1932. Introduced by Maurice Chevalier in (MM) *Love Me Tonight.* The song was then heard in (MM) *The Joker is Wild,* 1957, after which Chevalier sang it in (MM) *Pepe,* 1960. Chevalier recorded it as a single (Victor) and in numerous albums and/or anthologies of songs associated with him.

Mimi. w. Ballard MacDonald, m. Con Conrad, 1921. Featured by Frank Crumit and recorded by him with The Paul Biese Trio (Columbia). (Not to be confused with the 1932 "Mimi.")

Mind, Body and Soul. w/m Ronald Dunbar and Edith Wayne, 1969. Top 40 record by The Flaming Ember (Hot Wax).

Mind Games. w/m John Lennon, 1973. Top 20 U.S. record by John Lennon (Apple).

Mind If I Make Love to You. w/m Cole Porter, 1956. Introduced by Frank Sinatra in (MM) *High Society.*

Mindin' My Business. w. Gus Kahn, m. Walter Donaldson, 1924. Popularized and recorded by Frank Crumit accompanied by The Virginians (Victor), and by Ernest Hare (Okeh). Revived by Glen Gray and the Casa Loma Orchestra (Decca), 1938.

Mind Your Own Business. w/m Hank Williams, 1949, 1986. Introduced and recorded by Hank Williams (MGM). #1 Country chart record by Hank Williams, Jr., with "guest vocals" by Willie Nelson, Reba McEntire, and Reverend Ike (Warner Bros.), 1986.

Mine. w. Ira Gershwin, m. George Gershwin, 1933. Introduced by William Gaxton, Lois Moran, and ensemble in (TM) *Let 'Em Eat Cake.* The chorus of the song has a second patter melody that is sung or played contrapuntally with the main melody. In the 1945 George Gershwin screen biography (MM)

Rhapsody in Blue, it was performed by Robert Alda (as Gershwin) and Oscar Levant. It was interpolated in the 1952 revival of (TM) *Of Thee I Sing*. Recordings of note: the Arden-Ohman Orchestra (Brunswick); Harry Richman (Vocalion); Emil Coleman, coupled with the seldom heard title song, (Columbia); Horace Heidt (Victor); Dorothy Kirsten, with Percy Faith's Orchestra (Columbia); and in 1947, Bing Crosby and Judy Garland (Decca).

Mine, All Mine. w/m Lasses White, 1948. Hit Country chart record by Jimmy Wakely (Capitol).

Mine Alone. w. Mort Dixon, m. Allie Wrubel, 1935. Introduced by Everett Marshall in (MM) *I Live for Love* and recorded by him (Victor).

Mine for Me. w/m Paul McCartney, 1974. Recorded in England by Rod Stewart (Mercury).

Minimum Love. w/m Mac McAnally and Gerry Wexler, 1983. Recorded by Mac McAnally (Geffen).

Mini-Skirt Minnie. w/m Steve Cropper, Earl Cage, Jr., Lindell Hill, and George Jackson, 1969. Recorded by Wilson Pickett (Atlantic).

Minka. w/m Jay Milton, 1941. Introduced and recorded by Sammy Kaye, vocal by Tommy Ryan (Victor). Also recorded by Harry Sosnik, vocal by Bob Hannon (Decca); and Spike Jones and his Orchestra (V-Disc).

Minnie the Mermaid. w/m B. G. DeSylva, 1930. Introduced on radio by Rudy Vallee. Among recordings, the bands of: Bernie Cummins (Victor), Phil Harris (Victor), Pete Daily (Capitol).

Minnie the Moocher w/m Cab Calloway, Clarence Gaskill, and Irving Mills, 1931. Introduced at the Cotton Club in New York and recorded by Calloway (Columbia). He performed it with his Orchestra in (MM) *The Big Broadcast* in 1932. In 1937, Grace Moore sang an arrangement by Al Segal in (MM) *When*

You're in Love. Danny Kaye featured the song as an audience participation number in his appearances on stage and television.

Minnie the Moocher's Wedding Day. w. Ted Koehler, m. Harold Arlen, 1932. Introduced by Cab Calloway in the nightclub revue *Cotton Club Parade*. The Boswell Sisters had a popular record (Brunswick).

Minotaur, The. m. Dick Hyman, 1968. Top 40 instrumental by Dick Hyman and his Electric Eclectics (Command).

Minstrel in the Gallery. w/m Ian Anderson and Martin Barre, 1975. Chart record by the English group Jethro Tull (Chrysalis).

Minstrel Parade. w/m Irving Berlin, 1914. From (TM) *Watch Your Step*.

Minute by Minute. w. Lester Abrams and Michael McDonald, m. Michael McDonald, 1979. Recorded by the group The Doobie Brothers (Warner Bros.).

Minute of Your Time, A. w/m Clive Westlake, 1969. Recorded in England by the Welsh star Tom Jones (Parrot).

Minute You're Gone, The. w/m Jimmy Gateley, 1963. Recorded by Sonny James (Capitol).

Mira (Can You Imagine That?). w/m Bob Merrill, 1961. Introduced by Anna Maria Alberghetti in (TM) *Carnival*.

Miracle of Love. w/m Bob Merrill, 1956. Popular record by Eileen Rodgers (Columbia).

Miracle of Miracles. w. Sheldon Harnick, m. Jerry Bock, 1964. Introduced by Austin Pendleton in (TM) *Fiddler on the Roof*. In (MM) *Fiddler on the Roof*, 1971, it was sung by Leonard Frey and Rosalind Harris.

Miracles. w/m Martyn Buchwald, 1975. Recorded by the group Jefferson Starship (Grunt). Buchwald a.k.a. Marty Balin was one of the group's vocalists.

Miracles. w/m Bart Howard, 1960. Featured and recorded by Johnny Mathis (Columbia).

Mirage. w/m Ritchie Cordell and Bo Gentry, 1967. Hit record by Tommy James and The Shondells (Roulette).

Mirror, Mirror. w/m Michael Sembello and Dennis Matkosky, 1982. Top 10 record by Diana Ross (RCA).

Misery Loves Company. w/m Jerry Reed, 1962. Hit C&W record by Porter Wagoner (RCA).

Misirlou. w. Fred Wise, Milton Leeds, and S. K. (Bob) Russell, m. N. Roubanis, 1941. Original Greek words by Roubanis. Harry James's instrumental version was first U.S. recording to gain prominence (Columbia). Carol Bruce had an early vocal rendition (Decca). The orchestras led by Charlie Ventura (National) and Skitch Henderson (Capitol) showed other instrumental approaches. Organist Leon Berry later revived it with a chart record (Dot), 1953.

Misled. w/m Ronald Bell, "J. T." Taylor, Charles Smith, George Brown, Robert Bell, Curtis Williams, and James Bonneford, 1985. Top 10 record by Kool & The Gang (De-Lite).

Miss America. w/m Bernie Wayne, 1954. Long-time official song of the annual Miss America Pageant, taking place in Atlantic City, New Jersey, and televised nationally.

Miss Ann. w/m Richard Penniman and Enotris Johnson, 1957. Coupled with hit "Jenny, Jenny" by Little Richard (Specialty).

Miss Annabelle Lee. w/m Lew Pollack, Sidney Clare, and Harry Richman, 1927. Introduced by Harry Richman. Featured in vaudeville by James Barton. The orchestra played it in (MM) *Gentlemen Marry Brunettes*, 1955. Performed by Dick Shawn in (TM) *A Musical Jubilee*, 1975.

Miss Brown to You. w. Leo Robin, m. Ralph Rainger and Richard A. Whiting, 1935. Introduced by Ray Noble and his Orchestra, Bill Robinson, and the Nicholas Brothers in (MM) *The Big Broadcast of 1936*. The song is associated with Billie Holiday, who recorded it with Teddy Wilson's Orchestra (Brunswick).

Miss Celie's Blues. w. Lionel Richie, Quincy Jones, and Rod Temperton, m. Jones and Temperton, 1985. Introduced in (MP) *The Color Purple* by Tata Vega. Nominated for an Academy Award.

Missing in Action. w/m Helen Kaye and Arthur Q. Smith, 1952. Country hit by Ernest Tubb (Decca).

Missing You. w/m John Waite, Chas Sandford, and Mark Leonard, 1984. #1 single by the English-born John Waite, from his gold album "No Brakes" (EMI America).

Missing You. w/m Lionel Richie, 1984. Dedicated to the late singer, Marvin Gaye, who was killed in a family dispute earlier in the year. Introduced in the gold album "Swept Away" by Diana Ross and in the ensuing Top 10 single release (RCA).

Missing You. w/m Dan Fogelberg, 1982. Recorded by Dan Fogelberg (Full Moon).

Missing You. w/m Red Sovine and Dale Noe, 1957. C&W hit by Webb Pierce (Decca). Revived by Ray Peterson (Dunes), 1961.

Missionary Man. w/m Dave Stewart and Annie Lennox, 1986. Chart record written and recorded by the U.K. duo The Eurythmics (RCA).

Mission Bell. w/m William Michael, 1960. Popular record by Donnie Brooks (Era).

"Mission: Impossible" Theme. m. Lalo Schifrin, 1967. Theme of the series (TVP) "Mission: Impossible." Leading recording by the orchestra conducted by the Argentina-born composer/pianist Lalo Schifrin (Dot). Winner Grammy Award (NARAS) Best Instrumental Theme, 1967.

Mission to Moscow. m. Mel Powell, 1942. Instrumental, recorded by Benny Goodman and his Orchestra (Columbia).

Mississippi. w/m John Phillips, 1970. Top 40 record by John Phillips (Dunhill).

M-I-S-S-I-S-S-I-P-P-I. w/m Curley Williams and Billy Simmons, 1950. Introduced by Red Foley (Decca). Also recorded by Kay Starr (Capitol), Art Mooney and his Orchestra (MGM), Bill Darnel (Coral).

M-I-S-S-I-S-S-I-P-P-I. w. Bert Hanlon and Benny Ryan, m. Harry Tierney, 1916. This spelling song was introduced by Frances White in Ziegfeld's *Midnight Revue* on the New Amsterdam Theatre Roof. Grace La Rue then sang it in (TM) *Hitchy Koo of '17*.

Mississippi Basin. w. Andy Razaf, m. Reginald Forsythe, 1933. Recordings: Louis Armstrong (Victor); Bert Lown, vocal by Eddie Farley (Bluebird); Glen Gray and the Casa Loma Orchestra, vocal by Pee Wee Hunt (Brunswick).

Mississippi Cotton Picking Delta Town. w/m Harold Dorman and Wiley Gann, 1974. Crossover (Country/Pop) record by Charley Pride (RCA).

Mississippi Dream Boat. w. Lew Brown and Ralph Freed, m. Sammy Fain, 1943. Introduced by Marilyn Maxwell, with Kay Kyser's Orchestra, in (MM) *Swing Fever*.

Mississippi Goddam. w/m Nina Simone, 1964. Featured and recorded by Nina Simone (Philips).

Mississippi Mud. w. James Cavanaugh, m. Harry Barris, 1928. Made popular by the recording of Paul Whiteman's Orchestra, featuring the Rhythm Boys [Bing Crosby, Harry Barris, and Al Rinker] and Bix Beiderbecke (Victor). Also recorded by Frankie Trumbauer (Okeh); Lee Morse (Columbia); The Charleston Chasers (Columbia); and later, Connie Haines (Coral).

Mississippi Suite. See **Daybreak.**

Miss Marmelstein. w/m Harold Rome, 1962. Introduced by Barbra Streisand in (TM) *I Can Get It for You Wholesale*.

Miss Me Blind. w/m George "Boy George" O'Dowd, Jon Moss, Roy Hay, and Mikey Craig, 1984. Top 10 record written and performed by the British quartet The Culture Club (Epic/Virgin).

Miss Otis Regrets (She's Unable to Lunch Today). w/m Cole Porter, 1934. The sheet music reads "Dedicated to Elsa" [Maxwell]. Introduced by Douglas Byng in the London musical "Hi Diddle Diddle." In the Porter biography (MM) *Night and Day*, 1946, it was performed by Cary Grant and Monty Wooley. Among the recordings: Cab Calloway and his Orchestra (Brunswick); the Mills Brothers (Decca); Ethel Waters (Decca); Martha Raye, with Phil Moore (Discovery); the King Sisters, with Alvino Rey's Orchestra (Bluebird); Nat "King" Cole (Capitol).

Missouri. w/m Harry "Slim" Duncan and Hank Penny, 1946. Recorded by Hank Penny (King) and Merle Travis (Capitol).

Missouri Walking Preacher, The. w/m Willard Robison, 1949. Featured and recorded by Ray McKinley and his Orchestra (RCA Victor).

Missouri Waltz. w. J. R. Shannon, m. Frederick Knight Logan, 1916. Shannon, a pseudonym for James Royce, added the words to the melody that was originally published in 1914 and based on "an original melody procured by John Valentine Eppell." It became the official state song of Missouri and later was associated with President Harry Truman, who often would play it on the piano for guests at the White House.

Miss Sun. w/m David Paich and Boz Scaggs, 1980. Recorded by Box Scaggs, backup vocal by Lisa Dal Bello (Columbia).

Miss Wonderful. w. Eddie Ward, m. Alfred Bryan, 1930. Introduced by Jack Buchanan in (MM) *Paris*, which starred Irene Bordoni. The Cole Porter score of the Broadway show, on which this was based, was not used. Two popular recordings of this song were made by Hal Kemp and the Carolina Club Orchestra (Okeh), and Ted Weems's Orchestra, vocal by Parker Gibbs (Victor).

Miss You. w/m Mick Jagger and Keith Richards, 1978. #1 gold record by The Rolling Stones (Rolling Stones).

Miss You. w/m Harry Tobias, Charles Tobias, and Henry Tobias, 1929, 1942. Introduced and recorded by Rudy Vallee (Victor). Revived in 1942 in (MM) *Strictly in the Groove* and through recordings by Eddy Howard (Columbia), Freddy Martin (Bluebird), Harry Sosnik (Decca), and others. Song was on "Your Hit Parade" for eleven weeks.

Miss You Much. w/m James Harris III and Terry Lewis, 1989. Hit R&B and Pop chart single by Janet Jackson (A&M).

Mistakes. w. Edgar Leslie, m. Horatio Nicholls, 1929. Nicholls is a pseudonym for Lawrence Wright, the English writer and publisher. Records by Fred Rose (Brunswick), Blue Steele (Victor), Louise Massey (Okeh), Dennis Day (Victor), George Paxton's Orchestra (MGM).

Mister and Mississippi. w/m Irving Gordon, 1951. Best-selling records by Patti Page (Mercury), Dennis Day (RCA Victor), Tennessee Ernie Ford (Capitol).

Mister Chamberlain. w. P. G. Wodehouse, m. Jerome Kern, 1903. Written in London, this was Kern's first song success. It was a topical song about a well-known politician who was the father of the future Prime Minister, Neville Chamberlain.

Mister Custer. w/m Fred Darian, Al De Lory, and Joseph Van Winkle, 1960. #1 novelty record by Larry Verne (Era).

Mister Deep Blue Sea. w. Gene Austin, m. James P. Johnson, 1936. Sung by Mae West in (MM) *Klondike Annie*.

Mister Dooley. w. William Jerome, m. Jean Schwartz, 1902. A comedy song referring to newspaper columnist Peter Finley Dunne's character. Introduced by Thomas Q. Seabrooke in (TM) *A Chinese Honeymoon*. Leading recording by Dan Quinn (Victor).

Mister Five by Five. w/m Don Raye and Gene De Paul, 1942. Introduced in (MM) *Behind the Eight Ball* by Grace McDonald and Sonny Dunham's Orchestra. Song supposedly inspired by corpulent singer Jimmy Rushing, who recorded it (Columbia). Jane Frazee sang it in (MM) *Almost Married*, 1942, and The Andrews Sisters, who recorded it (Decca), sang it in (MM) *Always a Bridesmaid*, 1943. Freddie Slack with vocal by Ella Mae Morse (Capitol) had a popular record, but the #1 version was by Harry James and his Orchestra (Columbia).

Mister Gallagher and Mister Shean. w/m Ed Gallagher and Al Shean, 1922. A comedy patter song, introduced by the vaudeville team of Gallagher and Shean in (TM) *Ziegfeld Follies of 1922*. They also recorded it (Victor), as did another popular team, [Billy] Jones and [Ernie] Hare (Victor). It was sung by Charles Winninger and Al Shean in (MM) *Ziegfeld Girl*, 1941. Bing Crosby and Johnny Mercer had a popular version (Decca), 1938.

Misterioso. m. Thelonious Monk, 1948. Instrumental by Thelonious Monk (Blue Note).

Mister Johnson, Don't Get Gay. w/m Dave Reed, Jr., 1898.

Mister Johnson, Turn Me Loose. w/m Ben R. Harney, 1896. Introduced by May Irwin in (TM) *Courted into Court*. It then became one of the most popular routines of the ragtime pianist Ben Harney in vaudeville.

Mister Meadowlark. w. Johnny Mercer, m. Walter Donaldson, 1940. Donaldson's last hit. Best-selling records by Bing Crosby and Johnny Mercer (Decca); Ted Weems, vocal by Perry Como, whistling by Elmo Tanner (Decca).

Mister Moon. w/m Carl Smith, Autry Inman, and Shirley Lyn, 1951. Introduced and recorded by Carl Smith (Columbia).

Mister Sandman. w/m Pat Ballard, 1954. Introduced, featured, and #1 million-selling record by The Chordettes, with Archie Bleyer's Orchestra (Cadence). Revived by Emmylou Harris (Warner Bros.), 1981.

Mister Snow. w. Oscar Hammerstein II, m. Richard Rodgers, 1945. Introduced by Jean Darling in (TM) *Carousel*. Barbara Ruick sang it in the film version (MM) *Carousel*, 1957.

Mister Tap Toe. w/m Terry Gilkyson, Richard Dehr, and Frank Miller, 1952. Popular record by Doris Day, with The Norman Luboff Choir (Columbia).

Mist Is Over the Moon, A. w. Oscar Hammerstein, m. Ben Oakland, 1938. Introduced by Lanny Ross in (MM) *The Lady Objects*. Nominated for Academy Award, 1938.

Misto Cristofo Columbo. w/m Jay Livingston and Ray Evans, 1951. Introduced by Bing Crosby, Dorothy Lamour, Phil Harris, Louis Armstrong, and Cass Daley in (MM) *Here Comes the Groom*.

Mistrustin' Blues. w/m Johnny Otis, 1950. Hit R&B record by Little Esther, Mel Walker, and Johnny Otis (Savoy).

Misty. w. Johnny Burke, m. Erroll Garner, 1954. First recorded as an instrumental by the Erroll Garner Trio (Mercury). Garner recorded it again, this time featuring his piano with Mitch Miller's Orchestra (Columbia), 1956. Burke wrote a lyric and, in 1959, Johnny Mathis had the first vocal hit (Columbia). Among later chart records: Lloyd Price (Double-L), organist Richard "Groove" Holmes (Prestige), Ray Stevens (Barnaby).

Misty Blue. w/m Bob Montgomery, 1967. Country/Pop song recorded by Eddy Arnold (RCA) and Wilma Burgess (Decca). Revived with hit records by Dorothy Moore (Malaco) and Billie Jo Spears (United Artists), 1976.

Misunderstanding. w/m Phil Collins, 1980. Recorded by the British group, Genesis, of which Collins was lead singer/drummer (Atlantic).

Mixed Emotions. w/m Stuart F. Loucheim, 1951. Popularized by Rosemary Clooney, with Percy Faith's Orchestra (Columbia).

M'Lady. w/m Sylvester Stewart, 1968. Recorded by Sly and the Family Stone (Epic).

Moanin' in the Mornin'. w. E. Y. Harburg, m. Harold Arlen, 1937. Introduced by Vivian Vance in (TM) *Hooray for What!*

Moanin' Low. w. Howard Dietz, m. Ralph Rainger, 1929. Sung by Libby Holman and danced to by Clifton Webb in (TM) *The Little Show*. A torch song was needed for Holman to sing and none was forthcoming from the writers of the score. Rainger, one of the pit piano team, said he had a melody that might be appropriate. Dietz wrote the lyric, the song went in, the show opened, and a hit was born. Holman recorded it in a torchy coupling with "Am I Blue?" (q.v.) (Brunswick). It was performed by Harry James, dubbing on the soundtrack for Kirk Douglas, in (MM) *Young Man with a Horn* in 1950.

Moanin' the Blues. w/m Hank Williams, 1950. Recorded by Hank Williams (MGM).

Mockin' Bird Hill. w/m Vaughn Horton, 1951. Million-selling records by Les Paul and Mary Ford (Capitol) and Patti Page, with Jimmy Carroll's Orchestra (Mercury). Other popular versions by The Pinetoppers (Coral) and Russ Morgan, with his Orchestra (Decca).

Mockingbird. w/m Inez Foxx and Charlie Foxx, 1963. Introduced and Top 10 record by Inez Foxx, accompanied by brother Charlie Foxx (Symbol). Aretha Franklin had a chart record in 1967 (Columbia). Million-selling version by Carly Simon and James Taylor (Elektra), 1974.

Modern Girl. w/m Dominic Bugatti and Frank Musker, 1981. Recorded by the Scottish performer Sheena Easton (EMI America).

Modern Love. w/m David Bowie, 1983. Recorded by the English singer/songwriter David Bowie (EMI America).

Modern Woman. w/m Billy Joel, 1986. Introduced on the soundtrack of (MP) *Modern Woman*, and on a Top 10 single (Columbia) by Billy Joel.

Mohair Sam. w/m Dallas Frazier, 1965. Top 40 record by Charlie Rich (Smash).

Molly. w/m Steve Karliski, 1963. Popularized by Bobby Goldsboro (Laurie).

Molly Darling. w/m Eddy Arnold, 1948. Featured and recorded by Eddy Arnold (RCA Victor).

Molly Dear, It's You I'm After. w. Frank Wood, m. Henry E. Pether, 1915. Interpolated into the return Broadway engagement of the prior season's hit show (TM) *The Girl from Utah.*

Molly O! w/m William J. Scanlan, 1891. Introduced by Scanlan in (TM) *Mavourneen.*

Molly-O. See **Themes from "The Man with the Golden Arm."**

Mom and Dad's Waltz. w/m Lefty Frizzell, 1951. Introduced and recorded by Lefty Frizzell (Columbia).

Moment by Moment. w. Molly Ann Leiken, m. Lee Holdridge, 1978. Sung by Yvonne Elliman on the soundtrack of (MP) *Moment by Moment,* and on records (RSO).

Moments in the Moonlight. w/m Richard Himber, Irving Gordon, and Al Kaufman, 1940. Introduced by Richard Himber and his Orchestra. Recorded by the bands of Glenn Miller, vocal by Ray Eberle (Bluebird); Gene Krupa, vocal by Howard DuLany (Columbia); Bob Crosby, vocal by Marion Mann (Decca); Tommy Reynolds (Vocalion).

Moments Like This. w. Frank Loesser, m. Burton Lane, 1938. Introduced by Florence George in (MM) *College Swing.* Recorded by Maxine Sullivan (Victor); Dick Stabile and his Orchestra (Bluebird); Teddy Wilson, vocal by Nan Wynn (Brunswick). Included in Tony Bennett's album "The Art of Excellence" (Columbia), 1986.

Moments to Remember. w. Al Stillman, m. Robert Allen, 1955. Popularized via hit record by The Four Lads (Columbia). Revived by The Vogues in 1969 (Reprise).

Momma, Momma. w/m Harold Rome, 1962. Introduced by Elliott Gould and Lillian Roth in (TM) *I Can Get It for You Wholesale.*

Momma Look Sharp. w/m Sherman Edwards, 1969. Introduced by Scott Jarvis, William Duell, and B. J. Slater in (TM) *1776.*

Mommy for a Day. w/m Buck Owens and Harlan Howard, 1959. C&W hit by Kitty Wells (Decca).

Mona Lisa. w/m Jay Livingston and Ray Evans, 1950. From (MP) *Captain Carey, U.S.A.,* in which the song was never heard in its entirety. The fragments that were sung were in Italian. The song, however, won the Academy Award. Nat Cole's recording (Capitol) sold over three million copies and was the ninth best-seller in the first half of the century. Revived by rockabilly singer Carl Mann (Phillips), and country singer Conway Twitty (MGM), 1959.

Mona Lisa Lost Her Smile. w/m Johnny Cunningham, 1984. Top 10 Country chart record by actor/singer/composer David Allan Coe (Columbia).

Mon Amour Perdu (My Lost Love). w/m Richard M. Sherman and Robert B. Sherman, 1962. From (MP) *Big Red.*

Monday, Monday. w/m John Phillips, 1966. #1 gold record by The Mamas and the Papas (Dunhill).

Monday Date, A. w/m Earl Hines, 1928. Introduced and recorded by Louis Armstrong (Okeh). Also recorded by the composer (Okeh).

Money. w/m Roger Waters, 1973. Top 20 record by the British band Pink Floyd (Harvest).

Money. w/m John Sebastian, 1968. Recorded by The Lovin' Spoonful (Kama Sutra).

Money, Marbles, and Chalk. w/m Pop Eckler, 1949. Recorded by Patti Page, with Zeb Masher's Orchestra (Mercury).

Money, Money (Makes the World Go Round). w. Fred Ebb, m. John Kander, 1972. Specially written for the movie (MM) *Cabaret,* in which it was introduced by Joel Grey and Liza Minelli.

Money (That's What I Want). w/m Berry Gordy, Jr., and Janie Bradford, 1960. Crossover (R&B/Pop) hit by Barrett Strong (Anna), and later by The Kingsmen (Wand), 1964. Chart records by Jr. Walker and The All Stars (Soul), 1966; the British electronic recording production, The Flying Lizards (Virgin), 1980.

Money Burns a Hole in My Pocket. w. Bob Hilliard, m. Jule Styne, 1954. Introduced by Dean Martin in (MM) *Living It Up*, which was the film version of the Broadway play *Hazel Flagg*, which, in turn, was a musical based on the film *Nothing Sacred*. Some of the stage musical's songs were retained, but this was written for the film. Martin recorded it, with Dick Stabile's Orchestra (Capitol).

Money Changes Everything. w/m Thomas Gray, 1983. Introduced by The Brains on their self-named LP, 1980. Cyndi Lauper included it in her platinum album "She's So Unusual," from which it became one of five singles to reach the charts (Portrait).

Money for Nothing. w/m Mark Knopfler and Sting, 1985. #1 record by the group Dire Straits formed in London by Scottish-born Mark Knopfler (Warner Bros.).

Money Honey. w/m Eric Faulkner and Stuart Wood, 1976. Top 10 record by the Scottish group The Bay City Rollers (Arista).

Money Honey. w/m Jesse Stone, 1953. Hit record for Clyde McPhatter (Atlantic) and The Drifters (Atlantic). Recorded in 1956 by Elvis Presley (RCA Victor).

Money Is. w/m Quincy Jones, 1972. Performed by Little Richard on the soundtrack of (MP) *$(Dollars)*.

Money Is the Root of All Evil. w/m Joan Whitney and Alex Kramer, 1945. Recorded by The Andrews Sisters, with Guy Lombardo's Orchestra (Decca).

Money Song, The. w/m Harold Rome, 1948. From (TM) *That's the Ticket*, which closed in Philadelphia on its pre-Broadway tryout. The song gained popularity, however, through recordings by The Andrews Sisters (Decca) and Dean Martin and Jerry Lewis (Capitol).

Money Song, The (Sitting Pretty). w. Fred Ebb, m. John Kander, 1966. Introduced by Joel Grey and the Cabaret girls in (TM) *Cabaret*. The song was not included in the film version. See also "Money, Money" etc.

Money to Burn. w/m David Heneker, 1963. Sung by Tommy Steele and The Men in the Broadway production of the British musical (TM) *Half a Sixpence*, and in (MM) *Half a Sixpence*, 1967.

Money Tree, The. w. Cliff Ferre, m. Mark McIntyre, 1956. Introduced on records and best-seller by Margaret Whiting (Capitol). Popular record also by Patience and Prudence, whose father composed the song and conducted their orchestra (Liberty).

Monkey. w/m George Michael, 1988. Chart single from the album, "Faith," by the British singer/songwriter George Michael (Columbia).

Monkey Doodle Dandy. w. Jack Drislane, m. Henry Frantzen, 1909.

Monkey Time, The. w/m Curtis Mayfield, 1963. Introduced and hit record by Major Lance (Okeh). Revived by The Tubes (Capitol), 1983.

Monotonous. w. June Carroll, m. Arthur Siegel, 1952. Introduced by Eartha Kitt in (TM) *New Faces of 1952*, and repeated by her in (MM) *New Faces*, 1954.

Monster. w/m Jerry Edmonton and John Kay, 1970. Top 40 record by Steppenwolf (Dunhill).

Monster Mash. w/m Bobby Pickett and Leonard Capizzi, 1962. #1 million-selling novelty by Bobby "Boris" Pickett and The Crypt-Kickers (Garpax). The record had two chart reissues, 1970 and 1973, on another label (Parrot).

Montego Bay. w/m Jeff Barry and Bobby Bloom, 1970. Top 10 record by Bobby Bloom (L&R/MGM).

Monterey. w/m Eric Burdon, Victor Briggs, Barry Jenkins, Danny McCulloch, and Johnny Weide, 1968. Hit record by the English group Eric Burdon and The Animals (MGM).

Mony Mony. w/m Bobby Bloom, Ritchie Cordell, Bo Gentry, and Tommy James, 1968, 1987. The title came from the "MONY" electric sign atop the Mutual of New York building that faced the apartment of writer/singer Tommy James, who with The Shondells had a Top 10 record (Roulette). Revived by Billy Idol, who had a #1 single from his album "Vital Idol" (Chrysalis), 1987.

Mooche, The (a.k.a. **The Mooch**). m. Edward Kennedy "Duke" Ellington, 1928. Instrumental, first recorded by Duke Ellington (Okeh).

Mood Indigo. w/m Edward Kennedy "Duke" Ellington, Albany "Barney" Bigard, and Irving Mills, 1931. Introduced by Duke Ellington and his Orchestra under title "Dreamy Blues" a year earlier. This song became one of his greatest standards after the lyric to the Ellington-Bigard instrumental was retitled and written by Mitchell Parish under a "for hire" contract with the publisher, Mills Music. Parish received neither credit nor royalties for his contribution. Ellington recorded the new version (Victor), 1931, and later on another label (Decca). Among the many recordings are: The Boswell Sisters (Brunswick), Cab Calloway (Perfect), Jimmie Lunceford (Decca), Clyde McCoy (Columbia), Lee Morse (Columbia), Dinah Shore (Victor), Sonny Greer (Capitol). The Ellington orchestra played it on the soundtrack of (MM) *Paris Blues*, 1961.

Mood That I'm In, The. w/m Abner Silver and Al Sherman, 1937. Recorded by the bands or combos of: Teddy Wilson (Brunswick), Lionel Hampton (Victor), Eddie Farley (Decca), Dick McDonough (Melotone).

Moody Blue. w/m Mark James, 1976. Recorded by Elvis Presley (RCA).

Moody River. w/m Gary D. Bruce, 1961. #1 hit record by Pat Boone (Dot).

Moody Woman. w/m Theresa Bell, Jerry Butler, and Kenny Gamble, 1969. Top 40 record by Jerry Butler (Mercury).

Moon About Town. w/m Dana Suesse, 1934. Interpolated in (TM) *Ziegfeld Follies*. Recorded by Emil Coleman's Orchestra, vocal by Jerry Cooper (Columbia).

Moon and the Willow Tree, The. w. Johnny Burke, m. Victor Schertzinger, 1940. Introduced by Dorothy Lamour in (MM) *The Road to Singapore*. Recorded by Lamour (Bluebird), and Jack Teagarden, vocal by Kitty Kallen (Varsity).

Moonbeam, Kiss Her for Me. w. Mort Dixon, m. Harry Woods, 1927. Featured and recorded by Harry Richman (Vocalion).

Moonbeams. w. Henry Blossom, m. Victor Herbert, 1906. First sung by Augusta Greenleaf in (TM) *The Red Mill*.

Moonburn. w. Edward Heyman, m. Hoagy Carmichael, 1936. Introduced by Bing Crosby in (MM) *Anything Goes*.

Moon Country. w. Johnny Mercer, m. Hoagy Carmichael, 1934. First recorded by Hoagy Carmichael (Victor). Glen Gray and the Casa Loma Orchestra recorded it in 1934, vocal by Pee Wee Hunt (Brunswick), and again in 1939, vocal by the Merry Macs (Decca).

Moondance. w/m Van Morrison, 1977. Recorded by Van Morrison (Warner Bros.).

Moon-Faced, Starry-Eyed. w. Langston Hughes, m. Kurt Weill, 1947. Introduced by Danny Daniels and Sheila Bond in (TM) *Street Scene*. Most popular recordings by Freddy Martin, vocal by Murray Arnold (RCA Victor), and Benny Goodman, vocal by Johnny Mercer (Capitol).

Moonfall. w/m Rupert Holmes, 1985. Introduced by Patti Cohenour in (TM) *The Mystery of Edwin Drood*.

Moon Fell in the River, The. w. Mitchell Parish, m. Peter DeRose, 1940. From the Sonja Henie stage production (TM) *It Happens on*

Ice. Recorded by Ray Herbeck and his Orchestra (Okeh).

Moonglow. w/m Will Hudson, Eddie DeLange, and Irving Mills, 1934, 1956. Among the many recordings of this standard are: Glen Gray and the Casa Loma Orchestra (Brunswick); Guy Lombardo (Decca); Artie Shaw (Victor); Cab Calloway (Victor); Benny Goodman and band (Columbia), with quartet (Victor); King Sisters (Bluebird); Art Tatum (Decca); Art Mooney (MGM); Ethel Waters (Decca). The Hudson-DeLange Band, which was formed in 1936, did not record it. In 1956, it was heard in (MP) *Picnic* in counterpoint with "Theme from Picnic." Best-selling records of the coupling were made by Morris Stoloff and his Orchestra (Decca) and George Cates and his Orchestra (Coral).

Moon Got in My Eyes, The. w. Johnny Burke, m. Arthur Johnston, 1937. Introduced by Bing Crosby in (MM) *Double or Nothing.* Most popular records by Crosby (Decca) and Mildred Bailey (Vocalion).

Moon Has His Eyes on You, The. w. Billy Johnson, m. Albert Von Tilzer, 1905. Leading recordings by Frank Stanley and Corrinne Morgan (Victor) and Ada Jones (Edison).

Moon Is a Silver Dollar, The. w. Mitchell Parish, m. Sammy Fain, 1939.

Moon Is Blue, The. w. Sylvia Fine, m. Herschel Burke Gilbert, 1953. Title song of (MP) *The Moon Is Blue.* Nominated for Academy Award. Recorded by The Sauter-Finegan Orchestra, vocal by Sally Sweetland (RCA Victor).

Moon Is Grinning at Me, The. w. Irving Mills, m. Will Hudson, 1936. Introduced by the Hudson-DeLange Orchestra, vocal by Ruth Gaylor (Brunswick). Also recorded by Ben Pollack's Band (Variety) and the Mills Blue Rhythm Band, an all-star recording aggregation assembled by the publisher, Mills Music, to promote their songs (Columbia).

Moon Is Low, The. w. Arthur Freed, m. Nacio Herb Brown, 1930. Introduced by Cliff

"Ukulele Ike" Edwards in (MM) *Montana Moon*, which starred Joan Crawford. Among records concurrent with the film release were those by the orchestras of Guy Lombardo (Columbia), George Olsen (Victor), Roger Wolfe Kahn (Brunswick), Seger Ellis (Okeh).

Moon Is Still over Her Shoulder, The. w/m Hugh Prestwood, 1987. #1 Country chart record by Michael Johnson (RCA).

Moonlight. w. James O'Dea, m. Neil Moret, 1905. Popular instrumental by Sousa's Band (Victor).

Moonlight and Pretzels. w. E. Y. Harburg, m. Jay Gorney, 1933. Sung in a production number in (MM) *Moonlight and Pretzels.*

Moonlight and Roses. w. Ben Black, m. Neil Moret, a.k.a. Charles N. Daniels, 1925. Based on "Andantino in D Flat" by the British organist Edwin H. Lemare. Featured and recorded by John McCormack (Victor). Popularized and recorded by Lanny Ross, who used it as the theme song on his radio programs. Betty Grable sang it with a chorus in (MM) *Tin Pan Alley*, 1940. In 1943, Roy Rogers sang it in (MM) *Song of Texas* and Gloria Jean sang it in (MM) *Mr. Big.* Revived by Vic Dana (Dolton), 1965.

Moonlight and Shadows. w. Leo Robin, m. Frederick Hollander, 1937. Introduced by Dorothy Lamour in her first film (MP) *Jungle Princess* and sung by her on her first record release (Brunswick). Also recorded by the bands of Eddy Duchin (Victor) and Anson Weeks (Decca).

Moonlight Bay (a.k.a. **On Moonlight Bay**). w. Edward Madden, m. Percy Wenrich, 1912. Popular song and barbershop quartet favorite. First leading records by The American Quartet (Victor). The same performance was released on another label (Edison) under the name of The Premier Quartet. In films, Alice Faye sang it in (MM) *Tin Pan Alley*, 1940; it was heard in (MM) *Is Everybody Happy?*, 1943; it was sung by Doris Day in (MM) *On Moonlight Bay*, 1951. Top 20 record by Bing Crosby and Gary Crosby (Decca), 1951.

Moonlight Becomes You. w. Johnny Burke, m. James Van Heusen, 1942. Introduced by Bing Crosby in (MM) *Road to Morocco*. His record (Decca) became #1 in all categories, as did the song itself. Other chart records by Glenn Miller, vocal by Skip Nelson and The Modernaires (Victor); and Harry James, vocal by Johnny McAfee (Columbia).

Moonlight Cocktail. w. Kim Gannon, m. C. Luckeyth "Luckey" Roberts, 1942. Roberts adapted this from a ragtime instrumental of his, "Ripples of the Nile." #1 record by Glenn Miller, vocal by Ray Eberle (Bluebird).

Moonlight Feels Right. w/m Bruce Blackman, 1976. Top 10 record by the group Starbuck (Private Stock).

Moonlight Gambler. w. Bob Hilliard, m. Phil Springer, 1957. Popularized by Frankie Laine who had a hit record (Columbia).

Moonlighting. w. Al Jarreau, m. Lee Holdridge, 1986. Sung by Al Jarreau as the theme of the series (TVP) "Moonlighting," and on his chart single (MCA), 1987.

Moonlight in Vermont. w. John Blackburn, m. Karl Suessdorf, 1944. Title from but not used in film starring Ray Malone and Gloria Jean. Song became popular via recording by Billy Butterfield and an all-star orchestra, vocal by Margaret Whiting (Capitol). The record became a million-seller and helped establish Whiting as one of the top singers of her time. She recorded a new version, 1954, with Lou Busch's band accompanying (Capitol).

Moonlight Love. w. Mitchell Parish, m. adapted by Domenico Savino, 1956. Adapted from Claude Debussy's "Clair de Lune." Recorded by Perry Como (RCA).

Moonlight Masquerade. w. Jack Lawrence, m. Toots Camarata (adapted from Albeniz), 1941. An adaptation of the popular piano piece "Tango in D" by the Spanish composer Isaac Albeniz. Featured and recorded by Jimmy Dorsey, vocal by Bob Eberly (Decca).

Moonlight Mood. w. Harold Adamson, m. Peter De Rose, 1942. Popularized and recorded by Glenn Miller, vocal by Skip Nelson and the Modernaires (Victor); Kay Kyser and Orchestra (Columbia); Connee Boswell (Decca).

Moonlight on the Campus. w. Johnny Mercer, m. Richard A. Whiting, 1937. Introduced by Dick Powell in (MM) *Varsity Show* and recorded by him (Decca) and by the bands of Fred Waring (Decca) and Clyde Lucas (Vocalion).

Moonlight on the Colorado. w. Billy Moll, m. Robert A. King, 1930. Popular recordings by Nat Shilkret (Victor), Seger Ellis (Crown), Riley Puckett and Red Jones (Decca).

Moonlight on the Ganges. w. Chester Wallace, m. Sherman Myers, 1926. Upon publication, it was recorded by such prominent bands and singers as Sam Lanin (Perfect), Jack Denny (Brunswick), Freddie Rich (Columbia), Willard Robison (Perfect), the Revelers (Victor), Franklyn Baur (Brunswick). It was recorded later by Johnny Long (Decca), Glenn Miller (Columbia), Tommy Dorsey (Victor), Charlie Spivak (London), The Sauter-Finegan Band (Victor).

Moonlight Saving Time. w/m Irving Kahal and Harry Richman, 1931. Introduced by Richman. Recorded by Ruth Etting (Columbia), Guy Lombardo (Columbia), Maurice Chevalier (Victor), Annette Hanshaw (Velvetone), Dick Robertson (Melotone).

Moonlight Serenade. w. Mitchell Parish, m. Glenn Miller, 1939. Probably the most popular original theme song of the big band era. Miller composed it while studying composition with Joseph Schillinger, and while playing trombone with, and arranging for, Ray Noble's Orchestra. Edward Heyman wrote the original lyric, titled "Now I Lay Me Down to Weep." When Miller formed his own band, he felt the title was too negative and got Parish to write a new set of words. Miller coupled it with "Sunrise Serenade" (q.v.) for one of his earliest hit records (Bluebird). It was prominent in (MM) *The Glenn Miller Story*, 1954.

Moonlight Serenade

Moonlight Swim. w. Sylvia Dee, m. Ben Weisman, 1957. Recorded by Tony [Anthony] Perkins (RCA) and Nick Noble (Mercury).

Moon Love. w/m Mack David, Mack Davis, and André Kostalanetz, 1939. Adapted from the 1st theme of the 2nd Movement of Tchaikovsky's *Symphony No. 5 in E Minor*. The great airplay and numerous recordings resulted in twelve weeks on "Your Hit Parade," four times in the #1 position. Top recordings by Glenn Miller (Bluebird); Paul Whiteman, vocal by Joan Edwards (Decca); Horace Heidt (Brunswick); Mildred Bailey (Vocalion).

Moon Mist. m. Mercer Ellington, 1942. Introduced and recorded by Duke Ellington and his Orchestra (Victor).

Moon of Manakoora, The. w. Frank Loesser, m. Alfred Newman, 1937. Introduced by Dorothy Lamour in (MP) *The Hurricane* and recorded by her (Brunswick). Other recordings of note: Bing Crosby (Decca), and the bands of: Ray Noble, vocal by Tony Martin (Brunswick); Van Alexander (Bluebird); Ruby Newman (Decca).

Moon over Burma. w. Frank Loesser, m. Frederick Hollander, 1940. Sung by Dorothy Lamour in (MP) *Moon over Burma* and on discs (Bluebird). This was one of many "moon" songs recorded by her, e.g., "Moonlight and Shadows," "Moon of Manakoora," "Moon and the Willow Tree."

Moon over Miami. w. Edgar Leslie, m. Joe Burke, 1935. Popularized by airplay and recordings by Connie Boswell (Decca); Eddy Duchin (Victor); George Hall, vocal by Dolly Dawn (Brunswick); Jan Garber (Decca); Lud Gluskin (Brunswick). Theme song of Dean Hudson's Orchestra. Played under the credits in (MM) *Moon Over Miami*, 1941. Among later records: Vaughn Monroe (Victor), George Shearing (Discovery).

Moon Over Naples. See **Spanish Eyes.**

Moonraker. w. Hal David, m. John Barry, 1979. Sung on the soundtrack of (MP) *Moonraker* by Shirley Bassey.

Moonray. w/m Artie Shaw, Paul Madison, and Arthur Quenzer, 1939. Introduced and recorded by Artie Shaw, vocal by Helen Forrest (Bluebird), followed by Jack Jenney and his Orchestra (Vocalion).

Moonrise on the Lowlands. w. Al J. Neiburg, m. Jerry Livingston, 1936. Featured and recorded by: Willie Bryant (Bluebird), Jimmy Dorsey (Decca), Fletcher Henderson (Victor), Ruby Newman (Brunswick), Don Redman (Melotone).

Moon River. w. Johnny Mercer, m. Henry Mancini, 1961. Introduced by Audrey Hepburn in (MP) *Breakfast at Tiffany's*. Winner Academy Award and Grammy Award (NARAS) for Song of the Year. Top recordings by Henry Mancini and his Orchestra (RCA), Jerry Butler (Vee-Jay), Andy Williams (Columbia).

Moon Shadow. w/m Cat Stevens, 1971. Recorded in England by Cat Stevens (A&M). Top 40 on U.S. charts.

Moonshine Blues. w/m Gertrude "Ma" Rainey, 1924. Recorded by Ma Rainey (Paramount) and Bessie Smith (Columbia).

Moonshine Lullaby. w/m Irving Berlin, 1946. Introduced by Ethel Merman and children in (TM) *Annie Get Your Gun*. Song not used in film version.

Moonshine over Kentucky. w. Sidney D. Mitchell, m. Lew Pollack, 1938. From (MM) *Kentucky Moonshine*, sung by Tony Martin. Recorded by Jan Savitt, vocal by Bon Bon (Bluebird); Bunny Berigan, vocal by Ruth Gaylor (Victor); Charles "Buddy" Rogers and his Orchestra (Vocalion).

Moon Shines on the Moonshine, The. w. Francis DeWitt, m. Robin Hood Bowers, 1920. Satirical anti-prohibition song, introduced in the revue (TM) *Broadway Brevities of 1920* by Bert Williams.

Moon Song. w. Sam Coslow, m. Arthur Johnston, 1933. Introduced by Kate Smith in (MM) *Hello, Everybody!* She recorded it (Brunswick), as did Annette Hanshaw (Perfect), Frances Langford (Bluebird), Irene Beasley (Victor), Jack Denny (Victor), and Wayne King (Brunswick).

Moonstruck. w. Sam Coslow, m. Arthur Johnston, 1933. Introduced in (MM) *College Humor* and recorded by Bing Crosby (Brunswick).

Moon Talk. w/m Al Hoffman and Dick Manning, 1958. Top 40 record by Perry Como (RCA).

Moon Was Yellow, The. w. Edgar Leslie, m. Fred E. Ahlert, 1934. Featured and recorded by Bing Crosby (Decca) and the Dorsey Brothers Orchestra, vocal by Kay Weber (Decca). Later versions by Frances Langford (Mercury), Eddie Heywood (Victor), Les Brown (Coral), Buddy Cole (Capitol), and Al Haig (Pacific Jazz).

Moon Won't Talk, The. w. Charles Hathaway, m. Helen Bliss, 1940. Featured and recorded by Benny Goodman, vocal by Helen Forrest (Columbia); Bob Chester, vocal by Dolores O'Neill (Bluebird); Ginny Simms (Vocalion).

More. w. Tom Glazer, m. Alex Alstone, 1956. Popularized by Perry Como (RCA).

More, More, More. w/m Gregg Diamond, 1976. Top 10 gold record by The Andrea True Connection (Buddah).

More (Theme from "Mondo Cane"). w. Norman Newell (Engl.), m. Riz Ortolani and Nino Oliviero, 1963. Musical theme of Italian documentary film (MP) *Mondo Cane*, Italian words by M. Ciorciolini. Sung on the soundtrack of the film for the U.S. release by Kathina Ortolani. Nominated for Academy Award for best song, 1963. Hit instrumental record by Kai Winding (Verve). Best-selling and highest chart vocal version by Vic Dana (Dolton).

More and More. w/m Tommy Karen, Alan Reuss, and Rainey Robinson, 1967. Featured and recorded by Andy Williams (Columbia).

More and More. w/m Merle Kilgore and Webb Pierce, 1954. Million-selling #1 Coun-

try song featured and recorded by Webb Pierce (Decca). Not to be confused with similarly titled songs of 1944 or 1967.

More and More. w. E. Y. Harburg, m. Jerome Kern, 1944. Introduced by Deanna Durbin in (MM) *Can't Help Singing*, and recorded by her (Decca). Nominated for Academy Award. Tommy Dorsey, vocal by Bonnie Lou Williams (Victor), and Perry Como (Victor) had chart records.

More Beer. w/m Julian H. Miller, 1948. Adaptation of German song "Der Kreuzfidele Kupferschmied" ("The Jolly Coppersmith"). Most popular record was by The Andrews Sisters (Decca).

More Bounce to the Ounce. w/m Roger Troutman, 1980. Recorded by the band Zapp (Warner Bros.).

More I Cannot Wish You. w/m Frank Loesser, 1950. Introduced by Pat Rooney, Sr. in (TM) *Guys and Dolls*. Song not used in film version.

More I Know You, The. w. Benny Davis, m. J. Fred Coots, 1936. Introduced and recorded by Fats Waller (Victor).

More I See You, The. w. Mack Gordon, m. Harry Warren, 1945. Introduced as a duet by Dick Haymes and Betty Grable in (MM) *Billy Rose's Diamond Horseshoe*. Leading records by Haymes, with Victor Young's Orchestra (Decca), and Harry James, vocal by Buddy De Vito (Columbia). Top 20 record by Chris Montez (A&M), 1966.

More Love. w/m William "Smokey" Robinson, 1967. Top 40 record by "Smokey" Robinson and The Miracles (Tamla). Revived with Top 10 record by Kim Carnes (EMI America), 1980.

More Love Than Your Love. w. Dorothy Fields, m. Arthur Schwartz, 1954. Introduced by Wilbur Evans in (TM) *By the Beautiful Sea*. Recorded by Les Baxter and his Orchestra (Capitol).

More Than a Feeling. w/m Tom Scholz, 1976. Top 10 record by the group Boston (Epic).

More Than a Miracle. w/m Doc Pomus and Jerry Ragovoy, 1967. Leading record, instrumental by Roger Williams (Kapp).

More Than a Woman. w/m Barry Gibb, Maurice Gibb, and Robin Gibb, 1977. Introduced by The Bee Gees on the soundtrack of (MM) *Saturday Night Fever*. Leading record by the family group Tavares (Capitol).

More Than I Can Say. w/m Sonny Curtis and Jerry Allison, 1980. Introduced by Bobby Vee (Liberty), 1960. Top 10 gold record by English singer Leo Sayer (Warner Bros.), 1980.

More Than Just a Friend. w/m Richard Rodgers, 1962. Introduced by Tom Ewell in the third film version [second musical] (MM) *State Fair*.

More Than Just the Two of Us. w/m Michael Cary Schneider and Mitch Crane, 1981. Recorded by the sextet Sneaker (Handshake).

More Than the Eye Can See. w/m Bob Crewe and Larry Weiss, 1967. Recorded by Al Martino (Capitol).

More Than You Know. w. Edward Eliscu and William (Billy) Rose, m. Vincent Youmans, 1929. Introduced by Mayo Methot in (TM) *Great Day!* which, although it had a short run of thirty-six performances, spawned two other major standards, the title song and "Without a Song," (q.v.). This song, which has been recorded by almost every major vocalist, was interpolated in (MM) *Hit the Deck*, 1930, and again in the 1955 version, this time by Tony Martin. Gogi Grant, dubbing for Ann Blyth in the title role, sang it in (MM) *The Helen Morgan Story*, 1957; Barbra Streisand, as Fanny Brice, sang it in (MM) *Funny Lady*, 1975.

More Today Than Yesterday. w/m Pat Upton, 1969. Top 20 record by The Spiral Staircase, lead singer Pat Upton (Columbia).

More To Me. w/m Ben Peters, 1977. Country hit record by Charley Pride (RCA).

More You Do It, The (The More I Like It Done). w/m Charles Jackson, Jr. and Marvin Yancy, 1976. Recorded by Ronnie Dyson (Columbia).

Morgen (a.k.a. **One More Sunrise**). w. Noel Sherman (Engl.), and Peter Mosser, (Ger.), m. Peter Mosser, 1959. Hit record by the Yugoslav singer, Ivo Robic, singing in German (Laurie). Recorded with the English title and lyrics by Leslie Uggams (Columbia).

Moritat. See **Mack the Knife.**

Mornin'. w/m Al Jarreau, Jay Graydon, and David Foster, 1983. Recorded by Al Jarreau (Warner Bros.).

Mornin' Beautiful. w/m Dave Appell and Sandy Linzer, 1975. Top 20 record by Tony Orlando and Dawn (Elektra).

Morning. w. Frank L. Stanton, m. Oley Speaks, 1910.

Morning, Noon and Night. w. Arthur Swanstrom, m. Louis Alter, 1933.

Morning After. w. Dory Langdon Previn, m. Harold Arlen, 1962. Featured and recorded by Eileen Farrell (Columbia).

Morning After, The. w/m Al Kasha and Joel Hirshhorn, 1972. Introduced by Renée Armand, dubbing on the soundtrack for Carol Lynley, in (MP) *The Poseidon Adventure*. Academy Award-winning song. Maureen McGovern's first release became a #1 gold record (20th Century).

Morning After the Night Before, The. w. Ed Moran, m. J. Fred Helf, 1910.

Morning Dance. m. Jay Beckenstein, 1979. Instrumental by the Jazz/Pop band Spyro Gyra (Infinity).

Morning Desire. w/m Dave Loggins, 1985. #1 Country chart and Pop crossover record by Kenny Rogers (RCA).

Morning Dew. w/m Bonnie Dobson and Tim Rose, 1968. Based on the folk song and recorded by The Grateful Dead (Warner Bros.). Chart single by Lulu (Epic), 1968.

Morning Girl. w/m Tupper Saussy, 1969. Top 20 record by The Neon Philharmonic, comprised of musicians from the Nashville Symphony Orchestra, vocal by Don Gant, led by Saussy (Warner Bros.).

Morning Has Broken. w. Eleanor Farjeon, m. Cat Stevens, 1972. Top 10 record by Cat Stevens (A&M).

Morningside of the Mountain, The. w/m Dick Manning and Larry Stock, 1951, 1974. Leading records by Paul Weston and his Orchestra (Columbia); Tommy Edwards, who recorded it twice, 1951 and 1959 (MGM); Merv Griffin (RCA Victor); Jan Garber and his Orchestra (Capitol). Revived in 1974 with a Top 10 record by Donny and Marie Osmond (MGM). Note: Label credits have read "Morningside" and "Morning Side." The former is the writers' preference.

Morningtown Ride. w/m Malvina Reynolds, 1967. Recorded by the Australian group The Seekers (Capitol).

Morning Train (Nine to Five). w/m Florrie Palmer, 1981. #1 gold record by the Scottish singer Sheena Easton (EMI America).

Mornin' Mornin'. w/m Dennis Linde, 1970. C&W/Pop chart record by Bobby Goldsboro (United Artists).

Mornin' Ride. w/m Steve Bogard and Jeff Tweel, 1987. #1 Country chart record by Lee Greenwood (MCA).

Mosquito's Parade, The. m. Howard Whitney, 1899. Arranged by Theodore Bendix.

Most Beautiful Girl, The. w/m Rory Bourke, Billy Sherrill, and Norro Wilson, 1973. #1 record on both Country and Pop charts by Charlie Rich (Epic).

Most Beautiful Girl in the World, The. w. Lorenz Hart, m. Richard Rodgers, 1935. Introduced by Donald Novis and Gloria Grafton in Billy Rose's (TM) *Jumbo*. In the film version (MM) *Billy Rose's Jumbo*, 1962, it was sung by Stephen Boyd with a reprise by Jimmy

Durante. The song became associated with the pianist/singer/society bandleader Ted Straeter, who early in his career had been the rehearsal pianist for *Jumbo*. He recorded it three times (Liberty Music Shops, Columbia, MGM/Lion) and used it as his theme song.

Most Gentlemen Don't Like Love. w/m Cole Porter, 1938. Introduced by Sophie Tucker and ensemble in (TM) *Leave It to Me!* Mary Martin, who made her debut in this show with "My Heart Belongs to Daddy," (q.v.) recorded the two songs with Eddy Duchin and his Orchestra (Brunswick). The best-seller, nationally, was Larry Clinton and his Orchestra, vocal by Bea Wain, with the same coupling (Victor).

Most Happy Fella, The. w/m Frank Loesser, 1956. Introduced by Robert Weede in (TM) *The Most Happy Fella.*

Most Likely You Go Your Way (and I'll Go Mine). w/m Bob Dylan, 1974. Introduced by Bob Dylan in his album "Blonde on Blonde" (Columbia), 1966. The chart single with artistic credits, Bob Dylan/The Band, was a live recording from Dylan's 1973 tour (Asylum).

Most of All. w/m Harvey Fuqua and Alan Freed, 1955. Introduced and Top 10 R&B chart record by The Moonglows, of which Fuqua was a member (Chess). Revived by Jody Watley with a crossover [R&B/Pop charts] version (MCA), 1988.

Most People Get Married. w. Earl Shuman, m. Leon Carr, 1962. Introduced and recorded by Patti Page.

Moten Stomp. m. Bennie Moten, 1927. The theme of the legendary Kansas City pianist and bandleader, Bennie Moten, and recorded by him (Victor). See also "Moten Swing."

Moten Swing. m. Bennie Moten and Buster Moten, 1933. Basically the same as the 1927 "Moten Stomp," this became the theme of Bennie Moten during his last few years. He recorded this version, also (Victor). Among the many other releases of this jazz standard are those by: Count Basie (Okeh); Harry James, (Columbia Parts 1 & 2); Andy Kirk, featuring Mary Lou Williams on piano (Decca); Eddie Durham (Decca); Bernie Leighton (Key); Sam Donahue and the Navy Band (V-disc 12″); Jay McShann (Capitol). This was one of the early numbers to use the word "swing" in the stylistic context.

Moth and the Flame, The. w. George Taggart, m. Max S. Witt, 1898. Title suggested by Clude Fitch's play of the same name. Song introduced by Helene Mora.

Mother. w/m John Lennon, 1971. Leading records by John Lennon/Plastic Ono Band (Apple) and Barbra Streisand (Columbia).

Mother. w. Dorothy Donnelly, m. Sigmund Romberg, 1927. Introduced by Evelyn Herbert, as Barbara Frietchie, in (TM) *My Maryland*. This was the second song of this title to be written by Romberg.

Mother. w. Rida Johnson Young, m. Sigmund Romberg, 1916. From (TM) *Her Soldier Boy*.

M-O-T-H-E-R (A Word That Means the World to Me). w. Howard Johnson, m. Theodore F. Morse, 1915. Sophie Tucker popularized this spelling tribute in vaudeville. Henry Burr had the first popular recording (Victor). Bobby Breen, the boy tenor, later featured and recorded it (Decca), 1936.

Mother, the Queen of My Heart. w/m Hoyt Bryant and Jimmie Rodgers, 1933. Introduced and recorded by Jimmie Rodgers (Victor).

Mother and Child Reunion. w/m Paul Simon, 1972. Top 10 record by Paul Simon (Columbia).

Mother Earth and Father Time. w/m Richard M. Sherman and Robert B. Sherman, 1971. Sung on the soundtrack of the animated feature, (MM) *Charlotte's Web*, by Debbie Reynolds.

Mother-in-law. w/m Alan Toussaint, 1961. Hit record by Ernie K-Doe, with bass vocal by Benny Spellman (Minit).

Motherland Theme. See "Roots" Medley.

Mother Machree. w. Rida Johnson Young, m. Chauncey Olcott and Ernest R. Ball, 1910. Introduced by Olcott in (TM) *Barry of Ballymore* and sung by him again in (TM) *The Isle o' Dreams*, 1912. Dick Haymes sang it as Ernest R. Ball in his film biography (MM) *Irish Eyes Are Smiling*, 1944. Dennis Morgan, as Chauncey Olcott, sang it in his biography (MM) *My Wild Irish Rose, 1947*.

Mother Nature, Father Time. w/m Clyde Otis and Brook Benton, 1965. Introduced and recorded by Brook Benton (RCA).

Mother of Mine, I Still Have You. w. Grant Clarke, m. Lou Silvers and Al Jolson, 1927. Sung by Al Jolson in (MM) *The Jazz Singer*, and on records (Brunswick).

Mother Popcorn (You Got to Have a Mother for Me). w/m James Brown and Alfred Ellis, 1969. Top 20 record by James Brown (King).

Mother's Little Helper. w/m Mick Jagger and Keith Richards, 1966. Top 10 record by the British group The Rolling Stones (London).

Mother Was a Lady (or, If Jack Were Only Here). w. Edward B. Marks, m. Joseph W. Stern, 1896. Introduced by Lottie Gilson at Proctor's 58th Street Theatre in New York City.

Motorcycle Mama. w/m John Wyker, 1972. Top 20 record by the duo Sailcat (Elektra).

Mottoes Framed upon the Wall. w. William Devers, m. W. S. Mullaly, 1888.

Mountain Greenery. w. Lorenz Hart, m. Richard Rodgers, 1926. Sung by Sterling Holloway and Bobbie Perkins in (TM) *Garrick Gaieties*. In the Rodgers and Hart story, (MM) *Words and Music*, 1948, Perry Como and Allyn McLerie sang it. Frank Crumit (Victor) and

Roger Wolfe Kahn and his Orchestra (Victor) had popular recordings. A half-century later, Mel Tormé made a much admired and played recording of the song (Capitol).

Mountain High, Valley Low. w. Bernard Hanighen, m. Raymond Scott, 1946. Introduced by Mary Martin and Yul Brynner in (TM) *Lute Song*. Martin recorded it (Decca). Another version by Dorothy Collins, with the orchestra of her husband and composer of the song, Raymond Scott (MGM).

Mountain Music. w/m Randy Owen, 1982. #1 Country chart record by the group Alabama (RCA).

Mountain of Love. w/m Laura Martin and Venita Del Rio, 1963. Country record by David Houston (Epic). Revived by Bobby G. Rice (Royal American), 1971, and Charley Pride with a #1 record (RCA), 1982.

Mountain of Love. w/m Harold Dorman, 1960. Crossover [R&B/Pop] hit by Harold Dorman (Rita). Top 10 Pop chart hit by Johnny Rivers (Imperial), 1964. Chart record by Ronnie Dove (Diamond), 1968.

Mountain's High, The. w/m Dick St. John Gosting, 1961. Hit record by Dick and Deedee (Liberty).

Mounties, The (a.k.a. **Song of the Mounties**). w. Otto Harbach, Oscar Hammerstein II, m. Rudolf Friml and Herbert Stothart, 1924. Sung by Arthur Deagon in (TM) *Rose-Marie*. In the film version, (MM) *Rose Marie*, 1935, it was sung by Nelson Eddy and chorus; in the 1954 version by Howard Keel and chorus.

Move Away. w/m George O'Dowd, Roy Hay, Mikey Craig, Jon Moss, and Phil Pickett, 1986. Recorded by the British group Culture Club (Epic/Virgin).

Move 'Em Out. w. Leslie Bricusse, m. Henry Mancini, 1978. Sung on the soundtrack of (MP) *Revenge of the Pink Panther* by Lon Satton.

Move in a Little Closer, Baby. w/m Arnold Capitanelli and Robert O'Connor, 1969. Recorded by Mama Cass (Dunhill).

Move It On Over. w/m Hank Williams, 1947. Hank Williams's first hit as writer and singer (MGM).

Move It Over. w/m Sunny Skylar, 1942. Introduced and recorded by Ethel Merman (Victor).

Move On. w/m Stephen Sondheim, 1983. Introduced by Mandy Patinkin and Bernadette Peters in (TM) *Sunday in the Park with George*.

Move Over. w/m John Kay and Gabriel Mekler, 1969. Top 40 record by Steppenwolf (Dunhill).

Movin'. m. Randy Muller and Wade Williamston, 1976. Top 20 instrumental by The Brass Construction (United Artists).

Moving Day in Jungle Town. w. A. Seymour Brown, m. Nat D. Ayer, 1909. Introduced by Sophie Tucker in (TM) *Ziegfeld Follies of 1909*.

Movin' On. w/m Mick Ralphs, 1975. Written by the guitarist of the British group, Bad Company, which had a Top 10 U.S. record (Swan Song).

Movin' On Up. w/m Jeff Barry and Ja'net Dubois, 1975. Theme song of the series (TVP) "The Jeffersons," sung on the soundtrack by Ja'net Dubois and Oren Waters.

Movin' Out (Anthony's Song). w/m Billy Joel, 1978. Recorded by Billy Joel (Columbia).

Mozambique. w/m Bob Dylan and Jacques Levy, 1976. Recorded by Bob Dylan (Columbia).

Mr. and Mrs. Is the Name. w. Mort Dixon, m. Allie Wrubel, 1934. Introduced by Dick Powell and Ruby Keeler in (MM) *Flirtation Walk*. In addition to the recording by Powell (Brunswick), there were releases by George

Hall with vocal by Loretta Lee and Sunny Schuyler (Bluebird) and Victor Young's Orchestra (Decca).

Mr. and Mrs. Used to Be. w/m Joe Deaton, 1964. Country hit by Ernest Tubb and Loretta Lynn (Decca).

Mr. Big Stuff. w/m Joe Broussard, Carol Washington, and Ralph Williams, 1971. #1 R&B and Top 10 Pop record by Jean Knight (Stax). Winner Grammy Award (NARAS) Best Rhythm and Blues Song, 1971.

Mr. Blue. w/m Dewayne Blackwell, 1959. #1 record by The Fleetwoods (Dolton).

Mr. Bojangles. w/m Jerry Jeff Walker, 1968. Introduced and recorded by Jerry Jeff Walker (Atco). Featured and recorded by Sammy Davis, Jr. (Reprise) and Bobby Cole (Date). Top 10 record by The Nitty Gritty Dirt Band, featuring a prologue by Uncle Charlie and his Dog Teddy (Liberty), 1970.

Mr. Booze. w. Sammy Cahn, m. James Van Heusen, 1964. Introduced by Frank Sinatra, Bing Crosby, Dean Martin, and Sammy Davis, Jr. in (MM) *Robin and the Seven Hoods*.

Mr. Businessman. w/m Ray Stevens, 1968. Top 40 record by Ray Stevens (Monument).

Mr. Captain, Stop the Ship (I Want to Get Off and Walk). w. W. A. Archbold, m. Felix McGlennon, 1895.

Mr. Dieingly Sad. w/m Don Ciccone, 1966. Top 20 record by The Critters, the quintet of which the writer was lead singer (Kapp).

Mr. D.J. w/m Joyce Irby, Douglas Davies, and Dallas Austin, 1989. Hit R&B chart single by Joyce "Fenderella" Irby (Motown).

Mr. Dream Merchant. w/m Larry Weiss and Jerry Ross, 1967. Recorded by Jerry Butler (Mercury). Revived as "Dream Merchant" by the group New Birth (Buddah), 1975.

Mr. Freddie Blues. w/m J. H. "Freddie" Shayne, 1924. First recorded by Priscilla Stewart, with the composer at the piano (Para-

mount), and by pianist Jimmy Blythe (Paramount), 1926. Blues singer Victoria Spivey's 1936 recording (Vocalion) created new interest in the number furthered by Connie Boswell, with Ben Pollack's Orchestra, (Decca), 1938. Meade Lux Lewis cut it in 1941 (Decca).

Mr. Ghost Goes to Town. w. Mitchell Parish and Irving Mills, m. Will Hudson, 1937. Swing instrumental with lyrics added. Leading records by the bands of Hudson-DeLange (Brunswick), Tommy Dorsey (Victor), Louis Prima (Vocalion), Johnny Hamp (Bluebird), Mills Blue Rhythm Band (Columbia).

Mr. Jelly Lord. m. Ferdinand "Jelly Roll" Morton, 1924. Jazz instrumental. Recorded by Jelly Roll Morton's Steamboat Four (Paramount). Other versions by the pianist/composer: Jelly Roll Morton's Incomparables (Gennett), 1926; Jelly Roll Morton's Red Hot Peppers (Victor), 1927; "Interviews with Alan Lomax," piano and vocal by Jelly Roll Morton (Circle), 1938.

Mr. Lee. w/m Heather Dixon, Helen Gathers, Jannie Pought, Emma R. Pought, Laura Webb, 1957. Hit record by the vocal group, The Bobettes, comprised of the writers (Atlantic).

Mr. Lonely. w/m Bobby Vinton and Gene Allan, 1964. Introduced and recorded by Buddy Greco (Epic), 1962. Two years later, Bobby Vinton dubbed his voice on Greco's music track and had a #1 record hit (Epic).

Mr. Lucky. m. Henry Mancini, 1960. Theme from the series (TVP) "Mr. Lucky." Instrumental recording by Henry Mancini and his Orchestra (RCA).

Mr. Monotony. w/m Irving Berlin, 1988. Written as a non-production song in the forties, it was considered for the film version of *Annie Get Your Gun*, but dropped. It was rehearsed but cut from the Broadway productions of two other musicals, *Miss Liberty*, 1949, in which it was called "Mrs. Monotony," and *Call Me Madam*, 1950, both choreographed by Jerome Robbins. Debbie Shapiro introduced it in (TM) *Jerome Robbins' Broad-*

way, 1988, with dancing by Luis Perez, Jane Lanier, and Robert La Fosse.

Mr. Paganini. See **You'll Have to Swing It.**

Mr. Pitiful. w/m Otis Redding and Steve Cropper, 1965. Introduced and recorded by Otis Redding (Volt).

Mr. Roboto. w/m Dennis De Young, 1983. Top 10 gold record by the quintet Styx (A&M).

Mr. Spaceman. w/m Jim McGuinn, 1966. Top 40 record by the folk-rock group The Byrds, of which the writer was a member (Columbia).

Mr. Sun, Mr. Moon. w/m Mark Lindsay, 1969. Top 20 record by Paul Revere and The Raiders (Columbia).

Mr. Tambourine Man. w/m Bob Dylan, 1965. Introduced and recorded by Bob Dylan (Columbia). #1 hit by the folk-rock group The Byrds (Columbia).

Mr. Telephone Man. w/m Ray Parker, Jr., 1985. Recorded by the Boston teenage quintet New Edition (MCA).

Mr. Touchdown, U.S.A. w/m Ruth Roberts, Gene Piller, and William Katz, 1950. Popular record by Hugo Winterhalter and his Orchestra (RCA Victor).

Mr. Volunteer (or, You Don't Belong to the Regulars, You're Just a Volunteer). w/m Paul Dresser, 1901. Song was also used in Dresser's film biography (MM) *My Gal Sal*, 1942.

Mr. Walker, It's All Over. w/m Gene Crysler, 1969. Hit Country and Pop chart record by Billie Jo Spears (Capitol).

Mr. Wishing Well. w/m Laurence Weiss and Lockie Edwards, Jr., 1963. Recorded by Nat "King" Cole, coupled with the hit "That Sunday, That Summer" (q.v.) (Capitol).

Mr. Wonderful. w/m Jerry Bock, Larry Holofcener, and George David Weiss, 1956. Introduced by Olga James in (TM) *Mr. Wonderful*, which starred Sammy Davis, Jr. Leading

records by Sarah Vaughan (Mercury), Peggy Lee (Capitol), Teddi King (RCA).

Mrs. Brown, You've Got a Lovely Daughter. w/m Trevor Peacock, 1965. Introduced in a television play in England, it was recorded by Hermans' Hermits for a #1 record in the U.K. and the U.S. (MGM).

Mrs. Robinson. w/m Paul Simon, 1968. Introduced on the soundtrack of (MP) *The Graduate*, 1967, by Simon and Garfunkel. Their recording reached the #1 position in sales and performances and was awarded a gold record (Columbia), 1968, and won the Grammy Award (NARAS) for Record of the Year. Booker T. and The MG's had a Top 40 instrumental version (Stax), 1969.

Mrs. Worthington (Don't Put Your Daughter on the Stage). w/m Noël Coward, 1935. Introduced and featured by Noël Coward.

M.T.A., The. w/m Jacqueline Steiner and Bess Hawes, 1959. Based on the PD melody, "The Wreck of the Old '97," this was written as a protest song about the operations of the Boston, Massachusetts subway system, the Metropolitan Transport Authority. Hit record by The Kingston Trio (Capitol).

Mu-Cha-Cha. w. Betty Comden and Adolph Green, m. Jule Styne, 1956. Introduced by Judy Holliday and Peter Gennaro in (TM) *Bells Are Ringing*. A short version was danced in (MM) *Bells Are Ringing*, 1960.

Much More. w. Tom Jones, m. Harvey Schmidt, 1960. Introduced by Rita Gardner in (TM) *The Fantasticks*.

Muddy River. w/m James Hendricks, 1969. Recorded by Johnny Rivers (Imperial).

Muddy Water. w/m Roger Miller, 1985. Introduced by Ron Richardson and Daniel Jenkins in (TM) *Big River*.

Muddy Water. w. Jo Trent, m. Peter De-Rose and Harry Richman, 1926. Introduced, featured, and recorded by Harry Richman (Brunswick).

Mule Skinner Blues. See **Blue Yodel #8.**

Mule Train. w/m Johnny Lange, Hy Heath, and Fred Glickman, 1949. Frankie Laine (Mercury) had a #1 million-seller. Even though Bing Crosby (Decca), Tennessee Ernie Ford (Capitol), and Vaughn Monroe (RCA Victor) had popular records, this song was, and is, associated with Laine. Monroe sang it in (MM) *Singing Guns*, 1950, and Gene Autry in (MM) *Mule Train*, 1950. Nominated for Academy Award for being in, but not introduced in, *Singing Guns*.

Mull of Kintyre. w/m Denny Laine and Paul McCartney, 1977. Recorded by McCartney's group Wings (Capitol).

Multiplication. w/m Bobby Darin, 1961. Introduced by Bobby Darin on the soundtrack of (MP) *Come September*, in which he co-starred with Sandra Dee. Recorded by Darin (Atco).

Murder, He Says. w. Frank Loesser, m. Jimmy McHugh, 1943. Introduced by Betty Hutton in (MM) *Happy Go Lucky*. Dinah Shore had the best-selling record (Victor). It was played by Teddy Powell and his Orchestra in (MM) *Jam Session*, 1944.

Murphy's Law. w/m Geraldine Hunt and Daniel Joseph, 1982. Novelty, recorded by the Canadian duo Cheri (Venture).

Murphy's Romance. w/m Carole King, 1985. Introduced on the soundtrack of (MP) *Murphy's Romance* by Carole King.

Muscles. w/m Michael Jackson, 1982. Top 10 record by Diana Ross (RCA).

Museum. w/m Donovan Leitch, 1967. Recorded by the English group Herman's Hermits (MGM).

Music, Maestro, Please! w. Herb Magidson, m. Allie Wrubel, 1938. One of the biggest sheet music sellers of the year, it was on "Your Hit Parade" for twelve weeks, four times in the #1 position. Among the many recordings: Kay Kyser and his Orchestra (Brunswick), Tommy Dorsey (Victor), Art Kassel (Bluebird). This standard has also been recorded by the Benny Goodman Quintet (Capitol), Frankie Laine (Mercury), Sammy Kaye, vocal by Tony Alamo (Columbia).

Music, Music, Everywhere. w. Ted Koehler, m. Harold Arlen, 1932. Recordings by Art Jarrett (Columbia), Isham Jones (Victor), Will Osborne (Melotone).

Music! Music! Music! w/m Stephen Weiss and Bernie Baum, 1950. #1 million-selling record by Teresa Brewer (London). While there were many other recordings, the song is identified with Brewer.

Music and the Mirror, The. w. Edward Kleban, m. Marvin Hamlisch, 1975. Introduced in (TM) *A Chorus Line* by Donna McKechnie.

Music Box Dancer. m. Frank Mills, 1979. Gold instrumental record by the Canadian pianist Frank Mills (Polydor).

Music from Beyond the Moon. w. Jack Lawrence, m. Guy Wood, 1947. Popular records by Tony Martin (RCA Victor) and Jack Fina, vocal by Harry Prime (MGM). See also "My One and Only Love."

Music Goes 'Round and 'Round, The. w. "Red" Hodgson, m. Edward Farley and Michael Riley, 1935. Novelty describing a French horn swept the country during the last few weeks of 1935 and the early weeks of 1936. The publisher had to utilize four printing companies to accommodate the orders for sheet music, the sales of which went over two million copies in a month. Introduced at and broadcast from the Onyx Club on 52nd Street, New York by the Riley-Farley Band, and recorded by them for the best-selling record (Decca). Other big-selling discs by Tommy Dorsey's Clambake Seven, vocal by Edythe Wright (Victor); Hal Kemp, vocal by Saxie Dowell (Brunswick); Louis Armstrong (Decca); the Boswell Sisters (Decca); Wingy Manone (Vocalion). Performed by Riley and Farley with their Band in (MM) *The Music Goes Round*, 1936; by the Ritz Brothers in (MM) *Sing, Baby, Sing*, 1936; heard in (MM) *Tro-*

cadero, 1944; in (MM) *Holiday in Mexico*, 1946; sung by Danny Kaye and Susan Gordon in (MM) *The Five Pennies*, 1959.

Music in the Night. w. Oscar Hammerstein II, m. Erich Wolfgang Korngold, 1936. Sung by Jan Kiepura and Gladys Swarthout in (MM) *Give Us This Night*.

Music Makers. w. Don Raye, m. Harry James, 1941. Hit instrumental featured and recorded by Harry James and his Orchestra (Columbia).

Music Makes Me. w. Edward Eliscu and Gus Kahn, m. Vincent Youmans, 1933. Introduced by Ginger Rogers in (MM) *Flying Down to Rio*. Recorded by Fred Astaire, coupled with the title song of the first film in which he danced with Rogers (Columbia).

Music Makin' Mama from Memphis. w/m Hank Snow, 1951. Introduced and recorded by C&W star Hank Snow (RCA Victor).

Music Never Stopped, The. w/m John Barlow and Bob Weir, 1975. Recorded by The Grateful Dead (Grateful Dead).

Music of Goodbye, The. w. Alan Bergman and Marilyn Bergman, m. John Barry, 1986. Introduced by Al Jarreau and Melissa Manchester on the soundtrack of (MP) *Out of Africa*.

Music of Home, The. w/m Frank Loesser, 1959. Introduced by Anthony Perkins and Bruce MacKay in (TM) *Greenwillow*.

Music of Love (a.k.a. **The Bell Waltz).** w/m Guy Wood and Donald Voorhees, 1942. Theme song of the radio and television shows, "The Telephone Hour."

Music of the Night, The. w. Charles Hart and Richard Stilgoe, m. Andrew Lloyd Webber, 1988. Introduced in the U.S. by Michael Crawford in the Broadway production of the British musical (TM) *The Phantom of the Opera*.

Music Stopped, The. w. Harold Adamson, m. Jimmy McHugh, 1944. Introduced by Frank Sinatra in (MM) *Higher and Higher*.

Most popular record: Woody Herman, vocal by Frances Wayne (Decca).

Music That Makes Me Dance, The. w. Bob Merrill, m. Jule Styne, 1964. Introduced by Barbra Streisand in (TM) *Funny Girl*. The song was not used in the film version.

Music to Watch Girls By. w. Tony Velona, m. Sid Ramin, 1967. Based on the melody of a Diet Pepsi Cola radio and television jingle. Chart instrumental by The Bob Crewe Generation (Dyno-Voice). Chart vocal version by Andy Williams (Columbia).

Music Went out of My Life, The. w/m Peter Allen, 1988. Introduced by Julie Wilson in (TM) *Legs Diamond*.

Muskrat Love. w/m Willis Alan Ramsey, 1973, 1976. Introduced and chart record by the group, America (Warner Bros.), 1973. Gold record by The Captain and Tennille (A&M), 1976.

Muskrat (or Muskat) Ramble. w. Ray Gilbert, m. Edward "Kid" Ory, 1926. A popular jazz instrumental to which Gilbert added a lyric, 1950. Among the many recordings are those by Louis Armstrong (Okeh) (Decca), Bob Crosby (Decca), Eddie DeLange (Bluebird), Roy Eldridge (Varsity), Jimmy Dorsey (Columbia). More recent chart versions by The McGuire Sisters (Coral), 1954, and Freddy Cannon (Swan), 1961.

Mustang Sally. w/m Bonny Rice, 1966. Top 40 record by Wilson Pickett (Atlantic).

Must of Got Lost. w/m Seth Justman and Peter Wolf, 1974. Written by two members of The J. Geils Band. Top 20 record (Atlantic).

Must to Avoid, A. w/m P. F. Sloan and Steve Barri, 1966. Introduced in (MM) *Hold On!* and Top 10 record by Herman's Hermits (MGM).

Must We Say Goodnight So Soon? w/m Dorothy Dick, Nick Kenny, and Al Vann, 1934. Featured and recorded by the orchestras of Russ Morgan (Melotone) and Richard Himber (Victor), and singer Eddie Stone (Bluebird).

Mutiny in the Nursery. w/m Johnny Mercer, 1938. Sung by Louis Armstrong, Maxine Sullivan, Dick Powell, and Anita Louise in (MM) *Going Places.*

Mutiny in the Parlor. w. Edward Heyman, m. Vee Lawnhurst, 1936.

Mutual Admiration Society. w. Matt Dubey, m. Harold Carr, 1956. Introduced by Ethel Merman and Virginia Gibson in (TM) *Happy Hunting.* Popular records by Teresa Brewer (Coral), Eddy Arnold and Jaye P. Morgan (RCA).

My, How the Time Goes By. w. Harold Adamson, m. Jimmy McHugh, 1948. Introduced by Eddie Cantor in (MM) *If You Knew Suzie.*

My! My! w. Frank Loesser, m. Jimmy McHugh, 1940. Sung by Eddie "Rochester" Anderson in (MM) *Buck Benny Rides Again,* starring Jack Benny, and on records (Columbia). Among other versions: Glenn Miller, vocal by Marion Hutton (Bluebird); Tommy Dorsey, vocal by Jo Stafford and The Pied Pipers (Victor); Horace Heidt (Columbia).

My Adobe Hacienda. w/m Louise Massey and Lee Penny, 1947. First recorded by Louise Massey and The Westerners (Okeh), 1941. Song became hit in 1947 when Massey re-recorded it (Columbia). Biggest seller, however, was by Eddy Howard with his Orchestra (Majestic). Others: Dinning Sisters (Capitol), Billy Williams Quartet (RCA Victor), Kenny Baker, with Russ Morgan's Orchestra (Decca).

My Angel. See **Angela Mia.**

My Angel Baby. w/m Johnny Northern, 1978. Recorded by the quintet Toby Beau (RCA).

My Angeline. w. L. Wolfe Gilbert, m. Mabel Wayne, 1929. Introduced on radio and recorded by Frank Munn (Columbia). Also recorded by the Mississippi Maulers (Columbia) and the band of Henry Thies (Victor).

My Angeline. w. Harry B. Smith, m. Victor Herbert, 1895. Introduced in (TM) *The Wizard of the Nile.*

My Attorney, Bernie. w/m David Frishberg, 1982. Novelty, featured and recorded by Dave Frishberg in his LP, "The Dave Frishberg Songbook, Volume Two" (Omnisound).

My Babe. w/m Neil Diamond, 1967. Recorded by Ronnie Dove (Diamond).

My Babe. w/m Willie Dixon, 1955. #1 R&B hit by Little Walter (Checker).

My Baby. w/m Warren Moore, William Robinson, and Robert Rogers, 1965. Recorded by The Temptations (Gordy).

My Baby Just Cares for Me. w. Gus Kahn, m. Walter Donaldson, 1930. Introduced by Eddie Cantor in (MM) *Whoopee* and recorded by him (Victor). The song was heard in (MP) *Big City Blues,* 1932, starring Joan Blondell. Among recordings: Isham Jones (Brunswick), Smith Ballew (Okeh), Ted Weems, vocal by Art Jarrett. Later recordings: Joni James (MGM), Harry Cool (Mercury), Maurice Chevalier (MGM), Mel Tormé (Musicraft), Count Basie, vocal by Joe Williams (Polygram).

My Baby Left Me. w/m Arthur Crudup, 1956. First recorded by Arthur "Big Boy" Crudup (RCA Victor), 1950. It was coupled with "I Want You, I Need You, I Love You," (q.v.) a #1 hit record by Elvis Presley (RCA).

My Baby Loves Lovin'. w/m Roger Cook and Roger Greenaway, 1970. Recorded in England by White Plains, produced by the writers (Deram).

My Baby Loves Me. w/m Ivy Hunter, Sylvia Moy, and William Stevenson, 1966. Recorded by Martha and The Vandellas (Gordy).

My Baby Must Be a Magician. w/m William Robinson, 1968. Top 20 record by The Marvelettes (Tamla).

My Baby Said Yes. w/m Sid Robin, 1945. Introduced by Bob Haymes [appearing under the name of Bob Stanton] and Lynn Merrick in (MM) *Blonde from Brooklyn*. Popular records by Bing Crosby and Louis Jordan, with Jordan's Tympany Five (Decca); Charlie Spivak, vocal by Irene Daye (Victor).

My Baby's Arms. w. Joseph McCarthy, m. Harry Tierney, 1919. From (TM) *Ziegfeld Follies of 1919*.

My Baby's Coming Home. w/m William G. Leavitt, John C. Grady, and Sherm Feller, 1952. Popularized by Les Paul and Mary Ford (Capitol).

My Baby's Gone. w/m Hazel Houser, 1959. Leading C&W record by The Louvin Brothers (Capitol).

My Baby Walks All over Me. w/m Billy Mize, 1964. Country chart record by Johnny Sea (Philips).

My Back Pages. w/m Bob Dylan, 1964. Introduced and recorded by Bob Dylan (Columbia). Top 40 record by the folk-rock group The Byrds (Columbia), 1967.

My Beautiful Lady (Kiss Waltz). w. C. M. S. McLellan, m. Ivan Caryll, 1911. Introduced by William Elliott in (TM) *The Pink Lady*. This song was heard in Act III. "Kiss Waltz," with same melody, was heard in Act I (q.v.).

My Belgian Rose. w/m George Benoit, Robert Levenson and Ted Garton, 1918.

My Believing Heart. w/m Jimmy Crane and Al Jacobs, 1955. Leading recording by Joni James (MGM).

My Beloved. w/m Jay Livingston and Ray Evans, 1951. Introduced by Robert Merrill in (MM) *Aaron Slick from Punkin Crick*.

My Best Friend's Girl. w/m Ric Ocasek, 1978. Recorded by The Cars (Elektra).

My Best Girl. w/m Jerry Herman, 1966. Introduced by Frankie Michaels and Angela Lansbury in (TM) *Mame*. It was performed by Kirby Furlong and Lucille Ball in the film version, *Mame*, 1974.

My Best Girl. w/m Walter Donaldson, 1924. Featured and recorded by Georgie Price (Victor). Also recorded by Isham Jones and his Orchestra (Brunswick), Nick Lucas (Brunswick), Cliff Edwards (Path).

My Best Girl's a New Yorker (Corker). w/m John Stromberg, 1895. Both titles were used in this song, introduced by Lottie Gilson in her vaudeville act, said to be the first time a stooge in the balcony became part of a performer's routine.

My Bird of Paradise. w/m Irving Berlin, 1915. Featured by Blossom Seeley in vaudeville. Hit record by The Peerless Quartet (Victor).

My Blackbirds Are Bluebirds Now. w. Irving Caesar, m. Cliff Friend, 1928. Interpolated in (TM) *Whoopee*, during the run, by Eddie Cantor. George Jessel sang it in (MM) *Lucky Boy*, 1929. Recorded by Ruth Etting (Columbia) and Jean Goldkette (Victor).

My Blue Heaven. w. George Whiting, m. Walter Donaldson, 1927. Introduced two years earlier in vaudeville by George Whiting, but it was not until Eddie Cantor interpolated it in (TM) *Ziegfeld Follies of 1927* that it attained popularity. Gene Austin's recording (Victor) sold over five million copies and was the all-time best-seller until Bing Crosby's "White Christmas" fifteen years later. It was sung by Frances Langford in (MM) *Never a Dull Moment*, 1943; heard in (MM) *Moon Over Las Vegas*, 1944; sung as the title song in (MM) *My Blue Heaven* by Betty Grable and Dan Dailey, 1950; heard in the background in the Ruth Etting Story (MM) *Love Me or Leave Me*, 1955. Bob Crosby sang it in (MM) *The Five Pennies*, 1959. Fats Domino had a hit record (Imperial), 1956.

My Blue Ridge Mountain Home. w/m Carson J. Robison, 1927. Best-selling record by Vernon Dalhart (Victor). Dalhart also recorded it with Charlie Wells (Columbia).

My Bolero. w. Jimmy Kennedy, m. Nat Simon, 1949. Popular record by Vic Damone, with Glen Osser's Orchestra (Mercury).

My Bonnie Lassie. w/m Roy Bennett, Sid Tepper, and Marion McClurg, 1955. First published in Scotland. U.S. hit by The Ames Brothers (RCA Victor).

My Boomerang Won't Come Back. w/m Charlie Drake and Max Diamond, 1962. British novelty record by Charlie Drake (United Artists).

My Boy. w. Philip Coulter and Bill Martin (Engl.), m. Jean Bourtayre and Claude Francois, 1971. French song, lyrics by Yves Levot. Popular recordings by Richard Harris (Dunhill) and Elvis Presley (RCA), 1975.

My Boy—Flat Top. w/m John F. Young, Jr. and Boyd Bennett, 1955. Introduced by Boyd Bennett and His Rockets, vocal by Big Moe (King). Dorothy Collins had a Top 20 record (Coral).

My Boyfriend's Back. w/m Robert Feldman, Gerald Goldstein, and Richard Gottehrer, 1963. #1 hit record by The Angels (Smash).

My Boy Lollipop. w/m Johnny Roberts, Robert Spencer, and Morris Levy, 1964. Top 10 record by Millie Small (Smash).

My Buddy. w. Gus Kahn, m. Walter Donaldson, 1922. The first of over 100 songs written by this team and one of two smash hits in their first year of collaboration. The other was "Carolina in the Morning" (q.v.) The song was played by accompanying pianists to the showings of the hit silent film (MP) *Wings*, 1927, starring Clara Bow, Buddy Rogers, and Richard Arlen. It later became the theme song of Buddy Rogers's Orchestra. It served as the title song of (MP) *My Buddy*, 1944, in which it was sung by Donald Barry. Doris Day sang it in the film bio of Kahn, (MM) *I'll See You in My Dreams*, 1951.

My Cabin of Dreams. w/m Nat Madison, Al Frazzini, Charles Kenny, and Nick Kenny, 1937. Recorded by Frances Langford (Decca), Dick Robertson (Decca), Gus Arnheim (Brunswick), George Hall (Vocalion).

My Castle in Spain. w/m Isham Jones, 1926. Introduced by Dorothy Hurst in (TM) *By the Way*. Recorded by Frank Munn (Columbia), Van and Schenck (Victor), Isham Jones and his Orchestra (Brunswick).

My Castle on the Nile. w. James Weldon Johnson and Bob Cole, m. J. Rosamond Johnson, 1901. Comedy song featured by the team of Cole and Johnson [J. Rosamond], and Bert Williams in vaudeville.

My Cherie Amour. w/m Stevie Wonder, Henry Cosby, and Sylvia Moy, 1969. Top 10 record by Stevie Wonder (Tamla).

My Coloring Book. w. Fred Ebb, m. John Kander, 1962. Introduced by Kaye Ballard in nightclubs. Song made its national debut when sung by Sandy Stewart on (TVM) "The Perry Como Show." Stewart recorded it (Colpix), as did Kitty Kallen (RCA) and Barbra Streisand (Columbia).

My Cousin Carus'. w. Edward Madden, m. Gus Edwards, 1909. The success of the famous tenor Enrico Caruso was the inspiration for this song, which contained a strain of "Vesti la giubba" from *I Pagliacci*. It was interpolated in (TM) *Ziegfeld Follies of 1909*.

My Cousin in Milwaukee. w. Ira Gershwin, m. George Gershwin, 1933. Introduced by Lyda Roberti in (TM) *Pardon My English*, starring Jack Pearl. Ramona, with Roy Bargy's Orchestra, had a popular record (Victor).

My Cousin Louella. w/m Bernard Bierman and Jack Manus, 1947. Popular recording by Frank Sinatra, with instrumental trio (Columbia).

My Creole Sue. w/m Gussie L. Davis, 1898.

My Cup Runneth Over. w. Tom Jones, m. Harvey Schmidt, 1966. Introduced by Mary Martin and Robert Preston in (TM) *I Do! I Do!* Hit record by Ed Ames (RCA), 1967.

My Cutie's Due at Two to Two Today. w/m Albert Von Tilzer, Irving Bibo, and Leo Robin, 1926. Leading records by Jones [Billy] and

Hare [Ernie] (Columbia), Ted Weems's Orchestra, with vocal by Parker Gibbs (Victor), and Betty Hutton (Capitol).

My Dad. w/m Barry Mann and Cynthia Weil, 1962. Top 10 record by Paul Peterson (Colpix).

My Daddy Is Only a Picture. w/m Tommy Dilbeck, 1948. Eddy Arnold had a best-seller with this ballad (RCA Victor).

My Dancing Lady. w. Dorothy Fields, m. Jimmy McHugh, 1933. Introduced by Art Jarrett, singing, and Joan Crawford, dancing, in (MM) *Dancing Lady.*

My Darling. w. Edward Heyman, m. Richard Myers, 1932. Introduced by John Hale and Josephine Huston in (TM) *Earl Carroll Vanities, 10th Edition.*

My Darling, My Darling. w/m Frank Loesser, 1948. Introduced by Byron Palmer and Doretta Morrow in (TM) *Where's Charley?* Top recordings by Doris Day and Buddy Clark (Columbia), Jo Stafford and Gordon MacRae (Capitol), Peter Lind Hayes (Decca), Eve Young [Karen Chandler] and Jack Lathrop (RCA Victor). In the 1952 film version (MM) *Where's Charley?* it was sung by Robert Shackleton and Mary Germaine.

My Dearest Darling. w/m Paul Gayten and E. Bocage, 1960. Recorded by Etta James (Argo).

My Defenses Are Down. w/m Irving Berlin, 1946. Introduced by Ray Middleton in (TM) *Annie Get Your Gun.* It was sung by Howard Keel in the film version (MM) *Annie Get Your Gun,* 1950.

My Destiny. w. Sammy Cahn, m. Nicholas Brodsky, 1956. Introduced by Mario Lanza in (MM) *Serenade.*

My Devotion. w/m Roc Hillman and Johnny Napton, 1942. No. 1 record by Vaughn Monroe, vocal by Monroe (Victor). Other popular versions by the bands of Charlie Spivak, vocal by Garry Stevens (Columbia); Jimmy

Dorsey, vocal by Bob Eberly (Decca); The King Sisters, with Alvino Rey (Bluebird).

My Ding-A-Ling. w/m Chuck Berry, 1972. #1 gold record novelty by Chuck Berry (Chess).

My Dirty Stream (The Hudson River Song). w/m Pete Seeger, 1964. Written and introduced by Pete Seeger as an environmental admonishment.

My Dream Girl. w. Rida Johnson Young, m. Victor Herbert, 1924. Introduced by Walter Woolf in (TM) *The Dream Girl.* Herbert died three months before the show opened in New York.

My Dream Is Yours. w. Ralph Blane, m. Harry Warren, 1949. Introduced by Doris Day in (MM) *My Dream Is Yours.*

My Dream of the Big Parade. w. Al Dubin, m. Jimmy McHugh, 1926. Written as a promotional song for the silent film (MP) *The Big Parade.*

My Dreams Are Getting Better All the Time. w. Mann Curtis, m. Vic Mizzy, 1945. Introduced by Marion Hutton in (MM) *In Society,* starring Abbott and Costello. #1 record by Les Brown, vocal by Doris Day (Columbia). Others: Johnny Long, vocal by Dick Robertson (Decca); The Phil Moore Four, vocal by Moore and Billy Daniels (Victor).

My Dream Sonata. w. Mack David, m. James Van Heusen, 1956. Featured and recorded by Nat "King" Cole (Capitol).

My Dreamy China Lady. w. Gus Kahn, m. Egbert Van Alstyne, 1906. This was Kahn's first song to gain public acceptance.

My Ears Should Burn (When Fools Are Talked About). w/m Roger Miller, 1961. C&W chart hit by Claude Gray (Mercury).

My Elusive Dreams. w/m Curly Putman and Billy Sherrill, 1967. C&W/Pop hit by David Houston and Tammy Wynette (Epic). Revived by Bobby Vinton (Epic), 1970, and Charlie Rich (RCA), 1975.

My Empty Arms. w/m (adapted) Al Kasha and Hank Hunter, 1961. Based on an aria from Leoncavallo's opera *I Pagliacci*. Hit record by Jackie Wilson (Brunswick).

My Ever Changing Moods. w/m Paul Weller, 1984. Recorded by the English duo The Style Council (Geffen).

My Everything. w/m Marvin Lacy and Jim Wilson, 1954. Top 10 record by Eddy Arnold (RCA).

My Extraordinary Gal. w/m Terry Shand, 1931. Shand's first hit was introduced and featured by Guy Lombardo and the Royal Canadians (Brunswick).

My Eyes Adored You. w/m Bob Crewe and Kenny Nolan, 1975. #1 gold record by Frankie Valli (Private Stock).

My Eyes Can Only See As Far As You. w/m Naomi Martin and Jimmy Payne, 1976. Hit Country chart record by Charley Pride (RCA).

My Fair Lady. w/m Bob Hilliard and Carl Sigman, 1948. Popular record by Vic Damone, with Glen Osser's Orchestra (Mercury).

My Fair Share. w. Paul Williams, m. Charles Fox, 1977. Love theme of (MP) *One on One*, sung by Seals & Crofts on the soundtrack and on records (Warner Bros.).

My Faithful Stradivari. w. C. C. S. Cushing and E. P. Heath, m. Emmerich Kallman, 1913. From (TM) *Sari*.

My Fantasy. w/m Gene Griffin and William Aquart, 1989. From (MP) *Do the Right Thing*. Hit R&B chart single by Teddy Riley, featuring Guy (Motown).

My Fate Is in Your Hands. w. Andy Razaf, m. Thomas "Fats" Waller, 1929. Recordings by Guy Lombardo (Columbia), Gene Austin (Victor), Nat Shilkret (Victor), and Arthur Schutt (Okeh) and many radio performances made this a hit.

My Favorite Things. w. Oscar Hammerstein II, m. Richard Rodgers, 1959. Introduced by Patricia Neway and Mary Martin in (TM) *The Sound of Music*. Julie Andrews sang it in the film version (MM) *The Sound of Music*, 1965. Chart instrumental version by Herb Alpert and The Tijuana Brass (A&M), 1969.

My Filipino Rose. w/m C. E. Rose, 1949. Recorded by Country singer Ernest Tubb (Decca).

My Fine Feathered Friend. w. Harold Adamson, m. Jimmy McHugh, 1937. Sung by Alice Faye in (MM) *You're a Sweetheart*.

My First and Last Love. w. Remus Harris, m. Marvin Fisher, 1951. Music adapted from "The Young Prince and The Young Princess" theme from *Scheherezade* by Rimsky-Korsakoff. Recorded by Nat "King" Cole (Capitol).

My First Impression of You. w. Charles Tobias, m. Sam H. Stept, 1938. Among recordings: Fats Waller (Victor); Jimmy Dorsey and his Orchestra (Decca); Teddy Wilson (Brunswick); Dick Stabile, vocal by Paula Kelly (Bluebird); Pinky Tomlin (Brunswick).

My First Love Song. w/m Leslie Bricusse and Anthony Newley, 1964. Introduced by Anthony Newley and Joyce Jillson in (TM) *The Roar of the Greasepaint—The Smell of the Crowd*.

My Flaming Heart. w. Leo Robin, m. Nicholas Brodsky, 1953. Introduced by Nat Cole in (MM) *Small Time Girl*. Nominated for Academy Award, 1953.

My Foolish Heart. w. Ned Washington, m. Victor Young, 1949. Introduced by Susan Hayward in (MP) *My Foolish Heart*. Nominated for Academy Award. Billy Eckstine had a million-selling record (Mercury). Other hit versions by Gordon Jenkins, vocal by Eileen Wilson (Decca); Mindy Carson (RCA Victor).

My Forever Love. w/m Gerald Levert and Marc Gordon, 1987. Top 10 R&B chart record by the trio Levert (Atlantic).

My Friend. w/m Ervin Drake and Jimmy Shirl, 1954. Popular record by Eddie Fisher (RCA Victor).

My Friend, the Major. w/m E. W. Rogers, 1894.

My Friend on the Right. w/m Red Lane and Faron Young, 1964. Hit record by Country music star Faron Young (Mercury).

My Friends Are Gonna Be Strangers. w/m Liz Anderson, 1965. Country hit by Merle Haggard (Tally) and Roy Drusky (Mercury).

My Funny Valentine. w. Lorenz Hart, m. Richard Rodgers, 1937. Introduced by Mitzi Green in (TM) *Babes in Arms*. The song was not used in the film version but was interpolated in (MM) *Gentlemen Marry Brunettes* by Alan Young and Anita Ellis, the latter dubbing for Jeanne Crain, 1955. It was interpolated in (MM) *Pal Joey* by Trudy Erwin, dubbing for Kim Novak, 1957.

My Future Just Passed. w. George Marion, Jr., m. Richard A. Whiting, 1930. Sung by Charles "Buddy" Rogers in (MM) *Safety in Numbers* and recorded by him (Columbia).

My Future Star. w. Sidney Clare, m. Richard A. Whiting, 1934. Introduced by Alice Faye in (MM) *365 Nights in Hollywood*. Faye's recording was her first solo single (Melotone).

My Gal Is a High Born Lady. w/m Barney Fagan, 1896. A ragtime classic, it was introduced by Charles Ernest Haverly of Haverly's Minstrels and popularized by Clara Wieland.

My Gal Sal (or They Called Her Frivolous Sal). w/m Paul Dresser, 1905. Dresser's last hit, which became a two million-copy seller after his death. It was sung by Bobby Gordon, as the thirteen-year-old Jakie in (MM) *The Jazz Singer*, 1927. As the title song of the Dresser film biography (MM) *My Gal Sal*, it was sung by Nan Wynn, dubbing for Rita Hayworth, 1942.

My Galveston Gal. w/m Basil G. Adlam, 1933. Featured on radio and records by Harry Reser's Orchestra (Columbia). The band of Allen [Henry "Red"]-Hawkins [Coleman] also recorded it (Perfect).

My Generation. w/m Peter Townshend, 1966. Chart record by the British group, The Who, of which Townshend was a member (Decca).

My Girl. w/m William Robinson and Ronald White, 1965. Crossover (R&B/Pop) record, #1 on both charts, by The Temptations, produced by co-writer Smokey Robinson. Song is stepsister of "My Guy," which was sired by Robinson. Revivals: Bobby Vee in medley with "Hey, Girl" (Liberty), 1968; Daryl Hall, John Oates, with David Ruffin and Eddie Kendrick recorded it at the reopening of the Apollo Theatre in Harlem, N.Y. in a medley of two Temptations hits, which became a Top 20 single titled "A Nite at The Apollo Live! The Way You Do the Things You Do/My Girl" (RCA).

My Girl (Gone, Gone, Gone). w/m Bill Henderson and Brian McLeod, 1981. Recorded by the Canadian group Chilliwack (Millennium).

My Girl Bill. w/m Jim Stafford, 1974. Top 20 novelty record by Jim Stafford (MGM).

My Girl Has Gone. w/m Warren Moore, William Robinson, Marv Tarplin, and Ronald White, 1965. Recorded by The Miracles (Tamla).

My Girl Josephine. w/m Antoine "Fats" Domino and Dave Bartholomew, 1960. Hit record by Fats Domino (Imperial). Revived by Jerry Jaye (Hi), 1967.

My Girl Sloopy. See **Hang On Sloopy**.

My Greatest Mistake. w/m Jack Fulton and Jack O'Brien, 1940. A top 20 hit on its own, it was coupled with the #1 hit "We Three," by the Ink Spots (Decca).

My Guiding Star. w. Thurland Chattaway, m. Jean Schwartz, 1905.

My Guitar Is My Sweetheart. w/m Alfio Bargnesi and David Rhodes, 1947. Recorded by The Air Lane Trio, vocal by Ted Martin (DeLuxe).

My Guy. w/m William Robinson, 1964. #1 crossover hit (R&B/Pop) by Mary Wells, produced by William "Smokey" Robinson (Motown). Revived by Petula Clark (MGM), 1972, and Sister Sledge (Cotillion), 1982. Amii Stewart and Johnny Bristol combined it with "My Girl," of which Robinson was co-writer/producer (Handshake), 1980.

My Guy's Come Back. w. Ray McKinley, m. Mel Powell, 1945. Based on an instrumental Powell wrote and arranged for Glenn Miller's Air Force band of which he and McKinley were members. Powell arranged the new version, which was introduced and recorded by Benny Goodman, vocal by Liza Morrow (Columbia). Other recordings by Dinah Shore, with Russ Case's Orchestra (Victor); Helen Forrest (Decca) Thelma Carpenter (Majestic).

My Hang Up Is You. w/m Freddie Hart, 1972. Country hit by Freddie Hart (Capitol).

My Happiness. w. Betty Peterson, m. Borney Bergantine, 1948. This fifteen-year-old song became a #1, million-selling record for Jon and Sandra Steele (Damon). The recording by The Pied Pipers, with Paul Weston's Orchestra, also sold a million copies (Capitol). Ella Fitzgerald, with The Song Spinners, had a chart record (Decca). Revived by The Mulcays, a harmonica group (Cardinal), 1953, and by Connie Francis, who had a Top 10 recording (MGM), 1958.

My Happiness Forever. w/m Doc Pomus, 1956. Recorded by LaVern Baker (Atlantic).

My Hat's on the Side of My Head. w/m Harry Woods and Claude Hurlburt, 1933. First published in England. Two British recordings were well-received in the U.S., one by Ray Noble and his Band, with vocal by Freddy Gardner (Victor), the other by the American-born, London-based bandleader, Roy Fox (Brunswick).

My Hawaiian Sunrise. w/m L. Wolfe Gilbert and Carey Morgan, 1916. Leading recording by Henry Burr and Albert Campbell (Victor).

My Heart. w/m Don Pfrimmer and Charles Quillen, 1980. #1 Country chart record by Ronnie Milsap (RCA).

My Heart and I. w. Leo Robin, m. Frederick Hollander, 1936. Introduced in (MM) *Anything Goes* and recorded (Decca) by Bing Crosby.

My Heart Belongs to Daddy. w/m Cole Porter, 1938. Introduced by Mary Martin in (TM) *Leave It to Me*, in her Broadway debut. She then recorded it with Eddy Duchin's Orchestra (Brunswick). The best-selling record was Larry Clinton's, with vocal by Bea Wain (Victor). Mary Martin sang it in (MM) *Love Thy Neighbor*, 1940, and in the Porter story (MM) *Night and Day*, 1946. Another MM, Marilyn Monroe, sang it in (MM) *Let's Make Love*, 1960.

My Heart Belongs to Me. w/m Alan Gordon, 1977. Top 10 single by Barbra Streisand (Columbia).

My Heart Belongs to Only You. w/m Frank Daniels and Dorothy Daniels, 1953, 1964. First recording by Betty McLaurin (Derby). Popular version by June Christy, with Pete Rugolo's Orchestra (Capitol). Revived by Bobby Vinton, with a Top 10 record (Epic), 1964.

My Heart Belongs to You. w/m Arbee Stidham, 1948. #1 Country chart record by Arbee Stidham (Victor).

My Heart Can't Tell You No. w/m Simon Climie and Dennis Morgan, 1989. Hit record by Rod Stewart (Warner Bros.).

My Heart Cries for You. w/m Carl Sigman and Percy Faith, 1950. Adapted from an eighteenth-century French folk melody "Chanson de Marie Antoinette." Guy Mitchell's recording with Mitch Miller's Orchestra (Columbia) became his first million seller. Other Top 10 records by Dinah Shore (RCA Victor) and Vic Damone (Mercury).

My Heart Goes a-Gadding. w/m Larry Morey, 1950. Popular record by Jerry Wayne, with The Dell Trio (Columbia).

My Heart Goes Crazy. w. Johnny Burke, m. James Van Heusen, 1946. Featured and recorded by Paula Kelly and The Modernaires (Columbia), Charlie Spivak and his Orchestra (Victor), Pinky Tomlin (University).

My Heart Has a Mind of Its Own. w. Howard Greenfield, m. Jack Keller, 1960. Leading record by Connie Francis (MGM).

My Heart Has Learned to Love You, Now Do Not Say Goodbye. w. Dave Reed, m. Ernest R. Ball, 1910.

My Heart Is a Hobo. w. Johnny Burke, m. James Van Heusen, 1947. Introduced by Bing Crosby in (MM) *Welcome Stranger*. Records: Crosby (Decca), Tex Beneke and The Glenn Miller Band, vocal by the Mello-Larks (RCA Victor).

My Heart Is an Open Book. w. Hal David, m. Lee Pockriss, 1959. Top 10 record by Carl Dobkins, Jr. (Decca).

My Heart Is an Open Book. w/m Mack Gordon, 1935. Introduced by Joe Morrison in (MM) *Love in Bloom*.

My Heart Isn't in It. w/m Jack Lawrence, 1942. Among recordings: Charlie Barnet and his Orchestra (Decca) and Eddy Howard (Mercury). Interpolated in (MM) *Stars on Parade*, 1944.

My Heart Is Showing (Don't Look Now, But). w. Ann Ronell, m. Kurt Weill, 1948. Introduced by Ava Gardner (voice dubbed by Eileen Wilson), Dick Haymes, Robert Walker, and Olga San Juan in (MM) *One Touch of Venus*. In the original stage production a different lyric was sung. See also "Foolish Heart."

My Heart Is Singing. w. Gus Kahn, m. Bronislaw Kaper and Walter Jurmann, 1937. Sung by Deanna Durbin in her first feature film (MM) *Three Smart Girls*.

My Heart Is So Full of You. w/m Frank Loesser, 1956. Introduced by Robert Weede in (TM) *The Most Happy Fella*.

My Heart Is Taking Lessons. w. Johnny Burke, m. James V. Monaco, 1938. Introduced by Bing Crosby in (MM) *Doctor Rhythm*, and recorded by him with John Scott Trotter's Orchestra (Decca).

My Heart Reminds Me. See **And That Reminds Me.**

My Heart Sings. See **All of a Sudden My Heart Sings.**

My Heart Skips a Beat. w/m Buck Owens, 1964. Crossover [C&W/Pop] hit by Buck Owens (Capitol).

My Heart's Symphony. w/m Glen D. Hardin, 1966. Hit record by Gary Lewis and The Playboys (Liberty).

My Heart Still Clings to the Old First Love. w/m Paul Dresser, 1901.

My Heart Stood Still. w. Lorenz Hart, m. Richard Rodgers, 1927. The song was introduced in the London revue (TM) *One Dam Thing After Another*, by Jessie Matthews and Richard Dolman. Later in the year, it was introduced in the American musical (TM) *A Connecticut Yankee*, by William Gaxton and Constance Carpenter. It was played as background music in the Rodgers and Hart biography (MM) *Words and Music*, 1948.

My Heart Tells Me. w. Mack Gordon, m. Harry Warren, 1943. Introduced by Betty Grable in (MM) *Sweet Rosie O'Grady*. #1 hit record by Glen Gray and the Casa Loma Orchestra, vocal by Eugenie Baird (Hit).

My Heart Won't Say Goodbye. w. Leo Robin, m. Sigmund Romberg, 1954. Introduced by David Atkinson in (TM) *The Girl in Pink Tights*.

My Hero. w. Stanislaus Stange, m. Oscar Straus, 1909. Sung by Ida Brooks Hunt in (TM) *The Chocolate Soldier*. The song was also heard in the film version (MM) *The Chocolate Soldier* in 1941 and in (MM) *Two Weeks with Love*, 1950.

My Heroes Have Always Been Cowboys. w/m Sharon Vaughan, 1980. Introduced by

Willie Nelson in (MP) *The Electric Horseman,* and on records (Columbia).

My Hometown. w/m Bruce Springsteen, 1984. Top 10 single (1986) from the album by Bruce Springsteen "Born in the U.S.A." (Columbia).

My Home Town. w/m Ervin Drake, 1964. Introduced by Steve Lawrence in (TM) *What Makes Sammy Run?* and on records (Columbia).

My Home Town. w/m Paul Anka, 1960. Introduced and recorded by Paul Anka (ABC-Paramount).

My Home Town Is a One Horse Town (But It's Big Enough for Me). w. Alex Gerber, m. Abner Silver, 1920. Silver's first song success, featured in vaudeville by Van & Schenck.

My Honey Lou. w/m Thurland Chattaway, 1904.

My Honey's Lovin' Arms. w. Herman Ruby, m. Joseph Meyer, 1922. Isham Jones had a hit recording (Brunswick) of this jazz song, which was Meyer's first success. Many bands, such as the Original Memphis Five (Columbia), Red Nichols (Brunswick), Benny Goodman (Victor), Duke Ellington (Victor), and Red Nichols, on a 12″ V-disc [in W.W.II], recorded it. It was revived by Barbra Streisand (Columbia), 1963.

My Idaho Home. w/m Ronnie Blakely, 1975. Introduced by Ronnie Blakely in (MM) *Nashville.*

My Ideal. w. Leo Robin, m. Richard A. Whiting and Newell Chase, 1930. Introduced by Maurice Chevalier in (MM) *Playboy of Paris* and recorded by him (Victor). Isham Jones also had a popular release (Brunswick). In 1943, the composer's daughter, Margaret Whiting, had a hit record (Capitol).

My Irish Molly O. w. William Jerome, m. Jean Schwartz, 1905. Interpolated by Blanche Ring in the Broadway production of the English hit (TM) *Sergeant Brue.* Ring again interpolated it in (TM) *His Honor, The Mayor,* 1906. Popular recordings by Arthur Collins (Victor), Billy Murray (Edison), Harry Tally (Columbia), banjoist Vern Ossman (Victor).

My Isle of Golden Dreams. w. Gus Kahn, m. Walter Blaufuss, 1919. First known recording, Ben Selvin's Orchestra (Victor). The song became the theme song of Phil Spitalny and his All-Girl Orchestra on radio's "Hour of Charm" in the thirties and forties. Popular recordings by Glenn Miller and his Orchestra (Bluebird) and Bing Crosby (Decca), 1939.

My Jealous Eyes (That Turned from Blue to Green). w. Mack David, m. Martita (Margery S. Wolpin), 1953. Leading record by Patti Page (Mercury).

My Kinda Love. w. Jo Trent, m. Louis Alter, 1929. Bing Crosby sang this on his first solo record (Columbia). Also recorded by the Dorsey Brothers (Okeh) and Ben Pollack (Victor).

My Kind of Girl. w/m Leslie Bricusse, 1961. Hit record from England by Matt Monro (Warwick).

My Kind of Town (Chicago Is). w. Sammy Cahn, m. James Van Heusen, 1964. Introduced by Frank Sinatra in (MP) *Robin and the Seven Hoods,* and recorded by him (Reprise). Nominated for Academy Award.

My Kingdom for a Kiss. w/m Al Dubin, Harry Warren, and David Ormont, 1936. Introduced by Dick Powell in (MM) *Hearts Divided,* which co-starred Marion Davies. Powell recorded it, coupled with "Two Hearts Divided" from the same film (Decca).

My Lady Loves to Dance. w/m Sammy Gallop and Milton De Lugg, 1953. Featured and recorded by Julius La Rosa (Cadence).

My Last Affair. w/m Haven Johnson, 1936. Introduced by Billie Haywood in (TM) *New Faces of 1934,* but it did not become popular until this year when Jimmie Lunceford and his Band, with Dan Grissom doing the vocal, recorded it (Decca). The following year, the song was firmly established via recordings by Mildred Bailey (Vocalion), Teddy Wilson (Brunswick), Ella Fitzgerald (Decca), Lionel Hampton (Victor). Later records by Herbie Steward (Roost) and Gerald Wilson and his big band (United Artists).

My Last Date (with You). w. Boudleaux Bryant and Skeeter Davis, m. Floyd Cramer, 1961. Popular records by Skeeter Davis (RCA) and Joni James (MGM). See also "Last Date."

My Last Goodbye. w/m Eddy Howard, 1939. Introduced and recorded by Dick Jurgens, vocal by Eddy Howard (Vocalion).

My Last Love. w. Alan Jay Lerner, m. Frederick Loewe, 1943. Introduced in Lerner and Loewe's first Broadway show, (TM) *What's Up*, by Mary Roche, Larry Douglas, Lynn Gardner, Johnny Morgan, and William Tabbert.

My Life. w/m Billy Joel, 1978. Gold record by Billy Joel (Columbia).

My Life. w/m Bill Anderson, 1969. Country hit recorded by Bill Anderson (Decca).

My Lips Are Sealed. w/m Ben Weisman, Hal Blair, and Bill Peppers, 1956. Leading record by Jim Reeves (RCA).

My Little Bimbo Down on the Bamboo Isle. w. Grant Clarke, m. Walter Donaldson, 1920. Interpolated by Aileen Stanley in (TM) *Silks and Satins*. Featured and recorded by Frank Crumit (Columbia). Revived in the sixties by Burl Ives (Decca).

My Little Buckaroo. w. Jack Scholl, m. M. K. Jerome, 1937. Interpolated in (MP) *Cherokee Strip* by Dick Foran, 1940; by Roy Rogers in (MM) *Ridin' Down the Canyon*, 1942, and again by Rogers in (MM) *Don't Fence Me In*, 1945.

My Little Buttercup. w/m Randy Newman, 1987. Introduced by Randy Newman on the soundtrack of (MP) *Three Amigos* and the ensuing soundtrack album (Warner Bros.).

My Little Corner of the World. w. Bob Hilliard, m. Lee Pockriss, 1960. Recorded by Anita Bryant (Carlton).

My Little Cousin. w/m Happy Lewis, Sam Braverman, and Cy Coben, 1942. Recorded by Martha Raye (Decca); the orchestras of Benny Goodman, vocal by Peggy Lee (Okeh); Vaughn Monroe (Bluebird); Bunny Berigan (Elite).

My Little Georgia Rose. w. Robert F. Rosen, m. Max S. Witt, 1899.

My Little Girl. w. Sam M. Lewis and Will Dillon, m. Albert Von Tilzer, 1915. Popular records by the duets of Henry Burr and Albert Campbell (Victor), and Ada Jones and Will Robbins (Columbia).

My Little Grass Shack (in Kealakakua, Hawaii). w/m Billy Cogswell, Tom Harrison, and Johnny Noble, 1934. Featured and recorded by Ted Fio Rito's Orchestra (Brunswick) and Roy Smeck (Melotone).

My Little Lady. w/m Jimmie Rodgers, 1929. Introduced and recorded by Jimmie Rodgers (Victor).

My Little Nest of Heavenly Blue. w. Sigmund Spaeth, m. Franz Lehar, 1927. Spaeth added lyrics to Lehar's "Frasquita Serenade" from Lehar's 1923 operetta, *Frasquita*, which was produced in Vienna. The song was interpolated in (TM) *The Love Call*, which had a short run in New York. Herman Chittison, the jazz pianist, recorded the song under its original title (Brunswick), as did John Kirby's band (Okeh). Connee Boswell with Artie Shaw and The Gramercy Five performed it in (MM) *Rich, Young, and Pretty*, and on records (Decca), 1951.

My Little Red Book. w. Hal David, m. Burt Bacharach, 1965. From (MP) *What's New, Pussycat?* Recorded by the group Love (Elektra).

My Little Town. w/m Paul Simon, 1975. Top 10 record by Simon & Garfunkel (Columbia).

My Lost Love. See **Mon Amour Perdu**.

My Love. w/m Lionel Richie, 1983. Top 10 record by Lionel Richie (Motown).

My Love. w/m Paul McCartney and Linda McCartney, 1973. #1 gold record by Paul McCartney and Wings (Apple).

My Love. w/m Tony Hatch, 1966. #1 record by Petula Clark, produced by the writer (Warner Bros.).

My Love. w. Ned Washington, m. Victor Young, 1932. Recorded by Russ Columbo (Victor); Richard Himber's Orchestra, vocal by Joey Nash (Vocalion); Glen Gray and the Casa Loma Orchestra, vocal by Kenny Sargent (Brunswick). It was used as the theme song of the radio show sponsored by Pond's products.

My Love, Forgive Me (Amore, Scusami). w. Sydney Lee (Engl.), Vito Pallavicini (Ital.), m. Gino Mescoli, 1964. Introduced in the U.S. and recorded by Robert Goulet (Columbia).

My Love and Devotion. w/m Milton Carson, 1952. British song. Leading U.S. record by Perry Como (RCA Victor).

My Love for You. w. Sid Wayne, m. Abner Silver, 1960. Recorded by Johnny Mathis (Columbia).

My Love for You. w. Edward Heyman, m. Harry Jacobson, 1939. Recorded by Red Norvo, vocal by Terry Allen (Vocalion); Vincent Lopez, vocal by Sonny Schuyler (Bluebird); Jack Marshard, vocal by Vaughn Monroe (Brunswick); Clark Dennis (Tiffany).

My Love Is a Wanderer. w/m Bart Howard, 1953. Introduced in nightclubs by Portia Nelson. Sung by Polly Bergen in (TM) *John Murray Anderson's Almanac (1953)*. Recorded by Betty Clooney (Coral).

My Love Loves Me. w. and adapt. of m. Jay Livingston and Ray Evans, 1949. Words added to adaptation of the air, "Plaisir d'Amour," by J. P. E. Martini, which was heard in (MP) *The Heiress*.

My Love Parade. w. Clifford Grey, m. Victor Schertzinger, 1929. Introduced by Maurice Chevalier and Jeanette MacDonald, making her film debut in (MM) *The Love Parade*.

My Love's a Gentle Man. w. Roy Jordan, m. Ulpio Minucci, 1955. Featured and recorded by Felicia Sanders (Columbia).

My Lucky Star. w. B. G. DeSylva and Lew Brown, m. Ray Henderson, 1929. Sung by John Barker in (TM) *Follow Thru*. Two popular recordings [both coupled with "Button Up Your Overcoat" from the same show] by Fred Waring's Pennsylvanians (Victor) and Paul Whiteman's Orchestra (Columbia).

My Mammy. w. Sam M. Lewis and Joe Young, m. Walter Donaldson, 1918. Introduced in vaudeville by Paul Frawley. Al Jolson then interpolated it in New Haven in the pre-Broadway tryout of (TM) *Sinbad*. It stopped the show and from that moment on the song was identified with Jolson throughout his career as evidenced by the five films in which he sang it: (MM) *The Jazz Singer*, 1927, (MM) *The Singing Fool*, 1928, (MM) *Rose of Washington Square*, 1939, and on the soundtracks, dubbing the voice for Larry Parks, of (MM) *The Jolson Story*, 1946, and (MM) *Jolson Sings Again*, 1949. He recorded it twice (Brunswick, Decca). Revived by The Happenings, with a Top 20 record (B. T. Puppy), 1967.

My Man, a Sweet Man. w/m Norro Wilson, Billy Sherrill, and Carmol Taylor, 1972. C&W/R&B/Pop chart hit by Millie Jackson (Spring).

My Man (Mon Homme). w. Channing Pollock (Engl.), m. Maurice Yvain, 1921. A popular song from France, introduced by Mistinguett in a revue, *Paris Qui Jazz*. Original French lyrics by Albert Willemetz and Jacques Charles. Introduced in the U.S. in French by Irene Bordoni, and then by Fanny Brice in English in (TM) *Ziegfeld Follies of 1921*, in which, after playing comedy, and at Ziegfeld's insistence, she sang the ballad and created a sensation. She repeated it in (MM) *My Man*,

1929, and (MM) *The Great Ziegfeld*, 1936. Alice Faye sang it, as Brice, in (MM) *Rose of Washington Square*, 1939. It was interpolated by Barbra Streisand in (MM) *Funny Girl*, 1968, the film version of the Broadway production of the loosely based Brice biography. Diana Ross sang it in (MM) *Lady Sings the Blues*, 1972. Leading records: Fanny Brice (Victor); Teddy Wilson, vocal by Billie Holiday (Brunswick); Dinah Shore (Bluebird); Peggy Lee (Capitol), 1959; Barbra Streisand (Columbia), 1965.

My Man Is on the Make. w. Lorenz Hart, m. Richard Rodgers, 1929. Sung by Alice Boulden and danced by Atlas and LaMarr in (TM) *Heads Up!* Helen Kane performed it in (MM) *Heads Up!* 1930.

My Man's Gone Now. w. Du Bose Heyward, m. George Gershwin, 1935. Introduced by Ruby Elzy in (TM) *Porgy and Bess*. In the film version, 1959, (MM) *Porgy and Bess*, it was sung by Inez Matthews, dubbing for Ruth Attaway.

My Maria. w/m B. W. Stevenson and Daniel Moore, 1973. Top 10 record by B. W. Stevenson (RCA).

My Marie. w/m Tony Macaulay and Barry Mason, 1970. British song, recorded by Engelbert Humperdinck (Parrot).

My Mariuccia Take a Steamboat. w. George Ronklyn, m. Al Piantadosi, 1906.

My Melancholy Baby. w. George A. Norton, m. Ernie Burnett, 1912. This, an all-time standard, was the only hit written by the composer. Often recorded and used in motion pictures. Among the latter, it was sung by Bing Crosby in (MM) *The Birth of the Blues*, 1941; Gogi Grant, dubbing for Ann Blyth, in (MM) *The Helen Morgan Story*, 1957; Judy Garland in (MM) *A Star Is Born*, 1954. Tommy Edwards had a best-selling record (MGM), 1959.

My Melody of Love. w. Bobby Vinton (Engl.), George Buschor (Ger.), m. Henry Mayer, 1973. German song. Gold record English version by Bobby Vinton (ABC).

My Mistake (Was to Love You). w/m Gloria Jones and Pam Sawyer, 1974. Top 20 record by Diana Ross and Marvin Gaye (Motown).

My Mom. w/m Walter Donaldson, 1932. Introduced in vaudeville by Jackie Osterman. Recorded by Kate Smith (Victor), George Olsen and his Orchestra (Victor), Morton Downey (Hit of the Week). Revived in the early fifties by Eddie Fisher (Victor).

My Moonlight Madonna. w. Paul Francis Webster, m. William Scotti, 1933. The melody was adapted from "Poeme" by Zdenko Fibich. Popularized and recorded by Paul Whiteman (Victor), Rudy Vallee (Bluebird), Conrad Thibault (Victor), Victor Young's Orchestra (Brunswick), Jack Fulton (Decca).

My Most Important Moments Go By. w. Gretchen Cryer, m. Nancy Ford, 1970. Introduced by Fredericka Weber and Austin Pendleton in the off-Broadway (TM) *The Last Sweet Days of Isaac*.

My Mother's Eyes. w. L. Wolfe Gilbert, m. Abel Baer, 1929. Introduced by George Jessel in (MM) *Lucky Boy* and recorded by him (Victor). It was his trademark song throughout his long career. Revived by Bette Midler in (MM) *Divine Madness* and recorded by her (Atlantic), 1980.

My Mother's Lullaby. w. Charles Louis Ruddy, m. Harold Brown Freedman, 1917. Recorded by Billy Jones and Ernest Hare (Brunswick).

My Mother's Rosary (or, **Ten Baby Fingers and Ten Baby Toes**). w. Sam M. Lewis, m. George W. Meyer, 1915. Popular record by Henry Burr as Harry McClaskey (Columbia).

My Mother Would Love You. w/m Cole Porter, 1940. Introduced by Ethel Merman and James Dunn in (TM) *Panama Hattie*. Recorded by Freddy Martin and his Orchestra (Bluebird).

My Motter. w. Arthur Wimperis, m. Howard Talbot, 1910. Sung by Percival Knight in (TM) *The Arcadians*.

My Music. w/m Kenny Loggins and Jim Messina, 1973. Top 20 record by Loggins and Messina (Columbia).

My Name Is Mud. w/m Bill Anderson, 1962. Top 10 Country chart song by James O'Gwynn (Mercury).

My Ohio Home. w. Gus Kahn, m. Walter Donaldson, 1927. Featured in the media of vaudeville, radio, and records (Brunswick) by Nick Lucas.

My Oh My. w/m Noddy Holder and Jim Lea, 1984. Recorded by the English quartet Slade (CBS Associated).

My Old Flame. w. Sam Coslow, m. Arthur Johnston, 1934. Introduced by Mae West, with Duke Ellington and Orchestra in (MM) *Belle of the Nineties.* They later recorded it (Biltmore). Ellington also recorded it with vocal by Ivy Anderson (Victor). Other disk versions by Ted Lewis (Decca); Billie Holiday (Commodore); Herman Chittison (Brunswick); Stan Getz (New Jazz); Spike Jones (Victor); Benny Goodman, vocal by Peggy Lee (Columbia); Benny Morton (12″ Blue Note); Flip Phillips (Mercury).

My Old New Hampshire Home. w. Andrew B. Sterling, m. Harry Von Tilzer, 1898. Von Tilzer's first song hit. Popular recording by George J. Gaskin (Columbia).

My Old School. w/m Walter Becker and Donald Fagen, 1973. Written by the leaders of the group that recorded it, Steely Dan (ABC).

My One and Only. w. Ira Gershwin, m. George Gershwin, 1927. Introduced by Fred Astaire, Betty Compton, and Gertrude McDonald in (TM) *Funny Face.* Popular recordings by Jane Green (Victor) and Fred Astaire (Columbia). It was heard in the Gershwin biography (MM) *Rhapsody in Blue,* 1945. Tommy Tune and Charles "Honi" Coles performed it as the title song of (TM) *My One and Only,* 1983.

My One and Only Heart. w. Al Stillman, m. Robert Allen, 1953. Popular recording by Perry Como (RCA Victor).

My One and Only Highland Fling. w. Ira Gershwin, m. Harry Warren, 1949. Introduced by Fred Astaire and Ginger Rogers in (MM) *The Barkleys of Broadway.*

My One and Only Love. w. Robert Mellin, m. Guy Wood, 1953. Original melody, with new lyrics, of "Music From Beyond the Moon" (q.v.). First recorded by Frank Sinatra (Capitol).

My Own. w. Harold Adamson, m. Jimmy McHugh, 1938. Introduced by Deanna Durbin in (MM) *That Certain Age* and recorded by her (Decca). Among others to record this Academy Award nominee: Tommy Dorsey, vocal by Edythe Wright (Victor); Ozzie Nelson and his Orchestra (Bluebird); Gene Krupa, vocal by Irene Daye (Brunswick); Henry King and his Orchestra (Decca).

My Own Best Friend. w. Fred Ebb, m. John Kander, 1975. Introduced by Gwen Verdon and Chita Rivera in (TM) *Chicago.*

My Own Space. w. Fred Ebb, m. John Kander, 1977. Introduced by Liza Minnelli in (TM) *The Act.*

My Own True Love (Tara's Theme). w. Mack David, m. Max Steiner, 1954. David's lyrics added to "Tara's Theme" (q.v.) from (MP) *Gone With the Wind.* Leading records by Johnny Desmond (Coral) and Leroy Holmes's Orchestra (MGM).

My Own United States. w. Stanislaus Stange, m. Julian Edwards, 1902. From the musical (TM) *When Johnny Comes Marching Home.* Recorded by J. W. Myers (Columbia, Victor). Lawrence Tibbett sang his version in 1938 (Victor).

My Pajama Beauty. w. George V. Hobart, m. Mae A. Sloane, 1902. Sung to the pajama-clad chorus in (TM) *The Hall of Fame.*

My Paradise. w. Otto Harbach, m. Rudolf Friml, 1916. From (TM) *Katinka.*

My Pearl's a Bowery Girl. w. William Jerome, m. Andrew Mack, 1894,.

My Personal Possession. w/m Charles Singleton and Rose Marie McCoy, 1957. Featured and recorded by Nat "King" Cole (Capitol).

My Pet. w. Jack Yellen, m. Milton Ager, 1928.

My Pledge of Love. w/m Joseph Stafford, Jr., 1969. Top 20 record by The Joe Jeffrey Group (Wand).

My Pony Boy. w. Bobby Heath, m. Charles O'Donnell, 1908. From (TM) *Miss Innocence.* Recorded in 1909 by Ada Jones and the Peerless Quartet (Victor) and in 1939 by Freddie "Schnicklefritz" Fisher (Decca).

My Prayer. w. Jimmy Kennedy, m. Georges Boulanger and Jimmy Kennedy, 1939, 1956. Adapted [England] from the violin piece by Boulanger, "Avant de Mourir." Best-selling records by Glenn Miller, vocal by Ray Eberle (Bluebird) and The Ink Spots (Decca). The Platters (Mercury) revived it with a #1 record in 1956. Song on "Your Hit Parade" for fourteen weeks originally and eleven weeks in 1956.

My Prerogative. w/m Bobby Brown and Gene Griffin, 1989. Hit single by Bobby Brown (MCA).

My Rambler Rose. w. Gene Buck, m. Louis A. Hirsch and Dave Stamper, 1922. Introduced in song and dance by Andrew Tombes and Evelyn Law in (TM) *Ziegfeld Follies of 1922.*

My Resistance Is Low. w. Harold Adamson, m. Hoagy Carmichael, 1951. Introduced by Hoagy Carmichael in (MP) *The Las Vegas Story.*

My Resistance Is Low. w/m Orrin Tucker, 1941. Introduced by "Wee" Bonnie Baker, with Orrin Tucker's Orchestra in (MM) *You're the One,* and recorded by them (Columbia).

My Restless Lover (a.k.a. **Johnny Guitar**). w/m Pembroke Davenport, 1954. Original title of "Johnny Guitar" was changed to avoid conflict with film and song of same name. Popular record by Patti Page (Mercury).

My Reverie. w/m Larry Clinton, 1938. This was based on "Reverie" by Claude Debussy, the French composer. Clinton and his publisher were under the erroneous impression that the original work was in the public domain. After Clinton's recording, with vocal by Bea Wain (Victor), became a #1 hit, the Debussy estate sued for copyright infringement and was awarded royalties of over $60,000, an amount that exceeded Debussy's lifetime earnings from his collective works.

My Romance. w. Lorenz Hart, m. Richard Rodgers, 1935. Introduced by Donald Novis and Gloria Grafton in Billy Rose's (TM) *Jumbo.* Novis, with Paul Whiteman's Orchestra, which was also in the stage production, recorded it (Victor). Other releases by Arthur Tracy, "The Street Singer" (Brunswick); Jan Peerce (Brunswick); Morton Downey (Majestic); Eve Symington, with Cy Walter at the piano (Liberty Music Shops). Among later records, Margaret Whiting (Capitol); Dave Brubeck, piano solo (Fantasy). Doris Day sang it in (MM) *Billy Rose's Jumbo,* 1962.

My Rosary of Dreams. w/m C. M. Denison and E. F. Dusenberry, 1911.

My Rough and Rowdy Days. w/m Roger Murrah and Waylon Jennings, 1987. Country chart hit by Waylon Jennings (MCA).

My San Domingo Maid. w. Henry Blossom, m. Alfred George Robyn, 1903. From (TM) *The Yankee Consul.*

My Sharona. w/m Berton Averre and Doug Fieger, 1980. #1 gold record by the rock group The Knack (Capitol).

My Shawl. w. Stanley Adams (Engl.), Pedro Berrios (Sp.), m. Xavier Cugat, 1934. Cugat and his Orchestra recorded this twice (Victor, Columbia) and used it as their theme song. Also recorded by Jan August (Diamond) and Carol Bruce (Decca).

My Shining Hour. w. Johnny Mercer, m. Harold Arlen, 1943. Introduced by Fred Astaire in (MM) *The Sky's the Limit*. Nominated for Academy Award. Best-selling record by Glen Gray and the Casa Loma Orchestra, vocal by Eugenie Baird (Decca).

My Ship. w. Ira Gershwin, m. Kurt Weill, 1941. Introduced by Gertrude Lawrence in (TM) *Lady in the Dark* and recorded by her (Victor). Danny Kaye, appearing in the same show but not singing this song, recorded it (Columbia). Other than a few melodic bars, the song was not heard in the film version, 1944.

My Shoes Keep Walking Back to You. w/m Lee Ross and Bob Wills, 1957. C&W hit and Pop crossover by Ray Price (Columbia). Revived by Guy Mitchell with a Pop chart record in 1960 (Columbia).

My Shy Violet. w/m Earl Shuman and Leon Carr, 1968. Recorded by The Mills Brothers (Dot).

My Silent Love. w. Edward Heyman, m. Dana Suesse, 1932. The song was adapted from a theme from Suesse's instrumental "Jazz Nocturne." Among early recordings of this standard were those by the bands of Isham Jones (Brunswick), Roger Wolfe Kahn (Columbia), Ruby Newman (Victor), and the Washboard Rhythm Band (Victor). Later recordings include: Carmen Cavallaro (Decca); Dick Jurgens, vocal by Harry Cool (Okeh); Anita Boyer (V-disc 12″); Luis Russell (Apollo); Fran Warren (Victor); Paul Weston (Columbia).

My Sin. w. B. G. DeSylva and Lew Brown, m. Ray Henderson, 1929. First published as an independent song, then interpolated in (MM) *Showgirl in Hollywood*, which starred Alice White and Jack Mulhall. It was featured on radio, personal appearances, and recordings by Fred Waring's Pennsylvanians (Victor), Belle Baker (Brunswick), Franklyn Baur (Victor), and Jesse Crawford (Victor). In 1947, Julia Lee (Capitol) had a well-received, jazz-oriented recording and in the early fifties, Georgia Gibbs (Mercury) had a big-selling record.

My Sister and I. w/m Hy Zaret, Joan Whitney, and Alex Kramer, 1941. Title derived from the book of the same name by the Dutch victim of Nazi persecution, Dirk van der Heide. #1 on "Your Hit Parade," it was featured and recorded by Jimmy Dorsey, who had the best-selling record, vocal by Bob Eberly (Decca); Bea Wain (Victor); Bob Chester, vocal by Bill Darnell (Bluebird); Benny Goodman, vocal by Helen Forrest (Columbia); and others.

My Son, My Son. w. Bob Howard and Melville Farley, m. Eddie Calvert, 1954. English song popularized here via recording by Vera Lynn (London).

My Song. w/m Stonewall Jackson, 1968. Recorded by Aretha Franklin and coupled with the hit "See Saw" (q.v.) (Atlantic).

My Song. w. Lew Brown, m. Ray Henderson, 1931. Introduced by Ethel Merman and Rudy Vallee in (TM) *George White's Scandals, 11th Edition*. Featured on radio and records by Vallee (Victor).

My Song of the Nile. w. Alfred Bryan, m. George W. Meyer, 1929. Theme song of (MP) *Drag* starring Richard Barthelmess.

My Southern Rose. w/m Earl Taylor, 1909.

My Special Angel. w/m Jimmy Duncan, 1957, 1968. Hit C&W and Pop record by Bobby Helms (Decca). Revived with a Top 10 record by The Vogues (Reprise), 1968.

My State, My Kansas, My Home. w/m Meredith Willson, 1961. Introduced by Paul Reed, Arthur Rubin, Fred Gwynne, Janis Paige, and Cliff Hall in (TM) *Here's Love*, the musical version of the film *Miracle on 34th Street*. Willson had written the song to commemorate the Centennial of Kansas.

Mysterious Mose. w/m Walter Doyle, 1930. Recorded by composer Rube Bloom and his Bayou Boys (Columbia). The studio band, which was assembled for recordings, had among its personnel: Tommy Dorsey, Benny Goodman, Adrian Rollini, and Babe Russin.

Mystery Lady. w/m Keith Diamond, Billy Ocean, and James Woodley, 1985. Chart single from the album "Suddenly" by Billy Ocean (Jive).

Mystery Street. w. Bob Howard (Engl.), m. Jacques Plante and M. Philippe-Gerard, 1953. French song with English lyrics. Top records in the U.S. by June Valli (RCA Victor) and Jackie Gleason and his Orchestra (Capitol).

Mystery Train. w/m Sam C. Phillips and Herman Parker, Jr., 1956. Introduced and recorded by Elvis Presley (RCA Victor).

Mystic Eyes. w/m Van Morrison, 1965. Instrumental by the Northern Ireland rock group Them (Parrot).

My Sugar Is So Refined. w. Sylvia Dee, m. Sidney Lippman, 1946. Leading recording by Johnny Mercer (Capitol).

My Summer Love. w. Bob Hilliard, m. Mort Garson, 1963. Top 20 record by Ruby and The Romantics (Kapp).

My Sunny Tennessee. w/m Bert Kalmar, Harry Ruby, and Herman Ruby, 1921. Interpolated by Eddie Cantor in (TM) *The Midnight Rounders*. Fred Astaire and Red Skelton sang it in the film biography of Kalmar and Ruby (Harry), (MM) *Three Little Words*, 1950.

My Sunshine Jane. w. J. Keirn Brennan, m. Ernest R. Ball, 1917.

My Suppressed Desire. w. Ned Miller, m. Chester Conn, 1928. Popular recordings by Paul Whiteman, featuring the Rhythm Boys [Crosby, Barris, and Rinker] (Columbia), the Coon-Sanders Orchestra (Victor) and Abe Lyman's Orchestra (Brunswick).

My Sweet Adair. w. L. Wolfe Gilbert, m. Anatole Friedland, 1915. A barbershop quartet favorite.

My Sweeter Than Sweet. w. George Marion, Jr., m. Richard A. Whiting, 1929. Sung by Nancy Carroll in (MM) *Sweetie*. Popular recordings by the orchestras of Leo Reisman (Victor) and Frankie Trumbauer (Okeh), singer Sid Gary (Domino), and songwriter-singer Sammy Fain (Diva).

My Sweetheart's the Man in the Moon. w/m James Thornton, 1892. Inspired and featured by Bonnie (Mrs. James) Thornton at Tony Pastor's 14th Street Theatre in New York.

My Sweetie Turned Me Down. w. Gus Kahn, m. Walter Donaldson, 1925.

My Sweetie Went Away (She Didn't Say Where, When, or Why). w. Roy Turk, m. Lou Handman, 1923. Made popular via recordings by: Billy Murray and Ed Smalle (Victor), Ben Bernie (Vocalion), Dolly Kay (Columbia), Aileen Stanley (Victor).

My Sweet Lady. w/m John Denver, 1974. Introduced by Cliff De Young in (TVP) "Sunshine." His recording made the Top 20 (MCA). John Denver had a top 40 version (RCA), 1977.

My Sweet Lord. w/m George Harrison, 1970. #1 gold record by George Harrison, produced by Phil Spector and Harrison (Apple). Harrison also produced a recording by Billy Preston (Apple), 1971. The song was the subject of a lengthy and settled plagiarism suit by the copyright owners of the 1963 hit, "He's So Fine" (q.v.).

My Sweet Suzanne. w/m Blossom Seeley, 1911.

My Tears Are Overdue. w/m Freddie Hart, 1964. Leading C&W record by George Jones (United Artists).

My Time Is Your Time. w. Eric Little, m. Leo Dance, 1929. Pseudonyms for the British writers H. M. Tennent and R. S. Hooper, respectively. Rudy Vallee had heard the song in London four years earlier and secured the American rights. When he got his own coast-to-coast radio show, The Fleischmann Yeast Hour, he used it as the theme song. The song was heard on the soundtrack of (MM) *Margie* in 1946. Vallee recorded it (Victor) and used it as the title of his autobiography, published in 1962.

My Time of Day. w/m Frank Loesser, 1950. Introduced by Robert Alda in (TM) *Guys and Dolls*. Omitted from film version.

My Toot Toot. w/m Sidney Timien, 1985. Recorded by the New Orleans singer, Jean Knight (Mirage).

My Town, My Guy, and Me. w/m Bob Elgin, Lesley Gore, and Paul Kaufman, 1965. Top 40 record by Lesley Gore, produced by Quincy Jones (Mercury).

My Troubles Are Over. w. Edgar Leslie, m. James V. Monaco, 1929. Popular records by Ted Weems, with vocal by Parker Gibbs (Victor); Hal Kemp (Brunswick); and The Sunshine Boys [Joe and Danny Mooney] (Columbia).

My True Love. w/m Jack Scott, 1958. The first hit by singer/songwriter Jack Scott (Carlton).

My True Story. w/m Eugene Pitt and Oscar Waltzer, 1961. Top 10 record by The Jive Five (Beltone).

My Truly, Truly Fair. w/m Bob Merrill, 1951. Guy Mitchell, with Mitch Miller's Orchestra, had a million-seller (Columbia). Other Top 20 records by Vic Damone, with George Bassman's Orchestra (Mercury) and Freddy Martin, vocal by Merv Griffin (RCA Victor).

My Twilight Dream. m. Frederic Chopin, adapted by Eddy Duchin and Lew Sherwood, 1939. Theme song of Eddy Duchin's Orchestra, based on Chopin's "Nocturne in E Flat." Recorded (Columbia).

My Uncle Used to Love Me But She Died. w/m Roger Miller, 1966. Novelty record by Roger Miller (Smash).

My Very Good Friend, the Milkman. w. Johnny Burke, m. Harold Spina, 1935. Popularized by radio performances and recordings by Babs and Her Brothers (Decca); Dorsey Brothers Orchestra (Decca); George Hall, vocal by Dolly Dawn and Sonny Schuyler (Bluebird); Anson Weeks, vocal by Kay St. Germaine (Brunswick).

My Walking Stick. w/m Irving Berlin, 1938. Introduced by Ethel Merman in (MM) *Alexander's Ragtime Band*. Recorded by Tony Martin with Ray Noble's Orchestra (Brunswick); Ruby Newman's Orchestra (Decca); Roger Pryor's Orchestra (Vocalion).

My Way. w. Paul Anka (Engl.), m. Jacques Revaux and Claude François, 1969. Original French title, "Comme d'Habitude," lyrics by Gillis Thibault and Claude François. Introduced in France by François. English version popularized by and associated with Frank Sinatra (Reprise). Chart version by Brook Benton (Cotillion), 1970. Elvis Presley's performance of the song was recorded "live" on tour. Its posthumous single release was awarded a gold record (RCA), 1977.

My Way of Life. w. Carl Sigman, m. Bert Kaempfert and Herbert Rehbein, 1968. German song. English lyric version recorded by Frank Sinatra (Reprise).

My Whole World Ended (the Moment You Left Me). w/m Johnny Bristol, Harvey Fuqua, Jimmy Roach, and Pam Sawyer, 1969. Top 10 record by David Ruffin (Motown).

My Whole World Is Falling Down. w/m Bill Anderson and Jerry Crutchfield, 1963. Recorded by Brenda Lee (Decca).

My Wife's Gone to the Country, Hurrah! Hurrah! w. George Whiting and Irving Berlin, m. Ted Snyder, 1909. Comedy song, popular in vaudeville. Recordings by Arthur Collins and Byron Harlan (Columbia) and Bob Roberts (Indestructable).

My Wild Irish Rose. w/m Chauncey Olcott, 1899. One of the earliest Irish ballad successes to come out of Tin Pan Alley. It was introduced by Olcott in (TM) *A Romance of Athlone*. In 1947, Dennis Morgan playing Olcott, sang it as the title song in (MM) *My Wild Irish Rose*, the film biography of the famous tenor.

My Wish Came True. w/m Ivory Joe Hunter, 1959. Elvis Presley's first recording after his discharge from the Army (RCA).

My Woman, My Woman, My Wife. w/m Marty Robbins, 1970. Crossover (C&W/Pop) hit by Marty Robbins (Columbia). Winner Grammy Award (NARAS) for Country Song of the Year.

My Woman's Good to Me. w/m Billy Sherrill and Glenn Sutton, 1969. Hit Country record by David Houston (Epic).

My Wonderful Dream Girl. w. Oliver Morosco, m. Victor Schertzinger, 1913.

My Wonderful One, Let's Dance. w/m Arthur Freed, Roger Edens, and Nacio Herb Brown, 1940. Introduced by George Murphy and Lana Turner in (MM) *Two Girls on Broadway*, the re-make of the original *Broadway Melody*. It was heard orchestrally in (MM) *Two Girls and a Sailor*, 1944. Recordings by the bands of Ben Bernie (Vocalion) and Gene Krupa (Columbia).

My World. w/m Barry Gibb and Robin Gibb, 1972. Top 20 record by the British brother trio The Bee Gees (Atco).

My World Is Empty Without You. w/m Brian Holland, Eddie Holland, and Lamont Dozier, 1966. Top 10 record by The Supremes (Motown).

My Yiddishe Momme. w. Jack Yellen, m. Lew Pollack, 1925. Featured in vaudeville and on records by Willie Howard (Columbia) and Sophie Tucker (Columbia).

N

Nadia's Theme (The Young and the Restless). m. Barry DeVorzon and Perry Botkin, Jr., 1976. First used as theme music in (MP) *Bless the Beasts and Children*, 1972, followed by its usage as the theme for the series (TVP) "The Young and the Restless." Nadia Comaneci, the young Romanian gymnast, used the music in her successful championship pursuit in the 1976 Olympics. The instrumental recording by Barry DeVorzon and Perry Botkin, Jr. became a Top 10 gold record (A&M), 1976.

Nadine (Is It You?) w/m Chuck Berry, 1964. Top 40 record by Chuck Berry (Chess).

Nagasaki. w. Mort Dixon, m. Harry Warren, 1928. Introduced and recorded by Paul Mares and his Friars' Society Orchestra (Okeh). Among many other recordings are those by Don Redman (Brunswick); Fletcher Henderson (Columbia); Glen Gray and the Casa Loma Orchestra (Decca); Cab Calloway (Brunswick). Doris Day sang it in (MM) *My Dream Is Yours*, 1949.

Naked City Theme. m. Nelson Riddle, 1962. Theme of series (TVP) "Naked City." Recorded by Nelson Riddle (Capitol).

Name Game, The. w/m Shirley Elliston and Lincoln Chase, 1965. Hit record by Shirley Ellis (Congress).

Namely You. w. Johnny Mercer, m. Gene De Paul, 1956. Introduced by Edie Adams and Peter Palmer in (TM) *Li'l Abner*. Leading record by Don Cherry (Coral).

Name of the Game, The. w/m Benny Anderson, Stig Anderson, and Bjorn Ulvaeus, 1978. Recorded by the Swedish quartet Abba (Atlantic).

Name of the Game Was Love. w/m Cy Coben, 1969. Country chart record by Hank Snow (RCA).

Na Na Hey Hey (Kiss Him Goodbye). w/m Gary DeCarlo, Dale Frashuer, and Paul Leka, 1969. Gold record by the group Steam (Mercury). Revived by The Nylons, on a single from the album, "Happy Together" (Open Air), 1987.

Nancy (with the Laughing Face). w. Phil Silvers, m. James Van Heusen, 1945. Frank Sinatra recorded the song written about his two-year-old daughter (Columbia).

Nancy Brown. w/m Clifton Crawford, 1902. Introduced by interpolation in (TM) *The Wild Rose* by Marie Cahill. Leading record by J. W. Meyers (Columbia).

Napoleon. w. E. Y. Harburg, m. Harold Arlen, 1957. Based on the writers' earlier "Napoleon's a Pastry," introduced by June Clyde in (TM) *Hooray for What?*, 1937. The new version was introduced by Lena Horne in (TM) *Jamaica*.

Napoleon. w/m Vic Abrams, 1954. Vocal adaptation of music from Tchaikowsky's *1812 Overture* by Mitch Miller's Chorus and Orchestra (Columbia).

Nashville Cats. w/m John Sebastian, 1967. Top 10 record by The Lovin' Spoonful (Kama Sutra).

Nashville Nightingale. w. Irving Caesar, m. George Gershwin, 1923. From (TM) *Nifties of 1923*. Recorded in 1924 by The California Ramblers (Path) and The Charleston Seven, featuring trumpeter Red Nichols and clarinetist Miff Mole (Edison).

Nasty. w/m James Harris III, Terry Lewis, and Janet Jackson, 1986. Top 10 record by Janet Jackson (A&M)

Nasty Man. w. Jack Yellen and Irving Caesar, m. Ray Henderson, 1934. Introduced by Alice Faye, making her screen debut in (MM) *George White's Scandals*. Faye, who had been the vocalist with Rudy Vallee's orchestra, was a last-minute replacement, at Vallee's insistence, for Lillian Harvey who had quit the production. Recorded by Vallee (Victor) and Frances Langford (Melotone).

Nat'an, for What Are You Waitin', Nat'an. w/m James Kendis, 1916.

Nathan Jones. w/m Leonard Caston and Kathy Wakefield, 1971. Top 20 record by The Supremes (Motown).

National Emblem. m. E. E. Bagley, 1906. A march that became a staple in the repertoire of marching, circus, and carnival bands. A parody lyric was written that started with: "When the monkey wrapped his tail around the flagpole . . ."

Native New Yorker. w/m Sandy Linzer and Denny Randall, 1977. Recorded by the trio Odyssey (RCA).

Natural, The. m. Randy Newman, 1984. Theme from (MP) *The Natural*.

Natural High. w/m Freddy Powers, 1985. #1 Country chart song by Merle Haggard (Epic).

Natural High. w/m Charles McCormick, 1973. Top 10 hit by the group Bloodstone (London).

Naturally. w. Joseph McCarthy, m. Harry Barris, 1938. Featured and recorded by the bands of Louis Armstrong (Decca); Hal Kemp (Victor); Rudy Vallee (Bluebird); Orville Knapp (Decca); Al Donahue, vocal by Paula Kelly (Vocalion).

Naturally Stoned. w/m Chuck Woolery, 1968. Recorded by The Avant-Garde (Columbia).

Natural Man, A. w/m Bobby Hebb and Sandy Baron, 1971. Top 20 record by Lou Rawls (MGM).

Natural Woman, A (You Make Me Feel Like). w/m Gerry Goffin, Carole King, and Jerry Wexler, 1967. Hit record by Aretha Franklin (Atlantic). Carole King sang it on her album "Tapestry" (Ode), 1971.

Nature Boy. w/m Eden Ahbez, 1948. Nat "King" Cole had a million-selling record that was #1 on the charts eight weeks (Capitol). The song was on "Your Hit Parade" for ten weeks, six times in the #1 position.

Naughty, Naughty, Naughty. w. Harry Williams, m. Egbert Van Alstyne, 1911.

Naughty Angeline. w/m Allan Roberts and Lester Lee, 1947. Best-selling record by Dick Haymes (Decca).

Naughty Girls (Need Love Too). w/m Full Force, 1988. Popular single by Samantha Fox from the album of her name (Jive).

Naughty Lady of Shady Lane, The. w/m Sid Tepper and Roy C. Bennett, 1955. Hit record by The Ames Brothers (RCA Victor).

Navajo. w. Harry H. Williams, m. Egbert Van Alstyne, 1904. Interpolated by Marie Cahill in (TM) *Nancy Brown*. Leading recordings by Billy Murray (Columbia), Harry MacDonough (Victor), J. W. Myers (Columbia).

Navy Blue. w/m Bob Crewe, Edward Fluri, and Andrew Rachek, 1964. Top 10 record by Diane Renay (20th Century-Fox).

Neapolitan Love Song. w. Henry Blossom, m. Victor Herbert, 1915. Introduced in (TM) *The Princess Pat* by Joseph R. Lertora. Reinald Werrenrath, the famous baritone, recorded it (Victor) in 1915. Allan Jones sang it in (MM) *The Great Victor Herbert* in 1939.

Neapolitan Nights (Oh, Nights of Splendor). w. Harry D. Kerr, m. J. S. Zamecnik, 1925. Theme song of (MP) *Fazil*, starring Charles Farrell and Greta Nissen. Later used as the theme song of the radio series "The First Nighter."

Nearness of You, The. w. Ned Washington, m. Hoagy Carmichael, 1940. Among many recordings upon publication: Glenn Miller (Bluebird), Dinah Shore (Bluebird), Guy Lombardo (Decca), Larry Clinton (Victor), Connee (she changed spelling of her first name) Boswell (Decca), Ray Herbeck (Vocalion), Eddy Howard (Columbia).

Near You. w. Kermit Goell, m. Francis Craig, 1947. One of the top songs of the year, introduced by Francis Craig and his Orchestra, featuring Craig on piano (Bullet). Their record was #1 on the Billboard charts for seventeen weeks. Other hit records: The Andrews Sisters (Decca), Larry Green and his Orchestra (RCA Victor), Alvino Rey and his Orchestra (Capitol). Revived by Roger Williams (Kapp), 1958.

'Neath the Southern Moon, w. Rida Johnson Young, m. Victor Herbert, 1910. Introduced by Marie Duchene in (TM) *Naughty Marietta*. Nelson Eddy sang it in the film version (MM) *Naughty Marietta*, 1935.

'Neath the South Sea Moon. w. Gene Buck, m. Louis A. Hirsch and Dave Stamper, 1922. Gilda Gray had a show-stopping number with her shimmy performance in (TM) *Ziegfeld Follies of 1922*.

Necessity. w. E. Y. Harburg, m. Burton Lane, 1947. Introduced by Dolores Martin in (MM) *Finian's Rainbow*. Single record by Georgia Gibbs (Majestic). It was sung and prerecorded by Brenda Arnau and chorus for the film version (MM) *Finian's Rainbow*, 1968, issued on the soundtrack album, but not filmed.

Need for Love, The. See **Theme from "The Unforgiven."**

Needle in a Haystack. w/m Norman Whitfield and William Stevenson, 1964. Recorded by The Velvelettes (V.I.P.).

Needle in a Hay Stack, A. w. Herb Magidson, m. Con Conrad, 1934. Introduced by Fred Astaire in (MM) *The Gay Divorcée*. He can be heard singing it in the 4-LP set, "The Fred Astaire Story" (Mercury).

Needles and Pins. w/m Sonny Bono and Jack Nitzsche, 1963. Introduced and recorded by Jackie De Shannon (Liberty). Top 20 record by the English rock quartet, The Searchers (Kapp), 1964. Revived by Smokie, also an English rock quartet (RSO), 1977. Tom Petty, with The Heartbreakers and Stevie Nicks, had a Top 40 version (MCA), 1986.

Need to Be, The. w/m Jim Weatherly, 1974. Top 20 record by Jim Weatherly (Buddah).

Need You. w/m John Blackburn, Mitchell Tableporter, and Lew Porter, 1949. Popular recordings by Jo Stafford and Gordon MacRae (Capitol), and Guy Lombardo, vocal by Kenny Gardner (Decca).

Need Your Love So Bad. w/m John Metis, Jr., 1955. R&B hit by Little Willie John (King).

Need You Tonight. w/m Andrew Farriss and Michael Hutchence, 1987. Written by two members of the Australian sextet, INXS, which had a #1 single from their album "Kick" (Atlantic.

Nee Nee Na Na Na Na Nu Nu. w/m Eddie V. Deane and Al Dredick, 1958. Recorded by Dicky Doo and the Don'ts (Swan).

Neiani. w/m Axel Stordahl and Sy Oliver, 1941. Written by two arrangers for Tommy Dorsey and his Band who recorded it, vocal by Frank Sinatra (Victor). It was coupled with the hit "This Love of Mine" (q.v.).

Neighbor, Neighbor. w/m Alton J. Valier, 1966. Recorded by soul singer Jimmy Hughes (Fame).

Neighbors. w. Charles O'Flynn and James Cavanaugh, m. Frank Weldon, 1934. Featured and recorded by Isham Jones and his Orchestra (Victor).

Neither One of Us (Wants to Be the First to Say Goodbye). w/m Jim Weatherly, 1973. Top 10 record by Gladys Knight and The Pips (Soul).

Nel Blu, Dipinto di Blu. See **Volare.**

Nellie Kelly, I Love You. w/m George M. Cohan, 1922. Sung by Charles King in (TM) *Little Nellie Kelly.* It was revived by Judy Garland and Douglas MacPhail in (MM) *Little Nellie Kelly,* 1940. In 1968 it was sung in (TM) *George M!* by Joel Grey, Bernadette Peters, and company.

Neon Rainbow. w/m Wayne Thompson, 1967. Top 40 record by The Box Tops (Mala).

Nester, The. w/m Don Wayne, 1964. Country chart record by Lefty Frizzell (Columbia).

Neutron Dance. w/m Allee Willis and David Sembello, 1984. Introduced in the album "Breakout" by The Pointer Sisters (Planet), 1983. Then performed on the soundtrack of (MP) *Beverly Hills Cop* and released on the gold soundtrack album (MCA) and re-released as a Top 10 single (Planet), 1985.

Nevada. w. Mort Greene, m. Walter Donaldson, 1943. Donaldson's last song, introduced in (MM) *What's Buzzin', Cousin?* Two years later, Tommy Dorsey, with a vocal by Stuart Foster and The Sentimentalists, had a popular record (Victor).

Never. w/m Holly Knight, Walter Bloch, and Ann Wilson, 1985. Top 10 record and album cut by the group Heart (Capitol).

Never. w. Eliot Daniel, m. Lionel Newman, 1951. Introduced by Dennis Day in (MM) *Golden Girl,* and recorded by him (RCA Victor). Nominated for Academy Award.

Never, Never Gonna Give Ya Up. w/m Barry White, 1973. Top 10 R&B/Pop gold record by Barry White (20th Century).

Never As Good As the First Time. w/m Helen Folasade Adu and Stuart Matthewman, 1986. Co-written and recorded by the Nigerian-born Sade (Portrait).

Never Be Anyone Else But You. w/m Baker Knight, 1959. Hit record by Ricky Nelson (Imperial).

Never Been to Spain. w/m Hoyt Axton, 1970. Top 10 record by Three Dog Night (Dunhill).

Never Be the Same. w/m Christopher Geppert [Cross], 1980. Recorded by Christopher Cross (Warner Bros.).

Never Be You. w/m Tom Petty and Benmont Tench, 1986. #1 Country chart record by Roseanne Cash (Columbia).

Never Can Say Goodbye. w/m Clifton Davis, 1971. R&B/Pop hit by The Jackson 5 (Motown) and Isaac Hayes (Enterprise). Top 10 version by Gloria Gaynor (MGM), 1975.

Never Ending Song of Love. w/m Delaney Bramlett, 1971. Top 20 record by Delaney and Bonnie and Friends (Atco).

Never Ending Story. w/m Giorgio Moroder and Keith Forsey, 1985. Introduced on the soundtrack of (MP) *Never Ending Story.* Recorded by Limahl, an anagram of the last name of Chris Hamill (EMI America).

Never Give Anything Away. w/m Cole Porter, 1953. Introduced by Lilo in (TM) *Can-Can.* Not used in film version.

Never Give You Up. w/m Kenny Gamble, Leon Huff, and Jerry Butler, 1968. Top 20 record by Jerry Butler (Mercury).

Never Gonna Dance, w. Dorothy Fields, m. Jerome Kern, 1936. Introduced by Fred Astaire and Ginger Rogers in (MM) *Swing Time*. The original title of the film was *I Won't Dance*, then *Never Gonna Dance*. The producers felt each was too negative.

Never Gonna Fall in Love Again. w/m Eric Carmen, 1976. Top 20 record by Eric Carmen (Arista).

Never Gonna Give You Up. w/m Mike Stock, Matt Aitken, and Pete Waterman, 1988. #1 single by the British singer, Rick Astley, from his album "Whenever You Need Somebody" (RCA).

Never Gonna Let You Go. w. Cynthia Weil, m. Barry Mann, 1983. Top 10 record by Sergio Mendes, vocal by Joe Pizzulo and Leza Miller (A&M).

Never in a Million Years. w. Mack Gordon, m. Harry Revel, 1937. Introduced by Alice Faye and Buddy Clark, dubbing for Jack Haley, in (MM) *Wake Up and Live*. Faye recorded it (Brunswick); as did Bing Crosby, with Jimmy Dorsey's Orchestra (Decca); Mildred Bailey (Vocalion); Glen Gray and the Casa Loma Orchestra (Decca).

Never Knew Love Like This. w/m James Harris III and Terry Lewis, 1988. Top 10 R&B/Pop chart crossover record by Alexander O'Neal, featuring Cherrelle (Tabu).

Never Knew Love Like This Before. w/m James Mtume and Reginald Lucas, 1980. Top 10 gold record by Stephanie Mills (20th Century). Winner Grammy Award (NARAS) Rhythm and Blues Song of the Year.

Never Leave Me. w/m Gordon Jenkins, 1956. Developed from a theme from the original album by Gordon Jenkins with his orchestra, chorus, and narrator, "Manhattan Tower" (Decca), which was later expanded for a network TV show and new LP by Jenkins (Capitol). Recorded by Patti Page (Mercury), Dick Haymes (Capitol), Dick Hyman (MGM), and others.

Never Let Her Go. w/m Kay Twomey, Fred Wise, and Ben Weisman, 1952. Featured and recorded by Ray Bloch and his Orchestra (Coral).

Nevermore. w/m Noël Coward, 1934. Introduced in London and then in New York by Yvonne Printemps in (TM) *Conversation Piece*.

Never My Love. w/m Don Addrisi and Dick Addrisi, 1967. Gold record by The Association (Warner Bros.). Hit records by The 5th Dimension (Bell), 1971; the Swedish sextet, Blue Swede (Emi), 1974; the writers, the Addrisi Brothers, with their own version (Buddah), 1977.

Never Never Land. w. Betty Comden and Adolph Green, m. Jule Styne, 1954. Introduced by Mary Martin in (TM) *Peter Pan*.

Never on Sunday. w/ Billy Towne (Engl.), and Manos Hadjidakis (Gr.), m. Manos Hadjidakis, 1960. Introduced with Greek lyrics, and titled "Ta Pedia Tou Pirea" ("The Children of Piraeus") by Melina Mercouri in the Greek film (MP) *Never on Sunday*. Academy Award-winning song, 1960. Don Costa and his Orchestra had the leading instrumental recording (United Artists), and The Chordettes, the leading vocal (Cadence).

Never Say No to a Man. w/m Richard Rodgers, 1962. One of five songs Rodgers wrote for the second musical version of (MM) *State Fair*. This was sung by Alice Faye.

Never Should Have Told You. w/m Dave Franklin and Cliff Friend, 1937. Introduced and recorded by Benny Goodman and his Orchestra (Victor).

Never Surrender. w/m Corey Hart, 1985. Top 10 record by Canadian singer Corey Hart (EMI America).

Never Tear Us Apart. w/m Andrew Farriss and Michael Hutchence, 1988. Single from the album "Kick" by the Australian group INXS (Atlantic).

Nevertheless (I'm in Love with You). w. Bert Kalmar, m. Harry Ruby, 1931, 1950. Featured and recorded by the orchestras of Rudy Vallee (Victor) and Jack Denny (Brunswick). In the Kalmar and Ruby story, (MM) *Three Little Words*, 1950, it was sung by Fred Astaire, Red Skelton, and, dubbing for Vera-Ellen, Anita Ellis. This engendered new recordings and the song became a #1 hit. Best sellers by The Mills Brothers (Decca); Paul Weston (Columbia); Ray Anthony (Capitol); Ralph Flanagan, vocal by Harry Prime (Victor); Frank Sinatra (Columbia); Frankie Laine (Mercury).

Never the Luck. w/m Rupert Holmes, 1985. Introduced by Joe Grifasi in (TM) *The Mystery of Edwin Drood*.

Never Trust a Woman. w/m Jenny Lou Carson, 1948. Popular recordings by Red Foley (Decca) and Louis Jordan and his Tympany Five (Decca).

Never Will I Marry. w/m Frank Loesser, 1960. Introduced by Anthony Perkins in (TM) *Green Willow*.

'N' Everything. w/m Al Jolson, B. G. DeSylva, and Gus Kahn, 1917. Recorded by Al Jolson (Columbia), then interpolated the following year in (TM) *Sinbad*. It was DeSylva's first hit.

New Ashmolean Marching Society and Students' Conservatory Band. w/m Frank Loesser, 1948. Introduced by Byron Palmer, Allyn McLerie, Bobby Harrell, and Doretta Morrow in (TM) *Where's Charley?* In (MM) *Where's Charley?*, 1952, it was sung by Allyn McLerie and ensemble.

New Attitude. w/m Sharon Robinson, Jonathan Gilutin, and Bunny Hall, 1985. Top 10 crossover (R&B/Pop) chart record by Patti LaBelle (MCA).

New-Fangled Tango, A. w. Matt Dubey, m. Harold Carr, 1956. Introduced by Ethel Merman, Virginia Gibson, Leon Belasco, and the chorus in (TM) *Happy Hunting*.

New Fool at an Old Game. w/m R. Giles and S. Stephen, 1989. Hit Country single by Reba McEntire (MCA).

New Jole Blon. See **New Pretty Blonde.**

New Kid in Town. w/m Glenn Frey, Don Henlet, and John D. Souther, 1977. Recorded by the Eagles in their album "Hotel California" (Asylum). The single release became a #1 gold record.

New Look, The. w/m Barclay Allen, Roc Hillman, and Barney Ide, 1948. Title derived from the appellation given to the ladies' dress and coat styles of the day. Recorded by Freddy Martin and his Orchestra (RCA Victor).

New Moon and an Old Serenade, A. w/m Abner Silver, Sam Coslow, and Martin Block, 1939. Featured and recorded by the bands of Charlie Barnet (Bluebird) and Cab Calloway (Vocalion).

New Moon Is over My Shoulder, A. w. Arthur Freed, m. Nacio Herb Brown, 1934. Introduced by Phil Regan in (MM) *Student Tour*. Regan recorded it (Columbia). Others: Jane Froman (Decca); Johnny Green's Orchestra (Columbia); Isham Jones, vocal by Joe Martin (Victor); Georgie Price (Banner); Joe Reichman's Orchestra (Melotone); Anson Week's Orchestra (Brunswick).

New Moon on Sunday. w/m Duran Duran, 1984. Top 10 record by the English band Duran, Duran (Capitol).

New Mule Skinner Blues. See **Blue Yodel #8.**

New Orleans. w/m Frank Guida and Joseph Royster, 1960. Popularized by Top 10 record of Gary U.S. Bonds (Legrand). Revived by Eddie Hodges (Aurora), 1965, and Neil Diamond (Bang), 1968.

New Orleans. w. Gus Kahn, m. Arthur Johnston, 1935. Introduced in (MM) *Thanks a Million* and recorded by Ramona, with Paul Whiteman and his Orchestra (Victor).

New Orleans Bump. m. Ferdinand "Jelly Roll" Morton, 1929. Introduced and recorded by Jelly Roll Morton (Victor).

New Orleans Ladies. w/m H. Garrick and L. Medici, 1978. Recorded by the rock sextet, Louisiana's Le Roux (Capitol).

New Pair of Shoes, A. w/m Ervin Drake, 1963. Introduced by Steve Lawrence, Robert Alda, and chorus in (TM) *What Makes Sammy Run?*

New Pretty Blonde (a.k.a. **New Jole Blon**). w/m Lew Wayne and Moon Mullican, 1947. Cajun song introduced and recorded by Moon Mullican and the Showboys (King).

New San Antonio Rose. See **San Antonio Rose.**

New Sensation. w/m Andrew Farriss and Michael Hutchence, 1987. Single from the album "Kick" by the Australian group INXS (Atlantic).

New Sun in the Sky. w. Howard Dietz, m. Arthur Schwartz, 1931. Introduced by Fred Astaire in (TM) *The Band Wagon.* Astaire recorded it (Victor) with Leo Reisman's Orchestra. Betsy Drake sang it in (MM) *Dancing in the Dark* in 1949, and India Adams dubbed the vocal for Cyd Charisse in (MM) *The Band Wagon* in 1953.

New World Coming. w. Cynthia Weil, m. Barry Mann, 1970. Recorded by Mama Cass (Dunhill).

New World Man. w. Neil Peart, m. Alex Lifeson and Geddy Lee, 1982. Recorded by the Canadian trio Rush (Mercury).

New Year's Day. w/m Paul Hewson, Larry Mullen, Adam Clayton, and Dave Evans, 1983. Written and recorded by the Irish group U2 (Island).

New York, New York (The Bronx Is Up and the Battery Is Down). w. Betty Comden and Adolph Green, m. Leonard Bernstein, 1945. From the writers' first show score (TM) *On the Town,* and introduced by John Battles, Cris Alexander, and Adolph Green. In the film version (MM) *On the Town,* 1949, it was sung by Gene Kelly, Frank Sinatra, and Jules Munshin.

New York, New York. See **Theme from "New York, New York").**

New York Groove. w/m Russ Ballard, 1978. Recorded by guitarist/singer Ace Frehley (Casablanca).

New York Mining Disaster 1941 (Have You Seen My Wife, Mr. Jones?). w/m Barry Gibb, Maurice Gibb, and Robin Gibb, 1967. First U.S. chart hit by the English brother trio The Bee Gees (Atco).

New York's a Lonely Town. w/m Pete Andreoli and Vinnie Poncia, 1965. Top 40 record by The Trade Winds [the writers] (Red Bird).

New York's My Home. w/m Gordon Jenkins, 1946. Introduced by Beverly Mahr on the album "Manhattan Tower" (Decca). Later single releases by Patti Page (Mercury), Sammy Davis, Jr. (Decca), Ray Charles (Am-Par), Gordon Jenkins's Orchestra, with the Ralph Brewster Chorus (Capitol).

New York State of Mind. w/m Billy Joel, 1976. Introduced by Billy Joel in his album "Turnstiles" (Columbia).

Next Door to an Angel. w/m Howard Greenfield and Neil Sedaka, 1962. Introduced and recorded by Neil Sedaka (RCA).

Next in Line. w/m Wayne Kemp and Curtis Wayne, 1968. #1 Country chart record by Conway Twitty (Decca).

Next in Line. w/m Johnny Cash, 1957. C&W hit by Johnny Cash (Sun).

Next Plane to London. w/m Kenny Gist, Jr., 1967. Top 20 record by the quintet The Rose Garden (Atco).

Next Step Is Love, The. w/m Paul Evans and Paul Parnes, 1970. Recorded by Elvis Presley (RCA).

Next Time I Fall, The. w/m Bobby Caldwell and Paul Gordon, 1986. #1 chart record by Peter Cetera with Amy Grant (Full Moon).

Next Time It Happens, The. w. Oscar Hammerstein II, m. Richard Rodgers, 1955. Introduced by Judy Tyler and William Johnson in (TM) *Pipe Dream.*

Next Time You See Me. w/m Billy Harvey and Earl Forest, 1956. R&B chart record by Little Junior Parker (Duke).

Next to Lovin' (I Like Fightin'). w. Peter Udell, m. Garry Geld, 1975. Introduced by Jordan Suffin, Joel Higgins, Robert Rosen, Ted Agress, and David Russell in (TM) *Shenandoah.*

Next to Your Mother, Who Do You Love? w. Irving Berlin, m. Ted Snyder, 1909.

Nice, Nice, Very Nice. w. Kurt Vonnegut, Jr., B. Drummond, Chris North, David Pack, Joe Puerta, m. Drummond, North, Pack, and Puerta, 1975. Based on lyrics from Vonnegut's novel *Cat's Cradle.* Recorded by the trio Ambrosia (20th Century).

Nice 'n' Easy. w. Marilyn Keith Bergman and Alan Bergman, m. Lew Spence, 1960. Introduced and recorded by Frank Sinatra (Capitol).

Nice 'n Naasty. m. Vincent Montana, Jr., 1976. Recorded by The Salsoul Orchestra, led by Montana (Salsoul).

Nice to Be Around. w. Paul Williams, m. John Williams, 1973. Sung on the soundtrack of (MP) *Cinderella Liberty* by Paul Williams. Nominated for Academy Award. Recorded by Maureen McGovern (20th Century).

Nice to Be with You. w/m Jim Gold, 1972. Top 10 record by the sextet, Gallery, led by the writer (Sussex).

Nice Work If You Can Get It. w. Ira Gershwin, m. George Gershwin, 1937. Introduced by Fred Astaire, Jan Duggan, Mary Dean, Pearl Amatore, and ensemble in (MM) *A Damsel in Distress.* Astaire (Brunswick) and

the Andrews Sisters (Decca) had popular records. The latter was coupled with their phenomenal hit "Bei Mir Bist du Schoen" (q.v.) In 1951, Georges Guetary and Oscar Levant revived the number in (MM) *An American in Paris.*"

Nickel Song. w/m Melanie Safka, 1971. Recorded by The New Seekers (Elektra). Melanie had a Top 40 version (Buddah), 1972.

Nick Teen and Al K. Hall. w/m Rolf Harris, 1963. Australian novelty recorded by Rolf Harris (Epic).

Night. w/m Johnny Lehman and Herb Miller, 1960. Hit record by Jackie Wilson (Brunswick).

Night (Feel Like Getting Down). w/m Billy Ocean and Nigel Martinez, 1981. Top 10 R&B chart record by Billy Ocean (Epic).

Night and Day. w/m Cole Porter, 1932. Introduced by Fred Astaire and Claire Luce (TM) *Gay Divorce.* In the 1934 film version, retitled (MM) *The Gay Divorcée,* it was sung and danced by Fred Astaire and Ginger Rogers. Frank Sinatra sang it in (MM) *Reveille with Beverly* in 1943, and Deanna Durbin sang in it (MM) *Lady on a Train,* in 1945. In the Porter screen biography (MM) *Night and Day,* 1946, it was performed by Cary Grant, as Porter, and Alexis Smith. The song has been recorded by hundreds of singers, orchestras, and smaller groups and is considered to be one of the top standards of all American popular music.

Night Chicago Died, The. w/m Peter Callendar and Mitch Murray, 1974. #1 gold record by the English group Paper Lace (Mercury).

Nightfall. w/m Peter DeRose and Harold Lewis, 1932. Recorded by Paul Whiteman, vocal by Jack Fulton (Victor) and Freddy Martin and his Orchestra (Columbia).

Night Fever. w/m Barry Gibb, Maurice Gibb, and Robin Gibb, 1977. Sung by the Bee Gees on the soundtrack of (MM) *Saturday*

Night Fever. Their single became a #1 platinum record (RSO).

Night Has a Thousand Eyes, The. w/m Dottie Wayne, Marilynn Garrett, and Ben Weisman, 1963. Hit record by Bobby Vee (Liberty).

Night Has a Thousand Eyes, The. w. Buddy Bernier, m. Jerry Brainin, 1948. Title song for (MP) *The Night Has a Thousand Eyes.* Among recordings, Carl Ravazza with his Orchestra (Bluebird).

Night Hawk Blues. m. Joe Sanders, 1924. Introduced and recorded by the Coon-Sanders Night Hawks Orchestra (Victor).

Nightingale. w/m Carole King and David Palmer, 1975. Top 10 record by Carole King (Ode).

Nightingale. w. Fred Wise (Engl.), m. Xavier Cugat and George Rosner, 1942. Original Spanish words by Emilio de Torre. Introduced and recorded by Xavier Cugat, vocal by Lina Romay (Columbia).

Nightingale Sang in Berkeley Square, A. w. Eric Maschwitz, m. Manning Sherwin, 1940. From the London theatrical production *New Faces.* Glenn Miller's version, vocal by Ray Eberle (Bluebird), was the best-seller; followed by Guy Lombardo, vocal by brother Carmen (Decca); Ray Noble, vocal by Larry Stewart (Columbia); Sammy Kaye, vocal by Tommy Ryan (Victor).

Night in June, A. See **Give Me a Night in June.**

Night in Tunisia, A. w. Jon Hendricks, m. Frank Paparelli and John Birks "Dizzy" Gillespie, 1946. Early bop instrumental introduced by Dizzy Gillespie's band (Musicraft). Other recordings of note by Charlie Parker (Dial) and Lennie Tristano (V-Disc). Revived by Chaka Khan on her gold album "What Cha' Gonna Do for Me" (Warner Bros.), 1981.

Night Is Young, The. w. Oscar Hammerstein II, m. Sigmund Romberg, 1935. The title song of (MM) *The Night Is Young,* sung by Ramon Novarro and Evelyn Laye. Recorded by Paul Whiteman and his Orchestra (Victor).

Night Is Young and You're So Beautiful, The. w. Billy Rose and Irving Kahal, m. Dana Suesse, 1936. Popular waltz, first performed at Billy Rose's Casa Mañana in Fort Worth, Texas, as part of the Frontier Days Fair. Among recordings: Wayne King and his Orchestra (Victor), and Cliff "Ukulele Ike" Edwards (Decca).

Nightlife. w. Lee Adams, m. Charles Strouse, 1962. Introduced by Anita Gillette and chorus in (TM) *All American.*

Night Lights. w. Sammy Gallop, m. Chester Conn, 1956. Popular record by Nat "King" Cole (Capitol).

Nightmare. m. Artie Shaw, 1938. Featured and recorded theme of Artie Shaw and his Orchestra (Bluebird).

Night Moves. w/m Bob Seger, 1977. Top 10 hit record by Bob Seger (Capitol).

Night Must Fall. w. Barnett Shaw, m. Xavier Cugat, 1939. Introduced and recorded by Xavier Cugat and his Orchestra (Victor). Other band recordings by Blue Barron (Bluebird), Tommy Tucker (Vocalion), Art Mooney (MGM).

Night of My Nights. w/m Robert Wright and George Forrest, 1953. Adapted from Borodin's "Serenade," a piano piece. Introduced by Richard Kiley in (TM) *Kismet.* Sung by Vic Damone in (MM) *Kismet,* 1955.

Night on the Desert. w/m Billy Hill, 1934. Recorded by Ben Pollack's (Vocalion) and Richard Himber's (Victor) bands.

Night on the Water. w/m Carmen Lombardo, George Clarke, Bert Clarke, 1934. Recorded by Art Kahn, vocal by Helen Ward (Melotone), and Enoch Light and His Light Brigade (Bluebird). Revived in early fifties by the Andrews Sisters and Guy Lombardo's Orchestra (Decca).

Night Owl. w/m Herman Hupfeld, 1933. Introduced by Cliff "Ukulele Ike" Edwards in

(MM) *Take a Chance.* He recorded it (Vocalion) as did the bands of George Olsen (Columbia), Paul Whiteman (Victor), and Henry King (Vocalion).

Night Owls, The. w/m Graham Goble, 1981. Top 10 record by the Australian group Little River Band (Capitol).

Nights Are Forever Without You. w/m Parker McGee, 1976. Top 10 record by England Dan and John Ford Coley (Big Tree).

Nightshift. w/m Walter Orange, Dennis Lambert, and Franne Golde, 1985. #1 R&B, #3 Pop chart hit by The Commodores (Motown). Song written as tribute to the late singers Marvin Gaye and Jackie Wilson.

Nights in White Satin. w/m Justin Hayward, 1972. Gold record single released from the 1968 album by the British group The Moody Blues (Deram). The writer was lead singer/guitarist.

Nights on Broadway. w/m Barry Gibb, Maurice Gibb, and Robin Gibb, 1975. Top 10 record by the British brother-trio The Bee Gees (RSO).

Night Song. w. Lee Adams, m. Charles Strouse, 1964. Introduced by Sammy Davis, Jr., in (TM) *Golden Boy.*

Night the Lights Went Out in Georgia, The. w/m Bobby Russell, 1973. #1 gold record by Vicki Lawrence (Bell). Inspired film of same name, 1981.

Night They Drove Old Dixie Down, The. w/m Robbie Robertson, 1971. Introduced by The Band in its self-named album (Capitol), 1969. Gold record single by Joan Baez (Vanguard).

Night They Invented Champagne, The. w. Alan Jay Lerner, m. Frederick Loewe, 1958. Introduced by Leslie Caron [voice dubbed on soundtrack by Betty Wand], Louis Jourdan, and Hermione Gingold in (MM) *Gigi.* In the stage version, (TM) *Gigi,* 1973, it was performed by Maria Karnilova, Daniel Massey, and Karin Wolfe.

Night Time. w/m Robert Feldman, Richard Gottehrer, and Gerald Goldstein, 1966. Top 40 record by The Strangeloves [the writer/producers] (Bang).

Night Train. w. Oscar Washington and Lewis C. Simpkins, m. Jimmy Forrest, 1952. Instrumental introduced by Jimmy Forrest (United). Buddy Morrow had a hit with his big band version (RCA Victor). Other top records: The Viscounts (Madison), 1960; Richard Hayman (Mercury), 1961; James Brown (King), 1962.

Night Train to Memphis. w/m Beasley Smith, Marvin Hughes, and Owen Bradley, 1942. Hit record by Roy Acuff and His Smoky Mountain Boys (Okeh).

Night Was Made for Love, The. w. Otto Harbach, m. Jerome Kern, 1931. Introduced by George Meader in (TM) *The Cat and the Fiddle.* In the 1934 film adaptation (MM) *The Cat and the Fiddle,* it was sung by Ramon Novarro.

Night Watch, The. w/m Cindy Walker, 1954. Featured and recorded by Red Foley (Decca).

Night We Called It a Day, The. w. Tom Adair, m. Matt Dennis, 1942. Introduced by Frank Sinatra and recorded by him on his first solo single after leaving Tommy Dorsey's band (Bluebird). It was coupled with "Night and Day." Sung by Allan Jones in (MM) *Sing a Jingle,* 1944.

Night Wind. w. Bob Rothberg, m. David A. Pollack, 1935. Recorded by many jazz artists including: Taft Jordan (Melotone); Fats Waller (Victor); Benny Goodman, vocal by Helen Ward (Columbia); the Dorsey Brothers, vocal by Bob Crosby (Decca); Cosy Cole (Guild); Billy Taylor's Big Eight (Key). This Taylor was the bass player, not the pianist.

Nijinsky. w. Gene Buck, m. Dave Stamper, 1916. Introduced in (TM) *Ziegfeld Follies* by Fanny Brice in a tutu, spoofing the Ballet Russe. Brice continued to use the number in vaudeville.

Niki Hoeky. w/m Jim Ford, Lolly Vegas, and Pat Vegas, 1966. Top 40 record by P. J. Proby, né James M. Smith (Liberty).

Nikita. w/m Elton John and Bernie Taupin, 1986. Top 10 record by English singer/songwriter Elton John (Geffen).

Nina. w/m Cole Porter, 1948. Introduced by Gene Kelly in (MM) *The Pirate*.

Nina Never Knew. w. Milton Drake, m. Louis Alter, 1952. Popularized via recording by the Sauter-Finegan Orchestra, vocal by Joe Mooney (RCA Victor). Johnny Desmond also had a well-received version (Coral).

Nina Rosa. w. Irving Caesar, m. Sigmund Romberg, 1930. Introduced by Guy Robertson in (TM) *Nina Rosa*. Recorded by the piano team of Arden and Ohman (Victor).

Nine Little Miles from Ten-Ten-Tennessee. w. Al Sherman and Al Lewis, m. Con Conrad, 1930. Recorded by Duke Ellington, vocal by Smith Ballew (Victor), and Tom Gerun (Brunswick).

9 to 5. w/m Dolly Parton, 1980. Introduced by Dolly Parton in (MP) *9 to 5*. Winner Academy Award, Best Song. Parton's recording became a #1 gold record and Grammy Award (NARAS) Winner, Country Song of the Year, 1981.

992 Arguments. w/m Kenny Gamble and Leon Huff, 1972. Recorded by The O'Jays (Philadelphia International).

Nine Pound Hammer. w/m Merle Travis, 1947. Recorded by Merle Travis (Capitol); Ernest V. Stoneman and Eddie Stoneman (Vocalion).

19. w/m Paul Hardcastle, W. Coutourie, and J. McCord, 1985. Instrumental recorded by the London keyboardist Paul Hardcastle (Profile). Title refers to the average age of U.S. soldiers in Vietnam. Music written for background to a spoken section on (TVP) "Vietnam Requiem."

Nineteen Days. w/m Dave Clark and Denis Payton, 1966. Recorded by The Dave Clark Five (Epic).

1982. w/m James Blackmon and Carl Vipperman, 1986. Top 10 Country chart record by Randy Travis (Warner Bros.).

1999. w/m Prince Rogers Nelson, 1982. Recorded by Prince (Warner Bros.).

19th Nervous Breakdown. w/m Mick Jagger and Keith Richards, 1966. Hit record by the English group The Rolling Stones (London).

98.6. w. Tony Powers, m. George Fischoff, 1967. Top 10 record by Keith, backed by The Tokens (Mercury).

Ninety Miles an Hour on a Dead-End Street. w. Hal Blair and Don Robertson, m. Don Robertson, 1963. Recorded by Hank Snow (RCA). Included by Bob Dylan in his album "Down in the Groove" (Columbia), 1988.

99. w/m David Paich, 1980. Recorded by the group Toto (Columbia).

99 Miles from L.A. w. Hal David, m. Albert Hammond, 1975. Recorded by the British singer Albert Hammond (Mums).

Ninety-Nine out of a Hundred (Want to Be Loved). w/m Al Lewis and Al Sherman, 1931. Introduced, featured, and recorded by Rudy Vallee (Victor).

Ninety-Nine Ways. w/m Anthony September, 1957. Popular recording by Tab Hunter (Dot).

Ninety-Nine Years (Dead or Alive). w. Sid Wayne, m. John Benson Brooks, 1956. Popularized by Guy Mitchell (Columbia).

96 Tears. w/m Rudy Martinez, 1966. #1 record by ? (Question Mark) and The Mysterians (Cameo). Revived by Garland Jeffreys (Epic), 1981.

Nite and Day. w/m Al B. Sure and Kyle West, 1988. #1 R&B and Top 10 Pop chart record by Al B. Sure! [he bills himself with the "!"] (Warner Bros.).

Nitty Gritty, The. w/m Lincoln Chase, 1963. Top 10 record by Shirley Ellis (Congress). Revived with Top 20 version by Gladys Knight and The Pips (Soul), 1969.

No! No! a Thousand Times No! (You Shall Not Buy My Caress). w/m Al Sherman, Al Lewis, and Abner Silver, 1934. A gay nineties sing-along type song that caught the fancy of the public via performances and recordings by the orchestras of Ozzie Nelson, vocal by Harriet Hilliard (Brunswick); George Hall, vocal by Loretta Lee (Bluebird); and others.

No, No, Nanette. w. Otto Harbach, m. Vincent Youmans, 1925. Introduced by Louise Groody in (TM) *No, No, Nanette*. In the 1971 Broadway production it was sung by Susan Watson. It was Bernice Claire's song in (MM) *No, No, Nanette*, 1930; Anna Neagle's in the 1940 remake; and Doris Day's in (MM) *Tea for Two*, 1950. Sigmund Romberg's "One Kiss" from *The New Moon*, 1928, used the identical opening musical strain, but Youmans took no action, possibly because both songs were published by the same company, Harms, Inc.

No, No, Nora. w. Gus Kahn, m. Ted Fio Rito and Ernie Erdman, 1923. Introduced by Ted Fio Rio and his Orchestra. Hit record by Eddie Cantor (Columbia). Featured by Ruth Etting in vaudeville.

No, Not Much. w. Al Stillman, m. Robert Allen, 1956. Popularized by The Four Lads (Columbia). Revived with hit record by The Vogues (Reprise), 1969.

No Arms Can Ever Hold You. w/m Art Crafer and Jimmy Nebb, 1955. Best-selling records by Georgie Shaw (Decca) and Pat Boone (Dot).

Nobody. w/m Kye Fleming and Dennis Morgan, 1982. Crossover (C&W/Pop) gold record by country singer Sylvia (RCA).

Nobody. w. Alex Rogers, m. Bert Williams, 1905. The comedy song made famous by Bert Williams, while still a member of the vaudeville team of Williams and Walker. He interpolated it in (TM) *Ziegfeld Follies of 1910* when he became the first Negro to star with white performers in a Broadway musical. Bob Hope performed the song in (MM) *The Seven Little Foys*, 1955. Among recordings: Williams (Columbia), Phil Harris (Vocalion), Perry Como (Victor), Bing Crosby (Decca). Performed by Avon Long in (TM) *Bubbling Brown Sugar*, 1976.

Nobody But a Fool. w/m Bill Anderson, 1966. Country hit recorded by Connie Smith (RCA).

Nobody But Me. w/m O'Kelly Isley, Ronald Isley, and Rudolph Isley, 1968. Introduced by The Isley Brothers (Wand), 1963. Top 10 record by The Human Beinz (Capitol), 1968.

Nobody But You. w/m Dee Clark, 1958. Recorded by Dee Clark (Abner).

Nobody But You. w. Joe Goodwin, m. Gus Edwards, 1929. Introduced by Cliff "Ukulele Ike" Edwards [not related to the composer] in (MM) *Hollywood Revue of 1929*. Records by Frankie Trumbauer's Orchestra (Okeh), and the Les Paul Trio, vocal by Clancy Hayes (Mercury).

Nobody But You, Babe. w/m Willie Clarke and Clarence Reid, 1969. Top 40 record by Clarence Reid (Alston).

Nobody Cares. w/m Ray Charles, 1961. Recorded by Ray Charles (Atco).

Nobody Cares If I'm Blue. w. Grant Clarke, m. Harry Akst, 1930. Recordings: Meyer Davis (Brunswick), Marion Harris (Brunswick), Frank Luther with Johnny Hamp's Orchestra (Victor), Lee Morse (Columbia).

Nobody Does It Better. w. Carole Bayer Sager, m. Marvin Hamlisch, 1977. Sung on the soundtrack of the James Bond film (MP) *The Spy Who Loved Me* by Carly Simon. Nominated for an Academy Award. Simon's single reached #2 on the charts and was awarded a gold record (Elektra).

Nobody Else But Me. w. Oscar Hammerstein II, m. Jerome Kern, 1946. Kern's last song, written for the Broadway revival of (TM) *Show Boat*. It was sung by Jan Clayton and chorus. Recorded by Paul Weston, vocal by Lou Dinning (Capitol).

Nobody Falls Like a Fool. w/m Peter McCann and M. Wright, 1985. #1 Country chart record by Earl Thomas Conley (RCA).

Nobody I Know. w/m John Lennon and Paul McCartney, 1964. Popular record by the British duo Peter and Gordon (Capitol).

Nobody in His Right Mind Would've Left Her. w/m Dean Dillon, 1986. Country chart record by Dean Dillon (RCA), 1980. Revived with a #1 Country chart version by George Strait (MCA), 1986.

Nobody Knows, Nobody Cares. w/m Charles K. Harris, 1909.

Nobody Knows (and Nobody Seems to Care). w/m Irving Berlin, 1919. The year of publication, there were three recordings made of this song, which was highly unusual. They were: The Art Hickman Trio (Columbia), Irving and Jack Kaufman (Columbia), and Esther Walker (Victor). The song sold over a million copies of sheet music, yet it is one of the lesser-known Berlin songs today.

Nobody Knows What's Goin' On (in My Mind But Me). w/m Stephen Friedland, 1965. Recorded by The Chiffons (Laurie).

Nobody Knows You When You're Down and Out. w/m Jimmy Cox, 1923. Introduced in vaudeville by Jimmy Cox. First recorded by Bobby Baker (Path). Leading record by Bessie Smith (Columbia). Others: Pine Top Smith (Vocalion), Julia Lee (Capitol), Nina Simone (Colpix). It was sung by Linda Hopkins in the Bessie Smith musical (TM) *Me and Bessie*, 1975.

Nobody Likes Sad Songs. w/m Wayland Hollyfield and Bob McDill, 1979. Hit Country chart record by Ronnie Milsap (RCA).

Nobody Makes a Pass at Me. w/m Harold Rome, 1937. Introduced by Millie Weitz in (TM) *Pins and Needles*. Revived by Barbra Streisand in the early sixties (Columbia).

Nobody Said It Was Easy (Lookin' for the Lights). w/m Tony Haseldon, 1982. Recorded by the Louisiana sextet Le Roux (RCA).

Nobody's Baby Again. w/m Baker Knight, 1966. Featured and recorded by Dean Martin (Reprise).

Nobody's Chasing Me. w/m Cole Porter, 1950. Introduced by Charlotte Greenwood and ensemble in (TM) *Out of This World*. Popular record by Dinah Shore, with Henri René's Orchestra (RCA Victor).

Nobody's Darlin' But Mine. w/m Jimmie Davis, 1935. Introduced and recorded by Davis (Decca) and revived in 1949 by Bing Crosby (Decca).

Nobody Sees Us But the Man in the Moon. w/m J. Tim Brymn, 1900.

Nobody's Fool. w/m Kenny Loggins and Michael Towers, 1988. Sung on the soundtrack of (MP) *Caddyshack II* and its album by Kenny Loggins (Columbia).

Nobody's Fool. w/m Tom Kiefer, 1987. Recorded by Cinderella, from the album "Night Songs" (Mercury).

Nobody's Fool But Yours. w/m Buck Owens, 1962. Hit C&W record by Buck Owens (Capitol).

Nobody's Heart (Belongs to Me). w. Lorenz Hart, m. Richard Rodgers, 1942. Introduced by Constance Moore and reprised by Ray Bolger in (TM) *By Jupiter*.

Nobody's Little Girl. w. Jack Drislane, m. Theodore F. Morse, 1907. Popular recordings on three labels by Byron G. Harlan (Victor, Edison, Columbia).

Nobody's Sweetheart. w/m Elmer Schoebel, Ernie Erdman, Gus Kahn, and Billy Meyers, 1924. After its initial popularity, it was revived by the Mills Brothers in 1932, with their million-selling first release, coupled with "Tiger Rag" (q.v.) (Brunswick). The song was heard in (MM) *The Cuban Love Song*, 1932; sung by Constance Moore in (MM) *I'm Nobody's Sweetheart Now*, 1940; heard in (MM) *Stage Door Canteen* and (MM) *Hit Parade of 1943*, 1943; sung by Belle Baker in (MM) *Atlantic City*, 1944; sung by Doris Day in the Gus Kahn biography (MM) *I'll See You in My Dreams*, 1952.

Nobody There But Me. w/m Bruce Hornsby, 1987. Country chart single by Willie Nelson from his album "Island in the Sea" (Columbia).

Nobody Told Me. w/m John Lennon, 1984. Top 10 posthumous record by John Lennon, from a 1980 session (Polydor).

Nobody Told Me. w/m Richard Rodgers, 1962. Introduced by Richard Kiley and Diahann Carroll in (TM) *No Strings*.

Nobody Wants Me. w. Morrie Ryskind, m. Henry Souvaine, 1926. Introduced by Helen Morgan, atop an upright piano, in the first edition of the revue (TM) *Americana*.

Nobody Wants to Be Alone. w/m Michael Masser and Rhonda Fleming, 1985. Top 10 Country chart record by Crystal Gayle (Warner Bros.).

No Can Do. w. Charles Tobias, m. Nat Simon, 1945. Top record by Guy Lombardo, vocal by Don Rodney and Rose Marie Lombardo (Decca).

No Chance. w/m Moon Martin, 1979. Recorded by Moon Martin (Capitol).

No Charge. w/m Harlan Howard, 1975. Novelty, popularized by Country singer Melba Montgomery (Elektra). Gospel singer Shirley Caesar had a chart record (Hob/Scepter), 1975.

Noche de Amour. See **Valentino Tango, The.**

Noche de Ronda. See **Be Mine Tonight.**

No Chemise, Please. w/m Gerry Granahan, Jodi D'Amour, and Arnold Golan, 1958. Top 40 record by Gerry Granahan (Sunbeam).

Nodding Roses. w. Schuyler Greene and Herbert Reynolds, m. Jerome Kern, 1916. Introduced by Alice Dovey and Oscar Shaw in (TM) *Very Good Eddie*, one of Kern's Princess Theatre hits.

No Foolin'. w. Gene Buck, m. James F. Hanley, 1926. Introduced by Louise Brown in (TM) *No Foolin'*, which, after its opening, was retitled (TM) *Ziegfeld's American Revue of 1926*.

No Gettin' Over Me. See **There's No Gettin' Over Me.**

No Help Wanted. w/m Bill Carlisle, 1953. C&W hit by The Carlisles (Mercury), Hank Thompson (Capitol), Red Foley and Ernest Tubb (Decca). #10 pop chart record by Rusty Draper (Mercury).

Nola. m. Felix Arndt, 1916. Published as a piano solo, but has had many recordings in various forms. The song became associated with the orchestra of Vincent Lopez, who recorded it (Okeh), 1922, and used it as his theme in hotels, stage shows, and broadcasts. Among the many other recordings: Jan August (Mercury); Roy Bargy, with Paul Whiteman's Orchestra (Columbia); Isham Jones's Orchestra (Decca); whistler Elmo Tanner, with orchestra (Dot). A lyric was written by Sunny Skylar with popular recordings by Billy Williams (Coral), and The Morgan Brothers (MGM), 1959.

No Letter Today. w/m Frankie Brown, 1943. Top 10 record by Ted Daffan and His Texans (Okeh).

No Lies. w/m Carol Hall, 1978. Introduced by Carlin Glynn, Delores Hall, and the girls in (TM) *Best Little Whorehouse in Texas*.

No Love (But Your Love). w/m Billy Myles, 1957. Popularized by Johnny Mathis (Columbia).

No Love, No Nothin'. w. Leo Robin, m. Harry Warren, 1943. Introduced by Alice Faye in (MM) *The Gang's All Here*. Recordings, in order of popularity, sales, etc: Ella Mae Morse (Capitol); Johnny Long, vocal; Patti Dugan (Decca); Jan Garber, vocal; Liz Tilton (Hit); Judy Garland (Decca).

No Love at All. w/m Wayne Carson Thompson and Johnny Christopher, 1971. Top 20 record by B. J. Thomas (Scepter).

No Love Have I. w/m Tommy Collins, 1960. Crossover (C&W/Pop) chart record by Webb Pierce (Decca). Revived by Gail Davies (Lifesong), 1978.

No Man Is an Island. w/m Joan Whitney and Alex Kramer, 1950. Featured and recorded by Don Cornell (Coral).

No Matter What. w/m William Peter Ham, 1970. Top 10 U.S. release by the British quartet Badfinger (Apple).

No Matter What Shape (Your Stomach's In). w/m Sascha Burland, 1966. Instrumental and Top 10 hit based on an Alka-Seltzer jingle, recorded by The T-Bones (Liberty).

No Matter What Sign You Are. w/m Henry Crosby and Berry Gordy, Jr., 1969. Top 40 record by Diana Ross and The Supremes (Motown).

No Milk Today. w/m Graham Gouldman, 1967. Recorded in England by Herman's Hermits (MGM).

No Money Down. w/m Chuck Berry, 1956. Top 10 R&B record by Chuck Berry (Chess).

No Moon at All. w/m Redd Evans and Dave Mann, 1953. First popular recording four years earlier by Nat "King" Cole (Capitol). Chart record by The Ames Brothers, with Les Brown and his Orchestra (Coral).

No More (My Baby Don't Love Me). w. Julie De John and Dux De John, m. Leo J. De John, 1954. Introduced and recorded by The De John Sisters, with O. B. Massingill's Orchestra (Epic).

No More Doggin'. w/m Roscoe Gordon, 1952. R&B hit by Roscoe Gordon (RPM).

No More Lonely Nights. w/m Paul McCartney, 1984. Introduced by Paul McCartney in (MM) *Give My Regards to Broad Street* and his Top 10 record (Columbia).

No More Love. w. Al Dubin, m. Harry Warren, 1933. Ballad introduced by Ruth Etting in (MM) *Roman Scandals* and recorded by her (Brunswick). Other records: Irene Taylor (Vocalion), Barney Rapp (Bluebird), Joe Venuti, vocal by Howard Phillips (Melotone).

No More Songs for Me. w. Richard Maltby, Jr., m. David Shire, 1964. Introduced and recorded by Barbra Streisand (Columbia).

No More Tears. w. Arthur Freed, m. Burton Lane, 1937. From (MP) *Her Husband Lies*. Recorded by Artie Shaw and his Orchestra (Brunswick).

No More Tears (Enough Is Enough). w/m Paul Jabara and Bruce Roberts, 1979. #1 gold record by Barbra Streisand and Donna Summer (Columbia).

No Name Jive. m. Larry Wagner, 1940. Introduced and recorded by Glen Gray and the Casa Loma Orchestra (Decca, Parts 1 & 2). Composed by Wagner, a long-time arranger for the band, this became one of Casa Loma's biggest hits, and a rare case of a two-sided instrumental reaching the Top 10 on the charts. The band played it in (MM) *Jam Session*, 1944. Gene Krupa and his Orchestra had a version (Columbia), as did Charlie Barnet and his Orchestra (Bluebird, Parts 1 & 2).

Non Dimenticar (Don't Forget). w. Shelley Dobbins (Engl.), Michele Galdieri (It.), m. P. G. Redi, 1958. In the Italian film *Anna*, it was originally "T'ho Voluto Bene." Popular recording by Nat "King" Cole (Capitol).

None of My Business. w/m Jack Moran, 1969. Top 10 Country chart record by Henson Cargill (Monument).

No Night So Long. w. Will Jennings, m. Richard Kerr, 1980. Recorded by Dionne Warwick (Arista).

No No Song. w/m Hoyt Axton and David Jackson, Jr., 1975. Top 10 record by Ringo Starr (Apple).

Non-Stop Flight. m. Artie Shaw, 1938. Featured and recorded by Artie Shaw and his Orchestra (Bluebird).

Noodlin' Rag. w. Allan Roberts, m. Robert Allen, 1952. Recorded by Perry Como, with Mitchell Ayres's Orchestra (RCA Victor).

No One. w/m Doc Pomus and Mort Shuman, 1961. Introduced and Top 40 record by Connie Francis (MGM). Ray Charles followed with a popular version in 1963 (ABC-Paramount).

No One But You. w. Jack Lawrence, m. Nicholas Brodsky, 1954. From (MP) *Flame and the Flash*. Recorded by Charlie Applewhite, arranged and conducted by Jack Pleis (Decca).

No One Else But You. w/m Don Redman, 1929. Redman arranged the song's first recording for Louis Armstrong (Okeh).

No One Ever Loved You More Than I. w. Edward B. Marks, m. Joseph W. Stern, 1896.

No One Is Alone. w/m Stephen Sondheim, 1987. Introduced by Kim Crosby, Chip Zien, Ben Wright, and Danielle Ferland in (TM) *Into the Woods*.

No One Is to Blame. w/m Howard Jones, 1986. Top 10 record by the English singer/songwriter Howard Jones (Elektra).

No One Knows. w. Ken Hecht, m. Ernie Maresca, 1958. Top 40 record by Dion and The Belmonts (Laurie).

No One's Gonna Hurt You Anymore. w/m Steve Karliski and Ted Cooper, 1967. Country chart record by Bill Anderson (Decca).

No One to Cry To. w/m Foy Willing and Sid Robin, 1946. Popular recording by The Sons of the Pioneers (Victor).

No Orchids for My Lady. w. Alan Stranks, m. Jack Strachey, 1949. English song. Among U.S. recordings: Frank Sinatra (Columbia), The Ink Spots (Decca), Tony Martin (RCA Victor), Billy Eckstine (MGM).

No Other Arms, No Other Lips. w/m Joan Whitney, Alex Kramer, and Hy Zaret, 1959. Featured and recorded by The Chordettes, with Archie Bleyer's Orchestra (Cadence).

No Other Love. w. Oscar Hammerstein II, m. Richard Rodgers, 1953. Original music was the theme, "Beneath the Southern Cross," from the series, "Victory at Sea," telecast over the NBC-TV network for twenty-six weeks, 1952-1953. Lyrics were added, and as a song, it was introduced by Isabel Bigley and Richard Hayes in (TM) *Me and Juliet*. Perry Como had a #1 record (RCA Victor).

No Other Love. w. Tot Seymour, m. Vee Lawnhurst, 1935. Featured and recorded by Benny Goodman, vocal by Helen Ward (Victor); Babs and Her Brothers (Decca); Little Jack Little (Columbia).

No Other Love. w/m Bob Russell and Paul Weston, 1950. Based on Frederic Chopin's *Etude No. 3 in E*, Opus 10. Top records by Perry Como (RCA Victor), Helen O'Connell (Capitol), Bob Haymes (Bell).

No Other One. w/m Ivory Joe Hunter and Clyde Otis, 1956. Featured and recorded by Eddie Fisher (RCA).

No Particular Place to Go. w/m Chuck Berry, 1964. Top 10 record by Chuck Berry (Chess).

No Place Like Home. w/m Paul Overstreet, 1987. Top 10 Country chart single from the album "Storms of Life" by Randy Travis (Warner Bros.).

Nora Malone (Call Me by Phone). w. Junie McCree, m. Albert Von Tilzer, 1910.

Interpolated by Blanche Ring in (TM) *The Yankee Girl*, and recorded by her (Victor).

No Regrets. w. Harry Tobias, m. Roy Ingraham, 1936. Artie Shaw played clarinet in the band behind Billie Holiday's recording (Vocalion) and then recorded it with his own band on their first session (Brunswick). Tommy Dorsey, vocal by Jack Leonard (Victor); Frances Faye (Decca); Joe Haymes (Perfect); and Wingy Manone (Bluebird) also had records.

No Regrets (Non, Je Ne Regrette Rien). w. Hal David (Engl.), Michel Vaucaire (Fr.), m. Charles Dumont, 1961. French song introduced and recorded in Paris, 1960, by Edith Piaf. English lyric written in 1961. Leading record by Piaf (Capitol).

No Reply at All. w/m Tony Banks, Phil Collins, and Michael Rutherford, 1981. Recorded by the British group Genesis (Atlantic).

Norman. w/m John D. Loudermilk, 1962. Top 10 record by Sue Thompson (Hickory).

Normandy. w. Georgie Price, m. Abner Silver, 1927. Popular record by Ace Brigode's Band (Victor).

North to Alaska. w/m Mike Phillips, 1960. Introduced on the soundtrack of (MP) *North to Alaska* by Johnny Horton and recorded by him (Columbia).

North Wind. w/m Rodney Morris, 1953. Recorded by Slim Whitman (Imperial).

Norway. w. Joseph McCarthy, m. Fred Fisher, 1915.

Norwegian Wood. w/m John Lennon and Paul McCartney, 1965. From The Beatles LP "Rubber Soul" (Capitol).

No Sad Songs. w/m Darryl Carter, 1968. Recorded by Joe Simon (Sound Stage 7).

No Strings. w/m Richard Rodgers, 1962. Introduced by Richard Kiley and Diahann Carroll in (TM) *No Strings*.

No Strings (I'm Fancy Free). w/m Irving Berlin, 1935. Introduced in (MM) *Top Hat* and recorded by Fred Astaire (Brunswick).

Not a Day Goes By. w/m Stephen Sondheim, 1981. Introduced by Jim Walton in (TM) *Merrily We Roll Along*.

Not a Moment Too Soon. w/m Murray Grand, 1960. Featured and recorded by Mabel Mercer (Atlantic).

Not As a Stranger. w. Buddy Kaye, m. James Van Heusen, 1955. First heard as dance music on the soundtrack of (MP) *Not As a Stranger*. Recorded by Frank Sinatra (Capitol).

Not a Soul. w. Tennessee Williams, m. Kenyon Hopkins, 1960. Introduced by Marlon Brando in (MP) *The Fugitive Kind*.

Not Bad. w. James Dyrenforth, m. John Green, 1934. Recorded in England by Ray Noble, vocal by Al Bowlly (HMV/Victor).

No Tell Lover. w/m Peter Cetera, Lee Loughnane, and Danny Seraphine, 1979. Written by members of the group that recorded it, Chicago (Columbia).

Not Enough Indians. w/m Baker Knight, 1968. Featured and recorded by Dean Martin (Reprise).

Not Enough Love in the World. w/m Don Henley, Danny Kortchmar, and Ben Tench, 1985. Recorded by Don Henley (Geffen).

Not Fade Away. w/m Charles Hardin and Norman Petty, 1964. First U.S. chart record by the British group The Rolling Stones (London).

Not for All the Rice in China. w/m Irving Berlin, 1933. Introduced by Marilyn Miller and Clifton Webb in (TM) *As Thousands Cheer*. Bing Crosby sang it in (MM) *Blue Skies* in 1946. Webb recorded it with Leo Reisman's Orchestra (Victor) as did Ramona, with Roy Bargy's Orchestra (Victor).

Nothin' at All. w/m Mark Mueller, 1986. Top 10 single by the band Heart (Capitol).

Nothin' But a Good Time. w/m Bobby Dall, C. C. DeVille, Brett Michaels, and Ricki

Rockett, 1988. Single from the album "Open Up and Say Ahh!" by Poison (Capitol).

Nothin' for Nothin'. w. Dorothy Fields, m. Morton Gould, 1950. Introduced by Pearl Bailey in (TM) *Arms and the Girl*. Recorded by Pearl Bailey (Columbia), and Artie Shaw, vocal by Mary Ann McCall (Decca).

Nothing But a Heartache. w/m Wayne Bickerton and Tony Waddington, 1968. Recorded by the English group The Flirtations (Deram).

Nothing But Heartaches. w/m Eddie Holland, Lamont Dozier, and Brian Holland, 1965. Recorded by The Supremes (Motown).

Nothing Can Stop Me. w/m Curtis Mayfield, 1965. Recorded by Gene Chandler (Constellation).

Nothing Could Be Sweeter. See **Why, Oh Why?**

Nothing Ever Changes My Love for You. w. Jack Segal, m. Marvin Fisher, 1956. Recorded by Nat "King" Cole (Capitol).

Nothing From Nothing. w/m Billy Preston and Bruce Fisher, 1974. #1 gold record by Billy Preston (A&M).

Nothing I Can Do About It Now. w/m Beth Nielsen Chapman, 1989. Hit Country single by Willie Nelson (Columbia).

Nothing in Common. w/m Tom Bailey and Alannah Currie, 1986. Written and recorded by two-thirds of the British trio who called themselves The Thompson Twins (Arista). Said trio sang the song on the soundtrack of (MP) *Nothing in Common*.

Nothing New Beneath the Sun. w/m George M. Cohan, 1906. Originally written for the 1901 Cohan musical *The Governor's Son*, but not published until 1906, when it enjoyed some popularity.

Nothing's Gonna Change My Love for You. w/m Michael Masser, 1987. First recorded by George Benson on his album, 20/20 (Warner Bros.), 1985. Chart single by Glenn

Medeiros, from the album of his name (Amherst), 1987.

Nothing's Gonna Stop Us Now. w/m Diane Warren and Albert Hammond, 1987. #1 Pop chart record by the group, Starship, from the soundtrack of (MP) *Mannequin*. Nominated for an Academy Award.

Nothing's Too Good for My Baby. w/m Sylvia Moy, Henry Cosby, and William Stevenson, 1966. Top 20 record by Stevie Wonder (Tamla).

Nothing Takes the Place of You. w/m Toussaint McCall and Patrick Robinson, 1967. Recorded by R&B singer/organist Toussaint McCall (Ronn).

Nothin' Yet (We Ain't Got). See **We Ain't Got (Nothin' Yet).**

No Time. w/m Randy Bachman and Burton Cummings, 1970. Written by two members of the Canadian group, The Guess Who, which had a Top 10 record (RCA).

No Time at All. w/m Stephen Schwartz, 1972. Introduced by Irene Ryan and chorus in (TM) *Pippin*.

Not Me. w/m Gary Anderson and Frank Guida, 1960. Introduced and recorded by Gary U.S. Bonds (Legrand). Writer Anderson is singer Bonds. Popular record by The Orlons (Cameo), 1963.

Not Mine. w. Johnny Mercer, m. Victor Schertzinger, 1942. Introduced by Dorothy Lamour, Eddie Bracken, Betty Hutton, Jimmy Dorsey and his Orchestra, and Bob Eberly in (MM) *The Fleet's In*. Dorsey had a popular record, vocal by Bob Eberly and Helen O'Connell (Decca).

Notorious. w/m Simon LeBon, John Taylor, and Nick Rhodes, 1986. Top 10 record by the British group Duran Duran (Capitol).

Not Responsible. w/m Gordon Mills, 1966. Hit record by the Welsh singer Tom Jones (Parrot).

Not Since Nineveh. w/m Robert Wright and George Forrest, 1953. Adapted from a theme from Borodin's "Polovetsian Dances." Introduced by Joan Diener and Henry Calvin in (TM) *Kismet*. Recorded by Danny Kaye (Decca). Dolores Gray sang it in (MM) *Kismet*, 1955.

Not So Long Ago. w/m Marty Robbins, 1963. Country chart record by Marty Robbins (Columbia).

Not So Sweet Martha Lorraine. w/m Joe McDonald, 1967. Recorded by Country Joe [McDonald] and The Fish (Vanguard).

Not the Lovin' Kind. w/m Lee Hazlewood, 1965. Hit record by Dino, Desi, and Billy (Reprise).

Not What I Had in Mind. w/m Jack Clement, 1963. Country hit by George Jones (United Artists).

Not While I'm Around. w/m Stephen Sondheim, 1978. Introduced by Ken Jennings and Angela Lansbury in (MM) *Sweeney Todd, The Demon Barber of Fleet Street*.

No Two People. w/m Frank Loesser, 1951. Introduced by Danny Kaye and Jane Wyman in (MM) *Hans Christian Andersen*. Leading record by Doris Day and Donald O'Connor (Columbia).

No Vacancy. w/m Merle Travis and Cliffie Stone, 1946. Hit C&W record by Merle Travis (Capitol).

Now. w. Betty Comden and Adolph Green, m. adapted by Jule Styne, 1963. Written for the civil rights movement to an adaptation of the Israeli melody "Hava Nagila." Introduced and recorded by Lena Horne (20th Century-Fox).

Now and for Always. w/m Roy Alfred, 1958. Top 40 record by George Hamilton IV (ABC-Paramount).

Now and Forever. m. Bert Kaempfert, 1961. Instrumental, recorded in Germany by Bert Kaempfert and his Orchestra and released in the U.S. (Decca).

Now and Forever (You and Me). w/m David Foster, Jim Vallance, and Randy Goodrum, 1986. #1 Country chart song and Pop crossover by Canadian singer Anne Murray (Capitol).

No Way Out. w/m Paul Anka and Michael McDonald, 1987. Sung on the soundtrack of (MP) *No Way Out* by Julia Migenes and Paul Anka.

No Way Out. w/m Peter Wolf and Ina Wolf, 1984. Recorded by the group Jefferson Starship (Grunt).

No Wedding Bells for Me. w. E. P. Moran and Will A. Heelan, m. Seymour Furth, 1907. Sung by Flavia Arcaro in (TM) *The Orchid*. Recorded by Billy Murray (Victor) and Bob Roberts (Columbia).

Nowhere Man. w/m John Lennon and Paul McCartney, 1966. Gold record by The Beatles (Capitol). Song interpolated in their animated film (MM) *Yellow Submarine*, 1968.

Nowhere Road. w/m Steve Earle and Reno Kling, 1987. Country chart record by Steve Earle (MCA).

Nowhere to Run. w/m Brian Holland, Lamont Dozier, and Eddie Holland, 1965. Top 10 record by Martha and The Vandellas (Gordy).

Now I Have Everything. w. Sheldon Harnick, m. Jerry Bock, 1964. Introduced by Bert Convy and Julia Migenes in (TM) *Fiddler on the Roof*. Song not used in film version.

Now I Know. w. Stanley Gelber and Scott English, m. James Last, 1967. Recorded by Jack Jones (Kapp).

Now I Know. w. Ted Koehler, m. Harold Arlen, 1944. Introduced by Dinah Shore in (MM) *Up in Arms*. Nominated for Academy Award.

Now I Lay Me Down to Dream. w/m Ted Fio Rito and Eddy Howard, 1940. Popularized by the records of Bob Chester, vocal by Dolores O'Neill (Bluebird); Guy Lombardo, vocal by Kenny Gardner (Decca); Andy Kirk, vocal by Pha Terrell (Decca).

Now I'm a Lady. w/m Sam Coslow, Sammy Fain, and Irving Kahal, 1935. Introduced by Mae West in (MM) *Goin' to Town*. Recorded by Ramona, with Paul Whiteman's Orchestra (Victor), and by Joe Haymes's Orchestra (Bluebird).

Now Is the Hour (Maori Farewell Song). w/m Maewa Kaihan, Clement Scott, and Dorothy Stewart, 1948. Based on traditional New Zealand song. Original Maori title, "Haerere Ra." Gracie Fields revived it (London) and was covered by Bing Crosby, who had a million-seller (Decca). Other versions: Margaret Whiting (Capitol), Buddy Clark (Columbia), Eddy Howard (Majestic), Kate Smith (MGM).

Now It Can Be Told. w/m Irving Berlin, 1938. Introduced by Don Ameche and Alice Faye in (MM) *Alexander's Ragtime Band*. This Academy Award nominee was recorded by Tony Martin, with Ray Noble's Orchestra (Brunswick); Mildred Bailey, with Red Norvo's Orchestra (Vocalion); Teddy Wilson, vocal by Nan Wynn (Brunswick); Ruby Newman's Orchestra (Decca); and Roger Pryor's Orchestra (Vocalion).

No Wonder I'm Blue. w. Oscar Hammerstein II, m. Louis Alter, 1931. Introduced in (TM) *Ballyhoo* by Grace Hayes. Recorded by Frank Crumit (Columbia) and the New Orleans Ramblers (Melotone).

Now or Never. w. Sam M. Lewis, m. Peter De Rose, 1936.

Now Run and Tell That. w/m Denise LaSalle, 1972. Recorded by Denise LaSalle (Westbound).

Now's the Time. m. Charlie Parker, 1945. Introduced on records by Charlie Parker's group, which featured Miles Davis, Dizzy Gillespie, Max Roach, and Curly Russell (Savoy). Also recorded by Cozy Cole (Guild).

Now's the Time to Fall in Love (Potatoes Are Cheaper—Tomatoes Are Cheaper). w/m Al Sherman and Al Lewis, 1931. A novelty, stemming from the early years of the depression. Introduced by Eddie Cantor on his radio show. He sang it on the soundtrack for Keefe Brasselle in (MM) *The Eddie Cantor Story* in 1946, which was released on records (Decca).

Now That I'm in Love. w. Johnny Burke, m. G. Rossini, 1953. Adapted from Rossini's "William Tell Overture." Recorded by Patti Page (Mercury).

Now That I Need You (Where Are You). w/m Frank Loesser, 1949. Introduced by Betty Hutton in (MM) *Red, Hot, and Blue* (not to be confused with Broadway musical of same name). Leading recordings by Doris Day (Columbia) and Frankie Laine (Mercury).

Now That Summer Is Gone. w/m Seymour Simons, 1936. Introduced and featured on radio by Seymour Simons and his Orchestra. Recordings by the orchestras of Woody Herman (Decca), Red Norvo (Brunswick), and Shep Fields (Bluebird).

Now That We're in Love. w. Sammy Cahn, m. George Barrie, 1975. Introduced on the soundtrack of (MP) *Whiffs*. Nominated for an Academy Award.

Now That You're Gone. w. Gus Kahn, m. Ted Fio Rito, 1931. Featured and recorded by Ruth Etting (Columbia), Ted Black and his Orchestra (Victor), Guy Lombardo and the Royal Canadians (Columbia).

Now We Know. w. Ray Mayer, m. Willard Robison, 1940. Featured and recorded by Artie Shaw, vocal by Martha Tilton (Victor), and Ginny Simms (Okeh).

Now You Has Jazz. w/m Cole Porter, 1956. Introduced by Bing Crosby and Louis Armstrong in (MM) *High Society*, and on records (Capitol).

Now You're in My Arms. w. Morton Downey, m. Allie Wrubel, 1931. Wrubel's first song success. Introduced by Downey on his radio show. Recorded by Bert Lown and his Orchestra, vocal by Elmer Feldkamp (Victor); James Melton (Columbia).

Now You've Got Me Doing It. w. Johnny Burke, m. Harold Spina, 1935. Featured and recorded by Phil Harris (Decca).

#9 Dream. w/m John Lennon, 1975. Top 10 record by John Lennon (Apple).

Number 10 Lullaby Lane. w/m Bob Carlton, m. Bob Warren, 1941. Featured and re-

corded by Eddy Duchin, vocal by June Robbins (Columbia); Tony Pastor, vocal by Linda Keene (Bluebird); Joe Reichman's Orchestra (Victor).

Nutbush City Limits. w/m Tina Turner, 1973. Recorded by Ike and Tina Turner (United Artists). Bob Seger had a chart version (Capitol), 1976.

Nuttin' for Christmas. w/m Sid Tepper and Roy C. Bennett, 1955. Christmas novelty hit sung by seven-year-old Barry Gordon, with Art Mooney and his Orchestra (MGM).

O

O, Katharina! w. L. Wolfe Gilbert, m. Richard Fall, 1924. Popular records by the bands of Ted Lewis (Columbia), Lou Gold (Cameo), Ben Bernie (Vocalion), Vincent Lopez (Okeh), and later, on a 12″ record, "Jazz Session at Commodore" (CMS).

O (Oh!). w. Byron Gay, m. Byron Gay and Arnold Johnson, 1920. Recorded by Ted Lewis and his Band (Columbia). It was revived by Pee Wee Hunt and his Orchestra (Capitol), 1953.

Oakie Boogie. w/m Johnny Tyler, 1947. Records: Johnny Tyler (RCA Victor), Ella Mae Morse (Capitol).

Oak Tree, The. w/m Morris Day, 1985. Recorded by Morris Day (Warner Bros.).

Oasis. w/m M. Miller and M. Stevens, 1989. Hit R&B chart single by Roberta Flack (Atlantic).

Object of My Affection, The. w/m Pinky Tomlin, Coy Poe, and Jimmie Grier, 1934. Best-selling record by Pinky Tomlin, with Jimmie Grier's Orchestra (Brunswick). Other versions of this hit: the Boswell Sisters (Brunswick); Jan Garber, vocal by Lee Bennett (Victor); Archie Bleyer (Vocalion); Paul Pendarvis, vocal by Patricia Norman (Columbia); Joe Reichman, vocal by Paul Small (Banner). Lionel Hampton recorded it in 1937 (Victor). It was interpolated in (MP) *Time Square Lady* in 1937 and played by the Dorsey Brothers Band in (MM) *The Fabulous Dorseys* in 1947.

Ob-La-Di, Ob-La-Da. w/m John Lennon and Paul McCartney, 1969. Introduced and popularized by The Beatles in their "White Album" (Apple). First chart single of the song by Arthur Conley (Atco), 1969. The Beatles' cut from their album was released as a single (Capitol), 1976.

Obsession. w/m Holly Knight and Michael Desbarres, 1985. Top 10 record by the quintet Animotion (Mercury).

O Cangaceiro. See **Bandit, The.**

Ocarina, The. w/m Irving Berlin, 1950. Introduced by Galina Talva in (TM) *Call Me Madam*. Performed by Vera-Ellen in (MM) *Call Me Madam*, 1953.

Occasional Man, An. w/m Hugh Martin and Ralph Blane, 1955. Introduced by Gloria DeHaven in (MM) *The Girl Rush*. Leading record by Jeri Southern (Decca).

Occidental Woman (in an Oriental Mood for Love). w/m Gene Austin, 1936. Sung by Mae West in (MM) *Klondike Annie*.

Oceana Roll, The. w. Roger Lewis, m. Lucien Denni, 1911. Later recorded by Beatrice Kay (Columbia) and Teresa Brewer (London).

Ocean Front Property. w/m Dean Dillon, Chuck Cochran, and Royce Porter, 1987. #1 Country chart record by George Strait and title song of his platinum album (MCA).

Octoroon. m. Harry Warren, 1939. Featured and recorded by Artie Shaw (Bluebird) and Jack Teagarden (Brunswick) and their orchestras.

Odds and Ends. w. Hal David, m. Burt Bacharach, 1969. Recorded by Dionne Warwick (Scepter).

Odds and Ends, Bits and Pieces. w/m Harlan Howard, 1961. Hit on the Country charts by Warren Smith (Liberty).

Ode to Billy Joe. w/m Bobbie Gentry, 1967. #1 gold record by Bobbie Gentry (Capitol). Instrumental chart record by The Kingpins, featuring King Curtis (Atco). Bobbie Gentry re-recorded the song for the soundtrack of (MP) *Ode to Billy Joe*, 1976. Released as a single (Warner Bros.), it made the charts along with the re-release of her first record.

Ode to the Little Brown Shack Out Back. w/m Billy Edd Wheeler, 1964. Comedic crossover (C&W/Pop) chart hit by folk singer/composer Billy Edd Wheeler (Kapp).

O Dio Mio. w/m Al Hoffman and Dick Manning, 1960. Annette (Funicello) had a Top 10 record (Vista).

O Dry Those Tears! w/m Teresa Del Riego, 1901. Originally published in London, England.

Off on Your Own (Girl). w/m Al B. Sure and Kyle West, 1988. #1 R&B chart record by Al B. Sure! (Warner Bros.).

Off Shore. w. Steve Graham, m. Leo Diamond, 1953. Harmonicist Leo Diamond had first instrumental hit (Ambassador), followed by Richard Hayman (Mercury).

Off the Wall. w/m Rod Temperton, 1980. Top 10 single from the 1979 album "Off The Wall," by Michael Jackson, produced by Quincy Jones (Epic).

Of Thee I Sing. w. Ira Gershwin, m. George Gershwin, 1931. Introduced by William Gaxton, Lois Moran, and ensemble in (TM) *Of Thee I Sing*, the first musical to be awarded the Pulitzer Prize for drama. Recordings by the Arden-Ohman Orchestra (Victor), Sleepy Hall's Orchestra (Melotone), Paul Small

(Crown), and Jane Froman in a Gershwin medley (Victor 12″).

Oh, Babe! w/m Louis Prima and Milton Kabak, 1950. Introduced and recorded by Louis Prima, vocal by Keely Smith (Robin Hood), for their first chart record together. Top popular recordings by Kay Starr, with Frank DeVol's Orchestra (Capitol), The Ames Brothers (Coral), The Benny Goodman Sextet (Columbia), Ralph Flanagan, with vocal by Steve Benoric (RCA Victor).

Oh, Babe, What Would You Say? w/m E. B. Smith, 1973. Top 10 U.S. record by English singer/producer Hurricane Smith (Capitol).

Oh, Baby. w/m Owen Murphy, 1928. Interpolated in (TM) *Rain or Shine* starring Joe Cook. Among the jazz recordings are those by Ted Lewis (Columbia), Bobby Hackett (Columbia), Bud Freeman (Decca). Fletcher Henderson's Dixie Stompers (Harmony), Eddie Condon (Columbia), and Benny Goodman's two-sided 12″ recording (Columbia).

Oh, Baby Mine (I Get So Lonely). w/m Pat Ballard, 1954. Popular record by The Four Knights (Capitol).

Oh! Boy, What a Girl. w. Bud Green, m. Frank Wright Bessinger, 1925. Featured and recorded by Eddie Cantor (Columbia).

Oh, But I Do. w. Leo Robin, m. Arthur Schwartz, 1946. Introduced by Dennis Morgan in (MM) *The Time, The Place and the Girl*. Leading records by Margaret Whiting, with Jerry Gray's Orchestra (Capitol), and Tex Beneke, vocal by Artie Malvin (RCA Victor).

Oh, by Jingo! Oh, by Gee! (You're the Only Girl for Me). w. Lew Brown, m. Albert Von Tilzer, 1919. The hit song from (TM) *Linger Longer Letty* was introduced by Charlotte Greenwood. Betty Hutton sang it in the role of Texas Guinan in her film biography (MM) *Incendiary Blonde*, 1945. It was also interpolated by Vivian Blaine in (MM) *Skirts Ahoy*, starring Esther Williams, 1952.

Oh! Carol. w. Howard Greenfield, m. Neil Sedaka, 1959. First Top 10 recording by Neil Sedaka (RCA).

Oh! Darling. w/m John Lennon and Paul McCartney, 1978. Introduced by The Beatles in their album "Abbey Road," 1969. Sung by Robin Gibb in (MM) *Sgt. Pepper's Lonely Hearts Club Band*, and on Top 20 record (RSO), 1978.

Oh! Didn't He Ramble. w/m Bob Cole and J. Rosamond Johnson, 1902. The writers used the joint pseudonym of Will Handy on the song. (Not to be confused with W.C., "the father of the blues," who would achieve fame later.) It was introduced by George Primrose, the minstrel, and became a favorite with other minstrel acts and also jazz bands in New Orleans funeral processions. Among recordings: Dan Quinn (Victor), Kid Ory's Creole Jazz Band (Crescent), Jelly Roll Morton (Bluebird).

Oh, Didn't It Rain? w/m Eddie Leonard, 1923.

Oh, Donna Clara. w. Irving Caesar (Engl.), m. J. Petersburski, 1931. Austrian song with original German words by Beda Fritz Lohner. Introduced by Al Jolson in (TM) *The Wonder Bar.*

Oh! Frenchy. w. Sam Ehrlich, m. Con Conrad, 1918. Introduced by Arthur Fields (Victor). The song referred to American soldiers meeting French mademoiselles. It was sung by a chorus in (MM) *The Dolly Sisters*, 1945.

Oh, Happy Day. w/m Don Howard Koplow and Nancy Binns Reed, 1953. Million-selling record by the seventeen-year-old Don Howard (Essex). Other popular versions by Lawrence Welk, vocal by Larry Cooper (Coral), and The Four Knights (Capitol).

Oh, How I Hate to Get Up in the Morning. w/m Irving Berlin, 1918. Berlin wrote this song for and performed it in (TM) *Yip, Yip, Yaphank*, the cast of which was comprised of soldiers from Camp Upton, in Long Island, N.Y. The show then played thirty-two perfor-

mances in New York to raise money for various war charities. He again sang it in the 1942 [World War II] all-soldier show (TM) *This Is the Army*, which had a limited run of 113 performances on Broadway, before going on tour throughout the U.S. and Europe. In the scene in which it was done, Berlin was joined by some of the "Yaphank" veterans who originally performed it. He repeated it in the 1943 film version (MM) *This Is the Army*. All proceeds from the score and production went to the Army Emergency Relief fund. Jack Haley and chorus sang it in (MM) *Alexander's Ragtime Band*, 1938.

Oh, How I Long for Someone. w. Joseph Herbert, m. Efrem Zimbalist, 1920. from (TM) *Honeydew.*

Oh, How I Long to Belong to You. w. B. G. DeSylva, m. Vincent Youmans, 1932. Introduced by June Knight and Jack Whiting in (TM) *Take a Chance.*

Oh, How I Miss You Tonight. w/m Benny Davis, Joe Burke, and Mark Fisher, 1925. Introduced by Benny Davis in vaudeville. Featured and recorded by George Jessel (ARA).

Oh, How It Hurts. w/m Barbara Mason and Bernie Broomer, 1968. Recorded by Barbara Mason (Arctic).

Oh, How I Wish I Could Sleep Until My Daddy Comes Home. w. Sam M. Lewis and Joe Young, m. Pete Wendling, 1918. World War I ballad featured by Al Jolson and recorded by Henry Burr (Columbia).

Oh! How She Can Sing. w. Jack Yellen, m. Gus Van and Joe Schenck, 1919. Comedy song sung by Van and Schenck in (TM) *Ziegfeld Follies of 1919*, and recorded by them (Columbia).

Oh! How She Could Yacki, Hacki, Wicki, Wacki, Woo. w. Stanley Murphy and Charles McCarron, m. Albert Von Tilzer, 1916. Sub-titled "Love in Honolulu," this Hawaiian-influenced song was introduced by Eddie Cantor in one of Ziegfeld's *Midnight Frolics* on the New Amsterdam Theatre roof.

Recorded by Arthur Collins and Byron Harlan (Victor).

Oh, How That German Could Love. w/m Irving Berlin and Ted Snyder, 1910. Novelty song introduced by Irving Berlin in (TM) *The Girl and the Wizard*. This was also the first recording by Berlin (Columbia).

Oh, Isn't It Singular! w. J. P. Harrington, m. George LeBrunn, 1903.

Oh! Judge (He Treats Me Mean). w/m James F. Hanley, 1920. Featured and recorded by Marion Harris (Columbia).

Oh, Lady! Lady!! w. P. G. Wodehouse, m. Jerome Kern, 1918. Introduced by Carl Randall and a female chorus in (TM) *Oh, Lady! Lady!!*

Oh, Lady, Be Good! w. Ira Gershwin, m. George Gershwin, 1924. Introduced by Walter Catlett and ensemble in (TM) *Lady, Be Good!* It was interpolated in (MM) *Dancing Co-ed*, 1939; sung by Ann Sothern, Robert Young, Red Skelton, and John Carroll in (MM) *Lady Be Good*, 1941; performed by Joan Leslie in (MM) *Rhapsody in Blue*, 1945.

Oh, Lonesome Me. w/m Don Gibson, 1958. Hit C&W and Pop record by Don Gibson (RCA).

Oh, Look at Me Now. w. John De Vries, m. Joe Bushkin, 1941. Introduced, recorded, and popularized by Tommy Dorsey, vocal by Frank Sinatra, Connie Haines, and the Pied Pipers (Victor).

Oh! Ma-Ma (The Butcher Boy). w. Lew Brown, Rudy Vallee (Engl.), m. Paolo Citorello, 1938. Based on Italian song, "Luna Mezzo Mare," words and music by Citorello. Rudy Vallee and his Connecticut Yankees introduced the new version on radio and records (Bluebird). The Andrew Sisters also had a popular record (Decca). Lou Monte had a hit record (RCA), 1958, with a new lyric, "Lazy Mary (q.v.)."

Oh, Marie. w. William Jerome, m. Jean Schwartz, 1905. From (TM) *Lifting the Lid*.

Later successful recordings by Dean Martin (Capitol), Alan Dale (Coral), and Louis Prima (Majestic).

Oh, Mein Papa. See **Oh, My Papa.**

Oh, Miss Hannah! w. Thekla Hollingsworth, m. Jessie L. Deppen, 1925. Featured and recorded by the popular vocal group, The Revelers (Victor). Paul Whiteman revived it in 1929 with a recording featuring Bix Biederbecke on trumpet with an arrangement by Bill Challis (Columbia).

Oh! Miss Jaxon. w/m Edward Kennedy "Duke" Ellington, 1942. Popularized by Charlie Barnet, vocal by Peanuts Holland (Decca).

Oh, Monah. w/m Ted Weems and Joe "Country" Washburne, 1931. Novelty, introduced and recorded (Victor, Decca) by Ted Weems and his Orchestra. Also recorded by Joel Shaw (Crown); Billy Cotton, the English bandleader (Columbia); the Dinning Sisters (Capitol); Pee Wee King (Capitol).

Oh! Moytle. w. Charlie Tobias, m. Carmen Lombardo, 1945. Novelty featured and recorded by Guy Lombardo, vocal by Jimmy Brown (Decca).

Oh, Mr. Dream Man (Please Let Me Dream Some More). w/m James V. Monaco, 1911. Featured in vaudeville by the trio of baseball players, Jack Coombs, Chief Bender, and Cy Morgan (all pitchers!). Leading record by Ada Jones (Victor).

Oh, My Goodness. w. Mack Gordon, m. Harry Revel, 1936. Introduced by Shirley Temple in (MM) *Poor Little Rich Girl*.

Oh, My Papa. w. John Turner and Geoffrey Parsons (Engl.), Paul Burkhard, (Ger.), m. Paul Burkhard, 1954. Originally sung in German in Swiss musical *Fireworks*. First U.S. record release by trumpeter Eddie Calvert, with Norrie Paramor's Orchestra (Essex). Eddie Fisher, however, had his biggest-selling record, accompanied by Hugo Winterhalter and his Orchestra (RCA Victor).

Oh, Nights of Splendor. See **Neapolitan Nights.**

Oh! Oh! Delphine. w. M. S. McLellan, m. Ivan Caryll, 1912. From (TM) *Oh! Oh! Delphine.*

Oh, Pretty Woman. w/m Roy Orbison and William Dees, 1964. #1 gold record crossover (C&W/Pop) by Roy Orbison and The Candy Men (Monument). Revived by Van Halen (Warner Bros.), 1982.

Oh, Promise Me. w. Clement Scott, m. Reginald DeKoven, 1891. Sung by Jessie Bartlett Davis as an addition to the score of (TM) *Robin Hood,* having been published prior to and independently of the production. It has been a favorite wedding song ever since.

Oh, Sheila. w/m Melvin Riley, Gordon Strozier, and Gerald Valentine, 1985. #1 R&B and Pop chart record by the group Ready for the World (MCA).

Oh, Sherrie. w/m Steve Perry, Randy Goodrum, Bill Cuomo, and Craig Krampf, 1984. Top 10 record by Steve Perry (Columbia).

Oh, That Beautiful Rag. w. Irving Berlin, m. Ted Snyder, 1910. Performed by Berlin and Snyder in (TM) *Up and Down Broadway.*

Oh, That'll Be Joyful. w/m Jack McVea, Jake Porter, and Paul Campbell, 1954. Featured and recorded by The Four Lads, with Jimmy Carroll's Orchestra (Columbia).

Oh, What a Beautiful Mornin'. w. Oscar Hammerstein II, m. Richard Rodgers, 1943. The opening song of (TM) *Oklahoma,* introduced by Alfred Drake. Top popular recordings by Frank Sinatra (Columbia) and Bing Crosby (Decca). Gordon MacRae sang it in the film version (MM) *Oklahoma,* 1955.

Oh, What a Dream. w/m Chuck Willis, 1954. Top 10 R&B record by Ruth Brown and Her Rhythmakers (Atlantic).

Oh, What a Night. w/m Marvin Junior and John Funches, 1956, 1969. The writers were two of the original members of The Dells, the vocal group that had an R&B chart hit record of the song (Vee-Jay). The group's new version became a Pop chart hit (Cadet), 1969.

Oh, What a Pal Was Mary. w. Edgar Leslie and Bert Kalmar, m. Pete Wendling, 1919. Popular song with leading recordings by Henry Burr (Victor) and Edward Allen (Edison).

Oh, What a Thrill. w/m Al Hoffman, J. P. Murray, and Barry Trivers, 1931.

Oh! What It Seemed to Be. w/m Bennie Benjamin, George David Weiss, and Frankie Carle, 1946. Seventeen weeks on "Your Hit Parade," eight times as #1. Top records by Frankie Carle, vocal by daughter Marjorie Hughes (Columbia); Frank Sinatra, accompanied by Axel Stordahl's Orchestra (Columbia); Helen Forrest and Dick Haymes, with Earle Hagen's backing (Decca); Charlie Spivak, vocal by Jimmy Saunders (RCA Victor).

Oh, You Beautiful Doll. w. A. Seymour Brown, m. Nat D. Ayer, 1911. Long after song's first popularity it was interpolated in many films, such as: (MP) *Wharf Angel,* 1934; (MM) *The Story of Vernon and Irene Castle,* 1939; (MM) *For Me and My Gal,* sung by Judy Garland, 1942. It was the title song of Fred Fisher's film bio (MM) *Oh, You Beautiful Doll,* 1949. The unanswered question is: "Why was it used in that capacity when Fisher didn't write it?"

Oh! You Circus Day. w. Edith Maida Lessing, m. James V. Monaco, 1912. Introduced by Florence Moore and Billy Montgomery in (TM) *Hanky Panky.*

Oh, You Crazy Moon. w. Johnny Burke, m. James Van Heusen, 1939. This song marked the first collaboration of Burke and Van Heusen. Featured and recorded by top artists such as Tommy Dorsey, vocal by Jack Leonard (Victor); Glenn Miller, vocal by Ray Eberle (Bluebird); Bob Crosby and his Orchestra (Decca); Al Donahue and his Orchestra (Vocalion); Bea Wain (Victor).

Oh, You Cutie. w. Harry H. Williams, m. Nat D. Ayer, 1912.

Oh, You Million Dollar Baby. w. Eddie Doerr, m. Lou S. Lashley, 1912.

Oh, You Million Dollar Doll. w. Grant Clarke and Edgar Leslie, m. Maurice Abrahams, 1913.

Oh Bess, Oh Where's My Bess? See **Bess, Oh Where's My Bess?**

Oh Gee, Oh Gosh, Oh Golly, I'm in Love. w. Ole Olsen and Chic Johnson, m. Ernest Breuer, 1923. Introduced by Olsen and Johnson in (TM) *Ziegfeld Follies of 1922*. Featured in vaudeville and hit recordings by Eddie Cantor (Columbia) and Ernest Hare and Billy Jones (Edison).

Oh Gee! Oh Joy! w. Ira Gershwin and P. G. Wodehouse, m. George Gershwin, 1928. Introduced by Marilyn Miller and Jack Donahue in (TM) *Rosalie*. It was also heard in the Miller biography (MM) *Look for the Silver Lining*, 1949.

Oh Girl. w/m Eugene Record, 1972. #1 record by The Chi-Lites, of which Record was lead singer (Brunswick).

Oh Happy Day. w/m Edwin Hawkins, 1969. Gold record by The Edward Hawkins Singers (Pavillion).

Oh How Happy. w/m Charles Hatcher, 1966. Popular record by Shades of Blue (Impact). Revived by Edwin Starr [pseud. for Hatcher] and Blinky [pseud. for Sandra Williams] (Gordy).

Oh How I Laugh When I Think How I Cried About You. w. Roy Turk and George Jessel, m. Willy White, 1919. This was Turk's first published song success. Featured by Jessel in vaudeville. Popular recordings by Nora Bayes (Columbia) and Billy Murray and Rachel Grant [pseudonym for Gladys Rice] (Edison).

Ohio. w/m Neil Young, 1970. Top 20 record by Crosby, Stills, Nash, and Young. The song written after four students were killed at Kent State University in Ohio (Atlantic).

Ohio. w. Betty Comden and Adolph Green, m. Leonard Bernstein, 1953. Introduced by Rosalind Russell and Edith (Edie) Adams in (TM) *Wonderful Town*. Recorded by Lisa Kirk (RCA Victor).

Oh Johnny, Oh Johnny, Oh! w. Ed Rose, m. Abe Olman, 1917, 1939. Introduced by Harry Lewis in (TM) *Follow Me*, 1916. Written during World War I, the lyric read "Oh Johnny, Oh Johnny, how you can fight . . ." The song received no reaction whatsoever until the word "fight" was changed to "love," which gave it new meaning and immediate acclaim. Through top recordings by the American Quartette (Victor), the Joseph C. Smith Orchestra (Victor), and many vaudeville renditions, the song became a top sheet music seller. When Wee Bonnie Baker, singing with Orrin Tucker's band, had a million-selling record (Columbia), 1939, the song exceeded its original popularity and was on "Your Hit Parade" for eleven weeks.

Oh Julie. w/m Noel Ball and Kenneth R. Moffitt, 1957. Top recording by The Crescendos (Nasco), followed by Sammy Salvo (RCA). Revived by Barry Manilow (Arista), 1982.

Oh Me! Oh My! w. Ira Gershwin, m. Vincent Youmans, 1921. Gershwin wrote the lyrics under the pseudonym of Arthur Francis. This, the hit of (TM) *Two Little Girls in Blue*, sung by Marion Fairbanks and Oscar Shaw, was the first song success for both Gershwin and Youmans. Frank Crumit (Columbia) and Paul Whiteman and his Orchestra (Victor) had hit records. It was interpolated in (MM) *Tea for Two*, 1950, by Doris Day, Gene Nelson, and Patrice Wymore. It was featured in the title and production of the off-Broadway revue (TM) *Oh Me, Oh My, Oh Youmans*, 1981.

Oh Me Oh My (I'm a Fool for You, Baby). w/m Jim Doris, 1970. Top 40 record by Lulu (Atco), followed by Aretha Franklin (Atlantic), 1972.

Oh My My. w/m Vince Poncia and Ringo Starr, 1974. Top 10 record by Ringo Starr (Apple).

Oh No. w/m Lionel Richie, 1981. Top 10 record by The Commodores (Motown).

Oh No, Not My Baby. w/m Gerry Goffin and Carole King, 1964. Crossover (R&B/Pop) record by Maxine Brown (Wand). Revived by Rod Stewart (Mercury) and Merry Clayton (Ode), 1973.

Oh-Oh, I'm Falling in Love Again. w/m Al Hoffman, Dick Manning, and Mark Markwell, 1958. Markwell was a joint pseudonym for producer/arrangers Hugo Peretti and Luigi Creatore. Hit record by Jimmie Rodgers (Roulette).

Oh That's Good, No That's Bad. w/m Dewayne Blackwell, 1967. Recorded by Sam the Sham and The Pharaohs (MGM).

Oh Very Young. w/m Cat Stevens, 1974. Top 10 record from England by Cat Stevens (A&M).

Oh Well. w/m Peter Green, 1970. Recorded by the British blues band Fleetwood Mac (Reprise). Green was guitarist. The Rockets had a Top 40 version (RSO), 1979.

Oh What a Night for Dancing. w/m Barry White and Vance Wilson, 1978. Recorded by Barry White (20th Century).

Oh Yeah. m. Boris Blank and Dieter Meier, 1987. Chart novelty instrumental by the Swiss synthesizer trio, Yello, as played on the soundtrack of the films (MP) *Ferris Bueller's Day Off*, 1986, and (MP) *The Secret of My Success*, 1987.

Oh Yeah! w/m Ellas McDaniel, 1966. Recorded by The Shadows of Knight (Dunwich).

Okay Toots. w. Gus Kahn, m. Walter Donaldson, 1934. Introduced by Eddie Cantor in (MM) *Kid Millions* and recorded by him (Melotone). Other records: the bands of George Hall, vocal by Loretta Lee (Bluebird); Tom Coakley (Victor); Mal Hallett (Melotone).

Okie from Muskogee. w/m Merle Haggard and Roy Edward Burris, 1969. C&W/Pop hit record by Merle Haggard (Capitol).

Oklahoma. w. Oscar Hammerstein II, m. Richard Rodgers, 1943. The title song of (TM) *Oklahoma!* and first collaboration of the two writers was introduced by Alfred Drake, Joan Roberts, Betty Garde, Barry Kelley, Edwin Clay, and ensemble. In the film version (MM) *Oklahoma!*, it was sung by Gordon MacRae, Shirley Jones, Gene Nelson, Charlotte Greenwood, James Whitmore, Jay C. Flippen, and chorus.

Oklahoma Hills. w/m Leon Jerry (Jack) Guthrie and Woody Guthrie, 1945. Recorded by Jack Guthrie, cousin of Woody (Capitol). Revived by Hank Thompson (Capitol), 1961.

Old, Old Castle in Scotland, An. w. Herb Magidson, m. Ben Oakland, 1940. Recorded and popularized by Artie Shaw, vocal by Anita Boyer (Victor).

Old Acquaintance. w. Kim Gannon, m. Franz Waxman, 1943. Lyrics added to theme from (MP) *Old Acquaintance*. Popular record by Jo Stafford (Capitol).

Old Cape Cod. w/m Claire Rothrock, Milt Yakus, and Allan Jeffrey, 1957. Hit record by Patti Page (Mercury).

Old Curiosity Shop, An. w/m Abner Silver, Sam Coslow, and Guy Wood, 1939. Recorded by the bands of Gene Krupa (Brunswick), Shep Fields (Bluebird), Tommy Dorsey (Victor), Lawrence Welk (Vocalion).

Old Days. w/m James Pankow, 1975. Written by a member of the group, Chicago, which had a Top 10 record (Columbia).

Old Devil Moon. w. E. Y. Harburg, m. Burton Lane, 1947. Introduced by Donald Richards and Ella Logan in (TM) *Finian's Rainbow*. Sung by Petula Clark and Don Francks in (MM) *Finian's Rainbow*, 1968.

Old Devil Time. w/m Pete Seeger, 1970. Sung on the soundtrack of (MP) *Tell Me That You Love Me, Junie Moon*, by Pete Seeger.

Old Dogs, Children, and Watermelon Wine. w/m Tom T. Hall, 1973. Hit Country record by Tom T. Hall (Mercury).

Older and Bolder. w/m Cy Coben, 1952. Featured and recorded by Eddy Arnold (RCA Victor).

Older Women. w/m James O'Hara, 1981. #1 Country chart record by Ronnie McDowell (Epic).

Old Faithful. w/m Mel Tillis, 1969. Country chart record by Mel Tillis (Kapp). Also recorded by Tony Booth (Capitol), 1973.

Old-Fashioned Garden. w/m Cole Porter, 1919. This was Porter's first hit, introduced by Lillian Kemble Cooper in (TM) *Hitchy-Koo*. It was sung by Cary Grant and Selena Royle in the Porter film biography (MM) *Night and Day*, 1946.

Old Fashioned Love. w. Cecil Mack, m. James P. Johnson, 1923. Introduced by Adelaide Hall, Ina Duncan, and Arthur D. Porter in (TM) *Runnin' Wild*. Among the many recordings, in various styles, are those by Red Norvo (Columbia), Frank Crumit (Columbia), Noble Sissle and Eubie Blake (Victor), The Mills Brothers (Decca), Bob Willis (Columbia).

Old Fashioned Love Song, An. w/m Paul Williams, 1971. Top 10 record by Three Dog Night (Dunhill).

Old Fashioned Tune Is Always New, An. w/m Irving Berlin, 1939. Introduced by Rudy Vallee in (MM) *Second Fiddle*.

Old-Fashion Love. w/m Milan Williams, 1980. Recorded by The Commodores (Motown).

Old Flag Never Touched the Ground, The. w. James W. Johnson, m. J. Rosamond Johnson, 1901. Patriotic song interpolated in various theatrical productions.

Old Flame. w/m Donny Lowery and Mac McAnally, 1981. Country/Pop crossover hit by the group Alabama (RCA).

Old Flame Flickers and I Wonder Why, The. w/m Paul Dresser, 1898.

Old Flame Never Dies, An. w. Al Stillman, m. Arthur Schwartz, 1937. Introduced by Anne Booth in (TM) *Virginia*. Recorded by Tommy Dorsey, vocal by Jack Leonard (Victor), and Claude Thornhill, vocal by Barry McKinley (Brunswick).

Old Flames (Can't Hold a Candle to You). w/m Rosemary Sebert and Hugh Moffatt, 1978. Country chart records by Brian Collins (RCA), Joe Sun (Ovation), and Dolly Parton (RCA), 1980.

Old Folks. w/m Mike Reid, 1988. Top 10 Country chart record by Ronnie Milsap and Mike Reid (RCA).

Old Folks. w. Dedette Lee Hill, m. Willard Robison, 1938. Introduced and recorded by Mildred Bailey (Vocalion).

Old Grey Mare, The (She Ain't What She Used to Be). m. Frank Panella, 1915. Derived from the 1858 J. Warner song "Down in Alabam'." It has had many lyrics set to it including a Lincoln campaign song.

Old Hippie. w/m David Bellamy, 1985. Top 10 Country chart record by The Bellamy Brothers (MCA).

Old Lamp-Lighter, The. w. Charles Tobias, m. Nat Simon, 1946. #1 record by Sammy Kaye, vocal by Billy Williams (RCA Victor). Other chart versions by Hal Derwin, with Frank DeVol's Orchestra (Capitol); Morton Downey, with Jimmy Lytell's Orchestra (Majestic); Kay Kyser, vocal by Mike Douglas (Columbia); Kenny Baker, with Russ Morgan's Orchestra (Decca). Top 10 revival by The Browns (RCA), 1960.

Old MacDonald. w/m Randy Starr, 1967. Based on the traditional song, this version was featured by Elvis Presley in (MM) *Double Trouble* and on records (RCA).

Old Maid Boogie. w/m Jessie Mae Robinson, 1947. Popular record by Eddie "Cleanhead" Vinson and his Band (Mercury).

Old Man. w/m Neil Young, 1972. Top 40 record by Neil Young (Reprise).

Old Man Down the Road, The. w/m John Fogerty, 1985. Top 10 single from the #1 platinum album "Centerfield," by John Fogerty (Warner Bros.).

Old Man From the Mountain. w/m Merle Haggard, 1974. Country hit by Merle Haggard (Capitol).

Old Man Harlem. w/m Rudy Vallee and Hoagy Carmichael, 1933. Introduced on radio by Vallee and recorded by the bands of the Dorsey Brothers (Brunswick) and Eddie South (Victor).

Old Man of the Mountain. w. George Brown, m. Victor Young, 1932. Featured and recorded by Fred Waring and the Pennsylvanians (Victor). Best-selling record: The Mills Brothers (Brunswick). Also recorded by Lee Wiley (Coral), and Joe Haymes's Band (Columbia).

Old Man Sunshine, Little Boy Bluebird. w. Mort Dixon, m. Harry Warren, 1928. Featured and recorded by Lee Morse (Columbia).

Old Master Painter, The. w. Haven Gillespie, m. Beasley Smith, 1950. Introduced by Snooky Lanson, with Beasley Smith's Orchestra (London). Best-seller by Richard Hayes (Mercury); followed by Dick Haymes (Decca); Peggy Lee and Mel Tormé (Capitol); Phil Harris (RCA Victor); Frank Sinatra, with Paula Kelly and the Modernaires (Columbia).

Old Mill Wheel. w/m Milton Ager, Benny Davis, and Jesse Greer, 1939.

Old Moon. w. Waco Austin, m. O'Brien Fisher, 1959. C&W hit by Betty Foley (Bandera).

Old Music Master, The. w. Johnny Mercer, m. Hoagy Carmichael, 1943. Introduced by Dick Powell in (MM) *True to Life*. Recorded by Paul Whiteman and his Orchestra, vocal by Johnny Mercer and Jack Teagarden (Capitol).

Old Pal, Why Don't You Answer Me. w. Sam M. Lewis and Joe Young, m. M. K. Jerome, 1920. Recorded by Ernest Hare (Victor) and Henry Burr (Victor).

Old Piano Roll Blues, The. w/m Cy Coben, 1950. Leading record by Hoagy Carmichael and Cass Daly, with Matty Matlock's All-Stars (Decca). Among other chart versions: Lawrence "Piano Roll" Cook (Abbey); Eddie Cantor and Lisa Kirk, with Sammy Kaye's Orchestra (RCA Victor).

Old Playmate. w. Gus Kahn, m. Matty Malneck, 1931. Featured and recorded by the bands of Paul Whiteman, with vocal by Jack Fulton (Victor); Ted Lewis (Columbia); Ozzie Nelson (Brunswick).

Old Records. w/m Merle Kilgore and Arthur Thomas, 1963. Country hit by Margie Singleton (Mercury).

Old Refrain, The. m. Fritz Kreisler, 1915. Kreisler adapted this Viennese popular song for violin and piano from "Du Alter Stefansturm," from the operetta *Der Liebe Augustin* by Joseph Brandl.

Old Rivers. w/m Clifton Crofford, 1962. Top 10 record spoken by Walter Brennan (Liberty).

Old Rugged Cross, The. w/m Rev. George Bennard. This is considered to be the most popular of all Protestant hymns.

Old Showboat. w/m Marijohn Wilkin and Fred Burch, 1963. Top 10 C&W chart record by Stonewall Jackson (Columbia).

Old Smokey Locomotion. w/m adapted by Gerry Goffin and Carole King, 1963. New version of the traditional song, "On Top of Old Smoky," recorded by Little Eva (Dimension).

Old Soft Shoe, The. w. Nancy Hamilton, m. Morgan Lewis, 1946. Sung and danced by, and associated with, Ray Bolger, who introduced it in the revue (TM) *Three to Make Ready*.

Old Soldiers Never Die. w/m Tom Glazer, 1951. Inspired by the speech made by General Douglas MacArthur to Congress after he was recalled by President Harry Truman. Hit rec-

55555555

ord by Vaughn Monroe, with his Orchestra (RCA Victor).

Old Sombrero, An. w. Lew Brown, m. Ray Henderson, 1947. Recorded by Tex Beneke, vocal by Garry Stevens (RCA Victor); Alan Dale (Signature).

Old Songs, The. w/m David Pomeranz and Buddy Kaye, 1981. Introduced by David Pomeranz in his LP "The Truth of Us" (Pacific), 1980. Chart single by Barry Manilow (Arista), 1981.

Old Spinning Wheel, The. w/m Billy Hill, 1933. One of Hill's first hits. Early recordings by Frank Parker (Vocalion) and Riley Puckett (Bluebird). Bob Crosby had a popular record in 1937 (Decca).

Old Straw Hat, An. w. Mack Gordon, m. Harry Revel, 1938. Sung by Shirley Temple in (MM) *Rebecca of Sunnybrook Farm.*

Old Time Rock and Roll. w/m George Jackson and Tom Jones III, 1979. Top 40 record by Bob Seger and The Silver Bullet Band (Capitol). Featured in (MP) *Risky Business*, 1983, and re-released.

Old Water Mill, An. w/m Charles Tobias, Jack Scholl, and Murray Mencher, 1934. Featured and recorded by Vincent Lopez (Bluebird).

Ole Buttermilk Sky. w/m Hoagy Carmichael and Jack Brooks, 1946. Introduced by Hoagy Carmichael in (MP) *Canyon Passage.* Leading records by Kay Kyser, vocal by Mike Douglas; The Campus Kids (Columbia); and Hoagy Carmichael (ARA).

Ole Faithful. w/m Michael Carr and Joseph Hamilton Kennedy, 1935. Recorded by Gene Autry (Melotone), Roy Fox (Decca), Joe Morrison (Brunswick).

Ole Slew-Foot (a.k.a. **Slewfoot the Bear**). w/m Howard Hausey, 1961. Country song. Leading records by Johnny Horton (Columbia) and Porter Wagoner (RCA).

Ol' Man Mose. w/m Louis Armstrong and Zilner T. Randolph, 1938. Introduced and re-

corded by Louis Armstrong (Decca). The best-selling record was by Eddy Duchin and his Orchestra, vocal by Patricia Norman (Victor). The latter version caused a stir, which in turn created such a demand for the record that it became a best-seller. A line in the song went "Ol' Man Mose kicked the bucket,/Oh, bucket, buck, buck, bucket . . ." The record buyers were playing their discs at a slow tempo to hear Miss Norman's consonants.

Ol' Man River. w. Oscar Hammerstein II, m. Jerome Kern, 1928. This American classic was introduced by Jules Bledsoe in (TM) *Show Boat*. The first popular recording was by Paul Whiteman, vocal by Bing Crosby (Victor). Two months later, Whiteman re-recorded it with Paul Robeson and chorus (Victor). In the first film adaptation (MM) *Show Boat*, 1929, it was sung off-screen by Bledsoe. The 1936 production had Paul Robeson in the role of Joe, giving his memorable performance of the song. William Warfield sang it in the third film version, 1951. Caleb Peterson sang it and Frank Sinatra reprised it in the Kern story (MM) *Till the Clouds Roll By*, 1946.

Ol' Pappy. w. Marty Symes and Al J. Neiburg, m. Jerry Livingston, 1934. First recordings by Mildred Bailey, with Benny Goodman's Orchestra (Columbia), and Jack Teagarden, with his Orchestra (Brunswick).

O Lucky Man! w/m Alan Price, 1973. Introduced by Alan Price on the soundtrack of the British film (MP) *O Lucky Man!*

On a Blue and Moonless Night. w/m Will Osborne, Charles O'Flynn, Al Hoffman, 1930. Introduced and recorded by Will Osborne and his Orchestra (Columbia).

On a Carousel. w/m Allan Clarke, Tony Hicks, and Graham Nash, 1967. Hit record by the English group, The Hollies, of which the writers were members (Imperial). Revived by the quartet Glass Moon (Victor).

On Account of I Love You. w. James Dyrenforth, m. Phil Charig, 1931. Introduced by Fay Wray, Douglass Montgomery, Nathaniel

Wagner, and Archie Leach [Cary Grant] in (TM) *Nikki*.

On a Clear Day You Can See Forever. w. Alan Jay Lerner, m. Burton Lane, 1965. Introduced by John Cullum in (TM) *On a Clear Day You Can See Forever*. Sung by Yves Montand and reprised by Barbra Streisand in (MM) *On a Clear Day You Can See Forever*, 1970. Popular recordings by Johnny Mathis (Mercury) and Robert Goulet (Columbia).

On a Little Bamboo Bridge. w/m Archie Fletcher and Al Sherman, 1937. Recordings by Tommy Dorsey, vocal by Edythe Wright (Victor); Miff Mole (Brunswick); Abe Lyman, vocal by Sonny Schuyler (Decca).

On a Little Street in Singapore. w/m Peter DeRose and Billy Hill, 1940. Leading record by Jimmy Dorsey, vocal by Bob Eberly (Decca). Revived in 1944 via the release of a recording Frank Sinatra made with Harry James's band in October, 1939 (Columbia).

On and On. w/m Stephen Bishop, 1977. Recorded by Stephen Bishop (ABC).

On and On. w/m Curtis Mayfield, 1974. Introduced on the soundtrack of (MP) *Claudine*. Gold record by Gladys Knight and The Pips (Buddah).

On an Evening in Roma. w. Nan Frederics (Engl.), U. Bertini (Ital.), m. S. Taccani, 1959. Italian song "Sott'er Celo de Roma." Popularized in the U.S. by Dean Martin (Capitol).

On a Night Like This. w/m Bob Dylan, 1974. Recorded by Bob Dylan (Columbia).

On a Roof in Manhattan. w/m Irving Berlin, 1932. Introduced by J. Harold Murray and Katherine Harrington in (TM) *Face the Music*, which had a book by Moss Hart.

On a Slow Boat to China. w/m Frank Loesser, 1948. Best-selling record by Kay Kyser, vocal by Harry Babbitt and Gloria Wood (Columbia). Other hit records by Freddy Martin, vocal by Glen Hughes (RCA Victor); Eddy Howard, with his Orchestra (Mercury); Art Lund (MGM); Benny Goodman, vocal by Al Hendrickson (Capitol).

On a Sunday Afternoon. w. Arthur Freed, m. Nacio Herb Brown, 1935. Introduced by Buddy and Vilma Ebsen in (MM) *Broadway Melody of 1936*. Among records, the bands of Don Bestor (Brunswick), Archie Bleyer (Melotone), Richard Himber (Victor).

On a Sunday Afternoon. w. Andrew B. Sterling, m. Harry Von Tilzer, 1902. A song that sold two million copies of sheet music in the first year of its publication. It was later sung by Constance Moore in (MM) *Atlantic City*, 1944, and was also heard in Abbott and Costello's (MM) *The Naughty Nineties*, 1945.

On a Sunday by the Sea. w. Sammy Cahn, m. Jule Styne, 1947. Introduced by the ensemble in (TM) *High Button Shoes*.

On Behalf of the Visiting Firemen. w. Johnny Mercer, m. Walter Donaldson, 1940. Popular record by Bing Crosby and Johnny Mercer (Decca).

On Broadway. w/m Barry Mann, Cynthia Weil, Jerry Leiber, and Mike Stoller, 1963. Introduced and hit record by The Drifters (Atlantic). Revived with a Top 10 record by George Benson (Warner Bros.), 1978.

Once. w/m Ted Harris, 1967. Top 10 Country chart record by Ferlin Husky (Capitol).

Once. w. Bob Russell, m. Harold Spina, 1951. Featured and recorded by Billy Eckstine (MGM) and Jan Peerce (RCA Victor).

Once a Day. w/m Bill Anderson, 1964. Country hit by Connie Smith (RCA).

Once and for Always. w. Johnny Burke, m. James Van Heusen, 1949. Introduced by Bing Crosby and Rhonda Fleming in (MM) *A Connecticut Yankee in King Arthur's Court*.

Once Around the Moon. w. Bob Hilliard, m. Carl Sigman, 1947. From the revue (TM) *Angel in the Wings*. Recorded by Peggy Lee (Capitol).

Once Bitten, Twice Shy. w/m Jean Halversson, 1989. Hit record by Great White (Capitol).

Once Ev'ry Year. w/m Paul Dresser, 1894.

Once in a Blue Moon. w/m Tom Brasfield and Robert Byrne, 1986. #1 Country chart record by Earl Thomas Conley (RCA).

Once in a Blue Moon. w. Mack Gordon, m. Harry Revel, 1934. Introduced by Bing Crosby in (MM) *We're Not Dressing.*

Once in a Blue Moon. w. Anne Caldwell, m. Jerome Kern, 1923. Introduced by Roy Hoyer and Evelyn Herbert in (TM) *Stepping Stones.* Robert Russell Bennett, the noted composer and arranger, used this melody as the theme in his symphonic work, "Variations on a Theme by Jerome Kern," 1936.

Once in a Lifetime. w/m David Byrne, Chris Frantz, Jerry Harrison, Tina Weymouth, and Brian Eno, 1984. Written by [first four names] the quartet Talking Heads as part of their album, "Remain in Light," produced by Brian Eno (Sire), 1980. The group then recorded it at a "live" concert at the Pantages Theatre in Hollywood for their film and gold album (MM) *Stop Making Sense,* in 1984. The song was later featured in (MP) *Down and Out in Beverly Hills,* 1986, after which their chart single was released.

Once in a Lifetime. w/m Leslie Bricusse and Anthony Newley, 1962. Introduced by Anthony Newley in (TM) *Stop the World—I Want to Get Off.* Recorded by Newley in the cast album and released as a single (London). Featured and recorded by Sammy Davis, Jr. (Reprise).

Once in a Lifetime. w. Raymond Klages, m. Jesse Greer, 1928. Sung by Richard Bold in (TM) *Earl Carroll Vanities of 1928.* Recorded by Vincent Lopez's Orchestra (Brunswick); Johnny Johnson, vocal by Franklyn Baur (Victor); and Elmo Tanner (Vocalion).

Once in a While. w. Bud Green, m. Michael Edwards, 1937. In the #1 spot on "Your Hit Parade" seven times. Popularized and recorded by Tommy Dorsey and his Orchestra (Victor); Frances Langford (Decca); Louis Armstrong (Decca); Ozzie Nelson, vocal by Harriet Hilliard (Bluebird). Revived in 1950 by Harry James in (MM) *I'll Get By.* It was also heard in (MM) *New York, New York* in 1977. It was the last recording made by Bing Crosby, three days before he died of a heart attack on a golf course in Spain, 10/14/77.

Once in Love with Amy. w/m Frank Loesser, 1948. Introduced by Ray Bolger in (TM) *Where's Charley?* Bolger's recording (Decca) was the first hit single (10″ 78 rpm) over four minutes in length since discs replaced cylinders forty years earlier. Bolger repeated his role and the song in (MM) *Where's Charley,* in 1952.

Once Knew a Fella. w/m Harold Rome, 1959. Introduced by Andy Griffith and the men in (TM) *Destry Rides Again.*

Once Too Often. w. Mack Gordon, m. James V. Monaco, 1944. Introduced by Betty Grable, singing and dancing with choreographer Hermes Pan in (MM) *Pin-Up Girl.* Ella Fitzgerald had a popular recording (Decca).

Once Upon a Summertime. w. Johnny Mercer (Eng.), m. Michel Legrand and Eddie Barclay, 1962. First published in France, 1954, titled "La Valse des Lilas," lyric by Eddie Marnay. English version introduced by Tony Bennett (Columbia).

Once Upon a Time. w. Lee Adams, m. Charles Strouse, 1962. Introduced by Ray Bolger and Eileen Herlie in (TM) *All American.* Popularized by Tony Bennett (Columbia).

Once You Get Started. w/m Gavin Wright, 1975. Top 10 record by Rufus featuring Chaka Khan (ABC).

Once You've Had a Little Taste. w. Ben Tarver and John Clifton, m. John Clifton, 1966. Introduced by Alice Cannon in (TM) *Man with a Load of Mischief.*

Once You've Had the Best. w/m Johnny Paycheck, 1974. Hit Country record by George Jones (Epic).

One. w. Edward Kleban, m. Marvin Hamlisch, 1975. Introduced by the company in (TM) *A Chorus Line*, and in (MM) *A Chorus Line*, 1985.

One. w/m Harry Nilsson, 1969. Gold record by the group Three Dog Night (Dunhill).

(1–2–3–4–5–6–7) Count the Days. w/m Charlie Foxx, Brooks O'Dell, and Yvonne Williams, 1968. Chart record by Inez and Charlie Foxx (Dynamo).

1, 2, 3, Red Light. w/m Sal Trimachi and Bobbi Trimachi, 1968. Gold record by The 1910 Fruitgum Company (Buddah).

One, Two, Button Your Shoe. w. Johnny Burke, m. Arthur Johnston, 1936. Introduced by Bing Crosby in (MM) *Pennies from Heaven*, and recorded by him with Georgie Stoll's Orchestra (Decca). Other records by Ray Noble (Victor); Jimmy Dorsey, vocal by Bob Eberly (Decca); Billie Holiday (Vocalion); Joe Haymes (Perfect); Artie Shaw (Brunswick).

One, Two, Three (1–2–3). w/m Leonard Borisoff, Brian Holland, Eddie Holland, John Madara, 1965. Hit record by Len Barry (Decca). Ramsey Lewis had a popular instrumental version (Cadet), 1967.

One, Two, Three, Kick. w. Al Stillman, m. Xavier Cugat, 1939. Popular conga, introduced by Xavier Cugat and his Orchestra.

One Alone. w. Otto Harbach and Oscar Hammerstein II, m. Sigmund Romberg, 1926. Introduced by Robert Halliday in (TM) *The Desert Song*. In the film version (MM) *The Desert Song*, 1929, it was sung by John Boles. In the 1943 remake, by Dennis Morgan, and in the third version in 1952, by Gordon MacRae and Kathryn Grayson. The Romberg story, (MM) *Deep in My Heart*, 1954, featured the music in a *pas de deux* danced by Cyd Charisse and James Mitchell.

One and Only, The. w. Alan Bergman and Marilyn Bergman, m. Patrick Williams, 1978. Sung on the soundtrack of (MP) *The One and Only* by Kasey Ciszk.

One Bad Apple (Don't Spoil the Whole Bunch). w/m George Jackson, 1971. #1 gold record by The Osmonds (MGM).

One Boy. w. Lee Adams, m. Charles Strouse, 1960. Introduced in (TM) *Bye Bye Birdie* by Susan Watson, Jessica Albright, Sharon Lerit, and Chita Rivera. In the film version (MM) *Bye Bye Birdie*, 1963, it was sung by Ann-Margret and Janet Leigh, and as "One Girl," by Bobby Rydell.

One Broken Heart for Sale. w/m Otis Blackwell and Winfield Scott, 1963. Introduced by Elvis Presley in (MM) *It Happened at the World's Fair*, and on records (RCA).

One by One. w/m Johnnie Wright, Jack Anglin, and Jim Anglin, 1954. Hit C&W record by Kitty Wells and Red Foley (Decca).

One Called "Mother" and the Other "Home Sweet Home." w. William Cahill, m. Theodore F. Morse, 1905.

One Chain Don't Make No Prison. w/m Dennis Lambert and Brian Potter, 1974. Recorded by The Four Tops (Dunhill), and Santana (Columbia), 1979.

One Cigarette for Two. w/m Ros Metzger, Dan Dougherty, and Ben Ryan, 1940. Featured and recorded by Freddy Martin, vocal by Eddie Stone (Bluebird). The orchestras of Bobby Byrne (Decca) and Lennie Hayton, vocal by Linda Keene (Vocalion), also recorded it.

One Day at a Time. w/m Marijohn Wilkin and Kris Kristofferson, 1974, 1980. First recorded by Marilyn Sellars with a C&W/Pop crossover (Mega). Don Gibson's version then became a Country chart Top 10 record (Hickory). Revived with a #1 C&W chart record by Cristy Lane (United Artists), 1980.

One Day in June (It Might Have Been You). w. Joe Goodwin, m. James F. Hanley, 1918. Recorded by Henry Burr and Albert Campbell (Victor).

One Day of Your Life. w/m Neil Sedaka and Howard Greenfield, 1970. Recorded by Andy Williams (Columbia).

One Dozen Roses. w. Roger Lewis and Country Washburn, m. Dick Jurgens and Walter Donovan, 1942. Fourteen weeks on "Your Hit Parade," twice in the #1 position. Popularized via performances and recordings by Dick Jurgens, vocal by Buddy Moreno (Okeh); Harry James, vocal by Jimmy Saunders (Columbia); Dinah Shore (Victor); Glen Gray and the Casa Loma Orchestra, vocal by Pee Wee Hunt (Decca).

One Dyin' and a Buryin'. w/m Roger Miller, 1965. Introduced and recorded by Roger Miller (Smash).

One Early Morning. w/m Jon Hendricks and Stanley Meyer, 1969. Sung on the soundtrack of (MP) *Night of the Following Day* by Annie Ross.

One Fine Day. w/m Gerry Goffin and Carole King, 1963. Top 10 record by The Chiffons (Laurie). Revived by Julie Budd (Tom Cat), 1976; Rita Coolidge (A&M), 1979; Carole King (Capitol), 1980.

One Fine Morning. w/m Skip Prokop, 1971. Top 40 record by the Canadian group Lighthouse (Evolution).

One Finger Melody. w/m Al Hoffman, Kermit Goell, and Fred Spielman, 1950. Hit record by Frank Sinatra, with Axel Stordahl's Orchestra (Columbia).

One for My Baby (and One More for the Road). w. Johnny Mercer, m. Harold Arlen, 1943. Introduced by Fred Astaire in (MM) *The Sky's the Limit*. Among many recordings: Lena Horne, with Horace Henderson's Orchestra (Victor); Johnny Mercer (Capitol); Tony Bennett (Columbia); Frank Sinatra (Capitol); Mel Tormé (Musicraft); Fran Warren (Victor); Oscar Peterson (Clef); Ellis Larkins (Decca). It was sung by Ida Lupino in (MP) *Roadhouse*, 1948; Jane Russell in (MP) *Macao*, 1952; Frank Sinatra in (MM) *Young at Heart*, 1955.

One for the Money. w/m B. Moore and M. Williams, 1987. Country chart hit from the album of the same name by T. G. Sheppard (Columbia).

One Friend. w/m Dan Seals, 1987. #1 Country chart record by Dan Seals (Capitol).

One Girl, The. w. Oscar Hammerstein II, m. Vincent Youmans, 1928. Introduced by Allan Prior and male chorus in (TM) *Rainbow*. In the movie version (MM) *Song of the West*, 1930, it was sung by John Boles. Recorded by Boles (Victor) and Bert Lown's Orchestra (Perfect). It is also in the albums "Through the Years with Vincent Youmans" (Monmouth-Evergreen) and Ben Bagley's "Vincent Youmans Revisited" (Painted Smiles).

One Good Well. w/m Kent Robbins and Mike Reid, 1989. Hit Country record by Don Williams (RCA).

One Good Woman. w/m Peter Cetera and Patrick Leonard, 1988. Single by Peter Cetera from album "One More Story" (Full Moon).

One Hand, One Heart. w. Stephen Sondheim, m. Leonard Bernstein, 1957. Introduced by Larry Kent and Carol Lawrence in (TM) *West Side Story*. In the film version, 1961, it was sung by Marni Nixon and Jim Bryant, dubbing on the soundtrack for Natalie Wood and Richard Beymer, respectively.

One Has My Name, the Other Has My Heart. w/m Eddie Dean, Dearest Dean, and Hal Blair, 1948. Popularized by Jimmy Wakely (Capitol). Revived by Barry Young (Dot), 1965.

One Heartbeat. w. S. Legassick and B. Ray, 1987. Top 10 R&B and Pop chart single from the album of the same name by Smokey Robinson (Motown).

One Hell of a Woman. w/m Mac Davis and Mark James, 1974. Recorded by Mac Davis (Columbia).

(I'd Love to Spend). One Hour with You w. Leo Robin, m. Richard A. Whiting, 1932. Introduced by Jeanette MacDonald, Maurice Chevalier, Genevieve Tobin, Charles Ruggles, and Donald Novis in (MM) *One Hour with You*. MacDonald and Novis had individual singles (Victor). Other recordings by Morton Downey (Perfect), Jimmie Grier and his Band

(Victor), Andy Sanella (Hit of the Week). Eddie Cantor sang it as the closing theme on his weekly radio show for Chase and Sanborn coffee.

160 Acres. w/m David Kapp, 1947. Best-selling records by Bing Crosby and the Andrews Sisters (Decca), and The Sons of the Pioneers (Victor).

100% Chance of Rain. w/m Charlie Black and Austin Roberts, 1986. #1 Country chart record by Gary Morris (Warner Bros).

One Hundred Ways. w/m Tony Coleman, Kathy Wakefield, and Benjamin Wright, 1982. Recorded by Quincy Jones featuring James Ingram (A&M).

One I Love, The. w/m Bill Berry, Pete Buck, Mike Mills, and Michael Stipe, 1987. Top 10 single written and recorded by the group R.E.M. (I.R.S.).

One I Love, The (Belongs to Somebody Else). w. Gus Kahn, m. Isham Jones, 1924. Introduced by Isham Jones and his Orchestra (Brunswick). Among popular records: Al Jolson (Brunswick), Sophie Tucker (Okeh), Bing Crosby (Decca), Ella Fitzgerald (Decca). Judy Garland sang it in (MM) *Everybody Sing,* 1938; Doris Day sang it in the Gus Kahn story (MM) *I'll See You in My Dreams,* 1951; Gogi Grant sang it, dubbing for Ann Blyth in the title role of (MM) *The Helen Morgan Story,* 1957.

One I Loved Back Then, The (Corvette Song). w/m Gary Gentry, 1986. #1 Country chart record by George Jones (Epic).

One in a Million. w. Sidney D. Mitchell, m. Lew Pollack, 1937. Title song of Sonja Henie's first film (MM) *One in a Million.* Among records: Fats Waller (Victor), Bunny Berigan (Brunswick), Mal Hallett (Decca).

One in a Million You. w/m Sam Dees, 1980. Top 10 gold record by Larry Graham (Warner Bros.).

One Is a Lonely Number. w. Paul Francis Webster, m. Nicholas Brodsky, 1957. Introduced by Tony Martin in (MM) *Let's Be Happy.*

One Kiss. w. Oscar Hammerstein II, m. Sigmund Romberg, 1928. Sung by Evelyn Herbert in (TM) *The New Moon.* In the film adaptation (MM) *New Moon,* 1930 (the article was dropped from the film title), it was sung by Grace Moore. Jeanette MacDonald sang it in the remake, 1940. It was played orchestrally in the Romberg biography (MM) *Deep in My Heart,* 1954. The opening melodic line is identical to Vincent Youmans's "No, No, Nanette," which was composed in 1924 and published by the same firm, Harms, Inc. Youmans brought no legal action.

One Kiss for Old Times' Sake. w/m Artie Resnick and Kenny Young, 1965. Recorded by Ronnie Dove (Diamond).

One Kiss Too Many. w/m Steve Nelson, Ed Nelson, Jr., and Eddy Arnold, 1949. Leading record by Eddy Arnold (RCA Victor).

One Last Kiss. w/m Seth Justman and Peter Wolf, 1978. Written by two members of The J. Geils Band (EMI America).

One Last Kiss. w. Lee Adams, m. Charles Strouse, 1960. Introduced by Dick Gautier and ensemble in (TM) *Bye Bye Birdie.* In the film version (MM) *Bye Bye Birdie,* 1963, it was sung by Jesse Pearson.

One Less Bell to Answer. w. Hal David, m. Burt Bacharach, 1970. Gold record by The 5th Dimension (Bell).

One Less Set of Footsteps. w/m Jim Croce, 1973. Recorded by Jim Croce (ABC).

One Life to Live. w. Ira Gershwin, m. Kurt Weill, 1941. Introduced by Gertrude Lawrence and Danny Kaye in (TM) *Lady in the Dark.* Lawrence (Victor) and Kaye (Columbia) recorded the song singly. Ginger Rogers sang it in the film version (MM) *Lady in the Dark,* 1943.

One Little Candle. w. Joseph Maloy Roach, m. George Mysels, 1952. Featured and recorded by Perry Como (RCA Victor).

One Little Raindrop. w. Harry Richman and Jack Meskill, m. Jean Schwartz, 1931.

Introduced and featured by Little Jack Little. Recorded by the orchestras of Wayne King (Victor) and Seger Ellis (Brunswick).

One Little World Apart. w. Ronny Graham, m. Milton Schafer, 1962. Introduced by Michele Lee in (TM) *Bravo Giovanni.*

One Lonely Night. w/m Neal Doughty, 1985. Chart single by REO Speedwagon, from album "Wheels Are Turning" (Epic).

One Look at You. w. Ned Washington and Earl Carroll, m. Victor Young, 1940. From (MM) *A Night at Earl Carroll's.* First recording, Cab Calloway and his Orchestra (Vocalion); followed by Bobby Byrne, vocal by Jimmy Palmer (Decca); Bob Chester, vocal by Dolores O'Neill (Bluebird); Jack Leonard (Okeh).

One Love. w. Leo Robin, m. David Rose, 1946. Featured and recorded by Randy Brooks, vocal by Harry Prime (Decca).

One Love at a Time. w/m Paul Davis and Paul Overstreet, 1986. Top 10 Country chart record by Tanya Tucker (Capitol).

One Love in My Lifetime. w/m Larry Brown, Theresa McFaddin, and Leonard Perry, 1976. Recorded by Diana Ross (Motown).

One Lover at a Time. Top 10 R&B chart record and Pop chart entry by the band Atlantic Starr (Warner Bros.).

One Man Band. w/m Billy Fox, Tommy Kaye, and January Tyme, 1970. Top 20 record by Three Dog Night (Dunhill).

One Man Parade. w/m James Taylor, 1973. Recorded by James Taylor (Warner Bros.).

One Man Woman/One Woman Man. w/m Paul Anka, 1975. Top 10 record by Paul Anka, with backing vocal by Odia Coates (United Artists).

One Meat Ball. w. Hy Zaret, m. Lou Singer, 1945. Based on the mid-nineteenth century song, "The Lone Fish Ball," this novelty was introduced by folk/blues singer Josh White. It was featured in vaudeville and clubs by pantomimist Jimmy Savo who, of course, did not record it, but the Andrews Sisters did, coupled with "Rum and Coca Cola," which became a million-seller (Decca).

One Mint Julep. w/m Rudolph Toombs, 1952. Featured and recorded by The Clovers (Atlantic) and Buddy Morrow and his Orchestra (RCA Victor). Revived by Chet Atkins (RCA Victor), 1960; and Ray Charles, with a Top 10 hit (Impulse), 1961.

One Minute to One. w. Sam M. Lewis, m. J. Fred Coots, 1933. Introduced and featured by Harry Richman. Recorded by: Harry Sosnik, vocal by Bob Hannon (Bluebird); Enric Madriguera (Columbia); Joe Venuti (Melotone); Hal Kemp (Brunswick). It became the theme of Gray Gordon and his Tick-Tock Rhythm (Bluebird), 1938.

One Moment Alone. w. Otto Harbach, m. Jerome Kern, 1931. Introduced by Bettina Hall and Georges Metaxa in (TM) *The Cat and the Fiddle.* In the 1934 film version, (MM) *The Cat and the Fiddle*, it was sung by Jeanette MacDonald and Ramon Novarro.

One Moment in Time. w/m Albert Hammond and John Bettis, 1988. Written as a theme for the 1988 Olympic games. Leading record by Whitney Houston (Arista).

One Monkey Don't Stop No Show. w/m General Johnson and Greg S. Perry, 1971. Top 20 record by the female trio The Honey Cone (Hot Wax).

One More Heartache. w/m W. Moore, Robert Rogers, William Robinson, Marvin Taplin, Ronald White, 1966. R&B/Pop chart hit by Marvin Gaye (Tamla).

One More Hour. w/m Randy Newman, 1981. Introduced by Jennifer Warnes on the soundtrack of (MP) *Ragtime.* Nominated for an Academy Award.

One More Hour of Love. w. Clifford Grey, m. Oscar Straus, 1931. Introduced by Maurice Chevalier in (MM) *The Smiling Lieutenant.*

One More Mile. w/m Tom T. Hall, 1969. Country chart record by Dave Dudley (Mercury).

One More Mountain to Climb. w/m Al Kasha and Joel Hirschhorn, 1967. Recorded by Ronnie Dove (Diamond).

One More Night. w/m Phil Collins, 1985. #1 record by the English vocalist/drummer/ writer Phil Collins (Atlantic).

One More Sunrise. See **Morgen.**

One More Time. w/m Buzz Kohan and Bill Angelos, 1964. Recorded by the Ray Charles Singers (Command).

One More Time. w/m Mel Tillis, 1960. C&W chart hit by Ray Price (Columbia).

One More Time. w. B. G. DeSylva and Lew Brown; m. Ray Henderson, 1931. One of the last song collaborations by these writers. It was also the last recording by Bing Crosby before embarking on his career as a soloist. He recorded it as the band singer with Gus Arnheim and his Orchestra (Victor). Ted Lewis (Columbia), the Eubie Blake Orchestra (Crown), and later Phil Harris (Victor) also had records.

One More Tomorrow. w/m Ernesto Lecuona, Eddie DeLange, and Josef Myrow, 1946. Title song of (MP) *One More Tomorrow.* Featured and recorded by Frankie Carle and his Orchestra (Columbia).

One More Try. w/m George Michael, 1988. #1 R&B and Pop chart single by the British singer/writer, George Michael, the third hit from his album "Faith" (Columbia).

One More Walk Around the Garden. w. Alan Jay Lerner, m. Burton Lane, 1979. Introduced by Gordon Ramsey, Howard Ross, and Bernie Knee in (TM) *Carmelina.*

One Morning in May. w. Mitchell Parish, m. Hoagy Carmichael, 1934. Early recordings by Lanny Ross (Victor) and Wayne King's Orchestra (Brunswick). Among later standouts, Tommy Dorsey (Decca) and Sarah Vaughan (Mercury). This melody was one of Carmichael's favorites.

One Nation Under a Groove. w/m George Clinton, Gary Shider, and Walter Morrison, 1978. #1 R&B gold record by Funkadelic (Warner Bros.).

One Never Knows, Does One? w. Mack Gordon, m. Harry Revel, 1936. Introduced by Alice Faye in (MM) *Stowaway.* Popularized on radio and via recordings by Hal Kemp, vocal by Skinnay Ennis (Brunswick); Billie Holiday (Vocalion); the bands of Shep Fields (Bluebird), Mal Hallett (Bluebird), and Ruby Newman (Victor).

One Night. w/m Dave Bartholomew and Pearl King, 1958. Introduced in 1956 by Smiley Lewis (Imperial), who had an R&B chart record. Elvis Presley had a Top 10 record in 1958 (RCA).

One Night in Bangkok. w/m Tim Rice, Benny Anderson, and Bjorn Ulvaeus, 1985. From a forthcoming London and New York production, (TP) "Chess," this was first recorded by the British actor/singer, Murray Head, whose recorded version reached the Top 10 in the U.S. (RCA). Covered with a chart record by the Canadian-born model/actress Robey (Silver Blue).

One Night in June. w/m Charles K. Harris, 1899.

One Night in Monte Carlo. w. Al Sherman and Al Lewis, m. Abner Silver, 1936. Most popular records by the orchestras of Tommy Dorsey, vocal by Edythe Wright (Victor); Freddy Martin (Brunswick); and George Hall (Bluebird).

One Night of Love. w. Gus Kahn, m. Victor Schertzinger, 1934. Introduced by Grace Moore in (MM) *One Night of Love,* and recorded by her (Brunswick). Other recordings by Jack Fulton (Vocalion) and the orchestras of Freddy Martin (Brunswick) and Lud Gluskin (Columbia).

One Night Only. w. Tom Eyen, m. Henry Krieger, 1981. Introduced by Jennifer Holliday, Sheryl Lee Ralph, Loretta Devine, Deborah Burrell, and company in (TM) *Dreamgirls*. Recorded by Elaine Paige in the album "Stages" (Atlantic), 1987.

One Note Samba. w. Jon Hendricks (Engl.), Antonio Carlos Jobim and N. Medonca, (Port.), m. Jobim and Medonca, 1962. Brazilian song, introduced by Joao Gilberto (Capitol). First English version by Pat Thomas (Verve).

One O'Clock Jump. m. William "Count" Basie, 1937. Top swing standard, written, introduced, recorded by and theme of Count Basie and his Orchestra (Decca). Harry James had a big hand in the success of this number as he played trumpet on the hit 1938 recording with Benny Goodman (Victor), appeared with the Metronome All-Stars (Victor), and recorded it with his band (Columbia), coupled with "Two O'Clock Jump (q.v.)." It has been heard in the following films: (MM) *The Powers Girl*, 1943; (MM) *Reveille with Beverly*, 1943; (MM) *I Dood It*, 1943; (MM) *You Can't Ration Love*, 1944; (MM) *Night Club Girl*, 1944; (MM) *The Benny Goodman Story*, 1956.

One of a Kind (Love Affair). w/m Joseph B. Jefferson, 1973. #1 R&B, #11 Pop chart gold record by The Spinners (Atlantic).

One of the Boys. w. Fred Ebb, m. John Kander, 1981. Introduced by Lauren Bacall, Rex Everhart, and men in (TM) *Woman of the Year*.

One of the Living. w/m Holly Knight, 1985. Introduced by Tina Turner in the Australian film (MP) *Mad Max Beyond Thunderdome* and on records (Capitol).

One of These Days. w/m Marty Robbins, 1964. Top 10 Country chart record by Marty Robbins (Columbia). Chart version by Tompall and The Glaser Brothers (MGM), 1968. Revived with hit C&W record by Emmylou Harris (Reprise), 1976.

One of These Nights. w/m Glenn Frey and Don Henley, 1975. Written by two members of the group, The Eagles, which had a #1 single (Asylum).

One of Us (Will Weep Tonight). w/m Clint Ballard, Jr. and Fred Tobias, 1960. Recorded by Patti Page (Mercury).

One on One. w/m Daryl Hall, 1983. Top 10 record by Daryl Hall and John Oates (RCA).

One on the Right Is on the Left. w/m Jack Clement, 1966. Country and Pop chart record by Johnny Cash (Columbia).

One Owner Heart. w/m Walt Aldridge, Tom Brasfield, and Mac McAnally, 1985. Top 10 Country chart record by T. G. Sheppard (Warner Bros.).

One Piece at a Time. w/m Wayne Kemp, 1976. Novelty recorded by Johnny Cash and The Tennessee Three (Columbia).

One Promise Too Late. w/m Dave Loggins, Lisa Silver, and Don Schlitz, 1987. #1 Country chart single by Reba McEntire (MCA).

One Rose, The (That's Left in My Heart). w/m Del Lyon and Lani McIntyre, 1936. Popular Hawaiian song. Leading records by Larry Clinton and his Orchestra (Victor), Bing Crosby (Decca), Art Kassel and his Orchestra (Bluebird).

One Scotch, One Bourbon, One Beer. w/m Rudolph Toombs, 1953. R&B record by Amos Milburn (Aladdin).

One Song. w. Larry Morey, m. Frank Churchill, 1938. Introduced by Harry Stockwell, as the voice of the Prince, on the soundtrack of the animated feature (MM) *Snow White and the Seven Dwarfs*.

One's on the Way. w/m Shel Silverstein, 1971. Country hit by Loretta Lynn (Decca).

One Step Forward. w/m Chris Hillman and Bill Wildes, 1988. Top 10 Country chart record by The Desert Rose Band (MCA/Curb).

One Step to Heaven. w. Raymond Klages, m. Jesse Greer, 1928. From (TM) *Say When.*

One Step Up. w/m Bruce Springsteen, 1987. Popular track from the album "Tunnel of Love" by Bruce Springsteen (Columbia).

One Summer Night. w/m Danny Webb, 1958. First recorded by the R&B group The Danleers (AMP 3). The master was taken over by another label (Mercury), and the group's name was changed to The Dandleers. The Diamonds had a popular version in 1961 (Mercury).

One Sunny Day. w/m Bill Wolfer and Dean Pitchford, 1986. Introduced in medley with "Dueling Bikes from 'Quicksilver'" on the soundtrack of (MP) *Quicksilver* and on records (Atlantic) by Ray Parker, Jr. and Helen Terry.

One Sweet Letter from You. w. Lew Brown and Sidney Clare, m. Harry Warren, 1927. Originally recorded by Ted Lewis and his Band (Columbia), Gene Austin (Victor), Kate Smith (Columbia), Sophie Tucker (Okeh). Revived by the bands of Benny Goodman (Columbia), Lionel Hampton (Victor), and Jimmy Dorsey, with vocal by Helen O'Connell (Decca), 1939.

One That You Love, The. w/m Graham Russell, 1981. #1 gold record by the Australian duo, Graham Russell and Russ Hitchcock, calling themselves Air Supply (Arista).

One Thing Leads to Another. w/m Cy Curnin, Jamie West-Oram, Rupert Greenall, Adam Woods, Alfred Agius, 1983. Top 10 record by the English group The Fixx (MCA).

One Tin Soldier (The Legend of Billy Jack). w/m Dennis Lambert and Brian Potter, 1970. Sung on the soundtrack of (MP) *Billy Jack* by the quintet Coven. First recorded by The Original Caste (T-A). Leading record by Coven (Warner Bros.), 1971, (MGM), 1973.

One Toke Over the Line. w/m Mike Brewer and Tom Shipley, 1971. Top 10 record by Brewer and Shipley (Kama Sutra).

One Track Mind. w/m Bobby Lewis and Malou Ren, 1961. Top 10 record by Bobby Lewis (Beltone). Revived by The Knickerbockers (Challenge), 1966.

One Trick Pony. w/m Paul Simon, 1980. Introduced by Paul Simon in (MP) *One Trick Pony,* and on records (Warner Bros.).

1–2–3. w/m Gloria Estefan and Enrique Garcia, 1988. Pop and R&B chart hit by Gloria Estefan and Miami Sound Machine (Epic).

One Vision. w/m Queen, 1986. Introduced on the soundtrack of (MP) *Iron Eagle* and on records by the English group Queen (Capitol).

One Way or Another. w/m Nigel Harrison and Deborah Harry, 1979. Recorded by the group Blondie (Chrysalis).

One Who Really Loves You, The. w/m William Robinson, 1962. Top 10 hit on R&B and Pop charts by Mary Wells (Motown).

One You Love, The. w/m Glenn Frey and Jack Tempchin, 1982. Recorded by Glenn Frey (Asylum).

One You Slip Around With, The. w/m Harlan Howard and Fuzzy Owen, 1960. Country chart record by Jan Howard (Challenge).

One-zy Two-zy (I Love You-zy). w/m Dave Franklin and Irving Taylor, 1946. Novelty. Leading records by Phil Harris (ARA), Freddy Martin and his Orchestra (RCA Victor), Kay Kyser and his Orchestra (Columbia), Hildegarde with Guy Lombardo and his Royal Canadians (Decca).

On Green Dolphin Street. w. Ned Washington, m. Bronislaw Kaper, 1947. Adapted, with lyrics, from a theme from (MP) *Green Dolphin Street.* Most popular recording by Jimmy Dorsey, vocal by Bill Lawrence (MGM).

On London Bridge. w/m Sid Tepper and Roy C. Bennett, 1956. Leading record by Jo

Stafford, with Paul Weston's Orchestra (Columbia).

Only, Only One for Me, The. w. Bud Green, m. James V. Monaco and Harry Warren, 1942. Recorded by Gene Austin (Victor).

Only a Bowery Boy. w. Charles B. Ward, m. Gussie L. Davis, 1894.

Only a Lonely Heart Knows. w/m Dennis W. Morgan and Steve Davis, 1983. Top 10 Country chart record by Barbara Mandrell (MCA).

Only a Lonely Heart Sees. 1980. Recorded by Felix Cavaliere (Epic).

Only Another Boy and Girl. w/m Cole Porter, 1944. Introduced by Mary Roche and Bill Tabbert in (TM) *Seven Lively Arts*. Among recordings: Benny Goodman Quintet (Columbia); George Paxton, vocal by Alan Dale (Hit); Charlie Spivak and his Orchestra (Victor).

Only a Rose. w. Brian Hooker, m. Rudolf Friml, 1925. Introduced by Dennis King and Carolyn Thompson in (MM) *The Vagabond King*, and on records (Victor). It was heard in both film versions of (MM) *The Vagabond King*. In the 1930 production, King and Jeanette MacDonald sang it, and in the 1956 remake, it was sung by Oreste [Kirkop] and Kathryn Grayson.

Only Daddy That Will Walk the Line, The. w/m Ivy J. Bryant, 1968. Country hit recorded by Waylon Jennings (RCA).

Only Flame in Town, The w/m Elvis Costello, 1984. Recorded by the British singer Elvis Costello (Columbia).

Only Forever. w/m Johnny Burke, m. James V. Monaco, 1940. Introduced in (MM) *Rhythm on the River*, and on records (Decca) by Bing Crosby. Nominated for Academy Award.

Only in America. w/m Jerry Leiber, Mike Stoller, Barry Mann, and Cynthia Weil, 1963. Introduced and recorded by Jay and The Americans (United Artists).

Only in My Dreams. w/m Debbie Gibson, 1987. Top 10 single and first hit by the sixteen-year-old singer/songwriter Debbie Gibson (Atlantic).

Only Love Can Break a Heart. w. Hal David, m. Burt Bacharach, 1962. Hit record by Gene Pitney (Musicor). Later chart versions by Margaret Whiting (London) and Bobby Vinton (ABC).

Only Love Can Break Your Heart. w/m Neil Young, 1970. Top 40 record by Neil Young (Reprise).

Only Love Is Real. w/m Carole King, 1976. Recorded by Carole King (Ode).

Only Me. w. Walter H. Ford, m. John W. Bratton, 1894. Famous song about a neglected child.

Only One, The. w. Anne Croswell, m. Lee Pockriss, 1963. Introduced by Vivien Leigh in (TM) *Tovarich*.

Only One Girl in the World for Me. w/m Dave Marion, 1895.

Only One Love in My Life. w/m Royal C. Bannon and John Bettis, 1978. Country chart hit by Ronnie Milsap (RCA).

Only One You. w/m Michael Garvin and Bucky Jones, 1982. Country/Pop record by T.G. Sheppard (Warner Bros.).

Only Sixteen. w/m Sam Cooke, 1959, 1976. Introduced and hit R&B/Pop record by Sam Cooke (Keen). Top 10 gold record revival by the group Dr. Hook (Capitol), 1976.

Only Song I Know, The. w. J. Keirn Brennan, m. Ray Perkins, 1929. Introduced by Nick Lucas in (MM) *The Show of Shows*.

Only the Good Die Young. w/m Billy Joel, 1978. Recorded by Billy Joel (Columbia).

Only the Lonely. w/m Martha Davis, 1982. Top 10 record by the quintet, The Motels (Capitol), with Davis as lead singer.

Only the Lonely. w. Sammy Cahn, m. James Van Heusen, 1958. Introduced and recorded by Frank Sinatra (Capitol).

Only the Lonely (Know the Way I Feel). w/m Roy Orbison and Joe Melson, 1960. C&W and Pop chart hit by Roy Orbison (Monument). Revived on both charts by Sonny James (Capitol), 1969.

Only the Strong Survive. w/m Kenny Gamble, Leon Huff, and Jerry Butler, 1969. Top 10 record by Jerry Butler (Mercury).

Only the Young. w/m Steve Perry, Neal Schon, and Jonathan Cain, 1985. Introduced by the group Journey on the soundtrack of (MP) *Vision Quest*, and a Top 10 single, released from the soundtrack album (Geffen).

Only Time Will Tell. w/m John Wetton and Geoffrey Downes, 1982. Recorded by the British group Asia (Geffen).

Only Trust Your Heart. w. Sammy Cahn, m. Nicholas Brodszky, 1957. Introduced by Dean Martin, starring in his first film without Jerry Lewis, (MM) *Ten Thousand Bedrooms*.

Only When I Love. w/m Christopher Dunn, Tom Shapiro, and Holly Dunn, 1987. Top 10 Country chart record by Holly Dunn (MTM).

Only When You're in My Arms. w/m Bert Kalmar, Harry Ruby, Con Conrad, 1939. Introduced by Fred Astaire and Ginger Rogers in (MM) *The Story of Vernon and Irene Castle*.

Only with You. w/m Maury Yeston, 1982. Introduced by Raul Julia in (TM) *Nine*.

Only Women. w/m Alice Cooper and Dick Wagner, 1975. Top 20 record by Alice Cooper (Atlantic).

Only Yesterday. w/m John Bettis and Richard Carpenter, 1975. Top 10 record by The Carpenters (A&M).

Only You. w/m Buck Ram and Ande Rand, 1955. Introduced and top hit record by The Platters (Mercury), who had recorded an earlier unreleased version for Federal Rec-

ords. The Hilltoppers also had a popular version (Dot). The recording by the Platters was used on the soundtrack of (MP) *This Angry Age*, 1958. Franck Pourcel's French Fiddles recorded an instrumental version in France that has had lasting popularity in the U.S. (Capitol), 1959. Revived in 1974 by Ringo Starr (Apple), 1974, and Country singer Freddie Hart (Capitol), 1978.

Only You (Can Break My Heart). w/m Buck Owens, 1965. Hit Country record by Buck Owens (Capitol).

Only You Know and I Know. w/m Dave Mason, 1970. Recorded by Dave Mason (Blue Thumb), and Delaney and Bonnie (Atco), 1971.

On Miami Shore. w. William Le Baron, m. Victor Jacobi, 1919. Popular song with singers and hotel orchestras. Recorded as an instrumental by concert violinist/composer Fritz Kreisler (Victor). Sung by Phil Regan in (MM) *Las Vegas Nights*, 1941.

On Mobile Bay. w. Earle C. Jones, m. Charles N. Daniels, 1910.

On My Knees. w/m Charlie Rich, 1978. #1 Country chart crossover hit by Charlie Rich and Janie Frickie (Epic).

On My Mind Again. w/m Dean Beard, Elmer Ray, and Slim Willet, 1957. C&W chart record by Billy Walker (Columbia).

On My Own. w/m Burt Bacharach and Carole Bayer Sager, 1986. #1 gold record by Patti LaBelle and Michael McDonald (MCA). The two singers, who had sung their individual duet parts separately over prerecorded instrumental tracks, met for the first time when they performed their hit on The Johnny Carson TV show.

On Our Own. w/m Daryl Simmons, Kenny Edmonds, and Antonio Reid, 1989. Introduced on the soundtrack of (MP) *Ghostbusters II*. Hit single by Bobby Brown (MCA).

On Revival Day. w/m Andy Razaf, 1930. Introduced by Bessie Smith. Recorded by the star-stocked studio band, Rube Bloom and His Bayou Boys (Columbia), Ford Leary (Bluebird), Johnny Johnson's Band (Victor), Bob Howard (Decca).

On San Francisco Bay. w. Vincent Bryan, m. Gertrude Hoffman, 1906. Introduced in Florenz Ziegfeld's musical, (TM) *A Parisian Model*, which starred Anna Held.

On Tap, in the Can, Or in the Bottle. w. Hank Thompson, m. Dick Hart, 1968. Top 10 Country chart record by Hank Thompson (Dot).

On the Alamo. w. Gus Kahn, m. Isham Jones, 1922. Jones and his Orchestra recorded this big seller (Brunswick). The song was his first hit as a composer.

On the Atchison, Topeka, and the Santa Fe. w. Johnny Mercer, m. Harry Warren, 1946. The Academy Award-winning song was introduced by Judy Garland, Marjorie Main, Ray Bolger, Ben Carter, Virginia O'Brien, and the Harvey Girls in (MM) *The Harvey Girls*. No. 1 records by Johnny Mercer, with the Pied Pipers (Capitol), and Bing Crosby with Six Hits and a Miss (Decca). Also, top releases by Judy Garland, with the Merry Macs and Lyn Murray's Orchestra (Decca), and Tommy Dorsey, vocal by The Sentimentalists (Victor).

On the Banks of the Wabash Far Away. w/m Paul Dresser, 1897. An instant hit upon publication, it also became a favorite with the American troops in the Spanish-American War. Adopted as the official state song of Indiana in 1913. It was interpolated into Dresser's film biography, (MM) *My Gal Sal*, 1942, and (MM) *Wait Till the Sun Shines, Nellie*, 1952.

On the Beach. w. Steve Allen, m. Ernest Gold, 1959. Based on the theme music from (MP) *On the Beach*. The English orchestra leader, Frank Chacksfield, had a U.S. chart instrumental record (London), 1960.

On the Beach at Bali-Bali. w/m Al Sherman, Jack Meskill, and Abner Silver, 1936.

Popularized and recorded by Red Allen (Vocalion), Connie Boswell (Decca), Tommy Dorsey (Victor), Shep Fields (Bluebird), Jimmie Lunceford (Decca).

On the Beach at Waikiki. w. G. H. Stover, m. Henry Kailimai, 1915. An authentic Hawaiian song, first published in Honolulu.

On the Beach with You. w. Tot Seymour, m. Jesse Greer, 1931. Featured and recorded by the orchestras of Ozzie Nelson (Brunswick) and Johnny Hamp (Victor).

On the Benches in the Park. w/m James Thornton, 1896.

On the Boardwalk in Atlantic City. w. Mack Gordon, m. Josef Myrow, 1946. Introduced by Vera-Ellen, Vivian Blaine, and June Haver in (MM) *Three Little Girls in Blue*. Leading recordings by The Charioteers (Columbia) and Dick Haymes (Decca).

On the Border. w/m Al Stewart, 1977. Single from the album "Year of the Cat," by Scottish singer Al Stewart (Janus).

On the Bumpy Road to Love. w. Al Hoffman, Al Lewis, and Murray Mencher, 1938. Introduced by Judy Garland in (MM) *Listen, Darling*. Among recordings: Ozzie Nelson and his Orchestra (Brunswick); Teddy Wilson, vocal by Nan Wynn (Brunswick); Terry Shand (Decca); the Merry Macs (Decca).

On the Dark Side. w/m John Cafferty, 1984. Introduced by Eddie and The Cruisers (Scotti Brothers), 1983. Later in the year the song was used in the film titled (MP) *Eddie and The Cruisers*, after which the original record was re-released, with the artist credited as "John Cafferty and The Beaver Brown Band." The new release reached the Top 10, 1984.

On the 5:15. w. Stanley Murphy, m. Henry I. Marshall, 1914. The song referred to problems of a suburban commuter. Leading records by Arthur Collins and Byron Harlan (Columbia) and The American Quartet (Victor).

On the 'Gin, 'Gin, 'Ginny Shore. w. Edgar Leslie, m. Walter Donaldson, 1922. Popular song recorded by Ray Miller and his Orchestra (Columbia).

On the Good Ship Lollipop. w/m Sidney Clare and Richard A. Whiting, 1934. Introduced by Shirley Temple in (MM) *Bright Eyes.* In 1938, she sang it again, this time in a "medley of her past hits" (she was ten years old!) in (MM) *Rebecca of Sunnybrook Farms.* Shari Robinson and Dan Dailey sang it in (MM) *You're My Everything*, 1949. Tiny Tim featured it in the late sixties (Reprise).

On the Good Ship Mary Ann. w. Gus Kahn, m. Grace LeBoy, 1914.

On the Isle of May. w. Mack David, m. (adapt.) André Kostalanetz. 1940. Adapted from the Andante Cantabile movement of Tchaikowsky's *String Quartet in D Major.* Most popular records by Connee Boswell (Decca), and Dick Jurgens, vocal by Eddy Howard (Vocalion).

On the Mall. m. Edwin Franko Goldman, 1923. Goldman, a concert bandleader, wrote this popular march in recognition of his summer concerts played in the band shell on the Mall in Central Park, New York City.

On the Mississippi. w. Ballard MacDonald, m. Harry Carroll and Arthur Fields, 1912. This song appeared in two musicals in the same year, (TM) *The Whirl of Society* and (TM) *Hanky Panky.* It was heard in (MM) *The Dolly Sisters*, 1946, and sung by Mitzi Gaynor, as Eva Tanguay, in (MM) *The I Don't Care Girl*, 1953.

On the Nickel. w/m Tom Waits, 1980. Introduced by Tom Waits in his album "Heart-attack and Vine" (Asylum). Title song, used on soundtrack of (MP) *On the Nickel*, 1980.

On the Old Fall River Line. w. William Jerome and Andrew B. Sterling, m. Harry Von Tilzer, 1913. First recorded by Billy Murray (Victor).

On the Old Park Bench. w. Howard Dietz, m. Arthur Schwartz, 1940. Performed by Jackie Gleason and Larry Adler in (TM) *Keep Off the Grass.* Lawrence Welk and his Orchestra recorded it (Vocalion).

On the Old Spanish Trail. w/m Kenneth Leslie Smith and Jimmy Kennedy, 1947. English song recorded in the U.S. by Eddy Howard with his Orchestra (Majestic), Art Lund (MGM), Roy Rogers (RCA Victor), Andy Russell (Capitol).

On the Other Hand. w/m Paul Overstreet and Don Schlitz, 1986. Country singer Randy Travis's record was first released a year earlier. On its re-release, it reached #1 on the Country charts.

On the Outgoing Tide. w. Lew Brown, m. Mabel Wayne, 1950. Brown's last song success was recorded by Perry Como, with Mitchell Ayres's Orchestra (RCA Victor), and by Vera Lynn (London).

On the Radio. w. Donna Summer, m. Georgio Moroder, 1980. Gold record by Donna Summer (Casablanca).

On the Rebound. w/m Floyd Cramer, 1961. Featured and recorded by Floyd Cramer (RCA).

On the Rio Grande. w. Paul Green, m. Kurt Weill, 1936. Introduced by Gerrit (Tony) Kraber in (TM) *Johnny Johnson.* This was the first American show for which Weill wrote after leaving Germany because of the advent of Naziism.

On the Road Again. w/m Willie Nelson, 1980. Introduced by Willie Nelson in (MP) *Honeysuckle Rose.* [Film was retitled *On the Road Again* after success of the song.] Nominated for an Academy Award. Nelson's hit record (Columbia) won a Grammy Award (NARAS) for Country Song of the Year.

On the Road Again. w/m Alan Wilson and Floyd Jones, 1968. Top 20 record by the group, Canned Heat (Liberty). Not to be confused with Country song of the same title, 1980.

On the Road to Calais. w. Alfred Bryan, m. Al Jolson, 1918. Introduced, featured, and recorded by Al Jolson (Columbia). As with other songs, Jolson interpolated this in (TM) *Sinbad* during a post-Broadway tour.

On the Road to Home Sweet Home. w. Gus Kahn, m. Egbert Van Alstyne, 1918. Recorded by New Zealand-born singer, Percy Hemus (Victor). It attained popularity by being coupled with the major hit, "Just a Baby's Prayer at Twilight," sung by Henry Burr. It was not unusual to have a different artist on each side of a record.

On the Road to Mandalay. w. Rudyard Kipling, m. Oley Speaks, 1907. A popular musical setting of Kipling's poem from the collection, *Barrack Room Ballads.* It became a staple in the repertoire of baritones in concert and vaudeville. Sung by Lawrence Tibbett in (MM) *Metropolitan*, 1935.

On the Sentimental Side. w. Johnny Burke, m. James V. Monaco, 1938. Introduced by Bing Crosby and Mary Carlisle in (MM) *Doctor Rhythm.* Crosby recorded it with John Scott Trotter's Orchestra (Decca). Among other records: Billie Holiday (Vocalion), and Abe Lyman and his Orchestra (Bluebird).

On the South Side of Chicago. w/m Phillip Zeller, 1967.

On the Street of Regret. w. John Klenner, m. Pete Wendling, 1942. Best-selling recordings by Sammy Kaye, vocal by Tommy Ryan (Victor); Vaughn Monroe, vocal by Monroe (Bluebird); Connee Boswell (Decca); Kate Smith (Columbia); Eddy Duchin and his Orchestra (Columbia).

On the Street Where You Live. w. Alan Jay Lerner, m. Frederick Loewe, 1956. Introduced by Michael King in (TM) *My Fair Lady.* Best-selling record by Vic Damone, with Percy Faith's Orchestra (Columbia). Sung by Jeremy Brett in (MM) *My Fair Lady*, 1964.

On the Sunny Side of the Street. w. Dorothy Fields, m. Jimmy McHugh, 1930. Introduced by Harry Richman in (TM) Lew Leslie's *International Revue.* It was interpolated in (MM) *Nobody's Darling*, 1943; (MM) *Is Everybody Happy?*, 1943; (MM) *Swing Parade of 1946*; (MM) *Two Blondes and a Redhead*, 1947; (MM) *Make Believe Ballroom*, 1949; by Frankie Laine, who also had a hit record (Mercury), in (MM) *Sunny Side of the Street*, 1951; by Teddy Wilson in (MM) *The Benny Goodman Story*, 1956; by Gogi Grant, dubbing for Ann Blyth, in *The Helen Morgan Story*, 1957.

On the Trail. w. Harold Adamson, m. Ferde Grofé, 1933, 1946. From Grofé's orchestral "Grand Canyon Suite." Introduced on radio by Paul Whiteman and his Orchestra. For many years it was the theme song of the radio shows sponsored by Philip Morris cigarettes, over which "Johnny," the diminutive bellman, would page "Call for Philip Mor—ris." Grofé would use it as his theme song when he appeared with his Orchestra in theaters or on radio. Kay Kyser and his Band featured and recorded it with lyrics in 1946 (Columbia).

On the Twentieth Century. w. Betty Comden and Adolph Green, m. Cy Coleman, 1978. Introduced by John Cullum and Madeline Kahn in (TM) *On the Twentieth Century.*

On the Wings of a Nightingale. w/m Paul McCartney, 1984. Recorded by The Everly Brothers (Mercury). The record marked the reuniting of the brother act and their first chart record in seventeen years.

On the Wings of Love. w/m Peter Schless and Jeffrey Osborne, 1982. Crossover (R&B/Pop) record by Jeffrey Osborne (A&M).

On This Side of Goodbye. w/m Gerry Goffin and Carole King, 1966. Recorded by The Righteous Brothers (Verve).

On Top of Old Smoky. w/m Pete Seeger, 1951. Seeger's new words and arrangement of the American folk song were recorded on a million-seller by The Weavers, with Terry Gilkyson's Choir and Vic Schoen's Orchestra

(Decca). Other popular versions by Burl Ives, with Percy Faith's Orchestra (Columbia), and Vaughn Monroe with his Orchestra (RCA Victor).

On Top of Spaghetti. w/m adapted by Tom Glazer, 1963. Parody of the traditional song "On Top of Old Smoky." Introduced and recorded by Tom Glazer (Kapp).

On Treasure Island. w. Edgar Leslie, m. Joe Burke, 1935. Popularized by airplay and recordings of Louis Armstrong (Decca); Tommy Dorsey, vocal by Edythe Wright (Victor); Bob Crosby (Decca); Little Jack Little (Columbia); Jimmie Ray (Bluebird); Red Allen (Vocalion).

On Wisconsin. m. W. T. Purdy, 1909. A march and two-step that is now the official marching song of the University of Wisconsin.

On Your Toes. w. Lorenz Hart, m. Richard Rodgers, 1936. Introduced by Doris Carson, Ray Bolger, and David Morris in (TM) *On Your Toes*. In the film version (MM) *On Your Toes*, 1939, it was danced by Cyd Charisse, and in the Rodgers and Hart story, (MM) *Words and Music*, 1948, it was played instrumentally on the soundtrack.

Oo—Maybe It's You. w/m Irving Berlin, 1927. From (TM) *Ziegfeld Follies of 1927*. Recorded by the bands of Paul Whiteman (Victor), Ben Selvin (Brunswick), and Harry Reser (Columbia).

Oo! What You Do to Me. w/m Kay Twomey, Fred Wise, and Ben Weisman, 1953. Featured and recorded by Patti Page (Mercury).

Oodles of Noodles. m. Jimmy Dorsey, 1933. Jimmy Dorsey wrote this as a saxophone solo for himself when he was with the Dorsey Brothers Orchestra. In 1940, it served as the basis of "Contrasts (q.v.)" which was used as the theme of the new Jimmy Dorsey Orchestra (Decca).

Oogum Boogum Song, The. w/m Alfred J. Smith, 1967. Recorded pseudonymously by the writer as Brenton Wood (Double Shot).

Ooh! That Kiss. w. Mort Dixon and Joe Young, m. Harry Warren, 1931. Introduced by Jeanne Aubert, Lawrence Gray, and the ensemble in (TM) *The Laugh Parade*, which starred Ed Wynn. Popular recordings by the Dorsey Brothers (Columbia), Frank Luther (Victor), the Arden-Ohman Orchestra (Victor), Abe Lyman (Brunswick).

Ooh, What You Said! w. Johnny Mercer, m. Hoagy Carmichael, 1940. From (TM) *Walk with Music*. Most popular recording by Glenn Miller, vocal by Marion Hutton (Bluebird). Others: Hal Kemp, vocal by The Smoothies (Victor); Bob Crosby, vocal by Marion Mann (Decca).

Ooh Baby Baby. w/m William Robinson and Warren Moore, 1965. Hit record by The Miracles (Tamla). Popular version by The Five Stairsteps (Windy City), 1967. Revived with Top 10 hit by Linda Ronstadt (Asylum), 1979.

Ooh Boy. w/m Norman Whitfield, 1977. Recorded by the group Rose Royce (Whitfield).

O-O-H Child. w/m Stan Vincent, 1970. Top 10 record by The Five Stairsteps (Buddah).

Oooh! Look-a There, Ain't She Pretty? w. Clarence Todd, m. Carmen Lombardo, 1936. Introduced by Guy Lombardo and his Royal Canadians. Leading recordings: Larry Clinton (Decca), The Charioteers (Columbia), Clarence Williams (Vocalion).

Oooh, Oooh, Oooh. w/m Lloyd Price, 1952. Top 10 R&B record by Lloyd Price (Specialty).

Ooo La La La. w/m Teena Marie and Allen McGrier, 1988. #1 R&B chart record by Teena Marie, from her album "Naked to the World" (Epic).

Oo-oo Ernest, Are You Earnest with Me? w. Sidney Clare and Harry Tobias, m. Cliff Friend, 1922.

Oop Bop Sh' Bam. m. Walter G. Fuller, Jay Roberts, and John Dirks "Dizzy" Gillespie, 1946. Bop instrumental introduced by Dizzy Gillespie and his Orchestra (Musicraft). Among other recordings: Buddy Rich and his Orchestra (Mercury).

Oop Shoop. w/m Joe Josea, 1954. First recorded and a Top 10 R&B number by Shirley Gunter and The Queens (Flair). Covered and made into a Pop hit by The Crew Cuts (Mercury). Helen Grayco also had a chart version ("X").

Oo Wee Baby, I Love You. w/m Richard Parker, 1965. Top 40 record by soul singer Fred Hughes (Vee-Jay).

Open a New Window. w/m Jerry Herman, 1966. Introduced by Angela Lansbury and company in (TM) *Mame*. Lucille Ball and company sang it in the film version (MM) *Mame*, 1974.

Open Arms. w/m Steve Perry and Jonathan Cain, 1982. Top 10 record by the group Journey (Columbia).

Open Door, Open Arms. w. Buddy Kaye (Engl.), Erik Frykman and Fritz G. Sundelof, (Swed.), m. Frykman and Sundelof, 1950. Swedish song. Most popular U.S. recording by Kay Kyser, vocal by Mike Douglas (Columbia).

Open Sesame. w/m Robert Bell, Ronald Bell, George Brown, Charles Smith, Dennis Thomas, 1976. Instrumental heard on the soundtrack of (MM) *Saturday Night Fever* and on records by the group Kool and The Gang (De-Lite).

Open the Door, Richard. w. "Dusty" Fletcher and John Mason, m. Jack McVea and Dan Howell, 1947. #1 novelty hit of the year, based on old vaudeville routine performed for mainly black audiences by Fletcher and Mason. The first recording was by co-writer Jack McVea (Black and White). Hit records by Dusty Fletcher (National); Count Basie, vocal by Harry Edison and Bill Johnson (Victor); The Three Flames (Columbia); Louis Jordan and his Tympany Five (Decca).

Open the Door to Your Heart. w/m Darrell Banks and Donnie Elbert, 1966. Recorded by Darrell Banks (Revilot).

(Open Up the Door) Let the Good Times In. w/m Ramona Redd and Mitch Torok, 1966. Recorded by Dean Martin (Reprise).

Open Up Your Heart. w/m Buck Owens, 1966. C&W hit introduced and recorded by Buck Owens (Capitol).

Open Up Your Heart (and Let the Sunshine In). w/m Stuart Hamblen, 1953. First popular record of this song by Bing Crosby (Decca). Two years later, The Cowboy Church Sunday School had a best-selling version (Decca).

Open Your Heart. w/m Madonna, Gardner Cole, and Peter Rafelson, 1986. #1 single from the album "True Blue" by Madonna (Sire).

Operator. w/m Reggie Calloway, Vincent Calloway, Belinda Lipscomb, and Boaz Watson, 1985. Recorded by the group Midnight Star (Solar).

Operator. w/m William Spivey, 1975. First chart single by the group The Manhattan Transfer (Atlantic).

Operator (That's Not the Way It Feels). w/m Jim Croce, 1972. Top 20 record by Jim Croce (ABC).

Ophelia. w/m Robbie Robertson, 1976. Recorded by The Band, of which the writer was guitarist (Capitol).

Opportunities (Let's Make Lots of Money). w/m Nick Tennant and Chris Lowe, 1986. Written and Top 10 record by the British duo Pet Shop Boys (EMI America).

Optimistic. w/m Aubrey Freeman, 1961. Top 10 Country chart record by Skeeter Davis (RCA).

Opus No. 1. w. Sid Garris, m. Sy Oliver, 1945. Tommy Dorsey and his Orchestra's instrumental recording was voted the #12 all-time record in the Billboard poll (Victor). The Mills Brothers had the best-selling vocal (Decca). A version by Gene Krupa, vocal by Anita O'Day, also attained popularity (Columbia).

Opus 17 (Don't You Worry 'bout Me). w/m Sandy Linzer and Denny Randell, 1966. Hit record by The Four Seasons (Philips).

Orange Blossom Lane. w. Mitchell Parish and Nick Kenny, m. Peter De Rose, 1941. Featured and recorded by the bands of Glenn Miller, vocal by Ray Eberle (Bluebird), and Claude Thornhill (Columbia).

Orange Blossom Special. w/m Ervin T. Rouse, 1965. First popular recording of 1938 song, by Johnny Cash (Columbia).

Orange Blossom Time. w. Joe Goodwin, m. Gus Edwards, 1929. Sung by Charles King, danced by the Albertina Rasch Ballet and the Belcher Child Dancers in (MM) *Hollywood Revue of 1929*. Recorded by Cliff "Ukulele Ike" Edwards (Columbia), Tom Waring (Victor), Earl Burtnett (Brunswick).

Orange Colored Sky. w/m Milton De Lugg and William Stein, 1950. Introduced by Milton De Lugg and his Orchestra on Jerry Lester's "Broadway Open House," the forerunner to "The Tonight Show" on late-night television. Leading records by Nat "King" Cole with Stan Kenton's Orchestra (Capitol), Betty Hutton (RCA Victor), Jerry Lester (Coral).

Orange Grove in California, An. w/m Irving Berlin, 1923. Grace Moore, in her Broadway debut, and John Steel sang this in (TM) *Music Box Revue of 1923*. Popular recordings by John Steel (Victor), Paul Whiteman (Victor), The Golden Gate Orchestra (Perfect).

Orchids for Remembrance. w. Mitchell Parish, m. Peter De Rose, 1940. Most popular recording by Eddy Howard (Columbia). Others: Harry James, vocal by Dick Haymes (Varsity); Bob Chester, vocal by Dolores O'Neill (Bluebird); Bobby Byrne, vocal by Jimmy Palmer (Decca).

Orchids in the Moonlight. w. Edward Eliscu and Gus Kahn, m. Vincent You-

mans, 1933. Tango introduced by Raul Roulien, Fred Astaire, and Dolores Del Rio in (MM) *Flying Down to Rio*. This, one of four popular songs to come out of Youmans's last score, was featured and recorded by Rudy Vallee (Victor), Enric Madriguera (Brunswick), and later by Paul Weston (Capitol), André Kostalanetz (Columbia), and many others.

Orchid to You, An. w. Mack Gordon, m. Harry Revel, 1933. The title was inspired by Walter Winchell's newspaper column, in which he would give praise in the form of "an orchid."

Oregon Trail, The. w. Billy Hill, m. Peter De Rose, 1935. Among recordings: the orchestras of Victor Young (Decca), Ozzie Nelson (Brunswick), Dick Messner (Melotone).

Organ Grinder's Swing. w. Mitchell Parish and Irving Mills, m. Will Hudson, 1936. Instrumental hit, played by many bands. Among the recordings were: Hudson-DeLange (Brunswick), Jimmie Lunceford (Decca), Benny Goodman (Victor), Joe Haymes (Perfect), pianist Frank Froeba (Columbia). In 1937, Ella Fitzgerald recorded it with Chick Webb's Orchestra (Decca). It was sung by André DeShields, Jason Graae, and Jim Walton in (TM) *Stardust*, 1987.

Oriental. w/m Billy Meyers and Elmer Schoebel, 1922. Leading records by Paul Whiteman and his Orchestra (Victor) and The Friars' Society Orchestra (Gennett).

Original Dixieland One-step. w/m Joe Jordan, Nick LaRocca, J. Russell Robinson, 1918.

Orinoco: Jungle Rag Two-step. m. Cecil Duane Crabb, 1909. Issued originally on piano roll (QRS), played by the composer.

Ornithology. m. Charlie Parker and Benny Harris, 1946. Based on the chord progressions of "How High the Moon." Title suggested by Parker's nickname of "Bird." Recorded by Charlie Parker's Septet (Dial).

Or What Have You? w. Grace Henry, m. Morris Hamilton, 1929. Sung by Bettina Hall and John McCauley and danced by Clifton Webb and Joan Carter-Waddell in (TM) *The Little Show.* Recorded by Al Goodman's Orchestra (Brunswick).

Ostrich Walk. m. Edwin B. Edwards, Nick LaRocca, Tony Spargo, and Larry Shields, 1918. Written and recorded by members of the Original Dixieland Jazz Band (Victor).

Other Guy, The. w/m Graham Goble, 1983. Recorded by the Australian group Little River Band (Capitol).

Other Half of Me, The. w/m Jack Lawrence and Stan Freeman, 1964. Introduced by Richard Kiley in (TM) *I Had a Ball.*

Other Man's Grass Is Always Greener, The. w/m Tony Hatch and Jackie Trent, 1967. Top 40 hit recorded in England by Petula Clark (Warner Bros).

Other Side of the Mountain, Part 2. w. Mary Ann Leikin, m. Lee Holdridge, 1978. Sung by Merrily Webber on the soundtrack on (MP) *The Other Side of the Mountain, Part 2.*

Other Side of the Tracks, The. w. Carolyn Leigh, m. Cy Coleman, 1962. Introduced by Virginia Martin in (TM) *Little Me.*

Other Woman, The. w/m Ray Parker, Jr., 1982. Top 10 record by Ray Parker, Jr. (Arista).

Other Woman, The. w/m Don Rollins, 1965. Country hit by Ray Price (Columbia).

Other Woman, The. w/m Jessie Mae Robinson, 1956. Introduced and recorded by Sarah Vaughan (Mercury).

Oui, Oui, Marie. w. Alfred Bryan and Joseph McCarthy, m. Fred Fisher, 1918. Another song about World War I soldiers' experiences with mademoiselles. In 1920, it was interpolated into (TM) *Kissing Time.* The song was heard in the remake of (MP) *What Price Glory* in 1952, sung by Corinne Calvert in French, and by a male chorus in English.

Our Anniversary. w/m Jesse Murphy and James Freeman, 1962. Introduced by The Five Satins (Ember). Best-selling record by Shep and The Limelites (Hull), 1962.

Our Big Love Scene. w. Arthur Freed, m. Nacio Herb Brown, 1933. Introduced by Bing Crosby in (MM) *Going Hollywood.*

Our Concerto. w. Hal David (Engl.), Giorgio Calabrese (It.), m. Umberto Bindi, 1960. Original Italian title, "Il Nostro Concerto." First English recording by Al Martino (20th Fox). Recorded by Steve Lawrence (United Artists), 1962.

Our Country, May She Always Be Right. w/m Paul Dresser, 1898. Patriotic song written during Spanish-American war.

Our Day Will Come. w. Mort Garson, m. Bob Hilliard, 1962. #1 hit by Ruby and The Romantics (Kapp). Revived by Frankie Valli (Private Stock), 1975.

Our Director. m. F. E. Bigelow, 1926. A march that later became the Harvard University football song.

Our Everlasting Love. w. Earl Shuman, m. Leon Carr, 1964. Popularized by Ruby and The Romantics (Kapp).

Our House. w/m Christopher Foreman and Charles Smyth, 1983. Top 10 record by the British septet Madness (Geffen).

Our House. w/m Graham Nash, 1970. Top 40 record by Crosby, Stills, Nash & Young (Atlantic.)

Our Lady of Fatima. w/m Gladys Gollahon, 1950. Leading records by Kitty Kallen and Richard Hayes (Mercury); Red Foley, with The Anita Kerr Singers (Decca); Phil Spitalny, vocal by The Hour of Charm Choir (RCA Victor).

Our Lips Are Sealed. w/m Terry Hill and Jane Wiedlin, 1981. Recorded by the group The Go-Go's (I.R.S.).

Our Love. w/m Charles Jackson, Jr. and Marvin Yancy, 1978. Top 10 record by Natalie Cole (Capitol).

Our Love. w/m Larry Clinton, Buddy Bernier, and Bob Emmerich, 1939. Adapted from a theme in Tchaikovsky's *Romeo and Juliet Fantasy Overture*. Leading record by Tommy Dorsey, vocal by Stuart Foster (Victor).

Our Love Affair. w. Arthur Freed, m. Roger Edens, 1940. Introduced in a production number by Mickey Rooney and Judy Garland in (MM) *Strike Up the Band*. Nominated for Academy Award. Popular records by Tommy Dorsey, vocal by Frank Sinatra (Victor); Glenn Miller, vocal by Ray Eberle (Bluebird); Dick Jurgens, vocal by Harry Cool (Okeh).

(Our Love) Don't Throw It All Away. w/m Barry Gibb and Blue Weaver, 1978. Top 10 record by the British singer Andy Gibb (RSO).

Our Love Is Here to Stay. See **Love Is Here to Stay.**

Our Love Is on the Faultline. w/m Reece Kirk, 1983. Top 10 C&W chart record by Crystal Gayle (Warner Bros.).

Our Love Story. w/m Norma Newell and William Harrison, 1950. Featured and recorded by Herb Jeffries (Columbia).

Our Penthouse on Third Avenue. w. Lew Brown, m. Sammy Fain, 1937. Introduced by Harriet Hilliard in (MM) *New Faces of 1937*. Recorded by Hilliard with Ozzie Nelson's Orchestra (Bluebird); Tommy Dorsey, vocal by Jack Leonard (Victor); Gene Kardos, vocal by Bea Wain (Melotone).

Our Song. w. Dorothy Fields, m. Jerome Kern, 1937. Introduced by Grace Moore in (MM) *When You're in Love*. Recorded by Moore (Decca), and Eddy Duchin, vocal by Jerry Cooper (Victor).

Our Time. w/m Stephen Sondheim, 1981. Introduced by Jim Walton, Lonny Price, and Ann Morrison in (TM) *Merrily We Roll Along.*

Our Very Own. w. Jack Elliott, m. Victor Young, 1950. Title song of (MP) *Our Very Own*. Top record by Sarah Vaughan (Columbia).

Our Waltz. w. Nat Burton, m. David Rose, 1943. Theme song of David Rose's radio show. As instrumental, coupled with Rose's hit "Holiday for Strings" (Victor) (q.v.). Lyrics written later.

Our Winter Love. w. Bob Tubert, m. John Cowell, 1963. Top 10 instrumental recording by pianist Bill Pursell (Columbia). Leading vocal version by The Lettermen (Capitol), 1967.

Out and About. w/m Tommy Boyce and Bobby Hart, 1967. Recorded by Tommy Boyce and Bobby Hart (A&M).

Outa-Space. w/m Joseph Arthur Greene and Billy Preston, 1972. Gold record instrumental by Billy Preston (A&M).

Out Here on My Own. w/m Michael Gore and Lesley Gore, 1980. Introduced by Irene Cara in (MM) *Fame*, and on records (RSO). The song was an Academy Award nominee.

Out In the Cold Again. w. Ted Koehler, m. Rube Bloom, 1934. Featured, recorded, and popularized by Glen Gray and the Casa Loma Orchestra, vocal by Kenny Sargent (Brunswick); Rudy Vallee (Victor); the Dorsey Brothers Orchestra, vocal by Bob Crosby (Decca). Later records by Mindy Carson (Victor), Billy Eckstine (MGM), Sam Donahue and his Orchestra (Capitol).

Out In the Country. w. Paul Williams, m. Roger Nichols, 1970. Top 20 record by Three Dog Night (Dunhill).

Out In the Middle of the Night. w/m Harry Blum, 1954. Recorded by Karen Chandler, with Jack Pleis's Orchestra (Decca).

Outlaw Man. w/m David Blue, 1973. Introduced on records by David Blue, produced by Graham Nash (Asylum). Best-selling version by The Eagles (Asylum).

Out of Breath (and Scared to Death of You). w. Johnny Mercer, m. Everett Miller, 1930. Johnny Mercer's first published song. Introduced in (TM) *The Garrick Gaieties* by Sterling Holloway and Cynthia Rogers.

Out of Limits. w/m Michael Z. Gordon, 1963. Instrumental based on the theme of the series (TVP) "Outer Limits" by the surf quintet The Marketts (Liberty).

Out of My Dreams. w. Oscar Hammerstein II, m. Richard Rodgers, 1943. Introduced by Joan Roberts and female chorus in (TM) *Oklahoma!* and sung by Shirley Jones in the film version (MM) *Oklahoma!*

Out of My Head and Back in My Bed. w/m Peggy Forman, 1977. #1 Country chart record by Loretta Lynn (MCA).

Out of Nowhere. w. Edward Heyman, m. John Green, 1931. Introduced by Guy Lombardo and the Royal Canadians. It was heard in (MP) *Dude Ranch* in 1931; sung by Helen Forrest in (MP) *You Came Along* [title from first three words of song] in 1945; sung by Frank Sinatra in (MM) *The Joker Is Wild* in 1957; and heard in (MM) *The Five Pennies* in 1959, where Red Nichols dubbed in the cornet for Danny Kaye, who was portraying Nichols fronting the band. Many recordings include Lena Horne, with Teddy Wilson (Columbia); Harry James (Columbia); Martha Tilton (V-disc 12"); Artie Shaw (Bluebird); Jack Denny (Brunswick); Dick Hyman (MGM); Toots Thielemans (MGM).

Out of Sight, Out of Mind. w/m Ivory Joe Hunter and Clyde Otis, 1956. Popularized by the R&B group The Five Keys (Capitol). Revived in 1969 by Little Anthony and The Imperials (United Artists).

Out of Space. w/m Joe Bishop, Gene Gifford, and Winston Collins Tharp, 1934. Recorded by the orchestras of Isham Jones (Decca); Del Courtney (Vocalion); Hal Kemp, vocal by Nan Wynn (Victor); Glenn Miller, vocal by Ray Eberle (Bluebird).

Out of the Blue. w/m Debbie Gibson, 1988. Title song and single from the album by Debbie Gibson (Atlantic).

Out of the Blue. w/m Ritchie Cordell and Bo Gentry, 1967. Recorded by Tommy James and The Shondells (Roulette).

Out of the Question. w/m Raymond (Gilbert) O'Sullivan, 1973. Top 20 record, from England, by Gilbert O'Sullivan (MAM).

Out of the Silence. w/m Lloyd B. Norlind, 1941. From (MM) *All-Amerian Co-Ed.* Nominated for Academy Award.

Out of This World. w. Johnny Mercer, m. Harold Arlen, 1945. Bing Crosby dubbed his voice on the soundtrack of (MM) *Out of This World* for Eddie Bracken, who played the role of a crooning telegram delivery boy. Leading records by Crosby (Decca), Jo Stafford (Capitol), Tommy Dorsey, vocal by Stuart Foster (Victor).

Out of Time. w/m Mick Jagger and Keith Richards, 1975. First recorded by the English group The Rolling Stones in their album "Flowers" (London), 1966. Chart single (ABKCO) released 1975.

Out of Touch. w/m Daryl Hall and John Oates, 1984. #1 record by Daryl Hall and John Oates (RCA).

Out of Work. w/m Bruce Springsteen, 1982. Recorded by Gary U.S. Bonds (EMI America).

Out-o'-Town Gal. w/m Walter Donaldson, 1928. Introduced and recorded by Paul Whiteman, vocal by the Rhythm Boys [Bing Crosby, Harry Barris, and Al Rinker] (Columbia).

Outside. w/m Frank Flynn, 1929. Novelty song introduced by Rudy Vallee.

Outside of Heaven. w. Sammy Gallop, m. Chester Conn, 1952. Leading records by Eddie Fisher (RCA Victor); Margaret Whiting (Capitol).

Outside of Paradise. w. Jack Lawrence, m. Peter Tinturin, 1938. Introduced in (MM)

Outside of Paradise and on records (Brunswick) by Phil Regan. Other records: Al Bowlly (Bluebird) and Isham Jones's Band (Vocalion).

Outside of You. w. Al Dubin, m. Harry Warren, 1935. Introduced in (MM) *Broadway Gondolier* by Dick Powell and recorded by him with Victor Arden's Orchestra (Brunswick). Ted Fio Rito and his Band, who appeared in the film, also recorded it (Brunswick).

Outside the Gates of Heaven. w/m Twyla Herbert and Lou Christie, 1966. Recorded by Lou Christie (Co & Ce).

Out There in the Sunshine with You. w. J. Keirn Brennan, m. Ernest R. Ball, 1923.

Out Where the Blue Begins. w/m Cliff Friend, 1936. Featured and recorded by the tenor John Steel (Victor), and Ted Weems and his Orchestra, vocal by Perry Como (Decca).

Out Where the Blues Begin. w. Dorothy Fields, m. Jimmy McHugh, 1929. From (TM) *Hello, Daddy*. Recorded by two all-star bands, organized for recording: the publisher, Irving Mills and His Hotsy Totsy Gang, vocal by Smith Ballew (Brunswick); and the Louisiana Rhythm Kings, led by Red Nichols (Vocalion).

Out Where the West Begins. w. Arthur Chapman, m. Estelle Philleo, 1917.

Over and Over. w/m Robert Byrd, 1965. Introduced with chart record by Bobby Day (Class), 1958. The British group, The Dave Clark Five, had a #1 U.S. hit (Epic), 1965.

Overkill. w/m Colin Hay, 1983. Top 10 record by the Australian quintet Men At Work (Columbia).

Over My Head. w/m Christine McVie, 1975. Top 20 record by the British group Fleetwood Mac (Reprise). Song written by their keyboardist.

Over My Shoulder. w/m Harry Woods, 1935. Introduced by Jessie Matthews in the British film (MM) *Evergreen* and recorded by her in a medley from the film (Columbia, Engl.).

Overnight. w. Billy Rose and Charlotte Kent, m. Louis Alter, 1930. Introduced by Fanny Brice in (TM) *Sweet and Low*, produced by husband Billy Rose. Recordings include Belle Baker (Brunswick), Glen Gray and Casa Loma Orchestra (Okeh), High Hatters (Victor), Emil Coleman's Orchestra (Brunswick), and the earliest band recording that lists Benny Goodman as leader (Melotone).

Overnight Sensation (Hit Record). w/m Eric Carmen, 1974. Top 20 record by The Raspberries (Capitol).

Over Somebody Else's Shoulder. w/m Al Lewis and Al Sherman, 1934. Most popular recordings by Isham Jones and his Orchestra (Victor) and Eddie Cantor (Melotone).

Over the Hills and Far Away. w. William Jerome, m. Jean Schwartz, 1908.

Over the Mountain, Across the Sea. w/m Rex Garvin, 1957. Top 10 record by Johnnie and Joe (Chess). Top 40 record by Bobby Vinton (Epic), 1963.

Over the Rainbow. w. E. Y. Harburg, m. Harold Arlen, 1939. Introduced by Judy Garland in (MM) *The Wizard of Oz*. Garland recorded it (Decca) and it became her "theme song" for the rest of her career. Academy Award-winning song for the year. It was played by the band in (MM) *The Glenn Miller Story*, 1954; sung by Eileen Farrell, dubbing for Eleanor Parker, who portrayed the opera star Marjorie Lawrence in her story, (MM) *Interrupted Melody*, 1955; hummed by Elizabeth Hartman in (MP) *A Patch of Blue*, 1965.

Over There. w/m George M. Cohan, 1917. Undoubtedly, the song most identified with World War I. Charles King introduced it at a Red Cross benefit at the Hippodrome Theatre in New York. Nora Bayes recorded it (Victor) and featured it in her vaudeville act. Enrico Caruso recorded it, with choruses in English and French (Victor). The song swept the country, with sheet music sales in the millions. James Cagney and Frances Langford sang it in the Cohan screen biography (MM) *Yankee Doo-*

dle Dandy, 1942. Joel Grey sang it in the title role in (TM) *George M!*, at the Palace Theatre in New York, 1968. Patrice Munsel and chorus sang it in (TM) *A Musical Jubilee*, 1975.

Over the Rhythm of Raindrops. See **Rhythm of Raindrops, The.**

Over the Top. w. Tom Whitlock, m. Giorgio Moroder, 1987. Sung on the soundtrack of (MP) *Over the Top*, and on records by Kenny Loggins (Columbia).

Over Three Hills. w/m Ernest Benedict, Roy West, Lenny Sanders, and Dolly Kendall, 1949. C&W chart waltz, recorded by Ernie Benedict (RCA).

Overture from "Tommy" (A Rock Opera). m. Peter Townshend, 1970. Instrumental. Top 20 record by a studio group, The Assembled Multitide, arranged and conducted by Tom Sellers (Atlantic).

Over Under Sideways Down. w/m Chris Dreja, Keith Relf, Geoff Beck, Jim McCarty, and Paul Samwell-Smith, 1966. Written by members of the English group, The Yardbirds,

whose recording was in the Top 20 in the U.S. (Epic).

Over You. w/m Ray Parker, Carole Bayer Sager, and Burt Bacharach, 1987. Top 10 R&B chart record by Ray Parker with Natalie Cole (Geffen).

Over You. w/m Bobby Hart and Austin Roberts, 1983. From (MP) *Tender Mercies.* Nominated for an Academy Award.

Over You. w/m Jerry Fuller, 1968. Top 10 record by Gary Puckett and The Union Gap (Columbia).

Owner of a Lonely Heart w/m Jon Anderson, Trevor Horne, Trevor Rabin, and Chris Squire, 1983. #1 record by the English group Yes (Atlantic).

Oye Como Va. w/m Tito Puente, 1971. Top 20 hit by the Latin/rock group Santana (Columbia).

Ozarks Are Callin' Me Home, The. w/m Cole Porter, 1936. Introduced by Ethel Merman in (TM) *Red, Hot, and Blue!* Recorded by the popular pianist-singer Ramona (Liberty Music Shops).

P

Pack Up Your Sins and Go to the Devil. w/m Irving Berlin, 1922. Introduced by the McCarthy Sisters in (TM) *The Music Box Revue of 1922*. Recorded by the bands of Paul Whiteman (Victor) and Emil Coleman (Vocalion). Sung by Ethel Merman in (MM) *Alexander's Ragtime Band*, 1938.

Pack Up Your Sorrows. w/m Richard Faria and Pauline Marden, 1964. Featured and recorded by Joan Baez (Vanguard).

Pack Up Your Troubles in Your Old Kit Bag (and Smile, Smile, Smile). w. George Asaf, m. Felix Powell, 1915. An English war song that had equal popularity with the U.S. troops in World War I. Best-selling U.S. recordings by James F. Harrison and The Knickerbocker Quartet (Columbia), and Reinald Werrenrath (Victor), 1917. Sung by Julie Andrews in (MM) *Darling Lili*, 1970.

Pac-Man Fever. w/m Jerry Buckner and Gary Garcia, 1982. Gold record by Buckner and Garcia (Columbia). The novelty referred to the popular video game, Pac-Man.

Padam, Padam. w. Mann Holiner and Alberta Nichols (Engl.), m. Norbert Glanzberg, 1952. Original French lyrics by Henri Contet. Featured and recorded by Tony Martin (RCA Victor).

Paddlin' Madelin' Home. w/m Harry Woods, 1925. Established by the popular recordings of: Cliff "Ukulele Ike" Edwards (Pathé), Wendell Hall (Brunswick), George Olsen (Victor), Sam Lanin (Perfect).

Padre. w. Paul Francis Webster (Engl.), m. Alain C. Romans, 1958. Original French words by Marcel Algeron and Jacques Larue. Top 20 record by Toni Arden (Decca).

Pagan Love Song. w. Arthur Freed, m. Nacio Herb Brown, 1929. Sung by Ramon Novarro in (MM) *The Pagan* in 1929 and by Howard Keel in (MM) *The Pagan Love Song* in 1950. The screenplays were unrelated. The song was also heard in (MM) *Night Club Girl* in 1944.

Page Miss Glory. w. Al Dubin, m. Harry Warren, 1935. Introduced by Dick Powell and Marion Davies in (MP) *Page Miss Glory*.

Painted, Tainted Rose. w/m Peter De Angelis and Jean Sawyer, 1963. Recorded by Al Martino (Capitol).

Painting the Clouds with Sunshine. w. Al Dubin, m. Joe Burke, 1929. Introduced by Nick Lucas in (MM) *Gold Diggers of Broadway*, the hit film musical based on the 1923 silent film, *Gold Diggers*, which was adapted from Avery Hopwood's stage play of the same name. Leading records by Nick Lucas (Brunswick); and Jean Goldkette's Orchestra, conducted by Victor Young, with vocal by Frank Munn (Victor). In a 1950 remake, it became the title song of (MM) *Painting the Clouds with Sunshine*, sung by Dennis Morgan.

653

Paint It Black. w/m Mick Jagger and Keith Richards, 1966. #1 record by the British group The Rolling Stones (London).

Pair of Broken Hearts, A. w/m Jenny Lou Carson and Fred Rose, 1945. Most popular recording by Spade Cooley (Columbia).

Pale Moon. w. Jesse Glick, m. Frederick Knight Logan, 1920. Popular song. Instrumental version by Paul Whiteman (Victor), 1924.

Palesteena. w/m Con Conrad and J. Russell Robinson, 1920. Introduced and featured and recorded by Eddie Cantor (Emerson). Also recorded by The Original Dixieland Jazz Band (Victor) and Frank Crumit (Columbia).

Palisades Park. w/m Chuck Barris, 1962. Top 10 record by Freddy Cannon (Swan).

Pal of My Cradle Days. w. Marshall Montgomery, m. Al Piantadosi, 1925. Recorded by the popular tenor Lewis James (Columbia).

Paloma Blanca. w/m Johannes Bouwens, 1975. Popular U.S. release by the Dutch group, The George Baker Selection, led by Bouwens (Warner).

Pal That I Loved, The (Stole the Gal That I Loved). w. Harry Pease, m. Ed. G. Nelson, 1924. Recorded by Vernon Dalhart (Okeh) and Lewis James (Victor).

Pamela Throws a Party. w/m Robert Allen, 1957. Popularized via recording by Joe Reisman and his Orchestra (RCA).

Panama. w/m Eddie Van Halen, Alex Van Halen, Michael Anthony, and David Lee Roth, 1984. Written and recorded by the group Van Halen (Warner Bros.).

Panama. w. George V. Hobart, m. Raymond Hubbell, 1913. From (TM) *Ziegfeld Follies of 1913*.

Panamania. w. Sam Coslow, m. Al Siegel, 1937. Introduced in (MM) *Swing High, Swing Low* and recorded (Brunswick) by Dorothy Lamour.

Pan American. w/m Hank Williams, 1948. Country chart hit by Hawkshaw Hawkins (King).

Panamericana. m. Victor Herbert, 1901. Orchestral composition celebrating the Pan-American Exposition of 1901.

Pancho and Lefty. w/m Townes Van Zandt, 1983. First recorded by Emmylou Harris in her album "Luxury Liner" (Warner Bros.), 1977. #1 Country chart single by Willie Nelson and Merle Haggard (Epic), 1983.

Pancho Maximilian Hernandez. w/m Bob Hilliard and Al Frisch, 1947. Featured and recorded by Woody Herman and his Orchestra (Columbia).

Pandora's Golden Heebie Jeebies. w/m Gary Alexander, 1966. Top 40 record by The Association (Valiant).

Panhandle Rag. m. Leon McAuliffe, 1949. Instrumental, introduced by Leon McAuliffe and his Western Swing Band (Columbia) and covered by Gene Krupa and his Orchestra (RCA Victor).

Panic Is On, The. w/m George Clarke, Bert Clarke, Winston Tharp, and Thomas "Fats" Waller, 1936. Popularized and recorded by Fats Waller (Victor), Connie Boswell (Decca), Mezz Mezzrow (Bluebird).

Pansy. w. Jack Elliott (Engl.), Gigi Pisano (Ital.), m. Furio Rendine, 1958. Italian song, "La Pans," introduced in 1953 by Renato Carasone. His recording was released in the U.S. (Capitol). Among other recordings: The Gaylords (Mercury); Les Baxter (Capitol).

Papa, Can You Hear Me? w. Alan Bergman and Marilyn Bergman, m. Michel Legrand, 1983. Introduced by Barbra Streisand in (MM) *Yentl*. Nominated for an Academy Award.

Papa, Won't You Dance with Me? w. Sammy Cahn, m. Jule Styne, 1947. Introduced by Nanette Fabray and Jack McCauley in (TM) *High Button Shoes*. Doris Day, after leaving Les Brown's Orchestra, had her first chart record as a soloist with her version (Columbia).

Papa Don't Preach. w/m Brian Elliot and Madonna, 1986. #1 chart single from the album "True Blue," by Madonna (Sire).

(Down At) Papa Joe's. w/m Jerry Dean Smith, 1963. Hit record by the trio The Dixiebelles (Sound Stage).

Papa Loves Mambo. w/m Al Hoffman, Dick Manning, and Bix Reichner, 1954. Hit record by Perry Como (RCA Victor).

Papa Niccolini. w/m Anne Jean Edwards and Don George, 1941. Recorded and featured by Glenn Miller, vocal by Tex Beneke and The Modernaires (Bluebird).

Papa-Oom-Mow-Mow. w/m Al Frazier, John "Sonny" Harris, Carl White, Turner "Rocky" Wilson, Jr., 1962. Written and recorded by The Rivingtons (Liberty).

Papa's Got a Brand New Bag. w/m James Brown, 1965. James Brown's record was #1 on the R&B and in the Top 10 on the Pop charts (King, Part 1). Grammy Award winner (NARAS), Rhythm and Blues Song of the Year. Otis Redding had a Top 40 version (Atco), 1968.

Papa Was a Rollin' Stone. w/m Barrett Strong and Norman Whitfield, 1972. #1 chart record by The Temptations (Gordy). Winner Grammy Award (NARAS) Best Rhythm and Blues Song. Revived by Wolf [pseudonym for Bill Wolfer], who had a popular synthesized version (Constellation), 1983.

Papa Was Too. w/m Joe Tex, 1967. Introduced and recorded by Joe Tex (Dial).

Pa-Paya Mama. w/m George Sandler, Larry Coleman, and Norman Gimbel, 1953. Hit record by Perry Como (RCA Victor).

Paperback Writer. w/m John Lennon and Paul McCartney, 1966. #1 gold record by The Beatles (Capitol).

Paper Cup. w/m Jim Webb, 1967. Top 40 record by The 5th Dimension (Soul City).

Paper Doll. w/m Johnny S. Black, 1942. Published twelve years earlier and featured in nightclubs by Tommy Lyman, it did not catch on with the public until the Mills Brothers' colossal record hit in 1942 (Decca). Sales of over six million records to date, twelve weeks as #1 on The Billboard charts, #1 on "Your Hit Parade" for twenty-three weeks, and huge sheet music sales placed the song on Variety's "Fifty Year Hit Parade." The Delta Rhythm Boys sang it in (MM) *Hi, Good Lookin'*, 1944, and Lena Horne sang it in (MM) *Two Girls and a Sailor* that same year.

Paper in Fire. w/m John Cougar Mellencamp, 1987. Popular track and single from the album "The Lonesome Jubilee" by John Cougar Mellencamp (Mercury).

Paper Maché. w. Hal David, m. Burt Bacharach, 1970. Recorded by Dionne Warwick (Scepter).

Paper Mansions. w/m Ted Harris, 1967. Top 10 Country chart record by Dottie West (RCA).

Paper of Pins, A. See **Bus Stop Song, The**.

Paper Roses. w. Janice Torre, m. Fred Spielman, 1960, 1973. Popularized by Anita Bryant (Carlton). Marie Osmond revived it with a million-selling record (MGM), 1973.

Paper Sun. w/m Steve Winwood and Jim Capaldi, 1967. Recorded by the English rock band, Traffic, featuring Steve Winwood (United Artists).

Paper Tiger. w/m John D. Loudermilk, 1965. Recorded by Sue Thompson (Hickory).

Parade in Town, A. w/m Stephen Sondheim, 1964. Introduced by Angela Lansbury in (TM) *Anyone Can Whistle*.

Parade of the Wooden Soldiers. w. Ballard MacDonald (Engl.), Victor Oliver (Fr.), m. Leon Jessel, 1922. Introduced in the U.S.

in Nikita Balieff's Russian revue (TM) *Chauve Souris*, which was brought over from Paris. It was originally a German instrumental, "Die Parade der Holzsoldaten," 1911. Popular recordings by the orchestras of Vincent Lopez (Edison), Carl Fenton (Brunswick), Paul Whiteman (Victor).

Paradiddle Joe. w/m Johnny Morris, Fred Parries, and Jerry Pugsley, 1941. Most popular records by the bands of Tony Pastor (Bluebird) and Erskine Butterfield (Decca).

Paradise. w/m Folesade Adu, Paul Denman, Andrew Hale, and Stuart Matthewman, 1988. #1 R&B Pop chart crossover record by Sade [Folesade Adu], the Nigerian-born, London-raised singer/songwriter/clothing designer (Epic).

Paradise. w. Tanyayette Willoughby, m. Mauro Malavasi and David Romani, 1981. Recorded by the group Change (Atlantic).

Paradise. w. Nacio Herb Brown and Gordon Clifford, m. Nacio Herb Brown, 1932. A waltz introduced in the Pola Negri film (MP) *A Woman Commands*. The song was originally banned from being played on radio because the censors felt that the humming sections, indicated in the lyric, were liable to arouse the listener's prurient interest. The song was sung by Belita in a cabaret scene in (MP) *The Gangster*, 1947; by Gloria Grahame in (MP) *A Woman's Secret*, 1949; by Valentina Cortesa in (MP) *Malaya*, 1949; by Bob Crosby in (MM) *The Five Pennies*, 1959. Early popular records by Russ Columbo (Victor); Guy Lombardo (Brunswick); Morton Downey (Perfect); Phil Spitalny (Hit of the Week). Later records by Frank Sinatra (Columbia); Hal Kemp, vocal by Nan Wynn (Victor); Dorothy Lamour (Bluebird); Eddy Howard (Majestic); and many more.

Paradise by the Dashboard Light. w/m Jim Steinman, 1978. Novelty, recorded by Meatloaf with help from Ellen Foley as female vocalist, and Phil Rizzuto as baseball announcer (Epic).

Paradise Tonight. w/m Mark Wright and Bill Kenner, 1983. #1 Country chart record by Charly McClain and Mickey Gilley (Epic).

Pardon Came Too Late, The. w/m Paul Dresser, 1891.

Pardon Me, My Dear Alphonse, After You, My Dear Gaston. w. Vincent P. Bryan, m. Harry Von Tilzer, 1902. Based on the comic strip Gaston and Alphonse.

Pardon Me, Pretty Baby. w. Raymond Klages and Jack Meskill, m. Vincent Rose, 1931. Popularized by the bands of Freddie Rich (Columbia) and Sam Lanin (Hit of the Week). Later by Benny Carter (Decca) and Bobby Sherwood (Capitol).

Pardon My Love. w. Milton Drake, m. Oscar Levant, 1935. Introduced by Hal Kemp and his Orchestra, vocal by Skinnay Ennis. Best-selling record by Fats Waller (Victor).

Pardon My Southern Accent. w. Johnny Mercer, m. Matty Malneck, 1934. Top records by Paul Whiteman's Orchestra, vocal by Johnny Mercer (Victor); and Glen Gray and the Casa Loma Orchestra, vocal by Pee Wee Hunt (Brunswick).

Paree! w. Leo Robin, m. Jose Padilla, 1927. The English version of "Ca c'est Paris!"

Paree, What Did You Do to Me? w/m Cole Porter, 1929. Introduced by Betty Compton and Jack Thompson in (MM) *Fifty Million Frenchmen*.

Parents Just Don't Understand. w/m Jeff Townes, Will Smith, and Pete Q. Harris, 1988. Top 10 R&B crossover record by the rap duo, D. J. Jazzy Jeff and The Fresh Prince [Townes and Smith] (Jive).

Paris. m. Perez Prado, 1958. Instrumental recorded by Perez Prado and his Orchestra (RCA).

Paris. w. E. Ray Goetz, m. Louis Alter, 1928. Interpolated as the title song of (TM) *Paris*, starring Irene Bordoni.

Paris, Stay the Same. w. Clifford Grey, m. Victor Schertzinger, 1929. Introduced by Maurice Chevalier and Lupino Lane in (MM) *The Love Parade* and recorded by Chevalier (Victor).

Paris Blues. m. Edward Kennedy "Duke" Ellington, 1961. Introduced on the soundtrack of (MM) *Paris Blues* by Duke Ellington and his Orchestra.

Parisian Pierrot. w/m Noël Coward, 1924. Introduced by Gertrude Lawrence and cast members in the London production (TM) *London Calling!* 1923. Lawrence, with Barbara Roberts and Jill Williams, introduced it to the U.S. in (TM) *Charlot's Revue*. Julie Andrews and Daniel Massey sang it in the film loosely based on the career of Gertrude Lawrence (MM) *Star!*, 1968.

Paris in the Spring. w. Mack Gordon, m. Harry Revel, 1935. Introduced by Mary Ellis in (MM) *Paris in the Spring*. Among records: bands of Ray Noble (Victor), Freddy Martin (Brunswick), Frank Dailey (Bluebird).

Paris Is a Lonely Town. w. E. Y. Harburg, m. Harold Arlen, 1962. Introduced by Judy Garland singing on the soundtrack of the animated feature film (MM) *Gay Purr-ee*.

Paris Is a Paradise for Coons. w. Edward Madden, m. Jerome Kern, 1911. In the opening show of the Winter Garden Theatre in New York, it was sung by Al Jolson, making his musical comedy debut and portraying Erastus Sparkler, "a colored aristocrat of San Juan Hill, cutting a wide swath in Paris."

Paris Loves Lovers. w/m Cole Porter, 1955. Introduced by Don Ameche and Hildgarde Neff in (TM) *Silk Stockings*, the stage musical version of the Garbo film *Ninotchka*.

Paris Mist. m. Erroll Garner, 1963. From the music composed for and played by Erroll Garner on the soundtrack of (MP) *A New Kind of Love*.

Paris Original. w/m Frank Loesser, 1961. Introduced by Bonnie Scott, Claudette Sutherland, Mara Landi, and the company in (TM) *How to Succeed in Business Without Really Trying*. In the film version (MM) *How to Succeed in Business Without Really Trying*, 1967, it was heard orchestrally in the background.

Partin' Time. w/m B. B. King, 1960. B. B. King had an R&B Top 10 recording (Kent).

Partners. w/m Danny Dill, 1959. C&W hit record by Jim Reeves (RCA).

Partners After All. w/m Chips Moman and Bobby Emmons, 1987. Country chart record by Willie Nelson (Columbia).

Part of the Plan. w/m Dan Fogelberg, 1975. Recorded by Dan Fogelberg (Epic).

Part-Time Love. w. Elton John, m. Gary Osborne, 1978. Recorded by Elton John (MCA).

Part Time Love. w/m David Gates, 1975. Recorded by Gladys Knight and The Pips (Buddah).

Part Time Love. w/m Clay Hammond, 1963. Top 20 record by Little Johnny Taylor (Galaxy). Revived by Ann Peebles (Hi), 1970.

Part-Time Lover. w/m Stevie Wonder, 1985. #1 single from the album "In Square Circle," by Stevie Wonder (Motown).

Party All the Time. w/m Rick James, 1985. Top 10 gold record by comedian Eddie Murphy (Columbia).

Party Doll. w/m Jimmy Bowen and Buddy Knox, 1957. #1 hit by Buddy Knox (Roulette), but originally on another label (Triple-D). Other popular versions by Steve Lawrence (Coral) and Wingy Manone (Decca).

Party Lights. w/m Claudine Clark, 1962. Recorded by Claudine Clark (Chancellor).

Party's Over, The. w. Betty Comden and Adolph Green, m. Jule Styne, 1956. Introduced by Judy Holliday in (TM) *Bells Are*

Ringing, and sung by her in (MM) *Bells Are Ringing*, 1960. Leading record by Doris Day (Columbia), 1957.

Party Time. w/m Bruce Channel, 1981. #1 Country chart record by T. G. Sheppard (Warner Bros.).

Passé. w/m Joseph Meyer, Carl Sigman, and Eddie De Lange, 1946. Leading recordings by Tex Beneke, vocal by Lillian Lane (RCA Victor); Margaret Whiting (Capitol); Ray McKinley and his Orchestra (Majestic).

Passing By. w. Jack Lawrence (Engl.), m. John Hess and Paul Misraki, 1947. Original French title "Vous Qui Passez sans Me Voir," lyrics by Charles Trenet. This version was heard in (MP) *A Woman of My Own* and recorded by Jean Sablon (RCA Victor).

Passing Fancy. w/m Bob Hilliard and David Mann, 1947. Featured and recorded by Vaughn Monroe, with his Orchestra (RCA Victor).

Passing Strangers. w/m Rita Mann and Mel Mitchell, 1957. Recorded by Sarah Vaughan and Billy Eckstine (Mercury).

Passing Through. m. Erroll Garner, 1956. Instrumental introduced by pianist Erroll Garner.

Passion. w/m Rod Stewart, Phil Chen, Jim Cregan, Gary Grainger, and Kevin Savigar, 1980. Top 10 record by the English singer Rod Stewart (Warner Bros.).

Pass Me By. w. Carolyn Leigh, m. Cy Coleman, 1965. Sung on the soundtrack of (MP) *Father Goose*, starring Cary Grant, by Digby Wolfe. Song featured and recorded by Peggy Lee (Capitol).

Pass That Peace Pipe. w. Ralph Blane, m. Hugh Martin and Roger Edens, 1947. New song interpolated in (MM) *Good News*. Performed by Joan McCracken, Ray McDonald, and students. Nominated for Academy Award, 1947. Popular records by Margaret Whiting (Capitol) and Bing Crosby (Decca).

Pass the Booze. w/m Gene Northington and Ray Butts, 1965. C&W chart record by Ernest Tubb (Decca).

Pass the Dutchie. w/m Lloyd Ferguson, Jackie Mitoo, and Fitzroy Simpson, 1983. Top 10 record by Musical Youth, an English quintet comprised of schoolboys, ages eleven to sixteen (MCA). A Dutchie is a Jamaican cooking pot.

Password. w/m Herman Phillips, 1964. Country hit by Kitty Wells (Decca).

Pastel Blue. See **Why Begin Again?**

Pata Pata. w/m Miriam Makeba and Jerry Ragovoy, 1967. Top 10 record by the South African singer Miriam Makeba (Reprise).

Patches. w/m Barry Mann and Larry Kolber, 1962. Hit record by Dickey Lee (Smash).

Patches (I'm Depending on You). w/m General Johnson and Ronald Dunbar, 1970. Gold record by Clarence Carter (Atlantic). Winner Grammy Award (NARAS) for Best Rhythm and Blues Song, 1970.

Path That Leads the Other Way, The. w/m Paul Dresser, 1898.

Patience and Fortitude. w/m Blackie Warren and Billy Moore, 1945. Recorded instrumentally by Count Basie and his Orchestra (Columbia) and vocally by the Andrews Sisters (Decca).

Patricia. w. Bob Marcus, m. Perez Prado, 1958. #1 million-selling instrumental by Perez Prado and his Orchestra (RCA). Prado recorded a "twist" version in 1962 (RCA).

Patricia. w/m Benny Davis, 1950. Recorded by Perry Como, with Russ Case's Orchestra (RCA Victor).

Patty Cake, Patty Cake (Baker Man). w/m Andy Razaf, J. C. Johnson, and Thomas "Fats" Waller, 1938. Introduced and recorded by Fats Waller (Bluebird). Also recorded by Bunny Berigan (Victor).

Pavanne. m. Morton Gould, 1938. Adapted from a theme from Gould's "American Symphonette No. 2". Early leading recordings by the orchestras of Glenn Miller (Bluebird), 1939, and Jimmie Lunceford (Columbia), 1940.

Payback, The. w/m James Brown, Fred Wesley, and John Starks, 1974. Recorded by James Brown (Polydor).

Paying the Cost to Be Boss. w/m B. B. King, 1968. Top 10 R&B and Top 40 Pop chart recorded by B. B. King (Blues Way).

Pay to the Piper. w/m General Johnson, Greg S. Perry, and Ronald Dunbar, 1970. Top 20 record by Chairmen of the Board (Invictus).

Pay You Back with Interest. w/m Allan Clarke, Tony Hicks, and Graham Nash, 1967. Hit record by the English group, The Hollies, of which the writers were members (Imperial). Chart version by the Canadian singer Gary O'Connor, who billed himself as Gary O' (Capitol), 1970.

Peace, Brother. w. Eddie DeLange, m. James Van Heusen, 1939. Introduced by The Delta Rhythm Boys in (TM) *Swingin' the Dream*. Recorded by Benny Goodman, vocal by Mildred Bailey (Columbia).

Peace, Brother, Peace. w/m Barry Mann and Cynthia Weil, 1968. Recorded by Bill Medley (MGM).

Peaceful. w/m Kenny Rankin, 1973. Top 20 record by Helen Reddy (Capitol).

Peaceful Easy Feeling. w/m Jack Tempchin, 1973. Recorded by the quartet The Eagles (Asylum).

Peaceful Valley. w/m Willard Robison, 1925, 1942. Introduced by Willard Robison's Deep River Four. Revived via interpolation in (MP) *Arkansas Judge*, 1942. Recordings in both C&W and Pop fields by Charlie Barnet and his Orchestra (Bluebird); Christine and the Rangers (Decca); Red Nichols and his Five Pennies (Turntable).

Peace of Mind. w/m Mark Lindsay and Terry Melcher, 1967. Recorded by Paul Revere and The Raiders (Columbia).

Peace of Mind. w/m Riley (B. B.) King and Joe Josea, 1961. R&B Top 10 hit record by B. B. King (Kent).

Peace Train. w/m Cat Stevens, 1971. Written and recorded in England by Cat Stevens. Top 10 U.S. record (A&M).

Peace Will Come (According to Plan). w/m Melanie Safka, 1970. Top 40 record by Melanie (Buddah).

Peaches 'n Cream. w/m Steve Venet and Tommy Boyce, 1965. Recorded by The Ikettes, Ike and Tina Turner's trio (Modern).

Peach Picking Time Down in Georgia. w/m Jimmie Rodgers and C. "Pappy" McMichen, 1933. Written shortly before Rodgers died and recorded by him in his last session (Montgomery Ward). The song has three choruses, in which the title is used twice, but the word "down" does not appear.

Peanut Butter. w/m H. B. Barnum, Martin J. Cooper, Cliff Goldsmith, and Fred Smith, 1961. Recorded by The Olympics, who on this record used the name The Marathons (Arvee).

Peanuts. w/m Joe Cook, 1957. Top 40 record by Little Joe [Cook] and The Thrillers (Okeh). In 1961, Rick and The Keens had a chart version (Smash).

Peanut Vendor, The. w. Marion Sunshine and L. Wolfe Gilbert (Engl.), m. Moises Simons, 1930. A Cuban popular song entitled "El Manisero," introduced in the U.S., with the new English lyrics, by Don Azpiazu at the Palace Theatre in New York. The rhumba made an immediate impact and was recorded by Paul Whiteman (Victor), Guy Lombardo (Columbia), Louis Armstrong (Okeh), and Xavier Cugat (Victor), resulting in huge record and sheet music sales. It was interpolated into (MM) *The Cuban Love Song*, by Lawrence Tib-

659

bett, 1931; (MM) *Luxury Liner*, 1947, by Jane Powell; (MM) *A Star Is Born*, 1954, by Judy Garland. Among later recordings of note were those by Stan Kenton (Capitol), Desi Arnaz (Victor), Morton Gould (Columbia).

Pearl, Pearl, Pearl. w/m Paul Henning, 1963. Featured on the series (TVP) "The Beverly Hillbillies," and recorded by Lester Flatt and Earl Scruggs (Columbia).

Pearly Shells. w/m Webley Edwards and Leon Pober, 1964. Chart record by Burl Ives (Decca). Song heard in (MM) *Surf Party*.

Peckin'. w/m Ben Pollack and Harry James, 1937. Swing novelty, on which James performed [trumpet and vocal] with Ben Pollack's Band (Variety), and arranged for Benny Goodman (Victor). Cab Calloway also recorded it (Variety). It was featured in (MM) *New Faces of 1937*.

Pecos Bill. w. Johnny Lange, m. Eliot Daniel, 1948. Introduced in Walt Disney's animated film (MM) *Melody Time* by the voices of Roy Rogers and The Sons of the Pioneers, who also recorded it (RCA Victor).

Peek-A-Boo. w/m Jack Hammer, 1958. R&B and Pop chart record by The Cadillacs (Josie).

Peel Me a Grape. w/m Dave Frishberg, 1962. Featured and recorded in albums by Dave Frishberg and Blossom Dearie.

Peel Me a Nanner. w/m Bill Anderson, 1964. Country hit by Roy Drusky (Mercury).

Peg. w/m Walter Becker and Donald Fagen, 1978. Top 20 record by the group Steely Dan (ABC).

Peggy. w. Harry Williams, m. Neil Moret, 1919. Introduced by Dorothy Dickson in the revue (TM) *Century Midnight Whirl*.

Peggy O'Neil. w/m Harry Pease, Ed G. Nelson, and Gilbert Dodge, 1921. Popular song with vaudevillians and dance orchestras. Revived with hit records by The Harmonicats

(Vitacoustic) and Frankie Carle and his Orchestra (Columbia), 1947.

Peggy Sue. w/m Jerry Allison, Buddy Holly, and Norman Petty, 1957. Hit record by Buddy Holly (Coral). It was sung by Gary Busey in the title role of (MM) *The Buddy Holly Story*, 1976. Chart record by The Beach Boys (Brother), 1976.

Peg O' My Heart. w. Alfred Bryan, m. Fred Fisher, 1913, 1947. Introduced by José Collins in (TM) *Ziegfeld Follies of 1913*. The song was inspired by Laurette Taylor who starred in the Broadway play of the same name a year earlier. Charles Harrison (Victor) and Henry Burr (Columbia) had hit records. It was the title song of (MP) *Peg o' My Heart* starring Marion Davies, 1933, and was heard in Fisher's film bio (MM) *Oh, You Beautiful Doll*, 1949. Revived in 1947 with #1 records by The Harmonicats (Vitacoustic) and Buddy Clark (Columbia).

Peking Theme, The (So Little Time). w. Paul Francis Webster, m. Dimitri Tiomkin, 1963. Introduced on the soundtrack of (MP) *55 Days at Peking* by Andy Williams. Nominated for Academy Award, 1963. Recorded by Williams (Columbia).

Penguin at the Waldorf. w/m Jimmy Eaton, Larry Wagner, and Frank Shuman, 1947. Introduced and recorded by Frankie Carle and his Orchestra (Columbia).

Pennies from Heaven. w. Johnny Burke, m. Arthur Johnston, 1936. Introduced in (MM) *Pennies from Heaven* and recorded by Bing Crosby (Decca). One of the major hits of the year, it was nominated for an Academy Award and was on the "Your Hit Parade" for thirteen weeks, four times in the #1 position. Dick Haymes sang it in (MM) *Cruisin' Down the River*, 1953, and Crosby sang it again in (MM) *Pepe*, 1960. It was used as the title of (MP) *Pennies from Heaven*, 1981, starring Steve Martin, a film having nothing to do with the original.

Pennsylvania Polka. w/m Lester Lee and Zeke Manners, 1942. Introduced by The Andrews Sisters in (MM) *Give Out, Sisters.* They also had the hit record (Decca).

Pennsylvania 6–5000 w. Carl Sigman, m. Jerry Gray, 1940. Featured and recorded by Glenn Miller, unison vocal of the title by the band members (Bluebird). This million-seller derived its title from the telephone number of the Hotel Pennsylvania where, in its Café Rouge, the Miller band would play and broadcast. The number was performed in (MM) *The Glenn Miller Story*, 1954.

Penny a Kiss, a Penny a Hug, A. w/m Buddy Kaye and Ralph Care, 1951. Most popular recordings by Dinah Shore and Tony Martin (RCA Victor); Eddy Howard, with his Orchestra (Mercury); The Andrews Sisters (Decca).

Penny Candy. w. June Carroll, m. Arthur Siegel, 1952. Introduced by June Carroll (singing) and Carol Lawrence (dancing) in (TM) *New Faces of 1952*, and repeated by them in (MM) *New Faces*, 1954.

Penny Lane. w/m John Lennon and Paul McCartney, 1967. #1 gold record by The Beatles (Capitol).

Penny Lover. w/m Lionel Richie and Brenda Harvey-Richie, 1984. Top 10 record by Lionel Richie (Motown).

Penny Serenade. w. Hal Halifax, m. Melle Weersma, 1939. Steady airplay helped this song to spend eleven weeks on "Your Hit Parade."

Penthouse Serenade (a.k.a. **When We're Alone**). w/m Will Jason and Val Burton, 1931. After its initial popularity it was heard in (MM) *Sweetheart of Sigma Chi*, 1946; (MM) *Sarge Goes to College*, 1947; (MM) *Beau James*, 1957. Errol Garner (Savoy), Eddie Heywood (Signature 12″), and Sarah Vaughan (Musicraft) had notable recordings later on in the song's life.

Peony Bush, The. w/m Meredith Willson, 1949. Introduced and recorded by Danny Kaye (Decca).

People. w. Bob Merrill, m. Jule Styne, 1964. Hit song from (TM) *Funny Girl*, introduced by its star, Barbra Streisand. Her Grammy Award (NARAS) winning record was her first to reach the Top 10 (Columbia). Streisand also sang it in the film version (MM) *Funny Girl*, 1968. Top 40 record by the group, The Tymes (Columbia), 1968.

People, Get Ready. w/m Curtis Mayfield, 1965. Hit record by The Impressions (ABC-Paramount). Revived on the English recording by Jeff Beck and Rod Stewart (Epic), 1985.

People Alone. w. Will Jennings, m. Lalo Shifrin, 1980. From the film (MP) *The Competition*. Nominated for an Academy Award.

People Are People. w/m Martin Gore, 1985. Recorded by the all-synthesized English band Depeche Mode (Sire).

People Are Strange. w/m John Densmore, Robert Krieger, Raymond Manzarek, and James Morrison, 1967. Top 20 record by The Doors, the members of which wrote the song (Elektra).

People Gotta Move. w/m Gino Vannelli, 1974. Recorded by the Canadian singer Gino Vannelli (A&M).

People Got to Be Free. w. Felix Cavaliere, m. Eddie Brigati, 1968. #1 gold record by The Rascals (Atlantic).

People in Love. w/m Eric Stewart and Graham Gouldman, 1977. Recorded by the group 10cc (Mercury).

People Like You. w/m Larry Kusik and Eddie Snyder, 1967. Recorded by Eddie Fisher, arranged and conducted by Nelson Riddle (RCA).

People Like You and Me. w. Mack Gordon, m. Harry Warren, 1942. Introduced by Glenn Miller and his Orchestra, vocal by Marion Hutton, Tex Beneke, and The Modernaires in (MM) *Orchestra Wives*. Featured and recorded by Charlie Spivak and his Orchestra, coupled with "At Last" (q.v.) from the same film (Columbia).

People of the South Wind. w/m Kerry Livgren, 1979. Recorded by the group Kansas (Kirshner).

People Say. w/m Jeff Barry and Ellie Greenwich, 1964. Recorded by The Dixie Cups (Red Bird).

People Will Say We're in Love. w. Oscar Hammerstein II, m. Richard Rodgers, 1943. Introduced by Alfred Drake and Joan Roberts in (TM) *Oklahoma!* Their cast album performance was released as a single (Decca). In the film version (MM) *Oklahoma!*, it was sung by Gordon MacRae and Shirley Jones.

Pepe. w. Dory Langdon Previn, m. Hans Wittstatt, 1960. New lyric to a German song. Interpolated in (MM) *Pepe* by Shirley Jones. Popular instrumental recording by Duane Eddy (Jamie).

Pepino's Friend Pasqual (The Italian Pussy-Cat). w/m Ray Allen and Wanda Merrell, 1963. Sequel to hit, "Pepino the Italian Mouse," also recorded by Lou Monte (Reprise).

Pepino the Italian Mouse. w/m Ray Allen and Wanda Merrell, 1963. Novelty hit by Lou Monte (Reprise).

Pepper-Hot Baby. w/m Alicia Evelyn, 1955. Top record by Jaye P. Morgan (RCA). Popular version by Gisele MacKenzie, arranged and conducted by Richard Maltby ("X").

Peppermint Twist. w/m Joey Dee and Henry Glover, 1961. Joey Dee and The Starliters, who were the house band at The Peppermint Lounge in New York City, had a #1 record at the height of The Twist dance rage (Roulette).

Percolator. m. Lou Bideu and Ernie Freeman, 1962. Instrumental hit for the dance

rage, The Twist, recorded by Billy Joe and The Checkmates (Dore).

Perdido. w. Hans Lengsfelder and Ervin Drake, m. Juan Tizol, 1942. Instrumental introduced and recorded by Duke Ellington and his Orchestra (Victor). Outstanding version by Flip Phillips and Illinois Jacquet at "Jazz at the Philharmonic" concerts recorded by JATP on six sides (Mercury). Lyrics added in 1944. Among other notable versions: Dave Lambert and Buddy Stewart (Key); Oscar Pettiford (Manor); Gene Krupa Trio (Mercury); Stan Freeman (Columbia).

(Closest Thing to) Perfect. w/m Michael Omartian, Bruce Sudano, and Jermaine Jackson, 1980. From the soundtrack of (MP) *Perfect;* Jermaine Jackson had a chart record (Arista).

Perfect Day, A (The End of). w/m Carrie Jacobs-Bond, 1910. Introduced as a concert song by David Bispham, it has since been heard in almost every style of music.

Perfect Song, The. w. Clarence Lucas, m. Joseph Carl Breil, 1915. This was used as a promotional song and background music for the silent film (MP) *Birth of a Nation*. It later gained prominence as the theme song of the radio show "Amos 'n' Andy," which went on the air in 1928.

Perfect Strangers. w/m Rupert Holmes, 1985. Introduced by Betty Buckley and Patti Cohenour in (TM) *The Mystery of Edwin Drood*. Single record by Rupert Holmes and Rita Coolidge (Polygram).

Perfect Way. w/m Green Gartside and David Gamson, 1985. Recorded by the British trio Scritti Politti (Warner Bros.).

Perfect World. w/m Alex Call, 1988. Hit single and album title song by Huey Lewis & The News (Chrysalis).

Perfidia. w. Milton Leeds, m. Alberto Dominguez, 1941. Mexican song with original Spanish lyrics by Dominguez. Sixteen weeks on "Your Hit Parade" due to airplay, sheet music and record sales. Best-selling records by Glenn Miller, vocal by Dorothy Claire and the Modernaires (Bluebird); the orchestras of Xavier Cugat (Victor); Jimmy Dorsey (Decca); Benny Goodman, vocal by Helen Forrest (Columbia). The Four Aces (Decca) had a Top 10 record, 1952.

Perhaps, Perhaps, Perhaps. w. Joe Davis (Engl.), m. Osvaldo Farres, 1947. Cuban song, also played with Spanish title "Quizas, Quizas, Quizas" with lyrics by Farres.

Perhaps Love. w/m John Denver, 1982. Recorded by Placido Domingo and John Denver (Columbia).

Persian Rug. w. Gus Kahn, m. Neil Moret, 1927. Popular records by Louisiana Sugar Babies, featuring Fats Waller (Victor); The Dorsey Brothers [the band's first session], 1928 (Okeh); Jack Teagarden (Brunswick); Al Donahue (Vocalion); and Charley Straight (Brunswick).

Personality. w. Johnny Burke, m. James Van Heusen, 1946. Introduced by Dorothy Lamour in (MM) *Road to Utopia*. No. 1 record by Johnny Mercer (Capitol). Popular records by Bing Crosby, with Eddie Condon's Orchestra (Decca); Dinah Shore (Victor); Pearl Bailey (Columbia).

Personality (You've Got). w/m Lloyd Price and Harold Logan, 1959. Hit record by Lloyd Price (ABC-Paramount).

Personally. w/m Paul Kelly, 1982. Recorded by Karla Bonoff (Columbia).

Pessimistic Character, The (with the Crab Apple Face). w. Johnny Burke, m. James V. Monaco, 1940. Introduced by Bing Crosby in (MM) *If I Had My Way*, and on records (Decca).

Pete Kelly's Blues. w. Sammy Cahn, m. Ray Heindorf, 1955. Introduced by Ella Fitzgerald in (MM) *Pete Kelly's Blues*.

Peter Cottontail. w/m Jack Rollins and Steve Nelson, 1950. An Easter song, popularized by Gene Autry (Columbia); country

singer Mervin Shiner, who had a million-seller (Decca); Fran Allison (RCA Victor); Jimmy Wakely (Capitol).

Peter Gunn. m. Henry Mancini, 1959. Theme from series (TVP) "Peter Gunn." Leading record by Ray Anthony and his Orchestra (Capitol). Guitarist Duane Eddy had a chart record in 1960 (Jamie), and a new version with The Art of Noise in 1986 (China).

Peter Piper. w. Johnny Mercer, m. Richard A. Whiting, 1936. Featured and recorded by Red Norvo and his Orchestra (Brunswick).

Peter Rabbit. w/m Myron Wachendorf, 1966. Recorded by Dee Jay and The Runaways (Smash).

Petite Fleur. m. Sidney Bechet, 1959. Introduced in Paris in the early fifties by the great American soprano saxophonist Sidney Bechet. Hit record in the U.S. by the British Dixieland combo, Chris Barber's Jazz Band (Laurie).

Petite Waltz (La Petite Valse). w. E. A. Ellington and Phyllis Claire, m. Joe Heyne, 1950. First published in Belgium. Recorded in U.S., mostly as an instrumental, by Guy Lombardo, featuring his Twin Pianos (Decca); The Three Suns (RCA Victor); Jack Pleis and his Orchestra (London); Erroll Garner (Columbia); Jerry Murad's Harmonicats (Mercury); Richard Hayman (Mercury).

Pet Me, Poppa. w/m Frank Loesser, 1955. Introduced in (MM) *Guys and Dolls* by Vivian Blaine. Leading recording by Rosemary Clooney (Columbia).

Petticoat Junction. w/m Paul Henning and Curt Massey, 1963. Theme of the series (TVP) "Petticoat Junction." Introduced and recorded by Lester Flatt and Earl Scruggs (Columbia).

Petticoats of Portugal. w/m Michael Durso, Mel Mitchell, and Murl Kahn, 1956. Top recording by Dick Jacobs and his Orchestra (Coral), followed by Billy Vaughn and his Orchestra (Dot).

Pettin' in the Park. w. Al Dubin, m. Harry Warren, 1933. Introduced by Dick Powell, Ruby Keeler, and chorus in a production number in (MM) *Gold Diggers of 1933*. Recorded by Powell (Perfect).

Phantom of the Opera, The. w. Charles Hart and Richard Stilgoe, m. Andrew Lloyd Webber, 1988. Introduced in the U.S. by Michael Crawford and Sarah Brightman in the Broadway production of the British musical (TM) *The Phantom of the Opera*.

Phantom 309. w/m Tommy Faile, 1967. Top 10 Country chart record by Red Sovine (Starday).

Philadelphia. w/m Dave Crawford, 1975. Leading record: instrumental by B. B. King (ABC).

Philadelphia, U.S.A. w/m Anthony Antonucci and Bill Borrelli, Jr., 1958. First record by the Philadelphia string band, The Nu Tornados (Carlton). Art Lund had a chart version (Coral).

Philadelphia Freedom. w/m Elton John and Bernie Taupin, 1975. #1 gold record by The Elton John Band (MCA). The number was written for tennis star Billie Jean King, of whom John was a fan. At the time, King was player-coach of the team The Philadelphia Freedom.

Philadelphia Lawyer. w/m Woody Guthrie, 1949. Introduced by Woody Guthrie. Recorded by Rose Maddox (4 Star).

Philly Freeze, The. w. Otha Hayes, m. James L. Jones, 1966. Recorded by Alvin Cash and The Registers (Mar-V-Lus).

Phoenix Love Theme, The. w. Alec Wilder (Engl.), Gino Paoli (It.), m. Gino Paoli, 1966. Italian instrumental first introduced in the U.S. under title "Senza Fine." Played on soundtrack of (MP) *The Flight of the Phoenix*. Popular recording by The Brass Ring, a studio band under the direction of saxophonist Phil Bodner (Dunhill). Vocal recording in English by Peggy Lee (Capitol).

Photograph. w/m Steve Clark, Joe Elliott, Robert John, John Savage, and Pete Willis, 1983. Written and recorded by the English group Def Leppard (Mercury).

Photograph. w/m George Harrison and Ringo Starr, 1973. #1 gold record by Ringo Starr (Apple).

Physical. w/m Stephen Kipner and Terry Shaddick, 1981. A platinum award record by Olivia Newton-John, which was #1 on the charts for ten weeks (MCA).

Pianissimo. w/m Bennie Benjamin and George David Weiss, 1948. Featured and recorded by Perry Como (RCA Victor).

Piano Concerto In B♭. m. Peter I. Tchaikowsky, 1941. Hit record based on theme from 1st movement of composer's *Piano Concerto No. 1 in B♭ Minor*, recorded by Freddy Martin and his Orchestra, featuring Jack Fina on piano (Bluebird). See also "Tonight We Love," "Concerto for Two," and "Alone at Last".

Piano in the Dark. w/m Brenda Russell, Scott Cutler, and Jeff Hull, 1988. Top 10 R&B and Pop chart record by keyboardist/singer Brenda Russell featuring vocal by Joe Esposito (A&M).

Piano Man. w/m Billy Joel, 1974. Recorded by Billy Joel (Columbia).

Piano Man. w. Irving Berlin, m. Ted Snyder, 1910.

Piccolino, The. w/m Irving Berlin, 1935. Introduced by Fred Astaire, Ginger Rogers, and chorus in (MM) *Top Hat*.

Piccolo Pete. w/m Phil Baxter, 1929. Popularized by Ted Weems and his Orchestra, with vocal by Parker Gibbs (Victor). The recording was reissued in 1947, following the success of "Heartaches" (q.v.) by the same band, and received good air and juke-box play. The song was interpolated in (MM) *The Vagabond Lover* starring Rudy Vallee in 1929.

Pickin' Cotton. w. B. G. DeSylva and Lew Brown, m. Ray Henderson, 1928. Performed by Ann Pennington, Frances Williams, and Tom Patricola in (TM) *George White's Scandals of 1928*.

Pickin' Up Strangers. w/m Byron Hill, 1981. #1 Country chart record by Johnny Lee (Full Moon).

Pickin' Wild Mountain Berries. w/m Edward Thomas, Jr., Bob McRee, and Clifton Thomas, 1968.

Pick Me Up on Your Way Down. w/m Harlan Howard, 1959. C&W chart record by Charlie Walker (Columbia).

Pick of the Week. w/m Liz Anderson, 1964. Country hit by Roy Drusky (Mercury).

Pick-Pocket Tango. m. Albert Hague, 1959. Danced by the company, choreographed by Bob Fosse in (TM) *Redhead*.

Pick Up the Pieces. w/m Roger Ball and Hamish Stuart, 1975. #1 gold record, written by members of the Scottish group The Average White Band (Atlantic). The other members, Malcolm Duncan, Alan Gorrie, Robbie McIntosh, and Onnie McIntyre, are sometimes credited with authorship.

Pick Yourself Up. w. Dorothy Fields, m. Jerome Kern, 1936. Introduced by Fred Astaire and Ginger Rogers in (MM) *Swing Time*. First records by Astaire with Johnny Green's Orchestra (Brunswick) and Benny Goodman and his Orchestra (Victor). With the George Shearing Trio recording (MGM), circa 1949–1950, the song became a great favorite with jazz musicians.

Picnic for Two, A. w. Arthur J. Lamb, m. Albert Von Tilzer, 1905.

Picnic Song, The. w/m Carmen Dello and Theresa Dello, 1950. Most popular recording by Johnny Desmond (MGM).

Picture Me Without You. w. Ted Koehler, m. Jimmy McHugh, 1936. Sung by Shirley Temple in (MM) *Dimples*. Best-selling records: Ted Weems, vocal by Perry Como (Decca), and Red Norvo, vocal by Mildred Bailey (Brunswick).

Picture No Artist Can Paint, A. w/m J. Fred Helf, 1899.

Picture of You Without Me, A. w/m Cole Porter, 1935. Introduced by June Knight and Charles Walters in (TM) *Jubilee*. Heard in (MM) *At Long Last Love* in 1975. First recordings by the orchestras of Johnny Green (Brunswick) and George Hall (Bluebird).

Pictures of Lily. w/m Peter Townshend, 1967. Recorded by the British group, The Who, of which Townshend was a member (Decca).

Pictures of Matchstick Men. w/m Francis Michael Rossi, 1968. Top 20 U.S. record by the English group The Status Quo (Cadet Concept).

Picture That Is Turned Toward the Wall, The. w/m Charles Graham, 1891. Interpolated by Andrew Mack, an Irish tenor and actor, in (TM) *The City Directory*, in New York. Leading recordings by the Irish tenor George J. Gaskin (North American) and The Manhansett Quartette (North American). Revived by June Haver in (MM) *The Daughter of Rosie O'Grady*, 1950.

(My Heart Goes) Piddily Patter Patter. w/m Charles Singleton and Rose Marie McCoy, 1955. Introduced and hit R&B record by Nappy Brown (Savoy). Popular recording by Patti Page (Mercury).

Piece of My Heart. w/m Bert Berns and Jerry Ragovoy, 1967. Introduced and recorded by Erma Franklin (Shout). Hit record by Big Brother and The Holding Company, with Janis Joplin as lead singer (Columbia). Sammy Hagar had a chart version (Geffen), 1982.

Piece of the Action, A. w/m Curtis Mayfield, 1977. Sung by Mavis Staples on the soundtrack of (MP) *A Piece of the Action*.

Pieces of April. w/m Dave Loggins, 1972. Top 20 record by Three Dog Night (Dunhill).

Pieces of Dreams. w. Alan Bergman and Marilyn Bergman, m. Michel Legrand, 1970. Sung on the soundtrack of (MP) *Pieces of*

665

Dreams by Peggy Lee. Nominated for Academy Award, 1970. Recorded by Ferrante and Teicher (United Artists).

Pied Piper, The. w/m Artie Kornfeld and Steve Duboff, 1966. First recorded by the writers, under name of Changin' Times (Philips), 1965. Top 10 U.S. hit recorded in England by Crispian St. Peters (Jamie).

Pigeon Walk. m. James V. Monaco, 1914. An instrumental success. Later recorded by Jimmie Lunceford's band (Decca), 1938.

Pig Foot Pete. w. Don Raye, m. Gene De Paul, 1941. Introduced by Martha Raye in (MM) *Keep 'Em Flying*, starring Abbott and Costello, and recorded by her (Decca). Song nominated for Academy Award. Other records by Dolly Dawn (Bluebird), Ella Mae Morse (Capitol), Freddie Slack (Decca).

Pig Got Up and Slowly Walked Away, The. w/m Benjamin Hapgood Burt, 1933. Featured by Fred Waring and his Pennsylvanians.

Pigtails and Freckles. w/m Irving Berlin, 1962. Introduced by Jack Haskell and Anita Gillette in (TM) *Mr. President*, Irving Berlin's last Broadway musical score.

Pill, The. w/m Lorene Allen, T. D. Bayless, and Don McHan, 1975. Country/Pop chart record by Loretta Lynn (MCA).

Pillow Talk. w/m Sylvia Robinson and Michael Burton, 1973. Gold record by Sylvia (Vibration).

Pillow Talk. w/m Buddy Pepper and Inez James, 1959. Introduced by Doris Day and Rock Hudson in (MP) *Pillow Talk*.

Pillow That Whispers, The. w/m Cal Veale, 1964. Country chart record by Carl Smith (Columbia).

Pilot of the Airwaves. w/m Charmian Dore, 1980. Recorded by the female British singer/writer Charlie Dore (Island).

Pinball. w/m Brian Protheroe, 1975. Popular record by British actor/composer Brian Protheroe (Chrysalis).

Pinball Machine. w/m Lonnie Irving, 1960. Introduced and recorded by country singer Lonnie Irving (Starday).

Pinball Wizard. w/m Peter Townshend, 1969. Introduced by The Who in the album of the rock opera, *Tommy*, and Top 20 single (Decca).

Pinch Me. w/m Orrin Tucker, Everett Ralston, and Joey Simay, 1940. Featured and recorded by Orrin Tucker, vocal by "Wee" Bonnie Baker (Columbia).

Pineapple Princess. w/m Richard Sherman and Robert Sherman, 1960. Annette (Funicello) had a popular recording (Vista).

Pine Cones and Holly Berries. w/m Meredith Willson, 1963. Introduced by Laurence Naismith, Janis Paige, and Fred Gwynne in (TM) *Here's Love*.

Pinetop's Boogie. See **Boogie Woogie.**

Pine Top's Boogie Woogie. Clarence "Pine Top" Smith, 1929. Smith recorded this twice (Vocalion and Brunswick). It was the forerunner of Tommy Dorsey's "Boogie Woogie" (Victor) recorded in 1938 and re-released during a recording strike in 1943. The latter release established the number as a standard.

Piney Brown Blues. w/m Joe Turner and Pete Johnson, 1944. Written in Kansas City in the thirties and dedicated to two Piney Browns, "Big" and "Little," a politician and nightclub owner, respectively. Recorded by Joe Turner and his Fly Cats (Decca), 1940. Popular re-release with performers listed as Joe Turner and Pete Johnson (Decca), 1944.

Piney Ridge. w. Ballard MacDonald, m. Halsey K. Mohr, 1915.

Ping Pongo. w. Al Dubin, m. Joe Burke, 1929. Introduced by Winnie Lightner in (MM) *Show of Shows*.

Pinhead. w/m Douglas Colvin, John Cummings, Thomas Erdelyi, and Jeff Hyman, 1977. Introduced by The Ramones in their album "Leave Home" (Sire). Sung by them in (MM) *Rock 'n' Roll High School*, 1979.

Pink Cadillac. w/m Bruce Springsteen, 1988. Introduced on records by Bruce Springsteen (Columbia), 1983. Revived via hit single by Natalie Cole, from her album "Everlasting" (EMI), 1988.

Pink Champagne. w/m Joe Liggins, 1950. Writer-singer-pianist Joe Liggins's recording (Specialty) was #1 on the R&B chart for eleven weeks and reached the Top 40 on the Pop charts.

Pink Cocktail for a Blue Lady, A. w. Herb Magidson, m. Ben Oakland, 1943. Introduced and recorded by Glenn Miller and his Orchestra, vocal by Skip Nelson (Victor).

Pink Elephants. w. Mort Dixon, m. Harry Woods, 1932. Novelty song about the rigors of a hangover. Featured on radio by Ben Bernie and Rudy Vallee. Among recordings: The Joe Venuti-Eddie Lang Blue Five (Columbia) and Gene Kardos, vocal by Harry Goldfield (Banner).

Pink Houses. w/m John Cougar Mellencamp, 1983. Top 10 record by John Cougar Mellencamp (Riva).

Pink Lady Waltz, The. m. Ivan Caryll, 1911. Popular waltz from (TM) *The Pink Lady*.

Pink Panther Theme, The. w. Johnny Mercer, m. Henry Mancini, 1964. Theme from (MP) *The Pink Panther*. Hit instrumental by Henry Mancini and his Orchestra (RCA). Winner Grammy Award (NARAS) Best Instrumental Composition (Non-Jazz), 1964.

Pink Shoelaces. w/m Mickie Grant, 1959. Popular record by Dodie Stevens (Crystalette).

Pins and Needles (in My Heart). w/m Fred Rose, 1943. Best-selling records by the country vocal duo, Bob Atcher and Bonnie Blue Eyes (Okeh), and Roy Acuff (Columbia).

Pipe Dreaming. w/m Cole Porter, 1946. Introduced by Larry Laurence [Enzo Stuarti] in (TM) *Around the World*.

Pipeline. m. Bob Spickard and Brian Carman, 1963. Instrumental hit, recorded by The Chantays (Dot) and written by the guitarists in the group.

Pirate Jenny. w. Bertolt Brecht (Ger.), Marc Blitzstein (Engl.), m. Kurt Weill, 1954. Introduced by Lotte Lenya in the musical, "Die Dreigroschenoper," 1928, in Berlin. She sang it in the first film version (German), 1931. Lenya introduced it to the U.S. in the off-Broadway production of Marc Blitzstein's English version (TM) *The Threepenny Opera*, 1954. In (MM) *The Threepenny Opera*, 1964, it was sung in English by Martha Schlamme, dubbing for Hildegard Neff, and in German by Neff.

Pistol Packin' Mama. w/m Al Dexter, 1943. Introduced and recorded by Al Dexter and his Troopers (Okeh). Bing Crosby and The Andrews Sisters had a hit recording as well (Decca). It was heard in (MM) *Beautiful But Broke*, 1944.

Pittsburgh, Pennsylvania. w/m Bob Merrill, 1952. Leading record by Guy Mitchell, with Mitch Miller's Orchestra (Columbia).

Place in the Sun, A. w. Ronald Miller, m. Bryan Wells, 1966. Top 10 record by Stevie Wonder (Tamla). The song has no connection with the 1951 film of the same title.

Place to Fall Apart, A. w/m Merle Haggard, Willie Nelson, and Freddy Powers, 1985. #1 Country chart song by Merle Haggard and Janie Fricke (Epic).

Plain Brown Wrapper. w/m Gary Morris and Kevin Welch, 1987. Top 10 Country chart record by Gary Morris (Warner Bros.).

Plain Jane. w/m Doc Pomus and Mort Shuman, 1959. Recorded by Bobby Darin (Atco).

Planet Rock. w. E. Williams, A. H. Baker, J. Miller, B. Aasim, R. Allen, m. Baker, Miller, Aasim, Allen, and J. Robie, 1982. 12″ gold single by the rapper, Afrika Bambaataa & The Soul Sonic Force (Tommy Boy).

Plantation Boogie. m. Lenny Dee, 1955. Instrumental by organist Lenny Dee (Decca).

Plant a Watermelon on My Grave and Let the Juice Soak Through. w/m Frank Dumont and R. P. Lilly, 1910.

Play, Fiddle, Play. w. Jack Lawrence, m. Emery Deutsch and Arthur Altman, 1932. Lawrence's first success. Featured by Deutsch's Orchestra. Best-selling record by Arthur Tracy, "The Street Singer," (Brunswick).

Play, Guitar Play. w/m Conway Twitty, 1977. #1 Country chart record by Conway Twitty (MCA).

Play a Simple Melody. w/m Irving Berlin, 1914, 1950. Introduced by Sallie Fisher and Charles King in (TM) *Watch Your Step*. The chorus of the song is written with a counter melody and counterlyric. In 1950 a hit record (Decca) was made by Gary Crosby and friend [the friend was Gary's father, Bing.] The revived song was on the "Your Hit Parade" for eleven weeks. Ethel Merman and Dan Dailey performed it in (MM) *There's No Business Like Show Business*, 1954.

Playboy. w/m Gene Thomas, 1968. Top 20 record by Gene and Debbe (TRX).

Playboy. w/m Brian Holland, Robert Bateman, and William Stevenson, 1962. Hit record by The Marvelettes (Tamla).

Playboy Theme. w. Carolyn Leigh, m. Cy Coleman, 1960. Theme from series (TVM) "Playboy Penthouse Party." Recorded by Cy Coleman.

Playgirl. w/m Linda Colley and Keith Colley, 1969. Chart record by the quartet Thee Prophets (Kapp).

Playground in My Mind. w/m Paul Vance and Lee Pockriss, 1973. Gold record by Clint Holmes, with addition of child's voice of Philip Vance, the son of the co-writer/producer (Epic).

Play Gypsies, Dance Gypsies. w. Harry B. Smith, m. Emmerich Kallman, 1926. From Broadway production of the Viennese operetta (TM) *Countess Maritza*, introduced by Walter Woolf. Paul Whiteman had a popular record "Countess Maritza Medley" (Victor).

Playmates. w/m Saxie Dowell, 1940. Introduced and best-selling record by Kay Kyser, vocal by Harry Babbitt (Columbia). Mitchell Ayres, vocal by Mary Ann Mercer and Tommy Taylor, also had a popular version (Bluebird).

Playmates. w. Jack Yellen, m. Albert Gumble, 1917.

Playmates. w/m Harry Dacre, 1889. Sung by the author in English music halls and popularized in the U.S. by Eddie Leonard, the minstrel.

Play Me. w/m Neil Diamond, 1972. Top 20 record by Neil Diamond (Uni).

Play Me an Old Fashioned Melody. w. Mack Gordon, m. Harry Warren, 1945. Introduced by William Gaxton and Beatrice Kay in (MM) *Billy Rose's Diamond Horseshoe*.

Play Me Hearts and Flowers (I Wanna Cry). w. Mann Curtis, m. Sanford Green, 1955. Introduced by Johnny Desmond, as a record artist, on a dramatic show in the Philco Playhouse TV series. His recording then reached the Top 10 on the charts (Coral).

Play on Love. w/m Grace Slick and Pete Sears, 1976. Recorded by The Jefferson Starship and written by two of its members (Grunt).

Play That Barber Shop Chord. w. William Tracey and Ballard MacDonald, m. Lewis Muir, 1910. Introduced by Bert Williams at Hammerstein's Victoria Theatre in New York City. It was revived in the Judy Garland-Van Johnson film (MM) *In the Good Old Summertime* in 1949.

Play That Funky Music. w/m Robert Parissi, 1976. #1 platinum record by the band Wild Cherry (Epic).

Play the Game Tonight. w/m Kerry Livgren, Phil Ehart, Rich Williams, Robert Frazier, Danny Flower, 1982. Recorded by the group Kansas (Kirshner).

Play to Me, Gypsy. w. Jimmy Kennedy (Engl.), m. Karel Vacek, 1934. Original Czechoslovakian words by Beda (Beda Fritz Lohner).

Play with Fire. w/m Mick Jagger, Keith Richards, Bill Wyman, Brian Jones, Charlie Watts, 1965. Recorded by the British group, The Rolling Stones, who collaborated on the writing of the song (London).

Pleadin' for Love. w/m Larry Birdsong, 1956. R&B chart record by Larry Birdsong (Excello).

Pleasant Valley Sunday. w/m Gerry Goffin and Carole King, 1967. Hit record by The Monkees (Colgems).

Please. w. Leo Robin, m. Ralph Rainger, 1932. Introduced by Bing Crosby in (MM) *The Big Broadcast* and reprised in the finale by Crosby, Eddie Lang (guitarist), and Stuart Erwin. Crosby had a hit record (Brunswick). Also recorded concurrently with film release by George Olsen and his Band (Victor), Ray Noble (Victor), and Sam Coslow (Victor). Later recordings by Al Hibbler with Johnny Hodges' Orchestra (Mercury), and Giselle MacKenzie (Capitol).

Please, Mr. Sun. w. Sid Frank, m. Ray Getzov, 1952. Johnnie Ray's second successive million-seller (see "Cry"), orchestra conducted by Jimmy Carroll (Columbia). Other popular versions by Perry Como (RCA Victor) and Tommy Edwards (MGM). Revived by The Vogues (Co & Ce), 1966.

Please, Please, Please. w/m James Brown and Johnny Terry, 1956. Introduced and R&B hit by James Brown (Federal). In 1964, he recorded it again (King) with moderate success.

Please, Please Baby. 1987. Top 10 Country chart record by Dwight Yoakam (Reprise).

Please Be Kind. w. Sammy Cahn, m. Saul Chaplin, 1938. Introduced by Red Norvo and his Orchestra, vocal by Mildred Bailey (Brunswick). They had a two-sided hit, as it

was coupled with "The Weekend of a Private Secretary (q.v.)." Other records by Benny Goodman, vocal by Martha Tilton (Victor); Bob Crosby, vocal by Kay Weber (Decca); the Original Dixieland Band (Bluebird). Revived in 1946 by Charlie Ventura and his Orchestra (National).

Please Come and Play in My Yard. w. Edward Madden, m. Theodore F. Morse, 1904.

Please Come Home for Christmas. w/m Charles Brown and Gene Redd, 1960, 1978. Introduced on the R&B charts by singer/pianist Charles Brown (King), 1960. The following Christmas season, his record made the Pop charts. Revived with a Top 20 record by The Eagles (Asylum), 1978.

Please Come to Boston. w/m Dave Loggins, 1974. Top 10 record by Dave Loggins (Epic).

Please Don't Ask About Barbara. w/m Bill Buchanan and Jack Keller, 1962. Popularized by Bobby Vee (Liberty).

Please Don't Blame Me. w/m Marty Robbins, 1957. C&W chart record by Marty Robbins (Columbia).

Please Don't Eat the Daisies. w/m Joe Lubin, 1960. Introduced by Doris Day in (MP) *Please Don't Eat the Daisies* and on records (Columbia).

Please Don't Ever Leave Me. w/m Susan Haber, 1966. Featured by the Lafayette College group The Cyrkle (Columbia).

Please Don't Go. w/m Harry Wayne Casey and Richard Finch, 1979. #1 record, their last chart entry, by KC & The Sunshine Band (T.K.). Produced by Casey [KC] and Finch.

Please Don't Leave. w/m Lauren Wood, 1979. Recorded by Lauren Wood, harmony vocal by Michael McDonald (Warner Bros.).

Please Don't Leave Me. w/m Antoine "Fats" Domino, 1953. R&B hit by Fats Domino (Imperial).

Please Don't Let Me Love You. w/m Ralph Jones, 1949, C&W chart hit by George Morgan (Columbia). Version by Hank Williams released posthumously (MGM), 1955.

Please Don't Stop Loving Me. w/m Joy Byers, 1966. Introduced by Elvis Presley in (MM) *Frankie and Johnny* and on records (RCA).

Please Don't Take My Lovin' Man Away. w. Lew Brown, m. Albert Von Tilzer, 1912. Popular blues-type song. Leading recording by Elsie Baker (Victor).

Please Don't Talk About Me When I'm Gone. w. Sidney Clare, m. Sam H. Stept, 1931. Early records by Bert Lown (Victor); Ethel Waters (Columbia); the Eubie Blake Orchestra (Victor). It was heard in (MM) *Lullaby of Broadway* in 1951.

Please Don't Tell Me How the Story Ends. w/m Kris Kristofferson, 1974. Hit Country and Pop chart record by Ronnie Milsap (RCA).

Please Go 'Way and Let Me Sleep. w/m J. Tim Brymn and Harry Von Tilzer, 1902. Introduced by Arthur Deming, the minstrel, in vaudeville.

Please Handle with Care. w/m F. D. Ballard and Harry Stride, 1932. Popular recordings by the bands of Charles "Buddy" Rogers (Victor) and Enric Madriguera (Columbia).

Please Help Me, I'm Falling (a.k.a. **I Can't Help You, I'm Falling**). w/m Don Robertson and Hal Blair, 1960. Top 10 C&W and Pop recording by Hank Locklin (RCA). Skeeter Davis had a popular version under alternate title (RCA).

Please Keep Me in Your Dreams. w. Tot Seymour, m. Vee Lawnhurst, 1936. Featured and recorded by Billie Holiday (Vocalion); Al Donahue and his Orchestra (Decca); George Hall, vocal by Dolly Dawn (Bluebird).

Please Let Me Wonder. w/m Brian Wilson and Mike Love, 1965. Recorded by The Beach Boys (Capitol).

Please Love Me. w. Jules Taub, m. Riley (B. B.) King, 1953. Popular record by B. B. King (RPM).

Please Love Me Forever. w/m Johnny Malone and Ollie Blanchard, 1961, 1967. Introduced by Tommy Edwards (MGM), 1958. First hit by Cathy Jean and The Roommates (Valmor), 1961. Bobby Vinton had a Top 10 version (Epic), 1967.

Please Mr. Please. w/m John Rostill and Bruce Welch, 1975. Top 10 gold record by Olivia Newton-John (MCA).

Please Mr. Postman. w/m Brian Holland, Robert Bateman, and Fred Gorman, 1961, 1975. #1 record by The Marvelettes (Tamla). Revived in 1975 by The Carpenters, whose #1 recording sold over a million copies (A&M).

Please No Squeeza da Banana. w/m Jack Zero, Ben Jaffee, and Louis Prima, 1945. Italian dialect novelty recorded by Louis Prima, with his Orchestra (Majestic), and Tony Pastor, vocal by Charlie Trotta (Victor).

Please Pardon Us, We're in Love. w. Mack Gordon, m. Harry Revel, 1937. Introduced by Alice Faye in (MM) *You Can't Have Everything*.

Please Play Our Song (Mister Record Man). w/m Bob Marcus and Larry Stewart, 1953. Popular record by Don Cornell (Coral).

Please Please Me. w/m John Lennon and Paul McCartney, 1964. Top 10 record by The Beatles (Vee-Jay). Song used in (MM) *I Wanna Hold Your Hand*, 1978, a "Beatlemania" film in which the famed quartet did not appear.

Please Return Your Love to Me. w/m Norman Whitfield and Barrett Strong, 1968. Top 40 record by The Temptations (Gordy).

Please Say You're Foolin'. w/m Bobby Stevenson, 1966. Chart record by Ray Charles (ABC-Paramount).

Please Say You Want Me. w/m Donald Hayes, 1957. R&B chart record by The Schoolboys (Okeh).

Please Send Me Someone to Love. w/m Percy Mayfield, 1950. Recorded by Percy Mayfield (Specialty).

Please Stay. w. Bob Hilliard, m. Burt Bacharach, 1961. Popular record by The Drifters (Atlantic).

Please Talk to My Heart. w/m Jimmy Fautheree and "Country" Johnny Mathis, 1963. First recorded by "Country" Johnny Mathis (United Artists). Top 10 C&W chart record by Ray Price (Columbia), 1964. Chart version by Freddy Fender (Starflite), 1980.

Please Tell Me Why. w/m Dave Clark and Mike Smith, 1966. Recorded in England by The Dave Clark Five (Epic).

Pleasure Mad. w. Rousseau Simmons, m. Sidney Bechet, 1924. Recorded by Ethel Waters (Vocalion), Bennie Kreuger (Brunswick), and the State Street Ramblers (Gennett).

Pleasure Principle, The. w/m Monte Moir, 1987. #1 R&B chart record by Janet Jackson (A&M).

Pledging My Love. w/m Ferdinand Washington and Don D. Robey, 1955. Introduced by Johnny Ace, whose #1 R&B record made the Top 20 on the Pop charts (Duke). Covered and Pop hit by Teresa Brewer, with Jack Pleis's Orchestra (Decca). Later versions by Roy Hamilton (Epic), 1958, and Johnny Tillotson (Cadence), 1960.

Pocketful of Miracles. w. Sammy Cahn, m. James Van Heusen, 1961. Introduced by Frank Sinatra on the soundtrack of (MP) *Pocketful of Miracles*, and recorded by him (Reprise).

Poem Set to Music, A. w. Mack Gordon, m. Harry Warren, 1942. Introduced by Cesar Romero dancing to Hermes Pan's choreography, and Harry James and his Orchestra in (MM) *Springtime in the Rockies*. Recorded by James, vocal by Johnny McAfee (Columbia).

Poetry in Motion. w/m Paul Kaufman and Mike Anthony, 1960. Hit record by Johnny Tillotson (Cadence).

Poetry Man. w/m Phoebe Snow, 1975. Top 10 record by Phoebe Snow (Shelter).

Po' Folks. w/m Bill Anderson, 1961. Hit C&W record by Bill Anderson (Decca).

Poinciana (Song of the Tree). w. Buddy Bernier, m. Nat Simon, 1943. Original Spanish lyrics by Manuel Lliso. Best-selling record by Bing Crosby (Decca), followed by instrumental versions by Benny Carter and his Orchestra (Capitol) and David Rose and his Orchestra (Victor). Among others to record it were George Shearing (London); Steve Lawrence (King); The Four Freshmen (Capitol); Tex Beneke, vocal by Garry Stevens (Victor).

Point It Out. w/m William Robinson, Al Cleveland, and Marvin Taplin, 1970. Top 40 record by Smokey Robinson and The Miracles (Tamla).

Point of No Return. w/m Lewis Martine, 1987. This was a new Top 10 version of the 1985 disco hit by the trio Exposé (Arista).

Point of No Return. w/m Gerry Goffin and Carole King, 1962. Top 40 record by Gene McDaniels (Liberty).

Poison Ivy. w/m Jerry Leiber and Mike Stoller, 1959. Top 10 hit by The Coasters (Atco).

Poison Love. w/m Elmer Laird, 1951. Top 10 C&W chart record by Johnnie & Jack (RCA Victor). Revived by Gail Davies (Lifesong), 1978.

Politics and Poker. w. Sheldon Harnick, m. Jerry Bock, 1959. Introduced by Howard Da Silva and men in the Pulitzer Prize-winning musical (TM) *Fiorello!*

Polka Dots and Moonbeams. w. Johnny Burke, m. James Van Heusen, 1940. Popularized and leading records by Tommy Dorsey, vocal by Frank Sinatra (Victor), and Glenn Miller, vocal by Ray Eberle (Bluebird).

Polk Salad Annie. w/m Tony Joe White, 1969. Top 10 hit by the Bayou rock singer/writer Tony Joe White (Monument).

Pompanola. w. B. G. DeSylva and Lew Brown, m. Ray Henderson, 1928. Introduced by Dorothy Stone, Alan Edwards, and The Phelps Twins in (TM) *Three Cheers*, starring Will Rogers. Recorded by Ben Selvin, vocal by Larry Murphy (Columbia).

Pompton Turnpike. w/m Will Osborne and Dick Rogers, 1940. Best-selling record by Charlie Barnet, featuring trumpet solo by Billy May (Bluebird). Title derived from the site of Frank Dailey's Meadowbrook, a major restaurant-ballroom where the big bands played and broadcast, located on the Newark-Pompton Turnpike in New Jersey.

Pony Time. w/m Don Covay and John Berry, 1961. #1 record by Chubby Checker (Parkway). Also popular recording by The Goodtimers, a group led by writer Covay (Arnold).

Pool Shark, The. w/m Tom T. Hall, 1970. Hit Country record by Dave Dudley (Mercury).

Poor, Poor, Pitiful Me. w/m Warren Zevon, 1978. Sung by Linda Ronstadt in (MP) *FM* and on records (Asylum).

Poor Baby. w/m Tony Romeo, 1968. Recorded by The Cowsills (MGM).

Poor Boy. w. Mel Mitchell, m. David R. Sanderson, 1959. Instrumental recorded by The Royaltones (Jubilee).

Poor Boy. w/m Elvis Presley and Vera Matson, 1956. Introduced by Elvis Presley making his screen debut in (MM) *Love Me Tender*. He recorded it (RCA).

Poor Butterfly. w. John Golden, m. Raymond Hubbell, 1916. An all-time hit, both in performances and sheet music sales. It was introduced in (TM) *The Big Show*, at the Hippodrome Theatre in New York. That year Edna Brown and the Joseph C. Smith Orchestra both had successful records (Victor). Among the many other recordings over the years are those by such varied artists as Red Nichols (Brunswick), the Benny Goodman Sextet (Columbia), Deanna Durbin (Decca), Al Hibbler (Sunrise), Fritz Kreisler (Victor), and the recording that is considered by many to be the epitome of vocal interpretations, Sarah Vaughan's (Mercury).

Poor Fool. w/m Ike Turner, 1961. Recorded by Ike and Tina Turner (Sue).

Poor Jenny. w/m Boudleaux Bryant and Felice Bryant, 1959. Chart record by The Everly Brothers (Cadence).

Poor John. w. Fred W. Leigh, m. Henry E. Pether, 1906. Featured by Vesta Victoria in vaudeville in England and the U.S. Revived by Rita Hayworth in (MM) *Cover Girl*, 1944. Among recordings: Vesta Victoria (Victor); Gertrude Lawrence (Decca); Joan Morris (Nonesuch).

Poor Little Fool. w/m Shari Sheeley, 1958. #1 record by Ricky Nelson (Imperial).

Poor Little Hollywood Star. w. Carolyn Leigh, m. Cy Coleman, 1962. Introduced by Virginia Martin in (TM) *Little Me*.

Poor Little Puppet. w/m Howard Greenfield and Jack Keller, 1962. Recorded by Cathy Carroll (Warner Brothers).

Poor Little Rhode Island. w. Sammy Cahn, m. Jule Styne, 1944. Independent song interpolated by Ann Miller in (MM) *Carolina Blues*. Leading record by Guy Lombardo, vocal by Stuart Foster (Decca).

Poor Little Rich Girl. w/m Gerry Goffin and Carole King, 1963. Featured and recorded by Steve Lawrence (Columbia).

Poor Little Rich Girl. w/m Noël Coward, 1925. Introduced in the U.S. by Gertrude Lawrence in (TM) *Charlot's Revue*. She also recorded it (Columbia). This was Coward's first song success. Later recordings by Larry Clinton and His Orchestra (Victor) and Judy Garland (Decca). Sung by Tammy Grimes in (TM) *A Musical Jubilee*, 1975.

Poor Man's Riches. w/m Benny Barnes and Dee Marais, 1957. C&W chart record by Benny Barnes (Starday).

Poor Man's Roses, A (or a Rich Man's Gold). w. Bob Hilliard, m. Milton De

Lugg, 1957. Popular recording by Patti Page (Mercury).

Poor Me. w/m Dave Batholomew and Antoine "Fats" Domino, 1955. R&B chart record by Fats Domino (Imperial).

Poor Old Heartsick Me. w/m Helen Carter, 1959. C&W hit by Margie Bowes (Hickory).

Poor Papa (He's Got Nuthin' at All). w. Billy Rose, m. Harry Woods, 1926. Leading recording by "Whispering" Jack Smith (Victor).

Poor Pauline. w. Charles McCarron, m. Raymond Walker, 1914. The song was written to be played as background music for the popular silent screen serial (MP) *The Perils of Pauline*, starring Pearl White. The song was revived in the Betty Hutton film (MM) *The Perils of Pauline* in 1947.

Poor People of Paris, The. w. Jack Lawrence (Engl.), René Rouzoud (Fr.), m. Marguerite Monnot, 1956. Introduced in France as "Le Goualante de Pauvre Jean" by Edith Piaf. #1 record in U.S., instrumental by Les Baxter and his Orchestra (Capitol).

Poor Pierrot. w. Otto Harbach, m. Jerome Kern, 1931. Introduced by Lucette Valsy and Peter Chambers in (TM) *The Cat and the Fiddle*. It was sung by Jeanette MacDonald in the film version (MM) *The Cat and the Fiddle* in 1934.

Poor Side of Town. w/m Johnny Rivers and Lou Adler, 1966. #1 record by Johnny Rivers (Imperial). Revived by Al Wilson (Soul City), 1969.

Poor You. w. E. Y. Harburg, m. Burton Lane, 1942. Introduced by Frank Sinatra, Red Skelton, Virginia O'Brien, and Tommy Dorsey and his Orchestra in (MM) *Ship Ahoy*. Recorded by Dorsey/Sinatra (Victor).

Pop! Goes Your Heart. w. Mort Dixon, m. Allie Wrubel, 1934. Introduced by Dick Powell in (MM) *Happiness Ahead* and then recorded by him (Brunswick). Other recordings

by the orchestras of Ted Lewis (Decca); Raymond Paige (Victor); Vincent Rose, vocal by Chick Bullock (Melotone).

Pop a Top. w/m Nathan Stuckey, 1967. Country hit by Jim Ed Brown (RCA).

Popcorn. w. Gershon Kingsley, 1972. Top 10 instrumental by Hot Butter, the name under which Stan Free recorded on the Moog synthesizer (Musicor).

Popcorn, The. m. James Brown, 1969. Hit R&B/Pop instrumental by James Brown (King).

Popcorn Man. w/m Will Hudson, Lou Klein, and Bill Livingston, 1937. Leading record by Eddie DeLange and his Orchestra (Bluebird).

Popeye the Hitchhiker. w. Kal Mann, m. Dave Appell, 1962. Hit record by Chubby Checker (Parkway).

Popeye the Sailor Man. w/m Sammy Lerner, 1931. The theme song of the Max Fleischer animated cartoon *Popeye the Sailor*.

Pop Life. w/m Prince Rogers Nelson, 1985. Top 10 record by Prince (Paisley Park).

Pop Muzik. w/m Robin Scott, 1979. Under the name M, British musician Robin Scott produced the #1 gold record, which first was a hit in England and then in the U.S. (Sire).

Popo the Puppet. w/m Sylvia Fine, 1951. Performed by Danny Kaye in (MM) *On the Riviera*.

Poppa Don't Preach to Me. w/m Frank Loesser, 1947. Introduced by Betty Hutton in (MM) *The Perils of Pauline*, and recorded by her (Capitol).

Pops, We Love You (A Tribute to Father). w/m Marilyn McLeod and Pam Sawyer, 1979. Recorded by Diana Ross, Marvin Gaye, Smokey Robinson, and Stevie Wonder as a tribute to Berry Gordy, Sr., the father of the founder of the record company (Motown).

Popsicle. w/m Buzz Cason and Bobby Russell, 1966. Hit record by Jan and Dean (Liberty).

Popsicles and Icicles. w/m David Gates, 1963. Hit record by the teenage trio The Murmaids (Chattahoochee).

Popsicles in Paris. w. Sheldon Harnick, m. Jerry Bock, 1964. Introduced by the company in (TM) *To Broadway with Love*, at The New York World's Fair.

Popsicle Toes. w/m Michael Franks, 1976. Recorded by Michael Franks (Reprise).

Pore Jud Is Daid. w. Oscar Hammerstein II, m. Richard Rodgers, 1943. Introduced by Alfred Drake and Howard da Silva in (TM) *Oklahoma!* In the film (MM) *Oklahoma*, 1955, it was sung by Gordon MacRae and Rod Steiger.

Por Favor (Please). w/m Noel Sherman and Joe Sherman, 1955. Featured and recorded by Vic Damone (Mercury).

Porgy. w. Dorothy Fields, m. Jimmy McHugh, 1928. Introduced by Aida Ward and The Hall Johnson Choir in Lew Leslie's revue (TM) *Blackbirds of 1928*.

Port-au-Prince. w. Bernie Wayne and Miriam Lewis, m. Bernie Wayne, 1956. Instrumental recorded by Nelson Riddle and his Orchestra (Capitol).

Porter's Love Song to a Chambermaid, A. w. Andy Razaf, m. James P. Johnson, 1930. Recorded by Red Norvo (Brunswick), Jimmie Noone (Vocalion), Bob Howard (Decca), Pinky Tomlin (Brunswick).

Portrait of Jennie. w. Gordon Burge, m. J. Russel Robinson, 1948. Title suggested by the Robert Nathan book and the ensuing film. Leading records by Nat "King" Cole (Capitol) and Harry Babbitt (Seeco).

Portrait of My Love. w. David West, m. Cyril Ornadel, 1961. Hit record by Steve Lawrence (United Artists). Revived by The Tokens (Warner Brothers), 1967.

Portuguese Washerwomen, The. m. André Popp and Roger Lucchesi, 1956. Instrumental, composed and first published in France. Hit U.S. record by Joe "Fingers" Carr, pseudonym for pianist Lou Busch (Capitol).

Posin'. w. Sammy Cahn, m. Saul Chaplin, 1937. Featured and recorded by the bands of Jimmie Lunceford (Decca) and Tommy Dorsey (Victor).

Positively 4th Street. w/m Bob Dylan, 1965. Hit record by Bob Dylan (Columbia).

Pour Some Sugar on Me. w/m Steve Clark, Phil Collen, Joe Elliott, Robert John Lange, and Rick Savage, 1988. Hit single from the album "Hysteria" by Def Leppard (Mercury).

Powder Your Face with Sunshine (Smile! Smile! Smile!). w/m Carmen Lombardo and Stanley Rochinski, 1948. Introduced by Guy Lombardo, vocal by Carmen Lombardo (Decca). Hit records by Evelyn Knight, with The Starlighters (Decca); Dean Martin, with his first Top 10 record, while part of the comedy team of Martin and [Jerry] Lewis (Capitol); Sammy Kaye, vocal by the Three Kaydets (RCA Victor); Doris Day and Buddy Clark (Columbia); Blue Barron, vocal by ensemble (MGM).

Power. w/m John Hall and Johanna Hall, 1980. Sung by The Doobie Brothers, John Hall, and Carly Simon in (MM) *No Nukes*.

Powerful Stuff. w/m Robert Field, Michael Henderson, and Wally Wilson, 1988. Introduced on the soundtrack of (MP) *Cocktail* and its album by The Fabulous Thunderbirds (Elektra).

Powerhouse. m. Raymond Scott, 1937. Instrumental recorded by the Raymond Scott Quintette (Brunswick).

Power of Gold, The. w/m Dan Fogelberg, 1978. Recorded by Dan Fogelberg and Tim Weisberg (Full Moon).

Power of Love. w/m Kenny Gamble, Leon Huff, and Joe Simon, 1972. #1 R&B, Top 20 Pop, and gold record by Joe Simon (Spring).

Power of Love, The. w/m Candy Derouse, Gunther Mende, Mary Applegate, and Jennifer Rush, 1986. Recorded by Jennifer Rush (Epic). Also recorded by Laura Branigan (Atlantic), 1987.

Power of Love, The. w/m Chris Hayes, Huey Lewis, and Johnny Colla, 1985. Introduced by Huey Lewis in the film (MP) *Back to the Future*, and #1 single by Huey Lewis & The News (Chrysalis). Nominated for an Academy Award.

Power to the People. w/m John Lennon, 1971. Top 20 U.S. record by John Lennon/Plastic Ono Band (Apple).

Practice Makes Perfect. w/m Don Roberts and Ernest Gold, 1940. Leading recordings by Bob Chester, vocal by Al Stuart (Bluebird); Billie Holiday (Okeh); Al Kavelin, vocal by Bill Darnell (Okeh).

Praise the Lord and Pass the Ammunition. w/m Frank Loesser, 1942. Based on words spoken by United States Navy Chaplain William Maguire during Japanese attack on Pearl Harbor, this marked Loesser's first hit as writer of both lyrics and music. Kay Kyser's recording, with vocal by The Glee Club (Columbia) became a million-seller.

Pray for Peace. w/m Gene Bone and Howard Fenton, 1970. Originally recorded in a "religioso" version by Charles K. L. Davis, The Collegiate Chorale, and the Poliakin Orchestra as the title number of a sixties' album (Everest). Popular gospel version by The Edwin Hawkins Singers (Buddah).

Preacher, The. m. Horace Silver, 1956. Jazz instrumental recorded by pianist Horace Silver (Blue Note).

Preacher and the Bear, The. w/m Joe Arzonia, 1904. Novelty song, first recorded by Arthur Collins (Edison). It was the first two-million selling record. Collins also recorded it

for five other labels. Revived by Phil Harris on the radio and records (RCA Victor), 1947.

Precious and Few. w/m Walter Nims, 1972. Gold record by the quintet Climax (Carousel).

Precious Little Thing Called Love, A. w/m Lou Davis and J. Fred Coots, 1929. Written for and introduced by Nancy Carroll in (MP) *Shopworn Angel*. Hit recording by George Olsen's Orchestra, vocal by Ethel Shutta (Victor).

Precious Love. w/m Robert Welch, 1979. Recorded by Robert Welch (Capitol).

Prelude to a Kiss. w. Irving Gordon and Irving Mills, m. Edward Kennedy "Duke" Ellington, 1938. Introduced and recorded by Duke Ellington and his Orchestra (Brunswick). Also recorded by Johnny Hodges and his Orchestra (Vocalion), and in 1950 by Charlie Ventura's Band (Victor).

Prescription for the Blues. w/m Porter Grainger, 1924. Recorded by Clara Smith (Columbia).

Pressure. w/m Billy Joel, 1982. Recorded by Billy Joel (Columbia).

Pretend. w/m Lew Douglas, Cliff Parman, and Frank Levere, 1953. Nat "King" Cole, with Nelson Riddle's Orchestra, had a million-seller (Capitol). Ralph Marterie and his Orchestra (Mercury), and Eileen Barton with Jack Pleis's Orchestra (Coral) also had Top 20 records.

Pretender, The. w/m Jackson Browne, 1977. Recorded by Jackson Browne (Asylum).

Pretending. w. Marty Symes, m. Al Sherman, 1946. Recorded by Andy Russell, with Paul Weston's Orchestra (Capitol).

Pretend You Don't See Her. w/m Steve Allen, 1957. Leading record by Jerry Vale (Columbia). Bobby Vee had a chart version in 1964 (Liberty).

Pretty as You Feel. w/m Jack Casady, Joey Covington, and Jorma Kaukonen, 1971. Written by three members of the recording group Jefferson Airplane (Grunt).

Pretty Baby. w. Gus Kahn, m. Tony Jackson and Egbert Van Alstyne, 1916. Introduced in (TM) *A World of Pleasure*, 1915. The following year it became a hit via its interpolation by Dolly Hackett in (TM) *The Passing Show of 1916*. Among the dozen motion pictures in which this song has been heard are: (MM) *Is Everybody Happy?*, the Ted Lewis story, 1943; (MM) *Rose of Washington Square*, sung by Al Jolson, 1939; (MM) *Jolson Sings Again*, 1949, by Jolson on the soundtrack; by Danny Thomas in the Gus Kahn film bio (MM) *I'll See You in My Dreams*, 1951; by Charles Winninger and Gloria DeHaven in (MM) *Broadway Rhythm*, 1943; by Eddie Cantor dubbing on the soundtrack for Keefe Brasselle in (MM) *The Eddie Cantor Story*, 1953.

Pretty Ballerina. w/m Mike Brown, 1967. Recorded by the classical-influenced rock quintet The Left Banke (Smash).

Pretty Blue Eyes. w/m Teddy Randazzo and Bob Weinstein, 1959. Top 10 record by Steve Lawrence (ABC-Paramount).

Pretty Boy Floyd. w/m Woody Guthrie, 1961. Introduced, featured, and recorded by Woody Guthrie (Folkways). Bob Dylan sang it in his album "Folkways, A Vision Shared: A Tribute to Woody Guthrie and Leadbelly" (Columbia), 1988. Guthrie's version was re-released in the album "Dust Bowl Ballads" (Rounder), 1988.

Pretty Edelweiss. w. Matthew Woodward and Joseph Herbert, m. Franz Lehar, 1915. From (TM) *Alone At Last*.

Pretty Eyed Baby. w/m Mary Lou Williams, William Johnson, and Leo Mosely, 1951. Based on a piano instrumental "Satchel-Mouth Baby," recorded by Mary Lou Williams (Asch), 1944. Popularized by Frankie Laine and Jo Stafford (Columbia), and Al Trace, vocal by Lola Ameche (Mercury).

Pretty Flamingo. w/m Mark Barkan, 1966. Top 40 record by the British group Manfred Mann (United Artists). Included in Rod Stewart's album "A Night on the Town" (Warner Bros.), 1976.

Pretty Girl, A. w. J. Cheever Goodwin, m. Woolson Morse, 1891. Introduced by Della Morse in (TM) *Wang*.

Pretty Girl Is Like a Melody, A. w/m Irving Berlin, 1919. Probably the most representative of the songs from Ziegfeld's Follies. Introduced by John Steel in (MM) *Ziegfeld Follies of 1919* in a lavish production number. The song then became the theme of future Follies and of fashion shows and beauty pageants throughout the world. It was featured in (MM) *The Great Ziegfeld*, 1936, performed by Dennis Morgan, billed as Stanley Morner, with vocal dubbed on the soundtrack by Allan Jones; (MM) *Alexander's Ragtime Band*, 1938, by Ethel Merman; (MM) *Blue Skies*, 1946, by a quartet; (MM) *There's No Business Like Show Business*, 1954, by Alice Faye and Don Ameche.

Pretty Girl Milking Her Cow. w/m adapted by Roger Edens, 1940. Based on a traditional song, Edens adapted it for Judy Garland in (MM) *Little Nellie Kelly*. It was also heard in (MM) *Strictly in the Groove*, 1942.

Pretty Girls Everywhere. w/m Eugene Church and Thomas Williams, 1959. Introduced and recorded by Eugene Church and The Fellows (Class).

Pretty in Pink. w/m Richard Butler, Tim Butler, Vincent Ely, John Ashton, Duncan Kilburn, Roger Morris, 1986. Introduced in the LP "Talk, Talk, Talk" by the English group Psychedelic Furs (Columbia), 1981. Used in and title song of (MP) *Pretty in Pink*, 1986, which popularized single re-release.

Pretty Kitty Blue Eyes. w. Mann Curtis, m. Vic Mizzy, 1944. Featured and recorded by the Merry Macs (Decca).

Pretty Kitty Kelly. w. Harry Pease, m. Ed G. Nelson, 1920. Leading record by Charles Harrison (Victor).

Pretty Lips. w/m Walter Donaldson and Charley Straight, 1926. Introduced and recorded by Paul Whiteman, vocal by The Rhythm Boys [Bing Crosby, Harry Barris, and Al Rinker] (Victor).

Pretty Little Angel Eyes. w/m Tommy Boyce and Curtis Lee, 1961. Top 10 record by Curtis Lee (Dunes).

Pretty Little Baby. w/m Marvin Gaye, Dave Hamilton, and Clarence Paul, 1965. Recorded by Marvin Gaye (Tamla).

Pretty Mama Blues. w/m Ivory Joe Hunter, 1948. #1 R&B chart record by Ivory Joe Hunter (Pacific).

Pretty to Walk With. w. E. Y. Harburg, m. Harold Arlen, 1957. Introduced by Lena Horne in (TM) *Jamaica*.

Pretty Woman. See **Oh, Pretty Woman**.

Pretty Women. w/m Stephen Sondheim, 1978. Introduced by Edmund Lydeck, Len Cariou, and Victor Garber in (TM) *Sweeney Todd, The Demon Barber of Fleet Street*.

Pretzel Logic. w/m Walter Becker and Donald Fagen, 1974. Recorded by the studio band led by the writers, Steely Dan (ABC).

Pride. w/m Wayne P. Walker and Irene Stanton, 1963. Country chart hit by Ray Price (Columbia).

Pride, The. w/m Ernie Isley, Marvin Isley, O'Kelly Isley, Ronald Isley, Rudolph Isley, and Chris Jasper, 1977. Recorded by The Isley Brothers (T-Neck).

Pride (in the Name of Love). w/m Adam Clayton, Dave Evans, Paul Hewson, and Larry Mullen, Jr., 1984. Written and recorded by the Irish group U2 (Island).

Pride and Joy. w/m Marvin Gaye, William Stevenson, and Norman Whitfield, 1963. Introduced and recorded by Marvin Gaye (Tamla).

Pride Is Back, The. w/m Marc Blatte, Larry Gottlieb, and Alan Monde, 1986. Originally written as a commercial for Chrysler cars. Country chart record by Kenny Rogers with Nickie Ryder (RCA).

Primrose Lane. w/m George Callender and Wayne Shanklin, 1959. Top 10 record by Jerry Wallace, with The Jewels (Challenge).

Prince of Wails. m. Elmer Schoebel, 1924. Schoebel recorded this popular instrumental (Brunswick), as did Fletcher Henderson and his Orchestra (Paramount); The Cotton Pickers (Brunswick); Little Ramblers (Columbia); Bennie Moten (Victor); and Bud Freeman (Columbia).

Princess in Rags. w/m Roger Atkins and Helen Miller, 1965. Top 40 record by Gene Pitney (Musicor).

Princess of Pure Delight. w. Ira Gershwin, m. Kurt Weill, 1941. Introduced by Gertrude Lawrence in (TM) *Lady in the Dark* and recorded by her in an album of six songs from the production (Victor). Danny Kaye, who was in the show, also recorded it (Columbia).

Prisoner. See **Love Theme from "Eyes of Laura Mars."**

Prisoner of Hope. w/m Sterling Whipple and Gerald Metcalfe, 1981. Top 10 Country chart record by Johnny Lee (Full Moon).

Prisoner of Love. w. Leo Robin, m. Russ Columbo and Clarence Gaskill, 1931, 1946. Introduced, featured, and recorded by Russ Columbo (Victor). Revived by Perry Como, with a best-selling record (Victor). Song was on "Your Hit Parade" for fifteen weeks. Top 20 version by James Brown (King), 1963.

Prisoner's Song, The (a.k.a. **If I Had the Wings of an Angel**). w/m Guy Massey, 1924. This was Massey's only published song, but a major hit. The first release was by the country singer, Vernon Dalhart (Victor), whose record sold in the millions. He also recorded it for numerous other labels under pseudonyms. Bunny Berigan had an outstanding arrangement, which was coupled with his celebrated version of "I Can't Get Started with You" (Victor 12") (q.v.), 1938.

Private Dancer. w/m Mark Knopfler, 1985. Top 10 record by Tina Turner (Capitol).

Private Eyes. w/m Sara Allen, Janna Allen, Daryl Hall, and Warren Pash, 1981. #1 gold single title number from the platinum album by Daryl Hall & John Oates (RCA).

Private Idaho. w/m Fred Schneider, J. K. Strickland, Ricky Wilson, Cynthia Wilson, Kate Pierson, 1980. Recorded by the quintet The B-52's (Warner Bros.).

Private John Q. w/m Roger Miller, 1965. Featured and recorded by Glen Campbell (Capitol).

Problems. w/m Boudleaux Bryant and Felice Bryant, 1958. Top 10 record by The Everly Brothers (Cadence).

Prodigal Son, The. w/m Fred Rose, 1943. Best-seller by Roy Acuff (Okeh).

Prohibition Blues. w. Ring Lardner, m. Nora Bayes, 1919. Interpolated by Nora Bayes in the touring company of the woman's suffrage movement musical (TM) *Ladies First*, shortly before the enactment of the prohibition law. Recorded by Bayes (Columbia).

Promenade. See **Walking the Dog**.

Promised Land, The. w/m Chuck Berry, 1964. Introduced and recorded by Chuck Berry (Chess). Revived by Elvis Presley (RCA), 1974.

Promise Her Anything (But Give Her Love). w/m Roy Alfred, 1957. The phrase derived from an advertising slogan; "Arpege" was replaced by "love" in the song title. Recorded by Dean Martin (Capitol).

Promise Me Love. w/m Kay Thompson, 1958. Featured and recorded by Andy Williams (Cadence).

Promises. w/m Richard Feldman and Roger Linn, 1979. Recorded by British singer Eric Clapton (RSO).

Promises, Promises. w/m Pete Byrne and Rob Fisher, 1983. Written and recorded by the English duo Naked Eyes (EMI America).

Promises, Promises. w. Hal David, m. Burt Bacharach, 1968. Introduced by Jerry Orbach in (TM) *Promises, Promises*. Top 20 record by Dionne Warwick (Scepter).

Promises, Promises. w. William Smith, m. Carlisle Hughey, 1968. Top 10 Country record by Lynn Anderson (Chart).

Proud. w/m Barry Mann and Cynthia Weil, 1963. Recorded by Johnny Crawford (Del-Fi).

Proud Mary. w/m John C. Fogerty, 1969. Gold record by Creedance Clearwater Revival (Fantasy). Chart records by Solomon Burke (Bell) and The Checkmates, Ltd., featuring Sonny Charles (A&M). Ike and Tina Turner had a gold record version (Liberty), 1971.

Proud One, The. w/m Bob Crewe and Bob Gaudio, 1966, 1975. Introduced by Frankie Valli, produced by Bob Crewe (Philips), 1966. Revived by The Osmonds (MGM), 1975.

Proud Ones, The. See **Theme from "The Proud Ones."**

Prove It All Night. w/m Bruce Springsteen, 1978. Recorded by Bruce Springsteen (Columbia).

Prove Your Love. w/m Seth Swirsky and Arnie Roman, 1988. Recorded by Taylor Dayne (Arista).

(P.S.) I Love You. w/m John Lennon and Paul McCartney, 1964. Recorded by The Beatles (Tollie).

P.S. I Love You. w. Johnny Mercer, m. Gordon Jenkins, 1934. Best-selling records by Rudy Vallee (Victor), Glen Gray and the Casa Loma Orchestra (Decca), Eddie Stone (Bluebird), and Jack Fulton (Vocalion). It was revived by the Hilltoppers' hit single in 1953 (Dot).

Psychedelic Shack. w/m Barrett Strong and Norman Whitfield, 1970. Top 10 record by The Temptations (Gordy).

Psycho Killer. w/m David Byrne, Tina Weymouth, and Chris Frantz, 1978. Chart single from the album "Talking Heads" by the group of the same name (Sire), 1977.

Psychotic Reaction. w/m K. Ellner, R. Chaney, C. Atkinson, J. Byrne, and J. Michalski, 1966. The five San José, California, teenagers who wrote the Top 10 hit, recorded it as The Count Five (Double Shot).

P.T. 109. w/m Marijohn Wilkin and Fred Burch, 1962. The story of the heroism of John F. Kennedy after the destruction of his torpedo boat in World War II, recorded by Jimmy Dean (Columbia).

Pucker Up, Buttercup. w/m Johnny Bristol, Danny Coggins, and Harvey Fuqua, 1966. Top 40 record by Jr. Walker and The All Stars (Soul).

Pucker Up Your Lips, Miss Lindy. w. Eli Dawson, m. Albert Von Tilzer, 1912.

Puddin 'Head Jones. w. Alfred Bryan, m. Lou Handman, 1933. Featured and recorded by Rudy Vallee (Victor) and Fran Frey (Columbia).

Puff the Magic Dragon. w/m Peter Yarrow and Leonard Lipton, 1963. Hit record by Peter, Paul and Mary (Warner Bros.).

Pu-leeze, Mr. Hemingway. w. Walter Kent and Milton Drake, m. Abner Silver, 1932.

Pullman Porters on Parade, The. w. Ren G. May (Irving Berlin), m. Maurice Abrahams, 1913. Berlin's pseudonym is an anagram for "Germany," of which Berlin is the capital. Irving Berlin was changing publishing affiliations at the time and, because of contractual agreements, had to write the song under an alias. Al Jolson recorded the song in 1913 (Columbia).

Pull Over. w/m Marc Gordon and Gerald Levert, 1989. Hit R&B chart single by Levert (Atlantic).

Pump Up the Volume. w/m Steve Young and Andrew Biggs, 1988. Gold single by the Britain-based group, M/A/R/R/S (4th & Broadway).

Puppet Man. w/m Neil Sedaka and Howard Greenfield, 1970. Top 40 records by The 5th Dimension (Bell), and Tom Jones (Parrot), 1971.

Puppet on a String. w/m Sid Tepper and Roy Bennett, 1965. Introduced by Elvis Presley in (MM) *Girl Happy* and on records (RCA).

Puppy Love. w/m Barbara Lewis, 1964. Recorded by Barbara Lewis (Atlantic).

Puppy Love. w/m Paul Anka, 1960, 1972. Paul Anka had the first hit record (ABC-Paramount), followed twelve years later by Donny Osmond's million-seller (MGM).

Pure Love. w/m Eddie Rabbitt, 1974. Country hit by Ronnie Millsap (RCA).

Purlie. w. Peter Udell, m. Garry Geld, 1970. Introduced by Melba Moore in (TM) *Purlie*.

Purple Haze. w/m Jimi Hendrix, 1967. First chart single by The Jimi Hendrix Experience (Reprise). Dion recorded his version (Laurie), 1969.

Purple People Eater, The. w/m Sheb Wooley, 1958. #1 novelty hit by Sheb Wooley (MGM).

Purple Rain. w/m Prince Rogers Nelson, 1984. Top 10 gold record by Prince (Warner Bros.).

Push Dem Clouds Away. w/m Percy Gaunt, 1891. Introduced by George A. Beane in (TM) *A Trip to Chinatown*.

Pushin' Too Hard. w/m Sky Saxon, 1967. Top 40 record by The Seeds, the quartet of which Saxon, né Richard Marsh, was lead singer/bassist (GNP Crescendo).

Push It. w/m Herb Azor, 1988. R&B and Pop chart record by the rap trio Salt-N-Pepa (Next Plateau).

Pushover. w/m Roquel Davis and Tony Clarke, 1963. Featured and recorded by Etta James (Argo).

Push the Button. w. E. Y. Harburg, m. Harold Arlen, 1957. Introduced by Lena Horne in (TM) *Jamaica.*

Pussy Cat. w. Sunny Skylar, m. Tom Glazer, 1958. Featured and recorded by The Ames Brothers (RCA).

Pussy Cat Song, The (Nyow! Nyot Nyow!). w/m Dick Manning, 1949. Best-selling record of the novelty by Patti Andrews and Bob Crosby (Decca). Other chart versions by Perry Como (RCA Victor), Joy Nichols and Benny Lee (London), Jo Stafford and Gordon MacRae (Capitol).

Pussyfoot, The. w. Joan Ford, Walter Kerr, and Jean Kerr, m. Leroy Anderson, 1958. Introduced by Pat Stanley in (TM) *Goldilocks.*

Put a Light in the Window. w. Rhoda Roberts, m. Kenny Jacobson, 1957. Top 40 record by The Four Lads (Columbia).

Put a Little Love in Your Heart. w/m Jimmy Holiday, Randy Myers, and Jackie De-Shannon, 1969. Gold record by Jackie De-Shannon (Imperial). Sung on the soundtrack of (MP) *Scrooged* and its album (A&M) by Annie Lennox and Al Green, 1988.

Put Another Chair at the Table. w/m Richard Nelson and Cecil Gant, 1945. Featured and recorded by The Mills Brothers (Decca).

Put Away a Little Ray of Golden Sunshine (for a Rainy Day). w. Sam M. Lewis and Joe Young, m. Fred E. Ahlert, 1924. Recorded by the popular tenor Lewis James (Columbia).

Put 'Em in a Box, Tie 'Em with a Ribbon, and Throw 'Em in the Deep Blue Sea. w. Sammy Cahn, m. Jule Styne, 1948. Introduced by Doris Day with the Page Cavanaugh Trio in (MM) *Romance on the High Seas.* Top records by Doris Day (Columbia), Eddy Howard (Majestic), and Nat "King" Cole (Capitol).

Put It Off Until Tomorrow. w/m Dolly Parton and B. E. Owens, 1966. Country hit by Bill Phillips (Decca).

Put It There, Pal. w. Johnny Burke, m. James Van Heusen, 1945. Introduced by Bing Crosby and Bob Hope in (MM) *Road to Utopia* and recorded by them (Decca).

Put Me Off at Buffalo. w. Harry Dillon, m. John Dillon, 1895. Introduced in vaudeville by the Dillon Brothers.

Put Me to the Test. w. Ira Gershwin, m. Jerome Kern, 1944. Kern wrote a new melody for lyrics originally written for a George Gershwin tune for the film *Damsel in Distress.* The song was not used. The product of the new collaboration was sung by Gene Kelly and danced by Kelly and Rita Hayworth in (MM) *Cover Girl.*

Put On a Happy Face. w. Lee Adams, m. Charles Strouse, 1960. Introduced by Dick Van Dyke in (TM) *Bye Bye Birdie.* In the film version (MM) *Bye Bye Birdie,* 1963, it was sung by Van Dyke and Janet Leigh.

Put On Your Old Grey Bonnet. w. Stanley Murphy, m. Percy Wenrich, 1909. A favorite sing-a-long number. Recorded in many styles by many artists and jazz bands.

Put On Your Sunday Clothes. w/m Jerry Herman, 1964. Introduced by Charles Nelson Reilly, Jerry Dodge, Carol Channing, and Igors Gavon in (TM) *Hello, Dolly!* In (MM) *Hello, Dolly!,* 1969, it was sung by Barbra Streisand, Michael Crawford, Danny Lockin, and chorus.

Put That Ring on My Finger. w/m Sunny Skylar and Randy Ryan, 1945. Featured and recorded by Woody Herman, with his Orchestra (Columbia).

Put the Blame on Mame. w/m Allan Roberts and Doris Fisher, 1946. Introduced by Anita Ellis, dubbing on the soundtrack for Rita Hayworth, in (MP) *Gilda.* The song was heard again in (MM) *Betty Co-ed,* 1946. Featured and recorded by Janette Davis, accompanied by Archie Bleyer's Orchestra (Columbia).

Putting It Together. w/m Stephen Sondheim, 1984. Introduced by ten cast members in (TM) *Sunday in the Park with George*. Barbra Streisand recorded a revised version in "The Broadway Album" (Columbia).

Puttin' On the Ritz. w/m Irving Berlin, 1930, 1983. Introduced by Harry Richman in (MM) *Puttin' On the Ritz* and recorded by him (Brunswick). Clark Gable did a rendition of it in (MP) *Idiot's Delight*, 1939, which was included in (MM) *That's Entertainment*, 1974. Fred Astaire performed it in a spectacular Hermes Pan production in (MM) *Blue Skies*, 1945, and recorded the song (Decca). Revived by the Dutch/Indonesian singer, Taco [Ockerse], with a Top 10 record (RCA), 1983.

Put Your Arms Around Me, Honey. w. Junie McCree, m. Albert Von Tilzer, 1910. Introduced by Blossom Seeley in vaudeville. Interpolated during the run of (TM) *Madame Sherry* by Elizabeth M. Murray. Betty Grable sang it in (MM) *Coney Island*, 1943. It was used as a recurrent background theme in (MP) *In Old Oklahoma*, starring John Wayne, 1943. Judy Garland sang it in (MM) *In the Good Old Summertime* and on records with Georgie Stoll's Orchestra (MGM), 1949. It was interpolated by Judy Canova in (MM) *Louisiana Hayride*, 1944. The first hit recording was by Arthur Collins and Byron G. Harlan (Victor), 1911.

Put Your Dreams Away (for Another Day). w/m Ruth Lowe, Stephan Weiss, and Paul Mann, 1942. Frank Sinatra's radio theme. Recorded by him with Axel Stordahl's Orchestra (Columbia), 1945.

Put Your Hand in the Hand. w/m Gene Maclellan, 1971. Gold record by the Canadian quintet Ocean (Kama Sutra).

Put Your Hands Together. w/m Kenny Gamble and Leon Huff, 1974. Top 10 record by The O'Jays (Philadelphia International).

Put Your Head on My Shoulder. w/m Paul Anka, 1958. Hit record by Paul Anka, arranged and conducted by Don Costa (ABC-Paramount). Chart records in the next two decades by The Lettermen (Capitol), 1968, and by sixteen-year-old Leif Garrett (Atlantic), 1978.

Put Your Heart in a Song. w. Paul Francis Webster, m. Frank Churchill, 1938. Sung in (MM) *Breaking the Ice* and on records (Decca) by Bobby Breen.

Put Your Little Foot Right Out. w/m Larry Spier, 1940. Adapted from the French folk tune "Varsovienne." First recording by Louise Massey and The Westerners (Vocalion).

Put Your Mind at Ease. w/m Dennis Larden and Lorry Larden, 1967. Introduced and recorded by the quintet Every Mothers' Son (MGM). Written by brothers in the group.

Put Your Mouth on Me. w/m Jeffrey Cohen and Narada Michael Walden, 1989. Hit single by Eddie Murphy (Columbia).

Put Your Shoes On, Lucy. w/m Hank Fort, 1949. Featured and recorded by Beatrice Kay (Columbia).

Puzzlement, A. w. Oscar Hammerstein II, m. Richard Rodgers, 1951. Introduced by Yul Brynner in (TM) *The King and I*, and repeated by him in (MM) *The King and I*, 1956.

Pyramid. w. Irving Gordon, Irving Mills, m. Edward Kennedy "Duke" Ellington, 1938. Introduced and recorded by Duke Ellington and his Orchestra (Brunswick). Also recorded by the bands of Artie Shaw (Victor) and Johnny Hodges (Vocalion).

P.Y.T. (Pretty Young Thing). w/m James Ingram and Quincy Jones, 1983. Top 10 record by Michael Jackson (Epic).

Q

Quaker City Jazz.   m. Jan Savitt and Jimmy Schultz, 1937. Theme song of and recorded by Jan Savitt and his Top Hatters (Bluebird). Also recorded by Spud Murphy and his Band (Decca).

Quando, Quando, Quando (Tell Me When).   w. Pat Boone (Engl.), Alberto Testa (It.), m. Elio Cesari, 1962. Italian popular song, English version introduced by Pat Boone (Dot).

Quarter to Three.   w/m Gene Barge, Frank J. Guida, Joseph Royster, and Gary Anderson, 1961. Waltz, recorded by Gary U.S. Bonds (Legrand).

Queen Bee.   w/m Rupert Holmes, 1976. Introduced by Barbra Streisand in (MM) *A Star Is Born.*

Queen of Hearts.   w/m Hank DeVito, 1981. Top 10 gold record by Juice Newton (Capitol).

Queen of the Hop.   w/m Woody Harris and Bobby Darin, 1958. Hit record by Bobby Darin (Atco).

Queen of the House.   w/m Roger Miller, new lyrics by Mary Taylor, 1965. Answer song to Roger Miller's hit "King of the Road" (q.v.), recorded by Jody Miller (Capitol).

Queen of the Senior Prom.   w/m Ed Penney, Jack Richards, and Stella Lee, 1957. Leading recording by The Mills Brothers (Decca).

Queer Notions.   m. Coleman Hawkins, 1933. Introduced and recorded by Fletcher Henderson and his Orchestra, featuring the composer on tenor saxophone.

Quentin's Theme.   m. Robert W. Corbert, 1969. A theme from the series (TVP) "Dark Shadows." Top 20 instrumental record by The Charles Randolph Grean Sounde (Ranwood).

Que Sera, Sera (Whatever Will Be, Will Be).   w/m Jay Livingston and Ray Evans, 1956. Introduced by Doris Day in (MP) *The Man Who Knew Too Much.* Winner, Academy Award for Best Song, 1956. Doris Day had a top record in sales and plays (Columbia).

Quest, The. See **Impossible Dream, The.**

Question.   w/m Justin Hayward, 1970. Top 40 U.S. release by the English quintet The Moody Blues (Threshold). Hayward was lead singer and guitarist of the group.

Question.   w/m Lloyd Price and Harold Logan, 1960. Introduced and recorded by Lloyd Price (ABC-Paramount).

Question of Temperature, A.   w/m Michael Appel, Donald Henny, and Edward Schnug, 1968. Recorded by The Balloon Farm (Laurie).

Questions 67 and 68.   w/m Robert Lamm, 1969. Recorded by the jazz/rock group Chicago (Columbia). Single re-released in 1971, on the charts for ten weeks, reaching the Top 40.

Quick Joey Small (Run, Joey, Run). w/m Arthur Resnick and Joey Levine, 1968. Top 40 record by The Kasenetz-Katz Singing Orchestral Circus (Buddah).

Quicksand. w/m Brian Holland, Eddie Holland, and Lamont Dozier, 1963. Top 10 record by Martha and The Vandellas (Gordy).

Quicksilver. w/m Irving Taylor, George Wyle, and Edward Pola, 1950. Hit record by Bing Crosby and The Andrews Sisters (Decca). Popular version also by Doris Day, with The Country Cousins (Columbia).

Quien Sera. See **Sway.**

Quiet Girl, A. w. Betty Comden and Adolph Green, m. Leonard Bernstein, 1953. Introduced by George Gaynes in (TM) *Wonderful Town.*

Quiet Night. w. Lorenz Hart, m. Richard Rodgers, 1936. Sung by Earle MacVeigh and ensemble in (TM) *On Your Toes.* In the film version (MM) *On Your Toes,* 1939, it was played in the background.

Quiet Nights of Quiet Stars (Corcovado). w. Gene Lees (Engl.), Antonio Carlos Jobim (Port.), m. Antonio Carlos Jobim, 1962. Originally titled "Corcovado," recorded instrumentally by tenor saxophonist Stan Getz and guitarist Charlie Byrd (Verve). Vocal recording by Astrud Gilberto, with Stan Getz (Verve), 1964. Leading English lyric version recorded by Andy Williams (Columbia).

Quiet Storm. w/m Rose Ella Jones and William "Smokey" Robinson, 1976. Recorded by Smokey Robinson (Tamla).

Quiet Village. m. Les Baxter, 1959. Originally recorded by Les Baxter in the album "Le Sacre du Sauvage" (Capitol). Hit instrumental by Martin Denny and his Orchestra (Liberty).

Quiller Has the Brains. w. Harry B. Smith, m. Reginald DeKoven, 1900. From (TM) *Foxy Quiller.*

Quizas, Quizas, Quizas. See **Perhaps, Perhaps, Perhaps.**

R

Race Is On, The. w/m Don Rollins, 1965. Introduced by Country star George Jones (United Artists). Covered and hit record by Pop star Jack Jones (Kapp).

Racing with the Moon. w. Vaughn Monroe and Pauline Pope, m. Johnny Watson, 1941. Theme song of singing bandleader Vaughn Monroe. Through his recording (Bluebird), and radio, theatre, and ballroom performances, the song is solely associated with him. Watson, the composer, was arranger for the band at the time.

Rackety Coo. w. Otto Harbach, m. Rudolf Friml, 1916. Performed by Adele Rowland and chorus in (TM) *Katinka* with a flock of trained pigeons.

Radar Love. w/m Barry Hay and George Kooymans, 1974. Top 20 record from The Netherlands by the band Golden Earring (Track).

Radio Free Europe. w/m Michael Stipe, Pete Buck, Mike Mills, and Bill Berry, 1983. Written and recorded by the quartet R. E. M. (I.R.S.).

Radio Ga-Ga. w/m Roger Taylor, 1984. Recorded by the English group, Queen, of which Taylor was drummer (Capitol).

Radio Song, The. 1987. Popular track from the album "Got Any Gum?" by Joe Walsh (Warner Bros.).

Radio Waves. w/m Roger Waters, 1987. Popular track from the British album "Radio K.A.O.S." by Roger Waters, former member of the group, Pink Floyd (Columbia).

Rag, Mama, Rag. w/m Robbie Robertson, 1969. Chart record by The Band (Capitol).

Ragamuffin Romeo. w/m Harry De Costa and Mabel Wayne, 1930. Sung by Jeannie Lang in (MM) *King of Jazz.*

Rag Doll. w/m Bob Crewe and Bob Gaudio, 1964. #1 gold record by The Four Seasons (Philips).

Raggedy Ann. w. Anne Caldwell, m. Jerome Kern, 1923. Fred Stone and his daughter Dorothy sang and danced this number in the hit (TM) *Stepping Stones* with John Lambert and the John Tiller Sunshine Girls. Popular record by Paul Whiteman and his Orchestra (Victor).

Ragging the Scale. m. Edward B. Claypoole, 1915. Published and big seller as a piano instrumental. Popular recording by Conway's Band (Victor). Among later recordings: the orchestras of Vincent Lopez (Okeh), Jimmy Lunceford (Decca), Jack Pleis (London), Paul Whiteman (Decca).

Rag Mop. w/m Johnnie Lee Wills and Deacon Anderson, 1950. The Ames Brothers (Coral) had their first #1 million-seller. Other top recordings by Ralph Flanagan, vocal by Harry

Prime (RCA Victor); Lionel Hampton, vocal by The Hamptones (Decca); Johnnie Lee Wills (Bullet).

Rags to Riches. w/m Richard Adler and Jerry Ross, 1953. #1 record by Tony Bennett, with Percy Faith and his Orchestra (Columbia).

Ragtime Cowboy Joe. w. Grant Clarke, m. Maurice Abrahams and Lewis E. Muir, 1912. First hit record was by Bob Roberts (Victor), the year of publication. Sung by Alice Faye, Jack Oakie, and June Havoc in (MM) *Hello, Frisco, Hello*, 1943. Betty Hutton, as Texas Guinan, sang it in (MM) *Incendiary Blonde*, 1944. Hit recordings by Jo Stafford (Capitol), 1949, and The Chipmunks (Liberty), 1959.

Ragtime Jockey Man. w/m Irving Berlin, 1912. Introduced by Willie Howard in (TM) *The Passing Show of 1912*. Recorded by Maurice Burkhardt and The Peerless Quartet (Columbia).

Ragtime Violin, The. w/m Irving Berlin, 1911. Popular song with leading record by The American Quartet (Victor). In films, it was performed by Alice Faye, Dixie Dunbar, and Wally Vernon in (MM) *Alexander's Ragtime Band*, 1938, and in a medley by Judy Garland and Fred Astaire in (MM) *Easter Parade*, 1948.

Railroad Jim. w/m Nat H. Vincent, 1915.

Rain. w/m John Lennon and Paul McCartney, 1966. Recorded by The Beatles (Capitol).

Rain. w. Billy Hill, m. Peter DeRose, 1934. Featured and recorded by the bands of Jan Garber (Victor); Don Bestor (Brunswick); Larry Funk, vocal by Vaughn Monroe (Melotone).

Rain. w/m Eugene Ford, Carey Morgan, and Arthur Swanstrom, 1927. Recorded by Sam Lanin and his Orchestra (Banner) and Arnold Frank and his Rogers' Cafe Orchestra (Okeh).

Rain, Rain, Go Away! w. Edward Heyman and Mack David, m. John Green, 1932. Re-cordings by the bands of Art Kassel (Columbia) and Ted Black (Victor).

Rain, Rain Go Away. w/m Gloria Shayne and Noel Regney, 1962. Recorded by Bobby Vinton (Epic).

Rain, Rain, Rain. w/m Jay McConologue, 1954. Recorded by Frankie Laine and The Four Lads, with The Buddy Cole Quartet (Columbia).

Rain, The. w/m Vincent Bell, 1986. #1 R&B chart record from the album "Juice," by Oran "Juice" Jones (Def Jam).

Rain, the Park, and Other Things, The. w/m Artie Kornfeld and Steve Duboff, 1967. Gold record by The Cowsills, the Rhode Island family group (MGM).

Rainbow. w/m Russ Hamilton, 1957. Leading record by the English singer-writer Russ Hamilton (Kapp).

Rainbow at Midnight. w/m Lost John Miller, 1946. Ernest Tubb's recording (Decca) was so popular, that he followed it with "Answer to Rainbow at Midnight."

Rainbow Connection. w/m Kenny Ascher and Paul Williams, 1979. Introduced by Jim Henson, as Kermit the Frog, in (MM) *The Muppet Movie*. It was released as a single, artist credit: Kermit (Atlantic).

Rainbow in My Heart. w/m George Morgan, 1949. Top 10 C&W chart record by George Morgan (Columbia).

Rainbow in Your Eyes. w/m Leon Russell, 1976. Introduced and chart record by Leon and Mary Russell (Paradise). Al Jarreau's version made the R&B charts (Reprise).

Rainbow on the River. w. Paul Francis Webster, m. Louis Alter, 1936. Introduced by Bobby Breen in (MM) *Rainbow on the River*. Breen recorded it (Decca). Other popular versions by Guy Lombardo, vocal by Carmen Lombardo (Victor); Ted Weems, vocal by Perry Como (Decca); Tony Martin (Brunswick).

Rainbow Rhapsody. w. Allan Roberts, m. Benny Carter, 1943. Glenn Miller featured and recorded it as an instrumental (Victor).

Rainbow Ride. w/m Jeff Barry and Andy Kim, 1969. Recorded by Andy Kim (Steed).

Rainbows and Roses. w/m Ted Harris, 1966. Country record by Roy Drusky (Mercury).

Rainbow Valley. w. Edgar Leslie, m. Joe Burke, 1939. Popularized through recordings and airplay by the bands of Sammy Kaye, vocal by Tommy Ryan (Victor); Dick Jurgens, vocal by Eddy Howard (Vocalion); and Joseph Sudy (Bluebird).

Rain Dance. w/m Burt Cummings and Kurt Winter, 1971. Top 20 record by the Canadian group The Guess Who (RCA).

Raindrops. w/m Dee Clark, 1961. Top 10 record by Dee Clark (Vee-Jay).

Raindrops Keep Falling on My Head. w. Hal David, m. Burt Bacharach, 1969. Introduced on the soundtrack of (MP) *Butch Cassidy and the Sundance Kid* by B. J. Thomas. Winner Academy Award, 1969. Thomas's recording became a #1 gold record, one of the biggest sellers of the year, and helped establish the song as a standard.

Rain Forest. m. Paul Hardcastle, 1985. Title instrumental and single from the album by the British keyboardist Paul Hardcastle (Profile).

Rain in My Heart. w/m Teddy Randazzo and Victoria Pike, 1969. Leading record by Frank Sinatra (Reprise).

Rain in Spain, The. w. Alan Jay Lerner, m. Frederick Loewe, 1956. Introduced by Rex Harrison, Julie Andrews, and Robert Coote in (TM) *My Fair Lady*. In (MM) *My Fair Lady*, 1964, it was sung by Rex Harrison, Marni Nixon, dubbing for Audrey Hepburn, and Wilfred Hyde-White.

Rain on the Roof. w/m John Sebastian, 1966. Hit record by The Lovin' Spoonful (Kama Sutra).

Rain on the Roof. w/m Ann Ronell, 1932. Introduced by Paul Whiteman and his Orchestra. Recorded by Glen Gray and the Casa Loma Orchestra (Brunswick) and Nat Shilkret (Victor).

Rains Came, The. w/m Huey P. Meaux, 1962. Recorded by Big Sam and The House Wreckers (Eric), and later by The Sir Douglas Quintet (Tribe), 1966.

Rainy Day, A. w. Howard Dietz, m. Arthur Schwartz, 1932. Sung by Clifton Webb in (TM) *Flying Colors* and recorded by him with Leo Reisman's Orchestra (Victor).

Rainy Day People. w/m Gordon Lightfoot, 1975. Recorded by the Canadian singer/songwriter Gordon Lightfoot (Reprise).

Rainy Day Refrain, A. w. Eric Maschwitz (Engl.). Hermann Gaze (Ger.), m. Hermann Gaze, 1950. Original German song, "Schnurlregen." Most popular recordings in U.S. by Mary Martin and Arthur Godfrey (Columbia), Mindy Carson (RCA Victor), Vera Lynn (London).

Rainy Days and Mondays. w. Paul Williams, m. Roger Nichols, 1971. Gold record by The Carpenters (A&M).

Rainy Day Women No. 12 & 35. w/m Bob Dylan, 1966. Top 10 record by Bob Dylan (Columbia).

Rainy Night in Georgia, A. w/m Tony Joe White, 1970. Top 10 hit, for which Brook Benton's recording was awarded a gold record (Cotillion).

Rainy Night in Rio, A. w. Leo Robin, m. Arthur Schwartz, 1946. In a big production number in (MM) *The Time, the Place and the Girl*, this was sung by Jack Carson, Dennis Morgan, Janis Paige, and Martha Vickers, played on the piano by Carmen Cavallaro and embellished by the dancers.

Raised on Robbery. w/m Joni Mitchell, 1974. Recorded by Joni Mitchell (Asylum).

Raisin' the Rent. w. Ted Koehler, m. Harold Arlen, 1933. From *Cotton Club Pa-*

rade at the Cotton Club in Harlem, New York. Recorded by Duke Ellington, vocal by Ivy Anderson (Brunswick).

Ramblin' Gamblin' Man. w/m Bob Seger, 1969. Top 20 record by The Bob Seger System (Capitol).

Rambling Rose. w. Joseph Allan McCarthy, m. Joe Burke, 1948. Recorded by Perry Como, with Russ Case's Orchestra (RCA Victor); Gordon MacRae, with the Starlighters (Capitol); Phil Brito, with Richard Maltby's Orchestra (Musicraft). Not to be confused with hit song "Ramblin' Rose," 1962.

Ramblin' Man. w/m Dickey Betts, 1974. Written by the bassist of the combo that had the Top 10 record, The Allman Brothers Band (Capricorn).

Ramblin' Man. w/m Hank Williams, 1951. Introduced by Hank Williams (MGM). Sung by Hank Williams, Jr., dubbing on the soundtrack for George Hamilton in the Hank Williams story (MM) *Your Cheatin' Heart*, 1965.

Ramblin' Rose. w/m Noel Sherman and Joe Sherman, 1962. Hit record by Nat "King" Cole (Capitol).

Ramona. w. L. Wolfe Gilbert, m. Mabel Wayne, 1927. This was written to promote and accompany the silent film *Ramona*. The promotional technique was so successful that the song became a hit before the release of the film. With much fanfare, Dolores Del Rio, who starred in the film, sang the song on a coast-to-coast radio broadcast from Hollywood, accompanied by Paul Whiteman's Orchestra in New York. Gene Austin (Victor) and Whiteman with vocal by Austin Young (Victor) had best-selling records. Revived by Billy Walker with a Country chart hit (Monument), 1968.

Ramrod. m. Al Casey, 1958. Instrumental chart-maker by Duane Eddy (Jamie).

Rangers' Song, The. w. Joseph McCarthy, m. Harry Tierney, 1927. Sung by J. Harold Murray and Rangers Chorus in (TM) *Rio Rita*. In the film (MM) *Rio Rita*, 1929, it was sung

by John Boles and chorus, and in the 1942 version, by John Carroll.

Rang Tang Ding Dong (I Am the Japanese Sandman). w/m Alvin Williams, 1957. Recorded by the "doo-wop" vocal quintet The Cellos (Apollo).

Rapper, The. w/m Don Iris, 1970. Gold record awarded for the recording by The Jaggerz of which the writer was lead singer (Kama Sutra).

Rap Tap on Wood. w/m Cole Porter, 1936. Sung and danced by Eleanor Powell in (MM) *Born to Dance*. Frances Langford recorded it (Decca).

Rapture. w. Deborah Harry, m. Chris Stein, 1981. A #1 gold rap record by the group, Blondie, featuring the husband and wife writers (Chrysalis).

Raspberry Beret. w/m Prince Rogers Nelson, 1985. Top 10 record by Prince (Paisley Park).

Rastus on Parade. w. George Marion, m. Kerry Mills (Frederick Allen), 1895. Dave Genaro and wife Ray Bailey introduced this two-step, which became one of the earliest cakewalk successes.

Rated X. w/m Loretta Lynn, 1973. Country hit record by Loretta Lynn (MCA).

Ration Blues. w/m Louis Jordan, Anthonio Cosey, and Collenane Clark, 1943. Featured and recorded by Louis Jordan and his Tympany Five (Decca).

Raunchy. m. William E. Justis, Jr., and Sidney Manker, 1957. Hit instrumental by Bill Justis (Phillips). Other chart versions by Ernie Freeman (Imperial) and Billy Vaughn (Dot).

Rave On. w/m Norman Petty, Bill Tilghman, and Sonny West, 1958. Chart record by Buddy Holly (Coral). Revived by John Cougar Mellencamp in (MP) *Cocktail* and its album (Elektra), 1988.

Raw-Hide. m. Link Wray, 1959. Instrumental by guitarist Link Wray & His Men (Epic).

Rawhide. w. Ned Washington, m. Dimitri Tiomkin, 1958. Theme of series (TVP) "Rawhide," sung under titles by Frankie Laine.

Ray of Hope, A. w/m Felix Cavaliere and Eddie Brigati, 1968. Top 40 record by The Rascals (Atlantic).

Razzazza Mazzazza. m. Arthur Pryor, 1905. Band instrumental.

Razzle Dazzle. w. Fred Ebb, m. John Kander, 1975. Introduced by Jerry Orbach and company in (TM) *Chicago*.

Reach. w/m Johanna Hall and John Hall, 1977. Recorded by the group Orleans (Asylum).

Reaching for Someone (and Not Finding Anyone There). w. Edgar Leslie, m. Walter Donaldson, 1929. Popular records by Paul Whiteman, featuring Bix Beiderbecke, vocal by Bing Crosby (Columbia); George Olsen, vocal by Fran Frey (Victor); Frankie Trumbauer (Okeh); Cliff "Ukulele Ike" Edwards (Columbia).

Reaching for the Moon. w/m Irving Berlin, 1930. A waltz, originally sung by Bing Crosby in (MP) *Reaching for the Moon*, starring Douglas Fairbanks and Bebe Daniels. The vocal was deleted from the film before release, but the melody was retained in the background on the soundtrack. It was also interpolated in (MM) *Top Speed*, 1930.

Reaching for the Moon. w/m Benny Davis and Jesse Greer, 1926. Introduced by Benny Davis in vaudeville. Leading record by Ben Bernie, vocal by Paul Hagan (Brunswick). (Not to be confused with the film song of the same title.)

Reach Out, I'll Be There. w/m Brian Holland, Lamont Dozier, and Eddie Holland, 1966. #1 record by The Four Tops (Motown). Later chart records by Merrilee Rush

(AGP), 1968; Diana Ross (Motown), 1971; Gloria Gaynor (MGM), 1975.

Reach Out and Touch (Somebody's Hand). w/m Nicholas Ashford and Valerie Simpson, 1970. Hit record by Diana Ross, her first after leaving the Supremes (Motown).

Reach Out for Me. w. Hal David, m. Burt Bacharach, 1964. Recorded by Lou Johnson (Big Top), 1963. Top 20 record by Dionne Warwick (Scepter), 1964.

Reach Out of the Darkness. w/m Jim Post, 1968. Top 10 record by the husband and wife team of Jim and Cathy Post, billed as Friend and Lover (Verve Forecast).

Read 'Em and Weep. w/m Jim Steinman, 1983. Popularized by Barry Manilow (Arista).

Read My Lips. w/m Michael Franks, 1985. R&B chart record by Melba Moore (Capitol).

Ready. w/m Cat Stevens, 1975. Recorded by Cat Stevens (A&M).

Ready, Willing and Able. w/m Al Rinker, Floyd Huddleston, and Dick Gleason, 1954. Introduced by Doris Day in (MM) *Young at Heart*.

Ready for the River. w. Gus Kahn, m. Charles N. Daniels [a.k.a. Neil Moret], 1928. Featured and recorded by the Coon-Sanders Orchestra (Victor).

Ready for the Times to Get Better. w/m Allen Reynolds, 1978. Recorded by Crystal Gayle (United Artists).

Ready for the World. w/m Melvin Riley, 1986. Top 10 record by the sextet Ready for the World (MCA).

Ready or Not, Here I Come (Can't Hide from Love). w/m Thomas Bell and William Hart, 1968. Top 40 record by The Delfonics (Philly Groove).

Ready Teddy. w/m John Marascalo and Robert Blackwell, 1956. Featured and recorded by Little Richard (Specialty). He sang it in (MM) *The Girl Can't Help It*, 1957.

Ready to Take a Chance Again. w. Norman Gimbel, m. Charles Fox, 1978. Sung on the soundtrack of (MP) *Foul Play*, and on records by Barry Manilow (Arista). Song nominated for an Academy Award.

Real End, The. w/m Rickie Lee Jones, 1984. Recorded by Rickie Lee Jones (Warner Bros.).

Real Live Girl. w. Carolyn Leigh, m. Cy Coleman, 1962. Introduced by Sid Caesar in (TM) *Little Me*. Chart record by Steve Alaimo (ABC-Paramount), 1965.

Real Love. w/m André Cymone, 1989. Hit record by Jody Watley (MCA).

Real Love. w/m Patrick Henderson and Michael McDonald, 1980. Top 10 record by the group The Doobie Brothers (Warner Bros.).

Really Wanna Know You. w/m Gary Wright, m. Ali Thomson, 1981. Recorded by Gary Wright (Warner Bros.).

Real Man. w/m Todd Rundgren, 1975. Written and recorded by Todd Rundgren (Bearsville).

Real Me, The. w/m Peter Townshend, 1974. Recorded by the British group The Who (Track).

Real Nice Clambake, A. w. Oscar Hammerstein II, m. Richard Rodgers, 1945. Introduced by Jean Darling, Christine Johnson, Jan Clayton, and Eric Mattson in (TM) *Carousel*. In the 1956 film version (MM) *Carousel*, it was sung by Robert Rounseville, Barbara Ruick, Claramae Turner, and the ensemble.

Reaper, The. See **Don't Fear the Reaper**.

Reason to Believe. w/m Tim Hardin, 1971. Introduced by Tim Hardin in a self-named album (Verve-Forecast), 1966. Rod Stewart's version was the flip side of his hit "Maggie May" (q.v.) (Mercury), 1971.

Rebecca of Sunnybrook Farm. w. A. Seymour Brown, m. Albert Gumble, 1914. Inspired by Kate Douglas's novel. Recorded by the American Quartette (Victor).

Rebel-Rouser. m. Duane Eddy and Lee Hazlewood, 1958. Instrumental by Duane Eddy (Jamie).

Rebel Yell. w/m Billy Idol and Steve Stevens, 1984. Recorded by British singer Billy Idol (Chrysalis).

Recess in Heaven. w/m Johnnie Getz, 1948. Most popular record by The Deep River Boys (RCA Victor).

Recessional. w. Rudyard Kipling, m. Reginald DeKoven, 1898. DeKoven's setting of a poem by Kipling celebrating the Diamond Jubilee of Queen Victoria.

Reckless. w. Oscar Hammerstein II, m. Jerome Kern, 1935. The title song of (MP) *Reckless*, in which Virginia Verrill dubbed her voice on the soundtrack for Jean Harlow. Freddy Martin and his Orchestra recorded it with a vocal by Elmer Feldkamp (Brunswick).

Reconsider Baby. w/m Lowell Fulson, 1955. R&B hit by Lowell Fulson (Checker).

Reconsider Me. w/m Mira Smith and Margaret Lewis, 1969. Country and Pop hit by Johnny Adams (SSS International). Narvel Felts had a successful version in 1975 (ABC/Dot).

Recovery. w/m Billy Davis, Raynard Miner, and Carl William Smith, 1966. Recorded by Fontella Bass (Checker).

Red, Hot and Blue. w/m Cole Porter, 1936. Introduced by Ethel Merman and company in (TM) *Red, Hot and Blue*. Revived by Michael Feinstein in his Broadway show (TM) *Michael Feinstein in Concert . . . Isn't It Romantic*, 1988.

Red Ball Express, The. w/m Harold Rome, 1946. Introduced by Lawrence Winters in (TM) *Call Me Mister*. Song not used in the film version, 1951.

Red Bank Boogie. m. William "Count" Basie and Buck Clayton, 1943. Instrumental introduced and recorded by Count Basie and his Orchestra (Columbia) and named after his birthplace, Red Bank, New Jersey.

Red-Headed Music Maker. w/m Wendell Hall, 1924. Theme song of the popular ukulele-playing and singing radio and vaudeville performer Wendell Hall (Victor).

Red Headed Woman, A. w. Ira Gershwin, m. George Gershwin, 1935. Sung by Warren Coleman in (TM) *Porgy and Bess.* In the film version (MM) *Porgy and Bess,* 1959, it was sung by Brock Peters.

Red Hot Mama. w/m Gilbert Wells, Bud Cooper, and Fred Rose, 1924. In addition to Sophie Tucker (Okeh), with whom this song is associated, it has been recorded by Jimmy O'Bryant (Paramount), Freddie "Schnickelfritz" Fisher (Decca), Beatrice Kay (Columbia), and The Coon-Sanders Orchestra (Victor).

Red Lips Kiss My Blues Away. w. Alfred Bryan, m. James V. Monaco and Pete Wendling, 1927.

Redneck Friend. w/m Jackson Browne, 1973. Recorded by Jackson Browne (Asylum).

Rednecks, White Socks, and Blue Ribbon Beer. w/m Wayland D. Holyfield, Bob McDill, and Chuck Neese, 1973. Country hit by Johnny Russell (RCA).

Red Onion Rag. m. Abe Olman, 1911. Popular instrumental, first recorded by Roy Spangler (Rex).

Red Red Wine. w/m Neil Diamond, 1988. Recorded by Neil Diamond (Bang), 1962. The group, UB40, recorded a reggae version for their album "Labour of Love" (A&M), 1983, which, upon its re-release in 1988, resulted in a hit single of the song.

Red River Rock. m. Tom King, Ira Mack, and Fred Mendelsohn, 1959. Rock version of the traditional "Red River Valley," recorded as an instrumental by Johnny and The Hurricanes (Warwick).

Red River Rose. w/m Tommie Connor and Johnnie Reine, 1959. Featured and recorded by The Ames Brothers (RCA).

Red Roses for a Blue Lady. w/m Sid Tepper and Roy Brodsky, 1949, 1965. Top 10 records by Vaughn Monroe, with his Orchestra (RCA Victor), and Guy Lombardo and his Royal Canadians (Decca). Revived in 1965 with hit records by Vic Dana (Dolton); instrumental version by Bert Kaempfert and his Orchestra (Decca); Wayne Newton (Capitol).

Red Rubber Ball. w/m Paul Simon and Bruce Woodley, 1966. Hit record by The Cyrkle (Columbia).

Red Sails in the Sunset. w. Jimmy Kennedy, m. Will Grosz (pseud. Hugh Williams), 1935. English song, which became huge sheet music seller in U.S. via heavy airplay, many recordings, and its interpolation in (TM) *Provincetown Follies* by Phyllis Austen. Among recordings, then and later: Bing Crosby (Decca); Guy Lombardo and his Orchestra (Decca); Louis Armstrong (Decca); Frances Langford (Mercury); Lanny Ross (Brunswick); Montovani's Orchestra (Columbia); Gracie Fields (London); Mound City Blue Blowers (Champion); whistler Fred Lowery (Columbia); Les Brown and his Orchestra (Coral).

Red's Boogie. m. Willie Perryman, 1951. Featured and recorded by Piano Red (RCA Victor).

Red Silk Stockings and Green Perfume. w/m Bob Hilliard, Dick Sanford, and Sammy Mysels, 1947. Recorded by Sammy Kaye, vocal by Don Cornell (RCA Victor); Ray McKinley, with his Orchestra (Majestic); Tony Pastor, with his Orchestra (Columbia).

Redskin Rhumba. m. Charlie Barnet, 1940. Introduced and recorded by Charlie Barnet and his Orchestra (Bluebird).

Red Top. m. Gene Ammons, 1950. Tenor-saxophonist Ammons recorded his best-known jazz composition with his group (Mercury). There are other numbers with the same title.

Red Top. m. Lionel Hampton and Ben Kynard, 1947. Instrumental recorded by Lionel Hampton (Decca).

Red Wing (An Indian Fable). w. Thurland Chattaway, m. Kerry Mills, 1907. Novelty story song. Leading record by Frank Stanley and Henry Burr (Columbia).

Reefer Man. w. Andy Razaf, m. J. Russel Robinson, 1932. Recorded by Cab Calloway and his Orchestra (Brunswick) and performed by them in (MM) *International House* in 1933.

Reelin' and Rockin'. w/m Chuck Berry, 1965. First hit record by the English group The Dave Clark Five (Epic). The writer, Chuck Berry, revived it with a Top 40 version that was recorded live at a performance in Lanchester, England (Chess), 1973.

Reeling in the Years. w/m Donald Fagen and Walter Becker, 1973. Recorded by the group, Steely Dan, featuring the writers (ABC).

Re-enlistment Blues. w/m James Jones, Robert Wells, and Fred Karger, 1953. Introduced by Merle Travis in (MP) *From Here to Eternity*. Recorded by Buddy Morrow, vocal by Frankie Lester (RCA Victor).

Reflections. w/m Brian Holland, Lamont Dozier, and Eddie Holland, 1967. Top 10 record by The Supremes (Motown).

Reflections in the Water. w. Paul Francis Webster, m. John Jacob Loeb, 1933. Popular with orchestras and soloists on network radio programs. Arthur Tracy, "The Street Singer," had a successful recording (Brunswick).

Reflections of My Life. w/m William Campbell and Thomas McAleese, 1970. Top 10 record by the Scottish quintet The Marmalade (London).

Reflex, The. w/m Duran Duran, 1984. From the platinum LP "Seven and the Ragged Tiger," by the English group Duran Duran, the single became a #1 record (Capitol).

Refugee. w/m Tom Petty and Mike Campbell, 1980. Recorded by Tom Petty & The Heartbreakers (Backstreet).

Regency Rakes. w/m Noël Coward, 1934. From the London import (TM) *Conversation Piece*. Introduced in New York by George Sanders, Sidney Grammer, Antony Brian, and Pat Worsley.

Relax. w/m Peter Gill, William Johnson, and Mark O'Toole, 1985. The video version by the Liverpool, England, quartet Frankie Goes to Hollywood was banned by the British Broadcasting Company upon its initial release, 1984. The single was introduced in the U.S. the same year (Island). The record was used on the soundtrack of (MP), *Body Double*, 1985, and its re-release made the Top 10 on the charts.

Relax-Ay-Voo. w. Sammy Cahn, m. Arthur Schwartz, 1955. Sung by Dean Martin and Jerry Lewis in (MP) *You're Never Too Young*.

Release Me. w/m Eddie Miller and W. S. Stevenson, 1954, 1962, 1967. Originally a C&W chart maker by Ray Price (Columbia) and Kitty Wells (Decca). "Little Esther" Phillips had a Top 10 R&B and Pop chart record in 1962 (Lenox). Engelbert Humperdinck had a major hit, his first (Parrot), 1967.

Remember. w/m Irving Berlin, 1925. Another phenomenal ballad success for Berlin in this period. Originally copyrighted as "You Forgot to Remember." In films it was sung by Alice Faye in (MM) *Alexander's Ragtime Band*, 1938; Grace Moore in (MM) *So This Is Love*, 1953; the chorus in (MM) *There's No Business Like Show Business*, 1954.

Remember (Christmas). w/m Harry Nilsson, 1973. Introduced by Harry Nilsson in British film (MP) *Son of Dracula*, later retitled *Young Dracula*. Recorded by Nilsson (RCA).

Remember (the First Time). 1989. Hit R&B chart single by Eric Gable (Orpheus).

Remember (Walkin' in the Sand). w/m George F. Morton, 1964. Top 10 record by The Shangri-Las (Red Bird). Revived by Louise Goffin (Asylum), 1979, and the hard-rock band Aerosmith (Columbia), 1980.

Remember Me. w/m Nicholas Ashford and Valerie Simpson, 1971. Top 20 record by Diana Ross (Motown).

Remember Me? w. Al Dubin, m. Harry Warren, 1937. Introduced in (MP) *Mr. Dodds Takes the Air* by Kenny Baker. Leading record by Hal Kemp, vocal by Skinnay Ennis (Victor). Ennis again recorded it in the fifties with his own band (Signature). Nominated for Academy Award.

Remember Me (I'm the One Who Loves You). w/m Stuart Hamblen, 1950. Introduced and recorded by Stuart Hamblen (Columbia). Revived by Dean Martin (Reprise), 1965.

Remember Me (When the Candle Lights Are Gleaming). w/m Scott Wiseman, 1946. Popular recording by T. Texas Tyler (4 Star).

Remember Me to Carolina. w. Paul Francis Webster, m. Harry Revel, 1944. Introduced by Benny Fields and Judy Clark in (MM) *Minstrel Man*. Song nominated for Academy Award.

Remember My Forgotten Man. w. Al Dubin, m. Harry Warren, 1933. The stirring finale of (MM) *Gold Diggers of 1933* in which Etta Moten sang a plea for an understanding of veterans of World War I who were unemployed during the Depression. There were flashbacks of soldiers returning from the front juxtaposed with breadlines. Joan Blondell joined in the climax of the number.

Remember Poor Mother at Home. w/m James Thornton, 1890. Thornton's first published song.

Remember What I Told You to Forget. w/m Dennis Lambert and Brian Potter, 1975. Recorded by the group Tavares (Capitol).

Remember You're Mine. w/m Kal Mann and Bernie Lowe, 1957. Top 10 record by Pat Boone (Dot).

Rememb'ring. w/m Vivian and Rosetta Duncan, 1923. Performed by the Duncan Sisters in (TM) *Topsy and Eva*. Recorded by them, accompanied on the piano by Phil Ohman (Victor), and by Paul Ash and his Orchestra (Brunswick), 1924.

Remind Me. w. Dorothy Fields, m. Jerome Kern, 1940. Introduced by Peggy Moran in (MM) *One Night in the Tropics*, in which Abbott and Costello made their film debuts. Kern and Fields wrote the song some years earlier for an unproduced film. Mabel Mercer featured it in supper clubs and later recorded it in her album "Songs by Mabel Mercer" (Atlantic). It then started to receive recognition by other leading singers and musicians.

Reminiscing. w. Edgar Leslie, m. Harry Warren, 1930. Leading recording The California Ramblers with vocal by Arthur Fields (Harmony). Theme song of Joseph Sudy and his Orchestra. Later recording by Charlie Barnet, vocal by Mary Ann McCall (Bluebird), 1940.

Reminiscing in Tempo. m. Edward Kennedy "Duke" Ellington, 1935. Instrumental, introduced by Ellington and his Orchestra.

Remo's Theme (What If). w/m Tommy Shaw and Richie Cannata, 1985. From (MP) *Remo Williams: The Adventure Begins*. Recorded by guitarist Tommy Shaw (A&M).

Rendezvous. w/m Bruce Johnston, Bill Hudson, Brett Hudson, and Mark Hudson, 1975. Recorded by The Hudson Brothers (Rocket).

Rendezvous Time in Paree. w. Al Dubin, m. Jimmy McHugh, 1939. Introduced by Jean Sablon and Yvonne Bouvier in (TM) *Streets of Paris*.

Rendezvous with a Dream. w. Leo Robin, m. Ralph Rainger, 1936. Sung by Rochelle Hudson in (MP) *Poppy*, which starred W. C. Fields.

Renegade. w/m Tommy Shaw, 1979. Recorded by the quintet Styx (A&M).

Repeal the Blues. w. James Dyrenforth, m. John Green, 1934. Recorded by Lee Wiley with Johnny Green's Orchestra (Brunswick).

Repeat After Me. w/m Glenn Tubb, 1968. Top 10 Country chart record by Jack Reno (JAB). Revived by the Canadian group Family Brown (RCA), 1984.

Repeat After Me. w/m Gordon Jenkins, 1956. Introduced in the production of Gordon Jenkins's (TVM) "Manhattan Tower," and LP (Capitol). Single record by Patti Page (Mercury).

Repenting. w/m Gary Walker, 1957. Top 10 C&W record by Kitty Wells (Decca).

Rescue Me. w/m Carl William Smith and Raynard Miner, 1965. #1 R&B and Top 10 Pop chart record by Fontella Bass (Checker). Revived by Al B. Sure! in the album "In Effect Mode" (Warner Bros.), 1988.

Reservations for Two. w/m Tena Clark, Nathan East, and Gary Prim, 1987. R&B crossover chart record by Dionne Warwick and Kashif (Arista).

Respect. w/m Otis Redding, 1967. Introduced and recorded by Otis Redding (Volt), 1965. #1 gold record by Aretha Franklin (Atlantic). Winner, Grammy Award (NARAS) for Rhythm and Blues Song of the Year, 1967.

Respectable. w/m Barbara Baer, Elliot Greenberg, Doug Morris, and Robert Schwartz, 1966. Top 20 record by The Outsiders (Capitol).

Respect Yourself. w/m Luther Ingram and Mack Rice, 1971. Crossover R&B/Pop chart hit by the family gospel group The Staple Singers (Stax). Revived on the R&B charts by Bruce Willis (Motown) and J. Blackfoot (Edge), 1987.

Restless Heart. w/m John Waite, 1985. Recorded by British singer/songwriter John Waite (EMI America).

Restless Heart. w/m Harold Rome, 1954. Introduced by William Tabbert in (TM) *Fanny*.

Rest Your Love on Me. w/m Barry Gibb, 1981. Introduced by the British brother trio, The Bee Gees, on the flip side of their #1 Pop chart hit "Too Much Heaven" (RSO), 1978 (q.v.). Conway Twitty's version went to #1 on the Country charts (MCA), 1981.

Return of the Red Baron, The. w/m Phil Gernhard, James McCullough, and John McCullough, 1967. Sequel to the novelty hit "Snoopy Vs. The Red Baron," (q.v.) Also recorded by The Royal Guardsmen (Laurie).

Return to Me (Ritorna a Me). w/m Carmen Lombardo and Danny Di Minno, 1958. Popular record, sung in English and Italian, by Dean Martin (Capitol).

Return to Paradise. w. Ned Washington, m. Dimitri Tiomkin, 1953. Theme from (MM) *Return to Paradise*. Most popular record: Nat "King" Cole (Capitol). Instrumental versions by the orchestras of Percy Faith (Columbia) and Camarata (Decca).

Return to Sender. w/m Otis Blackwell and Winfield Scott, 1962. Introduced by Elvis Presley in (MM) *Girls! Girls! Girls!* Presley's recording was a million-plus seller (RCA).

Reuben and Cynthia. w. Charles Hoyt, m. Percy Gaunt, 1891. New words and adapted melody of old tune, introduced in (TM) *A Trip to Chinatown*. Sometimes referred to by its opening line, "Reuben, Reuben, I've been thinking . . ."

Reunited. w/m Dino Fekaris and Freddie Perren, 1979. #1 platinum R&B and Pop record by the duo Peaches & Herb (Polydor).

Reveille Rock. m. Ira Mack, Tom King, and I. Conatser, 1959. Rock version of the Army bugle call "Reveille." Instrumental by Johnny and The Hurricanes (Warwick).

Revenge. w/m Brook Benton, Marnie Ewald, and Oliver Hall, 1961. Introduced and recorded by Brook Benton (Mercury).

Revenge. w. Sam M. Lewis and Joe Young, m. Harry Akst, 1928.

Reverend Mr. Black. w/m Billy Edd Wheeler, 1962. Featured and Top 10 record by The Kingston Trio (Capitol).

Revolution. w/m John Lennon and Paul McCartney, 1968. Recorded by The Beatles, coupled with the hit "Hey Jude" (Capitol).

Rhapsody in Blue. m. George Gershwin, 1924. Paul Whiteman commissioned Gershwin to compose a piece for a concert he was presenting, *Experiment in Modern Music*, at Aeolian Hall in New York, on February 12th. The composer, because of the conflict of other assignments, wrote this in a short period of time and called in Ferde Grofé to orchestrate it. It has remained the most significant composition involving jazz in the "serious" form of concert music. Its "slow" theme became the signature of Paul Whiteman's Orchestra. In 1930, the Rhapsody was played in (MM) *The King of Jazz* by Whiteman and his Orchestra, with dancers in the foreground. A small section of the piece was heard in (MM) *The Great Ziegfeld*, 1935. It became the title of the Gershwin story (MM) *Rhapsody in Blue*, 1945, performed by Oscar Levant and, again, Whiteman's Orchestra. It also was played in (MM) *Sincerely Yours*, 1955, this time by Liberace.

Rhapsody in the Rain. w. Lou Christie, m. Twyla Herbert, 1966. Top 20 record by Lou Christie (MGM).

Rhiannon (Will You Ever Win). w/m Stevie Nicks, 1976. Top 20 record by the British group Fleetwood Mac (Reprise).

Rhinestone Cowboy. w/m Larry Weiss, 1975. Introduced by Larry Weiss in his album "Black and Blue Suite" (20th Century), 1974. Recorded by Glen Campbell for the biggest hit of his career (Capitol). His version, a #1 gold record, was on the Pop charts for twenty-three weeks. The film (MP) *Rhinestone*, 1984, was based on the song.

Rhode Island Is Famous for You. w. Howard Dietz, m. Arthur Schwartz, 1948. Introduced by Jack Haley and Estelle Loring in

(TM) *Inside U.S.A.* A single of the song was released from the cast album (RCA Victor).

Rhumba Boogie. w/m Hank Snow, 1951. Top C&W records by Hank Snow (RCA Victor) and Spade Cooley (Decca).

Rhumba Girl. w/m Jesse Winchester, 1979. Recorded by Nicolette Larson (Warner Bros.).

Rhumboogie. w/m Don Raye and Hughie Prince, 1940. Introduced by the Andrews Sisters in their film debut in (MM) *Argentine Nights*. Their recording (Decca) was the bestseller, followed by Ray McKinley with Will Bradley and his Orchestra (Columbia), and piano playing-bandleader Bob Zurke (Victor).

Rhymes Have I. w/m Robert Wright and George Forrest, 1953. Based on music by Alexander Borodin in (TM) *Kismet*, it was introduced by Alfred Drake and Doretta Morrow. Howard Keel sang it in (MM) *Kismet*, 1955.

Rhythm. w/m Curtis Mayfield, 1964. Crossover (R&B/Pop) hit by Major Lance (Okeh).

Rhythm and Romance. w. George Whiting and Nat Burton, m. J. C. Johnson, 1935. Introduced, recorded, and popularized by Fats Waller (Victor).

Rhythm in My Nursery Rhymes. w. Sammy Cahn and Don Raye, m. Jimmie Lunceford and Saul Chaplin, 1935. Introduced and recorded by Jimmie Lunceford and his Orchestra (Decca). Other records of note: Tommy Dorsey's Clambake Seven, vocal by Edythe Wright (Victor); Wingy Manone (Vocalion); Joe Haymes (Melotone); Teddy Wilson (Brunswick).

Rhythm Is Gonna Get You. w/m Gloria Estefan and Enrique Garcia, 1987. Top 10 single by Gloria Estefan and The Miami Sound Machine (Epic).

Rhythm Is Our Business. w. Sammy Cahn, m. Jimmie Lunceford and Saul Chaplin, 1935. While numerous bands had arrangements of this number, it is most associated with Jimmie Lunceford, who introduced it, recorded it (Decca), and used it as one of his theme songs.

Rhythm King. w. Jo Trent, m. J. Russel Robinson, 1928. Robinson composed this under the pseudonym of Joe Hoover. First recorded by Bix Beiderbecke and his Gang (Okeh). Others: Ben Bernie and His Hotel Roosevelt Orchestra, vocal by Ben Bernie and His Speed Boys (Brunswick); and The Coon-Sanders Orchestra, vocal by Carlton Coon (Victor).

Rhythm 'n' Blues (Mama's Got the Rhythm, Papa's Got the Blues). w/m Jules Loman and Buddy Kaye, 1955. Recorded by The McGuire Sisters, coupled with the hit "Something's Gotta Give" (Coral).

Rhythm of Life, The. w. Dorothy Fields, m. Cy Coleman, 1966. Introduced by Harold Pierson, Eddie Gasper, Arnold Soboloff, and chorus in (TM) *Sweet Charity*. Sung by Sammy Davis, Jr., and chorus in (MM) *Sweet Charity*, 1969, and recorded as a single by Davis (Reprise).

Rhythm of Raindrops, The (a.k.a. **Over the Rhythm of Raindrops**). w/m Larry Wagner, Guy Wood, and Jimmy Eaton, 1957. Leading records by the orchestras of Frankie Carle (Victor), Jack Pleis (Decca), Frank Fields (Dot), vocal version by Connie Francis (MGM).

Rhythm of the Night. w/m Diane Warren, 1985. From the Berry Gordy film (MP) *The Last Dragon*. Top 10 single from the album "Rhythm of the Night," by the family group DeBarge (Gordy).

Rhythm of the Rain. w/m John Gummoe, 1963. Hit record by The Valiants (Valiant). Revived by Gary Lewis and The Playboys (Liberty), 1969.

Rhythm of the Rain. w. Jack Meskill, m. Jack Stern, 1935. Introduced by Maurice Chevalier and Ann Sothern in (MM) *Folies Ber-*

gere. Recorded by the bands of the Dorsey Brothers, vocal by Kay Weber (Decca); Abe Lyman (Brunswick); Vincent Rose (Banner).

Rhythm on the River. w. Johnny Burke, m. James V. Monaco, 1940. Introduced by Bing Crosby in (MM) *Rhythm on the River*, and recorded by him (Decca); also by Wingy Manone and his Orchestra (Bluebird).

Rhythm Saved the World. w. Sammy Cahn, m. Saul Chaplin, 1936. Recorded by Bunny Berigan and his Orchestra (Vocalion), coupled with his first version of "I Can't Get Started With You" (q.v.). Other discs of note: Louis Armstrong (Decca); Tommy Dorsey and the Clambake Seven, vocal by Edythe Wright (Victor); The Mills Brothers (Decca); Wingy Manone and his Orchestra (Bluebird).

Ribbon of Darkness. w/m Gordon Lightfoot, 1965. #1 Country chart record by Marty Robbins (Columbia). Connie Smith had a C&W chart version (RCA), 1969.

Ribbons Down My Back. w/m Jerry Herman, 1964. Introduced by Eileen Brennan in (TM) *Hello, Dolly!* Sung by Marianne McAndrew in (MM) *Hello, Dolly!* 1969.

Rice Is Nice. w/m Paul Leka and Shelley Pinz, 1968. Recorded by The Lemon Pipers (Buddah).

Richard's Window. w. Norman Gimbel, m. Charles Fox, 1975. Sung on the soundtrack of (MP) *Other Side of the Mountain* by Olivia Newton-John.

Richest Man, The (in the World). w/m Boudleaux Bryant, 1955. Featured and recorded by Eddy Arnold (RCA).

Rich Girl. w/m Daryl Hall, 1977. #1 gold record by Daryl Hall and John Oates (RCA).

Rickety Rickshaw Man, The. w/m Ervin Drake, 1946. Top 10 record by Eddy Howard, with his Orchestra (Majestic).

Ricochet (Rick-O-Shay). w/m Larry Coleman, Joe Darion, and Norman Gimbel, 1953.

Million-seller for Teresa Brewer, with Jack Pleis's Orchestra (Decca).

Ride! w/m John Sheldon and David Leon, 1962. Hit record by Dee Dee Sharp (Cameo).

Ride, Cossack, Ride. w. Bob Wright and Chet Forrest, m. Herbert Stothart, 1940. Introduced by Nelson Eddy in (MM) *Balalaika*.

Ride, Ride, Ride. w/m Liz Anderson, 1967. Hit Country/Pop record by Brenda Lee (Decca).

Ride, Tenderfoot, Ride. w. Johnny Mercer, m. Richard A. Whiting, 1938. Introduced by Dick Powell in (MM) *Cowboy from Brooklyn*. Recorded by Powell (Decca) and Dick Todd (Victor). Also by the bands of Eddy Duchin (Brunswick), Freddy Martin (Bluebird), Orrin Tucker (Vocalion), Guy Lombardo (Victor).

Ride Away. w/m Roy Orbison and Bill Dees, 1965. Introduced and recorded by Roy Orbison (MGM).

Ride 'Em Cowboy. w/m Paul Davis, 1974. Recorded by Paul Davis (Bang).

Ride Like the Wind. w/m Christopher Geppert [Cross], 1980. Top 10 record by Christopher Cross, vocal backing by Michael McDonald (Warner Bros.).

Ride On, Ride On. w. Henry Hart Milman, m. John Prindle Scott, 1918. Recorded by June Richmond with Andy Kirk's Orchestra in 1943 (Decca).

Riders in the Sky (a Cowboy Legend) (a.k.a. Ghost Riders in the Sky). w/m Stan Jones, 1949. Original recording by Burl Ives (Decca). #1 record in plays and sales by Vaughn Monroe, with his Orchestra (RCA Victor). Other hit records by Peggy Lee (Capitol) and Bing Crosby (Decca). Chart revivals by The Ramrods (Bell), 1961; The Baja Marimba Band (A&M), 1966; The Outlaws (Arista), 1981.

Riders on the Storm. w/m John Densmore, Robbie Krieger, Ray Manzarek, and Jim Morrison, 1971. Written and Top 20 record by The Doors (Elektra).

Ride Your Pony. w/m Naomi Neville, 1965. Recorded by Lee Dorsey (Amy).

Ridin' Around in the Rain. w/m Gene Austin and Carmen Lombardo, 1934. Best-selling records by Bing Crosby (Brunswick); the bands of Glen Gray, vocal by Pee Wee Hunt (Brunswick); Earl Burtnett (Columbia); Isham Jones, vocal by Eddie Stone (Victor); Vincent Lopez (Bluebird).

Ridin' High. w/m Cole Porter, 1936. Introduced by Ethel Merman in (TM) *Red, Hot and Blue!*

Ridin' My Thumb to Mexico. w/m Johnny Rodriguez, 1973. Recorded by Johnny Rodriguez (Mercury).

Riff Song, The (Ho!). w. Otto Harbach and Oscar Hammerstein II, m. Sigmund Romberg, 1926. Sung by Robert Halliday and William O'Neal in (TM) *The Desert Song*. The first film version (MM) *The Desert Song*, 1929, had John Boles and chorus doing the song. In the 1943 remake, it was sung by Dennis Morgan, and in the 1953 remake sung by Gordon MacRae.

Rigamarole. m. Harold Mooney, 1936. Published as a piano solo, then became a swing band instrumental introduced by Ozzie Nelson and his Orchestra. First record by Willie Bryant (Victor) in 1935. Jimmy Dorsey had a popular record (Decca) in 1939. One of two successful instrumentals by Mooney this year. See also "Swamp Fire."

Right as the Rain. w. E. Y. Harburg, m. Harold Arlen, 1944. Introduced by Celeste Holm and David Brooks in (TM) *Bloomer Girl*, and recorded by them on a single (Decca).

Right Back Where We Started From. w/m Vincent Edwards and Pierre Tubbs, 1976. Top 10 gold record by the English singer Maxine Nightingale (United Artists).

Right Down the Line. w/m Gerry Rafferty, 1978. Recorded by the Scottish singer/songwriter Gerry Rafferty (United Artists).

Right From the Start. w/m Earl Thomas Conley, 1987. #1 Country chart by Earl Thomas Conley (RCA).

Right Girl, The. w/m Stephen Sondheim, 1971. Introduced by Gene Nelson in (TM) *Follies*.

Right Girl for Me, The. w. Betty Comden and Adolph Green, m. Roger Edens, 1949. Introduced by Frank Sinatra in (MM) *Take Me Out to the Ball Game*. Recorded by Sammy Kaye, vocal by Tony Alamo (RCA Victor).

Right Hand Man. w/m Gary Scruggs, 1987. Top 10 Country chart single and title song of album by Eddy Raven (RCA).

Right Here Waiting. w/m Richard Marx, 1989. Hit record by Richard Marx (EMI).

Right Next Door (Because of Me). w/m Dennis Walker, 1987. Chart single from the album "Strong Persuader" by The Robert Cray Band (Mercury).

Right on Track. w/m Steve Bray and Steve Gilroy, 1987. Top 10 chart record by The Breakfast Club (MCA).

Right or Wrong. w/m Wanda Jackson, 1961. Introduced and recorded by Wanda Jackson (Capitol). Popular version by Ronnie Dove (Diamond), 1964.

Right Place, Wrong Time. w/m Mac Rebennack, 1973. Recorded by the writer under the name of Dr. John (Atco).

Right Somebody to Love, The. w. Jack Yellen, m. Lew Pollack, 1936. Introduced by Shirley Temple in (MM) *Captain January*.

Right Thing to Do, The. w/m Carly Simon, 1973. Top 20 record by Carly Simon (Elektra).

Right Time, The. w/m Ozzie Cadena and Lew Herman, 1959. Top 10 R&B record by Ray Charles (Atlantic).

Right Time of the Night. w/m Peter McCann, 1977. Top 10 record by Jennifer Warnes (Arista).

Rikki Don't Lose That Number. w/m Walter Becker and Donald Fagen, 1974. Top 10 record by Fagen and Becker's studio group Steeley Dan (ABC).

Ring-a-Ling-a-Lario. w/m Gerry Grant, Arthur Kent, and Joe Reisman, 1959. Recorded by Jimmie Rodgers, with Joe Reisman's Orchestra (Roulette).

Ring Dang Doo. w/m Joy Byers and Robert F. Tubert, 1965. Chart record by Sam the Sham and The Pharaohs (MGM).

Ring Dem Bells. w/m Edward Kennedy "Duke" Ellington and Irving Mills, 1930. Ellington and his Orchestra performed the number in the Amos 'n' Andy film (MM) *Check and Double Check*. He then recorded it (Victor) coupled with "Three Little Words," (q.v.) the hit song from the movie.

Ring My Bell. w/m Frederick Knight, 1979. #1 R&B and Pop chart record by Anita Ward, written, produced, all percussion instruments and male backup vocals by Frederick Knight (Juana).

Ringo. w. Hal Blair and Don Robertson, m. Don Robertson, 1964. Hit record spoken by Lorne Green (RCA).

Ring of Fire. w/m June Carter and Merle Kilgore, 1963. Crossover (C&W/Pop) hit by Johnny Cash (Columbia).

Ring on Her Finger, Time on Her Hands. w/m Don Goodman, Mary Ann Kennedy, and Pam Rose, 1982. Country chart hit by Lee Greenwood (MCA).

Ring on the Finger Is Worth Two on the Phone, A w. Jack Mahoney, m. George W. Meyer, 1911.

Ringo's Theme (This Boy). w/m John Lennon and Paul McCartney, 1964. From (MM) *A Hard Day's Night*, starring The Beatles. Instrumental recording by George Martin and his Orchestra (United Artists).

Rings. w/m Alex Harvey and Eddie Reeves, 1971. Top 20 record by the trio Cymarron (Entrance). Other chart versions by Lobo

(Big Three) and Reuben Howell (Motown), 1974.

Rings of Gold. w/m Gene Edward Thomasson, 1969. Hit Country record by Dottie West and Don Gibson (RCA).

Rings On My Fingers. See **I've Got Rings On My Fingers.**

Ring the Living Bell. w/m Melanie Safka, 1972. Recorded by Melanie (Neighborhood).

Rinky Dink. m. Paul Winley and David Clowney, 1962. Instrumental hit by organist Dave "Baby" Cortez (Chess).

Rio. w/m Duran Duran, 1983. Recorded by the English group Duran Duran (Capitol).

Rio Bravo. w. Paul Francis Webster, m. Dimitri Tiomkin, 1959. Title song of (MP) *Rio Bravo*, sung by Dean Martin.

Rio De Janeiro. w. Ned Washington (Engl.), m. Ary Barroso, 1944. Original Portuguese words by Barroso. Introduced in (MM) *Brazil*, and nominated for an Academy Award.

Rio Rita. w. Joseph McCarthy, m. Harry Tierney, 1927. The title and hit song from (TM) *Rio Rita* was sung as a duet by J. Harold Murray and Ethelind Terry. In the first film adaptation (MM) *Rio Rita*, 1929, it was sung by John Boles and in the 1943 remake, by John Carroll.

Rip It Up. w/m John Marascalco and Robert A. Blackwell, 1956. #1 R&B and high Pop chart record by Little Richard (Specialty). Bill Haley and his Comets also had a popular version (Decca). It was heard in (MM) *Elvis* in 1979.

Rip Off. 1972. Crossover (R&B/Pop) hit record by soul singer Laura Lee (Hot Wax).

Riptide. w. Gus Kahn, m. Walter Donaldson, 1934. Promotional song for (MP) *Riptide*, starring Norma Shearer, Herbert Marshall, and Robert Montgomery. Recordings: The Pickens Sisters (Victor); the bands of Vincent Lopez (Brunswick), Benny Kruger (Columbia), Guy Lombardo (Melotone), Nye Mayhew (Vo-

calion), Eddy Duchin (Victor). Revived by Robert Palmer in his album "Riptide" (Island), 1985.

Rip Van Winkle Was a Lucky Man. w. William Jerome, m. Jean Schwartz, 1901. Introduced by Harry Bolger in (TM) *The Sleeping Beauty and the Beast.*

Rise. m. Andy Armer and Randy Badazz, 1979. #1 gold record instrumental by Herb Alpert (A&M). The record's popularity was enhanced by its use on the daytime serial (TVP) "General Hospital."

Rise 'n' Shine. w. B. G. DeSylva, m. Vincent Youmans, 1932. Introduced by Ethel Merman in (TM) *Take A Chance*. It was sung by Lillian Roth in the film version (MM) *Take A Chance* in 1933. Paul Whiteman and his Orchestra had a popular recording (Victor). The song has long been a favorite "opener" for nightclub acts and with tap dancers, acrobats, and jugglers.

River, Stay 'Way from My Door. w. Mort Dixon, m. Harry Woods, 1931. Featured and recorded by Kate Smith (Velvetone), Phil Harris (Victor), Art Jarrett with vocal with Jimmie Noone's band (Brunswick), Paul Robeson (Victor), Singin' Sam, the Barbasol Man (Conqueror), Erno Rapee and his Orchestra (Hit of the Week). The song received additional popularity with the pantomime performance of Jimmy Savo in his one-man revue "Mum's the Word." Savo made it a highlight of his vaudeville and nightclub act.

River, The. w/m Bruce Springsteen. 1980. Title song of Bruce Springsteen's LP, "The River" (Columbia).

River and Me, The. w. Al Dubin, m. Harry Warren, 1931. Recorded by Duke Ellington (Victor).

River Boat. w/m Bill Anderson, 1960. Hit C&W record by Faron Young (Capitol).

Riverboat Shuffle. m. Hoagy Carmichael and Irving Mills, 1925. This was Carmichael's first success, recorded by the Wolverines, featuring Bix Beiderbecke (Gennett). A publishing contract was signed with a New York publisher (Mills) after the recording had achieved popularity. Recorded in 1938 by Carmichael, backed with "Hong Kong Blues" (q.v.) (Brunswick). Lyrics were later added by Mitchell Parish.

River Deep—Mountain High. w/m Jeff Barry, Ellie Greenwich, and Phil Spector, 1966. Introduced on records by Ike and Tina Turner (Philles). Other chart records by the British group Deep Purple (Tetragrammaton), 1969; The Supremes and The Four Tops (Motown), 1970. Performed by Darlene Love in (TP) *Leader of the Pack*, 1985.

River in the Rain. w/m Roger Miller, 1985. Introduced by Daniel Jenkins and Ron Richardson in (TM) *Big River*.

River Is Wide, The. w/m Gary Knight and Billy Joe Admire, 1967. Recorded by the trio Forum (Mira) and The Grass Roots (Dunhill), 1969.

River Kwai March. w/m Malcolm Arnold, 1958. Based on "Colonel Bogey," a march from World War I, this was featured in (MP) *The Bridge on the River Kwai*. Mitch Miller and his Orchestra had a hit record (Columbia). See also "Colonel Bogey."

River of No Return. w. Ken Darby, m. Lionel Newman, 1954. Introduced by Marilyn Monroe and Tennessee Ernie Ford in (MP) *River of No Return*. Monroe (RCA Victor) and Ford (Capitol) recorded it individually.

River Seine, The (a.k.a. **La Seine.**) w. Allan Roberts and Alan Holt (Engl.), m. Guy La Farge, 1949. French song popularized in U.S. by Johnny Desmond (Coral) and Guy Lombardo and his Orchestra (Decca).

Rivers of Babylon. w/m Frank Farian, G. Reyam, B. Dowe, and F. McNaughton, 1978. Recorded by the West Indian vocal group, Boney M, in Germany (Sire).

River Song. w/m Richard M. Sherman and Robert B. Sherman, 1973. Musical theme of the film (MM) *Tom Sawyer*, sung on the soundtrack by Charley Pride.

Riviera, The. w. Joseph Allan McCarthy, m. Cy Coleman, 1956. Written for and recorded by Mabel Mercer (Atlantic). Also featured and recorded by Bobby Short (Atlantic).

Roadhouse Blues. w/m John Densmore, Robby Krieger, Ray Manzarek, and Jim Morrison, 1970. Recorded by the Doors, of which the writers were the members (Elektra).

Road Runner. w/m Eugene McDaniels, 1960. Introduced by Bo Diddley (Checker). Revived by The Gants (Liberty), 1965.

Road to Hong Kong, The. w. Sammy Cahn, m. James Van Heusen, 1962. Introduced by Bob Hope and Bing Crosby in the last of their "road" films (MM) *The Road to Hong Kong*.

Road to Morocco. w. Johnny Burke, m. James Van Heusen, 1942. Introduced by Bing Crosby and Bob Hope in (MM) *Road to Morocco*. They had a popular record three years later (Decca).

Road to Paradise, The. w. Rida Johnson Young, m. Sigmund Romberg, 1917. Peggy Wood and Charles Purcell introduced it in (TM) *Maytime*. In the 1937 film version (MM) *Maytime*, it was sung by Jeanette MacDonald and Nelson Eddy. Vic Damone sang it in Romberg's film biography (MM) *Deep in My Heart* in 1954.

Road You Didn't Take, The. w/m Stephen Sondheim, 1971. Introduced by John McMartin in (TM) *Company*.

Roamin' in the Gloamin'. w/m Harry Lauder, 1911. Introduced, popularized, and recorded by Harry Lauder, the eminent Scottish performer (Victor).

Robbers' March, The. m. Frederic Norton, 1917. From (TM) *Chu Chin Chow*.

Robbin' the Cradle. w/m Anthony J. Bellusci, 1959. Chart record by Tony Bellus, the writer of the song (NRC).

Robbins Nest. m. Sir Charles Thompson and Illinois Jacquet, 1947. Dedicated to New York disc jockey Fred Robbins. First record by Illinois Jacquet and his Orchestra (Apollo).

Co-composer Thompson was pianist with band. Among other recordings: Count Basie and his Orchestra (Columbia), Claude Thornhill and his Orchestra (Columbia), Errol Garner (Columbia), Oscar Peterson (Mercury). For song version, see "Just When We're Falling in Love."

Robin Hood. w/m Louis Prima and Bob Miketta, 1944. Recorded by the bands of Louis Prima (Hit), Les Brown (Columbia), Glen Gray and the Casa Loma Orchestra (Decca), Jimmy Palmer (Mercury).

Robins and Roses. w. Edgar Leslie, m. Joe Burke, 1936. Introduced, featured, and recorded by Bing Crosby (Decca). Other records and airplay enabled this to be on "Your Hit Parade" for eleven weeks. Among those who contributed: Jimmy Dorsey, vocal by Kay Weber (Decca); Tommy Dorsey, vocal by Edythe Wright (Victor); Stuff Smith's Combo featuring Jonah Jones (Vocalion); Dolly Dawn (Bluebird); Orville Knapp and his Orchestra (Brunswick).

Rock-a-Billy. w/m Eddie V. Deane and Woody Harris, 1957. Hit record by Guy Mitchell (Columbia).

Rock-a-Bye Bay. w. Mann Curtis, m. Guy Wood, 1942. Top recordings by Claude Thornhill and his Orchestra (Columbia); Glen Gray and The Case Loma Orchestra (Decca); Ray McKinley and his Orchestra (Decca).

Rock-a-Bye Moon. w/m Howard E. Johnson. 1932. Popular records by George Olsen's Orchestra, vocal by Ethel Shutta; Johnny Marvin (Melotone); Donald Novis (Brunswick).

Rock-a-Bye Your Baby with a Dixie Melody. w. Sam M. Lewis and Joe Young, m. Jean Schwartz, 1918, 1956. Introduced by Al Jolson in (TM) *Sinbad* at the Winter Garden where it was an immediate hit, as was his recording (Victor). It became a staple of his repertoire. He also sang it in (MM) *Rose of Washington Square*, 1939; (MM) *The Jolson Story*, 1946; and (MM) *Jolson Sings Again*, 1949. In the latter two, he dubbed in his voice

on the soundtrack for Larry Parks who portrayed Jolson on the screen. It was also heard in (MM) *The Show of Shows*, 1929, and (MM) *The Merry Monahans*, 1944. In 1956, Jerry Lewis, with Jack Pleis's Orchestra, had a hit record that was on the charts for over three months (Decca).

Rock-a-Hula Baby. w/m Fred Wise, Ben Weisman, and Dolores Fuller, 1962. Introduced by Elvis Presley in (MM) *Blue Hawaii* and on records (RCA).

Rock and Roll. w. Sidney Clare, m. Richard A. Whiting, 1934. The title refers to the setting, rather than presaging a style of music to become popular twenty years later. It was introduced in (MM) *Transatlantic Merry-Go-Round* by the Boswell Sisters who also recorded it (Brunswick).

Rock and Roll, Hoochie Koo. w/m Rick Derringer, 1974. Leading record by Rick Derringer (Blue Sky). First recorded by Johnny Winter (Columbia) and Edgar Winter (Epic).

Rock and Roll All Nite. w/m Stanley Eisen and Gene Simmons, 1976. First recorded in a studio session by the rock band Kiss (Casablanca). That single reached the "Top 100" and remained on the charts for six weeks. Later in the same year, a "live" recording from a concert appearance was released and reached the Top 20 and remained on the charts for fourteen weeks.

Rock and Roll Girls. w/m John Fogerty, 1985. Chart single by John Fogerty, coupled with title song from his album, "Center Field" (Warner Bros.).

Rock and Roll Heaven. w/m John Stevenson and Alan O'Day, 1974. Top 10 record by The Righteous Brothers (Haven).

Rock and Roll Is Here to Stay. w/m David White, 1958. Recorded by Danny and The Juniors, with Freddy Cannon (ABC-Paramount).

Rock and Roll Lullaby. w/m Barry Mann and Cynthia Weil, 1972. Top 20 record by B.

J. Thomas, featuring Duane Eddy on guitar (Scepter).

Rock and Roll Music. w/m Chuck Berry, 1957. Hit record by Chuck Berry (Chess). Revived by The Beach Boys (Brother), 1976.

Rock and Roll Never Forgets. w/m Bob Seger, 1977. Recorded by Bob Seger (Capitol).

Rock and Roll Part 2. m. Gary Glitter and Mike Leander, 1972. Top 10 U.S. instrumental recorded in England by Gary Glitter (Bell).

Rock and Roll Waltz, The. w. Roy Alfred, m. Shorty Allen, 1956. #1 record by Kay Starr (RCA).

Rock and Rye Polka. w/m Tex Ritter, Frank Harford, and Edyth Bergdahl, 1948. Hit C&W chart record by Tex Ritter (Capitol).

Rock and Rye Rag. w/m Al Dexter, 1948. C&W chart record by Al Dexter (Columbia).

Rock Around the Clock (We're Gonna). w/m Max Freedman and Jimmy De Knight, 1955. De Knight is a pseudonym for the publisher, James E. Myers. First released by Bill Haley and His Comets (Decca), 1954. When re-released and played under the credits on the soundtrack of (MP) *The Blackboard Jungle*, it emerged as the first major rock and roll hit, eventually selling over twenty-five million records in over thirty languages throughout the world. The Haley Band played it in (MM) *Rock Around the Clock*, 1956, and in (MM) *Don't Knock the Rock*, 1957. Song heard in (MP) *American Graffiti*, 1973, and (MP) *Superman*, 1978.

Rockaway. w/m Howard Johnson, Alex Rogers, and C. Luckeyth (Luckey) Roberts, 1917.

Rockaway Beach. w/m Douglas Colvin, John Cummings, Thomas Erdelyi, and Jeff Hyman, 1978. Recorded by The Ramones (Sire).

Rocket "88." w/m Jackie Brenston, 1951. #1 R&B record by Jackie Brenston (Chess).

Rocket Man. w/m Elton John and Bernie Taupin, 1972. Top 10 record by the British singer/writer Elton John (Uni).

Rocket 2 U. w/m Bobby Nunn, 1988. Top 10 R&B/Pop chart single from the album "Magic," by the family band, The Jets (MCA).

Rockford Files, The. m. Peter Carpenter and Mike Post, 1975. Theme of the series (TVP) "The Rockford Files." Top 10 instrumental record by Mike Post (MGM).

Rockhouse. m. Ray Charles, 1958. Two-sided instrumental recorded by Ray Charles (Atlantic).

Rockin' All Over the World. w/m John Fogerty, 1975. Recorded by John Fogerty (Asylum).

Rockin' Blues. w/m Johnny Otis, 1951. Hit R&B chart record by The Johnny Otis Orchestra, vocal by Mel Walker (Savoy).

Rockin' Chair. w/m Willie Clark and Clarence Reid, 1975. Top 10 record by Gwen McCrae, vocally backedup by George McCrae (Cat).

Rockin' Chair. w/m Hoagy Carmichael, 1930. Introduced by Mildred Bailey (Victor) and re-recorded by her (Vocalion, Decca [twice]), including her LP titled "The Rockin' Chair Lady." It was also her theme song. In 1930, Carmichael recorded it (Victor) with band featuring Bix Beiderbecke, Benny and Harry Goodman, Eddie Lang, Joe Venuti, and Gene Krupa. Among other top recordings: Louis Armstrong's All-stars (Victor); Red Nichols (Brunswick); Gene Krupa's Orchestra (Okeh); Roy Eldridge (Decca); Jack Teagarden (Commodore 12″); Larry Clinton (Victor); Duke Ellington (Brunswick); Paul Robeson (Victor); Lee Sims, piano solo (Brunswick).

Rockin' Good Way (to Mess Around and Fall in Love), A. w/m Brook Benton, Clyde Otis, and Gladyces De Jesus, 1960. Top 10 hit by Dinah Washington and Brook Benton (Mercury).

Rockin' in Rhythm. m. Edward Kennedy "Duke" Ellington and Irving Mills, 1931. Instrumental recorded by Ellington (Brunswick).

Rockin' Pneumonia and the Boogie Woogie Flu. w/m Huey Smith and John Vincent, 1957, 1972. Introduced by Huey Smith and The Clowns (Ace). Johnny Rivers had a gold record (United Artists), 1972.

Rockin' Robin. w/m Jimmie Thomas. 1958, 1972. Hit record by Bobby Day (Class). Revived by thirteen-year-old Michael Jackson with a Top 10 record in 1972 (Motown).

Rockin' Roll Baby. w/m Linda Creed and Thom Bell, 1973. Top 20 record by The Stylistics (Avco).

Rockin' Soul. w/m Waldo Holmes, Bruno Pallini, and Lorenzo Raggi, 1974. Top 20 successor to the hit "Rock the Boat" (q.v.) by The Hues Corporation (RCA).

Rockin' With the Rhythm of the Rain. w/m Don Schlitz and Brent Maher, 1986. #1 Country chart hit by the mother/daughter duo The Judds (RCA).

Rock Island Line. w/m Lonnie Donegan, 1956. Traditional American folk song, formerly associated with Huddie Ledbetter (Leadbelly). Lonnie Donegan and His Skiffle Group recorded their version in England, which became a hit there and in the U.S. (London). Don Cornell had a chart record (Coral). Johnny Cash's 1956 recording was released in 1970 (Sun).

Rockit. w/m Herbie Hancock, Bill Laswell, and Michael Beinhorn, 1983. Popular instrumental by jazz keyboardist Herbie Hancock (Columbia).

Rock It for Me. w/m Kay Werner and Sue Werner, 1937. First recording by Teddy Grace (Decca), although it was introduced by Chick Webb, with vocal by Ella Fitzgerald, who recorded it (Decca) a year later. Others: Hot Lips Page (Bluebird) and Jimmie Lunceford (Columbia) with their bands.

Rock Lobster. w/m Fred Schneider and Ricky Wilson, 1980. Novelty by the quintet The B-52's (Warner Bros.).

Rock Love. w/m Henry Glover, 1955. Top 20 record by The Fontane Sisters, with Billy Vaughn's Orchestra (Dot).

Rock Me. w/m John Kay, 1968. Introduced in (MP) *Candy*. Top 10 record by the quintet Steppenwolf, of which the writer was a member (Dunhill).

Rock Me All Night Long. w/m Jimmy Ricks and Bill Sanford, 1952. Top 10 R&B record by The Ravens (Mercury).

Rock Me Amadeus. w/m Rob Bolland, Ferdi Bolland, and Falco, 1986. International hit by the Austrian singer/songwriter Falco (né Johann Holzel). Its U.S. release became a #1 chart record (A&M).

Rock Me Gently. w/m Andy Kim, 1974. #1 gold record by Andy Kim (Capitol). The release was coupled with an instrumental version of the song.

Rock Me on the Water. w/m Jackson Browne, 1972. Recorded by Jackson Browne (Asylum), and Linda Ronstadt (Capitol).

Rock Me Tonight (for Old Times Sake). w/m Paul Laurence, 1985. #1 chart crossover record by Freddie Jackson (Capitol).

Rock Me Tonite. w/m Billy Squier, 1984. Recorded by Billy Squier (Capitol).

Rock'n Me. w/m Steve Miller, 1976. A #1 single from the Album "Fly Like an Eagle," by Steve Miller (Capitol).

Rock 'n' Roll (I Gave You the Best Years of My Life). w/m Kevin Johnson, 1973. Introduced by the Australian singer/writer Kevin Johnson (Mainstream). Top 20 version by Mac Davis (Columbia), 1975.

Rock 'n' Roll Fantasy. w/m Paul Rodgers, 1979. Recorded by the British group Bad Company (Swan Song).

Rock 'n' Roll Fantasy, A. w/m Ray Davies, 1978. Introduced and chart record by the British group, The Kinks, of which the writer was lead singer (Arista).

Rock 'n' Roll Is King. w/m Jeff Lynne, 1983. Recorded by the trio, ELO, an off-shoot of The Electric Light Orchestra (Jet).

Rock 'n' Roll Woman. w/m Stephen Stills, 1967. Recorded by the group, Buffalo Springfield, of which Stills was a member (Atco).

Rock of Ages. w/m Steve Clark, Robert John Lange, and Joe Elliott, 1983. Recorded by the English quintet Def Leppard (Mercury).

Rock of Gibraltar, The. w/m Terry Gilkyson, 1952. Popularized and recorded by Frankie Laine, with Jimmy Carroll's Orchestra (Mercury).

Rock of Rages. w/m Ellie Greenwich and Jeff Kent, 1985. Introduced by Dinah Manoff in (TM) *Leader of the Pack.*

Rock On. w/m David Essex, 1974. Gold record by the English actor/singer/writer David Essex (Columbia).

Rock Steady. w/m L. A. Reid, Babyface, and B. Watson, 1987. #1 R&B and Top 10 Pop chart record by The Whispers (Solar).

Rock Steady. w/m Aretha Franklin, 1971. Top 10 record by Aretha Franklin (Atlantic).

Rock the Boat. w/m Waldo Holmes, 1974. #1 gold record by The Hues Corporation (RCA).

Rock the Casbah. w/m Topper Headon, Mick Jones, Paul Simon, and Joe Strummer, 1982. Top 10 by the British quartet The Clash (Epic).

Rock This Town. w/m Brian Setzer, 1982. Top 10 record by the trio Stray Cats (EMI America).

Rock with Me. w/m Curtis Mayfield, 1976. Introduced by Irene Cara and Lonette McKee in (MM) *Sparkle.*

Rock with You. w/m Rod Temperton, 1980. #1 gold record single from the

1979 album "Off The Wall," by Michael Jackson, produced by Quincy Jones (Epic).

Rocky. w/m Jay Stevens, 1975. Top 10 record by Austin Roberts (Private Stock).

Rocky Mountain High. w/m John Denver and Michael Taylor, 1972. Top 10 record by John Denver (RCA).

Rocky Mountain Way. w/m Joe Walsh, Roche Grace, Kenny Passarelli, and Joey Vitale, 1973. Recorded by Joe Walsh (Dunhill).

Rock You Like a Hurricane. w/m Klaus Meine, Herman Rarebell, and Rudolf Schenker, 1984. Recorded by the German quintet The Scorpions (Mercury).

Rock Your Baby. w/m Harry Wayne Casey and Richard Finch, 1974. #1 R&B/Pop chart record by George McCrae (T.K.).

Rock Your Little Baby to Sleep. w/m Buddy Knox, 1957. Top 40 record by Buddy Knox (Roulette).

Rocky Raccoon. w/m John Lennon and Paul McCartney, 1969. Popular cut from The Beatle's two-disc album, often referred to as the "White Album" a.k.a. "The Beatles" (Apple).

Rocky Road Blues. w/m Bill Monroe, 1946. Featured and recorded by Bill Monroe and The Blue Grass Boys (Columbia).

Rodger Young. w/m (Private) Frank Loesser, 1945. Loesser wrote this while serving in the U.S. Army and dedicated it to Private Rodger Young, an infantryman who was killed at Guadalcanal in the Solomon Islands and posthumously awarded the Medal of Honor. It was introduced on radio by Earl Wrightson, and recorded by Burl Ives (Decca) and noted baritone John Charles Thomas (Victor).

Rogue Song, The. w. Clifford Grey, m. Herbert Stothart, 1930. Sung by Lawrence Tibbett in his film debut in (MM) *The Rogue Song.* He also recorded it (Victor).

Rolene. w/m Moon Martin, 1979. Recorded by Moon Martin (Capitol).

Roll Along, Covered Wagon. w/m Jimmy Kennedy, 1935.

Roll Along, Prairie Moon. w/m Albert Von Tilzer, Harry McPherson, and Ted Fio Rito, 1935. Introduced by Harry Stockwell in (MM) *Here Comes the Band*. Among recordings: Al Bowlly (Victor); the bands of Smith Ballew (Melotone) and Henry "Red" Allen (Vocalion). This was Von Tilzer's last song success.

Roll Along Kentucky Moon. w/m Bill Halley (William H. Heagney), 1932. Featured and recorded by Singin' Sam, the Barbasol Man (Oriole).

Roll Dem Roly Boly Eyes. w/m Eddie Leonard, 1912. Featured by Leonard in his vaudeville minstrel shows. He also performed it in (MM) *Melody Lane*, 1929.

Roll 'Em. m. Mary Lou Williams, 1937. The jazz pianist and composer, Mary Lou Williams, arranged her instrumental for Benny Goodman's Band, which had the best-selling record (Victor). Williams later recorded it on a 12″ record (Asch).

Roll 'Em Girls, Roll Your Own. w/m Archie Fletcher and Bobby Heath, 1925. Recorded by Jack Shilkret (Victor) and Paul Specht (Columbia).

Roll 'Em Pete. w/m Pete Johnson and Joe Turner, 1941. Johnson, playing boogie-woogie piano, and Turner, blues singing, performed this number together for many years before recording it (Vocalion). Count Basie and his Band also recorded their version (Clef).

Rollin' Down the River. w. Stanley Adams, m. Thomas "Fats" Waller, 1930. This was Adams's first successful song, written for a Connie's Inn revue. Gene Austin (Victor) and Tom Gerun and his Band recorded it (Victor).

Rolling Stones. w. Edgar Leslie, m. Archie Gottler, 1916. Popular recording by the American Quartette (Victor).

Rollin' in My Sweet Baby's Arms. w/m Buck Owens, 1971. Hit Country record by Buck Owens (Capitol).

Rollin' Plains. w/m Walter G. Samuels, Leonard Whitcup, and Teddy Powell, 1937. Title song of (MM) *Rollin' Plains*, sung by Tex Ritter. Recorded by Dick Robertson (Decca) and Jimmy Ray (Bluebird).

Rollin' Stone. w/m Robert S. Riley, 1955. Popular record by The Fontane Sisters (Dot).

Rollin' with the Flow. w/m Jerry Hayes, 1977. Country chart hit by Charlie Rich (Epic).

Roll Muddy River. w/m Betty Sue Perry, 1963. Country hit by The Wilburn Brothers (Decca).

Roll On, Mississippi, Roll On. w/m James McCaffrey, Eugene West, and Dave Ringle, 1931. Popular recordings by the Boswell Sisters (Brunswick), Grace Johnston (Melotone), and the bands of Noble Sissle (Brunswick) and Ray Noble (Victor).

Roll On Big Mama. w/m Danny Darst, 1975. Hit Country record by Joe Stampley (Epic).

Roll On Down the Highway. w/m Charles Turner and Randy Bachman, 1975. Top 20 record by the Canadian group Bachman-Turner Overdrive (Mercury).

Roll Over Beethoven. w/m Chuck Berry, 1956. Hit record by Chuck Berry (Chess). In 1964, a Beatles version was released (Capitol of Canada) with moderate success. The Electric Light Orchestra had a bona fide revival in 1973 (United Artists).

Roll Them Cotton Bales. w. James Weldon Johnson, m. J. Rosamond Johnson, 1914.

Roll Up the Carpet. w. Raymond Klages, m. Raymond Klages, Al Goodhart, and Al Hoffman, 1933. Records: Ray Noble, vocal by Al Bowlly (HMV-Victor); and Paul Specht (Columbia).

Roll with It. w. Will Jennings, m. Steve Winwood, 1988. Hit single and album title song by Steve Winwood (Virgin).

Roly Poly. w/m Fred Rose, 1946. Hit record by Bob Wills and his Texas Playboys (Columbia).

Romance. w/m Bill Berry, Pete Buck, Mike Mills, and Michael Stipe, 1987. Performed on the soundtrack and album of (MP) *Made in Heaven* (Elektra).

Romance. w. Edgar Leslie, m. Walter Donaldson, 1929. Sung by J. Harold Murray in (MM) *Cameo Kirby*, a musical remake of the silent film starring John Gilbert. The song was recorded by John Boles (Victor) and was an early recording by the Casa Loma Orchestra (Okeh). Ten years later, it became the theme song of Ray Herbeck's Orchestra.

Romance. w. Otto Harbach and Oscar Hammerstein II, m. Sigmund Romberg, 1926. Introduced by Vivienne Segal in (TM) *The Desert Song*. In the first film version (MM) *The Desert Song*, 1929, it was sung by Carlotta King. In the 1943 version by Irene Manning and in the 1952 remake by Kathryn Grayson.

Romance in the Dark. w/m Lil Green, 1940. Leading record by Lil Green, with Big Bill Broonzy's Band (Bluebird). Other versions by Billie Holiday (Okeh) and Larry Clinton, with vocal by Bea Wain (Victor).

Romance Runs in the Family. w/m Al Goodhart, Al Hoffman, and Manny Kurtz, 1939.

Romancing the Stone. w/m Eddy Grant, 1984. Recorded in Barbados by Eddy Grant (Portrait). Written for the film of the same name but not included.

Romantic Guy, I, A. w/m Del Sharbutt, Richard Uhl, and Frank H. Stanton, 1941. Featured by Lanny Ross on his radio show. It later was used as the theme of the Bob Cummings Show, a popular television series in the mid-fifties.

(Just Like) Romeo and Juliet. w/m Bob Hamilton and Freddy Gorman, 1964. Top 10 record by The Reflections (Golden World). Revived by Sha Na Na (Kama Sutra), 1975.

Romeo Smith and Juliet Jones. w. Johnny Burke, m. James Van Heusen, 1941. Introduced by Kay Kyser and his Orchestra, Ginny Simms, and Harry Babbitt in (MM) *Playmates* and recorded by them (Columbia).

Romeo's Tune. w/m Steve Forbert, 1980. Top 20 record by Steve Forbert (Nemperor).

Roni. w/m Kenneth Edmonds and Darnel Bristol, 1989. Hit R&B chart single by Bobby Brown (MCA).

Ronnie. w/m Bob Crewe and Bob Gaudio, 1964. Hit record by The Four Seasons (Philips).

Ronnie, Call Me When You Get a Chance. w/m Mike Anthony and Ted Cooper, 1963. Recorded by Shelley Fabares (Colpix).

Room Full of Roses. w/m Tim Spencer, 1949. Best-selling records by Sammy Kaye, vocal by Don Cornell (RCA Victor); Eddy Howard, with his Orchestra (Mercury); Dick Haymes, with Sonny Burke's Orchestra (Decca). Revived by Mickey Gilley with a #1 Country chart version (Playboy), 1974.

Room in Your Heart. w/m Frances Long and Sonny James, 1966. Hit Country song. Introduced and best-selling record by Sonny James (Capitol).

Room with a View, A. w. Al Stillman, m. E. A. Swan, 1938. Leading records by Helen Forrest (Bluebird) and Seger Ellis (Brunswick).

Room with a View, A. w/m Noël Coward, 1928. Introduced in the U.S. by the composer in the American production of the hit English revue (TM) *This Year of Grace*. Recorded by Ben Selvin (Columbia). Revived by Tommy Dorsey, vocal by Jack Leonard (Victor), 1939.

Room Without Windows, A. w/m Ervin Drake, 1964. Introduced by Steve Lawrence and Sally Ann Howes in (TM) *What Makes Sammy Run?* Recorded by Steve Lawrence (Columbia).

Roosevelt and Ira Lee (Night of the Moccasin). w/m Tony Joe White, 1969. Recorded by Tony Joe White (Monument).

Roots, Rock, Reggae. w/m Vincent Ford, 1976. Recorded by the Jamaican reggae band Bob Marley and The Wailers (Island).

"Roots" Medley. m. Gerald Fried, 1977. "Motherland" and "Roots Mural Theme" from the series (TVP) "Roots," recorded by Quincy Jones and his Orchestra (A&M).

Roots of My Raising, The. w/m Tommy Collins, 1976. Hit Country chart record by Merle Haggard (Capitol).

Ro-Ro-Rollin' Along. w/m Murray Mencher, Harry Richman, and Billy Moll, 1930. Featured and recorded (Brunswick) by Harry Richman. Also recorded by songwriter Sammy Fain (Harmony), and Meyer Davis and his Orchestra (Brunswick).

Rosalie. w/m Judy Henske and Craig Doerge, 1974. Recorded by Sam Neely (Capitol).

Rosalie. w/m Cole Porter, 1937. Introduced by Nelson Eddy in (MM) *Rosalie.* This became a #1 hit, despite the fact that Porter had written five previous versions of the title tune that had proved unsatisfactory to producer Sam Goldwyn. Porter then wrote what he considered a "cliche-filled, typical Tin Pan alley hack song." To his surprise, it was accepted by the producer and became a big hit with the public.

Rosalita. w/m Al Dexter, 1943. Introduced and recorded by Al Dexter and his Troopers (Okeh).

Rosanna. w/m David Paich, 1982. Top 10 record by the group Toto (Columbia). Winner, Grammy Award (NARAS) Record of the Year.

Rosanna's Going Wild. w/m Anita Carter, Helen Carter, and June Carter, 1968. C&W/Pop chart record by Johnny Cash (Columbia).

Rosanne. w/m Dick Manning, Glenn Osser, and Edna Osser, 1952. Popular record by Vic Damone, with Norman Leyden's Orchestra (Mercury).

Rosary, The. w. Robert Cameron Rogers, m. Ethelbert Nevin, 1898. A concert song that became a popular favorite. Among the many recordings: Henry Burr (Columbia), William H. Thompson (Edison), Alan Turner (Victor), Ernestine Schumann-Heink (Victor), John McCormack (Victor).

Rose, Rose, I Love You. w. Wilfred Thomas, m. arr. by Chris Langdon, 1951. Based on a traditional Chinese melody, the leading recordings were by Frankie Laine, with Mitch Miller's Orchestra (Columbia); Buddy Morrow and his Orchestra (RCA Victor); Gordon Jenkins, vocal by Cisco Houston (Decca).

Rose, The. w/m Amanda McBroom, 1979. Introduced by Bette Midler in (MM) *The Rose,* and recorded by her for a Top 10 gold record (Atlantic).

Rose and a Baby Ruth, A. w/m John Loudermilk, 1956. First and biggest hit by George Hamilton IV (ABC-Paramount).

Rose and a Prayer, A. w/m Remus Harris, Dan Woodward, and Chester Conn, 1941. Featured and recorded by Charlie Spivak, vocal by Garry Stevens (Okeh).

Rose Ann of Charing Cross. w. Kermit Goell, m. Mabel Wayne, 1942. American song, but most popular recording by British bandleader Peter Piper (Hit).

(I Never Promised You a) Rose Garden. w/m Joe South, 1971. Crossover (C&W/Pop) gold record by Lynn Anderson (Columbia). Title came from Hannah Green's best-selling book of same name.

Rose in Her Hair, The. w. Al Dubin, M. Harry Warren, 1935. Introduced by Dick Powell in (MM) *Broadway Gondolier* and recorded by Powell (Brunswick). Ted Fio Rito, whose band appeared in the film, also recorded it (Brunswick).

Rose in Paradise. w/m Stewart Harris and Jim McBride, 1987. #1 Country chart record by Waylon Jennings, from his album "Hangin' Tough" (MCA).

Rose-Marie. w. Otto Harbach and Oscar Hammerstein II, m. Rudolf Friml, 1924. Introduced by Dennis King and Arthur Deagon in (TM) *Rose-Marie.* In the 1935 (MM) *Rose Marie* (Hollywood dropped the hyphen), it was sung by Nelson Eddy. Howard Keel sang it in the 1954 remake. Slim Whitman had a hit recording that same year (Imperial).

Rosemary. w/m Jimmy Dodd and John Jacob Loeb, 1945. Featured and recorded by Kay Kyser, vocal by Mike Douglas and the Campus Kids (Columbia).

Rose O'Day (The Filla-ga-dusha Song). w/m Charles Tobias and Al Lewis, 1941. Top Ten song in all categories, i.e., sheet music and record sales, radio performances, and juke-box plays. Freddy Martin's recording, vocal by Eddie Stone (Bluebird), was the most played, but Kate Smith's was the best-seller, due to coupling with the big hit, "The White Cliffs of Dover" (q.v.) (Columbia). Woody Herman, vocal by Herman and Carolyn Grey (Decca), and the King Sisters with Alvino Rey's Orchestra (Bluebird) also had chart records.

Rose of No Man's Land, The. w. Jack Caddingan, m. Joseph A. Brennan, 1918. A World War I tribute to the Red Cross nurse. The song was revived in (MP) *The Cockeyed World* starring Victor McLaglen and Edmond Lowe, 1929.

Rose of the Rio Grande. w. Edgar Leslie, m. Harry Warren and Ross Gorman, 1922. This hit was Warren's first published song. Introduced by Paul Whiteman.

Rose of the World. w. Glen MacDonough, m. Victor Herbert, 1908. Introduced by Ida

Brooks in (TM) *Algeria* and sung by her in the 1909 revised and retitled (TM) *The Rose of Algeria.* The song was also heard in (MM) *The Great Victor Herbert* in 1939.

Rose of Washington Square. w. Ballard MacDonald, m. James F. Hanley, 1920. Introduced by Fannie Brice in (TM) *Ziegfeld Midnight Frolic.* Alice Faye sang it in (MM) *Rose of Washington Square*, 1939; Millie Slavin sang it in (TM) *To Broadway with Love*, at the New York World's Fair, 1964; Ann Dee sang it in (MM) *Thoroughly Modern Millie*, 1967.

Rose Room. w. Harry Williams, m. Art Hickman, 1918. Introduced by the Art Hickman Band at the New Amsterdam Roof where (TM) *Ziegfeld Midnight Frolic* was being presented. The song has been heard in (MM) *Ziegfeld Girl*, 1941; (MM) *The Merry Monahans*, 1944; (MM) *The Strip*, 1951; (MM) *Somebody Loves Me*, 1952. It has been recorded by many bands, among them the Joseph C. Smith Orchestra (Victor), Duke Ellington (Brunswick), Jimmy Lunceford (Decca), Fletcher Henderson (Vocalion), Artie Shaw (Bluebird), The Benny Goodman Sextet (Columbia).

Roses. w/m Tim Spencer and Glenn Spencer, 1950. A C&W and Pop hit, introduced by The Sons of the Pioneers. Its most popular recordings were by Sammy Kaye, vocal by The Three Kaydets (RCA Victor); Ray Anthony, vocal by Ronnie Deauville (Capitol); Dick Haymes, with Gordon Jenkins's Orchestra (Decca).

Roses Are Forget-Me-Nots. w/m Al Hoffman, Charles O'Flynn, and Will Osborne, 1930.

Roses Are Red (My Love). w/m Al Byron and Paul Evans, 1962. Million-seller by Bobby Vinton (Epic). See also "Long as the Rose Is Red."

Roses Bring Dreams of You. w/m Herbert Ingraham, 1908.

Roses in December. w/m George Jessel and Ben Oakland, 1937. Introduced by Harriet Hilliard and Gene Raymond in (MM) *Life of the Party*. Hilliard recorded it with Ozzie Nelson's Orchestra (Brunswick).

Roses in the Rain. w. Fred Wise and Al Frisch, m. Frankie Carle, 1947. Introduced and recorded by Frankie Carle and his Orchestra (Columbia).

Roses of Picardy. w. Frederick E. Weatherley, m. Haydn Wood, 1916. Originally a concert song recorded by such singers as John McCormack (Victor), but adapted into other styles by boogie-woogie pianist Albert Ammons and his Rhythm Kings (Mercury), Red Nichols (Brunswick), George Shearing (MGM), and Bobby Darin (Atco).

Roses of Yesterday. w/m Irving Berlin, 1928. Early recordings by Lewis James (Victor), Fred Waring's Pennsylvanians (Victor), and B. A. Rolfe's Orchestra (Edison). Tony Bennett recorded it in the late fifties (Columbia).

Rose Tattoo, The. w. Jack Brooks, m. Harry Warren, 1955. Written as a title song for the film *The Rose Tattoo* but not used. Recorded by Perry Como (RCA).

Rosetta. w/m Earl Hines and Henri Woode, 1933. Earl "Fatha" Hines recorded this (Brunswick) and again in 1935 (Decca). Among the many others to cut this standard were: Henry "Red" Allen (Vocalion), Charlie Shavers (Key 12″), Muggsy Spanier (Commodore), Frankie Newton (Bluebird), Dexter Gordon (Mercury 12″), Benny Goodman (Victor), Teddy Wilson (Columbia), Fats Waller (Victor), Art Tatum (Decca), Jazz at the Philharmonic (Parts 1 & 2, Disc), Bob Wills, The King of Western Swing (Vocalion).

Rosewood Spinet, A. w. Charles Tobias, m. Nat Simon, 1948. Featured and recorded by Eddy Howard, with his Orchestra (Mercury) and by Dinah Shore (Columbia).

Rosie. w. Lee Adams, m. Charles Strouse, 1960. Introduced by Dick Van Dyke and Chita Rivera in (TM) *Bye Bye Birdie*. In (MM) *Bye Bye Birdie*, it was sung by Van Dyke, Janet Leigh, and Bobby Rydell.

Rosie Lee. w/m Jerry Carr, 1957. Chart record by The Mello-Tones (Gee).

Rosie the Riveter. w/m Redd Evans and John Jacob Loeb, 1943. A World War II song describing Rosie's contribution to the war effort. Recorded by The Four Vagabonds (Bluebird). Interpolated in (MM) *Follow the Band* by the King Sisters, with Alvino Rey's Orchestra, 1943. Title song of (MP) *Rosie the Riveter*, 1944.

Rosita, La. w. Allan Stuart, m. Paul Dupont, 1923.

Rough Boys. w/m Pete Townshend, 1980. Recorded by the British singer and songwriter Pete Townshend (Atco).

Roundabout. w/m Jon Anderson and Steve Howe, 1972. Recorded in England by the group, Yes, of which the writers were members (Atlantic).

Roundabout. w. Ogden Nash, m. Vernon Duke, 1952. Originally sung by Dolores Gray in (TM) *Sweet Bye and Bye*, which closed before reaching Broadway, 1946. Ellen Hanley introduced it in New York in the revue (TM) *Two's Company*.

'Round About Midnight. m. Thelonious Monk, 1946. Jazz instrumental featured and recorded by Charlie Parker's group, Tempo Jazzmen (Dial).

Round and Round. w/m Warren DeMartini, Stephen Pearcy, and Robbin Crosby, 1984. Recorded by the quintet Ratt (Elektra).

Round and Round. w/m Lou Stallman and Joe Shapiro, 1956. #1 hit by Perry Como (RCA).

Round Every Corner. w/m Tony Hatch, 1965. English song and recording by Petula Clark (Warner Bros.).

'Round Her Neck She Wears (Wore) a Yellow Ribbon. See **She Wore a Yellow Ribbon.**

Round on the End and High in the Middle (O-Hi-O). w/m Alfred Bryan and Bert Hanlon, 1922. Introduced and featured by Al Jolson.

Round the Old Deserted Farm. w/m Willard Robison, 1936. Recorded by Bunny Berigan, vocal by Ruth Gaylor (Victor).

(Get Your Kicks On) Route 66. w/m Robert Troup, 1946. Big hit for The King Cole Trio (Capitol). Bing Crosby and The Andrews Sisters also had a popular version (Decca).

Route 66 Theme. m. Nelson Riddle, 1962. From the series (TVP) "Route 66." Recorded by Nelson Riddle and his Orchestra (Capitol).

Roving Kind, The. w/m Jessie Cavanaugh and Arnold Stanton, 1950. Adapted from the English folk song known as "The Pirate Ship," "The Rakish Kind," and other titles. Leading records by Guy Mitchell, with Mitch Miller's Orchestra (Columbia); The Weavers, with Leroy Holmes's Orchestra (Decca); Rex Allen, with Lew Douglas's Orchestra (Mercury).

Row, Row, Row. w. William Jerome, m. James V. Monaco, 1912. Introduced in (TM) *Ziegfeld Follies of 1912* by Lillian Lorraine. Ada Jones had a popular recording (Victor) that year. Betty Hutton sang it in (MM) *Incendiary Blonde*, 1944. Eddie Cantor, dubbing for Keefe Brasselle, sang it in (MM) *The Eddie Cantor Story*, 1953; Bob Hope, with a group of children, sang it in (MM) *The Seven Little Foys*, 1955.

Roxanne. w/m Gordon "Sting" Sumner, 1979. Recorded by the English trio Police (A&M).

Roxanne, Roxanne. w/m UTFO, 1985. Recorded by the rap/break trio listing themselves collectively as UTFO and individually as The Kangol Kid, Doctor Ice, and The Educated Rapper (Select).

Royal Garden Blues. w/m Clarence Williams and Spencer Williams, 1921. Standard, multi-recorded jazz composition. Early recordings by The Original Dixieland Jazz Band,

vocal by Al Bernard (Victor); Mamie Smith and Her Jazz Hounds (Okeh). Among the myriad of other versions: Bix Beiderbecke (Okeh), Duke Ellington (Victor), Count Basie (Columbia), Benny Goodman (Columbia).

Rub-a-Dub-Dub. w/m Hank Thompson, 1953. Introduced and featured by Hank Thompson, the C&W star (Capitol). Ralph Flanagan and his Orchestra had a popular version (RCA Victor).

Rubber Ball. w/m Aaron Schroeder and Anne Orlowski, 1960. Hit record by Bobby Vee (Liberty).

Rubberband Man, The. w/m Thom Bell and Linda Creed, 1976. Gold record R&B/Pop chart record by The Spinners (Atlantic).

Rubber Biscuit. w/m Nat Epps, Charles Johnson, Shedrick Lincoln, and Samuel Strain, 1979. Novelty by the Blues Brothers [John Belushi and Dan Aykroyd] (Atlantic).

Rubber Bullets. w/m Loi Creme, Kevin Godley, and Graham Gouldman, 1973. Written and recorded in England by the group 10cc (UK).

Rubber Duckie. w/m Jeffrey Moss, 1970. Introduced by Ernie, the Muppet whose voice was Jim Henson, on (TVM) "Sesame Street." His recording made the Top 20 on the charts (Columbia).

Rubberneckin'. w. Dory Jones, m. Bunny Warren, 1969. Introduced by Elvis Presley in (MP) *Change of Habit*, and coupled with the gold record hit "Don't Cry Daddy" (q.v.) (RCA).

Ruben James. w/m Barry Etris and Alex Harvey, 1969. Top 40 by Kenny Rodgers and The First Edition (Reprise).

Rub It In. w/m Layng Martine, 1974. Introduced and recorded by Layng Martine (Barnaby), 1971. Billy "Crash" Craddock popularized it with a Top 20 record (ABC), 1974.

Ruby. w. Mitchell Parish, m. Heinz Roemheld, 1953. Theme from (MP) *Ruby Gentry*. Leading recordings by harmonicist Richard Hayman and his Orchestra (Mercury); and Less Baxter and his Orchestra, harmonica solo by Danny Welton (Capitol).

Ruby, Don't Take Your Love to Town. w/m Mel Tillis, 1969. Major Country/Pop song with many recordings and performances. Kenny Rodgers and The First Edition had the best-selling version (Reprise).

Ruby, My Dear. m. Thelonious Monk, 1947. Jazz instrumental introduced and recorded by Thelonious Monk (Blue Note).

Ruby and the Pearl, The. w/m Jay Livingston and Ray Evans, 1952. Introduced in (MP) *Thunder in the East*. Popular record by Nat "King" Cole, accompanied by Les Baxter's Orchestra (Capitol).

Ruby Ann. w/m Lee Emerson, 1962. Crossover (C&W/Pop) chart record by Marty Robbins (Columbia).

Ruby Baby. w/m Jerry Leiber and Mike Stoller, 1963. Top 10 record by Dion (Columbia). Revived by Billy "Crash" Craddock (ABC), 1974.

Ruby Duby Du. w. Sunny Skylar, m. Charles Wolcott, 1960. From (MP) *Key Witness*. Leading recordings, instrumentals by guitarist Tobin Matthews and Co. (Chief); and Charles Wolcott (Warner Brothers).

Ruby Tuesday. w/m Mick Jagger and Keith Richards, 1967. #1 gold record by The Rolling Stones, the British group of which the writers were members (London). Chart record by Melanie (Buddah), 1971.

Rudolph the Red-Nosed Reindeer. w/m Johnny Marks, 1949. The recording by Gene Autry, with The Pinafores (Columbia), sold over eight million copies and is listed as the second biggest-selling record during the first half of the 20th century, surpassed only by Bing Crosby's "White Christmas," which sold over thirty million. The song has had sheet music sales of over five million copies and has been translated into dozens of languages.

Rufus Rastus Johnson Brown. See **What You Goin' to Do When the Rent Comes 'Round**?

Rug Cutter's Swing. m. Horace Henderson, 1934. "Rug cutting" referred to dancing in this instrumental that was introduced and recorded by Fletcher Henderson's Band (Decca). Henry "Red" Allen also recorded it (Perfect). Revived by Glenn Miller, with an arrangement by Bill Finegan (Bluebird), 1940.

Rules of the Road, The. w. Carolyn Leigh, m. Cy Coleman, 1963. Introduced and recorded by Tony Bennett (Columbia). Nat "King" Cole also had a popular version (Capitol).

Rum and Coca-Cola. w/m Morey Amsterdam, Paul Baron, and Jeri Sullivan, 1945. As proven in a plagiarism suit, music was adapted from a calypso melody written in Trinidad in 1906. The original owners, publisher Maurice Baron and writers Massie Patterson and Lionel Belasco, received a financial settlement and waived their future writing and publishing credits. The new version, based on calypso lyrics sung in Trinidad during World War II, was popularized by The Andrews Sisters (Decca).

Rumble. m. Sy Oliver, 1958. Top 20 instrumental by guitarist Link Wray and His Ray Men (Cadence). Another chart record by keyboardist/arranger Jack Nitzche (Reprise), 1963.

Rumble, Rumble, Rumble. w/m Frank Loesser, 1947. Introduced by Betty Hutton in (MM) *The Perils of Pauline* and recorded by her (Capitol).

Rumors. w/m Alex Hill, Michael Marshall, and Marcus Thompson, 1986. #1 R&B chart and Top 10 Pop chart record by The California rap group, Timex Social Club, led by Marshall (Jay).

Rumors Are Flying. w/m Bennie Benjamin and George David Weiss, 1946. #1 song, fifteen weeks on "Your Hit Parade." Top recordings by Frankie Carle, vocal by Marjorie

Hughes (Columbia); The Andrews Sisters with Les Paul (Decca).

Run, Baby, Run (Back into My Arms). w/m Joe Melson and Don Gant, 1965. Recorded by The Newbeats (Hickory).

Run, Rabbit, Run. w. Noel Gay and Ralph T. Butler, m. Noel Gay, 1939. Introduced in the London musical (TM) *The Little Dog Laughed.* Featured and recorded in the U.S. by Bob Crosby, vocal by Marion Mann (Decca), and Enoch Light and his Light Parade (Bluebird).

Run, Run, Look and See. w/m Marty Cooper and Ray Whitley, 1966. Recorded by Brian Hyland (Philips).

Run, Runaway. w/m Noddy Holder and Jim Lea, 1984. Recorded by the British quartet Slade (CBS Associated).

Run, Woman, Run. w/m Ann Booth, Duke Goff, and Dan Hoffman, 1970. C&W/Pop crossover by Tammy Wynette (Epic).

Runaround. w/m Cirino Celacrai, 1954. Popular record by The Three Chuckles ("X").

Runaround Sue. w/m Dion Di Mucci and Ernest Maresca, 1961. #1 record by Dion (Laurie). Revived by Leif Garrett (Atlantic), 1977.

Runaway. w/m Jon Bon Jovi and George Karak, 1984. First chart record by the quintet Bon Jovi (Mercury).

Runaway. w/m Nicholas Dewey, 1978. Recorded by the group Jefferson Starship (Grunt).

Runaway. w. Del Shannon, m. Max Crook and Del Shannon, 1961. #1 record by Del Shannon (Big Top). Twenty-five years later, Shannon sang it, with lyric changes, as the opening theme of the series (TVP) "Crime Story." Bonnie Raitt had a chart revival (Warner Bros.), 1977.

Run Away, Little Tears. w/m Dallas Frazier, 1968. Top 10 Country chart record by Connie Smith (RCA).

Run Away Child, Running Wild. w/m Barrett Strong and Norman Whitfield, 1969. Top 10 record by The Temptations (Gordy).

Runaway Train. w/m John Stewart, 1988. #1 Country chart record by Roseanne Cash (Columbia).

Run for the Roses. w/m Dan Fogelberg, 1982. Recorded by Dan Fogelberg (Full Moon).

Run Joe. w/m Walt Herrick, Joe Willoughby, and Louis Jordan, 1947. Popular record by Louis Jordan and his Tympany Five (Decca).

Run Joey Run. w/m Jack Perricone and Paul Vance, 1975. Top 10 record by David Geddes (Big Three).

Runner, The. w/m Ian Thomas, 1984. Recorded by the English group, Manfred Mann's Earth Band (Arista).

Runnin' Away. w/m Sylvester Stewart, 1972. Recorded by Sly & The Family Stone (Epic).

Running Bear. w/m J. P. Richardson, 1959. #1 hit by Johnny Preston, with Indian sounds by The Big Bopper [J. P. Richardson] and George Jones (Mercury). Revived by Sonny James (Capitol), 1969.

Running Between the Raindrops. w. James Dyrenforth, m. Carroll Gibbons, 1931. Popular recordings by Guy Lombardo, vocal by Carmen Lombardo (Columbia); Bert Lown and his Orchestra (Victor); Andy Sannella's Orchestra (Perfect).

Running in the Family. w/m Wally Badarou, Phil Gould, and Mark King, 1987. Recorded by the group, Level 42, as title song of their album (Polydor).

Running on Empty. w/m Jackson Browne, 1978. Top 20 hit by Jackson Browne (Asylum).

Running Scared. w/m Roy Orbison and Joe Melson, 1961. Crossover hit (C&W/Pop) by Roy Orbison (Monument).

Running Through My Mind. w/m Charles Kenny and Nick Kenny, 1939. Records: Jan Savitt, vocal by Phil Brito (Decca); Barry Wood (Vocalion).

Running Up That Hill. w/m Kate Bush, 1985. Recorded by the English singer Kate Bush (EMI America).

Running With the Night. w. Cynthia Weil, m. Lionel Richie, 1983. Recorded by Lionel Richie (Motown).

Runnin' Out of Fools. w/m Richard Ahlert and Kay Rogers, 1964. Featured and recorded by Aretha Franklin (Columbia).

Runnin' Wild! w. Joe Grey and Leo Wood, m. A. Harrington Gibbs, 1922. A hit number recorded by Ted Lewis and his Band (Columbia). Among later recordings: the Benny Goodman Quartet (Victor), Jimmie Lunceford (Decca), Glenn Miller (Bluebird). Its film history included (MM) *The Fabulous Dorseys*, 1959, performed by The Dorsey Brothers Band; (MM) *The Five Pennies*, 1959, played by the Five Pennies; (MP) *Some Like It Hot*, 1959, sung by Marilyn Monroe.

Run Run Run. w/m Domenic Troiano and Roy Kenner, 1972. Recorded by the quartet Jo Jo Gunne (Asylum).

Run Samson Run. w. Howard Greenfield, m. Neil Sedaka, 1960. Introduced and recorded by Neil Sedaka (RCA).

Run Through the Jungle. w/m John Fogerty, 1970. Recorded by Creedence Clearwater Revival (Fantasy).

Run to Him. w/m Gerry Goffin and Jack Keller, 1961. Hit record by Bobby Vee (Liberty).

Run to Me. w/m Barry Gibb, Maurice Gibb, and Robin Gibb, 1972. Top 20 record by the British brother trio The Bee Gees (Atco). R&B chart records by Candi Staton (Warner Bros.), 1976, and by Angela Winbush (Mercury), 1988.

Run to You. w/m Bryan Adams and Jim Vallance, 1985. Top 10 record by the Canadian singer Bryan Adams (A&M).

Rush on Me, A (You're Puttin'). See **You're Puttin' a Rush on Me**.

Russian Lullaby. w/m Irving Berlin, 1927. The recordings of Franklyn Baur (Victor); Jesse Crawford, the organist (Victor); the bands of Roger Wolfe Kahn (Victor) and Ernie Golden (Brunswick); and many vaudeville and radio performances made this another hit for Berlin. Bing Crosby revived it in (MM) *Blue Skies*, 1946. Among other notable recordings through the years: Bunny Berigan (Victor); Red Nichols (Brunswick); Benny Goodman (Victor); Joan Edwards (Decca); Dave Pell (Trend); Mary Lou Williams (Asch); and, during World War II, a 12″ V-disc by Teddy Wilson.

Russians. w/m Sting, 1986. Recorded by the British singer/guitarist, Sting, né Gordon Sumner (A&M).

Rusty Bells. w/m Richard Ahlert and Eddie Snyder, 1965. Recorded by Brenda Lee (Decca).

Rusty Dusty Blues. w/m J. Mayo Williams, 1943. Featured and recorded by Count Basie, vocal by Jimmy Rushing, arranged by Buster Harding (Columbia).

Ruthless. w/m Bobby Braddock, 1967. Country chart record by The Statler Brothers (Columbia).

S

Sabbath Prayer. w. Sheldon Harnick, m Jerry Bock, 1964. Introduced by Zero Mostel, Maria Karnilova, and chorus in (TM) *Fiddler on the Roof*. In the film version (MM) *Fiddler on the Roof*, 1971, it was sung by Topol, Norma Crane, and chorus.

Sabre Dance. m. Aram Khatchaturian, 1948. Adapted from "Sabre (Sword) Dance" from his *Gayne, Ballet Suite*. Leading recordings: Oscar Levant (Columbia), Woody Herman and his Orchestra (Columbia), The Andrews Sisters (Decca), The Harmonicats (Mercury).

Sabre Dance Boogie. m. Aram Khatchaturian, 1948. Based on "Sabre (or Sword) Dance" from *Gayne, Ballet Suite* by Khatchaturian. Top 10 record by Freddy Martin and his Orchestra (RCA Victor).

Sacred. w. William Landau, m. Adam Ross, 1961. Recorded by The Castells (Era).

Sad, Sad Girl. w/m Barbara Mason, 1965. Written and recorded by eighteen-year-old Barbara Mason (Arctic).

Sad Eyes. w/m Robert John, 1979. #1 gold record by Robert John (EMI America).

Sad Girl. w/m Lloyd Smith and Jay Wiggins, 1969. Recorded by The Intruders (Gamble). Revived by GQ (Arista), 1982.

Sad Hours. w/m Walter Jacobs, 1952. Featured and recorded by Little Walter (Checker).

Sadie, Sadie. w. Bob Merrill, m. Jule Styne, 1964. Introduced by Barbra Streisand and ensemble in (TM) *Funny Girl*, and then in (MM) *Funny Girl*, 1968.

Sadie Salome, Go Home! w. Edgar Leslie, m. Irving Berlin, 1909. Featured and recorded by the comic singers, Edward M. Favor (Edison) and Bob Roberts (Columbia).

Sadie's Shawl. m. Nico Carstens and Sam Lorraine, 1956. Instrumental success from England, recorded by Bob Sharples and his Orchestra (London).

Sadie Thompson's Song. w. Ned Washington, m. Lester Lee, 1953. From (MP) *Miss Sadie Thompson*. Popular instrumental by Richard Hayman and his Orchestra (Mercury).

Sad Movies (Make Me Cry). w/m John D. Loudermilk, 1961. Hit record by Sue Thompson (Hickory). Chart version by The Lennon Sisters (Dot).

Sad Songs (Say So Much). w. Bernie Taupin, m. Elton John, 1984. Top 10 record by English singer/songwriter Elton John (Geffen).

Sad Tomorrows. w/m Gerald Marcellino and John Greenbach, 1965. Featured and recorded by Trini Lopez (Reprise).

Safe in My Garden. w/m John Phillips, 1968. Recorded by The Mamas and The Papas (Dunhill).

Safety Dance, The. w/m Ivan Doroschuk, 1983. Top 10 record by the Canadian trio Men Without Hats (Backstreet).

Saga of Jenny, The. See **Jenny**.

Saginaw, Michigan. w/m Don Wayne and Bill Anderson, 1964. Hit Country record by Lefty Frizzell (Columbia).

Said I to My Heart, Said I. w. E. Y. Harburg, m. Earl Robinson, 1946. Introduced by Barbara Stanwyck in (MM) *California*.

Sail Along, Silv'ry Moon w. Harry Tobias, m. Percy Wenrich, 1937, 1958. Wenrich's last song success in a three-decade career. First recorded by Gene Autry (Vocalion), Red McKenzie (Vocalion), and Horace Heidt and his Musical Knights (Brunswick). In 1958, Billy Vaughn and his Orchestra revived it with a Top Ten instrumental version (Dot).

Sail Away. w/m Noël Coward, 1961. Originally sung by Graham Payn in a 1950 musical in London, *Ace of Clubs*. Coward used the song as the title number in (TM) *Sail Away*, introduced in the U.S. by James Hurst.

Sailboat in the Moonlight, A. w/m John Jacob Loeb and Carmen Lombardo, 1937. Introduced and recorded by Guy Lombardo, vocal by Carmen Lombardo (Victor). Also recorded by Billie Holiday (Vocalion); Dick Robertson (Decca); Johnny Hodges, vocal by Buddy Clark (Variety); Emery Deutsch and his Orchestra (Brunswick).

Sailin' Away on the Henry Clay. w. Gus Kahn, m. Egbert Van Alstyne, 1917. Introduced by Elizabeth Murray in (TM) *Goodnight, Paul*. The Marx Brothers often performed it in their vaudeville act.

Sailing. w/m Christopher Cross, 1980. #1 single from the platinum album "Christopher Cross" (Warner Bros.), resulting in three awards in the Grammy (NARAS) voting: Album of the Year; Song of the Year; Record of the Year.

Sailing. w/m Gavin Sutherland, 1975. Leading recording by Rod Stewart (Warner Bros.).

Sailing Down the Chesapeake Bay. w. Jean C. Havez, m. George Botsford, 1913.

Sail On. w/m Lionel Richie, 1979. Recorded by The Commodores (Motown).

Sail on Sailor. w. Jack Rieley and Ray Kennedy, m. Brian Wilson and Tandyn Almer, 1973. Recorded by The Beach Boys (Brother).

Sailor (Your Home Is the Sea). w. Alan Holt (Engl.), Fini Busch (Ger), m. Werner Scharfenberger, 1960. Austrian song titled "Seemann." Recorded in Germany by Lolita [Ditta]. Her record reached the Top 10 on the American charts (Kapp).

Sailor Beware. w. Leo Robin, m. Richard A. Whiting, 1936. Introduced by Bing Crosby in the first film version (MM) *Anything Goes*. Crosby recorded it, with orchestra under direction of Georgie Stoll (Decca).

Sailor Boy. w/m Gerry Goffin and Russ Titelman, 1964. Recorded by The Chiffons (Laurie).

St. Elmo's Fire (Man in Motion). w/m David Foster and John Parr, 1985. #1 record based on theme from (MP) *St. Elmo's Fire* by John Parr (Atlantic).

St. Elmo's Fire. See also **Love Theme from "St. Elmo's Fire."**

St. George and the Dragonet. w. Stan Freberg and Daws Butler, m. Walter Schumann, 1953. #1 best-selling record, parody of the TV show "Dragnet," by Stan Freberg, with speaking voices by Daws Butler and June Foray (Capitol).

St. James Infirmary. w/m Joe Primrose, 1930. Adapted from traditional folk number. This version first recorded by King Oliver (Victor), but most popular release by Cab Calloway (Brunswick) the following year. Artie Shaw had a two-sided arrangement in 1941 (Victor), and in 1948 Louis Armstrong had a lasting interpretation, featuring Earl Hines on piano (Victor). The song was interpolated in (TM) Lew Leslie's *Blackbirds of 1934*.

Bing Crosby sang it in (MM) *Birth of the Blues* in 1941.

St. Louis Blues. w/m W. C. Handy, 1914. Undoubtedly the most renowned, most played, and best-selling blues song ever written. It has been performed and used as background music in many films, including (MM) *Is Everybody Happy?* by Ted Lewis and Band, 1929; Nan Wynn in the film bio of Lewis, (MM) *Is Everybody Happy?*, 1943; (MM) *The Birth of the Blues*, sung by Ruby Elzy, 1941; two films titled (MM) *St. Louis Blues*, the first featuring Maxine Sullivan, 1939, and the second starring Nat "King" Cole as Handy, 1958. In (MM) *The Glenn Miller Story*, 1954, it was played as the "St. Louis Blues March." Among the hundreds of recordings are those by The Original Dixieland Jazz Band (Victor), Ted Lewis (Columbia), Benny Goodman (Victor), Roy Eldridge (Key), and at least three by W. C. Handy, playing trumpet with band (Paramount, Okeh, Varsity).

St. Therese of the Roses. w. Remus Harris, m. Arthur Strauss, 1956. Hit record by Billy Ward and His Dominoes (Decca). Jackie Wilson was lead singer at the time.

St. Thomas. m. Sonny Rollins, 1963. Jazz instrumental introduced by Sonny Rollins (Prestige). Among recordings is that of Herbie Mann (United Artists).

Sally. w. Clifford Grey, m. Jerome Kern, 1921. Introduced By Irving Fisher and ensemble in (TM) *Sally*, starring Marilyn Miller. Miller, starring in the film version, (MM) *Sally*, 1929, was sung to by a chorus.

Sally, Go Round the Roses. w/m Zell Sanders and Lona Spector, 1963. Hit record by The Jaynetts (Tuff).

Sally, Won't You Come Back. w. Gene Buck, m. Dave Stamper, 1921. Introduced by Joe Schenck in (TM) *Ziegfeld Follies of 1921*. Recorded instrumentally by Ted Lewis and his Orchestra (Columbia).

Sally G. w/m Paul McCartney and Linda McCartney, 1975. Recorded by Paul Mc-

Cartney and Wings, coupled with the hit "Junior's Farm" (Apple).

Salome. m. William Loraine, 1898. Piano solo.

Salt in My Tears, The. w/m Martin Briley, 1983. Recorded by Martin Briley (Mercury).

Salt Peanuts. w/m John Birks "Dizzy" Gillespie and Kenneth Clarke, 1945. Recorded by Dizzy Gillespie and his All-Star quintet, vocal by Gillespie and the Band. Among other recordings: The Auld-Webster-Hawkins Saxtet (Apollo) and The Nutty Squirrels (Hanover).

Sam. w/m Don Black, John Farrar, and Hank Marvin, 1977. English song recorded by Olivia Newton-John (MCA).

Sam, The Old Accordion Man. w/m Walter Donaldson, 1927. Featured, recorded, and made popular by Ruth Etting (Columbia). It was heard in (MM) *Glorifying the American Girl*, 1929, and sung by Doris Day, as Ruth Etting, in her story (MM) *Love Me or Leave Me*, 1955.

Sam, You Made the Pants Too Long. See **Lawd, You Made the Night Too Long**.

Sam and Delilah. w. Ira Gershwin, m. George Gershwin, 1930. Introduced by Ethel Merman and ensemble in (TM) *Girl Crazy*. Recordings of note by Duke Ellington and his Orchestra, vocal by Chick Bullock (Victor) and Lee Wiley (Liberty Music Shop).

Samba de Orfeo. w. Antonio Maria, m. Luis Bonfa, 1960. Portuguese song from the Academy Award-winning French film (MP) *Black Orpheus*.

Same Old Lang Syne. w/m Dan Fogelberg, 1980. Top 10 record by Dan Folgelberg (Full Moon).

Same Old Me, The. w/m Fuzzy Owen, 1960. C&W hit by Ray Price (Columbia). Pop version by Guy Mitchell (Columbia).

Same Old Moon, The. w. Bert Kalmar and Otto Harbach, m. Harry Ruby, 1927. Introduced by Joseph Santley and Ivy Sawyer in (TM) *Lucky*. Leading record by Carl Fenton, vocal by Frank Munn (Brunswick).

Same Old Saturday Night. w. Sammy Cahn, m. Frank Reardon, 1955. Featured and recorded by Frank Sinatra, with Nelson Riddle's Orchestra (Capitol).

Same Old Story, The. w/m Michael Field and Newt Oliphant, 1940. Most played records: Frankie Masters, singing with his Orchestra (Vocalion); Eddy Duchin, vocal by Johnny Drake (Columbia).

Same Ole Me. w/m Paul Overstreet, 1982. Top 10 Country chart record by George Jones (Epic).

Same Sort of Girl. w. Harry B. Smith, m. Jerome Kern, 1914. Introduced by Julia Sanderson and Donald Brian in (TM) *The Girl from Utah*. Julia Sanderson and her husband, Frank Crumit, featured it on their radio show and recorded it (Decca), 1941.

Same Sweet Girl To-day, The. w/m Dan W. Quinn, 1895.

Sam Hill. w/m Tommy Collins, 1964. Country chart records by Claude King (Columbia) and Merle Haggard (Tally).

Sammy. w. James O'Dea, m. Edward Hutchinson, 1903. Interpolated by Anna Laughlin and Paula Edwards in (TM) *The Wizard of Oz*. Popular recording by Henry Burr (Columbia).

Sam's Place. w. Red Simpson, m. Buck Owens, 1967. Crossover (C&W/Pop) chart hit by Buck Owens (Capitol).

Sam's Song. w. Jack Elliott, m. Lew Quadling, 1950. Coupled with "Play a Simple Melody" (q.v.) this was a hit for the singers billed as "Gary Crosby and Friend," who were Bing and son Gary (Decca). A popular record was cut by Joe "Fingers" Carr [pseudonym of pianist Lou Busch] (Capitol). Dean Martin and Sammy Davis, Jr. revived it in 1962 (Reprise).

San. w/m Lindsay McPhail and Walter Michels, 1920. Instrumental hit. First popular recording by The Benson Orchestra of Chicago (Victor), 1921. Ted Lewis and his Orchestra had two well accepted versions (Columbia), 1924 and 1930. Song was coupled with "Oh!" (q.v.) on a gold record by Pee Wee Hunt and his Orchestra (Capitol), 1953.

San Antonio. w. Harry H. Williams, m. Egbert Van Alstyne, 1907. A successor to the same writers' American Indian songs, "Navajo" and "Cheyenne."

San Antonio Rose (a.k.a. New San Antonio Rose). w/m Bob Wills, 1940. Introduced and recorded by Bob Wills and his Texas Playboys (Okeh), and covered for the best-selling record by Bing Crosby (Decca). Both releases had the adjective "New" as the first word of the title, which word has since been dropped. Many versions have been played and sung including those by Tito Guizar (Victor), The Dinning Sisters (Capitol), Tex Ritter (Capitol), Ken Griffin (Columbia), the Firehouse Five Plus Two (Good Time Jazz), Joe "Fingers" Carr (Capitol), Floyd Cramer (RCA). It was the title song of (MM) *San Antonio Rose*, 1941.

San Antonio Stroll. w/m Peter Noah, 1975. Hit Country record by Tanya Tucker (MCA).

Sanctified Lady. w/m Marvin Gaye and Gordon Banko, 1985. Posthumous R&B chart Top 10 record by Marvin Gaye (Columbia).

Sanctify Yourself. w/m Jim Kerr, Michael MacNeil, Charles Burchill, Mel Gaynor, John Gibbin, 1986. Recorded by the Scottish group Simple Minds (A&M).

Sand and the Sea, The. w/m Hal Hester and Barry Parker, 1955. Recorded by Nat "King" Cole (Capitol).

Sand in My Shoes. w. Frank Loesser, m. Victor Schertzinger, 1941. Introduced by Connee Boswell in (MM) *Kiss the Boys Goodbye* and on records (Decca). Also recorded by Helen Morgan (Bluebird); Sammy Kaye, vocal by Tommy Ryan (Victor); Sonny Dunham and his Orchestra (Bluebird).

Sandman. w/m Ralph Freed and Bonnie Lake, 1935. Theme song of the Dorsey Brothers Orchestra. Recorded by them (Decca), with vocal by Kay Weber. Benny Goodman featured and recorded a Fletcher Henderson arrangement (Victor).

Sands of Gold. w/m Webb Pierce, Hal Eddy, and Cliff Parman, 1963. Hit Country record by Webb Pierce (Decca).

Sands of Time, The. w/m Robert Wright and George Forrest, 1953. From a theme of Borodin's *In the Steppes of Central Asia*. Introduced by Alfred Drake, Doretta Morrow, and Richard Oneto in (TM) *Kismet*. In the film version (MM) *Kismet*, 1955, it was sung by Howard Keel.

Sandy. w. Scott Simon, m. Louis St. Louis, 1978. Introduced by John Travolta in (MM) *Grease*.

Sandy. w/m Terry Fell, 1959. Recorded by Larry Hall (Strand). Revived by Ronny and The Daytonas (Mala), 1965.

San Fernando Valley. w/m Gordon Jenkins, 1943. Bing Crosby had a #1 recording (Decca). Popular versions, also, by Johnny Mercer (Capitol) and Roy Rogers (Victor). Latter sang it in (MP) *San Fernando Valley*, 1944.

San Franciscan Nights. w/m Eric Burdon, Victor Briggs, Barry Jenkins, Danny McCulloch, John Weider, 1967. Top 10 record by the British group The Animals (MGM).

San Francisco. w. Gus Kahn, m. Bronislaw Kaper and Walter Jurmann, 1936. Introduced by Jeanette MacDonald in (MM) *San Francisco*. It was sung by a chorus in (MM) *Hello, Frisco, Hello* in 1943; heard in the background of (MM) *Nob Hill* in 1945, and in the Kahn biography (MM) *I'll See You in My Dreams* in 1952.

San Francisco (Be Sure to Wear Some Flowers in Your Hair). w/m John Phillips, 1967. Top 10 record by Scott McKenzie (Ode).

San-Ho-Zay. m. Freddy King and Sonny Thompson, 1961. Instrumental by Freddy King (Federal).

Santa Baby. w/m Joan Javits, Phil Springer, and Tony Springer, 1953. Hit record by Eartha Kitt, with Henri René's Orchestra (RCA Victor).

Santa Claus Is Comin' to Town. w/m Haven Gillespie and J. Fred Coots, 1934. This Christmas standard was introduced on radio by Ethel Shutta, singing with George Olsen's Orchestra. First popular recording by George Hall, vocal by Sonny Schuyler (Bluebird). The best-selling record was by Bing Crosby and the Andrews Sisters (Decca), 1947. Revived by Bruce Springsteen (Columbia), 1985.

Santa Claus Is Riding the Trail. w. Jack Meskill, m. Archie Gottler, 1943.

Santa Claus Is Watching You. w/m Ray Stevens, 1962. Novelty chart Christmas single by Ray Stevens (Mercury).

Sara. w/m Ina Wolf and Peter Wolf, 1986. #1 single by the group Starship (Grunt).

Sara. w/m Stevie Nicks, 1980. Top 10 record by the British group Fleetwood Mac (Warner Bros.).

Sarafina. w/m Hugh Masakela, 1987. Introduced by the cast in the musical (TM) *Sarafina*.

Sara Smile, w/m Daryl Hall and John Oates, 1976. Top 10 gold record by Daryl Hall and John Oates (RCA).

Saskatchewan. w. Irving Caesar and Sammy Lerner, m. Gerald Marks, 1936. Featured by Rudy Vallee and his Orchestra on his weekly radio show.

Satan Never Sleeps. w. Harold Adamson and Leo McCarey, m. Harry Warren, 1962. Title song of (MP) *Satan Never Sleeps*. Recorded by Timi Yuro (Liberty).

Satan's Holiday. w. Irving Kahal, m. Sammy Fain, 1930. As a last-minute replacement for Ruth Etting, Ethel Merman made her screen debut by introducing the song in (MM) *Follow the Leader*, the film version of the Broadway musical, *Manhattan Mary*.

Satan's Little Lamb. w. E. Y. Harburg and Johnny Mercer, m. Harold Arlen, 1932. Sung by Francetta Malloy and The Musketeers, danced by Doris Humphrey, José Limon, and Charles Weidman in (TM) *Americana*. Ethel Merman recorded it (Victor).

Satan Takes a Holiday. m. Larry Clinton, 1937. Hit instrumental by Tommy Dorsey and his Orchestra (Victor). Other popular versions by Eddie Stone and his Orchestra (Vocalion), and as "Spooky Takes a Holiday," by the bands of Ozzie Nelson (Bluebird), Edgar Hayes (Decca), and recorded in London by Nat Gonella and his Georgians (Parlophone).

Satellite. w/m Rob Hyman, Eric Bazilian, and Rick Chertoff, 1987. Popular single and album cut from "One Way Home" by The Hooters (Columbia). The lyric took a stand against TV evangelists such as the discredited Jim and Tammy Bakker.

Satin and Silk. w/m Cole Porter, 1955. Introduced by Gretchen Wyler in (TM) *Silk Stockings*. Janis Paige performed the number in the film version (MM) *Silk Stockings*, 1956.

Satin Doll. w. Johnny Mercer, m. Billy Strayhorn and Edward Kennedy "Duke" Ellington, 1958. First recorded as an instrumental by Duke Ellington and his Orchestra, featuring piano solo by Ellington (Capitol), 1953. With Mercer's lyric added, song became a standard with a myriad of vocal and instrumental recordings.

Satin Pillows. w/m Bob Tubert, m. Sonny James, 1966. Top 40 record by Bobby Vinton (Epic).

Satin Soul. m. Barry White, 1975. Instrumental recorded by Love Unlimited Orchestra, arranged and conducted by Barry White (20th Century).

Satisfaction Guaranteed. w/m Kay Twomey, Fred Wise, and Ben Weisman, 1953. Country hit by Carl Smith (Columbia).

Satisfied. w/m Martha Carson, 1951. Introduced and recorded by Martha Carson (RCA Victor).

Satisfied! w. Irving Caeser, m. Cliff Friend, 1929.

Satisfied Mind, A. w/m J. H. Hays and Jack Rhodes, 1955. C&W hit with records by Red and Betty Foley (Decca), Porter Wagoner (RCA), Jean Shepard (Capitol). Revived in 1966 by Bobby Hebb (Philips).

Satisfied with You. w/m Dave Clark and Denis Payton, 1966. Recorded by The English group The Dave Clark Five (Epic).

Saturday. w. Sidney D. Mitchell, m. Harry Brooks, 1921. Introduced by Nora Bayes in the revue (TM) *Snapshots of 1921* and on records (Columbia).

Saturday Date. w/m Jack Brooks, 1947. Recorded by Kay Kyser, vocal by Harry Babbit and Gloria Wood (Columbia).

Saturday in the Park. w/m Robert Lamm, 1972. Gold record by the group, Chicago, of which Lamm was keyboardist (Columbia).

Saturday Love. w/m James Harris III and Terry Lewis, 1986. Recorded by Cherrelle with Alexander O'Neal (Tabu).

Saturday Night. w/m Phil Coulter and Bill Martin, 1975. #1 gold record by the Scottish group The Bay City Rollers (Arista).

Saturday Night. w/m Randy Sparks, 1963. Hit recording by The New Christy Minstrels (Columbia).

Saturday Night (Is the Loneliest Night in the Week). w. Sammy Cahn, m. Jule Styne, 1944. Frank Sinatra, accompanied by Axel Stordahl's Orchestra, had the best-selling record (Columbia). Among others were: Sammy Kaye, vocal by Nancy Norman (Victor); Frankie Carle, vocal by Phyllis Lynne (Columbia); Woody Herman, vocal by Frances Wayne (Decca); The King Sisters (Victor).

Saturday Night at the Movies. w/m Barry Mann and Cynthia Weil, 1964. Recorded by The Drifters (Atlantic).

Saturday Night Fish Fry. w. Ellis Walsh and Louis Jordan, 1949. Featured and recorded by Louis Jordan and his Tympany Five (Decca).

Saturday Night Function. m. Albany "Barney" Bigard and Edward Kennedy "Duke" Ellington, 1929. Recorded by the orchestras of Duke Ellington (Victor) and Sonny Greer (Columbia).

Saturday Night's Alright for Fighting. w/m Elton John and Bernie Taupin,1973. Top 20 record from England by Elton John (MCA).

Saturday Night Special. w/m Edward King and Ronnie Van Zant, 1975. Recorded by the group Lynyrd Skynyrd (MCA).

Saturday Nite. w/m Philip Bailey, Albert McKay, and Maurice White, 1976. Popular record by the group Earth, Wind & Fire (Columbia).

Sausalito Summernight. w/m Marc Boon Lucian and Robert Vundernik, 1981. Record by the group from the Netherlands, Diesel (Regency).

Savannah. w/m E. Y. Harburg, m. Harold Arlen, 1957. Introduced by Ricardo Montalban in (TM) *Jamaica.*

Savannah. w/m Fred Fisher, 1924.

Save a Prayer. w/m Duran Duran, 1985. Recorded by the English band Duran Duran (Capitol).

Save It, Pretty Mama. w/m Don Redman, 1929. Recorded by McKinney's Cotton Pickers, arranged by Redman (Victor); Louis Armstrong (Okeh); the Varsity Seven (Varsity); Sidney Bechet (Victor); and in 1940 by Lionel Hampton (Victor) and Walter "Foots" Thomas (Joe Davis).

Save It for a Rainy Day. w/m Stephen Bishop, 1977. Recorded by Stephen Bishop, with guitar solo by Eric Clapton and background vocal by Chaka Khan (ABC).

Save It for Me. w/m Bob Crewe and Bob Gaudio, 1964. Top 10 record by The Four Seasons (Philips).

Save Me, Sister. w. E. Y. Harburg, m. Harold Arlen, 1936. Sung by Al Jolson, Cab Calloway, and Wini Shaw in (MM) *The Singing Kid.*

Save the Bones for Henry Jones ('Cause Henry Don't Eat Meat). w/m Danny Barker and Michael H. Goldsen, 1947. Recorded by Johnny Mercer and The King Cole Trio (Capitol).

Save the Country. w/m Laura Nyro, 1968. Introduced and recorded by Laura Nyro (Columbia). Chart records by The 5th Dimension (Bell) and Thelma Houston (Dunhill), 1970.

Save the Last Dance for Me. w/m Doc Pomus and Mort Shuman, 1960. Hit record by The Drifters (Atlantic). Answer song, "I'll Save the Last Dance for You," by Damita Jo (Mercury). Revived by the De Franco Family (20th Century), 1974.

Save the Last Dance for Me. w. Walter Hirsch, m. Frank Magine and Phil Spitalny, 1931. Popularized by Russ Columbo on radio and recording (Victor). Also featured and recorded by Arthur Tracy, "The Street Singer" (Brunswick), Morton Downey (Perfect), and Erno Rapee and his Orchestra (Hit of the Week).

Save the Overtime for Me. w. Bubba Knight, Gladys Knight, Sam Dees, m. Rickey Smith, Joey Gallo, 1983. #1 R&B chart record by Gladys Knight and The Pips (Columbia).

Save Your Heart for Me. w/m Gary Geld and Peter Udell, 1965. Hit record by Gary Lewis and The Playboys (Liberty).

Save Your Kisses for Me. w/m Tony Hiller, Martin Lee, and Lee Sheridan, 1976. Hit record by the British studio group The Brotherhood of Man (Pye). Chart U.S. cover record by Bobby Vinton (ABC).

Save Your Sorrow (for Tomorrow). w. B. G. DeSylva, m. Al Sherman, 1925. This was Sherman's first song success. Popular recordings by The Shannon Four (Columbia), Ray Miller (Brunswick), Gene Austin (Victor).

Saving All My Love for You. w/m Gerry Goffin and Michael Masser, 1985. Originally recorded by Marilyn McCoo and Billy Davis, Jr. (ABC), 1977, the song was revised and became the first #1 hit for Whitney Houston (Arista).

Saving My Love for You. w/m Ron Hoffman, 1954. Top 10 R&B number by Johnny Ace (Duke).

Saving Myself for You. w. Sammy Cahn, m. Saul Chaplin, 1938. Featured and recorded by Benny Goodman and his Orchestra (Victor).

Savin' My Love for You. w/m Mike Clark, 1986. Top 10 Country chart record by Pake McEntire (RCA).

Sawmill. w/m Horace Wheatley and Melvin Tillis, 1963. Recorded by Webb Pierce (Decca).

Say, Darling. w. Betty Comden and Adolph Green, m. Jule Styne, 1958. Introduced in (TM) *Say, Darling* by Johnny Desmond.

Say, Has Anybody Seen My Sweet Gypsy Rose. w/m Irwin Levine and L. Russell Brown, 1973. Gold record successor to "Tie a Yellow Ribbon, etc." (q.v.) by Dawn, featuring Tony Orlando (Bell).

Say, Man. w/m Ellas McDaniel. 1959. Top 40 novelty by Bo Diddley (Checker).

Say a Little Prayer for Me. w/m Horatio Nicholls and Joseph Gilbert, 1931. Popularized and recorded by Jack Denny and his Orchestra (Brunswick), Morton Downey (Victor), and Smith Ballew (Columbia).

Say a Prayer for Me Tonight. w. Alan Jay Lerner, m. Frederick Loewe, 1958. Introduced by Leslie Caron [voice dubbed on soundtrack by Betty Wand] in (MM) *Gigi.*

Say a Prayer for the Boys Over There. w. Herb Magidson, m. Jimmy McHugh, 1943. Introduced by Deanna Durbin in (MM) *Hers to Hold,* and recorded by her with Victor Young's Orchestra (Decca). Nominated for Academy Award.

Say "Au Revoir" But Not "Goodbye." w/m Harry Kennedy, 1893. Kennedy introduced it at the end of his career, after which Helene Mora, the "female baritone," featured and popularized it. She appropriately sang it at the composer's funeral.

Say Goodbye to Hollywood. w/m Billy Joel, 1981. Top 20 single taken from the album "Turnstiles," 1976, by Billy Joel (Columbia).

Say I Am (What I Am). w/m George Tomsco and Barbara Tomsco, 1966. Recorded by Tommy James and The Shondells (Roulette).

Say It. w. Nat Burton, m. Basil G. Adlam, 1934. Featured and recorded by Isham Jones and his Orchestra (Victor).

Say It (Over and Over Again). w. Frank Loesser, m. Jimmy McHugh, 1940. Introduced by Ellen Drew, Virginia Dale, and Lillian Cornell, performing as a vocal trio in a nightclub scene in (MM) *Buck Benny Rides Again.* Leading recording by Glenn Miller, vocal by Ray Eberle (Bluebird); Tommy Dorsey, vocal by Frank Sinatra (Victor).

Say It Again. w/m Bunny Sigler and Carol Davis, 1988. R&B and Pop chart record by Jermaine Stewart (Arista).

Say It Again. w/m Bob McDill, 1976. Hit Country record by Don Williams (ABC/Dot).

Say It Isn't So. w/m Daryl Hall, 1983. Top 10 record by Daryl Hall & John Oates (RCA). Not to be confused with Irving Berlin's standard of the same title.

Say It Isn't So. w/m Irving Berlin, 1932. Introduced by Rudy Vallee (Columbia) and followed by George Olsen, vocal by Paul Small (Victor), Ozzie Nelson (Brunswick), Connie Boswell (Brunswick), Annette Hanshaw (Mercury), Will Osborne (Melotone), Sam Coslow (Victor). Among later recordings: Georgia Gibbs (Mercury), Stan Kenton (Capitol), Lawrence Welk (Coral).

Say It Loud—I'm Black and I'm Proud. w/m James Brown and Alfred Ellis, 1968. Top 10 record by James Brown (King, Part 1).

Say It's Not You. w/m Dallas Frazier, 1968. Top 10 Country chart record by George Jones (Musicor).

Say It While Dancing. w. Bennie Davis, m. Abner Silver, 1922.

Say It with a Kiss. w. Johnny Mercer, m. Harry Warren, 1938. Introduced in (MM) *Going Places* and on records (Victor) by Maxine Sullivan. Other releases: Teddy Wilson (Brunswick); Gene Krupa, vocal by Irene Daye (Brunswick); Artie Shaw, vocal by Helen Forrest (Bluebird).

Say It with Music. w/m Irving Berlin, 1921. Introduced by Wilda Bennett and Paul Frawley in (TM) *The Music Box Revue*, which opened the threater of the same name. John Steel (Victor) and Paul Whiteman (Victor) both had popular records of the song, which, with the success of the show, aided in the creation of another Berlin standard. Ethel Merman sang it in (MM) *Alexander's Ragtime Band*, 1938.

Say It with Your Heart. w/m Norman Kaye and Steve Nelson, 1953. Popular record by Bob Carroll, with Jimmy Leyden's Orchestra (Derby).

Say Not Love Is a Dream. w. Basil Hood, m. Franz Lehar, 1912. From (TM) *The Count of Luxembourg.*

Sayonara. w/m Irving Berlin, 1957. From (MP) *Sayonara.* Recorded by Eddie Fisher (RCA Victor).

Say Say Say. w/m Paul McCartney and Michael Jackson, 1983. #1 gold record by Paul McCartney and Michael Jackson (Columbia).

Say "Si Si." w. Al Stillman (Engl.), Francia Luban (Sp.), m. Ernesto Lecuona, 1940. Original title "Paro Vigo Me Voy." Introduced and recorded by Xavier Cugat, vocal by Lina Romay (Victor), 1936. In 1940, hit records by The Andrews Sisters (Decca), Glenn Miller, vocal by Marion Hutton (Bluebird), and others, plus the re-release of Cugat's disc, established the number as a Latin-American standard. It was heard in (MM) *When My Baby Smiles at Me*, 1948, and had popular versions by the Mills Brothers (Decca) and Eugenie Baird (Vinrob), 1953.

Says My Heart. w. Frank Loesser, m. Burton Lane, 1938. Introduced by Harriet Hilliard, accompanied by Harry Owens's Orchestra in (MM) *Cocoanut Grove.* Hilliard then recorded it with Ozzie Nelson's Orchestra (Bluebird). Other records included Billie Holiday (Vocalion), Tommy Dorsey (Victor), Jimmie Grier (Decca), George Hall, vocal by Dolly Dawn (Conqueror). The song was on "Your Hit Parade" for twelve weeks, four times in the #1 position.

Say Something Funny. w. Bernice Ross, m. Lor Crane, 1965. The natural title for a follow-up to "Don't Just Stand There" (q.v.) by Patty Duke (United Artists).

Say Something Sweet to Your Sweetheart. w/m Sid Tepper and Roy Brodsky, 1948. Leading records by Joe Stafford and Gordon MacRae (Capitol), The Ink Spots (Decca), Vic Damone and Patti Page (Mercury).

Says Who? Says You, Says I! w. Johnny Mercer, m. Harold Arlen, 1941. Introduced by Will Osborne and his Orchestra in (MM) *Blues in the Night.*

Say When. w. Ted Koehler, m. Ray Henderson, 1934. Introduced in (TM) *Say When* and recorded by Harry Richman (Columbia).

Say Wonderful Things. w/m Norman Newell and Phil Green, 1963. Introduced in England and released in the U.S. by Ronnie Carroll (Philips). Popular U.S. version by Patti Page (Columbia).

Say You. w/m Johnnie B. Hicks, 1964. Recorded by Ronnie Dove (Diamond).

Say You, Say Me (under title song of White Nights). w/m Lionel Richie, 1985. Introduced on soundtrack of (MP) *White Nights* and

721

on a #1 gold record by Lionel Richie (Motown). Because of contractual differences, the song was excluded from the soundtrack album (Atlantic). Winner Academy Award, Best Song.

Say You'll Be Mine. w/m Christopher Cross, 1981. Recorded by Christopher Cross (Warner Bros.).

Say You'll Stay Until Tomorrow. w/m Roger Greenaway and Barry Mason, 1976. Top 20 English song by Tom Jones (Epic).

Say You Love Me. w/m Christine McVie, 1976. Top 20 record by the British group, Fleetwood Mac, and written by the keyboardist (Reprise).

Say You're Mine Again. w/m Charles Nathan and Dave Heisler, 1953. Top 10 record by Perry Como (RCA Victor). June Hutton had a popular version, with Axel Stordahl's Orchestra (Capitol).

(Say) You're My Girl. w/m Roy Orbison and Bill Dees, 1965. Introduced and recorded by Roy Orbison.

Say You Will. w/m Mick Jones and Lou Gramm, 1988. Chart single for the album "Inside Information" by the Anglo-American group Foreigner (Atlantic).

Scarborough Fair—Canticle. w/m Paul Simon and Art Garfunkel, 1966. Simon and Garfunkel introduced it in their album "Parsley, Sage, Rosemary and Thyme" (Columbia). Song sometimes known by the album title. The duo sang it on the soundtrack of the 1967 film (MP) *The Graduate*. Single hits in 1968 by Simon and Garfunkel (Columbia) and Sergio Mendes and Brasil '66 (A&M).

Scarlet Ribbons. w. Jack Segal, m. Evelyn Danzig, 1949. First recording by Juanita Hall (RCA Victor). Jo Stafford's Top 20 version (Capitol), 1950, and Harry Belafonte's performances and popular recording (RCA Victor), 1952, helped the ballad attain the level of a standard. The Browns had a Top 20 record (RCA), 1959.

Scarlett O'Hara. m. Jerry Lordan, 1963. Instrumental written and first recorded in England. Popular U.S. version by Lawrence Welk and his Orchestra (Dot) and Bobby Gregg and His Friends (Epic).

Scat Song, The. w. Mitchell Parish, m. Frank Perkins and Cab Calloway, 1932. Introduced and recorded by Cab Calloway (Brunswick).

Scatterbrain. w/m Johnny Burke, Carl Bean, Kahn Keene, and Frankie Masters, 1939. Introduced, recorded by, and theme of Frankie Masters and his Orchestra (Vocalion). The song, which became #1 on "Your Hit Parade," was performed by Kay Kyser and his Band in (MM) *That's Right—You're Wrong*, 1939, and as a production number in (MM) *Scatterbrain*, starring Judy Canova, 1940.

Scattered Toys. w/m Charles Kenny and Nick Kenny, 1950. Featured and recorded by Arthur Godfrey, with Archie Bleyer's Orchestra (Columbia) and Ray Anthony and his Orchestra (Capitol).

Scattin' at the Kit Kat. w. Irving Mills, m. Edward Kennedy "Duke" Ellington, 1937. Instrumental, recorded twice by Duke Ellington and his Orchestra (Master and Brunswick).

Schnitzelbank. w. Anonymous, 1906. Based on the 1863 song "Johnny Schmoker." This became a favorite with male glee clubs, camp, college, fireside, and tavern (especially German) sings.

Schön Rosmarin (Fair Rosmarin). m. Fritz Kreisler, 1910. One of five popular violin and piano compositions written by Kreisler during this calendar year.

School Day. w/m Chuck Berry, 1957. Hit record by Chuck Berry (Chess). Played on the soundtrack of (MM) *Rock 'n' Roll High School*, 1979.

School Days (When We Were a Couple of Kids). w. Will D. Cobb, m. Gus Edwards, 1907. Title song of Gus Edwards's vaudeville act, which featured child stars such as Lila Lee, George Jessel, Eddie Cantor, and Georgie Price. The song was Edward's greatest hit, selling over three million copies of sheet music. Byron G. Harlan's recording was one of the biggest sellers to date (Victor). It was sung by Bing Crosby in the film based on the life of Gus Edwards (MM) *The Star Maker*, 1939. Gale Storm and Phil Regan sang it in (MM) *Sunbonnet Sue*, 1945.

Schoolhouse Blues. w/m Irving Berlin, 1921. Introduced by The Brox Sisters in (TM) *Music Box Revue*, and recorded by them (Brunswick).

School Is Out. w/m Gary Anderson and Gene Barge, 1961. U.S. Bonds [writer Gary Anderson], a.k.a. Garry U.S. Bonds, had a Top 10 recording (Legrand).

School's Out. w/m Alice Cooper and Michael Bruce, 1972. Top 10 record by Alice Cooper (Warner Bros.). Heard on the soundtrack of (MM) *Rock 'n' Roll High School*, 1979. Revived by the Swiss heavy-metal band Krokus (Arista), 1986.

Scorpio. m. Dennis Coffey, 1971. Gold record instrumental by Dennis Coffey and The Detroit Guitar Band (Sussex).

Scotch and Soda. w/m adapted by Dave Guard, 1962. New lyrics to traditional song recorded by The Kingston Trio (Capitol). Country chart versions by Mac Wiseman (Churchill), 1979, and Ray Price (Viva), 1983.

Scrounch. See **Skrontch**.

Scrub Me Mama with a Boogie Beat. w/m Don Raye, 1940. A boogie-woogie version of the traditional song "The Irish Washerwoman." Best-selling records by Will Bradley, vocal by Ray McKinley (Columbia) and The Andrews Sisters (Decca).

Sealed with a Kiss. w. Peter Udell, m. Gary Geld,1962. Top 10 record by Brian Hyland (ABC-Paramount). Chart records by Gary

Lewis and The Playboys (Liberty), 1968, and Bobby Vinton (Epic), 1972.

Seal It with a Kiss. w. Edward Heyman, m. Arthur Schwartz, 1937. Introduced by Lily Pons in (MM) *That Girl from Paris*.

Seaman's Blues. w/m Ernest Tubb and Talmadge "Billy" Tubb, 1948. Top 10 C&W chart record by Ernest Tubb (Decca).

Sea of Heartbreak. w. Hal David, m. Paul Hampton, 1961. Featured and recorded by Don Gibson (RCA).

Sea of Love. w/m Phil Battiste and George Khoury, 1959. Top 10 record by Phil Phillips and The Twilights (Mercury). Del Shannon had a chart version in 1982 (Network) and The Honeydrippers had a Top 10 record in 1985 (Es Paranza).

Sea of the Moon, The. w. Arthur Freed, m. Harry Warren, 1950. Introduced by Esther Williams in (MM) *Pagan Love Song*.

Searchin'. w/m Jerry Leiber and Mike Stoller, 1957. The first hit record by The Coasters (Atco).

Searching for My Love. w/m Robert Moore, 1966. R&B/Pop hit by Bobby Moore and The Rhythm Aces (Checker).

Searching Wind, The. w. Edward Heyman, m. Victor Young, 1946. Lyrics added to the theme from (MP) *The Searching Wind*.

Search Is Over, The. w/m Frankie Sullivan and Jim Petrik, 1985. Top 10 record by the group, Survivor, of which the writers were members (Scotti Brothers).

Search Is Through, The. w. Ira Gershwin, m. Harold Arlen, 1954. Introduced by Bing Crosby in (MM) *The Country Girl*.

Seasons. w/m Grace Slick, 1980. Chart record by Grace Slick (RCA).

Seasons Change. w/m Lewis Martine, 1987. #1 single from the album "Exposure" by the female trio Expose (Arista).

Seasons in the Sun. w. Rod McKuen (Engl.), Jacques Brel (Fr.), m. Jacques Brel, 1964, 1974. Introduced in France as "Le Moribond" by Jacques Brel. English version introduced and recorded in the U.S. by The Kingston Trio (Captitol). #1 gold record by the Canadian singer Terry Jacks (Bell), 1974.

Seasons of My Heart. w/m George Jones and Darrell Edwards, 1956. Top 10 Country record by Jimmy Newman (Dot). Revived by Johnny Cash (Columbia), 1960.

Seattle. w/m Jack Keller, Hugo Montenegro, and Ernie Sheldon, 1969. From the series (TVP) "Here Come the Brides." Top 40 record by Perry Como (RCA).

Second Avenue. w/m Tim Moore, 1974. Introduced and recorded by Tim Moore (Asylum). Best-selling record by Art Garfunkel (Columbia).

Second Chance, A. w. Dory Langdon Previn, m. André Previn, 1962. From (MP) *Two for The Seesaw*. Nominated for Academy Award, 1962.

Second Fiddle (to an Old Guitar). w/m Betty Amos, 1964. Country hit recorded by Jean Shepard (Capitol).

Second Hand Love. w/m Phil Spector and Hank Hunter, 1962. Top 10 record by Connie Francis (MGM).

Second Hand Rose. w. Grant Clarke, m. James F. Hanley, 1921. Associated with and introduced by Fanny Brice in (TM) *Ziegfeld Follies of 1921*, and on records (Columbia). She sang it in (MM) *My Man*, 1929. Barbra Streisand revived it with a hit record (Columbia), 1966, and, as Brice, sang it in (MM) *Funny Girl*, 1968.

Second Hand Rose (Second Hand Heart). w/m Harlan Howard, 1963. Country chart hit by Roy Drusky (Decca). Not to be confused with the 1921 standard.

Second Time Around, The. w/m William Shelby and Leon Sylvers, 1980. Gold record by the trio Shalamar (Solar).

Second Time Around, The. w. Sammy Cahn, m. James Van Heusen, 1960. Introduced by Bing Crosby in (MM) *High Time*. Nominated for Academy Award, 1960. Leading record by Frank Sinatra (Reprise), 1961.

Secret, The. w/m Joe Lubin and I. J. Roth, 1958. Featured and recorded by Gordon MacRae (Capitol).

Secret Agent Man. w/m Phil Sloan and Steve Barri, 1966. From the series (TVP) "Secret Agent." Leading records by Johnny Rivers (Imperial) and instrumental version by The Ventures (Dolton).

Secretary Song, The. w/m Sammy Fain and Jack Barnett, 1947. Featured and recorded by Ted Weems, vocal by Shirley Richards (Mercury), and Tony Pastor, vocal by The Clooney Sisters, Rosemary and Betty (Columbia).

Secret Lady. w/m La La, 1987. Top 10 R&B chart record by Stephanie Mills (MCA).

Secret Love. w. Paul Francis Webster, m. Sammy Fain, 1953. Introduced by Doris Day in (MM) *Calamity Jane*. Winner Academy Award. Day's record was the biggest hit of her career, a #1 million-seller (Columbia). Hit revivals by Billy Stewart (Chess), 1966, and Freddy Fender (ABC-Dot), 1975.

Secret Lovers. w/m David Lewis and Wayne Lewis,1986. Top 10 record by the group, Atlantic Starr, of which the Lewis brothers were lead singers (A&M).

Secretly. w/m Al Hoffman, Dick Manning, and Mark Markwell, 1958. Top 10 record by Jimmie Rodgers (Roulette). Revived by The Lettermen (Capitol), 1965.

Secret of Christmas, The. w. Sammy Cahn, m. James Van Heusen, 1959. Introduced by Bing Crosby in (MP) *Say One for Me*.

Secret of My Success, The. w/m Jack Blades, David Foster, Tom Keane, and Mike Landau, 1987. Sung by the group, Night Ranger, on the soundtrack and album of the film (MP) *Night Ranger* (MCA/Camel).

Secret Separation. w/m Jeanette Obstoj, Cy Curnin, Jamie West-Oram, Rupert Greenall, 1986. Recorded by the London group The Fixx (MCA).

Secret Service, The. w/m Irving Berlin, 1962. Introduced by Anita Gillette in (TM) *Mr. President*, Berlin's last Broadway score.

Secrets in the Moonlight. w/m Mack Gordon, 1940. Featured and recorded by Harry James, vocal by Dick Haymes (Varsity); Jan Savitt, vocal by Bon Bon (Decca); Al Donahue, vocal by Phil Brito (Vocalion).

Security. w/m Otis Redding, 1968. Recorded by Otis Redding (Volt), 1964. Top 40 by Etta James (Cadet), 1968.

Seduction, The (Love Theme from "American Gigolo"). m. Giorgio Moroder, 1980. Love theme from (MP) *American Gigolo*. Instrumental by the German arranger/conductor James Last (Polydor).

See. w/m Felix Cavaliere, 1969. Top 40 record by The Rascals (Atlantic).

See, Saw, Margery Daw. w/m Arthur West, 1893. Still popular with children at play.

Seeing You Like This. w. Ray Errol Fox (Engl.), m. G. Fusco, 1966. Song based on the theme from the French/Swedish (MP) *La Guerre Est Finie*. Recorded by Roger Williams, vocal by Laura Williams (RCA), 1971.

Seein' the Right Love Go Wrong. w/m Aaron Schroeder and Joey Brooks, 1965. Recorded by Jack Jones (Kapp).

Seeker, The. w/m Dolly Parton, 1975. Hit Country record by Dolly Parton (RCA).

Seeker, The. w/m Peter Townshend, 1970. Recorded by the English group The Who (Decca).

See Me, Feel Me. w/m Peter Townshend, 1970. The British group, The Who, introduced it in the rock opera *Tommy* (Decca), 1969, then had a hit single release, 1970. The New Seekers had a Top 40 version, in medley with "Pinball Wizard," also from *Tommy* (Verve), 1973.

Seems Like Old Times. w/m Carmen Lombardo and John Jacob Loeb, 1946. Introduced and recorded by Guy Lombardo, vocal by Carmen Lonbardo (Decca). The song was a moderate success when first released, but it became a standard when Arthur Godfrey chose it as the theme song for his radio and TV programs. In addition to two network TV evening shows, he headed an hour-and-a-half radio and television show that was simulcast five mornings a week. The song not only opened and closed the show, but was played at the beginning and end of each fifteen-minute segment, giving it theretofore unheard of exposure.

See Ruby Fall. w/m Johnny Cash and Roy Orbison, 1969. Recorded by Johnny Cash on the reverse side of "Blistered" (Columbia).

See Saw. w/m Don Covay and Steve Cropper, 1965. Introduced by Don Covay and The Goodtimers (Atlantic). R&B/Pop gold record by Aretha Franklin (Atlantic), 1968.

See Saw. w/m Roquel Davis, Charles Sutton, and Harry Pratt, 1956. R&B/Pop charts crossover by the The Moonglows (Chess). Popular record by Don Cornell (Coral).

See See Rider Blues (a.k.a. **C. C. Rider**). w/m Gertrude "Ma" Rainey, 1925, 1943. Ma Rainey's interpretation of a traditional blues was recorded by her in 1925 (Paramount) and became the accepted version. Among many other recordings were those by Helen Humes (Philo), Bunk Johnson (American Music 12"), Big Bill Broonzy (Perfect). Bea Booze (Decca) had a chart-maker in 1943. Chuck Willis's hit 1957 recording (Atlantic) started "The Stroll" dance craze. Top 40 version by LaVern Baker (Atlantic), 1963, followed by a Top 10 hit by The Animals (MGM), 1966.

See the Big Man Cry. w/m Ed Bruce, 1965. Hit Country record by Charlie Louvin (Capitol).

See the Funny Little Clown. w/m Bobby Goldsboro, 1964. Hit crossover (C&W/Pop) record by Bobby Goldsboro (United Artists).

See the U.S.A. in Your Chevrolet. w/m Leon Carr and Leo Corday, 1948. Based on the radio and television jingle sung by Dinah Shore.

See What It Gets You. w/m Stephen Sondheim, 1964. Introduced by Lee Remick in (TM) *Anyone Can Whistle*.

See What the Boys in the Back Room Will Have. See **Boys in the Back Room, The**.

See You in September. w. Sid Wayne, m. Sherman Edwards, 1959. Top 40 record by The Tempos (Climax). The Happenings had a Top 10 hit in 1966 (B. T. Puppy).

See You Later, Alligator. w/m Robert Guidry, 1956. Introduced by Bill Haley and His Comets in (MM) *Rock Around the Clock*, the first rock and roll movie. The Haley recording (Decca) was in the Top 10 in all categories.

Se La. w/m Greg Phillinganes and Lionel Richie, 1987. R&B and Pop chart record by Lionel Ritchie (Motown).

Self Control. w. Steve Piccolo (Eng.) and Raffaele Riefoli (It.), m. Raffaele Riefoli and Giancarlo Bigazzi, 1984. Top 10 record by Laura Branigan (Atlantic).

Send a Little Love My Way. w. Hal David, m. Henry Mancini, 1973. Sung by Anne Murray on the soundtrack of (MP) *Oklahoma Crude*, and on records (Capitol).

Send for Me. w/m Ollie Jones, 1957. Hit record by Nat "King" Cole (Capitol).

Send for Me. w. Lorenz Hart, m. Richard Rodgers, 1930. Introduced by Doreen Leslie, Alan Edwards, and a female chorus in (TM) *Simple Simon*, starring Ed Wynn. The melody was used in a prior Rodgers and Hart show *Chee-Chee*, under title of "I Must Love You" (q.v.).

Send Her My Love. w/m Steve Perry and Jonathan Cain, 1983. Recorded by the group Journey (Columbia).

Send in the Clowns. w/m Stephen Sondheim, 1973. Introduced by Glynis Johns in (TM) *A Little Night Music*. Leading records by Judy Collins (Elektra) and Frank Sinatra (Reprise). Collins's version made the Top 40, and its re-release in 1975 made the Top 20. It won a Grammy Award (NARAS) for Song of the Year, 1975, although the song was introduced in a hit musical and had the two major recordings two years earlier. Sung by Elizabeth Taylor in the film version (MM) *A Little Night Music*, 1977.

Send Me Away with a Smile. w/m Louis Weslyn and Al Piantadosi, 1917. A World War I ballad. Popular recording by John McCormack (Victor).

Send Me No Flowers. w. Hal David, m. Burt Bacharach, 1964. Introduced by Doris Day in (MP) *Send Me No Flowers* and recorded by her (Columbia).

Send Me Some Lovin'. w/m Leo Price and John Marascalco, 1957. Coupled with the hit "Lucille," by Little Richard (Specialty). Revived by Sam Cooke, with a Top 20 record (RCA).

Send Me the Pillow You Dream On. w/m Hank Locklin, 1958. Crossover (C&W/Pop) chart records by Hank Locklin (RCA), 1958, the Browns (RCA), 1960, Johnny Tillotson (Cadence), 1962. Top 40 Pop hit by Dean Martin (Reprise), 1965.

Send My Baby Back to Me. w. Bob Hilliard, m. Milton De Lugg, 1953. Leading records by Billy Eckstine, with Nelson Riddle's Orchestra (MGM) and Sunny Gale (RCA Victor).

Send One Your Love. w/m Stevie Wonder, 1979. Top 10 record by Stevie Wonder (Tamla).

Send Ten Pretty Flowers (to My Girl in Tennessee). w/m Steve Nelson and Ed

Nelson, Jr., 1949. Featured and recorded by Spade Cooley (RCA Victor).

Sent for You Yesterday, and Here You Come Today. w/m William "Count" Basie, Eddie Durham, and Jimmy Rushing, 1939. Introduced and recorded by Count Basie, vocal by Jimmy Rushing (Decca); followed by Benny Goodman, with vocal by Johnny Mercer (Victor). Al Hibbler had a later version with the Basie Band (Mercury).

Sentimental and Melancholy. w. Johnny Mercer, m. Richard A. Whiting, 1937. Introduced by Winifred Shaw in (MM) *Ready, Willing and Able*. Recordings: Glen Gray and the Casa Loma Orchestra (Decca), Phil Harris (Vocalion), Teddy Wilson (Brunswick).

Sentimental Gentleman from Georgia. w. Mitchell Parish, m. Frank Perkins, 1932. In addition to the recording by Isham Jones and his Orchestra, with vocal by Eddie Stone (Victor), the song has been recorded by three groups of sisters, the Boswells (Brunswick), the Pickens (Victor), and the Dinnings (Capitol).

Sentimental Journey. w. Bud Green, m. Les Brown and Ben Homer, 1945. Released in 1944, but became a hit in 1945. Ben Homer's arrangement for Les Brown's Orchestra with vocal by Doris Day combined for a million-seller (Columbia) and was instrumental in the song's sixteen weeks' stay on "Your Hit Parade," five weeks as #1. Ella Fitzgerald, with Eddie Heywood's Orchestra, had a popular version (Decca), 1947, as did The Ames Brothers and Les Brown's Band (Coral), 1951. Title song of and featured in (MP) *Sentimental Journey*, 1946.

Sentimental Lady. w/m Bob Welch, 1977. Introduced by Fleetwood Mac in the album "Bare Trees" (Warner Bros.), 1972. The writer, Bob Welch, who had been a vocalist with the group, recorded a single that made the Top 10 (Capitol), 1977.

Sentimental Me. w/m James T. Morehead and James Cassin, 1950. Hit record, coupled with "Rag Mop," (q.v.) by The Ames Brothers (Coral). Chart records by the bands of Ray Anthony (Capitol) and Russ Morgan (Decca).

Sentimental Me. w. Lorenz Hart, m. Richard Rodgers, 1925. Sung by June Cochrane, Edith Meiser, James Norris, and Sterling Holloway in (TM) *Garrick Gaieties*. Leading recordings, both instrumental, by the orchestras of Ben Selvin (Brunswick) and Arden and Ohman (Columbia).

Sentimental Rhapsody. See **Street Scene**.

Sentimental Street. w/m Jack Blades and Alan "Fitz" Gerald, 1985. Top 10 single by the quintet Night Ranger (MCA/Camel).

Senza Fine See **Phoenix Love Theme, The.**

Separate Lives (Love Theme from "White Nights"). w/m Stephen Bishop, 1985. Introduced in (MP) *White Nights*. Via the recording by Phil Collins and Marilyn Martin (Atlantic), the song became the second #1 record from the same film (see **Say You, Say Me**). Nominated for an Academy Award.

Separate Ways. w/m Steve Perry and Jonathan Cain, 1983. Top 10 record by the group Journey (Columbia).

Separate Ways. w/m Bobby West and Richard Mainegra, 1973. Performed by Elvis Presley in the documentary (MM) *Elvis On Tour*, 1972. Top 20 record by Presley (RCA), 1973.

September. w/m Albert McKay, Maurice White, and Alle Wills, 1979. Gold record by the R&B group Earth, Wind & Fire (ARC).

September in the Rain. w. Al Dubin, m. Harry Warren, 1937. Originally written for the 1935 film (MM) *Stars Over Broadway*, starring James Melton. It was heard only as background music, but was sung by Melton in his third and last film (MM) *Melody for Two*, 1937. Melton recorded it (Decca), but the song lasted much longer than his film career. It was the first hit for The George Shearing trio [really a quartet] (MGM), 1949, which established them and insured the status of a standard for the song. Dinah Washington had a Top 40 record in 1961 (Mercury).

September Morn. w. Neil Diamond (Engl.), Gilbert Becaud (Fr.), m. Gilbert Becaud, 1979. Recorded in English by Neil Diamond (Columbia).

September of My Years. w. Sammy Cahn, m. James Van Heusen, 1965. Introduced by Frank Sinatra (Reprise).

September Song. w. Maxwell Anderson, m. Kurt Weill, 1938. Introduced by Walter Huston in (TM) *Knickerbocker Holiday*, followed by his classic recording (Brunswick). Charles Coburn sang it in the film version (MM) *Knickerbocker Holiday*, 1944. In (MP) *September Affair*, 1951, it was played as a recurrent theme, with Huston's recorded voice on the soundtrack. Maurice Chevalier sang it in (MM) *Pepe*, 1960. The song, an all-time standard, has been performed by most leading singers and musicians. Top records by Huston; Frank Sinatra (Columbia), 1946; Stan Kenton and his Orchestra (Capitol), 1951; Jimmy Durante (Warner Bros.), 1963.

Sequel. w/m Harry Chapin, 1980. Harry Chapin's last chart record, written as a "sequel" to his first chart record "Taxi" (Boardwalk).

Serenade. w. Dorothy Donnelly, m. Sigmund Romberg, 1924. Sung by Howard Marsh and other principals in the closing scene of Act I of (TM) *The Student Prince*. Popular recording by the violinist Efrem Zimbalist (Victor). In (MM) *The Student Prince*, 1954, it was sung on the soundtrack by Mario Lanza, dubbing for Edmund Purdom. William Olvis sang it in the Romberg film biography (MM) *Deep in My Heart*, 1954. Larry Kert sang it in (TM) *A Musical Jubilee*, 1975.

Serenade. m. Riccardo Drigo, 1901. Also known as "Drigo's Serenade." Written for violin and piano, excerpted from the composer's ballet, *Les Ballet d'Arlequin*, produced in St. Petersburg, Russia in 1900.

Serenade for a Wealthy Widow. m. Reginald Foresythe, 1934. A piano instrumental arranged for bands. Recorded by Foresythe in England and released in the U.S. (Columbia). Fats Waller (Victor) and Paul Whiteman (Victor) both had popular versions.

Serenade in Blue. w. Mack Gordon, m. Harry Warren, 1942. Introduced by Glenn Miller and his Orchestra, vocal by Ray Eberle and the Modernaires in (MM) *Orchestra Wives* and on records (Victor).

Serenade in the Night. w/m C. A. Bixio and B. Cherubini; Engl. w. and musical adaptation Jimmy Kennedy, 1937. Popular tango.

Serenade of the Bells. w/m Kay Twomey, Al Goodhart, and Al Urbano, 1947. Popular recordings by Jo Stafford (Capitol); Sammy Kaye, vocal by Don Cornell (RCA Victor); Kay Kyser, vocal by Harry Babbitt (Columbia).

Serenade to a Maid. w/m John Jacob Loeb, 1942, Novelty, recorded by Teddy Powell and his Band, with help from Ruth Gaylor and the composer (Bluebird). A take-off on the sweet bands of the day, such as Sammy Kaye, Kay Kyser, Blue Barron, and Ray Herbeck, who inserted spoken introductions of song and singer over musical signatures before the chorus.

Serenade to an Old-Fashioned Girl, A. w/m Irving Berlin, 1946. Introduced by Joan Caulfield in (MM) *Blue Skies*.

Serenade to the Stars, A. w. Harold Adamson, m. Jimmy McHugh, 1938. Introduced by Deanna Durbin in (MM) *Mad About Music*.

Serenata. w. Mitchell Parish, m. Leroy Anderson, 1950. Introduced and recorded as an instrumental by Leroy Anderson and his Orchestra (Decca).

Sergeant Pepper's Lonely Hearts Club Band. See **Sgt. Pepper's Lonely Hearts Club Band**.

Sermonette. w. Jon Hendricks, m. Julian Adderley, 1959. Originally an instrumental introduced by Julian "Cannonball" Adderley, 1956. Featured and recorded by Lambert, Hendricks and Ross (Columbia). Della Reese also had a popular vocal version (Jubilee).

Serpentine Fire. w/m Reginald Burke, Maurice White, and Verdine White, 1977. Recorded by the group Earth, Wind & Fire (Columbia).

Sesame Street. See **This Way to Sesame Street.**

Set 'Em Up Joe. w/m Hank Cochran, Vern Gosdin, Dean Dillon, and Buddy Cannon, 1988. #1 Country chart record by Vern Gosdin (Columbia).

Set Him Free. w/m Mary Depew, Marie Wilson, and Helen Moyers, 1959. Hit C&W record by Skeeter Davis (RCA).

Set Me Free. w/m Todd Rundgren, Roger Powell, Kasim Sulton, and John Wilcox, 1980. Written and recorded by the group Utopia (Bearsville).

Set Me Free. w/m Ray Davies, 1965. Written by the lead singer of the British group The Kinks (Reprise).

Set Me Free (Rosa Lee). w/m Cesar Rosas, 1987. Popular track of the album "By the Light of the Moon" by the group Los Lobos (Slash). The composer was singer/guitarist with Los Lobos.

Settin' the Woods on Fire. w/m Fred Rose and Ed. G. Nelson, 1952. Leading recording by Hank Williams (MGM).

Set You Free This Time. w/m Gene Clark, 1966. The writer was the percussionist for the group that recorded the song, The Byrds (Columbia).

7 and 7 Is. w/m Arthur Lee, 1966. Top 40 record by the writer-led group Love (Elektra).

Seven Days. w/m Willis Carroll and Carmen Taylor, 1956. Hit R&B and Pop crossover by Clyde McPhatter (Atlantic). Pop chart records by The Crew-Cuts (Mercury) and Dorothy Collins (Coral).

Seven Day Weekend. w/m Doc Pomus and Mort Shuman, 1962. Popular record by Gary U. S. Bonds (Legrand).

Seven Deadly Virtues, The. w. Alan Jay Lerner, m. Frederick Loewe, 1960. Introduced by Roddy McDowall in (TM) *Camelot.* Not used in film version.

Seven Little Girls Sitting in the Back Seat. w. Bob Hilliard, m. Lee Pockriss, 1959. Top 10 record by Paul Evans, with The Curls (Guaranteed).

Seven Lonely Days. w/m Earl Shuman, Alden Shuman, and Marshall Brown, 1953. Most popular record by Georgia Gibbs, with The Yale Brothers (Mercury).

Seven Long Days. w/m Jessie Mae Robinson, 1951. Chart R&B record by Charles Brown (Aladdin).

Seven or Eleven (My Dixie Pair o' Dice). w/m Brian Holland, Lamont Dozier, and Eddie Holland, 1967. Top 20 record by The Four Tops (Motown).

7 Rooms of Gloom. w/m Brian Holland, Lamont Dozier, and Eddie Holland, 1967. Top 20 record by The Four Tops (Motown).

Seven Spanish Angels. w/m Troy Seals and Eddie Setser, 1985. One of the cuts from the album "Friendship," in which Ray Charles sang duets with ten Country stars (Columbia).

Seventeen. w/m Rick James, 1984. Top 10 R&B and Pop chart record by Rick James (Gordy).

Seventeen. w/m John Young, Jr., Chuck Gorman, and Boyd Bennett, 1955. Hit records by Boyd Bennett, who introduced it (King), and The Fontane Sisters (Dot). Rusty Draper also had a chart version (Mercury).

Seventh Dawn, The. w. Paul Francis Webster, m. Riz Ortolani, 1964. Song adapted from a theme from (MP) *The Seventh Dawn.*

Most popular record by Ferrante and Teicher (United Artists).

Seventh Heaven. w. Sidney D. Mitchell, m. Lew Pollack, 1937. Theme song of (MP) *Seventh Heaven*, starring James Stewart. It was sung by a chorus in the background.

Seventh Son. w/m Willie Dixon, 1965. Top 10 hit by Johnny Rivers (Imperial).

720 in the Books. w. Harold Adamson, m. Jan Savitt and Leo Watson, 1940. Introduced and recorded by Jan Savitt and his Orchestra (Decca) for their biggest instrumental hit. Charlie Barnet followed with a vocal by Mary Ann McCall (Bluebird). Revived a decade later by Art Mooney and his Orchestra (MGM).

77 Sunset Strip. w/m Mack David and Jerry Livingston, 1959. Theme from the series (TVP) "77 Sunset Strip." Leading recording, instrumental version, by Don Ralke and his Orchestra (Warner Brothers).

Seventy-Six Trombones. w/m Meredith Willson, 1957. Introduced by Robert Preston in (TM) *The Music Man*. Preston repeated his role and the song in (MM) *The Music Man*, 1962.

Seven Wonders. w/m Sandy Stewart and Stevie Nicks, 1987. Popular airplay track from the album "Tango in the Night" by the group Fleetwood Mac (Warner Bros.).

Seven Year Ache. w/m Rosanne Cash, 1981. Crossover (C&W/Pop) record by Rosanne Cash (Columbia).

Seven Years with the Wrong Woman. w/m Bob Miller, 1932.

Sewing Machine, The. w/m Frank Loesser, 1947. Introduced by Betty Hutton in (MM) *The Perils of Pauline*, and on records (Capitol).

Sex (I'm a . . .). w/m John Crawford, Terri Nunn, and David Diamond, 1983. Recorded by the trio Berlin (Geffen).

Sexual Healing. w/m Marvin Gaye, 1982. Marvin Gaye's recording of his song was #1 on the R&B charts for ten weeks and reached #3 on the Pop charts (Columbia).

Sexy Eyes. w/m Christopher Dunn, Robert Mather, and Keith Stegall, 1980. Top 10 gold record by the group Dr. Hook (Capitol).

Sexy Girl. w/m Glenn Frey and Jack Tempchin, 1984. Recorded by Glenn Frey (MCA).

Sexy Mama. w/m Willie Goodman, Harry Ray, and Sylvia Robinson, 1973. Top 20 record by The Moments (Stang).

Sexy + 17 (She's). See **(She's) Sexy + 17.**

Sexy Ways. w/m Hank Ballard, 1954. R&B record by The Midnighters (Federal).

Sgt. Pepper's Lonely Hearts Club Band. w/m John Lennon and Paul McCartney, 1967. Introduced by The Beatles in their album of the same name (Capitol); sung by them in the animated film (MM) *Yellow Submarine*, 1968; chart single, sung in medley with "With a Little Help from My Friends" (q.v.) (Capitol), 1978.

Shaddap You Face. w/m Joe Dolce, 1981. Novelty Italian-American song by Joe Dolce (MCA).

Shade of the Palm, The. w. Owen Hall, m. Leslie Stuart (Thomas A. Barrett), 1900. From the New York production of the 1899 London hit (TM) *Floradora*.

Shadow Dancing. w/m Barry Gibb, Maurice Gibb, Robin Gibb, and Andy Gibb, 1978. Platinum record by Barry Gibb became the #1 single of the year (RSO).

Shadow of Your Smile, The. w. Paul Francis Webster, m. Johnny Mandel, 1965. Introduced by a chorus under the final credits of (MP) *The Sandpiper*, starring Elizabeth Taylor and Richard Burton. Academy Award-winning song, 1965. Leading record by Tony Bennett (Columbia). Grammy Award (NARAS) for Song of the Year. Popular instrumental by saxophonist Boots Randolph (Monument), 1967.

Shadow on My Heart. w/m Ted Daffan, 1945. Leading recording by Ted Daffan (Okeh).

Shadows in the Moonlight. w/m Charlie Black and Rory Bourke, 1979. Recorded by the Canadian singer Anne Murray (Capitol).

Shadows of the Night. w/m David Leigh Byron, 1982. Recorded by Pat Benatar (Chrysalis).

Shadows on the Swanee. w. Joe Young and Johnny Burke m. Harold Spina, 1933. Leading recordings: Irving Aaronson and his Commanders, vocal by Dick Robertson (Vocalion); Allen [Henry "Red"]-Hawkins [Coleman] Orchestra (Perfect); Paul Ash (Columbia); Hal Kemp, vocal by Skinnay Ennis (Brunswick); Irene Taylor (Vocalion); Ethel Waters (Brunswick).

Shadow Waltz. w. Al Dubin, m. Harry Warren, 1933. Introduced by Dick Powell, Ruby Keeler, and chorus in (MM) *The Golddiggers of 1933*. It was interpolated in (MM) *Cain and Mabel* starring Clark Gable and Marion Davies in 1936. Performed by Tammy Grimes and the ladies in (TM) *42nd Street*, 1980.

Shadow Woman. w/m Arthur Hamilton, 1954. Introduced and recorded by Julie London (Liberty).

Shadrach (Meshach, Abednigo). w/m Robert MacGimsey, 1938. Published in 1931 but received major recognition through records of Larry Clinton and his Orchestra, vocal by Ford Leary (Victor) and Louis Armstrong (Decca) in 1938. Robert Merrill (Victor) recorded it in the forties.

Shady Lady Bird. w/m Ralph Blane and Hugh Martin. Introduced by Maureen Cannon in (TM) *Best Foot Forward*. Recorded by Benny Goodman and his Orchestra (Columbia).

Shake. w/m Joey Levine and Kris Resnick, 1968. Recorded by The Shadows of Knight (Team).

Shake. w/m Sam Cooke, 1964. Hit record and last to be released by Sam Cooke before

his death (RCA). Popular version by Otis Redding (Volt), 1967.

Shake, Rattle and Roll. w/m Charles Calhoun, 1954. One of the earliest rock and roll hits. Introduced by Joe Turner (Atlantic). Million-selling record by Bill Haley and his Comets (Decca). Revived by Arthur Conley (Atco), 1967.

(Shake, Shake, Shake) Shake Your Booty. w/m Harry Wayne Casey and Richard Finch, 1976. #1 record by KC & The Sunshine Band (T.K.).

Shake a Hand. w/m Joe Morris, 1953. R&B singer Faye Adams had a #1 record (Herald), followed by jazz/R&B singer Savannah Churchill (Decca). Chart version by Jackie Wilson and Linda Hopkins (Brunswick) in 1963.

Shake a Tail Feather. w. Verlie Rice, m. André Williams and Otha Hayes, 1963. Introduced by The Five Du-Tones (One-derful!). Top 40 version by James and Bobby Purify (Bell), 1967.

Shake and Fingerpop. w/m Autry DeWalt, Lawrence Horn, and Willie Woods, 1965. R&B/Pop chart hit by Jr. Walker [DeWalt] and The All Stars (Soul).

Shakedown. w/m Harold Faltermeyer, Keith Forsey, and Bob Seger, 1987. Introduced by Bob Seger on the soundtrack of (MP) *Beverly Hills Cop II*. Nominated for an Academy Award. Seger's single became a #1 bestseller (MCA).

Shake Down the Stars. w. Eddie DeLange, m. James Van Heusen, 1940. Leading records by Glenn Miller and his Orchestra (Bluebird) and Ella Fitzgerald (Decca).

Shake It. w/m Terence Boylan, 1978. Top 20 record by English singer Ian Matthews (Mushroom).

Shake It Up. w/m Ric Ocasek, 1982. Top 10 record by the group The Cars (Elektra).

Shake It Up Tonight. w/m Michael Sutton and Brenda Sutton, 1981. Crossover (R&B/Pop) hit by Cheryl Lynn (Columbia).

Shake It Well. w/m Donald Davie and Eddie Robinson, 1977. Recorded by The Dramatics (ABC).

Shake Me, Wake Me (When It's Over). w/m Eddie Holland, Lamont Dozier, and Brian Holland, 1966. Top 20 record by The Four Tops (Motown).

Shake Me I Rattle (Squeeze Me I Cry). w/m Hal Hackady and Charles Naylor, 1963. Introduced by The Lennon Sisters on the Lawrence Welk TV show. Popular record by Marion Worth (Columbia).

Shake Sherry. w/m Berry Gordy, Jr., 1963. Recorded by the vocal sextet The Contours (Gordy).

Shakey Ground. w/m Jeffrey Bowen, Alphonso Boyd, and Edward Hazel, 1975. #1 R&B record by The Temptations (Gordy). Phoebe Snow had a chart version (Columbia), 1977.

Shake You Down. w/m Gregory Abbott, 1986. #1 record by Gregory Abbott on both the R&B and the Pop charts (Columbia).

Shake Your Body (Down to the Ground). w/m Michael Jackson and Stephen Jackson, 1979. R&B/Pop platinum record by The Jacksons (Epic).

Shake Your Booty. See **(Shake, Shake, Shake) Shake Your Booty.**

Shake Your Groove Thing. w/m Dino Fekaris and Freddie Perren, 1979. Top 10 gold record by Peaches & Herb (Polydor).

Shake Your Love. w/m Debbie Gibson, 1987. Top 10 single by Debbie Gibson (Atlantic).

Shake Your Rump to the Funk. w/m The Bar-Kays, 1976. Hit R&B/Pop chart record by the group The Bar-Kays (Mercury).

Shakin' All Over. w/m Johnny Kidd, 1965. Recorded by the Canadian Group The Guess Who (Scepter).

Shaking the Blues Away. w/m Irving Berlin, 1927. Introduced by Ruth Etting in (TM) *Ziegeld Follies of 1927*. It was recorded by Etting (Columbia), and the orchestras of Paul Whiteman (Victor), Harry Reser (Columbia), and Ben Selvin (Brunswick). Ann Miller sang and danced the number in (MM) *Easter Parade*, 1948; and Doris Day, as Ruth Etting, sang it in (MM) *Love Me or Leave Me*, 1955.

Sha-La-La. w. Robert Mosley, m. Robert Taylor, 1964. Introduced and recorded by The Shirelles (Scepter). Hit record by the English group Manfred Mann (Ascot).

Sha-La-La (Make Me Happy). w/m Al Green, 1974. R&B and Pop chart gold record hit by Al Green (Hi).

Shall We Dance? w. Oscar Hammerstein II, m. Richard Rodgers, 1951. Introduced by Yul Brynner and Gertrude Lawrence in (TM) *The King and I*. Brynner performed it with Deborah Kerr in (MM) *The King and I*, 1956.

Shall We Dance. w. Ira Gershwin, m. George Gershwin, 1937. Introduced by Fred Astaire and Ginger Rogers in (MM) *Shall We Dance?* Astaire recorded it with Johnny Green and his Orchestra (Brunswick).

Shalom. w/m Jerry Herman, 1961. Introduced by Robert Weede and Mimi Benzell in (TM) *Milk and Honey*. Sung by Leslie Uggams in the all-Jerry Herman revue (TM) *Jerry's Girls*, 1985.

Shambala. w/m Daniel Moore, 1973. Popular records by Three Dog Night (Dunhill) and B. W. Stevenson (RCA).

Shame. w/m John Fitch and Reuben Cross, 1977. Top 10 gold record by Evelyn "Champagne" King (RCA).

Shame, Shame. w/m Keith Colley, Linda Colley, and Knox Henderson, 1967. Record by the English quartet The Magic Lanterns (Atlantic).

Shame, Shame, Shame. w/m Sylvia Robinson, 1975. Top 20 record by Shirley & Company, male vocal by Jesus Alvarez (Vibration).

Shame on Me. w/m Lawton Williams and Bill Enis, 1962. Introduced by Lawton Williams (King). Hit record by Bobby Bare (RCA). Revived by Chuck Jackson (Wand), 1967.

Shame on the Moon. w/m Rodney Crowell, 1982. Top 10 record by Bob Seger and The Silver Bullet Band (Capitol).

Shame on You. w/m Spade Cooley, 1944. C&W song that crossed over to Pop as indicated by its recordings: Spade Cooley (Columbia); Red Foley, with Lawrence Welk and his Orchestra (Decca); Lisa Kirk (Victor); Peggy Lee (Capitol).

Shame on You. w. Edward Heyman, m. Harold Arlen, 1933. Recorded by Rudy Vallee, vocal by Alice Faye (Bluebird), and Freddy Martin, vocal by Terry Shand (Brunswick).

Shane. w. Mack David, m. Victor Young, 1953. Also known as "The Call of the Far-Away Hills," this was a theme from (MP) *Shane*. Leading recording by Paul Weston and his Orchestra (Columbia).

Shanghai. w/m Bob Hilliard and Milton De Lugg, 1951. Leading record by Doris Day, with Paul Weston's Orchestra (Columbia). Other chart versions by The Billy Williams Quartet (MGM); Bing Crosby (Decca); Bob Crosby, with his Orchestra (Capitol).

Shanghai Breezes. w/m John Denver, 1982. Recorded by John Denver (RCA).

Shanghai Lil. w. Al Dubin, m. Harry Warren, 1933. Introduced by James Cagney, Ruby Keeler, and chorus in the big Busby Berkeley finale of (MM) *Footlight Parade*.

Shanghai Shuffle. w/m Larry Conley and Gene Rodemich, 1924. Introduced and recorded by Gene Rodemich's Orchestra (Brunswick). Other records by Fletcher Henderson (Decca) and Buster Bailey (Vocalion).

Shangri-La. w. Carl Sigman, m. Matt Malneck and Robert Maxwell, 1946. Introduced as instrumental by harpist Robert Maxwell with Matty Malneck's Orchestra (Columbia, Parts 1&2). Revived vocally by The Four Coins (Epic), 1957; Vic Dana (Dolton), 1964; The Letterman (Capitol), 1969.

Shannon. w/m Henry Gross, 1976. Top 10 record by Henry Gross (Lifesong).

Shanty in Old Shanty Town, A. See **In a Shanty in Old Shanty Town.**

Shape of Things, The. w/m Sheldon Harnick, 1956. Comedy quasi-folk song introduced by Charlotte Rae in (TM) *The Littlest Revue*.

Shape of Things to Come. w/m Barry Mann and Cynthia Weil, 1968. Sung by Christopher Jones in (MP) *Wild in the Streets*. Top 40 record by Max Frost and The Troopers (Tower). "Frost" was a pseudonym for Jones.

Shape of Things to Come, The. w/m George Boyter, Malcolm Calum, Brian Lewis, and Davey Ross, 1979. Recorded by the Scottish quartet The Headboys (RSO).

Shapes of Things. w/m Paul Samwell-Smith, Keith Relf, and James McCarty, 1966. Hit record by the British group The Yardbirds (Epic).

Share the Land. w/m Burton Cummings, 1970. Top 10 record by the Canadian group Guess Who (RCA).

Share Your Love with Me. w/m Al Bragg and Deadric Malone, 1964. Introduced by Bobby Bland (Duke). Top 20 records by Aretha Franklin (Atlantic), 1969, and Kenny Rogers (Liberty), 1981.

Sharing the Night Together. w/m Ava Alderidge and Edward Struzick, 1978. Gold record by the group Dr. Hook (Columbia).

Sharp Dressed Man. w/m Billy Gibbons, Dusty Hill, and Frank Beard, 1983. Written and recorded by the trio ZZ Top (Warner Bros.).

Shattered. w/m Mick Jagger and Keith Richards, 1979. Recorded by The Rolling Stones (Rolling Stones).

Shattered Dreams. w/m Clark Datchler, 1988. Popular single from the album, "Turn Back the Clock" by the British group Johnny Hates Jazz (Virgin).

Shauny O'Shay. w/m Hugh Martin, 1948. Introduced by Don Liberto and Virginia Gorski in (TM) *Look Ma, I'm Dancin'!* Recorded by Jack Smith (Capitol) and Elliot Lawrence and his Orchestra (Columbia).

Shaving Cream. w/m Benny Bell, 1975. A novelty dialect record by Benny Bell (Vanguard), originally released in 1946 and rediscovered 29 years later by disc jockey Dr. Demento.

Shazam! w/m Lee Hazelwood and Duane Eddy, 1960. Instrumental introduced in (MM) *Because They're Young* by Duane Eddy and recorded by him (Jamie).

Sh-Boom (Life Could Be a Dream). w/m James Keys, Claude Feaster, Carl Feaster, Floyd F. McRae, and James Edwards, 1954. Introduced and recorded by The Chords (Cat), the members of the R&B group having written the song. It was covered by The Crew-Cuts (Mercury) who made it the first #1 rock and roll song. Later that year, Stan Freberg, with The Toads and Billy May's Orchestra, had a hit parody version (Capitol).

She. w/m Ritchie Cordell, Tommy James, Jerry Kasenetz, Jeff Katz, and Mike Vale, 1970. Recorded by Tommy James and The Shondells (Roulette).

She and I. w/m Dave Loggins, 1986. #1 record on the Country charts by the group Alabama (RCA).

She Believes in Me. w/m Steve Gibb, 1979. Top 10 gold record by Kenny Rogers (United Artists).

She Belongs to Me. w/m Bob Dylan, 1969. Introduced and first recorded in an album by Bob Dylan (Columbia), 1965. Top 40 single by Rick Nelson (Decca), 1969.

She Blew A Good Thing. w/m Ronnie Lewis and Henry Murray, Jr., 1966. Recorded by The Poets (Symbol).

She Blinded Me with Science. w/m Thomas Dolby and Joe Kerr, 1983. Recorded by the British singer/writer Thomas Dolby (Capitol).

She Bop. w/m Cyndi Lauper, Richard Chertoff, Gary Corbett, and Stephen Lunt, 1984. Top 10 hit by Cyndi Lauper (Portrait).

She Broke My Heart in Three Places. w/m Milton Drake, Al Hoffman, and Jerry Livingston, 1944. The three places were three different cities!

She Called Me Baby. w/m Harlan Howard, 1974. Crossover (C&W/Pop) hit by Charlie Rich (RCA).

She Came in Through the Bathroom Window. w/m John Lennon and Paul McCartney, 1969. Introduced by The Beatles in their album "Abbey Road" (Apple). Top 30 single by Joe Cocker (A&M), 1970.

She Can't Find Her Keys. w. Roy Alfred, m. Wally Gold, 1962. Recorded by Paul Petersen (Colpix).

She Can't Say That Anymore. w/m John Conlee, 1980. Top 10 Country chart record by John Conlee (MCA), 1980.

She Comes to Me (When She Needs Good Lovin'). See **(When She Needs Good Lovin') She Comes to Me.**

She Cried (a.k.a. **He Cried**). w/m Ted Darryl and Greg Richards, 1962. Introduced by Ted Darryl (Utopia). Top 10 record by Jay and The Americans (United Artists). Revived by The Letterman (Capitol), 1970. Recorded by The Shangri-Las under title of "He Cried" (Red Bird) 1966.

She Did It. w/m Eric Carmen, 1977. Recorded by Eric Carmen (Arista), followed by Michael Damian (Leg), 1981.

She Didn't Say "Yes." w. Dorothy Fields, m. Jerome Kern, 1931. Introduced by Bettina Hall in (TM) *The Cat and the Fiddle.* Jeanette MacDonald sang it in the film adaptation (MM) *The Cat and the Fiddle* in 1934. In the Kern screen biography (MM) *Till the Clouds Roll By* in 1946, it was sung by the Wilde Twins.

She Don't Love Nobody. w/m John Hiatt, 1989. Hit Country record by The Desert Rose Band (MCA/Curb).

She'd Rather Be with Me. w/m Garry Bonner and Alan Gordon, 1966. Top 10 record by The Turtles (White Whale).

She Drives Me Crazy. w/m David Steele and Roland Gift, 1989. Hit record by Fine Young Cannibals (I.R.S.).

Sheena Is a Punk Rocker. w/m Douglas Colvin, John Cummings, Thomas Erdelyi, and Jeff Hyman, 1977. Recorded by the group The Ramones (Sire). Sung by them in (MM) *Rock 'n' Roll High School*, 1979.

She Even Woke Me Up to Say Goodbye. w/m Douglas Gilmore and Mickey Newbury, 1970. Country chart hit by Jerry Lee Lewis (Smash).

She Got the Goldmine (I Got the Shaft). w/m Tim DuBois, 1982. Country/Pop novelty by Jerry Reed (RCA).

She Had to Go and Lose It at the Astor. w/m Don Raye and Hugh Prince, 1939. Hit record by Johnny Messner and his Orchestra (Varsity).

Sheik of Araby, The. w. Harry B. Smith and Francis Wheeler, m. Ted Snyder, 1921. Inspired by the silent film *The Sheik*, starring Rudolph Valentino. Eddie Cantor interpolated it in (TM) *Make It Snappy*, 1922. It was revived with a comedy treatment by Alice Faye, Betty Grable, Billy Gilbert, and the Nicholas Brothers in (MM) *Tin Pan Alley*, 1940.

Sheik of Avenue B, The. w. Bert Kalmar, m. Harry Ruby, 1924. Introduced, performed, and recorded (Victor) by Fanny Brice.

Sheila. w/m Tommy Roe, 1962. #1 chart record by Tommy Roe (ABC-Paramount).

She Is More to Be Pitied Than Censured. w/m William B. Gray, 1895. A well-known sentimental ballad of the 1890s with the claim that a man was the cause of her downfall. Leading recording by the vaudevillian, Steve Porter (Columbia). It was sung satirically by a chorus in (MM) *Cruisin' Down the River*, 1953.

She Is My Daisy. w. Harry Lauder and J. D. Harper, m. Harry Lauder, 1905. Introduced and featured by Lauder in vaudeville and on a 12″ 78 RPM record (Victor).

She Is Not Thinking of Me. See **Waltz at Maxim's.**

She Is Still a Mystery. w/m John Sebastian, 1967. Top 40 record by The Lovin' Spoonful (Kama Sutra).

She Is the Belle of New York. w/m Hugh Morton, m. Gustav Kerker, 1898. Introduced by Edna May in (TM) *The Belle of New York*.

She Is the Sunshine of Virginia. w. Ballard MacDonald, m. Harry Carroll, 1916.

She Keeps the Home Fires Burning. w/m Dennis Morgan, Don Pfrimmer, and Mike Reid, 1985. #1 Country chart record by Ronnie Milsap (RCA).

She Left Love All over Me. w/m Chester Lester, 1983. #1 Country chart record by Razzy Bailey (RCA).

She'll Always Remember. w/m Edward Pola and Johnny Marks, 1942. Featured and recorded by Woody Herman, vocal by Carolyn Grey (Decca); Dolly Dawn (Elite); Earl Hines, vocal by Billy Eckstine (Bluebird).

She Loves Me. w. Sheldon Harnick, m. Jerry Bock, 1963. Introduced by Daniel Massey in (TM) *She Loves Me*.

She Loves You. w/m John Lennon and Paul McCartney. 1964. #1 chart record by The Beatles (Swan), and sung by them in (MM) *A Hard Day's Night*. They also recorded a German version, "Sie Liebt Dich" (Swan).

Shelter of Your Arms, The. w/m Jerry Samuels, 1964. Hit record by Sammy Davis, Jr. (Reprise).

She May Have Seen Better Days. w/m James Thornton, 1894.

She Needs Someone to Hold Her (When She Cries). w/m Raymond Smith, 1973. #1 Country chart record by Conway Twitty (Decca).

Shepherd Serenade. w. Kermit Goell, m. Fred Spielman, 1941. Popularized and recorded by Bing Crosby (Decca); Horace Heidt, vocal by Gordon MacRae; Larry Cotton, and whistling by Fred Lowery (Columbia); Art Jarrett, vocal by Jarrett and The Smoothies (Victor).

Shepherd's Serenade, The. w. Clifford Grey, m. Herbert Stothart, 1930. Sung by Ramon Novarro in (MM) *Devil May Care.* Frank Munn (Brunswick) and Leo Reisman and his Orchestra (Victor) both coupled their recordings with "Charming" (q.v.) from the same film. Smith Ballew also recorded it (Okeh).

She Reminds Me of You. w. Mack Gordon, m. Harry Revel, 1934. Introduced by Bing Crosby in (MM) *We're Not Dressing.* Crosby recorded it (Brunswick) as did Eddy Duchin's Orchestra, with vocal by Lew Sherwood (Victor).

Sherry. w/m Bob Gaudio, 1962. The first #1 record by the vocal group The Four Seasons (Vee-Jay).

She's a Bad Mama Jama (She's Built, She's Stacked). w/m Leon Haywood, 1981. Top 10 crossover (R&B/Pop) record by Carl Carlton (20th Century).

She's a Beauty. w/m David Foster, Steve Lukather, and Fee Waybill, 1983. Top 10 record by the group The Tubes (Capitol).

She's About a Mover. w/m Doug Sahm, 1965. Introduced and recorded by "Tex-Mex" rock group, The Sir Douglas [Sahm] Quintet (Tribe).

She's Actin' Single (I'm Drinkin' Doubles). w/m Wayne Carson Thompson, 1975. #1 Country chart record by Gary Stewart (RCA).

She's a Fool. w/m Ben Raleigh and Mark Barkan, 1963. Top 10 record by Lesley Gore (Mercury).

She's a Great, Great Girl. w/m Harry Woods, 1928.

She's a Heartbreaker. w/m Charlie Foxx and Jerry Williams, 1968. Top 20 record by Gene Pitney (Musicor).

She Said She Said. w/m John Lennon and Paul McCartney, 1966. Introduced by The Beatles in their album "Revolver" (Capitol).

She's a Lady. w/m Paul Anka, 1971. Gold record by Welsh singer Tom Jones (Parrot).

She's a Lady. w/m John Sebastian, 1969. Recorded by John Sebastian (Kama Sutra).

She's a Latin from Manhattan. w. Al Dubin, m. Harry Warren, 1935. Introduced by Al Jolson, who was joined by Ruby Keeler in a production number in (MM) *Go Into Your Dance.* Jack Carson and Joan Leslie sang it in (MP) *The Hard Way* in 1942 and Jolson, dubbing for Larry Parks, sang it again, this time with Evelyn Keyes, in (MM) *The Jolson Story* in 1946.

She's All I Got. w/m Gary Bonds and Jerry Williams, Jr., 1971. Country/Pop chart records by Freddie North (Mankind) and Johnny Paycheck (Epic).

She's Always a Woman. w/m Billy Joel, 1978. Recorded by Billy Joel (Columbia).

She's a Miracle. w/m J. P. Pennington and Sonny Lemaire, 1985. #1 Country chart record by the band Exile (Epic).

She's a Rainbow. w/m Mick Jagger and Keith Richards, 1968. Record by The Rolling Stones (London).

She's a Woman. w/m John Lennon and Paul McCartney, 1964. Hit record by The Beatles (Capitol).

She Say (Oom Dooby Doom). w/m Barry Mann and Mike Anthony, 1959. Popular record by The Diamonds (Mercury).

She Sells Sea Shells. w. Terry Sullivan, m. Harry Gifford, 1909. Recorded by Ada Jones and Billy Murray (Victor).

She's Everybody's Sweetheart (But Nobody's Gal). w. Billy Rose, m. Con Conrad, 1924. Introduced and recorded by Ted Lewis and his Band (Columbia).

She's Funny That Way (I Got a Woman, Crazy for Me). w. Richard A. Whiting, m. Neil Moret, 1928. A rare case of Whiting writing the lyric to someone else's melody. Popular records by Gene Austin (Victor) and Ted Lewis and his Band (Columbia). The song was heard in (MP) *The Postman Always Rings Twice*, starring Lana Turner and John Garfield, 1946. Sung by Frank Sinatra in (MM) *Meet Danny Wilson* and by Frankie Laine in (MM) *Rainbow 'round My Shoulder*, 1952.

She's Gone. w/m Daryl Hall and John Oates, 1974. Introduced by Hall and Oates (Atlantic). Also recorded by the family group Tavares (Capitol). Hall and Oates had their version re-released in 1976, with their record reaching the Top 10 on the Pop charts.

She's Gone Gone Gone. w/m Harlan Howard, 1965. C&W chart record by Lefty Frizzell (Columbia). Revived by Carl Jackson (Columbia), 1984.

She's Got a Single Thing in Mind. w/m Walt Aldredge, 1989. Hit Country chart record by Conway Twitty (MCA).

She's Got a Way. w/m Billy Joel, 1981. Introduced by Billy Joel in his first album "Cold Spring Harbor" (Columbia), 1971. A single was released and made the Top 40 (Columbia), 1981.

She's Got It. w/m Richard Penniman, 1956. Top 10 R&B chart record by Little Richard (Specialty). He sang it in (MM) *The Girl Can't Help It*, 1957.

She's Got to Be a Saint. w/m Mario Dinapoli and Joe Paulini, 1973. C&W/Pop record by Ray Price (Columbia).

She's Got You. w/m Hank Cochran, 1962. Crossover hit (C&W and Pop) by Patsy Cline (Decca). Revived by Loretta Lynn (MCA), 1977.

She Shall Have Music. w/m Maurice Sigler, Al Goodhart, and Al Hoffman, 1936. Popularized in the U.S. by the English bandleader, Jack Hylton, who was appearing on a weekly network radio show. His recording (Victor) and that of Rudy Vallee (Melotone) were the best-selling versions.

She's Having a Baby. w/m Dave Wakeling and Ian Ritchie, 1988. Introduced on the soundtrack of (MP) *She's Having a Baby* by Dave Wakeling.

She's Just a Whole Lot Like You. w/m Hank Thompson, 1960. Featured and recorded by Hank Thompson (Capitol).

She's Just My Style. w/m Gary Lewis, Thomas Lesslie, Al Capps, and Leon Russell, 1966. Top 10 hit by Gary Lewis and The Playboys (Liberty).

She's Like the Wind. w/m Patrick Swayze and Stacey Widelitz, 1987. Sung on the soundtrack of (MP) *Dirty Dancing* and on a Top 10 record by Patrick Swayze with Wendy Fraser (RCA).

She's Lookin' Good. w/m Rodger Collins, 1968. Hit record by Wilson Pickett (Atlantic).

She's Mine, All Mine. w/m Bert Kalmar and Harry Ruby, 1921. Revived by male quartet in (MM) *Three Little Words*, the biographical film based on the careers of Kalmar and Ruby, 1950.

She's My Girl. w/m Garry Bonner and Alan Gordon, 1967. Top 40 record by The Turtles (White Whale).

She's My Love. w/m Bob Merrill, 1961. Introduced by Jerry Orbach in (TM) *Carnival*.

She's No Lady. w/m Lyle Lovett, 1988. Country chart record by Lyle Lovett (MCA/Curb).

She's Not Just Another Woman. w/m Ronald Dunbar and Clyde Wilson, 1971. Hit record by a Detroit studio group The 8th Day (Invictus).

She's Not Really Cheatin' (She's Just Gettin' Even). w/m Randy Shaffer, 1982. Top 10 Country chart record by Moe Bandy (Columbia).

She's Not There. w/m Rod Argent, 1964. Introduced by the British group The Zombies (Parrot). Re-popularized by the U.S. group Santana (Columbia) 1977.

She's Not You. w/m Doc Pomus, Jerry Leiber, and Mike Stoller, 1962. Hit record by Elvis Presley (RCA).

She's Out of My Life. w/m Tom Bahler, 1980. Recorded by Michael Jackson (Epic).

She's Pulling Me Back Again. w/m Jerry Foster and Wilburn Rice, 1977. #1 Country chart record by Mickey Gilley (Playboy).

(She's) Sexy + 17. w/m Brian Setzer, 1983. Recorded by the trio Stray Cats (EMI America).

She's Single Again. w/m Charlie Craig and Peter McCann, 1985. Top 10 Country chart record by Janie Fricke (Columbia).

She's So Cold. w/m Mick Jagger and Keith Richards, 1980. Recorded by The Rolling Stones (Rolling Stones).

She's Strange. w/m Larry Blackmon, Charlie Singleton, Nathan Leftenant, and Tomi Jenkins, 1984. Recorded by the Blackmon-led group Cameo (Atlanta Artists).

She's Such a Comfort to Me. w. Douglas Furber, Max Lief, Nathaniel Lief, and Donovan Parsons, m. Arthur Schwartz, 1930. Introduced in London in (TM) *The House That Jack Built* by Jack Hulburt. Jack Buchanan introduced it in the U.S. when the song was added to the mostly Cole Porter score for the revue (TM) *Wake Up and Dream*.

She's the Daughter of Mother Machree. w. Jeff T. Branen, m. Ernest R. Ball, 1915. The lyricist reversed his name to Nenarb on the title page credits. This song was an attempt to follow Ball's successful "Mother Machree" (q.v.). Popular records by Charles Harrison (Victor) and Manuel Romain (Columbia).

She's the Fairest Little Flower Dear Old Dixie Ever Grew. w. Ashley S. Johnson, m. Theodore F. Morse, 1907.

She's Too Good to Be True. w/m Sonny LeMaire and J. P. Pennington, 1987. #1 Country chart song by the group Exile (Epic).

She Sure Got Away with My Heart. w/m James Aldridge and Howard Brasfield, 1984.

Top 10 Country chart record by John Anderson (Warner Bros.).

She's Way Up Thar. w/m Lew Brown, 1934. Lew Brown performed this novelty song in (MM) *Stand Up and Cheer*. It was recorded by Clyde Lucas and his Band (Columbia) and Frank Luther (Melotone).

She Thinks I Still Care. w/m Dickey Lee, 1962. #1 Country hit by George Jones (United Artists). Revived by Elvis Presley (RCA), 1977.

She Took Mother's Advice. w. Stanley Murphy, m. Percy Wenrich, 1910.

She Touched Me. w. Ira Levin, m. Milton Schafer, 1965. Introduced by Elliott Gould in (TM) *Drat! The Cat!* Barbra Streisand had a popular recording titled "He Touched Me" (Columbia).

She Understands Me (a.k.a. **Dum-De-Da**). w/m Merle Kilgore and Margie Singleton, 1964. Introduced by Johnny Tillotson (MGM). Top 40 version under title "Dum-De-Da" by Bobby Vinton (Epic), 1966.

She Used to Be Somebody's Baby. w/m Larry Gatlin, 1986. Top 10 Country chart record by Larry, Steve, Rudy: The Gatlin Brothers (Columbia).

She Waits by the Deep Blue Sea. w. Edward Madden, m. Theodore F. Morse, 1905.

She Was a Dear Little Girl. w. Irving Berlin, m. Ted Snyder, 1909. In the first stage musical to contain a Berlin song (TM) *The Boys and Betty*, this was introduced by Marie Cahill.

She Was Bred in Old Kentucky. w. Harry Braisted, m. Stanley Carter, 1898. Written by comedy writers Harry B. Berdan and Frederick J. Redcliffe under the above pseudonyms and featured by Lottie Gilson.

She Was Happy Till She Met You. w. Charles Graham, m. Monroe H. Rosenfeld, 1899.

She Was Hot. w/m Mick Jagger and Keith Richards, 1984. Recorded by The Rolling Stones (Rolling Stones).

She Wasn't You. w. Alan Jay Lerner, m. Burton Lane, 1965. Introduced by Clifford David in (TM) *On a Clear Day You Can See Forever*. In the film version (MM) *On a Clear Day You Can See Forever*, 1970, Barbra Streisand sang the song, now retitled "He Isn't You."

She Was Only Seventeen (He Was One Year More). w/m Marty Robbins, 1958. Introduced and hit C&W and Pop record by Marty Robbins (Columbia).

She Went a Little Bit Farther. w/m Mack Vickery and Merle Kilgore, 1968. Country chart record by Faron Young (Mercury).

She Went to the City. w/m Paul Dresser, 1904.

She Wore a Yellow Ribbon (a.k.a. 'Round Her Neck She Wears (Wore) a Yellow Ribbon). w/m George A. Norton, 1917, 1949. Most popular version of American folk song. Song was sung in (MP) *She Wore a Yellow Ribbon*, starring John Wayne, 1949. Hit records by Eddie "Piano" Miller (Rainbow) and The Andrews Sisters with Russ Morgan and his Orchestra (Decca).

She Works Hard for the Money. w/m Donna Summer and Michael Omartian, 1983. Top 10 R&B/Pop chart record (Mercury).

Shifting, Whispering Sands, The. w. V. C. Gilbert, m. Mary M. Hadler, 1955. Hit records by Rusty Draper, with David Carroll's Orchestra (Mercury); Billy Vaughn, narration by Ken Nordine (Dot, Parts 1 & 2).

Shilo. w/m Neil Diamond, 1970. Top 40 record by Neil Diamond (Bang).

Shim-Me-Sha-Wabble. m. Spencer Williams, 1917. An instrumental based on the dances, the shimmy and the wobble, numbered among its many recordings, McKinney's Cotton Pickers (Victor), 1928, and Don Redman and his Orchestra (Bluebird), 1940.

Shimmy, Shimmy, Ko-Ko-Bop. w/m Bob Smith, 1959. Hit record by Little Anthony and The Imperials (End).

Shine. w. Cecil Mack and Lew Brown, m. Ford T. Dabney, 1924. Featured and recorded by Van and Schenck (Columbia). The song has had many recordings in the jazz and popular fields. Among the standouts are Louis Armstrong (Okeh); Art Hodes with Sidney Bechet (Brunswick); Jack Teagarden (HRS); The Benny Goodman Sextette (Columbia); Ella Fitzgerald (Decca); Frankie Laine (Mercury). It was played as an instrumental in (MM) *The Birth of the Blues*, 1941; performed by John W. Bubbles in (MM) *Cabin in the Sky*, 1942; played in (MM) *The Benny Goodman Story*, 1955, and (MM) *The Eddy Duchin Story*, 1956.

Shine, Shine, Shine. w/m Bud McGuire and Ken Bell, 1987. #1 Country chart record by Eddy Raven from his album "Right Hand Man" (RCA).

Shine a Little Love. w/m Jeff Lynne, 1979. Top 10 record by the English group Electric Light Orchestra (Jet).

Shine It On. w. Fred Ebb, m. John Kander, 1977. Introduced by Liza Minnelli and company in (TM) *The Act*.

Shine On, Harvest Moon. w. Jack Norworth, m. Nora Bayes and Jack Norworth, 1908. Introduced by Nora Bayes in (TM) *Ziegfeld Follies of 1908*, and, oddly, also sung by Anna Held in (TM) *Miss Innocence* later the same year. Ruth Etting sang it in (TM) *Ziegfeld Follies of '31*. It was the title song in (MM) *Shine On, Harvest Moon*, 1944, in which Ann Sheridan and Dennis Morgan played the roles of the authors. The song was also used as background music in (MP) *Ever Since Eve*, 1937.

Shine On Your Shoes, A w. Howard Dietz, m. Arthur Schwartz, 1932. Introduced by Vilma and Buddy Ebsen, Monette Moore, and Larry Adler in (TM) *Flying Colors*. Performed by Fred Astaire in (MM) *The Band Wagon* in 1953.

Shining Star. w/m Paul Richmond and Leo Graham, Jr., 1980. Crossover (R&B/Pop) Top 10 hit by The Manhattans (Columbia).

Shining Star. w/m Philip Bailey and

Maurice White, 1975. Introduced by the group Earth, Wind & Fire in (MP) *Shining Star*, originally titled "That's the Way of the World." The recording became a #1 gold record (Columbia).

Shinin' On. w/m Mark Farner and Don Brewer, 1974. Top 20 record by the group Grand Funk (Capitol).

Ship Ahoy!—All the Nice Girls Love a Sailor. w. A. J. Mills, m. Bennett Scott, 1909.

Ship of Fools (Save Me from Tomorrow). w/m Karl Wallinger, 1987. Led by Wallinger, the U.K. group World Party had a chart record (Chysalis).

Ships. w/m Ian Hunter, 1979. Top 10 U.S. record of the English song by Barry Manilow (Arista).

Ship Without a Sail, A. w. Lorenz Hart, m. Richard Rodgers, 1929. Sung by Jack Whiting and sailors in (TM) *Heads Up!* In the film version (MM) *Heads Up!*, 1930, it was sung by Charles "Buddy" Rogers. Recorded by Libby Holman (Brunswick).

Shirley. w/m Warner Webster, 1957. R&B/Pop chart crossover record by The Schoolboys (Okeh).

Shock the Monkey. w/m Peter Gabriel, 1982. Written and recorded by the English singer Peter Gabriel (Geffen).

Shoe Goes on the Other Foot Tonight, The. w/m Buddy R. Mize, 1967. Country chart hit by Marty Robbins (Columbia).

Shoein' the Mare. w. Ira Gershwin and E. Y. Harburg, m. Harold Arlen, 1934. Sung by Adrienne Matzenauer and danced by Esther Junger and Ofelia & Pimento in (TM) *Life Begins at 8:40.*

Shoeless Joe from Hannibal, Mo. w/m Richard Adler and Jerry Ross, 1955. Introduced by Rae Allen and The Baseball Players in (TM) *Damn Yankees*, and repeated by them in (MM) *Damn Yankees*, 1958.

Shoes. w/m Eric Beam, 1975. Recorded by Reparata (Polydor).

Shoeshine Boy. w/m Linda Allen and Harry Booker, 1975. #1 R&B and Top 20 Pop chart record by Eddie Kendricks (Tamla).

Shoe Shine Boy. w. Sammy Cahn, m. Saul Chaplin, 1936. Introduced in a revue at Connie's Inn, in New York, by Louis Armstrong and his Orchestra. The best-selling record, however, was by the Mills Brothers (Decca). This was the first hit for both Cahn and Chaplin.

Shoes of a Fool. w. Jimmy Day and Jim Coleman, 1963. C&W chart record by Bill Goodwin (Vee Jay).

Shoes with Wings On. w. Ira Gershwin, m. Harry Warren, 1949. Introduced by Fred Astaire in (MM) *The Barkleys of Broadway.*

Shogun (Mariko's Theme). m. Maurice Jarre, 1980. Instrumental based on the love theme from the mini-series (TVP) "Shogun," recorded by Meco (RSO).

Shoo-Be-Doo-Be-Doo-Da-Day. w/m Henry Cosby, Stevie Wonder, and Sylvia Moy, 1968. Top 10 record by Stevie Wonder (Tamla).

Shoo-Fly Pie and Apple Pan Dowdy. w. Sammy Gallop, m. Guy Wood, 1946. Stan Kenton, vocal by June Christy, had a million-seller (Capitol) and Dinah Shore had a hit, with Sonny Burke's Orchestra accompanying (Columbia).

Shoop Shoop Song, The (It's in His Kiss). w/m Rudy Clark, 1964. Hit record by Betty Everett (Vee-Jay).

Shoo-Shoo Baby. w/m Phil Moore, 1943. A #1 wartime hit ("—your papa's off to the seven seas"), it was featured in six movies, five in a space of three years: (MM) *Beautiful But Broke*, 1943; (MM) *Trocadero*, sung by Ida James, 1944; (MM) *Follow the Boys*, sung by The Andrews Sisters, 1944; (MM) *South of Dixie*, sung by Ella Mae Morse, 1944; (MM) *Billy Rose's Diamond Horseshoe*, interpolated by Betty Grable, 1945. The Page Cavanaugh

Trio performed it in (MM) *Big City*, 1948. The Andrews Sisters' record (Decca) was #1 for nine weeks! Ella Mae Morse had a Top 10 record (Capitol).

Shoot 'Em Up, Baby. w/m Jeff Barry and Andy Kim, 1968. Top 40 record by Andy Kim (Steed).

Shoot the Sherbet to Me, Herbert. w/m Ben Homer, 1939. Popular records by the Merry Macs (Decca) and Tommy Dorsey's Clambake Seven (Victor).

Shoot Your Shot. w/m Autry DeWalt, James Graves, and Lawrence Horn, 1967. Recorded by Jr. Walker [DeWalt] and The All Stars (Soul).

Shop Around. w/m Berry Gordy, Jr. and William "Smokey" Robinson, 1961, 1976. Introduced and Top 10 record by The Miracles (Tamla). Revived and million-selling record by Captain and Tennille (A&M), 1976. See also **Don't Let Him Shop Around**.

Short Fat Fannie. w/m Larry Williams, 1957. Featured and recorded by Larry Williams (Specialty).

Short'nin' Bread. w/m Jacques Wolfe, 1928. A concert song written in the style of a Negro spiritual. Various black composers claimed to have written it originally, but the most likely was Reese d'Pree in 1905. Whether Wolfe's was a transcription or an arrangement, it became a favorite of baritone singers in concert, vaudeville, and radio. Lawrence Tibbett introduced it and recordings by Nelson Eddy (Columbia), Conrad Thibaut (Victor), and Fats Waller (Bluebird) followed. Paul Robeson sang it in (MM) *Jericho*, made in England in 1937; and in the 1946 Disney animated film (MM) *Make Mine Music*, Nelson Eddy sang it as the voice of Willie, the opera-singing whale.

Short People. w/m Randy Newman, 1978. Novelty gold record by Randy Newman (Warner Bros.).

Short Shorts. w. Bob Gaudio and Bill Dalton, m. Tom Austin and Bill Crandall, 1958. The writers comprised the vocal group,

The Royal Teens, who had a hit recording of the topical song referring to a current dress vogue (ABC-Paramount).

Shotgun. w/m Autry DeWalt, 1965. R&B/Pop Top 10 hit by Jr. Walker [DeWalt] and The All Stars (Soul).

Shot Gun Boogie. w/m Tennessee Ernie Ford, 1951. Introduced and recorded by Tennessee Ernie Ford (Capitol).

Should I? w. Arthur Freed, m. Nacio Herb Brown, 1929. Introduced by Charles Kayley and reprised by Ethelind Terry in (MM) *Lord Byron of Broadway*. It was revived by Debbie Reynolds in (MM) *Singin' in the Rain* in 1952. Among the early recordings were Jack Fulton with Paul Whiteman's Orchestra (Columbia) and the Arden and Ohman Orchestra (Victor).

Should I Be Sweet? w. B. G. DeSylva, m. Vincent Youmans 1932. Introduced by June Knight in (TM) *Take a Chance* and sung by her in the film version (MM) *Take a Chance* in 1933. Millie Slavin recorded it in the LP "Through the Years with Vincent Youmans" (Monmouth-Evergreen).

Should I Do It. w/m Layng Martine, Jr., 1982. Recorded by The Pointer Sisters (Planet).

Should I Tell You I Love You? w/m Cole Porter, 1946. Introduced by Mary Healy in (TM) *Around the World*. First record by Monica Lewis (Signature).

Should've Known Better. w/m Richard Marx, 1987. Top 10 record by Richard Marx from the album of his name (Manhattan).

Should've Never Let You Go. w/m Neil Sedaka and Phil Cody, 1980. Recorded by Neil Sedaka and his daughter, Dara (Elektra).

Shout. w/m Roland Orzabel and Ian Stanley, 1985. #1 single from the album "Songs from the Big Chair" by the English duo Tears for Fears (Mercury).

Shout. w/m O'Kelly Isley, Ronald Isley, and Rudolph Isley, 1959. Introduced by the Isley Brothers (RCA, Part 1). Top 10 hit by Joey Dee and The Starliters (Roulette, Part 1),

1962. Other chart records by Lulu and The Luvers (Parrot), 1964, and The Chambers Brothers (Vault, Part 1), 1969.

Shout! Shout! (Knock Yourself Out). w/m Ernie Maresca and Thomas F. Bogdany, 1962. Top 10 record by Ernie Maresca (Seville).

Shout, Sister, Shout. w/m J. Tim Brymn, Alexander Hill, and Clarence Williams, 1932. First recorded by Eva Taylor with her husband Clarence Williams accompanying (Perfect). Sung by The Boswell Sisters in (MM) *The Big Broadcast of 1932.* Also recorded in the forties by Lucky Millinder, vocal by Sister Rosetta Tharpe (Decca).

Shout for Joy. m. Albert Ammons, 1941. Introduced and recorded by boogie-woogie pianist Albert Ammons (Vocalion).

Show, The. w/m Douglas David and Ricky Walters, 1985. Recorded by the rap trio Doug E. Fresh and The Get Fresh Crew (Reality).

Show and Tell. w/m Jerry Fuller, 1973. #1 gold record by Al Wilson (Rocky Road).

Show Biz Kids. w/m Walter Becker and Donald Fagen, 1973. Recorded by the group Steely Dan (ABC).

Showboat Shuffle. m. Edward Kennedy "Duke" Ellington, 1935. Recorded by Duke Ellington and his Orchestra (Brunswick) and the Mills Blue Ribbon Band (Columbia). Eight years earlier, King Oliver (Vocalion) had a record released with the same title.

Show Business. w/m June Jackson, 1967. Featured and recorded by Lou Rawls (Capitol).

Shower Me with Your Love. w/m Bernard Leon Jackson, Jr., 1989. Hit R&B chart single by Surface (Columbia).

Shower the People. w/m James Taylor, 1976. Recorded by James Taylor (Warner Bros.).

Show Her. w/m Ronnie Milsap, 1984. #1 Country chart record by Ronnie Milsap (RCA).

Show Me. w/m Chrissie Hynde, 1984. Recorded by The Pretenders (Sire).

Show Me. w/m Joe Tex, 1967. C&W/Pop chart record by Joe Tex (Dial).

Show Me. w. Alan Jay Lerner, m. Frederick Loewe, 1956. Introduced by Julie Andrews in (TM) *My Fair Lady.* In the film version (MM) *My Fair Lady,* 1964, it was sung on the soundtrack by Marni Nixon, dubbing for Audrey Hepburn, with Jeremy Brett.

Show Me the Way. w/m Junior Potts, Joey Gallo, and Angela Winbush, 1987. Top 10 R&B chart record by Regina Belle (Columbia).

Show Me the Way. w/m Peter Frampton, 1976. Top 10 record by the British singer Peter Frampton (A&M).

Show Me the Way Back to Your Heart. w/m Steve Nelson, Ed Nelson, Jr., Zel Soehnel, and Eddy Arnold, 1949. Top 10 C&W record by Eddy Arnold (RCA).

Show Me the Way to Get Out of This World ('Cause That's Where Everything Is). w. Les Clark, m. Matt Dennis, 1950. Introduced in clubs by Matt Dennis. Top 10 record by Peggy Lee, with Dave Barbour's Orchestra (Capitol).

Show Me the Way to Go Home. w/m Reg Connelly and Jimmy Campbell, 1925. The English writer-publishers, using the pseudonym of Irving King, adapted this from a song with folk origins. It has a post-carousal connotation.

Show Must Go On, The. w/m David Courtney and Leo Sayer, 1974. Gold record by the group Three Dog Night (Dunhill).

Show the White of Yo' Eye. w/m Stanley Crawford, 1903.

Shrimp Boats. w/m Paul Mason Howard and Paul Weston, 1951. Jo Stafford, with the Norman Luboff Choir and Paul Weston's Orchestra, had a million-selling record (Capitol).

Shrine of Saint Cecilia, The. w. Carroll Loveday, m. Nils Johan Perne, a.k.a. "Jokern," 1941. Swedish song with English lyrics, popularized and recorded by The Andrews Sisters (Decca); Sammy Kaye, vocal by Allan Foster (Victor); Vaughn Monroe with his Orchestra (Bluebird).

Shuffle Along. w/m Noble Sissle and Eubie Blake, 1921. Introduced by Charles Davis as title song of the revue (TM) *Shuffle Along.*

Shuffle Off to Buffalo. w. Al Dubin, m. Harry Warren, 1933. Introduced by Ginger Rogers, Una Merkel, Ruby Keeler, and Clarence Nordstrom in (MM) *Forty-Second Street.* It was featured in the stage version (TM) *42nd Street,* 1980, by Karen Prunscik, Joseph Bova, Carole Cook, and girls.

Shut Down. w. Roger Christian, m. Brian Wilson, 1963. Popular record by The Beach Boys (Capitol).

Shutters and Boards. w/m Audie Murphy and Scott Turner, 1962. Top 40 record by Jerry Wallace (Challenge).

Shut That Gate. w/m Ted Daffan and Dick James, 1946. Introduced and recorded by Ted Daffan and His Texans (Columbia).

Siam. w. Howard Johnson, m. Fred Fisher, 1915.

Siamese Cat Song, The. w/m Peggy Lee and Sonny Burke, 1955. Introduced by Peggy Lee on the soundtrack of the Disney full-length cartoon feature (MM) *The Lady and the Tramp.*

Siberia. w/m Cole Porter, 1955. Comedy song introduced by Henry Lascoe, Leon Belasco, and David Opatoshu in (TM) *Silk Stockings.* In (MM) *Silk Stockings,* 1957, it was sung by Peter Lorre, Jules Munshin, and Joseph Buloff.

Siboney. w. Dolly Morse (Theodora Morse), m. Ernesto Lecuona, 1929. Originally published in Cuba as "Canto Siboney" with Spanish words by the composer. Early recordings by Jessica Dragonette (Victor); Enric Madriguera and his Orchestra (Columbia); the Anglo-Persians [Nick Lucas and recording group] (Brunswick). Frances Wayne with Neal Hefti's Band recorded it in the fifties (Coral). In motion pictures, Grace Moore sang it in

(MM) *When You're in Love* in 1937, Gloria Jean in (MM) *Get Hep to Love* in 1942, and it was heard in (MM) *Babes on Swing Street* in 1944.

Sick, Sober and Sorry. w/m Tex Atchinson and Eddie Hazelwood, 1951. Top 10 C&W chart record by Johnny Bond (Columbia).

Side by Side. w/m Harry Woods, 1927, 1953. One of the biggest hits of the year in sheet music and record sales. Leading recordings by Nick Lucas (Brunswick); Paul Whiteman, with The Rhythm Boys [Bing Crosby, Al Rinker, and Harry Barris] (Victor); Aileen Stanley and Johnny Marvin (Victor); Cliff "Ukulele Ike" Edwards (Perfect). Revived in 1953 by Kay Starr, with a best-selling record (Capitol). Frankie Laine sang it in (MM) *Bring Your Smile Along,* 1955.

Side by Side by Side. w/m Stephen Sondheim, 1970. Introduced by Dean Jones and cast in (TM) *Company.* The song inspired the title of the all-Sondheim revue (TM) *Side by Side by Sondheim,* 1977.

Sideshow. w/m Vinnie Barrett and Bobby Eli, 1974. #1 R&B and Top 10 Pop chart gold record by the group Blue Magic (Atco).

Sidewalks of Cuba. w/m Mitchell Parish, Ben Oakland, and Irving Mills, 1934. Introduced in the nightclub revue *Cotton Club Parade* in Harlem, New York. Woody Herman and his band had a popular revival (Columbia), 1946. In the 1987 Mitchell Parish musical (TM) *Stardust,* it was sung by Kim Criswell and Jason Graae.

Sidewalks of New York, The. w/m James W. Blake and Charles B. Lawlor, 1894. Introduced by Lottie Gilson at the Old London Theater in the Bowery, New York. Leading recordings by George J. Gaskin (Chicago), J. W. Myers (Columbia), Dan Quinn (Columbia). It was the campaign song of Alfred E. Smith, the Democratic nominee for President, 1924. The song was not used in the Broadway musical of the same name. Betty Grable and June Haver sang it in (MM) *The Dolly Sisters,* 1945,

743

and Jimmy Durante and Bob Hope performed it in the New York City Mayor Jimmy Walker story (MM) *Beau James*, 1957.

Sidewalk Talk. w/m Madonna, 1986. Recorded by Jellybean, pseudonym for John Benitez, a record producer and engineer (EMI America).

Sierra Sue. w/m Joseph Buell Carey, 1916, 1940. Publisher Elliot Shapiro revived the song in 1940 and it reached #1 on "Your Hit Parade." There were three hit recordings that year: Bing Crosby (Decca), Glen Gray and the Casa Loma Orchestra with a vocal by Kenny Sargent (Decca), and Glenn Miller with a vocal by Ray Eberle (Bluebird). Gene Autry sang it in (MM) *Sierra Sue*, 1941.

Signed, Sealed, and Delivered. w/m Cowboy Copas and Lois Mann, 1948. Hit record by Cowboy Copas (King) and re-recorded (Starday), 1961. Other chart records by Rusty Draper (Mercury), 1961, and James Brown (King), 1963.

Signed, Sealed, Delivered I'm Yours. w/m Lee Garrett, Lila Mae Hardaway, Stevie Wonder, and Syreeta Wright, 1970. #1 R&B and Top 20 Pop chart record by Stevie Wonder (Tamla).

Sign of the Times, A. w/m Tony Hatch, 1966. Top 20 record by Petula Clark (Warner Bros.).

Sign O' the Times. w/m Prince Rogers Nelson, 1987. Title song of (MP) *Sign O' the Times*, sung on the soundtrack and #1 R&B and Top 10 Pop chart record by Prince (Paisley Park).

Signs. w/m Arthur Thomas, 1971. Gold record by the Canadian group Five Man Electrical Band (Lionel).

Sign Your Name. w/m Terence Trent D'Arby, 1988. Top 10 R&B and Pop chart record by Terence Trent D'Arby (Columbia).

Silence Is Golden. w/m Bob Crewe and Bob Gaudio, 1967. Recorded by the English quartet The Tremeloes (Epic).

Silent Running. w. Diane Lampert, m. Peter Schickele, 1971. Title song of (MP) *Silent Running*, sung on the soundtrack by Joan Baez.

Silent Running (On Dangerous Ground). w/m Mike Rutherford and Brian Robertson, 1985. Top 10 record by the British quintet Mike + The Mechanics (Atlantic).

Silent Treatment. w/m Earl Thomas Conley, 1981. Top 10 Country chart record by Earl Thomas Conley (Sunbird).

Silhouetted in the Moonlight. w. Johnny Mercer, m. Richard A. Whiting, 1938. Introduced by Frances Langford and Jerry Cooper in (MM) *Hollywood Hotel*. Recorded by Langford (Decca) and Glenn Miller and his Orchestra (Brunswick).

Silhouettes. w/m Frank Slay and Bob Crewe, 1957, 1965. Hit record by The Rays (Cameo), and chart record by The Diamonds (Mercury); Steve Gibson and The Redcaps (ABC-Paramount). Revived in 1965 by the British group, Herman's Hermits, who had a Top 10 record in the U.S. (MGM).

Silk Stockings. w/m Cole Porter, 1955. Introduced by Don Ameche in (TM) *Silk Stockings*. In the film version, (MM) *Silk Stockings*, 1956, it was danced by Cyd Charisse, with Carole Richards overdubbing the vocal.

Silly Love Songs. w/m Paul McCartney and Linda McCartney, 1976. #1 record by McCartney's group Wings (Capitol).

Silly People. w/m Stephen Sondheim, 1982. Introduced by Craig Lucas in the off-Broadway (TM) *Marry Me a Little*.

Silver and Gold. w. Henry Prichard, m. Del Sharbutt and Bob Crosby, 1952. Best-selling record by Pee Wee King (RCA Victor). Other popular versions by Jack Haskell, with Richard Maltby's Orchestra (Coral); Alan Dale (Decca); Billy May and his Orchestra (Capitol).

Silver Bell. w. Edward Madden, m. Percy Wenrich, 1910.

Silver Bells. w/m Jay Livingston and Ray Evans, 1951. Introduced by Bob Hope and Marilyn Maxwell in (MP) *The Lemon Drop Kid*. Bing Crosby and Carol Richards recorded it two years later (Decca) and gave the song the impetus to join the list of Christmas standards. It since has sold millions of copies of sheet music and records.

Silver Dew on the Blue Grass Tonight. w/m Ed Burt, 1945. Best-selling record by Bob Wills and his Texas Playboys (Columbia). Among others: Denver Darling (Decca); Don Cherry (Decca).

Silver Moon. w/m Michael Nesmith, 1970. Recorded by Michael Nesmith and The First National Band (RCA).

Silver Moon. w. Dorothy Donnelly, m. Sigmund Romberg, 1927. Introduced by Evelyn Herbert and Nathaniel Wagner in (TM) *My Maryland*. Popular record by Paul Whiteman and his Orchestra (Victor).

Silver on the Sage. w. Leo Robin, m. Ralph Rainger, 1938. Introduced on the soundtrack of (MP) *The Texans*. Recorded by the bands of Dick Jurgens (Vocalion), Art Kassel (Bluebird), Will Osborne (Decca).

Silver Shadows and Broken Dreams. w. Charles Newman, m. Lew Pollack, 1944. An Academy Award nominee from (MM) *Lady Let's Dance*.

Siver Threads and Golden Needles. w/m Dick Reynolds and Jack Rhodes, 1962. Bestseller by the English trio The Springfields (Phillips). Later chart records by Jody Miller (Capitol), 1965; The Cowsills (MGM), 1969; Linda Ronstadt (Asylum), 1974.

Silver Wings in the Moonlight. w/m Hugh Charles, Sonny Miller, and Leo Towers, 1943. English wartime song popularized in the U.S. by Freddie Slack, vocal by Margaret Whiting (Capitol).

Similau. w/m Harry Coleman and Arden Clar, 1949. Featured and recorded by Peggy Lee (Capitol).

Simon Says. w/m Elliot Chiprut, 1968. Gold record by The 1910 Fruitgum Company (Buddah).

Simple. w/m Maury Yeston, 1982. Introduced by Anita Morris in (TM) *Nine*.

Simple and Sweet. w. Irving Kahal, m. Sammy Fain, 1934. From (MM) *Harold Teen*, starring Hal LeRoy, Rochelle Hudson, and Patricia Ellis. Recorded by the bands of: Bunny Berigan (Victor), Ted Weems (Decca), Ray Herbeck (Vocalion), Kay Kyser (Brunswick), Will Osborne (Melotone).

Simple Joys of Maidenhood, The. w. Alan Jay Lerner, m. Frederick Loewe, 1960. Introduced by Julie Andrews in (TM) *Camelot*. In (MM) *Camelot*, 1967, it was sung by Vanessa Redgrave.

Simple Little Things. w. Tom Jones, m. Harvey Schmidt, 1963. Introduced by Inga Swenson in (TM) *110 in the Shade*.

Simple Song of Freedom. w/m Bobby Darin,1969. Recorded by Tim Hardin (Columbia).

Simple Things in Life, The. w. Ted Koehler, m. Ray Henderson, 1935. Rochelle Hudson introduced this in the Shirley Temple film, (MM) *Curly Top*, the first remake of *Daddy Long Legs*, which starred Mary Pickford.

Simply Irresistible. w/m Robert Palmer, 1988. From the album "Irresistible" by the English singer/songwriter Robert Palmer (Island).

Simply Meant to Be. w. George Merrill and Shannon Rubicam, m. Henry Mancini, 1987. Sung by Jennifer Warnes and Gary Morris on the soundtrack of (MP) *Blind Date*.

Sin. w. Chester R. Shull, m. George Hoven, 1951. The Four Aces first recorded this in their home town of Chester, Pa., for a small label (Victoria). It became a million-seller and was covered by numerous performers including Eddy Howard (Mercury) and Savannah Churchill (Columbia).

Since Father Went to Work. w/m William Cahill, 1906.

Since I Don't Have You. w. The Skyliners [see below], m. Joseph Rock and Lennie Martin, 1959. Recorded by The Skyliners (Calico). The personnel of the quintet, James Beaumont, Walter Lester, John Taylor, Joseph VerScharen, and Janet Vogel, wrote the lyrics. Later chart records by Chuck Jackson (Wand), 1964; Eddie Holman (ABC), 1970; Art Garfunkel (Columbia), 1979; Don McLean (Millennium), 1981.

Since I Fell for You. w/m Buddy Johnson, 1948, 1963. Top 20 record by the jazz pianist Paul Gayten and his Trio, vocal by Annie Laurie (Dixie). Singer Lenny Welch, in 1963, had a Top 10 recording (Cadence), which led to later popular version by Mel Tormé and George Shearing (Capitol), Laura Lee (Hot Wax), and Charlie Rich (Epic).

Since I Kissed My Baby Goodbye. w/m Cole Porter, 1941. Sung by The Delta Rhythm Boys and sung and danced by Fred Astaire in (MM) *You'll Never Get Rich*, and recorded by Astaire (Decca). Song nominated for Academy Award.

Since I Lost My Baby. w/m William Robinson and Warren Moore, 1965. R&B/Pop hit by The Temptations (Gordy).

Since I Made You Cry. w/m Mayme Watts and Robert Mosely, 1960. Recorded by The Rivieras (Co-ed).

Since I Met You Baby. w/m Ivory Joe Hunter, 1956. Introduced and Top 20 record by Ivory Joe Hunter (Atlantic). Top 40 record by Mindy Carson (Columbia). Revived by Sonny James (Capitol), 1969, and Freddy Fender (GRT), 1975.

Sincerely. w/m Harvey Fuqua and Alan Freed, 1955. The Moonglows first recorded the number (Chess) with success on the R&B charts. The McGuire Sisters covered it with their biggest hit, #1 in all categories (Coral).

Sincerely Yours. w. Paul Francis Webster, m. Liberace, 1955. Introduced by Liberace in (MM) *Sincerely Yours*.

Since Sister Nell Heard Paderewski Play. w. William Jerome, m. Jean Schwartz, 1902.

Since You're Gone. w/m Ric Ocasek, 1982. Recorded by The Cars (Elektra).

Since You Showed Me How to Be Happy. w/m Gary Jackson, Gerald Sims, and Floyd Smith, 1967. Top 40 record by Jackie Wilson (Brunswick).

Since You've Been Gone (Sweet, Sweet Baby). See **(Sweet, Sweet Baby) Since You've Been Gone.**

Sing, Baby, Sing. w. Jack Yellen, m. Lew Pollack, 1936. Introduced by Tony Martin and Alice Faye in (MM) *Sing, Baby, Sing*.

Sing, My Heart. w. Ted Koehler, m. Harold Arlen, 1939. Sung by Irene Dunne in (MP) *Love Affair*, co-starring Charles Boyer.

Sing, Sing, Sing. w/m Louis Prima, 1936. Although introduced by Louis Prima, recorded early by Jimmy Dorsey (Decca) and Fletcher Henderson (Victor), Benny Goodman made it all his own in 1937 by recording Jimmy Mundy's arrangement on two sides of a 12" 78 RPM record (Victor) and creating a swing classic. His now famous Carnegie Hall Jazz Concert of January 16th, 1938 was recorded (Columbia, 2 LPs) and contains the concert-stopping version he and the band played that night.

Sing (Sing a Song). w/m Joe Raposo, 1972. Introduced by Bob McGrath in the children's series (TVM) "Sesame Street." Barbara Streisand recorded it in medley with "Make Your Own Kind of Music" (Columbia). The Carpenters had a gold record version (A&M), 1973.

Sing a Little Jingle. w. Mort Dixon, m. Harry Warren, 1931. From Billy Rose's (TM) *Crazy Quilt*. Recorded by Hal Kemp's Carolina Club Orchestra, with vocal by Skinnay Ennis, (Melotone).

Sing a Little Love Song. w. Sidney D. Mitchell, m. Con Conrad and Archie Gottler, 1929. Performed by Glenn Tryon in (MM) *Broadway*, the musical film version of Phillip Dunning and George Abbott's 1927 stage hit.

Sing a Little Low Down Tune. w. Charles Tobias and Jack Scholl, m. Murray Mencher, 1933.

Sing a Little Song of Heartache. w/m Del Reeves and Ellen Reeves, 1963. Country chart hit by Rose Maddox (Capitol).

Sing a New Song. w. Ned Wever, m. Milton Ager, 1932. Recorded by the bands of Art Kassel (Columbia), Bennie Krueger (Brunswick), and Coon-Sanders (Victor).

Sing an Old Fashioned Song (to a Young Sophisticated Lady). w. Joe Young, m. Fred E. Ahlert, 1936. Popularized by radio performances and Red McKenzie's recording (Decca).

Sing a Rainbow. w/m Arthur Hamilton, 1955. Introduced by Peggy Lee in (MM) *Pete Kelly's Blues*.

Sing a Sad Song. w/m Wynn Stewart, 1963. First C&W chart record by Buddy Cagle (Capitol). Also recorded by Merle Haggard (Tally). Revived by the writer, Wynn Stewart (Playboy), 1976.

Sing a Song. w/m Albert McKay and Maurice White, 1975. R&B/Pop hit by Earth, Wind & Fire (Columbia).

Sing a Song of Sunbeams. w. Johnny Burke, m. James V. Monaco, 1939. Introduced by Bing Crosby in (MM) *East Side of Heaven*, and recorded by him (Decca). Also recorded by Bob Crosby and the Bob Cats, vocal by Marion Mann (Decca) and Gray Gordon, vocal by Cliff Grass (Victor).

Sing a Tropical Song. w. Frank Loesser, m. Jimmy McHugh, 1943. Introduced by Dick Powell and Eddie Bracken in (MM) *Happy Go Lucky*. Best-selling records by The Andrews Sisters (Decca) and Jack Smith (Hit).

Sing Before Breakfast. w. Arthur Freed, m. Nacio Herb Brown, 1935. Introduced by Eleanor Powell, and Vilma and Buddy Ebsen in (MM) *Broadway Melody of 1936*.

Sing Boy Sing. w/m Tommy Sands and Rod McKuen, 1958. Introduced by Tommy Sands in (MM) *Sing Boy Sing*, and on records (Capitol).

Singer and the Song, The. w. Will D. Cobb, m. Gus Edwards, 1899.

Singer in the Balcony, The. w/m Harry A. Mayo, 1895. Title refers to boy stooges who would sing reprises, from the balcony, of a number sung by a vaudevillian on stage.

Sing for the Day. w/m Tommy Shaw, 1979. Recorded by the quintet, Styx, coupled with "Renegade" (A&M).

Sing for Your Supper. w. Lorenz Hart, m. Richard Rodgers, 1938. Introduced by Muriel Angelus, Marcy Westcott, Wynn Murray, and the ladies' chorus in (TM) *The Boys from Syracuse*. In the film version (MM) *The Boys from Syracuse*, 1940, it was sung by Martha Raye.

Singing a Song to the Stars. w. Howard Johnson, m. Joseph Meyer, 1930.

Singing a Vagabond Song. w/m Val Burton, Harry Richman, and Sam Messenheimer, 1930. Introduced by Harry Richman in (MM) *Puttin' on the Ritz* and recorded by him (Brunswick). The song, which became associated with Richman, as well as his theme song in nightclubs and on radio, was parodied by the Ritz Brothers in (MM) *Sing, Baby, Sing* in 1936.

Singing Hills, The. w/m Mack David, Sammy Mysels, and Dick Sanford, 1940. Bing Crosby (Decca) had the best-seller, followed by Dick Todd (Bluebird), Eddy Howard (Columbia), and Gene Autry (Conqueror).

Singing My Song. w/m Tammy Wynette, Billy Sherrill, and Glenn Sutton, 1969. C&W/Pop hit by Tammy Wynette (Epic).

Singing the Blues. w/m Melvin Endsley, 1957. Introduced and recorded by Marty Robbins (Columbia). This C&W hit was covered by Guy Mitchell who had a #1 Pop record in all categories (Columbia).

Singin' in the Bathtub. w/m Herb Magidson, Ned Washington, and Michael H. Cleary, 1929. Sung by Winnie Lightner in (MM) *The Show of Shows*.

Singin' in the Rain. w. Arthur Freed, m. Nacio Herb Brown, 1929. Introduced by Cliff "Ukulele Ike" Edwards who was joined by Marion Davies, Joan Crawford, Buster Keaton, George K. Arthur, Nacio Herb Brown, and the Brox Sisters in (MM) *Hollywood Revue of 1929*. Judy Garland sang it in (MM) *Little Nellie Kelly*, 1940. It was the title song of (MM) *Singin' in the Rain*, 1952, and was sung and danced by Gene Kelly in a memorable five-minute production number. The scene was shown as one of the highlights of (MM) *That's Entertainment*, 1974. It was in the England and U.S. stage version (TM) *Singing in the Rain*, which opened on Broadway, 1985.

Singin' the Blues. w. Dorothy Fields, m. Jimmy McHugh, 1931. Interpolated in the play with songs (TP) *Singin' the Blues*.

Singin' the Blues (Till My Daddy Comes Home). w. Sam M. Lewis and Joe Young, m. Con Conrad and J. Russell Robinson, 1920. Featured and recorded by many bands over the years. Among more popular versions: Fletcher Henderson's Connie's Inn Orchestra (Melotone and Victor); Lionel Hampton (Victor); Frankie Trumbauer, featuring Bix Beiderbecke (Okeh); Adrian Rollini, vocal by Pat Hoke (Decca); Nat Gonella (Parlophone).

Single Girl. w/m Martha Sharp, 1966. Hit record by Tennessee singer Sandy Posey (MGM).

Single Life. w/m Larry Blackmon and Thomas Jenkins, 1985. Top 10 R&B chart record by the group Cameo (Atlanta Artists).

Sing Me a Baby Song. w. Gus Kahn, m. Walter Donaldson, 1927. Most popular records: Nick Lucas (Brunswick), Vaughn De-

Leath (Victor), and Fred Waring, with a vocal by brother Tom (Victor).

Sing Me a Song of the Islands. w. Mack Gordon, m. Harry Owens, 1942. Introduced by Betty Grable and Hilo Hattie in (MM) *Song of the Islands*. Bing Crosby had a popular record (Decca).

Sing Me a Song with Social Significance. w/m Harold Rome, 1937. Sung by the chorus in (TM) *Pins and Needles*.

Sing Me a Swing Song. w. Stanley Adams, m. Hoagy Carmichael, 1936. Recorded by Benny Goodman (Victor) and Chick Webb and his Orchestra, vocal by Ella Fitzgerald (Decca). Fitzgerald, eighteen years old at the time of the recording, had been with the band for two years.

Sing Me Back Home. w/m Merle Haggard, 1968. #1 Country chart record by Merle Haggard (Capitol).

Sing Something Simple. w/m Herman Hupfeld, 1930. The hit song from (TM) *The Second Little Show* was introduced by Ruth Tester. There were recordings by Leo Reisman and his Orchestra (Victor), Fred Rich (Columbia), the Revelers (Victor), and Maxine Sullivan (Victor) in 1939.

Sing Song Girl. w. Joseph McCarthy, m. James F. Hanley, 1931.

Sing You Sinners. w/m W. Franke Harling and Sam Coslow, 1930. Sung by Lillian Roth in (MM) *Honey*, which starred Nancy Carroll. Belle Baker recorded the song (Brunswick) and featured it in vaudeville and on radio. In the early fifties, it was revived by Tony Bennett (Columbia). Billy Daniels sang it in (MM) *Cruisin' Down the River*, 1953, and Susan Hayward, portraying Roth, sang it in her story (MM) *I'll Cry Tomorrow*, 1955.

Sink the Bismarck. w/m Tillman Franks and Johnny Horton, 1960. Title derived from the film of the same name. Hit record by Johnny Horton (Columbia).

Sinner Kissed an Angel, A. w. Mack David, m. Larry Shayne, 1941. Most popular records by Harry James, vocal by Dick Haymes (Columbia), and Tommy Dorsey, vocal by Frank Sinatra (Victor). Publisher Shayne wrote music under pseudonym of Ray Joseph.

Sinner Man. w/m Billy Barberis, Bobby Hart, Teddy Randazzo, Bobby Weinstein, and Trini Lopez, 1965. Introduced by Trini Lopez on the soundtrack of (MP) *Marriage on the Rocks*, and recorded by him (Reprise).

Sinner or Saint. w/m Irving Gordon, 1952. Recorded by Sarah Vaughan, with Percy Faith's Orchestra (Columbia).

Sioux City Sue. w. Ray Freedman, m. Dick Thomas, 1946. Introduced and recorded by Dick Thomas (National). Song covered by the hit record of Bing Crosby, with The Jesters and Bob Haggart's Orchestra (Decca). Tony Pastor, with his Orchestra, also had a popular version (Cosmo). C&W hit version by Zeke Manners (Victor).

Sipping Cider Thru a Straw. w/m Carey Morgan and Lee David, 1919. Popular tongue-twisting novelty.

Sir Duke. w/m Stevie Wonder, 1977. Written as a tribute to Duke Ellington, Stevie Wonder's recording was #1 on both the R&B and Pop charts (Tamla).

Siren's Song, The. w. P. G. Wodehouse, m. Jerome Kern, 1917. Sung by Edith Hallor in (TM) *Leave It to Jane*.

Sister. w/m Jim Wann, 1981. Introduced by Cass Morgan and Debra Monk in the off-Broadway hit (TM) *Pump Boys and Dinettes*.

Sister Christian. w/m Kelly Keagy, 1984. Top 10 record by the quintet Night Ranger (MCA/Camel).

Sister Golden Hair. w/m Gerry Beckley, 1975. Originally from the album "Hearts," by the trio America (Warner Bros.). A single was released and reached #1 on the charts.

Sisters. w/m Irving Berlin, 1954. Introduced by Rosemary Clooney and Vera-Ellen, and reprised by Bing Crosby and Danny Kaye, miming to the voices of the female stars, in (MM) *White Christmas*. Popular recording by Rosemary and Betty Clooney, accompanied by Paul Weston and his Orchestra (Columbia).

Sisters Are Doin' It for Themselves. w/m Annie Lennox and Dave Stewart, 1985. Written by the U.K. duo, the Eurythmics, who recorded it with Aretha Franklin (RCA).

Sisters of Mercy. w/m Leonard Cohen, 1967. First recorded by Judy Collins in her album "Wildflowers" (Elektra). Leonard Cohen sang it in his album "Songs of Leonard Cohen" (Columbia). He also sang it on the soundtrack of (MP) *McCabe and Mrs. Miller*, 1971.

Sister Susie's Sewing Shirts for Soldiers. w. R. P. Weston, m. Herman E. Darewski, 1914. Pre-World War I song of the tongue-twisting genre. Featured and recorded by Al Jolson (Columbia). Billy Murray also had a popular version (Victor).

Sit Down, I Think I Love You. w/m Stephen A. Sills, 1967. Recorded by the quartet The Mojo Men (Reprise).

Sit Down, You're Rocking the Boat. w/m Frank Loesser, 1950. Introduced by Stubby Kaye in (TM) *Guys and Dolls*. Kaye repeated his role and the song in (MM) *Guys and Dolls*, 1955.

Sit Down, You're Rocking the Boat! w. William Jerome and Grant Clarke, m. Jean Schwartz, 1913. Hit record by Billy Murray (Victor).

Sitting. w/m Cat Stevens, 1972. Top 20 record by the English-born Cat Stevens (A&M).

Sitting by the Window. w/m Paul Insetta, 1949. Featured and recorded by Vic Damone (Mercury), Billy Eckstine (MGM), the bands of Ray Anthony (Capitol) and Jerry Gray (Decca).

Sitting in Limbo. w/m Jimmy Cliff and Gilly Bright-Plummer, 1973. Sung by Jimmy

Cliff in the Jamaican film (MP) *The Harder They Come*. Don Brown had a chart version (1st American), 1978.

Sitting in the Park. w/m Billy Stewart, 1965. Crossover (R&B/Pop) hit by Billy Stewart (Chess).

Sittin' in a Corner. w. Gus Kahn, m. George W. Meyer, 1923.

Sittin' in an All Nite Cafe. w/m James W. Glaser, 1965. Hit Country song by Warner Mack (Decca).

Sittin' in the Balcony. w/m John D. Loudermilk, 1957. Introduced and recorded by Johnny Dee, Loudermilk's pseudonym (Colonial). Hit record by Eddie Cochran (Liberty).

Sittin' on a Backyard Fence. w. Irving Kahal, m. Sammy Fain, 1933. Introduced by Ruby Keeler in (MM) *Footlight Parade*. Best-selling recordings: Paul Whiteman (Victor) and Freddy Martin, vocal by Terry Shand (Brunswick).

Sittin' on a Log (Pettin' My Dog). w. Byron Gay, m. Edward "Zez" Confrey, 1934. Introduced by Jack Denny and his Orchestra, vocal by the baby-voiced Jeanie Lang. Recordings: Fran Frey (Columbia); the bands of Isham Jones (Victor), Sam Robbins (Bluebird), and Anson Weeks with vocal by Bob Crosby (Brunswick).

Sittin' on a Rock (Cryin' in a Creek). w. Jimmy Louis and Mart Melshee, m. Mart Melshee, 1966. Top 10 Country chart record by Warner Mack (Decca).

Sittin' on It All the Time. w/m Lois Mann and Henry Bernard, 1950. R&B chart hit by Wynonie Harris (King).

(Sittin' on) the Dock of the Bay. w/m Otis Redding and Steve Cropper, 1968. One of the biggest hits of the year and winner of the Grammy Award (NARAS) for best R&B Song of the Year. Otis Redding's recording was cut three years before and released one month after his death in the crash of his private plane. It became the #1 song in the country

and his recording sold over four million copies (Volt). There have been numerous other versions, vocal and instrumental. The last chart record was by a group that called itself The Reddings, comprised of Otis Redding's sons, Dexter and Otis III, and a cousin, Mark Locket (Believe).

Si Tu Partais. See **If You Go.**

Sit Yourself Down. w/m Stephen Stills, 1971. Recorded by Stephen Stills (Atlantic).

Six Boys and Seven Girls. w/m Carl Sigman, 1959. Popular recording by Anita Bryant (Carlton).

Six Days on the Road. w/m Earl Green and Carl Montgomery, 1963. Crossover (C&W/Pop) hit by Dave Dudley (Golden Wing).

Six Flats Unfurnished. m. Richard Maltby, 1942. Instrumental, introduced and recorded by Benny Goodman and his Orchestra (Columbia). Richard Maltby and his Orchestra recorded it ("X"), 1955.

Six Lessons from Madame La Zonga. w. Charles Newman, m. James V. Monaco, 1940. Hit record by Jimmy Dorsey, vocal by Helen O'Connell (Decca). It was the title song of (MM) *Six Lessons from Madame La Zonga*, 1941, starring Lupe Velez.

Six Little Wives. w. Harry Greenbank and Adrian Ross, m. Sidney Jones, 1899. From (TM) *San Toy*.

Six Man Band. w/m Terry Kirkman, 1986. Recorded by The Association, a six-man band, of which Kirkman was a member (Warner Bros.).

Six O'Clock. w/m John Sebastian, 1967. Recorded by The Lovin' Spoonful (Kama Sutra).

16 Candles. w/m Luther Dixon and Allyson R. Khent, 1959. Top 10 record by The Crests (Co-ed).

Sixteen Going on Seventeen. w. Oscar Hammerstein II, m. Richard Rodgers,

1959. Introduced by Lauri Peters and Brian Davies in (TM) *The Sound of Music*. In the film version (MM) *The Sound of Music*, 1965, it was sung by Charmian Carr and Daniel Truhitte.

Sixteen Reasons. w/m Bill Post and Doree Post, 1960. Top 10 record by Connie Stevens (Warner Bros.). Revived by LaVerne and Shirley [Penny Marshall and Cindy Williams] (Atlantic), 1976.

Sixteen Tons. w/m Merle Travis, 1955. Introduced and first recorded by the composer/singer Merle Travis, the son of a Kentucky coal miner (Capitol), 1947. Tennessee Ernie Ford recorded it in 1955 (Capitol) and the song became a #1 hit in all categories. Revivals by Tom Jones (Parrot), 1967, and The Don Harrison Band (Atlantic), 1976.

634–5789 (Soulsville U.S.A.). w/m Steve Cropper and Eddie Floyd, 1966. Top 20 record by Wilson Pickett (Atlantic).

'65 Love Affair. w/m Paul Davis, 1981. Top 10 record by Paul Davis (Arista).

Sixty Minute Man. w/m Billy Ward and Rose Marks, 1951. A million-seller and #1 R&B record by The Dominoes, featuring Clyde McPhatter as lead singer and Billy Ward on piano (Federal).

Sixty Seconds Every Minute (I Think of You). w. Irving Caesar and John Murray Anderson, m. Louis A. Hirsch, 1922. Introduced by Carl Randall and Marjorie Peterson in *Greenwich Village Follies of 1922*. Recorded instrumentally by The Colombians (Columbia).

Sixty Seconds Got Together. w. Mack David, m. Jerry Livingston, 1938. Popular records by Dick Todd (Victor), and the bands of George Olsen, vocal by Eddy Howard (Decca), Gray Gordon (Bluebird), Kay Kyser (Brunswick).

Skateaway. w/m Mark Knopfler, 1981. Recorded by the English group Dire Straits (Warner Bros.).

Skeleton in the Closet, The. w. Johnny Burke, m. Arthur Johnson, 1936. Introduced by Louis Armstrong in (MM) *Pennies from Heaven*. Armstrong recorded it (Decca) as did Artie Shaw (Brunswick).

Skeletons. w/m Stevie Wonder, 1987. #1 R&B chart record by Stevie Wonder (Motown).

Skid Row Joe. w/m Freddie Hart, 1966. Country chart record by Porter Wagoner (RCA).

Skinny Legs and All. w/m Joe Tex, 1967. Gold record by Joe Tex (Dial).

Skinny Minnie. w/m Bill Haley, Arrett "Rusty" Keefer, Catherine Williamson, and Milt Gabler, 1958. Top 40 record by Bill Haley and His Comets (Decca).

Skin Tight. w/m Marshall Jones, Marvin Pierce, Leroy Bonner, Jimmy Williams, Ralph Middlebrook, and Clarence Satchell, 1974. Crossover (R&B/Pop) gold record by The Ohio Players (Mercury).

Skip a Rope. w/m Jack Moran and Glenn D. Tubb, 1968. C&W/Pop hit by Henson Cargill (Monument).

Skokiaan. w. Tom Glazer, m. Msarurgwa, 1954. Name derived from a Zulu tribal drink. This South African song was first recorded by the Bulawayo Sweet Rhythms Band in their country. The record was then released in the U.S. (London). The best-seller was by the orchestra of Ralph Marterie (Mercury). The leading vocal recording in sales and performances was the The Four Lads, with Neal Hefti's Orchestra (Columbia).

Skrontch. w. Henry Nemo and Irving Mills, m. Edward Kennedy "Duke" Ellington, 1938. Originally recorded as "Scrounch" by Duke Ellington and his Orchestra (Brunswick). Fats Waller recorded it under new spelling and pronunciation when lyrics were added later in the year (Victor).

Skybird. w/m Neil Diamond, 1974. Sung on the soundtrack of (MP) *Jonathan Livingston Seagull* and on records by Neil Diamond (Columbia), also by Tony Orlando and Dawn (Arista), 1975.

Sky Fell Down, The. w. Edward Heyman, m. Louis Alter, 1940. Featured and recorded by Benny Goodman, vocal by Helen Forrest (Columbia); Al Donahue, vocal by Phil Brito (Vocalion); Woody Herman's Orchestra (Decca).

Sky High. w/m Des Dyer and Clive Scott, 1975. Hit record by the English quartet Jigsaw (Chelsea) from the soundtrack of (MP) *Man from Hong Kong*, originally titled *The Dragon Flies*. The writers were members of the recording group.

Skylark. w. Johnny Mercer, m. Hoagy Carmichael, 1942. Almost three months on "Your Hit Parade," this standard-to-be was featured and recorded by Glenn Miller, vocal by Ray Eberle (Bluebird); Dinah Shore (Bluebird); Harry James, vocal by Helen Forrest (Columbia); Bing Crosby (Decca).

Skyliner. m. Charlie Barnet, 1944. Famous instrumental by Charlie Barnet and his Orchestra (Decca).

Sky Pilot. w/m Eric Burdon, Victor Briggs, Johnny Weider, Barry Jenkins, D. McCulloch, 1968. Top 20 record by the English group, Eric Burdon and The Animals (MGM, Part 1).

Slap Polka, The. w. Paul Francis Webster, m. Harry Revel, 1943. Introduced by Ginny Simms in (MM) *Hit the Ice*. June Preisser performed it in (MM) *I'll Tell the World*, 1945.

Slap That Bass. w. Ira Gershwin, m. George Gershwin, 1937. Introduced by Fred Astaire in (MM) *Shall We Dance*, and recorded by him with Johnny Green's Orchestra (Brunswick).

Slaughter on Tenth Avenue. m. Richard Rodgers, 1936. Rodgers' ballet was first danced in (TM) *On Your Toes* by Ray Bolger (Hoofer), Tamara Geva (Stip-tease girl), and George Church (Boss). In the film version, it was danced by Eddie Albert and Zorina, and in the Rodgers and Hart story, (MM) *Words and Music*, by Gene Kelly and Vera-Ellen. In 1950, Les Brown and his Band recorded the music (Columbia, Parts 1 & 2).

Sledgehammer. w/m Peter Gabriel, 1986. #1 Pop chart record by the British singer Peter Gabriel (Geffen).

Sleep. w/m Earl Lebieg, 1923. Based on a theme from Lebieg's earlier piano composition, "Visions of Sleep," which was published under the reverse pseudonym of "Geibel." The version was recorded by Fred Waring's Pennsylvanians, vocal by Fred and Tom Waring (Victor). It became the Waring signature theme for his ensuing career of over sixty years. While others, such as Tommy Dorsey (Victor), Benny Carter (Vocalion), and Les Paul (Capitol) had releases, the song is indelibly associated with Waring.

Sleep, Come On and Take Me. w/m Joe Young and Boyd Bunch, 1932. Introduced and featured by Guy Lombardo and His Royal Canadians.

Sleepin' Bee, A. w. Truman Capote and Harold Arlen, m. Harold Arlen, 1954. Introduced by Diahann Carrol in (TM) *House of Flowers*.

Sleeping Bag. w/m Billy Gibbons, Dusty Hill, and Frank Beard, 1985. Top 10 single, written and recorded by the trio ZZ Top (Warner Bros.).

Sleeping Single in a Double Bed. w/m Key Fleming and Dennis Morgan, 1978. Country chart hit by Barbara Mandrell (ABC).

Sleep Walk. m. Ann Farina, John Farina, and Santo Farina, 1959. #1 instrumental hit by Santo and Johnny (Canadian-American).

Sleepwalker. w/m Ray Davies, 1977. Recorded by the British group The Kinks (Arista).

Sleepy-Eyed John. w/m Tex Atcheson, 1961. Posthumous release of a Johnny Horton recording (Columbia).

Sleepy Head. w. Gus Kahn, m. Walter Donaldson, 1934. Theme song of (MP) *Operator 13*, starring Gary Cooper and Marion Davies. Recorded by the Mills Brothers (Melotone) (Brunswick); the bands of Vincent Lopez (Bluebird) and Ben Pollack (Columbia). The latter had a vocal by Joe Harris.

Sleepy Head. w. Benny Davis, m. Jesse Greer, 1926. Popularized by the team of Ford and Glenn (Columbia).

Sleepy Lagoon. w. Jack Lawrence, m. Eric Coates, 1942. Adapted from a symphonic work *By a Sleepy Lagoon*, by the British composer Coates. Harry James and his Orchestra's instrumental version was the best-seller (Columbia). Lyrics were added in 1942. Other well-received releases were made by Xavier Cugat and his Orchestra (Columbia); Dinah Shore, with Leonard Joy's Orchestra (Victor); Beryl Davis, with David Rose's Orchestra (MGM); Toots Thielemans (Columbia); Meredith Willson and his Orchestra (Decca).

Sleepy Man. w. Alfred Uhry, m. Robert Waldman, 1975. Introduced by Rhonda Coullette in (TM) *The Robber Bridegroom*.

Sleepy Serenade. w. Mort Greene, m. Lou Singer, 1941. Woody Herman (Decca) and Claude Thornhill (Okeh) and their orchestras recorded this as an instrumental. The vocal version was introduced by the Andrews Sisters, accompanied by Ted Lewis and his Orchestra in (MM) *Hold That Ghost* later in 1941 and then recorded by them (Decca).

Sleepy Time Gal. w. Joseph R. Alden and Raymond B. Egan, m. Ange Lorenzo and Richard A. Whiting, 1925. Ben Bernie and his Orchestra had a popular record (Victor) followed by many others. It has always been a favorite sing-along tune. It was the title song of (MM) *Sleepy Time Gal*, 1942, starring Judy Canova and Tom Brown. Frances Langford sang it in (MM) *Never a Dull Moment*, 1943.

Sleigh Ride. w. Mitchell Parish, m. Leroy Anderson, 1949. First recorded by The Boston Pops Orchestra under the direction of Arthur Fiedler (RCA Victor), for which Anderson was arranger. Anderson, with his own orchestra, had a popular recording a year later (Decca), after which Parish added lyrics. The composition is now a "winter" standard.

Sleighride in July. w. Johnny Burke, m. James Van Heusen, 1944. Introduced by Dinah Shore in (MM) *Belle of the Yukon*. Song nominated for Academy Award. Shore had the best-selling record (Victor), followed by Bing Crosby (Decca); Tommy Dorsey, vocal by Bonnie Lou Williams (Victor); Les Brown, vocal by Gordon Drake (Columbia).

Slewfoot the Bear. See Ole Slew-Foot.

Slide. m. Walter Lewis Wagner, 1977. Instrumental by the funk band, Slave (Cotillion).

Slide, Kelly Slide. w/m John W. Kelly, 1889. The first popular song hit about baseball, inspired by Mike (King) Kelly [no relation], the versatile major league ballplayer.

Slider. w. Fred Wise, m. Boyd Raeburn and George Temple, 1949. Featured and recorded by Ray Anthony and his Orchestra (Capitol).

Slightly Less Than Wonderful. w. George Marion, Jr., m. Thomas "Fats" Waller, 1943. Introduced by Jane Deering and George Zoritch in (TM) *Early to Bed*. The songs in this musical were the last written by Waller, who died during the run.

Slightly Out of Tune. w. Jon Hendricks and Jessie Cavanaugh, m. Antonio Carlos Jobim, 1962. English words written to the Brazilian "Desifinado." Cavanaugh is reportedly a pseudonym for music publisher Howard S. Richmond. Recorded by Pat Thomas (MGM). See also "Desifinado".

Slip Away. w/m William Armstrong, Marcus Daniel, and Wilbur Terrell, 1968. Top 10 record by Clarence Carter (Atlantic).

Slip-In Mules (No High-heel Sneakers). w/m Billy Davis and Robert Higginbotham, 1964. An indirect referral to the hit "Hi-Heel Sneakers." Recorded by R&B singer Sugar Pie DeSanto (Checker).

Slip of the Lip, A. w/m Mercer Ellington and Luther Henderson, 1942. Introduced and recorded by Duke Ellington, vocal by Ray Nance (Victor).

Slipper and the Rose Waltz, The. w/m Richard M. Sherman and Robert B. Sherman, 1977. Introduced by Gemma Craven in (MM) *The Slipper and the Rose*. Nominated for an Academy Award.

Slippery Horn. m. Edward Kennedy "Duke" Ellington, 1933. Introduced and recorded by Duke Ellington and his Orchestra (Brunswick).

Slippery When Wet. w/m William King, Ronald LaPread, Thomas McClary, Walter Orange, Lionel Richie, and Milan Williams, 1975. Written and recorded by The Commodores (Motown).

Slippin' and Slidin' (Peepin' and Hidin'). w/m Richard Penniman, Edwin Bocage, James Smith, and Albert Collins, 1956. R&B and Pop chart success by Little Richard (Specialty), coupled with the hit, "Long Tall Sally" (q.v.).

Slipping Around. w/m Floyd Tillman, 1949. Margaret Whiting and Jimmy Wakely had a #1 and million-selling record (Capitol). Also, big sellers by Ernest Tubb (Decca); Floyd Tillman (Columbia).

Slipping Away. w/m Bill Anderson, 1973. Hit country record by Jean Shepard (United Artists).

Slippin' into Darkness. w/m Dee Allen, B. B. Dickerson, Lee Oskar, Howard Scott, and Lonnie Jordan, 1972. Top 20 record by War, members of whom wrote the song (United Artists).

Slip Slidin' Away. w/m Paul Simon. Top 10 record by Paul Simon (Columbia).

Sloop John B. See **Wreck of the John B.**

Slow Burn. w/m Tommy Rocco and Charlie Black, 1983. #1 Country chart record by T. G. Sheppard (Warner Bros.).

Slow But Sure. w/m Charlie Agnew, Audree Collins, and Charles Newman, 1931. Recorded by Red Nichols, with vocal by Smith Ballew (Brunswick) and by Benny Goodman, in an early session under his name (Melotone).

Slow Dancing. See **Swayin' to the Music.**

Slow Dancin' Don't Turn Me On. w/m Dick Addrisi and Don Addrisi, 1977. Top 20 record by The Addrisi Brothers (Buddah).

Slow Down. w/m Lawrence E. Williams, 1964. Recorded by The Beatles (Capitol).

Slow Freight. w. Lupin Fien and Irving Mills, m. Buck Ram, 1940. Introduced and recorded by Benny Carter and his Orchestra (Vocalion). Best-selling record by Glenn Miller and his Orchestra (Bluebird).

Slow Hand. w. John Bettis, m. Michael Clark, 1981. Top 10 gold R&B/Pop chart record by The Pointer Sisters (Planet).

Slowly. w/m Tommy Hill and Webb Pierce, 1954. Introduced and recorded by Webb Pierce (Decca).

Slowly. w. Kermit Goell, m. David Raksin, 1946. Introduced on the soundtrack of (MP) *Fallen Angel* by Dick Hymes, and recorded by him with Victor Young's Orchestra (Decca). Kay Kyser, with vocal by Mike Douglas, also had a well-received version (Columbia).

Slowly, with Feeling. w. Don George, m. Moose Chalap, 1955. Recorded by Sarah Vaughan (Mercury).

Slow Poke. w/m Pee Wee King, Red Stewart, and Chilton Price, 1951. Pee Wee King, vocal by Redd Stewart [King], had a million-selling record (RCA Victor). Other top versions by Roberta Lee, with Neal Hefti's Orchestra (Decca); Ralph Flanagan's Orchestra (RCA Victor); Helen O'Connell (Capitol); Arthur Godfrey (Columbia).

Slow Ride. w/m Dave Peverett, 1976. Top 20 record by the quartet, Foghat, led by "Lonesome" Dave Peverett (Bearsville).

Slow River. w. Henry Myers, m. Charles M. Schwab, 1927. From (TM) *The New Yorkers.* [Not to be confused with the 1930 Cole Porter musical of the same name.] The song was recorded by the bands of Jean Goldkette (Victor), Gerald Marks (Columbia), Noble Sissle and Eubie Blake (Okeh), and Clarence Williams (Brunswick).

Slow Twistin'. w/m Kal Mann, 1962. Hit record by Chubby Checker, with a vocal assist by Dee Dee Sharp (Parkway).

Slow Walk. w/m Sil Austin, Irving Siders, and Connie Moore, 1956. Instrumental first recorded by Sil Austin (Mercury). Both his group and that of Bill Doggett (King) had Top 20 records.

Sluefoot. w/m Johnny Mercer, 1955. Introduced by Fred Astaire and company, with Ray Anthony and his Orchestra in (MM) *Daddy Long Legs.*

Slumming on Park Avenue. w/m Irving Berlin, 1937. Introduced by Alice Faye and the Ritz Brothers in (MM) *On the Avenue.* Recorded by Faye (Brunswick); Ray Noble, vocal by the Merry Macs (Victor); Red Norvo, vocal by Mildred Bailey (Brunswick); and Jimmie Lunceford's Band (Decca).

Smack Dab in the Middle. w/m Charles E. Calhoun, 1955. Introduced and featured by Count Basie, vocal by Joe Williams. Ray Charles had a popular record in 1964 (ABC-Paramount).

Smackwater Jack. w. Gerry Goffin, m. Carole King, 1971,. Recorded by Carole King, coupled with "So Far Away" (q.v.) (Ode).

Small Craft Warnings. w. Barry Harman, m. Keith Hermann, 1988. Introduced by Deborah Graham and Robert Hoshour in (TM) *Romance, Romance.*

Small Fry. w. Frank Loesser, m. Hoagy Carmichael, 1938. Introduced in (MM) *Sing You Sinners* by Bing Crosby, Fred MacMurray, and Donald O'Connor. Hit record by Bing Crosby and Johnny Mercer (Decca). This year

marked the emergence of Loesser as a major writer with an output that included at least six songs that became hits or standards.

Small Paradise. w/m John Cougar Mellencamp, 1980. Recorded by John Cougar (Riva).

Small Talk. w/m Richard Adler and Jerry Ross, 1954. Introduced by Janis Paige and John Raitt in (TM) *The Pajama Game.* Sung by Doris Day in the film version (MM) *The Pajama Game,* 1957.

Small Town. w/m John Cougar Mellencamp, 1985. Top 10 single by John Cougar Mellencamp (Riva).

Smalltown Boy. w/m Jimmy Somerville, Steve Bronski, and Larry Steinbachek, 1985. Written and recorded by the British trio Bronski Beat (MCA).

Small Town Girl. w/m John Jarvis and Don Cook, 1987. #1 country chart song by Steve Wariner, from his album "It's a Crazy World" (MCA).

Small World. w. Stephen Sondheim, m. Jule Styne, 1959. Introduced by Ethel Merman and Jack Klugman in (TM) *Gypsy.* Leading recording by Johnny Mathis (Columbia). In the film version (MM) *Gypsy,* 1962, it was sung by Rosalind Russell and Karl Malden. Russell's vocals were partially dubbed by Lisa Kirk.

Smarty. w. Ralph Freed, m. Burton Lane, 1937. Sung in (MM) *Double or Nothing* and on records (Decca) by Bing Crosby. Also recorded by the Count Basie Band (Decca).

Smarty. w. Jack Norworth, m. Albert Von Tilzer, 1908. Introduced and featured by Jack Norworth in vaudeville. Recorded by Ada Jones and Billy Murray (Victor).

Smellin' of Vanilla (Bamboo Cage). w. Truman Capote and Harold Arlen, m. Harold Arlen, 1954. Introduced by Dolores Harper, Enid Mosier, and Ada Moore in (TM) *House of Flowers.*

Smile. w. John Turner and Geoffrey Parsons, m. Charles Chaplin, 1954. Music originally written by Chaplin for the score of his 1936 film *Modern Times*. In the new form, the leading records were by Nat "King" Cole, with Nelson Riddle's Orchestra (Capitol); Sunny Gale (RCA Victor); David Whitfield, with Eric Rogers' Orchestra (London); Ferrante and Teicher (United Artists).

Smile, Darn Ya, Smile. w. Charles O'Flynn and Jack Meskill, m. Max Rich, 1931. A popular song, usually played in a quasi-march tempo.

Smile, Smile, Smile. See **Pack Up Your Troubles in Your Old Kit Bag.**

Smile a Little Smile for Me. w/m Tony Macaulay and Geoff Stephens, 1969. Gold record by the British quintet The Flying Machine (Congress).

Smile and Show Your Dimple. w/m Irving Berlin, 1917. World War I farewell song. Recorded by Sam Ash (Columbia). The melody became the basis of Berlin's future standard "Easter Parade" (q.v.).

Smile for Me. w/m Phil Baxter, 1932. Theme song for "The Fitch Bandwagon," a weekly radio network musical show.

Smile Right Back at the Sun. w. Johnny Burke, m. James Van Heusen, 1947. Introduced by Bing Crosby in (MM) *Welcome Stranger*.

Smiles. w. J. Will Callahan, m. Lee G. Roberts, 1918. A big favorite toward the end of World War 1 and an everlasting standard. Introduced by Neil Carrington and a chorus of girls in (TM) *The Passing Show of 1918*, it had many recordings and large sales of sheet music and piano rolls. Judy Garland sang it in (MM) *For Me and My Gal*, 1942. It was also heard in (MM) *Tin Pan Alley*, 1940, (MM) *The Dolly Sisters*, 1946, (MM) *Somebody Loves Me*, 1952, and (MM) *The Eddy Duchin Story*, 1956.

Smile She Means for You, The. w. Otto Harbach, m. Karl Hoschna, 1910. Sung by Lina Abarbanell, Frances Demarest, Elizabeth Murray, Jack Gardner, Carl Martens, and Ralph C. Herz in (TM) *Madame Sherry*.

Smile Will Go a Long, Long Way, A. w. Benny Davis, m. Harry Akst, 1923. Recorded by Ted Weems and his Orchestra (Victor), The Peerless Quartet (Victor), Sam Lanin's Orchestra (Okeh).

Smilin'. w/m Sylvester Stewart, 1972. Recorded by Sly and The Family Stone (Epic).

Smiling Irish Eyes. w. Herman Ruby, m. Ray Perkins, 1929. Introduced by Colleen Moore and James Hall in (MM) *Smiling Irish Eyes*.

Smilin' Through. w/m Arthur A. Penn, 1919. Inspired by the hit play of the same name, starring Jane Cowl. Popular recording by Reinald Werrenrath (Victor). The film, (MP) *Smilin' Through*, 1932, starring Norma Shearer and Leslie Howard, used the melody as a recurrent theme in the background. It was later heard in the Jeanette MacDonald-Brian Aherne-Gene Raymond musical version (MM) *Smilin' Through*, 1941.

Smoke! Smoke! Smoke! (That Cigarette). w/m Merle Travis and Tex Williams, 1947. Tex Williams and The Western Caravan had the hit record, which sold over two million copies (Capitol). Phil Harris had a popular version (RCA Victor).

Smoke Dreams. w/m John Klenner, Lloyd Shaffer, and Ted Steele, 1947. Introduced by Jo Stafford as the theme of the network radio show, "The Chesterfield Supper Club," with orchestra conducted by Lloyd Shaffer. Stafford recorded it (Capitol).

Smoke Dreams. w. Arthur Freed, m. Nacio Herb Brown, 1937. From (MP) *After the Thin Man*, starring William Powell and Myrna Loy. Featured and recorded by Benny Goodman, Helen Ward vocal (Victor); Red Norvo (Brunswick); Abe Lyman, vocal by Sonny Schuyler (Decca); Johnny Hamp (Bluebird).

Smoke from a Distant Fire. w/m Ed Sanford, John Townsend, and Steven Stewart, 1977. Top 10 record by The Sanford/Townsend Band (Warner Bros.).

Smoke Gets in Your Eyes. w. Otto Harbach, m. Jerome Kern, 1933, 1959. Introduced by Tamara in (TM) *Roberta*. In the Kern biography (MM) *Till the Clouds Roll By*, 1946, it was performed by Cyd Charisse and Gower Champion. In the remake of *Roberta*, (MM) *Lovely to Look At*, 1952, Kathryn Grayson sang it while Marge and Gower Champion danced. The Platters had a #1 record in 1958-1959 (Mercury) and the English group Blue Haze had a best-seller in 1972 (A&M).

Smoke on the Water. w/m Richard Blackmore, Ian Gillian, Roger Glover, Jon Lord, and Ian Paice, 1973. Written and gold record by the British hard-rock band Deep Purple (Warner Bros.).

Smoke on the Water. w/m Earl Nunn and Zeke Clements, 1944. One of the the major C&W hits of the year, recorded by Red Foley (Decca).

Smoke Rings. w. Ned Washington, m. Gene Gifford, 1932. Introduced by and the theme song of Glen Gray and the Casa Loma Orchestra, of which Gifford was the chief arranger. The band recorded it (Brunswick) (Decca) (Capitol). Revived in the early fifties by Les Paul and Mary Ford (Capitol).

Smokey Mountain Boogie. w/m Tennessee Ernie Ford and Cliffie Stone, 1949. Top 10 C&W chart record by Tennessee Ernie Ford (Capitol).

Smokey Mountain Rain. w/m Kye Fleming and Dennis Morgan, 1980. Recorded by Ronnie Milsap (RCA).

Smokey the Bear. w/m Steve Nelson and Jack Rollins, 1952. A forest fire-prevention song promoted in conjunction with campaign organized by the U.S. Forestry Service.

Smokie—Part 2. m. William P. Black, 1959. Instrumental hit by Bill Black's Combo (Hi).

Smoking Gun. w/m Bruce Bromberg, Robert Cray, and Richard Cousins, 1987. Chart record by the blues-oriented Robert Cray Band (Mercury).

Smokin' in the Boys' Room. w/m Cub Koda and Michael Lutz, 1974. Written by two members of the trio, Brownsville Station, who received a gold record for their version (Big Tree). Revived by the group Motley Crue with a Top 20 record (Elektra), 1985.

Smoky Mokes (a.k.a. **Smokey Mokes**). w/m Abe Holzmann, 1899. Cakewalk. Among recordings: Len Spencer (Columbia), Graeme Bell and The Australian Jazz Band (ReZono), Vess L. Ossman (His Master's Voice and three other labels), Lu Watters (Jazz Man).

Smoky Places. w/m Abner Spector, 1962. Recorded by The Corsairs (Tuff).

Smooth Operator. w/m Helen Folasade Adu and St. John, 1985. Top 10 record by Nigerian-born, London-raised Sade, née Adu (Portrait).

Smooth Sailing. w/m Arnett Cobb, 1951. Many composers and arrangers have written a version of "Smooth Sailing." Cobb is listed as composer on Ella Fitzgerald's chart-making record (Decca), in her inimitable style of scat-singing.

Smooth Sailin' Tonight. w/m Angela Winbush, 1987. Top 10 R&B record by The Isley Brothers and title song of their album (Warner Bros.).

Smuggler's Blues. w/m Glenn Frey and Jack Tempchin, 1985. Chart single by Glenn Frey, from his album The Allnighter (MCA). Featured in an episode of (TVP) "Miami Vice."

Snag It. m. Joseph "King" Oliver, 1926. Jazz instrumental, first recorded by King Oliver and His Dixie Syncopators (Brunswick).

Snake, The. w/m Oscar Brown, Jr., 1966. Leading record by Al Wilson (Soul City).

Snake Charmer, The. w/m Leonard Whitcup and Teddy Powell, 1937. Recorded by Jerry Blaine and His Streamline Rhythm (Bluebird).

Snap Your Fingers. w/m Grady Martin and Alex Zanetis, 1962. Hit R&B and Pop chart record by Joe Henderson (Todd), then Barbara Lewis (Atlantic), 1964. Country chart records by Dick Curless (Capitol), 1971, and Don Gibson (Hickory), 1974. #1 Country record by Ronnie Milsap (RCA), 1987.

Snap Your Fingers and Away You Go. w. William Jerome, m. Harry Von Tilzer, 1912. Featured and recorded by Al Jolson (Victor).

Snatch and Grab It. w/m Sharon Pease, 1947. Recorded by Julia Lee and Her Boy Friends (Capitol).

Snatching It Back. w/m George Jackson and Clarence Carter, 1969. Top 40 record by Clarence Carter (Atlantic).

Sneaky Pete. w/m Lucius "Lucky" Millinder and Sally Nix, 1948. Hit R&B chart record by Bull Moose Jackson (King).

Sneaky Snake. w/m Tom T. Hall, 1975. Country/Pop chart record by Tom T. Hall (Mercury).

Snookeroo. w/m Elton John and Bernie Taupin, 1975. Recorded by Ringo Starr (Apple).

Snookey Ookums. w/m Irving Berlin, 1913. A comedy baby talk number introduced by Natalie Normandie. Hit phonograph records by the comedy team of Arthur Collins and Byron Harlan (Columbia), and Billy Murray (Victor). Fred Astaire and Judy Garland performed the song in a medley in (MM) *Easter Parade*, 1948.

Snoops, The Lawyer. w. Bert Kalmar, m. Harry Ruby, 1921. Comedy song recorded by Beatrice Lillie (Gramophone) in London, but popular in the U.S.

Snoopy vs. the Red Baron. w/m Phil Gernhard and Richard L. Holler, 1967. Novelty hit (gold record) by the sextet The Royal Guardsmen (Laurie).

Snowball. w/m Hoagy Carmichael, 1933. Introduced on a solo piano and vocal recording by Hoagy Carmichael (Victor). Also recorded by Louis Armstrong (Victor).

Snowbird. w/m Gene Maclellan, 1970. Gold record by the Canadian singer Anne Murray (Capitol).

Snow Blind Friend. w/m Hoyt Axton, 1971. Recorded by the quintet Steppenwolf (Dunhill).

Snowfall. m. Claude Thornhill, 1941. Theme of Claude Thornhill and his Orchestra (Columbia).

Snow Flake. w/m Ned Miller, 1966. Posthumous crossover (C&W/Pop) hit by Jim Reeves (RCA).

Snug as a Bug in a Rug. w. Frank Loesser, m. Matty Malneck, 1939. Featured and recorded by Jan Savitt, vocal by Bon Bon (Decca).

Snuggled on Your Shoulder. w. Joe Young, m. Carmen Lombardo, 1932. Introduced, featured, and recorded by Guy Lombardo and the Royal Canadians, vocal by Carmen (Columbia). Among other popular records: Jack Denny (Victor), Morton Downey (Banner), Eddy Duchin (Columbia), Kate Smith (Columbia). Revived by Kay Starr in the late fifties (Capitol).

So Am I. w. Ira Gershwin, m. George Gershwin, 1924. Performed by Alan Edwards and Adele Astaire in (TM) *Lady, Be Good!*

So At Last It's Come to This. w. Gus Kahn, m. Matty Malneck and Frank Signorelli, 1932. Featured and recorded by Paul Whiteman and his Orchestra, vocal by Irene Taylor (Victor).

So Bad. w/m Paul McCartney, 1984. Recorded by Paul McCartney (Columbia).

Sobbin' Blues. w/m Art Kassel, 1923. Written by the Chicago-based sweet music bandleader, it has been recorded by numerous jazz or swing bands such as King Oliver's Creole Jazz Band (Okeh), The New Orleans

Rhythm Kings (Gennett), Ted Lewis (Columbia), Les Brown (Bluebird), Bunny Berigan (Victor), Artie Shaw and his Strings (Brunswick).

Sobbin' Women. w. Johnny Mercer, m. Gene De Paul, 1954. The film (MM) *Seven Brides for Seven Brothers* was based on a story by Stephen Vincent Benet called "The Sobbin' Women." Howard Keel and the six other brothers, Jeff Richards, Russ Tamblyn, Tommy Rall, Marc Platt, Matt Mattox, and Jacques D'Amboise, introduced the song.

So Beats My Heart for You. w/m Pat Ballard, Charles Henderson, and Tom Waring, 1930. Popular recordings by Will Osborne (Columbia) and Fred Waring (Victor).

So Blue. w. B. G. DeSylva and Lew Brown, m. Ray Henderson, 1927. This non-production song was recorded by Harry Richman (Vocalion); Annette Hanshaw, accompanied by J. Russel Robinson (Perfect); Nick Lucas (Brunswick); Paul Whiteman (Victor). Pee Wee Hunt and his Band revived it (Capitol), 1954.

Society (Oh! I Love Society). w. Aubrey Hopwood and Harry Greenbank, m. Lionel Monckton, 1898. From (TM) *A Runaway Girl.*

Society's Child (Baby, I've Been Thinking). w/m Janis Ian, 1967. Hit record by Janis Ian (Verve).

Sock It to Me, Baby! w/m Bob Crewe and L. Russell Brown, 1967. Top 10 record by Mitch Ryder and The Detroit Wheels (New Voice).

So Close. w/m Jake Holmes, 1970. Recorded by Jake Holmes (Polydor).

So Close. w/m Brook Benton, Clyde Otis, and Luther Dixon, 1959. Introduced and recorded by Brook Benton (Mercury).

So Doggone Lonesome. w/m Johnny Cash, 1956. Introduced and recorded by Johnny Cash (Sun).

So Do I. w. Johnny Burke, m. Arthur Johnston, 1936. Introduced by Bing Crosby in (MM) *Pennies from Heaven* and recorded by him with Georgie Stoll's Orchestra (Decca). Tony Martin (Brunswick) and Eddy Duchin and his Orchestra (Victor) also recorded it.

So Do I. w. B. G. DeSylva, m. Vincent Youmans, 1932. Introduced by Jack Whiting and June Knight in (TM) *Take a Chance.*

So Emotional. w/m Billy Steinberg and Tom Kelly, 1987. Sixth consecutive #1 record by Whitney Houston, from her album "Whitney" (Arista).

So Excited. w/m Riley B. "B. B." King and Gerald Jemmott, 1970. Recorded by B. B. King (Blues Way).

So Far. w. Oscar Hammerstein II, m. Richard Rodgers, 1947. Introduced by Gloria Wills in (TM) *Allegro.* Most popular recordings by Frank Sinatra (Columbia) and Perry Como (RCA Victor).

So Far, So Good. w. Jack Lawrence, m. Jimmy Mundy and Eddie White, 1940. Leading recordings by Bob Crosby, vocal by Marion Mann; Duke Ellington and his Orchestra (Victor); Will Bradley, vocal by Carlotta Dale (Columbia); Charlie Barnett, vocal by Mary Ann McCall (Bluebird).

So Far Away. w/m Mark Knopfler, 1986. Recorded by the British group Dire Straits, of which Knopfler was lead singer and producer (Warner Bros.).

So Far Away. w/m Carole King, 1971. Recorded by Carole King (Ode).

So Far So Good. w/m Tom Snow and Cynthia Weil, 1986. Introduced by Sheena Easton on the soundtrack of (MP) *About Last Night* and on records (EMI America).

So Fine. w/m Johnny Otis, 1959. R&B chart record by The Fiestas (Old Town). Revived with Top 10 R&B chart record by Howard Johnson (A&M), 1982.

Soft. w/m Tiny Bradshaw, 1953. Introduced and recorded by Tiny Bradshaw (King). Revived by Bill Doggett (King), 1957.

Soft and Wet. w/m Christopher Moon and Prince Roger Nelson, 1978. First chart record by Prince (Warner Bros.).

Soft as Spring. w/m Alec Wilder, 1941. Introduced and recorded by Benny Goodman, vocal by Peggy Lee (Columbia).

Soft Lights and Sweet Music. w/m Irving Berlin, 1932. Introduced by J. Harold Murray and Katherine Carrington in (TM) *Face the Music*.

Softly, As I Leave You. w. Harold Shaper (Engl.), Giorgio Calabrese (It.), m. Antonio De Vita, 1964. Italian song, originally titled "Piano." Popularized by Frank Sinatra (Reprise).

Softly, As in a Morning Sunrise. w. Oscar Hammerstein II, m. Sigmund Romberg, 1928. Introduced by William O'Neal in (TM) *The New Moon*. It was omitted from the first film adaptation, 1930. Nelson Eddy sang it in the second film version (MM) *New Moon*, 1940. In the Romberg biography (MM) *Deep in My Heart*, 1954, it was sung by Helen Traubel. Artie Shaw and his Orchestra had a hit record (Bluebird), 1938.

Softly and Tenderly (I'll Hold You in My Arms). w. Red Bailey, m. Jim Howell, 1960. Top 10 C&W chart record by Lewis Pruitt (Decca).

Softly Thro' the Summer Night. w. C. C. S. Cushing and E. P. Heath, m. Emmerich Kallman, 1914. From (TM) *Sari*.

Soft Rain. w/m Ray Price, 1962. Country chart hit by Ray Price (Columbia).

Soft Sands. w/m Carroll Coates, m. Lou Stein, 1957. Featured and recorded by The Chordettes (Cadence).

Soft Summer Breeze. w. Judy Spencer, m. Eddie Heywood, 1956. Top 20 instrumental by Eddie Heywood (Mercury). The Diamonds had the leading vocal recording (Mercury).

Soft Winds. w. Fred Royal, m. Benny Goodman, 1940. Recorded by The Benny Goodman Sextet (Columbia).

So Good. w/m Peter Vale, Stephen Waters, and Sue Shifrin, 1989. Hit R&B chart single by Al Jarreau (Reprise).

So Good (You Make Me Feel). See **(You Make Me Feel) So Good.**

So Good Together. w/m Jeff Barry and Andy Kim, 1969. Top 40 record by Andy Kim (Steed).

So Help Me. w/m Irving Berlin, 1934. Recorded by Freddy Martin, vocal by Elmer Feldkamp (Brunswick); Paul Hamilton, vocal by Chick Bullock (Vocalion); Emil Coleman (Columbia). Revived in the mid-fifties by Paul Weston's Orchestra, featuring a whistling solo by Fred Lowery (Columbia).

So Help Me (If I Don't Love You). w. Eddie DeLange, m. James Van Heusen, 1938.

So I Can Love You. w/m Sheila Hutchinson, 1969. Written by one of the trio, The Emotions, who had a Top 40 record (Volt).

So in Love. w/m OMD and Steve Hague, 1985. Recorded by the British quartet Orchestral Manoeuvres in the Dark [OMD] (A&M). Song not to be confused with the "Kiss Me Kate" standard.

So in Love. w/m Cole Porter, 1949. Introduced by Patricia Morrison and reprised by Alfred Drake in (TM) *Kiss Me Kate*. Recorded by Drake (Victor). Best sellers: Patti Page (Mercury), Gordon MacRae (Capitol), Dinah Shore (Columbia). In (MM) *Kiss Me Kate*, 1953, it was sung by Kathryn Grayson and Howard Keel.

So in to You. w/m Buddy Buie, Dean Daughtry, and Robert Nix, 1977. Top 10 record by The Atlanta Rhythm Section (Polydor).

Soldier Boy. w/m Luther Dixon and Florence Green, 1962. #1 hit record by The Shirelles (Scepter).

Soldiers in the Park, The. w. Lionel Monckton, Aubrey Hopwood, and Harry Greenbank, m. Ivan Caryll, 1898. From (TM) *A Runaway Girl*.

Soldier's Last Letter. w/m Ernest Tubb and (Sgt.) Henry Stewart, 1944. Ernest Tubb had the premier recording (Decca).

Sole Sole Sole. w. Hal David (Engl.), Laura Zanin (Ital.), m. Arturo Casadei, 1964. Recorded in Italy by the Swedish female singer Siw Malmkvist and the Italian male singer Umberto Marcato (Jubilee). English version by Sarah Vaughan (Mercury).

Solid. w/m Nick Ashford and Valerie Simpson, 1984. Recorded by Ashford and Simpson (Capitol).

Soliloquy. w. Oscar Hammerstein II, m. Richard Rodgers, 1945. Introduced by John Raitt in (TM) *Carousel*, and sung by Gordon MacRae in the film version (MM) *Carousel*, 1956. Frank Sinatra has featured the song in concert and club appearances and on records (Columbia).

Soliloquy. m. Rube Bloom, 1927. This piano solo was well recorded in its debut year. In addition to the solo performance by Bloom (Harmony), the orchestras of Don Voorhees (Columbia), Paul Whiteman (Victor), and, on a 12″ disc, Ben Bernie (Brunswick) recorded it.

Solitaire. w. Diane Warren (Eng.), Martine Clemenceau (Fr.), Martine Clemenceau, 1983. Top 10 record by Laura Branigan (Atlantic).

Solitaire. w/m Neil Sedaka and Phil Cody, 1975. Popularized by the Top 20 record by The Carpenters (A&M).

Solitaire. w/ Steve Allen, m. Erroll Garner, 1955. Originally an instrumental, and introduced by Erroll Garner. Allen wrote the lyric later.

Solitaire. w. Reneé Borek and Carl Nutter, m. King Guion, 1951. Leading record by Tony Bennett, with Percy Faith's Orchestra (Columbia).

Solitary Man. w/m Neil Diamond, 1966. Neil Diamond's first chart record (Bang). Reissued and Top 40 rating, 1970.

So Little Time. See **Peking Theme, The.**

Solitude. w. Eddie DeLange and Irving Mills, m. Edward Kennedy "Duke" Ellington, 1934. Introduced by Duke Ellington and recorded twice within a year by his band (Brunswick) (Victor). The song won a special ASCAP prize as Best Song of the Year. The Dorsey Brothers recorded it on a 12″ record in 1935 (Decca).

Solo Flight. m. Charlie Christian, Jimmy Mundy, and Benny Goodman, 1944. Featured and recorded by Benny Goodman and his Orchestra (Columbia).

So Long. w/m Antoine "Fats" Domino and Dave Batholomew, 1956. Introduced and recorded by Fats Domino (Imperial).

So Long. w/m Russ Morgan, Remus Harris, and Irving Melsher, 1940. Introduced and recorded by Russ Morgan and his Orchestra (Decca). Featured and recorded by Gene Krupa's Band (Columbia) and The Charioteers (Columbia). Revived by The Four Aces, arranged and conducted by Jack Pleis (Decca), 1954.

So Long, Big Time! w. Dory Langdon Previn, m. Harold Arlen, 1964. Introduced and featured by Tony Bennett.

So Long, Dearie. w/m Jerry Herman, 1964. Introduced by Carol Channing in (TM) *Hello, Dolly!* Sung by Barbra Streisand in (MM) *Hello, Dolly!* 1969.

So Long, Mary. w/m George M. Cohan, 1906. Introduced by Donald Brian in (TM) *Forty-five Minutes from Broadway*. Sung by Irene Manning and chorus in (MM) *Yankee Doodle Dandy*, the Cohan film biography, 1942. Revived in (TM) *George M!*, 1968, by Joel Grey, Harvey Evans, Loni Ackerman, Danny Carroll, and Angela Martin.

So Long, Oo Long. w. Bert Kalmar, m. Harry Ruby, 1920. Kalmar and Ruby "sat in " with the bearded act, The House of David Band, at the Palace Theatre and sang and danced the number, after which they pulled off their false beards and received an ovation.

Isham Jones had a popular recording (Brunswick). Fred Astaire and Red Skelton performed it as Kalmar and Ruby in their film bio (MM) *Three Little Words*, 1950.

So Long, Pal. w/m Al Dexter, 1944. #1 C&W hit of the year, recorded by Al Dexter (Okeh).

So Long, Sally. w/m Bob Merrill, 1950. Featured and recorded by The Norman Luboff Choir (Columbia) and Curt Massey (London).

So Long (It's Been Good to Know Yuh). w/m Woody Guthrie, 1951. Guthrie wrote this in the thirties about leaving the Oklahoma "Dust Bowl" during the depression. The Weavers, with Gordon Jenkins's Orchestra, had the first hit record (Decca). Others: Paul Weston (Columbia), Ralph Marterie (Mercury) and their orchestras.

So Long Dixie. w. Cynthia Weil, m. Barry Mann, 1972. Recorded by the group Blood, Sweat & Tears (Columbia).

So Long Letty. w/m Earl Carroll, 1916. From (TM) *So Long Letty*, sung by Charlotte Greenwood, Sydney Grant, and chorus. Leading recordings by Prince's Band (Columbia) and Olive Kline and Lambert Murphy under the pseudonyms of Alice Green and Raymond Dixon (Victor). It served as the title song for (MM) *So Long Letty*, 1930.

Solsbury Hill. w/m Peter Gabriel, 1977. Recorded by the English singer Peter Gabriel (Atco). A live concert version reached the charts in 1983 (Geffen).

So Madly in Love. w/m Kim Gannon and Mabel Wayne, 1952. Popular record by Georgia Gibbs (Mercury).

So Many Times. w. Don DeVito, m. Jimmy Dorsey, 1939. Introduced and recorded by Jimmy Dorsey and his Orchestra (Decca). Other versions by Tommy Dorsey, vocal by Jack Leonard (Victor); Jack Teagarden, vocal by Kitty Kallen (Columbia); Tommy Tucker, vocal by Amy Arnell (Vocalion).

So Many Ways. w/m Bobby Stevenson, 1959. Featured and recorded by Brook Benton (Mercury).

Somebody. w/m Bryan Adams and Jim Vallance, 1985. Recorded by the Canadian singer/songwriter Bryan Adams (A&M).

Somebody. w. Jack Brooks, m. Harry Warren, 1960. Introduced by Jerry Lewis in (MP) *Cinderfella*. Recorded by Tony Bennett (Columbia).

Somebody Bad Stole de Wedding Bell (Who's Got de Ding Dong?) w. Bob Hilliard, m. Dave Mann, 1954. From the New York City *Copacabana* nightclub show. Leading record by Eartha Kitt (RCA Victor), followed by Georgia Gibbs (Mercury).

Somebody Bigger Than You and I. w/m Johnny Lange, Hy Heath, and Sonny Burke, 1951. Introduced by Gene Autry in (MM) *The Old West*.

Somebody Done Change the Lock. w/m William Weldon, 1945. Popularized by Louis Jordan and his Tympany Five (Decca).

Somebody Else. w. Anne Caldwell, m. Raymond Hubbell, 1927. From (TM) *Yours Truly*.

Somebody Else, It's Always Somebody Else. w. Jack Drislane, m. George W. Meyer, 1910.

Somebody Else Is Taking My Place. w/m Dick Howard, Russ Morgan, and Bob Ellsworth, 1937, 1942. Popular in its year of release, it attained #1 status on "Your Hit Parade" in 1942, triggered by the success of the recordings by Russ Morgan and his Orchestra (Decca) and Benny Goodman, vocal by Peggy Lee (Okeh). It was interpolated in (MM) *Strictly in the Groove* and (MM) *Call of the Canyon* in 1942 and by Russ Morgan in (MM) *Sarge Goes to College* in 1947.

Somebody Else's Guy. w/m Jocelyn Brown and Annette Brown, 1984. Top 10 R&B chart record by Jocelyn Brown (Vinyl Dreams).

Somebody from Somewhere. w. Ira Gershwin, m. George Gershwin, 1931. Introduced by Janet Gaynor in (MM) *Delicious*. Recorded by Bob Causer, with vocal by Kenny Sargent (Perfect). Sharon Bolin recorded it in 1955 (Vanguard).

Somebody Help Me. w/m Jackie Edwards, 1967. Recorded in England by The Spencer Davis Group (United Artists).

Somebody Lied. w/m J. Chambers and L. Jenkins, 1987. #1 Country chart hit by Ricky Van Shelton (Columbia).

Somebody Like Me. w/m Wayne Carson, 1966. Crossover (C&W/Pop) chart hit by Eddy Arnold (RCA).

Somebody Loves Me. w. Ballard Mac-Donald and B. G. DeSylva, m. George Gershwin, 1924. Introduced by Winnie Lightner and Tom Patricola in (TM) *George White's Scandals of 1924*. This classic had been often recorded and featured in motion pictures. Among the latter are (MM) *Broadway Rhythm*, 1943, sung by Lena Horne; (MM) *Rhapsody in Blue*, 1945, by Oscar Levant and Tom Patricola; (MM) *Lullaby of Broadway*, 1951; (MM) *Somebody Loves Me*, the Blossom Seely bio, 1952; (MM) *Pete Kelly's Blues*, 1955, sung by Peggy Lee. Among the first recordings [1924] are Marion Harris (Brunswick) and Paul Whiteman (Victor).

Somebody Loves You. w. Charles Tobias, m. Pete De Rose, 1932.

Somebody Nobody Loves. w/m Seymour Miller, 1942. Featured and recorded by Dinah Shore (Bluebird), and the bands of Benny Goodman (Okeh), Vincent Lopez (Elite), Lou Breese (Decca).

Somebody's Baby. w/m Jackson Browne and Danny Kotchmar, 1982. Introduced on the soundtrack of (MP) *Fast Times at Ridgemont High* and on a Top 10 record by Jackson Browne (Asylum).

Somebody's Back in Town. w/m Don Helms, Teddy Wilburn, and Doyle Wilburn, 1959. C&W hit by The Wilburn Brothers (Decca).

Somebody's Been Beatin' My Time. w/m Zeke Clements, 1951. C&W hit by Eddy Arnold (RCA Victor), covered by Bob Eberly, with Les Baxter's Orchestra (Capitol).

Somebody's Been Sleeping (in My Bed). w/m Angelo Bond, General Johnson, and Greg S. Perry, 1970. R&B/Pop gold record by the group, 100 Proof Aged in Soul (Hot Wax).

Somebody's Coming to My House. w/m Irving Berlin, 1913.

Somebody's Gonna Love You. w/m Don Cook and Rafe Van Hoy, 1983. Country/Pop chart record by Lee Greenwood (MCA).

Somebody Should Leave. w/m Harlan Howard and Chick Rains, 1985. #1 Country chart record by Reba McEntire (MCA).

Somebody's Knockin'. w/m Ed Penney and Jerry Gillespie, 1981. Crossover hit (C&W/Pop) record by Terri Gibbs, produced by Ed Penney (MCA).

Somebody's Needin' Somebody. w/m Len Chera, 1984. #1 Country chart record by Conway Twitty (RCA).

Somebody Somewhere. w/m Frank Loesser, 1956. Introduced by Jo Sullivan in (TM) *The Most Happy Fella*.

Somebody Somewhere (Don't Know What He's Missin' Tonight). w/m Lola Jean Dillon, 1976. Hit country record by Loretta Lynn (MCA).

Somebody's Stolen My Honey. w/m Boudleaux Bryant, 1951. Featured and recorded by Ernest Tubb (Decca).

Somebody Stole My Gal. w/m Leo Wood, 1922. While published four years earlier, it first found popularity this year. Now a standard, its many recordings include those by Bix Beiderbecke (Okeh), Benny Goodman (Columbia), Fletcher Henderson (Columbia), Ted Weems (Columbia), and Buddy Cole (Capitol).

Somebody's Waiting for You. w. Vincent Bryan, m. Albert Gumble, 1907. Popularized in vaudeville. Leading record by Frank Stanley (Columbia).

Somebody's Watching Me. w/m Rockwell, 1984. #1 R&B gold record by Rockwell, vocal background by Michael Jackson (Motown). Rockwell was pseudonym for Kennedy Gordy, the son of the Motown founder, Berry Gordy, Jr.

Somebody to Love. w/m Freddie Mercury, 1977. Top 10 record by the English rock group Queen (Elektra).

Somebody to Love. w/m Darby Slick, 1967. First hit record by the group Jefferson Airplane (RCA).

Somebody Touched Me. w/m Ahmet Ertegun, 1958. Popular record by Buddy Knox and the Rhythm Orchids (Roulette) and Ruth Brown (Atlantic).

Somebody Up There Likes Me. w. Sammy Cahn, m. Bronislau Kaper, 1956. From (MP) *Somebody Up There Likes Me*. Recorded by Perry Como (RCA).

Some Broken Hearts Never Mend. w/m Wayland Holyfield, 1977. Hit Country chart record by Don Williams (RCA).

Someday. w/m Alan Frew, Sam Reid, Al Connelly, Wayne Parker, Michael Hanson, and Jim Vallance, 1986. Top 10 record by the Canadian quintet Glass Tiger (Manhattan).

Some Day. w. Brian Hooker, m. Rudolf Friml, 1925. Introduced by Carolyn Thompson in (TM) *The Vagabond King*. In the first film version, (MM) *The Vagabond King*, 1930, it was sung by Jeanette MacDonald, and in the 1956 remake, by Kathryn Grayson. Revived by Tony Martin (RCA Victor), 1952, and Frankie Laine (Columbia), 1954.

Someday, Someway. w/m Marshall Crenshaw, 1981. First recording by Robert Gordon (RCA). Best-selling recording by Marshall Crenshaw (Warner Bros.), 1982.

Someday, Somewhere (We'll Meet Again). w. Lew Pollack, m. Erno Rapee, 1928. Theme song of (MP) *The Red Dance*, starring Charles Farrell and Dolores Del Rio.

Someday (You'll Want Me to Want You). w/m Jimmie Hodges, 1940, 1949. Introduced by Elton Britt (Victor). #1 record in 1949 by Vaughn Monroe (RCA Victor). Among many other versions: Eddy Arnold (RCA Victor), The Mills Brothers (Decca), Ricky Nelson (Imperial), The Ames Brothers (RCA Victor).

Someday I'll Find You. w/m Noël Coward, 1930. Sung by Noël Coward and Gertrude Lawrence in (TP) *Private Lives*. They recorded it in London (HMV), 1931. Lawrence later recorded it (Decca) in the U.S. and Coward included it in his LP (Columbia).

Someday I'll Meet You Again. w. Ned Washington, m. Max Steiner, 1944. From (MP) *Passage to Marseilles*. Leading record: The Ink Spots (Decca).

Someday My Prince Will Come. w. Larry Morey, m. Frank Churchill, 1938. Introduced by the voice of Adriana Caselotti, as Snow White, in the feature-length animated cartoon (MM) *Snow White and the Seven Dwarfs*.

Someday Never Comes. w/m John Fogerty, 1972. Recorded by Creedence Clearwater Revival, lead singer, Fogerty (Fantasy).

Someday Soon. w/m Ian Tyson, 1969. Recorded by folksinger Judy Collins (Elektra).

Someday Sweethheart. w/m John Spikes and Benjamin Spikes, 1919. A jazz standard. Among the many recordings: King Oliver (Vocalion), Gene Austin (Victor), Mildred Bailey (Vocalion), Bing Crosby (Decca), Count Basie (Columbia), Woody Herman (Columbia).

Someday We'll Be Together. w/m Jack Beavers, Johnny Bristol, and Harvey Fuqua, 1969. #1 record hit by The Supremes (Motown).

Someday We'll Look Back. w/m Merle Haggard, 1971. Hit country record by Merle Haggard (Capitol).

Someday We're Gonna Love Again. w/m Sharon McMahan, 1964. Recorded by the English rock quartet The Searchers (Kapp).

Someday When Things Are Good. w/m Merle Haggard and Leona Williams, 1984. #1 Country chart record by Merle Haggard (Epic).

Some Enchanted Evening. w. Oscar Hammerstein II, m. Richard Rodgers, 1949. Introduced by Ezio Pinza in (TM) *South Pacific*. Pinza's single, from the cast album, was a million-seller (Columbia), as was Perry Como's recording (RCA Victor). Other best-sellers by Joe Stafford (Capitol), Frank Sinatra (Columbia), Bing Crosby (Decca). In (MM) *South Pacific*, 1958, it was sung by Giorgio Tozzi, dubbing for Rossano Brazzi, and Mitzi Gaynor. Later popular record by Jay and The Americans (United Artists), 1965, and Jane Olivor (Columbia), 1977.

Some Guys Have All the Luck. w/m Jeff Fortgang, 1973, 1984. Top 10 R&B and Top 40 Pop chart hit by The Persuaders (Atco). Revived with Top 10 record by Rod Stewart (Warner Bros.), 1984.

Somehow. w/m Mort Maser, 1949. Leading record by Billy Eckstine (MGM).

Somehow It Seldom Comes True. w. Arthur J. Jackson and B. G. DeSylva, m. George Gershwin, 1919. Introduced in (TM) *La, La, Lucille* by Jane Verlie.

Some Kind of Friend. w. Adrienne Anderson, m. Barry Manilow, 1983. Recorded by Barry Manilow (Arista).

Some Kind-a Wonderful (a.k.a. **Some Kind of Wonderful**). w/m Gerry Goffin and Carole King, 1961, 1975. Recorded by The Drifters (Atlantic). Under the alternate title, the group Grand Funk had a Top 10 version (Capitol), 1975.

Some Like It Hot. w/m Andy Taylor, John Taylor, and Robert Palmer, 1985. Written by three quarters of the quartet, Power Station, the group that had a Top 10 record (Capitol).

Some Little Bug Is Going to Find You. w. Benjamin Hapgood Burt and Roy Atwell, m. Silvio Hein, 1915. This song satirized the influenza epidemic of that year. The song was interpolated in and became the hit of Franz Lehar's (TM) *Alone At Last*.

Some of Shelly's Blues. w/m Michael Nesmith, 1971. Recorded by The Nitty Gritty Dirt Band (United Artists).

Some of These Days. w/m Shelton Brooks, 1910. Sophie Tucker introduced this song that became not only her theme song but the title of her autobiography in 1945. She sang it in (MM) *Honky Tonk*, 1929; in (MM) *Broadway Melody of '38*; in (MM) *Follow the Boys*, 1944. The song was interpolated in (MM) *Animal Crackers*, 1930; in (MM) *Rose Marie*, 1930; in (MM) *Broadway*, 1942; danced by Sandahl Bergman in (MM) *All That Jazz*, 1979.

Someone Before Me. w/m Bob Hicks, 1966. Country hit by The Wilburn Brothers (Decca).

Someone Could Lose a Heart Tonight. w/m David Malloy, Even Stevens, and Eddie Rabbitt, 1982. Country/Pop hit by Eddie Rabbitt (Elektra).

Someone Else May Be There (While I'm Gone). w/m Irving Berlin, 1917. Al Jolson featured and recorded this song about a soldier's fear in World War I (Columbia).

Someone Is Sending Me Flowers. w. Sheldon Harnick, m. David Baker, 1955. Introduced by Dody Goodman in (TM) *Shoestring Revue*.

Someone Like You. w. Ralph Blane, m. Harry Warren, 1949. Introduced by Doris Day in (MM) *My Dream Is Yours*.

Someone Like You. w. Robert B. Smith, m. Victor Herbert, 1919. From (TM) *Angel Face*.

Someone Loves You After All. w. Joseph McCarthy, m. Harry Tierney, 1923. Introduced by Eddie Cantor and Mary Eaton in (TM) *Kid Boots*. Recorded by Paul Whiteman and his Orchestra (Victor).

Someone Nice Like You. w/m. Leslie Bricusse and Anthony Newley, 1962. Introduced by Anthony Newley in (TM) *Stop the World—I Want to Get Off*.

Someone Saved My Life Tonight. w/m Elton John and Bernie Taupin, 1975. Recorded in England by Elton John (MCA).

Someone's Rocking My Dreamboat. w/m Leon René, Otis René, and Emerson Scott, 1941. The vocal group, The Ink Spots, had the top record (Deccca).

Someone Stole Gabriel's Horn. w. Ned Washington, Edgar Hayes, and Irving Mills, 1932. Recorded by Bing Crosby (Brunswick), Jack Teagarden (Columbia), and the Washboard Rhythm Kings (Victor).

Someone's Waiting for You. w. Carol Connors and Ayn Robbins, m. Sammy Fain, 1977. Sung by Shelby Flint on the soundtrack of (MP) *The Rescuers*. Nominated for an Academy Award.

Someone That I Used to Love. w. Gerry Goffin, m. Michael Masser, 1980. Recorded by Natalie Cole (Capitol).

Someone to Care for Me. w/m Gus Kahn, Bronislaw Kaper, and Walter Jurmann, 1937. Introduced in (MM) *Three Smart Girls* and recorded by Deanna Durbin on her first commercial release (Decca).

Someone to Lay Down Beside Me. w/m Karla Bonoff, 1976. Recorded by Linda Ronstadt (Asylum).

Someone to Watch over Me. w. Ira Gershwin, m. George Gershwin, 1926. Gertrude Lawrence, in her first appearance in an American musical, introduced this future evergreen in (TM) *Oh, Kay!* Frank Sinatra sang it in (MM) *Young at Heart*, 1942. It was in a montage in (MM) *Rhapsody in Blue*, 1946; per-

formed by Marge and Gower Champion in (MM) *Three for the Show*, 1955; sung on the soundtrack by Gogi Grant for Ann Blyth in (MM) *The Helen Morgan Story*, 1957; sung by Vera Miles in (MM) *Beau James*, 1957.

Someone You Love. w/m Steven Michaels, 1955. Featured and recorded by Nat "King" Cole (Capitol).

Some Other Spring. w. Arthur Herzog, Jr., m. Irene Kitchings, 1939. Recorded by Billie Holiday (Vocalion) and Teddy Wilson (Columbia).

Some Other Time. w. Betty Comden and Adolph Green, m. Leonard Bernstein, 1945. Introduced by Betty Comden, Adolph Green, Nancy Walker, and Cris Alexander in (TM) *On the Town*.

Some Other Time. w. Sammy Cahn, m. Jule Styne, 1944. Introduced by Frank Sinatra in (MM) *Step Lively*, a musical remake of (TM) *Room Service*.

Some People. w. Stephen Sondheim, m. Jule Styne, 1959. Introduced by Ethel Merman in (TM) *Gypsy*. In the film version (MM) *Gypsy*, 1962, it was sung by Rosalind Russell, whose vocals were partially dubbed by Lisa Kirk.

Some Sort of Somebody. w. Elsie Janis, m. Jerome Kern, 1915. Introduced by Elsie Janis in (MM) *Miss Information*. Two months later it was heard again, via its interpolation by Ann Orr, in a new musical (MM) *Very Good, Eddie*, at the Princess Theatre.

Some Sunday Morning. w. Ted Koehler, m. M. K. Jerome and Ray Heindorf, 1945. Introduced by Alexis Smith in (MP) *San Antonio*, starring Errol Flynn. Nominated for Academy Award. Popular records by Helen Forrest and Dick Haymes, with Gordon Jenkins's Orchestra (Decca) and Louis Prima and his Band (Majestic).

Some Sunday Morning. w. Gus Kahn and Raymond Egan, m. Richard A. Whiting, 1917. Popular song with recording by Ada

Jones and M. J. O'Connell (Columbia). Jones also recorded it with Billy Murray (Victor); Joseph C. Smith's Orchestra [instrumental] (Victor).

Some Sunny Day. w/m Irving Berlin, 1922. Popular records by Marion Harris (Columbia) and Paul Whiteman and his Orchestra (Victor).

Some Sweet Day. w/m Nat Shilkret and Lew Pollack, 1929. Theme song of (MP) *Children of the Ritz*, starring Dorothy Mackail. Recorded by Nat Shilkret and The Victor Orchestra, vocal by Franklin Baur (Victor).

Some Sweet Day. w. Gene Buck, m. Dave Stamper and Louis A. Hirsch, 1923. Introduced in (TM) *Ziegfeld Follies of 1922*.

Something. w/m George Harrison, 1969. #1 gold record by The Beatles (Apple). Among many recordings, chart versions by Shirley Bassey (United Artists); instrumental by Booker T. and The MG's (Stax), 1970; and Johnny Rodriguez (Mercury), 1974.

Something About Love. w. Lou Paley, m. George Gershwin, 1919. Introduced by Adele Rowland and Donald MacDonald in (TM) *The Lady in Red*. It was interpolated in the London production of (TM) *Lady Be Good*, 1926.

Something About You. w/m Mark Lindup, Phil Gould, Boon Gould, Mark King, and Walter Badarou, 1986. Top 10 record by the British group Level 42 (Polydor).

Something About You. w/m Eddie Holland, Lamont Dozier, and Brian Holland, 1965. Hit record by The Four Tops (Motown). Revived by LeBlanc and Carr (Big Tree), 1977.

Something Better to Do. w/m John Farrar, 1975. Top 20 record by Olivia Newton-John (MCA).

Something for the Boys. w/m Cole Porter, 1943. Introduced by Ethel Merman in (TM) *Something for the Boys*. Sung by Vivian Blaine in the film version (MM) *Something for the Boys*, 1944. This was the only song retained from the stage show.

Something Had to Happen. w. Oscar Hammerstein II, m. Jerome Kern, 1933. Sung by Lydia Roberti, Bob Hope, and Ray Middleton in (TM) *Roberta*. Ramona recorded it (Victor).

Something He Can Feel. w/m Curtis Mayfield, 1976. Introduced by Irene Cara and Lonette McKee in (MM) *Sparkle*. Chart record by Aretha Franklin (Atlantic).

Something I Dreamed Last Night. w. Herb Magidson and Jack Yellen, m. Sammy Fain, 1939. Introduced by Ella Logan in (TM) *George White's Scandals, 1939 Edition*. Logan recorded it (Columbia) as did Teddy Wilson (Musicraft), and later, Anita O'Day (London).

Something in My Heart. w/m Wayland Patton, 1985. Country chart hit by Ricky Skaggs (Epic).

Something in the Air. w/m John Keene, 1969. From the British comedy (MP) *The Magic Christian*. Top 40 record by Thunderclap Newman (Track).

Something in the Wind. w. Leo Robin, m. John Green, 1947. Introduced by Deanna Durbin in (MM) *Something in the Wind* and recorded by her (Decca). Also recorded by The Modernaires with Paula Kelly (Columbia).

Something in Your Eyes. w/m Richard Carpenter and Pamela Philips Oland, 1987. Recorded by Richard Carpenter and Dusty Springfield as part of the album "Time" (A&M).

Something Just Ain't Right. w/m Keith Sweat and Teddy Riley, 1988. Top 10 R&B chart record by Keith Sweat (Vintertainment).

Something Old, Something New. w/m Cy Coben and Charles Green, 1951. Top 10 C&W chart record by Eddy Arnold (RCA).

Something Old, Something New. w/m Ramez Idriss and George Tibbles, 1946. Featured and recorded by Frank Sinatra (Columbia).

Something Pretty. w/m Charlie Williams and Buddy Wayne, 1968. Top 10 Country chart record by Wynn Stewart (Capitol).

Some Things Are Better Left Unsaid. w/m Daryl Hall, 1985. Recorded by Daryl Hall and John Oates (RCA).

Something's Burning. w/m Mac Davis, 1970. Top 20 record by Kenny Rogers and The First Edition (Reprise).

Something's Coming. w. Stephen Sondheim, m. Leonard Bernstein, 1957. Introduced by Larry Kert in (TM) *West Side Story*. In the film version (MM) *West Side Story*, 1961, it was sung by Jim Bryant, dubbing on the soundtrack for Richard Beymer.

Something Seems Tingle-Ingling. w. Otto Harbach, m. Rudolf Friml, 1913. Sung by Burrell Barbaretto and Elaine Hammerstein in (TM) *High Jinks*.

Something's Got a Hold on Me. w/m Pearl Woods, Etta James, and Leroy Kirkland, 1962. Crossover (R&B/Pop) hit by Etta James (Argo).

Something's Gotta Give. w/m Johnny Mercer, 1955. Introduced by Fred Astaire vocally, and then danced by Astaire and Leslie Caron in (MM) *Daddy Long Legs*. Hit records by The McGuire Sisters (Coral) and Sammy Davis, Jr. (Decca).

Something's on Your Mind. w/m Hubert Eaves III and James Williams, 1984. Top 10 R&B chart record by "D" Train, pseudonym for co-writer Williams (Prelude).

Something Sort of Grandish. w. E. Y. Harburg, m. Burton Lane, 1947. Introduced by David Wayne and Ella Logan in (TM) *Finian's Rainbow*. In (MM) *Finian's Rainbow*, 1968, it was sung by Don Francks and Petula Clark.

Something So Strong. w/m Neil Finn and Mitchell Froom, 1987. Top 10 single from the album of their name by the Australian/New Zealand group Crowded House (Chrysalis).

Something's Wrong with Me. w/m Bobby Hart and Danny Janssen, 1972. Top 20 record by Austin Roberts (Chelsea).

Some Things You Never Get Used To. w/m Nicholas Ashford and Valerie Simpson, 1968. Top 40 record by Diana Ross and The Supremes (Motown).

Something Tells Me. w/m Hugh Martin and Timothy Gray, 1964. Introduced by Tammy Grimes in (TM) *High Spirits*.

Something Tells Me. w. Johnny Mercer, m. Harry Warren, 1938. Non-movie number featured and recorded by Louis Armstrong (Decca) and Kay Kyser (Brunswick).

Something to Grab For. w/m Ric Ocasek, 1983. Recorded by Ric Ocasek (Geffen).

Something to Live For. w. Edward Eliscu, m. Joseph Meyer, 1929. From (TM) *Lady Fingers*, starring Eddie Buzzell.

Something to Remember You By. w. Howard Dietz, m. Arthur Schwartz, 1930. The melody was first performed in a London musical, *Little Tommy Tucker*, with the title of "I Have No Words to Say How Much I Love You." With new lyrics, it was introduced by Libby Holman in (TM) *Three's a Crowd*. She sang it to a sailor, whose back was to the audience during the entire song. The sailor was the then unknown Fred MacMurray, who was part of the California Collegians, the stage band in the revue. Holman had a two-sided hit record (Brunswick), coupled with the even bigger hit from the same show, "Body and Soul" (q.v.).

Something to Shout About. w/m Cole Porter, 1943. Title song of (MM) *Something to Shout About*, sung by Jack Oakie, Don Ameche, William Gaxton, Janet Blair, Veda Ann Borg, and ensemble.

Something Very Strange. w/m Noël Coward, 1961. Introduced by Elaine Stritch in (TM) *Sail Away*.

Something Wonderful. w. Oscar Hammerstein II, m. Richard Rodgers, 1951.

Introduced by Dorothy Sarnoff in (TM) *The King and I*. In (MM) *The King and I*, 1956, it was sung by Terry Saunders.

Something You Got. w/m Chris Kenner, 1964. Chart records by Alvin Robinson (Tiger); as an instrumental, Ramsey Lewis (Argo); Chuck Jackson and Maxine Brown (Wand), 1965.

Something You Never Had Before. w. Howard Dietz, m. Arthur Schwartz, 1961. Introduced by Barbara Cook in (TM) *The Gay Life*.

Somethin' Stupid. w/m C. Carson Parks, 1967. #1 gold record by Nancy Sinatra and Frank Sinatra (Reprise)

Sometime. w. Gus Kahn, m. Ted Fio Rito, 1925. Introduced by Ted Fio Rito and his Orchestra.

Sometime. w. Rida Johnson Young, m. Rudolf Friml, 1918. Introduced by Francine Larrimore in (TM) *Sometime*, which also featured Ed Wynn and Mae West.

Sometimes. w/m Bill Anderson, 1975. Hit Country record by Bill Anderson and Mary Lou Turner (MCA). Pop chart version by the trio Facts of Life (Kayvette), 1977.

Sometimes a Lady. w/m Eddy Raven and Frank Myers, 1986. Top 10 Country chart record by Eddy Raven (RCA).

Sometimes Good Guys Don't Wear White. w/m Ed Cobb, 1966. Recorded by the punk rock quartet The Standells (Tower).

Sometimes I'm Happy. w. Irving Caesar, m. Vincent Youmans, 1927. This had some false starts before becoming a major standard. It originally had a lyric that Oscar Hammerstein wrote for (TM) *Mary Jane McKane*, 1923, titled "Come On and Pet Me." The song was published but dropped from the show before the opening. Caesar created its present title and words for (TM) *A Night Out*, which closed in Philadelphia during a pre-Broadway tryout, 1925. Two years later Louise Groody and Charles King introduced it in (TM) *Hit the*

Deck and the song was finally established. It received another boost in 1935, when Benny Goodman recorded Fletcher Henderson's great arrangement, backed with "King Porter Stomp," (q.v.) for his first big seller (Victor). It was the second number on the program of Goodman's famous Carnegie Hall concert in 1938. It was sung by Polly Walker and Jack Oakie in (MM) *Hit the Deck*, 1930, and by Jane Powell and Vic Damone in the 1955 remake. It was also in (MM) *The Benny Goodman Story*, 1955.

Sometimes When We Touch. w. Dan Hill, m. Barry Mann, 1978. Top 10 gold record by Dan Hill (20th Century).

Some Velvet Morning. w/m Lee Hazlewood, 1967. Top 40 record by Nancy Sinatra and Lee Hazlewood (Reprise).

Somewhere. w. Stephen Sondheim, m. Leonard Bernstein, 1957. Danced by the company and sung by Reri Grist in (TM) *West Side Story*. In the film version, (MM) *West Side Story*, 1961, it was sung by Marni Nixon and Jim Bryant, dubbing on the soundtrack for Natalie Wood and Richard Beymer. Chart singles by P. J. Proby (Liberty), 1965, Len Barry (Decca), 1967, Barbra Streisand (Columbia), 1986.

Somewhere Along the Way. w. Sammy Gallop, m. Kurt Adams, 1952. Popularized by Nat "King" Cole (Capitol).

Somewhere a Voice Is Calling. w. Eileen Newton, m. Arthur F. Tate, 1911.

Somewhere Down the Line. w/m Lewis Anderson and Casey Kelly, 1984. Introduced and first Country chart record by The Younger Brothers [James and Michael] (MCA), 1983. Top 10 follow-up by T. G. Sheppard (Warner Bros.), 1984.

Somewhere Down the Road. w/m Cynthia Weil, m. Tom Snow, 1981. Recorded by Barry Manilow (Arista).

Somewhere in France Is the Lily. w. Philander Johnson, m. Joseph E. Howard, 1918.

World War I song about flowers of the Allies. Leading recordings by Henry Burr (Columbia) and Charles Hart (Victor).

Somewhere in Old Wyoming. w. Charles Tobias, m. Peter De Rose, 1930. Early recordings by Carson Robison and Red Billings (Victor) and Andy Sanella and his Orchestra (Crown).

Somewhere in the Night. w/m Richard Kerr and Will Jennings, 1975. First chart record by the duo Batdorf & Rodney (Arista). Top 20 record by Helen Reddy (Capitol), 1976, and Top 10 version by Barry Manilow (Arista), 1979.

Somewhere in the Night. w. Milton Raskin, m. Billy May, 1962. Based on the theme of the series (TVP) "Naked City." Lyric version introduced by Teri Thornton (Dauntless).

Somewhere in the Night. w. Mack Gordon, m. Josef Myrow, 1946. Introduced by Vivian Blaine in (MM) *Three Little Girls in Blue*. Leading recordings by Betty Jane Rhodes (Victor), Ginny Simms (ARA), Martha Tilton (Capitol).

Somewhere My Love (Lara's Theme). w. Paul Francis Webster, m. Maurice Jarre, 1966. Based on theme from (MP) *Dr. Zhivago*, 1965. Top 10 vocal record by The Ray Conniff Singers (Columbia). Leading instrumental ("Lara's Theme") by Roger Williams (Kapp).

Somewhere Out There. w/m James Horner, Barry Mann, and Cynthia Weil, 1986. Introduced by Linda Ronstadt and James Ingram on the soundtrack of the animated film (MP) *An American Tail* and on a Top 10 single (MCA). Nominated for an Academy Award. Winner Grammy Award (NARAS), Song of the Year, 1987.

Somewhere That's Green. w. Howard Ashman, m. Alan Menken, 1982. Introduced by Ellen Greene in (TM) *Little Shop of Horrors*. She also sang it in the film version (MM) *Little Shop of Horrors*, 1986.

Somewhere There Is Someone. w/m Charles Nathan and Dave Heisler, 1954. Recorded by Lou Monte, with Henri René's Orchestra (RCA Victor).

Somewhere There's a Someone. w/m Baker Knight, 1966. Featured and recorded by Dean Martin (Reprise).

Somewhere Tonight. w/m Harlan Howard and Rodney Crowell, 1987. #1 Country chart song by the quartet, Highway 101, from the album of their name (Warner Bros.).

So Much in Love. w. William Jackson and George Williams, m. Roy Straigis, 1963. Hit record by The Tymes (Parkway). Revived in (MM) *Fast Times at Ridgemont High* and recorded by Timothy B. Schmit (Full Moon), 1982.

Sonata. w. Ervin Drake and Jimmy Shirl, m. Alex Alstone, 1947. Popular records by Perry Como (Victor) and Jo Stafford (Capitol).

So Near and Yet So Far. w/m Cole Porter, 1941. Introduced by Fred Astaire in (MM) *You'll Never Get Rich*.

Song Angels Sing, The. w. Paul Francis Webster, m. adapted by Irving Aaronson, 1952. Based on the 1st theme of the 3rd movement of Brahms's *Symphony No. 3 in F*. Introduced by Mario Lanza in (MM) *Because You're Mine*. Lanza recorded it (RCA Victor), as did John Raitt (Decca).

Songbird. m. Kenny Gorelik, 1987. Hit instrumental record by saxophonist Kenny G (Arista).

Songbird. w/m Dave Wolfert and Stephen Nelson, 1978. Recorded by Barbra Streisand (Columbia).

Song for a Summer Night. w/m Robert Allen, 1956. Introduced by Mitch Miller and his Orchestra in the Westinghouse "Studio One" production (TVP) "Song for a Summer Night." Miller's instrumental made the Top 10 on the popularity charts (Columbia).

Song from M*A*S*H (Suicide Is Painless). w/m Michael Altman and Johnny Mandel, 1970. Theme from (MP) "M*A*S*H." Instrumental recording by orchestra under direction of Al DeLory (Capitol). Later used as theme of long-running series (TVP) "M*A*S*H."

Song from "Moulin Rouge," The (a.k.a. Where Is Your Heart?). w. William Engvick, m. Georges Auric, 1953. Theme from (MP) *Moulin Rouge*. Original French title, "Le Long de la Seine," words by Jacques Larue. Percy Faith and his Orchestra, featuring the English vocal by Felicia Sanders, had a #1 million-selling record (Columbia).

Song from "Some Came Running" (a.k.a. To Love and Be Loved). w. Sammy Cahn, m. James Van Heusen, 1958. From (MP) *Some Came Running*. Nominated for Academy Award, 1958. Recorded by Frank Sinatra (Capitol).

Song from "10." See **It's Easy to Say.**

Song from "Two for the Seesaw." See **Second Chance, A.**

Song I Love, The. w. B. G. De Sylva and Lew Brown, m. Ray Henderson, 1928. Featured and recorded by Fred Waring's Pennsylvanians (Victor).

Song Is Ended, The (But the Melody Lingers On). w/m Irving Berlin, 1927. Featured and recorded by Ruth Etting (Columbia) and "Whispering" Jack Smith (Victor). Nellie Lutcher and Her Rhythm revived it (Capitol), 1947. It is interesting to note that, except for its use in the background of (MM) *Blue Skies*, 1946, this Berlin ballad has not been heard in any other film.

Song Is You, The. w. Oscar Hammerstein II, m. Jerome Kern, 1932. Introduced by Tullio Carminati and reprised by him with Natalie Hall in (TM) *Music in the Air*. In the film adaptation (MM) *Music in the Air*, 1934, it was sung by John Boles. Outstanding later recordings were made by Tommy Dorsey and his Orchestra (Victor) and Frank Sinatra (Bluebird). Sung by John Raitt in (TM) *A Musical Jubilee*, 1975.

Song of Delilah. w. Jay Livingston and Ray Evans, m. Victor Young, 1950. Title song of (MP) *Samson and Delilah*.

Song of India. m. Nicholas Rimsky-Korsakoff, 1937. On one of the all-time biggest record sellers, Tommy Dorsey and his Orchestra (Victor) coupled a swing arrangement of this classic Russian composition with a revival and new treatment of Irving Berlin's "Marie."

Song of Joy. w. Orbe (Sp.), Ross Parker (Engl.), m. Ludwig von Beethoven, 1970. Adapted from the last movement of Beethoven's *Ninth Symphony*. Top 20 record by Miguel Rios, conducted by Waldo de los Rios (A&M).

Song of Love. w. Dorothy Donnelly, m. Sigmund Romberg, 1921. Introduced by Bertram Peacock, in the role of Franz Schubert, and Olga Cook in (TM) *Blossom Time*. The melody was based on the 2nd theme from the 1st movement of Schubert's *Symphony No. 8 in B Minor*, the "Unfinished."

Song of New Orleans. w/m Sunny Skylar, 1947. Featured and recorded by Larry Green and his Orchestra (RCA Victor).

Song of Persia. w. David E. Radford and Raymond B. Egan, m. Richard A. Whiting, 1922. Popular record by Edwin Dale (Columbia).

Song of Raintree County, The. w. Paul Francis Webster, m. John Green, 1957. Sung by Nat "King" Cole under the credits, on the soundtrack of (MP) *Raintree County*. Recorded by Cole (Capitol).

Song of Songs, The. w. Clarence Lucas, m. Harold Vicars, 1914. An English translation of the French "Chanson du Coeur Brise." The original French words were by Maurice Vancaire.

Song of Surrender. w. Jay Livingston and Ray Evans, m. Victor Young, 1949. Title song of (MP) *Song of Surrender*, sung by Buddy Clark (Columbia).

Song of Surrender. w. Al Dubin, m. Harry Warren, 1934. Introduced by the Boswell Sisters in (MM) *Moulin Rouge* and recorded by them (Brunswick). Other records of note by the bands of: Eddy Duchin (Victor), Wayne King

(Brunswick), Ted Weems (Bluebird), Emil Coleman (Columbia).

Song of the Bayou. w/m Rube Bloom, 1929. Piano solo introduced by the composer on radio. Later recorded by Jack Fina (MGM) and Hal McIntyre and his Orchestra (Cosmo).

Song of the Dawn. w. Jack Yellen, m. Milton Ager, 1930. Sung by John Boles in (MM) *King of Jazz* and recorded by him (Victor).

Song of the Dreamer. w/m Eddie "Tex" Curtis, 1955. Featured and recorded by Eddie Fisher (RCA).

Song of the Flame. w. Otto Harbach and Oscar Hammerstein II, m. George Gershwin and Herbert Stothart, 1925. Sung by Tessa Kosta, Greek Evans, and the Russian Art Choir in (TM) *Song of the Flame*. Recorded by the Ipana Troubadors (Columbia), Vincent Lopez and his Orchestra (Okeh), The Victor Light Opera Company (Victor).

Song of the Fool. w. Sam M. Lewis, m. Jesse Greer, 1930. Featured in vaudeville, radio, and recorded (Brunswick) by Georgie Price.

Song of the Islands. w/m Charles E. King, 1915. Probably the most representative and most popular of the Hawaiian songs extant. This was first published in Honolulu. Harry Owens, popular Hawaiian bandleader, played it in (MM) *Song of the Islands*, 1942. It was also heard in (MM) *Melody Lane*, 1929, and in (MM) *Ice-Capades Revue*, 1942. The famed Ben Pollack's Band used it as its theme song and recorded it twice (Decca) (Brunswick). Among other recordings are Count Basie (Vocalion), Harry Owens (Decca), Bobby Breen (Bluebird), and Jesse Crawford, the organist (Victor).

Song of the Marines, The. w. Al Dubin, m. Harry Warren, 1937. Introduced in (MM) *The Singing Marine* and recorded (Decca) by Dick Powell.

Song of the Metronome. w/m Irving Berlin, 1939. Sung by the Brian Sisters and chorus in (MM) *Second Fiddle*.

Song of the Moonbeams. w. Harry Tobias, m. Vincent Rose, 1929. From (TM) *Earl Carroll's Sketch Book*. The orchestras of George Olsen, with vocal by Fran Frey (Victor) and Fred Rich, featuring Jimmy and Tommy Dorsey (Columbia), helped popularize the song.

Song of the Mounties. See **Mounties, The.**

Song of the Open Road. w/m Albert Hay Malotte, 1935. Sung by John Carroll in (MM) *Hi Gaucho!*

Song of the Shirt, The. w. Clifford Grey, m. Herbert Stothart, 1930. Introduced by Lawrence Tibbett in (MM) *The Rogue Song*.

Song of the South. w. Sam Coslow, m. Arthur Johnston, 1946. Heard on the soundtrack as title song of (MM) *Song of the South*.

Song of the Vagabonds. w. Brian Hooker, m. Rudolf Friml, 1925. Introduced by Dennis King and chorus in (TM) *The Vagabond King*. King sang it in the first film version (MM) *The Vagabond King*, 1930, and Oreste [Kirkop] sang it in the remake, 1956. Leading records by King (Victor) and Vincent Lopez and his Orchestra (Okeh).

Song of the Wanderer. w/m Neil Moret, 1926. Leading record by Erskine Hawkins and his Orchestra (Bluebird), 1941.

Song on the Radio. w/m Al Stewart, 1979. Recorded by the Scottish singer Al Stewart (Arista).

Song on the Sand. w/m Jerry Herman, 1983. Introduced by Gene Barry, and reprised by Barry and George Hearn in (TM) *La Cage aux Folles*.

Song's Gotta Come from the Heart, The. w. Sammy Cahn, m. Jule Styne, 1947. Introduced as a duet by Jimmy Durante and Frank Sinatra in (MM) *It Happened in Brooklyn*.

Song Sung Blue. w/m Neil Diamond, 1972. #1 gold record by Neil Diamond (Uni).

Song Was Born, A. w/m Don Raye and Gene de Paul, 1948. Introduced by The Golden Gate Quartet, Virginia Mayo (voice dubbed by Jeri Sullivan), and members of the "faculty," Louis Armstrong, Benny Goodman, Tommy Dorsey, Lionel Hampton, Charlie Barnet, and Mel Powell, in (MM) *A Song Is Born.*

So Nice Seeing You Again. w. Mort Dixon, m. Allie Wrubel, 1935. Popular recordings by Phil Regan (Columbia), Enric Madriguera (Victor), Chick Bullock (Melotone).

Sonny Boy. w/m Al Jolson, B. G. DeSylva, Lew Brown, and Ray Henderson, 1928. Al Jolson sang this, which the sheet music lists as the "theme song," in (MM) *The Singing Fool.* His record (Brunswick) sold a million copies. He sang it again on the soundtrack, dubbing for Larry Parks, in (MM) *The Jolson Story* in 1946. His new recording (Decca) again was a million-seller. In (MM) *Jolson Sings Again,* 1949, a montage from the 1946 film was shown that included "Sonny Boy." It was sung in the DeSylva, Brown, and Henderson bio (MM) *The Best Things in Life Are Free,* 1956, by Gordon MacRae, Ernest Borgnine, Dan Dailey, and Norman Brooks, the first three as the writers, and Brooks as Jolson. Hit record by The Andrews Sisters (Decca), 1941.

Son-of-a Preacher Man. w/m John Hurley and Ronnie Wilkins, 1968. English song. Top 10 record by Dusty Springfield (Atlantic).

Son of a Travelin' Man. w/m Robert I. Allen, Mauro Lusini, and Francesco Migliacci, 1969. Recorded by Ed Ames (RCA).

Son of Hickory Holler's Tramp, The. w/m Dallas Frazier, 1968. C&W/Pop hit. Leading record by O. C. Smith (Columbia).

Sons of . . . w. Mort Shuman and Eric Blau (Engl.), m. Gerard Jouannest, 1968. Original French title, "Fils de . . .," words by Jacques Brel. Introduced by him in France, 1967. The English version was introduced in the off-Broadway revue, *Jacques Brel Is Alive and Well in Paris,* by Elly Stone.

Sons of Katie Elder, The. w. Ernie Sheldon, m. Elmer Bernstein, 1965. Based on theme from (MP) *The Sons of Katie Elder.* Recorded by Johnny Cash (Columbia).

Soon. w. Lorenz Hart, m. Richard Rodgers, 1935. Introduced by Bing Crosby in (MM) *Mississippi* and recorded by him (Decca).

Soon. w. Ira Gershwin, m. George Gershwin, 1930. Introduced by Jerry Goff and Margaret Schilling in (TM) *Strike Up the Band.* George used a four-bar section of the Act I finale of the original production [which did not reach Broadway] as the basis for this melody.

Soon (I'll Be Home Again). w/m Bob Crewe and Bob Gaudio, 1963. Recorded by The Four Seasons (Vee-Jay).

Sooner or Later. w/m Edward Townsend, 1975. Recorded by The Impressions (Curtom).

Sooner or Later. w/m Alan Zekley, Mitch Bottler, Adenaye Paris, Ted McNamara, and Ekundayo Paris, 1971. Top 10 record by The Grass Roots (Dunhill).

Sooner or Later. w. Ray Gilbert, m. Charles Wolcott, 1946. Introduced by Hattie McDaniel in (MM) *Song of the South.* Popular recordings by Sammy Kaye, vocal by Betty Barclay (RCA Victor); Les Brown, vocal by Doris Day (Columbia).

Soon It's Gonna Rain. w. Tom Jones, m. Harvey Schmidt, 1960. Introduced by Kenneth Nelson and Rita Gardner in (TM) *The Fantasticks.*

So-o-o-o-o in Love. w. Leo Robin, m. David Rose, 1945. Introduced by Vera-Ellen [voice dubbed on soundtrack by June Hutton] in (MM) *Wonder Man,* starring Danny Kaye. Nominated for Academy Award. Recorded by Ray Noble and his Orchestra (Columbia).

Soothe Me. w/m Joe Greene, 1947. Featured and recorded by Stan Kenton, vocal by June Christy (Capitol).

Sophisticated Cissy. m. Arthur Neville, Leo Nocentelli, George Porter, and Joseph Modeliste, 1969. Instrumental by the New Orleans R&B group The Meters (Josie).

Sophisticated Lady. w. Mitchell Parish and Irving Mills, m. Edward Kennedy "Duke" Ellington, 1933. Introduced by Duke Ellington and his Orchestra as an instrumental (Brunswick). Sung in (TM) *Bubbling Brown Sugar* in 1976 by Chip Garnett. In the all-Ellington musical (TM) *Sophisticated Ladies*, 1981, it was performed by Gregory Hines. Ellington's Band played it on the soundtrack of (MM) *Paris Blues* in 1961. Among the many recordings: The Boswell Sisters (Brunswick); Don Redman [under pseudonym of Earl Harlan] (Melotone); Art Tatum (Brunswick); Willie "The Lion" Smith (Mercury 12"); Duke Ellington and Jimmy Blanton (Victor); Glen Gray and the Casa Loma Orchestra (Decca); Jimmy Lunceford, arranged by Edwin Wilcox (Decca); Morton Gould (Victor); George Shearing (Savoy); Stan Kenton, arranged by Pete Rugolo (Capitol).

Sophisticated Lady (She's a Different Lady). w/m Natalie Cole, Charles Jackson, Jr., and Marvin Yancy, 1976. Recorded by Natalie Cole (Capitol).

Sophisticated Swing. m. Mitchell Parish, m. Will Hudson, 1937. Introduced by and theme song of the Hudson-DeLange Orchestra (Brunswick). Also recorded by the bands of Les Brown (Columbia); Bunny Berigan (Victor); Ozzie Nelson (Brunswick); and in 1957, coupled with the hit revival "So Rare," by the Jimmy Dorsey Band (Fraternity).

So Rare. w. Jack Sharpe, m. Jerry Herst, 1937, 1957. Originally introduced by Jimmy Dorsey and his Orchestra. The song, through numerous recordings and sustained airplay, became #1 and was on "Your Hit Parade" for eleven weeks. Twenty years later, via the Jimmy Dorsey Band pseudo-rock recording (Fra-

ternity), the song again became a "Hit Parader," and again for eleven weeks! Dorsey was awarded a gold record for his million-seller shortly before he died of cancer.

Sorghum Switch. m. Jesse Stone, 1942. Instrumental, first recorded by Doc Wheeler and his Sunset Orioles (Bluebird), 1941. Popular record by Jimmy Dorsey and his Orchestra (Decca). See also **Cole Slaw.**

So Round, So Firm, So Fully Packed. w/m Merle Travis, Cliffie Stone, and Eddie Kirk, 1947. Title derived from a major cigarette advertising slogan, but had a different connotation in the song. Merle Travis's recording was #1 on the Country charts (Capitol).

Sorrow on the Rocks. w/m Tony Moon, 1964. Hit Country record by Porter Wagoner (RCA).

Sorry. w. Buddy Pepper, m. Richard A. Whiting, 1950. Posthumous song of Whiting's, introduced and recorded by his daughter, Margaret Whiting (Capitol). Popular record by Frank Sinatra, with Paula Kelly and the Modernaires (Columbia).

Sorry, I Ran All the Way Home. w/m Harry Giosasi and Artie Zwirn, 1959. Top 10 record by The Impalas (Cub).

Sorry I Ain't Got It, You Could Have It, etc. See **All in Down and Out.**

Sorry Seems to Be the Hardest Word. w/m Elton John and Bernie Taupin, 1976. Top 10 gold record by British singer Elton John (MCA/Rocket).

Sorta on the Border. w/m Irving Gordon, 1953. Leading record by Tony Martin (RCA Victor).

S.O.S. w/m Benny Anderson, Stig Anderson, and Bjorn Ulvaeus, 1975. Recorded by the Swedish quartet Abba (Atlantic).

So Sad (to Watch Good Love Go Bad). w/m Don Everly, 1960. Top 10 record by The Everly Brothers (Warner Brothers).

So Sad the Song. w/m Gerry Goffin and Michael Masser, 1976. Introduced by Gladys Knight and The Pips on the soundtrack of (MP) *Pipe Dreams*, and on records (Buddah).

So the Bluebirds and the Blackbirds Got Together. w. Billy Moll, m. Harry Barris, 1929. Introduced by Paul Whiteman's Rhythm Boys [Bing Crosby, Harry Barris, and Al Rinker] (Columbia). They then sang it in (MM) *The King of Jazz*, 1930.

So This Is Love. w/m Herbert Newman, 1962. Recorded by The Castells (Era).

So This Is Love. w/m E. Ray Goetz, 1923. Introduced by Irene Bordoni in (TP) *Little Miss Bluebeard*. The French star also recorded it (Victor).

So Tired. w/m Russ Morgan and Jack Stuart, 1949. Introduced, featured, and recorded by Russ Morgan, with his orchestra (Decca). Kay Starr followed it with one of her first hit records (Capitol). Freddy Martin, vocal by Merv Griffin, also had a popular version (RCA Victor).

So Tired. w/m George A. Little and Arthur Sizemore, 1927. Recorded by Jean Goldkette's Band with vocal by Hoagy Carmichael (Victor); Art Gillham (Columbia); Fred Rose (Brunswick); and Elmo Tanner (Vocalion).

Soul and Inspiration (You're My). See **(You're My) Soul and Inspiration.**

Soul Coaxing. See **Ame Caline.**

Soul Deep. w/m Wayne Carson Thompson, 1969. Top 20 record by The Box Tops (Mala).

Soul Finger. m. James Alexander, Ronnie Caldwell, Ben Cauley, Carl Cunningham, Jimmy King, and Phalon Jones, 1967. Top 20 instrumental written and recorded by The Bar-Kays (Volt).

Soulful Strut (a.k.a. **Am I the Same Girl?**). w/m Eugene Record and William Sanders, 1968. Gold record instrumental by Young-Holt Unlimited (Brunswick). A vocal version was created by Barbara Acklin, re-placing the solo piano track with her voice (Brunswick), 1969.

Soul Hootenanny. w/m Eugene Dixon (a.k.a. Gene Chandler), 1964. Chart record by Gene Chandler (Constellation—Part 1).

Soul Je T'Aime. See **Je T'Aime . . . Moi Non Plus.**

Soul Kiss. w/m Mark Goldenberg, 1985. Recorded by Olivia Newton-John (MCA).

Soul-Limbo. w/m Booker T. Jones, Steve Cropper, Donald Dunn, and Al Jackson, 1968. Top 20 instrumental by Booker T. and The MG's (Stax).

Soul Makossa. m. Manu Dibango, 1973. Instrumental recorded by the African saxophonist Manu Dibango (Atlantic) and the band Afrique (Mainstream).

Soul Man. w/m Isaac Hayes and David Porter, 1967. Gold record by Sam and Dave, produced by the writers (Stax). Instrumental chart version by pianist Ramsey Lewis (Cadet). Top 20 revival by The Blues Brothers [John Belushi and Dan Akroyd] (Atlantic), 1979. Sung by Lou Reed and Sam Moore in (MP) *Soul Man* and on the soundtrack album (A&M), 1986.

Soul Power. w/m James Brown, 1971. Hit R&B/Pop record by James Brown (King).

Souls. w/m Rick Springfield, 1983. Recorded by the Australian singer/songwriter Rick Springfield (RCA).

Soul Serenade. w/m Curtis Ousley and Luther Dixon, 1964. Instrumental, first recorded by R&B saxophonist King Curtis [pseud. for Ousley] (Capitol). Hit revival by keyboardist Willie Mitchell (HI), 1968.

Soul Shake. w/m Mira Smith and Margaret Lewis, 1969. Popular recordings by Peggy Scott and Jo Jo Benson (SSS International), and Delaney & Bonnie and Friends (Atco), 1970.

Soul Sister, Brown Sugar. w/m Isaac Hayes and David Porter, 1969. Recorded by Sam and Dave (Atlantic).

Soul Train '75. w/m Donald Cornelius and Dick Griffey, 1975. Recorded by The Soul Train Gang, comprised of studio singers from the syndicated show (TVM) "Soul Train" (Soul Train).

Soul Twist. m. Curtis Ousley, 1962. Instrumental hit by King Curtis (Enjoy).

Sound Off. w/m Willie Lee Duckworth, 1951. Duckworth is credited on the published song version of the number. Col. Bernard Lentz, U.S.A., Ret., is credited in a manual of close order drill cadences. The basic concept developed as an oral marching cadence chanted by black U.S. Army troops before integration took place in the early days of World War II. This version was later used as a radio and TV commercial for Chesterfield cigarettes. Vaughn Monroe, with his Orchestra, had a popular recording (RCA Victor).

Sound of Goodbye, The. w/m Hugh Prestwood, 1984. Country/Pop chart record by Crystal Gayle (Warner Bros.).

Sound of Love. w/m John Durrill, Norman Ezell, and Mike Rabon, 1967. Recorded by The Five Americans (Abnak).

Sound of Music, The. w. Oscar Hammerstein II, m. Richard Rodgers, 1959. Introduced by Mary Martin in (TM) *The Sound of Music.* Julie Andrews sang it in the film version (MM) *The Sound of Music,* 1965.

Sound of Surf, The. m. Charles Albertine, 1963. Instrumental recorded by Percy Faith and his Orchestra (Columbia).

Sounds. w. Will Holt, m. Gary William Friedman, 1970. Introduced by Hattie Wilson and Beverly Ann Bremers in (TM) *The Me Nobody Knows.*

Sounds of Silence, The. w/m Paul Simon, 1964. #1 gold record by Simon and Garfunkel (Columbia). The artists sang it on the soundtrack of (MP) *The Graduate,* 1967.

Soup for One. w/m Bernard Edwards and Nile Rodgers, 1982. Theme of (MP) *Soup for One* and recorded by the group, Chic, produced and performed by the writers (Mirage).

Sous Les Ponts de Paris. See **Under the Bridges of Paris.**

Sous Les Toits de Paris (Under a Roof in Paree). w. Irving Caesar (Engl.), Rene Nazelles (Fr.), m. Raoul Moretti, 1931. From the 1930 French film (MM) *Sous les Toits de Paris.* The English words were written a year later.

South. m. Bennie Moten and Thamon Hayes, 1924. Instrumental recorded twice by Moten's band, in 1924 (Okeh), 1928 (Victor). Some other standouts are: Woody Herman and the Woodchoppers (Decca), Hot Lips Page (Decca), Kid Ory (Crescent), Pete Daily (Capitol), the Riley-Farley Band (Decca), Bob Scobey (Good Time Jazz), the Lawson-Haggart Band (Decca), Les Paul (Capitol).

South America, Take it Away. w/m Harold Rome, 1946. Introduced by Betty Garrett in the revue (TM) *Call Me Mister.* Hit record by Bing Crosby and The Andrews Sisters (Decca). Also popular record by Xavier Cugat, vocal by Buddy Clark (Columbia).

South American Joe. w/m Irving Caesar and Cliff Friend, 1934.

South American Way. w. Al Dubin, m. Jimmy McHugh, 1939. Sung by Carmen Miranda [first U.S. show], Ramon Vinay, the Hylton Sisters, and Della Lind; danced by Jo and Jeanne Readinger and Gower (Champion) and Jeanne (Tyler) in (TM) *Streets of Paris.* Miranda then sang it in her first film (MM) *Down Argentine Way,* 1940, and recorded it (Decca). Other popular disc versions by The Andrews Sisters (Decca); the bands of Ozzie Nelson, vocal by Harriet Hilliard (Bluebird); Ray Noble, vocal by Larry Stewart (Brunswick); Desi Arnaz (Columbia).

South Central Rain (I'm Sorry). w/m Bill Berry, Pete Buck, Mike Mills, and Michael Stipe, 1984. Written and recorded by the quartet R.E.M. (I.R.S.).

Southern Cross. w/m Steve Stills, Richard Curtis, and Michael Curtis, 1982. Recorded by Crosby, Stills and Nash (Atlantic).

Southern Fried. w/m Harlan Leonard, James Ross, and Fred Culliver, 1940. First recorded by Harlan Leonard and his Orchestra (Bluebird). Most popular recordings by the bands of Charlie Barnett (Bluebird), Al Donahue (Okeh), Terry Shand (Decca).

Southern Nights. w/m Allen Toussaint, 1977. First recorded by Toussaint in an album (Warner Bros.), 1975; the song was picked up by Glen Campbell, whose version became a #1 gold record (Capitol).

Southern Rains. w/m Roger Murrah, 1981. #1 Country record by Mel Tillis (Elektra).

South of the Border (Down Mexico Way). w/m Jimmy Kennedy and Michael Carr, 1939. Introduced and recorded by Gene Autry (Okeh) and then sung as title song by Autry in (MM) *South of the Border*, 1939. The song was the No. 1 sheet music seller of the year and a top record seller, with Autry's record leading such other hit versions as Sammy Kaye (Victor), Kenny Baker (Victor), Benny Goodman (Columbia), Horace Heidt (Columbia), and Shep Fields (Bluebird). Alec Templeton had a novelty version, "Opera Presentation of 'South of the Border' " (Victor). Bing Crosby sang it in (MM) *Pepe*, 1960.

South Rampart Street Parade. w. Steve Allen, m. Ray Bauduc and Bob Haggart, 1939. Introduced and recorded by Bob Crosby and his Orchestra (Decca). Among other recordings: Phil Napoleon (Swan), Nappy Lamare (Capitol), Jimmy Dorsey (Columbia). Lyrics added in 1952.

South Sea Island Magic. w/m Andy Iona Long, 1936. Top records by Artie Shaw, vocal by Peg La Centra (Brunswick) and George Hall and his Orchestra (Bluebird).

South Sea Isles (a.k.a. **Sunny South Sea Islands**). w. Arthur Jackson, m. George Gershwin, 1921. Introduced by Charles King

and Ann Pennington in (TM) *George White's Scandals*.

South's Gonna Do It, The. w/m Charlie Daniels, 1975. Recorded by The Charlie Daniels Band (Kama Sutra).

South Street. w. Kal Mann, m. Dave Appell, 1963. Hit record by The Orlons (Cameo).

Southtown, U.S.A. w/m Billy Sherrill, 1964. Top 40 record by The Dixiebelles (Sound Stage).

Souvenir d'Italie. w. Carl Sigman (Engl.), m. L. Luttazzi, 1957. Original Italian words by Scarnicci Tarabusi. Sung in the Italian film of (MP) *Souvenir d'Italie* and in the British film (MP) *Danger, Girl at Play*. Leading U.S. records by Tony Martin (RCA), Toni Arden (Decca), and Leroy Holmes (MGM).

So Very Hard to Go. w/m Emilio Castillo and Stephen Kupka, 1973. Recorded by Tower of Power (Warner Bros.).

So Would I. w. Johnny Burke, m. James Van Heusen, 1946. Recorded by Georgia Gibbs (Majestic); Paul Weston, vocal by Matt Dennis (Capitol); Skinnay Ennis, with his Orchestra (Signature).

So You Want to Be a Rock 'n' Roll Star. w/m Jim McGuinn and Chris Hillman, 1967. Written by two members of The Byrds, who had a Top 40 record (Columbia).

Spaceballs. w/m Jeffrey Pescetto, Clyde Lieberman, and Mel Brooks, 1987. Sung by The Spinners on the soundtrack of the Mel Brooks film (MP) *Spaceballs*.

Spaceman. w/m Harry Nilsson, 1972. Recorded by Nilsson (RCA).

Space Oddity. w/m David Bowie, 1973. Written and recorded in England by David Bowie (RCA).

Space Race. m. Billy Preston, 1973. Keyboard instrumental hit by Billy Preston (A&M).

Spain. w. Gus Kahn, m. Isham Jones, 1924. One of numerous successes by the team. Introduced and hit record by Isham Jones and his Orchestra (Brunswick).

Spaniard That Blighted My Life, The. w/m Billy Merson, 1911. Introduced by Al Jolson in (TM) *The Honeymoon Express*. It was sung by Jolson in (MM) *The Singing Fool*, 1928, and, dubbing for Larry Parks, with chorus in (MM) *The Jolson Story*, 1946. Recorded by Jolson (Victor), 1913, and with Bing Crosby (Decca), 1947.

Spanish Eddie. w/m David Palmer and Chuck Cochran, 1985. Recorded by Laura Branigan (Atlantic).

Spanish Eyes. w. Charles Singleton and Eddie Snyder, m. Bert Kaempfert, 1965, 1966. German composition, introduced instrumentally in the U.S. by Bert Kaempfert and his Orchestra (Decca) under title of "Moon Over Naples." Al Martino popularized the lyric version (Capitol), 1966.

Spanish Fire Ball. w/m Daniel James Welch, 1953. To 10 C&W record by Hank Snow (RCA).

Spanish Flea. m. Julius Wechter, 1966. Instrumental hit by Herb Alpert and The Tijuana Brass (A&M). Theme song of the game show (TVP) *The Dating Game*.

Spanish Harlem. w/m Jerry Leiber and Phil Spector, 1961, 1971. Introduced and hit record by Ben E. King (Atco). Saxophonist King Curtis had a popular instrumental version (Atco), 1966. Revived by Aretha Franklin with a million-selling record (Atlantic), 1971.

Spanish Love. w/m Vincent Bryan, Ted Snyder, and Irving Berlin, 1911. Introduced by Ethel Levey in vaudeville. Interpolated in the revue (TM) *Folies Bergere*. Leading recording by the male singer, Andrea Sarto (Columbia).

Spanish Rose. w. Lee Adams, m. Charles Strouse, 1960. Introduced by Chita Rivera in (TM) *Bye Bye Birdie*. Song not used in film version.

Spare Parts. w/m Bruce Springsteen, 1987. Popular track of the Bruce Springsteen album "Tunnel of Love" (Columbia)

Sparrow in the Tree Top. w/m Bob Merrill, 1951. Popularized and recorded by Guy Mitchell, with Mitch Miller's Orchestra (Columbia), Bing Crosby and The Andrews Sisters (Decca), Rex Allen (Mercury).

Speaking Confidentially. w. Dorothy Fields, m. Jimmy McHugh, 1935. Introduced by Frances Langford, Alice Faye, and Patsy Kelly in (MM) *Every Night at Eight*, and recorded by Langford (Brunswick).

Speaking of Heaven. w. Mack Gordon, m. James Van Heusen, 1939. Recordings: the bands of Glenn Miller (Bluebird), Eddie Duchin (Columbia), Will Bradley (Vocalion), Bobby Byrne (Decca), Reggie Childs (Varsity).

Speaking of the Weather. w. E. Y. Harburg, m. Harold Arlen, 1937. Sung in (MM) *Gold Diggers of 1937* and on records by Dick Powell (Decca).

Speak Low. w. Ogden Nash, m. Kurt Weill, 1943. Introduced by Mary Martin, and reprised by Kenny Baker and Martin in (TM) *One Touch of Venus*. In the film version (MM) *One Touch of Venus*, 1948, it was sung by Dick Haymes and, dubbing for Ava Gardner, Eileen Wilson.

Speak Softly Love. See **Love Theme from "The Godfather."**

Speak to Me of Love. w. Bruce Siever (Engl.), Jean Lenoir (Fr.), m. Jean Lenoir, 1932. French song, originally titled "Parlez-Moi d'Amour." Featured by Irene Bordoni, Lucienne Boyer, and other French performers on stage, radio, and in nightclubs. Bob Crosby and the Bob Cats had a popular version in 1939 (Decca).

Speak to the Sky. w/m Rick Springfield, 1972. Top 20 record by Rick Springfield (Capitol).

Special Delivery. w/m Bo Gentry and Bobby Bloom, 1969. Recorded by The 1910 Fruitgum Company (Buddah).

Special Lady. w/m Harry Ray, Al Goodman, and Billy Brown, 1980. #1 R&B, #5 Pop chart gold record by the trio, Ray, Goodman & Brown (Polydor).

Special Occasion. w/m Alfred Cleveland and William Robinson, 1968. Top 40 record by Smokey Robinson and The Miracles.

Speedoo. w/m Esther Navarro, 1955. Hit record for The Cadillacs (Josie). Title comes from the nickname of the lead singer of the group, Earl Carroll.

Speedy Gonzales. w/m Buddy Kaye, David Hess, and Ethel Lee, 1962. Novelty hit popularized by Pat Boone (Dot).

Spellbound (a.k.a. **Spellbound Concerto**). w. Mack David, m. Miklos Rozsa, 1945. Based on the theme from (MP) *Spellbound*. Recorded by Eddie Safranski and Vido Musso (Savoy), and from the soundtrack of the film, the orchestra led by Ray Heindorf (Warner Bros.).

Spend the Night (Ce Soir). w/m Angela Lisa Winbush, 1989. Hit R&B chart single by The Isley Brothers (Warner Bros.).

Spiders and Snakes. w/m Jim Stafford and David Bellamy, 1974. Featured and gold record by Jim Stafford (MGM).

Spies Like Us. w/m Paul McCartney, 1986. Sung by Paul McCartney on the soundtrack of (MP) *Spies Like Us* and on a Top 10 single (Capitol).

Spill the Wine. w/m Dee Allen, Harold Brown, B. B. Dickerson, Lonnie Jordan, L. O. Levitin, and Howard Scott, 1970. Gold record by Eric Burdon and War (MGM).

Spinning Wheel. w/m David Clayton-Thomas, 1969. Gold record by the group, Blood, Sweat & Tears, of which the writer was lead singer (Columbia).

Spinout. w/m Darrell Fuller, Sid Wayne, and Ben Weisman, 1966. Introduced by Elvis Presley in (MM) *Spinout* and on records (RCA).

Spirit in the Dark. w/m Aretha Franklin, 1970. Introduced and recorded by Aretha Franklin (Atlantic).

Spirit in the Night. w/m Bruce Springsteen, 1972. Introduced by Springsteen in his album "Greetings from Asbury Park" (Columbia). Best-selling single by the English group, Manfred Mann's Earth Band (Warner Bros.), 1977.

Spirit in the Sky. w/m Norman Greenbaum, 1970. Gold record by Norman Greenbaum (Reprise). Revived by the English sextet, Doctor and The Medics (I.R.S.), 1986.

Spirit of Radio, The. w. Neil Peart, m. Geddy Lee and Alex Lifeson, 1980. Written and recorded by the Canadian trio Rush (Mercury).

Spirit of the Boogie. w/m Robert "Kool" Bell & The Gang, 1975. Written and recorded by Kool & The Gang (De-Lite).

Spirits in the Material World. w/m Sting, 1982. Recorded by the English trio, Police; vocalist, Sting (A&M).

Splish Splash. w/m Bobby Darin and Jean Murray, 1958. Top 10 record by Bobby Darin (Atco). This was Darin's first hit record.

Spooky. w. Buddy Buie and J. R. Cobb, m. Harry Middlebrooks and Mike Sharpe, 1968. Instrumental by saxophonist Mike Sharpe (Liberty), 1967. Hit record by Classics IV (Imperial). Revived by The Atlanta String Section (Polydor), 1979.

Spooky Ookum. w. Henry Blossom, m. Victor Herbert, 1919. From (TM) *The Velvet Lady*.

Spooky Takes a Holiday. See **Satan Takes a Holiday.**

Spoonful of Sugar, A. w/m Richard M. Sherman and Robert B. Sherman, 1963. Introduced by Julie Andrews in (MM) *Mary Poppins*.

S'posin'. w. Andy Razaf, m. Paul Denniker, 1929. Recorded by many, over the years, including Seger Ellis (Okeh), Bob Haring (Brunswick), Erskine Hawkins (Bluebird), Al Hibbler (Aladdin), Andy Kirk (Decca), and Jack Leonard (Majestic). In 1948, it was revived by Donald O'Connor in (MM) *Feudin', Fussin', and A-Fightin'*.

Spread a Little Sunshine. w/m Stephen Schwartz, 1972. Introduced by Leland Palmer in (TM) *Pippin*.

Spreadin' Rhythm Around. w. Ted Koehler, m. Jimmy McHugh, 1936. Introduced in (MM) *King of Burlesque* and recorded (Decca) by Alice Faye. Fats Waller had a popular recording (Victor). It was performed by the company at the beginning of Act II of the Waller musical (TM) *Ain't Misbehavin'*, 1978, with additional lyrics by Richard Maltby, Jr.

Spread It on Thick. w/m Bill Cates, John Hurley, and Ronnie Wilkins, 1966. Recorded by The Gentrys (MGM).

Spring, Beautiful Spring. m. Paul Lincke, 1903. See also **Chimes of Spring**.

Spring, Spring, Spring. w. Johnny Mercer, m. Gene De Paul, 1954. Introduced by Jane Powell and the brothers in (MM) *Seven Brides for Seven Brothers*.

Spring Can Really Hang You Up the Most. w. Fran Landesman, m. Tommy Wolf, 1955.

Spring Has Sprung. w. Charles Tobias, m. Peter De Rose, 1952. From (MM) *About Face*, which was based on the Broadway play and later film, *Brother Rat*.

Spring in Maine. w. Carolyn Leigh, m. Steve Allen, 1956. Introduced and recorded by Margaret Whiting (Capitol).

Spring Is Here. w. Lorenz Hart, m. Richard Rodgers, 1938. Introduced by Dennis King and Vivienne Segal in (TM) *I Married an Angel*. Jeanette MacDonald and Nelson Eddy sang it in the film version (MM) *I Married an Angel*, 1942, and Mickey Rooney, as Lorenz Hart, sang it in the Rogers and Hart story, (MM) *Words and Music*, 1948.

Springtime of Life, The. w. Robert B. Smith, m. Victor Herbert, 1914. From (TM) *The Debutante*.

Spring Will be a Little Late This Year. w/m Frank Loesser, 1944. Introduced by Deanna Durbin in (MP) *Christmas Holiday*. She recorded it, coupled with the other song from the film, Irving Berlin's "Always" (q.v.) (Decca).

Square Biz. w/m Mary Brockert and Allen McGrier, 1981. Crossover (R&B/Pop) record by Teena Marie [Brockert's pseudonym] (Gordy).

Square in the Social Circle, A. w/m Jay Livingston and Ray Evans, 1945. Introduced by Betty Hutton in (MM) *The Stork Club*.

Squeeze Box. w/m Peter Townshend, 1976. Top 20 record by the British group The Who (MCA).

Squeeze Me. w. Clarence Williams, m. Thomas "Fats" Waller, 1928. This was Waller's first song success. After Clarence Williams's initial recording (Okeh), it was followed by Louis Armstrong (Okeh), The Louisiana Rhythm Kings (Brunswick), Bessie Smith (Columbia), Chick Webb (Decca), Lena Horne (Black and White), Mildred Bailey (Decca), Bob Crosby (Decca), Art Hodes on a 12″ disc (Banner), Red Nichols (Brunswick), and many more. Armelia McQueen sang it in (TM) *Ain't Misbehavin'*, 1978.

Stagger Lee. w/m Lloyd Price and Harold Logan, 1958. #1 record by Lloyd Price (ABC-Paramount). Later popular versions by Wilson Pickett (Atlantic), 1967, and Tommy Roe (ABC), 1971.

Stairway of Love. w/m Sid Tepper and Roy C. Bennett, 1958. C&W and Pop chart song by Marty Robbins (Columbia).

Stairway to Heaven. w. Howard Greenfield, m. Neil Sedaka, 1960. Top 10 record by Neil Sedaka (RCA).

Stairway to the Stars. w. Mitchell Parish, m. Matty Malneck and Frank Signorelli, 1939.

The melody was a theme from the composers' 1935 instrumental suite, "Park Avenue Fantasy." As a song with Parish's lyrics, it became one of the top hits of the year, spending twelve weeks on "Your Hit Parade," four as #1. Malneck and his Orchestra recorded it with its original title (Columbia). Top records by the bands of Glenn Miller, vocal by Ray Eberle (Bluebird); Sammy Kaye (Victor); Kay Kyser (Brunswick); Al Donahue (Vocalion); singers Martha Raye (Brunswick) and Kenny Baker (Victor).

Stamp Out Loneliness. w/m Carl Belew and Van Givens, 1967. Country chart record by Stonewall Jackson (Columbia).

Stand! w/m Sylvester Stewart, 1969. Top 40 record by Sly and The Family Stone (Epic).

Stand Back. w/m Stevie Nicks and Prince Rodgers Nelson, 1983. Top 10 record by Stevie Nicks (Modern).

Stand Beside Me. w/m Tompall Glaser, 1966. Hit country record by Jimmy Dean (RCA).

Stand by Me. w/m Ben E. King, Jerry Leiber, and Mike Stoller, 1961. Introduced and first hit record by Ben E. King (Atco) [See answer song, "I'll Be There."] Among many recordings: novelty, by Spyder Turner giving impressions of five record stars (MGM), 1967; John Lennon (Apple), 1975; Mickey Gilley (Full Moon), 1980. Song heard in (MP) *Urban Cowboy*, 1980. King's original recording was featured in (MP) *Stand by Me*, 1986, and was then re-released and became a Top 10 hit for the second time (Atlantic).

Stand by Your Man. w/m Tammy Wynette and Billy Sherrill, 1968. #1 Country and Top 20 Pop chart hit by Tammy Wynette, produced by Billy Sherrill (Epic). Candi Staton had a Top 40 record (Fame), 1970.

Standing in the Shadows. w/m Hank Williams, Jr., 1966. Hit Country record by Hank Williams, Jr. (MGM).

Standing in the Shadows of Love. w/m Brian Holland, Lamont Dozier, and Eddie Holland, 1967. Top 10 record by The Four Tops (Motown).

Standing on the Corner. w/m Frank Loesser, 1956. Introduced by Shorty Long, John Henson, Alan Gilbert, and Roy Lazarus in (TM) *The Most Happy Fella*.

Standing on the Top. w/m Rick James, 1982. R&B Top 10 and Pop chart crossover record by The Temptations featuring Rick James (Gordy).

Stand or Fall. w/m Charles Barrett, Cy Curnin, Peter Greenall, Jamie West-Oram, and Adam Woods. Recorded by the London group The Fixx (MCA).

Stand Tall. w/m Burton Cummings, 1976. Top 10 gold record by Canadian singer/writer Burton Cummings (Portrait).

Stand Up and Cheer. w. Lew Brown, m. Harry Akst, 1934. Title song of (MM) *Stand Up and Cheer*.

Stanley Steamer, The. w. Ralph Blane, m. Harry Warren, 1947. Introduced by Gloria De Haven, Mickey Rooney, Agnes Moorhead, Selena Royle, Walter Huston, and Jackie "Butch" Jenkins in (MM) *Summer Holiday*. Leading record by Jo Stafford (Capitol).

Star! w. Sammy Cahn, m. James Van Heusen, 1968. Introduced by Julie Andrews in the Gertrude Lawrence story (MM) *Star!* Song nominated for Academy Award. Recorded by Frank Sinatra, arranged by Nelson Riddle (Reprise).

Starbright. w/m Lee Pockriss and Paul Vance, 1960. Featured and recorded by Johnny Mathis (Columbia).

Star Dust. w. Mitchell Parish, m. Hoagy Carmichael, 1927. At a class reunion at the University of Indiana, Carmichael originally composed it as a fast-tempo piano instrumental, which a fellow alumnus titled for him. It didn't catch on with the public until Isham Jones and his Orchestra recorded Victor Young's slower-tempo arrangement (Brunswick). Parish then wrote a lyric for it, which version was recorded by Bing Crosby (Brunswick) and Louis Armstrong (Columbia, Okeh). Artie Shaw's recording (Victor), 1941, sold more than two million copies. It has since become one of the all-time most recorded and performed American songs.

Stardust on the Moon. w/m Emery Deutsch and Jimmy Rogan, 1937. Popularized and recorded by Emery Deutsch and his Orchestra (Brunswick).

Star Eyes. w/m Don Raye and Gene De Paul, 1943. Introduced by Jimmy Dorsey and his Orchestra, vocal by Helen O'Connell and Bob Eberly, in (MM) *I Dood It*, starring Red Skelton. The top recording was by Dorsey, vocal by Kitty Kallen [O'Connell left the band after the completion of the film] and Bob Eberly (Decca).

Star Fell Out of Heaven, A. w. Mack Gordon, m. Harry Revel, 1936. One of the few songs by these writers, together or with other collaborators, not from a production. Popular recordings by Tony Martin (Decca), and the bands of Charlie Barnet (Bluebird) and Ben Bernie (Decca).

Star Gazing. w. Marty Symes and Al J. Neiburg, m. Jerry Livingston, 1935. Featured and recorded by Kay Kyser and his Orchestra (Brunswick).

Starlight. w. Joe Young, m. Bernice Petkere, 1932. Featured and recorded by Bing Crosby (Brunswick); Singin' Sam, the Barbasol Man (Oriole); Jack Denny's Orchestra (Victor); and Glen Gray and the Casa Loma Orchestra (Brunswick).

Starlight. w. Edward Madden, m. Theodore F. Morse, 1905.

Starlight Express. w. Richard Stilgoe, m. Andrew Lloyd Webber, 1987. Introduced in the U.S. by Greg Mowry in the Broadway production of the London musical (TM) *Starlight Express*.

Starlit Hour, The. w. Mitchell Parish, m. Peter DeRose, 1940. Introduced in (TM) *Earl Carroll Vanities*. Popular recordings by Glenn

Miller, vocal by Ray Eberle (Bluebird); Tommy Dorsey, vocal by Jack Leonard (Victor); Ella Fitzgerald (Decca); Kenny Baker (Victor).

Starman. w/m David Bowie, 1972. Recorded in England by David Bowie (RCA)

Starry Eyed. w. Earl Shuman, m. Mort Garson, 1959. Recorded by Gary Stites (Carlton).

Stars and Stripes Forever. m. John Philip Sousa, 1897. The most famous of Sousa's marches, and possibly of all American marches. Sousa's Band had three successful recordings, with three different companies: (Columbia), 1897; (Gram-o-Phone), 1901; (Victor), 1917. It was featured in the Sousa biographical film (MM) *Stars and Stripes Forever*, with Clifton Webb portraying the noted bandleader/composer, 1952.

Stars and Stripes on Iwo Jima. w/m Bob Wills and Cliff Johnsen, 1945. #1 C&W hit by Bob Wills and His Texas Playboys (Okeh). Also recorded by The Sons of the Pioneers (Victor).

Stars Fell on Alabama. w. Mitchell Parish, m. Frank Perkins, 1934. Associated with Jack Teagarden, whose two recordings with his band featured his vocal and trombone solos (Brunswick) (Capitol). Among the many other recordings are: Guy Lombardo, vocal by Carmen Lombardo (Decca); Freddy Martin, vocal by Buddy Clark (Brunswick); Richard Himber (Victor); the Vincent Rose studio band, led by Benny Goodman (Melotone); Woody Herman (Columbia); Montovani (London); Eddie Condon (Decca); Stan Getz (Mercury); Toots Thielemans (Columbia); Johnny Guarnieri (Majestic); Al Haig (New Jazz). Jim Walton and Maureen Brennan sang it in the Mitchell Parish musical (TM) *Stardust*, 1987.

Stars in My Eyes. w. Dorothy Fields, m. Fritz Kreisler, 1936. A new lyric to the melody of "Who Can Tell," (q.v.) from Kreisler's (TM) *Apple Blossoms*, 1919. This version was introduced by Grace Moore in (MM) *The King Steps Out*.

Stars in Your Eyes (a.k.a. **Mars**). w. Mort Greene (Engl.), R. Lopez Mendez (Sp.), m. Gabriel Ruiz, 1945. Sometimes performed under its original Mexican title, "Mars." The English version was introduced by Chuy Castillon in (MM) *Pan-Americana.*

Starting All Over Again. w/m Phillip Mitchell, 1972. Top 20 record by Mel and Tim (Stax).

Starting Over (Just Like). See **(Just Like) Starting Over.**

Starting Over Again. w/m Donna Summer and Bruce Sudano, 1980. Recorded by Dolly Parton (RCA).

Start Me Up. w/m Mick Jagger and Keith Richards, 1981. Top 10 record by The Rolling Stones (Rolling Stones).

Start Movin' (in My Direction). w/m David Hill and Bobby Stevenson, 1957. Popular record by Sal Mineo (Epic).

Start of a Romance. w/m Joseph F. Williams and Thomas G. McConnell, 1989. Hit R&B chart single by Skyy (Atlantic).

Start the Day Right. w/m Al Lewis, Maurice Spitalny, and Charles Tobias, 1939.

"Star Wars" Title Theme. m. John Williams, 1977. Introduced on the soundtrack of (MP) *Star Wars* by the London Symphony Orchestra conducted by the composer, John Williams. Their recording became a Top 10 single (20th Century). For another version, Meco [Monardo] recorded themes from the film and those played by a bar band. The instrumental was called " 'Star Wars' Theme/ Cantina Band." It became a #1 platinum record (Millennium).

State of Shock. w/m Michael Jackson and Randy Hansen, 1984. Gold record by The Jacksons, lead vocals by Michael Jackson and Mick Jagger (Epic).

Statue of a Fool. w/m Jan Crutchfield, 1969. #1 Country chart record by Jack Greene (Decca). Revived by Brian Collins (Dot), 1974, and by Bill Medley (United Artists), 1979.

Stay. w/m Maurice Williams, 1960. Introduced and #1 hit record by Maurice Williams and The Zodiacs (Herald). Revived with high chart records by The Four Seasons (Vee-Jay), 1964, and Jackson Browne (Asylum), 1978.

Stay. w/m Sid Tepper and Roy C. Bennett, 1958. Recorded by The Ames Brothers (RCA).

Stay a Little Longer. w/m Bob Wills and Tommy Duncan, 1947. Featured and recorded by Bob Wills and his Texas Playboys (Columbia).

Stay As Sweet As You Are. w. Mack Gordon, m. Harry Revel, 1934. Introduced by Lanny Ross in (MM) *College Rhythm* and on records (Brunswick). Also recorded by the bands of Guy Lombardo (Decca), Little Jack Little (Columbia), Art Kassel (Bluebird), Jimmie Grier (Brunswick), Jolly Coburn (Victor), Archie Bleyer (Vocalion). Frankie Laine revived it in 1947 (Mercury). Nat Cole had a popular version later (Capitol).

Stay Away from My Baby. w/m Ray Pennington, 1965. R&B song, recorded by Ted Taylor (Okeh).

Stay Awhile. w/m Ken Tobias, 1971. Gold record by the Canadian quintet The Bells (Polydor).

Stay Awhile. w. Mike Hawker, m. Ivor Raymonde, 1964. Recorded in England by Dusty Springfield (Philips). Later version by The Continental Miniatures (London), 1978.

Stay Here with Me. w. Milt Gabler, m. Domenico Modugno, 1957. Original Italian title, "Resta Cu'mme," words by Verde and Modugno. Sung in (MP) *Bay of Naples.* Recorded in English and Italian by Modugno (Decca).

Stayin' Alive. w/m Barry Gibb, Maurice Gibb, and Robin Gibb, 1977. Sung on the soundtrack of (MM) *Saturday Night Fever* by The Bee Gees. Their single earned a platinum record and was one of three #1 chart hits by them from the same film (RSO).

Staying Young. w/m Bob Merrill, 1959. Introduced by Jackie Gleason and Walter Pidgeon in (TM) *Take Me Along.*

Stay in My Corner. w/m Wade Flemmons, Bobby Miller, and Barrett Strong, 1965. Hit record on the R&B charts by The Dells (Vee Jay). Re-released in 1968 on different label (Cadet), and became #1 R&B and Top 10 Pop record.

Stay in Your Own Back Yard. w. Karl Kennett, m. Lyn Udall, 1899.

Stay on the Right Side, Sister. w. Ted Koehler, m. Rube Bloom, 1933. Introduced by Ruth Etting. Recorded by Bing Crosby (Brunswick). Sung by Doris Day, as Etting, in her biography (MM) *Love Me or Leave Me* in 1955.

Stay the Night. w/m Peter Cetera and David Foster, 1984. Recorded by the group Chicago (Full Moon).

Stay Well. w. Maxwell Anderson, m. Kurt Weill, 1949. Introduced by Inez Matthews in (TM) *Lost in the Stars.* Leading recording by Vera Lynn (London). Song not used in film version.

Stay with Me. w/m Rod Stewart and Ron Wood, 1972. Recorded in England by the writers with the group Faces (Warner Bros.).

Stay with Me. w. Carolyn Leigh, m. Jerome Moross, 1963. Based on a theme from (MP) *The Cardinal.* Song introduced and recorded by Frank Sinatra (Reprise).

Stay with Me Tonight. w/m Raymond Jones, 1983. Top 10 R&B crossover (Pop chart) record by Jeffrey Osborne (A&M).

Stay with the Happy People. w. Bob Hilliard, m. Jule Styne, 1950. Introduced by Lina Romay in (TM) *Michael Todd's Peep Show.* Recorded by Art Mooney and his Orchestra (MGM).

Steady. w/m Jules Shear and Cyndi Lauper, 1985. Recorded by Jules Shear (EMI America).

Steal Away. w/m Robbie Dupree, m. Rick Chudacoff, 1980. Top 10 record by Robbie Dupree (Elektra).

Steal Away. w/m Jimmy Hughes, 1963. Hit crossover [Gospel/R&B/Pop] records by Jimmy Hughes (Fame) and revived by Johnny Taylor (Stax), 1970.

Stealin' Apples. w. Andy Razaf, m. Thomas "Fats" Waller, 1936. Introduced and recorded by Fletcher Henderson and his Orchestra (Vocalion). Recorded by Benny Goodman and his Orchestra (Columbia), 1940, and by his Septet in the fifties (Capitol).

Stealing in the Name of the Lord. w/m Paul Kelly, 1970. Recorded by Paul Kelly (Happy Tiger).

Steal On Home. w/m Berry Gordy and Ron Miller, 1976. Sung by Thelma Houston on the soundtrack of (MP) *The Bingo Long Traveling All-Star and Motor Kings.*

Steamboat. w/m Buddy Lucas, 1956. R&B chart record by The Drifters (Atlantic).

Steamboat Bill. w. Ren Shields, m. Bert Leighton and Frank Leighton, 1910. Introduced by the Leighton Brothers in vaudeville.

Steam Heat. w/m Richard Adler and Jerry Ross, 1954. Introduced by Carol Haney, Peter Gennaro, and Buzz Miller in (TM) *The Pajama Game.* The song had been written for the revue *John Murray's Almanac* a year earlier but was not used. In the film version (MM) *The Pajama Game,* 1957, it was performed by Carol Haney, Buzz Miller, and Kenneth Leroy.

Steamroller Blues. w/m James Taylor, 1973. Introduced by James Taylor in his album "Sweet Baby James" (Warner Bros.), 1969. Hit single, from a live concert performance in Hawaii, by Elvis Presley (RCA).

Steel Guitar Rag. w. Merle Travis and Cliffie Stone, m. Leon McAuliffe, 1941. Originally an instrumental. First record by Bob

Wills (Vocalion), an instrumental on which McAuliffe played the steel guitar. Merle Travis later recorded it (Capitol).

Steel Men. w/m David Martins, 1962. Recorded by Jimmy Dean (Columbia).

Steel Rail Blues. w/m Gordon Lightfoot, 1966. Country chart record by George Hamilton IV (RCA).

Stein Song, A (It's Always Fair Weather When Good Fellows Get Together). w. Richard Hovey, m. Frederick Field Bullard, 1898. A favorite with male quartets.

Stein Song (University of Maine). w. Lincoln Colcord, m. E. A. Fenstad (arr. by A. W. Sprague), 1910, 1930. The melody was written as a march in 1901. The lyrics and new arrangement were written in 1910 and became the official song of the University of Maine. In 1930, Rudy Vallee played it on his network radio show and at the Paramount Theatre in New York. The song became a best-seller and has remained one of the best known college songs.

Stella. w/m Al Jolson, Benny Davis, and Harry Akst, 1923. Introduced, featured, and recorded by Al Jolson (Columbia).

Stella by Starlight. w. Ned Washington, m. Victor Young, 1946. Song based on theme from (MP) *The Uninvited*, 1944. Victor Young and his Orchestra (Decca) were the first to record what was to become a standard. Popular versions by Harry James, as an instrumental (Columbia); and Frank Sinatra, as a vocal (Columbia), both in 1947. Among many others, Billy Butterfield (Capitol), Buddy Greco (London), Charlie Parker (Mercury).

Step by Step. w/m Eddie Rabbitt, Even Stevens, and David Malloy, 1981. Country/Pop Top 10 record by Eddie Rabbitt (Elektra).

Step by Step. w/m Ollie Jones and Billy Dawn Smith, 1960. Recorded by The Crests (Coed).

Step in Time. w/m Richard M. Sherman and Robert B. Sherman, 1964. Introduced by Dick Van Dyke, Julie Andrews, and the Chimney Sweeps in (MM) *Mary Poppins*.

Step out of Your Mind. w/m Al Gorgoni and Chip Taylor, 1966. Top 40 record by The American Breed (Acta).

Steppin' in a Slide Zone. w/m John Lodge, 1978. Recorded by the English group The Moody Blues (London).

Steppin' Into Swing Society. w. Henry Nemo and Irving Mills, m. Edward Kennedy "Duke" Ellington, 1938. Introduced and recorded by Duke Ellington and his Orchestra (Brunswick).

Steppin' Out. w/m Joe Jackson, 1982. Top 10 record by the English-born singer/pianist Joe Jackson (A&M).

Steppin' Out. w/m Paul Revere and Mark Lindsay, 1965. Recorded by Paul Revere and The Raiders (Columbia).

Steppin' Out. w. John S. Howard, m. Con Conrad, 1923. Recorded by Vincent Lopez (Okeh) and Al Jolson (Brunswick).

Steppin' Out (Gonna Boogie Tonight). w/m Irwin Levine and L. Russell Brown, 1974. Top 10 record by Tony Orlando and Dawn (Bell).

Steppin' Out with My Baby. w/m Irving Berlin, 1948. Introduced by Fred Astaire in (MM) *Easter Parade*.

Step That Step. w/m Mark Miller, 1985. #1 Country chart record by the group named after two streets in Nashville, Sawyer Brown (Capitol).

Step to the Rear. w. Carolyn Leigh, m. Elmer Bernstein, 1967. Introduced by Tony Roberts, Charlotte Jones, and company in (TM) *How Now, Dow Jones*.

Stereophonic Sound. w/m Cole Porter, 1955. Introduced by Gretchen Wyler in (TM) *Silk Stockings*. Fred Astaire and Janis Paige performed it in (MM) *Silk Stockings*, 1957.

785

Sticks and Stones. w/m Titus Turner, 1960. Recorded by Ray Charles (ABC-Paramount).

Stick Shift. m. Henry Bellinger, 1961. Instrumental by The Duals (Sue).

Stick-Up. w/m Angelo Bond, General Johnson, and Greg S. Perry, 1971. Hit record by the female trio The Honey Cone (Hot Wax).

Still. w/m Lionel Richie, 1979. #1 R&B and Pop chart record by The Commodores (Motown). John Schneider had a chart version (Scotti Brothers), 1982.

Still. w/m Dorian Burton and Howard Plummer, Jr., 1956. Introduced and recorded by LaVern Baker (Atlantic), and covered by The Fontane Sisters (Dot).

Still (I Love You). w/m Bill Anderson, 1963. Bill Anderson's crossover record was #1 on the Country charts, and Top 10 on the Pop charts (Decca).

Still a Thrill. w/m André Cymone and Jody Watley, 1987. Top 10 R&B chart record by Jody Watley (MCA).

Still Crazy After All These Years. w/m Paul Simon. 1976. Single taken from the album of the same name by Paul Simon (Columbia), 1975.

Still in Saigon. w/m Dan Daley, 1982. Recorded by The Charlie Daniels Band (Epic).

Still Losing You. w/m Mike Reid, 1984. #1 Country chart song by Ronnie Milsap (RCA).

Still of the Night. w/m David Coverdale and John Sykes, 1987. Chart record by the British quintet Whitesnake (Geffen).

Stillsane. w/m Carolyne Mas, 1979. Written and recorded by singer/guitarist Carolyne Mas (Mercury).

Still Taking Chances. w/m Michael Murphey, 1983. Top 10 Country crossover record by Michael Murphey (Liberty).

Still the Bluebird Sings. w. Johnny Burke, m. James V. Monaco, 1939. Introduced in (MM) *The Star Maker* and on records by Bing Crosby (Decca).

Still the One. w/m John Hall and Johanna Hall, 1976. Top 10 record by the group Orleans (Asylum).

Still the Same. w/m Bob Seger, 1978. Top 10 record by Bob Seger and The Silver Bullet Band (Capitol).

Still They Ride. w/m Steve Perry, Neal Schon, and Jonathan Cain, 1982. Recorded by the group Journey (Columbia).

Still Waiting. w/m Prince Rogers Nelson, 1987. R&B chart record from the album "Sweetheart" by Rainy Davis (Columbia).

Still Water (Love). w/m William "Smokey" Robinson and Frank Wilson, 1970. Top 20 record by The Four Tops (Motown).

Stir It Up. w/m Allee Willis and Michael Sembello, 1985. Introduced by Patti LaBelle in (MP) *Beverly Hills Cop* and recorded by her (MCA).

Stir It Up. w/m Bob Marley, 1973. Top 20 version of the Jamaican song, recorded by Johnny Nash (Epic).

Stockholm. m. George Cates, 1964. Instrumental recorded by Lawrence Welk and his Orchestra (Dot).

Stolen Moments. w. Sid Wayne, m. Joe Sherman, 1957. Featured and recorded by Hank Snow (RCA Victor).

Stomp! w/m George Johnson, Louis Johnson, Valerie Johnson, and Rod Temperton, 1980. Top 10 record by the duo The Brothers Johnson (A&M).

Stompin' at the Savoy. w. Andy Razaf, m. Benny Goodman, Chick Webb, and Edgar Sampson, 1936. One of the top numbers to come out of the Swing Era, usually done as an instrumental. It was introduced by Chick Webb and his Orchestra (Columbia), 1934, with an arrangement by Edgar Sampson who then did the same for Benny Goodman's Band two years later, which turned out to be the hit record (Victor). The Goodman Quartet recorded it in 1937 (Victor). Among many other recordings: Jimmy Dorsey (Decca), Ben Pollack (Savoy), Jonah Jones (Commodore), Art Tatum (Decca), Teddy Wilson (Musicraft), Woody Herman (Mars), Charlie Ventura (Lamplighter, 1 & 2), Babs' 3 Bips and a Bop (Blue Note), Charlie Christian (Vox Album, 1, 2 & 3), Eddie South (Columbia), Chicago Rhythm Kings (Bluebird).

Stompy Jones. m. Edward Kennedy "Duke" Ellington, 1934. Recorded by Duke Ellington (Victor), Sidney Bechet (Victor), Barney Bigard (Variety).

Stone Cold. w/m Ritchie Blackmore, Roger Glover, and Joe Lynn Turner, 1982. Recorded by the British band Rainbow (Mercury).

Stone Cold Dead in de Market. w/m Wilmoth Houdini, 1946. Calypso song introduced by Houdini. Popular recording by Ella Fitzgerald and Louis Jordan (Decca).

Stoned Love. w/m Yennik Samoht and Frank Wilson, 1970. Top 10 record by The Supremes (Motown).

Stoned Soul Picnic. w/m Laura Nyro, 1968. Introduced by Laura Nyro in her album "Eli and the Thirteenth Confession" (Columbia). The 5th Dimension's single version became their first gold record (Soul City).

Stone Love. w/m Charles Smith, James Taylor, and Kool & The Gang, 1987. Top 10 R&B and Pop chart record by Kool & The Gang (Mercury).

Stones. w/m Neil Diamond, 1971. Top 20 record by Neil Diamond (Uni).

Stoney End. w/m Laura Nyro, 1970. Introduced by Laura Nyro in her first album "More Than a New Discovery" (Verve), 1966. Top 10 single by Barbra Streisand (Columbia), 1970.

Stood Up. w/m Willis Dickerson and Erma Herrold, 1958. Hit record by Ricky Nelson (Imperial).

Stop! and Think It Over. w/m Sid Tepper and Roy C. Bennett, 1967. Featured and recorded by Perry Como (RCA).

Stop! in the Name of Love. w/m Brian Holland, Eddie Holland, and Lamont Dozier, 1965. The fourth in the string of five consecutive #1 hits by The Supremes (Motown). Revived by Margie Joseph (Volt), 1971, and The Hollies (Atlantic), 1983.

Stop! It's Wonderful. w. Bickley Reichner, m. Clay Boland, 1939. Recorded and popularized by Orrin Tucker's band, vocal by Wee Bonnie Baker (Columbia) as a follow-up to their hit record of "Oh Johnny, Oh Johnny, Oh!" (q.v.).

Stop, Stop, Stop. w/m Allan Clarke, Tony Hicks, and Graham Nash, 1966. Top 10 record in the U.S. by the British group The Hollies (Imperial).

Stop! You're Breakin' My Heart. w. Ted Koehler, m. Burton Lane, 1936. Introduced by Judy Canova and Ben Blue in (MM) *Artists and Models*. Popular recordings by Hal Kemp, vocal by Skinnay Ennis (Victor); and Claude Thornhill's combo, vocal by Maxine Sullivan (Vocalion).

Stop and Smell the Roses. w/m Mac Davis and Doc Severinsen, 1974. Top 10 record by Mac Davis (Columbia).

Stop and Think It Over. w/m Jake Graffagnino, 1964. Top 10 record by Dale and Grace (Montel).

Stop Beatin' round the Mulberry Bush. w. Bickley Reichner, m. Clay Boland, 1938. Written for the Mask and Wig Club show at the University of Pennsylvania. Recorded and popularized by Tommy Dorsey and his Orchestra (Victor) and The Merry Macs (Decca).

Stop Doggin' Me Around. See **Doggin' Around.**

Stop Draggin' My Heart Around. w/m Tom Petty and Mike Campbell, 1981. Top 10 record by Stevie Nicks with Tom Petty and The Heartbreakers (Modern).

Stop Her on Sight (S.O.S.). w/m Al Hamilton, Charles Hatcher, and Richard Morris, 1966. Recorded by Edwin Starr (Ric-Tic).

Stop Kicking My Heart Around. w. George Jessel, m. Paul Fredericks, 1939. Featured and recorded by Kenny Baker (Victor) and Jack Teagarden, vocal by Kitty Kallen (Columbia).

Stop the Start (of Tears in My Heart). w/m Fred Carr, Ken Milburn, Dan Rose, and Johnny Dollar, 1966. Country chart record by Johnny Dollar (Columbia).

Stop the World (and Let Me Off). w. W. S. Stevenson, m. Carl Belew, 1958. Hit C&W single by Johnnie and Jack (RCA). Revived with chart records by Waylon Jennings (RCA), 1965; Susan Raye (Capitol), 1974; Donny King (Warner Bros.), 1976.

Stop to Love. w/m Luther Vandross and Nat Adderly, Jr., 1987. Chart record by Luther Vandross (Epic).

Stop Yer Tickling, Jock! w. Harry Lauder and Frank Folley, m. Harry Lauder, 1910. An import from Great Britain and featured by the Scottish performer, Harry Lauder, in vaudeville.

Stop Your Sobbing. w/m Ray Davies, 1980. Recorded by the Anglo-American quartet The Pretenders (Sire).

Stormy. w/m Buddy Buie and James B. Cobb, 1968. Gold record hit by The Classics IV, featuring Dennis Yost (Imperial). Revived with a Top 40 record by the group, Santana (Columbia), 1979.

Stormy Monday Blues. w/m Earl Hines, Billy Eckstine, and Bob Crowder, 1942. Chart record by Earl Hines, vocal by Billy Eckstine (Bluebird).

Stormy Weather. w. Ted Koehler, m. Harold Arlen, 1933. Written for Cab Calloway, while the writers were creating material for the Cotton Club revues in Harlem, New York City. As Calloway was not appearing in the 1933 edition, the song was given to Ethel Waters. Before the new revue opened, Arlen recorded it vocally with Leo Reisman's Orchestra (Victor). It became an immediate best-seller. By the time Waters sang it in the revue, the song was already a hit, but became identified with her. Lena Horne recorded it later (Victor) and then, in 1943, sang it in (MM) *Stormy Weather*, while Katherine Dunham and her troupe danced. Connee Boswell sang it in (MM) *Swing Parade* in 1946. Lena Horne featured it in her Broadway theatrical revue (TM) *Lena Horne: A Lady and Her Music* in 1981, and in the album of the show. Larry Kert sang it in (TM) *A Musical Jubilee*, 1975.

Storybook Children (Daybreak). w/m Spencer Proffer and David Pomerantz, 1977. Recorded by Bette Midler (Atlantic).

Storybook Love. w/m Willy DeVille, 1987. Introduced by Willy DeVille on the soundtrack of (MP) *The Princess Bride*. Nominated for an Academy Award.

Story Goes On, The. w. Richard Maltby, Jr., m. David Shire, 1983. Introduced by Liz Callaway in (TM) *Baby*.

Story in Your Eyes. w/m Justin Hayward, 1971. Written by the lead vocalist/guitarist of the English group, The Moody Blues, which had a popular U.S. release (Threshold).

Story of a Starry Night, The. w/m Jerry Livingston, Al Hoffman, and Mann Curtis, 1942. Adapted from the second phrase of the second theme of the 1st movement of *Symphony No. 6, in B Minor*, the *Pathétique*, by Tchaikowsky. Best-seller by Glenn Miller, vocal by Ray Eberle (Bluebird).

Story of Isaac. w/m Leonard Cohen, 1968. First recorded by Judy Collins in her album "Who Knows Where the Time Goes" (Elektra). Leonard Cohen recorded it in his "Songs from a Room" LP (Columbia).

Story of Love, The. w. George Thorn (Engl.), Carlos Almaran, (Sp.), m. Carlos Almaran, 1956. Original Spanish title: "Historia de un Amor." Popular Bolero from Mexico.

Story of My Life, The. w. Hal David, m. Burt Bacharach, 1957. C&W and Pop hit recording by Marty Robbins (Columbia).

Story of My Love, The. w/m Jack Nance and Conway Twitty, 1959. Introduced and recorded by Conway Twitty (MGM).

Story of Our Love, The. w. Tony Piano, m. Michael Colicchio, 1959. Recorded by Johnny Mathis (Columbia).

Story of Rock and Roll, The. w/m Harry Nilsson, 1968. Recorded by The Turtles (White Whale).

Story Untold, A. w/m LeRoy Griffin and Marty Wilson, 1955. Introduced by R&B group The Nutmegs (Herald). Covered by Pop group The Crew Cuts (Mercury).

Stouthearted Men. w. Oscar Hammerstein II, m. Sigmund Romberg, 1928. Introduced by Robert Halliday and a male chorus in (TM) *The New Moon*. In the 1930 film (MM) *New Moon*, it was sung by Lawrence Tibbett and, in the 1940 remake, by Nelson Eddy, both with male choruses. In the Romberg biography (MM) *Deep in My Heart*, 1954, it was sung, not by a baritone, but by operatic soprano Helen Traubel. The number, normally a rouser, was recorded effectively as a ballad by Barbra Streisand (Columbia), 1967.

Straight, No Chaser. m. Thelonious Monk, 1951. Instrumental, introduced and recorded by Thelonious Monk (Blue Note).

Straighten Up and Fly Right. w/m Nat "King" Cole and Irving Mills, 1944. The first big hit for The King Cole Trio (Capitol), following their introducing it in (MM) *Here Comes Elmer*, 1943. The Andrews Sisters had a popular record (Decca) and then performed it in (MM) *Her Lucky Night*, 1945.

Straight from the Heart. w/m Bryan Adams and Eric Kagna, 1989. Recorded by the Canadian singer Bryan Adams (A&M).

Straight from the Shoulder (Right from the Heart). w. Mack Gordon, m. Harry Revel, 1934. Introduced by Bing Crosby and

Kitty Carlisle in (MM) *She Loves Me Not*. Crosby's record was coupled with the hit "Love in Bloom" (q.v.) (Brunswick). Hal Kemp and his Orchestra recorded the same coupling for the same label (Brunswick).

Straight Life, The. w/m Sonny Curtis, 1968. Hit Country and Pop record by Bobby Goldsboro (United Artists).

Straight On. w/m Ann Wilson and Nancy Wilson, 1978. Recorded by the group Heart (Portrait).

Straight Up. w/m Elliott Wolff, 1989. Top Pop chart record by Paula Abdul (Virgin).

Stranded in the Jungle. w/m Ernestine Smith and James Johnson, 1956. Novelty introduced and recorded by The Jayhawks, of which Johnson was a member (Flash). Covered and best-selling record by The Cadets (Modern). Chart record also by The Gadabouts (Mercury).

Strange. w. John La Touche, m. Marvin Fisher, 1953. Recorded by Nat "King" Cole, with Nelson Riddle's Orchestra (Capitol).

Strange and Sweet. w/m Gene Bone and Howard Fenton, 1948. Recorded by Tex Beneke, vocal by Gary Stevens (RCA Victor).

Strange Are the Ways of Love. w. Paul Francis Webster, m. Sammy Fain, 1972. From (MP) *The Stepmother*. Nominated for an Academy Award.

Strange Are the Ways of Love. w. Ned Washington, m. Dimitri Tiomkin, 1959. Introduced by Randy Sparks in (MP) *The Young Land*. Nominated for Academy Award. Recorded by Gogi Grant (Era).

Strange As It Seems. w. Andy Razaf, m. Thomas "Fats" Waller, 1932. Recorded by Adelaide Hall (Brunswick) and Harlan Lattimore (Columbia).

Strange Enchantment. w. Frank Loesser, m. Frederick Hollander, 1939. Introduced by Dorothy Lamour in (MM) *Man About Town*. Records: Lamour (Bluebird); Skinnay Ennis

(Victor); Bob Crosby, vocal by Marion Mann (Decca).

Strange Fruit. w/m Lewis Allan, 1939. Title taken from the book by Lillian Smith that tells the story of the lynching of a black man in the southern U.S. Introduced and recorded by Billie Holiday (Commodore Music Shop). Diana Ross sang it as Billie Holiday in her story (MM) *Lady Sings the Blues* in 1972.

Strange I Know. w/m Brian Holland, Freddy Gorman, and Lamont Dozier, 1962. Crossover (R&B/Pop) hit by The Marvelettes (Tamla).

Strange Interlude. w. Ben Bernie and Walter Hirsch, m. Phil Baker, 1932. Introduced by Ben Bernie and his Band. Morton Downey, accompanied by the composer, comedian Phil Baker on accordian, recorded it (Perfect) as did the orchestras of Ruby Newman (Victor) and Anson Weeks (Brunswick). Title from the play by Eugene O'Neill. Theme song of Bill McCune and his Orchestra.

Strange Lady in Town. w. Ned Washington, m. Dimitri Tiomkin, 1955. From the film (MP) *Strange Lady in Town*, starring Greer Garson and Dana Andrews. Recorded by Frankie Laine (Columbia).

Strange Little Girl. w/m Jerry Ross and Richard Adler, 1951. First song success for the writers. Featured and recorded by Eddy Howard with his Orchestra (Mercury), and Tennessee Ernie Ford (Capitol).

Strange Loneliness, A. w/m Sammy Mysels and Bob Burke, 1937. Introduced and recorded by Artie Shaw, vocal by Dolores O'Neill (Brunswick).

Strange Love. w. Edward Heyman, m. Miklos Rozsa, 1946. Based on the theme from (MP) *The Strange Love of Martha Ivers*. Recorded by the orchestras of Randy Brooks (Decca) and Elliot Lawrence (Columbia).

Strange Magic. w/m Jeff Lynne, 1976. Recorded by the English group Electric Light Orchestra (United Artists).

Strange Music. w/m Robert Wright and George Forrest, 1944. Based on a nocturne and the piano piece, "Wedding Day at Troldhaugen" by Edvard Grieg, this was introduced in (TM) *Song of Norway* by Lawrence Brooks [as Grieg] and Helena Bliss. Most popular recordings by Bing Crosby (Decca), James Melton (Victor 12″), Lanny Ross (Silvertone 12″).

Stranger in My House. w/m Mike Reid, 1983. Crossover (C&W/Pop) hit by Ronnie Milsap. Winner Grammy Award (NARAS), Country Song of the Year.

Stranger in Paradise. w/m Robert Wright and George Forrest, 1953. Based on the 1st theme from the Polovetsian Dances from the opera *Prince Igor*, by Alexander Borodin, this was introduced by Richard Kiley and Doretta Morrow in (TM) *Kismet*. Hit recordings by Tony Bennett, with Percy Faith's Orchestra (Columbia), and The Four Aces, with Jack Pleis's Orchestra (Decca).

Stranger in Town. w/m Del Shannon, 1965. Introduced and recorded by Del Shannon (Amy).

Stranger in Town, A. w/m Mel Tormé, 1945. Introduced and recorded by Mel Tormé (Decca), who recorded it again as a single for another label (Capitol). Martha Tilton, accompanied by Eddie Miller's Orchestra, had a popular early version (Capitol).

Stranger on the Shore. w. Robert Mellin, m. Acker Bilk, 1962. English instrumental originally titled "Jenny." Retitled for use as theme for British series (TVP) "Stranger on the Shore." U.S. release by Mr. Acker Bilk became million-seller in the U.S. (Atco). Lyric version recorded by Andy Williams (Columbia).

Strangers. w. Charles O'Flynn, m. J. Fred Coots, 1932. Popular records by Sleepy Hall (Melotone), Art Kassel's Orchestra (Columbia), Mildred Bailey (Victor), and Phil Spitalny (Hit of the Week). Later versions by Tommy Dorsey with vocal by Don Cherry (Decca), and Buddy Morrow with vocal by Tommy Mercer (Victor).

Strangers in the Night. w. Charles Singleton and Eddie Snyder, m. Bert Kaempfert, 1966. Adapted from a theme from (MP) *A Man Could Get Killed*, starring James Garner. #1 record by Frank Sinatra, and voted Grammy Award Winner (NARAS) Record of the Year (Reprise). Bert Kaempfert and his Orchestra had a popular instrumental version (Decca).

Stranger Song, The. w/m Leonard Cohen, 1968. Introduced by poet/folksinger Leonard Cohen in his album "Songs of Leonard Cohen" (Columbia). He sang it on the soundtrack of (MP) *McCabe and Mrs. Miller*, 1971.

Strange Sensation. w/m Kay Twomey, Fred Wise, and Ben Weisman, 1952. Based on the tango "La Cumparsita." Recorded by June Valli (RCA Victor).

Strange Things Are Happening (Ho Ho, Hee Hee, Ha Ha). w/m Red Buttons, Elliot Lawrence, and Allan Walker, 1953. Featured on Red Buttons' TV show and recorded by him with Elliot Lawrence's Orchestra, and coupled with "The Ho Ho Song" (q.v.) (Columbia).

Strange Way. w/m Rick Roberts, 1978. Recorded by the group Firefall (Atlantic).

Strawberry Fields Forever. w/m John Lennon and Paul McCartney, 1967. Top 10 hit, coupled with the gold record recording of "Penny Lane" (q.v.) by The Beatles. An area, "Strawberry Fields," is dedicated to the memory of John Lennon in Central Park, New York City.

Strawberry Letter 23. w/m Shuggie Otis, 1977. Gold record by the duo The Brothers Johnson (A&M).

Strawberry Shortcake. w/m Maurice Irby, Jr., 1968. Recorded by Jay and The Techniques (Smash).

Stray Cat Strut. w/m Brian Setzer, 1983. Top 10 record by the trio The Stray Cats (EMI America).

Streak, The. w/m Ray Stevens, 1974. "Inspired" by the interloper who streaked nude across the stage while actor David Niven was presenting an Oscar during the internationally televised Academy Awards show, this hastily written and released novelty performed by Stevens became a #1 Country and Pop chart gold record (Barnaby).

Street Corner. w/m Nick Ashford and Valerie Simpson, 1982. Top 10 R&B chart record by Ashford and Simpson (Capitol).

Street Fighting Man. w/m Mick Jagger and Keith Richards, 1968. Recorded by the British group The Rolling Stones (London).

Street of Dreams. w. Sam M. Lewis, m. Victor Young, 1933. Ballad standard, popularized on radio and records by Bing Crosby (Brunswick), Morton Downey (Perfect), and Russ Columbo (Victor). Among later recordings: Tommy Dorsey and his Orchestra, vocal by Frank Sinatra (Victor); the Ink Spots (Decca); Stan Kenton and his Orchestra (Capitol).

Street Scene. m. Alfred Newman, 1931. The theme from (MP) *Street Scene* that has been heard in numerous films as background music in big city sequences. In 1942, Harold Adamson wrote a lyric to the melody and the new song was titled "Sentimental Rhapsody."

Streets of Bakersfield. w/m Homer Joy, 1988. #1 Country chart single by Dwight Yoakam and Buck Owens (Warner Bros.).

Streets of Baltimore. w/m Tompall Glaser and Harlan Howard, 1966. Hit Country record by Bobby Bare (RCA).

Streets of Cairo (She Never Saw the). w/m James Thornton, 1893. The song, which opens with a direct musical quote from the "Hootchy-Kootchy," was written as a spoof of Little Egypt who was appearing at the Chicago World's Fair.

Streets of Laredo, The. w. Ray Evans, m. Jay Livingston, 1948. Featured and recorded by Dennis Day (RCA Victor) and Ray Noble and his Orchestra (Columbia).

Streets of New York, The (or, **In Old New York**). w. Henry Blossom, m. Victor Herbert, 1906. Sung by Fred Stone, David Montgomery, and chorus in (TM) *The Red Mill*.

Strictly Instrumental. w/m Eddie Seiler, Sol Marcus, Bennie Benjamin, and Edgar Battle, 1942. Harry James and his Orchestra's hit record (Columbia) was on the charts for three months.

Strictly U.S.A. w/m Roger Edens, Betty Comden, and Adolph Green, 1949. Sung by Frank Sinatra, Gene Kelly, Esther Williams, and Betty Garrett as the finale of (MM) *Take Me Out to the Ball Game*.

Strike Me Pink. w. Lew Brown, m. Ray Henderson, 1933. Title song of (TM) *Strike Me Pink*, sung by Johnny Downs and Dorothy Dare and danced by Hal LeRoy. Frank Luther recorded it (Victor).

Strike Up the Band. w. Ira Gershwin, m. George Gershwin, 1930. First sung by Max Hoffman, Jr., and ensemble in (TM) *Strike Up the Band*, 1927. This production never reached New York. In the revised Broadway version, 1930, it was sung by Jerry Goff and ensemble. This was the first of two Gershwin musicals this year that had Red Nichols' pit band, numbering among its musicians Benny Goodman, Glenn Miller, Gene Krupa, Jack Teagarden, and Jimmy Dorsey. The other, later in the theatrical season, was *Girl Crazy*. In 1936, Ira wrote special lyrics for U. C. L. A., and the Gershwins donated their royalties to the university. The title was used for the Mickey Rooney-Judy Garland film (MM) *Strike Up the Band*, 1939. Busby Berkely staged the number as a rousing finale. Revived by Tommy Tune in (TM) *My One and Only*, 1983.

Strike Up the Band, Here Comes a Sailor. w. Andrew B. Sterling, m. Charles B. Ward, 1900. Originally a hit in vaudeville. It was performed by Jack Oakie with a female chorus in (MM) *Hello, Frisco, Hello*, 1943, and was also interpolated in (MM) *In Old Sacramento*, 1946.

String Along. w/m Dave Coleman, 1952. Leading record by The Ames Brothers, with Ray Bloch's Orchestra (Coral).

String of Pearls, A. w. Eddie DeLange, m. Jerry Gray, 1941. A #1 instrumental hit introduced and recorded by Glenn Miller and his Orchestra (Bluebird), composed by his arranger, Jerry Gray. A year later, Benny Goodman recorded it, coupled with his #1 hit "Jersey Bounce" (q.v.) (Okeh). The number was prominently featured in (MM) *The Glenn Miller Story*, 1954.

Stripper, The. m. David Rose, 1962. Hit instrumental by David Rose and his Orchestra (MGM).

Strip Polka, The. w/m Johnny Mercer, 1942. Novelty with self-explanatory subtitle "Take It Off! Take It Off!" was introduced and recorded by Johnny Mercer (Capitol), whose record was on the charts for three months. Other hit versions by Kay Kyser, vocal by Jack Martin (Columbia); The Andrews Sisters (Decca); Alvino Rey, vocal by The Four King Sisters (Bluebird). Song was arbitrarily kept off "Your Hit Parade" because of subject matter.

Stroke, The. w/m Billy Squier, 1981. Recorded by Billy Squier (Capitol).

Stroll, The. w/m Nancy Lee and Clyde Otis, 1958. Hit record by The Diamonds (Mercury).

Strong Enough to Bend. w/m Beth Neilsen-Chapman and Don Schlitz, 1988. #1 Country record and album title song by Tanya Tucker (Capitol).

Strong Heart. w/m Tommy Rocco, Charlie Black, and Austin Roberts, 1986. #1 Country chart record by T. G. Sheppard (Columbia).

Strung Out. w/m Paul Laurence, 1986. Recorded by Paul Laurence (Capitol).

Strut. w/m Charlene Dore and J. Littman, 1984. Top 10 record by Scottish singer Sheena Easton (EMI America).

Strut Miss Lizzie. w. Henry Creamer, m. Turner Layton, 1921. The title song of the all-

Negro show (TM) *Strut Miss Lizzie*. It was performed by the writers and company. Recorded by The American Quartet (Victor).

Struttin'. m. Billy Preston, 1975. Instrumental by singer/pianist Billy Preston (A&M).

Struttin' with Some Barbecue. w/m Louis Armstrong and Lillian Hardin Armstrong, 1927. A dixieland number that the Armstrongs recorded (Okeh). Louis recorded it again in 1938 (Decca). It has also been done by Bobby Hackett (Columbia), Jimmy Dorsey (Columbia), Pete Fountain (Southland), Turk Murphy (Good Time Jazz).

Stubborn Kind of Fellow. w/m William Stevenson, Marvin Gaye, and George Gordy, 1962. Recorded by Marvin Gaye, backed by Martha and The Vandellas (Tamla).

Stuck in the Middle with You. w/m Joe Egan and Gerry Rafferty, 1973. Written by the two leaders of the British group, Stealers Wheel, who had a Top 10 U.S. release (A&M).

Stuck on You. w/m Lionel Richie, 1984. Top 10 Pop and R&B chart record by Lionel Richie (Motown).

Stuck on You. w/m Aaron Schroeder and J. Leslie McFarland, 1960. Elvis Presley's first recording after his release from the Army became a #1 record on the Pop charts (RCA).

Stuck with You. w/m Chris Hayes and Huey Lewis, 1986. #1 single by Huey Lewis and The News (Chrysalis).

Study in Brown, A. m. Larry Clinton, 1937. Theme song of Larry Clinton and his Orchestra. In addition to Clinton's recording (Victor), there were releases by the bands of Bunny Berigan (Victor), Teddy Hill (Bluebird), and Eddie Stone (Perfect), who coupled it with another Clinton instrumental "Satan Takes a Holiday" (q.v.).

Stuff Like That. w/m Nicholas Ashford, Valerie Simpson, S. Gadd, E. Gale, Quincy Jones, M. MacDonald, and R. Tee, 1978. Recorded by Quincy Jones, vocal by Ashford and Simpson and Chaka Khan (A&M).

Stuff Like That There. w. Ray Evans, m. Jay Livingston, 1945. Introduced by The King Sisters in (MM) *On Stage Everybody*. Betty Hutton had a Top 10 recording (Capitol).

Stuff That Dreams Are Made Of. w/m Carly Simon, 1987. Popular track from the album "Coming Around Again" by Carly Simon (Arista).

Stumbling. w/m Zez Confrey, 1922. A popular comment on popular dances of the twenties. Hit records by Paul Whiteman and his Orchestra (Victor), Billy Murray (Victor), Frank Crumit (Columbia). Revived in (MM) *Thoroughly Modern Millie*, 1967, by Julie Andrews and Mary Tyler Moore.

Stumblin' In. w/m Mike Chapman and Nicky Chinn, 1979. Recorded by Suzi Quatro and Chris Norman (RSO).

Stupid Cupid. w. Howard Greenfield, m. Neil Sedaka, 1958. Featured and recorded by Connie Francis (MGM).

Style. w. Sammy Cahn, m. James Van Heusen, 1964. Introduced by Frank Sinatra, Bing Crosby, and Dean Martin in (MM) *Robin and the Seven Hoods*.

Suavecito. w/m Richard Bean, Pablo Tellez, and Abel Zarate, 1972. Top 20 record by the Latin-rock band Malo (Warner Bros.).

Substitute. w/m Peter Townshend, 1978. Introduced by the British group, The Who (Decca), 1966. Best-selling records by The Clout (Epic) and Gloria Gaynor (Polydor), 1978.

Subterranean Homesick Blues. w/m Bob Dylan, 1965. First chart single by Bob Dylan (Columbia).

Success. w/m Johnny Mullins, 1962. C&W hit by Loretta Lynn (Decca).

(Such An) Easy Question. w/m Otis Blackwell and Winfield Scott, 1965. Introduced in a 1962 LP by Elvis Presley. Hit single in 1965 (RCA).

Such a Night. w/m Mac Rebennack, 1973. Recorded by Dr. John (Atco).

Such a Night. w/m Lincoln Chase, 1954. Introduced and #2 on the R&B charts by Clyde McPhatter and The Drifters (Atlantic). Top Pop record by Johnny Ray, with Joe Reisman's Orchestra (Columbia). Also recorded by Bunny Paul, with Sy Oliver's Orchestra (Essex). Elvis Presley had a hit single, 1964, from an LP cut in 1960 (RCA Victor).

Sud Bustin' Blues. w/m Steve Lewis, Peter Bocage, and A. J. Piron, 1924. Recorded and featured by Piron's New Orleans Band (Columbia).

Suddenly. w/m Keith Diamond and Billy Ocean, 1985. Top 10 single by Billy Ocean (Jive).

Suddenly. w/m John Farrar, 1980. Introduced by Olivia Newton-John and Cliff Richard in (MM) *Xanadu* and on records (MCA).

Suddenly. w. E. Y. Harburg, m. Vernon Duke, 1934. Introduced by Jane Froman and Everett Marshall in (TM) *Ziegfeld Follies*. Revived by Les Baxter's Orchestra (Capitol) and Beryl Davis (MGM) in the fifties.

Suddenly I'm All Alone. w/m Van McCoy, 1964. Recorded by Walter Jackson (Okeh).

Suddenly It's Spring. w. Johnny Burke, m. James Van Heusen, 1944. Introduced by Ginger Rogers in (MM) *Lady in the Dark*. Leading records by Glen Gray and the Casa Loma Orchestra, vocal by Eugenie Baird (Decca) and Hildegarde (Decca).

Suddenly Last Summer. w/m Martha Davis, 1983. Top 10 record by the quintet The Motels (Capitol). Song has no connection with the Tennessee Williams play and film of the same title.

Suddenly There's a Valley. w/m Chuck Meyer and Biff Jones, 1955. Top 40 records by Gogi Grant, with Buddy Bregman's Orchestra (Era); Jo Stafford, with Paul Weston's Orchestra (Columbia); Julius LaRosa, with Archie Bleyer's Orchestra (Cadence).

Suddenly You Love Me. w. Peter Callander (Engl.), D. Pace (It.), m. D. Pace, M.

Panzeri, L. Pilat, 1968. Originally an Italian song, "Uno Tranquillo." English version recorded by The Tremeloes (Epic).

Sue Me. w/m Frank Loesser, 1950. Introduced by Sam Levene and Vivian Blaine in (TM) *Guys and Dolls*. In (MM) *Guys and Dolls*, 1955, it was sung by Frank Sinatra and Jean Simmons.

Sugar. w/m Maceo Pinkard and Sidney D. Mitchell, 1928. The first recording of this standard was by Ethel Waters (Columbia). Among the many that followed are Bennie Moten (Victor); Paul Whiteman, featuring Bix Beiderbecke (Columbia); Count Basie (Victor); Teddy Wilson (Brunswick); Louis Armstrong (Victor). In (MM) *Pete Kelly's Blues*, 1955, it was sung by Peggy Lee with Matty Matlock's Dixielanders.

Sugar, Sugar. w/m Jeff Barry and Andy Kim, 1969. Gold record by The Archies (Calendar). Wilson Pickett had a Top 40 version (Atlantic), 1970.

Sugar and Spice. w/m Fred Nightingale, 1964. First recorded in England by The Searchers and released in the U.S. (Liberty). Chart version by The Cyran' Shames (Destination), 1966.

Sugar Blues. w. Lucy Fletcher, m. Clarence Williams, 1923. This song is irrevocably associated with trumpet-playing band leader Clyde McCoy and his "wah-wah" sound. It became his theme song and was recorded by him four times (Columbia) (Decca) (Mercury) (Capitol). The first known recording was by Leona Williams and Her Dixie Band (Columbia), 1922. The composer, Clarence Williams, recorded it (Vocalion), 1934. Among others: Ella Fitzgerald (Decca), 1940; Johnny Mercer, accompanied by Paul Weston and his Orchestra (Capitol), 1947.

Sugarbush. w/m Josef Marais, 1952. Published ten years earlier in a collection of South African songs, "Songs from the Veld." Updated words and music were recorded by Doris Day and Frankie Laine, with The Norman Luboff Choir and Carl Fischer's Orchestra (Columbia).

Sugar Daddy. w/m David Bellamy, 1984. #1 Country chart record by The Bellamy Brothers (Warner Bros.).

Sugar Daddy. w/m Berry Gordy, Jr., Fonce Mizell, Freddie Perren, and Deke Richards, 1971. Top 10 record by The Jackson 5 (Motown).

Sugar Dumpling. w/m Sam Cooke, 1965. Top 40 record by Sam Cooke (RCA).

Sugaree. w/m Jerry Garcia and Robert Hunter, 1972. Recorded by Jerry Garcia (Warner Bros.).

Sugarfoot Rag. w. George Vaughn, m. Hank Garland, 1950. Leading record by Red Foley, featuring a guitar solo by Garland (Decca). Popular record by Art Lund, with Leroy Holmes's Orchestra (MGM).

Sugar Foot Stomp. w. Walter Melrose, m. Joseph "King" Oliver, 1925. Under this title (title changed from "Dipper Mouth Blues" when lyrics were written) it was recorded by Fletcher Henderson (Columbia), Jan Savitt (Bluebird), Artie Shaw (Brunswick), Benny Goodman (Victor), Bob Crosby (Decca), Art Hodes on a 12″ 78 RPM disc (Blue Note), and many others.

Sugar Lips. w/m Buddy Killen and Billy Sherrill, 1964. Instrumental hit by trumpeter Al Hirt, with his Orchestra (RCA).

Sugar Magnolia. w/m Robert Hunter and Bob Weir, 1973. Recorded by The Grateful Dead (Warner Bros.).

Sugar Moon. w/m Danny Wolfe, 1958. Hit record by Pat Boone (Dot).

Sugar Moon. w/m Bob Wills and Cindy Walker, 1947. #1 C&W chart hit by Bob Wills and His Texas Playboys (Columbia).

Sugar Moon. w. Stanley Murphy, m. Percy Wenrich, 1910. Comedy hit recorded by Arthur Collins and Byron Harland (Victor). They

recorded it for numerous other labels as was the custom of the period.

Sugar on Sunday. w/m Tommy James and Mike Vale, 1969. Top 40 record by The Clique (White Whale).

Sugar Plum. w. Gus Kahn, m. Arthur Johnston, 1935. Introduced by Ann Dvorak and Patsy Kelly in (MM) *Thanks a Million*.

Sugar Shack. w/m Keith McCormack and Faye Voss, 1963. #1 million-seller by The Fireballs, with Jimmy Gilmer (Dot).

Sugartime. w/m Charlie Phillips and Odis Echols, 1958. Featured and hit record by The McGuire Sisters (Coral).

Sugar Town. w/m Lee Hazlewood, 1966. Top 10 gold record by Nancy Sinatra, produced by Lee Hazlewood (Reprise).

Sugar Walls. w/m Prince Rogers Nelson, 1985. Top 10 record by the Scottish singer, Sheena Easton, written and produced by Prince using pseudonym of Alexander Nevermind (EMI America).

Suicide is Painless. See **Song from M*A*S*H.**

Suitcase Blues. m. Hersal Thomas, 1924. Albert Ammons had a popular recording of this jazz instrumental in 1939 (Blue Note).

Sukiyaki. w. Tom Leslie and Buzz Cason (Eng.), m. Hachidai Nakamura and Rokusuke Ei, 1963. Japanese song titled "Ue O Muite Aruko" ("I Look Up When I Walk"), words by the composers. Japanese record released in the U.S. by Kyu Sakamoto (Capitol) and reached the #1 position on the charts. Revived with English lyrics by the American quartet, A Taste of Honey (Capitol), 1981.

Sultans of Swing. w/m Mark Knopfler, 1979. Top 10 record by the London group Dire Straits (Warner Bros.).

Summer. w/m Dee Allen, Harold Brown, B. B. Dickerson, Jerry Goldstein, Lonnie Jordan, Lee Oskar, Charles Miller, and Howard

Scott, 1976. Top 10 record written and recorded by the group War (United Artists).

Summer Breeze. w. Jimmy Seals, m. Dash Crofts, 1972. Top 10 record by Seals and Crofts (Warner Bros.). Chart version by The Isley Brothers (T-Neck), 1974.

Summer in the City. w/m John B. Sebastian, Mark Sebastian, and Steve Boone, 1966. Gold record by The Lovin' Spoonful (Kama Sutra).

Summer Is A-Comin' In. w. John Latouche, m. Vernon Duke, 1941. First heard in the short-lived musical (TM) *The Lady Comes Across*, sung by The Four Martins. It was revived by Charlotte Rae in (TM) *The Littlest Revue*, 1956.

Summer Love. w/m George David Weiss, 1957. Featured and recorded by Joni James (MGM).

Summer Me, Winter Me. w. Marilyn Bergman and Alan Bergman, m. Michel Legrand, 1969. Based on the main theme from (MP) *Picasso Summer*. A favorite with singers, although no chart versions.

Summer Night. w. Al Dubin, m. Harry Warren, 1936. Introduced by James Melton in (MM) *Sing Me a Love Song* and recorded by him (Decca). Other records: Enoch Light (Perfect); Abe Lyman, vocal by Sonny Schuyler (Decca); Dick Stabile (Bluebird). Later records by Hal McIntyre (Cosmo), Ralph Marterie (Mercury), Clark Dennis (Capitol).

Summer Nights. w/m Jim Jacobs and Warren Casey, 1972. Introduced by Carole Demas, Barry Bostwick, and cast members in (TM) *Grease*. Sung by Olivia Newton-John, John Travolta, and cast members in the film version (MM) *Grease*, 1978, and on the gold record single from the cast album (RSO).

Summer Nights. w/m Brian Henderson and Liza Strike, 1965. Recorded by the English singer Marianne Faithful (London).

Summer of '69. w/m Bryan Adams and Jim Vallance, 1985. Top 10 record by Canadian singer/songwriter Bryan Adams (A&M).

Summer Rain. w/m James Hendricks, 1967. Top 20 record by Johnny Rivers (Imperial).

Summer Samba (So Nice). w. Norman Gimbel (Engl.), Marcos Valle and Paulo Sergio, (Port.) m. Valle and Sergio, 1966. Brazilian composition, "Samba de Verao." Top 40 instrumental record by organist/pianist Walter Wanderley (Verve).

Summer's Gone. w/m Paul Anka, 1960. Recorded by Paul Anka (ABC-Paramount).

Summer Song, A. w/m Clive Metcalfe, Keith Noble, and David Stuart, 1964. Recorded in England by the duo Chad and Jeremy (World Artists).

Summer Sounds. w/m Sid Tepper and Roy C. Bennett, 1965. Popularized by Robert Goulet (Columbia).

Summer Souvenirs. w/m Paul Evans and Jimmy Krondes, 1961. Introduced and recorded by Karl Hammel, Jr. (Arliss).

Summertime. w. Du Bose Heyward, m. George Gershwin, 1935. Introduced by Abbie Mitchell in (TM) *Porgy and Bess*. First popular recording by Billie Holiday (Vocalion). In the film version (MM) *Porgy and Bess*, 1959, it was sung by Loulie Jean Norman, dubbing for Diahann Carroll. Anne Brown, who played Bess in the original stage production, sang it in the Gershwin biography (MM) *Rhapsody in Blue*, 1945. The song was later used as the theme of Bob Crosby's Orchestra. There are many recordings of this major standard.

Summertime, Summertime. w/m Tom Jameson and Sherm Feller, 1958. Hit record by The Jamies (Epic).

Summertime Blues. w/m Eddie Cochrane and Jerry Capehart, 1958. Top 10 record by Eddie Cochran (Liberty). Later high chart records by Blue Cheer (Phillips), 1968, and The Who (Decca), 1970.

Summertime in Venice. w. Carl Sigman (Engl.), Pinchi (It.), m. Icini, 1955. Italian title, "Tempo d'Estate (A Venzia)." Love theme from (MP) *Summertime*, starring Katharine Hepburn and Rossano Brazzi, based on the play, *The Time of the Cuckoo*. Among recordings: Rossano Brazzi (RCA), Jane Froman (Capitol), Gracie Fields (Decca), David Rose and his Orchestra (MGM).

Summertime Lies. w/m Alan Hood and Richard Loring, 1958. Recorded by The Four Preps (Capitol).

Summertime Love. w/m Frank Loesser, 1960. Introduced by Anthony Perkins in (TM) *Greenwillow*.

Summer Wind. w/m Chris Hillman and Steve Hill, 1988. Top 10 Country chart record by The Desert Rose Band (MCA/Curb).

Summer Wind. w. Johnny Mercer (Engl.), Hans Bradtke (Ger.), m. Henry Mayer, 1965. German song. First U.S. recording with English lyrics by Wayne Newton (Capitol). Best-selling record by Frank Sinatra (Reprise), 1966.

Summer Wine. w/m Lee Hazlewood, 1967. Recorded by Nancy Sinatra and Lee Hazlewood, coupled with hit "Sugar Town" (q.v.) (Reprise).

Summit Ridge Drive. m. Artie Shaw, 1944. Instrumental by Artie Shaw and his Gramercy Five (Victor), first released 1940–1941 but reissued during the record strike of 1943–1944 when it established itself as one of the all-time favorite recordings.

Sun Ain't Gonna Shine Anymore, The. w/m Bob Crewe and Bob Gaudio, 1966. Hit record by The Walker Brothers (Smash). Revived by the vocal duo, Nielsen/Pearson (Capitol), 1981.

Sun Always Shines on T.V., The. w/m Pal Waaktaar, 1986. Recorded by the Norwegian trio A-Ha (Warner Bros.)

Sun Arise. w/m Rolf Harris and Harry Butler, 1963. Australian song, recorded in England by Rolf Harris (Epic).

Sunbonnet Sue. w. Will D. Cobb, m. Gus Edwards, 1906. Seventeen years after its ini-

tial popular success, it became the title song of (TM) *Sunbonnet Sue* on Broadway. It served the same purpose in (MM) *Sunbonnet Sue*, 1945, when it was sung by Gale Storm and Phil Regan. Bing Crosby sang it earlier, 1939, in the Gus Edwards story (MM) *The Star Maker*. Bob Wills had a big-selling record (Vocalion), 1937.

Sun City. w/m Steven Van Zant, 1985. Recorded by Artists Against Apartheid, made up of forty-nine top singers, groups, rap, street, pop, and jazz musicians to raise money to benefit political prisoners in South Africa (Manhattan).

Sunday. w/m Stephen Sondheim, 1981. Introduced by the company in (TM) *Sunday in the Park with George*.

Sunday. w. Oscar Hammerstein II, m. Richard Rodgers, 1958. Introduced by Pat Suzuki and Larry Blyden in (TM) *Flower Drum Song*. In the film version (MM) *Flower Drum Song*, 1961, it was performed by Nancy Kwan (vocal dubbed by B. J. Baker) and Jack Soo.

Sunday. w. Clifford Grey, m. J. Fred Coots, 1926. Popular song from the short-lived (TM) *The Merry World*.

Sunday. w. Ned Miller, m. Jule Styne and Bennie Krueger, 1926. Jule Styne's first hit, written while he was pianist/arranger for Arnold Johnson's Orchestra in Chicago. Leading recordings by Cliff Edwards (Perfect); Gene Austin (Victor); Jean Goldkette and his Orchestra (Victor). It was used as the theme song of The Phil Harris-Alice Faye radio show, 1947–1954.

Sunday, Monday, or Always. w. Johnny Burke, m. James Van Heusen, 1943. Introduced by Bing Crosby in (MM) *Dixie*. His recording was #1 for seven weeks (Decca). Frank Sinatra also had a Top 10 version (Columbia). Song was on "Your Hit Parade" for eighteen weeks, six in the #1 position. It was later interpolated in (MM) *Take It Big*, 1944.

Sunday and Me. w/m Neil Diamond, 1965. Hit record by Jay and The Americans (United Artists).

Sunday Down in Tennessee. w/m Beasley Smith, 1949. Leading recorded version by Red Foley (Decca).

Sunday for Tea. w/m Carter-Lewis, 1967. Recorded by the British team of Peter and Gordon (Capitol).

Sunday in New York. w/m Portia Nelson, 1958. Introduced by Ceil Cabot and Gerry Matthews in Julius Monk's nightclub revue *Demi-Dozen*. Featured and recorded by Mabel Mercer (Atlantic).

Sunday in the Park. w/m Harold Rome, 1937. Sung by the company in Rome's first success (TM) *Pins and Needles*.

Sunday in the South. 1989. Hit country single by Shenandoah (Columbia).

Sunday Kind of Love, A. w/m Barbara Belle, Anita Leonard, Stan Rhodes, and Louis Prima, 1946. Introduced and hit recording by Claude Thornhill, with vocal by Fran Warren (Columbia). Revived by Jan and Dean (Liberty), 1962; Lenny Welch (Atco), 1972. Top 10 Country chart version by Reba McEntire (MCA), 1986.

Sunday Mornin'. w/m Margo Guryan, 1968. Top 40 records by Spanky and Our Gang (Mercury) and Oliver (Crewe), 1969.

Sunday Mornin' Comin' Down. w/m Kris Kristofferson, 1970. First recorded by Ray Stevens (Monument), 1969. Popularized by Johnny Cash (Columbia), 1970.

Sunday Morning Sunshine. w/m Harry Chapin, 1972. Recorded by Harry Chapin (Elektra).

Sunday School to Broadway. w/m Daniel Hice and Ruby Hice, 1976. Country chart songs by Sammi Smith (Elektra), 1976, and Anne Murray (Capitol), 1977.

Sunday Sun. w/m Neil Diamond, 1968. Recorded by Neil Diamond (Uni).

Sunday Will Never Be the Same. w/m Gene Pistilli and Terry Cashman, 1967. Top 10 record by Spanky and Our Gang (Mercury).

Sundown. w/m Gordon Lightfoot, 1974. #1 gold record by the Canadian singer/composer Gordon Lightfoot (Reprise).

Sunflower. w/m Neil Diamond, 1977. Recorded by Glen Campbell (Capitol).

Sunflower. w/m Mack David, 1949. Bestseller by Russ Morgan, with his Orchestra (Decca). Other chart records by Jack Fulton (Tower), Jack Smith (Capitol), Frank Sinatra (Columbia). It was selected as the official state song of Kansas. Fifteen years after its initial popularity, the writer received a reputed $250,000.00 in a plagiarism case against the song "Hello Dolly" (q.v.).

Sunglasses at Night. w/m Corey Hart, 1984. Top 10 record by Corey Hart (EMI America).

Sunny. w/m Bobby Hebb, 1966. Introduced and gold record by Bobby Hebb (Philips).

Sunny. w. Otto Harbach and Oscar Hammerstein II, m. Jerome Kern, 1925. Introduced by Paul Frawley in (TM) *Sunny*, starring Marilyn Miller. The song was in both film versions of (MM) *Sunny*, 1930 and 1941. In the Kern biography (MM) *Till the Clouds Roll By*, 1946, it was sung by Judy Garland, and in the Marilyn Miller film story (MM) *Look for the Silver Lining*, 1949, it was sung by June Haver in the role of Miller.

Sunny Afternoon. w/m Ray Davis, 1966. Written by the lead singer of the British group, The Kinks, who had a Top 20 U.S. release (Reprise).

Sunny Disposish. w. Ira Gershwin, m. Philip Charig, 1926. Introduced by Arline and Edgar Gardiner in (TM) *Americana*. It was recorded by Frank Crumit (Victor), Jean Goldkette (Victor), and later Ziggy Elman (MGM).

Sunny Side of Life. w/m Shel Silverstein, 1973. Sung by Rip Torn in (MP) *Payday*.

Sunny Side of Things, The. w. Paul Francis Webster, m. Frank Churchill, 1938. Introduced by Bobby Breen in (MM) *Breaking the*

Ice and recorded by Breen (Decca) and Charles "Buddy" Rogers and his Orchestra (Vocalion).

Sunny Side Up. w. B. G. DeSylva and Lew Brown, m. Ray Henderson, 1929. Sung by Janet Gaynor and the neighbors in (MM) *Sunny Side Up.* In 1956, it was performed in the DeSylva, Brown, and Henderson biography (MM) *The Best Things in Life Are Free*, by Gordon MacRae, Ernest Borgnine, and Dan Dailey respectively, playing the writers, and Sheree North.

Sunrise, Sunset. w. Sheldon Harnick, m. Jerry Bock, 1964. Introduced by Zero Mostel, Maria Karnilova, and chorus in (TM) *Fiddler on the Roof.* Popular recordings by pianist Roger Williams (Kapp) and Eddie Fisher (Dot). In the film version (MM) *Fiddler on the Roof*, 1971, it was sung by Topol, Norma Crane, and chorus.

Sunrise and You. w/m Arthur A. Penn, 1918.

Sunrise Serenade. w. Jack Lawrence, m. Frankie Carle, 1939. Instrumental hit introduced by Glen Gray and the Casa Loma Orchestra (Decca). Double-sided record bestseller [with "Moonlight Serenade"] (q.v.) by Glenn Miller (Bluebird). Lyrics were added and it was recorded by Connie Boswell (Decca). Fifteen weeks on "Your Hit Parade." Pianist-composer Carle, after leaving Horace Heidt and starting his own band, used the song as his theme (Columbia).

Sunset Grill. w/m Don Henley, Dan Kortchmar, and Ben Tench, 1985. Recorded by Don Henley (Geffen).

Sunshine. w/m Andy Kim, 1972. Top 10 record by Jonathan Edwards (Capricorn).

Sunshine. w/m Irving Berlin, 1928. Recorded by Vaughn DeLeath (Edison), Wendell Hall (Victor), Scrappy Lambert (Vocalion), Whispering Jack Smith (His Master's Voice), and Paul Whiteman's Orchestra (Victor).

Sunshine, Lollipops, and Rainbows. w. Howard Liebling, m. Marvin Hamlisch, 1964.

Introduced by Lesley Gore in (MM) *Ski Party*, and on records (Mercury).

Sunshine and Roses. w. Gus Kahn, m. Egbert Van Alstyne, 1913. Recorded by Edna Brown and James F. Harrison (Victor).

Sunshine Cake. w. Johnny Burke, m. James Van Heusen, 1950. Introduced by Bing Crosby in (MM) *Riding High.*

Sunshine Girl. w/m Jerry Riopelle, Fred "Smokey" Roberds, and Murray MacLeod, 1967. Top 20 record by The Parade (A&M).

Sunshine Girl (Has Raindrops in Her Eyes). w/m Bob Merrill, 1957. Introduced by Del Anderson, Eddie Phillips, and Mark Dawson in (TM) *New Girl in Town.*

Sunshine of Paradise Alley, The. w. Walter H. Ford, m. John W. Bratton, 1895. Introduced by Lottie Gilson at the Casino Roof Garden in New York.

Sunshine of Your Love. w Peter Brown, Jack Bruce, and Eric Clapton, 1968. Gold record by the British group Cream (Atco).

Sunshine of Your Smile, The. w. Leonard Cooke, m. Lillian Ray, 1915. Recorded by John McCormack (Victor). Revived by Meredith Willson and his Orchestra (Decca), 1941.

Sunshine on My Shoulders. w/m John Denver, Richard L. Kniss, and Michael Taylor, 1974. #1 gold record by John Denver (RCA).

Sunshine Smiles. w. Betty Box and Joe Camp, m. Evel Box, 1977. Sung by Charlie Rich on the soundtrack of (MP) *For the Love of Benji.*

Sunshine Superman. w/m Donovan Leitch, 1966. #1 chart record by the Scottish writer/ singer Donovan (Epic).

Sun Showers. w. Arthur Freed, m. Nacio Herb Brown, 1937. Introduced by Eleanor Powell in (MM) *Gold Diggers of '38.*

Super Bad. w/m James Brown, 1970. #1 R&B, Top 10 Pop chart record by James Brown (King).

Super Bowl Shuffle. w/m Lloyd Barry, Bobby Daniels, Richard Meyer, and Melvin Owens, 1986. Chart record by The Chicago Bears Shufflin' Crew, comprised of ten members of the Super Bowl XX champions (Red Label).

Supercalifragilisticexpialidocious. w/m Richard M. Sherman and Robert B. Sherman, 1964. Introduced by Julie Andrews, Dick Van Dyke, and the animated Pearlies in (MM) *Mary Poppins.*

Superfly. w/m Curtis Mayfield, 1972. Sung on the soundtrack of (MP) *Superfly* by Curtis Mayfield, and on a Top 10 record (Curtom).

"Superman," Love Theme From. See **Can You Read My Mind.**

Supernatural Thing—Part 1. w/m Patrick Grant and Gwen Guthrie, 1975. Top 10 record by Ben E. King (Atlantic).

Superstar. w. Tim Rice, m. Andrew Lloyd Webber, 1971. Sung by Ben Vereen and chorus in (TM) *Jesus Christ Superstar.* First popular single by the British singer/actor, Murray Head, with The Trinidad Singers (Decca). In the film version (MM) *Jesus Christ Superstar,* 1973, it was sung by Carl Anderson.

Superstar. w/m Bonnie Bramlett and Leon Russell, 1971. Gold record by The Carpenters (A&M).

Superstar (Remember How You Got Where You Are). w/m Barrett Strong and Norman Whitfield, 1971. Top 20 record by The Temptations (Gordy).

Superstition. w/m Stevie Wonder, 1973. #1 R&B and Pop chart hit by Stevie Wonder (Tamla). Winner Grammy Award (NARAS), Best Rhythm and Blues Song.

Superwoman. w/m Antonio Reid, Kenneth Edmonds, and Daryl Simmons, 1989. #1 R&B chart single by Karyn White (Warner Bros.)

Superwoman (Where Were You When I Needed You). w/m Stevie Wonder, 1972. Recorded by Stevie Wonder (Tamla).

Supper Time. w/m Irving Berlin, 1933. Introduced by Ethel Waters in (TM) *As Thousands Cheer.* Recorded by Gertrude Niesen (Victor) and Leo Reisman's Orchestra, vocal by Clifton Webb (Vocalion).

Sure As I'm Sittin' Here. w/m John Hiatt, 1974. Top 20 record by Three Dog Night (Dunhill).

Sure Gonna Miss Her. w/m Bobby Russell, 1966. Top 10 record by Gary Lewis and the Playboys (Liberty).

Sure Thing. w. Ira Gershwin, m. Jerome Kern, 1944. Introduced by Martha Mears, dubbing for Rita Hayworth, in (MM) *Cover Girl.* First recorded by Glen Gray and the Casa Loma Orchestra (Decca).

(We've Got a) Sure Thing. w. Johnny Burke, m. James Van Heusen, 1950. Introduced by Bing Crosby in (MM) *Riding High.*

Surf City. w/m Jan Berry and Brian Wilson, 1963. #1 chart hit by Jan and Dean (Liberty).

Surfer Girl. w/m Brian Wilson, 1963. Top 10 record by The Beach Boys (Capitol).

Surfer Joe. w/m Ron Wilson, 1963. Record by The Surfaris, coupled with their hit "Wipe Out" (Dot).

Surfin' Bird. w/m Al Frazier, John Earl Harris, Carl White, and Turner Wilson, 1964. Top 10 record by The Trashmen (Garrett). Sung by Pee Wee Herman in (MP) *Back to the Beach,* 1987.

Surfin' Safari. w/m Mike Love and Brian Wilson, 1962. Featured and recorded by The Beach Boys (Capitol).

Surfin' U.S.A. w/m Chuck Berry, 1963. Revision by Brian Wilson of Chubby Checker's 1958 hit, "Sweet Little Sixteen," (q.v.) for the group, The Beach Boys, of which Wilson was a member (Capitol). Their record was revived in 1974. Top 20 version by Leif Garrett (Atlantic), 1977.

Surrender. w/m Rick Nielsen, 1978. Recorded by the quartet Cheap Trick (Epic).

Surrender. w. (Engl.) and m. (adaptation) Doc Pomus and Mort Shuman, 1961. Adapted from Italian song, "Torna a Sorrento" ["Come Back to Sorrento," w. G. Battista De Curtis, m. Ernesto De Curtis]. #1 record by Elvis Presley (RCA).

Surrender. w/m Bennie Benjamin and George David Weiss, 1947. Leading record by Perry Como (RCA Victor), followed by Woody Herman with his Orchestra (Columbia).

Surrey with the Fringe on Top, The. w. Oscar Hammerstein II, m. Richard Rodgers, 1943. Introduced by Alfred Drake, Joan Roberts, and Betty Garde in (TM) *Oklahoma!* In the film version, 1955, (MM) *Oklahoma!*, it was sung by Gordon MacRae, Shirley Jones, and Charlotte Greenwood.

Surround Me with Love. w/m Wayne Hollyfield and Norro Wilson, 1981. Top 10 Country chart record by Charly McClain (Epic).

Susan. w/m Gary Beisbier, James Guercio, and James Holvay, 1968. Hit record by The Buckinghams (Columbia).

Susie Darlin'. w/m Robin Luke, 1958. Top 10 record by sixteen-year-old Robin Luke (Dot). Tommy Roe had a chart record in 1962 (ABC-Paramount).

Susie-Q. w/m Dale Hawkins, Stanley Lewis, and Eleanor Broadwater, 1957. First popularized by Dale Hawkins (Checker). Top 20 record by Creedence Clearwater Revival in 1968 (Fantasy, Part 1).

Suspicion. w/m Doc Pomus and Mort Shuman, 1964. Hit record by Terry Stafford (Crusader).

Suspicion. w/m Les Paul and Foster Carling, 1948. Leading records by Tex Williams (Capitol) and Jo Stafford (Capitol).

Suspicions. w/m David Malloy, Randy McCormick, Eddie Rabbitt, and Even Stevens, 1979. Recorded by Country/Pop singer/writer Eddie Rabbitt (Elektra).

Suspicious Minds. w/m Mark James, 1969. #1 gold record by Elvis Presley (RCA). Dee Dee Warwick recorded a chart version (Atco), 1971.

Sussudio. w/m Phil Collins, 1985. #1 single from the Album by Phil Collins "No Jacket Required" (Atlantic). The title verbalizes, to Collins, the drum roll he used in recording.

Suzanne. w/m Steve Perry and Jonathan Cain, 1986. Recorded by the Trio Journey (Columbia).

Suzanne. w/m Leonard Cohen, 1967. First recorded by Judy Collins in her album "In My Life" (Elektra), 1966. Noel Harrison popularized it with a chart single (Reprise), 1967. Cohen sang it in his album "Songs of Leonard Cohen" (Columbia), 1968.

Suzanne (Ev'ry Night When the Sun Goes Down). w/m Harry Belafonte and Millard Thomas, 1953. Adaptation of an American folk song. Harry Belafonte introduced it and sang it in his screen debut (MP) *Bright Road.*

Suzie Wong. See **Love Theme from "Suzie Wong."**

Swamp Fire. m. Harold Mooney, 1936. Mooney had two hit instrumentals this year (see "Rigamarole"). This was introduced by Ozzie Nelson and his Orchestra and subsequently recorded by Shep Fields (Bluebird), Lou Breese (Varsity), Les Brown (Decca), Jimmy Dorsey (Decca), André Kostalanetz (Brunswick), Duke Ellington (Victor).

Swamp Girl. w/m Michael Brown, 1950. Introduced by Frankie Laine with Harry Geller's Orchestra (Mercury).

Swanee. w. Irving Caesar, m. George Gershwin, 1919. This was the first hit for both Gershwin and Caesar. It was introduced by Muriel DeForrest in a lavish production that opened the Capitol Theatre in New York. The song made little impact until Al Jolson sang it in a Sunday night show at the Winter Garden and then added it to the score of the road tour of (TM) *Sinbad* in which he was starring. The song sold over a million copies of sheet music and Jolson's recording (Columbia), 1920, was also a best-seller. Jolson sang it in the George Gershwin film biography (MM) *Rhapsody in Blue*, 1945. He dubbed in the vocal for Larry Parks in (MM) *The Jolson Story*, 1946, which version was reproduced in (MM) *Jolson Sings Again*, 1949. Judy Garland sang it in (MM) *A Star Is Born*, 1954.

Swanee Butterfly. w. Billy Rose, m. Walter Donaldson, 1925. Recorded by the orchestras of Isham Jones (Brunswick), Fred Waring (Victor), William F. Wirges (Perfect), solo vocal by Georgie Price (Victor).

Swanee River Moon. w/m H. Pitman Clarke, 1921.

Swanee River Rock (Talkin' 'bout That River). w/m Ray Charles, 1957. Based on Stephen Foster's "Old Folks at Home." This was one of Ray Charles's earliest Pop chart records.

Swanee Shuffle. w/m Irving Berlin, 1929. Sung and danced by Nina Mae McKinney in (MM) *Hallelujah.*

Sway (a.k.a. Quien Sera). w. Norman Gimbel (Engl.), Pablo Beltran Ruiz (Sp.), m. Pablo Beltran Ruiz, 1954. Mexican song. Leading records by Dean Martin, with Dick Stabile's Orchestra (Capitol); Eileen Barton, with Terry Gibbs's Sextet (Coral).

Swayin' to the Music (a.k.a. Slow Dancing). w/m Jack Tempchin, 1977. Introduced and chart record under title of "Slow Dancing" by The Funky Kings (Arista), a septet led by the writer, 1976. Top 10 record by Johnny Rivers (Big Tree), 1977.

Swearin' to God. w/m Bob Crewe and Denny Randell, 1975. Top 10 record by Frankie Valli (Private Stock).

Swedish Pastry. m. Barney Kessel, 1948. Jazz instrumental featured and recorded by the combos of Stan Hasselgard (Capitol), George Shearing (MGM), Red Norvo (Discovery).

Swedish Rhapsody (a.k.a. Midsummer Vigil). m. Hugo Alfven, adapted by Percy Faith, 1953. Popularized by Percy Faith and his Orchestra, coupled with his hit record "Song from Moulin Rouge" (q.v.) (Columbia).

Sweepin' the Clouds Away. w/m Sam Coslow, 1930. Sung by Maurice Chevalier in (MM) *Paramount on Parade* and on records (Victor). Also recorded by Charles "Buddy" Rogers and his Band (Columbia).

Sweet, Sweet Baby (I'm Falling). w/m Maria McKee, Steve Van Zant, and Ben Tench, 1985. Recorded by the quartet Lone Justice (Geffen).

(Sweet, Sweet Baby) Since You've Been Gone. w/m Aretha Franklin and Ted White, 1968. Gold record by Aretha Franklin (Atlantic).

Sweet, Sweet Love. w/m Mary Vesta Williams-White, Attala Zane Gales, and William Osborne, 1989. Hit R&B chart single by Vesta (A&M).

Sweet Adeline (or You're the Flower of My Heart). w. Richard H. Gerard [Richard Gerard Husch], m. Harry Armstrong, 1903. One of the most successful of barber-shop quartet songs. Originally titled "Down Home in New England," then "You're the Flower of My Heart, Sweet Rosalie." The "Adeline" was substituted as a tribute to Adelina Patti, the Italian opera star. The number was introduced by the Quaker City Four at Hammerstein's Victoria Theatre in New York. In 1906 it served as the campaign song for John F. "Honey" Fitzgerald in his race for mayor of Boston.

Sweet and Gentle. w. George Thorn (Engl.), Otilio Portal (Sp.), m. Otilio Portal, 1955. Original Cuban title "Me Lo Dijo Adela." A cha cha, popularized by the hit records of Alan Dale (Coral) and Georgia Gibbs (Mercury).

Sweet and Hot. w. Jack Yellen, m. Harold Arlen, 1931. Introduced by Lyda Roberti,

Peggy Bernier, and Hughie Clarke in (TM) *You Said It*, starring Lou Holtz. The song made a headliner out of Roberti, and her performance caused the show to be billed as "The Sweet and Hot Musical." Arlen recorded it with Red Nichols' Band (Brunswick), as did Fletcher Henderson (Columbia) and Ben Pollack (Perfect).

Sweet and Innocent. w/m Rick Hall and Billy Sherrill, 1971. Top 10 record by Donny Osmond (MGM).

Sweet and Lovely. w/m Gus Arnheim, Harry Tobias, and Jules Lemare, 1931. Introduced by Arnheim's Orchestra on broadcasts from the Cocoanut Grove in Los Angeles, California, and recorded by him (Victor). Russ Columbo then had a hit record (Victor), which firmly established the singer and the song. It became the theme song of Arnheim's Orchestra. The reverse side of Columbo's record, "You Call It Madness," (q.v.) became Columbo's theme. "Sweet and Lovely" was performed by June Allyson, Gloria De Haven, and Harry James and his Orchestra in (MM) *Two Girls and a Sailor* in 1944. It was also heard in (MP) *Battleground* in 1949 and (MP) *This Earth Is Mine* in 1959.

Sweet and Low-Down. w. Ira Gershwin, m. George Gershwin, 1925. Introduced by Harry Watson, Lovey Lee, Amy Revere, and the Ensemble in (TM) *Tip-Toes*. It was performed by Charles "Honi" Coles, Tommy Tune, and Twiggy in the all-Gershwin musical (TM) *My One and Only* in 1983.

Sweet Annie Moore. w/m John H. Flynn, 1900. Hit song from (TM) *The Casino Girl*.

Sweet as a Song. w. Mack Gordon, m. Harry Revel, 1938. Introduced by Tony Martin in (MM) *Sally, Irene and Mary*.

Sweet Baby. w/m George Duke, 1981. Recorded by the jazz/rock musicians, bassist Stanley Clarke and keyboardist George Duke (Epic).

Sweet Beginning. w/m Leslie Bricusse and Anthony Newley, 1965. Introduced as the finale of (TM) *The Roar of the Greasepaint—The Smell of the Crowd* by Anthony Newley, Cyril Ritchard, and chorus.

Sweet Blindness. w/m Laura Nyro, 1968. Introduced by Laura Nyro in her album "Eli and the Thirteenth Confession" (Columbia). The 5th Dimension had a Top 20 single (Soul City), 1968.

Sweet Bunch of Daisies. w/m Anita Owen, 1894.

Sweet Caroline (Good Times Never Seemed So Good). w/m Neil Diamond, 1969. Top 10 record by Neil Diamond (Uni).

Sweet Cherry Wine. w/m Tommy James and Richie Grasso, 1969. Top 10 record by Tommy James and The Shondells (Roulette).

Sweet Child O'Mine. w/m Guns N' Roses, 1988. Hit single by Guns N' Roses from the album "Appetite for Destruction" (Geffen).

Sweet City Woman. w/m Rick Dodson, 1971. Top 10 record by the Calgary, Alberta trio, The Stampeders (Bell).

Sweet Cream Ladies, Forward March. w/m Bobby Weinstein and Jon Stroll, 1969. Top 40 record by The Box Tops (Mala).

Sweet Danger. w/m Robert Wright and George Forrest, 1961. Introduced by Joan Weldon and Alfred Drake in (TM) *Kean*.

Sweet Desire. w/m Jeannie Kuykendall, 1978. Recorded by the Nashville father and daughter duo The Kendalls (Ovation).

Sweet Dreams. w/m Graham Russell, 1982. Top 10 record by the Australian duo Air Supply (Arista).

Sweet Dreams. w/m Don Gibson, 1956. First hit record by C&W singer Faron Young (Capitol). Don Gibson had a chart record (RCA), 1960; Patsy Cline had a C&W/Pop crossover hit (Decca), 1963; Tommy McLain had a Top 20 Pop record (MSL), 1966. Country chart record by Emmylou Harris (Reprise), 1976. Title song of the Patsy Cline film biography (MM) *Sweet Dreams*, 1985, starring Hope Lange as Cline.

Sweet Dreams, Sweetheart. w. Ted Koehler, m. M. K. Jerome, 1944. Introduced by Kitty Carlisle and Joan Leslie in (MM) *Hollywood Canteen*. Song nominated for Academy Award. Recorded by Carlisle (Decca) and Ray Noble and his Orchestra, vocal by Larry Stewart (Columbia).

Sweet Dreams (Are Made of This). w/m Annie Lennox and David Stewart, 1983. Written and #1 gold record by the U.K. duo, The Eurythmics (RCA).

Sweet Eloise. w. Mack David, m. Russ Morgan, 1942. Introduced and recorded by Russ Morgan and his Orchestra (Decca). Bestseller by Glenn Miller, vocal by Ray Eberle and The Modernaires (Victor). Also recorded by Chico Marx and his Orchestra (Hit).

Sweet Emalina, My Gal. w/m Henry Creamer and Turner Layton, 1917.

Sweeter He Is, The. w/m Isaac Hayes and David Porter, 1969. Recorded by The Soul Children (Stax, Part 1).

Sweeter Than the Flowers. w/m Morry Burns, Ervin Rouse, and Lois Mann, 1947. C&W chart hits by Moon Mullican (King) and Shorty Long and The Sante Fe Rangers (Decca).

Sweeter Than the Sweetest. w. Neil Lawrence, m. Willie "The Lion" Smith, 1941. Featured and recorded by Glenn Miller with vocal by the Modernaires, arranged by Billy May (Bluebird).

Sweeter Than You. w/m Baker Knight, 1959. Recorded by Ricky Nelson (Imperial).

Sweetest Flower the Garden Grew, The. w/m Thurland Chattaway, 1907.

Sweetest Gift, The. w/m J. B. Coats, 1975. Introduced by Linda Ronstadt in her album "Prisoner in Disguise" (Asylum). Country chart single by Linda Ronstadt and Emmylou Harris (Asylum), 1976.

Sweetest Maid of All. w. Joseph Herbert, m. Oscar Straus, 1908. From (TM) *The Waltz Dream*.

Sweetest Music This Side of Heaven, The. w/m Carmen Lombardo and Cliff Friend, 1934. Introduced by Guy Lombardo and the Royal Canadians in (MM) *Many Happy Returns*, starring Burns and Allen. The song title was the "slogan" of the Lombardo band, recorded by them (Melotone) and co-written by brother Carmen.

Sweetest Sounds, The. w/m Richard Rodgers, 1962. Introduced by Diahann Carroll and Richard Kiley in (TM) *No Strings*.

Sweetest Taboo, The. w/m Helen Folasade Adu and Martin Ditcham, 1986. Top 10 record by the singer Sade (Portrait).

Sweetest Thing (I've Ever Known), The. w/m Otha Young, 1981. Top 10 record by Juice Newton (Capitol).

Sweetest Thing This Side of Heaven, The. w/m Van McCoy, 1967. Top 40 record by soul singer Chris Bartley (Vando).

Sweet Fire of Love. w/m Robbie Robertson and U2, 1987. Popular track from the co-writer's album "Robbie Robertson" (Geffen).

Sweet Freedom. w/m Rod Temperton, 1986. Introduced by Michael McDonald on the soundtrack of (MP) *Running Scared* and on a Top 10 single (MCA).

Sweet Georgia Brown. w/m Ben Bernie, Maceo Pinkard, and Ken Casey, 1925. Introduced and featured by Ben Bernie and his Orchestra. In later years, the song was associated with the popular touring basketball team, the Harlem Globetrotters, who used it as background music for their exhibition of ball-handling in arenas and on T.V. The song was heard in (MM) *Broadway*, 1942; (MM) *Follow the Boys*, 1944; (MM) *Some Like It Hot*, 1959; and (MM) *Jazz on a Summer's Day*, 1960. It was sung by Vivian Reed in (TM) *Bubbling Brown Sugar*, 1976.

Sweet Harmony. w/m William "Smokey" Robinson, 1973. Recorded by Smokey Robinson (Tamla).

Sweet Hawaiian Moonlight. w. Harold G. Frost, m. F. H. Klickmann, 1919. Popular record by Vivian Holt and Lillian Rosedale (Victor). Revived and recorded by Harry Owens and his Orchestra (Decca), 1939.

Sweetheart. w/m Frankie Previte and W. Elworthy, 1981. Top 10 record by the quintet Franke and The Knockouts (Millennium).

Sweetheart, We Need Each Other. w. Joseph McCarthy, m. Harry Tierney, 1927. From (TM) *Rio Rita*. Ben Pollack had a popular record (Victor).

Sweet Heartache. w. Ned Washington, m. Sam H. Stept, 1937. Introduced in (MM) *The Hit Parade* and recorded (Decca) by Frances Langford.

Sweet Heartaches. w/m Nat Simon and Jimmy Kennedy, 1956. Popular record by Eddie Fisher (RCA).

Sweetheart Darlin'. w. Gus Kahn, m. Herbert Stothart, 1933. Featured and recorded by Morton Downey (Melotone), Annette Hanshaw (Perfect), Ted Fio Rito (Brunswick), Jack Hylton (Br. Decca), and Adrian Schubert, vocal by Elmer Feldkamp (Crown).

Sweetheart Like You. w/m Bob Dylan, 1984. Chart single from the album "Infidels," by Bob Dylan (Columbia).

Sweetheart of All My Dreams (I Love You, I Love You, I Love You). w/m Art Fitch, Kay Fitch, and Bert Lowe, 1928. A popular song of the year that was then sung by Helen Morgan in (MM) *Applause*, 1929. It originally was recorded by Rudy Vallee, under the pseudonym of Frank Mater (Harmony); Irving Aaronson and His Commanders (Victor); Art Gillham (Columbia), and others. It was revived in (MP) *Thirty Seconds Over Tokyo*, 1944, starring Spencer Tracy and Van Johnson, which led to new recordings by Benny Goodman (Columbia), Carmen Cavallero (Decca), The King Sisters (Victor), and Charlie Spivak's Band (Victor).

Sweetheart of My Student Days. w. Gus Kahn, m. Seymour Simons, 1930. Featured and recorded by Belle Baker (Brunswick).

Sweetheart of Sigma Chi, The. w. Byron D. Stokes, m. F. Dudleigh Vernor, 1912. A college favorite that was the title song for (MM) *The Sweetheart of Sigma Chi*, 1946.

Sweetheart of the Year. w/m Van Givens and Clyde Pitts, 1969. Country chart record by Ray Price (Columbia).

Sweethearts. w. Robert B. Smith, m. Victor Herbert, 1913. Introduced by Christie MacDonald in (TM) *Sweethearts*. It was sung by Jeanette MacDonald in the film version (MM) *Sweethearts*, 1938.

Sweethearts Forever. w. Irving Caesar, m. Cliff Friend, 1932. Introduced by Brick Holton, dubbing for David Manners, in the title role of (MM) *Crooner*. Most popular recording by Wayne King's Orchestra (Victor).

Sweethearts On Parade. w. Charles Newman, m. Carmen Lombardo, 1928. The first big hit for each writer. Introduced, featured, and recorded by Guy Lombardo and his Orchestra (Columbia). It was the title song of (MM) *Sweethearts on Parade*, 1930, and was also heard in (MM) *Swingin' on a Rainbow*, 1945.

Sweethearts or Strangers. w/m Jimmie Davis and Lou Wayne, 1941. The sheet music credits read: "Revised edition by Don Marcotte." Among recordings: Connee Boswell (Decca), Jimmie Davis (Decca), Lawrence Welk and his Orchestra (Decca). It was featured in (MM) *Strictly in the Groove*, 1942.

Sweetheart Tree, The. w. Johnny Mercer, m. Henry Mancini, 1965. Introduced by Jackie Ward, dubbing on the soundtrack for Natalie Wood, in (MP) *The Great Race*. Nominated for Academy Award. Leading record by Johnny Mathis (Mercury).

Sweet Hitch-hiker. w/m John Fogerty, 1971. Top 10 record by Creedence Clearwater Revival (Fantasy).

Sweet Home Alabama. w/m Edward King, Gary Rossington, and Ronnie Van Zant, 1974. Top 10 record by the group, Lynyrd Skynyrd (MCA).

Sweetie Pie. w/m John Jacob Loeb, 1934. Featured and recorded by Fats Waller and his Rhythm (Victor), and Anson Weeks, vocal by Kay St. Germaine (Brunswick). Stan Getz, the tenor sax star, revived it with his group in 1950 (Roost).

Sweet Indiana Home. w/m Walter Donaldson, 1922. Recorded by Aileen Stanley (Victor).

Sweet Inspiration. w/m Dan Pennington and Dewey Lindon Oldham, 1968. Top 20 record by the vocal group The Sweet Inspirations (Atlantic). Barbra Streisand sang it in medley with "Where You Lead" (Columbia), 1972.

Sweet Is the Word for You. w. Leo Robin, m. Ralph Rainger, 1937. Introduced in (MM) *Waikiki Wedding* and recorded (Decca) by Bing Crosby. Other records by Hal Kemp, vocal by Bob Allen (Brunswick), and Tommy Dorsey, vocal by Jack Leonard (Victor).

Sweet Jennie Lee. w/m Walter Donaldson, 1930. Featured and recorded by Isham Jones and his Orchestra (Brunswick), and Harry Reser and his Orchestra (Hit of the Week).

Sweet Katie Connor. w/m Harry Dacre, 1890.

Sweet Kentucky Ham. w/m Dave Frishberg, 1987. Recorded by singer/pianist/songwriter Dave Frishberg on his album "Can't Take You Nowhere" (Fantasy).

Sweet Kentucky Lady. w. William Jerome, m. Louis A. Hirsch, 1914.

Sweet Lady. w. Howard Johnson, m. Frank Crumit and Dave Zoob, 1921. The hit song from (TM) *Tangerine*, introduced by Julia Sanderson and Frank Crumit. Crumit recorded it that year (Columbia).

Sweet Leilani. w/m Harry Owens, 1937. Introduced in (MM) *Waikiki Wedding* by Bing Crosby. His recording (Decca) was a million-seller. The song was the 1937 Academy Award winner.

Sweet Life. w/m Susan Collins and Paul Davis, 1978. Recorded by Paul Davis (Bang).

Sweet Lips. w/m Webb Pierce, Glenn D. Tubb, and Wayne P. Walker, 1961. C&W hit introduced and recorded by Webb Pierce (Decca).

Sweet Little Buttercup. w. Alfred Bryan, m. Herman Paley, 1917.

Sweet Little Sixteen. w/m Chuck Berry, 1958. Introduced and Top 10 record by Chuck Berry (Chess).

Sweet Little You. w/m Barry Mann and Larry Kolber, 1961. Recorded by Neil Sedaka (RCA).

Sweet Lorraine. w. Mitchell Parish, m. Cliff Burwell, 1928. An all-time hit with hundreds of recordings by pianists, groups, and bands. The composer was playing piano for Rudy Vallee's Band when he wrote this. Vallee introduced and recorded it (Victor). Jimmy Noone, the clarinetist, had a jazz hit (Vocalion), 1928, and Nat Cole had a chart record over twenty-five years later (Capitol).

Sweet Love. w/m Anita Baker, Louis A. Johnson, and Gary Bias, 1986. Hit R&B and Pop chart record by Anita Baker (Elektra). Winner Grammy Award (NARAS) Rhythm and Blues Song of the Year, 1986.

Sweet Love. w/m William King, Ronald La Pread, Thomas McClary, Walter Orange, Lionel Richie, and Milan Williams, 1975. Top 10 record, written and recorded by The Commodores (Motown).

Sweet Madness. w. Ned Washington, m. Victor Young, 1933. From Earl Carroll's (TM) *Murder at the Vanities* and the 1934 film version (MM) *Murder at the Vanities*. Recorded by Adrian Rollini's (Melotone) and Leo Reisman's orchestras (Victor).

Sweet Magnolia Blossom. w/m Gayle Barnhill and Rory Bourke, 1974. Hit Country record by Billy "Crash" Craddock (MCA).

Sweet Marie. w. Cy Warman, m. Raymond Moore, 1893. Introduced by Moore in a minstrel show at the Euclid Opera House in Cleveland, Ohio.

Sweet Mary. w/m Steve Jablecki, 1971. Top 10 record by Wadsworth Mansion (Sussex).

Sweet Memories. w/m Mickey Newbury, 1968. Recorded by Andy Williams (Columbia).

Sweet Music. w. Al Dubin, m. Harry Warren, 1935. Introduced in (MM) *Sweet Music* and recorded by Rudy Vallee (Victor). Among other recordings: the orchestras of Will Osborne (Melotone), Archie Bleyer (Vocalion), Lud Gluskin, vocal by Buddy Clark (Columbia), Freddy Martin (Brunswick), Victor Young (Decca).

Sweet Nothin's. w/m Ronnie Self and Dub Allbritten, 1960. Top 10 record by Brenda Lee (Decca).

Sweet Old Fashioned Girl, A. w/m Bob Merrill, 1956. Popular record by Teresa Brewer, with Dick Jacobs's Orchestra (Coral).

Sweet Pea. w/m Tommy Roe, 1966. Gold record by Tommy Roe (ABC-Paramount).

Sweet Potato Piper. w. Johnny Burke, m. James V. Monaco, 1940. Introduced by Bing Crosby, Bob Hope, and Dorothy Lamour in the first of their "road" pictures (MM) *The Road to Singapore*. Crosby, with The Foursome, recorded it (Decca). Lamour also had a single (Bluebird).

Sweet Rosie Jones. w/m Buck Owens, 1968. Top 10 Country record by Buck Jones and The Buckaroos (Capitol).

Sweet Rosie O'Grady. w/m Maude Nugent, 1896. Introduced and featured by Nugent at the Abbey, then at Tony Pastor's, both night entertainment clubs in New York. This waltz, one of the most successful of the "gay nineties," was the title song of the film (MM) *Sweet Rosie O'Grady*, 1943.

Sweet Savannah. w/m Paul Dresser, 1898.

Sweet Savannah Sue. w. Andy Razaf, m. Thomas "Fats" Waller and Harry Brooks, 1929. From (TM) *Hot Chocolates*. Recorded by Louis Armstrong (Okeh); Irving Mills and his Hotsy Totsy Gang, a recording band (Brunswick); Fats Waller, piano solo coupled with "Ain't Misbehavin'" (Victor); and Fess Williams (Victor).

Sweet Seasons. w/m Carole King and Toni Stern, 1972. Top 10 record by Carole King (Ode).

Sweet Sensation. w/m James Mtume and Reggie Lucas, 1980. Recorded by Stephanie Mills (20th Century).

Sweets for My Sweet. w/m Doc Pomus and Mort Shuman, 1961. Hit record by The Drifters (Atlantic). Revived by Tony Orlando (Casablanca), 1979.

Sweet Sixteen. w/m Billy Idol, 1987. Chart single from the album "Whiplash Smile" by Billy Idol (Chrysalis).

Sweet Sixteen. w/m Riley "B. B." King and Joe Josea, 1960. Top 10 R&B chart record by B. B. King (Kent). King recorded a new version that reached the R&B and Pop charts (ABC), 1972.

Sweet Sixteen. w/m Ahmet Ertegun, 1952. Top 10 R&B record by Joe Turner (Atlantic).

Sweet Sixteen. w. Gene Buck, m. Dave Stamper, 1919. Introduced by Marilyn Miller in (TM) *Ziegfeld Follies of 1919*.

Sweet Sixteen Bars. m. Ray Charles, 1962. Instrumental introduced by Ray Charles. Best-selling record by Earl Grant (Decca).

Sweet Slumber. w/m Al J. Neiburg, Henri Woode, and Lucky Millinder, 1943. Introduced and recorded by Lucky Millinder, vocal by Trevor Bacon (Decca).

Sweet Someone. w. Mack Gordon, m. Harry Revel, 1938. Introduced by Simone Simon in (MM) *Love and Hisses*. Recorded by Bob Crosby, vocal by Kay Weber (Decca), and Isham Jones's Orchestra (Vocalion).

Sweet Soul Music. w/m Arthur Conley, Sam Cooke, and Otis Redding, 1967. #1 gold record by Arthur Conley (Atco). Music originally written by Sam Cooke as "Yeah Man."

Sweet Sticky Thing. w/m Billy Beck, Leroy Bonner, Marshall Jones, Ralph Middlebrook, Marvin Pierce, Clarence Satchell, and Jimmy Williams, 1975. Recorded by The Ohio Players (Mercury).

Sweet Stranger. w/m Milton Ager, Jerry Livingston, and Ned Wever, 1938. Featured and recorded by Glenn Miller, vocal by Kathleen Lane (Brunswick); Al Bowlly (Bluebird); Reggie Childs and his Orchestra (Decca).

Sweet Sue (Just You). w. Will J. Harris, m. Victor Young, 1928. Supposedly inspired by the movie actress Sue Carol. A multirecorded song by singers, instrumentalists, groups, and bands. Artie Shaw and his Orchestra played it in (MM) *Second Chorus*, 1941. The next year the Mills Brothers, who had a hit record of it early in their career (Brunswick), sang it in (MM) *Rhythm Parade*. In (MM) *The Eddy Duchin Story*, Carmen Cavallero played it on the soundtrack, dubbing for Tyrone Power in the title role, 1956. It was also heard in (MM) *Some Like It Hot*, 1959.

Sweet Summer Lovin'. w/m Blaise Tosti, 1979. Recorded by Dolly Parton (RCA).

Sweet Surrender. w/m John Denver, 1975. Featured and Top 20 record by John Denver (RCA).

Sweet Surrender. w/m David Gates, 1972. Recorded by the group Bread (Elektra).

Sweet Talkin' Guy. w/m Barbara Baer, Elliot Greenberg, Doug Morris, and Robert Schwartz, 1966. Top 10 record by The Chiffons (Laurie).

Sweet Talkin' Woman. w/m Jeff Lynne, 1978. Recorded by the British group Electric Light Orchestra (Jet).

Sweet Temptation. w/m Merle Travis and Cliffie Stone, 1947. Introduced by Merle Travis (Capitol); also recorded later by Tennessee Ernie Ford (Capitol).

Sweet Thang. w/m Nat Stuckey, 1966. Country hit by Nat Stuckey (Paula).

Sweet Thing. w/m Chaka Khan and Tony Maiden, 1976. Gold record by Rufus featuring Chaka Khan (ABC).

Sweet Thoughts of Home. w. Stanislaus Stange, m. Julian Edwards, 1904. From (TM) *Love's Lottery*.

Sweet Thursday. w. Oscar Hammerstein II, m. Richard Rodgers, 1955. Introduced by Helen Traubel in (TM) *Pipe Dream*. Johnny Mathis had a popular single in 1962 (Columbia).

Sweet Time. w. Robert Brittan, m. Judd Woldin, 1973. Introduced by Ernestine Jackson and Joe Morton in (TM) *Raisin*.

Sweet Violets. w/m adapted by Cy Coben and Charles Grean, 1951. Based on traditional folk song. Most popular record by Dinah Shore (RCA Victor).

Sweet William. w/m Buddy Kaye and Philip Springer, 1964. Recorded by Millie Small (Smash).

Sweet Woman Like You, A. w/m Joe Tex, 1966. Top 40 record by Joe Tex (Dial).

Swept Away. w/m Sara Allen and Daryl Hall, 1984. Recorded by Diana Ross and produced by Daryl Hall (RCA).

Swing, Brother, Swing. w/m Walter Bishop, Lewis Raymond, and Clarence Williams, 1936. Featured and recorded by Wingy Manone and his Orchestra (Okeh) and Willie "The Lion" Smith (Decca).

Swing High, Swing Low. w. Ralph Freed, m. Burton Lane, 1937. Introduced by Dorothy Lamour in (MP) *Swing High, Swing Low*, a remake of *Dance of Life*, starring Nancy Carroll, adapted from the play *Burlesque*. A third remake, (MM) *When My Baby Smiles at Me*, starring Betty Grable, was made in 1948. Recordings by Lamour (Brunswick), The Ink Spots (Decca), Phil Harris (Vocalion), Ruby Newman, vocal by Ray Heatherton (Victor).

Swingin'. w/m John Anderson and Lionel Delmore, 1983. Gold record crossover (C&W/Pop) record by John Anderson (Warner Bros.).

Swingin' a Dream. w. Eddie DeLange, m. James Van Heusen, 1939. "Almost" title-song of (TM) "Swingin' the Dream," introduced by the Dandridge Sisters [Dorothy, Etta, and Vivian], Maxine Sullivan, and the Deep River Boys. Will Bradley and his Band recorded it (Vocalion).

Swingin' Down the Lane. w. Gus Kahn, m. Isham Jones, 1923. A big hit in its first year when it was recorded by Isham Jones and his Orchestra (Brunswick), Ben Bernie and his Orchestra (Vocalion), and the Columbians (Columbia). The song has remained a standard and has numerous other recordings. Doris Day and Danny Thomas sang it in the Kahn film bio (MM) *I'll See You in My Dreams*, 1951. It was also heard in (MM) *The Great American Broadcast*, 1941.

Swinging Doors. w/m Merle Haggard, 1966. Hit country record by Merle Haggard (Capitol).

Swinging in a Hammock. w. Tot Seymour and Charles O'Flynn, m. Pete Wendling, 1930. Popular records by Guy Lombardo and the Royal Canadians (Columbia) and Leo Reisman and his Orchestra (Victor).

Swinging on a Star. w. Johnny Burke, m. James Van Heusen, 1944. Introduced by Bing Crosby and the Robert Mitchell Boys' Choir in (MM) *Going My Way*. Academy Award Winner for Best Song, 1944. Crosby's recording, with The Williams Brothers [including Andy] and John Scott Trotter's Orchestra, coupled with the title song of the film, was a million-seller (Decca). Frank Sinatra sang it in (MM) *The Joker Is Wild*, with additional lyrics by Harry Harris, 1957.

Swingin' on a Rainbow. w/ Bob Marcucci, m. Pete De Angelis, 1960. Recorded by Frankie Avalon, coupled with his #1 hit, "Why" (Chancellor).

Swingin' Safari, A. m. Bert Kaempfert, 1962. Recorded by Billy Vaughn and his Orchestra (Dot).

Swingin' School. w. Kal Mann, m. Bernie Loewe and Dave Appell, 1960. From (MP) *Because They're Young*. Top 10 record by Bobby Rydell (Cameo).

Swingin' Shepherd Blues, The. w. Rhoda Roberts and Kenny Jacobson, m. Moe Koffman, 1958. Top 40 instrumental by Canadian flutist Moe Koffman's Quartette (Jubilee).

Swingin' the Blues. w. William "Count" Basie and Eddie Durham, 1938. Instrumental, introduced and recorded by Count Basie and his Band (Decca).

Swingin' the Jinx Away. w/m Cole Porter, 1936. Introduced by Frances Langford, Eleanor Powell, Buddy Ebsen, and dancers as the finale of (MM) *Born to Dance*. Recorded by Frances Langford (Decca).

Swing Is Here to Sway. w. Mack Gordon, m. Harry Revel, 1937. From the Eddie Cantor film (MM) *Ali Baba Goes to Town*. In 1938, it was recorded by Sammy Kaye and his "Swing and Sway" Orchestra (Vocalion).

Swingtime in the Rockies. m. Jimmy Mundy and Benny Goodman, 1936. Mundy's arrangement for Benny Goodman's Band became one of their biggest instrumental hits, and representative of big band swing (Victor).

Swingtown. w/m Chris McCarty and Steve Miller, 1977. Recorded by Steve Miller Band (Capitol).

Swingy Little Thingy. w. Bud Green, m. Sam H. Stept, 1933. Performed by Max Hoffman, Jr., Audrey Christie, and Lester Allen in (TM) *Shady Lady.*

Swiss Boy, The. w/m Lawrence Duchow and Buck Leverton, 1947. Polka, featured by Lawrence Duchow's Red Raven Orchestra (RCA Victor).

Swiss Miss. w. Ira Gershwin, m. George Gershwin, 1924. Introduced by Fred and Adele Astaire in (TM) *Lady, Be Good!*

Switch-A-Roo, The. w/m Al Kasha, Gordon Evans, and Alonzo Tucker, 1961. Recorded by Hank Ballard and The Midnighters.

'S Wonderful. w. Ira Gershwin, m. George Gershwin, 1927. The hit song from (TM) *Funny Face* was sung by Allen Kearns and Adele Astaire. It was heard in the George Gershwin bio (MM) *Rhapsody in Blue*, 1945; sung by Doris Day in a cameo appearance in (MM) *Starlift*, 1951; performed by Gene Kelly and Georges Guetary in (MM) *An American in Paris*, 1951; performed by Fred Astaire and Audrey Hepburn in (MM) *Funny Face* in 1956. It was sung and danced by Tommy Tune and Twiggy in (TM) *My One and Only*, 1983.

Sylvia. w. Paul Francis Webster, m. David Raksin, 1965. Introduced on the soundtrack of (MP) *Sylvia* by Paul Anka.

Sylvia. w. Clinton Scollard, m. Oley Speaks, 1914. A concert song that became popular through performances by male vocal groups and solo tenors in vaudeville and on records.

Sylvia's Mother. w/m Shel Silverstein, 1972. Gold record by Dr. Hook and The Medicine Show (Columbia).

Sympathy. w. Otto Harbach, m. Rudolf Friml, 1912. Introduced by Audrey Maple and Melville Stewart in (TM) *The Firefly*. It was later heard in the Jeanette MacDonald-Allan Jones film (MM) *The Firefly*, 1937, and interpolated in the score of (MM) *The Chocolate Soldier*, 1941.

Symphony. w. Jack Lawrence (Engl.), m. Alex Alstone, 1945. A French song, "Symphonie," with original lyrics by André Tabet and Roger Bernstein. Best-selling record by Freddy Martin, vocal by Clyde Rogers (Victor). Others: Benny Goodman, vocal by Liza Morrow (Columbia); Bing Crosby (Decca); Jo Stafford (Capitol); Marlene Dietrich (Decca).

Symphony for Susan, A. w/m Bill Stegmeyer, 1966. Recorded by the two-pair-of-brothers quartet The Arbors (Mercury).

Symphony in Riffs. m. Benny Carter and Irving Mills, 1934. Introduced and recorded by Benny Carter and his Orchestra (Columbia). Tommy Dorsey and his Orchestra recorded it (Victor), 1939, followed a year later by Gene Krupa and his Orchestra (Columbia).

Synchronicity II. w/m Sting, 1983. Recorded by the British trio Police (A&M).

Syncopated Clock, The. m. Leroy Anderson, 1951. Anderson's first major hit as a composer and orchestra leader. His instrumental version sold over a million copies (Decca). Also recorded by The Boston Pops Orchestra, for whom he was arranger (RCA Victor), and organist Ethel Smith (Decca). It was the theme of TV's "The Late Show."

Syncopated Vamp, The. w/m Irving Berlin, 1920. From (TM) *Ziegfeld Follies of 1920.*

Syncopated Walk. w/m Irving Berlin, 1914. From (TM) *Watch Your Step.*

S.Y.S.L.J.F.M. (The Letter Song). w/m Joe Tex, 1966. Top 40 record by Joe Tex (Dial).

System of Survival. w/m Skylark, 1987. #1 R&B chart record by the group Earth, Wind & Fire (Columbia).

T

Table in the Corner, A. w. Sam Coslow, m. Dana Suesse, 1939. Recorded by Jimmy Dorsey, vocal by Bob Eberly (Decca); Artie Shaw, vocal by Helen Forrest (Bluebird); Jack Teagarden, vocal by Kitty Kallen (Columbia); Larry Clinton, vocal by Terry Allen (Victor); Del Courtney's Band (Vocalion).

Taboo. w. S. K. "Bob" Russell, m. Margarita Lecuona, 1942. Original Cuban title "Tabu," Spanish words by the composer. Instrumental version first recorded in U.S. by Vic Berton and his Orchestra (Vocalion), 1935. Enric Madriguera and his Orchestra had a popular record (Brunswick), 1939, as well as Sammy Kaye, with Tommy Ryan singing the English lyric (Victor), 1942. Many other treatments followed including those by the bands of Desi Arnaz (Victor), Stan Kenton (Capitol), Johnny Smith (Roost).

Tabu. See **Taboo.**

Tainted Love. w/m Ed Cobb, 1982. Top 10 record by the British duo Soft Cell (Sire).

'Taint Nobody's Bizness If I Do. w/m Clarence Williams, Porter Grainger, and Graham Prince, 1922. Recorded by Bessie Smith (Columbia), Alberta Hunter (Paramount), Frank Froeba (Columbia), and "Fats" Waller, in his first recording (Victor). Linda Hopkins sang it in (TM) *Me and Bessie*, 1975. André de Shields sang it in the Fats Waller musical (TM) *Ain't Misbehavin'* in 1978. Diana Ross sang it in (MM) *Lady Sings the Blues* in 1972.

Tain't No Sin (to Take Off Your Skin and Dance Around in Your Bones). w. Edgar Leslie, m. Walter Donaldson, 1929. Novelty, featured in vaudeville and on records by Lee Morse and Her Blue Grass Boys (Columbia) and Fred Hall's Sugar Babies (Okeh).

'Taint No Use. w. Herb Magidson, m. Burton Lane, 1936. Featured and recorded by Benny Goodman and his Orchestra, vocal by Benny Goodman (Victor).

'Tain't So, Honey, 'Tain't So. w/m Willard Robison, 1928. Popularly recorded by Paul Whiteman's Orchestra featuring Bing Crosby, with a Bill Challis arrangement (Victor).

'Taint What You Do (It's the Way That'Cha Do It). w/m Sy Oliver and James "Trummy" Young, 1939. Introduced and recorded by Jimmie Lunceford and his Orchestra, arranged by Sy Oliver. Also recorded by Chick Webb's Band, vocal by Ella Fitzgerald (Decca); and The Ramblers (Decca).

Take a Chance on Me. w/m Benny Anderson and Bjorn Ulvaeus, 1978. Top 10 gold record by the Swedish quartet Abba (Atlantic).

Take a Day Off, Mary Ann. w. Edward Harrigan, m. David Braham, 1891. From (TM) *The Last of the Hogans.*

Take a Lesson from the Lark. w. Leo Robin, m. Ralph Rainger, 1934. Introduced by Ben Bernie and his Orchestra in (MM) *Shoot the Works*.

Take a Letter, Maria. w/m R. B. Greaves, 1969. Gold record by R. B. Greaves (Atco).

Take a Letter, Miss Gray. w/m Justin Tubb, 1963. Hit Country record by Justin Tubb (Groove).

Take a Little One-Step. w. Zelda Sears, m. Vincent Youmans, 1924. Introduced by Ada May and Harry Puck in (TM) *Lollipop*. It was interpolated by Ruby Keeler, Patsy Kelly, and the company in the 1971 Broadway revival (TM) *No, No, Nanette*.

Take a Little Rhythm. w/m Ali Thompson, 1980. Recorded by the Scottish singer/songwriter Ali Thompson (A&M).

Take a Message to Mary. w/m Boudleaux Bryant and Felice Bryant, 1959. Recorded by The Everly Brothers (Cadence).

Take Another Guess. w/m Murray Mencher, Charles Newman, and Al Sherman, 1936. Featured and recorded by Chick Webb, vocal by Ella Fitzgerald (Decca), and Benny Goodman and his Orchestra (Victor).

Take a Number from One to Ten. w. Mack Gordon, m. Harry Revel, 1934. Introduced by Lyda Roberti and Jack Oakie in (MM) *College Rhythm*. Roberti (Columbia) and Oakie (Perfect) recorded the song individually. Kay Thompson, in her first recording, was heard with Tom Coakley's Band (Victor). The bands of Art Kassel (Bluebird) and Jimmie Grier (Brunswick) also cut it.

Take a Seat, Old Lady. w/m Paul Dresser, 1894. A ballad made popular by Meyer Cohen.

Take Back Your Gold. w/m Monroe H. Rosenfeld, 1897. Louis W. Pritzkow, a popular minstrel, was originally given credit for the words in return for introducing the song. It was popularized by Emma Carus and Imogene Comer in vaudeville.

Take Back Your Mink. w/m Frank Loesser, 1950. Introduced by Vivian Blaine in (TM) *Guys and Dolls*, and also sung by her in (MM) *Guys and Dolls*, 1955.

Take Care (When You Say "Te Quiero"). w/m Henry Pritchard, 1946. Introduced and recorded by Guy Lombardo and his Royal Canadians (Decca).

Take Care of Your Homework. w/m Homer Banks, Don Davis, Raymond Jackson, and Thomas Kelly, 1969. Top 20 record by Johnnie Taylor (Stax).

Take Five. w. Iola Brubeck, m. Paul Desmond, 1961. Instrumental hit, which would become a jazz standard, introduced by The Dave Brubeck Quartet (Columbia). Lyric added a year later and recorded by Carmen McRae with The Dave Brubeck Quartet (Columbia). Featured and recorded by Al Jarreau (Warner Bros.), 1977.

Take Good Care of Her. w/m Edward C. Warren and Arthur Kent, 1961. Top 10 record by Adam Wade (Coed). Later chart versions by Mel Carter (Imperial), 1966, and Elvis Presley (RCA), 1974.

Take Good Care of My Baby. w/m Gerry Goffin and Carole King, 1961. #1 record by Bobby Vee (Liberty). Revived by Bobby Vinton (Epic), 1968.

Take In the Sun, Hang Out the Moon. w. Sam M. Lewis and Joe Young, m. Harry Woods, 1926.

Take It Away. w/m Paul McCartney, 1982. Top 10 record by Paul McCartney (Columbia).

Take It Easy. w/m Andy Taylor and Steve Jones, 1986. Introduced by the English singer/guitarist Andy Taylor on the soundtrack of (MP) *American Anthem*, and on records (Atlantic).

Take It Easy. w/m Jackson Browne and Glenn Frey, 1972. Top 20 record by The Eagles (Asylum).

Take It Easy. w/m Albert DeBrue, Irving Taylor, and Vic Mizzy, 1943. Featured and recorded by Guy Lombardo and his Orchestra (Decca). Interpolated in (MM) *Two Girls and a Sailor* by Virginia O'Brien and Lina Romay with Xavier Cugat and his Orchestra, 1944. The same year, it was sung by Marion Hutton with Freddie Slack's Orchestra in (MM) *Babes on Swing Street*.

Take It Easy. w. Dorothy Fields, m. Jimmy McHugh, 1935. Sung by Alice Faye, Frances Langford, and Patsy Kelly in (MM) *Every Night at Eight*.

Take It Easy on Me. w/m Graham Goble, 1982. Top 10 record by the Australian group Little River Band (Capitol).

Take It from Me. w. Stanley Adams, m. Thomas "Fats" Waller, 1931. Among the recordings of note were those by Leo Reisman's Orchestra, vocal by Lee Wiley (Victor); The Sunshine Boys [Joe and Danny Mooney] (Columbia); Roy Fox, vocal by Al Bowlly (Br. Decca, released in the U.S.).

Take It on the Run. w/m Gary Richrath, 1982. Written by the lead guitarist of the group, REO Speedwagon, which had a Top 10 record (Epic).

Take It Slow, Joe. w. E. Y. Harburg, m. Harold Arlen, 1957. Introduced by Lena Horne in (TM) *Jamaica*.

Take It to the Limit. w/m Don Henley and Randy Meisner, 1976. Top 10 record by The Eagles (Asylum).

Take Me. w/m George Jones and Leon Payne, 1966. Hit Country record by George Jones (Musicor).

Take Me. w. Mack David, m. Rube Bloom, 1942. Featured and recorded by Tommy Dorsey, vocal by Frank Sinatra (Victor); Jimmy Dorsey, vocal by Helen O'Connell (Decca); Benny Goodman, vocal by Dick Haymes (Columbia).

Take Me (Just As I Am). w/m Dewey Lindon Oldham and Dan Pennington, 1967. Recorded by Solomon Burke (Atlantic).

Take Me Along. w/m Bob Merrill, 1959. Introduced by Jackie Gleason and Walter Pidgeon in (TM) *Take Me Along*.

Take Me Around Again. w. Ed Rose, m. Kerry Mills, 1907.

Take Me As I Am (or Let Me Go). w/m Boudleaux Bryant, 1968. Top 10 Country chart record by Ray Price (Columbia). Revived by Mack White (Commercial), 1976, and by Bobby Bare (Columbia), 1981.

Take Me Back. w/m Teddy Randazzo, 1965. Hit record by Little Anthony and The Imperials (DCP).

Take Me Back to Manhattan. w/m Cole Porter, 1930. Sung by Frances Williams in (TM) *The New Yorkers*.

Take Me Back to My Boots and Saddle. w/m Walter G. Samuels, Leonard Whitcup, and Teddy Powell, 1935. Introduced and recorded by Gene Autry (Vocalion). Among other recordings of note: Red Allen (Vocalion), John Charles Thomas (Victor), Victor Young's Orchestra (Decca), Jimmy Ray (Bluebird), whistler Fred Lowery (Columbia).

Take Me Back to New York Town. w. Andrew B. Sterling, m. Harry Von Tilzer, 1907.

Take Me Back to the Garden of Love. w. E. Ray Goetz, m. Nat Osborne, 1911.

Take Me Back to Your Heart Again. w. Collin Davis, m. Frank J. Richmond, 1905.

Take Me Down. w/m Mark Gray and James Pennington, 1982. #1 Country and Top 20 Pop hit recorded by the quartet Alabama (RCA).

Take Me for a Buggy Ride. w/m Wesley Wilson, 1933. Introduced and recorded by Bessie Smith (Okeh).

Take Me for a Little While. w/m Trade Martin, 1967. R&B and Pop chart record by Patti LaBelle and The Blue Belles (Atlantic). Top 40 version by Vanilla Fudge (Atco), 1968.

Take Me Home. w/m Phil Collins, 1986. Top 10 record by the English singer Phil Collins (Atlantic).

Take Me Home. w/m Michele Aller and Bob Esty, 1979. Top 10 gold record by Cher (Casablanca).

Take Me Home, Country Roads. w/m Bill Danoff, John Denver, and Taffy Nivert, 1971. John Denver's first gold record hit, back-up vocals by Fat City, the other two writers (RCA).

Take Me Home Tonight. w/m Mike Leeson, Peter Vale, Ellie Greenwich, Jeff Barry, and Phil Spector, 1986. Top 10 record by Eddie Money, with Ronnie Spector singing lines from her 1963 hit while lead singer of the Ronettes, "Be My Baby" (q.v.) (Columbia).

Take Me in Your Arms. w. Mitchell Parish (Engl.), m. Fred Markush, 1932. Original German words by Fritz Rotter and Markush. The song has been heard in (MM) *Hi, Buddy*, 1943, and (MM) *On Stage Everybody*, 1945. Featured on radio by Frank Parker, who later recorded it with Marion Marlowe (Columbia), and Arthur Tracy, "The Street Singer" (Brunswick). Subsequently revived by Don Cornell (Victor), Les Paul and Mary Ford (Capitol), Vic Damone (Mercury), Doris Day (Columbia), Hazel Scott (Decca).

Take Me in Your Arms (Rock Me). w/m Brian Holland, Lamont Dozier, and Eddie Holland, 1965, 1975. R&B/Pop record by Kim Weston (Gordy). Hit record by The Doobie Brothers (Warner Bros.), 1975.

Take Me in Your Arms and Hold Me. w/m Cindy Walker, 1950. Established by Eddy Arnold (RCA Victor) and followed two years later by Les Paul and Mary Ford with a Top 20 record (Capitol).

Take Me Out to the Ballgame. w. Jack Norworth, m. Albert Von Tilzer, 1908. One of Von Tilzer's (né Albert Gumm) most popular and long-lasting songs, which is still the anthem of "America's pastime." It was heard in the film biography of Nora Bayes and Jack Norworth (MM) *Shine On, Harvest Moon*, 1944. It also was the title song of the film (MM) *Take Me Out to the Ballgame*, 1949, featuring Gene Kelly, Frank Sinatra, and Esther Williams.

Take Me to Heart. w/m Marv Ross, 1983. Recorded by the group Quarterflash (Geffen).

Take Me to the Next Phase. w/m Ernie Isley, Marvin Isley, O'Kelly Isley, Ronald Isley, Rudolph Isley, and Chris Jasper, 1978. #1 R&B chart record by The Isley Brothers (T-Neck).

Take Me to the River. w/m Al Green and Mabon Hodges, 1973. Introduced by Al Green and his album "Call Me" (Hi). Popular single by Syl Johnson (Hi), 1975. Revived by The Talking Heads (Sire), 1978.

Take Me to Your World. w/m Billy Sherrill and Glen Sutton, 1968. #1 Country chart record by Tammy Wynette (Epic).

Take Me Up with You, Dearie. w. Junie McCree, m. Albert Von Tilzer, 1909.

Take My Breath Away (Love Theme from "Peter Gunn"). w/m Giorgio Moroder and Tom Whitlock, 1986. #1 hit single by the trio, Berlin, from the soundtrack of (MP) *Peter Gunn* (Columbia). Winner Academy Award, Best Song, 1986.

Take My Hand, Paree. w. E. Y. Harburg, m. Harold Arlen, 1961. Dubbed on the soundtrack by Judy Garland in the cartoon feature-length film (MM) *Gay Purr-ee*.

Take My Heart (and Do with It What You Please). w. Joe Young, m. Fred E. Ahlert, 1936. Featured and recorded by the bands of Eddy Duchin, vocal by Jerry Cooper (Victor); Nat Brandwynne (Brunswick); Jan Garber (Decca); Red Allen (Vocalion); pianist Lee Sims (Decca); later, singer Toni Arden (Columbia).

Take My Heart (You Can Have It If You Want It). w/m George Brown, Eumir Deodato, Charles Smith, James Taylor, 1981. Recorded by Kool & The Gang (De-Lite).

Take My Love (I Want to Give It All to You). w/m Mertis John, Jr., 1961. Crossover record (R&B/Pop) by Little Willie John (King).

Take My Ring off Your Finger. w/m Benny Joy and Hugh X. Lewis, 1964. Country hit record by Carl Smith (Columbia).

Taken In. w/m Mike Rutherford and Christopher Neil, 1986. Recorded by the quintet Mike + The Mechanics (Atlantic).

Take Off. w/m K. Crawford, M. Giacommelli, J. Goldsmith, Rick Moranis, Dave Thomas, 1982. Novelty record by the Canadian comedian/writers, Moranis and Thomas, recording as Bob and Doug McKenzie (Mercury).

Take on Me. w/m Pal Waaktaar, Mags Furuholem, and Morten Harket, 1985. #1 hit, written and recorded by the Norwegian trio A-Ha (Warner Bros.).

Taker, The. w/m Kris Kristofferson and Shel Silverstein, 1970. C&W/Pop chart hit by Waylon Jennings (RCA).

Takes Two to Make a Bargain. w. Mack Gordon, m. Harry Revel, 1935. Introduced in (MM) *Two for Tonight* and recorded (Decca) by Bing Crosby.

Takes Two to Tango. w/m Al Hoffman and Dick Manning, 1952. Hit record by Pearl Bailey, with Don Redman's Orchestra (Coral). Louis Armstrong also had a popular version (Decca).

Take Ten. m. Paul Desmond, 1963. Jazz instrumental by saxophonist Paul Desmond (RCA).

Take the "A" Train. w/m Billy Strayhorn, 1941. Strayhorn, arranging for the Duke Ellington Band, composed this reference to the Harlem express on the Eighth Avenue Line of the New York subway system. Ellington's recording (Victor) was a chart maker when first released, and again after he and the band performed it in (MM) *Reveille with Beverly*,

1943. It was the Ellington band theme for many years.

Take the Long Way Home. w/m Rick Davies and Roger Hodgson, 1979. Top 10 record by the British quintet Supertramp (A&M).

Take the Moment. w. Stephen Sondheim, m. Richard Rodgers, 1965. Introduced by Sergio Franchi in (TM) *Do I Hear a Waltz?*

Take the Money and Run. w/m Steve Miller, 1976. Recorded by Steve Miller (Capitol).

Take These Chains from My Heart. w/m Fred Rose and Hy Heath, 1953. Country hit by Hank Williams (MGM). Revived by Ray Charles, with a Top 10 hit (ABC-Paramount), 1963.

Take This Heart of Mine. w/m Warren Moore, William Robinson, and Marv Tarplin, 1966. Chart record by Marvin Gaye (Tamla).

Take This Job and Shove It. w/m David Allan Coe, 1977. Hit Country record by Johnny Paycheck (Epic).

Take Time. w/m Mel Tillis and Marijohn Wilkin, 1962. C&W hit by Webb Pierce (Decca).

Take Time to Know Her. w/m Steve Davis, 1968. Top 20 record by Percy Sledge (Atlantic).

Take Your Girlie to the Movies (If You Can't Make Love at Home). w. Edgar Leslie and Bert Kalmar, m. Pete Wendling, 1919. Popular recordings by Billy Murray (Victor) and Irving Kaufman (Columbia). Revived by Kay Kyser and his Orchestra in 1935 (Brunswick).

Take Your Time (Do It Right). w/m Harold Clayton and Sigidi, 1980. #1 R&B, #3 Pop chart platinum record by The S.O.S. Band (Tabu).

Take Your Tomorrow (and Give Me Today). w. Andy Razaf, m. J. C. Johnson, 1928. Popular record by Frankie Trumbauer, featuring cornetist Bix Beiderbecke (Okeh).

Takin' Care of Business. w/m Randy Bachman, 1974. Top 20 record from Canada by Bachman-Turner Overdrive (Mercury).

Taking a Chance on Love. w. John Latouche and Ted Fetter, m. Vernon Duke, 1940, 1943. Introduced by Ethel Waters in (TM) *Cabin in the Sky*, and reprised by her and Dooley Wilson. The song was added to the score three days before the Broadway opening. Duke and Fetter had written an earlier version titled "Fooling Around with Love," which Latouche, the lyricist for the show, altered to fit the character and the scene. It was sung by Waters and Eddie "Rochester" Anderson in the film version (MM) *Cabin in the Sky*, 1943, after which the revived song spent seventeen weeks on "Your Hit Parade."

Taking in the Town. w. Edward Harrigan, m. David Braham, 1890. From (TM) *Reilly and the 400*.

Takin' It Easy. w/m Lacy J. Dalton, Billy Sherrill, and Mark Sherrill, 1981. Introduced with Country chart record by Joey Davis (MRC), 1978. Lacy J. Dalton's version reached the #2 position (Columbia), 1981.

Takin' It to the Streets. w/m Michael McDonald, 1976. Written by the lead vocalist/keyboardist of the group, The Doobie Brothers, which had a Top 20 recording (Warner Bros.).

Tale of a Bumble Bee, The. w. Frank Pixley, m. Gustav Luders, 1901. One of the numerous titles by these writers starting with "The Tale of—." This one is from (TM) *King Dodo*.

Tale of an Oyster, The. w/m Cole Porter, 1929. Sung by Helen Broderick in (TM) *Fifty Million Frenchmen*.

Tale of the Kangaroo, The. w. Frank Pixley, m. Gustav Luders, 1900. From (TM) *The Burgomaster*. This was the first of this writing team's four hit song titles that started with "The Tale of—."

Tale of the Seashell. w. Frank Pixley, m. Gustav Luders, 1902. Sung by Arthur Donald-son and Lillian Coleman in (TM) *The Prince of Pilsen*.

Tale of the Turtle Dove, The. w. Frank Pixley, m. Gustav Luders, 1904. Another "Tale" song by the same writing team, this one from (TM) *Woodlands*, introduced by Margaret Sayre.

Talk, Talk. w/m Sean Bonniwell, 1966. Recorded by The Music Machine, quintet of which writer was lead singer (Original Sound).

Talk Back Trembling Lips. w/m John D. Loudermilk, 1963. First chart record by Ernest Ashworth (Hickory). Crossover (C&W/Pop) hit by Johnny Tillotson (MGM), 1964.

Talk Dirty to Me. w/m Bobby Dall, C. C. DeVille, Bret Michaels, and Rikki Rocket, 1987. Top 10 single by the quartet Poison (Enigma).

Talking in Your Sleep. w/m Jimmy Marinos, Wally Palmar, Mile Skill, Coz Canler, and Pete Solley, 1983. Top 10 record by the quartet The Romantics (Nemperor).

Talking in Your Sleep. w/m Roger Cook and Bobby Wood, 1978. C&W/Pop chart record by Crystal Gayle (United Artists).

Talkin' to My Heart. w/m Jimmy Dorsey and Anthony J. Franchini, 1940. Introduced and recorded by Jimmy Dorsey, vocal by Bob Eberly (Decca). Also recorded by Hal Kemp, with vocal by Janet Blair (Victor), and Bob Chester, with vocal by Dolores O'Neill (Bluebird).

Talkin' to Myself. w. Herb Magidson, m. Con Conrad, 1934. From (MM) *Gift of Gab*. Among band recordings: the California Ramblers, vocal by Sid Gary (Perfect); Orville Knapp (Decca); Leo Reisman (Brunswick); Ted Weems (Columbia); Raymond Paige (Victor).

Talkin' to the Wall. w/m Warner McPherson, 1966. Hit Country record by Warner Mack (Decca).

Talk It Over in the Morning. w/m Roger Nichols and Paul Williams, 1971. Recorded by Anne Murray (Capitol).

Talk Talk. w/m Edwin Hollis and Mark Hollis, 1982. Recorded by the British rock band Talk Talk with lead singer Mark Hollis (EMI America).

Talk That Talk. w/m Sid Wyche, 1959. Featured and recorded by Jackie Wilson (Brunswick).

Talk to Me. w/m Chas Sandford, 1985. Top 10 record by Stevie Nicks (Modern).

Talk to Me. w/m Eddie Snyder and Stanley J. Kahan, 1959. Top 40 record by Frank Sinatra (Capitol).

Talk to Me, Baby. w. Johnny Mercer, m. Robert Emmett Dolan, 1964. Introduced by Julienne Marie and John Davidson in (TM) *Foxy*. Recorded by Frank Sinatra (Reprise).

Talk to Me, Talk to Me. w/m Joe Seneca, 1958, 1963. Top 40 record by Little Willie John (King). Sunny and The Sunglows had a Top 20 record (Tear Drop) in 1963.

Talk to the Animals. w/m Leslie Bricusse, 1967. Introduced by Rex Harrison in (MM) *Doctor Doolittle*. Academy Award winner, 1967.

Tall, Dark Stranger. w/m Buck Owens, 1969. Hit Country record by Buck Owens and His Buckaroos (Capitol).

Tallahassee. w/m Frank Loesser, 1947. Introduced by Dorothy Lamour and Alan Ladd in (MM) *Variety Girl*. Popular records by Bing Crosby and The Andrews Sisters (Decca), and Dinah Shore and Woody Herman (Columbia).

Tallahassee Lassie. w/m Frank C. Slay, Jr., Bob Crewe, and Frederick A. Picariello, 1959. Top 10 record by Freddy Cannon (Swan).

Tall Hope. w. Carolyn Leigh, m. Cy Coleman, 1960. Introduced in (TM) *Wildcat* by Bill Walker, Swen Swenson, Ray Mason, Charles Braswell, and the Crew.

Tall Paul. w/m Bob Roberts, Robert Sherman, and Richard Sherman, 1959. First record success by Annette [Funicello] (Disneyland).

Tambourin Chinois. m. Fritz Kreisler, 1910. One of the five popular pieces for violin and piano Kreisler composed this year. It was interpolated in (TM) *Apple Blossoms*, 1919, and danced to by Fred and Adele Astaire.

T.A.M.I. Show Theme. See **(Here They Come) from All over the World.**

Tamiami Trail. w/m Cliff Friend and Joseph H. Santly, 1926. Popular song with vaudeville performers. Leading record, Ben Selvin and his Orchestra (Vocalion).

Tammany. w. Vincent P. Bryan, m. Gus Edwards, 1905. The song was interpolated in (TM) *Fantana* by Jefferson De Angelis. It was originally written, satirically, for a political party in New York City. The melody later became familiar to wide audiences as the theme song for "Singin' Sam, the Barbasol Man" who was sponsored by the shaving cream company on radio in the thirties.

Tammy. w/m Jay Livingston and Ray Evans, 1957. Introduced by Debbie Reynolds in (MP) *Tammy and the Bachelor*. Nominated for Academy Award, 1957. Reynolds had her only #1 hit record with this song (Coral). The Ames Brothers (RCA) also had a popular version.

Tampico. w/m Allan Roberts and Doris Fisher, 1945. Stan Kenton, with vocal by June Christy, had a million-seller with their recording (Capitol).

Tangerine. w. Johnny Mercer, m. Victor Schertzinger, 1942. Introduced by Jimmy Dorsey and his Orchestra, vocal by Bob Eberly and Helen O'Connell in (MM) *The Fleet's In*. Their record was one of the biggest hits of the year (Decca). Revived with an instrumental disco version by The Salsoul Orchestra (Salsoul), 1976.

Tangled Mind. w/m Ted Daffan and Herman Shoss, 1957. Recorded by Hank Snow. (RCA).

Tangled Up in Blue. w/m Bob Dylan, 1975. Chart single by Bob Dylan (Columbia).

Tapestry. w/m Carole King, 1971. Title song of Carole King's album (Ode).

Tapioca Tundra. w/m Michael Nesmith, 1968. Recorded by The Monkees (Colgems).

Tar and Cement. w. Lee Pockriss and Paul Vance (Engl.), m. Adriano Celentano, 1966. Original Italian title "Il Ragazzo della Via Gluck," lyrics by Luciano Beretta and Michel Del Prete. U.S. Top 40 record by Verdelle Smith (Capitol).

Ta-Ra-Ra-Boom-De-Re. w/m Henry J. Sayers, 1891. This song, while written in St. Louis, was introduced in London, England by Lottie Collins. In 1892, her performances at Koster and Bial's Theatre in New York launched its U.S. success. As some folk material has been found in an old German song book, numerous authors and composers have made slight alterations in the song and spelling of the title and have claimed authorship. Best-selling recordings by Len Spencer (Columbia) and the U.S. Marine Band, directed by John Philip Sousa (Columbia). It has been heard in (MM) *Happy Go Lucky*, 1943, and under the titles in (MM) *Mother Wore Tights*, 1947.

Tara's Theme. m. Max Steiner, 1939. Prominent theme from (MP) *Gone with the Wind*. Lyrics written in 1954 by Mack David, under new title (see "My Own True Love").

Tara Talara Tala. w/m Marty Symes and Johnny Farrow, 1948. Featured and recorded by Dennis Day (Victor) and Frankie Laine (Mercury).

Tarkio Road. w/m Charles Brewer and Thomas Shipley, 1971. Recorded by Brewer and Shipley (Kama Sutra).

Tar Paper Stomp. m. Joe Garland and Wingy Manone, 1937. Instrumental recorded by Wingy Manone and his Band (Champion). A revision of this number by Garland became the famous "In The Mood" (q.v.).

Tarzan Boy. w/m Naimy Hackett and Maurizio Bassi, 1986. Recorded by Baltimore, pseudonym for Northern Irish singer Jimmy McShane (Manhattan).

Taste of Honey, A. w. Ric Marlow, m. Bobby Scott, 1962. Music introduced by pianist/composer Bobby Scott and his Combo on Broadway in (TP) *A Taste of Honey*. Instrumental chart records by The Victor Feldman Quartet (Infinity) and Martin Denny and his Orchestra (Liberty). First chart vocal record by Tony Bennett (Columbia), 1964. Hit recording and triple Grammy Award (NARAS) winner by Herb Alpert and The Tijuana Brass (A&M), 1965.

Taste of Your Love. w/m Marvin Ennis, Harold Lloyd, and Steven Franco, 1989. Hit R&B chart single by E.U. (Virgin).

Tasty Love. w/m Paul Laurence and Freddie Jackson, 1986. Single from the album "Just Like the First Time," by Freddie Jackson (Capitol).

Ta Ta. w/m Clyde McPhatter and Jimmy Oliver, 1960. Introduced and recorded by Clyde McPhatter (Mercury).

Taurus. m. Dennis Coffey, 1972. Instrumental by Dennis Coffey and The Detroit Guitar Band (Sussex).

Taxi. w/m Homer Banks and Charles Brooks, 1984. Recorded by J. Blackfoot (Sound Town).

Taxi. w/m Harry Chapin, 1972. Recorded by Harry Chapin (Elektra).

Tchaikowsky (and Other Russians). w. Ira Gershwin, m. Kurt Weill, 1941. The number that made Danny Kaye a star when he introduced it in (TM) *Lady in the Dark*. It was based on a humorous poem, "The Music Hour," which seventeen years earlier, Ira Gershwin, under the pseudonym of Arthur Francis, wrote for a popular magazine. In it he listed the names of forty-nine Russian composers. The song was not included in the film version . . . nor was Danny Kaye! His performance was preserved on records (Decca).

Teacher, Teacher. w. Al Stillman, m. Robert Allen, 1958. Popularized by Johnny Mathis (Columbia).

Teacher's Pet. w/m Joe Lubin, 1958. Introduced by Doris Day in (MP) *Teacher's Pet*, starring Day and Clark Gable. Recorded by Day (Columbia).

Teacher Teacher. w/m Bryan Adams and James Vallance, 1984. From (MP) *Teachers*. Recorded by the sextet 38 Special (A&M).

Teach Me Tonight. w. Sammy Cahn, m. Gene de Paul, 1954. First record by Janet Brace, with Jack Pleis's Orchestra (Decca). Jo Stafford had a hit record (Capitol), followed a year later by the De Castro Sisters (Abbott).

Teach Your Children. w/m Graham Nash, 1970. Top 20 record by Crosby, Stills, Nash & Young (Atlantic).

Tea for Two. w. Irving Caesar, m. Vincent Youmans, 1925. This, one of the most performed songs of all time, was introduced by Louise Groody, Jack Barker, and chorus in (TM) *No, No, Nanette*, with hit records by Marion Harris (Brunswick), The Benson Orchestra (Victor), and Ben Bernie and his Orchestra (Vocalion). The latter two were instrumentals. In the 1971 Broadway production, it was sung by Susan Watson, Roger Rathburn, and chorus. It has been recorded hundreds of times and translated into dozens of languages. In 1958, Warren Covington and his Orchestra (Decca) had a #1 hit, "Tea for Two Cha Cha." It has been heard in many films including (MM) *No, No, Nanette*, 1930 and 1940; (MM) *Tea for Two*, 1950, performed by Doris Day, Gordon MacRae, and Gene Nelson; (MM) *With a Song in My Heart*, 1952, the Jane Froman story in which she dubbed her voice on the soundtrack for Susan Hayward; (MM) *Sincerely Yours*, 1955; (MM) *Jazz on a Summer's Day*, 1960.

Tea Leaves. w/m Morty Berk, Frank Capano, and Max C. Freedman, 1948. Leading records by Jack Smith (Capitol); the a capella group, The Emile Cote Serenaders (Columbia); Ella Fitzgerald (Decca).

Tea Leaves. w. Raymond B. Egan, m. Richard A. Whiting, 1921. Featured and recorded by Nora Bayes (Columbia).

Teamwork. w. Sammy Cahn, m. James Van Heusen, 1962. Introduced by Bing Crosby, Bob Hope, and Joan Collins in (MM) *The Road to Hong Kong*.

Tea on the Terrace. w/m Sam Coslow, 1937. Introduced and recorded by Tommy Dorsey, vocal by Edythe Wright (Victor).

Tear Drop. m. Ann Farina, John Farina, and Santo Farina, 1959. Instrumental recorded by Santo and Johnny (Canadian-American).

Teardrops from My Eyes. w/m Rudolph Toombs, 1950. R&B hit by Ruth Brown (Atlantic).

Teardrops in My Heart. w/m Vaughn Horton, 1947. Hit record by The Sons of the Pioneers (Victor). Revived by Rex Allen, Jr. (Warner Bros.), 1976, and Marty Robbins (Columbia), 1981.

Teardrops on Your Letter. w/m Henry Glover, 1959. Recorded by Hank Ballard and The Midnighters (King).

Teardrops Will Fall. w/m Marion Smith and Dave Alldred, 1959. Featured by Dicky Doo [Dave Alldred] and The Don'ts (Swan).

Tear Fell, A. w/m Dorian Burton and Eugene Randolph, 1956. Top 10 record by Teresa Brewer (Coral). Revived in 1964 by Ray Charles (ABC-Paramount).

Tears and Laughter. w/m Miriam Lewis, 1962. Introduced and recorded by Dinah Washington (Mercury).

Tears Broke Out on Me. w/m Hank Cochran, 1962. C&W hit by Eddy Arnold (RCA).

Tears from My Inkwell. w. Mort Dixon, m. Harry Warren, 1939. Dixon's last popular song. Popularized by the recording and performances of Glen Gray and the Casa Loma Orchestra, vocal by Kenny Sargent (Decca). Red Nichols and his Band also had a well-received version (Bluebird).

Tears of a Clown, The. w/m Henry Cosby, William "Smokey" Robinson, and Stevie

Wonder, 1970. #1 record by The Miracles (Tamla).

Tears of Rage. w. Bob Dylan, m. Richard Manuel, 1968. Recorded in albums by The Band (Capitol), Ian and Sylvia (MGM), Joan Baez (Vanguard).

Tears of the Lonely. w/m Wayland Holyfield, 1982. Top 10 Country chart record by Mickey Gilley (Epic).

Tears on My Pillow. w/m Sylvester Bradford and Al Lewis, 1958. Hit record by Little Anthony and The Imperials (End).

Tears on My Pillow. w/m Gene Autry and Fred Rose, 1941. Introduced and recorded by Gene Autry (Okeh). Louise Massey and The Westerners also had a popular record (Okeh).

Tear the Roof Off the Sucker (Give Up the Funk). w/m George Clinton, Bootsie Collins, and Jerome Brailey, 1976. R&B/Pop chart gold record by the group Parliament (Casablanca).

Tear Time. w/m Jan Crutchfield, 1967, 1978. Country chart record by Wilma Burgess (Decca). Revived with #1 C&W chart record by the trio Dave & Sugar (RCA), 1978.

Teasin'. w/m Bob Carlton, J. Brandon Walsh, and Paul Biese, 1922. Featured and recorded by Vincent Lopez and his Orchestra (Okeh).

Teasing. w. Cecil Mack, m. Albert Von Tilzer, 1904.

Teasin' You. w/m Earl King Johnson, 1965. Recorded by Willie Tee (Atlantic).

Teddy. w/m Paul Anka, 1959. Recorded by Connie Francis (MGM).

Teddy Bear. w/m Red Sovine, Billy Joe Burnette, Tommy Hill, and Dale Royal, 1976. Spoken word C&W/Pop chart gold record by Red Sovine (Starday).

(Let Me Be Your) Teddy Bear. w/m Kal Mann and Bernie Lowe, 1957. Introduced by Elvis Presley in (MM) *Loving You*, and on #1 record (RCA).

Teddy Bears' Picnic, The. w/m John W. Bratton and James B. Kennedy, 1913.

Teen Age Crush. w/m Audrey Allison and Joe Allison, 1957. Introduced by Tommy Sands in (TVM) "The Singing Idol." His recording became the #2 best-seller and his biggest hit (Capitol).

Teen Age Idol. w/m Jack Lewis, 1962. Top 10 record by Ricky Nelson (Imperial).

Teen Age Prayer. w/m Bix Reichner and Bernie Lowe, 1956. Hit record by Gale Storm (Dot).

Teenager in Love, A. w/m Doc Pomus and Mort Shuman, 1959. Top 10 hit by Dion and The Belmonts (Laurie).

Teenager's Romance, A. w/m David Gillam, 1957. Ricky Nelson's first hit record (Verve).

Teen Angel. w/m Jean Surrey and Red Surrey, 1960. Hit record by Mark Dinning (MGM). Revived by the quartet Wednesday (Sussex), 1974.

Teen Beat. m. Sander Nelson and Arthur Egnoian, 1959. Instrumental record by R&R drummer Sandy Nelson (Original Sound). Nelson recorded a later version called "Teen Beat," 1965 (Imperial).

Teeter Totter Tessie. w. Nancy Hamilton, m. Morgan Lewis, 1939. Introduced by Grace McDonald and Gene Kelly in (TM) *One for the Money*. Recorded by Ted Straeter (Liberty Music Shops).

Telefone (Long Distance Love Affair). w/m Gregory Mathieson and Trevor Veitch, 1983. Top 10 record by the Scottish singer Sheena Easton (EMI America).

Telephone Hour, The. w. Lee Adams, m. Charles Strouse, 1960. Introduced by the teenagers from Sweet Apple, Ohio, in (TM) *Bye Bye Birdie*, and by Bobby Rydell and the teenagers in (MM) *Bye Bye Birdie*, 1963.

Telephone Line. w/m Jeff Lynne, 1977. Top 10 gold record by the British group Electric Light Orchestra (United Artists).

Telephone Man. w/m Meri Wilson, 1977. Novelty hit by Meri Wilson (GRT).

Tell All the Folks in Kentucky. w/m Irving Berlin, 1923.

Tell All the People. w/m Robbie Krieger, 1969. Recorded by The Doors (Elektra).

Tell Another Lie. w. Randy Starr and Fred Wise, m. Christian Bruhn, 1965. Introduced and recorded by Country singer Connie Smith (RCA).

Tell Her About It. w/m Billy Joel, 1983. From his album "An Innocent Man," Billy Joel's single became a #1 record (Columbia).

Tell Her for Me. w/m Selma Craft and Morty Craft, 1960. Recorded by Adam Wade (Coed).

Tell Her in the Springtime. w/m Irving Berlin, 1924. Introduced by Grace Moore in (TM) *Music Box Revue of 1924*. Recorded by Moore (Victor), Paul Whiteman and his Orchestra (Victor), Sam Lanin (Columbia).

Tell Her No. w/m Rod Argent, 1964. Recorded in England by The Zombies, rock quintet of which the writer was a member. Top 10 U.S. record (Parrot). Revived by Juice Newton (Capitol), 1983.

Tell Her So. w/m Glenn D. Tubb, 1963. Country chart records by The Wilburn Brothers (Decca) and Ernest Tubb (Decca).

Tell Her You Love Her Each Day. See **Tell Her You Love Her Every Day.**

Tell Her You Love Her Every Day. w/m Gil Ward and Charles Watkins, 1965. Featured and recorded by Frank Sinatra (Reprise).

Tell Him. w/m Bert Russell, 1963. Top 10 record by The Exciters (United Artists).

Tell Him No. w/m Travis Pritchett, 1959. Introduced and leading record by Travis and Bob (Sandy). Also recorded by Dean and Marc (Bullseye).

Telling It to the Daisies. w. Joe Young, m. Harry Warren, 1930. Popular records by Gene Austin (Victor), Annette Hanshaw (Harmony), Nick Lucas (Brunswick).

Telling Me Lies. w/m Linda Thompson and Betsy Cook, 1987. English song introduced by co-writer Linda Thompson on the album "Can't Stop the Girl" (Warner Bros.), 1986. Hit Country chart version by Dolly Parton, Linda Ronstadt, and Emmylou Harris, from their album "Trio" (Warner Bros.).

Tell It All Brother. w/m Alex Harvey, 1970. Top 20 record by Kenny Rogers and The First Edition (Reprise).

Tell It All Over Again. w. Henry Blossom, m. Victor Herbert, 1914. From (TM) *The Only Girl*.

Tell It Like It Is. w/m George Davis and Lee Diamond, 1967. Hit record by Aaron Neville (Par-Lo). Revived by Andy Williams (Columbia), 1976, and by the Top 10 record of the rock band Heart (Epic), 1980.

Tell It to My Heart. w/m Seth Swirsky and Ernie Gold, 1987. Top 10 record by the female disco singer Taylor Dayne (Arista).

Tell It to the Rain. w/m Mike Petrillo and Chubby Cifelli, 1967. Top 10 record by The Four Seasons (Philips).

Tell Laura I Love Her. w/m Jeff Barry and Ben Raleigh, 1960. Introduced and Top 10 record by Ray Peterson (RCA).

Tell Mama. w/m Clarence Carter, Marcus Daniel, and Wilbur Terrell, 1969. Top 40 record by Etta James (Cadet).

Tell Me. w/m Dick St. John Gosting, 1962. Recorded by Dick and Deedee (Liberty).

Tell Me, Dusky Maiden, w. Bob Cole and James W. Johnson, m. J. Rosamond Johnson, 1902. From (TM) *Sleeping Beauty and the Beast*. Popular recording by Arthur Collins and Joe Natus (Edison).

Tell Me, Little Gypsy. w/m Irving Berlin, 1920. Sung by John Steel in (TM) *Ziegfeld Follies of 1920*. Recorded by John Steel (Victor) and Art Hickman and his Orchestra (Columbia).

Tell Me, Tell Me Evening Star. w. E. Y. Harburg, m. Harold Arlen, 1944. Introduced by Marlene Dietrich in (MP) *Kismet*. This third non-musical film version of the Arabian Nights-type tale is not to be confused with the stage and screen musical of the fifties.

Tell Me, What Is Love? w/m Noël Coward, 1929. Introduced in the U.S. By Evelyn Laye in (TM) *Bitter Sweet*, after its London production, in which it was sung by Peggy Wood. Anna Neagle sang it in the first film version [British], 1933, and Jeanette MacDonald and Nelson Eddy sang a duet in (MM) *Bitter Sweet*, 1940.

Tell Me (Why Nights Are Lonely). w. J. Will Callahan, m. Max Kortlander, 1919. The song was revived in Ted Lewis's screen biography (MM) *Is Everybody Happy?*, 1943, and in (MM) *On Moonlight Bay*, 1951, in which it was sung by Doris Day.

Tell Me (You're Coming Back). w/m Mick Jagger and Keith Richards, 1964. Early hit record by the British group The Rolling Stones (London).

Tell Me a Bedtime Story. w/m Irving Berlin, 1923. Grace Moore made her debut singing this in the opening scene of (TM) *Music Box Revue of 1923*.

Tell Me a Lie. w/m Barbara Wyrick and Mickey Buckins, 1974. Country/Pop crossover record by Sami Jo [Cole] (MGM South). Janie Fricke revived it with a #1 Country chart version (Columbia).

Tell Me a Story. w/m Terry Gilkyson, 1953. Hit record by Frankie Laine and Jimmy Boyd (Columbia).

Tell Me a Story. w. Maurice Sigler, m. Larry Stock, 1948. Featured and recorded by Sammy Kaye, vocal by Don Cornell (RCA Victor).

Tell Me Daddy. w/m Bobby Black, 1948. Recorded by Julia Lee (Capitol).

Tell Me on a Sunday. w. Don Black, m. Andrew Lloyd Webber, 1985. Introduced in

London by Marti Webb in (TM) *Tell Me on a Sunday*. Introduced in the U.S. by Bernadette Peters in (TM) *Song and Dance*.

Tell Me Pretty Maiden (Are There Any More at Home Like You?). w. Owen Hall, m. Leslie Stuart (Thomas A. Barrett), 1900. The famous sextet from (TM) *Florodora*, the English operetta of 1889, which was a hit in New York the following year. Popular records by Byron G. Harlan and Joe Belmont and The Florodora Girls (Columbia), and Harry MacDonough and Grace Spencer (Edison).

Tell Me Something Good. w/m Stevie Wonder, 1974. Gold record by the soul group Rufus (ABC).

Tell Me That You Love Me. w. Al Stillman (Engl.), m. C. A. Bixio, 1935. Original Italian song, "Parlami d'Amore, Mariu," had lyrics by Ennio Neri. This was Stillman's first song success, written under name of Silverman. Song introduced in the U. S. on radio by Frank Parker. Lily Pons was among artists who recorded it (Columbia).

Tell Me the Truth. w/m George Harold Jackson and Dimple Marcene Jackson, 1963. Introduced and recorded by Nancy Wilson (Capitol).

Tell Me Tomorrow. w/m Gary Goetzman and Mike Piccirillo, 1982. Recorded by Smokey Robinson (Tamla).

Tell Me to My Face. w/m Allan Clarke, Tony Hicks, and Graham Nash, 1967. Written and published in England and recorded in the U.S. by the Philadelphian, Keith (Mercury).

Tell Me What It's Like. w/m Ben Peters, 1979. Top 10 Country chart record by Brenda Lee (MCA).

Tell Me Why. w/m John Lennon and Paul McCartney, 1964. Introduced by The Beatles in (MM) *A Hard Day's Night*.

Tell Me Why. w/m Titus Turner, 1956. Chart records by The Crew Cuts (Mercury) and Gale Storm (Dot). Revived by Elvis Presley (RCA), 1966.

Tell Me Why. w. Al Alberts, m. Marty Gold, 1952. Million-selling records by The Four Aces, of whom Alberts was lead singer (Decca); and Eddie Fisher, with Hugo Winterhalter's Orchestra (RCA Victor). Revived by Bobby Vinton (Epic), 1964.

Tell Me Why. w. Milt Gabler, m. Maurice Hartmann, 1949. Featured and recorded by Eddy Howard (Mercury).

Tell Me Why You Smile, Mona Lisa. w. Raymond B. Egan (Engl.), Walter Reisch (Ger.), m. Robert Stolz, 1932. The original German title was "Warum lächelst du, Mona Lisa?" Featured by Frank Munn and recorded by him with Victor Young's Orchestra (Brunswick).

Tell Me With a Love Song. w. Ted Koehler, m. Harold Arlen, 1931. Introduced by Kate Smith on radio and recorded by Paul Whiteman and his Orchestra, with vocal by Jack Fulton (Victor).

Tell Me You Love Me. w/m Sammy Kaye, 1951. Adapted from the aria "Vesti la Giubba," from Leoncavallo's opera *I Pagliacci*. Leading record by Vic Damone (Mercury).

Tell Me You're Mine. w. Ronnie Vincent (Engl.), m. D. Vasin, 1953. Original Italian song, "Per un Bacio d'Amore," words by U. Bertini. Million-seller by The Gaylords (Mercury).

Telstar. m. Joe Meek, 1962. Instrumental by the British surf-rock group The Tornadoes (London).

Temma Harbour. w/m Philamore Lincoln, 1970. Top 40 record from England by Mary Hopkin (Apple).

Tempo of the Times, The. w. Carolyn Leigh, m. Cy Coleman, 1960. Introduced in the cabaret revue *Medium Rare*, starring Stiller and Meara, and Bobo Lewis, at the Happy Medium in Chicago, Ill.

Temptation. w. Arthur Freed, m. Nacio Herb Brown, 1933. Introduced by Bing Crosby in (MM) *Going Hollywood*, and on a best-selling record (Brunswick). Later heard in (MM) *A Date with Judy*, 1948; (MM) *The Seven Hills of Rome*, sung by Mario Lanza, 1958; (MM) *Viva Las Vegas*, 1964. In 1947 Jo Stafford, under the pseudonym of Cinderella G. Stump, with Red Ingle and His Natural Seven recorded a #1 novelty hit version, "Timtayshun" (Capitol). Top 40 record by The Everly Brothers (Warner Bros.), 1961.

Temptation Eyes. w/m Harvey Price and Dan Walsh, 1971. Top 20 record by The Grass Roots (Dunhill).

Tempted. w/m Chris Difford and Glenn Tilbrook, 1981. Recorded by the writer-led British quintet, Squeeze, vocal by Paul Carrack (A&M).

Ten Cents a Dance. w. Lorenz Hart, m. Richard Rodgers, 1930. Introduced by Ruth Etting in (TM) *Simple Simon* starring Ed Wynn. Etting also recorded it (Columbia). Doris Day sang it as Ruth Etting in her film biography (MM) *Love Me or Leave Me*, 1955.

Tender Is the Night. w/m Russ Kunkel, Danny Kortchmar, and Jackson Browne, 1983. Recorded by Jackson Browne (Asylum).

Tender Is the Night. w. Paul Francis Webster, m. Sammy Fain, 1962. Introduced by Earl Grant in (MP) *Tender Is the Night*, starring Jennifer Jones and Jason Robards. Song nominated for Academy Award, 1962.

Tender Is the Night. w. Harold Adamson, m. Walter Donaldson, 1935. Introduced by Harry Stockwell and Virginia Bruce in (MM) *Here Comes the Band*.

Tender Lie, A. w/m Randy Sharp, 1988. #1 Country chart record by the group Restless Heart (RCA).

Tender Love. w/m James Harris III and Terry Lewis, 1986. Introduced by the soul/rap quintet, Force M.D.'s, in (MM) *Krush Groove*, 1985. Their single, included in their album "Chillin'," was a Top 10 R&B and Pop chart entry (Warner Bros.).

Tenderly. w. Jack Lawrence, m. Walter Gross, 1946. Major standard introduced by Clark Dennis (Capitol). Often recorded by singers and jazz musicians. Sarah Vaughan had an early popular recording (Musicraft). Rosemary Clooney's 1952 version was a million-seller over a period of time (Columbia). The song was played in (MM) *Torch Song*, starring Joan Crawford, 1953.

Tender Shepherd. w. Carolyn Leigh, m. Moose Charlap, 1954. Introduced by Margalo Gillmore, Robert Harrington, Kathy Nolan, and Joseph Stafford in (TM) *Peter Pan*.

Tender Trap, The. w. Sammy Cahn, m. James Van Heusen, 1955. Introduced by Frank Sinatra in (MP) *The Tender Trap*, and hit recording by him (Capitol). Nominated for Academy Award.

Tender Years. w/m Darrell Edwards, 1961. Crossover (C&W/Pop) record by George Jones (Mercury).

Tend to Your Business. w/m Dave Bartholomew, 1951. R&B record by James Waynes (Sittin' in).

Ten Little Bottles. w. Ballard MacDonald, m. James V. Monaco, 1920. Comedy song featured in vaudeville and recorded by Bert Williams (Columbia). Johnny Bond, Western movie and radio actor, recorded it twice: (Columbia), 1945, and (Starday), 1965.

Ten Little Fingers and Ten Little Toes (Down in Tennessee). w. Harry Pease and Johnny White, m. Ira Schuster and Ed. G. Nelson, 1921. Popular records by Irving Kaufman (Columbia) and Billy Murray and Ed Smalle (Victor).

Ten Little Miles from Town. w. Gus Kahn, m. Elmer Schoebel, 1928.

Tennessee Birdwalk. w/m Jack Blanchard, 1970. Hit C&W/Pop novelty record by Jack Blanchard and Misty Morgan (Wayside).

Tennessee Border. w/m Jimmy Work, 1949. Introduced by Jimmy Work (Bullet). Red Foley (Decca) had the best-seller.

Tennessee Border No. 2. w. Henry B. Haynes [Homer] and Kenneth C. Burns [Jethro], m. Jimmy Work, 1950. Homer and Jethro's follow-up to "Tennessee Border." Best-seller by Red Foley and Ernest Tubb (Decca).

Tennessee Fish Fry. w. Oscar Hammerstein II, m. Arthur Schwartz, 1940. From the New York World's Fair production (TM) *American Jubilee*. Leading recordings by Mildred Bailey (Columbia), Kay Kyser and his Orchestra (Columbia).

Tennessee Flat-Top Box. w/m Johnny Cash, 1962, 1987. Introduced and recorded by Johnny Cash (Columbia). Cash's daughter, Roseanne Cash, had a #1 Country chart record fifteen years later (Columbia).

Tennessee Homesick Blues. w/m Dolly Parton, 1984. #1 Country chart record by Dolly Parton (RCA).

Tennessee Moon. w/m Jean Branch and Cowboy Copas, 1948. C&W chart hit by Cowboy Copas (King).

Tennessee Polka. w/m Pee Wee King, 1949. Leading recordings by Red Foley (Decca) and Pee Wee King (RCA Victor).

Tennessee River. w/m Randy Owen, 1980. The first of twenty-one consecutive #1 Country chart records by the quartet, Alabama, of which Owen was guitarist (RCA).

Tennessee Saturday Night. w/m Billy Hughes, 1949. Hit song by Red Foley (Decca), followed by Ella Mae Morse (Capitol), and The Pied Pipers (RCA Victor).

Tennessee Stud. w/m Jimmy Driftwood, 1959. Hit C&W and Pop chart record by Eddy Arnold (RCA).

Tennessee Tango. w/m Redd Stewart and Pee Wee King, 1952. One of four C&W chart "Tennessee" songs by King, "Tennessee Waltz," "Tennessee Polka," and "Tennessee Tears" (q.v.) being the others. This was introduced and recorded by Pee Wee King, vocal by Redd Stewart (RCA Victor). Also recorded by Eileen Barton (Coral) and Francis Craig and his Orchestra (MGM).

Tennessee Tears. w/m Pee Wee King and Ernie Lee, 1949. Leading record by Pee Wee King (RCA Victor).

Tennessee Waltz. w/m Redd Stewart and Pee Wee King, 1950. Introduced and recorded (RCA Victor) by Pee Wee King, vocal by Redd Stewart, 1948. Two years later Patti Page's recording (Mercury) sold three million copies. The song was on "Your Hit Parade" for fifteen weeks, six times as #1, and with many recordings by top artists. Fifteen years later it became Tennessee's official state song. Later chart records by Bobby Comstock (Blaze), 1959; Jerry Fuller (Challenge), 1959; Sam Cooke (RCA), 1964.

Tennessee Wig Walk. w. Norman Gimbel, m. Larry Coleman, 1953. C&W chart record by Bonnie Lou (King).

Ten Pins in the Sky. w. Joseph McCarthy, m. Milton Ager, 1938. Introduced by Judy Garland in (MM) *Listen, Darling*. Recorded by Clyde McCoy and his Orchestra (Decca).

Tenth Avenue Freeze-Out. w/m Bruce Springsteen. 1976. Recorded by Bruce Springsteen (Columbia).

Ten Thousand Drums. w/m Mel Tillis and Carl Smith, 1959. Crossover hit by C&W star Carl Smith (Columbia).

Ten Thousand Years from Now. w. J. Keirn Brennan, m. Ernest R. Ball, 1923.

Tequila. m. Chuck Rio, 1958. Instrumental hit, #1 on Pop and R&B charts by The Champs (Challenge). Winner Grammy Award (NARAS) for Rhythm and Blues Song of the Year.

Tequila Sunrise. w/m Glenn Frey and Don Henley, 1973. Recorded by The Eagles (Asylum).

Teresa. w. Jack Hoffman, m. Babe Russin, 1948. Popularized by Dick Haymes and The Andrews Sisters (Decca).

Terry Theme, The. See **Eternally**.

Tessie, You Are the Only, Only, Only. w/m Will R. Anderson, 1902. Interpolated in the English import (TM) *The Silver Slipper*.

Tess's Torch Song. w. Ted Koehler, m. Harold Arlen, 1943. Introduced by Dinah Shore in (MM) *Up in Arms*. Ella Mae Morse had the best-selling record (Capitol).

Texarkana Baby. w/m Fred Rose and Cottonseed Clark, 1948. Leading record by Eddy Arnold (RCA Victor).

Texas Blues. w/m Cottonseed Clark and Foy Willing, 1944. Best-selling Country hit records by Foy Willing (Capitol) and Bob Wills (MGM).

Texas Tornado. w. Sidney D. Mitchell, m. Lew Pollack, 1936. One of three songs sung by Judy Garland in her first feature film (MM) *Pigskin Parade*, in which she was given ninth billing.

T for Texas (a.k.a. **Blue Yodel No. 1**). w/m Jimmie Rodgers, 1963. This version of "Blue Yodel" (q.v.) by Grandpa Jones became a Country chart hit (Monument). Revived by Tompall and His Outlaw Band (Polydor), 1976.

Thank God I'm a Country Boy. w/m John Martin Sommers, 1975. Originally recorded by John Denver for his album "Back Home Again" (RCA), 1974. Written by Denver's guitarist, the single version was next recorded live at Denver's concert performance at the Universal Amphitheatre in California and became a #1 gold record.

Thank God It's Friday. w/m Robert Costandinos, 1978. Introduced by the studio group Love and Kisses in (MP) *Thank God It's Friday* and on records (Casablanca).

Thank Heaven for Little Girls. w. Alan Jay Lerner, m. Frederick Loewe, 1958. Introduced by Maurice Chevalier in (MM) *Gigi*. In the stage version (TM) *Gigi*, 1973, it was sung by Alfred Drake.

Thanks. w. Sam Coslow, m. Arthur Johnston, 1933. Introduced by Bing Crosby, with Judith Allen, in (MM) *Too Much Harmony.* Crosby recorded it with Jimmie Grier's Orchestra (Brunswick). Cover records: Will Osborne (Melotone); Irving Aaronson and his Commanders (Vocalion); Victor Young's Orchestra, vocal by Scrappy Lambert; Meyer Davis's Orchestra (Columbia).

Thanks, Mister Florist. w/m Roy C. Bennett and Sid Tepper, 1950. Featured and recorded by Vaughn Monroe, with his Orchestra (RCA Victor).

Thanks a Lot. w/m Don Sessions and Eddie Miller, 1963. Introduced by Ernest Tubb (Decca). Best-selling record by Brenda Lee (Decca), 1965.

Thanks a Lot, But No Thanks. w/m Betty Comden and Adolph Green, 1954. Introduced by Dolores Gray in (MM) *It's Always Fair Weather.*

Thanks a Million. w. Gus Kahn, m. Arthur Johnston, 1935. Introduced by Dick Powell in (MM) *Thanks a Million.* Popular records by Powell (Decca); The Mound City Blowers (Champion); the bands of Paul Whiteman (Victor), Johnny Hamp (Melotone), and Paul Pendarvis (Columbia).

Thanks for Ev'rything. w. Mack Gordon, m. Harry Revel, 1938. Introduced by Tony Martin in (MM) *Thanks for Everything.* The "title song" although with its apostrophe it differs from the film title. Recorded by Connie Boswell, with Woody Herman's Orchestra (Decca) and by Artie Shaw (Bluebird).

Thanks for Saving My Life. w/m Kenny Gamble and Leon Huff, 1974. Recorded by Billy Paul (Philadelphia International).

Thanks for the Buggy Ride. w/m Jules Buffano, 1926. Featured and recorded by Fred Waring's Pennsylvanians (Victor), Paul Ash (Columbia), Billy Jones and Ernie Hare (Banner), Johnny Marvin (Columbia). The Andrews Sisters sang it in (MM) *Always a Bridesmaid,* 1943.

Thanks for the Memory. w. Leo Robin, m. Ralph Rainger, 1938. This Academy Award winner was introduced by Bob Hope, in his film debut, and Shirley Ross in (MM) *The Big Broadcast of 1938.* Hope and Ross had a best-selling record (Decca), and the song became Hope's theme song for the rest of his long career. Later in the year, it was the title song of (MP) *Thanks for the Memory.*

Thanksgivin'. w. Johnny Mercer, m. Hoagy Carmichael, 1932. Recorded by Carmichael (Victor).

Thanks to You. w. Grant Clarke, m. Pete Wendling, 1931. Recorded by Gus Arnheim's Orchestra. The vocal was by Bing Crosby, his last as a band singer before becoming a solo performer.

Thank the Lord for the Night Time. w/m Neil Diamond, 1967. Top 20 record by Neil Diamond (Bang).

Thank You (Falettinme Be Mice Elf Agin). w/m Sylvester Stewart, 1970. #1 gold record by Sly [Stewart] and The Family Stone (Epic).

Thank You for a Lovely Evening. w. Dorothy Fields, m. Jimmy McHugh, 1934. Introduced by Phil Harris and his Band, with vocal by Leah Ray and Harris, who were making their New York debut in a nightclub revue at the Palais Royale. The song was heard in (MP) *Have a Heart* and (MP) *Girl from Missouri,* both 1934.

Thank You for Being a Friend. w/m Andrew Gold, 1978. Recorded by Andrew Gold (Asylum).

Thank You for Calling. w/m Cindy Walker, 1954. C&W that crossed over and became a Pop song, with the leading recording by Jo Stafford (Columbia).

Thank You Girl. w/m John Lennon and Paul McCartney, 1963. Recorded by The Beatles (Vee-Jay).

Thank You Pretty Baby. w/m Clyde Otis and Brook Benton, 1959. Popular recording by Brook Benton (Mercury).

Thank Your Father. w. B. G. DeSylva and Lew Brown, m. Ray Henderson, 1930. Sung by Oscar Shaw and Grace Brinkley in (TM) *Flying High.* Early recordings include those by Helen Kane (Victor), Fred Waring (Victor), Al Goodman (Brunswick), The Knickerbockers (Columbia).

Thank Your Lucky Stars. w. Frank Loesser, m. Arthur Schwartz, 1943. Title song introduced by Dinah Shore in (MM) *Thank Your Lucky Stars.*

Thank You So Much, Mrs. Lowsborough-Goodby. w/m Cole Porter, 1934. One of Porter's few songs to be published independently of a production. Porter sang and played it [piano] on a recording (Victor).

Thank You Very Much. w/m Leslie Bricusse, 1970. Introduced by Albert Finney and Anton Rogers in (MM) *Scrooge.* Nominated for Academy Award, 1970.

That Ain't Love. w/m Kevin Cronin, 1987. Top 10 single from the album "Life as We Know It" by REO Speedwagon (Epic).

That Ain't Right. w/m Nat "King" Cole and Irving Mills, 1943. Recorded by The King Cole Trio (Decca) and Slim Gaillard (Majestic). Revived in (TM) *Ain't Misbehavin',* 1978, by André de Shields, Armelia McQueen, and the cast, with new lyrics by Richard Maltby, Jr. and Murray Horwitz.

That Blue-Eyed Baby from Memphis. w/m unknown, 1929. First recorded by studio group led by Paul Whiteman, featuring Bix Beiderbecke on cornet, Benny Goodman on clarinet, Frankie Trumbauer on C-melody saxophone, and vocal by Bing Crosby (Victor); also recorded by Don Redman, vocal by Harlan Lattimore (Brunswick), 1933.

That Certain Feeling. w. Ira Gershwin, m. George Gershwin, 1925. Introduced by Allen Kearns and Queenie Smith in (TM) *Tip-Toes.* It was the title song and was sung by Pearl Bailey, reprised by Bob Hope and Eva Marie Saint in (MP) *That Certain Feeling,* 1956.

That Certain Party. w. Gus Kahn, m. Walter Donaldson, 1925. Hit song, featured by Ted Lewis (Columbia) and Ernest Hare and Billy Jones (Victor). Revived, 1948, by Benny Strong and his Orchestra (Tower), Buddy Clark and Doris Day (Columbia), Dean Martin and Jerry Lewis (Capitol).

That Chick's Too Young to Fry. w/m Tommy Edwards and Jimmy Hilliard, 1946. Coupled with the hit "Choo Choo Ch'boogie" (q.v.) by Louis Jordan and his Tympany Five (Decca).

That Da Da Strain. w. Mamie Medina, m. Edgar Dowell, 1922. A favorite with jazz musicians. Among the recordings are those by Mamie Smith (Okeh), Muggsy Spanier (Bluebird), The Louisiana Rhythm Kings (Vocalion), Bud Freeman (Columbia), and Ben Pollack (Savoy).

That Dallas Man. w/m Harvey O. Brooks and Ben Ellison, 1933. Sung by Mae West in (MM) *I'm No Angel.* Recorded by Irene Taylor (Vocalion) and Isham Jones and his Orchestra (Victor).

That Do Make It Nice. w/m Eddy Arnold, Fred Ebb, and Paul Klein, 1955. Introduced and recorded by Eddy Arnold (RCA).

That Face. w. Alan Bergman and Lew Spence, m. Lew Spence, 1957. Introduced by Fred Astaire on television.

That Feeling in the Moonlight. See **Did You Ever Get That Feeling in the Moonlight?**

That Foolish Feeling. w. Harold Adamson, m. Jimmy McHugh, 1937. Introduced by Ella Logan in (MM) *Top of the Town.* Leading recording by Tommy Dorsey, vocal by Edythe Wright (Victor).

That Girl. w/m Stevie Wonder, 1981. #1 R&B, Top 10 Pop chart hit by Stevie Wonder (Tamla).

That Girl Could Sing. w/m Jackson Browne, 1980. Recorded by Jackson Browne (Asylum).

That Glory Bound Train. w/m Roy Acuff and Odell McLeod, 1944. C&W song, featured and recorded by Roy Acuff (Okeh).

That Great Come-and-Get-It Day. w. E. Y. Harburg, m. Burton Lane, 1947. Introduced by Ella Logan, Donald Richards, and chorus in (TM) *Finian's Rainbow*. In the film version (MM) *Finian's Rainbow*, 1968, it was sung by Petula Clark, Don Francks, and chorus.

That Happy Feeling. m. Guy Warren, 1962. Instrumental by Bert Kaempfert and his Orchestra (Decca).

That Haunting Melody. w/m George M. Cohan, 1911. Introduced by Al Jolson in (TM) *Vera Violetta*.

That Heart Belongs to Me. w/m Webb Pierce, 1952. Introduced and recorded by Webb Pierce (Decca).

That Hound Dog in the Window. w/m Bob Merrill, 1953. Homer and Jethro, the country comedy team, had a hit parody of "The Doggie in the Window" (q.v.) (RCA Victor).

That International Rag. w/m Irving Berlin, 1913.

That Lady. w/m Christopher Isley, Ernest Isley, and Marvin Isley, 1973. Hit record by The Isley Brothers (T-Neck).

That Little Dream Got Nowhere. w. Johnny Burke, m. James Van Heusen, 1946. Introduced by Betty Hutton in (MM) *Cross My Heart*. Recorded by Ray McKinley and his Orchestra (Majestic).

That'll Be the Day. w/m Jerry Allison, Buddy Holly, and Norman Petty, 1957. First hit and #1 million-seller by Buddy Holly and The Crickets (Brunswick). Linda Rondstadt had a Top 20 version in 1976 (Asylum). It was sung by Gary Busey in the title role of (MM) *The Buddy Holly Story*, 1978.

That'll Show Him. w/m Stephen Sondheim, 1962. Introduced by Preshy Marker in (TM) *A Funny Thing Happened on the Way to the Forum*.

That Lost Barbershop Chord. w. Ira Gershwin, m. Phil Charig, 1926. Introduced by Louis Lazarin and The Pan-American Quartet in the revue (TM) *Americana*.

That Lovin' Rag. w. Victor H. Smalley, m. Bernie Adler, 1907. Introduced by Sophie Tucker.

That Lucky Fellow. w. Oscar Hammerstein II, m. Jerome Kern, 1939. Introduced by Robert Shackleton and reprised as "That Lucky Lady" by Grace McDonald in (TM) *Very Warm for May*. Leading record by Tommy Dorsey, vocal by Jack Leonard (Victor), coupled with "All the Things You Are" (q.v.). Also recorded by Paul Whiteman, vocal by Hal Dickinson (Decca).

That Lucky Old Sun (Just Rolls Around Heaven All Day). w. Haven Gillespie, m. Beasley Smith, 1949. A #1 song on all the charts. Frankie Laine had a million-seller (Mercury). It was followed by Vaughn Monroe (RCA Victor); Sarah Vaughan (Columbia); Frank Sinatra (Columbia); Louis Armstrong, accompanied by Gordon Jenkins' Orchestra (Decca).

That Mellow Melody. w. Sam M. Lewis, m. George W. Meyer, 1912.

That Mesmerizing Mendelssohn Tune. w/m Irving Berlin, 1909. This, a ragtime treatment of Mendelssohn's "Spring Song," was one of the first Berlin "words and music" song successes. Popular records by Arthur Collins and Byron Harlan (Columbia) and Billy Murray (Victor).

That Minor Strain. w. Cecil Mack, m. Ford Dabney, 1910.

That Moment of Moments. w. Ira Gershwin, m. Vernon Duke, 1936. Sung by Gertrude Niesen and Rodney McLennan and danced by Harriet Hoctor in (TM) *Ziegfeld Follies of 1936*. Recorded by Hal Kemp's Band (Brunswick).

That Mysterious Rag. w/m Irving Berlin and Ted Snyder, 1911. Written for the production (TM) *Real Girl*. Leading records by Arthur

Collins and Albert Campbell (Columbia) and The American Quartet (Victor). Revived by Joan Morris and William Bolcomb in their all-Irving Berlin album "The Girl on the Magazine Cover" (RCA), 1979.

That Naughty Waltz. w. Edwin Stanley, m. Sol P. Levy, 1919. Recorded and made popular by Ben Selvin's Novelty Orchestra (Victor).

That Old Black Magic. w. Johnny Mercer, m. Harold Arlen, 1942. Introduced by Johnny Johnson singing, and Vera Zorina dancing, in (MM) *Star Spangled Rhythm*. Glenn Miller's recording, with vocal by Skip Nelson and the Modernaires (Victor), helped the song become a #1 hit. In other films, it was sung by Bing Crosby in (MM) *Here Come the Waves*, 1944; Frances Langford in (MM) *Radio Stars on Parade*, 1945; Billy Daniels in (MM) *When You're Smiling*, 1950; Frank Sinatra in (MM) *Meet Danny Wilson*, 1952; Louis Prima and Keely Smith in (MM) *Senior Prom*, 1958; Marilyn Monroe in (MP) *Bus Stop*, 1956. Billy Daniels became associated with the song, featuring it in nightclubs and on television. He recorded it twice (Mercury). Chart records for Sammy Davis, 1955 (Decca); Louis Prima and Keely Smith (Capitol), 1958; Bobby Rydell (Cameo), 1961.

That Old Feeling. w. Lew Brown, m. Sammy Fain, 1937. Introduced by Virginia Verrill in (MM) *Vogues of 1938*. One of the top hits of the year in sheet music and record sales and nominated for an Academy Award. Jane Froman, dubbing her voice on the soundtrack for Susan Hayward, sang it in the Froman story (MM) *With a Song in My Heart*, 1952.

That Old Gang of Mine. w. Billy Rose and Mort Dixon, m. Ray Henderson, 1923. Popularized by Van and Schenck in vaudeville. They then interpolated it in (TM) *Ziegfeld Follies of 1923* during its run.

That Old Girl of Mine. w. Earle C. Jones, m. Egbert Van Alstyne, 1912. Popular song with vaudeville performers. Leading record by The American Quartet (Columbia).

That Old Irish Mother of Mine. w. William Jerome, m. Harry Von Tilzer, 1920. Popular ballad. Recorded by Charles Harrison (Columbia).

That Ole Devil Called Love. w/m Allan Roberts and Doris Fisher, 1945. Best-selling record by Billie Holiday, with Toots Camarata's Orchestra (Decca).

That Once in a Lifetime. w/m Dino Fekaris and Freddie Perren, 1978. Recorded by the Greek singer Demis Roussos (Mercury).

That Railroad Rag. w. Nat Vincent, m. Ed Bimberg, 1911.

That Revolutionary Rag. w/m Irving Berlin, 1919. From the Cohan and Harris production (TM) *The Royal Vagabond*. Berlin was severing connections with his music publishing firm and played this for Max Dreyfus, head of T. B. Harms, who wanted to publish it. Berlin explained that he couldn't notate it and Dreyfus said, "I have a kid here who can do it." The kid who put this song on paper was George Gershwin.

That Rock Won't Roll. w/m John Scott Sherrill and Bob Dipiero, 1986. #1 Country chart record by the group Restless Heart (RCA).

That's a Good Girl. w/m Irving Berlin, 1926. Leading record by Ben Selvin and his Orchestra, vocal by Selvin (Brunswick).

That's All. w/m Tony Banks, Phil Collins, and Mike Rutherford, 1983. Written and recorded by the British trio Genesis (Atlantic).

That's All. w. Alan Brandt, m. Bob Haymes, 1952. Song has achieved the status of "standard" by being included in the repertoire of many singers and musicians, Pop and jazz. Among the artists who recorded the song are Bob Haymes (Bell), Tommy Edwards (MGM), Nat "King" Cole (Capitol), Ben Webster (Norgran), Rick Nelson (Imperial).

That's All. w/m Merle Travis, 1946. Introduced by Merle Travis (Capitol). Revived by Tennessee Ernie Ford (Capitol), 1956. Not to be confused with Bob Haymes's song of same title.

That's All in the Movies. w/m Merle Haggard and Kelli Haggard, 1975. Hit Country record by Merle Haggard (Capitol).

That's All I Want from You. w/m M. Rotha, 1954. Popularized by Jaye P. Morgan's most successful recording (RCA Victor).

That's All Right. w/m Arthur Crudup, 1947. Introduced by Big Boy [Arthur] Crudup and revived by Elvis Presley on his first commercial recording (Sun), 1954. Marty Robbins' cover record reached the Top 10 on the C&W charts (Columbia).

That's All That Matters. w/m Hank Cochran, 1963, 1980. Country chart song recorded by Ray Price (Columbia). Revived with a #1 version by Mickey Gilley (Epic), 1980.

That's All There Is to That. w/m Clyde Otis and Kelly Owens, 1956. Leading record by Nat "King" Cole and The Four Knights (Capitol).

That's All You Gotta Do. w/m Jerry Reed, 1960. Hit record by Brenda Lee (Decca).

That's Amore. w. Jack Brooks, m. Harry Warren, 1953. Introduced by Dean Martin in the Martin and Lewis film (MP) *The Caddy*. Nominated for Academy Award. Martin had a million-selling record (Capitol).

That's a No No. w/m Ben Peters, 1969. Hit Country record by Lynn Anderson (Chart).

That's A-Plenty. m. Lew Pollack, 1914. One of the most performed and recorded jazz standards. Among the many recordings are those by Prince's Orchestra (Columbia), New Orleans Rhythm Kings (Gennett), Miff Mole (Okeh), Jan Savitt (Bluebird), Hoagy Carmichael (Decca), Phil Napoleon (Swan), Tommy Dorsey (Victor), Earl "Fatha" Hines (Decca).

That's A-Plenty. w. Henry A. Creamer, m. Bert Williams, 1909. A popular song recorded by singer Arthur Collins (Victor and Colum-

bia). Note: Not to be confused with jazz standard of same title.

That's Enough. w/m Ray Charles, 1959. Introduced and recorded by Ray Charles (Atlantic). Leading record by Roscoe Robinson (Wand), 1966.

That's Entertainment. w. Howard Dietz, m. Arthur Schwartz, 1953. Introduced by Fred Astaire, Cyd Charisse [vocal dubbed on soundtrack by India Adams], Nanette Fabray, Jack Buchanan, and Oscar Levant in (MM) *The Band Wagon*. Used as the title song of (MM) *That's Entertainment*, 1974, and (MM) *That's Entertainment, Part Two*, 1976.

That Sentimental Sandwich. w. Frank Loesser, m. Frederick Hollander, 1939. Introduced by Dorothy Lamour and Phil Harris in (MM) *Man About Town*. Recorded by Lamour (Bluebird).

That's for Me. w. Oscar Hammerstein II, m. Richard Rodgers, 1945. Introduced by Vivian Blaine and reprised by Louanne Hogan in (MM) *State Fair*. Pat Boone sang it in the remake (MM) *State Fair*, 1962. Best-selling records by Jo Stafford (Capitol), Dick Haymes (Decca), Kay Kyser, vocal by Mike Douglas and the Campus Kids (Columbia).

That's for Me. w. Johnny Burke, m. James V. Monaco, 1940. Introduced by Bing Crosby in (MM) *Rhythm on the River*, and on records, coupled with the title song of the film (Decca).

That's Him. w. Ogden Nash, m. Kurt Weill, 1943. Introduced by Mary Martin in (TM) *One Touch of Venus*. Ann Ronell wrote new lyrics for the song for the film version (MM) *One Touch of Venus*, 1948, which was sung by Eileen Wilson [dubbing for Ava Gardner], Olga San Juan, and Eve Arden.

That's How I Need You. w. Joseph McCarthy and Joe Goodwin, m. Al Piantadosi, 1912. Recorded by Henry Burr (Victor).

That's How It Went All Right. w. Dory Langdon Previn, m. André Previn, 1960. Introduced by Bobby Darin, Shirley Jones, Matt Mattox, and Michael Callan in (MM) *Pepe*.

That's How Much I Love You. w/m Eddy Arnold, Wally Fowler, and J. Graydon Hall, 1947. Introduced by Eddy Arnold (Victor). Popular records by Bing Crosby, with Bob Crosby's Orchestra (Decca); Frank Sinatra, with The Page Cavanaugh Trio (Columbia); Louis Prima, with his Orchestra (Majestic).

That's How the Shannon Flows. w. J. Keirn Brennan, m. Ernest R. Ball, 1915. Recorded (Columbia) and featured by Chauncey Olcott.

That Silver Haired Daddy of Mine. w/m Jimmy Long and Gene Autry, 1932. Introduced and recorded by Gene Autry (Vocalion).

That's Life. w/m Dean Kay and Kelly Gordon, 1966. Hit record by Frank Sinatra (Reprise). Later chart versions by O. C. Smith (Columbia), 1967; David Lee Roth (Warner Bros.), 1986.

(But as They Say) That's Life. w/m Moose Charlap and Jack Pleis, 1957. Popular instrumental recording by Jack Pleis and his Orchestra. Title sung as last line of song by Al Hibbler but not credited on label (Decca).

That's Love. w. Lorenz Hart, m. Richard Rodgers, 1934. Introduced by Anna Sten in (MP) *Nana*. Recorded by the orchestras of Enric Madriguera (Vocalion) and Harry Sosnik, vocal by Bob Hanlon (Victor).

That Sly Old Gentleman (from Featherbed Lane). w. Johnny Burke, m. James V. Monaco, 1939. Sung by Bing Crosby in (MM) *East Side of Heaven* and on records (Decca).

That's Me Without You. w/m J. D. Miller and Bennett Wyatt, 1952. Country song recorded by Webb Pierce (Decca).

That's My Desire. w. Carroll Loveday, m. Helmy Kresa, 1947. Introduced on radio by Lanny Ross, 1931. Frankie Laine revived it with a million-selling record (Mercury) in 1947, establishing it as a standard.

That's My Kind of Love. w/m Marion Worth, 1960. Top 10 C&W chart record by Marion Worth (Guyden).

That's My Pa. w/m Sheb Wooley, 1962. Novelty record by Sheb Wooley (MGM).

That's My Weakness Now. w/m Bud Green and Sam H. Stept, 1928. Stept's first song success. It was introduced by Helen Kane who was appearing with Paul Ash's Orchestra at the Paramount Theatre in New York. Her added "boop-oop-a-doops" made the song a hit, and her a star. Her recording (Victor) was a top-seller, as were those by Cliff "Ukulele Ike" Edwards (Columbia) and Paul Whiteman (Victor). Revived by Russ Morgan, vocal by The Morganaires (Decca), 1949.

That's Old Fashioned (That's the Way Love Should Be). w/m Bill Giant, Bernie Baum, and Florence Kaye, 1962. Top 10 hit by The Everly Brothers (Warner Bros.).

That Soldier of Mine. w. Paul Herrick, m. Matt Dennis, 1942. Featured and recorded by Harry James, vocal by Helen Forrest (Columbia).

That's Rock 'n' Roll. w/m Eric Carmen, 1977. Gold record by Shaun Cassidy (Warner Bros.).

That's Sabotage. w. Mack Gordon, m. Harry Warren, 1942. Introduced by Glenn Miller, vocal by Marion Hutton, in (MM) *Orchestra Wives* and on records (Victor).

That's the Beginning of the End. w/m Joan Whitney and Alex Kramer, 1947. Popular records by Perry Como (Victor); Benny Goodman, vocal by Karen Chandler [under name of Eve Young] (Columbia); Cass Daley (Decca).

That's the Chance You Take. w. Sylvia Dee, m. Sidney Lippman, 1952. Popularized and recorded by Eddie Fisher, with Hugo Winterhalter's Orchestra (RCA Victor).

That's the Kind of Baby for Me. w/m Jack Egan and Alfred Harrison, 1917. Introduced by Eddie Cantor in (TM) *Ziegfeld Follies of 1917*.

That's the Rhythm of the Day. w. Lorenz Hart, m. Richard Rodgers, 1933. Introduced by Nelson Eddy in the production number finale of (MM) *Dancing Lady*.

That's the Thing About Love. w/m Gary Nicholson and Richard Leigh, 1984. #1 Country chart record by Don Williams (MCA), 1984.

That's the Way (I Like It). w/m Harry Wayne Casey and Richard Finch, 1975. #1 R&B/Pop chart record by KC and The Sunshine Band (T.K.).

That's the Way I've Always Heard It Should Be. w. Jacob Brackman, m. Carly Simon, 1971. Top 10 record by Carly Simon, her first hit single (Elektra).

That's the Way Love Goes. w/m Lefty Frizzell and Whitey Shafer, 1974, 1984. #1 Country chart record by Johnny Rodriguez (Mercury). #1 Revival by Merle Haggard (Epic), 1984.

That's the Way Love Is. w/m Norman Whitfield and Barrett Strong, 1969. Top 10 record by Marvin Gaye (Tamla).

That's the Way Love Is. w/m Deadric Malone, 1963. Leading record by Bobby Bland (Duke).

That's the Way of the World. w/m Philip Bailey, Larry Dunn, and Maurice White, 1975. Introduced by the group Earth, Wind & Fire in (MP) *Shining Star*, originally titled *That's the Way of the World*. Top 20 record by the group (Columbia).

That Sunday, That Summer. w. George David Weiss, m. Joe Sherman, 1963. Popularized by Nat "King" Cole (Capitol).

That's What Friends Are For. w. Carole Bayer Sager, m. Burt Bacharach, 1985. Originally written for (MP) *Night Shift*, 1982, and recorded by Rod Stewart (Warner Bros.). #1 gold record by Dionne Warwick and Friends (Arista), 1985. The "friends" were Elton John, Gladys Knight, and Stevie Wonder, who collaborated vocally. Proceeds were contributed to AIDS research. Winner Grammy Award (NARAS) for Song of the Year, 1986.

That's What Girls Are Made For. w/m

Harvey Fuqua and Gwen Gordy, 1961. Introduced and recorded by The Spinners (Tri-Phi).

That's What I Like. w. Bob Hilliard, m. Jule Styne, 1954. Introduced by Dean Martin in the Martin and Lewis film (MM) *Living It Up*. Popular record by Don, Dick 'N' Jimmy (Crown).

That's What I Like About the West. w/m Robert MacGimsey and Edith Bergdahl, 1947. C&W hit, recorded by Tex Williams (Capitol Americana).

That's What I Like 'bout the South. w/m Andy Razaf, 1944. Title was published with the apostrophe in "about," although the "a" appears in most recorded versions. Song identified with Phil Harris who has performed it on radio and television, and in nightclubs and theaters, and recorded it twice (Okeh) (Victor).

That's What It's Like to Be Lonesome. w/m Bill Anderson, 1959. C&W hit by Ray Price (Columbia).

That's What I Want for Christmas. w. Irving Caesar, m. Gerald Marks, 1936. Introduced by Shirley Temple in (MM) *Stowaway*.

That's What Love Is All About. w/m Michael Bolton and Eric Kaz, 1987. Chart record by Michael Bolton (Columbia).

That's What Makes Paris Paree. w. Sammy Cahn, m. Vernon Duke, 1952. Introduced by Doris Day and Claude Dauphin in (MM) *April in Paris*.

That's What the Daisy Said, w/m Albert Von Tilzer, 1903.

That's What You're Doing to Me. w/m Rose Marks and Billy Ward, 1952. Top R&B record by The Dominoes (Federal).

That's What You Think. w/m Truman "Pinky" Tomlin, Raymond Jasper, and Coy Poe, 1935. Introduced by Pinky Tomlin in (MM) *King Solomon of Broadway*. Recorded by Tomlin (Brunswick), Red McKenzie (Decca), Will Osborne (Columbia), Gene Krupa, vocal by Anita O'Day (Columbia).

That's When I See the Blues (in Your

Pretty Brown Eyes). w/m Carl Belew, Tommy Blake, and W. S. Stevenson, 1968. Top 10 Country chart record by Jim Reeves (RCA).

That's When She Started to Stop Loving You. w/m Wayne Kemp, 1970. Top 10 Country chart record by Conway Twitty (Decca).

That's When the Music Takes Me. w/m Neil Sedaka, 1975. Recorded by Neil Sedaka (Rocket).

That's Where I Came In. w. Charles Tobias, m. Peter De Rose, 1947. Popularized by Perry Como (RCA Victor).

That's Why (I Love You So). w/m Berry Gordy, Jr., Gwendolyn Gordy, and Tyran Carlo, 1959. Featured and recorded by Jackie Wilson (Brunswick).

That's Why Darkies Were Born. w/m Lew Brown and Ray Henderson, 1931. Sung by Everett Marshall in (TM) *George White's Scandals, Eleventh Edition* and recorded by him with the Victor Young Orchestra (Victor). The song is no longer sung, for good and obvious reasons.

That's Why I Love You. w. Paul Ash, m. Walter Donaldson, 1926. Featured and recorded by Johnny Hamp, vocal by Charles Buckwalter, Frank Master, and Elwood Groff (Victor).

That's Why I Was Born. w/m O. O. Merritt and Vin Roddie, 1957. Introduced and recorded by Janice Harper (Prep).

That's You, Baby. w. Sidney D. Mitchell, m. Con Conrad and Archie Gottler, 1929. Introduced as a production number by most of the large cast in (MM) *Fox Movietone Follies of 1929.*

That Tumble-Down Shack in Athlone. w. Richard W. Pascoe, m. Monte Carlo and Alma M. Sanders, 1918. Sentimental song in the Irish genre with leading recordings by John McCormack (Victor) and The Sterling Trio (Columbia). Later featured and recorded by Phil Regan (Decca) and Bing Crosby (Decca).

That Was a Close One. w/m Robert Byrne, 1987. #1 Country chart song by Earl Thomas Conley (RCA).

That Was Before I Met You. w. Alfred Bryan, m. George W. Meyer, 1911.

That Was Then, This Is Now. w/m Vance Brescia and Ed Davis, 1986. First chart record in sixteen years by The Monkees (Arista).

That Was Yesterday. w/m Mick Jones and Lou Gramm, 1985. Recorded by the Anglo-American group Foreigner (Atlantic).

That Was Yesterday. w/m Donna Fargo, 1977. Hit Country record by Donna Fargo (Warner Bros.).

That Was Yesterday. w/m Jerry Herman, 1961. Introduced by Mimi Benzell and company in (TM) *Milk and Honey.*

That Wild and Wicked Look in Your Eye. w/m Sam Nichols, 1948. Hit C&W record by Ernest Tubb (Decca).

That Wonderful Mother of Mine. w. Clyde Hager, m. Walter Goodwin, 1918. Featured in vaudeville by Frank Morrell. Popular recording by Henry Burr (Victor).

That Wonderful Something. w. Joe Goodwin, m. Louis Alter, 1929. From (MP) *Untamed* starring Joan Crawford. Recorded by Nat Shilkret (Victor); Joe Venuti, vocal by Smith Ballew (Okeh); Irving Kaufman (Perfect).

Thee I Love. See **Friendly Persuasion.**

Theme from "Adventures in Paradise." w. Dorcas Cochrane, m. Lionel Newman, 1960. Theme from series (TVP) "Adventures in Paradise." Recorded as instrumental by Jerry Byrd (Monument).

Theme from "A Summer Place." m. Max Steiner, 1960. Theme from (MP) *A Summer Place.* #1 million-seller by Percy Faith and his Orchestra (Columbia). Later popular recordings by Dick Roman (Harmon), 1962, and The Letterman (Capitol), 1965.

Theme from "Baby Doll." See **Baby Doll.**

Theme from "Ben Casey." m. David Raksin, 1962. Theme of the series (TVP) "Ben Casey." Popular instrumental by pianist Valjean (Carlton).

Theme from "Caddyshack." See **I'm Alright.**

Theme from "Carnival." See **Love Makes the World Go 'Round.**

Theme from "Charlie's Angels." m. Jack Elliot, 1977. Music introduced on series (TVP) "Charlie's Angels," 1976. Popular instrumental record by Henry Mancini and his Orchestra (RCA).

Theme from "Cleopatra Jones." w/m Joe Simon, 1973. From the film (MP) *Cleopatra Jones.* Top 20 record by Joe Simon (Spring).

Theme from "Close Encounters of the Third Kind." m. John Williams, 1978. From the film of the same title. Leading recordings were John Williams, from the soundtrack (Arista), and Meco (Millennium).

Theme from "Come September." m. Bobby Darin, 1962. From (MP) *Come September,* starring Bobby Darin and Sandra Dee. Recorded by Bobby Darin and his Orchestra (Atco).

Theme from "Doctor Detroit." w/m Gerald Casale and Mark Mothersbaugh, 1983. From (MP) *Doctor Detroit.* Chart record by the group Devo (Backstreet).

Theme from "Dr. Kildare." See **Three Stars Will Shine Tonight.**

Theme from "Dukes of Hazzard" (Good Ol' Boys). w/m Waylon Jennings, 1979. From the series (TVP) "Dukes of Hazzard." Recorded by Waylon Jennings (RCA), 1980.

Theme from "Dynasty." m. Bill Conti, 1982. From the series (TVP) "Dynasty." Recorded by the composer/conductor Bill Conti (Arista).

Theme from "East of Eden." m. Leonard Rosenman, 1956. From (MP) *East of Eden.* Most popular recording by Dick Jacobs and his Orchestra (Decca).

Theme from "Goodbye Again." m. Georges Auric, 1961. From (MP) *Goodbye Again,* starring Ingrid Bergman. Leading recording by the two-piano team of Ferrante and Teicher (United Artists).

Theme from "Hatari." See **Baby Elephant Walk.**

Theme from "Hill Street Blues." m. Mike Post, 1981. From the series (TVP) "Hill Street Blues." Instrumental record by the composer, Mike Post, featuring guitarist Larry Carlton (Elektra).

Theme from "Jaws" (Main Title). m. John Williams, 1975. Introduced by the orchestra under the direction of the composer John Williams on the soundtrack of (MP) "Jaws," and on records (MCA).

Theme from "Lawrence of Arabia." m. Maurice Jarre, 1963. Recorded by the two-piano team of Ferrante and Teicher (United Artists).

Theme from "Love Story" (Lyric Version: Where Do I Begin). w. Carl Sigman, m. Francis Lai, 1970. Title theme of (MP) *Love Story.* Leading recordings in 1971 by Andy Williams [lyric version] (Columbia); Henry Mancini (RCA) and Francis Lai (Paramount) [both instrumental].

Theme from "Magnum P. I." m. Mike Post and Pete Carpenter, 1982. From the series (TVP) "Magnum P. I." Instrumental recorded by Mike Post (Elektra).

Theme from "Mahogany" (Do You Know Where You're Going To?). w. Gerry Goffin, m. Michael Masser, 1975. Words to the theme music of (MP) *Mahogany,* starring Diana Ross and Billy Dee Williams. Ross's record became a #1 best-seller (Motown).

Theme from "Naked City." See **Somewhere in the Night.**

Theme from "New York, New York." w. Fred Ebb, m. John Kander, 1977. Introduced by Liza Minnelli in (MM) *New York, New York*. Leading records by Minnelli (United Artists), 1977, and Frank Sinatra (Reprise), 1980. Chosen as official song of The City of New York.

Theme from "Picnic." w. Steve Allen, m. George Duning, 1956. From (MP) *Picnic*, played in counterpoint with 1934 song "Moonglow." [For further information see "Moonglow."] The McGuire Sisters had a popular vocal version of the "Picnic" song (Cadence).

Theme from "Shaft." w/m Isaac Hayes, 1971. Sung by Isaac Hayes on the soundtrack of (MP) *Shaft*, and #1 on the charts (Enterprise). Winner, Academy Award, 1971.

Theme from "Summer of '42." m. Michel Legrand, 1971. Main theme of (MP) *Summer of '42*, scored and conducted by Michel Legrand. Instrumental recordings by Peter Nero (Columbia), 1971, and a disco version recorded in London by The Biddu Orchestra (Epic), 1975.

Theme from S.W.A.T. m. Barry De-Vorzon, 1975. The first #1 hit from a television series (TVP) theme. This dance version was recorded by a studio group, Rhythm Heritage (ABC).

Theme from "Taras Bulba" (The Wishing Star). w. Mack David, m. Franz Waxman, 1962. From (MP) *Taras Bulba*. Recorded by Jerry Butler (Vee-Jay).

Theme from "The Apartment." m. Charles Williams, 1960. From (MP) *The Apartment*. Originally a British song titled "Jealous Lover" (q.v.). Popular instrumental by the piano duo of Ferrante and Teicher (United Artists).

Theme from "The Dark at the Top of the Stairs." m. Max Steiner, 1960. From (MP) *The Dark at the Top of the Stairs*. Leading record by Ernie Freeman and his Orchestra (Imperial).

Theme from "The Greatest American Hero" (Believe It or Not). w. Stephen Geyer, m. Mike Post, 1981. From series (TVP) "The Greatest American Hero." Top 10 gold record by Joey Scarbury (Elektra).

Theme from "The Men." m. Isaac Hayes and Ronny Scaife, 1972. Theme from the series (TVP) "The Men." Isaac Hayes had a popular instrumental record (Enterprise).

Theme from "The Misfits." m. Alex North, 1961. From (MP) *The Misfits*. Leading record by Don Costa (United Artists).

Theme from "The Proud Ones." m. Ruth Keddington, 1956. Theme from the (MP) *The Proud Ones*. Leading records by the orchestras of Nelson Riddle (Capitol), Lionel Newman with whistling by Muzzy Marcellino (Columbia), Leroy Holmes (MGM).

Theme from "The Sundowners." m. Dimitri Tiomkin, 1960. From (MP) *The Sundowners*. Leading instrumentals by the orchestras of Billy Vaughn (Dot), Felix Slatkin (Liberty), Mantovani (London).

Theme from "The Thomas Crown Affair." See **Windmills of Your Mind, The.**

Theme from "The Unforgiven" (The Need for Love). w. Ned Washington, m. Dimitri Tiomkin, 1960. Theme from (MP) *The Unforgiven*. Recorded instrumentally by Don Costa and his Orchestra (United Artists) and vocally by the McGuire Sisters (Coral).

Theme from "Valley of the Dolls." w. Dory Previn, m. André Previn, 1967. Sung on the soundtrack of (MP) *Valley of the Dolls*, by Dionne Warwick, who then had a hit single (Scepter), 1968. Chart instrumental version by King Curtis (Atco), 1968.

Themes from "The Man with the Golden Arm." m. Elmer Bernstein, 1956. From (MP) *The Man with the Golden Arm*, starring Frank Sinatra and Kim Novak. Best-selling record, containing "Main Title Theme," "Molly-O," and "Delilah Jones," by Richard Maltby and his Orchestra (Vik).

Theme Song from "Which Way Is Up?" w/m Norman Whitfield, 1977. From the film of the same title. Recorded by the female trio Stargard (MCA).

Them There Eyes. w/m Maceo Pinkard, William Tracey, and Doris Tauber, 1930. First recorded by Gus Arnheim and his Orchestra (Victor). Billie Holiday's recording (Vocalion), 1939, remains, with Louis Armstrong's version (Okeh), 1931, the disc performances most associated with the song. Diana Ross, as Holiday, sang it in her story (MM) *Lady Sings the Blues*, 1972.

Then and Only Then. w/m Bill Anderson, 1965. Hit country record by Connie Smith (RCA).

Then a Tear Fell. w/m Warner McPherson, 1962. Top 10 C&W chart record by Earl Scott (Kapp).

Then Came You. w/m Sherman Marshall and Phil Pugh, 1974. #1 gold record by Dionne Warwick and The Spinners (Atlantic).

Then He Kissed Me. w/m Jeff Barry, Ellie Greenwich, and Phil Spector, 1963. Introduced and Top 10 record by The Crystals (Philles).

(I Wanna Go Where You Go, Do What You Do) Then I'll Be Happy. w. Sidney Clare and Lew Brown, m. Cliff Friend, 1926. Leading record by "Whispering" Jack Smith (Victor).

Then I'll Be Tired of You. w. E. Y. Harburg, m. Arthur Schwartz, 1934. Originally recorded by the bands of Isham Jones, vocal by Joe Martin (Decca); Freddy Martin, vocal by Elmer Feldkamp (Brunswick); Ambrose, whose English recording was released in the U.S. (Decca).

Then I'll Stop Loving You. w/m Jim Reeves, 1954. Top 10 Country chart record by Jim Reeves (Abbott). Revived by The Browns (RCA), 1964.

(If It Isn't Pain) Then It Isn't Love. w. Leo Robin, m. Ralph Rainger, 1937. Introduced by Carole Lombard in (MM) *Swing High, Swing Low*. Originally written for Marlene Dietrich in the film *The Devil Is a Woman*, in 1935, but cut from final print.

Then It's Love. w/m Dennis Linde, 1987. Top 10 Country chart record by Don Williams (Capitol).

Then I Turned and Walked Slowly Away. w/m Arnold "Red" Fortner and Eddy Arnold, 1949. Featured and recorded by Eddy Arnold (RCA Victor).

Then You Can Tell Me Goodbye. w/m John D. Loudermilk, 1967. Hit record by The Casinos (Fraternity). Other chart versions by Eddy Arnold (RCA), 1968; Glen Campbell, in medley with "Don't Pull Your Love" (q.v.) (Capitol), 1976; the quintet Toby Beau (RCA), 1979.

Then You May Take Me to the Fair. w. Alan Jay Lerner, m. Frederick Loewe, 1960. Introduced by Julie Andrews, John Cullum, James Gannon, and Bruce Yarnell in (TM) *Camelot*. In (MM) *Camelot*, 1967, it was sung by Vanessa Redgrave.

Then You've Never Been Blue. w. Sam M. Lewis and Joe Young, m. Ted Fio Rito, 1929. Recorded by Ted Fio Rito (Columbia), Frances Williams (Brunswick), and Roger Wolfe Kahn's Orchestra (Brunswick). Sung by Frances Langford in (MM) *Every Night at Eight*, 1935, and recorded by her (Brunswick). Later recorded by Kay Starr, arranged and conducted by Frank DeVol (Capitol); Martha Lou Harp, arranged and conducted by Richard Maltby (Decca).

There, I've Said It Again. w/m Redd Evans and Dave Mann, 1945. Introduced four years earlier by Benny Carter and his band (Bluebird), but it was not until Vaughn Monroe with the Norton Sisters and his Orchestra had a hit record that the song was established (Victor). Jimmy Dorsey, vocal by Teddy Walters (Decca), and The Modernaires with Paula Kelly (Columbia) also had popular recordings. Bobby Vinton revived it with a #1 record (Epic), 1964.

There Ain't No Easy Run. w/m Dave Dudley and Tom T. Hall, 1968. Top 10 Country chart record by Dave Dudley (Mercury).

There Ain't No Maybe in My Baby's Eyes. w. Gus Kahn and Raymond B. Egan, m. Walter Donaldson, 1926. Popularized by "Whispering" Jack Smith (Victor).

There Ain't No Sweet Man (Worth the Salt of My Tears). w/m Fred Fisher, 1928. First recorded by the Rhythm Boys [Crosby, Barris, and Rinker] with Paul Whiteman's Orchestra. Also by Libby Holman (Brunswick) and Kay Starr (Capitol).

There Are Such Things. w/m Stanley Adams, Abel Baer, and George W. Meyer, 1942. The last hit song for each of the writers . . . but what a hit! Tommy Dorsey's record with vocal by Frank Sinatra and The Pied Pipers (Victor) was on the charts for six months, six weeks as #1. The song was on "Your Hit Parade" for eighteen weeks, also six weeks as #1.

There But for Fortune. w/m Phil Ochs, 1965. Introduced by folk singer Phil Ochs. Chart single by Joan Baez (Vanguard).

There But for You Go I. w. Alan Jay Lerner, m. Frederick Loewe, 1947. Introduced by David Brooks in (TM) *Brigadoon*. Sung by Gene Kelly in the film version (MM) *Brigadoon*, 1955.

There Goes My Baby. w/m Benjamin Nelson, Lover Patterson, George Treadwell, Jerry Leiber, Mike Stoller, 1959. Top 10 record by The Drifters (Atlantic). Revived by Donna Summer (Geffen), 1984.

There Goes My Everything. w/m Dallas Frazier, 1967. Crossover (C&W/Pop) hit by drummer/singer Jack Greene (Decca). Top 20 hit by Engelbert Humperdinck (Parrot). Top 10 record by Elvis Presley (RCA), 1971.

There Goes My Heart. w. Benny Davis, m. Abner Silver, 1934. Featured and recorded by Isham Jones, vocal by Joe Martin (Victor), and Enric Madriguera's Orchestra (Columbia). Later recordings of note by Louis Jordan (Dec-

ca), Herb Jeffries (Columbia), and Julia Lee (Capitol).

There Goes That Song Again. w. Sammy Cahn, m. Jule Styne, 1944. Introduced by Kay Kyser and his Orchestra, vocal by Georgia Carroll in (MM) *Carolina Blues* and recorded by them (Columbia). Other top recordings by Russ Morgan, with his Orchestra (Decca); Sammy Kaye, vocal by Nancy Norman (Victor); Billy Butterfield, vocal by Margaret Whiting, coupled with million-selling "Moonlight in Vermont" (q.v.) (Capitol); Kate Smith (Columbia).

There I Go. w. Hy Zaret, m. Irving Weiser, 1940. The first hit for Zaret and for the singing-bandleader Vaughn Monroe (Bluebird). Additional recordings by Tommy Tucker, vocal by Amy Arnell (Okeh); Kenny Baker (Victor); Woody Herman (Decca); and Will Bradley (Columbia).

There I Go Dreaming Again. w. Lew Brown, m. Ray Henderson, 1932. Featured by George Olsen's Orchestra, vocal by Ethel Shutta (Victor).

There Is. w/m Bobby Miller and Raynard Miner, 1968. Hit record by The Dells (Cadet).

There Is a Mountain. w/m Donovan Leitch, 1967. Top 20 hit by the Scottish singer Donovan (Epic).

There Is Love. See **Wedding Song.**

There Is No Breeze. w/m Alex Alstone, Dorothy Dick, Roger Bernstein, and André Tabet, 1946. French song with new English lyrics. Recordings: Judy Garland (Decca); Tommy Dorsey, vocal by Stuart Foster (Victor); Gene Krupa, vocal by Carolyn Grey (Columbia); Eddy Howard and his Orchestra (Majestic); Griff Williams and his Orchestra (Sonora).

There Is No Greater Love. w. Marty Symes, m. Isham Jones, 1936. Introduced and recorded by Isham Jones and his Orchestra, vocal by Woody Herman (Decca). Guy Lombardo and his Royal Canadians had a popular record (Victor). Later versions by Billie Holiday (Decca); Al Hibbler, with Johnny Hodges' Orchestra (Mercury); Jimmy Dorsey, vocal by Bob Carroll (MGM); Billy May (Capitol); and many other performances in albums.

There Is Nothin' Like a Dame. w. Oscar Hammerstein II, m. Richard Rodgers, 1949. Introduced by the sailors and marines in (TM) *South Pacific*, and in the film version (MM) *South Pacific*, 1958.

There Isn't Any Limit to My Love. w/m Al Hoffman, Al Goodhart, and Maurice Sigler, 1936. Introduced by Jack Buchanan in the British film (MM) *This'll Make You Whistle*, in which he repeated his stage role. Recorded by the Gene Kardos Band, with vocal by Bea Wain, one of her first commercial releases (Melotone).

There'll Always Be an England. w/m Ross Parker and Hugh Charles, 1939. English success, written at the outset of World War II. Well-received in the United States.

There'll Be No Teardrops Tonight. w/m Hank Williams and Nelson King, 1949. Introduced by Hank Williams (MGM). Tony Bennett had a 1954 Top 10 record (Columbia).

There'll Be Sad Songs (to Make You Cry). w/m Wayne Brathwaite, Barry Eastmond, and Billy Ocean, 1986. #1 chart record from the album "Love Zone" by Billy Ocean (Jive).

There'll Be Some Changes Made. w. Billy Higgins, m. W. Benton Overstreet, 1924. Introduced by vaudevillian/writer Billy Higgins. First recording by Ethel Waters (Black Swan). Among the many others: Marion Harris (Brunswick); Mildred Bailey (Vocalion); Ted Lewis (Columbia); Bunny Berigan (Victor); Sophie Tucker (Okeh); The Boswell Sisters (Brunswick); Gene Krupa, vocal by Irene Daye (Okeh); Vaughn Monroe (Bluebird); Benny Goodman (Victor). Sung by Dolores Gray in (MP) *Designing Woman*, 1957. Performed by Ann Reinking in the Bob Fosse film (MM) *All That Jazz*, 1979.

There'll Come a Time. w/m Eugene B. Record and Floyd Smith, 1969. Top 40 record by Betty Everett (Uni).

There'll Come a Time. w/m Shelton Brooks, 1911.

There'll Come a Time. w/m Charles K. Harris, 1895.

There'll Soon Be a Rainbow. w/m Henry Nemo and David Saxon, 1943. One of Perry Como's earliest chart singles (Victor).

There Must Be a Way. w/m Sammy Gallop and David Saxon, 1945. Leading records by Charlie Spivak, vocal by Jimmy Saunders (Victor), and by Johnnie (Johnny) Johnston (Capitol).

There Must Be More to Love Than This. w/m William E. Taylor and LaVerne Thomas, 1970. Hit Country chart record by Jerry Lee Lewis (Mercury).

There Must Be Somethin' Better Than Love. w. Dorothy Fields, m. Morton Gould, 1950. Introduced by Pearl Bailey in (TM) *Arms and the Girl*. Leading records by Pearl Bailey (Columbia); Artie Shaw, vocal by Mary Ann McCall (Decca).

There Never Was a Girl Like You. w. Harry H. Williams, m. Egbert Van Alstyne, 1907.

There Never Was a Time. w/m Mira Smith and Margaret Lewis, 1969. Recorded by Jeannie C. Riley (Plantation).

There Once Was a Man. w/m Richard Adler and Jerry Ross, 1954. Introduced by John Raitt and Janis Paige in (TM) *The Pajama Game*. In (MM) *The Pajama Game*, 1957, it was sung by John Raitt and Doris Day.

There Once Was an Owl. w. Harry B. Smith, m. Victor Herbert, 1903. Vocal sextet from (TM) *Babette*. Allan Jones and Mary Martin sang it in (MM) *The Great Victor Herbert*, 1939.

There's a Big Wheel. w/m Don Gibson, 1960. Hit C&W record by Wilma Lee and Stoney Cooper (Hickory).

There's a Bluebird at My Window. w. Mack Gordon, m. Harry Revel, 1933. Sung by Jack Oakie in (MM) *Sitting Pretty*.

There's a Boat Dat's Leavin' Soon for New York. w. Ira Gershwin, m. George Gershwin, 1935. Introduced by John W. Bubbles and Anne Brown in (TM) *Porgy and Bess*. In the film version (MM) *Porgy and Bess*, 1959, it was sung by Sammy Davis, Jr.

There's a Boy in Harlem. w. Lorenz Hart, m. Richard Rodgers, 1938. Introduced by Jeni LeGon in (MM) *Fools for Scandal*. Recorded by Tommy Dorsey with vocal by Edythe Wright (Victor), and Bob Crosby and his Band (Decca).

There's a Bridle Hangin' on the Wall. w/m Carson Robison, 1936. Featured by the composer.

There's a Broken Heart for Every Light on Broadway. w. Howard Johnson, m. Fred Fisher, 1915. A popular vaudeville song of its day. Leading record by Elsie Baker (Victor). The song was heard in the Fisher film biography (MM) *Oh, You Beautiful Doll*. 1949.

There's a Cabin in the Pines. w/m Billy Hill, 1933. Introduced on radio by George Hall's Orchestra, vocal by Loretta Lee. Among recordings: Mildred Bailey (Brunswick), Ray Noble (HMV-Victor), Johnny Mercer (Varsity).

There's a Chill on the Hill Tonight. w. Jimmie Davis and Nelson Cogane, m. Dick Robertson and Sammy Mysels, 1944. Recorded by Jimmie Davis (Decca).

There's a Cradle in Caroline. w. Sam M. Lewis and Joe Young, m. Fred E. Ahlert, 1927.

There's a Dixie Girl Who's Longing for a Yankee Doodle Boy. w. Robert F. Roden, m. George W. Meyer, 1911.

There's a Far Away Look in Your Eye. w. Irving Taylor, m. Vic Mizzy, 1938. Mizzy's first song success. Introduced and recorded by Jimmy Dorsey and his Orchestra (Decca).

There's a Girl in Havana. w/m Irving Berlin, Ted Snyder, and E. Ray Goetz, 1911. Sung by Will Archie and Helen Hayes in (TM) *The Never Homes*. The sheet music credited E.

Ray Goetz and A. Baldwin Sloane as the writers, but Berlin and Snyder, with Goetz, contributed the song that became the show-stopper.

There's a Girl in the Heart of Maryland (With a Heart That Belongs to Me). w. Ballard MacDonald, m. Harry Carroll, 1913.

There's a Girl in This World for Every Boy, and a Boy for Every Girl. w. Will D. Cobb, m. Ted Snyder, 1907.

There's a Gold Mine in the Sky. w/m Charles Kenny and Nick Kenny, 1938. Used as title song of (MP) *There's a Gold Mine in the Sky*, sung and recorded by Gene Autry (Vocalion). Among other recordings: Bing Crosby (Decca), Horace Heidt (Brunswick), Isham Jones (Vocalion), and singer Kate Smith (Victor).

There's a Great Day Coming Mañana. w. E. Y. Harburg, m. Burton Lane, 1940. Introduced by Al Jolson in (TM) *Hold on to Your Hats*.

There's a Honky Tonk Angel (Who'll Take Me Back In). w/m Troy Seals and Denzil Rice, 1974. Hit Country record by Conway Twitty (MCA).

There's a Kind of Hush (All over the World). w/m Les Reed and Geoff Stevens, 1966. Written and recorded in England. Herman's Hermits were awarded a gold record for their U.S. release (MGM). Revived by The Carpenters (A&M), 1976.

There's a Light in Your Eyes. w. P. G. Wodehouse, m. Ivan Caryll, 1918. From (TM) *The Girl Behind the Gun*.

There's a Little Bit of Bad in Every Good Little Girl. w. Grant Clarke, m. Fred Fisher, 1916. Irving Kaufman (Columbia) and Billy Murray (Victor) both had popular recordings.

There's a Little Bit of Everything in Texas. w/m Ernest Tubb, 1946. Recorded by Ernest Tubb (Decca).

There's a Little Bit of You in Every Love Song. w. E. Y. Harburg, m. Sammy Fain,

1933. Sung by Roger Pryor in (MM) *Moonlight and Pretzels.*

There's a Little Lane Without a Turning on the Way to Home, Sweet Home. w. Sam M. Lewis, m. George W. Meyer, 1915.

There's a Little Spark of Love Still Burning. w. Joseph McCarthy, m. Fred Fisher, 1914. Recorded by Henry Burr (Victor).

There's a Little Star Shining for You. w/m James Thornton, 1897. Hit song with leading recording by Dan Quinn (Edison).

There's a Long, Long Trail. w. Stoddard King, m. Zo Elliott, 1917. This song became a great favorite with British and American troops in World War I, though written in 1913 by two seniors at Yale.

There's a Lull in My Life. w. Mack Gordon, m. Harry Warren, 1937. Introduced by Alice Faye in (MM) *Wake Up and Live* and recorded by her, coupled with the title song (Brunswick). Other popular versions by Teddy Wilson (Brunswick); George Hall, vocal by Dolly Dawn (Variety); Duke Ellington, vocal by Ivie Anderson (Master).

There's a Lump of Sugar Down in Dixie. w. Alfred Bryan and Jack Yellen, m. Albert Gumble, 1918. Featured and recorded by Al Jolson (Columbia). Best-selling record by Marion Harris (Victor).

There's a Moon Out Tonight. w/m Alfred Striano, Joseph Luccisano, and Alfonso Gentile, 1961. Hit record by The Capris (Old Town).

There's a New Moon Over My Shoulder. w/m Jimmie Davis, Ekko Whelan, and Lee Blastic, 1944. Country song introduced and recorded by Jimmie Davis (Decca). Tex Ritter (Capitol) had the best-seller.

There's a New Star in Heaven Tonight— Rudolph Valentino. w. J. Keirn Brennan and Irving Mills, m. Jimmy McHugh, 1926. Vernon Dalhart (Columbia) (Victor) (Edison) (Edison Amberol) (Gennett) (Banner) (Domino) (Harmony) (Regal) and Frank Munn (Brunswick) recorded this musical reference to the death of the motion picture star.

There's a Place. w/m John Lennon and Paul McCartney, 1963. Coupled with the hit "Twist and Shout," (q.v.) by The Beatles (Tollie).

There's a Quaker Down in Quaker Town. w. David Berg, m. Alfred Solman, 1916. Recorded by Albert Campbell and Henry Burr (Victor).

There's a Rainbow 'round My Shoulder. w/m Dave Dreyer, Billy Rose and Al Jolson, 1928. Sung by Al Jolson in (MM) *The Singing Fool.* Jolson again sang it in (MM) *The Jolson Story* in 1946, dubbing on the soundtrack for Larry Parks in the title role. It was heard as the title song of (MM) *Rainbow 'round My Shoulder* featuring Frankie Laine and Billy Daniels in 1952.

There's a Small Hotel. w. Lorenz Hart, m. Richard Rodgers, 1936. Originally written for Billy Rose's 1935 musical *Jumbo,* but dropped before the opening. Introduced by Ray Bolger and Doris Carson in (TM) *On Your Toes.* It was played in the background for the film version (MM) *On Your Toes,* 1939; sung by Betty Garrett in the Rodgers and Hart story, (MM) *Words and Music,* 1948; sung by Frank Sinatra in (MM) *Pal Joey,* 1957.

There's a Star Spangled Banner Waving Somewhere. w/m Paul Roberts and Shelby Darnell, 1942. Best-selling record by Elton Britt (Bluebird). Jimmy Wakely also had a popular version (Decca). Revived by Red River Dave (Savoy) in 1950 as "There's a Star Spangled Banner Waving #2 (The Ballad of Francis Powers)." Powers, a U-2 pilot, was shot down in Russia two years before.

There's a Wah-wah Gal in Agua Caliente. w/m Walter Donaldson, 1930. Recordings by the bands of: Ben Pollack (Perfect), Johnny Johnson (Victor), Rube Bloom and his Bayou Boys (Columbia), Isham Jones (Brunswick).

There's Been a Change in Me. w/m Cy Coben, 1951. Featured and recorded by Eddy Arnold (RCA Victor).

There's Danger in Your Eyes, Cherie. w/m Pete Wendling, Harry Richman, and Jack Meskill, 1930. Introduced by Harry Richman in (MM) *Puttin' on the Ritz* and recorded by him (Brunswick). Coinciding with the issuance of the film, there were recordings by Fred Waring's Pennsylvanians (Victor); Sid Gary (Harmony); Smith Ballew, with Ed Lloyd's Orchestra (Okeh); Guy Lombardo, vocal by Carmen Lombardo (Columbia); Vincent Lopez (Perfect); James Melton (Victor); Irving Kaufman (Columbia). Danielle Darrieux sang it in (MM) *Rich, Young and Pretty*, 1951.

There's Everything Nice About You (There's Something Nice About Everyone). w. Arthur Terker and Alfred Bryan, m. Pete Wendling, 1927.

There's Frost on the Moon. w. Joe Young, m. Fred E. Ahlert, 1937. Featured and recorded by Tommy Dorsey, vocal by Edythe Wright (Victor).

There's Gonna Be a Showdown. w/m Kenny Gamble and Leon Huff, 1969. Top 40 record by Archie Bell and The Drells (Atlantic).

There's Good Blues Tonight. w/m Abe Osser and Edna Osser, 1946. Recorded by Tommy Dorsey's Clambake Seven, vocal by Sy Oliver (Victor).

There's Gotta Be Something Better Than This. w. Dorothy Fields, m. Cy Coleman, 1966. Introduced by Gwen Verdon, Helen Gallagher, and Thelma Oliver in (TM) *Sweet Charity*. In the film version (MM) *Sweet Charity*, 1969, it was performed by Shirley MacLaine, Chita Rivera, and Paula Kelly.

There's Got to Be a Word. w/m Don Ciccone, 1966. Recorded by The Innocence (Kama Sutra).

There Shall Be No Night. w. Gladys Shelley, m. Abner Silver, 1940. Recorded by Joan Edwards (Decca) and the bands of Duke Ellington, vocal by Herb Jeffries (Victor); Dick Jurgens, vocal by Harry Cool (Okeh); Bob Chester, vocal by Dolores O'Neill (Bluebird).

There She Goes. w/ Eddie Miller, Durward Haddock, and W. S. Stevenson, 1955. Introduced and recorded by Carl Smith (Columbia). Revived by Jerry Wallace in 1960 (Challenge).

There's Honey on the Moon Tonight. w. Haven Gillespie and Mack David, m. J. Fred Coots, 1938. Featured and recorded by Fats Waller (Victor).

There's Life in the Old Dog Yet. w. P. G. Wodehouse, m. Ivan Caryll, 1918. From (TM) *The Girl Behind the Gun.*

There's More to the Kiss Than the X-X-X. w. Irving Caesar, m. George Gershwin, 1919. Interpolated by Mollie King in the Broadway production of the English musical (TM) *Good Morning Judge*. With a slight title alteration to "There's More to the Kiss than the Sound," it was sung by Helen Clark and ensemble in (TM) *La, La, Lucille*, 1919. The only known recording extant is by Barbara Cook, Elaine Stritch, Anthony Perkins, and Bobby Short in the album "Ben Bagley's George Gershwin Revisited" (MGM).

There's No Business Like Show Business. w/m Irving Berlin, 1946. Introduced by William O'Neal, Ray Middleton, Marty May, and Ethel Merman in (TM) *Annie Get Your Gun*. In the film version (MM) *Annie Get Your Gun*, 1950, it was performed by Betty Hutton, Howard Keel, Louis Calhern, and Keenan Wynn. It was sung as the title song in (MM) *There's No Business Like Show Business*, 1954, by Ethel Merman, Dan Dailey, Donald O'Connor, Johnny Ray, and Marilyn Monroe. This rousing number is considered to be the anthem of the theatrical world.

(There's) No Gettin' Over Me. w/m Tom Brasfield and Walt Aldridge, 1981. C&W/Pop chart hit by Ronnie Milsap (RCA).

There's No Holding Me. w. Ira Gershwin, m. Arthur Schwartz, 1946. Introduced by Ray McDonald and Martha Stewart in (TM) *Park Avenue*. Featured and recorded by Hildegarde (Decca).

There's No Livin' Without Your Lovin'. w/m Paul Kaufman and Jerry Harris, 1966. Recorded by the British duo Peter and Gordon (Capitol).

There's No Me Without You. w/m Edward Bivins, 1973. Top 10 R&B record and crossover Pop chart entry by The Manhattans (Columbia). Written by a member of the group.

There's No North or South Today. w/m Paul Dresser, 1901. Dresser wrote this about the country's unity in the Spanish-American War.

There's No One But You. w/m Austen Croom-Johnson and Redd Evans, 1946. Originally titled "The Prince George Hotel," as a radio jingle for the New York hotel of that name. Commercial recordings by The Mills Brothers (Decca) and Hal McIntyre, vocal by Frankie Lester (Cosmo).

There's No Other (Like My Baby). w/m Phil Spector and Leroy Bates, 1961. Popular record by The Crystals (Philles).

There's No Place Like Your Arms. w. Bickley Reichner, m. Clay Boland, 1938. Featured and recorded by Jan Savitt, vocal by Bon Bon (Bluebird); Tommy Dorsey and his Orchestra (Victor); Arthur Godfrey (Bluebird).

There's No Reason in the World. w/m Jerry Herman, 1961. Introduced by Robert Weede in (TM) *Milk and Honey*.

There's Not a Thing (I Wouldn't Do for You). w/m Billy Hughes, 1949. Hit C&W chart record by Eddy Arnold (Victor).

There's Nothing Better Than Love. w/m Luther Vandross and J. Skip Anderson, 1987. #1 R&B chart record and Pop chart entry by Luther Vandross with Gregory Hines (Epic).

There's Nothing Like a Model "T". w. Sammy Cahn, m. Jule Styne, 1947. Introduced by Jack McCauley, Nanette Fabray, and company in (TM) *High Button Shoes*. Their cast album performance was released as a single (Victor).

There's Nothing Too Good for My Baby. w/m Harry Akst, Benny Davis, and Eddie Cantor, 1931. Sung by Cantor in (MM) *Palmy Days*. Leo Reisman and his Orchestra recorded it (Victor) with an uncredited vocal by Eddie Cantor.

There's Nothing Wrong with a Kiss. w. Irving Caesar and Graham John, m. Oscar Levant, 1930. Sung by Paula Stone and Eddie Foy, Jr. in (TM) *Ripples*.

There's No Tomorrow. w. and adaptation of music by Al Hoffman, Leon Carr, and Leo Corday, 1949. Based on the Italian song, "O Sole Mio," music by Edoardo di Capua. Tony Martin had a hit record (RCA Victor) and then sang it in (MM) *Two Tickets to Broadway*, 1951.

There's No Two Ways About Love. w. Ted Koehler, m. James P. Johnson and Irving Mills, 1943. Introduced by Lena Horne, Bill Robinson, and Cab Calloway in (MM) *Stormy Weather*. Horne, with Calloway and his Orchestra, recorded it for the Armed Forces overseas (V-disc 12").

There's No Wings on My Angel. w/m Cy Coben, Irving Melsher, and Eddy Arnold, 1949. From the film (MP) *Feudin' Rhythm*. Recorded by Eddy Arnold (RCA).

There's No You. w. Tom Adair, m. Hal Hopper, 1944. Jo Stafford had the first popular recording (Capitol). Others: Charlie Barnet and his Orchestra (Decca), Bill Doggett (King), Martha Stewart (Victor).

There's Oceans of Love by the Beautiful Sea. w/m J. Fred Coots and Little Jack Little, 1932. Popularized on radio. Among recordings: Alex Bartha and his Hotel Traymore [Atlantic City] Orchestra (Victor); Joe Haymes, vocal by Larry Murphy (Electradisk); Dick Robertson and his Orchestra (Melotone).

There's Only One of You. w. Al Stillman, m. Robert Allen, 1958. Popular record by The Four Lads (Columbia).

There's Something About an Old Love. w. Irving Mills and Lupin Fein, m. Will Hudson, 1938. Introduced and recorded by Will Hudson and his Orchestra (Brunswick). Other records: the Blue Barron (Bluebird) and Benny Strong (Capitol) bands.

There's Something About a Rose (That Reminds Me of You). w. Irving Kahal and Francis Wheeler, m. Sammy Fain, 1928.

There's Something About a Soldier. w/m Noel Gay, 1933. An English song from the musical production *Soldiers of the King*. The writer used the name as a pseudonym for Reginald M. Armitrage. Featured on radio and in theaters by Rudy Vallee, Ben Bernie, and other performing bands.

There's Something About a Uniform. w/m George M. Cohan, 1909. From (TM) *The Man Who Owns Broadway*.

There's Something in the Air. w. Harold Adamson, m. Jimmy McHugh, 1936. Introduced by Tony Martin in (MM) *Banjo on My Knee*. Martin recorded it (Brunswick), as did Ruth Etting (Decca), Ray Noble with vocal by Al Bowlly (Victor), and Mal Hallett's Orchestra (Decca).

There's Something on Your Mind. w/m Jay McNeely, 1959. Introduced and recorded by Big Jay McNeely and Band, vocal by Sonny Warner (Swingin'). Chart records by Bobby Marchan (Fire), 1960, and Baby Ray (Imperial), 1966.

There Stands the Glass. w/m Mary Jean Schurz, Russ Hull, and Audrey Grisham, 1954. Leading C&W record by Webb Pierce (Decca).

There's the Girl. w/m Holly Knight and Nancy Wilson, 1987. Recorded by the band, Heart, from their album "Bad Animals" (Capitol).

There's Where My Heart Is Tonight. w/m Paul Dresser, 1899.

There's Yes! Yes! in Your Eyes. w. Cliff Friend, m. Joseph H. Santly, 1924. Among recordings: Paul Whiteman (Victor), Art Kahn (Columbia), Guy Lombardo (Decca), Artie Shaw (Columbia), Eddy Howard (Mercury).

There Was a Crooked Man. w. Lee Adams, m. Charles Strouse, 1970. Sung by Trini Lopez on the soundtrack of (MP) *There Was a Crooked Man*.

There Was a Time. w/m James Brown and Buddy Hobgood, 1968. Introduced and recorded by James Brown (King). Chart version by Gene Chandler (Brunswick).

There Will Come a Day (I'm Gonna Happen to You). w/m Brenda Sutton, Michael Sutton, and Kathleen Wakefield, 1977. Recorded by Smokey Robinson (Tamla).

There Will Never Be Another You. w. Mack Gordon, m. Harry Warren, 1942. Introduced by Joan Merrill, accompanied by Sammy Kaye's Orchestra in (MM) *Iceland*, starring Sonja Henie and John Payne. Top recordings: Woody Herman, vocal by Herman (Decca); Sammy Kaye, vocal by Nancy Norman (Victor). Dennis Day sang it in (MM) *I'll Get By*, 1950, and recorded it (Victor). Revived by Chris Montez (A&M), 1966.

There Won't Be Anymore. w/m Charlie Rich, 1974. Top 20 record by Charlie Rich (RCA).

There Won't Be Trumpets. w/m Stephen Sondheim, 1964. Introduced by Lee Remick in (TM) *Anyone Can Whistle*. It was sung by Millicent Martin, Julia McKenzie, and David Kernan in (TM) *Side by Side by Sondheim*, 1974.

There You Go. w/m Johnny Cash, 1957. Introduced and recorded by Johnny Cash (Sun).

These Are Not My People. w/m Joe South, 1967. Leading record by Johnny Rivers (Imperial).

These Boots Are Made for Walking. w/m Lee Hazlewood, 1966. #1 gold record by Nancy Sinatra, produced by Lee Hazlewood (Reprise).

These Dreams. w/m Bernie Taupin and Martin Page, 1986. #1 single by the group, Heart, from the album of their name (Capitol).

These Eyes. w/m Randy Bachman and Burton Cummings, 1969. Hit records by The Guess Who (RCA) and Jr. Walker and The All Stars (Soul).

These Foolish Things (Remind Me of You). w. Holt Marvell (Erich Maschwitz), m. Jack Strachey and Harry Link, 1936. Introduced in the London revue *Spread It Abroad*.

The great airplay, sheet music, and record sales enabled it to become the #1 song and be on "Your Hit Parade" for thirteen weeks. Among top recordings: Benny Goodman, a Jimmy Mundy arrangement, with vocal by Helen Ward (Victor); Nat Brandwynne (Brunswick); Mark Warnow (Victor); Joe Sanders (Decca); Lee Sims (Decca). Outstanding later versions: Art Pepper (Discovery), Gene Krupa (Victor), Thelma Carpenter (Majestic), the Benny Goodman Sextet (Columbia), Herb Jeffries (Exclusive), Lester Young (Philo), the Norman Luboff Choir (Columbia). Song heard in (MP) *A Yank in the R.A.F.*, starring Tyrone Power and Betty Grable, 1941; (MP) *Ghost Catchers*, starring Olsen and Johnson, 1944; (MP) *Tokyo Rose*, starring Humphrey Bogart, 1949.

These Hands. w/m Eddie Noack, 1956. Hit C&W record by Hank Snow (RCA). Pop record by Len Dresslar (Mercury).

These Lonely Hands of Mine. w/m Lamar Morris and Charles E. Norrell, 1969. Top 10 Country chart record by Mel Tillis (Kapp).

These Things I Offer You (for a Lifetime). w/m Morty Nevins, Bennie Benjamin, and George David Weiss, 1951. Leading records by Sarah Vaughan, with Percy Faith's Orchestra (Columbia); Ray Anthony, vocal by Tommy Mercer and the Skyliners (Capitol); Patti Page, with Joe Reisman's Orchestra (Mercury).

These Things You Left Me. w. Hal Dickinson, m. Sidney Lippman, 1940. Introduced and recorded by Benny Goodman, vocal by Helen Forrest (Columbia). Among other recordings: Charlie Barnet, vocal by Bob Carroll (Bluebird); Gene Krupa, vocal by Howard DuLany (Okeh); Ginny Simms, with Eddie South's Orchestra (Okeh).

These Will Be the Best Years of Our Lives. w. Bob Hilliard, m. David Mann, 1949. Leading record by Jo Stafford (Capitol).

The Touch (Le Grisbi). w. Norman Gimbel (Engl.), Marc Lanjean (Fr.), m. Jean Wiener, 1954. Played by harmonicist Wiener on the soundtrack of the French film *Touchez*

Pas au Grisbi. Among recordings: harmonicists Richard Hayman (Mercury) and Larry Adler (Angel); orchestras led by Sy Oliver (New Disc), Harry James (Columbia), and Ted Heath (London).

They All Laughed. w. Ira Gershwin, m. George Gershwin, 1937. Introduced by Fred Astaire and Ginger Rogers in (MM) *Shall We Dance*. Recorded by Astaire, with Johnny Green's Orchestra (Brunswick), and the bands of Tommy Dorsey, vocal by Edythe Wright (Victor); Jimmy Dorsey (Decca); Ozzie Nelson (Bluebird).

They Call It Dancing. w/m Irving Berlin, 1921. In a spoof of current dance forms, this was introduced by Sam Bernard and René Riano in (TM) *The Music Box Revue*.

They Call Me Sister Honky Tonk. w/m Gladys DuBois, Ben Ellison, and Harvey O. Brooks, 1933. Sung by Mae West in (MM) *I'm No Angel*.

They Call the Wind Maria. w. Alan Jay Lerner, m. Frederick Loewe, 1951. Introduced by Rufus Smith in (TM) *Paint Your Wagon*. In (MM) *Paint Your Wagon*, 1969, it was sung by Harve Presnell and chorus.

They Came to Cordura. w. Sammy Cahn, m. James Van Heusen, 1959. From (MP) *They Came to Cordura*. Recorded by Frank Sinatra (Capitol).

They Can't Convince Me. w/m Allan Roberts and Doris Fisher, 1947. Introduced by Rita Hayworth, with voice dubbed on the soundtrack by Anita Ellis, in (MM) *Down to Earth*. Records: Mel Tormé (Musicraft) and Elliot Lawrence and his Orchestra (Columbia).

They Can't Take That Away from Me. w. Ira Gershwin, m. George Gershwin, 1937. Sung by Fred Astaire to Ginger Rogers on a ferryboat in (MM) *Shall We Dance*, and recorded by Astaire, with Johnny Green's Orchestra (Brunswick). It was the only George Gershwin song to be nominated for an Academy Award. Astaire interpolated it in (MM) *The Barclays of Broadway*, 1949.

They Cut Down the Old Pine Tree. w/m Edward Eliscu, William J. (Billy) Hill, Willie Raskin, 1930. This was Hill's first song success. On first copies of the sheet music, the name "George Brown" appears. Hill was known to have sold some of his early songs outright. Gene and Glenn had a popular recording (Victor).

They Didn't Believe Me. w. Michael E. Rourke, m. Jerome Kern, 1914. Kern's first major hit, one of seven Kern songs added to the Broadway production of the London hit (TM) *The Girl from Utah*, was sung by Julia Sanderson and Donald Brian. Rourke used the pseudonym of Herbert Reynolds on his credits. In the Kern screen biography (MM) *Till the Clouds Roll By*, it was sung by Dinah Shore, 1946. Mario Lanza and Kathryn Grayson sang it in (MM) *That Midnight Kiss*, 1949. Tammy Grimes sang it in (TM) *A Musical Jubilee*, 1975.

They Don't Know. w/m Kirsty MacColl, 1984. Top 10 record by British actress/singer Tracey Ullman (MCA).

They Don't Make Them Like They Used To. w/m Burt Bacharach and Carole Bayer Sager, 1986. Introduced by Kenny Rogers on the soundtrack of (MP) *Tough Guys*, starring Burt Lancaster and Kirk Douglas.

They Go Wild, Simply Wild, Over Me. w. Joseph McCarthy, m. Fred Fisher, 1917. Featured and recorded by Marion Harris (Victor). Performed by Gene Kelly in (MM) *For Me and My Gal*, 1943.

They Just Can't Stop It (The Games People Play). w/m Bruce Hawes, Joseph Jefferson, and Charles Simmons, 1975. #1 R&B, #5 Pop gold record by The Spinners (Atlantic).

(They Long to Be) Close to You. w. Hal David, m. Burt Bacharach, 1970. #1 gold record by The Carpenters (A&M). Other recordings by Jerry Butler and Brenda Lee Eager (Mercury), 1972, and B. T. Express (Roadshow), 1976.

They Love Me. w/m Irving Berlin, 1962. Introduced by Nanette Fabray in Berlin's last musical score (TM) *Mr. President*.

They Met in Rio. w. Mack Gordon, m. Harry Warren, 1941. Introduced by Alice Faye and Don Ameche in (MM) *That Night in Rio*.

They Needed a Song Bird in Heaven (So God Took Caruso Away). w. George A. Little, m. Jack Stanley, 1921. From an idea suggested by George Walter Brown following the death of the famous tenor, Enrico Caruso, this song attained some popularity. Recorded by Sam Ash (Grey Gull) and Anthony Urato (Cardinal).

They Never Tell All What They Know. w. Edward Harrigan, m. David Braham, 1893.

They're All Sweeties. w. Andrew B. Sterling, m. Harry Von Tilzer, 1919. Recorded by Van and Schenck (Columbia) and featured by them in vaudeville.

They're Coming to Take Me Away, Ha-Haaa! w/m Jerry Samuels, 1966. Top 10, novelty hit by Napoleon XIV (Warner Bros.). Napoleon is New York recording engineer/writer Samuels.

They're Either Too Young or Too Old. w. Frank Loesser, m. Arthur Schwartz, 1943. Introduced by Bette Davis in (MM) *Thank Your Lucky Stars*. Hit record by Jimmy Dorsey, vocal by Kitty Kallen (Decca). Nominated for Academy Award.

They're Playing Our Song. w. Carole Bayer Sager, m. Marvin Hamlisch, 1979. Introduced by Robert Klein and Lucie Arnaz in (TM) *They're Playing Our Song*.

They're Wearing 'Em Higher in Hawaii. w. Joe Goodwin, m. Halsey K. Mohr, 1916. A comedy song popular with vaudevillians. Featured by Eddie Cantor and Al Jolson. Recordings: Arthur Collins and Byron Harlan (Victor), Morton Harvey (Columbia).

They Say. w. Edward Heyman, m. Paul Mann and Stephan Weiss, 1938. Popular recordings by Artie Shaw, vocal by Helen Forrest (Bluebird); Connie Boswell, with Woody Herman's Orchestra (Decca); Sammy Kaye, vocal by Tommy Ryan (Victor); Ted Fio Rito, vocal by Muzzy Marcelino (Decca); Ethel Waters (Bluebird).

They Say It's Wonderful. w/m Irving Berlin, 1946. The popular ballad from the hit-filled score of (TM) *Annie Get Your Gun*, introduced by Ethel Merman and Ray Middleton. Best-selling records by Frank Sinatra, coupled with "The Girl That I Marry" (q.v.) from the same show (Columbia); Perry Como (RCA Victor); Andy Russell (Capitol); Bing Crosby (Decca).

They Took the Stars out of Heaven. w/m Floyd Tillman, 1943. Hit Country record by Floyd Tillman (Decca).

They Want Money. w/m Mohandas Dewese and Edward Riley, 1989. Hit R&B chart record by Kool Moe Dee (Jive).

They Were All Out of Step But Jim. w/m Irving Berlin, 1918. Popular vaudeville song. Featured and recorded by Van & Schenck (Columbia) and Billy Murray (Victor).

They Were Doin' the Mambo. w/m Don Raye and Sonny Burke, 1954. Popularized by Vaughn Monroe with his Orchestra (RCA Victor).

They Were You. w. Tom Jones, m. Harvey Schmidt, 1960. Introduced by Kenneth Nelson and Rita Gardner in (TM) *The Fantasticks*.

Thicker Than Water. See **(Love Is) Thicker Than Water**.

Thief in the Night. w. Howard Dietz, m. Arthur Schwartz, 1935. Introduced by Ethel Waters in (TM) *At Home Abroad*.

Thine Alone. w. Henry Blossom, m. Victor Herbert, 1917. Introduced by Grace Breen and Walter Scanlon in (TM) *Eileen*. Allan Jones and Mary Martin sang it in (MM) *The Great Victor Herbert* in 1939.

Thing, The. w/m Charles R. Grean, 1950. Novelty. Phil Harris, with Walter Scharf's Orchestra (RCA Victor) had a #1 million-seller. Other leading versions by Arthur Godfrey, with Archie Bleyer's Orchestra (Columbia); The Ames Brothers, with Roy Ross's Orchestra (Coral).

Things. w/m Bobby Darin, 1962. Top 10 record by Bobby Darin (Atco). Revived by Anne Murray (Capitol), 1976.

Things Ain't What They Used to Be. m. Mercer Ellington and Edward Kennedy "Duke" Ellington, 1941. Introduced by Duke Ellington and his Orchestra. First recorded by Johnny Hodges' Band (Bluebird). Performed by the Ellington band in (MM) *Cabin in the Sky*, 1942. Other records: Cootie Williams (Hit) and Wild Bill Davis (Mercer). See also "Time's A-wastin'."

Things Are Looking Up. w. Ira Gershwin, m. George Gershwin, 1937. Introduced by Fred Astaire and Joan Fontaine in (MM) *A Damsel in Distress*. Astaire recorded it (Brunswick).

Things Can Only Get Better. w/m Howard Jones, 1985. Top 10 record by English singer Howard Jones (Elektra).

Things Have Gone to Pieces. w/m Leon Payne, 1965. Introduced by Leon Payne (D Records), 1964. Top 10 Country chart record by George Jones (Musicor).

Things I'd Like to Say. w. Ronald Rice, m. Leslie Kummel, 1969. Top 20 record by The New Colony Six (Mercury).

Things I Love, The. w. Lew Harris, m. Harold Barlow, 1941. Adapted from Tchaikowsky's *Melody*, Opus 42, No. 3. Introduced and recorded by Barry Wood (Victor). Best-selling record by Jimmy Dorsey, vocal by Bob Eberly (Decca).

Things I Should Have Said. w/m P. F. Sloan and Steve Barri, 1967. Top 40 record by The Grass Roots (Dunhill).

Things Might Have Been So Different. w. Sam M. Lewis, m. J. Fred Coots, 1935. Featured and recorded by Ruth Etting (Columbia) and Richard Himber and his Orchestra, vocal by Joey Nash (Victor).

Things That I Used to Do, The. w/m Eddie "Guitar Slim" Jones, 1954. Million-selling R&B hit by Guitar Slim, accompanied on piano by Ray Charles (Specialty).

Things That Might Have Been. w/m Bob Miller, 1939. Introduced and recorded by Roy Acuff (Okeh).

Things That Were Made for Love, The (You Can't Take Away). w. Charles Tobias and Irving Kahal, m. Peter De Rose, 1930. Recorded by Sammy Fain (Diva), Sid Gary (Perfect), Nat Shilkret (Victor).

Things We Did Last Summer, The. w. Sammy Cahn, m. Jule Styne, 1946. Leading recording by Frank Sinatra (Columbia).

Things We Do for Love, The. w/m Graham Gouldman and Eric Stewart, 1977. Gold record by the English group 10cc (Mercury).

Think. w/m Aretha Franklin and Ted White, 1968. Introduced and gold record by Aretha Franklin (Atlantic).

Think. w/m Lowman Pauling, 1957. Introduced by The "5" Royales (King). James Brown recorded the song four times, all chartmakers: (Federal), 1960; (King), 1967; two versions with Vicki Anderson (Polydor), 1973.

Think (About It). w/m James Brown, 1972. Recorded by Lyn Collins (People).

Think About Love (Think About Me). w/m Richard Brannon and Tom Campbell, 1986. #1 Country chart record by Dolly Parton (RCA).

Think About Me. w/m Christine McVie, 1980. Recorded by the British group Fleetwood Mac (Warner Bros.).

Think I'll Go Somewhere and Cry Myself to Sleep. w/m Bill Anderson, 1966. Top 40 record by Al Martino (Capitol).

Think I'm in Love. w/m Eddie Money and Randy Oda, 1982. Recorded by Eddie Money (Columbia).

Thinking of a Rendezvous. w/m Bobby Braddock and Sonny Throckmorton, 1976. Hit Country record by Johnny Duncan (Columbia).

Thinking of You. w/m Jim Messina, 1973. Top 20 record by Loggins and Messina (Columbia).

Thinking of You. w. Bert Kalmar, m. Harry Ruby, 1927, 1950. Introduced by Mary Eaton and Oscar Shaw in (TM) *The Five O'Clock Girl*. Fred Astaire and Vera-Ellen performed it in the Kalmar and Ruby biography, (MM) *Three Little Words*, 1950, followed by new popular recordings by Don Cherry (Decca); Eddie Fisher, with his first chart record (RCA Victor); Sarah Vaughan (Columbia).

(I've Grown So Lonesome) Thinking of You. w. Paul Ash, m. Walter Donaldson, 1926. Recorded by Ruth Etting (Columbia); Paul Ash and his Orchestra (Columbia); Willard Robison (Perfect). Kay Kyser and his Orchestra revived it (Brunswick), 1935. It became his theme and was used in his "singing song titles." At the start of each number, the band would play a few bars and then Kyser, over the theme, would announce the title of the song, and the singer.

Think Nothing About It. w/m Curtis Mayfield, 1964. Recorded by Gene Chandler (Constellation).

Think of Me (When You're Lonely). w. Estella Olsen, m. Don Rich, 1966. Country hit, recorded by Buck Owens (Capitol).

Think Twice. w/m Joe Shapiro, Jimmy Williams, and Clyde Otis, 1961. Introduced by Brook Benton (Mercury). Revived by Jackie Wilson and LaVern Baker (Brunswick), 1966.

Thin Line Between Love and Hate. w/m Richard Poindexter, Robert Poindexter, and Jackie Members, 1971. #1 R&B and Top 20 Pop gold record by The Persuaders (Atco). Revived by The Pretenders (Sire), 1984.

847

Third Man Theme. m. Anton Karas, 1950. Introduced by Anton Karas playing the zither on the soundtrack of (MP) *The Third Man*. Karas's #1 recording sold over two million copies (London). Guy Lombardo, with Don Rodney on guitar, had a one million-seller (Decca). Revived by Herb Alpert and The Tijuana Brass (A&M), 1965.

Third Rate Romance. w/m Russell Smith, 1975. Top 20 record by The Amazing Rhythm Aces (ABC).

Third Time Lucky (First Time I Was a Fool). w/m Dave Peverett, 1979. Recorded by the group Foghat (Bearsville).

Thirty One Flavors. w. Mack David, m. Ernest Gold, 1963. Introduced on the soundtrack of (MP) *It's a Mad, Mad, Mad, Mad World* by The Shirelles, who also recorded it (Scepter).

This Bitter Earth. w/m Clyde Otis, 1960. Introduced and recorded by Dinah Washington (Mercury). Revived by The Satisfactions (Lionel), 1970.

This Boy. See **Ringo's Theme**.

This Can't Be Love. w. Lorenz Hart, m. Richard Rodgers, 1938. Introduced by Marcy Westcott and Eddie Albert in (TM) *The Boys from Syracuse*. Rosemary Lane sang it in (MM) *The Boys from Syracuse*, 1940. Doris Day interpolated it in (MM) *Jumbo*, 1962.

This Changing World. w. Harold Adamson, m. Dana Suesse, 1940. Among recordings: Kay Kyser, vocal by Ginny Simms (Columbia); Will Bradley, vocal by Carlotta Dale (Vocalion); Will Osborne, with his Orchestra (Varsity); Barry Wood (Columbia).

This Could Be the Night. w/m Paul Dean, Jonathan Cain, Mike Reno, and Bill Wray, 1986. Top 10 single from the album "Lovin' Every Minute of It" by the Canadian group Loverboy (Columbia).

This Could Be the Start of Something. w/m Steve Allen, 1956. Introduced on Steve Allen's Sunday night TV show by Les Brown

and his Orchestra. The song became Allen's theme and has been heavily performed, with many recordings. It is a good example of an important standard without a hit record.

This Crazy Love. w/m Roger Murrah and J. Hicks, 1987. #1 Country chart hit by The Oak Ridge Boys, from their album "Where the Fast Love Ends (RCA).

This Diamond Ring. w/m Al Kooper, Irwin Levine, and Bob Brass, 1965. #1 gold record by Gary Lewis and The Playboys (Liberty).

This Door Swings Both Ways. w/m Estelle Levitt and Don Thomas, 1966. Recorded by Herman's Hermits (MGM).

This Friendly World. w/m Ken Darby, 1959. Introduced by Fabian in (MM) *Hound Dog Man*, and on records (Chancellor).

This Funny World. w. Lorenz Hart, m. Richard Rodgers, 1926. Introduced by Belle Baker in (TM) *Betsy*, a short-lived Ziegfeld-produced musical that opened on Broadway one night after the writers' hit show, *Peggy-Ann*, made its debut.

This Girl Is a Woman Now. w/m Abe Bernstein and Victor Millrose, 1969. Top 10 record by Gary Puckett and The Union Gap.

This Girl's in Love with You. See: **This Guy's (Girl's) in Love with You**.

This Guy's (Girl's) in Love with You. w. Hal David, m. Burt Bacharach, 1968. #1 gold record by Herb Alpert (vocal) and The Tijuana Brass (A&M). Dionne Warwick recorded a Top 10 girl's version (Scepter), 1969.

This Happy Feeling. w/m Jay Livingston and Ray Evans, 1958. Introduced by Debbie Reynolds in (MP) *This Happy Feeling*.

This Heart of Mine. w. Arthur Freed, m. Harry Warren, 1946. Performed by Fred Astaire and Lucille Bremer in (MM) *Ziegfeld Follies*. Judy Garland recorded it prior to the release of the film (Decca). It was heard orchestrally in (MM) *The Barkleys of Broadway*, 1949.

This Is a Great Country. w/m Irving Berlin, 1962. Introduced by Robert Ryan in (TM) *Mr. President.*

This Is All I Ask. w/m Gordon Jenkins, 1963. Recorded by Tony Bennett (Columbia). Spoken word version by Burl Ives (Decca).

This Is Always. w. Mack Gordon, m. Harry Warren, 1946. Introduced by June Haver in (MM) *Three Little Girls in Blue.* Leading records by Dick Haymes (Decca); Jo Stafford (Capitol); Harry James, vocal by Buddy Di Vito (Columbia); Ginny Simms (ARA); Betty Rhodes (Victor).

This Is It. w/m Kenny Loggins and Michael McDonald, 1979. Recorded by Kenny Loggins (Columbia).

This Is It. w/m Cindy Walker, 1965. Crossover (C&W/Pop) hit record by Jim Reeves (RCA).

This Is It. w. Dorothy Fields, m. Arthur Schwartz, 1939. Introduced by Ethel Merman, with Walter Cassel, Robert Shanley, Edward Kane, and Davis Cunningham in (TM) *Stars in Your Eyes.* Recordings: Merman (Liberty Music Shops), Frances Langford (Decca), Artie Shaw (Bluebird).

This Is My Country. w/m Curtis Mayfield, 1968. Top 40 record by The Impressions (Curtom).

This Is My Country. w. Don Raye, m. Al Jacobs, 1940. Introduced and featured by Fred Waring and his Pennsylvanians.

(This Is My) Lucky Day. See **Lucky Day (This Is My).**

This Is My Night to Dream. w. Johnny Burke, m. James V. Monaco, 1938. Introduced in (MM) "Doctor Rhythm" and on records (Decca) by Bing Crosby. Abe Lyman and his Orchestra featured it on his radio program and recorded it (Bluebird). Nat "King" Cole had a later version (Capitol).

This Is My Song. w. Will Holt, m. Gary William Friedman, 1983. Sung by the company in the off-Broadway (TM) *Taking My Turn.*

This Is My Song. w/m Charles Chaplin, 1967. Theme from Charles Chaplin's last film as director and actor [cameo role] (MP) *A Countess in Hong Kong.* Top 10 record by Petula Clark (Warner Bros.).

This Is My Song. w/m Dick Charles, 1952. Written for and recorded by Patti Page (Mercury), who used it as the theme of her NBC-TV series.

This Is New. w. Ira Gershwin, m. Kurt Weill, 1941. Introduced by Gertrude Lawrence in (TM) *Lady in the Dark.* It was sung by Ginger Rogers in the film version (MM) *Lady in the Dark,* 1943. Gertrude Lawrence recorded four singles from the show, of which this was one (Victor). Helen Forrest also sang it with Benny Goodman's Orchestra (Columbia).

This Is No Dream. w. Benny Davis, m. Ted Shapiro and Tommy Dorsey, 1939. Introduced and recorded by Tommy Dorsey, vocal by Jack Leonard (Victor). Brother Jimmy [Dorsey] cut his version with vocal by Bob Eberly (Decca), as did Horace Heidt, vocal by Larry Cotton (Brunswick).

This Is No Laughing Matter. w. Buddy Kaye, m. Al Frisch, 1941. Most popular recordings—in order: Charlie Spivak, vocal by Garry Stevens (Okeh); Glenn Miller, vocal by Ray Eberle (Bluebird); Jimmy Dorsey, vocal by Bob Eberly (Decca).

This Is Not America. w/m Pat Metheny and Lyle Mays, 1985. Theme from (MP) *The Falcon and the Snowman.* Top 10 record by David Bowie and jazz guitarist/composer Pat Metheny's Group (EMI America).

This Isn't Heaven. w/m Richard Rodgers, 1962. Introduced by Bobby Darin as one of five new songs written by Rodgers for the second musical film version of (MM) *State Fair.*

This Is Our Last Night Together. w/m Jay Gorney and Lew Brown, 1934. Sung by Sylvia Froos and John Boles in (MM) *Stand Up and Cheer.*

This Is Romance. w. Edward Heyman, m. Vernon Duke, 1933. Featured and recorded by Glen Gray and the Casa Loma Orchestra, vocal by Kenny Sargent (Brunswick); Ben Bernie (Columbia); Jack Fulton (Vocalion); Ray Noble, vocal by Al Bowlly (HMV-Victor); Nye Mayhew (Perfect). Artie Shaw revived it in 1941 (Victor).

This Is the Army, Mr. Jones. w/m Irving Berlin, 1942. Sung by the full company in the all-soldier show (TM) *This Is the Army*, and in the film version (MM) *This Is the Army*, both produced to raise money for the Army Emergency Relief Fund. Proceeds from the music also went to AER.

This Is the Beginning of the End. w/m Mack Gordon, 1940. Introduced by Dorothy Lamour in (MP) *Johnny Apollo* and recorded by her (Bluebird). Among other records: Tommy Dorsey, vocal by Frank Sinatra (Victor); Buddy Clark (Varsity); Al Donahue, vocal by Paula Kelly (Vocalion). Revived by Don Cornell (Coral), 1952.

This Is the Life. w. Lee Adams, m. Charles Strouse, 1964. Introduced by Billy Daniels, Sammy Davis, Jr., and company in (TM) *Golden Boy*.

This Is the Life. w/m Irving Berlin, 1914. Introduced and made popular by Al Jolson at the Winter Garden in New York. Recorded by Billy Murray (Victor) and The Peerless Quartet (Columbia).

This Is the Missus. w/m Lew Brown and Ray Henderson, 1931. Introduced by Rudy Vallee in (TM) *George White's Scandals*, Eleventh Edition and recorded by him (Victor). Ernest Borgnine sang it in (MM) *The Best Things in Life Are Free*, the DeSylva, Brown and Henderson biography.

This Is the Moment. w. Leo Robin, m. Frederick Hollander, 1948. Introduced by Betty Grable in (MM) *That Lady in Ermine*. Nominated for Academy Award.

This Is the Night. w/m Redd Evans and Lewis Bellin, 1946. Featured and recorded by Frank Sinatra (Columbia).

This Is the Night. w. Sam Coslow, m. Ralph Rainger, 1932. From (MM) *This Is the Night* starring Cary Grant and Thelma Todd.

This Is the Thanks I Get (for Loving You). w/m Tommy Dilbeck and Eddy Arnold, 1954. Hit country record by Eddy Arnold (RCA Victor).

This Is the Time. w/m Billy Joel, 1986. Single by Billy Joel from his album "The Bridge" (Columbia).

This I Swear. w/m Joseph Rock and The Skyliners, 1959. Recorded by The Skyliners, whose writer/singer personnel consisted of James Beaumont, Janet Vogel, Walter Lester, John Taylor, and Joseph VerScharen (Calico).

This Is What I Call Love. w. Matt Dubey, m. Harold Carr, 1956. Introduced by Ethel Merman in (TM) *Happy Hunting*.

This Is Worth Fighting For. w. Eddie De-Lange, m. Sam H. Stept, 1942. Introduced in (MM) *When Johnny Comes Marching Home*, by Allan Jones. Most popular records: Jimmy Dorsey, vocal by Bob Eberly (Decca); Shep Fields, vocal by Ken Curtis (Bluebird); Ray McKinley, with his Orchestra (Hit).

This Land Is Mine. See **Exodus**.

This Land Is Your Land. w/m Woody Guthrie, 1956. Adapted from a folk melody. Introduced and featured by The Weavers. The New Christy Minstrels (Columbia) and Ketty Lester (Era) both had popular records in 1962. It was the title number of an LP of songs written and sung by Guthrie issued the year of his death, 1967 (Folkways).

This Little Bird. w/m John D. Loudermilk, 1965. Top 40 record by Marianne Faithfull (London).

This Little Girl. w/m Bruce Springsteen, 1981. Recorded by Gary U.S. Bonds (EMI America).

This Little Girl. w/m Gerry Goffin and Carole King, 1963. Recorded by Dion (Laurie).

This Little Girl of Mine. w/m Ray Charles, 1955, 1958. Initially on the R&B charts by

Ray Charles (Atlantic). Top 40 Pop record by The Everly Brothers (Cadence), 1958.

This Little Girl's Gone Rockin'. w/m Bobby Darin and Mann Curtis, 1958. Leading record by Ruth Brown (Atlantic).

This Little Piggie Went to Market. w. Sam Coslow, m. Harold "Lefty" Lewis, 1933. Featured and recorded by Ruth Etting (Brunswick); George Olsen and his Orchestra, vocal by Ethel Shutta (Columbia); Annette Hanshaw (Vocalion); and Victor Young's Orchestra, vocal by Peg La Centra, under pseudonym of Jane Vance (Brunswick). Revived by the Andrews Sisters in 1939 (Decca).

This'll Make You Whistle. w/m Al Goodhart, Al Hoffman, and Maurice Sigler, 1936. Title song of the British film (MM) *This'll Make You Whistle*, sung by Jack Buchanan.

This Love of Mine. w. Frank Sinatra, m. Sol Parker and Henry Sanicola, 1941. A big hit for Tommy Dorsey, vocal by Frank Sinatra (Victor).

This Magic Moment. w/m Doc Pomus and Mort Shuman, 1960, 1969. First hit record by The Drifters (Atlantic). Revived in 1969 by Jay and the Americans, whose record sold over a million copies (United Artists).

This Masquerade. w/m Leon Russell, 1976. Top 10 record by George Benson (Warner Bros.). Winner Grammy Award (NARAS) for Record of the Year.

This Missin' You Heart of Mine. w/m Woody Mullis and Mike Geiger, 1988. Top 10 Country chart record by Sawyer Brown (Capitol).

This Nearly Was Mine. w. Oscar Hammerstein II, m. Richard Rodgers, 1949. Introduced by Ezio Pinza in (TM) *South Pacific*. In the film version (MM) *South Pacific*, 1958, it was sung on the soundtrack by Giorgio Tozzi, dubbing for Rossano Brazzi.

This Never Happened Before. w. Harold Adamson, m. Jimmy McHugh, 1937. Introduced by Lily Pons in (MM) *Hitting a New High*. The orchestras of Leo Reisman (Victor) and Johnny Long (Vocalion) recorded it.

This Night Will Be My Souvenir. w. Gus Kahn, m. Harry Warren, 1939. Introduced in (MM) *Honolulu*. Records: Glen Gray and the Casa Loma Orchestra (Decca), Tommy Dorsey and his Orchestra (Victor).

This Night Won't Last Forever. w/m Ron Freeland and Bill LaBounty, 1978. Introduced by Bill LaBounty (Warner Bros.). Top 20 record by Michael Johnson (EMI America), 1979.

This Ol' Cowboy. w/m Toy Caldwell, 1975. Written by the lead guitarist of The Marshall Tucker Band (Capricorn).

This Old Heart of Mine (Is Weak for You). w/m Brian Holland, Lamont Dozier, and Eddie Holland, 1966. Top 20 record by The Isley Brothers (Tamla). Chart versions by Tammi Terrell (Motown), 1969; Rod Stewart (Warner Bros.), 1976.

This Old Man. See **Children's Marching Song**.

This Ole House. w/m Stuart Hamblen, 1954. Introduced and recorded by the composer, Stuart Hamblen (RCA Victor). The bestseller, however, was recorded by Rosemary Clooney on a two-sided hit, coupled with "Hey There" (q.v.) (Columbia).

This One's for You. w/m Barry Manilow and Marty Panzer, 1976. Recorded by Barry Manilow (Arista).

This Orchid Means Goodbye. w/m Buck Bryant and Mark Webb, 1953. Top 10 C&W chart by Carl Smith (Columbia).

This Should Go On Forever. w/m J. Miller and B. Jolivette, 1959. Chart record by Rod Bernard (Argo).

This Song. w/m George Harrison, 1976. Recorded by former Beatle, George Harrison (Dark Horse).

This Time. w/m Charlie Singleton, 1989. R&B chart hit single by Kiara, in duet with Shanice Wilson (Arista).

This Time. w/m Bryan Adams and Jim Vallance, 1983. Recorded by Canadian singer/songwriter Bryan Adams (A&M).

This Time. w/m Waylon Jennings, 1974. This "This Time" was a Country hit song recorded by Waylon Jennings (RCA).

This Time. w/m Chips Moman, 1961. Pop/Country hit by Troy Shondell (Liberty).

This Time (Is the Last Time). w/m Irving Berlin, 1942. Sung by the company as the finale of the all-soldier show (TM) *This is the Army*, and the film version (MM) *This is the Army*, 1943.

This Time I'm in It for Love. w/m Steve Pippin and Larry Keith, 1978. Hit record by the group Player (RSO).

This Time It's Love. w. Sam M. Lewis, m. J. Fred Coots, 1933. Among the many recordings upon publication: Adelaide Hall, accompanied by Art Tatum (Brunswick); Art Jarrett (Columbia); the bands of Nye Mayhew (Perfect), Red McKenzie (Vocalion), George Olsen (Columbia), Jacques Renard (Vocalion), and Sam Robbins (Bluebird).

This Time It's True Love. w/m Noël Coward, 1963. Introduced by José Ferrer and Florence Henderson in (TM) *The Girl Who Came to Supper*.

This Time the Dream's on Me. w. Johnny Mercer, m. Harold Arlen, 1941. Introduced by Priscilla Lane in (MM) *Blues in the Night*. Most popular records by Woody Herman, vocal by Herman (Decca), and Glenn Miller, vocal by Ray Eberle (Bluebird).

This Town. w/m Lee Hazlewood, 1967. Introduced in (MM) *The Cool Ones*. Leading record by Frank Sinatra (Reprise).

This Way to Sesame Street. w/m Joe Raposo and Jeffrey Moss, 1970. Sung by the children as the theme of (TVM) "Sesame Street."

This White Circle on My Finger. w/m Margie Bainbridge and Dorothy Lewis, 1964. C&W hit by Kitty Wells (Decca).

This Will Be (an Everlasting Love). w/m Charles Jackson, Jr. and Marvin Yancy, 1975. Top 10 record by Natalie Cole (Capitol).

This Woman. w/m Barry Gibb and Albhy Galuten, 1984. Recorded by Kenny Rogers (RCA).

This Woman's Work. w/m Kate Bush, 1988. Introduced by Kate Bush on the soundtrack of (MP) *She's Having a Baby* and the soundtrack album (I.R.S.).

This Year's Kisses. w/m Irving Berlin, 1937. Introduced in (MM) *On the Avenue* and recorded by Alice Faye (Brunswick).

Tho' I Tried (I Can't Forget You). w/m Gene Autry, Oakley Haldeman, and Smokey Rogers, 1946. C&W chart hit record by Wesley Tuttle (Capitol).

Thoroughly Modern Millie. w. Sammy Cahn, m. James Van Heusen, 1967. Introduced by Julie Andrews in (MM) *Thoroughly Modern Millie* and recorded by her (Decca). Nominated for Academy Award.

Those Lazy-Hazy-Crazy Days of Summer. w. Charles Tobias, m. Hans Carste, 1963. English lyrics to the melody of a German song. Hit record by Nat "King" Cole (Capitol).

Those Oldies But Goodies (Remind Me of You). w/m Paul Politti and Nick Curinga, 1961. Top 10 record by Little Caesar and The Romans (Del-Fi).

Those Things Money Can't Buy. w. Ruth Poll, m. Al Goodhart, 1947. Chart records by Nat "King" Cole (Capitol), and Buddy Clark, with Ray Noble and his Orchestra (Columbia).

Those Were the Days. w. Lee Adams, m. Charles Strouse, 1971. Theme song of the long-running series (TVP) "All in the Family," performed at the opening of each show by Carroll O'Connor and Jean Stapleton, who also had a popular recording (Atlantic).

Those Were the Days. w/m Gene Raskin, 1968. Based on a Russian folk song "Darogoi Dlimmoya [Dear for Me]," it was first recorded by The Limelighters (RCA). The Welsh singer Mary Hopkin recorded it under the aegis of Paul McCartney (Apple). It became an international hit and was awarded a gold record in the U.S.

Those Were the Happy Days. w. Glen MacDonough, m. A. Baldwin Sloane, 1910. From (TM) *The Summer Widowers*.

Those Wonderful Years. w/m Webb Pierce and Don Schroeder, 1963. Country hit by Webb Pierce (Decca).

Thoughtless. w. Buddy Kaye, m. Carl Lampl, 1948. Records: The Buddy Kaye Quintet (MGM), Vic Damone (Mercury), Guy Lombardo and his Orchestra (Decca), Doris Day (Columbia), Gordon MacRae (Capitol).

Thousand Goodnights, A. w/m Walter Donaldson, 1934. Among recordings: Paul Small (Melotone); and the bands of Don Bestor (Victor), Bennie Krueger (Columbia), Adrian Rollini (Vocalion).

Thousand Islands Song, The (I Left My Love on One of the Thousand Islands). w/m Bob Hilliard and Carl Sigman, 1947. Comedy song introduced by Hank Ladd in revue (TM) *Angel in the Wings*. Popular records by Arthur Godfrey (Columbia) and Johnny Mercer (Capitol).

Thousand Miles Ago, A. w/m Mel Tillis and Webb Pierce, 1959. C&W hit by Webb Pierce (Decca).

Thousand Miles Away, A. w/m James Sheppard and William H. Miller, 1957. Top R&B hit by The Heartbeats (Rama).

Thousand Stars, A. w/m Eugene Pearson, 1960. Hit record by Kathy Young and The Innocents (Indigo).

Thousand Violins, A. w/m Jay Livingston and Ray Evans, 1951. From (MP) *The Great Lover*. Leading records by Tony Martin (RCA Victor); Russ Case, vocal by Stuart Foster (MGM); Victor Young and his Orchestra (Decca).

Thou Shalt Not Steal. w/m John D. Loudermilk, 1962. Introduced by John D. Loudermilk (RCA). Hit record by Dick and Deedee (Warner Bros.), 1964.

Thou Swell. w. Lorenz Hart, m. Richard Rodgers, 1927. Sung by William Gaxton and Constance Carpenter in (TM) *A Connecticut Yankee*. In the Rodgers and Hart story (MM) *Words and Music*, it was performed by June Allyson and the Blackburn Twins, 1948.

Three A.M. w/m Bill Anderson and Jerry Todd, 1965. Top 10 Country chart record by Bill Anderson (Decca).

Three Bells, The (a.k.a. **Jimmy Brown Song, The**). w. Bert Reisfeld (Engl.), (Fr.), m. Jean Villard [Gilles], 1952, 1959. Original French title, "Les Trois Cloche." Introduced in France by Edith Piaf and Les Compagnons de la Chanson, 1948. In 1952, Les Compagnons had an American hit record (Columbia) that established the singing group and the song in the U.S. Revived with a #1 record by The Browns (RCA), 1959.

Three B's, The. w/m Hugh Martin and Ralph Blane, 1941. Introduced by Victoria Schools, June Allyson, and Nancy Walker in (TM) *Best Foot Forward*. In the film version (MM) *Best Foot Forward*, 1943, Gloria De Haven joined Allyson and Walker in the song.

Three Caballeros, The. w. Ray Gilbert (Engl.), Ernesto M. Cortazar (Sp.), m. Manuel Esperon, 1944. Original Mexican title: "Ay, Jalisco No Te Rajes (Los Tres Caballeros)." It became song of the title characters of the Disney cartoon film (MM) *The Three Caballeros*, introduced by the voices of Clarence Nash (Donald Duck), José Olivera (Joe Carioca), and Joaquin Garay (Panchito). Popular record by Bing Crosby and the Andrews Sisters (Decca).

Three Coins in the Fountain. w. Sammy Cahn, m. Jule Styne, 1954. Sung under the title credits of (MP) *Three Coins in the Fountain* by Frank Sinatra, who recorded it with Nelson Riddle's Orchestra (Capitol). The best-selling record was by The Four Aces, with

Jack Pleis's Orchestra (Decca). Winner, Academy Award for Best Song.

Three Days. w/m Willie Nelson and Faron Young, 1962. Hit C&W record by Faron Young (Capitol). Revived by k. d. lang in the album "Absolute Torch and Twang" (Sire), 1989.

Three for Jack. w. Frederick Edward Weatherley, m. W. H. Squire, 1904. A London-originated song that gained popularity in the U.S.

Three Hearts in a Tangle. w/m Ray Pennington and Sonny Thompson, 1961. Recorded by Roy Drusky (Decca).

Three Little Fishies. w/m Saxie Dowell, 1939. Introduced and recorded by Hal Kemp, vocal by Saxie Dowell and the Smoothies (Victor). This novelty hit was also recorded by Kay Kyser, vocal by Ish Kabibble [Merwyn Bogue] (Brunswick); Paul Whiteman, vocal by the Modernaires (Decca); the Hoosier Hot Shots (Vocalion); Spike Jones [late '40s] (Victor). Revived by Mitch Ryder and The Detroit Wheels in medley with "Too Many Fish in the Sea" (q.v.) (New Voice), 1967.

Three Little Sisters. w/m Irving Taylor and Vic Mizzy, 1942. Introduced by The Andrews Sisters in (MM) *Private Buckaroo*, and recorded by them (Decca). Other versions: Vaughn Monroe, with his Orchestra (Bluebird), Horace Heidt and his Orchestra (Columbia).

Three Little Words. w. Bert Kalmar, m. Harry Ruby, 1930. From the Amos 'n' Andy film (MM) *Check and Double Check*. Records by Duke Ellington (Victor) and Ethel Waters (Columbia) helped popularize the song. In the Kalmar and Ruby story (MM) *Three Little Words*, 1950, Fred Astaire, as Kalmar, sang the title song.

Three Nights a Week. w/m Antoine "Fats" Domino, 1960. Introduced and recorded by Fats Domino (Imperial).

Three O'Clock Blues. w. Jules Taub, m. Riley King, 1952. #1 R&B record by B. B. King (RPM).

Three O'Clock in the Morning. w. Dorothy Terris (pseud. for Theodora Morse), m. Julian Robledo, 1921. This waltz was first published as a piano piece three years earlier in New Orleans, after which Morse set her words to it. The song then became the hit finale of (TM) *Greenwich Village Follies of 1921*. Frank Crumit recorded it (Columbia), followed by Paul Whiteman and his Orchestra (Victor), whose instrumental version sold over three and a half million records, while the sheet music sold over a million copies. The song was sung by Judy Garland in (MM) *Presenting Lily Mars*, 1943; played by the orchestra in an ice skating number in (MM) *Margie*, 1946; sung by J. Carrol Naish in (MM) *That Midnight Kiss*, 1949; played by the orchestra in (MM) *The Eddy Duchin Story*, 1956. Trumpeter Monty Kelly with his Orchestra had a Top 40 instrumental record (Essex), 1953. Revived by Bert Kaempfert and his Orchestra (Decca), and Lou Rawls (Capitol), 1965.

Three on a Match. w. Raymond B. Egan, m. Ted Fio Rito, 1932. From the Robert Montgomery-Marion Davies-Jimmy Durante-Billie Dove film (MM) *Blondie of the Follies*. Leading recordings: Paul Whiteman, vocal by Red McKenzie (Victor); Freddy Martin (Columbia); Will Osborne (Melotone); Anson Weeks (Brunswick).

Three Rivers, The (the Allegheny, Susquehanna, and the Old Monongahela). w. Paul Francis Webster, m. Hoagy Carmichael, 1949. Recorded by Margaret Whiting (Capitol).

Three's a Crowd. w. Al Dubin and Irving Kahal, m. Harry Warren, 1932. Introduced by David Manners in (MM) *The Crooner*. Featured on radio and records by Rudy Vallee (Columbia) and Wayne King (Victor).

Three's Company. w. Don Nicholl, m. Joe Raposo, 1977. From the series (TVP) "Three's Company."

Three Shades of Blue. w. Ferde Grofé, 1927. A suite for solo piano containing three sections: (1) Indigo, (2) Alice Blue, (3) Heliotrope.

Three Stars. w/m Tommy Dee, 1959. A tribute to Buddy Holly, Ritchie Valens, and The Big Bopper who were killed in an airplane accident. Narrated by disc jockey Tommy Dee and sung by Carol Kay and the Teen-Aires (Crest).

Three Stars Will Shine Tonight (Theme from "Dr. Kildare"). w. Hal Winn, m. Jerrald Goldsmith and Pete Rugolo, 1962. Theme from series (TVP) "Dr. Kildare." Hit record by Richard Chamberlain (MGM).

Three Steps to the Phone. w/m Harlan Howard, 1961. C&W chart hit by George Hamilton IV (RCA).

3:10 to Yuma. w. Ned Washington, m. George Duning, 1957. Introduced on the soundtrack of (MP) *3:10 to Yuma* by Frankie Laine.

Three Time Loser. w/m Dan Seals, 1987. #1 Country chart record by Dan Seals (EMI America).

Three Times a Lady. w/m Lionel Richie, 1978. #1 record by The Commodores (Motown).

Three Times in Love. w/m Tommy James and Rick Serota, 1980. Recorded by Tommy James (Millennium).

Three Times Seven. w/m Merle Travis and Cliffie Stone, 1947. Leading recording by Merle Travis (Capitol).

Three Window Coupe. w/m Jan Berry and Roger Christian, 1964. Recorded by The Rip Chords (Columbia).

Three Wishes. w/m George Posford and Douglas Furber, 1933. An English success. Imported records by Ray Noble, vocal by Al Bowlly (Victor), and Jessie Matthews (Columbia). Freddy Martin had a well-received American recording (Brunswick).

Three Wonderful Letters from Home. w. Joe Goodwin and Ballard MacDonald, m. James F. Hanley, 1918. A popular ballad from World War I.

Thrilled. w. Mort Greene, m. Harry Barris, 1935.

Thriller. w/m Rod Temperton, 1984. Title song and Top 10 single from Michael Jackson's platinum album (Epic).

Thrill Is Gone, The. w/m Lew Brown and Ray Henderson, 1931. Sung by Everett Marshall, with Rudy Vallee and Ross McLean, and danced by Dorothy and Harry Dixon in (TM) *George White's Scandals*, eleventh edition. Marshall recorded it with the Victor Young Orchestra (Victor) and Vallee with his own band (Victor). Ella Mae Morse had a popular record with Freddie Slack's Band (Capitol), 1942. Revived by Top 20 record of B. B. King (Blues Way), 1970.

Thrill of a Lifetime. w/m Sam Coslow, Frederick Hollander, and Carmen Lombardo, 1938. Title song of (MM) *Thrill of a Lifetime*, sung by Dorothy Lamour.

Through (How Can You Say We're Through?). w. Joseph McCarthy, m. James V. Monaco, 1929. Recorded by the Casa Loma Orchestra (Okeh); Roger Wolfe Kahn, vocal by Franklyn Baur (Brunswick); Ted Lewis (Columbia); Leo Reisman (Victor); Sid Gary (Perfect).

Through a Long and Sleepless Night. w. Mack Gordon, m. Alfred Newman, 1949. From (MP) *Come to the Stable*. Nominated for Academy Award. Leading recording by Bill Farrell (MGM).

Through a Thousand Dreams. w. Leo Robin, m. Arthur Schwartz, 1946. Introduced by Dennis Morgan, Martha Vickers, and pianist Carmen Cavallaro in (MM) *The Time, the Place and the Girl*. Among recordings: the orchestras of Desi Arnaz (Victor) and George Olsen (Majestic).

Through the Eyes of Love. w. Albert Beach, m. Sidney Lippman, 1957. Recorded by Doris Day (Columbia).

Through the Fire. w/m David Foster, Tom Keene, and Cynthia Weil, 1985. Recorded by Chaka Khan (Warner Bros.).

Through the Years. w/m Steve Dorff and Marty Panzer, 1982. Recorded by Kenny Rogers, produced by Lionel Richie (Liberty). Song not to be confused with the standard of the same name.

Through the Years. w. Edward Heyman, m. Vincent Youmans, 1932. Introduced by Natalie Hall and Michael Bartlett in (TM) *Through the Years*, the musical version of the play *Smilin' Through*. This standard, one of Youmans's later songs, was also said to be his favorite. Among the numerous recordings are those by Nelson Eddy (Victor), Risë Stevens (Columbia), Gladys Swarthout (Victor), Mark Warnow's Orchestra (MGM), and Artie Shaw (Victor).

Throw Another Log on the Fire. w. Jack Scholl, Charles Tobias, m. Murray Mencher, 1934.

Throw Him Down McCloskey. w. John M. Kelly, 1890. Introduced by Maggie Cline at Tony Pastor's in New York.

Throwing It All Away. w/m Tony Banks, Phil Collins, and Michael Rutherford, 1986. Top 10 record by the English group Genesis (Atlantic).

Throwin' Stones at the Sun. w/m Nat Simon, Billy Hueston, and Sammy Mysels, 1935. Featured and recorded by Benny Goodman, vocal by Helen Ward (Columbia); Freddy Martin (Brunswick); Willie Bryant (Victor); Archie Bleyer (Vocalion); Bob Howard (Decca); Joe Haymes (Melotone).

Throw Me a Kiss. w. Gene Buck, m. Louis A. Hirsch and Dave Stamper, 1922. Introduced by Mary Eaton in (TM) *Ziegfeld Follies of 1922*.

Throw Me a Rose. w. P. G. Wodehouse and Herbert Reynolds, m. Emmerich Kallman, 1916. From (TM) *Miss Springtime*.

Throw Your Love My Way. w/m Ernest Tubb and Loys Southerland, 1950. C&W chart hit by Ernest Tubb (Decca).

Thru the Courtesy of Love. w. Jack Scholl, m. M. K. Jerome, 1936. From (MP) *Here Comes Carter*.

Thumbelina. w/m Frank Loesser, 1952. Introduced by Danny Kaye in (MM) *Hans Christian Andersen*, and recorded by him with Gordon Jenkins' Orchestra (Decca).

Thunder and Lightning. w/m Chi Coltrane, 1972. Top 20 record by Chi Coltrane (Columbia).

Thunderball. w. Don Black, m. John Barry, 1965. Title song of the James Bond movie (MP) *Thunderball*, sung on the soundtrack by Tom Jones and recorded by him (Parrot).

Thunder Island. w/m Jay Ferguson, 1978. Top 10 record by Jay Ferguson (Asylum).

Thunder over Paradise. w. Leo Robin, m. Ralph Rainger, 1936. From (MM) *Rose of the Rancho*, starring John Boles, Gladys Swarthout, and Willie Howard. Recorded by Isham Jones, vocal by Woody Herman (Decca).

Thursday's Child. w. Elisse Boyd and Murray Grand, m. Murray Grand, 1958. Leading recordings by Eartha Kitt (RCA) and Chris Connor (Atlantic).

Ticket Agent, Ease Your Window Down. w/m Spencer Williams, 1924. Recorded by Bessie Smith (Columbia).

Ticket to Ride. w/m John Lennon and Paul McCartney, 1965. Introduced by The Beatles in (MM) *Help!* and on their #1 record (Capitol). Also recorded by The Carpenters (A&M), 1970.

Tickle Toe. m. Lester Young, 1940. Jazz instrumental, introduced and recorded by Count Basie and his Orchestra (Columbia).

Tickle Toe, The (Everybody Ought to Know How to Do). w. Otto Harbach, m. Louis A. Hirsch, 1918. Introduced by Edith Day, Allen Fagan, and ensemble in (TM) *Going Up*.

Tico-Tico. Ervin Drake (Engl.), Aloysio Oliviera (Port.), m. Zequinha Abreu, 1944.

First heard in Disney's cartoon film (MM) *Saludos Amigos*, 1943. In same year it was danced by Maxine Barrett and Don Loper in (MM) *Thousands Cheer*. Organist Ethel Smith performed it in (MM) *Bathing Beauty*, 1944, and established song and her identification with it. Her recording with Bando Carioca (Decca) outsold earlier releases by Charles Wolcott and his Orchestra (Decca) and The Andrews Sisters (Decca). It was heard again in (MM) "Kansas City Kitty," 1944 and sung by Carmen Miranda in (MM) *Copacabana*, 1947, and recorded by her (Decca).

Tide Is High, The. w/m John Holt, 1980. #1 gold record from the platinum album by the group Blondie (Chrysalis).

Tie a String Around Your Finger. w. Zelda Sears, m. Vincent Youmans, 1924. Sung by Ada May and Harry Puck in (TM) *Lollipop*.

Tie a Yellow Ribbon Round the Ole Oak Tree. w/m Irwin Levine and L. Russell Brown, 1973. #1 gold record and biggest hit of the year, recorded by Dawn, featuring Tony Orlando (Bell).

Tie Me Kangaroo Down, Sport. w/m Rolf Harris, 1963. Novelty hit recorded in Australia by Rolf Harris (Epic).

Tie Me to Your Apron Strings Again. w. Joe Goodwin, m. Larry Shay, 1925.

Tiger. w/m Ollie Jones, 1959. Recorded by Fabian (Chancellor).

Tiger Rag. w. Harry De Costa, m. Edwin B. Edwards, Nick La Rocca, Tony Spargo, Larry Shields, 1918. The composers of this jazz standard were members of "The Original Dixieland Jazz Band" whose recording (Victor) introduced the number. Among other recordings are those by Kid Ory (Columbia), Isham Jones (Decca), Ted Lewis (Columbia), Sidney Bechet (Brunswick), Tommy Dorsey (Victor), Les Paul and Mary Ford (Capitol), and The Mills Brothers (Brunswick), their first commercially released record, 1931. They also sang it in (MM) *The Big Broadcast* that same year. As an instrumental, it was heard in (MM) *Is Everybody Happy?* 1929; (MM) *The Birth of the Blues*, 1941; (MM) *Night Club Girl*, 1944; (MM) *Jazz on a Summer Day*, 1960.

Tiger Rose. w/m Gene Buck, 1917.

Tiger Woman. w/m Merle Kilgore and Claude King, 1965. Hit Country record by Claude King (Columbia).

Tighten Up. w/m Archie Bell and Billy Buttier, 1968. Gold record by Archie Bell and The Drells (Atlantic).

Tighter, Tighter. w/m Tommy James and Bob King, 1970. Top 10 record by the group Alive and Kicking (Roulette).

Tight Fittin' Jeans. w/m Mike Huggman, 1981. #1 Country chart record by Conway Twitty (MCA).

Tight Rope. w/m Leon Russell, 1972. Top 20 record by Leon Russell (Shelter).

Tijuana Jail, The. w/m Denny Thompson, 1959. Featured and recorded by The Kingston Trio (Capitol).

Tijuana Taxi. m. Bud Coleman, 1966. Top 40 instrumental by Herb Alpert and The Tijuana Brass (A&M).

'Til I Can Make It on My Own. w/m George Richey, Billy Sherrill, and Tammy Wynette, 1976. Country hit and Pop chart record by Tammy Wynette (Epic). Dottie West and Kenny Rogers combined for another hit Country version (United Artists), 1979.

'Til I Gain Control Again. w/m Rodney Crowell, 1982. First Country chart record by Bobby Bare (Columbia), 1979. #1 revival by Crystal Gayle (Elektra), 1982.

'Til I Get It Right. w/m Red Lane and Larry Henley, 1973. Country chart hit by Tammy Wynette (Epic).

'Til I Kissed You. w/m Don Everly, 1959. Introduced and recorded by The Everly Brothers (Cadence).

Till. w. Carl Sigman, m. Charles Danvers, 1957. Leading records by Roger Williams (Kapp) and Percy Faith (Columbia). Leading revivals by The Angels (Caprice), 1961; The Vogues (Reprise), 1968; Tom Jones (Parrot), 1971.

Till I Waltz Again with You. w/m Sidney Prosen, 1952. Teresa Brewer with Jack Pleis's Orchestra had a #1 record, with sales of over a million discs (Coral).

Till Love Touches Your Life. w. Arthur Hamilton, m. Riz Ortolani, 1970. Sung on the soundtrack on (MP) *Madron* by Richard Williams. Nominated for Academy Award, 1970.

Till the Clouds Roll By. w. P. G. Wodehouse, Guy Bolton, and Jerome Kern, m. Jerome Kern, 1917. Introduced by Anna Wheaton and Tom Powers in the Princess Theatre production of (TM) *Oh, Boy!* In the screen bio of Kern (MM) *Till the Clouds Roll By*, 1946, the title song was performed by June Allyson, Kathryn Grayson, Virginia O'Brien, Frank Sinatra, Ray McDonald, Tony Martin, and Johnny Johnston.

Till the End of the Day. w/m Ray Davies, 1966. Written by the lead singer of The Kinks, the British group that recorded the song (Reprise).

Till the End of the World. w/m Vaughn Horton, 1949. Popularized by Jimmy Wakely (Capitol) and revived by hit record of Bing Crosby, with Grady Martin and his Slew Foot Five (Decca), 1952.

Till the End of Time. w/m Buddy Kaye and Ted Mossman, 1945. Adapted from *Polonaise in A Flat Major*, Opus 53, by Frederic Chopin that was featured in the Chopin story, (MM) *A Song to Remember*, featuring Cornel Wilde as the composer, Merle Oberon, and Paul Muni. Perry Como's record of the song adaptation (Victor) sold two million copies. Other top records by Les Brown, vocal by Doris Day (Columbia); Dick Haymes (Decca). Song on "Your Hit Parade" for nineteen weeks, seven times as #1. It was the title song of (MP) *Till the End of Time*, 1946.

Till Then. w/m Eddie Seiler, Sol Marcus, and Guy Wood, 1944, 1954. Hit record by The Mills Brothers (Decca). Revived in 1954 by The Hilltoppers, with a Top 10 record (Dot).

Till the Real Thing Comes Along. See **Until the Real Things Comes Along**.

Till There Was You. w/m Meredith Willson, 1957. Popular ballad from (TM) *The Music Man*, introduced by Barbara Cook and Robert Preston. In (MM) *The Music Man*, 1962, it was sung by Shirley Jones and Robert Preston. Best-selling single record by Anita Bryant (Carlton), 1959.

Till the Rivers All Run Dry. w/m Wayland Holyfield and Don Williams, 1976. Hit Country record by Don Williams (ABC/Dot).

Till the Sands of the Desert Grow Cold. w. George Graff, Jr., m. Ernest R. Ball, 1911. Popularized by Wilfred Glenn's recording (Victor). Alfred Drake recorded it in the forties (Decca).

Till We Meet Again. w. Raymond B. Egan, m. Richard A. Whiting, 1918. A major ballad hit in World War I, with many recordings and massive sheet music sales. In films it was sung by Judy Garland in (MM) *For Me and My Gal*, 1942, and by Gordon MacRae and Doris Day in (MM) *On Moonlight Bay*, 1951.

Till We Two Are One. w. Tom Glazer, m. Billy Martin and Larry Martin, 1954. Popular records by Georgie Shaw (Decca) and Eddy Howard (Mercury).

Till You're Gone. w/m James Aldridge and Tom Brasfield, 1982. #1 Country chart song by Barbara Mandrell (MCA).

'Til My Baby Comes Home. w/m Luther Vandross and Marcus Miller, 1985. Crossover (R&B/Pop) chart record by Luther Vandross (Epic).

Til Reveille (Lights Out—). w/m Stanley Cowan, m. Bobby Worth, 1941. Leading recordings of this early wartime song by Bing Crosby (Decca) and Kay Kyser, vocal by Harry

Babbit, Ginny Simms, and company (Columbia).

Til Tomorrow. w. Sheldon Harnick, m. Jerry Bock, 1959. Introduced by Ellen Hanley and company in (TM) *Fiorello!*

Timber. w. Bob Emmerich, m. Billy Hill, 1937.

Timber, I'm Falling. w/m Dallas Frazier and Ferlin Husky, 1963. Country hit record by Ferlin Husky (Capitol).

Timber, I'm Falling in Love. w/m Ferlin Husky and Dalton Timbur, 1989. Hit Country record by Patty Loveless (MCA).

Timber Trail, The. w/m Tim Spencer, 1942. Introduced and recorded by The Sons of the Pioneers (Victor).

Timbrook. w/m James G. Howell and Don Pierce, 1960. Country hit by Lewis Pruitt (Decca).

Timbuctoo. w. Bert Kalmar, m. Harry Ruby, 1920. Featured by Frank Crumit and recorded by him with The Paul Biese Trio (Columbia).

Time. w/m Eric Woolfson and Alan Parsons, 1981. Written and recorded by the British duo The Alan Parsons Project (Arista).

Time. w/m Michael Dee Merchant, 1966. Recorded by the Texas trio The Pozo-Seco Singers (Columbia).

Time After Time. w/m Cyndi Lauper and Rob Hyman, 1983. #1 single from the platinum album "She's So Unusual," by Cyndi Lauper (Portrait). Song not to be confused with the Cahn-Styne standard.

Time After Time. w. Sammy Cahn, m. Jule Styne, 1947. Introduced by Frank Sinatra in (MM) *It Happened in Brooklyn* and on records (Columbia). Revived with chart records by Frankie Ford (Ace), 1960, and Chris Montez (A&M), 1966.

Time Alone Will Tell. w. Mack Gordon, m. James V. Monaco, 1944. From (MM) *Pin-Up Girl.* Recorded by Ella Fitzgerald (Decca).

Time and Love. w/m Laura Nyro, 1969. Introduced by Laura Nyro in her album "New York Tendaberry" (Columbia). Chart single by Barbra Streisand (Columbia), 1971.

Time and the Place and the Girl, The. w. Henry Blossom, m. Victor Herbert, 1905. In one of three musicals to open on Christmas night, this was introduced by Walter Percival in (TM) *Mlle. Modiste.*

Time and the River. w/m Aaron Schroeder and Wally Gold, 1960. Featured and recorded by Nat "King" Cole (Capitol).

Time for Livin'. w/m Don Addrisi and Dick Addrisi, 1968. Top 40 record by The Association (Warner Bros.).

Time for Livin' (Time for Givin'). w/m Sylvester Stewart, 1974. Recorded by Sly and The Family Stone (Epic).

Time for Love, A. w. Paul Francis Webster, m. Johnny Mandel, 1966. Sung by Jackie Ward, dubbing on the soundtrack for Janet Leigh, in (MP) *An American Dream.* Nominated for Academy Award, 1966. Popular record by Tony Bennett (Columbia).

Time for Me to Fly. w/m Kevin Cronin, 1978. Recorded by the quintet REO Speedwagon (Epic).

Time for Parting. w. Betty Comden, m. Adolph Green, 1955. Introduced by Gene Kelly, Dan Dailey, Michael Kidd, and some help from David Burns in (MM) *It's Always Fair Weather.*

Time for Us, A. See **Love Theme from "Romeo and Juliet."**

Time Has Come Today. w. Joe Chambers, m. Willie Chambers, 1968. Top 20 record by The Chambers Brothers (Columbia).

Time in a Bottle. w/m Jim Croce, 1973. #1 gold record by Jim Croce (ABC).

Time Is on My Side. w/m Jerry Ragovoy, 1964. Top 10 record by British group The Rolling Stones (London).

Time Is Tight. m. Booker T. Jones, Al Jackson, Jr., Steve Cropper, and Donald V. Dunn, 1969. From the soundtrack of (MP) *Up Tight.* Top 10 instrumental recorded by Booker T. and The MG's (Stax).

Time Is Time. w/m Andy Gibb and Barry Gibb, 1980. Recorded by the British singer Andy Gibb (RSO).

Time Machine. w/m Mark Farner, 1969. Written by the guitarist of Grand Funk Railroad. This was the group's first chart record (Capitol).

Time of My Life, The. See **(I've Had) the Time of My Life.**

Time of the Season. w/m Rod Argent, 1969. Gold record by The Zombies (Date). Written by the keyboardist/singer of the British quintet.

Time on My Hands. w. Harold Adamson and Mack Gordon, m. Vincent Youmans, 1930. Introduced by Paul Gregory in (TM) *Smiles.* He sang it to the star, Marilyn Miller, for whom the song was written but who had refused to perform it. She did, however, sing a chorus of it with a different lyric by Ring Lardner, titled "What Can I Say?" The latter version has not been heard since. Ironically, "Time on My Hands" was sung by June Haver, portraying Marilyn Miller in her film biography (MM) *Look for the Silver Lining,* 1949. Kathryn Grayson sang it in the Grace Moore story (MM) *So This Is Love,* 1953. A major standard, it has been recorded hundreds of times.

Time Out for Tears. w/m Abe Schiff and Irving Berman, 1948. Top 20 record by Savannah Churchill, with The Four Tunes (Manor).

Time Passages. w/m Al Stewart and Peter White, 1978. Top 10 record by Scottish singer Al Stewart (Arista).

Time's A-Wastin' w. Don George, m. Mercer Ellington and Edward Kennedy "Duke" Ellington, 1946. Originally instrumental titled "Things Ain't What they Used to Be," (q.v.). New version recorded by Duke Ellington and his Orchestra (Victor).

Times of Your Life. w/m William Lane and Roger Nichols, 1976. Top 10 record by Paul Anka (United Artists).

Times They Are A-Changin', The. w/m Bob Dylan, 1964. Introduced and recorded by Bob Dylan, and title of one of his albums (Columbia).

Time to Bum Again. w/m Harlan Howard, 1966. Country chart record by Waylon Jennings (RCA).

Time to Care, A. w. Al Jarreau, m. Henry Mancini, 1982. Introduced by Al Jarreau on the soundtrack of (MP) *Better Late Than Never,* starring David Niven, Art Carney, and Maggie Smith.

Time Waits for No One. w. Charles Tobias, m. Cliff Friend, 1944. Introduced in (MM) *Shine on Harvest Moon.* Top recordings: Helen Forrest (Decca) and Johnny Long and his Orchestra (Decca). Revived by the Hilltoppers (Dot), 1954.

Time Was. w. S. K. (Bob) Russell (Engl.), m. Miguel Prado, 1941. Original Mexican song, Spanish lyrics by Gabriel Luna, titled "Duerme." Top Ten record by Jimmy Dorsey, vocal by Bob Eberly and Helen O'Connell (Decca).

Time Will Reveal. w/m Bunny DeBarge and Eldra DeBarge, 1983. Recorded by the family quintet DeBarge (Gordy).

Time Will Tell. w. Raymond Klages, m. J. Fred Coots, 1922. Introduced by Eddie Dowling and Edna Morn in (TM) "Sally, Irene and Mary." This show marked the start of Coots's professional songwriting career.

Time Won't Let Me. w. Chet Kelley, m. Tom King, 1966. Top 10 record by The Outsiders (Capitol).

Timothy. w/m Rupert Holmes, 1971. Top 20 record by The Buoys (Scepter).

Timtayshun. See **Temptation.**

Tina Marie. w/m Bob Merrill, 1955. Top 10 record by Perry Como (RCA Victor).

Ting-a-Ling. w/m Ahmet Ertegun, 1952. Hit R&B record by The Clovers (Atlantic).

Ting-a-Ling (the Waltz of the Bells). w. Addy Britt, m. Jack Little, 1926. Introduced and featured by Little Jack Little.

Tin Man. w/m Lee Bunnell, 1974. Top 10 record by the group America (Warner Bros.).

Tin Roof Blues. m. Paul Mares, Walter Melrose, Ben Pollack, Mel Stitzel, George Brunies, and Leon Rappolo, 1923. A favorite jazz instrumental written by members of the New Orleans Rhythm Kings [excepting Melrose] who first recorded it (Gennett). The Original Memphis Five (Victor) and the Original Indiana Five (Perfect) also had releases that same year. Many other discs have been cut since. Lyrics were added in 1954 for Jo Stafford's hit record. See **Make Love to Me**, 1954.

Tiny Bubbles. w/m Leon Prober, 1966. Popular Hawaiian song recorded by Don Ho and The Aliis (Reprise).

Tiny Dancer. w/m Elton John and Bernie Taupin, 1972. English song recorded by Elton John (Uni).

Tiny Little Fingerprints. w/m Charles Newman, Sam H. Stept, and Charles Tobias, 1935.

Ti-Pi-Tin. w. Raymond Leveen (Engl.), Maria Grever (Sp.), m. Maria Grever, 1938. Mexican song recorded and popularized by Horace Heidt (Brunswick) and Guy Lombardo (Victor) and their orchestras. Revived by Jan August, with the Harmonicats in 1947 (Mercury).

Tip of My Fingers, The. w/m Bill Anderson, 1960. Hit Country records by Bill Anderson (Decca), 1960; Roy Clark (Capitol), 1963; Eddy Arnold (RCA), 1966.

Tippin' In. w. Marty Symes, m. Bobby Smith, 1945. Erskine Hawkins and his Orchestra had a Top 10 hit with this jazz instrumental. The lyrics were added later.

Tippy Toeing. w/m Bobby Harden, 1966. Recorded by The Harden Trio (Columbia).

Tip Toe Through the Tulips with Me. w. Al Dubin, m. Joe Burke, 1929. Introduced by Nick Lucas in (MM) *Gold Diggers of Broadway*. Leading recordings by Lucas (Brunswick) and Jean Goldkette's Orchestra, conducted by Victor Young with vocal by Frank Munn (Victor). The song was sung in another adaptation of the original Avery Hopwood *Gold Diggers*, (MM) *Painting the Clouds with Sunshine*, 1951, by Lucille Norman, Virginia Mayo, Virginia Gibson, and Gene Nelson. Tiny Tim revived it with a hit recording (Reprise), 1968.

Tip-Top Tipperary Mary. w. Ballard MacDonald, m. Harry Carroll, 1914.

Tired. w/m Alan Roberts and Doris Fisher, 1947. Sung in (MM) *Variety Girl* and recorded (Columbia) by Pearl Bailey.

Tired of Being Alone. w/m Al Green, 1971. Top 20 record by Al Green (Hi).

Tired of It All. w. Bert Kalmar, m. Harry Ruby, 1934. Introduced by Ruth Etting in (MM) *Hips, Hips, Hooray*. Etting recorded it (Brunswick) as did Glen Gray and the Casa Loma Orchestra, vocal by Kenny Sargent (Brunswick); and George Hall and his Orchestra (Bluebird).

Tired of Toein' the Line. w/m Rocky Burnette and Ron Coleman, 1980. Top 10 record by Rocky Burnette (EMI America).

Tired of Waiting for You. w/m Roy Davies, 1965. Hit record by the English group The Kinks (Reprise).

'Tis Autumn. w/m Henry Nemo, 1941. Most popular recording by Woody Herman, vocal by Herman and Carolyn Grey (Decca), followed by Les Brown, vocal by Ralph Young (Okeh).

Tishomingo Blues. m. Spencer Williams, 1918. Leading recording by Duke Ellington and his Orchestra (Brunswick), 1928.

Titina. w/m W. C. Duncan, A. G. Leblond, H. A. Lemonnier, L. Maubon, and F. J. Niquet, 1925. A French import introduced by Elsie Janis in (TM) *Puzzles of 1925*. It was popularized via a hit record (Regal) by Billy Jones and Ernie Hare, coupled with "Who Takes Care of the Caretaker's Daughter While the Caretaker's Busy Taking Care?" (q.v.). Charlie Chaplin performed it, while singing a gibberish lyric in (MP) *Modern Times*, 1936.

T.L.C. Tender Love and Care. w/m Herb Clarke, Stan Lebowsky, and Johnny Lehmann, 1960. Featured and recorded by Jimmie Rodgers (Roulette).

"T" 99 Blues. w/m Jules Taub and Jimmy Nelson, 1951. Recorded by Jimmy Nelson (RPM).

To All the Girls I've Loved Before. w. Hal David, m. Albert Hammond, 1984. Top 10 gold record by Julio Iglesias and Willie Nelson (Columbia).

Toast and Marmalade for Two. w/m Steve Groves, 1971. Top 20 U.S. release by the Australian duo Tin Tin (Atco).

To a Sweet Pretty Thing. w. Joe Young, m. Fred E. Ahlert, 1937. Among recordings: the orchestras of Mitchell Ayres, vocal by Ruth Gaylor (Varsity); Nat Brandwynne, vocal by Buddy Clark (Melotone); Eddie Farley (Decca); Ozzie Nelson (Bluebird).

Tobacco Road. w/m John D. Loudermilk, 1964. Hit record, recorded in London by the British rock sextet The Nashville Teens (London).

To Be a Lover. w/m William Bell and Booker T. Jones, 1967, 1986. Top 10 R&B chart record and Pop crossover by Gene Chandler (Checker), 1967. Revived with a Top 10 record by the British singer, Billy Idol (Chrysalis), 1986.

To Be in Love. w. Roy Turk, m. Fred E. Ahlert, 1929.

To Be Loved. w/m Tyran Carlo, Berry Gordy, Jr., and Gwen Gordy, 1958. Top 40 record by Jackie Wilson (Brunswick).

Tobermory. w/m Harry Lauder, 1901. Written and performed by the great Scottish entertainer.

To Be Young, Gifted and Black. w/m Weldon J. Irvine, Jr. and Nina Simone, 1969. Introduced and recorded by Nina Simone (RCA). The title came from the autobiography of the late playwright Lorraine Hansberry.

To Daddy. w/m Dolly Parton, 1977. Hit Country record by Emmylou Harris (Warner Bros.).

Today. w/m Randy Sparks, 1964. Introduced on the soundtrack of (MP) *Advance to the Rear*. Popular record by The New Christy Minstrels (Columbia).

Today I Love Everybody. w. Dorothy Fields, m. Harold Arlen, 1953. Introduced by Betty Grable in (MM) *The Farmer Takes a Wife*.

Today I Sing the Blues. w/m Curtis R. Lewis, 1947. Introduced and recorded by Helen Humes (Mercury).

Today's the Day. w/m Dan Peek, 1976. Recorded by the group America (Warner Bros.).

To Each His Own. w/m Van McCoy, 1975. Recorded by Faith, Hope and Charity (RCA).

To Each His Own. w. Ray Evans, m. Jay Livingston, 1946. The first of many movie song hits for the writing team. This was written to publicize (MP) *To Each His Own*, starring Olivia De Havilland and John Lund, though not used in the film. Song became one of the biggest hits of the year, with three different recordings selling over a million copies: Eddy Howard (Majestic), The Ink Spots (Decca), Freddy Martin, vocal by Stuart Wade (RCA Victor). There were also Top 10 records by Tony Martin (Mercury) and The Modernaires with Paula Kelly (Columbia). Revived with chart records by The Platters (Mercury), 1960, The Tymes (RCA), 1964, Frankie Laine (ABC), 1968.

Together. w. B. G. DeSylva and Lew Brown, m. Ray Henderson, 1928, 1944. This was one of the few DeSylva, Brown and Henderson songs not from a production. It became a hit through the recordings and performances of Paul Whiteman, vocal by Jack Fulton (Victor); Cliff "Ukulele Ike" Edwards (Columbia); Franklyn Baur (Victor). It was featured in (MP) *Since You Went Away*, 1944, and its new popularity got it on "Your Hit Parade" for twelve weeks. Dan Dailey, as Henderson, performed it in the biography of the three writers (MM) *The Best Things in Life Are Free*, 1956. Revived by Connie Francis (MGM), 1961; The Intruders (Gamble), 1967; the septet Tierra (Boardwalk), 1980.

Together Again. w/m Buck Owens, 1964. Country hit, introduced by Buck Owens (Capitol). Ray Charles had a Top 20 version (ABC-Paramount), 1966. Revived with the Country chart hit by Emmylou Harris (Reprise), 1976.

Together Forever. w/m Mike Stock, Matt Aitken, and Pete Waterman, 1988. #1 hit single from the album "Whenever You Need Somebody" by the British singer Rick Astley (RCA).

Togetherness. w/m Russell Faith, 1960. Popularized by Frankie Avalon (Chancellor).

Together Through the Years. w/m Charles Fox, 1986. Sung by Roberta Flack as the title song of the series (TVP) "Valerie."

Together We Two. w/m Irving Berlin, 1927. Popular records by Harry Archer (Brunswick), Vaughn DeLeath (Victor), Willard Robison (Perfect), and Johnny Johnson's Orchestra (Victor).

Together Wherever We Go. w. Stephen Sondheim, m. Jule Styne, 1959. Introduced by Ethel Merman, Jack Klugman, and Sandra Church in (TM) *Gypsy*. In (MM) *Gypsy*, 1962, it was sung by Rosalind Russell [partially dubbed by Lisa Kirk], Karl Malden, and Natalie Wood. The song was deleted from the film by some distributors "for reasons of brevity."

To Give (the Reason I Live). w/m Bob Crewe and Bob Gaudio, 1968. Popular record by Frankie Valli (Philips).

To Have, to Hold, to Love. w. Darl MacBoyle, m. Ernest R. Ball, 1913.

Tokay. w/m Noël Coward, 1929. Introduced by Gerald Nodin in the U.S. in (TM) *Bitter Sweet* and in the London production, earlier, by Georges Metaxa, whom Nodin understudied. Nelson Eddy sang it in the second film version (MM) *Bitter Sweet* in 1940.

To Keep My Love Alive. w. Lorenz Hart, m. Richard Rodgers, 1944. Hart's last Broadway show lyric was introduced by Vivienne Segal in the revival of (TM) *A Connecticut Yankee*.

To Kill a Mockingbird. w. Mack David, m. Elmer Bernstein, 1963. Based on a theme from (MP) *To Kill a Mockingbird*. First recording by Vincent Edwards (Decca).

To Know Him Is to Love Him. w/m Phil Spector, 1958, 1987. Hit record by The Teddy Bears (Dore). As "To Know You Is to Love You," Peter and Gordon (Capitol), 1965, and Bobby Vinton (Epic), 1969, had chart versions. Revived, under the original title, with a #1 Country chart record by Dolly Parton, Linda Ronstadt, and Emmylou Harris, from their album "Trio" (Warner Bros.), 1987.

To Know You Is to Love You. w. Allan Roberts, m. Robert Allen, 1952. Featured and recorded by Perry Como (RCA Victor).

To Know You Is to Love You. w. B. G. De Sylva and Lew Brown, m. Ray Henderson, 1930. Introduced by Jack Whiting and Ona Munson in (TM) *Hold Everything*.

To Know You Is to Love You. See **To Know Him Is to Love Him.**

To Life. w. Sheldon Harnick, m. Jerry Bock, 1964. Introduced by Zero Mostel, Michael Granger, and men in (TM) *Fiddler on the Roof*. In the film version (MM) *Fiddler on the Roof*, 1971, it was sung by Topol, Paul Mann, and men.

To Live and Die in L.A. w/m Wang Chung, 1985. Written and introduced in (MP) *To Live and Die in L.A.*, and recorded by the British group Wang Chung (Geffen).

To Look Upon My Love. w/m Robert Wright and George Forrest, 1961. Introduced by Alfred Drake and Truman Smith in (TM) *Kean.*

To Love Again. w. Ned Washington, m. Morris Stoloff and George Sidney, 1956. Based on Chopin's *E-Flat Nocturne*, which had been the theme song of Eddy Duchin's Orchestra. Performed on the soundtrack of (MM) *The Eddy Duchin Story*, by Carmen Cavallaro, dubbing for Tyrone Power in the role of Duchin. Hit record by The Four Aces, arranged and conducted by Jack Pleis (Decca).

To Love and Be Loved. See **Song from "Some Came Running."**

To Love Somebody. w/m Barry Gibb, Maurice Gibb, and Robin Gibb, 1967. Top 20 record by the English brother trio The Bee Gees (Atco). Chart record by The Sweet Inspirations (Atlantic), 1968.

To Love You and to Lose You. w. Edward Heyman, m. Kurt Weill, 1936. New version, for popular publication, of "Listen to My Song (Johnny's Song)," which was sung by Russell Collins in (TM) *Johnny Johnson*. The original lyrics were by Paul Green. The new version was first recorded by Ray Noble and his Orchestra (Victor).

To Make a Man (Feel Like a Man). w/m Loretta Lynn, 1969. Country hit by Loretta Lynn (Decca).

To Make Love Sweeter for You. w/m Glenn Sutton and Jerry Kennedy, 1969. #1 Country chart record by Jerry Lee Lewis (Smash).

Tomb of the Unknown Love. w/m Michael Smotherman, 1986. #1 Country chart record by Kenny Rogers, from his album "The Heart of the Matter" (RCA).

Tomboy. w/m Joe Farrell and Jim Conway, 1959. Introduced and recorded by Perry Como (RCA).

Tombstone Every Mile, A. w/m Daniel B. Fulkerson, 1965. Hit Country record by Dick Curless (Tower).

Tom Dooley, w/m Traditional. Arranged by Dave Guard, 1958. Based on a folk song telling the story of a murder in North Carolina in the mid-1860s. Guard, a member of The Kingston Trio, arranged the number that became a #1 million-seller and the first hit for the group (Capitol). The song was voted a Grammy Award by the members of NARAS for Country Song of the Year.

To Me. w/m Mack David and Mike Reid, 1983. Top 10 Country chart record by Barbara Mandrell and Lee Greenwood (MCA).

To Me. w. Don George, m. Allie Wrubel, 1947. Introduced by Janet Blair, William Lundigan, and Tommy Dorsey and his Orchestra in (MM) *The Fabulous Dorseys.*

Tommy, Lad! w. Edward Teschemacher, m. E. J. Margetson, 1907. Originally published in London, England.

Tomorrow. w. Martin Charnin, m. Charles Strouse, 1977. Introduced by Andrea McArdle in (TM) *Annie.* Sung by Aileen Quinn in (MM) *Annie,* 1982.

Tomorrow. w/m Edward C. King and Mark Weitz, 1968. Recorded by The Strawberry Alarm Clock (Uni).

Tomorrow. w/m Gordon Jenkins, 1947. Best-selling record by Charlie Spivak, vocal by Rusty Nichols (Victor).

Tomorrow, Tomorrow. w/m Barry Gibb and Maurice Gibb, 1969. Recorded by The Bee Gees (Atco).

Tomorrow Belongs to Me. w. Fred Ebb, m. John Kander, 1966. Introduced by Robert Sharp and Joel Grey in (TM) *Cabaret.* In (MM) *Cabaret,* 1972, it was sung by Mark Lambert, dubbing for Oliver Collignon.

Tomorrow Is Forever. w. Charles Tobias, m. Max Steiner, 1946. Adaptation of Steiner's theme from (MP) *Tomorrow Is Forever*. Leading recordings by Dick Haymes and Helen Forrest (Decca) and Martha Stewart (Victor).

Tomorrow Is the First Day of the Rest of My Life. w/m Peter Link and C. C. Courtney, 1969. Sung by the company as the finale of the off-Broadway musical (TM) *Salvation*.

Tomorrow Mountain. w. John Latouche, m. Edward Kennedy "Duke" Ellington, 1947. Introduced by Alfred Drake in (TM) *Beggar's Holiday*.

Tomorrow Never Comes. w/m Ernest Tubb and Johnny Bond, 1945. Hit record by Country singer Ernest Tubb (Decca).

Tomorrow Night. w. Sam Coslow, m. Will Grosz, 1939, 1948. Popularized by Horace Heidt, vocal by The Heidt-Lites (Columbia). Revived in 1948 by blues singer and guitarist Lonnie Johnson, who had a hit record at the age of 59 (King).

Tom Sawyer. w. Neil Peart and Pye Dubois, m. Geddy Lee and Alex Lifeson, 1981. Recorded by the Canadian trio Rush (Mercury).

Tom Sawyer. w/m Richard M. Sherman and Robert B. Sherman, 1973. Introduced in (MM) *Tom Sawyer* by Celeste Holm.

Tom Thumb's Tune. w/m Peggy Lee, 1958. Introduced by Russ Tamblyn in the title role of (MM) *Tom Thumb*.

To My Mammy. w/m Irving Berlin, 1930. Sung by Al Jolson in (MM) *Mammy*. Gene Austin (Victor) and Sid Gary (Velvetone) recorded the song.

To My Sorrow. w/m Vernice McAlpin, 1947. C&W hit by Eddy Arnold (Victor). Revived by Johnny Duncan (Columbia), 1968.

Tonight. w/m Kool and The Gang, 1984. Recorded by Kool and The Gang (De-Lite).

Tonight. w. Stephen Sondheim, m. Leonard Bernstein, 1957. Introduced by Larry Kert and Carol Lawrence in (TM) *West Side Story*. In the film version (MM) *West Side Story*, 1961, it was sung by Jim Bryant and Marni Nixon, dubbing on the soundtrack for Richard Beymer and Natalie Wood, respectively. Leading records by Ferrante and Teicher (United Artists), Eddie Fisher (RCA Victor).

Tonight, Tonight, Tonight. w/m Tony Banks, Phil Collins, and Mike Rutherford, 1987. Top 10 chart hit, written and recorded by the British trio Genesis (Atlantic). Popularity enhanced by use on a Michelob beer TV commercial.

Tonight at Eight. w. Sheldon Harnick, m. Jerry Bock, 1963. Introduced by Daniel Massey in (TM) *Tonight at Eight*.

Tonight Carmen. w/m Marty Robbins, 1967. #1 Country chart record by Marty Robbins (Columbia).

Tonight I Celebrate My Love. w. Gerry Goffin, m. Michael Masser, 1983. Recorded by Peabo Bryson and Roberta Flack (Capitol).

Tonight I'll Be Staying Here with You. w/m Bob Dylan, 1969. Recorded by Bob Dylan (Columbia).

Tonight I'll Say a Prayer. w. R. I. Allen (Engl.), Alberto Testa (Ital.), m. Tony Renis, 1970. Italian song, "Il Posto Mio." Leading U.S. record by Eydie Gormé (RCA).

Tonight I'm Yours (Don't Hurt Me). w. Rod Stewart, m. Jim Cregan and Kevin Savigar, 1982. Recorded by the English singer Rod Stewart (Warner Bros.).

Tonight Is Mine. w. Gus Kahn, m. W. Franke Harling, 1934. Introduced by Irene Dunne in (MP) *Stingaree*.

Tonight Is What It Means to Be Young. w/m Jim Steinman, 1984. Introduced in the "rock 'n' roll fable," (MM) *Streets of Fire*, by the group assembled for the film Fire Inc. (MCA).

Tonight She Comes. w/m Ric Ocasek, 1985. Top 10 record by The Cars (Elektra).

Tonight's the Night. w/m Don Covay and Solomon Burke, 1965. Introduced and recorded by Solomon Burke (Atlantic).

Tonight's the Night (Gonna Be Alright). w/m Rod Stewart, 1976. #1 gold record single from the album "A Night on the Town," by the English singer Rod Stewart (Warner Bros.). Because of "sexually explicit" lyrics, the song at first received very little airplay until the public's demand forced the program directors to relent.

Tonight We Love. w. Bobby Worth, m. Freddy Martin and Ray Austin, 1941. Vocal version of Freddy Martin's hit instrumental based on Tchaikowsky's *Piano Concerto No. 1 in B Flat Minor.* This recording (Bluebird) was sung by Clyde Rogers. (See also "Concerto for Two," "Piano Concerto in B Flat," and "Alone at Last.")

Tonight Will Live. w. Ned Washington and Agustin Lara, 1938. Sung by Dorothy Lamour, Elvira Rios, and Tito Guizar in (MM) *Tropic Holiday* and recorded by Lamour, with Herbie Kay's Orchestra (Brunswick).

Tonight You Belong to Me. w. Billy Rose, m. Lee David, 1926, 1956. Recorded by Irving Kaufman (Banner) (Domino) (Harmony) (Regal); Gene Austin (Victor); Franklyn Baur (Brunswick); Sam Lanin's Orchestra (Cameo). Revived by Frankie Laine (Columbia), 1953 and, in 1956, by Patience and Prudence who had a million-seller (Liberty). Other popular versions: The Lennon Sisters with Lawrence Welk's Orchestra (Coral); and Karen Chandler and Jimmy Wakely, arranged and conducted by Jack Pleis (Decca).

Tony's Wife. w. Harold Adamson, m. Burton Lane, 1933. Recorded and featured by Gertrude Niesen (Columbia).

Too Beautiful for Words. w/m Bernie Grossman, Russ Columbo, and Jack Stern, 1934. Russ Columbo introduced this in (MM) *Wake Up and Dream,* his last film before his tragic fatal accident.

Too Busy Thinking About My Baby. w/m Janie Bradford, Barrett Strong, and Norman Whitfield, 1969. Top 10 record by Marvin Gaye (Tamla).

Too Close for Comfort. w/m Jerry Bock, Larry Holofcener, and George David Weiss, 1956. Introduced by Sammy Davis, Jr. in (TM) *Mr. Wonderful.* Best-selling record by Eydie Gormé (ABC-Paramount).

Too Close to Paradise. w. Bruce Roberts and Carole Bayer Sager, m. Bill Conti, 1978. Introduced by Sylvester Stallone in (MP) Paradise Alley.

Too Darn Hot. w/m Cole Porter, 1949. Introduced by Lorenzo Fuller, Eddie Sledge, and Fred Davis in (TM) *Kiss Me Kate.* Sung and danced by Ann Miller in (MM) *Kiss Me Kate,* 1953.

Toodle-Oo. w. Oscar Hammerstein II and W. C. Duncan, m. Vincent Youmans and Herbert Stothart, 1924. Sung by Mary Hay and Stanley Ridges in (TM) *Mary Jane McKane.*

Too Fat Polka. w/m Ross MacLean and Arthur Richardson, 1947. First hit record by Arthur Godfrey (Columbia).

Too Gone Too Long. w/m Gene Pistilli, 1988. #1 Country chart single from the album "Always and Forever" by Randy Travis (Warner Bros.).

Too Good for the Average Man. w. Lorenz Hart, m. Richard Rodgers, 1936. Introduced by Luella Gear and Monty Wooley in (TM) *On Your Toes.* Ramona, the singer-pianist, recorded it (Liberty Music Shops). In the 1983 revival, it was sung by George S. Irving and Dina Merrill.

Too Hot. w/m George Brown, 1980. Top 10 record by the group Kool and The Gang (De-Lite).

Too Hot Ta Trot. w/m William King, Ronald LaPread, Thomas McClary, Walter Orange, Lionel Ritchie, and Milan Williams, 1978. Recorded by The Commodores (Motown) and performed by them in (MP) *Thank God It's Friday.*

Too Late. w/m Jimmy Wakely, 1941. Best-selling records by Wakely (Decca) and Gene Autry (Okeh).

Too Late. w. Sam M. Lewis, m. Victor Young, 1931. Introduced by Bing Crosby on his radio program. Featured and recorded by Mildred Bailey (Victor). Best-selling record by Kate Smith with Guy Lombardo and His Royal Canadians (Columbia).

Too Late. m. D. C. Nelson and Joe "King" Oliver, 1929. Recorded by King Oliver's Orchestra (Victor).

Too Late for Goodbyes. w/m Julian Lennon, 1985. Top 10 single by Julian Lennon (Atlantic).

Too Late Now. w. Alan Jay Lerner, m. Burton Lane, 1951. Introduced by Jane Powell in (MM) *Royal Wedding*. Song nominated for Academy Award. Powell recorded it (MGM), as did Toni Arden (Columbia), Dick Haymes (Decca), Dinah Shore (RCA Victor). Song has become a standard.

Too Late to Try Again. w/m Carl Butler, 1964. Top 10 Country chart record by Carl Butler and Pearl (Columbia).

Too Late to Turn Back Now. w/m Eddie Cornelius, 1972. Gold record by the family trio The Cornelius Brothers and Sister Rose (United Artists).

Too Late to Worry, Too Blue to Cry. w/m Al Dexter, 1944. Recorded by Al Dexter and his Troopers (Okeh).

Toolie Oolie Doolie (The Yodel Polka). w. Vaughn Horton (Engl.), Arthur Beul (Ger.), m. Arthur Beul, 1948. Original Swiss-German title "Nach em Rage Schint Sunne." Introduced on records in the U.S. by Vaughn Horton and his Polka Debs (Continental). Top 10 hit by The Andrews Sisters (Decca) and popular recording by The Sportsmen (Capitol). Gene Autry sang it in (MP) *Riders of the Whistling Pines*, 1949.

Too Long at the Fair. w/m Billy Barnes, 1959. Introduced by Joyce Jameson and Jackie Joseph in (TM) *The Billy Barnes Revue*. Featured and recorded by Felicia Sanders (Decca) and Barbra Streisand (Columbia).

Too Many Fish in the Sea. w/m Eddie Holland and Norman Whitfield, 1965. Crossover (R&B/Pop) hit by The Marvelettes (Tamla). Chart record, in medley with "Three Little Fishies," (q.v.) by Mitch Ryder and The Detroit Wheels (New Voice), 1967.

Too Many Lovers. w/m Mark True, Ted Lindsay, and Sam Hogin, 1981. #1 Country chart record by Crystal Gayle (Columbia).

Too Many Mornings. w/m Stephen Sondheim, 1971. Introduced by John McMartin and Dorothy Collins in (TM) *Follies*.

Too Many Rings Around Rosie. w. Irving Caesar, m. Vincent Youmans, 1925. Introduced by Josephine Whittell and chorus in (TM) *No, No, Nanette*. In the 1971 Broadway production, it was performed by Helen Gallagher and chorus.

Too Many Rivers. w/m Harlan Howard, 1965. Hit record by Brenda Lee (Decca).

Too Many Tears. w. Al Dubin, m. Harry Warren, 1932. Introduced and popularized by Guy Lombardo and the Royal Canadians (Brunswick). Also recorded by the Pickens Sisters (Victor).

Too Many Times. w/m Michael Smotherman, Scott Page, and Tony McShear, 1986. Top 10 Country chart song by Earl Thomas Conley and Anita Pointer (RCA).

Too Many Times. w/m Don Winters, 1961. Top 10 Country chart record by Don Winters (Decca).

Too Marvelous for Words. w. Johnny Mercer, m. Richard A. Whiting, 1937. In (MM) *Ready, Willing and Able*, it was introduced by Ross Alexander [voice dubbed by James Newill] and Wini Shaw, then sung by Ruby Keeler and danced by her with Lee Dixon on a giant typewriter. It was heard in (MP) *Dark Passage* in 1947; in (MM) *Young Man* *with a Horn*, 1950; sung by Frankie Laine in (MP) *On the Sunny Side of the Street*, 1951.

Too Much. w/m Bernard Weinman, 1957. #1 hit by Elvis Presley (RCA).

Too Much, Too Little, Too Late. w/m Nat Kipner and John Vallins, 1978. #1 gold record by Johnny Mathis and Deniece Williams (Columbia).

Too Much Heaven. w/m Barry Gibb, Maurice Gibb, and Robin Gibb, 1979. #1 platinum record, with all royalties donated to UNICEF by The Bee Gees, the British brother trio who wrote and recorded the song (RSO).

Too Much in Love. w. Kim Gannon, m. Walter Kent, 1944. Introduced by Jane Powell in her screen debut in (MM) *Song of the Open Road*. Nominated for Academy Award, 1944.

Too Much Is Not Enough. w/m David Bellamy and Ron Taylor, 1986. #1 Country chart record by The Bellamy Brothers with The Forester Sisters (Curb).

Too Much Lovin' w/m Lowman Pauling, 1953. R&B success by The "5" Royales (Apollo).

Too Much Monkey Business. w/m Chuck Berry, 1956. R&B hit by Chuck Berry (Chess).

Too Much of Nothing. w/m Bob Dylan, 1967. Top 40 record by Peter, Paul and Mary (Warner Bros.).

Too Much on My Heart. w/m Lester Fortune, 1985. #1 Country chart song by The Statler Brothers (Mercury).

Too Much Talk. w/m Mark Lindsay, 1968. Top 20 record by Paul Revere and The Raiders (Columbia). Lindsay was lead singer.

Too Much Tequila. m. Dave Burgess, 1959. Instrumental by The Champs (Challenge).

Too Much Time on My Hands. w/m Tommy Shaw ,1981. Top 10 record by the quintet Styx (A&M).

Too Much to Lose. w/m Tommy Blake and Lester Vanadore, 1960. C&W hit by Carl Belew (Decca).

Too Old to Cut the Mustard. w/m Bill Carlisle, 1952. Hit Pop record by Marlene Dietrich and Rosemary Clooney (Columbia). Hit C&W record by Red Foley and Ernest Tubb (Decca).

Too-Ra-Loo-Ra-Loo-Ral (That's an Irish Lullaby). w/m James Royce Shannon, 1914, 1944. Introduced by Chauncey Olcott. It was revived by Bing Crosby in (MM) *Going My Way* in 1944. Crosby's recording (Decca) sold over a million copies and enabled this thirty-year-old song to get on "Your Hit Parade."

Too Romantic. w. Johnny Burke, m. James V. Monaco, 1940. Introduced by Bing Crosby and Dorothy Lamour in (MM) *Road to Singapore*. Because of contractual arrangements, Crosby (Decca) and Lamour (Bluebird) recorded the song individually.

Too Shy. w/m Limahl and Nick Beggs, 1983. Top 10 record by the English quintet Kajagoogoo (EMI America).

Toot, Toot, Tootsie, Goodbye. w/m Ted Fio Rito, Robert A. King, Gus Kahn, and Ernie Erdman, 1922. Al Jolson interpolated this during the run of (TM) *Bombo* at the Winter Garden in New York, and it was a show stopper. His record followed (Columbia). Jolson sang the song in (MM) *The Jazz Singer*, 1927; (MM) *Rose of Washington Square*, 1939; (MM) *The Jolson Story*, 1946; (MM) *Jolson Sings Again*, 1949. In the latter two, he dubbed his voice on the soundtrack for Larry Parks. The song was also heard in the Kahn film biography (MM) *I'll See You in My Dreams*, 1951.

Too Tight. w/m Michael Cooper, 1981. Recorded by the band Con Funk Shun (Mercury).

Tootin' Through the Roof. m. Edward Kennedy "Duke" Ellington, 1939. Swing instrumental introduced and recorded by Duke Ellington (Columbia).

Too True. w. Jack Heinz, m. Robert Lissauer, 1955. Recorded by Karen Rich, with Larry Wagner's Orchestra (Decca).

Too Weak to Fight. w/m Clarence Carter, Rick Hall, George Jackson, and John Keyes, 1968. Hit record by Clarence Carter (Atlantic).

Too Young. w. Sylvia Dee, m. Sidney Lippman, 1951. The recording by Nat "King" Cole, with Les Baxter's Orchestra (Capitol), was the #1 song in all categories for the year. It was also #1 on "Your Hit Parade" twelve times, an unequaled record. Revived by Donny Osmond (MGM), 1972.

Too Young to Go Steady. w. Harold Adamson, m. Jimmy McHugh, 1955. Popular records by Nat "King" Cole (Capitol); Patti Page (Mercury); Connie Stevens (Warner Bros.), 1960.

Top Hat, White Tie and Tails. w/m Irving Berlin, 1935. Introduced by Fred Astaire in (MM) *Top Hat*. Astaire recorded it (Brunswick), as did the Boswell Sisters (Decca), and the bands of Archie Bleyer (Melotone), the Dorsey Brothers (Decca), Phil Ohman (Columbia).

Topkapi. w. Noel Sherman, m. Manos Hadjidakis, 1964. Composition based on a theme from (MP) *Topkapi*. Leading record by jazz organist Jimmy McGriff (Sue).

Top of the Town. w. Harold Adamson, Jimmy McHugh, 1937. Introduced in (MM) *Top of the Town* and on records by Gertrude Niesen (Brunswick). Also recorded by Clarence Williams and his Washboard Band, vocal by Eva Taylor (Bluebird).

Top of the World. w/m John Bettis and Richard Carpenter, 1973. Popular records by The Carpenters (A&M), and Lynn Anderson (Columbia).

Topsy II. m. Edgar Battle and Eddie Durham, 1958. Instrumental hit based on "Topsy," a section from an earlier piece, "Uncle Tom's Cabin," by the same writers. Drummer Cozy Cole had a Top 10 record of the new version (Love).

Torch Song, The. w. Mort Dixon and Joe Young, m. Harry Warren, 1931. Sung by Bartlett Robinson in (TM) *The Laugh Parade*.

Torero. w. Al Hoffman and Dick Manning (Engl.), Nisa (Ital.), m. Renato Carosone, 1958. Popularized in the U.S. by the Italian recording of Renato Carosone (Capitol). Among other versions, Julius LaRosa (RCA).

Tormented. w/m Will Hudson, 1936. Introduced and recorded by the Hudson-DeLange Orchestra, vocal by Ruth Gaylor (Brunswick). The bands of Richard Himber [Bunny Berigan and Artie Shaw played on the recording] (Victor), Isham Jones (Decca), Wingy Manone (Bluebird), and jazz harpist Caspar Reardon (Liberty Music Shops) also recorded it.

Torn Between Two Lovers. w/m Phil Jarrell and Peter Yarrow, 1977. #1 gold record by Mary MacGregor (Ariola America).

Torture. w/m John D. Loudermilk, 1962. Crossover (C&W/Pop) chart record by Kris Jensen (Hickory).

To See My Angel Cry. w/m Conway Twitty, Carlton Haney, and L. E. White, 1969. #1 Country chart record by Conway Twitty (Decca).

To Sir with Love. w. Don Black, m. Marc London and R. Granier, 1967. Sung by the Scottish singer/actress Lulu, under the credits on the soundtrack of (MP) *To Sir with Love*, and on her #1 gold record (Epic). Instrumental chart record by flutist Herbie Mann (Atlantic).

Tossin' and Turnin'. w/m Malou Ren and Ritchie Adams, 1961. Bobby Lewis's record was #1 on the R&B and Pop charts (Beltone).

To Susan on the West Coast Waiting. w/m Donovan Leitch, 1969. Top 40 record by Donovan (Epic).

Total Eclipse of the Heart. w/m Jim Steinman, 1983. #1 gold record by the Welsh-born singer Bonnie Tyler (Columbia).

Totem Tom-Tom. w. Oscar Hammerstein II and Otto Harbach, m. Rudolf Friml, 1924. Introduced by Pearl Regay and chorus in (TM) *Rose-Marie*. It was sung by the chorus in (MM) *Rose Marie*, 1935, and in its remake, 1954. Tammy Grimes and female ensemble sang it in (TM) *A Musical Jubilee*, 1975.

To the Aisle. w/m Billy Dawn Smith and Stuart Wiener, 1957. Top 10 R&B and Top 40 Pop chart record by The Five Satins (Ember).

To the Door of the Sun (Alle Porte del Sole). w. Norman Newell (Engl.), m. Mario Panzeri, Lorenzo Pilat, and Corrado Conti, 1975. Original Italian words by Daniele Pace. Featured and Top 20 record by Al Martino (Capitol).

To the Land of My Own Romance. w. Harry B. Smith, m. Victor Herbert, 1911. A waltz introduced by Kitty Gordon in (TM) *The Enchantress*. In (MM) *The Great Victor Herbert*, 1939, it was sung by Susanna Foster and Allan Jones.

To Think You've Chosen Me. w/m Bennie Benjamin and George Weiss, 1950. Leading record by Eddy Howard, with his Orchestra (Mercury).

Touch a Four Leaf Clover. w/m David Lewis and Wayne Lewis, 1983. Recorded by the band Atlantic Starr (A&M).

Touch a Hand, Make a Friend. w/m Homer Banks, Carl Hampton, and Raymond Jackson, 1985. Adapted from the traditional song, The Oak Ridge Boys had a #1 Country chart record (MCA).

Touch a Hand, Make a Friend. Traditional, 1974. Gospel song recorded by the family group The Staple Singers (Stax).

Touch Me. w/m Raymond Fenwick and Mike Hurst, 1974. Recorded by the English quartet Fancy (Big Tree).

Touch Me. w/m John Densmore, Robert Krieger, Raymond Manzarek, and James Morrison, 1969. Written and gold record by The Doors (Elektra).

Touch Me. w/m Willie Nelson, 1962. Top 10 Country chart record by Willie Nelson (Liberty). Revived by Howdy Glenn (Warner Bros.), 1977, and the group Bandana (Warner Bros.), 1986.

Touch Me (I Want Your Body). w/m M. Shreeve, J. Astrop, and P. Q. Harris, 1987. Top 10 record by Samantha Fox (Jive).

Touch Me in the Morning. w/m Michael Masser and Ronald Miller, 1973. #1 record by Diana Ross (Motown).

Touch Me When We're Dancing. w/m Kenneth Bell, Terry Skinner, and J. L. Wallace, 1981, 1986. First recorded by the Alabama studio session band Bama (Free Flight), 1979. Best-selling record by The Carpenters (A&M). #1 Country chart record by the group Alabama (RCA), 1986.

Touch My Heart. w/m Aubrey Mayhew and Donny Young, 1967. Hit Country record by Ray Price (Columbia).

Touch of God's Hand, The. w/m Bob Nolan, 1936. Introduced and featured by the Sons of the Pioneers.

Touch of Grey. w. Robert Hunter, m. Jerry Garcia, 1987. Top 10 single by the group, The Grateful Dead, from their album "In the Dark" (Arista).

Touch of Pink, A. w/m Diane Lampert and Richard Loring, 1959. From (MP) *The Wild and the Innocent*. Leading record by Jerry Wallace (Challenge).

Touch of Texas, A. w. Frank Loesser, m. Jimmy McHugh, 1942. Introduced by Freddy Martin and his Orchestra in (MM) *Seven Days Leave*, and recorded by him, vocal by Eddie Stone and Glen Hughes (Victor). Song also heard in (MM) *Moon Over Las Vegas*, 1944.

Touch of Your Hand, The. w. Otto Harbach, m. Jerome Kern, 1933. Introduced by Tamara and William Hain in (TM) *Roberta*. Ginger Rogers sang it in (MM) *Roberta* in 1934. In the second film version, retitled (MM) *Lovely to Look At*, 1952, it was sung by Howard Keel and Kathryn Grayson.

Touch of Your Lips, The. w/m Ray Noble, 1936. Introduced, featured, and recorded by Ray Noble and his Orchestra, vocal by Al Bowlly (Victor). Also recorded by the orchestras of Hal Kemp (Brunswick) and Stew Pletcher (Bluebird) and later by accordionist Art Van Damme (Capitol).

Touch Your Woman. w/m Dolly Parton, 1972. Top 10 Country chart record by Dolly Parton (RCA).

Tower of Strength. w. Bob Hilliard, m. Burt Bacharach, 1961. Hit record by Gene McDaniels (Liberty).

To Whom It May Concern, w. Sidney D. Mitchell, m. George W. Meyer and Archie Gottler, 1930. Featured and recorded by Ben Bernie and his Orchestra (Brunswick).

Town Where I Was Born, The. w/m Paul Dresser, 1905.

Town Without Pity. w. Ned Washington, m. Dimitri Tiomkin, 1961. Sung by Gene Pitney on the soundtrack of (MP) *Town Without Pity*. Nominated for Academy Award, 1961. Top 40 record by Pitney (Musicor).

Toyland. w. Glen MacDonough, m. Victor Herbert, 1903. Introduced by Bessie Wynn in (TM) *Babes in Toyland*. The song was also used in the film versions (MM) *Babes in Toyland*, 1934 and 1961.

Toy Monkey, The. w. Harry Greenbank, m. Lionel Monckton, 1896. Introduced in (TM) *The Geisha* in London in April and in New York in September of the same year.

To You. w. Benny Davis, m. Ted Shapiro and Tommy Dorsey, 1939. Introduced and recorded by Tommy Dorsey and his Band (Victor). Also recorded by Glenn Miller (Bluebird), Al Donahue (Vocalion), and Paul Whiteman, with vocal by Joan Edwards (Decca).

To You, My Love. w. Jack Lawrence (Engl.), Louis Gaste (Fr.), m. Louis Gaste, 1956. French song. Recorded by Nick Noble (Mercury), Georgie Shaw (Decca).

To You, Sweetheart, Aloha. w/m Harry Owens, 1936. Introduced and featured by its composer, Harry Owens and his Royal Hawaiians, at the Royal Hawaiian Hotel in Honolulu. Recorded by Del Courtney and his Orchestra, who also performed at the hotel (Vocalion), Louis Armstrong (Decca), and Gray Gordon (Victor).

Toys. w/m Bob Merrill, 1953. Popular record by Eileen Barton, with Jack Pleis's Orchestra (Decca).

Toys in the Attic. w/m George Duning, Joe Sherman, and George David Weiss, 1963. Theme from (MP) *Toys in the Attic*. Instrumental recording by Joe Sherman and his Orchestra (World), and vocal version by Jack Jones (Kapp).

Toy Soldiers. w/m Michael Jary and Marta Marrero, 1989. Hit record by Martika (Columbia).

Toy Trumpet, The. w. Sidney D. Mitchell and Lew Pollack, m. Raymond Scott, 1937. The instrumental version was introduced and recorded by the Raymond Scott Quintette (Brunswick). Other popular versions by Horace Heidt and his Musical Knights (Brunswick), the Milt Herth Trio (Decca), and Frank Dailey and his Orchestra (Bluebird). It was interpolated in (MM) *Rebecca of Sunnybrook Farm*, 1938, in which it was sung by Shirley Temple, danced by Bill Robinson, and played by the Scott group.

Traces. w/m Buddy Buie, James B. Cobb, Jr., and Emory Gordy, Jr., 1969. Hit record by Classics IV, featuring Dennis Yost (Imperial). The Lettermen had a chart version in medley with "Memories" (Capitol), 1970, (q.v.).

Tracks of My Tears, The. w/m Warren Moore, William Robinson, and Marv Taplin, 1965. Introduced by The Miracles, the R&B group of which writers "Smokey" Robinson and "Pete" Moore were members (Tamla). Later hit records by Johnny Rivers (Imperial), 1967, and Linda Ronstadt (Asylum), 1976.

Tracy. w/m Lee Pockriss and Paul Vance, 1969. Top 10 record by The Cuff Links (Decca). The "group" was comprised of overdubbed voices by Ron Dante.

Tracy's Theme.   m. Robert Ascher, 1960. From (TVP) "The Philadelphia Story." Popular instrumental by Spencer Ross and his Orchestra (Columbia). Ross was pseudonym for Robert Mersey.

Trade Mark.   w/m Porter Wagoner and Gary Walker, 1953. Hit Country record by Carl Smith (Columbia).

Trade Winds.   w. Charles Tobias, m. Cliff Friend, 1940. A #1 song on all the charts, most popular records by Bing Crosby (Decca), and Tommy Dorsey with vocal by Frank Sinatra (Victor).

Tradition.   w. Sheldon Harnick, m. Jerry Bock, 1964. Introduced by Zero Mostel and the villagers in (TM) *Fiddler on the Roof*. In the film version (MM) *Fiddler on the Roof*, 1971, it was performed by Topol and the villagers, with Isaac Stern on the soundtrack as the fiddler.

Traffic Jam.   m. Teddy McRae and Artie Shaw, 1939. Instrumental featured by Artie Shaw and his Orchestra (Bluebird).

Tragedy.   w/m Barry Gibb, Maurice Gibb, and Robin Gibb, 1979. The fourth consecutive #1 platinum record by the British brother trio The Bee Gees (RSO).

Tragedy.   w/m Gerald H. Nelson and Fred B. Burch, 1959. First hit record by Thomas Wayne (Fernwood). Others: The Fleetwoods (Dolton), 1961; and Bryan Hyland (Dot), 1969.

Trail of Broken Treaties.   w/m Steve Van Zant, 1987. Popular album track from "Freedom—No Compromise" (Manhattan).

Trail of the Lonesome Pine, The.   w. Ballard MacDonald, m. Harry Carroll, 1913.

Train in Vain (Stand by Me).   w/m Mick Jones and Joe Strummer, 1980. Recorded by the London, England, group The Clash (Epic).

Train of Love.   w/m Johnny Cash, 1956. Introduced and recorded by Johnny Cash (Sun).

Trains and Boats and Planes.   w. Hal David, m. Burt Bacharach, 1965. Popular records by Billy J. Kramer and The Dakotas (Imperial), and Dionne Warwick (Scepter), 1967.

Train Whistle Blues.   w/m Jimmie Rodgers, 1930. Introduced and recorded by Rodgers (Victor).

Tra La La.   w/m Johnny Parker, 1956. Introduced by LaVern Baker in (MM) *Rock, Rock, Rock* and recorded by her with The Gliders (Atlantic). Best-selling version by Georgia Gibbs (Mercury).

Tra-La-La.   w. Ira Gershwin, m. George Gershwin, 1922. Ira wrote the lyrics under the pseudonym of Arthur Francis. The song was introduced in (TM) *For Goodness Sake* by Marjorie Gateson and John E. Hazzard. Revived by Gene Kelly and Oscar Levant in (MM) *An American in Paris*, 1951.

Tra-La-La-La   w. Mack Gordon, m. Harry Warren, 1940. Sung by Shirley Temple, Jack Oakie, and Charlotte Greenwood in (MM) *Young People*. It was interpolated in (MM) *Mother Wore Tights*, starring Betty Grable and Dan Dailey, 1947.

Tramp.   w/m Lowell Fulson and J. McCracklin, 1967. Introduced and chart record by Lowell Fulson (Kent). Covered by Otis [Redding] and Carla [Thomas] with a Top 40 record (Stax).

Tramp! Tramp! Tramp!   w. Rida Johnson Young, m. Victor Herbert, 1910. Introduced by Orville Harrold and chorus in (TM) *Naughty Marietta*. In the film version of (MM) *Naughty Marietta* it was sung by Nelson Eddy and male chorus.

Tramps at Sea.   w/m Dorothy Fields, Jimmy McHugh, and Herbert Stothart, 1932. Sung by Lawrence Tibbett in (MM) *The Cuban Love Song* and recorded by him (Victor), coupled with the title song.

Transblucency. m. Edward Kennedy "Duke" Ellington and Lawrence Brown, 1946. Based on a theme from the instrumental "Blue Lights," recorded by Duke Ellington, 1939 (Brunswick). This was composed with trombonist Brown as a piece for voice as an instrument, and orchestra. Vocalist on the recording was Kay Davis (Victor).

Transfusion. w/m Jimmy Drake, 1956. Novelty hit by Nervous Norvus, pseudonym for Drake (Dot).

Transistor Sister. w/m Frank C. Slay, Jr. and Chuck Dougherty, 1961. Recorded by Freddy Cannon (Swan).

Trapped by a Thing Called Love. w/m Denise LaSalle, 1971. Top 20 record by Denise LaSalle (Westbound).

Travelin' Band. w/m John Fogerty, 1970. Gold record by Creedence Clearwater Revival (Fantasy).

Travelin' Blues. w/m Jimmie Rodgers and Shelly Lee Alley, 1931. Introduced by Rodgers (Victor). Revived in 1951 by Lefty Frizzell (Columbia).

Travelin' Blues. w/m unknown, 1925. Recorded by Lovie Austin (Paramount); Ma Rainey (Paramount); Slim Gaillard, with vocal by Leo Watson (Queen).

Traveling Down a Lonely Road. See **Love Theme from "La Strada."**

Travelin' Light. w. Sidney Clare, m. Harry Akst, 1937. Introduced by Anthony (Tony) Martin in (MM) *Sing and Be Happy.*

Travelin' Man. w/m Jerry Fuller, 1961. Popularized by Ricky Nelson's #1 million-selling record (Imperial).

Travelin' Prayer. w/m Billy Joel, 1973. Recorded by Billy Joel (Columbia).

Travelin' Shoes. w/m Elvin Bishop, 1974. Recorded by Elvin Bishop (Capricorn).

Trav'lin' All Alone. w/m J. C. Johnson, 1930. Outstanding recordings by McKinney's Cotton Pickers (Victor), the Boswell Sisters (Brunswick), Billie Holiday, with Claude Thornhill at the piano (Vocalion).

Trav'lin' Light. w. Johnny Mercer, m. Jimmy Mundy and Trummy Young, 1943. Recorded by Paul Whiteman and his Orchestra, vocal by Billie Holiday, who was listed only as "Lady Day" (Capitol).

Travlin' Man. w. Ronald Miller, m. Bryan Wells, 1967. Top 40 record by Stevie Wonder (Tamla).

Treasure of Love. w/m Lou Stallman and Joe Shapiro, 1956. Hit record by Clyde McPhatter (Atlantic).

Treasure of Sierra Madre, The. w. Buddy Kaye, m. Dick Manning, 1947. Based on the title and written to promote the film of the same name. Leading records by Buddy Clark, with Ray Noble and his Orchestra (Columbia); Freddy Martin and his Orchestra (RCA Victor); Dick Haymes (Decca).

Treat Her Like a Lady. w/m Eddie Cornelius, 1971. Gold record by The Cornelius Brothers and Sister Rose (United Artists).

Treat Her Right. w/m Roy Head, 1965. Hit Pop and R&B record by Roy Head and The Traits (Back Beat).

Treat Me Nice. w/m Mike Stoller and Jerry Leiber, 1957. Introduced by Elvis Presley in (MM) *Jailhouse Rock*, and coupled by Presley with the hit title song (RCA).

Treat Me Right. w/m Doug Lubahn, 1981. Recorded by Pat Benatar (Chrysalis).

Treat Me Rough. w. Ira Gershwin, m. George Gershwin, 1930. Introduced by William Kent and ensemble in (TM) *Girl Crazy*. It was omitted from the first screen version, 1932, but included in the second (MM) *Girl Crazy*, 1943, and sung by Mickey Rooney and June Allyson. Sue Ann Langdon sang it in another version (MM) *When the Boys Meet the Girls*, 1966.

Tree in the Meadow, A. w/m Billy Reid, 1948. Margaret Whiting recorded this British song for her first million-seller and #1 hit

(Capitol). Although there are many other versions, it is associated with her.

Tree in the Park, A. w. Lorenz Hart, m. Richard Rodgers, 1926. Introduced by Helen Ford and Lester Cole in (MM) *Peggy-Ann.* Recorded by Helen Morgan (Brunswick), and Frank Black and his Orchestra (Brunswick).

Trees. w. Joyce Kilmer, m. Otto Rasbach, 1922, 1931. Rasbach set Kilmer's poem to music in the form of a concert song, recorded by John Charles Thomas (Victor), Nelson Eddy (Victor), and Paul Robeson (Victor). The popular acceptance occurred with the release of the recording by Isham Jones and his Orchestra (Brunswick), 1931, coupled with the famous arrangement of "Star Dust" (q.v.). In films, it was sung in (MM) *The Big Broadcast,* 1932, by Donald Novis who also recorded it (Brunswick), and by Fred Waring's Pennsylvanians in (MM) *Melody Time,* 1948. Later recorded by such diverse musical aggregations as Bunny Berigan and his Band (Victor), Claude Hopkin's Band (Decca), and the Country group The Sons of the Pioneers (Victor).

Tree Was a Tree, A. w. Mack Gordon, m. Harry Revel, 1933. Most popular record was by Isham Jones (Victor).

Tres Palabras. See **Without You.**

Triangle. w/m Jean Chapel and Robert Taubert, 1964. Hit country record by Carl Smith (Columbia).

Triflin' Gal. w/m Cindy Walker, 1945. Leading record by Al Dexter (Okeh).

Triplets. w. Howard Dietz, m. Arthur Schwartz, 1937. Introduced by The Tune Twisters in (TM) *Between the Devil.* In (MM) *The Band Wagon,* 1953, it was interpolated by Fred Astaire, Jack Buchanan, and Nanette Fabray.

Tripoli (The Shores of). w. Paul Cunningham and Al Dubin, m. Irving Weill, 1920.

Trip to Heaven. w/m Freddie Hart, 1973. Hit Country record by Freddie Hart (Capitol).

Troglodyte (Cave Man). w/m Jimmy Castor, Gerry Thomas, Lenny Fridie, Jr., Harry Jensen, Bobby Manigault, and Doug Gibson, 1972. Novelty gold record, written and recorded by The Jimmy Castor Bunch (RCA).

Trolley Song, The. w/m Hugh Martin and Ralph Blane, 1944. Introduced by Judy Garland in (MM) *Meet Me in St. Louis.* Song nominated for Academy Award. Other versions, in addition to Garland's recording (Decca): The Pied Pipers (Capitol); The King Sisters (Bluebird); Vaughn Monroe, vocal by Monroe and Marilyn Duke (Victor); Guy Lombardo, vocal by Stuart Foster (Decca). Song on "Your Hit Parade" for fourteen weeks, five times as #1. Revived by Donna Kane and the company in (TM) *Meet Me in St. Louis,* 1989.

Tropical Magic. w. Mack Gordon, m. Harry Warren, 1941. Introduced by Alice Faye in (MM) *Week-end in Havana.* Among recordings: Gene Krupa, vocal by Johnny Desmond (Okeh); Dick Todd (Bluebird).

Tropicana. m. Bernie Wayne, 1953. Instrumental, recorded by trumpeter Monty Kelly and his Orchestra (Essex).

Trouble. w/m Lindsey Buckingham, 1981. Top 10 record by Lindsey Buckingham (Asylum).

Trouble in Mind. w/m Richard M. Jones, 1926. Jones first recorded this with his band (Bluebird). It was followed by Bertha "Chippie" Hill (Okeh); Jay McShann, vocal by Julia Lee (Capitol); Victoria Spivey (Vocalion); Sister Rosetta Tharpe with Lucky Millinder's Band (Decca); Nina Simone (Colpix); Aretha Franklin (Columbia); Ray Charles (Atlantic). It was sung by Marianne Faithfull as the title song of (MP) *Trouble in Mind* and recorded on the soundtrack album (Island), 1986.

Trouble in Paradise. w/m Allison R. Khent and Billy Dawn Smith, 1960. Popular record by The Crests, featuring Johnny Mastro (Coed).

Trouble in Paradise. w. Ned Wever, m. Milton Ager and Arthur Schwartz, 1933. Recorded by the bands of Ted Weems (Bluebird), Charlie Agnew (Columbia), and Freddy Martin and the Hotel Bossert Orchestra (Melotone).

Trouble in the Fields. w/m Nanci Griffith and Rick West, 1987. Country chart record by Nanci Griffith, from the album "Lone Star State of Mind" (MCA).

Trouble Is a Man. w/m Alec Wilder, 1944. Introduced and featured Mabel Mercer.

Trouble Man. w/m Marvin Gaye, 1972. Sung on the soundtrack of (MP) *Trouble Man* by Marvin Gaye, who also had a Top 10 recording (Tamla).

Trouble's Back in Town. w/m Dick Flood, 1962. Hit record on the C&W charts by The Wilburn Brothers (Decca).

Trouble with Harry, The. w. Floyd Huddleston and Herb Eiseman, m. Mark McIntyre, 1956. Novelty, inspired by the film *The Trouble with Harry*. Leading records by Alfi and Harry (Liberty) and Les Baxter and his Orchestra (Capitol).

Truck Drivers Blues. w/m Ted Daffan, 1939. Popular Country and Western song.

Truck Drivin' Son-of-a-Gun. w/m Dixie Deen and Ray King, 1965. Country hit by Dave Dudley (Mercury).

Truckin'. w/m Jerry Garcia, Robert Hunter, Billy Kruetzmann, Philip Lesh, Bob Weir, 1971. Written by members of the group, The Grateful Dead, which recorded the song (Warner Bros.). Not to be confused with the 1935 hit.

Truckin'. w. Ted Koehler, m. Rube Bloom, 1935. Introduced in the Cotton Club revue in Harlem, New York. Among top recordings: Fats Waller (Victor); Duke Ellington, vocal by Ivy Anderson (Brunswick); Red Allen (Vocalion); Johnny "Scat" Davis (Decca); Little Ramblers (Bluebird); Mills Blue Rhythm Band (Columbia).

Truck Stop. m. Jerry Dean Smith, 1969. Instrumental recorded by Jerry Smith and His Pianos (ABC).

True. w/m Gary Kemp, 1983. Top 10 record written by the guitarist of the English quintet Spandau Ballet (Chrysalis).

True. w/m Walter G. Samuels and Leonard Whitcup, 1934. Popularized by Paul Whiteman, vocal by Jack Fulton (Victor); Guy Lombardo (Brunswick); Chick Webb (Vocalion); Ted Black (Bluebird). Andy Russell, with orchestra conducted by Paul Weston, revived it in the mid-forties (Capitol).

True, True Love, A. w/m Bobby Darin, 1962. Love theme from (MP) *If a Man Answers*, starring Bobby Darin and Sandra Dee. Darin's recording was coupled with the more popular title song (Capitol) (q.v.).

True Blue. w/m Madonna and Steve Bray, 1986. Top 10 single from the album of the same name by Madonna (Sire).

True Blue Lou. w/m Sam Coslow, Leo Robin, and Richard A. Whiting, 1929. Introduced by Hal Skelly in (MM) *Dance of Life*, the film adaptation of the Broadway success, *Burlesque*. Popular recordings by Meyer Davis's Orchestra (Brunswick) and Johnny Marvin (Victor).

True Colors. w/m Tom Kelly and Billy Steinberg, 1986. #1 single from the album of the same name by Cyndi Lauper (Portrait).

True Confession. w/m Sam Coslow and Frederick Hollander, 1937. Theme song of (MP) *True Confession*, which starred Carole Lombard and Fred MacMurray. Many recordings, including: Dorothy Lamour (Brunswick), coupled with "Moon of Manakoora," (q.v.) and the bands: Larry Clinton, vocal by Bea Wain (Victor); Don Bestor (Bluebird); Sammy Kaye (Vocalion); Russ Morgan (Brunswick).

True Grit. w. Don Black, m. Elmer Bernstein, 1969. Introduced by Glen Campbell in (MP) *True Grit*, and on his Top 40 record (Capitol).

True Love. w/m Cole Porter, 1956. Introduced by Bing Crosby and Grace Kelly in (MM) *High Society*. Nominated for Academy Award. Crosby and Kelly's recording was a best-seller (Capitol).

True Love Goes On and On. w/m Richard Adler and Jerry Ross, 1954. Popularized by Burl Ives, with Gordon Jenkins' Orchestra (Decca).

True Love's a Blessing. w. Carole Smith, m. Sonny James, 1966. Country hit record by Sonny James (Capitol).

True Love Ways. w/m Norman Petty and Buddy Holly, 1965. Hit record by the British duo Peter and Gordon (Capitol). Revived by Mickey Gilley (Epic), 1980.

Truly. w/m Lionel Richie, 1982. #1 gold single by Lionel Richie, from his platinum self-named LP (Motown).

Trumpet Blues. m. Harry James and Jack Matthias, 1942. Introduced and recorded by Harry James and his Orchestra, coupled with his big hit "Sleepy Lagoon" (q.v.).

Trust in Me. w. Ned Wever, m. Milton Ager and Jean Schwartz, 1937. Featured and recorded by Mildred Bailey (Vocalion); Bobby Hayes, vocal by Don Cornell (Melotone); Wayne King (Victor); Abe Lyman, vocal by Sonny Schuyler (Decca). The song reached #2 on "Your Hit Parade." Chart revivals: Eddie Fisher (Victor), Roy Rogers (Decca), 1952, Chris Connor (Atlantic), 1957, Patti Page (Mercury), 1959, Etta James (Argo), 1961.

Try Again. w/m Michael Day, Rocky Maffit, and Dana Walden, 1983. Recorded by the sextet Champaign (Columbia).

Try a Little Kindness. w/m Bobby Austin and Thomas Sapaugh, 1969. Country and Pop hit by Glen Campbell (Capitol).

Try a Little Tenderness. w/m Harry Woods, Jimmy Campbell, and Reg Connelly, 1933. First published in England [Campbell and Connelly were British writer/publishers], it became a hit on two continents. Introduced and recorded in the U.S. by Ruth Etting (Melotone). Other popular records by Ray Noble (Victor), Eddy Duchin (Brunswick), Ted Lewis (Columbia). Top 40 records were made by Otis Redding (Volt), 1967, and Three Dog Night (Dunhill), 1969. With more

than a touch of irony, the song was played under the title of (MP) *Dr. Strangelove*, 1964. The film depicted events leading to a nuclear destruction.

Trying. w/m Billy Vaughn, 1952. Top records by The Hilltoppers (Dot), Ella Fitzgerald (Decca), Johnny Desmond (Coral).

Trying to Hold On to My Woman. w/m McKinley Jackson and James Reddick, 1974. Top 20 record by songwriter/producer Lamont Dozier (ABC).

Trying to Love Two Women. w/m James Throckmorton, 1980. #1 Country record by The Oak Ridge Boys (MCA).

Tryin' to Beat the Morning Home. w/m Elroy Kahaneck, T. G. Sheppard, and Red Williams, 1975. Recorded by T. G. Sheppard (Melodyland).

Tryin' to Get the Feeling Again. w/m David Pomeranz, 1976. Top 10 record by Barry Manilow (Arista).

Tryin' to Love Two. w/m William Bell and Paul Mitchell, 1977. Top 10 record by William Bell (Mercury).

Try It Baby. w/m Berry Gordy, Jr., 1964. Hit record by Marvin Gaye (Tamla).

Try Me. w/m James Brown, 1959. #1 R&B record by James Brown and The Famous Flames (Federal).

Try Me One More Time. w/m Ernest Tubb, 1943. Introduced and recorded by Ernest Tubb (Decca).

Try to Forget. w. Otto Harbach, m. Jerome Kern, 1931. Introduced by Bettina Hall, Eddie Foy, Jr., and Doris Carson in (TM) *The Cat and the Fiddle*. In the 1934 film version (MM) *The Cat and the Fiddle*, it was sung by Jeanette MacDonald and Ramon Novarro.

Try Too Hard. w/m Dave Clark and Mike Smith, 1966. Top 20 hit by the British group The Dave Clark Five (Epic).

Try to Remember. w. Tom Jones, m. Harvey Schmidt, 1960, 1965. Introduced by

Jerry Orbach in (TM) *The Fantasticks*. Ed Ames popularized the song with his 1965 recording (RCA). The Brothers Four (Columbia) and Roger Williams (Kapp) also had chart records. Gladys Knight and The Pips, who sang it in a medley with "The Way We Were" (q.v.) (Buddah), 1975, had a hit record.

Try to See It My Way. w. Mort Dixon, m. Allie Wrubel, 1934. Introduced by Dick Powell and Joan Blondell in (MM) *Dames*.

TSOP (The Sound of Philadelphia). w/m Kenny Gamble and Leon Huff, 1974. Theme of the television show "Soul Train." #1 gold record by the interracial studio band, MFSB [stands for Mothers, Fathers, Sisters, Brothers], featuring The Three Degrees (Philadelphia International).

Tubular Bells. m. Mike Oldfield, 1973. Theme from (MP) *The Exorcist*. Top 10 instrumental record by Mike Oldfield (Virgin). Chart record by The Champs' Boys Orchestra (Janus), 1976.

Tuck Me to Sleep in My Old 'Tucky Home. w. Sam H. Lewis and Joe Young, m. George W. Meyer, 1921. Introduced by Al Jolson. Leading records by Ernest Hare (Pathé), Billy Jones (Okeh), Vernon Dalhart (Victor).

Tuesday Afternoon (Forever Afternoon). w/m Justin Hayward, 1968. Written by the lead singer/guitarist of the British group that recorded the song, The Moody Blues (Deram).

Tuff. m. Ace Cannon, 1962. Hit instrumental by saxophonist Ace Cannon (Hi).

Tuff Enuff. w/m Kim Wilson, 1986. Top 10 record by the quartet The Fabulous Thunderbirds with Kim Wilson as lead singer (CBS Associated). Song heard in (MP) *Tough Guys* and (MP) *Gung Ho*.

Tulip or Turnip. w. Don George, m. Edward Kennedy "Duke" Ellington, 1946. Introduced and recorded by Duke Ellington, vocal by Ray Nance (Musicraft).

Tulips and Heather. w/m Milton Carson, 1952. Popularized by Perry Como, with Mitchell Ayres' Orchestra (RCA Victor).

Tulip Time. w. Gene Buck, m. Dave Stamper, 1919. Sung by John Steel and Delyle Alda in (TM) *Ziegfeld Follies of 1919*. Steel recorded it (Victor), backed with "A Pretty Girl Is Like a Melody" (q.v) from the same show.

Tulsa Time. w/m Danny Flowers, 1978. Country chart record by Don Williams (ABC). Also recorded by Eric Clapton (RSO), 1980.

Tumblin' Down. w/m David Nesta Marley and Tyrone Ralph Downie, 1989. Single hit record by Ziggy Marley and The Melody Makers (Virgin).

Tumbling Dice. w/m Mick Jagger and Keith Richards, 1972. Top 10 record by The Rolling Stones (Rolling Stones). Revived by Linda Ronstadt (Asylum), 1978.

Tumbling Tumbleweeds. w/m Bob Nolan, 1934. Sung by Gene Autry in (MM) *Tumbling Tumbleweeds*. The Sons of the Pioneers, whose theme song this became, performed it in (MM) *Hollywood Canteen* in 1944, and Roy Rogers sang it in (MM) *Don't Fence Me In* in 1945. Recordings: Autry (Perfect); Sons of the Pioneers (Decca); Bing Crosby (Decca); Glen Gray and the Casa Loma Orchestra, vocal by Kenny Sargent (Decca); Larry Cotton and Fred Lowery (Columbia); Patti Page (Mercury); Jo Stafford (Capitol).

Tune For Humming, A. w/m Frank Loesser, 1947. Leading records by Eddy Howard (Majestic) and Bob Houston (MGM).

Tunnel of Love. w/m Bruce Springsteen, 1987. Popular airplay and record sales number by Bruce Springsteen (Columbia).

Tunnel of Love, The. w/m Frank Loesser, 1950. Introduced by Fred Astaire and Betty Hutton in (MM) *Let's Dance*.

Tupelo County Jail. w/m Webb Pierce and Mel Tillis, 1958. C&W record by Webb Pierce (Decca).

Tupelo Honey. w/m Van Morrison, 1972. Recorded by Van Morrison (Warner Bros.).

Turn! Turn! Turn! w/m Pete Seeger, 1965. Seeger adapted the words from the Book of Ecclesiastes, and introduced it (Columbia), 1962. The Byrds had a #1 chart record, produced by Terry Melcher (Columbia), 1965. Judy Collins also had a popular version (Elektra), 1969.

Turn Around. w/m Harry Belafonte, Alan Greene, and Malvina Reynolds, 1964. Top 40 record by Dick and Deedee (Warner Bros.).

Turn Around, Look at Me. w/m Jerry Capehart, 1968. First recorded by Glen Campbell (Crest), 1961. The Vogues (Reprise) had a gold record hit, 1968.

Turn Back the Hands of Time. w/m Jack Daniels and Bonnie Thompson, 1970. Gold record by Tyrone Davis (Dakar). Not to be confused with earlier song of same title.

Turn Back the Hands of Time. w/m Jimmy Eaton, Larry Wagner, and Con Hammond, 1951. Popularized by Eddie Fisher, with Hugo Winterhalter's Orchestra (RCA Victor).

Turn Back the Universe and Give Me Yesterday. w. J. Keirn Brennan, m. Ernest R. Ball, 1916. Hit record by The Orpheus Quartet (Victor).

Turn-Down Day. w/m David Blume and Jerry Kelly, 1966. Top 20 record by the Lafayette College group The Cyrkle (Columbia).

Turned Away. w/m Eugene Booker, 1989. R&B chart hit single by Chuckii Booker (Atlantic).

Turning Japanese. w/m David Fenton, 1981. Recorded by the British quartet, The Vapors, with Fenton as lead singer (Liberty).

Turn It Loose. w/m Craig Bickhardt, Brent Maher, and Don Schlitz, 1988. #1 Country chart record by the mother/daughter duo The Judds (RCA).

Turn Loose of My Leg. w/m Willie Hammond and Jim Stafford, 1977. Novelty record by Jim Stafford (Warner Bros.).

Turn Me Around. w. Norman Gimbel, m. Dominic Frontiere, 1970. Sung on the soundtrack of the Western film (MP) *Chisum* by Merle Haggard.

Turn Me Loose. w/m Doc Pomus and Mort Shuman, 1959. Top 10 record by Fabian (Chancellor).

Turn Off the Moon. w/m Sam Coslow, 1937. Introduced by Kenny Baker in (MM) *Turn Off the Moon*. Recorded by Mal Hallett, vocal by Teddy Grace (Decca); Little Jack Little (Vocalion); Clarence Williams (Bluebird).

Turn Off Your Light, Mr. Moon Man. w/m Nora Bayes, Jack Norworth, 1911. From (TM) *Little Miss Fix-it*.

Turn On the Heat. w. B. G. DeSylva and Lew Brown, m. Ray Henderson, 1929. Sung by Sharon Lynn in a big production number in (MM) *Sunny Side Up*. Recordings by Lloyd Keating's Orchestra with vocal by songwriter Sammy Fain (Harmony); Frankie Trumbauer's Orchestra with vocal by jazz violinist Joe Venuti; the Charleston Chasers featuring Eva Taylor (Columbia); Earl Burtnett's Orchestra who recorded four songs from the film (Brunswick).

Turn On the Old Music Box. w. Ned Washington, m. Leigh Harline, 1939. Sung on the soundtrack by Cliff "Ukulele Ike" Edwards, as the voice of Jiminy Cricket, in the feature-length cartoon film (MM) *Pinocchio*. Edwards also recorded it (Decca).

Turn On the Sunshine. w. Howard Greenfield, m. Neil Sedaka, 1960. Introduced by Connie Francis in (MM) *Where the Boys Are*.

Turn On Your Lovelight. w/m Deadric Malone and Joseph Scott, 1962. Introduced and recorded by Bobby Bland (Duke).

Turn Out the Light and Love Me Tonight. w/m Bob McDill, 1975. Country hit record by Don Williams (ABC/Dot).

Turntable Song, The. w. Leo Robin, m. John Green, 1947. Introduced by Deanna Durbin in (MM) *Something in the Wind*. Leading record by The Modernaires with Paula Kelly (Columbia).

Turn the Beat Around. w/m Gerald Jackson and Peter Jackson, 1976. Top 10 disco vocal record by Vicki Sue Robinson (RCA).

Turn the World Around the Other Way. w/m Ben Peters, 1967. C&W/Pop hit by Eddy Arnold (RCA).

Turn to Stone. w/m Jeff Lynne, 1978. Recorded by the British group The Electric Light Orchestra (Jet).

Turn to Stone. w/m Joe Walsh and Terry Trebandt, 1975. Recorded by Joe Walsh (Dunhill).

Turn Your Love Around. w/m Bill Champlin, Jay Graydon, and Steve Lukather, 1981. #1 R&B, Top 10 Pop chart record by George Benson (Warner Bros.). Winner, Grammy Award (NARAS), Rhythm and Blues Song of the Year, 1982.

Tush. w/m Billy Gibbons, Dusty Hill, and Frank Beard, 1975. Written and recorded by the trio ZZ Top (London).

Tusk. w/m Lindsay Buckingham, 1979. Top 10 record by the group, Fleetwood Mac, with the University of Southern California Trojan Marching Band, recorded live at Dodger Stadium, Los Angeles (Warner Bros.).

Tutti Frutti. w. Richard Penniman, D. La Bostrie, and Joe Lubin, 1956. Introduced by Little Richard (Specialty) and covered by Pat Boone (Dot), both of whom had hit records.

Tutti-Frutti. w/m Doris Fisher and Slim Gaillard, 1938. Introduced by Slim [Gaillard] and Slam [Stewart] (Vocalion), following their big hit "Flat Foot Floogie" (q.v.). Also recorded by Gene Krupa, vocal by Leo Watson (Brunswick), and the Jackson-Harris Herd (Mercury).

Tuxedo Junction. w. Buddy Feyne, m. Erskine Hawkins, William Johnson, and Julian Dash, 1940. Introduced by Erskine Hawkins and his Band at the Savoy Ballroom in New York City and on records (Bluebird), 1939. The instrumental, named after a railroad junction in Alabama, was then recorded

by Glenn Miller on the same label (Bluebird), and it became one of his band's biggest hits. Lyrics were added and were sung by the Andrews Sisters on their version (Decca). Jan Savitt and his Orchestra also had a popular arrangement (Decca). The number was featured by the band in (MM) *The Glenn Miller Story*, 1953.

TVC 15. w/m David Bowie, 1976. Recorded by the English performer David Bowie (RCA).

'Twas Not So Long Ago. w. Oscar Hammerstein II, m. Jerome Kern, 1929. Introduced by Helen Morgan in (TM) *Sweet Adeline*. Irene Dunne sang it in (MM) *Sweet Adeline* in 1935.

Tweedle Dee. w/m Winfield Scott, 1955. Introduced and recorded by LaVern Baker, who had a Top 10 R&B hit (Atlantic). Covered by Georgia Gibbs, who had a Top 10 Pop hit (Mercury). The Lancers, with Dick Jacobs' Orchestra, had a popular version (Coral). Revived in 1973 by Little Jimmy Osmond (MGM).

Tweedle-O-Twill. w/m Gene Autry and Fred Rose, 1943. Autry sang it in (MP) *Home in Wyoming* and recorded it (Okeh).

Twelfth of Never, The. w. Paul Francis Webster, m. Jerry Livingston, 1957. Adapted from "The Riddle Song," a folk song of unproven regional origin. Johnny Mathis had a hit record (Columbia). Country chart version by Slim Whitman (Imperial), 1966. Top 10 Pop chart revival by Donny Osmond (MGM), 1973.

Twelfth Street Rag. m. Euday L. Bowman, 1914, 1948. A ragtime classic, first published as a piano solo. One set of lyrics was added by James S. Sumner, 1916, another by Spencer Williams, 1929, and a third set by Andy Razaf, 1942. In 1948, Pee Wee Hunt and his Orchestra had a best-seller (Capitol) and the thirty-four-year-old number became "Top 10." Among earlier recordings were those by Earl Fuller's Novelty Orchestra (Columbia), Fats Waller (Victor), Sidney Bechet (Victor), Count Basie (Vocalion), Duke Ellington (Brunswick).

Twelve O'Clock at Night. w. Herman Ruby and Billy Rose, m. Lou Handman, 1923. Introduced and recorded by Sophie Tucker (Okeh).

Twelve Thirty (Young Girls Are Coming to the Canyon). w/m John Philips, 1967. Top 20 record by The Mamas and The Papas (Dunhill).

Twenty Feet of Muddy Water. w/m Bill Smith, 1956. Featured and recorded by Sonny James (Capitol).

Twenty-Five Miles. w/m Bert Berns, Johnny Bristol, Harvey Fuqua, Edwin Starr, Jerry Wexler, 1969. Top 10 record by Edwin Starr (Gordy).

25 or 6 to 4. w/m Robert Lamm, 1970. Top 10 record by Chicago (Columbia), and re-recorded (Full Moon), 1986.

Twenty-Four Hours a Day. w. Arthur Swanstrom, m. James F. Hanley, 1935. Sung by Frank Parker in (MM) *Sweet Surrender*. Jan Garber (Bluebird), Al Donahue (Decca), Teddy Wilson (Brunswick) and their bands recorded the song.

24 Hours a Day (365 a Year). w/m Rudy Toombs and Henry Glover, 1955. Popular record by Georgia Gibbs (Mercury).

Twenty-Four Hours from Tulsa. w. Hal David, m. Burt Bacharach, 1963. Top 20 record by Gene Pitney (Musicor).

Twenty-Four Hours of Lovin'. w/m Carol Hall, 1978. Introduced by Delores Hall and The Girls in (TM) *Best Little Whorehouse in Texas*.

Twenty-Four Hours of Sunshine. w. Carl Sigman, m. Peter De Rose, 1949. Popular recording by Art Mooney and his Orchestra (MGM).

Twenty Miles. w. Kal Mann, m. Bernie Lowe, 1963. Featured and recorded by Chubby Checker (Parkway).

Twenty-One Dollars a Day—Once a Month. w. Raymond Klages, m. Felix Bernard, 1941. Title referred to a rookie's starting salary at the outset of World War II. Tony Pastor with his Orchestra helped popularize it (Bluebird).

Twenty-One Years. w/m Bob Miller, 1931. Recorded by Carson Robinson (Perfect) and Red Nichols (Brunswick).

Twenty-Six Miles (Santa Catalina). w/m Bruce Bell and Glen Larson, 1958. Written by two of The Four Preps who had a Top 10 record (Capitol).

Twenty Years Ago. w/m Wood Newton, Michael Noble, Michael Spriggs, and Daniel Tyler, 1987. Popular recording by Kenny Rogers, from his album "They Don't Make Them Like They Used To" (RCA).

Twice As Much. w/m Royce Swain, 1953. Recorded by The Mills Brothers, with Sonny Burke's Orchestra (Decca).

Twilight in Turkey. m. Raymond Scott, 1937. Instrumental, introduced and recorded by the Raymond Scott Quintette (Brunswick) who also performed it in (MM) *Ali Baba Goes to Town*, starring Eddie Cantor. Other records by Tommy Dorsey and his Clambake Seven (Victor), Stuff Smith (Decca), Teddy Hill (Bluebird), Isham Jones (Vocalion).

Twilight on the Trail. w. Sidney D. Mitchell, m. Louis Alter, 1936. Introduced by Fuzzy Knight in (MP) *Trail of the Lonesome Pine*. In 1941 it was the title song of (MP) *Twilight on the Trail*, starring William Boyd, who later became known as Hopalong Cassidy. Bing Crosby (Decca) had the hit recording, which was a favorite of President Franklin D. Roosevelt. A gift to the president, through Mrs. Roosevelt, of Alter's manuscript and Crosby's record now are part of the collection of the FDR Museum in Hyde Park, New York.

Twilight Time. w/m Buck Ram, Morty Nevins, and Artie Dunn, 1944, 1958. Introduced, recorded by, and the theme song of The Three Suns (Hit) (Victor). Les Brown had a popular instrumental version (Decca), 1945, as did Johnny Maddox and his Orchestra (Dot), 1953. Revived in 1958 by The Platters, whose record

(Mercury) was #1 on all charts and was responsible for the song reaching #1 on "Your Hit Parade."

Twilight Zone. w/m George Kooymans, 1983. Top 10 record by the Dutch band Golden Earring (21 Records). The writer was vocalist/guitarist with the group.

Twine Time. m. André Williams and Verlie Rice, 1965. Instrumental by Alvin Cash and The Crawlers (Mar-V-Lus).

Twinkle, Twinkle, Little Star. w. Herb Magidson, m. Ben Oakland, 1936. Introduced by John Payne and Mae Clarke in (MM) *Hats Off.*

Twinkle, Twinkle, Lucky Star. w/m Merle Haggard, 1987. #1 Country chart record by Merle Haggard (Epic).

Twinkle Toes. w/m Roy Orbison and Bill Dees, 1966. Top 40 record by Roy Orbison (MGM).

Twist, The. w/m Hank Ballard, 1960. Introduced by Hank Ballard and The Midnighters and released in February, 1959 as the "B" side of "Teardrops on My Letter" (King). After being re-released during the summer of 1960 as the "A" side and beginning to catch on with the public, it was covered by Chubby Checker (Parkway), whose version quickly became #1 in the U.S. It was responsible for the new dance craze named after the song. A year later, his record became #1 on the charts again.

Twist, Twist Señora. w/m Frank J. Guida, Gene Barge, and Joseph Royster, 1962. Hit record by Gary U.S. Bonds (Legrand).

Twist and Shout. w/m Bert Russell and Phil Medley, 1962. First hit by The Isley Brothers (Wand). In 1964, The Beatles had one of their early hits (Tollie), which was reissued in 1986, (Capitol), after the song was heard in (MP) *Ferris Bueller's Day Off* and (MP) *Back to School.*

Twisted. w. Annie Ross, m. Wardell Gray, 1953. First recorded by saxophonist Wardell Gray and combo (New Jazz). Annie Ross wrote lyrics to it and recorded the new version (Prestige); also featured and recorded by Lambert, Hendricks, and Ross (Columbia), Bette Midler (Atlantic), and Joni Mitchell (Asylum).

Twisting Matilda. w/m Norman Span, 1963. Based on "Matilda, Matilda!," the 1953 calypso song. This version was popularized by Jimmy Soul (S.P.Q.R.).

Twistin' the Night Away. w/m Sam Cooke, 1962. Introduced and Top 10 record by Sam Cooke (RCA). Revived by the English recording star Rod Stewart (Mercury), 1973.

Twistin' U.S.A. w/m Kal Mann, 1960. Top 40 record by Danny and The Juniors (Swan).

Twist of Fate. w/m Steven Kipner and Peter Beckett, 1983. Introduced by Olivia Newton-John in (MP) *Two of a Kind* and on a Top 10 record (MCA).

Twixt Twelve and Twenty. w/m Aaron Schroeder and Fredda Gold, 1959. Top 20 record by Pat Boone (Dot).

Two-Bit Manchild. w/m Neil Diamond, 1968. Recorded by Neil Diamond (Uni).

Two Blind Loves. w. E. Y. Harburg, m. Harold Arlen, 1939. Introduced by Kenny Baker and Florence Rice in (MM) *At the Circus,* starring the Marx Brothers. Recorded by Baker (Victor); Ted Weems, vocal by Perry Como (Decca); Jack Teagarden, vocal by Kitty Kallen (Columbia).

Two Blue Eyes, Two Little Baby Shoes. w. Edward Madden, m. Theodore F. Morse, 1907.

Two Bouquets. w. Jimmy Kennedy, m. Michael Carr, 1938. British song recorded in the U.S. by the bands of Guy Lombardo (Victor), Russ Morgan (Brunswick), Jerry Blaine (Bluebird).

Two Buck Tim from Timbuctoo. w. Edward Heyman, m. Al Goodhart and Al Hoffman, 1933.

Two by Two. w. Martin Charnin, m. Richard Rodgers, 1970. Introduced by Danny Kaye and "family" in (TM) *Two by Two.*

Two Cigarettes in the Dark. w. Paul Francis Webster, m. Lew Pollack, 1934. Introduced by Gloria Grafton in (MP) *Kill That Story.* Recordings: Morton Downey (Perfect); Glen Gray and the Casa Loma Orchestra, vocal by Kenny Sargent (Brunswick); Joe Morrison (Brunswick); Johnny Green's Orchestra (Columbia); Ted Straeter (Crown); Skitch Henderson (Capitol).

Two Different Worlds. w. Sid Wayne, m. Al Frisch, 1956. Hit record by Don Rondo (Jubilee). Chart records by Roger Williams and Jane Morgan (Kapp), and Dick Haymes (Capitol). Revived by Lenny Welch (Kapp) 1965.

Two Divided by Love. w/m Dennis Lambert, Marty Kupps, and Brian Potter, 1971. Top 20 record by The Grass Roots (Dunhill).

Two Doors Down. w/m Dolly Parton, 1978. Hit Country/Pop chart record by Dolly Parton (RCA), and Country hit by Zella Lehr (RCA).

Two Dreams Met. w. Mack Gordon, m. Harry Warren, 1940. Introduced by Betty Grable, Don Ameche, and the vocal group Six Hits and a Miss in (MM) *Down Argentine Way.* Most popular recordings by Mitchell Ayres, vocal by Mary Ann Mercer (Bluebird); Tommy Dorsey, vocal by Connie Haines (Victor); Eddy Duchin, vocal by Johnny Drake (Columbia).

Two Faces Have I. w/m Twyla Herbert and Lou Sacco, 1963. Recorded by Lou Christie (Roulette).

Two for Tonight. w. Mack Gordon, m. Harry Revel, 1935. Title song of (MM) *Two for Tonight,* introduced by Bing Crosby in film and on records (Decca).

Two Guitars. m. arranged by Harry Horlick, 1925. Based on a Russian gypsy air. Horlick was conductor of The A&P Gypsies, the orchestra on the popular radio program sponsored by the food chain. It was recorded by them (Brunswick) and used as their theme song. Morton Gould and his Orchestra later recorded it (Columbia).

Two Hearts. w/m Phil Collins and Lamont Dozier, 1988. Introduced by Phil Collins on the soundtrack of (MP) *Buster.* Nominated for an Academy Award.

Two Hearts. w/m Otis Williams and Henry Stone, 1955. Pat Boone's first chart record (Dot).

Two Hearts in Three-Quarter Time. w. Joe Young (Engl.), W. Reisch and A. Robinson (Ger.), m. Robert Stolz, 1930. Original title "Zwei Herzen im Dreivierteltakt" from the German film of the same name.

Two Hearts That Pass in the Night. w. Forman Brown (Engl.), Ernesto Lecuona (Sp.), m. Ernesto Lecuona, 1941. Adapted from the Spanish song "Dame de Tus Rosas." Recorded by the bands of Bobby Byrne (Decca), Teddy Powell (Bluebird), Sammy Kaye (Victor), Charlie Spivak (Okeh), Orrin Tucker (Columbia).

Two in Love. w/m Meredith Willson, 1941. Introduced and recorded by Tommy Dorsey, vocal by Frank Sinatra (Victor).

Two Ladies in de Shade of de Banana Tree. w. Truman Capote and Harold Arlen, m. Harold Arlen, 1954. Introduced by Ada Moore and Enid Mosier in (TM) *House of Flowers.*

Two Laughing Irish Eyes. w. Henry Blossom, m. Victor Herbert, 1915. From (TM) *The Princess Pat.*

Two Little Babes in the Wood. w/m Cole Porter, 1928. Introduced vocally by Julia Silvers and Georgie Hale, danced by The Dolly Sisters, James Clemons, and James Naulty in (TM) *Greenwich Follies of '24.* Interpolated by Irene Bordoni in (TM) *Paris,* 1928.

Two Little Bluebirds. w. Otto Harbach and Oscar Hammerstein II, m. Jerome Kern, 1925. Introduced by Clifton Webb and Mary

Hay in (TM) *Sunny*. It was also in both film versions, (MM) *Sunny*, 1930 and 1941.

Two Little Blue Little Eyes. w/m John Jacob Loeb, Rudy Vallee, and Paul Francis Webster, 1931. Introduced, featured, and recorded by Rudy Vallee (Victor).

Two Little Girls in Blue. w/m Charles Graham, 1893. Popularized in vaudeville by Lottie Gilson. Not to be confused with the Vincent Youmans-Ira Gershwin musical of 1921.

Two Little Kids. w/m Barbara Acklin, Carl H. Davis, and Eugene Record, 1968. Top 40 record by Peaches and Herb (Date).

Two Little Love Bees. w. Robert B. Smith, m. Heinrich Reinhardt, 1911. From (TM) *The Spring Maid*, which opened December 26, 1910.

Two Lost Souls. Richard Adler and Jerry Ross, 1955. Introduced by Gwen Verdon and Stephen Douglass in (TM) *Damn Yankees*. Sung by Gwen Verdon and Tab Hunter in (MM) *Damn Yankees*, 1958.

Two Lovers. w/m William Robinson, 1963. Crossover hit (R&B/Pop) by Mary Wells (Motown).

Two Loves Have I. w. J. P. Murray, Barry Trivers (Engl.), m. Vincent Scotto, 1931. Original French words by Georges Koger and H. Varna, titled "J'ai Deux Amours." Josephine Baker introduced it in Paris and Irene Bordoni in the U.S. Recorded by Frank Munn with Ted Black's Orchestra (Victor), and Paul Small with Vincent Rose's Orchestra (Banner).

Two More Bottles of Wine. w/m Delbert McClinton, 1978. Hit Country record by Emmylou Harris (Elektra).

Two O'Clock Jump. m. Harry James, William "Count" Basie, and Benny Goodman, 1941. Sequel to "One O'Clock Jump" (q.v.). Harry James and his Music Makers introduced and recorded it (Columbia) and performed it in (MM) *Best Foot Forward*, 1943.

Two of a Kind. w. Johnny Mercer, m. Bobby Darin, 1963. Written as title number of an album sung by Mercer and Darin (Atco).

Two of Hearts. w/m John Mitchell, Sue Gatlin, and Tim Greene, 1986. Top 10 record by the disco singer Stacey Q [pseudonym for Stacey Swain] (Atlantic).

Two Out of Three Ain't Bad. w/m Jim Steinman, 1978. Hit record by Meat Loaf né Marvin Lee Aday (Epic).

Two Shadows on Your Window. w/m Mickey Baker and Robert Taylor, 1957. Hit C&W record by Jim Reeves (RCA).

Two Silhouettes. w. Ray Gilbert, m. Charles Wolcott, 1946. Sung on the soundtrack by Dinah Shore and danced by Tatiana Riabouchinska and David Lichine in Disney's (MM) *Make Mine Music*.

Two Sleepy People. w. Frank Loesser, m. Hoagy Carmichael, 1938. Introduced by Bob Hope and Shirley Ross in (MM) *Thanks for the Memory* and recorded by them (Decca). Among other recordings: Hoagy Carmichael and Ella Logan (Brunswick), Fats Waller (Bluebird), Lawrence Welk (Vocalion), Sammy Kaye (Victor), Kay Kyser (Brunswick). Armelia McQueen and Ken Page revived it in the Fats Waller musical (TM) *Ain't Misbehavin'*, 1978.

Two Story House. w/m Glen Tubb, David Lindsey, and Tammy Wynette, 1980. Top 10 Country chart record by George Jones and Tammy Wynette (Epic).

Two Tickets to Georgia. w/m Joe Young, Charles Tobias, and J. Fred Coots, 1933.

Two Tickets to Paradise. w/m Eddie Money, 1978. Recorded by Eddie Money (Columbia).

Two Together. w. Gus Kahn, m. Arthur Johnston, 1935. Roger Pryor and Ann Sothern introduced this in (MM) *The Girl Friend*, which had no connection with the Rodgers and Hart 1926 Broadway musical.

Two Tribes. w/m Peter Gill, William Johnson, and Mark O'Toole, 1984. Recorded by the British quintet Frankie Goes to Hollywood (Island).

Typewriter, The. m. Leroy Anderson, 1953. Instrumental recorded by Leroy Anderson and his Orchestra, featuring the clicking of a typewriter's keys and the bell indicating the end of a line (Decca).

Typically English. w/m Leslie Bricusse and Anthony Newley, 1961. Introduced by Anna Quayle in (TM) *Stop the World—I Want to Get Off*.

Typical Male. w/m Terry Britten and Graham Lyle, 1986. English song recorded by Tina Turner in her album "Break Every Rule" (Capitol). Her single release made the Top 10 on the R&B and Pop charts.

Tzena, Tzena, Tzena. w. Mitchell Parish (Engl.), m. Issachar Miron (Michrovsky) and Julius Grossman, 1950. Parts A and B of the melody were written by Miron, and part C by Grossman. First published in Israel. English version had hit records by The Weavers, with Gordon Jenkins' Orchestra (Decca), a million-seller; Mitch Miller and his Orchestra (Columbia); and Vic Damone (Mercury).

U

U.S. Male. w/m Jerry Reed, 1968. Introduced by Jerry Reed, but popularized by Elvis Presley (RCA).

U Got the Look. w/m Prince Rogers Nelson, 1987. Top 10 single by Prince (Paisley Park), from his concert film (MM) *Sign o' the Times.*

Ugly Chile (a.k.a. **You're Some Pretty Doll).** w/m Clarence Williams, 1917. Originally recorded by Sam Ash (Columbia) under alternate title. George Brunis and an all-star group recorded it (Commodore Music Shop) in the forties. Johnny Mercer had a popular version (Capitol), 1946.

Ugly Duckling, The. w/m Frank Loesser, 1952. Introduced by Danny Kaye in (MM) *Hans Christian Andersen.*

Uh! Oh! w/m Granville "Sascha" Burland and Don Elliott, 1959. Novelty jazz hit by The Nutty Squirrels (Hanover). The writer/singers employed the "speeded-up" effect associated with the Chipmunks. This was in two parts, both sides making the charts. Part 2 became a Top 10 record and has since been recorded by numerous jazz combos and/or bands.

Ukulele Lady. w. Gus Kahn, m. Richard Whiting, 1925. Featured and popularized by Vaughn DeLeath on her radio show and in vaudeville. She also recorded it (Columbia).

Um, Um, Um, Um, Um, Um. w/m Curtis Mayfield, 1963. Crossover (R&B/Pop) chart hit by Major Lance (Okeh).

Umbrella Man, The. w. James Cavanaugh, m. Vincent Rose and Larry Stock, 1938. Introduced and recorded by Guy Lombardo and his Royal Canadians (Decca). Among other recordings: Connie Boswell, with Woody Herman's Orchestra (Decca); Kay Kyser (Brunswick); Lawrence Welk (Vocalion); Dizzy Gillespie (DeeGee).

Umbriago. w/m Irving Caesar and Jimmy Durante, 1944. Sung by Jimmy Durante in (MM) *Music for Millions* and on records (Decca).

Unborn Child. w/m Louise Bogan and James Seals, 1974. Recorded by Seals and Crofts (Warner Bros.).

Unchained Melody. w. Hy Zaret, m. Alex North, 1955. Theme from (MP) *Unchained.* Leading instrumental record by Les Baxter and his Orchestra (Capitol); leading vocal by Al Hibbler, arranged and conducted by Jack Pleis (Decca). Revived by The Righteous Brothers (Philles), 1965.

Unchain My Heart. w/m Teddy Powell and Bobby Sharp, 1962. Hit record by Ray Charles (ABC-Paramount). In 1968, jazz flutist Herbie Mann and his combo had a chart recording (A&M).

Uncle Albert/Admiral Halsey. w/m Paul McCartney and Linda McCartney, 1971. #1 U.S. gold record in England by Paul and Linda McCartney (Apple).

Uncle John's Band. w/m Jerry Garcia and Robert Hunter, 1970. Recorded by The Grateful Dead (Warner Bros).

Uncle Pen. w/m Bill Monroe, 1956, 1984. C&W Top 10 record by Porter Wagoner (RCA Victor). Revived with a #1 C&W chart version by Ricky Skaggs (Sugar Hill), 1984.

Uncle Remus Said. w/m Johnny Lange, Hy Heath, and Eliot Daniel, 1946. Introduced by The Hall Johnson Choir in (MM) *Song of the South*. Recorded by Woody Herman and his Orchestra (Columbia).

Uncle Sam Rag, The. w. Dorothy Fields, m. Albert Hague, 1959. Introduced by Leonard Stone and the ensemble in (TM) *Redhead*.

Undecided. w. Sid Robin, m. Charlie Shavers, 1939, 1951. Introduced and first recorded by John Kirby and "The Biggest Little Band in the Land," arranged by Charlie Shavers and featuring him on trumpet (Decca). Hit record by Chick Webb, vocal by Ella Fitzgerald (Decca). Other popular versions by Benny Goodman and his Orchestra (Victor), and Fats Waller (Bluebird). Revived in 1951 by The Ames Brothers' million-seller, with Les Brown's Orchestra (Coral).

Under a Blanket of Blue. w. Marty Symes and Al J. Neiburg, m. Jerry Livingston, 1933. Glen Gray and the Casa Loma Orchestra, with vocal by Kenny Sargent, introduced, recorded, and popularized this ballad. Among other recordings: Don Bestor (Victor), George Hall (Bluebird), Will Osborne (Melotone).

Under Any Old Flag At All. w/m George M. Cohan, 1907. From (TM) *The Talk of New York*.

Under a Roof in Paree. See **Sous Les Toits de Paris.**

Under a Strawberry Moon. w. Al Lewis, m. Mabel Wayne, 1943. Featured and recorded by Mitchell Ayres, vocal by Meredith Blake (Bluebird), The Merry Macs (Decca), Dick Robertson (Decca).

Under a Texas Moon. w/m Ray Perkins, 1930. Introduced by Frank Fay in (MM) *Under a Texas Moon*. Popular recordings by Gene Austin (Victor), Guy Lombardo (Columbia), Seger Ellis (Okeh), Ted Fio Rito (Victor), Lee Sims (Brunswick), and later, Dale Evans (Majestic).

Undercover Angel. w/m Alan O'Day, 1977. #1 gold record by Alan O'Day (Pacific).

Undercover of the Night. w/m Mick Jagger and Keith Richards, 1983. Top 10 record by The Rolling Stones (Rolling Stones).

Underground. w/m David Bowie, 1986. Introduced by David Bowie in the film (MP) *Labyrinth*.

Underneath the Arches. w/m Reg Connelly and Bud Flanagan. [Additional lyrics in U.S. by Joseph McCarthy], 1933, 1948. Introduced in London by the comedy team Flanagan and Allen. Best-selling record in U.S. by George Olsen and his Orchestra, vocal by Ethel Shutta (Victor). Revived in 1948 via the hit import, Primo Scala's Banjo and Accordion Orchestra (London). The Andrews Sisters' version (Decca), and Andy Russell's, with the Pied Pipers (Capitol), helped the song reach "Your Hit Parade."

Underneath the Harlem Moon. w. Mack Gordon, m. Harry Revel, 1932. Leading records by the bands of Don Redman (Brunswick), Fletcher Henderson (Columbia), Peter DeRose (Electrodisk), and the Washboard Rhythm Kings (Victor).

Underneath the Japanese Moon. w. Gene Buck, m. Gus Haenschen, 1914.

Underneath the Russian Moon. w. James Kendis and Frank Samuels, m. Meyer Gusman, 1929. Featured and recorded by Belle Baker (Brunswick).

Underneath the Stars. w. Fleta Jan Brown, m. Herbert Spencer, 1915. Recorded by Raymond Dixon (Victor).

Under Paris Skies. w. Kim Gannon (Engl.), Jean Drejac (Fr.), m. Hubert Giraud, 1953. Original French title, "Sous le Ciel de Paris," from the French film of the same name. Among popular recordings: Mitch Miller and his Orchestra (Columbia), Georgia Gibbs (Mercury), The Three Suns (RCA Victor).

Under Pressure. w/m David Bowie, m. Queen, 1982. Recorded by the English group Queen, and David Bowie (Elektra).

Understanding. w/m Bob Seger, 1984. Introduced in (MP) *Teachers*, and recorded by Bob Seger and The Silver Bullet Band (Capitol).

Understanding. w/m Ray Charles and Jimmy Holiday, 1968. Recorded by Ray Charles, coupled with "Eleanor Rigby" (q.v.) (ABC/TRC).

Understand Your Man. w/m Johnny Cash, 1964. Crossover (C&W/Pop) hit record by Johnny Cash (Columbia).

Under the Anheuser Bush. w. Andrew B. Sterling, m. Harry Von Tilzer, 1904. Sequel to the hit "Down Where the Wurzburger Flows" (q.v.). Popular vaudeville song. Recorded by Arthur Collins and Byron Harlan (Victor) and Billy Murray (Columbia). The song was well-received in London where the title was changed to the pub-related "Down at the Old Bull and Bush." Stanley Holloway included the latter version in his album "Join in the Chorus" (Vanguard).

Under the Bamboo Tree (If You Lak-a Me Like I Lak-a You). w/m Bob Cole and J. Rosamond Johnson, 1902. Sung by Marie Cahill in (TM) *Sally in Our Alley*. It was revived by Judy Garland and Margaret O'Brien in (MM) *Meet Me in St. Louis*, 1944, and by Louise Albritton, impersonating Lillian Russell, in (MM) *Bowery to Broadway*, 1944. Revived by the company in (TM) *Meet Me in St. Louis*, 1989.

Under the Boardwalk. w/m Artie Resnick and Kenny Young, 1964. Hit record by The Drifters (Atlantic). Recorded by TV star Bruce Willis (Motown), 1987. Sung by Bette Midler in (MP) *Beaches*, 1988. Country chart record by Lynn Anderson (Mercury), 1988.

Under the Bridges of Paris. w. Dorcas Cochran (Engl.), J. Rodor (Fr.), m. Vincent Scotto, 1953. Original French title, "Sous les Ponts de Paris."

Under the Covers. w/m Janis Ian, 1981. Recorded by Janis Ian (Columbia).

Under the Influence of Love. w/m Buck Owens and Harlan Howard, 1961. C&W chart hit by Buck Owens (Capitol).

Under the Moon. w. Francis Wheeler and E. E. Lynn, m. Ted Snyder, 1927. Recorded by Johnny Marvin and Aileen Stanley (Victor) and the orchestras of Frank Black (Brunswick), Jan Garber (Victor), and Guy Lombardo (Columbia).

Under the Sea. w. Howard Ashman, m. Alan Menken, 1989. From the animated feature film (MM) *The Little Mermaid*. Winner Academy Award, Best Song.

Under the Yum-Yum Tree. w. Sammy Cahn, m. James Van Heusen, 1963. Title song of (MP) *Under the Yum-Yum Tree*. Recorded by Robert Goulet (Columbia).

Under the Yum-Yum Tree. w. Andrew B. Sterling, m. Harry Von Tilzer, 1910. Arthur Collins and Byron Harlan recorded their comedy hit for five different labels (Columbia) (Victor) (Edison) (Amberol) (Indestructable) (U.S.) (Everlasting). The song was used in (MP) *Wharf Angel* in 1934.

Under Your Spell. w. Howard Dietz, m. Arthur Schwartz, 1937. Sung by Lawrence Tibbett in (MM) *Under Your Spell*. The song originally was heard in the radio series, "The Gibson Family," sung by Conrad Thibaut.

Under Your Spell Again. w/m Buck Owens, 1965. Hit record by Johnny Rivers (Imperial).

Under Your Spell Again. w/m Dusty Rhodes and Buck Owens, 1959. recorded by C&W singers, Buck Owens (Capitol), and Ray Price (Columbia).

Undisputed Truth, The. w/m Barrett Strong and Norman Whitfield, 1971. Top 10 R&B/Pop chart record by The Undisputed Truth (Gordy).

Undun. w/m Randy Bachman, 1969. Top 40 record by The Guess Who (RCA).

Uneasy Rider. w/m Charlie Daniels, 1973. Top 10 novelty record by The Charlie Daniels Band (Kama Sutra).

Unexpected Song. w. Don Black, m. Andrew Lloyd Webber, 1985. Introduced in the U.S. by Bernadette Peters in (TM) *Song and Dance*.

Unforgettable. w/m Irving Gordon, 1951. Hit record by Nat "King" Cole, with Nelson Riddle's Orchestra (Capitol). The Dick Hyman Trio had a popular instrumental version (MGM), 1954, and Dinah Washington revived it (Mercury), 1959.

Unforgiven, The. See **Theme from "The Unforgiven."**

Unicorn, The. w/m Shel Silverstein, 1968. Top 10 record by The Irish Rovers (Decca).

Union Man. w/m Earl Cate and Ernie Cate, 1976. Recorded by The Cate Brothers (Asylum).

Union of the Snake. w/m Duran Duran, 1983. Written and Top 10 record by the British band Duran Duran (Capitol).

United (a.k.a. **We'll Be United**). w/m Kenny Gamble and Leon Huff, 1966. Introduced by The Intruders (Gamble). Leading record by Peaches and Herb (Date). Chart instrumental by The Music Makers (Gamble, Part 1).

United Nations on the March. w. Harold Rome, m. Dmitri Shostakovich, 1943. Rome's English words and adaptation of music by the Russian composer Shostakovich was intro-

duced by Kathryn Grayson, accompanied by José Iturbi in (MM) *Thousands Cheer*.

United Together. w/m Chuck Jackson and Phil Perry, 1980. Top 10 R&B, crossover Pop chart record of the redundantly titled song by Aretha Franklin (Arista).

United We Stand. w/m Tony Hiller and Peter Simons, 1970. Top 20 record by the British group The Brotherhood of Man (Deram).

Universal Soldier, The. w/m Buffy Sainte-Marie, 1963. Introduced and recorded by Buffy Sainte-Marie (Vanguard). 1965 chart record by Glen Campbell (Capitol) and Donovan (Hickory).

Unknown Soldier. w/m John Densmore, Robert Krieger, Raymond Manzarek, and James Morrison, 1968. Written and recorded by The Doors (Elektra).

Unless. w/m Stanley J. Damerell, Tolchard Evans, Robert Hargreaves, Henry B. Tilsley, 1934, 1951. An English popular song, revived in 1951 by Guy Mitchell (Columbia), Eddie Fisher (Victor), Gordon Jenkins with vocal by Bob Stephens (Decca).

Unless You Care. w/m Philip Sloan and Steve Barri, 1964. Recorded by Terry Black (Tollie).

Unloved, Unwanted. w/m Wayne P. Walker and Irene Stanton, 1962. Country hit record by Kitty Wells (Decca).

Unloved and Unclaimed. w/m Roy Acuff and Vito Pelletieri, 1948. Introduced and recorded by C&W singer Roy Acuff (Columbia).

Unmitigated Gall. w/m Mel Tillis, 1966. Top 10 Country chart record by Faron Young (Mercury).

Unsquare Dance. m. Dave Brubeck, 1962. Instrumental, recorded by The Dave Brubeck Quartet (Columbia).

Unsuspecting Heart. w. Freddy James, m. Joe Beal, Bob Singer, and Joe Shank, 1955. Leading records by Sunny Gale (RCA) and Georgie Shaw (Decca).

Until. w/m Jack Fulton and Bob Crosby, 1948. Featured and recorded by Tommy Dorsey, vocal by Harry Prime (Victor).

Until. w. Edward Teschemacher, m. Wilfred Sanderson, 1918.

Until I Met You. w/m Hank Riddle, 1986. #1 Country chart song by Judy Rodman (MTM).

Until It's Time for You to Go. w/m Buffy Sainte-Marie, 1967. Introduced by Buffy Sainte-Marie (Vanguard). Chart records by Neil Diamond (Uni), 1970; Elvis Presley (RCA), 1972; the vocal group, New Birth (RCA), 1973.

Until My Dreams Come True. w/m Dallas Frazier, 1969. #1 Country chart record by Jack Greene (Decca).

Until Sunrise. w. Jack Wolf Fine, m. Marie Moss and Will Collins, 1954. Recorded by Joe "Fingers" Carr, with The Carr-Hops (Capitol).

Until the Real Thing Comes Along (It Will Have to Do). w/m Mann Holiner, Alberta Nichols, Sammy Cahn, Saul Chaplin, and L. E. Freeman, 1936. An earlier version was introduced as "Till the Real Thing, etc." by Ethel Waters and reprised by the Berry Brothers in (TM) *Rhapsody in Black*, 1931. The new version was introduced by the makers of the hit recording, Andy Kirk and his Clouds of Joy, vocal by Pha Terrell (Decca). It then became their theme. Fats Waller also had a hit version (Victor).

Until Today. w. Benny Davis, m. J. Fred Coots and Oscar Levant, 1936. Recorded by Ted Weems and his Orchestra, vocal by Perry Como (Decca).

Until Tomorrow. w/m Sammy Kaye, 1940. Introduced and best-seller recorded by Sammy Kaye and his Orchestra (Victor).

Until You Come Back to Me (That's What I'm Gonna Do). w/m Morris Broadnax, Clarence Paul, and Stevie Wonder, 1974. Gold record by Aretha Franklin (Atlantic).

Untouchables, The. m. Nelson Riddle, 1959. Theme music of the series (TVP) "The Untouchables."

Unwanted Sign upon Your Heart. w/m Hank Snow, 1951. Hit C&W chart record by Hank Snow (RCA Victor).

Up, Up, Up in My Aeroplane. w. Edward Madden, m. Gus Edwards, 1909. Introduced by Lillian Lorraine in (TM) *Ziegfeld Follies of 1909*, while flying over the heads of the audience in a simulated plane.

Up Above My Head, I Hear Music in the Air. w/m Sister Rosetta Tharpe, 1949. Recorded by Sister Rosetta Tharpe, teamed vocally with Marie Knight, and backed by The Sam Price Trio (Decca).

Up and Down. w/m Dennis Lambert and Louis Pegues, 1966. Recorded by The McCoys (Bang).

Up Around the Bend. w/m John Fogerty, 1970. Gold record by Creedence Clearwater Revival (Fantasy).

Up in a Balloon. w. Ren Shields, m. Percy Wenrich, 1908.

Up in a Puff of Smoke. w/m Gerald Shury and Philip Swern, 1975. Top 20 record by British singer Polly Brown (GTO).

Up in the Clouds. w. Bert Kalmar, m. Harry Ruby, 1927. Introduced by Mary Eaton and Oscar Shaw in (TM) *The Five O'Clock Girl*. It was sung by the chorus in the Kalmar and Ruby biography (MM) *Three Little Words*, 1950.

Up on Cripple Creek. w/m Robbie Robertson, 1969. Top 40 record by The Band (Capitol).

Up on the Mountain. w/m Nathaniel Montague and Ewart G. Abner, Jr., 1956. Top 10 R&B chart record by The Magnificents (Vee-Jay).

Up on the Roof. w/m Gerry Goffin and Carole King, 1963. Hit record by The Drifters (Atlantic). Later chart versions by The Cryan'

Shames (Columbia), 1968; Laura Nyro (Columbia), 1970; James Taylor (Columbia), 1979.

Upper Ten, Lower Five. w/m James Thornton, 1888. Title refers to class distinctions, not Pullman berths. Introduced by Lawlor and Thornton in vaudeville.

Ups and Downs. w/m Mark Lindsay and Terry Melcher, 1967. Top 40 record by Paul Revere and The Raiders (Columbia).

Upside Down. w/m Bernard Edwards and Nile Rodgers, 1980. #1 gold record by Diana Ross (Motown).

Up the Ladder to the Roof. w/m Vincent Dimirco and Frank Wilson, 1970. Top 10 record by The Supremes (Motown).

Uptight (Everything's Alright). w/m Sylvia Moy, Stevie Wonder, and Henry Cosby, 1966. Hit record by Stevie Wonder (Tamla). Instrumental chart records by Ramsey Lewis (Cadet), The Jazz Crusaders (Pacific Jazz), vocal record by Nancy Wilson (Capitol). Bill Cosby had a Top 10 novelty version entitled "Little Ole Man (Uptight—Everything's Alright)" (Warner Bros.), 1967.

Up to My Neck in High Muddy Water. w/m John Herald, Robert Yellin, and Frank Wakefield, 1968. Chart record by Linda Ronstadt and The Stone Poneys (Capitol).

Uptown. w/m Barry Mann and Cynthia Weil, 1962. Recorded by The Crystals (Philles).

Uptown Girl. w/m Billy Joel, 1983. Top 10 gold record by Billy Joel (Columbia).

Uptown Saturday Night. w/m Tom Scott and Morgan Ames, 1974. Sung on the soundtrack of (MP) *Uptown Saturday Night* by Dobie Gray.

Up—Up and Away. w/m Jim Webb, 1967. Hit record by The 5th Dimension (Soul City). Grammy Award (NARAS) for Song of the Year and Record of the Year, 1967.

Up Where We Belong. w/m Will Jennings, Jack Nitzsche, and Buffy Sainte-Marie, 1982. Introduced by Joe Cocker and Jennifer Warnes on the soundtrack of (MP) *An Officer and a Gentleman*. Winner Academy Award, Best Song, 1982. Cocker and Warnes's recording became a #1 record (Island).

Up with the Lark. w. Leo Robin, m. Jerome Kern, 1946. From Kern's last score (MM) *Centennial Summer*, sung by Louanne Hogan [dubbing on the soundtrack for Jeanne Crain], Constance Bennett, Dorothy Gish, and Buddy Swan.

Urge for Going. w/m Joni Mitchell, 1967. Top 10 Country chart record by George Hamilton IV (RCA).

Urgent. w/m Mick Jones, 1981. Top 10 record by the Anglo-American group Foreigner (Atlantic).

Used to Blue. w/m Fred Knobloch and Bill LaBounty, 1985. Top 10 Country chart record by the group Sawyer Brown (Capitol).

Used to You. w/m B. G. DeSylva, Lew Brown, Ray Henderson, and Al Jolson, 1929. Sung by Jolson in (MM) *Say It with Songs*.

Useless Waltz, w. Dave Frishberg, m. Bob Brookmeyer, 1983. Jazz piece, featured and recorded by Dave Frishberg (Omnisound).

Use Me. w/m Bill Withers, 1972. Gold record by Bill Withers (Sussex).

Use ta Be My Girl. w/m Kenny Gamble and Leon Huff, 1978. #1 R&B crossover gold record by The O'Jays (Philadelphia International).

Use Your Head. w/m Chuck Barksdale, Wade Flemons, and Barrett Strong, 1964. Leading record by Mary Wells (20th Century).

Use Your Imagination. w/m Cole Porter, 1950. Introduced by William Redfield and Priscilla Gillette in the finale of (TM) *Out of This World*. Early recording by Jimmy McPartland and his Combo, featuring Marian McPartland on piano (Prestige).

Use Your Noggin'. w. Sammy Cahn, m. James Van Heusen, 1964. Introduced by Louise Troy, Sharon Dierking, and Gretchen Van Aken in (TM) *Walking Happy.*

Uska Dara (A Turkish Tale). w/m Stella Lee, 1953. This adaptation of a Turkish song was introduced by Eydie Gormé (Coral). She and Eartha Kitt, who had the best-seller (RCA Victor), both sang in Turkish and English.

Us on a Bus. w. Tot Seymour, m. Vee Lawnhurst, 1936. Novelty built on the familiar four-note automobile horn. Featured and recorded by Rudy Vallee (Melotone), Shep Fields (Bluebird), Fats Waller (Victor).

Utopia. w/m Aaron Schroeder, Wally Gold, and Martin Kalmanoff, 1961. Recorded by Frank Gari (Crusade).

V

Vacation. w. Charlotte Caffey, Jane Wiedlin, m. Kathy Valentine, 1982. Top 10 record by the quintet The Go-Go's (I.R.S.).

Vacation. w/m Hank Hunter, Connie Francis, and Harold Temklin, 1962. Recorded by Connie Francis (MGM).

Vagabond Dreams. w. Jack Lawrence, m. Hoagy Carmichael, 1939. Recordings by the bands of Benny Carter (Vocalion), Gene Krupa (Columbia), Glenn Miller (Bluebird), Russ Morgan (Decca), and by singer Barry Wood (Columbia).

Vagabond Shoes. w. Sammy Gallop, m. David Saxon, 1950. Most popular recordings by Vic Damone with Glenn Osser's Orchestra (Mercury), Pearl Bailey (Columbia), Harry Babbitt (Coral).

Vahevela. w/m Danny Loggins and Daniel Lottermoser, 1972. Recorded by Loggins and Messina (Columbia).

Valencia. w. Lucien Jean Boyer, Jacques Charles (Fr.), Clifford Grey (Engl.), m. José Padilla, 1926. French lyrics to a Spanish song introduced by Mistinguett at the Moulin Rouge in Paris. Introduced in the U.S. by Hazel Dawn and company in (TM) *Great Temptations*. Paul Whiteman had a big-selling record (Victor). The song had at least eight recordings in its first year.

Valentine. w. Albert Willemetz (Fr.), Herbert Reynolds (Engl.), m. Henri Christin, 1929. Maurice Chevalier is identified with this song in the U.S., as he performed it in (MM) *Innocents of Paris* and in (MM) *Folies Bergere*, 1935, in addition to recording it (Victor) and

performing it on stage, radio, and T.V. The title has the French pronunciation of four syllables.

Valentino Tango, The (Noche de Amour). w. Jack Lawrence, m. Heinz Roemheld, 1950. Used in (MP) *Valentino*. Recorded by: Tony Bennett (Columbia), Victor Young and the Castilians (Decca), Buddy Morrow and his Orchestra (Mercury).

Valerie. w. Will Jennings, m. Steve Winwood, 1982. Chart record by the English singer/songwriter Steve Winwood (Island). Included in two subsequent albums of his.

Valleri. w/m Tommy Boyce and Bobby Hart, 1968. Top 10 hit by The Monkees (Colgems).

Valley Girl. w/m Frank Zappa and Moon Unit Zappa, 1982. Novelty record by Frank Zappa, featuring his daughter, Moon Unit Zappa (Barking Pumpkin).

Valley of Tears, w/m Antoine "Fats" Domino and Dave Bartholomew, 1957. Introduced and hit record by Fats Domino (Imperial).

Valley Road, The. w/m Bruce Hornsby and John Hornsby, 1988. Chart single from the album "Scenes from the Southside" by Bruce Hornsby and The Range (RCA).

Valotte. w/m Julian Lennon, Justin Clayton, and Carlton Morales, 1984. Top 10 record by Julia Lennon (Atlantic).

Vamp, The. w/m Byron Gay, 1919. Popular song with an oriental flavor. Leading records by Joseph C. Smith's Orchestra, vocal by Billy Murray and Harry MacDonough (Victor), and

The Waldorf-Astoria Dance Orchestra, directed by Joseph Knecht, vocal by Irving and Jack Kaufman (Columbia).

Vanessa. m. Bernie Wayne, 1952. Instrumental dedicated to film actress Vanessa Brown. Popular recording by Hugo Winterhalter and his Orchestra (RCA Victor).

Vanity. w. Jack Manus and Bernard Bierman, m. Guy Wood, 1951. Leading records by Don Cherry, with Sy Oliver's Orchestra (Decca); Tony Martin, with Henri René's Orchestra (RCA Victor); Sarah Vaughan, with Paul Weston's Orchestra (Columbia).

Vanna, Pick Me a Letter. See **Letter, The.**

Varsity Drag, The. w. B. G. DeSylva and Lew Brown, m. Ray Henderson, 1927. Introduced by Zelma O'Neal with backing by George Olsen's Orchestra in (TM) *Good News.* Olsen recorded four songs from the show (this, "Good News," "Lucky in Love, and The Best Things in Life Are Free") on two records (Victor). In the first film version (MM) *Good News,* 1930, it was sung by Dorothy McNulty [later known as Penny Singleton] and Billy Taft. In the 1947 remake, it was performed by June Allyson and Peter Lawford. It was also heard in (MM) *You're My Everything,* 1949.

Vaya Con Dios (May God Be with You). w/m Larry Russell, Inez James, and Buddy Pepper, 1953. Les Paul and Mary Ford had one of their biggest hit records (Capitol).

Vehicle. w/m Jim Peterik, 1970. Top 10 record by The Ides of March, of which Peterik was lead singer (Warner Bros.).

Velvet Glove, The. m. Harold Spina, 1953. Popular instrumental by Hugo Winterhalter and his Orchestra, featuring Henri René playing the musette accordion (RCA Victor).

Velvet Moon. w. Eddie DeLange, m. Josef Myrow, 1943. Harry James and his Orchestra's instrumental was a top-seller (Columbia).

Vengeance, w/m Carly Simon, 1979. Recorded by Carly Simon (Elektra).

Ventura Highway. w/m Lee Bunnell, 1972. Top 10 record by the trio America (Warner Bros.).

Venus. w/m Robbie van Leeuwen, 1970. Gold record by the Dutch group, The Shocking Blue, of which the composer was guitarist (Colossus). Revived by the female English trio, Bananarama, with a #1 U.S. hit (London), 1986.

Venus. w/m Ed Marshall, 1959. #1 hit by Frankie Avalon (Chancellor). Avalon recorded a disco version that attained popularity in 1976 (De-Lite).

Venus and Mars Rock Show. w/m Paul McCartney, 1975. Top 20 record by Paul McCartney's group Wings (Capitol).

Venus in Blue Jeans. w/m Howard Greenfield and Jack Keller, 1962. Top 10 record by Jimmy Clanton (Ace).

Venus Waltz. w. C. M. S. McLellan, m. Ivan Caryll, 1912. Introduced by Octavia Broske in (TM) *Oh! Oh! Delphine.*

Verdict, The. w. Glen Moore, m. Alan Freed, 1955. Recorded by The Five Keys (Capitol).

Very Next Man, The (I'll Marry). w. Sheldon Harnick, m. Jerry Bock, 1959. Introduced by Patricia Wilson in (TM) *Fiorello!*

Very Precious Love, A. w. Paul Francis Webster, m. Sammy Fain, 1958. From (MP) *Marjorie Morningstar.* Nominated for Academy Award, 1958. Best-selling record by The Ames Brothers (RCA).

Very Special. w/m William Jeffrey and Lisa Peters, 1981. Recorded by Debra Laws, male vocal by Ronnie Laws (Elektra).

Very Special Day, A. w. Oscar Hammerstein II, m. Richard Rodgers, 1953. Introduced by Isabel Bigley in (TM) *Me and Juliet.*

Very Special Love, A. w/m Robert Allen, 1957. Introduced on Playhouse 90 (TVP) "The Ninth Day." First recorded instrumentally by Mitch Miller and his Orchestra (Columbia). Popular vocal recordings by Debbie Reynolds (Coral) and Johnny Nash (ABC-Paramount).

Very Special Love Song, A. w/m Billy Sherrill and Norro Wilson, 1974. Crossover (Country/Pop) hit by Charlie Rich (Epic). Winner Grammy Award (NARAS), Country and Western Song of the Year.

Very Thought of You, The. w/m Ray Noble, 1934. Introduced, recorded by, and the theme song of Ray Noble and his Orchestra (Victor). Other recordings: Kitty Carlisle (Decca), Benny Carter (Bluebird), Carmen Cavallaro (Decca), Billie Holiday (Vocalion), Joe Reichman (Victor). Doris Day sang it in (MM) *Young Man with a Horn,* 1950.

Victoria. w/m Ray Davies, 1970. English song recorded by The Kinks (Reprise).

Victory. w/m Ronald Bell and James Taylor, 1986. Top 10 single from the album "Forever," by Kool and The Gang (Mercury).

Vict'ry Polka. w. Sammy Cahn, m. Jule Styne, 1943. Hit record by Bing Crosby and The Andrews Sisters (Decca).

Video Killed the Radio Star. w/m Geoff Downes, Trevor Horne, and Bruce Wooley, 1979. Leading record by the British duo, The Buggles, comprised of Downes and Horne (Island). Also recorded by the third writer, Bruce Wooley (Columbia).

Vieni, Vieni. w. George Koger and Henri Varna (It. and Fr.), Rudy Vallee (Engl.), m. Vincent Scotto, 1937. Featured and recorded by Rudy Vallee and his Orchestra (Bluebird) who were responsible for the song attaining a #1 position on charts and surveys.

Vieni Su (Say You Love Me Too). w/m Johnny Cola, 1949. Based on a public domain Italian song. Top record by Vaughn Monroe, with his Orchestra (RCA Victor). Other popular recordings by Dean Martin, with Paul Weston's Orchestra (Capitol); Carl Ravazza, who used it as his theme, with his Orchestra (Decca); Phil Brito, with Walter Gross's Orchestra (MGM); Frankie Carle, vocal by Marjorie Hughes (Columbia).

Vienna Calling. w/m Rob Bolland, Ferdi Bolland, and Johann Holzel, 1986. Chart single by the Austrian singer Falco [Holzel], from the album "Falco" (A&M).

Vienna Dreams. w. Irving Caesar, m. Rudolf Sieczynski, 1937. The original Austrian song, "Wien, du Stadt meiner Traume," 1914, had lyrics by Sieczynski. English version first published as "Someone Will Make You Smile," also with lyrics by Caesar, 1923.

Viet Nam Blues. w/m Kris Kristofferson, 1966. Country/Pop crossover record by Dave Dudley (Mercury).

View to a Kill, A. w/m Duran Duran, m. John Barry, 1985. Title song and #1 chart record from the James Bond film (MP), "A View to a Kill," by the British group Duran Duran (Capitol).

Vilia. w. Adrian Ross, m. Franz Lehar, 1907. Sung by Ethel Jackson in (TM) *The Merry Widow.* Jeanette MacDonald sang it in (MM) *The Merry Widow,* 1934, with new lyrics by Lorenz Hart. Fernando Lamas sang it in the 1952 remake with new lyrics by Paul Francis Webster. See also "I Love You So."

Village of St. Bernadette, The. w/m Eula Parker, 1960. English song popularized in the U.S. by Andy Williams (Cadence).

Vincent. w/m Don McLean, 1972. Top 20 recording by Don McLean of song written as tribute to Dutch painter Vincent Van Gogh (United Artists).

Violet and a Rose, The. w/m Mel Tillis, Bud Augue, and John Reinfeld, 1958. Introduced by Mel Tillis (Columbia). Other Country chart records by "Little" Jimmy Dickens (Columbia), 1962, and Wanda Jackson (Capitol), 1964.

Violets. w. Julian Fane, m. Ellen Wright, 1900. The words were adapted from a poem of the German poet Heinrich Heine. The song was introduced by Sydney Barraclough in (TM) *The Little Duchess.*

Violets for Your Furs. w. Tom Adair, m. Matt Dennis, 1941. Introduced, recorded, and popularized by Tommy Dorsey, vocal by Frank Sinatra (Victor).

Violins from Nowhere. w. Herb Magidson, m. Sammy Fain, 1950. Introduced by Arthur Carroll in (TM) *Michael Todd's Peep Show.*

Viper's Drag. m. Thomas "Fats" Waller, 1940. Based on the traditional "The Reefer Song," this version was introduced by Fats Waller. Revived by André De Shields and Company in the Waller musical (TM) *Ain't Misbehavin'*, 1978.

Virginia (Don't Go Too Far). w. B. G. DeSylva, m. George Gershwin, 1924. Sung by Constance Binney and ensemble in (TM) *Sweet Little Devil*.

Virgin Man. w/m William "Smokey" Robinson and Rose Ella Jones, 1974. Recorded by Smokey Robinson (Tamla).

Vision of Salome, A. m. J. Bodewalt Lampe, 1908. An instrumental.

Viva Las Vegas. w/m Doc Pomus and Mort Shuman, 1964. Introduced by Elvis Presley in (MM) *Viva Las Vegas*, and on records (RCA).

Viva Tirado. m. Gerald Wilson, 1970. Top 40 instrumental, recorded by the band El Chicano (Kapp, Part 1).

Vodka. w. Otto Harbach and Oscar Hammerstein II, m. George Gershwin and Herbert Stothart, 1926. Introduced by Dorothy Mackaye in (TM) *Song of the Flame*.

Vo-Do-Do-De-O Blues. w. Jack Yellen, m. Milton Ager, 1927. This was recorded by Vaughn DeLeath (Okeh), Van and Schenck (Columbia), and the Goofus Five (Okeh).

Voice, The. w/m Justin Hayward, 1981. Recorded by the English group The Moody Blues (Threshold).

Voice in My Heart, The. w/m Dave Franklin, 1958. Recorded by Eydie Gormé, with Don Costa's Orchestra (ABC-Paramount).

Voice in the Old Village Choir, The. w. Gus Kahn, m. Harry Woods, 1932. Featured and recorded by Paul Whiteman, vocal by Jack Fulton (Victor), Donald Novis (Victor), and organist Lew White (Brunswick).

Voice of America's Sons. w/m John Cafferty, 1986. Introduced by John Cafferty and The Beaver Brown Band on the soundtrack of (MP) *Cobra*, and on a chart single from the soundtrack album (Scotti Brothers).

Voice of the Hudson, The. w/m Paul Dresser, 1903.

Voices Carry. w/m Aimee Mann, Michael Hausmann, Robert Holmes, and Joey Pesce, 1985. Top 10 record by the group 'Til Tuesday (Epic).

Volare (a.k.a. **Nel Blu, Dipinto di Blu**). w. Mitchell Parish (Engl.), m. Domenico Modugno, 1958. Italian words by Franci Migliacci and Modugno. The song was winner of First Prize at the San Remo (Italy) Festival of Music. Domenico Modugno's recording, under title of "Nel Blu, etc.," sold nearly a million copies in Italy, after which it was released in the U.S. (Decca) and became not only the #1 best-seller of the year, selling over three million discs, but it was voted Song of the Year, Record of the Year, and Best Male Vocal Performance at the first Grammy Awards presentation under the aegis of NARAS. Under "Volare" title with English lyrics by Parish, Dean Martin had a Top 20 version (Capitol). In 1960, Bobby Rydell had a popular recording (Cameo).

Volcano. w/m Jimmy Buffett, Keith Sykes, and H. Dailey, 1979. Recorded by Jimmy Buffett (MCA).

Volunteer, The. w/m Autry Inman, 1963. Country record by Autry Inman (Sims).

Volunteer Organist, The. w. William B. Gray (Glenroy), m. Henry Lamb (Spaulding), 1893.

Volunteers. w/m Marty Balin and Paul Kantner, 1969. Recorded by Jefferson Airplane (RCA).

Vol Vistu Gaily Star. w/m Slim Gaillard and Bud Green, 1938. Introduced by Slim [Gaillard] and Slam [Stewart] (Vocalion). Also recorded by Tommy Dorsey (Victor), Emery Deutsch (Bluebird), The Merry Macs (Decca), The Smoothies (Bluebird).

Voodoo Man, The. w. George Walker, m. Bert Williams, 1900.

Voodoo Woman, w/m Bobby Goldsboro, 1965. Introduced and recorded by Bobby Goldsboro.

W

Wabash Blues. w. Dave Ringle, m. Fred Meinken, 1921. The song had two hit records in its first year, Isham Jones (Brunswick) and the Benson Orchestra (Victor). The composition was considered to be a Tin Pan Alley, or a commercial blues, rather than an authentic one. However, it has enjoyed ongoing popularity.

Wabash Moon. w/m Dave Dreyer and Morton Downey, 1931. Introduced, popularized, and recorded (Victor) by Morton Downey. It was not his theme, however, as frequently misstated. [See "Carolina Moon."] Other recordings by Wayne King (Victor), Nick Lucas (Brunswick), Roy Smeck (Crown).

Wack Wack. m. Eldee Young, Isaac Holt, and Don Walker, 1967. Instrumental by the Young Holt Trio (Brunswick).

Wacky Dust. w. Stanley Adams, m. Oscar Levant, 1938. Best-selling records by Chick Webb, vocal by Ella Fitzgerald (Decca) and Bunny Berigan, vocal by Ruth Gaylor (Victor).

Wade in the Water. Traditional, 1966. Mid-nineteenth-century slave song. Revived via instrumental recordings by The Ramsey Lewis Trio (Cadet), and Herb Alpert and The Tijuana Brass (A&M), 1967.

Wagon Train. w. Bob Russell, m. Henri René, 1957. Title theme of TV series "Wagon Train."

Wagon Wheels. w. Billy Hill, m. Peter De-Rose, 1934. Introduced by Everett Marshall in (TM) *Ziegfeld Follies*. Popular recordings by the bands of: George Olsen (Victor), Spade Cooley (Victor), Sy Oliver (Decca), Tommy Dorsey (Victor), and by singers Frank Luther (Melotone), Paul Robeson (Victor).

Wah-Hoo! w/m Cliff Friend, 1936. Popularized and recorded by Jimmy Dorsey and his Orchestra (Decca), the Hoosier Hot Shots (Melotone), and Joe Haymes and his Orchestra (Perfect). The Andrews Sisters revived it in (MM) *Moonlight and Cactus* in 1944.

Wah Watusi, The. w. Kal Mann, m. Dave Appell, 1962. Hit record by The Orlons (Cameo).

Wail of the Winds. m. Harry Warren, 1932. Red Nichols and his Orchestra used this instrumental as his theme song, and recorded it in 1939 (Bluebird) and again later (Capitol). It was played by the band in (MM) *The Five Pennies*, the film biography of Nichols, 1959.

Wait. w/m Vito Bratta and Mike Tramp, 1988. Single from the album "Pride" by White Lion (Atlantic).

Wait and See. w. Johnny Mercer, m. Harry Warren, 1946. Introduced by Kenny Baker, Cyd Charisse [voice dubbed on soundtrack by Betty Russell], and Angela Lansbury in (MM) *The Harvey Girls*. Recorded by Judy Garland (Decca) and Johnny Johnston (Capitol).

Waiter and the Porter and the Upstairs Maid, The. w/m Johnny Mercer, 1941. Introduced by Bing Crosby, Mary Martin, and Jack Teagarden in (MM) *Birth of the Blues.*

Wait for Me. w/m Daryl Hall, 1979. Recorded by Hall and Oates (RCA).

Wait for Me, Mary. w/m Charles Tobias, Nat Simon, and Harry Tobias, 1943. Most popular version by Dick Haymes with the Song Spinners (Decca), coupled with his #1 hit "You'll Never Know" (q.v.).

Waitin' at the Gate for Katy. w. Gus Kahn, m. Richard A. Whiting, 1934. Introduced by John Boles in (MM) *Bottoms Up.* Recorded by Anson Weeks and his Orchestra, vocal by Bob Crosby (Brunswick); Earl Burtnett's Orchestra (Columbia); Adrian Rollini, vocal by Joey Nash (Vocalion); Paul Small (Melotone). In 1947, it was played by the band in (MM) *The Fabulous Dorseys.*

Waitin' for the Evening Train. w. Howard Dietz, m. Arthur Schwartz, 1963. Introduced by Mary Martin and George Wallace in (TM) *Jennie.*

Waitin' for the Train to Come In. w/m Sunny Skylar and Martin Block, 1945. Popularized by Peggy Lee on her first solo chartmaking single (Capitol). Other popular versions by Harry James, vocal by Kitty Kallen (Columbia); and Johnny Long, vocal by Dick Robertson (Decca).

Waiting. w. Otto Harbach, m. Louis A. Hirsch, 1920. From (TM) *Mary.*

Waiting. w. Harry L. Cort and George E. Stoddard, m. Harold Orlob, 1918. A 1909 copyright that was sung in (TM) *Listen Lester* in 1918.

Waiting, The. w/m Tom Petty, 1981. Recorded by Tom Petty and The Heartbreakers (Backstreet).

Waiting at the Church. w. Fred W. Leigh, m. Henry E. Pether, 1906. English song, featured and recorded by Vesta Victoria (Victor). Ada Jones also had a popular version (Victor).

Sung by Mary Martin in (MM) *Birth of the Blues,* 1941.

Waiting at the End of the Road. w/m Irving Berlin, 1929. Sung by the Dixie Jubilee Singers in (MM) *Hallelujah.*

Waiting for a Girl Like You. w/m Mick Jones and Lou Gramm, 1981. Top 10 gold record by the Anglo-American group Foreigner (Atlantic).

Waiting for a Star to Fall. w/m George Merrill and Shannon Rubicam, 1989. Hit record by Boy Meets Girl (RCA).

Waiting for the Robert E. Lee. w. L. Wolfe Gilbert, m. Lewis F. Muir, 1912. Introduced by Al Jolson at the Winter Garden in New York. Also featured in vaudeville by Ruth Roye. In films, it was sung by Bobbie Gordon in (MM) *The Jazz Singer,* 1927; Fred Astaire and Ginger Rogers performed it in (MM) *The Story of Vernon and Irene Castle,* 1939; Judy Garland sang it in (MM) *Babes on Broadway,* 1941; Al Jolson dubbed in the voice for Larry Parks in (MM) *The Jolson Story,* 1946.

Waiting for the Sun to Come Out. w. Arthur Francis (Ira Gershwin), m. George Gershwin, 1920. Introduced by Helen Ford and Joseph Lertora in (TM) *The Sweetheart Shop.* Recorded by Lambert Murphy (Victor).

Waiting Game, The. w. Bob Hilliard, m. Robert Allen, 1958. Recorded by Harry Belafonte (RCA).

Waiting in the Lobby of Your Heart. w/m Billy Gray and Hank Thompson, 1952. Introduced and recorded by Hank Thompson (Capitol).

Waiting on a Friend. w/m Mick Jagger and Keith Richards, 1981. Recorded by The Rolling Stones (Rolling Stones).

Waitin' in School. w/m Johnny Burnette and Dorsey Burnette, 1958. Coupled with the hit "Stood Up" (q.v.) by Ricky Nelson (Imperial).

Waitin' in Your Welfare Line. w. Nat Stuckey, m. Don Rich and Buck Owens,

1966. C&W/Pop chart hit by Buck Owens (Capitol).

Wait Till She Sees You in Your Uniform. w. Edgar Leslie, m. John Jacob Loeb, 1942. Introduced and recorded by The McFarland Twins and their Orchestra (Okeh).

Wait Till the Cows Come Home. w. Anne Caldwell, m. Ivan Caryll, 1917. The hit song from (TM) *Jack 'O Lantern*, starring Fred Stone.

Wait Till the Sun Shines, Nellie. w. Andrew B. Sterling, m. Harry Von Tilzer, 1905. One of the biggest post-turn-of-the-century hits. Leading recordings by Byron G. Harlan (Columbia) (Edison). Mary Martin and Bing Crosby performed a memorable duet in (MM) *The Birth of the Blues*, 1941, that was released on record (Decca). It was also in (MM) *Rhythm Parade*, starring Gale Storm, 1942, and was the title song in the David Wayne-Jean Peters film (MP) *Wait Till the Sun Shines, Nellie*, 1952.

Wait Till You Get Them Up in the Air, Boys. w. Lew Brown, m. Harry Von Tilzer, 1919. Recorded by Billy Murray (Columbia). The other side of the record was Al Jolson's recording of Irving Berlin's "I've Got My Captain Working for Me Now" (q.v.). It was not uncustomary to find the coupling of artists in this fashion.

Wait Till You See Her. w. Lorenz Hart, m. Richard Rodgers, 1942. Introduced by Ronald Graham in (TM) *By Jupiter*.

Wait 'Til My Bobby Gets Home. w/m Phil Spector, Ellie Greenwich, and Jeff Barry, 1963. Recorded by Darlene Love (Philles).

Wait 'Til You See Ma Cherie. w. Leo Robin, m. Richard A. Whiting, 1929. Sung by Maurice Chevalier in his first American full-length film (MM) *Innocents of Paris* and recorded by him (Victor).

Wait Until Your Daddy Comes Home. w/m Irving Berlin, 1912.

Wake Me Up Before You Go-Go. w/m George Michael, 1984. #1 gold record by the British duo Wham! (Columbia).

Wake Me When It's Over. w. Sammy Cahn, m. James Van Heusen, 1960. Introduced in (MP) *Wake Me When It's Over*. Recorded by Andy Williams (Cadence).

Wake the Town and Tell the People. w. Sammy Gallop, m. Jerry Livingston, 1955. Best-selling records by Les Baxter, vocal by The Notables (Capitol) and Mindy Carson (Columbia).

Wake Up, America! w. George Graff, Jr., m. Jack Glogau, 1916. An American pro-intervention song, written just prior to its entry into World War I. Best-selling recording by James F. Harrison, under pseudonym of Frederick J. Wheeler (Victor).

Wake Up, Irene. w/m John Hathcock and Weldon Allard, 1954. C&W hit by Hank Thompson (Capitol).

Wake Up (Next to You). w/m Graham Parker, 1985. Written and recorded by British singer Graham Parker and The Shot (Elektra).

Wake Up and Live. w. Mack Gordon, m. Harry Revel, 1937. Introduced by Alice Faye and Jack Haley in (MM) *Wake Up and Live*. Faye recorded it (Brunswick), as did Leon Belasco and his Orchestra, vocal by the Andrews Sisters (Brunswick). This marked the sisters' last recording before going on their own.

Wake Up and Sing. w/m Cliff Friend, Carmen Lombardo, and Charles Tobias, 1936. Introduced by Guy Lombardo and his Royal Canadians. Also recorded by Eddy Duchin (Victor) and Bob Howard (Decca).

Wake Up Everybody. w/m Vic Carstarphen, Gene McFadden, and John Whitehead, 1976. Recorded by Harold Melvin and The Blue Notes (Philadelphia International).

Wake Up Little Susie. w/m Boudleaux Bryant and Felice Bryant, 1957. #1 hit by The Everly Brothers (Cadence).

Wal, I Swan! (or, Ebenezer Frye). w/m Benjamin Hapgood Burt, 1907. A rustic comedy song containing the catch-line, "Giddyap, Napoleon, it looks like rain." It was sung by Raymond Hitchcock in (TM) *A Yankee Tourist*.

Walk, Don't Run. w/m Johnny Smith, 1960. Hit record by the instrumental group, The Ventures (Dolton), who recorded a successful new version four years later titled "Walk, Don't Run '64" (Dolton).

Walk a Mile in My Shoes. w/m Joe Smith, 1969. Top 20 record by Joe South (Capitol).

Walk Away from Love. w/m Charles Kipps, 1975. #1 R&B, Top 10 Pop record by David Ruffin (Motown).

Walk Away Renee. w/m Mike Brown, Tony Sansone, and Bob Calilli, 1966. Top 10 hit by The Left Banke (Smash). Revived by The Four Tops (Motown), 1968; and Southside Johnny and The Jukes (Atlantic), 1986.

Walk Hand in Hand. w/m Johnny Cowell, 1956. Hit record by Tony Martin (RCA). Andy Williams sang it on his first chart record (Cadence). First recorded by Denny Vaughn (Kapp).

Walk Him Up the Stairs. w. Peter Udell, m. Gary Geld, 1970. Sung as the opening number of (TM) *Purlie* by Linda Hopkins and company, and as the finale by Cleavon Little and company.

Walkin', Talkin', Cryin', Barely Beatin', Broken Heart. w/m Justin Tubb and Roger Miller, 1964. Country chart record by Johnny Wright (Decca).

Walkin' a Broken Heart. w/m Alan Rush and Dennis Linde, 1985. Hit Country single by Don Williams (MCA).

Walkin' After Midnight. w. Don Hecht, m. Alan Block, 1957. C&W and Pop hit by Patsy Cline (Decca).

Walkin' Back to Happiness. w. John Schroeder, m. Mike Hawker, 1961. From the British film (MP) *Look at Life*. Recorded in London by Helen Shapiro and released in the U.S. (Capitol).

Walkin' Down to Washington. w/m Dick Sanford and Sammy Mysels, 1960. Recorded by Mitch Miller, his Orchestra and chorus (Columbia).

Walking Along with Billy. w. Mack Gordon, m. Josef Myrow, 1950. Introduced by Betty Grable in (MM) *Wabash Avenue*.

Walking Happy. w. Sammy Cahn, m. James Van Heusen, 1966. Originally written seven years earlier for an abandoned Fred Astaire film project, it became the title song of the Broadway musical (TM) *Walking Happy*, introduced by Norman Wisdom, Louise Troy, and ensemble.

Walking in Rhythm. w/m Barney Perry, 1975. Top 10 record by The Blackbyrds (Fantasy).

Walking in Space. w. Gerome Ragni and James Rado, m. Galt MacDermot, 1967. Sung by the company in the off-Broadway production of (TM) *Hair*, and the Broadway production of (TM) *Hair*, 1968.

Walking in the Rain. w/m Barry Mann, Cynthia Weil, and Phil Spector, 1964. Top 40 records by The Ronettes (Philles), and Jay and The Americans (United Artists), 1970.

Walking in the Sunshine. w/m Roger Miller, 1967. Country and Pop hit record by Roger Miller (Smash).

Walking on a Thin Line. w/m André Pessis and Kevin Wells, 1984. Recorded by Huey Lewis and The News (Chrysalis).

Walking on New Grass. w/m Ray Pennington, 1966. Country hit by Ray Price (Boone).

Walking on Sunshine. w/m Kimberly Rew, 1985. Top 10 record by Katrina and The Waves (Capitol).

Walking on Thin Ice. w/m Yoko Ono, 1981. Recorded by Yoko Ono (Geffen).

Walking Proud. w/m Gerry Goffin and Carole King, 1963. Featured and recorded by Steve Lawrence (Columbia).

Walking Tall. w/m Walter Scharf and Don Black, 1973. Sung on the soundtrack of (MP) *Walking Tall* by Johnny Mathis.

Walking the Dog. w/m Rufus Thomas, 1963. Introduced and Top 10 crossover (R&B/Pop) record by Rufus Thomas (Stax).

Walking the Dog (a.k.a. **Promenade**). m. George Gershwin, 1937. Music composed for scene with Fred Astaire and Ginger Rogers promenading their dogs on shipboard in (MM) *Shall We Dance*.

Walking the Floor over You. w/m Ernest Tubb, 1941. Major country hit written and recorded by Ernest Tubb (Decca). Bing Crosby teamed up with his brother Bob's band for a popular version (Decca).

Walking the Streets. w/m Gene Evans, Jimmy Fields, and Jimmy Littlejohn, 1961. Country hit record by Webb Pierce.

Walking to New Orleans. w/m Antoine "Fats" Domino, 1960. Hit record by Fats Domino (Imperial).

Walking with Susie. w. Sidney D. Mitchell, m. Con Conrad and Archie Gottler, 1929. From (MM) *Fox Movietone Follies of 1929*. Also recorded by Fran Frey with George Olsen's Orchestra (Victor), Milt Shaw (Columbia), Hal Kemp's Carolina Club Orchestra (Okeh).

Walkin' in the Rain with the One I Love. w/m Barry White, 1972. Gold record by the female trio Love Unlimited (Uni).

Walkin' My Baby Back Home. w/m Roy Turk and Fred Ahlert, 1931, 1952. Introduced by Harry Richman. Among records: Nick Lucas (Brunswick); Louis Armstrong (Okeh); Maurice Chevalier (Victor); Ted Weems, vocal by Parker Gibbs (Victor). Johnny Ray revived it with a million-seller (Columbia), 1952, and the song reached #1 on "Your Hit Parade." Nat "King" Cole (Capitol) and Dean Martin

(Apollo) also had big-selling releases in the renascence. Donald O'Connor sang it as the title song of (MM) *Walkin' My Baby Back Home*, 1953.

Walkin' My Cat Named Dog. w/m Norma Tanega, 1966. Top 40 record by Norma Tanega (New Voice).

Walk in the Black Forest. m. Horst Jankowski, 1962. German instrumental, originally titled "Eine Schwarzwaldfahrt." Recorded in Germany by jazz pianist/composer Horst Jankowski (Mercury).

Walkin' to Missouri. w/m Bob Merrill, 1952. Featured and recorded by Sammy Kaye, vocal by Tony Russo (Columbia).

Walk Like a Man. w/m Bob Crewe and Bob Gaudio, 1963. #1 chart hit by The Four Seasons (Vee-Jay). Revived by the group, Grand Funk Railroad (Capitol), 1974.

Walk Like an Egyptian. w/m Liam Sternberg, 1986. #1 record by the female quartet The Bangles (Columbia).

Walk Me to the Door. w/m Conway Twitty, 1963. Country chart hit by Ray Price (Columbia).

Walk of Life. w/m Mark Knopfler, 1985. Written by the lead singer and founder of the British group Dire Straits (Warner Bros.).

Walk On. w/m Neil Young, 1974. Recorded by Neil Young (Reprise).

Walk On, Boy. w/m Mel Tillis and Wayne P. Walker, 1960. Recorded by Mel Tillis (Columbia) and Jimmy Dean (Columbia).

Walk on By. w. Hal David, m. Burt Bacharach, 1964. Top 10 record by Dionne Warwick (Scepter). Isaac Hayes had a Top 40 version (Enterprise), 1969.

Walk on By. w/m Kendall Hayes, 1961. Top 10 record by Leroy Van Dyke (Mercury).

Walk on Out of My Mind. w/m Red Lane, 1968. Top 10 Country chart record by Waylon Jennings (RCA).

Walk on the Wild Side. w/m Lou Reed, 1973. Top 20 record by Lou Reed (RCA). Not to be confused with earlier novel, film, or song of same title.

Walk on the Wild Side. w. Mack David, m. Elmer Bernstein, 1962. From (MP) *Walk on the Wild Side*. Nominated for Academy Award, 1962. Instrumental hit by Jimmy Smith (Verve, Part 1). First popular vocal recording by Brook Benton (Mercury).

Walk on Water. w/m Neil Diamond, 1972. Recorded by Neil Diamond (Uni).

Walk Out Backwards. w/m Bill Anderson, 1961. Introduced and recorded by Bill Anderson (Decca).

Walk Right Back. w/m Sonny Curtis, 1961. Top 10 record by The Everly Brothers, coupled with hit "Ebony Eyes" (q.v.) (Warner Bros.).

Walk Right In. w. Gus Cannon, m. Hosie Woods, 1930, 1963. First recorded by Gus Cannon's Jug Stompers (Victor). The Rooftop Singers had a #1 record in 1963 and firmly reestablished the song (Vanguard).

Walk Tall. w/m Don Wayne, 1965. Top 10 Country chart record by Faron Young (Mercury).

Walk This Way. w/m Joe Perry and Steve Tyler, 1977, 1986. Top 10 record by the hard-rock band Aerosmith (Columbia). Revived with hit rap record by the trio, Run-D.M.C., with Aerosmith writers Perry and Tyler on vocals and guitar, respectively (Profile).

Walk Through This World with Me. w/m Sandra Seamons and Kay Jeanne Savage, 1967. Country hit recorded by George Jones (Musicor).

Wallflower. See **Dance with Me Henry.**

Wall to Wall Love. w/m Helen Carter and June Carter, 1962. Country hit record by Bob Gallion (Hickory).

Walter Winchell Rhumba. w. Carl Sigman, m. Noro Morales, 1964. Introduced in (MM) *Holiday in Mexico* by Xavier Cugat and his Orchestra.

Waltz At Maxim's (a.k.a. **She Is Not Thinking of Me**). w. Alan Jay Lerner, m. Frederick Loewe, 1958. Introduced by Louis Jourdan in (MM) *Gigi*. Daniel Massey sang it in the stage version (TM) *Gigi*, 1973.

Waltz for Debby. w. Gene Lees, m. Bill Evans, 1964. Originally a jazz instrumental, introduced by pianist Bill Evans. Vocal version featured and recorded by Tony Bennett (Columbia).

Waltz Huguette. See **Huguette Waltz.**

Waltzing in a Dream. w. Ned Washington and Bing Crosby, m. Victor Young, 1932. Recorded by Bing Crosby (Brunswick).

Waltzing in the Clouds. w. Gus Kahn, m. Robert Stolz, 1940. Introduced in (MM) *Spring Parade* and recorded by Deanna Durbin (Decca). Nominated for Academy Award.

Waltzing Matilda. w. A. B. Paterson, m. Marie Cowan, arr. by Orrie Lee, 1941. An Australian "bush song," adopted by the Australian Army in World War II. Folk singer Josh White helped popularize it in the U.S. Song featured in (MP) *On the Beach*, 1959. Jimmie Rodgers had a popular record in 1960 (Roulette).

Waltz in Swingtime. w. Dorothy Fields, m. Jerome Kern, 1936. Danced by Fred Astaire and Ginger Rogers in (MM) *Swing Time*.

Waltz Me Around Again, Willie ('Round, 'Round, 'Round). w. Will D. Cobb, m. Ren Shields, 1906. Introduced by Blanche Ring in (TM) *His Honor, The Mayor*. Leading record by Billy Murray and The Haydn Quartet (Victor).

Waltz of Long Ago, The. w/m Irving Berlin, 1923. Introduced by Grace Moore in (TM) *Music Box Revue of 1923*. Recorded by Paul Specht and his Orchestra (Columbia).

Waltz of the Wind. w/m Fred Rose, 1947. Featured and recorded by Roy Acuff (Columbia).

Waltz Was Born in Vienna, A. w. Earle Crooker, m. Frederick Loewe, 1936. Loewe's first song success. A non-production song, although interpolated in some revues. Leading recordings by the orchestras of Paul Whiteman (Victor), Henry King (Decca), and Leo Reisman (Brunswick).

Waltz You Saved for Me, The. w. Gus Kahn, m. Wayne King and Emil Flindt, 1930. Introduced by bandleader Wayne King who recorded it (Victor) and used it as his theme.

Wanderer, The. w. Donna Summer, m. Giorgio Moroder, 1980. Top 10 gold record by Donna Summer (Geffen).

Wanderer, The. w/m Ernest Maresca, 1962, 1988. Hit record by Dion (Laurie). Revived by Leif Garrett (Atlantic), 1978. #1 Country chart single from the album "I Wanna Dance with You" by Eddie Rabbitt (MCA), 1988.

Wanderin'. w/m Traditional, 1950. Adapted from an American folk song discovered by Carl Sandburg and first published in his "American Songbag," 1927. Edward Jackson and Sammy Kaye had their adaptations published in 1950. Kaye's version, with vocal by Tony Alamo (RCA Victor), was the most popular recording.

Wanderlust. m. Edward Kennedy "Duke" Ellington and Johnny Hodges, 1939. Recorded by Johnny Hodges and his Orchestra (Vocalion).

Wand'rin Star. w. Alan Jay Lerner, m. Frederick Loewe, 1951. Introduced by Rufus Smith, Robert Penn, and Jared Reed in (TM) *Paint Your Wagon*. In (MM) *Paint Your Wagon*, 1969, it was sung by Lee Marvin.

Wang, Wang Blues, The. w. Leo Wood, m. Gus Mueller, Buster Johnson, and Henry Busse, 1921. Busse, the noted trumpet player and future bandleader, wrote this with two other members of Paul Whiteman's Orchestra, Mueller, a clarinetist, and Johnson, a trombonist. Both Whiteman (Victor), and later, Busse (Decca) had big-selling records.

Wang Dang Doodle. w/m Willie Dixon, 1966. Recorded by Ko Ko Taylor (Checker). Revived by The Pointer Sisters (Blue Thumb), 1974.

Wango Tango. w/m Ted Nugent, 1980. Recorded by Ted Nugent (Epic).

Wanna Be Startin' Somethin'. w/m Michael Jackson, 1983. Top 10 R&B/Pop chart record by Michael Jackson (Epic).

Want Ads. w/m General Johnson, Barney Perkins, and Greg S. Perry, 1971. #1 gold record by the female trio The Honey Cone (Hot Wax).

Wanted. w/m Jack Fulton and Lois Steele, 1954. #1 million-selling record by Perry Como, with Hugo Winterhalter's Orchestra (RCA Victor).

Wanted Dead or Alive. w/m Bon Jovi and Richie Sambora, 1987. Top 10 single by Bon Jovi (Mercury).

Wanting You. w. Oscar Hammerstein II, m. Sigmund Romberg, 1928. Introduced by Evelyn Herbert and Robert Halliday in (TM) *The New Moon*. In the film adaptation, (MM) *New Moon*, 1930, it was sung by Lawrence Tibbett and Grace Moore, and in the 1940 remake, by Jeanette MacDonald and Nelson Eddy.

War. w/m Barrett Strong and Norman Whitfield, 1970. #1 record by Edwin Starr (Gordy). Revived by Bruce Springsteen and The E Street Band (Columbia), 1986.

War and Peace. w. Wilson Stone, m. Nino Rota, 1965. Melody from a theme from (MP) *War and Peace*. Leading record by Vic Damone (Columbia).

War Dance for Wooden Indians. m. Raymond Scott, 1938. Introduced in (MM) *Happy Landings*, danced by the Condos Brothers to the playing of the Raymond Scott Quintette, who recorded it (Brunswick).

War Is Hell (on the Homefront Too). w/m Curly Putman, Dan Wilson, and Bucky Jones, 1982. #1 Country chart record by T. G. Sheppard (Warner Bros.).

Warm. w. Sid Jacobson, m. Jimmy Krondes, 1957. Introduced and recorded by Johnny Mathis (Columbia).

Warm All Over. w/m Frank Loesser, 1956. Introduced by Jo Sullivan In (TM) *The Most Happy Fella.*

Warm and Tender Love. w/m Bobby Robinson and Ida Irral Berger, 1966. Top 20 record by Percy Sledge (Atlantic).

Warmer Than a Whisper. w. Sammy Cahn, m. James Van Heusen, 1962. Introduced by Dorothy Lamour in the last of the Bob Hope-Bing Crosby "road" pictures (MM) *The Road to Hong Kong.*

Warm Red Wine. w/m Cindy Walker, 1949. Hit C&W chart record by Ernest Tubb (Decca). Revived by Wes Buchanan (Columbia), 1968.

Warm Valley. m. Edward Kennedy "Duke" Ellington, 1940. Instrumental introduced and recorded by Duke Ellington and his Orchestra (Victor). Later recorded by André Previn (Sunset).

Warning Sign. w/m Eddie Rabbitt and Even Stevens, 1985. Top 10 Country chart song by Eddie Rabbitt (Warner Bros.).

Warrior, The. w/m Holly Knight and Nick Gilder, 1984. Top 10 record by the group Scandal (Columbia).

Warsaw Concerto. m. Richard Adinsell, 1942. From the British film (MP) *Suicide Squadron,* later retitled (MP) *Warsaw Concerto,* after the popularity of the composition. It was performed by the pianist Louis Kentner [dubbing for the star of the film, Anton Walbrook], and the London Symphony Orchestra, conducted by Muir Mathieson. In addition to the British soundtrack record, it was recorded by Alec Templeton (Decca 1 & 2) and Freddy Martin, piano solo by Jack Fina (Victor). Later

versions by pianist-bandleaders Claude Thornhill (Columbia) and Carmen Cavallaro (Decca). See also "World Outside, The."

War Song. w/m Neil Young, 1972. Recorded by Neil Young and Graham Nash (Reprise).

Washboard Blues. m. Hoagy Carmichael and Irving Mills, 1925. After his first success, "Riverboat Shuffle" (q.v.) Carmichael wrote this and recorded it as pianist for Hitch's Happy Harmonists, backed with another original, "Boneyard Shuffle" (q.v.) (Gennett). He also recorded it, as pianist, on a 12″ record with Paul Whiteman and his Orchestra (Victor), 1927. Other records: Red Nichols and his Five Pennies (Brunswick), Mildred Bailey (Vocalion).

Washington and Lee Swing. w. C. A. Robbins, m. Thornton W. Allen and M. W. Sheafe, 1910. One of the most popular of the college marches.

Washington Post March m. John Philip Sousa, 1890. Popular march featured and recorded by the U.S. Marine Band, under the direction of John Philip Sousa (Columbia). The piece was commissioned for the annual awards ceremonies given by the newspaper, The Washington Post. The number was performed in (MM) *Stars and Stripes Forever,* the Sousa story, 1952.

Washington Square w/m Bob Goldstein and David Shire, 1963. Hit instrumental by The Village Stompers (Epic). Marilyn May recorded it vocally (RCA).

Washington Twist, The. w/m Irving Berlin, 1962. Introduced by Anita Gillette in (TM) *Mr. President.*

Was It a Dream? w/m Larry Spier and Sam Coslow, 1928.

Was I to Blame for Falling in Love with You? w. Charles Newman and Gus Kahn, m. Victor Young, 1930. Glen Gray and the Casa Loma Orchestra used this as a theme song before "Smoke Rings." An arrangement of it by Larry Wagner appears in the Casa Loma LP "Solo Spotlight" (Capitol).

Was It Rain? w. Walter Hirsch, m. Lou Handman, 1937. Introduced by Frances Langford and Phil Regan in (MM) *The Hit Parade*, and recorded by them on separate labels, (Decca) and (Brunswick), respectively.

Wasn't It Beautiful While It Lasted? w. B. G. DeSylva and Lew Brown, m. Ray Henderson, 1930. Introduced by Grace Brinkley and Oscar Shaw in (TM) *Flying High*.

Wasn't It You? w. Ben Raleigh, m. Bernie Wayne, 1941. Recorded by Jimmy Dorsey, Vocal by Bob Eberly (Decca); Sammy Kaye, vocal by Tommy Ryan (Victor); Charlie Barnet, vocal by Bob Carroll (Bluebird); Dick Todd (Bluebird).

Was She Prettier Than I? w/m Hugh Martin and Timothy Gray, 1964. Introduced by Louise Troy in (TM) *High Spirits*.

Wasted Days and Wasted Nights. w/m Freddy Fender and Wayne Duncan, 1975. Originally recorded by Freddy Fender (Duncan), 1959. His new version became a Country/Pop gold record hit (ABC/Dot).

Wasted on the Way. w/m Graham Nash, 1982. Top 10 record by Crosby, Stills & Nash (Atlantic).

Wasted Words. w/m Don Gibson, 1957. Popular country record by Ray Price (Columbia).

Was That the Human Thing to Do? w. Joe Young, m. Sammy Fain, 1932. Featured and recorded by: Bert Lown, vocal by Elmer Feldkamp (Victor); Singin' Sam, The Barbasol Man (Oriole); The Pickens Sisters (Victor); Arthur Schutt (Crown); Benny Krueger's Band (Brunswick); Rudy Vallee (Hit of the Week).

Watch Closely Now. w/m Kenny Ascher and Paul Williams, 1976. Introduced by Kris Kristofferson in (MM) *A Star Is Born*, and recorded by him (Columbia).

Watch Her Ride, w/m Paul Kantner, 1968. Written by a member of The Jefferson Airplane who recorded it (RCA).

Watching My Dreams Go By. w. Al Dubin, m. Joe Burke, 1930. Sung by Winnie Lightner in (MM) *She Couldn't Say No.* Recorded by Vincent Lopez and his Orchestra (Perfect).

Watching the Clouds Roll By. w. Bert Kalmar, m. Harry Ruby, 1928. Introduced by Bernice Ackerman and Milton Watson in (TM) *Animal Crackers*, which starred The Four Marx Brothers. It was also heard in (MM) *Animal Crackers*, 1930.

Watching the River Flow. w/m Bob Dylan, 1971. Recorded by Bob Dylan (Columbia).

Watching the River Run. w/m Kenny Loggins and Jim Messina, 1974. Recorded by Loggins and Messina (Columbia).

Watching the Wheels. w/m John Lennon, 1981. Top 10 record by John Lennon (Geffen).

Watching You. w/m Mark Adams, Steve Arrington, Raye Turner, Dan Webster, Steve Washington, 1981. Recorded by the group Slave (Cotillion).

Watchin' Scotty Grow. w/m Mac Davis, 1971. Top 20 record by Bobby Goldsboro (United Artists).

Watch Out for Lucy. w/m Eric Clapton, 1979. Recorded by Eric Clapton (RSO).

Watch the Flowers Grow. w/m L. Russell Brown and Raymond Bloodworth, 1967. Top 40 record by The Four Seasons (Philips).

Watch What Happens. w. Norman Gimbel (Engl.), Jacques Demy (Fr.), m. Michel Legrand, 1964. Originally a theme from a French film, "Lola," 1960. Titled "Lola's Theme," it was sung by Georges Blanes, dubbing for Marc Michel, in the French film (MM) *The Umbrellas of Cherbourg*. Among many recordings were those by Jean-Paul Vignon (Columbia) and Lena Horne (Skye).

Watch Where You're Going. w/m Don Gibson, 1965. Top 10 Country record by Don Gibson (RCA).

We Don't Need Another Hero (Thunderdome). w/m Terry Britten and Graham Lyle, 1985. Introduced by Tina Turner in the Australian film (MP) *Mad Max Beyond Thunderdome*, and on the Top 10 record (Capitol).

We Don't Talk Anymore. w/m Al Tarney, 1979. Recorded by British singer/actor Cliff Richard (EMI America).

We Don't Want the Bacon, What We Want Is a Piece of the Rhine. w/m Howard Carr, Harry Russell, and Jimmie Havens, 1918.

Wee Baby Blues. w/m Pete Johnson and Joe Turner, 1944. Written in the thirties, but Turner's vocal with Art Tatum's group (Decca) gave the number a wider audience.

Wee Deoch-An-Doris, A. w. Gerald Grafton, m. Harry Lauder, 1911.

Weekend, The. w/m Bill LaBounty and Brent Maher, 1987. #1 Country chart record by Steve Wariner (MCA).

Week-end in Havana, A. w. Mack Gordon, m. Harry Warren, 1941. Introduced by Carmen Miranda in (MM) *Week-end in Havana* and on records (Decca). Bob Crosby, with vocal by Liz Tilton, also recorded it (Decca).

Weekend in New England. w/m Randy Edelman, 1977. Top 10 record by Barry Manilow (Arista).

Weekend in the Country, A. w/m Stephen Sondheim, 1973. Introduced by the company in (TM) *A Little Night Music*. It also was a cast number in (MM) *A Little Night Music*, 1977.

Weekend in the Country, A. w. Ira Gershwin, m. Harry Warren, 1949. Introduced by Fred Astaire, Ginger Rogers, and Oscar Levant in (MM) *The Barkleys of Broadway*.

Weekend of a Private Secretary, The. w. Johnny Mercer, m. Bernard Hanighen, 1938. Introduced, featured, and recorded by Mildred Bailey, with Red Norvo's Orchestra (Brunswick).

Week in a Country Jail, A. w/m Tom T. Hall, 1970. Country hit by Tom T. Hall (Mercury).

Week in the Country, A. w/m Baker Knight, 1964. Country hit record by Ernest Ashworth (Hickory).

Weepin' and Cryin'. w/m Tommy Brown, 1952. Leading record by The Griffin Brothers, featuring Tommy Brown (Dot).

Weep No More, My Baby. w. Edward Heyman, m. John Green, 1933. Introduced by Una Vallon and Billy House in (TM) *Murder at the Vanities*.

Weep No More, My Darlin'. w. Irmgard Baker, m. Elton Britt, 1949. Introduced and recorded by Elton Britt (Bluebird).

We Fight Tomorrow, Mother. w/m Paul Dresser, 1898. Spanish-American war song.

We Got Love. w. Kal Mann, m. Bernie Lowe, 1959. Top 10 record by Bobby Rydell (Cameo).

We Got More Soul. w/m Arlester Christian, 1969. Top 40 record by Dyke [Christian] and The Blazers (Original Sound).

We Gotta Get Out of This Place. w/m Barry Mann and Cynthia Weil, 1965. Top 20 record by the British group The Animals (MGM).

We Gotta Get You a Woman. w/m Todd Rundgren, 1970. Top 40 record by Runt [Todd Rundgren] (Ampex).

We Got the Beat. w/m Charlotte Caffey, 1982. Top 10 gold record by The Go-Go's (I.R.S.).

We Got Us. w/m Walter Marks, 1968. Introduced by Steve Lawrence and Scott Jacoby, and reprised by Lawrence, Jacoby, and Eydie Gormé in (TM) *Golden Rainbow*. Featured and recorded by Steve Lawrence and Eydie Gormé (United Artists).

We Go Well Together. w. Sid Robin, m. Arthur Kent, 1941. Featured and recorded by the bands of Cab Calloway (Okeh) and Fletcher Henderson (Columbia).

Weight, The. w/m Robbie Robertson, 1968. Leading records by Jackie DeShannon (Imperial); The Band, of which the writer was a member (Capitol); Aretha Franklin (Atlantic), 1969; Diana Ross & The Supremes and The Temptations (Motown), 1969.

Weird Science. w/m Danny Elfman, 1985. Introduced by the group, Oingo Boingo, as title song of (MP) *Weird Science*, and on records (MCA). Elfman was the lead singer.

We Just Couldn't Say Goodbye. w/m Harry Woods, 1932. One of the big popular hits of the year. Among its recordings: Paul Whiteman, vocal by Mildred Bailey (Victor); Guy Lombardo (Brunswick); Freddy Martin (Columbia); Russ Carlson (Crown); Chick Bullock (Perfect); Annette Hanshaw (Melotone). Hal Derwin revived it in the early fifties (Capitol).

We Just Disagree. w/m Jim Krueger, 1977. Recorded by English singer/guitarist Dave Mason (Columbia).

We Kiss in a Shadow. w. Oscar Hammerstein, m. Richard Rodgers, 1951. Introduced by Doretta Morrow and Larry Douglas in (TM) *The King and I*. In (MM) *The King and I*, 1956, it was sung by Rita Moreno and Carlos Rivas.

Welcome Back. w/m John Sebastian, 1976. Written and sung as the theme song of the series (TVP) "Welcome Back, Kotter" by John Sebastian, who then sang a lengthened commercial record version that became a #1 gold record (Reprise).

Welcome Home. w/m Harold Rome, 1954. Introduced by Ezio Pinza in (TM) *Fanny*.

Welcome Me, Love. w/m Tony Romeo, 1969. Recorded by Brooklyn Bridge (Buddah).

Welcome to L.A. w/m Richard Baskin, 1977. Sung by Richard Baskin on soundtrack of (MP) *Welcome to L.A.*

Welcome to My Dream. w. Johnny Burke, m. James Van Heusen, 1945. Introduced by Bing Crosby in (MM) *Road to Utopia*. Leading records by Crosby (Decca), and Woody Herman with vocal by Frances Wayne (Columbia).

Welcome to My World. w/m Ray Winkler and John Hathcock, 1964. C&W chart hit by Jim Reeves (RCA).

Welcome to the Boomtown. w/m David Baerwald and David Ricketts, 1986. Written and recorded by David and David (A&M).

Welcome to the Pleasuredome. w/m William Johnson, Mark O'Toole, Peter Gill, and Brian Nash, 1984. Recorded by the British group Frankie Goes to Hollywood (Island).

Welcome to the Theatre. w. Lee Adams, m. Charles Strouse, 1970. Introduced by Lauren Bacall in (TM) *Applause*.

Welfare Cadillac. w/m Guy Drake, 1970. Comedy record by Guy Drake (Royal American).

We Live for Love. w/m Neil Geraldo, 1980. Recorded by Pat Benatar (Chrysalis).

We Live in Two Different Worlds. w/m Fred Rose, 1943. Top C&W recordings by Roy Acuff (Columbia) and Tex Ritter (Capitol).

Well, All Right! w/m Frances Faye, David Kapp, and Don Raye, 1939. The Andrews Sisters had the best-selling record, coupled with "Beer Barrel Polka" (q.v.). Others, by bands of Eddy Duchin (Brunswick) and Tommy Tucker (Vocalion).

Well, Did You Evah? (What a Swell Party This Is). w/m Cole Porter, 1939. First performed by Betty Grable and Charles Walters in (TM) *DuBarry Was a Lady*. Bing Crosby and Frank Sinatra, with revised lyrics, sang it in (MM) *High Society*, 1956, and on records (Capitol). It was heard in (MM) *At Long Last Love*, 1975.

Well, Git It! m. Sy Oliver, 1942. Instrumental arranged by Oliver for Tommy Dorsey's Orchestra (Victor).

Well, Oh Well. w/m Tiny Bradshaw, Lois Mann, and Henry Bernard, 1950. Hit R&B recording by Tiny Bradshaw (King).

Well, You Needn't! m. Thelonious Monk, 1947. Jazz instrumental recorded by Thelonious Monk (Blue Note).

We'll Be the Same. w. Lorenz Hart, m. Richard Rodgers, 1931. Sung by Harriette Lake (Ann Sothern) and Jack Whiting and reprised by Whiting and Gus Shy in (TM) *America's Sweetheart*. Recorded by the orchestras of Arden and Ohman, vocal by Frank Luther (Victor), and Emil Coleman (Brunswick).

We'll Be Together. w/m Sting, 1987. Top 10 single from the album "Nothing Like the Sun" by Sting (A&M).

We'll Be Together Again. w. Frankie Laine, m. Carl Fischer, 1945. Frankie Laine introduced and recorded his song and had the best-seller (Mercury). Other versions by Les Brown and his Orchestra (Columbia); The Pied Pipers, with June Hutton (Capitol); later, The Four Freshman (Capitol).

(We'll Be) United. See **United**

We'll Gather Lilacs (Now That You're Home Once More). w/m Ivor Novello, 1945. A post-war English song introduced in the London musical (TM) *Perchance to Dream*. Recorded in the United States by Tommy Dorsey, vocal by Stuart Foster (Victor); and Gene Krupa, vocal by Buddy Stewart (Columbia).

We'll Have a Jubilee in My Old Kentucky Home. w. Coleman Goetz, m. Walter Donaldson, 1915. Recorded by the Peerless Quartette (Victor).

We'll Have a Kingdom. w. Otto Harbach and Oscar Hammerstein II, m. Rudolf Friml, 1926. Introduced by Desiree Ellinger and Joseph Santley in (TM) *The Wild Rose*.

We'll Make Hay While the Sun Shines. w. Arthur Freed, m. Nacio Herb Brown, 1933. Introduced by Bing Crosby in (MM) *Going Hollywood*. Crosby recorded it (Brunswick) backed with "Temptation" (q.v.) the hit song from the film, as did Nye Mayhew and his Orchestra (Vocalion).

We'll Meet Again. w. Hugh Charles, m. Albert R. Parker, 1941. British song, a favorite ballad of World War II, popularized in the U.S. by Kay Kyser, vocal by Harry Babbitt and Ginny Simms (Columbia); Guy Lombardo, vocal by Carmen Lombardo (Decca); Benny Goodman, vocal by Peggy Lee (Okeh). The English singer, Vera Lynn, revived it in 1954 (London). That recording was heard at the climax of (MM) *Dr. Strangelove*, 1964.

We'll Never Have to Say Goodbye Again. w/m Jeff Comanor, 1978. Introduced by the team of Deardorff & Joseph (Arista), 1977. Popularized by the Top 10 record of England Dan [Seals] and John Ford Coley (Big Tree).

Well Respected Man, A. w/m Ray Davies, 1966. Written by the lead voice of the British group, The Kinks, whose U.S. release was in the Top 20 (Reprise).

We'll Sing in the Sunshine. w/m Gale Garnett, 1964. Introduced and hit record by Gale Garnett (RCA).

We Love You. w/m Mick Jagger and Keith Richards, 1967. Recorded by The Rolling Stones (London).

We Love You Beatles. w. Lee Adams, m. Charles Strouse, 1964. Based on "We Love You, Conrad!" from the film *Bye Bye Birdie*, this novelty was recorded by the British group The Carefrees (London International).

We May Never Love Like This Again. w/m Joel Hirschhorn and Al Kasha, 1974. Sung by Maureen McGovern on the soundtrack of (MP) *The Towering Inferno*, and on records (20th Century). Winner Academy Award.

We May Never Pass This Way (Again). w/m Jimmy Seals and Dash Crofts, 1973. Recorded by Seals and Crofts (Warner Bros.).

We Might As Well Forget It. w/m Johnny Bond, 1944. Featured and recorded by Bob Wills and his Texas Playboys, vocal by Leon Huff (Okeh).

We Missed You. w/m Bill Anderson, 1963. Hit C&W record by Kitty Wells.

We Must Be Vigilant. w. Edgar Leslie, m. E. H. Meacham and Joe Burke, 1942. Burke adapted the 1880s march of Meacham's "American Patrol." This version was popularized and recorded by Phil Spitalny and his "Hour of Charm" all-girl Orchestra (Columbia), who also performed it in (MM) *When Johnny Comes Marching Home*, 1943. See also "American Patrol."

We Must Have Been out of Our Minds. w/m Melba Montgomery, 1963. Hit country record by George Jones and Melba Montgomery (United Artists).

We Mustn't Say Goodbye. w. Al Dubin, m. James V. Monaco, 1943. Featured in (MM) *Stage Door Canteen*. Nominated for an Academy Award.

Wendy. w. Betty Comden and Adolph Green, 1954. Introduced by Mary Martin and Kathy Nolan in (TM) *Peter Pan*.

We Need a Little Christmas. w/m Jerry Herman, 1966. Introduced by Angela Lansbury, Frankie Michaels, Jane Connell, and Sab Shimono in (TM) *Mame*. Lucille Ball and company performed it in the film version (MM) *Mame*, 1974.

We Never Talk Much. w. Sammy Cahn, m. Nicholas Brodsky, 1951. Introduced by Danielle Darrieux and Fernando Lamas in (MM) *Rich, Young and Pretty*, and reprised by Jane Powell and Vic Damone.

We Open in Venice. w/m Cole Porter, 1949. Introduced by Alfred Drake, Patricia Morison, Lisa Kirk, and Harold Lang in (TM) *Kiss Me Kate*. In (MM) *Kiss Me Kate*, 1953, it was sung by Howard Keel, Kathryn Grayson, Ann Miller, and Tommy Rall.

We're All Alone. w/m Boz Scaggs, 1977. First recorded by Frankie Valli (Private Stock), 1976. Rita Coolidge's version became a Top 10 gold record (A&M), 1977.

We're All Playing in the Same Band. w/m Bert Sommer, 1970. Recorded by Bert Sommer (Eleuthera).

We're an American Band. w/m Don Brewer, 1973. #1 gold record by the group, Grand Funk (Capitol).

We're a Winner. w/m Curtis Mayfield, 1968. Top 20 record by The Impressions (ABC).

We're Friends Again. w. Roy Turk, m. Fred E. Ahlert, 1930.

We're Getting Careless with Our Love. w/m Frank Johnson and Donald David, 1974. Recorded by Johnnie Taylor (Stax).

We're Going All the Way. w. Cynthia Weil, m. Barry Mann, 1984. Recorded by Jeffrey Osborne (A&M).

We're Going Over. w. Andrew B. Sterling and Bernard Grossman, m. Arthur Lange, 1917.

We're Gonna Make It. w/m Gene Barge, Billy Davis, Raynard Miner, and Carl William Smith 1965. Chart hit by Little Milton (Checker).

We're Gonna Make It (After All). w/m Ellie Greenwich, 1985. Finale of (TM) *Leader of the Pack*, sung by Ellie Greenwich, Darlene Love, Annie Golden, and company.

(We're Gonna) Rock Around the Clock. See **Rock Around the Clock**.

We're Having a Baby (My Baby and Me). w. Harold Adamson, m. Vernon Duke, 1942. Introduced by Eddie Cantor and June Clyde in (TM) *Banjo Eyes*, the musical based on the play *Three Men on a Horse*. Cantor sang it with Nora Martin in (MM) *Hollywood Canteen*, 1944.

We're in Business. w. Dorothy Fields, m. Harold Arlen, 1953. Introduced by Betty

Grable and Dale Robertson in (MM) *The Farmer Takes a Wife*, the musical film based upon the 1935 movie and earlier stage play of the same name.

We're in the Money (a.k.a. **The Gold Diggers' Song**). w. Al Dubin, m. Harry Warren, 1933. Introduced by Ginger Rogers in (MM) *Gold Diggers of 1933*. Recorded by Dick Powell (Perfect) and Leo Reisman and his Orchestra (Victor). It was later heard in (MM) *We're in the Money*, 1935; in (MM) *The Jolson Story*, 1946, sung by Evelyn Keyes; in (MM) *Painting the Clouds with Sunshine*, 1951. In (TM) *42nd Street*, 1980, it was performed by Karen Prunczik, Wanda Richert, Ginny King, Jeri Kansas, Lee Roy Reams, and ensemble.

We're in This Love Together. w/m Roger Murrah and Keith Stegall, 1981. Top 10 R&B and Pop chart record by Al Jarreau (Warner Bros.).

We're Off to See the Wizard. w. E. Y. Harburg, m. Harold Arlen, 1939. Sung by Judy Garland, Ray Bolger, Jack Haley, and Bert Lahr in (MM) *The Wizard of Oz*.

We're on Our Way to France. w/m Irving Berlin, 1918. Introduced by the company in the finale of the all-soldier show (TM) *Yip, Yip, Yaphank*. The company did ship out to France, marking the end of the service-benefiting run. The scene depicting the departure of the troops through the theater in which it was performing was reenacted in (MM) *Alexander's Ragtime Band*, 1938, and in (MM) *This Is the Army*, 1943. In the latter it was sung by George Murphy, George Tobias, Alan Hale, and the company.

We're Ready. w/m Tom Scholz, 1987. Top 10 single by the group, Boston, from their album "Third Stage" (MCA).

We're the Couple in the Castle. w. Frank Loesser, m. Hoagy Carmichael, 1941. From the animated cartoon (MM) *Mr. Bug Goes to Town*. Leading record by Glenn Miller, vocal by Ray Eberle (Bluebird).

We're the Talk of the Town. w. Buck Owens, m. Rollie Weber, 1963. C&W chart record by Buck Owens and Rose Maddox (Capitol).

Were Thine That Special Face. w/m Cole Porter, 1949. Introduced by Alfred Drake in (TM) *Kiss Me Kate*. Sung by Howard Keel in (MM) *Kiss Me Kate*, 1953.

Werewolf. w/m Les Emmerson, 1974. Recorded by the Canadian group Five Man Electrical Band (Polydor).

Werewolves of London. w/m Leroy Marinell, Robert Wachtel, and Warren Zevon, 1978. Recorded by Warren Zevon (Asylum). Zevon sang it on the soundtrack of (MP) *The Color of Money*. A new version is on the soundtrack album (Warner Bros.).

Were You Foolin'? w. Edgar Leslie, m. Fred E. Ahlert, 1934. Popular recordings by the bands of Ted Fio Rito (Brunswick), Richard Himber (Victor), Johnny "Scat" Davis (Decca), Johnny Green (Columbia).

Were Your Ears Burning? w. Mack Gordon, m. Harry Revel, 1934. Introduced by Ben Bernie and his Band in (MM) *Shoot the Works*.

Were You Sincere? w. Jack Meskill, m. Vincent Rose, 1931. Introduced and recorded by Bing Crosby (Brunswick).

We Saw the Sea. w/m Irving Berlin, 1936. Introduced by Fred Astaire and chorus in (MM) *Follow the Fleet*. Astaire recorded it (Brunswick).

We Shall Overcome. Anonymous, 1963. Based on a folk song of obscure origin, C. Albert Tindley copyrighted it as a hymn, "I'll Overcome Some Day," 1901. In the early days of Franklin D. Roosevelt's administration (1933), West Virginia coal miners altered the words and started singing the optimistic new words. The song became the theme of the Civil Rights movement in 1963. Joan Baez recorded it live at Miles College in Birmingham, Alabama. Her version gained wide popularity (Vanguard), 1963.

West End Girls. w/m Neil Tennant and Chris Lowe, 1986. Written and #1 record by the British duo The Pet Shop Boys (EMI America).

Western Movies. w. Cliff Goldsmith, m. Fred Smith, 1958. Novelty hit by The Olympics (Liberty).

Western Union. w/m Mike Rabon, Norman Ezell, and John Durrill, 1967. Hit record by The Five Americans (Abnak).

West L.A. Fadeaway. w/m Jerry Garcia and Robert Hunter, 1987. Popular airplay track from the album "In the Dark" by The Grateful Dead (Arista).

West of the Great Divide. w. George Whiting, m. Ernest R. Ball, 1924. Leading record by Henry Burr (Victor).

Westwind. w. Ogden Nash, m. Kurt Weill, 1943. Introduced by John Boles in (TM) *One Touch of Venus*. Coincidentally, thirteen years earlier Boles introduced Hammerstein and Youmans's "West Wind" (q.v.) in the film *Song of the West*.

West Wind. w. Oscar Hammerstein II, m. Vincent Youmans, 1930. Sung by John Boles in (MM) *Song of the West*, the film version of the stage musical, *Rainbow*. Boles recorded it (Victor).

We Sure Can Love Each Other. w/m Billy Sherrill and Tammy Wynette, 1971. Hit Country record by Tammy Wynette (Epic).

We Three (My Echo, My Shadow, and Me). w/m Nelson Cogane, Sammy Mysels, and Dick Robertson, 1940. #1 on the charts and "Your Hit Parade." Best-seller: The Ink Spots (Decca), followed by Tommy Dorsey's version with vocal by Frank Sinatra (Victor).

We Two Shall Meet Again. w. Harry B. Smith, m. Emmerich Kallman, 1927. From (TM) *The Circus Princess* starring Desiree Tabor and Guy Robertson.

We've Been Chums for Fifty Years. w/m Thurland Chattaway, 1906.

We've Come a Long Way Together. w. Ted Koehler, m. Sam H. Stept, 1939. Featured and recorded by Sammy Kaye, vocal by Tommy Ryan (Victor).

We've Come Too Far to End It Now. w/m Wade Brown, Jr., Johnny Bristol, and David Jones, 1972. Recorded by The Miracles (Tamla).

We've Gone Too Far. w/m Hank Thompson and Billy Gray, 1954. C&W record by Hank Thompson (Capitol).

We've Got a Good Fire Goin'. w/m Dave Loggins, 1986. Top 10 Country chart hit by Don Williams (Capitol).

(We've Got) Honey Love. w/m Sylvia Moy and Richard Morris, 1969. Recorded by Martha and The Vandellas (Gordy).

We've Got Tonight. w/m Bob Seger, 1979, 1983. Top 20 record by Bob Seger (Capitol). In 1983, Kenny Rogers and Sheena Easton teamed up for a #1 Country, Top 10 Pop version (Liberty).

We've Only Just Begun. w/m Paul Williams and Roger Nichols, 1970. Gold record by The Carpenters (A&M).

We've Only Just Begun (The Romance Is Not Over). w/m Timmy Allen and Glenn Jones, 1987. Top 10 R&B chart record by Glenn Jones (Jive).

We Were the Best of Friends. w. Sam M. Lewis, m. Pete Wendling and George W. Meyer, 1933. Best-selling record by Glen Gray and the Casa Loma Orchestra (Brunswick).

We Will Always Be Sweethearts. w. Leo Robin, m. Oscar Straus, 1932. Introduced by Jeanette MacDonald and Maurice Chevalier in (MM) *One Hour with You*.

Whale of a Tale, A. w/m Al Hoffman and Norman Gimbel, 1953. Introduced by Kirk Douglas in (MP) *20,000 Leagues under the Sea*.

Wham. w/m Eddie Durham and Joseph Taps Miller, 1940. Classic recording by Jimmie Lunceford and his Orchestra (Vocalion).

Others: Glenn Miller and his Orchestra (Bluebird); Jack Teagarden, vocal by Kitty Kallen (Varsity); Andy Kirk, vocal by June Richmond (Decca).

Wham Bam (Shang-A-Lang). w/m Richard Giles, 1976. Top 20 record by the quartet Silver (Arista).

What a Beautiful Beginning. w. Sidney Clare, m. Harry Akst, 1937. Introduced by Anthony [Tony] Martin in (MM) *Sing and Be Happy*.

What About Love? w/m Sharon Alton, Brian Allen, and Jim Vallance, 1985. Recorded by the group Heart (Capitol).

What About Me. w/m Scott McKenzie, 1973. Recorded by Anne Murray (Capitol).

What a Day! w/m Harry Woods, 1929. Best-selling record by Ted Weems' Orchestra, with vocal by Parker Gibbs (Victor). Also songwriter-singer Sammy Fain (Velvetone); Carl Fenton (Brunswick), and the band assembled for recording, the Mason-Dixon Orchestra (Columbia).

What a Diff'rence a Day Made (a.k.a. **What a Diff'rence a Day Makes).** w. Stanley Adams (Engl.), Maria Grever (Sp.), m. Maria Grever, 1934. This Mexican song was originally titled "Cuando Vuelva a Tu Lado." Popular records by Richard Himber, vocal by Joey Nash (Victor); Freddy Martin, vocal by Elmer Feldkamp (Brunswick); Art Kassel (Hit); the Dorsey Brothers, vocal by Bob Crosby (Decca); Benny Carter, vocal by Maxine Sullivan, 1941 (Bluebird); Charlie Barnet, vocal by Kay Starr, 1944 (Decca). Dinah Washington had a Top 10 record in 1959 (Mercury) and Little Esther Phillips' version made the Top 20 in 1975 (Kudu).

What a Diff'rence a Day Makes. See **What a Diff'rence a Day Made**.

What a Difference You've Made in My Life. w/m Archie Jordan, 1977. Country/Popular chart record by Ronnie Milsap (RCA).

What a Dream. See **Oh, What a Dream**.

What a Fool Believes. w/m Michael McDonald and Kenny Loggins, 1979. #1 gold record by The Doobie Brothers (Warner Bros.). Winner of both Grammy Awards (NARAS) for Song of the Year and Record of the Year.

What a Life! w. Charlotte Kent, m. Louis Alter, 1932. Recorded by the Coon-Sanders Orchestra (Victor), Isham Jones (Brunswick), Art Kassel (Columbia), Andy Kirk, vocal by Pha Terrell, 1939 (Decca).

What a Little Moonlight Can Do. w/m Harry Woods, 1935. Woods spent a period in the mid-thirties writing for English films. This was in one titled *Roadhouse Nights*. It is, however, associated with Billie Holiday who made the classic recording with Teddy Wilson's all-star band, featuring Benny Goodman, Roy Eldridge, Ben Webster, and others (Brunswick). Goodman and his Band, with vocal by Helen Ward, recorded it fifteen years later (Columbia). Diana Ross sang it as Billie Holiday, in her film story (MM) *Lady Sings the Blues*, 1972.

What Am I Going to Do Without Your Love? w/m William Stevenson and Sylvia Moy, 1966. Recorded by Martha and The Vandellas (Gordy).

What Am I Gonna Do About You. w/m Doug Gilmore, Bob Simon, and Jim Allison, 1986. First recorded by country singer, Con Hunley (Capitol), 1985. #1 Country chart hit by Reba McEntire (MCA), 1986.

What Am I Gonna Do About You? w. Sammy Cahn, m. Jule Styne, 1946. Introduced by Eddie Bracken and Virginia Welles in (MM) *Ladies' Man*. Recorded by Harry James, vocal by Art Lund (Columbia); Joan Edwards (Vogue).

What Am I Gonna Do with You. w/m Barry White, 1975. Top 10 record by Barry White (20th Century).

What Am I Living For? w/m Fred Jay and Art Harris, 1958. Hit record by Chuck Willis (Atlantic). Later chart records by Conway

Twitty (MGM), 1960; Percy Sledge (Atlantic), 1967; Ray Charles (ABC-TRC), 1972.

What Am I Worth. w/m Darrell Edwards and George Jones, 1955. Top 10 C&W chart record by George Jones (Starday).

What a Perfect Combination. w. Bert Kalmar and Irving Caesar, m. Harry Akst and Harry Ruby, 1932. Introduced by Eddie Cantor in (MM) *The Kid from Spain* and on records (Columbia). Ozzie Nelson's Band also had a record release (Brunswick).

What a Piece of Work Is Man. w. William Shakespeare, m. Galt MacDermot, 1968. The words are from *Hamlet*. Sung in the Broadway production of (TM) *Hair* by Ronald Dyson and Walter Harris.

What Are We Doin' in Love? w/m Randy Goodrum, 1981. Country/Pop hit by Dottie West, backup vocal by Kenny Rogers (Liberty).

What Are You Doing New Year's Eve? w/m Frank Loesser, 1947. Introduced and recorded by Margaret Whiting (Capitol).

What Are You Doing the Rest of Your Life? w. Marilyn Bergman and Alan Bergman, m. Michel Legrand, 1969. Introduced on the soundtrack of (MP) *The Happy Ending* by Michael Dees. This is an example of a modern song becoming a standard without a hit record.

What a Sweet Thing That Was. w/m Gerry Goffin and Carole King, 1961. Recorded by The Shirelles (Scepter).

What a Woman in Love Won't Do. w/m John D. Loudermilk, 1967. Top 40 record by Sandy Posey (MGM).

What a Wonderful Mother You'd Be. w. Joe Goodwin, m. Al Piantadosi, 1915.

What a Wonderful World. w/m George David Weiss and Robert Thiele, 1968. Recorded by and associated with Louis Armstrong (ABC). Armstrong's record was played on the soundtrack of (MP) *Good Morning Vietnam*, 1986, after which the song and record gained new popularity.

What a Wonderful World. w. Howard Dietz, m. Arthur Schwartz, 1935. Introduced by Eleanor Powell, Woods Miller, and the Sue Hastings Marionettes in (TM) *At Home Abroad*.

(What a) Wonderful World. w/m Barbara Campbell, Lou Adler, and Herb Alpert, 1960. First hit recording by Sam Cooke (Keen); then by Herman's Hermits (MGM), 1965; and Art Garfunkel, with James Taylor and Paul Simon (Columbia), 1978.

What Becomes of the Brokenhearted? w/m James Dean, Paul Riser, and William Weatherspoon, 1966. Top 10 record by Jimmy Ruffin (Soul).

What Can I Do? w. Harold Rome (Engl.), Edith Piaf (Fr.), m. Henri Betti, 1949. Originally "Mais Qu'est-ce que J'ai." Introduced in France by Edith Piaf and featured by her and Yves Montand in U.S. appearances, record albums, etc.

What Can I Say After I Say I'm Sorry. See **After I Say I'm Sorry**.

What Can You Say in a Love Song? w. Ira Gershwin and E. Y. Harburg, m. Harold Arlen, 1934. Sung by Josephine Huston and Bartlett Simmons in (TM) *Life Begins at 8:40*.

Whatcha Gonna Do? w/m Cory Lerios and Dave Jenkins, 1977. Top 10 record by the quartet Pablo Cruise (A&M).

What'cha Gonna Do? w/m Ahmet Ertegun, 1955. Introduced and recorded by The Drifters, featuring Clyde McPhatter (Atlantic).

What Cha' Gonna Do for Me. w/m James Stuart and Ned Doheny, 1981. Recorded by Chaka Khan (Warner Bros.).

Whatcha Gonna Do Now? w/m Tommy Collins, 1954. Top 10 C&W record by Tommy Collins (Capitol).

Whatcha' Gonna Do When Your Baby Leaves You. w/m Chuck Willis, 1956. Recorded by Chuck Willis.

What Cha Gonna Do with My Lovin'. w/m Reggie Lucas and James Mtune, 1979. Chart record by Stephanie Mills (20th Century).

Whatcha Know, Joe? w/m James "Trummy" Young, 1940. Introduced and recorded by Jimmie Lunceford and his Orchestra (Columbia), with whom Young was trombonist. Other popular recordings by Erskine Butterfield and his combo (Decca); Tommy Dorsey (Victor); The King Sisters, with Alvino Rey and his Orchestra (Bluebird); Charlie Barnet, vocal by Ford Leary (Bluebird).

Whatcha See Is What You Get. w/m Tony Hester, 1971. Top 10 record by The Dramatics (Volt).

What Color (Is a Man). w/m Marge Barton, 1965. Top 40 record by Bobby Vinton (Epic).

What Did I Do? w. Mack Gordon, m. Josef Myrow, 1948. Introduced in the Betty Grable-Dan Dailey starring film (MM) *When My Baby Smiles at Me.* Leading record by Harry James, vocal by Marion Morgan (Columbia).

What Did I Ever See in Him? w. Lee Adams, m. Charles Strouse, 1960. Introduced by Chita Rivera and Susan Watson in (TM) *Bye Bye Birdie.* Song not used in film version.

What Did I Have That I Don't Have. w. Alan Jay Lerner, m. Burton Lane, 1965. Introduced by Barbara Harris in (TM) *On a Clear Day You Can See Forever.* Barbra Streisand sang it in (MM) *On a Clear Day You Can See Forever,* 1970.

What'd I Say. w/m Ray Charles, 1959. Introduced and recorded by Ray Charles (Atlantic). Charles sang it in (MM) *Swingin' Along,* 1962. Jerry Lee Lewis (Sun), 1961, and Bobby Darin (Atco, Part 1), 1962, had Top 40 versions. In 1964, Elvis Presley sang it in (MM) *Viva Las Vegas,* and recorded it (RCA).

What Does It Matter? w/m Irving Berlin, 1927. Introduced on radio by the opera star Lucrezia Bori. Among recordings: Paul Ash (Columbia), Franklyn Baur (Columbia), Henry Burr (Victor), Harry Richman (Brunswick).

What Does It Take. w/m Derry Grehan, 1986. Written by the guitarist of the Canadian

quintet, Honeymoon Suite, the group that introduced it on the soundtrack of (MP) *One Crazy Summer,* and on records (Warner Bros.).

What Does It Take (to Keep a Man Like You Satisfied)? w/m James W. Glaser, 1967. Country hit by Skeeter Davis (RCA).

What Does It Take (to Win Your Love)? w/m Johnny Bristol, Vernon Bullock, and Harvey Fuqua, 1969. #1 R&B and #4 Pop chart hit by Jr. Walker and The All Stars (Soul).

What Do I Care? w/m Johnny Cash, 1958. Introduced and recorded by Johnny Cash (Columbia).

What Do I Care What Somebody Said? w. Sidney Clare, m. Harry Woods, 1927.

What Do I Have to Do to Make You Love Me? w/m Inez James and Sidney Miller, 1948. Written for (MM) *Are You with It?,* based on the Broadway musical of the same name. Leading recording by Vaughn Monroe with his Orchestra (RCA Victor).

What Do the Simple Folks Do? w. Alan Jay Lerner, m. Frederick Loewe, 1960. Introduced by Julie Andrews and Richard Burton in (TM) *Camelot.* Sung by Vanessa Redgrave and Richard Harris in the film version (MM) *Camelot,* 1967.

What Do You Do in the Infantry? w/m Frank Loesser, 1943. Introduced by Bing Crosby on his network radio show.

What Do You Do Sunday, Mary? w. Irving Caesar, m. Stephen Jones, 1923. Introduced by Luella Gear and Robert Woolsey in (TM) *Poppy.* Recorded by The American Quartet (Victor).

What Do You Think I Am? w/m Hugh Martin and Ralph Blane, 1941. Sung by June Allyson and Kenneth Bowers in (TM) *Best Foot Forward.* Recorded by Nancy Walker (Bluebird).

What Do You Want to Make Those Eyes at Me For? w. Joseph McCarthy and Howard Johnson, m. James V. Monaco, 1916. First recording by Ada Jones and Billy Murray (Victor). The song was heard in (MM) *The Merry Monahans*, starring Donald O'Connor and Peggy Ryan and in the Texas Guinan screen bio (MM) *Incendiary Blonde* starring Betty Hutton, 1944.

What Do You Want with Me? w/m Chad Stuart and Jeremy Clyde, 1965. Recorded by the British duo Chad and Jeremy (World Artists).

What D'ya Say? w. B. G. DeSylva and Lew Brown, m. Ray Henderson, 1928. Introduced by Frances Williams and Harry Richman in (TM) *George White's Scandals of 1928*.

Whatever Gets You Through the Night. w/m John Lennon, 1974. #1 record by John Lennon with the Plastic Ono Nuclear Band, and Elton John backing vocals (Apple).

Whatever Happened to Old Fashioned Love. w/m Lewis Anderson, 1983. Recorded by B. J. Thomas (Cleveland International).

Whatever Happened to Saturday Night. w/m Richard O'Brien, 1975. Introduced by Meat Loaf in (TM) *The Rocky Horror Show*.

Whatever Lola Wants (Lola Gets). w/m Richard Adler and Jerry Ross, 1955. Introduced by Gwen Verdon in (TM) *Damn Yankees*, and repeated by her in (MM) *Damn Yankees*, 1958. Leading recordings by Sarah Vaughan (Mercury) and Dinah Shore (RCA).

Whatever Will Be, Will Be. See **Que Sera, Sera**.

What Every Girl Should Know. w. Robert Wells, m. David Holt, 1954.

What Goes On. w/m John Lennon and Paul McCartney, 1966. Recorded by The Beatles, coupled with the hit "Nowhere Man" (q.v.) (Capitol).

What Goes On Here in My Heart? w. Leo Robin, m. Ralph Rainger, 1938. Introduced by Jack Whiting and Betty Grable in (MM) *Give Me a Sailor*. Recordings by the orchestras

of Henry Busse (Decca), Frank Dailey (Bluebird), Dick Jurgens (Vocalion), Gene Krupa (Brunswick).

What Goes On When the Sun Goes Down. w/m John Schweers, 1976. #1 Country chart record by Ronnie Milsap (RCA).

What Goes Up Must Come Down. w. Ted Koehler, m. Rube Bloom, 1939. Popular records by Count Basie, vocal by Helen Humes (Vocalion); Les Brown (Bluebird); Horace Heidt (Brunswick); Ginny Simms (Vocalion). In World War II, Kay Starr with Les Paul recorded it on V-discs.

What Good Am I Without You? w/m Milton Ager, 1931. Introduced and recorded by Fletcher Henderson's Orchestra (Columbia). Also recorded by Duke Ellington, with Dick Robertson as vocalist. Revived in the early fifties by Bill Farrell (MGM).

What Good Would the Moon Be? w. Langston Hughes, m. Kurt Weill, 1947. Introduced by Ann Jeffreys in (TM) *Street Scene*. Recorded by Freddy Martin, vocal by Murray Arnold (RCA Victor).

What Has Become of Hinky Dinky Parlay Voo? w/m Al Dubin, Jimmy McHugh, Irwin Dash, and Irving Mills, 1924. Featured by Billy Jones and Ernie Hare, The Happiness Boys.

What Have I Done to Deserve This? w/m Neil Tennant, Chris Lowe, and Allee Willis, 1987. Top 10 single by the British duo The Pet Shop Boys with Dusty Springfield (EMI American).

What Have They Done to My Song, Ma. See **Look What They've Done**, etc.

What Have They Done to the Rain? w/m Malvina Reynolds, 1965. Popularized by the British quartet The Searchers (Kapp).

What Have We Got to Lose? w. Gus Kahn and Charlotte Kent, m. Louis Alter, 1933. Best-selling records: Ben Bernie (Brunswick), Phil Harris (Columbia).

What Have You Done for Me Lately. w/m James Harris III and Terry Lewis, 1986. #1 R&B chart and Top 10 Pop chart record by Janet Jackson (A&M).

What Have You Got That Gets Me? w. Leo Robin, m. Ralph Rainger, 1938. Performed by the Yacht Club Boys, Joyce Compton, Jack Benny, and Joan Bennett in (MM) *Artists and Models Abroad*. Recorded by Bob Crosby with vocal by Marion Mann (Decca), and Kay Kyser with vocal by Ginny Simms (Brunswick).

What I Did for Love. w. Edward Kleban, m. Marvin Hamlisch, 1975. Introduced by Priscilla Lopez and company in (TM) *A Chorus Line*. In (MM) *A Chorus Line*, 1985, it was sung by Alyson Reed.

What I Didn't Do. w/m Wood Newton and Michael Noble, 1985. Top 10 Country chart record by Steve Wariner (MCA).

What I Feel in My Heart (How Can I Write on Paper). w/m Don Carter, Danny Harrison, George Kent, and Jim Reeves, 1961. Introduced and recorded by Jim Reeves (RCA).

What I Need Most. w/m Hugh X. Lewis, 1965. Country chart record by Hugh X. Lewis (Kapp).

What in the World's Come Over You? w/m Jack Scott, 1960. Top 10 record by Jack Scott (Top Rank).

What Is a Man? w. Lorenz Hart, m. Richard Rodgers, 1940. Vivienne Segal introduced the number under the title "Love Is My Friend" in (TM) *Pal Joey*. Shortly after the show opened on Broadway, Hart wrote a new lyric, with the new title. In the successful 1952 revival, Segal again appeared in the same role and also recorded the song (Columbia).

What Is Hip? w/m Emilio Castillo, John Garibaldi, and Stephen Kupka, 1974. Recorded by the band Tower of Power (Warner Bros.).

What Is It? w. Harry Tobias, m. Harry Barris, 1931. Chief recordings by Gene Austin (Perfect) and Smith Ballew (Columbia).

What Is Life. w/m George Harrison, 1971. Top 10 record by George Harrison (Apple).

What Is Life Without Love? w/m Eddy Arnold, Owen Bradley, and Vernice McAlpin, 1947. #1 C&W chart record by Eddy Arnold (Victor).

What Is Love? w/m Lee Pockriss and Paul Vance, 1959. Recorded by The Playmates (Roulette).

What Is There to Say? w. E. Y. Harburg, m. Vernon Duke, 1934. Introduced by Jane Froman and Everett Marshall in (TM) *Ziegfeld Follies*. The song reached a standard plateau in 1941 when recorded by such bands as Artie Shaw (Victor), Jack Jenney (Vocalion), Bud Freeman (Decca), and subsequently, Coleman Hawkins (Capitol), and Bobby Hackett (Brunswick).

What Is This Thing Called Love? w/m Cole Porter, 1930. In the London production of (TM) *Wake Up and Dream*, this was sung by Elsie Carlisle and danced by Tilly Losch, Toni Birkmayer, Alanova, and William Cavanagh. In the Broadway production, it was sung by Frances Shelley and danced by Miss Losch and Mr. Birkmayer. It was heard in (MM) *You're a Lucky Fellow, Mr. Smith*, 1942; sung by Ginny Simms in the Cole Porter story (MM) *Night and Day*, 1945; sung by Lucille Norman and Gordon MacRae in (MM) *Starlift*, 1951; played in (MM) *The Eddy Duchin Story*, 1956.

What Is Truth. w/m Johnny Cash, 1970. Hit C&W and Pop record by Johnny Cash (Columbia).

What Kinda Deal Is This? w/m Wayne Gilbreath, 1966. Country hit by Bill Carlisle (Hickory).

What Kind of Fool. w/m Barry Gibb and Albhy Galuten, 1981. Top 10 record by Barbra Streisand and Barry Gibb (Columbia).

What Kind of Fool (Do You Think I Am?).
w/m Ray Whitley, 1964. Crossover (R&B/Pop)
Top 10 record by The Tams (ABC-Paramount).
Bill Deal and The Rhondels had a Top 40
version (Heritage), 1969.

What Kind of Fool Am I? w/m Leslie Bricusse and Anthony Newley, 1962. Introduced
by Anthony Newley in the New York production of the English musical (TM) *Stop the
World—I Want to Get Off*. Winner of Grammy
Award (NARAS) for Song of the Year. Leading
records: Sammy Davis, Jr. (Reprise), Anthony
Newley (London), Robert Goulet (Columbia).
Revived by Rick Springfield (RCA), 1982.

What Kind of Love Is This? w/m Johnny
Nash, 1963. From (MM) *Two Tickets to Paris*.
Recorded by Joey Dee and The Starliters (Rou-
lette).

What'll I Do? w/m Irving Berlin, 1924.
One of Berlin's ballad classics. It was published as a non-production song and is listed
that way in the Berlin catalog, even though it
was interpolated by Grace Moore in (TM) *Music Box Revue* after the opening. The song was
sung by a chorus in (MM) *Alexander's Ragtime
Band*, 1938; sung by Danny Thomas in (MM)
Big City, 1948; and was prominently used as
the background theme throughout (MP) *The
Great Gatsby*, 1974. Among the many recordings are those by Paul Whiteman (Victor)
(Decca), Henry Burr and Marcia Freer (Victor), Art Lund (MGM), Nat "King" Cole (Capitol), Frank Sinatra (Columbia), Giselle
McKenzie (Capitol).

**What'll We Do on a Saturday Night When
the Town Goes Dry?** w/m Harry Ruby,
1919. This was one of the first songs written
referring to the advent of Prohibition.

What Makes a Man Wander. w/m Harlan
Howard, 1958. Jimmie Skinner's Top 10 C&W
record introduced the song (Mercury). Jan
Howard, then the wife of the composer, had a
popular Country chart version (Decca), 1965.

What Makes the Sunset? w. Sammy Cahn,
m. Jule Styne, 1944. Introduced by Frank
Sinatra in (MM) *Anchors Aweigh* and on records (Columbia).

What More Can a Woman Do? w/m Peggy
Lee and Dave Barbour, 1945. One of Peggy
Lee's earliest recordings of her own composi-
tions (Capitol). Also cut by Sarah Vaughan
(Continental).

What More Can I Ask? w. A. E. Wilkins,
m. Ray Noble, 1933. Introduced and recorded
by Ray Noble and his Orchestra (HMV-
Victor).

What Now My Love. w. Carl Sigman
(Engl.), P. Dalanoe (Fr.), m. Gilbert Be-
caud, 1966. Introduced in France in 1962 by
Gilbert Becaud. Leading U.S. records: instru-
mental by Herb Alpert and The Tijuana Brass
(A&M); vocal by Sonny and Cher (Atco); Mitch
Ryder (DynoVoice).

**What's a Memory Like You (Doing in a
Love Like This).** w/m Charles Quillen and
John Jarrard, 1986. #1 Country chart record
by John Schneider (MCA).

**What's Easy for Two Is So Hard for
One.** w/m William Robinson, 1963. Top 40
record by Mary Wells (Motown).

What's Forever For. w/m Rafe Van
Hoy, 1982. #1 Country chart crossover record
by Michael Murphey (Liberty).

What's Going On. w/m Renaldo Benson,
Al Cleveland, and Marvin Gaye, 1971. #1
R&B and #2 Pop chart record by Marvin Gaye
(Tamla). Chart single by Cyndi Lauper, from
her album "True Colors" (Portrait), 1987.

What's Going On in Your World? w/m
O'Brien Fisher, Royce Porter, and David
Chamberlain, 1989. Hit Country chart record
by George Strait (MCA).

What's Good About Goodbye? w. Leo
Robin, m. Harold Arlen, 1948. Introduced by
Tony Martin in (MM) *Casbah* and on records
(RCA Victor). Most popular recording by Mar-
garet Whiting (Capitol).

What's He Doin' in My World? w/m Carl
Belew, Eddie Bush, Barry Moore, W. S. Stev-
enson, Betty J. Robinson, 1965. Country and
Pop chart hit by Eddy Arnold (RCA).

What She Is (Is a Woman in Love). w/m Bob McDill and Paul Harrison, 1988. #1 Country chart record by Earl Thomas Conley (RCA).

What's It Gonna Be? w/m Mort Shuman and Jerry Ragovoy, 1967. Recorded by English singer Dusty Springfield (Philips).

What's Love Got to Do with It. w/m Terry Britten and Graham Lyle, 1984. #1 gold record by Tina Turner (Capitol). English song produced by co-writer Terry Britten. Winner Grammy Awards (NARAS) for Song of the Year and Record of the Year.

What's Made Milwaukee Famous (Has Made a Loser out of Me). w/m Glenn Sutton, 1968. Recorded by Jerry Lee Lewis (Smash).

What's New? w. Johnny Burke, m. Bob Haggart, 1939. Introduced as an instrumental, "I'm Free," by Bob Crosby and his Orchestra the prior year. Haggart was bass player in the band. Trumpeter Billy Butterfield had an outstanding solo and later recorded the song with Jess Stacy's Band (Varsity) and his own band (Capitol), for which it was the theme. Among other recordings: Benny Goodman (Columbia); Bing Crosby (Decca); Kay Kyser, vocal by Ginny Simms (Columbia); Stan Getz (Prestige); Maynard Ferguson (Capitol); Milt Jackson (Blue Note). Revived by Linda Ronstadt (Asylum), 1983.

What's New, Pussycat? w. Hal David, m. Burt Bacharach, 1965. Introduced in (MP) *What's New, Pussycat?* Nominated for Academy Award. Hit record by Tom Jones (Parrot).

What's New at the Zoo? w. Betty Comden and Adolph Green, m. Jule Styne, 1960. Introduced by Nancy Dussault in (TM) *Do Re Mi.*

What's on Your Mind (Pure Energy). w/m Paul Robb and Kurt Valaquen, 1988. Recorded by Information Society from the album of their name (Reprise).

What's the Matter Now? w/m Clarence Williams and Spencer Williams, 1926.

What's the Matter with Father. w. Harry H. Williams, m. Egbert Van Alstyne, 1910.

What's the Matter with Me? w. Al Lewis, m. Terry Shand, 1940. Featured and recorded by Glenn Miller, vocal by Marion Hutton (Bluebird).

What's the Name of That Song? w. Tot Seymour, m. Vee Lawnhurst, 1936. Featured by the bands of Ozzie Nelson (Brunswick) and Bob Crosby (Decca).

What's the Reason (I'm Not Pleasin' You)? w/m Coy Poe, Jimmie Grier, Truman "Pinky" Tomlin, and Earl Hatch, 1935. Introduced by Pinky Tomlin in (MP) *Times Square Lady.* Tomlin recorded it with Jimmie Grier's Orchestra (Brunswick). Other popular versions by Fats Waller (Victor), Guy Lombardo (Decca), the Mills Brothers (Decca), Jimmy Dorsey and his Orchestra (Decca).

What's the Use? w. Charles Newman, m. Isham Jones, 1930.

What's the Use of Breaking Up? w/m Kenny Gamble, Jerry Butler, and Theresa Bell, 1969. Top 20 record by Jerry Butler (Mercury).

What's the Use of Dreaming? w/m Will M. Hough and Joseph E. Howard, 1906. Introduced by Mabel Barrison in Chicago in (TM) *The District Leader.* Recorded by Joe Howard with the Elm City Four and The Floradora Girls (DeLuxe). It was included in the Howard film biography (MM) *I Wonder Who's Kissing Her Now,* 1942.

What's the Use of Loving If You Can't Love All the Time? w. Joseph Mittenthal, m. Harry Armstrong, 1906.

What's the Use of Wond'rin'? w. Oscar Hammerstein II, m. Richard Rodgers, 1945. Introduced by Jan Clayton in (TM) *Carousel.* Shirley Jones sang it in the film version (MM) *Carousel,* 1956.

What's This? w/m Dave Lambert, 1945. Introduced by Gene Krupa, vocal by Dave Lambert and Buddy Stewart (Columbia) and considered by jazz historian Leonard Feather to be the first recorded bop vocal.

What's Wrong with Me? w. Edward Heyman, m. Nacio Herb Brown, 1948. Introduced by Kathryn Grayson in (MM) *The Kissing Bandit* and recorded by her with Georgie Stoll's Orchestra (MGM).

What's Your Mama's Name, Child? w/m Dallas Frazier and Earl Montgomery, 1973. Country hit and Pop chart record by Tanya Tucker (Columbia).

What's Your Name. w/m Gary Rossington and Ronnie Van Zant, 1978. Top 20 record by the group Lynyrd Skynyrd (MCA).

What's Your Name? w/m Claude Johnson, 1962. Hit record by Don and Juan (Big Top). Revived in 1974 by Andy and David Williams, the fourteen-year-old twin nephews of singer Andy Williams (Barnaby).

What's Your Story, Morning Glory? w/m Jack Lawrence, Paul Webster, Mary Lou Williams, 1938. Introduced and recorded by Andy Kirk and his Clouds of Joy (Decca). Mary Lou Williams, the pianist and composer, arranged the number. Paul Webster was an active trumpet player with big bands, and is not to be confused with the writer whose middle name is Francis.

What Takes My Fancy. w. Carolyn Leigh, m. Cy Coleman, 1960. Introduced by Lucille Ball and Don Tomkins in (TM) *Wildcat*.

What the World Needs Now Is Love. w. Hal David, m. Burt Bacharach, 1965. Top 10 record by Jackie DeShannon (Imperial). Tom Clay, a disc jockey, narrated a Top 10 version in medley with "Abraham, Martin and John," vocal backup by The Blackberries (Mowest), 1971.

What to Do. w/m Sid Robin, 1942. Introduced by the Andrews Sisters in (MM) *What's Cookin'?*

What We're Fighting For. w/m Tom T. Hall, 1965. Country chart hit by Dave Dudley (Mercury).

What Will I Tell My Heart? w/m Jack Lawrence, Peter Tinturin, and Irving Gordon, 1937. Leading recordings by Bing Crosby (Decca); Hal Kemp, vocal by Bob Allen (Brunswick); Eddy Howard (Mercury); Andy Kirk, vocal by Pha Terrell (Decca); Art Tatum (Decca); Roy Smeck (Decca).

What Will My Mary Say? w/m Paul Vance and Eddie Snyder, 1963. Popularized by Johnny Mathis (Columbia).

What Would I Care? w. Bert Kalmar, m. Harry Ruby, 1930. Sung by Paul Frawley and Irene Delroy in (TM) *Top Speed*, which opened on Christmas night, 1929. In the film (MM) *Top Speed*, 1930, it was sung by Jack Whiting and Bernice Claire.

What Wouldn't I Do for That Man? w. E. Y. Harburg, m. Jay Gorney, 1929. Introduced by Helen Morgan in (MM) *Applause* and sung again a year later, this time perched on a white piano, in (MM) *Glorifying the American Girl*. She recorded it (Victor) on a hit record coupled with "More Than You Know" (q.v.) It was also done by Annette Hanshaw, under pseudonym of Gay Ellis (Harmony); and by the Charleston Chasers, featuring Eva Taylor [vocal] and Clarence Williams [piano] (Columbia).

What Would You Do? w/m Richard Adler and Jerry Ross, 1952. Recorded by Rosemary Clooney (Columbia).

What Would You Do? w. Leo Robin, m. Richard A. Whiting, 1932. Introduced by Maurice Chevalier in (MM) *One Hour with You*, and recorded by him (Victor).

What You Gave Me. w/m Nicholas Ashford and Valerie Simpson, 1969. Recorded by Marvin Gaye and Tammi Terrell (Tamla).

What You Get Is What You See. w/m Terry Britten and Graham Lyle, 1987. British song recorded by Tina Turner (Capitol).

What You Goin' to Do When the Rent Comes 'Round? (or, **Rufus Rastus Johnson Brown**). w. Andrew B. Sterling, m. Harry Von Tilzer, 1905. First recorded by Arthur Collins (Columbia). Later featured and recorded by Jimmy Durante and Eddie Jackson (MGM) and Beatrice Kay (Columbia).

What You Need. w/m Andrew Farriss and Michael Hutchence, 1986. Top 10 record by the Australian sextet INXS (Atlantic).

What You Won't Do for Love. w/m Bobby Caldwell and Alfons Kettner, 1979. Top 10 record by Bobby Caldwell (Clouds).

Wheel in the Sky. w/m Robert Fleischman, Neal Schon, and Diane Valory, 1978. Recorded by the group Journey (Columbia).

Wheel of Fortune. w/m Bennie Benjamin and George David Weiss, 1952. Kay Starr had a million-selling record (Capitol). Other hit versions by Bobby Wayne (London), The Bell Sisters (RCA Victor), Eddie Wilcox Orchestra with Sunny Gale (Derby).

Wheel of Hurt, The. w/m Charles Singleton and Eddie Snyder, 1966. Top 40 record by Margaret Whiting (London); chart version by Al Martino (Capitol).

Wheels. w/m Dave Loggins, 1987. #1 Country chart record by the quintet Restless Heart (RCA).

Wheels. w/m Jimmy Torres and Richard Stephens, 1961. Introduced and recorded by the instrumental quintet, The String-a-Longs, two of whom were the writers (Warwick). Popular instrumental also by Billy Vaughn and his Orchestra (Dot).

When. w/m Paul Evans and Jack Reardon, 1958. Hit record by The Kalin Twins, arranged and conducted by Jack Pleis (Decca). The song became a #1 hit in England, France, Italy, Germany, the Benelux and Scandinavian countries, and Australia, with many recordings. Revived with Country chart hit by Slim Whitman (Cleveland International), 1980.

When. w. Bob Schafer and Andy Razaf, m. J. C. Johnson, 1928. Paul Whiteman's Orchestra, with Bix Beiderbecke and the Rhythm Boys featured, had a popular recording (Victor).

When a Fellah Has Turned Sixteen. w/m E. W. Rogers, 1898.

When a Fellow's on the Level with a Girl's That on the Square. w/m George M. Cohan, 1907. Introduced by Victor Moore in (TM) *The Talk of New York*.

When a Gypsy Makes His Violin Cry. w. Dick Smith, Frank Winegar, and Jimmy Rogan, m. Emery Deutsch, 1935. Introduced, featured on radio, in theaters and hotels, recorded (Majestic), and used as a theme song by Emery Deutsch and his Orchestra. Enric Madriguera and his Orchestra (Victor) and the Pickens Sisters (Columbia) also had well-received recordings.

When a Lady Meets a Gentleman Down South. w/m Michael Cleary, Jacques Krakeur, and David Oppenheim, 1936. Recorded by Ted Weems and his Orchestra (Decca); Benny Goodman, vocal by Helen Ward; Lee Wiley (Coral).

When Alexander Takes His Ragtime Band to France. w. Alfred Bryan and Edgar Leslie, m. Cliff Hess, 1918. World War I song featured and recorded by Marion Harris (Victor).

When a Maid Comes Knocking at Your Heart. w. Otto Harbach, m. Rudolf Friml, 1912. Introduced in (TM) *The Firefly* by Emma Trentini. Jeanette MacDonald sang it in the film version (MM) *The Firefly*, 1937.

When a Man (Woman) Loves a Woman (Man). w/m Calvin H. Lewis and Andrew Wright, 1966. #1 gold record by Percy Sledge (Atlantic). Female lyric chart records by Esther Phillips (Atlantic), 1966, and Bette Midler (Atlantic), 1980. Midler sang it in (MM) *The Rose*, 1979.

When a Prince of a Fella Meets a Cinderella. w. Manny Kurtz, m. James Van Heusen, 1938. Recorded by the bands of Bunny Berigan (Victor); Kay Kyser, vocal by Harry Babbitt; Gray Gordon, vocal by Cliff Grass (Vocalion).

When a Woman Loves a Man. w. Johnny Mercer, m. Bernard Hanighen and Gordon Jenkins, 1934. The definitive recording was made by Billie Holiday (Vocalion), 1938. Among later interpretations were those by pianist Beryl Booker (MGM) and singer Julia Lee (Capitol).

When a Woman Loves a Man. w. Billy Rose, m. Ralph Rainger, 1930. Introduced by Fanny Brice in (MM) *Be Yourself*. Brice's recording (Victor) was coupled with "Cooking Breakfast for the One I Love" (q.v.) from the same film. Two other recordings, Libby Holman with Roger Wolfe Kahn's Orchestra (Brunswick), and Annette Hanshaw (Okeh), had the same couplings.

When Big Profundo Sang Low "C". w. Marion T. Bohannon, m. George Botsford, 1921.

When Buddha Smiles. w. Arthur Freed, m. Nacio Herb Brown, 1921. The first hit for this team. Paul Whiteman had a big-selling record (Victor).

When Day Is Done. w. B. G. DeSylva, m. Robert Katscher, 1926. German song, originally titled "Madonna, Du Bist Schöner als der Sonnenschein!" with lyrics by Katscher. Introduced in the U.S. by Paul Whiteman and his Orchestra on a 12″ record (Victor). A favorite standard with singers and musicians in all categories. Among the host of recordings are those by organists Jesse Crawford (Victor) and Lew White (Brunswick); singers Mildred Bailey (Vocalion), Dennis Day (Capitol), Arthur Tracy (London), Jack Fulton (Decca); bands of Henry Busse, who used it as his theme (Decca), and Coleman Hawkins (Bluebird).

When de Moon Comes Up Behind de Hill. w/m Paul Dresser, 1900.

When Did I Fall in Love? w. Sheldon Harnick, m. Jerry Bock, 1959. Introduced by Ellen Hanley in (TM) *Fiorello!*

When Did You Leave Heaven? w. Walter Bullock, m. Richard A. Whiting, 1936. Introduced by Tony Martin and Alice Faye in (MM) *Sing, Baby, Sing* and recorded by Martin (Decca). Featured and recorded by Ben Bernie and "all the lads" (Decca) and Charlie Barnet

and his Orchestra (Bluebird). Nominated for Academy Award.

When Doves Cry. w/m Prince Rogers Nelson, 1984. Introduced in (MM) *Purple Rain* by Prince. The #1 platinum single and the #1 platinum album, "Purple Rain" by Prince, became the top-sellers of the year (Warner Bros.).

Whenever a Teenager Cries. w/m Ernie Maresca, 1965. Recorded by Reparata and The Delrons (World Artists).

Whenever He Holds You (a.k.a. **Whenever She Holds You).** w/m Bobby Goldsboro, 1964. Introduced and hit record by Bobby Goldsboro (United Artists). Recorded by Patty Duke as "Whenever She Holds You" (United Artists), 1966.

Whenever I Call You "Friend." w/m Melissa Manchester and Kenny Loggins, 1978. Top 10 record by Kenny Loggins, vocal harmony by Stevie Nicks (Columbia).

Whenever You're Away from Me. w/m John Farrar, 1980. Introduced by Olivia Newton-John and Gene Kelly in (MM) *Xanadu*.

When Francis Dances with Me. w. Ben Ryan, m. Sol Violinsky (Sol Ginsberg), 1921. Novelty recorded by Ada Jones and Billy Murray (Victor). Later version by Benay Venuta (Mercury). Interpolated in (MM) *Give My Regards to Broadway*, starring Dan Dailey, 1948.

When Hearts Are Young. w. Cyrus Wood, m. Sigmund Romberg and Al Goodman, 1922. Interpolated in and sung by Wilda Bennett in (TM) *The Lady in Ermine*. It was recorded by Paul Whiteman and his Orchestra (Victor) and the Joseph C. Smith Orchestra (Brunswick).

When He Comes Home to Me. w. Leo Robin, m. Sam Coslow, 1934. Sung by Helen Morgan in (MP) *You Belong to Me*.

When He Touches Me (Nothing Else Matters). w/m Carolyn Varga, 1969. Recorded by Peaches and Herb (Date).

When I Die. w/m Steve Kennedy and William Smith, 1969. Top 20 record by the Canadian quartet Motherlode (Buddah).

When I Die Just Let Me Go to Texas. w/m Bobby Borchers, Ed Bruce, and Patsy Bruce, 1977. Hit Country record by Tanya Tucker (MCA).

When I Dream. w/m V. Stephenson, 1979. First recorded by Jack Clement (Epic), 1978. Top 10 Country and Pop crossover record by Crystal Gayle (United Artists).

When I Dream in the Gloaming of You. w/m Herbert Ingraham, 1909. Leading records by Walter Van Brunt (Victor) and Harry Tally (Columbia).

When I Fall in Love. w. Edward Heyman, m. Victor Young, 1952. From (MP) *One Minute to Zero*. Top 20 record by Doris Day (Columbia), followed by Nat "King" Cole (Capitol) and Jeri Southern (Decca). Revived via hit record by The Lettermen (Capitol), 1962.

When I Fall in Love. w/m Albert Selden, 1948. Introduced in (TM) *Small Wonder* by Marilyn Day.

When I Get Back Again to Bonnie Scotland. w/m Harry Lauder, 1908. Featured and recorded by Scottish star Harry Lauder (Victor).

When I Get Back to the U.S.A. w/m Irving Berlin, 1915. From the musical (TM) *Stop! Look! Listen!* Recorded by Billy Murray (Victor).

When I Get Through with You (You'll Love Me Too). w/m Harlan Howard, 1962. Popularized by Patsy Cline (Decca).

When I Get You Alone Tonight. w. Joseph McCarthy and Joe Goodwin, m. Fred Fisher, 1912. Popular record by Ada Jones and Walter Van Brunt (Columbia).

When I Go A-Dreamin'. w. Bickley Reichner, m. Clay Boland, 1938. Recorded by Benny Goodman, vocal by Martha Tilton (Victor); Kay Kyser, vocal by Harry Babbit (Victor); Jan Savitt (Bluebird); Dick Todd (Victor).

When I Go on the Stage. w. Lorenz Hart, m. Richard Rodgers, 1928. Introduced by Beatrice Lillie in (TM) *She's My Baby*.

When I Grow Too Old to Dream. w. Oscar Hammerstein II, m. Sigmund Romberg, 1935. Sung by Evelyn Laye and Ramon Novarro in (MM) *The Night Is Young*. José Ferrer sang it as Romberg in his film biography (MM) *Deep in My Heart*, 1954. One of Romberg's most recorded songs, done by such varied artists as: Glen Gray and The Casa Loma Orchestra, vocal by Kenny Sargent (Decca); Irene Dunne (Brunswick); Nelson Eddy (Victor); Robert Merrill and Dorothy Kirsten (Victor); Allan Jones (Victor); Rose Murphy (Majestic); Jane Pickens (Columbia). Also by the orchestras of Al Goodman (Columbia); George Hall, vocal by Sonny Schuyler (Bluebird); Jerry Jerome (Asch); Arnett Cobb (Apollo, Parts 1 & 2); Lt. Bob Crosby (V-Disc). Revived by Nat "King" Cole (Capitol), 1951, and Ed Townsend (Capitol), 1958.

When I Grow Up. w. Edward Heyman, m. Ray Henderson, 1935. Sung by Shirley Temple in (MM) *Curly Top*.

When I Grow Up (to Be a Man). w/m Brian Wilson, 1964. Top 10 record by The Beach Boys (Capitol).

When I Leave the World Behind. w/m Irving Berlin, 1915. Henry Burr popularized the song with his recording (Victor). Revived by Bob Chester, vocal by Dolores O'Neill (Bluebird), 1940.

When I Look at You. w. Paul Francis Webster, m. Walter Jurmann, 1943. Introduced by Judy Garland in (MM) *Presenting Lily Mars*.

When I Look in Your Eyes. w/m Leslie Bricusse, 1967. Introduced by Rex Harrison in (MM) *Doctor Doolittle*.

When I Lost You. w/m Irving Berlin, 1912. Berlin wrote this ballad after the death of his young bride, who died shortly after their honeymoon. It had a tremendous sheet music sale and remains one of Berlin's most moving songs. Henry Burr had a successful record (Victor).

When I'm Away from You. w/m Frankie Miller, 1983. #1 Country chart record by The Bellamy Brothers (Elektra).

When I'm Away from You, Dear. w/m Paul Dresser, 1904.

When I'm Gone. w/m William Robinson, 1965. Recorded by Brenda Holloway (Tamla).

When I'm Gone I Won't Forget. w. Ivan Reid, m. Peter DeRose, 1920.

When I'm Gone You'll Soon Forget. w/m E. Austin Keith, 1920.

When I'm Looking at You. w. Clifford Grey, m. Herbert Stothart, 1930. Sung by Lawrence Tibbett in (MM) *The Rogue Song*.

When I'm Not Near the Girl I Love. w. E. Y. Harburg, m. Burton Lane, 1947. Introduced by David Wayne in (TM) *Finian's Rainbow*. Tommy Steele sang it in (MM) *Finian's Rainbow*, 1968.

When I'm 64. w/m John Lennon and Paul McCartney, 1967. Introduced by The Beatles in their album "Sgt. Pepper's Lonely Hearts Club Band" (Capitol). They sang it in their animated cartoon film (MM) *Yellow Submarine*, 1968. Revived by Sandy Farina in (MM) *Sgt. Pepper's Lonely Hearts Club Band*, 1978.

When I'm the President. w/m Al Sherman and Al Lewis, 1931. Introduced and featured by Eddie Cantor on his radio show. It was during this "campaign" that the musical cry of "We Want Cantor" started, based on the root tones of the I VI II V chords.

When I'm with You. w. Mack Gordon, m. Harry Revel, 1936. Introduced by Tony Martin in an unbilled spot as a radio singer, followed by Shirley Temple with a different set of lyrics to sing to her father and later reprised by Alice Faye in (MM) *Poor Little Rich Girl*. Most popular recording by Ray Noble and his Orchestra, vocal by Al Bowlly (Victor).

When I'm Wrong. w/m B. B. King, 1976. R&B hit by B. B. King (ABC).

When I Need You. w. Carole Bayer Sager, m. Albert Hammond, 1977. #1 single from the album "Endless Flight," by Leo Sayer (Warner Bros.).

When in Rome (I Do As the Romans Do). w. Carolyn Leigh, m. Cy Coleman, 1964. Introduced and recorded by Barbra Streisand (Columbia).

When Irish Eyes Are Smiling. w. Chauncey Olcott and George Graff, Jr., m. Ernest R. Ball, 1912. Composer Ball dedicated the song to his wife, actress Maude Lambert. Olcott introduced it in (TM) *The Isle o' Dreams*. Leading recordings by Chauncey Olcott (Columbia) and Harry MacDonough (Victor). Dick Haymes sang it in the role of the composer in (MM) *Irish Eyes Are Smiling*, 1944; Dennis Morgan, as Chauncey Olcott, sang it in (MM) *My Wild Irish Rose*, 1947.

When I See an Elephant Fly. w. Ned Washington, m. Oliver Wallace, 1941. Sung by Cliff Edwards, as the voice of The Crow, on the soundtrack of the full-length movie cartoon (MM) *Dumbo*. Jane Froman recorded it (Columbia).

When I See You Smile. w/m Diane Warren, 1989. Hit record by the group Bad English (Epic).

When Is Sometime? w. Johnny Burke, m. James Van Heusen, 1949. Introduced by Rhonda Fleming in (MM) *A Connecticut Yankee in King Arthur's Court*.

When I Take My Sugar to Tea. w/m Sammy Fain, Irving Kahal, and Pierre Norman Connor, 1931. Successful records by Glen Gray and the Casa Loma Orchestra, vocal by Pee Wee Hunt (Brunswick); Bert Lown and his Orchestra (Victor); the Melotone Boys, featuring Joe Mooney (Melotone). Later recordings by the King Cole Trio (Capitol), Don Cornell (Victor), Billy May's band (Capitol). The song was heard in (MP) *Monkey Business*, 1931, and in (MP) *The Mating Game*, 1951.

When I Think of You. w/m James Harris III, Terry Lewis, and Janet Jackson, 1986. #1 record by Janet Jackson (A&M).

When It's All Goin' Out, and Nothin' Comin' In. w/m Bert Williams and George Walker, 1902. Interpolated into (TM) *Sally in Our Alley*.

When It's Apple Blossom Time in Normandy. w/m Harry Gifford, Tom Mellor, and Huntley Trevor, 1912. Melody based on Beethoven's *Minuet in G*, it was introduced by Nora Bayes in the Broadway production (TM) *Roly Poly*. Popular recordings by Edna Brown (pseudonym for Elsie Baker) and James F. Harrison (Columbia), and Harry Mac-Donough and Marguerite Dunlap (Victor). Sung by Ann Sheridan and Dennis Morgan in (MM) *Shine On, Harvest Moon*, the film biography of Nora Bayes, 1944.

When It's Lamp Lightin' Time in the Valley. w/m Joe Lyons, Sam C. Hart, Herald Goodman, Dean Upoon, and Curt Poulton, 1933. Popular records by Singin' Sam (Melotone), Tex Ritter (Decca).

When It's Love. w/m Alex Van Halen, Eddie Van Halen, Sammy Hagar, and Michael Anthony, 1988. Chart single by the group Van Halen (Warner Bros.).

When It's Moonlight on the Prairie. w. Robert F. Roden, m. S. R. Henry, 1908. Popular with vaudeville performers. Leading record by The Haydn Quartet (Victor).

When It's Nightime Down in Burgundy. w. Alfred Bryan, m. Herman Paley, 1914.

When It's Night Time in Dixie Land. w/m Irving Berlin, 1914.

When It's Night Time in Italy, It's Wednesday over Here. w/m James Kendis and Lew Brown, 1924. Introduced by Jimmy Kendis on radio. Featured and recorded by Lew Holtz and his Orchestra (Victor).

When It's Round-Up Time in Heaven. w/m Jimmie Davis, 1936. One of the early song successes of the Country and Western singing star and future governor of Louisiana, Jimmie Davis.

When It's Sleepy Time Down South. w/m Leon René, Otis René, and Clarence Muse, 1931. Among the early hit records of this standard were those by Louis Armstrong (Okeh) and Paul Whiteman (Victor). The song became associated with Armstrong, who used it as his theme song and recorded it again (Decca).

When It's Springtime in Alaska. w/m Tillman Franks, 1959. C&W hit by Johnny Horton (Columbia).

When It's Springtime in the Rockies. w. Mary Hale Woolsey and Milton Taggert, m. Robert Sauer, 1930. Featured and recorded by Gene and Glenn (Columbia), Ben Selvin (Columbia), Carson Robison (Perfect), organist Lew White (Brunswick), Roy Smeck (Regal). The song was not used in the film based on its title.

When I Waltz With You. w. Alfred Bryan, m. Albert Gumble, 1912. Popular record by Helen Clark (Victor).

When I Wanted You. w/m Gino Cunico, 1980. Recorded by Barry Manilow (Arista).

When I Was a Little Cuckoo. w/m Cole Porter, 1944. Comedy number written for and performed by Beatrice Lillie in (TM) *Seven Lively Arts*.

When I Was Twenty-One and You Were Sweet Sixteen. w. Harry H. Williams, m. Egbert Van Alstyne, 1911.

When I Was Young. w/m Eric Burdon, Victor Briggs, Barry Jenkins, Danny McCulloch, John Weider, 1967. Hit U.S. record by the British group The Animals (MGM).

When Julie Comes Around. w/m Lee Pockriss and Paul Vance, 1970. Chart record by The Cuff Links (Decca).

When Kate and I Were Comin' Thro' the Rye. w. Andrew B. Sterling, m. Harry Von Tilzer, 1902. Ballad popularized via vaudeville performances and recording by Harry MacDonough (Victor).

When Kentucky Bids the World "Good Morning." w. Edgar Leslie, m. Mabel Wayne, 1930. Popular record by Red Nichols (Brunswick).

When Lights Are Low. w. Spencer Williams, m. Benny Carter, 1936. Introduced and recorded by Benny Carter and his Band in England, vocal by Elizabeth Welch (Br. Decca). Lionel Hampton recorded it (Victor). The song's popularity was greatly helped by George Shearing's recording (MGM), as it was coupled with the pianist's big hit "Lullaby of Birdland" (q.v.).

When Lights Are Low. w. Gus Kahn and Ted Koehler, m. Ted Fio Rito, 1923. Introduced by Ted Fio Rito and his Orchestra.

When Liking Turns to Loving. w/m Kenny Young and Jay Fishman, 1966. Top 20 hit by Ronnie Dove (Diamond).

When Love Beckoned. w/m Cole Porter, 1939. Introduced by Ethel Merman in (TM) *DuBarry Was a Lady*. Recorded by Leo Reisman, vocal by Gertrude Niesen (Victor) and Artie Shaw and Band (Bluebird).

When Love Comes Swinging Along. w. Ted Koehler, m. Ray Henderson, 1934. Introduced by Harry Richman and Lillian Emerson in (TM) *Say When*. Richman recorded it (Columbia), as did Victor Young's Orchestra, vocal by Al Bowlly (Decca), and Richard Himber, vocal by Joey Nash (Victor).

When Love Goes Wrong. w. Harold Adamson, m. Hoagy Carmichael, 1953. Introduced by Marilyn Monroe and Jane Russell in (MM) *Gentlemen Prefer Blondes*.

When Love Is Young in Springtime. w. Rida Johnson Young, m. Melville Ellis, 1906.

When Love Knocks at Your Heart. w/m Billy Hill and Peter DeRose, 1935. Among recordings are the bands of: Jan Garber, vocal by Lee Bennett (Victor); Teddy Hill, vocal by Bill Dillard (Melotone); Freddy Martin

(Brunswick); Victor Young, vocal by Jimmy Ray (Decca).

When Mabel Comes in the Room. w/m Jerry Herman, 1975. Introduced by Stanley Simmonds in (TM) *Mack and Mabel*.

When Mexican Joe Met Jole Blon. w/m Sheb Wooley, 1953. Hank Snow recorded this follow-up to Jim Reeves's hit "Mexican Joe" (q.v.) (RCA Victor).

When Mr. Shakespeare Comes to Town. w. William Jerome, m. Jean Schwartz, 1901. Comedy song from (TM) *Hoity Toity*. Recorded by Dan Quinn (Edison).

When My Baby Smiles at Me. w. Andrew B. Sterling and Ted Lewis, m. Bill Munro, 1920. Introduced by Ted Lewis, with his band in (TM) *Greenwich Village Follies of 1919*, and recorded by them (Columbia) that same year with sales reaching the hit level in 1920. It was associated with Lewis for his entire career and became his theme song. The Ritz Brothers sang it in (MM) *Sing, Baby, Sing*, 1936. It was the title song of (MM) *When My Baby Smiles at Me*, 1949, sung by Dan Dailey. It was also heard in (MP) *Hold That Ghost*, starring Abbott and Costello in 1941, and (MM) *Behind the Eight Ball*, 1942.

When My Blue Moon Turns to Gold Again. w/m Wiley Walker and Gene Sullivan, 1941. Popular recordings by Gene Autry (Okeh) and Tex Ritter (Capitol).

When My Dreamboat Comes Home. w/m Cliff Friend and Dave Franklin, 1936. Introduced, popularized, and recorded by Guy Lombardo and his Royal Canadians, vocal by Carmen Lombardo (Victor).

When My Dreams Come True. w/m Irving Berlin, 1929. Introduced by Mary Eaton and Oscar Shaw in (MM) *The Cocoanuts* starring the Marx Brothers.

When My Little Girl Is Smiling. w/m Gerry Goffin and Carole King, 1961. Popular records by The Drifters (Atlantic) and Steve Alaimo (Entrance).

When My Man Comes Home. w. J. Mayo Williams, m. Buddy Johnson, 1944. Introduced and recorded by Buddy Johnson, vocal by Ella Johnson (Decca).

When My Ship Comes In. w. Gus Kahn, m. Walter Donaldson, 1934. Introduced by Eddie Cantor in (MM) *Kid Millions.* Cantor recorded it (Melotone) coupled with "Okay, Toots" (q.v.) from the same film. Band recordings: Mal Hallett (Melotone), George Hall (Bluebird), Emil Coleman (Columbia).

When My Sugar Walks Down the Street. w/m Gene Austin, Jimmy McHugh, and Irving Mills, 1924. Introduced by Gene Austin and recorded by him with Aileen Stanley (Victor). Featured by Phil Harris and his Orchestra in theaters and on The Jack Benny Show (radio).

When Old Bill Bailey Plays the Ukulele. w/m Charles McCarron and Nat Vincent, 1916. Featured and recorded by Nora Bayes (Victor). The Peerless Quartet had a popular record on two labels (Columbia and Victor).

When Shall I Again See Ireland? w. Henry Blossom, m. Victor Herbert, 1917. From (TM) *Eileen.*

When Shall We Meet Again? w. Raymond B. Egan, m. Richard A. Whiting, 1921. Interpolated in (TM) *Tip Top* by The Duncan Sisters.

(When She Needs Good Lovin') She Comes to Me. w/m Jerry Leiber and Mike Stoller, 1966. Recorded by The Chicago Loop (DynoVoice).

When She Was My Girl. w/m Marc Blatte and Larry Gottlieb, 1980. #1 R&B crossover record by The Four Tops (Casablanca).

When Smokey Sings. w/m Martin Fry and Mark White, 1987. A tribute to the American singer/songwriter Smokey Robinson. Top 10 chart record by the British group ABC (Mercury).

When Something Is Wrong with My Baby. w/m David Porter and Isaac Hayes, 1967. Recorded by Sam and Dave, produced by Hayes and Porter (Stax).

When Summer Is Gone. w. Charlie Harrison, m. Monte Wilhite, 1929. Introduced and recorded by Franklyn Baur (Victor). Also recorded by Meyer Davis (Brunswick), Lee Sims (Brunswick), Lou Gold (Diva); and in the late forties, by Tex Beneke's Orchestra with vocal by Garry Stevens. Song is not to be confused with Hal Kemp's theme "(Oh, How I'll Miss You) When Summer Is Gone."

When Summer Is Gone (Oh, How I'll Miss You). w/m Hal Kemp, 1937. Hal Kemp and his Orchestra used this as their closing theme on broadcasts and band engagements.

When Sunny Gets Blue. w. Jack Segal, m. Marvin Fisher, 1956. Jazz standard, with many vocal and instrumental recordings. Popularized by Johnny Mathis (Columbia).

When Sweet Marie Was Sweet Sixteen. w. Raymond Moore, m. Ernest R. Ball, 1907.

When the Angelus Is Ringing. w. Joe Young, m. Bert Grant, 1914. Recorded by The Peerless Quartet (Columbia).

When the Bees Are in the Hive. w. Alfred Bryan, m. Kerry Mills, 1904.

When the Bell in the Lighthouse Rings Ding Dong. w. Arthur J. Lamb, m. Alfred Solman, 1905.

When the Birds Have Sung Themselves to Sleep. w/m Paul Dresser, 1901.

When the Birds in Georgia Sing of Tennessee. w. Arthur J. Lamb, m. Ernest R. Ball, 1907.

When the Black Sheep Returns to the Fold. w/m Irving Berlin, 1916. Introduced by the Avon Comedy Four (Victor).

When the Bloom Is on the Sage. w/m Nat Vincent and Fred Howard Wright, 1931. Theme song of the radio series "Tom Mix and His Straight Shooters."

When the Blue Sky Turns to Gold. w/m Thurland Chattaway, 1901.

When the Boy in Your Arms (Is the Boy in Your Heart). w/m Sid Tepper and Roy C. Bennett, 1962. Top 10 record by Connie Francis (MGM).

When the Boys Come Home. w. John Hay, m. Oley Speaks, 1917.

When the Boys Talk About the Girls. w/m Bob Merrill, 1958. Popularized by Valerie Carr (Roulette).

When the Cherry Blossoms Fall. w. Stephen Ivor Szinnyey and William Cary Duncan, m. Anselm Goetzel, 1919.

When the Fog Rolls In to San Francisco. w/m Joseph Liebman, 1966. Featured and recorded by Damita Jo, coupled with "If You Go Away" (q.v.) (Epic).

When the Folks High-up Do the Mean Low-down. w/m Irving Berlin, 1931. Introduced by Bebe Daniels and Bing Crosby in (MP) *Reaching for the Moon.* This marked Crosby's film debut.

When the Going Gets Tough, the Tough Get Going. w/m Wayne Brathwaite, Barry Eastmond, Robert John "Mutt" Lange, Billy Ocean, 1985. Introduced in (MP) *Jewel of the Nile.* Top 10 record by Billy Ocean (Jive). Included in Ocean's album "Love Zone."

When the Grass Grows over Me. w/m Don Chapel, 1969. Top 10 Country chart record by George Jones (Musicor).

When the Grown-Up Ladies Act Like Babies (I've Got to Love 'Em, That's All). w. Joe Young and Edgar Leslie, m. Maurice Abrahams, 1915. Featured by Al Jolson. Leading record by Billy Murray (Victor).

When the Harvest Days Are Over, Jessie Dear. w. Howard Graham, m. Harry Von Tilzer, 1900.

When the Heart Rules the Mind. w/m Steve Hackett and Steve Howe, 1986. Recorded by the British quintet GTR, of which the writers were members (Arista).

When the Honeymoon Was Over. w/m Fred Fisher, 1921.

When the Idle Poor Become the Idle Rich. w. E. Y. Harburg, m. Burton Lane, 1947. Introduced by Ella Logan and chorus in (TM) *Finian's Rainbow.* Sung in the film version (MM) *Finian's Rainbow,* 1968, by Fred Astaire, Petula Clark, and chorus.

When the Leaves Come Tumbling Down. w/m Richard Howard, 1922. Recorded by Paul Specht and his Orchestra (Columbia).

When the Lights Go On Again (All Over the World). w/m Eddie Seiler, Sol Marcus, and Bennie Benjamin, 1942. World War II ballad of optimism featured and recorded by vocalist-bandleaders Vaughn Monroe (Victor) and Lucky Millinder (Decca).

When the Midnight Choo Choo Leaves for Alabam'. w/m Irving Berlin, 1912. Arthur Collins and Byron G. Harlan recorded the song for two labels the same year (Victor and Columbia). A recording by the Victor Military Band added to its instant popularity. It was sung by Alice Faye in (MM) *Alexander's Ragtime Band,* 1944; by Fred Astaire and Judy Garland in (MM) *Easter Parade,* 1948; by Ethel Merman, Dan Dailey, Mitzi Gaynor, and Donald O'Connor in (MM) *There's No Business Like Show Business,* 1954.

When the Mighty Organ Plays the Song of Songs for Me. w/m John Klenner, 1934. Sentimental waltz, introduced by Guy Lombardo and his Orchestra.

When the Mocking Birds Are Singing in the Wildwood. w. Arthur J. Lamb, m. H. B. Blake, 1905.

When the Moon Comes Over Madison Square. w. Johnny Burke, m. James V. Monaco, 1940. Sung by Bing Crosby in (MM) *Rhythm on the River* and on records (Decca).

When the Moon Comes Over the Mountain. w/m Howard Johnson, Harry Woods, and Kate Smith, 1931. Introduced and recorded (Clarion) (Columbia) by Kate Smith. It became her theme song for future radio shows and other appearances. She sang it in (MM) *The Big Broadcast* in 1932.

When the Morning Comes. w/m Hoyt Axton, 1971. Recorded by Hoyt Axton (A&M).

When the Morning Glories Wake Up in the Morning. w. Billy Rose, m. Fred Fisher, 1927. This song was sub-titled, "Then I'll Kiss Your Two Lips Goodbye." Recorded by Don Voorhees, vocal by Irving Kaufman, featuring trumpeter Red Nichols and trombonist Miff Mole (Columbia).

When the One You Love Loves You. w/m Cliff Friend, Paul Whiteman, and Abel Baer, 1924. Introduced and recorded by Paul Whiteman and his Orchestra (Victor).

When the Organ Played at Twilight. w. Raymond Wallace, m. Jimmy Campbell and Reg Connelly, 1930. An English song introduced in the U.S. and recorded by organist Jesse Crawford (Victor).

When the Red, Red Robin Comes Bob, Bob, Bobbin' Along. w/m Harry Woods, 1926. One of the biggest hits of the year. It was introduced by Sophie Tucker at the Woods [no relation to the composer] Theatre in Chicago and also featured in vaudeville by Lillian Roth. Among leading records: Al Jolson (Victor) and Paul Whiteman (Victor). Jolson sang it on the soundtrack for Larry Parks in (MM) *Jolson Sings Again*, 1949. It was heard in (MM) *Has Anybody Seen My Gal?* 1952, and in (MM) *I'll Cry Tomorrow*, in which Susan Hayward sang it, portraying Lillian Roth, 1955.

When There's a Breeze on Lake Louise. w. Mort Greene, m. Harry Revel, 1942. Introduced by Joan Merrill, with Freddy Martin and his Orchestra, in (MM) *The Mayor of 44th Street*. They also had a popular recording (Bluebird).

When There's No You. w/m Les Reed and Jackie Reed, 1971. A British song derived from the operatic aria, "Vesti la Giubba" from Leoncavallo's *I Pagliacci*. Recorded by Engelbert Humperdinck (Parrot).

When the Roll Is Called Up Yonder (I'll Be There). w/m James M. Black, 1893. Hymn.

When the Roses Bloom Again. w. Nat Burton, m. Walter Kent, 1942. Featured and recorded by Jimmy Dorsey, vocal by Bob Eberly (Decca).

When the Shepherd Leads the Sheep Back Home. w. Edgar Leslie, m. Harry Warren, 1931. Recorded by Guy Lombardo and the Royal Canadians (Columbia) and Paul Small, with Nat Shilkret's Orchestra (Victor).

When the Ship Comes In. w/m Bob Dylan, 1963. Introduced by Bob Dylan (Columbia). Best-selling record by Peter, Paul and Mary (Warner Bros.), 1965.

When the Snow Is on the Roses. w. Larry Kusik and Eddie Snyder (Engl.), Ernst Bader (Ger), m. James Last, 1967. German song. English version featured and recorded by Ed Ames (RCA).

When the Sun Comes Out. w. Ted Koehler, m. Harold Arlen, 1941. Jimmy Dorsey, vocal by Helen O'Connell (Decca), had an early success. Other bands to feature and record it were Benny Goodman, vocal by Helen Forrest (Columbia); Harry James (Columbia); Charlie Barnet, vocal by Bob Carroll (Bluebird); Charlie Spivak (Okeh).

When the Sun Goes Down. w/m Anonymous, 1922. Many arrangers and writers lay claim to this blues. The date is an arbitrary choice, based on some performances and recordings. It later was recorded by such diverse artists as Leroy Carr (Bluebird), Count Basie, piano solo with rhythm section (Decca), and Libby Holman with Josh White (Decca).

When the Swallows Come Back to Capistrano. w/m Leon René, 1940. Recorded by a cross-section of artists, among whom are: The Ink Spots (Decca) and Glenn Miller, vocal by Ray Eberle (Bluebird), the best-sellers; Gene Autry (Okeh); Xavier Cugat, vocal by Dinah Shore (Victor); Gene Krupa, vocal by Howard DuLany (Columbia); Guy Lombardo, vocal by Carmen Lombardo (Decca); Ray Herbeck and his Orchestra (Vocalion); later, Billy May and his Band (Capitol).

When the Wind Was Green. w/m Don Hunt, 1950. Leading records by Dick Haymes (Decca), David Rose and his Orchestra (MGM), Hugo Winterhalter and his Orchestra (Columbia). It was heard in (MM) *When You're Smiling*, 1950.

When the World Was Young (Ah, the Apple Trees). w. Johnny Mercer (Engl.), Angela Vannier (Fr.), m. M. Philippe-Gerard, 1950. Original French title "Le Chevalier de Paris (Les Pommiers Doux)." First U.S. recording by Peggy Lee (Capitol).

When They Ask About You. w/m Sam H. Stept, 1943. Jimmy Dorsey, vocal by Kitty Kallen, had a Top 10 record (Decca). It was then heard in (MM) *Stars on Parade*, 1944.

When They Played the Polka. w. Lou Holzer, m. Fabian André, 1938. Introduced and recorded by Horace Heidt, vocal by the King Sisters (Brunswick). Also recorded by Freddie "Schnicklefritz" Fisher and his Band (Decca).

When Tomorrow Comes. w. Irving Kahal, m. Sammy Fain, 1934. From the film (MP) *Mandalay*. Recorded by Freddy Martin's (Brunswick) and Enoch Light's (Bluebird) orchestras.

When Twilight Comes. w/m Peter DeRose and Billy Hill, 1938. Records: Jan Savitt, vocal by Carlotta Dale (Bluebird); Will Osborne and his Orchestra (Decca).

When Two Worlds Collide. w/m Roger Miller and Bill Anderson, 1962. Country hit by Roger Miller (RCA).

When Uncle Joe Plays a Rag on His Old Banjo. w/m Theodore F. Morse, 1912. Recorded by Arthur Collins (Victor).

When We Get Married. w/m Donald Hogan, 1961. Hit record by The Dreamlovers (Heritage). Later chart versions by The Intruders (Gamble), 1970, and Larry Graham (Warner Bros.), 1980.

When We Make Love. w/m Troy Seals and Mentor Williams, 1984. #1 Country chart and Pop crossover record by the quartet Alabama (RCA).

When We're Alone. See **Penthouse Serenade**.

When We Were a Couple of Kids. See **School Days**.

When Will I Be Loved? w/m Phil Everly, 1960, 1975. Top 10 record by The Everly Brothers (Cadence). Linda Ronstadt had a hit C&W/Pop version (Capitol), 1975.

When Will I See You Again? w/m Kenny Gamble and Leon Huff, 1974. R&B/Pop gold record by The Three Degrees (Philadelphia International).

When Winter Comes. w/m Irving Berlin, 1939. Introduced by Sonja Henie and Rudy Vallee in (MM) *Second Fiddle*. Recordings by the bands of: Vallee (Decca); Artie Shaw (Bluebird); Hal Kemp, vocal by Nan Wynn (Victor); Frankie Masters (Vocalion).

When Yankee Doodle Learns to Parlez-Vous Francais. w. Will Hart, m. Ed G. Nelson, 1917. World War I novelty sung by Elsie Janis and recorded by Arthur Fields (Columbia).

When You Ain't Got No More Money, Well, You Needn't Come 'Round. w. Clarence S. Brewster, m. A. Baldwin Sloane, 1898.

When You and I Were Seventeen. w. Gus Kahn, m. Charles Rosoff, 1924. Popularized by Ruth Etting in vaudeville and by Marion Harris on records (Brunswick).

When You and I Were Young, Maggie, Blues. w/m Jack Frost and Jimmy McHugh, 1923, 1951. As sung in the lyrics, "Now that Maggie tune, is a raggie tune," this was a jazz derivation of the 1866 song by J. A. Butterfield and George Johnson, "When You and I Were Young, Maggie," and first popularized by Van and Schenk in vaudeville and on records (Columbia), 1923. It was revived with hit records by Bing and Gary Crosby (Decca) and Margaret Whiting and Jimmy Wakely (Capitol) in 1951.

When You Close Your Eyes. w/m Jack Blades, Alan Fitzgerald, and Brad Gillis, 1984. Recorded by the quintet, Night Ranger (MCA/Camel).

When You Come Back. w/m George M. Cohan, 1918. It is included here only to note that it was written as a sequel to Cohan's tremendous hit "Over There." The song attained little popularity.

When You Come Back They'll Wonder Who the ———— You Are. w/m Paul Dresser, 1902. Song was commentary on the complacency of the public after the Spanish-American War.

When You Dance. w/m Andrew Jones and Leroy Kirkland, 1955. Introduced and recorded by the R&B group The Turbans (Herald). Revived in 1969 by Jay and The Americans (United Artists).

When You Dream About Hawaii. w. Bert Kalmar and Sid Silvers, m. Harry Ruby, 1937. Featured and recorded by Bing Crosby (Decca).

When You First Kiss the Last Girl You Loved. w. Will M. Hough and Frank R. Adams, m. Joseph E. Howard, 1909. From (TM) *A Stubborn Cinderella*.

When You Hear Love's Hello. w. E. Ray Goetz, m. Louis A. Hirsch, 1911. From (TM) *Vera Violetta*.

When You Hear the Time Signal. w. Johnny Mercer, m. Victor Schertzinger, 1942. Mercer's title emanates from the radio announcers' phrase to preface the giving of the correct time. Introduced by Dorothy Lamour in (MM) *The Fleet's In*.

When You Know You're Not Forgotten by the Girl You Can't Forget. w. Ed. Gardenier, m. J. Fred Helf, 1906.

When You Leave, Don't Slam the Door. w/m Joe Allison, 1946. Popular C&W record by Tex Ritter (Capitol).

When You Look in the Heart of a Rose. w. Marian Gillespie, m. Florence Methuen, 1919. Popularized via recordings by John McCormack (Victor) and Charles Harrison (Columbia).

When You Play in the Game of Love. w. Joe Goodwin, m. Al Piantadosi, 1913.

When You're All Dressed Up and No Place to Go. w. Benjamin Hopgood, m. Silvio Hein, 1914. From (TM) *The Beauty Shop*.

When You're a Long, Long Way from Home. w. Sam M. Lewis, m. George W. Meyer, 1914.

When You're Away. w. Henry Blossom, m. Victor Herbert, 1914. One of Herbert's more popular waltzes, introduced by Wilda Bennett in (TM) *The Only Girl*.

When You're Away. w. A. Seymour Brown and Joe Young, m. Bert Grant, 1911.

When You're Down in Louisville (Call on Me). w/m Irving Berlin, 1916. Featured in vaudeville by Belle Baker and Nora Bayes. Leading record by Anna Chandler (Columbia).

When You're Hot, You're Hot. w/m Jerry Reed, 1971. Crossover (Country/Pop) hit record by Jerry Reed (RCA).

When You're in Love. w. Johnny Mercer, m. Gene De Paul, 1954. Introduced by Jane Powell and Howard Keel in (MM) *Seven Brides for Seven Brothers*.

When You're in Love with a Beautiful Woman. w/m Even Stevens, 1979. Top 10 gold record by the group Dr. Hook (Capitol).

When You're in Love with Someone (Who Is Not in Love with You). w. Grant Clarke, m. Al Piantadosi, 1916. Popular records by Henry Burr and Miriam [pseudonym for Helen] Clark (Columbia), and Charles Harrison (Victor).

When You're in Town. w/m Irving Berlin, 1911. From (TM) *A Real Girl*, which closed in its pre-Broadway tryout. Popular record by Henry Burr and Elise Stevenson (Victor).

When You're over Sixty, and You Feel Like Sweet Sixteen. w/m Little Jack Little, Dave Oppenheim, and Ira Schuster, 1933. Introduced and featured on radio by Little Jack Little.

When You're Smiling (the Whole World Smiles with You). w/m Mark Fisher, Joe Goodwin, and Larry Shay, 1928. Louis Armstrong's recording (Okeh) helped establish this standard. Among the many other disc preservations were those by King Oliver (Victor), Cab Calloway (Brunswick), Teddy Wilson (Brunswick), Clyde McCoy (Mercury), Skitch Henderson (Capitol). It was the title song for (MM) *When You're Smiling*, 1950, and was sung by Frank Sinatra in (MM) *Meet Danny Wilson*, 1952.

When You're Wearing the Ball and Chain. w. Harry B. Smith, m. Victor Herbert, 1914. From (TM) *The Only Girl*.

When You're Young and in Love. w/m Van McCoy, 1964. Hit record by Ruby and The Romantics (Kapp), followed by The Marvelettes (Tamla), 1967.

When Your Hair Has Turned to Silver (I Will Love You Just the Same). w. Charles Tobias, m. Peter DeRose, 1930. Popular song on radio. Leading recording by "Bud and Joe Billings," pseudonyms for Frank Luther and Carson Robison (Victor).

When Your Heart Is Weak. w/m Peter Kingsbery, 1989. Recorded by the quartet Cock Robin (Columbia).

When Your Love Grows Cold. w/m Charles Miller, 1895.

When Your Lover Has Gone. w/m E. A. Swan, 1931. Featured and recorded by Louis Armstrong (Okeh), Bert Lown (Victor), Johnny Walker [studio band led by Benny Goodman] (Columbia), Harry Richman (Brunswick). Among later releases: Roy Eldridge (Mercury), Frank Sinatra (Columbia), Stan Kenton (Capitol), George Shearing (MGM).

When You Say Nothing At All. w/m Paul Overstreet and Don Schlitz, 1988. #1 Country chart record by Keith Whitley (RCA).

When You've Got a Little Springtime in Your Heart. w/m Harry Woods, 1935. Introduced by Jessie Matthews in the British film (MM) *Evergreen*, from which she recorded a medley of songs (Columbia Br.).

When You've Had a Little Love You Want a Little More. w. Arthur Lamb, m. John T. Hall, 1912.

When You Walked Out, Someone Else Walked Right In. w/m Irving Berlin, 1923. Introduced, featured, and recorded by Frank Crumit (Columbia). Popular instrumental version by Isham Jones and his Orchestra (Brunswick).

When You Want 'Em, You Can't Get 'Em (When You Got 'Em, You Don't Want 'Em). w. Murray Roth, m. George Gershwin, 1916. Gershwin's first published song, written while he was working as a song demonstrator for the Jerome Remick publishing company. They did not publish it, however, making it clear that Gershwin was paid to play piano, not compose. Harry Von Tilzer's firm published it and gave him a five-dollar advance. The sheet music royalties did not equal the advance.

When You Were Mine. w/m Prince Rogers Nelson, 1983. Introduced by Prince on his album "Dirty Mind," 1980. Chart record by Mitch Ryder (Riva), 1983.

When You Were Sweet Sixteen. w/m James Thornton, 1898. Thornton's last success, which became a perennial barber-shop quartet favorite.

When You Wish Upon a Star. w. Ned Washington, m. Leigh Harline, 1940. Sung on the soundtrack by Cliff Edwards as "Jiminy Cricket," in the Walt Disney feature-length cartoon (MM) *Pinocchio*. Academy Award winning song. Revised by Ringo Starr in his album "Stay Awake" (A&M), 1988.

When You Wore a Pinafore. w. Edward Madden, m. Theodore F. Morse, 1908.

When You Wore a Tulip and I Wore a Big Red Rose. w. Jack Mahoney, m. Percy

Wenrich, 1914, 1942. An immediate hit in vaudeville and recorded by the American Quartette (Victor). In 1942, Gene Kelly and Judy Garland sang it in (MM) *For Me and My Gal*. Their Decca record, with the film title song on the other side, was one of the biggest selling records of the year. The song was used in an ice skating medley in (MM) *Hello, Frisco, Hello*, 1943, and also interpolated in (MM) *The Merry Monahans*, 1944, and (MM) *Has Anybody Seen My Gal?*, 1952.

When Yuba Plays the Rhumba on the Tuba. w/m Herman Hupfeld, 1931. Introduced by Walter O'Keefe in (TM) *The Third Little Show*. Featured and recorded by Rudy Vallee (Victor).

Where, Oh Where? w/m Cole Porter, 1950. Waltz, introduced by Barbara Ashley in (TM) *Out of This World*.

Where Am I? w. Al Dubin, m. Harry Warren, 1935. Introduced by James Melton who with Jane Froman made their film debuts in (MM) *Stars Over Broadway*. Melton (Victor), Ray Noble and his Orchestra (Victor), and Little Jack Little (Columbia) made recordings.

Where Am I Going? w. Dorothy Fields, m. Cy Coleman, 1966. Introduced by Gwen Verdon in (TM) *Sweet Charity*. Popular record by Barbra Streisand (Columbia). Sung by Shirley MacLaine in (MM) *Sweet Charity*, 1969.

Where Are the Friends of Other Days? w/m Paul Dresser, 1903.

Where Are You? w. Harold Adamson, m. Jimmy McHugh, 1937. Introduced in (MM) *Top of the Town* and on records (Brunswick) by Gertrude Niesen. Many recordings of the hit song of the film, among which were those by: Tommy Dorsey, vocal by Jack Leonard (Victor); Connie Boswell, with Ben Pollack's Orchestra (Decca); Bunny Berigan (Brunswick); Barry Wood (Variety); Will Osborne (Decca). Les Brown and his Band revived it in 1948 (Columbia).

Where Are You Going. w. Danny Meehan, m. Bobby Scott, 1970. Sung on the soundtrack of (MP) *Joe* and on records by Jerry Butler (Mercury).

Where Can I Go Without You? w. Peggy Lee, m. Victor Young, 1954. Recorded by Peggy Lee, with Victor Young's Orchestra (Decca).

Where Did I Go Wrong. w/m Bill La Bounty and Steve Wariner, 1989. Hit Country single by Steve Wariner (MCA).

Where Did Our Love Go. w/m Brian Holland, Eddie Holland, and Lamont Dozier, 1964. Recorded by The Supremes, for their first #1 record (Motown). Revived by Donnie Elbert (All Platinum), 1971; The J. Geils Band (Atlantic), 1976.

Where Did Robinson Crusoe Go with Friday on Saturday Night? w. Sam M. Lewis and Joe Young, m. George W. Meyer, 1916. Introduced by Al Jolson in (TM) *Robinson Crusoe, Jr.*, and also recorded by him (Victor).

Where Did the Good Times Go? w/m Richard M. Sherman and Robert B. Sherman, 1974. Introduced by Patty Andrews in (TM) *Over Here*.

Where Did the Night Go? w/m Harold Rome, 1952. Introduced by Jack Cassidy and Patricia Marand in (TM) *Wish You Were Here*.

Where Did They Go, Lord. w/m Dallas Frazier and A. L. "Doodle" Owens, 1971. Hit C&W/Pop record by Elvis Presley (RCA).

Where Did You Get That Girl? w. Bert Kalmar, m. Harry Puck, 1913. Popular recording by tenor Walter Van Brunt (Victor).

Where Did You Get That Hat? w/m Joseph J. Sullivan, 1888. Introduced at Miner's Eighth Avenue Theatre in New York City.

Where Did You Learn to Love? w/m Sammy Cahn, Jule Styne, and Harry Harris, 1946. Featured and recorded by Tommy Dorsey, vocal by Stuart Foster (Victor).

Where Did Your Heart Go? w/m David Weiss and Donald Fagenson, 1986. Chart record by the British duo Wham! (Columbia).

Where Do Broken Hearts Go. w/m Frank Wildhorn and Chuck Jackson, 1988. The 4th #1 single from the album "Whitney" by Whitney Houston (Arista).

Where Does a Little Tear Come From? w/m Marge Barton and Fred Macrae, 1964. Country chart hit by George Jones (United Artists).

Where Does the Good Times Go? w/m Buck Owens, 1967. Hit Country record by Buck Owens (Capitol).

Where Do I Begin. See **Theme from "Love Story."**

Where Do I Go? w. Gerome Ragni and James Rado, m. Galt MacDermot, 1967. Introduced by Walker Daniels and company in the off-Broadway musical (TM) *Hair*. In the Broadway production (TM) *Hair*, 1968, it was sung by James Rado and company. Chart records by Carla Thomas (Stax), 1968, and The Happenings, who sang it in medley with "Be-In"/"Hare Krishna" (q.v.) from the same show (Jubilee), 1969.

Where Do I Go from You? w. Walter Bullock, m. Allie Wrubel, 1940. Leading recording: Orrin Tucker, vocal by "Wee" Bonnie Baker (Columbia). Others: Hal Kemp, vocal by Bob Allen (Victor); Guy Lombardo, vocal by Carmen Lombardo (Decca); Mitchell Ayres (Bluebird); and Lou Breese (Varsity).

Where Do I Put Her Memory? w/m James Weatherly, 1979. #1 Country chart record by Charley Pride (RCA).

Where Do the Children Go? w/m Rob Hyman and Eric Bazilian, 1986. Written by the leaders of the recording quintet The Hooters (Columbia).

Where Do the Nights Go. w/m Mike Reid and Rory Bourke, 1987. #1 Country chart record by Ronnie Milsap (RCA).

Where Do They Go When They Row, Row, Row? w. Bert Kalmar and George Jessel, m. Harry Ruby, 1920.

Where Do We Go from Here? w. Howard Johnson, m. Percy Wenrich, 1917. A popular World War I song referring to the #1 question of rookies. Judy Garland sang it in (MM) *For Me and My Gal* in 1942.

Where Do You Come From? w/m Ruth Batchelor and Bob Roberts, 1962. Introduced by Elvis Presley in (MM) *Girls! Girls! Girls!* and on records (RCA).

Where Do You Go? w/m Sonny Bono, 1965. Recorded by Cher (Imperial).

Where Do You Work-a, John? (On the Delaware Lackawan'). w. Mortimer Weinberg and Charley Marks, m. Harry Warren, 1926. A popular novelty featured and recorded by Fred Waring's Pennsylvanians (Victor).

Where'd You Get Those Eyes? w/m Walter Donaldson, 1926. Featured and recorded by Ted Lewis and his Orchestra (Columbia).

Where Everybody Knows Your Name. w/m Gary Portnoy and Judy Hart Angelo, 1983. Theme from the series (TVP) "Cheers." Recorded by Gary Portnoy (Applause).

"Where Has My Hubby Gone?" Blues. w. Irving Caesar, m. Vincent Youmans, 1925. Introduced as "Who's the Who?" by Josephine Whittell and male chorus in (TM) *No, No Nanette*. In the 1971 Broadway revival, it was sung by Helen Gallagher.

Where Have All the Flowers Gone? w/m Pete Seeger, 1962. Pete Seeger, the folksinger and member of The Weavers, got the title from the novel *And Quiet Flows the Don*, by Mikhail Sholokhov. The Kingston Trio (Capitol) popularized the song. Johnny Rivers revived it in 1965 (Capitol).

Where Have We Met Before? w. E. Y. Harburg, m. Vernon Duke, 1932. Introduced by John Hundley and Sue Hicks in (MM) *Walk a Little Faster*. Recorded by Victor Young's Orchestra (Brunswick).

Where Have You Been? w/m Cole Porter, 1930. Introduced by Charles King and

Whistling Away the Dark. w. Johnny Mercer, m. Henry Mancini, 1970. Introduced by Julie Andrews in (MM) *Darling Lili*. Nominated for Academy Award, 1970.

Whistling Boy, The. w. Dorothy Fields, m. Jerome Kern, 1937. Introduced in (MM) *When You're in Love* and on records (Decca) by Grace Moore.

Whistling Coon, The. w/m Sam Devere, 1888. Introduced by Devere, a banjo-playing minstrel. George Washington Johnson, who was born into slavery, became one of the first well-known recording stars, and his cylinder containing this song was a big seller (Columbia).

Whistling in the Dark. w. Allen Boretz, m. Dana Suesse, 1931. Featured and recorded by Guy Lombardo and the Royal Canadians (Columbia).

Whistling Rag. w/m Irving Berlin, 1911.

Whistling Rufus. w. W. Murdock Lind, m. Kerry Mills, 1899. Originally an instrumental two-step. With Lind's words, it became popular in minstrel shows and vaudeville.

White Bird. w/m David Laflamme and Linda Laflamme, 1977. Originally recorded in the album by his group, "It's a Beautiful Day," 1969, David Laflamme had a chart single (Amherst), 1977.

White Christmas. w/m Irving Berlin, 1942. Introduced by Bing Crosby and Marjorie Reynolds in (MM) *Holiday Inn*. Academy Award winner, 1942. During World War II, it was a great favorite with members of the armed forces in the Pacific. It has become the most famous and biggest selling Christmas song of the twentieth century, translated into dozens of languages. Crosby's record (Decca), alone, has sold over thirty million copies. Also sung by Crosby in (MM) *Blue Skies*, 1946, and as title song in (MM) *White Christmas*, 1954.

White Cliffs of Dover, The (There'll Be Bluebirds Over). w. Nat Burton, m. Walter Kent, 1941. American song of optimism about the plight of England in the early days of World War II. The song was on "Your Hit Parade" for seventeen weeks, six times in the #1 spot. Best-selling records by Kay Kyser, vocal by Harry Babbitt (Columbia); Glenn Miller, vocal by Ray Eberle (Bluebird); Kate Smith (Columbia); Sammy Kaye, vocal by Arthur Wright (Victor); Jimmy Dorsey, vocal by Bob Eberly (Decca).

White Dove, The. w. Clifford Grey, m. Franz Lehar, 1930. Sung by Lawrence Tibbett in (MM) *The Rogue Song* and recorded by him (Victor). Originally in a Viennese operetta, *Zigeunerliebe*, which had an English-language version, *Gypsy Love*, presented in the U.S. in 1911. The song was titled "The Melody of Love," with lyrics by Harry B. and Robert B. Smith.

White Heat. m. Will Hudson, 1934. Featured and recorded by Jimmie Lunceford and his Orchestra (Victor).

White Horse. w/m Tim Stahl and John Guldberg, 1984. Written and recorded by the Danish duo Laid Back (Sire).

White Jazz. m. Gene Gifford, 1933. Coupled with "Blue Jazz" on the recording by Glen Gray and the Casa Loma Orchestra (Brunswick). The same coupling was made by the British band of Lew Stone (Decca). Gifford, the chief arranger for Casa Loma, also wrote "Black Jazz" as an instrumental for the band.

White Knight, The. w/m Jay Huguely, 1976. Top 20 novelty record by Cledus Maggard and The Citizen's Band (Mercury). Maggard was the writer's pseudonym.

White Lightning. w/m J. P. Richardson, 1959. Chart record, written by The Big Bopper (Richardson's performing pseudonym) and recorded by George Jones (Mercury).

White on White. w. Bernice Ross, m. Lor Crane, 1964. Top 10 record by Danny Williams (United Artists).

White Rabbit. w/m Grace Slick, 1967. Top 10 record by the group Jefferson Airplane (RCA). The group, renamed Jefferson Starship, performed it on the soundtrack of the Vietnam War film (MP) *Platoon*, 1987.

White Room. w/m Pete Brown and Jack Bruce, 1968. Top 10 U.S. release by The British group Cream (Atco).

White Rose of Athens, The. w. Norman Newell (Engl.), Nikos Gatsos (Gr.), m. Manos Hadjidakis, 1962. Originally titled "Weisse Rosen aus Athen," words by Hans Bradtke, from the German film (MP) *Dreamland of Desire*. Introduced by Nana Mouskouri (Riverside). Leading record by David Carroll and his Orchestra (Mercury).

Whiter Shade of Pale, A. w/m Gary Brooker and Keith Reid, 1967. Hit record by the British rock group Procol Harum (Deram).

White Sails. w/m Harry Archer, Nick Kenny, and Charles Kenny, 1939. Archer's last song. Featured and recorded by Kenny Baker (Victor) and the bands of Al Donahue, vocal by Paula Kelly (Vocalion); Sammy Kaye (Victor); Jack Teagarden, vocal by Linda Keene (Brunswick); Ozzie Nelson (Bluebird).

White Silver Sands. w/m Charles Matthews and Gladys Reinhardt, 1957. Introduced and recorded by Dave Gardner (OJ). Top 10 record by Don Rondo (Jubilee) and chart version by The Owen Bradley Quintet, vocal by The Anita Kerr Quartet (Decca). Bill Black's Combo had a Top 10 instrumental in 1960 (Hi), and a "twistin'" version in 1962 (Hi).

White Sport Coat, A (and a Pink Carnation). w/m Marty Robbins, 1957. Hit C&W and Pop crossover record by Marty Robbins (Columbia).

White Wedding. w/m Billy Idol, 1983. Recorded by the English singer Billy Idol (Chrysalis).

Who? w. Otto Harbach and Oscar Hammerstein II, m. Jerome Kern, 1925. In this major standard, Kern wrote the music first and presented the lyric writers with a problem. The opening note of the song and subsequent sequential passages were held for nine beats, or two and a quarter measures. Harbach and Hammerstein agreed that it had to be a singable vowel sound with continuing interest to the listener, ergo the title. It was introduced by Marilyn Miller and Paul Frawley in (TM) *Sunny*. George Olsen's Orchestra, with a male trio doing the vocal, had a hit record (Victor) and popularized the song. It was sung by Marilyn Miller and Lawrence Gray in (MM) *Sunny*, 1930, and by Anna Neagle and John Carroll in the remake, 1941. Judy Garland sang it in the Kern movie bio (MM) *Till the Clouds Roll By*, 1946, and Ray Bolger performed it in the Marilyn Miller story (MM) *Look for the Silver Lining*, 1949.

Whoa! Sailor! w/m Hank Thompson, 1949. C&W chart hit by Hank Thompson (Capitol).

Who Am I? w/m Tony Hatch and Jackie Trent, 1966. Popular record made in England by Petula Clark (Warner Bros.).

Who Am I? w. Walter Bullock, m. Jule Styne, 1940. Styne's first song success was nominated for an Academy Award after being introduced by Frances Langford and Kenny Baker in (MM) *Hit Parade of 1941*. Recorded by Langford (Decca); Count Basie, vocal by Helen Humes (Okeh); Charlie Barnet, vocal by Dolores O'Neill (Bluebird).

Who Are You. w/m Peter Townshend, 1978. Recorded by the English rock group The Who (MCA).

Who Are You Now? w. Bob Merrill, m. Sammy Cahn, 1964. Introduced by Barbra Streisand in (TM) *Funny Girl*. Song not used in film version.

Who Are You With Tonight? w. Harry Williams, m. Egbert Van Alstyne, 1910.

Who Ate Napoleons with Josephine When Bonaparte Was Far Away? w. Alfred Bryan, m. E. Ray Goetz, 1920. Novelty, introduced in (TM) *As You Were*.

Who Can It Be Now? w/m Colin Hay, 1982. #1 record by the Australian group Men at Work (Columbia).

Who Can I Turn To? w. Bill Engvick, m. Alec Wilder, 1942. Featured and recorded by

Why. w. Bob Marcucci, m. Peter De Angelis, 1960. #1 chart record by Frankie Avalon (Chancellor). Revived by Donny Osmond (MGM), 1972.

Why. w. Buddy Feyne, m. Maurice Shapiro, 1954. Top 40 records by Karen Chandler (Coral) and Nat "King" Cole (Capitol).

Why? w. Arthur Swanstrom and Benny Davis, m. J. Fred Coots, 1929. Introduced by Lily Damita and Jack Donahue in (TM) *Sons o' Guns*.

Why, Baby, Why? w/m George Jones and Darrell Edwards, 1955. Leading C&W chart record by Red Sovine and Webb Pierce (Decca).

Why, Oh Why? w. Leo Robin and Clifford Grey, m. Vincent Youmans, 1927. Introduced by Madeline Cameron in (TM) *Hit the Deck*. Four months after the show opened, a new lyric titled "Nothing Could Be Sweeter" (q.v.) was written for the original melody and replaced this in the production. However, in both the 1930 and 1955 film productions of (MM) *Hit the Deck*, the original title and lyrics were sung. In the latter version it was performed by Tony Martin, Jane Powell, Russ Tamblyn, Vic Damone, Debbie Reynolds, and Ann Miller.

Why, Why. w/m Wayne P. Walker and A. R. Peddy, 1958. C&W hit by Carl Smith (Columbia).

Why Baby Why. w/m Luther Dixon and Larry Harrison, 1957. Top 10 record by Pat Boone (Dot).

Why Begin Again? (a.k.a. **Pastel Blue**). w. Don Raye, m. Artie Shaw and Charlie Shavers, 1939, 1943. As instrumental "Pastel Blue," it was recorded by John Kirby and his Band (Decca) and Artie Shaw and his Band (Bluebird) in 1939. Lyrics were added and it was recorded under new title by Shaw (Victor), Tommy Dorsey (Victor), and Dick Todd (Victor).

Why Can't I? w. Lorenz Hart, m. Richard Rodgers, 1929. Introduced by Inez Courtney and Lillian Taiz in (TM) *Spring Is Here*. Interpolated by Doris Day and Martha Raye in (MM) Billy Rose's *Jumbo*, 1962.

(If You Let Me Make Love to You Then) Why Can't I Touch You. w/m C. C. Courtney and Peter Link, 1969. Introduced by the company in the off-Broadway musical (TM) *Salvation*. Top 10 record by Ronnie Dyson (Columbia), 1970.

Why Can't I Touch You. See **(If You Let Me Make Love to You Then) Why Can't I Touch You**.

Why Can't the English? w. Alan Jay Lerner, m. Frederick Loewe, 1956. Introduced by Rex Harrison in (TM) *My Fair Lady*. Harrison repeated his performance in (MM) *My Fair Lady*, 1964.

Why Can't This Be Love. w/m Alex Van Halen, Eddie Van Halen, Michael Anthony, and Sammy Hagar, 1986. Top 10 record by the band Van Halen (Warner Bros.).

Why Can't This Night Go On Forever? w. Charles Newman, m. Isham Jones, 1933. Introduced and featured by Jane Froman. Popular recordings by the orchestras of Isham Jones (Victor) and Jack Denny (Victor).

Why Can't We Be Friends? w/m Dee Allen, Harold Brown, B. B. Dickerson, Jerry Goldstein, Lonnie Jordan, Charles Miller, Lee Oskar, and Howard Scott, 1975. Written by the members of the group, War, which was awarded a gold record for their Top 10 recording (United Artists).

Why Can't We Live Together. w/m Timmy Thomas, 1972. #1 R&B, #3 Pop chart hit by Timmy Thomas (Glades).

Why Can't You? w/m B. G. DeSylva, Lew Brown, Ray Henderson, and Al Jolson, 1929. Sung by Jolson in (MM) *Say It with Songs*.

Why Can't You Behave? w/m Cole Porter, 1949. Introduced by Lisa Kirk and Harold Lang in (TM) *Kiss Me Kate*. Sung by Ann Miller in (MM) *Kiss Me Kate*, 1953.

Why Can't You Feel Sorry for Me? w/m Merle Kilgore and Marvin Rainwater, 1964. Introduced and recorded by Carl Smith (Columbia).

Why Couldn't It Be Poor Little Me? w. Gus Kahn, m. Isham Jones, 1924.

Why Dance? w. Roy Turk, m. Fred E. Ahlert, 1931.

Why Did I Kiss That Girl? w. Lew Brown, m. Robert A. King and Ray Henderson, 1924. Popularized by Paul Whiteman and his Orchestra (Victor).

Why Does It Get So Late So Early? w. Allie Wrubel and John Lehmann, m. Allie Wrubel, 1946. Leading record by Helen Forrest and Dick Haymes (Decca).

Why Does It Have to Be (Wrong or Right). w/m Randy Sharp and Donny Lowery, 1987. #1 Country chart record by the group Restless Heart (RCA).

Why Does It Have to Rain on Sunday? w/m Bob Merrill and Vi Ott, 1947. Merrill's first song success. Leading records by Freddy Martin and his Orchestra (Victor), Snooky Lanson (Mercury).

Why Doesn't Somebody Tell Me These Things? w. Jimmy Eaton, m. Terry Shand, 1938. Introduced and recorded by Bunny Berigan and his Orchestra (Victor).

Why Do Fools Fall in Love? w/m Frank Lymon and Morris Levy, 1956. Hit by The Teenagers, featuring Frankie Lymon (Gee). The billing was reversed on later records. Gale Storm had a popular version (Dot), as did The Diamonds (Mercury). Song was used in (MM) *American Hot Wax* in 1978. Revived by Diana Ross with a Top 10 record in 1981 (RCA).

Why Do I Dream Those Dreams? w. Al Dubin, m. Harry Warren, 1934. Introduced by Dick Powell in (MM) *Wonder Bar* and recorded (Brunswick).

Why Do I Love You? w. Oscar Hammerstein II, m. Jerome Kern, 1928. Sung by Norma Terris, Howard Marsh, Edna May Oliver, and Charles Winninger in (TM) *Show Boat*. The song was not used in the first film adaptation, 1929, and used only in the background of the second version (MM) *Show Boat*, 1936. In (MM) *Show Boat*, 1951, it was sung by Kathryn Grayson and Howard Keel.

Why Do I Love You? w. B. G. DeSylva and Ira Gershwin, m. George Gershwin, 1925. Esther Howard and Lou Holtz sang this in a musical originally titled in its pre-Broadway tryout, *My Fair Lady*, which name was changed to (TM) *Tell Me More!* Not to be confused with the song of the same name from *Show Boat*.

Why Do Lovers Break Each Other's Hearts? w/m Ellie Greenwich, Tony Powers, and Phil Spector, 1962. Top 40 record by Bob B. Soxx and The Blue Jeans (Philles).

Why Don't They Understand. w/m Jack Fishman and Joe Henderson, 1958. Popularized by George Hamilton IV (ABC-Paramount).

Why Don't We Do This More Often? w. Charles Newman, m. Allie Wrubel, 1941. Most popular recordings by Kay Kyser, vocal by Ginny Simms and Harry Babbitt (Columbia); and Freddy Martin, vocal by Eddie Stone (Bluebird).

Why Don't You? w. Joseph McCarthy, m. Harry Tierney, 1920. Interpolated by Alice Delysia in the English/French import (TM) *Afgar*.

Why Don't You Believe Me. w/m Lew Douglas, King Laney, and Roy Rodde, 1952. Joni James, with Lew Douglas's Orchestra, had a #1 record (MGM).

Why Don't You Do Right? w/m Joe McCoy, 1942. Introduced and recorded by blues singer Lil Green (Bluebird). Benny Goodman, with vocal by Peggy Lee, covered the record for Lee's first big hit (Columbia). Goodman and Lee performed it in (MM) *Stage Door Canteen*, 1943. Lee recorded a solo version, with husband Dave Barbour's accompaniment (Capitol), mid-forties.

(As Long As You're Not in Love with Anyone Else) Why Don't You Fall in Love with Me? w. Al Lewis, m. Mabel Wayne, 1942. Best-selling records: Dinah Shore (Victor); Dick Jurgens, vocal by Harry Cool (Columbia); Johnny Long, vocal by Bob Houston and Johnny Long (Decca); Connee Boswell (Decca).

Why Don't You Haul Off and Love Me? w/m Wayne Raney and Lonnie Glosson, 1949. Popular country record by singer-harmonicist Wayne Raney (King).

Why Don't You Love Me? w/m Hank Williams, 1950. Introduced and recorded by Hank Williams (MGM).

Why Don't You Practice What You Preach? w/m Al Goodhart, Al Hoffman, and Maurice Sigler, 1934. Best-selling record by the Boswell Sisters (Brunswick).

Why Don't You Spend the Night. w/m Bob McDill, 1980. #1 Country chart record by Ronnie Milsap (RCA).

Why Don't You Write Me? w/m Laura Hollins, 1955. R&B success by The Jacks (RPM).

Why Do the Wrong People Travel? w/m Noël Coward, 1961. Introduced by Elaine Stritch in (TM) *Sail Away*.

Why Do They All Take the Night Boat to Albany? w. Joe Young and Sam M. Lewis, m. Jean Schwartz, 1918. Interpolated by Al Jolson in (TM) *Sinbad* at the Winter Garden.

Why Do Things Happen to Me? w/m Roy Hawkins, 1950. Popular R&B record by Roy Hawkins (Modern).

Why Do Ya Roll Those Eyes? w. Morrie Ryskind, m. Philip Charig, 1926. Introduced by Helen Morgan, Lyman Byck, Evelyn Bennett, and Betty Compton in the revue (TM) *Americana of 1926*.

Why Do You Suppose? w. Lorenz Hart, m. Richard Rodgers, 1929. Introduced by Barbara Newberry and Jack Whiting in (TM) *Heads Up!* Nat Shilkret had a popular record

(Victor). Note: The song has the same melody as "How Was I to Know," which was cut from the musical *She's My Baby* (1928).

Why Dream? w/m Leo Robin, Ralph Rainger, and Richard A. Whiting, 1935. Introduced by Henry Wadsworth in (MM) *The Big Broadcast of 1936*. Featured and recorded by Ray Noble and his Orchestra, vocal by Al Bowlly and arranged by Glenn Miller (Victor); Little Jack Little (Columbia); Jack Oakie (Melotone). Noble, with his band, and Oakie appeared in the film.

Why'd You Come Here Lookin' Like That. w/m R. Thomas and B. Carlisle, 1989. Hit Country record by Dolly Parton (Columbia).

Why Fight the Feeling? w/m Frank Loesser, 1950. Introduced by Betty Hutton in (MM) *Let's Dance*.

Why Have You Left the One You Left Me For. w/m Christopher True, 1979. #1 Country chart record by Crystal Gayle (United Artists).

Why Him? w. Alan Jay Lerner, m. Burton Lane, 1979. Introduced by Georgia Brown in (TM) *Carmelina*.

Why I'm Walkin'. w/m Stonewall Jackson and Melvin Endsley, 1960. Crossover record, C&W and Pop, by Stonewall Jackson (Columbia).

Why I Sing the Blues. w/m B. B. King and Dave Clark, 1969. Recorded by B. B. King (Blues Way).

Why Lady Why. w/m Randy Owen. 1980. #1 Country chart record by the group Alabama (RCA). Gary Morris had a Top 10 version (Warner Bros.), 1984.

Why Me? w/m Tony Carey, 1983. Recorded by Irene Cara (Geffen).

Why Me. w/m Kris Kristofferson, 1973. Gold record crossover Country/Pop record by Kris Kristofferson (Monument).

Why Not Me. w/m Fred Knoblock and Carson Whitsett, 1980. Recorded by Fred Knoblock (Scotti Brothers).

Why Not String Along with Me? w. Lew Brown, m. Lew Pollack, 1938. Sung by Ethel Merman in (MM) *Straight, Place and Show.*

Why Not Tonight? w/m Jimmy Gilreath, 1967. Recorded by Jimmy Hughes (Fame).

Why Should I Cry? w/m Zeke Clements, 1950. Hit C&W record by Eddy Arnold (RCA Victor).

Why Should I Cry over You? w. Ned Miller, m. Chester Conn, 1925. This song has had many recordings, among them: Billy Jones (Victor); Ace Brigode (Vocalion); Johnny Johnston (MGM); Curt Massey (Coast); and Johnny Mercer and The Pied Pipers (Capitol).

Why Shouldn't I? w/m Cole Porter, 1935. Introduced by Margaret Adams in (TM) *Jubilee.* Recorded by Paul Whiteman, vocal by Ramona (Victor); Ted Black, vocal by Frank Parker (Perfect); Jimmy Dorsey, vocal by Kay Weber (Decca); Johnny Green's Orchestra (Brunswick). Later recordings by Artie Shaw (Victor), Mary Martin (Decca), and Bobby Short (Atlantic).

Why Should We Try Anymore? w/m Hank Williams, 1950. Introduced and recorded by Hank Williams (MGM).

Why Stars Come Out at Night. w/m Ray Noble, 1935. Introduced by Ray Noble and his Orchestra in (MM) *The Big Broadcast of 1936* and recorded by him (Victor).

Why Talk About Love? w. Sidney D. Mitchell, m. Lew Pollack, 1937. From (MM) *One in a Million.* This was the first record by the Andrews Sisters (Decca).

Why Try to Change Me Now? w. Joseph Allan McCarthy, m. Cy Coleman, 1952. The first song success for each of the writers. Introduced and recorded by Frank Sinatra (Capitol).

Why Was I Born? w. Oscar Hammerstein II, m. Jerome Kern, 1929. Introduced by Helen Morgan in (TM) *Sweet Adeline.* In the film version (MM) *Sweet Adeline*, 1935, it was sung by Irene Dunne. Lena Horne sang it in the Kern biography (MM) *Till the Clouds Roll By*, 1946, as did Ida Lupino in (MM) *The Man I Love* that same year. In 1957, Gogi Grant, dubbing for Ann Blyth in the title role, sang it in (MM) *The Helen Morgan Story.* Patrice Munsel sang it in (TM) *A Musical Jubilee,* 1975.

Why Worry? w/m Seymour Simons, 1920. Introduced by Nora Bayes in (TM) *Her Family Tree* and on records (Columbia).

Why You Treat Me So Bad. w/m Jay King, Thomas McElroy, and David Foster, 1987. Top 10 R&B chart and Pop crossover record by the disco group Club Nouveau (Warner Bros.).

Wichita Lineman. w/m Jim Webb, 1969. Introduced and gold record by Glen Campbell (Capitol). Chart version by Sergio Mendes and Brasil '66 (A&M).

Wiederseh'n. w. Milt Gabler (Engl.), m. Bert Kaempfert and Herbert Rehbein, 1966. German song. English version recorded by Al Martino (Capitol).

Wigwam. w/m Bob Dylan, 1970. Recorded by Bob Dylan (Columbia).

Wild, Wild, Women Are Making a Wild Man of Me, The. w/m Henry Lewis, Al Wilson, and Al Piantadosi, 1917. Novelty song, revived via the recording by Freddie "Schnickelfritz" Fisher and his Orchestra (Decca), 1938.

Wild, Wild West. w/m The Escape Club, 1988. Chart single and album title song by The Escape Club (Atlantic).

Wild, Wild West, The. w. Johnny Mercer, m. Harry Warren, 1946. Introduced in (MM) *The Harvey Girls* and on records by Virginia O'Brien (Decca).

Wild, Wild Young Men. w/m Ahmet Ertegun, 1953. Top 10 R&B record by Ruth Brown (Atlantic).

Wild As a Wild Cat. w/m Carmol Taylor, 1965. Top 10 Country record by Charlie Walker (Epic).

Wild Boys, The. w/m Duran Duran, 1984. Top 10 record by the British band Duran Duran (Capitol).

Wildest Gal in Town, The. w. Jack Yellen, m. Sammy Fain, 1947. Popular recording by Billy Eckstine (MGM).

Wildfire. w/m Larry Cansler and Michael Murphey, 1975. Top 10 gold C&W/Pop record by Michael Murphey (Epic).

Wildflower. w/m David Richardson and Doug Edwards, 1973. Top 10 record by the Canadian quartet Skylark (Capitol). Chart version by vocal group, The New Birth (RCA), 1974.

Wildflower. w. Otto Harbach and Oscar Hammerstein, m. Vincent Youmans and Herbert Stothart, 1923. Introduced by Guy Robertson in (TM) *Wildflower*. Popular instrumental record by Ben Bernie and his Orchestra (Vocalion). This was the first major success for Hammerstein, who co-wrote the book and lyrics.

Wildflowers. w/m Dolly Parton, 1988. Top 10 Country chart record by Dolly Parton, Linda Ronstadt, and Emmylou Harris, from their album "Trio" (Warner Bros.).

Wild Honey. w/m Brian Wilson and Mike Love, 1967. Top 40 record by The Beach Boys (Capitol).

Wild Honey. w/m George Hamilton, Harry Tobias, and Charles N. Daniels [Neil Moret], 1934. Introduced by George Hamilton and his Orchestra. Leading records by the bands of Jan Garber (Victor); Joe Haymes (Melotone); Dick Jurgens, vocal by Eddy Howard (Decca); Archie Bleyer (Vocalion). John Arcesi (Don Darcy) revived it in the late forties (Capitol).

Wild Horses. w/m Mick Jagger and Keith Richards, 1971. Top 40 record by The Rolling Stones (Rolling Stones).

Wild Horses. w/m Johnny Burke, 1953. Adapted from "Wilder Reiter" ("Wild Horseman") by Robert Schumann. Leading recordings by Perry Como (RCA Victor); and Ray Anthony, vocal by Jo Ann Greer (Capitol).

Wild in the Country. w/m George David Weiss, Hugo Peretti, and Luigi Creatore, 1961. Introduced by Elvis Presley in (MM) *Wild in the Country*, and on records (RCA).

Wild Is the Wind. w. Ned Washington, m. Dimitri Tiomkin, 1957. Title song of (MP) *Wild Is the Wind*. Nominated for Academy Award. Popularized by Johnny Mathis (Columbia).

Wild Man Blues. m. Louis Armstrong and Ferdinand "Jelly Roll" Morton, 1927. Louis Armstrong and His Hot Seven (Okeh) and Jelly Roll Morton's Red Hot Peppers (Victor) both recorded this jazz instrumental, as did Johnny Dodds' Black Bottom Stompers (Brunswick), Sidney Bechet (Victor), and Bob Scobey (Triton).

Wild Night. w/m Van Morrison, 1971. Recorded by Van Morrison (Warner Bros.).

Wild One. w/m William Stevenson and Ivy Hunter, 1965. Recorded by Martha and The Vandellas (Gordy).

Wild One. w/m Bernie Lowe, Kal Mann, and Dave Appell, 1960. Hit record by Bobby Rydell (Cameo).

Wild Rose. w. Clifford Grey, m. Jerome Kern, 1920. Introduced by Marilyn Miller in (TM) *Sally*. She also sang it in (MM) *Sally*, 1929. June Haver, playing Miller, sang it in her film biography (MM) *Look for the Silver Lining*, 1949.

Wild Rose, The. w. Otto Harbach and Oscar Hammerstein II, m. Rudolf Friml, 1926. Title song of (TM) *The Wild Rose*.

Wild Side of Life, The. w/m William Warren and A. A. Carter, 1952. Featured and recorded by Hank Thompson (Capitol).

Wild Thing. w/m M. Young, Anthony Smith, and M. Dike, 1989. Hit record by Tone Loc (Delicious Vinyl).

Wild Thing. w/m Chip Taylor, 1966. #1 record by the British quartet Troggs (Fontana, Atco). Hit comedy record by Senator Bobby, pseudonym for Bill Minkin (Parkway), 1967.

Revived by the British rock quartet, Fancy (Big Tree), 1974. Sung on the soundtrack of (MP) *Something Wild* by Sister Carol; included in the soundtrack album (MCA).

Wild Week-end. w/m Bill Anderson, 1968. Country hit by Bill Anderson (Decca).

Wild Weekend. w/m Tom Shannon and Phil Todaro, 1963. Instrumental hit by The Rebels (Swan). Theme song of Buffalo, N.Y., disc jockey Tom Shannon, who wrote the song with producer Phil Todaro.

Wildwood Days. w. Kal Mann, m. Dave Appell, 1963. Featured and recorded by Bobby Rydell (Cameo).

Wildwood Flower. w/m Hank Thompson, 1955. Introduced and Top 10 C&W chart record by Hank Thompson (Capitol). Revived instrumentally by Roy Clark (Churchill), 1983.

Wildwood Weed. w/m Dan Bowman and Jim Stafford, 1974. Top 10 novelty record by Jim Stafford (MGM).

Wild World. w/m Cat Stevens, 1971. Top 20 record by Cat Stevens (A&M).

Wilhelmina. w. Mack Gordon, m. Josef Myrow, 1950. From the film starring Betty Grable, *Wabash Avenue*. Nominated for Academy Award. Leading records by Art Lund, with Leroy Holmes' Orchestra (MGM); Kay Kyser, vocal by Mike Douglas (Columbia).

Wilkes-Barre, Pa. w. Anne Croswell, m. Lee Pockriss, 1963. Introduced by Vivien Leigh and Byron Mitchell in (TM) *Tovarich*.

Will He Like Me? w. Sheldon Harnick, m. Jerry Bock, 1963. Introduced by Barbara Cook in (TM) *She Loves Me*.

Willie and the Hand Jive. w/m Johnny Otis, 1958. Hit R&B/Pop record by The Johnny Otis Show (Capitol). Chart records by Eric Clapton (RSO), 1974; George Thorogood and The Destroyers (EMI America), 1985.

Willie the Weeper. w/m Billy Walker and Freddie Hart, 1962. Top 10 Country chart record by Billy Walker (Decca).

Will I Ever Know? w. Mack Gordon, m. Harry Revel, 1936. Introduced in (MM) *Palm Springs* and recorded by Frances Langford (Decca).

Willing and Eager. w/m Richard Rodgers, 1962. One of five songs by Rodgers (w/m) written for the second musical version of (MM) *State Fair*. Introduced by Pat Boone and Ann-Margret.

Willingly. w/m Hank Cochran, 1962. Top 10 Country chart record by Willie Nelson and Shirley Collie (Liberty).

Will It Go Round in Circles. w/m Billy Preston and Bruce Fisher, 1973. #1 gold record by Billy Preston (A&M).

Willkommen. w. Fred Ebb, m. John Kander, 1966. Introduced by Joel Grey and company in (TM) *Cabaret*. Grey repeated his performance with chorus in (MM) *Cabaret*, 1972.

Will Love Find a Way? w/m Brooks Bowman, 1935. The third song from the Princeton Triangle Club show, *Stags at Bay*, to attain public acceptance. (See: Brooks Bowman, Section III.) Most popular recordings by Glen Gray and the Casa Loma Orchestra, vocal by Kenny Sargent (Decca) and Hal Kemp, vocal by Deane Janis (Brunswick). Kemp recorded all three songs from the college show.

Willow Weep for Me. w/m Ann Ronell, 1932. Introduced and recorded (Victor) by Paul Whiteman and his Orchestra, vocal by Irene Taylor. Ted Fio Rito and his Band had a popular recording (Brunswick). Later singles attaining popular acceptance: Cab Calloway (Okeh); Harry James (Columbia); Pete Rugolo's arrangement for Stan Kenton's band, vocal by June Christy (Capitol). The song was heard in the Marx Brothers film (MP) *Love Happy*, 1949. Hit record by Chad and Jeremy (World Artists), 1964.

Will Santy Come to Shanty Town? w/m Eddy Arnold, Steve Nelson, and Ed Nelson, Jr., 1949. Featured and recorded by Eddy Arnold (RCA Victor).

Will the Wolf Survive? w/m David Hidalgo and Louie Perez, 1985. Chart record by the Hispanic-American quintet Los Lobos (Slash). Waylon Jennings had a Top 10 Country chart record, which then became the title song of his album (MCA), 1986.

Will You Be Staying After Sunday? w/m Al Kasha and Joel Hirschhorn, 1969. Top 40 record by The Peppermint Rainbow (Decca).

Will You Love Me in December As You Do in May? w. James J. Walker, m. Ernest R. Ball, 1905. The lyrics were written by the future mayor of New York and introduced by Janet Allen of the vaudeville team of Allen and McShane, who became the first Mrs. James J. Walker. The song was in the Bob Hope film based on the life of Walker (MM) *Beau James*, 1954, and (MM) *The Eddy Duchin Story*, 1956.

Will You Love Me Tomorrow? w/m Gerry Goffin and Carole King, 1961. #1 hit by The Shirelles (Scepter). Other later chart recordings by The Four Seasons (Phillips), 1968, Roberta Flack (Atlantic), 1972, Melanie (Neighborhood), 1979, Dave Mason (Columbia), 1978.

Will You Remember. w. Dusty Negulesco, m. Marguerite Monnot, 1962. Introduced by Maurice Chevalier in (MP) *Jessica.*

Will You Remember? w. Rida Johnson Young, m. Sigmund Romberg, 1917. Introduced by Peggy Wood and Charles Purcell in (TM) *Maytime.* Nelson Eddy and Jeanette MacDonald sang it in the movie version (MM) *Maytime*, 1937. Jane Powell and Vic Damone sang it in the Romberg screen bio (MM) *Deep in My Heart*, 1954.

Will Your Lawyer Talk to God? w/m Harlan Howard and Richard Johnson, 1962. Top 10 Country chart record by Kitty Wells (Decca).

Will You Still Be Mine? w. Tom Adair, m. Matt Dennis, 1941. Introduced by Tommy Dorsey with vocal by Connie Haines. Their record was re-released in 1944 (Victor).

Will You Still Love Me? w/m David Foster, Tom Keane, and Richard Baskin, 1986. Top 10 single by the group Chicago (Full Moon).

Wimoweh. w/m Paul Campbell, 1952. Campbell is a pseudonym for the four members of The Weavers, the singing group comprised of Pete Seeger, Fred Hellerman, Lee Hays, and Ronnie Gilbert. Gilbert adapted and arranged the South African Zulu song, "Mbube," and recorded it with Gordon Jenkins' Orchestra (Decca). See also "Lion Sleeps Tonight, The."

Winchester Cathedral. w/m Geoff Stephens, 1966. #1 gold record in U.S. by The New Vaudeville Band, a recording group assembled by the British composer (Fontana).

Wind Beneath My Wings (a.k.a. **Hero).** w/m Larry Henley and Jeff Silbar, 1983, 1988. Country chart hit by Gary Morris (Warner Bros.). R&B/Pop chart record by Lou Rawls (Epic). Under the title, "Hero," Gladys Knight and The Pips had a chart version (Columbia). Other renditions by Willie Nelson (Columbia), Sheena Easton (EMI America). Sung by Bette Midler on the soundtrack of (MP) *Beaches*, 1988, and on her hit single (Atlantic).

Wind in the Willows, The. w/m Vivian Ellis and Desmond Carter, 1931.

Windmills of Your Mind, The. w. Marilyn Bergman and Alan Bergman, m. Michel Legrand, 1968. Introduced by Noel Harrison on the soundtrack of (MP) *The Thomas Crown Affair.* Academy Award-winning song, 1968. Leading record by Dusty Springfield (Atlantic), 1969.

Windmill Under the Stars. w. Johnny Mercer, m. Jerome Kern, 1942. Probably written for but not used in the film *You Were Never Lovelier.* Featured and recorded by Russ Morgan and his Orchestra (Decca) and Johnny Johnston (Capitol).

Windows of the World, The. w. Hal David, m. Burt Bacharach, 1967. Recorded by Dionne Warwick (Scepter).

Window Up Above, The. w/m George Jones, 1961. Hit country record by George Jones (Mercury). Revived by Mickey Gilley (Playboy), 1975.

Windy. w/m Ruthann Friedman, 1967. #1 gold record by The Association (Warner Bros.). Chart instrumental by guitarist Wes Montgomery (A&M).

Wine, Women and Song. w/m Betty Sue Perry, 1964. Country hit recorded by Loretta Lynn (Decca).

Wine, Women and Song. w/m Al Dexter and Aubrey Gass, 1946. Introduced and recorded by Al Dexter (Vocalion).

Wine Me Up. w/m Faron Young and Billy Beaton, 1969. Top 10 Country chart record by Faron Young (Mercury).

Wings. w. Ballard Macdonald, m. J. S. Zamecnik, 1928. The love theme from (MP) *Wings.* Featured on radio and recorded by The Cliquot Club Eskimos, directed by Harry Reser (Columbia).

Wings of a Dove. w/m Bob Ferguson, 1960. Crossover (C&W/Pop) hit by Ferlin Husky (Capitol).

Winners and Losers. w/m Ann Hamilton and Dan Hamilton, 1975. Recorded by Hamilton, Joe Frank & Reynolds (Playboy).

Winner Takes It All. w/m Giorgio Moroder and Thom Whitlock, 1987. Sung by Sammy Hagar on the soundtrack and album of (MP) *Over the Top.* Not to be confused with the Abba hit of 1981.

Winner Takes It All, The. w/m Benny Anderson and Bjorn Ulvaeus, 1980. Top 10 record by the Swedish group Abba (Atlantic).

Winning. w/m Russ Ballard, 1981. Recorded by the group Santana (Columbia).

Winter. w. Alfred Bryan, m. Albert Gumble, 1910.

Winter Garden Rag. m. Abe Olman, 1908. Popular instrumental. Recorded by Lee Stafford (Castle), 1950.

Wintergreen for President. w. Ira Gershwin, m. George Gershwin, 1931. Sung by the ensemble in the Pulitzer Prize-winning musical (TM) *Of Thee I Sing.*

Winter Lady. w/m Leonard Cohen, 1968. Introduced by Leonard Cohen and sung in his album *Songs of Leonard Cohen* (Columbia). Cohen sang it on the soundtrack of (MP) *McCabe and Mrs. Miller,* 1971.

Winter Weather. w/m Ted Shapiro, 1941. Most popular records: Benny Goodman, vocal by Peggy Lee and Art Lund (Okeh); Fats Waller (Bluebird); Tommy Dorsey, vocal by Jo Stafford and the Pied Pipers (Victor).

Winter Wonderland. w. Richard B. Smith, m. Felix Bernard, 1934. This perennial seasonal success has been recorded by almost every singer and orchestra who has made a Christmas album. Early records by Ted Weems, vocal by Parker Gibbs (Columbia); Archie Bleyer (Vocalion); Richard Himber, vocal by Joey Nash. It was heard in (MM) *Lake Placid Serenade* in 1944. The Andrews Sisters, with Guy Lombardo's Orchestra, had a hit record in 1950 (Decca).

Winter World of Love. w/m Les Reed and Barry Mason, 1970. English song. Engelbert Humperdinck's recording was a Top 20 hit in the U.S. (Parrot).

Win Your Love for Me. w/m L. C. Cooke, 1958. Introduced and Top 40 record by Sam Cooke (Keen).

Wipe Out. w. Robert Berryhill, Patrick Connolly, James Fuller, and Ron Wilson, 1963. Written by four-fifths of the quintet, The Surfaris, whose instrumental version reached the #2 position on the charts (Dot). Its rerelease in 1966 reached the Top 20. Revived by The Fat Boys, backed by the Beach Boys, on the soundtrack of (MP) *Disorderlies,* 1987. The single was an R&B and Pop chart hit (Tin Pan).

Wise Old Owl, The. w/m Joe Ricardel, 1940. Leading records by the bands of Kay Kyser (Columbia), Teddy Powell (Bluebird), Al Donahue (Okeh).

Wishful, Sinful. w/m John Densmore, Robert Krieger, Raymond Manzarek, and James Morrison, 1969. Written and recorded by The Doors (Elektra).

Wishful Thinking. w/m Wynn Stewart, 1960. Popular Country record by Wynn Stewart (Challenge).

Wishin' and Hopin'. w. Hal David, m. Burt Bacharach, 1964. Hit record by Dusty Springfield (Philips).

Wishing (Will Make It So). w/m B. G. DeSylva, 1939. DeSylva's last hit, and a rare case of his writing both words and music. Introduced by Irene Dunne in (MP) *Love Affair*, the song was nominated for an Academy Award. Glenn Miller and his Orchestra had the top recording (Bluebird). Other popular versions by the bands of Russ Morgan (Decca); Skinnay Ennis, vocal by Ennis (Victor); Ted Straeter (Liberty Music Shops). Rose Murphy revived it in the late forties. Ethel Smith performed it on the organ in (MM) *George White's Scandals of '45*.

Wishing and Waiting for Love. w. Grant Clarke, m. Harry Akst, 1929. Introduced by Alice White in (MM) *Broadway Babies*. Grant Withers and Sue Carol performed it in *Dancing Sweeties* in 1930.

Wishing Doll, The. w. Mack David, m. Elmer Bernstein, 1966. Introduced in (MP) *Hawaii*. Nominated for Academy Award.

Wishing for Your Love. w/m Sampson Horton, 1958. Recorded by The Voxpoppers (Mercury).

Wishing Ring. w/m Al Britt and Pee Wee Maddux, 1952. Recorded by Joni James, with Lew Douglas's Orchestra (MGM).

Wishing Well. w/m Terence Trent D'Arby and Sean Oliver, 1988. #1 single, recorded in England by the American, Terence Trent D'Arby, from the album "Introducing the Hardine According to Terence Trent D'Arby" (Columbia).

Wishing Well (Down in the Well), The. w/m Peter Hiscock, 1965. Hank Snow had a

Top 10 Country chart record of this Australian song (RCA).

Wishing You Were Here. w/m Peter Cetera, 1974. Top 20 record by Chicago (Columbia).

Wish Me a Rainbow. w/m Jerry Livingston and Ray Evans, 1966. Introduced by Mary Badham in (MP) *This Property Is Condemned*, a film based on Tennessee Williams' one-act play. Popular recording by The Gunter Kallmann Chorus (4 Corners of the World).

Wish That I Wish Tonight, The. w. Jack Scholl, m. M. K. Jerome, 1945. From (MP) *Christmas in Connecticut*. Leading records by the orchestras of Russ Morgan (Decca) and Ray Noble (Columbia).

Wish You Didn't Have to Go. w/m Dan Pennington and Dewey Lindon Oldham, 1967. Top 40 record by James and Bobby Purify (Bell).

Wish You Were Here. w/m Harold Rome, 1952. Introduced by Jack Cassidy in (TM) *Wish You Were Here*. #1 hit record by Eddie Fisher, with Hugo Winterhalter's Orchestra (RCA Victor). Jane Froman, with Sid Feller's Orchestra, also had a popular version (Capitol).

Wish You Were Here Buddy. w/m Pat Boone, 1966. Introduced and recorded by Pat Boone (Dot).

Wistful and Blue. w/m Ruth Etting and Morrey Davidson, 1927. Recorded by Paul Whiteman, vocal by Al Rinker (Victor), Abe Lyman and his California Orchestra (Brunswick), and The Original Memphis Five, vocal by Annette Hanshaw (Paramount). In 1937, it was recorded by Glenn Miller, vocal by Doris Kerr (Decca).

Witchcraft. w. Carolyn Leigh, m. Cy Coleman, 1958. Popularized by Frank Sinatra (Capitol).

Witchcraft. w/m Dave Bartholomew and Pearl King, 1956. #5 on the R&B charts by The Spiders (Imperial). Revived by Elvis Presley with a Top 40 record on the Pop charts, 1963 (RCA). Not to be confused with the Sinatra hit of the same title.

Witch Doctor. w/m Ross Bagdasarian, 1958. Novelty hit by David Seville [Bagdasarian's pseudonym] (Liberty).

Witch Queen of New Orleans, The. w/m Lolly Vegas and Pat Vegas, 1971. Hit record by Redbone (Epic).

With a Banjo on My Knee. w. Harold Adamson, m. Jimmy McHugh, 1936. Performed by Buddy Ebsen and Walter Brennan in (MM) *Banjo on My Knee.*

With a Girl Like You. w/m Reg Presley, 1966. Recorded by the English group, The Troggs, of which the writer was lead singer (Fontana, Atco).

With a Hey and a Hi and a Ho-Ho-Ho. w. Mann Curtis, m. Vic Mizzy, 1947. Introduced and recorded by Louis Prima and his Orchestra (Victor).

With a Little Bit of Luck. w. Alan Jay Lerner, m. Frederick Loewe, 1956. Introduced by Stanley Holloway in (TM) *My Fair Lady*, and sung by him in the film (MM) *My Fair Lady*, 1964. Popular recordings by Percy Faith and his Orchestra, as an instrumental (Columbia); and Jo Stafford, with Paul Weston's Orchestra (Columbia).

With a Little Help from My Friends. w/m John Lennon and Paul McCartney, 1967. Introduced by The Beatles in their album "Sgt. Pepper's Lonely Hearts Club Band" (Capitol); sung by them in their animated film (MM) *Yellow Submarine*, 1968. Leading single by Joe Cocker (A&M), 1968. Sung by Peter Frampton and The Bee Gees on the soundtrack of (MM) *Sgt. Pepper's Lonely Hearts Club Band*, 1978.

With a Little Luck. w/m Paul McCartney, 1978. #1 single from the album "London Town," recorded in a 24-track studio aboard a yacht anchored in the Virgin Islands, by McCartney's group, Wings (Capitol).

With All Her Faults I Love Her Still. w/m Monroe H. Rosenfeld, 1888. Introduced by the Primrose and West Minstrels.

With All My Heart. w. Bob Marcucci and Pete De Angelis, m. Pete De Angelis, 1957. Top 20 record by Jodie Sands (Chancellor).

With All My Heart. w. Gus Kahn, m. Jimmy McHugh, 1936. From (MM) *Her Master's Voice*. Recorded by Glen Gray and the Casa Loma Orchestra (Decca), Lee Morse (Puritan), and Dick Robertson (Champion).

With a Smile and a Song. w. Larry Morey, m. Frank Churchill, 1938. Sung by Adriana Caselotti as Snow White in the feature-length animated cartoon (MM) *Snow White and the Seven Dwarfs.*

With a Song in My Heart. w. Lorenz Hart, m. Richard Rodgers, 1929. Introduced by John Hundley and Lillian Taiz in (TM) *Spring Is Here*. It was sung in the 1930 film version (MM) *Spring Is Here* by Bernice Claire and Frank Albertson; in a two-reel version of the film re-titled *Yours Sincerely*, 1933, starring Lanny Ross, which was part of the *Broadway Brevities* series; in (MM) *This Is the Life* by Donald O'Connor and Susanna Foster, 1944; in the Rodgers and Hart biography (MM) *Words and Music* by Perry Como, 1948; it was heard in (MM) *Young Man with a Horn*, 1950; sung by Dennis Morgan and Lucille Norman in (MM) *Painting the Clouds with Sunshine*, 1951; as the title song in the Jane Froman story (MM) *With a Song in My Heart*, 1952, sung by Froman on the soundtrack for Susan Hayward.

Wither Thou Goest. w/m Guy Singer, 1954. Leading records by Les Paul and Mary Ford (Capitol).

With Every Breath I Take. w. Leo Robin, m. Ralph Rainger, 1934. Sung by Bing Crosby in (MM) *Here Is My Heart* and on records (Decca).

With My Eyes Wide Open I'm Dreaming. w. Mack Gordon, m. Harry Revel, 1934. Introduced by Dorothy Dell and Jack

Oakie in (MM) *Shoot the Works*. In 1953, Dean Martin sang it in (MM) *The Stooge*, co-starring Jerry Lewis. Patti Page had her first million-seller, on which she overdubbed on four tracks and was billed as "The Patti Page Quartet" (Mercury), 1950.

With My Head in the Clouds. w/m Irving Berlin, 1942. Introduced in the all-soldier show (TM) *This Is the Army* by Private Robert Shanley. Sung in the musical version (MM) *This Is the Army* by Sergeant Robert Shanley, 1943. [Not only the song was promoted.]

With One Exception. w/m Billy Sherrill and Glenn Sutton, 1967. #1 Country chart record by David Houston (Epic).

With or Without You. w/m U2, 1987. #1 single from the album "The Joshua Tree" by the Irish group U2 (Island).

Without a Song. w. Edward Eliscu and William (Billy) Rose, m. Vincent Youmans, 1929. Introduced by baritone Lois Deppe and Russell Wooding's Jubilee Singers in (TM) *Great Day!* in 1931, Lawrence Tibbett sang it in (MM) *The Prodigal* [originally called *The Southerner*] and recorded it (Victor). This was one of three major standards (the others: "Great Day!" and "More Than You Know" [q.v.]) to come from the short-lived show. Among the many recordings: Paul Whiteman with vocal by Bing Crosby (Columbia), Nelson Eddy (Columbia), Perry Como (Victor), Tommy Dorsey's Orchestra on a 12″ disc with vocal by Frank Sinatra (Victor), solo by Sinatra (Reprise), Jan Peerce (Royale), Wild Bill Davis (Okeh), Eddie Heywood (Columbia), Rex Stewart (Bluebird), Ray McKinley (Capitol).

Without a Word of Warning. w. Mack Gordon, m. Harry Revel, 1935. Introduced in (MM) *Two for Tonight* and recorded by Bing Crosby (Decca).

Without Her. w/m Harry Nilsson, 1969. Introduced by Harry Nilsson. First recorded by Blood, Sweat & Tears in an album (Columbia), 1968. Chart single by Herb Alpert and The Tijuana Brass (A&M), 1969.

Without Love. w/m Cole Porter, 1955. Introduced by Hildegarde Neff in (TM) *Silk Stockings*, and performed by Fred Astaire and Cyd Charisse [vocal dubbed by Carole Richards] in (MM) *Silk Stockings*, 1957.

Without Love. w. B. G. DeSylva and Lew Brown, m. Ray Henderson, 1930. Sung by Grace Brinkley, Oscar Shaw, and Kate Smith in (TM) *Flying High*. Song was not retained in 1931 film adaptation. Eileen Wilson dubbed it on the soundtrack for Sheree North in the biography of the writing team (MM) *The Best Things in Life*, 1957. Among recordings: Al Goodman's Orchestra (Brunswick), Fred Waring's Pennsylvanians (Victor), Margaret Whiting, with Billy Butterfield's Orchestra (Capitol).

Without Love (There Is Nothing). w/m Danny Small, 1957, 1970. First hit recording by Clyde McPhatter (Atlantic). Chart records by Ray Charles (ABC-Paramount), 1963; and Oscar Toney, Jr. (Bell), 1968. Tom Jones had a million-seller (Parrot), 1970.

Without That Certain Thing. w. Max and Harry Nesbitt, 1934. An English hit, introduced and recorded by Ambrose and his Orchestra (Brunswick), followed by Ted Black (Bluebird) and Emil Coleman (Columbia) and their orchestras.

Without That Gal. w/m Walter Donaldson, 1931. Featured by Leo Reisman and his Orchestra (Victor); and Scrappy Lambert, with Vincent Rose and his Orchestra (Banner).

Without You. w/m Thomas Evans and Peter Ham, 1972. #1 gold record by Harry Nilsson (RCA).

Without You. w/m Johnny Tillotson, 1961. Top 10 record by Johnny Tillotson (Cadence).

Without You. w/m J. D. Miller, 1956. Popular record by Eddie Fisher (RCA).

Without You (a.k.a. **Tres Palabras**). w. Ray Gilbert (Engl.), m. Osvaldo Farres, 1946. Sung on the soundtrack by Andy Russell in an animated segment of the Disney film (MM)

Make Mine Music. Original Spanish lyrics for this Mexican import by Farres.

Without Your Love. w/m Billy Nicholls, 1980. Recorded by the English singer Roger Daltrey (Polydor).

Without Your Love. w. Johnny Lange, m. Fred Stryker, 1937. From (MM) *Pick a Star*. Recordings: Billie Holiday (Vocalion); Eddy Duchin, vocal by Jerry Cooper (Victor); Grace Moore and Richard Crooks (Victor).

With Pen in Hand. w/m Bobby Goldsboro, 1968. First chart record by Billy Vera (Atlantic); followed by Vicki Carr (Liberty), 1969; and the writer, Bobby Goldsboro (United Artists), 1972.

With Plenty of Money and You. w. Al Dubin, m. Harry Warren, 1937. Introduced in (MM) *Gold Diggers of 1937* and on records (Decca) by Dick Powell. Recorded by many, but outstanding version by Art Tatum (Decca). Interpolated in (MM) *My Dream Is Yours* by Lee Bowman in 1949, and by Doris Day in (MM) *She's Working Her Way Through College*, 1952.

With So Little to Be Sure Of. w/m Stephen Sondheim, 1964. Introduced by Lee Remick and Harry Guardino in (TM) *Anyone Can Whistle*.

With Thee I Swing. w/m Basil G. "Buzz" Adlam, Alex Hyde, Al Stillman, 1936. Recorded by the bands of Riley-Farley (Decca) and Teddy Wilson (Brunswick).

With These Hands. w. Benny Davis, m. Abner Silver, 1953. Introduced two years earlier on recording by Nelson Eddy and Jo Stafford (Columbia). Hit records by Eddie Fisher, with Hugo Winterhalter's Orchestra (RCA Victor); and Johnny Ray, with The Four Lads and Buddy Cole's Quintet (Columbia). Revived by Tom Jones (Parrot), 1965.

With the Wind and the Rain in Your Hair. w/m Jack Lawrence and Clara Edwards, 1940. Lawrence adapted Edward's ten-year-old concert song into a popular form. Featured and recorded by Bob Crosby, vocal by Marion Mann (Decca); Kay Kyser, vocal by Ginny Simms (Columbia); Bob Chester, vocal by Dolores O'Neill (Bluebird). Revived by Pat Boone (Dot), 1959.

With This Ring. w/m Luther Dixon, Anthony Hester, and Richard Wylie, 1967. Top 20 record by The Platters (Musicor).

With You. w/m Irving Berlin, 1930. Introduced by Harry Richman in (MM) *Puttin' On the Ritz* and recorded by him (Brunswick). Fred Waring (Victor) and Guy Lombardo (Columbia) also had popular recordings.

With You I'm Born Again. w. Carol Connors, m. David Shire, 1979. Sung on the soundtrack of (MP) *Fast Break*, and on records by Billy Preston and Syreeta (Motown).

With You on My Mind. w. Charlotte Hawkins, m. Nat "King" Cole, 1957. Introduced and recorded by Nat "King" Cole (Capitol).

With Your Love. w/m Martyn Buchwald, Joey Covington, and Victor Smith, 1976. Top 20 record by The Jefferson Starship (Grunt).

Wives and Lovers. w. Hal David, m. Burt Bacharach, 1963. From the film title of the same name. Top 20 record by Jack Jones (Kapp).

WKRP In Cincinnati. w/m James Thomas Wells and Hugh Wilson, 1981. Signature song of the series (TVP) "WKRP in Cincinnati," sung under the titles and on records by Steve Carlisle (MCA).

Woke Up This Morning. w/m Riley King and Jules Taub, 1953. Leading R&B record by B. B. King (RPM).

W-O-L-D. w/m Harry Chapin, 1974. Recorded by Harry Chapin (Elektra).

Wolverine Blues. w/m Ferdinand "Jelly Roll" Morton, Benjamin F. Spikes, John C. Spikes, 1923. The New Orleans Rhythm Kings recorded this (Gennett) followed by many others including Jelly Roll Morton (Victor) and Larry Clinton (Victor).

Wolverton Mountain. w/m Merle Kilgore and Claude King, 1962. Crossover (Country/Pop) hit, introduced and recorded by Claude King (Columbia). See also "(I'm the Girl on) Wolverton Mountain."

Woman. w/m John Lennon, 1981. Gold single by John Lennon from the platinum album "Double Fantasy" (Geffen).

Woman. w/m Paul McCartney, 1966. Top 20 song recorded by the British duo Peter [Asher] and Gordon [Waller] (Capitol).

Woman, a Lover, a Friend, A. w/m Sid Wyche, 1960. Top 20 record by Jackie Wilson (Brunswick).

Woman, Woman. w/m Charles Anderson, 1967. Gold record by Gary Puckett and The Union Gap (Columbia).

Woman (Sensuous Woman). w/m Gary S. Paxton, 1972. Hit Country record by Don Gibson (Hickory).

Woman (Uh-Huh!). w/m Dick Gleason, 1953. First recorded by Johnny Desmond (Coral). The best-seller was recorded by José Ferrer, with Norman Leyden's Orchestra and chorus (Columbia).

Woman Always Knows, A. w/m Billy Sherrill, 1971. Hit Country record by David Houston (Epic).

Woman Don't Go Astray. w/m King Floyd, 1972. Recorded by King Floyd (Chimneyville).

Woman from Tokyo. w/m Richard Blackmore, Ian Gillian, Roger Glover, Jon Lord, Ian Paice, 1973. Recorded by the British group Deep Purple (Warner Bros.).

Woman Helping Man. w/m Mark Charron, 1969. Recorded by The Vogues (Reprise).

Woman in Love. w/m Barry Gibb and Robin Gibb, 1980. #1 gold single from the platinum album "Guilty," by Barbra Streisand (Columbia).

Woman in Love, A. w/m Charles Anderson, 1967. Top 10 Country chart record by Bonnie Guitar (Dot).

Woman in Love, A. w/m Frank Loesser, 1955. Introduced by Marlon Brando and Jean Simmons in (MM) *Guys and Dolls*. Best-selling records by The Four Aces (Decca) and Frankie Laine (Mercury).

Woman in the Moon, The. w/m Kenny Ascher and Paul Williams, 1976. Introduced by Barbra Streisand in (MM) *A Star Is Born*.

Woman in You, The. w/m Barry Gibb, Robin Gibb, and Maurice Gibb, 1983. Recorded by the British brother trio The Bee Gees (RSO).

Woman Is a Sometime Thing, A. w. DuBose Heyward, m. George Gershwin, 1935. Introduced by Edward Matthews and chorus in (TM) *Porgy and Bess*. In the film version (MM) *Porgy and Bess*, 1959, it was sung by Leslie Scott, Sammy Davis, Jr., and Loulie Jean Norman, dubbing for Diahann Carroll.

Woman Is Only a Woman, But a Good Cigar Is a Smoke, A. w. Harry B. Smith, m. Victor Herbert, 1905. Based on a line from Kipling's "The Betrothed," this comedy song was introduced by Melville Stewart in (TM) *Miss Dolly Dollars*.

Woman Lives for Love, A. w/m George Richey, Norro Wilson, and Glenn Sutton, 1970. Country chart record by Wanda Jackson (Capitol).

Woman Needs Love, A (Just Like You Do). w/m Ray Parker, Jr., 1981. Top 10 record by Ray Parker, Jr. & Raydio (Arista).

Woman of the World (Leave My World Alone). w/m Sharon Higgins, 1969. #1 Country chart record by Loretta Lynn (Decca).

Woman's Got Soul. w/m Curtis Mayfield, 1965. Top 40 record by The Impressions (ABC-Paramount).

Woman's Gotta Have It. w/m Darryl Carter, Linda Cooke, and Bobby Womack, 1972. Recorded by Bobby Womack (United Artists).

Woman's Intuition, A. w/m Madeline Burroughs, 1960. Country hit by the Wilburn Brothers (Decca).

959

Woman's Prerogative, A. w. Johnny Mercer, m. Harold Arlen, 1946. Introduced by Pearl Bailey in (TM) *St. Louis Woman.*

Women Do Funny Things to Me. w/m Larry Kingston, 1966. Top 10 Country record by Del Reeves (United Artists).

Women I've Never Had. w/m Hank Williams, Jr., 1980. Recorded by Country singer Hank Williams, Jr. (Elektra).

Women's Love Rights. w/m Angelo Bond and William Weatherspoon, 1971. Recorded by Laura Lee (Hot Wax).

Wonder Bar. w. Al Dubin, m. Harry Warren, 1934. Introduced by Al Jolson in (MM) *Wonder Bar.*

Wonder Could I Live There Anymore. w/m Bill Rice, 1970. Hit Country and chart Pop record by Charley Pride (RCA).

Wonderful! Wonderful! w. Ben Raleigh, m. Sherman Edwards, 1956. Popularized by Johnny Mathis on his first chart record (Columbia). Revived with a hit record in 1963 by the Philadelphia soul group The Tymes (Parkway).

Wonderful, Wonderful Day. w. Johnny Mercer, m. Gene De Paul, 1954. Introduced by Jane Powell in (MM) *Seven Brides for Seven Brothers.*

Wonderful Baby. w/m Don McLean, 1975. Written and recorded as a tribute to Fred Astaire by Don McLean (United Artists).

Wonderful Copenhagen. w/m Frank Loesser, 1951. Introduced by Danny Kaye in (MM) *Hans Christian Andersen.*

Wonderful Day Like Today, A. w/m Leslie Bricusse and Anthony Newley, 1964. Introduced by Cyril Ritchard and the chorus in (TM) *The Roar of the Greasepaint—The Smell of the Crowd.*

Wonderful Guy, A. w. Oscar Hammerstein II, m. Richard Rodgers, 1949. Introduced by Mary Martin in (TM) *South Pacific.* Mitzi Gaynor sang it in the film version (MM) *South Pacific,* 1958.

Wonderful One (My). w. Dorothy Terris (pseud. for Theodora Morse), m. Paul Whiteman, Ferde Grofé, 1922. Adapted from a theme by Marshall Neilan. Whiteman had a successful (Victor) recording. It later became the theme song of the popular radio singer Al Shayne. Judy Garland sang it in (MM) *Strike Up the Band,* 1940. It was heard in (MM) *Margie,* 1940, and (MM) *The Great American Broadcast,* 1941.

Wonderful Summer. w/m Gil Garfield and Perry Botkin, Jr., 1963. Recorded by Robin Ward (Dot).

Wonderful to Be Young. w. Hal David, m. Burt Bacharach, 1962. Introduced by Cliff Richard in the British film (MM) *Wonderful to Be Young.*

Wonderful Tonight. w/m Eric Clapton, 1978. Recorded by the English singer Eric Clapton (RSO).

Wonderful World, Beautiful People. w/m Jimmy Cliff, 1970. Top 40 record by the Jamaican reggae singer/composer Jimmy Cliff (A&M).

Wonderful World (What a). See **(What a) Wonderful World.**

Wonderful World of the Young, The. w/m Sid Tepper and Roy C. Bennett, 1962. Featured and recorded by Andy Williams (Columbia).

Wonderful You. w. Jack Meskill and Max Rich, m. Pete Wendling, 1929.

Wondering. w/m Jack Schafer, 1957. Recorded by Patti Page (Mercury).

Wondering. w/m Joe Werner, 1952. Country hit recorded by Webb Pierce (Decca).

Wondering Where the Lions Are. w/m Bruce Cockburn, 1980. Recorded by the Canadian singer/songwriter Bruce Cockburn (Millennium).

Wonderland. w/m Milan Williams, 1980. Recorded by The Commodores (Motown).

Wonderland by Night. w. Lincoln Chase, m. Klauss-Gunter Neuman, 1961. Original German title, "Wunderland bei Nacht." German instrumental recording released in U.S. by Bert Kaempfert, with trumpet solo by Charly Tabor, became a #1 best-seller (Decca). Louis Prima and his Orchestra also had a chart record (Dot). First vocal recording by Anita Bryant (Carlton).

Wonder of You, The. w/m Baker Knight, 1959. First hit record by Ray Peterson (RCA). Revived by Elvis Presley, recorded live at Las Vegas (RCA), 1970, earning a gold record.

Wonder When My Baby's Coming Home. w. Kermit Goell, m. Arthur Kent, 1942. Among recordings: Sammy Kaye, vocal by Nancy Norman (Victor); Jimmy Dorsey, vocal by Helen O'Connell (Decca).

Wonder Why. w. Sammy Cahn, m. Nicholas Brodsky, 1951. Introduced by Jane Powell in (MM) *Rich, Young and Pretty*. Nominated for Academy Award.

Won't You Be My Honey? w. Jack Drislane, m. Theodore F. Morse, 1907. Popular record by Ada Jones and Billy Murray (Victor). Contrary to later record business practice, they each recorded solo versions for another label (Columbia).

Won't You Be My Little Girl. w. Isaac G. Reynolds, m. Homer Tourjee, 1896.

Won't You Be My Sweetheart? w. J. G. Judson, m. H. C. Verner, 1893.

Won't You Come Over to My House? w. Harry H. Williams, m. Egbert Van Alstyne, 1906.

Won't You Waltz "Home Sweet Home" with Me? w/m Herbert Ingraham, 1907.

Wood. w/m Jimmy Durante, 1930. Interpolated into the otherwise all-Cole Porter score for (TM) *The New Yorkers* by Clayton, Jackson, and Durante. The song extolled the virtues of wood and ended Act 1 by filling the stage with a vast amount of lumber.

Woodchopper's Ball. m. Woody Herman and Joe Bishop, 1939. Instrumental featured by Woody Herman and his Orchestra; recorded by them twice, 1939 (Decca) and 1947 (Columbia).

Wooden Heart. w/m (adapted) Bert Kaempfert, Kay Twomey, Ben Weisman, and Fred Wise, 1960. Based on a German folk song, "Muss I Denn zum Stadtele Haus." Introduced by Elvis Presley in (MM) *G. I. Blues*, and recorded by him (RCA). The #1 record was by Joe Dowell (Smash), 1961. Revived by Bobby Vinton (ABC), 1975.

Wooden Soldier and the China Doll, The. w. Charles Newman, m. Isham Jones, 1932. Most popular recordings: Ben Bernie (Brunswick), Nat Shilkret (Victor), Rudy Vallee (Hit of the Week), Sleepy Hall (Melotone).

Woodman, Woodman, Spare That Tree. w/m Irving Berlin, 1911. Based on the George Pope Morris/Henry Russell song of 1837, Berlin wrote this for Bert Williams who introduced it in (TM) *Ziegfeld Follies of 1911*. It then became a staple of William's vaudeville act. Leading records by Bert Williams (Columbia) and Bob Roberts (Victor).

Woodpecker Song, The. w. Harold Adamson (Engl.), m. Eldo di Lazzaro, 1940. Not to be confused with "Woody Woodpecker." This Italian song, originally titled "Reginella Campagnola," had words by C. Bruno and the composer. In the U.S. it was introduced by Will Glahe and his Musette Orchestra (Victor). The leading records were by Glenn Miller, vocal by Marion Hutton (Bluebird); the Andrews Sisters (Decca); Kate Smith (Columbia).

Woodstock. w/m Joni Mitchell, 1970. Written about the Woodstock, N.Y., festival, 1969. Hit record by Crosby, Stills, Nash, and Young (Atlantic). Among other versions, Joni Mitchell, in her album "Ladies of the Canyon" (Reprise); The Assembled Multitude (Atlantic). Top 40 single by the English group, Matthew's Southern Comfort (Decca), 1971.

Woody Woodpecker. w/m George Tibbles and Ramez Idriss, 1948. Based on the character in the Walter Lantz cartoon film, *Wet Blanket Policy*, and future Woody Woodpecker shorts. #1 hit record by Kay Kyser, his Orchestra, and singers (Columbia). Mel Blanc, whose voice was heard as the tree-pecking bird in the films, recorded it with The Sportsmen (Capitol).

Woo-Hoo. w/m George Donald McGraw, 1959. Instrumental recorded by sextet The Rock-a-Teens (Roulette).

Wooly Bully. w/m Domingo "Sam" Samudio, 1965. Gold record by Sam the Sham and The Pharoahs (MGM).

Words. w/m Barry Gibb, Robin Gibb, and Maurice Gibb, 1968. Written and Top 20 record by the British brother trio The Bee Gees (Atco). Hit Country record revival by Susie Allanson (Elektra), 1979.

Words. w/m Tommy Boyce and Bobby Hart, 1967. Top 20 side, coupled with "Pleasant Valley Sunday" (q.v.), by The Monkees (Colgems).

Words Are in My Heart, The. w. Al Dubin, m. Harry Warren, 1935. Introduced by Dick Powell and fifty-six girls at fifty-six pianos in a Busby Berkeley production number in (MM) *The Gold Diggers of 1935*. Powell also recorded it (Brunswick).

Words Get in the Way. w/m Gloria Estefan, 1986. Top 10 record by Miami Sound Machine, with Estefan as lead singer (Epic).

Words I'm Gonna Have to Eat. w/m Liz Anderson, 1967. Top 10 Country record by Bill Phillips (Decca).

Words of Love. w/m John Phillips, 1967. Top 10 record by The Mamas and The Papas (Dunhill).

Words Without Music. w. Ira Gershwin, m. Vernon Duke, 1936. Sung by Gertrude Niesen and danced by Harriet Hoctor in (TM) *Ziegfeld Follies, 1936 Edition*.

Word Up. w/m Larry Blackmon and Tomi Jenkins, 1986. Top 10 record by the group Cameo (Atlanta Artists).

Workin' at the Car Wash Blues. w/m Jim Croce, 1974. Recorded by Jim Croce (ABC).

Workin' for the Man. w/m Roy Orbison, 1962. Recorded by Roy Orbison (Monument).

Working Class Hero. w/m John Lennon, 1970. Introduced by John Lennon in "Plastic Ono Band" album (Apple). Chart single by Tommy Roe (MGM), 1973.

Working for the Weekend. w/m Paul Dean, Matt Frenette, and Mike Reno, 1982. Recorded by the Canadian quintet Loverboy (Columbia).

"Working Girl" Theme. See **Let the River Run**.

Working in the Coal Mine. w/m Allen Toussaint, 1966. Top 10 record by Lee Dorsey (Amy). Revived in (MM) *Heavy Metal*, 1981, and recorded by the rock group Devo (Full Moon).

Working Man Blues. w/m Merle Haggard, 1969. Hit Country record by Merle Haggard (Capitol).

Workin' on a Groovy Thing. w/m Neil Sedaka and Roger Atkins, 1968. First chart record by Patti Drew (Capitol), followed in 1969 by a Top 20 version by The 5th Dimension (Soul City).

Work Song, The. w. Oscar Brown, Jr., m. Nat Adderley, 1966. Jazz instrumental to which a lyric was added for recording by Oscar Brown, Jr. (Columbia). Herb Alpert and The Tijuana Brass had a Top 40 instrumental in 1966 (A&M).

Work with Me Annie. w/m Hank Ballard, 1954. Top 10 R&B record by The Midnighters (Federal).

World. 1969. Top 10 R&B and Top 40 Pop chart record by James Brown (King).

World Is a Ghetto, The. w/m Dee Allen, Harold Brown, B. B. Dickerson, Lonnie Jordan, Charles Miller, Lee Oskar, and Howard Scott, 1972. Written and gold record by War (United Artists).

World Is in My Arms, The. w. E. Y. Harburg, m. Burton Lane, 1940. Introduced by Jack Whiting and Eunice Healey in (TM) *Hold On to Your Hats.* Recorded by Tommy Dorsey, vocal by Frank Sinatra (Victor).

World Is Mine, The. w. Holt Marvell (Eric Maschwitz), m. George Posford, 1936. This English song was introduced by Nino Martini in (MM) *The Gay Desperado.* Recorded by Tony Martin (Decca); and Richard Himber, vocal by Allen Stuart (Victor).

World Is Mine, The. w. E. Y. Harburg, m. John Green, 1934. From (MP) *The Count of Monte Cristo.* Recorded by Lanny Ross (Brunswick) and Archie Bleyer's Orchestra (Vocalion).

World Is Round, The. w/m Tony Senn, Tommy Stough, and Henry Paul Johnson, 1966. Top 10 Country chart record by Roy Drusky (Mercury).

World Is Waiting for the Sunrise, The. w. Eugene Lockhart, m. Ernest Seitz, 1919, 1951. The lyricist later had a notable acting career on stage and screen as Gene Lockhart. The song, written as what used to be called a "big ballad," became a favorite of jazz musicians. John Steel (Victor) and Isham Jones and his Orchestra (Brunswick) had the first hit records. Among the many jazz versions were those by Jack Teagarden (HRS), Bob Crosby (Decca), and Duke Ellington with Al Hibbler (Columbia). The biggest success, however, was the 1951 recording by Les Paul and Mary Ford (Capitol), which sold over a million copies and helped the song become a "Hit Parader."

World I Used to Know, The. w/m Rod McKuen, 1964. Leading record by Jimmy Rodgers (Dot).

World of Fantasy. w/m Clarence Burke and Gregory Fowler, 1966. Recorded by The Five Stairsteps (Windy C).

World of Make Believe. w/m Pete McCord, Marion Carpenter, Pee Wee Maddux, and H. E. Smith, 1974. Country record hit by Bill Anderson (Decca).

World of Our Own, A. w/m Tom Springfield, 1965. Popularized by the Australian group The Seekers (Capitol). Revived by Country singer Sonny James (Capitol), 1968.

World Outside, The. w. Carl Sigman, m. Richard Adinsell, 1958. Lyrics added to the 1942 composition "Warsaw Concerto" (q.v.) from the film (MP) *Suicide Squadron.* This version recorded by The Four Aces, with Jack Pleis's Orchestra (Decca).

World Owes Me a Living, The. w. Larry Morey, m. Leigh Harline, 1934. From the cartoon musical film (MM) *The Grasshopper and the Ants.*

World So Full of Love, A. w/m Roger Miller and Faron Young, 1960. Leading C&W chart record by Ray Sanders (Liberty). Also recorded by co-composer Faron Young (Capitol).

World Weary. w/m Noël Coward, 1928. Introduced by Beatrice Lillie in the Broadway production of (TM) *This Year of Grace!* The song was not in the London production, which was the predecessor. Coward recorded the song coupled with his "Zigeuner" (q.v.) (Victor).

World We Knew, The (Over and Over). w. Carl Sigman (Engl.), m. Bert Kaempfert and Herbert Rehbein, 1967. German song. Top 40 English version by Frank Sinatra (Reprise).

World Where You Live. w/m Neil Finn, 1987. Popular track and single from the album "Crowded House" by the Australian group of the same name (Chrysalis).

World Without Heroes, A. w/m Bob Ezrin, Lou Reed, Gene Simmons, and Paul Stanley, 1982. Recorded by the rock band Kiss (Casablanca).

World Without Love, A. w/m John Lennon and Paul McCartney, 1964. #1 record by the British team of Peter and Gordon (Capitol). Chart record by Bobby Rydell (Cameo).

Worried Guy. w/m Jack Reardon and Paul Evans, 1964. Top 40 record by Johnny Tillotson (MGM).

Worried Man, A. w/m Dave Guard and Tom Glazer, 1959. Based on American folk song. Top 40 record by The Kingston Trio (Capitol).

Worried Mind. w/m Jimmie Davis and Ted Daffan, 1941. Two-market song, Country and Pop. Introduced in first category by Ted Daffan and His Texans (Okeh); followed by Bob Wills and His Texans, vocal by Tommy Duncan (Okeh); and later, Roy Acuff (Conqueror). In the Pop field, outstanding records by Larry Clinton, vocal by Butch Stone (Bluebird); Wayne King and his Orchestra (Victor); The Milt Herth Trio (Decca).

Worry, Worry, Worry. w/m Ramez Idriss and George Tibbles, 1948. Recorded by Hal Derwin (Capitol), and Kay Kyser and his Orchestra (Columbia).

Worry Song, The. w. Ralph Freed, m. Sammy Fain, 1945. Sung and danced by Gene Kelly and the cartoon character Jerry [of Tom and Jerry] in (MM) *Anchors Aweigh*.

Worst That Could Happen, The. w/m Jim Webb, 1967. Hit record by The Brooklyn Bridge (Buddah).

Wot's It to Ya. w/m Robbie Nevil and Broek Walsh, 1987. Recorded by Robbie Nevil (Manhattan).

Would I Lie to You? w/m Annie Lennox and David Stewart, 1985. Written and Top 10 record by the British duo The Eurythmics (RCA).

Would I Love You (Love You, Love You). w. Bob Russell, m. Harold Spina, 1951. Patti Page had a million-seller (Mercury). Other Top 20 versions by Doris Day, with Harry James's Orchestra (Columbia); Helen O'Connell (Capitol); Tony Martin (RCA Victor).

Would'ja for a Big Red Apple? w. Johnny Mercer, m. Henry Souvaine, 1932. Introduced by Peggy Cartwright and Gordon Smith in (TM) *Americana*.

Would Jesus Wear a Rolex. w/m Chet Atkins and Margaret Archer, 1987. Novelty Country chart single by Ray Stevens, from his album "Crackin' Up" (MCA).

Wouldn't It Be Loverly? w. Alan Jay Lerner, m. Frederick Loewe, 1956. Introduced by Julie Andrews in (TM) *My Fair Lady*. Sung by Marni Nixon on the soundtrack, dubbing for Audrey Hepburn, in (MM) *My Fair Lady*, 1964.

Wouldn't It Be Nice? w. Tony Asher and Brian Wilson, m. Brian Wilson, 1966. Top 10 record by The Beach Boys (Capitol).

Wouldn't It Be Wonderful? w. Grant Clarke, m. Harry Akst, 1929. Introduced by Ted Lewis in (MM) *Is Everybody Happy?* and recorded by him (Columbia).

Would There Be Love? w. Mack Gordon, m. Harry Revel, 1935. From (MM) *Stolen Harmony*, starring Ben Bernie and his Orchestra, George Raft, and Grace Bradley. Recordings: Morton Downey (Melotone); Gertrude Niesen (Columbia); the bands of Will Osborne (Banner) and Paul Pendarvis (Columbia).

Would You. w. Johnny Burke, m. James Van Heusen, 1946. Introduced by Dorothy Lamour in (MM) *Road to Utopia*. Not to be confused with the Freed-Brown song of the same title.

Would You? w. Arthur Freed, m. Nacio Herb Brown, 1936. Introduced by Jeanette MacDonald in (MM) *San Francisco*. In 1952, Debbie Reynolds and Gene Kelly revived it in (MM) *Singin' in the Rain*. Bing Crosby had a popular version with Victor Young's Orchestra (Decca). The song was in the score of the Broadway production (TM) *Singin' in the Rain*, 1985.

Would You Believe It. w/m Bart Howard, 1958. Introduced, featured, and recorded by Mabel Mercer (Atlantic).

Would You Believe Me? w. Charles Tobias, m. M. K. Jerome and Ray Heindorf, 1947. Introduced in (MM) *Love and Learn* by Martha Vickers performing it, while her voice was dubbed on the soundtrack by Trudy Erwin. Recorded by Claude Thornhill, vocal by Fran Warren (Columbia); Skitch Henderson, vocal by Eileen Barton (Capitol).

Would You Care? w/m Charles K. Harris, 1905. Popular song, featured and recorded by Bryon G. Harlan (Victor).

Would You Catch a Falling Star. w/m Bobby Braddock, 1982. Top 10 Country chart record by John Anderson (Warner Bros.).

Would You Hold It Against Me? w/m Bill West and Dottie West, 1966. Hit Country record by Dottie West (RCA).

Would You Lay with Me (in a Field of Stone). w/m David Allan Coe, 1974. Hit Country record by Tanya Tucker (Columbia).

Would You Like to Take a Walk? w. Mort Dixon and Billy Rose, m. Harry Warren, 1930. Introduced by Hannah Williams and Hal Thompson in (TM) *Sweet and Low*, produced by Billy Rose. It was retained for the revue *Billy Rose's Crazy Quilt*, 1931. Popular recordings by Frank Crumit and Julia Sanderson (Victor), Hal Kemp (Brunswick), Rudy Vallee (Victor), Annette Hanshaw (Velvetone).

Would You Rather Be a Colonel with an Eagle on Your Shoulder or a Private with a Chicken on Your Knee? w. Sidney D. Mitchell, m. Archie Gottler, 1918. Performed by Eddie Cantor in (TM) *Ziegfeld Follies of 1918*.

Wound Time Can't Erase, A. w/m William D. Johnson, 1962. Country hit by Stonewall Jackson (Columbia).

Wrap Her Up. w/m Dave Johnstone, Bernie Taupin, Elton John, 1985. English song, recorded by Elton John (Geffen).

Wrap It Up. w/m Isaac Hayes and David Porter, 1970, 1986. Introduced by Archie Bell and The Drells (Atlantic), 1970. Revived by the quartet The Fabulous Thunderbirds (CBS Associated), 1986.

Wrapped Around Your Finger. w/m Sting, 1984. Top 10 record by the British trio Sting (A&M).

Wrappin' It Up. m. Fletcher Henderson, 1934. Instrumental, recorded first by Fletcher Henderson's Band (Decca). Benny Goodman had the best-selling version (Victor), 1938.

Wrap Your Arms Around Me. w/m Harry Wayne Casey and Richard Finch, 1978. Recorded by KC and The Sunshine Band (T.K.).

Wrap Your Troubles in Dreams. w. Ted Koehler and Billy Moll, m. Harry Barris, 1931. Introduced, featured, and recorded by Bing Crosby (Victor). It was heard in (MM) *Top Man* in 1943, and sung by Frankie Laine in (MM) *Rainbow Round My Shoulder* in 1952. Laine's version was released as a record (Mercury).

Wreck of the Edmund Fitzgerald, The. w/m Gordon Lightfoot, 1976. Top 10 record by the Canadian singer/writer, Gordon Lightfoot, based on the actual story of an ore vessel that sank in Lake Superior the prior year (Reprise).

Wreck of the John B (a.k.a. **Sloop John B**). w/m Traditional (Bahamanian), 1964. The two most popular versions were recorded by Jimmie Rodgers (Roulette), 1964, and with alternate title by The Beach Boys, adapted by Brian Wilson (Capitol), 1966.

Wreck of the Old '97. w/m Henry C. Work, 1924. Work, basing this on a 19th-century song, "The Ship That Never Returned," wrote this reference to a 1903 train wreck in Virginia. Vernon Dalhart recorded it, coupled with "The Prisoner's Song" (q.v.) (Victor), and it became one of the biggest sellers up to that time. It was first recorded by Henry Whittier, a Country singer (Okeh). Carl Fenton (Brunswick), and later, Muggsy Spanier (Decca) had recorded versions.

Wreck of the Shenandoah, The. w/m Carson Robison, 1925. Robison, under the pseudonym of Maggie Andrews, wrote this song about the wreck of a U.S. Army dirigible in Ohio. Vernon Dalhart cornered the market by recording it for eleven labels: (Victor), (Columbia), (Edison), and eight others.

Wreck on the Highway. w/m Dorsey Dixon, 1946. C&W hit for Roy Acuff (Okeh). Revived by Wilma Lee and Stoney Cooper (Hickory), 1961.

Wringle Wrangle. w/m Stan Jones, 1956. Introduced by Fess Parker in (MP) *Westward Ho the Wagons*, and recorded by him (Disneyland). Also recorded by Bill Hayes (ABC-Paramount).

Write Me a Letter. w/m Howard Biggs, 1947. R&B hit by The Ravens (National).

Write Me Sweetheart. w/m Roy Acuff, 1943. Wartime Country ballad by Roy Acuff (Okeh).

Writing on the Wall, The. w/m Mark Barkan, Sandy Baron, and George Paxton, 1961. Top 10 record by Adam Wade (Coed).

Written on the Wind. w/m Sammy Cahn, m. Victor Young, 1956. Sung on the soundtrack, behind the opening titles of (MP) *Written on the Wind*, by The Four Aces and recorded by them (Decca). Song nominated for Academy Award, 1956.

Wrong for Each Other. w/m Doc Pomus and Mort Shuman, 1964. Featured and recorded by Andy Williams (Columbia).

Wrong Note Rag. w. Betty Comden and Adolph Green, m. Leonard Bernstein, 1953. Show-stopping number introduced by Rosalind Russell and Edie Adams in (TM) *Wonderful Town*.

Wunderbar. w/m Cole Porter, 1949. Introduced by Alfred Drake and Patricia Morison in (TM) *Kiss Me Kate*, and sung by Howard Keel and Kathryn Grayson in (MM) *Kiss Me Kate*, 1953.

Wurlitzer Prize, The (I Don't Want to Get Over You). w/m Chips Moman and Bobby Emmons, 1977. Hit Country record by Waylon Jennings (RCA).

X

Xanadu. w/m Jeff Lynne, 1980. Introduced in (MM) *Xanadu* and on Top 10 record (MCA) by Olivia Newton-John and The Electric Light Orchestra.

Y

Yaaka Hula Hickey Dula. w/m E. Ray Goetz, Joe Young, and Pete Wendling, 1916. Introduced by Al Jolson in (TM) *Robinson Crusoe, Jr.* During its first year it was recorded by the Avon Comedy Four (Victor), Arthur Collins and Bryon G. Harlan (Victor), and Al Jolson (Columbia). The song was revived in the Helen Morgan film (MM) *Applause*, 1929.

Ya Got Me. w. Betty Comden and Adolph Green, m. Leonard Bernstein, 1945. Introduced by Nancy Walker, Betty Comden, Adolph Green, and Cris Alexander in (TM) *On the Town.*

Ya Got Me. w. Bickley Reichner, m. Clay Boland, 1938. Introduced and recorded by Jan Savitt, vocal by Bon Bon (Bluebird). Also recorded by the bands of Tommy Dorsey (Victor) and Clyde McCoy (Decca).

Ya Gotta Know How to Love. w. Bud Green, m. Harry Warren, 1926. Recorded by Gene Austin (Victor), Irving Aaronson and His Commanders (Victor), the California Ramblers (Columbia), and Fess Williams (Gennett).

Yah Mo B There. w/m James Ingram, Michael McDonald, Rod Temperton, and Quincy Jones, 1984. Crossover (R&B/Pop) hit by James Ingram with Michael McDonald (Qwest).

Yah-Ta-Ta, Yah-Ta-Ta (Talk, Talk, Talk) w. Johnny Burke, James Van Heusen, 1945. Recorded by Bing Crosby and Judy Garland (Decca).

Yakety Axe. See **Yakety Sax**.

Yakety Sax. m. James Rich and Boots Randolph, 1963. Instrumental hit, recorded by saxophonist Boots Randolph (Monument). Guitarist Chet Atkins recorded it as "Yakety Axe" (RCA), 1965.

Yakety Yak. w/m Jerry Leiber and Mike Stoller, 1958. #1 hit record by The Coasters (Atco).

Yam, The. w/m Irving Berlin, 1938. Introduced by Fred Astaire and Ginger Rogers in (MM) *Carefree*. Rogers recorded it (Bluebird). Best-selling record by Jimmy Dorsey's Orchestra (Decca).

Yama Yama Man, The. w. Collin Davis, m. Karl Hoschna, 1908. Sung by Bessie McCoy in (TM) *The Three Twins*. Popular record by Ada Jones and The Victor Light Opera Co. (Victor). It was performed by Ginger Rogers in (MM) *The Story of Vernon and Irene Castle*, 1939, and by June Haver in the Marilyn Miller biography (MM) *Look for the Silver Lining*, 1949.

Yancey Special. w. Andy Razaf, m. Meade "Lux" Lewis, 1938. Introduced by pianist Lewis (Decca). Best-selling record by Bob Crosby, featuring Bub Zurke on piano (Decca). Tune was dedicated to boogie-woogie composer and pianist Jimmy Yancey.

Yankee Doodle Blues. w. Irving Caesar and B. G. DeSylva, m. George Gershwin,

1922. Introduced by Georgie Price in (TM) *Spice of 1922*. Joan Leslie and Hazel Scott performed it in the George Gershwin film biography (MM) *Rhapsody in Blue*, 1945. It was sung by June Haver, Gloria De Haven, and chorus in (MM) *I'll Get By*, 1950.

Yankee Doodle Boy, The. w/m George M. Cohan, 1904. Introduced by Cohan in the title role of (TM) *Little Johnny Jones*. Eddie Buzzell performed it in the film version (MM) *Little Johnny Jones*, 1929. James Cagney performed it in (MM) *Yankee Doodle Dandy*, 1942, and in (MM) *The Seven Little Foys*, 1955. It was also sung by Joel Grey in (TM) *George M!*, 1968, at the Palace Theatre in New York.

Yankee Doodle Never Went to Town. w. Ralph Freed, m. Bernard Hanighen, 1935. Featured and recorded by Benny Goodman, vocal by Helen Ward (Victor); Babs and Her Brothers [The Smoothies] (Decca); Glen Gray and the Casa Loma Orchestra, vocal by Pee Wee Hunt (Decca); Joe Venuti's Orchestra (Columbia); Teddy Wilson (Brunswick).

Yankee Rose. w. Sidney Holden, m. Abe Frankel, 1926. Recorded by Sam Lanin's Orchestra with vocal by Vaughn DeLeath (Okeh).

Yank Me, Crank Me. w/m Ted Nugent, 1978. Recorded by Ted Nugent (Epic).

Yardbird Suite. m. Charlie Parker, 1946. Alto saxophone great Charlie Parker, with group that included Miles Davis on trumpet, had first recording (Dial). Among other versions: Al Haig (Pacific Jazz), Earl Coleman (Dial).

Yard Went On Forever, The. w/m Jim Webb, 1968. Leading record by Richard Harris (Dunhill).

Ya Wanna Buy a Bunny? w/m Carl Hoefle and Del Porter, 1949. Easter novelty recorded by Spike Jones and his City Slickers, vocal by George Rock (RCA Victor).

Yawning Song, The. w/m Kermit Goell and Fred Spielman, 1958. Performed by a puppet, with the voice of Stan Freberg on the soundtrack in (MM) *Tom Thumb*.

Ya Ya. w/m Lee Dorsey, Clarence Lewis, and Morgan Robinson, 1961. Hit record by Lee Dorsey (Fury).

Yearning (Just for You). w. Benny Davis, m. Joe Burke, 1925. A popular song on radio and records, featured and recorded by Gene Austin (Victor), Roger Wolfe Kahn (Victor), Harry Reser (Columbia), William F. Wirges (Perfect). Revived by Tommy Dorsey, vocal by Jack Leonard (Victor), 1938.

Yearning for Love. w. Mitchell Parish and Irving Mills, m. Edward Kennedy "Duke" Ellington, 1936. Originally written as an instrumental featuring trombonist Lawrence Brown, long-time member of the Ellington band, and titled "Lawrence's Concerto." Lyrics were added, the title changed, and the record released (Brunswick).

Yearning for Your Love. w/m Ronnie Wilson and Oliver Scott, 1981. Recorded by The Gap Band (Mercury).

Year of the Cat. w/m Al Stewart and Peter Wood, 1977. Recorded in England; Top 10 U.S. record by Al Stewart (Janus).

Years. w/m Kye Fleming and Dennis Morgan, 1980. First recorded by Barbara Mandrell (ABC), 1979. Chart cover record by Wayne Newton (Aries II).

Year That Clayton Delaney Died, The. w/m Tom T. Hall, 1971. Country and Pop chart hit by Tom T. Hall (Mercury).

Yeh! Yeh! w. Jon Hendricks, m. Rodgers Grant and Pat Patrick, 1963. Instrumental, introduced and chart record by Mongo Santamaria and his Band (Battle). Top 40 release in the U.S. by the English pianist/singer Georgie Fame, backed by The Blue Flames (Imperial), 1965.

Yellow Balloon, The. w/m Dick St. John, Jay Lee, and Gary Zekley, 1967. Top 40 record by The Yellow Balloon (Canterbury).

Yellow Bandana, The. w/m Al Gorgoni, Steve Karliski, and Larry Kolber, 1963. Hit C&W chart record by Faron Young (Mercury).

Yellow Bird. w/m Alan Bergman, Marilyn Keith, and Norman Luboff, 1961. Adapted from a West Indian folk song. First popular record by The Mills Brothers (Dot), 1959. Hit instrumental by Arthur Lyman (Hi Fi).

Yellow Dog Blues, The. w/m W. C. Handy, 1928. This blues was written fourteen years earlier, but it did not receive public acceptance until this period. Among recordings: Duke Ellington (Brunswick), Ted Lewis (Columbia), Bessie Smith (Columbia), and W. C. Handy (Lyratone).

Yellow River. w/m Jeff Christie, 1970. Recorded by the English trio Christie (Epic).

Yellow Rose, The. w/m John Wilder, 1984. Theme song of the series (TVP) "The Yellow Rose." #1 Country chart record by Johnny Lee with Lane Brody (Warner Bros.).

Yellow Rose of Texas, The. w/m adapted by Don George, 1955. Based on a mid-nineteenth-century song often heard in minstrel shows. It was sung by both sides in the Civil War, in its original form and parodied. This version was recorded by Mitch Miller's Orchestra and chorus (Columbia) and became a #1 best-seller. Johnny Desmond had a popular vocal, with Dick Jacob's Orchestra (Coral).

Yellow Roses. w/m Kenny Devine and Sam Nichols, 1955. Hit country record by Hank Snow (RCA Victor).

Yellow Submarine. w/m John Lennon and Paul McCartney, 1966. Gold record by The Beatles (Capitol). Sung on the soundtrack of their animated film (MM) *Yellow Submarine*, 1968.

Yes, I Know Why. w/m Webb Pierce, 1956. Introduced and recorded by Webb Pierce (Decca).

Yes, I'm Lonesome Tonight. w/m Roy Turk and Lou Handman, 1961. Answer song to Elvis Presley's revival of "Are You Lonesome Tonight?" (q.v.). Recorded by Thelma Carpenter (Coral) and Dodie Stevens (Dot).

Yes, I'm Ready. w/m Barbara Mason, 1965. Top 10 record by Barbara Mason (Arctic). Revived with a gold record by Teri DeSario with K.C. (Casablanca), 1979.

Yes, Indeed! w/m Sy Oliver, 1941. Featured and hit record by Tommy Dorsey, vocal by Jo Stafford and Sy Oliver (Victor). Bing Crosby and Connee Boswell had a popular version (Decca).

Yes, Mr. Peters. w/m Steve Karliski and Larry Kolber, 1965. #1 Country chart record by Roy Drusky and Priscilla Mitchell (Mercury).

Yes, My Darling Daughter. w/m Jack Lawrence, 1940. Based on a Ukrainian folk song. Most popular recordings by Dinah Shore (Bluebird); Glenn Miller, vocal by Marion Hutton (Bluebird); Benny Goodman, vocal by Helen Forrest (Columbia).

Yes, My Heart. w/m Bob Merrill, 1961. Introduced by Anna Maria Alberghetti and chorus in (TM) *Carnival*.

Yes! We Have No Bananas. w/m Frank Silver and Irving Cohn, 1923. One of the biggest novelty hits of the twenties, it was introduced by Eddie Cantor who, in Philadelphia, interpolated it in the revue (TM) *Make It Snappy*. The show had a short New York run the prior year. The song was such a success that Cantor kept it as a staple of his vaudeville act. There were many recordings of it, the best-seller being Billy Jones (Vocalion). Another indication of the song's impact was the recording made by Eddie Cantor and Belle Baker, titled "I've Got the Yes! We Have No Bananas Blues" (q.v.). A French version, "Les Ananas," was sung by Maurice Chevalier in (MM) *Innocents of Paris*, 1929. Al Jolson sang the lyrics to the melodies of famous operatic arias in (MM) *Mammy*, 1930. The Pied Pipers sang it in (MM) *Luxury Liner*, 1948. Eddie Cantor, dubbing for Keefe Brasselle, sang it on the soundtrack of (MM) *The Eddie Cantor Story*, 1953.

Yes, Yes, Yes. w/m Michael Hazlewood, 1976. Comedy song recorded by Bill Cosby (Capitol).

Yes It Is. w/m John Lennon and Paul McCartney, 1965. Recorded by The Beatles (Capitol).

Yes Sir! That's My Baby. w. Gus Kahn, m. Walter Donaldson, 1925. Featured by Eddie Cantor. Hit records by Ben Bernie (Vocalion), Ace Brigode (Victor), Gene Austin (Victor), Coon-Sanders' Original Nighthawk Orchestra (Victor). Interpolated in (MM) *Broadway*, 1942; sung by Donald O'Connor, Gloria De Haven, Charles Coburn, Barbara Brown, and Joshua Shelley in (MM) *Yes Sir, That's My Baby*, 1949; sung by Doris Day and Danny Thomas in the Kahn bio (MM) *I'll See You in My Dreams*, 1951; by Cantor, dubbing for Keefe Brasselle who portrayed him, in (MM) *The Eddie Cantor Story*, 1953.

Yesterday. w/m John Lennon and Paul McCartney, 1965. Gold record and one of the biggest hits by The Beatles (Capitol). Among the many other recordings, the leading seller was by Ray Charles (ABC/TRC), 1967.

Yesterday, When I Was Young. w. Herbert Kretzmer (Engl.), Charles Aznavour, (Fr.), m. Aznavour, 1969. Introduced in France as "Hier Encore" by Charles Aznavour. Hit U.S. English version by Roy Clark (Dot).

Yesterday and You. See **Armen's Theme**.

Yesterday Once More. w/m John Bettis and Richard Carpenter, 1973. Gold record by The Carpenters (A&M). Revived by The Spinners, in medley with "Nothing Remains the Same" (Atlantic), 1981.

Yesterdays. w. Otto Harbach, m. Jerome Kern, 1933. Introduced by Fay Templeton in (TM) *Roberta*. In the first film version (MM) *Roberta*, 1935, it was sung by Irene Dunne and Helen Westley; and in the remake, retitled (MM) *Lovely to Look At*, 1952, by Kathryn Grayson and danced by Marge and Gower Champion. It was sung by a chorus in the Kern biography (MM) *Till the Clouds Roll By*, 1946.

Yesterday's Dreams. w/m Vernon Bullock, Jack Goga, Ivy Hunter, and Pamela Sawyer, 1968. Recorded by The Four Tops (Motown).

Yesterday's Gardenias. w/m Dick Robertson, Nelson Cogane, and Sammy Mysels, 1942. Featured and recorded by Glenn Miller, vocal by Ray Eberle and the Modernaires (Bluebird), and Charlie Spivak, vocal by Garry Stevens (Columbia).

Yesterday's Girl. w/m Billy Gray and Hank Thompson, 1953. Introduced and recorded by Hank Thompson (Capitol).

Yesterday's Hero. w/m Harry Vanda and John Paul Young, 1976. Introduced and recorded by the Australian singer/songwriter John Paul Young (Ariola America); followed by the Scottish group, The Bay City Rollers (Arista), 1977.

Yesterday's Memories. w/m Hank Cochran, 1962. Country chart record by Eddy Arnold (RCA).

Yesterday's Roses. w/m Gene Autry and Fred Rose, 1942. Recorded by Gene Autry (Okeh).

Yesterday's Songs. w/m Neil Diamond, 1981. Recorded by Neil Diamond (Columbia).

Yesterday's Tears. w/m Ernest Tubb, 1943. Introduced and recorded by Ernest Tubb (Decca).

Yester Love. w/m William "Smokey" Robinson and Alfred Cleveland, 1968. Top 40 record by Smokey Robinson and The Miracles (Tamla).

Yester-Me, Yester-You, Yesterday. w. Ronald Miller, m. Bryan Wells, 1969. Top 10 record by Stevie Wonder (Tamla).

Yesterthoughts. w. Stanley Adams, m. Victor Herbert, 1940. Adapted from an instrumental of Herbert's published forty years earlier. Featured and recorded by Glenn Miller, vocal by Ray Eberle (Bluebird), and Kenny Baker (Victor).

Yes Tonight, Josephine. w/m Winfield Scott and Dorothy Goodman, 1957. Featured and recorded by Johnnie Ray (Columbia).

Yes to You. w. Sidney Clare, m. Richard A. Whiting, 1934. Introduced by Alice Faye in (MM) *365 Nights in Hollywood* and recorded by her (Melotone).

Yes We Can Can. w/m Allan Toussaint, 1973. Top 20 record by The Pointer Sisters (Blue Thumb).

Yet . . . I Know. w. Don Raye (Engl.), Charles Aznavour (Fr.), m. Georges Garvarentz, 1964. French song, "Et Pourtant." Introduced in France by Charles Aznavour. English version introduced and recorded by Steve Lawrence (Columbia).

Yiddle on Your Fiddle Play Some Ragtime. w/m Irving Berlin, 1910. Novelty featured by Fanny Brice in vaudeville. Brice revived it in (MM) *The Great Ziegfeld*, 1936.

Yip-I-Addy-I-Ay! w. Will D. Cobb, m. John H. Flynn, 1908. Introduced and made into a hit by Blanche Ring who brought the song with her when she replaced the star of the already running musical (TM) *The Merry Widow Burlesque.* Her recording became a top seller (Victor). The song was interpolated in (MP) *New York Town*, 1941; (MM) *Bowery to Broadway*, 1944; (MM) *Sunbonnet Sue*, 1945.

Y.M.C.A. w/m Henri Belolo, Jacques Morali, and Victor Willis, 1979. Platinum record by the group Village People (Casablanca).

Yogi. w/m Lou Stallman, Sid Jacobson, and Charles Koppelman, 1960. Novelty based on the character from the TV cartoon show "Huckleberry Hound." Top 10 record by The Ivy Three (Shell).

Yolanda. w. Arthur Freed, m. Harry Warren, 1945. Introduced by Fred Astaire in (MM) *Yolanda and the Thief.* Featured and recorded by Artie Shaw and his Orchestra (Victor).

Yonder Comes a Sucker. w/m Jim Reeves, 1955. Introduced and recorded by Jim Reeves (RCA).

Yoo-Hoo. w. B. G. DeSylva, m. Al Jolson, 1921. Interpolated by Al Jolson in (TM) *Bombo* and recorded by him (Columbia).

You. w/m George Harrison, 1975. Top 20 record by George Harrison (Apple).

You. w/m Jeffrey Bowen, Jack Goga, and Ivy Hunter, 1968. Top 40 record by Marvin Gaye (Tamla).

You. w. Harold Adamson, m. Walter Donaldson, 1936. Sung by the chorus in a production number in (MM) *The Great Ziegfeld.* Jimmy Dorsey and his Band, with vocal by Bob Eberly, recorded it as their first release, backed with "You Never Looked So Beautiful" from the same film (Decca).

You, I. w/m Steve McNicol, 1969. Top 40 record by The Rugbys (Amazon).

You, Me and He. w/m James Mtume, 1984. Recorded by the band led by Mtume (Epic).

You, You Darlin'. w. Jack Scholl, m. M. K. Jerome, 1940. Featured on radio and recorded by Kay Kyser, vocal by Ginny Simms (Columbia); Bob Crosby, vocal by Marion Mann (Decca); Duke Ellington, vocal by Herb Jeffries (Victor).

You, You, You. w. Robert Mellin (Engl.), m. Lotar Elias, 1953. Original German words by Walter Rothenberg. Hit record by The Ames Brothers, accompanied by Hugo Winterhalter and his Orchestra (RCA Victor). Revived by Mel Carter (Imperial), 1966.

You, You, You Are the One. w. Fred Wise and Milton Leeds, m. Tetos Demey, 1949. Derived from the German song, "Du, Du, Liegst Mir im Herzen." Russ Morgan with vocal by The Skylarks (Decca) had the best seller, followed by The Ames Brothers (Coral), The Three Suns (RCA Victor), organist Ken Griffin (Rondo).

You Again. w/m Don Schlitz and Paul Overstreet, 1987. #1 Country chart record by The Forester Sisters (Warner Bros.).

You Ain't Going Nowhere. w/m Bob Dylan, 1968. Leading single by The Byrds (Columbia). Among album inclusions: Joan Baez (Vanguard), Bob Dylan (Columbia).

You Ain't Heard Nothing Yet. w/m Al Jolson, Gus Kahn, and B. G. DeSylva, 1919. The title comes from Jolson's favorite statement to his audiences upon receiving an ovation at the conclusion of a song. He interpolated it in the touring company of (TM) *Sinbad*, and recorded it (Columbia).

You Ain't Seen Nothing Yet. w/m Randy Bachman, 1974. #1 gold record by the Canadian group Bachman-Turner Overdrive (Mercury).

You Ain't Woman Enough. w/m Loretta Lynn, 1966. Hit Country record by Loretta Lynn (Decca).

You Alone (Solo Tu). w. Al Stillman, m. Robert Allen, 1953. Popularized by Perry Como (RCA Victor).

You Always Come Back (to Hurting Me). w/m Tom T. Hall and Johnny Rodriguez, 1973. Country/Pop chart record by Johnny Rodriguez (Mercury).

You Always Hurt the One You Love. w/m Allan Roberts and Doris Fisher, 1944. The Mills Brothers had a million-selling record that was on the charts for thirty-three weeks, five times as #1. To point out fallacies in surveys, the song was never on "Your Hit Parade."

You and I. w/m Frank Myers, 1982. Crossover (Country-Pop) hit by Eddie Rabbitt and Crystal Gayle (Elektra).

You and I. w/m James Johnson, Jr. (a.k.a. Rick James), 1978. Recorded by Rick James (Gordy).

You and I. w/m Meredith Willson, 1941. Nineteen weeks on "Your Hit Parade," five weeks in the #1 spot, song was featured and recorded by Glenn Miller, vocal by Ray Eberle (Bluebird); Bing Crosby (Decca); Tommy Dorsey, vocal by Frank Sinatra (Victor).

You and I. w. Harlan Thompson, m. Harry Archer, 1924. From (TM) *My Girl*.

You and I Know. w. Al Stillman, m. Arthur Schwartz, 1937. Introduced by Anne Booth and Ronald Graham in (TM) *Virginia*. Claude Thornhill, with vocal by Barry McKinley, recorded it (Brunswick).

You and Me. w/m Alice Cooper and Dick Wagner, 1977. Top 10 record by Alice Cooper (Warner Bros.).

You and Me. w/m George Richey and Billy Sherrill, 1976. Country record hit by Tammy Wynette (Epic).

You and Me. w/m Johnnie Wright, Jack Anglin, and Jim Anglin, 1956. Popular C&W record by Red Foley and Kitty Wells (Decca).

You and Me Against the World. w/m Kenny Ascher and Paul Williams 1974. Top 10 record by Helen Reddy (Capitol).

You and Me That Used to Be, The. w. Walter Bullock, m. Allie Wrubel, 1937. Featured and recorded by Kay Kyser, vocal by Harry Babbitt (Brunswick).

You and Me Tonight. w/m Eban Kelly, Jimi Randolph, and K. Moore, 1987. Top 10 R&B chart and Pop chart entry by the duo Deja (Virgin).

You and the Night and the Music. w. Howard Dietz, m. Arthur Schwartz, 1934. The music was originally heard in the background during the nighttime radio serial "The Gibson Family." The song was introduced by Georges Metaxa and Libby Holman in (TM) *Revenge with Music*. In (MM) *The Band Wagon*, 1953, it was sung by the chorus.

You and Your Beautiful Eyes w. Mack David, m. Jerry Livingston, 1950. Introduced by Dean Martin in (MP) *At War with the Army*.

You and Your Love. w. Johnny Mercer, m. John Green, 1939. Featured and recorded by Count Basie, vocal by Helen Humes (Vocalion); Bob Crosby, vocal by Teddy Grace (Decca); Gene Krupa, vocal by Irene Daye (Brunswick); Ozzie Nelson, vocal by Harriet Hilliard (Bluebird).

You Are. w/m Lionel Richie and Brenda Richie, 1983. Top 10 R&B and Pop record by Lionel Richie (Motown).

You Are a Song. w/m James Weatherly, 1975. Recorded by the duo Batdorf and Rodney (Arista).

You Are Beautiful. w. Oscar Hammerstein II, m. Richard Rodgers, 1958. Introduced in (TM) *Flower Drum Song* by Juanita Hall and Ed Kenney. Most popular record by Johnny Mathis (Columbia). Sung by James Shigeta in (MM) *Flower Drum Song*.

You Are Everything. w/m Linda Creed and Thom Bell, 1971. R&B/Pop gold record by The Stylistics (Avco).

You Are Free. w. William Le Baron, m. Victor Jacobi, 1919. Sung by John Charles Thomas and Wilda Bennett in (TM) *Apple Blossoms*.

You Are Love. w. Oscar Hammerstein II, m. Jerome Kern, 1928. Introduced by Howard Marsh and Norma Terris in (TM) *Show Boat*. In the second film adaptation (MM) *Show Boat*, 1936, it was sung by Allan Jones and Irene Dunne. Howard Keel and Kathryn Grayson sang it in the 1951 version (MM) *Show Boat*. Sung by Patrice Munsel and John Raitt in (TM) *A Musical Jubilee*, 1975.

Your Are My Destiny. w/m Paul Anka, 1958. Top 10 record by Paul Anka (ABC-Paramount).

You Are My Flower. w/m A. P. Carter, 1939. Introduced and featured by The Carter Family. Country chart record by Lester Flatt and Earl Scruggs (Columbia), 1964.

You Are My Lady. w/m Barry Eastmond, 1985. #1 R&B chart crossover record by Freddie Jackson (Capitol).

You Are My Love. w/m Jimmie Nabbie, 1955. Popularized by Joni James (MGM).

You Are My Lucky Star. w. Arthur Freed, m. Nacio Herb Brown, 1935. Introduced by Dick Powell and Frances Langford in (MM) *Broadway Melody of 1936*. It was used in other films: sung by Betty Jaynes in (MM) *Babes in Arms*, 1939; heard in (MM) *Born to Sing*, 1942; played as a recurrent theme in the background of (MP) *The Stratton Story*, 1949; sung by Phil Regan in (MM) *Three Little Words*, 1950, the Kalmar-Ruby biography, although this was not a K & R song; sung by Gene Kelly and Debbie Reynolds in (MM) *Singin' in the Rain*, 1952; heard in (MM) *The Boy Friend*, 1971, and in (MM) *New York, New York*, 1977. Among recordings: The Dorsey Brothers Orchestra, vocal by Bob Eberly (Victor); Eleanor Powell with Tommy Dorsey's Orchestra (Victor); the bands of Don Bestor (Brunswick), Archie Bleyer (Melotone), and Eddy Duchin (Victor).

You Are My Miracle. w/m Roger Whittaker, 1979. Recorded by British singer Roger Whittaker (RCA).

You Are My Sunshine. w/m Jimmie Davis and Charles Mitchell, 1940. C&W standard, sung by Tex Ritter in (MM) *Take Me Back to Oklahoma*. Hit records by Bing Crosby (Decca), Bob Atcher (Columbia), and Gene Autry (Okeh). It was the campaign song for Davis's successful quest of the governorship of Louisiana in 1944. In 1962, Ray Charles had a Top 10 record (ABC-Paramount). Sung by Bette Midler, Barbara Hersey, and Catherine Johnston in (MP) *Beaches*, 1988.

You Are My Treasure. w/m Cindy Walker, 1968. #1 Country chart record by Jack Greene (Decca).

You Are Never Away. w. Oscar Hammerstein II, m. Richard Rodgers, 1947. Introduced by John Battles and chorus in (TM) *Allegro*. Popular recordings by Buddy Clark (Columbia), Clark Dennis (Capitol), Charlie Spivak with vocal by Tommy Mercer (Victor).

You Are Not My First Love. w/m Bart Howard and Peter Windsor, 1953. Introduced and featured by Mabel Mercer.

You Are So Beautiful. w/m Billy Preston and Bruce Fischer, 1975. Top 10 record by Joe Cocker (A&M).

You Are the Girl. w/m Ric Ocasek, 1987. Popular airplay track and single from the album "Door to Door" by The Cars (Elektra).

You Are the Ideal of My Dreams. w/m Herbert Ingraham, 1910.

You Are the One. w/m Mitchell Torok, 1956. Recorded by Carl Smith (Columbia).

You Are the Sunshine of My Life. w/m Stevie Wonder, 1973. #1 record by Stevie Wonder (Tamla).

You Are the Woman. w/m Rick Roberts, 1976. Top 10 record by the group, Firefall, of which Roberts was lead singer (Atlantic).

You Are Too Beautiful. w. Lorenz Hart, m. Richard Rodgers, 1933. Introduced by Al Jolson in (MM) *Hallelujah, I'm a Bum.* Jolson recorded it (Brunswick). Dick Haymes had a popular recording (Decca), 1946.

You Are Woman, I Am Man. w. Bob Merrill, m. Jule Styne, 1964. Introduced by Sydney Chaplin and Barbra Streisand in (TM) *Funny Girl.* In (MM) *Funny Girl*, 1968, it was sung by Omar Sharif and Barbra Streisand.

You Baby. w/m P. F. Sloan and Steve Barri, 1966. Hit record by The Turtles (White Whale).

You Beat Me to the Punch. w/m William Robinson and Ronald White. 1962. Top 10 hit by Mary Wells (Motown).

You Belong to Me. w. Carly Simon, m. Michael McDonald, 1978. Top 10 record by Carly Simon (Elektra). The Doobie Brothers had a chart version (Warner Bros.), 1983.

You Belong to Me. w/m Pee Wee King, Redd Stewart, and Chilton Price, 1952. One of the biggest hits of the year. Song was on "Your Hit Parade" for nineteen weeks, nine times in the #1 position. Jo Stafford's record (Columbia) sold two million copies and was #1 on the charts for twelve weeks. Patti Page (Mercury) and Dean Martin (Capitol) also had chart versions. Revived ten years later by The Duprees, who had a Top 10 record (Coed).

You Belong to Me. w. Harry B. Smith, m. Victor Herbert, 1916. From (TM) *The Century Girl.*

You Belong to My Heart. w. Ray Gilbert (Engl.), Augustin Lara (Sp.), m. Augustin Lara, 1944. Mexican song known as "Solamente Una Vez." Introduced by Dora Luz in Disney's cartoon film (MM) *The Three Caballeros.* Top-selling record by Bing Crosby with Xavier Cugat's Orchestra (Decca). Ezio Pinza sang it in his screen debut in (MM) *Mr. Imperium*, which was retitled in Great Britain, *You Belong to My Heart*, 1951.

You Belong to the City. w/m Glenn Frey, 1985. Introduced by Glenn Frey in the series (TVP) "Miami Vice," and on a Top 10 single (MCA).

You Better Get It. w/m Joe Tex, 1965. Introduced and recorded by Joe Tex (Dial).

You Better Go Now. w. Bickley Reichner, m. Irvin Graham, 1936. Introduced by Nancy Noland and Tom Rutherford in Leonard Sillman's *New Faces of 1936.* Among recordings: Billie Holiday, in the mid-forties (Decca); Beryl Booker (Mercury); and Jeri Sothern, who had a hit record (Decca) in the fifties.

You Better Know It. w/m Jackie Wilson and Norm Henry, 1959. From (MM) *Go, Johnny, Go.* Recorded by Jackie Wilson (Brunswick).

You Better Not Do That. w/m Tommy Collins, 1954. Top 10 C&W record by Tommy Collins (Capitol).

You Better Run. w/m Eddie Brigati and Felix Cavaliere, 1966. Top 20 record by The Young Rascals (Atlantic) and written by two members of the group. Revived by Pat Benatar (Chrysalis), 1980.

You Better Sit Down Kids. w/m Sonny Bono, 1967. Top 10 record by Cher (Imperial).

You Better Think Twice. w/m Jim Messina, 1970. Recorded by the group, Poco, and written by the lead guitarist (Epic).

You Better Watch Your Step. See **Watch Your Step**.

You Better You Bet. w/m Peter Townshend, 1981. Recorded by the British group The Who (Warner Bros.).

You Broke the Only Heart That Ever Loved You. w. Teddy Powell, m. Jack Little, 1946. Popular recording by Elliot Lawrence, vocal by Rosalind Patton and Jack Hunter (Columbia).

You Broke Your Promise. w/m Irving Taylor, George Wyle, and Edward Pola, 1949. Featured and recorded by The Pied Pipers (RCA Victor).

You Brought a New Kind of Love to Me. w/m Sammy Fain, Irving Kahal, and Pierre Norman, 1930. Introduced by Maurice Chevalier in (MM) *The Big Pond*, recorded by him (Victor), and associated with him. It was used as the underlying theme for (MP) *A New Kind of Love*, 1963, and was played in (MM) *New York, New York*, 1977.

You Call Everybody Darling. w/m Sam Martin, Ben Trace, and Clem Watts, 1948. Al Trace and his Orchestra had a #1 hit record (Regent) and re-recorded it later the same year (Sterling). Song was on "Your Hit Parade" for sixteen weeks, due in part to the multitude of recordings. Among them: Anne Vincent (Mercury), The Andrews Sisters (Decca), Jack Smith (Capitol), Jerry Wayne (Columbia), Art Lund (MGM), Bruce Hayes (De Luxe).

You Call It Madness (But I Call It Love). w/m Con Conrad, Gladys Du Bois, Russ Columbo, and Paul Gregory, 1931. Russ Columbo had the top record (Victor) and used the song as his radio theme. Among the many recordings in addition were: Smith Ballew (Columbia), Bert Lown and his Orchestra (Victor), Kate Smith (Columbia), Phil Spitalny [all-male orchestra!] (Perfect). Later notable renditions by Dick Stabile (Bluebird); Nat Cole (Capitol); Stuart Allen, with Richard Himber's Orchestra (Victor); Don Byas (Jamboree).

You Came Along (From out of Nowhere). See **Out of Nowhere.**

You Came a Long Way from St. Louis. w. Bob Russell, m. John Benson Brooks, 1948. Featured and hit record by Ray McKinley and his Orchestra (RCA Victor).

You Came to My Rescue. w. Leo Robin, m. Ralph Rainger, 1936. Introduced by Shirley Ross and Frank Forrest in (MM) *The Big Broadcast of 1937*.

You Can Call Me Al. w/m Paul Simon, 1986. Chart single from the album "Graceland" by Paul Simon (Warner Bros.).

You Can Dance with Any Girl At All. w. Irving Caesar, m. Vincent Youmans, 1925. Introduced by Josephine Whittell and Wellington Cross in (TM) *No, No, Nanette*. Helen Gallagher and Bobby Van performed it in the 1971 production.

You Can Depend on Me. w/m Earl Hines, Charles Carpenter, and Luis Dunlap, 1932. Among many recordings are those by: Louis Armstrong (Columbia) (Okeh); Fletcher Henderson (Victor); Earl "Fatha" Hines (Bluebird); Count Basie, vocal by Jimmy Rushing (Decca); Orrin Tucker, vocal by Bonnie Baker (Columbia); Art Jarrett (Victor); Pinky Tomlin (Brunswick); Dinah Washington (Mercury). Brenda Lee had a Top 10 record (Decca), 1961.

You Can Do Magic. w/m Russ Ballard, 1982. Top 10 record by the group America (Capitol).

You Can Do No Wrong. w/m Cole Porter, 1948. Introduced by Judy Garland in (MM) *The Pirate*, and on records (MGM). Also recorded by Harry James, vocal by Marion Morgan (Columbia).

You Can Dream of Me. w/m Steve Wariner and John Hall, 1985. #1 Country chart record by Steve Wariner (MCA).

You Can Get It If You Really Want. w/m Jimmy Cliff, 1973. Sung by Jimmy Cliff in the Jamaican film (MP) *The Harder They Come*.

You Can Have Her (a.k.a. You Can Have Him). w/m Billy Cook, 1961. Hit record by Roy Hamilton (Epic). Three chart records in 1965: The Righteous Brothers (Moonglow); and changing "her" to "him" in the title, Dionne Warwick (Scepter); and Timi Yoro (Mercury). Sam Neely had a Top 40 version in 1974 (A&M).

You Can Have Him. w/m Irving Berlin, 1949. Introduced by Mary McCarty and Allyn McLerie in (TM) *Miss Liberty*.

You Can Have Him, I Don't Want Him, Didn't Love Him Anyhow Blues! w. William Tracey, m. Dan Dougherty, 1922. Popular recordings by Van and Schenck (Columbia) and Mamie Smith and Her Jazz Hounds (Okeh).

You Can Make My Life a Bed of Roses. w. Lew Brown, m. Ray Henderson, 1932. Introduced by June Knight and Charles "Buddy" Rogers in (TM) *Hot-cha*. Recorded by George Olsen and his Orchestra, vocal by Fran Frey (Victor).

You Cannot Make Your Shimmy Shake on Tea. w. Rennold Wolf, m. Irving Berlin, 1919. Bert Williams performed this prohibition protest in (TM) *Ziegfeld Follies of 1919*.

You Can't Always Get What You Want. w/m Mick Jagger and Keith Richards, 1969. Released by The Rolling Stones as the flip side of the gold record hit "Honky Tonk Woman" (London). Re-released and chart record, 1973.

You Can't Be a Beacon (If Your Light Don't Shine). w/m Martin Cooper, 1974. Popular record by Donna Fargo (Dot).

You Can't Be True, Dear. w. Hal Cotton (Engl.), m. Ken Griffin (adapt.), Hans Otten, 1948. Original German title "Du kannst nicht treu sein," lyrics by Gerhard Ebeler. Ken Griffin, with vocal by Jerry Wayne, had a million-selling #1 hit (Rondo). Three months later Griffin recorded it as an instrumental that reached the #2 chart position.

You Can't Break My Heart ('Cause It's Already Broken). w/m Henry Sweesy and Gary Garrett, 1946. Popular record by Spade Cooley (Columbia).

You Can't Brush Me Off. w/m Irving Berlin, 1940. Introduced by April Ames, Nick Long, Jr., and The Martins [Hugh Martin, Ralph Blane, and others) in (TM) *Louisiana Purchase*.

You Can't Change That. w/m Ray Parker, Jr., 1979. Recorded by the band, Raydio, formed by guitarist Parker (Arista).

You Can't Do That. w/m John Lennon and Paul McCartney, 1964. Recorded by The Beatles, coupled with the hit "Cant' Buy Me Love" (q.v.) (Capitol).

You Can Tell She Comes from Dixie. w. Marty Symes, m. Milton Ager, 1937. Popularized and recorded by Phil Harris (Vocalion), Artie Shaw (Brunswick), and Anson Weeks (Decca).

You Can't Get Along with 'Em or Without 'Em. w. Grant Clarke, m. Fred Fisher, 1917. Popularized by Anna Chandler in vaudeville and on records (Columbia).

You Can't Get a Man with a Gun. w/m Irving Berlin, 1946. Introduced by Ethel Merman in (TM) *Annie Get Your Gun*. In the film version (MM) *Annie Get Your Gun*, 1950, it was sung by Betty Hutton.

You Can't Get That No More. w/m Sam Theard and Louis Jordan, 1944. Recorded by Louis Jordan and his Tympani Five (Decca).

You Can't Get What You Want (Till You Know What You Want). w/m Joe Jackson, 1984. Recorded by Joe Jackson (A&M).

You Can't Have Everything. w. Mack Gordon, m. Harry Revel, 1937. Introduced by Alice Faye in (MM) *You Can't Have Everything*. Among leading recordings: Louis Prima and his Band (Vocalion); Bob Crosby, vocal by Kay Weber (Decca); Judy Garland, whose record was coupled with her hit version of the standard, "You Made Me Love You" (q.v.) (Decca).

You Can't Have My Love. w/m Chuck Harding, Marty Roberts, Hank Thompson, and Billy Gray, 1954. Top 10 C&W chart record by Wanda Jackson and Billy Gray (Decca).

You Can't Hold a Memory in Your Arms. w. Hy Zaret, title by Thekla Hollingsworth, m. Arthur Altman, 1942. Introduced by Jane

977

Frazee, with Woody Herman and his Orchestra, in (MM) *What's Cookin'?* Recorded by Herman (Decca); Art Jarrett (RCA Victor); later, Steve Lawrence (King).

You Can't Hurry Love. w/m Brian Holland, Lamont Dozier, and Eddie Holland, 1966. #1 record by The Supremes (Motown). Revived by the British singer Phil Collins, whose record reached the Top 10 in the U. S. (Atlantic), 1983.

You Can't Keep a Good Man Down. w/m M. F. Carey, 1900. A "blues" of the day. Recorded by Mamie Smith (Okeh).

You Can't Lose the Blues with Colors. w/m Irving Berlin, 1957. Recorded by Rosemary Clooney (Columbia). This was Berlin's last published non-production song.

You Can't Pick a Rose in December. w/m Leo Payne, 1961. Country hit recorded by Ernest Ashworth (Decca).

You Can't Play Every Instrument in the Band. w. Joseph Cawthorn, m. John L. Golden, 1913. From (TM) *The Sunshine Girl.*

You Can't Pull the Wool Over My Eyes. w/m Milton Ager, Charles Newman, and Murray Mencher, 1936. Introduced by George Hall, vocal by Dolly Dawn (Victor). Bestselling record by Benny Goodman, vocal by Helen Ward (Victor); and Ted Weems, vocal by Perry Como (Decca).

You Can't Roller Skate in a Buffalo Herd. w/m Roger Miller, 1966. Novelty hit by Roger Miller (Smash).

You Can't Run Away from It. w. Johnny Mercer, m. Gene De Paul, 1956. From (MP) *You Can't Ran Away from It.* Popular record by The Four Aces, arranged and conducted by Jack Pleis (Decca).

You Can't Say No to a Soldier. w. Mack Gordon, m. Harry Warren, 1942. Introduced by Joan Merrill in (MM) *Iceland* and on records (Bluebird).

You Can't See the Sun When You're Cryin.' w/m Allan Roberts and Doris Fish-

er, 1947. Top recordings: The Ink Spots (Decca) and Vaughn Monroe, with his Orchestra (RCA Victor).

You Can't Sit Down. w/m Dee Clark, Cornell Muldrow, and Kal Mann, 1961. Introduced as an instrumental on the Top 40 record by The Philip Upchurch Combo (Boyd). Vocal hit by The Dovells (Parkway), 1963.

You Can't Stop Me from Loving You. w. Mann Holiner, m. Alberta Nichols, 1931. Originally written for Billy Rose's revue, *Corned Beef and Roses*, which closed in Philadelphia before Broadway opening. Interpolated in Lew Leslie's revue (TM) *Rhapsody in Black* by Ethel Waters and Blue McAllister.

You Can't Turn Me Off (in the Middle of Turning Me On). w/m Marilyn McLeod and Pam Sawyer, 1977. R&B/Pop chart hit by the female group High Inergy (Gordy).

You Cheated. w/m Don Burch, 1958. Introduced and recorded by The Slades, a group of which the writer was lead singer (Domino). The record was covered by The Shields (Dot), a group formed solely for this recording. The latter had the bigger seller.

You Comb Her Hair. w/m Harlan Howard and Hank Cochran, 1963. Country hit record by George Jones (United Artists).

You Could Drive a Person Crazy. w/m Stephen Sondheim, 1970. Introduced by Donna McKechnie, Susan Browning, and Pamela Myers in (TM) *Company.*

You Could Have Been With Me. w/m Lea Maalfried, 1981. Recorded by the Scottish singer Sheena Easton (EMI America).

You Couldn't Be Cuter. w. Dorothy Fields, m. Jerome Kern, 1938. Introduced by Irene Dunne in (MM) *Joy of Living.*

You Darlin'. w/m Harry Woods, 1930.

You'd Be So Nice to Come Home To. w/m Cole Porter, 1943. Introduced by Don Ameche and Janet Blair in (MM) *Something to Shout About.* Nominated for Academy Award. Dinah Shore had the best-selling record, accompanied by Paul Weston's Orchestra (Victor); followed by Six Hits and a Miss (Capitol); and Dick Jurgens, vocal by Harry Cool (Columbia).

You'd Be Surprised. w/m Irving Berlin, 1919, 1940. Eddie Cantor introduced this in (TM) *Ziegfeld Folllies of 1919* and recorded it (Victor), which was to be his only million-seller. Bonnie Baker, vocalist with Orrin Tucker's Orchestra, revived the song with a hit recording (Columbia), 1940. Olga San Juan sang it in (MM) *Blue Skies*, 1946, and Dan Dailey sang it in (MM) *There's No Business Like Show Business*, 1954.

You'd Better Come Home. w/m Tony Hatch, 1965. Recorded in England by Petula Clark, produced by Tony Hatch (Warner Bros.).

You'd Better Love Me. w/m Hugh Martin and Timothy Gray, 1964. Introduced by Tammy Grimes in (TM) *High Spirits*.

You'd Better Watch Yourself. w/m Walter Jacobs, 1954. Top 10 R&B chart record by Little Walter (Checker).

You Decorated My Life. w/m Deborah Kay Hupp and Robert Morrison, 1979. Hit record by Kenny Rogers (United Artists). Winner Grammy Award (NARAS), Country Song of the Year.

You Didn't Have to Be So Nice. w/m John Sebastian and Steve Boone, 1965. Written by two members of The Lovin' Spoonful, the group that had their second successive Top 10 record with this song (Kama Sutra).

You Didn't Have to Tell Me (I Knew It All the Time). w/m Walter Donaldson, 1931. Early recording by Benny Goodman (Melotone). Later versions by Johnny Messner (Vocalion) and Don Cherry (Decca).

You Didn't Know the Music. w/m Sam Coslow, 1931. Featured and recorded by Leo Reisman's Orchestra, with Eddy Duchin on piano (Victor).

You Didn't Want Me When You Had Me (So Why Do you Want Me Now?). w. Beneé Russell and Bernie Grossman, m. George J. Bennett, 1919. Popular song in vaudeville and records. Revived by The Mills Brothers (Decca), 1954.

You Do. w. Mack Gordon, m. Josef Myrow, 1947. Introduced by Betty Grable and Dan Dailey in (MM) *Mother Wore Tights*. Nominated for Academy Award, 1947. Top 10 records by Dinah Shore (Columbia); Vaughn Monroe, with his Orchestra (RCA Victor); Margaret Whiting (Capitol); Vic Damone (Mercury); Bing Crosby (Decca).

You Done Me Wrong. w/m Ray Price and Shirley Jones, 1956. Introduced and recorded by Ray Price (Columbia).

You Don't Bring Me Flowers. w. Alan Bergman, Marilyn Bergman, Neil Diamond, m. Neil Diamond, 1978. Barbara Streisand and Neil Diamond had each recorded the song on their own albums. Gary Guthrie, a Louisville, Kentucky, disc jockey, after noting that both singers had done the song in the same key, synchronized the two performances on tape and then played the newly formed duet on the air. The response was so favorable that the record company (Columbia) brought the two stars into their studio and re-recorded the song. The Streisand/Diamond single became a #1 gold record.

You Don't Care What Happens to Me. w/m Fred Rose, 1945. C&W hit record by Bob Wills and His Texas Playboys (Columbia). Revived by Wynn Stewart (Capitol), 1970.

You Don't Have to Be a Baby to Cry. w/m Terry Shand and Bob Merrill, 1950. Leading records by Tennessee Ernie Ford (Capitol) and Jimmy Dorsey and his Orchestra (Columbia).

You Don't Have to Be a Star (to Be in My Show). w/m James Dean and John Glover, 1976. #1 gold record by Marilyn McCoo and Billy Davis, Jr. (ABC).

You Don't Have to Cry. w/m Ren Moore and Angela Winbush, 1986. Top 10 R&B

chart crossover record by the duo Ren and Angela (Mercury).

You Don't Have to Go. w/m Matcher James Reed, 1955. Top 10 R&B record by Jimmy Reed (Vee-Jay).

You Don't Have to Know the Language. w. Johnny Burke, m. James Van Heusen, 1948. Introduced by Bing Crosby and The Andrews Sisters in (MM) *Road to Rio*, and recorded by them (Decca).

You Don't Have to Paint Me a Picture. w/m Thomas Garrett, Leon Russell, and Roger Carroll Tillison, 1966. Top 20 record by Gary Lewis and The Playboys (Liberty).

You Don't Have to Say You Love Me. w. Vicki Wickham and Simon Napier-Bell (Engl.), m. P. Donaggio, 1966. Italian song originally titled "Io Che Non Vivo (Senza Te)," lyrics by V. Pallavicini. Hit English version by Dusty Springfield (Philips). Revived by Elvis Presley (RCA), 1970.

You Don't Hear. w/m Jerry Huffman and Tom Cash, 1965. Hit Country record by Kitty Wells (Decca).

You Don't Know. w/m Meredith Willson, 1963. Introduced by Janis Paige in (MM) *Here's Love.*

You Don't Know Him. w/m Jay Livingston and Ray Evans, 1958. Introduced by Jacquelyn McKeever and Abbe Lane in (TM) *Oh, Captain!*

(You Don't Know) How Glad I Am. w/m Jimmy Williams and Larry Harrison, 1964. Introduced and Top 20 record by Nancy Wilson (Capitol). Grammy Award (NARAS) winner Rhythm and Blues Song of the Year. Revived by the English singer Kiki Dee (Rocket), 1975.

You Don't Know Like I Know. w/m David Porter and Isaac Hayes, 1966. Produced by the writers and recorded by Sam and Dave (Stax).

You Don't Know Me. w/m Cindy Walker and Eddy Arnold, 1956, 1962. Introduced and

recorded by Eddy Arnold (Victor). Jerry Vale had a Top 20 record on the Pop charts (Columbia). Revived in 1962 by Ray Charles, with a #2 record (ABC-Paramount). Popular versions by Elvis Presley (RCA), 1967, and Mickey Gilley (Epic), 1981.

You Don't Know Paree. w/m Cole Porter, 1929. Introduced by William Gaxton in (TM) *Fifty Million Frenchmen.*

You Don't Know What Love Is. w/m Don Raye and Gene De Paul, 1941. Introduced by Carol Bruce in (MM) *Keep 'em Flying*, and sung again by her in (MM) *Behind the Eight Ball* the following year. She also recorded it (Columbia). Among the many other versions on records: Dick Haymes (Columbia) (Capitol), Ella Fitzgerald (Decca), Billy Eckstine and Earl Hines (RCA Victor), Dinah Washington (Mercury), Miles Davis (Prestige).

You Don't Know What You Mean to Me. w/m Eddie Floyd and Steve Cropper, 1968. Recorded by Sam and Dave (Atlantic).

You Don't Know What You've Got (Until You Lose It). w/m Paul Hampton and George Burton, 1961. Top 10 record by Ral Donner (Gone).

You Don't Like It—Not Much. w. Ned Miller, m. Chester Conn and Art Kahn, 1927. Novelty song featured and recorded by The Happiness Boys, Billy Jones and Ernie Hare (Victor).

You Don't Love Me Anymore. w/m Alan Ray and Jeffrey Raymond, 1978. Recorded by Eddie Rabbitt (Elektra).

You Don't Mess Around with Jim. w/m Jim Croce, 1972. Top 10 record by Jim Croce (ABC).

You Don't Owe Me a Thing. w/m Marty Robbins, 1957. Introduced and recorded by Marty Robbins (Columbia). Best-seller by Johnny Ray (Columbia).

You Don't Own Me. w/m John Madera and David White, 1964. Hit record by Lesley Gore (Mercury). Song heard on the soundtrack of (MP) *Dirty Dancing*, 1987.

You Don't Remind Me. w/m Cole Porter, 1950. Introduced by George Jongeyans in (TM) *Out of This World*. Leading record by Jo Stafford (Columbia).

You Don't Want Me Anymore. w/m Kenneth Goorabian, 1982. Recorded by the sextet Steel Breeze (RCA).

You Don't Want My Love. w/m Roger Miller, 1961. Leading record by Andy Williams (Cadence).

You Do Something to Me. w/m Cole Porter, 1929. Introduced by William Gaxton and Genevieve Tobin in (TM) *Fifty Million Frenchmen*. In the Porter biography (MM) *Night and Day*, 1945, it was sung by Jane Wyman; in (MM) *Starlift*, 1951, by Doris Day; Mario Lanza sang it in (MM) *Because You're Mine*, and recorded it (Victor), 1952. It was interpolated in (MM) *Can-Can*, 1960, and sung by Louis Jourdan. Recordings by Leo Reisman's Orchestra (Victor); Marion Harris (Brunswick); Marlene Dietrich (British Brunswick), and in the U.S. (Brunswick).

You Do the Darndest Things, Baby. w. Sidney D. Mitchell, m. Lew Pollack, 1936. Sung by Jack Haley in (MM) *Pigskin Parade*. Recorded by Charlie Barnet (Bluebird) and Joe Sanders, "The Old Lefthander" (Decca), and their orchestras.

You Dropped Me Like a Red Hot Penny. w. Joe Young, m. Fred E. Ahlert, 1936.

You Fascinate Me So. w. Carolyn Leigh, m. Cy Coleman, 1958. Introduced in the nightclub revue *Julius Monk's Demi-Dozen* by Jean Arnold. Popularized and recorded by Mabel Mercer (Atlantic).

You Fit into the Picture. w. Bud Green, m. Jesse Greer, 1935. Fats Waller (Victor) and Bob Howard (Decca) recorded the song.

You Forgot About Me. w/m Dick Robertson, James F. Hanley, Sammy Mysels, 1940. Leading record by Bob Crosby, vocal by Crosby and the Bob-o-Links (Decca). Among others: Connee Boswell (Decca); the bands of Larry Clinton (Bluebird), Artie Shaw (Victor), and Gene Krupa (Okeh).

You Forgot Your Gloves. w. Edward Eliscu, m. Ned Lehac, 1931. Introduced by Constance Carpenter and Carl Randall in (TM) *The Third Little Show*.

You Gave Me a Mountain. w/m Marty Robbins, 1969. Top 40 record by Frankie Laine, produced by Jimmy Bowen (ABC).

You Give Good Love. w/m La Forrest Cope, a.k.a. La La, 1985. #1 R&B, Top 10 Pop chart by Whitney Houston (Arista).

You Give Love a Bad Name. w/m Jon Bon Jovi, Richie Sambora, and Desmond Child, 1986. #1 single from the album "Slippery When Wet" by the band Bon Jovi (Mercury).

You Got It All. w/m Rupert Holmes, 1987. Top 10 chart record by The Jets (MCA).

You Got Lucky. w/m Tom Petty and Mike Campbell, 1983. Recorded by Tom Petty and The Heartbreakers (Backstreet).

You Got Me Dizzy. w/m Jimmy Reed and Ewart Abner, Jr., 1957. Hit R&B record by Jimmy Reed (Vee-Jay).

You Go to My Head. w. Haven Gillespie, m. J. Fred Coots, 1938. Introduced and recorded by Glen Gray and the Casa Loma Orchestra, vocal by Kenny Sargent (Decca). First recording by Larry Clinton, vocal by Bea Wain (Victor). A cross section of recordings of this all-time standard: Frank Sinatra (Columbia); Marlene Dietrich (Decca); Mitchell Ayres, who used it as his Orchestra's theme (Bluebird); Lena Horne (Black & White); Teddy Wilson, vocal by Nan Wynn (Brunswick); John Kirby, vocal by Sarah Vaughan (Crown); Kay Kyser, vocal by Ginny Simms (Brunswick); Zoot Sims (Prestige); Bud Powell (Blue Note). Interpolated in (TM) *A Musical Jubilee* by John Raitt, 1975.

You Gotta Be a Football Hero. w/m Al Lewis, Al Sherman, and Buddy Fields, 1933. Featured and recorded by Ben Bernie and his Orchestra (Columbia) and Harry Reser and his Orchestra (Melotone).

You Gotta Be My Baby. w/m George Jones, 1956. Introduced and recorded by George Jones (Starday).

You Gotta Fight for Your Right to Party. See **Fight for Your Right** etc.

You Gotta Love Everybody. w/m Bill Norvas and Kay Thompson, 1958. Featured and recorded by Della Reese (Jubilee).

You Gotta S-M-I-L-E to be H-A-Double P-Y. w/m Mack Gordon and Harry Revel, 1936. Introduced by Shirley Temple in (MM) *Stowaway*.

You Got the Love. w/m Chaka Khan and Ray Parker, Jr., 1974. Top 20 record by Rufus featuring Chaka Khan (ABC).

You Got to Me. w/m Neil Diamond, 1967. Top 20 record by Neil Diamond (Bang).

You Got What It Takes. w/m Berry Gordy, Jr., Gwen Gordy, and Tyran Carlo, 1959. Hit record by Marv Johnson (United Artists). Revived with a Top 10 record by the British group, The Dave Clark Five (Epic), 1967.

You Got Yours and I'll Get Mine. w/m William Hart and Thomas R. Bell, 1969. Top 40 record by The Delfonics (Philly Groove).

You Go Your Way (and I'll Go Crazy). w. Mort Greene, m. Harry Revel, 1941. Introduced by Ray Bolger in (MM) *Four Jacks and a Jill*. In (MM) *Make Mine Laughs*, 1949, a film clip of Bolger's previous performance was inserted.

You Grow Sweeter As the Years Go By. w/m Johnny Mercer, 1939. Recorded by Glen Gray and the Casa Loma Orchestra, vocal by Kenny Sargent (Decca); Artie Shaw, vocal by Helen Forrest (Bluebird); Connie Boswell (Decca).

You Haven't Changed At All. w. Alan Jay Lerner, m. Frederick Loewe, 1945. Introduced by Irene Manning and Bill Johnson in (TM) *The Day Before Spring*.

You Haven't Done Nothin'. w/m Stevie Wonder, 1974. #1 record by Stevie Wonder, background vocal by The Jackson 5 (Tamla).

You Have Taken My Heart. w. Johnny Mercer, m. Gordon Jenkins, 1934. Popular song on radio. Leading record by Glen Gray and the Casa Loma Orchestra, vocal by Kenny Sargent (Brunswick).

You Have the Choice. w. Harold Pinter, m. Maurice Jarre, 1976. Sung on the soundtrack of (MP) *The Last Tycoon* by Jeanne Moreau.

You Hit the Spot. w. Mack Gordon, m. Harry Revel, 1936. Introduced by Frances Langford, with assistance from Jack Oakie and Mack Gordon in (MM) *Collegiate*. Langford recorded it (Decca), as did Kay Thompson (Brunswick); Richard Himber's Orchestra, vocal by Allen Stuart (Victor); Bob Howard (Decca); and The Mound City Blue Blowers (Champion). The song was revived in the Martin and Lewis film (MM) *Scared Stiff*, 1953.

You Keep Coming Back Like a Song. w/m Irving Berlin, 1946. Introduced by Bing Crosby and Joan Caulfield in (MM) *Blue Skies*. Nominated for Academy Award. Leading recordings, in addition to Crosby (Decca), by Dinah Shore (Columbia) and Jo Stafford (Capitol).

You Keep Me Hangin' On. w/m Eddie Holland, Lamont Dozier, and Brian Holland, 1966, 1987. #1 record by The Supremes (Motown). The rock quartet Vanilla Fudge (Atco) and Joe Simon (Sound Stage) had hit versions in 1968. #1 hit single by the British singer, Kim Wilde (MCA), 1987.

You Keep Running Away. w/m Eddie Holland, Lamont Dozier, and Brian Holland, 1967. Top 20 record by The Four Tops (Motown).

You Keep Sending 'Em Over and We'll Keep Knocking 'Em Down. w. Sidney D. Mitchell, m. Harry Ruby, 1918. Military song sung by Eddie Cantor in (TM) *Ziegfeld Follies of 1918*.

You Know and I Know. w. Schuyler Greene, m. Jerome Kern, 1915. Introduced by Alice Dovey and George Anderson in Kern's first Princess Theatre production (TM) *Nobody Home.*

You Know I Love You. w. Riley King, m. Jules Taub, 1952. #1 R&B record by B. B. King (RPM).

You Know I Love You . . . Don't You? w/m Howard Jones, 1986. Chart record by the English singer/songwriter Howard Jones (Elektra).

You Know What I Mean. w/m Garry Bonner and Alan Gordon, 1967. Popular record by The Turtles (White Whale).

You Know You Belong to Somebody Else (So Why Don't You Leave Me Alone). w. Eugene West, m. James V. Monaco, 1922. Introduced, featured, and recorded by Nora Bayes (Columbia).

You Leave Me Breathless. w. Ralph Freed, m. Frederick Hollander, 1938. Introduced by Fred MacMurray and Harriet Hilliard in (MM) *Cocoanut Grove.* Hilliard recorded it with Ozzie Nelson's Orchestra (Bluebird). Others: Tommy Dorsey, vocal by Jack Leonard (Victor); George Hall, vocal by Dolly Dawn (Conqueror); Jimmie Grier and his Orchestra (Decca).

You Let Me Down. w. Al Dubin, m. Harry Warren, 1935. Introduced by Jane Froman in (MM) *Stars Over Broadway.* Among recordings: Kay Thompson (Brunswick); the bands of Jimmie Lunceford with vocal by Dan Grissom (Vocalion), and Wingy Manone (Vocalion).

You Light Up My Life. w/m Joe Brooks, 1977. Introduced by Kasey Cisyk, dubbing for Didi Conn in (MP) *You Light Up My Life.* Winner Academy Award. Debby Boone's platinum record was the #1 single of the year, holding the top position for ten weeks (Warner Bros.).

You Little Trustmaker. w/m Christopher Jackson, 1974. Top 20 record by The Tymes (RCA).

You'll Accomp'ny Me. w/m Bob Seger, 1980. Recorded by Bob Seger (Capitol).

You'll Always Be Just Sweet Sixteen to Me. w. Paul West, m. John Bratton, 1908.

You'll Always Be the Same Sweet Girl. w. Andrew B. Sterling, m. Harry Von Tilzer, 1915. Recorded by James F. Harrison and James Reed (Victor and Columbia).

You'll Answer to Me. w. Hal David, m. Sherman Edwards, 1961. Recorded by Patti Page (Mercury).

You'll Be Back (Every Night in My Dreams). w/m Johnny Russell and Wayland Holyfield, 1982. First Country chart record by Johnny Russell (Polydor), 1978. Top 10 version by The Statler Brothers (Mercury), 1982.

You'll Be Sorry When I'm Gone. w/m Gene Autry and Fred Rose, 1942. Recorded by Gene Autry (Okeh) and The Sons of the Pioneers (Victor).

You'll Drive Me Back (into Her Arms Again). w/m Merle Kilgore and Jill Jackson, 1963. Country song recorded by Faron Young (Mercury).

You'll Get By. w. Roy Turk, m. J. Fred Coots, 1932. By the lyricist of the 1928 hit "I'll Get By," (q.v.) but without the same success. Recorded by Fred Waring's Pennsylvanians (Victor).

You'll Have to Swing It (Mr. Paganini). w/m Sam Coslow, 1936. Martha Raye introduced this in her first film (MM) *Rhythm on the Range.* She made the song, and the song made her. Raye recorded it (Brunswick); as did Ella Fitzgerald, with Chick Webb's Orchestra (Decca); and jazz harpist Caspar Reardon (Liberty Music Shops).

You'll Lose a Good Thing. w/m Barbara Lynn Ozen, 1962. Introduced and Top 10 record by Barbara Lynn (Jamie). Revived by Freddy Fender (ABC-Dot), 1976.

You'll Never Find Another Love Like Mine. w/m Kenny Gamble and Leon Huff, 1976. R&B/Pop gold record by Lou Rawls (Philadelphia International).

You'll Never Get Away. w/m Joan Whitney, Alex Kramer, and Hy Zaret, 1952. Popular recording by Teresa Brewer and Don Cornell, arranged and conducted by Jack Pleis (Coral).

You'll Never Get Away from Me. w. Stephen Sondheim, m. Jule Styne, 1959. Introduced by Ethel Merman and Jack Klugman in (TM) *Gypsy*. In (MM) *Gypsy*, 1962, it was sung by Rosalind Russell [with help on the soundtrack from Lisa Kirk] and Karl Malden. The music, with lyrics by Leo Robin and called "I'm in Pursuit of Happiness," was originally sung in (TVM) "Ruggles of Red Gap" by Michael Redgrave.

You'll Never Get to Heaven. w. Hal David, m. Burt Bacharach, 1964. Recorded by Dionne Warwick (Scepter). Revived by The Stylistics (Avco), 1973.

You'll Never Know. w. Mack Gordon, m. Harry Warren, 1943. Introduced by Alice Faye in (MM) *Hello, Frisco, Hello*. Winner Academy Award for Best Song, 1943. Faye reprised it in (MM) *Four Jills in a Jeep*, 1944. Dick Haymes, backed by the Song Spinners, had the #1 record (Decca), followed by Frank Sinatra, with The Bobby Tucker Singers (Columbia). Because of a musicians' strike, the singing was a cappella. Revived by Rosemary Clooney, with Harry James's Orchestra (Columbia), 1953, and The Platters' hit version (Mercury), 1956.

You'll Never Know That Old Home Town of Mine. w. Howard Johnson, m. Walter Donaldson, 1915. One of Donaldson's first hits. Introduced by Al Jolson in (TM) *Dancing Around*. Featured by Van and Schenck at The Palace in New York and on tour.

You'll Never Walk Alone. w. Oscar Hammerstein II, m. Richard Rodgers, 1945. Introduced by Christine Johnson in (TM) *Carousel* and sung by Claramae Turner in the film version (MM) *Carousel*, 1957. Leading recordings by Frank Sinatra (Columbia) and Judy Garland (Decca). Revivals: Roy Hamilton (Epic), 1954; Patti LaBelle and the Blue Belles (Park-way), 1964; Gerry and the Pacemakers (Laurie), 1965; Elvis Presley (RCA), 1968; Brooklyn Bridge (Buddha), 1969.

You Look Marvelous. w. Billy Crystal, m. Paul Shaffer, 1985. Actor Fernando Lamas impersonation by comedian Billy Crystal (A&M).

You Look So Good in Love. w/m Glen Ballard, Rory Bourke, and Kerry Chater, 1984. #1 Country record by George Strait (MCA).

You Love Me. w. Anne Croswell, m. Lee Pockriss, 1963. Introduced by Vivien Leigh and Jean Pierre Aumont in (TM) *Tovarich*.

You Lucky People, You. w. Johnny Burke, m. James Van Heusen, 1941. Introduced by Bing Crosby in (MM) *Road to Zanzibar* and records (Decca).

You Made Me Believe in Magic. w/m Leonard Boone, 1977. Top 10 record by The Bay City Rollers (Arista).

You Made Me Love You (I Didn't Want to Do It). w. Joseph McCarthy, m. James V. Monaco, 1913. Of all the recordings released during the year of its publication, Al Jolson's made the biggest impact (Columbia). The song became a staple of his Winter Garden performances and his future appearances in all media. Judy Garland, in (MM) *The Broadway Melody of '38*, sang it to a photograph of Clark Gable, after which her version ("Dear Mr. Gable") was recorded (Decca). Harry James had a million-selling record (Columbia), 1941. Jolson sang it on the soundtrack of (MM) *The Jolson Story*, 1946, which was then used in a montage in (MM) *Jolson Sings Again*, 1949. Doris Day, as Ruth Etting, sang it in (MM) *Love Me or Leave Me*, 1955. The song was also heard in (MM) *Syncopation*, 1942, and (MM) *Private Buckaroo*, 1945.

You Make Loving Fun. w/m Christine McVie, 1977. Top 10 record by the group Fleetwood Mac (Warner Bros.).

You Make Me Feel Brand New. w/m Linda Creed and Thom Bell, 1974. R&B/Pop gold record by The Stylistics (Avco).

You Make Me Feel Like Dancing. w/m Leo Sayer and Vini Poncia, 1977. #1 gold record by British-born Leo Sayer (Warner Bros.). While Sayer's record only reached #43 on the R&B charts, the song won the Grammy Award (NARAS) for Rhythm and Blues Song of the Year.

(You Make Me Feel) So Good. w/m Doc Pomus, Mort Shuman, Jerry Goldstein, and Richard Gottehrer, 1966. Recorded by The McCoys (Bang).

You Make Me Feel So Young. w. Mack Gordon, m. Josef Myrow, 1946. Introduced by Del Porter and Carol Stewart, dubbing on the soundtrack for Charles Smith and Vera-Ellen, but danced by the principals in (MM) *Three Little Girls in Blue*. Sung by Dennis Day in (MM) *I'll Get By*, 1950. Number has been a favorite of nightclub performers and jazz musicians.

You Make Me Real. w/m Jim Morrison, 1970. Recorded by The Doors (Elektra).

You Make Me Want to Make You Mine. w/m Dave Loggins, 1985. #1 Country chart record by Juice Newton (RCA).

You Make My Dreams. w. John Oates, Sara Allen, and Daryl Hall, m. Daryl Hall, 1981. Top 10 record by Daryl Hall and John Oates (RCA).

You May Be Right. w/m Billy Joel, 1980. Recorded by Billy Joel (Columbia).

You Mean Everything to Me. w/m Neil Sedaka and Howard Greenfield, 1960. Introduced and recorded by Neil Sedaka (RCA).

You Mean the World to Me. w/m Billy Sherrill and Glenn Sutton, 1967. Crossover (C&W/Pop) hit by David Houston (Epic).

You Met Your Match. w/m Lula Hardaway, Don Hunter, and Stevie Wonder, 1968. Top 40 record by Stevie Wonder (Tamla).

You Might Have Belonged to Another. w/m Pat West and Lucille Harmon, 1941. Best-selling record by Tommy Dorsey, vocal by Frank Sinatra, Connie Haines, and the Pied Pipers (Victor).

You Might Think. w/m Ric Ocasek, 1984. Top 10 record by the group, The Cars, for which Ocasek was lead singer (Elektra).

You Must Have Been a Beautiful Baby. w. Johnny Mercer, m. Harry Warren, 1938. Introduced by Dick Powell in (MM) *Hard to Get*. Doris Day sang it in (MM) *My Dream Is Yours*, 1949, and Eddie Cantor dubbed his voice on the soundtrack for Keefe Brasselle in (MM) *The Eddie Cantor Story*, 1953. It was revived by Bobby Darin, who had a Top Ten record (Atco), 1961, and by the British group, The Dave Clark Five (Epic), 1967.

You Mustn't Be Discouraged. w. Betty Comden and Adolph Green, m. Jule Styne, 1964. Introduced by Carol Burnett and Tiger Haynes in (TM) *Fade Out—Fade In*.

You Mustn't Kick It Around. w. Lorenz Hart, m. Richard Rodgers, 1940. Introduced by Gene Kelly, June Havoc, Diane Sinclair, Sondra Barrett, and chorus in (TM) *Pal Joey*.

You Nearly Lose Your Mind. w/m Ernest Tubb, 1943. Introduced and recorded by Ernest Tubb (Decca). Connie Haines recorded it in the early fifties (Coral).

You Needed Me. w/m Randy Goodrum, 1978. A #1 gold record, this was the biggest hit by Anne Murray (Capitol).

You Need Hands. w/m Roy Irwin, 1957. English song popularized in the U.S. by Eydie Gormé (ABC-Paramount).

You Never Done It Like That. w/m Howard Greenfield and Neil Sedaka, 1978. Top 10 record by The Captain and Tennille (A&M).

You Never Gave Up on Me. w/m Leslie Pearl, 1982. Top 10 Country chart record by Crystal Gayle (Columbia).

You Never Miss a Real Good Thing. w/m Bob McDill, 1976. Country record hit by Crystal Gayle (United Artists).

You Never Miss the Water Till the Well Runs Dry. w. Paul Secon, m. Arthur Kent, 1946. Featured and recorded by The Mills Brothers (Decca).

Young Americans. w/m David Bowie, 1975. Chart record from England by David Bowie (RCA).

Young and Foolish. w. Arnold B. Horwitt, m. Albert Hague, 1955. Hit song from (TM) *Plain and Fancy.* Introduced by David Daniels and Gloria Marlowe.

Young and Healthy. w. Al Dubin, m. Harry Warren, 1933. Introduced by Dick Powell, Toby Wing, and chorus in (MM) *Forty-Second Street.* Revived by Lee Roy Reams and Wanda Richert in (TM) *42nd Street,* 1980.

Young and in Love. w/m Hal Hester and Danny Apolinar, 1968. Introduced by Tom Ligon in the off-Broadway production of (TM) *Your Own Thing.*

Young and in Love. w/m Dick St. John, 1963. Hit record by Dick and Deedee (Warner Bros.).

Young and the Restless, The. See **Nadia's Theme.**

Young and Warm and Wonderful. w. Hy Zaret, m. Lou Singer, 1958. Featured and recorded by Tony Bennett (Columbia).

Young at Heart. w. Carolyn Leigh, m. Johnny Richards, 1954. Lyric written to a melody called "Moonbeam," which Richards had composed fifteen years earlier. Frank Sinatra's recording with Nelson Riddle's Orchestra (Capitol) became a million-seller and established the song as a standard. The title was given to the 1955 film (MM) *Young at Heart,* starring Sinatra and Doris Day. Sinatra sang it under the titles and in the last scene.

Young Blood. w/m Rickie Lee Jones, 1979. Recorded by Rickie Lee Jones (Warner Bros.).

Young Blood. w/m Jerry Leiber, Mike Stoller, and Doc Pomus, 1957. Top 10 record by The Coasters (Atco). Revived in 1976 by the British group Bad Company (Swan Song).

Young Country. w/m Hank Williams, Jr., 1988. Top 10 Country chart record by Hank Williams, Jr., and a chorus of Country stars (Warner Bros.).

Young Emotions. w. Mack David, m. Jerry Livingston, 1960. Top 40 record by Ricky Nelson (Imperial).

Younger Girl. w/m John Sebastian, 1966. Recorded by The Critters (Kapp) and The Hondells (Mercury).

Younger Than Springtime. w. Oscar Hammerstein II, m. Richard Rodgers, 1949. Introduced by William Tabbert in (TM) *South Pacific.* In (MM) *South Pacific,* 1958, it was sung by Bill Lee, dubbing for John Kerr.

Young Girl. w/m Jerry Fuller, 1968. Gold record by Gary Puckett and The Union Gap (Columbia).

Young Girl, A. w. Oscar Brown, Jr. (Engl.), Charles Aznavour (Fr.), m. Aznavour and R. Chauvigny, 1965. Introduced in France as "Une Enfant" by Charles Aznavour. Leading English vocal by Noel Harrison (London).

Young Hearts Run Free. w/m Dave Crawford, 1976. #1 R&B and Top 20 Pop chart record by Candi Staton (Warner Bros.).

Young Ideas. w. Chuck Sweeney, m. Moose Charlap, 1956. Introduced in (TVM) "The King and Mrs. Candle." First recorded by Tony Martin (RCA). In 1959, Chico Holiday had a popular record (RCA).

Young Love. w/m Ric Cartey and Carole Joyner, 1957. Hit records by Tab Hunter (Dot) and Sonny James (Capitol). The Crew-Cuts also had a chart record (Mercury).

Young Love (Strong Love). w/m Paul Kennerley and Kent Robbins, 1989. Hit Country record by The Judds (RCA).

Young Lovers. w/m Ray Hildebrand and Jill Jackson, 1963. Top 10 record by Paul and Paula (Philips).

Young Man's Fancy, A. w. John Murray Anderson and Jack Yellen, m. Milton Ager, 1920. The hit song, sung by Rosalind Fuller, from the revue (TM) *What's in a Name?*

Young Man with a Horn, The. w. Ralph Freed, m. George Stoll, 1944. Introduced by June Allyson and Harry James and his Orchestra in (MM) *Two Girls and a Sailor.* Allyson and James performed it again in (MM) *The Opposite Sex*, a musicalization of the stage and screen play *The Women*, 1956.

Young New Mexican Puppeteer, The. w. Earl Shuman, m. Leon Carr, 1972. Recorded by Tom Jones (Parrot).

Young Turks. w. Rod Stewart, m. Carmen Appice, Duane Hitchings, and Kevin Savigar, 1981. Top 10 record by Rod Stewart (Warner Bros.).

Young World. w/m Jerry Fuller, 1962. Hit record by Rick Nelson (Imperial).

You Only Live Twice. w/m Leslie Bricusse and John Barry, 1967. Title song of the British film (MP) *You Only Live Twice.* Popular record by Nancy Sinatra (Reprise).

You-oo Just You. w. Irving Caesar, m. George Gershwin, 1918. Introduced by Adele Rowland in (TM) *Hitchy-Koo.*

You or No One. w. Bob Rothberg, m. Peter Tinturin, 1933. Introduced and featured by Guy Lombardo and His Royal Canadians.

You Oughta Be in Pictures. w. Edward Heyman, m. Dana Suesse, 1934. Jane Froman interpolated it during the run of (TM) *Ziegfeld Follies.* Doris Day and Gordon MacRae sang it in (MM) *Starlift*, 1951. Popular recordings by Guy Lombardo, vocal by Carmen Lombardo (Melotone); George Hall (Bluebird); Little Jack Little (Columbia); the Boswell Sisters (Brunswick); Al Bowlly (Decca).

You Oughta See My Baby. w. Roy Turk, m. Fred E. Ahlert, 1920. This was Ahlert's first song success.

You Ought to Be with Me. w/m Al Green, Willie Mitchell, and Al Jackson, 1972. Gold record by Al Green (Hi).

You Planted a Rose in the Garden of Love. w. J. Will Callahan, m. Ernest R. Ball, 1914.

(I'll Be Glad When You're Dead) You Rascal You. w/m Sam Theard. Sometimes credited: w/m Charles "Cow Cow" Davenport, 1931. When first published, recorded by many bands and singers, among them: Louis Armstrong (Okeh), Red Nichols (Brunswick), Jack Teagarden (Columbia), Mound City Blowers (Okeh), Fletcher Henderson's Connie's Inn Orchestra (Crown), Cab Calloway (Brunswick), Tampa Red and Georgia Tom (Vocalion). Armstong recorded it again (Decca), 1941, and then with Louis Jordan (Decca).

Your Bulldog Drinks Champagne. w/m David Bellamy and Jim Stafford, 1975. Novelty record by Jim Stafford (MGM).

Your Cash Ain't Nothin' But Trash. w/m Charles Calhoun, 1954. R&B chart-maker by The Clovers (Atlantic). Revived by The Steve Miller Band (Capitol), 1974.

Your Cheatin' Heart. w/m Hank Williams, 1952. Introduced and recorded by Hank Williams (MGM). Hit records by Joni James (MGM) and Frankie Laine (Columbia). It became the title song of the film biography of Williams (MM) *Your Cheatin' Heart*, 1965, with Hank Williams, Jr., singing on the soundtrack for George Hamilton, who portrayed the composer.

Your Dad Gave His Life for His Country. w. Harry J. Breen, m. T. Mayo Geary, 1903.

You're a Builder Upper. w. Ira Gershwin and E. Y. Harburg, m. Harold Arlen, 1934. Introduced by Ray Bolger and Dixie Dunbar in (TM) *Life Begins at 8:40.* Popular recordings by Glen Gray and the Casa Loma Orchestra, vocal by Pee Wee Hunt (Decca); Ethel Merman, with Johnny Green's Orchestra (Brunswick); Richard Himber, vocal by Joey Nash (Victor); Joe Reichman's Orchestra (Melotone).

You're a Friend of Mine. w/m Narada Michael Walden and Jeffrey Cohen, 1986. Chart single from the album "Hero" by Clarence Clemons and Jackson Browne, added vocal by actress Daryl Hannah (Columbia).

You're a Good Man, Charlie Brown. w/m Clark Gesner, 1967. Sung by the company in the off-Broadway musical (TM) *You're a Good Man, Charlie Brown.*

You're a Grand Old Flag. w/m George M. Cohan, 1906. Introduced by Cohan in (TM) *George Washington, Jr.* Originally, the title contained the noun "rag," referring to the tattered remnants after a battle. Some patriotic groups misunderstood the allusion and Cohan was forced to change it to "flag." He sang it in (MM) *The Phantom President*, 1932, as did James Cagney in (MM) *Yankee Doodle Dandy*, 1924. Joel Gray performed it in (TM) *George M!*, 1968.

You're a Great Big Blue-Eyed Baby. w/m A. Seymour Brown, Jr., 1913.

You're a Heavenly Thing. w. Joe Young, m. Little Jack Little, 1935. Introduced by Little Jack Little on radio and recorded by Benny Goodman (Victor) and Orville Knapp (Decca) and their orchestras.

You're All I Need. w. Gus Kahn, m. Bronislaw Kaper and Walter Jurmann, 1935. From (MP) *Escapade* and recorded by the Dorsey Brothers, vocal by Bob Eberly (Decca) and Ted Fio Rito's Orchestra (Brunswick).

You're All I Need to Get By. w/m Nicholas Ashford and Valerie Simpson, 1968. Top 10 hit by Marvin Gaye and Tammi Terrell (Tamla). Other chart records by Aretha Franklin (Atlantic), 1971; Tony Orlando and Dawn (Elektra), 1975; Johnny Mathis and Deniece Williams (Columbia), 1978.

You're All I Want for Christmas. w/m Glen Moore and Seger Ellis, 1948. Introduced by Frank Gallagher (Dana). Seasonal hit by Frankie Laine, with Carl Fisher's Orchestra (Mercury).

You're All the World to Me. w. Alan Jay Lerner, m. Burton Lane, 1951. Melody originally heard in (TM) *Kid Millions* as "I Want to Be a Minstrel Man." This version was played while Fred Astaire did his celebrated dance on the walls and ceiling in (MM) *Royal Wedding*.

You Really Got Me. w/m Ray Davies, 1964. Hit record by the British group, The Kinks, of which the writer was lead singer (Reprise). Revived with Top 40 record by Van Halen (Warner Bros.), 1978.

You Really Know How to Hurt a Guy. w/m Jan Berry, Jill Gibson, and Roger Christian, 1965. Top 40 record by Jan and Dean (Liberty).

You're a Lucky Guy. w. Sammy Cahn, m. Saul Chaplin, 1939. Featured and recorded by Billie Holiday (Vocalion). Also by the bands: Louis Armstrong (Decca); Roy Eldridge (Varsity); Gene Krupa, vocal by Irene Daye (Columbia); Artie Shaw (Bluebird).

You're Always in My Arms. w. Joseph McCarthy, m. Harry Tierney, 1927. Introduced by Ethelind Terry in (TM) *Rio Rita.* In the film (MM) *Rio Rita*, 1929, it was sung by Bebe Daniels, who then recorded it (Victor).

You're Always There. w/m Don Marcotte and Nat Miles, 1950. Featured and recorded by Benny Goodman, vocal by Buddy Greco (Capitol).

You're a Million Miles from Nowhere (When You're One Little Mile from Home). w. Sam Lewis and Joe Young, m. Walter Donaldson, 1919. Post World War I sentimental ballad.

You're an Angel. w. Dorothy Fields, m. Jimmy McHugh, 1935. Introduced by Gene Raymond and Ann Sothern in (MM) *Hooray for Love.* Morton Downey had a popular record (Melotone).

You're an Old Smoothie. w/m B. G. DeSylva, Richard A. Whiting, and Nacio Herb Brown, 1932. Introduced by Jack Haley and Ethel Merman in (TM) *Take a Chance.* It was recorded by and became the theme song of the vocal group, The Smoothies, also known as Babs and Her Brothers (Bluebird), and by Lee Wiley, with Victor Young's Orchestra (Brunswick).

You're a Part of Me. w/m Kim Carnes, 1975. First recorded by Susan Jacks (Mercury). Revived by Gene Cotton with Kim Carnes (Ariola), 1978.

You're a Queer One, Julie Jordan. w. Oscar Hammerstein II, m. Richard Rodgers, 1945. Introduced by Jean Darling and Jan Clayton in (TM) *Carousel*. Sung in the film version (MM) *Carousel*, 1957, by Shirley Jones and Barbara Ruick.

You're a Special Part of Me. w/m Harold Johnson, Andrew Porter, and Gregory Wright, 1973. Top 20 record by Diana Ross and Marvin Gaye (Motown).

You're As Pretty As a Picture. w. Harold Adamson, m. Jimmy McHugh, 1938. Introduced by Deanna Durbin in (MM) *That Certain Age*. Among recordings: Tommy Dorsey, vocal by Edythe Wright (Victor); George Hall, vocal by Dolly Dawn (Vocalion); Henry King and his Orchestra (Decca).

You're a Sweetheart. w. Harold Adamson, m. Jimmy McHugh, 1937. Sung and danced by Alice Faye and George Murphy in (MM) *You're a Sweetheart*. Frank Sinatra sang it in (MM) *Meet Danny Wilson*, 1952.

You're a Sweet Little Headache. w. Leo Robin, m. Ralph Rainger, 1938. Introduced by Bing Crosby in (MM) *Paris Honeymoon* and recorded by him (Decca). Artie Shaw, vocal by Helen Forrest (Bluebird), and Nan Wynn (Vocalion) also had popular recordings.

You're As Welcome As the Flowers in May. w/m Dan J. Sullivan, 1901.

You're a Wonderful One. w/m Brian Holland, Eddie Holland, and Lamont Dozier, 1964. Crossover (R&B/Pop) hit by Marvin Gaye (Tamla).

You're Blasé. w. Bruce Sievier, m. Ord Hamilton, 1932. This British hit had great popularity in the United States, despite its erudite lyrics and French adjective in the title. The recordings of English bandleaders Ambrose (HMV-Victor) and Jack Hylton (Brunswick) introduced it to this country, followed by American bandleader Gus Arnheim (Victor) and many radio performances. Sara Vaughan,

with George Auld's Band, had a standout release in the early fifties (Musicraft).

You're Breaking My Heart. w/m Pat Genaro and Sunny Skylar, 1948. Based on "La Mattinata ('Tis the Day) by Leoncavallo, 1904, Vic Damone had a million-selling #1 Narecord (Mercury). Hit records were also made by Buddy Clark (Columbia) and The Ink Spots (Decca).

You're Dangerous. w. Johnny Burke, m. James Van Heusen, 1941. Introduced by Bing Crosby in (MM) *Road to Zanzibar*. Recorded by Crosby (Decca) and by the bands: Benny Goodman (Columbia); Tommy Dorsey, vocal by Connie Haines (Victor); Tommy Tucker, vocal by Amy Arnell (Okeh).

You're De Apple of My Eye. w. George H. Emerick, m. Herbert Dillea, 1896.

You're Devastating. w. Otto Harbach, m. Jerome Kern, 1933. Introduced by Bob Hope and reprised by Tamara in (TM) *Roberta*. The song was not in the first film version of the stage show, but was sung in the remake (MM) *Lovely to Look At*, 1952, by Howard Keel and Kathryn Grayson. Kern had used this melody in a 1928 London musical *Blue Eyes*. It was titled "Do I Do Wrong?" with lyrics by Graham John.

You're Driving Me Crazy. w/m Walter Donaldson, 1930. Introduced and recorded by Guy Lombardo (Columbia) and featured and recorded by Rudy Vallee (Victor). It was interpolated by Adele Astaire and Eddie Foy, Jr., in (TM) *Smiles*. The song was included in (MM) *Gentlemen Marry Brunettes*, 1955.

You're Easy to Dance With. w/m Irving Berlin, 1942. Introduced by Fred Astaire singing, then dancing in turn with Virginia Dale and Marjorie Reynolds in (MM) *Holiday Inn*. Recorded by Dick Stabile, vocal by Gracie Barrie (Decca); Shep Fields, vocal by Ken Curtis (Bluebird).

You're Everywhere. w. Edward Heyman, m. Vincent Youmans, 1932. Introduced by Natalie Hall and Michael Bartlett in (TM) *Through the Years*.

You're Fooling You. w/m The Dramatics. 1976. Top 10 R&B chart record by The Dramatics (ABC).

You're For Me. w/m Tommy Collins and A. E. Owens, Jr., 1964. Top 10 Country chart record by Buck Owens (Capitol).

You're Free to Go. w/m Don Robertson and Louis Herscher, 1955. Top 10 C&W record by Carl Smith (Columbia). Revived by Sonny James (Columbia).

You're Getting to Be a Habit with Me. w. Al Dubin, m. Harry Warren, 1933. Introduced by Dick Powell and Bebe Daniels in (MM) *Forty-Second Street*. Bing Crosby had a best-selling record (Brunswick). In (MM) *Lullaby of Broadway*, 1951, Doris Day sang it and danced to it with Gene Nelson. In the Broadway musical version (TM) *42nd Street*, 1980, it was performed by Tammy Grimes, Lee Roy Reams, Wanda Richert, and ensemble.

You're Going Far Away, Lad (or I'm Still Your Mother, Dear). w/m Paul Dresser, 1897.

You're Gonna Change (or I'm Gonna Leave). w/m Hank Williams, 1949. Introduced and hit Country record by Hank Williams (MGM).

You're Gonna Get What's Coming. w/m Robert Palmer, 1980. Recorded by Bonnie Raitt (Warner Bros.).

You're Gonna Hear from Me. w. Dory Previn, m. André Previn, 1966. Introduced in (MP) *Inside Daisy Clover*, sung by Jackie Ward, dubbing for Natalie Wood. Featured and recorded by Andy Williams (Columbia).

You're Gonna Hurt Yourself. w/m Bob Crewe and Charles Calello, 1966. Recorded by Frankie Valli (Smash).

You're Gonna Lose Your Gal. w. Joe Young, m. James V. Monaco, 1933. Popularized by Glen Gray and the Casa Loma Orchestra, vocal by Pee Wee Hunt (Brunswick) and Jan Garber's Orchestra (Victor). Doris Day sang it in (MM) *Starlift*, 1961.

You're Gonna Make Me Cry. w/m Deadric Malone, 1965. Recorded by R&B singer O. V. Wright (Back Beat).

You're Gonna Miss Me. w/m Eddie Curtis, 1959. Popularized by Connie Francis (MGM).

(You're) Having My Baby. See **Having My Baby (You're).**

You're Here and I'm Here. w. Harry B. Smith, m. Jerome Kern, 1914. From (TM) *The Marriage Market*.

You're in Love. w. Otto Harbach and Edward Clark, m. Rudolf Friml, 1917. Introduced by Lawrence Wheat, Marie Flynn, and chorus in (TM) *You're in Love*. Recorded by Harry MacDonough and the Lyric Quartette (Victor).

You're in Love with Someone. w/m Rod Stewart, 1977. Top 10 gold record by Rod Stewart (Warner Bros.).

You're in My Heart (The Final Acclaim). w/m Rod Stewart, 1977. Top 10 gold record by Rod Stewart (Warner Bros.).

You're in My Power (Ha, Ha, Ha). w/m Al Hoffman, James Cavanaugh, and Nat Simon, 1934.

You're in the Right Church, But the Wrong Pew. w. Cecil Mack, m. Chris Smith, 1980. Popularized by Bert Williams.

You're Just a Dream Come True. w. Charles Newman, m. Isham Jones, 1931. This became the theme song of Isham Jones and his Orchestra, after recording it in 1930 (Brunswick).

You're Just a Flower from an Old Bouquet. w. Gwynne Denni, m. Lucien Denni, 1924. Recorded and featured by Vincent Lopez and his Orchestra (Okeh), by Lewis James, the popular tenor (Columbia), and later Carmen Cavallaro (Decca).

You're Just in Love. w/m Irving Berlin, 1951. Introduced by Ethel Merman and Russell Nype in (TM) *Call Me Madam*. Hit record by Perry Como, with The Fontane Sisters

(RCA Victor). Other popular versions by Rosemary Clooney and Guy Mitchell (Columbia), and Ethel Merman and Dick Haymes, with Gordon Jenkins' Orchestra (Decca). In (MM) *Call Me Madam*, 1953, it was sung by Ethel Merman and Donald O'Connor.

You're Just the Kind. w. Bill Carey, m. Carl Fischer, 1949. Introduced and recorded by Frankie Laine (Mercury).

You're Laughing at Me. w/m Irving Berlin, 1937. Introduced by Dick Powell in (MM) *On the Avenue*. Best-selling records by Mildred Bailey (Vocalion), Fats Waller (Victor), and Wayne King (Victor).

You're Lonely and I'm Lonely. w/m Irving Berlin, 1940. Performed by Victor Moore and Vera Zorina in (TM) *Louisiana Purchase*, and again in the film version (MM) *Louisiana Purchase*, 1942.

You're Lookin' at Country. w/m Loretta Lynn, 1970. Country hit by Loretta Lynn (Decca).

You're Lucky to Me. w. Andy Razaf, m. Eubie Blake, 1930. Ethel Waters sang it in Lew Leslie's (TM) *Blackbirds of 1930* and recorded it (Victor). Among other recordings: Louis Armstrong (Okeh), the Charleston Chasers (Columbia), Duke Ellington (Victor), Tom Gerun (Brunswick), Will Bradley (Columbia).

You're Making a Fool out of Me. w/m Tompall Glaser, 1959. Hit C&W record by Jimmy Newman (MGM).

You Remind Me of My Mother. w/m George M. Cohan, 1922. Introduced by Elizabeth Hines and Charles King in (TM) *Little Nellie Kelly*.

You Remind Me of the Girl That Used to Go to School with Me! w. Jack Drislane, m. Charles Miller, 1910.

You're Mine, You. w. Edward Heyman, m. John Green, 1933. Popularized by Ray Noble (HMV-Victor), Guy Lombardo (Brunswick), Gertrude Niesen (Columbia). Among the many subsequent recordings: Artie Shaw, arranged by Gordon Jenkins (Decca); Carmen

Cavallaro (Decca); Delta Rhythm Boys (Victor); Horace Henderson (Vocalion); Mary Ann McCall (Discovery); Ziggy Elman (Bluebird); Lonnie Johnson, the blues singer-guitarist (King).

You're More Than the World to Me. w. Jeff Branen, m. Alfred Solman, 1914.

You're Movin' Out Today. w/m Carole Bayer Sager, Bruce Roberts, and Bette Midler, 1977. Recorded by Bette Midler (Atlantic) and Carole Bayer Sager (Elektra).

You're My Baby. w. A. Seymour Brown, m. Nat D. Ayer, 1912. Recorded by the American Quartet (Victor).

You're My Best Friend. w/m John Deacon, 1976. Top 20 record by the British group Queen (Elektra).

You're My Best Friend. w/m Wayne Holyfield, 1975. Hit Country record by Don Williams (ABC/Dot).

You're My Dish. w. Harold Adamson, m. Jimmy McHugh, 1937. From (MM) *Merry-Go-Round of '38*.

You're My Everything. w/m Cornelius Grant, Roger Penzabene, and Norman Whitfield, 1967. Top 10 record by The Temptations (Gordy).

You're My Everything. w. Mort Dixon and Joe Young, m. Harry Warren, 1931. Introduced by Jeanne Aubert and Lawrence Gray in (MM) *The Laugh Parade*, starring Ed Wynn. Dan Dailey sang it in (MM) *You're My Everything*, 1949. It was also heard in (MM) *Painting the Clouds with Sunshine*, 1951, and in (MM) *The Eddy Duchin Story*, 1956.

You're My First Lady. w/m Mac McAnally, 1987. Top 10 Country chart record by T. G. Sheppard (Columbia).

You're My Girl (Say). See **(Say) You're My Girl**.

You're My Jamaica. w/m Kent Robbins, 1979. #1 Country chart record by Charley Pride (RCA).

You're My Latest, My Greatest Inspiration. w/m Kenny Gamble and Leon Huff, 1982. R&B/Pop chart by Teddy Pendergrass (Philadelphia International).

You're My Man. w/m Glenn Sutton, 1971. Country and Pop hit by Lynn Anderson (Columbia).

You're My Past, Present and Future. w. Mack Gordon, m. Harry Revel, 1933. Sung by Russ Columbo in (MM) *Broadway Thru a Keyhole*. Recorded by the bands of Isham Jones (Victor) and Richard Himber (Vocalion).

(You're My) Soul and Inspiration. w/m Barry Mann and Cynthia Weil, 1966. #1 gold record by the Righteous Brothers (Verve). Revived by Donny and Marie Osmond (Polydor), 1977.

You're My Thrill. w. Ned Washington, m. Burton Lane, 1935. Introduced by Ted Lewis in (MM) *Here Comes the Band*.

You're My Thrill. w. Sidney Clare, m. Jay Gorney, 1934. Associated with Billie Holiday (Decca), though there were many earlier versions. Isham Jones and his Orchestra also recorded it (Victor), 1934. Lena Horne, with Charlie Barnet's Band, had an outstanding record (Bluebird), 1941.

You're My World. w. Carl Sigman (Engl.), Gino Paoli (It.), m. Umberto Bindi, 1964. Original Italian title "Il Mio Mondo." Hit record by British singer Cilla Black (Capitol). Revived by Helen Reddy (Capitol), 1977.

You're Nearer. w. Lorenz Hart, m. Richard Rodgers, 1940. Written for the Broadway musical's film version (MM) *Too Many Girls*, it was sung by Trudi Erwin, [dubbing on the soundtrack for Lucille Ball], and Frances Langford, Ann Miller, and Libby Bennett.

You're Never Too Old for Young Love. w/m Rick Giles and Frank Myers, 1987. Top 10 Country record by Eddy Raven, from the album "Right Hand" (RCA).

You're Nobody Till Somebody Loves You. w/m Russ Morgan, Larry Stock, and James Cavanaugh, 1944. Introduced and recorded by Russ Morgan, with his Orchestra (Decca). Revived by Dean Martin (Reprise), 1965.

You're No Good. w/m Clint Ballard, Jr., 1975. Chart record by Betty Everett (Vee-Jay), 1969. #1 record by Linda Ronstadt (Capitol), 1975.

You're Not Mine Anymore. w/m Webb Pierce, Doyle Wilburn, and Teddy Wilburn, 1955. C&W success by Webb Pierce (Decca).

You're Not So Easy to Forget. w. Herb Magidson, m. Ben Oakland, 1947. From (MP) *Song of the Thin Man*. Popular records by Claude Thornhill, vocal by Fran Warren (Columbia), and Johnny Johnston (MGM).

You're Not the Kind. w/m Will Hudson and Irving Mills, 1936. Introduced and recorded by the Hudson-DeLange Orchestra, vocal by Ruth Gaylor (Brunswick). Other records: Frances Faye (Decca), Fats Waller (Victor), Pinky Tomlin (Brunswick), Red Allen (Vocalion), Sarah Vaughan (Musicraft).

You're Not the Only Oyster in the Stew. w. Johnny Burke, m. Harold Spina, 1934. Top records by Fats Waller and His Rhythm (Victor) and Ozzie Nelson and his Orchestra (Brunswick).

You're Only Lonely. w/m J. D. Souther, 1979. Top 10 record by J. D. Souther (Columbia).

(You're Puttin') a Rush on Me. w/m Timmy Allen and Paul Laurence, 1987. #1 single by Stephanie Mills (MCA).

You're Running Wild. w/m Ray Edenton and Don Winters, 1956. Top 10 C&W record by The Louvin Brothers (Capitol).

You're Sensational. w/m Cole Porter, 1956. Introduced by Frank Sinatra in (MM) *High Society* and on records (Capitol).

You're Simply Delish. w. Arthur Freed, m. Joseph Meyer, 1930. Sung by Cliff Edwards and Fifi d'Orsay in (MP) *Those Three French Girls*. Recorded by Bert Lown and his Orchestra (Victor) and Smith Ballew (Columbia).

You're Sixteen. w/m Richard Sherman and Robert Sherman, 1960, 1974. Top 10 record by Johnny Burnette (Liberty). Revived by Ringo Starr, with a #1 record (Apple), 1974.

You're Slightly Terrific. w. Sidney D. Mitchell, m. Lew Pollack, 1936. Sung by Tony Martin and Dixie Dunbar in (MM) *Pigskin Parade*. Martin recorded it (Decca) as did the band of Joe Sanders (Decca).

You're So Darn Charming. w. Johnny Burke, m. Harold Spina, 1935. Featured and recorded by Fats Waller (Victor), the Dorsey Brothers (Decca), Babs and her Brothers [The Smoothies] (Decca).

You're So Desirable. w/m Ray Noble, 1939. Introduced and recorded by Ray Noble, vocal by Howard Barrie (Brunswick). Other versions by Red Norvo, vocal by Terry Allen (Vocalion); Red Nichols, vocal by Bill Darnell (Bluebird); Gray Gordon, vocal by Cliff Grass (Victor); Jimmy Dorsey and his Orchestra (Decca).

You're So Fine. w/m Lance Finney, Willie Schofield, and Bob West, 1959. Chart record by the R&B group The Falcons (Unart).

You're So Much a Part of Me. w/m Richard Adler and Jerry Ross, 1953. Introduced by Carleton Carpenter and Elaine Dunn in (TM) *John Murray Anderson's Almanac*.

(You're So Square) Baby, I Don't Care. See **Baby, I Don't Care.**

You're So Understanding. w. Ben Raleigh, m. Bernie Wayne, 1949. Highest chart record by Evelyn Knight, with Four Hits and a Miss (Decca). Others: Russ Carlyle (Coral); Ralph Flanagan and his Orchestra (Bluebird).

You're So Vain. w/m Carly Simon, 1973. #1 gold record by Carly Simon (Elektra).

You're Still a Young Man. w. Emilio Castillo and Stephen Kupka, 1972. Recorded by Tower of Power (Warner Bros.).

You're Still Mine. w. Eddie Thorpe, m. Faron Young, 1956. Introduced and recorded by Faron Young (Capitol).

You're Still My Baby. w/m Chuck Willis, 1954. Introduced and Top 10 R&B record by Chuck Willis (Okeh).

You're Such a Comfort to Me. w. Mack Gordon, m. Harry Revel, 1934. Introduced by Ginger Rogers, Jack Oakie, Thelma Todd, and Jack Haley in (MM) *Sitting Pretty*. Recordings: the Pickens Sisters (Victor); George Hall, vocal by Loretta Lee (Bluebird); Leo Reisman and his Orchestra (Victor).

You're the Best Break This Old Heart Ever Had. w/m Robert Hatch and Wayland Holyfield, 1982. #1 Country chart record by Ed Bruce (MCA).

You're the Best Thing That Ever Happened to me. See **Best Thing That**, etc.

You're the Cats. w. Lorenz Hart, m. Richard Rodgers, 1931. Sung by Ben Lyon and Ona Munson in (MM) *The Hot Heiress*.

You're the Cause of It All. w. Sammy Cahn, m. Jule Styne, 1946. From Danny Kaye in (MM) *The Kid from Brooklyn*. Popular recordings by Fred Martin, vocal by Clyde Rogers (Victor); Kay Kyser, vocal by Lucy Ann Polk (Columbia).

You're the Cream in My Coffee. w. B. G. DeSylva and Lew Brown, m. Ray Henderson, 1928. Introduced by Jack Whiting and Ona Munson in (TM) *Hold Everything*. Leading records by Ben Selvin, vocal by Jack Palmer (Columbia); Ted Weems and his Orchestra (Victor); Ruth Etting (Columbia). It was interpolated into (MP) *The Cockeyed World*, a quasi-musical, 1929.

You're the Cure for What Ails Me. w. E. Y. Harburg, m. Harold Arlen, 1936. Sung by Al Jolson, Edward Everett Horton, Sybil Jason, and Allen Jenkins in (MM) *The Singing Kid*.

You're the Devil in Disguise. w/m Bill Giant, Bernie Baum, and Florence Kaye, 1963. Top 10 record by Elvis Presley (RCA).

You're the First, the Last, My Everything. w/m Barry White, Tony Sepe, and

993

Peter Radcliffe, 1974. Gold record by Barry White (20th Century).

You're the First Time I've Thought About Leaving. w/m Dickey Betts and Kerry Chater, 1983. #1 Country chart record by Reba McEntire (Mercury).

You're the Flower of My Heart. See **Sweet Adeline.**

You're the Inspiration. w/m Peter Cetera and David Foster, 1984. Top 10 record by the group Chicago (Full Moon).

You're the Last Thing I Needed Tonight. w/m Allee Wills and Don Pfrimmer, 1986. #1 Country chart record by John Schneider (MCA).

You're the Love. w/m Louie Shelton and David Batteau, 1978. Recorded by Seals and Crofts (Warner Bros.).

You're the Nearest Thing to Heaven. w. Johnny Cash, m. Hoydt Johnson and Jim Atkins, 1958. Popular record by Johnny Cash (Sun).

You're the One. w/m Petula Clark and Tony Hatch, 1965. Written in England, recorded and Top 10 single by the American vocal group The Vogues (Co & Ce).

You're the One. w. Johnny Mercer, m. Jimmy McHugh, 1941. Introduced by "Wee" Bonnie Baker, with Orrin Tucker's Orchestra in (MM) *You're the One*, and recorded by them (Columbia).

You're the One (I Need). w/m William Robinson, 1966. Recorded by The Marvelettes (Tamla).

You're the One (You Beautiful Son-of-a-Gun). w. Buddy Fields, m. Gerald Marks, 1932. Interpolated by Harry Richman in (TM) *George White's Music Hall Varieties*. Marks originally wrote this as a "schottische," but bandleader Fred Waring, who was at the publisher's office to hear Marks demonstrate the song, suggested the tempo be changed to 6/8 time. Marks tried it and immediately ef-

fected the change. Richman sang it in the show and recorded it (Brunswick), and Waring then recorded it, with a vocal by Johnny "Scat" Davis (Victor). Rudy Vallee also had a hand in the song's popularity via his numerous radio performances.

You're the One I Care For. w. Harry Link, m. Bert Lown and Chauncey Gray, 1930. Popular song featured and recorded by Bert Lown and his Orchestra (Victor) and Belle Baker (Brunswick).

You're the One That I Want. w/m John Farrar, 1978. Introduced in (MM) *Grease* by Olivia Newton-John and John Travolta. Their recording became a #1 platinum hit (MCA).

You're the Only Good Thing (That's Happened to Me). w/m Chuck Gregory, 1960. Country hit by George Morgan (Columbia).

You're the Only One. w/m Bruce Roberts and Carole Bayer Sager, 1979. Recorded by Dolly Parton (RCA).

You're the Only One. w/m Seth Justman and Peter Wolf, 1977. Written by two members of the band credited only as Geils (Atlantic).

You're the Only Star (in My Blue Heaven). w/m Gene Autry, 1938. Introduced and recorded by Gene Autry (Conqueror). Other versions: Roy Acuff (Vocalion), Patsy Montana (Conqueror), Barry Wood (Brunswick).

You're the Only Woman (You and I). w/m David Pack, 1980. Recorded by the trio Ambrosia (Warner Bros.).

You're the Only World I Know. w/m Sonny James and Robert F. Tubert, 1964. Crossover (C&W/Pop) hit by Sonny James (Capitol).

You're the Reason. w/m Bobby Edwards, Mildred Imes, Fred Henley, and Terry Fell, 1961. Crossover (C&W/Pop) hit by Bobby Edwards (Crest).

You're the Reason (I'm in Love). w/m Jack Morrow, 1957. Popular record by Sonny James (Capitol).

You're the Reason God Make Oklahoma. w/m Larry Collins and Sandy Pinkard, 1980. From the film (MP) *Any Which Way You Can.* Country chart hit by David Frizzell and Shelly West (Warner Bros.).

You're the Reason I'm Living. w/m Bobby Darin, 1963. Top 10 record by Bobby Darin (Capitol).

You're the Top. w/m Cole Porter, 1934. Introduced by William Gaxton and Ethel Merman in (TM) *Anything Goes.* Merman sang it in (MM) *Anything Goes,* 1936. In the Porter biography (MM) *Night and Day,* 1946, it was sung by Cary Grant as Porter, and Ginny Simms. Bing Crosby and Mitzi Gaynor sang it in the 1956 remake of (MM) *Anything Goes,* and it was sung in (MM) *At Long Last Love,* 1975, by Burt Reynolds, Madeline Kahn, Duilio Del Prete, and Cybill Shepherd. Ethel Merman, with Johnny Green's Orchestra, recorded it (Brunswick) as did Cole Porter, singing it at the piano (Victor).

You're Too Dangerous, Cherie. See **La Vie en Rose.**

Your Eyes Have Told Me So. w. Gus Kahn, m. Egbert Van Alstyne, 1919. Grace LaRue featured it in vaudeville. James Melton sang it in (MM) *Sing Me a Love Song* in 1936 and Doris Day and Gordon MacRae sang it in (MM) *By the Light of the Silvery Moon* in 1952. It was used as background music in the Kahn film bio (MM) *I'll See You in My Dreams* in 1951.

Your Father's Moustache. w/m Bill Harris and Woody Herman, 1945. Introduced and recorded by Woody Herman and his Orchestra (Columbia).

Your Feet's Too Big. w/m Ada Benson and Fred Fisher, 1936. Introduced, featured, and recorded by Fats Waller. Ken Page performed it in the 1978 Waller musical (TM) *Ain't Misbehavin'.*

Your God Comes First, Your Country Next, Then Mother Dear. w/m Paul Dresser, 1898.

Your Good Girl's Gonna Go Bad. w/m Billy Sherrill and Glenn Sutton, 1967. Country record hit by Tammy Wynette (Epic).

Your Good Thing Is About to End. w/m Isaac Hayes and David Porter, 1969. Introduced by Mable John (Stax), 1966. Hit record by Lou Rawls (Capitol).

Your Head on My Shoulder. w. Harold Adamson, m. Burton Lane, 1934. The ballad hit of the Eddie Cantor musical (MM) *Kid Millions,* sung by Ann Sothern and George Murphy. Among recordings: Dorsey Brothers, vocal by Kay Weber (Decca); Anson Weeks, vocal by Kay St. Germaine (Brunswick); George Hall (Bluebird); Tom Coakley, vocal by Carl Ravazza (Victor); Mal Hallett (Melotone).

Your Heart Turned Left (and I Was on the Right). w/m Harlan Howard, 1964. Hit country record by George Jones (United Artists).

Your Husband—My Wife. w/m Toni Wine and Irwin Levine, 1969. Recorded by the group Brooklyn Bridge (Buddah).

Your Land and My Land. w. Dorothy Donnelly, m. Sigmund Romberg, 1927. Sung by Nathaniel Wagner and the company in (TM) *My Maryland.* In the film biography of Romberg (MM) *Deep in My Heart,* 1954, it was sung by Howard Keel.

Your Love. w/m John Spinks, 1986. Top 10 record by the British trio, The Outfield, of which Spinks was guitarist (Columbia).

Your Love. w/m H. B. Barnum and Walter Johnson, 1977. Top 20 record by Marilyn McCoo and Billy Davis, Jr. (ABC).

Your Love. w. Ned Washington, m. Walter Gross, 1934. Leading recording by Freddy Martin, vocal by Elmer Feldkamp (Brunswick).

Your Love Is All That I Crave. w/m Al Dubin, Perry Bradford, and Jimmy Johnson, 1929. Introduced by Frank Fay, with composer Harry Akst at the piano, in (MM) *Show of Shows.*

Your Love Is Driving Me Crazy. w/m Sammy Hagar, 1983. Recorded by Sammy Hagar (Geffen).

(Your Love Keeps Lifting Me) Higher and Higher. w/m Gary L. Jackson, Raynard Miner, and Carl Smith, 1967. Hit record by Jackie Wilson (Brunswick). Revived by Rita Coolidge, whose gold record version was slightly retitled "(Your Love Has Lifted Me) Higher and Higher" (A&M), 1977.

Your Love's on the Line. w/m Earl Thomas Conley and Randy Scruggs, 1983. #1 Country chart record by Earl Thomas Conley (RCA).

Your Mama Don't Dance. w/m Kenny Loggins and Jim Messina, 1973. Gold record by Loggins and Messina (Columbia).

Your Mother and Mine. w. Joe Goodwin, m. Gus Edwards, 1929. Introduced by Charles King, Jack Benny, Karl Dane, and George K. Arthur in (MM) *Hollywood Revue of 1929*. It was also interpolated in (MM) *The Show of Shows* later that same year.

Your Mother's Son-in-Law. w. Mann Holiner, m. Alberta Nichols, 1933. Introduced by John Mason, Edith Wilson, Toni Ellis, and Martha Thomas in Lew Leslie's (TM) *Blackbirds (1933-1934 Edition)*. Billie Holiday recorded it with Benny Goodman's Orchestra in 1933 (Columbia).

Your Name Is Beautiful. w/m Diane Lampert and John Gluck, 1958. C&W and Pop chart record by Carl Smith (Columbia).

Your Old Love Letters. w/m Johnny Bond, 1961. Hit Country record by Porter Wagoner (RCA).

Your Old Standby. w/m Janie Bradford and William Robinson, 1963. Crossover (R&B/Pop) hit by Mary Wells (Motown).

Your Old Used to Be. w. Hilda M. Young, m. Faron Young, 1960. Hit C&W record by Faron Young (Capitol).

Your Other Love. w. Ben Raleigh, m. Claus Ogerman, 1963. Introduced and recorded by Connie Francis (MGM).

Your Own Back Yard. w/m Dion DiMucci and Tony Fasce, 1970. Recorded by Dion (Warner Bros.).

Your Own Special Way. w/m Michael Rutherford, 1977. Recorded by the English group Genesis (Atco).

Your Own Thing. w/m Hal Hester and Danny Apolinar, 1969. Introduced by Danny Apolinar, Michael Valenti, and John Kuhner in the off-Broadway musical (TM) *Your Own Thing*.

Your Precious Love. w/m Valerie Simpson and Nicholas Ashford, 1967. Top 10 hit by Marvin Gaye and Tammi Terrell (Tamla).

Your Red Wagon. w. Don Raye, m. Richard M. Jones and Gene De Paul, 1940. Based on a blues instrumental by Jones. Most popular records: The Andrews Sisters (Decca), and the bands of Ray McKinley (Majestic) and Tony Pastor (Columbia).

Yours. w. Jack Sherr (Engl.), Augustin Rodriguez (Sp.), m. Gonzalo Roig, 1941. Cuban song, originally titled "Quierme Mucho." Dinah Shore recorded it (Victor), 1939, but song became major hit via recording by Jimmy Dorsey, vocal by Bob Eberly and Helen O'Connell (Decca) in 1941. Other popular versions by Benny Goodman and his Orchestra (Columbia); Tito Guizar, in Spanish (Victor); Vaughn Monroe, with his Orchestra (Victor). Vera Lynn revived it with a hit record (London), 1952, followed by Les Baxter and his Orchestra (Capitol).

Yours, Love. w/m Harlan Howard, 1969. Hit Country record by Dolly Parton and Porter Wagoner (RCA). Pop chart version by Joe Simon (Sound Stage), 1970.

Yours and Mine. w. Arthur Freed, m. Nacio Herb Brown, 1937. Introduced by Judy Garland, Eleanor Powell, and the Robert Mitchell Boys' Choir in (MM) *Broadway Melody of '38*.

Yours for a Song. w. Ted Fetter and Billy Rose, m. Dana Suesse, 1939. Sung by Morton Downey and swum to by Eleanor Holm in Billy

Rose's *Aquacade* at the New York World's Fair.

Yours Is My Heart Alone. w. Harry B. Smith (Engl.), m. Franz Lehar, 1931. This Austrian song had the original title of "Dein ist Mein Ganzes Herz," with German lyrics by Ludwig Herzer and Fritz Löhner. It was introduced by Richard Tauber in the operetta *Das Land das Lächelns (The Land of Smiles)* in Germany. Featured in the U.S. and recorded by James Melton (Victor); Frank Munn, with Leo Reisman's Orchestra (Victor); Jack Hylton, the English bandleader (Victor 12″). Later recordings by Everett Marshall (Decca), Glenn Miller (Bluebird), Jan August (Mercury).

Your Smile. w/m Ren Moore and Angela Winbush, 1986. #1 R&B chart record by Ren and Angela (Mercury).

Your Smiles, Your Tears. w. Irving Caesar, m. Sigmund Romberg, 1930. Introduced by Ethelind Terry and Guy Robertson in (MM) *Nina Rosa.*

Your Smiling Face. w/m James Taylor, 1977. Recorded by James Taylor (Columbia).

Your Socks Don't Match. w/m Leon Carr and Leo Corday, 1941. Introduced by Fats Waller. His 1943 recording (Bluebird) reached the popularity charts less than three months before his death. Bing Crosby and Louis Jordan had the best-selling version of the song (Decca).

Your Song. w/m Elton John and Bernie Taupin, 1970. First U.S. Top 10 record by the British singer/writer Elton John (Uni).

Yours Sincerely. w. Lorenz Hart, m. Richard Rodgers, 1929. Introduced by Glenn Hunter and Lillian Taiz in (TM) *Spring Is Here.* In the film adaptation (MM) *Spring Is Here,* 1930, it was sung by Alexander Gray and Bernice Claire. It was heard again in a two-reel version called *Yours Sincerely,* 1933, which was part of the *Broadway Brevities* series, starring Lanny Ross.

Yours Truly Is Truly Yours, w. Benny Davis, m. J. Fred Coots and Ted Fio Rito, 1936. Introduced and recorded by Ted Fio Rito and his Orchestra (Decca). Other recordings by Ray Noble, vocal by Al Bowlly (Victor), and Gene Kardos, vocal by Bea Wain (Melotone).

Your Tender Loving Care. w/m Buck Owens, 1967. Country hit, recorded by Buck Owens (Capitol).

Your Time to Cry. w/m Joe Simon, Raeford Gerald, and Dock Price, Jr., 1970. Top 40 record by Joe Simon (Spring).

Your True Love. w/m Carl Lee Perkins, 1957. C&W chart record by Carl Perkins (Sun).

Your Unchanging Love. w/m Brian Holland, Lamont Dozier, and Eddie Holland, 1967. Recorded by Marvin Gaye (Tamla).

Your Used to Be. w/m Howard Greenfield and Jack Keller, 1962. Popular recording by Brenda Lee (Decca).

Your Wildest Dreams. w/m Justin Hayward, 1986. Top 10 record by the British group The Moody Blues (Threshold).

You Said a Bad Word. w/m Joe Tex, 1972. Recorded by Joe Tex (Dial).

You Said It. w. Jack Yellen, m. Harold Arlen, 1931. Introduced by Mary Lawlor and Stanley Smith in (TM) *You Said It,* starring Lou Holtz. Arlen recorded it with Red Nichols's Band (Brunswick).

You Said It. w. Bert Kalmar and Eddie Cox, m. Henry W. Santly, 1919.

You Say the Nicest Things, Baby. w. Harold Adamson, m. Jimmy McHugh, 1948. Introduced by Betty Jane Watson and Bill Callahan and reprised by Irene Rich and Bobby Clark in (TM) *As the Girls Go.*

You Say the Sweetest Things, Baby. w. Mack Gordon, m. Harry Warren, 1940. Introduced by Alice Faye, John Payne, and Jack

Oakie in (MM) *Tin Pan Alley*. Popular recordings by Glen Gray and the Casa Loma Orchestra, vocal by Pee Wee Hunt (Decca); Tommy Dorsey, vocal by Connie Haines (Victor).

You'se Just a Little Nigger, Still You're Mine, All Mine. w/m Paul Dresser, 1898.

You Send Me. w/m L. C. Cooke, 1957. Sam Cooke had a #1 hit record of this song, written by his brother (Keen). Teresa Brewer had a Top 40 version (Coral). Revived by Aretha Franklin (Atlantic), 1968.

You Send Me. w. Harold Adamson, Jimmy McHugh, 1944. Introduced by Dick Haymes in (MM) *Four Jills in a Jeep*.

You Sexy Thing. w/m Errol Brown and Anthony Wilson, 1975. Gold record by the British group Hot Chocolate (Big Tree).

You Shook Me All Night Long. w/m Angus Young, Malcolm Young, and Brian Johnson, 1980. Written by members of the Australian group AC/DC (Atlantic).

You Should Be Dancing. w/m Barry Gibb, Maurice Gibb, and Robin Gibb, 1976. #1 gold record by the British brother trio The Bee Gees (RSO).

You Should Be Mine (the Woo Woo Song). w/m Andy Goldmark and Bruce Roberts, 1986. Crossover Country/Pop hit record by Jeffrey Osborne (A&M).

You Should Have Been Gone By Now. w/m Eddy Raven, Frank Myers, and Don Pfrimmer, 1986. Top 10 Country chart record by Eddy Raven (RCA).

You Should Hear How She Talks About You. w/m Tom Snow and Dean Pitchford, 1982. Top 10 record by Melissa Manchester (Arista).

You Should See Yourself. w. Dorothy Fields, m. Cy Coleman, 1966. Introduced by Gwen Verdon in (TM) *Sweet Charity*. Song not used in film version.

You Showed Me. w/m Gene Clark and Jim McGuinn, 1969. Top 10 record by The Turtles (White Whale).

You Showed Me the Way. w/m Ella Fitzgerald, Bud Green, Teddy McRae, and Chick Webb, 1937. Introduced, recorded, and popularized by Chick Webb, vocal by Ella Fitzgerald (Decca). Among other popular band records: Fats Waller (Victor), Frankie Newton (Vocalion), Teddy Wilson (Brunswick), Gene Kardos (Melotone).

You Spin Me Round Like a Record. w/m Peter Burns, Steven Coy, Timothy Lever, and Michael Percy, 1985. Recorded by the British quartet Dead or Alive (Epic).

You Splash Me and I'll Splash You. w. Arthur J. Lamb, m. Alfred Solman, 1907.

You Started Me Dreaming. w. Benny Davis, m. J. Fred Coots, 1936.

You Started Something. w/m Al Rinker and Floyd Huddleston, 1947. Featured and recorded by Tony Pastor, with his Orchestra (Columbia).

You Started Something. w. Leo Robin, m. Ralph Rainger, 1941. Introduced by Betty Grable, Don Ameche, and Robert Cummings in (MM) *Moon Over Miami*. Among recordings: Jan Savitt, vocal by Bon Bon (Bluebird); Art Jarrett, vocal by The Smoothies (Victor); Larry Clinton, vocal by Peggy Mann (Bluebird); Bea Wain (Victor); Tommy Tucker and his Orchestra (Okeh).

You Stayed Away Too Long. w. George Whiting and Nat Schwartz, m. J. C. Johnson, 1936. Introduced and recorded by Fats Waller (Victor). Also recorded by the Original Dixieland Jazz Band (Vocalion) and Dick Messner's Orchestra (Melotone).

You Stepped into My Life. w/m Barry Gibb, Maurice Gibb, and Robin Gibb, 1979. Chart records by Melba Moore (Epic) and Wayne Newton (Aries II).

You Stepped Out of a Dream. w. Gus Kahn, m. Nacio Herb Brown, 1941. Introduced by Tony Martin in (MM) *Ziegfeld Girl* and on records (Decca). Other records: Kay Kyser, vocal by Harry Babbitt (Columbia); Glenn Miller, vocal by the Modernaires (Bluebird); Guy Lombardo, vocal by Carmen Lombardo (Decca).

You Still Move Me. w/m Dan Seals, 1987. #1 Country chart record by Dan Seals from the album "On the Front Line" (EMI America).

You Take Me for Granted. w/m Leona Williams, 1983. #1 Country chart song by Merle Haggard (Epic).

You Take My Breath Away. w. Bruce Hart, m. Stephen Lawrence, 1979. Introduced by Rex Smith in (MP) *Sooner or Later*, 1978, followed by his gold record (Columbia).

You Talk Too Much. w/m Joe Jones and Reginald Hall, 1960. Top 40 record by pianist/singer Joe Jones (Roulette).

You Taught Me How to Love You, Now Teach Me to Forget. w. Jack Drislane and Alfred Bryan, m. George W. Meyer, 1909. Popular ballad recorded by Joe Maxwell (Edison Amberol).

You Taught Me to Love Again. w. Charles Carpenter, m. Tommy Dorsey and Henri Woode, 1939. Introduced and recorded by Tommy Dorsey, vocal by Jack Leonard (Victor). Also recorded by Gene Krupa, vocal by Irene Daye (Brunswick), and Jan Savitt, vocal by Carlotta Dale (Decca).

You Tell Her, I S-t-u-t-t-e-r. Billy Rose, m. Cliff Friend, 1922. Featured and recorded by Van and Schenck (Columbia) and Ernest Hare and Billy Jones (Edison).

You Tell Me Why. w/m Ronald Elliott, 1965. Recorded by The Beau Brummels (Autumn).

You Tell Me Your Dream. w. Seymour A. Rice and Al H. Brown, m. Neil Moret, 1908.

You Think of Ev'rything. w. Joseph McCarthy and Billy Rose, m. James Van Heusen, 1940. Introduced at the New York World's Fair [second season] in Billy Rose's *Aquacade*, starring Eleanor Holm. Recorded by Tommy Dorsey, vocal by Connie Haines (Victor).

You Told a Lie (I Believed You). w/m Lew Porter and Mitchell Tableportor, 1949.

Featured and recorded by Marjorie Hughes with Hugo Winterhalter and his Orchestra (RCA Victor).

You Took Advantage of Me. w. Lorenz Hart, m. Richard Rodgers, 1928. Introduced by Joyce Barbour, Busby Berkeley [who also choreographed the show], and the ensemble in (TM) *Present Arms*. The film version, 1930, was renamed (MM) *Leathernecking [Present Arms* in Great Britain], and the song was performed by Lilyan Tashman and Fred Santley. The jazz band played it in (MM) *Young Man with a Horn*, 1950. It was sung by Judy Garland in the "Born in a Trunk" number in (MM) *A Star Is Born*, 1954.

You Took Her off My Hands (Now Please Take Her off My Mind). w/m Wynn Stewart, Skeets McDonald, and Harlan Howard, 1963. Hit C&W record by Ray Price (Columbia).

You Took the Words Right Out of My Heart. w. Leo Robin, m. Ralph Rainger, 1937. Sung by Dorothy Lamour, with Leif Ericson, in (MM) *The Big Broadcast of '38*. Lamour recorded it (Brunswick) coupled with "Thanks for the Memory," (q.v.) the big hit from the same film, although she did not sing the latter in the movie.

You Took the Words Right Out of My Mouth. w/m Jim Steinman, 1978. Recorded by Meat Loaf, né Marvin Lee Aday (Epic).

You Took the Words Right Out of My Mouth. w. Harold Adamson, m. Burton Lane, 1935. Introduced by Maurice Chevalier in (MM) *Folies Bergere*.

You Try Somebody Else. w. B. G. DeSylva and Lew Brown, m. Ray Henderson, 1931. Introduced by Belle Baker. Bestselling records by Russ Columbo (Victor) and Guy Lombardo, with vocal by Carmen Lombardo (Columbia). Sung by Sheree North and Roxanne Arlen in the DeSylva, Brown and Henderson story (MM) *The Best Things in Life Are Free*, 1956.

You Turned My World Around. w. K. C. Ellingson, D. Ellingson, m. Burt Kaempfert and Herbert Rehbein, 1974. Recorded by Frank Sinatra (Reprise).

You Turned the Tables on Me. w. Sidney D. Mitchell, m. Louis Alter, 1936. Introduced by Alice Faye in (MM) *Sing, Baby, Sing*. Best-selling record by Benny Goodman, vocal by Helen Ward (Victor). Among later versions: Ella Fitzgerald (Decca), Merry Macs (Majestic), and Gene Krupa, with vocal by Dolores Hawkins (Columbia).

You Turn Me On (The Turn On Song). w/m Ian Whitcomb, 1965. Written and recorded in England by Ian Whitcomb and Bluesville (Tower).

You Turn Me On, I'm a Radio. w/m Joni Mitchell, 1972. Recorded by Joni Mitchell (Asylum).

You Two-Timed Me One Time Too Often. w/m Jenny Lou Carson, 1945. Featured and recorded by Tex Ritter (Capitol).

You Upset Me, Baby. w. Maxwell Davis, m. Joe Josea, 1954. R&B record by B. B. King (RPM).

You've Been Cheatin'. w/m Curtis Mayfield, 1965. Top 40 record by The Impressions (ABC-Paramount).

You've Been Doing Wrong for So Long. w/m Frank Johnson and Terry Woodford, 1974. R&B chart record by Thelma Houston (Motown).

You've Been in Love Too Long. w/m Ivy Hunter, Clarence Paul, and William Stevenson, 1965. Hit record by Martha and The Vandellas (Gordy).

You've Changed. w. Bill Carey, m. Carl Fischer, 1942. Leading records by Harry James, vocal by Dick Haymes (Columbia). Bill Farrell, with Russ Case's Orchestra (MGM) had a popular version, 1949, as did Connie Russell, with Harold Mooney's Orchestra (Capitol), 1954.

You've Come Home. w. Carolyn Leigh, m. Cy Coleman, 1960. Introduced by Keith Andes in (TM) *Wildcat*, starring Lucille Ball.

You've Got a Friend. w/m Carole King, 1971. Introduced by Carole King in her album "Tapestry" (Ode). #1 gold record by James Taylor (Warner Bros.). Chart version by Roberta Flack and Donny Hathaway (Atlantic). Winner Grammy Award (NARAS), Song of the Year.

You've Got Another Thing Comin'. w/m Rob Halford, K. K. Downing, and Glenn Tipton, 1981. Recorded by the English rock quintet Judas Priest (Columbia).

You've Got Everything. w. Gus Kahn, m. Walter Donaldson, 1933. Introduced in (MP) *The Prizefighter and the Lady*, starring heavyweight boxing champion Max Baer and Myrna Loy. Featured and recorded by the bands of Jan Garber (Victor); Anson Weeks, vocal by Bob Crosby (Brunswick); Bernie Cummins (Columbia).

You've Got Me Crying Again. w. Charles Newman, m. Isham Jones, 1933. Another much-recorded standard composed by Jones. He recorded this twice, with his old band (Victor) and later with Curt Massey doing the vocal (Coast). Ruth Etting featured it when new. Numbered among the leading records are those by: Phil Harris (Columbia), Hal Kemp (Victor), Sammy Kaye (Columbia), Teresa Brewer (London), Billy Eckstine (MGM), Coleman Hawkins (Roost), Boyd Raeburn (Guild), Buddy Rich (Mercury).

(You've Got Me) Dangling on a String. w/m Ronald Dunbar and Edythe Wayne, 1970. Top 40 record by the vocal group Chairman of the Board (Invictus).

You've Got Me in the Palm of Your Hand. w. Cliff Friend and Edgar Leslie, m. James V. Monaco, 1932.

You've Got Me Out on a Limb. w. Joseph McCarthy, m. Harry Tierney, 1940. The last produced song written by each of the successful team. This was added to the original stage score for the film version (MM) *Irene*. It was recorded by Harry James, vocal by Dick Haymes (Columbia), and Charlie Barnet, vocal by Mary Ann McCall (Bluebird).

Zonky. w. Andy Razaf, m. Thomas "Fats" Waller, 1930. Introduced in the revue, *Load of Coal*, at Connie's Inn in Harlem. This jazz piece was recorded by McKinney's Cotton Pickers (Victor); Clarence Williams and his Band (Columbia); Six Men and a Girl, the latter being pianist Mary Lou Williams (Varsity); Nat Jaffe (Signature).

Zoot Suit, A (for My Sunday Girl). w/m Ray Gilbert and Bob O'Brien, 1942. Featured and recorded by Kay Kyser, vocal by Sully Mason, Jack Martin, Max Williams, and Trudy (Columbia); Benny Goodman, vocal by Art Lund (Okeh).

Zorba the Greek. m. Mikis Theodorakis, 1965. Theme from (MP) *Zorba the Greek*. Hit instrumental by Herb Alpert and The Tijuana Brass (A&M).

Zorro. w. Norman Foster, m. George Bruns, 1958. Theme of series (TVP) "Zorro." Leading record by The Chordettes (Cadence).

Zsa Zsa. m. Bernie Wayne, 1953. An instrumental dedicated to the Gabor of the same name. Recorded by Bernie Wayne and his Orchestra (Coral).

Section II

THE YEARS

(Arranged Chronologically)

DADDY WOULDN'T BUY ME A BOW-WOW

DAISY BELL (or BICYCLE BUILT FOR TWO)

MAN THAT BROKE THE BANK AT MONTE CARLO, THE

MY SWEETHEART'S THE MAN IN THE MOON

1893

CAT CAME BACK, THE

DECEMBER AND MAY (or, MOLLIE NEWELL DON'T BE CRUEL)

DO, DO, MY HUCKLEBERRY DO

FATAL WEDDING, THE

HAPPY BIRTHDAY TO YOU

I LONG TO SEE THE GIRL I LEFT BEHIND

LITTLE ALABAMA COON

LOVE ME LITTLE, LOVE ME LONG

MAMIE, COME KISS YOUR HONEY

SAY "AU REVOIR" BUT NOT "GOODBYE"

SEE, SAW, MARGERY DAW

STREETS OF CAIRO (SHE NEVER SAW THE)

SWEET MARIE

THEY NEVER TELL ALL WHAT THEY KNOW

TWO LITTLE GIRLS IN BLUE

VOLUNTEER ORGANIST, THE

WHEN THE ROLL IS CALLED UP YONDER (I'LL BE THERE)

WON'T YOU BE MY SWEETHEART?

1894

AIRY, FAIRY LILLIAN

AND HER GOLDEN HAIR WAS HANGING DOWN HER BACK

COMRADES

DON'T GO OUT TONIGHT, BOY

FORGOTTEN

HER EYES DON'T SHINE LIKE DIAMONDS

HIS LAST THOUGHTS WERE OF YOU

HONEYMOON, THE

I DON'T WANT TO PLAY IN YOUR YARD

I'LL BE TRUE TO MY HONEY BOY

KATHLEEN

LITTLE LOST CHILD, THE

LONG AGO IN ALCALA

MY FRIEND, THE MAJOR

MY PEARL'S A BOWERY GIRL

ONCE EV'RY YEAR

ONLY A BOWERY BOY

ONLY ME

SHE MAY HAVE SEEN BETTER DAYS

SIDEWALKS OF NEW YORK, THE

SWEET BUNCH OF DAISIES

TAKE A SEAT, OLD LADY

1895

ALGY, THE PICCADILLY JOHNNY WITH THE LITTLE GLASS EYE

BAND PLAYED ON, THE

BELLE OF AVENOO A, THE

BY THE SAD SEA WAVES

CRISTOFO COLUMBO

DON'T GIVE UP THE OLD LOVE FOR NEW

DOWN IN POVERTY ROW

DREAM, A

HANDICAP, THE

HAND THAT ROCKS THE CRADLE, THE

HOT TAMALE ALLEY

I WAS LOOKING FOR MY BOY, SHE SAID (or, DECORATION DAY)

JEAN

JUST TELL HER THAT YOU SAW ME

KING COTTON

MR. CAPTAIN, STOP THE SHIP (I WANT TO GET OFF AND WALK)

MY ANGELINE

MY BEST GIRL'S A NEW YORKER (CORKER)

ONLY ONE GIRL IN THE WORLD FOR ME

PUT ME OFF AT BUFFALO

RASTUS ON PARADE

SAME SWEET GIRL TO-DAY, THE
SHE IS MORE TO BE PITIED THAN
  CENSURED
SINGER IN THE BALCONY, THE
SUNSHINE OF PARADISE ALLEY, THE
THERE'LL COME A TIME
WHEN YOUR LOVE GROWS COLD
ZENDA WALTZES

1896

ALL COONS LOOK ALIKE TO ME
AMOROUS GOLDFISH, THE
BELOVED, IT IS MORN
CHIN-CHIN-CHINAMAN
CHON KINA
DON'T TELL HER THAT YOU LOVE HER
DREAM OF MY BOYHOOD DAYS, A
EL CAPITAN
ELI GREEN'S CAKEWALK
ELSIE FROM CHELSEA
GOING FOR A PARDON
HAPPY DAYS IN DIXIE
HE BROUGHT HOME ANOTHER
HE FOUGHT FOR A CAUSE HE THOUGHT
  WAS RIGHT
HOT TIME IN THE OLD TOWN TONIGHT
I CAN'T THINK OF NUTHIN' ELSE BUT
  YOU
I LOVE YOU IN THE SAME OLD WAY—
  DARLING SUE
IN THE BAGGAGE COACH AHEAD
I'SE YOUR NIGGER IF YOU WANTS ME,
  LIZA JANE
IT DON'T SEEM LIKE THE SAME OLD
  SMILE
I WISH THAT YOU WERE HERE TONIGHT
I WONDER IF SHE'LL EVER COME BACK
  TO ME
JEWEL OF ASIA, THE
KENTUCKY BABE
LAUGH AND THE WORLD LAUGHS WITH
  YOU
LOVE MAKES THE WORLD GO 'ROUND

LUCKY JIM
MISTER JOHNSON, TURN ME LOOSE
MOTHER WAS A LADY (or, IF JACK
  WERE ONLY HERE)
MY GAL IS A HIGH BORN LADY
NO ONE EVER LOVED YOU MORE
  THAN I
ON THE BENCHES IN THE PARK
SWEET ROSIE O'GRADY
TOY MONKEY, THE
WHISPER YOUR MOTHER'S NAME
WON'T YOU BE MY LITTLE GIRL
YOU'RE DE APPLE OF MY EYE

1897

ASLEEP IN THE DEEP
AT A GEORGIA CAMP MEETING
BADINAGE
BEAUTIFUL ISLE OF SOMEWHERE
BREAK THE NEWS TO MOTHER
CUPID AND I
DANNY DEEVER
FACE TO FACE
IF YOU SEE MY SWEETHEART
I'VE JUST COME BACK TO SAY GOOD-
  BYE
JUST FOR THE SAKE OF OUR DAUGHTER
LET BYGONES BE BYGONES
MAMMY'S LITTLE PUMPKIN COLORED
  COON
ON THE BANKS OF THE WABASH FAR
  AWAY
STARS AND STRIPES FOREVER
TAKE BACK YOUR GOLD
THERE'S A LITTLE STAR SHINING FOR
  YOU
WEDDING OF THE WINDS
YOU'RE GOING FAR AWAY, LAD (or I'M
  STILL YOUR MOTHER, DEAR)

1898

BABY'S PRAYER

BECAUSE

BOY GUESSED RIGHT, THE

COME TELL ME WHAT'S YOUR ANSWER, YES OR NO

DON'T LEAVE ME DOLLY

EVERY NIGHT THERE'S A LIGHT

GOLD WILL BUY MOST ANYTHING BUT A TRUE GIRL'S HEART

GOOD NIGHT, LITTLE GIRL, GOOD NIGHT

GYPSY LOVE SONG (SLUMBER ON, MY LITTLE GYPSY SWEETHEART)

I GUESS I'LL HAVE TO TELEGRAPH MY BABY

JUST AS THE SUN WENT DOWN

JUST ONE GIRL

KISS ME, HONEY, DO

LITTLE BIRDIES LEARNING HOW TO FLY

'MID THE GREEN FIELDS OF VIRGINIA

MISTER JOHNSON, DON'T GET GAY

MOTH AND THE FLAME, THE

MY CREOLE SUE

MY OLD NEW HAMPSHIRE HOME

OLD FLAME FLICKERS AND I WONDER WHY, THE

OUR COUNTRY, MAY SHE ALWAYS BE RIGHT

PATH THAT LEADS THE OTHER WAY, THE

RECESSIONAL

ROSARY, THE

SALOME

SHE IS THE BELLE OF NEW YORK

SHE WAS BRED IN OLD KENTUCKY

SOCIETY (OH! I LOVE SOCIETY)

SOLDIERS IN THE PARK, THE

STEIN SONG, A (IT'S ALWAYS FAIR WEATHER WHEN GOOD FELLOWS GET TOGETHER)

SWEET SAVANNAH

WE FIGHT TOMORROW, MOTHER

WHEN A FELLAH HAS TURNED SIXTEEN

WHEN YOU AIN'T GOT NO MORE MONEY, WELL, YOU NEEDN'T COME 'ROUND

WHEN YOU WERE SWEET SIXTEEN

1899

ABSENT

ALWAYS

BEN HUR CHARIOT RACE

COME HOME, DEWEY, WE WON'T DO A THING TO YOU

CURSE OF THE DREAMER, THE

DOAN YE CRY, MAH HONEY

FACE TO FACE

HANDS ACROSS THE SEA

HEART OF MY HEART, I LOVE YOU (THE STORY OF THE ROSE)

HEARTS AND FLOWERS

HELLO, MA BABY

I'D LEAVE MY HAPPY HOME FOR YOU

IF ONLY YOU WERE MINE

IN GOOD OLD NEW YORK TOWN

I'VE WAITED, HONEY, WAITED LONG FOR YOU

I WONDER IF SHE'S WAITING

I WONDER WHERE SHE IS TONIGHT

MANDY LEE

MAPLE LEAF RAG

MOSQUITO'S PARADE, THE

MY LITTLE GEORGIA ROSE

MY WILD IRISH ROSE

ONE NIGHT IN JUNE

PICTURE NO ARTIST CAN PAINT, A

SHE WAS HAPPY TILL SHE MET YOU

SINGER AND THE SONG, THE

SIX LITTLE WIVES

SMOKEY MOKES

STAY IN YOUR OWN BACK YARD

THERE'S WHERE MY HEART IS TONIGHT

WE CAME FROM THE SAME OLD STATE

WHERE THE SWEET MAGNOLIAS GROW

WHISTLING RUFUS

WHO DAT SAY CHICKEN IN DIS CROWD

YOUR GOD COMES FIRST, YOUR COUNTRY NEXT, THEN MOTHER DEAR

YOU'SE JUST A LITTLE NIGGER, STILL
   YOU'RE MINE, ALL MINE

ZIZZY, ZE ZUM, ZUM!

1900

ABSENCE MAKES THE HEART GROW
   FONDER

BIRD IN A GILDED CAGE, A

BLUE AND THE GRAY (or, MOTHER'S
   GIFT TO HER COUNTRY, A)

BRIDGE OF SIGHS

CALLING TO HER BOY JUST ONCE AGAIN

COME BACK, MY HONEY BOY, TO ME

CREOLE BELLE

DOWN BY THE RIVERSIDE

EVERY RACE HAS A FLAG BUT THE
   COON

FATAL ROSE OF RED, THE

FOR OLD TIME'S SAKE

GOOD-BYE, DOLLY GRAY

I CAN'T TELL WHY I LOVE YOU, BUT I
   DO

I'D STILL BELIEVE YOU TRUE

IN THE HOUSE OF TOO MUCH TROUBLE

I'VE A LONGING IN MY HEART FOR
   YOU, LOUISE

I WON'T BE AN ACTOR NO MORE

JUST BECAUSE SHE MADE THEM GOO-
   GOO EYES

LIFT EVERY VOICE AND SING

MA BLUSHIN' ROSIE

MIDNIGHT FIRE ALARM

NOBODY SEES US BUT THE MAN IN THE
   MOON

QUILLER HAS THE BRAINS

SHADE OF THE PALM, THE

STRIKE UP THE BAND, HERE COMES A
   SAILOR

SWEET ANNIE MOORE

TALE OF THE KANGAROO, THE

TELL ME PRETTY MAIDEN (ARE THERE
   ANY MORE AT HOME LIKE YOU?)

VIOLETS

VOODOO MAN, THE

WHEN DE MOON COMES UP BEHIND DE
   HILL

WHEN THE HARVEST DAYS ARE OVER,
   JESSIE DEAR

YOU CAN'T KEEP A GOOD MAN DOWN

1901

AIN'T DAT A SHAME?

ALL THAT GLITTERS IS NOT GOLD

AMERICAN PATROL

ANY OLD PLACE I HANG MY HAT IS
   HOME SWEET HOME TO ME

BEAUTIFUL ISLE OF SOMEWHERE

BILLBOARD, THE

BLAZE AWAY!

COON! COON! COON!

DAVEY JONES' LOCKER

DON'T PUT ME OFF AT BUFFALO ANY
   MORE

DOWN WHERE THE COTTON BLOSSOMS
   GROW

EYES OF BLUE, EYES OF BROWN

GO WAY BACK AND SIT DOWN

HELLO CENTRAL, GIVE ME HEAVEN

HIGH SOCIETY

I JUST WANT TO GO BACK AND START
   THE WHOLE THING OVER

I'LL BE WITH YOU WHEN THE ROSES
   BLOOM AGAIN

I'M TIRED

IN A COSY CORNER

IN THE GREAT SOMEWHERE

I'VE GROWN SO USED TO YOU

JOSEPHINE, MY JO

JUST A-WEARYIN' FOR YOU

MAIDEN WITH THE DREAMY EYES

MAMIE

MIGHTY LAK' A ROSE

MR. VOLUNTEER (or, YOU DON'T
   BELONG TO THE REGULARS, YOU'RE
   JUST A VOLUNTEER)

MY CASTLE ON THE NILE

MY HEART STILL CLINGS TO THE OLD
  FIRST LOVE
O DRY THOSE TEARS!
OLD FLAG NEVER TOUCHED THE
  GROUND, THE
PANAMERICANA
RIP VAN WINKLE WAS A LUCKY MAN
SERENADE
TALE OF A BUMBLE BEE, THE
THERE'S NO NORTH OR SOUTH TODAY
TOBERMORY
WE SHALL OVERCOME
WHEN MR. SHAKESPEARE COMES TO
  TOWN
WHEN THE BIRDS HAVE SUNG
  THEMSELVES TO SLEEP
WHEN THE BLUE SKY TURNS TO GOLD
WHERE THE SILV'RY COLORADO WENDS
  ITS WAY
YOU'RE AS WELCOME AS THE FLOWERS
  IN MAY

1902

ANY RAGS?
BECAUSE
BILL BAILEY, WON'T YOU PLEASE COME
  HOME
BIRD THAT NEVER SINGS, THE
COME DOWN MA' EVENIN' STAR
DOWN ON THE FARM (THEY ALL ASK
  FOR YOU)
DOWN WHERE THE WURZBURGER
  FLOWS
ENTERTAINER, THE
GOOD MORNING, CARRIE
HEIDELBERG STEIN SONG
IF MONEY TALKS, IT AIN'T ON SPEAKING
  TERMS WITH ME
I'M UNLUCKY
IN DEAR OLD ILLINOIS
IN THE GOOD OLD SUMMERTIME
IN THE SWEET BYE AND BYE
JENNIE LEE

LAND OF HOPE AND GLORY, THE
LITTLE GYPSY MAID, THE
MANSION OF ACHING HEARTS, THE
MISTER DOOLEY
MY OWN UNITED STATES
MY PAJAMA BEAUTY
NANCY BROWN
OH! DIDN'T HE RAMBLE
ON A SUNDAY AFTERNOON
PARDON ME, MY DEAR ALPHONSE,
  AFTER YOU, MY DEAR GASTON
PLEASE GO 'WAY AND LET ME SLEEP
SINCE SISTER NELL HEARD
  PADEREWSKI PLAY
TALE OF THE SEASHELL
TELL ME, DUSKY MAIDEN
TESSIE, YOU ARE THE ONLY, ONLY,
  ONLY
UNDER THE BAMBOO TREE (IF YOU
  LAK-A ME LIKE I LAK-A YOU)
WAY DOWN IN OLD INDIANA
WHEN IT'S ALL GOIN' OUT, AND NOTHIN'
  COMIN' IN
WHEN KATE AND I WERE COMIN' THRO'
  THE RYE
WHEN YOU COME BACK THEY'LL
WONDER WHO THE ——— YOU ARE
WHERE THE SUNSET TURNS THE
  OCEAN'S BLUE TO GOLD

1903

AIN'T IT FUNNY WHAT A DIFFERENCE
  JUST A FEW HOURS MAKE?
ALWAYS IN THE WAY
ALWAYS LEAVE THEM LAUGHING WHEN
  YOU SAY GOOD-BYE
BEDELIA
BEER THAT MADE MILWAUKEE FAMOUS,
  THE
BOYS ARE COMING HOME TODAY, THE
BURNING OF ROME, THE
BY THE SYCAMORE TREE
CARISSIMA

CONGO LOVE SONG
DEAR OLD GIRL
GOOD-BYE, ELIZA JANE
HANNAH!
HIAWATHA
HURRAH FOR BAFFIN'S BAY!
I CAN'T DO THIS SUM
IDA! SWEET AS APPLE CIDER!
I'M ON THE WATER WAGON NOW
IN THE MERRY MONTH OF MAY
KASHMIRI SONG
LAUGHING WATER
LAZY MOON
LINCOLN, GRANT OR LEE
MARCH OF THE TOYS, THE
MELODY OF LOVE
MESSAGE OF THE VIOLET, THE
MISTER CHAMBERLAIN
MY SAN DOMINGO MAID
OH, ISN'T IT SINGULAR!
SAMMY
SHOW THE WHITE OF YO' EYE
SPRING, BEAUTIFUL SPRING
SWEET ADELINE (or, YOU'RE THE
   FLOWER OF MY HEART)
THAT'S WHAT THE DAISY SAID
THERE ONCE WAS AN OWL
TOYLAND
VOICE OF THE HUDSON, THE
WHERE ARE THE FRIENDS OF OTHER
   DAYS?
YOUR DAD GAVE HIS LIFE FOR HIS
   COUNTRY

1904

ABSINTHE FRAPPE
ALEXANDER, DON'T YOU LOVE YOUR
   BABY NO MORE?
AL FRESCO
ALL ABOARD FOR DREAMLAND
BACK, BACK, BACK TO BALTIMORE

BLUE BELL
COME, TAKE A TRIP IN MY AIRSHIP
COME BACK TO SORRENTO
DOWN ON THE BRANDYWINE
EV'RY LITTLE BIT HELPS
FASCINATION
FOU THE NOO (or, SOMETHING IN THE
   BOTTLE FOR THE MORNING)
GHOST THAT NEVER WALKED, THE
GIVE MY REGARDS TO BROADWAY
GOLD AND SILVER
GOOD-BYE, FLO
GOODBYE, LITTLE GIRL, GOODBYE
GOODBYE, MY LADY LOVE
GOODNIGHT, MY OWN TRUE LOVE
HANNAH, WON'T YOU OPEN THAT
   DOOR?
I CAN'T TAKE MY EYES OFF YOU
I MAY BE CRAZY BUT I AIN'T NO FOOL
IN ZANZIBAR—MY LITTLE CHIMPANZEE
I'VE GOT A FEELING FOR YOU (or, WAY
   DOWN IN MY HEART)
KNOT OF BLUE, A
LIFE'S A FUNNY PROPOSITION AFTER
   ALL
LITTLE BOY CALLED "TAPS"
MAN WITH THE LADDER AND THE HOSE
MEET ME IN ST. LOUIS, LOUIS
MY HONEY LOU
NAVAJO
PLEASE COME AND PLAY IN MY YARD
PREACHER AND THE BEAR, THE
SHE WENT TO THE CITY
SWEET THOUGHTS OF HOME
TALE OF THE TURTLE DOVE, THE
TEASING
THREE FOR JACK
UNDER THE ANHEUSER BUSH
WHEN I'M AWAY FROM YOU, DEAR
WHEN THE BEES ARE IN THE HIVE
WHERE THE SOUTHERN ROSES GROW
YANKEE DOODLE BOY, THE

1905

BANDANNA LAND

BOWL OF ROSES, A

DAY THAT YOU GREW COLDER, THE

DEARIE

DOWN WHERE THE SILV'RY MOHAWK FLOWS

EVERYBODY WORKS BUT FATHER

GOODBYE, SWEETHEART, GOODBYE

HE'S ME PAL

HOW'D YOU LIKE TO SPOON WITH ME?

I DON'T CARE

IF A GIRL LIKE YOU LOVED A BOY LIKE ME

IF THE MAN IN THE MOON WERE A COON

IN DEAR OLD GEORGIA

IN MY MERRY OLDSMOBILE

IN THE SHADE OF THE OLD APPLE TREE

JELLY ROLL BLUES

JIM JUDSON FROM THE TOWN OF HACKENSACK

JUST A LITTLE ROCKING CHAIR AND YOU

KEEP A LITTLE COZY CORNER IN YOUR HEART FOR ME

LEADER OF THE GERMAN BAND, THE

LONGING FOR YOU

MAKING EYES

MARY'S A GRAND OLD NAME

MOON HAS HIS EYES ON YOU, THE

MOONLIGHT

MY GAL SAL (or, THEY CALLED HER FRIVOLOUS SAL)

MY GUIDING STAR

MY IRISH MOLLY O

NOBODY

OH, MARIE

ONE CALLED "MOTHER" AND THE OTHER "HOME SWEET HOME"

PICNIC FOR TWO, A

RAZZAZZA MAZZAZZA

SHE IS MY DAISY

SHE WAITS BY THE DEEP BLUE SEA

STARLIGHT

TAKE ME BACK TO YOUR HEART AGAIN

TAMMANY

TIME AND THE PLACE AND THE GIRL, THE

TOWN WHERE I WAS BORN, THE

WAIT TILL THE SUN SHINES, NELLIE

WHAT YOU GOIN' TO DO WHEN THE RENT COMES 'ROUND? (or, RUFUS RASTUS JOHNSON BROWN)

WHEN THE BELL IN THE LIGHTHOUSE RINGS DING DONG

WHEN THE MOCKING BIRDS ARE SINGING IN THE WILDWOOD

WHERE THE MORNING GLORIES TWINE AROUND THE DOOR

WHERE THE RIVER SHANNON FLOWS

WHISTLER AND HIS DOG, THE

WILL YOU LOVE ME IN DECEMBER AS YOU DO IN MAY?

WOMAN IS ONLY A WOMAN, BUT A GOOD CIGAR IS A SMOKE, A

WOULD YOU CARE?

1906

AIN'T YOU COMING BACK TO OLD NEW HAMPSHIRE, MOLLY?

ALL IN DOWN AND OUT (SORRY, I AIN'T GOT IT, YOU COULD HAVE IT, ETC., BLUES)

ANCHORS AWEIGH

ARRAH WANNA

AT DAWNING

BAKE DAT CHICKEN PIE

BECAUSE YOU'RE YOU

BELLE OF THE BALL, THE

BIRD ON NELLIE'S HAT, THE

BLOW THE SMOKE AWAY

CHEYENNE (SHY ANN)

COLLEGE LIFE

DADDY'S LITTLE GIRL

DON'T GO IN THE LION'S CAGE TONIGHT

DREAMING

EVERY DAY IS LADIES' DAY WITH ME

FORTY-FIVE MINUTES FROM BROADWAY

GOOD OLD U.S.A., THE

HE'S A COUSIN OF MINE

HE WALKED RIGHT IN, TURNED AROUND AND WALKED RIGHT OUT AGAIN

IF WASHINGTON SHOULD COME TO LIFE

I JUST CAN'T MAKE MY EYES BEHAVE

I LOVE A LASSIE (or, MA SCOTCH BLUEBELL)

I LOVE YOU TRULY

ISLE OF OUR DREAMS, THE

I WANT WHAT I WANT WHEN I WANT IT

I WAS BORN IN VIRGINIA

KEEP ON THE SUNNY SIDE

KISS ME AGAIN

LEMON IN THE GARDEN OF LOVE, A

LET IT ALONE

LINGER LONGER GIRL, THE

LOVE ME AND THE WORLD IS MINE

MEET ME DOWN AT THE CORNER

MOONBEAMS

MY DREAMY CHINA LADY

MY MARIUCCIA TAKE A STEAMBOAT

NATIONAL EMBLEM

NOTHING NEW BENEATH THE SUN

ON SAN FRANCISCO BAY

POOR JOHN

SCHNITZELBANK

SINCE FATHER WENT TO WORK

SO LONG, MARY

STREETS OF NEW YORK, THE (or, IN OLD NEW YORK)

SUNBONNET SUE

WAITING AT THE CHURCH

WALTZ ME AROUND AGAIN, WILLIE ('ROUND, 'ROUND, 'ROUND)

WE'VE BEEN CHUMS FOR FIFTY YEARS

WHAT'S THE USE OF DREAMING?

WHAT'S THE USE OF LOVING IF YOU CAN'T LOVE ALL THE TIME?

WHEN LOVE IS YOUNG IN SPRINGTIME

WHEN YOU KNOW YOU'RE NOT FORGOTTEN BY THE GIRL YOU CAN'T FORGET

WON'T YOU COME OVER TO MY HOUSE?

YOU'RE A GRAND OLD FLAG

1907

AND A LITTLE BIT MORE

AS LONG AS THE WORLD ROLLS ON

BECAUSE I'M MARRIED NOW

BE MY LITTLE TEDDY BEAR

BEST I GET IS MUCH OBLIGED TO YOU, THE

BON BON BUDDY

BUDWEISER'S A FRIEND OF MINE

BYE BYE DEARIE

COME TO THE LAND OF BOHEMIA

DARLING SUE

EVERY LITTLE BIT ADDED TO WHAT YOU'VE GOT MAKES JUST A LITTLE BIT MORE

FLUFFY RUFFLES

GLOW-WORM, THE

HE GOES TO CHURCH ON SUNDAY

HONEY BOY

I'D RATHER BE A LOBSTER THAN A WISE GUY

IF I'M GOING TO DIE I'M GOING TO HAVE SOME FUN

I LOVE YOU SO (THE MERRY WIDOW WALTZ)

I'M AFRAID TO COME HOME IN THE DARK

I'M A POPULAR MAN

IN THE WILDWOOD WHERE THE BLUEBELLS GROW

IT'S DELIGHTFUL TO BE MARRIED

IT'S GREAT TO BE A SOLDIER MAN

I WANT YOU

I WISH I HAD A GIRL

LET'S TAKE AN OLD-FASHIONED WALK

MARIE FROM SUNNY ITALY

MAXIM'S

NOBODY'S LITTLE GIRL

NO WEDDING BELLS FOR ME

ON THE ROAD TO MANDALAY

RED WING (AN INDIAN FABLE)

SAN ANTONIO

SCHOOL DAYS (WHEN WE WERE A COUPLE OF KIDS)

SHE'S THE FAIREST LITTLE FLOWER DEAR OLD DIXIE EVER GREW

SOMEBODY'S WAITING FOR YOU

SWEETEST FLOWER THE GARDEN GREW, THE

TAKE ME AROUND AGAIN

TAKE ME BACK TO NEW YORK TOWN

THAT LOVIN' RAG

THERE NEVER WAS A GIRL LIKE YOU

THERE'S A GIRL IN THIS WORLD FOR EVERY BOY, AND A BOY FOR EVERY GIRL

TOMMY, LAD!

TWO BLUE EYES, TWO LITTLE BABY SHOES

UNDER ANY OLD FLAG AT ALL

VILIA

WAL, I SWAN! (or, EBENEZER FRYE)

WHEN A FELLOW'S ON THE LEVEL WITH A GIRL THAT'S ON THE SQUARE

WHEN SWEET MARIE WAS SWEET SIXTEEN

WHEN THE BIRDS IN GEORGIA SING OF TENNESSEE

WON'T YOU BE MY HONEY?

WON'T YOU WALTZ "HOME SWEET HOME" WITH ME?

YOU SPLASH ME AND I'LL SPLASH YOU

1908

ALL FOR LOVE OF YOU

ALOHA OE (FAREWELL TO THEE)

ANY OLD PORT IN A STORM

ARE YOU SINCERE?

ASK HER WHILE THE BAND IS PLAYING

COME ON DOWN TOWN

CONSOLATION

CUDDLE UP A LITTLE CLOSER, LOVEY MINE

DAISIES WON'T TELL

DON'T TAKE ME HOME

DOWN AMONG THE SUGAR CANE

DOWN IN JUNGLE TOWN

DUSTY RAG

GOLLIWOG'S CAKE WALK

GOODBYE, MR. RAGTIME

GOOD EVENING, CAROLINE

HARRIGAN

HOO-OO, AIN'T YOU COMING OUT TONIGHT?

I DON'T WANT ANOTHER SISTER

IF I HAD A THOUSAND LIVES TO LIVE

IF YOU CARED FOR ME

IF YOU WERE I AND I WERE YOU

I HEAR YOU CALLING ME

I'LL BE MARRIED TO THE MUSIC OF A MILITARY BAND

IN THE GARDEN OF MY HEART

IT LOOKS TO ME LIKE A BIG NIGHT TONIGHT

IT'S MOONLIGHT ALL THE TIME ON BROADWAY

I'VE TAKEN QUITE A FANCY TO YOU

KISS YOUR MINSTREL BOY GOODBYE

LAND OF THE HEART'S DESIRE, THE

LANKY YANKEE BOYS IN BLUE, THE

LONGEST WAY 'ROUND IS THE SHORTEST WAY HOME, THE

LOVE DAYS

LOVE IS LIKE A CIGARETTE

LOVE'S ROUNDELAY

MAKE BELIEVE

MEET ME TONIGHT IN DREAMLAND

MY PONY BOY

OVER THE HILLS AND FAR AWAY

ROSE OF THE WORLD

ROSES BRING DREAMS OF YOU

SHINE ON, HARVEST MOON

SMARTY

SWEETEST MAID OF ALL

TAKE ME OUT TO THE BALLGAME

UP IN A BALLOON

VISION OF SALOME, A

WHEN I GET BACK AGAIN TO BONNIE
  SCOTLAND

WHEN IT'S MOONLIGHT ON THE PRAIRIE

WHEN YOU WORE A PINAFORE

WINTER GARDEN RAG

YAMA YAMA MAN, THE

YIP-I-ADDY-I-AY!

YOU'LL ALWAYS BE JUST SWEET
  SIXTEEN TO ME

YOU'RE IN THE RIGHT CHURCH, BUT
  THE WRONG PEW

YOU TELL ME YOUR DREAM

1909

BEAUTIFUL EYES

BY THE LIGHT OF THE SILVERY MOON

CARRIE (MARRY HARRY)

CASEY JONES

COME AFTER BREAKFAST, BRING 'LONG
  YOUR LUNCH AND LEAVE 'FORE
  SUPPER TIME

COME ON AND PLAY BALL WITH ME

CUBANOLA GLIDE, THE

DEAR OLD BROADWAY

DIXIE LAND, I LOVE YOU

DOWN AT THE HUSKIN' BEE

FOR YOU ALONE

FROM THE LAND OF THE SKY-BLUE
  WATER

GARDEN OF ROSES, THE

GIRL WITH A BROGUE, THE

HAT MY FATHER WORE ON ST.
  PATRICK'S DAY, THE

HONEY GAL

I LOVE MY WIFE, BUT OH, YOU KID!

I'M AWFULLY GLAD I MET YOU

I'VE GOT A PAIN IN MY SAWDUST

I'VE GOT RINGS ON MY FINGERS (or,
  MUMBO JUMBO JIJIBOO J. O'SHEA)

I WISH I HAD MY OLD GIRL BACK
  AGAIN

I WONDER WHO'S KISSING HER NOW

LETTER SONG, THE

LONESOME

MAN WHO OWNS BROADWAY, THE

MEET ME IN ROSE-TIME, ROSIE

MONKEY DOODLE DANDY

MOVING DAY IN JUNGLE TOWN

MY COUSIN CARUS'

MY HERO

MY PONY BOY

MY SOUTHERN ROSE

MY WIFE'S GONE TO THE COUNTRY,
  HURRAH! HURRAH!

NEXT TO YOUR MOTHER, WHO DO YOU
  LOVE?

NOBODY KNOWS, NOBODY CARES

ON WISCONSIN

ORINOCO: JUNGLE RAG TWO-STEP

PUT ON YOUR OLD GREY BONNET

SADIE SALOME, GO HOME!

SHE SELLS SEA SHELLS

SHE WAS A DEAR LITTLE GIRL

SHIP AHOY!—ALL THE NICE GIRLS LOVE
  A SAILOR

TAKE ME UP WITH YOU, DEARIE

THAT MESMERIZING MENDELSSOHN
  TUNE

THAT'S A-PLENTY

THERE'S SOMETHING ABOUT A UNIFORM

UP, UP, UP IN MY AEROPLANE

WHEN I DREAM IN THE GLOAMING OF
  YOU

WHEN YOU FIRST KISS THE LAST
  GIRL YOU LOVED

WHERE MY CARAVAN HAS RESTED

WHIFFENPOOF SONG, THE

YOU TAUGHT ME HOW TO LOVE YOU,
  NOW TEACH ME TO FORGET

1910

AH! SWEET MYSTERY OF LIFE
ALEXANDER AND HIS CLARINET
ALL ABOARD FOR BLANKET BAY
ALL THAT I ASK OF YOU IS LOVE
ALMA, WHERE DO YOU LIVE?
ANGEL EYES
ANY LITTLE GIRL THAT'S A NICE LITTLE
    GIRL IS THE RIGHT LITTLE GIRL FOR
    ME
AS DEEP AS THE DEEP BLUE SEA
BACK TO MY OLD HOME TOWN
BANJO SONG, A
BIG BASS VIOL, THE
BIRTH OF PASSION, THE
BRING ME A ROSE
CALL ME UP SOME RAINY AFTERNOON
CAPRICE VIENNOIS
CHANTICLEER RAG, THE
CHICKEN REEL
CHINATOWN, MY CHINATOWN
COME, JOSEPHINE, IN MY FLYING
    MACHINE
COME ALONG, MY MANDY
CONSTANTLY
DAY DREAMS
DON'T WAKE ME UP, I'M DREAMING
DOWN BY THE OLD MILL STREAM
EVERY LITTLE MOVEMENT (HAS A
    MEANING ALL ITS OWN)
FOUNTAIN FAY
GEE, BUT IT'S GREAT TO MEET A
    FRIEND FROM YOUR HOME TOWN
GOODBYE, ROSE
GOODY GOODY GUMDROPS
GRIZZLY BEAR
HAS ANYBODY HERE SEEN KELLY?
HAVANA
HEAVEN WILL PROTECT THE WORKING
    GIRL
I'D LOVE TO LIVE IN LOVELAND
IF HE COMES IN, I'M GOING OUT
IF I WAS A MILLIONAIRE

I'LL LEND YOU EVERYTHING I'VE GOT
    EXCEPT MY WIFE
I'LL MAKE A RING AROUND ROSIE
I LOVE IT
I LOVE THE NAME OF MARY
I'M FALLING IN LOVE WITH SOMEONE
I'M LOOKING FOR A NICE YOUNG
    FELLOW WHO IS LOOKING FOR A
    NICE YOUNG GIRL
IN THE SHADOWS
ITALIAN STREET SONG
I'VE GOT THE TIME, I'VE GOT THE
    PLACE, BUT IT'S HARD TO FIND THE
    GIRL
KISS ME, MY HONEY, KISS ME
LET ME CALL YOU SWEETHEART
LIEBESFREUD
LIEBESLIED
LIFE IS ONLY WHAT YOU MAKE IT,
    AFTER ALL
MACUSHLA
MORNING
MORNING AFTER THE NIGHT BEFORE,
    THE
MOTHER MACHREE
MY HEART HAS LEARNED TO LOVE
    YOU, NOW DO NOT SAY GOODBYE
MY MOTTER
'NEATH THE SOUTHERN MOON
NORA MALONE (CALL ME BY PHONE)
OH, HOW THAT GERMAN COULD LOVE
OH, THAT BEAUTIFUL RAG
1, 2, 3, RED LIGHT
ON MOBILE BAY
PERFECT DAY, A (THE END OF)
PIANO MAN
PLANT A WATERMELON ON MY GRAVE
    AND LET THE JUICE SOAK THROUGH
PLAY THAT BARBER SHOP CHORD
PUT YOUR ARMS AROUND ME, HONEY
SCHON ROSMARIN (FAIR ROSMARIN)
SHE TOOK MOTHER'S ADVICE
SILVER BELL
SIMON SAYS

RACKETY COO

ROLLING STONES

ROSES OF PICARDY

SHE IS THE SUNSHINE OF VIRGINIA

SIERRA SUE

SO LONG LETTY

THERE'S A LITTLE BIT OF BAD IN
EVERY GOOD LITTLE GIRL

THERE'S A QUAKER DOWN IN QUAKER
TOWN

THEY'RE WEARING 'EM HIGHER IN
HAWAII

THROW ME A ROSE

TURN BACK THE UNIVERSE AND GIVE
ME YESTERDAY

WAKE UP, AMERICA!

WHAT DO YOU WANT TO MAKE THOSE
EYES AT ME FOR?

WHEN OLD BILL BAILEY PLAYS THE
UKULELE

WHEN THE BLACK SHEEP RETURNS TO
THE FOLD

WHEN YOU'RE DOWN IN LOUISVILLE
(CALL ON ME)

WHEN YOU'RE IN LOVE WITH SOMEONE
(WHO IS NOT IN LOVE WITH YOU)

WHEN YOU WANT 'EM, YOU CAN'T GET
'EM (WHEN YOU GOT 'EM, YOU DON'T
WANT 'EM)

WHERE DID ROBINSON CRUSOE GO
WITH FRIDAY ON SATURDAY NIGHT?

WHERE THE BLACK-EYED SUSANS
GROW

YAAKA HULA HICKEY DULA

YOU BELONG TO ME

1917

ALL THE WORLD WILL BE JEALOUS
OF ME

AMERICA, HERE'S MY BOY

AMERICAN PATROL

ANY TIME'S KISSING TIME

AU REVOIR, BUT NOT GOODBYE,
SOLDIER BOY

BEALE STREET BLUES

BELLS OF SAINT MARY'S, THE

BRING BACK MY DADDY TO ME

CLEOPATTERER

COBBLER'S SONG, THE

COME AND HAVE A SWING WITH ME

COME TO THE FAIR

DARKTOWN STRUTTERS' BALL, THE

DEEP RIVER

EILEEN ALANA ASTHORE

EVERYBODY'S GONE CRAZY 'BOUT THE
DOGGONE BLUES

FOR ME AND MY GAL

FOR YOU A ROSE

GIVE A MAN A HORSE HE CAN RIDE

GIVE ME THE MOONLIGHT, GIVE ME
THE GIRL

GOODBYE, MA! GOODBYE, PA!
GOODBYE, MULE!

GOODBYE BROADWAY, HELLO FRANCE

HAIL, HAIL, THE GANG'S ALL HERE

HAVE A HEART

HAWAIIAN BUTTERFLY

HINDUSTAN

HOMING

HUCKLEBERRY FINN

I CAN DANCE WITH EVERYONE BUT
MY WIFE

I'D LOVE TO BE A MONKEY IN THE ZOO

I DON'T KNOW WHERE I'M GOING BUT
I'M ON MY WAY

I DON'T WANT TO GET WELL (I'M IN
LOVE WITH A BEAUTIFUL NURSE)

IF YOU LOOK IN HER EYES

I'M ALL BOUND 'ROUND WITH THE
MASON DIXON LINE

I'M ALWAYS CHASING RAINBOWS

I MAY BE GONE FOR A LONG, LONG
TIME

INDIANA (BACK HOME AGAIN IN)

INDIANOLA

JOAN OF ARC, THEY ARE CALLING YOU

JOHNSON RAG

JUMP JIM CROW

LAND WHERE THE GOOD SONGS GO, THE

LEAVE IT TO JANE

LIBERTY BELL, IT'S TIME TO RING AGAIN

LILY OF THE VALLEY

LITTLE MOTHER OF MINE

LITTLE SIR ECHO

LIVERY STABLE BLUES

LORRAINE, MY BEAUTIFUL ALSACE LORRAINE

MACNAMARA'S BAND

MADEMOISELLE FROM ARMENTIERES (HINKY DINKY PARLAY VOO)

MAGIC OF YOUR EYES, THE

MEET ME AT THE STATION, DEAR

MY MOTHER'S LULLABY

MY SUNSHINE JANE

'N' EVERYTHING

OH JOHNNY, OH JOHNNY, OH!

OUT WHERE THE WEST BEGINS

OVER THERE

PLAYMATES

ROAD TO PARADISE, THE

ROBBERS' MARCH, THE

ROCKAWAY

SAILIN' AWAY ON THE HENRY CLAY

SEND ME AWAY WITH A SMILE

SHE WORE A YELLOW RIBBON

SHIM-ME-SHA-WABBLE

SIREN'S SONG, THE

SMILE AND SHOW YOUR DIMPLE

SOMEONE ELSE MAY BE THERE (WHILE I'M GONE)

SOME SUNDAY MORNING

SWEET EMALINA, MY GAL

SWEET LITTLE BUTTERCUP

THAT'S THE KIND OF BABY FOR ME

THERE'S A LONG, LONG TRAIL

THEY GO WILD, SIMPLY WILD, OVER ME

THINE ALONE

TIGER ROSE

TILL THE CLOUDS ROLL BY

UGLY CHILE

WAIT TILL THE COWS COME HOME

WE'RE GOING OVER

WHEN SHALL I AGAIN SEE IRELAND?

WHEN THE BOYS COME HOME

WHEN YANKEE DOODLE LEARNS TO PARLEZ-VOUS FRANCAIS

WHERE DO WE GO FROM HERE?

WHERE THE MORNING GLORIES GROW

WHOSE LITTLE HEART ARE YOU BREAKING NOW?

WILD, WILD, WOMEN ARE MAKING A WILD MAN OF ME, THE

WILL YOU REMEMBER?

YOU CAN'T GET ALONG WITH 'EM OR WITHOUT 'EM

YOU'RE IN LOVE

1918

AFTER YOU'VE GONE

AT THE JAZZ BAND BALL

BAGDAD

BEAUTIFUL OHIO

BLUE DEVILS OF FRANCE, THE

CAISSONS GO ROLLING ALONG, THE (OVER HILL, OVER DALE)

CAN YOU TAME WILD WIMMEN?

CLARINET MARMALADE

COME ON, PAPA

DALLAS BLUES

DAUGHTER OF ROSIE O'GRADY, THE

DEAR LITTLE BOY OF MINE

DEAR OLD PAL OF MINE

EVERYTHING IS PEACHES DOWN IN GEORGIA

GARDEN OF MY DREAMS

GOING UP

GOOD MAN IS HARD TO FIND, A

GOOD MORNING, MR. ZIP-ZIP-ZIP! (WITH YOUR HAIR CUT JUST AS SHORT AS MINE)

HELLO, CENTRAL, GIVE ME NO MAN'S LAND

I CAN ALWAYS FIND A LITTLE SUNSHINE IN THE Y.M.C.A.

I'D LIKE TO SEE THE KAISER WITH A LILY IN HIS HAND

IF HE CAN FIGHT LIKE HE CAN LOVE, GOOD NIGHT GERMANY

I FOUND THE END OF THE RAINBOW

I HATE TO LOSE YOU

I'LL SAY SHE DOES

I'M GONNA PIN MY MEDAL ON THE GIRL I LEFT BEHIND

I'M SORRY I MADE YOU CRY

IN THE LAND OF BEGINNING AGAIN

JA-DA

JUST A BABY'S PRAYER AT TWILIGHT

JUST LIKE WASHINGTON CROSSED THE DELAWARE, GENERAL PERSHING WILL CROSS THE RHINE

K-K-K-KATY

MADELON

MAMMY'S CHOCOLATE SOLDIER

MICKEY

MY BELGIAN ROSE

MY MAMMY

OH! FRENCHY

OH, HOW I HATE TO GET UP IN THE MORNING

OH, HOW I WISH I COULD SLEEP UNTIL MY DADDY COMES HOME

OH, LADY! LADY!!

ONE DAY IN JUNE (IT MIGHT HAVE BEEN YOU)

ON THE ROAD TO CALAIS

ON THE ROAD TO HOME SWEET HOME

ORIGINAL DIXIELAND ONE-STEP

OSTRICH WALK

OUI, OUI, MARIE

RIDE ON, RIDE ON

ROCK-A-BYE YOUR BABY WITH A DIXIE MELODY

ROSE OF NO MAN'S LAND, THE

ROSE ROOM

SMILES

SOMETIME

SOMEWHERE IN FRANCE IS THE LILY

SUNRISE AND YOU

THAT TUMBLE-DOWN SHACK IN ATHLONE

THAT WONDERFUL MOTHER OF MINE

THERE'S A LIGHT IN YOUR EYES

THERE'S A LUMP OF SUGAR DOWN IN DIXIE

THERE'S LIFE IN THE OLD DOG YET

THEY WERE ALL OUT OF STEP BUT JIM

THREE WONDERFUL LETTERS FROM HOME

TICKLE TOE, THE (EVERYBODY OUGHT TO KNOW HOW TO DO)

TIGER RAG

TILL WE MEET AGAIN

TISHOMINGO BLUES

UNTIL

WAITING

WATERS OF VENICE (or, FLOATING DOWN THE SLEEPY LAGOON)

WE DON'T WANT THE BACON, WHAT WE WANT IS A PIECE OF THE RHINE

WE'RE ON OUR WAY TO FRANCE

WHEN ALEXANDER TAKES HIS RAGTIME BAND TO FRANCE

WHEN YOU COME BACK

WHY DO THEY ALL TAKE THE NIGHT BOAT TO ALBANY?

WOULD YOU RATHER BE A COLONEL WITH AN EAGLE ON YOUR SHOULDER OR A PRIVATE WITH A CHICKEN ON YOUR KNEE?

YOU KEEP SENDING 'EM OVER AND WE'LL KEEP KNOCKING 'EM DOWN

YOU-OO JUST YOU

1919

AIN'T YOU COMIN' BACK, MARY ANN,
   TO MARYLAND?

ALCOHOLIC BLUES, THE

ALICE BLUE GOWN

ALL THE QUAKERS ARE SHOULDER
   SHAKERS DOWN IN QUAKER TOWN

AND HE'D SAY "OO-LA-LA! WEE-WEE"

ANY OLD PLACE WITH YOU

ASK THE STARS

BABY

BABY'S PRAYER WILL SOON BE
   ANSWERED

BARNYARD BLUES

BEST OF EVERYTHING, THE

BLUES MY NAUGHTY SWEETIE GIVES TO
   ME, THE

BREEZE (BLOW MY BABY BACK TO ME)

BRING BACK THOSE WONDERFUL DAYS

BUDDHA

CAROLINA SUNSHINE

CASTLE OF DREAMS

CHINESE LULLABY

COME TO THE MOON

DADDY LONG LEGS

DARDANELLA

DON'T CRY, FRENCHY, DON'T CRY

DREAMY ALABAMA

FLOATIN' DOWN TO COTTON TOWN

FRECKLES

HOW YA GONNA KEEP 'EM DOWN ON
   THE FARM? (AFTER THEY'VE SEEN
   PAREE)

I AIN'T GONNA GIVE NOBODY NONE O'
   THIS JELLY ROLL

I'LL BE HAPPY WHEN THE PREACHER
   MAKES YOU MINE

I'LL REMEMBER YOU

I'M FOREVER BLOWING BUBBLES

I MIGHT BE YOUR ONCE-IN-A-WHILE

I'M IN LOVE

I'M LIKE A SHIP WITHOUT A SAIL

INDIAN SUMMER

IRENE

IT'S NOBODY'S BUSINESS BUT MY OWN

I'VE GOT MY CAPTAIN WORKING FOR
   ME NOW

JUST LIKE A GYPSY

KID DAYS

LAMPLIT HOUR, THE

LETTER SONG

LET THE REST OF THE WORLD GO BY

LITTLE CHURCH AROUND THE CORNER,
   THE

LITTLE GIRLS, GOODBYE

LOVE SENDS A LITTLE GIFT OF ROSES

MAMMY O' MINE

MANDY

MEET ME IN BUBBLE LAND

MY BABY'S ARMS

MY ISLE OF GOLDEN DREAMS

NOBODY KNOWS (AND NOBODY SEEMS
   TO CARE)

OH! HOW SHE CAN SING

OH, BY JINGO! OH, BY GEE! (YOU'RE
   THE ONLY GIRL FOR ME)

OH, WHAT A PAL WAS MARY

OH HOW I LAUGH WHEN I THINK HOW I
   CRIED ABOUT YOU

OLD-FASHIONED GARDEN

ON MIAMI SHORE

PEGGY

PRETTY GIRL IS LIKE A MELODY, A

PROHIBITION BLUES

SIPPING CIDER THRU A STRAW

SMILIN' THROUGH

SOMEDAY SWEETHEART

SOMEHOW IT SELDOM COMES TRUE

SOMEONE LIKE YOU

SOMETHING ABOUT LOVE

SPOOKY OOKUM

SWANEE

SWEET HAWAIIAN MOONLIGHT

SWEET SIXTEEN

TAKE YOUR GIRLIE TO THE MOVIES (IF
   YOU CAN'T MAKE LOVE AT HOME)

TELL ME (WHY NIGHTS ARE LONELY)

THAT NAUGHTY WALTZ

THAT REVOLUTIONARY RAG

THERE'S MORE TO THE KISS THAN THE X-X-X

THEY'RE ALL SWEETIES

TULIP TIME

VAMP, THE

WAIT TILL YOU GET THEM UP IN THE AIR, BOYS

WHAT'LL WE DO ON A SATURDAY NIGHT WHEN THE TOWN GOES DRY?

WHEN THE CHERRY BLOSSOMS FALL

WHEN YOU LOOK IN THE HEART OF A ROSE

WHO CAN TELL

WORLD IS WAITING FOR THE SUNRISE, THE

YOU AIN'T HEARD NOTHING YET

YOU ARE FREE

YOU CANNOT MAKE YOUR SHIMMY SHAKE ON TEA

YOU'D BE SURPRISED

YOU DIDN'T WANT ME WHEN YOU HAD ME (SO WHY DO YOU WANT ME NOW?)

YOU'RE A MILLION MILES FROM NOWHERE (WHEN YOU'RE ONE LITTLE MILE FROM HOME)

YOUR EYES HAVE TOLD ME SO

YOU SAID IT

1920

AFTER YOU GET WHAT YOU WANT, YOU DON'T WANT IT

ALL SHE'D SAY WAS "UMH HUM"

ALL THAT I WANT IS YOU

ANGEL FACE

AT THE MOVING PICTURE BALL

AUNT HAGAR'S BLUES

AVALON

BEAUTIFUL FACES NEED BEAUTIFUL CLOTHES

BELIEVE ME, BELOVED

BROADWAY ROSE

CARESSES

CHILI BEAN

COUNTRY COUSIN, THE

DADDY, YOU'VE BEEN A MOTHER TO ME

DEEP IN YOUR EYES

DOWN BY THE O-HI-O

DO YOU EVER THINK OF ME?

FEATHER YOUR NEST

GIRLS OF MY DREAMS, THE

HIAWATHA'S MELODY OF LOVE

HOLD ME

HUMMING

I'D LOVE TO FALL ASLEEP AND WAKE UP IN MY MAMMY'S ARMS

I'LL BE WITH YOU IN APPLE BLOSSOM TIME

I'LL SEE YOU IN C-U-B-A

I LOST THE BEST PAL THAT I HAD

I LOVE THE LAND OF OLD BLACK JOE

I'M AN INDIAN

I'M A LONESOME LITTLE RAINDROP (LOOKING FOR A PLACE TO FALL)

I'M A VAMP FROM EAST BROADWAY

IN A PERSIAN MARKET

I NEVER KNEW I COULD LOVE ANYBODY (LIKE I'M LOVING YOU)

I USED TO LOVE YOU (BUT IT'S ALL OVER NOW)

JAPANESE SANDMAN, THE

LA VEEDA

LEFT ALL ALONE AGAIN BLUES

LITTLE TOWN IN THE OULD COUNTY DOWN

LONG GONE

LOVE BOAT, THE

LOVE NEST, THE

MAH LINDY LOU

MARGIE

MARY

MOON SHINES ON THE MOONSHINE, THE

MY HOME TOWN IS A ONE HORSE TOWN (BUT IT'S BIG ENOUGH FOR ME)

MY LITTLE BIMBO DOWN ON THE BAMBOO ISLE

O (OH!)

OH! JUDGE (HE TREATS ME MEAN)

OH, HOW I LONG FOR SOMEONE

OLD PAL, WHY DON'T YOU ANSWER ME

PALE MOON

PALESTEENA

PRETTY KITTY KELLY

ROSE OF WASHINGTON SQUARE

SAN

SINGIN' THE BLUES (TILL MY DADDY COMES HOME)

SO LONG, OO LONG

SYNCOPATED VAMP, THE

TELL ME, LITTLE GYPSY

TEN LITTLE BOTTLES

THAT OLD IRISH MOTHER OF MINE

TIMBUCTOO

TRIPOLI (THE SHORES OF)

WAITING

WAITING FOR THE SUN TO COME OUT

WHEN I'M GONE I WON'T FORGET

WHEN I'M GONE YOU'LL SOON FORGET

WHEN MY BABY SMILES AT ME

WHERE DO THEY GO WHEN THEY ROW, ROW, ROW?

WHISPERING

WHO ATE NAPOLEONS WITH JOSEPHINE WHEN BONAPARTE WAS FAR AWAY?

WHOSE BABY ARE YOU?

WHY DON'T YOU?

WHY WORRY?

WILD ROSE

YOUNG MAN'S FANCY, A

YOU OUGHTA SEE MY BABY

1921

AIN'T WE GOT FUN?

ALL BY MYSELF

ANY TIME

APRIL SHOWERS

ARKANSAS BLUES

BANDANA DAYS

BIMINI BAY

BLUE DANUBE BLUES

BRIGHT EYES

BY THE WATERS OF MINNETONKA

CHERIE

CRAZY BLUES

DAPPER DAN (THE SHEIK OF ALABAM')

DEAR OLD SOUTHLAND

DOLLY

DOWN HOME BLUES

DOWN THE OLD CHURCH AISLE

DOWN YONDER

EVERYBODY STEP

GEORGIA ROSE

GIVE ME MY MAMMY

GOOD MORNING, DEARIE

HOME AGAIN BLUES

I AIN'T NOBODY'S DARLING

I FOUND A ROSE IN THE DEVIL'S GARDEN

I'LL FORGET YOU

I'M GOIN' SOUTH

I'M GOING TO WEAR YOU OFF MY MIND

I'M JUST WILD ABOUT HARRY

I'M MISSIN' MAMMY'S KISSIN' (AND I KNOW SHE'S MISSIN' MINE)

I'M NOBODY'S BABY

IN THE LITTLE RED SCHOOL HOUSE

I WONDER IF YOU STILL CARE FOR ME

JAZZ ME BLUES

KA-LU-A

KITTEN ON THE KEYS

LEARN TO SMILE

LEAVE ME WITH A SMILE

LOOK FOR THE SILVER LINING

LOVELESS LOVE (a.k.a. CARELESS LOVE)

LOVE WILL FIND A WAY

MA! (HE'S MAKING EYES AT ME)

MAKE BELIEVE

MANDY 'N' ME

MIMI

MY MAN (MON HOMME)

MY SUNNY TENNESSEE

OH ME! OH MY!

PEGGY O'NEIL

ROYAL GARDEN BLUES

SALLY

SALLY, WON'T YOU COME BACK

SATURDAY

SAY IT WITH MUSIC

SCHOOLHOUSE BLUES

SECOND HAND ROSE

SHEIK OF ARABY, THE

SHE'S MINE, ALL MINE

SHUFFLE ALONG

SNOOPS, THE LAWYER

SONG OF LOVE

SOUTH SEA ISLES (a.k.a. SUNNY SOUTH
    SEA ISLANDS)

STRUT MISS LIZZIE

SWANEE RIVER MOON

SWEET LADY

TEA LEAVES

TEN LITTLE FINGERS AND TEN LITTLE
    TOES (DOWN IN TENNESSEE)

THEY CALL IT DANCING

THEY NEEDED A SONG BIRD IN HEAVEN
    (SO GOD TOOK CARUSO AWAY)

THREE O'CLOCK IN THE MORNING

TUCK ME TO SLEEP IN MY OLD 'TUCKY
    HOME

WABASH BLUES

WANG, WANG BLUES, THE

WHEN BIG PROFUNDO SANG LOW "C"

WHEN BUDDHA SMILES

WHEN FRANCIS DANCES WITH ME

WHEN SHALL WE MEET AGAIN?

WHEN THE HONEYMOON WAS OVER

WHIP-POOR-WILL

WHO'LL BE THE NEXT ONE? (TO CRY
    OVER YOU)

YOO-HOO

1922

AIN'T IT A SHAME

ALL OVER NOTHING AT ALL

ANGEL CHILD

AS LONG AS I HAVE YOU

BABY, WON'T YOU PLEASE COME HOME

BABY BLUE EYES

BEAUTIFUL GIRLS

BEE'S KNEES

BLUE (AND BROKEN HEARTED)

BROKEN HEARTED MELODY

BROWN BIRD SINGING, A

BY AND BY

CAROLINA IN THE MORNING

CAROLINA SHOUT

CHICAGO

CHINA BOY

COAL BLACK MAMMY

CRINOLINE DAYS

DANCING FOOL

DIXIE HIGHWAY

DO IT AGAIN!

DOWN THE WINDING ROAD OF DREAMS

DREAMY MELODY

EVERY DAY

FAREWELL BLUES

GEE, BUT I HATE TO GO HOME ALONE

GEORGETTE

GEORGIA

GOIN' HOME

HE MAY BE YOUR MAN (BUT HE COMES
    TO SEE ME SOMETIMES)

HOMESICK

HOT LIPS

I GAVE YOU UP JUST BEFORE YOU
    THREW ME DOWN

I'LL BUILD A STAIRWAY TO PARADISE

I LOVE HER, SHE LOVES ME (I'M HER HE, SHE'S MY SHE)

I WISH I COULD SHIMMY LIKE MY SISTER KATE

I WONDER WHY

JOURNEY'S END

KISS IN THE DARK, A

LADY IN ERMINE, THE

LADY LUCK, SMILE ON ME

LADY OF THE EVENING

L'AMOUR, TOUJOURS, L'AMOUR (LOVE EVERLASTING)

LET'S KISS AND MAKE UP

LONESOME MAMA BLUES

LOVESICK BLUES

LOVIN' SAM, THE SHEIK OF ALABAM'

MARY, DEAR

MISTER GALLAGHER AND MISTER SHEAN

MY BUDDY

MY HONEY'S LOVIN' ARMS

MY RAMBLER ROSE

'NEATH 'NEATH THE SOUTH SEA MOON

NELLIE KELLY, I LOVE YOU

ON THE ALAMO

ON THE 'GIN, 'GIN, 'GINNY SHORE

OO-OO ERNEST, ARE YOU EARNEST WITH ME?

ORIENTAL

PACK UP YOUR SINS AND GO TO THE DEVIL

PARADE OF THE WOODEN SOLDIERS

ROSE OF THE RIO GRANDE

ROUND ON THE END AND HIGH IN THE MIDDLE (O-HI-O)

RUNNIN' WILD!

SAY IT WHILE DANCING

SIXTY SECONDS EVERY MINUTE (I THINK OF YOU)

SOMEBODY STOLE MY GAL

SOME SUNNY DAY

SOME SWEET DAY

SONG OF PERSIA

STUMBLING

SWEET INDIANA HOME

'TAINT NOBODY'S BIZNESS IF I DO

TEASIN'

THAT DA DA STRAIN

THROW ME A KISS

TIME WILL TELL

TOOT, TOOT, TOOTSIE, GOODBYE

TRA-LA-LA

TREES

'WAY DOWN YONDER IN NEW ORLEANS

WHEN HEARTS ARE YOUNG

WHEN THE LEAVES COME TUMBLING DOWN

WHEN THE SUN GOES DOWN

WHO CARES?

WONDERFUL ONE (MY)

YANKEE DOODLE BLUES

YOU CAN HAVE HIM, I DON'T WANT HIM, DIDN'T LOVE HIM ANYHOW BLUES!

YOU KNOW YOU BELONG TO SOMEBODY ELSE (SO WHY DON'T YOU LEAVE ME ALONE)

YOU REMIND ME OF MY MOTHER

YOU TELL HER, I S-T-U-T-T-E-R

1923

AGGRAVATIN' PAPA (DON'T YOU TRY TO TWO-TIME ME)

AIN'T YOU ASHAMED?

ALIBI BABY

ANNABELLE

ANNABEL LEE

BAMBALINA

BARNEY GOOGLE

BEALE STREET MAMA

BEBE

BESIDE A BABBLING BROOK

BIG FOOT HAM

BUGLE CALL RAG

CHARLESTON

CIELITO LINDO (AY, AY, AY, AY)

COME ON, SPARK PLUG!

COVERED WAGON DAYS

DEAREST (YOU'RE THE NEAREST TO MY HEART)

DIRTY HANDS, DIRTY FACE

DIZZY FINGERS

DOWN BY THE RIVER

DOWN HEARTED BLUES

DREAM DADDY

FIRST, LAST, AND ALWAYS

FROM BROADWAY TO MAIN STREET

GEORGIA BLUES

GULF COAST BLUES

HAPPY ENDING

I CRIED FOR YOU

I LOVE LIFE

I LOVE YOU

I'M SITTING PRETTY IN A PRETTY LITTLE CITY

INDIANA MOON

IN LOVE WITH LOVE

IT AIN'T GONNA RAIN NO MO'

IT WAS MEANT TO BE

I'VE GOT THE YES! WE HAVE NO BANANAS BLUES

IVY, CLING TO ME

I WON'T SAY I WILL, BUT I WON'T SAY I WON'T

JUST A GIRL THAT MEN FORGET

JUST HOT!

KANSAS CITY STOMP(S)

LAST NIGHT ON THE BACK PORCH (I LOVED HER BEST OF ALL)

LEARN TO DO THE STRUT

LINGER AWHILE

LITTLE BUTTERFLY

LOUISVILLE LOU

LOVEY CAME BACK

MAMA GOES WHERE PAPA GOES (OR PAPA DON'T GO OUT TONIGHT)

MAMA LOVES PAPA (PAPA LOVES MAMA)

MEXICALI ROSE

MY SWEETIE WENT AWAY (SHE DIDN'T SAY WHERE, WHEN OR WHY)

NASHVILLE NIGHTINGALE

NO, NO, NORA

NOBODY KNOWS YOU WHEN YOU'RE DOWN AND OUT

OH, DIDN'T IT RAIN!

OH GEE, OH GOSH, OH GOLLY, I'M IN LOVE

OLD FASHIONED LOVE

ONCE IN A BLUE MOON

ON THE MALL

ORANGE GROVE IN CALIFORNIA, AN

OUT THERE IN THE SUNSHINE WITH YOU

RAGGEDY ANN

REMEMB'RING

ROSITA, LA

SEVEN OR ELEVEN (MY DIXIE PAIR O' DICE)

SITTIN' IN A CORNER

SLEEP

SMILE WILL GO A LONG, LONG WAY, A

SOBBIN' BLUES

SOMEONE LOVES YOU AFTER ALL

SOME SWEET DAY

SO THIS IS LOVE

STELLA

STEPPIN' OUT

SUGAR BLUES

SWINGIN' DOWN THE LANE

TELL ALL THE FOLKS IN KENTUCKY

TELL ME A BEDTIME STORY

TEN THOUSAND YEARS FROM NOW

THAT OLD GANG OF MINE

TIN ROOF BLUES

TWELVE O'CLOCK AT NIGHT

WALTZ OF LONG AGO, THE

WEARY BLUES

WHAT DO YOU DO SUNDAY, MARY?

WHEN LIGHTS ARE LOW

WHEN YOU AND I WERE YOUNG, MAGGIE, BLUES

WHEN YOU WALKED OUT, SOMEONE
  ELSE WALKED RIGHT IN
WHO'LL BUY MY VIOLETS?
WHO'S SORRY NOW?
WILDFLOWER
WOLVERINE BLUES
YES! WE HAVE NO BANANAS
YOU'VE GOT TO SEE MAMMA EV'RY
  NIGHT, (OR YOU CAN'T SEE MAMMA
  AT ALL)

1924

ADORING YOU
ALL ALONE
ATLANTA BLUES
BACK O' TOWN BLUES
BAGDAD
BATTLESHIP KATE
BIG BOY
BOOZE AND BLUES
BO-WEAVIL BLUES
CAKE WALKING BABIES FROM HOME
CALIFORNIA, HERE I COME
CALL OF THE SOUTH, THE
CANAL STREET BLUES
CAROLINA ROLLING STONE
CHARLESTON CRAZY
CHARLEY, MY BOY
COPENHAGEN
COUNTING THE BLUES
COVER ME UP WITH THE SUNSHINE OF
  VIRGINIA
DANCING TIME
DEEP IN MY HEART
DEEP IN MY HEART, DEAR
DOES THE SPEARMINT LOSE ITS FLAVOR
  ON THE BEDPOST OVER NIGHT?
DON'T MIND THE RAIN
DOODLE DOO DOO
DOOR OF MY DREAMS, THE
DOO WACKA DOO
DOWN IN THE MOUTH BLUES

DRINKING SONG (DRINK! DRINK! DRINK!)
DYING GAMBLER'S BLUES
EVERYBODY LOVES MY BABY (BUT MY
  BABY DON'T LOVE NOBODY BUT ME)
FASCINATING RHYTHM
FIDGETY FEET
FLANNEL PETTICOAT GAL
FOLLOW THE SWALLOW
GHOST OF THE BLUES
GOLDEN DAYS
GRAVEYARD BOUND BLUES
GRAVIER STREET BLUES
HALF OF IT, DEARIE, BLUES, THE
HANG ON TO ME
HARD HEARTED HANNAH (THE VAMP
  OF SAVANNAH)
HAUNTED HOUSE BLUES
HONEST AND TRULY
HONEY-BUN
HOODOO MAN, THE
HOW COME YOU DO ME LIKE YOU DO?
HOW DO YOU DO (EVERYBODY)
I CAN'T GET THE ONE I WANT
IF YOUR HEART'S IN THE GAME
I'LL SEE YOU IN MY DREAMS
I'M A LITTLE BLACKBIRD LOOKING FOR
  A BLUEBIRD
I'M IN LOVE AGAIN
INDIAN LOVE CALL
IN SHADOWLAND
IN THE EVENING
IN THE GARDEN OF TOMORROW
IT HAD TO BE YOU
I WONDER WHAT'S BECOME OF SALLY
I WONDER WHO'S DANCING WITH YOU
  TONIGHT
JAIL HOUSE BLUES
JAPANESE SUNSET, A
JEALOUS
JIG WALK
JIMTOWN BLUES
JUNE BROUGHT THE ROSES

JUNE NIGHT

JUST WE TWO

KEEP YOUR EYE ON THE BALL

KEEP YOUR TEMPER

KING PORTER STOMP

LAZY

LENOX AVENUE SHUFFLE

LET ME LINGER LONGER IN YOUR ARMS

LIMEHOUSE BLUES

LISTENING

LITTLE JAZZ BIRD

LITTLE OLD CLOCK ON THE MANTEL, THE

LONELY LITTLE MELODY

MAH JONG

MAMA'S GONE, GOODBYE

MANDALAY

MANDY, MAKE UP YOUR MIND

ME AND THE BOY FRIEND

MEMORY LANE

MINDIN' MY BUSINESS

MOONSHINE BLUES

MOUNTIES, THE

MR. FREDDIE BLUES

MR. JELLY LORD

MY BEST GIRL

MY DREAM GIRL

NIGHT HAWK BLUES

NOBODY'S SWEETHEART

O, KATHARINA!

OH, LADY BE GOOD!

ONE I LOVE, THE (BELONGS TO SOMEBODY ELSE)

ONLY, ONLY ONE FOR ME, THE

PAL THAT I LOVED, THE (STOLE THE GAL THAT I LOVED)

PARISIAN PIERROT

PLEASURE MAD

PRESCRIPTION FOR THE BLUES

PRINCE OF WAILS

PRISONER'S SONG, THE (a.k.a. IF I HAD THE WINGS OF AN ANGEL)

PUT AWAY A LITTLE RAY OF GOLDEN SUNSHINE (FOR A RAINY DAY)

RED-HEADED MUSIC MAKER

RED HOT MAMA

RHAPSODY IN BLUE

ROSE-MARIE

SAVANNAH

SERENADE

SHANGHAI SHUFFLE

SHE'S EVERYBODY'S SWEETHEART (BUT NOBODY'S GAL)

SHINE

SO AM I

SOMEBODY LOVES ME

SOUTH

SPAIN

SUD BUSTIN' BLUES

SUITCASE BLUES

SWISS MISS

TAKE A LITTLE ONE-STEP

TELL HER IN THE SPRINGTIME

THERE'LL BE SOME CHANGES MADE

THERE'S YES! YES! IN YOUR EYES

TICKET AGENT, EASE YOUR WINDOW DOWN

TIE A STRING AROUND YOUR FINGER

TOODLE-OO

TOTEM TOM-TOM

VIRGINIA (DON'T GO TOO FAR)

WEST OF THE GREAT DIVIDE

WHAT HAS BECOME OF HINKY DINKY PARLAY VOO?

WHAT'LL I DO?

WHEN IT'S NIGHT TIME IN ITALY, IT'S WEDNESDAY OVER HERE

WHEN MY SUGAR WALKS DOWN THE STREET

WHEN THE ONE YOU LOVE LOVES YOU

WHEN YOU AND I WERE SEVENTEEN

WHERE IS THAT OLD GIRL OF MINE?

WHERE THE LAZY DAISIES GROW

WHY COULDN'T IT BE POOR LITTLE ME?

WHY DID I KISS THAT GIRL?
WRECK OF THE OLD '97
YOU AND I
YOU'RE JUST A FLOWER FROM AN OLD
    BOUQUET

1925

ALABAMY BOUND
ALONE AT LAST
ALWAYS
ANGRY
ARE YOU SORRY?
AT THE END OF THE ROAD
BABY!
BAM, BAM, BAMY SHORE
BONEYARD SHUFFLE
BROWN EYES, WHY ARE YOU BLUE?
BYE AND BYE
CECILIA
CHEATIN' ON ME
CLAP HANDS! HERE COMES CHARLEY!
COLLEGIATE
DAVENPORT BLUES
DEATH OF FLOYD COLLINS, THE
DINAH
DON'T BRING LULU
DON'T WAKE ME UP, LET ME DREAM
DOWN BY THE WINEGAR WOIKS
DRIFTING AND DREAMING
D'YE LOVE ME?
EVERYTHING IS HOTSY TOTSY NOW
FIVE FOOT TWO, EYES OF BLUE (HAS
    ANYBODY SEEN MY GIRL)
FRESHIE
GIGOLETTE
GOT NO TIME
GRANDPA'S SPELLS
HEADIN' FOR LOUISVILLE
HELLO 'TUCKY
HERE IN MY ARMS (IT'S ADORABLE)
HILLS OF HOME, THE

HUGS AND KISSES
HUGUETTE WALTZ
IF I HAD A GIRL LIKE YOU
IF YOU KNEW SUSIE (LIKE I KNOW
    SUSIE)
I LOVE MY BABY (MY BABY LOVES ME)
I'M GONNA CHARLESTON BACK TO
    CHARLESTON
I MISS MY SWISS (MY SWISS MISS MISSES
    ME)
I'M KNEE DEEP IN DAISIES (AND HEAD
    OVER HEELS IN LOVE)
I'M SITTING ON TOP OF THE WORLD
I'M TIRED OF EVERYTHING BUT YOU
I NEVER KNEW (THAT ROSES GREW)
IN THE MIDDLE OF THE NIGHT
ISN'T SHE THE SWEETEST THING? (OH
    MAW, OH PAW)
IT MUST BE LOVE
I WANT TO BE HAPPY
I WONDER WHERE MY BABY IS
    TONIGHT
JALOUSIE (JEALOUSY)
JUST A COTTAGE SMALL (BY A
    WATERFALL)
JUST AROUND THE CORNER
KEEP SMILING AT TROUBLE
KEEP YOUR SKIRTS DOWN, MARY ANN
KENTUCKY'S WAY OF SAYING GOOD
    MORNIN'
KICKIN' THE CLOUDS AWAY
KIDS IN AMERICA
LET IT RAIN! LET IT POUR! (I'LL BE IN
    VIRGINIA IN THE MORNING)
LET'S SAY GOOD NIGHT TILL IT'S
    MORNING
LITTLE BUNGALOW, A
LITTLE PEACH
LONESOMEST GIRL IN TOWN, THE
LOVE FOR SALE
LOVE ME TONIGHT
LUCKY BOY
MANHATTAN

MIAMI

MILENBERG JOYS

MOONLIGHT AND ROSES

MY SWEETIE TURNED ME DOWN

MY YIDDISHE MOMME

NEAPOLITAN NIGHTS (OH, NIGHTS OF
    SPLENDOR)

NO, NO, NANETTE

OH! BOY, WHAT A GIRL

OH, HOW I MISS YOU TONIGHT

OH, MISS HANNAH!

ONLY A ROSE

PADDLIN' MADELIN' HOME

PAL OF MY CRADLE DAYS

PEACEFUL VALLEY

POOR LITTLE RICH GIRL

REMEMBER

RIVERBOAT SHUFFLE

ROLL 'EM GIRLS, ROLL YOUR OWN

SAVE YOUR SORROW (FOR TOMORROW)

SEE SEE RIDER (BLUES) (a.k.a. C. C.
    RIDER)

SENTIMENTAL ME

SHOW ME THE WAY TO GO HOME

SLEEPY TIME GAL

SOME DAY

SOMETIME

SONG OF THE FLAME

SONG OF THE VAGABONDS

SUGAR FOOT STOMP

SUNNY

SWANEE BUTTERFLY

SWEET AND LOW-DOWN

SWEET GEORGIA BROWN

TEA FOR TWO

THAT CERTAIN FEELING

THAT CERTAIN PARTY

TIE ME TO YOUR APRON STRINGS AGAIN

TITINA

TOO MANY RINGS AROUND ROSIE

TRAVELIN' BLUES

TWO GUITARS

TWO LITTLE BLUEBIRDS

UKULELE LADY

WASHBOARD BLUES

WATERS OF THE PERKIOMEN

"WHERE HAS MY HUBBY GONE?" BLUES

WHO?

WHO TAKES CARE OF THE
    CARETAKER'S DAUGHTER?

WHY DO I LOVE YOU?

WHY SHOULD I CRY OVER YOU?

WRECK OF THE SHENANDOAH, THE

YEARNING (JUST FOR YOU)

YES SIR! THAT'S MY BABY

YOU CAN DANCE WITH ANY GIRL AT
    ALL

1926

ACE IN THE HOLE

AFTER I SAY I'M SORRY (WHAT CAN I
    SAY?)

ALABAMA STOMP

ALL ALONE MONDAY

AM I WASTING MY TIME ON YOU?

AT PEACE WITH THE WORLD

BABY

BABY FACE

BARCELONA

BECAUSE I LOVE YOU

BIG BUTTER AND EGG MAN, THE

BIRTH OF THE BLUES, THE

BLACK BOTTOM

BLACK BOTTOM STOMP

BLOWIN' THE BLUES AWAY

BLUE ROOM, THE

BREEZIN' ALONG WITH THE BREEZE

BRING BACK THOSE MINSTREL DAYS

BUT I DO, YOU KNOW I DO

BYE BYE BLACKBIRD

CHERIE, I LOVE YOU

CLAP YO' HANDS

CLIMBING UP THE LADDER OF LOVE

COSSACK LOVE SONG (DON'T FORGET ME)

CROSS YOUR HEART

CUP OF COFFEE, A SANDWICH AND YOU, A

DEAR LITTLE GIRL

'DEED I DO

DESERT SONG, THE

DO, DO, DO

DON'T BE ANGRY WITH ME

DREAMING

EAST ST. LOUIS TOODLE-OO

EVERYTHING'S GONNA BE ALL RIGHT

FIDGETY FEET

FLAMIN' MAMIE

FLAPPERETTE

FLORIDA, THE MOON AND YOU

FOR MY SWEETHEART

FRENCH MILITARY MARCHING SONG

GANG THAT SANG HEART OF MY HEART, THE

GENTLEMEN PREFER BLONDES

GIMME A LITTLE KISS, WILL YA, HUH?

GIN HOUSE BLUES, THE

GIRL FRIEND, THE

GIRL IS YOU AND THE BOY IS ME, THE

HEEBIE JEEBIES

HELLO, ALOHA, HOW ARE YOU?

HELLO BLUEBIRD

HI-DIDDLE-DIDDLE

HORSES

HOW MANY TIMES?

HUGS AND KISSES

I'D CLIMB THE HIGHEST MOUNTAIN

I'D RATHER BE THE GIRL IN YOUR ARMS

I FOUND A NEW BABY

I KNOW THAT YOU KNOW

I LOVE THE COLLEGE GIRLS

I'M JUST WILD ABOUT ANIMAL CRACKERS

I'M ON MY WAY HOME

IN A LITTLE SPANISH TOWN

I NEED LOVIN'

IT ALL DEPENDS ON YOU

IT MADE YOU HAPPY WHEN YOU MADE ME CRY

I'VE GOT THE GIRL

JERSEY WALK

JUST A BIRD'S EYE VIEW OF MY OLD KENTUCKY HOME

KATINKA

LANTERN OF LOVE

LET'S TALK ABOUT MY SWEETIE

LIKE HE LOVES ME

LITTLE BIRDIE TOLD ME SO, A

LITTLE WHITE HOUSE, THE (AT THE END OF HONEYMOON LANE)

LONESOME AND SORRY

LOOKING AT THE WORLD THROUGH ROSE COLORED GLASSES

LOOKING FOR A BOY

LUCKY DAY (THIS IS MY)

MA CURLY HEADED BABBY

MARY LOU

MAYBE

ME TOO (HO, HO, HA, HA)

MOONLIGHT ON THE GANGES

MOUNTAIN GREENERY

MUDDY WATER

MUSKRAT (or MUSKAT) RAMBLE

MY CASTLE IN SPAIN

MY CUTIE'S DUE AT TWO TO TWO TODAY

MY DREAM OF THE BIG PARADE

NOBODY WANTS ME

NO FOOLIN'

ONE ALONE

OUR DIRECTOR

PLAY GYPSIES, DANCE GYPSIES

POOR PAPA (HE'S GOT NUTHIN' AT ALL)

PRETTY LIPS

REACHING FOR THE MOON

RIFF SONG, THE

ROMANCE

SLEEPY HEAD

SNAG IT

SOMEONE TO WATCH OVER ME

SONG OF THE WANDERER

SUNDAY

SUNDAY

SUNNY DISPOSISH

TAKE IN THE SUN, HANG OUT THE
MOON

TAMIAMI TRAIL

THANKS FOR THE BUGGY RIDE

THAT LOST BARBERSHOP CHORD

THAT'S A GOOD GIRL

THAT'S WHY I LOVE YOU

(I WANNA GO WHERE YOU GO, DO
WHAT YOU DO) THEN I'LL BE HAPPY

THERE AIN'T NO MAYBE IN MY BABY'S
EYES

THERE'S A NEW STAR IN HEAVEN
TONIGHT—RUDOLPH VALENTINO

(I'VE GROWN SO LONESOME) THINKING
OF YOU

THIS FUNNY WORLD

TING-A-LING (THE WALTZ OF THE
BELLS)

TONIGHT YOU BELONG TO ME

TREE IN THE PARK, A

TROUBLE IN MIND

VALENCIA

VODKA

WE'LL HAVE A KINGDOM

WHAT'S THE MATTER NOW?

WHEN DAY IS DONE

WHEN THE RED, RED ROBIN COMES
BOB, BOB, BOBBIN' ALONG

WHERE DO YOU WORK-A, JOHN? (ON
THE DELAWARE LACKAWAN')

WHERE'D YOU GET THOSE EYES?

WHY DO YA ROLL THOSE EYES?

WILD ROSE, THE

YA GOTTA KNOW HOW TO LOVE

YANKEE ROSE

YOU WILL, WON'T YOU?

1927

ABDUL ABULBUL AMIR

AIN'T SHE SWEET?

AIN'T THAT A GRAND AND GLORIOUS
FEELING?

ALLIGATOR CRAWL

AMONG MY SOUVENIRS

ARE YOU LONESOME TONIGHT?

AT SUNDOWN

AWAY DOWN SOUTH IN HEAVEN

AY, AY, AY

BABBITT AND THE BROMIDE, THE

BARBARA

BEAUTIFUL

BEST THINGS IN LIFE ARE FREE, THE

BLACK AND TAN FANTASY

BLESS THIS HOUSE

BLUE RIVER

BLUE SKIES

BROADWAY

(HERE AM I) BROKEN HEARTED

BY THE BEND OF THE RIVER

CALINDA, THE (BOO-JOOM, BOO-JOOM,
BOO!)

C'EST VOUS (IT'S YOU)

CHANGES

CHANSONETTE

CHARMAINE

CHLO-E

COVER ME UP WITH SUNSHINE

CRAZY WORDS, CRAZY TUNE
(VO-DO-DE-O-DO)

CREOLE LOVE CALL

DANCING TAMBOURINE

DANCING THE DEVIL AWAY

DAWN

DEAR EYES THAT HAUNT ME

(WHAT DO WE DO ON A) DEW-
DEW-DEWY DAY

DIANE (I'M IN HEAVEN WHEN I SEE YOU
SMILE)

DID YOU MEAN IT?

DIXIE VAGABOND

DOCTOR JAZZ

DOLL DANCE, THE

EVERYTHING'S MADE FOR LOVE

EVERY TUB

EVERYWHERE YOU GO

FIFTY MILLION FRENCHMEN (CAN'T BE WRONG)

FOLLOWING THE SUN AROUND

FORGIVE ME

FOUR OR FIVE TIMES

FUNNY FACE

GID-AP GARIBALDI

GIRL OF MY DREAMS

GIVE ME A NIGHT IN JUNE

GONNA GET A GIRL

GOOD NEWS

HALLELUJAH!

HEADING FOR HARLEM

HELLO, SWANEE, HELLO!

HE LOVES AND SHE LOVES

HERE COMES THE SHOW BOAT

HE'S THE LAST WORD

HIGH, HIGH, HIGH UP IN THE HILLS

HIGHWAYS ARE HAPPY WAYS

HOOSIER SWEETHEART

HOT HEELS

I CAN'T BELIEVE THAT YOU'RE IN LOVE WITH ME

I FEEL AT HOME WITH YOU

IF YOU'RE IN LOVE, YOU'LL WALTZ

IF YOU SEE SALLY

I LEFT MY SUGAR STANDING IN THE RAIN

I'LL TAKE CARE OF YOUR CARES

I'M COMING VIRGINIA

I'M GONNA MEET MY SWEETIE NOW

I MIGHT FALL BACK ON YOU

I'M LOOKING OVER A FOUR LEAF CLOVER

I'M TELLIN' THE BIRDS, I'M TELLIN' THE BEES (HOW I LOVE YOU)

I'M WAITING FOR SHIPS THAT NEVER COME IN

IN A MIST

I NEVER SEE MAGGIE ALONE

I SCREAM, YOU SCREAM (WE ALL SCREAM FOR ICE CREAM)

IS EVERYBODY HAPPY NOW?

IS IT POSSIBLE?

IS SHE MY GIRL FRIEND?

IT ALL BELONGS TO ME

IT'S A MILLION TO ONE YOU'RE IN LOVE

IT WAS ONLY A SUN SHOWER

IT WON'T BE LONG NOW

JACK IN THE BOX

JUST A MEMORY

JUST ANOTHER DAY WASTED AWAY (WAITING FOR YOU)

JUST IMAGINE

JUST LIKE A BUTTERFLY (THAT'S CAUGHT IN THE RAIN)

JUST ONCE AGAIN

KANSAS CITY SHUFFLE

KEEP SWEEPING THE COBWEBS OFF THE MOON

KICKIN' THE CAT

KINKAJOU, THE

KRAZY KAT

LANE IN SPAIN, A

LAZY WEATHER

LET'S KISS AND MAKE UP

LOVE AND KISSES

LUCKY IN LOVE

LUCKY LINDY

MANHATTAN MARY

(WHAT ARE YOU WAITING FOR) MARY

ME AND MY SHADOW

MISS ANNABELLE LEE

MOONBEAM, KISS HER FOR ME

MOTEN STOMP

MOTHER

MOTHER OF MINE, I STILL HAVE YOU

MY BLUE HEAVEN

MY BLUE RIDGE MOUNTAIN HOME
MY HEART STOOD STILL
MY LITTLE NEST OF HEAVENLY BLUE
MY OHIO HOME
MY ONE AND ONLY
NORMANDY
ONE SWEET LETTER FROM YOU
OO—MAYBE IT'S YOU
PAREE!
PERSIAN RUG
RAIN
RAMONA
RANGERS' SONG, THE
RED LIPS KISS MY BLUES AWAY
RIO RITA
RUSSIAN LULLABY
SAM, THE OLD ACCORDION MAN
SAME OLD MOON, THE
SHAKING THE BLUES AWAY
SIDE BY SIDE
SILVER MOON
SING ME A BABY SONG
SLOW RIVER
SO BLUE
SOLILOQUY
SOMEBODY ELSE
SOMETIMES I'M HAPPY
SONG IS ENDED, THE (BUT THE MELODY
    LINGERS ON)
SO TIRED
STAR DUST
STRUTTIN' WITH SOME BARBECUE
SWEETHEART, WE NEED EACH OTHER
'S WONDERFUL
THERE'S A CRADLE IN CAROLINE
THERE'S EVERYTHING NICE ABOUT YOU
    (THERE'S SOMETHING NICE ABOUT
    EVERYONE)
THINKING OF YOU
THOU SWELL
THREE SHADES OF BLUE

TOGETHER WE TWO
UNDER THE MOON
UP IN THE CLOUDS
VARSITY DRAG, THE
VO-DO-DO-DE-O BLUES
WE TWO SHALL MEET AGAIN
WHAT DOES IT MATTER?
WHAT DO I CARE WHAT SOMEBODY
    SAID?
WHEN THE MORNING GLORIES WAKE UP
    IN THE MORNING
WHERE'S THAT RAINBOW?
WHY, OH WHY?
WILD MAN BLUES
WISTFUL AND BLUE
YOU DON'T LIKE IT—NOT MUCH
YOU'RE ALWAYS IN MY ARMS
YOUR LAND AND MY LAND

1928

AFTER MY LAUGHTER CAME TEARS
ALABAMA SONG
AMERICAN TUNE
ANGELA MIA (MY ANGEL)
ANYTHING YOU SAY
AVALON TOWN
BABY!
BABY'S BEST FRIEND, A
BACK IN YOUR OWN BACK YARD
BASIN STREET BLUES
BECAUSE MY BABY DON'T MEAN
    "MAYBE" NOW
BELOVED
BILL
BLUE SHADOWS
BLUE YODEL
CAN'T HELP LOVIN' DAT MAN
CHERRY
CHIQUITA
COLLEGIANA

C-O-N-S-T-A-N-T-I-N-O-P-L-E

COQUETTE

COW COW BLUES

CRAZY RHYTHM

DANCE, LITTLE LADY

DANCE OF THE PAPER DOLLS

DEAR, ON A NIGHT LIKE THIS

DIGA DIGA DOO

DO I HEAR YOU SAYING, "I LOVE YOU"?

DOIN' THE NEW LOW-DOWN

DOIN' THE RACCOON

DON'T BE LIKE THAT

DON'T HOLD EVERYTHING

DON'T LOOK AT ME THAT WAY

DOWN WHERE THE SUN GOES DOWN

DREAM HOUSE

DUSKY STEVEDORE

EMPTY BED BLUES

EVENING STAR

FEELING I'M FALLING

FOR OLD TIMES' SAKE

FOUR WALLS

FROM MONDAY ON

GAY CABALLERO, A

GET OUT AND GET UNDER THE MOON

GIVE ME ONE HOUR

GLORY ROAD, DE

GOLDEN GATE

GUESS WHO'S IN TOWN

HALF-WAY TO HEAVEN

HAPPY GO LUCKY LANE

HAY, STRAW

HEAH ME TALKIN' TO YA

HEIGH-HO, EVERYBODY, HEIGH-HO

HELLO, MONTREAL

HENRY'S MADE A LADY OUT OF LIZZIE

HIGH UP ON A HILL TOP

HOORAY FOR CAPTAIN SPAULDING

HOT AND BOTHERED

HOT HEELS

HOW ABOUT ME?

HOW LONG HAS THIS BEEN GOING ON?

I CAN'T DO WITHOUT YOU

I CAN'T GIVE YOU ANYTHING BUT LOVE

I DON'T THINK I'LL FALL IN LOVE
TODAY

I'D RATHER BE BLUE OVER YOU (THAN
BE HAPPY WITH SOMEBODY ELSE)

I FAW DOWN AN' GO BOOM!

IF YOU WANT THE RAINBOW (YOU MUST
HAVE THE RAIN)

I JUST ROLL ALONG

I'LL GET BY

IMAGINATION

I'M BRINGING A RED, RED ROSE

I'M ON THE CREST OF A WAVE

I'M SORRY, SALLY

I MUST BE DREAMING

I MUST HAVE THAT MAN

I MUST LOVE YOU

I'M WILD ABOUT HORNS ON
AUTOMOBILES THAT GO "TA-TA-
TA-TA"

IN A GREAT BIG WAY

IN THE JAILHOUSE NOW

I STILL LOVE YOU

IT GOES LIKE THIS (THAT FUNNY
MELODY)

I WANNA BE LOVED BY YOU

I WANT A MAN

I WANT TO BE BAD

JAPANSY

JEANNINE, I DREAM OF LILAC TIME

(I'M) JIMMY, THE WELL-DRESSED MAN

JUST LIKE A MELODY OUT OF THE SKY

KING FOR A DAY

K-RA-ZY FOR YOU

LAST NIGHT I DREAMED YOU KISSED ME

LAUGH, CLOWN, LAUGH

LET A SMILE BE YOUR UMBRELLA

LET'S DO IT (LET'S FALL IN LOVE)

LET'S MISBEHAVE

LIFE UPON THE WICKED STAGE

LONELY MELODY

LONESOME IN THE MOONLIGHT

LONESOME ROAD, THE

LOOKING AT YOU

LOUISIANA

LOVE ME OR LEAVE ME

LOVER, COME BACK TO ME

MA BELLE

MAKE BELIEVE

MAKIN' WHOOPEE

MANHATTAN SERENADE

MAN I LOVE, THE

MARCH OF THE MUSKETEERS

MARIANNE

MARIE

MARY ANN

MASQUERADE

ME AND THE MAN IN THE MOON

MEMORIES OF FRANCE

MISSISSIPPI MUD

MONDAY DATE, A

MOOCHE, THE

MY BLACKBIRDS ARE BLUEBIRDS NOW

MY PET

MY SUPPRESSED DESIRE

NAGASAKI

OH, BABY

OH GEE! OH JOY!

OLD MAN SUNSHINE, LITTLE BOY
   BLUEBIRD

OL' MAN RIVER

ONCE IN A LIFETIME

ONE GIRL, THE

ONE KISS

ONE STEP TO HEAVEN

OUT-O'-TOWN GAL

PARIS

PICKIN' COTTON

POMPANOLA

PORGY

READY FOR THE RIVER

REVENGE

RHYTHM KING

ROOM WITH A VIEW, A

ROSES OF YESTERDAY

SHE'S A GREAT, GREAT GIRL

SHE'S FUNNY THAT WAY (I GOT A
   WOMAN, CRAZY FOR ME)

SHORT'NIN' BREAD

SOFTLY, AS IN A MORNING SUNRISE

SOMEDAY, SOMEWHERE (WE'LL MEET
   AGAIN)

SONG I LOVE, THE

SONNY BOY

SQUEEZE ME

STOUTHEARTED MEN

SUGAR

SUNSHINE

SWEETHEART OF ALL MY DREAMS (I
   LOVE YOU, I LOVE YOU, I LOVE YOU)

SWEETHEARTS ON PARADE

SWEET LORRAINE

SWEET SUE (JUST YOU)

'TAIN'T SO, HONEY, 'TAIN'T SO

TAKE YOUR TOMORROW (AND GIVE ME
   TODAY)

TEN LITTLE MILES FROM TOWN

THAT'S MY WEAKNESS NOW

THERE AIN'T NO SWEET MAN (WORTH
   THE SALT OF MY TEARS)

THERE'S A RAINBOW 'ROUND MY
   SHOULDER

THERE'S SOMETHING ABOUT A ROSE
   (THAT REMINDS ME OF YOU)

TOGETHER

TWO LITTLE BABES IN THE WOOD

WANTING YOU

WAS IT A DREAM?

WATCHING THE CLOUDS ROLL BY

WHAT D'YA SAY?

WHEN

WHEN I GO ON THE STAGE

WHEN YOU'RE SMILING (THE WHOLE
   WORLD SMILES WITH YOU)

WHERE IS THE SONG OF SONGS FOR
   ME?

WHERE THE SHY LITTLE VIOLETS GROW

WHERE WERE YOU—WHERE WAS I?
  (EXACTLY WHERE WE ARE)
WHY DO I LOVE YOU?
WINGS
WORLD WEARY
YELLOW DOG BLUES, THE
YOU ARE LOVE
YOU'LL GET BY
YOU'RE THE CREAM IN MY COFFEE
YOU TOOK ADVANTAGE OF ME

1929

AIN'T MISBEHAVIN'
ALBUM OF MY DREAMS, THE
ALL BY YOURSELF IN THE MOONLIGHT
ALL THAT I'M ASKING IS SYMPATHY
AM I BLUE?
AWFUL SAD
BABY'S AWAKE NOW
BARNACLE BILL THE SAILOR
BESIDE AN OPEN FIREPLACE
BIFF'LY BLUES
BIG CITY BLUES
BIGGER AND BETTER THAN EVER
BIRMINGHAM BERTHA
BLACK AND BLUE
BLONDY
BOOGIE WOOGIE
BREAKAWAY, THE
BROADWAY MELODY
BUILDING A NEST FOR MARY
BUNDLE OF OLD LOVE LETTERS, A
BUTTON UP YOUR OVERCOAT
(I CAN DO WITHOUT BROADWAY, BUT)
  CAN BROADWAY DO WITHOUT ME?
CAN'T WE BE FRIENDS?
CAN'T YOU UNDERSTAND?
CAROLINA MOON
CHANT OF THE JUNGLE
CORRINE, CORRINA (CORINNA,
  CORINNA)
CRAZE-OLOGY
CROSS YOUR FINGERS

DANCE AWAY THE NIGHT
DEAR LITTLE CAFE
DEEP NIGHT
DICTY GLIDE, THE
DOIN' THE VOOM VOOM
DON'T EVER LEAVE ME
DON'T HANG YOUR DREAMS ON A
  RAINBOW
DO SOMETHING
DO WHAT YOU DO
DREAM LOVER
DREAM TRAIN
DUKE STEPS OUT, THE
EVANGELINE
EV'RYBODY LOVES YOU
EV'RY DAY AWAY FROM YOU
FANCY OUR MEETING
FEELING DROWSY
FIND ME A PRIMITIVE MAN
FUTURISTIC RHYTHM
GARDEN IN THE RAIN, A
GEE BABY, AIN'T I GOOD TO YOU?
GLAD RAG DOLL
GOIN' TO TOWN
GOOD LITTLE, BAD LITTLE YOU
GOTTA FEELIN' FOR YOU
GRAND PIANO BLUES
GREAT DAY!
GYPSY DREAM ROSE
HAPPY DAYS AND LONELY NIGHTS
HAPPY DAYS ARE HERE AGAIN
HAUNTED NIGHTS
HEIGH-HO, EVERYBODY, HEIGH-HO
HERE AM I
HERE COMES MY BALL AND CHAIN
HERE WE ARE
HE'S A GOOD MAN TO HAVE AROUND
HE'S SO UNUSUAL
HITTIN' THE CEILING
HONEY
HONEYSUCKLE ROSE
HOW AM I TO KNOW?
HOW LONG, HOW LONG BLUES

I CAN GET IT FOR YOU WHOLESALE

ICH LIEBE DICH (I LOVE YOU)

I DON'T WANT YOUR KISSES (IF I CAN'T HAVE YOUR LOVE)

IF HE CARED

IF I CAN'T HAVE YOU

IF I COULD LEARN TO LOVE (AS WELL AS I FIGHT)

IF I HAD A TALKING PICTURE OF YOU

IF I HAD YOU

IF I'M DREAMING, DON'T WAKE ME TOO SOON

IF LOVE WERE ALL

IF YOU BELIEVED IN ME

IF YOU COULD ONLY COME WITH ME

I GET THE BLUES WHEN IT RAINS

I GOT A CODE IN MY DOSE

I GUESS I'LL HAVE TO CHANGE MY PLAN (THE BLUE PAJAMA SONG)

I HAVE TO HAVE YOU

I KISS YOUR HAND, MADAME

I'LL ALWAYS BE IN LOVE WITH YOU

I'LL NEVER ASK FOR MORE

I'LL SEE YOU AGAIN

I'M A DREAMER, AREN'T WE ALL?

I MAY BE WRONG (BUT I THINK YOU'RE WONDERFUL)

I'M IN LOVE WITH YOU

I'M IN SEVENTH HEAVEN

I'M JUST A VAGABOND LOVER

I'M STILL CARING

I'M THE LAST OF THE RED HOT MAMMAS

I'M THE MEDICINE MAN FOR THE BLUES

I'M UNLUCKY AT GAMBLING

IN THE BOTTLE BLUES

I UPS TO HIM AND HE UPS TO ME

IT'S HARD TO LAUGH OR SMILE

I'VE GOT A FEELING I'M FALLING

JERICHO

JUNE MOON

JUNIOR

JUST AN HOUR OF LOVE

JUST YOU, JUST ME

KANSAS CITY KITTY

KEEPIN' MYSELF FOR YOU

LADY LUCK

LET'S SIT AND TALK ABOUT YOU

LITTLE BY LITTLE

LITTLE KISS EACH MORNING, A LITTLE KISS EACH NIGHT, A

LITTLE PAL

LIZA (ALL THE CLOUDS'LL ROLL AWAY)

LONELY TROUBADOUR

LOUISE

LOVABLE AND SWEET

LOVE, YOUR MAGIC SPELL IS EVERYWHERE

LOVE AIN'T NOTHIN' BUT THE BLUES

LOVE BOAT

LOW DOWN RHYTHM

MAMA DON'T ALLOW IT

MARCH OF THE GRENADIERS

MEAN TO ME

MISS YOU

MISTAKES

MOANIN' LOW

MORE THAN YOU KNOW

MY ANGELINE

MY FATE IS IN YOUR HANDS

MY KINDA LOVE

MY LITTLE LADY

MY LOVE PARADE

MY LUCKY STAR

MY MAN IS ON THE MAKE

MY MOTHER'S EYES

MY SIN

MY SONG OF THE NILE

MY SWEETER THAN SWEET

MY TIME IS YOUR TIME

MY TROUBLES ARE OVER

NEW ORLEANS BUMP

NOBODY BUT YOU

NO ONE ELSE BUT YOU

ONLY SONG I KNOW, THE

ORANGE BLOSSOM TIME

OR WHAT HAVE YOU?

OUTSIDE

OUT WHERE THE BLUES BEGIN

PAGAN LOVE SONG

PAINTING THE CLOUDS WITH SUNSHINE

PAREE, WHAT DID YOU DO TO ME?

PARIS, STAY THE SAME

PICCOLO PETE

PINE TOP'S BOOGIE WOOGIE

PING PONGO

PRECIOUS LITTLE THING CALLED LOVE, A

REACHING FOR SOMEONE (AND NOT FINDING ANYONE THERE)

ROMANCE

SATISFIED!

SATURDAY NIGHT FUNCTION

SAVE IT, PRETTY MAMA

SHE'S SUCH A COMFORT TO ME

SHIP WITHOUT A SAIL, A

SHOULD I?

SIBONEY

SING A LITTLE LOVE SONG

SINGIN' IN THE BATHTUB

SINGIN' IN THE RAIN

SMILING IRISH EYES

SOME SWEET DAY

SOMETHING TO LIVE FOR

SONG OF THE BAYOU

SONG OF THE MOONBEAMS

SO THE BLUEBIRDS AND THE BLACKBIRDS GOT TOGETHER

S'POSIN

SUNNY SIDE UP

SWANEE SHUFFLE

SWEET SAVANNAH SUE

TAIN'T NO SIN (TO TAKE OFF YOUR SKIN AND DANCE AROUND IN YOUR BONES)

TALE OF AN OYSTER, THE

TELL ME, WHAT IS LOVE?

THAT BLUE-EYED BABY FROM MEMPHIS

THAT'S YOU, BABY

THAT WONDERFUL SOMETHING

THEN YOU'VE NEVER BEEN BLUE

THROUGH (HOW CAN YOU SAY WE'RE THROUGH?)

TIP TOE THROUGH THE TULIPS WITH ME

TO BE IN LOVE

TOKAY

TOO LATE

TRUE BLUE LOU

TURN ON THE HEAT

'TWAS NOT SO LONG AGO

UNDERNEATH THE RUSSIAN MOON

USED TO YOU

VALENTINE

WAITING AT THE END OF THE ROAD

WAIT 'TIL YOU SEE MA CHERIE

WALKING WITH SUSIE

WAY I FEEL TODAY, THE

WEARY RIVER

WEDDING BELLS ARE BREAKING UP THAT OLD GANG OF MINE

WEDDING OF THE PAINTED DOLL, THE

WHAT A DAY!

WHAT WOULDN'T I DO FOR THAT MAN?

WHEN MY DREAMS COME TRUE

WHEN SUMMER IS GONE

WHERE IS THE SONG OF SONGS FOR ME?

WHERE THE SWEET FORGET-ME-NOTS REMEMBER

WHERE WOULD YOU GET YOUR COAT?

WHO WILL BE WITH YOU WHEN I'M FAR AWAY?

WHO WOULDN'T BE JEALOUS OF YOU?

WHY?

WHY CAN'T I?

WHY CAN'T YOU?

WHY DO YOU SUPPOSE?

WHY WAS I BORN?

WISHING AND WAITING FOR LOVE

WITH A SONG IN MY HEART

WITHOUT A SONG
WONDERFUL YOU
WOULDN'T IT BE WONDERFUL?
YOU DON'T KNOW PAREE
YOU DO SOMETHING TO ME
YOUR LOVE IS ALL THAT I CRAVE
YOUR MOTHER AND MINE
YOURS SINCERELY
YOU'VE GOT THAT THING
YOU'VE MADE ME HAPPY TODAY
YOU WERE MEANT FOR ME
YOU WOULDN'T FOOL ME, WOULD YOU?
ZIGEUNER

1930

ABSENCE MAKES THE HEART GROW
   FONDER (FOR SOMEBODY ELSE)
AIN'TCHA?
ALL THE KING'S HORSES
ALWAYS IN ALL WAYS
ANDALUCIA
AND THEN YOUR LIPS MET MINE
ANY OLD TIME
AROUND THE CORNER
AU REVOIR, PLEASANT DREAMS
BABY'S BIRTHDAY PARTY
BENCH IN THE PARK, A
BETTY CO-ED
BETWEEN THE DEVIL AND THE DEEP
   BLUE SEA
BEYOND THE BLUE HORIZON
BIDIN' MY TIME
BLUE, TURNING GREY OVER YOU
BLUE AGAIN
BLUE IS THE NIGHT
BODY AND SOUL
BOY! WHAT LOVE HAS DONE TO ME!
BUT NOT FOR ME
BUTTON UP YOUR HEART
BYE BYE BLUES
CAN THIS BE LOVE?

CASA LOMA STOMP
CHARMING
CHEERFUL LITTLE EARFUL
CHEER UP
CHIMES OF SPRING
COME OUT OF THE KITCHEN, MARY
   ANN
CONGRATULATIONS
COOKING BREAKFAST FOR THE ONE I
   LOVE
COTTAGE FOR SALE, A
CRYIN' FOR THE CAROLINES
CRYING MYSELF TO SLEEP
DANCING ON THE CEILING
DANCING WITH TEARS IN MY EYES
DON'T TELL HER WHAT HAPPENED TO
   ME
DOUBLE CHECK STOMP
DOWN THE RIVER OF GOLDEN DREAMS
DO YA LOVE ME?
DUST
ELEVEN MORE MONTHS AND TEN MORE
   DAYS
EMBRACEABLE YOU
EXACTLY LIKE YOU
FINE AND DANDY
FREE AND EASY, THE
FROGGY BOTTOM
FUNNY, DEAR, WHAT LOVE CAN DO
GEE, I'D LIKE TO MAKE YOU HAPPY
GEORGIA ON MY MIND
GET HAPPY
GIRL TROUBLE
GIVE ME A MOMENT PLEASE
GO HOME AND TELL YOUR MOTHER
GOOD FOR YOU—BAD FOR ME
GREAT INDOORS, THE
HANGIN' ON THE GARDEN GATE
HAPPY FEET
HARMONICA HARRY
HAVE A LITTLE FAITH IN ME
HERE COMES EMILY BROWN

HERE COMES THE SUN

HIGH SOCIETY BLUES

HITTIN' THE BOTTLE

I AM ONLY HUMAN AFTER ALL

I DON'T MIND WALKING IN THE RAIN

IF I COULD BE WITH YOU (ONE HOUR TONIGHT)

IF I WERE KING

I GOT RHYTHM

I LIKE TO DO THINGS FOR YOU

I'LL BE BLUE, JUST THINKING OF YOU

I LOVE YOU SO MUCH

I'M A DING DONG DADDY FROM DUMAS

I'M ALONE BECAUSE I LOVE YOU

I'M CONFESSIN' THAT I LOVE YOU

I'M FOLLOWING YOU

I'M GETTING MYSELF READY FOR YOU

I'M IN THE MARKET FOR YOU

I MISS A LITTLE MISS

I'M THINKING TONIGHT OF MY BLUE EYES

I'M TICKLED PINK WITH A BLUE-EYED BABY

I'M YOURS

IN MY LITTLE HOPE CHEST

INTO MY HEART

I STILL GET A THRILL (THINKING OF YOU)

IS THAT RELIGION?

IT HAPPENED IN MONTEREY

IT MUST BE TRUE

IT'S A GREAT LIFE (IF YOU DON'T WEAKEN)

IT SEEMS TO BE SPRING

I'VE GOT A CRUSH ON YOU

I WANT A LITTLE GIRL

JUNGLE DRUMS

JUST A GIGOLO

JUST A LITTLE CLOSER

KEEP YOUR UNDERSHIRT ON

KING'S HORSES, THE (AND THE KING'S MEN)

KISS WALTZ, THE

LADY, PLAY YOUR MANDOLIN

LAZY LOU'SIANA MOON

LET ME SING AND I'M HAPPY

LET'S FLY AWAY

LET'S GO EAT WORMS IN THE GARDEN

'LEVEN-THIRTY SATURDAY NIGHT

LIES

LINDA

LITTLE THINGS IN LIFE, THE

LITTLE WHITE LIES

LIVIN' IN THE SUNLIGHT, LOVIN' IN THE MOONLIGHT

LONELY

LONESOME LOVER

LOOKING AT YOU

LOOKING AT YOU (ACROSS THE BREAKFAST TABLE)

LOVE AIN'T NOTHIN' BUT THE BLUES

LOVE FOR SALE

LUCKY ME, LOVABLE YOU

LUCKY SEVEN

MADEMOISELLE IN NEW ROCHELLE

MALAGUEÑA

MAN FROM THE SOUTH, THE (WITH A BIG CIGAR IN HIS MOUTH)

MANHATTAN RAG

MARCH OF TIME, THE

MEMORIES OF YOU

MINNIE THE MERMAID

MISS WONDERFUL

MOON IS LOW, THE

MOONLIGHT ON THE COLORADO

MORE THAN YOU KNOW

MY BABY JUST CARES FOR ME

MY FUTURE JUST PASSED

MY IDEAL

MYSTERIOUS MOSE

NINA ROSA

NINE LITTLE MILES FROM TEN-TEN-TENNESSEE

NOBODY CARES IF I'M BLUE

ON A BLUE AND MOONLESS NIGHT

ON REVIVAL DAY

ON THE SUNNY SIDE OF THE STREET

OUT OF BREATH (AND SCARED TO DEATH OF YOU)

OVERNIGHT

PEANUT VENDOR, THE

PORTER'S LOVE SONG TO A CHAMBERMAID, A

PUTTIN' ON THE RITZ

RAGAMUFFIN ROMEO

REACHING FOR THE MOON

REMINISCING

RING DEM BELLS

ROCKIN' CHAIR

ROGUE SONG, THE

ROLLIN' DOWN THE RIVER

RO-RO-ROLLIN' ALONG

ROSES ARE FORGET-ME-NOTS

ST. JAMES INFIRMARY

SAM AND DELILAH

SATAN'S HOLIDAY

SEND FOR ME

SHEPHERD'S SERENADE, THE

SHE'S SUCH A COMFORT TO ME

SINGING A SONG TO THE STARS

SINGING A VAGABOND SONG

SING SOMETHING SIMPLE

SING YOU SINNERS

SO BEATS MY HEART FOR YOU

SOMEDAY I'LL FIND YOU

SOMETHING TO REMEMBER YOU BY

SOMEWHERE IN OLD WYOMING

SONG OF THE DAWN

SONG OF THE FOOL

SONG OF THE SHIRT, THE

SOON

SPRING, BEAUTIFUL SPRING

STEIN SONG (UNIVERSITY OF MAINE)

STRIKE UP THE BAND

SWEEPIN' THE CLOUDS AWAY

SWEETHEART OF MY STUDENT DAYS

SWEET JENNIE LEE

SWINGING IN A HAMMOCK

TAKE ME BACK TO MANHATTAN

TAMMANY

TELLING IT TO THE DAISIES

TEN CENTS A DANCE

THANK YOUR FATHER

THEM THERE EYES

THERE'S A WAH-WAH GAL IN AGUA CALIENTE

THERE'S DANGER IN YOUR EYES, CHERIE

THERE'S NOTHING WRONG WITH A KISS

THEY CUT DOWN THE OLD PINE TREE

THINGS THAT WERE MADE FOR LOVE, THE (YOU CAN'T TAKE AWAY)

THREE LITTLE WORDS

TIME ON MY HANDS

TO KNOW YOU IS TO LOVE YOU

TO MY MAMMY

TO WHOM IT MAY CONCERN

TRAIN WHISTLE BLUES

TRAV'LIN' ALL ALONE

TREAT ME ROUGH

TWO HEARTS IN THREE-QUARTER TIME

UNDER A TEXAS MOON

WALK RIGHT IN

WALTZ YOU SAVED FOR ME, THE

WAS I TO BLAME FOR FALLING IN LOVE WITH YOU?

WASN'T IT BEAUTIFUL WHILE IT LASTED?

WATCHING MY DREAMS GO BY

WE'RE FRIENDS AGAIN

WEST WIND

WHAT IS THIS THING CALLED LOVE?

WHAT'S THE USE?

WHAT WOULD I CARE?

WHEN A WOMAN LOVES A MAN

WHEN I'M LOOKING AT YOU

WHEN IT'S SPRINGTIME IN THE ROCKIES

WHEN KENTUCKY BIDS THE WORLD "GOOD MORNING"

WHEN THE ORGAN PLAYED AT
   TWILIGHT
WHEN YOUR HAIR HAS TURNED TO
   SILVER (I WILL LOVE YOU JUST THE
   SAME)
WHERE HAVE YOU BEEN?
WHITE DOVE, THE
WHY, OH WHY?
WITHOUT LOVE
WITH YOU
WOOD
WOULD YOU LIKE TO TAKE A WALK?
YOU BROUGHT A NEW KIND OF LOVE
   TO ME
YOU DARLIN'
YOU'RE DRIVING ME CRAZY
YOU'RE LUCKY TO ME
YOU'RE SIMPLY DELISH
YOU'RE THE ONE I CARE FOR
YOUR SMILES, YOUR TEARS
YOU WILL REMEMBER VIENNA
ZONKY

1931

ADIOS
ALL OF ME
AS TIME GOES BY
AT YOUR COMMAND
BEAUTIFUL LOVE
BEGGING FOR LOVE
BEND DOWN, SISTER
BLAH, BLAH, BLAH
BLUE KENTUCKY MOON
BLUES IN MY HEART
BLUE YODEL #8
BUILDING A HOME FOR YOU
BUSINESS IN F
BY MY SIDE
BY SPECIAL PERMISSION OF THE
   COPYRIGHT OWNERS, I LOVE YOU
BY THE RIVER SAINTE MARIE
BY THE SYCAMORE TREE

CALL ME DARLING
CAN'T YOU SEE?
COME TO ME
CONCENTRATIN' (ON YOU)
CREOLE RHAPSODY
CROSBY, COLUMBO, AND VALLEE
CUBAN LOVE SONG
DANCING IN THE DARK
DELISHIOUS
DO THE NEW YORK
DREAM A LITTLE DREAM OF ME
EGYPTIAN ELLA
ELIZABETH
FADED SUMMER LOVE, A
FALLING IN LOVE AGAIN (CAN'T HELP
   IT)
FIESTA
FOR YOU
GIVE ME YOUR AFFECTION, HONEY
GOIN' TO TOWN
GOODBYE TO LOVE
GOOD EVENING, FRIENDS
GOODNIGHT MOON
GOODNIGHT SWEETHEART
GOT A DATE WITH AN ANGEL
GOT THE BENCH, GOT THE PARK (BUT I
   HAVEN'T GOT YOU)
GREEN EYES
GUILTY
HALF CASTE WOMAN
HANG OUT THE STARS IN INDIANA
HAVE A HEART
HAVE YOU FORGOTTEN (THE THRILL)?
HEARTACHES
HELLO, BEAUTIFUL
HELLO, MY LOVER, GOODBYE
HELP YOURSELF TO HAPPINESS
HIGH AND LOW
HO-HUM
HOME
HOUR OF PARTING, THE
I APOLOGIZE

STRANGERS

SWEETHEARTS FOREVER

TAKE ME IN YOUR ARMS

TELL ME WHY YOU SMILE, MONA LISA

THANKSGIVIN'

THAT SILVER HAIRED DADDY OF MINE

THERE I GO DREAMING AGAIN

THERE'S OCEANS OF LOVE BY THE
    BEAUTIFUL SEA

THIS IS THE NIGHT

THREE ON A MATCH

THREE'S A CROWD

THROUGH THE YEARS

TOO MANY TEARS

TRAMPS AT SEA

UNDERNEATH THE HARLEM MOON

VOICE IN THE OLD VILLAGE CHOIR, THE

WAIL OF THE WINDS

WALTZING IN A DREAM

WAS THAT THE HUMAN THING TO DO?

WE JUST COULDN'T SAY GOODBYE

WE WILL ALWAYS BE SWEETHEARTS

WHAT A LIFE!

WHAT A PERFECT COMBINATION

WHAT WOULD YOU DO?

WHERE HAVE WE MET BEFORE?

WHERE THE BLUE OF THE NIGHT MEETS
    THE GOLD OF THE DAY

WILLOW WEEP FOR ME

WOODEN SOLDIER AND THE CHINA
    DOLL, THE

WOULD'JA FOR A BIG RED APPLE?

YOU CAN DEPEND ON ME

YOU CAN MAKE MY LIFE A BED OF
    ROSES

YOU'LL GET BY

YOU'RE AN OLD SMOOTHIE

YOU'RE BLASE

YOU'RE EVERYWHERE

YOU'RE THE ONE (YOU BEAUTIFUL
    SON-OF-A-GUN)

YOU'VE GOT ME IN THE PALM OF YOUR
    HAND

1933

ADORABLE

AFTER ALL, YOU'RE ALL I'M AFTER

AFTER SUNDOWN

AH, BUT IS IT LOVE?

AH, THE MOON IS HERE

AIN'TCHA GLAD?

AND SO GOODBYE

ANNIE DOESN'T LIVE HERE ANYMORE

ARE YOU MAKIN' ANY MONEY?

BEAUTIFUL GIRL

BLACK EYED SUSAN BROWN

BLACK MOONLIGHT

BLESS YOUR HEART

BLUE HOURS

BLUE LOU

BLUE PRELUDE

BUILD A LITTLE HOME

BY A WATERFALL

CARIOCA

CAVERNISM

CINDERELLA'S FELLA

COME UP AND SEE ME SOMETIME

COUNT YOUR BLESSINGS

(WHEN IT'S) DARKNESS ON THE DELTA

DAY YOU CAME ALONG, THE

DEEP FOREST

DID YOU EVER SEE A DREAM WALKING?

DINNER AT EIGHT

DOIN' THE UPTOWN LOWDOWN

DON'T BLAME ME

DOWN A CAROLINA LANE

DOWN THE OLD OX ROAD

DO YOUR DUTY

DROP ME OFF IN HARLEM

EASTER PARADE

EEL, THE

EMPEROR JONES

EVERYTHING I HAVE IS YOURS

FAREWELL TO ARMS

FLYING DOWN TO RIO

FOOL IN LOVE, A

FORTY-SECOND STREET

GATHER LIP ROUGE WHILE YOU MAY

GIMME A PIGFOOT

GIVE ME LIBERTY OR GIVE ME LOVE

GOING, GOING, GONE

GOOD MORNING GLORY

GOODNIGHT LITTLE GIRL OF MY
  DREAMS

GRASS IS GETTING GREENER ALL THE
  TIME, THE

GUY WHAT TAKES HIS TIME, A

HALLELUJAH, I'M A BUM

HANDFUL OF KEYS

HAPPY AS THE DAY IS LONG

HARLEM ON MY MIND

HARLEM SPEAKS

HAVE YOU EVER BEEN LONELY? (HAVE
  YOU EVER BEEN BLUE?)

HEAT WAVE

HEIGH HO, THE GANG'S ALL HERE

HERE YOU COME WITH LOVE

HEY, YOUNG FELLA

HOLD ME

HOLD YOUR MAN

HONEYMOON HOTEL

HOW COULD WE BE WRONG

HOW'S CHANCES?

HUSTLIN' AND BUSTLIN' FOR BABY

I CAN'T REMEMBER

I COULDN'T TELL THEM WHAT TO DO

I COVER THE WATERFRONT

I DON'T STAND A GHOST OF A CHANCE
  WITH YOU

IF I FORGET YOU

IF I LOVE AGAIN

IF IT'S TRUE

I GUESS IT HAD TO BE THAT WAY

I LIKE MOUNTAIN MUSIC

I'LL BE FAITHFUL

I'LL BE HARD TO HANDLE

I'LL TAKE AN OPTION ON YOU

I MAY BE DANCING WITH SOMEBODY
  ELSE

I'M DOWN IN THE DUMPS

I'M NO ANGEL

I'M SATISFIED

I'M YOUNG AND HEALTHY

IN THE PARK IN PAREE

IN THE VALLEY OF THE MOON

I RAISED MY HAT

ISN'T IT A PITY?

ISN'T IT HEAVENLY?

ISN'T THIS A NIGHT FOR LOVE?

IT ISN'T FAIR

IT MIGHT HAVE BEEN A DIFF'RENT
  STORY

IT'S ONLY A PAPER MOON

IT'S THE TALK OF THE TOWN

IT'S WITHIN YOUR POWER

IT WAS A NIGHT IN JUNE

I'VE GOTTA GET UP AND GO TO WORK

I'VE GOT THE WORLD ON A STRING

I'VE GOT TO PASS YOUR HOUSE (TO GET
  TO MY HOUSE)

I'VE GOT TO SING A TORCH SONG

I WAKE UP SMILING

I WANNA BE LOVED

I WANT YOU, I NEED YOU

JONNY

KEEP YOUNG AND BEAUTIFUL

LAST ROUND-UP, THE

LAZYBONES

LEARN TO CROON

LET ME GIVE MY HAPPINESS TO YOU

LET'S BEGIN

LET'S CALL IT A DAY

LET'S GO BAVARIAN

LONELY HEART

LONELY LANE

LOOK WHAT I'VE GOT

LOOK WHO'S HERE

LOUISVILLE LADY

LOVE IS THE SWEETEST THING

LOVE IS THE THING

LOVELY

LOVE SONGS OF THE NILE

LUCKY FELLA

MAN ON THE FLYING TRAPEZE, THE

MARCHING ALONG TOGETHER

MAYBE IT'S BECAUSE I LOVE YOU TOO
    MUCH

MINE

MISSISSIPPI BASIN

MOONLIGHT AND PRETZELS

MOON SONG

MOONSTRUCK

MORNING, NOON AND NIGHT

MOTEN SWING

MOTHER, THE QUEEN OF MY HEART

MUSIC MAKES ME

MY COUSIN IN MILWAUKEE

MY DANCING LADY

MY GALVESTON GAL

MY HAT'S ON THE SIDE OF MY HEAD

MY MOONLIGHT MADONNA

NIGHT OWL

NO MORE LOVE

NOT FOR ALL THE RICE IN CHINA

OLD MAN HARLEM

OLD SPINNING WHEEL, THE

ONE MINUTE TO ONE

ON THE TRAIL

OODLES OF NOODLES

ORCHIDS IN THE MOONLIGHT

ORCHID TO YOU, AN

OUR BIG LOVE SCENE

PEACH PICKING TIME DOWN IN
    GEORGIA

PETTIN' IN THE PARK

PIG GOT UP AND SLOWLY WALKED
    AWAY, THE

PUDDIN' HEAD JONES

QUEER NOTIONS

RAISIN' THE RENT

REFLECTIONS IN THE WATER

REMEMBER MY FORGOTTEN MAN

ROLL UP THE CARPET

ROSETTA

SHADOWS ON THE SWANEE

SHADOW WALTZ

SHAME ON YOU

SHANGHAI LIL

SHUFFLE OFF TO BUFFALO

SING A LITTLE LOW DOWN TUNE

SITTIN' ON A BACKYARD FENCE

SITTIN' ON A LOG (PETTIN' MY DOG)

SLIPPERY HORN

SMOKE GETS IN YOUR EYES

SNOWBALL

SOMETHING HAD TO HAPPEN

SOPHISTICATED LADY

STAY ON THE RIGHT SIDE, SISTER

STORMY WEATHER

STREET OF DREAMS

STRIKE ME PINK

SUPPER TIME

SWEETHEART DARLIN'

SWEET MADNESS

SWINGY LITTLE THINGY

TAKE ME FOR A BUGGY RIDE

TEMPTATION

THANKS

THAT DALLAS MAN

THAT'S THE RHYTHM OF THE DAY

THERE'S A BLUEBIRD AT MY WINDOW

THERE'S A CABIN IN THE PINES

THERE'S A LITTLE BIT OF YOU IN
    EVERY LOVE SONG

THERE'S SOMETHING ABOUT A SOLDIER

THEY CALL ME SISTER HONKY TONK

THIS IS ROMANCE

THIS LITTLE PIGGIE WENT TO MARKET

THIS TIME IT'S LOVE

THREE WISHES

TONY'S WIFE

TOUCH OF YOUR HAND, THE

TREE WAS A TREE, A

TROUBLE IN PARADISE

TRY A LITTLE TENDERNESS

TWO BUCK TIM FROM TIMBUCTOO
TWO TICKETS TO GEORGIA
UNDER A BLANKET OF BLUE
UNDERNEATH THE ARCHES
WEEP NO MORE, MY BABY
WE'LL MAKE HAY WHILE THE SUN SHINES
WE'RE IN THE MONEY (THE GOLD DIGGERS' SONG)
WE WERE THE BEST OF FRIENDS
WHAT HAVE WE GOT TO LOSE?
WHAT MORE CAN I ASK?
WHEN IT'S LAMP LIGHTIN' TIME IN THE VALLEY
WHEN YOU'RE OVER SIXTY, AND YOU FEEL LIKE SWEET SIXTEEN
WHITE JAZZ
WHO'S AFRAID OF THE BIG BAD WOLF?
WHY CAN'T THIS NIGHT GO ON FOREVER?
YESTERDAYS
YOU ARE TOO BEAUTIFUL
YOU GOTTA BE A FOOTBALL HERO
YOUNG AND HEALTHY
YOU OR NO ONE
YOU'RE DEVASTATING
YOU'RE GETTING TO BE A HABIT WITH ME
YOU'RE GONNA LOSE YOUR GAL
YOU'RE MINE, YOU
YOU'RE MY PAST, PRESENT, AND FUTURE
YOUR MOTHER'S SON-IN-LAW
YOU'VE GOT EVERYTHING
YOU'VE GOT ME CRYING AGAIN

1934

ALICE IN WONDERLAND
ALL I DO IS DREAM OF YOU
ALL THROUGH THE NIGHT
AND I STILL DO
ANYTHING GOES

AS LONG AS I LIVE
BABY, TAKE A BOW
BAD IN EVERY MAN, THE
BEAT OF MY HEART, THE
BELIEVE IT, BELOVED
BE STILL, MY HEART
BIG BAD WOLF WAS DEAD, THE
BIG JOHN'S SPECIAL
BLAME IT ON MY YOUTH
BLOW, GABRIEL, BLOW
BLUEBIRD OF HAPPINESS
BLUE FEELING
BLUE INTERLUDE
BLUE LAMENT
BLUE MOON
BLUE SKY AVENUE
BORN TO BE KISSED
BOULEVARD OF BROKEN DREAMS, THE
BREAKFAST BALL
BREEZE, THE (THAT'S BRINGIN' MY HONEY BACK TO ME)
BROADWAY'S GONE HILLBILLY
BUTTERFINGERS
CARRY ME BACK TO THE LONE PRAIRIE
CATTLE CALL, THE
CHAMPAGNE WALTZ, THE
CHIME BELLS
CHRISTMAS NIGHT IN HARLEM
COCKTAILS FOR TWO
COFFEE IN THE MORNING, KISSES IN THE NIGHT
COLLEGE RHYTHM
CONTINENTAL, THE
CROSS-EYED KELLY (FROM PENN-SYL-VAN-EYE-AY)
DAMES
DANCING IN THE MOONLIGHT
DAYBREAK EXPRESS
DEEP PURPLE
DON'T LET IT BOTHER YOU
DON'T LET YOUR LOVE GO WRONG
DON'T SAY GOODNIGHT

I FOUND A DREAM
IF THE MOON TURNS GREEN
IF YOU WERE MINE
I GOT LOVE
I GOT PLENTY O' NUTTIN'
I LIVE FOR LOVE
I'LL NEVER SAY "NEVER AGAIN" AGAIN
I LOVES YOU, PORGY
I'M A HUNDRED PERCENT FOR YOU
I'M GOIN' SHOPPIN' WITH YOU
I'M GROWING FONDER OF YOU
I'M IN THE MOOD FOR LOVE
I'M JUST AN ORDINARY HUMAN
I'M KEEPING THOSE KEEPSAKES FOR YOU
I'M LIVIN' IN A GREAT BIG WAY
I'M ON A SEE-SAW
I'M PAINTING THE TOWN RED
I'M SITTING HIGH ON A HILLTOP
I'M THE ECHO (YOU'RE THE SONG)
IN A BLUE AND PENSIVE MOOD
IN A LITTLE GYPSY TEA ROOM
I NEVER SAW A BETTER NIGHT
IN THE MIDDLE OF A KISS
I SAW HER AT EIGHT O'CLOCK
ISLE OF CAPRI
ISN'T LOVE THE GRANDEST THING?
ISN'T THIS A LOVELY DAY?
I SOLD MY HEART TO THE JUNK MAN
IT AIN'T NECESSARILY SO
I THREW A BEAN BAG AT THE MOON
IT MUST HAVE BEEN A DREAM
IT'S AN OLD SOUTHERN CUSTOM
IT'S EASY TO REMEMBER
IT'S THE ANIMAL IN ME
I'VE GOT A FEELIN' YOU'RE FOOLIN'
I'VE GOT AN INVITATION TO A DANCE
I'VE GOT A POCKETFUL OF SUNSHINE
I WAS LUCKY
I WISHED ON THE MOON
I WISH I WERE ALADDIN

I WOKE UP TOO SOON
I WON'T DANCE
JOCKEY ON THE CAROUSEL, THE
JUNE IN JANUARY
JUST ONCE AROUND THE CLOCK
JUST ONE OF THOSE THINGS
LADY IN RED, THE
LET'S DANCE
LIFE IS A SONG (LET'S SING IT TOGETHER)
LIGHTS OUT
LIKE A BOLT FROM THE BLUE
LITTLE BIT INDEPENDENT, A
LITTLE BROWN GAL
LITTLE GIRL BLUE
LITTLE THINGS YOU USED TO DO, THE
LITTLE WHITE GARDENIA, A
LOUISIANA FAIRY TALE
LOVE AND A DIME
LOVE DROPPED IN FOR TEA
LOVE IS A DANCING THING
LOVE IS JUST AROUND THE CORNER
LOVELY TO LOOK AT
LOVE ME FOREVER
LOVE PASSES BY
LULLABY OF BROADWAY
LULU'S BACK IN TOWN
MAD ABOUT THE BOY
MARCH WINDS AND APRIL SHOWERS
ME AND MARIE
MIDNIGHT IN PARIS
MINE ALONE
MISS BROWN TO YOU
MOON OVER MIAMI
MOST BEAUTIFUL GIRL IN THE WORLD, THE
MRS. WORTHINGTON (DON'T PUT YOUR DAUGHTER ON THE STAGE)
MUSIC GOES 'ROUND AND 'ROUND, THE
MY HEART IS AN OPEN BOOK
MY MAN'S GONE NOW

MY ROMANCE
MY VERY GOOD FRIEND, THE MILKMAN
NEW ORLEANS
NIGHT IS YOUNG, THE
NIGHT WIND
NOBODY'S DARLIN' BUT MINE
NO OTHER ONE
NO STRINGS (I'M FANCY FREE)
NOW I'M A LADY
NOW YOU'VE GOT ME DOING IT
OLE FAITHFUL
ON A SUNDAY AFTERNOON
ON TREASURE ISLAND
OREGON TRAIL, THE
OUTSIDE OF YOU
OVER MY SHOULDER
PAGE MISS GLORY
PARDON MY LOVE
PARIS IN THE SPRING
PICCOLINO, THE
PICTURE OF YOU WITHOUT ME, A
RECKLESS
RED HEADED WOMAN, A
RED SAILS IN THE SUNSET
REMINISCING IN TEMPO
RHYTHM AND ROMANCE
RHYTHM IN MY NURSERY RHYMES
RHYTHM IS OUR BUSINESS
RHYTHM OF THE RAIN
ROLL ALONG, COVERED WAGON
ROLL ALONG, PRAIRIE MOON
ROSE IN HER HAIR, THE
ROSETTA
SANDMAN
SHE'S A LATIN FROM MANHATTAN
SHOWBOAT SHUFFLE
SIMPLE THINGS IN LIFE, THE
SING BEFORE BREAKFAST
SONG OF THE OPEN ROAD
SO NICE SEEING YOU AGAIN
SOON
SPEAKING CONFIDENTIALLY

STAR GAZING
SUGAR PLUM
SUMMERTIME
SWEET MUSIC
TAKE IT EASY
TAKE ME BACK TO MY BOOTS AND
    SADDLE
TAKES TWO TO MAKE A BARGAIN
TELL ME THAT YOU LOVE ME
TENDER IS THE NIGHT
THANKS A MILLION
THAT'S WHAT YOU THINK
THERE'S A BOAT DAT'S LEAVIN' SOON
    FOR NEW YORK
THIEF IN THE NIGHT
THINGS MIGHT HAVE BEEN SO
    DIFFERENT
THRILLED
THROWIN' STONES AT THE SUN
TINY LITTLE FINGERPRINTS
TOP HAT, WHITE TIE AND TAILS
TRUCKIN'
TWENTY-FOUR HOURS A DAY
TWO FOR TONIGHT
TWO TOGETHER
WAY BACK HOME
WHAT A LITTLE MOONLIGHT CAN DO
WHAT A WONDERFUL WORLD
WHAT'S THE REASON (I'M NOT PLEASIN'
    YOU)?
WHEN A GYPSY MAKES HIS VIOLIN CRY
WHEN I GROW TOO OLD TO DREAM
WHEN I GROW UP
WHEN LOVE KNOCKS AT YOUR HEART
WHEN THE SUN GOES DOWN
WHEN YOU'VE GOT A LITTLE
    SPRINGTIME IN YOUR HEART
WHERE AM I?
WHOSE BIG BABY ARE YOU?
WHOSE HONEY ARE YOU?
WHY DREAM?
WHY SHOULDN'T I?
WHY STARS COME OUT AT NIGHT

WILL LOVE FIND A WAY?
WITHOUT A WORD OF WARNING
WOMAN IS A SOMETIME THING, A
WORDS ARE IN MY HEART, THE
WOULD THERE BE LOVE?
YANKEE DOODLE NEVER WENT TO
   TOWN
YOU ARE MY LUCKY STAR
YOU FIT INTO THE PICTURE
YOU LET ME DOWN
YOU'RE A HEAVENLY THING
YOU'RE ALL I NEED
YOU'RE AN ANGEL
YOU'RE MY THRILL
YOU'RE SO DARN CHARMING
YOU TOOK THE WORDS RIGHT OUT OF
   MY MOUTH
ZING! WENT THE STRINGS OF MY HEART

1936

AFTERGLOW
AH STILL SUITS ME
ALABAMA BARBECUE
ALL MY LIFE
AM I GONNA HAVE TROUBLE WITH
   YOU?
AT THE CODFISH BALL
AWAKE IN A DREAM
BALBOA
BEAUTIFUL LADY IN BLUE, A
BIG CHIEF DE SOTA
BLUE PRAIRIE
BLUE RHYTHM FANTASY
BOJANGLES OF HARLEM
BREAKIN' IN A PAIR OF SHOES
BROKEN RECORD, THE
BUT DEFINITELY
BUT WHERE ARE YOU?
BYE BYE BABY
CHRISTOPHER COLUMBUS
CLARINET LAMENT
CLING TO ME

CLOSE TO ME
COOL WATER
COPPER-COLORED GAL
CRAZY WITH LOVE
CROSS PATCH
DANCING UNDER THE STARS
DARLING, NOT WITHOUT YOU
DAY I LET YOU GET AWAY, THE
DID I REMEMBER?
DID YOUR MOTHER COME FROM
   IRELAND?
DINNER FOR ONE, PLEASE JAMES
DOES YOUR HEART BEAT FOR ME?
DOIN' THE SUSI-Q
DOWN IN THE DEPTHS (ON THE
   NINETIETH FLOOR)
EARLY BIRD
EASY TO LOVE
ECHOES OF HARLEM
EMPTY SADDLES
EVERY MINUTE OF THE HOUR
EVERYTHING'S IN RHYTHM WITH MY
   HEART
FANCY MEETING YOU
FINE ROMANCE, A
FLOATIN' DOWN TO COTTON TOWN
FOLLOW YOUR HEART
GAY RANCHERO, A (LAS ALTENITAS)
GET THEE BEHIND ME SATAN
GIVE ME A HEART TO SING TO
GLAD TO BE UNHAPPY
GLOOMY SUNDAY
GLORY OF LOVE, THE
GOODNIGHT, MY LOVE
GOODY GOODY
GUESS WHO
HARLEM SPEAKS
HAWAIIAN WAR CHANT
HEART IS QUICKER THAN THE EYE, THE
HE HASN'T A THING EXCEPT ME
HERE'S LOVE IN YOUR EYE
HEY, BABE, HEY

HEY, WHAT DID THE BLUEBIRD SAY?

HILLS OF OLD WYOMIN', THE

I CAN'T ESCAPE FROM YOU

I CAN'T GET STARTED

I DON'T WANT TO MAKE HISTORY (I JUST WANT TO MAKE LOVE)

I'D RATHER DRINK MUDDY WATER

I'D RATHER LEAD A BAND

I FEEL LIKE A FEATHER IN THE BREEZE

IF YOU LOVE ME

I HOPE GABRIEL LIKES MY MUSIC

I'LL NEVER TELL YOU I LOVE YOU

I'LL SING YOU A THOUSAND LOVE SONGS

I'LL STAND BY

I LOVE TO SING-A

I'M A FOOL FOR LOVING YOU

I'M AN OLD COW HAND (FROM THE RIO GRANDE)

I'M BUILDING UP TO AN AWFUL LETDOWN

I'M GONNA CLAP MY HANDS

I'M GONNA SIT RIGHT DOWN AND WRITE MYSELF A LETTER

I'M IN A DANCING MOOD

I'M PUTTING ALL MY EGGS IN ONE BASKET

I'M SHOOTING HIGH

IN A SENTIMENTAL MOOD

I NEARLY LET LOVE GO SLIPPING THROUGH MY FINGERS

IN THE CHAPEL IN THE MOONLIGHT

I'SE A-MUGGIN'

IS IT TRUE WHAT THEY SAY ABOUT DIXIE?

ISLAND IN THE WEST INDIES

ISN'T LOVE THE STRANGEST THING?

IT'S A SIN TO TELL A LIE

IT'S DE-LOVELY

IT'S GOT TO BE LOVE

IT'S GREAT TO BE IN LOVE AGAIN

IT'S LOVE I'M AFTER

IT'S NO FUN

I'VE GOT MY FINGERS CROSSED

I'VE GOT TO GET HOT

I'VE GOT YOU UNDER MY SKIN

I WANNA GO TO THE ZOO

I WISHED ON THE MOON

KING OF SWING

KNICK KNACKS ON THE MANTEL

KNOCK, KNOCK, WHO'S THERE?

LADY DANCES, THE

LAST NIGHT WHEN WE WERE YOUNG

LAUGHING IRISH EYES

LET MY SONG FILL YOUR HEART

LET'S CALL A HEART A HEART

LET'S FACE THE MUSIC AND DANCE

LET'S SING AGAIN

LET YOURSELF GO

LIFE BEGINS AT SWEET SIXTEEN

LIFE BEGINS WHEN YOU'RE IN LOVE

LITTLE HOUSE THAT LOVE BUILT, THE

LITTLE ROSE OF THE RANCHO

LITTLE SKIPPER FROM HEAVEN ABOVE, A

LONG AGO AND FAR AWAY

LOST

LOVE CAME OUT OF THE NIGHT

LOVE IS LIKE A CIGARETTE

LOVELY LADY

MAGNOLIAS IN THE MOONLIGHT

MAKE BELIEVE BALLROOM

MANHATTAN MERRY-GO-ROUND

MARY HAD A LITTLE LAMB

ME AND THE MOON

MELODY FROM THE SKY, A

MIDNIGHT BLUE

MILKMAN'S MATINEE, THE

MISTER DEEP BLUE SEA

MOONBURN

MOON IS GRINNING AT ME, THE

MOONRISE ON THE LOWLANDS

MORE I KNOW YOU, THE

MUSIC IN THE NIGHT

MUTINY IN THE PARLOR

MY HEART AND I

MY KINGDOM FOR A KISS

MY LAST AFFAIR

NEVER GONNA DANCE

NIGHT IS YOUNG AND YOU'RE SO BEAUTIFUL, THE

NO REGRETS

NOW OR NEVER

NOW THAT SUMMER IS GONE

OCCIDENTAL WOMAN (IN AN ORIENTAL MOOD FOR LOVE)

OH, MY GOODNESS

ONE, TWO, BUTTON YOUR SHOE

ONE NEVER KNOWS, DOES ONE?

ONE NIGHT IN MONTE CARLO

ONE ROSE, THE (THAT'S LEFT IN MY HEART)

ON THE BEACH AT BALI-BALI

ON THE RIO GRANDE

ON YOUR TOES

OOOH! LOOK-A THERE, AIN'T SHE PRETTY?

ORGAN GRINDER'S SWING

OUT WHERE THE BLUE BEGINS

OZARKS ARE CALLIN' ME HOME, THE

PANIC IS ON, THE

PENNIES FROM HEAVEN

PETER PIPER

PICK YOURSELF UP

PICTURE ME WITHOUT YOU

PLEASE KEEP ME IN YOUR DREAMS

QUIET NIGHT

RAINBOW ON THE RIVER

RAP TAP ON WOOD

RED, HOT AND BLUE

RENDEZVOUS WITH A DREAM

RHYTHM SAVED THE WORLD

RIDIN' HIGH

RIGAMAROLE

RIGHT SOMEBODY TO LOVE, THE

ROBINS AND ROSES

'ROUND THE OLD DESERTED FARM

SAILOR BEWARE

SAN FRANCISCO

SASKATCHEWAN

SAVE ME, SISTER

SHE SHALL HAVE MUSIC

SHOE SHINE BOY

SING, BABY, SING

SING, SING, SING

SING AN OLD FASHIONED SONG (TO A YOUNG SOPHISTICATED LADY)

SING ME A SWING SONG

SKELETON IN THE CLOSET, THE

SLAUGHTER ON TENTH AVENUE

SO DO I

SOUTH SEA ISLAND MAGIC

SPREADIN' RHYTHM AROUND

STAR FELL OUT OF HEAVEN, A

STARS IN MY EYES

STEALIN' APPLES

STOMPIN' AT THE SAVOY

STOP! YOU'RE BREAKIN' MY HEART

SUMMER NIGHT

SWAMP FIRE

SWING, BROTHER, SWING

SWINGIN' THE JINX AWAY

SWINGTIME IN THE ROCKIES

'TAINT NO USE

TAKE ANOTHER GUESS

TAKE MY HEART (AND DO WITH IT WHAT YOU PLEASE)

TEXAS TORNADO

THAT MOMENT OF MOMENTS

THAT'S WHAT I WANT FOR CHRISTMAS

THERE IS NO GREATER LOVE

THERE ISN'T ANY LIMIT TO MY LOVE

THERE'S A BRIDLE HANGIN' ON THE WALL

THERE'S A SMALL HOTEL

THERE'S SOMETHING IN THE AIR

THESE FOOLISH THINGS (REMIND ME OF YOU)

THIS'LL MAKE YOU WHISTLE

THRU THE COURTESY OF LOVE
THUNDER OVER PARADISE
TO LOVE YOU AND TO LOSE YOU
TOO GOOD FOR THE AVERAGE MAN
TORMENTED
TOUCH OF GOD'S HAND, THE
TOUCH OF YOUR LIPS, THE
TO YOU, SWEETHEART, ALOHA
TWILIGHT ON THE TRAIL
TWINKLE, TWINKLE, LITTLE STAR
UNTIL THE REAL THING COMES ALONG
   (IT WILL HAVE TO DO)
UNTIL TODAY
US ON A BUS
WAH-HOO!
WAKE UP AND SING
WALTZ IN SWINGTIME
WALTZ WAS BORN IN VIENNA, A
WAY YOU LOOK TONIGHT, THE
WE SAW THE SEA
WHAT'S THE NAME OF THAT SONG?
WHEN A LADY MEETS A GENTLEMAN
   DOWN SOUTH
WHEN DID YOU LEAVE HEAVEN?
WHEN I'M WITH YOU
WHEN IT'S ROUND-UP TIME IN HEAVEN
WHEN LIGHTS ARE LOW
WHEN MY DREAMBOAT COMES HOME
WHERE THE LAZY RIVER GOES BY
WHIFFENPOOF SONG, THE
WILL I EVER KNOW?
WITH A BANJO ON MY KNEE
WITH ALL MY HEART
WITH THEE I SWING
WORDS WITHOUT MUSIC
WORLD IS MINE, THE
WOULD YOU?
YEARNING FOR LOVE
YOU
YOU BETTER GO NOW
YOU CAME TO MY RESCUE
YOU CAN'T PULL THE WOOL OVER MY
   EYES

YOU DO THE DARNDEST THINGS, BABY
YOU DROPPED ME LIKE A RED HOT
   PENNY
YOU GOTTA S-M-I-L-E TO BE
   H-A-DOUBLE P-Y
YOU HIT THE SPOT
YOU'LL HAVE TO SWING IT (MR.
   PAGANINI)
YOU'RE NOT THE KIND
YOU'RE SLIGHTLY TERRIFIC
YOU'RE THE CURE FOR WHAT AILS ME
YOUR FEET'S TOO BIG
YOURS TRULY IS TRULY YOURS
YOU STARTED ME DREAMING
YOU STAYED AWAY TOO LONG
YOU TURNED THE TABLES ON ME
YOU WERE THERE

1937

AFRAID TO DREAM
AFTER YOU
ALIBI BABY
ALLEGHENY AL
ALL GOD'S CHILLUN GOT RHYTHM
ALL'S FAIR IN LOVE AND WAR
ALL YOU WANT TO DO IS DANCE
ALWAYS AND ALWAYS
AM I IN LOVE?
AZURE
BABES IN ARMS
(I'VE GOT) BEGINNER'S LUCK
BEI MIR BIST DU SCHOEN (MEANS THAT
   YOU'RE GRAND)
BIG APPLE, THE
BIG BOY BLUE
BLACK BUTTERFLY
BLAME IT ON THE RHUMBA
BLOSSOMS ON BROADWAY
BLUE HAWAII
BLUE VENETIAN WATERS
BOB WHITE (WHATCHA GONNA SWING
   TONIGHT?)

BOO-HOO
BY STRAUSS
CAN I FORGET YOU?
CARAVAN
CARELESSLY
CAUSE MY BABY SAYS IT'S SO
CRESCENDO IN BLUE
CUBAN PETE
DANCING UNDER THE STARS
DANGER—LOVE AT WORK
DEDICATED TO YOU
DIMINUENDO IN BLUE
DIPSY DOODLE, THE
DONKEY SERENADE
DON'T EVER CHANGE
DOWN WITH LOVE
DUSK IN UPPER SANDUSKY
DUSK ON THE DESERT
EASY LIVING
EBB TIDE
EVERYBODY SING
EVERYTHING YOU SAID CAME TRUE
FAREWELL TO DREAMS
FIFI
FIRST TIME I SAW YOU, THE
FOGGY DAY, A (IN LONDON TOWN)
FOLKS WHO LIVE ON THE HILL, THE
FOOLIN' MYSELF
FOR DANCERS ONLY
GEE, BUT YOU'RE SWELL
GEORGIANNA
GETTING SOME FUN OUT OF LIFE
GIRL ON THE POLICE GAZETTE, THE
GOD'S COUNTRY
GONE WITH THE WIND
GOOD-BYE JONAH
GOOD MORNIN'
GONNA GOO, THE
GOT A PAIR OF NEW SHOES
GREAT SPECKLED BIRD
HARBOR LIGHTS
HAVE YOU GOT ANY CASTLES, BABY?

HAVE YOU MET MISS JONES?
HEAD OVER HEELS IN LOVE
HE AIN'T GOT RHYTHM
HEART OF STONE, A
HEAVEN HELP THIS HEART OF MINE
HERE'S LOVE IN YOUR EYE
HIGH, WIDE AND HANDSOME
HORSE WITH THE DREAMY EYES, THE
HOW COULD YOU?
HOW YA BABY?
I CAN'T BE BOTHERED NOW
I CAN'T LOSE THAT LONGING FOR YOU
I DOUBLE DARE YOU
I'D RATHER BE RIGHT
IF IT'S THE LAST THING I DO
IF MY HEART COULD ONLY TALK
I HIT A NEW HIGH
I KNOW NOW
I'LL TAKE ROMANCE
IMAGE OF YOU, THE
I'M FEELIN' LIKE A MILLION
I'M WISHING
IN A LITTLE DUTCH KINDERGARTEN
IN A LITTLE HULA HEAVEN
IN THE SHADE OF THE NEW APPLE
  TREE
IN THE STILL OF THE NIGHT
IN YOUR OWN LITTLE WAY
I SEE YOUR FACE BEFORE ME
I STILL LOVE TO KISS YOU GOODNIGHT
IT LOOKS LIKE RAIN IN CHERRY
  BLOSSOM LANE
IT'S RAINING SUNBEAMS
IT'S SWELL OF YOU
IT'S THE NATURAL THING TO DO
I'VE A STRANGE NEW RHYTHM IN MY
  HEART
I'VE GONE ROMANTIC ON YOU
I'VE GOT A NEW LEASE ON LOVE
I'VE GOT MY HEART SET ON YOU
I'VE GOT MY LOVE TO KEEP ME WARM
I'VE GOT TO BE A RUG CUTTER

I WANT YOU FOR CHRISTMAS

I WAS SAYING TO THE MOON

I WISH I WERE IN LOVE AGAIN

JAMBOREE

JOHNNY ONE NOTE

JOHN'S IDEA

JOINT IS JUMPIN', THE

JOSEPHINE

JUST A MOOD

JUST A QUIET EVENING

LADY IS A TRAMP, THE

LAST NIGHT I DREAMED OF YOU

LEANING ON THE LAMP POST

LET'S CALL THE WHOLE THING OFF

LET'S GIVE LOVE ANOTHER CHANCE

LET'S HAVE ANOTHER CIGARETTE

LET'S PUT OUR HEADS TOGETHER

LIFE GOES TO A PARTY

LISTEN MY CHILDREN AND YOU SHALL
    HEAR

LITTLE OLD LADY

LITTLE ROCK GETAWAY

LOCH LOMOND

LOVE AND LEARN

LOVE BUG WILL BITE YOU, THE (IF YOU
    DON'T WATCH OUT)

LOVE IS A MERRY-GO-ROUND

LOVE IS NEVER OUT OF SEASON

LOVE IS ON THE AIR TONIGHT

LOVELINESS OF YOU, THE

LOVELY ONE

LOVE SONG OF LONG AGO, A

MAY I HAVE THE NEXT ROMANCE WITH
    YOU?

ME, MYSELF AND I (ARE ALL IN LOVE
    WITH YOU)

MEANEST THING YOU EVER DID WAS
    KISS ME, THE

MELODY FOR TWO

MERRY-GO-ROUND BROKE DOWN, THE

MILLER'S DAUGHTER MARIANNE, THE

MOANIN' IN THE MORNIN'

MOOD THAT I'M IN, THE

MOON GOT IN MY EYES, THE

MOONLIGHT AND SHADOWS

MOONLIGHT ON THE CAMPUS

MOON OF MANAKOORA, THE

MR. GHOST GOES TO TOWN

MY CABIN OF DREAMS

MY FINE FEATHERED FRIEND

MY FUNNY VALENTINE

MY HEART IS SINGING

MY LITTLE BUCKAROO

NEVER IN A MILLION YEARS

NEVER SHOULD HAVE TOLD YOU

NICE WORK IF YOU CAN GET IT

NOBODY MAKES A PASS AT ME

NO MORE TEARS

OLD FLAME NEVER DIES, AN

ON A LITTLE BAMBOO BRIDGE

ONCE IN A WHILE

ONE IN A MILLION

ONE O'CLOCK JUMP

OUR PENTHOUSE ON THIRD AVENUE

OUR SONG

PANAMANIA

PECKIN'

PLEASE PARDON US, WE'RE IN LOVE

POPCORN MAN

POSIN'

POWERHOUSE

QUAKER CITY JAZZ

REMEMBER ME?

ROCK IT FOR ME

ROLL 'EM

ROLLIN' PLAINS

ROSALIE

ROSES IN DECEMBER

SAIL ALONG, SILV'RY MOON

SAILBOAT IN THE MOONLIGHT, A

SATAN TAKES A HOLIDAY

SCATTIN' AT THE KIT KAT

SEAL IT WITH A KISS

YAM, THE
YANCEY SPECIAL
YOU COULDN'T BE CUTER
YOU GO TO MY HEAD
YOU LEAVE ME BREATHLESS
YOU MUST HAVE BEEN A BEAUTIFUL
   BABY
YOU'RE AS PRETTY AS A PICTURE
YOU'RE A SWEET LITTLE HEADACHE
YOU'RE THE ONLY STAR (IN MY BLUE
   HEAVEN)

1939

ADDRESS UNKNOWN
AFTER ALL
ALL IN FUN
ALL I REMEMBER IS YOU
ALL THE THINGS YOU ARE
ANATOLE (OF PARIS)
AND THE ANGELS SING
APPLE FOR THE TEACHER, AN
ARE YOU HAVIN' ANY FUN?
ARMY AIR CORPS, THE
AT LEAST YOU COULD SAY HELLO
AT THE BALALAIKA
BABALU
BABY, DON'T TELL ON ME
BABY, WHAT ELSE CAN I DO?
BABY ME
BACK TO BACK
BEER BARREL POLKA
BLAME IT ON MY LAST AFFAIR
BLESS YOU
BLUE EVENING
BLUE ORCHIDS
BLUE RAIN
BOLERO AT THE SAVOY
BOOGIE WOOGIE MAXIXE
BOY MEETS HORN
BOYS IN THE BACK ROOM, THE
BUT IN THE MORNING, NO!

CAN I HELP IT?
CARELESS
CHEW, CHEW, CHEW, CHEW YOUR
   BUBBLE GUM
CINDERELLA, STAY IN MY ARMS
COMES LOVE
CONCERT IN THE PARK
COULD BE
CUCKOO IN THE CLOCK
DARN THAT DREAM
DAY IN—DAY OUT
DEEP PURPLE
DING-DONG! THE WITCH IS DEAD
DO I LOVE YOU?
DON'T WORRY 'BOUT ME
DON'T YOU MISS YOUR BABY?
DRUMMIN' MAN
EAST SIDE OF HEAVEN
EL RANCHO GRANDE
ESPECIALLY FOR YOU
FAITHFUL FOREVER
FIDGETY JOE
FLYIN' HOME
FRIENDSHIP
GIVE IT BACK TO THE INDIANS
GOD BLESS AMERICA
GO FLY A KITE
GOOD FOR NOTHIN' BUT LOVE
GOOD MORNING
GOODNIGHT, MY BEAUTIFUL
GOTTA GET SOME SHUT-EYE
HANG YOUR HEART ON A HICKORY
   LIMB
HAPPY BIRTHDAY TO LOVE
HAVE MERCY
HEAVEN CAN WAIT
HEAVEN IN MY ARMS
HOLD TIGHT—HOLD TIGHT (WANT SOME
   SEA FOOD, MAMA)
HOME IN THE CLOUDS, A
HONG KONG BLUES
HONKY TONK TRAIN

HONOLULU
HOW STRANGE?
HUCKLEBERRY DUCK
I CAN'T AFFORD TO DREAM
I DIDN'T KNOW WHAT TIME IT WAS
IF I DIDN'T CARE
IF I HAD MY LIFE TO LIVE OVER
IF I KNEW THEN (WHAT I KNOW NOW)
IF I ONLY HAD A BRAIN
IF I ONLY HAD A HEART
IF I ONLY HAD THE NERVE
IF I WERE SURE OF YOU
IF YOU EVER CHANGE YOUR MIND
I GET ALONG WITHOUT YOU VERY WELL
I LIKE TO RECOGNIZE THE TUNE
I'LL KEEP ON LOVING YOU
I'LL REMEMBER
I'M CHECKING OUT—GO'OM BYE
I'M FIT TO BE TIED
I'M IN LOVE WITH THE HONORABLE MR. SO AND SO
I'M SORRY FOR MYSELF
IN AN EIGHTEENTH CENTURY DRAWING ROOM
INDIAN SUMMER
I NEVER KNEW HEAVEN COULD SPEAK
IN THE MOOD
I ONLY WANT A BUDDY, NOT A SWEETHEART
I POURED MY HEART INTO A SONG
IS IT POSSIBLE?
I THOUGHT ABOUT YOU
IT MAKES NO DIFFERENCE NOW
IT'S A HUNDRED TO ONE
IT'S ALL YOURS
IT'S FUNNY TO EVERYONE BUT ME
IT'S MY TURN NOW
IT'S NEVER TOO LATE (TO SAY YOU'RE SORRY)
I WANT MY SHARE OF LOVE
I WON'T BELIEVE IT
JITTERBUG, THE

JUMPIN' AT THE WOODSIDE
JUMPIN' JIVE, THE
JUST A DREAM
JUST FOR A THRILL
KATIE WENT TO HAITI
LADY'S IN LOVE WITH YOU, THE
LAMP IS LOW, THE
LAST NIGHT
LAST TWO WEEKS IN JULY, THE
LET'S MAKE MEMORIES TONIGHT
LET'S SAY GOODBYE
LET'S STOP THE CLOCK
LILACS IN THE RAIN
LITTLE MAN WHO WASN'T THERE, THE
LITTLE RED FOX, THE (N'YA, N'YA, YA CAN'T CATCH ME)
LITTLE SIR ECHO
LOVE NEVER WENT TO COLLEGE
LOVER IS BLUE, A
LOW DOWN RHYTHM IN A TOP HAT
LYDIA, THE TATTOOED LADY
MAKE WITH THE KISSES
MAN AND HIS DREAM, A
MAN WITH THE MANDOLIN, THE
MANY DREAMS AGO
MARY'S IDEA
MASQUERADE IS OVER, THE
MELANCHOLY LULLABY
MELANCHOLY MOOD
MILE AFTER MILE
MOON IS A SILVER DOLLAR, THE
MOONLIGHT SERENADE
MOON LOVE
MOONRAY
MY LAST GOODBYE
MY LOVE FOR YOU
MY PRAYER
MY TWILIGHT DRAM
NEAPOLITAN LOVE SONG
NEW MOON AND AN OLD SERENADE, A
NIGHT MUST FALL
OCTOROON

OH, YOU CRAZY MOON

OH JOHNNY, OH JOHNNY, OH!

OLD CURIOSITY SHOP, AN

OLD FASHIONED TUNE IS ALWAYS NEW, AN

OLD MILL WHEEL

ONE, TWO, THREE, KICK

ONLY WHEN YOU'RE IN MY ARMS

OUR LOVE

OVER THE RAINBOW

PEACE, BROTHER

PENNY SERENADE

RAINBOW VALLEY

RENDEZVOUS TIME IN PAREE

ROMANCE RUNS IN THE FAMILY

RUN, RABBIT, RUN

RUNNING THROUGH MY MIND

SCATTERBRAIN

SENT FOR YOU YESTERDAY, AND HERE YOU COME TODAY

SHE HAD TO GO AND LOSE IT AT THE ASTOR

SHOOT THE SHERBET TO ME, HERBERT

SING, MY HEART

SING A SONG OF SUNBEAMS

SING SOMETHING SIMPLE

SNUG AS A BUG IN A RUG

SO LONG, IT'S BEEN GOOD TO KNOW YOU

SO MANY TIMES

SOME OTHER SPRING

SOMETHING I DREAMED LAST NIGHT

SONG OF THE METRONOME

SOUTH AMERICAN WAY

SOUTH OF THE BORDER (DOWN MEXICO WAY)

SOUTH RAMPART STREET PARADE

SPEAKING OF HEAVEN

SPEAK TO ME OF LOVE

STAIRWAY TO THE STARS

START THE DAY RIGHT

STILL THE BLUEBIRD SINGS

STOP! IT'S WONDERFUL

STOP KICKING MY HEART AROUND

STRANGE ENCHANTMENT

STRANGE FRUIT

SUNRISE SERENADE

SWINGIN' A DREAM

TABLE IN THE CORNER, A

TAINT WHAT YOU DO (IT'S THE WAY THAT'CHA DO IT)

TARA'S THEME

TEARS FROM MY INKWELL

TEETER TOTTER TESSIE

THAT LUCKY FELLOW

THAT SENTIMENTAL SANDWICH

THAT SLY OLD GENTLEMAN (FROM FEATHERBED LANE)

THERE'LL ALWAYS BE AN ENGLAND

THINGS THAT MIGHT HAVE BEEN

THIS IS IT

THIS IS NO DREAM

THIS NIGHT WILL BE MY SOUVENIR

THREE LITTLE FISHIES

TOMORROW NIGHT

TOOTIN' THROUGH THE ROOF

TO YOU

TRAFFIC JAM

TRUCK DRIVERS BLUES

TURN ON THE OLD MUSIC BOX

TWO BLIND LOVES

UNDECIDED

VAGABOND DREAMS

WANDERLUST

WELL, ALL RIGHT!

WELL, DID YOU EVAH? (WHAT A SWELL PARTY THIS IS)

WE'RE OFF TO SEE THE WIZARD

WE'VE COME A LONG WAY TOGETHER

WHAT A LIFE!

WHAT GOES UP MUST COME DOWN

WHAT'S NEW?

WHEN LOVE BECKONED

WHEN WINTER COMES

WHITE SAILS

WHY BEGIN AGAIN? (PASTEL BLUE)
WISHING (WILL MAKE IT SO)
WOODCHOPPER'S BALL
YOU AND YOUR LOVE
YOU ARE MY FLOWER
YOU GROW SWEETER AS THE YEARS
  GO BY
YOU'RE A LUCKY GUY
YOU'RE SO DESIRABLE
YOURS FOR A SONG
YOU TAUGHT ME TO LOVE AGAIN
YOU WILL REMEMBER VIENNA

1940

ACCIDENT'LY ON PURPOSE
AFTER HOURS
ALL THIS AND HEAVEN TOO
ALL TOO SOON
ALONG THE SANTA FE TRAIL
AM I PROUD?
AND SO DO I
ANGEL
ANGEL IN DISGUISE
APPLE BLOSSOMS AND CHAPEL BELLS
APRIL PLAYED THE FIDDLE
BABY, I DONE GOT WISE
BACK BEAT BOOGIE
BACK IN THE SADDLE AGAIN
BAD HUMOR MAN, THE
BALLAD FOR AMERICANS
BEAT ME DADDY, EIGHT TO THE BAR
BECAUSE OF YOU
BETWEEN 18TH AND 19TH ON CHESTNUT
  STREET
BIG NOISE FROM WINNETKA
BLUEBIRDS IN THE MOONLIGHT
BLUE LOVEBIRD
BLUEBERRY HILL
BLUES ON PARADE
BOOG-IT

BREEZE AND I, THE
BUDS WON'T BUD
CABIN IN THE SKY
CALL OF THE CANYON
CAN'T GET INDIANA OFF MY MIND
CHARMING LITTLE FAKER
CLEAR OUT OF THIS WORLD
CONFUCIUS SAY
CORN SILK
COTTON TAIL
CROSSTOWN
DANCING ON A DIME
DAY DREAMS COME TRUE AT NIGHT
DEAREST, DAREST I?
DEN OF INIQUITY
DEVIL MAY CARE
DOLIMITE
DOWN ARGENTINA WAY
DO YOU CALL THAT A BUDDY?
DO YOU KNOW WHY?
DREAMING OUT LOUD
DREAM VALLEY
EASY DOES IT
EV'RY SUNDAY AFTERNOON
FABLE OF THE ROSE
FALLING LEAVES
FERRYBOAT SERENADE, THE
FIFTEEN MINUTE INTERMISSION
FINE AND MELLOW
FIVE O'CLOCK WHISTLE, THE
FLOWER OF DAWN
FOOLS RUSH IN
FRENESI
FROM ANOTHER WORLD
GAUCHO SERENADE, THE
GIVE A LITTLE WHISTLE
GOODBYE, LITTLE DARLIN', GOODBYE
GOODY GOODBYE
HANDFUL OF STARS, A
HAPPY HUNTING HORN
HARLEM AIR SHAFT
HARLEM NOCTURNE

HEAR MY SONG, VIOLETTA

HE'S MY UNCLE

HIGH ON A WINDY HILL

HONESTLY

HONEY IN THE HONEYCOMB

HOW CAN I EVER BE ALONE?

HOW DID HE LOOK?

HOW HIGH THE MOON

I AM AN AMERICAN

I CAN'T LOVE YOU ANYMORE (ANY MORE THAN I DO)

I CAN'T REMEMBER TO FORGET

I CAN'T RESIST YOU

I CONCENTRATE ON YOU

I COULD KISS YOU FOR THAT

I COULD MAKE YOU CARE

I'D KNOW YOU ANYWHERE

IF IT'S YOU

IF IT WASN'T FOR THE MOON

I GIVE YOU MY WORD

I HAVEN'T TIME TO BE A MILLIONAIRE

I HEAR A RHAPSODY

I HEAR MUSIC

I'LL NEVER SMILE AGAIN

I'LL PRAY FOR YOU

I LOVE YOU MUCH TOO MUCH

IMAGINATION

I'M GONNA MOVE TO THE OUTSKIRTS OF TOWN

I MISS YOU SO

I'M LOOKING FOR A GUY WHO PLAYS ALTO AND BARITONE AND DOUBLES ON A CLARINET AND WEARS A SIZE 37 SUIT

I'M NOBODY'S BABY

I'M STEPPING OUT WITH A MEMORY TONIGHT

IN A MELLOW TONE

IN AN OLD DUTCH GARDEN (BY AN OLD DUTCH MILL)

IN CHI CHI CASTENANGO

IN THE COOL OF THE EVENING

I SHOULD HAVE KNOWN YOU YEARS AGO

ISN'T THAT JUST LIKE LOVE

IS THERE SOMEBODY ELSE?

IT NEVER ENTERED MY MIND

IT'S A BIG, WIDE, WONDERFUL WORLD

IT'S A BLUE WORLD

IT'S A GREAT DAY FOR THE IRISH

IT'S A HAP-HAP-HAPPY DAY

IT'S A LOVELY DAY TOMORROW

IT'S A WONDERFUL WORLD

IT'S EIGHT O'CLOCK

IT'S MAKE BELIEVE BALLROOM TIME

IT'S THE SAME OLD SHILLELAGH

I UNDERSTAND

I'VE GOT A ONE TRACK MIND

I'VE GOT MY EYES ON YOU

I WALK WITH MUSIC

I WANNA WRAP YOU UP

I WANT MY MAMA (MAMA YO QUIERO)

I WOULDN'T TAKE A MILLION

JACK THE BEAR

JUST TO EASE MY WORRIED MIND

LATINS KNOW HOW

LATIN TUNE, A MANHATTAN MOON AND YOU, A

LEANIN' ON THE OLE TOP RAIL

LET'S BE BUDDIES

LET THERE BE LOVE

LITTLE CURLY HAIR IN A HIGH CHAIR

LOUISIANA PURCHASE

LOVE IS ALL

LOVE LIES

LOVE OF MY LIFE

LOVER'S LULLABY, A

MAKE-BELIEVE ISLAND

MAKE IT ANOTHER OLD-FASHIONED PLEASE

MAN WHO COMES AROUND, THE

MAYBE

MAY I NEVER LOVE AGAIN

MEET THE SUN HALF WAY

MILLION DREAMS AGO, A

MISTER MEADOWLARK

MOMENTS IN THE MOONLIGHT

MOON AND THE WILLOW TREE, THE

MOON FELL IN THE RIVER, THE

MOON OVER BURMA

MOON WON'T TALK, THE

MY! MY!

MY GREATEST MISTAKE

MY MOTHER WOULD LOVE YOU

MY WONDERFUL ONE, LET'S DANCE

NEARNESS OF YOU, THE

NIGHTINGALE SANG IN BERKELEY
  SQUARE, A

NO NAME JIVE

NOW I LAY ME DOWN TO DREAM

NOW WE KNOW

OLD, OLD CASTLE IN SCOTLAND, AN

ON A LITTLE STREET IN SINGAPORE

ON BEHALF OF THE VISITING FIREMEN

ONE CIGARETTE FOR TWO

ONE LOOK AT YOU

ONLY FOREVER

ON THE ISLE OF MAY

ON THE OLD PARK BENCH

OOH, WHAT YOU SAID!

ORCHIDS FOR REMEMBRANCE

OUR LOVE AFFAIR

PENNSYLVANIA 6-5000

PESSIMISTIC CHARACTER, THE (WITH
  THE CRAB APPLE FACE)

PINCH ME

PLAYMATES

POLKA DOTS AND MOONBEAMS

POMPTON TURNPIKE

PRACTICE MAKES PERFECT

PRETTY GIRL MILKING HER COW

PUT YOUR LITTLE FOOT RIGHT OUT

REDSKIN RHUMBA

REMIND ME

RHUMBOOGIE

RHYTHM ON THE RIVER

RIDE, COSSACK, RIDE

ROMANCE IN THE DARK

SAME OLD STORY, THE

SAN ANTONIO ROSE

SAY IT (OVER AND OVER AGAIN)

SAY "SI SI"

SCRUB ME MAMA WITH A BOOGIE BEAT

SECRETS IN THE MOONLIGHT

720 IN THE BOOKS

SHAKE DOWN THE STARS

SIERRA SUE

SINGING HILLS, THE

SIX LESSONS FROM MADAME LA ZONGA

SKY FELL DOWN, THE

SLOW FREIGHT

SO FAR, SO GOOD

SOFT WINDS

SO LONG

SOMEDAY (YOU'LL WANT ME TO WANT
  YOU)

SOUTHERN FRIED

STARLIT HOUR, THE

SWEET POTATO PIPER

TAKING A CHANCE ON LOVE

TALKIN' TO MY HEART

TENNESSEE FISH FRY

THAT'S FOR ME

THERE I GO

THERE'S A GREAT DAY COMING
  MAÑANA

THERE SHALL BE NO NIGHT

THESE THINGS YOU LEFT ME

THIS CHANGING WORLD

THIS IS MY COUNTRY

THIS IS THE BEGINNING OF THE END

TICKLE TOE

TOO ROMANTIC

TRADE WINDS

TRA-LA-LA-LA

TUXEDO JUNCTION

TWO DREAMS MET

UNTIL TOMORROW

VIPER'S DRAG

WALTZING IN THE CLOUDS

WARM VALLEY

WE COULD MAKE SUCH BEAUTIFUL MUSIC

WE THREE (MY ECHO, MY SHADOW, AND ME)

WHAM

WHATCHA KNOW, JOE

WHAT IS A MAN?

WHAT'S THE MATTER WITH ME?

WHAT'S YOUR STORY, MORNING GLORY?

WHEN THE MOON COMES OVER MADISON SQUARE

WHEN THE SWALLOWS COME BACK TO CAPISTRANO

WHEN YOU WISH UPON A STAR

WHERE DO I GO FROM YOU?

WHERE WAS I?

WHISPERING GRASS (DON'T TELL THE TREES)

WHO AM I?

WHO'S YEHOODI?

WISE OLD OWL, THE

WITH THE WIND AND THE RAIN IN YOUR HAIR

WOODPECKER SONG, THE

WORLD IS IN MY ARMS, THE

YES, MY DARLING DAUGHTER

YESTERTHOUGHTS

YOU, YOU DARLING

YOU ARE MY SUNSHINE

YOU CAN'T BRUSH ME OFF

YOU'D BE SURPRISED

YOU FORGOT ABOUT ME

YOU MUSTN'T KICK IT AROUND

YOU'RE LONELY AND I'M LONELY

YOUR RED WAGON

YOU'RE NEARER

YOU SAY THE SWEETEST THINGS, BABY

YOU THINK OF EV'RYTHING

YOU'VE GOT ME OUT ON A LIMB

YOU'VE GOT ME THIS WAY (WHATTA YA GONNA DO ABOUT IT?)

YOU WALK BY

ZIP

1941

ACE IN THE HOLE

ADIOS

AIR MAIL SPECIAL

ALEXANDER THE SWOOSE (HALF SWAN—HALF GOOSE)

ALL THAT MEAT AND NO POTATOES

ALWAYS ALONE

AMAPOLA (PRETTY LITTLE POPPY)

ANGELS CAME THRU, THE

ANNIVERSARY WALTZ, THE

ANY BONDS TODAY?

ARMS FOR THE LOVE OF AMERICA (THE ARMY ORDNANCE SONG)

AS WE WALK INTO THE SUNSET

AU REET

AURORA

BABY MINE

BEAR MASH BLUES

BEAU NIGHT IN HOTCHKISS CORNERS

BE HONEST WITH ME

BELLS OF SAN RAQUEL, THE

BEWITCHED, BOTHERED, AND BEWILDERED

BI-I-BI

BLESS 'EM ALL

BLUE CHAMPAGNE

BLUES IN THE NIGHT

BOOGIE WOOGIE BUGLE BOY (OF COMPANY B)

BOOGIE WOOGIE PRAYER

BOOGLIE WOOGLIE PIGGY, THE

BOUNCE ME BROTHER WITH A SOLID FOUR

BUCKLE DOWN, WINSOCKI

BY-U, BY-O (THE LOU'SIANA LULLABY)

CAE CAE

CANCEL THE FLOWERS

CAN THIS BE THE END OF THE
RAINBOW?

CELERY STALKS AT MIDNIGHT

CHARLESTON ALLEY

CHATTANOOGA CHOO CHOO

CHELSEA BRIDGE

CHERRY BLOSSOMS ON CAPITOL HILL

CHERRY RED

CHICA CHICA BOOM CHIC

CHIN UP, CHEERIO, CARRY ON!

CHOCOLATE SHAKE

CITY CALLED HEAVEN

CONCERTO FOR CLARINET

CONCERTO FOR TWO

CONFESSIN' THE BLUES

CONTRASTS

COWBOY SERENADE, THE

DADDY

DAY DREAMING

DEAR MOM

DEEP IN THE HEART OF TEXAS

DELILAH

DO I WORRY?

DOLORES

DON'T CRY, CHERIE

DON'T LET JULIA FOOL YA

DON'T TAKE YOUR LOVE FROM ME

DOWN THE ROAD A PIECE

DO YOU CARE?

DREAM DANCING

DREAMSVILLE, OHIO

DRUMBOOGIE

EASY STREET

ELMER'S TUNE

EVERYTHING HAPPENS TO ME

EV'RYTHING I LOVE

EV'RY TIME

FAN IT

FIVE GUYS NAMED MOE

FLAMINGO

FRIENDLY TAVERN POLKA

FROM ONE LOVE TO ANOTHER

G'BYE NOW

GOD BLESS THE CHILD

GOIN' TO CHICAGO BLUES

GOODBYE DEAR, I'LL BE BACK IN A
YEAR

GREEN EYES

HAPPY IN LOVE

HE'S 1-A IN THE ARMY AND HE'S A-1 IN
MY HEART

HI, NEIGHBOR!

HOW ABOUT YOU?

HUT-SUT SONG, THE

I, YI, YI, YI, YI (I LIKE YOU VERY
MUCH)

I CAME, I SAW, I CONGA'D

I COULD WRITE A BOOK

I DON'T WANT TO SET THE WORLD ON
FIRE

I DREAMT I DWELT IN HARLEM

I FOUND YOU IN THE RAIN

I GOT IT BAD AND THAT AIN'T GOOD

I GUESS I'LL HAVE TO DREAM THE REST

I KNOW WHY (AND SO DO YOU)

I'LL NEVER LET A DAY PASS BY

I'M THRILLED

I'M TRUSTING IN YOU

INTERMEZZO

I SAID NO

I SEE A MILLION PEOPLE (BUT ALL I
CAN SEE IS YOU)

IT ALL COMES BACK TO ME NOW

IT HAPPENED IN SUN VALLEY

I THINK OF YOU

IT'S ALWAYS YOU

IT'S SO PEACEFUL IN THE COUNTRY

I WENT OUT OF MY WAY

I WONDER WHY YOU SAID "GOODBYE"

JAVA JIVE

JENNY (THE SAGA OF)

JERSEY BOUNCE

JIM

JOLTIN' JOE DI MAGGIO

JUMP FOR JOY

JUST A LITTLE BIT SOUTH OF NORTH CAROLINA

JUST A LITTLE JOINT WITH A JUKE BOX

KEY TO THE HIGHWAY

KING JOE

KISS POLKA, THE

KISS THE BOYS GOODBYE

LAMENT TO LOVE

LAST TIME I SAW PARIS, THE

LEAP FROG

LET ME OFF UPTOWN

LET'S GET AWAY FROM IT ALL

LET'S NOT TALK ABOUT LOVE

LITTLE MAN WITH A CANDY CIGAR

MA! I MISS YOUR APPLE PIE

MAKE LOVE TO ME

MARIA ELENA

MIDNIGHT SPECIAL

MINKA

MISIRLOU

MOONLIGHT MASQUERADE

MUSIC MAKERS

MY RESISTANCE IS LOW

MY SHIP

MY SISTER AND I

NEIANI

NUMBER 10 LULLABY LANE

OH, LOOK AT ME NOW

ONE LIFE TO LIVE

ORANGE BLOSSOM LANE

OUT OF THE SILENCE

PAPA NICCOLINI

PARADIDDLE JOE

PERFIDIA

PIANO CONCERTO IN B♭

PIG FOOT PETE

PRINCESS OF PURE DELIGHT

RACING WITH THE MOON

ROLL 'EM PETE

ROMANTIC GUY, I, A

ROMEO SMITH AND JULIET JONES

ROSE AND A PRAYER, A

ROSE O'DAY (THE FILLA-GA-DUSHA SONG)

SAND IN MY SHOES

SAYS WHO? SAYS YOU, SAYS I!

SHEPHERD SERENADE

SHOUT FOR JOY

SHRINE OF SAINT CECILIA, THE

SINCE I KISSED MY BABY GOODBYE

SINNER KISSED AN ANGEL, A

SLEEPY SERENADE

SNOWFALL

SOFT AS SPRING

SOMEONE'S ROCKING MY DREAMBOAT

SO NEAR AND YET SO FAR

STEEL GUITAR RAG

STRING OF PEARLS, A

SUMMER IS A-COMIN' IN

SWEETER THAN THE SWEETEST

SWEETHEARTS OR STRANGERS

TAKE THE "A" TRAIN

TCHAIKOWSKY (AND OTHER RUSSIANS)

TEARS ON MY PILLOW

THEY MET IN RIO

THINGS AIN'T WHAT THEY USED TO BE

THINGS I LOVE, THE

THIS IS NEW

THIS IS NO LAUGHING MATTER

THIS IS ROMANCE

THIS LOVE OF MINE

THIS TIME THE DREAM'S ON ME

THREE B'S, THE

'TIL REVEILLE (LIGHTS OUT- -)

TIME WAS

'TIS AUTUMN

TONIGHT WE LOVE

TOO LATE

TROPICAL MAGIC

TWENTY-ONE DOLLARS A DAY—ONCE A MONTH

TWO HEARTS THAT PASS IN THE NIGHT

TWO IN LOVE

TWO O'CLOCK JUMP

VIOLETS FOR YOUR FURS

WAITER AND THE PORTER AND THE UPSTAIRS MAID, THE

WALKING THE FLOOR OVER YOU

WALTZING MATILDA

WASN'T IT YOU?

WEEK-END IN HAVANA, A

WE GO WELL TOGETHER

WE'LL MEET AGAIN

WE'RE THE COUPLE IN THE CASTLE

WHAT DO YOU THINK I AM?

WHEN I SEE AN ELEPHANT FLY

WHEN MY BLUE MOON TURNS TO GOLD AGAIN

WHEN THE SUN COMES OUT

WHEN THE SUN GOES DOWN

WHITE CLIFFS OF DOVER, THE (THERE'LL BE BLUEBIRDS OVER)

WHY DON'T WE DO THIS MORE OFTEN?

WILL YOU STILL BE MINE?

WINTER WEATHER

WORRIED MIND

YES, INDEED!

YOU AND I

YOU DON'T KNOW WHAT LOVE IS

YOU GO YOUR WAY (AND I'LL GO CRAZY)

YOU LUCKY PEOPLE, YOU

YOU MIGHT HAVE BELONGED TO ANOTHER

YOU'RE DANGEROUS

YOU'RE THE ONE

YOURS

YOUR SOCKS DON'T MATCH

YOU STARTED SOMETHING

YOU STEPPED OUT OF A DREAM

1942

AIN'T GOT A DIME TO MY NAME

ALL I NEED IS YOU

ALWAYS IN MY HEART

AMEN (YEA-MAN)

AMERICAN PATROL

ARTHUR MURRAY TAUGHT ME DANCING IN A HURRY

AS TIME GOES BY

AT LAST

AT THE CROSSROADS

AUTUMN NOCTURNE

BARRELHOUSE BESSIE FROM BASIN STREET

BE CAREFUL, IT'S MY HEART

BLUE FLAME

BOY IN KHAKI, A GIRL IN LACE, A

CALIFORNIA MELODIES

CAN'T GET OUT OF THIS MOOD

CAPTAINS OF THE CLOUDS

CHIU, CHIU

CIMARRON (ROLL ON)

C-JAM BLUES (OR, "C" JAM BLUES)

CONCHITA, MARQUITA, LOLITA, PEPITA, ROSITA, JUANITA LOPEZ

CONSTANTLY

COW-COW BOOGIE

CRYING MYSELF TO SLEEP

DANCE OF THE SPANISH ONION

DAYBREAK

DEARLY BELOVED

DER FUEHRER'S FACE

DON'T GET AROUND MUCH ANYMORE

DON'T SIT UNDER THE APPLE TREE (WITH ANYONE ELSE BUT ME)

DUSTY RAG

END OF THE WORLD, THE

EPISTROPHY

EVERYBODY'S MAKING MONEY BUT TCHAIKOVSKY

EVERY DAY OF MY LIFE

EV'RY NIGHT ABOUT THIS TIME

EV'RYTHING I'VE GOT

FAT MEAT IS GOOD MEAT

FLEET'S IN, THE

FULL MOON (NOCHE DE LUNA)

GOING UP

GOODBYE MAMA, I'M OFF TO YOKOHAMA

GOT THE MOON IN MY POCKET

HAPPY HOLIDAY

HARVARD BLUES

HAYFOOT, STRAWFOOT

HEAVENLY HIDEAWAY

HE LOVED ME TILL THE ALL-CLEAR CAME

HERE YOU ARE

HEREAFTER

HE'S MY GUY

HE WEARS A PAIR OF SILVER WINGS

HIP, HIP. HOORAY

HIT THE ROAD TO DREAMLAND

HOOTIE BLUES

HOUSE I LIVE IN, THE (THAT'S AMERICA TO ME)

HOW DO I KNOW IT'S REAL?

HOW LONG DID I DREAM?

HUMPTY DUMPTY HEART

I CAME HERE TO TALK FOR JOE

IDAHO

I DON'T WANT TO WALK WITHOUT YOU

IF I CARED A LITTLE BIT LESS

IF YOU ARE BUT A DREAM

IF YOU BUILD A BETTER MOUSETRAP

I GET THE NECK OF THE CHICKEN

I HAD THE CRAZIEST DREAM

I HANG MY HEAD AND CRY

I HUNG MY HEAD AND CRIED

I LEFT MY HEART AT THE STAGE DOOR CANTEEN

I'LL ALWAYS BE GLAD TO TAKE YOU BACK

I'LL NEVER FORGET

I'LL PRAY FOR YOU

I'LL REMEMBER APRIL

I'LL TAKE TALLULAH

I LOST MY SUGAR IN SALT LAKE CITY

I MARRIED AN ANGEL

I MET HER ON MONDAY

I'M GETTING TIRED SO I CAN SLEEP

I'M GLAD THERE IS YOU

I'M GONNA MOVE TO THE OUTSKIRTS OF TOWN

I'M OLD FASHIONED

I'M SENDING YOU RED ROSES

I'M THINKING TONIGHT OF MY BLUE EYES

IN THE BLUE OF EVENING

I REMEMBER YOU

I SAID NO!

I THREW A KISS IN THE OCEAN

IT MUST BE JELLY ('CAUSE JAM DON'T SHAKE LIKE THAT)

IT STARTED ALL OVER AGAIN

IT WON'T BE LONG (TILL I'LL BE LEAVING)

I'VE GOT A GAL IN KALAMAZOO

I'VE GOT TO SING A TORCH SONG

JINGLE, JANGLE, JINGLE

JITTERBUG WALTZ, THE

JOHNNY DOUGHBOY FOUND A ROSE IN IRELAND

JUKE BOX SATURDAY NIGHT

JUST AS THOUGH YOU WERE HERE

JUST PLAIN LONESOME

KILLE KILLE (INDIAN LOVE TALK)

KNOCK ME A KISS

LAMPLIGHTER'S SERENADE, THE

LAMP OF MEMORY, THE

LAST CALL FOR LOVE

LET'S START THE NEW YEAR RIGHT

LILY OF LAGUNA

LONELY RIVER

LONG BEFORE YOU CAME ALONG

LOVE IS A SONG

LOVER MAN (OH, WHERE CAN I BE?)

LOW AND LONELY

MAD ABOUT HIM, SAD ABOUT HIM, HOW CAN I BE GLAD ABOUT HIM BLUES

MANDY IS TWO

MANHATTAN SERENADE

MARCHING THROUGH BERLIN

MASSACHUSETTS

ME AND MY MELINDA

MISSION TO MOSCOW

MISS YOU

MISTER FIVE BY FIVE

MOONLIGHT BECOMES YOU

MOONLIGHT MOOD

MOON MIST

MOVE IT OVER

MY DEVOTION

MY HEART ISN'T IN IT

MY LITTLE COUSIN

NIGHTINGALE

NIGHT TRAIN TO MEMPHIS

NIGHT WE CALLED IT A DAY, THE

NOBODY'S HEART (BELONGS TO ME)

NOT MINE

OH! MISS JAXON

ONE DOZEN ROSES

ON THE STREET OF REGRET

PAPER DOLL

PEACEFUL VALLEY

PENNSYLVANIA POLKA

PEOPLE LIKE YOU AND ME

PERDIDO

POEM SET TO MUSIC, A

POOR YOU

PRAISE THE LORD AND PASS THE
  AMMUNITION

PUT YOUR DREAMS AWAY (FOR
  ANOTHER DAY)

ROAD TO MOROCCO

ROCK-A-BYE BAY

ROSE ANN OF CHARING CROSS

SERENADE IN BLUE

SERENADE TO A MAID

SHE'LL ALWAYS REMEMBER

SING ME A SONG OF THE ISLANDS

SIX FLATS UNFURNISHED

SKYLARK

SLEEPY LAGOON

SLIP OF THE LIP, A

SOMEBODY ELSE IS TAKING MY PLACE

SOMEBODY NOBODY LOVES

SORGHUM SWITCH

STORMY MONDAY BLUES

STORY OF A STARRY NIGHT, THE

STRICTLY INSTRUMENTAL

STRIP POLKA, THE

SWEET ELOISE

TABOO

TAKE ME

TANGERINE

THAT OLD BLACK MAGIC

THAT SOLDIER OF MINE

THAT'S SABOTAGE

THERE ARE SUCH THINGS

THERE'S A STAR SPANGLED BANNER
  WAVING SOMEWHERE

THERE WILL NEVER BE ANOTHER YOU

THIS IS THE ARMY, MR. JONES

THIS IS WORTH FIGHTING FOR

THIS TIME (IS THE LAST TIME)

THREE LITTLE SISTERS

TIMBER TRAIL, THE

TOUCH OF TEXAS, A

TRUMPET BLUES

WAIT TILL SHE SEES YOU IN YOUR
  UNIFORM

WAIT TILL YOU SEE HER

WARSAW CONCERTO

WELL, GIT IT!

WE MUST BE VIGILANT

WE'RE HAVING A BABY (MY BABY
  AND ME)

WHAT TO DO

WHEN THE LIGHTS GO ON AGAIN (ALL
  OVER THE WORLD)

WHEN THERE'S A BREEZE ON LAKE
  LOUISE

WHEN THE ROSES BLOOM AGAIN

WHEN YOU HEAR THE TIME SIGNAL

WHEN YOU WORE A TULIP AND I WORE
  A BIG RED ROSE

WHERE THE MOUNTAINS MEET THE SKY

WHISPER THAT YOU LOVE ME

WHITE CHRISTMAS

WHO CAN I TURN TO?

WHO WOULDN'T LOVE YOU?

WHY DON'T YOU DO RIGHT?

(AS LONG AS YOU'RE NOT IN LOVE WITH ANYONE ELSE) WHY DON'T YOU FALL IN LOVE WITH ME?

WINDMILL UNDER THE STARS

WITH MY HEAD IN THE CLOUDS

WONDER WHEN MY BABY'S COMING HOME

YESTERDAY'S GARDENIAS

YESTERDAY'S ROSES

YOU CAN'T HOLD A MEMORY IN YOUR ARMS

YOU CAN'T SAY NO TO A SOLDIER

YOU'LL BE SORRY WHEN I'M GONE

YOU'RE EASY TO DANCE WITH

YOU'VE CHANGED

YOU WERE NEVER LOVELIER

ZOOT SUIT, A (FOR MY SUNDAY GIRL)

1943

ACROSS THE TRACK BLUES

AIN'T THAT JUST LIKE A MAN?

ALL ER NOTHIN'

ALL OR NOTHING AT ALL

AND SO LITTLE TIME

APOLLO JUMP

ARMY AIR CORPS, THE

BESAME MUCHO

BOOGIE WOOGIE

BORN TO LOSE

BRANDED WHEREVER I GO

BRAZIL

BY THE MISSISSINEWAH

BY THE RIVER OF THE ROSES

CAN'T YOU DO A FRIEND A FAVOR

CHANGE OF HEART, A

CLOSE TO YOU

COLUMBUS STOCKADE BLUES

COMIN' IN ON A WING AND A PRAYER

COULD IT BE YOU

DEACON JONES

DO NOTHIN' TILL YOU HEAR FROM ME

DON'T BELIEVE EVERYTHING YOU DREAM

DON'T CRY, BABY

DON'T SWEETHEART ME

DREAMER, THE

EL CUMBANCHERO

FELLOW ON A FURLOUGH, A

FOOLISH HEART

FOR ME AND MY GAL

FOR THE FIRST TIME (I'VE FALLEN IN LOVE)

FUDDY DUDDY WATCHMAKER, THE

GERTIE FROM BIZERTE

GOODBYE SUE

HANG YOUR HEAD IN SHAME (DON'T YOUR CONSCIENCE EVER BOTHER YOU)

HAPPINESS IS JUST A THING CALLED JOE

HAPPY GO LUCKY

HAVE I STAYED AWAY TOO LONG?

HEY, GOOD-LOOKIN'

HOLIDAY FOR STRINGS

HOME IN SAN ANTONE

HOW SWEET YOU ARE

I ALWAYS KNEW

I CAIN'T SAY NO

I DUG A DITCH (IN WICHITA)

IF YOU PLEASE

I HEARD YOU CRIED LAST NIGHT

I'LL BE AROUND

I'LL BE HOME FOR CHRISTMAS

I LOVE YOU

I'M A STRANGER HERE MYSELF

I'M LIKE A FISH OUT OF WATER

I'M RIDIN' FOR A FALL

I NEVER MENTION YOUR NAME

IN MY ARMS

IS MY BABY BLUE TONIGHT?

IT CAN'T BE WRONG

I'VE GOT SIXPENCE

I'VE HAD THIS FEELING BEFORE

I'VE HEARD THAT SONG BEFORE

I WANT TO BE WANTED

I WISH THAT I COULD HIDE INSIDE THIS LETTER

JEALOUS HEART

JOHNNY ZERO

JOINT IS REALLY JUMPIN' AT CARNEGIE HALL

JOURNEY TO A STAR, A

JUMP TOWN

KANSAS CITY (EVERYTHING'S UP TO DATE IN)

LATER TONIGHT

LET'S GET LOST

LOT IN COMMON, A

MANY A NEW DAY

MEADOWLAND

MEXICO JOE

MISSISSIPPI DREAM BOAT

MURDER, HE SAYS

MY HEART TELLS ME

MY LAST LOVE

MY SHINING HOUR

NEVADA

NO LETTER TODAY

NO LOVE, NO NOTHIN'

OH, WHAT A BEAUTIFUL MORNIN'

OKLAHOMA

OLD ACQUAINTANCE

OLD MUSIC MASTER, THE

ONE FOR MY BABY (AND ONE MORE FOR THE ROAD)

OUR WALTZ

OUT OF MY DREAMS

PEOPLE WILL SAY WE'RE IN LOVE

PINK COCKTAIL FOR A BLUE LADY, A

PINS AND NEEDLES (IN MY HEART)

PISTOL PACKIN' MAMA

POINCIANA (SONG OF THE TREE)

PORE JUD IS DAID

PRODIGAL SON, THE

RAINBOW RHAPSODY

RATION BLUES

RED BANK BOOGIE

ROSALITA

ROSIE THE RIVETER

RUSTY DUSTY BLUES

SAN FERNANDO VALLEY

SANTA CLAUS IS RIDING THE TRAIL

SAY A PRAYER FOR THE BOYS OVER THERE

SEE SEE RIDER (BLUES) a.k.a. C. C. RIDER

SHOO-SHOO BABY

SILVER WINGS IN THE MOONLIGHT

SING A TROPICAL SONG

SLAP POLKA, THE

SLIGHTLY LESS THAN WONDERFUL

SOMETHING FOR THE BOYS

SOMETHING TO SHOUT ABOUT

SPEAK LOW

STAR EYES

SUNDAY, MONDAY OR ALWAYS

SURREY WITH THE FRINGE ON TOP, THE

SWEET SLUMBER

TAKE IT EASY

TAKING A CHANCE ON LOVE

TELL ME (WHY NIGHTS ARE LONELY)

TESS'S TORCH SONG

THANK YOUR LUCKY STARS

THAT AIN'T RIGHT

THAT'S HIM

THERE'LL SOON BE A RAINBOW

THERE'S NO TWO WAYS ABOUT LOVE

THEY'RE EITHER TOO YOUNG OR TOO OLD

THEY TOOK THE STARS OUT OF HEAVEN

TRAV'LIN' LIGHT

TRY ME ONE MORE TIME

TWEEDLE-O-TWILL

UNDER A STRAWBERRY MOON

UNITED NATIONS ON THE MARCH

VELVET MOON

VICT'RY POLKA

WAIT FOR ME, MARY

WE LIVE IN TWO DIFFERENT WORLDS

WE MUSTN'T SAY GOODBYE

WESTWIND

WHAT DO YOU DO IN THE INFANTRY?

WHEN I LOOK AT YOU

WHEN THEY ASK ABOUT YOU

WHILE WE'RE YOUNG

WHO DID? I DID

WHY BEGIN AGAIN?

WRITE ME SWEETHEART

YESTERDAY'S TEARS

YOU'D BE SO NICE TO COME HOME TO

YOU'LL NEVER KNOW

YOU NEARLY LOSE YOUR MIND

1944

AC-CENT-TCHU-ATE THE POSITIVE

ALWAYS

AMOR

AND HER TEARS FLOWED LIKE WINE

AND THEN YOU KISSED ME

ANGELINA (THE WAITRESS AT THE PIZZERIA)

ANY MOMENT NOW

ARTISTRY IN RHYTHM

AS LONG AS THERE'S MUSIC

BLUEBIRDS IN MY BELFRY

BLUES IN MY MIND

BOY NEXT DOOR, THE

CALIFORN-I-AY

CANDY

CAN'T HELP SINGING

COME OUT, COME OUT, WHEREVER YOU ARE

CORNS FOR MY COUNTRY

DANCE WITH A DOLLY (WITH A HOLE IN HER STOCKING)

DAY AFTER FOREVER, THE

DIZZY ATMOSPHERE

DON'T FENCE ME IN

DON'T YOU KNOW I CARE (OR DON'T YOU CARE TO KNOW?)

DREAM

EACH MINUTE SEEMS A MILLION YEARS

EACH NIGHT AT NINE

EAGLE AND ME, THE

EVELINA

EVIL GAL BLUES

EV'RYTIME WE SAY GOODBYE

FIRST CLASS PRIVATE MARY BROWN

FOR THE FIRST HUNDRED YEARS

FUZZY WUZZY

G.I. BLUES

G.I. JIVE

GOING MY WAY

GONNA BUILD A BIG FENCE AROUND TEXAS

GOOD, GOOD, GOOD (THAT'S YOU— THAT'S YOU)

GOOD BAIT

GOOD EARTH, THE

GOODNIGHT, WHEREVER YOU ARE

GREAT LIE, THE

HAMP'S BOOGIE WOOGIE

HAVE YOURSELF A MERRY LITTLE CHRISTMAS

HIS ROCKING HORSE RAN AWAY

HOT TIME IN THE TOWN OF BERLIN, A (WHEN THE YANKS GO MARCHING IN)

HOUR NEVER PASSES, AN

HOW BLUE THE NIGHT

HOW LITTLE WE KNOW

HOW MANY HEARTS HAVE YOU BROKEN?

HOW MANY TIMES DO I HAVE TO TELL YOU?

HURRY, HURRY
I AIN'T GOT NOTHIN' BUT THE BLUES
I CAN COOK TOO
I CAN'T SEE FOR LOOKIN'
I COULDN'T SLEEP A WINK LAST NIGHT
I DIDN'T KNOW ABOUT YOU
I DON'T WANT TO LOVE YOU (LIKE I DO)
I DREAM OF YOU
I HAD A LITTLE TALK WITH THE LORD
I LEARNED A LESSON I'LL NEVER
   FORGET
I'LL BE SEEING YOU
I'LL FORGIVE YOU, BUT I CAN'T FORGET
I'LL GET BY
I'LL REMEMBER SUZANNE
I'LL WALK ALONE
I LOVE YOU
I'M BEGINNING TO SEE THE LIGHT
I'M LOST
I'M MAKING BELIEVE
I'M WASTIN' MY TEARS ON YOU
IN A MOMENT OF MADNESS
IN THE MIDDLE OF NOWHERE
INTO EACH LIFE SOME RAIN MUST FALL
INVITATION TO THE BLUES
I PROMISE YOU
IRRESISTIBLE YOU
IS YOU IS OR IS YOU AIN'T MY BABY?
IT COULD HAPPEN TO YOU
IT HAD TO BE YOU
IT'S LOVE, LOVE, LOVE
I WANNA GET MARRIED
I WONDER
KENTUCKY
LET ME LOVE YOU TONIGHT
LET'S TAKE THE LONG WAY HOME
LIKE SOMEONE IN LOVE
LILI MARLENE
LINDA
LITTLE ON THE LONELY SIDE, A
LONG AGO AND FAR AWAY
LOOK WHO'S TALKIN'
LOVE I LONG FOR, THE

LOVE LIKE OURS, A
LOVELY WAY TO SPEND AN EVENING, A
MAD ABOUT YOU
MAGIC IS THE MOONLIGHT
MAIN STEM
MAIRZY DOATS
MAKE WAY FOR TOMORROW
MILKMAN, KEEP THOSE BOTTLES QUIET
MOONLIGHT IN VERMONT
MORE AND MORE
MUSIC STOPPED, THE
NOW I KNOW
ONCE TOO OFTEN
ONLY ANOTHER BOY AND GIRL
PINEY BROWN BLUES
POOR LITTLE RHODE ISLAND
PRETTY KITTY BLUE EYES
PUT ME TO THE TEST
REMEMBER ME TO CAROLINA
RIGHT AS THE RAIN
RIO DE JANEIRO
ROBIN HOOD
SHAME ON YOU
SHE BROKE MY HEART IN THREE
   PLACES
SILVER SHADOWS AND BROKEN
   DREAMS
SKYLINER
SLEIGHRIDE IN JULY
SMOKE ON THE WATER
SOLDIER'S LAST LETTER
SOLO FLIGHT
SO LONG, PAL
SOMEDAY I'LL MEET YOU AGAIN
SOME OTHER TIME
SPRING WILL BE A LITTLE LATE THIS
   YEAR
STRAIGHTEN UP AND FLY RIGHT
STRANGE MUSIC
SUDDENLY IT'S SPRING
SUMMIT RIDGE DRIVE
SURE THING
SWEET DREAMS, SWEETHEART

AREN'T YOU KIND OF GLAD WE DID?

ASK ANYONE WHO KNOWS

AS LONG AS I'M DREAMING

AT THE CANDLELIGHT CAFE

BACK BAY POLKA

BALLERINA

BEGAT, THE

BEG YOUR PARDON

BELLA BELLA MARIE

BESIDE YOU

BEWARE MY HEART

BEYOND THE SEA

BIG BRASS BAND FROM BRAZIL, THE

BLOOP, BLEEP!

BLUE MOON OF KENTUCKY

BOB WILLS BOOGIE

BOOGIE WOOGIE BLUE PLATE

BORN TO BE BLUE

BRIGADOON

BROOKLYN BRIDGE

CHANGING MY TUNE

CHI-BABA, CHI-BABA (MY BAMBINA GO
    TO SLEEP)

CHRISTMAS DREAMING

CHRISTMAS ISLAND

CIGARETTES, WHUSKY, AND WILD,
    WILD WOMEN

CIVILIZATION (BONGO, BONGO, BONGO)

COME TO ME, BEND TO ME

COME TO THE MARDI GRAS

CONNECTICUT

COUNTRY STYLE

DARK AS A DUNGEON

DEEP SONG

DONNA LEE

DON'T BE SO MEAN TO BABY ('CAUSE
    BABY'S SO GOOD TO YOU)

DON'T CALL IT LOVE

DON'T LOOK NOW (BUT YOUR BROKEN
    HEART IS SHOWIN')

DON'T TELL ME

DON'T YOU LOVE ME ANYMORE?

DOWN AT THE ROADSIDE INN

DOWN IN HONKY TONKY TOWN

DO YOU KNOW WHAT IT MEANS TO MISS
    NEW ORLEANS?

DREAM OF OLWEN, THE

DREAMS ARE A DIME A DOZEN

DUM-DOT SONG

ECHO SAID "NO," THE

EGG AND I, THE

EITHER IT'S LOVE OR IT ISN'T

EVERY SO OFTEN

FELLOW NEEDS A GIRL, A

FEUDIN' AND FIGHTIN'

FOOTPRINTS IN THE SNOW

FOREVER AMBER

FOR ONCE IN YOUR LIFE

FORSAKING ALL OTHERS

FOR YOU, FOR ME, FOREVER MORE

FREE

FREEDOM TRAIN, THE

FRENCH LESSON, THE

FUN AND FANCY FREE

GENTLEMAN IS A DOPE, THE

GOLDEN EARRINGS

GOTTA GIMME WHATCHA GOT

GUILTY

HAND IN HAND

HARMONY

HEARTACHES

HEARTBREAKER

HEATHER ON THE HILL, THE

HERE COMES SANTA CLAUS (DOWN
    SANTA CLAUS LANE)

HE'S A REAL GONE GUY

HIS FEET TOO BIG FOR DE BED

HOODLE ADDLE

HOW ARE THINGS IN GLOCCA MORRA?

HOW LUCKY YOU ARE

HOW SOON (WILL I BE SEEING YOU?)

HURRY ON DOWN

I BELIEVE

I'D TRADE ALL OF MY TOMORROWS (FOR JUST ONE YESTERDAY)

I FEEL SO SMOOCHIE

IF I HAD MY LIFE TO LIVE OVER

IF I ONLY HAD A MATCH

IF THIS ISN'T LOVE

IF YOU'RE EVER DOWN IN TEXAS, LOOK ME UP

I GOTTA GAL I LOVE (IN NORTH AND SOUTH DAKOTA)

I HAVE BUT ONE HEART

I'LL CLOSE MY EYES

I'LL DANCE AT YOUR WEDDING

I'LL GO HOME WITH BONNIE JEAN

I'LL HATE MYSELF IN THE MORNING

I'LL HOLD YOU IN MY HEART (TILL I CAN HOLD YOU IN MY ARMS)

I'LL STEP ASIDE

I LOVE YOU, YES I DO

I'M SO RIGHT TONIGHT (BUT I'VE BEEN SO WRONG FOR SO LONG)

IN A LITTLE BOOKSHOP

I STILL GET JEALOUS

I TIPPED MY HAT (AND SLOWLY RODE AWAY)

I TOLD YA I LOVE YA, NOW GET OUT

IT'S A GOOD DAY

IT'S A SIN

IT'S DREAMTIME

IT'S THE SAME OLD DREAM

IT'S THE SENTIMENTAL THING TO DO

IT TAKES A LONG, LONG TRAIN WITH A RED CABOOSE (TO CARRY MY BLUES AWAY)

IT TAKES TIME

I'VE GOT ME

I'VE ONLY MYSELF TO BLAME

IVY

I WANT TO BE LOVED (BUT ONLY BY YOU)

I WANT TO THANK YOUR FOLKS

I WISH I DIDN'T LOVE YOU SO

I WONDER, I WONDER, I WONDER

JACK! JACK! JACK!

JACK, YOU'RE DEAD

JE VOUS AIME

JUMPIN' AT THE WOODSIDE

KATE (HAVE I COME TOO EARLY TOO LATE)

KING SIZE PAPA

KOKOMO, INDIANA

LADY FROM 29 PALMS, THE

LAZY COUNTRYSIDE

LAZY MOOD

LIFE CAN BE BEAUTIFUL

LINDA

LITTLE OLD MILL, THE (WENT ROUND AND ROUND)

LOOK TO THE RAINBOW

LOVE AND THE WEATHER

LOVE FOR LOVE

LOVE SOMEBODY

MAHARAJAH OF MAGADOR, THE

MAKIN' LOVE, MOUNTAIN STYLE

MAM'SELLE

MANAGUA NICARAGUA

ME AND THE BLUES

MEET ME AT NO SPECIAL PLACE (AND I'LL BE THERE AT NO PARTICULAR TIME)

MENTION MY NAME IN SHEBOYGAN

MERRY CHRISTMAS BABY

MIAMI BEACH RHUMBA

MIDNIGHT SUN

MOON-FACED, STARRY-EYED

MOVE IT ON OVER

MUSIC FROM BEYOND THE MOON

MY ADOBE HACIENDA

MY COUSIN LOUELLA

MY GUITAR IS MY SWEETHEART

MY HEART IS A HOBO

MY SIN

MY WILD IRISH ROSE

NAUGHTY ANGELINE

NEAR YOU

TWELFTH STREET RAG

UNDERNEATH THE ARCHES

UNLOVED AND UNCLAIMED

UNTIL

WHAT DID I DO?

WHAT DO I HAVE TO DO TO MAKE YOU LOVE ME?

WHAT'S GOOD ABOUT GOODBYE?

WHAT'S WRONG WITH ME?

WHEN I FALL IN LOVE

WHERE IS THE ONE?

WOODY WOODPECKER

WORRY, WORRY, WORRY

YOU CALL EVERYBODY DARLING

YOU CAME A LONG WAY FROM ST. LOUIS

YOU CAN DO NO WRONG

YOU CAN'T BE TRUE, DEAR

YOU DON'T HAVE TO KNOW THE LANGUAGE

YOU'RE ALL I WANT FOR CHRISTMAS

YOU'RE BREAKING MY HEART

YOU SAY THE NICEST THINGS, BABY

YOU WERE ONLY FOOLING (WHILE I WAS FALLING IN LOVE)

1949

AGAIN

ALL RIGHT, LOUIE, DROP THE GUN

ALL SHE WANTS TO DO IS ROCK

ALWAYS TRUE TO YOU IN MY FASHION

ANOTHER OP'NIN', ANOTHER SHOW

A-SLEEPIN' AT THE FOOT OF THE BED

AT THE CAFE RENDEZVOUS

"A"—YOU'RE ADORABLE (THE ALPHABET SONG)

BABY, IT'S COLD OUTSIDE

BALI HA'I

BAR ROOM POLKA

BEANS AND CORN BREAD

BEFORE YOU CALL

BIANCA

BIG MOVIE SHOW IN THE SKY

BLACK LACE

BLACK VELVET

BLAME MY ABSENT-MINDED HEART

BLOODY MARY

BLOSSOMS ON THE BOUGH, THE

BLUE AND LONESOME

BLUEBIRD ON YOUR WINDOWSILL (THERE'S A)

BLUES, STAY AWAY FROM ME

BOOGIE CHILLEN'

BOPLICITY

BRUSH UP YOUR SHAKESPEARE

BUSY DOING NOTHING

BYE BYE BABY

CABARET

CANDY STORE BLUES

CARELESS HANDS

CIRCUS

C-H-R-I-S-T-M-A-S

COCK-EYED OPTIMIST, A

COLE SLAW

COMME ÇI, COMME ÇA

CONGRATULATIONS

COPPER CANYON

COUNTRY BOY

CRAZY, HE CALLS ME

CRUISING DOWN THE RIVER (ON A SUNDAY AFTERNOON)

CRY-BABY HEART

DEACON'S HOP

DEATH OF LITTLE KATHY FISCUS, THE

DETOUR AHEAD

DIAMONDS ARE A GIRL'S BEST FRIEND

DID YOU SEE JACKIE ROBINSON HIT THAT BALL?

DIME A DOZEN

DITES-MOI

DON'T CRY, JOE (LET HER GO, LET HER GO, LET HER GO)

DON'T PUT ME DOWN

DON'T ROB ANOTHER MAN'S CASTLE

DORMI, DORMI

DREAM IS A WISH YOUR HEART MAKES, A

DREAMER'S HOLIDAY, A

DREAMER WITH A PENNY

DREAM OF YOU

DRINKIN' WINE, SPO-DEE-O-DEE

EARLY AUTUMN

ECHO OF YOUR FOOTSTEPS, THE

ENVY

FAR AWAY PLACES

FAREWELL

FAREWELL AMANDA

FIDDLE DEE DEE

FOOL'S PARADISE

FOREVER AND EVER

FOUR WINDS AND THE SEVEN SEAS

GALWAY BAY

GIRLS WERE MADE TO TAKE CARE OF BOYS

GIVE ME YOUR HAND

GIVE ME YOUR TIRED, YOUR POOR

GODCHILD

GOODBYE, JOHN

HAPPY TALK

HAPPY TIMES

HAVIN' A WONDERFUL WISH

HERE'S TO LOVE

HOMEWORK

HONEY BUN

HOP-SCOTCH POLKA (SCOTCH HOT)

HOT CANARY, THE

HOW IT LIES, HOW IT LIES, HOW IT LIES!

I CAN DREAM, CAN'T I?

I DON'T SEE ME IN YOUR EYES ANYMORE

IF I EVER LOVE AGAIN

IF YOU STUB YOUR TOE ON THE MOON

I GOTTA HAVE MY BABY BACK

I HATE MEN

I JUST DON'T LIKE THIS KIND OF LIVIN'

I'LL NEVER SLIP AROUND AGAIN

I'LL WAIT

I'M BITIN' MY FINGERNAILS AND THINKING OF YOU

I'M GONNA WASH THAT MAN RIGHT OUTA MY HAIR

I'M SO LONESOME I COULD CRY

I'M THROWING RICE (AT THE GIRL I LOVE)

I NEVER SEE MAGGIE ALONE

IN THE LAND OF OO-BLA-DEE

IT HAPPENS EVERY SPRING

IT ONLY HAPPENS ONCE

IT'S A GREAT FEELING

IT'S DELIGHTFUL DOWN IN CHILE

IT'S GREAT TO BE ALIVE

IT'S MIDNIGHT

I'VE COME TO WIVE IT WEALTHILY IN PADUA

I'VE GOT A LOVELY BUNCH OF COCONUTS (ROLL OR BOWL A BALL, A PENNY A PITCH)

I WANNA GO HOME

I WISH I HAD A NICKEL

I YUST GO NUTS AT CHRISTMAS

JEALOUS HEART

JERU

JOHNSON RAG

JUDY

JUST ONE WAY TO SAY I LOVE YOU

KID'S A DREAMER, THE

KISS ME SWEET

LAST MILE HOME, THE

LATE NOW

LAUGHING BOY

LAVENDER BLUE (DILLY DILLY)

LEMON DROP

LET'S TAKE AN OLD FASHIONED WALK

LITTLE GIRL, DON'T CRY

LITTLE GIRL FROM LITTLE ROCK, A

LITTLE GRAY HOUSE, THE

LONELY NIGHT

'LONG ABOUT MIDNIGHT

LOOK AT ME

LOST HIGHWAY

LOST IN A DREAM

LOST IN THE STARS

LOVE ME! LOVE ME! LOVE ME!

LOVER'S GOLD

LOVESICK BLUES

LUSH LIFE

MAMA AND DADDY BROKE MY HEART

MARRIAGE VOW

MAYBE IT'S BECAUSE

MEADOWS OF HEAVEN, THE

MIND YOUR OWN BUSINESS

MISSOURI WALKING PREACHER, THE

MONEY, MARBLES, AND CHALK

MULE TRAIN

MY BOLERO

MY DREAM IS YOURS

MY FILIPINO ROSE

MY FOOLISH HEART

MY LOVE LOVES ME

MY ONE AND ONLY HIGHLAND FLING

NEED YOU

NO ORCHIDS FOR MY LADY

NOW THAT I NEED YOU (WHERE ARE YOU)

ONCE AND FOR ALWAYS

ONE KISS TOO MANY

OVER THREE HILLS

PANHANDLE RAG

PEONY BUSH, THE

PHILADELPHIA LAWYER

PLEASE DON'T LET ME LOVE YOU

PUSSY CAT SONG, THE (NYOW! NYOT NYOW!)

PUT YOUR SHOES ON, LUCY

RAINBOW IN MY HEART

RED ROSES FOR A BLUE LADY

RIDERS IN THE SKY (A COWBOY LEGEND)

RIGHT GIRL FOR ME, THE

RIVER SEINE, THE

ROOM FULL OF ROSES

RUDOLPH THE RED-NOSED REINDEER

SATURDAY NIGHT FISH FRY

SCARLET RIBBONS

SEND TEN PRETTY FLOWERS (TO MY GIRL IN TENNESSEE)

SHE WORE A YELLOW RIBBON

SHOES WITH WINGS ON

SHOW ME THE WAY BACK TO YOUR HEART

SIMILAU

SLEIGH RIDE

SLIDER

SLIPPING AROUND

SMOKEY MOUNTAIN BOOGIE

SO IN LOVE

SOMEDAY (YOU'LL WANT ME TO WANT YOU)

SOME ENCHANTED EVENING

SOMEHOW

SOMEONE LIKE YOU

SONG OF SURRENDER

SO TIRED

STAY WELL

STRICTLY U.S.A.

SUNDAY DOWN IN TENNESSEE

SUNFLOWER

TELL ME WHY

TENNESSEE BORDER

TENNESSEE POLKA

TENNESSEE SATURDAY NIGHT

TENNESSEE TEARS

THAT LUCKY OLD SUN (JUST ROLLS AROUND HEAVEN ALL DAY)

THEN I TURNED AND WALKED SLOWLY AWAY

THERE IS NOTHIN' LIKE A DAME

THERE'LL BE NO TEARDROPS TONIGHT

THERE'S NOT A THING (I WOULDN'T DO FOR YOU)

THERE'S NO TOMORROW

THERE'S NO WINGS ON MY ANGEL

THESE WILL BE THE BEST YEARS OF OUR LIVES

THIS NEARLY WAS MINE

THREE RIVERS, THE (THE ALLEGHENY, SUSQUEHANNA, AND THE OLD MONONGAHELA)

THROUGH A LONG AND SLEEPLESS NIGHT

TILL THE END OF THE WORLD

TOO DARN HOT

TWENTY-FOUR HOURS OF SUNSHINE

UP ABOVE MY HEAD, I HEAR MUSIC IN THE AIR

VIENI SU (SAY YOU LOVE ME TOO)

WARM RED WINE

WEDDING BELLS

WEDDING OF LILI MARLENE, THE

WEEKEND IN THE COUNTRY, A

WEEP NO MORE, MY DARLIN'

WE OPEN IN VENICE

WERE THINE THAT SPECIAL FACE

WHAT CAN I DO?

WHEN IS SOMETIME?

WHERE IS THE LIFE THAT LATE I LED?

WHIRLWIND

WHISPERING HOPE

WHOA! SAILOR!

WHO DO YOU KNOW IN HEAVEN (THAT MADE YOU THE ANGEL YOU ARE?)

WHO SHOT THE HOLE IN MY SOMBRERO?

WHY CAN'T YOU BEHAVE?

WHY DON'T YOU HAUL OFF AND LOVE ME?

WILL SANTY COME TO SHANTY TOWN?

WONDERFUL GUY, A

WUNDERBAR

YA WANNA BUY A BUNNY?

YOU, YOU, YOU ARE THE ONE

YOU BROKE YOUR PROMISE

YOU CAN HAVE HIM

YOUNGER THAN SPRINGTIME

YOU'RE GONNA CHANGE (OR I'M GONNA LEAVE)

YOU'RE IN LOVE WITH SOMEONE

YOU'RE JUST THE KIND

YOU'RE SO UNDERSTANDING

YOU TOLD A LIE (I BELIEVED YOU)

YOU'VE GOT TO BE CAREFULLY TAUGHT

YOU WAS

1950

ACCIDENTS WILL HAPPEN

ADELAIDE'S LAMENT

ALL MY LOVE

AMERICAN BEAUTY ROSE

AND YOU'LL BE HOME

ANTICIPATION BLUES

ANY TIME, ANY PLACE, ANYWHERE

BABY, WON'T YOU SAY YOU LOVE ME?

BAD, BAD WHISKEY

BAMBOO

BE MINE

BELOVED, BE FAITHFUL

BEST THING FOR YOU, THE

BEWITCHED, BOTHERED AND BEWILDERED

BEYOND THE REEF

BIBBIDI-BOBBIDI-BOO

BILLBOARD, THE

BIRMINGHAM BOUNCE

BLOODSHOT EYES

BLUE LIGHT BOOGIE

BLUE SHADOWS

BONAPARTE'S RETREAT

BOULEVARD OF BROKEN DREAMS, THE

BOUTONNIERE

BROKEN DOWN MERRY-GO-ROUND

BUSHEL AND A PECK, A

CALYPSO BLUES

CAN ANYONE EXPLAIN? (NO! NO! NO!)

CANDY AND CAKE

CARELESS KISSES

C'EST SI BON

CHATTANOOGIE SHOE SHINE BOY
CHOO'N GUM
CHRISTMAS IN KILLARNEY
CINCINNATI DANCING PIG
COME DANCE WITH ME
COUNT EVERY STAR
CRY, CRY BABY
CRY OF THE WILD GOOSE, THE
CUDDLE BUGGIN' BABY
CUPID'S BOOGIE
DADDY'S LITTLE GIRL
DARN IT BABY, THAT'S LOVE
DEAR HEARTS AND GENTLE PEOPLE
DEARIE
DECEIVIN' BLUES
DON'CHA GO 'WAY MAD
DON'T ROCK THE BOAT, DEAR
DO SOMETHING FOR ME
DOUBLE CROSSING BLUES
DREAM A LITTLE LONGER
ECHOES
ENCLOSED, ONE BROKEN HEART
END OF A LOVE AFFAIR, THE
ENJOY YOURSELF (IT'S LATER THAN YOU THINK)
EVERY DAY I HAVE THE BLUES
FAIRY TALES
FAT MAN, THE
FOGGY DAY, A (IN LONDON TOWN)
FOLLOW THE FOLD
FRIENDLY STAR
FROSTY THE SNOWMAN
FUGUE FOR TINHORNS
GOD'S COUNTRY
GODS WERE ANGRY WITH ME, THE
GONE FISHIN'
GOODNIGHT, IRENE
GO TO SLEEP, GO TO SLEEP, GO TO SLEEP
GUYS AND DOLLS
HALF A HEART IS ALL YOU LEFT ME (WHEN YOU BROKE MY HEART IN TWO)

HARBOR LIGHTS
HARD LUCK BLUES
HEAVENLY MUSIC
HIGH ON THE LIST
HILLBILLY FEVER
HILLBILLY FEVER, NO. 2
HOME COOKIN'
HOOP-DE-DOO
HORSE TOLD ME, THE
HOSTESS WITH THE MOSTES' ON THE BALL, THE
I ALMOST LOST MY MIND
I AM LOVED
I CAN SEE YOU
I CROSS MY FINGERS
I DIDN'T SLIP, I WASN'T PUSHED, I FELL
I DON'T CARE IF THE SUN DON'T SHINE
IF I KNEW YOU WERE COMIN' I'D'VE BAKED A CAKE
IF I WERE A BELL
IF YOU FEEL LIKE SINGING, SING
IF YOU'VE GOT THE MONEY (I'VE GOT THE TIME)
I'LL ALWAYS LOVE YOU
I'LL GET ALONG SOMEHOW
I'LL KNOW
I'LL NEVER BE FREE
I'LL SAIL MY SHIP ALONE
I LOVE A NEW YORKER
I LOVE THE GUY
I LOVE YOU BECAUSE
I'M GONNA LIVE TILL I DIE
I'M MOVIN' ON
I'M YOURS TO KEEP
I NEED YOU SO
I NEVER HAD A WORRY IN THE WORLD
INFORMATION BLUES
I QUIT MY PRETTY MAMA
I REMEMBER THE CORNFIELDS
I SAID MY PAJAMAS (AND PUT ON MY PRAY'RS)
I STILL FEEL THE SAME ABOUT YOU
I TAUT I SAW A PUDDY TAT

IT ISN'T FAIR

IT'S A LOVELY DAY TODAY

IT'S SO NICE TO HAVE A MAN AROUND THE HOUSE

I'VE NEVER BEEN IN LOVE BEFORE

I WANNA BE LOVED

JET

JUST SAY I LOVE HER

LA VIE EN ROSE

LAZIEST GAL IN TOWN, THE

LET'S DO IT AGAIN

LET'S GO TO CHURCH (NEXT SUNDAY MORNING)

LET'S GO WEST AGAIN

LETTERS HAVE NO ARMS

LIFE IS SO PECULIAR

LILAC WINE

LITTLE ANGEL WITH A DIRTY FACE

LONELY WINE

LONG GONE LONESOME BLUES

LOVEBUG ITCH, THE

LOVE DON'T LOVE NOBODY

LUCK BE A LADY

MAMBO JAMBO

MARRYING FOR LOVE

MAY THE GOOD LORD BLESS AND KEEP YOU

MELANCHOLY RHAPSODY

MERRY CHRISTMAS POLKA, THE

M-I-S-S-I-S-S-I-P-P-I

MISTRUSTING' BLUES

MOANIN' THE BLUES

MONA LISA

MORE I CANNOT WISH YOU

MR. TOUCHDOWN, U.S.A.

MUSIC! MUSIC! MUSIC!

MY HEART CRIES FOR YOU

MY HEART GOES A-GADDING

MY TIME OF DAY

NEVERTHELESS (I'M IN LOVE WITH YOU)

NOBODY'S CHASING ME

NO MAN IS AN ISLAND

NO OTHER LOVE

NOTHIN' FOR NOTHIN'

OCARINA, THE

OH, BABE!

OLD MASTER PAINTER, THE

OLD PIANO ROLL BLUES, THE

ONE FINGER MELODY

ON THE OUTGOING TIDE

OPEN DOOR, OPEN ARMS

ORANGE COLORED SKY

OUR LADY OF FATIMA

OUR LOVE STORY

OUR VERY OWN

PATRICIA

PETER COTTONTAIL

PETITE WALTZ (LA PETITE VALSE)

PICNIC SONG, THE

PINK CHAMPAGNE

PLAY A SIMPLE MELODY

PLEASE SEND ME SOMEONE TO LOVE

QUICKSILVER

RAG MOP

RAINY DAY REFRAIN, A

RED TOP

REMEMBER ME (I'M THE ONE WHO LOVES YOU)

ROSES

ROVING KIND, THE

SAM'S SONG

SCATTERED TOYS

SEA OF THE MOON, THE

SENTIMENTAL ME

SERENATA

SHOW ME THE WAY TO GET OUT OF THIS WORLD ('CAUSE THAT'S WHERE EVERYTHING IS)

SIT DOWN, YOU'RE ROCKIN' THE BOAT

SITTING BY THE WINDOW

SITTIN' ON IT ALL THE TIME

SO LONG, IT'S BEEN GOOD TO KNOW YOU

SO LONG, SALLY

SONG OF DELILAH
SORRY
STAY WITH THE HAPPY PEOPLE
SUE ME
SUGARFOOT RAG
SUNSHINE CAKE
SURE THING (WE'VE GOT A)
SWAMP GIRL
TAKE BACK YOUR MINK
TAKE ME IN YOUR ARMS AND HOLD ME
TEARDROPS FROM MY EYES
TENNESSEE BORDER NO. 2
TENNESSEE WALTZ
THANKS, MISTER FLORIST
THERE MUST BE SOMETHIN' BETTER
  THAN LOVE
THING, THE
THINKING OF YOU
THIRD MAN THEME
THROW YOUR LOVE MY WAY
TO THINK YOU'VE CHOSEN ME
TUNNEL OF LOVE, THE
TZENA, TZENA, TZENA
USE YOUR IMAGINATION
VAGABOND SHOES
VALENTINO TANGO, THE (NOCHE DE
  AMOUR)
VIOLINS FROM NOWHERE
WALKING ALONG WITH BILLY
WANDERIN'
WE JUST COULDN'T SAY GOODBYE
WELL, OH WELL
WHEN THE WIND WAS GREEN
WHEN THE WORLD WAS YOUNG (AH,
  THE APPLE TREES)
WHERE, OH WHERE?
WHY DON'T YOU LOVE ME?
WHY DO THINGS HAPPEN TO ME?
WHY FIGHT THE FEELING?
WHY SHOULD I CRY?
WHY SHOULD WE TRY ANYMORE?
WILHELMINA

YOU AND YOUR BEAUTIFUL EYES
YOU DON'T HAVE TO BE A BABY TO
  CRY
YOU DON'T REMIND ME
YOU'RE ALWAYS THERE
YOU WONDERFUL YOU

1951

ABA DABA HONEYMOON, THE
ALICE IN WONDERLAND
ALL NIGHT LONG
ALWAYS LATE (WITH YOUR KISSES)
ANDIAMO
AND SO TO SLEEP AGAIN
ANOTHER AUTUMN
ANY TIME
BABY, LET ME HOLD YOUR HAND
BECAUSE OF YOU
BELLE, BELLE, MY LIBERTY BELLE
BLACK NIGHT
BLUEBIRD ISLAND
BLUE VELVET
BLUE VIOLINS
BONNE NUIT—GOODNIGHT
BRING BACK THE THRILL
CALLA CALLA
CASTLE ROCK
CHAINS OF LOVE
CHARMAINE
CHEROKEE BOOGIE (EH-OH-ALEENA)
CHICA BOO
CHICKEN SONG, THE (I AIN'T GONNA
  TAKE IT SETTIN' DOWN)
COLD, COLD HEART
COME ON-A MY HOUSE
CRAZY HEART
CRY
CRYING HEART BLUES
DARK IS THE NIGHT
DEAR JOHN
DEAR OLD STOCKHOLM

DESTINATION MOON

DIDJA EVER?

DOMINO

DON'T YOU KNOW I LOVE YOU?

DOWN THE TRAIL OF ACHIN' HEARTS

DOWN YONDER

DUSTY RAG

FOOL, FOOL, FOOL

GEE, BABY

GET OUT THOSE OLD RECORDS

GETTING TO KNOW YOU

GOLDEN ROCKET

GOT HER OFF MY HANDS BUT CAN'T GET HER OFF MY MIND

HEART STRINGS

HELLO, YOUNG LOVERS

HELLO AND GOODBYE

HERE'S TO MY LADY

HEY, GOOD LOOKIN'

HOLD ME—HOLD ME—HOLD ME

HOT ROD RACE

HOW COULD YOU BELIEVE ME WHEN I SAID I LOVE YOU WHEN YOU KNOW I'VE BEEN A LIAR ALL MY LIFE

HOW D'YA LIKE YOUR EGGS IN THE MORNING?

HOW HIGH THE MOON

HOWLIN' AT THE MOON

I APOLOGIZE

I CAN'T HELP IT (IF I'M STILL IN LOVE WITH YOU)

IF

IF TEARDROPS WERE PENNIES

IF YOU TURN ME DOWN

IF YOU WANT TO BE A TOP BANANA

I GET IDEAS (WHEN I DANCE WITH YOU)

I GOT LOADED

I HAVE DREAMED

I LEFT MY HAT IN HAITI

I LIKE IT, I LIKE IT

I'LL BUY YOU A STAR

I LOVE THE SUNSHINE OF YOUR SMILE

I LOVE THE WAY YOU SAY GOODNIGHT

I LOVE YOU A THOUSAND WAYS

I'M A FOOL TO WANT YOU

I'M IN LOVE AGAIN

I'M IN THE MOOD

I'M LATE

I'M LIKE A NEW BROOM

I'M ON MY WAY

I'M WAITING JUST FOR YOU

I'M YOURS TO COMMAND

INCH WORM

IN THE COOL, COOL, COOL OF THE EVENING

INVITATION TO A BROKEN HEART

I RAN ALL THE WAY HOME

I STILL SEE ELISA

I TALK TO THE TREES

IT IS NO SECRET (WHAT GOD CAN DO)

IT'S ALL IN THE GAME

IT'S BEGINNING TO LOOK A LOT LIKE CHRISTMAS

I WANNA PLAY HOUSE WITH YOU

I WANT TO BE WITH YOU ALWAYS

I WHISTLE A HAPPY TUNE

I WILL WAIT

I WISH I HAD A GIRL

I WISH I WUZ

I WON'T CRY ANYMORE

JALOUSIE (JEALOUSY)

JEZEBEL

KISSES SWEETER THAN WINE

KISSIN' BUG BOOGIE

KISS TO BUILD A DREAM ON, A

LEAN BABY

LET ME IN

LET OLD MOTHER NATURE HAVE HER WAY

LET'S LIVE A LITTLE

LIFE IS A BEAUTIFUL THING

LITTLE WHITE CLOUD THAT CRIED, THE

LONELY LITTLE ROBIN

LONGING FOR YOU

SATIN AND SILK
SATISFIED MIND, A
SEVENTEEN
SHIFTING, WHISPERING SANDS, THE
SHOELESS JOE FROM HANNIBAL, MO
SIAMESE CAT SONG, THE
SIBERIA
SILK STOCKINGS
SINCERELY
SINCERELY YOURS
SING A RAINBOW
SIXTEEN TONS
SLOWLY, WITH FEELING
SLUEFOOT
SMACK DAB IN THE MIDDLE
SOLITAIRE
SOMEONE IS SENDING ME FLOWERS
SOMEONE YOU LOVE
SOMETHING'S GOTTA GIVE
SONG OF THE DREAMER
SPEEDOO
SPRING CAN REALLY HANG YOU UP THE
    MOST
STEREOPHONIC SOUND
STORY UNTOLD, A
STRANGE LADY IN TOWN
SUDDENLY THERE'S A VALLEY
SUMMERTIME IN VENICE
SWEET AND GENTLE
SWEET THURSDAY
TENDER TRAP, THE
THAT DO MAKE IT NICE
THAT'S ALL RIGHT
THERE SHE GOES
THIS LITTLE GIRL OF MINE
TIME FOR PARTING
TINA MARIE
TOO TRUE
TOO YOUNG TO GO STEADY
TWEEDLE DEE
24 HOURS A DAY (365 A YEAR)
TWO HEARTS

TWO LOST SOULS
UNCHAINED MELODY
UNSUSPECTING HEART
VERDICT, THE
WAKE THE TOWN AND TELL THE
    PEOPLE
WHAT AM I WORTH
WHAT'CHA GONNA DO?
WHATEVER LOLA WANTS (LOLA GETS)
WHEN YOU DANCE
WHERE IS THAT SOMEONE FOR ME?
WHO'S GOT THE PAIN?
WHY, BABY, WHY?
WHY DON'T YOU WRITE ME?
WILDWOOD FLOWER
WITHOUT LOVE
WOMAN IN LOVE, A
YELLOW ROSE OF TEXAS, THE
YELLOW ROSES
YONDER COMES A SUCKER
YOU ARE MY LOVE
YOU DON'T HAVE TO GO
YOUNG AND FOOLISH
YOU'RE FREE TO GO
YOU'RE NOT MINE ANYMORE
ZAMBEZI

1956

A.B.C.'S OF LOVE, THE
AFTER THE LIGHTS GO DOWN LOW
AIN'T GOT NO HOME
ALLEGHENY MOON
ANGELS IN THE SKY
ANY WAY YOU WANT ME (THAT'S HOW I
    WILL BE)
APRIL IN FAIRBANKS
ARE YOU SATISFIED?
ARMEN'S THEME (YESTERDAY AND YOU)
ASK ME
AUTUMN WALTZ, THE
AWAY ALL BOATS

BABY DOLL

BAD LUCK

BEAUTIFUL LIES

BE-BOP-A-LULA

BELLS ARE RINGING

BIG D

BLACKBOARD OF MY HEART

BLUEBERRY HILL

BLUE SUEDE SHOES

BOPPIN' THE BLUES

BORN TO BE WITH YOU

BO WEEVIL

BUS STOP SONG, THE (A PAPER OF PINS)

CANADIAN SUNSET

CAN I STEAL A LITTLE LOVE?

CAN'T WE BE SWEETHEARTS

CAN YOU FIND IT IN YOUR HEART

CASUAL LOOK, A

CHAIN GANG

CHINCHERINCHEE

CHURCH BELLS MAY RING

CINDY, OH CINDY

CITY OF ANGELS

CONSCIENCE, I'M GUILTY

CRAZY ARMS

DELILAH JONES

DON'T BE CRUEL

DON'T CRY

DON'T GO TO STRANGERS

DOWN IN MEXICO

DREAM ALONG WITH ME (I'M ON MY
  WAY TO A STAR)

DREAMY

DROWN IN MY OWN TEARS

EARTHBOUND

EAT, DRINK AND BE MERRY

EDDIE, MY LOVE

11TH HOUR MELODY

ELOISE

ENGLISH MUFFINS AND IRISH STEW

EVERY DAY OF MY LIFE

FABULOUS CHARACTER

FEVER

FIRST BORN

FIRST WARM DAY IN MAY

FLOWERS MEAN FORGIVENESS

FOLSOM PRISON BLUES

FOOL, THE

FOREVER DARLING

FOR RENT

FORTY DAYS AND FORTY NIGHTS

FRIENDLY PERSUASION (THEE I LOVE)

FROM THE CANDY STORE ON THE
  CORNER TO THE CHAPEL ON THE
  HILL

FROM THE FIRST HELLO TO THE LAST
  GOODBYE

GAME OF LOVE, THE

GARDEN OF EDEN, THE

GET ME TO THE CHURCH ON TIME

GHOST TOWN

GIANT

GIVE US THIS DAY

GLENDORA

GONNA GET ALONG WITHOUT YA NOW

GO ON WITH THE WEDDING

GRADUATION DAY

GREAT PRETENDER, THE

GREEN DOOR, THE

HALLELUJAH I LOVE HER SO

HANDS OFF

HAPPINESS STREET (CORNER SUNSHINE
  SQUARE)

HAPPY TO MAKE YOUR ACQUAINTANCE

HAPPY WHISTLER

HEARTBREAK HOTEL

HEY, DOLL BABY

HEY! JEALOUS LOVER

HIGH SOCIETY CALYPSO

HIGH STEEL

HIS NAME WAS DEAN

HOLD EVERYTHING

HONKY TONK

HONKY TONK MAN

HOPING THAT YOU'RE HOPING

HOT DIGGITY (DOG ZIGGITY BOOM)

HOUND DOG

HOUSE WITH LOVE IN IT, A

HOW FAR IS HEAVEN?

HOW LITTLE WE KNOW (HOW LITTLE IT MATTERS)

I CAN'T LOVE YOU ENOUGH

I COULD HAVE DANCED ALL NIGHT

I DON'T BELIEVE YOU'VE MET MY BABY

I DREAMED

IF I HAD MY DRUTHERS

IF'N

I FORGOT TO REMEMBER TO FORGET

I'LL BE HOME

I'LL CRY TOMORROW

I LOVE YOU, SAMANTHA

I'M AN ORDINARY MAN

I'M AVAILABLE

I'M GONNA LAUGH YOU RIGHT OUT OF MY LIFE

I'M IN LOVE AGAIN

IMPOSSIBLE

I'M SO IN LOVE WITH YOU

I NEVER FELT THIS WAY BEFORE

IN THE MIDDLE OF THE HOUSE

IN THE STILL OF THE NITE (I'LL REMEMBER)

I PROMISE TO REMEMBER

ISN'T HE ADORABLE?

I TAKE THE CHANCE

ITALIAN THEME, THE

IT ISN'T RIGHT

IT ONLY HURTS FOR A LITTLE WHILE

IT'S A GREAT LIFE

IT'S BETTER IN THE DARK

IT'S TOO LATE

I'VE BEEN SEARCHING

I'VE GOT FIVE DOLLARS AND IT'S SATURDAY NIGHT

I'VE GROWN ACCUSTOMED TO HER FACE

IVORY TOWER

I WALK THE LINE

I WANNA DO MORE

I WANT YOU, I NEED YOU, I LOVE YOU

I WANT YOU TO BE MY GIRL

I WAS THE ONE

JIVIN' AROUND

JOEY, JOEY, JOEY

JOHNNY CONCHO THEME (WAIT FOR ME)

JUBILATION T. CORNPONE

JUKE BOX BABY

JULIE

JUST IN TIME

JUST WALKING IN THE RAIN

JUST YOU WAIT

KA-DING-DONG (MY HEART GOES)

KISS ME ANOTHER

KNEE DEEP IN THE BLUES

LATE, LATE SHOW, THE

LAY DOWN YOUR ARMS

LET THE GOOD TIMES ROLL

LIPSTICK AND CANDY AND RUBBERSOLE SHOES

LISBON ANTIGUA (IN OLD LISBON)

LITTLE CHILD

LITTLE GIRL OF MINE

LITTLE ROSA

LONG BEFORE I KNEW YOU

LONG TALL SALLY

LOVE IN A HOME

LOVE ME

LOVE ME, TENDER

LOVE, LOVE, LOVE

LULLABY IN BLUE

MACK THE KNIFE (MORITAT)

MADLY IN LOVE

MAGIC TOUCH, THE (YOU'VE GOT)

MAMA, TEACH ME TO DANCE

MAMA FROM THE TRAIN

MAN WITH THE GOLDEN ARM, THE

MAN WITH THE GOLDEN ARM, THE (MAIN TITLE)

MARRIED I CAN ALWAYS GET
MEMORIES ARE MADE OF THIS
MIND IF I MAKE LOVE TO YOU
MIRACLE OF LOVE
MONEY TREE, THE
MOONGLOW
MOONLIGHT LOVE
MORE
MOST HAPPY FELLA, THE
MR. WONDERFUL
MU-CHA-CHA
MUTUAL ADMIRATION SOCIETY
MY BABY LEFT ME
MY DESTINY
MY DREAM SONATA
MY HAPPINESS FOREVER
MY HEART IS SO FULL OF YOU
MY LIPS ARE SEALED
MY PRAYER
MYSTERY TRAIN
NAMELY YOU
NEVER LEAVE ME
NEW-FANGLED TANGO, A
NEXT TIME YOU SEE ME
NIGHT LIGHTS
NINETY-NINE YEARS (DEAD OR ALIVE)
NO, NOT MUCH
NO MONEY DOWN
NO OTHER ONE
NOTHING EVER CHANGES MY LOVE FOR
  YOU
NOW YOU HAS JAZZ
OH, WHAT A NIGHT
ON LONDON BRIDGE
ON THE STREET WHERE YOU LIVE
OTHER WOMAN, THE
OUT OF SIGHT, OUT OF MIND
PARTY'S OVER, THE
PASSING THROUGH
PETTICOATS OF PORTUGAL
PLEADIN' FOR LOVE
PLEASE, PLEASE, PLEASE

POOR BOY
POOR PEOPLE OF PARIS, THE
PORT-AU-PRINCE
PORTUGUESE WASHERWOMEN, THE
PREACHER, THE
QUE SERA, SERA (WHATEVER WILL BE,
  WILL BE)
RAIN IN SPAIN, THE
READY TEDDY
REPEAT AFTER ME
RIP IT UP
ROCK-A-BYE YOUR BABY WITH A DIXIE
  MELODY
ROCK AND ROLL WALTZ, THE
ROCK ISLAND LINE
ROLL OVER BEETHOVEN
ROSE AND A BABY RUTH, A
ROUND AND ROUND
SADIE'S SHAWL
ST. THERESE OF THE ROSES
SEASONS OF MY HEART
SEE SAW
SEE YOU LATER, ALLIGATOR
SEVEN DAYS
SHAPE OF THINGS, THE
SHE'S GOT IT
SHOW ME
SINCE I MET YOU BABY
SLIPPIN' AND SLIDIN' (PEEPIN' AND
  HIDIN')
SLOW WALK
SO DOGGONE LONESOME
SO LONG
SOFT SUMMER BREEZE
SOMEBODY SOMEWHERE
SOMEBODY UP THERE LIKES ME
SONG FOR A SUMMER NIGHT
SPRING IN MAINE
STANDING ON THE CORNER
STEAMBOAT
STILL
STORY OF LOVE, THE

STRANDED IN THE JUNGLE
SWEET DREAMS
SWEET HEARTACHES
SWEET OLD FASHIONED GIRL, A
TEAR FELL, A
TEEN AGE PRAYER
TELL ME WHY
THAT'S ALL THERE IS TO THAT
THEME FROM "EAST OF EDEN"
THEME FROM "PICNIC"
THEME FROM "THE PROUD ONES"
THEMES FROM "THE MAN WITH THE
    GOLDEN ARM"
THESE HANDS
THIS COULD BE THE START OF
    SOMETHING
THIS IS WHAT I CALL LOVE
THIS LAND IS YOUR LAND
TO LOVE AGAIN
TONIGHT YOU BELONG TO ME
TOO CLOSE FOR COMFORT
TOO MUCH MONKEY BUSINESS
TO YOU, MY LOVE
TRAIN OF LOVE
TRA LA LA
TRANSFUSION
TREASURE OF LOVE
TROUBLE WITH HARRY, THE
TRUE LOVE
TUTTI FRUTTI
TWENTY FEET OF MUDDY WATER
TWO DIFFERENT WORLDS
UNCLE PEN
UP ON THE MOUNTAIN
WALK HAND IN HAND
WAR AND PEACE
WARM ALL OVER
WAYWARD WIND, THE
WHATCHA' GONNA DO WHEN YOUR
    BABY LEAVES YOU
WHEN SUNNY GETS BLUE
WHO WANTS TO BE A MILLIONAIRE?

WHY CAN'T THE ENGLISH?
WHY DO FOOLS FALL IN LOVE?
WITCHCRAFT
WITH A LITTLE BIT OF LUCK
WITHOUT YOU
WONDERFUL! WONDERFUL!
WOULDN'T IT BE LOVERLY?
WRINGLE WRANGLE
WRITTEN ON THE WIND
YES, I KNOW WHY
YOU AND ME
YOU ARE THE ONE
YOU CAN'T RUN AWAY FROM IT
YOU DONE ME WRONG
YOU DON'T KNOW ME
YOU GOTTA BE MY BABY
YOUNG IDEAS
YOU'RE RUNNING WILD
YOU'RE SENSATIONAL
YOU'RE STILL MINE

1957

ACCORDING TO MY HEART
AFFAIR TO REMEMBER, AN
AFTER SCHOOL
AIN'T IT DE TRUTH?
AIN'T THAT LOVE
ALL SHOOK UP
ALL THE WAY
ALMOST PARADISE
ALONE (WHY MUST I BE ALONE)
AMERICA
ANASTASIA
AND THAT REMINDS ME
APRIL LOVE
AROUND THE WORLD
BANANA BOAT SONG, THE (DAY-O)
BE-BOP BABY
BERNADINE
BLACK SLACKS
BLUE MONDAY

BON VOYAGE
BONY MORONIE
BOY ON A DOLPHIN
BUTTERFLY
BUZZ-BUZZ-BUZZ
BYE BYE LOVE
ÇA, C'EST L'AMOUR
CALYPSO MELODY
CARIBBEAN COCKTAIL
C'EST L'AMOUR
CHANCES ARE
CHANTEZ, CHANTEZ
CINCO ROBLES (FIVE OAKS)
COCOANUT SWEET
COCOANUT WOMAN
COME GO WITH ME
COME TO ME
COMMENT ALLEZ-VOUS?
COOL
COULD THIS BE MAGIC
DARK MOON
DIANA
DID YOU CLOSE YOUR EYES? (WHEN WE KISSED)
DO I LOVE YOU BECAUSE YOU'RE BEAUTIFUL
DON'T
DON'T FORBID ME
DON'T LAUGH
DON'T LET GO
EMPTY ARMS
EVERYONE'S LAUGHING
FABULOUS
FALLEN STAR, A
FARTHER UP THE ROAD
FASCINATION
FIRST DATE, FIRST KISS, FIRST LOVE
FLINGS
FORGOTTEN DREAMS
FOUR WALLS
FRAULEIN
FREIGHT TRAIN

GEE, OFFICER KRUPKE
GIRL CAN'T HELP IT, THE
GIRL WITH THE GOLDEN BRAIDS, THE
GIRL WITH THE HEATHER GREEN EYES, THE
GO AWAY WITH ME
GONE
GONNA FIND ME A BLUEBIRD
GOODNIGHT MY LOVE (PLEASANT DREAMS)
GOODNIGHT MY SOMEONE
GREAT BALLS OF FIRE
HAPPY, HAPPY BIRTHDAY BABY
HEY, SCHOOLGIRL
HONEST I DO
HONEYCOMB
HONKY TONK SONG
HULA LOVE
I FEEL PRETTY
I FOUND MY GIRL IN THE U.S.A.
I HEARD THE BLUEBIRDS SING
I JUST DON'T KNOW
I LIKE YOUR KIND OF LOVE
I'LL REMEMBER TODAY
I'M A ONE WOMAN MAN
I'M AVAILABLE
I'M COMING HOME
I'M GONNA SIT RIGHT DOWN AND WRITE MYSELF A LETTER
I MISS YOU ALREADY
I'M JUST A COUNTRY BOY
I'M STICKIN' WITH YOU
I'M TIRED
I'M WALKING
INDEPENDENT (ON MY OWN)
I NEVER FELT MORE LIKE FALLING IN LOVE
IN MY OWN LITTLE CORNER
IN THE MIDDLE OF AN ISLAND
IS IT WRONG (FOR LOVING YOU)
ISLAND IN THE SUN
IT HURTS TO BE IN LOVE

IT'S GOOD TO BE ALIVE

IT'S NOT FOR ME TO SAY

IT'S YOU

IT'S YOU I LOVE

I'VE GOT A NEW HEARTACHE

IVY ROSE

I WON'T BE THE FOOL ANYMORE

JAILHOUSE ROCK

JAMAICA FAREWELL

JENNY, JENNY

JIM DANDY

JINGLE BELL ROCK

JOEY'S SONG

JOKER, THE (THAT'S WHAT THEY CALL ME)

JUST BECAUSE

JUST BETWEEN YOU AND ME

JUST BORN (TO BE YOUR BABY)

JUST MY LUCK

JUST ONE MORE

KEEP A KNOCKIN'

KISSES SWEETER THAN WINE

LADDER OF LOVE, THE

LASTING LOVE

LET IT BE ME

LET THE FOUR WINDS BLOW

LIDA ROSE

LIECHTENSTEINER POLKA

LIPS OF WINE

LITTLE BISCUIT

LITTLE BITTY PRETTY ONE

LITTLE DARLIN'

LONELY ISLAND

LONG LONELY NIGHTS

LOOK AT 'ER

LOOK HOMEWARD, ANGEL

LOVE IS A GOLDEN RING

LOVE IS STRANGE

LOVE LETTERS IN THE SAND

LOVELY NIGHT, A

LOVE ME FOREVER

LOVE ME TO PIECES

LOVING YOU

LUCILLE

LUCKY LIPS

MAMA GUITAR

MAMA LOOK A BOOBOO

MANGOS

MARIA

MARIANNE

MARIAN THE LIBRARIAN

MEANING OF THE BLUES, THE

MELODIE D'AMOUR

MI CASA, SU CASA (MY HOUSE IS YOUR HOUSE)

MISS ANN

MISSING YOU

MOONLIGHT GAMBLER

MOONLIGHT SWIM

MR. LEE

MY PERSONAL POSSESSION

MY SHOES KEEP WALKING BACK TO YOU

MY SPECIAL ANGEL

NAPOLEON

NEXT IN LINE

NINETY-NINE WAYS

NO LOVE (BUT YOUR LOVE)

OH JULIE

OLD CAPE COD

ON MY MIND AGAIN

ONE HAND, ONE HEART

ONE IS A LONELY NUMBER

ONLY TRUST YOUR HEART

OVER THE MOUNTAIN, ACROSS THE SEA

PAMELA THROWS A PARTY

PARTY DOLL

PASSING STRANGERS

PEANUTS

PEGGY SUE

PLEASE DON'T BLAME ME

PLEASE SAY YOU WANT ME

POOR MAN'S RICHES

POOR MAN'S ROSES, A (OR A RICH MAN'S GOLD)

PRETEND YOU DON'T SEE HER

PRETTY TO WALK WITH

PROMISE HER ANYTHING (BUT GIVE HER LOVE)

PUSH THE BUTTON

PUT A LIGHT IN THE WINDOW

QUEEN OF THE SENIOR PROM

RAINBOW

RANG TANG DING DONG (I AM THE JAPANESE SANDMAN)

RAUNCHY

REMEMBER YOU'RE MINE

REPENTING

RHYTHM OF RAINDROPS, THE

ROCK-A-BILLY

ROCK AND ROLL MUSIC

ROCKIN' PNEUMONIA AND THE BOOGIE WOOGIE FLU

ROCK YOUR LITTLE BABY TO SLEEP

ROSIE LEE

SAVANNAH

SAYONARA

SCHOOL DAY

SEARCHIN'

SEND FOR ME

SEND ME SOME LOVIN'

SEVENTY-SIX TROMBONES

SHIRLEY

SHORT FAT FANNIE

SICK AND TIRED

SILHOUETTES

SINGING THE BLUES

SITTIN' IN THE BALCONY

SOFT SANDS

SOMETHING'S COMING

SOMEWHERE

SONG OF RAINTREE COUNTY, THE

SO RARE

SOUVENIR D'ITALIE

START MOVIN' (IN MY DIRECTION)

STAY HERE WITH ME

STOLEN MOMENTS

STORY OF MY LIFE, THE

SUMMER LOVE

SUNSHINE GIRL (HAS RAINDROPS IN HER EYES)

SUSIE-Q

SWANEE RIVER ROCK (TALKIN' 'BOUT THAT RIVER)

TAKE IT SLOW, JOE

TAMMY

TANGLED MIND

(LET ME BE YOUR) TEDDY BEAR

TEEN AGE CRUSH

TEENAGER'S ROMANCE, A

THAT FACE

THAT'LL BE THE DAY

(BUT AS THEY SAY) THAT'S LIFE

THAT'S WHY I WAS BORN

THERE YOU GO

THINK

THOUSAND MILES AWAY, A

3:10 TO YUMA

THROUGH THE EYES OF LOVE

TILL

TILL THERE WAS YOU

TONIGHT

TOO MUCH

TO THE AISLE

TREAT ME NICE

TWELFTH OF NEVER, THE

TWO SHADOWS ON YOUR WINDOW

VALLEY OF TEARS

VERY SPECIAL LOVE, A

WAGON TRAIN

WAKE UP LITTLE SUSIE

WALKIN' AFTER MIDNIGHT

WARM

WASTED WORDS

WHISPERING BELLS

WHITE SILVER SANDS

WHITE SPORT COAT, A (AND A PINK CARNATION)

WHOLE LOT-TA SHAKIN' GOIN' ON

WHO NEEDS YOU?

WHY BABY WHY

WILD IS THE WIND

WITH ALL MY HEART

WITHOUT LOVE (THERE IS NOTHING)

WITH YOU ON MY MIND

WONDERING

YES TONIGHT, JOSEPHINE

YOU CAN'T LOSE THE BLUES WITH
   COLORS

YOU DON'T OWE ME A THING

YOU GOT ME DIZZY

YOU NEED HANDS

YOU SEND ME

YOU'RE THE REASON (I'M IN LOVE)

YOUR TRUE LOVE

YOUNG BLOOD

YOUNG LOVE

1958

ALL GROWN UP

ALL I HAVE TO DO IS DREAM

ALL OF THESE AND MORE

ALL OVER AGAIN

ALL THE TIME

ALMOST IN YOUR ARMS (LOVE SONG
   FROM "HOUSEBOAT")

ALONE WITH YOU

ANGEL BABY

ANGEL SMILE

ANNA MARIE

ANOTHER TIME, ANOTHER PLACE

ARE YOU REALLY MINE?

ARE YOU SINCERE?

AT THE HOP

BALLAD OF A TEENAGE QUEEN

BALLAD OF PALADIN, THE

BEEP BEEP

BELIEVE WHAT YOU SAY

BIG DADDY

BIG GUITAR, THE

BIG MAN

BILLY BAYOU

BIMBOMBEY

BING! BANG! BONG!

BIRD DOG

BLOB, THE

BLUE, BLUE DAY

BLUEBELL

BOOK OF LOVE

BORN TOO LATE

BREATHLESS

CALL ME

CANNONBALL

CAROL

CATCH A FALLING STAR

CERTAIN SMILE, A

CERVEZA

CHA-HUA-HUA

CHANSON D'AMOUR (SONG OF LOVE)

CHANTILLY LACE

CHILDREN'S MARCHING SONG, THE
   (THIS OLD MAN)

CHIPMUNK SONG, THE (CHRISTMAS
   DON'T BE LATE)

CITY LIGHTS

C'MON EVERYBODY

COLONEL BOGEY

COME ON, LET'S GO

COME PRIMA (FOR THE FIRST TIME)

COME TO ME

CRAZY LOVE

CURTAIN IN THE WINDOW

DANCE, EVERYONE, DANCE

DAY THE RAINS CAME, THE

DEDE DINAH

DEVOTED TO YOU

DONCHA' THINK IT'S TIME

DONDE ESTA SANTA CLAUS? (WHERE IS
   SANTA CLAUS?)

DONNA

DON'T ASK ME WHY

DORMI, DORMI, DORMI

DOWN THE AISLE OF LOVE

DO YOU WANT TO DANCE? (DO YOU WANNA DANCE?)

DRIP DROP

EARLY IN THE MORNING

EL RANCHO ROCK

ENCHANTED ISLAND

END, THE (AT THE END OF THE RAINBOW)

ENDLESS SLEEP

EVERYBODY LOVES A LOVER

FALLIN'

FALLING BACK TO YOU

FATE

FEMININITY

FEVER

FIREFLY

FORGET ME NOT

FOR MY GOOD FORTUNE

FOR YOUR LOVE

FOR YOUR PRECIOUS LOVE

GEE, BUT IT'S LONELY

GEISHA GIRL

GET A JOB

GIGI

GINGER BREAD

GIRL ON PAGE 44, THE

GIVE IT ALL YOU'VE GOT

GIVE MYSELF A PARTY

GOOD GOLLY MISS MOLLY

GRANT AVENUE

GUAGLIONE (THE MAN WHO PLAYS THE MANDOLINO)

GUESS THINGS HAPPEN THAT WAY

HALF A MIND

HANG UP MY ROCK AND ROLL SHOES

HARD HEADED WOMAN

HE'S GOT THE WHOLE WORLD IN HIS HANDS

HIBISCUS

HIDEAWAY

HIGH SCHOOL CONFIDENTIAL

HOLIDAY FOR LOVE

HOME OF THE BLUES

HOW THE TIME FLIES

HULA HOOP SONG, THE

HUNDRED MILLION MIRACLES, A

I BEG OF YOU

I BELIEVE IN YOU

I CAN'T STOP LOVING YOU

I CRIED A TEAR

I ENJOY BEING A GIRL

IF DREAMS COME TRUE

IF I HAD A HAMMER

I GOT A FEELING

I GOT STUNG

I KNOW WHERE I'M GOIN'

I'LL COME RUNNING BACK TO YOU

I'LL WAIT FOR YOU

I'M GLAD I'M NOT YOUNG ANYMORE

I REMEMBER IT WELL

IT AMAZES ME

ITCHY TWITCHY FEELING

IT'S A BORE

IT'S ALL IN THE GAME

IT'S JUST ABOUT TIME

IT'S ONLY MAKE BELIEVE

I WONDER WHY

JENNIE LEE

JO-ANN

JOHNNY B. GOODE

JUMPING JACK

JUST A DREAM

JUST YOUNG

KATHY O'

KEWPIE DOLL

LA DEE DAH

LAZY MARY

LAZY SUMMER NIGHT

LEFT RIGHT OUT OF YOUR HEART

LET THE BELLS KEEP RINGING

LIGHT OF LOVE

LI'L DARLIN'

LITTLE BLUE MAN, THE

LITTLE DRUMMER BOY, THE

LITTLE STAR

LOLLIPOP

LONELY TEARDROPS

LONESOME TOWN

LONG HOT SUMMER, THE

LONG LEGGED LADIES OF LABRADOR

LOOKING BACK

LOVE, LOOK AWAY

LOVE EYES

LOVE IS ALL WE NEED

LOVE MAKES THE WORLD GO 'ROUND

LOVE YOU MOST OF ALL

LUCKY LADYBUG

MAGIC MOMENTS

MANDOLINS IN THE MOONLIGHT

MAVERICK

MAYBE

MOON TALK

MY TRUE LOVE

NEE NEE NA NA NA NA NU NU

NIGHT THEY INVENTED CHAMPAGNE,
  THE

NOBODY BUT YOU

NO CHEMISE, PLEASE

NON DIMENTICAR (DON'T FORGET)

NO ONE KNOWS

NOW AND FOR ALWAYS

OH, LONESOME ME

OH-OH, I'M FALLING IN LOVE AGAIN

ONE NIGHT

ONE SUMMER NIGHT

ONLY THE LONELY

PADRE

PANSY

PARIS

PATRICIA

PEEK-A-BOO

PHILADELPHIA, U.S.A.

POOR LITTLE FOOL

PROBLEMS

PROMISE ME LOVE

PURPLE PEOPLE EATER, THE

PUSSY CAT

PUSSYFOOT, THE

PUT YOUR HEAD ON MY SHOULDER

QUEEN OF THE HOP

RAMROD

RAVE ON

RAWHIDE

REBEL-ROUSER

RETURN TO ME (RITORNA A ME)

RIVER KWAI MARCH

ROCK AND ROLL IS HERE TO STAY

ROCKHOUSE

ROCKIN' ROBIN

RUMBLE

SAIL ALONG, SILV'RY MOON

SATIN DOLL

SAY, DARLING

SAY A PRAYER FOR ME TONIGHT

SECRET, THE

SECRETLY

SEND ME THE PILLOW YOU DREAM ON

SHE WAS ONLY SEVENTEEN (HE WAS
  ONE YEAR MORE)

SHORT SHORTS

SING BOY SING

SKINNY MINNIE

SOMEBODY TOUCHED ME

SONG FROM "SOME CAME RUNNING"
  (TO LOVE AND BE LOVED)

SPLISH SPLASH

STAGGER LEE

STAIRWAY OF LOVE

STAY

STOOD UP

STOP THE WORLD (AND LET ME OFF)

STROLL, THE

STUPID CUPID

SUGAR MOON

SUGARTIME

SUMMERTIME, SUMMERTIME

SUMMERTIME BLUES

SUMMERTIME LIES
SUNDAY
SUNDAY IN NEW YORK
SUSIE DARLIN'
SWEET LITTLE SIXTEEN
SWINGIN' SHEPHERD BLUES, THE
TALK TO ME, TALK TO ME
TEACHER, TEACHER
TEACHER'S PET
TEARS ON MY PILLOW
TEQUILA
THANK HEAVEN FOR LITTLE GIRLS
THERE'S ONLY ONE OF YOU
THIS HAPPY FEELING
THIS LITTLE GIRL OF MINE
THIS LITTLE GIRL'S GONE ROCKIN'
THURSDAY'S CHILD
TO BE LOVED
TO KNOW HIM IS TO LOVE HIM
TOM DOOLEY
TOM THUMB'S TUNE
TOPSY II
TORERO
TUPELO COUNTY JAIL
TWENTY-SIX MILES (SANTA CATALINA)
TWILIGHT TIME
VERY PRECIOUS LOVE, A
VIOLET AND A ROSE, THE
VOICE IN MY HEART, THE
VOLARE (NEL BLU, DIPINTO DI BLU)
WAITING GAME, THE
WAITIN' IN SCHOOL
WALTZ AT MAXIM'S (SHE IS NOT
  THINKING OF ME)
WAYS OF A WOMAN IN LOVE, THE
WEAR MY RING AROUND YOUR NECK
WE BELONG TOGETHER
WEDDING, THE
WESTERN MOVIES
WHAT AM I LIVING FOR?
WHAT DO I CARE?
WHAT MAKES A MAN WANDER

WHEN
WHEN THE BOYS TALK ABOUT THE
  GIRLS
WHOLE LOTTA LOVING
WHO'S SORRY NOW?
WHY, WHY
WHY DON'T THEY UNDERSTAND
WILLIE AND THE HAND JIVE
WIN YOUR LOVE FOR ME
WISHING FOR YOUR LOVE
WITCHCRAFT
WITCH DOCTOR
WORLD OUTSIDE, THE
YAKETY YAK
YAWNING SONG, THE
YOU ARE BEAUTIFUL
YOU ARE MY DESTINY
YOU CHEATED
YOU DON'T KNOW HIM
YOU FASCINATE ME SO
YOU GOTTA LOVE EVERYBODY
YOUNG AND WARM AND WONDERFUL
YOU'RE THE NEAREST THING TO
  HEAVEN
YOUR NAME IS BEAUTIFUL
ZORRO

1959

ALL-AMERICAN BOY, THE
ALL I NEED IS THE GIRL
ALL MY TOMORROWS
ALMOST GROWN
ALONG CAME JONES
ALVIN'S HARMONICA
AM I THAT EASY TO FORGET?
ANGELS LISTENED IN, THE
ANYONE WOULD LOVE YOU
BABY TALK
BACK IN THE U.S.A.
BALLAD OF THE SAD YOUNG MEN, THE
BATTLE OF KOOKAMONGA, THE

BATTLE OF NEW ORLEANS, THE
BE MY GUEST
BEST IS YET TO COME, THE
BEST OF EVERYTHING, THE
BETTY MY ANGEL
BIG HUNK O'LOVE, A
BIG HURT, THE
BIG MIDNIGHT SPECIAL
BILLY
BOBBY SOX TO STOCKINGS
BONGO ROCK
BOY WITHOUT A GIRL, A
BROKEN-HEARTED MELODY
CHARLIE BROWN
CIAO, CIAO, BAMBINA
CLIMB EV'RY MOUNTAIN
COME INTO MY HEART
COME SOFTLY TO ME
COME TO ME
COME WALK WITH ME
COUNTRY GIRL
COUNTRY MUSIC IS HERE TO STAY
CROSSFIRE
DANCE WITH ME
DARK HOLLOW
DECK OF CARDS, THE
DIARY, THE
DON'T PITY ME
DON'T TAKE YOUR GUNS TO TOWN
DON'T TELL ME YOUR TROUBLES
DON'T YOU KNOW
DO-RE-MI
DREAM LOVER
EL PASO
ENCHANTED
ENCHANTED SEA, THE
ENDLESSLY
ERBIE FITCH'S TWITCH
EVERYBODY LIKES TO CHA CHA CHA
EVERYTHING'S COMING UP ROSES
FAIR WARNING
FIRST ANNIVERSARY

FIRST NAME INITIAL
FIVE FEET HIGH AND RISING
FIVE PENNIES, THE
FOOLS' HALL OF FAME
FOOL SUCH AS I, A (NOW AND THEN
    THERE'S)
FOR A PENNY
FORTY MILES OF BAD ROAD
FRANKIE
FRENCH FOREIGN LEGION
GENTLEMAN JIMMY
GIDGET
GO, JIMMY, GO
GOODBYE BABY
GOODBYE JIMMY, GOODBYE
GOTTA TRAVEL ON
GRIN AND BEAR IT
HANGING TREE, THE
HAPPIEST MOMENTS IN LIFE, THE
HAPPY ANNIVERSARY
HAPPY ORGAN, THE
HAWAIIAN WEDDING SONG, THE
HEARTACHES BY THE NUMBER
HERE COMES SUMMER
HEY, LITTLE GIRL
HEY, LITTLE LUCY! (DON'TCHA PUT NO
    LIPSTICK ON)
HIGH HOPES
HOME
HOUND DOG MAN
HUSHABYE
I AIN'T NEVER
I CAN'T GET YOU OUT OF MY HEART
IF I HAD A GIRL
I GO APE
I GOT A WIFE
I GOT STRIPES
I'LL BE SATISFIED
I'M A MAN
I'M GONNA BE A WHEEL SOMEDAY
I'M GONNA GET MARRIED
I'M IN LOVE AGAIN

I'M LOOKING OUT THE WINDOW

I'M READY

I NEED YOUR LOVE TONIGHT

I NEED YOUR LOVIN'

I SAY HELLO

IT DOESN'T MATTER ANYMORE

IT'S JUST A MATTER OF TIME

IT'S LATE

IT'S ONLY THE BEGINNING

IT'S TIME TO CRY

IT WAS I

I'VE COME OF AGE

I'VE HAD IT

I'VE RUN OUT OF TOMORROWS

I WAITED TOO LONG

I WANT TO WALK YOU HOME

JUST A LITTLE TOO MUCH

JUST ASK YOUR HEART

JUST AS MUCH AS EVER

JUST FOR ONCE

JUST KEEP IT UP

KANSAS CITY

KISSIN' TIME

KOOKIE, KOOKIE (LEND ME YOUR COMB)

LA BAMBA

LA PLUME DE MA TANTE

LAST RIDE, THE

LAUGH, I THOUGHT I'D DIE

LET ME ENTERTAIN YOU

LET'S LOVE

LIFE TO GO

LIKE YOUNG

LIPSTICK ON YOUR COLLAR

LITTLE DIPPER

LITTLE LAMB

LITTLE SPACE GIRL

LIVING DOLL

LONELY BOY (I'M JUST A)

LONELY FOR YOU

LONELY GOATHERD, THE

LONELY ONE, THE

LONELY STREET

LONG BLACK VEIL

LOVE POTION NUMBER NINE

LOVER'S QUESTION, A

LULLABY IN RAGTIME

LUTHER PLAYED THE BOOGIE

M.T.A., THE

MACK THE KNIFE

MAKIN' LOVE

MANHATTAN SPIRITUAL

MARIA

MARINA

MARY LOU

MATING GAME, THE

MAY YOU ALWAYS

MIDNIGHT FLYER

MOMMY FOR A DAY

MORGEN (ONE MORE SUNRISE)

MR. BLUE

M.T.A., THE

MUSIC OF HOME, THE

MY BABY'S GONE

MY FAVORITE THINGS

MY HEART IS AN OPEN BOOK

MY WISH CAME TRUE

NEVER BE ANYONE ELSE BUT YOU

NO OTHER ARMS, NO OTHER LIPS

OH! CAROL

OLD MOON

ON AN EVENING IN ROMA

ONCE KNEW A FELLA

ONLY SIXTEEN

ON THE BEACH

PARTNERS

(YOU'VE GOT) PERSONALITY

PETER GUNN

PETITE FLEUR

PICK ME UP ON YOUR WAY DOWN

PICK-POCKET TANGO

PILLOW TALK

PINK SHOELACES

PLAIN JANE

POISON IVY

POLITICS AND POKER

POOR BOY
POOR JENNY
POOR OLD HEARTSICK ME
PRETTY BLUE EYES
PRETTY GIRLS EVERYWHERE
PRIMROSE LANE
QUIET VILLAGE
RAW-HIDE
RED RIVER ROCK
RED RIVER ROSE
REVEILLE ROCK
RIGHT TIME, THE
RING-A-LING-A-LARIO
RIO BRAVO
ROBBIN' THE CRADLE
RUNNING BEAR
SANDY
SAY, MAN
SEA OF LOVE
SECRET OF CHRISTMAS, THE
SEE YOU IN SEPTEMBER
SERMONETTE
SET HIM FREE
SEVEN LITTLE GIRLS SITTING IN THE
  BACK SEAT
77 SUNSET STRIP
SHE SAY (OOM DOOBY DOOM)
SHIMMY, SHIMMY, KO-KO-BOP
SHOUT
SINCE I DON'T HAVE YOU
SIX BOYS AND SEVEN GIRLS
16 CANDLES
SIXTEEN GOING ON SEVENTEEN
SLEEP WALK
SMALL WORLD
SMOKE GETS IN YOUR EYES
SMOKIE—PART 2
SO CLOSE
SO FINE
SO MANY WAYS
SOMEBODY'S BACK IN TOWN
SOME PEOPLE
SORRY, I RAN ALL THE WAY HOME

SOUND OF MUSIC, THE
STARRY EYED
STAYING YOUNG
STORY OF MY LOVE, THE
STORY OF OUR LOVE, THE
STRANGE ARE THE WAYS OF LOVE
SWEETER THAN YOU
TAKE A MESSAGE TO MARY
TAKE ME ALONG
TALK THAT TALK
TALK TO ME
TALLAHASSEE LASSIE
TALL PAUL
TEAR DROP
TEARDROPS ON YOUR LETTER
TEARDROPS WILL FALL
TEDDY
TEENAGER IN LOVE, A
TEEN BEAT
TELL HIM NO
TENNESSEE STUD
TEN THOUSANDS DRUMS
THANK YOU PRETTY BABY
THAT'S ENOUGH
THAT'S WHAT IT'S LIKE TO BE
  LONESOME
THAT'S WHY (I LOVE YOU SO)
THERE GOES MY BABY
THERE'S SOMETHING ON YOUR MIND
THEY CAME TO CORDURA
THIS FRIENDLY WORLD
THIS I SWEAR
THIS SHOULD GO ON FOREVER
THOUSAND MILES AGO, A
THREE BELLS, THE (THE JIMMY
  BROWN SONG)
THREE STARS
TIGER
TIJUANA JAIL, THE
'TIL I KISSED YOU
TIL TOMORROW
TOGETHER WHEREVER WE GO
TOMBOY

TOO LONG AT THE FAIR

TOO MUCH TEQUILA

TOUCH OF PINK, A

TRAGEDY

TRY ME

TURN ME LOOSE

TWIXT TWELVE AND TWENTY

UH! OH!

UNCLE SAM RAG, THE

UNDER YOUR SPELL AGAIN

UNTOUCHABLES, THE

VENUS

VERY NEXT MAN, THE (I'LL MARRY)

WAIL OF THE WINDS

WATERLOO

WE GOT LOVE

WHAT IS LOVE?

WHAT'D I SAY

WHEN DID I FALL IN LOVE?

WHEN IT'S SPRINGTIME IN ALASKA

WHERE WERE YOU (ON OUR WEDDING DAY)?

WHICH ONE IS TO BLAME?

WHITE LIGHTNING

WHO CARES FOR ME?

WHO SHOT SAM?

WONDER OF YOU, THE

WOO-HOO

WORRIED MAN, A

YOU BETTER KNOW IT

YOU GOT WHAT IT TAKES

YOU'LL NEVER GET AWAY FROM ME

YOU'RE GONNA MISS ME

YOU'RE MAKING A FOOL OUT OF ME

YOU'RE SO FINE

YOU WERE MINE

1960

ABOVE AND BEYOND (THE CALL OF LOVE)

ADAM AND EVE

ALABAM

ALLEY OOP

ALL I COULD DO WAS CRY

ALL MY LOVE (YOU WERE MADE FOR)

ALL YOU NEED IS A QUARTER

ALONE AT LAST

ALVIN'S ORCHESTRA

AMIGO'S GUITAR

AM I LOSING YOU?

ANGEL BABY

ANOTHER

ANOTHER SLEEPLESS NIGHT

ANYBODY BUT ME

ANYMORE

ANY WAY THE WIND BLOWS

APPLE GREEN

ARE YOU LONESOME TONIGHT?

ARE YOU WILLING, WILLIE?

ARTIFICIAL FLOWERS

ASK ANYONE IN LOVE

ASKING FOR YOU

BABY, TALK TO ME

BABY (YOU'VE GOT WHAT IT TAKES)

BABY SITTIN' BOOGIE

BAD MAN BLUNDER

BALLAD OF THE ALAMO

BALLAD OF WILD RIVER, THE

BANJO BOY

BEATNIK FLY

BECAUSE THEY'RE YOUNG

BELLY UP TO THE BAR, BOYS

BEYOND THE SEA

BIG IRON

BLUE ANGEL

BLUE RONDO A LA TURK

BONNIE CAME BACK

BURNING BRIDGES

CAMELOT

CATHY'S CLOWN

CHAIN GANG

CHERRY PIE

CHINA DOLL

CHING-CHING AND A DING DING DING

CLEMENTINE

CORRINE, CORRINA (CORINNA, CORINNA)

CRADLE OF LOVE

CRUEL LOVE

CRY LIKE THE WIND

DELAWARE

DEVIL OR ANGEL

DING-A-LING

DIS-DONC, DIS-DONC

DOGGIN' AROUND

DOLCE FAR NIENTE

DOLLAR DOWN, A

DONDI

DON'T COME KNOCKIN'

DON'T CRY NO MORE

DO YOU MIND?

DREAMIN'

DREAMY

EACH MOMENT (SPENT WITH YOU)

EARLY IN THE MORNING (DOWN BY THE STATION)

EVERYBODY'S SOMEBODY'S FOOL

FACE TO THE WALL

FACTS OF LIFE, THE

FAME AND FORTUNE

FAMILY BIBLE

FAMILY MAN

FANNIE MAE

FARAWAY PART OF TOWN, THE

FEEL SO FINE

FINGER POPPIN' TIME

FINGS AIN'T WOT THEY USED T'BE

FIREWORKS

FOLLOW ME

FOOL IN LOVE, A

FOOTSTEPS

FOREVER

GEORGIA ON MY MIND

GIMME THAT WINE

GIVE A LITTLE WHISTLE

GLORIA'S THEME

GOOD CLEAN FUN

GOOD TIMIN'

GREENFIELDS

GREEN LEAVES OF SUMMER, THE

GUENEVERE

HANDBAG IS NOT A PROPER MOTHER, A

HANDY MAN

HAPPY-GO-LUCKY ME

HEARTBREAK (IT'S HURTING ME)

HEART TO HEART TALK

HE'LL HAVE TO GO

HE'LL HAVE TO STAY

HE WILL BREAK YOUR HEART
  a.k.a. HE DON'T LOVE YOU—(LIKE I LOVE YOU)

HEY, LOOK ME OVER!

HONESTLY SINCERE

HOT ROD LINCOLN

HOUSE OF BAMBOO

HOW LOVELY TO BE A WOMAN

HOW TO HANDLE A WOMAN

HYMN FOR A SUNDAY EVENING

I AIN'T DOWN YET

I CAN SEE IT

IF EVER I WOULD LEAVE YOU

IF I CAN'T HAVE YOU

IF I KNEW

I GOTTA KNOW

I KNOW ABOUT LOVE

I KNOW ONE

I'LL BE THERE

I'LL NEVER SAY NO

I'LL TAKE CARE OF YOU

I LOVED YOU ONCE IN SILENCE

I LOVE THE WAY YOU LOVE

IMAGE OF A GIRL

I'M GETTIN' BETTER

I'M GONNA GO FISHIN'

I MISSED ME

I'M SORRY

IRMA LA DOUCE

IT'S NOW OR NEVER
ITSY BITSY TEENIE WEENIE YELLOW
  POLKA DOT BIKINI
I WANT TO BE WANTED
I WANT TO KNOW
I WISH I'D NEVER BEEN BORN
I WONDER WHAT THE KING IS DOING
  TONIGHT
JEALOUS LOVER (THEME FROM "THE
  APARTMENT")
JUMP OVER
JUST A LITTLE BIT
JUST COME HOME
JUST ONE TIME
KIDDIO
KIDS
KOOKIE LITTLE PARADISE, A
LADY LUCK
LAST DATE
LEFT TO RIGHT
LET HER DANCE
LET'S GO, LET'S GO, LET'S GO
LET'S THINK ABOUT LIVING
LIKE LOVE
LITTLE BITTY GIRL
LITTLE OLD NEW YORK
LITTLE SUSIE
LOCO WEED
LONELY BLUE BOY
LONELY WEEKENDS
LONELY WOMAN
LOT OF LIVIN' TO DO, A
LOVE HAS MADE YOU BEAUTIFUL
LOVELY WORK OF ART, A
LOVE THEME FROM "SUZIE WONG"
LOVE YOU SO
LUSTY MONTH OF MAY, THE
MADISON, THE
MADISON TIME
MAGNIFICENT SEVEN, THE
MAKE SOMEONE HAPPY
MAMA

MANHA DE CARNAVAL
MANY TEARS AGO
MESS OF BLUES, A
MIDNIGHT LACE
MILLER'S CAVE
MILLION TO ONE, A
MIRACLES
MISSION BELL
MISTER CUSTER
MONEY (THAT'S WHAT I WANT)
MOUNTAIN OF LOVE
MR. LUCKY
MUCH MORE
MY DEAREST DARLING
MY GIRL JOSEPHINE
MY HEART HAS A MIND OF ITS OWN
MY HOME TOWN
MY LITTLE CORNER OF THE WORLD
MY LOVE FOR YOU
NEVER ON SUNDAY
NEVER WILL I MARRY
NEW ORLEANS
NICE 'N' EASY
NIGHT
NO LOVE HAVE I
NORTH TO ALASKA
NOT A MOMENT TOO SOON
NOT A SOUL
NOT ME
O DIO MIO
ONE BOY
ONE LAST KISS
ONE MORE TIME
ONE OF US (WILL WEEP TONIGHT)
ONE YOU SLIP AROUND WITH, THE
ONLY THE LONELY (KNOW THE WAY I
  FEEL)
OUR CONCERTO
PAPER ROSES
PARTIN' TIME
PEPE
PINBALL MACHINE
PINEAPPLE PRINCESS

PLAYBOY THEME
PLEASE COME HOME FOR CHRISTMAS
PLEASE DON'T EAT THE DAISIES
PLEASE HELP ME, I'M FALLING
POETRY IN MOTION
PUPPY LOVE
PUT ON A HAPPY FACE
QUESTION
RIVER BOAT
ROAD RUNNER
ROCKIN' GOOD WAY, A (TO MESS
    AROUND AND FALL IN LOVE)
ROSIE
RUBBER BALL
RUBY DUBY DU
RUN SAMSON RUN
SAILOR (YOUR HOME IS THE SEA)
SAMBA DE ORFEO
SAME OLD ME, THE
SAVE THE LAST DANCE FOR ME
SECOND TIME AROUND, THE
SEVEN DEADLY VIRTUES, THE
SHAZAM!
SHE'S JUST A WHOLE LOT LIKE YOU
SIMPLE JOYS OF MAIDENHOOD, THE
SINCE I MADE YOU CRY
SINK THE BISMARCK
SIXTEEN REASONS
SOFTLY AND TENDERLY (I'LL HOLD YOU
    IN MY ARMS)
SOMEBODY
SOON IT'S GONNA RAIN
SO SAD (TO WATCH GOOD LOVE GO
    BAD)
SPANISH ROSE
STAIRWAY TO HEAVEN
STARBRIGHT
STAY
STEP BY STEP
STICKS AND STONES
STUCK ON YOU
SUMMER'S GONE
SUMMERTIME LOVE

SWEET NOTHIN'S
SWEET SIXTEEN
SWINGIN' ON A RAINBOW
SWINGIN' SCHOOL
TALL HOPE
TA TA
TEEN ANGEL
TELEPHONE HOUR, THE
TELL HER FOR ME
TELL LAURA I LOVE HER
TEMPO OF THE TIMES, THE
THAT'S ALL YOU GOTTA DO
THAT'S HOW IT WENT ALL RIGHT
THAT'S MY KIND OF LOVE
THEME FROM "ADVENTURES IN
    PARADISE"
THEME FROM "A SUMMER PLACE"
THEME FROM "THE APARTMENT"
THEME FROM "THE DARK AT THE TOP
    OF THE STAIRS"
THEME FROM "THE SUNDOWNERS"
THEME FROM "THE UNFORGIVEN" (THE
    NEED FOR LOVE)
THEN YOU MAY TAKE ME TO THE FAIR
THERE'S A BIG WHEEL
THEY WERE YOU
THIS BITTER EARTH
THIS MAGIC MOMENT
THOUSAND STARS, A
THREE NIGHTS A WEEK
TIMBROOK
TIME AND THE RIVER
TIP OF MY FINGERS, THE
T.L.C. TENDER LOVE AND CARE
TOGETHERNESS
TOO MUCH TO LOSE
TRACY'S THEME
TROUBLE IN PARADISE
TRY TO REMEMBER
TURN ON THE SUNSHINE
TWIST, THE
TWISTIN' U.S.A.
VILLAGE OF ST. BERNADETTE, THE

WAKE ME WHEN IT'S OVER
WALK, DON'T RUN
WALKIN' DOWN TO WASHINGTON
WALKING TO NEW ORLEANS
WALK ON, BOY
'WAY DOWN YONDER IN NEW ORLEANS
WAY OF A CLOWN, THE
(WHAT A) WONDERFUL WORLD
WHAT DID I EVER SEE IN HIM?
WHAT DO THE SIMPLE FOLKS DO?
WHAT IN THE WORLD'S COME OVER
  YOU?
WHAT'S NEW AT THE ZOO?
WHAT TAKES MY FANCY
WHEN WILL I BE LOVED?
WHERE THE BOYS ARE
WHO WAS THAT LADY?
WHY
WHY I'M WALKIN'
WILD ONE
WINGS OF A DOVE
WISHFUL THINKING
WOMAN, A LOVER, A FRIEND, A
WOMAN'S INTUITION, A
WOODEN HEART
WORLD SO FULL OF LOVE, A
YOGI
YOU MEAN EVERYTHING TO ME
YOUNG EMOTIONS
YOU'RE SIXTEEN
YOU'RE THE ONLY GOOD THING (THAT'S
  HAPPENED TO ME)
YOUR OLD USED TO BE
YOU TALK TOO MUCH
YOU'VE COME HOME

1961

AFRICAN WALTZ
AIR MAIL TO HEAVEN
ALL IN MY MIND
APACHE

ASIA MINOR
AS IF I DIDN'T KNOW
ASK ME NICE
AS SIMPLE AS THAT
BABY, YOU'RE RIGHT
BACHELOR IN PARADISE
BARBARA ANN
BEAUTIFUL CANDY
BEFORE THIS DAY ENDS
BEGGAR TO A KING
BE QUIET, MIND
BERLIN MELODY, THE
BIG BAD JOHN
BIG BOSS MAN
BIG COLD WIND
BIG JOHN
BIG RIVER, BIG MAN
BILBAO SONG, THE
BLACKLAND FARMER
BLESS YOU
BLIZZARD, THE
BLUE MOON
BOLL WEEVIL SONG, THE
BONANZA!
BREAKIN' IN A BRAND NEW BROKEN
  HEART
BRIGHT LIGHTS, BIG CITY
BRISTOL STOMP
BROKEN HEART AND A PILLOW FILLED
  WITH TEARS
BROTHERHOOD OF MAN
BUT I DO
BUZZ BUZZ A-DIDDLE IT
CALCUTTA
CALENDAR GIRL
CALIFORNIA SUN
CANDY MAN
CATERINA
CERTAIN GIRL, A
CHERIE
COMANCHEROS, THE
COMES ONCE IN A LIFETIME

COMPANY WAY, THE
CRAZY
CRYING
CUPID
DADDY'S HOME
DANCE ON, LITTLE GIRL
DEDICATED TO THE ONE I LOVE
DON'T BET MONEY, HONEY
DON'T CRY, BABY
DON'T LET HIM SHOP AROUND
DON'T READ THE LETTER
DON'T WORRY
DREAMBOAT (HE'S MY)
DREAMSTREET
DRIVING WHEEL
DUM DUM
EBONY EYES
ELENA
EMOTIONS
EMPTY POCKETS FILLED WITH LOVE
EVENTUALLY
EVERLOVIN'
EVERY BEAT OF MY HEART
EVERY BREATH I TAKE
EVERYTHING BEAUTIFUL
EXCUSE ME (I THINK I'VE GOT A
   HEARTACHE)
EXODUS
FALLEN ANGEL
FIND ANOTHER GIRL
FIRST LADY WALTZ
FISH, THE
FLAT TOP
FLY, THE
FLY BY NIGHT
FOOLIN' AROUND
FOOL #1
FOR MY BABY
FROG AND THE GROG, THE
GEE WHIZ! (LOOK AT HIS EYES)
GO HOME
GOODBYE AGAIN

GOODBYE CRUEL WORLD
GOOD TIME BABY
GRAND OLD IVY
GREENER PASTURES
GUILTY OF LOVING YOU
GUNS OF NAVARONE, THE
GYPSY WOMAN
HALFWAY TO PARADISE
HAPPY BIRTHDAY, SWEET SIXTEEN
HAPPY TIMES (ARE HERE TO STAY)
HATS OFF TO LARRY
HEARTBREAK, U.S.A.
HEART OVER MIND
HELLO, MARY LOU
HELLO FOOL
HELLO WALLS
HER FACE
HER ROYAL MAJESTY
HIDE AWAY
HIS LATEST FLAME (MARIE'S THE NAME)
HIT THE ROAD, JACK
HOLLYWOOD
(HOW CAN I WRITE ON PAPER) WHAT I
   FEEL IN MY HEART
HOW CAN YOU DESCRIBE A FACE?
HOW MANY TEARS
HOW TO
HUNDRED POUNDS OF CLAY, A
HURT
I BELIEVE IN YOU
I DON'T BELIEVE I'LL FALL IN LOVE
   TODAY
I DON'T MIND
I DON'T WANT TO CRY
I'D RATHER LOAN YOU OUT
I FALL TO PIECES
I JUST DON'T UNDERSTAND
I KNOW (YOU DON'T WANT ME NO
   MORE)
I LIKE IT LIKE THAT
I'LL BE THERE
I'LL JUST HAVE A CUP OF COFFEE
   (THEN I'LL GO)

I LOVE HOW YOU LOVE ME

I'M GONNA KNOCK ON YOUR DOOR

I'M HURTIN'

IN THE MIDDLE OF A HEARTACHE

I PITY THE FOOL

I THINK I KNOW

IT'S ALL OVER NOW

IT'S GONNA WORK OUT FINE

IT'S YOUR WORLD

I UNDERSTAND JUST HOW YOU FEEL

I WENT OUT OF MY WAY (TO MAKE YOU HAPPY)

I WILL FOLLOW YOU

I WISH I COULD FALL IN LOVE TODAY

JEREMIAH PEABODY'S POLYUNSATURATED QUICK DISSOLVING FAST ACTING PLEASANT TASTING GREEN AND PURPLE PILLS

JIMMY'S GIRL

JUST FOR OLD TIME'S SAKE

KISSIN' ON THE PHONE

LA DOLCE VITA (THE SWEET LIFE)

LA PACHANGA

LAST NIGHT

LET FORGIVENESS IN

LET ME BELONG TO YOU

LET'S GET TOGETHER

LET'S NOT WASTE A MOMENT

LET'S TWIST AGAIN

LET THERE BE DRUMS

LIKE A YOUNG MAN

LION SLEEPS TONIGHT, THE (WIMOWEH)

LITTLE BIT OF SOAP, A

LITTLE BOY SAD

LITTLE DEVIL

LITTLE SISTER

LONELY TEENAGER

LONELYVILLE

LONESOME NUMBER ONE

LONESOME WHISTLE BLUES

LOOK IN MY EYES

LOSING YOUR LOVE

LOUISIANA MAN

LOVE FROM A HEART OF GOLD

LOVE MAKES THE WORLD GO 'ROUND

(I WANNA) LOVE MY LIFE AWAY

LOVE THEME FROM "EL CID" (THE FALCON AND THE DOVE)

LOVE THEME FROM "ONE EYED JACKS"

LOVING YOU (WAS WORTH THIS BROKEN HEART)

MAGIC MOMENT

MAMA SAID

MARRIAGE-GO-ROUND, THE

MENTAL CRUELTY

MEWSETTE

MEXICO

MICHAEL (ROW THE BOAT ASHORE)

MILK AND HONEY

MILORD

MIRA (CAN YOU IMAGINE THAT?)

MOODY RIVER

MOON RIVER

MOTHER-IN-LAW

MOUNTAIN'S HIGH, THE

MULTIPLICATION

MY EARS SHOULD BURN (WHEN FOOLS ARE TALKED ABOUT)

MY EMPTY ARMS

MY KIND OF GIRL

MY LAST DATE (WITH YOU)

MY STATE, MY KANSAS, MY HOME

MY TRUE STORY

NOBODY CARES

NO ONE

NO REGRETS (NON, JE NE REGRETTE RIEN)

NOW AND FOREVER

ODDS AND ENDS, BITS AND PIECES

OLE SLEW-FOOT (SLEWFOOT THE BEAR)

ONE TRACK MIND

ON THE REBOUND

OPTIMISTIC

PARIS BLUES
PARIS ORIGINAL
PEACE OF MIND
PEANUT BUTTER
PEPPERMINT TWIST
PLEASE LOVE ME FOREVER
PLEASE MR. POSTMAN
PLEASE STAY
POCKETFUL OF MIRACLES
PO' FOLKS
PONY TIME
POOR FOOL
PORTRAIT OF MY LOVE
PRETTY BOY FLOYD
PRETTY LITTLE ANGEL EYES
QUARTER TO THREE
RAINDROPS
REVENGE
RIGHT OR WRONG
RUNAROUND SUE
RUNAWAY
RUNNING SCARED
RUN TO HIM
SACRED
SAD MOVIES (MAKE ME CRY)
SAIL AWAY
SAN-HO-ZAY
SCHOOL IS OUT
SEA OF HEARTBREAK
SHALOM
SHE'S MY LOVE
SHOP AROUND
SLEEPY-EYED JOHN
SOME KIND-A WONDERFUL
SOMETHING VERY STRANGE
SOMETHING YOU NEVER HAD BEFORE
SPANISH HARLEM
STAND BY ME
STICK SHIFT
SUMMER SOUVENIRS
SURRENDER
SWEET DANGER

SWEET LIPS
SWEET LITTLE YOU
SWEETS FOR MY SWEET
SWITCH-A-ROO, THE
TAKE FIVE
TAKE GOOD CARE OF HER
TAKE GOOD CARE OF MY BABY
TAKE MY HAND, PAREE
TAKE MY LOVE (I WANT TO GIVE IT ALL
  TO YOU)
TENDER YEARS
THAT'S WHAT GIRLS ARE MADE FOR
THAT WAS YESTERDAY
THEME FROM "GOODBYE AGAIN"
THEME FROM "THE MISFITS"
THERE'S A MOON OUT TONIGHT
THERE'S NO OTHER (LIKE MY BABY)
THERE'S NO REASON IN THE WORLD
THINK TWICE
THIS TIME
THOSE OLDIES BUT GOODIES (REMIND
  ME OF YOU)
THREE HEARTS IN A TANGLE
THREE STEPS TO THE PHONE
TO LOOK UPON MY LOVE
TOO MANY TIMES
TOSSIN' AND TURNIN'
TOWER OF STRENGTH
TOWN WITHOUT PITY
TRANSISTOR SISTER
TRAVELIN' MAN
TYPICALLY ENGLISH
UNDER THE INFLUENCE OF LOVE
UTOPIA
WALKIN' BACK TO HAPPINESS
WALKING THE STREETS
WALK ON BY
WALK OUT BACKWARDS
WALK RIGHT BACK
WHAT A SWEET THING THAT WAS
WHEELS
WHEN MY LITTLE GIRL IS SMILING

WHEN WE GET MARRIED
WHERE SHALL I FIND HIM?
WHO KNOWS WHAT MIGHT HAVE BEEN?
WHO PUT THE BOMP (IN THE BOMP, BOMP, BOMP)
WHY DO THE WRONG PEOPLE TRAVEL?
WILD IN THE COUNTRY
WILL YOU LOVE ME TOMORROW?
WINDOW UP ABOVE, THE
WITHOUT YOU
WONDERLAND BY NIGHT
WRITING ON THE WALL, THE
YA YA
YELLOW BIRD
YES, I'M LONESOME TONIGHT
YES, MY HEART
YOU CAN HAVE HER
YOU CAN'T PICK A ROSE IN DECEMBER
YOU CAN'T SIT DOWN
YOU DON'T KNOW WHAT YOU'VE GOT (UNTIL YOU LOSE IT)
YOU DON'T WANT MY LOVE
YOU'LL ANSWER TO ME
YOU'RE THE REASON
YOUR OLD LOVE LETTERS

1962

ABOVE THE STARS
ACHING, BREAKING HEART
ADIOS AMIGO
AFRIKAAN BEAT
AFTER LOVING YOU
AHAB THE ARAB
AIN'T NOTHING BUT A MAN
AIN'T THAT LOVING YOU
ALADDIN
AL DI LA
ALL ALONE AM I
ALLA MY LOVE
ALLEY CAT
ANNA (GO TO HIM)

ANNIE GET YOUR YO-YO
ANYTHING THAT'S PART OF YOU
BABY, IT'S YOU
BABY ELEPHANT WALK (THEME FROM "HATARI")
BACHELOR BOY
BACKTRACK
BALLAD OF JED CLAMPETT
BALLAD OF PALADIN, THE
BE A PERFORMER
BEAUTIFUL
BEECHWOOD 4-5789
BEING IN LOVE
BEST DRESSED BEGGAR (IN TOWN), THE
BIG GIRLS DON'T CRY
BIRD MAN, THE
BLUE HAWAII
BOBBY'S GIRL
BOYS' NIGHT OUT, THE
BREAKING UP IS HARD TO DO
BREAK IT TO ME GENTLY
BRING IT ON HOME TO ME
BROWN BABY
BURNING OF ATLANTA, THE
CAJUN QUEEN, THE
CALL ME MR. IN-BETWEEN
CAN'T HELP FALLING IN LOVE
CAST YOUR FATE TO THE WIND
CHA CHA CHA, THE
CHAINS
CHAPEL BY THE SEA
CHARLIE'S SHOES
CHIP CHIP
CINDY'S BIRTHDAY
CLOSE TO CATHY
COLD DARK WATERS
COME AWAY MELINDA
COMEBACK, THE
COMEDY TONIGHT
COMIN' HOME BABY
CONSCIENCE
COTTONFIELDS

COW TOWN

CRAZY WILD DESIRE

CRISS-CROSS

CROWD, THE

CRYING IN THE RAIN

CRY TO ME

CUTTIN' IN

DANCIN' PARTY

DAY INTO NIGHT

DAYS OF WINE AND ROSES

DEAR IVAN

DEAR LADY TWIST

DEAR LONELY HEARTS

DEAR ONE

DEEP DOWN INSIDE

DESIFINADO

DEVIL WOMAN

DOES HE MEAN THAT MUCH TO YOU?

DON'T ASK ME TO BE FRIENDS

DON'T BREAK THE HEART THAT LOVES YOU

DON'T GO NEAR THE INDIANS

DON'T HANG UP

DON'T PLAY THAT SONG (YOU LIED)

DON'T YOU BELIEVE IT

DO YOU HEAR WHAT I HEAR?

DO YOU LOVE ME?

DREAM BABY (HOW LONG MUST I DREAM)

DUKE OF EARL

ESO BESO (THAT KISS)

EVERYBODY BUT ME

EVERYBODY LOVES ME BUT YOU

EVERYBODY OUGHT TO HAVE A MAID

FIESTA

FOLLOWED CLOSELY BY TEARDROPS

FOLLOW THE BOYS

FOOTSTEPS OF A FOOL

FORTUNETELLER

FROM THE BOTTOM OF MY HEART (DAMMI, DAMMI, DAMMI)

FUNNY HOW TIME SLIPS AWAY (FUNNY)

FUNNY WAY OF LAUGHIN'

GET A LITTLE DIRT ON YOUR HANDS

GIFT TODAY, A (THE BAR MITZVAH SONG)

GINA

GINNY COME LATELY

GIRL I USED TO KNOW, A

GLAD TO BE HOME

GONNA BUILD A MOUNTAIN

GOOD LUCK CHARM

GRAVY (FOR MY MASHED POTATOES)

GREEN ONIONS

GUITAR MAN (DANCE WITH THE)

HAPPY BIRTHDAY TO ME

HAPPY JOURNEY

HARMONY

HAVE I TOLD YOU LATELY?

HAVING A PARTY

HEARTACHE FOR A KEEPSAKE

HEART IN HAND

HERE'S TO US

HE'S A REBEL

HE'S SO HEAVENLY

HEY! BABY

HOLLY, JOLLY CHRISTMAS, A

HOW CAN I MEET HER?

HOW DO YOU TALK TO A BABY?

I CAN MEND YOUR BROKEN HEART

I CAN'T STOP LOVING YOU

IF A MAN ANSWERS

IF A WOMAN ANSWERS (HANG UP THE PHONE)

IF I DIDN'T HAVE A DIME (TO PLAY THE JUKEBOX)

IF I HAD A HAMMER

I FOUND A LOVE

IF YOU DON'T KNOW, I AIN'T GONNA TELL YOU

I GUESS I'LL NEVER LEARN

I KEEP FORGETTIN' (EVERY TIME YOU'RE NEAR)

I LEFT MY HEART IN SAN FRANCISCO

I'LL NEVER DANCE AGAIN

I'LL TRY SOMETHING NEW

IMAGINE THAT

I'M BLUE (THE GONG-GONG SONG)

I'M FASCINATING

I'M GONNA CHANGE EVERYTHING

I'M GONNA GET HIM

(I'M THE GIRL ON) WOLVERTON
   MOUNTAIN

IT IS BETTER TO LOVE

IT KEEPS RIGHT ON A-HURTIN' (SINCE I
   LEFT)

IT MIGHT AS WELL RAIN UNTIL
   SEPTEMBER

IT STARTED ALL OVER AGAIN

IT'S THE LITTLE THINGS IN TEXAS

I'VE BEEN EVERYWHERE

I'VE GOT BONNIE

I'VE GOT JUST ABOUT EVERYTHING

I'VE GOT YOUR NUMBER

I'VE JUST SEEN HER (AS NOBODY ELSE
   HAS SEEN HER)

I WISH THAT WE WERE MARRIED

JAILER, BRING ME WATER

JAMES (HOLD THE LADDER STEADY)

JAMIE

JESSICA

JOEY BABY

JOHN BIRCH SOCIETY, THE

JOHNNY ANGEL

JOHNNY GET ANGRY

JOHNNY LOVES ME

JOHNNY'S THEME

JUST TELL HER JIM SAID HELLO

KEEP YOUR HANDS OFF MY BABY

KING OF CLOWNS

KING OF THE WHOLE WIDE WORLD

LA LA LA

LEMON TREE

LEONA

LET ME DO IT MY WAY

LET ME GO THE RIGHT WAY

LET ME IN

LET'S DANCE

LET'S GO BACK TO THE WALTZ

LET'S NOT BE SENSIBLE

LETTER FULL OF TEARS

LIE TO ME

LIMBO ROCK

LIPSTICK TRACES (ON A CIGARETTE)

LITTLE BITTY TEAR, A

LITTLE BLACK BOOK

LITTLE BOXES

LITTLE DIANE

LITTLE DROPS OF RAIN

LITTLE HEARTACHE, A

LITTLE ME

LOADS OF LOVE

LOCO-MOTION, THE

LOLITA YA-YA

LOLLIPOPS AND ROSES

LONELY BULL, THE

LONELY TEARDROPS

LONG AS THE ROSE IS RED

LONGEST DAY, THE

LOOKIN' FOR A LOVE

LOOK NO FURTHER

LOST SOMEONE

LOVE, I HEAR

LOVE CAME TO ME

LOVELY

LOVE ME WARM AND TENDER

LOVE ON MY MIND

LOVER, PLEASE

LOVER COME BACK

LOVERS WHO WANDER

LOVE SONG FROM "MUTINY ON THE
   BOUNTY"

MADE TO LOVE (GIRLS, GIRLS, GIRLS)

MAINE

MAKE IT EASY ON YOURSELF

MAMA SANG A SONG

MAN OF CONSTANT SORROW

MAN WHO SHOT LIBERTY VALANCE, THE

MARY'S LITTLE LAMB

MASHED POTATO TIME

MIDNIGHT IN MOSCOW

MISERY LOVES COMPANY

MISS MARMELSTEIN

MOMMA, MOMMA

MON AMOUR PERDU (MY LOST LOVE)

MONSTER MASH

MORE THAN JUST A FRIEND

MORNING AFTER

MOST PEOPLE GET MARRIED

MY BOOMERANG WON'T COME BACK

MY COLORING BOOK

MY DAD

MY NAME IS MUD

NAKED CITY THEME

NEVER SAY NO TO A MAN

NEXT DOOR TO AN ANGEL

NIGHTLIFE

NOBODY'S FOOL BUT YOURS

NOBODY TOLD ME

NORMAN

NO STRINGS

OLD RIVERS

ONCE IN A LIFETIME

ONCE UPON A SUMMERTIME

ONCE UPON A TIME

ONE LITTLE WORLD APART

ONE NOTE SAMBA

ONE WHO REALLY LOVES YOU, THE

ONLY LOVE CAN BREAK A HEART

OTHER SIDE OF THE TRACKS, THE

OUR ANNIVERSARY

OUR DAY WILL COME

PALISADES PARK

PAPA-OOM-MOW-MOW

PARIS IS A LONELY TOWN

PARTY LIGHTS

PATCHES

PEEL ME A GRAPE

PERCOLATOR

PIGTAILS AND FRECKLES

PLAYBOY

PLEASE DON'T ASK ABOUT BARBARA

POINT OF NO RETURN

POOR LITTLE HOLLYWOOD STAR

POOR LITTLE PUPPET

POPEYE THE HITCHHIKER

P.T. 109

QUANDO, QUANDO, QUANDO (TELL ME WHEN)

QUIET NIGHTS OF QUIET STARS (CORCOVADO)

RAIN, RAIN GO AWAY

RAINS CAME, THE

RAMBLIN' ROSE

REAL LIVE GIRL

RELEASE ME

RETURN TO SENDER

REVEREND MR. BLACK

RIDE!

RINKY DINK

ROAD TO HONG KONG, THE

ROCK-A-HULA BABY

ROSES ARE RED (MY LOVE)

ROUTE 66 THEME

RUBY ANN

SANTA CLAUS IS WATCHING YOU

SATAN NEVER SLEEPS

SCOTCH AND SODA

SEALED WITH A KISS

SECOND CHANCE, A

SECOND HAND LOVE

SECRET SERVICE, THE

SEVEN DAY WEEKEND

SHAME ON ME

SHE CAN'T FIND HER KEYS

SHE CRIED (HE CRIED)

SHEILA

SHERRY

SHE'S GOT YOU

SHE'S NOT YOU

SHE THINKS I STILL CARE

SHOUT! SHOUT! (KNOCK YOURSELF OUT)

SHUTTERS AND BOARDS

SILVER THREADS AND GOLDEN
    NEEDLES

SLIGHTLY OUT OF TUNE

SLOW TWISTIN'

SMOKY PLACES

SNAP YOUR FINGERS

SOFT RAIN

SOLDIER BOY

SOMEONE NICE LIKE YOU

SOMETHING'S GOT A HOLD ON ME

SOMEWHERE IN THE NIGHT

SO THIS IS LOVE

SOUL TWIST

SPEEDY GONZALES

STEEL MEN

STRANGE I KNOW

STRANGER ON THE SHORE

STRIPPER, THE

STUBBORN KIND OF FELLOW

SUCCESS

SURFIN' SAFARI

SWEETEST SOUNDS, THE

SWEET SIXTEEN BARS

SWINGIN' SAFARI, A

TAKE TIME

TASTE OF HONEY, A

TEAMWORK

TEARS AND LAUGHTER

TEARS BROKE OUT ON ME

TEEN AGE IDOL

TELL ME

TELSTAR

TENDER IS THE NIGHT

TENNESSEE FLAT-TOP BOX

THAT HAPPY FEELING

THAT'LL SHOW HIM

THAT'S MY PA

THAT'S OLD FASHIONED (THAT'S THE
    WAY LOVE SHOULD BE)

THEME FROM "BEN CASEY"

THEME FROM "COME SEPTEMBER"

THEME FROM "TARAS BULBA" (THE
    WISHING STAR)

THEN A TEAR FELL

THEY LOVE ME

THINGS

THIS IS A GREAT COUNTRY

THIS ISN'T HEAVEN

THOU SHALT NOT STEAL

THREE DAYS

THREE STARS WILL SHINE TONIGHT
    (THEME FROM "DR. KILDARE")

TORTURE

TOUCH ME

TROUBLE'S BACK IN TOWN

TRUE, TRUE LOVE, A

TUFF

TURN ON YOUR LOVELIGHT

TWIST, TWIST SEÑORA

TWIST AND SHOUT

TWISTIN' THE NIGHT AWAY

UNCHAIN MY HEART

UNLOVED, UNWANTED

UNSQUARE DANCE

UPTOWN

VACATION

VENUS IN BLUE JEANS

WAH WATUSI, THE

WALK IN THE BLACK FOREST

WALK ON THE WILD SIDE

WALL TO WALL LOVE

WANDERER, THE

WARMER THAN A WHISPER

WASHINGTON TWIST, THE

WAY DOWN EAST

WHAT KIND OF FOOL AM I?

WHAT'S YOUR NAME?

WHEN I GET THROUGH WITH YOU
    (YOU'LL LOVE ME TOO)

WHEN THE BOY IN YOUR ARMS (IS THE BOY IN YOUR HEART)

WHEN TWO WORLDS COLLIDE

WHERE DO YOU COME FROM?

WHERE HAVE ALL THE FLOWERS GONE?

WHERE I OUGHTA BE

WHITE ROSE OF ATHENS, THE

WHO'S PERFECT?

WHY DO LOVERS BREAK EACH OTHER'S HEARTS?

WILLIE THE WEEPER

WILLING AND EAGER

WILLINGLY

WILL YOU REMEMBER

WILL YOUR LAWYER TALK TO GOD?

WONDERFUL TO BE YOUNG

WONDERFUL WORLD OF THE YOUNG, THE

WORKIN' FOR THE MAN

WOUND TIME CAN'T ERASE, A

YESTERDAY'S MEMORIES

YOU BEAT ME TO THE PUNCH

YOU DON'T KNOW ME

YOU'LL LOSE A GOOD THING

YOUNG WORLD

YOUR USED TO BE

1963

ABILENE

ACT NATURALLY

AIN'T GOT TIME FOR NOTHIN'

ALICE IN WONDERLAND

ALL OVER THE WORLD

ALLY ALLY OXEN FREE

AMEN

AMY

ANOTHER BRIDGE TO BURN

ANOTHER SATURDAY NIGHT

ANY DAY NOW

ARM IN ARM

AS LONG AS HE NEEDS ME

AS LONG AS I KNOW HE'S MINE

AS USUAL

BABY WORKOUT

BAD GIRL

BEFORE I KISS THE WORLD GOODBYE

BEGGING TO YOU

BE MY BABY

BE TRUE TO YOUR SCHOOL

BIG WIDE WORLD

BIRD'S THE WORD, THE

BLAME IT ON THE BOSSA NOVA

BLOWIN' IN THE WIND

BLUE BAYOU

BLUE ON BLUE

BLUESETTE

BLUE VELVET

BLUE WINTER

BORNING DAY, THE

BOSSA NOVA BABY

BOSSA NOVA U.S.A.

BOSS GUITAR

BUSTED

BYE BYE BIRDIE

CALL ME IRRESPONSIBLE

CALL ON ME

CANDY GIRL

CAN I GET A WITNESS

CAN'T GET USED TO LOSING YOU

CHARADE

CHARMS

CINNAMON CINDER, THE (IT'S A VERY NICE DANCE)

COLD AND LONELY (IS THE FORECAST FOR TONIGHT)

COME AND GET THESE MEMORIES

CONSIDER YOURSELF

COWBOY BOOTS

CRY BABY

DA DOO RON RON (WHEN HE WALKED ME HOME)

DANKE SCHOEN

DARKEST STREET IN TOWN

DAYS GONE BY

DEAR FRIEND

DEEP PURPLE

DENISE

DETROIT CITY

DID YOU HAVE A HAPPY BIRTHDAY?

D. J. FOR A DAY

DOMINIQUE

DONNA THE PRIMA DONNA

DON'T BE AFRAID, LITTLE DARLIN'

DON'T CALL ME FROM A HONKY TONK

DON'T LET ME CROSS OVER

DON'T MAKE ME OVER

DON'T MAKE MY BABY BLUE

DON'T SAY NOTHIN' BAD (ABOUT MY BABY)

DON'T TAKE OUR CHARLIE FOR THE ARMY

DON'T THINK TWICE, IT'S ALL RIGHT

DON'T TRY TO FIGHT IT, BABY

DON'T WAIT TOO LONG

DON'T YOU FORGET IT

DO THE BIRD

DOWN BY THE RIVER

DRIP DROP

DROWNIN' MY SORROWS

EASIER SAID THAN DONE

EASY COME—EASY GO

8 X 10

EIGHTEEN YELLOW ROSES

EL WATUSI

END OF THE WORLD, THE

EVERYBODY

EVERY STEP OF THE WAY

EVERYTHING BEAUTIFUL HAPPENS AT NIGHT

FADED LOVE

FALLING

FINE, FINE BOY, A

FINGERTIPS

FIVE HUNDRED MILES AWAY FROM HOME

FOOD, GLORIOUS FOOD

FOOLISH LITTLE GIRL

FORGET HIM

FOUR STRONG WINDS

FROM A JACK TO A KING

FROM ME TO YOU

GIRL FROM SPANISH TOWN, THE

GIVE US YOUR BLESSING

GO AWAY LITTLE GIRL

GOING THROUGH THE MOTIONS (OF LIVING)

GOOD LIFE, THE

GOTTA MOVE

GRAND KNOWING YOU

GRASS IS GREENER, THE

GRAVY WALTZ

GREEN, GREEN

GREENBACK DOLLAR

GUILTY

HAPPY TO BE UNHAPPY

HARD RAIN'S A-GONNA FALL

HEART (I HEAR YOU BEATING)

HEART BE CAREFUL

HEAT WAVE

HELLO HEARTACHE, GOODBYE LOVE

HELLO MUDDUH, HELLO FADDUH! (A LETTER FROM CAMP)

HELLO OUT THERE

HELLO STRANGER

HELLO TROUBLE

HERE AND NOW

HERE'S LOVE

HE'S A BAD BOY

HE'S SO FINE

HE'S SURE THE BOY I LOVE

HEY GIRL

HEY LITTLE GIRL

HEY PAULA

HEY THERE LONELY BOY (GIRL)

HOBO FLATS

HONOLULU LULU

HOPELESS

HOTEL HAPPINESS
HOT PASTRAMI
HOW MUCH CAN A LONELY HEART
    STAND?
I (WHO HAVE NOTHING)
I ADORE HIM
I CAN'T STAY MAD AT YOU
I COULD GO ON SINGING
I'D DO ANYTHING
I DON'T CARE MUCH
IF AND WHEN
IF I HAD A HAMMER
IF YOU NEED ME
IF YOU WANNA BE HAPPY
I KNOW THE FEELING
ILONA
I'LL REMEMBER HER
I'LL TAKE YOU HOME
I LOVE TO LAUGH
I LOVE YOU BECAUSE
I'M A WOMAN
I'M GONNA BE STRONG
I'M GONNA BE WARM THIS WINTER
I'M LEAVING IT (ALL) UP TO YOU
I'M SAVING MY LOVE
IN DREAMS
IN MY ROOM
IN THE SUMMER OF HIS YEARS
I PUT MY HAND IN
I SAW LINDA YESTERDAY
I SAW ME
IS IT REALLY ME?
IS THIS ME?
I STILL LOOK AT YOU THAT WAY
IT'S ALL RIGHT
IT'S A MAD, MAD, MAD, MAD WORLD
IT'S MY PARTY
IT'S TOO LATE
IT'S UP TO YOU
I'VE BEEN INVITED TO A PARTY
I'VE ENJOYED AS MUCH OF THIS AS I
    CAN STAND

I WANNA BE AROUND
I WANT TO STAY HERE
I WILL FOLLOW HIM
I WILL LIVE MY LIFE FOR YOU
I WILL LOVE YOU
JAMES BOND THEME, THE
JOLLY HOLIDAY
JUDY'S TURN TO CRY
JUST ONE LOOK
KEEPING UP WITH THE JONESES
KICKIN' OUR HEARTS AROUND
KIND OF BOY YOU CAN'T FORGET, THE
LAND OF 1000 DANCES
LAUGHING BOY
LEAVIN' ON YOUR MIND
LET'S GO FLY A KITE
LET'S GO STEADY AGAIN
LET'S INVITE THEM OVER
LET'S TURKEY TROT
LITTLE LATIN LUPE LU
LITTLE OLE YOU
LITTLE RED ROOSTER
LITTLE TOWN FLIRT
LOCK, STOCK AND TEARDROPS
LOCKING UP MY HEART
LODDY LO
LONDON IS A LITTLE BIT OF ALL RIGHT
LONESOME 7-7203
LOOP DE LOOP
LOSING YOU
LOUIE, LOUIE
LOVE, DON'T TURN AWAY
LOVE (MAKES THE WORLD GO 'ROUND)
LOVE ME WITH ALL YOUR HEART
    (CUANDO CALIENTE EL SOL)
LOVE OF MY MAN, THE
LOVE'S GONNA LIVE HERE
LOVE SHE CAN COUNT ON, A
MAKE THE WORLD GO AWAY
MAMA DIDN'T LIE
MAN WHO ROBBED THE BANK AT
    SANTA FE, THE

MARLENA

MARTIAN HOP

MARVELOUS TOY, THE

MASTERS OF WAR

MATADOR, THE

MEAN WOMAN BLUES

MECCA

MEDITATION (MEDITACAO)

MEMPHIS

MICKEY'S MONKEY

MIDNIGHT MARY

MILLION YEARS OR SO, A

MINUTE YOU'RE GONE, THE

MOCKINGBIRD

MOLLY

MONEY TO BURN

MONKEY TIME, THE

MORE (THEME FROM "MONDO CANE")

MOUNTAIN OF LOVE

MR. WISHING WELL

MY BOYFRIEND'S BACK

MY SUMMER LOVE

MY WHOLE WORLD IS FALLING DOWN

NEEDLES AND PINS

NEW PAIR OF SHOES, A

NICK TEEN AND AL K. HALL

NIGHT HAS A THOUSAND EYES, THE

NINETY MILES AN HOUR ON A DEAD-END STREET

NITTY GRITTY, THE

NOT SO LONG AGO

NOT WHAT I HAD IN MIND

NOW!

OLD RECORDS

OLD SHOWBOAT

OLD SMOKEY LOCOMOTION

ON BROADWAY

ONE BROKEN HEART FOR SALE

ONE FINE DAY

ONLY IN AMERICA

ONLY ONE, THE

ON TOP OF SPAGHETTI

OUR WINTER LOVE

OUT OF LIMITS

PAINTED, TAINTED ROSE

(DOWN AT) PAPA JOE'S

PARIS MIST

PART TIME LOVE

PEARL, PEARL, PEARL

PEKING THEME, THE (SO LITTLE TIME)

PEPINO'S FRIEND PASQUAL (THE ITALIAN PUSSY-CAT)

PEPINO THE ITALIAN MOUSE

PETTICOAT JUNCTION

PINE CONES AND HOLLY BERRIES

PIPELINE

PLEASE TALK TO MY HEART

POOR LITTLE RICH GIRL

POPSICLES AND ICICLES

PRIDE

PRIDE AND JOY

PROUD

PUFF THE MAGIC DRAGON

PUSHOVER

QUICKSAND

RHYTHM OF THE RAIN

RING OF FIRE

ROLL MUDDY RIVER

RONNIE, CALL ME WHEN YOU GET A CHANCE

RUBY BABY

RULES OF THE ROAD, THE

ST. THOMAS

SALLY, GO ROUND THE ROSES

SANDS OF GOLD

SATURDAY NIGHT

SAWMILL

SAY WONDERFUL THINGS

SCARLETT O'HARA

SECOND HAND ROSE (SECOND HAND HEART)

SHAKE A TAIL FEATHER

SHAKE ME I RATTLE (SQUEEZE ME I CRY)

SHAKE SHERRY
SHE LOVES ME
SHE'S A FOOL
SHOES OF A FOOL
SHUT DOWN
SIMPLE LITTLE THINGS
SINCE I FELL FOR YOU
SING A LITTLE SONG OF HEARTACHE
SING A SAD SONG
SIX DAYS ON THE ROAD
SO MUCH IN LOVE
SOON (I'LL BE HOME AGAIN)
SOUND OF SURF, THE
SOUTH STREET
SPOONFUL OF SUGAR, A
STAY WITH ME
STEAL AWAY
STILL (I LOVE YOU)
SUGAR SHACK
SUKIYAKI
SUN ARISE
SURF CITY
SURFER GIRL
SURFER JOE
SURFIN' U.S.A.
TAKE A LETTER, MISS GRAY
TAKE TEN
TALK BACK TREMBLING LIPS
TALK TO ME, TALK TO ME
TELL HER SO
TELL HIM
TELL ME THE TRUTH
T FOR TEXAS (BLUE YODEL NO. 1)
THANKS A LOT
THANK YOU GIRL
THAT'S ALL THAT MATTERS
THAT'S THE WAY LOVE IS
THAT SUNDAY, THAT SUMMER
THEME FROM "LAWRENCE OF ARABIA"
THEN HE KISSED ME
THERE'S A PLACE
THIRTY ONE FLAVORS

THIS IS ALL I ASK
THIS LITTLE GIRL
THIS TIME IT'S TRUE LOVE
THOSE LAZY-HAZY-CRAZY DAYS OF SUMMER
THOSE WONDERFUL YEARS
TIE ME KANGAROO DOWN, SPORT
TIMBER, I'M FALLING
TO KILL A MOCKINGBIRD
TONIGHT AT EIGHT
TOYS IN THE ATTIC
TWENTY-FOUR HOURS FROM TULSA
TWENTY MILES
TWISTING MATILDA
TWO FACES HAVE I
TWO LOVERS
TWO OF A KIND
UM, UM, UM, UM, UM, UM
UNDER THE YUM-YUM TREE
UNIVERSAL SOLDIER, THE
UP ON THE ROOF
VOLUNTEER, THE
WAITIN' FOR THE EVENING TRAIN
WAIT 'TIL MY BOBBY GETS HOME
WALKING PROUD
WALKING THE DOG
WALK LIKE A MAN
WALK ME TO THE DOOR
WALK RIGHT IN
WASHINGTON SQUARE
WATERMELON MAN
WE MISSED YOU
WE MUST HAVE BEEN OUT OF OUR MINDS
WE'RE THE TALK OF THE TOWN
WE SHALL OVERCOME
WHAT KIND OF LOVE IS THIS?
WHAT'S EASY FOR TWO IS SO HARD FOR ONE
WHAT WILL MY MARY SAY?
WHEN THE SHIP COMES IN
WHERE IS LOVE?

1963

WHO'S BEEN CHEATIN' WHO?
WHO WILL BUY?
WILD WEEKEND
WILDWOOD DAYS
WILKES-BARRE, PA.
WILL HE LIKE ME?
WIPE OUT
WIVES AND LOVERS
WONDERFUL SUMMER
YAKETY SAX
YEH! YEH!
YELLOW BANDANA, THE
YOU COMB HER HAIR
YOU DON'T KNOW
YOU'LL DRIVE ME BACK (INTO HER
    ARMS AGAIN)
YOU LOVE ME
YOUNG AND IN LOVE
YOUNG LOVERS
YOU'RE THE DEVIL IN DISGUISE
YOU'RE THE REASON I'M LIVING
YOUR OLD STANDBY
YOUR OTHER LOVE
YOU TOOK HER OFF MY HANDS (NOW
    PLEASE TAKE HER OFF MY MIND)
YOU'VE REALLY GOT A HOLD ON ME

1964

ABSENT MINDED ME
AIN'T NOTHING YOU CAN DO
AIN'T THAT JUST LIKE ME
ALL CRIED OUT
ALL MY LOVING
ALMOST THERE
ALWAYS SOMETHING THERE TO REMIND
    ME (THERE'S)
ANAHEIM, AZUSA AND CUCAMONGA
    SEWING CIRCLE, BOOK REVIEW AND
    TIMING ASSOCIATION
AND I LOVE HER
ANGELITO

ANOTHER CUP OF COFFEE
ANYONE CAN WHISTLE
ANYONE WHO HAD A HEART
ANY WAY YOU WANT IT
ASK ME
AS TEARS GO BY
BABY, I LOVE YOU
BABY, I NEED YOUR LOVING
BABY LOVE
BAD NEWS
BAD TO ME
BALLAD OF IRA HAYES, THE
BALTIMORE
BARRY'S BOYS
BEACH GIRL
BEANS IN MY EARS
BECAUSE
BEFORE I'M OVER YOU
BEFORE THE PARADE PASSES BY
BIG MAN IN TOWN
BITS AND PIECES
B.J. THE D.J.
BORN TO WANDER
BOY TEN FEET TALL, A
BREAD AND BUTTER
BREAKFAST WITH THE BLUES
BURNING MEMORIES
CAN'T BUY ME LOVE
CAN'T GET OVER (THE BOSSA NOVA)
CAN'T YOU SEE IT?
CAN'T YOU SEE THAT SHE'S MINE?
CARNY TOWN
CAT, THE
CHAPEL OF LOVE
CHIM CHIM CHEREE
CHIMES OF FREEDOM
CHUG-A-LUG
CIRCUMSTANCES
CLINGING VINE
CLOSE HARMONY
CLOSEST THING TO HEAVEN, THE
C'MON AND SWIM

1158

COME A LITTLE BIT CLOSER
COME HOME
COME ON, DO THE JERK
COME SEE ABOUT ME
CORNET MAN
COTTON CANDY
COTTON MILL MAN
COWBOY IN THE CONTINENTAL SUIT, THE
CROSS THE BRAZOS AT WACO
DANCE, DANCE, DANCE
DANCING IN THE STREET
DANG ME
DAWN (GO AWAY)
DAYS OF THE WALTZ, THE
DEAD MAN'S CURVE
DEAR HEART
DERN YA
DODO, THE
DO IT RIGHT
DON'T BOTHER ME
DON'T FORGET I STILL LOVE YOU
DON'T FORGET 127TH STREET
DON'T LET THE RAIN COME DOWN (CROOKED LITTLE MAN)
DON'T LET THE SUN CATCH YOU CRYING
DON'T RAIN ON MY PARADE
DON'T THROW YOUR LOVE AWAY
DON'T WORRY BABY
DOOR IS STILL OPEN TO MY HEART, THE
DO-WACKA-DO
DO WAH DIDDY DIDDY
DO YOU LOVE ME?
DO YOU WANT TO KNOW A SECRET?
DRAG CITY
EMILY
EVERYBODY KNOWS
EVERYBODY KNOWS (I STILL LOVE YOU)
EVERYBODY LOVES SOMEBODY
EVERYBODY SAYS DON'T
FADE OUT—FADE IN

FAITH
FAR FROM THE HOME I LOVE
FEED THE BIRDS
FIDDLER ON THE ROOF
FIVE LITTLE FINGERS
FOOL NEVER LEARNS, A
FOREVER AND A DAY
FOR YOU
FRIENDLIEST THING, THE
FROM A WINDOW
FROM RUSSIA WITH LOVE
FUN, FUN, FUN
FUNNY GIRL
GIRL FROM IPANEMA
GIVE ME 40 ACRES
GIVING UP
GLAD ALL OVER
GO, CAT GO
GOIN' OUT OF MY HEAD
GOLDEN BOY
GONNA SEND YOU BACK TO GEORGIA
GOOD NEWS
G.T.O.
HARD DAY'S NIGHT, A
HARLEM SHUFFLE
HAUNTED HOUSE
HAVE I THE RIGHT?
HELLO, DOLLY!
HERE COMES MY BABY BACK AGAIN
HE'S A GOOD GUY (YES HE IS)
HE SAYS THE SAME THINGS TO ME
HE'S MY FRIEND
HEY, LITTLE COBRA
HEY BOBBA NEEDLE
HI-HEEL SNEAKERS
HIPPY HIPPY SHAKE
HOUSE IS NOT A HOME, A
HOUSE OF THE RISING SUN
HOW DO YOU DO IT
I CAN
I DON'T LOVE YOU ANYMORE
I DON'T WANNA BE A LOSER

I DON'T WANT TO SEE YOU AGAIN

I FEEL FINE

IF I FELL

IF I GAVE YOU

IF I WERE A RICH MAN

I GET AROUND

I GOT EVERYTHING I WANT

I GUESS I'M CRAZY (FOR LOVING YOU)

I HAD A BALL

I KNEW IT ALL THE TIME

I KNOW YOUR HEART

I LIKE TO LEAD WHEN I DANCE

I'LL CRY INSTEAD

I'LL GO DOWN SWINGING

I'LL KEEP YOU SATISFIED

I LOVE TO DANCE WITH ANNIE

I LOVE YOU MORE AND MORE EVERY
   DAY

I'M CRYING

I'M HAPPY JUST TO DANCE WITH YOU

I'M INTO SOMETHING GOOD

I'M ON THE OUTSIDE (LOOKING IN)

I'M SO PROUD

I'M THE GREATEST STAR

I'M THE LONELY ONE

I'M WITH YOU

IN MY LONELY ROOM

IN THE MISTY MOONLIGHT

IN THE NAME OF LOVE

INVISIBLE TEARS

I ONLY WANT TO BE WITH YOU

I SAW HER STANDING THERE

I SHOULD HAVE KNOWN BETTER

IT AIN'T ME, BABE

I THANK MY LUCKY STARS

IT HAPPENED JUST THAT WAY

IT HURTS TO BE IN LOVE

IT ONLY TAKES A MOMENT

IT'S ALL OVER

IT'S FOR YOU

IT'S GOT THE WHOLE WORLD SHAKIN'

IT'S OVER

IT TAKES A WOMAN

I'VE GOT SAND IN MY SHOES

I'VE GOT YOU TO LEAN ON

I WANNA LOVE HIM SO BAD

I WANT TO BE WITH YOU

I WANT TO HOLD YOUR HAND

I WANT YOU TO MEET MY BABY

I WOULDN'T TRADE YOUR FOR THE
   WORLD

JAMAICA SKA

JAVA

JERK, THE

KEEP ON PUSHING

KEEP SEARCHIN' (WE'LL FOLLOW THE
   SUN)

KISS ME, SAILOR

KISS ME NO KISSES

KISS ME QUICK

KISSIN' COUSINS

LA LA LA LA LA

LAST DAY IN THE MINES

LAST KISS

LAST THING ON MY MIND, THE

LAY DOWN YOUR WEARY TUNE

LEADER OF THE PACK

LIFE I LEAD, THE

LITTLE BOY

LITTLE CHILDREN

LITTLE HONDA

LITTLE OLD LADY (FROM PASADENA),
   THE

LIVE WIRE

LOOKING FOR LOVE

LOOKING FOR MORE IN '64

LORNA'S HERE

L-O-V-E

LOVE IS NO EXCUSE

LOVE LOOKS GOOD ON YOU

LOVE ME DO

LOVE WITH THE PROPER STRANGER

LUMBERJACK, THE

MAD

MATADOR, THE

MATCHBOX

MATCHMAKER, MATCHMAKER

MAYBE I KNOW

MAYBE SOME OTHER TIME

ME

MEMORY NO. 1

MERCY, MERCY

MEXICAN DRUMMER MAN

MEXICAN SHUFFLE

MIRACLE OF MIRACLES

MISSISSIPPI GODDAM

MR. AND MRS. USED TO BE

MR. BOOZE

MR. LONELY

MUSIC THAT MAKES ME DANCE, THE

MY BABY WALKS ALL OVER ME

MY BACK PAGES

MY BOY LOLLIPOP

MY DIRTY STREAM (THE HUDSON RIVER
    SONG)

MY FIRST LOVE SONG

MY FRIEND ON THE RIGHT

MY GUY

MY HEART BELONGS TO ONLY YOU

MY HEART SKIPS A BEAT

MY HOME TOWN

MY KIND OF TOWN (CHICAGO IS)

MY LOVE, FORGIVE ME (AMORE,
    SCUSAMI)

MY TEARS ARE OVERDUE

NADINE (IS IT YOU?)

NAVY BLUE

NEEDLE IN A HAYSTACK

NESTER, THE

NIGHT SONG

NOBODY I KNOW

NOR MORE SONGS FOR ME

NO PARTICULAR PLACE TO GO

NOT FADE AWAY

NOW I HAVE EVERYTHING

ODE TO THE LITTLE BROWN SHACK OUT
    BACK

OH, PRETTY WOMAN

OH NO, NOT MY BABY

ONCE A DAY

ONE MORE TIME

ONE OF THESE DAYS

OTHER HALF OF ME, THE

OUR EVERLASTING LOVE

PACK UP YOUR SORROWS

PARADE IN TOWN, A

PASSWORD

PEARLY SHELLS

PEEL ME A NANNER

PEOPLE

PEOPLE SAY

PICK OF THE WEEK

PILLOW THAT WHISPERS, THE

PINK PANTHER THEME, THE

PLEASE PLEASE ME

POPSICLES IN PARIS

PROMISED LAND, THE

(P.S.) I LOVE YOU

PUPPY LOVE

PUT ON YOUR SUNDAY CLOTHES

RAG DOLL

REACH OUT FOR ME

REMEMBER (WALKIN' IN THE SAND)

RHYTHM

RIBBONS DOWN MY BACK

RINGO

RINGO'S THEME (THIS BOY)

(JUST LIKE) ROMEO AND JULIET

RONNIE

ROOM WITHOUT WINDOWS, A

RUNNIN' OUT OF FOOLS

SABBATH PRAYER

SADIE, SADIE

SAGINAW, MICHIGAN

SAILOR BOY

SAM HILL

SATURDAY NIGHT AT THE MOVIES

SAVE IT FOR ME

SAY YOU

SEASONS IN THE SUN

SECOND FIDDLE (TO AN OLD GUITAR)

SEE THE FUNNY LITTLE CLOWN

SEE WHAT IT'GETS YOU

SEND ME NO FLOWERS

SEVENTH DAWN, THE

SHA-LA-LA

SHARE YOUR LOVE WITH ME

SHE LOVES YOU

SHELTER OF YOUR ARMS, THE

SHE'S A WOMAN

SHE'S NOT THERE

SHE UNDERSTANDS ME (DUM-DE-DA)

SHOOP SHOOP SONG, THE (IT'S IN HIS KISS)

SLIP-IN MULES (NO HIGH-HEEL SNEAKERS)

SLOW DOWN

SOFTLY, AS I LEAVE YOU

SOLE SOLE SOLE

SO LONG, BIG TIME!

SO LONG, DEARIE

SOMEDAY WE'RE GONNA LOVE AGAIN

SOMETHING TELLS ME

SOMETHING YOU GOT

SORROW ON THE ROCKS

SOUL HOOTENANNY

SOUL SERENADE

SOUNDS OF SILENCE, THE

SOUTHTOWN U.S.A.

STAY AWHILE

STEP IN TIME

STOCKHOLM

STOP AND THINK IT OVER

STYLE

SUDDENLY I'M ALL ALONE

SUGAR AND SPICE

SUGAR LIPS

SUMMER SONG, A

SUNRISE, SUNSET

SUNSHINE, LOLLIPOPS AND RAINBOWS

SUPERCALIFRAGILISTICEXPIALIDOCIOUS

SURFIN' BIRD

SUSPICION

SWEET WILLIAM

TAKE MY RING OFF YOUR FINGER

TALK TO ME, BABY

TELL HER NO

TELL ME (YOU'RE COMING BACK)

TELL ME WHY

THERE WON'T BE TRUMPETS

THINK NOTHING ABOUT IT

THIS IS THE LIFE

THIS WHITE CIRCLE ON MY FINGER

THREE WINDOW COUPE

TIME IS ON MY SIDE

TIMES THEY ARE A-CHANGIN', THE

TOBACCO ROAD

TODAY

TOGETHER AGAIN

TO LIFE

TOO LATE TO TRY AGAIN

TOPKAPI

TRADITION

TRIANGLE

TRY IT BABY

TURN AROUND

UNDERSTAND YOUR MAN

UNDER THE BOARDWALK

UNLESS YOU CARE

USE YOUR HEAD

USE YOUR NOGGIN'

VIVA LAS VEGAS

WALKIN', TALKIN', CRYIN', BARELY BEATIN' BROKEN HEART

WALKING IN THE RAIN

WALK ON BY

WALTZ FOR DEBBY

WAS SHE PRETTIER THAN I?

WATCH WHAT HAPPENS

WAY YOU DO THE THINGS YOU DO, THE

WEDDING, THE (LA NOVIA)

WEEK IN THE COUNTRY, A
WELCOME TO MY WORLD
WE'LL SING IN THE SUNSHINE
WE LOVE YOU BEATLES
WHAT KIND OF FOOL (DO YOU THINK I AM)?
WHENEVER HE (SHE) HOLDS YOU
WHEN I GROW UP (TO BE A MAN)
WHEN IN ROME (I DO AS THE ROMANS DO)
WHEN YOU'RE YOUNG AND IN LOVE
WHERE DID OUR LOVE GO
WHERE DOES A LITTLE TEAR COME FROM?
WHERE LOVE HAS GONE
WHILE THE CITY SLEEPS
WHITE ON WHITE
WHO ARE YOU NOW?
WHO CAN I TURN TO (WHEN NOBODY NEEDS ME)
WHO'S BEEN SLEEPING IN MY BED?
WHY
WHY CAN'T YOU FEEL SORRY FOR ME?
WINE, WOMEN, AND SONG
WISHIN' AND HOPIN'
WITH SO LITTLE TO BE SURE OF
WONDERFUL DAY LIKE TODAY, A
WORLD I USED TO KNOW, THE
WORLD WITHOUT LOVE, A
WORRIED GUY
WRONG FOR EACH OTHER
YET . . . I KNOW
YOU ARE WOMAN, I AM MAN
YOU CAN'T DO THAT
YOU'D BETTER LOVE ME
(YOU DON'T KNOW) HOW GLAD I AM
YOU DON'T OWN ME
YOU'LL NEVER GET TO HEAVEN
YOU MUSTN'T BE DISCOURAGED
YOU REALLY GOT ME
YOU'RE A WONDERFUL ONE
YOU'RE FOR ME

YOU'RE MY WORLD
YOU'RE THE ONLY WORLD I KNOW
YOUR HEART TURNED LEFT (AND I WAS ON THE RIGHT)
YOU WERE ON MY MIND

1965

ACTION
AGENT DOUBLE-O-SOUL
AIN'T IT TRUE?
AIN'T THAT LOVE
AIN'T THAT PECULIAR?
ALL DAY AND ALL OF THE NIGHT
ALL I REALLY WANT TO DO
AND I LOVE HIM
AND ROSES AND ROSES
ANGEL
ANNIE FANNY
ANOTHER GIRL
ANYTIME AT ALL
APACHE '65
APPLE OF MY EYE
ARTIFICIAL ROSE
ASK THE LONELY
AT THE CLUB
BABY, DON'T GO
BABY, I'M YOURS
BABY, THE RAIN MUST FALL
BACK IN MY ARMS AGAIN
BALLAD OF CAT BALLOU, THE
BEFORE AND AFTER
BEFORE YOU GO
BEHIND THE TEARS
BELLES OF SOUTHERN BELL
BIRDS AND THE BEES, THE
BLIND MAN
BLUE KENTUCKY GIRL
BOO-GA-LOO
BOY FROM NEW YORK CITY, THE
BREAK AWAY (FROM THAT BOY)
BRIDGE WASHED OUT, THE

BUCKAROO
BUCKET "T"
BUMBLE BEE
BUT YOU'RE MINE
BYE, BYE, BABY (BABY GOODBYE)
CALIFORNIA GIRLS
CAN'T YOU HEAR MY HEARTBEAT?
CAN YOU JERK LIKE ME
CARA-LIN
CARA MIA
CATCH THE WIND
CATCH US IF YOU CAN
CERTAIN
CHANGE IS GONNA COME, A
CINCINNATI KID, THE
CLAPPING SONG, THE (CLAP PAT CLAP
    SLAP)
CLEO'S BACK
COME AND STAY WITH ME
COME BACK TO ME
COME ON OVER TO MY PLACE
COME SEE
COME TOMORROW
CONCRETE AND CLAY
COUNT ME IN
CRYSTAL CHANDELIER
DANGER HEARTBREAK DEAD AHEAD
DAWN OF CORRECTION
DAY TRIPPER
DEAR LOVER
D.J. CRIED, THE
DO I HEAR A WALTZ?
DON'T COME RUNNING BACK TO ME
DON'T JUST STAND THERE
DON'T LET ME BE MISUNDERSTOOD
DON'T MESS UP A GOOD THING
DON'T TALK TO STRANGERS
DO THE BOOMERANG
DO THE CLAM
DO THE FREDDIE
DO WHAT YOU DO DO WELL
DOWN IN THE BOONDOCKS

DOWNTOWN
DO YOU BELIEVE IN MAGIC?
DREAM ON LITTLE DREAMER
DRIVE MY CAR
DUCK, THE
EARLY MORNIN' RAIN
EIGHT DAYS A WEEK
ENGINE, ENGINE NUMBER NINE
ENGLAND SWINGS
ENTERTAINER, THE
EVE OF DESTRUCTION
EVERYBODY LOVES A CLOWN
EVERYONE'S GONE TO THE MOON
EVERYTHING MAKES MUSIC WHEN
    YOU'RE IN LOVE
FANCY PANTS
FELLING GOOD
FERRY ACROSS THE MERSEY
FIRST I LOOK AT THE PURSE
FIRST THING EVERY MORNING (AND
    THE LAST THING EVERY NIGHT), THE
FIVE O'CLOCK WORLD
FLOWERS ON THE WALL
FORGET DOMANI
FOR LOVIN' ME
FOR MAMA
FOR YOUR LOVE
GAME OF LOVE, THE
GET OFF OF MY CLOUD
GET TOGETHER
GIRL COME RUNNING
GIRL DON'T COME
GIRL ON THE BILLBOARD
GIVE HIM A GREAT BIG KISS
GLORIA
GOLDFINGER
GO NOW!
GOODBYE MY LOVER, GOODBYE
GOOD LOVIN'
GOODNIGHT
GOT TO GET YOU OFF MY MIND
HALF A SIXPENCE

HANG ON SLOOPY

HAPPINESS IS

HAVE YOU LOOKED INTO YOUR HEART?

HAWAII TATTOO

HE AIN'T NO ANGEL

HEART FULL OF SOUL

HEART OF STONE

HELP!

HELP ME, RHONDA

HERE COMES THE NIGHT

HERE I AM

HERE IT COMES AGAIN

(HERE THEY COME) FROM ALL OVER THE WORLD

HICKTOWN

HIGHWAY 61 REVISITED

HOLD WHAT YOU'VE GOT

HOLE IN THE WALL

HOME OF THE BRAVE

HOME YOU'RE TEARING DOWN, THE

HOUSTON

HOW SWEET IT IS (TO BE LOVED BY YOU)

HUNG ON YOU

HUNGRY FOR LOVE

HURRY, IT'S LOVELY UP HERE

HURT SO BAD

HUSH, HUSH, SWEET CHARLOTTE

I CAN NEVER GO HOME ANYMORE

I CAN'T EXPLAIN

(I CAN'T GET NO) SATISFACTION

I CAN'T HELP MYSELF (SUGAR PIE, HONEY BUNCH)

I CAN'T REMEMBER

I CAN'T STOP THINKING OF YOU

I CAN'T WORK NO LONGER

I DO

I DO LOVE YOU

I DON'T CARE (JUST AS LONG AS YOU LOVE ME)

I DON'T WANNA LOSE YOU, BABY

I DON'T WANT TO SPOIL THE PARTY

IF I DIDN'T LOVE YOU

IF I RULED THE WORLD

IF IT PLEASES YOU

I FOUND A GIRL

I FOUND A LOVE, OH WHAT A LOVE

IF THE RAIN'S GOT TO FALL

IF THIS IS GOODBYE

IF YOU'VE GOT A HEART

I GO TO PIECES

I GOT YOU BABE

I HEAR A SYMPHONY

I KNEW YOU WHEN

I KNOW A PLACE

IKO IKO

I'LL ALWAYS LOVE YOU

I'LL BE DOGGONE

I'LL KEEP HOLDING ON

I'LL KEEP HOLDING ON (JUST TO YOUR LOVE)

I'LL MAKE ALL YOUR DREAMS COME TRUE

I'LL NEVER FIND ANOTHER YOU

I'LL REPOSSESS MY HEART

I'LL TAKE YOU WHERE THE MUSIC'S PLAYING

I'M A FOOL

I'M A HAPPY MAN

I'M ALL SMILES

I'M A MAN

I'M HENERY VIII, I AM

IMPOSSIBLE DREAM, THE (THE QUEST)

I'M SO MISERABLE WITHOUT YOU

I'M TELLING YOU NOW

I MUST BE SEEING THINGS

I'M YOURS

"IN" CROWD, THE

I NEED YOU

IN THE MIDNIGHT HOUR

IS IT REALLY OVER?

IT'S ALL OVER NOW, BABY BLUE

IT'S ALRIGHT

IT'S A MAN DOWN THERE

IT'S ANOTHER WORLD
IT'S GONNA BE ALL RIGHT
IT'S GONNA TAKE A MIRACLE
IT'S GROWING
IT'S JUST A LITTLE BIT TOO LATE
IT'S MY LIFE
IT'S NOT UNUSUAL
IT'S THE SAME OLD SONG
IT'S TOO LATE, BABY, TOO LATE
I'VE BEEN LOVING YOU TOO LONG (TO STOP NOW)
I'VE GOT A TIGER BY THE TAIL
I'VE GOT NEWS FOR YOU
I WANT CANDY
I WANT TO (DO EVERYTHING FOR YOU)
I WILL
I WILL WAIT FOR YOU
I WON'T FORGET YOU
JENNY REBECCA
JOKER, THE
JOLLY GREEN GIANT
JU JU HAND
JUST A LITTLE
JUST A LITTLE BIT BETTER
JUST ONCE IN MY LIFE
JUST YOU
KANSAS CITY STAR
KEEP ON DANCING
KID AGAIN, A
KING OF THE ROAD
KISS AWAY
LAST CHANCE TO TURN AROUND
LAST TIME, THE
LAUGH AT ME
LAUGH, LAUGH
LAURIE (STRANGE THINGS HAPPEN)
LEADER OF THE LAUNDROMAT
LESS AND LESS
LET ME BE
LET'S DO THE FREDDIE
LET'S HANG ON

LET'S LOCK THE DOOR (AND THROW AWAY THE KEY)
LIAR, LIAR
LIES
LIFETIME OF LONELINESS, A
LIKE A ROLLING STONE
LITTLE BIT OF HEAVEN, A
LITTLE GIRL I ONCE KNEW, THE
LITTLE LONELY ONE
LITTLE THINGS
LITTLE YOU
LONELINESS OF EVENING
L-O-N-E-L-Y
LOOK AT THAT FACE
LOOKING THROUGH THE EYES OF LOVE
LOOK OF LOVE
LOVE MINUS ZERO—NO LIMIT
LOVER'S CONCERTO, A
MAKE ME YOUR BABY
MARRIED MAN, A
MATAMOROS
MAY THE BIRD OF PARADISE FLY UP YOUR NOSE
MEETING OVER YONDER
MELINDA
MEXICAN PEARLS
MICHAEL
MOHAIR SAM
MOTHER NATURE, FATHER TIME
MR. PITIFUL
MRS. BROWN, YOU'VE GOT A LOVELY DAUGHTER
MR. TAMBOURINE MAN
MY BABY
MY FRIENDS ARE GONNA BE STRANGERS
MY GIRL
MY GIRL HAS GONE
MY LITTLE RED BOOK
MYSTIC EYES
MY TOWN, MY GUY AND ME
NAME GAME, THE

NEW YORK'S A LONELY TOWN
NOBODY KNOWS WHAT'S GOIN' ON (IN
    MY MIND BUT ME)
NORWEGIAN WOOD
NOTHING BUT HEARTACHES
NOTHING CAN STOP ME
NOT THE LOVIN' KIND
NOWHERE TO RUN
ON A CLEAR DAY YOU CAN SEE
    FOREVER
1-2-3
ONE DYIN' AND A BURYIN'
ONE KISS FOR OLD TIMES' SAKE
ONLY YOU (CAN BREAK MY HEART)
OOH BABY BABY
OO WEE BABY, I LOVE YOU
ORANGE BLOSSOM SPECIAL
OTHER WOMAN, THE
OVER AND OVER
PAPA'S GOT A BRAND NEW BAG
PAPER TIGER
PASS ME BY
PASS THE BOOZE
PEACHES 'N' CREAM
PEOPLE, GET READY
PLAY WITH FIRE
PLEASE LET ME WONDER
POSITIVELY 4TH STREET
PRETTY LITTLE BABY
PRINCESS IN RAGS
PRIVATE JOHN Q
PUPPET ON A STRING
QUEEN OF THE HOUSE
QUEST, THE
RACE IS ON, THE
RED ROSES FOR A BLUE LADY
REELIN' AND ROCKIN'
RESCUE ME
RIBBON OF DARKNESS
RIDE AWAY
RIDE YOUR PONY
RING DANG DOO

ROUND EVERY CORNER
RUN, BABY, RUN (BACK INTO MY ARMS)
RUSTY BELLS
SAD, SAD GIRL
SAD TOMORROWS
SAVE YOUR HEART FOR ME
SAY SOMETHING FUNNY
(SAY) YOU'RE MY GIRL
SEEIN' THE RIGHT LOVE GO WRONG
SEE SAW
SEE THE BIG MAN CRY
SEPTEMBER OF MY YEARS
SET ME FREE
SEVENTH SON
SHADOW OF YOUR SMILE, THE
SHAKE
SHAKE AND FINGERPOP
SHAKIN' ALL OVER
SHE'S ABOUT A MOVER
SHE'S GONE GONE GONE
SHE TOUCHED ME
SHE WASN'T YOU
SHOTGUN
SILHOUETTES
SINCE I LOST MY BABY
SINNER MAN
SITTING IN THE PARK
SITTIN' IN AN ALL NITE CAFE
SOMETHING ABOUT YOU
SONS OF KATIE ELDER, THE
STAY AWAY FROM MY BABY
STAY IN MY CORNER
STEPPIN' OUT
STOP! IN THE NAME OF LOVE
STRANGER IN TOWN
SUBTERRANEAN HOMESICK BLUES
(SUCH AN) EASY QUESTION
SUGAR DUMPLING
SUMMER NIGHTS
SUMMER SOUNDS
SUMMER WIND
SUNDAY AND ME

SWEET BEGINNING

SWEETHEART TREE, THE

SYLVIA

TAKE ME BACK

TAKE ME IN YOUR ARMS (ROCK ME)

TAKE THE MOMENT

TEASIN' YOU

TELL ANOTHER LIE

TELL HER YOU LOVE HER EVERY DAY

TEN LITTLE BOTTLES

THEN AND ONLY THEN

THERE BUT FOR FORTUNE

THINGS HAVE GONE TO PIECES

THIS DIAMOND RING

THIS IS IT

THIS LITTLE BIRD

THREE A.M.

THUNDERBALL

TICKET TO RIDE

TIGER WOMAN

TIRED OF WAITING FOR YOU

TOMBSTONE EVERY MILE, A

TONIGHT'S THE NIGHT

TOO MANY FISH IN THE SEA

TOO MANY RIVERS

TRACKS OF MY TEARS, THE

TRAINS AND BOATS AND PLAINS

TREAT HER RIGHT

TRUCK DRIVIN' SON-OF-A-GUN

TRUE LOVE WAYS

TRY TO REMEMBER

TURN! TURN! TURN!

TWINE TIME

UNDER YOUR SPELL AGAIN

VOODOO WOMAN

WALK TALL

WATCH WHERE YOU'RE GOING

WE GOTTA GET OUT OF THIS PLACE

WE'RE GONNA MAKE IT

WHAT COLOR (IS A MAN)

WHAT DID I HAVE THAT I DON'T HAVE

WHAT DO YOU WANT WITH ME?

WHAT HAVE THEY DONE TO THE RAIN?

WHAT I NEED MOST

WHAT'S HE DOIN' IN MY WORLD?

WHAT'S NEW, PUSSYCAT?

WHAT THE WORLD NEEDS NOW IS LOVE

WHAT WE'RE FIGHTING FOR

WHENEVER A TEENAGER CRIES

WHEN I'M GONE

WHERE DO YOU GO?

WHERE WERE YOU WHEN I NEEDED YOU?

WHIPPED CREAM

WHO'LL BE THE NEXT IN LINE?

WHO'S CHEATING WHO?

WHOSE HEART ARE YOU BREAKING TONIGHT?

WILD AS A WILD CAT

WILD ONE

WISHING WELL, THE (DOWN IN THE WELL)

WOMAN'S GOT SOUL

WOOLY BULLY

WORLD OF OUR OWN, A

YES, I'M READY

YES, MR. PETERS

YES IT IS

YESTERDAY

YOU BETTER GET IT

YOU DIDN'T HAVE TO BE SO NICE

YOU'D BETTER COME HOME

YOU DON'T HEAR

YOUNG GIRL, A

YOU REALLY KNOW HOW TO HURT A GUY

YOU'RE GONNA MAKE ME CRY

YOU'RE THE ONE

YOU TELL ME WHY

YOU TURN ME ON (THE TURN ON SONG)

YOU'VE BEEN CHEATIN'

YOU'VE BEEN IN LOVE TOO LONG

YOU'VE GOT TO HIDE YOUR LOVE AWAY

PAPERBACK WRITER
PETER RABBIT
PHILLY FREEZE, THE
PHOENIX LOVE THEME, THE
PIED PIPER, THE
PLACE IN THE SUN, A
PLEASE DON'T EVER LEAVE ME
PLEASE DON'T STOP LOVING ME
PLEASE SAY YOU'RE FOOLIN'
PLEASE TELL ME WHY
POOR SIDE OF TOWN
POPSICLE
PRETTY FLAMINGO
PROUD ONE, THE
PSYCHOTIC REACTION
PUCKER UP, BUTTERCUP
PUT IT OFF UNTIL TOMORROW
RAIN
RAINBOWS AND ROSES
RAIN ON THE ROOF
RAINY DAY WOMEN NO. 12 AND 35
REACH OUT, I'LL BE THERE
RECOVERY
RED RUBBER BALL
RESPECTABLE
RHAPSODY IN THE RAIN
RHYTHM OF LIFE, THE
RIVER DEEP—MOUNTAIN HIGH
ROOM IN YOUR HEART
RUN, RUN, LOOK AND SEE
SATIN PILLOWS
SATISFIED WITH YOU
SAY I AM (WHAT I AM)
SCARBOROUGH FAIR—CANTICLE
SEARCHING FOR MY LOVE
SECRET AGENT MAN
SEEING YOU LIKE THIS
SET YOU FREE THIS TIME
7 AND 7 IS
SHAKE ME, WAKE ME (WHEN IT'S OVER)
SHAPES OF THINGS
SHE BLEW A GOOD THING

SHE'D RATHER BE WITH ME
SHE SAID SHE SAID
SHE'S JUST MY STYLE
SIGN OF THE TIMES, A
SINGLE GIRL
SITTIN' ON A ROCK (CRYIN' IN A CREEK)
634-5789 (SOULSVILLE U.S.A.)
SKID ROW JOE
SNAKE, THE
SNOW FLAKE
SOLITARY MAN
SOMEBODY LIKE ME
SOMEONE BEFORE ME
SOMETIMES GOOD GUYS DON'T WEAR WHITE
SOMEWHERE MY LOVE (LARA'S THEME)
SOMEWHERE THERE'S A SOMEONE
SPANISH EYES
SPANISH FLEA
SPINOUT
SPREAD IT ON THICK
STAND BESIDE ME
STANDING IN THE SHADOWS
STEEL RAIL BLUES
STEP OUT OF YOUR MIND
STOP, STOP, STOP
STOP HER ON SIGHT (S.O.S.)
STOP THE START (OF TEARS IN MY HEART)
STRANGERS IN THE NIGHT
STREETS OF BALTIMORE
SUGAR TOWN
SUMMER IN THE CITY
SUMMER SAMBA (SO NICE)
SUN AIN'T GONNA SHINE ANYMORE, THE
SUNNY
SUNNY AFTERNOON
SUNSHINE SUPERMAN
SURE GONNA MISS HER
SWEET PEA
SWEET TALKIN' GUY

SWEET THANG

SWEET WOMAN LIKE YOU, A

SWINGING DOORS

SYMPHONY FOR SUSAN, A

S.Y.S.L.J.F.M. (THE LETTER SONG)

TAKE ME

TAKE THIS HEART OF MINE

TALK, TALK

TALKIN' TO THE WALL

TAR AND CEMENT

THAT'S LIFE

THERE'S A KIND OF HUSH (ALL OVER THE WORLD)

THERE'S GOTTA BE SOMETHING BETTER THAN THIS

THERE'S GOT TO BE A WORD

THERE'S NO LIVIN' WITHOUT YOUR LOVIN'

THESE BOOTS ARE MADE FOR WALKING

THEY'RE COMING TO TAKE ME AWAY, HA-HAAA!

THINK I'LL GO SOMEWHERE AND CRY MYSELF TO SLEEP

THINK OF ME (WHEN YOU'RE LONELY)

THIS DOOR SWINGS BOTH WAYS

THIS OLD HEART OF MINE (IS WEAK FOR YOU)

TIJUANA TAXI

TILL THE END OF THE DAY

TIME

TIME FOR LOVE, A

TIME TO BUM AGAIN

TIME WON'T LET ME

TINY BUBBLES

TIPPY TOEING

TOMORROW BELONGS TO ME

TRUE LOVE'S A BLESSING

TRY TOO HARD

TURN-DOWN DAY

TWINKLE TOES

UNMITIGATED GALL

UP AND DOWN

UPTIGHT (EVERYTHING'S ALRIGHT)

VIET NAM BLUES

WADE IN THE WATER

WAITIN' IN YOUR WELFARE LINE

WALK AWAY RENEE

WALKING HAPPY

WALKING ON NEW GRASS

WALKIN' MY CAT NAMED DOG

WANG DANG DOODLE

WARM AND TENDER LOVE

WAY TO SURVIVE, A

WE CAN WORK IT OUT

(WE'LL BE) UNITED

WELL RESPECTED MAN, A

WE NEED A LITTLE CHRISTMAS

WHAT AM I GOING TO DO WITHOUT YOUR LOVE?

WHAT BECOMES OF THE BROKENHEARTED?

WHAT GOES ON

WHAT KINDA DEAL IS THIS?

WHAT NOW MY LOVE

WHEEL OF HURT, THE

WHEN A MAN (WOMAN) LOVES A WOMAN (MAN)

WHEN LIKING TURNS TO LOVING

(WHEN SHE NEEDS GOOD LOVIN') SHE COMES TO ME

WHEN THE FOG ROLLS IN TO SAN FRANCISCO

WHERE AM I GOING?

WHISPERS (GETTIN' LOUDER)

WHO AM I?

WHOLE LOT OF SHAKIN' IN MY HEART (SINCE I MET YOU)

WIEDERSEH'N

WILD THING

WILLKOMMEN

WINCHESTER CATHEDRAL

WISHING DOLL, THE

WISH ME A RAINBOW

WISH YOU WERE HERE, BUDDY

WITH A GIRL LIKE YOU

WOMAN

WOMEN DO FUNNY THINGS TO ME

WORKING IN THE COAL MINE

WORK SONG, THE

WORLD IS ROUND, THE

WORLD OF FANTASY

WOULDN'T IT BE NICE?

WOULD YOU HOLD IT AGAINST ME?

YELLOW SUBMARINE

YOU AIN'T WOMAN ENOUGH

YOU BABY

YOU BETTER RUN

YOU CAN'T HURRY LOVE

YOU CAN'T ROLLER SKATE IN A
   BUFFALO HERD

YOU DON'T HAVE TO PAINT ME A
   PICTURE

YOU DON'T HAVE TO SAY YOU LOVE ME

YOU DON'T KNOW LIKE I KNOW

YOU KEEP ME HANGIN' ON

(YOU MAKE ME FEEL) SO GOOD

YOUNGER GIRL

YOU'RE GONNA HEAR FROM ME

YOU'RE GONNA HURT YOURSELF

(YOU'RE MY) SOUL AND INSPIRATION

YOU'RE THE ONE (I NEED)

YOU SHOULD SEE YOURSELF

YOU'VE GOT POSSIBILITIES

YOU WON'T SEE ME

YOU WOULDN'T LISTEN

1967

A BANDA (PARADE)

AIN'T GOT NO

AIN'T NO MOUNTAIN HIGH ENOUGH

AIR

AIRPLANE SONG (MY AIRPLANE)

ALICE'S RESTAURANT

ALL I NEED

ALL THE TIME

ALL YOU NEED IS LOVE

AND GET AWAY

ANGEL OF THE MORNING

ANOTHER DAY, ANOTHER HEARTACHE

ANYTHING YOUR HEART DESIRES

APPLES, PEACHES, PUMPKIN PIE

AQUARIUS

ARE YOU LONELY FOR ME?

AT THE ZOO

BABY, PLEASE COME BACK HOME

BABY, YOU'RE A RICH MAN

BABY, YOU'VE GOT IT

BABY I LOVE YOU

BACK ON THE STREET AGAIN

BALLAD OF THE CHRISTMAS DONKEY,
   THE

BALLAD OF YOU AND ME AND POONEIL

BARE NECESSITIES, THE

BEAT GOES ON, THE

BEAUTIFUL PEOPLE

BEG, BORROW, AND STEAL

BEGGIN'

BERNADETTE

BLUEBIRD

BOOGALOO DOWN BROADWAY

BOWLING GREEN

BRANDED MAN

BREAK MY MIND

BRING IT UP

BROWN EYED GIRL

BUY ME FOR THE RAIN

BY THE TIME I GET TO PHOENIX

CALIFORNIA NIGHTS

CAN'T SEEM TO MAKE YOU MINE

CAN'T TAKE MY EYES OFF YOU

CARRIE-ANNE

CASINO ROYALE

CAT IN THE WINDOW, THE (THE BIRD IN
   THE SKY)

CHILD OF CLAY

CHOKIN' KIND, THE

CINCINNATI, OHIO

C'MON MARIANNE

COLD HARD FACTS OF LIFE

COLD SWEAT

COLOR MY WORLD

COME BACK WHEN YOU GROW UP

COME ON DOWN TO MY BOAT

COME TO THE SUNSHINE

COMMUNICATION BREAKDOWN

COULD I FALL IN LOVE?

COVER ME

CREEQUE ALLEY

DANDELION

DARLING BE HOME SOON

DAYDREAM BELIEVER

DEAD END STREET

DEAR ELOISE

DEDICATED TO THE ONE I LOVE

DIFFERENT DRUM

DIRTY MAN

DIS-ADVANTAGES OF YOU, THE

DOES MY RING HURT YOUR FINGER?

DO IT AGAIN, A LITTLE BIT SLOWER

DON'T BLAME THE CHILDREN

DON'T COME HOME A-DRINKIN' (WITH LOVIN' ON YOUR MIND)

DON'T GO OUT INTO THE RAIN (YOU'RE GONNA MELT)

DON'T LET THE RAIN FALL DOWN ON ME

DON'T SLEEP IN THE SUBWAY

DON'T SQUEEZE MY SHARMON

DON'T YOU CARE

DRIFTING APART

DRY YOUR EYES

EASY TO BE HARD

EIGHT MEN, FOUR WOMEN

EPISTLE TO DIPPY

EVEN THE BAD TIMES ARE GOOD

EVERLASTING LOVE

EVERYBODY NEEDS LOVE

EVERYBODY NEEDS SOMEBODY TO LOVE

EXPLOSION IN MY SOUL

EXPRESSWAY TO YOUR HEART

EYES OF LOVE, THE (CAROL'S THEME)

FAKIN' IT

FEEL SO BAD

FEEL SO GOOD

FIRE

59TH STREET BRIDGE SONG, THE (FEELIN' GROOVY)

FLIM FLAM MAN

FOOL, FOOL, FOOL

FOR ONCE IN MY LIFE

FOR WHAT IT'S WORTH (STOP, HEY WHAT'S THAT SOUND)

FRANK MILLS

FRIDAY ON MY MIND

FUGITIVE, THE (I'M A LONESOME FUGITIVE)

FUNKY BROADWAY

FUNNY, FAMILIAR, FORGOTTEN FEELINGS

GAME OF TRIANGLES, THE

GENTLE ON MY MIND

GET IT TOGETHER

GET ME TO THE WORLD ON TIME

GET ON UP

GETTIN' TOGETHER

GET WHILE THE GETTIN'S GOOD

GIMME LITTLE SIGN

GIMME SOME LOVIN'

GIRL, YOU'LL BE A WOMAN SOON

GIRL I KNEW SOMEWHERE, THE

GIRL I NEVER LOVED, THE

GIRL LIKE YOU, A

GIRLS IN LOVE

GONNA GIVE HER ALL THE LOVE I'VE GOT

GOOD DAY SUNSHINE

GOOD MORNING STARSHINE

GOOD THING

GO WHERE YOU WANNA GO

GROOVIN'

HA HA SAID THE CLOWN

HAIR

HAPPENING, THE

HAPPY

HAPPY JACK

HAPPY TOGETHER

HARE KRISHNA (BE-IN)

HELLO, GOODBYE

HELLO, HELLO

HERE COMES MY BABY

HERE COMES THE RAIN, BABY

HERE WE GO AGAIN

HEROES AND VILLAINS

HEY, BABY (THEY'RE PLAYIN' OUR SONG)

HEY, LEROY, YOUR MAMA'S CALLIN' YOU

HEY, THAT'S NO WAY TO SAY GOODBYE

HIM OR ME, WHAT'S IT GONNA BE?

HIP HUG-HER

HOLIDAY

HOMBURG

HONEY CHILE

HOW CAN I BE SURE?

HOW DO YOU CATCH A GIRL?

HOW LONG WILL IT TAKE

HURT HER ONCE FOR ME

HYPNOTIZED

I AM THE WALRUS

I CAN SEE FOR MILES

I CAN'T GET THERE FROM HERE

I DIG ROCK AND ROLL MUSIC

I DON'T WANNA PLAY HOUSE

I-FEEL-LIKE-I'M-FIXIN'-TO-DIE RAG

IF I COULD BUILD MY WHOLE WORLD AROUND YOU

IF I KISS YOU (WILL YOU GO AWAY?)

IF THIS IS LOVE (I'D RATHER BE LONELY)

IF YOU'RE NOT GONE TOO LONG

I GOT LIFE

I HAD A DREAM

I HAD TOO MUCH TO DREAM (LAST NIGHT)

I HEARD IT THROUGH THE GRAPEVINE

I LIKE THE WAY

I'LL COME RUNNING

I'LL NEVER FALL IN LOVE AGAIN

I'LL PLANT MY OWN TREE

I'LL TAKE CARE OF YOUR CARES

I'LL TRY ANYTHING

I MAKE A FOOL OF MYSELF

I'M A MAN

I'M IN LOVE

I'M NOT YOUR STEPPIN' STONE

I'M STILL NOT OVER YOU

I'M WONDERING

IN AND OUT OF LOVE

INCENSE AND PEPPERMINTS

INDESCRIBABLY BLUE

I NEVER LOVED A MAN (THE WAY I LOVE YOU)

IN THE HEAT OF THE NIGHT

I SAY A LITTLE PRAYER

I SECOND THAT EMOTION

I TAKE IT BACK

I TAKE WHAT I WANT

ITCHYCOO PARK

I THINK WE'RE ALONE NOW

I THREW AWAY THE ROSE

IT MUST BE HIM

IT'S NOW WINTER'S DAY

IT TAKES TWO

I'VE BEEN LONELY TOO LONG

I'VE GOT TO HAVE A REASON

I'VE PASSED THIS WAY BEFORE

I WANNA TESTIFY

I WAS KAISER BILL'S BATMAN

I WAS MADE TO LOVE HER

I WON'T COME IN WHILE HE'S THERE

JACKSON

JIMMY MACK

JOY

JUDY IN DISGUISE (WITH GLASSES)

KEEP THE BALL ROLLIN'

KENTUCKY WOMAN

KIND OF A DRAG

KNIGHT IN RUSTY ARMOUR

LADY

LADY BIRD

LADY CAME FROM BALTIMORE, THE

LAST WALTZ, THE

LAURA (WHAT'S HE GOT THAT I AIN'T
  GOT?)

LAZY DAY

LEOPARD-SKIN PILL-BOX HAT

LET LOVE COME BETWEEN US

LET'S LIVE FOR TODAY

LET'S SPEND THE NIGHT TOGETHER

LETTER, THE

LET THE SUNSHINE IN (THE FLESH
  FAILURES)

LET YOURSELF GO

LIFE TURNED HER THAT WAY

LIGHT MY FIRE

LIGHTNING'S GIRL

(LIGHTS WENT OUT IN) MASSACHUSETTS

LIKE AN OLD TIME MOVIE

LITTLE BIT ME, A LITTLE BIT YOU, A

LITTLE BIT O' SOUL

LITTLE GAMES

LITTLE OLE WINEDRINKER ME

LIVE FOR LIFE

(LONELINESS MADE ME REALIZE) IT'S
  YOU I NEED

LONELY IS THE NAME

LONG-LEGGED GUITAR PICKIN' MAN

LOOK OF LOVE, THE

LOOK WHAT YOU'VE DONE

LOSER'S CATHEDRAL

LOVE BUG LEAVE MY HEART ALONE

LOVE EYES

LOVE I SAW IN YOU WAS JUST A
  MIRAGE, THE

LOVE IS HERE AND NOW YOU'RE GONE

LOVELY RITA (METER MAID)

LOVE POWER

LOVIN' YOU

LUCY IN THE SKY WITH DIAMONDS

MAGICAL MYSTERY TOUR, THE

MAKE ME YOURS

MAKING EVERY MINUTE COUNT

MAKING MEMORIES

MAMA SPANK

MARY IN THE MORNING

MELANCHOLY MUSIC MAN

MEMPHIS SOUL STEW

MERCY, MERCY, MERCY

MICHAEL FROM MOUNTAINS

MIRAGE

"MISSION: IMPOSSIBLE" THEME

MISTY BLUE

MORE AND MORE

MORE LOVE

MORE THAN A MIRACLE

MORE THAN THE EYE CAN SEE

MORNINGTOWN RIDE

MR. DREAM MERCHANT

MUSEUM

MUSIC TO WATCH GIRLS BY

MY BABE

MY ELUSIVE DREAMS

NASHVILLE CATS

NATURAL WOMAN, A (YOU MAKE ME
  FEEL LIKE)

NEON RAINBOW

NEVER MY LOVE

NEW YORK MINING DISASTER 1941
  (HAVE YOU SEEN MY WIFE, MR.
  JONES?)

NEXT PLANE TO LONDON

98.6

NO MILK TODAY

NO ONE'S GONNA HURT YOU ANYMORE

NOTHING TAKES THE PLACE OF YOU

NOT SO SWEET MARTHA LORRAINE

NOW I KNOW

ODE TO BILLY JOE

OH THAT'S GOOD, NO THAT'S BAD

OLD MACDONALD
ON A CAROUSEL
ONCE
ONE MORE MOUNTAIN TO CLIMB
ON THE SOUTH SIDE OF CHICAGO
OOGUM BOOGUM SONG, THE
OTHER MAN'S GRASS IS ALWAYS
  GREENER, THE
OUT AND ABOUT
OUT OF THE BLUE
PAPA WAS TOO
PAPER CUP
PAPER MANSIONS
PAPER SUN
PATA PATA
PAY YOU BACK WITH INTEREST
PEACE OF MIND
PENNY LANE
PEOPLE ARE STRANGE
PEOPLE LIKE YOU
PHANTOM 309
PICTURES OF LILY
PIECE OF MY HEART
PLEASANT VALLEY SUNDAY
PLEASE LOVE ME FOREVER
POP A TOP
PRETTY BALLERINA
PURPLE HAZE
PUSHIN' TOO HARD
PUT YOUR MIND AT EASE
RAIN, THE PARK AND OTHER THINGS,
  THE
REFLECTIONS
RELEASE ME
RESPECT
RETURN OF THE RED BARON, THE
RIDE, RIDE, RIDE
RIVER IS WIDE, THE
ROCK 'N' ROLL WOMAN
RUBY TUESDAY
RUTHLESS
SAM'S PLACE

SAN FRANCISCAN NIGHTS
SAN FRANCISCO (BE SURE TO WEAR
  SOME FLOWERS IN YOUR HAIR)
7 ROOMS OF GLOOM
SGT. PEPPER'S LONELY HEARTS CLUB
  BAND
SHAME, SHAME
SHE IS STILL A MYSTERY
SHE'S MY GIRL
SHOE GOES ON THE OTHER FOOT
  TONIGHT, THE
SHOOT YOUR SHOT
SHOW BUSINESS
SHOW ME
SILENCE IS GOLDEN
SINCE YOU SHOWED ME HOW TO BE
  HAPPY
SISTERS OF MERCY
SIT DOWN, I THINK I LOVE YOU
SIX O'CLOCK
SKINNY LEGS AND ALL
SNOOPY VS. THE RED BARON
SOCIETY'S CHILD (BABY, I'VE BEEN
  THINKING)
SOCK IT TO ME, BABY!
SOMEBODY HELP ME
SOMEBODY TO LOVE
SOMETHIN' STUPID
SOME VELVET MORNING
SOUL FINGER
SOUL MAN
SOUND OF LOVE
SO YOU WANT TO BE A ROCK 'N' ROLL
  STAR
STAMP OUT LONELINESS
STANDING IN THE SHADOWS OF LOVE
STEP TO THE REAR
STOP! AND THINK IT OVER
STRAWBERRY FIELDS FOREVER
SUMMER RAIN
SUMMER WINE
SUNDAY FOR TEA

SUNDAY WILL NEVER BE THE SAME

SUNSHINE GIRL

SUZANNE

SWEETEST THING THIS SIDE OF
  HEAVEN, THE

SWEET SOUL MUSIC

TAKE ME (JUST AS I AM)

TAKE ME FOR A LITTLE WHILE

TALK TO THE ANIMALS

TEAR TIME

TELL IT LIKE IT IS

TELL IT TO THE RAIN

TELL ME TO MY FACE

THANK THE LORD FOR THE NIGHT TIME

THEME FROM "VALLEY OF THE DOLLS"

THEN YOU CAN TELL ME GOODBYE

THERE GOES MY EVERYTHING

THERE IS A MOUNTAIN

THESE ARE NOT MY PEOPLE

THINGS I SHOULD HAVE SAID

THIS IS MY SONG

THIS TOWN

THOROUGHLY MODERN MILLIE

TO BE A LOVER

TO LOVE SOMEBODY

TONIGHT CARMEN

TOO MUCH OF NOTHING

TO SIR WITH LOVE

TOUCH MY HEART

TRAMP

TRAVELIN' MAN

TURN THE WORLD AROUND THE OTHER
  WAY

TWELVE THIRTY (YOUNG GIRLS ARE
  COMING TO THE CANYON)

UNTIL IT'S TIME FOR YOU TO GO

UPS AND DOWNS

UP—UP AND AWAY

URGE FOR GOING

WACK WACK

WALKING IN SPACE

WALKING IN THE SUNSHINE

WALK THROUGH THIS WORLD WITH ME

WATCH THE FLOWERS GROW

(WE AIN'T GOT) NOTHIN' YET

WEAR YOUR LOVE LIKE HEAVEN

WE LOVE YOU

WESTERN UNION

WHAT A WOMAN IN LOVE WON'T DO

WHAT DOES IT TAKE (TO KEEP A
  WOMAN LIKE YOU SATISFIED?)

WHAT'S IT GONNA BE?

WHEN I LOOK IN YOUR EYES

WHEN I'M 64

WHEN I WAS YOUNG

WHEN SOMETHING IS WRONG WITH MY
  BABY

WHEN THE SNOW IS ON THE ROSES

WHERE DOES THE GOOD TIMES GO?

WHERE DO I GO?

WHERE WILL THE WORDS COME FROM?

WHITE RABBIT

WHITER SHADE OF PALE, A

WHOLE WORLD IS A STAGE, THE

WHO NEEDS MONEY?

WHY NOT TONIGHT?

WILD HONEY

WINDOWS OF THE WORLD, THE

WINDY

WISH YOU DIDN'T HAVE TO GO

WITH A LITTLE HELP FROM MY FRIENDS

WITH ONE EXCEPTION

WITH THIS RING

WOMAN, WOMAN

WOMAN IN LOVE, A

WORDS

WORDS I'M GONNA HAVE TO EAT

WORDS OF LOVE

WORLD WE KNEW, THE (OVER AND
  OVER)

WORST THAT COULD HAPPEN, THE

YELLOW BALLOON, THE

YOU BETTER SIT DOWN KIDS

YOU GOT TO ME

YOU KEEP RUNNING AWAY

YOU KNOW WHAT I MEAN

YOU MEAN THE WORLD TO ME

YOU ONLY LOVE TWICE

YOU'RE A GOOD MAN, CHARLIE BROWN

YOU'RE MY EVERYTHING

YOUR GOOD GIRL'S GONNA GO BAD

(YOUR LOVE KEEPS LIFTING ME)
  HIGHER AND HIGHER

YOUR PRECIOUS LOVE

YOUR TENDER LOVING CARE

YOUR UNCHANGING LOVE

YOU'VE GOT TO PAY THE PRICE

YOU'VE MADE ME SO VERY HAPPY

YOU WANTED SOMEONE TO PLAY WITH
  (I WANTED SOMEONE TO LOVE)

ZIP CODE

1968

ABRAHAM, MARTIN, AND JOHN

AIN'T NOTHING LIKE THE REAL THING

AIN'T NO WAY

ALICE LONG (YOU'RE STILL MY
  FAVORITE GIRLFRIEND)

ALL ALONG THE WATCHTOWER

ALL TOGETHER NOW

ALMOST IN LOVE

ALREADY IT'S HEAVEN

ALWAYS TOGETHER

AME CALINE (SOUL COAXING)

AMEN

AMERICA IS MY HOME

AMSTERDAM

AND SUDDENLY

ANOTHER PLACE, ANOTHER TIME

AS LONG AS I LIVE

AUTUMN OF MY LIFE

BABY, COME BACK

BABY, LET'S WAIT

BABY, MAKE YOUR OWN SWEET MUSIC

BABY, NOW THAT I'VE FOUND YOU

BABY, YOU COME ROLLIN 'CROSS MY
  MIND

BABY'S BACK AGAIN

BALLAD OF BONNIE AND CLYDE, THE

BALLAD OF FORTY DOLLARS

BALL AND CHAIN

BANG-SHANG-A-LANG

BEAUTIFUL MORNING, A

BEND ME, SHAPE ME

BEST OF BOTH WORLDS

BIRD ON THE WIRE

BORN TO BE WILD

BOTH SIDES NOW (a.k.a. FROM BOTH
  SIDES NOW)

BOTTLE OF WINE

BOXER, THE

BREAK YOUR PROMISE

BROOKLYN ROADS

BROWN EYED WOMAN

CAB DRIVER

CAJUN STRIPPER, THE

CALL ME LIGHTNING

CAROUSEL

CARPET MAN

CHAINED

CHAIN OF FOOLS

CHEWY CHEWY

CHILD OF THE UNIVERSE

CHITTY CHITTY BANG BANG

CHOO CHOO TRAIN

CINNAMON

CLASSICAL GAS

CLOUD NINE

CONDITION RED

COUNTRY GIRL—CITY MAN

COURT OF LOVE

COWBOYS TO GIRLS

CROSSTOWN TRAFFIC

CRY LIKE A BABY

CYCLES

DANCE TO THE MUSIC

DANCING BEAR

DARLIN'
DAY THE WORLD STOOD STILL, THE
DEAR PRUDENCE
DELILAH
D-I-V-O-R-C-E
DOES YOUR MAMA KNOW ABOUT ME?
DO IT AGAIN
DON'T GIVE UP
DON'T PUT IT DOWN
DON'T TAKE IT SO HARD
DO SOMETHING TO ME
DO THE CHOO CHOO
DOWN AT LULU'S
DOWN ON ME
DO YOU KNOW THE WAY TO SAN JOSÉ?
DREAM A LITTLE DREAM OF ME
DREAMS OF THE EVERYDAY
  HOUSEWIFE
D. W. WASHBURN
EASY PART'S OVER, THE
ELENORE
ELI'S COMING
END OF OUR ROAD, THE
EVERYTHING THAT TOUCHES YOU
EYES OF A NEW YORK WOMAN, THE
FACE IT GIRL, IT'S OVER
FIRE!
FIST CITY
FLOWER OF LOVE
FOGGY MOUNTAIN BREAKDOWN
FOLSOM PRISON BLUES
FOOL FOR YOU
FOOL ON THE HILL, THE
FOREVER CAME TODAY
FOR LOVE OF IVY
1432 FRANKLIN PIKE CIRCLE HERO
FOXEY LADY
FRIENDS
FUNKY JUDGE
FUNKY STREET
GIRLS CAN'T DO WHAT THE GUYS DO
GIRL WATCHER

GIVE A DAMN
GOIN' BACK
GOIN' OUT OF MY HEAD
GOOD, THE BAD AND THE UGLY, THE
GOODBYE, MY LOVE
GOODY GOODY GUMDROPS
GRAZING IN THE GRASS
GREEN LIGHT
GREEN TAMBOURINE
GUITAR MAN
HANG 'EM HIGH
HAPPY SONG (DUM DUM), THE
HAPPY STATE OF MIND
HARPER VALLEY P.T.A.
HAVE A LITTLE FAITH
HEAVEN SAYS HELLO
HELLO, I LOVE YOU
HELP YOURSELF
HELTER SKELTER
HERE COMES HEAVEN
HERE COMES THE JUDGE
HERE I AM BABY
HEY, WESTERN UNION MAN
HIP CITY
HIS EYES—HER EYES
HITCH IT TO THE HORSE
HOLD ME TIGHT
HOLDING ON TO NOTHING
HONEY
HORSE, THE
HORSE FEVER
HOUSE THAT JACK BUILT, THE
HOW'D WE EVER GET THIS WAY?
HOW LONG WILL MY BABY BE GONE?
HURDY GURDY MAN
HUSHABYE MOUNTAIN
I AINT GOT TO LOVE NOBODY ELSE
I BELIEVE IN LOVE
I CAN TAKE OR LEAVE YOUR LOVING
I CAN'T BELIEVE I'M LOSING YOU
I CAN'T DANCE TO THAT MUSIC
  YOU'RE PLAYIN'

I CAN'T QUIT HER

I CAN'T STAND MYSELF (WHEN YOU TOUCH ME)

I CAN'T STOP DANCING

I CAN'T TURN YOU LOOSE

I COULD NEVER LOVE ANOTHER (AFTER LOVING YOU)

IF I CAN DREAM

I FOUND A TRUE LOVE

IF THIS WORLD WERE MINE

IF WE ONLY HAVE LOVE

IF YOU CAN WANT

IF YOU DON'T WANT MY LOVE

I GET THE SWEETEST FEELING

I GOT THE FEELIN'

I GOT YOU

I HEARD A HEART BREAK LAST NIGHT

I JUST CAME TO GET MY BABY

I'LL BE YOUR BABY TONIGHT

I'LL NEVER FALL IN LOVE AGAIN

I LOVE YOU

I'M A MIDNIGHT MOVER

I MET HER IN CHURCH

I'M GONNA MAKE YOU LOVE ME

I'M GONNA MOVE ON

I'M SORRY

IN-A-GADDA-DA-VIDA

INDIAN LAKE

INDIAN RESERVATION (THE LAMENT OF THE CHEROKEE RESERVATION INDIAN)

INNER LIGHT, THE

I SHALL BE RELEASED

IT SHOULD HAVE BEEN ME

IT'S NICE TO BE WITH YOU

IT'S WONDERFUL

I'VE GOT DREAMS TO REMEMBER

I'VE GOTTA BE ME

I'VE GOTTA GET A MESSAGE TO YOU

I'VE NEVER FOUND A GIRL (TO LOVE ME LIKE YOU DO)

I WALK ALONE

I WANNA LIVE

I WILL ALWAYS THINK ABOUT YOU

I WISH IT WOULD RAIN

I WONDER WHAT SHE'S DOING TONIGHT

JEALOUS LOVE

JELLY JUNGLE (OF ORANGE MARMALADE)

JENNIFER ECCLES

JENNIFER JUNIPER

JOHN WESLEY HARDING

JOURNEY TO THE CENTER OF THE MIND

JULIA

JUMPIN' JACK FLASH

JUST DROPPED IN (TO SEE WHAT CONDITION MY CONDITION WAS IN)

JUST FOR YOU

KEEP ON LOVIN' ME HONEY

KEEP THE ONE YOU GOT

KISS ME GOODBYE

KNOWING WHEN TO LEAVE

LADY MADONNA

LADY WILLPOWER

LA LA MEANS I LOVE YOU

LALENA

L. DAVID SLOANE

LEGEND OF BONNIE AND CLYDE, THE

LES BICYCLETTES DE BELSIZE

LESSON, THE

LET THE WORLD KEEP ON A TURNIN'

LICKING STICK—LICKING STICK

LIFE OF THE PARTY, THE

LIKE TO GET TO KNOW YOU

LISTEN HERE

LITTLE ARROWS

LITTLE GREEN APPLES

LIVING IN THE U.S.A.

LONG TIME GONE

LOOKING AT THE WORLD THROUGH A WINDSHIELD

LOOK TO YOUR SOUL

LOVE CHILD

LOVE IN EVERY ROOM

LOVE IS ALL AROUND

LOVE IS BLUE

LOVE IS IN THE AIR

(LOVE IS LIKE A) BASEBALL GAME

LOVE MAKES A WOMAN

LOVE ME TWO TIMES

LOVER'S HOLIDAY

LOVE TAKES CARE OF ME

MACARTHUR PARK

MADELEINE

MAGIC BUS, THE

MAGIC CARPET RIDE

MAMA TRIED

MAN AND A HALF, A

MAN WITHOUT LOVE, A

MARIEKE

MASTER JACK

MAYBE JUST TODAY

MEN ARE GETTIN' SCARCE

MIDNIGHT CONFESSIONS

MIGHTY QUINN (QUINN, THE ESKIMO)

MINOTAUR, THE

M'LADY

MONEY

MONTEREY

MONY MONY

MORNING DEW

MR. BOJANGLES

MR. BUSINESSMAN

MRS. ROBINSON

MY BABY MUST BE A MAGICIAN

MY SHY VIOLET

MY SONG

MY SPECIAL ANGEL

MY WAY OF LIFE

NATURALLY STONED

NEVER GIVE YOU UP

NEXT IN LINE

NOBODY BUT ME

NO SAD SONGS

NOT ENOUGH INDIANS

NOTHING BUT A HEARTACHE

OH, HOW IT HURTS

1-2-3-4-5-6-7 COUNT THE DAYS

1, 2, 3, RED LIGHT

ONLY DADDY THAT WILL WALK THE LINE, THE

ON TAP, IN THE CAN, OR IN THE BOTTLE

ON THE ROAD AGAIN

OVER YOU

PAYING THE COST TO BE BOSS

PEACE, BROTHER, PEACE

PEOPLE GOT TO BE FREE

PICKIN' WILD MOUNTAIN BERRIES

PICTURES OF MATCHSTICK MEN

PLAYBOY

PLEASE RETURN YOUR LOVE TO ME

POOR BABY

PROMISES, PROMISES

QUESTION OF TEMPERATURE, A

QUICK JOEY SMALL (RUN, JOEY, RUN)

RAY OF HOPE, A

REACH OUT OF THE DARKNESS

READY OR NOT, HERE I COME (CAN'T HIDE FROM LOVE)

REPEAT AFTER ME

REVOLUTION

RICE IS NICE

ROCK ME

ROSANNA'S GOING WILD

RUN AWAY, LITTLE TEARS

SAFE IN MY GARDEN

SAVE THE COUNTRY

SAY IT LOUD—I'M BLACK AND I'M PROUD

SAY IT'S NOT YOU

SECURITY

SHAKE

SHAPE OF THINGS TO COME

SHE'S A HEARTBREAKER

SHE'S A RAINBOW

SHE'S LOOKIN' GOOD

SHE WENT A LITTLE BIT FARTHER

SHOO-BE-DOO-BE-DOO-DA-DAY

SHOOT'EM UP, BABY

SIMON SAYS

SING ME BACK HOME

(SITTIN' ON) THE DOCK OF THE BAY

SIX MAN BAND

SKIP A ROPE

SKY PILOT

SLIP AWAY

SOMETHING PRETTY

SOME THINGS YOU NEVER GET USED TO

SON-OF-A-PREACHER MAN

SON OF HICKORY HOLLER'S
  TRAMP, THE

SONS OF . . .

SOULFUL STRUT (AM I THE SAME GIRL?)

SOUL-LIMBO

SPECIAL OCCASION

SPOOKY

STAND BY YOUR MAN

STAR!

STONED SOUL PICNIC

STORMY

STORY OF ISAAC

STORY OF ROCK AND ROLL, THE

STRAIGHT LIFE, THE

STRANGER SONG, THE

STRAWBERRY SHORTCAKE

STREET FIGHTING MAN

SUDDENLY YOU LOVE ME

SUNDAY MORNIN'

SUNDAY SUN

SUNSHINE OF YOUR LOVE

SUSAN

(SWEET, SWEET BABY) SINCE YOU'VE
  BEEN GONE

SWEET BLINDNESS

SWEET INSPIRATION

SWEET MEMORIES

SWEET ROSIE JONES

TAKE ME AS I AM (OR LET ME GO)

TAKE ME TO YOUR WORLD

TAKE TIME TO KNOW HER

TAPIOCA TUNDRA

TEARS OF RAGE

TELL MAMA

THAT'S WHEN I SEE THE BLUES (IN
  YOUR PRETTY BROWN EYES)

THERE AIN'T NO EASY RUN

THERE IS

THERE WAS A TIME

THINK

THIS GUY'S IN LOVE WITH YOU

THIS IS MY COUNTRY

THOSE WERE THE DAYS

TIGHTEN UP

TIME FOR LIVIN'

TIME HAS COME TODAY

TO GIVE (THE REASON I LIVE)

TOMORROW

TOO MUCH TALK

TOO WEAK TO FIGHT

TUESDAY AFTERNOON (FOREVER
  AFTERNOON)

TURN AROUND, LOOK AT ME

TWO-BIT MANCHILD

TWO LITTLE KIDS

UNDERSTANDING

UNICORN, THE

UNKNOWN SOLDIER

UP TO MY NECK IN HIGH MUDDY
  WATER

U.S. MALE

VALLERI

WALK ON OUT OF MY MIND

WATCH HER RIDE

WEAR IT ON OUR FACE

WE CAN FLY

WE GOT US

WEIGHT, THE

WE'RE A WINNER

WHAT A PIECE OF WORK IS MAN

WHAT A WONDERFUL WORLD

WHAT'S MADE MILWAUKEE FAMOUS
 (HAS MADE A LOSER OUT OF ME)
WHITE ROOM
WHO IS GONNA LOVE ME?
WHO KNOWS WHERE THE TIME GOES?
WHO'S MAKING LOVE?
WHO WILL ANSWER?
WILD WEEK-END
WINDMILLS OF YOUR MIND, THE
WINTER LADY
WITH PEN IN HAND
WORDS
WORKIN' ON A GROOVY THING
YARD WENT ON FOREVER, THE
YESTERDAY'S DREAMS
YESTER LOVE
YOU
YOU AIN'T GOING NOWHERE
YOU ARE MY TREASURE
YOU DON'T KNOW WHAT YOU MEAN
 TO ME
YOU MET YOUR MATCH
YOUNG AND IN LOVE
YOUNG GIRL
YOU'RE ALL I NEED TO GET BY
YOU'VE JUST STEPPED IN (FROM
 STEPPING OUT ON ME)
YOU'VE STILL GOT A PLACE IN MY
 HEART
YUMMY, YUMMY, YUMMY
ZABADAK

1969

ABERGAVENNY
AIN'T IT FUNKY NOW
ALL FOR THE LOVE OF A GIRL
ALL I HAVE TO OFFER YOU IS ME
AND WHEN I DIE
APRICOT BRANDY
APRIL FOOLS, THE
ARE YOU HAPPY?
ATLANTIS

BABY, BABY, DON'T CRY
BABY, I LOVE YOU
BABY, I'M FOR REAL
BACKFIELD IN MOTION
BACK IN THE U.S.S.R.
BAD MOON RISING
BADGE
BALLAD OF EASY RIDER
BALLAD OF JOHN AND YOKO, THE
BALL OF FIRE
BEGINNING OF MY END, THE
BE GLAD
BELLA LINDA
BIG WIND
BIRTHDAY
BLACK PEARL
BLESSED IS THE RAIN
BLISTERED
BORN AGAIN
BOY NAMED SUE, A
BRAND NEW ME, A
BROTHER LOVE'S TRAVELLING
 SALVATION SHOW
BUILD ME UP, BUTTERCUP
BUT YOU KNOW I LOVE YOU
BUYING A BOOK
CAJUN BABY
CALIFORNIA GIRL AND THE TENNESSEE
 SQUARE
CALIFORNIA SOUL
CAN I CHANGE MY MIND?
CAN'T FIND THE TIME
CARROLL COUNTY ACCIDENT
CARRY ME BACK
CHANGE OF HEART
CHELSEA MORNING
CHERRY HILL PARK
CHOICE OF COLORS
CISSY STRUT
CLEAN UP YOUR OWN BACK YARD
COCO
COLD TURKEY

COLOR HIM FATHER

COME SATURDAY MORNING

COME TOGETHER

COMMOTION

COMPOSER, THE

CRIMSON AND CLOVER

CROSSROADS

CRUMBS OFF THE TABLE

CRYSTAL BLUE PERSUASION

DADDY SANG BASS

DADDY'S LITTLE MAN

DARLING, YOU KNOW I WOULDN'T LIE

DAY AFTER DAY (IT'S SLIPPIN' AWAY)

DAY IS DONE

DAYS OF SAND AND SHOVELS, THE

DEAR WORLD

DELTA LADY

DIDN'T WE

DID YOU SEE HER EYES?

DIZZY

DOES ANYBODY KNOW I'M HERE?

DOGGONE RIGHT

DOIN' OUR THING

DON'T CRY DADDY

DON'T GIVE IN TO HIM

DON'T IT MAKE YOU WANT TO
GO HOME?

DON'T LET HIM TAKE YOUR LOVE
FROM ME

DON'T LET LOVE HANG YOU UP

DON'T LET ME DOWN

DON'T LET THE JONESES GET YOU
DOWN

DON'T WAKE ME UP IN THE MORNING,
MICHAEL

DOWN ON THE CORNER

DO YOUR THING

EARLY IN THE MORNING

ECHO PARK

EVERYBODY'S TALKING

EVERYDAY PEOPLE

EVERYDAY WITH YOU GIRL

EVIL WOMAN, DON'T PLAY YOUR GAMES
WITH ME

FANCY

FEELIN' ALRIGHT

FIRST OF MAY

FORTUNATE SON

FREE AGAIN

FRIEND, LOVER, WOMAN, WIFE

FRIENDSHIP TRAIN

GABRIELLE

GALVESTON

GAMES PEOPLE PLAY

GET BACK

GET TOGETHER (LET'S)

GIMME, GIMME GOOD LOVIN'

GIMME SHELTER

GIRL FROM THE NORTH COUNTRY

GIRL MOST LIKELY, THE

GITARZAN

GIVE IT UP OR TURNIT A LOOSE

GIVE PEACE A CHANCE

GOING IN CIRCLES

GOING UP THE COUNTRY

GOODBYE

GOODBYE, COLUMBUS

GOOD LOVIN' AIN'T EASY TO COME BY

GOOD TIME CHARLIES

GOOD TIMES, BAD TIMES

GOO GOO BARABAJAGAL (LOVE IS HOT)

GREEN RIVER

GRITS AIN'T GROCERIES (ALL AROUND
THE WORLD)

GROOVY GRUBWORM

HAPPY HEART

HAWAII FIVE-O

HEATHER HONEY

HEAVEN

HEAVEN KNOWS

HERE I GO AGAIN

HERE'S TO LOVE

HOLLY HOLY

HOME COOKIN'

HONKY TONK WOMEN

HOOKED ON A FEELING

HOT FUN IN THE SUMMERTIME

HOT SMOKE AND SASSAFRAS

HUNGRY EYES

I CAN HEAR MUSIC

I CAN'T GET NEXT TO YOU

I CAN'T SEE MYSELF LEAVING YOU

I COULD NEVER BE PRESIDENT

I COULD NEVER LIE TO YOU

I DON'T KNOW WHY

I DON'T WANT NOBODY TO GIVE ME NOTHING (OPEN UP THE DOOR, I'LL GET IT MYSELF)

I'D RATHER BE AN OLD MAN'S SWEETHEART (THAN A YOUNG MAN'S FOOL)

I'D RATHER BE GONE

I'D WAIT A MILLION YEARS

IF NOT FOR YOU

I FORGOT TO BE YOUR LOVER

(IF YOU LET ME MAKE LOVE TO YOU THEN) WHY CAN'T I TOUCH YOU?

I GOT A LINE ON YOU

I GUESS THE LORD MUST BE IN NEW YORK CITY

I LIKE WHAT YOU'RE DOING (TO ME)

I'LL HOLD OUT MY HAND

I'LL SHARE MY WORLD WITH YOU

I'LL TRY SOMETHING NEW

I LOVE YOU MORE TODAY

I'M A BETTER MAN (FOR HAVING LOVED YOU)

I'M A DRIFTER

I'M DOWN TO MY LAST "I LOVE YOU"

I'M FREE

I'M GONNA MAKE YOU MINE

I'M LIVIN' IN SHAME

IN A MOMENT

INDIAN GIVER

IN THE GHETTO

IN THE YEAR 2525 (EXORDIUM AND TERMINUS)

IS IT SOMETHING YOU'VE GOT?

ISRAELITES

I STARTED A JOKE

IS THAT ALL THERE IS?

I THANK YOU

I THREW IT ALL AWAY

IT'S GETTING BETTER

IT'S NEVER TOO LATE

IT'S ONLY LOVE

IT'S YOUR THING

I TURNED YOU ON

I'VE BEEN HURT

I WANT TO TAKE YOU HIGHER

I WANT YOU BACK

I WASN'T BORN TO FOLLOW

JAM UP JELLY TIGHT

JEALOUS KIND OF FELLA

JEAN

JESUS IS A SOUL MAN

JE T'AIME . . . MOI NON PLUS

JINGLE JANGLE

JOHNNY ONE TIME

KAY

KEEM-O-SABE

KISS HER NOW

KOZMIC BLUES

KUM BA YAH

LA, LA, LA (IF I HAD YOU)

LAUGHING

LAY, LADY, LAY

LEAVING ON A JET PLANE

LEAVE MY DREAM ALONE

LET A WOMAN BE A WOMAN, LET A MAN BE A MAN

LET ME

LITTLE WOMAN

LODI

LO MUCHO TE QUIERO (THE MORE I LOVE YOU)

LOOK-KA PY PY

LOVE (CAN MAKE YOU HAPPY)

LOVE IS JUST A FOUR-LETTER WORD

LOVE ME TONIGHT

LOVE THEME FROM "ROMEO AND JULIET" (A TIME FOR US)

LOVE WILL FIND A WAY

LOVIN' THINGS, THE

LOWDOWN POPCORN

MAH-NA-MAH-NA

MAKE BELIEVE

MAKE YOUR OWN KIND OF MUSIC

MALINDA

MARGIE'S AT THE LINCOLN PARK INN

MARRAKESH EXPRESS

MAY I

MEDICINE MAN

MEMORIES

MEMPHIS UNDERGROUND

MENDOCINO

MERCY

MIDNIGHT COWBOY

MIND, BODY, AND SOUL

MINI-SKIRT MINNIE

MINUTE OF YOUR TIME, A

MOMMA LOOK SHARP

MOODY WOMAN

MORE TODAY THAN YESTERDAY

MORNING GIRL

MOTHER POPCORN (YOU GOT TO HAVE A MOTHER FOR ME)

MOVE IN A LITTLE CLOSER, BABY

MOVE OVER

MR. SUN, MR. MOON

MR. WALKER, IT'S ALL OVER

MUDDY RIVER

MY CHERIE AMOUR

MY LIFE

MY PLEDGE OF LOVE

MY WAY

MY WHOLE WORLD ENDED (THE MOMENT YOU LEFT ME)

MY WOMAN'S GOOD TO ME

NAME OF THE GAME WAS LOVE

NA NA HEY HEY (KISS HIM GOODBYE)

NOBODY BUT YOU, BABE

NO MATTER WHAT SIGN YOU ARE

NONE OF MY BUSINESS

OB-LA-DI, OB-LA-DA

ODDS AND ENDS

OH, WHAT A NIGHT

OH HAPPY DAY

OKIE FROM MUSKOGEE

OLD FAITHFUL

ONE

ONE EARLY MORNING

ONE MORE MILE

ONLY THE STRONG SURVIVE

PINBALL WIZARD

PLAYGIRL

POLK SALAD ANNIE

POPCORN, THE

PROUD MARY

PUT A LITTLE LOVE IN YOUR HEART

QUENTIN'S THEME

QUESTIONS 67 AND 68

RAG, MAMA, RAG

RAINBOW RIDE

RAINDROPS KEEP FALLING ON MY HEAD

RAIN IN MY HEART

RAMBLIN' GAMBLIN' MAN

RECONSIDER ME

RINGS OF GOLD

ROCKY RACCOON

ROOSEVELT AND IRA LEE (NIGHT OF THE MOCCASIN)

RUBBERNECKIN'

RUBEN JAMES

RUBY, DON'T TAKE YOUR LOVE TO TOWN

RUN AWAY CHILD, RUNNING WILD

SAD GIRL

SEATTLE

SEE

SEE RUBY FALL

SHE BELONGS TO ME

SHE CAME IN THROUGH THE
  BATHROOM WINDOW

SHE'S A LADY

SIMPLE SONG OF FREEDOM

SINGING MY SONG

SMILE A LITTLE SMILE FOR ME

SNATCHING IT BACK

SO GOOD TOGETHER

SO I CAN LOVE YOU

SOMEDAY SOON

SOMEDAY WE'LL BE TOGETHER

SOMETHING

SOMETHING IN THE AIR

SON OF A TRAVELIN' MAN

SOPHISTICATED CISSY

SOUL DEEP

SOUL SHAKE

SOUL SISTER, BROWN SUGAR

SPECIAL DELIVERY

SPINNING WHEEL

STAND!

STATUE OF A FOOL

SUGAR, SUGAR

SUGAR ON SUNDAY

SUITE: JUDY BLUE EYES

SUMMER ME, WINTER ME

SUSPICIOUS MINDS

SWEET CAROLINE (GOOD TIMES NEVER
  SEEMED SO GOOD)

SWEET CHERRY WINE

SWEET CREAM LADIES, FORWARD
  MARCH

SWEETER HE IS, THE

SWEETHEART OF THE YEAR

TAKE A LETTER, MARIA

TAKE CARE OF YOUR HOMEWORK

TALL, DARK STRANGER

TELL ALL THE PEOPLE

THAT'S A NO NO

THAT'S THE WAY LOVE IS

THERE'LL COME A TIME

THERE NEVER WAS A TIME

THERE'S GONNA BE A SHOWDOWN

THESE EYES

THESE LONELY HANDS OF MINE

THINGS I'D LIKE TO SAY

THIS GIRL IS A WOMAN NOW

THIS MAGIC MOMENT

TIME AND LOVE

TIME IS TIGHT

TIME MACHINE

TIME OF THE SEASON

TO BE YOUNG, GIFTED, AND BLACK

TO MAKE A MAN (FEEL LIKE A MAN)

TO MAKE LOVE SWEETER FOR YOU

TOMORROW, TOMORROW

TOMORROW IS THE FIRST DAY OF THE
  REST OF MY LIFE

TONIGHT I'LL BE STAYING HERE
  WITH YOU

TOO BUSY THINKING ABOUT MY BABY

TO SEE MY ANGEL CRY

TO SUSAN ON THE WEST COAST
  WAITING

TOUCH ME

TRACES

TRACY

TRUCK STOP

TRUE GRIT

TRY A LITTLE KINDNESS

TWENTY-FIVE MILES

UNDUN

UNTIL MY DREAMS COME TRUE

UP ON CRIPPLE CREEK

VOLUNTEERS

WALK A MILE IN MY SHOES

WAY IT USED TO BE, THE

WAYS TO LOVE A MAN, THE

WE GOT MORE SOUL

WEDDING BELL BLUES

WELCOME ME, LOVE

(WE'VE GOT) HONEY LOVE

WHAT ARE YOU DOING THE REST OF
  YOUR LIFE?

WHAT DOES IT TAKE (TO WIN YOUR LOVE)?

WHAT'S THE USE OF BREAKING UP?

WHAT YOU GAVE ME

WHEN HE TOUCHES ME (NOTHING ELSE MATTERS)

WHEN I DIE

WHEN THE GRASS GROWS OVER ME

WHERE'S THE PLAYGROUND SUSIE

WHERE THE BLUE AND LONELY GO

WHICH WAY YOU GOIN' BILLY?

WHOLE LOTTA LOVE

WHO'S GONNA MOW YOUR GRASS?

WHO'S JULIE?

WHY I SING THE BLUES

WICHITA LINEMAN

WILL YOU BE STAYING AFTER SUNDAY?

WINE ME UP

WISHFUL, SINFUL

WITHOUT HER

WOMAN HELPING MAN

WOMAN OF THE WORLD (LEAVE MY WORLD ALONE)

WORKING MAN BLUES

WORLD

YESTERDAY, WHEN I WAS YOUNG

YESTER-ME, YESTER-YOU, YESTERDAY

YOU, I

YOU CAN'T ALWAYS GET WHAT YOU WANT

YOU GAVE ME A MOUNTAIN

YOU GOT YOURS AND I'LL GET MINE

YOUR GOOD THING IS ABOUT TO END

YOUR HUSBAND—MY WIFE

YOUR OWN THING

YOURS, LOVE

YOU SHOWED ME

1970

ABC

ADD SOME MUSIC TO YOUR DAY

AFTER MIDNIGHT

"AIRPORT" LOVE THEME

ALL FOR THE LOVE OF SUNSHINE

ALL RIGHT NOW

ALPHAGENESIS

ANOTHER HUNDRED PEOPLE

ARE YOU READY?

ARIZONA

BABY, BABY (I KNOW YOU'RE A LADY)

BABY, TAKE ME IN YOUR ARMS

BALL OF CONFUSION (THAT'S WHAT THE WORLD IS TODAY)

BAND OF GOLD

BARCELONA

BEING ALIVE

BELLS, THE

BENEATH STILL WATERS

BEYOND THE VALLEY OF THE DOLLS

BIG YELLOW TAXI

BLACK MAGIC WOMAN

BLOWING AWAY

BOOZERS AND LOSERS

BORDER SONG

BRIDGE OVER TROUBLED WATER

BRIGHTON HILL

BROTHER RAPP

BUFFALO SOLDIER

CALL ME

CANDIDA

CAN'T STOP LOVING YOU

CECILIA

CELEBRATE

CINNAMON GIRL

CIRCLE GAME, THE

COME AND GET IT

COME RUNNING

COMPARED TO WHAT

COURT OF THE CRIMSON KING

CRACKLIN' ROSIE

DADDY WAS AN OLD TIME PREACHER MAN

DARKNESS, DARKNESS

DAUGHTER OF DARKNESS

DECLARATION

DIDN'T I (BLOW YOUR MIND THIS TIME)

DOES ANYBODY REALLY KNOW WHAT TIME IT IS?

DON'T TRY TO LAY NO BOOGIE WOOGIE ON THE KING OF ROCK AND ROLL

DOWN BY THE RIVER

DREAM BABIES

EASY COME, EASY GO

EL CONDOR PASA

EMPTY PAGES

ENGINE NUMBER 9 (GET ME BACK ON TIME)

EVERYBODY IS A STAR

EVERYBODY'S GOT THE RIGHT TO LOVE

EVERYBODY'S OUT OF TOWN

EVERYTHING IS BEAUTIFUL

EVIL WAYS

EXPRESS YOURSELF

FIFTEEN YEARS AGO

FIGHTIN' SIDE OF ME, THE

FIRE AND RAIN

5-10-15-20 (25-30 YEARS OF LOVE)

FOR ALL WE KNOW

FOR THE LOVE OF HIM

FOR YASGUR'S FARM

FOR YOU BLUE

FREE THE PEOPLE

GET READY

GET UP (I FEEL LIKE BEING A SEX MACHINE)

GIMME DAT DING

GIVE ME JUST A LITTLE MORE TIME

GO BACK

GOD, LOVE, AND ROCK AND ROLL

GOOD TIMES ARE COMING, THE

GOOD YEAR FOR THE ROSES, A

GOTTA HOLD ON TO THIS FEELING

GREEN-EYED LADY

GROOVE ME

GROOVY SITUATION

GYPSY WOMAN

HANDBAGS AND GLADRAGS

HAND ME DOWN WORLD

HE AIN'T HEAVY . . . HE'S MY BROTHER

HEARTBREAKER

HEAVEN HELP US ALL

HELLO, IT'S ME

HELLO DARLIN'

HE LOVES ME ALL THE WAY

HELP ME MAKE IT THROUGH THE NIGHT

HI, MOM!

HI-DE-HO

HITCHIN' A RIDE

HONEY COME BACK

HOW I FEEL

I CAN'T BELIEVE THAT YOU'VE STOPPED LOVING ME

I DO NOT KNOW A DAY I DID NOT LOVE YOU

I DON'T KNOW HOW TO LOVE HIM

IF YOU WERE MINE

I GOT LOVE

I JUST CAN'T HELP BELIEVING

I'LL BE THERE

I'LL PAINT YOU A SONG

I'LL SEE HIM THROUGH

I'M JUST ME

INDIANA WANTS ME

INSTANT KARMA (WE ALL SHINE ON)

IN THE SUMMERTIME

INTO THE MYSTIC

IS ANYBODY GOIN' TO SAN ANTONE?

IS IT BECAUSE I'M BLACK?

ISN'T IT A PITY

I THINK I LOVE YOU

IT'S A SHAME

I'VE LOST YOU

I WANT TO WALK TO SAN FRANCISCO

I WOULD BE IN LOVE (ANYWAY)

JERUSALEM

JESUS IS JUST ALRIGHT

JOANNE

JOSHUA

JULIE, DO YA LOVE ME

KANSAS CITY SONG

KENTUCKY RAIN

KNOCK THREE TIMES

LADIES WHO LUNCH, THE

LAY DOWN (CANDLES IN THE WIND)

LET IT BE

LET ME GO TO HIM

LIVING LOVING MAID (SHE'S JUST A WOMAN)

LOLA

LONG AND WINDING ROAD, THE

LONG LONG TIME

LOOKIN' OUT MY BACK DOOR

LOOK WHAT THEY'VE DONE TO MY SONG, MA

LOVE BONES

LOVE GROWS (WHERE MY ROSEMARY GROWS)

LOVE IS A SOMETIMES THING

LOVE LAND

LOVE ON A TWO-WAY STREET

LOVE OR LET ME BE LONELY

LOVE YOU SAVE, THE

LUCIFER

MA BELLE AMIE

MAKE IT WITH YOU

MAKE ME SMILE

MAMA LIKED THE ROSES

MAMA TOLD ME (NOT TO COME)

ME AND MY ARROW

MEMO FROM TURNER

MILL VALLEY

MISSISSIPPI

MONSTER

MONTEGO BAY

MORNIN' MORNIN'

MY BABY LOVES LOVIN'

MY MARIE

MY MOST IMPORTANT MOMENTS GO BY

MY WOMAN, MY WOMAN, MY WIFE

NEVER BEEN TO SPAIN

NEW WORLD COMING

NEXT STEP IS LOVE, THE

NO MATTER WHAT

NO TIME

OHIO

OH ME OH MY (I'M A FOOL FOR YOU, BABY)

OH WELL

OLD DEVIL TIME

ONE DAY OF YOUR LIFE

ONE LESS BELL TO ANSWER

ONE MAN BAND

ONE TIN SOLDIER (THE LEGEND OF BILLY JACK)

ONLY LOVE CAN BREAK YOUR HEART

ONLY YOU KNOW AND I KNOW

O-O-H CHILD

OUR HOUSE

OUT IN THE COUNTRY

OVERTURE FROM "TOMMY" (A ROCK OPERA)

PAPER MACHE

PATCHES (I'M DEPENDING ON YOU)

PAY TO THE PIPER

PEACE WILL COME (ACCORDING TO PLAN)

PIECES OF DREAMS

POINT IT OUT

POOL SHARK, THE

PRAY FOR PEACE

PSYCHEDELIC SHACK

PUPPET MAN

PURLIE

QUESTION

RAINY NIGHT IN GEORGIA, A

RAPPER, THE

REACH OUT AND TOUCH (SOMEBODY'S HAND)

REFLECTIONS OF MY LIFE

ROADHOUSE BLUES

RUBBER DUCKIE

RUN, WOMAN, RUN
RUN THROUGH THE JUNGLE
SEEKER, THE
SEE ME, FEEL ME
SHARE THE LAND
SHE
SHE EVEN WOKE ME UP TO SAY
    GOODBYE
SHILO
SIDE BY SIDE BY SIDE
SIGNED, SEALED, DELIVERED I'M YOURS
SILVER MOON
SNOWBIRD
SO CLOSE
SO EXCITED
SOMEBODY'S BEEN SLEEPING (IN
    MY BED)
SOMETHING'S BURNING
SONG FROM M*A*S*H (SUICIDE IS
    PAINLESS)
SONG OF JOY
SOUNDS
SPILL THE WINE
SPIRIT IN THE DARK
SPIRIT IN THE SKY
STEALING IN THE NAME OF THE LORD
STILL WATER (LOVE)
STONED LOVE
STONEY END
SUNDAY MORNIN' COMIN' DOWN
SUPER BAD
TAKER, THE
TEACH YOUR CHILDREN
TEARS OF A CLOWN, THE
TELL IT ALL BROTHER
TEMMA HARBOUR

TENNESSEE BIRDWALK

THANK YOU (FALETTINME BE MICE ELF
    AGIN)

THANK YOU VERY MUCH

THAT'S WHEN SHE STARTED TO STOP
    LOVING YOU

THEME FROM "LOVE STORY" (WHERE
    DO I BEGIN)
THERE MUST BE MORE TO LOVE
    THAN THIS
THERE WAS A CROOKED MAN
(THEY LONG TO BE) CLOSE TO YOU
THIS WAY TO SESAME STREET
TIGHTER, TIGHTER
TILL LOVE TOUCHES YOUR LIFE
TONIGHT I'LL SAY A PRAYER
TRAVELIN' BAND
TURN BACK THE HANDS OF TIME
TURN ME AROUND
25 OR 6 TO 4
TWO BY TWO
UNCLE JOHN'S BAND
UNITED WE STAND
UP AROUND THE BEND
UP THE LADDER TO THE ROOF
VEHICLE
VENUS
VICTORIA
VIVA TIRADO
WALK HIM UP THE STAIRS
WAR
WEEK IN A COUNTRY JAIL, A
WE GOTTA GET YOU A WOMAN
WELCOME TO THE THEATRE
WELFARE CADILLAC
WE'RE ALL PLAYING IN THE
    SAME BAND
WE'VE ONLY JUST BEGUN
WHAT IS TRUTH
WHEN JULIE COMES AROUND
WHERE ARE YOU GOING
WHISTLING AWAY THE DARK
WHO'LL STOP THE RAIN
WHOSE GARDEN WAS THIS
WIGWAM

WINTER WORLD OF LOVE

WITHOUT LOVE (THERE IS NOTHING)

WOMAN LIVES FOR LOVE, A

WONDER COULD I LIVE THERE
  ANYMORE

WONDERFUL WORLD, BEAUTIFUL
  PEOPLE

WOODSTOCK

WORKING CLASS HERO

WRAP IT UP

YELLOW RIVER

YOU BETTER THINK TWICE

YOU COULD DRIVE A PERSON CRAZY

YOU MAKE ME REAL

YOU'RE LOOKIN' AT COUNTRY

YOUR OWN BACK YARD

YOUR SONG

YOUR TIME TO CRY

(YOU'VE GOT ME) DANGLING ON
  A STRING

YOU WANNA GIVE ME A LIFT

1971

AFTER THE FIRE IS GONE

AGE OF NOT BELIEVING

AIN'T NO SUNSHINE

ALL HIS CHILDREN

ALL I EVER NEED IS YOU

AMAZING GRACE

AMERICAN TRILOGY, AN

AMOS MOSES

ANOTHER DAY

ANOTHER TIME, ANOTHER PLACE

APEMAN

ASK ME NO QUESTIONS

BABY, I'M A-WANT YOU

BANGLA-DESH

BED OF ROSE'S

BEGINNINGS

BEHIND BLUE EYES

BEIN' GREEN

BELL BOTTOM BLUES

BE NICE TO ME

BETTER MOVE IT ON HOME

BLESS THE BEASTS AND CHILDREN

BLUE MONEY

BORN TO WANDER

BRAND NEW KEY

BREAKDOWN

BRING THE BOYS HOME

BROADWAY BABY

BROWN SUGAR

CALL ME UP IN DREAMLAND

CANDY MAN, THE

CAREY

CAROLINA DAY

CAROLYN

CHANGE PARTNERS

CHARITY BALL

CHERISH

CHICAGO

CHICK-A-BOOM (DON'T YA JES' LOVE IT)

CHIRPY CHIRPY CHEEP CHEEP

CLEAN UP WOMAN

CLOWNS, THE

COAL MINER'S DAUGHTER

COAT OF MANY COLORS

COUNTRY ROAD

CRAZY LOVE

CRIED LIKE A BABY

DADDY FRANK (THE GUITAR MAN)

DADDY'S GONE A-HUNTING

DAY BY DAY

DEEP BLUE

DIAMONDS ARE FOREVER

DOESN'T SOMEBODY WANT TO
  BE WANTED

DOLLY DAGGER

DON'T CHANGE ON ME

DON'T KEEP ME HANGING ON

DON'T KNOCK MY LOVE

DON'T LET THE GREEN GRASS
  FOOL YOU

DON'T PULL YOUR LOVE

DON'T WANT TO LIVE INSIDE MYSELF

DOUBLE LOVIN'

DO YOU KNOW WHAT I MEAN

DRAGGIN' THE LINE

DROWNING IN THE SEA OF LOVE

EASY LOVING

EIGHTEEN

EMPTY ARMS

EVERYBODY'S EVERYTHING

EVERYTHING'S ALRIGHT

FAMILY AFFAIR

FIRST TIME EVER I SAW YOUR FACE, THE

FOLLOW ME

FOR THE GOOD TIMES

FREE

FREEDOM

FRESH AS A DAISY

FRIENDS

FRIENDS WITH YOU

FUNKY NASSAU

GEORGE JACKSON

GET IT WHILE YOU CAN

GHETTO WOMAN

GO AWAY LITTLE GIRL

GO DOWN GAMBLIN'

GOODBYE, SO LONG

GOOD LOVIN' (MAKES IT RIGHT)

GOT TO BE THERE

GRANDMA'S HANDS

GREEN GRASS STARTS TO GROW, THE

GYPSYS

HAPPIEST GIRL IN THE WHOLE U.S.A.

HAVE YOU EVER SEEN THE RAIN

HAVE YOU SEEN HER?

HAVING MYSELF A FINE TIME

HE GIVES US ALL HIS LOVE

HERE COMES THAT RAINY DAY FEELING AGAIN

HERE COMES THE SUN

HEY BIG BROTHER

HILL WHERE THE LORD HIDES

HOT PANTS (SHE GOT TO USE WHAT SHE GOT TO GET WHAT SHE WANTS)

HOUSE AT POOH CORNER

HOW CAN I UNLOVE YOU

HOW CAN YOU MEND A BROKEN HEART

HOW MUCH MORE CAN SHE STAND?

I AM . . . I SAID

I DON'T BLAME YOU AT ALL

I DON'T WANT TO DO WRONG

I'D RATHER BE SORRY

I'D RATHER LOVE YOU

IF

I FEEL THE EARTH MOVE

IF I WERE YOUR WOMAN

IF NOT FOR YOU

IF YOU COULD READ MY MIND

IF YOU REALLY LOVE ME

I HEAR YOU KNOCKING

I'LL MEET YOU HALFWAY

I LOVE YOU FOR ALL SEASONS

IMAGINE

I'M GONNA BE A COUNTRY GIRL AGAIN

IMMIGRANT SONG

I'M STILL HERE

IN BUDDY'S EYES

INDIAN RESERVATION (THE LAMENT OF THE CHEROKEE RESERVATION INDIAN)

INNER CITY BLUES (MAKE ME WANNA HOLLER)

IN THE QUIET MORNING

I SAW THE LIGHT

IT DON'T COME EASY

IT'S FOUR IN THE MORNING

IT'S IMPOSSIBLE

IT'S TOO LATE

I'VE FOUND SOMEONE OF MY OWN

I WANNA BE FREE

I WOKE UP IN LOVE THIS MORNING

I WON'T MENTION IT AGAIN

JENNIFER

JOY TO THE WORLD

JUST MY IMAGINATION (RUNNING AWAY WITH ME)

KISS AN ANGEL GOOD MORNIN'

LAST TIME I SAW RICHARD, THE

LAYLA

LEAD ME ON

LEVON

LIAR

LIFE IS A CARNIVAL

LIFE IS WHAT YOU MAKE IT

LIGHT SINGS

LILLY DONE THE ZAMPOUGHI EVERY TIME I PULLED HER COATTAIL

LONELY DAYS

LONG AGO TOMORROW

LOSING MY MIND

LOST HER LOVE ON OUR LAST DATE

LOVE HAS DRIVEN ME SANE

LOVE HER MADLY

LOVE'S LINES, ANGLES AND RHYMES

LOVE THE ONE YOU'RE WITH

LOVING HER WAS EASIER (THAN ANYTHING I'LL EVER DO AGAIN)

LUCKY MAN

MAGGIE MAY

MAKE ME THE WOMAN THAT YOU GO HOME TO

MAMA'S PEARL

MAMMY BLUE

MAN IN BLACK

ME AND BOBBY MCGEE

ME AND YOU AND A DOG NAMED BOO

MERCY, MERCY ME (THE ECOLOGY)

MOON SHADOW

MOTHER

MOTHER EARTH AND FATHER TIME

MR. BIG STUFF

MY BOY

NATHAN JONES

NATURAL MAN, A

NEVER CAN SAY GOODBYE

NEVER ENDING SONG OF LOVE

NICKEL SONG

NIGHT THEY DROVE OLD DIXIE DOWN, THE

NO LOVE AT ALL

OLD FASHIONED LOVE SONG, AN

ONE BAD APPLE (DON'T SPOIL THE WHOLE BUNCH)

ONE FINE MORNING

ONE MONKEY DON'T STOP NO SHOW

ONE'S ON THE WAY

ONE TOKE OVER THE LINE

OYE COMO VA

PEACE TRAIN

POWER TO THE PEOPLE

PRETTY AS YOU FEEL

PUT YOUR HAND IN THE HAND

RAIN DANCE

RAINY DAYS AND MONDAYS

REASON TO BELIEVE

REMEMBER ME

RESPECT YOURSELF

RIDERS ON THE STORM

RIGHT GIRL, THE

RINGS

ROAD YOU DIDN'T TAKE, THE

ROCK STEADY

ROLLIN' IN MY SWEET BABY'S ARMS

(I NEVER PROMISED YOU A) ROSE GARDEN

SCORPIO

SHE'S A LADY

SHE'S ALL I GOT

SHE'S NOT JUST ANOTHER WOMAN

SIGNS

SILENT RUNNING

SIT YOURSELF DOWN

SMACKWATER JACK

SNOW BLIND FRIEND

SO FAR AWAY

SOMEDAY WE'LL LOOK BACK

SOME OF SHELLY'S BLUES

SOONER OR LATER

SOUL POWER

SPANISH HARLEM

STAY AWHILE
STICK-UP
STONES
STORY IN YOUR EYES
SUPERSTAR
SUPERSTAR
SUPERSTAR (REMEMBER HOW YOU GOT
   WHERE YOU ARE)
SWEET AND INNOCENT
SWEET CITY WOMAN
SWEET HITCH-HIKER
SWEET MARY
TAKE ME HOME, COUNTRY ROADS
TALK IT OVER IN THE MORNING
TAPESTRY
TARKIO ROAD
TEMPTATION EYES
THAT'S THE WAY I'VE ALWAYS HEARD
   IT SHOULD BE
THEME FROM "SHAFT"
THEME FROM "SUMMER OF '42"
THIN LINE BETWEEN LOVE AND HATE
THOSE WERE THE DAYS
TIMOTHY
TIRED OF BEING ALONE
TOAST AND MARMALADE FOR TWO
TOO MANY MORNINGS
TRAPPED BY A THING CALLED LOVE
TREAT HER LIKE A LADY
TRUCKIN'
TWO DIVIDED BY LOVE
UNCLE ALBERT/ADMIRAL HALSEY
UNDISPUTED TRUTH, THE
WANT ADS
WATCHING THE RIVER FLOW
WATCHIN' SCOTTY GROW
WEDDING SONG (THERE IS LOVE)
WE SURE CAN LOVE EACH OTHER
WHATCHA SEE IS WHAT YOU GET
WHAT IS LIFE
WHAT'S GOING ON
WHEN THE MORNING COMES

WHEN THERE'S NO YOU
WHEN YOU'RE HOT, YOU'RE HOT
WHERE DID THEY GO, LORD
WHERE YOU LEAD
WILD HORSES
WILD NIGHT
WILD WORLD
WITCH QUEEN OF NEW ORLEANS, THE
WOMAN ALWAYS KNOWS, A
WOMEN'S LOVE RIGHTS
YEAR THAT CLAYTON DELANEY
   DIED, THE
YOU ARE EVERYTHING
YOU'RE MY MAN
YOU'VE GOT A FRIEND
YO-YO

1972

ACROSS 110TH STREET
AIN'T LOVE GRAND
AIN'T UNDERSTANDING MELLOW
AIN'T WASTIN' TIME NO MORE
ALL THE YOUNG DUDES
ALONE AGAIN (NATURALLY)
AMERICA
AMERICAN CITY SUITE
AMERICAN PIE
AND YOU AND I
ANTICIPATION
BABY BLUE
BABY DON'T GET HOOKED ON ME
BABY LET ME TAKE YOU IN MY ARMS
BACK OFF BOOGALOO
BACK STABBERS
BANG A GONG (GET IT ON)
BEAUTIFUL SUNDAY
BEAUTY SCHOOL DROPOUT
BEEN TO CANAAN
BEN
BETCHA BY GOLLY, WOW
BLACK AND WHITE

BLACK DOG

BLESS YOUR HEART

BRANDY (YOU'RE A FINE GIRL)

BRIAN'S SONG

BURNING LOVE

CASTLES IN THE AIR

CHANGES

CISCO KID, THE

CITY OF NEW ORLEANS, THE

CLAIR

COCONUT

COLORADO

COME BACK, CHARLESTON BLUE

COME FOLLOW, FOLLOW ME

CONQUISTADOR

CORNER OF THE SKY

COTTON JENNY

COULD IT BE I'M FALLING IN LOVE?

COWBOY'S WORK IS NEVER DONE, A

CRAZY HORSES

CRAZY MAMA

DADDY, DON'T YOU WALK SO FAST

DANCING IN THE MOONLIGHT

DAY AFTER DAY

DAY DREAMING

DELTA DAWN

DIARY

DOCTOR MY EYES

DO IT AGAIN

DO IT TO IT

DON'T BOTHER ME, I CAN'T COPE

DON'T EVER BE LONELY (A POOR
    LITTLE FOOL LIKE ME)

DON'T SAY YOU DON'T REMEMBER

DO THE FUNKY PENGUIN

DOWN BY THE LAZY RIVER

DUELING BANJOS

DUNCAN

ELEVEN ROSES

EVERYBODY PLAYS THE FOOL

FAMILY OF MAN, THE

FLOY JOY

FOR EMILY, WHENEVER I MAY
    FIND HER

FOR THE ROSES

FREDDIE'S DEAD

GARDEN PARTY

GERONIMO'S CADILLAC

GET ON THE GOOD FOOT

GIVE IRELAND BACK TO THE IRISH

GO ALL THE WAY

GOODBYE TO LOVE

GOOD-HEARTED WOMAN, A

GOOD TIME CHARLIE'S GOT THE BLUES

GRANDMA HARP

GROWIN' UP

GUITAR MAN

HAPPY

HAPPY (LOVE THEME FROM "LADY
    SINGS THE BLUES")

HEARSAY

HEART OF GOLD

HERE I AM AGAIN

HOLD HER TIGHT

HOLD YOUR HEAD UP

HONKY CAT

HORSE WITH NO NAME, A

HOT 'N' NASTY

HOT ROD LINCOLN

HOW DO YOU DO?

HURTING EACH OTHER

I AM WOMAN

I BELIEVE IN MUSIC

I CAN SEE CLEARLY NOW

I'D LIKE TO TEACH THE WORLD TO SING
    (IN PERFECT HARMONY)

I'D LOVE YOU TO WANT ME

(IF LOVING YOU IS WRONG) I DON'T
    WANT TO BE RIGHT

IF I COULD REACH YOU

IF YOU DON'T KNOW ME BY NOW

I GOTCHA

I GOTTA KEEP MOVIN'

I'LL BE AROUND

I'LL TAKE YOU THERE

I'M GONNA TEAR YOUR PLAYHOUSE DOWN

I'M STILL IN LOVE WITH YOU

I'M STONE IN LOVE WITH YOU

I NEED YOU

IN THE RAIN

ISN'T LIFE STRANGE?

I TAKE IT ON HOME

IT NEVER RAINS IN SOUTHERN CALIFORNIA

IT'S ALWAYS LOVE

IT'S GOING TO TAKE SOME TIME

IT'S GONNA TAKE A LITTLE BIT LONGER

IT'S NOT LOVE (BUT IT'S NOT BAD)

IT'S NOT WHERE YOU START

I WANNA BE WHERE YOU ARE

JOIN TOGETHER

JOY

JUMP INTO THE FIRE

JUNGLE FEVER

KEEPER OF THE CASTLE

LEAN ON ME

LET IT RAIN

LET'S STAY TOGETHER

LION SLEEPS TONIGHT, THE (WIMOWEH)

LISTEN TO THE MUSIC

LIVING IN A HOUSE DIVIDED

LIVING IN THE PAST

LONG COOL WOMAN (IN A BLACK DRESS)

LOOKIN' THROUGH THE WINDOWS

LOOK WHAT YOU DONE FOR ME

LOST HORIZON

LOVE AND LIBERTY

LOVE JONES

LOVE THEME FROM "THE GODFATHER" (SPEAK SOFTLY LOVE)

MADE IN JAPAN

MANDY (BRANDY)

MARMALADE, MOLASSES, AND HONEY

MARY HAD A LITTLE LAMB

MAYBE THIS TIME

ME AND JULIO DOWN BY THE SCHOOLYARD

ME AND MRS. JONES

MELISSA

MIDNIGHT RIDER

MONEY, MONEY (MAKES THE WORLD GO ROUND)

MONEY IS

MORNING AFTER, THE

MORNING HAS BROKEN

MOTHER AND CHILD REUNION

MOTORCYCLE MAMA

MY DING-A-LING

MY HANG UP IS YOU

MY MAN, A SWEET MAN

MY WORLD

NICE TO BE WITH YOU

NIGHTS IN WHITE SATIN

992 ARGUMENTS

NO TIME AT ALL

NOW RUN AND TELL THAT

OH GIRL

OLD MAN

OPERATOR (THAT'S NOT THE WAY IT FEELS)

OUTA-SPACE

PAPA WAS A ROLLIN' STONE

PIECES OF APRIL

PLAY ME

POPCORN

POWER OF LOVE

PRECIOUS AND FEW

PUPPY LOVE

RING THE LIVING BELL

RIP OFF

ROCK AND ROLL LULLABY

ROCK AND ROLL PART 2

ROCKET MAN

ROCKIN' PNEUMONIA AND THE BOOGIE WOOGIE FLU

ROCKIN' ROBIN

ROCK ME ON THE WATER

ROCKY MOUNTAIN HIGH

ROUNDABOUT

RUNNIN' AWAY

RUN RUN RUN

RUN TO ME

SATURDAY IN THE PARK

SCHOOL'S OUT

SING (SING A SONG)

SITTING

SLIPPIN' INTO DARKNESS

SMILIN'

SO LONG DIXIE

SOMEDAY NEVER COMES

SOMETHING'S WRONG WITH ME

SONG SUNG BLUE

SPACEMAN

SPEAK TO THE SKY

SPIRIT IN THE NIGHT

SPREAD A LITTLE SUNSHINE

STARMAN

STARTING ALL OVER AGAIN

STAY WITH ME

STRANGE ARE THE WAYS OF LOVE

SUAVECITO

SUGAREE

SUMMER BREEZE

SUMMER NIGHTS

SUNDAY MORNING SUNSHINE

SUNSHINE

SUPERFLY

SUPERWOMAN (WHERE WERE YOU
  WHEN I NEEDED YOU)

SWEET SEASONS

SWEET SURRENDER

SYLVIA'S MOTHER

TAKE IT EASY

TAURUS

TAXI

THEME FROM "THE MEN"

THINK (ABOUT IT)

THUNDER AND LIGHTNING

TIGHT ROPE

TINY DANCER

TOO LATE TO TURN BACK NOW

TOUCH YOUR WOMAN

TROGLODYTE (CAVE MAN)

TROUBLE MAN

TUMBLING DICE

TUPELO HONEY

USE ME

VAHEVELA

VENTURA HIGHWAY

VINCENT

WALKIN' IN THE RAIN WITH THE ONE
  I LOVE

WALK ON WATER

WAR SONG

WAY OF LOVE, THE

WE COULD BE CLOSE

WE'VE COME TOO FAR TO END IT NOW

WHERE IS THE LOVE

WHO'S GONNA PLAY THIS OLD PIANO?

WHY CAN'T WE LIVE TOGETHER

WITHOUT YOU

WOMAN (SENSUOUS WOMAN)

WOMAN DON'T GO ASTRAY

WOMAN'S GOTTA HAVE IT

WORLD IS A GHETTO, THE

YOU DON'T MESS AROUND WITH JIM

YOUNG NEW MEXICAN PUPPETEER, THE

YOU OUGHT TO BE WITH ME

YOU'RE STILL A YOUNG MAN

YOU SAID A BAD WORD

YOU TURN ME ON, I'M A RADIO

YOU WEAR IT WELL

1973

AIN'T NO WOMAN LIKE THE ONE I GOT

ALAIYO

ALL I KNOW

ALL THAT LOVE WENT TO WASTE

AMAZING LOVE

AND I LOVE YOU SO

ANGEL

ANGIE

ARE YOU MAN ENOUGH?

AUBREY

AVENGING ANNIE

BACK WHEN MY HAIR WAS SHORT

BAD, BAD LEROY BROWN

BASKETBALL JONES FEATURING TYRONE
   SHOELACES

BE

BEHIND CLOSED DOORS

BELIEVE IN HUMANITY

BIG CITY MISS RUTH ANN

BILLION DOLLAR BABIES

BITTER BAD

BLOOD RED AND GOIN' DOWN

BOOGIE WOOGIE BUGLE BOY (OF
   COMPANY B)

BREAK UP TO MAKE UP

BROTHER LOUIE

BROTHER SUN, SISTER MOON

CALIFORNIA SAGA (ON MY WAY TO
   SUNNY CALIFORN-I-A)

CALL ME (COME BACK HOME)

CHEAPER TO KEEP HER

CHINA GROVE

COME GET TO THIS

COME LIVE WITH ME

COOK WITH HONEY

CORAZON

COUNTRY SUNSHINE

COVER OF "ROLLING STONE," THE

CROCODILE ROCK

DADDY COULD SWEAR, I DECLARE

DAISY A DAY

DANIEL

DANNY'S SONG

DEAD SKUNK

DESPERADO

DESPERADOES WAITING FOR A TRAIN

DIAMOND GIRL

DON'T EXPECT ME TO BE YOUR FRIEND

DON'T FIGHT THE FEELINGS OF LOVE

DON'T LET ME BE LONELY TONIGHT

DREIDEL

DRIFT AWAY

D'YER MAKER

EVERYBODY'S HAD THE BLUES

FEELIN' STRONGER EVERY DAY

FRANKENSTEIN

FREEBOOTIN'

FREE RIDE

FRIENDS

FUNKY WORM

FUNNY FACE

GET DOWN

GIVE IT TO ME

GIVE ME LOVE (GIVE ME PEACE ON
   EARTH)

GIVING IT ALL AWAY

GOODBYE YELLOW BRICK ROAD

GYPSY MAN

HALF-BREED

HARDER THEY COME, THE

HEARTBEAT—IT'S A LOVEBEAT

HELLO—HOORAY

HERE I AM (COME AND TAKE ME)

HE'S GOOD FOR ME

HEY GIRL (I LIKE YOUR STYLE)

HEY YOU! GET OFF MY MOUNTAIN

HI, HI, HI

HIGHER GROUND

HOCUS POCUS

HUMMINGBIRD

HURTS SO GOOD

I BELIEVE IN YOU (YOU BELIEVE IN ME)

I CAN'T STAND THE RAIN

IF TEARDROPS WERE PENNIES

IF WE TRY

IF YOU'RE READY (COME GO WITH ME)

IF YOU WANT ME TO STAY

I GOT A NAME

I'M DOIN' FINE NOW

I'M GONNA LOVE YOU JUST A LITTLE BIT MORE, BABY

I'M JUST A SINGER (IN A ROCK AND ROLL BAND)

I NEVER SAID GOODBYE

I'VE GOT TO USE MY IMAGINATION

IT WOULD HAVE BEEN WONDERFUL

I WANNA BE WITH YOU

JEREMY

JESSE

JESSICA

JOKER, THE

JUST YOU 'N' ME

KEEP ME IN MIND

KEEP ON TRUCKIN'

KIDS SAY THE DARNDEST THINGS

KILLING ME SOFTLY WITH HIS SONG

KNOCKIN' ON HEAVEN'S DOOR

KODACHROME

L. A. FREEWAY

LA GRANGE

(LAST NIGHT) I DIDN'T GET TO SLEEP AT ALL

LAST SONG

LAST TANGO IN PARIS

LEAVE ME ALONE (RUBY RED DRESS)

LEAVING ME

LET ME SERENADE YOU

LET ME TRY AGAIN

LET'S GET IT ON

LITTLE WILLY

LIVE AND LET DIE

LIVING FOR THE CITY

LIVING TOGETHER, GROWING TOGETHER

LONG TRAIN RUNNIN'

LORD KNOWS I'M DRINKING, THE

LOVE

LOVE, REIGN O'ER ME

LOVE HAS NO PRIDE

LOVE I LOST, THE

LOVE IS THE FOUNDATION

LOVES ME LIKE A ROCK

LOVE TRAIN

LOVING ARMS

LOVIN' YOU MORE

MAN AND A TRAIN, A

MANY RIVERS TO CROSS

ME AND BABY BROTHER

MIDNIGHT TRAIN TO GEORGIA

MIND GAMES

MONEY

MOST BEAUTIFUL GIRL, THE

MUSKRAT LOVE

MY LOVE

MY MARIA

MY MELODY OF LOVE

MY MUSIC

MY OLD SCHOOL

NATURAL HIGH

NEITHER ONE OF US (WANTS TO BE THE FIRST TO SAY GOODBYE)

NEVER, NEVER GONNA GIVE YA UP

NICE TO BE AROUND

NIGHT THE LIGHTS WENT OUT IN GEORGIA, THE

NUTBUSH CITY LIMITS

OH, BABE, WHAT WOULD YOU SAY?

OLD DOGS, CHILDREN, AND WATERMELON WINE

O LUCKY MAN!

ONE LESS SET OF FOOTSTEPS

ONE MAN PARADE

ONE OF A KIND (LOVE AFFAIR)

OUTLAW MAN

OUT OF THE QUESTION

PAPER ROSES

PEACEFUL

PEACEFUL EASY FEELING

PHOTOGRAPH

PILLOW TALK

PLAYGROUND IN MY MIND

RATED X

REDNECK FRIEND

REDNECKS, WHITE SOCKS, AND BLUE
   RIBBON BEER

REELING IN THE YEARS

REMEMBER (CHRISTMAS)

RIDIN' MY THUMB TO MEXICO

RIGHT PLACE, WRONG TIME

RIGHT THING TO DO, THE

RIVER SONG

ROCKIN' ROLL BABY

ROCK 'N' ROLL (I GAVE YOU THE BEST
   YEARS OF MY LIFE)

ROCKY MOUNTAIN WAY

RUBBER BULLETS

SAIL ON SAILOR

SATURDAY NIGHT'S ALRIGHT FOR
   FIGHTING

SAY, HAS ANYBODY SEEN MY SWEET
   GYPSY ROSE

SEND A LITTLE LOVE MY WAY

SEND IN THE CLOWNS

SEPARATE WAYS

SEXY MAMA

SHAMBALA

SHE NEEDS SOMEONE TO HOLD HER
   (WHEN SHE CRIES)

SHE'S GOT TO BE A SAINT

SHOW AND TELL

SHOW BIZ KIDS

SITTING IN LIMBO

SLIPPING AWAY

SMOKE ON THE WATER

SOME GUYS HAVE ALL THE LUCK

SOUL MAKOSSA

SO VERY HARD TO GO

SPACE ODDITY

SPACE RACE

STEAMROLLER BLUES

STIR IT UP

STUCK IN THE MIDDLE WITH YOU

SUCH A NIGHT

SUGAR MAGNOLIA

SUNNY SIDE OF LIFE

SUPERSTITION

SWEET HARMONY

SWEET TIME

TAKE ME TO THE RIVER

TEQUILA SUNRISE

THAT LADY

THEME FROM "CLEOPATRA JONES"

THERE'S NO ME WITHOUT YOU

THINKING OF YOU

TIE A YELLOW RIBBON ROUND THE OLE
   OAK TREE

'TIL I GET IT RIGHT

TIME IN A BOTTLE

TOM SAWYER

TOP OF THE WORLD

TOUCH ME IN THE MORNING

TRAVELIN' PRAYER

TRIP TO HEAVEN

TUBULAR BELLS

UNEASY RIDER

WALKING TALL

WALK ON THE WILD SIDE

WAY WE WERE, THE

WE DID IT

WEEKEND IN THE COUNTRY, A

WE MAY NEVER PASS THIS WAY (AGAIN)

WE'RE AN AMERICAN BAND

WHAT ABOUT ME

WHAT'S YOUR MAMA'S NAME, CHILD?

WHERE PEACEFUL WATERS FLOW

WHY ME

WILDFLOWER

WILL IT GO ROUND IN CIRCLES

WOMAN FROM TOKYO

YESTERDAY ONCE MORE

YES WE CAN CAN

YOU ALWAYS COME BACK (TO HURTING
   ME)

YOU ARE THE SUNSHINE OF MY LIFE

YOU CAN GET IT IF YOU REALLY WANT

YOU'RE A SPECIAL PART OF ME
YOU'RE SO VAIN
YOUR MAMA DON'T DANCE
YOU'VE NEVER BEEN THIS FAR BEFORE

1974

AFTER THE GOLDRUSH
AIR THAT I BREATHE, THE
ALL IN LOVE IS FAIR
ALREADY GONE
AMERICAN TUNE
ANGIE BABY
ANNIE'S SONG
ANOTHER LONELY SONG
BABY COME CLOSE
BACK HOME AGAIN
BAND ON THE RUN
BEACH BABY
BENNIE AND THE JETS
BEST THING THAT EVER HAPPENED
  TO ME
BE THANKFUL FOR WHAT YOU'VE GOT
BILLY, DON'T BE A HERO
BLACK FRIDAY
BLAZING SADDLES
BOOGIE BANDS AND ONE NIGHT STANDS
BOOGIE DOWN
BOOGIE ON REGGAE WOMAN
BUNGLE IN THE JUNGLE
CALL ON ME
CAN'T GET ENOUGH
CAN'T GET ENOUGH OF YOUR LOVE,
  BABE
CAREFREE HIGHWAY
CAT'S IN THE CRADLE
CHICO AND THE MAN (MAIN THEME)
CHRISTMAS DREAM
CLAP FOR THE WOLFMAN
COME AND GET YOUR LOVE
COME MONDAY
CRUDE OIL BLUES, THE

DADDY, WHAT IF
DANCIN' FOOL
DANCING MACHINE
DARK HORSE
DARK LADY
DO IT ('TIL YOU'RE SATISFIED)
DO IT BABY
DON'T EAT THE YELLOW SNOW
DON'T LET THE SUN GO DOWN ON ME
DON'T YOU WORRY 'BOUT A THING
DOO DOO DOO DOO DOO
  (HEARTBREAKER)
DREAM ON
DRINKIN' THING
EARACHE MY EYE FEATURING ALICE
  BOWIE
EASE ON DOWN THE ROAD
ENTERTAINER, THE
ERES TU (TOUCH THE WIND)
FAIRYTALE
FEEL LIKE MAKIN' LOVE
FINALLY GOT MYSELF TOGETHER (I'M A
  CHANGED MAN)
FOR A DANCER
FOR THE LOVE OF MONEY
FREE BIRD
FREE MAN IN PARIS
GEORGIA PORCUPINE
GET DANCIN'
GET OUT OF DENVER
GIVE IT TO THE PEOPLE
GOLDEN AGE OF ROCK 'N' ROLL
GOOD TIMES
HANG ON IN THERE BABY
HAPPY DAYS
HAVEN'T GOT TIME FOR THE PAIN
(YOU'RE) HAVING MY BABY
HEARTBREAK KID, THE
HEART LIKE A WHEEL
HELEN WHEELS
HELP ME

HEY, LORETTA

HOLLYWOOD SWINGING

HOMELY GIRL

HOOKED ON A FEELING

HOUSTON (I'M COMIN' TO SEE YOU)

I CAN HELP

I FEEL LOVE (BENJI'S THEME)

IF WE MAKE IT THROUGH DECEMBER

IF YOU LOVE ME (LET ME KNOW)

IF YOU TALK IN YOUR SLEEP

IF YOU WANNA GET TO HEAVEN

I HONESTLY LOVE YOU

I'LL HAVE TO SAY I LOVE YOU IN A SONG

I LOVE

I LOVE MY FRIEND

I'M A RAMBLIN' MAN

I'M COMING HOME

I'M STILL LOVING YOU

I OVERLOOKED AN ORCHID

I SEE THE WANT IN YOUR EYES

I SHALL SING

I SHOT THE SHERIFF

IT'S BEEN A LONG TIME

IT'S ONLY ROCK 'N' ROLL (BUT I LIKE IT)

(I'VE BEEN) SEARCHIN' SO LONG

I'VE GOT THE MUSIC IN ME

I WILL ALWAYS LOVE YOU

I WON'T LAST A DAY WITHOUT YOU

I WOULDN'T TREAT A DOG (THE WAY YOU TREATED ME)

JAMES DEAN

JAZZMAN

JET

JOLENE

JUNGLE BOOGIE

JUNIOR'S FARM

JUST DON'T WANT TO BE LONELY TONIGHT

KEEP ON SINGING

KEEP ON SMILIN'

KUNG FU FIGHTING

LAST LOVE SONG, THE

LAST TIME I SAW HIM

(I'D BE) LEGEND IN MY TIME, A

LET IT RIDE

LET ME BE THERE

LET'S PUT IT ALL TOGETHER

LIFE IS A ROCK (BUT THE RADIO ROLLED ME)

LITTLE PRINCE, THE (FROM WHO KNOWS WHERE)

LIVIN' FOR YOU

LOCO-MOTION, THE

LONGFELLOW SERENADE

LOOKIN' FOR A LOVE

LOOKING BACK

LOVE DON'T LOVE NOBODY

LOVE IS LIKE A BUTTERFLY

LOVE ME FOR A REASON

LOVE SONG, A

LOVE'S THEME

MACHINE GUN

MANDY (BRANDY)

MARIE LAVEAU

MIDNIGHT, ME AND THE BLUES

MIDNIGHT AT THE OASIS

MIGHTY LOVE, A

MINE FOR ME

MISSISSIPPI COTTON PICKING DELTA TOWN

MORNINGSIDE OF THE MOUNTAIN, THE

MOST LIKELY YOU GO YOUR WAY (AND I'LL GO MINE)

MUST OF GOT LOST

MY GIRL BILL

MY MISTAKE (WAS TO LOVE YOU)

MY SWEET LADY

NEED TO BE, THE

NIGHT CHICAGO DIED, THE

NOTHING FROM NOTHING

OH MY MY

OH VERY YOUNG

OLD MAN FROM THE MOUNTAIN

ON AND ON

ON A NIGHT LIKE THIS

ONCE YOU'VE HAD THE BEST

ONE CHAIN DON'T MAKE NO PRISON

ONE DAY AT A TIME

ONE HELL OF A WOMAN

OVERNIGHT SENSATION (HIT RECORD)

PAYBACK, THE

PEOPLE GOTTA MOVE

PIANO MAN

PLEASE COME TO BOSTON

PLEASE DON'T TELL ME HOW THE
    STORY ENDS

PRETZEL LOGIC

PURE LOVE

PUT YOUR HANDS TOGETHER

RADAR LOVE

RAISED ON ROBBERY

RAMBLIN' MAN

REAL ME, THE

RIDE 'EM COWBOY

RIKKI DON'T LOSE THAT NUMBER

ROCK AND ROLL, HOOCHIE KOO

ROCK AND ROLL HEAVEN

ROCKIN' SOUL

ROCK ME GENTLY

ROCK ON

ROCK THE BOAT

ROCK YOUR BABY

ROSALIE

RUB IT IN

SEASONS IN THE SUN

SECOND AVENUE

SHA-LA-LA (MAKE ME HAPPY)

SHE CALLED ME BABY

SHE'S GONE

SHININ' ON

SHOW MUST GO ON, THE

SIDESHOW

SKIN TIGHT

SKYBIRD

SMOKIN' IN THE BOYS' ROOM

SPIDERS AND SNAKES

STEPPIN' OUT (GONNA BOOGIE TONIGHT)

STOP AND SMELL THE ROSES

STREAK, THE

SUNDOWN

SUNSHINE ON MY SHOULDERS

SURE AS I'M SITTIN' HERE

SWEET HOME ALABAMA

SWEET MAGNOLIA BLOSSOM

TAKIN' CARE OF BUSINESS

TELL ME A LIE

TELL ME SOMETHING GOOD

THANKS FOR SAVING MY LIFE

THAT'S THE WAY LOVE GOES

THEN CAME YOU

THERE'S A HONKY TONK ANGEL
    (WHO'LL TAKE ME BACK IN)

THERE WON'T BE ANYMORE

THIS TIME

TIME FOR LIVIN' (TIME FOR GIVIN')

TIN MAN

TOUCH A HAND, MAKE A FRIEND

TOUCH ME

TRAVELIN' SHOES

TRYING TO HOLD ON TO MY WOMAN

TSOP (THE SOUND OF PHILADELPHIA)

UNBORN CHILD

UNTIL YOU COME BACK TO ME (THAT'S
    WHAT I'M GONNA DO)

UPTOWN SATURDAY NIGHT

VERY SPECIAL LOVE SONG, A

VIRGIN MAN

WALK ON

WATCHING THE RIVER RUN

WATERLOO

WE MAY NEVER LOVE LIKE THIS AGAIN

WE'RE GETTING CARELESS WITH OUR
    LOVE

WEREWOLF

WHATEVER GETS YOU THROUGH THE
    NIGHT

WHAT IS HIP?

WHEN WILL I SEE YOU AGAIN?

WHERE DID THE GOOD TIMES GO?

WHEREVER LOVE TAKES ME

WHO DO YOU THINK YOU ARE?

WILDWOOD WEED

WISHING YOU WERE HERE

W-O-L-D

WORKIN' AT THE CAR WASH BLUES

WORLD OF MAKE BELIEVE

WOULD YOU LAY WITH ME (IN A FIELD
   OF STONE)

YOU AIN'T SEEN NOTHING YET

YOU AND ME AGAINST THE WORLD

YOU CAN'T BE A BEACON (IF YOUR
   LIGHT DON'T SHINE)

YOU GOT THE LOVE

YOU HAVEN'T DONE NOTHIN'

YOU LITTLE TRUSTMAKER

YOU MAKE ME FEEL BRAND NEW

YOU'RE SIXTEEN

YOU'RE THE FIRST, THE LAST, MY
   EVERYTHING

YOU TURNED MY WORLD AROUND

YOU'VE BEEN DOING WRONG FOR
   SO LONG

1975

AARON LOVES ANGELA

AIN'T NO WAY TO TREAT A LADY

ALL THAT JAZZ

ALMOST SATURDAY NIGHT

ALWAYS WANTING YOU

AMIE

ANYTIME (I'LL BE THERE)

APPLE DUMPLING GANG, THE

ARE YOU SURE HANK DONE IT
   THIS WAY?

ART FOR ART'S SAKE

AS LONG AS HE TAKES CARE OF HOME

AT SEVENTEEN

AT THE BALLET

ATTITUDE DANCING

AUTOBAHN

AWAY FROM YOU

BABY THAT'S BACKATCHA

BAD BLOOD

BAD LUCK

BAD TIME

BALLROOM BLITZ

BARGAIN STORE, THE

BEFORE THE NEXT TEARDROP FALLS

BERTHA BUTT BOOGIE, THE

BEST OF MY LOVE

BLACK SUPERMAN—"MUHAMMAD ALI"

BLACK WATER

BLANKET ON THE GROUND

BLOODY WELL RIGHT

BLUEBIRD

BLUE EYES CRYING IN THE RAIN

BORN TO RUN

BROKEN LADY

CALYPSO

CAN'T GET IT OUT OF MY HEAD

CAN'T SMILE WITHOUT YOU

CAROLINA IN THE PINES

CHAMPAGNE

CHARMER

CHEVY VAN

CHICKEN SOUP WITH RICE

COULD IT BE MAGIC

COUNTRY BOY (YOU GOT YOUR FEET
   IN L.A.)

CUT THE CAKE

DAISY JANE

DANCE: TEN; LOOKS: THREE

DANCE WITH ME

DAS SWEET DREAMER

DEVIL IN THE BOTTLE

DIAMONDS AND RUST

DISCO QUEEN

DOCTOR'S ORDERS

DO IT ANY WAY YOU WANNA

DON'T CALL US, WE'LL CALL YOU

DON'T IT MAKE YOU WANNA DANCE?

DON'T TELL ME GOODNIGHT

DYNOMITE

EIGHTEEN WITH A BULLET

EMMA

EMOTION (AMOREUSE)

EVERY TIME YOU TOUCH ME (I GET HIGH)

EXPRESS

FALLIN' IN LOVE

FAME

FEELINGS

FEELIN'S

FEEL LIKE MAKIN' LOVE

FIGHT THE POWER

FIRE

FLY, ROBIN, FLY

FOR THE LOVE OF YOU

FOX ON THE RUN

FRIEND OF MINE IS GOING BLIND, A

GET DOWN, GET DOWN (GET ON THE FLOOR)

GET DOWN TONIGHT

GIVE THE PEOPLE WHAT THEY WANT

GONE AT LAST

GOT TO GET YOU INTO MY LIFE

HANK WILLIAMS, YOU WROTE MY LIFE

HAPPY PEOPLE

HARRY TRUMAN

HAVE YOU NEVER BEEN MELLOW

HE DON'T LOVE YOU (LIKE I LOVE YOU)

HELLO TWELVE, HELLO THIRTEEN, HELLO LOVE

(HEY, WONT YOU PLAY) ANOTHER SOMEBODY DONE SOMEBODY WRONG SONG

HEY YOU

HIJACK

HOLDIN' ON TO YESTERDAY

HOPE THAT WE CAN BE TOGETHER SOON

HOPE YOU'RE FEELIN' ME LIKE I'M FEELIN' YOU

HOPPY, GENE AND ME

HOW LONG

HOW LONG (BETCHA' GOT A CHICK ON THE SIDE)

HOW LUCKY CAN YOU GET

HUSTLE, THE

I AM LOVE

I BELIEVE I'M GONNA LOVE YOU

(I BELIEVE) THERE'S NOTHING STRONGER THAN OUR LOVE

I BELONG TO YOU

I CAN DO THAT

I CARE

I DON'T LIKE TO SLEEP ALONE

I DON'T WANT TO TALK ABOUT IT

I DREAMED LAST NIGHT

IF I COULD ONLY WIN YOUR LOVE

IF I EVER LOSE THIS HEAVEN

I GOT STONED AND I MISSED IT

I JUST CAN'T GET HER OUT OF MY MIND

I'LL GO TO MY GRAVE LOVING YOU

I'LL PLAY FOR YOU

I'M EASY

IMMIGRANT, THE

I'M NOT IN LOVE

I'M NOT LISA

I'M ON FIRE

I'M SORRY

I'VE BEEN THIS WAY BEFORE

ISLAND GIRL

ISN'T IT LONELY TOGETHER

IT DON'T WORRY ME

IT ONLY TAKES A MINUTE

IT'S A MIRACLE

IT'S A SIN WHEN YOU LOVE SOMEBODY

IT'S ALL DOWN TO GOODNIGHT VIENNA

IT'S TIME TO PAY THE FIDDLER

I WANNA DANCE WIT' CHOO (DOO DAT DANCE)

I WANT'A DO SOMETHING FREAKY TO YOU

I WANT TO HOLD YOU IN MY DREAMS TONIGHT

JACKIE BLUE

JIVE TALKIN'

JUST A LITTLE BIT OF YOU

JUST GET UP AND CLOSE THE DOOR

JUST TOO MANY PEOPLE

KATMANDU

KEEP YOUR EYE ON THE SPARROW
(BARETTA'S THEME)

KILLER QUEEN

LADY

LADY BLUE

LADY MARMALADE

LAST FAREWELL, THE

LAST GAME OF THE SEASON, THE (A
BLIND MAN IN THE BLEACHERS)

LAUGHTER IN THE RAIN

LET'S DO IT AGAIN

LETTER THAT JOHNNY WALKER
READ, THE

LINDA ON MY MIND

LISTEN TO WHAT THE MAN SAID

LIZZIE AND THE RAINMAN

LONG HAIRED COUNTRY BOY

LONG TALL GLASSES (I CAN DANCE)

LOOK AT ME (I'M IN LOVE)

LOOK IN MY EYES PRETTY WOMAN

L-O-V-E (LOVE)

LOVE DON'T YOU GO THROUGH NO
CHANGES ON ME

LOVE IS A ROSE

LOVE MACHINE

LOVE POWER

LOVE PUT A SONG IN MY HEART

LOVE WILL KEEP US TOGETHER

LOVE WON'T LET ME WAIT

LOVIN' YOU

LOW RIDER

LUCKY LADY

LYIN' EYES

MAGIC

MEXICO

MIDNIGHT BLUE

MINSTREL IN THE GALLERY

MIRACLES

MORNIN' BEAUTIFUL

MORNINGSIDE OF THE MOUNTAIN

MOVIN' ON

MOVIN' ON UP

MUSIC AND THE MIRROR, THE

MUSIC NEVER STOPPED, THE

MY EYES ADORED YOU

MY IDAHO HOME

MY LITTLE TOWN

MY OWN BEST FRIEND

NEXT TO LOVIN' (I LIKE FIGHTIN')

NICE, NICE, VERY NICE

NIGHTINGALE

NIGHTS ON BROADWAY

99 MILES FROM L.A.

NO CHARGE

NO NO SONG

NOW THAT WE'RE IN LOVE

#9 DREAM

OLD DAYS

ONCE YOU GET STARTED

ONE

ONE MAN WOMAN/ONE WOMAN MAN

ONE OF THESE NIGHTS

ONLY WOMEN

ONLY YESTERDAY

OPERATOR

OUT OF TIME

OVER MY HEAD

PALOMA BLANCA

PART OF THE PLAN

PART TIME LOVE

PHILADELPHIA

PHILADELPHIA FREEDOM

PICK UP THE PIECES

PINBALL

PLEASE MR. PLEASE

PLEASE MR. POSTMAN

POETRY MAN

PROUD ONE, THE

RAINY DAY PEOPLE

RAZZLE DAZZLE

READY

REAL MAN

REMEMBER WHAT I TOLD YOU TO FORGET

RENDEZVOUS

RHINESTONE COWBOY

RICHARD'S WINDOW

ROCKFORD FILES, THE

ROCKIN' ALL OVER THE WORLD

ROCKIN' CHAIR

ROCKY

ROLL ON BIG MAMA

ROLL ON DOWN THE HIGHWAY

RUN JOEY RUN

SAILING

SALLY G

SAN ANTONIO STROLL

SATIN SOUL

SATURDAY NIGHT

SATURDAY NIGHT SPECIAL

SEEKER, THE

SHAKEY GROUND

SHAME, SHAME, SHAME

SHAVING CREAM

SHE'S ACTIN' SINGLE (I'M DRINKIN' DOUBLES)

SHINING STAR

SHOES

SHOESHINE BOY

SING A SONG

SISTER GOLDEN HAIR

SKY HIGH

SLEEPY MAN

SLIPPERY WHEN WET

SNEAKY SNAKE

SNOOKEROO

SOLITAIRE

SOME KIND OF WONDERFUL

SOMEONE SAVED MY LIFE TONIGHT

SOMETHING BETTER TO DO

SOMETIMES

SOMEWHERE IN THE NIGHT

SOONER OR LATER

S.O.S.

SOUL TRAIN '75

SOUTH'S GONNA DO IT, THE

SPIRIT OF THE BOOGIE

STRUTTIN'

SUPERNATURAL THING—PART 1

SWEARIN' TO GOD

SWEETEST GIFT, THE

SWEET LOVE

SWEET STICKY THING

SWEET SURRENDER

TAKE ME IN YOUR ARMS (ROCK ME)

TANGLED UP IN BLUE

THANK GOD I'M A COUNTRY BOY

THAT'S ALL IN THE MOVIES

THAT'S THE WAY (I LIKE IT)

THAT'S THE WAY OF THE WORLD

THAT'S WHEN THE MUSIC TAKES ME

THEME FROM "JAWS" (MAIN TITLE)

THEME FROM "MAHOGANY" (DO YOU KNOW WHERE YOU'RE GOING TO?)

THEME FROM S.W.A.T.

THEY JUST CAN'T STOP IT (THE GAMES PEOPLE PLAY)

THIRD RATE ROMANCE

THIS OL' COWBOY

THIS WILL BE (AN EVERLASTING LOVE)

TO EACH HIS OWN

TO THE DOOR OF THE SUN (ALLE PORTE DEL SOLE)

TRYIN' TO BEAT THE MORNING HOME

TURN OUT THE LIGHT AND LOVE ME TONIGHT

TURN TO STONE

TUSH

UP IN A PUFF OF SMOKE

VENUS AND MARS ROCK SHOW

WALK AWAY FROM LOVE

WALKING IN RHYTHM
WASTED DAYS AND WASTED NIGHTS
WAY I WANT TO TOUCH YOU, THE
WHAT AM I GONNA DO WITH YOU
WHATEVER HAPPENED TO SATURDAY
   NIGHT
WHAT I DID FOR LOVE
WHEN MABEL COMES IN THE ROOM
WHEN WILL I BE LOVED?
WHO LOVES YOU
WHY CAN'T WE BE FRIENDS?
WILDFIRE
WINNERS AND LOSERS
WONDERFUL BABY
YOU
YOU ARE A SONG
YOU ARE SO BEAUTIFUL
YOUNG AMERICANS
YOUR BULLDOG DRINKS CHAMPAGNE
YOU'RE A PART OF ME
YOU'RE MY BEST FRIEND
YOU'RE NO GOOD
YOU SEXY THING

1976

ACTION
ADVENTURES IN PARADISE
AFTER ALL THE GOOD IS GONE
ALL BY MYSELF
ALL I CAN DO
ALL THESE THINGS
ALWAYS AND FOREVER
ARE YOU READY FOR THE COUNTRY?
ARMS OF MARY
AVE SATANI
BABY, I LOVE YOUR WAY
BABY BOY
BACK TO THE ISLAND
BALLAD OF GATOR MCCLUSKY
BEST DISCO IN TOWN, THE
BETH
BETTER DAYS

BETTER PLACE TO BE
BOHEMIAN RHAPSODY
BOOGIE FEVER
BOYS ARE BACK IN TOWN, THE
BREAK AWAY
BREEZIN'
BROKEN DOWN IN TINY PIECES
CHEROKEE MAIDEN
CHRYSANTHEMUM TEA
COME ON OVER
COME TO ME
CONVOY
CRAZY ON YOU
DAZZ
DECEMBER 1963 (OH, WHAT A NIGHT)
DETROIT ROCK CITY
DEVIL WOMAN
DISCO DUCK
DISCO LADY
DO IT TO MY MIND
(DON'T FEAR) THE REAPER
DON'T GO BREAKING MY HEART
DON'T STOP BELIEVIN'
DON'T THE GIRLS ALL GET PRETTIER AT
   CLOSING TIME?
DON'T TOUCH ME THERE
DOOR'S ALWAYS OPEN, THE
DO YOU FEEL LIKE WE DO
DREAM ON
DREAM WEAVER
DROPKICK ME, JESUS
EL PASO CITY
EMPTY TABLES
ENJOY YOURSELF
EVERGREEN (LOVE THEME FROM "A
   STAR IS BORN")
EVIL WOMAN
FANNY (BE TENDER WITH MY LOVE)
FASTER HORSES
FERNANDO
FEZ, THE
FIFTH OF BEETHOVEN, A

50 WAYS TO LEAVE YOUR LOVER
FLY AWAY
FOOLED AROUND AND FELL IN LOVE
FOOL TO CRY
GAMES THAT DADDIES PLAY, THE
GETAWAY
GET CLOSER
GET UP AND BOOGIE (THAT'S RIGHT)
GOLDEN RING
GOLDEN YEARS
GOOD WOMAN BLUES
GROW SOME FUNK OF YOUR OWN
HAPPY MUSIC
HEART HEELER
HEAVEN MUST BE MISSING AN ANGEL
HELLO OLD FRIEND
HERE'S SOME LOVE
HOOKED ON YOUR LOVE
HOT LINE
HOT STUFF
HUNGRY YEARS, THE
HURRICANE
I BELIEVE IN LOVE
I CAN'T BELIEVE SHE GIVES IT ALL
   TO ME
I CAN'T HEAR YOU NO MORE
I DO, I DO, I DO, I DO, I DO
I DON'T WANT TO HAVE TO MARRY YOU
I'D REALLY LOVE TO SEE YOU TONIGHT
I FEEL LIKE A BULLET (IN THE GUN OF
   ROBERT FORD)
IF YOU KNOW WHAT I MEAN
IF YOU LEAVE ME NOW
I HOPE WE GET TO LOVE IN TIME
I'LL BE GOOD TO YOU
I'LL GET OVER YOU
I LOVE MUSIC
I'M A STAND BY MY WOMAN MAN
I'M FEELING FINE
I'M MANDY, FLY ME
I NEED TO BE IN LOVE
I NEVER CRY

IN FRANCE THEY KISS ON MAIN STREET
IN MY LONELINESS
INSEPARABLE
IT KEEPS YOU RUNNING
IT'S OVER
I WANT TO GET NEXT TO YOU
I WANT YOU
I WRITE THE SONGS
JUMP
JUNK FOOD JUNKIE
JUST TO BE CLOSE TO YOU
KID CHARLEMAGNE
KISS AND SAY GOODBYE
LAST CHILD
LET 'EM IN
LET HER IN
LET IT SHINE
LET IT SHINE
LET YOUR LOVE FLOW
LIKE A SAD SONG
LITTLE BIT MORE, A
LIVIN' FOR THE WEEKEND
LIVIN' THING
LONELY NIGHT (ANGEL FACE)
LOOKING FOR SPACE
LOOK INTO YOUR HEART
LOST WITHOUT YOUR LOVE
LOVE BALLAD
"LOVE BOAT" THEME
LOVE HANGOVER
LOVE HURTS
LOVE IN THE SHADOWS
LOVE IS ALIVE
LOVE IS THE DRUG
LOVE ME
LOVE REALLY HURTS WITHOUT YOU
LOVE ROLLERCOASTER
LOVE SO RIGHT
LOVE TO LOVE YOU, BABY
LOWDOWN
MAGIC MAN
MAKING OUR DREAMS COME TRUE

MAMMA MIA

MAN SMART, WOMAN SMARTER

MESSAGE IN OUR MUSIC

MILES AND MILES OF TEXAS

MONEY HONEY

MOODY BLUE

MOONLIGHT FEELS RIGHT

MORE, MORE, MORE

MORE THAN A FEELING

MORE YOU DO IT, THE (THE MORE I LIKE IT DONE)

MOVIN'

MOZAMBIQUE

MUSKRAT LOVE

MY EYES CAN ONLY SEE AS FAR AS YOU

NADIA'S THEME (THE YOUNG AND THE RESTLESS)

NEVER GONNA FALL IN LOVE AGAIN

NEW YORK STATE OF MIND

NICE 'N NAASTY

NIGHTS ARE FOREVER WITHOUT YOU

ONE LOVE IN MY LIFETIME

ONE PIECE AT A TIME

ONLY LOVE IS REAL

ONLY SIXTEEN

OPEN SESAME

OPHELIA

PLAY ON LOVE

PLAY THAT FUNKY MUSIC

POPSICLE TOES

QUEEN BEE

QUIET STORM

RAINBOW IN YOUR EYES

RHIANNON (WILL YOU EVER WIN)

RIGHT BACK WHERE WE STARTED FROM

ROCK AND ROLL ALL NITE

ROCK'N ME

ROCK WITH ME

ROOTS, ROCK, REGGAE

ROOTS OF MY RAISING, THE

RUBBERBAND MAN, THE

SARA SMILE

SATURDAY NITE

SAVE YOUR KISSES FOR ME

SAY IT AGAIN

SAY YOU'LL STAY UNTIL TOMORROW

SAY YOU LOVE ME

(SHAKE, SHAKE, SHAKE) SHAKE YOUR BOOTY

SHAKE YOUR RUMP TO THE FUNK

SHANNON

SHOP AROUND

SHOWER THE PEOPLE

SHOW ME THE WAY

SILLY LOVE SONGS

SLOW RIDE

SOMEBODY SOMEWHERE (DON'T KNOW WHAT HE'S MISSIN' TONIGHT)

SOMEONE TO LAY DOWN BESIDE ME

SOMETHING HE CAN FEEL

SOPHISTICATED LADY (SHE'S A DIFFERENT LADY)

SORRY SEEMS TO BE THE HARDEST WORD

SO SAD THE SONG

SQUEEZE BOX

STAND TALL

STEAL ON HOME

STILL CRAZY AFTER ALL THESE YEARS

STILL THE ONE

STRANGE MAGIC

SUMMER

SUNDAY SCHOOL TO BROADWAY

SWEET THING

TAKIN' IT TO THE STREETS

TAKE IT TO THE LIMIT

TAKE THE MONEY AND RUN

TEAR THE ROOF OFF THE SUCKER (GIVE UP THE FUNK)

TEDDY BEAR

TENTH AVENUE FREEZE-OUT

THINKING OF A RENDEZVOUS

THIS MASQUERADE

THIS ONE'S FOR YOU

THIS SONG

TILL THE RIVERS ALL RUN DRY

TIMES OF YOUR LIFE

TODAY'S THE DAY

TONIGHT'S THE NIGHT (GONNA BE
  ALRIGHT)

TRYIN' TO GET THE FEELING AGAIN

TURN THE BEAT AROUND

TVC 15

UNION MAN

WAKE UP EVERYBODY

WATCH CLOSELY NOW

WE CAN'T HIDE IT ANYMORE

WELCOME BACK

WHAM BAM (SHANG-A-LANG)

WHAT GOES ON WHEN THE SUN GOES
  DOWN

WHEN I'M WRONG

WHITE KNIGHT, THE

WHO'D SHE COO?

WITH YOUR LOVE

WOMAN IN THE MOON, THE

WRECK OF THE EDMUND FITZGERALD,
  THE

YES, YES, YES

YESTERDAY'S HERO

YOU AND ME

YOU ARE THE WOMAN

YOU DON'T HAVE TO BE A STAR (TO BE
  IN MY SHOW)

YOU HAVE THE CHOICE

YOU'LL NEVER FIND ANOTHER LOVE
  LIKE MINE

YOU NEVER MISS A REAL GOOD THING

YOUNG HEARTS RUN FREE

YOU'RE FOOLING YOU

YOU'RE MY BEST FRIEND

YOU SHOULD BE DANCING

1977

AFTERNOON DELIGHT

AFTER THE LOVIN'

AIN'T GONNA BUMP NO MORE (WITH NO
  BIG FAT WOMAN)

ANGEL IN YOUR ARMS

ARIEL

ARRESTED FOR DRIVING WHILE BLIND

AT MIDNIGHT (MY LOVE WILL LIFT YOU
  UP)

BABY, WHAT A BIG SURPRISE

BANDIT, THE

BARRACUDA

BELLE

BEST OF MY LOVE

BLACK BETTY

BLINDED BY THE LIGHT

BLUE BAYOU

BOBO'S

BOOGIE CHILD

BOOGIE NIGHTS

BOOGIE SHOES

BREAKDOWN

BREAK IT TO ME GENTLY

BRICK HOUSE

BROOKLYN

CALLING DR. LOVE

CALLING OCCUPANTS OF
  INTERPLANETARY CRAFT

CANDLE ON THE WATER

CAN'T STOP DANCIN'

CARRY ON, WAYWARD SON

CAR WASH

CAT SCRATCH FEVER

CHANGES IN LATITUDES, CHANGES IN
  ATTITUDES

CHRISTINE SIXTEEN

COLD AS ICE

COME IN FROM THE RAIN

COME SAIL AWAY

COULDN'T GET IT RIGHT

COWBOY AND THE LADY, THE

CRACKERBOX PALACE

DA DOO RON RON (WHEN HE WALKED
  ME HOME)

DANCE, DANCE, DANCE (YOWSAH, YOWSAH, YOWSAH)

DANCING QUEEN

DANCIN' MAN

DARLIN' DARLIN' BABY (SWEET, TENDER LOVE)

DAYBREAK

DAYTIME FRIENDS

DEVIL'S GUN

DISCO INFERNO

DON'T ASK TO STAY UNTIL TOMORROW

DON'T GIVE UP ON US

DON'T IT MAKE MY BROWN EYES BLUE

DON'T LEAVE ME THIS WAY

DON'T STOP

DO YA

DO YA WANNA GET FUNKY WITH ME

DO YA WANNA MAKE LOVE?

DREAMBOAT ANNIE

DREAMS

DUSIC

EARLY IN THE MORNING

EAST BOUND AND DOWN

EASY STREET

ECHOES OF LOVE

EVERYBODY OUGHT TO BE IN LOVE

(EVERY TIME I TURN AROUND) BACK IN LOVE AGAIN

FALLING

FEELS LIKE THE FIRST TIME

FIRST CUT IS THE DEEPEST, THE

FLOAT ON

FLY LIKE AN EAGLE

FREE

FROM GRACELAND TO THE PROMISED LAND

GIRLS' SCHOOL

GIVE A LITTLE BIT

GLORIA

GONE TOO FAR

GONNA FLY NOW (THEME FROM "ROCKY")

GOT TO GIVE IT UP

GO YOUR OWN WAY

GREATEST LOVE OF ALL, THE

HANDY MAN

HARD LUCK WOMAN

HEARD IT IN A LOVE SONG

HEAVEN ON THE SEVENTH FLOOR

HEAVEN'S JUST A SIN AWAY

HELP IS ON ITS WAY

HERE COME THOSE TEARS AGAIN

HERE YOU COME AGAIN

HEY THERE, GOOD TIMES

HIGH SCHOOL DANCE

HOLD BACK THE NIGHT

HOOKED ON YOU

HOTEL CALIFORNIA

HOW DEEP IS YOUR LOVE

HOW MUCH LOVE

I BELIEVE YOU

I CAN'T GET OVER YOU

I DON'T NEED ANYTHING BUT YOU

I FEEL LOVE

IF I CAN'T HAVE YOU

IF WE'RE NOT BACK IN LOVE BY MONDAY

I GO TO RIO

I JUST WANT TO BE YOUR EVERYTHING

I LIKE DREAMIN'

I'LL BE LEAVING ALONE

"I LOVE LUCY" THEME (DISCO LUCY)

I LOVE MY WIFE

I'M DREAMING

I'M IN YOU

I'M THE ONLY HELL (MAMA EVER RAISED)

I'M YOUR BOOGIE MAN

ISN'T IT TIME

IT COULDN'T HAVE BEEN ANY BETTER

IT FEELS SO GOOD TO BE LOVED SO BAD

IT'S ECSTASY WHEN YOU LAY DOWN NEXT TO ME

(OUR LOVE) DON'T THROW IT ALL AWAY
PARADISE BY THE DASHBOARD LIGHT
PART-TIME LOVE
PEG
PLEASE COME HOME FOR CHRISTMAS
POOR, POOR, PITIFUL ME
POWER OF GOLD, THE
PRETTY WOMEN
PROVE IT ALL NIGHT
PSYCHO KILLER
READY FOR THE TIMES TO GET BETTER
READY TO TAKE A CHANCE AGAIN
RIGHT DOWN THE LINE
RIVERS OF BABYLON
ROCKAWAY BEACH
ROCK 'N' ROLL FANTASY, A
RUNAWAY
RUNNING ON EMPTY
SANDY
SHADOW DANCING
SHAKE IT
SHARING THE NIGHT TOGETHER
SHE'S ALWAYS A WOMAN
SHORT PEOPLE
SLEEPING SINGLE IN A DOUBLE BED
SOFT AND WET
SOMETIMES WHEN WE TOUCH
SONGBIRD
STEPPIN' IN A SLIDE ZONE
STILL THE SAME
STRAIGHT ON
STRANGE WAY
STUFF LIKE THAT
SUBSTITUTE
SURRENDER
SWEET DESIRE
SWEET LIFE
SWEET TALKIN' WOMAN
TAKE A CHANCE ON ME
TAKE ME TO THE NEXT PHASE
TALKING IN YOUR SLEEP

TEAR TIME
THANK GOD IT'S FRIDAY
THANK YOU FOR BEING A FRIEND
THAT ONCE IN A LIFETIME
THEME FROM "CLOSE ENCOUNTERS OF
    THE THIRD KIND"
THIS NIGHT WON'T LAST FOREVER
THIS TIME I'M IN IT FOR LOVE
THREE TIMES A LADY
THUNDER ISLAND
TIME FOR ME TO FLY
TIME PASSAGES
TOO CLOSE TO PARADISE
TOO HOT TA TROT
TOO MUCH, TOO LITTLE, TOO LATE
TULSA TIME
TURN TO STONE
TWENTY-FOUR HOURS OF LOVIN'
TWO DOORS DOWN
TWO MORE BOTTLES OF WINE
TWO OUT OF THREE AIN'T BAD
TWO TICKETS TO PARADISE
USE TA BE MY GIRL
WAVELENGTH
WE ARE THE CHAMPIONS
WE'LL NEVER HAVE TO SAY GOODBYE
    AGAIN
WEREWOLVES OF LONDON
WHAT'S YOUR NAME
WHEEL IN THE SKY
WHENEVER I CALL YOU "FRIEND"
WHO ARE YOU
WITH A LITTLE LUCK
WONDERFUL TONIGHT
WRAP YOUR ARMS AROUND ME
YANK ME, CRANK ME
YOU AND I
YOU BELONG TO ME
YOU DON'T BRING ME FLOWERS
YOU DON'T LOVE ME ANYMORE
YOU NEEDED ME

YOU NEVER DONE IT LIKE THAT
YOU'RE THE LOVE
YOU'RE THE ONE THAT I WANT
YOU TOOK THE WORDS RIGHT OUT OF
   MY MOUTH

1979

AFTER THE LOVE HAS GONE
AIN'T LOVE A BITCH
AIN'T NO STOPPIN' US NOW
ALL THE GOLD IN CALIFORNIA
AMANDA
ARROW THROUGH ME
BABE
BABY I'M BURNIN'
BAD CASE OF LOVING YOU (DOCTOR,
   DOCTOR)
BAD GIRLS
BAKER STREET
BETTER LOVE NEXT TIME
BETTER THAN EVER
BIG SHOT
BLOW AWAY
BLUE MORNING, BLUE DAY
BOOGIE WONDERLAND
BORN TO BE ALIVE
BOSS, THE
BROKEN HEARTED ME
BUENOS AIRES
BUSTIN' LOOSE
BUSTIN' OUT
CAME SO FAR FOR BEAUTY
CAN YOU READ MY MIND (LOVE THEME
   FROM "SUPERMAN")
CHIQUITITA
CHUCK E.'S IN LOVE
COCA COLA COWBOY
COME TO ME
COME WITH ME
COOL CHANGE
COWARD OF THE COUNTRY
CRAZY LOVE

CRUEL SHOES
CRUEL TO BE KIND
CRUISIN'
DAMNED IF I DO
DANCE AWAY
DANCE THE NIGHT AWAY
DANCIN' SHOES
DAYS GONE DOWN (STILL GOT THE
   LIGHT IN YOUR EYES)
DEEPER THAN THE NIGHT
DEJA VU
DEPENDIN' ON YOU
DEVIL WENT DOWN TO GEORGIA, THE
DIFFERENT WORLDS
DIM ALL THE LIGHTS
DIRTY WHITE BOY
DISCO NIGHTS (ROCK-FREAK)
DOES YOUR MOTHER KNOW?
DO IT OR DIE
DON'T BRING ME DOWN
DON'T CRY FOR ME, ARGENTINA
DON'T CRY OUT LOUD
DON'T DO ME LIKE THAT
DON'T STOP 'TIL YOU GET ENOUGH
DON'T TAKE IT AWAY
DO THAT TO ME ONE MORE TIME
DO YA THINK I'M SEXY?
DO YOU LOVE WHAT YOU FEEL?
DO YOU THINK I'M DISCO?
DREAMING
DRIVER'S SEAT
ESCAPE (THE PIÑA COLADA SONG)
EVERY TIME I THINK OF YOU
FAMILY TRADITION
FIGHT
FINS
5:15
FOREVER IN BLUE JEANS
FREDERICK
GET IT RIGHT NEXT TIME
GETTING CLOSER
GET USED TO IT

GIMME MICK
GIRL OF MY DREAMS
GIRLS TALK
GOLD
GOODBYE STRANGER
GOOD GIRLS DON'T
GOODNIGHT TONIGHT
GOOD TIMES
GOOD TIMES ROLL
GOT TO BE REAL
HALF THE WAY
HAPPY BIRTHDAY DARLIN'
HARD TIMES FOR LOVERS
HEAD GAMES
HEARTACHE TONIGHT
HEART OF GLASS
HEART OF THE NIGHT
HEAVEN KNOWS
HE'S THE GREATEST DANCER
HIGHWAY TO HELL
HOLD ON
HONESTY
HOT NUMBER
HOT STUFF
I CALL YOUR NAME
I CHEATED ME RIGHT OUT OF YOU
I DON'T KNOW IF IT'S RIGHT
I DON'T LIKE MONDAYS
I DO THE ROCK
I'D RATHER LEAVE WHILE I'M IN LOVE
IF I SAID YOU HAVE A BEAUTIFUL BODY, WOULD YOU HOLD IT AGAINST ME?
IF YOU REMEMBER ME
I GOT MY MIND MADE UP (YOU CAN GET IT GIRL)
I JUST FALL IN LOVE AGAIN
I KNOW A HEARTACHE WHEN I SEE ONE
I'LL BE COMING BACK FOR MORE
I'LL NEVER LOVE THIS WAY AGAIN
I'LL NEVER SAY GOODBYE

I MAY NEVER GET TO HEAVEN
I'M SO ANXIOUS
I NEED A LOVER
IN THE NAVY
ISN'T IT ALWAYS LOVE
IS SHE REALLY GOING OUT WITH HIM?
IT GOES LIKE IT GOES
IT MUST BE LOVE
IT'S ALL I CAN DO
IT'S EASY TO SAY (SONG FROM "10")
I WANNA BE SEDATED
I WANT YOUR LOVE
I WANT YOU TONIGHT
I WANT YOU TO WANT ME
I WAS MADE FOR DANCIN'
I WAS MADE FOR LOVIN' YOU
I WILL SURVIVE
JANE
JUST GOOD OL' BOYS
JUST WHEN I NEEDED YOU THE MOST
KNEE DEEP (NOT JUST)
LADIES NIGHT
LADY
LADY WRITER
LAST CHEATER'S WALTZ
LEAD ME ON
LET'S GO
LIFE DURING WARTIME (THIS AIN'T NO PARTY . . . THIS AIN'T NO DISCO . . . THIS AIN'T NO FOOLIN' AROUND)
LITTLE MORE LOVE, A
LIVIN' IT UP (FRIDAY NIGHT)
LOGICAL SONG, THE
LONESOME LOSER
LONG LIVE ROCK
LOOKING THROUGH THE EYES OF LOVE
LOTTA LOVE
LOVE BALLAD
LOVE IS THE ANSWER
LOVE TAKES TIME
LOVE YOU INSIDE OUT
LOVIN', TOUCHIN', SQUEEZIN'

MAIN EVENT, THE

MAKIN' IT

MAMA CAN'T BUY YOU LOVE

MAN WITH THE CHILD IN HIS EYES, THE

MARIANNE

MARRIED MEN

MAYBE I'M A FOOL

MEATBALLS

MESSAGE IN A BOTTLE

MINUTE BY MINUTE

MOONRAKER

MORNING DANCE

MUSIC BOX DANCER

NOBODY LIKES SAD SONGS

NO CHANCE

NO MORE TEARS (ENOUGH IS ENOUGH)

NO TELL LOVER

OLD TIME ROCK AND ROLL

ONE MORE WALK AROUND THE GARDEN

ONE WAY OR ANOTHER

PEOPLE OF THE SOUTH WIND

PLEASE DON'T GO

PLEASE DON'T LEAVE

POP MUZIK

POPS, WE LOVE YOU (A TRIBUTE TO FATHER)

PRECIOUS LOVE

PROMISES

RAINBOW CONNECTION

RENEGADE

REUNITED

RHUMBA GIRL

RING MY BELL

RISE

ROCK 'N' ROLL FANTASY

ROLENE

ROSE, THE

ROXANNE

RUBBER BISCUIT

SAD EYES

SAIL ON

SEND ONE YOUR LOVE

SEPTEMBER

SEPTEMBER MORN

SHADOWS IN THE MOONLIGHT

SHAKE YOUR BODY (DOWN TO THE GROUND)

SHAKE YOUR GROOVE THING

SHAPE OF THINGS TO COME, THE

SHATTERED

SHE BELIEVES IN ME

SHINE A LITTLE LOVE

SHIPS

SING FOR THE DAY

SONG ON THE RADIO

STILL

STILLSANE

STUMBLIN' IN

SULTANS OF SWING

SUSPICIONS

SWEET SUMMER LOVIN'

TAKE ME HOME

TAKE THE LONG WAY HOME

TELL ME WHAT IT'S LIKE

THEME FROM "DUKES OF HAZZARD" (GOOD OL' BOYS)

THEY'RE PLAYING OUR SONG

THIRD TIME LUCKY (FIRST TIME I WAS A FOOL)

THIS IS IT

TOO MUCH HEAVEN

TRAGEDY

TUSK

VENGEANCE

VIDEO KILLED THE RADIO STAR

VOLCANO

WAIT FOR ME

WATCH OUT FOR LUCY

WE ARE FAMILY

WE DON'T TALK ANYMORE

WE'VE GOT TONIGHT

WHAT A FOOL BELIEVES

WHAT CHA GONNA DO WITH MY LOVIN'

WHAT YOU WON'T DO FOR LOVE

HEADACHE TOMORROW, A (or A
    HEARTACHE TONIGHT)
HEARTBREAK HOTEL
HEART IN NEW YORK, A
HEARTS
HEARTS ON FIRE
HEAVY METAL (TAKING A RIDE)
HERE I AM (JUST WHEN I THOUGHT I
    WAS OVER YOU)
HER TOWN TOO
HILLS OF TOMORROW, THE
HOLD ON TIGHT
HOOKED ON MUSIC
HOW 'BOUT US
HURRICANE
I CAN'T STAND IT
I CAN'T STAND IT
I COULD NEVER MISS YOU MORE THAN I
    DO
I DON'T NEED YOU
IF WE WERE IN LOVE
I LOVED 'EM EVERY ONE
I LOVE YOU
I'M GONNA LOVE HER FOR THE BOTH
    OF US
I'M IN LOVE
I'M JUST AN OLD CHUNK OF COAL (BUT
    I'M GONNA BE A DIAMOND SOME DAY)
I'M SO GLAD I'M STANDING HERE
    TODAY
IN THE AIR TONIGHT
IN THE DARK
IN YOUR LETTER
IS IT YOU
I STILL BELIEVE IN WALTZES
IT DIDN'T TAKE LONG
IT DON'T HURT ME HALF AS BAD
I THINK I'LL JUST STAY HERE AND
    DRINK
I TOLD YOU SO
IT'S A LOVE THING
I WAS COUNTRY WHEN COUNTRY
    WASN'T COOL

JESSIE'S GIRL
JOSÉ CUERVO
JUST THE TWO OF US
KEEP ON LOVING YOU
KISS ON MY LIST
LADY (YOU BRING ME UP)
LADY DOWN ON LOVE
LET'S GROOVE
LIMELIGHT
LITTLE IN LOVE, A
LIVING INSIDE MYSELF
LONELY NIGHTS
LONG NIGHT, A
MAGIC MAN
MAKE THAT MOVE
MAMAW
MARRY ME A LITTLE
MODERN GIRL
MORE THAN JUST THE TWO OF US
MORNING TRAIN (NINE TO FIVE)
MY GIRL (GONE, GONE, GONE)
NIGHT (FEEL LIKE GETTING DOWN)
NIGHT OWLS, THE
NO REPLY AT ALL
NOT A DAY GOES BY
OH NO
OLDER WOMEN
OLD FLAME
OLD SONGS, THE
ONE MORE HOUR
ONE NIGHT ONLY
ONE OF THE BOYS
ONE THAT YOU LOVE, THE
OUR LIPS ARE SEALED
OUR TIME
PARADISE
PARTY TIME
PHYSICAL
PICKIN' UP STRANGERS
PRISONER OF HOPE
PRIVATE EYES
QUEEN OF HEARTS

RAPTURE

REALLY WANNA KNOW YOU

REST YOUR LOVE ON ME

SAUSALITO SUMMERNIGHT

SAY GOODBYE TO HOLLYWOOD

SAY YOU'LL BE MINE

SEVEN YEAR ACHE

SHADDAP YOU FACE

SHAKE IT UP TONIGHT

SHE'S A BAD MAMA JAMA (SHE'S BUILT, SHE'S STACKED)

SHE'S GOT A WAY

SILENT TREATMENT

SISTER

'65 LOVE AFFAIR

SKATEAWAY

SLOW HAND

SOMEBODY'S KNOCKIN'

SOMEDAY, SOMEWAY

SOMEWHERE DOWN THE ROAD

SOUTHERN RAINS

SQUARE BIZ

START ME UP

STEP BY STEP

STOP DRAGGIN' MY HEART AROUND

STROKE, THE

SUNDAY

SURROUND ME WITH LOVE

SWEET BABY

SWEETEST THING (I'VE EVER KNOWN), THE

SWEETHEART

TAKE MY HEART (YOU CAN HAVE IT IF YOU WANT IT)

TAKIN' IT EASY

TEMPTED

THAT GIRL

THEME FROM "HILL STREET BLUES"

THEME FROM "THE GREATEST AMERICAN HERO" (BELIEVE IT OR NOT)

(THERE'S) NO GETTIN' OVER ME

THIS LITTLE GIRL

TIGHT FITTIN' JEANS

TIME

TOM SAWYER

TOO MANY LOVERS

TOO MUCH TIME ON MY HANDS

TOO TIGHT

TOUCH ME WHEN WE'RE DANCING

TREAT ME RIGHT

TROUBLE

TURNING JAPANESE

TURN YOUR LOVE AROUND

UNDER THE COVERS

URGENT

VERY SPECIAL

VOICE, THE

WAITING, THE

WAITING FOR A GIRL LIKE YOU

WAITING ON A FRIEND

WALKING ON THIN ICE

WATCHING THE WHEELS

WATCHING YOU

WE'RE IN THIS LOVE TOGETHER

WHAT ARE WE DOIN' IN LOVE?

WHAT CHA' GONNA DO FOR ME

WHAT KIND OF FOOL

WHILE YOU SEE A CHANCE

WHO'S CHEATIN' WHO

WHO'S CRYING NOW

WINNING

WKRP IN CINCINNATI

WOMAN

WOMAN NEEDS LOVE, A (JUST LIKE YOU DO)

YEARNING FOR YOUR LOVE

YESTERDAY'S SONGS

YOU BETTER YOU BET

YOU COULD HAVE BEEN WITH ME

YOU MAKE MY DREAMS

YOUNG TURKS

YOU'VE GOT ANOTHER THING COMIN'

1982

ABRACADABRA

AFRICA

ALWAYS ON MY MIND

AMERICAN HEARTBEAT

AMERICAN MUSIC

AND I AM TELLING YOU I'M NOT GOING

ANGEL IN BLUE

ANOTHER HONKY TONK NIGHT ON
  BROADWAY

ANOTHER SLEEPLESS NIGHT

ARE THE GOOD TIMES REALLY OVER (I
  WISH A BUCK WAS STILL SILVER)

ATHENA

(YOU'RE SO SQUARE) BABY, I DON'T
  CARE

BACK WHERE YOU BELONG

BE ITALIAN (TI VOGLIO BENE)

BIG CITY

BIG FUN

BIG LOG

BIG OLE BREW

BLUE EYES

BOBBIE SUE

BODY LANGUAGE

BORN TO RUN

BREAKIN' AWAY

CALL ME

CAN'T EVEN GET THE BLUES

CAT PEOPLE (PUTTING OUT FIRE)

CAUGHT UP IN YOU

CHICAGO, ILLINOIS

CIRCLES

CLOWN, THE

CONTROVERSY

COOL

COUNTRY BOY CAN SURVIVE, A

CRYING MY HEART OUT OVER YOU

CUTIE PIE

DANCE FLOOR

DANCE WIT' ME

DANCING YOUR MEMORY AWAY

DID IT IN A MINUTE

DIRTY LAUNDRY

DON'T FIGHT IT

DON'T TALK TO STRANGERS

DON'T WORRY 'BOUT ME BABY

DON'T YOU WANT ME

DOWN UNDER

DO YOU BELIEVE IN LOVE

DO YOU WANNA TOUCH ME (OH YEAH)

EARLY IN THE MORNING

EBONY AND IVORY

EDGE OF SEVENTEEN (JUST LIKE THE
  WHITE WINGED DOVE)

867-5309/JENNY

EMPTY GARDEN (HEY HEY JOHNNY)

EVEN THE NIGHTS ARE BETTER

EVERYBODY WANTS YOU

EYE IN THE SKY

EYE OF THE TIGER

FAKING LOVE

FANTASY

FEED ME: GIT IT

FIND ANOTHER FOOL

FOLIES BERGERE

FOOL FOR YOUR LOVE

FOOL HEARTED MEMORY

FOR ALL THE WRONG REASONS

FORGET ME NOTS

FREEZE-FRAME

GENIUS OF LOVE

GET CLOSER

GET DOWN ON IT

GIGOLO, THE

GIRL IS MINE, THE

GLORIA

GOIN' DOWN

GOODY TWO SHOES

GUS THE THEATRE CAT

HAND TO HOLD ON TO

HANG FIRE

HAPPY MAN

HARD TO SAY I'M SORRY

HEARTBREAKER

HEART TO HEART

HEAT OF THE MOMENT

HIT AND RUN

HOLD ME

HOLD ON

HOT IN THE CITY

HOW DO YOU KEEP THE MUSIC
PLAYING?

HURT SO GOOD

I CAN'T GO FOR THAT (NO CAN DO)

I DON'T KNOW WHERE TO START

I DON'T THINK SHE'S IN LOVE ANYMORE

IF HOLLYWOOD DON'T NEED YOU

IF IT AIN'T ONE THING . . . IT'S
ANOTHER

IF YOU'RE THINKING YOU WANT A
STRANGER (THERE'S ONE COMING
HOME)

I.G.Y. (WHAT A BEAUTIFUL WORLD)

I KEEP FORGETTIN' (EVERY TIME
YOU'RE NEAR)

I KNOW THERE'S SOMETHING GOING ON

I KNOW WHAT BOYS LIKE

I LIE

I LOVE ROCK 'N' ROLL

I'M GONNA HIRE A WINO TO DECORATE
OUR HOME

I'M NOT THAT LONELY YET

I RAN (SO FAR AWAY)

I REALLY DON'T NEED NO LIGHT

IT AIN'T ENOUGH

IT'S RAINING AGAIN

I'VE NEVER BEEN TO ME

I WON'T BE HOME TONIGHT

I WOULDN'T HAVE MISSED IT FOR THE
WORLD

JACK AND DIANE

JUKE BOX HERO

JUMP TO IT

JUST BE YOURSELF

JUST TO SATISFY YOU

KEEP THE FIRE BURNIN'

KEY LARGO

LEADER OF THE BAND

LEATHER AND LACE

LET IT WHIP

LET ME GO

LET ME TICKLE YOUR FANCY

LET THE FEELING FLOW

LOOK OF LOVE

LORD, I HOPE THIS DAY IS GOOD

LOVE COME DOWN

LOVE IN THE FIRST DEGREE

LOVE IS ALRIGHT TONITE

LOVE IS IN CONTROL (FINGER ON THE
TRIGGER)

LOVE ME TOMORROW

LOVE NEVER GOES AWAY

LOVE PLUS ONE

LOVE'S BEEN A LITTLE BIT HARD ON ME

LOVE'S COMIN' AT YA

LOVE WILL TURN YOU AROUND

MAKE A MOVE ON ME

MAKE UP YOUR MIND

MAKING LOVE

MAMA USED TO SAY

MANEATER

MAN ON THE CORNER

MAN ON YOUR MIND

MEEK SHALL INHERIT, THE

MEMORY

MESSAGE, THE

MICKEY

MIRROR, MIRROR

MISSING YOU

MOUNTAIN MUSIC

MURPHY'S LAW

MUSCLES

MY ATTORNEY, BERNIE

NEW WORLD MAN

1982

1999

WHERE EVERYBODY KNOWS YOUR NAME

WHITE WEDDING

WHY ME?

WIND BENEATH MY WINGS (HERO)

WOMAN IN YOU, THE

YOU ARE

YOU GOT LUCKY

YOU'RE THE FIRST TIME I'VE THOUGHT ABOUT LEAVING

YOUR LOVE IS DRIVING ME CRAZY

YOUR LOVE'S ON THE LINE

YOU TAKE ME FOR GRANTED

1984

ADULT EDUCATION

AFTER ALL THESE YEARS

AGAINST ALL ODDS (TAKE A LOOK AT ME NOW)

ALL I NEED

ALL MY ROWDY FRIENDS ARE COMING OVER TONIGHT

ALL OF YOU

ALL THE CHILDREN IN A ROW

ALL THROUGH THE NIGHT

ALMOST PARADISE . . . LOVE THEME FROM "FOOTLOOSE"

APPLE DOESN'T FALL, THE

ARE WE OURSELVES?

AUTHORITY SONG, THE

AUTOMATIC

BABY, I'M HOOKED (RIGHT INTO YOUR LOVE)

BABY BYE BYE

BEAT STREET BREAKDOWN

BLUE JEAN

BOP 'TIL YOU DROP

BORDERLINE

BORN IN THE U.S.A.

BOYS OF SUMMER, THE

BREAKDANCE

BREAKIN' . . . THERE'S NO STOPPING US

BRINGIN' ON THE HEARTBREAK

BRUCE

CARELESS WHISPER

CARIBBEAN QUEEN (NO MORE LOVE ON THE RUN)

CENTIPEDE

CITY OF NEW ORLEANS, THE

COLORED LIGHTS

COOL IT NOW

COVER ME

CRUEL SUMMER

DANCE HALL DAYS

DANCING IN THE DARK

DANCING IN THE SHEETS

DESERT MOON

DOCTOR! DOCTOR!

DON'T LET GO

DON'T LOOK ANY FURTHER

DON'T MAKE IT EASY FOR ME

DON'T WALK AWAY

DON'T WASTE YOUR TIME

DO THEY KNOW IT'S CHRISTMAS?

DO WHAT YOU DO

DRIVE

DYNAMITE

EASY LOVER

EAT IT

ELIZABETH

ENCORE

EYES WITHOUT A FACE

FAITHLESS LOVE

FEELS SO REAL (WON'T LET GO)

FIELDS OF FIRE

FINE FINE DAY, A

FOOTLOOSE

FOR A ROCKER

FREAKSHOW ON THE DANCE FLOOR

GHOSTBUSTERS

GIRL IN TROUBLE (IS A TEMPORARY THING), A

GIRLS

GIRLS JUST WANT TO HAVE FUN

GIVE IT UP

GIVE ME ONE MORE CHANCE

GLAMOROUS LIFE, THE

GOD BLESS THE U.S.A.

GOT A HOLD ON ME

HAPPY BIRTHDAY, DEAR HEARTACHE

HARD HABIT TO BREAK

HEAD OVER HEELS

HEART OF ROCK AND ROLL, THE

HELLO

HERE COMES THE RAIN AGAIN

HIGH ON EMOTION

HOLD ME NOW

HOLDING OUT FOR A HERO

HONEY (OPEN THAT DOOR)

I CAN DREAM ABOUT YOU

I CAN TELL BY THE WAY YOU DANCE
    (YOU'RE GONNA LOVE ME TONIGHT)

I CAN'T HOLD BACK

I DON'T KNOW A THING ABOUT LOVE

I DON'T WANNA LOSE YOUR LOVE

I FEEL FOR YOU

IF EVER YOU'RE IN MY ARMS AGAIN

IF THIS IS IT

IF YOU'RE GONNA PLAY IN TEXAS (YOU
    GOTTA HAVE A FIDDLE IN THE BAND)

I GOT MEXICO

I GUESS IT NEVER HURTS TO HURT
    SOMETIMES

I JUST CALLED TO SAY I LOVE YOU

I'LL WAIT

I'M SO EXCITED

INFATUATION

IN MY EYES

INNOCENT MAN, AN

IT'S A MIRACLE

I'VE BEEN AROUND LONG ENOUGH TO
    KNOW

I WANT A NEW DRUG

I WILL FOLLOW

I WOULD DIE 4 U

JAMIE

JAM ON IT

JOYSTICK

JUMP

JUMP (FOR MY LOVE)

JUST THE WAY YOU LIKE IT

LADY TAKES THE COWBOY EVERY
    TIME, THE

LANGUAGE OF LOVE, THE

LEFT IN THE DARK

LEGS

LET'S FALL TO PIECES TOGETHER

LET'S GO CRAZY

LET'S HEAR IT FOR THE BOY

LET'S STOP TALKIN' ABOUT IT

LET THE MUSIC PLAY

LIGHTS OUT

LIKE A VIRGIN

LIVIN' FOR YOUR LOVE

LONGEST TIME, THE

LONG HARD ROAD (THE
    SHARECROPPER'S DREAM)

LOVE HAS FINALLY COME AT LAST

LOVE LIGHT IN FLIGHT

LOVERBOY

LOVE SOMEBODY

LUCKY STAR

MAGIC

MAKE MY DAY

MIDDLE OF THE ROAD

MISSING YOU

MISSING YOU

MISS ME BLIND

MONA LISA LOST HER SMILE

MY EVER CHANGING MOODS

MY HOMETOWN

MY OH MY

NATURAL, THE

NEUTRON DANCE

NEW MOON ON SUNDAY

NOBODY TOLD ME

NO MORE LONELY NIGHTS

NO WAY OUT
OH, SHERRIE
ONCE IN A LIFETIME
ONLY FLAME IN TOWN, THE
ON THE DARK SIDE
ON THE WINGS OF A NIGHTINGALE
OUT OF TOUCH
PANAMA
PENNY LOVER
PRIDE (IN THE NAME OF LOVE)
PURPLE RAIN
PUTTING IT TOGETHER
RADIO GA-GA
REAL END, THE
REBEL YELL
REFLEX, THE
ROCK ME TONITE
ROCK YOU LIKE A HURRICANE
ROMANCING THE STONE
ROUND AND ROUND
RUN, RUNAWAY
RUNAWAY
RUNNER, THE
SAD SONGS (SAY SO MUCH)
SELF CONTROL
17
SEXY GIRL
SHE BOP
SHE'S STRANGE
SHE SURE GOT AWAY WITH MY HEART
SHE WAS HOT
SHOW HER
SHOW ME
SISTER CHRISTIAN
SO BAD
SOLID
SOMEBODY ELSE'S GUY
SOMEBODY'S NEEDIN' SOMEBODY
SOMEBODY'S WATCHING ME
SOMEDAY WHEN THINGS ARE GOOD
SOME GUYS HAVE ALL THE LUCK

SOMETHING'S ON YOUR MIND
SOMEWHERE DOWN THE LINE
SOUND OF GOODBYE, THE
SOUTH CENTRAL RAIN (I'M SORRY)
STATE OF SHOCK
STAY THE NIGHT
STILL LOSING YOU
STRUT
STUCK ON YOU
SUGAR DADDY
SUNGLASSES AT NIGHT
SWEETHEART LIKE YOU
SWEPT AWAY
TAXI
TEACHER TEACHER
TENDER SHEPHERD
TENNESSEE HOMESICK BLUES
THAT'S THE THING ABOUT LOVE
THAT'S THE WAY LOVE GOES
THEY DON'T KNOW
THIS WOMAN
THRILLER
TO ALL THE GIRLS I'VE LOVED BEFORE
TONIGHT
TONIGHT IS WHAT IT MEANS TO BE
  YOUNG
TWO TRIBES
UNCLE PEN
UNDERSTANDING
VALOTTE
WAKE ME UP BEFORE YOU GO-GO
WALKING ON A THIN LINE
WARRIOR, THE
WE BELONG
WELCOME TO THE PLEASUREDOME
WE'RE GOING ALL THE WAY
WHAT'S LOVE GOT TO DO WITH IT
WHEN DOVES CRY
WHEN WE MAKE LOVE
WHEN YOU CLOSE YOUR EYES
WHITE HORSE
WHO'S THAT GIRL?

WHO WEARS THESE SHOES?
WILD BOYS, THE
WRAPPED AROUND YOUR FINGER
YAH MO B THERE
YELLOW ROSE, THE
YOO, ME AND HE
YOU CAN'T GET WHAT YOU WANT (TILL YOU KNOW WHAT YOU WANT)
YOU LOOK SO GOOD IN LOVE
YOU MIGHT THINK
YOU'RE GETTIN' TO ME AGAIN
YOU'RE THE INSPIRATION

1985

AFTER THE FIRE
AIN'T NO ROAD TOO LONG
AIN'T SHE SOMETHIN' ELSE
ALIVE AND KICKING
ALL I NEED
ALL SHE WANTS TO DO IS DANCE
ALL YOU ZOMBIES
ALONG COMES A WOMAN
AMERICA IS
AND SHE WAS
AND WE DANCED
ANGEL
AS LONG AS WE GOT EACH OTHER
AXEL F
BABY'S GOT HER BLUE JEANS ON
BACK IN STRIDE
BEAT OF A HEART
BE NEAR ME
BE YOUR MAN
BETWEEN BLUE EYES AND JEANS
BIG TRAIN (FROM MEMPHIS)
BIT BY BIT
BROKEN WINGS
BURNING HEART
CALIFORNIA GIRLS
CALL ME
CALL TO THE HEART

CAN'T FIGHT THIS FEELING
CARAVAN OF LOVE
CARELESS WHISPER
CENTERFIELD
CHAIR, THE
CHERISH
C-I-T-Y
(CLOSEST THING TO) PERFECT
(COME ON) SHOUT
CONGA
COUNT ME OUT
COUNTRY BOY
COUNTRY GIRLS
COWBOY RIDES AWAY, THE
CRAZY
CRAZY FOR YOU
CRAZY IN THE NIGHT (BARKING AT AIRPLANES)
CRY
DARE ME
DEEP PURPLE
DON'T CALL HIM A COWBOY
DON'T CALL IT LOVE
DON'T COME AROUND HERE NO MORE
DON'T LOSE MY NUMBER
DON'T YOU (FORGET ABOUT ME)
DOWN ON LOVE
DOWN ON THE FARM
DRESS YOU UP
EASY LOVER
ELECTION DAY
EMERGENCY
EVERYBODY DANCE
EVERYBODY WANTS TO RULE THE WORLD
EVERYTHING I NEED
EVERYTHING SHE WANTS
EVERYTIME YOU GO AWAY
FACE THE FACE
FOOLISH HEART
FOREVER MAN
FORGIVING YOU WAS EASY

FORTRESS AROUND YOUR HEART

40 HOUR WEEK (FOR A LIVIN')

FOUR IN THE MORNING (I CAN'T TAKE
  IT ANYMORE)

FRANKIE

FREEDOM

FREEWAY OF LOVE

FRESH

FRIGHT NIGHT

GETCHA BACK

GIRL'S NIGHT OUT, A

GLORY DAYS

GOONIES 'R' GOOD ENOUGH, THE

GOTTA GET YOU HOME TONIGHT

HANGIN' ON A STRING
  (CONTEMPLATING)

HAVE MERCY

HEAT IS ON, THE

HEAVEN

HIGH ON YOU

HIGH SCHOOL NIGHTS

HIGHWAYMAN

HOW'M I DOIN'

I DON'T KNOW WHY YOU DON'T WANT
  ME

I DON'T MIND THE THORNS (IF YOU'RE
  THE ROSE)

IF I HAD A ROCKET LAUNCHER

IF YOU LOVE SOMEBODY SET THEM
  FREE

I'LL NEVER STOP LOVING YOU

I'M FOR LOVE

I'M GOIN' DOWN

I MISS YOU

I'M ON FIRE

I'M YOUR MAN

IN A NEW YORK MINUTE

I NEED MORE OF YOU

IN MY HOUSE

INVINCIBLE

IT'S ONLY LOVE

I WANT TO KNOW WHAT LOVE IS

I WONDER IF I TAKE YOU HOME

JESSE

JUNGLE LOVE

JUST ANOTHER NIGHT

JUST AS I AM

JUST ONE OF THE GUYS

KAYLEIGH

KEEPING THE FAITH

LASSO THE MOON

LAY YOUR HANDS ON ME

LET HIM GO

LIE TO YOU FOR YOUR LOVE

LIFE IN ONE DAY

LONELY OL' NIGHT

LOST IN THE FIFTIES TONIGHT (IN THE
  STILL OF THE NIGHT)

LOVE BIZARRE, A

LOVE IS ALIVE

LOVE IS THE SEVENTH WAVE

LOVERGIRL

LOVE THEME FROM "ST. ELMO'S FIRE"

LOVIN' EVERY MINUTE OF IT

MAKE MY LIFE WITH YOU

MAKE NO MISTAKE HE'S MINE

MATERIAL GIRL

MEN ALL PAUSE, THE

METHOD OF MODERN LOVE

MIAMI VICE THEME

MISLED

MISS CELIE'S BLUES

MONEY FOR NOTHING

MOONFALL

MORNING DESIRE

MR. TELEPHONE MAN

MUDDY WATER

MURPHY'S ROMANCE

MYSTERY LADY

MY TOOT TOOT

NATURAL HIGH

NEVER

NEVER ENDING STORY

NEVER SURRENDER

NEVER THE LUCK

NEW ATTITUDE

NIGHTSHIFT

19

NOBODY FALLS LIKE A FOOL

NOBODY WANTS TO BE ALONE

NOT ENOUGH LOVE IN THE WORLD

OAK TREE, THE

OBSESSION

OH, SHEILA

OLD HIPPIE

OLD MAN DOWN THE ROAD, THE

ONE LONELY NIGHT

ONE MORE NIGHT

ONE NIGHT IN BANGKOK

ONE OF THE LIVING

ONE OWNER HEART

ONLY THE YOUNG

OPERATOR

PART-TIME LOVER

PARTY ALL THE TIME

PEOPLE ARE PEOPLE

PERFECT STRANGERS

PERFECT WAY

PLACE TO FALL APART, A

POP LIFE

POWER OF LOVE, THE

PRIVATE DANCER

RAIN FOREST

RASPBERRY BERET

READ MY LIPS

RELAX

REMO'S THEME (WHAT IF)

RESTLESS HEART

RHYTHM OF THE NIGHT

RIVER IN THE RAIN

ROCK AND ROLL GIRLS

ROCK ME TONIGHT (FOR OLD TIMES SAKE)

ROCK OF RAGES

ROXANNE, ROXANNE

RUNNING UP THAT HILL

RUN TO YOU

ST. ELMO'S FIRE (MAN IN MOTION)

SANCTIFIED LADY

SAVE A PRAYER

SAVING ALL MY LOVE FOR YOU

SAY YOU, SAY ME (UNDER TITLE SONG OF "WHITE NIGHTS")

SEARCH IS OVER, THE

SENTIMENTAL STREET

SEPARATE LIVES (LOVE THEME FROM "WHITE NIGHTS")

SEVEN SPANISH ANGELS

SHE KEEPS THE HOME FIRES BURNING

SHE'S A MIRACLE

SHE'S SINGLE AGAIN

SHOUT

SHOW, THE

SILENT RUNNING (ON DANGEROUS GROUND)

SINGLE LIFE

SISTERS ARE DOIN' IT FOR THEMSELVES

SLEEPING BAG

SMALL TOWN

SMALLTOWN BOY

SMOOTH OPERATOR

SMUGGLER'S BLUES

SO IN LOVE

SOMEBODY

SOMEBODY SHOULD LEAVE

SOME LIKE IT HOT

SOMETHING IN MY HEART

SOME THINGS ARE BETTER LEFT UNSAID

SOUL KISS

SPANISH EDDIE

SPIES LIKE US

STEADY

STEP THAT STEP

STIR IT UP

SUDDENLY

SUGAR WALLS

SUMMER OF '69

SUN CITY

SUNSET GRILL

SUSSUDIO

SWEET, SWEET BABY (I'M FALLING)

TAKE ON ME

TALK TO ME

TELL ME ON A SUNDAY

THAT'S WHAT FRIENDS ARE FOR

THAT WAS YESTERDAY

THINGS CAN ONLY GET BETTER

THIS IS NOT AMERICA

THROUGH THE FIRE

'TIL MY BABY COMES HOME

TO LIVE AND DIE IN L.A.

TONIGHT SHE COMES

TOO LATE FOR GOODBYES

TOO MUCH ON MY HEART

TOUCH A HAND, MAKE A FRIEND

UNEXPECTED SONG

USED TO BLUE

VIEW TO A KILL, A

VOICES CARRY

WAKE UP (NEXT TO YOU)

WALKIN' A BROKEN HEART

WALKING ON SUNSHINE

WALK OF LIFE

WARNING SIGN

WAYS TO BE WICKED

WE ARE THE WORLD

WE BUILT THIS CITY

WE DON'T NEED ANOTHER HERO
(THUNDERDOME)

WEIRD SCIENCE

WE'RE GONNA MAKE IT (AFTER ALL)

WHAT ABOUT LOVE?

WHAT I DIDN'T DO

WHEN THE GOING GETS TOUGH, THE
TOUGH GET GOING

WHO'S HOLDING DONNA NOW?

WHO'S ZOOMIN' WHO

WILL THE WOLF SURVIVE?

WOULD I LIE TO YOU?

WRAP HER UP

YOU ARE MY LADY

YOU BELONG TO THE CITY

YOU CAN DREAM OF ME

YOU GIVE GOOD LOVE

YOU LOOK MARVELOUS

YOU MAKE ME WANT TO MAKE YOU
MINE

YOU SPIN ME ROUND LIKE A RECORD

YOU WEAR IT WELL

1986

ABSOLUTE BEGINNERS

ADDICTED TO LOVE

AIN'T NOTHIN' GOIN' ON BUT THE RENT

ALL CRIED OUT

ALL I NEED

ALL I WANTED

ALL THE LOVE IN THE WORLD

ALWAYS HAVE ALWAYS WILL

AMANDA

AMERICAN STORM

AT THIS MOMENT

BABY LOVE

BAD BOY

BE GOOD TO YOURSELF

BEAT'S SO LONELY

BEST MAN IN THE WORLD, THE

BEST OF ME, THE

BOP

BORN YESTERDAY

BRAND NEW LOVER

BRAND NEW WORLD

CAJUN MOON

CALLING AMERICA

CAN'T WAIT ANOTHER MINUTE

CAPTAIN OF HER HEART, THE

CAUGHT UP IN THE RAPTURE

CLUB PARADISE

COME BACK WITH THE SAME LOOK IN
YOUR EYES

COME ON IN (YOU DID THE BEST YOU
COULD DO)

COMING AROUND AGAIN

COUNT YOUR BLESSINGS

CRACK KILLED APPLEJACK

CRAZAY

CRUSH ON YOU

CRY MYSELF TO SLEEP

DADDY'S HANDS

DANCING ON THE CEILING

DANGER ZONE

DAY BY DAY

DEAR MR. JESUS

DESPERADO LOVE

DIAMONDS ON THE SOLES OF HER
SHOES

DIGGING YOUR SCENE

DIGGIN' UP BONES

DO ME BABY

DOMINOES

DON'T GET ME WRONG

DON'T SAY NO TONIGHT

DON'T UNDERESTIMATE MY LOVE
FOR YOU

DOWNTOWN TRAIN

DO YOU GET ENOUGH LOVE

DREAMTIME

EDGE OF HEAVEN, THE

EMOTION IN MOTION

EVERYBODY HAVE FUN TONIGHT

EVERYTHING THAT GLITTERS (IS NOT
GOLD)

FALLING

FALL ON ME

FEEL IT AGAIN

FINE MESS, A

FINEST, THE

FIRE WITH FIRE

FREEDOM OVERSPILL

FRENCH KISSIN'

FRIENDS AND LOVERS

FUTURE'S SO BRIGHT, I GOTTA WEAR
SHADES

GIVE ME THE REASON

GIVE ME WINGS

GLORY OF LOVE

GO HOME

GOIN' TO THE BANK

GOODBYE

GOOD FRIENDS

GOOD TO GO

GOT MY HEART SET ON YOU

GRACELAND

GRANDPA (TELL ME 'BOUT THE GOOD
OLD DAYS)

GREAT GOSH A'MIGHTY! (IT'S A MATTER
OF TIME)

GUITARS, CADILLACS, ETC., ETC.

GUITAR TOWN

HALF PAST FOREVER (TILL I'M BLUE IN
THE HEART)

HANDS ACROSS AMERICA

HARLEM SHUFFLE

HEADLINES

HEARTBEAT

HEARTBEAT IN THE DARKNESS

HEARTS AREN'T MADE TO BREAK
(THEY'RE MADE TO LOVE)

HEAVEN IN YOUR EYES

HELL AND HIGH WATER

HIGHER LOVE

HIP TO BE SQUARE

HOLDING BACK THE YEARS

HOLIER THAN THOU

(HOW TO BE A) MILLIONAIRE

HOW WILL I KNOW

HUMAN

HYPERACTIVE

I AM BY YOUR SIDE

I CAN'T WAIT

I CAN'T WAIT

I DIDN'T MEAN TO TURN YOU ON

I DO WHAT I DO

IF YOU LEAVE

I HAVE LEARNED TO RESPECT THE
POWER OF LOVE

I KNEW HIM SO WELL

I'LL BE OVER YOU

I'LL COME BACK AS ANOTHER WOMAN

I'M FOR REAL

I MUST BE DREAMING

IN LOVE

IN THE SHAPE OF A HEART

INVISIBLE TOUCH

IN YOUR EYES

IS IT LOVE

IS THIS LOVE

IT AIN'T COOL TO BE CRAZY ABOUT YOU

I THINK IT'S LOVE

IT'LL BE ME

IT'S IN THE WAY YOU USE IT

I WANNA BE A COWBOY

I WANT TO MAKE THE WORLD TURN AROUND

I WISH THAT I COULD HURT THAT WAY AGAIN

JUST ANOTHER LOVE

JUST IN CASE

KEEP YOUR HANDS TO YOURSELF

KING FOR A DAY

KISS

KYRIE

LADY SOUL

LAMBETH WALK

LAND OF CONFUSION

LEAVE ME LONELY

LET ME BE THE ONE

LET ME DOWN EASY

LET'S GO ALL THE WAY

LIFE IN A LOOKING GLASS

LIFE IN A NORTHERN TOWN

LIFE'S HIGHWAY

LIKE A ROCK

LIKE NO OTHER NIGHT

LISTEN LIKE THIEVES

LITTLE BIT MORE, A

LITTLE BIT OF LOVE (IS ALL IT TAKES), A

LITTLE ROCK

LIVE TO TELL

LIVING IN AMERICA

LIVING IN THE PROMISELAND

LONELY ALONE

LOVE IS FOREVER

LOVE TOUCH (THEME FROM "LEGAL EAGLES")

LOVE WALKS IN

LOVE WILL CONQUER ALL

LOVE ZONE

MAD ABOUT YOU

MAKIN' UP FOR LOST TIME (THE "DALLAS" LOVERS' SONG)

MAMA'S NEVER SEEN THOSE EYES

MANIC MONDAY

MAN SIZE LOVE

MATTER OF TRUST, A

MEAN GREEN MOTHER FROM OUTER SPACE

MIND YOUR OWN BUSINESS

MISSIONARY MAN

MODERN WOMAN

MOONLIGHTING

MOVE AWAY

MUSIC OF GOODBYE, THE

NASTY

NEVER AS GOOD AS THE FIRST TIME

NEVER BE YOU

NEXT TIME I FALL, THE

NIKITA

1982

NOBODY IN HIS RIGHT MIND WOULD'VE LEFT HER

NO ONE IS TO BLAME

NOTHIN' AT ALL

NOTHING IN COMMON

NOTORIOUS

NOW AND FOREVER (YOU AND ME)

ONCE IN A BLUE MOON

100% CHANCE OF RAIN

ONE I LOVED BACK THEN, THE (THE
    CORVETTE SONG)

ONE LOVE AT A TIME

ONE SUNNY DAY

ONE VISION

ON MY OWN

ON THE OTHER HAND

OPEN YOUR HEART

OPPORTUNITIES (LET'S MAKE LOTS OF
    MONEY)

PAPA DON'T PREACH

POWER OF LOVE, THE

PRETTY IN PINK

PRIDE IS BACK, THE

RAIN, THE

READY FOR THE WORLD

ROCKIN' WITH THE RHYTHM OF THE
    RAIN

ROCK ME AMADEUS

RUMORS

RUSSIANS

SANCTIFY YOURSELF

SARA

SATURDAY LOVE

SAVIN' MY LOVE FOR YOU

SECRET LOVERS

SECRET SEPARATION

SHAKE YOU DOWN

SHE AND I

SHE USED TO BE SOMEBODY'S BABY

SIDEWALK TALK

SLEDGEHAMMER

SO FAR AWAY

SO FAR SO GOOD

SOMEDAY

SOMETHING ABOUT YOU

SOMETIMES A LADY

SOMEWHERE OUT THERE

SPIES LIKE US

STRONG HEART

STRUNG OUT

STUCK WITH YOU

SUN ALWAYS SHINES ON T.V., THE

SUPER BOWL SHUFFLE

SUZANNE

SWEETEST TABOO, THE

SWEET FREEDOM

SWEET LOVE

TAKE IT EASY

TAKE ME HOME

TAKE ME HOME TONIGHT

TAKE MY BREATH AWAY (LOVE THEME
    FROM "PETER GUNN")

TAKEN IN

TARZAN BOY

TASTY LOVE

TENDER LOVE

THAT ROCK WON'T ROLL

THAT WAS THEN, THIS IS NOW

THERE'LL BE SAD SONGS (TO MAKE YOU
    CRY)

THESE DREAMS

THEY DON'T MAKE THEM LIKE THEY
    USED TO

THINK ABOUT LOVE (THINK ABOUT ME)

THIS COULD BE THE NIGHT

THIS IS THE TIME

THROWING IT ALL AWAY

TO BE A LOVER

TOGETHER THROUGH THE YEARS

TOMB OF THE UNKNOWN LOVE

TOO MANY TIMES

TOO MUCH IS NOT ENOUGH

TOUCH ME WHEN WE'RE DANCING

TRUE BLUE

TRUE COLORS

TUFF ENUFF

TWO OF HEARTS

TYPICAL MALE

UNDERGROUND

UNTIL I MET YOU

VICTORY

VIENNA CALLING

1987

CATCH ME (I'M FALLING)

CAUSING A COMMOTION

C'EST LA VIE

CHANGE OF HEART

CHERRY BOMB

CINDERELLA

COLD HEARTS/CLOSED MINDS

COME AS YOU ARE

COME GO WITH ME

CONTROL

CRAZY

CRAZY FROM THE HEART

CRAZY OVER YOU

CROSS MY BROKEN HEART

CRY FREEDOM

CRYING SHAME

DADDIES NEED TO GROW UP TOO

DAY-IN DAY-OUT

DEAR GOD

DEEPER LOVE

DIAMONDS

DIDN'T WE ALMOST HAVE IT ALL

DINNER WITH GERSHWIN

DOING IT ALL FOR MY BABY

DOMESTIC LIFE

DON'T DISTURB THIS GROOVE

DON'T DREAM IT'S OVER

DON'T GIVE UP

DON'T GO

DON'T GO TO STRANGERS

DON'T MAKE ME WAIT FOR LOVE

DON'T MEAN NOTHING

DON'T YOU WANT ME

DO YA'

DO YOU BELIEVE ME NOW?

DREAM WARRIORS

DRINK WITH ME TO DAYS GONE BY

DUDE (LOOKS LIKE A LADY)

EVERCHANGING TIMES

EVERY LITTLE KISS

EVERYWHERE

FACE IN THE CROWD, A

FAITH

FAKE

FALLIN' FOR YOU FOR YEARS

(YOU GOTTA) FIGHT FOR YOUR RIGHT
    (TO PARTY)

FINAL COUNTDOWN, THE

FINER THINGS, THE

FIRST WE TAKE MANHATTAN

FISHIN' IN THE DARK

FLAMES OF PARADISE

FOREVER AND EVER, AMEN

GIRLFRIEND

GIRLS, GIRLS, GIRLS

GIRLS I NEVER KISSED, THE

GIVE TO LIVE

GOD WILL

GOODBYE SAVING GRACE

GOOD TIMES

GO SEE THE DOCTOR

GOT MY MIND SET ON YOU

GOTTA SERVE SOMEBODY

HAD A DREAM ABOUT YOU, BABY

HAND THAT ROCKS THE CRADLE, THE

HAPPY

HAVE YOU EVER LOVED SOMEBODY

HEAD TO TOE

HEART AND SOUL

HEARTBREAK BEAT

HEARTS ON FIRE

HEAT OF THE NIGHT

HEAVEN IS A PLACE ON EARTH

HELL IN A BUCKET

HERE I GO AGAIN

HOLD ME

HOLIDAY

HONEYTHIEF, THE

HOURGLASS

HOUSEQUAKE

HOW DO I TURN YOU ON

HOW SOON WE FORGET

HUNGRY EYES

FLAME, THE

FOOLISH BEAT

GET OUTTA MY DREAMS, GET INTO MY
CAR

GIVE A LITTLE LOVE

GIVING YOU THE BEST THAT I GOT

GOING BACK TO CALI

GOIN' GONE

GONNA TAKE A LOT OF RIVER

GROOVY KIND OF LOVE, A

HAIRSPRAY

HANDS TO HEAVEN

HE'S BACK AND I'M BLUE

HOLD ME

HOLD ON TO THE NIGHTS

HONKY TONK MOON

HYSTERIA

I COULDN'T LEAVE YOU IF I TRIED

I DON'T WANNA GO ON WITH YOU LIKE
THAT

I DON'T WANNA LIVE WITHOUT YOUR
LOVE

I DON'T WANT TO LIVE WITHOUT YOU

IF IT DON'T COME EASY

IF IT ISN'T LOVE

IF YOU AIN'T LOVIN' (YOU AIN'T LIVIN')

IF YOU CHANGE YOUR MIND

I GET WEAK

I HATE MYSELF FOR LOVING YOU

I KNOW HOW HE FEELS

I LIVE FOR YOUR LOVE

I'LL ALWAYS COME BACK

I'LL ALWAYS LOVE YOU

I'LL LEAVE THIS WORLD LOVING YOU

I'M GONNA GET YOU

I'M GONNA MISS YOU, GIRL

I'M REAL

I'M YOUR MAN

IN MY DARKEST HOUR

I SHOULD BE SO LUCKY

I SHOULD BE WITH YOU

I STILL BELIEVE

I TOLD YOU SO

IT'S SUCH A SMALL WORLD

I'VE BEEN LOOKIN'

I WANNA DANCE WITH YOU

I WANT HER

I WON'T TAKE LESS THAN YOUR LOVE

JOE KNOWS HOW TO LIVE

JOY

JUST GOT PAID

JUST LIKE PARADISE

(DO YOU LOVE ME) JUST SAY YES

KISSING A FOOL

KOKOMO

LATE NITE COMIC

LET THE RIVER RUN

LIFE TURNED HER THAT WAY

LITTLE BIT IN LOVE, A

LITTLE WALTER

LOCO-MOTION, THE

LOOK WHAT YOU STARTED

LOOSEY'S RAP

LOVE BITES

LOVE OVERBOARD

LOVE SUPREME, A

LOVE WILL FIND ITS WAY TO YOU

LOVE WILL SAVE THE DAY

LOVIN' ON NEXT TO NOTHIN'

MAKE IT LAST FOREVER

MAKE IT REAL

MAKE ME LOSE CONTROL

MAMACITA

MAN IN THE MIRROR

MERCEDES BOY

MONKEY

MR. MONOTONY

MUSIC OF THE NIGHT, THE

MUSIC WENT OUT OF MY LIFE, THE

NAUGHTY GIRLS (NEED LOVE TOO)

NEVER GONNA GIVE YOU UP

NEVER KNEW LOVE LIKE THIS

NEVER TEAR US APART

NITE AND DAY

NOBODY'S FOOL

NOTHIN' BUT A GOOD TIME

OFF ON YOUR OWN (GIRL)

OLD FOLKS

ONE FRIEND

ONE GOOD WOMAN

ONE MOMENT IN TIME

ONE MORE TRY

ONE STEP FORWARD

1—2—3

OOO LA LA LA

OUT OF THE BLUE

PARADISE

PARENTS JUST DON'T UNDERSTAND

PERFECT WORLD

PHANTOM OF THE OPERA, THE

PIANO IN THE DARK

PINK CADILLAC

POUR SOME SUGAR ON ME

POWERFUL STUFF

PROVE YOUR LOVE

PUMP UP THE VOLUME

PUSH IT

RED RED WINE

ROCKET 2 U

ROLL WITH IT

RUNAWAY TRAIN

SAY IT AGAIN

SAY YOU WILL

SET 'EM UP JOE

SHATTERED DREAMS

SHE'S HAVING A BABY

SHE'S NO LADY

SIGN YOUR NAME

SIMPLY IRRESISTIBLE

SOMETHING JUST AIN'T RIGHT

STREETS OF BAKERSFIELD

STRONG ENOUGH TO BEND

SUMMER WIND

SWEET CHILD O' MINE

TENDER LIE, A

THIS MISSIN' YOU HEART OF MINE

THIS WOMAN'S WORK

TOGETHER FOREVER

TOO GONE TOO LONG

TURN IT LOOSE

TWO HEARTS

VALLEY ROAD, THE

WAIT

WANDERER, THE

WE BELIEVE IN HAPPY ENDINGS

WHAT SHE IS (IS A WOMAN IN LOVE)

WHAT'S ON YOUR MIND (PURE ENERGY)

WHEN IT'S LOVE

WHEN YOU SAY NOTHING AT ALL

WHERE DO BROKEN HEARTS GO

WILD, WILD WEST

WILDFLOWERS

WIND BENEATH MY WINGS (HERO)

WISHING WELL

YOUNG COUNTRY

YOU WILL KNOW

1989

ABOVE AND BEYOND

AFTER ALL THIS TIME

ALL I WANT IS FOREVER

ARE YOU EVER GONNA LOVE ME

BABY, I LOVE YOUR WAY

BABY COME TO ME

BABY'S GOTTEN GOOD AT GOODBYE

BACK TO LIFE

BATDANCE

BAYOU BOYS

BETTER LOVE NEXT TIME, A

BETTER MAN

BIG WHEELS IN THE MOONLIGHT

BLAME IT ON THE RAIN

BORN TO BE MY BABY

BUFFALO STANCE

BURNIN' OLD MEMORIES

BUST A MOVE

CAN'T GET OVER YOU

CAN U READ MY LIPS
CAN YOU STAND THE RAIN
CATHY'S CLOWN
CHURCH ON CUMBERLAND ROAD, THE
CLOSER THAN FRIENDS
COLD HEARTED
COME FROM THE HEART
CONGRATULATIONS
DIAL MY HEART
DON'T MAKE ME OVER
DON'T RUSH ME
DON'T WANNA LOSE YOU
DON'T YOU EVER GET TIRED (OF
   HURTING ME)
DREAMIN'
ETERNAL FLAME
EVERY LITTLE STEP
EVERY ROSE HAS ITS THORN
EVERYTHING I MISS AT HOME
FOREVER YOUR GIRL
FROM THE WORD GO
GIRL, YOU KNOW IT'S TRUE
GIRL I'M GONNA MISS YOU
GIVE ME HIS LAST CHANCE
GOOD THING
HANGIN' TOUGH
HAVE YOU HAD YOUR LOVE TODAY
(I WISH I HAD A) HEART OF STONE
HEAVEN
HEY BOBBY
HIGH COTTON
HIGHWAY ROBBERY
HIM OR ME
HOUSTON SOLUTION
HOW CAN I FALL
IF I COULD TURN BACK TIME
IF YOU DON'T KNOW ME BY NOW
I GOT DREAMS
I LIKE
I'LL BE LOVING YOU (FOREVER)
I'LL BE THERE FOR YOU
I'M NO STRANGER TO THE RAIN

I'M STILL CRAZY
IN A LETTER TO YOU
I SANG DIXIE
I STILL BELIEVE IN YOU
IT'S NO CRIME
I WONDER DO YOU THINK OF ME
JUST BECAUSE
JUST COOLIN'
KEEP ON MOVIN'
KILLIN' TIME
LET GO
LET ME TELL YOU ABOUT LOVE
LIKE A PRAYER
LISTEN TO YOUR HEART
LIVING PROOF
LIVING YEARS, THE
LOOK, THE
LOOK AWAY
LOST IN YOUR EYES
LOVE HAS NO RIGHT
LOVE OUT LOUD
LOVER IN ME, THE
LOVE SAW IT
LOVE SHACK
LOVIN' ONLY ME
LUCKY CHARM
ME MYSELF AND I
MISS YOU MUCH
MR. D.J.
MY FANTASY
MY HEART CAN'T TELL YOU NO
MY PREROGATIVE
NEW FOOL AT AN OLD GAME
NOTHING I CAN DO ABOUT IT NOW
OASIS
ONCE BITTEN, TWICE SHY
ONE GOOD WELL
ON OUR OWN
PULL OVER
PUT YOUR MOUTH ON ME
REAL LOVE
REMEMBER (THE FIRST TIME)

RIGHT HERE WAITING

RONI

SHE DON'T LOVE NOBODY

SHE DRIVES ME CRAZY

SHE'S GOT A SINGLE THING IN MIND

SHOWER ME WITH YOUR LOVE

SO GOOD

SPEND THE NIGHT (CE SOIR)

START OF A ROMANCE

STRAIGHT UP

SUNDAY IN THE SOUTH

SUPERWOMAN

SWEET, SWEET LOVE

TASTE OF YOUR LOVE

THEY WANT MONEY

THIS TIME

TIMBER, I'M FALLING IN LOVE

TOY SOLDIERS

TUMBLIN' DOWN

TURNED AWAY

WAITING FOR A STAR TO FALL

WHEN I SEE YOU SMILE

WHO YOU GONNA BLAME IT ON THIS
TIME

WHY'D YOU COME HERE LOOKIN' LIKE
THAT

WILD THING

YOUNG LOVE (STRONG LOVE)

Section III

THE WRITERS
(Alphabetically)

Aaronson, Irving

LOVELIEST NIGHT IN THE YEAR,
   THE
SONG ANGELS SING, THE

Aasim, B.

PLANET ROCK

Abbott, Charlie

AS WE WALK INTO THE SUNSET
FIVE SALTED PEANUTS

Abbott, Gregory

I GOT THE FEELIN' (IT'S OVER)
SHAKE YOU DOWN

Abner, Buford

DADDY O

Abner, Ewart G., Jr.

AT MY FRONT DOOR (CRAZY LITTLE
   MAMA SONG)
HONEST I DO
UP ON THE MOUNTAIN
YOU GOT ME DIZZY

Abrahams, Maurice

HE'D HAVE TO GET UNDER—GET
   OUT AND GET UNDER
HIGH, HIGH, HIGH UP IN THE HILLS
HITCHY-KOO
OH, YOU MILLION DOLLAR DOLL
PULLMAN PORTERS ON PARADE,
   THE
RAGTIME COWBOY JOE
WHEN THE GROWN-UP LADIES ACT
   LIKE BABIES (I'VE GOT TO LOVE
   'EM, THAT'S ALL)

Abrams, Colonel

HOW SOON WE FORGET

Abrams, Lester

MINUTE BY MINUTE

Abrams, Rita

MILL VALLEY

Abrams, Vic

NAPOLEON

Abreu, Zequinha

TICO-TICO

Ackerman, Jack

LASTING LOVE

Acklin, Barbara

HAVE YOU SEEN HER?
TWO LITTLE KIDS
WHISPERS (GETTIN' LOUDER)

Acuff, Roy

AS LONG AS I LIVE
BRANDED WHEREVER I GO
IT WON'T BE LONG (TILL I'LL BE
   LEAVING)
JUST TO EASE MY WORRIED MIND
THAT GLORY BOUND TRAIN
UNLOVED AND UNCLAIMED
WRITE ME SWEETHEART

Adair, Tom

EVERYTHING HAPPENS TO ME
IN THE BLUE OF EVENING
JULIE
LET'S GET AWAY FROM IT ALL
NIGHT WE CALLED IT A DAY, THE
THERE'S NO YOU
VIOLETS FOR YOUR FURS
WILL YOU STILL BE MINE?

Adams, A. Emmett

BELLS OF SAINT MARY'S, THE

Adams, Bryan

BACK TO PARADISE
HEARTS ON FIRE
HEAT OF THE NIGHT

HEAVEN
IT'S ONLY LOVE
LET ME DOWN EASY
RUN TO YOU
SOMEBODY
STRAIGHT FROM THE HEART
SUMMER OF '69
TEACHER TEACHER
THIS TIME

Adams, Dick

BEWARE (BROTHER, BEWARE)

Adams, Frankie

BEAUTIFUL EYES

Adams, Frank R.

BLOW THE SMOKE AWAY
I WONDER WHO'S KISSING HER
   NOW
WHEN YOU FIRST KISS THE LAST
   GIRL YOU LOVED

Adams, Kevin

COME ON EILEEN

Adams, Kurt

FOOL WAS I, A
SOMEWHERE ALONG THE WAY

Adams, Lee

BABY, TALK TO ME
BEFORE THE PARADE PASSES BY
BYE BYE BIRDIE
CAN'T YOU SEE IT?
DON'T FORGET 127TH STREET
GOLDEN BOY
HONESTLY SINCERE
HOW LOVELY TO BE A WOMAN
HYMN FOR A SUNDAY EVENING
I'M FASCINATING
I'VE JUST SEEN HER (AS NOBODY
   ELSE HAS SEEN HER)
I WANT TO BE WITH YOU
KIDS
LORNA'S HERE
LOT OF LIVIN' TO DO, A

MATING GAME, THE
NIGHTLIFE
NIGHT SONG
ONCE UPON A TIME
ONE BOY
ONE LAST KISS
PUT ON A HAPPY FACE
ROSIE
SPANISH ROSE
TELEPHONE HOUR, THE
THERE WAS A CROOKED MAN
THIS IS THE LIFE
THOSE WERE THE DAYS
WELCOME TO THE THEATRE
WE LOVE YOU BEATLES
WHAT DID I EVER SEE IN HIM?
WHILE THE CITY SLEEPS
YOU'VE GOT POSSIBILITIES

Adams, Marie

I'M GONNA PLAY THE HONKY
   TONKS

Adams, Mark

WATCHING YOU

Adams, Patrick

IN THE BUSH

Adams, Ritchie

AFTER THE LOVIN'
FLY BY NIGHT
HAPPY SUMMER DAYS
TOSSIN' AND TURNIN'

Adams, Stanley

DUEL IN THE SUN
HEARTSTRINGS
I COULDN'T BE MEAN TO YOU
I THREW A BEAN BAG AT THE
   MOON
JUBILEE
LA CUCARACHA
LITTLE OLD LADY
MY SHAWL
ROLLIN' DOWN THE RIVER
SING ME A SWING SONG
TAKE IT FROM ME

THERE ARE SUCH THINGS
WACKY DUST
WHAT A DIFF'RENCE A DAY MADE
   (A.K.A. WHAT A DIFF'RENCE A
   DAY MAKES)
YESTERTHOUGHTS

Adams, Wesley

HIM OR ME

Adamson, Harold

720 IN THE BOOKS
AFFAIR TO REMEMBER, AN
AROUND THE WORLD
AS THE GIRLS GO
AURORA
BLAME IT ON THE RHUMBA
CHANGE OF HEART, A
COMIN' IN ON A WING AND A
   PRAYER
DAYBREAK
DID I REMEMBER?
DIG YOU LATER (A HUBBA-HUBBA-
   HUBBA)
DON'T BELIEVE EVERYTHING YOU
   DREAM
EVERYTHING I HAVE IS YOURS
EVERYTHING'S BEEN DONE BEFORE
FERRYBOAT SERENADE, THE
GIGI
HAVE A HEART
HEIGH HO, THE GANG'S ALL HERE
HERE COMES HEAVEN AGAIN
HERE'S HOPING
HOW BLUE THE NIGHT
HOW MANY TIMES DO I HAVE TO
   TELL YOU?
I COULDN'T SLEEP A WINK LAST
   NIGHT
I DON'T CARE WHO KNOWS IT
I GOT LUCKY IN THE RAIN
I HIT A NEW HIGH
"I LOVE LUCY" THEME
IN THE MIDDLE OF NOWHERE
IT'S A MOST UNUSUAL DAY
IT'S A WONDERFUL WORLD
IT'S BEEN SO LONG
I WALKED IN
I WANT TO BE A MINSTREL MAN
JAMBOREE
LEGEND OF WYATT EARP, THE

LET'S GIVE LOVE ANOTHER CHANCE
LET'S GO BAVARIAN
LIFE CAN BE BEAUTIFUL
LIKE ME A LITTLE BIT LESS (LOVE
   ME A LITTLE BIT MORE)
LITTLE MAN WHO WASN'T THERE,
   THE
LOOK WHO'S HERE
LOVELY WAY TO SPEND AN
   EVENING, A
MANHATTAN SERENADE
MOONLIGHT MOOD
MUSIC STOPPED, THE
MY, HOW THE TIME GOES BY
MY FINE FEATHERED FRIEND
MY OWN
MY RESISTANCE IS LOW
ON THE TRAIL
SATAN NEVER SLEEPS
SERENADE TO THE STARS, A
TENDER IS THE NIGHT
THAT FOOLISH FEELING
THERE'S SOMETHING IN THE AIR
THIS CHANGING WORLD
THIS NEVER HAPPENED BEFORE
TIME ON MY HANDS
TONY'S WIFE
TOO YOUNG TO GO STEADY
TOP OF THE TOWN
WE'RE HAVING A BABY (MY BABY
   AND ME)
WHEN LOVE GOES WRONG
WHERE ARE YOU?
WHERE THE LAZY RIVER GOES BY
WITH A BANJO ON MY KNEE
WOODPECKER SONG, THE
YOU
YOU'RE AS PRETTY AS A PICTURE
YOU'RE A SWEETHEART
YOU'RE MY DISH
YOUR HEAD ON MY SHOULDER
YOU SAY THE NICEST THINGS, BABY
YOU SEND ME
YOU TOOK THE WORDS RIGHT OUT
   OF MY MOUTH

Adderley, Julian

SERMONETTE

Adderley, Nat

WORK SONG, THE

Allen, Timmy

(YOU'RE PUTTIN') A RUSH ON ME
I'M IN LOVE
WE'VE ONLY JUST BEGUN (THE
    ROMANCE IS NOT OVER)

Aller, Michele

TAKE ME HOME

Alley, Shelly Lee

TRAVELIN' BLUES

Allison, Andrew K.

DOWN ON THE FARM IN HARVEST
    TIME

Allison, Audrey

HE'LL HAVE TO GO
HE'LL HAVE TO STAY
IT'S A GREAT LIFE
TEEN AGE CRUSH

Allison, Jerry

MORE THAN I CAN SAY
PEGGY SUE
THAT'LL BE THE DAY

Allison, Jim

WHAT AM I GONNA DO ABOUT YOU

Allison, Joe

HE'LL HAVE TO GO
HE'LL HAVE TO STAY
IT'S A GREAT LIFE
LIVE FAST, LOVE HARD, DIE YOUNG
TEEN AGE CRUSH
WHEN YOU LEAVE, DON'T SLAM
    THE DOOR

Allison, Mose

ASK ME NICE

Allman, Greg

AIN'T WASTIN' TIME NO MORE
MELISSA
MIDNIGHT RIDER

Allsup, Joyce Ann

D. J. CRIED, THE

Almaran, Carlos

STORY OF LOVE, THE

Almeda, Margarite

CALLA CALLA

Almer, Tandyn

ALONG COMES MARY
SAIL ON SAILOR

Alomar, Carlos

FAME

Alpert, Herb

JERUSALEM
MAGIC MAN
(WHAT A) WONDERFUL WORLD

Alstone, Alex

DANCIN' WITH SOMEONE (LONGIN'
    FOR YOU)
MORE
SONATA
SYMPHONY
THERE IS NO BREEZE

Alter, Louis

BLUE SHADOWS
CIRCUS
COME UP AND SEE ME SOMETIME
DOLORES
DO YOU KNOW WHAT IT MEANS TO
    MISS NEW ORLEANS?
GOTTA FEELIN' FOR YOU
HUGS AND KISSES
IF I HAD A WISHING RING

I'M ONE OF GOD'S CHILDREN (WHO
    HASN'T GOT WINGS)
ISN'T LOVE THE GRANDEST THING?
LOVE AIN'T NOTHIN' BUT THE
    BLUES
MANHATTAN SERENADE
MELODY FROM THE SKY, A
MORNING, NOON AND NIGHT
MY KINDA LOVE
NINA NEVER KNEW
NO WONDER I'M BLUE
OVERNIGHT
PARIS
RAINBOW ON THE RIVER
SKY FELL DOWN, THE
THAT WONDERFUL SOMETHING
TWILIGHT ON THE TRAIL
WHAT A LIFE!
WHAT HAVE WE GOT TO LOSE?
YOU TURNED THE TABLES ON ME

Altfeld, Don

ANAHEIM, AZUSA AND CUCAMONGA
    SEWING CIRCLE, BOOK REVIEW
    AND TIMING ASSOCIATION
BUCKET "T"
LITTLE OLD LADY (FROM
    PASADENA), THE

Altman, Arthur

ALL ALONE AM I
ALL OR NOTHING AT ALL
AMERICAN BEAUTY ROSE
GREEN YEARS
I FALL IN LOVE WITH YOU EVERY
    DAY
I'LL PRAY FOR YOU
I WILL FOLLOW HIM
PLAY, FIDDLE, PLAY
YOU CAN'T HOLD A MEMORY IN
    YOUR ARMS

Altman, Michael

SONG FROM M*A*S*H (SUICIDE IS
    PAINLESS)

Altman, Robert

BLACK SHEEP

Alton, Alvin

MAMA, COME GET YOUR BABY BOY

Alton, Sharon

WHAT ABOUT LOVE?

Alvaeus, Bjorn

DOES YOUR MOTHER KNOW?
MAMA MIA

Amadeo, Jim

ARE YOU MINE?

Ames, Morgan

KEEP YOUR EYE ON THE SPARROW
  (BARETTA'S THEME)
UPTOWN SATURDAY NIGHT

Ammons, Albert

BOOGIE WOOGIE PRAYER
SHOUT FOR JOY

Ammons, Gene

RED TOP

Amos, Betty

SECOND FIDDLE (TO AN OLD
  GUITAR)

Amsterdam, Morey

RUM AND COCA-COLA

Amway, Jack

DOGGONE IT, BABY, I'M IN LOVE

Anders, Scott

HIGH COTTON

Anderson, Adrienne

COULD IT BE MAGIC
DAYBREAK

DEJA VU
I GO TO RIO
SOME KIND OF FRIEND

Anderson, Bette

I CAN'T REMEMBER

Anderson, Bill

8 X 10
BAD SEED
CERTAIN
CINCINNATI, OHIO
CITY LIGHTS
COLD HARD FACTS OF LIFE
EASY COME—EASY GO
FACE TO THE WALL
FIVE LITTLE FINGERS
GET A LITTLE DIRT ON YOUR
  HANDS
GET WHILE THE GETTIN'S GOOD
HAPPY BIRTHDAY TO ME
HAPPY STATE OF MIND
I CAN'T REMEMBER
I DON'T LOVE YOU ANYMORE
I GET THE FEVER
I'LL GO DOWN SWINGING
I-LOVE-   YOU DROPS
I MAY NEVER GET TO HEAVEN
I MISSED ME
I'VE ENJOYED AS MUCH OF THIS AS
  I CAN STAND
LORD KNOWS I'M DRINKING, THE
LOSING YOUR LOVE
MAMA SANG A SONG
MY LIFE
MY NAME IS MUD
MY WHOLE WORLD IS FALLING
  DOWN
NOBODY BUT A FOOL
ONCE A DAY
PEEL ME A NANNER
PO' FOLKS
RIVER BOAT
SAGINAW, MICHIGAN
SLIPPING AWAY
SOMETIMES
STILL (I LOVE YOU)
THAT'S WHAT IT'S LIKE TO BE
  LONESOME
THEN AND ONLY THEN

THINK I'LL GO SOMEWHERE AND
  CRY MYSELF TO SLEEP
THREE A.M.
TIP OF MY FINGERS, THE
WALK OUT BACKWARDS
WE MISSED YOU
WHEN TWO WORLDS COLLIDE
WILD WEEK-END

Anderson, Casey

FUGITIVE, THE (A.K.A. I'M A
  LONESOME FUGITIVE)

Anderson, Charles

I BELIEVE IN LOVE
WOMAN, WOMAN
WOMAN IN LOVE, A

Anderson, Deacon

RAG MOP

Anderson, Edmund

FLAMINGO

Anderson, Frank

LOVE ME! LOVE ME! LOVE ME!

Anderson, Gary

NOT ME
QUARTER TO THREE

Anderson, Ian

BUNGLE IN THE JUNGLE
LIVING IN THE PAST
MINSTREL IN THE GALLERY

Anderson, John

SWINGIN'

Anderson, John Murray

ANNABEL LEE
SIXTY SECONDS EVERY MINUTE (I
  THINK OF YOU)

YOUNG MAN'S FANCY, A

Anderson, Jon

AND YOU AND I
CHARIOTS OF FIRE (RACE TO THE END)
OWNER OF A LONELY HEART
ROUNDABOUT

Anderson, J. Skip

THERE'S NOTHING BETTER THAN LOVE

Anderson, Leroy

BELLE OF THE BALL
BLUE TANGO
FIDDLE FADDLE
FORGOTTEN DREAMS
PUSSYFOOT, THE
SERENATA
SLEIGH RIDE
SYNCOPATED CLOCK, THE
TYPEWRITER, THE

Anderson, Lewis

SOMEWHERE DOWN THE LINE
WHATEVER HAPPENED TO OLD FASHIONED LOVE

Anderson, Liz

BE QUIET, MIND
FUGITIVE, THE (A.K.A. I'M A LONESOME FUGITIVE)
IF I KISS YOU (WILL YOU GO AWAY)?
MAMA SPANK
MY FRIENDS ARE GONNA BE STRANGERS
PICK OF THE WEEK
RIDE, RIDE, RIDE
WORDS I'M GONNA HAVE TO EAT

Anderson, Maxwell

IT NEVER WAS YOU
LITTLE GRAY HOUSE, THE
LOST IN THE STARS
SEPTEMBER SONG
STAY WELL

Anderson, Melvin

I WONDER WHY

Anderson, R. Alex

COCKEYED MAYOR OF KAUNAKAKAI

Anderson, Robert

HE'S BACK AND I'M BLUE

Anderson, Stig

DANCING QUEEN
FERNANDO
I DO, I DO, I DO, I DO, I DO
KNOWING ME, KNOWING YOU
MAMA MIA
NAME OF THE GAME, THE
S.O.S.
WATERLOO

Anderson, Terry

BATTLESHIP CHAINS

Anderson, Will R.

TESSIE, YOU ARE THE ONLY, ONLY, ONLY

Andersson, Benny

CHIQUITITA
DANCING QUEEN
DOES YOUR MOTHER KNOW?
FERNANDO
I DO, I DO, I DO, I DO, I DO
I KNEW HIM SO WELL
KNOWING ME, KNOWING YOU
MAMMA MIA
NAME OF THE GAME, THE
ONE NIGHT IN BANGKOK
S.O.S.
TAKE A CHANCE ON ME
WATERLOO
WINNER TAKES IT ALL, THE

André, Fabian

DREAM A LITTLE DREAM OF ME
WHEN THEY PLAYED THE POLKA

Andreoli, Pete

NEW YORK'S A LONELY TOWN

Andreolli, John

HI, MOM!

Andrews, Chris

GIRL DON'T COME
IT'S ALRIGHT

Andrews, Lee

LONG LONELY NIGHTS

Andrews, Reginald

LET IT WHIP
LET'S WAIT AWHILE

Angelo, Judy Hart

WHERE EVERYBODY KNOWS YOUR NAME

Angelos, Bill

ONE MORE TIME

Anglin, Jack

ONE BY ONE
YOU AND ME

Anglin, Jim

ONE BY ONE
YOU AND ME

Angulo, Hector

GUANTANAMERA

Anisfield, Fred

BACKSTAGE

Anka, Paul

ADAM AND EVE
ANYTIME (I'LL BE THERE)

BROKEN HEART AND A PILLOW
   FILLED WITH TEARS
CRAZY LOVE
DANCE ON, LITTLE GIRL
DIANA
DID YOU HAVE A HAPPY BIRTHDAY?
EVERYBODY OUGHT TO BE IN LOVE
(YOU'RE) HAVING MY BABY
I DON'T LIKE TO SLEEP ALONE
IT DOESN'T MATTER ANYMORE
IT'S TIME TO CRY
JOHNNY'S THEME
LET ME TRY AGAIN
LET THE BELLS KEEP RINGING
LONELY BOY (I'M JUST A)
LONGEST DAY, THE
LOVE (MAKES THE WORLD GO
   'ROUND)
LOVE ME WARM AND TENDER
MY HOME TOWN
MY WAY
NO WAY OUT
ONE MAN WOMAN/ONE WOMAN
   MAN
PUPPY LOVE
PUT YOUR HEAD ON MY SHOULDER
SHE'S A LADY
SUMMER'S GONE
TEDDY
(I BELIEVE) THERE'S NOTHING
   STRONGER THAN OUR LOVE
YOU ARE MY DESTINY

Anonymous

DRILL, YE TARRIERS, DRILL
MADEMOISELLE FROM
   ARMENTIERES (HINKY DINKY
   PARLAY VOO)
SCHNITZELBANK
WE SHALL OVERCOME
WHEN THE SUN GOES DOWN

Ant, Adam

GOODY TWO SHOES

Anthony, John

KEEP ON SMILIN'

Anthony, Michael

AND THE CRADLE WILL ROCK
DANCE THE NIGHT AWAY
DREAMS
I'LL WAIT
JUMP
LOVE WALKS IN
PANAMA
WHEN IT'S LOVE
WHY CAN'T THIS BE LOVE

Anthony, Mike

GRASS IS GREENER, THE
I'LL NEVER DANCE AGAIN
POETRY IN MOTION
RONNIE, CALL ME WHEN YOU GET
   A CHANCE
SHE SAY (OOM DOOBY DOOM)

Anthony, Ray

BUNNY HOP, THE

Anton, Emil

DEAR LONELY HEARTS

Antonucci, Anthony

PHILADELPHIA, U.S.A.

Apolinar, Danny

YOUNG AND IN LOVE
YOUR OWN THING

Appel, Mike

DOESN'T SOMEBODY WANT TO BE
   WANTED
QUESTION OF TEMPERATURE, A

Appell, Dave

BRISTOL STOMP
CHA CHA CHA, THE
CHERIE
DANCIN' PARTY
DING-A-LING
DON'T HANG UP
DO THE BIRD

FISH, THE
GOOD TIME BABY
GRAVY (FOR MY MASHED POTATOES)
HEY BOBBA NEEDLE
LET'S DO THE FREDDIE
LET'S TWIST AGAIN
LODDY LO
MORNIN' BEAUTIFUL
POPEYE THE HITCHHIKER
SOUTH STREET
SWINGIN' SCHOOL
WAH WATUSI, THE
WILD ONE
WILDWOOD DAYS

Appice, Carmen

DO YA THINK I'M SEXY?
DO YOU THINK I'M DISCO?
YOUNG TURKS

Applegate, Mary

POWER OF LOVE, THE

Aquart, William

MY FANTASY

Aquaviva, Nick

AM I IN LOVE?
GHOST TOWN
IN THE MIDDLE OF AN ISLAND

Archbold, W. A.

MR. CAPTAIN, STOP THE SHIP (I
   WANT TO GET OFF AND WALK)

Archer, Harry

FROM BROADWAY TO MAIN STREET
I'D RATHER BE THE GIRL IN YOUR
   ARMS
I LOVE YOU
IT MUST BE LOVE
WHITE SAILS
YOU AND I

Archer, Margaret

WOULD JESUS WEAR A ROLEX

Babyface

DON'T BE CRUEL
GIRLFRIEND
I LOVE YOU BABE
ROCK STEADY

Bach, J. S.

JOY

Bacharach, Burt

ALFIE
ALWAYS SOMETHING THERE TO
    REMIND ME (THERE'S)
ANOTHER NIGHT
ANY DAY NOW
ANYONE WHO HAD A HEART
APRIL FOOLS, THE
ARE YOU THERE (WITH ANOTHER
    GIRL)?
ARTHUR'S THEME (THE BEST THAT
    YOU CAN DO)
BABY, IT'S YOU
BLOB, THE
BLUE ON BLUE
CASINO ROYALE
(THEY LONG TO BE) CLOSE TO YOU
DON'T MAKE ME OVER
DON'T YOU BELIEVE IT
DO YOU KNOW THE WAY TO SAN
    JOSE?
EVERCHANGING TIMES
EVERYBODY'S OUT OF TOWN
GREEN GRASS STARTS TO GROW,
    THE
HERE I AM
HOUSE IS NOT A HOME, A
I JUST DON'T KNOW WHAT TO DO
    WITH MYSELF
I'LL NEVER FALL IN LOVE AGAIN
I'M A BETTER MAN (FOR HAVING
    LOVED YOU)
I SAY A LITTLE PRAYER
KNOWING WHEN TO LEAVE
LET ME GO TO HIM
LIFETIME OF LONELINESS, A
LIVING TOGETHER, GROWING
    TOGETHER
LONG AGO TOMORROW
LOOK OF LOVE, THE
LOST HORIZON

LOVE POWER
MAGIC MOMENTS
MAKE IT EASY ON YOURSELF
MAKING LOVE
MAN WHO SHOT LIBERTY VALANCE,
    THE
MESSAGE TO MICHAEL
MY LITTLE RED BOOK
ODDS AND ENDS
ONE LESS BELL TO ANSWER
ONLY LOVE CAN BREAK A HEART
ON MY OWN
OVER YOU
PAPER MACHÉ
PLEASE STAY
PROMISES, PROMISES
RAINDROPS KEEP FALLING ON MY
    HEAD
REACH OUT FOR ME
SEND ME NO FLOWERS
STORY OF MY LIFE, THE
THAT'S WHAT FRIENDS ARE FOR
THEY DON'T MAKE THEM LIKE
    THEY USED TO
THIS GUY'S (GIRL'S) IN LOVE WITH
    YOU
TOWER OF STRENGTH
TRAINS AND BOATS AND PLANES
TWENTY-FOUR HOURS FROM TULSA
WALK ON BY
WHAT'S NEW, PUSSYCAT?
WHAT THE WORLD NEEDS NOW IS
    LOVE
WHO IS GONNA LOVE ME?
WHO'S BEEN SLEEPING IN MY BED?
WINDOWS OF THE WORLD, THE
WISHIN' AND HOPIN'
WIVES AND LOVERS
WONDERFUL TO BE YOUNG
YOU'LL NEVER GET TO HEAVEN

Bachelor, Ruth

KING OF THE WHOLE WIDE WORLD

Bachman, Randy

HEY YOU
LAUGHING
LET IT RIDE
NO TIME
ROLL ON DOWN THE HIGHWAY
TAKIN' CARE OF BUSINESS

THESE EYES
UNDUN
YOU AIN'T SEEN NOTHING YET

Backer, William

I'D LIKE TO TEACH THE WORLD TO
    SING (IN PERFECT HARMONY)

Badarou, Wally

LESSONS IN LOVE
RUNNING IN THE FAMILY

Badazz, Randy

RISE

Bader, Ernst

WHEN THE SNOW IS ON THE ROSES

Badger, Ronald

I WANT TO KNOW

Baer, Abel

DON'T WAKE ME UP, LET ME
    DREAM
GEE, BUT YOU'RE SWELL
HARRIET
HELLO, ALOHA, HOW ARE YOU?
HIGH UP ON A HILL TOP
IF YOU BELIEVED IN ME
I'LL LOVE YOU IN MY DREAMS
I MISS MY SWISS (MY SWISS MISS
    MISSES ME)
I'M SITTING PRETTY IN A PRETTY
    LITTLE CITY
IT'S THE GIRL
JUNE NIGHT
LAST TWO WEEKS IN JULY, THE
LET ME LINGER LONGER IN YOUR
    ARMS
LONESOME IN THE MOONLIGHT
LUCKY LINDY
MAMA LOVES PAPA (PAPA LOVES
    MAMA)
MY MOTHER'S EYES
THERE ARE SUCH THINGS
WHEN THE ONE YOU LOVE LOVES
    YOU

Baer, Barbara

RESPECTABLE ·
SWEET TALKIN' GUY

Baerwald, David

WELCOME TO THE BOOMTOWN

Baez, Joan

DIAMONDS AND RUST

Bagdasarian, Ross

ALVIN'S HARMONICA
ALVIN'S ORCHESTRA
ARMEN'S THEME
CHIPMUNK SONG, THE (CHRISTMAS
  DON'T BE LATE)
COME ON-A MY HOUSE
WITCH DOCTOR

Bagley, E. E.

NATIONAL EMBLEM

Baham, Roy

CHARLIE'S SHOES

Bahler, Tom

JULIE, DO YA LOVE ME
LIVING IN A HOUSE DIVIDED
SHE'S OUT OF MY LIFE

Bailey, Jim

EVERYBODY PLAYS THE FOOL

Bailey, Phil

EASY LOVER

Bailey, Philip

SATURDAY NITE
SHINING STAR
THAT'S THE WAY OF THE WORLD

Bailey, Red

SOFTLY AND TENDERLY (I'LL HOLD
  YOU IN MY ARMS)

Bailey, Tom

DOCTOR! DOCTOR!
HOLD ME NOW
KING FOR A DAY
LAY YOUR HANDS ON ME
LOVE ON YOUR SIDE
NOTHING IN COMMON

Bainbridge, Margie

THIS WHITE CIRCLE ON MY FINGER

Baird, Dan

KEEP YOUR HANDS TO YOURSELF

Baird, Tom

BORN TO WANDER
DOES YOUR MAMA KNOW ABOUT
  ME?

Baker, A. H.

PLANET ROCK

Baker, Anita

GIVING YOU THE BEST THAT I GOT
SWEET LOVE
WATCH YOUR STEP

Baker, David

SOMEONE IS SENDING ME FLOWERS

Baker, Don

BLESS YOU

Baker, Irmgard

WEEP NO MORE, MY DARLIN'

Baker, Jack

I HEAR A RHAPSODY

Baker, James

IT'S BEEN A LONG TIME

Baker, LaVern

I CAN'T LOVE YOU ENOUGH

Baker, Mickey

LOVE IS STRANGE
TWO SHADOWS ON YOUR WINDOW

Baker, Phil

DID YOU MEAN IT?
INVITATION TO A BROKEN HEART
LOVE AND KISSES
STRANGE INTERLUDE

Baker, Yvonne

LET ME IN

Balderrana, R.

I NEED SOMEBODY

Baldridge, Fanny

LET'S DANCE

Baldwin, Donald

HAPPY PEOPLE

Baldwin, John

D'YER MAKER

Balfe, David

BEAUTIFUL SUNDAY

Balin, Marty

VOLUNTEERS

Ball, Ernest R.

AFTER THE ROSES HAVE FADED
  AWAY
ALL FOR LOVE OF YOU

ALL THE WORLD WILL BE JEALOUS
   OF ME
AS LONG AS THE WORLD ROLLS ON
DEAR LITTLE BOY OF MINE
DOWN THE WINDING ROAD OF
   DREAMS
FOR DIXIE AND UNCLE SAM
GOODBYE, GOOD LUCK, GOD BLESS
   YOU
I'LL FORGET YOU
I LOVE THE NAME OF MARY
IN THE GARDEN OF MY HEART
IRELAND IS IRELAND TO ME
ISLE O'DREAMS, THE
LETTER SONG
LET THE REST OF THE WORLD GO
   BY
LITTLE BIT OF HEAVEN, A (SHURE
   THEY CALLED IT IRELAND)
LOVE ME AND THE WORLD IS MINE
MOTHER MACHREE
MY HEART HAS LEARNED TO LOVE
   YOU, NOW DO NOT SAY GOODBYE
MY SUNSHINE JANE
OUT THERE IN THE SUNSHINE WITH
   YOU
SHE'S THE DAUGHTER OF MOTHER
   MACHREE
TEN THOUSAND YEARS FROM NOW
THAT'S HOW THE SHANNON FLOWS
TILL THE SANDS OF THE DESERT
   GROW COLD
TO HAVE, TO HOLD, TO LOVE
TURN BACK THE UNIVERSE AND
   GIVE ME YESTERDAY
WEST OF THE GREAT DIVIDE
WHEN IRISH EYES ARE SMILING
WHEN SWEET MARIE WAS SWEET
   SIXTEEN
WHEN THE BIRDS IN GEORGIA SING
   OF TENNESSEE
WILL YOU LOVE ME IN DECEMBER
   AS YOU DO IN MAY?
YOU PLANTED A ROSE IN THE
   GARDEN OF LOVE

Ball, Kenny

MIDNIGHT IN MOSCOW

Ball, Noel

OH JULIE

Ball, Roger

CUT THE CAKE
PICK UP THE PIECES

Ballard, Clint, Jr.

GAME OF LOVE, THE
GINGER BREAD
GOOD TIMIN'
I'M ALIVE
IT'S JUST A LITTLE BIT TOO LATE
JUMPING JACK
LADDER OF LOVE, THE
LITTLE BITTY GIRL
ONE OF US (WILL WEEP TONIGHT)
YOU'RE NO GOOD

Ballard, F. D.

PLEASE HANDLE WITH CARE

Ballard, Glen

ALL I NEED
MAN IN THE MIRROR
YOU LOOK SO GOOD IN LOVE

Ballard, Hank

DANCE WITH ME HENRY
FINGER POPPIN' TIME
LET'S GO, LET'S GO, LET'S GO
SEXY WAYS
TWIST, THE
WORK WITH ME ANNIE

Ballard, Pat

MISTER SANDMAN
OH, BABY MINE (I GET SO LONELY)
SO BEATS MY HEART FOR YOU

Ballard, Russ

BORDER, THE
I KNOW THERE'S SOMETHING GOING
   ON
LIAR
NEW YORK GROOVE
WINNING
YOU CAN DO MAGIC

Ballman, Wanda

IF YOU'RE NOT GONE TOO LONG

Balthrop, J. A.

FAMILY MAN

Banko, Gordon

SANCTIFIED LADY

Banks, Anthony

FOLLOW YOU FOLLOW ME

Banks, Darrell

OPEN THE DOOR TO YOUR HEART

Banks, Homer

I COULD NEVER BE PRESIDENT
(IF LOVING YOU IS WRONG) I DON'T
   WANT TO BE RIGHT
IF YOU'RE READY (COME GO WITH
   ME)
I LIKE WHAT YOU'RE DOING (TO ME)
TAKE CARE OF YOUR HOMEWORK
TAXI
TOUCH A HAND, MAKE A FRIEND
WHO'S MAKING LOVE?

Banks, Larry

GO NOW

Banks, Tony

IN TOO DEEP
INVISIBLE TOUCH
LAND OF CONFUSION
NO REPLY AT ALL
THAT'S ALL
THROWING IT ALL AWAY
TONIGHT, TONIGHT, TONIGHT

Bannon, Royal C.

ONLY ONE LOVE IN MY LIFE

Bar-Kays, The

FREAKSHOW ON THE DANCE FLOOR
HIT AND RUN
SHAKE YOUR RUMP TO THE FUNK

Barbarin, Paul

BOURBON STREET PARADE

Barbata, John

ELENORE

Barberis, Billy

BIG WIDE WORLD
HAVE YOU LOOKED INTO YOUR
    HEART?
SINNER MAN

Barbieri, Gato

LAST TANGO IN PARIS

Barbosa, Chris

LET THE MUSIC PLAY

Barbour, Dave

DON'T BE SO MEAN TO BABY
    ('CAUSE BABY'S SO GOOD TO
    YOU)
I DON'T KNOW ENOUGH ABOUT YOU
IT'S A GOOD DAY
MAÑANA (IS SOON ENOUGH FOR ME)
WHAT MORE CAN A WOMAN DO?

Barcelata, Lorenzo

BELLS OF SAN RAQUEL, THE
MARIA ELENA

Barclay, Eddie

ONCE UPON A SUMMERTIME

Bare, Bobby

FIVE HUNDRED MILES AWAY FROM
    HOME
HAPPY TO BE UNHAPPY

Barefoot, Nathan C., Jr.

DANGER! HEARTBREAK AHEAD

Barer, Marshall

I'M JUST A COUNTRY BOY

Barge, Gene

QUARTER TO THREE
TWIST, TWIST SENORA
WE'RE GONNA MAKE IT

Barge, M.

LEAVING ME

Bargnesi, Alfio

MY GUITAR IS MY SWEETHEART

Bargoni, Camillo

AND THAT REMINDS ME (A.K.A. MY
    HEART REMINDS ME)

Barish, Jeff

HEARTS

Barish, Jesse

COUNT ON ME

Barkan, Mark

I DON'T WANNA BE A LOSER
IF I DIDN'T LOVE YOU
I'LL TRY ANYTHING
I'M GONNA BE WARM THIS WINTER
PRETTY FLAMINGO
SHE'S A FOOL
WRITING ON THE WALL, THE

Barker, Aaron

BABY BLUE

Barker, Bobby

I CHEATED ME RIGHT OUT OF YOU

Barker, Danny

SAVE THE BONES FOR HENRY
    JONES ('CAUSE HENRY DON'T EAT
    MEAT)

Barker, Rocco

I GO CRAZY

Barksdale, Chuck

USE YOUR HEAD

Barlow, Harold

I FOUND YOU IN THE RAIN
MAMA
THINGS I LOVE, THE

Barlow, John

MUSIC NEVER STOPPED, THE

Barnes, Benny

POOR MAN'S RICHES

Barnes, Billy

TOO LONG AT THE FAIR

Barnes, David

BUFFALO SOLDIER

Barnes, Don

IF I'D BEEN THE ONE
LIKE NO OTHER NIGHT

Barnes, F. J.

I'VE GOT RINGS ON MY FINGERS
    (OR, MUMBO JUMBO JIJIBOO J.
    O'SHEA)

Barnes, Howard

BLOSSOM FELL, A
I REALLY DON'T WANT TO KNOW

Belafonte, Harry

COCOANUT WOMAN
ISLAND IN THE SUN
SUZANNE (EV'RY NIGHT WHEN THE
 SUN GOES DOWN)
TURN AROUND

Belew, Carl

AM I THAT EASY TO FORGET?
DON'T SQUEEZE MY SHARMON
LONELY STREET
STAMP OUT LONELINESS
STOP THE WORLD (AND LET ME
 OFF)
THAT'S WHEN I SEE THE BLUES (IN
 YOUR PRETTY BROWN EYES)
WHAT'S HE DOIN' IN MY WORLD?

Bell, Anthony

I'M STONE IN LOVE WITH YOU

Bell, Archie

JAPANESE SUNSET, A
TIGHTEN UP

Bell, Bruce

TWENTY-SIX MILES (SANTA
 CATALINA)

Bell, Ken

SHINE, SHINE, SHINE

Bell, Kenneth

EVEN THE NIGHTS ARE BETTER
TOUCH ME WHEN WE'RE DANCING

Bell, Leroy

LIVIN' IT UP (FRIDAY NIGHT)
MAMA CAN'T BUY YOU LOVE

Bell, Robert

HOLLYWOOD SWINGING
LADIES NIGHT
MISLED

OPEN SESAME

Bell, Ronald

CELEBRATION
HOLLYWOOD SWINGING
LADIES NIGHT
MISLED
OPEN SESAME
VICTORY

Bell, Theresa

ARE YOU HAPPY?
BRAND NEW ME, A
MOODY WOMAN
WHAT'S THE USE OF BREAKING UP?

Bell, Thom

BETCHA BY GOLLY, WOW
BREAK UP TO MAKE UP
DIDN'T I (BLOW YOUR MIND THIS
 TIME)
I'M COMING HOME
I'M DOIN' FINE NOW
I'M STONE IN LOVE WITH YOU
ROCKIN' ROLL BABY
RUBBERBAND MAN, THE
YOU ARE EVERYTHING
YOU MAKE ME FEEL BRAND NEW

Bell, Thomas

I'M SORRY
LA LA MEANS I LOVE YOU
READY OR NOT, HERE I COME
 (CAN'T HIDE FROM LOVE)
YOU GOT YOURS AND I'LL GET MINE

Bell, Vincent

RAIN, THE

Bell, William

I FORGOT TO BE YOUR LOVER
TO BE A LOVER
TRYIN' TO LOVE TWO

Bellamy, David

CRAZY FROM THE HEART

DANCIN' COWBOYS
FEELIN' THE FEELIN'
FOR ALL THE WRONG REASONS
IF I SAID YOU HAVE A BEAUTIFUL
 BODY, WOULD YOU HOLD IT
 AGAINST ME?
I NEED MORE OF YOU
KIDS OF THE BABY BOOM
LIE TO YOU FOR YOUR LOVE
OLD HIPPIE
SPIDERS AND SNAKES
SUGAR DADDY
TOO MUCH IS NOT ENOUGH
YOUR BULLDOG DRINKS
 CHAMPAGNE

Bellamy, Howard

LIE TO YOU FOR YOUR LOVE

Belland, Bruce

BIG MAN
EARLY IN THE MORNING (DOWN BY
 THE STATION)

Belle, Barbara

SUNDAY KIND OF LOVE, A

Bellin, Lewis

THIS IS THE NIGHT

Bellinger, Henry

STICK SHIFT

Bellis, Hal

CORN SILK

Bellmon, Johnnie

DON'T LET THE GREEN GRASS FOOL
 YOU

Bellotte, Pete

HEAVEN KNOWS
HOT STUFF
I FEEL LOVE

IT'S ALL WRONG, BUT IT'S ALL
RIGHT
LOVE TO LOVE YOU, BABY

Bellusci, Anthony J.

ROBBIN' THE CRADLE

Belmonte, José

ECSTASY TANGO

Belolo, Henri

BEST DISCO IN TOWN, THE
IN THE NAVY
MACHO MAN
Y.M.C.A.

Belvin, Jesse

DREAM GIRL
EARTH ANGEL (WILL YOU BE MINE)

Benatar, Pat

FIRE AND ICE

Benedict, Ernest

I'M BITIN' MY FINGERNAILS AND
THINKING OF YOU
OVER THREE HILLS

Benjamin, Bennie

CAN ANYONE EXPLAIN? (NO! NO!
NO!)
CANCEL THE FLOWERS
CONFESS
CROSS OVER THE BRIDGE
DANCIN' WITH SOMEONE (LONGIN'
FOR YOU)
DON'T CALL MY NAME
DON'T LET ME BE MISUNDERSTOOD
ECHOES
FUN AND FANCY FREE
GIRL!, A GIRL!, A (ZOOM-BA DI ALLI
NELLA)
HOW IMPORTANT CAN IT BE?
I DON'T SEE ME IN YOUR EYES
ANYMORE

I DON'T WANT TO SET THE WORLD
ON FIRE
I'LL NEVER BE FREE
I RAN ALL THE WAY HOME
I WANT TO THANK YOUR FOLKS
JET
MELODY TIME
OH! WHAT IT SEEMED TO BE
PIANISSIMO
RUMORS ARE FLYING
STRICTLY INSTRUMENTAL
SURRENDER
THESE THINGS I OFFER YOU (FOR A
LIFETIME)
TO THINK YOU'VE CHOSEN ME
WHEEL OF FORTUNE
WHEN THE LIGHTS GO ON AGAIN
(ALL OVER THE WORLD)

Bennard, Rev. George

OLD RUGGED CROSS, THE

Bennett, Boyd

MY BOY—FLAT TOP
SEVENTEEN

Bennett, Dave

BYE BYE BLUES

Bennett, George J.

YOU DIDN'T WANT ME WHEN YOU
HAD ME (SO WHY DO YOU WANT
ME NOW?)

Bennett, Joe

BLACK SLACKS
FUNNY, DEAR, WHAT LOVE CAN DO

Bennett, Milton

GO NOW

Bennett, Richard

FOREVER IN BLUE JEANS

Bennett, Rodney Richard

BROWN BIRD SINGING, A

Bennett, Roy C.

ALL THAT I AM
DON'T COME RUNNING BACK TO ME
IF I HAD A GIRL
KEWPIE DOLL
MY BONNIE LASSIE
NAUGHTY LADY OF SHADY LANE,
THE
NUTTIN' FOR CHRISTMAS
ON LONDON BRIDGE
PUPPET ON A STRING
STAIRWAY OF LOVE
STAY
STOP! AND THINK IT OVER
SUMMER SOUNDS
THANKS, MISTER FLORIST
WHEN THE BOY IN YOUR ARMS (IS
THE BOY IN YOUR HEART)
WONDERFUL WORLD OF THE
YOUNG, THE

Benoit, George

MY BELGIAN ROSE

Benson, Ada

YOUR FEET'S TOO BIG

Benson, Arthur C.

LAND OF HOPE AND GLORY, THE

Benson, Gary

LET HER IN

Benson, Ray

LETTER THAT JOHNNY WALKER
READ, THE

Benson, Renaldo

WHAT'S GOING ON

Bently, Gus

IF IT'S TRUE

Benton, Brook

BOLL WEEVIL SONG, THE
ENDLESSLY
FOR MY BABY
I'LL TAKE CARE OF YOU
IT'S JUST A MATTER OF TIME
KIDDIO
LIE TO ME
LOOKING BACK
LOVER'S QUESTION, A
MOTHER NATURE, FATHER TIME
REVENGE
ROCKIN' GOOD WAY (TO MESS
 AROUND AND FALL IN LOVE), A
SO CLOSE
THANK YOU PRETTY BABY

Berg, David

THERE'S A QUAKER DOWN IN
 QUAKER TOWN

Berg, Harold

FRESHIE

Berg, Matraca

FAKING LOVE
LAST ONE TO KNOW, THE

Bergantine, Borney

MY HAPPINESS

Bergdahl, Edith

ROCK AND ROLL POLKA
THAT'S WHAT I LIKE ABOUT THE
 WEST

Berger, Ida Irral

WARM AND TENDER LOVE

Bergere, Roy

HOW COME YOU DO ME LIKE YOU
 DO?

Bergman, Alan

ALL HIS CHILDREN
FIFTY PERCENT
GIRL WHO USED TO BE ME, THE
GOOD TIMES
GUAGLIONE (A.K.A. THE MAN WHO
 PLAYS THE MANDOLINO)
HIS EYES—HER EYES
HOW DO YOU KEEP THE MUSIC
 PLAYING?
I BELIEVE IN LOVE
IF WE WERE IN LOVE
I'LL NEVER SAY GOODBYE
I LOVE TO DANCE
IN THE HEAT OF THE NIGHT
IT MIGHT BE YOU
JERUSALEM
LAST TIME I FELT LIKE THIS, THE
MARMALADE, MOLASSES, AND
 HONEY
MARRIAGE-GO-ROUND, THE
MUSIC OF GOODBYE, THE
NICE 'N' EASY
ONE AND ONLY, THE
PAPA, CAN YOU HEAR ME?
PIECES OF DREAMS
SUMMER ME, WINTER ME
THAT FACE
WAY HE MAKES ME FEEL, THE
WAY WE WERE, THE
WHAT ARE YOU DOING THE REST
 OF YOUR LIFE?
WINDMILLS OF YOUR MIND, THE
YELLOW BIRD
YOU DON'T BRING ME FLOWERS

Bergman, Marilyn

ALL HIS CHILDREN
FIFTY PERCENT
GIRL WHO USED TO BE ME, THE
GOOD TIMES
GUAGLIONE (A.K.A. THE MAN WHO
 PLAYS THE MANDOLINO)
HIS EYES—HER EYES
HOW DO YOU KEEP THE MUSIC
 PLAYING?

I BELIEVE IN LOVE
IF WE WERE IN LOVE
I'LL NEVER SAY GOODBYE
I LOVE TO DANCE
IN THE HEAT OF THE NIGHT
IT MIGHT BE YOU
JERUSALEM
LAST TIME I FELT LIKE THIS, THE
MARMALADE, MOLASSES, AND
 HONEY
MARRIAGE-GO-ROUND, THE
MUSIC OF GOODBYE, THE
NICE 'N' EASY
ONE AND ONLY, THE
PAPA, CAN YOU HEAR ME?
PIECES OF DREAMS
SUMMER ME, WINTER ME
WAY HE MAKES ME FEEL, THE
WAY WE WERE, THE
WHAT ARE YOU DOING THE REST
 OF YOUR LIFE?
WINDMILLS OF YOUR MIND, THE
YOU DON'T BRING ME FLOWERS

Berk, Morty

EVERY DAY OF MY LIFE
HEARTBREAKER
TEA LEAVES

Berkeley, Charles W.

HAND THAT ROCKS THE CRADLE,
 THE

Berle, Milton

I

Berlin, Irving

ACROSS THE BREAKFAST TABLE
 (LOOKING AT YOU)
AFTER YOU GET WHAT YOU WANT,
 YOU DON'T WANT IT
ALEXANDER AND HIS CLARINET
ALEXANDER'S BAG-PIPE BAND
ALEXANDER'S RAGTIME BAND
ALL ALONE
ALL BY MYSELF
ALL OF MY LIFE
ALONG CAME RUTH
ALWAYS

ANY BONDS TODAY?
ANYTHING YOU CAN DO
ARABY
ARMS FOR THE LOVE OF AMERICA
(THE ARMY ORDNANCE SONG)
AT PEACE WITH THE WORLD
AT THE DEVIL'S BALL
BACK TO BACK
BEAUTIFUL FACES NEED BEAUTIFUL
CLOTHES
BE CAREFUL, IT'S MY HEART
BECAUSE I LOVE YOU
BEGGING FOR LOVE
BEST THING FOR YOU, THE
BEST THINGS HAPPEN WHILE
YOU'RE DANCING, THE
BETTER LUCK NEXT TIME
BLUE DEVILS OF FRANCE, THE
BLUE SKIES
BUTTERFINGERS
BUT WHERE ARE YOU?
CALL ME UP SOME RAINY
AFTERNOON
CALL OF THE SOUTH, THE
CHANGE PARTNERS
CHEEK TO CHEEK
CHICKEN WALK, THE
COHEN OWES ME NINETY-SEVEN
DOLLARS
COUNT YOUR BLESSINGS (INSTEAD
OF SHEEP)
COUPLE OF SONG AND DANCE MEN,
A
COUPLE OF SWELLS, A
CRINOLINE DAYS
DOIN' WHAT COMES NATUR'LLY
DO IT AGAIN
EASTER PARADE
EMPTY POCKETS FILLED WITH LOVE
EPHRAHAM PLAYED UPON THE
PIANO
EVERYBODY KNEW BUT ME
EVERYBODY'S DOIN' IT NOW
EVERYBODY STEP
FELLA WITH AN UMBRELLA, A
FOR THE VERY FIRST TIME
FREEDOM TRAIN, THE
GET THEE BEHIND ME SATAN
GIRL ON THE MAGAZINE COVER,
THE
GIRL ON THE POLICE GAZETTE,
THE
GIRLS OF MY DREAMS, THE

GIRL THAT I MARRY, THE
GIVE ME YOUR TIRED, YOUR POOR
GLAD TO BE HOME
GOD BLESS AMERICA
GRIZZLY BEAR
HAPPY HOLIDAY
HARLEM ON MY MIND
HE AIN'T GOT RHYTHM
HEAT WAVE
HE'S A DEVIL IN HIS OWN HOME
TOWN
HE'S A RAG PICKER
HOME AGAIN BLUES
HOMESICK
HOMEWORK
HOSTESS WITH THE MOSTES' ON
THE BALL, THE
HOW ABOUT ME?
HOW DEEP IS THE OCEAN?
HOW MANY TIMES?
HOW'S CHANCES?
I CAN ALWAYS FIND A LITTLE
SUNSHINE IN THE Y.M.C.A.
I CAN'T DO WITHOUT YOU
I CAN'T REMEMBER
I'D RATHER LEAD A BAND
IF YOU DON'T WANT MY PEACHES
(YOU'D BETTER STOP SHAKING
MY TREE)
I GOT LOST IN HIS ARMS
I GOT THE SUN IN THE MORNING
I LEFT MY HEART AT THE STAGE
DOOR CANTEEN
I'LL SEE YOU IN C-U-B-A
I LOVE A PIANO
I'M AN INDIAN TOO
I'M A VAMP FROM EAST BROADWAY
I'M GETTING TIRED SO I CAN SLEEP
I'M GONNA GET HIM
I'M GONNA PIN MY MEDAL ON THE
GIRL I LEFT BEHIND
I'M ON MY WAY HOME
I'M PLAYING WITH FIRE
I'M PUTTING ALL MY EGGS IN ONE
BASKET
I'M SORRY FOR MYSELF
I NEVER HAD A CHANCE
IN FLORIDA AMONG THE PALMS
IN MY HAREM
I POURED MY HEART INTO A SONG
I SAY IT'S SPINACH
ISN'T THIS A LOVELY DAY?
IT ALL BELONGS TO ME

I THREW A KISS IN THE OCEAN
IT ONLY HAPPENS WHEN I DANCE
WITH YOU
IT'S A LOVELY DAY TOMORROW
I'VE GOT MY CAPTAIN WORKING
FOR ME NOW
I'VE GOT MY LOVE TO KEEP ME
WARM
I USED TO BE COLOR BLIND
I WANT TO GO BACK TO MICHIGAN,
DOWN ON THE FARM
JUST A BLUE SERGE SUIT
JUST ONE WAY TO SAY I LOVE YOU
KATE (HAVE I COME TOO EARLY
TOO LATE)
KISS ME, MY HONEY, KISS ME
LADY OF THE EVENING
LATINS KNOW HOW
LAZY
LEARN TO DO THE STRUT
LET ME SING AND I'M HAPPY
LET'S FACE THE MUSIC AND DANCE
LET'S GO BACK TO THE WALTZ
LET'S GO WEST AGAIN
LET'S HAVE ANOTHER CUP OF
COFFEE
LET'S START THE NEW YEAR RIGHT
LET'S TAKE AN OLD FASHIONED
WALK
LET YOURSELF GO
LISTENING
LITTLE BUNGALOW, A
LITTLE BUTTERFLY
LITTLE THINGS IN LIFE, THE
LONELY HEART
LOOKING AT YOU (ACROSS THE
BREAKFAST TABLE)
LOUISIANA PURCHASE
LOVE, YOU DIDN'T DO RIGHT BY ME
LOVE AND THE WEATHER
LUCKY BOY
MANDY
MARIE
MARIE FROM SUNNY ITALY
MARRYING FOR LOVE
MAYBE IT'S BECAUSE I LOVE YOU
MUCH
ME
ME AND MY MELINDA
MINSTREL PARADE
MOONSHINE LULLABY
MR. MONOTONY
MY BIRD OF PARADISE

MY DEFENSES ARE DOWN
MY WALKING STICK
MY WIFE'S GONE TO THE COUNTRY, HURRAH! HURRAH!
NEXT TO YOUR MOTHER, WHO DO YOU LOVE?
NOBODY KNOWS (AND NOBODY SEEMS TO CARE)
NO STRINGS (I'M FANCY FREE)
NOT FOR ALL THE RICE IN CHINA
NOW IT CAN BE TOLD
OCARINA, THE
OH, HOW I HATE TO GET UP IN THE MORNING
OH, HOW THAT GERMAN COULD LOVE
OH, THAT BEAUTIFUL RAG
OLD FASHIONED TUNE IS ALWAYS NEW, AN
ON A ROOF IN MANHATTAN
OO—MAYBE IT'S YOU
ORANGE GROVE IN CALIFORNIA, AN
PACK UP YOUR SINS AND GO TO THE DEVIL
PIANO MAN
PICCOLINO, THE
PIGTAILS AND FRECKLES
PLAY A SIMPLE MELODY
PRETTY GIRL IS LIKE A MELODY, A
PULLMAN PORTERS ON PARADE, THE
PUTTIN' ON THE RITZ
RAGTIME VIOLIN, THE
REACHING FOR THE MOON
REMEMBER
ROSES OF YESTERDAY
RUSSIAN LULLABY
SADIE SALOME, GO HOME!
SAY IT ISN'T SO
SAY IT WITH MUSIC
SAYONARA
SECRET SERVICE, THE
SERENADE TO AN OLD-FASHIONED GIRL
SHAKING THE BLUES AWAY
SHE WAS A DEAR LITTLE GIRL
SISTERS
SLUMMING ON PARK AVENUE
SMILE AND SHOW YOUR DIMPLE
SNOOKEY OOKUMS
SOFT LIGHTS AND SWEET MUSIC
SO HELP ME
SOMEBODY'S COMING TO MY HOUSE

SOMEONE ELSE MAY BE THERE (WHILE I'M GONE)
SOME SUNNY DAY
SONG IS ENDED, THE (BUT THE MELODY LINGERS ON)
SONG OF THE METRONOME
SPANISH LOVE
STEPPIN' OUT WITH MY BABY
SUNSHINE
SUPPER TIME
SWANEE SHUFFLE
SYNCOPATED VAMP, THE
SYNCOPATED WALK
TELL ALL THE FOLKS IN KENTUCKY
TELL HER IN THE SPRINGTIME
TELL ME, LITTLE GYPSY
TELL ME A BEDTIME STORY
THAT INTERNATIONAL RAG
THAT MESMERIZING MENDELSSOHN TUNE
THAT MYSTERIOUS RAG
THAT REVOLUTIONARY RAG
THAT'S A GOOD GIRL
THERE'S A GIRL IN HAVANA
THERE'S NO BUSINESS LIKE SHOW BUSINESS
THEY CALL IT DANCING
THEY LOVE ME
THEY SAY IT'S WONDERFUL
THEY WERE ALL OUT OF STEP BUT JIM
THIS IS A GREAT COUNTRY
THIS IS THE ARMY, MR. JONES
THIS IS THE LIFE
THIS TIME (IS THE LAST TIME)
THIS YEAR'S KISSES
TOGETHER WE TWO
TO MY MAMMY
TOP HAT, WHITE TIE AND TAILS
WAITING AT THE END OF THE ROAD
WAIT UNTIL YOUR DADDY COMES HOME
WALTZ OF LONG AGO, THE
WASHINGTON TWIST, THE
WE'RE ON OUR WAY TO FRANCE
WE SAW THE SEA
WHAT DOES IT MATTER?
WHAT'LL I DO?
WHEN I GET BACK TO THE U.S.A.
WHEN I LEAVE THE WORLD BEHIND
WHEN I LOST YOU
WHEN IT'S NIGHT TIME IN DIXIE LAND

WHEN MY DREAMS COME TRUE
WHEN THE BLACK SHEEP RETURNS TO THE FOLD
WHEN THE FOLKS HIGH-UP DO THE MEAN LOW-DOWN
WHEN THE MIDNIGHT CHOO CHOO LEAVES FOR ALABAM'
WHEN WINTER COMES
WHEN YOU'RE DOWN IN LOUISVILLE (CALL ON ME)
WHEN YOU'RE IN TOWN
WHEN YOU WALKED OUT, SOMEONE ELSE WALKED RIGHT IN
WHERE IS THE SONG OF SONGS FOR ME?
WHISTLING RAG
WHITE CHRISTMAS
WHO DO YOU LOVE, I HOPE?
WHOSE LITTLE HEART ARE YOU BREAKING NOW?
WITH MY HEAD IN THE CLOUDS
WITH YOU
WOODMAN, WOODMAN, SPARE THAT TREE
YAM, THE
YIDDLE ON YOUR FIDDLE PLAY SOME RAGTIME
YOU CAN HAVE HIM
YOU CANNOT MAKE YOUR SHIMMY SHAKE ON TEA
YOU CAN'T BRUSH ME OFF
YOU CAN'T GET A MAN WITH A GUN
YOU CAN'T LOSE THE BLUES WITH COLORS
YOU'D BE SURPRISED
YOU KEEP COMING BACK LIKE A SONG
YOU'RE EASY TO DANCE WITH
YOU'RE JUST IN LOVE
YOU'RE LAUGHING AT ME
YOU'RE LONELY AND I'M LONELY
YOU'VE GOT YOUR MOTHER'S BIG BLUE EYES

Berlin, Murray

LATE, LATE SHOW, THE

Berline, Byron

APPLE DUMPLING GAME, THE

Berman, Irving

TIME OUT FOR TEARS

Bernard, Andrew

JUDY IN DISGUISE (WITH GLASSES)

Bernard, Felix

DARDANELLA
TWENTY-ONE DOLLARS A DAY—
   ONCE A MONTH
WINTER WONDERLAND

Bernard, Henry

I'LL SAIL MY SHIP ALONE
SITTIN' ON IT ALL THE TIME
WELL, OH WELL

Bernard, L. R.

BOB WILLS BOOGIE

Bernie, Ben

I CAN'T BELIEVE IT'S TRUE
STRANGE INTERLUDE
SWEET GEORGIA BROWN
WHO'S YOUR LITTLE WHO-ZIS?

Bernie, Saul

DON'T CRY, BABY

Bernier, Buddy

BAMBOO
BIG APPLE, THE
HEAR MY SONG, VIOLETTA
HURRY HOME
MILE AFTER MILE
NIGHT HAS A THOUSAND EYES, THE
OUR LOVE
POINCIANA (SONG OF THE TREE)

Berns, Bert

ARE YOU LONELY FOR ME?
EVERYBODY NEEDS SOMEBODY TO
   LOVE
HERE COMES THE NIGHT

I'LL TAKE GOOD CARE OF YOU
I WANT CANDY
PIECE OF MY HEART
TWENTY-FIVE MILES

Bernstein, Abe

THIS GIRL IS A WOMAN NOW

Bernstein, Alan

AFTER THE LOVIN'

Bernstein, Elmer

BABY, THE RAIN MUST FALL
BIRD MAN, THE
DELILAH JONES
LOVE WITH THE PROPER STRANGER
MAGNIFICENT SEVEN, THE
MAN WITH THE GOLDEN ARM, THE
MEATBALLS
SONS OF KATIE ELDER, THE
STEP TO THE REAR
THEME FROM "THE MAN WITH THE
   GOLDEN ARM"
TO KILL A MOCKINGBIRD
TRUE GRIT
WALK ON THE WILD SIDE
WHEREVER LOVE TAKES ME
WISHING DOLL, THE

Bernstein, Leonard

AMERICA
COOL
GEE, OFFICER KRUPKE
I CAN COOK TOO
I FEEL PRETTY
I GET CARRIED AWAY
IT'S LOVE
LITTLE BIT IN LOVE
LONELY TOWN
LUCKY TO BE ME
MARIA
NEW YORK, NEW YORK (THE
   BRONX IS UP AND THE BATTERY
   IS DOWN)
OHIO
ONE HAND, ONE HEART
QUIET GIRL, A
SOME OTHER TIME
SOMETHING'S COMING

SOMEWHERE
TONIGHT
WRONG NOTE RAG
YA GOT ME

Bernstein, Roger

THERE IS NO BREEZE

Berrios, Pedro

MY SHAWL

Berry, Bill

FALL ON ME
IT'S THE END OF THE WORLD AS
   WE KNOW IT (AND I FEEL FINE)
ONE I LOVE, THE
RADIO FREE EUROPE
ROMANCE
SOUTH CENTRAL RAIN (I'M SORRY)

Berry, Chuck

ALMOST GROWN
BACK IN THE U.S.A.
CAROL
JOHNNY B. GOODE
MAYBELLENE
MEMPHIS
MY DING-A-LING
NADINE (IS IT YOU?)
NO MONEY DOWN
NO PARTICULAR PLACE TO GO
PROMISED LAND, THE
REELIN' AND ROCKIN'
ROCK AND ROLL MUSIC
ROLL OVER BEETHOVEN
SURFIN' U.S.A.
SWEET LITTLE SIXTEEN
TOO MUCH MONKEY BUSINESS

Berry, Jan

ANAHEIM, AZUSA AND CUCAMONGA
   SEWING CIRCLE, BOOK REVIEW
   AND TIMING ASSOCIATION
DEAD MAN'S CURVE
DRAG CITY
HONOLULU LULU
I ADORE HIM
JENNIE LEE

SURF CITY
THREE WINDOW COUPE
YOU REALLY KNOW HOW TO HURT
A GUY

Berry, Jeff

RAINBOW RIDE

Berry, John

PONY TIME

Berry, Leon

CHRISTOPHER COLUMBUS

Berry, Richard

LOUIE, LOUIE

Berryhill, Robert

WIPE OUT

Bertini, U.

ON AN EVENING IN ROMA

Berton, Charles

DEAR OLD BROADWAY

Berzas, Carol

I'LL PIN A NOTE ON YOUR PILLOW

Bessinger, Frank Wright

OH! BOY, WHAT A GIRL

Best, Denzil

BEMSHA SWING

Best, Pat

I UNDERSTAND JUST HOW YOU FEEL

Best, William

FOR SENTIMENTAL REASONS (I LOVE
YOU)

Bestor, Don

CONTENTED
DOWN BY THE WINEGAR WOIKS

Betti, Henri

C'EST SI BON
WHAT CAN I DO?

Bettis, John

AS LONG AS WE GOT EACH OTHER
CRAZY FOR YOU
GOODBYE TO LOVE
HUMAN NATURE
I NEED TO BE IN LOVE
ONE MOMENT IN TIME
ONLY ONE LOVE IN MY LIFE
ONLY YESTERDAY
SLOW HAND
TOP OF THE WORLD
YESTERDAY ONCE MORE

Bettis, Jon

LIKE NO OTHER NIGHT

Betts, Dickey

JESSE
RAMBLIN' MAN
YOU'RE THE FIRST TIME I'VE
THOUGHT ABOUT LEAVING

Beul, Arthur

TOOLIE OOLIE DOOLIE (THE YODEL
POLKA)

Beverly, Frankie

BACK IN STRIDE
CAN'T GET OVER YOU

Bias, Gary

SWEET LOVE

Bibo, Irving

AM I WASTING MY TIME ON YOU?
CHERIE
MY CUTIE'S DUE AT TWO TO TWO
TODAY

Bickerton, Wayne

CAN'T STOP LOVING YOU
NOTHING BUT A HEARTACHE

Bickhardt, Craig

I KNOW WHERE I'M GOING
TURN IT LOOSE

Bideu, Lou

PERCOLATOR

Bierman, Arthur

MIDNIGHT MASQUERADE

Bierman, Bernard

MIDNIGHT MASQUERADE
MY COUSIN LOUELLA
VANITY

Biese, Paul

TEASIN'

Bigard, Albany "Barney"

"C"-JAM BLUES (OR "C" JAM BLUES)
CLARINET LAMENT
DOUBLE CHECK STOMP
MOOD INDIGO
SATURDAY NIGHT FUNCTION

Big Country

FIELDS OF FIRE
IN A BIG COUNTRY

Bigazzi, Giancarlo

GLORIA
SELF CONTROL

Bigelow, Bob

HARD HEARTED HANNAH (THE
    VAMP OF SAVANNAH)

Bigelow, F. E.

OUR DIRECTOR

Biggs, Andrew

PUMP UP THE VOLUME

Biggs, Cynthia

IF ONLY YOU KNEW

Biggs, Howard

GOT YOU ON MY MIND
MELANCHOLY ME
WRITE ME A LETTER

Bilk, Acker

STRANGER ON THE SHORE

Bimberg, Ed

THAT RAILROAD RAG

Bindi, Umberto

OUR CONCERTO
YOU'RE MY WORLD

Binnick, Bernard

KEEM-O-SABE

Biondi, Ray

BOOGIE BLUES

Birdsong, Edwin

ME, MYSELF, AND I

Birdsong, Larry

PLEADIN' FOR LOVE

Birtles, Beeb

HAPPY ANNIVERSARY

Bishop, Elvin

FOOLED AROUND AND FELL IN
    LOVE
TRAVELIN' SHOES

Bishop, Joe

BLUE EVENING
BLUE LAMENT
BLUE PRELUDE
OUT OF SPACE
WOODCHOPPER'S BALL

Bishop, Stephen

ANIMAL HOUSE
ON AND ON
SAVE IT FOR A RAINY DAY
SEPARATE LIVES (LOVE THEME
    FROM "WHITE NIGHTS")

Bishop, Walter

JACK, YOU'RE DEAD
MAD ABOUT YOU
SWING, BROTHER, SWING

Bivens, Burke

DON'T LET JULIA FOOL YA
JOSEPHINE

Bivins, Edward

THERE'S NO ME WITHOUT YOU

Bixio, C. A.

MAMA
SERENADE IN THE NIGHT
TELL ME THAT YOU LOVE ME

Bjorn, Frank

ALLEY CAT

Black, Ben

HOLD ME
MOONLIGHT AND ROSES

Black, Bobby

TELL ME DADDY

Black, Charlie

100% CHANCE OF RAIN
ANOTHER SLEEPLESS NIGHT
BLESSED ARE THE BELIEVERS
I KNOW A HEARTACHE WHEN I SEE
    ONE
LITTLE GOOD NEWS, A
SHADOWS IN THE MOONLIGHT
SLOW BURN
STRONG HEART

Black, Clint Patrick

BETTER MAN
KILLIN' TIME

Black, Don

BEN
BEST OF BOTH WORLDS
BORN FREE
COME BACK WITH THE SAME LOOK
    IN YOUR EYES
COME TO ME
DIAMONDS ARE FOREVER
FOR MAMA
SAM
TELL ME ON A SUNDAY
THUNDERBALL
TO SIR WITH LOVE
TRUE GRIT
UNEXPECTED SONG
WALKING TALL
WHEREVER LOVE TAKES ME

Black, Gene

LOVE TOUCH (THEME FROM "LEGAL
    EAGLES")

Black, James M.

WHEN THE ROLL IS CALLED UP
    YONDER (I'LL BE THERE)

Black, Johnny S.

DARDANELLA
PAPER DOLL
WHO'LL BE THE NEXT ONE? (TO
    CRY OVER YOU)

Black, William P.

SMOKIE—PART 2

Blackburn, Brian

LOVE IS BLUE

Blackburn, John

MOONLIGHT IN VERMONT
NEED YOU

Blackman, Bruce

MOONLIGHT FEELS RIGHT

Blackmon, James

1982

Blackmon, Larry

BACK AND FORTH
CANDY
FREAKY DANCIN'
JUST BE YOURSELF
SHE'S STRANGE
SINGLE LIFE
WORD UP

Blackmore, Richard

DEEP PURPLE
SMOKE ON THE WATER
STONE COLD
WOMAN FROM TOKYO

Blackwell, DeWayne

I'M GONNA HIRE A WINO TO
    DECORATE OUR HOME
MAKE MY DAY
MR. BLUE
OH THAT'S GOOD, NO THAT'S BAD

Blackwell, Otis

ALL SHOOK UP
BREATHLESS
DON'T BE CRUEL
(SUCH AN) EASY QUESTION
FOR MY GOOD FORTUNE
GREAT BALLS OF FIRE
HANDY MAN
HEY, LITTLE GIRL
JUST KEEP IT UP
ONE BROKEN HEART FOR SALE
RETURN TO SENDER

Blackwell, Robert

GOOD GOLLY MISS MOLLY
READY TEDDY

Blackwell, Robert A.

LONG TALL SALLY
RIP IT UP

Blackwell, Ronald

HAIR ON MY CHINNY-CHIN-CHIN,
    THE
HOW DO YOU CATCH A GIRL?
LI'L RED RIDING HOOD

Blades, Jack

FOUR IN THE MORNING (I CAN'T
    TAKE IT ANYMORE)
GOODBYE
SECRET OF MY SUCCESS, THE
SENTIMENTAL STREET
WHEN YOU CLOSE YOUR EYES

Blaha, Vaclav

BLUE SKIRT WALTZ, THE

Blaikley, Alan

HAVE I THE RIGHT?
I'VE LOST YOU

Blaikley, Howard

HAVE I THE RIGHT?
ZABADAK

Blair, Hal

GO BACK YOU FOOL
I'M YOURS
I WAS THE ONE
MY LIPS ARE SEALED
NINETY MILES AN HOUR ON A
    DEAD-END STREET
ONE HAS MY NAME, THE OTHER
    HAS MY HEART
PLEASE HELP ME, I'M FALLING
    (A.K.A. I CAN'T HELP YOU, I'M
    FALLING)
RINGO

Blaisch, Lois

COULD'VE BEEN

Blake, Charlotte

HARBOR OF LOVE, THE

Blake, Eubie

AIN'T YOU COMIN' BACK, MARY
    ANN, TO MARYLAND?
BANDANA DAYS
BUGLE CALL RAG
I'M JUST WILD ABOUT HARRY
LOVE WILL FIND A WAY
MEMORIES OF YOU
SHUFFLE ALONG
YOU'RE LUCKY TO ME

Blake, George

COME DANCE WITH ME

Blake, H. B.

WHEN THE MOCKING BIRDS ARE
    SINGING IN THE WILDWOOD

Blake, James W.

SIDEWALKS OF NEW YORK, THE

Blake, Tommy

THAT'S WHEN I SEE THE BLUES (IN
    YOUR PRETTY BROWN EYES)
TOO MUCH TO LOSE

Blakely, Ronnie

MY IDAHO HOME

Blanchard, Jack

TENNESSEE BIRDWALK

Blanchard, Ollie

PLEASE LOVE ME FOREVER

Blandon, Richard

COULD THIS BE MAGIC

Blane, Ralph

BIRMIN'HAM
BOY NEXT DOOR, THE
BUCKLE DOWN, WINSOCKI
COMMENT ALLEZ-VOUS? (HOW ARE
    THINGS WITH YOU?)
CONNECTICUT
DON'T ROCK THE BOAT, DEAR
EV'RY TIME
GIRLS WERE MADE TO TAKE CARE
    OF BOYS
HAVE YOURSELF A MERRY LITTLE
    CHRISTMAS
I LOVE A NEW YORKER
JOINT IS REALLY JUMPIN' AT
    CARNEGIE HALL
JUST A LITTLE JOINT WITH A JUKE
    BOX
LOVE
LOVE ON A GREYHOUND BUS
MY DREAM IS YOURS
OCCASIONAL MAN, AN
PASS THAT PEACE PIPE
SHADY LADY BIRD
SOMEONE LIKE YOU
STANLEY STEAMER, THE

THREE B'S, THE
TROLLEY SONG, THE
WHAT DO YOU THINK I AM?

Blank, Boris

OH YEAH

Blanvillain, Jean Marie

ALL OF A SUDDEN MY HEART SINGS

Blasingame, Al

BREAKIN' THE RULES

Blastic, Lee

THERE'S A NEW MOON OVER MY
    SHOULDER

Blatte, Marc

HANDS ACROSS AMERICA
PRIDE IS BACK, THE
WHEN SHE WAS MY GIRL

Blau, Eric

AMSTERDAM
CAROUSEL
IF WE ONLY HAVE LOVE
MADELEINE
MARIEKE
SONS OF . . .

Blaufuss, Walter

MY ISLE OF GOLDEN DREAMS

Blevins, Paul

LET ME BE THE ONE

Bleyer, Archie

BUSINESS IN F
EH, CUMPARI!

Bliss, Helen

I WENT OUT OF MY WAY
MOON WON'T TALK, THE

Bliss, Paul

HOW DO I SURVIVE?

Blitzstein, Marc

MACK THE KNIFE (A.K.A. MORITAT)
PIRATE JENNY

Bloch, Ray

IN MY LITTLE RED BOOK

Bloch, Walter

NEVER

Block, Alan

WALKIN' AFTER MIDNIGHT

Block, Martin

I GUESS I'LL HAVE TO DREAM THE
    REST
IT'S MAKE BELIEVE BALLROOM
    TIME
I WON'T BELIEVE IT
NEW MOON AND AN OLD
    SERENADE, A
WAITIN' FOR THE TRAIN TO COME
    IN

Bloodworth, Raymond

C'MON MARIANNE
JOY
WATCH THE FLOWERS GROW

Bloom, Bobby

INDIAN GIVER
MONTEGO BAY
MONY, MONY
SPECIAL DELIVERY

Bloom, Marty

DOES THE SPEARMINT LOSE ITS
    FLAVOR ON THE BEDPOST OVER
    NIGHT?

Bloom, Rube

COTTON
DAY IN—DAY OUT
DON'T WORRY 'BOUT ME
FEELIN' HIGH AND HAPPY
FOOLS RUSH IN
GIVE ME THE SIMPLE LIFE
HERE'S TO MY LADY
I CAN'T FACE THE MUSIC (WITHOUT
    SINGING THE BLUES)
IF I WERE SURE OF YOU
IT HAPPENS TO THE BEST OF
    FRIENDS
I WISH I COULD TELL YOU
LOST IN A DREAM
LOVE IS A MERRY-GO-ROUND
MAN FROM THE SOUTH, THE (WITH
    A BIG CIGAR IN HIS MOUTH)
MAYBE YOU'LL BE THERE
OUT IN THE COLD AGAIN
SOLILOQUY
SONG OF THE BAYOU
STAY ON THE RIGHT SIDE, SISTER
TAKE ME
TRUCKIN'
WHAT GOES UP MUST COME DOWN

Bloom, Vera

JALOUSIE (JEALOUSY)

Bloom, William

DOUBLE DUTCH BUS

Blossom, Henry

AIN'T IT FUNNY WHAT A
    DIFFERENCE JUST A FEW HOURS
    MAKE?
ALL FOR YOU
BECAUSE YOU'RE YOU
EILEEN ALANA ASTHORE
EVERY DAY IS LADIES' DAY WITH
    ME
IF YOU WERE I AND I WERE YOU
I'LL BE MARRIED TO THE MUSIC OF
    A MILITARY BAND
ISLE OF OUR DREAMS, THE
I WANT WHAT I WANT WHEN I
    WANT IT
KISS ME AGAIN

LOVE IS THE BEST OF ALL
MOONBEAMS
MY SAN DOMINGO MAID
NEAPOLITAN LOVE SONG
SPOOKY OOKUM
STREETS OF NEW YORK, THE (OR,
    IN OLD NEW YORK)
TELL IT ALL OVER AGAIN
THINE ALONE
TIME AND THE PLACE AND THE
    GIRL, THE
TWO LAUGHING IRISH EYES
WHEN SHALL I AGAIN SEE
    IRELAND?
WHEN YOU'RE AWAY

Blue, David

OUTLAW MAN

Blum, Harry

OUT IN THE MIDDLE OF THE NIGHT

Blume, David

TURN-DOWN DAY

Blunt, Robbie

BIG LOG

Bobbitt, C.

GIVE IT UP OR TURNIT A LOOSE

Bobyn, Alfred G.

AIN'T IT FUNNY WHAT A
    DIFFERENCE JUST A FEW HOURS
    MAKE?

Bocage, Edwin

MY DEAREST DARLING
SLIPPIN' AND SLIDIN' (PEEPIN' AND
    HIDIN')

Bocage, Peter

MAMA'S GONE, GOODBYE
SUD BUSTIN' BLUES

Bock, Jerry

ALL OF THESE AND MORE
ARTIFICIAL FLOWERS
DAYS GONE BY
DEAR FRIEND
DO YOU LOVE ME?
FAR FROM THE HOME I LOVE
FIDDLER ON THE ROOF
GENTLEMAN JIMMY
GOOD CLEAN FUN
GRAND KNOWING YOU
IF I WERE A RICH MAN
ILONA
I'M AVAILABLE
JUST MY LUCK
LITTLE OLD NEW YORK
MATCHMAKER, MATCHMAKER
MIRACLE OF MIRACLES
MR. WONDERFUL
NOW I HAVE EVERYTHING
POLITICS AND POKER
POPSICLES IN PARIS
SABBATH PRAYER
SHE LOVES ME
SUNRISE, SUNSET
TIL TOMORROW
TO LIFE
TONIGHT AT EIGHT
TOO CLOSE FOR COMFORT
TRADITION
VERY NEXT MAN, THE (I'LL MARRY)
WHEN DID I FALL IN LOVE?
WILL HE LIKE ME?

Bogan, Louise

UNBORN CHILD

Bogard, Steve

MORNIN' RIDE

Bogdany, Thomas F.

SHOUT! SHOUT! (KNOCK YOURSELF
    OUT)

Bohannon, Marion T.

BIG BASS VIOL, THE
WHEN BIG PROFUNDO SANG
    LOW "C"

Bolan, Marc

BANG A GONG (GET IT ON)

Boland, Clay

GYPSY IN MY SOUL, THE
I LIVE THE LIFE I LOVE
STOP! IT'S WONDERFUL
STOP BEATIN' ROUND THE
    MULBERRY BUSH
THERE'S NO PLACE LIKE YOUR
    ARMS
WHEN I GO A-DREAMIN'
YA GOT ME

Bolland, Ferdi

ROCK ME AMADEUS
VIENNA CALLING

Bolland, Rob

ROCK ME AMADEUS
VIENNA CALLING

Bolton, Guy

TILL THE CLOUDS ROLL BY

Bolton, Michael

HOW AM I SUPPOSED TO LIVE
    WITHOUT YOU?
I FOUND SOMEONE
THAT'S WHAT LOVE IS ALL ABOUT

Bon Jovi, Jon

BAD MEDICINE
I'LL BE THERE FOR YOU
LIVIN' ON A PRAYER
RUNAWAY
WANTED DEAD OR ALIVE
YOU GIVE LOVE A BAD NAME

Bond, Angelo

BRING THE BOYS HOME
SOMEBODY'S BEEN SLEEPING (IN
    MY BED)
STICK-UP
WOMEN'S LOVE RIGHTS

Bond, Johnny

CIMARRON (ROLL ON)
DON'T LIVE A LIE
FOREVER IS ENDING TODAY
I'LL STEP ASIDE
TOMORROW NEVER COMES
WE MIGHT AS WELL FORGET IT
YOUR OLD LOVE LETTERS

Bonds, Gary

SHE'S ALL I GOT

Bone, Gene

PRAY FOR PEACE
STRANGE AND SWEET

Bonfa, Luiz

ALMOST IN LOVE
DAY IN THE LIFE OF A FOOL, A
MANHA DE CARNAVAL
SAMBA DE ORFEO

Bonfire, Mars

BORN TO BE WILD

Bonham, John

D'YER MAKER
GOOD TIMES, BAD TIMES
HEARTBREAKER
WHOLE LOTTA LOVE

Bonime, Joseph

LET'S DANCE

Bonneford, James

MISLED

Bonner, Garry

CAT IN THE WINDOW (THE BIRD IN
    THE SKY)
CELEBRATE
GIRLS IN LOVE
HAPPY TOGETHER
MELANCHOLY MUSIC MAN

SHE'D RATHER BE WITH ME
SHE'S MY GIRL
YOU KNOW WHAT I MEAN

Bonner, Leroy

FIRE
FUNKY WORM
LOVE ROLLERCOASTER
SKIN TIGHT
SWEET STICKY THING
WHO'D SHE COO

Bonniwell, Sean

TALK, TALK

Bono, Sonny

BABY, DON'T GO
BANG, BANG (MY BABY SHOT ME
    DOWN)
BEAT GOES ON, THE
BUT YOU'RE MINE
COWBOY'S WORK IS NEVER DONE, A
HAVE I STAYED TOO LONG?
I GOT YOU BABE
IT'S THE LITTLE THINGS
JUST YOU
LAUGH AT ME
LITTLE MAN
NEEDLES AND PINS
WHERE DO YOU GO?
YOU BETTER SIT DOWN KIDS

Bonoff, Karla

I CAN'T HOLD ON
ISN'T IT ALWAYS LOVE
LOSE AGAIN
SOMEONE TO LAY DOWN BESIDE ME

Bonura, Carl

I'VE HAD IT

Bonx, Nat

COLLEGIATE
IF YOU ARE BUT A DREAM
I LOVE THE COLLEGE GIRLS

Booker, Eugene

TURNED AWAY

Booker, Gary

CONQUISTADOR

Booker, Harry

SHOESHINE BOY

Boone, Charles E. (Pat)

EXODUS
QUANDO, QUANDO, QUANDO (TELL ME WHEN)
WISH YOU WERE HERE BUDDY

Boone, Claude

WEDDING BELLS

Boone, Larry

BURNIN' OLD MEMORIES

Boone, Leonard

YOU MADE ME BELIEVE IN MAGIC

Boone, Richard

BALLAD OF PALADIN, THE

Boone, Steve

SUMMER IN THE CITY
YOU DIDN'T HAVE TO BE SO NICE

Booth, Ann

RUN, WOMAN, RUN

Boothe, James

JINGLE BELL ROCK

Borch, Michael

YOU WOULDN'T LISTEN

Borchers, Bobby

I'M THE ONLY HELL (MAMA EVER RAISED)
WHEN I DIE JUST LET ME GO TO TEXAS

Borek, Renee

SOLITAIRE

Boretz, Allen

WHISTLING IN THE DARK

Borisoff, Bernice

KEEM-O-SABE

Borisoff, Leonard

ONE, TWO, THREE (1-2-3)

Borrelli, Bill

HERE IN MY HEART
PHILADELPHIA, U.S.A.

Borsdorf, Thomas

FIND YOUR WAY BACK

Boshell, Bias

I'VE GOT THE MUSIC IN ME

Bostic, Earl

LET ME OFF UPTOWN

Botkin, Perry, Jr.

BLESS THE BEASTS AND CHILDREN
NADIA'S THEME (THE YOUNG AND THE RESTLESS)
WONDERFUL SUMMER

Botkin, Roy

AMIGO'S GUITAR
COLD AND LONELY (IS THE FORECAST FOR TONIGHT)
LOVEBUG ITCH, THE

Botsford, George

GRIZZLY BEAR
SAILING DOWN THE CHESAPEAKE BAY
WHEN BIG PROFUNDO SANG LOW "C"

Bottler, Mitch

SOONER OR LATER

Boublil, A.

DRINK WITH ME TO DAYS GONE BY
I DREAMED A DREAM

Boulanger, Georges

MY PRAYER

Bourgeois, Brent

I DON'T MIND AT ALL

Bourke, Rory

ANGEL
ANOTHER SLEEPLESS NIGHT
BABY I LIED
BLESSED ARE THE BELIEVERS
I KNOW A HEARTACHE WHEN I SEE ONE
LET'S STOP TALKIN' ABOUT IT
LITTLE GOOD NEWS, A
MOST BEAUTIFUL GIRL, THE
SHADOWS IN THE MOONLIGHT
SWEET MAGNOLIA BLOSSOM
WHERE DO THE NIGHTS GO
YOU LOOK SO GOOD IN LOVE

Bourtayre, Jean

MY BOY

Bousquet, Louis

MADELON

Boutelje, Phil

CHINA BOY

Bouwens, Johannes

PALOMA BLANCA

Bovington, Jay

HEART BE CAREFUL

Bowen, Jeffrey

HAPPY PEOPLE
SHAKEY GROUND
YOU

Bowen, Jimmy

I'M STICKIN' WITH YOU
PARTY DOLL

Bower, Maurice "Bugs"

CATERINA

Bowers, Frederick V.

ALWAYS
BECAUSE

Bowers, Robin Hood

CHINESE LULLABY
MOON SHINES ON THE MOONSHINE,
THE

Bowie, David

ABSOLUTE BEGINNERS
ALL THE YOUNG DUDES
BLUE JEAN
CAT PEOPLE (PUTTING OUT FIRE)
CHANGES
CHINA GIRL
DAY-IN DAY-OUT
FAME
GOLDEN YEARS
LET'S DANCE
MODERN LOVE
SPACE ODDITY
STARMAN
TVC 15
UNDERGROUND
UNDER PRESSURE
YOUNG AMERICANS

Bowles, Rick

I CAN'T WIN FOR LOSING YOU
I KNOW HOW HE FEELS

Bowling, Roger

BLANKET ON THE GROUND
COWARD OF THE COUNTY
LUCILLE

Bowman, Brooks

EAST OF THE SUN (AND WEST OF
THE MOON)
LOVE AND A DIME
WILL LOVE FIND A WAY?

Bowman, Dan

WILDWOOD WEED

Bowman, Don

ANITA, YOU'RE DREAMING
JUST TO SATISFY YOU

Bowman, Elmer

ALL IN DOWN AND OUT (SORRY, I
AIN'T GOT IT, YOU COULD HAVE
IT, ETC.)
BEANS! BEANS!! BEANS!!!
GO WAY BACK SIT DOWN

Bowman, Euday L.

TWELFTH STREET RAG

Bowman, Priscilla

HANDS OFF

Bowne, Jerry

FRIENDLY TAVERN POLKA

Box, Betty

I FEEL LOVE (BENJI'S THEME)
SUNSHINE SMILES

Box, Elton

I'VE GOT SIXPENCE
JUST A LITTLE FOND AFFECTION

Box, Euel

I FEEL LOVE (BENJI'S THEME)
SUNSHINE SMILES

Boyce, Henry

(I'VE GOT A) HUMPTY DUMPTY
HEART

Boyce, Tommy

ACTION
ALICE LONG (YOU'RE STILL MY
FAVORITE GIRLFRIEND)
BE MY GUEST
COME A LITTLE BIT CLOSER
GREEN GRASS
I'M NOT YOUR STEPPIN' STONE
I WONDER WHAT SHE'S DOING
TONIGHT
LAST TRAIN TO CLARKSVILLE
OUT AND ABOUT
PEACHES 'N CREAM
PRETTY LITTLE ANGEL EYES
VALLERI
WORDS

Boyd, Alphonso

SHAKEY GROUND

Boyd, Eddie

FIVE LONG YEARS

Boyd, Elisse

GUESS WHO I SAW TODAY?
THURSDAY'S CHILD

Boyd, Tony

5-10-15-20 (25-30 YEARS OF LOVE)

Boyer, Lucien Jean

VALENCIA

Boylan, John

ALL I WANT IS YOU

Boylan, Terence

SHAKE IT

Boyter, George

SHAPE OF THINGS TO COME, THE

Brackman, Jacob

ATTITUDE DANCING
HAVEN'T GOT TIME FOR THE PAIN
THAT'S THE WAY I'VE ALWAYS
   HEARD IT SHOULD BE

Bradbury, Stan

I'VE GOT SIXPENCE

Braddock, Bobby

BALLAD OF TWO BROTHERS
D-I-V-O-R-C-E
FAKING LOVE
GOLDEN RING
HE STOPPED LOVING HER TODAY
I FEEL LIKE LOVING YOU AGAIN
RUTHLESS
THINKING OF A RENDEZVOUS
WOULD YOU CATCH A FALLING STAR

Bradford, Janie

HIP CITY—PT. 2
MONEY (THAT'S WHAT I WANT)
TOO BUSY THINKING ABOUT MY
   BABY
YOUR OLD STANDBY

Bradford, Johnny

FANDANGO

Bradford, Perry

CRAZY BLUES
YOUR LOVE IS ALL THAT I CRAVE

Bradford, Sylvester

I'M READY
TEARS ON MY PILLOW

Bradley, Owen

ALL ALONE IN THIS WORLD
   WITHOUT YOU
NIGHT TRAIN TO MEMPHIS
WHAT IS LIFE WITHOUT LOVE?

Bradley, Will

CELERY STALKS AT MIDNIGHT

Bradshaw, Tiny

JERSEY BOUNCE
SOFT
WELL, OH WELL

Bradtke, Hans

SUMMER WIND

Bragg, Al

SHARE YOUR LOVE WITH ME

Bragg, Johnny

JUST WALKING IN THE RAIN

Braham, David

DE RAINBOW ROAD
HATS OFF TO ME
I'VE COME HERE TO STAY
KNIGHTS OF THE MYSTIC STAR
MAGGIE MURPHY'S HOME
TAKE A DAY OFF, MARY ANN
TAKING IN THE TOWN
THEY NEVER TELL ALL WHAT THEY
   KNOW

Braham, Philip

LIMEHOUSE BLUES

Brailey, Jerome

TEAR THE ROOF OFF THE SUCKER
   (GIVE UP THE FUNK)

Brainin, Jerome

DON'T LET JULIA FOOL YA
NIGHT HAS A THOUSAND EYES, THE

Braisted, Harry

SHE WAS BRED IN OLD KENTUCKY
WHISPER YOUR MOTHER'S NAME

Braithwaite, Wayne

COLOUR OF LOVE, THE
LOVE ZONE

Bramlett, Bonnie

SUPERSTAR

Bramlett, Delaney

NEVER ENDING SONG OF LOVE

Brammer, Julius

JUST A GIGOLO

Braña, Hernan

HIS FEET TOO BIG FOR DE BED

Branch, Jean

TENNESSEE MOON

Brand, Oscar

GUY IS A GUY, A

Brandow, Jerry

HOLD TIGHT—HOLD TIGHT (WANT
   SOME SEA FOOD, MAMA)

Brandt, Alan

THAT'S ALL

Brandt, Edward

ALL THE KING'S HORSES

Branen, Jeff T.

I'M LOOKING FOR A NICE YOUNG
FELLOW WHO IS LOOKING FOR A
NICE YOUNG GIRL
SHE'S THE DAUGHTER OF MOTHER
MACHREE
YOU'RE MORE THAN THE WORLD TO
ME

Brannon, Richard

THINK ABOUT LOVE (THINK ABOUT
ME)

Brantley, James

BABY BYE BYE

Brantley, Vincent

COOL IT NOW
COUNT ME OUT

Brasfield, Howard

SHE SURE GOT AWAY WITH MY
HEART

Brasfield, Tom

ANGEL IN YOUR ARMS
HALF PAST FOREVER (TILL I'M BLUE
IN THE HEART)
(THERE'S) NO GETTIN' OVER ME
ONCE IN A BLUE MOON
ONE OWNER HEART
TILL YOU'RE GONE

Brass, Bob

I MUST BE SEEING THINGS
LITTLE LONELY ONE
THIS DIAMOND RING

Brathwaite, Wayne

THERE'LL BE SAD SONGS (TO MAKE
YOU CRY)

WHEN THE GOING GETS TOUGH,
THE TOUGH GET GOING

Bratta, Vito

WAIT

Bratton, John W.

I LOVE YOU IN THE SAME OLD
WAY—DARLING SUE
I'M ON THE WATER WAGON NOW
IN A COSY CORNER
ONLY ME
SUNSHINE OF PARADISE ALLEY,
THE
TEDDY BEARS' PICNIC, THE
YOU'LL ALWAYS BE JUST SWEET
SIXTEEN TO ME

Braverman, Sam

MY LITTLE COUSIN

Bray, Stephen

BABY LOVE
CROSS MY BROKEN HEART

Bray, Steve

ANGEL
CAUSING A COMMOTION
RIGHT ON TRACK
TRUE BLUE

Brazilian, Eric

ALL YOU ZOMBIES

Breau, Louis

HUMMING

Brecht, Bertolt

ALABAMA SONG
BILBAO SONG, THE
MACK THE KNIFE (A.K.A. MORITAT)
PIRATE JENNY

Breeland, Walt

FAMILY BIBLE

Breen, Harry J.

YOUR DAD GAVE HIS LIFE FOR HIS
COUNTRY

Breil, Joseph Carl

PERFECT SONG, THE

Brel, Jacques

AMSTERDAM
CAROUSEL
DAYS OF THE WALTZ, THE
IF WE ONLY HAVE LOVE
IF YOU GO AWAY
MADELEINE
MARIEKE
SEASONS IN THE SUN

Brennan, J. Keirn

ALL OVER NOTHING AT ALL
DEAR LITTLE BOY OF MINE
EMPTY SADDLES
FOR DIXIE AND UNCLE SAM
GOODBYE, GOOD LUCK, GOD BLESS
YOU
IRELAND IS IRELAND TO ME
LET THE REST OF THE WORLD GO
BY
LITTLE BIT OF HEAVEN, A (SHURE
THEY CALLED IT IRELAND)
MY SUNSHINE JANE
ONLY SONG I KNOW, THE
OUT THERE IN THE SUNSHINE WITH
YOU
TEN THOUSAND YEARS FROM NOW
THAT'S HOW THE SHANNON FLOWS
THERE'S A NEW STAR IN HEAVEN
TONIGHT—RUDOLPH VALENTINO
TURN BACK THE UNIVERSE AND
GIVE ME YESTERDAY

Brennan, James A.

IN THE LITTLE RED SCHOOL HOUSE

Brennan, Joseph A.

ROSE OF NO MAN'S LAND, THE

Brenston, Jackie

ROCKET "88"

Brent, Earl K.

ANGEL EYES
HOW STRANGE?
LOVE IS WHERE YOU FIND IT

Brescia, Vance

THAT WAS THEN, THIS IS NOW

Bresler, Jerry

FIVE GUYS NAMED MOE

Bretton, Elise

FOR HEAVEN'S SAKE

Breuer, Ernest

DOES THE SPEARMINT LOSE ITS
    FLAVOR ON THE BEDPOST OVER
    NIGHT?
OH GEE, OH GOSH, OH GOLLY, I'M
    IN LOVE

Brewer, Charles

TARKIO ROAD

Brewer, Don

SHININ' ON
WE'RE AN AMERICAN BAND

Brewer, Mike

ONE TOKE OVER THE LINE

Brewster, Clarence S.

WHEN YOU AIN'T GOT NO MORE
    MONEY, WELL, YOU NEEDN'T
    COME ROUND

Brewster, Jimmy

IF I GIVE MY HEART TO YOU

Brice, Monty C.

DAUGHTER OF ROSIE O'GRADY, THE

Brickman, James

AS LONG AS THE SHAMROCK
    GROWS GREEN

Bricusse, Leslie

CANDY MAN, THE
CAN YOU READ MY MIND (LOVE
    THEME FROM "SUPERMAN")
CHICAGO, ILLINOIS
CRAZY WORLD
FEELING GOOD
GOLDFINGER
GONNA BUILD A MOUNTAIN
IF I RULED THE WORLD
JOKER, THE
LIFE IN A LOOKING GLASS
LOOK AT THAT FACE
MOVE 'EM OUT
MY FIRST LOVE SONG
MY KIND OF GIRL
ONCE IN A LIFETIME
SOMEONE NICE LIKE YOU
SWEET BEGINNING
TALK TO THE ANIMALS
THANK YOU VERY MUCH
TYPICALLY ENGLISH
WHAT KIND OF FOOL AM I?
WHEN I LOOK IN YOUR EYES
WHO CAN I TURN TO (WHEN
    NOBODY NEEDS ME)
WONDERFUL DAY LIKE TODAY, A
YOU ONLY LIVE TWICE

Bridges, Alicia

I LOVE THE NIGHTLIFE (DISCO
    ROUND)

Bridges, Jo

DO THE FUNKY PENGUIN

Brigati, Eddie

BEAUTIFUL MORNING, A
GIRL LIKE YOU, A
GROOVIN'
HOW CAN I BE SURE?
IT'S WONDERFUL
I'VE BEEN LONELY TOO LONG
PEOPLE GOT TO BE FREE
RAY OF HOPE, A
YOU BETTER RUN

Briggs, David

HAPPY ANNIVERSARY
LONESOME LOSER

Briggs, Fred

CONDITION RED

Briggs, Victor

MONTEREY
SAN FRANCISCAN NIGHTS
SKY PILOT
WHEN I WAS YOUNG

Brigham, Townsend

LITTLE MAN WITH A CANDY CIGAR

Bright-Plummer, Gilly

SITTING IN LIMBO

Briley, Martin

SALT IN MY TEARS, THE

Brine, Mary D.

HEARTS AND FLOWERS

Brislane, Jack

MAKE BELIEVE

Bristol, Darnel

RONI

Bristol, Johnny

DADDY COULD SWEAR, I DECLARE
DO IT TO MY MIND
GOTTA HOLD ON TO THIS FEELING
HANG ON IN THERE BABY
I DON'T WANT TO DO WRONG
IF I COULD BUILD MY WHOLE
    WORLD AROUND YOU
MY WHOLE WORLD ENDED (THE
    MOMENT YOU LEFT ME)
PUCKER UP, BUTTERCUP
SOMEDAY WE'LL BE TOGETHER
TWENTY-FIVE MILES
WE'VE COME TOO FAR TO END IT
    NOW
WHAT DOES IT TAKE (TO WIN YOUR
    LOVE)?

Briston, Johnny

LOVE ME FOR A REASON

Brito, Phil

MAMA

Britt, Addy

AGGRAVATIN' PAPA (DON'T YOU TRY
    TO TWO-TIME ME)
HELLO, SWANEE, HELLO!
TING-A-LING (THE WALTZ OF THE
    BELLS)

Britt, Al

WISHING RING

Britt, Elton

CHIME BELLS
WEEP NO MORE, MY DARLIN'

Brittan, Robert

ALAIYO
SWEET TIME

Britten, Terry

DEVIL WOMAN
TYPICAL MALE

WE DON'T NEED ANOTHER HERO
    (THUNDERDOME)
WHAT'S LOVE GOT TO DO WITH IT
WHAT YOU GET IS WHAT YOU SEE

Broadnax, Morris

UNTIL YOU COME BACK TO ME
    (THAT'S WHAT I'M GONNA DO)

Broadwater, Eleanor

SUSIE-Q

Brock, Bill

I'LL JUST HAVE A CUP OF COFFEE
    (THEN I'LL GO)

Brockert, Mary

SQUARE BIZ

Brockman, James

DOWN AMONG THE SHELTERING
    PALMS
FEATHER YOUR NEST
I FAW DOWN AN' GO BOOM!
I'M LIKE A SHIP WITHOUT A SAIL

Brodsky, Nicholas

BECAUSE YOU'RE MINE
BELOVED
BE MY LOVE
DARK IS THE NIGHT
HOW D'YA LIKE YOUR EGGS IN THE
    MORNING?
I CAN SEE YOU
I'LL NEVER STOP LOVING YOU
I'LL WALK WITH GOD
MY DESTINY
MY FLAMING HEART
NO ONE BUT YOU
ONE IS A LONELY NUMBER
ONLY TRUST YOUR HEART
WE NEVER TALK MUCH
WONDER WHY

Brodsky, Roy

RED ROSES FOR A BLUE LADY

SAY SOMETHING SWEET TO YOUR
    SWEETHEART

Bromberg, Bruce

SMOKING GUN

Bronner, René

AS DEEP AS THE DEEP BLUE SEA

Bronski, Steve

SMALLTOWN BOY

Brooker, Gary

HOMBURG
WHITER SHADE OF PALE, A

Brookmeyer, Bob

USELESS WALTZ

Brooks, Arthur

FOR YOUR PRECIOUS LOVE

Brooks, Charles

TAXI

Brooks, Harry

BLACK AND BLUE
SATURDAY
SWEET SAVANNAH SUE

Brooks, Harvey O.

I'M NO ANGEL
I WANT YOU, I NEED YOU
LITTLE BIRD TOLD ME, A
THAT DALLAS MAN
THEY CALL ME SISTER HONKY
    TONK

Brooks, Harry

AIN'T MISBEHAVIN'

Brooks, Jack

AM I IN LOVE?
INNAMORATA (SWEETHEART)
IT'S DREAMTIME
LOOK AT ME
OLE BUTTERMILK SKY
ROSE TATTOO, THE
SATURDAY DATE
SOMEBODY
THAT'S AMORE
YOU WONDERFUL YOU

Brooks, Joe

IF EVER I SEE YOU AGAIN
SEEIN' THE RIGHT LOVE GO WRONG
YOU LIGHT UP MY LIFE

Brooks, John Benson

BOY FROM TEXAS, A GIRL FROM
    TENNESSEE, A
DOOR WILL OPEN, A
JUST AS THOUGH YOU WERE HERE
NINETY-NINE YEARS (DEAD OR
    ALIVE)
YOU CAME A LONG WAY FROM ST.
    LOUIS

Brooks, Johnny

WHO THREW THE WHISKEY IN THE
    WELL?

Brooks, Mel

BLAZING SADDLES
SPACEBALLS

Brooks, Randy

GRANDMA GOT RUN OVER BY A
    REINDEER

Brooks, Richard

FOR YOUR PRECIOUS LOVE

Brooks, Ruth

IN SHADOWLAND

Brooks, Shelton

ALL NIGHT LONG
DARKTOWN STRUTTERS' BALL, THE
HONEY GAL
SOME OF THESE DAYS
THERE'LL COME A TIME

Broomer, Bernie

OH, HOW IT HURTS

Broomfield, Ron

DON'T SAY NO TONIGHT
GOTTA GET YOU HOME TONIGHT

Broones, Martin

BRING BACK THOSE MINSTREL DAYS
ICH LIEBE DICH (I LOVE YOU)
I DON'T WANT YOUR KISSES (IF I
    CAN'T HAVE YOUR LOVE)

Broonzy, Bill

BABY, I DONE GOT WISE
JUST A DREAM
KEY TO THE HIGHWAY

Broughton, Bruce

LOVE LIVES ON

Broughton, Philip

FUNNY (NOT MUCH)

Broussard, Joe

MR. BIG STUFF

Browd, Wade, Jr.

LOVE ME FOR A REASON

Brown, Adam

ARE WE OURSELVES?

Brown, Al

JUST BECAUSE

MADISON, THE

Brown, Alfred

IN A MOMENT

Brown, Al H.

YOU TELL ME YOUR DREAM

Brown, Al W.

AIN'T IT A SHAME

Brown, Annette

SOMEBODY ELSE'S GUY

Brown, Arthur

FIRE!

Brown, A. Seymour

DIXIE LAND, I LOVE YOU
MOVING DAY IN JUNGLE TOWN
OH, YOU BEAUTIFUL DOLL
REBECCA OF SUNNYBROOK FARM
WHEN YOU'RE AWAY
YOU'RE A GREAT BIG BLUE-EYED
    BABY
YOU'RE MY BABY

Brown, A. W.

LONESOME MAMA BLUES

Brown, Billie

LONESOME MAMA BLUES

Brown, Billie Jean

HERE COMES THE JUDGE

Brown, Billy

SPECIAL LADY

Brown, Bobby

MY PREROGATIVE

Brown, Boots

CERVEZA

Brown, Charles

PLEASE COME HOME FOR
CHRISTMAS

Brown, Chuck

BUSTIN' LOOSE

Brown, Dan K.

ARE WE OURSELVES?

Brown, Danny Joe

FLIRTIN' WITH DISASTER

Brown, Earl

IF I CAN DREAM

Brown, Elkin

BLUES PLUS BOOZE (MEANS I LOSE)

Brown, Errol

BROTHER LOUIE
DISCO QUEEN
EMMA
EVERY 1'S A WINNER
YOU SEXY THING

Brown, Fleta Jan

UNDERNEATH THE STARS

Brown, Forman

TWO HEARTS THAT PASS IN THE
NIGHT

Brown, Frankie

BORN TO LOSE
NO LETTER TODAY

Brown, Gayle Candis

IT'S TOO LATE, BABY, TOO LATE

Brown, George

HOLLYWOOD SWINGING
LADIES NIGHT
MISLED
OLD MAN OF THE MOUNTAIN
TAKE MY HEART (YOU CAN HAVE IT
IF YOU WANT IT)
TOO HOT

Brown, H.

GYPSY MAN

Brown, Harold

CISCO KID, THE
L. A. SUNSHINE
LOW RIDER
ME AND BABY BROTHER
SPILL THE WINE
SUMMER
WHY CAN'T WE BE FRIENDS?
WORLD IS A GHETTO, THE

Brown, J.

CRYING HEART BLUES (A.K.A.
CRYIN' HEART BLUES)

Brown, James

AIN'T IT FUNKY NOW
AIN'T THAT A GROOVE
AMERICA IS MY HOME
BABY, YOU'RE RIGHT
BRING IT UP
BROTHER RAPP
COLD SWEAT
DON'T BE A DROP-OUT
GET IT TOGETHER
GET ON THE GOOD FOOT
GET UP (I FEEL LIKE BEING A SEX
MACHINE)
GOODBYE, MY LOVE
HOT PANTS (SHE GOT TO USE WHAT
SHE GOT TO GET WHAT SHE
WANTS)

I CAN'T STAND MYSELF (WHEN YOU
TOUCH ME)
I DON'T MIND
I DON'T WANT NOBODY TO GIVE ME
NOTHING (OPEN UP THE DOOR,
I'LL GET IT MYSELF)
I GOT THE FEELIN'
I GOT YOU (I FEEL GOOD)
I'M REAL
IT'S A MAN'S, MAN'S, MAN'S WORLD
LET YOURSELF GO
LICKING STICK—LICKING STICK
LOST SOMEONE
LOWDOWN POPCORN
MOTHER POPCORN (YOU GOT TO
HAVE A MOTHER FOR ME)
PAPA'S GOT A BRAND NEW BAG
PAYBACK, THE
PLEASE, PLEASE, PLEASE
POPCORN, THE
SAY IT LOUD—I'M BLACK AND I'M
PROUD
SOUL POWER
SUPER BAD
THERE WAS A TIME
THINK (ABOUT IT)
TRY ME
WORLD

Brown, Jimmy

DUSIC

Brown, Jocelyn

SOMEBODY ELSE'S GUY

Brown, Larry

ONE LOVE IN MY LIFETIME

Brown, Lawrence

TRANSBLUCENCY

Brown, Lawrence Russell

BON BON VIE (GIMME THE GOOD
LIFE)
JOY

Brown, Les

ABILENE
LITTLE PAL
SENTIMENTAL JOURNEY

Brown, Lew

AIN'T YOU ASHAMED?
AMERICAN TUNE
ANNABELLE
AU REVOIR, BUT NOT GOODBYE,
  SOLDIER BOY
BABY, TAKE A BOW
BEER BARREL POLKA
BEST THINGS IN LIFE ARE FREE,
  THE
BIRTH OF THE BLUES, THE
BLACK BOTTOM
BROADWAY
BROADWAY'S GONE HILLBILLY
(HERE AM I) BROKEN HEARTED
CHILI BEAN
COMES LOVE
COME TO ME
DAPPER DAN (THE SHEIK OF
  ALABAM')
DON'T BRING LULU
DON'T CRY, CHERIE
DON'T HOLD EVERYTHING
DON'T SIT UNDER THE APPLE TREE
  (WITH ANYONE ELSE BUT ME)
DON'T TELL HER WHAT HAPPENED
  TO ME
FIRST YOU HAVE ME HIGH (THEN
  YOU HAVE ME LOW)
FOR OLD TIMES' SAKE
GEORGETTE
GIRL IS YOU AND THE BOY IS ME,
  THE
GIVE ME THE MOONLIGHT, GIVE ME
  THE GIRL
GOOD FOR YOU—BAD FOR ME
GOOD NEWS
I CAME HERE TO TALK FOR JOE
I CAN'T AFFORD TO DREAM
I DUG A DITCH (IN WICHITA)
I'D CLIMB THE HIGHEST MOUNTAIN
IF I HAD A TALKING PICTURE OF
  YOU
IF YOU HAVEN'T GOT LOVE
I'M A DREAMER, AREN'T WE ALL?

I MAY BE GONE FOR A LONG, LONG
  TIME
I'M LAUGHIN'
I'M ON THE CREST OF A WAVE
I'M TELLIN' THE BIRDS, I'M TELLIN'
  THE BEES (HOW I LOVE YOU)
I'M THE LONESOMEST GAL IN TOWN
IT ALL DEPENDS ON YOU
IT WON'T BE LONG NOW
I USED TO LOVE YOU (BUT IT'S ALL
  OVER NOW)
I'VE GOT THE YES WE HAVE NO
  BANANAS BLUES
I'VE GOT TO PASS YOUR HOUSE (TO
  GET TO MY HOUSE)
I WANT TO BE BAD
JUST A MEMORY
JUST IMAGINE
KENTUCKY SUE
LADY DANCES, THE
LAST NIGHT ON THE BACK PORCH (I
  LOVED HER BEST OF ALL)
LET'S CALL IT A DAY
LET'S MAKE MEMORIES TONIGHT
LIFE BEGINS WHEN YOU'RE IN LOVE
LIFE IS JUST A BOWL OF CHERRIES
LITTLE PAL
LOVE IS NEVER OUT OF SEASON
LUCKY DAY (THIS IS MY)
LUCKY IN LOVE
MANHATTAN MARY
MISSISSIPPI DREAM BOAT
MY LUCKY STAR
MY SIN
MY SONG
OH, BY JINGO! OH, BY GEE!
  (YOU'RE THE ONLY GIRL FOR ME)
OH! MA-MA (THE BUTCHER BOY)
OLD SOMBRERO, AN
ONE MORE TIME
ONE SWEET LETTER FROM YOU
ON THE OUTGOING TIDE
OUR PENTHOUSE ON THIRD AVENUE
PICKIN' COTTON
PLEASE DON'T TAKE MY LOVIN'
  MAN AWAY
POMPANOLA
SHE'S WAY UP THAR
SHINE
SO BLUE
SONG I LOVE, THE
SONNY BOY
STAND UP AND CHEER

STRIKE ME PINK
SUNNY SIDE UP
THANK YOUR FATHER
THAT OLD FEELING
THAT'S WHY DARKIES WERE BORN
(I WANNA GO WHERE YOU GO, DO
  WHAT YOU DO) THEN I'LL BE
  HAPPY
THERE I GO DREAMING AGAIN
THIS IS OUR LAST NIGHT TOGETHER
THIS IS THE MISSUS
THRILL IS GONE, THE
TOGETHER
TO KNOW YOU IS TO LOVE YOU
TURN ON THE HEAT
USED TO YOU
VARSITY DRAG, THE
WAIT TILL YOU GET THEM UP IN
  THE AIR, BOYS
WASN'T IT BEAUTIFUL WHILE IT
  LASTED?
WHAT D'YA SAY?
WHEN IT'S NIGHT TIME IN ITALY,
  IT'S WEDNESDAY OVER HERE
WHY CAN'T YOU?
WHY DID I KISS THAT GIRL?
WHY NOT STRING ALONG WITH ME?
WITHOUT LOVE
YOU CAN MAKE MY LIFE A BED OF
  ROSES
YOU'RE THE CREAM IN MY COFFEE
YOU TRY SOMEBODY ELSE
YOU WOULDN'T FOOL ME, WOULD
  YOU?

Brown, L. Russell

C'MON MARIANNE
I WOKE UP IN LOVE THIS MORNING
KNOCK THREE TIMES
SAY, HAS ANYBODY SEEN MY
  SWEET GYPSY ROSE
SOCK IT TO ME, BABY!
STEPPIN' OUT (GONNA BOOGIE
  TONIGHT)
TIE A YELLOW RIBBON ROUND THE
  OLE OAK TREE
WATCH THE FLOWERS GROW

Brown, Marshall

BANJO'S BACK IN TOWN, THE
SEVEN LONELY DAYS

Brown, Maxine

ALL IN MY MIND

Brown, Michael

JOHN BIRCH SOCIETY, THE
LIZZIE BORDEN
SWAMP GIRL

Brown, Mike

AND SUDDENLY
PRETTY BALLERINA
WALK AWAY RENEE

Brown, Milton

ANOTHER HONKY TONK NIGHT ON
    BROADWAY
BAR ROOM BUDDIES
EVERYBODY'S EVERYTHING
EVERY WHICH WAY BUT LOOSE
HOPPY, GENE, AND ME
LASSO THE MOON

Brown, Nacio Herb

AFTER SUNDOWN
ALL I DO IS DREAM OF YOU
ALONE
AVALON TOWN
BEAUTIFUL GIRL
BLONDY
BROADWAY MELODY
BROADWAY RHYTHM
BUNDLE OF OLD LOVE LETTERS, A
CHANT OF THE JUNGLE
CINDERELLA'S FELLA
DOLL DANCE, THE
EADIE WAS A LADY
EVERYBODY SING
GOOD MORNING
GOT A PAIR OF NEW SHOES
HOLD YOUR MAN
HOODOO MAN, THE
I'M FEELIN' LIKE A MILLION
I'VE GOT A FEELIN' YOU'RE FOOLIN'
LATER TONIGHT
LOVE BOAT
LOVE IS WHERE YOU FIND IT
LOVE SONGS OF THE NILE
MOON IS LOW, THE

MY WONDERFUL ONE, LET'S DANCE
NEW MOON IS OVER MY SHOULDER,
    A
ON A SUNDAY AFTERNOON
OUR BIG LOVE SCENE
PAGAN LOVE SONG
PARADISE
SHOULD I?
SING BEFORE BREAKFAST
SINGIN' IN THE RAIN
SMOKE DREAMS
SUN SHOWERS
TEMPTATION
WEDDING OF THE PAINTED DOLL,
    THE
WE'LL MAKE HAY WHILE THE SUN
    SHINES
WHAT'S WRONG WITH ME?
WHEN BUDDHA SMILES
WOULD YOU?
YOU ARE MY LUCKY STAR
YOU'RE AN OLD SMOOTHIE
YOURS AND MINE
YOU STEPPED OUT OF A DREAM
YOU WERE MEANT FOR ME

Brown, Nacio Herb, Jr.

JUST BECAUSE YOU'RE YOU

Brown, Nappy

DON'T BE ANGRY

Brown, Ollie

BREAKIN' . . . THERE'S NO
    STOPPING US

Brown, Oscar, Jr.

BROWN BABY
SNAKE, THE
WORK SONG, THE
YOUNG GIRL, A

Brown, Paula

MAD ABOUT YOU

Brown, Pete

WHITE ROOM

Brown, Peter

DANCE WITH ME
DO YA WANNA GET FUNKY WITH
    ME
MATERIAL GIRL
SUNSHINE OF YOUR LOVE

Brown, Ray

GRAVY WALTZ

Brown, Richard, Jr.

HAPPY MUSIC

Brown, Roy

GOOD ROCKIN' TONIGHT
HARK LUCK BLUES
LOLLY POP MAMA
'LONG ABOUT MIDNIGHT

Brown, Seymour

AT THE MISSISSIPPI CABARET

Brown, T. Graham

HELL AND HIGH WATER

Brown, Tommy

WEEPIN' AND CRYIN'

Brown, Wade, Jr.

WE'VE COME TOO FAR TO END IT
    NOW

Brown, Walter

CONFESSIN' THE BLUES

Brown, Walter H.

LITTLE MOTHER OF MINE

Brown, William

LOOK AT ME (I'M IN LOVE)

Browne, Jackson

BOULEVARD
DOCTOR MY EYES
FOR A DANCER
FOR A ROCKER
HERE COME THOSE TEARS AGAIN
IN THE SHAPE OF A HEART
JAMES DEAN
LAWYERS IN LOVE
LOAD-OUT, THE
PRETENDER, THE
REDNECK FRIEND
ROCK ME ON THE WATER
RUNNING ON EMPTY
SOMEBODY'S BABY
TAKE IT EASY
TENDER IS THE NIGHT
THAT GIRL COULD SING

Browne, Porter Emerson

COLLEGE LIFE

Browne, Raymond A.

DOWN ON THE FARM (THEY ALL ASK FOR YOU)

Browne, Tom

FUNKIN' FOR JAMAICA (N.Y.)

Browner, Rudolph

JEALOUS KIND OF FELLA

Browning, Bill

DARK HOLLOW

Brownlee, Larry

MICHAEL

Brubeck, Dave

BLUE RONDO A LA TURK

BOSSA NOVA U.S.A.
UNSQUARE DANCE

Brubeck, Iola

TAKE FIVE

Bruce, Ed

MAMMAS, DON'T LET YOUR BABIES
GROW UP TO BE COWBOYS
SEE THE BIG MAN CRY
WHEN I DIE JUST LET ME GO TO
TEXAS

Bruce, Gary D.

MOODY RIVER

Bruce, Jack

SUNSHINE OF YOUR LOVE
WHITE ROOM

Bruce, Michael

BILLION DOLLAR BABIES
EIGHTEEN

Bruce, Patsy

MAMMAS, DON'T LET YOUR BABIES
GROW UP TO BE COWBOYS
WHEN I DIE JUST LET ME GO TO
TEXAS

Bruce, Robert

AFTER HOURS
CHARLESTON ALLEY

Bruford, Bill

AND YOU AND I

Bruhn, Christian

TELL ANOTHER LIE

Bruner, Cliff

I HUNG MY HEAD AND CRIED

Brunies, George

MAKE LOVE TO ME
TIN ROOF BLUES

Brunies, Henry

ANGRY

Bruno, Tony

LAST CHANCE TO TURN AROUND

Bruns, George

LOVE
ZORRO

Bryan, Alfred

AFTER THAT I WANT A LITTLE
MORE
AND A LITTLE BIT MORE
ANGEL EYES
ARE YOU SINCERE?
BLUE RIVER
BRING BACK MY GOLDEN DREAMS
BROWN EYES, WHY ARE YOU BLUE?
COME, JOSEPHINE, IN MY FLYING
MACHINE
COME BACK TO ARIZONA
COUNTRY COUSIN, THE
GIVE ME YOUR AFFECTION, HONEY
HIAWATHA'S MELODY OF LOVE
I DIDN'T RAISE MY BOY TO BE A
SOLDIER
IF I CAN'T HAVE YOU
IN A LITTLE DUTCH KINDERGARTEN
JAPANSY
JOAN OF ARC, THEY ARE CALLING
YOU
JUST AN HOUR OF LOVE
LONESOME LOVER
LORRAINE, MY BEAUTIFUL ALSACE
LORRAINE
MADELON
MISS WONDERFUL
MY SONG OF THE NILE
ON THE ROAD TO CALAIS
OUI, OUI, MARIE
PEG O' MY HEART

PUDDIN' HEAD JONES
RED LIPS KISS MY BLUES AWAY
ROUND ON THE END AND HIGH IN
   THE MIDDLE (O-HI-O)
SWEET LITTLE BUTTERCUP
THAT WAS BEFORE I MET YOU
THERE'S A LUMP OF SUGAR DOWN
   IN DIXIE
THERE'S EVERYTHING NICE ABOUT
   YOU (THERE'S SOMETHING NICE
   ABOUT EVERYONE)
WHEN ALEXANDER TAKES HIS
   RAGTIME BAND TO FRANCE
WHEN IT'S NIGHTTIME DOWN IN
   BURGUNDY
WHEN I WALTZ WITH YOU
WHEN THE BEES ARE IN THE HIVE
WHO ATE NAPOLEONS WITH
   JOSEPHINE WHEN BONAPARTE
   WAS FAR AWAY?
WHO PAID THE RENT FOR MRS. RIP
   VAN WINKLE?
WINTER
YOU TAUGHT ME HOW TO LOVE
   YOU, NOW TEACH ME TO FORGET

Bryan, Bill

I'LL BE BACK

Bryan, Vincent P.

BE MY LITTLE TEDDY BEAR
BUDWEISER'S A FRIEND OF MINE
CUBANOLA GLIDE, THE
DON'T TAKE ME HOME
DOWN ON THE BRANDYWINE
DOWN WHERE THE WURZBURGER
   FLOWS
EPHRAHAM PLAYED UPON THE
   PIANO
HE GOES TO CHURCH ON SUNDAY
HE'S ME PAL
HURRAH FOR BAFFIN'S BAY!
IN MY MERRY OLDSMOBILE
IN THE SWEET BYE AND BYE
ON SAN FRANCISCO BAY
PARDON ME, MY DEAR ALPHONSE,
   AFTER YOU, MY DEAR GASTON
SOMEBODY'S WAITING FOR YOU
SPANISH LOVE

TAMMANY

Bryant, Boudleaux

ALL I HAVE TO DO IS DREAM
BACK UP, BUDDY
BALTIMORE
BIRD DOG
BREAK AWAY (FROM THAT BOY)
BYE BYE LOVE
COME LIVE WITH ME
COUNTRY BOY
DEVOTED TO YOU
HAVE A GOOD TIME
HAWK-EYE
HEY JOE
I LOVE TO DANCE WITH ANNIE
IT'S A LOVELY, LOVELY WORLD
I'VE BEEN THINKING
JUST WAIT 'TIL I GET YOU ALONE
LET'S THINK ABOUT LIVING
LOVE HURTS
MEXICO
MIDNIGHT
MY LAST DATE (WITH YOU)
POOR JENNY
PROBLEMS
RICHEST MAN, THE (IN THE WORLD)
SOMEBODY'S STOLEN MY HONEY
TAKE A MESSAGE TO MARY
TAKE ME AS I AM (OR LET ME GO)
WAKE UP LITTLE SUSIE

Bryant, Buck

THIS ORCHID MEANS GOODBYE

Bryant, D.

DON'T YOU WANT ME

Bryant, Donald

I CAN'T STAND THE RAIN

Bryant, Felice

BALTIMORE
BREAK AWAY (FROM THAT BOY)
BYE BYE LOVE
COME LIVE WITH ME
COUNTRY BOY
HAVE A GOOD TIME

I LOVE TO DANCE WITH ANNIE
JUST WAIT 'TIL I GET YOU ALONE
POOR JENNY
PROBLEMS
TAKE A MESSAGE TO MARY
WAKE UP LITTLE SUSIE

Bryant, Francis J.

CRISTOFO COLUMBO

Bryant, Hoyt

MOTHER, THE QUEEN OF MY
   HEART

Bryant, Ivy J.

ONLY DADDY THAT WILL WALK THE
   LINE, THE

Bryant, Ray

LITTLE SUSIE
MADISON TIME

Bryant, Willie

DO YOU WANNA JUMP, CHILDREN?
IT'S OVER BECAUSE WE'RE
   THROUGH

Brymn, J. Tim

COME AFTER BREAKFAST, BRING
   'LONG YOUR LUNCH AND LEAVE
   'FORE SUPPER TIME
GHOST OF THE BLUES
JOSEPHINE, MY JO
NOBODY SEES US BUT THE MAN IN
   THE MOON
PLEASE GO 'WAY AND LET ME
   SLEEP
SHOUT, SISTER, SHOUT

Bryon, Morty

I WANNA GO BACK

Bryon, Richard

LOVE IS LIKE A CIGARETTE

Bryson, Peabo

LET THE FEELING FLOW

Buarque de Hollanda, Chico

A BANDA (PARADE)

Buchanan, Bessie

AFTER THE ROSES HAVE FADED
   AWAY

Buchanan, Bill

PLEASE DON'T ASK ABOUT
   BARBARA

Buchwald, Martyn

MIRACLES
WITH YOUR LOVE

Buck, Gene

DADDY HAS A SWEETHEART (AND
   MOTHER IS HER NAME)
FLORIDA, THE MOON AND YOU
GARDEN OF MY DREAMS
HAVE A HEART
HELLO, FRISCO!
LONELY LITTLE MELODY
LOVE BOAT, THE
MY RAMBLER ROSE
'NEATH THE SOUTH SEA MOON
NIJINSKY
NO FOOLIN'
SALLY, WON'T YOU COME BACK
SWEET SIXTEEN
THROW ME A KISS
TIGER ROSE
TULIP TIME
UNDERNEATH THE JAPANESE MOON

Buck, Pete

FALL ON ME
IT'S THE END OF THE WORLD AS
   WE KNOW IT (AND I FEEL FINE)
ONE I LOVE, THE
RADIO FREE EUROPE
ROMANCE

SOUTH CENTRAL RAIN (I'M SORRY)

Buck, Richard

KENTUCKY BABE

Buck, Richard Henry

DEAR OLD GIRL
WHERE THE SOUTHERN ROSES
   GROW

Buck, Verne

DOWN WHERE THE SUN GOES
   DOWN

Buckingham, Jan

I DON'T MIND THE THORNS (IF
   YOU'RE THE ROSE)

Buckingham, Lindsay

BIG LOVE
GO YOUR OWN WAY
TROUBLE
TUSK

Buckins, Mickey

DOUBLE LOVIN'
TELL ME A LIE

Buckner, Eva Fern

WHERE THE SUNSET TURNS THE
   OCEAN'S BLUE TO GOLD

Buckner, Jerry

PAC-MAN FEVER

Buckner, Milt

HAMP'S BOOGIE WOOGIE

Buckshon, James

IT'S ONLY MAKE BELIEVE

Buff, Wade

IT'S ALMOST TOMORROW

Buffano, Jules

THANKS FOR THE BUGGY RIDE

Buffett, Jimmy

CHANGES IN LATITUDES, CHANGES
   IN ATTITUDES
CHEESEBURGER IN PARADISE
COME MONDAY
FINS
LIVINGSTON SATURDAY NIGHT
MAÑANA
MARGARITAVILLE
VOLCANO

Bugatti, Dominic

EVERY WOMAN IN THE WORLD
HEAVEN ON THE SEVENTH FLOOR
MARRIED MEN
MODERN GIRL

Buie, Buddy

CHAMPAGNE JAM
CHANGE OF HEART
DO IT OR DIE
EVERYDAY WITH YOU GIRL
IMAGINARY LOVER
I'M NOT GONNA LET IT BOTHER ME
   TONIGHT
SO IN TO YOU
SPOOKY
STORMY
TRACES

Buie, Perry C.

I TAKE IT BACK

Bulger, Harry

HEY, RUBE!

Bulhoes, Max

COME TO THE MARDI GRAS

Bullard, Frederick Field

STEIN SONG, A (IT'S ALWAYS FAIR
　　WEATHER WHEN GOOD FELLOWS
　　GET TOGETHER)

Bullock, Jeff

GIRL'S NIGHT OUT, A

Bullock, Vernon

IF I COULD BUILD MY WHOLE
　　WORLD AROUND YOU
WHAT DOES IT TAKE (TO WIN YOUR
　　LOVE)?
YESTERDAY'S DREAMS

Bullock, Walter

I COULD USE A DREAM
IN THE COOL OF THE EVENING
I STILL LOVE TO KISS YOU
　　GOODNIGHT
MAGNOLIAS IN THE MOONLIGHT
WHEN DID YOU LEAVE HEAVEN?
WHERE DO I GO FROM YOU?
WHO AM I?
YOU AND ME THAT USED TO BE,
　　THE

Bunch, Boyd

BROKEN RECORD, THE
DAY I LET YOU GET AWAY, THE
SLEEP, COME ON AND TAKE ME

Bunch, Pat

I'LL STILL BE LOVING YOU

Bunetta, P.

LOOK WHAT YOU STARTED

Bunnell, Dewey

BORDER, THE

Bunnell, Lee

HORSE WITH NO NAME, A

TIN MAN
VENTURA HIGHWAY

Burch, Don

YOU CHEATED

Burch, Fred

DREAM ON LITTLE DREAMER
OLD SHOWBOAT
P.T. 109
TRAGEDY

Burchill, Charles

ALIVE AND KICKING
SANCTIFY YOURSELF

Burdon, Eric

I'M CRYING
INSIDE—LOOKING OUT
MONTEREY
SAN FRANCISCAN NIGHTS
SKY PILOT
WHEN I WAS YOUNG

Burello, Tony

GOD BLESS US ALL

Burge, Gordon

PORTRAIT OF JENNIE

Burgers, Jan

MIDNIGHT IN MOSCOW

Burgess, Dave

EVERLOVIN'
EVERYBODY BUT ME
I'M AVAILABLE
LONELYVILLE
TOO MUCH TEQUILA

Burgie, Irving L. (Lord Burgess)

ISLAND IN THE SUN
JAMAICA FAREWELL

Burke, Bob

DADDY'S LITTLE GIRL
STRANGE LONELINESS, A

Burke, Clarence

WORLD OF FANTASY

Burke, Delores

GOT TO GET YOU OFF MY MIND

Burke, Joe

ALL THAT I'M ASKING IS SYMPATHY
AT A PERFUME COUNTER
BY THE RIVER OF THE ROSES
CAROLINA MOON
CLING TO ME
CROSBY, COLUMBO, AND VALLEE
DANCING WITH TEARS IN MY EYES
DREAM VALLEY
FOR YOU
GETTING SOME FUN OUT OF LIFE
GOODNIGHT LITTLE GIRL OF MY
　　DREAMS
HOW CAN YOU SAY "NO" (WHEN
　　ALL THE WORLD IS SAYING
　　"YES")?
IF I'M DREAMING, DON'T WAKE ME
　　TOO SOON
IN A LITTLE GYPSY TEA ROOM
IN THE VALLEY OF THE MOON
IT LOOKS LIKE RAIN IN CHERRY
　　BLOSSOM LANE
KISS WALTZ, THE
LITTLE BIT INDEPENDENT, A
MANY HAPPY RETURNS OF THE
　　DAY
MIDNIGHT BLUE
MOON OVER MIAMI
OH, HOW I MISS YOU TONIGHT
ON TREASURE ISLAND
PAINTING THE CLOUDS WITH
　　SUNSHINE
PING PONGO
RAINBOW VALLEY
RAMBLING ROSE
ROBINS AND ROSES
TIP TOE THROUGH THE TULIPS
　　WITH ME
WATCHING MY DREAMS GO BY

WE MUST BE VIGILANT
YEARNING (JUST FOR YOU)

Burke, Johnny

ACCIDENTS WILL HAPPEN
AIN'T GOT A DIME TO MY NAME
ALL YOU WANT TO DO IS DANCE
AND YOU'LL BE HOME
ANNIE DOESN'T LIVE HERE
   ANYMORE
APALACHICOLA, FLA.
APPLE FOR THE TEACHER, AN
APRIL PLAYED THE FIDDLE
AREN'T YOU GLAD YOU'RE YOU?
AS LONG AS I'M DREAMING
BEAT OF MY HEART, THE
BETWEEN A KISS AND A SIGH
BLUEBIRDS IN MY BELFRY
BUSY DOING NOTHING
BUT BEAUTIFUL
CHARMING LITTLE FAKER
CHICAGO STYLE
CONSTANTLY
COUNTRY STYLE
DAY AFTER FOREVER, THE
DEAREST, DAREST I?
DEVIL MAY CARE
DON'T LET THAT MOON GET AWAY
DO YOU KNOW WHY?
EAST SIDE OF HEAVEN
EXPERIENCE
FOR THE FIRST HUNDRED YEARS
FRIEND OF YOURS, A
FROM THE FIRST HELLO TO THE
   LAST GOODBYE
GO FLY A KITE
GOING MY WAY
GOOD-TIME CHARLEY
GOT THE MOON IN MY POCKET
GRASS IS GETTING GREENER ALL
   THE TIME, THE
HANG YOUR HEART ON A HICKORY
   LIMB
HARD WAY, THE
HARMONY
HERE'S THAT RAINY DAY
HIGH ON THE LIST
HIS ROCKING HORSE RAN AWAY
HORSE TOLD ME, THE
HOW LONG DID I DREAM?
HUMPTY DUMPTY HEART
IF YOU PLEASE

IF YOU STUB YOUR TOE ON THE
   MOON
I HAVEN'T TIME TO BE A
   MILLIONAIRE
IMAGINATION
IRRESISTIBLE
ISN'T THAT JUST LIKE LOVE
IT COULD HAPPEN TO YOU
I THOUGHT ABOUT YOU
IT'S ALWAYS YOU
IT'S ANYBODY'S SPRING
IT'S DARK ON OBSERVATORY HILL
IT'S THE NATURAL THING TO DO
I'VE GOT A POCKETFUL OF DREAMS
I'VE GOT A WARM SPOT IN MY
   HEART FOR YOU
I WAS SAYING TO THE MOON
JUST MY LUCK
JUST PLAIN LONESOME
KISS IN YOUR EYES, THE
LAUGH AND CALL IT LOVE
LET'S CALL A HEART A HEART
LIFE IS SO PECULIAR
LIKE SOMEONE IN LOVE
LOVE DROPPED IN FOR TEA
LOVE IS THE DARNDEST THING
MAN AND HIS DREAM, A
MEET THE SUN HALF WAY
MISTY
MOON AND THE WILLOW TREE, THE
MOON GOT IN MY EYES, THE
MOONLIGHT BECOMES YOU
MY HEART GOES CRAZY
MY HEART IS A HOBO
MY HEART IS TAKING LESSONS
MY VERY GOOD FRIEND, THE
   MILKMAN
NOW THAT I'M IN LOVE
NOW YOU'VE GOT ME DOING IT
OH, YOU CRAZY MOON
ONCE AND FOR ALWAYS
ONE, TWO, BUTTON YOUR SHOE
ONLY FOREVER
ON THE SENTIMENTAL SIDE
PENNIES FROM HEAVEN
PERSONALITY
PESSIMISTIC CHARACTER, THE
   (WITH THE CRAB APPLE FACE)
POLKA DOTS AND MOONBEAMS
PUT IT THERE, PAL
RHYTHM OF THE RIVER
ROAD TO MOROCCO
ROMEO SMITH AND JULIET JONES

SCATTERBRAIN
SHADOWS ON THE SWANEE
SING A SONG OF SUNBEAMS
SKELETON IN THE CLOSET, THE
SLEIGHRIDE IN JULY
SMILE RIGHT BACK AT THE SUN
SO DO I
SO WOULD I
STILL THE BLUEBIRD SINGS
SUDDENLY IT'S SPRING
SUNDAY, MONDAY, OR ALWAYS
SUNSHINE CAKE
(WE'VE GOT A) SURE THING
SWEET POTATO PIPER
SWINGING ON A STAR
THAT LITTLE DREAM GOT NOWHERE
THAT'S FOR ME
THAT SLY OLD GENTLEMAN (FROM
   FEATHERBED LANE)
THIS IS MY NIGHT TO DREAM
TOO ROMANTIC
WELCOME TO MY DREAM
WHAT'S NEW?
WHEN IS SOMETIME?
WHEN THE MOON COMES OVER
   MADISON SQUARE
WILD HORSES
WOULD YOU
YAH-TA-TA, YAH-TA-TA (TALK, TALK,
   TALK)
YOU DON'T HAVE TO KNOW THE
   LANGUAGE
YOU LUCKY PEOPLE, YOU
YOU'RE DANGEROUS
YOU'RE NOT THE ONLY OYSTER IN
   THE STEW
YOU'RE SO DARN CHARMING

Burke, Reginald

SERPENTINE FIRE

Burke, Solomon

EVERYBODY NEEDS SOMEBODY TO
   LOVE
GOT TO GET YOU OFF MY MIND
TONIGHT'S THE NIGHT

Burke, Sonny

BLACK COFFEE
HE'S A TRAMP

HOW IT LIES, HOW IT LIES, HOW IT LIES!
MERRY CHRISTMAS POLKA, THE
MIDNIGHT SUN
SIAMESE CAT SONG, THE
SOMEBODY BIGGER THAN YOU AND I
THEY WERE DOIN' THE MAMBO
YOU WAS

Burke, Thomas

LAMPLIT HOUR, THE

Burkhard, Paul

OH, MY PAPA

Burkhart, Addison

GOODBYE, ROSE

Burland, Granville "Sascha"

NO MATTER WHAT SHAPE (YOUR STOMACH'S IN)
UH! OH!

Burleigh, Harry T.

DEEP RIVER
LITTLE MOTHER OF MINE

Burnett, Ernie

MY MELANCHOLY BABY

Burnette, Billy Joe

TEDDY BEAR

Burnette, Dorsey

BELIEVE WHAT YOU SAY
CATCH A LITTLE RAINDROP
IT'S LATE
WAITIN' IN SCHOOL

Burnette, Johnny

BELIEVE WHAT YOU SAY
JUST A LITTLE TOO MUCH

WAITIN' IN SCHOOL

Burnette, O'Bryan, II

GIGOLO, THE

Burnette, Rocky

TIRED OF TOEIN' THE LINE

Burns, Annelu

I'LL FORGET YOU

Burns, Kenneth C.

TENNESSEE BORDER NO. 2

Burns, Morry

I'LL SAIL MY SHIP ALONE
SWEETER THAN THE FLOWERS

Burns, Peter

BRAND NEW LOVER
YOU SPIN ME ROUND LIKE A RECORD

Burns, Ralph

BIJOU
EARLY AUTUMN

Burnside, R. H.

LADDER OF ROSES, THE

Burr, Gary

LOVE'S BEEN A LITTLE BIT HARD ON ME
MAKE MY LIFE WITH YOU

Burris, James Henry

BALLIN' THE JACK
COME AFTER BREAKFAST, BRING 'LONG YOUR LUNCH AND LEAVE 'FORE SUPPER TIME
CONSTANTLY

Burris, Roy Edward

OKIE FROM MUSKOGEE

Burroughs, Madeline

WOMAN'S INTUITION, A

Burrows, Abe

LEAVE US FACE IT

Burrs, Glenn

ALEXANDER THE SWOOSE (HALF SWAN—HALF GOOSE)

Burt, Benjamin Hapgood

BEST I GET IS MUCH OBLIGED TO YOU, THE
PIG GOT UP AND SLOWLY WALKED AWAY, THE
SOME LITTLE BUG IS GOING TO FIND YOU
WAL, I SWAN! (OR, EBENEZER FRYE)

Burt, Ed

SILVER DEW ON THE BLUE GRASS TONIGHT

Burtnett, Earl

CANADIAN CAPERS
DO YOU EVER THINK OF ME?
LEAVE ME WITH A SMILE
'LEVEN-THIRTY SATURDAY NIGHT
MANDALAY

Burton, China

JESSE

Burton, Dorian

I CAN'T LOVE YOU ENOUGH
STILL
TEAR FELL, A

Burton, Eddie

DANCING YOUR MEMORY AWAY

Burton, George

YOU DON'T KNOW WHAT YOU'VE
GOT (UNTIL YOU LOSE IT)

Burton, Lori

BABY, LET'S WAIT

Burton, Michael

PILLOW TALK

Burton, Nat

OUR WALTZ
RHYTHM AND ROMANCE
SAY IT
WHEN THE ROSES BLOOM AGAIN
WHITE CLIFFS OF DOVER, THE
(THERE'LL BE BLUEBIRDS OVER)

Burton, Ray

I AM WOMAN

Burton, Val

BIG BAD WOLF WAS DEAD, THE
ISN'T THIS A NIGHT FOR LOVE?
PENTHOUSE SERENADE (A.K.A.
WHEN WE'RE ALONE)
SINGING A VAGABOND SONG

Burwell, Cliff

SWEET LORRAINE

Busch, Fini

SAILOR (YOUR HOME IS THE SEA)

Busch, Lou

HELLO MUDDAH, HELLO FADDUH!
(A LETTER FROM CAMP)

Buschor, George

MY MELODY OF LOVE

Bush, Eddie

WHAT'S HE DOIN' IN MY WORLD?

Bush, Kate

MAN WITH THE CHILD IN HIS EYES,
THE
RUNNING UP THAT HILL
THIS WOMAN'S WORK

Bushkin, Joe

BOOGIE WOOGIE BLUE PLATE
HOT TIME IN THE TOWN OF BERLIN,
A (WHEN THE YANKS GO
MARCHING IN)
OH, LOOK AT ME NOW

Buskirk, Paul

FAMILY BIBLE

Busse, Henry

HOT LIPS
WANG, WANG BLUES, THE

Butcher, Jon

GOODBYE SAVING GRACE

Butler, Billy

HONKY TONK

Butler, Carl

CRYING MY HEART OUT OVER YOU
IF TEARDROPS WERE PENNIES
IF TEARDROPS WERE SILVER
TOO LATE TO TRY AGAIN

Butler, Christopher

I KNOW WHAT BOYS LIKE

Butler, Daws

ST. GEORGE AND THE DRAGONET

Butler, Harry

SUN ARISE

Butler, Jerry

ARE YOU HAPPY?
BRAND NEW ME, A
DON'T LET LOVE HANG YOU UP
FIND ANOTHER GIRL
FOR YOUR PRECIOUS LOVE
HE DON'T LOVE YOU (LIKE I LOVE
YOU)
HE WILL BREAK YOUR HEART
(A.K.A. HE DON'T LOVE YOU—
LIKE I LOVE YOU)
HEY, WESTERN UNION MAN
I'VE BEEN LOVING YOU TOO LONG
(TO STOP NOW)
MOODY WOMAN
NEVER GIVE YOU UP
ONLY THE STRONG SURVIVE
WHAT'S THE USE OF BREAKING UP?

Butler, Jonathan

LIES

Butler, Larry

ANOTHER SOMEBODY DONE
SOMEBODY WRONG SONG
JUST FOR YOU
LULLABY OF LOVE

Butler, Pearl

KISSES DON'T LIE

Butler, Ralph T.

RUN, RABBIT, RUN

Butler, Richard

HEARTBREAK BEAT
LOVE MY WAY
PRETTY IN PINK

Butler, Tim

HEARTBREAK BEAT
LOVE MY WAY
PRETTY IN PINK

Butler, William B.

MATADOR, THE

Buttier, Billy

TIGHTEN UP

Buttolph, David

MAVERICK

Buttons, Red

HO HO SONG, THE
STRANGE THINGS ARE HAPPENING
   (HO HO, HEE HEE, HA HA)

Butts, Ray

PASS THE BOOZE

Buxton, Glen

EIGHTEEN

Byers, Joy

HERE COMES HEAVEN
PLEASE DON'T STOP LOVING ME
RING DANG DOO

Bynum, Hal

LUCILLE

Byrd, Bobby

LICKING STICK—LICKING STICK
LOST SOMEONE

Byrd, R.

BUZZ-BUZZ-BUZZ

Byrd, Robert

LITTLE BITTY PRETTY ONE
OVER AND OVER

Byrne, David

AND SHE WAS
BURNING DOWN THE HOUSE
LIFE DURING WARTIME (THIS AIN'T
   NO PARTY . . . THIS AIN'T NO
   DISCO . . . THIS AIN'T NO FOOLIN'
   AROUND)
ONCE IN A LIFETIME
PSYCHO KILLER

Byrne, J.

PSYCHOTIC REACTION

Byrne, Pete

PROMISES, PROMISES

Byrne, Robert

HOW DO I TURN YOU ON
I CAN'T WIN FOR LOSING YOU
ONCE IN A BLUE MOON
THAT WAS A CLOSE ONE

Byron, Al

LONG AS THE ROSE IS RED
ROSES ARE RED (MY LOVE)

Byron, David Leight

SHADOWS OF THE NIGHT

Caddigan, Jack

CAROLINA, I'M COMING BACK TO
   YOU
ROSE OF NO MAN'S LAND, THE

Cadena, Ozzie

RIGHT TIME, THE

Cadman, Charles Wakefield

AT DAWNING
FROM THE LAND OF THE SKY-BLUE
   WATER

Caesar, Irving

ANIMAL CRACKERS IN MY SOUP
ANNABEL LEE
BIGGER AND BETTER THAN EVER
CHANSONETTE
COUNT YOUR BLESSINGS
CRAZY RHYTHM
DEAR, ON A NIGHT LIKE THIS
DUST OFF THAT OLD PIANNA (OH,
   SUZANNA)
ELIZABETH
GIGOLETTE
GOOD EVENING, FRIENDS
HOLD MY HAND
IF I FORGET YOU
I LOVE HER, SHE LOVES ME (I'M
   HER HE, SHE'S MY SHE)
IMAGINATION
IS IT TRUE WHAT THEY SAY ABOUT
   DIXIE?
IT GOES LIKE THIS (THAT FUNNY
   MELODY)
I WANT TO BE HAPPY
JUST A GIGOLO
LADY, PLAY YOUR MANDOLIN
LOOK WHAT YOU'VE DONE
MY BLACKBIRDS ARE BLUEBIRDS
   NOW
NASHVILLE NIGHTINGALE
NASTY MAN
NINA ROSA
OH, DONNA CLARA
SASKATCHEWAN
SATISFIED!
SIXTY SECONDS EVERY MINUTE (I
   THINK OF YOU)
SOMETIMES I'M HAPPY
SOUS LES TOITS DE PARIS (UNDER A
   ROOF IN PAREE)
SOUTH AMERICAN JOE
SWANEE
SWEETHEARTS FOREVER
TEA FOR TWO
THAT'S WHAT I WANT FOR
   CHRISTMAS

THERE'S MORE TO THE KISS THAN
THE X-X-X
THERE'S NOTHING WRONG WITH A
KISS
TOO MANY RINGS AROUND ROSIE
UMBRIAGO
VIENNA DREAMS
WHAT A PERFECT COMBINATION
WHAT DO YOU DO SUNDAY, MARY?
"WHERE HAS MY HUBBY GONE?"
BLUES
YANKEE DOODLE BLUES
YOU CAN DANCE WITH ANY GIRL
AT ALL
YOU-OO JUST YOU
YOUR SMILES, YOUR TEARS

Cafferty, John

C-I-T-Y
ON THE DARK SIDE
VOICE OF AMERICA'S SONS

Caffey, Charlotte

HEAD OVER HEELS
VACATION
WE GOT THE BEAT

Cage, Earl, Jr.

MINI-SKIRT MINNIE

Cagle, Joseph

HEAVEN

Cahill, William

ONE CALLED "MOTHER" AND THE
OTHER "HOME SWEET HOME"
SINCE FATHER WENT TO WORK

Cahn, Sammy

ALL MY TOMORROWS
ALL THAT LOVE WENT TO WASTE
ALL THE WAY
AND THEN YOU KISSED ME
ANYWHERE
AS LONG AS THERE'S MUSIC
AT THE CAFE RENDEVOUS
BECAUSE YOU'RE MINE

BEI MIR BIST DU SCHOEN (MEANS
THAT YOU'RE GRAND)
BE MY LOVE
BEST OF EVERYTHING, THE
BLAME MY ABSENT-MINDED HEART
BOYS' NIGHT OUT, THE
BROOKLYN BRIDGE
CALL ME IRRESPONSIBLE
CAN THIS BE THE END OF THE
RAINBOW?
CAN'T YOU READ BETWEEN THE
LINES?
CHARM OF YOU, THE
COME OUT, COME OUT, WHEREVER
YOU ARE
DARK IS THE NIGHT
DAY BY DAY
DEDICATED TO YOU
DORMI, DORMI, DORMI
EVERYTHING MAKES MUSIC WHEN
YOU'RE IN LOVE
EV'RY DAY I LOVE YOU (JUST A
LITTLE BIT MORE)
FACE TO FACE
FIDDLE DEE DEE
FIVE MINUTES MORE
FOREVER DARLING
GO TO SLEEP, GO TO SLEEP, GO TO
SLEEP
GUESS I'LL HANG MY TEARS OUT TO
DRY
HEY! JEALOUS LOVER
HIGH HOPES
HOW D'YA LIKE YOUR EGGS IN THE
MORNING?
HOW D'YA TALK TO A GIRL
I BEGGED HER
I BELIEVE
I CAN SEE YOU
I COULD MAKE YOU CARE
I DON'T CARE IF IT RAINS ALL
NIGHT
I DON'T THINK I'M IN LOVE
I FALL IN LOVE TOO EASILY
IF AND WHEN
IF IT'S THE LAST THING I DO
I GOTTA GAL I LOVE (IN NORTH
AND SOUTH DAKOTA)
I LIKE TO LEAD WHEN I DANCE
I'LL NEVER STOP LOVING YOU
I'LL WALK ALONE
I LOVE AN OLD FASHIONED SONG
I'M GLAD I WAITED FOR YOU

I'M IN LOVE
IMPATIENT YEARS, THE
INDISCRETION
I SHOULD CARE
I STILL GET JEALOUS
IT'S A GREAT FEELING
IT'S A WOMAN'S WORLD
IT'S BEEN A LONG, LONG TIME
IT'S BETTER IN THE DARK
IT'S MAGIC
IT'S MY TURN NOW
IT'S THE SAME OLD DREAM
IT'S YOU OR NO ONE
I'VE HEARD THAT SONG BEFORE
I'VE NEVER FORGOTTEN
I WANT MY SHARE OF LOVE
JOSEPH! JOSEPH!
LATELY SONG, THE
LET IT SNOW! LET IT SNOW! LET IT
SNOW!
LET ME TRY AGAIN
LET'S NOT BE SENSIBLE
LONG HOT SUMMER, THE
LOVE AND MARRIAGE
LOVE ME
MAKE HER MINE
MAN WITH THE GOLDEN ARM, THE
MELANCHOLY RHAPSODY
MR. BOOZE
MY DESTINY
MY KIND OF TOWN (CHICAGO IS)
NOW THAT WE'RE IN LOVE
ON A SUNDAY BY THE SEA
ONLY THE LONELY
ONLY TRUST YOUR HEART
PAPA, WON'T YOU DANCE WITH ME?
PETE KELLY'S BLUES
PLEASE BE KIND
POCKETFUL OF MIRACLES
POOR LITTLE RHODE ISLAND
POSIN'
PUT 'EM IN A BOX, TIE 'EM WITH A
RIBBON, AND THROW 'EM IN THE
DEEP BLUE SEA
RELAX-AY-VOO
RHYTHM IN MY NURSERY RHYMES
RHYTHM IS OUR BUSINESS
RHYTHM SAVED THE WORLD
ROAD TO HONG KONG, THE
SAME OLD SATURDAY NIGHT
SATURDAY NIGHT (IS THE
LONELIEST NIGHT IN THE WEEK)
SAVING MYSELF FOR YOU

SECOND TIME AROUND, THE
SECRET OF CHRISTMAS, THE
SEPTEMBER OF MY YEARS
SHOE SHINE BOY
SOMEBODY UP THERE LIKES ME
SOME OTHER TIME
SONG FROM "SOME CAME RUNNING"
   (A.K.A. TO LOVE AND BE LOVED)
SONG'S GOTTA COME FROM THE
   HEART, THE
STAR!
STYLE
TEACH ME TONIGHT
TEAMWORK
TENDER TRAP, THE
THAT'S WHAT MAKES PARIS PAREE
THERE GOES THAT SONG AGAIN
THERE'S NOTHING LIKE A
   MODEL "T"
THEY CAME TO CORDURA
THINGS WE DID LAST SUMMER, THE
THOROUGHLY MODERN MILLIE
THREE COINS IN THE FOUNTAIN
TIME AFTER TIME
UNDER THE YUM-YUM TREE
UNTIL THE REAL THING COMES
   ALONG (IT WILL HAVE TO DO)
USE YOUR NOGGIN'
VICT'RY POLKA
WAKE ME WHEN IT'S OVER
WALKING HAPPY
WARMER THAN A WHISPER
WE NEVER TALK MUCH
WHAT AM I GONNA DO ABOUT YOU?
WHAT MAKES THE SUNSET?
WHERE DID YOU LEARN TO LOVE?
WHERE LOVE HAS GONE
WHO ARE YOU NOW?
WHO DID? I DID
WHO WAS THAT LADY?
WONDER WHY
WRITTEN ON THE WIND
YOU'RE A LUCKY GUY
YOU'RE THE CAUSE OF IT ALL

Cain, Jonathan

BE GOOD TO YOURSELF
DON'T STOP BELIEVIN'
FAITHFULLY
I'LL BE ALRIGHT WITHOUT YOU
ONLY THE YOUNG
OPEN ARMS

SEND HER MY LOVE
SEPARATE WAYS
STILL THEY RIDE
SUZANNE
THIS COULD BE THE NIGHT
WHO'S CRYING NOW

Calabrese, Giorgio

OUR CONCERTO
SOFTLY, AS I LEAVE YOU

Caldwell, Anne

BAGDAD
BLUE DANUBE BLUES
COME AND HAVE A SWING WITH
   ME
GOOD MORNING, DEARIE
I KNOW THAT YOU KNOW
IN LOVE WITH LOVE
KA-LU-A
LEFT ALL ALONE AGAIN BLUES
LIKE HE LOVES ME
LOOK AT THE WORLD AND SMILE
ONCE IN A BLUE MOON
RAGGEDY ANN
SOMEBODY ELSE
WAIT TILL THE COWS COME HOME
WHOSE BABY ARE YOU?
YOU WILL, WON'T YOU?

Caldwell, Bobby

NEXT TIME I FALL, THE
WHAT YOU WON'T DO FOR LOVE

Caldwell, Gayle

CYCLES

Caldwell, Gloria

DON'T LET ME BE MISUNDERSTOOD

Caldwell, Ronnie

SOUL FINGER

Caldwell, Toy

HEARD IT IN A LOVE SONG
THIS OL' COWBOY

Cale, J. J.

AFTER MIDNIGHT

Calello, Charles

YOU'RE GONNA HURT YOURSELF

Calhoun, Charles

FLIP FLOP AND FLY
SHAKE, RATTLE AND ROLL
YOUR CASH AIN'T NOTHIN' BUT
   TRASH

Calhoun, Charles E.

SMACK DAB IN THE MIDDLE

Calhoun, Floride

HILLS OF HOME, THE

California, Randy

I GOT A LINE ON YOU

Calilli, Bob

WALK AWAY RENEE

Calis, Jo

DON'T YOU WANT ME

Call, Alex

867-5309/JENNY
LITTLE TOO LATE
PERFECT WORLD

Call, Michael

CINDERELLA, STAY IN MY ARMS

Callahan, J. Will

SMILES
TELL ME (WHY NIGHTS ARE
   LONELY)
YOU PLANTED A ROSE IN THE
   GARDEN OF LOVE

Cargill, Ike

FOREVER IS ENDING TODAY

Carin

LEARNING TO FLY

Carl, Billy

GOODY GOODY GUMDROPS

Carle, Frankie

FALLING LEAVES
GEORGIANNA
LOVER'S LULLABY, A
OH! WHAT IT SEEMED TO BE
ROSES IN THE RAIN
SUNRISE SERENADE

Carle, Richard

LEMON IN THE GARDEN OF LOVE, A

Carleton, Bob

JA-DA
TEASIN'
WHERE THE BLUES WERE BORN IN
    NEW ORLEANS

Carlin, Fred

COME SATURDAY MORNING

Carling, Foster

SUSPICION

Carlisi, Jeff

CAUGHT UP IN YOU
IF I'D BEEN THE ONE
LIKE NO OTHER NIGHT

Carlisi, Sammy

LOVE I YOU (YOU I LOVE)

Carlisle, B.

WHY'D YOU COME HERE LOOKIN'
    LIKE THAT

Carlisle, Bill

IS ZAT YOU, MYRTLE?
KNOTHOLE
NO HELP WANTED
TOO OLD TO CUT THE MUSTARD

Carlisle, Una Mae

I SEE A MILLION PEOPLE (BUT ALL I
    CAN SEE IS YOU)

Carlo, Monte

LITTLE TOWN IN THE OULD
    COUNTRY DOWN
THAT TUMBLE-DOWN SHACK IN
    ATHLONE

Carlo, Tyran

I'LL BE SATISFIED
LONELY TEARDROPS
THAT'S WHY (I LOVE YOU SO)
TO BE LOVED
YOU GOT WHAT IT TAKES

Carlton, Bob

NUMBER 10 LULLABY LANE

Carlton, Harry

C-O-N-S-T-A-N-T-I-N-O-P-L-E

Carlyle, Russ

IF I EVER LOVE AGAIN

Carman, Brian

PIPELINE

Carmen, Albert

APACHE '65

Carmen, Eric

ALL BY MYSELF
ALMOST PARADISE . . . LOVE
    THEME FROM "FOOTLOOSE"
BOATS AGAINST THE CURRENT
CHANGE OF HEART
GO ALL THE WAY
HEY DEANIE
I WANNA BE WITH YOU
MAKE ME LOSE CONTROL
NEVER GONNA FALL IN LOVE AGAIN
OVERNIGHT SENSATION (HIT
    RECORD)
SHE DID IT
THAT'S ROCK 'N' ROLL

Carmichael, Hoagy

AFTER TWELVE O'CLOCK
APRIL IN MY HEART
BALTIMORE ORIOLE
BLUE ORCHIDS
BONEYARD SHUFFLE
BUBBLE LOO, BUBBLE LOO
CAN'T GET INDIA OFF MY MIND
COLLEGE SWING
DOWN T'UNCLE BILL'S
GEORGIA ON MY MIND
HEART AND SOUL
HONG KONG BLUES
HOW LITTLE WE KNOW
I GET ALONG WITHOUT YOU VERY
    WELL
IN THE COOL, COOL, COOL OF THE
    EVENING
I SHOULD HAVE KNOWN YOU YEARS
    AGO
IVY
I WALK WITH MUSIC
JUBILEE
JUDY
KINDA LONESOME
LAMPLIGHTER'S SERENADE, THE
LAZYBONES
LAZY RIVER
LITTLE OLD LADY
MANHATTAN RAG
MEMPHIS IN JUNE
MOONBURN
MOON COUNTRY
MY RESISTANCE IS LOW
NEARNESS OF YOU, THE

OLD MAN HARLEM
OLD MUSIC MASTER, THE
OLE BUTTERMILK SKY
ONE MORNING IN MAY
OOH, WHAT YOU SAID!
RIVERBOAT SHUFFLE
ROCKIN' CHAIR
SING ME A SWING SONG
SKYLARK
SMALL FRY
SNOWBALL
STAR DUST
THANKSGIVIN'
THREE RIVERS, THE (THE
    ALLEGHENY, SUSQUEHANNA,
    AND THE OLD MONONGAHELA)
TWO SLEEPY PEOPLE
VAGABOND DREAMS
WASHBOARD BLUES
WATERMELON WEATHER
WE'RE THE COUPLE IN THE
    CASTLE
WHEN LOVE GOES WRONG

Carnelia, Craig

JUST A HOUSEWIFE

Carnes, John

HANDS ACROSS AMERICA

Carnes, Kim

CRAZY IN THE NIGHT (BARKING AT
    AIRPLANES)
DON'T FALL IN LOVE WITH A
    DREAMER
MAKE NO MISTAKE HE'S (SHE'S)
    MINE
YOU'RE A PART OF ME

Carnes, Rich

CAN'T EVEN GET THE BLUES

Carosone, Renato

TORERO

Carpenter, Bob

BABY'S GOT A HOLD ON ME

I'LL COME BACK AS ANOTHER
    WOMAN

Carpenter, Charles

BOLERO AT THE SAVOY
LOVER IS BLUE, A
YOU CAN DEPEND ON ME
YOU TAUGHT ME TO LOVE AGAIN

Carpenter, Imogene

BORN TO SING THE BLUES

Carpenter, Marion

WORLD OF MAKE BELIEVE

Carpenter, Michael

CAN U READ MY LIPS

Carpenter, Moneen

WAY TO SURVIVE, A

Carpenter, Peter

ROCKFORD FILES, THE
THEME FROM "MAGNUM P. I."

Carpenter, Richard

GOODBYE TO LOVE
I NEED TO BE IN LOVE
ONLY YESTERDAY
SOMETHING IN YOUR EYES
TOP OF THE WORLD
YESTERDAY ONCE MORE

Carr, Fred

STOP THE START (OF TEARS IN MY
    HEART)

Carr, Harold

GAME OF LOVE, THE
IF'N
MUTUAL ADMIRATION SOCIETY
NEW-FANGLED TANGO, A
THIS IS WHAT I CALL LOVE

Carr, Howard

WE DON'T WANT THE BACON, WHAT
    WE WANT IS A PIECE OF THE
    RHINE

Carr, Jerry

ROSIE LEE

Carr, Leon

ANOTHER CUP OF COFFEE
BELL BOTTOM BLUES
CLINGING VINE
GINA
HEY THERE LONELY BOY (A.K.A.
    HEY THERE LONELY GIRL)
HOTEL HAPPINESS
MOST PEOPLE GET MARRIED
MY SHY VIOLET
OUR EVERLASTING LOVE
SEE THE U.S.A. IN YOUR
    CHEVROLET
THERE'S NO TOMORROW
YOUNG NEW MEXICAN PUPPETEER,
    THE
YOUR SOCKS DON'T MATCH

Carr, Leroy

HOW LONG, HOW LONG BLUES

Carr, Michael

BANDIT, THE
DID YOUR MOTHER COME FROM
    IRELAND?
DINNER FOR ONE, PLEASE JAMES
GENTLEMAN OBVIOUSLY DOESN'T
    BELIEVE, THE
HE WEARS A PAIR OF SILVER
    WINGS
HOME TOWN
OLE FAITHFUL
SOUTH OF THE BORDER (DOWN
    MEXICO WAY)
TWO BOUQUETS

Carr, Robert

I BELIEVE IN YOU
WE BELONG TOGETHER

Channel, Bruce

DON'T WORRY 'BOUT ME BABY
HEY! BABY
PARTY TIME

Chapel, Don

WHEN THE GRASS GROWS OVER ME

Chapel, Jean

GOING THROUGH THE MOTIONS (OF
LIVING)
LONELY AGAIN
TRIANGLE

Chapin, Harry

BETTER PLACE TO BE
CAT'S IN THE CRADLE
SEQUEL
SUNDAY MORNING SUNSHINE
TAXI
W-O-L-D

Chapin, Sandra

CAT'S IN THE CRADLE

Chaplin, Charles

ETERNALLY (A.K.A. LIMELIGHT OR
THE TERRY THEME)
SMILE
THIS IS MY SONG

Chaplin, Saul

ANNIVERSARY SONG
BEI MIR BIST DU SCHOEN (MEANS
THAT YOU'RE GRAND)
CAN THIS BE THE END OF THE
RAINBOW?
DEDICATED TO YOU
I COULD MAKE YOU CARE
IF IT'S THE LAST THING I DO
IT'S MY TURN NOW
I WANT MY SHARE OF LOVE
JOSEPH! JOSEPH!
PLEASE BE KIND
POSIN'
RHYTHM IN MY NURSERY RHYMES

RHYTHM IS OUR BUSINESS
RHYTHM SAVED THE WORLD
SAVING MYSELF FOR YOU
SHOE SHINE BOY
UNTIL THE REAL THING COMES
ALONG (IT WILL HAVE TO DO)
YOU'RE A LUCKY GUY
YOU WONDERFUL YOU

Chapman, Arthur

OUT WHERE THE WEST BEGINS

Chapman, Beth Nielsen

NOTHING I CAN DO ABOUT IT NOW

Chapman, G.

I PREFER THE MOONLIGHT

Chapman, Mike

BALLROOM BLITZ
HEART AND SOUL
KISS YOU ALL OVER
LIVING NEXT DOOR TO ALICE
LOVE IS A BATTLEFIELD
LOVE TOUCH (THEME FROM "LEGAL
EAGLES")
MICKEY
STUMBLIN' IN

Chapman, Tracy

FAST CAR

Chaquico, Craig

FIND YOUR WAY BACK
JANE

Charig, Phil

BLOWIN' THE BLUES AWAY
FANCY OUR MEETING
I WANNA GET MARRIED
ON ACCOUNT OF I LOVE YOU
SUNNY DISPOSISH
THAT LOST BARBERSHOP CHORD
WHY DO YA ROLL THOSE EYES?

Charlap, Moose

ENGLISH MUFFINS AND IRISH STEW
I'M FLYING
I'VE GOTTA CROW
I WON'T GROW UP
LOVE EYES
SLOWLY, WITH FEELING
TENDER SHEPHERD
(BUT AS THEY SAY) THAT'S LIFE
YOUNG IDEAS

Charles, Beau

LIES

Charles, Dick

ALONG THE NAVAJO TRAIL
CORNS FOR MY COUNTRY
I TIPPED MY HAT (AND SLOWLY
RODE AWAY)
IT TAKES A LONG, LONG TRAIN
WITH A RED CABOOSE (TO
CARRY MY BLUES AWAY)
MAD ABOUT HIM, SAD ABOUT HIM,
HOW CAN I BE GLAD ABOUT HIM
BLUES
MAY YOU ALWAYS
THIS IS MY SONG

Charles, Ernest

LET MY SONG FILL YOUR HEART

Charles, Hugh

I WON'T TELL A SOUL
SILVER WINGS IN THE MOONLIGHT
THERE'LL ALWAYS BE AN ENGLAND
WE'LL MEET AGAIN

Charles, Jacques

VALENCIA

Charles, Lee

HERE I AM (COME AND TAKE ME)

Charles, Les

LOVE REALLY HURTS WITHOUT YOU

Charles, Ray

AIN'T THAT LOVE
BABY, LET ME HOLD YOUR HAND
COME BACK
DON'T YOU KNOW
FOOL FOR YOU, A
HALLELUJAH I LOVE HER/HIM SO
I CHOSE TO SING THE BLUES
I GOT A WOMAN (I GOT A SWEETIE)
LOVE ON MY MIND
NOBODY CARES
ROCKHOUSE
SWANEE RIVER ROCK (TALKIN'
    'BOUT THAT RIVER)
SWEET SIXTEEN BARS
THAT'S ENOUGH
THIS LITTLE GIRL OF MINE
UNDERSTANDING
WHAT'D I SAY

Charles, Ray

FRENESI

Charnin, Martin

EASY STREET
I DO NOT KNOW A DAY I DID NOT
    LOVE YOU
I DON'T NEED ANYTHING BUT YOU
IT'S THE HARD KNOCK LIFE
MAYBE
TOMORROW
TWO BY TWO

Charron, Mark

BILLY AND SUE
MAMA
WOMAN HELPING MAN

Chase, Clifton

MESSAGE, THE

Chase, Lincoln

CINNAMON SINNER
CLAPPING SONG, THE (CLAP PAT
    CLAP SLAP)
JIM DANDY
NAME GAME, THE

NITTY GRITTY, THE
SUCH A NIGHT
WONDERLAND BY NIGHT

Chase, Newell

IF I WERE KING
IT'S A GREAT LIFE (IF YOU DON'T
    WEAKEN)
MY IDEAL

Chater, Kerry

I KNOW A HEARTACHE WHEN I SEE
    ONE
I.O.U.
YOU LOOK SO GOOD IN LOVE
YOU'RE THE FIRST TIME I'VE
    THOUGHT ABOUT LEAVING

Chatman, Bo

CORRINE, CORRINA (CORINNA,
    CORINNA)

Chatman, Peter, Jr.

BLUE AND LONESOME
EVERY DAY I HAVE THE BLUES
    (A.K.A. EVERY DAY)

Chattaway, Thurland

CAN'T YOU TAKE IT BACK AND
    CHANGE IT?
I'VE GROWN SO USED TO YOU
MANDY LEE
MY GUIDING STAR
MY HONEY LOU
RED WING (AN INDIAN FABLE)
SWEETEST FLOWER THE GARDEN
    GREW, THE
WE'VE BEEN CHUMS FOR FIFTY
    YEARS
WHEN THE BLUE SKY TURNS TO
    GOLD

Chatton, Brian

I WANNA BE A COWBOY

Chauncey, Danny

I WANNA GO BACK

Chauvigny, R.

YOUNG GIRL, A

Chayefsky, Paddy

MARTY

Chazon, Samuel Marvin

ANDREA

Chen, Phil

PASSION

Chera, Len

SOMEBODY'S NEEDIN' SOMEBODY

Cherne, Leo M.

I'LL NEVER FORGET

Chertoff, Rick

DAY BY DAY
SATELLITE
SHE BOP

Cherubini, B.

MAMA
SERENADE IN THE NIGHT

Chesnut, Jerry

ANOTHER PLACE, ANOTHER TIME
GOOD TIME CHARLIES
GOOD YEAR FOR THE ROSES, A
HOLDING ON TO NOTHING
IF NOT FOR YOU
IT'S FOUR IN THE MORNING
LOOKING AT THE WORLD THROUGH
    A WINDSHIELD

Chessler, Deborah

IT'S TOO SOON TO KNOW

Chiarelli, Jack

IN THE MISSION OF ST. AUGUSTINE

Chiate, Lloyd

MAYBE I'M A FOOL

Child, Desmond

ANGEL
BAD MEDICINE
BORN TO BE MY BABY
DUDE (LOOKS LIKE A LADY)
I HATE MYSELF FOR LOVING YOU
I WAS MADE FOR LOVIN' YOU
LIVIN' ON A PRAYER
YOU GIVE LOVE A BAD NAME

Chinn, Nicky

BALLROOM BLITZ
HEART AND SOUL
KISS YOU ALL OVER
LIVING NEXT DOOR TO ALICE
MICKEY
STUMBLIN' IN

Chiprut, Elliot

SIMON SAYS

Chisolm, Ed

LET THE MUSIC PLAY

Choate, Donald

IT'S TIME TO PAY THE FIDDLER

Chong, Tommy

BASKETBALL JONES FEATURING
  TYRONE SHOELACES
DOES YOUR MAMA KNOW ABOUT
  ME?
EARACHE MY EYE FEATURING
  ALICE BOWIE

Chopin, Frederic

MY TWILIGHT DREAM

Christenson, Laurie

IN THE MIDDLE OF A HEARTACHE

**Christian, Arlester
"Dyke"**

FUNKY BROADWAY
LET A WOMAN BE A WOMAN, LET A
  MAN BE A MAN
WE GOT MORE SOUL

Christian, Charlie

AIR MAIL SPECIAL
SOLO FLIGHT

Christian, Rick

I DON'T NEED YOU

Christian, Roger

ANAHEIM, AZUSA AND CUCAMONGA
  SEWING CIRCLE, BOOK REVIEW
  AND TIMING ASSOCIATION
BUCKET "T"
DEAD MAN'S CURVE
DON'T WORRY BABY
DRAG CITY
HONOLULU LULU
LITTLE OLD LADY (FROM
  PASADENA), THE
SHUT DOWN
THREE WINDOW COUPE
YOU REALLY KNOW HOW TO HURT
  A GUY

Christie, George

BABY ROSE

Christie, Jeff

YELLOW RIVER

Christie, Lou

LIGHTNIN' STRIKES

OUTSIDE THE GATES OF HEAVEN
RHAPSODY IN THE RAIN

Christin, Henri

VALENTINE

Christopher, Gretchen

COME SOFTLY TO ME

Christopher, Johnny

ALWAYS ON MY MIND
BETTER LOVE NEXT TIME, A
IF YOU TALK IN YOUR SLEEP
MAMA LIKED THE ROSES
NO LOVE AT ALL

Chudacoff, Rick

LOOK WHAT YOU STARTED
STEAL AWAY

Chung, Wang

EVERYBODY HAVE FUN TONIGHT
LET'S GO!
TO LIVE AND DIE IN L.A.

Church, Eugene

PRETTY GIRLS EVERYWHERE

Church, Gary

I ALWAYS GET LUCKY WITH YOU

Churchill, Frank

BABY MINE
HEIGH-HO
I'M WISHING
LOVE IS A SONG
ONE SONG
PUT YOUR HEART IN A SONG
SOMEDAY MY PRINCE WILL COME
SUNNY SIDE OF THINGS, THE
WHISTLE WHILE YOU WORK
WHO'S AFRAID OF THE BIG BAD
  WOLF?
WITH A SMILE AND A SONG

Churchill, Savannah

I WANT TO BE LOVED (BUT BY ONLY
    YOU)

Cicchetti, Carl

BEEP BEEP

Ciccone, Don

MR. DIEINGLY SAD
THERE'S GOT TO BE A WORD

Ciccone, Madonna

LIKE A PRAYER
LIVE TO TELL
LUCKY STAR

Cicognini, Alessandro

INDISCRETION

Cifelli, Chubby

TELL IT TO THE RAIN

Citorello, Paolo

LAZY MARY
OH! MA-MA (THE BUTCHER BOY)

Claire, Phyllis

PETITE WALTZ (LA PETITE VALSE)

Clanton, Jimmy

JUST A DREAM

Clapp, Sunny

BUNDLE OF SOUTHERN SUNSHINE,
    A
GIRL OF MY DREAMS

Clapps, Donald

BEEP BEEP

Clapton, Eric

BADGE
BELL BOTTOM BLUES
BLUES POWER
HELLO OLD FRIEND
I CAN'T STAND IT
IT'S IN THE WAY YOU USE IT
LAY DOWN SALLY
LAYLA
SUNSHINE OF YOUR LOVE
WATCH OUT FOR LUCY
WONDERFUL TONIGHT

Clar, Arden

SIMILAU

Clare, Sidney

BIG BUTTER AND EGG MAN, THE
I'D CLIMB THE HIGHEST MOUNTAIN
I'M MISSIN' MAMMY'S KISSIN' (AND I
    KNOW SHE'S MISSIN' MINE)
IT WAS SWEET OF YOU
KEEPIN' MYSELF FOR YOU
LOVABLE AND SWEET
MA! (HE'S MAKING EYES AT ME)
ME AND THE BOY FRIEND
MISS ANNABELLE LEE
MY FUTURE STAR
ONE SWEET LETTER FROM YOU
ON THE GOOD SHIP LOLLIPOP
OO-OO ERNEST, ARE YOU EARNEST
    WITH ME?
PLEASE DON'T TALK ABOUT ME
    WHEN I'M GONE
ROCK AND ROLL
(I WANNA GO WHERE YOU GO, DO
    WHAT YOU DO) THEN I'LL BE
    HAPPY
TRAVELIN' LIGHT
WHAT A BEAUTIFUL BEGINNING
WHAT DO I CARE WHAT SOMEBODY
    SAID?
YES TO YOU
YOU'RE MY THRILL

Clark, Billy

I LOVE MY WIFE, BUT OH, YOU KID!

Clark, Claudine

PARTY LIGHTS

Clark, Collenane

RATION BLUES

Clark, Cottonseed

TEXARKANA BABY
TEXAS BLUES

Clark, Dave

ANY WAY YOU WANT IT
AT THE SCENE
BECAUSE
BITS AND PIECES
CAN'T YOU SEE THAT SHE'S MINE?
CATCH US IF YOU CAN
COME HOME
EVERYBODY KNOWS (I STILL LOVE
    YOU)
GHETTO WOMAN
GLAD ALL OVER
I'VE GOT TO HAVE A REASON
NINETEEN DAYS
PLEASE TELL ME WHY
SATISFIED WITH YOU
TRY TOO HARD
WHY I SING THE BLUES

Clark, Dee

NOBODY BUT YOU
RAINDROPS
YOU CAN'T SIT DOWN

Clark, Edward

YOU'RE IN LOVE

Clark, Freddie

BEANS AND CORN BREAD

Clark, Gary

MARY'S PRAYER

Clark, Gene

EIGHT MILES HIGH
SET YOU FREE THIS TIME
YOU SHOWED ME

Clark, Guy

BABY I'M YOURS
DESPERADOES WAITING FOR A
   TRAIN
L. A. FREEWAY

Clark, Les

SHOW ME THE WAY TO GET OUT OF
   THIS WORLD ('CAUSE THAT'S
   WHERE EVERYTHING IS)

Clark, Louie

LET OLD MOTHER NATURE HAVE
   HER WAY

Clark, Michael

SLOW HAND

Clark, Mike

SAVIN' MY LOVE FOR YOU

Clark, Petula

YOU'RE THE ONE

Clark, Randy

DO IT RIGHT

Clark, Rudy

EVERYBODY PLAYS THE FOOL
GOOD LOVIN'
GOT MY MIND SET ON YOU
SHOOP SHOOP SONG, THE (IT'S IN
   HIS KISS)

Clark, S.

COME FROM THE HEART

Clark, Stanley

I'M FOR REAL

Clark, Steve

ANIMAL
BRINGIN' ON THE HEARTBREAK
FOOLIN'
HYSTERIA
LOVE BITES
PHOTOGRAPH
POUR SOME SUGAR ON ME
ROCK OF AGES

Clark, Tena R.

CONGRATULATIONS
RESERVATIONS FOR TWO

Clark, Willie

ROCKIN' CHAIR

Clark, Willie J.

GIRLS CAN'T DO WHAT THE GUYS
   DO

Clarke, Allan

CARRIE-ANNE
DEAR ELOISE
JENNIFER ECCLES
LONG COOL WOMAN (IN A BLACK
   DRESS)
ON A CAROUSEL
PAY YOU BACK WITH INTEREST
STOP, STOP, STOP
TELL ME TO MY FACE

Clarke, Bert

NIGHT ON THE WATER
PANIC IS ON, THE

Clarke, Elizabeth

BLUEBIRD ON YOUR WINDOWSILL
   (THERE'S A)

Clarke, George

NIGHT ON THE WATER
PANIC IS ON, THE

Clarke, Grant

AM I BLUE?
AVALON TOWN
BACK TO THE CAROLINA YOU LOVE
BEATRICE FAIRFAX, TELL ME WHAT
   TO DO!
BIRMINGHAM BERTHA
BLUE (AND BROKEN HEARTED)
EVERYTHING IS PEACHES DOWN IN
   GEORGIA
HE'D HAVE TO GET UNDER—GET
   OUT AND GET UNDER
HE'S A DEVIL IN HIS OWN HOME
   TOWN
IF HE CAN FIGHT LIKE HE CAN
   LOVE, GOOD NIGHT GERMANY
I HATE TO LOSE YOU
I LOVE THE LADIES
I LOVE THE LAND OF OLD BLACK
   JOE
I'M A LITTLE BLACKBIRD LOOKING
   FOR A BLUEBIRD
I'M THE MEDICINE MAN FOR THE
   BLUES
IN THE LAND OF BEGINNING AGAIN
MANDY, MAKE UP YOUR MIND
MOTHER OF MINE, I STILL HAVE
   YOU
MY LITTLE BIMBO DOWN ON THE
   BAMBOO ISLE
NOBODY CARES IF I'M BLUE
OH, YOU MILLION DOLLAR DOLL
RAGTIME COWBOY JOE
SECOND HAND ROSE
SIT DOWN, YOU'RE ROCKING THE
   BOAT!
THANKS TO YOU
THERE'S A LITTLE BIT OF BAD IN
   EVERY GOOD LITTLE GIRL
WEARY RIVER
WHEN YOU'RE IN LOVE WITH
   SOMEONE (WHO IS NOT IN LOVE
   WITH YOU)
WISHING AND WAITING FOR LOVE
WOULDN'T IT BE WONDERFUL?
YOU CAN'T GET ALONG WITH 'EM
   OR WITHOUT 'EM

Clarke, Herb

T.L.C. TENDER LOVE AND CARE

Clarke, H. Pitman

SWANEE RIVER MOON

Clarke, Kenny

EPISTROPHY
SALT PEANUTS

Clarke, Robert Coningby

BOWL OF ROSES, A

Clarke, S.

LIVING PROOF

Clarke, Tony

ENTERTAINER, THE
PUSHOVER

Clarke, Willie

CLEAN UP WOMAN
NOBODY BUT YOU, BABE

Clarkson, Geoffrey

GOODBYE TO LOVE
HOME

Clarkson, Harry

GOODBYE TO LOVE
HOME

Clasky, Richard

IMAGE OF A GIRL

Clauson, William

LA BAMBA

Claypoole, Edward B.

RAGGING THE SCALE

Clayton, Adam

I WILL FOLLOW
NEW YEAR'S DAY
PRIDE (IN THE NAME OF LOVE)

Clayton, Buck

RED BANK BOOGIE

Clayton, Harold

TAKE YOUR TIME (DO IT RIGHT)

Clayton, Justin

VALOTTE

Clayton, Paul

GOTTA TRAVEL ON

Clayton-Thomas, David

SPINNING WHEEL

Cleary, Michael

HERE IT IS MONDAY AND I'VE STILL
GOT A DOLLAR
SINGIN' IN THE BATHTUB
WHEN A LADY MEETS A
GENTLEMAN DOWN SOUTH

Clemenceau, Martine

SOLITAIRE

Clement, Doris

DOES MY RING HURT YOUR
FINGER?

Clement, Jack H.

BALLAD OF A TEENAGE QUEEN
CALIFORNIA GIRL AND THE
TENNESSEE SQUARE
GIRL I USED TO KNOW, A
GUESS THINGS HAPPEN THAT WAY
I KNOW ONE
IT'S JUST ABOUT TIME
JUST BETWEEN YOU AND ME

MILLER'S CAVE
NOT WHAT I HAD IN MIND

Clement, Jake

ONE ON THE RIGHT IS ON THE
LEFT

Clements, Zeke

JUST A LITTLE LOVIN' (WILL GO A
LONG, LONG WAY)
SMOKE ON THE WATER
SOMEBODY'S BEEN BEATIN' MY
TIME
WHY SHOULD I CRY?

Clempson, Clem

HOT 'N' NASTY

Clesi, N. J.

I'M SORRY I MADE YOU CRY

Cleveland, Alfred

BABY, BABY, DON'T CRY
COME BACK, CHARLESTON BLUE
DOGGONE RIGHT
HERE I GO AGAIN
I SECOND THAT EMOTION
MALINDA
POINT IT OUT
SPECIAL OCCASION
WHAT'S GOING ON
YESTER LOVE

Cliff, Jimmy

BREAKDOWN
CLUB PARADISE
HARDER THEY COME, THE
MANY RIVERS TO CROSS
SITTING IN LIMBO
WONDERFUL WORLD, BEAUTIFUL
PEOPLE
YOU CAN GET IT IF YOU REALLY
WANT

Cliff, Laddie

COAL BLACK MAMMY

Clifford, Buzz

ECHO PARK

Clifford, Gordon

I SURRENDER, DEAR
IT MUST BE TRUE
PARADISE

Clifton, John

ANY OTHER WAY
COME TO THE MASQUERADE
HULLA-BALOO-BALAY
MAN WITH A LOAD OF MISCHIEF
ONCE YOU'VE HAD A LITTLE TASTE

Climie, Simon

I KNEW YOU WERE WAITING FOR
ME
INVINCIBLE
MY HEART CAN'T TELL YOU NO

Clinton, George

AQUA BOOGIE (A PSYCHOALPHADIS-
COBETABIOAQUADOLOOP)
FLASH LIGHT
I WANNA TESTIFY
KNEE DEEP (NOT JUST)
ME, MYSELF, AND I
ONE NATION UNDER A GROOVE
TEAR THE ROOF OFF THE SUCKER
(GIVE UP THE FUNK)

Clinton, Larry

CALYPSO MELODY
DIPSY DOODLE, THE
DUSK IN UPPER SANDUSKY
MY REVERIE
OUR LOVE
SATAN TAKES A HOLIDAY
STUDY IN BROWN, A

Clowney, David

HAPPY ORGAN, THE
RINKY DINK

Clutsam, George H.

MA CURLY HEADED BABBY

Clyde, Jeremy

WHAT DO YOU WANT WITH ME?

Coates, Carroll

SOFT SANDS

Coates, Eric

SLEEPY LAGOON

Coates, Maurice

DRY YOUR EYES

Coates, Paul

IF THE MOON TURNS GREEN

Coats, J. B.

SWEETEST GIFT, THE

Cobb, Arnett

SMOOTH SAILING

Cobb, Ed

DIRTY WATER
SOMETIMES GOOD GUYS DON'T
WEAR WHITE
TAINTED LOVE

Cobb, George L.

ALABAMA JUBILEE
ALL ABOARD FOR DIXIELAND
ARE YOU FROM DIXIE ('CAUSE I'M
FROM DIXIE TOO)

Cobb, J. R.

CHAMPAGNE JAM
DO IT OR DIE
SPOOKY

Cobb, James B.

CHANGE OF HEART
EVERYDAY WITH YOU GIRL
I TAKE IT BACK
STORMY
TRACES

Cobb, Margaret

HEY! BABY

Cobb, Will D.

FOR YOU A ROSE
GOOD-BYE, DOLLY GRAY
GOODBYE, LITTLE GIRL, GOODBYE
I CAN'T TELL WHY I LOVE YOU, BUT
I DO
IF A GIRL LIKE YOU LOVED A BOY
LIKE ME
IF I WAS A MILLIONAIRE
I JUST CAN'T MAKE MY EYES
BEHAVE
I'LL BE WITH YOU WHEN THE
ROSES BLOOM AGAIN
I'LL GET YOU
IN ZANZIBAR—MY LITTLE
CHIMPANZEE
MAMIE
MEET ME DOWN AT THE CORNER
SINGER AND THE SONG, THE
SUNBONNET SUE
THERE'S A GIRL IN THIS WORLD
FOR EVERY BOY, AND A BOY FOR
EVERY GIRL
WALTZ ME AROUND AGAIN, WILLIE
('ROUND, 'ROUND, 'ROUND)
YIP-I-ADDY-I-AY!

Coben, Cy

BEWARE OF IT
EASY ON THE EYES
EDDY'S SONG
FREE HOME DEMONSTRATION
GAME OF TRIANGLES, THE
HEP CAT BABY
I LOVE THE GUY
I WANNA PLAY HOUSE WITH YOU
LADY'S MAN
LONELY LITTLE ROBIN
MY LITTLE COUSIN

Coben, Cy

NAME OF THE GAME WAS LOVE
OLDER AND BOLDER
OLD PIANO ROLL BLUES, THE
SOMETHING OLD, SOMETHING NEW
SWEET VIOLETS
THERE'S BEEN A CHANGE IN ME
THERE'S NO WINGS ON MY ANGEL

Coburn, Ray

FEEL IT AGAIN

Coburn, Richard

WHISPERING

Cochran, Chuck

OCEAN FRONT PROPERTY
SPANISH EDDIE

Cochran, Dorcas

AGAIN
CINCINNATI KID, THE
HERE
I GET IDEAS (WHEN I DANCE WITH
    YOU)
THEME FROM "ADVENTURES IN
    PARADISE"
UNDER THE BRIDGES OF PARIS

Cochran, Eddie

C'MON EVERYBODY

Cochran, Garland

WHO YOU GONNA BLAME IT ON
    THIS TIME

Cochran, Hank

CHAIR, THE
DON'T TOUCH ME
DON'T YOU EVER GET TIRED OF
    HURTING ME?
FUNNY WAY OF LAUGHIN'
I FALL TO PIECES
IT'S NOT LOVE (BUT IT'S NOT BAD)
IT'S ONLY LOVE
I WANT TO GO WITH YOU
LITTLE BITTY TEAR, A

MAKE THE WORLD GO AWAY
SET 'EM UP JOE
SHE'S GOT YOU
TEARS BROKE OUT ON ME
THAT'S ALL THAT MATTERS
WAY TO SURVIVE, A
WILLINGLY
YESTERDAY'S MEMORIES
YOU COMB HER HAIR

Cochran, Wayne

LAST KISS

Cochrane, Eddie

SUMMERTIME BLUES

Cockburn, Bruce

IF I HAD A ROCKET LAUNCHER
WONDERING WHERE THE LIONS
    ARE

Cody, Phil

BAD BLOOD
DOING IT ALL FOR MY BABY
IMMIGRANT, THE
LAUGHTER IN THE RAIN
LOVE IN THE SHADOWS
SHOULD'VE NEVER LET YOU GO
SOLITAIRE

Coe, David Allan

TAKE THIS JOB AND SHOVE IT
WOULD YOU LAY WITH ME (IN A
    FIELD OF STONE)

Coffey, Dennis

TAURUS

Cogane, Nelson

IS THERE SOMEBODY ELSE?
THERE'S A CHILL ON THE HILL
    TONIGHT
WE THREE (MY ECHO, MY SHADOW,
    AND ME)
YESTERDAY'S GARDENIAS

Coggins, Danny

PUCKER UP, BUTTERCUP

Cogswell, Billy

MY LITTLE GRASS SHACK (IN
    KEALAKAKUA, HAWAII)

Cohan, George M.

ALWAYS LEAVE THEM LAUGHING
    WHEN YOU SAY GOOD-BYE
ANY PLACE THE OLD FLAG FLIES
BARNUM HAD THE RIGHT IDEA
COME ON DOWN TOWN
FORTY-FIVE MINUTES FROM
    BROADWAY
GIVE MY REGARDS TO BROADWAY
GOOD-BYE, FLO
HARRIGAN
HELLO, BROADWAY!
HOT TAMALE ALLEY
IF WASHINGTON SHOULD COME TO
    LIFE
I GUESS I'LL HAVE TO TELEGRAPH
    MY BABY
I'M A POPULAR MAN
I WANT YOU
I WAS BORN IN VIRGINIA
I WON'T BE AN ACTOR NO MORE
LIFE'S A FUNNY PROPOSITION
    AFTER ALL
MAN WHO OWNS BROADWAY, THE
MARY'S A GRAND OLD NAME
NELLIE, KELLY, I LOVE YOU
NOTHING NEW BENEATH THE SUN
OVER THERE
SO LONG, MARY
THAT HAUNTING MELODY
THERE'S SOMETHING ABOUT A
    UNIFORM
UNDER ANY OLD FLAG AT ALL
WHEN A FELLOW'S ON THE LEVEL
    WITH A GIRL'S THAT ON THE
    SQUARE
WHEN YOU COME BACK
WHERE WERE YOU—WHERE WAS I
    (EXACTLY WHERE WE ARE)
YANKEE DOODLE BOY, THE
YOU'RE A GRAND OLD FLAG
YOU REMIND ME OF MY MOTHER

Cohen, Henry

CANADIAN CAPERS

Cohen, Jeffrey

BABY COME TO ME
FREEWAY OF LOVE
JIMMY LEE
PUT YOUR MOUTH ON ME
YOU'RE A FRIEND OF MINE

Cohen, Jerry

AIN'T NO STOPPIN' US NOW

Cohen, Leonard

AIN'T NO CURE FOR LOVE
BIRD ON THE WIRE
CAME SO FAR FOR BEAUTY
FIRST WE TAKE MANHATTAN
HEY, THAT'S NO WAY TO SAY
    GOODBYE
I'M YOUR MAN
SISTERS OF MERCY
STORY OF ISAAC
STRANGER SONG, THE
SUZANNE
WINTER LADY

Cohn, Irving

YES! WE HAVE NO BANANAS

Cola, Johnny

HEART OF ROCK AND ROLL, THE
VIENI SU (SAY YOU LOVE ME TOO)

Colahan, Dr. Arthur

GALWAY BAY

Colbert, John

HEARSAY

Colby, Robert

FREE AGAIN
JILTED

Colclough, Mildred

I WILL WAIT

Colcord, Lincoln

STEIN SONG (UNIVERSITY OF
    MAINE)

Cole, Bob

CONGO LOVE SONG
LAZY MOON
MAIDEN WITH THE DREAMY EYES
MY CASTLE ON THE NILE
OH! DIDN'T HE RAMBLE
TELL ME, DUSKY MAIDEN
UNDER THE BAMBOO TREE (IF YOU
    LAK-A ME LIKE I LAK-A YOU)

Cole, D.

LOVE SUPREME, A

Cole, Gardner

OPEN YOUR HEART

Cole, Nat

CALYPSO BLUES
I'M A SHY GUY
STRAIGHTEN UP AND FLY RIGHT
THAT AIN'T RIGHT
WITH YOU ON MY MIND

Cole, Natalie

SOPHISTICATED LADY (SHE'S A
    DIFFERENT LADY)

Coleman, Bud

TIJUANA TAXI

Coleman, Cy

AUTUMN WALTZ, THE
BAD IS FOR OTHER PEOPLE
BE A PERFORMER
BEST IS YET TO COME, THE
BIG SPENDER
BOOZERS AND LOSERS

COLORS OF MY LIFE, THE
DEEP DOWN INSIDE
EARLY MORNING BLUES
FIREFLY
GIVE A LITTLE WHISTLE
HERE'S TO US
HE'S GOOD FOR ME
HEY, LOOK ME OVER!
HEY THERE, GOOD TIMES
HIBISCUS
IF MY FRIENDS COULD SEE ME NOW
I LOVE MY WIFE
I'M GONNA LAUGH YOU RIGHT OUT
    OF MY LIFE
ISN'T HE ADORABLE?
IT AMAZES ME
IT'S NOT WHERE YOU START
I'VE GOT YOUR NUMBER
LEGACY, THE
LITTLE ME
LOVE MAKES SUCH FOOLS OF US
    ALL
ON THE TWENTIETH CENTURY
OTHER SIDE OF THE TRACKS, THE
PASS ME BY
PLAYBOY THEME
POOR LITTLE HOLLYWOOD STAR
REAL LIVE GIRL
RHYTHM OF LIFE, THE
RIVIERA, THE
RULES OF THE ROAD, THE
TALL HOPE
TEMPO OF THE TIMES, THE
THERE'S GOTTA BE SOMETHING
    BETTER THAN THIS
WHAT TAKES MY FANCY
WHEN IN ROME (I DO AS THE
    ROMANS DO)
WHERE AM I GOING?
WHY TRY TO CHANGE ME NOW?
WITCHCRAFT
YOU FASCINATE ME SO
YOU SHOULD SEE YOURSELF
YOU'VE COME HOME

Coleman, Dave

BACKWARD, TURN BACKWARD
STRING ALONG

Coleman, Harry

SIMILAU

Coleman, James

HELLO FOOL
SHOES OF A FOOL

Coleman, Larry

BIG GUITAR, THE
CHANGING PARTNERS
JUST AS MUCH AS EVER
PA-PAYA MAMA
RICOCHET (RICK-O-SHAY)
TENNESSEE WIG WALK

Coleman, Lonnie

BOOM BOOM BOOMERANG

Coleman, Marty

IF THIS IS LOVE (I'D RATHER BE
LONELY)

Coleman, Ornette

LONELY WOMAN

Coleman, Ron

TIRED OF TOEIN' THE LINE

Coleman, Tony

ONE HUNDRED WAYS

Coletharp, Ruth E.

LET'S LIVE A LITTLE

Coley, John Ford

GONE TOO FAR

Colicchio, Michael

STORY OF OUR LOVE, THE

Colla, John

IF THIS IS IT
POWER OF LOVE, THE

Collen, Phil

ANIMAL
HYSTERIA
LOVE BITES
POUR SOME SUGAR ON ME

Colley, Keith

PLAYGIRL
SHAME, SHAME

Colley, Linda

PLAYGIRL
SHAME, SHAME

Collins, Aaron

EDDIE, MY LOVE

Collins, Albert

LUCILLE
SLIPPIN' AND SLIDIN' (PEEPIN' AND
HIDIN')

Collins, Allen

BABY, I LOVE YOUR WAY
FREE BIRD

Collins, Audree

SLOW BUT SURE

Collins, Bootsie

TEAR THE ROOF OFF THE SUCKER
(GIVE UP THE FUNK)

Collins, G.

FOR YASGUR'S FARM

Collins, Larry

DELTA DAWN
YOU'RE THE REASON GOD MADE
OKLAHOMA

Collins, Phil

AGAINST ALL ODDS (TAKE A LOOK
AT ME NOW)
DON'T LOSE MY NUMBER
EASY LOVER
FOLLOW YOU FOLLOW ME
IN THE AIR TONIGHT
IN TOO DEEP
INVISIBLE TOUCH
LAND OF CONFUSION
MAN ON THE CORNER
MISUNDERSTANDING
NO REPLY AT ALL
ONE MORE NIGHT
SUSSUDIO
TAKE ME HOME
THAT'S ALL
THROWING IT ALL AWAY
TONIGHT, TONIGHT, TONIGHT
TWO HEARTS

Collins, Roger

SHE'S LOOKIN' GOOD

Collins, Susan

SWEET LIFE

Collins, Tommy

CAROLYN
IF YOU AIN'T LOVIN' (YOU AIN'T
LIVIN')
IF YOU CAN'T BITE, DON'T GROWL
IT TICKLES
NO LOVE HAVE I
ROOTS OF MY RAISING, THE
SAM HILL
WHATCHA GONNA DO NOW?
YOU BETTER NOT DO THAT
YOU'RE FOR ME

Collins, Wanda

IT TICKLES

Collins, Will

UNTIL SUNRISE

Collins, William

AQUA BOOGIE (A PSYCHOALPHADIS-
   COBETABIOAQUADOLOOP)
FLASH LIGHT

Colter, Jessi

I'M NOT LISA

Colton, Tony

COUNTRY BOY
I'M NO ANGEL

Coltrane, Chi

THUNDER AND LIGHTNING

Coltrane, John

LOVE SUPREME, A

Columbo, Russ

I'M YOURS TO COMMAND
PRISONER OF LOVE
TOO BEAUTIFUL FOR WORDS
YOU CALL IT MADNESS (BUT I CALL
   IT LOVE)

Colvin, Douglas

I WANNA BE SEDATED
PINHEAD
ROCKAWAY BEACH
SHEENA IS A PUNK ROCKER

Coman, Thomas

C'MON AND SWIM

Comanor, Jeff

WE'LL NEVER HAVE TO SAY
   GOODBYE AGAIN

Comden, Betty

ALL YOU NEED IS A QUARTER
ASKING FOR YOU
BELLS ARE RINGING

CLOSE HARMONY
COMES ONCE IN A LIFETIME
CRY LIKE THE WIND
DISTANT MELODY
FADE OUT—FADE IN
FIREWORKS
FRENCH LESSON, THE
HOLD ME—HOLD ME—HOLD ME
HOW CAN YOU DESCRIBE A FACE?
I CAN COOK TOO
I GET CARRIED AWAY
I KNOW ABOUT LOVE
I LIKE MYSELF
I'M WITH YOU
INDEPENDENT (ON MY OWN)
IT'S LOVE
JUST IN TIME
LEGACY, THE
LITTLE BIT IN LOVE
LONELY TOWN
LONG BEFORE I KNEW YOU
LOOKING BACK
LUCKY TO BE ME
MAKE SOMEONE HAPPY
MU-CHA-CHA
NEVER NEVER LAND
NEW YORK, NEW YORK (THE
   BRONX IS UP AND THE BATTERY
   IS DOWN)
NOW
OHIO
ON THE TWENTIETH CENTURY
PARTY'S OVER, THE
QUIET GIRL, A
RIGHT GIRL FOR ME, THE
SAY, DARLING
SOME OTHER TIME
STRICTLY U.S.A.
THANKS A LOT, BUT NO THANKS
TIME FOR PARTING
WENDY
WHAT'S NEW AT THE ZOO?
WHO KNOWS WHAT MIGHT HAVE
   BEEN?
WRONG NOTE RAG
YA GOT ME
YOU MUSN'T BE DISCOURAGED

Compton, Harry

HOW MUCH MORE CAN SHE STAND?

Compton, Lewis

I'VE RUN OUT OF TOMORROWS

Conatser, I.

REVEILLE ROCK

Confrey, Zez

DIZZY FINGERS
JACK IN THE BOX
KITTEN ON THE KEYS
SITTIN' ON A LOG (PETTIN' MY DOG)
STUMBLING

Conlee, John

DOMESTIC LIFE
SHE CAN'T SAY THAT ANYMORE

Conley, Arthur

FUNKY STREET
SWEET SOUL MUSIC

Conley, David

HAPPY
LATELY

Conley, Earl Thomas

DON'T MAKE IT EASY FOR ME
FIRE AND SMOKE
I HAVE LOVED YOU, GIRL (BUT NOT
   LIKE THIS BEFORE)
RIGHT FROM THE START
SILENT TREATMENT
YOUR LOVE'S ON THE LINE

Conley, Larry

COTTAGE FOR SALE, A
SHANGHAI SHUFFLE

Conley, William Lee

JUST A DREAM

Conn, Chester

DON'T MIND THE RAIN

FORGIVE MY HEART
MAKE HER MINE
MY SUPPRESSED DESIRE
NIGHT LIGHTS
OUTSIDE OF HEAVEN
ROSE AND A PRAYER, A
WHY SHOULD I CRY OVER YOU?
YOU DON'T LIKE IT—NOT MUCH

Connell, Andy

BREAKOUT

Connell, Jane

JOEY BABY

Connelly, Al

SOMEDAY

Connelly, Reg

BY THE FIRESIDE (IN THE
   GLOAMING)
GOODNIGHT SWEETHEART
IF I HAD YOU
JUST AN ECHO IN THE VALLEY
SHOW ME THE WAY TO GO HOME
TRY A LITTLE TENDERNESS
UNDERNEATH THE ARCHES
WHEN THE ORGAN PLAYED AT
   TWILIGHT

Connolly, Brian

ACTION
FOX ON THE RUN

Connolly, Patrick

WIPE OUT

Connor, Pierre Norman

WHEN I TAKE MY SUGAR TO TEA

Connor, Thomas

BIGGEST ASPIDASTRA IN THE
   WORLD, THE

Connor, Tommie

ANGELINA
I SAW MOMMY KISSING SANTA
   CLAUS
LILI MARLENE
RED RIVER ROSE
WEDDING OF LILI MARLENE, THE

Connors, Carol

DON'T ASK TO STAY UNTIL
   TOMORROW
GONNA FLY NOW (THEME FROM
   "ROCKY")
HEY, LITTLE COBRA
SOMEONE'S WAITING FOR YOU
WITH YOU I'M BORN AGAIN

Connors, Marshall

HEY, LITTLE COBRA

Conrad, Con

BARNEY GOOGLE
BEND DOWN, SISTER
BIG CITY BLUES
BLUE SKY AVENUE
BREAKAWAY, THE
CHAMPAGNE WALTZ, THE
COME ON, SPARK PLUG!
CONTINENTAL, THE
DEAR, ON A NIGHT LIKE THIS
DOWN IN DEAR OLD NEW ORLEANS
HERE COMES EMILY BROWN
HERE'S TO ROMANCE
HITTIN' THE CEILING
LONESOME AND SORRY
LONESOME ME
MA! (HE'S MAKING EYES AT ME)
MAH JONG
MANDY 'N' ME
MARGIE
MEMORY LANE
MIAMI
MIDNIGHT IN PARIS
MIMI
NEEDLE IN A HAY STACK, A
NINE LITTLE MILES FROM TEN-TEN-
   TENNESSEE
OH! FRENCHY
ONLY WHEN YOU'RE IN MY ARMS

PALESTEENA
SHE'S EVERYBODY'S SWEETHEART
   (BUT NOBODY'S GAL)
SING A LITTLE LOVE SONG
SINGIN' THE BLUES (TILL MY
   DADDY COMES HOME)
STEPPIN' OUT
TALKIN' TO MYSELF
THAT'S YOU, BABY
WALKING WITH SUSIE
YOU CALL IT MADNESS (BUT I CALL
   IT LOVE)
YOU'VE GOT TO SEE MAMMA EV'RY
   NIGHT (OR YOU CAN'T SEE
   MAMMA AT ALL)

Conrad, Jack

EVERY TIME I THINK OF YOU
FAMILY OF MAN, THE
ISN'T IT TIME

Contet, Henri

ALL MY LOVE

Conti, Bill

EVERCHANGING TIMES
FOR YOUR EYES ONLY
GONNA FLY NOW (THEME FROM
   "ROCKY")
THEME FROM "DYNASTY"
TOO CLOSE TO PARADISE

Conti, Corrado

TO THE DOOR OF THE SUN (ALLE
   PORTE DEL SOLE)
WAY IT USED TO BE, THE

Conway, Jim

TOMBOY

Cook, Betsy

TELLING ME LIES

Cook, Bill

FORGIVE THIS FOOL

YOU CAN HAVE HER (A.K.A. YOU
CAN HAVE HIM)

Cook, Don

JULIA
LADY LAY DOWN
SMALL TOWN GIRL
SOMEBODY'S GONNA LOVE YOU

Cook, Joe

PEANUTS

Cook, Mercer

IS I IN LOVE? I IS

Cook, Robert

ARE THESE REALLY MINE?

Cook, Roger

DOCTOR'S ORDERS
HERE COMES THAT RAINY DAY
FEELING AGAIN
I BELIEVE IN YOU
I'D LIKE TO TEACH THE WORLD TO
SING (IN PERFECT HARMONY)
I WAS KAISER BILL'S BATMAN
I WISH THAT I COULD HURT THAT
WAY AGAIN
LONG COOL WOMAN (IN A BLACK
DRESS)
LOVE IS ON A ROLL
MY BABY LOVES LOVIN'
TALKING IN YOUR SLEEP
WAY IT USED TO BE, THE
YOU'VE GOT YOUR TROUBLES

Cook, Will Marion

BON BON BUDDY
I'M COMING VIRGINIA
LITTLE GYPSY MAID, THE

Cooke, Charles L.

I WONDER WHERE MY LOVIN' MAN
HAS GONE

Cooke, L. C.

WIN YOUR LOVE FOR ME
YOU SEND ME

Cooke, Leonard

SUNSHINE OF YOUR SMILE, THE

Cooke, Leslie

LOVE SENDS A LITTLE GIFT OF
ROSES

Cooke, Linda

WOMAN'S GOTTA HAVE IT

Cooke, Sam

ANOTHER SATURDAY NIGHT
BRING IT ON HOME TO ME
CHAIN GANG
CHANGE IS GONNA COME, A
CUPID
GOOD NEWS
HAVING A PARTY
I'LL COME RUNNING BACK TO YOU
IT'S GOT THE WHOLE WORLD
SHAKIN'
ONLY SIXTEEN
SHAKE
SUGAR DUMPLING
SWEET SOUL MUSIC
TWISTIN' THE NIGHT AWAY

Cooler, Whey

CATCH ME (I'M FALLING)

Cooley, Eddie

FEVER

Cooley, Spade

MAMA AND DADDY BROKE MY
HEART
SHAME ON YOU

Coolidge, Edwina

ALONG THE SANTA FE TRAIL

Coon, Carleton

HI-DIDDLE-DIDDLE

Cooper, Alice

BILLION DOLLAR BABIES
EIGHTEEN
HOW YOU GONNA SEE ME NOW
I NEVER CRY
ONLY WOMEN
YOU AND ME

Cooper, Bernadette

ACTION JACKSON
JUST THAT TYPE OF GIRL
MEN ALL PAUSE, THE

Cooper, Bud

RED HOT MAMA

Cooper, Colin

COULDN'T GET IT RIGHT

Cooper, Gary

LET'S GO ALL THE WAY

Cooper, George

DON'T GO OUT TONIGHT, BOY

Cooper, Joe

I'M A FOOL
I'VE BEEN FLOATING DOWN THE
OLD GREEN RIVER

Cooper, John

DO YOU EVER THINK OF ME?

Cooper, Martin

IF YOU LEAVE
YOU CAN'T BE A BEACON (IF YOUR
LIGHT DON'T SHINE)

Cooper, Martin J.

PEANUT BUTTER

Cooper, Marty

RUN, RUN, LOOK AND SEE

Cooper, Michael

FFUN
TOO TIGHT

Cooper, Richard

DREAM NEVER DIES, THE

Cooper, Sandra

IN THE BUSH

Cooper, Sarah Jane

YOU WILL HAVE TO PAY (FOR YOUR
    YESTERDAY)

Cooper, Steve

HOLE IN THE WALL

Cooper, Ted

NO ONE'S GONNA HURT YOU
    ANYMORE
RONNIE, CALL ME WHEN YOU GET
    A CHANCE

Cooper, Wilma Lee

BIG MIDNIGHT SPECIAL

Coots, J. Fred

ALABAMA BARBECUE
BEAUTIFUL LADY IN BLUE, A
COPPER-COLORED GAL
CROSS YOUR FINGERS
DOIN' THE RACCOON
DOIN' THE SUSI-Q
ENCORE, CHERIE
FOR ALL WE KNOW
GOODBYE MAMA, I'M OFF TO
    YOKOHAMA

HERE COMES MY BALL AND CHAIN
HERE'S HOPING
I KNEW YOU WHEN
I'LL STAND BY
I MISS A LITTLE MISS
I'M MADLY IN LOVE WITH YOU
IN YOUR OWN LITTLE WAY
ISN'T LOVE THE STRANGEST THING?
I STILL GET A THRILL (THINKING
    OF YOU)
I WONDER WHY
LATE NOW
LET'S STOP THE CLOCK
LOUISIANA FAIRY TALE
LOVE LETTERS IN THE SAND
MORE I KNOW YOU, THE
ONE MINUTE TO ONE
PRECIOUS LITTLE THING CALLED
    LOVE, A
SANTA CLAUS IS COMIN' TO TOWN
STRANGERS
SUNDAY
THERE'S HONEY ON THE MOON
    TONIGHT
THERE'S OCEANS OF LOVE BY THE
    BEAUTIFUL SEA
THINGS MIGHT HAVE BEEN SO
    DIFFERENT
THIS TIME IT'S LOVE
TIME WILL TELL
TWO TICKETS TO GEORGIA
UNTIL TODAY
WHOSE HONEY ARE YOU?
WHY?
YOU GO TO MY HEAD
YOU'LL GET BY
YOURS TRULY IS TRULY YOURS
YOU STARTED ME DREAMING

Copas, Cowboy

ALABAM
FLAT TOP
SIGNED, SEALED AND DELIVERED
TENNESSEE MOON

Cope, La Forrest (a.k.a. La La)

(IF YOU) LOVE ME JUST A LITTLE
YOU GIVE GOOD LOVE

Copeland, Allan

MAKE LOVE TO ME

Copeland, Greg

BUY ME FOR THE RAIN

Copeland, Leon C.

LEAD ME ON

Coquatrix, Bruno

COMME ÇI, COMME ÇA
COUNT EVERY STAR

Cor, Peter

GETAWAY

Corbert, Robert W.

QUENTIN'S THEME

Corbett, Gary

SHE BOP

Corbetta, Jerry

DON'T CALL US, WE'LL CALL YOU
GREEN-EYED LADY

Corcoran, Tom

FINS

Corday, Leo

LEAP FROG
SEE THE U.S.A. IN YOUR
    CHEVROLET
THERE'S NO TOMORROW
YOUR SOCKS DON'T MATCH

Cordell, Ritchie

GET OUT NOW
GETTIN' TOGETHER
GIMME, GIMME GOOD LOVIN'
I LIKE THE WAY
INDIAN GIVER

I THINK WE'RE ALONE NOW
MIRAGE
MONY, MONY
OUT OF THE BLUE

Cordle, Larry

HIGHWAY 40 BLUES

Corles, Rick

COME ON IN (YOU DID THE BEST
YOU COULD DO)

Cormier, Ray

HIT AND RUN AFFAIR

Cornelius, Don

GIGOLO, THE
SOUL TRAIN '75

Cornelius, Eddie

DON'T EVER BE LONELY (A POOR
LITTLE FOOL LIKE ME)
TOO LATE TO TURN BACK NOW
TREAT HER LIKE A LADY

Cornelius, Harold

BLOSSOM FELL, A

Cornett, Alice

ALL THAT GLITTERS IS NOT GOLD

Cort, Harry L.

WAITING

Cortazar, Ernesto M.

THREE CABALLEROS, THE

Cory, Charles B.

DREAM, A

Cory, George

DEEP SONG

I LEFT MY HEART IN SAN
FRANCISCO
YOU WILL WEAR VELVET

Cosby, Henry

DO THE BOOMERANG
FINGERTIPS
HOME COOKIN'
I'M LIVIN' IN SHAME
I'M WONDERING
I WAS MADE TO LOVE HER
MY CHERIE AMOUR
NOTHING'S TOO GOOD FOR MY
BABY
SHOO-BE-DOO-BE-DOO-DA-DAY
TEARS OF A CLOWN, THE
UPTIGHT (EVERYTHING'S ALRIGHT)

Cosey, Antonio

RATION BLUES

Coslow, Sam

AFTER YOU
BEBE
BESIDE A MOONLIT STREAM
BEWARE MY HEART
BLACK MOONLIGHT
BLUE MIRAGE (DON'T GO)
COCKTAILS FOR TWO
DAY YOU CAME ALONG, THE
DOWN THE OLD OX ROAD
DREAMING OUT LOUD
EBONY RHAPSODY
EVERY DAY'S A HOLIDAY
FIFI
GOOD MORNIN'
HAVE YOU FORGOTTEN SO SOON?
HEAVENLY MUSIC
HELLO, SWANEE, HELLO!
IF I WERE KING
I GUESS IT HAD TO BE THAT WAY
I'M IN LOVE WITH THE HONORABLE
MR. SO AND SO
I'M JUST WILD ABOUT ANIMAL
CRACKERS
IN MY LITTLE HOPE CHEST
IN THE MIDDLE OF A KISS
IT'S RAINING SUNBEAMS
JE VOUS AIME
JUST ONE MORE CHANCE

KINDA LONESOME
LEARN TO CROON
LITTLE WHITE GARDENIA, A
LIVE AND LOVE TONIGHT
LONELY MELODY
MAKE-BELIEVE ISLAND
MOON SONG
MOONSTRUCK
MY OLD FLAME
NEW MOON AND AN OLD
SERENADE, A
NOW I'M A LADY
OLD CURIOSITY SHOP, AN
PANAMANIA
SING YOU SINNERS
SONG OF THE SOUTH
SWEEPIN' THE CLOUDS AWAY
TABLE IN THE CORNER, A
TEA ON THE TERRACE
THANKS
THIS IS THE NIGHT
THIS LITTLE PIGGIE WENT TO
MARKET
THRILL OF A LIFETIME
TOMORROW NIGHT
TRUE BLUE LOU
TRUE CONFESSION
TURN OFF THE MOON
WAS IT A DREAM?
WHEN HE COMES HOME TO ME
YOU DIDN'T KNOW THE MUSIC
YOU'LL HAVE TO SWING IT (MR.
PAGANINI)

Costa, Don

BECAUSE THEY'RE YOUNG
I CAN'T BELIEVE I'M LOSING YOU

Costandinos, Robert

THANK GOD IT'S FRIDAY

Costello, Bartley

EL RANCHO GRANDE

Costello, Elvis

EVERY DAY I WRITE THE BOOK
GIRLS TALK
ONLY FLAME IN TOWN, THE

Cotton, Hal

YOU CAN'T BE TRUE, DEAR

Cotton, Paul

HEART OF THE NIGHT

Couch, Orville

HELLO TROUBLE

Coulter, Phil

MY BOY
SATURDAY NIGHT

Cour, Pierre

LOVE IS BLUE

Courtney, Alan

HEREAFTER
JOLTIN' JOE DIMAGGIO

Courtney, C. C.

TOMORROW IS THE FIRST DAY OF
    THE REST OF MY LIFE
(IF YOU LET ME MAKE LOVE TO YOU
    THEN) WHY CAN'T I TOUCH YOU

Courtney, David

GIVING IT ALL AWAY
LONG TALL GLASSES (I CAN DANCE)
SHOW MUST GO ON, THE

Courtney, Lou

DO THE FREDDIE

Cousins, Richard

SMOKING GUN

Coutourie, W.

19

Covay, Don

CHAIN OF FOOLS
LETTER FULL OF TEARS
LIGHTS OUT
MERCY, MERCY
PONY TIME
SEE SAW
TONIGHT'S THE NIGHT

Coverdale, David

HERE I GO AGAIN
IS THIS LOVE
STILL OF THE NIGHT

Covington, Joey

PRETTY AS YOU FEEL
WITH YOUR LOVE

Cowan, Joel

CABARET
IT'S LIKE TAKING CANDY FROM A
    BABY

Cowan, Lynn

DREAM HOUSE
I'M IN LOVE WITH YOU

Cowan, Marie

WALTZING MATILDA

Cowan, Stanley

DO I WORRY?
TIL REVEILLE (LIGHTS OUT—)

Coward, Noël

DANCE, LITTLE LADY
DEAR LITTLE CAFE
DON'T TAKE OUR CHARLIE FOR THE
    ARMY
HALF CASTE WOMAN
HERE AND NOW
IF LOVE WERE ALL
IF YOU COULD ONLY COME WITH
    ME
I'LL FOLLOW MY SECRET HEART

I'LL REMEMBER HER
I'LL SEE YOU AGAIN
I'VE BEEN INVITED TO A PARTY
LET'S SAY GOODBYE
LONDON IS A LITTLE BIT OF ALL
    RIGHT
MAD ABOUT THE BOY
MAD DOGS AND ENGLISHMEN
MRS. WORTHINGTON (DON'T PUT
    YOUR DAUGHTER ON THE STAGE)
NEVERMORE
PARISIAN PIERROT
POOR LITTLE RICH GIRL
REGENCY RAKES
ROOM WITH A VIEW, A
SAIL AWAY
SOMEDAY I'LL FIND YOU
SOMETHING VERY STRANGE
TELL ME, WHAT IS LOVE?
THIS TIME IT'S TRUE LOVE
TOKAY
WHERE SHALL I FIND HIM?
WHY DO THE WRONG PEOPLE
    TRAVEL?
WORLD WEARY
YOU WERE THERE
ZIGEUNER

Cowart, W. D.

LEAVING LOUISIANA IN THE BROAD
    DAYLIGHT

Cowell, John

OUR WINTER LOVE
WALK HAND IN HAND

Cowell, Rodney

LEAVING LOUISIANA IN THE BROAD
    DAYLIGHT

Cowles, Eugene

FORGOTTEN

Cowsill, Bill

WE CAN FLY

Cowsill, Bob

WE CAN FLY

Cox, Desmond

I'VE GOT SIXPENCE
JUST A LITTLE FOND AFFECTION

Cox, Eddie

YOU SAID IT

Cox, Herbert

CAN'T WE BE SWEETHEARTS
LITTLE GIRL OF MINE

Cox, Jimmy

NOBODY KNOWS YOU WHEN YOU'RE
   DOWN AND OUT

Cox, Peter

CALL ME

Cox, Roy E., Jr.

HOT SMOKE AND SASSAFRAS

Coy, Steven

BRAND NEW LOVER
YOU SPIN ME ROUND LIKE A
   RECORD

Crabb, Cecil Duane

FLUFFY RUFFLES
KLASSICLE RAG
ORINOCO: JUNGLE RAG TWO-STEP

Crafer, Art

NO ARMS CAN EVER HOLD YOU

Craff, George, Jr.

ISLE O'DREAMS, THE

Craft, Morton

ALONE (WHY MUST I BE ALONE)
CHURCH BELLS MAY RING
TELL HER FOR ME

Craft, Paul

DROPKICK ME, JESUS
HANK WILLIAMS, YOU WROTE MY
   LIFE

Craft, Selma

ALONE (WHY MUST I BE ALONE)
TELL HER FOR ME

Craig, Charlie

SHE'S SINGLE AGAIN

Craig, Francis

BEG YOUR PARDON
NEAR YOU

Craig, Mikey

CHURCH OF THE POISON MIND
DO YOU REALLY WANT TO HURT ME
I'LL TUMBLE 4 YA
IT'S A MIRACLE
KARMA CHAMELEON
MISS ME BLIND
MOVE AWAY

Crain, Tom

DEVIL WENT DOWN TO GEORGIA,
   THE
IN AMERICA

Cramer, Floyd

FANCY PANTS
LAST DATE
LOST HER LOVE ON OUR LAST DATE
MY LAST DATE (WITH YOU)
ON THE REBOUND

Crandall, Bill

SHORT SHORTS

Crane, Jimmie

EVERY DAY OF MY LIFE
HURT
I CAN'T GET YOU OUT OF MY
   HEART
IF I GIVE MY HEART TO YOU
I NEED YOU NOW
MY BELIEVING HEART

Crane, Lor

DON'T JUST STAND THERE
SAY SOMETHING FUNNY
WHITE ON WHITE

Crane, Mitch

MORE THAN JUST THE TWO OF US

Crane, Vincent

FIRE!

Crawford, Blackie

ALWAYS LATE (WITH YOUR KISSES)

Crawford, Cliff

CHIP CHIP

Crawford, Clifton

NANCY BROWN

Crawford, Dave

PHILADELPHIA
YOUNG HEARTS RUN FREE

Crawford, John

METRO, THE
SEX (I'M A . . .)

Crawford, K.

TAKE OFF

Crawford, Robert M.

ARMY AIR CORPS, THE

Crawford, Stanley

SHOW THE WHITE OF YO' EYE

Cray, Robert

SMOKING GUN

Creamer, Henry

AFTER YOU'VE GONE
ALABAMA STOMP
DEAR OLD SOUTHLAND
DOWN BY THE RIVER
EVERYBODY'S GONE CRAZY 'BOUT
    THE DOGGONE BLUES
IF I COULD BE WITH YOU (ONE
    HOUR TONIGHT)
I NEED LOVIN'
JERSEY WALK
STRUT MISS LIZZIE
SWEET EMALINA, MY GAL
THAT'S A-PLENTY
WAY DOWN YONDER IN NEW
    ORLEANS

Creatore, Luigi

BIMBOMBEY
CAN'T HELP FALLING IN LOVE
CRAZY OTTO RAG, THE
EXPERIENCE UNNECESSARY
HELLO HEARTACHE, GOODBYE
    LOVE
LET'S PUT IT ALL TOGETHER
LION SLEEPS TONIGHT, THE
WILD IN THE COUNTRY

Creed, Linda

BETCHA BY GOLLY, WOW
BREAK UP TO MAKE UP
GREATEST LOVE OF ALL, THE
I'M COMING HOME
I'M STONE IN LOVE WITH YOU
ROCKIN' ROLL BABY
RUBBERBAND MAN, THE
YOU ARE EVERYTHING
YOU MAKE ME FEEL BRAND NEW

Cregan, Jim

PASSION

TONIGHT I'M YOURS (DON'T HURT
ME)

Creme, Lol

CRY
RUBBER BULLETS

Crenshaw, Marshall

FAVORITE WASTE OF TIME
SOMEDAY, SOMEWAY

Cretecos, Jimmy

DOESN'T SOMEBODY WANT TO BE
    WANTED

Crewe, Bob

BIG GIRLS DON'T CRY
BUZZ BUZZ A-DIDDLE IT
BYE, BYE, BABY (BABY GOODBYE)
CAN'T TAKE MY EYES OFF YOU
GET DANCIN'
GIRL COME RUNNING
I MAKE A FOOL OF MYSELF
I WANNA DANCE WIT' CHOO (DOO
    DAT DANCE)
JUMP OVER
LA DEE DAH
LADY MARMALADE
LET'S HANG ON
LUCKY LADYBUG
MORE THAN THE EYE CAN SEE
MY EYES ADORED YOU
NAVY BLUE
PROUD ONE, THE
RAG DOLL
RONNIE
SAVE IT FOR ME
SILENCE IS GOLDEN
SILHOUETTES
SOCK IT TO ME, BABY!
SOON (I'LL BE HOME AGAIN)
SUN AIN'T GONNA SHINE ANYMORE,
    THE
SWEARIN' TO GOD
TALLAHASSEE LASSIE
TO GIVE (THE REASON I LIVE)
WALK LIKE A MAN
YOU'RE GONNA HURT YOURSELF

Crier, Keith

DISCO NIGHTS (ROCK-FREAK)

Criss, Peter

BETH

Croce, Jim

BAD, BAD LEROY BROWN
I'LL HAVE TO SAY I LOVE YOU IN A
    SONG
ONE LESS SET OF FOOTSTEPS
OPERATOR (THAT'S NOT THE WAY IT
    FEELS)
TIME IN A BOTTLE
WORKIN' AT THE CAR WASH BLUES
YOU DON'T MESS AROUND WITH JIM

Crockett, George L.

IT'S A MAN DOWN THERE

Crofford, Clifton

BAR ROOM BUDDIES
OLD RIVERS

Crofts, Dash

DIAMOND GIRL
GET CLOSER
HUMMINGBIRD
I'LL PLAY FOR YOU
SUMMER BREEZE
WE MAY NEVER PASS THIS WAY
    (AGAIN)

Crompton, William

HOUSE OF BAMBOO
WHY

Cronin, Kevin

CAN'T FIGHT THIS FEELING
IN MY DREAMS
KEEP ON LOVING YOU
KEEP THE FIRE BURNIN'
THAT AIN'T LOVE
TIME FOR ME TO FLY

Crook, Max

RUNAWAY

Crooker, Earle

WALTZ WAS BORN IN VIENNA, A

Croom-Johnson, Austen

GEORGIANNA
JUST THE OTHER DAY
LAST NIGHT
THERE'S NO ONE BUT YOU

Cropper, Steve

634-5789 (SOULSVILLE U.S.A.)
FA-FA-FA-FA-FA (SAD SONG)
GREEN ONIONS
HAPPY SONG (DUM, DUM), THE
HIP HUG-HER
IN THE MIDNIGHT HOUR
KNOCK ON WOOD
MINI-SKIRT MINNIE
MR. PITIFUL
SEE SAW
SOUL-LIMBO
(SITTIN' ON) THE DOCK OF THE BAY
TIME IS TIGHT
YOU DON'T KNOW WHAT YOU MEAN
    TO ME

Crosby, Bing

AT YOUR COMMAND
FROM MONDAY ON
I DON'T STAND A GHOST OF A
    CHANCE WITH YOU
LOVE ME TONIGHT
WALTZING IN A DREAM
WHERE THE BLUE OF THE NIGHT
    MEETS THE GOLD OF THE DAY

Crosby, Bob

BIG NOISE FROM WINNETKA
BOOGIE WOOGIE MAXIXE
SILVER AND GOLD
UNTIL

Crosby, David

EIGHT MILES HIGH
LONG TIME GONE

Crosby, Henry

NO MATTER WHAT SIGN YOU ARE

Crosby, Robbin

ROUND AND ROUND

Cross, Christopher

ALL RIGHT
ARTHUR'S THEME (THE BEST THAT
    YOU CAN DO)
SAILING
SAY YOU'LL BE MINE

Cross, Douglass

DEEP SONG
I LEFT MY HEART IN SAN
    FRANCISCO
YOU WILL WEAR VELVET

Cross, Reuben

SHAME

Cross, T.

FAMILY MAN

Croswell, Anne

HANDBAG IS NOT A PROPER
    MOTHER, A
I KNOW THE FEELING
ONLY ONE, THE
WILKES-BARRE, PA.
YOU LOVE ME

Crowder, Bob

STORMY MONDAY BLUES

Crowell, Rodney

AFTER ALL THIS TIME
AMERICAN DREAM, AN

EVEN COWGIRLS GET THE BLUES
I AIN'T LIVING LONG LIKE THIS
I COULDN'T LEAVE YOU IF I TRIED
I DON'T KNOW WHY YOU DON'T
    WANT ME
IT'S SUCH A SMALL WORLD
LONG HARD ROAD (THE
    SHARECROPPER'S DREAM)
SHAME ON THE MOON
SOMEWHERE TONIGHT
'TILL I GAIN CONTROL AGAIN

Crowley, John Charles

BABY, COME BACK

Crozier, Jim

ALPHAGENESIS
DECLARATION

Crudup, Arthur

MY BABY LEFT ME
THAT'S ALL RIGHT

Crumit, Frank

ABDUL ABULBUL AMIR
GAY CABALLERO, A
SWEET LADY

Crutcher, Bettye

I COULD NEVER BE PRESIDENT
I LIKE WHAT YOU'RE DOING (TO ME)
WHO'S MAKING LOVE?

Crutchfield, Jan

DOWN BY THE RIVER
DREAM ON LITTLE DREAMER
I'M LIVING IN TWO WORLDS
STATUE OF A FOOL
TEAR TIME

Crutchfield, Jerry

MY WHOLE WORLD IS FALLING
    DOWN

Crutchfield, John

DOES MY RING HURT YOUR
    FINGER?

Cryer, Gretchen

I WANT TO WALK TO SAN
    FRANCISCO
MY MOST IMPORTANT MOMENTS GO
    BY

Crysler, Gene

MR. WALKER, IT'S ALL OVER

Crystal, Billy

YOU LOOK MARVELOUS

Cuffley, John

COULDN'T GET IT RIGHT

Cugat, Xavier

MY SHAWL
NIGHTINGALE
NIGHT MUST FALL
ONE, TWO, THREE, KICK

Culhan, George M.

WHEN WE ARE M-A-RRIED

Culliver, Fred

SOUTHERN FRIED

Cummings, Burton

CLAP FOR THE WOLFMAN
LAUGHING
NO TIME
RAIN DANCE
SHARE THE LAND
STAND TALL
THESE EYES

Cummings, John

I WANNA BE SEDATED
PINHEAD

ROCKAWAY BEACH
SHEENA IS A PUNK ROCKER

Cummings, Margery

LAST CALL FOR LOVE

Cunico, Gino

WHEN I WANTED YOU

Cunningham, Carl

SOUL FINGER

Cunningham, James

JO-ANN

Cunningham, John

JO-ANN
MONA LISA LOST HER SMILE

Cunningham, Paul

ALL OVER NOTHING AT ALL
FROM THE VINE CAME THE GRAPE
HARRIET
I AM AN AMERICAN
TRIPOLI (THE SHORES OF)

Cuomo, Bill

OH, SHERRIE

Curb, Mike

ALL FOR THE LOVE OF SUNSHINE
BLUE'S THEME

Curiel, Gonzalo

FULL MOON (NOCHE DE LUNA)
LAMP OF MEMORY, THE

Curinga, Nick

THOSE OLDIES BUT GOODIES
    (REMIND ME OF YOU)

Curnin, Cy

ARE WE OURSELVES?
ONE THING LEADS TO ANOTHER
SECRET SEPARATION
STAND OR FALL

Currie, Alannah

DOCTOR! DOCTOR!
HOLD ME NOW
KING FOR A DAY
LAY YOUR HANDS ON ME
LOVE ON YOUR SIDE
NOTHING IN COMMON

Currie, Jimmie

I'LL NEVER FALL IN LOVE AGAIN

Curry, Tim

I DO THE ROCK

Curtis, Eddie

JOKER, THE
YOU'RE GONNA KISS ME

Curtis, Eddie "Tex"

SONG OF THE DREAMER

Curtis, Loyal

DRIFTING AND DREAMING

Curtis, Mann

ANEMA E CORE (WITH ALL MY
    HEART AND SOUL)
APPLE BLOSSOMS AND CHAPEL
    BELLS
CHOO'N GUM
DIDJA EVER?
FOOLED
I HAD A LITTLE TALK WITH THE
    LORD
I LIKE IT, I LIKE IT
I'M GONNA LIVE TILL I DIE
JONES BOY, THE
LET IT BE ME

MY DREAMS ARE GETTING BETTER
   ALL THE TIME
PLAY ME HEARTS AND FLOWERS (I
   WANNA CRY)
PRETTY KITTY BLUE EYES
ROCK-A-BYE BABY
STORY OF A STARRY NIGHT, THE
THIS LITTLE GIRL'D GONE ROCKIN'
WHOLE WORLD IS SINGING MY
   SONG, THE
WITH A HEY AND A HI AND A HO-
   HO-HO

Curtis, Memphis

LOVEY DOVEY

Curtis, Michael

SOUTHERN CROSS

Curtis, Richard

SOUTHERN CROSS

Curtis, Sonny

FOOL NEVER LEARNS, A
I FOUGHT THE LAW
I'M NO STRANGER TO THE RAIN
MORE THAN I CAN SAY
STRAIGHT LIFE, THE
WALK RIGHT BACK
WHERE WILL THE WORDS COME
   FROM?

Curtiss, Jimmy

CHILD OF CLAY

Cushing, C. C. S.

L'AMOUR, TOUJOURS, L'AMOUR
   (LOVE EVERLASTING)
LOVE HAS WINGS
LOVE'S OWN SWEET SONG
MY FAITHFUL STRADIVARI
SOFTLY THRO' THE SUMMER NIGHT

Cutler, Scott

PIANO IN THE DARK

Cutter, Bob (a.k.a. Robert C. Haring)

GERTIE FROM BIZERTE

Cymbal, Johnny

CINNAMON
MARY IN THE MORNING

Cymone, André

LOOKING FOR A NEW LOVE
REAL LOVE
STILL A THRILL

Dabney, Ford T.

SHINE
THAT MINOR STRAIN

D'Abo, Michael

BUILD ME UP, BUTTERCUP
HANDBAGS AND GLADRAGS

Dacre, Harry

DAISY BELL (OR, BICYCLE BUILT
   FOR TWO)
ELSIE FROM CHELSEA
I CAN'T THINK OB NUTHIN' ELSE
   BUT YOU
PLAYMATES
SWEET KATIE CONNOR

Dacris, Desmond

ISRAELITES

Daffan, Ted

ALWAYS ALONE
HEADIN' DOWN THE WRONG
   HIGHWAY
I'M A FOOL TO CARE
I'VE GOT FIVE DOLLARS AND IT'S
   SATURDAY NIGHT
LAST RIDE, THE
LOOK WHO'S TALKIN'
SHADOW ON MY HEART
SHUT THAT GATE
TANGLED MIND

TRUCK DRIVERS BLUES
WORRIED MIND

Dahl, Steve

DO YOU THINK I'M DISCO?

Dahlstrom, Patti

EMOTION (AMOREUSE)

Dailey, H.

VOLCANO

Dailey, J. Anton

DREAMING

Dain, Irving

COCA COLA COWBOY

Dair, Marquis

DEAD GIVEAWAY

Dale, Bill

GOIN' GONE

Dale, Jim

GEORGY GIRL
JUST SAY I LOVE HER

Daley, Dan

STILL IN SAIGON

Dall, Bobby

I WON'T FORGET YOU
NOTHIN' BUT A GOOD TIME
TALK DIRTY TO ME

Dall and Daville

EVERY ROSE HAS ITS THORN

Dallin, Sarah

I HEARD A RUMOR

Dalton, Bill
SHORT SHORTS

Dalton, Lacy J.
TAKIN' IT EASY

Daly, Joseph M.
CHICKEN REEL
DALY'S REEL

Daly, William
EVERY DAY

Damato, Pete
JUST ASK YOUR HEART

Damerell, Stanley
IF
LADY OF SPAIN
LET'S ALL SING LIKE THE BIRDIES
   SING
UNLESS

Dameron, Tadd
GOOD BAIT
IF YOU COULD SEE ME NOW

Damon, Russ
COTTON CANDY

D'Amour, Jodi
NO CHEMISE, PLEASE

Damphier, Thomas William
CAN'T EVEN GET THE BLUES
I LIE

Damrosch, Walter
DANNY DEEVER

Dana, Walter
LONGING FOR YOU

Dance, Leo
MY TIME IS YOUR TIME

Daniel, Eliot
BLUE SHADOWS ON THE TRAIL
"I LOVE LUCY" THEME
LAVENDER BLUE (DILLY DILLY)
NEVER
PECOS BILL
UNCLE REMUS SAID

Daniel, Marcus
SLIP AWAY
TELL MAMA

Daniels, Bobby
SUPER BOWL SHUFFLE

Daniels, Charles N. (Neil Moret)
HERE YOU COME WITH LOVE
ON MOBILE BAY
READY FOR THE RIVER
WILD HONEY

Daniels, Charlie
DEVIL WENT DOWN TO GEORGIA, THE
IN AMERICA
LONG HAIRED COUNTRY BOY
SOUTH'S GONNA DO IT, THE
UNEASY RIDER

Daniels, Dorothy
MY HEART BELONGS TO ONLY YOU

Daniels, Elliot
DANSERO

Daniels, Frank
MY HEART BELONGS TO ONLY YOU

Daniels, Jack
IT'S A MAN DOWN THERE
TURN BACK THE HANDS OF TIME

Danko, Rick
LIFE IS A CARNIVAL

Danoff, Bill
AFTERNOON DELIGHT
FRIENDS WITH YOU
TAKE ME HOME, COUNTRY ROADS

Danoff, Sidney
DANCE, EVERYONE, DANCE

Danvers, Charles
TILL

Danzig, Evelyn
SCARLET RIBBONS

Darby, Ken
BUS STOP SONG, THE (A.K.A. PAPER OF PINS, A)
RIVER OF NO RETURN
THIS FRIENDLY WORLD

D'Arby, Terence Trent
SIGN YOUR NAME
WISHING WELL

Darewski, Herman E.
SISTER SUSIE'S SEWING SHIRTS FOR SOLDIERS

Darian, Fred
MISTER CUSTER

Darin, Bobby

DREAM LOVER
EARLY IN THE MORNING
EIGHTEEN YELLOW ROSES
IF A MAN ANSWERS
I'LL BE THERE
JAILER, BRING ME WATER
MULTIPLICATION
QUEEN OF THE HOP
SIMPLE SONG OF FREEDOM
SPLISH SPLASH
THEME FROM "COME SEPTEMBER"
THINGS
THIS LITTLE GIRL'S GONE ROCKIN'
TRUE, TRUE LOVE, A
TWO OF A KIND
YOU'RE THE REASON I'M LIVING

Darion, Joe

CHANGING PARTNERS
HO HO SONG, THE
IMPOSSIBLE DREAM, THE (THE
    QUEST)
RICOCHET (RICK-O-SHAY)

Darling, Denver

CHOO CHOO CH'BOOGIE

Darling, Erik

BANANA BOAT SONG (A.K.A. DAY-O)

Darnell, Larry

I'LL GET ALONG SOMEHOW

Darnell, Shelby

THERE'S A STAR SPANGLED BANNER
    WAVING SOMEWHERE

Darst, Daniel

BLACK SHEEP
ROLL ON BIG MAMA

D'Artega, Alfred A.

IN THE BLUE OF EVENING

Daryll, Ted

COUNTRY GIRL—CITY MAN

Dash, Irwin

WHAT HAS BECOME OF HINKY
    DINKY PARLAY VOO?

Dash, Julian

TUXEDO JUNCTION

Datchler, Clark

SHATTERED DREAMS

Daugherty, Doc

I'M CONFESSIN' THAT I LOVE YOU

Daughtry, Dean

IMAGINARY LOVER
I'M NOT GONNA LET IT BOTHER ME
    TONIGHT
SO IN TO YOU

Davenport, Charles

COW COW BLUES
MAMA DON'T ALLOW IT

Davenport, John

FEVER

Davenport, Pembroke

MY RESTLESS LOVER (A.K.A.
    JOHNNY GUITAR)

David, Bobby

DEVIL IN THE BOTTLE
HOPE YOU'RE FEELIN' ME LIKE I'M
    FEELIN' YOU

David, Donald

WE'RE GETTING CARELESS WITH
    OUR LOVE

David, Douglas

SHOW, THE

David, Hal

99 MILES FROM L.A.
ALFIE
ALWAYS SOMETHING THERE TO
    REMIND ME (THERE'S)
AMERICA IS
AMERICAN BEAUTY ROSE
ANOTHER NIGHT
ANYONE WHO HAD A HEART
APRIL FOOLS, THE
ARE YOU THERE (WITH ANOTHER
    GIRL)?
BELL BOTTOM BLUES
BLUE ON BLUE
BROKEN-HEARTED MELODY
CASINO ROYALE
(THEY LONG TO BE) CLOSE TO YOU
DON'T MAKE ME OVER
DO YOU KNOW THE WAY TO SAN
    JOSE?
EVERYBODY'S OUT OF TOWN
FOUR WINDS AND THE SEVEN SEAS
GOOD TIMES ARE COMING, THE
GREEN GRASS STARTS TO GROW,
    THE
HERE I AM
HOUSE IS NOT A HOME, A
I JUST DON'T KNOW WHAT TO DO
    WITH MYSELF
I'LL NEVER FALL IN LOVE AGAIN
I'M A BETTER MAN (FOR HAVING
    LOVED YOU)
I SAY A LITTLE PRAYER
IT WAS ALMOST LIKE A SONG
JOHNNY GET ANGRY
KNOWING WHEN TO LEAVE
LET ME GO TO HIM
LIFETIME OF LONELINESS, A
LIVING TOGETHER, GROWING
    TOGETHER
LONG AGO TOMORROW
LOOK OF LOVE, THE
LOST HORIZON
MAGIC MOMENTS
MAKE IT EASY ON YOURSELF
MAN AND A TRAIN, A
MAN WHO SHOT LIBERTY VALANCE,
    THE

MESSAGE TO MICHAEL
MOONRAKER
MY HEART IS AN OPEN BOOK
MY LITTLE RED BOOK
NO REGRETS (NON, JE NE
   REGRETTE RIEN)
ODDS AND ENDS
ONE LESS BELL TO ANSWER
ONLY LOVE CAN BREAK A HEART
OUR CONCERTO
PAPER MACHÉ
PROMISES, PROMISES
RAINDROPS KEEP FALLING ON MY
   HEAD
REACH OUT FOR ME
SEA OF HEARTBREAK
SEND A LITTLE LOVE MY WAY
SEND ME NO FLOWERS
SOLE SOLE SOLE
STORY OF MY LIFE, THE
THIS GUY'S (GIRL'S) IN LOVE WITH
   YOU
TO ALL THE GIRLS I'VE LOVED
   BEFORE
TRAINS AND BOATS AND PLANES
TWENTY-FOUR HOURS FROM TULSA
WALK ON BY
WHAT'S NEW, PUSSYCAT?
WHAT THE WORLD NEEDS NOW IS
   LOVE
WHO IS GONNA LOVE ME?
WHO'S BEEN SLEEPING IN MY BED?
WINDOWS OF THE WORLD, THE
WISHIN' AND HOPIN'
WIVES AND LOVERS
WONDERFUL TO BE YOUNG
YOU'LL ANSWER TO ME
YOU'LL NEVER GET TO HEAVEN

David, Hod

HERE'S TO LOVE

David, John

HIGH SCHOOL NIGHTS

David, L.

IF YOU DON'T WANT MY LOVE

David, Lee

HOT HEELS
SIPPING CIDER THRU A STRAW
TONIGHT YOU BELONG TO ME

David, Mack

77 SUNSET STRIP
AT THE CANDLELIGHT CAFE
BABY, BABY, BABY
BABY, IT'S YOU
BACHELOR IN PARADISE
BALLAD OF CAT BALLOU, THE
BIBBIDI-BOBBIDI-BOO
BIMBOMBEY
BIRD MAN, THE
BLOB, THE
BLUE AND SENTIMENTAL
CANDY
CHERRY PINK AND APPLE BLOSSOM
   WHITE
CHI-BABA, CHI-BABA (MY BAMBINA
   GO TO SLEEP)
DON'T YOU KNOW I CARE (OR,
   DON'T YOU CARE TO KNOW)?
DON'T YOU LOVE ME ANYMORE?
DREAM IS A WISH YOUR HEART
   MAKES, A
FALLING LEAVES
GLORIA'S THEME
HANGING TREE, THE
HAPPY BIRTHDAY, DEAR
   HEARTACHE
HUSH, HUSH, SWEET CHARLOTTE
I DON'T CARE IF THE SUN DON'T
   SHINE
I'M JUST A LUCKY SO AND SO
IT MUST BE HIM
IT ONLY HURTS FOR A LITTLE
   WHILE
IT'S A MAD, MAD, MAD, MAD
   WORLD
IT'S LOVE, LOVE, LOVE
JOHNNY ZERO
JUST A KID NAMED JOE
LA VIE EN ROSE
LESSON, THE
MOON LOVE
MY DREAM SONATA
MY JEALOUS EYES (THAT TURNED
   FROM BLUE TO GREEN)

MY OWN TRUE LOVE (TARA'S
   THEME)
ON THE ISLE OF MAY
RAIN, RAIN, GO AWAY!
SHANE
SINGING HILLS, THE
SINNER KISSED AN ANGEL, A
SIXTY SECONDS GOT TOGETHER
SPELLBOUND (A.K.A. SPELLBOUND
   CONCERTO)
SUNFLOWER
SWEET ELOISE
TAKE ME
THEME FROM "TARAS BULBA" (THE
   WISHING STAR)
THERE'S HONEY ON THE MOON
   TONIGHT
THIRTY ONE FLAVORS
TO KILL A MOCKINGBIRD
TO ME
WALK ON THE WILD SIDE
WISHING DOLL, THE
YOU AND YOUR BEAUTIFUL EYES
YOUNG EMOTIONS

David, Sunny

LOVE, LOVE, LOVE
WHOLE LOT-TA SHAKIN' GOIN' ON

Davidson

WISTFUL AND BLUE

Davidson, Eduardo

LA PACHANGA

Davidson, Lenny

AT THE SCENE
CATCH US IF YOU CAN
EVERYBODY KNOWS (I STILL LOVE
   YOU)
I'VE GOT TO HAVE A REASON

Davie, Donald

SHAKE IT WELL

Davies, Bill

KNOCK, KNOCK, WHO'S THERE?

Davies, Douglas

MR. D.J.

Davies, I.

CRAZY

Davies, Ian

ELECTRIC BLUE

Davies, Louis "Chip"

CONVOY

Davies, Ray

ALL DAY AND ALL OF THE NIGHT
APEMAN
COME DANCING
DANDY
DEDICATED FOLLOWER OF FASHION
LOLA
ROCK 'N' ROLL FANTASY, A
SET ME FREE
SLEEPWALKER
STOP YOUR SOBBING
TILL THE END OF THE DAY
TIRED OF WAITING FOR YOU
VICTORIA
WELL RESPECTED MAN, A
WHO'LL BE THE NEXT IN LINE?
YOU REALLY GOT ME

Davies, Richard

BLOODY WELL RIGHT

Davies, Rick

DREAMER
GIVE A LITTLE BIT
GOODBYE STRANGER
IT'S RAINING AGAIN
LOGICAL SONG, THE
TAKE THE LONG WAY HOME

Davis, Benny

ALABAMA BARBECUE
ALL I NEED IS YOU
ALL THAT I'M ASKING IS SYMPATHY

ANGEL CHILD
ARE YOU SORRY?
BABY FACE
CAROLINA MOON
CHASING SHADOWS
COPPER-COLORED GAL
CROSS YOUR FINGERS
DEAREST (YOU'RE THE NEAREST TO
    MY HEART)
DOIN' THE SUSI-Q
DON'T BREAK THE HEART THAT
    LOVES YOU
EVERYTHING'S GONNA BE ALL
    RIGHT
FIRST, LAST AND ALWAYS
FOLLOW THE BOYS
GOODBYE BROADWAY, HELLO
    FRANCE
I HATE MYSELF (FOR BEING SO
    MEAN TO YOU)
I LAUGHED AT LOVE
I'LL STAND BY
I'M GONNA MEET MY SWEETIE NOW
I'M MADLY IN LOVE WITH YOU
I'M NOBODY'S BABY
ISN'T LOVE THE STRANGEST THING?
I STILL GET A THRILL (THINKING
    OF YOU)
IT'S A MILLION TO ONE YOU'RE IN
    LOVE
LONESOME AND SORRY
MAKE BELIEVE
MARGIE
MARY ANN
MORE I KNOW YOU, THE
OH, HOW I MISS YOU TONIGHT
OLD MILL WHEEL
PATRICIA
REACHING FOR THE MOON
SAY IT WHILE DANCING
SLEEPY HEAD
SMILE WILL GO A LONG, LONG
    WAY, A
STELLA
THERE GOES MY HEART
THERE'S NOTHING TOO GOOD FOR
    MY BABY
THIS IS NO DREAM
TO YOU
UNTIL TODAY
WHOSE HEART ARE YOU BREAKING
    TONIGHT?
WHY?

WITH THESE HANDS
YEARNING (JUST FOR YOU)
YOURS TRULY IS TRULY YOURS
YOU STARTED ME DREAMING

Davis, Bernice

LONG LONELY NIGHTS

Davis, Bessie

KENTUCKY BABE

Davis, Bill

COUNTRY SUNSHINE

Davis, Billy

RECOVERY
SLIP-IN MULES (NO HIGH-HEEL
    SNEAKERS)
WE'RE GONNA MAKE IT
WHO'S CHEATING WHO?

Davis, Bob

GREEN DOOR, THE

Davis, Carl

DEAR LOVER
LOVE MAKES A WOMAN
MATADOR, THE

Davis, Carl H.

TWO LITTLE KIDS

Davis, Carol

SAY IT AGAIN

Davis, Charlie

COPENHAGEN

Davis, Clifton

LOOKIN, THROUGH THE WINDOWS
NEVER CAN SAY GOODBYE

Davis, Collin

TAKE ME BACK TO YOUR HEART
   AGAIN
YAMA, YAMA MAN, THE

Davis, Denny

INDIANA MOON

Davis, Dixie

MENTAL CRUELTY

Davis, Don

DISCO LADY
I BELIEVE IN YOU (YOU BELIEVE IN
   ME)
LOVE BONES
LOVE IS BETTER IN THE A.M.
TAKE CARE OF YOUR HOMEWORK
WHO'S MAKING LOVE?

Davis, Donald

BABY, PLEASE COME BACK HOME
CONDITION RED
I'LL LOVE YOU FOREVER

Davis, Doris

LITTLE GIRL, DON'T CRY

Davis, Douglas

LOVIN' EVERY MINUTE OF IT
   (CYCLONE RIDGE)

Davis, Ed

THAT WAS THEN, THIS IS NOW

Davis, Gene

I WON'T COME IN WHILE HE'S
   THERE

Davis, George

TELL IT LIKE IT IS

Davis, Gussie L.

DOWN IN POVERTY ROW
FATAL WEDDING, THE
IN THE BAGGAGE COACH AHEAD
MY CREOLE SUE
ONLY A BOWERY BOY

Davis, Hal

DANCING MACHINE
I'LL BE THERE

Davis, Herman

GROOVY SITUATION

Davis, Jay

BABY JANE

Davis, Jimmie

COLUMBUS STOCKADE BLUES
GRIEVIN' MY HEART OUT FOR YOU
HOW FAR IS HEAVEN?
I HUNG MY HEAD AND CRIED
IT MAKES NO DIFFERENCE NOW
NOBODY'S DARLIN' BUT MINE
SWEETHEARTS OR STRANGERS
THERE'S A CHILL ON THE HILL
   TONIGHT
THERE'S A NEW MOON OVER MY
   SHOULDER
WHEN IT'S ROUND-UP TIME IN
   HEAVEN
WORRIED MIND
YOU ARE MY SUNSHINE

Davis, Jimmy

LOVER MAN (OH, WHERE CAN YOU
   BE?)

Davis, Joe

ALLIGATOR CRAWL
I LEARNED A LESSON I'LL NEVER
   FORGET
JACK! JACK! JACK!
JOY
MILKMAN'S MATINEE, THE
PERHAPS, PERHAPS, PERHAPS

Davis, June

I SAW ME

Davis, Katherine

LITTLE DRUMMER BOY, THE

Davis, Larry

MENTAL CRUELTY

Davis, Link

BIG MAMOU

Davis, Lou

ALBUM OF MY DREAMS, THE
HERE COMES MY BALL AND CHAIN
HOT LIPS
I'M SITTING PRETTY IN A PRETTY
   LITTLE CITY
PRECIOUS LITTLE THING CALLED
   LOVE, A

Davis, Mac

BABY DON'T GET HOOKED ON ME
DADDY'S LITTLE MAN
FRIEND, LOVER, WOMAN, WIFE
HOOKED ON MUSIC
I BELIEVE IN MUSIC
I'LL PAINT YOU A SONG
ONE HELL OF A WOMAN
SOMETHING'S BURNING
STOP AND SMELL THE ROSES
WATCHIN' SCOTTY GROW

Davis, Mack

I NEVER MENTION YOUR NAME
MOON LOVE

Davis, Martha

ONLY THE LONELY
SUDDENLY LAST SUMMER

Davis, Maxwell

EDDIE, MY LOVE
YOU UPSET ME, BABY

Davis, Miles

BOPLICITY

Davis, Paul

'65 LOVE AFFAIR
BOP
COOL NIGHT
DO RIGHT
I GO CRAZY
JUST ANOTHER LOVE
LOVE ME LIKE YOU USED TO
ONE LOVE AT A TIME
RIDE 'EM COWBOY
SWEET LIFE

Davis, Ray

SUNNY AFTERNOON

Davis, Roquel

ALL I COULD DO WAS CRY
I'D LIKE TO TEACH THE WORLD TO
    SING (IN PERFECT HARMONY)
PUSHOVER
SEE SAW

Davis, Scott

CLEAN UP YOUR OWN BACK YARD
DON'T CRY DADDY
IN THE GHETTO
MEMORIES

Davis, Sheila

WHO WILL ANSWER?

Davis, Skeeter

MY LAST DATE (WITH YOU)

Davis, Spencer

GIMME SOME LOVIN'

Davis, Steve

ONLY A LONELY HEART KNOWS
TAKE TIME TO KNOW HER

Davis, Tex

BE-BOP-A-LULA

Davis, Thomas Maxwell

BAD, BAD WHISKEY

Davis, Warren

BOOK OF LOVE

Davis, William

GEE!

Dawes, Charles G.

IT'S ALL IN THE GAME
MELODY

Dawn, Billy

ANGEL SMILE

Dawson, Eli

PUCKER UP YOUR LIPS, MISS LINDY

Day, Bobby

GIVE US THIS DAY

Day, Jimmy

SHOES OF A FOOL

Day, Joey

BEG, BORROW, AND STEAL

Day, Michael

TRY AGAIN

Day, Mike

LITTLE WILLY

Day, Morris

FISHNET
JUNGLE LOVE

OAK TREE, THE

Deacon, John

ANOTHER ONE BITES THE DUST
YOU'RE MY BEST FRIEND

Dean, Dearest

ONE HAS MY NAME, THE OTHER
    HAS MY HEART

Dean, Debbie

I CAN'T DANCE TO THAT MUSIC
    YOU'RE PLAYIN'

Dean, Eddie

I DREAMED OF A HILLBILLY
    HEAVEN
I'LL BE BACK
ONE HAS MY NAME, THE OTHER
    HAS MY HEART

Dean, James

I HOPE WE GET TO LOVE IN TIME
I'VE PASSED THIS WAY BEFORE
WHAT BECOMES OF THE
    BROKENHEARTED?
YOU DON'T HAVE TO BE A STAR (TO
    BE IN MY SHOW)

Dean, Jimmy

BIG BAD JOHN
DEAR IVAN
FIRST THING EVERY MORNING (AND
    THE LAST THING EVERY NIGHT),
    THE
LITTLE BLACK BOOK

Dean, Mary

HALF-BREED

Dean, Paul

HEAVEN IN YOUR EYES
HOT GIRLS IN LOVE
THIS COULD BE THE NIGHT
WORKING FOR THE WEEKEND

Dean, Robert, Jr.

I WANT TO HOLD YOU IN MY
    DREAMS TONIGHT

Dean, Steve

HEARTS AREN'T MADE TO BREAK
    (THEY'RE MADE TO LOVE)
IT TAKES A LITTLE RAIN (TO MAKE
    LOVE GROW)

Deane, Eddie V.

HAPPIEST MOMENTS OF LIFE, THE
MAKE ME THRILL
MEN IN MY LITTLE GIRL'S LIFE, THE
NEE NEE NA NA NA NA NU NU
ROCK-A-BILLY

DeAngelis, Peter

DEDE DINAH
I'LL WAIT FOR YOU
PAINTED, TAINTED ROSE
SWINGIN' ON A RAINBOW
WHY
WITH ALL MY HEART

Deaton, Joe

MR. AND MRS. USED TO BE

DeBarge, Bobby

LOVE OVER AND OVER AGAIN

DeBarge, Bunny

LOVE OVER AND OVER AGAIN
TIME WILL REVEAL

DeBarge, Chico

YOU WEAR IT WELL

DeBarge, Eldra

ALL THIS LOVE
TIME WILL REVEAL
YOU WEAR IT WELL

deBarrio, Eddie

FANTASY

DeBrue, Albert

TAKE IT EASY

DeBuhr, Alice

CHARITY BALL

DeBurgh, Chris

DON'T PAY THE FERRYMAN
HIGH ON EMOTION
LADY IN RED, THE

Debussy, Claude

GOLLIWOG'S CAKE WALK

DeCarlo, Gary

NA NA HEY HEY (KISS HIM
    GOODBYE)

Decker, Carol

HEART AND SOUL

DeCosta, Harry

MARY, DEAR
RAGAMUFFIN ROMEO
TIGER RAG

de Crescenzo, V.

LUNA ROSSA (A.K.A. BLUSHING
    MOON)

de Curtis, Ernesto

COME BACK TO SORRENTO

de Curtis, G. Battista

COME BACK TO SORRENTO

Dee, Buddy

HOLD EVERYTHING

Dee, Joey

PEPPERMINT TWIST

Dee, Lenny

PLANTATION BOOGIE

Dee, Sylvia

AFTER GRADUATION DAY
CHICKERY CHICK
END OF THE WORLD, THE
HOUSE WITH LOVE IN IT, A
I'M THRILLED
IT COULDN'T BE TRUE (OR COULD
    IT?)
LAROO, LAROO, LILLI BOLERO
MOONLIGHT SWIM
MY SUGAR IS SO REFINED
THAT'S THE CHANCE YOU TAKE
TOO YOUNG

Dee, Tommy

THREE STARS

Deen, Dixie

TRUCK DRIVIN' SON-OF-A-GUN

Dees, Bill

COMMUNICATION BREAKDOWN
GOODNIGHT
IT'S OVER
RIDE AWAY
TWINKLE TOES
(SAY) YOU'RE MY GIRL

Dees, Rick

DISCO DUCK

Dees, Sam

IN LOVE
ONE IN A MILLION YOU
SAVE THE OVERTIME FOR ME

Dees, William

OH, PRETTY WOMAN

DeHaven, Carter

BEAUTIFUL EYES

Dehr, Richard

GREENFIELDS
LOVE IS A GOLDEN RING
MARIANNE
MEMORIES ARE MADE OF THIS
MISTER TAP TOE

DeJesus, Gladyces

ROCKIN' GOOD WAY (TO MESS
    AROUND AND FALL IN LOVE), A

DeJohn, Dux

NO MORE (MY BABY DON'T LOVE
    ME)

DeJohn, Julie

NO MORE (MY BABY DON'T LOVE
    ME)

DeJohn, Leo J.

NO MORE (MY BABY DON'T LOVE
    ME)

DeKnight, Jimmy

ROCK AROUND THE CLOCK (WE'RE
    GONNA)

DeKoven, Reginald

BROWN OCTOBER ALE
OH, PROMISE ME
QUILLER HAS THE BRAINS
RECESSIONAL

DeLachau, Countess Ada

L'IL LIZA JANE

Delahunty, Michael

HOW CAN I FALL

Delaney, Tom

DOWN HOME BLUES
JAZZ ME BLUES

DeLange, Eddie

ALL I REMEMBER IS YOU
ALL THIS AND HEAVEN TOO
ALONG THE NAVAJO TRAIL
AND SO DO I
AT YOUR BECK AND CALL
CAN I HELP IT?
DARN THAT DREAM
DEEP IN A DREAM
DO YOU KNOW WHAT IT MEANS TO
    MISS NEW ORLEANS?
FLOWER OF DAWN
GOOD FOR NOTHIN' BUT LOVE
HAUNTING ME
HEAVEN CAN WAIT
HOW WAS I TO KNOW?
IF I'M LUCKY
I WISH I WERE TWINS
JUST AS THOUGH YOU WERE HERE
LOST APRIL
MAN WITH A HORN
MOONGLOW
ONE MORE TOMORROW
PASSÉ
PEACE, BROTHER
SHAKE DOWN THE STARS
SO HELP ME (IF I DON'T LOVE YOU)
SOLITUDE
STRING OF PEARLS, A
SWINGIN' A DREAM
THIS IS WORTH FIGHTING FOR
VELVET MOON
WHO THREW THE WHISKEY IN THE
    WELL?

Delanoe, Pierre

DAY THE RAINS CAME, THE
WHAT NOW MY LOVE

DeLeon, Robert

CAN'T GET INDIA OFF MY MIND

Delettre, Jean

HANDS ACROSS THE TABLE

Dello, Carmen

PICNIC SONG, THE

Dello, Theresa

PICNIC SONG, THE

Delmore, Alton

BLUES, STAY AWAY FROM ME

Delmore, Lionel

SWINGIN'

Delmore, Rabon

BLUES, STAY AWAY FROM ME

DeLorme, Gaye

EARACHE MY EYE FEATURING
    ALICE BOWIE

DeLory, Al

MISTER CUSTER

Delp, Brad

CAN'TCHA SAY (YOU BELIEVE IN
    ME)

del Riego, Teresa

HOMING
O DRY THOSE TEARS!

Del Rio, Venita

MOUNTAIN OF LOVE

DeLugg, Milton

BE MY LIFE'S COMPANION
HOOP-DE-DOO
JUST ANOTHER POLKA
MY LADY LOVES TO DANCE
ORANGE COLORED SKY
POOR MAN'S ROSES, A (OR A RICH
    MAN'S GOLD)
SEND MY BABY BACK TO ME

SHANGHAI

DeMartini, Warren

ROUND AND ROUND

Demetrius, Claude

AIN'T THAT JUST LIKE A WOMAN
HARD HEADED WOMAN
I WAS THE ONE

Demey, Tetos

YOU, YOU, YOU ARE THE ONE

Dempsey, Greg

BOOGIE BANDS AND ONE NIGHT
    STANDS

Dempsey, J. E.

GARDEN OF ROSES, THE

Dempsey, James E.

ACE IN THE HOLE

Demy, Jacques

I WILL WAIT FOR YOU
WATCH WHAT HAPPENS

DeNicola, John

HUNGRY EYES
(I'VE HAD) THE TIME OF MY LIFE

Denison, C. M.

LAND OF GOLDEN DREAMS, THE
MY ROSARY OF DREAMS

Denman, Paul

PARADISE

Denni, Gwynne

YOU'RE JUST A FLOWER FROM AN
    OLD BOUQUET

Denni, Lucien

OCEANA ROLL, THE
YOU'RE JUST A FLOWER FROM AN
    OLD BOUQUET

Denniker, Paul

BESIDE AN OPEN FIREPLACE
MAKE BELIEVE BALLROOM
MILKMAN'S MATINEE, THE
S'POSIN'

Dennis, Matt

ANGEL EYES
EVERYTHING HAPPENS TO ME
LET'S GET AWAY FROM IT ALL
LITTLE MAN WITH A CANDY CIGAR
NIGHT WE CALLED IT A DAY, THE
SHOW ME THE WAY TO GET OUT OF
    THIS WORLD ('CAUSE THAT'S
    WHERE EVERYTHING IS)
THAT SOLDIER OF MINE
VIOLETS FOR YOUR FURS
WHO'S YEHOODI?
WILL YOU STILL BE MINE?

Denny, Jim

LOCO WEED

Denny, Joy

FRANKIE

Denny, Sandy

WHO KNOWS WHERE THE TIME
    GOES?

DeNota, Diane

JUST ASK YOUR HEART

Densmore, John

HELLO, I LOVE YOU
LIGHT MY FIRE
LOVE HER MADLY
LOVE ME TWO TIMES
PEOPLE ARE STRANGE
RIDERS ON THE STORM

ROADHOUSE BLUES
TOUCH ME
UNKNOWN SOLDIER
WISHFUL, SINFUL

Denson, William

MAMA SAID

Denson, Willie

BACKSTAGE

Denton, Jimmy

BLACK SLACKS

Denver, John

ANNIE'S SONG
BACK HOME AGAIN
CALYPSO
FLY AWAY
FOLLOW ME
FOR BABY (A.K.A. FOR BOBBIE)
I'M SORRY
LEAVING ON A JET PLANE
LOOKING FOR SPACE
MY SWEET LADY
PERHAPS LOVE
ROCKY MOUNTAIN HIGH
SHANGHAI BREEZES
SUNSHINE ON MY SHOULDERS
SWEET SURRENDER
TAKE ME HOME, COUNTRY ROADS

Deodato, Eumir

TAKE MY HEART (YOU CAN HAVE IT
    IF YOU WANT IT)

DeOliviera, Milton

COME TO THE MARTI GRAS

dePasse, Suzanne

HERE COMES THE JUDGE

De Paul, Gene

AIN'T THAT JUST LIKE A MAN?
BLESS YORE BEAUTIFUL HIDE

COW-COW BOOGIE
DADDY-O (I'M GONNA TEACH YOU
    SOME BLUES)
HE'S MY GUY
IF I HAD MY DRUTHERS
I'LL REMEMBER APRIL
IRRESISTIBLE YOU
IT'S WHATCHA DO WITH WHATCHA
    GOT
JUBILATION T. CORNPONE
JUDALINE
LONESOME POLECAT
LOVE IN A HOME
MILKMAN, KEEP THOSE BOTTLES
    QUIET
MISTER FIVE BY FIVE
NAMELY YOU
PIG FOOT PETE
SOBBIN' WOMEN
SONG WAS BORN, A
SPRING, SPRING, SPRING
STAR EYES
TEACH ME TONIGHT
WHEN YOU'RE IN LOVE
WONDERFUL, WONDERFUL DAY
YOU CAN'T RUN AWAY FROM IT
YOU DON'T KNOW WHAT LOVE IS
YOUR RED WAGON

Depew, Mary

SET HIM FREE

Deppen, Jessie L

IN THE GARDEN OF TOMORROW
JAPANESE SUNSET, A
OH, MISS HANNAH!

Dermer, Larry

BAD BOY

DeRosa, Francis

BIG GUITAR, THE

De Rose, Peter

ALL I NEED IS YOU
ANGEL
AUTUMN SERENADE
CLOSE TO ME

DEEP PURPLE
HAVE YOU EVER BEEN LONELY?
    (HAVE YOU EVER BEEN BLUE?)
IF YOU TURN ME DOWN
I JUST ROLL ALONG
LAMP IS LOW, THE
LAZY WEATHER
LILACS IN THE RAIN
LOUISVILLE LADY
LOVE YA
MARSHMALLOW WORLD, A
MOON FELL IN THE RIVER, THE
MOONLIGHT MOOD
MUDDY WATER
NIGHTFALL
NOW OR NEVER
ON A LITTLE STREET IN SINGAPORE
ORANGE BLOSSOM LANE
ORCHIDS FOR REMEMBRANCE
OREGON TRAIL, THE
RAIN
SOMEBODY LOVES YOU
SOMEWHERE IN OLD WYOMING
SPRING HAS SPRUNG
STARLIT HOUR, THE
THAT'S WHERE I CAME IN
THEN TWILIGHT COMES
THINGS THAT WERE MADE FOR
    LOVE, THE (YOU CAN'T TAKE
    AWAY)
TWENTY-FOUR HOURS OF SUNSHINE
WAGON WHEELS
WHEN I'M GONE I WON'T FORGET
WHEN LOVE KNOCKS AT YOUR
    HEART
WHEN YOUR HAIR HAS TURNED TO
    SILVER (I WILL LOVE YOU JUST
    THE SAME)
WHO DO YOU KNOW IN HEAVEN
    (THAT MADE YOU THE ANGEL
    YOU ARE)?

Derosier, Michael

BARRACUDA

Derouse, Candy

POWER OF LOVE, THE

D'Errico, Carl

IT'S MY LIFE

Derringer, Rick

ROCK AND ROLL, HOOCHIE KOO

Desautels, John

LOVE THEME FROM "EYES OF
    LAURA MARS" (A.K.A. PRISONER)

Des Barres, Michael

I DO WHAT I DO
OBSESSION

DeShannon, Jackie

BETTE DAVIS EYES
BRIGHTON HILL
COME AND STAY WITH ME
DUM DUM
HEART IN HAND
HE'S SO HEAVENLY
LOVE WILL FIND A WAY
PUT A LITTLE LOVE IN YOUR HEART

Desmond, Paul

TAKE FIVE
TAKE TEN

Despenza, Barry

CAN I CHANGE MY MIND?

DeSylva, B. G.

ALABAMY BOUND
AMERICAN TUNE
APRIL SHOWERS
AVALON
BABY!
BEST OF EVERYTHING, THE
BEST THINGS IN LIFE ARE FREE,
    THE
BIRTH OF THE BLUES, THE
BLACK BOTTOM
BROADWAY
(HERE AM I) BROKEN HEARTED
CALIFORNIA, HERE I COME
COME TO ME
CROSS YOUR HEART
DO IT AGAIN!
DON'T HOLD EVERYTHING

DON'T TELL HER WHAT HAPPENED
  TO ME
EADIE WAS A LADY
FOR OLD TIMES' SAKE
GATHER LIP ROUGE WHILE YOU
  MAY
GENTLEMEN PREFER BLONDES
GIRL IS YOU AND THE BOY IS ME,
  THE
GIVE ME MY MAMMY
GOOD FOR YOU—BAD FOR ME
GOOD NEWS
HEADIN' FOR LOUISVILLE
HELLO 'TUCKY
IF I HAD A TALKING PICTURE OF
  YOU
IF YOU HAVEN'T GOT LOVE
IF YOU KNEW SUSIE (LIKE I KNOW
  SUSIE)
I'LL BUILD A STAIRWAY TO
  PARADISE
I'LL SAY SHE DOES
I'M A DREAMER, AREN'T WE ALL?
I'M IN SEVENTH HEAVEN
I'M ON THE CREST OF A WAVE
IT ALL DEPENDS ON YOU
IT WON'T BE LONG NOW
I WANT TO BE BAD
I WANT TO BE WITH YOU
I WON'T SAY I WILL, BUT I WON'T
  SAY I WON'T
JUST A COTTAGE SMALL (BY A
  WATERFALL)
JUST A MEMORY
JUST IMAGINE
KEEP SMILING AT TROUBLE
KICKIN' THE CLOUDS AWAY
KISS IN THE DARK, A
LIFE IS JUST A BOWL OF CHERRIES
LITTLE PAL
LOOK FOR THE SILVER LINING
LUCKY DAY (THIS IS MY)
LUCKY IN LOVE
MANHATTAN MARY
MEMORY LANE
MIAMI
MINNIE THE MERMAID
MY LUCKY STAR
MY SIN
'N' EVERYTHING
OH, HOW I LONG TO BELONG TO
  YOU
ONE MORE TIME

PICKIN' COTTON
POMPANOLA
RISE 'N' SHINE
SAVE YOUR SORROW (FOR
  TOMORROW)
SHOULD I BE SWEET?
SO BLUE
SO DO I
SOMEBODY LOVES ME
SOMEHOW IT SELDOM COMES TRUE
SONG I LOVE, THE
SONNY BOY
SUNNY SIDE UP
THANK YOUR FATHER
TOGETHER
TO KNOW YOU IS TO LOVE YOU
TURN ON THE HEAT
USED TO YOU
VARSITY DRAG, THE
VIRGINIA (DON'T GO TOO FAR)
WASN'T IT BEAUTIFUL WHILE IT
  LASTED?
WHAT D'YA SAY?
WHEN DAY IS DONE
WHIP-POOR-WILL
WHY CAN'T YOU?
WHY DO I LOVE YOU?
WISHING (WILL MAKE IT SO)
WITHOUT LOVE
YANKEE DOODLE BLUES
YOO-HOO
YOU AIN'T HEARD NOTHING YET
YOU'RE AN OLD SMOOTHIE
YOU'RE THE CREAM IN MY COFFEE
YOU TRY SOMEBODY ELSE
YOU WOULDN'T FOOL ME, WOULD
  YOU?

Deutsch, Emery

PLAY, FIDDLE, PLAY
STARDUST ON THE MOON
WHEN A GYPSY MAKES HIS VIOLIN
  CRY

Deutsch, Helen

HI-LILI, HI-LO

Devaney, Don

CRY, CRY, CRY

Devaney, Yvonne

MILLION AND ONE

DeVaughn, William

BE THANKFUL FOR WHAT YOU'VE
  GOT

Devere, Sam

WHISTLING COON, THE

Devers, William

MOTTOES FRAMED UPON THE WALL

Deville, C. C.

I WON'T FORGET YOU
NOTHIN' BUT A GOOD TIME
TALK DIRTY TO ME

DeVille, Willy

I MUST BE DREAMING
STORYBOOK LOVE

Devine, Kenny

YELLOW ROSES

DeVita, Antonio

SOFTLY, AS I LEAVE YOU

DeVito, Don

SO MANY TIMES

DeVito, Hank

IF YOU CHANGED YOUR MIND
QUEEN OF HEARTS

DeVol, Frank

BLUES FROM "KISS ME DEADLY"
  (A.K.A. I'D RATHER HAVE THE
  BLUES)
FRIENDLY TAVERN POLKA
HAPPENING, THE
HUSH, HUSH, SWEET CHARLOTTE

De Voll, Cal

LOVER COME BACK
MAN AND A TRAIN, A

De Voll, Cal

HOW DO YOU DO (EVERYBODY)

DeVorzon, Barry

BLESS THE BEASTS AND CHILDREN
DREAMIN'
I WILL LOVE YOU
NADIA'S THEME (THE YOUNG AND
   THE RESTLESS)
THEME FROM "S.W.A.T."

DeVries, John

BOOGIE WOOGIE BLUE PLATE
HOT TIME IN THE TOWN OF BERLIN,
   A (WHEN THE YANKS GO
   MARCHING IN)
OH, LOOK AT ME NOW

de Waal, Anton

ZAMBEZI

DeWalt, Autry

CLEO'S BACK
CLEO'S MOOD
DO THE BOOMERANG
HIP CITY—PT. 2
SHAKE AND FINGERPOP
SHOOT YOUR SHOT
SHOTGUN

DeWese, Mohandas

GO SEE THE DOCTOR
THEY WANT MONEY

Dewey, Nicholas

RUNAWAY

DeWitt, Francis

MOON SHINES ON THE MOONSHINE,
   THE

DeWitt, Lewis

FLOWERS ON THE WALL

Dexter, Al

CALICO RAG
DOWN AT THE ROADSIDE INN
GUITAR POLKA
HONEY, DO YOU THINK IT'S
   WRONG?
I'M LOSING MY MIND OVER YOU
IT'S UP TO YOU
PISTOL PACKIN' MAMA
ROCK AND RYE RAG
ROSALITA
SO LONG, PAL
TOO LATE TO WORRY, TOO BLUE TO
   CRY
WINE, WOMEN AND SONG

Dexter, Johnny

HEAVEN IN YOUR EYES

Dey, Richard

JUST LIKE ME

DeYoung, Dennis

BABE
BEST OF TIMES, THE
COME SAIL AWAY
DESERT MOON
DON'T LET IT END
LADY
MR. ROBOTO

d'Hardelot, Guy

BECAUSE

Diamond, David

SEX (I'M A . . .)

Diamond, Gregg

MORE, MORE, MORE

Diamond, Keith

CARIBBEAN QUEEN (NO MORE LOVE
   ON THE RUN)
MYSTERY LADY
SUDDENLY

Diamond, Lee

TELL IT LIKE IT IS

Diamond, Leo

OFF SHORE

Diamond, Max

MY BOOMERANG WON'T COME BACK

Diamond, Michael

(YOU GOTTA) FIGHT FOR YOUR
   RIGHT (TO PARTY)

Diamond, Neil

AMERICA
BE
BROOKLYN ROADS
BROTHER LOVE'S TRAVELLING
   SALVATION SHOW
CHERRY, CHERRY
CRACKLIN' ROSIE
DESIREE
FOREVER IN BLUE JEANS
GIRL, YOU'LL BE A WOMAN SOON
HELLO AGAIN
HOLLY HOLY
I AM . . . I SAID
IF YOU KNOW WHAT I MEAN
I GOT THE FEELIN' (OH NO, NO)
I'M A BELIEVER
I'VE BEEN THIS WAY BEFORE
KENTUCKY WOMAN
LITTLE BIT ME, A LITTLE BIT YOU,
   A
LONGFELLOW SERENADE
LOVE ON THE ROCKS
MY BABE
PLAY ME
RED RED WINE
SEPTEMBER MORN
SHILO

SKYBIRD
SOLITARY MAN
SONG SUNG BLUE
STONES
SUNDAY AND ME
SUNDAY SUN
SUNFLOWER
SWEET CAROLINE (GOOD TIMES
   NEVER SEEMED SO GOOD)
THANK THE LORD FOR THE NIGHT
   TIME
TWO-BIT MANCHILD
WALK ON WATER
YESTERDAY'S SONGS
YOU DON'T BRING ME FLOWERS
YOU GOT TO ME

Diamond, Steve

DON'T UNDERESTIMATE MY LOVE
   FOR YOU
I'VE GOT A ROCK AND ROLL HEART

Dibango, Manu

SOUL MAKOSSA

di Cicco, Richard

BOBBY SOX TO STOCKINGS

Dick, Dorothy

BY MY SIDE
CALL ME DARLING
MUST WE SAY GOODNIGHT SO
   SOON?
THERE IS NO BREEZE

Dickerson, B. B.

CISCO KID, THE
L. A. SUNSHINE
LOW RIDER
ME AND BABY BROTHER
SLIPPIN' INTO DARKNESS
SPILL THE WINE
SUMMER
WHY CAN'T WE BE FRIENDS?
WORLD IS A GHETTO, THE

Dickerson, Dez

COOL

Dickerson, R.

GYPSY MAN

Dickerson, Willis

STOOD UP

Dickinson, Hal

THESE THINGS YOU LEFT ME

DiCola, Vince

FAR FROM OVER

Didier, Julie

ANYONE WHO ISN'T ME TONIGHT

Dietz, Howard

ALIBI BABY
ALL THE KING'S HORSES
ALONE TOGETHER
BEFORE I KISS THE WORLD
   GOODBYE
BY MYSELF
DANCING IN THE DARK
DANCING TIME
DICKEY-BIRD SONG, THE
FAREWELL, MY LOVELY
FEELIN' HIGH
GOT A BRAN' NEW SUIT
HAUNTED HEART
HIGH AND LOW
HOTTENTOT POTENTATE, THE
IF THERE IS SOMEONE LOVELIER
   THAN YOU
I GUESS I'LL HAVE TO CHANGE MY
   PLAN (THE BLUE PAJAMA SONG)
I LOVE LOUISA
I SEE YOUR FACE BEFORE ME
I STILL LOOK AT YOU THAT WAY
JUNGLE FEVER
LOUISIANA HAYRIDE
LOVE I LONG FOR, THE
LOVE IS A DANCING THING
LUCKY SEVEN

MAGIC MOMENT
MOANIN' LOW
NEW SUN IN THE SKY
ON THE OLD PARK BENCH
RAINY DAY, A
RHODE ISLAND IS FAMOUS FOR YOU
SHINE ON YOUR SHOES, A
SOMETHING TO REMEMBER YOU BY
SOMETHING YOU NEVER HAD
   BEFORE
THAT'S ENTERTAINMENT
THIEF IN THE NIGHT
TRIPLETS
UNDER YOUR SPELL
WAITIN' FOR THE EVENING TRAIN
WHAT A WONDERFUL WORLD
YOU AND THE NIGHT AND THE
   MUSIC

Dieval, Jacques

WAY OF LOVE, THE

Difford, Chris

HOURGLASS
TEMPTED

DiFranco, Paul

LIFE IS A ROCK (BUT THE RADIO
   ROLLED ME)

DiGregorio, Joel

IN AMERICA

DiGregorio, Taz

DEVIL WENT DOWN TO GEORGIA,
   THE

Dike, M.

BUST A MOVE
WILD THING

diLazzaro, Eldo

FERRYBOAT SERENADE, THE
WOODPECKER SONG, THE

Dilbeck, Tommy

I'LL HOLD YOU IN MY HEART (TILL I
CAN HOLD YOU IN MY ARMS)
MY DADDY IS ONLY A PICTURE
THIS IS THE THANKS I GET (FOR
LOVING YOU)

Dill, Danny

COMEBACK, THE
DETROIT CITY
LONG BLACK VEIL
PARTNERS

Dillea, Herbert

ABSENCE MAKES THE HEART GROW
FONDER
YOU'RE DE APPLE OF MY EYE

Dillon, Dean

BY NOW
CHAIR, THE
FAMOUS LAST WORDS OF A FOOL
IT AIN'T COOL TO BE CRAZY ABOUT
YOU
NOBODY IN HIS RIGHT MIND
WOULD'VE LEFT HER
OCEAN FRONT PROPERTY
SET 'EM UP JOE

Dillon, Harry

DO, DO, MY HUCKLEBERRY DO
PUT ME OFF AT BUFFALO

Dillon, John

DO, DO, MY HUCKLEBERRY DO
IF YOU WANNA GET TO HEAVEN
PUT ME OFF AT BUFFALO

Dillon, Lawrence

EVERY LITTLE BIT ADDED TO WHAT
YOU'VE GOT MAKES JUST A
LITTLE BIT MORE

Dillon, Lola Jean

SOMEBODY SOMEWHERE (DON'T
KNOW WHAT HE'S MISSIN'
TONIGHT)

Dillon, William A.

ALL ALONE
EVERY LITTLE BIT ADDED TO WHAT
YOU'VE GOT MAKES JUST A
LITTLE BIT MORE
GOODBYE, BOYS
IT'S THE IRISH IN YOUR EYES, IT'S
THE IRISH IN YOUR SMILE
I WANT A GIRL (JUST LIKE THE
GIRL THAT MARRIED DEAR OLD
DAD)
MY LITTLE GIRL

DiMinno, Danny

FROM THE BOTTOM OF MY HEART
(DAMMI, DAMMI, DAMMI)
I CAN'T GET YOU OUT OF MY
HEART
RETURN TO ME (RITORNA A ME)

Dimirco, Vincent

UP THE LADDER TO THE ROOF

DiMucci, Dion

DONNA THE PRIMA DONNA
LITTLE DIANE
LOVE CAME TO ME
LOVERS WHO WANDER
RUNAROUND SUE
YOUR OWN BACK YARD

Dinapoli, Mario

SHE'S GOT TO BE A SAINT

Dino, Ralph

DO WHAT YOU DO

di Paola, V.

COME PRIMA (FOR THE FIRST TIME)

DiPaoli, Alfred

LONELY TEENAGER

Dipiero, Robert

AMERICAN MADE
CHURCH ON CUMBERLAND ROAD,
THE
(DO YOU LOVE ME) JUST SAY YES
LITTLE ROCK
THAT ROCK WON'T ROLL

Discant, Mack

GIRL WITH THE HEATHER GREEN
EYES
LONG LEGGED LADIES OF
LABRADOR

Dispenza, Barry

IS IT SOMETHING YOU'VE GOT?

Distel, Sacha

GOOD LIFE, THE

Ditcham, Martin

SWEETEST TABOO, THE

DiTomaso, Larry

DO WHAT YOU DO

Dixon, Cliff

WHERE THE BLUES WERE BORN IN
NEW ORLEANS

Dixon, Dave

I DIG ROCK AND ROLL MUSIC

Dixon, Dorsey

WRECK ON THE HIGHWAY

Dixon, Eugene (a.k.a. Gene Chandler)

DUKE OF EARL

Dixon, Eugene (a.k.a. Gene Chandler)

I FOOLED YOU THIS TIME
SOUL HOOTENANNY

Dixon, Floyd

CALL OPERATOR 210

Dixon, Heather

MR. LEE

Dixon, Jerry

HEAVEN

Dixon, Julius

DIM, DIM, THE LIGHTS (I WANT
SOME ATMOSPHERE)
IT HURTS TO BE IN LOVE
LET ME DO IT MY WAY
LOLLIPOP

Dixon, Luther

16 CANDLES
ANGEL SMILE
BIG BOSS MAN
HUNDRED POUNDS OF CLAY, A
I DON'T WANT TO CRY
I LOVE YOU 1000 TIMES
JUST BORN (TO BE YOUR BABY)
MAMA SAID
SO CLOSE
SOLDIER BOY
SOUL SERENADE
WHY BABY WHY
WITH THIS RING

Dixon, Mort

BAM, BAM, BAMY SHORE
BYE BYE BLACKBIRD
COVER ME UP WITH SUNSHINE
FARE THEE WELL, ANNABELLE
FLIRTATION WALK
FOLLOW THE SWALLOW
HAPPINESS AHEAD
HELLO, MONTREAL
I CAN'T LOSE THAT LONGING FOR
YOU
IF I HAD A GIRL LIKE YOU

I FOUND A MILLION DOLLAR BABY
(IN A FIVE AND TEN CENT
STORE)
IF YOU WANT THE RAINBOW (YOU
MUST HAVE THE RAIN)
I LIVE FOR LOVE
I'LL TAKE CARE OF YOUR CARES
I'M LOOKING OVER A FOUR LEAF
CLOVER
I SEE TWO LOVERS
IS IT POSSIBLE?
I WONDER WHO'S DANCING WITH
YOU TONIGHT
JUST LIKE A BUTTERFLY (THAT'S
CAUGHT IN THE RAIN)
LADY IN RED, THE
MINE ALONE
MOONBEAM, KISS HER FOR ME
MR. AND MRS. IS THE NAME
NAGASAKI
OLD MAN SUNSHINE, LITTLE BOY
BLUEBIRD
OOH! THAT KISS
PINK ELEPHANTS
POP! GOES YOUR HEART
RIVER, STAY 'WAY FROM MY DOOR
SING A LITTLE JINGLE
SO NICE SEEING YOU AGAIN
TEARS FROM MY INKWELL
THAT OLD GANG OF MINE
TORCH SONG, THE
TRY TO SEE IT MY WAY
WHERE THE SWEET FORGET-ME-
NOTS REMEMBER
WOULD YOU LIKE TO TAKE A WALK?
YOU'RE MY EVERYTHING

Dixon, Willie

DONCHA' THINK IT'S TIME
I'M READY
I'M YOUR HOOCHIE COOCHE MAN
LITTLE RED ROOSTER
MY BABE
SEVENTH SON
WANG DANG DOODLE

D'Lorah, Juan Y.

LA CUCARACHA

Dobbins, Shelley

NON DIMENTICAR (DON'T FORGET)

Dobson, Bonnie

MORNING DEW

Dodd, Bonnie

YOU WILL HAVE TO PAY (FOR YOUR
YESTERDAY)

Dodd, Jimmy

ROSEMARY

Dodge, Gilbert

PEGGY O'NEIL

Dodson, Rick

SWEET CITY WOMAN

Doerge, Craig

CRIED LIKE A BABY
ROSALIE

Doerr, Eddie

OH, YOU MILLION DOLLAR BABY

Doggett, Bill

HONKY TONK

Doheny, Ned

WHAT CHA' GONNA DO FOR ME

Doherty, Dennis

I SAW HER AGAIN

Dolan, Robert Emmett

BIG MOVIE SHOW IN THE SKY
IT'S GREAT TO BE ALIVE
LITTLE BY LITTLE
TALK TO ME, BABY

Dolby, Thomas

SHE BLINDED ME WITH SCIENCE

Dolce, Joe

SHADDAP YOU FACE

Dollar, Johnny

STOP THE START (OF TEARS IN MY
HEART)

Dollison, Maurice

JEALOUS KIND OF FELLA

Dolph, Norman

LIFE IS A ROCK (BUT THE RADIO
ROLLED ME)

Dolphin, John

JIVIN' AROUND

Dominguez, Alberto

FRENESI
PERFIDIA

Domino, Antoine "Fats"

AIN'T THAT A SHAME (A.K.A. AIN'T
IT A SHAME)
ALL BY MYSELF
BE MY GUEST
BLUE MONDAY
BO WEEVIL
DON'T COME KNOCKIN'
FAT MAN, THE
GOIN' HOME
GOIN' TO THE RIVER
I'M GONNA BE A WHEEL SOMEDAY
I'M IN LOVE AGAIN
I'M READY
I'M WALKING
IT'S YOU I LOVE
I WANT TO WALK YOU HOME
LAND OF 1000 DANCES
LET THE FOUR WINDS BLOW
MY GIRL JOSEPHINE
PLEASE DON'T LEAVE ME

POOR ME
SO LONG
THREE NIGHTS A WEEK
VALLEY OF TEARS
WALKING TO NEW ORLEANS
WHOLE LOTTA LOVING

Donaggio, P.

YOU DON'T HAVE TO SAY YOU LOVE
ME

Donahue, Al

DON'T CROSS YOUR FINGERS, CROSS
YOUR HEART
LOW DOWN RHYTHM IN A TOP HAT

Donaldson, B. B. B.

I FAW DOWN AN' GO BOOM!

Donaldson, Walter

AFTER I SAY I'M SORRY (WHAT CAN
I SAY?)
ANYTHING YOU SAY
AT SUNDOWN
BACK HOME IN TENNESSEE
BECAUSE MY BABY DON'T MEAN
"MAYBE" NOW
BESIDE A BABBLING BROOK
BLUE KENTUCKY MOON
BUT I DO, YOU KNOW I DO
CAROLINA IN THE MORNING
CHANGES
CLOUDS
COULD BE
CUCKOO IN THE CLOCK
DANCING IN THE MOONLIGHT
DAUGHTER OF ROSIE O'GRADY, THE
DID I REMEMBER?
DIXIE HIGHWAY
DIXIE VAGABOND
DON'T BE ANGRY WITH ME
DON'T CRY, FRENCHY, DON'T CRY
EARFUL OF MUSIC, AN
FEELIN' HIGH
FOR MY SWEETHEART
GEORGIA
GIVE ME MY MAMMY
GOODNIGHT MOON
GOTTA GET SOME SHUT-EYE

HELLO BEAUTIFUL
HE'S THE LAST WORD
HORSE WITH THE DREAMY EYES,
THE
HOW YA GONNA KEEP 'EM DOWN
ON THE FARM (AFTER THEY'VE
SEEN PAREE)?
IF YOU SEE SALLY
I'LL BE HAPPY WHEN THE
PREACHER MAKES YOU MINE
I LOVE THE LAND OF OLD BLACK
JOE
I'M BRINGING A RED, RED ROSE
I'M FIT TO BE TIED
IN THE EVENING
IN THE MIDDLE OF THE NIGHT
ISN'T SHE THE SWEETEST THING?
(OH MAW, OH PAW)
IT MADE YOU HAPPY WHEN YOU
MADE ME CRY
IT'S BEEN SO LONG
I'VE GOT THE GIRL
I'VE HAD MY MOMENTS
I WONDER WHERE MY BABY IS
TONIGHT
JUNGLE FEVER
JUNIOR
JUST A BIRD'S EYE VIEW OF MY
OLD KENTUCKY HOME
JUST LIKE A MELODY OUT OF THE
SKY
JUST ONCE AGAIN
KANSAS CITY KITTY
LAZY LOU'SIANA MOON
LET IT RAIN! LET IT POUR! (I'LL BE
IN VIRGINIA IN THE MORNING)
LET'S TALK ABOUT MY SWEETIE
LITTLE WHITE LIES
LOVE ME OR LEAVE ME
MAKIN' WHOOPEE
(WHAT ARE YOU WAITING FOR)
MARY
MINDIN' MY BUSINESS
MISTER MEADOWLARK
MY BABY JUST CARES FOR ME
MY BEST GIRL
MY BLUE HEAVEN
MY BUDDY
MY LITTLE BIMBO DOWN ON THE
BAMBOO ISLE
MY MAMMY
MY MOM
MY OHIO HOME

MY SWEETIE TURNED ME
    DOWN
NEVADA
OKAY TOOTS
ON BEHALF OF THE VISITING
    FIREMEN
ON THE 'GIN, 'GIN, 'GINNY SHORE
OUT-O'-TOWN GAL
PRETTY LIPS
REACHING FOR SOMEONE (AND NOT
    FINDING ANYONE THERE)
RIPTIDE
ROMANCE
SAM, THE OLD ACCORDION MAN
SING ME A BABY SONG
SLEEPY HEAD
SWANEE BUTTERFLY
SWEET INDIANA HOME
SWEET JENNIE LEE
TAIN'T NO SIN (TO TAKE OFF YOUR
    SKIN AND DANCE AROUND IN
    YOUR BONES)
TENDER IS THE NIGHT
THAT CERTAIN PARTY
THAT'S WHY I LOVE YOU
THERE AIN'T NO MAYBE IN MY
    BABY'S EYES
THERE'S A WAH-WAH GAL IN AGUA
    CALIENTE
(I'VE GROWN SO LONESOME)
    THINKING OF YOU
THOUSAND GOODNIGHTS, A
WE'LL HAVE A JUBILEE IN MY OLD
    KENTUCKY HOME
WHEN MY SHIP COMES IN
WHERE'D YOU GET THOSE EYES?
WITHOUT THAT GAL
YES SIR! THAT'S MY BABY
YOU
YOU DIDN'T HAVE TO TELL ME (I
    KNEW IT ALL THE TIME)
YOU'LL NEVER KNOW THAT OLD
    HOME TOWN OF MINE
YOU'RE A MILLION MILES FROM
    NOWHERE (WHEN YOU'RE ONE
    LITTLE MILE FROM HOME)
YOU'RE DRIVING ME CRAZY
YOU'VE GOT EVERYTHING

Donaldson, Will

DOO WACKA DOO
I CAN'T RESIST YOU

Donegan, Lonnie

I'LL NEVER FALL IN LOVE AGAIN
ROCK ISLAND LINE

Donida, Carlo

AL DI LA
HELP YOURSELF
I (WHO HAVE NOTHING)

Donna, James J.

LIAR, LIAR

Donnelly, Dorothy

DEEP IN MY HEART, DEAR
DRINKING SONG (DRINK! DRINK!
    DRINK!)
GOLDEN DAYS
JUST WE TWO
MOTHER
SERENADE
SILVER MOON
SONG OF LOVE
YOUR LAND AND MY LAND

Donny, Harold

ALLA MY LOVE

Donovan, Michael

HURTS SO GOOD

Donovan, Walter

ABA DABA HONEYMOON, THE
DOWN BY THE WINEGAR WOIKS
ONE DOZEN ROSES

Dore, Charlene

STRUT

Dore, Charmian

PILOT OF THE AIRWAVES

Dorel, Francis

GARDEN OF YOUR HEART, THE

Dorff, Stephen

ANOTHER HONKY TONK NIGHT ON
    BROADWAY
AS LONG AS WE GOT EACH OTHER
BAR ROOM BUDDIES
COCA COLA COWBOY
COWBOYS AND CLOWNS
DON'T UNDERESTIMATE MY LOVE
    FOR YOU
EVERY WHICH WAY BUT LOOSE
HOPPY, GENE, AND ME
I JUST FALL IN LOVE AGAIN
LASSO THE MOON
THROUGH THE YEARS

Doris, Jim

OH ME OH MY (I'M A FOOL FOR
    YOU, BABY)

Dorman, Harold

MISSISSIPPI COTTON PICKING DELTA
    TOWN
MOUNTAIN OF LOVE

Dornackle, Jane

DON'T TOUCH ME THERE

Doroschuk, Ivan

SAFETY DANCE, THE

Dorough, Bob

COMIN' HOME BABY
I'M HIP
I'VE GOT JUST ABOUT EVERYTHING

Dorset, Ray

IN THE SUMMERTIME

Dorsey, Jimmy

CONTRASTS
DUSK IN UPPER SANDUSKY
I'M GLAD THERE IS YOU
IT'S THE DREAMER IN ME
JOHN SILVER
OODLES OF NOODLES

SO MANY TIMES
TALKIN' TO MY HEART

Dorsey, Lee

YA YA

Dorsey, Tommy

THIS IS NO DREAM
TO YOU
YOU TAUGHT ME TO LOVE AGAIN

Dougall, Bernard

I'LL BE HARD TO HANDLE

Dougherty, Chuck

TRANSISTOR SISTER

Dougherty, Dan

GLAD RAG DOLL
ONE CIGARETTE FOR TWO
YOU CAN HAVE HIM, I DON'T WANT
   HIM, DIDN'T LOVE HIM ANYHOW
   BLUES!

Doughty, Neal

ONE LONELY NIGHT

Douglas, Carl

KUNG FU FIGHTING

Douglas, Glenn

HOME OF THE BLUES

Douglas, Greg

JUNGLE LOVE

Douglas, Lew

ALMOST ALWAYS
HAVE YOU HEARD?
PRETEND
WHY DON'T YOU BELIEVE ME

DoVale, A.

LISBON ANTIGUA (IN OLD LISBON)

Dowe, B.

RIVERS OF BABYLON

Dowell, Edgar

THAT DA DA STRAIN

Dowell, Saxie

PLAYMATES
THREE LITTLE FISHIES

Dowling, Eddie

HEADING FOR HARLEM
JERSEY WALK
LITTLE WHITE HOUSE, THE (AT THE
   END OF HONEYMOON LANE)

Downes, Geoff

DON'T CRY
HEAT OF THE MOMENT
ONLY TIME WILL TELL
VIDEO KILLED THE RADIO STAR

Downey, Morton

NOW YOU'RE IN MY ARMS
WABASH MOON

Downie, Tyrone Ralph

TUMBLIN' DOWN

Downing, K. K.

YOU'VE GOT ANOTHER THING
   COMIN'

Downing, Phil

LOVE SUPREME, A

Doyle, Walter

EGYPTIAN ELLA
MYSTERIOUS MOSE

Dozier, Lamont

BABY, I NEED YOUR LOVING
BABY LOVE
BACK IN MY ARMS AGAIN
BERNADETTE
CAN I GET A WITNESS
COME AND GET THESE MEMORIES
COME SEE ABOUT ME
DARLING BABY
FOREVER CAME TODAY
HAPPENING, THE
HEAT WAVE
HEAVEN MUST HAVE SENT YOU
HOW SWEET IT IS (TO BE LOVED BY
   YOU)
I CAN'T HELP MYSELF (SUGAR PIE,
   HONEY BUNCH)
I GUESS I'LL ALWAYS LOVE YOU
I HEAR A SYMPHONY
I'M READY FOR LOVE
(COME 'ROUND HERE) I'M THE ONE
   YOU NEED
IN AND OUT OF LOVE
IN MY LONELY ROOM
IT'S THE SAME OLD SONG
JIMMY MACK
LA LA LA LA LA
LITTLE DARLING, I NEED YOU
LIVE WIRE
LOCKING UP MY HEART
LOVE IS HERE AND NOW YOU'RE
   GONE
LOVE IS LIKE AN ITCHING IN MY
   HEART
MICKEY'S MONKEY
MY WORLD IS EMPTY WITHOUT YOU
NOTHING BUT HEARTACHES
NOWHERE TO RUN
QUICKSAND
REACH OUT, I'LL BE THERE
REFLECTIONS
(I'M A) ROAD RUNNER
SEVEN OR ELEVEN (MY DIXIE PAIR
   O' DICE)
SHAKE ME, WAKE ME (WHEN IT'S
   OVER)
SOMETHING ABOUT YOU
STANDING IN THE SHADOWS OF
   LOVE
STOP! IN THE NAME OF LOVE
STRANGE I KNOW
TAKE ME IN YOUR ARMS (ROCK ME)

THIS OLD HEART OF MINE (IS WEAK
    FOR YOU)
TWO HEARTS
WHERE DID OUR LOVE GO
YOU CAN'T HURRY LOVE
YOU KEEP ME HANGIN' ON
YOU KEEP RUNNING AWAY
YOU'RE A WONDERFUL ONE
YOUR UNCHANGING LOVE

Drake, Charlie

MY BOOMERANG WON'T COME BACK

Drake, Ervin

AL DI LA
BELOVED, BE FAITHFUL
CASTLE ROCK
COME TO THE MARTI GRAS
FRIENDLIEST THING, THE
GOOD MORNING HEARTACHE
HAYFOOT, STRAWFOOT
I BELIEVE
IT WAS A VERY GOOD YEAR
KISS ME NO KISSES
MAYBE SOME OTHER TIME
MY FRIEND
MY HOME TOWN
NEW PAIR OF SHOES, A
PERDIDO
RICKETY RICKSHAW MAN, THE
ROOM WITHOUT WINDOWS, A
SONATA
TICO-TICO

Drake, Guy

WELFARE CADILLAC

Drake, Jimmy

TRANSFUSION

Drake, Milton

ASHBY DE LA ZOOCH
BLESS YOUR HEART
CHAMPAGNE WALTZ, THE
FUZZY WUZZY
IF IT'S YOU
I'M A BIG GIRL NOW
I'M COUNTING ON YOU

JAVA JIVE
KISS ME SWEET
MAIRZY DOATS
NINA NEVER KNEW
PARDON MY LOVE
PU-LEEZE, MR. HEMINGWAY
SHE BROKE MY HEART IN THREE
    PLACES

Drake, Tom

ALLY ALLY OXEN FREE

Drakeford, Lee

HIM OR ME

Dramatics, The

HEY YOU! GET OFF MY MOUNTAIN
I CAN'T GET OVER YOU

Draper, Guy

BEGINNING OF MY END, THE
COURT OF LOVE

Draper, Terry

CALLING OCCUPANTS OF
    INTERPLANETARY CRAFT

Drayton, Victor

DON'T LET THE GREEN GRASS FOOL
    YOU

Dredick, Al

NEE NEE NA NA NA NA NU NU

Dreja, Chris

OVER UNDER SIDEWAYS DOWN

Drejac, Jean

UNDER PARIS SKIES

Dresser, Paul

BLUE AND THE GRAY (OR,
    MOTHER'S GIFT TO HER
    COUNTRY, A)
BOYS ARE COMING HOME TODAY,
    THE
CALLING TO HER BOY JUST ONCE
    AGAIN
COME HOME, DEWEY, WE WON'T
    DO A THING TO YOU
COME TELL ME WHAT'S YOUR
    ANSWER, YES OR NO
CONVICT AND THE BIRD, THE
CURSE OF THE DREAMER, THE
DAY THAT YOU GREW COLDER,
    THE
DON'T TELL HER THAT YOU LOVE
    HER
DREAM OF MY BOYHOOD DAYS, A
EVERY NIGHT THERE'S A LIGHT
HE BROUGHT HOME ANOTHER
HE FOUGHT FOR A CAUSE HE
    THOUGHT WAS RIGHT
HERE LIES AN ACTOR
I'D STILL BELIEVE YOU TRUE
IF YOU SEE MY SWEETHEART
I JUST WANT TO GO BACK AND
    START THE WHOLE THING OVER
IN DEAR OLD ILLINOIS
IN GOOD OLD NEW YORK
    TOWN
IN THE GREAT SOMEWHERE
I'SE YOUR NIGGER IF YOU WANTS
    ME, LIZA JANE
I WAS LOOKING FOR MY BOY, SHE
    SAID (OR, DECORATION DAY)
I WISH THAT YOU WERE HERE
    TONIGHT
I WONDER IF SHE'LL EVER COME
    BACK TO ME
I WONDER WHERE SHE IS TONIGHT
JEAN
JIM JUDSON FROM THE TOWN OF
    HACKENSACK
JUST TELL HER THAT YOU
    SAW ME
LINCOLN, GRANT, OR LEE
MR. VOLUNTEER (OR, YOU DON'T
    BELONG TO THE REGULARS,
    YOU'RE JUST A VOLUNTEER)
MY GAL SAL (OR, THEY CALLED
    HER FRIVOLOUS SAL)

MY HEART STILL CLINGS TO THE
   OLD FIRST LOVE
OLD FLAME FLICKERS AND I
   WONDER WHY, THE
ONCE EV'RY YEAR
ON THE BANKS OF THE WABASH
   FAR AWAY
OUR COUNTRY, MAY SHE ALWAYS BE
   RIGHT
PARDON CAME TOO LATE, THE
PATH THAT LEADS THE OTHER WAY,
   THE
SWEET SAVANNAH
TAKE A SEAT, OLD LADY
THERE'S NO NORTH OR SOUTH
   TODAY
TOWN WHERE I WAS BORN, THE
VOICE OF THE HUDSON, THE
WAY DOWN IN OLD INDIANA
WE CAME FROM THE SAME OLD
   STATE
WE FIGHT TOMORROW, MOTHER
WHEN DE MOON COMES UP BEHIND
   DE HILL
WHEN I'M AWAY FROM YOU, DEAR
WHEN THE BIRDS HAVE SUNG
   THEMSELVES TO SLEEP
WHEN YOU COME BACK THEY'LL
   WONDER WHO THE —— YOU
   ARE
WHERE ARE THE FRIENDS OF
   OTHER DAYS?
YOU'RE GOING FAR AWAY, LAD (OR
   I'M STILL YOUR MOTHER, DEAR)
YOUR GOD COMES FIRST, YOUR
   COUNTRY NEXT, THEN MOTHER
   DEAR
YOU'SE JUST A LITTLE NIGGER,
   STILL YOU'RE MINE, ALL MINE

Drewery, Corinne

BREAKOUT

Dreyer, Dave

BACK IN YOUR OWN BACK YARD
CECILIA
FOUR WALLS
GOLDEN GATE
I'LL CRY TOMORROW
I'M FOLLOWING YOU
I'M KEEPING COMPANY

I WANNA SING ABOUT YOU
ME AND MY SHADOW
THERE'S A RAINBOW 'ROUND MY
   SHOULDER
WABASH MOON

Driftwood, Jimmy

BATTLE OF KOOKAMONGA, THE
BATTLE OF NEW ORLEANS, THE
TENNESSEE STUD

Driggs, Carlos

GET OFF

Drigo, Riccardo

I
SERENADE

Drislane, Jack

AFTER ALL THAT I'VE BEEN TO YOU
ARRAH WANNA
DEAR OLD ROSE
GOOD OLD U.S.A., THE
HONEY-LOVE
I'M AWFULLY GLAD I MET YOU
IT'S GREAT TO BE A SOLDIER MAN
JUST A LITTLE ROCKING CHAIR
   AND YOU
KEEP A LITTLE COZY CORNER IN
   YOUR HEART FOR ME
KEEP ON THE SUNNY SIDE
LONGING FOR YOU
MONKEY DOODLE DANDY
NOBODY'S LITTLE GIRL
SOMEBODY ELSE, IT'S ALWAYS
   SOMEBODY ELSE
WON'T YOU BE MY HONEY?
YOU REMIND ME OF THE GIRL THAT
   USED TO GO TO SCHOOL WITH
   ME!
YOU TAUGHT ME HOW TO LOVE
   YOU, NOW TEACH ME TO FORGET

Drummie, Richard

CALL ME

Drummond, B.

NICE, NICE, VERY NICE

Drummond, Neil

BLUES IN ADVANCE

Drusky, Roy

ALONE WITH YOU
ANOTHER
ANYMORE
BEFORE THIS DAY ENDS
COUNTRY GIRL
I'D RATHER LOAN YOU OUT
I WENT OUT OF MY WAY (TO MAKE
   YOU HAPPY)

Dubey, Matt

GAME OF LOVE, THE
IF'N
MUTUAL ADMIRATION SOCIETY
NEW-FANGLED TANGO, A
THIS IS WHAT I CALL LOVE

Dubin, Al

ABOUT A QUARTER TO NINE
ALL'S FAIR IN LOVE AND WAR
ALL THE WORLD WILL BE JEALOUS
   OF ME
ALONG THE SANTA FE TRAIL
AM I IN LOVE?
ANGELS CAME THRU, THE
ANNIVERSARY WALTZ, THE
BOULEVARD OF BROKEN DREAMS,
   THE
BUILD A LITTLE HOME
CAUSE MY BABY SAYS IT'S SO
CLEAR OUT OF THIS WORLD
COFFEE IN THE MORNING, KISSES
   IN THE NIGHT
CONFIDENTIALLY
CROSBY, COLUMBO, AND VALLEE
CUP OF COFFEE, A SANDWICH AND
   YOU, A
DAMES
DANCING WITH TEARS IN MY EYES
DON'T GIVE UP THE SHIP
   (SHIPMATES ALL FOREVER)
DON'T SAY GOODNIGHT

EV'RYBODY LOVES YOU
FAIR AND WARMER
FEUDIN' AND FIGHTIN'
FORTY-SECOND STREET
FOR YOU
GARDEN OF THE MOON
GIRL AT THE IRONING BOARD, THE
GIRL FRIEND OF THE WHIRLING
   DERVISH, THE
GOIN' TO HEAVEN ON A MULE
GO INTO YOUR DANCE
GOOD OLD FASHIONED COCKTAIL, A
   (WITH A GOOD OLD FASHIONED
   GIRL)
HALF-WAY TO HEAVEN
HONEYMOON HOTEL
HOW CAN YOU SAY "NO" (WHEN
   ALL THE WORLD IS SAYING
   "YES")?
HOW COULD YOU?
I'D LOVE TO TAKE ORDERS FROM
   YOU
I'D RATHER LISTEN TO YOUR EYES
IF I'M DREAMING, DON'T WAKE ME
   TOO SOON
I KNOW NOW
I'LL SING YOU A THOUSAND LOVE
   SONGS
I'LL STRING ALONG WITH YOU
I'M GOIN' SHOPPIN' WITH YOU
I MUST BE DREAMING
I'M YOUNG AND HEALTHY
INDIAN SUMMER
I ONLY HAVE EYES FOR YOU
IS IT POSSIBLE?
I'VE GOT TO SING A TORCH SONG
I WANNA GO BACK TO BALI
JUST A GIRL THAT MEN FORGET
KEEP YOUNG AND BEAUTIFUL
KISS WALTZ, THE
LATIN TUNE, A MANHATTAN MOON,
   AND YOU, A
LITTLE HOUSE THAT LOVE BUILT,
   THE
LITTLE THINGS YOU USED TO DO,
   THE
LONESOMEST GIRL IN TOWN, THE
LOVE IS WHERE YOU FIND IT
LULLABY OF BROADWAY
LULU'S BACK IN TOWN
MANY HAPPY RETURNS OF THE
   DAY
MELODY FOR TWO

MEMORIES OF FRANCE
MY DREAM OF THE BIG PARADE
MY KINGDOM FOR A KISS
NO MORE LOVE
OUTSIDE OF YOU
PAGE MISS GLORY
PAINTING THE CLOUDS WITH
   SUNSHINE
PETTIN' IN THE PARK
PING PONGO
REMEMBER ME?
REMEMBER MY FORGOTTEN MAN
RENDEZVOUS TIME IN PAREE
RIVER AND ME, THE
ROSE IN HER HAIR, THE
SEPTEMBER IN THE RAIN
SHADOW WALTZ
SHANGHAI LIL
SHE'S A LATIN FROM MANHATTAN
SHUFFLE OFF TO BUFFALO
SONG OF SURRENDER
SONG OF THE MARINES, THE
SOUTH AMERICAN WAY
SUMMER NIGHT
SWEET MUSIC
THREE'S A CROWD
TIP TOE THROUGH THE TULIPS
   WITH ME
TOO MANY TEARS
TRIPOLI (THE SHORES OF)
WATCHING MY DREAMS GO BY
WATERS OF THE PERKIOMEN
WE MUSN'T SAY GOODBYE
WE'RE IN THE MONEY (A.K.A. THE
   GOLD DIGGERS' SONG)
WHAT HAS BECOME OF HINKY
   DINKY PARLAY VOO?
WHERE AM I?
WHERE WAS I?
WHY DO I DREAM THOSE DREAMS?
WITH PLENTY OF MONEY AND YOU
WONDER BAR
WORDS ARE IN MY HEART, THE
YOU LET ME DOWN
YOUNG AND HEALTHY
YOU'RE GETTING TO BE A HABIT
   WITH ME
YOUR LOVE IS ALL THAT I CRAVE

Duboff, Steve

PIED PIPER, THE

RAIN, THE PARK, AND OTHER
   THINGS, THE
WE CAN FLY

DuBois, Gladys

I'M NO ANGEL
THEY CALL ME SISTER HONKY
   TONK
YOU CALL IT MADNESS (BUT I CALL
   IT LOVE)

Dubois, James

LOVE IN THE FIRST DEGREE

Dubois, Ja'net

MOVIN' ON UP

Dubois, Pye

TOM SAWYER

Dubois, Tim

BLUEST EYES IN TEXAS
SHE GOT THE GOLDMINE (I GOT
   THE SHAFT)

Duchow, Lawrence

SWISS BOY, THE

Duckworth, Willie Lee

SOUND OFF

Duddy, Lyn

DARN IT BABY, THAT'S LOVE
JOHNNY ANGEL
LET IT RING
LET'S MAKE UP BEFORE WE SAY
   GOODNIGHT

Dudley, Dave

THERE AIN'T NO EASY RUN

Dudley, T.

CUTIE PIE

Duke, Billy

I CRIED

Duke, George

SWEET BABY

Duke, M.

DOING IT ALL FOR MY BABY

Duke, Vernon

APRIL IN PARIS
AUTUMN IN NEW YORK
CABIN IN THE SKY
HE HASN'T A THING EXCEPT ME
HONEY IN THE HONEYCOMB
I AM ONLY HUMAN AFTER ALL
I CAN'T GET STARTED
I LIKE THE LIKES OF YOU
ISLAND IN THE WEST INDIES
JUST LIKE A MAN
LOVE I LONG FOR, THE
MADLY IN LOVE
ROUNDABOUT
SUDDENLY
SUMMER IS A-COMIN' IN
TAKING A CHANCE ON LOVE
THAT MOMENT OF MOMENTS
THAT'S WHAT MAKES PARIS PAREE
THIS IS ROMANCE
WATER UNDER THE BRIDGE
WE'RE HAVING A BABY (MY BABY
    AND ME)
WHAT IS THERE TO SAY?
WHERE HAVE WE MET BEFORE?
WORDS WITHOUT MUSIC

Dull, Sunny

WHICH ONE IS TO BLAME?

Dumont, Charles

I'VE BEEN HERE!
NO REGRETS (NON, JE NE
    REGRETTE RIEN)

Dumont, Frank

BAKE DAT CHICKEN PIE

PLANT A WATERMELON ON MY
    GRAVE AND LET THE JUICE SOAK
    THROUGH

Dunaway, Dennis

EIGHTEEN

Dunbar, Paul Lawrence

WHO DAT SAY CHICKEN IN DIS
    CROWD

Dunbar, Ronald

BAND OF GOLD
CRUMBS OFF THE TABLE
DANGLING ON A STRING (YOU'VE
    GOT ME)
MIND, BODY AND SOUL
PATCHES (I'M DEPENDING ON YOU)
PAY TO THE PIPER
SHE'S NOT JUST ANOTHER WOMAN

Duncan, D.

LET GO

Duncan, Harry "Slim"

MISSOURI

Duncan, Jimmy

EVERYBODY KNOWS
MY SPECIAL ANGEL

Duncan, Johnny

I'D RATHER LOVE YOU

Duncan, Malcolm

CUT THE CAKE

Duncan, Rosetta

REMEMB'RING

Duncan, Tommy

BUBBLES IN MY BEER
STAY A LITTLE LONGER

Duncan, Vivian

REMEMB'RING

Duncan, W. C.

FLANNEL PETTICOAT GAL
TITINA
TOODLE-OO
WHEN THE CHERRY BLOSSOMS
    FALL

Duncan, Wayne

WASTED DAYS AND WASTED NIGHTS

Dundas, David

JEANS ON

Dunham, Bev

CITY OF ANGELS

Dunham, "By"

AH, BUT IT HAPPENS
ANY WAY THE WIND BLOWS
IF YOU'RE EVER DOWN IN TEXAS,
    LOOK ME UP
I'M SO RIGHT TONIGHT (BUT I'VE
    BEEN SO WRONG FOR SO LONG)

Dunham, Kaye

BLACK BETTY

Duning, George

3:10 TO YUMA
I CAN'T REMEMBER TO FORGET
LOVE THEME FROM "SUZIE WONG"
THEME FROM "PICNIC"
TOYS IN THE ATTIC

Dunlap, George

I BELIEVE IN YOU

Dunlap, Luis

YOU CAN DEPEND ON ME

Dunn, Artie

TWILIGHT TIME

Dunn, Christopher

FROM THE WORD GO
HIP HUG-HER
SEXY EYES
SOUL-LIMBO

Dunn, Donald V.

TIME IS TIGHT

Dunn, Holly

DADDY'S HANDS
LOVE SOMEONE LIKE ME

Dunn, Larry

THAT'S THE WAY OF THE WORLD

Dupont, Paul

LA ROSITA

Dupree, Harry

LISBON ANTIGUA (IN OLD LISBON)

Dupree, Robbie

STEAL AWAY

Durand, Paul

ALL MY LOVE
MADEMOISELLE DE PAREE

Durand, Robert

DON'T TALK TO STRANGERS
JUST A LITTLE

Duran Duran

HUNGRY LIKE THE WOLF
IS THERE SOMETHING I SHOULD
　KNOW
NEW MOON ON SUNDAY

REFLEX, THE
RIO
SAVE A PRAYER
UNION OF THE SNAKE
VIEW TO KILL, A
WILD BOYS, THE

Durante, Jimmy

(I CAN DO WITHOUT BROADWAY,
　BUT) CAN BROADWAY DO
　WITHOUT ME?
INKA DINKA DOO
I UPS TO HIM AND HE UPS TO ME
(I'M) JIMMY, THE WELL-DRESSED
　MAN
UMBRIAGO
WHO WILL BE WITH YOU WHEN I'M
　FAR AWAY?
WOOD

Durden, Tommy

HEARTBREAK HOTEL

Durham, Eddie

DON'T YOU MISS YOUR BABY?
EVERY TUB
GOOD MORNING BLUES
I DON'T WANT TO SET THE WORLD
　ON FIRE
JOHN'S IDEA
SENT FOR YOU YESTERDAY, AND
　HERE YOU COME TODAY
SWINGIN' THE BLUES
TOPSY II
WHAM

Durrill, John

DARK LADY
I SEE THE LIGHT
SOUND OF LOVE
WESTERN UNION
ZIP CODE

Durso, Michael

PETTICOATS OF PORTUGAL

Dusenberry, E. F.

LAND OF GOLDEN DREAMS, THE
MY ROSARY OF DREAMS

Dyer, Desmond

SKY HIGH
WHO DO YOU THINK YOU ARE?

Dyer, Jan

EVERYTIME TWO FOOLS COLLIDE

Dylan, Bob

ALL ALONG THE WATCHTOWER
ALL I REALLY WANT TO DO
BLOWIN' IN THE WIND
CAN YOU PLEASE CRAWL OUT YOUR
　WINDOW?
CHIMES OF FREEDOM
DON'T THINK TWICE, IT'S ALL
　RIGHT
GEORGE JACKSON
GIRL FROM THE NORTH COUNTRY
GOTTA SERVE SOMEBODY
HAD A DREAM ABOUT YOU, BABY
HARD RAIN'S A-GONNA FALL
HIGHWAY 61 REVISITED
HURRICANE
IF NOT FOR YOU
I'LL BE YOUR BABY TONIGHT
I SHALL BE RELEASED
IT AIN'T ME, BABE
I THREW IT ALL AWAY
IT'S ALL OVER NOW, BABY BLUE
I WANT YOU
JAMMIN' ME
JOHN WESLEY HARDING
JUST LIKE A WOMAN
KNOCKIN' ON HEAVEN'S DOOR
LAY, LADY, LAY
LAY DOWN YOUR WEARY TUNE
LEOPARD-SKIN PILL-BOX HAT
LIKE A ROLLING STONE
LOVE IS JUST A FOUR-LETTER
　WORD
LOVE MINUS ZERO—NO LIMIT
MASTERS OF WAR
MIGHTY QUINN (QUINN, THE
　ESKIMO)

MOST LIKELY YOU GO YOUR WAY
   (AND I'LL GO MINE)
MOZAMBIQUE
MR. TAMBOURINE MAN
MY BACK PAGES
ON A NIGHT LIKE THIS
POSITIVELY 4TH STREET
RAINY DAY WOMEN NO. 12 & 35
SHE BELONGS TO ME
SUBTERRANEAN HOMESICK BLUES
SWEETHEART LIKE YOU
TANGLED UP IN BLUE
TEARS OF RAGE
TIMES THEY ARE A-CHANGIN', THE
TONIGHT I'LL BE STAYING HERE
   WITH YOU
TOO MUCH OF NOTHING
WATCHING THE RIVER FLOW
WHEN THE SHIP COMES IN
WIGWAM
YOU AIN'T GOING NOWHERE

Dyrenforth, James

GARDEN IN THE RAIN, A
I'M FOR YOU ONE HUNDRED
   PERCENT
NOT BAD
ON ACCOUNT OF I LOVE YOU
REPEAL THE BLUES
RUNNING BETWEEN THE
   RAINDROPS

Dyson, Hal

LONELY MELODY

Eager, Edward

GOODBYE, JOHN

Eardley-Wilmot, D.

LITTLE GREY HOME IN THE WEST

Earl, Mary

DREAMY ALABAMA

Earl, Raymond

I GOT MY MIND MADE UP (YOU CAN
   GET IT GIRL)

Earle, Steve

GUITAR TOWN
I AIN'T EVER SATISFIED
LITTLE BIT IN LOVE, A
NOWHERE ROAD

East, Nathan

EASY LOVER
RESERVATIONS FOR TWO

Eastman, Barry

DOMINOES

Eastmond, Barry

COLOUR OF LOVE, THE
HAVE YOU EVER LOVED SOMEBODY
LOVE IS FOREVER
LOVE ZONE
THERE'LL BE SAD SONGS (TO MAKE
   YOU CRY)
WHEN THE GOING GETS TOUGH,
   THE TOUGH GET GOING
YOU ARE MY LADY

Easton, Lynn

ANNIE FANNY
JOLLY GREEN GIANT

Eaton, Jimmy

BLUE CHAMPAGNE
CRY BABY CRY
DANCE WITH A DOLLY (WITH A
   HOLE IN HER STOCKING)
I DOUBLE DARE YOU
I'M GONNA LOCK MY HEART (AND
   THROW AWAY THE KEY)
LOW DOWN RHYTHM IN A TOP HAT
PENGUIN AT THE WALDORF
RHYTHM OF RAINDROPS, THE
   (A.K.A. OVER THE RHYTHM OF
   RAINDROPS)
TURN BACK THE HANDS OF TIME
WHY DOESN'T SOMEBODY TELL ME
   THESE THINGS?

Eaves, Hubert, III

SOMETHING'S ON YOUR MIND

Ebb, Fred

AFTER ALL THESE YEARS
ALL THAT JAZZ
ALL THE CHILDREN IN A ROW
APPLE DOESN'T FALL, THE
BOBO'S
CABARET
COLORED LIGHTS
GRASS IS ALWAYS GREENER, THE
HOW LUCKY CAN YOU GET
I DON'T CARE MUCH
IF YOU COULD SEE HER (THE
   GORILLA SONG)
I TOLD YOU SO
IT'S THE STRANGEST THING
KISS ME ANOTHER
LIFE OF THE PARTY, THE
LITTLE BLUE MAN, THE
LUCKY LADY
MARRIED (HEIRATEN)
MAYBE THIS TIME
MEESKITE
MONEY, MONEY (MAKES THE
   WORLD GO ROUND)
MONEY SONG, THE (SITTING
   PRETTY)
MY COLORING BOOK
MY OWN BEST FRIEND
MY OWN SPACE
ONE OF THE BOYS
RAZZLE DAZZLE
SHINE IT ON
THAT DO MAKE IT NICE
THEME FROM "NEW YORK, NEW
   YORK"
TOMORROW BELONGS TO ME
WE CAN MAKE IT
WILLKOMMEN

Ebbins, Milt

HIP, HIP, HOORAY

Eberhart, Nelle Richmond

AT DAWNING

FROM THE LAND OF THE SKY-BLUE
    WATER

Echols, Odis

SUGARTIME

Eckler, Pop

MONEY, MARBLES, AND CHALK

Eckstine, Billy

STORMY MONDAY BLUES

Eddy, Duane

BONNIE COME BACK
BOSS GUITAR
CANNONBALL
FORTY MILES OF BAD ROAD
(DANCE WITH THE) GUITAR MAN
LONELY ONE, THE
REBEL-ROUSER

Eddy, Hal

SANDS OF GOLD

Ede, Nick

I'VE BEEN IN LOVE BEFORE

Edelman, Randy

WEEKEND IN NEW ENGLAND

Edens, Roger

FRENCH LESSON, THE
IN-BETWEEN
IT'S A GREAT DAY FOR THE IRISH
JOINT IS REALLY JUMPIN' AT
    CARNEGIE HALL
MY WONDERFUL ONE, LET'S DANCE
OUR LOVE AFFAIR
PASS THAT PEACE PIPE
PRETTY GIRL MILKING HER COW
RIGHT GIRL FOR ME, THE
STRICTLY U.S.A.

Edenton, Ray

YOU'RE RUNNING WILD

Edmonds, Kenneth

DIAL MY HEART
EVERY LITTLE STEP
IT'S NO CRIME
LOVER IN ME, THE
LOVE SAW IT
LUCKY CHARM
RONI
SUPERWOMAN

Edmonds, Kenny

I'D STILL SAY YES
ON OUR OWN

Edmonton, Jerry

MONSTER

Edmunds, Dave

HIGH SCHOOL NIGHTS

Edmunson, Travis

CLOUDY SUMMER AFTERNOON
    (RAINDROPS)

Edwards, Anne Jean

PAPA NICCOLINI

Edwards, Bernard

DANCE, DANCE, DANCE (YOWSAH,
    YOWSAH, YOWSAH)
GOOD TIMES
HE'S THE GREATEST DANCER
I'M COMING OUT
I WANT YOUR LOVE
LE FREAK
SOUP FOR ONE
UPSIDE DOWN
WE ARE FAMILY

Edwards, Bobby

YOU'RE THE REASON

Edwards, Clara

BY THE BEND OF THE RIVER
WITH THE WIND AND THE RAIN IN
    YOUR HAIR

Edwards, Darrell

SEASONS OF MY HEART
TENDER YEARS
WHAT AM I WORTH
WHO SHOT SAM?
WHY, BABY, WHY?

Edwards, Doug

WILDFLOWER

Edwards, Earl

DUKE OF EARL

Edwards, Edwin B.

AT THE JAZZ BAND BALL
BARNYARD BLUE
CLARINET MARMALADE
FIDGETY FEET
OSTRICH WALK
TIGER RAG

Edwards, Fred

DEVIL WENT DOWN TO GEORGIA,
    THE
IN AMERICA

Edwards, Gus

BY THE LIGHT OF THE SILVERY
    MOON
COME ON AND PLAY BALL WITH ME
FOR YOU A ROSE
GOODBYE, LITTLE GIRL, GOODBYE
HE'S ME PAL
I CAN'T TELL WHY I LOVE YOU, BUT
    I DO
IF A GIRL LIKE YOU LOVED A BOY
    LIKE ME
IF I WAS A MILLIONAIRE
I JUST CAN'T MAKE MY EYES
    BEHAVE

I'LL BE WITH YOU WHEN THE
   ROSES BLOOM AGAIN
I'LL GET YOU
IN MY MERRY OLDSMOBILE
IN ZANZIBAR—MY LITTLE
   CHIMPANZEE
JIMMY VALENTINE
MAMIE
MY COUSIN CARUS'
NOBODY BUT YOU
ORANGE BLOSSOM TIME
SINGER AND THE SONG, THE
SUNBONNET SUE
TAMMANY
UP, UP, UP IN MY AEROPLANE
YOUR MOTHER AND MINE

Edwards, Jackie

SOMEBODY HELP ME

Edwards, James

SH-BOOM (LIFE COULD BE A
   DREAM)

Edwards, Joan

DARN IT BABY, THAT'S LOVE
LET IT RING
LET'S MAKE UP BEFORE WE SAY
   GOODNIGHT

Edwards, Julian

MY OWN UNITED STATES
SWEET THOUGHTS OF HOME

Edwards, Leo

I'M AN INDIAN
ISLE D'AMOUR

Edwards, Lockie, Jr.

MR. WISHING WELL

Edwards, Michael

ONCE IN A WHILE

Edwards, Raymond W.

GET A JOB

Edwards, Sherman

BROKEN-HEARTED MELODY
DUNGAREE DOLL
FOR HEAVEN'S SAKE
JOHNNY GET ANGRY
MOMMA LOOK SHARP
SEE YOU IN SEPTEMBER
WONDERFUL! WONDERFUL!
YOU'LL ANSWER TO ME

Edwards, Tommy

THAT CHICK'S TOO YOUNG TO FRY

Edwards, Vincent

RIGHT BACK WHERE WE STARTED
   FROM

Edwards, Webley

PEARLY SHELLS

Egan, Jack

BE STILL, MY HEART
THAT'S THE KIND OF BABY FOR ME

Egan, Joe

STUCK IN THE MIDDLE WITH YOU

Egan, Raymond B.

AIN'T WE GOT FUN?
AND THEY CALLED IT DIXIELAND
   (THEY MADE IT TWICE AS NICE
   AS PARADISE)
BIMINI BAY
IF YOU SEE SALLY
I NEVER KNEW I COULD LOVE
   ANYBODY (LIKE I'M LOVING YOU)
JAPANESE SANDMAN, THE
KNICK KNACKS ON THE MANTEL
MAMMY'S LITTLE COAL BLACK ROSE
SLEEPY TIME GAL
SOME SUNDAY MORNING
SONG OF PERSIA

TEA LEAVES
TELL ME WHY YOU SMILE, MONA
   LISA
THERE AIN'T NO MAYBE IN MY
   BABY'S EYES
THREE ON A MATCH
TILL WE MEET AGAIN
WHEN SHALL WE MEET AGAIN?
WHERE THE MORNING GLORIES
   GROW

Egan, Walter

HOT SUMMER NIGHTS
MAGNET AND STEEL

Egnoian, Arthur

BONGO ROCK
TEEN BEAT

Ehart, Phil

PLAY THE GAME TONIGHT

Ehrlich, Larry

GOTTA TRAVEL ON

Ehrlich, Sam

OH! FRENCHY

Ei, Rokusuke

SUKIYAKI

Eiseman, Herb

TROUBLE WITH HARRY, THE

Eisen, Stanley

ROCK AND ROLL ALL NITE

Elbert, Donnie

OPEN THE DOOR TO YOUR HEART

Elfman, Danny

WEIRD SCIENCE

Elgar, Edward

LAND OF HOPE AND GLORY, THE

Elgin, Bob

BIG COLD WIND
COME TOMORROW
HUNDRED POUNDS OF CLAY, A
LAST CHANCE TO TURN AROUND
MY TOWN, MY GUY, AND ME

Eli, Bobby

JUST DON'T WANT TO BE LONELY
  TONIGHT
LOVE WON'T LET ME WAIT
SIDESHOW

Elias, Jonathan

I DO WHAT I DO

Elias, Lotar

YOU, YOU, YOU

Elias, Michael

I CRIED

Eliot, T. S.

GUS THE THEATRE CAT
MEMORY

Eliscu, Edward

CARIOCA
FLYING DOWN TO RIO
GREAT DAY!
MORE THAN YOU KNOW
MUSIC MAKES ME
ORCHIDS IN THE MOONLIGHT
SOMETHING TO LIVE FOR
THEY CUT DOWN THE OLD PINE
  TREE
WITHOUT A SONG
YOU FORGOT YOUR GLOVES

Ellefson, Dave

IN MY DARKEST HOUR

Ellen, Mack

CRY, CRY BABY

Ellen, Robert

CRY, CRY BABY

Ellingson, D.

YOU TURNED MY WORLD AROUND

Ellingson, Dave

DON'T FALL IN LOVE WITH A
  DREAMER

Ellingson, K. C.

YOU TURNED MY WORLD AROUND

Ellington, E. A.

PETITE WALTZ (LA PETITE VALSE)

Ellington, Edward Kennedy "Duke"

ACROSS THE TRACK BLUES
ALL TOO SOON
AWFUL SAD
AZURE
BABY, WHEN YOU AIN'T THERE
BEST WISHES
BLACK AND TAN FANTASY
BLACK BUTTERFLY
BLUE FEELING
BOY MEETS HORN
CARAVAN
CARNEGIE BLUES
CHOCOLATE SHAKE
"C"-JAM BLUES (OR "C" JAM BLUES)
CLARINET LAMENT
COTTON TAIL
CREOLE LOVE CALL
CREOLE RHAPSODY
CRESCENDO IN BLUE
DAYBREAK EXPRESS
DICTY GLIDE, THE
DIMINUENDO IN BLUE
DOIN' THE VOOM VOOM
DO NOTHIN' TILL YOU HEAR FROM
  ME

DON'T GET AROUND MUCH
  ANYMORE
DON'T YOU KNOW I CARE (OR,
  DON'T YOU CARE TO KNOW)?
DROP ME OFF IN HARLEM
DUKE STEPS OUT, THE
DUSK ON THE DESERT
EAST ST. LOUIS TOODLE-OO
ECHOES OF HARLEM
EIGHTH VEIL, THE
EVERYTHING BUT YOU
GOING UP
GOIN' TO TOWN
GYPSY WITHOUT A SOUL, A
HARLEM AIR SHAFT
HARLEM SPEAKS
HARMONY IN HARLEM
HAUNTED NIGHTS
HOT AND BOTHERED
I AIN'T GOT NOTHIN' BUT THE
  BLUES
I DIDN'T KNOW ABOUT YOU
IF YOU WERE IN MY PLACE
I GOT IT BAD AND THAT AIN'T
  GOOD
I LET A SONG GO OUT OF MY
  HEART
I'M BEGINNING TO SEE THE LIGHT
I'M CHECKING OUT—GO'OM BYE
I'M GONNA GO FISHIN'
I'M JUST A LUCKY SO AND SO
I'M SATISFIED
IN A MELLOW TONE
IN A SENTIMENTAL MOOD
IT DON'T MEAN A THING (IF IT
  AIN'T GOT THAT SWING)
IT SHOULDN'T HAPPEN TO A DREAM
I'VE GOT ME
I'VE GOT TO BE A RUG CUTTER
JACK THE BEAR
JEEP'S BLUES
JIG WALK
JUMP FOR JOY
JUST A-SITTIN' AND A-ROCKIN'
JUST SQUEEZE ME (BUT DON'T
  TEASE ME)
LAZY RHAPSODY
LOST IN MEDITATION
MAIN STEM
MOOCHE, THE (A.K.A. THE MOOCH)
MOOD INDIGO
OH! MISS JAXON
PARIS BLUES

PRELUDE TO A KISS
PYRAMID
REMINISCING IN TEMPO
RING DEM BELLS
ROCKIN' IN RHYTHM
SATIN DOLL
SATURDAY NIGHT FUNCTION
SCATTIN' AT THE KIT KAT
SHOWBOAT SHUFFLE
SKRONTCH
SLIPPERY HORN
SOLITUDE
SOPHISTICATED LADY
STEPPIN' INTO SWING SOCIETY
STOMPY JONES
THINGS AIN'T WHAT THEY USED TO
 BE
TIME'S A-WASTIN'
TOMORROW MOUNTAIN
TOOTIN' THROUGH THE ROOF
TRANSBLUCENCY
TULIP OR TURNIP
WANDERLUST
WARM VALLEY
YEARNING FOR LOVE

Ellington, Mercer

MOON MIST
SLIP OF THE LIP, A
THINGS AIN'T WHAT THEY USED TO
 BE
TIME'S A-WASTIN'

Elliot, Brian

PAPA DON'T PREACH

Elliott, Don

UH! OH!

Elliott, Jack

BE MINE
DO YOU CARE?
I THINK OF YOU
IT'S SO NICE TO HAVE A MAN
 AROUND THE HOUSE
OUR VERY OWN
PANSY
SAM'S SONG
THEME FROM "CHARLIE'S ANGELS"

WEAVER OF DREAMS, A

Elliott, Joe

BRINGIN' ON THE HEARTBREAK
FOOLIN'
HYSTERIA
LOVE BITES
PHOTOGRAPH
POUR SOME SUGAR ON ME
ROCK OF AGES

Elliott, Ron

DON'T TALK TO STRANGERS
JUST A LITTLE
LAUGH, LAUGH
YOU TELL ME WHY

Elliott, Zo

THERE'S A LONG, LONG TRAIL

Ellis, Alfred

COLD SWEAT
GET IT TOGETHER
LICKING STICK—LICKING STICK
MOTHER POPCORN (YOU GOT TO
 HAVE A MOTHER FOR ME)
SAY IT LOUD—I'M BLACK AND I'M
 PROUD

Ellis, Barbara

COME SOFTLY TO ME

Ellis, Herb

DETOUR AHEAD
I TOLD YA I LOVE YA, NOW GET
 OUT

Ellis, Jack

I CAN GET IT FOR YOU WHOLESALE

Ellis, Jonah

DON'T STOP THE MUSIC
DON'T WASTE YOUR TIME

Ellis, Melville

WHEN LOVE IS YOUNG IN
 SPRINGTIME

Ellis, Norman

CARELESSLY

Ellis, Seger

LITTLE JACK FROST GET LOST
YOU'RE ALL I WANT FOR
 CHRISTMAS

Ellis, Ted

DREAMIN'

Ellis, Vivian

I'M ON A SEE-SAW
WIND IN THE WILLOWS, THE

Ellison, Ben

I'M NO ANGEL
I WANT YOU, I NEED YOU
THAT DALLAS MAN
THEY CALL ME SISTER HONKY
 TONK

Elliston, Shirley

NAME GAME, THE

Ellner, K.

PSYCHOTIC REACTION

Ellstein, Abraham

WEDDING SAMBA, THE

Ellsworth, Bob

SOMEBODY ELSE IS TAKING MY
 PLACE

Elman, Ziggy

AND THE ANGELS SING

Elrod, Jean

I WENT OUT OF MY WAY (TO MAKE
YOU HAPPY)

Elston, Harry

GRAZING IN THE GRASS

Elworthy, W.

SWEETHEART

Ely, Vincent

LOVE MY WAY
PRETTY IN PINK

Emer, Michel

IF YOU GO

Emerick, George H.

YOU'RE DE APPLE OF MY EYE

Emerson, Ida

HELLO, MA BABY

Emerson, Lee

RUBY ANN

Emery, Mac

ALL SHE'D SAY WAS "UMH HUM"

Emmerich, Bob

BIG APPLE, THE
HEAR MY SONG, VIOLETTA
HURRY HOME
OUR LOVE
TIMBER

Emmerson, Les

WEREWOLF

Emmons, Bobby

LOVE ME LIKE YOU USED TO

LUCKENBACH, TEXAS (BACK TO THE
BASICS OF LOVE)
PARTNERS AFTER ALL
WURLITZER PRIZE, THE (I DON'T
WANT TO GET OVER YOU)

Endor, Chick

WHO TAKES CARE OF THE
CARETAKER'S DAUGHTER?

Endsley, Melvin

I LIKE YOUR KIND OF LOVE
KNEE DEEP IN THE BLUES
LOVE ME TO PIECES
SINGING THE BLUES
WHY I'M WALKIN'

Engelmann, H.

MELODY OF LOVE
WHISPER THAT YOU LOVE ME

English, D.

I'M ON FIRE

English, Scott

BEND ME, SHAPE ME
HELP ME, GIRL
MANDY (A.K.A. BRANDY)
NOW I KNOW

Engvick, William

ANNA
BONNIE BLUE GAL
I'LL REMEMBER TODAY
SONG FROM "MOULIN ROUGE," THE
(A.K.A. WHERE IS YOUR HEART?)
WHILE WE'RE YOUNG
WHO CAN I TURN TO?

Enis, Bill

SHAME ON ME

Ennis, Marvin

TASTE OF YOUR LOVE

Ennis, Sue

BEST MAN IN THE WORLD, THE
EVEN IT UP

Eno, Brian

ONCE IN A LIFETIME

Enston, Duke

BLESS YOUR HEART

Epps, Nat

RUBBER BISCUIT

Epps, Preston

BONGO ROCK

Erdelyi, Thomas

PINHEAD
ROCKAWAY BEACH
SHEENA IS A PUNK ROCKER

Erdman, Ernie

NO, NO, NORA
NOBODY'S SWEETHEART
TOOT, TOOT, TOOTSIE, GOODBYE

Erickson, Jack

MAY I NEVER LOVE AGAIN

Ertegun, Ahmet

CHAINS OF LOVE
DON'T PLAY THAT SONG (YOU LIED)
DON'T YOU KNOW I LOVE YOU?
FOOL, FOOL, FOOL
GOOD LOVIN'
HEY, MISS FANNIE
LITTLE MAMA
LOVEY DOVEY
MIDDLE OF THE NIGHT
SOMEBODY TOUCHED ME
SWEET SIXTEEN
TING-A-LING
WHAT'CHA GONNA DO?
WILD, WILD YOUNG MEN

Ertel, Jay

BOWLING GREEN

Erving, B.

I NEED LOVE

Erwin, Lee

DANCE ME LOOSE

Erwin, Ralph

I KISS YOUR HAND, MADAME

Escape Club, The

WILD, WILD WEST

Escovedo, Sheila

HOLD ME
LOVE BIZARRE, A

Eskridge, Ralph

LOVE JONES

Esperon, Manuel

THREE CABALLEROS, THE

Espinosa, J. J.

GAY RANCHERO, A (LAS ALTENITAS)

Esposito, Joe

BAD GIRLS

Esposito, Michael

(WE AIN'T GOT) NOTHIN' YET

Esrom, D. A.

HAIL, HAIL, THE GANG'S ALL HERE

Essex, David

ROCK ON

Estefan, Gloria

1-2-3
ANYTHING FOR YOU
CAN'T STAY AWAY FROM YOU
DON'T WANNA LOSE YOU
RHYTHM IS GONNA GET YOU
WORDS GET IN THE WAY

Esty, Bob

FIGHT
MAIN EVENT, THE
TAKE ME HOME

Etris, Barry

RUBEN JAMES

Etting, Ruth

WISTFUL AND BLUE

Etts, S.

I NEED LOVE

Eugene, Jayne

HANGIN' ON A STRING
  (CONTEMPLATING)

Evans, Bill

WALTZ FOR DEBBY

Evans, Dale

BIBLE TELLS ME SO, THE
I WISH I HAD NEVER MET
  SUNSHINE

Evans, Dave

I WILL FOLLOW
NEW YEAR'S DAY
PRIDE (IN THE NAME OF LOVE)

Evans, Gene

WALKING THE STREETS

Evans, George

COME, TAKE A TRIP IN MY AIRSHIP
COME TO THE LAND OF BOHEMIA
I'LL BE TRUE TO MY HONEY BOY
IN THE GOOD OLD SUMMERTIME
IN THE MERRY MONTH OF MAY

Evans, Gordon

SWITCH-A-ROO, THE

Evans, Mitchell Young

MAD ABOUT YOU

Evans, Paul

FOLLOWED CLOSELY BY TEARDROPS
HAPPINESS IS
HAPPY-GO-LUCKY ME
I GOTTA KNOW
LONG AS THE ROSE IS RED
NEXT STEP IS LOVE, THE
ROSES ARE RED (MY LOVE)
SUMMER SOUVENIRS
WHEN
WORRIED GUY

Evans, Ray

ALL THE TIME
ALMOST IN YOUR ARMS (A.K.A.
  LOVE SONG FROM "HOUSEBOAT")
ANGEL
ANOTHER TIME, ANOTHER PLACE
BESIDE YOU
BING! BANG! BONG!
BONANZA!
BONNE NUIT—GOODNIGHT
BUTTONS AND BOWS
CAT AND THE CANARY, THE
COPPER CANYON
DEAR HEART
ERES TU (TOUCH THE WIND)
EVERYTHING BEAUTIFUL
FEMININITY
G'BYE NOW
GIVE IT ALL YOU'VE GOT
GOLDEN EARRINGS
HAVIN' A WONDERFUL WISH
HERE'S TO LOVE
HOME COOKIN'

I'LL ALWAYS LOVE YOU
IN THE ARMS OF LOVE
LIFE IS A BEAUTIFUL THING
MARSHMALLOW MOON
MISTO CRISTOFO COLUMBO
MONA LISA
MY BELOVED
MY LOVE LOVES ME
QUE SERA SERA (WHATEVER WILL
    BE, WILL BE)
RUBY AND THE PEARL, THE
SILVER BELLS
SONG OF DELILAH
SONG OF SURRENDER
SQUARE IN THE SOCIAL CIRCLE, A
STREETS OF LAREDO, THE
STUFF LIKE THAT THERE
TAMMY
THIS HAPPY FEELING
THOUSAND VIOLINS, A
TO EACH HIS OWN
WISH ME A RAINBOW
YOU DON'T KNOW HIM

Evans, Redd

AMERICAN BEAUTY ROSE
DON'T GO TO STRANGERS
FRIM FRAM SAUCE, THE
HE'S 1-A IN THE ARMY AND HE'S
    A-1 IN MY HEART
I'VE ONLY MYSELF TO BLAME
JUST THE OTHER DAY
LET ME OFF UPTOWN
NO MOON AT ALL
ROSIE THE RIVETER
THERE, I'VE SAID IT AGAIN
THERE'S NO ONE BUT YOU
THIS IS THE NIGHT

Evans, Rick

IN THE YEAR 2525 (EXORDIUM AND
    TERMINUS)

Evans, Thomas

WITHOUT YOU

Evans, Tolchard

BARCELONA
IF

LADY OF SPAIN
LET'S ALL SING LIKE THE BIRDIES
    SING
UNLESS

Evans, Willie

METRO POLKA

Evelyn, Alicia

I GET THE SWEETEST FEELING
PEPPER-HOT BABY

Everette, Bill

GITARZAN

Everly, Don

BORN YESTERDAY
CATHY'S CLOWN
SO SAD (TO WATCH GOOD LOVE GO
    BAD)
'TIL I KISSED YOU

Everly, Phil

CATHY'S CLOWN
GEE, BUT IT'S LONELY
MADE TO LOVE (GIRLS, GIRLS,
    GIRLS)
WHEN WILL I BE LOVED?

Evoy, Larry

LAST SONG

Ewald, Marnie

REVENGE

Eyen, Tom

AND I AM TELLING YOU I'M NOT
    GOING
CADILLAC CAR
ONE NIGHT ONLY

Eyton, Frank

BODY AND SOUL

Ezell, Norman

I SEE THE LIGHT
SOUND OF LOVE
WESTERN UNION
ZIP CODE

Ezrin, Bob

BETH
DETROIT ROCK CITY
LEARNING TO FLY
WORLD WITHOUT HEROES, A

Faber, William E.

I'M A LONELY LITTLE PETUNIA (IN
    AN ONION PATCH)
YOU WERE ONLY FOOLING (WHILE I
    WAS FALLING IN LOVE)

Fagan, Barney

MY GAL IS A HIGH BORN LADY

Fagen, Donald

BLACK FRIDAY
CENTURY'S END
DEACON BLUES
DO IT AGAIN
FEZ, THE
FM (NO STATIC AT ALL)
HEY NINETEEN
I.G.Y. (WHAT A BEAUTIFUL WORLD)
JOSIE
KID CHARLEMAGNE
MY OLD SCHOOL
PEG
PRETZEL LOGIC
REELING IN THE YEARS
RIKKI DON'T LOSE THAT NUMBER
SHOW BIZ KIDS

Fagenson, Donald

WHERE DID YOUR HEART GO?

Fahey, Siobhan

I HEARD A RUMOR

Faile, Tommy

PHANTOM 309

Fain, Sammy

AH, THE MOON IS HERE
ALICE IN WONDERLAND
ALL THE TIME
AM I GONNA HAVE TROUBLE WITH
    YOU?
AND THERE YOU ARE
APRIL LOVE
ARE YOU HAVIN' ANY FUN?
BY A WATERFALL
CERTAIN SMILE, A
DEAR HEARTS AND GENTLE PEOPLE
DICKEY-BIRD SONG, THE
EV'RY DAY
FACE TO FACE
GOODNIGHT, MY BEAUTIFUL
HAPPY IN LOVE
HOW DO I KNOW IT'S SUNDAY?
HUMMIN' TO MYSELF (I'VE GOT THE
    WORDS—I'VE GOT THE TUNE)
I CAN DREAM, CAN'T I?
I LEFT MY SUGAR STANDING IN THE
    RAIN
I'LL BE SEEING YOU
I'M LATE
I SPEAK TO THE STARS
LATELY, SONG, THE
LET A SMILE BE YOUR UMBRELLA
LITTLE LOVE CAN GO A LONG,
    LONG WAY, A
LONELY LANE
LOVE IS A MANY-SPLENDORED
    THING
LOVE IS NEVER OUT OF SEASON
MISSISSIPPI DREAM BOAT
MOON IS A SILVER DOLLAR, THE
NOW I'M A LADY
OUR PENTHOUSE ON THIRD AVENUE
SATAN'S HOLIDAY
SECRETARY SONG, THE
SECRET LOVE
SIMPLE AND SWEET
SITTIN' ON A BACKYARD FENCE
SOMEONE'S WAITING FOR YOU
SOMETHING I DREAMED LAST
    NIGHT
STRANGE ARE THE WAYS OF LOVE
TENDER IS THE NIGHT

THAT OLD FEELING
THERE'S A LITTLE BIT OF YOU IN
    EVERY LOVE SONG
THERE'S SOMETHING ABOUT A ROSE
    (THAT REMINDS ME OF YOU)
VERY PRECIOUS LOVE, A
VIOLINS FROM NOWHERE
WAS THAT THE HUMAN THING TO
    DO?
WEDDING BELLS ARE BREAKING UP
    THAT OLD GANG OF MINE
WHEN I TAKE MY SUGAR TO TEA
WHEN TOMORROW COMES
WILDEST GAL IN TOWN, THE
WORRY SONG, THE
YOU BROUGHT A NEW KIND OF
    LOVE TO ME

Fairbarn, Bruce

HOT GIRLS IN LOVE

Fairburn, Lewi Werly

I FEEL LIKE CRYIN'

Fairburn, Werly

I GUESS I'M CRAZY (FOR LOVING
    YOU)

Fairfax, Reuben

BELLE

Fairman, George

I DON'T KNOW WHERE I'M GOING
    BUT I'M ON MY WAY

Faith, Percy

MY HEART CRIES FOR YOU
SWEDISH RHAPSODY (A.K.A.
    MIDSUMMER VIGIL)

Faith, Russell

BOBBY SOX TO STOCKINGS
TOGETHERNESS

Falbo, John

LOVE CAME TO ME

Falco

DER KOMMISSAR
ROCK ME AMADEUS

Fall, Richard

O, KATHARINA!

Fallenstein, Peter Bischof

GIRL I'M GONNA MISS YOU

Faltermeyer, Harold

AXEL F
BIT BY BIT
HEAT IS ON, THE
HOT STUFF
SHAKEDOWN

Fane, Julian

VIOLETS

Faraci, Silvio

LONELY TEENAGER

Fargo, Donna

FUNNY FACE
HAPPIEST GIRL IN THE WHOLE
    U.S.A.
THAT WAS YESTERDAY

Faria, Richard

PACK UP YOUR SORROWS

Farian, Frank

GIRL I'M GONNA MISS YOU
RIVERS OF BABYLON

Farina, Ann

SLEEP WALK

TEAR DROP

Farina, John

SLEEP WALK
TEAR DROP

Farina, Mimi

IN THE QUIET MORNING

Farina, Peggy

BEGGIN'

Farina, Santo

SLEEP WALK
TEAR DROP

Farjeon, Eleanor

MORNING HAS BROKEN

Farley, Eddie

I'M GONNA CLAP MY HANDS
MUSIC GOES 'ROUND AND 'ROUND,
THE

Farley, Melville

MY SON, MY SON

Farmer, Steve

JOURNEY TO THE CENTER OF THE
MIND

Farner, Mark

BAD TIME
SHININ' ON
TIME MACHINE

Farnsworth, Nancy

HERE COME THOSE TEARS AGAIN

Farrar, Don

SAM

Farrar, John

DON'T STOP BELIEVIN'
HAVE YOU NEVER BEEN MELLOW
HOPELESSLY DEVOTED TO YOU
LITTLE MORE LOVE, A
MAGIC
MAKE A MOVE ON ME
SOMETHING BETTER TO DO
SUDDENLY
WHENEVER YOU'RE AWAY FROM ME
YOU'RE THE ONE THAT I WANT

Farrar, Walter

I CROSS MY FINGERS

Farrar, Walton

LAST MILE HOME, THE

Farrell, Joe

TOMBOY

Farrell, Joseph C.

HANNAH!

Farrell, Wes

COME A LITTLE BIT CLOSER
COME ON DOWN TO MY BOAT
DOESN'T SOMEBODY WANT TO BE
WANTED
HANG ON SLOOPY
HAPPY SUMMER DAYS
I'LL MAKE ALL YOUR DREAMS
COME TRUE
I'LL MEET YOU HALFWAY
LET'S LOCK THE DOOR (AND THROW
AWAY THE KEY)
LOOK WHAT YOU'VE DONE

Farres, Osvaldo

COME CLOSER TO ME
PERHAPS, PERHAPS, PERHAPS
WITHOUT YOU (A.K.A. TRES
PALABRAS)

Farriss, Andrew

DEVIL INSIDE
NEED YOU TONIGHT
NEVER TEAR US APART
NEW SENSATION
WHAT YOU NEED

Farrow, Johnny

I HAVE BUT ONE HEART
TARA TALARA TALA

Fasce, Tony

YOUR OWN BACK YARD

Fassert, Fred

BARBARA ANN

Faulkner, Eric

MONEY HONEY

Faust, Sid

ANGELS LISTENED IN, THE

Fautheree, Jack

CRADLE OF LOVE

Fautheree, Jimmy

PLEASE TALK TO MY HEART

Fay, Martin

(HOW TO BE A) MILLIONAIRE

Faye, Frances

WELL, ALL RIGHT!

Fearis, J. S.

LITTLE SIR ECHO

Fearman, Eric

JOYSTICK

Feaster, Carl

SH-BOOM (LIFE COULD BE A
DREAM)

Feaster, Claude

SH-BOOM (LIFE COULD BE A
DREAM)

Feather, Leonard

EVIL GAL BLUES
MIGHTY LIKE THE BLUES

Feathers, Charles A. L.

I FORGOT TO REMEMBER TO
FORGET

Fein, Lupin

THERE'S SOMETHING ABOUT AN
OLD LOVE

Fekaris, Dino

HEY BIG BROTHER
I PLEDGE MY LOVE
I WILL SURVIVE
MAKIN' IT
REUNITED
SHAKE YOUR GROOVE THING
THAT ONCE IN A LIFETIME

Felder, Don

HEAVY METAL (TAKING A RIDE)
HOTEL CALIFORNIA

Feldman, Al (a.k.a. Van Alexander)

A-TISKET A-TASKET

Feldman, Bob

CARA-LIN
I WANT CANDY

Feldman, Jack

COPACABANA (AT THE COPA)

I MADE IT THROUGH THE RAIN

Feldman, Nick

HYPNOTIZE ME

Feldman, Richard

PROMISES

Feldman, Robert

MY BOYFRIEND'S BACK
NIGHT TIME

Feldman, Steven

MERCY

Feliciano, Janna

AARON LOVES ANGELA

Feliciano, José

AARON LOVES ANGELA
CHICO AND THE MAN (MAIN
THEME)

Fell, Terry

DON'T DROP IT
SANDY
YOU'RE THE REASON

Feller, Dick

BANDIT, THE
EAST BOUND AND DOWN

Feller, Sherm

MY BABY'S COMING HOME
SUMMERTIME, SUMMERTIME

Fenceton, Donald

I AM LOVE

Fender, Freddy

WASTED DAYS AND WASTED NIGHTS

Fenderetta

I'D STILL SAY YES

Fenn, R.

FAMILY MAN

Fennelly, Mike

GO BACK

Fenstad, E. A.

STEIN SONG (UNIVERSITY OF
MAINE)

Fenton, David

TURNING JAPANESE

Fenton, George

CRY FREEDOM

Fenton, Howard

PRAY FOR PEACE
STRANGE AND SWEET

Fenton, Mack

BY-U, BY-O (THE LOU'SIANA
LULLABY)

Fenwick, Raymond

TOUCH ME

Ferguson, Bob

CARROLL COUNTY ACCIDENT
WINGS OF A DOVE

Ferguson, Celia

EAT, DRINK AND BE MERRY

Ferguson, Jay

THUNDER ISLAND

Ferguson, Lloyd

PASS THE DUTCHIE

Ferguson, Sandra

EAT, DRINK AND BE MERRY

Fernandez, C.

CIELITO LINDO (AY, AY, AY, AY)

Ferrao, Raul

APRIL IN PORTUGAL

Ferrari, Louis

DOMINO

Ferraris, Richie

LET'S LOVE

Ferre, Cliff

MONEY TREE, THE

Ferris, John S.

BEAUTIFUL ISLE OF SOMEWHERE

Ferry, Bryan

DANCE AWAY

Fetter, Ted

TAKING A CHANCE ON LOVE
YOURS FOR A SONG

Feyne, Buddy

AFTER HOURS
DOLIMITE
TUXEDO JUNCTION
WHY

Fidie, Lenny, Jr.

TROGLODYTE (CAVE MAN)

Fieger, Doug

GOOD GIRLS DON'T
MY SHARONA

Field, Carl

GOODBYE TO LOVE

Field, Eugene

LITTLE BOY BLUE

Field, Michael

SAME OLD STORY, THE

Field, Robert

POWERFUL STUFF

Fields, Arthur

ABA DABA HONEYMOON, THE
ELEVEN MORE MONTHS AND TEN
   MORE DAYS
I GOT A CODE IN MY DOSE
ON THE MISSISSIPPI

Fields, Buddy

YOU GOTTA BE A FOOTBALL HERO
YOU'RE THE ONE (YOU BEAUTIFUL
   SON-OF-A-GUN)

Fields, Dorothy

ALONE TOO LONG
ANDIAMO
BABY!
BIG SPENDER
BLUE AGAIN
BOJANGLES OF HARLEM
BUTTON UP YOUR HEART
CLOSE AS PAGES IN A BOOK
COLLEGIANA
CUBAN LOVE SONG
DIGA DIGA DOO
DINNER AT EIGHT
DOIN' THE NEW LOW-DOWN
DON'T BLAME ME
DON'T MENTION LOVE TO ME
ERBIE FITCH'S TWITCH

EXACTLY LIKE YOU
FINE ROMANCE
FUTURISTIC RHYTHM
GO HOME AND TELL YOUR MOTHER
GOODBYE BLUES
HANG UP
HAPPY HABIT
HE'S GOOD FOR ME
HEY, YOUNG FELLA
HOORAY FOR LOVE
I CAN'T GIVE YOU ANYTHING BUT
   LOVE
I DREAM TOO MUCH
I FEEL A SONG COMIN' ON
IF MY FRIENDS COULD SEE ME NOW
I GOT LOVE
I'LL BUY YOU A STAR
I'M IN THE MOOD FOR LOVE
I'M LIKE A NEW BROOM
I'M LIVIN' IN A GREAT BIG WAY
I'M THE ECHO (YOU'RE THE SONG)
I MUST HAVE THAT MAN
IN A GREAT BIG WAY
IT'S ALL YOURS
IT'S NOT WHERE YOU START
IT'S THE DARNDEST THING
I WON'T DANCE
JOCKEY ON THE CAROUSEL, THE
JUST FOR ONCE
JUST LET ME LOOK AT YOU
LET'S SIT AND TALK ABOUT YOU
LOOK WHO'S DANCING
LOST IN A FOG
LOVE IS THE REASON
LOVELY TO LOOK AT
LUCKY FELLA
MAKE THE MAN LOVE ME
MORE LOVE THAN YOUR LOVE
MY DANCING LADY
NEVER GONNA DANCE
NOTHIN' FOR NOTHIN'
ON THE SUNNY SIDE OF THE
   STREET
OUR SONG
OUT WHERE THE BLUES BEGIN
PICK YOURSELF UP
PORGY
REMIND ME
RHYTHM OF LIFE, THE
SHE DIDN'T SAY "YES"
SINGIN' THE BLUES
SPEAKING CONFIDENTIALLY
STARS IN MY EYES

TAKE IT EASY
THANK YOU FOR A LOVELY
   EVENING
THERE MUST BE SOMETHIN' BETTER
   THAN LOVE
THERE'S GOTTA BE SOMETHING
   BETTER THAN THIS
THIS IS IT
TODAY I LOVE EVERYBODY
TRAMPS AT SEA
UNCLE SAM RAG, THE
WALTZ IN SPRINGTIME
WAY YOU LOOK TONIGHT, THE
WE'RE IN BUSINESS
WHERE AM I GOING?
WHISTLING BOY, THE
YOU COULDN'T BE CUTER
YOU'RE AN ANGEL
YOU SHOULD SEE YOURSELF

Fields, Harold

BE MINE!

Fields, Irving

CHANTEZ, CHANTEZ
MANAGUA NICARAGUA
MIAMI BEACH RHUMBA

Fields, Jimmy

WALKING THE STREETS

Fields, Philip

ARE YOU SINGLE?

Fields, Richard "Dimples"

IF IT AIN'T ONE THING . . . IT'S
   ANOTHER

Fien, Lupin

SLOW FREIGHT

Fina, Jack

BUMBLE BOOGIE

Finch, Dick

JEALOUS

Finch, Richard

BOOGIE SHOES
GET DOWN TONIGHT
I'M YOUR BOOGIE MAN
KEEP IT COMIN' LOVE
PLEASE DON'T GO
ROCK YOUR BABY
(SHAKE, SHAKE, SHAKE) SHAKE
   YOUR BOOTY
THAT'S THE WAY (I LIKE IT)
WRAP YOUR ARMS AROUND ME

Finck, Herman

IN THE SHADOWS

Finckel, Eddie

WHERE IS THE ONE?

Findon, Benjamin

LOVE REALLY HURTS WITHOUT YOU

Fine, Jack Wolf

UNTIL SUNRISE

Fine, Sylvia

ANATOLE (OF PARIS)
DELILAH JONES
FIVE PENNIES, THE
HAPPY TIMES
LULLABY IN RAGTIME
MOON IS BLUE, THE
POPO THE PUPPET

Finesilver

FIRE!

Fink, Henry

CURSE OF AN ACHING HEART, THE
   (OR, YOU MADE ME WHAT I AM
   TODAY)

Finley, John

LET ME SERENADE YOU

Finn, Neil

DON'T DREAM IT'S OVER
I GOT YOU
SOMETHING SO STRONG
WORLD WHERE YOU LIVE

Finneran, John Lawrence

DEAR ONE

Finneran, Vince

DEAR ONE
HURT HER ONCE FOR ME

Finney, Lance

YOU'RE SO FINE

Fiorino, Vincent

BLUE CANARY

Fio Rito, Ted

ALONE AT A TABLE FOR TWO
ALONE AT LAST
CHARLEY, MY BOY
HANGIN' ON THE GARDEN GATE
I'M SORRY, SALLY
I NEVER KNEW (THAT ROSES GREW)
KING FOR A DAY
KNICK KNACKS ON THE MANTEL
LAUGH, CLOWN, LAUGH
LILY OF LAGUNA
LITTLE OLD CLOCK ON THE
   MANTEL, THE
NO, NO, NORA
NOW I LAY ME DOWN TO DREAM
NOW THAT YOU'RE GONE
ROLL ALONG, PRAIRIE MOON
SOMETIME
THEN YOU'VE NEVER BEEN BLUE
THREE ON A MATCH
TOOT, TOOT, TOOTSIE, GOODBYE
WHEN LIGHTS ARE LOW
YOURS TRULY IS TRULY YOURS

Fischer, Carl

BLACK LACE
IT STARTED ALL OVER AGAIN
WE'LL BE TOGETHER AGAIN
WHO WOULDN'T LOVE YOU?
YOU'RE JUST THE KIND
YOU'VE CHANGED

Fischer, Robert

I BELIEVE YOU

Fischer, Tony

GOOD TO GO

Fischoff, George

98.6
AIN'T GONNA LIE
GEORGIA PORCUPINE
LAZY DAY

Fish

KAYLEIGH

Fisher, Bruce

NOTHING FROM NOTHING
WILL IT GO ROUND IN CIRCLES
YOU ARE SO BEAUTIFUL

Fisher, Dan

GOOD MORNING HEARTACHE

Fisher, Dave

MICHAEL (ROW THE BOAT ASHORE)

Fisher, Doris

ANGELINA (THE WAITRESS AT THE
    PIZZERIA)
EITHER IT'S LOVE OR IT ISN'T
GOOD, GOOD, GOOD (THAT'S YOU—
    THAT'S YOU)
INTO EACH LIFE SOME RAIN MUST
    FALL
INVITATION TO THE BLUES
I WISH

PUT THE BLAME ON MAME
TAMPICO
THAT OLE DEVIL CALLED LOVE
THEY CAN'T CONVINCE ME
TIRED
TUTTI-FRUTTI
WHISPERING GRASS (DON'T TELL
    THE TREES)
YOU ALWAYS HURT THE ONE YOU
    LOVE
YOU CAN'T SEE THE SUN WHEN
    YOU'RE CRYIN'

Fisher, Fred

AFTER THAT I WANT A LITTLE
    MORE
AND A LITTLE BIT MORE
ANGELS WITH DIRTY FACES
ANY LITTLE GIRL THAT'S A NICE
    LITTLE GIRL IS THE RIGHT
    LITTLE GIRL FOR ME
BLUE IS THE NIGHT
CHICAGO
COME, JOSEPHINE, IN MY FLYING
    MACHINE
DADDY, YOU'VE BEEN A MOTHER
    TO ME
DARDANELLA
DUST
FIFTY MILLION FRENCHMEN (CAN'T
    BE WRONG)
GIRL TROUBLE
HAPPY DAYS AND LONELY NIGHTS
ICH LIEBE DICH (I LOVE YOU)
I DON'T WANT YOUR KISSES (IF I
    CAN'T HAVE YOUR LOVE)
I'D RATHER BE BLUE OVER YOU
    (THAN BE HAPPY WITH
    SOMEBODY ELSE)
I FOUND A ROSE IN THE DEVIL'S
    GARDEN
IF THE MAN IN THE MOON WERE A
    COON
IRELAND MUST BE HEAVEN, FOR
    MY MOTHER CAME FROM THERE
LORRAINE, MY BEAUTIFUL ALSACE
    LORRAINE
NORWAY
OUI, OUI, MARIE
PEG O' MY HEART
SAVANNAH
SIAM

THERE AIN'T NO SWEET MAN
    (WORTH THE SALT OF MY TEARS)
THERE'S A BROKEN HEART FOR
    EVERY LIGHT ON BROADWAY
THERE'S A LITTLE BIT OF BAD IN
    EVERY GOOD LITTLE GIRL
THERE'S A LITTLE SPARK OF LOVE
    STILL BURNING
THEY GO WILD, SIMPLY WILD,
    OVER ME
WHEN I GET YOU ALONE TONIGHT
WHEN THE HONEYMOON WAS OVER
WHEN THE MORNING GLORIES
    WAKE UP IN THE MORNING
WHISPERING GRASS (DON'T TELL
    THE TREES)
WHO PAID THE RENT FOR MRS. RIP
    VAN WINKLE?
YOU CAN'T GET ALONG WITH 'EM
    OR WITHOUT 'EM
YOUR FEET'S TOO BIG

Fisher, Herb

I'M YOURS TO KEEP

Fisher, Mark

EVERYWHERE YOU GO
OH, HOW I MISS YOU TONIGHT
WHEN YOU'RE SMILING (THE
    WHOLE WORLD SMILES WITH
    YOU)

Fisher, Marvin

CAPTAIN KIDD
DESTINATION MOON
FOR ONCE IN YOUR LIFE
IT'S THE SENTIMENTAL THING TO
    DO
MY FIRST AND LAST LOVE
NOTHING EVER CHANGES MY LOVE
    FOR YOU
STRANGE
WHEN SUNNY GETS BLUE

Fisher, Mike

CRAZY ON YOU

Fisher, O'Brien

OLD MOON
WHAT'S GOING ON IN YOUR WORLD?

Fisher, Rob

PROMISES, PROMISES

Fisher, Roger

BARRACUDA

Fisher, Shug

CINCINNATI LOU

Fisher, William Arms

GOIN' HOME

Fishman, Jack

HELP YOURSELF
LOVE IN EVERY ROOM
WHY DON'T THEY UNDERSTAND

Fishman, Jay

WHEN LIKING TURNS TO LOVING

Fitch, Art

SWEETHEART OF ALL MY DREAMS
(I LOVE YOU, I LOVE YOU, I LOVE
YOU)

Fitch, Clyde

LOVE MAKES THE WORLD GO
'ROUND

Fitch, John

I DON'T KNOW IF IT'S RIGHT
SHAME

Fitch, Kay

SWEETHEART OF ALL MY DREAMS
(I LOVE YOU, I LOVE YOU, I LOVE
YOU)

Fitzgerald, Alan

WHEN YOU CLOSE YOUR EYES

Fitzgerald, Ella

A-TISKET A-TASKET
CHEW, CHEW, CHEW, CHEW YOUR
BUBBLE GUM
YOU SHOWED ME THE WAY

Fitzgerald, Tyrone

FUNKY NASSAU

Fitzgibbon, Bert

JUST A LITTLE ROCKING CHAIR
AND YOU

Fitzsimmons, Dale

CALIFORNIA POLKA

Five Star

CAN'T WAIT ANOTHER MINUTE

Flanagan, Bud

UNDERNEATH THE ARCHES

Flanagan, Ralph

HOT TODDY

Fleeson, Neville

AS LONG AS I HAVE YOU
I'LL BE WITH YOU IN APPLE
BLOSSOM TIME
WATERS OF VENICE (OR, FLOATING
DOWN THE SLEEPY LAGOON)

Fleetwood, Ansley

JUST GOOD OL' BOYS

Fleischman, Robert

WHEEL IN THE SKY

Fleming, George

FREEDOM OVERSPILL

Fleming, Kye

I WAS COUNTRY WHEN COUNTRY
WASN'T COOL
I WOULDN'T HAVE MISSED IT FOR
THE WORLD
NOBODY
SLEEPING SINGLE IN A DOUBLE BED
SMOKEY MOUNTAIN RAIN
YEARS

Fleming, Phil

HOW DO YOU DO (EVERYBODY)

Fleming, Rhonda

NOBODY WANTS TO BE ALONE

Flemmons, Wade

STAY IN MY CORNER
USE YOUR HEAD

Fletcher, Archie

ON A LITTLE BAMBOO BRIDGE
ROLL 'EM GIRLS, ROLL YOUR OWN

Fletcher, Donald

DANCING MACHINE

Fletcher, "Dusty"

OPEN THE DOOR, RICHARD

Fletcher, E.

MESSAGE, THE

Fletcher, Lucy

SUGAR BLUES

Flindt, Emil

WALTZ YOU SAVED FOR ME, THE

Flint, Shelby

I WILL LOVE YOU

Flood, Dick

TROUBLE'S BACK IN TOWN

Flower, Danny

PLAY THE GAME TONIGHT

Flowers, Danny

TULSA TIME

Floyd, Eddie

634-5789 (SOULSVILLE U.S.A.)
I'VE NEVER FOUND A GIRL (TO
  LOVE ME LIKE YOU DO)
KNOCK ON WOOD
YOU DON'T KNOW WHAT YOU MEAN
  TO ME

Floyd, King

GROOVE ME
WOMAN DON'T GO ASTRAY

Fluri, Edward

NAVY BLUE

Flynn, Allan

BE STILL, MY HEART
MAYBE

Flynn, Frank

OUTSIDE

Flynn, Jimmy

GEORGIA ROSE

Flynn, John H.

SWEET ANNIE MOORE
YIP-I-ADDY-I-AY!

Flynn, Joseph

DOWN WENT MCGINTY
I NEVER LIKED O'REGAN

Fogarty, J. Paul

BETTY CO-ED

Fogelberg, Dan

HEART HOTELS
LANGUAGE OF LOVE, THE
LEADER OF THE BAND
LONGER
MAKE LOVE STAY
MISSING YOU
PART OF THE PLAN
POWER OF GOLD, THE
RUN FOR THE ROSES
SAME OLD LANG SYNE

Fogerty, John

ALMOST SATURDAY NIGHT
BAD MOON RISING
BIG TRAIN (FROM MEMPHIS)
CENTERFIELD
COMMOTION
DOWN ON THE CORNER
FORTUNATE SON
GREEN RIVER
HAVE YOU EVER SEEN THE RAIN
LODI
LOOKIN' OUT MY BACK DOOR
OLD MAN DOWN THE ROAD, THE
PROUD MARY
ROCK AND ROLL GIRLS
ROCKIN' ALL OVER THE WORLD
RUN THROUGH THE JUNGLE
SOMEDAY NEVER COMES
SWEET HITCH-HIKER
TRAVELIN' BAND
UP AROUND THE BEND
WHO'LL STOP THE RAIN

Foley, John

MAMAW

Foley, Red

I'LL NEVER LET YOU WORRY MY
  MIND

Folley, Frank

STOP YER TICKLING, JOCK!

Fonfara, Michael

APRICOT BRANDY

Fontenoy, Marc

CHOO CHOO TRAIN (CH-CH-FOO)

Forbert, Steve

ROMEO'S TUNE

Forbes, Alexandra

DON'T RUSH ME

Ford, Eugene

RAIN

Ford, Jim

NIKI HOEKY

Ford, Joan

PUSSYFOOT, THE

Ford, Lena Guilbert

KEEP THE HOME FIRES BURNING

Ford, Nancy

I WANT TO WALK TO SAN
  FRANCISCO
MY MOST IMPORTANT MOMENTS GO
  BY

Ford, Naomi

FOOL, THE

Ford, Robert

BREAKS, THE

Ford, Tennessee Ernie

ANTICIPATION BLUES
BLACKBERRY BOOGIE
SHOT GUN BOOGIE
SMOKEY MOUNTAIN BOOGIE

Ford, Vincent

ROOTS, ROCK, REGGAE

Ford, Walter H.

I LOVE YOU IN THE SAME OLD
   WAY—DARLING SUE
ONLY ME
SUNSHINE OF PARADISE ALLEY,
   THE

Fordon, Irving

SINNER OR SAINT

Foreman, Charles E.

GOLD WILL BUY MOST ANYTHING
   BUT A TRUE GIRL'S HEART

Foreman, Christopher

OUR HOUSE

Forest, Earl

NEXT TIME YOU SEE ME

Foresythe, Reginald

DEEP FOREST
DODGING A DIVORCEE
MISSISSIPPI BASIN
SERENADE FOR A WEALTHY WIDOW

Forman, Peggy

OUT OF MY HEAD AND BACK IN MY
   BED

Forrest, Ben

ALEXANDER THE SWOOSE (HALF
   SWAN—HALF GOOSE)

Forrest, George

ALWAYS AND ALWAYS
AND THIS IS MY BELOVED
AT THE BALALAIKA
BAUBLES, BANGLES AND BEADS
DONKEY SERENADE
ELENA
FATE
FROG AND THE GROG, THE
HORSE WITH THE DREAMY EYES,
   THE
IF THIS IS GOODBYE
I LOVE YOU
IT'S A BLUE WORLD
NIGHT OF MY NIGHTS
NOT SINCE NINEVEH
RHYMES HAVE I
RIDE, COSSACK, RIDE
SANDS OF TIME, THE
STRANGE MUSIC
STRANGER IN PARADISE
SWEET DANGER
TO LOOK UPON MY LOVE

Forrest, Jimmy

NIGHT TRAIN

Forsey, Keith

BEAT'S SO LONELY
DON'T YOU (FORGET ABOUT ME)
FLASHDANCE . . . WHAT A FEELING
HEAT IS ON, THE
HOT STUFF
NEVER ENDING STORY
SHAKEDOWN

Fort, Hank

PUT YOUR SHOES ON, LUCY

Fortgang, Jeff

SOME GUYS HAVE ALL THE LUCK

Fortner, Arnold "Red"

THEN I TURNED AND WALKED
   SLOWLY AWAY

Fortune, Jimmy

ELIZABETH

Fortune, Lester

TOO MUCH ON MY HEART

Foster, David

AFTER THE LOVE HAS GONE
BEST OF ME, THE
BREAKDOWN DEAD AHEAD
GLORY OF LOVE
GOT TO BE REAL
HARD TO SAY I'M SORRY
HEART TO HEART
I AM LOVE
LET ME BE THE ONE
LOOK WHAT YOU'VE DONE TO ME
LOVE ME TOMORROW
LOVE THEME FROM "ST. ELMO'S
   FIRE"
MORNIN'
NOW AND FOREVER (YOU AND ME)
SECRET OF MY SUCCESS, THE
SHE'S A BEAUTY
STAY THE NIGHT
ST. ELMO'S FIRE (MAN IN MOTION)
THROUGH THE FIRE
WHO'S HOLDING DONNA NOW?
WHY YOU TREAT ME SO BAD
WILL YOU STILL LOVE ME?
YOU'RE THE INSPIRATION

Foster, Denzil

LITTLE WALTER

Foster, Fred L.

ME AND BOBBY MCGEE

Foster, G.

LOVE IS A HOUSE

Foster, Jerry

AIN'T SHE SOMETHIN' ELSE
DAY THE WORLD STOOD STILL, THE
EASY PART'S OVER, THE
GIVING UP EASY
SHE'S PULLING ME BACK AGAIN

Foster, Norman

ZORRO

Foster, Radney

CRAZY OVER YOU
LOVE SOMEONE LIKE ME

Foster, Warren

I TAUT I SAW A PUDDY TAT

Fotine, Larry

YOU WERE ONLY FOOLING (WHILE I
 WAS FALLING IN LOVE)

Fowler, Gregory

FALLIN' AGAIN
WORLD OF FANTASY

Fowler, Lem

HE MAY BE YOUR MAN (BUT HE
 COME TO SEE ME SOMETIMES)
HOW'M I DOIN'? (HEY, HEY!)

Fowler, T. J.

CROSSFIRE

Fowler, Wallace

I'M SENDING YOU RED ROSES
THAT'S HOW MUCH I LOVE YOU

Fox, Billy

ONE MAN BAND

Fox, Charles

DIFFERENT WORLDS

HAPPY DAYS
I GOT A NAME
JOHN WAYNE
KILLING ME SOFTLY WITH HIS SONG
"LOVE BOAT" THEME
MAKING OUR DREAMS COME TRUE
MY FAIR SHARE
READY TO TAKE A CHANCE AGAIN
RICHARD'S WINDOW
TOGETHER THROUGH THE YEARS

Fox, Oscar J.

HILLS OF HOME, THE

Fox, Ray Errol

CLOWNS, THE
HERE'S TO LOVE
SEEING YOU LIKE THIS

Foxe, Earl

DREAM HOUSE

Foxx, Charlie

(1-2-3-4-5-6-7) COUNT THE DAYS
MOCKINGBIRD
SHE'S A HEARTBREAKER

Foxx, Inez

MOCKINGBIRD

Fragos, George

I HEAR A RHAPSODY

Frampton, Peter

BABY, I LOVE YOUR WAY
DO YOU FEEL LIKE WE DO
I CAN'T STAND IT
I'M IN YOU
SHOW ME THE WAY

Franceschi, Kendall

LOVE, YOU AIN'T SEEN THE LAST
 OF ME
WHOEVER'S IN NEW ENGLAND

Franchini, Anthony J.

TALKIN' TO MY HEART

Francis, Connie

VACATION

Francis, Mary

WHISKEY, IF YOU WERE A WOMAN

Franco, Steven

TASTE OF YOUR LOVE

Francois, Claude

MY BOY
MY WAY

Frank, David

DON'T DISTURB THIS GROOVE

Frank, J. L.

I'LL FORGIVE YOU, BUT I CAN'T
 FORGET

Frank, Sid

PLEASE, MR. SUN

Frankel, Abe

YANKEE ROSE

Franklin, Aretha

CALL ME
DAY DREAMING
ROCK STEADY
(SWEET, SWEET BABY) SINCE
 YOU'VE BEEN GONE
SPIRIT IN THE DARK
THINK
WHO'S ZOOMIN' WHO

Franklin, Carolyn

AIN'T NO WAY

Franklin, Dave

ANNIVERSARY WALTZ, THE
BLUE LAMENT
BREAKIN' IN A PAIR OF SHOES
CONCERT IN THE PARK
EVERYTHING YOU SAID CAME TRUE
GIVE A BROKEN HEART A BREAK
HAPPY BIRTHDAY TO LOVE
I AIN'T LAZY—I'M JUST DREAMIN'
I HOPE GABRIEL LIKES MY MUSIC
I MUST SEE ANNIE TONIGHT
IT'S FUNNY TO EVERYONE BUT ME
I WOKE UP TOO SOON
LILY BELLE
MERRY-GO-ROUND BROKE DOWN,
    THE
NEVER SHOULD HAVE TOLD YOU
ONE-ZY TWO-ZY (I LOVE YOU-ZY)
VOICE IN MY HEART, THE
WHEN MY DREAMBOAT COMES
    HOME

Franks, Michael

POPSICLE TOES
READ MY LIPS

Franks, Tillman

COMANCHEROS, THE
HONKY TONK MAN
HOW FAR IS HEAVEN?
SINK THE BISMARCK
WHEN IT'S SPRINGTIME IN ALASKA

Frantz, Chris

AND SHE WAS
BURNING DOWN THE HOUSE
ONCE IN A LIFETIME
PSYCHO KILLER

Frantzen, Henry

COLLEGE LIFE
HANNAH!
MONKEY DOODLE DANDY

Franzel, Jeffrey

DON'T RUSH ME

Franzese, Pat

IN THE MIDDLE OF A HEARTACHE

Fraser, Andy

ALL RIGHT NOW
EVERY KINDA PEOPLE

Frashuer, Dale

NA NA HEY HEY (KISS HIM
    GOODBYE)

Frato, Russ

MAYBELLENE

Frayn, Chris

LETTER THAT JOHNNY WALKER
    READ, THE

Frazier, Al

BIRD'S THE WORD, THE
PAPA-OOM-MOW-MOW
SURFIN' BIRD

Frazier, Dallas

AIN'T HAD NO LOVIN'
ALLEY OOP
ALL I HAVE TO OFFER YOU IS ME
BENEATH STILL WATERS
ELVIRA
FOURTEEN CARAT MIND
I CAN'T BELIEVE THAT YOU'VE
    STOPPED LOVING ME
I CAN'T GET THERE FROM HERE
I'M A PEOPLE
JOHNNY ONE TIME
MOHAIR SAM
RUN AWAY, LITTLE TEARS
SAY IT'S NOT YOU
SON OF HICKORY HOLLER'S TRAMP,
    THE
THERE GOES MY EVERYTHING
TIMBER, I'M FALLING
UNTIL MY DREAMS COME TRUE
WHAT'S YOUR MAMA'S NAME,
    CHILD?
WHERE DID THEY GO, LORD

Frazier, Eddie

HARVARD BLUES

Frazier, James

KISSIN' TIME

Frazier, Leonard

KISSIN' TIME

Frazier, Robert

PLAY THE GAME TONIGHT

Frazzini, Al

MY CABIN OF DREAMS

Freberg, Stan

ST. GEORGE AND THE DRAGONET

Fred, John

JUDY IN DISGUISE (WITH GLASSES)

Frederick, M.

LAUGHING WATER

Fredericks, Nan

ON AN EVENING IN ROMA

Fredericks, Paul

STOP KICKING MY HEART AROUND

Freed, Alan

MAYBELLENE
MOST OF ALL
SINCERELY
VERDICT, THE

Freed, Arthur

AFTER SUNDOWN
ALL I DO IS DREAM OF YOU
ALONE
ANGEL

Freed, Arthur

BEAUTIFUL GIRL
BLONDY
BROADWAY MELODY
BROADWAY RHYTHM
BUNDLE OF OLD LOVE LETTERS, A
CHANT OF THE JUNGLE
CINDERELLA'S FELLA
COFFEE TIME
EVERYBODY SING
FIT AS A FIDDLE
GOOD MORNING
GOT A PAIR OF NEW SHOES
HOLD YOUR MAN
I CRIED FOR YOU
I'M FEELIN' LIKE A MILLION
IT'S WINTER AGAIN
IT WAS SO BEAUTIFUL
I'VE GOT A FEELIN' YOU'RE FOOLIN'
LOVE BOAT
LOVE SONGS OF THE NILE
MOON IS LOW, THE
MY WONDERFUL ONE, LET'S DANCE
NEW MOON IS OVER MY SHOULDER, A
NO MORE TEARS
ON A SUNDAY AFTERNOON
OUR BIG LOVE SCENE
OUR LOVE AFFAIR
PAGAN LOVE SONG
SEA OF THE MOON, THE
SHOULD I?
SING BEFORE BREAKFAST
SINGIN' IN THE RAIN
SMOKE DREAMS
SUN SHOWERS
TEMPTATION
THIS HEART OF MINE
WEDDING OF THE PAINTED DOLL, THE
WE'LL MAKE HAY WHILE THE SUN SHINES
WHEN BUDDHA SMILES
WOULD YOU?
YOLANDA
YOU ARE MY LUCKY STAR
YOU'RE SIMPLY DELISH
YOURS AND MINE
YOU WERE MEANT FOR ME

Freed, Ralph

ADIOS AMIGO
ALL THE TIME

GUESS WHO
HAWAIIAN WAR CHANT
HOW ABOUT YOU?
I DUG A DITCH (IN WICHITA)
I'LL REMEMBER
IN A MOMENT OF MADNESS
I NEVER FELT MORE LIKE FALLING IN LOVE
LISTEN MY CHILDREN AND YOU SHALL HEAR
LITTLE DUTCH MILL
LOVE LIES
LOVELIGHT IN THE STARLIGHT
MISSISSIPPI DREAM BOAT
SANDMAN
SMARTY
SWING HIGH, SWING LOW
WHO WALKS IN WHEN I WALK OUT?
WORRY SONG, THE
YANKEE DOODLE NEVER WENT TO TOWN
YOU LEAVE ME BREATHLESS
YOUNG MAN WITH A HORN, THE

Freedland, Judy

DREAMSVILLE, OHIO

Freedman, Harold Brown

MY MOTHER'S LULLABY

Freedman, Max C.

HEARTBREAKER
ROCK AROUND THE CLOCK (WE'RE GONNA)
TEA LEAVES

Freedman, Ray

SIOUX CITY SUE

Freeland, Beverly

BI-I-BI

Freeland, Judy

BI-I-BI

Freeland, Ron

THIS NIGHT WON'T LAST FOREVER

Freeman, Aubrey

OPTIMISTIC

Freeman, Bobby

DO YOU WANT TO DANCE? (A.K.A. DO YOU WANNA DANCE?)

Freeman, Bud

EEL, THE

Freeman, Donald

DON'T YOU GET SO MAD

Freeman, Ernie

JIVIN' AROUND
PERCOLATOR

Freeman, James

OUR ANNIVERSARY

Freeman, John

JUST DON'T WANT TO BE LONELY TONIGHT

Freeman, Lawrence "Bud"

CRAZE-OLOGY

Freeman, L. E.

UNTIL THE REAL THING COMES ALONG (IT WILL HAVE TO DO)

Freeman, Myrna

LAST WALTZ, THE

Freeman, Stan

FAITH
I GOT EVERYTHING I WANT

I HAD A BALL
OTHER HALF OF ME, THE

Freiberg, David

JANE

Freire, Osman Perez

AY, AY, AY

Frenette, Matt

WORKING FOR THE WEEKEND

Frew, Alan

SOMEDAY

Frey, Glenn

BEST OF MY LOVE
DESPERADO
HEARTACHE TONIGHT
HOTEL CALIFORNIA
I CAN'T TELL YOU WHY
JAMES DEAN
LIFE IN THE FAST LANE
LYIN' EYES
NEW KID IN TOWN
ONE OF THESE NIGHTS
ONE YOU LOVE, THE
SEXY GIRL
SMUGGLER'S BLUES
TAKE IT EASY
TEQUILA SUNRISE
YOU BELONG TO THE CITY

Fricker, Sylvia

YOU WERE ON MY MIND

Fried, Gerald

"ROOTS" MEDLEY

Fried, Martin

BROADWAY ROSE

Friedhofer, Hugh

LOVE THEME FROM "ONE EYED
JACKS"

Friedland, Anatole

LILY OF THE VALLEY
MY SWEET ADAIR

Friedland, Stephen

NOBODY KNOWS WHAT'S GOIN' ON
(IN MY MIND BUT ME)

Friedman, Charles

KISS ME ANOTHER

Friedman, Dean

ARIEL

Friedman, Gary William

DO YOU REMEMBER?
DREAM BABIES
HOW I FEEL
LIGHT SINGS
SOUNDS
THIS IS MY SONG

Friedman, Leo

COON! COON! COON!
LET ME CALL YOU SWEETHEART
MEET ME TONIGHT IN DREAMLAND

Friedman, Rob

DON'T SHED A TEAR

Friedman, Ruthann

WINDY

Friedman, Stanleigh P.

DOWN THE FIELD

Friend, Cliff

BIG BUTTER AND EGG MAN, THE
BIGGER AND BETTER THAN EVER
BROKEN RECORD, THE
CONCERT IN THE PARK
CONFUCIUS SAY
DON'T SWEETHEART ME
EVERYTHING YOU SAID CAME TRUE
GIVE ME A NIGHT IN JUNE
GONNA BUILD A BIG FENCE
    AROUND TEXAS
HELLO BLUEBIRD
HUNKADOLA
I'M TELLIN' THE BIRDS, I'M TELLIN'
    THE BEES (HOW I LOVE YOU)
I MUST SEE ANNIE TONIGHT
IT GOES LIKE THIS (THAT FUNNY
    MELODY)
I WANNA SING ABOUT YOU
JUNE NIGHT
JUST BECAUSE YOU'RE YOU
LET IT RAIN! LET IT POUR! (I'LL BE
    IN VIRGINIA IN THE MORNING)
LET ME LINGER LONGER IN YOUR
    ARMS
LET'S HAVE A PARTY
LIGHTS ARE LOW, THE MUSIC IS
    SWEET, THE
LOVESICK BLUES
MAMA LOVES PAPA (PAPA LOVES
    MAMA)
MERRY-GO-ROUND BROKE DOWN,
    THE
MY BLACKBIRDS ARE BLUEBIRDS
    NOW
NEVER SHOULD HAVE TOLD YOU
OO-OO ERNEST, ARE YOU EARNEST
    WITH ME?
OUT WHERE THE BLUE BEGINS
SATISFIED!
SOUTH AMERICAN JOE
SWEETEST MUSIC THIS SIDE OF
    HEAVEN, THE
SWEETHEARTS FOREVER
TAMIAMI TRAIL
(I WANNA GO WHERE YOU GO, DO
    WHAT YOU DO) THEN I'LL BE
    HAPPY
THERE'S YES! YES! IN YOUR EYES
TIME WAITS FOR NO ONE
TRADE WINDS
WAH-HOO!

WAKE UP AND SING
WHEN MY DREAMBOAT COMES
   HOME
WHEN THE ONE YOU LOVE LOVES
   YOU
WHERE THE LAZY DAISIES GROW
YOU TELL HER, I S-T-U-T-T-E-R
YOU'VE GOT ME IN THE PALM OF
   YOUR HAND

Fries, Bill

CONVOY

Friga, John

AFTER THE FALL

Frigo, John

DETOUR AHEAD
I TOLD YA I LOVE YA, NOW GET
   OUT

Friml, Rudolf

ALLAH'S HOLIDAY
BUBBLE, THE
CHANSONETTE
DONKEY SERENADE
DOOR OF MY DREAMS, THE
FLORIDA, THE MOON AND YOU
GIANNINA MIA
GIVE ME ONE HOUR
HUGUETTE WALTZ
INDIAN LOVE CALL
I WANT TO MARRY A MALE
   QUARTETTE
KATINKA
L'AMOUR TOUJOURS, L'AMOUR (LOVE
   EVERLASTING)
LOVE FOR SALE
LOVE IS LIKE A FIREFLY
LOVE ME TONIGHT
MA BELLE
MARCH OF THE MUSKETEERS
MOUNTIES, THE (A.K.A. SONG OF
   THE MOUNTIES)
MY PARADISE
ONLY A ROSE
RACKETY COO
ROSE-MARIE
SOME DAY

SOMETHING SEEMS TINGLE-INGLING
SOMETIME
SONG OF THE VAGABONDS
SYMPATHY
TOTEM TOM-TOM
WE'LL HAVE A KINGDOM
WHEN A MAID COMES KNOCKING
   AT YOUR HEART
WILD ROSE, THE
YOU'RE IN LOVE

Frisch, Al

ALL OVER THE WORLD
CONGRATULATIONS TO SOMEONE
FLOWERS MEAN FORGIVENESS
HERE COMES THAT HEARTACHE
   AGAIN
I WON'T CRY ANYMORE
MELANCHOLY MINSTREL, THE
PANCHO MAXIMILIAN HERNANDEZ
ROSES IN THE RAIN
THIS IS NO LAUGHING MATTER
TWO DIFFERENT WORLDS

Frisch, Billy

I'D LIKE TO SEE THE KAISER WITH
   A LILY IN HIS HAND

Frishberg, Dave

I'M HIP
MY ATTORNEY, BERNIE
PEEL ME A GRAPE
SWEET KENTUCKY HAM
USELESS WALTZ
YOU WOULD RATHER HAVE THE
   BLUES

Fritts, Donnie

CHOO CHOO TRAIN

Frizzell, Lefty

ALWAYS LATE (WITH YOUR KISSES)
DON'T STAY AWAY
FOREVER AND ALWAYS
GIVE ME MORE, MORE, MORE OF
   YOUR KISSES
IF YOU'VE GOT THE MONEY (I'VE
   GOT THE TIME)

I LOVE YOU A THOUSAND WAYS
I'M AN OLD, OLD MAN
I WANT TO BE WITH YOU ALWAYS
MOM AND DAD'S WALTZ
THAT'S THE WAY LOVE GOES

Froeba, Frank

JUMPIN' JIVE, THE

Frontiere, Dominic

HANG 'EM HIGH
TURN ME AROUND

Froom, Mitchell

SOMETHING SO STRONG

Frost, Harold G.

SWEET HAWAIIAN MOONLIGHT

Frost, Jack

FLOATIN' DOWN TO COTTON TOWN
WHEN YOU AND I WERE YOUNG,
   MAGGIE, BLUES

Fry, Martin

BE NEAR ME
LOOK OF LOVE (PART ONE)
WHEN SMOKEY SINGS

Fryberg, Mart

CALL ME DARLING

Frye, M.

FAMILY MAN

Frykman, Erik

OPEN DOOR, OPEN ARMS

Fucilli, Guiseppe

GUAGLIONE (A.K.A. THE MAN WHO
   PLAYS THE MANDOLINO)

Fulkerson, Daniel B.

TOMBSTONE EVERY MILE, A

Fuller, Craig

AMIE

Fuller, Darrell

SPINOUT

Fuller, Dolores

DO THE CLAM
ROCK-A-HULA BABY

Fuller, James

WIPE OUT

Fuller, Jerry

BETTY MY ANGEL
GUILTY OF LOVING YOU
IT'S UP TO YOU
LADY WILLPOWER
OVER YOU
SHOW AND TELL
TRAVELIN' MAN
YOUNG GIRL
YOUNG WORLD

Fuller, Walter G.

OOP BOP SH' BAM

Full Force

ALL CRIED OUT
HEAD TO TOE
I'M REAL
I WONDER IF I TAKE YOU HOME
LOST IN EMOTION
NAUGHTY GIRLS (NEED LOVE TOO)

Fullylove, Leroy

BUMBLE BEE

Fulson, Lowell

RECONSIDER BABY

TRAMP

Fulton, Jack

IF YOU ARE BUT A DREAM
IVORY TOWER
MY GREATEST MISTAKE
UNTIL
WANTED

Fulton, Kathryn R.

FOOL #1

Funches, John

OH, WHAT A NIGHT

Fuqua, Harvey

IF I CAN'T HAVE YOU
IF I COULD BUILD MY WHOLE
    WORLD AROUND YOU
MOST OF ALL
MY WHOLE WORLD ENDED (THE
    MOMENT YOU LEFT ME)
PUCKER UP, BUTTERCUP
SINCERELY
SOMEDAY WE'LL BE TOGETHER
THAT'S WHAT GIRLS ARE MADE FOR
TWENTY-FIVE MILES
WHAT DOES IT TAKE (TO WIN YOUR
    LOVE)?

Furber, Douglas

BELLS OF SAINT MARY'S, THE
FANCY OUR MEETING
HOLD MY HAND
LAMBETH WALK
LET ME GIVE MY HAPPINESS TO
    YOU
LIMEHOUSE BLUES
SHE'S SUCH A COMFORT TO ME
THREE WISHES

Furin, Matt

LATE NOW

Furlett, Frank

ALEXANDER THE SWOOSE (HALF
    SWAN—HALF GOOSE)

Furst, William

LOVE MAKES THE WORLD GO
    'ROUND

Furth, Seymour

BUDWEISER'S A FRIEND OF MINE
NO WEDDING BELLS FOR ME

Furuholem, Mags

TAKE ON ME

Fusco, G.

SEEING YOU LIKE THIS

Fysher, Nilson

LITTLE LOVE, A LITTLE KISS, A

Gabbard, Rusty

I'LL BE THERE IF YOU EVER WANT
    ME

Gabler, Milt

CHOO CHOO CH'BOOGIE
DANKE SCHOEN
IN A MELLOW TONE
L-O-V-E
SKINNY MINNIE
STAY HERE WITH ME
TELL ME WHY
WIEDERSEH'N

Gabriel, Charles H.

BRIGHTEN THE CORNER WHERE
    YOU ARE

Gabriel, Gilbert

LIFE IN A NORTHERN TOWN

Gabriel, Peter

BIG TIME
DON'T GIVE UP
GAMES WITHOUT FRONTIERS
IN YOUR EYES
SHOCK THE MONKEY
SLEDGEHAMMER
SOLSBURY HILL

Gadd, S.

STUFF LIKE THAT

Gade, Jacob

JALOUSIE (JEALOUSY)

Gailbraith, Gordon

I GOT YOU

Gaillard, Slim

CEMENT MIXER (PUT-TI, PUT-TI)
DOWN BY THE STATION
FLAT FOOT FLOOGIE, THE
TUTTI-FRUTTI
VOL VISTU GAILY STAR

Gaines, Lee

JUST A-SITTIN' AND A-ROCKIN'
JUST SQUEEZE ME (BUT DON'T
    TEASE ME)

Gainsbourg, Serge

JE T'AIME . . . MOI NON PLUS

Gaitsch, Bruce

BOYS NIGHT OUT
DON'T MEAN NOTHING

Galdieri, M.

LOVE THEME FROM "LA STRADA"

Galdieri, Michele

NON DIMENTICAR (DON'T FORGET)

Galdo, Joe

BAD BOY

Gale, E.

STUFF LIKE THAT

Gales, Attala Zane

SWEET, SWEET LOVE

Galhardo, J.

LISBON ANTIGUA (IN OLD LISBON)

Gall, Robert

FOR MAMA

Gallagher, Benny

BREAK AWAY
HEART IN NEW YORK, A

Gallagher, Ed

MISTER GALLAGHER AND MISTER
    SHEAN

Gallagher, Michael

DO YOU FEEL LIKE WE DO

Gallo, Joey

DEAD GIVEAWAY
SAVE THE OVERTIME FOR ME
SHOW ME THE WAY

Gallop, Sammy

AUTUMN SERENADE
BLOSSOMS ON THE BOUGH, THE
BOOGIE WOOGIE MAXIXE
COUNT EVERY STAR
ELMER'S TUNE
FORGIVE MY HEART
FREE
MAYBE YOU'LL BE THERE
MY LADY LOVES TO DANCE
NIGHT LIGHTS
OUTSIDE OF HEAVEN

SHOO-FLY PIE AND APPLE PAN
    DOWDY
SOMEWHERE ALONG THE WAY
THERE MUST BE A WAY
VAGABOND SHOES
WAKE THE TOWN AND TELL THE
    PEOPLE

Galloway, Tod B.

WHIFFENPOOF SONG, THE

Galuten, Albhy

THIS WOMAN
WHAT KIND OF FOOL

Gamble, Kenny

992 ARGUMENTS
ARE YOU HAPPY?
(LOVE IS LIKE A) BASEBALL GAME
BRAND NEW ME, A
BREAK UP TO MAKE UP
CLOSE THE DOOR
COWBOYS TO GIRLS
DARLIN' DARLIN' BABY (SWEET,
    TENDER LOVE)
DON'T LEAVE ME THIS WAY
DON'T LET LOVE HANG YOU UP
DO THE CHOO CHOO
DO YOU GET ENOUGH LOVE
DROWNING IN THE SEA OF LOVE
ENGINE NUMBER 9 (GET ME BACK
    ON TIME)
ENJOY YOURSELF
EXPLOSION IN MY SOUL
EXPRESSWAY TO YOUR HEART
FOR THE LOVE OF MONEY
GIRL, DON'T LET IT GET YOU DOWN
GIVE THE PEOPLE WHAT THEY
    WANT
HEY, WESTERN UNION MAN
HOPE THAT WE CAN BE TOGETHER
    SOON
I CAN'T STOP DANCING
IF ONLY YOU KNEW
IF YOU DON'T KNOW ME BY NOW
I LOVE MUSIC
I'M GONNA MAKE YOU LOVE ME
LET ME TOUCH YOU
LET'S CLEAN UP THE GHETTO
LIVIN' FOR THE WEEKEND

LOVE I LOST, THE
LOVE TRAIN
LOVIN' YOU
ME AND MRS. JONES
MESSAGE IN OUR MUSIC
MOODY WOMAN
NEVER GIVE YOU UP
ONLY THE STRONG SURVIVE
POWER OF LOVE
PUT YOUR HANDS TOGETHER
THANKS FOR SAVING MY LIFE
THERE'S GONNA BE A SHOWDOWN
TSOP (THE SOUND OF
  PHILADELPHIA)
UNITED (A.K.A. WE'LL BE UNITED)
USE TA BE MY GIRL
WHAT'S THE USE OF BREAKING UP?
WHEN WILL I SEE YOU AGAIN?
YOU'LL NEVER FIND ANOTHER
  LOVE LIKE MINE
YOU'RE MY LATEST, MY GREATEST
  INSPIRATION

Gamse, Albert

AMAPOLA (PRETTY LITTLE POPPY)
CHANTEZ, CHANTEZ
FROM ONE LOVE TO ANOTHER
MANAGUA NICARAGUA
MARIA FROM BAHIA
MIAMI BEACH RUMBA

Gamson, David

PERFECT WAY

Gann, Wiley

MISSISSIPPI COTTON PICKING DELTA
  TOWN

Gannon, Kim

ALWAYS IN MY HEART
ANGEL IN DISGUISE
AUTUMN NOCTURNE
CROCE DI ORO (CROSS OF GOLD)
DREAMER'S HOLIDAY, A
ENDLESSLY
FIVE O'CLOCK WHISTLE, THE
I'LL BE HOME FOR CHRISTMAS
I'LL PRAY FOR YOU
IT CAN'T BE WRONG

I UNDERSTAND
I WANT TO BE WANTED
MAKE LOVE TO ME
MOONLIGHT COCKTAIL
OLD ACQUAINTANCE
SO MADLY IN LOVE
TOO MUCH IN LOVE
UNDER PARIS SKIES

Gant, Cecil

I WONDER
PUT ANOTHER CHAIR AT THE TABLE

Gant, Don

RUN, BABY, RUN (BACK INTO MY
  ARMS)

Gantry, Chris

DREAMS OF THE EVERYDAY
  HOUSEWIFE

Garcia, Enrique

1-2-3
CONGA
RHYTHM IS GONNA GET YOU

Garcia, Gary

PAC-MAN FEVER

Garcia, Jerry

HELL IN A BUCKET
SUGAREE
TOUCH OF GREY
TRUCKIN'
UNCLE JOHN'S BAND
WEST L.A. FADEAWAY

Gardenier, Ed

FATAL ROSE OF RED, THE
WHEN YOU KNOW YOU'RE NOT
  FORGOTTEN BY THE GIRL YOU
  CAN'T FORGET

Gardes, G.

FOR YASGUR'S FARM

Gardner, Don

ALL I WANT FOR CHRISTMAS (IS MY
  TWO FRONT TEETH)

Gardner, William H.

CAN'T YOU HEAR ME CALLIN',
  CAROLINE?
DON T LEAVE ME DOLLY

Garfield, Gil

WONDERFUL SUMMER

Garfunkel, Art

HEY, SCHOOLGIRL
SCARBOROUGH FAIR—CANTICLE

Gari, Brian

CLARA'S DANCING SCHOOL
LATE NITE COMIC

Garibaldi, John

WHAT IS HIP?

Garland, Hank

SUGARFOOT RAG

Garland, Joe

IN THE MOOD
LEAP FROG
TAR PAPER STOMP

Garner, Erroll

DREAMSTREET
DREAMY
MISTY
PARIS MIST
PASSING THROUGH
SOLITAIRE

Garnett, Gale

WE'LL SING IN THE SUNSHINE

Garrett, Gary

YOU CAN'T BREAK MY HEART
 ('CAUSE IT'S ALREADY BROKEN)

Garrett, Lee

IT'S A SHAME
LET'S GET SERIOUS
MAYBE I'M A FOOL
SIGNED, SEALED, DELIVERED I'M
 YOURS

Garrett, Lloyd

DALLAS BLUES

Garrett, Marilynn

NIGHT HAS A THOUSAND EYES, THE

Garrett, Siedah

MAN IN THE MIRROR

Garrett, Snuff

ANOTHER HONKY TONK NIGHT ON
 BROADWAY
BAR ROOM BUDDIES
COWBOYS AND CLOWNS
EVERY WHICH WAY BUT LOOSE
HOPPY, GENE, AND ME
YOU DON'T HAVE TO PAINT ME A
 PICTURE

Garrick, H.

NEW ORLEANS LADIES

Garris, Sid

OPUS NO. 1

Garrity, Freddie

I'M TELLING YOU NOW

Garron, Joe

JUST A GIRL THAT MEN FORGET

Garson, Mort

DONDI
LEFT RIGHT OUT OF YOUR HEART
MY SUMMER LOVE
OUR DAY WILL COME
STARRY EYED

Garton, Ted

MY BELGIAN ROSE

Gartside, Green

PERFECT WAY

Garufalo, Bryan

LOAD-OUT, THE

Garvarentz, Georges

YET . . . I KNOW

Garvin, Michael

DESPERADO LOVE
FROM THE WORD GO
IN A NEW YORK MINUTE
ONLY ONE YOU

Garvin, Rex

OVER THE MOUNTAIN, ACROSS THE
 SEA

Garvin and Jones

HIGHWAY ROBBERY

Gaskill, Clarence

DOO WACKA DOO
I CAN'T BELIEVE THAT YOU'RE IN
 LOVE WITH ME
I'M WILD ABOUT HORNS ON
 AUTOMOBILES THAT GO "TA-TA-TA-
 TA"
MINNIE THE MOOCHER (THE HO DE
 HO SONG)
PRISONER OF LOVE

Gaspar, David

HANDS TO HEAVEN

Gasparre, Dick

I HEAR A RHAPSODY

Gass, Aubrey

DEAR JOHN
WINE, WOMEN AND SONG

Gaste, Louis

TO YOU, MY LOVE

Gaston, Lyle

BLACKBOARD OF MY HEART

Gately, Jimmy

ALLA MY LOVE
MINUTE YOU'RE GONE, THE

Gately, Mike

IF YOU DON'T WANT MY LOVE

Gates, David

AUBREY
BABY, I'M A-WANT YOU
DIARY
GOODBYE GIRL
GUITAR MAN
HOOKED ON YOU
IF
LOST WITHOUT YOUR LOVE
MAKE IT WITH YOU
PART TIME LOVE
POPSICLES AND ICICLES
SWEET SURRENDER

Gathers, Helen

MR. LEE

Gatlin, Larry

ALL THE GOLD IN CALIFORNIA
BROKEN LADY

I JUST CAN'T GET HER OUT OF MY
   MIND
I JUST WISH YOU WERE SOMEONE I
   LOVE
LADY TAKES THE COWBOY EVERY
   TIME, THE
SHE USED TO BE SOMEBODY'S BABY

Gatlin, Sue

TWO OF HEARTS

Gatling, Tim

I LIKE

Gatsos, Nikos

WHITE ROSE OF ATHENS, THE

Gaudio, Bob

BEGGIN'
BIG GIRLS DON'T CRY
BIG MAN IN TOWN
BYE, BYE, BABY (BABY GOODBYE)
CAN'T TAKE MY EYES OFF YOU
DAWN (GO AWAY)
DECEMBER 1963 (OH, WHAT A
   NIGHT)
GIRL COME RUNNING
I MAKE A FOOL OF MYSELF
I WOULD BE IN LOVE (ANYWAY)
MARLENA
PROUD ONE, THE
RAG DOLL
RONNIE
SAVE IT FOR ME
SHERRY
SHORT SHORTS
SILENCE IS GOLDEN
SOON (I'LL BE HOME AGAIN)
SUN AIN'T GONNA SHINE ANYMORE,
   THE
TO GIVE (THE REASON I LIVE)
WALK LIKE A MAN
WHO LOVES YOU

Gaunt, Percy

BOWERY, THE
LOVE ME LITTLE, LOVE ME LONG
PUSH DEM CLOUDS AWAY

REUBEN AND CYNTHIA

Gay, Byron

FOUR OR FIVE TIMES
HORSES
O (OH!)
SITTIN' ON A LOG (PETTIN' MY DOG)
VAMP, THE

Gay, Noel

HOLD MY HAND
KING'S HORSES, THE (AND THE
   KING'S MEN)
LAMBETH WALK
LEANING ON THE LAMP POST
RUN, RABBIT, RUN
THERE'S SOMETHING ABOUT A
   SOLDIER

Gayden, Mac

EVERLASTING LOVE
IT'S ALRIGHT

Gaye, Anna

BABY, I'M FOR REAL
BELLS, THE

Gaye, Marvin

BABY, I'M FOR REAL
BEECHWOOD 4-5789
BELLS, THE
COME GET TO THIS
DANCING IN THE STREET
GOT TO GIVE IT UP
IF THIS WORLD WERE MINE
INNER CITY BLUES (MAKE ME
   WANNA HOLLER)
LET'S GET IT ON
MERCY, MERCY ME (THE ECOLOGY)
PRETTY LITTLE BABY
PRIDE AND JOY
SANCTIFIED LADY
SEXUAL HEALING
STUBBORN KIND OF FELLOW
TROUBLE MAN
WHAT'S GOING ON

Gayle, Tim

LATE NOW

Gaylord, Ronnie

CUDDLE ME

Gaynor, Mel

ALIVE AND KICKING
SANCTIFY YOURSELF

Gayten, Paul

MY DEAREST DARLING

Gaze, Heino

ASK ME
BERLIN MELODY, THE
CALCUTTA
FIESTA

Gaze, Hermann

RAINY DAY REFRAIN, A

Geary, T. Mayo

MAN WITH THE LADDER AND THE
   HOSE
YOUR DAD GAVE HIS LIFE FOR HIS
   COUNTRY

Gebest, Charles J.

I LOVE LOVE

Geddins, Robert

HAUNTED HOUSE
I WANT TO KNOW

Gee, Jack

DYING GAMBLER BLUES

Geehl, Henry E.

FOR YOU ALONE

Geiger, Mike

DARLENE
THIS MISSIN' YOU HEART OF MINE

Geitsch, Bruce

LA ISLA BONITA

Gelber, Stanley

NOW I KNOW

Geld, Gary

GINNY COME LATELY
HE SAYS THE SAME THINGS TO ME
HURTING EACH OTHER
I GOT LOVE
LET ME BELONG TO YOU
NEXT TO LOVIN' (I LIKE FIGHTIN')
PURLIE
SAVE YOUR HEART FOR ME
WALK HIM UP THE STAIRS

Geldof, Bob

DO THEY KNOW IT'S CHRISTMAS?
I DON'T LIKE MONDAYS

Genaro, Pat

HERE IN MY HEART
YOU'RE BREAKING MY HEART

Genovese, Robert

BIG GUITAR, THE

Gensler, Lewis

BY SPECIAL PERMISSION OF THE
    COPYRIGHT OWNERS, I LOVE
    YOU
CROSS YOUR HEART
ENDING WITH A KISS
FATAL FASCINATION
GENTLEMEN PREFER BLONDES
HOW DO YOU DO IT?
I NEVER SAW A BETTER NIGHT
KEEP SMILING AT TROUBLE
LOVE IS JUST AROUND THE CORNER
MELODY IN SPRING

Gentile, Alfonso

THERE'S A MOON OUT TONIGHT

Gentry, Bo

GET OUT NOW
I LIKE THE WAY
INDIAN GIVER
MAKE BELIEVE
MIRAGE
MONY, MONY
OUT OF THE BLUE
SPECIAL DELIVERY

Gentry, Bobbie

FANCY
ODE TO BILLY JOE

Gentry, Gary

ONE I LOVED BACK THEN, THE
    (CORVETTE SONG)

Gentry, Teddy

FALLIN' AGAIN

George, Barbara

I KNOW (YOU DON'T WANT ME NO
    MORE)

George, Don

CALYPSO BLUES
DOOR WILL OPEN, A
EVERYTHING BUT YOU
FORSAKING ALL OTHERS
I AIN'T GOT NOTHIN' BUT THE
    BLUES
I'M BEGINNING TO SEE THE LIGHT
I NEVER MENTION YOUR NAME
IT SHOULDN'T HAPPEN TO A DREAM
LOVE SONG, A
PAPA NICCOLINI
SLOWLY, WITH FEELING
TIME'S A-WASTIN'
TO ME
TULIP OR TURNIP
YELLOW ROSE OF TEXAS, THE

George, Jimmy

I'LL ALWAYS LOVE YOU
I WONDER WHO SHE'S SEEING NOW
JUST TO SEE HER

George, Steve

BROKEN WINGS
IS IT LOVE
KYRIE

Geppert, Christopher

NEVER BE THE SAME
RIDE LIKE THE WIND

Gerald, Alan "Fitz"

SENTIMENTAL STREET

Gerald, J.

HONEY LOVE

Gerald, Raeford

GET DOWN, GET DOWN (GET ON
    THE FLOOR)
YOUR TIME TO CRY

Geraldo, Neil

WE LIVE FOR LOVE

Gerard, Philippe

MAGIC TANGO, THE

Gerard, Richard H.

SWEET ADELINE (OR, YOU'RE THE
    FLOWER OF MY HEART)

Gerber, Alex

LITTLE CHURCH AROUND THE
    CORNER, THE
MY HOME TOWN IS A ONE HORSE
    TOWN (BUT IT'S BIG ENOUGH FOR
    ME)

Gerhard, Ake

LAY DOWN YOUR ARMS

Gerlach, Horace

DADDY'S LITTLE GIRL

Gernhard, Phil

RETURN OF THE RED BARON, THE
SNOOPY VS. THE RED BARON

Gershwin, Arthur

INVITATION TO THE BLUES

Gershwin, George

AREN'T YOU KING OF GLAD WE
    DID?
BABBITT AND THE BROMIDE, THE
BABY!
BACK BAY POLKA
(I'VE GOT) BEGINNER'S LUCK
BESS, OH WHERE'S MY BESS?
BESS, YOU IS MY WOMAN NOW
BEST OF EVERYTHING, THE
BIDIN' MY TIME
BLAH, BLAH, BLAH
BOY! WHAT LOVE HAS DONE TO ME!
BUT NOT FOR ME
BY AND BY
BY STRAUSS
CHANGING MY TUNE
CLAP YO' HANDS
COME TO THE MOON
COSSACK LOVE SONG (DON'T
    FORGET ME)
DEAR LITTLE GIRL
DELISHIOUS
DO, DO, DO
DO IT AGAIN!
DO WHAT YOU DO
EMBRACEABLE YOU
FASCINATING RHYTHM
FEELING I'M FALLING
FIDGETY FEET
FOGGY DAY, A (IN LONDON TOWN)
FOR YOU, FOR ME, FOREVER MORE
FUNNY FACE
HALF OF IT, DEARIE, BLUES, THE
HANG ON TO ME

HE LOVES AND SHE LOVES
HOW LONG HAS THIS BEEN GOING
    ON?
I CAN'T BE BOTHERED NOW
I DON'T THINK I'LL FALL IN LOVE
    TODAY
I GOT PLENTY O' NUTTIN'
I GOT RHYTHM
I'LL BUILD A STAIRWAY TO
    PARADISE
I LOVES YOU, PORGY
ISN'T IT A PITY?
IT AIN'T NECESSARILY SO
I'VE GOT A CRUSH ON YOU
I WAS DOING ALL RIGHT
I WON'T SAY I WILL, BUT I WON'T
    SAY I WON'T
KICKIN' THE CLOUDS AWAY
KING OF SWING
K-RA-ZY FOR YOU
LET'S CALL THE WHOLE THING OFF
LET'S KISS AND MAKE UP
LITTLE JAZZ BIRD
LIZA (ALL THE CLOUDS'LL ROLL
    AWAY)
LOOKING FOR A BOY
LOVE IS HERE TO STAY
LOVE IS SWEEPING THE COUNTRY
LOVE WALKED IN
MADEMOISELLE IN NEW ROCHELLE
MAN I LOVE, THE
MAYBE
MINE
MY COUSIN IN MILWAUKEE
MY MAN'S GONE NOW
MY ONE AND ONLY
NASHVILLE NIGHTINGALE
NICE WORK IF YOU CAN GET IT
OF THEE I SING
OH! LADY BE GOOD!
OH GEE! OH JOY!
RED HEADED WOMAN, A
RHAPSODY IN BLUE
SAM AND DELILAH
SHALL WE DANCE
SLAP THAT BASS
SO AM I
SOMEBODY FROM SOMEWHERE
SOMEBODY LOVES ME
SOMEHOW IT SELDOM COMES TRUE
SOMEONE TO WATCH OVER ME
SOMETHING ABOUT LOVE
SONG OF THE FLAME

SOON
SOUTH SEA ISLES (A.K.A. SUNNY
    SOUTH SEA ISLANDS)
STRIKE UP THE BAND
SUMMERTIME
SWANEE
SWEET AND LOW-DOWN
SWISS MISS
'S WONDERFUL
THAT CERTAIN FEELING
THERE'S A BOAT DAT'S LEAVIN'
    SOON FOR NEW YORK
THERE'S MORE TO THE KISS THAN
    THE X-X-X
THEY ALL LAUGHED
THEY CAN'T TAKE THAT AWAY
    FROM ME
THINGS ARE LOOKING UP
TRA-LA-LA
TREAT ME ROUGH
VIRGINIA (DON'T GO TOO FAR)
VODKA
WAITING FOR THE SUN TO COME
    OUT
WALKING THE DOG (A.K.A.
    PROMENADE)
WHEN YOU WANT 'EM, YOU CAN'T
    GET 'EM (WHEN YOU GOT 'EM,
    YOU DON'T WANT 'EM)
WHO CARES?
WHY DO I LOVE YOU?
WINTERGREEN FOR PRESIDENT
WOMAN IS A SOMETIME THING, A
YANKEE DOODLE BLUES
YOU-OO JUST YOU

Gershwin, Ira

ALL AT ONCE
AREN'T YOU KIND OF GLAD WE
    DID?
BABBITT AND THE BROMIDE, THE
BABY!
BACK BAY POLKA
(I'VE GOT) BEGINNER'S LUCK
BESS, OH WHERE'S MY BESS?
BESS, YOU IS MY WOMAN NOW
BIDIN' MY TIME
BLAH, BLAH, BLAH
BLOWIN' THE BLUES AWAY
BOY! WHAT LOVE HAS DONE TO ME!
BUT NOT FOR ME
BY STRAUSS

CHANGING MY TUNE
CHEERFUL LITTLE EARFUL
CLAP YO' HANDS
DEAR LITTLE GIRL
DELISHIOUS
DISSERTATION ON THE STATE OF
   BLISS (A.K.A. LOVE AND LEARN)
DO, DO, DO
DOLLY
DON'T BE A WOMAN IF YOU CAN
DO WHAT YOU DO
EMBRACEABLE YOU
FASCINATING RHYTHM
FEELING I'M FALLING
FIDGETY FEET
FOGGY DAY, A (IN LONDON TOWN)
FOR YOU, FOR ME, FOREVER MORE
FUNNY FACE
FUN TO BE FOOLED
GOTTA HAVE ME GO WITH YOU
HALF OF IT, DEARIE, BLUES, THE
HANG ON TO ME
HE HASN'T A THING EXCEPT ME
HE LOVES AND SHE LOVES
HERE'S WHAT I'M HERE FOR
HOW LONG HAS THIS BEEN GOING
   ON?
I AM ONLY HUMAN AFTER ALL
I CAN'T BE BOTHERED NOW
I CAN'T GET STARTED
I DON'T THINK I'LL FALL IN LOVE
   TODAY
I GOT PLENTY O' NUTTIN'
I GOT RHYTHM
I'LL BUILD A STAIRWAY TO
   PARADISE
I LOVES YOU, PORGY
IN THE MERRY MONTH OF MAYBE
ISLAND IN THE WEST INDIES
ISN'T IT A PITY?
IT AIN'T NECESSARILY SO
IT'S A NEW WORLD
I'VE GOT A CRUSH ON YOU
I WAS DOING ALL RIGHT
I WON'T SAY I WILL, BUT I WON'T
   SAY I WON'T
JENNY (THE SAGA OF)
KICKIN' THE CLOUDS AWAY
K-RA-ZY FOR YOU
LET'S CALL THE WHOLE THING OFF
LET'S KISS AND MAKE UP
LET'S TAKE A WALK AROUND THE
   BLOCK

LITTLE JAZZ BIRD
LIZA (ALL THE CLOUDS'LL ROLL
   AWAY)
LONG AGO AND FAR AWAY
LOOKING FOR A BOY
LOSE THAT LONG FACE
LOVE IS HERE TO STAY
LOVE IS SWEEPING THE COUNTRY
LOVE WALKED IN
MADEMOISELLE IN NEW ROCHELLE
MAKE WAY FOR TOMORROW
MAN I LOVE, THE
MAN THAT GOT AWAY, THE
MAYBE
MINE
MY COUSIN IN MILWAUKEE
MY ONE AND ONLY
MY ONE AND ONLY HIGHLAND
   FLING
MY SHIP
NICE WORK IF YOU CAN GET IT
OF THEE I SING
OH! LADY BE GOOD!
OH GEE! OH JOY!
OH ME! OH MY!
ONE LIFE TO LIVE
PRINCESS OF PURE DELIGHT
PUT ME TO THE TEST
RED HEADED WOMAN, A
SAM AND DELILAH
SEARCH IS THROUGH, THE
SHALL WE DANCE
SHOEIN' THE MARE
SHOES WITH WINGS ON
SLAP THAT BASS
SO AM I
SOMEBODY FROM SOMEWHERE
SOMEONE TO WATCH OVER ME
SOON
STRIKE UP THE BAND
SUNNY DISPOSISH
SURE THING
SWEET AND LOW-DOWN
SWISS MISS
'S WONDERFUL
TCHAIKOWSKY (AND OTHER
   RUSSIANS)
THAT CERTAIN FEELING
THAT LOST BARBERSHOP CHORD
THAT MOMENT OF MOMENTS
THERE'S A BOAT DAT'S LEAVIN'
   SOON FOR NEW YORK
THERE'S NO HOLDING ME

THEY ALL LAUGHED
THEY CAN'T TAKE THAT AWAY
   FROM ME
THINGS ARE LOOKING UP
THIS IS NEW
TRA-LA-LA
TREAT ME ROUGH
WAITING FOR THE SUN TO COME
   OUT
WEEKEND IN THE COUNTRY, A
WHAT CAN YOU SAY IN A LOVE
   SONG?
WHO CARES?
WHY DO I LOVE YOU?
WINTERGREEN FOR PRESIDENT
WORDS WITHOUT MUSIC
YOU'RE A BUILDER UPPER

Gerst, Harvey

IT WON'T BE WRONG

Gesner, Clark

YOU'RE A GOOD MAN, CHARLIE
   BROWN

Gessle, Per

LISTEN TO YOUR HEART
LOOK, THE

Getz, Johnnie

RECESS IN HEAVEN

Getz, Stan

DEAR OLD STOCKHOLM

Getzov, Ray

PLEASE, MR. SUN

Geyer, Stephen

HOT ROD HEARTS
THEME FROM "THE GREATEST
   AMERICAN HERO" (BELIEVE IT
   OR NOT)

Giacalone, Paul

YOU WERE MINE

Giacomazzi, Angelo

ITALIAN THEME, THE

Giacommelli, M.

TAKE OFF

Giant, Bill

ASK ME
THAT'S OLD FASHIONED (THAT'S THE WAY LOVE SHOULD BE)
YOU'RE THE DEVIL IN DISGUISE

Gibb, Andy

SHADOW DANCING
(LOVE IS) THICKER THAN WATER
TIME IS TIME

Gibb, Barry

BOOGIE CHILD
COME ON OVER
DESIRE
(OUR LOVE) DON'T THROW IT ALL AWAY
DON'T WANT TO LIVE INSIDE MYSELF
EMOTION
EVERLASTING LOVE, AN
FANNY (BE TENDER WITH MY LOVE)
FIRST OF MAY
GREASE
GUILTY
HEARTBREAKER
HOLIDAY
HOW CAN YOU MEND A BROKEN HEART
HOW DEEP IS YOUR LOVE
I CAN'T HELP IT
IF I CAN'T HAVE YOU
I JUST WANT TO BE YOUR EVERYTHING
ISLANDS IN THE STREAM
I STARTED A JOKE
I'VE GOTTA GET A MESSAGE TO YOU
JIVE TALKIN'

LONELY DAYS
LOVE ME
LOVE SO RIGHT
LOVE YOU INSIDE OUT
(LIGHTS WENT OUT IN) MASSACHUSETTS
MORE THAN A WOMAN
MY WORLD
NEW YORK MINING DISASTER 1941 (HAVE YOU SEEN MY WIFE, MR. JONES?)
NIGHT FEVER
NIGHTS ON BROADWAY
REST YOUR LOVE ON ME
RUN TO ME
SHADOW DANCING
STAYIN' ALIVE
(LOVE IS) THICKER THAN WATER
THIS WOMAN
TIME IS TIME
TO LOVE SOMEBODY
TOMORROW, TOMORROW
TOO MUCH HEAVEN
TRAGEDY
WHAT KIND OF FOOL
WOMAN IN LOVE
WOMAN IN YOU, THE
WORDS
YOU SHOULD BE DANCING
YOU STEPPED INTO MY LIFE
YOU WIN AGAIN

Gibb, Maurice

BOOGIE CHILD
DESIRE
FANNY (BE TENDER WITH MY LOVE)
FIRST OF MAY
GUILTY
HEARTBREAKER
HOLIDAY
HOW DEEP IS YOUR LOVE
IF I CAN'T HAVE YOU
ISLANDS IN THE STREAM
I STARTED A JOKE
I'VE GOTTA GET A MESSAGE TO YOU
JIVE TALKIN'
LONELY DAYS
LOVE ME
LOVE SO RIGHT
LOVE YOU INSIDE OUT
(LIGHTS WENT OUT IN) MASSACHUSETTS

MORE THAN A WOMAN
NEW YORK MINING DISASTER 1941 (HAVE YOU SEEN MY WIFE, MR. JONES?)
NIGHT FEVER
NIGHTS ON BROADWAY
RUN TO ME
SHADOW DANCING
STAYIN' ALIVE
TO LOVE SOMEBODY
TOMORROW, TOMORROW
TOO MUCH HEAVEN
TRAGEDY
WOMAN IN YOU, THE
WORDS
YOU SHOULD BE DANCING
YOU STEPPED INTO MY LIFE
YOU WIN AGAIN

Gibb, Robin

BOOGIE CHILD
COME ON OVER
DESIRE
EMOTION
FANNY (BE TENDER WITH MY LOVE)
FIRST OF MAY
GUILTY
HEARTBREAKER
HOLD ON TO MY LOVE
HOLIDAY
HOW CAN YOU MEND A BROKEN HEART
HOW DEEP IS YOUR LOVE
IF I CAN'T HAVE YOU
ISLANDS IN THE STREAM
I STARTED A JOKE
I'VE GOTTA GET A MESSAGE TO YOU
JIVE TALKIN'
LONELY DAYS
LOVE ME
LOVE SO RIGHT
LOVE YOU INSIDE OUT
(LIGHTS WENT OUT IN) MASSACHUSETTS
MORE THAN A WOMAN
MY WORLD
NEW YORK MINING DISASTER 1941 (HAVE YOU SEEN MY WIFE, MR. JONES?)
NIGHT FEVER
NIGHTS ON BROADWAY
RUN TO ME

I MISS MY SWISS (MY SWISS MISS
   MISSES ME)
JEANNINE, I DREAM OF LILAC TIME
LILY OF THE VALLEY
LUCKY LINDY
MAMA INEZ
MAMMY JINNY'S JUBILEE
MARIA, MY OWN
MARTA
MY ANGELINE
MY HAWAIIAN SUNRISE
MY MOTHER'S EYES
MY SWEET ADAIR
O, KATHARINA!
PEANUT VENDOR, THE
RAMONA
WAITING FOR THE ROBERT E. LEE

Gilbert, Mary Margaret Hadler

CHAPEL BY THE SEA

Gilbert, Ray

AND ROSES AND ROSES
BLAME IT ON THE SAMBA
CUANTO LE GUSTA (LA PARRANDA)
EVERYBODY HAS A LAUGHING
   PLACE
JOHNNY FEDORA AND ALICE BLUE
   BONNET
MUSKRAT (OR MUSKAT) RAMBLE
SOONER OR LATER
THREE CABALLEROS, THE
TWO SILHOUETTES
WITHOUT YOU (A.K.A. TRES
   PALABRAS)
YOU BELONG TO MY HEART
ZIP-A-DEE-DOO-DAH
ZOOT SUIT (FOR MY SUNDAY GIRL)

Gilbert, Ronald

(WE AIN'T GOT) NOTHIN' YET

Gilbert, Tim

INCENSE AND PEPPERMINTS

Gilbert, V. C.

SHIFTING, WHISPERING SANDS, THE

Gilbert, Vivian

CHAPEL BY THE SEA

Gilbreath, Wayne

WHAT KINDA DEAL IS THIS?

Gilder, Nick

HOT CHILD IN THE CITY
WARRIOR, THE

Giles, R.

NEW FOOL AT AN OLD GAME

Giles, Richard

WHAM BAM (SHANG-A-LANG)

Giles, Rick

YOU'RE NEVER TOO OLD FOR
   YOUNG LOVE

Gilkyson, Neal

GIRL IN THE WOOD

Gilkyson, Stuart

GIRL IN THE WOOD

Gilkyson, Terry

BARE NECESSITIES, THE
CRY OF THE WILD GOOSE, THE
DAY OF JUBILO
GIRL IN THE WOOD
GREENFIELDS
LOVE IS A GOLDEN RING
MARIANNE
MEMORIES ARE MADE OF THIS
MISTER TAP TOE
ROCK OF GIBRALTAR, THE
TELL ME A STORY

Gill, Geoff

HEARTBREAKER

Gill, Peter

RELAX
TWO TRIBES
WELCOME TO THE PLEASUREDOME

Gill, Vince

CINDERELLA

Gillam, David

TEENAGER'S ROMANCE, A

Gillan, Ian

DEEP PURPLE

Gillespie, Arthur

ABSENCE MAKES THE HEART GROW
   FONDER

Gillespie, Haven

BEAUTIFUL
BEAUTIFUL LOVE
BREEZIN' ALONG WITH THE BREEZE
BY THE SYCAMORE TREE
DO YA LOVE ME?
DRIFTING AND DREAMING
GOD'S COUNTRY
HONEY
IT'S THE LITTLE THINGS THAT
   COUNT
LET'S STOP THE CLOCK
LOUISIANA FAIRY TALE
OLD MASTER PAINTER, THE
SANTA CLAUS IS COMIN' TO TOWN
THAT LUCKY OLD SUN (JUST ROLLS
   AROUND HEAVEN ALL DAY)
THERE'S HONEY ON THE MOON
   TONIGHT
WHOSE HONEY ARE YOU?
WHO WOULDN'T BE JEALOUS OF
   YOU?
YOU GO TO MY HEAD

Gillespie, Jerry

HEAVEN'S JUST A SIN AWAY
SOMEBODY'S KNOCKIN'

Gillespie, John Birks "Dizzy"

DIZZY ATMOSPHERE
EMANON
GROOVIN' HIGH
MANTECA
NIGHT IN TUNISIA, A
OOP BOP SH' BAM
SALT PEANUTS

Gillespie, Marian

WHEN YOU LOOK IN THE HEART OF
  A ROSE

Gillette, Stephen

BACK ON THE STREET AGAIN

Gillian, Ian

SMOKE ON THE WATER
WOMAN FROM TOKYO

Gillis, Brad

WHEN YOU CLOSE YOUR EYES

Gilmore, Billy

CHERRY HILL PARK

Gilmore, Douglas

SHE EVEN WOKE ME UP TO SAY
  GOODBYE
WHAT AM I GONNA DO ABOUT YOU

Gilmore, Raymond

DAWN OF CORRECTION

Gilmour, David

LEARNING TO FLY

Gilreath, Jimmy

WHY NOT TONIGHT?

Gilroy, John

DON'T GO IN THE LION'S CAGE
  TONIGHT

Gilroy, Steve

RIGHT ON TRACK

Gilutin, Jonathan

NEW ATTITUDE

Gimbel, Norman

BLUESETTE
CANADIAN SUNSET
DIFFERENT WORLDS
GIRL FROM IPANEMA
HAPPY DAYS
I GOT A NAME
IT GOES LIKE IT GOES
I WILL FOLLOW HIM
I WILL WAIT FOR YOU
KILLING ME SOFTLY WITH HIS SONG
LAND OF DREAMS
LIVE FOR LIFE
LOVE AMONG THE YOUNG
LOVE EYES
MAKING OUR DREAMS COME TRUE
MEATBALLS
MEDITATION (MEDITACAO)
PA-PAYA MAMA
READY TO TAKE A CHANCE AGAIN
RICHARD'S WINDOW
RICOCHET (RICK-O-SHAY)
SUMMER SAMBA (SO NICE)
SWAY (A.K.A. QUIEN SERA)
TENNESSEE WIG WALK
THE TOUCH (LE GRISBI)
TURN ME AROUND
WATCH WHAT HAPPENS
WHALE OF A TALE, A

Gins, Marilyn

CAN'T GET OVER (THE BOSSA NOVA)

Ginsburg, Arnie

JENNIE LEE

Giosasi, Harry

SORRY, I RAN ALL THE WAY HOME

Giraldo

BACK TO PARADISE

Giraud, Hubert

MAMMY BLUE
UNDER PARIS SKIES

Giscombe, Junior

MAMA USED TO SAY

Gish, Billy

CYNTHIA'S IN LOVE

Gist, Kenny, Jr.

NEXT PLANE TO LONDON

Giuffria, Gregg

CALL TO THE HEART

Givens, Van

DON'T SQUEEZE MY SHARMON
STAMP OUT LONELINESS
SWEETHEART OF THE YEAR

Gladston, Phil

IT'S NOT OVER ('TIL IT'S OVER)

Gladstone, Harvey

I DIDN'T WANT TO DO IT

Glanzberg, Norbert

PADAM, PADAM

Glasco, Waymon

FANNIE MAE

Glaser, James W.

SITTIN' IN AN ALL NITE CAFE
WHAT DOES IT TAKE (TO KEEP A
   MAN LIKE YOU SATISFIED)?

Glaser, Tompall

STAND BESIDE ME
STREETS OF BALTIMORE
YOU'RE MAKING A FOOL OUT OF ME

Glasper, David

HOW CAN I FALL

Glass, Preston

DON'T MAKE ME WAIT FOR LOVE
JIMMY LEE
WE DON'T HAVE TO TAKE OUR
   CLOTHES OFF
WHO'S ZOOMIN' WHO

Glasser, Dick

ANGELS IN THE SKY
COME RUNNIN' BACK
I WILL

Glassmeyer, Steven

LOVE OR SOMETHING LIKE IT

Glazer, Tom

MAMA GUITAR
MELODY OF LOVE
MORE
OLD SOLDIERS NEVER DIE
ON TOP OF SPAGHETTI
PUSSY CAT
SKOKIAAN
TILL WE TWO ARE ONE
WORRIED MAN, A

Gleason, Dick

WOMAN (UH-HUH!)

Gleason, Jackie

MELANCHOLY SERENADE

Glen, Catherine Young

ABSENT

Glen, Garry

CAUGHT UP IN THE RAPTURE

Glenn, Artie

CRYING IN THE CHAPEL

Glenn, Darrell

BEAR WITH ME A LITTLE LONGER
INDESCRIBABLY BLUE

Glenn, Lloyd C.

BLUE SHADOWS
CHICA BOO

Glick, Elmo

DANCE WITH ME

Glick, Jesse

KID DAYS
PALE MOON

Glickman, Fred

MULE TRAIN

Glitter, Gary

DO YOU WANNA TOUCH ME (OH
   YEAH)
ROCK AND ROLL PART 2

Glogau, Jack

WAKE UP, AMERICA!

Glosson, Lonnie

WHY DON'T YOU HAUL OFF AND
   LOVE ME?

Glover, Henry

24 HOURS A DAY (365 DAYS A
   YEAR)
ALL MY LOVE BELONGS TO YOU
ANNIE HAD A BABY
BLUES, STAY AWAY FROM ME
CALIFORNIA SUN
DROWN IN MY OWN TEARS
HONKY TONK
I CAN'T GO ON WITHOUT YOU
I'LL DROWN MY TEARS
I LOVE YOU, YES I DO
I'M WAITING JUST FOR YOU
I WANT A BOWLEGGED WOMAN
LET HER DANCE
PEPPERMINT TWIST
ROCK LOVE
TEARDROPS ON YOUR LETTER

Glover, John Henry

I HOPE WE GET TO LOVE IN TIME
YOU DON'T HAVE TO BE A STAR (TO
   BE IN MY SHOW)

Glover, Melvin

BEAT STREET BREAKDOWN
MESSAGE, THE

Glover, Roger

DEEP PURPLE
SMOKE ON THE WATER
STONE COLD
WOMAN FROM TOKYO

Gluck, John, Jr.

BLUE WINTER
IT'S MY PARTY
MECCA
YOUR NAME IS BEAUTIFUL

Gmeiner, Tom

HEART HEELER

Goble, Graham

LADY
NIGHT OWLS, THE

OTHER GUY, THE
TAKE IT EASY ON ME

Godard, Benjamin Louis

IN THE MOON MIST

Godley, Kevin

CRY
I'M MANDY, FLY ME
RUBBER BULLETS

Godwin, Mable

LING, TING, TONG

Goehring, George

LIPSTICK ON YOUR COLLAR

Goell, Kermit

HUGGIN' AND CHALKIN' (A.K.A.
A-HUGGIN' AND A-CHALKIN')
LUNA ROSSA (A.K.A. BLUSHING
MOON)
NEAR YOU
ONE FINGER MELODY
ROSE ANN OF CHARING CROSS
SHEPHERD SERENADE
SLOWLY
WONDER WHEN MY BABY'S COMING
HOME
YAWNING SONG, THE

Goering, Al

WHO'S YOUR LITTLE WHO-ZIS?

Goetschius, Marjorie

I DREAM OF YOU
LAST TIME I SAW YOU, THE

Goetz, Coleman

CONGRATULATIONS
WE'LL HAVE A JUBILEE IN MY OLD
KENTUCKY HOME

Goetz, E. Ray

ALEXANDER'S BAG-PIPE BAND
ASIA
DON'T GO IN THE LION'S CAGE
TONIGHT
FOR ME AND MY GAL
HAVANA
HE GOES TO CHURCH ON SUNDAY
I LOVE IT
IN THE SHADOWS
PARIS
SO THIS IS LOVE
TAKE ME BACK TO THE GARDEN OF
LOVE
THERE'S A GIRL IN HAVANA
WHEN YOU HEAR LOVE'S HELLO
WHO ATE NAPOLEONS WITH
JOSEPHINE WHEN BONAPARTE
WAS FAR AWAY?
WHO'LL BUY MY VIOLETS?
YAAKA HULA HICKEY DULA

Goetzel, Anselm

WHEN THE CHERRY BLOSSOMS
FALL

Goetzman, Gary

TELL ME TOMORROW

Goff, Duke

RUN, WOMAN, RUN

Goffin, Gerry

AT THE CLUB
CHAINS
DON'T ASK ME TO BE FRIENDS
DON'T BRING ME DOWN
DON'T SAY NOTHIN' BAD (ABOUT MY
BABY)
DON'T TRY TO FIGHT IT, BABY
EVERY BREATH I TAKE
GO AWAY LITTLE GIRL
GOIN' BACK
HALFWAY TO PARADISE
HAPPY TIMES (ARE HERE TO STAY)
HER ROYAL MAJESTY
HE'S A BAD BOY
HEY GIRL

HI-DE-HO
HOW CAN I MEET HER?
HOW MANY TEARS
HUNG ON YOU
I CAN'T HEAR YOU NO MORE
I CAN'T STAY MAD AT YOU
I'LL MEET YOU HALFWAY
I'M INTO SOMETHING GOOD
IT MIGHT AS WELL RAIN UNTIL
SEPTEMBER
IT STARTED ALL OVER AGAIN
I'VE GOT BONNIE
I'VE GOT TO USE MY IMAGINATION
I WANT TO STAY HERE
I WASN'T BORN TO FOLLOW
JUST ONCE IN MY LIFE
KEEP YOUR HANDS OFF MY BABY
LET'S TURKEY TROT
LOCO-MOTION, THE
NATURAL WOMAN, A (YOU MAKE
ME FEEL LIKE)
OH NO, NOT MY BABY
OLD SMOKEY LOCOMOTION
ONE FINE DAY
ON THIS SIDE OF GOODBYE
PLEASANT VALLEY SUNDAY
POINT OF NO RETURN
POOR LITTLE RICH GIRL
RUN TO HIM
SAILOR BOY
SAVING ALL MY LOVE FOR YOU
SMACKWATER JACK
SOME KIND-A WONDERFUL (A.K.A.
SOME KIND OF WONDERFUL)
SOMEONE THAT I USED TO LOVE
SO SAD THE SONG
TAKE GOOD CARE OF MY BABY
THEME FROM "MAHOGANY" (DO
YOU KNOW WHERE YOU'RE
GOING TO?)
THIS LITTLE GIRL
TONIGHT I CELEBRATE MY LOVE
UP ON THE ROOF
WALKING PROUD
WHAT A SWEET THING THAT WAS
WHEN MY LITTLE GIRL IS SMILING
WILL YOU LOVE ME TOMORROW?

Goga, Jack

YESTERDAY'S DREAMS
YOU

Goggin, Dan

HOLIER THAN THOU

Golan, Arnold

NO CHEMISE, PLEASE

Gold, Andrew

LONELY BOY
THANK YOU FOR BEING A FRIEND

Gold, Bert

DOGFACE SOLDIER

Gold, Ernest

ACCIDENT'LY ON PURPOSE
EXODUS
IT'S A MAD, MAD, MAD, MAD
   WORLD
ON THE BEACH
PRACTICE MAKES PERFECT
THIRTY ONE FLAVORS

Gold, Ernie

TELL IT TO MY HEART

Gold, Fredda

TWIXT TWELVE AND TWENTY

Gold, Jim

NICE TO BE WITH YOU

Gold, Marty

TELL ME WHY

Gold, Wally

BECAUSE THEY'RE YOUNG
FOOLS' HALL OF FAME
GOOD LUCK CHARM
IT'S MY PARTY
IT'S NOW OR NEVER
LOOK HOMEWARD ANGEL
SHE CAN'T FIND HER KEYS
TIME AND THE RIVER

UTOPIA

Goldberg, Barry

I'VE GOT TO USE MY IMAGINATION

Golde, Franne

BE THERE
BIT BY BIT
DON'T LOOK ANY FURTHER
DON'T YOU WANT ME
FALLING
GOIN' TO THE BANK
NIGHTSHIFT

Golden, John

GOODBYE, GIRLS, I'M THROUGH
I CAN DANCE WITH EVERYONE BUT
   MY WIFE
POOR BUTTERFLY
YOU CAN'T PLAY EVERY
   INSTRUMENT IN THE BAND

Goldenberg, Billy

FIFTY PERCENT
I LOVE TO DANCE

Goldenberg, Mark

ALONG COMES A WOMAN
AUTOMATIC
SOUL KISS

Goldman, Edwin Franko

ON THE MALL

Goldman, James

BEAUTIFUL
HARMONY

Goldman, Steve

HOW MANY TIMES CAN WE SAY
   GOODBYE?

Goldman, William

BEAUTIFUL
HARMONY

Goldmark, Andy

DYNAMITE
FLAMES OF PARADISE
GOIN' TO THE BANK
YOU SHOULD BE MINE (THE WOO
   WOO SONG)

Goldner, George

A.B.C.'S OF LOVE, THE
CAN'T WE BE SWEETHEARTS
I WANT YOU TO BE MY GIRL
LITTLE GIRL OF MINE
MAYBE

Goldsboro, Bobby

AUTUMN OF MY LIFE
BLUE AUTUMN
COWBOY AND THE LADY, THE
IF YOU'VE GOT A HEART
I'M A DRIFTER
LITTLE THINGS
SEE THE FUNNY LITTLE CLOWN
VOODOO WOMAN
WHENEVER HE HOLDS YOU (A.K.A.
   WHENEVER SHE HOLDS YOU)
WITH PEN IN HAND

Goldsen, Michael H.

SAVE THE BONES FOR HENRY
   JONES ('CAUSE HENRY DON'T EAT
   MEAT)

Goldsmith, Cliff

PEANUT BUTTER
WESTERN MOVIES

Goldsmith, J.

TAKE OFF

Goldsmith, Jerry

AMEN

AVE SATANI
THREE STARS WILL SHINE TONIGHT
(THEME FROM "DR. KILDARE")

Goldstein, Bob

WASHINGTON SQUARE

Goldstein, Jerry

CARA-LIN
COME ON DOWN TO MY BOAT
IT'S NICE TO BE WITH YOU
I WANT CANDY
L. A. SUNSHINE
MY BOYFRIEND'S BACK
NIGHT TIME
(YOU MAKE ME FEEL) SO GOOD
SUMMER
WHY CAN'T WE BE FRIENDS?

Gollahon, Gladys

OUR LADY OF FATIMA

Gomez, Johnny

KING SIZE PAPA

Gomm, Ian

CRUEL TO BE KIND
HOLD ON

Gonzalez, Bob

LITTLE GIRL

Goodhart, Al

AUF WIEDERSEHEN, MY DEAR
BLACK EYED SUSAN BROWN
CRAZY WITH LOVE
EVERYTHING'S IN RHYTHM WITH
MY HEART
FIT AS A FIDDLE
HAPPY-GO-LUCKY YOU (AND
BROKEN HEARTED ME)
I APOLOGIZE
I'M IN A DANCING MOOD
IN A LITTLE BOOKSHOP
I SAW STARS
IT'S WINTER AGAIN

JIMMY HAD A NICKEL
JOHNNY DOUGHBOY FOUND A ROSE
IN IRELAND
ROLL UP THE CARPET
ROMANCE RUNS IN THE FAMILY
SERENADE OF THE BELLS
SHE SHALL HAVE MUSIC
THERE ISN'T ANY LIMIT TO MY
LOVE
THIS'LL MAKE YOU WHISTLE
THOSE THINGS MONEY CAN'T BUY
TWO BUCK TIM FROM TIMBUCTOO
WHO WALKS IN WHEN I WALK OUT?
WHY DON'T YOU PRACTICE WHAT
YOU PREACH?

Goodman, Al

LADY IN ERMINE, THE
LOOK AT ME (I'M IN LOVE)
SPECIAL LADY
WHEN HEARTS ARE YOUNG

Goodman, Benny

AIR MAIL SPECIAL
DON'T BE THAT WAY
FLYIN' HOME
GEORGIA JUBILEE
HOME IN THE CLOUDS, A
IF DREAMS COME TRUE
LIFE GOES TO A PARTY
LULLABY IN RHYTHM
SOFT WINDS
SOLO FLIGHT
STOMPIN' AT THE SAVOY
SWINGTIME IN THE ROCKIES
TWO O'CLOCK JUMP

Goodman, Bob

CLOSE TO CATHY

Goodman, Don

FEELIN'S
I'LL PIN A NOTE ON YOUR PILLOW
RING ON HER FINGER, TIME ON
HER HANDS

Goodman, Dorothy

YES TONIGHT, JOSEPHINE

Goodman, Herald

WHEN IT'S LAMP LIGHTIN' TIME IN
THE VALLEY

Goodman, Lillian Rosedale

CHERIE, I LOVE YOU

Goodman, Robert

HIDEAWAY

Goodman, Steve

CITY OF NEW ORLEANS, THE

Goodman, Willie

SEXY MAMA

Goodrum, Randy

BEFORE MY HEART FINDS OUT
BLUER THAN BLUE
BROKEN HEARTED ME
FOOLISH HEART
IF SHE WOULD HAVE BEEN
FAITHFUL
I'LL BE OVER YOU
IT'S SAD TO BELONG
LESSON IN LEAVIN', A
NOW AND FOREVER (YOU AND ME)
OH, SHERRIE
WHAT ARE WE DOIN' IN LOVE?
WHO'S HOLDING DONNA NOW?
YOU NEEDED ME

Goodwin, J. Cheever

ASK THE MAN IN THE MOON
PRETTY GIRL, A

Goodwin, Joe

ALL THAT I WANT IS YOU
BABY SHOES
BILLY (FOR WHEN I WALK)
BREEZE (BLOW MY BABY BACK TO
ME)
EVERYWHERE YOU GO

GEE, BUT I HATE TO GO HOME
ALONE
GIRLIE WAS JUST MADE TO LOVE, A
HOOSIER SWEETHEART
I'M A LONESOME LITTLE RAINDROP
(LOOKING FOR A PLACE TO FALL)
I'M KNEE DEEP IN DAISIES (AND
HEAD OVER HEELS IN LOVE)
LIBERTY BELL, IT'S TIME TO RING
AGAIN
LITTLE HOUSE UPON THE HILL, THE
LOVE, HONOR AND OBEY
LOVE AIN'T NOTHIN' BUT THE
BLUES
NOBODY BUT YOU
ONE DAY IN JUNE (IT MIGHT HAVE
BEEN YOU)
ORANGE BLOSSOM TIME
THAT'S HOW I NEED YOU
THAT WONDERFUL SOMETHING
THEY'RE WEARING 'EM HIGHER IN
HAWAII
THREE WONDERFUL LETTERS FROM
HOME
TIE ME TO YOUR APRON STRINGS
AGAIN
WHAT A WONDERFUL MOTHER
YOU'D BE
WHEN I GET YOU ALONE TONIGHT
WHEN YOU PLAY IN THE GAME OF
LOVE
WHEN YOU'RE SMILING (THE
WHOLE WORLD SMILES WITH
YOU)
YOUR MOTHER AND MINE

Goodwin, Walter

THAT WONDERFUL MOTHER OF
MINE

Goorabian, Kenneth

YOU DON'T WANT ME ANYMORE

Gordon, Alan

CAT IN THE WINDOW (THE BIRD IN
THE SKY)
CELEBRATE
GIRLS IN LOVE
HAPPY TOGETHER
MELANCHOLY MUSIC MAN

MY HEART BELONGS TO ME
SHE'D RATHER BE WITH ME
SHE'S MY GIRL
YOU KNOW WHAT I MEAN

Gordon, Billy

BOO-GA-LOO

Gordon, Del

JUST A LITTLE BIT

Gordon, Irving

BE ANYTHING (BUT BE MINE)
CHRISTMAS DREAMING
DELAWARE
DON'T BURN THE CANDLE AT BOTH
ENDS
GYPSY WITHOUT A SOUL, A
KENTUCKIAN SONG, THE
MAMA FROM THE TRAIN
ME, MYSELF AND I (ARE ALL IN
LOVE WITH YOU)
MISTER AND MISSISSIPPI
MOMENTS IN THE MOONLIGHT
PRELUDE TO A KISS
PYRAMID
SORTA ON THE BORDER
UNFORGETTABLE
WHAT WILL I TELL MY HEART?

Gordon, Jim

LAYLA

Gordon, Kelly

THAT'S LIFE

Gordon, Mack

AFRAID TO DREAM
AIN'TCHA?
AND SO TO BED
ARE YOU IN THE MOOD FOR
MISCHIEF?
AT LAST
BABY, WON'T YOU SAY YOU LOVE
ME?
BOY AND A GIRL WERE DANCING, A
BUT DEFINITELY

BY THE WAY
CHATTANOOGA CHOO CHOO
CHICA CHICA BOOM CHIC
COLLEGE RHYTHM
DANGER—LOVE AT WORK
DID YOU EVER SEE A DREAM
WALKING?
DOIN' THE UPTOWN LOWDOWN
DON'T LET IT BOTHER YOU
DOWN ARGENTINA WAY
FRIENDLY STAR
FROM THE TOP OF YOUR HEAD TO
THE TIP OF YOUR TOES
GOOD MORNING GLORY
GOOD NIGHT, LOVELY LITTLE LADY
GOODNIGHT, MY LOVE
GOT ME DOIN' THINGS
GOT MY MIND ON MUSIC
HEAD OVER HEELS IN LOVE
HELP YOURSELF TO HAPPINESS
(LOOKIE, LOOKIE, LOOKIE) HERE
COMES COOKIE
I, YI, YI, YI, YI (I LIKE YOU VERY
MUCH)
I CAN'T BEGIN TO TELL YOU
I FEEL LIKE A FEATHER IN THE
BREEZE
IF YOU FEEL LIKE SINGING, SING
I HAD THE CRAZIEST DREAM
I KNOW WHY (AND SO DO YOU)
I'M HUMMIN'—I'M WHISTLIN'—I'M
SINGIN'
I'M MAKING BELIEVE
IN ACAPULCO
IN AN OLD DUTCH GARDEN (BY AN
OLD DUTCH MILL)
I NEVER FELT THIS WAY BEFORE
I NEVER KNEW HEAVEN COULD
SPEAK
IN OLD CHICAGO
I PLAYED FIDDLE FOR THE CZAR
IT HAPPENED IN SUN VALLEY
IT HAPPENS EVERY SPRING
IT'S SWELL OF YOU
IT'S THE ANIMAL IN ME
IT'S WITHIN YOUR POWER
IT WAS A NIGHT IN JUNE
I'VE GOT A DATE WITH A DREAM
I'VE GOT A GAL IN KALAMAZOO
I'VE GOT MY HEART SET ON YOU
I WANNA BE IN WINCHELL'S
COLUMN
I WANNA GO TO THE ZOO

I WISH I KNEW
I WISH I WERE ALADDIN
I WOULDN'T TAKE A MILLION
KISS POLKA, THE
KOKOMO, INDIANA
LADY LOVES, A
LET'S GIVE THREE CHEERS FOR
    LOVE
LET'S K-NOCK K-NEES
LISTEN TO THE GERMAN BAND
LOVELINESS OF YOU, THE
LOVE THY NEIGHBOR
LULLABY IN BLUE
MAM'SELLE
MAY I?
MAY I HAVE THE NEXT ROMANCE
    WITH YOU?
MEET THE BEAT OF MY HEART
MORE I SEE YOU, THE
MY HEART IS AN OPEN BOOK
MY HEART TELLS ME
NEVER IN A MILLION YEARS
OH, MY GOODNESS
OLD STRAW HAT, AN
ONCE IN A BLUE MOON
ONCE TOO OFTEN
ONE NEVER KNOWS, DOES ONE?
ON THE BOARDWALK IN ATLANTIC
    CITY
ORCHID TO YOU, AN
PARIS IN THE SPRING
PEOPLE LIKE YOU AND ME
PLAY ME AN OLD FASHIONED
    MELODY
PLEASE PARDON US, WE'RE IN
    LOVE
POEM SET TO MUSIC, A
SECRETS IN THE MOONLIGHT
SERENADE IN BLUE
SHE REMINDS ME OF YOU
SING ME A SONG OF THE ISLANDS
SOMEWHERE IN THE NIGHT
SPEAKING OF HEAVEN
STAR FELL OUT OF HEAVEN, A
STAY AS SWEET AS YOU ARE
STRAIGHT FROM THE SHOULDER
    (RIGHT FROM THE HEART)
SWEET AS A SONG
SWEET SOMEONE
SWING IS HERE TO STAY
TAKE A NUMBER FROM ONE TO TEN
TAKES TWO TO MAKE A BARGAIN
THANKS FOR EV'RYTHING

THAT'S SABOTAGE
THERE'S A BLUEBIRD AT MY
    WINDOW
THERE'S A LULL IN MY LIFE
THERE WILL NEVER BE ANOTHER
    YOU
THEY MET IN RIO
THIS IS ALWAYS
THIS IS THE BEGINNING OF THE
    END
THROUGH A LONG AND SLEEPLESS
    NIGHT
TIME ALONE WILL TELL
TIME ON MY HANDS
TRA-LA-LA-LA
TREE WAS A TREE, A
TROPICAL MAGIC
TWO DREAMS MET
TWO FOR TONIGHT
UNDERNEATH THE HARLEM
    MOON
WAKE UP AND LIVE
WALKING ALONG WITH BILLY
WEEK-END IN HAVANA, A
WERE YOUR EARS BURNING?
WHAT DID I DO?
WHEN I'M WITH YOU
WILHELMINA
WILL I EVER KNOW?
WITH MY EYES WIDE OPEN I'M
    DREAMING
WITHOUT A WORD OF WARNING
WOULD THERE BE LOVE?
YOU CAN'T HAVE EVERYTHING
YOU CAN'T SAY NO TO A SOLDIER
YOU DO
YOU GOTTA S-M-I-L-E TO BE H-A-
    DOUBLE P-Y
YOU HIT THE SPOT
YOU'LL NEVER KNOW
YOU MAKE ME FEEL SO YOUNG
YOU'RE MY PAST, PRESENT AND
    FUTURE
YOU'RE SUCH A COMFORT TO ME
YOU SAY THE SWEETEST THINGS,
    BABY

Gordon, Marc

MAMACITA
MY FOREVER LOVE
PULL OVER

Gordon, Michael Z.

OUT OF LIMITS

Gordon, Paul

FRIENDS AND LOVERS
NEXT TIME I FALL, THE

Gordon, Roscoe

BOOTED
NO MORE DOGGIN'

Gordy, Berry, Jr.

ABC
ALL I COULD DO WAS CRY
BELLS, THE
COME TO ME
DON'T LET HIM SHOP AROUND
DO YOU LOVE ME?
I'LL BE SATISFIED
I'LL BE THERE
I LOVE THE WAY YOU LOVE
I'M LIVIN' IN SHAME
I WANT YOU BACK
LET ME GO THE RIGHT WAY
LONELY TEARDROPS
LOVE YOU SAVE, THE
MAMA'S PEARL
MONEY (THAT'S WHAT I WANT)
NO MATTER WHAT SIGN YOU ARE
SHAKE SHERRY
SHOP AROUND
STEAL ON HOME
SUGAR DADDY
THAT'S WHY (I LOVE YOU SO)
TO BE LOVED
TRY IT BABY
YOU GOT WHAT IT TAKES
YOU'VE MADE ME SO VERY HAPPY

Gordy, Emory, Jr.

TRACES

Gordy, George

BEECHWOOD 4-5789
STUBBORN KIND OF FELLOW

Gordy, Gwen

ALL I COULD DO WAS CRY
I'LL BE SATISFIED
LONELY TEARDROPS
THAT'S WHAT GIRLS ARE MADE FOR
THAT'S WHY (I LOVE YOU SO)
TO BE LOVED
YOU GOT WHAT IT TAKES

Gore, Al

DIGGIN' UP BONES

Gore, Charlie

CRYIN', PRAYIN', WISHIN', WAITIN'
DADDY O

Gore, Lesley

MY TOWN, MY GUY, AND ME
OUT HERE ON MY OWN

Gore, Martin

PEOPLE ARE PEOPLE

Gore, Michael

FAME
OUT HERE ON MY OWN

Gorelik, Kenny

SONGBIRD

Gorgoni, Al

I CAN'T LET GO
I'LL HOLD OUT MY HAND
STEP OUT OF YOUR MIND
YELLOW BANDANA, THE

Gorman, Chuck

SEVENTEEN

Gorman, Freddy

PLEASE MR. POSTMAN
(JUST LIKE) ROMEO AND JULIET
STRANGE I KNOW

Gorman, Ross

ROSE OF THE RIO GRANDE

Gorman, Vinny

HAPPY

Gormé, Eydie

CAN'T GET OVER (THE BOSSA NOVA)

Gorney, Jay

AH, BUT IS IT LOVE
BABY, TAKE A BOW
BROADWAY'S GONE HILLBILLY
BROTHER, CAN YOU SPARE A DIME?
I FOUND A DREAM
I'M LAUGHIN'
IN CHI CHI CASTENANGO
MOONLIGHT AND PRETZELS
THIS IS OUR LAST NIGHT TOGETHER
WHAT WOULDN'T I DO FOR THAT
    MAN?
YOU'RE MY THRILL

Gorrell, Stuart

GEORGIA ON MY MIND

Gorrie, Alan

CUT THE CAKE

Gosdin, Rebe

DON'T LAUGH

Gosdin, Vern

CHISELED IN STONE
DO YOU BELIEVE ME NOW?
I'M STILL CRAZY
SET 'EM UP JOE

Gosh, Bobby

LITTLE BIT MORE, A

Gosting, Dick St. John

MOUNTAIN'S HIGH, THE

TELL ME

Gottehrer, Richard

CARA-LIN
I WANT CANDY
MY BOYFRIEND'S BACK
NIGHT TIME
(YOU MAKE ME FEEL) SO GOOD

Gottler, Archie

AMERICA, I LOVE YOU
BABY ME
BIG CITY BLUES
BREAKAWAY, THE
DON'T BE LIKE THAT
HITTIN' THE CEILING
I HATE TO LOSE YOU
I'M GONNA MAKE HAY WHILE THE
    SUN SHINES IN VIRGINIA
IN THE GOLD FIELDS OF NEVADA
IS IT ANY WONDER?
MAMMY'S CHOCOLATE SOLDIER
ROLLING STONES
SANTA CLAUS IS RIDING THE TRAIL
SING A LITTLE LOVE SONG
THAT'S YOU, BABY
TO WHOM IT MAY CONCERN
WALKING WITH SUSIE
WOULD YOU RATHER BE A COLONEL
    WITH AN EAGLE ON YOUR
    SHOULDER OR A PRIVATE WITH
    A CHICKEN ON YOUR KNEE?

Gottlieb, Larry

HANDS ACROSS AMERICA
PRIDE IS BACK, THE
WHEN SHE WAS MY GIRL

Gottschalk, Louis

LAUGH AND THE WORLD LAUGHS
    WITH YOU

Gould, Boon

SOMETHING ABOUT YOU

Gould, Morton

NOTHIN' FOR NOTHIN'

PAVANNE
THERE MUST BE SOMETHIN' BETTER
  THAN LOVE

Gould, Phil

LESSONS IN LOVE
RUNNING IN THE FAMILY
SOMETHING ABOUT YOU

Gould, Sam

HIGH SCHOOL NIGHTS

Goulding, Edmund

LOVE, YOUR MAGIC SPELL IS
  EVERYWHERE
MAM'SELLE

Gouldman, Graham

ART FOR ART'S SAKE
BUS STOP
DREADLOCK HOLIDAY
FOR YOUR LOVE
HEART FULL OF SOUL
I'M MANDY, FLY ME
I'M NOT IN LOVE
LISTEN, PEOPLE
LOOK THROUGH ANY WINDOW
NO MILK TODAY
PEOPLE IN LOVE
RUBBER BULLETS
THINGS WE DO FOR LOVE, THE

Grace, Roche

ROCKY MOUNTAIN WAY

Grady, John C.

MY BABY'S COMING HOME

Graff, George, Jr.

AS LONG AS THE WORLD ROLLS ON
I LOVE THE NAME OF MARY
IN THE GARDEN OF TOMORROW
TILL THE SANDS OF THE DESERT
  GROW COLD
WAKE UP, AMERICA!
WHEN IRISH EYES ARE SMILING

Graffagnino, Jake

STOP AND THINK IT OVER

Grafton, Gerald

FOU THE NOO (OR, SOMETHING IN
  THE BOTTLE FOR THE MORNING)
I LOVE A LASSIE (OR, MA SCOTCH
  BLUEBELL)
WEE DEOCH-AN-DORIS

Graham, Berkeley

IF I CARED A LITTLE BIT LESS

Graham, Charles

PICTURE THAT IS TURNED TOWARD
  THE WALL, THE
SHE WAS HAPPY TILL SHE MET YOU
TWO LITTLE GIRLS IN BLUE

Graham, Dick

FLAME, THE

Graham, Harry

KING'S HORSES, THE (AND THE
  KING'S MEN)

Graham, Howard

WHEN THE HARVEST DAYS ARE
  OVER, JESSIE DEAR

Graham, Irvin

I BELIEVE
YOU BETTER GO NOW

Graham, Leo, Jr.

SHINING STAR

Graham, Roger

I AIN'T GOT NOBODY

Graham, Ronny

I'M IN LOVE WITH MISS LOGAN

ONE LITTLE WORLD APART

Graham, Steve

INTERMISSION RIFF
OFF SHORE

Grainger, Gary

AIN'T LOVE A BITCH
I WAS ONLY JOKING
PASSION

Grainger, M.

BLACK IS BLACK

Grainger, Porter

CHARLESTON CRAZY
PRESCRIPTION FOR THE BLUES
'TAINT NOBODY'S BIZNESS IF I DO

Gramm, Lou

BLUE MORNING, BLUE DAY
COLD AS ICE
DIRTY WHITE BOY
DOUBLE VISION
DOWN ON LOVE
HEAD GAMES
HOT BLOODED
JUKE BOX HERO
LONG, LONG WAY FROM HOME
MIDNIGHT BLUE
SAY YOU WILL
THAT WAS YESTERDAY
WAITING FOR A GIRL LIKE YOU

Granahan, Gerry

NO CHEMISE, PLEASE

Granata, Rocco

MARINA

Grand, Murray

APRIL IN FAIRBANKS
BOOZERS AND LOSERS
COME BY SUNDAY
COMMENT ALLEZ-VOUS?

GOOD FRIENDS
GUESS WHO I SAW TODAY?
NOT A MOMENT TOO SOON
THURSDAY'S CHILD

Grande, Vincent

BLUES SERENADE, A

Granier, R.

TO SIR WITH LOVE

Grant, Bert

ALONG THE ROCKY ROCK TO
    DUBLIN
ARRAH GO ON, I'M GONNA GO
    BACK TO OREGON
DON'T BLAME IT ALL ON BROADWAY
IF I KNOCK THE "L" OUT OF KELLY
WHEN THE ANGELUS IS RINGING
WHEN YOU'RE AWAY

Grant, Cornelius

I KNOW I'M LOSING YOU
YOU'RE MY EVERYTHING

Grant, Eddy

BABY, COME BACK
ELECTRIC AVENUE
ROMANCING THE STONE

Grant, Gerry

RING-A-LING-A-LARIO

Grant, Harold

HERE

Grant, Ian

LET THERE BE LOVE

Grant, Marshall

LONG-LEGGED GUITAR PICKIN' MAN

Grant, Micki

CLEANIN' WOMEN
DON'T BOTHER ME, I CAN'T COPE
I GOTTA KEEP MOVIN'
PINK SHOELACES

Grant, Patrick

LOVE DON'T YOU GO THROUGH NO
    CHANGES ON ME
SUPERNATURAL THING—PART 1

Grant, Rodgers

YEH! YEH!

Grant, Thomas

DANCING YOUR MEMORY AWAY

Grantham, Bill

'LEVEN-THIRTY SATURDAY NIGHT

Grashey, Don

ARE YOU MINE?

Grasso, Richie

SWEET CHERRY WINE

Graves, Burkett

COME WALK WITH ME

Graves, James

SHOOT YOUR SHOT

Graves, Pete

BUMMIN' AROUND

Gray, Billy

BREAKIN' THE RULES
GOLDEN GUITAR
WAITING IN THE LOBBY OF YOUR
    HEART
WE'VE GONE TOO FAR
YESTERDAY'S GIRL

YOU CAN'T HAVE MY LOVE

Gray, Charles

MEXICAN RADIO

Gray, Chauncey

BYE BYE BLUES
BY MY SIDE
YOU'RE THE ONE I CARE FOR

Gray, Claude

FAMILY BIBLE
I NEVER HAD THE ONE I WANTED

Gray, Dobie

GOT MY HEART SET ON YOU

Gray, Ed

CRYSTAL BLUE PERSUASION

Gray, J.

BUZZ-BUZZ-BUZZ
JIVIN' AROUND

Gray, Jerry

I DREAMT I DWELT IN HARLEM
PENNSYLVANIA 6-5000
STRING OF PEARLS, A

Gray, Mark

TAKE ME DOWN

Gray, Thomas J.

ANY LITTLE GIRL THAT'S A NICE
    LITTLE GIRL IS THE RIGHT
    LITTLE GIRL FOR ME
GOODNIGHT, NURSE

Gray, Thomas

MONEY CHANGES EVERYTHING

1407

Gray, Timothy

FOREVER AND A DAY
IF I GAVE YOU
I KNOW YOUR HEART
SOMETHING TELLS ME
WAS SHE PRETTIER THAN I?
YOU'D BETTER LOVE ME

Gray, Wardell

TWISTED

Gray, Wayne

CRADLE OF LOVE

Gray, William B.

SHE IS MORE TO BE PITIED THAN
    CENSURED
VOLUNTEER ORGANIST, THE

Gray, Yvonne

DANCIN' MAN
LADY LOVE

Graydon, Jay

AFTER THE LOVE HAS GONE
BREAKIN' AWAY
MORNIN'
TURN YOUR LOVE AROUND
WHO'S HOLDING DONNA NOW?

Grean, Charles R.

EDDY'S SONG
FREE HOME DEMONSTRATION
HE'LL HAVE TO STAY
I DREAMED
SOMETHING OLD, SOMETHING NEW
SWEET VIOLETS
THING, THE

Greaves, R. B.

TAKE A LETTER, MARIA

Green, Adolph

ALL YOU NEED IS A QUARTER

ASKING FOR YOU
BELLS ARE RINGING
CLOSE HARMONY
COMES ONCE IN A LIFETIME
CRY LIKE THE WIND
DISTANT MELODY
FADE OUT—FADE IN
FIREWORKS
FRENCH LESSON, THE
HOLD ME—HOLD ME—HOLD ME
HOW CAN YOU DESCRIBE A FACE?
I CAN COOK TOO
I GET CARRIED AWAY
I KNOW ABOUT LOVE
I LIKE MYSELF
I'M WITH YOU
INDEPENDENT (ON MY OWN)
IT'S LOVE
JUST IN TIME
LEGACY, THE
LITTLE BIT IN LOVE
LONELY TOWN
LONG BEFORE I KNEW YOU
LOOKING BACK
LUCKY TO BE ME
MAKE SOMEONE HAPPY
MU-CHA-CHA
NEVER NEVER LAND
NEW YORK, NEW YORK (THE
    BRONX IS UP AND THE BATTERY
    IS DOWN)
NOW
OHIO
ON THE TWENTIETH CENTURY
PARTY'S OVER, THE
QUIET GIRL, A
RIGHT GIRL FOR ME, THE
SAY, DARLING
SOME OTHER TIME
STRICTLY U.S.A.
THANKS A LOT, BUT NO THANKS
TIME FOR PARTING
WENDY
WHAT'S NEW AT THE ZOO?
WHO KNOWS WHAT MIGHT HAVE
    BEEN?
WRONG NOTE RAG
YA GOT ME
YOU MUSN'T BE DISCOURAGED

Green, Al

BELLE

CALL ME (COME BACK HOME)
I'M STILL IN LOVE WITH YOU
LET'S STAY TOGETHER
LIVIN' FOR YOU
LOOK WHAT YOU DONE FOR ME
L-O-V-E (LOVE)
SHA-LA-LA (MAKE ME HAPPY)
TAKE ME TO THE RIVER
TIRED OF BEING ALONE
YOU OUGHT TO BE WITH ME

Green, Bud

AFTER ALL
ALABAMY BOUND
AWAY DOWN SOUTH IN HEAVEN
CONGRATULATIONS
DAY AFTER DAY
DO SOMETHING
FLAT FOOT FLOOGIE, THE
GOOD LITTLE, BAD LITTLE YOU
HONESTLY
IF YOU EVER CHANGE YOUR MIND
I'LL ALWAYS BE IN LOVE WITH YOU
I LOVE MY BABY (MY BABY LOVES
    ME)
MAN WHO COMES AROUND, THE
OH! BOY, WHAT A GIRL
ONCE IN A WHILE
ONLY, ONLY ONE FOR ME, THE
SENTIMENTAL JOURNEY
SWINGY LITTLE THING
THAT'S MY WEAKNESS NOW
VOL VISTU GAILY STAR
YA GOTTA KNOW HOW TO LOVE
YOU FIT INTO THE PICTURE
YOU SHOWED ME THE WAY

Green, Earl

SIX DAYS ON THE ROAD

Green, Eddie

GOOD MAN IS HARD TO FIND, A

Green, Florence

SOLDIER BOY

Green, G.

CUTIE PIE

Green, Garfield

JEALOUS KIND OF FELLA

Green, George Michael

HURT SO GOOD

Green, George

COME ON IN (YOU DID THE BEST
YOU COULD DO)

Green, Harold

I GUESS I'LL HAVE TO DREAM THE
REST
IT'S MAKE BELIEVE BALLROOM
TIME

Green, J.

CAN'TCHA SAY (YOU BELIEVE IN
ME)

Green, Joe

ACROSS THE ALLEY FROM THE
ALAMO

Green, John

BODY AND SOUL
COQUETTE
EASY COME, EASY GO
HELLO, MY LOVER, GOODBYE
I COVER THE WATERFRONT
I'M YOURS
I WANNA BE LOVED
NOT BAD
OUT OF NOWHERE
RAIN, RAIN, GO AWAY!
REPEAL THE BLUES
SOMETHING IN THE WIND
SONG OF RAINTREE COUNTY, THE
TURNTABLE SONG, THE
WEEP NO MORE, MY BABY
WORLD IS MINE, THE
YOU AND YOUR LOVE
YOU'RE MINE, YOU

Green, Kathe

LOVE'S GOT A LINE ON YOU

Green, Leo

DISCO INFERNO

Green, Lil

ROMANCE IN THE DARK

Green, Marlin

COVER ME

Green, Mort

YOU GO YOUR WAY (AND I'LL GO
CRAZY)

Green, Paul

ON THE RIO GRANDE

Green, Peter

BEAUTIFUL SUNDAY
BLACK MAGIC WOMAN
OH WELL

Green, Phil

SAY WONDERFUL THINGS

Green, Sanford

AM I WASTING MY TIME?
PLAY ME HEARTS AND FLOWERS (I
WANNA CRY)

Green, Schuyler

IN ARCADY
ISN'T IT GREAT TO BE MARRIED?

Green, Tony

COME TO ME

Green, Viviane

LOVE ME! LOVE ME! LOVE ME!

Greenall, Peter

STAND OR FALL

Greenall, Rupert

ONE THING LEADS TO ANOTHER
SECRET SEPARATION

Greenaway, Roger

DOCTOR'S ORDERS
HERE COMES THAT RAINY DAY
FEELING AGAIN
I'D LIKE TO TEACH THE WORLD TO
SING (IN PERFECT HARMONY)
IT'S LIKE WE NEVER SAID
GOODBYE
JEANS ON
LONG COOL WOMAN (IN A BLACK
DRESS)
MY BABY LOVES LOVIN'
SAY YOU'LL STAY UNTIL TOMORROW
YOU'VE GOT YOUR TROUBLES

Greenbach, John

SAD TOMORROWS

Greenbank, Harry

AMOROUS GOLDFISH, THE
CHIN-CHIN-CHINAMAN
CHON KINA
JEWEL OF ASIA, THE
SIX LITTLE WIVES
SOCIETY (OH! I LOVE SOCIETY)
SOLDIERS IN THE PARK, THE
TOY MONKEY, THE

Greenbaum, Norman

EGGPLANT THAT ATE CHICAGO, THE
SPIRIT IN THE SKY

Greenberg, Abner

C'EST VOUS (IT'S YOU)

Greenberg, Elliot

RESPECTABLE
SWEET TALKIN' GUY

Greenberg, Steven

FUNKYTOWN

Greene, Alan

TURN AROUND

Greene, Earl

GIVE ME 40 ACRES

Greene, Joe

AND HER TEARS FLOWED LIKE WINE
DON'T LET THE SUN CATCH YOU CRYIN'
SOOTHE ME

Greene, John

GIVE ME 40 ACRES

Greene, Joseph Arthur

OUTA-SPACE

Greene, Mort

NEVADA
SLEEPY SERENADE
STARS IN YOUR EYES (A.K.A. MARS)
THRILLED
WHEN THERE'S A BREEZE ON LAKE LOUISE

Greene, Schuyler

BABES IN THE WOOD
DOLLY
MAGIC MELODY, THE
NODDING ROSES
YOU KNOW AND I KNOW

Greene, Tim

TWO OF HEARTS

Greenebaum, John

DOWN ON THE FARM
HEART HEELER

Greenfield, Howard

ALICE IN WONDERLAND

ANOTHER SLEEPLESS NIGHT
BAD GIRL
BREAKING UP IS HARD TO DO
BREAKIN' IN A BRAND NEW BROKEN HEART
CALENDAR GIRL
CHARMS
CLOSEST THING TO HEAVEN, THE
CRYING IN THE RAIN
DARKEST STREET IN TOWN
DIARY, THE
DID YOU HAVE A HAPPY BIRTHDAY?
DON'T READ THE LETTER
EVERYBODY'S SOMEBODY'S FOOL
FALLIN'
FOOLISH LITTLE GIRL
FRANKIE
HAPPY BIRTHDAY, SWEET SIXTEEN
HUNGRY YEARS, THE
I GO APE
IT HURTS TO BE IN LOVE
I WAITED TOO LONG
I WISH I'D NEVER BEEN BORN
KING OF CLOWNS
LET'S GO STEADY AGAIN
LITTLE DEVIL
LOVE WILL KEEP US TOGETHER
MY HEART HAS A MIND OF ITS OWN
NEXT DOOR TO AN ANGEL
OH! CAROL
ONE DAY OF YOUR LIFE
POOR LITTLE PUPPET
PUPPET MAN
RUN SAMSON RUN
STAIRWAY TO HEAVEN
STUPID CUPID
TURN ON THE SUNSHINE
VENUS IN BLUE JEANS
WAY OF A CLOWN, THE
WHERE THE BOYS ARE
YOU MEAN EVERYTHING TO ME
YOU NEVER DONE IT LIKE THAT
YOUR USED TO BE

Greenway, Roger

I WAS KAISER BILL'S BATMAN
WAY IT USED TO BE, THE

Greenwich, Ellie

BABY, I LOVE YOU
BE MY BABY

CHAPEL OF LOVE
DA DOO RON RON (WHEN HE WALKED ME HOME)
DO WAH DIDDY DIDDY
FINE, FINE BOY, A
GIVE US YOUR BLESSING
HANKY PANKY
HE AIN'T NO ANGEL
I CAN HEAR MUSIC
I'LL TAKE YOU WHERE THE MUSIC'S PLAYING
I WANNA LOVE HIM SO BAD
KIND OF BOY YOU CAN'T FORGET, THE
LEADER OF THE PACK
LITTLE BOY
LOOK OF LOVE
MAYBE I KNOW
PEOPLE SAY
RIVER DEEP—MOUNTAIN HIGH
ROCK OF AGES
TAKE ME HOME TONIGHT
THEN HE KISSED ME
WAIT 'TIL MY BOBBY GETS HOME
WE'RE GONNA MAKE IT (AFTER ALL)
WHY DO LOVERS BREAK EACH OTHER'S HEARTS?

Greenwood, Lee

GOD BLESS THE U.S.A.

Greer, Dan

LET ME LOVE YOU TONIGHT

Greer, Jesse

BABY BLUE EYES
BUILDING A NEST FOR MARY
CHEER UP
CLIMBING UP THE LADDER OF LOVE
FLAPPERETTE
FRESHIE
I CAN'T LOSE THAT LONGING FOR YOU
I COULDN'T BE MEAN TO YOU
I'M GONNA MEET MY SWEETIE NOW
JUST YOU, JUST ME
LOW DOWN RHYTHM
OLD MILL WHEEL
ONCE IN A LIFETIME

ONE STEP TO HEAVEN
ON THE BEACH WITH YOU
REACHING FOR THE MOON
SLEEPY HEAD
SONG OF THE FOOL
YOU FIT INTO THE PICTURE

Gregory, Chuck

YOU'RE THE ONLY GOOD THING
   (THAT'S HAPPENED TO ME)

Gregory, Paul

YOU CALL IT MADNESS (BUT I CALL
   IT LOVE)

Grehan, Derry

WHAT DOES IT TAKE

Greiner, Al

DONDE ESTA SANTA CLAUS?
   (WHERE IS SANTA CLAUS?)

Grenet, Eliseo

MAMA INEZ

Grever, Maria

HEARTSTRINGS
MAGIC IS THE MOONLIGHT
TI-PI-TIN
WHAT A DIFF'RENCE A DAY MADE
   (A.K.A. WHAT A DIFF'RENCE A
   DAY MAKES)

Grey, Clifford

CHARMING
DREAM LOVER
GOT A DATE WITH AN ANGEL
HALLELUJAH!
IF HE CARED
IF YOU WERE THE ONLY GIRL IN
   THE WORLD
LONELY
MA BELLE
MARCH OF THE GRENADIERS
MARCH OF THE MUSKETEERS
MY LOVE PARADE

ONE MORE HOUR OF LOVE
PARIS, STAY THE SAME
ROGUE SONG, THE
SALLY
SHEPHERD'S SERENADE, THE
SONG OF THE SHIRT, THE
SUNDAY
VALENCIA
WHEN I'M LOOKING AT YOU
WHILE HEARTS ARE SINGING
WHITE DOVE, THE
WHY, OH WHY?
WILD ROSE

Grey, Joe

RUNNIN' WILD!

Grey, Zane

EVERY TIME I TURN AROUND (BACK
   IN LOVE AGAIN)

Grier, Jimmie

DON'T BE AFRAID TO TELL YOUR
   MOTHER
OBJECT OF MY AFFECTION, THE
WHAT'S THE REASON (I'M NOT
   PLEASIN' YOU)?

Griff, Ray

BETTER MOVE IT ON HOME
IT COULDN'T HAVE BEEN ANY
   BETTER
WHO'S GONNA PLAY THIS OLD
   PIANO?

Griffey, Dana

IT'S A LOVE THING

Griffey, Dick

SOUL TRAIN '75

Griffin, Bill

LOVE MACHINE

Griffin, Gene

HIM OR ME
I LIKE
JUST GOT PAID
MY FANTASY
MY PREROGATIVE

Griffin, Howard

BOPPIN' THE BLUES

Griffin, Ken

YOU CAN'T BE TRUE, DEAR

Griffin, LeRoy

STORY UNTOLD, A

Griffin, Melvin

LOVE IS BETTER IN THE A.M.

Griffin, Paul

FEZ, THE

Griffin, Reggie

BEAT STREET BREAKDOWN

Griffin, Rex

JUST CALL ME LONESOME
LET FORGIVENESS IN

Griffin, Trevor

LOVE IS LIKE OXYGEN

Griffith, Nanci

COLD HEARTS/CLOSED MINDS
TROUBLE IN THE FIELDS

Grimaldi, Jerry

I CAN NEVER GO HOME ANYMORE

Grimsley, C. W.

I'M WALKING THE DOG

Grimsley, E. M.

I'M WALKING THE DOG

Grisham, Audrey

THERE STANDS THE GLASS

Griswold, Earl

GAL WHO INVENTED KISSIN', THE

Groce, Larry

JUNK FOOD JUNKIE

Grofé, Ferde

COUNT YOUR BLESSINGS
DAYBREAK
ON THE TRAIL
THREE SHADES OF BLUE
WONDERFUL ONE (MY)

Grogan, Phil

ESPECIALLY FOR YOU

Gross, Henry

SHANNON

Gross, Larry

BELLA LINDA

Gross, Walter

TENDERLY
YOUR LOVE

Grossman, Bernard

TOO BEAUTIFUL FOR WORDS
WE'RE GOING OVER
YOU DIDN'T WANT ME WHEN YOU
   HAD ME (SO WHY DO YOU WANT
   ME NOW?)

Grossman, Julius

TZENA, TZENA, TZENA

Grossmith, George

DANCING TIME

Grosz, Will

ALONG THE SANTA FE TRAIL
IN AN OLD DUTCH GARDEN (BY AN
   OLD DUTCH MILL)
ISLE OF CAPRI
MAKE-BELIEVE ISLAND
MILLER'S DAUGHTER MARIANNE,
   THE
RED SAILS IN THE SUNSET
TOMORROW NIGHT

Grouya, Ted

FLAMINGO
I HEARD YOU CRIED LAST NIGHT
IN MY ARMS

Groves, Steve

TOAST AND MARMALADE FOR TWO

Grown, George

OPEN SESAME

Gruber, Edmund L.

CAISSONS GO ROLLING ALONG, THE
   (OVER HILL, OVER DALE)

Grudeff, Marian

ALL
MARRIED MAN, A

Grusin, Dave

CHILD OF THE UNIVERSE
GOOD TIMES
IT MIGHT BE YOU
KEEP YOUR EYE ON THE SPARROW
   (BARETTA'S THEME)

Gruska, Jay

FRIENDS AND LOVERS

Guaraldi, Vincent

CAST YOUR FATE TO THE WIND

Guard, Dave

WORRIED MAN, A

Guare, John

LOVE HAS DRIVEN ME SANE

Guercio, James

DISTANT SHORES
SUSAN

Guess Who, The

DANCIN' FOOL

Guest, Edgar

COUNT YOUR BLESSINGS

Guest, William

I DON'T WANT TO DO WRONG

Guida, Carmela

IF YOU WANNA BE HAPPY

Guida, Frank J.

DEAR LADY TWIST
IF YOU WANNA BE HAPPY
NEW ORLEANS
NOT ME
QUARTER TO THREE
TWIST, TWIST SENORA

Guidry, Greg

GOIN' DOWN

Guidry, Robert

BUT I DO
SEE YOU LATER, ALLIGATOR

Guiffre, Jimmy

FOUR BROTHERS

Guinn, Janis Lee

CHICK-A-BOOM (DON'T YA JES' LOVE
   IT)

Guion, King

SOLITAIRE

Guldberg, John

WHITE HORSE

Gumble, Albert

ARE YOU SINCERE?
AT THE MISSISSIPPI CABARET
CHANTICLEER RAG, THE
HOW'S EVERY LITTLE THING IN
   DIXIE?
PLAYMATES
REBECCA OF SUNNYBROOK FARM
SOMEBODY'S WAITING FOR YOU
THERE'S A LUMP OF SUGAR DOWN
   IN DIXIE
WHEN I WALTZ WITH YOU
WINTER

Gummoe, John

RHYTHM OF THE RAIN

Gundry, Bob

IF YOU EVER CHANGE YOUR MIND

Guns N' Roses

SWEET CHILD O' MINE

**Gunter, Sid
"Hardrock"**

BIRMINGHAM BOUNCE

Gurd, Geoff

LOVE IS A HOUSE

Gurnee, Hal

DRIFTING APART

Gurvitz, Paul

WHO FOUND WHO

Guryan, Margo

LONELY WOMAN
SUNDAY MORNIN'

Gusman, Meyer

GYPSY DREAM ROSE
UNDERNEATH THE RUSSIAN MOON

Gussin, David

ENVY

Guthrie, Arlo

ALICE'S RESTAURANT

Guthrie, Beverly

LOVE ME FOREVER

Guthrie, Gwen

AIN'T NOTHIN' GOIN' ON BUT THE
   RENT
LOVE DON'T YOU GO THROUGH NO
   CHANGES ON ME
SUPERNATURAL THING—PART 1

**Guthrie, Leon Jerry
(Jack)**

OKLAHOMA HILLS

Guthrie, Woody

OKLAHOMA HILLS
PHILADELPHIA LAWYER
PRETTY BOY FLOYD
SO LONG (IT'S BEEN GOOD TO KNOW
   YUH)
THIS LAND IS YOUR LAND

Guy, Billy

AIN'T THAT JUST LIKE ME

Guzman, Connie

HOLD ME

Gwangwa, Jonas

CRY FREEDOM

Haber, Susan

PLEASE DON'T EVER LEAVE ME

Haberman, William

I'M HAPPY THAT LOVE HAS FOUND
   YOU

Hackady, Hal

SHAKE ME I RATTLE (SQUEEZE ME I
   CRY)

Hackett, Naimy

TARZAN BOY

Hackett, Steve

WHEN THE HEART RULES THE
   MIND

Haddock, Durward

THERE SHE GOES

Hadjidakis, Manos

ALL ALONE AM I
NEVER ON SUNDAY
TOPKAPI
WHITE ROSE OF ATHENS, THE

Hadler, Mary M.

SHIFTING, WHISPERING SANDS, THE

Haenschen, Gustave

MANHATTAN (MERRY-GO-ROUND)

UNDERNEATH THE JAPANESE MOON

Hagar, Sammy

DREAMS
GIVE TO LIVE
LOVE WALKS IN
WHEN IT'S LOVE
WHY CAN'T THIS BE LOVE
YOUR LOVE IS DRIVING ME CRAZY

Hagen, Earle

HARLEM NOCTURNE

Hager, Clyde

THAT WONDERFUL MOTHER OF
   MINE

Hager, W.

LAUGHING WATER

Haggard, Kelli

THAT'S ALL IN THE MOVIES

Haggard, Merle

ARE THE GOOD TIMES REALLY
   OVER (I WISH A BUCK WAS STILL
   SILVER)
AWAYS WANTING YOU
BIG CITY
BOTTLE LET ME DOWN, THE
BRANDED MAN
DADDY FRANK (THE GUITAR MAN)
EVERYBODY'S HAD THE BLUES
FIGHTIN' SIDE OF ME, THE
FROM GRACELAND TO THE
   PROMISED LAND
GRANDMA HARP
HUNGRY EYES
I'D RATHER BE GONE
IF WE MAKE IT THROUGH
   DECEMBER
I THINK I'LL JUST STAY HERE AND
   DRINK
I THREW AWAY THE ROSE
LEGEND OF BONNIE AND CLYDE,
   THE
MAMA TRIED

OKIE FROM MUSKOGEE
OLD MAN FROM THE MOUNTAIN
PLACE TO FALL APART, A
SING ME BACK HOME
SOMEDAY WE'LL LOOK BACK
SOMEDAY WHEN THINGS ARE GOOD
SWINGING DOORS
THAT'S ALL IN THE MOVIES
TWINKLE, TWINKLE, LUCKY STAR
WORKING MAN BLUES

Haggart, Bob

BIG NOISE FROM WINNETKA
I'M PRAYIN' HUMBLE
SOUTH RAMPART STREET PARADE
WHAT'S NEW?

Hague, Albert

ERBIE FITCH'S TWITCH
IT'S A HELLUVA WAY TO RUN A
   LOVE AFFAIR
JUST FOR ONCE
PICK-POCKET TANGO
UNCLE SAM RAG, THE
YOUNG AND FOOLISH

Hague, Steve

SO IN LOVE

Haig, Bernhardt

BY THE BEND OF THE RIVER

Haines, W. G.

BIGGEST ASPIDASTRA IN THE
   WORLD, THE

Halcomb, Robert

LAST RIDE, THE

Haldeman, Oakley

BRUSH THOSE TEARS FROM YOUR
   EYES
HERE COMES SANTA CLAUS (DOWN
   SANTA CLAUS LANE)
I WISH I HAD NEVER MET
   SUNSHINE

THO' I TRIED (I CAN'T FORGET YOU)

Hale, Andrew

PARADISE

Haley, Bill

CRAZY, MAN, CRAZY
SKINNY MINNIE

Halford, Rob

YOU'VE GOT ANOTHER THING
   COMIN'

Halifax, Hal

PENNY SERENADE

Hall, Aaron

I LIKE

Hall, Bunny

BREAKDANCE
NEW ATTITUDE

Hall, Carol

BALLAD OF THE CHRISTMAS
   DONKEY, THE
DOATSY MAE
HARD CANDY CHRISTMAS
JENNY REBECCA
NO LIES
TWENTY-FOUR HOURS OF LOVIN'

Hall, Dan

CAN'T WE TRY

Hall, Daryl

ADULT EDUCATION
DID IT IN A MINUTE
DREAMTIME
EVERYTHING YOUR HEART DESIRES
EVERYTIME YOU GO AWAY
I CAN'T GO FOR THAT (NO CAN DO)
IT'S A LAUGH
KISS ON MY LIST

MANEATER
METHOD OF MODERN LOVE
ONE ON ONE
OUT OF TOUCH
PRIVATE EYES
RICH GIRL
SARA SMILE
SAY IT ISN'T SO
SHE'S GONE
SOME THINGS ARE BETTER LEFT
　UNSAID
SWEPT AWAY
WAIT FOR ME
YOU MAKE MY DREAMS

Hall, Fred

ELEVEN MORE MONTHS AND TEN
　MORE DAYS
I GOT A CODE IN MY DOSE

Hall, Guy H.

JOHNSON RAG

Hall, Jack

KEEP ON SMILIN'

Hall, James

KEEP ON SMILIN'

Hall, J. Graydon

THAT'S HOW MUCH I LOVE YOU

Hall, Johanna

DANCE WITH ME
POWER
REACH
STILL THE ONE

Hall, John T.

WEDDING OF THE WINDS
WHEN YOU'VE HAD A LITTLE LOVE
　YOU WANT A LITTLE MORE

Hall, John

DANCE WITH ME

POWER
REACH
STILL THE ONE
YOU CAN DREAM OF ME

Hall, Oliver

REVENGE

Hall, Owen

SHADE OF THE PALM, THE
TELL ME PRETTY MAIDEN (ARE
　THERE ANY MORE AT HOME
　LIKE YOU?)

Hall, Reginald

YOU TALK TOO MUCH

Hall, Rich

COWBOY SERENADE, THE

Hall, Rick

SWEET AND INNOCENT
TOO WEAK TO FIGHT

Hall, Roe E.

ACHING, BREAKING HEART

Hall, Ruth

BLOODSHOT EYES

Hall, Tom T.

ARTIFICIAL ROSE
BACK POCKET MONEY
BALLAD OF FORTY DOLLARS
D. J. FOR A DAY
FASTER HORSES
HARPER VALLEY P.T.A.
I CARE
I LOVE
MAD
MARGIE'S AT THE LINCOLN PARK
　INN
ONE MORE MILE
POOL SHARK, THE
SNEAKY SNAKE

THERE AIN'T NO EASY RUN
WEEK IN A COUNTRY JAIL, A
WHAT WE'RE FIGHTING FOR
YEAR THAT CLAYTON DELANEY
　DIED, THE
YOU ALWAYS COME BACK (TO
　HURTING ME)

Hall, Wendell

IT AIN'T GONNA RAIN NO MO'
RED-HEADED MUSIC MAKER

Hall, William C.

LOVE IS THE FOUNDATION

Halle, R. L.

BABY'S PRAYER

Halley, Bill

ROLL ALONG KENTUCKY MOON

Halley, Bob

DEAR LONELY HEARTS

Halversson, Jean

ONCE BITTEN, TWICE SHY

Ham, William Peter

BABY BLUE
DAY AFTER DAY
NO MATTER WHAT
WITHOUT YOU

Hamati, Sandor

BLUEBIRD OF HAPPINESS

Hamblen, Stuart

IT IS NO SECRET (WHAT GOD CAN
　DO)
MAINLINER (THE HAWK WITH
　SILVER WINGS)
OPEN UP YOUR HEART (AND LET
　THE SUNSHINE IN)

REMEMBER ME (I'M THE ONE WHO
   LOVES YOU)
THIS OLE HOUSE

Hamilton, Al

HUNGRY FOR LOVE
STOP HER ON SIGHT (S.O.S.)

Hamilton, Ann

FALLIN' IN LOVE
WINNERS AND LOSERS

Hamilton, Arthur

CRY ME A RIVER
HE NEEDS ME
SHADOW WOMAN
SING A RAINBOW
TILL LOVE TOUCHES YOUR LIFE

Hamilton, Bob

HUNGRY FOR LOVE
(JUST LIKE) ROMEO AND JULIET

Hamilton, Clyde

ITALIAN THEME, THE

Hamilton, Dan

FALLIN' IN LOVE
WINNERS AND LOSERS

Hamilton, Dave

PRETTY LITTLE BABY

Hamilton, George

WILD HONEY

Hamilton, George, IV

IF YOU DON'T KNOW, I AIN'T GONNA
   TELL YOU

Hamilton, Geraldine

IF YOU DON'T, SOMEBODY ELSE
   WILL

Hamilton, Morris

OR WHAT HAVE YOU?

Hamilton, Nancy

HOW HIGH THE MOON
OLD SOFT SHOE, THE
TEETER TOTTER TESSIE

Hamilton, Ord

HEART OF STONE, A
YOU'RE BLASE

Hamilton, Ronald

IN A MOMENT

Hamilton, Russ

RAINBOW

Hamlin, Rose

ANGEL BABY

Hamlisch, Marvin

AT THE BALLET
BETTER THAN EVER
BREAK IT TO ME GENTLY
CALIFORNIA NIGHTS
DANCE: TEN; LOOKS: THREE
GIRL WHO USED TO BE ME, THE
HELLO TWELVE, HELLO THIRTEEN,
   HELLO LOVE
I CAN DO THAT
IF HE REALLY KNEW ME
IF YOU REMEMBER ME
I STILL BELIEVE IN LOVE
JUST FOR TONIGHT
LAST TIME I FELT LIKE THIS, THE
LIFE IS WHAT YOU MAKE IT
LOOKING THROUGH THE EYES OF
   LOVE
MUSIC AND THE MIRROR, THE
NOBODY DOES IT BETTER
ONE
SUNSHINE, LOLLIPOPS, AND
   RAINBOWS
THEY'RE PLAYING OUR SONG
WAY WE WERE, THE

WHAT I DID FOR LOVE

Hamm, Fred

BYE BYE BLUES

Hammer, Jack

GREAT BALLS OF FIRE
PEEK-A-BOO

Hammer, Jan

MIAMI VICE THEME

Hammerstein, Arthur

BECAUSE OF YOU

Hammerstein, Oscar, II

AH STILL SUITS ME
ALL AT ONCE YOU LOVE HER
ALLEGHENY AL
ALL ER NOTHIN'
ALL IN FUN
ALL THE THINGS YOU ARE
ALL THROUGH THE DAY
AND LOVE WAS BORN
BALI HA'I
BAMBALINA
BILL
BLOODY MARY
CAN I FORGET YOU?
CAN'T HELP LOVIN' DAT MAN
CLIMB EV'RY MOUNTAIN
COCK-EYED OPTIMIST, A
COSSACK LOVE SONG (DON'T
   FORGET ME)
DANCE, MY DARLINGS
DESERT SONG, THE
DITES-MOI
DO I LOVE YOU BECAUSE YOU'RE
   BEAUTIFUL?
DON'T EVER LEAVE ME
DOOR OF MY DREAMS, THE
DO-RE-MI
D'YE LOVE ME?
EVERYBODY'S GOT A HOME BUT ME
EVERYTHING'S UP TO DATE IN
   (KANSAS CITY)
FELLOW NEEDS A GIRL, A
FLANNEL PETTICOAT GAL

FOLKS WHO LIVE ON THE HILL,
 THE
FRENCH MILITARY MARCHING SONG
GENTLEMAN IS A DOPE, THE
GETTING TO KNOW YOU
GRAND AVENUE
HAPPY TALK
HAY, STRAW
HEAVEN IN MY ARMS
HELLO, YOUNG LOVERS
HERE AM I
HIGH, WIDE AND HANDSOME
HONEY BUN
HOW CAN I EVER BE ALONE?
HUNDRED MILLION MIRACLES, A
I BUILT A DREAM ONE DAY
I CAIN'T SAY NO
I ENJOY BEING A GIRL
IF I LOVED YOU
I HAVE DREAMED
I HAVEN'T GOT A WORRY IN THE
 WORLD
I'LL TAKE ROMANCE
I'M GONNA WASH THAT MAN RIGHT
 OUTA MY HAIR
I MIGHT FALL BACK ON YOU
I'M ONE OF GOD'S CHILDREN (WHO
 HASN'T GOT WINGS)
I'M YOUR GIRL
INDIAN LOVE CALL
IN EGERN ON THE TEGERN SEE
IN MY OWN LITTLE CORNER
ISN'T IT KINDA FUN?
IT MIGHT AS WELL BE SPRING
IT'S A GRAND NIGHT FOR SINGING
I'VE TOLD EV'RY LITTLE STAR
I WANT A MAN
I WHISTLE A HAPPY TUNE
JUNE IS BUSTIN' OUT ALL OVER
JUST ONCE AROUND THE CLOCK
KANSAS CITY (EVERYTHING'S UP TO
 DATE IN)
KEEP IT GAY
KISS TO BUILD A DREAM ON, A
LAST TIME I SAW PARIS, THE
LET'S SAY GOODNIGHT 'TIL IT'S
 MORNING
LIFE UPON THE WICKED STAGE
LONELINESS OF EVENING
LONELY GOATHERD, THE
LOVE, LOOK AWAY
LOVELY NIGHT, A
LOVER, COME BACK TO ME

MAKE BELIEVE
MANY A NEW DAY
MARIA
MARIANNE
MARRIAGE TYPE LOVE
MISTER SNOW
MIST IS OVER THE MOON, A
MOUNTIES, THE (A.K.A. SONG OF
 THE MOUNTIES)
MUSIC IN THE NIGHT
MY FAVORITE THINGS
NEXT TIME IT HAPPENS, THE
NIGHT IS YOUNG, THE
NOBODY ELSE BUT ME
NO OTHER LOVE
NO WONDER I'M BLUE
OH, WHAT A BEAUTIFUL MORNIN'
OKLAHOMA
OL' MAN RIVER
ONE ALONE
ONE GIRL, THE
ONE KISS
OUT OF MY DREAMS
PEOPLE WILL SAY WE'RE IN LOVE
PORE JUD IS DAID
PUZZLEMENT, A
REAL NICE CLAMBAKE, A
RECKLESS
RIFF SONG, THE (HO!)
ROMANCE
ROSE-MARIE
SHALL WE DANCE?
SIXTEEN GOING ON SEVENTEEN
SO FAR
SOFTLY, AS IN A MORNING SUNRISE
SOLILOQUY
SOME ENCHANTED EVENING
SOMETHING HAD TO HAPPEN
SOMETHING WONDERFUL
SONG IS YOU, THE
SONG OF THE FLAME
SOUND OF MUSIC, THE
STOUTHEARTED MEN
SUNDAY
SUNNY
SURREY WITH THE FRINGE ON TOP,
 THE
SWEET THURSDAY
TENNESSEE FISH FRY
THAT LUCKY FELLOW
THAT'S FOR ME
THERE IS NOTHIN' LIKE A DAME
THIS NEARLY WAS MINE

TOODLE-OO
TOTEM TOM-TOM
'TWAS NOT SO LONG AGO
TWO LITTLE BLUEBIRDS
VERY SPECIAL DAY, A
VODKA
WANTING YOU
WE KISS IN A SHADOW
WE'LL HAVE A KINGDOM
WEST WIND
WHAT'S THE USE OF WOND'RIN?
WHEN I GROW TOO OLD TO DREAM
WHO?
WHY DO I LOVE YOU?
WHY WAS I BORN?
WILDFLOWER
WILD ROSE, THE
WONDERFUL GUY, A
YOU ARE BEAUTIFUL
YOU ARE LOVE
YOU ARE NEVER AWAY
YOU'LL NEVER WALK ALONE
YOUNGER THAN SPRINGTIME
YOU'RE A QUEER ONE, JULIE
 JORDAN
YOU'VE GOT TO BE CAREFULLY
 TAUGHT
YOU WILL REMEMBER VIENNA

Hammond, Albert

99 MILES FROM L.A.
GIMME DAT DING
I DON'T WANNA LIVE WITHOUT
 YOUR LOVE
I NEED TO BE IN LOVE
IT NEVER RAINS IN SOUTHERN
 CALIFORNIA
LITTLE ARROWS
NOTHING'S GONNA STOP US NOW
ONE MOMENT IN TIME
TO ALL THE GIRLS I'VE LOVED
 BEFORE
WHEN I NEED YOU

Hammond, Barry

EIGHTEEN WITH A BULLET

Hammond, Clay

PART TIME LOVE

Hammond, Con

TURN BACK THE HANDS OF TIME

Hammond, Ronnie

DO IT OR DIE

Hammond, Willie

TURN LOOSE OF MY LEG

Hammonds, Jake, Jr.

GONNA SEND YOU BACK TO
GEORGIA (A.K.A. GONNA SEND
YOU BACK TO WALKER)

Hamner, Curley

HEY! BA-BA-RE-BOP

Hampton, Bill

I CAN'T REMEMBER TO FORGET

Hampton, Carl

(IF LOVING YOU IS WRONG) I DON'T
WANT TO BE RIGHT
IF YOU'RE READY (COME GO WITH
ME)
TOUCH A HAND, MAKE A FRIEND

Hampton, Lionel

EVIL GAL BLUES
FLYIN' HOME
HAMP'S BOOGIE WOOGIE
HEY! BA-BA-RE-BOP
MIDNIGHT SUN
RED TOP

Hampton, Paul

SEA OF HEARTBREAK
YOU DON'T KNOW WHAT YOU'VE
GOT (UNTIL YOU LOSE IT)

Hancock, Herbie

ROCKIT
WATERMELON MAN

Hancock, James S.

BIGGEST ASPIDASTRA IN THE
WORLD, THE

Handman, Lou

ARE YOU LONESOME TONIGHT?
BABY ME
BLUE (AND BROKEN HEARTED)
BYE BYE BABY
DON'T EVER CHANGE
I CAN'T GET THE ONE I WANT
I'M GONNA CHARLESTON BACK TO
CHARLESTON
IS MY BABY BLUE TONIGHT?
LAST NIGHT I DREAMED OF YOU
LOVEY CAME BACK
ME AND THE MOON
MY SWEETIE WENT AWAY (SHE
DIDN'T SAY WHERE, WHEN, OR
WHY)
PUDDIN' HEAD JONES
TWELVE O'CLOCK AT NIGHT
WAS IT RAIN?
YES, I'M LONESOME TONIGHT

Handy, W. C.

ATLANTA BLUES
AUNT HAGAR'S BLUES
BEALE STREET BLUES
JOE TURNER BLUES
LONG GONE
LOVELESS LOVE (CARELESS LOVE)
MEMPHIS BLUES
ST. LOUIS BLUES
YELLOW DOG BLUES, THE

Haney, Carlton

TO SEE MY ANGEL CRY

Hanighen, Bernard

BABY DOLL
BOB WHITE (WHATCHA GONNA
SWING TONIGHT?)
DIXIELAND BAND
FARE-THEE-WELL TO HARLEM
HERE COME THE BRITISH
IF THE MOON TURNS GREEN

LITTLE MAN WHO WASN'T THERE,
THE
MOUNTAIN HIGH, VALLEY LOW
WEEKEND OF A PRIVATE
SECRETARY, THE
WHEN A WOMAN LOVES A MAN
YANKEE DOODLE NEVER WENT TO
TOWN

Hanks, Len

EVERY TIME I TURN AROUND (BACK
IN LOVE AGAIN)

Hanley, James F.

AT THE END OF THE ROAD
BREEZE (BLOW MY BABY BACK TO
ME)
GEE, BUT I HATE TO GO HOME
ALONE
HEADING FOR HARLEM
HIGH SOCIETY BLUES
I'M A LONESOME LITTLE RAINDROP
(LOOKING FOR A PLACE TO FALL)
I'M IN THE MARKET FOR YOU
(BACK HOME AGAIN IN) INDIANA
I'VE GOT THE YES WE HAVE NO
BANANAS BLUES
JERSEY WALK
JUST A COTTAGE SMALL (BY A
WATERFALL)
LITTLE WHITE HOUSE, THE (AT THE
END OF HONEYMOON LANE)
NO FOOLIN'
OH! JUDGE (HE TREATS ME MEAN)
ONE DAY IN JUNE (IT MIGHT HAVE
BEEN YOU)
ROSE OF WASHINGTON SQUARE
SECOND HAND ROSE
SING SONG GIRL
THREE WONDERFUL LETTERS FROM
HOME
TWENTY-FOUR HOURS A DAY
YOU FORGOT ABOUT ME
ZING! WENT THE STRINGS OF MY
HEART

Hanlon, Bert

I'D LOVE TO BE A MONKEY IN THE
ZOO
M-I-S-S-I-S-S-I-P-P-I

ROUND ON THE END AND HIGH IN
   THE MIDDLE (O-HI-O)

Hann, W. A.

AIN'T IT A SHAME

Hanna, Jeff

BABY'S GOT A HOLD ON ME
I'VE BEEN LOOKIN'

Hanner, Dave

BEAUTIFUL YOU
LORD, I HOPE THIS DAY IS GOOD

Hansen, Randy

STATE OF SHOCK

Hanson, Michael

SOMEDAY

Harbach, Otto

ALLAH'S HOLIDAY
BAMBALINA
BIRTH OF PASSION, THE
BUBBLE, THE
COSSACK LOVE SONG (DON'T
   FORGET ME)
CUDDLE UP A LITTLE CLOSER,
   LOVEY MINE
DANCING THE DEVIL AWAY
DESERT SONG, THE
DOOR OF MY DREAMS, THE
D'YE LOVE ME?
EVERY GIRLIE LOVES ME BUT THE
   GIRLIE I LOVE
EVERY LITTLE MOVEMENT (HAS A
   MEANING ALL ITS OWN)
FRENCH MILITARY MARCHING SONG
GIANNINA MIA
GOING UP
IF YOU LOOK IN HER EYES
INDIAN LOVE CALL
I WANT TO MARRY A MALE
   QUARTETTE
KATINKA
LEARN TO SMILE
LET'S BEGIN

LET'S SAY GOODNIGHT 'TIL IT'S
   MORNING
LOVE IS LIKE A FIREFLY
LOVE NEST, THE
MARY
MOUNTIES, THE (A.K.A. SONG OF
   THE MOUNTIES)
MY PARADISE
NIGHT WAS MADE FOR LOVE, THE
NO, NO, NANETTE
ONE ALONE
ONE MOMENT ALONE
POOR PIERROT
RACKETY COO
RIFF SONG, THE (HO!)
ROMANCE
ROSE-MARIE
SAME OLD MOON, THE
SMILE SHE MEANS FOR YOU, THE
SMOKE GETS IN YOUR EYES
SOMETHING SEEMS TINGLE-INGLING
SONG OF THE FLAME
SUNNY
SYMPATHY
TICKLE TOE, THE (EVERYBODY
   OUGHT TO KNOW HOW TO DO)
TOTEM TOM-TOM
TOUCH OF YOUR HAND, THE
TRY TO FORGET
TWO LITTLE BLUEBIRDS
VODKA
WAITING
WE'LL HAVE A KINGDOM
WHEN A MAID COMES KNOCKING
   AT YOUR HEART
WHO?
WILDFLOWER
WILD ROSE, THE
YESTERDAY
YOU'RE DEVASTATING
YOU'RE IN LOVE
YOU WILL, WON'T YOU?

Harburg, E. Y.

AH, BUT IS IT LOVE?
AIN'T IT DE TRUTH?
ANY MOMENT NOW
APRIL IN PARIS
BEGAT, THE
BROTHER, CAN YOU SPARE A DIME?
BUDS WON'T BUD
CALIFORN-I-AY

CAN'T HELP SINGING
CHIN UP, CHEERIO, CARRY ON!
COCOANUT SWEET
DING-DONG! THE WITCH IS DEAD
DOWN WITH LOVE
EAGLE AND ME, THE
EVELINA
FANCY MEETING YOU
FUN TO BE FOOLED
GOD'S COUNTRY
HAPPINESS IS JUST A THING
   CALLED JOE
HOW ARE THINGS IN GLOCCA
   MORRA?
HOW DO YOU DO IT?
I AM ONLY HUMAN AFTER ALL
I COULD GO ON SINGING
IF I DIDN'T HAVE YOU
IF I ONLY HAD A BRAIN
IF I ONLY HAD A HEART
IF I ONLY HAD THE NERVE
IF THIS ISN'T LOVE
I LIKE THE LIKES OF YOU
I'LL TAKE TALLULAH
I LOVE TO SING-A
I'M YOURS
IN THE SHADE OF THE NEW APPLE
   TREE
ISN'T IT HEAVENLY?
IT'S ONLY A PAPER MOON
I'VE GONE ROMANTIC ON YOU
JITTERBUG, THE
LAST CALL FOR LOVE
LAST NIGHT WHEN WE WERE
   YOUNG
LET'S PUT OUR HEADS TOGETHER
LET'S TAKE A WALK AROUND THE
   BLOCK
LITTLE BISCUIT
LITTLE DROPS OF RAIN
LONG BEFORE YOU CAME ALONG
LOOK TO THE RAINBOW
LYDIA, THE TATTOOED LADY
MAKE WAY FOR TOMORROW
MEWSETTE
MOANIN' IN THE MORNIN'
MOONLIGHT AND PRETZELS
MORE AND MORE
NAPOLEON
NECESSITY
OLD DEVIL MOON
OVER THE RAINBOW
PARIS IS A LONELY TOWN

POOR YOU
PRETTY TO WALK WITH
PUSH THE BUTTON
RIGHT AS THE RAIN
SAID I TO MY HEART, SAID I
SATAN'S LITTLE LAMB
SAVANNAH
SAVE ME, SISTER
SHOEIN' THE MARE
SOMETHING SORT OF GRANDISH
SPEAKING OF THE WEATHER
SUDDENLY
TAKE IT SLOW, JOE
TAKE MY HAND, PAREE
TELL ME, TELL ME EVENING STAR
THAT GREAT COME-AND-GET-IT DAY
THEN I'LL BE TIRED OF YOU
THERE'S A GREAT DAY COMING
   MAÑANA
THERE'S A LITTLE BIT OF YOU IN
   EVERY LOVE SONG
TWO BLIND LOVES
WATER UNDER THE BRIDGE
WE'RE OFF TO SEE THE WIZARD
WHAT CAN YOU SAY IN A LOVE
   SONG?
WHAT IS THERE TO SAY?
WHAT WOULDN'T I DO FOR THAT
   MAN?
WHEN I'M NOT NEAR THE GIRL I
   LOVE
WHEN THE IDLE POOR BECOME
   THE IDLE RICH
WHERE HAVE WE MET BEFORE?
WORLD IS IN MY ARMS, THE
WORLD IS MINE, THE
YOU'RE A BUILDER UPPER
YOU'RE THE CURE FOR WHAT AILS
   ME

Hardaway, Lila Mae

SIGNED, SEALED, DELIVERED I'M
   YOURS

Hardaway, Lula

I DON'T KNOW WHY
I WAS MADE TO LOVE HER
YOU MET YOUR MATCH

Hardcastle, Paul

19
RAIN FOREST

Hardeman, Annette

I FEEL GOOD ALL OVER

Hardeman, Gabe

I FEEL GOOD ALL OVER

Harden, Bobby

TIPPY TOEING

Hardgrave, Ron

HIGH SCHOOL CONFIDENTIAL

Hardin, Charles

NOT FADE AWAY

Hardin, Glen D.

COUNT ME IN
MY HEART'S SYMPHONY
WHERE WILL THE WORDS COME
   FROM?

Hardin, Mel

BACKFIELD IN MOTION

Hardin, Tim

IF I WERE A CARPENTER
LADY CAME FROM BALTIMORE, THE
REASON TO BELIEVE

Harding, Chuck

HONKY TONK GIRL
YOU CAN'T HAVE MY LOVE

Hardy, Bill

AMEN (YEA-MAN)

Harford, Frank

I'M WASTIN' MY TEARS ON YOU
LONG TIME GONE
ROCK AND RYE POLKA

Harford, Harold

I HEAR YOU CALLING ME

Hargis, Reggie

DAZZ

Hargreaves, Robert

IF
LADY OF SPAIN
LET'S ALL SING LIKE THE BIRDIES
   SING
UNLESS

Hargrove, Linda

JUST GET UP AND CLOSE THE DOOR
LET IT SHINE

Haring, Bob

CROCE DI ORO (CROSS OF GOLD)

Harju, Gary

COWBOYS AND CLOWNS

Harket, Morten

TAKE ON ME

Harline, Leigh

GIVE A LITTLE WHISTLE
TURN ON THE OLD MUSIC BOX
WHEN YOU WISH UPON A STAR
WORLD OWES ME A LIVING, THE

Harling, W. Franke

ALWAYS IN ALL WAYS
BEYOND THE BLUE HORIZON
GIVE ME A MOMENT PLEASE
IN MY LITTLE HOPE CHEST
SING YOU SINNERS

TONIGHT IS MINE
WHERE WAS I?

Harman, Barry

SMALL CRAFT WARNINGS

Harmon, Lucille

YOU MIGHT HAVE BELONGED TO
ANOTHER

Harney, Ben R.

MISTER JOHNSON, TURN ME LOOSE

Harnick, Sheldon

ALL OF THESE AND MORE
ARTIFICIAL FLOWERS
AWAY FROM YOU
BOSTON BEGUINE
DAYS GONE BY
DEAR FRIEND
DO YOU LOVE ME?
FAR FROM THE HOME I LOVE
FIDDLER ON THE ROOF
GENTLEMAN JIMMY
GOOD CLEAN FUN
GRAND KNOWING YOU
IF I WERE A RICH MAN
ILONA
JUST MY LUCK
LITTLE OLD NEW YORK
MATCHMAKER, MATCHMAKER
MERRY LITTLE MINUET
MIRACLE OF MIRACLES
NOW I HAVE EVERYTHING
POLITICS AND POKER
POPSICLES IN PARIS
SABBATH PRAYER
SHAPE OF THINGS, THE
SHE LOVES ME
SOMEONE IS SENDING ME FLOWERS
SUNRISE, SUNSET
TIL TOMORROW
TO LIFE
TONIGHT AT EIGHT
TRADITION
VERY NEXT MAN, THE (I'LL MARRY)
WHEN DID I FALL IN LOVE?
WILL HE LIKE ME?

Harold, William

GOOFUS

Harper, J. D.

SHE IS MY DAISY

Harper, Wally

IT'S BETTER WITH A BAND

Harrigan, Edward

DE RAINBOW ROAD
HATS OFF TO ME
I'VE COME HERE TO STAY
KNIGHTS OF THE MYSTIC STAR
MAGGIE MURPHY'S HOME
TAKE A DAY OFF, MARY ANN
TAKING IN THE TOWN
THEY NEVER TELL ALL WHAT THEY
KNOW

Harriman, Al

IN THE TOWN WHERE I WAS BORN

Harrington, J. P.

OH, ISN'T IT SINGULAR!

Harris

HAND THAT ROCKS THE CRADLE,
THE

Harris, Art

WHAT AM I LIVING FOR?

Harris, Benny

ORNITHOLOGY

Harris, Bill

YOUR FATHER'S MOUSTACHE

Harris, Bob

LOLITA YA-YA
JOYSTICK

Harris, Charles K.

AFTER THE BALL
ALWAYS IN THE WAY
BELLE OF THE BALL, THE
BREAK THE NEWS TO MOTHER
FOR OLD TIME'S SAKE
HELLO CENTRAL, GIVE ME HEAVEN
I'VE A LONGING IN MY HEART FOR
YOU, LOUISE
I'VE JUST COME BACK TO SAY
GOOD-BYE
KISS AND LET'S MAKE UP
'MID THE GREEN FIELDS OF
VIRGINIA
NOBODY KNOWS, NOBODY CARES
ONE NIGHT IN JUNE
THERE'LL COME A TIME
WOULD YOU CARE?

Harris, Don F.

I'M LEAVING IT (ALL) UP TO YOU
JOLLY GREEN GIANT

Harris, Eddie

LISTEN HERE

Harris, George

CELERY STALKS AT MIDNIGHT

Harris, Harry

BABY ME
HIGHWAYS ARE HAPPY WAYS
WHERE DID YOU LEARN TO LOVE?

Harris, James, III

CAN YOU STAND THE RAIN
CONTROL
DIAMONDS
ENCORE
EVERYTHING I MISS AT HOME
FAKE
FINEST, THE
FISHNET
HUMAN
I DIDN'T MEAN TO TURN YOU ON
IF IT ISN'T LOVE
IN A MOMENT

JUST BE GOOD TO ME
JUST THE FACTS
JUST THE WAY YOU LIKE IT
KEEP YOUR EYE ON ME
LET'S WAIT AWHILE
MISS YOU MUCH
NASTY
NEVER KNEW LOVE LIKE THIS
SATURDAY LOVE
TENDER LOVE
WHAT HAVE YOU DONE FOR ME
   LATELY
WHEN I THINK OF YOU

Harris, Jerry

THERE'S NO LIVIN' WITHOUT YOUR
   LOVIN'

Harris, John E.

BIRD'S THE WORD, THE
SURFIN' BIRD

Harris, John "Sonny"

PAPA-OOM-MOW-MOW

Harris, Lew

THINGS I LOVE, THE

Harris, Lewis

MAHARAJAH OF MAGADOR, THE

Harris, Maury Coleman

DEAR MOM

Harris, Pete Q.

PARENTS JUST DON'T UNDERSTAND
TOUCH ME (I WANT YOUR BODY)

Harris, Reggie

DUSIC

Harris, Remus

CRY BABY CRY

I WANNA WRAP YOU UP
MY FIRST AND LAST LOVE
ROSE AND A PRAYER, A
SO LONG
ST. THERESE OF THE ROSES

Harris, Rolf

NICK TEEN AND AL K. HALL
SUN ARISE
TIE ME KANGAROO DOWN, SPORT

Harris, Stewart

HURRICANE
ROSE IN PARADISE

Harris, Ted

CRYSTAL CHANDELIER
ONCE
PAPER MANSIONS
RAINBOWS AND ROSES

Harris, Will J.

SWEET SUE (JUST YOU)

Harris, Woody

CLEMENTINE
EARLY IN THE MORNING
QUEEN OF THE HOP
ROCK-A-BILLY

Harris, Wynonie

ALL SHE WANTS TO DO IS ROCK
A-SLEEPIN' AT THE FOOT OF THE
   BED

Harrison, Alfred

THAT'S THE KIND OF BABY FOR ME

Harrison, Betty E.

HOPING THAT YOU'RE HOPING

Harrison, Charles

HOW DO YOU DO (EVERYBODY)

Harrison, Charlie

WHEN SUMMER IS GONE

Harrison, Danny

FOOTSTEPS OF A FOOL
(HOW CAN I WRITE ON PAPER)
   WHAT I FEEL IN MY HEART

Harrison, George

ALL THOSE YEARS AGO
BADGE
BANGLA-DESH
BLOW AWAY
BREATH AWAY FROM HEAVEN
CRACKERBOX PALACE
DARK HORSE
DEEP BLUE
DON'T BOTHER ME
FOR YOU BLUE
GIVE ME LOVE (GIVE ME PEACE ON
   EARTH)
HERE COMES THE SUN
I NEED YOU
INNER LIGHT, THE
ISN'T IT A PITY
MY SWEET LORD
PHOTOGRAPH
SOMETHING
THIS SONG
WHAT IS LIFE
YOU

Harrison, Jerry

AND SHE WAS
BURNING DOWN THE HOUSE
ONCE IN A LIFETIME

Harrison, Larry

(YOU DON'T KNOW) HOW GLAD I AM
WHY BABY WHY

Harrison, Neil

I COULD NEVER MISS YOU MORE
   THAN I DO

Harrison, Nigel

ONE WAY OR ANOTHER

Harrison, Paul

WHAT SHE IS (IS A WOMAN IN
LOVE)

Harrison, Tom

MY LITTLE GRASS SHACK (IN
KEALAKAKUA, HAWAII)

Harrison, William

OUR LOVE STORY

Harry, Deborah

ATOMIC
CALL ME
DREAMING
FRENCH KISSIN'
HARDEST PART, THE
HEART OF GLASS
ONE WAY OR ANOTHER
RAPTURE

Hart, Bobby

ALICE LONG (YOU'RE STILL MY
FAVORITE GIRLFRIEND)
COME A LITTLE BIT CLOSER
DOMINOES
HURT SO BAD
I'M NOT YOUR STEPPIN' STONE
I WONDER WHAT SHE'S DOING
TONIGHT
KEEP ON SINGING
LAST TRAIN TO CLARKSVILLE
OUT AND ABOUT
OVER YOU
SINNER MAN
SOMETHING'S WRONG WITH ME
VALLERI
WORDS

Hart, Bruce

YOU TAKE MY BREATH AWAY

Hart, Charles

ALL I ASK OF YOU
MUSIC OF THE NIGHT, THE
PHANTOM OF THE OPERA, THE

Hart, Corey

I AM BY YOUR SIDE
IT AIN'T ENOUGH
NEVER SURRENDER
SUNGLASSES AT NIGHT

Hart, Dick

ON TAP, IN THE CAN, OR IN THE
BOTTLE

Hart, Freddie

BLESS YOUR HEART
EASY LOVING
LOOSE TALK
MY HANG UP IS YOU
MY TEARS ARE OVERDUE
SKID ROW JOE
TRIP TO HEAVEN
WILLIE THE WEEPER

Hart, Ken Woodrow

DOGFACE SOLDIER

Hart, Lorenz

ANY OLD PLACE WITH YOU
BABES IN ARMS
BABY'S AWAKE NOW
BABY'S BEST FRIEND, A
BAD IN EVERYMAN, THE
BEWITCHED, BOTHERED, AND
BEWILDERED
BLUE MOON
BLUE ROOM, THE
BYE AND BYE
CAN'T YOU DO A FRIEND A FAVOR
CIRCUS IS ON PARADE, THE
DANCING ON THE CEILING
DEN OF INIQUITY
DO I HEAR YOU SAYING, "I LOVE
YOU"?
DOWN BY THE RIVER
EV'RY SUNDAY AFTERNOON

EV'RYTHING I'VE GOT
FALLING IN LOVE WITH LOVE
FROM ANOTHER WORLD
GIRL FRIEND, THE
GIVE IT BACK TO THE INDIANS
GLAD TO BE UNHAPPY
HALLELUJAH, I'M A BUM
HAPPY HUNTING HORN
HAVE YOU MET MISS JONES?
HEART IS QUICKER THAN THE EYE,
THE
HERE IN MY ARMS (IT'S ADORABLE)
HOW CAN YOU FORGET?
HOW TO WIN FRIENDS AND
INFLUENCE PEOPLE
I COULD WRITE A BOOK
I DIDN'T KNOW WHAT TIME IT WAS
I'D RATHER BE RIGHT
I FEEL AT HOME WITH YOU
I LIKE TO RECOGNIZE THE TUNE
I MARRIED AN ANGEL
I MUST LOVE YOU
ISN'T IT ROMANTIC?
IT NEVER ENTERED MY MIND
IT'S EASY TO REMEMBER
IT'S GOT TO BE LOVE
I'VE GOT FIVE DOLLARS
I WISH I WERE IN LOVE AGAIN
JOHNNY ONE NOTE
LADY IS A TRAMP, THE
LIKE ORDINARY PEOPLE DO
LITTLE BIRDIE TOLD ME SO, A
LITTLE GIRL BLUE
LOVE ME TONIGHT
LOVE NEVER WENT TO COLLEGE
LOVER
MANHATTAN
MIMI
MOST BEAUTIFUL GIRL IN THE
WORLD, THE
MOUNTAIN GREENERY
MY FUNNY VALENTINE
MY HEART STOOD STILL
MY MAN IS ON THE MAKE
MY ROMANCE
NOBODY'S HEART (BELONGS TO ME)
ON YOUR TOES
QUIET NIGHT
SEND FOR ME
SENTIMENTAL ME
SHIP WITHOUT A SAIL, A
SING FOR YOUR SUPPER
SOON

Hathcock, John

I GUESS I'LL NEVER LEARN
WAKE UP, IRENE
WELCOME TO MY WORLD

Hattori, Raymond

GOMEN NASAI (FORGIVE ME)

Hauenschild, Clara

GOING FOR A PARDON

Haugh, Felix

CAPTAIN OF HER HEART, THE

Hausey, Howard

ALL GROWN UP
HONKY TONK MAN
OLE SLEW-FOOT (A.K.A. SLEWFOOT
   THE BEAR)

Hausmann, Michael

VOICES CARRY

Havens, Jimmie

WE DON'T WANT THE BACON, WHAT
   WE WANT IS A PIECE OF THE
   RHINE

Havens, Richie

LIGHT AT THE END OF THE TUNNEL

Havez, Jean

EVERYBODY WORKS BUT FATHER
I'LL LEND YOU EVERYTHING I'VE
   GOT EXCEPT MY WIFE
SAILING DOWN THE CHESAPEAKE
   BAY

Hawes, Bess

M.T.A., THE

Hawes, Bruce

MIGHTY LOVE, A
THEY JUST CAN'T STOP IT (THE
   GAMES PEOPLE PLAY)

Hawker, Mike

I ONLY WANT TO BE WITH YOU
STAY AWHILE
WALKIN' BACK TO HAPPINESS

Hawkins, Charlotte

WITH YOU ON MY MIND

Hawkins, Coleman

QUEER NOTIONS

Hawkins, Dale

SUSIE-Q

Hawkins, Edwin

OH HAPPY DAY

Hawkins, Erskine

TUXEDO JUNCTION

Hawkins, Hawkshaw

DOGHOUSE BOOGIE

Hawkins, Ronnie

MARY LOU

Hawkins, Roy

WHY DO THINGS HAPPEN TO ME?

Hay, Barry

RADAR LOVE

Hay, Colin

DOWN UNDER
EVERYTHING I NEED
IT'S A MISTAKE

OVERKILL
WHO CAN IT BE NOW?

Hay, John

WHEN THE BOYS COME HOME

Hay, Roy

CHURCH OF THE POISON MIND
DO YOU REALLY WANT TO HURT ME
I'LL TUMBLE 4 YA
MISS ME BLIND
MOVE AWAY

Haycock, Peter

COULDN'T GET IT RIGHT

Hayden, Joe

HOT TIME IN THE OLD TOWN
   TONIGHT

Hayes, Alfred

JOE HILL

Hayes, Billy

BLUE CHRISTMAS
WHO SHOT THE HOLE IN MY
   SOMBRERO?

Hayes, Chris

I KNOW WHAT I LIKE
I WANT A NEW DRUG
POWER OF LOVE, THE
STUCK WITH YOU

Hayes, Clancy

HUGGIN' AND CHALKIN'

Hayes, Donald

PLEASE SAY YOU WANT ME

Hayes, Edgar

SOMEONE STOLE GABRIEL'S HORN

Hayes, Isaac

B-A-B-Y
BORN AGAIN
DEJA VU
HOLD ON! I'M COMIN'
I TAKE WHAT I WANT
I THANK YOU
LET ME BE GOOD TO YOU
SOUL MAN
SOUL SISTER, BROWN SUGAR
SWEETER HE IS, THE
THEME FROM "SHAFT"
THEME FROM "THE MEN"
WHEN SOMETHING IS WRONG WITH
    MY BABY
WRAP IT UP
YOU DON'T KNOW LIKE I KNOW
YOUR GOOD THING IS ABOUT TO
    END

Hayes, Jerry

ROLLIN' WITH THE FLOW
WHO'S CHEATIN' WHO

Hayes, Julia M.

GOOD NIGHT, LITTLE GIRL, GOOD
    NIGHT

Hayes, Kendall

WALK ON BY

Hayes, Otha

PHILLY FREEZE, THE
SHAKE A TAIL FEATHER

Hayes, Peter Lind

COME TO ME

Hayes, Red

HOLD EVERYTHING

Hayes, Robert

IS IT ANY WONDER?

Hayes, Thamon

SOUTH

Hayes, Tony

BLACK IS BLACK

Hayman, Richard

DANSERO

Haymes, Bob

LIPSTICK AND CANDY AND
    RUBBERSOLE SHOES
THAT'S ALL

Haymes, Joe

LET'S HAVE A PARTY

Haynes, Henry B.

TENNESSEE BORDER NO. 2

Haynes, Tony

HYPERACTIVE

Haynes, Walter

8 X 10
GIRL ON THE BILLBOARD
IT'S TIME TO PAY THE FIDDLER

Hays, Billy

EVERY DAY OF MY LIFE

Hays, J. H.

SATISFIED MIND, A

Hays, Lee

BAD MAN BLUNDER
IF I HAD A HAMMER

Hayward, Charles

DEVIL WENT DOWN TO GEORGIA,
    THE

IN AMERICA

Hayward, Justin

I DREAMED LAST NIGHT
NIGHTS IN WHITE SATIN
QUESTION
STORY IN YOUR EYES
TUESDAY AFTERNOON (FOREVER
    AFTERNOON)
VOICE, THE
YOUR WILDEST DREAMS

Haywood, Leon

DON'T PUSH IT, DON'T FORCE IT
I WANT'A DO SOMETHING FREAKY
    TO YOU
SHE'S A BAD MAMA JAMA (SHE'S
    BUILT, SHE'S STACKED)

Hazard, Robert

GIRLS JUST WANT TO HAVE FUN

Hazel, Edward

SHAKEY GROUND

Hazelwood, Eddie

SICK, SOBER AND SORRY

Hazlewood, Albert

AIR THAT I BREATHE, THE

Hazlewood, Lee

BONNIE COME BACK
BOSS GUITAR
CANNONBALL
FRIDAY'S CHILD
(DANCE WITH THE) GUITAR MAN
HOUSTON
HOW DOES THAT GRAB YOU,
    DARLING?
IN OUR TIME
LADY BIRD
LIGHTNING'S GIRL
LONELY ONE, THE
LOVE EYES
NOT THE LOVIN' KIND

REBEL-ROUSER
SOME VELVET MORNING
SUGAR TOWN
SUMMER WINE
THESE BOOTS ARE MADE FOR
    WALKING
THIS TOWN

Hazlewood, Mike

AIR THAT I BREATHE, THE
GIMME DAT DING
IT NEVER RAINS IN SOUTHERN
    CALIFORNIA
LITTLE ARROWS
YES, YES, YES

Hazzard, Anthony

HA HA SAID THE CLOWN

Head, Roy

APPLE OF MY EYE
TREAT HER RIGHT

Headon, Topper

ROCK THE CASBAH

Heard, Dick

KENTUCKY RAIN

Heath, Bobby

MY PONY BOY
ROLL 'EM GIRLS, ROLL YOUR OWN

Heath, E. P.

LOVE HAS WINGS
LOVE'S OWN SWEET SONG
MY FAITHFUL STRADIVARI
SOFTLY THRO' THE SUMMER NIGHT

Heath, Hy

DEACON JONES
I'D NEVER STAND IN YOUR WAY
LITTLE RED FOX, THE (N'YA, N'YA,
    YA CAN'T CATCH ME)
MULE TRAIN

SOMEBODY BIGGER THAN YOU
    AND I
TAKE THESE CHAINS FROM MY
    HEART
UNCLE REMUS SAID

Heatherton, Fred

I'VE GOT A LOVELY BUNCH OF
    COCONUTS (ROLL OR BOWL A
    BALL, A PENNY A PITCH)

Hebb, Bobby

NATURAL MAN, A
SUNNY

Hecht, Don

WALKIN' AFTER MIDNIGHT

Hecht, Ken

IT'S EIGHT O'CLOCK
NO ONE KNOWS

Heelan, Will A.

EVERY RACE HAS A FLAG BUT THE
    COON
I'D LEAVE MY HAPPY HOME FOR
    YOU
IN THE HOUSE OF TOO MUCH
    TROUBLE
NO WEDDING BELLS FOR ME

Hefti, Neal

BATMAN THEME
GOOD EARTH, THE
LI'L DARLIN'

Hegel, Robert

JUST AS I AM

Heidt, Horace

I'LL LOVE YOU IN MY DREAMS

Hein, Silvio

HE'S A COUSIN OF MINE

SOME LITTLE BUG IS GOING TO
    FIND YOU
WHEN YOU'RE ALL DRESSED UP
    AND NO PLACE TO GO

Heindorf, Ray

HOLD ME IN YOUR ARMS
MELANCHOLY RHAPSODY
PETE KELLY'S BLUES
SOME SUNDAY MORNING
WOULD YOU BELIEVE ME?

Heinz, Jack

HIGH STEEL
LIE DETECTOR
TOO TRUE

Heinzman, John

DOWN WHERE THE SILV'RY
    MOHAWK FLOWS

Heinzman, Otto

DOWN WHERE THE SILV'RY
    MOHAWK FLOWS

Heiser, L. W.

DREAMING

Heisler, Dave

SAY YOU'RE MINE AGAIN
SOMEWHERE THERE IS SOMEONE

Held, Anna

IT'S DELIGHTFUL TO BE MARRIED

Helf, J. Fred

AIN'T YOU COMING BACK TO OLD
    NEW HAMPSHIRE, MOLLY?
EVERY RACE HAS A FLAG BUT THE
    COON
FATAL ROSE OF RED, THE
IF MONEY TALKS, IT AIN'T ON
    SPEAKING TERMS WITH ME
IN THE HOUSE OF TOO MUCH
    TROUBLE

THANK YOUR FATHER
THAT OLD GANG OF MINE
THAT'S WHY DARKIES WERE BORN
THERE I GO DREAMING AGAIN
THIS IS THE MISSUS
THRILL IS GONE, THE
TOGETHER
TO KNOW YOU IS TO LOVE YOU
TURN ON THE HEAT
USED TO YOU
VARSITY DRAG, THE
WASN'T IT BEAUTIFUL WHILE IT
    LASTED?
WHAT D'YA SAY?
WHEN I GROW UP
WHEN LOVE COMES SWINGING
    ALONG
WHOSE BIG BABY ARE YOU?
WHY CAN'T YOU?
WHY DID I KISS THAT GIRL?
WITHOUT LOVE
YOU CAN MAKE MY LIFE A BED OF
    ROSES
YOU'RE THE CREAM IN MY COFFEE
YOU TRY SOMEBODY ELSE
YOU WOULDN'T FOOL ME, WOULD
    YOU?

Hendler, Herb

HOT TODDY

Hendricks, Belford

CALL ME
I'M TOO FAR GONE (TO TURN
    AROUND)
IT'S JUST A MATTER OF TIME
LOOKING BACK
MARCHING THROUGH BERLIN

Hendricks, James

LOOK TO YOUR SOUL
MUDDY RIVER
SUMMER RAIN

Hendricks, Jon

BIJOU
EVERY TUB
FOUR BROTHERS
GIMME THAT WINE

I WANT YOU TO BE MY BABY
NIGHT IN TUNISIA, A
ONE EARLY MORNING
ONE NOTE SAMBA
SERMONETTE
SLIGHTLY OUT OF TUNE
YEH! YEH!

Hendrix, Jimi

CROSSTOWN TRAFFIC
DOLLY DAGGER
FIRE
FOXEY LADY
FREEDOM
PURPLE HAZE

Heneker, David

DIS-DONC, DIS-DONC
HALF A SIXPENCE
IF THE RAIN'S GOT TO FALL
IRMA LA DOUCE
MONEY TO BURN

Henley, Cherokee Jack

DON'T JUST STAND THERE (WHEN
    YOU FEEL LIKE YOU'RE IN LOVE)

Henley, Don

BEST OF MY LOVE
BOYS OF SUMMER, THE
DESPERADO
DIRTY LAUNDRY
HEARTACHE TONIGHT
HOTEL CALIFORNIA
I CAN'T TELL YOU WHY
JAMES DEAN
LIFE IN THE FAST LANE
LYIN' EYES
NEW KID IN TOWN
NOT ENOUGH LOVE IN THE WORLD
ONE OF THESE NIGHTS
SUNSET GRILL
TAKE IT TO THE LIMIT
TEQUILA SUNRISE

Henley, Fred

YOU'RE THE REASON

Henley, Larry

HE'S A HEARTACHE (LOOKING FOR
    A PLACE TO HAPPEN)
LIZZIE AND THE RAINMAN
'TILL I GET IT RIGHT
WIND BENEATH MY WINGS (A.K.A.
    HERO)

Henley, Mark

GONNA TAKE A LOT OF RIVER

Henley, W. E.

BOWL OF ROSES, A

Henning, Paul

BALLAD OF JED CLAMPETT
PEARL, PEARL, PEARL
PETTICOAT JUNCTION

Henning, Robert

INTERMEZZO

Henny, Donald

QUESTION OF TEMPERATURE, A

Henry, Clarence

AIN'T GOT NO HOME
EVIL WAYS

Henry, Francis

LITTLE GIRL

Henry, Grace

OR WHAT HAVE YOU?

Henry, Norm

YOU BETTER KNOW IT

Henry, Shifte

LET ME GO HOME, WHISKEY

Henry, S. R.

BY HECK
I'M LOOKING FOR A NICE YOUNG
   FELLOW WHO IS LOOKING FOR A
   NICE YOUNG GIRL
I'VE GOT THE TIME, I'VE GOT THE
   PLACE, BUT IT'S HARD TO FIND
   THE GIRL
WHEN IT'S MOONLIGHT ON THE
   PRAIRIE

Henske, Judy

ROSALIE

Herald, John

UP TO MY NECK IN HIGH MUDDY
   WATER

Herbert, Arthur

BROKEN DOWN MERRY-GO-ROUND

Herbert, Joseph

BELIEVE ME, BELOVED
LOVE'S ROUNDELAY
OH, HOW I LONG FOR SOMEONE
PRETTY EDELWEISS
SWEETEST MAID OF ALL

Herbert, Twyla

LIGHTNIN' STRIKES
OUTSIDE THE GATES OF HEAVEN
RHAPSODY IN THE RAIN
TWO FACES HAVE I

Herbert, Victor

ABSINTHE FRAPPE
AH! SWEET MYSTERY OF LIFE
AL FRESCO
ALL FOR YOU
ANGEL FACE
ANGELUS, THE
ASK HER WHILE THE BAND IS
   PLAYING
BADINAGE
BAGDAD
BANDANNA LAND

BECAUSE YOU'RE YOU
CRICKET ON THE HEARTH, THE
CUPID AND I
EILEEN ALANA ASTHORE
EVERY DAY IS LADIES' DAY WITH
   ME
GYPSY LOVE SONG (SLUMBER ON,
   MY LITTLE GYPSY SWEETHEART)
I CAN'T DO THIS SUM
IF ONLY YOU WERE MINE
IF YOU WERE I AND I WERE YOU
I'LL BE MARRIED TO THE MUSIC OF
   A MILITARY BAND
I'M FALLING IN LOVE WITH
   SOMEONE
I MIGHT BE YOUR ONCE-IN-A-WHILE
INDIAN SUMMER
ISLE OF OUR DREAMS, THE
ITALIAN STREET SONG
I WANT WHAT I WANT WHEN I
   WANT IT
JUMP JIM CROW
KISS IN THE DARK, A
KISS ME AGAIN
KNOT OF BLUE, A
LOVE BOAT, THE
LOVE IS LIKE A CIGARETTE
LOVE IS THE BEST OF ALL
MARCH OF THE TOYS, THE
MY ANGELINE
MY DREAM GIRL
NEAPOLITAN LOVE SONG
'NEATH THE SOUTHERN MOON
PANAMERICANA
ROSE OF THE WORLD
SOMEONE LIKE YOU
SPOOKY OOKUM
SPRINGTIME OF LIFE, THE
STREETS OF NEW YORK, THE (OR,
   IN OLD NEW YORK)
SWEETHEARTS
TELL IT ALL OVER AGAIN
THERE ONCE WAS AN OWL
THINE ALONE
TIME AND THE PLACE AND THE
   GIRL, THE
TO THE LAND OF MY OWN
   ROMANCE
TOYLAND
TRAMP! TRAMP! TRAMP!
TWO LAUGHING IRISH EYES
WHEN SHALL I AGAIN SEE
   IRELAND?

WHEN YOU'RE AWAY
WHEN YOU'RE WEARING THE BALL
   AND CHAIN
WOMAN IS ONLY A WOMAN, BUT A
   GOOD CIGAR IS A SMOKE, A
YESTERTHOUGHTS
YOU BELONG TO ME

Herbstritt, Larry

COWBOYS AND CLOWNS
I JUST FALL IN LOVE AGAIN

Herman, Jerry

AS SIMPLE AS THAT
BEFORE THE PARADE PASSES BY
BEST OF TIMES, THE
DEAR WORLD
HELLO, DOLLY!
I AM WHAT I AM
IF HE WALKED INTO MY LIFE
I PUT MY HAND IN
IT ONLY TAKES A MOMENT
IT TAKES A WOMAN
I WILL FOLLOW YOU
KISS HER NOW
LET'S NOT WASTE A MOMENT
LIKE A YOUNG MAN
LOOK OVER THERE
MAME
MARIANNE
MILK AND HONEY
MY BEST GIRL
OPEN A NEW WINDOW
PUT ON YOUR SUNDAY CLOTHES
RIBBONS DOWN MY BACK
SHALOM
SO LONG, DEARIE
SONG ON THE SAND
THAT WAS YESTERDAY
THERE'S NO REASON IN THE
   WORLD
WE NEED A LITTLE CHRISTMAS
WHEN MABEL COMES IN THE ROOM

Herman, Lew

RIGHT TIME, THE

Herman, Pinky

MANHATTAN MERRY-GO-ROUND

Herman, Reba Nell

KISS GOODNIGHT, A

Herman, Woody

APPLE HONEY
BLUES ON PARADE
EARLY AUTUMN
WOODCHOPPER'S BALL
YOUR FATHER'S MOUSTACHE

Hermann, Keith

SMALL CRAFT WARNINGS

Hernandez, Patrick

BORN TO BE ALIVE

Hernandez, Rafael

EL CUMBANCHERO

Herpin, Henri

ALL OF A SUDDEN MY HEART SINGS

Herrera, René

ANGELITO
LO MUCHO TE QUIERO (THE MORE I
LOVE YOU)

Herrick, Paul

THAT SOLDIER OF MINE

Herrick, Walt

RUN JOE

Herrold, Erma

STOOD UP

Herron, Joel

I'M A FOOL TO WANT YOU

Herschell, William

GOODBYE, MA! GOODBYE, PA!
GOODBYE, MULE!

Herscher, Louis

DREAM DADDY
YOU'RE FREE TO GO

Hershey, June

DEEP IN THE HEART OF TEXAS

Herst, Jerry

SO RARE

Herzer, Wallie

EVERYBODY TWO-STEP

Herzog, Arthur, Jr.

DON'T EXPLAIN
GOD BLESS THE CHILD
SOME OTHER SPRING

Hess, Cliff

FRECKLES
HUCKLEBERRY FINN
WHEN ALEXANDER TAKES HIS
RAGTIME BAND TO FRANCE

Hess, David

SPEEDY GONZALES

Hess, John

PASSING BY

Hester, Hal

SAND AND THE SEA, THE
YOUNG AND IN LOVE
YOUR OWN THING

Hester, Tony

HEY, YOU! GET OFF MY MOUNTAIN
IN THE RAIN

WHATCHA SEE IS WHAT YOU GET
WITH THIS RING

Heuberger, Richard

KISS IN YOUR EYES, THE

Hewett, Howard

I'M FOR REAL

Hewson, Paul "Bono"

DESIRE
I WILL FOLLOW
NEW YEAR'S DAY
PRIDE (IN THE NAME OF LOVE)

Heyman, Edward

AFTER ALL, YOU'RE ALL I'M AFTER
ALIBI BABY
BLAME IT ON MY YOUTH
BLUEBIRD OF HAPPINESS
BLUE STAR (THE MEDIC THEME)
BODY AND SOUL
BOO-HOO
DARLING, NOT WITHOUT YOU
DRUMS IN MY HEART
EASY COME, EASY GO
HAVE YOU FORGOTTEN SO SOON?
HELLO, MY LOVER, GOODBYE
HO-HUM
I COVER THE WATERFRONT
I WANNA BE LOVED
JONNY
KINDA LIKE YOU
LOVE AND LEARN
LOVE LETTERS
MELANCHOLY LULLABY
MOONBURN
MUTINY IN THE PARLOR
MY DARLING
MY LOVE FOR YOU
MY SILENT LOVE
OUT OF NOWHERE
RAIN, RAIN, GO AWAY!
SEARCHING WIND, THE
SHAME ON YOU
SKY FELL DOWN, THE
STRANGE LOVE
THEY SAY
THIS IS ROMANCE
THROUGH THE YEARS

TO LOVE YOU AND TO LOSE YOU
TWO BUCK TIM FROM TIMBUCTOO
WEEP NO MORE, MY BABY
WHAT'S WRONG WITH ME?
WHEN I FALL IN LOVE
WHEN I GROW UP
YOU OUGHTA BE IN PICTURES
YOU'RE EVERYWHERE
YOU'RE MINE, YOU

Heymann, Werner R.

HA-CHA-CHA

Heyne, Joe

PETITE WALTZ (LA PETITE VALSE)

Heyward, DuBose

BESS, OH WHERE'S MY BESS?
BESS, YOU IS MY WOMAN NOW
I GOT PLENTY O' NUTTIN'
I LOVES YOU, PORGY
MY MAN'S GONE NOW
SUMMERTIME
WOMAN IS A SOMETIME THING, A

Heyward, Nick

LOVE PLUS ONE

Heywood, Donald

I'M COMING VIRGINIA

Heywood, Eddie

CANADIAN SUNSET
LAND OF DREAMS
SOFT SUMMER BREEZE

Hiatt, John

SHE DON'T LOVE NOBODY
SURE AS I'M SITTIN' HERE
WAY WE MAKE A BROKEN HEART,
  THE

Hice, Daniel

SUNDAY SCHOOL TO BROADWAY

Hice, Ruby

SUNDAY SCHOOL TO BROADWAY

Hickey, Emily

BELOVED, IT IS MORN

Hickey, Ersel

DON'T LET THE RAIN COME DOWN
  (CROOKED LITTLE MAN)

Hickman, Art

HOLD ME
ROSE ROOM

Hicks, Bob

SOMEONE BEFORE ME

Hicks, J.

THIS CRAZY LOVE

Hicks, Johnnie B.

SAY YOU

Hicks, Tony

CARRIE-ANNE
DEAR ELOISE
ON A CAROUSEL
PAY YOU BACK WITH INTEREST
STOP, STOP, STOP
TELL ME TO MY FACE

Hidalgo, David

WILL THE WOLF SURVIVE?

Higginbotham, Irene

FAT MEAT IS GOOD MEAT
GOOD MORNING HEARTACHE

Higginbotham, Robert

HI-HEEL SNEAKERS
SLIP-IN MULES (NO HIGH-HEEL
  SNEAKERS)

Higgins, Bertie

KEY LARGO

Higgins, Billy

GEORGE BLUES
THERE'LL BE SOME CHANGES MADE

Higgins, Sharon

WOMAN OF THE WORLD (LEAVE MY
  WORLD ALONE)

Hildebrand, Ray

HEY PAULA
YOUNG LOVERS

Hilderbrand, Diane

EASY COME, EASY GO

Hill, Al

LET ME GO, LOVER!

Hill, Alex

(I WOULD DO) ANYTHING FOR YOU
I'M CRAZY 'BOUT MY BABY
LONG ABOUT MIDNIGHT
RUMORS
SHOUT, SISTER, SHOUT

Hill, B.

CAN'T WE TRY

Hill, Billy

ALL ASHORE
ALONE AT A TABLE FOR TWO
CALL OF THE CANYON
CLOUDS WILL SOON ROLL BY, THE
EMPTY SADDLES
GLORY OF LOVE, THE
HAVE YOU EVER BEEN LONELY?
  (HAVE YOU EVER BEEN BLUE?)
IN THE CHAPEL IN THE MOONLIGHT
LAST ROUND-UP, THE
LIGHTS OUT
LOUISVILLE LADY

MILLER'S DAUGHTER MARIANNE,
    THE
NIGHT ON THE DESERT
OLD SPINNING WHEEL, THE
ON A LITTLE STREET IN SINGAPORE
OREGON, TRAIL, THE
RAIN
THERE'S A CABIN IN THE PINES
THEY CUT DOWN THE OLD PINE
    TREE
TIMBER
WAGON WHEELS
WHEN LOVE KNOCKS AT YOUR
    HEART
WHEN TWILIGHT COMES

Hill, Bunny

LET ME BE YOUR ANGEL

Hill, Byron

FOOL HEARTED MEMORY
PICKIN' UP STRANGERS

Hill, Dan

SOMETIMES WHEN WE TOUCH

Hill, David

I GOT STUNG
START MOVIN' (IN MY DIRECTION)

Hill, Dedette Lee

ADDRESS UNKNOWN
OLD FOLKS

Hill, Dusty

GIMME ALL YOUR LOVIN'
LEGS
SHARP DRESSED MAN
SLEEPING BAG
TUSH

Hill, Joe

ARRESTED FOR DRIVING WHILE
    BLIND
LA GRANGE

Hill, John

ARE YOU READY?

Hill, Lindell

MINI-SKIRT MINNIE

Hill, Mildred J.

HAPPY BIRTHDAY TO YOU

Hill, Patty Smith

HAPPY BIRTHDAY TO YOU

Hill, Robert

KISS OF FIRE

Hill, Stanley

I'LL PRAY FOR YOU

Hill, Stephen

I STILL BELIEVE IN YOU
LOVE REUNITED

Hill, Steve

SUMMER WIND

Hill, Teddy

BLUE RHYTHM FANTASY

Hill, Terry

OUR LIPS ARE SEALED

Hill, Tommy

FLAT TOP
GIDDYUP GO
SLOWLY
TEDDY BEAR

Hiller, Tony

SAVE YOUR KISSES FOR ME
UNITED WE STAND

Hilliard, Bob

ALICE IN WONDERLAND
ALONE AT LAST
ANY DAY NOW
AUTUMN WALTZ, THE
BE MY LIFE'S COMPANION
BIG BRASS BAND FROM BRAZIL,
    THE
BOUQUET OF ROSES
BOUTONNIERE
CARELESS HANDS
CIVILIZATION (BONGO, BONGO,
    BONGO)
COFFEE SONG, THE (THEY'VE GOT
    AN AWFUL LOT OF COFFEE IN
    BRAZIL)
DEAR HEARTS AND GENTLE
    PEOPLE
DEARIE
DON'T YOU BELIEVE IT
DOWNHEARTED
ENGLISH MUFFINS AND IRISH STEW
EV'RY STREET'S A BOULEVARD IN
    OLD NEW YORK
FROM THE CANDY STORE ON THE
    CORNER TO THE CHAPEL ON
    THE HILL
HOW DO YOU SPEAK TO AN ANGEL?
I FEEL LIKE I'M GONNA LIVE
    FOREVER
I'M LATE
IN THE MIDDLE OF THE HOUSE
IN THE WEE SMALL HOURS OF THE
    MORNING
KOOKIE LITTLE PARADISE, A
MENTION MY NAME IN SHEBOYGAN
MONEY BURNS A HOLE IN MY
    POCKET
MOONLIGHT GAMBLER
MY FAIR LADY
MY LITTLE CORNER OF THE WORLD
MY SUMMER LOVE
ONCE AROUND THE MOON
OUR DAY WILL COME
PANCHO MAXIMILIAN HERNANDEZ
PASSING FANCY
PLEASE STAY
POOR MAN'S ROSES, A (OR A RICH
    MAN'S GOLD)
RED SILK STOCKINGS AND GREEN
    PERFUME
SEND MY BABY BACK TO ME

SEVEN LITTLE GIRLS SITTING IN
  THE BACK SEAT
SHANGHAI
SOMEBODY BAD STOLE DE
  WEDDING BELL (WHO'S GOT DE
  DING DONG?)
STAY WITH THE HAPPY PEOPLE
THAT'S WHAT I LIKE
THESE WILL BE THE BEST YEARS
  OF OUR LIVES
THOUSAND ISLANDS SONG, THE (I
  LEFT MY LOVE ON ONE OF THE
  THOUSAND ISLANDS)
TOWER OF STRENGTH
WAITING GAME, THE
ZAMBEZI

Hilliard, Jimmy

THAT CHICK'S TOO YOUNG TO FRY

Hillman, Chris

I STILL BELIEVE IN YOU
LOVE REUNITED
ONE STEP FORWARD
SO YOU WANT TO BE A ROCK 'N'
  ROLL STAR
SUMMER WIND

Hillman, Roc

MY DEVOTION
NEW LOOK, THE

Hillman (and Perrin)

MAMMY'S LITTLE PUMPKIN
  COLORED COON

Hilton, Eddie

COVER ME

Himber, Richard

DAY AFTER DAY
IT ISN'T FAIR
MOMENTS IN THE MOONLIGHT

Hines, Earl

CAVERNISM

DEEP FOREST
GRAND PIANO BLUES
MONDAY DATE, A
ROSETTA
STORMY MONDAY BLUES
YOU CAN DEPEND ON ME

Hinton, Eddie

CHOO CHOO TRAIN

Hinton, Joe

GOTTA HOLD ON TO THIS FEELING

Hirsch, Ken

I'VE NEVER BEEN TO ME

Hirsch, Louis A.

ANNABEL LEE
COME AND DANCE WITH ME
GABY GLIDE, THE
GOING UP
HELLO, FRISCO!
IF YOU LOOK IN HER EYES
LEARN TO SMILE
LOVE NEST, THE
MARY
MY RAMBLER ROSE
'NEATH THE SOUTH SEA MOON
SIXTY SECONDS EVERY MINUTE (I
  THINK OF YOU)
SWEET KENTUCKY LADY
THROW ME A KISS
TICKLE TOE, THE (EVERYBODY
  OUGHT TO KNOW HOW TO DO)
WAITING
WEDDING GLIDE, THE
WHEN YOU HEAR LOVE'S HELLO

Hirsch, Maurice

KEEP ON SMILIN'

Hirsch, Walter

BABY, WHAT ELSE CAN I DO?
BABY BLUE EYES
BYE BYE BABY
CAROLINA SUNSHINE
'DEED I DO

DON'T EVER CHANGE
JOE TURNER BLUES
LAST NIGHT I DREAMED OF YOU
LULLABY IN RHYTHM
ME AND THE MOON
SAVE THE LAST DANCE FOR ME
STRANGE INTERLUDE
WAS IT RAIN?
WHO'S YOUR LITTLE WHO-ZIS?

Hirschhorn, Joel

CANDLE ON THE WATER
LET'S START ALL OVER AGAIN
LOVE NEVER GOES AWAY
MORNING AFTER, THE
ONE MORE MOUNTAIN TO CLIMB
WE MAY NEVER LOVE LIKE THIS
  AGAIN
WILL YOU BE STAYING AFTER
  SUNDAY?

Hiscock, Peter

WISHING WELL (DOWN IN THE
  WELL), THE

Hitchings, Duane

DON'T LOOK ANY FURTHER
YOUNG TURKS

Hite, Les

IT MUST HAVE BEEN A DREAM

Hludeck, David

FLIRTIN' WITH DISASTER

Hobart, George V.

ALMA, WHERE DO YOU LOVE?
BY THE SYCAMORE TREE
HELLO, HONEY
MY PAJAMA BEAUTY
PANAMA

Hobbs, Becky

I WANT TO KNOW YOU BEFORE WE
  MAKE LOVE

Hobgood, Bud

GET IT TOGETHER
LET YOURSELF GO
THERE WAS A TIME

Hobson, Joe

LET ME BE THE ONE
MAKING BELIEVE

Hodges, Johnny

HARMONY IN HARLEM
I'M BEGINNING TO SEE THE LIGHT
IT SHOULDN'T HAPPEN TO A DREAM
JEEP'S BLUES
WANDERLUST

Hodges, Mabon

I TAKE WHAT I WANT
L-O-V-E (LOVE)
TAKE ME TO THE RIVER

Hodgson, "Red"

MUSIC GOES 'ROUND AND 'ROUND,
  THE

Hodgson, Roger

BLOODY WELL RIGHT
DREAMER
GIVE A LITTLE BIT
GOODBYE STRANGER
IT'S RAINING AGAIN
LOGICAL SONG, THE
TAKE THE LONG WAY HOME

Hoefle, Carl

YA WANNA BUY A BUNNY?

Hoffman, Al

ALLEGHENY MOON
APPLE BLOSSOMS AND CHAPEL
  BELLS
ARE YOU REALLY MINE?
ASHBY DE LA ZOOCH
AUF WIEDERSEHEN, MY DEAR
BIBBIDI-BOBBIDI-BOO

BLACK EYED SUSAN BROWN
CHI-BABA, CHI-BABA (MY BAMBINA
  GO TO SLEEP)
CLOSE TO YOU
CRAZY WITH LOVE
DENNIS THE MENACE
DON'T STAY AWAY TOO LONG
DON'T YOU LOVE ME ANYMORE?
DREAM IS A WISH YOUR HEART
  MAKES, A
EVERYTHING'S IN RHYTHM WITH
  MY HEART
FIT AS A FIDDLE
FUZZY WUZZY
GILLY, GILLY, OSSENFEFFER,
  KATSENELLEN BOGEN BY THE
  SEA
GOODNIGHT, WHEREVER YOU ARE
HAPPY-GO-LUCKY YOU (AND
  BROKEN HEARTED ME)
HAWAIIAN WEDDING SONG, THE
HEARTACHES
HOT DIGGITY (DOG ZIGGITY BOOM)
I APOLOGIZE
I CAN'T TELL A WALTZ FROM A
  TANGO
I DON'T MIND WALKING IN THE
  RAIN
IF I KNEW YOU WERE COMIN' I'D'VE
  BAKED A CAKE
I'M A BIG GIRL NOW
I'M GONNA LIVE TILL I DIE
I'M IN A DANCING MOOD
I SAW STARS
IT'S WINTER AGAIN
IVY ROSE
JIMMY HAD A NICKEL
LA PLUME DE MA TANTE
LITTLE MAN, YOU'VE HAD A BUSY
  DAY
MAIRZY DOATS
MAKIN' FACES AT THE MAN IN THE
  MOON
MAMA, TEACH ME TO DANCE
MI CASA, SU CASA (MY HOUSE IS
  YOUR HOUSE)
MOON TALK
O DIO MIO
OH, WHAT A THRILL
OH-OH, I'M FALLING IN LOVE AGAIN
ON A BLUE AND MOONLESS NIGHT
ONE FINGER MELODY
ON THE BUMPY ROAD TO LOVE

PAPA LOVES MAMBO
ROLL UP THE CARPET
ROMANCE RUNS IN THE FAMILY
ROSES ARE FORGET-ME-NOTS
SECRETLY
SHE BROKE MY HEART IN THREE
  PLACES
SHE SHALL HAVE MUSIC
STORY OF A STARRY NIGHT, THE
TAKES TWO TO TANGO
THERE ISN'T ANY LIMIT TO MY
  LOVE
THERE'S NO TOMORROW
THIS'LL MAKE YOU WHISTLE
TORERO
TWO BUCK TIM FROM TIMBUCTOO
WHALE OF A TALE, A
WHO WALKS IN WHEN I WALK OUT?
WHY DON'T YOU PRACTICE WHAT
  YOU PREACH?
YOU'RE IN MY POWER (HA, HA, HA)

Hoffman, Dan

RUN, WOMAN, RUN

Hoffman, Gertrude

ON SAN FRANCISCO BAY

Hoffman, Henry

BOBBY'S GIRL

Hoffman, Jack

I LOVE THE SUNSHINE OF YOUR
  SMILE
TERESA

Hoffman, Max

BE MY LITTLE TEDDY BEAR

Hoffman, Ron

SAVING MY LOVE FOR YOU

Hoffmann, Max

BY THE SYCAMORE TREE

Hoffs, Susanna

ETERNAL FLAME

Hogan, Billy

EACH MOMENT (SPENT WITH YOU)

Hogan, Donald

WHEN WE GET MARRIED

Hogan, Ernest

ALL COONS LOOK ALIKE TO ME

Hogin, Sam

I BELIEVE IN YOU
TOO MANY LOVERS

Hoier, Thomas

DON'T BITE THE HAND THAT'S
   FEEDING YOU

Hokenson, Eddie

BAD GIRLS

Holden, Mark

LADY SOUL

Holden, Ron

LOVE YOU SO

Holden, Sidney

YANKEE ROSE

Holder, Noddy

CUM ON FEEL THE NOIZE
MY OH MY
RUN, RUNAWAY

Holdridge, Lee

EIGHT IS ENOUGH
JEREMY
MOMENT BY MOMENT

MOONLIGHTING
OTHER SIDE OF THE MOUNTAIN

Holiday, Billie

DON'T EXPLAIN
FINE AND MELLOW
GOD BLESS THE CHILD

Holiday, Jimmy

ALL I EVER NEED IS YOU
BRIGHTON HILL
DON'T CHANGE ON ME
I CHOSE TO SING THE BLUES
LOVE WILL FIND A WAY
PUT A LITTLE LOVE IN YOUR HEART
UNDERSTANDING

Holiner, Mann

I JUST COULDN'T TAKE IT, BABY
LOVE LIKE OURS, A
PADAM, PADAM
UNTIL THE REAL THING COMES
   ALONG (IT WILL HAVE TO DO)
YOU CAN'T STOP ME FROM LOVING
   YOU
YOUR MOTHER'S SON-IN-LAW

Hollan, Eddie

AIN'T TOO PROUD TO BEG

Holland, Brian

BABY, I NEED YOUR LOVING
BABY LOVE
BACK IN MY ARMS AGAIN
BERNADETTE
CAN I GET A WITNESS
COME AND GET THESE MEMORIES
COME SEE ABOUT ME
DARLING BABY
FOREVER CAME TODAY
GIVE ME JUST A LITTLE MORE TIME
HAPPENING, THE
HEAT WAVE
HEAVEN MUST HAVE SENT YOU
HOW SWEET IT IS (TO BE LOVED BY
   YOU)
I CAN'T HELP MYSELF (SUGAR PIE,
   HONEY BUNCH)

I GUESS I'LL ALWAYS LOVE YOU
I HEAR A SYMPHONY
I'M READY FOR LOVE
(COME 'ROUND HERE) I'M THE ONE
   YOU NEED
IN AND OUT OF LOVE
IN MY LONELY ROOM
IT'S THE SAME OLD SONG
JIMMY MACK
JUST A LITTLE BIT OF YOU
LA LA LA LA LA
LITTLE DARLING, I NEED YOU
LIVE WIRE
LOCKING UP MY HEART
LOVE IS HERE AND NOW YOU'RE
   GONE
LOVE IS LIKE AN ITCHING IN MY
   HEART
MICKEY'S MONKEY
MY WORLD IS EMPTY WITHOUT YOU
NOTHING BUT HEARTACHES
NOWHERE TO RUN
ONE, TWO, THREE (1-2-3)
PLAYBOY
PLEASE MR. POSTMAN
QUICKSAND
REACH OUT, I'LL BE THERE
REFLECTIONS
(I'M A) ROAD RUNNER
SEVEN OR ELEVEN (MY DIXIE PAIR
   O' DICE)
SHAKE ME, WAKE ME (WHEN IT'S
   OVER)
SOMETHING ABOUT YOU
STANDING IN THE SHADOWS OF
   LOVE
STOP! IN THE NAME OF LOVE
STRANGE I KNOW
TAKE ME IN YOUR ARMS (ROCK ME)
THIS OLD HEART OF MINE (IS WEAK
   FOR YOU)
WHERE DID OUR LOVE GO
YOU CAN'T HURRY LOVE
YOU KEEP ME HANGIN' ON
YOU KEEP RUNNING AWAY
YOU'RE A WONDERFUL ONE
YOUR UNCHANGING LOVE

Holland, Eddie

ALL I NEED
BABY, I NEED YOUR LOVING
BABY LOVE

BACK IN MY ARMS AGAIN
BEAUTY IS ONLY SKIN DEEP
BERNADETTE
CAN I GET A WITNESS
COME AND GET THESE MEMORIES
COME SEE ABOUT ME
DARLING BABY
EVERYBODY NEEDS LOVE
FOREVER CAME TODAY
HAPPENING, THE
HEAT WAVE
HEAVEN MUST HAVE SENT YOU
HOW SWEET IT IS (TO BE LOVED BY
    YOU)
I CAN'T HELP MYSELF (SUGAR PIE,
    HONEY BUNCH)
I GUESS I'LL ALWAYS LOVE YOU
I HEAR A SYMPHONY
I KNOW I'M LOSING YOU
I'M READY FOR LOVE
(COME 'ROUND HERE) I'M THE ONE
    YOU NEED
IN AND OUT OF LOVE
IN MY LONELY ROOM
IT'S THE SAME OLD SONG
JIMMY MACK
JUST A LITTLE BIT OF YOU
LA LA LA LA LA
LITTLE DARLING, I NEED YOU
LIVE WIRE
LOCKING UP MY HEART
LONELINESS MADE ME REALIZE
    (IT'S YOU I NEED)
LOVE IS HERE AND NOW YOU'RE
    GONE
LOVE IS LIKE AN ITCHING IN MY
    HEART
MICKEY'S MONKEY
MY WORLD IS EMPTY WITHOUT YOU
NOTHING BUT HEARTACHES
NOWHERE TO RUN
ONE, TWO, THREE (1-2-3)
QUICKSAND
REACH OUT, I'LL BE THERE
REFLECTIONS
(I'M A) ROAD RUNNER
SEVEN OR ELEVEN (MY DIXIE PAIR
    O' DICE)
SHAKE ME, WAKE ME (WHEN IT'S
    OVER)
SOMETHING ABOUT YOU
STANDING IN THE SHADOWS OF
    LOVE

STOP! IN THE NAME OF LOVE
TAKE ME IN YOUR ARMS (ROCK ME)
THIS OLD HEART OF MINE (IS WEAK
    FOR YOU)
TOO MANY FISH IN THE SEA
WHERE DID OUR LOVE GO
YOU CAN'T HURRY LOVE
YOU KEEP ME HANGIN' ON
YOU KEEP RUNNING AWAY
YOU'RE A WONDERFUL ONE
YOUR UNCHANGING LOVE

Holland, Randy

GIVING YOU THE BEST THAT I GOT

Hollander, Frederick

AWAKE IN A DREAM
BESIDE A MOONLIT STREAM
BLACK MARKET
BOYS IN THE BACK ROOM, THE
FALLING IN LOVE AGAIN (CAN'T
    HELP IT)
IT'S RAINING SUNBEAMS
JONNY
LOVELIGHT IN THE STARLIGHT
MOONLIGHT AND SHADOWS
MOON OVER BURMA
MY HEART AND I
STRANGE ENCHANTMENT
THAT SENTIMENTAL SANDWICH
THIS IS THE MOMENT
THRILL OF A LIFETIME
TRUE CONFESSION
WHISPERS IN THE DARK
YOU LEAVE ME BREATHLESS

Holler, Richard L.

ABRAHAM, MARTIN, AND JOHN
SNOOPY VS. THE RED BARON

Hollingsworth, Thekla

OH, MISS HANNAH!

Hollins, Laura

WHY DON'T YOU WRITE ME?

Hollis, Edwin

TALK TALK

Hollis, Mark

TALK TALK

Holloman, Rodney

GIRL, YOU KNOW IT'S TRUE

Holloway, Brenda

YOU'VE MADE ME SO VERY HAPPY

Holloway, Dean

BIG CITY

Holloway, Patrice

YOU'VE MADE ME SO VERY HAPPY

Holly, Buddy

LOVE'S MADE A FOOL OF YOU
PEGGY SUE
THAT'LL BE THE DAY
TRUE LOVE WAYS

Holmes, Jack

BLACKSMITH BLUES, THE

Holmes, Jake

I WOULD BE IN LOVE (ANYWAY)
SO CLOSE

Holmes, Malcolm

IF YOU LEAVE

Holmes, Robert

VOICES CARRY

Holmes, Rupert

ESCAPE (THE PIÑA COLADA SONG)
HIM
LETTERS THAT CROSS IN THE MAIL

MOONFALL
NEVER THE LUCK
PERFECT STRANGERS
QUEEN BEE
TIMOTHY
YOU GOT IT ALL

Holmes, Waldo

ROCKIN' SOUL
ROCK THE BOAT

Holmes, William H.

HAND THAT ROCKS THE CRADLE,
THE

Holofcener, Larry

I'M AVAILABLE
MR. WONDERFUL
TOO CLOSE FOR COMFORT

Holt, Alan

RIVER SEINE, THE (A.K.A. LA
SEINE)
SAILOR (YOUR HOME IS THE SEA)

Holt, David

WHAT EVERY GIRL SHOULD KNOW

Holt, Derek

COULDN'T GET IT RIGHT
I LOVE YOU

Holt, Isaac

WACK WACK

Holt, John

TIDE IS HIGH, THE

Holt, Will

DAYS OF THE WALTZ, THE
DO YOU REMEMBER?
DREAM BABIES
HOW I FEEL
LEMON TREE

LIGHT SINGS
SOUNDS
THIS IS MY SONG

Holvay, James

DON'T YOU CARE
HEY, BABY (THEY'RE PLAYIN' OUR
SONG)
KIND OF A DRAG
SUSAN

Holyfield, D.

(I WISH I HAD A) HEART OF STONE

Holyfield, Wayland

COULD I HAVE THIS DANCE
I'LL BE LEAVING ALONE
NOBODY LIKES SAD SONGS
REDNECKS, WHITE SOCKS, AND
BLUE RIBBON BEER
SOME BROKEN HEARTS NEVER
MEND
SURROUND ME WITH LOVE
TEARS OF THE LONELY
TILL THE RIVERS ALL RUN DRY
YOU'LL BE BACK (EVERY NIGHT IN
MY DREAMS)
YOU'RE MY BEST FRIEND
YOU'RE THE BEST BREAK THIS OLD
HEART EVER HAD

Holzel, Johann

VIENNA CALLING

Holzer, Lou

WHEN THEY PLAYED THE POLKA

Holzmann, Abe

BLAZE AWAY!
SMOKY MOKES (A.K.A. SMOKEY
MOKES)

Homer, Ben

JOLTIN' JOE DIMAGGIO
SENTIMENTAL JOURNEY

SHOOT THE SHERBERT TO ME,
HERBERT

Homer, Escamilla

ARE YOU SATISFIED?

Homer, Sidney

BANJO SONG, A

Honeyman-Scott, James

BRASS IN POCKET (I'M SPECIAL)

Hood, Alan

SUMMERTIME LIES

Hood, Basil

SAY NOT LOVE IS A DREAM

Hooker, Brian

BY AND BY
GIVE ME ONE HOUR
HUGUETTE WALTZ
LOVE FOR SALE
LOVE ME TONIGHT
ONLY A ROSE
SOME DAY
SONG OF THE VAGABONDS

Hooker, Jake

FREEDOM OVERSPILL
I LOVE ROCK 'N' ROLL

Hooker, John Lee

BOOGIE CHILLEN'
I'M IN THE MOOD

Hooper, Paul

BACK TO LIFE

Hooven, Jeff

CINDY'S BIRTHDAY

Hooven, Joseph

ANY WAY THE WIND BLOWS
BABY, YOU'VE GOT IT
GIMME LITTLE SIGN

Hooven, Marilyn

ANY WAY THE WIND BLOWS

Hope, Dorothy Jo

DADDY WAS AN OLD TIME
PREACHER MAN

Hope, Laurence

KASHMIRI SONG

Hopgood, Benjamin

WHEN YOU'RE ALL DRESSED UP
AND NO PLACE TO GO

Hopkins, Claude

(I WOULD DO) ANYTHING FOR YOU

Hopkins, Kenyon

BABY DOLL
NOT A SOUL

Hopkins, Sam "Lightnin' "

FEEL SO BAD

Hoppen, Lance

LOVE TAKES TIME

Hopper, Hal

THERE'S NO YOU

Hopper, Sean

HIP TO BE SQUARE

Hopwood, Aubrey

SOCIETY (OH! I LOVE SOCIETY)

SOLDIERS IN THE PARK, THE

Horlick, Harry

TWO GUITARS

Horn, Lawrence

SHAKE AND FINGERPOP
SHOOT YOUR SHOT

Horncastle, George

ACTIONS SPEAK LOUDER THAN
WORDS

Horne, Trevor

OWNER OF A LONELY HEART
VIDEO KILLED THE RADIO STAR

Horner, James

SOMEWHERE OUT THERE

Hornez, Andrez

C'EST SI BON

Hornsby, Bruce

EVERY LITTLE KISS
JACOB'S LADDER
MANDOLIN RAIN
NOBODY THERE BUT ME
VALLEY ROAD, THE
WAY IT IS, THE

Hornsby, John

JACOB'S LADDER
MANDOLIN RAIN
VALLEY ROAD, THE

Horovitz, Adam

(YOU GOTTA) FIGHT FOR YOUR
RIGHT (TO PARTY)

Horther, George

DOO WACKA DOO

Horton, Johnny

ALL FOR THE LOVE OF A GIRL
HONKY TONK MAN
I'M A ONE WOMAN MAN
I'M COMING HOME
SINK THE BISMARCK

Horton, McKinley

DON'T SAY NO TONIGHT
GOTTA GET YOU HOME TONIGHT

Horton, Sampson

WISHING FOR YOUR LOVE

Horton, Vaughn

BAR ROOM POLKA
CHOO CHOO CH'BOOGIE
HILLBILLY FEVER
HILLBILLY FEVER, NO. 2
METRO POLKA
MOCKIN' BIRD HILL
TEARDROPS IN MY HEART
TILL THE END OF THE WORLD
TOOLIE OOLIE DOOLIE (THE YODEL
POLKA)

Horton, William F.

GET A JOB

Horwitt, Arnold B.

ARE YOU WITH IT?
I FELL IN LOVE WITH YOU
IT'S A HELLUVA WAY TO RUN A
LOVE AFFAIR
JUST BEYOND THE RAINBOW
YOUNG AND FOOLISH

Horwitz, Charles

ALWAYS
BECAUSE
LUCKY JIM

Horwitz, Murray

HANDFUL OF KEYS

Hoschna, Karl

BIRTH OF PASSION, THE
CUDDLE UP A LITTLE CLOSER,
   LOVEY MINE
EVERY GIRLIE LOVES ME BUT THE
   GIRLIE I LOVE
EVERY LITTLE MOVEMENT (HAS A
   MEANING ALL ITS OWN)
SMILE SHE MEANS FOR YOU, THE
YAMA, YAMA MAN, THE

Hou, Philemon

GRAZING IN THE GRASS

Houdini, Wilmoth

STONE COLD DEAD IN DE MARKET

Hough, Will M.

BLOW THE SMOKE AWAY
I WONDER WHO'S KISSING HER
   NOW
WHAT'S THE USE OF DREAMING?
WHEN YOU FIRST KISS THE LAST
   GIRL YOU LOVED

House, Bob

COULD I HAVE THIS DANCE

House, Gerry

LITTLE ROCK
MIDNIGHT, ME AND THE BLUES

Houser, Hazel

MY BABY'S GONE

Houston, Cisco

BAD MAN BLUNDER
DOLLAR DOWN, A

Hoven, George

SIN

Hovey, Richard

STEIN SONG, A (IT'S ALWAYS FAIR
   WEATHER WHEN GOOD FELLOWS
   GET TOGETHER)

Howard, Bart

FIRST WARM DAY IN MAY, THE
FLY ME TO THE MOON (IN OTHER
   WORDS)
LET ME LOVE YOU
MIRACLES
MY LOVE IS A WANDERER
WOULD YOU BELIEVE IT
YOU ARE NOT MY FIRST LOVE

Howard, Bob

MY SON, MY SON
MYSTERY STREET

Howard, Chuck

COME WITH ME
HAPPY BIRTHDAY DARLIN'
I'M ALWAYS ON A MOUNTAIN WHEN
   I FALL

Howard, Dick

IN THE TOWN WHERE I WAS BORN
SOMEBODY ELSE IS TAKING MY
   PLACE

Howard, Eddy

CARELESS
IF I KNEW THEN (WHAT I KNOW
   NOW)
MILLION DREAMS AGO, A
MY LAST GOODBYE
NOW I LAY ME DOWN TO DREAM

Howard, Harlan

ABOVE AND BEYOND (THE CALL OF
   LOVE)
AIN'T GOT TIME FOR NOTHIN'
ANOTHER BRIDGE TO BURN
BLIZZARD, THE

BUSTED
CALL ME MR. IN-BETWEEN
CHOKIN' KIND, THE
DON'T CALL ME FROM A HONKY
   TONK
EVIL ON YOUR MIND
EXCUSE ME (I THINK I'VE GOT A
   HEARTACHE)
FOOLIN' AROUND
GO, CAT, GO
HEARTACHES BY THE NUMBER
HEARTBREAK, U.S.A.
HURTIN'S ALL OVER, THE
I DON'T BELIEVE I'LL FALL IN LOVE
   TODAY
I DON'T KNOW A THING ABOUT
   LOVE
I FALL TO PIECES
I'VE GOT A TIGER BY THE TAIL
I WISH I COULD FALL IN LOVE
   TODAY
I WON'T FORGET YOU
LIFE TURNED HER THAT WAY
MOMMY FOR A DAY
NO CHARGE
ODDS AND ENDS, BITS AND
   PIECES
ONE YOU SLIP AROUND WITH, THE
PICK ME UP ON YOUR WAY DOWN
SECOND HAND ROSE (SECOND
   HAND HEART)
SHE CALLED ME BABY
SHE'S GONE GONE GONE
SOMEBODY SHOULD LEAVE
SOMEWHERE TONIGHT
STREETS OF BALTIMORE
THREE STEPS TO THE PHONE
TIME TO BUM AGAIN
TOO MANY RIVERS
UNDER THE INFLUENCE OF LOVE
WHAT MAKES A MAN WANDER
WHEN I GET THROUGH WITH YOU
   (YOU'LL LOVE ME TOO)
WHERE I OUGHTA BE
WILL YOUR LAWYER TALK
   TO GOD?
YOU COMB HER HAIR
YOUR HEAD TURNED LEFT (AND I
   WAS ON THE RIGHT)
YOURS, LOVE
YOU TOOK HER OFF MY HANDS
   (NOW PLEASE TAKE HER OFF MY
   MIND)

Howard, Jan

LOVE IS A SOMETIMES THING

Howard, Jerome

MIDNIGHT LACE

Howard, John S.

STEPPIN' OUT

Howard, Joseph E.

BLOW THE SMOKE AWAY
GOODBYE, MY LADY LOVE
HELLO, MA BABY
I WONDER WHO'S KISSING HER
    NOW
SOMEWHERE IN FRANCE IS THE
    LILY
WHAT'S THE USE OF DREAMING?
WHEN YOU FIRST KISS THE LAST
    GIRL YOU LOVED

Howard, Ken

I'VE LOST YOU

Howard, Mel

DANCE ME LOOSE

Howard, Paul Mason

GANDY DANCERS' BALL, THE
SHRIMP BOATS

Howard, Richard

FACE TO FACE WITH THE GIRL OF
    MY DREAMS
GOODBYE, LITTLE GIRL OF MY
    DREAMS
WHEN THE LEAVES COME
    TUMBLING DOWN

Howard, Robert

DIGGING YOUR SCENE

Howe, Steve

AND YOU AND I
ROUNDABOUT
WHEN THE HEART RULES THE
    MIND

Howell, Dan

BIG BOY BLUE
FAN IT
OPEN THE DOOR, RICHARD

Howell, James G.

TIMBROOK

Howell, Jim

SOFTLY AND TENDERLY (I'LL HOLD
    YOU IN MY ARMS)

Hoyer, Mike

LOOKING AT THE WORLD THROUGH
    A WINDSHIELD

Hoyles, C.

HEARTBREAK (IT'S HURTING ME)

Hoyt, Charles H.

BOWERY, THE
REUBEN AND CYNTHIA

Hoyt, Harry

MEET ME DOWN AT THE CORNER

Huang, Nancy

COMING TO AMERICA

Hubbell, Raymond

HELLO, HONEY
LADDER OF ROSES, THE
LOOK AT THE WORLD AND SMILE
PANAMA
POOR BUTTERFLY
SOMEBODY ELSE

Hucknall, Mick

HOLDING BACK THE YEARS

Huddleston, Floyd

LOVE
TROUBLE WITH HARRY, THE
YOU STARTED SOMETHING

Hudson, Al

CUTIE PIE

Hudson, Bill

RENDEZVOUS

Hudson, Brett

RENDEZVOUS

Hudson, G.

CUTIE PIE

Hudson, Howard

LADY (YOU BRING ME UP)

Hudson, James

GOODNIGHT, WELL IT'S TIME TO GO

Hudson, Mark

RENDEZVOUS

Hudson, Susan

GREEN GRASS

Hudson, Will

HOBO ON PARK AVENUE
HOW WAS I TO KNOW?
I'LL NEVER TELL YOU I LOVE YOU
JAZZNOCRACY
MOONGLOW
MOON IS GRINNING AT ME, THE
MR. GHOST GOES TO TOWN
ORGAN GRINDER'S SWING
POPCORN MAN

Hunter, Alberta

DOWN HEARTED BLUES

Hunter, Don

I DON'T KNOW WHY
YOU MET YOUR MATCH

Hunter, Hank

BORN TO BE IN LOVE WITH YOU
FOOTSTEPS
GINGER BREAD
I'M GONNA BE WARM THIS WINTER
JUMPING JACK
JUST FOR OLD TIME'S SAKE
LOOKING FOR LOVE
MY EMPTY ARMS
SECOND HAND LOVE
VACATION

Hunter, Ian

GOLDEN AGE OF ROCK 'N' ROLL
SHIPS

Hunter, Ivory Joe

DON'T FALL IN LOVE WITH ME
EMPTY ARMS
I ALMOST LOST MY MIND
I NEED YOU SO
I QUIT MY PRETTY MAMA
IT MAY SOUND SILLY
MY WISH CAME TRUE
NO OTHER ONE
OUT OF SIGHT, OUT OF MIND
PRETTY MAMA BLUES
SINCE I MET YOU BABY

Hunter, Ivy

ASK THE LONELY
CAN YOU JERK LIKE ME
DANGER HEARTBREAK DEAD
   AHEAD
I'LL ALWAYS LOVE YOU
I'LL KEEP HOLDING ON
LOVING YOU IS SWEETER THAN
   EVER
MY BABY LOVES ME
WILD ONE

YESTERDAY'S DREAMS
YOU
YOU'VE BEEN IN LOVE TOO LONG

Hunter, Robert

HELL IN A BUCKET
SUGAREE
SUGAR MAGNOLIA
TOUCH OF GREY
TRUCKIN'
UNCLE JOHN'S BAND
WEST L.A. FADEAWAY

Hupfeld, Herman

ARE YOU MAKIN' ANY MONEY?
AS TIME GOES BY
CALINDA, THE (BOO-JOOM, BOO-
   JOOM, BOO!)
I'VE GOTTA GET UP AND GO TO
   WORK
LET'S PUT OUT THE LIGHTS AND GO
   TO SLEEP
NIGHT OWL
SING SOMETHING SIMPLE
WHEN YUBA PLAYS THE RHUMBA
   ON THE TUBA

Hupp, Deborah Kay

ARE YOU ON THE ROAD TO LOVIN'
   ME AGAIN?
DON'T CALL HIM A COWBOY
YOU DECORATED MY LIFE

Hurdon, Basil

ALADDIN
FORTUNETELLER

Hurdon, Dyer

ALADDIN
FORTUNETELLER

Hurlburt, Claude

MY HAT'S ON THE SIDE OF MY
   HEAD

Hurley, John

LAND OF MILK AND HONEY, THE
SON-OF-A-PREACHER MAN
SPREAD IT ON THICK

Hurst, Mike

TOUCH ME

Hurt, Jim

I KEEP COMING BACK
LOVE IN THE FIRST DEGREE

Hurtt, Phil

BEST DISCO IN TOWN, THE

Husky, Ferlin

COUNTRY MUSIC IS HERE TO STAY
TIMBER, I'M FALLING
TIMBER, I'M FALLING IN LOVE

Huston, Paul

ME, MYSELF, AND I

Huston, Rex

FAMOUS LAST WORDS OF A FOOL

Hutch, Willie

I'LL BE THERE
LOVE POWER

Hutchence, Michael

DEVIL INSIDE
NEED YOU TONIGHT
NEVER TEAR US APART
NEW SENSATION
WHAT YOU NEED

Hutcheson, Susan

I LOVE THE NIGHTLIFE (DISCO
   ROUND)

Hutchings, Duane

INFATUATION

Hutchins, Daryl

I WONDER, I WONDER, I WONDER

Hutchinson, Edward

SAMMY

Hutchinson, Sheila

SO I CAN LOVE YOU

Hutter, Ralf

AUTOBAHN

Hutton, Leo

FUNKY JUDGE

Hyde, Alex

WITH THEE I SWING

Hyde, Madeline

LITTLE GIRL

Hyman, Dick

MINOTAUR, THE

Hyman, Jeff

I WANNA BE SEDATED
PINHEAD
ROCKAWAY BEACH
SHEENA IS A PUNK ROCKER

Hyman, Rob

ALL YOU ZOMBIES
AND WE DANCED
DAY BY DAY
SATELLITE
TIME AFTER TIME
WHERE DO THE CHILDREN GO?

Hynde, Chrissie

BACK ON THE CHAIN GANG
BRASS IN POCKET (I'M SPECIAL)
DON'T GET ME WRONG
MIDDLE OF THE ROAD
SHOW ME

Ian, Janis

AT SEVENTEEN
JESSE
SOCIETY'S CHILD (BABY, I'VE BEEN
    THINKING)
UNDER THE COVERS

Ibarra, Sammy

LO MUCHO TE QUIERO (THE MORE I
    LOVE YOU)

Ibbotson, J.

I'VE BEEN LOOKIN'

Icini

SUMMERTIME IN VENICE

Ide, Barney

NEW LOOK, THE

Idol, Billy

EYES WITHOUT A FACE
HOT IN THE CITY
REBEL YELL
SWEET SIXTEEN
WHITE WEDDING

Idriss, Ramez

SOMETHING OLD, SOMETHING NEW
WOODY WOODPECKER
WORRY, WORRY, WORRY

Iglesias, Julio

ALL OF YOU

Ilda, Lewis

JUST A LITTLE FOND AFFECTION
LITTLE OLD MILL, THE (WENT
    ROUND AND ROUND)

Imes, Mildred

YOU'RE THE REASON

Immel, Jerrold

DALLAS

Imus, Fred

I DON'T WANT TO HAVE TO MARRY
    YOU

Ingle, Doug

IN-A-GADDA-DA-VIDA

Ingraham, Herbert

ALL THAT I ASK OF YOU IS LOVE
BECAUSE I'M MARRIED NOW
DON'T WAKE ME UP, I'M DREAMING
GOODBYE, ROSE
HOO-OO, AIN'T YOU COMING OUT
    TO-NIGHT!
ROSES BRING DREAMS OF YOU
WHEN I DREAM IN THE GLOAMING
    OF YOU
WON'T YOU WALTZ "HOME SWEET
    HOME" WITH ME?
YOU ARE THE IDEAL OF MY
    DREAMS

Ingraham, Roy

NO REGRETS

Ingram, Arnold

FLOAT ON

Ingram, James

P.Y.T. (PRETTY YOUNG THING)
YAH MO B THERE

Ingram, Luther

RESPECT YOURSELF

Inman, Autry

I DON'T BELIEVE YOU'VE MET MY
  BABY
IT'S BEEN SO LONG
MISTER MOON
VOLUNTEER, THE

Innis, Dave

DARE ME

Innis, Louis

DADDY O

Insetta, Paul

SITTING BY THE WINDOW

Instone, Anthony Gordon

HERE COMES THAT RAINY DAY
  FEELING AGAIN

INXS

LISTEN LIKE THIEVES

Ioannides, Jean

ALL ALONE AM I

Irby, Jerry

DRIVIN' NAILS IN MY COFFIN'
KEEPER OF MY HEART

Irby, Joyce

MR. D.J.

Irby, Maurice, Jr.

APPLES, PEACHES, PUMPKIN PIE
STRAWBERRY SHORTCAKE

Iris, Don

RAPPER, THE

Irons, Eddie

DAZZ

Irvine, Weldon J., Jr.

TO BE YOUNG, GIFTED AND BLACK

Irving, Lonnie

PINBALL MACHINE

Irving, Roy

YOU NEED HANDS

Irwin, Gene

FIVE O'CLOCK WHISTLE, THE

Irwin, May

MAMIE, COME KISS YOUR HONEY

Isbell, Alvertis

I'LL TAKE YOU THERE
I'VE NEVER FOUND A GIRL (TO
  LOVE ME LIKE YOU DO)
LOVE BONES

Isley, Christopher

THAT LADY

Isley, Ernest

BETWEEN THE SHEETS
CARAVAN OF LOVE
DON'T SAY GOODNIGHT (IT'S TIME
  FOR LOVE)
FIGHT THE POWER
FOR THE LOVE OF YOU
PRIDE, THE
TAKE ME TO THE NEXT PHASE
THAT LADY

Isley, Marvin

BETWEEN THE SHEETS
CARAVAN OF LOVE
DON'T SAY GOODNIGHT (IT'S TIME
  FOR LOVE)
FIGHT THE POWER
FOR THE LOVE OF YOU
PRIDE, THE
TAKE ME TO THE NEXT PHASE
THAT LADY

Isley, O'Kelly

BETWEEN THE SHEETS
DON'T SAY GOODNIGHT (IT'S TIME
  FOR LOVE)
FIGHT THE POWER
FOR THE LOVE OF YOU
IT'S YOUR THING
I TURNED YOU ON
NOBODY BUT ME
PRIDE, THE
SHOUT
TAKE ME TO THE NEXT PHASE

Isley, Ronald

BETWEEN THE SHEETS
DON'T SAY GOODNIGHT (IT'S TIME
  FOR LOVE)
FIGHT THE POWER
FOR THE LOVE OF YOU
IT'S YOUR THING
I TURNED YOU ON
NOBODY BUT ME
PRIDE, THE
SHOUT
TAKE ME TO THE NEXT PHASE

Isley, Rudolph

BETWEEN THE SHEETS
DON'T SAY GOODNIGHT (IT'S TIME
  FOR LOVE)
FIGHT THE POWER
FOR THE LOVE OF YOU
IT'S YOUR THING
I TURNED YOU ON
NOBODY BUT ME
PRIDE, THE
SHOUT
TAKE ME TO THE NEXT PHASE

Ivey, Herbert

ANGEL IN YOUR ARMS

Ivory, J.

ARE YOU SINGLE?

Iyall, Debora

GIRL IN TROUBLE, A (IS A
    TEMPORARY THING)

Jaarczyk, Herbert

I'M ALWAYS HEARING WEDDING
    BELLS

Jabara, Paul

FIGHT
IT'S RAINING MEN
LAST DANCE, THE
MAIN EVENT, THE
NO MORE TEARS (ENOUGH IS
    ENOUGH)

Jablecki, Steve

SWEET MARY

Jacks, Terry

WHICH WAY YOU GOIN' BILLY?

Jackson, Al

CALL ME (COME BACK HOME)
HOLE IN THE WALL
I'M STILL IN LOVE WITH YOU
LET'S STAY TOGETHER
LOOK WHAT YOU DONE FOR ME
SOUL-LIMBO
YOU OUGHT TO BE WITH ME

Jackson, Al, Jr.

GREEN ONIONS
HIP HUG-HER
TIME IS TIGHT

Jackson, Anthony

FOR THE LOVE OF MONEY

Jackson, Arthur

BEST OF EVERYTHING, THE
EVERY DAY
SOUTH SEA ISLES (A.K.A. SUNNY
    SOUTH SEA ISLANDS)

Jackson, Arthur J.

SOMEHOW IT SELDOM COMES TRUE

Jackson, Bernard

HAPPY
LATELY

Jackson, Bernard Leon, Jr.

CLOSER THAN FRIENDS
SHOWER ME WITH YOUR LOVE

Jackson, Billy

DON'T THROW YOUR LOVE AWAY

Jackson, Charles, Jr.

INSEPARABLE
I'VE GOT LOVE ON MY MIND
MORE YOU DO IT, THE (THE MORE I
    LIKE IT DONE)
OUR LOVE
SOPHISTICATED LADY (SHE'S A
    DIFFERENT LADY)
THIS WILL BE (AN EVERLASTING
    LOVE)

Jackson, Christopher

YOU LITTLE TRUSTMAKER

Jackson, Chuck

HERE I AM (COME AND TAKE ME)
I DON'T WANT TO CRY
UNITED TOGETHER
WHERE DO BROKEN HEARTS GO

Jackson, David, Jr.

NO NO SONG

Jackson, Deon

LOVE MAKES THE WORLD GO
    'ROUND

Jackson, Dimple Marcene

TELL ME THE TRUTH

Jackson, Freddie

JAM TONIGHT
TASTY LOVE

Jackson, Gary

SINCE YOU SHOWED ME HOW TO BE
    HAPPY

Jackson, Gary L.

(YOUR LOVE KEEPS LIFTING ME)
    HIGHER AND HIGHER

Jackson, George

DOUBLE LOVIN'
I'D RATHER BE AN OLD MAN'S
    SWEETHEART (THAN A YOUNG
    MAN'S FOOL)
MAN AND A HALF, A
MINI-SKIRT MINNIE
OLD TIME ROCK AND ROLL
ONE BAD APPLE (DON'T SPOIL THE
    WHOLE BUNCH)
SNATCHING IT BACK
TOO WEAK TO FIGHT

Jackson, George Harold

TELL ME THE TRUTH

Jackson, Gerald

TURN THE BEAT AROUND

Jackson, Howard M.

LAZY RHAPSODY

Jackson, Janet

CONTROL
LET'S WAIT AWHILE
NASTY
WHEN I THINK OF YOU

Jackson, Jermaine

I THINK IT'S LOVE
LET ME TICKLE YOUR FANCY
(CLOSEST THING TO) PERFECT

Jackson, Jill

YOU'LL DRIVE ME BACK (INTO HER
ARMS AGAIN)
YOUNG LOVERS

Jackson, J. J.

BUT IT'S ALRIGHT
LONG LIVE OUR LOVE

Jackson, Joanne

HUNGRY FOR LOVE

Jackson, Joe

BREAKING US IN TWO
IS SHE REALLY GOING OUT WITH
HIM?
STEPPIN' OUT
YOU CAN'T GET WHAT YOU WANT
(TILL YOU KNOW WHAT YOU
WANT)

Jackson, June

SHOW BUSINESS

Jackson, Marlon

DON'T GO

Jackson, Martin

BREAKOUT

Jackson, McKinley

TRYING TO HOLD ON TO MY
WOMAN

Jackson, Michael

BAD
BEAT IT
BILLE JEAN
CENTIPEDE
DIRTY DIANA
DON'T STOP 'TIL YOU GET ENOUGH
GIRL IS MINE, THE
HEARTBREAK HOTEL
I JUST CAN'T STOP LOVING YOU
LOVELY ONE
MUSCLES
SAY SAY SAY
SHAKE YOUR BODY (DOWN TO THE
GROUND)
STATE OF SHOCK
WANNA BE STARTIN' SOMETHIN'
WAY YOU MAKE ME FEEL, THE
WE ARE THE WORLD

Jackson, Mike

KNOCK ME A KISS

Jackson, Milt

BAGS' GROOVE

Jackson, Paul M., Jr.

LET ME TICKLE YOUR FANCY

Jackson, Peter

TURN THE BEAT AROUND

Jackson, Randy

LOVELY ONE

Jackson, Ray

I COULD NEVER BE PRESIDENT
I DON'T WANT TO BE RIGHT (IF
LOVING YOU IS WRONG)
IF YOU'RE READY (COME GO WITH
ME)

I LIKE WHAT YOU'RE DOING (TO ME)
TAKE CARE OF YOUR HOMEWORK
TOUCH A HAND, MAKE A FRIEND
WHO SHOT SAM?
WHO'S MAKING LOVE?

Jackson, Rudy

HEARTS OF STONE

Jackson, Stephen

SHAKE YOUR BODY (DOWN TO THE
GROUND)

Jackson, Stonewall

MY SONG
WHY I'M WALKIN'

Jackson, Tony

PRETTY BABY

Jackson, Wanda

IN THE MIDDLE OF A HEARTACHE
KICKIN' OUR HEARTS AROUND
RIGHT OR WRONG

Jackson, William

SO MUCH IN LOVE

Jacobi, Victor

DEEP IN YOUR EYES
LITTLE GIRLS, GOODBYE
ON MIAMI SHORE
YOU ARE FREE

Jacobs, Al

BUT I DID
EVERY DAY OF MY LIFE
HURT
IF I GIVE MY HEART TO YOU
I'M JUST AN ORDINARY HUMAN
I NEED YOU NOW
MY BELIEVING HEART
THIS IS MY COUNTRY

Jacobs, Jacob

BEI MIR BIST DU SCHOEN (MEANS
    THAT YOU'RE GRAND)

Jacobs, Jim

BEAUTY SCHOOL DROPOUT
SUMMER NIGHTS

Jacobs, Walter

JUKE
SAD HOURS
YOU'D BETTER WATCH YOURSELF

Jacobs-Bond, Carrie

I LOVE YOU TRULY
JUST A-WEARYIN' FOR YOU
PERFECT DAY, A (THE END OF)

Jacobson, Arthur

I'M HAPPY THAT LOVE HAS FOUND
    YOU

Jacobson, Harry

MY LOVE FOR YOU

Jacobson, Kenny

PUT A LIGHT IN THE WINDOW
SWINGIN' SHEPHERD BLUES, THE

Jacobson, Sid

BOY WITHOUT A GIRL, A
DON'T PITY ME
END, THE (A.K.A. AT THE END OF
    THE RAINBOW)
I'VE COME OF AGE
WARM
YOGI

Jacquet, Illinois

BLACK VELVET
DON'CHA GO 'WAY MAD
JUST WHEN WE'RE FALLING IN
    LOVE
ROBBINS NEST

Jaffe, Moe

BELL BOTTOM TROUSERS
COLLEGIATE
GYPSY IN MY SOUL, THE
IF I HAD MY LIFE TO LIVE OVER
IF YOU ARE BUT A DREAM
I LOVE THE COLLEGE GIRLS
I'M MY OWN GRANDPAW
    (GRANDMAW)

Jaffee, Ben

PLEASE NO SQUEEZA DA BANANA

Jagger, Mick

19TH NERVOUS BREAKDOWN
ANGIE
AS TEARS GO BY
BEAST OF BURDEN
BROWN SUGAR
CRAZY MAMA
DANDELION
DOO DOO DOO DOO DOO
    (HEARTBREAKER)
EMOTIONAL RESCUE
FOOL TO CRY
GET OFF MY CLOUD
GIMME SHELTER
HANG FIRE
HAPPY
HAVE YOU SEEN YOUR MOTHER,
    BABY, STANDING IN THE
    SHADOW?
HEART OF STONE
HONKY TONK WOMEN
HOT STUFF
I CAN'T GET NO SATISFACTION
IT'S ONLY ROCK 'N' ROLL (BUT I
    LIKE IT)
JUMPIN' JACK FLASH
JUST ANOTHER NIGHT
LADY JANE
LAST TIME, THE
LET'S SPEND THE NIGHT TOGETHER
LET'S WORK
MEMO FROM TURNER
MISS YOU
MOTHER'S LITTLE HELPER
OUT OF TIME
PAINT IT BLACK
PLAY WITH FIRE

RUBY TUESDAY
SHATTERED
SHE'S A RAINBOW
SHE'S SO COLD
SHE WAS HOT
START ME UP
STREET FIGHTING MAN
TELL ME (YOU'RE COMING BACK)
TUMBLING DICE
UNDERCOVER OF THE NIGHT
WAITING ON A FRIEND
WE LOVE YOU
WILD HORSES
YOU CAN'T ALWAYS GET WHAT YOU
    WANT

Jam, Jimmy

MAKING LOVE IN THE RAIN

Jamerson, James, Jr.

DON'T HOLD BACK

James, Arthur

FOR ALL WE KNOW

James, Casey

LIVIN' IT UP (FRIDAY NIGHT)
MAMA CAN'T BUY YOU LOVE

James, Dick

SHUT THAT GATE

James, Doug

HOW AM I SUPPOSED TO LIVE
    WITHOUT YOU?

James, Etta

DANCE WITH ME HENRY
IF I CAN'T HAVE YOU
SOMETHING'S GOT A HOLD ON ME

James, Freddy

UNSUSPECTING HEART

James, Harry

BACK BEAT BOOGIE
EVERY DAY OF MY LIFE
EVERYTHING BUT YOU
I'M BEGINNING TO SEE THE LIGHT
JUMP TOWN
LIFE GOES TO A PARTY
MUSIC MAKERS
PECKIN'
TRUMPET BLUES
TWO O'CLOCK JUMP

James, Inez

COME TO BABY, DO
PILLOW TALK
VAYA CON DIOS (MAY GOD BE WITH
 YOU)
WHAT DO I HAVE TO DO TO MAKE
 YOU LOVE ME?

James, Jesse

BOOGALOO DOWN BROADWAY
HITCH IT TO THE HORSE
HORSE, THE
HORSE FEVER

James, Marguerite

LOVE HAS JOINED US TOGETHER

James, Mark

ALWAYS ON MY MIND
EYES OF A NEW YORK WOMAN,
 THE
HOOKED ON A FEELING
IT'S ONLY LOVE
MOODY BLUE
ONE HELL OF A WOMAN
SUSPICIOUS MINDS

James, Palmer E.

BACK UP TRAIN

James, Paul

CAN THIS BE LOVE?
CAN'T WE BE FRIENDS?
FINE AND DANDY

FREIGHT TRAIN
LET'S GO EAT WORMS IN THE
 GARDEN

James, Rich

LOOSEY'S RAP

James, Rick

COLD BLOODED
DANCE WIT' ME
GIVE IT TO ME BABY
IN MY HOUSE
PARTY ALL THE TIME
SEVENTEEN
STANDING ON THE TOP

James, Sonny

DON'T KEEP ME HANGING ON
I'LL KEEP HOLDING ON (JUST TO
 YOUR LOVE)
I'M SO IN LOVE WITH YOU
ROOM IN YOUR HEART
SATIN PILLOWS
TRUE LOVE'S A BLESSING
YOU'RE THE ONLY WORLD I KNOW

James, Tommy

BALL OF FIRE
CRIMSON AND CLOVER
CRYSTAL BLUE PERSUASION
DRAGGIN' THE LINE
MONY, MONY
SUGAR ON SUNDAY
SWEET CHERRY WINE
THREE TIMES IN LOVE
TIGHTER, TIGHTER

Jameson, Tom

SUMMERTIME, SUMMERTIME

Janis, Elsie

LOVE, YOUR MAGIC SPELL IS
 EVERYWHERE
SOME SORT OF SOMEBODY

Jankel, Chaz

AI NO CORRIDA

Jankowski, Horst

WALK IN THE BLACK FOREST

Jans, Tom

LOVING ARMS

Jansen, Bernard

LONGING FOR YOU

Janssen, Danny

KEEP ON SINGING
LA, LA, LA (IF I HAD YOU)
LITTLE WOMAN
SOMETHING'S WRONG WITH ME

Jardine, Alan

ALMOST SUMMER
FRIENDS

Jarrard, John

LONELY ALONE
WHAT'S A MEMORY LIKE YOU
 (DOING IN A LOVE LIKE THIS)
"YOU'VE GOT" THE TOUCH

Jarre, Maurice

MARMALADE, MOLASSES, AND
 HONEY
SHOGUN (MARIKO'S THEME)
SOMEWHERE MY LOVE (LARA'S
 THEME)
THEME FROM "LAWRENCE OF
 ARABIA"
YOU HAVE THE CHOICE

Jarreau, Al

BREAKIN' AWAY
MOONLIGHTING
MORNIN'
TIME TO CARE, A

Jarrell, Phil

TORN BETWEEN TWO LOVERS

Jarrett, Ted

IT'S LOVE, BABY
LOVE, LOVE, LOVE

Jarrett, Tommy

HOW THE TIME FLIES

Jarvis, John

JULIA
SMALL TOWN GIRL

Jary, Michael

TOY SOLDIERS

Jason, Will

BIG BAD WOLF WAS DEAD, THE
ISN'T THIS A NIGHT FOR LOVE?
PENTHOUSE SERENADE (A.K.A.
  WHEN WE'RE ALONE)

Jasper, Christopher

BETWEEN THE SHEETS
CARAVAN OF LOVE
DON'T SAY GOODNIGHT (IT'S TIME
  FOR LOVE)
PRIDE, THE
TAKE ME TO THE NEXT PHASE

Jasper, Raymond

THAT'S WHAT YOU THINK

Javits, Joan

SANTA BABY

Jaxon, Frankie

FAN IT

Jay, Fred

HAPPY JOURNEY

I CRIED A TEAR
WEDDING, THE (LA NOVIA)
WHAT AM I LIVING FOR?

Jay, Jimmy

AT EASE, HEART

Jay, Penny

DON'T LET ME CROSS OVER

Jaye, Miles

LET'S START LOVE OVER

Jefferson, Joseph

LOVE DON'T LOVE NOBODY
THEY JUST CAN'T STOP IT (THE
  GAMES PEOPLE PLAY)

Jefferson, Joseph B.

MIGHTY LOVE, A
ONE OF A KIND (LOVE AFFAIR)

Jeffrey, Allan

OLD CAPE COD

Jeffrey, William

VERY SPECIAL

Jeffreys, Alan

HOPELESS

Jeffries, Herb

CANDY STORES BLUES

Jemmott, Gerald

SO EXCITED

Jenkins, Andrew

DEATH OF FLOYD COLLINS, THE

Jenkins, Barry

MONTEREY
SAN FRANCISCAN NIGHTS
SKY PILOT
WHEN I WAS YOUNG

Jenkins, David

COOL LOVE
DON'T WANT TO LIVE WITHOUT IT
I WANT YOU TONIGHT
LOVE WILL FIND A WAY
WHATCHA GONNA DO?

Jenkins, Floyd

HOME IN SAN ANTONE
LOW AND LONELY

Jenkins, Gordon

BLUE EVENING
BLUE PRELUDE
GOODBYE
HOMESICK—THAT'S ALL
MARRIED I CAN ALWAYS GET
NEVER LEAVE ME
NEW YORK'S MY HOME
P.S. I LOVE YOU
REPEAT AFTER ME
SAN FERNANDO VALLEY
THIS IS ALL I ASK
TOMORROW
WHEN A WOMAN LOVES A MAN
YOU HAVE TAKEN MY HEART

Jenkins, L.

SOMEBODY LIED

Jenkins, Thomas

SINGLE LIFE

Jenkins, Tomi

BACK AND FORTH
CANDY
FREAKY DANCIN'
JUST BE YOURSELF
SHE'S STRANGE
WORD UP

Jenney, Jack

MAN WITH A HORN

Jennings, Dick

LITTLE OLD WINEDRINKER ME

Jennings, Waylon

AIN'T NO ROAD TOO LONG
ANITA, YOU'RE DREAMING
ARE YOU SURE HANK DONE IT THIS
 WAY?
GOOD-HEARTED WOMAN, A
I'VE ALWAYS BEEN CRAZY
JUST TO SATISFY YOU
MY ROUGH AND ROWDY DAYS
THEME FROM "DUKES OF
 HAZZARD" (GOOD OL' BOYS)
THIS TIME

Jennings, Will

BACK IN THE HIGH LIFE AGAIN
BOYS NIGHT OUT
DIDN'T WE ALMOST HAVE IT ALL
DON'T YOU KNOW WHAT THE NIGHT
 CAN DO?
FEELIN'S
FINER THINGS, THE
HIGHER LOVE
I'LL NEVER LOVE THIS WAY AGAIN
I'M SO GLAD I'M STANDING HERE
 TODAY
LOOKS LIKE WE MADE IT
LOVE LIVES ON
NO NIGHT SO LONG
PEOPLE ALONE
ROLL WITH IT
SOMEWHERE IN THE NIGHT
UP WHERE WE BELONG
VALERIE
WHILE YOU SEE A CHANCE

Jennings, Willie

I NEED YOUR LOVIN'

Jensen, Harry

TROGLODYTE (CAVE MAN)

Jentes, Harry

I DON'T WANT TO GET WELL (I'M IN
 LOVE WITH A BEAUTIFUL NURSE)

Jeopardi, Jeff

I WANNA BE A COWBOY

Jerome, Jerome

LOVE IS LIKE A CIGARETTE

Jerome, John

CHINCHERINCHEE

Jerome, M. K.

BRIGHT EYES
IF I COULD LEARN TO LOVE (AS
 WELL AS I FIGHT)
JUST A BABY'S PRAYER AT
 TWILIGHT
MARY, DEAR
MY LITTLE BUCKAROO
OLD PAL, WHY DON'T YOU ANSWER
 ME
SOME SUNDAY MORNING
SWEET DREAMS, SWEETHEART
THRU THE COURTESY OF LOVE
WHO CARES WHAT PEOPLE SAY?
WISH THAT I WISH TONIGHT, THE
WOULD YOU BELIEVE ME?
YOU, YOU DARLIN'

Jerome, William

AND THE GREEN GRASS GREW ALL
 AROUND
ANY OLD PLACE I HANG MY HAT IS
 HOME SWEET HOME TO ME
BACK HOME IN TENNESSEE
BEDELIA
CHINATOWN, MY CHINATOWN
DON'T PUT ME OFF AT BUFFALO
 ANY MORE
GET OUT AND GET UNDER THE
 MOON
GHOST THAT NEVER WALKED, THE
GOODBYE, MR. RAGTIME
GOODNIGHT, MY OWN TRUE LOVE

HAT MY FATHER WORE ON ST.
 PATRICK'S DAY, THE
I'LL MAKE A RING AROUND ROSIE
I'M TIRED
I'M UNLUCKY
KISS YOUR MINSTREL BOY
 GOODBYE
LITTLE BUNCH OF SHAMROCKS, A
LOVE DAYS
MEET ME IN ROSE-TIME, ROSIE
MISTER DOOLEY
MY IRISH MOLLY O
MY PEARL'S A BOWERY GIRL
OH, MARIE
ON THE OLD FALL RIVER LINE
OVER THE HILLS AND FAR AWAY
ROW, ROW, ROW
SINCE SISTER NELL HEARD
 PADEREWSKI PLAY
SIT DOWN, YOU'RE ROCKING THE
 BOAT!
SNAP YOUR FINGERS AND AWAY
 YOU GO
SWEET KENTUCKY LADY
THAT OLD IRISH MOTHER OF MINE
WHEN MR. SHAKESPEARE COMES
 TO TOWN

Jessel, George

AND HE'D SAY "OO-LA-LA! WEE-
 WEE"
BABY BLUE EYES
OH HOW I LAUGH WHEN I THINK
 HOW I CRIED ABOUT YOU
ROSES IN DECEMBER
STOP KICKING MY HEART AROUND
WHERE DO THEY GO WHEN THEY
 ROW, ROW, ROW?

Jessel, Leon

PARADE OF THE WOODEN SOLDIERS

Jessel, Raymond

ALL
MARRIED MAN, A

Jett, Joan

I HATE MYSELF FOR LOVING YOU

Jiles, Jimmie

LEAVING ME

Jobe, Steve

WHERE WERE YOU WHEN I WAS
    FALLING IN LOVE

Jobim, Antonio Carlos

DESIFINADO
GIRL FROM IPANEMA
MEDITATION (MEDITACAO)
ONE NOTE SAMBA
QUIET NIGHTS OF QUIET STARS
    (CORCOVADO)
SLIGHTLY OUT OF TUNE

Jodges, Jimmie

SOMEDAY (YOU'LL WANT ME TO
    WANT YOU)

Joel, Billy

ALLENTOWN
BABY GRAND
BIG SHOT
DON'T ASK ME WHY
ENTERTAINER, THE
GOODNIGHT SAIGON
HONESTY
INNOCENT MAN, AN
IT'S STILL ROCK AND ROLL TO ME
JUST THE WAY YOU ARE
KEEPING THE FAITH
LONGEST TIME, THE
MATTER OF TRUST, A
MODERN WOMAN
MOVIN' OUT (ANTHONY'S SONG)
MY LIFE
NEW YORK STATE OF MIND
ONLY THE GOOD DIE YOUNG
PIANO MAN
PRESSURE
SAY GOODBYE TO HOLLYWOOD
SHE'S ALWAYS A WOMAN
SHE'S GOT A WAY
TELL HER ABOUT IT
THIS IS THE TIME
TRAVELIN' PRAYER
UPTOWN GIRL

YOU MAY BE RIGHT

John, Dominic

BLOSSOM FELL, A

John, Elton

BENNIE AND THE JETS
BITCH IS BACK, THE
BLUE EYES
BORDER SONG
CANDLE IN THE WIND
CROCODILE ROCK
DANIEL
DON'T GO BREAKING MY HEART
DON'T LET THE SUN GO DOWN ON
    ME
EMPTY GARDEN (HEY HEY JOHNNY)
FRIENDS
GOODBYE YELLOW BRICK ROAD
GROW SOME FUNK OF YOUR OWN
HONKY CAT
I DON'T WANNA GO ON WITH YOU
    LIKE THAT
I FEEL LIKE A BULLET (IN THE GUN
    OF ROBERT FORD)
I GUESS THAT'S WHY THEY CALL IT
    THE BLUES
I'M STILL STANDING
ISLAND GIRL
KISS THE BRIDE
LEVON
LITTLE JEANNIE
NIKITA
PART-TIME LOVE
PHILADELPHIA FREEDOM
ROCKET MAN
SAD SONGS (SAY SO MUCH)
SATURDAY NIGHT'S ALRIGHT FOR
    FIGHTING
SNOOKEROO
SOMEONE SAVED MY LIFE TONIGHT
SORRY SEEMS TO BE THE HARDEST
    WORD
TINY DANCER
WHO WEARS THESE SHOES?
WRAP HER UP
YOUR SONG

John, Graham

THERE'S NOTHING WRONG WITH A
    KISS
YOU'VE MADE ME HAPPY TODAY

John, Mertis, Jr.

TAKE MY LOVE (I WANT TO GIVE IT
    ALL TO YOU)

John, Robert

PHOTOGRAPH
SAD EYES

Johns, Al

GO WAY BACK SIT DOWN

Johns, Leo

MELODIE D'AMOUR

Johns, Sammy

CHEVY VAN
COMMON MAN
DESPERADO LOVE

Johnsen, Cliff

STARS AND STRIPES ON IWO JIMA

Johnson, Arnold

DOES YOUR HEART BEAT FOR ME?
DON'T HANG YOUR DREAMS ON A
    RAINBOW
GOODBYE BLUES
O (OH!)

Johnson, Arthur

SKELETON IN THE CLOSET, THE

Johnson, Ashley S.

SHE'S THE FAIREST LITTLE FLOWER
    DEAR OLD DIXIE EVER GREW

Johnson, Billy

ALL IN DOWN AND OUT (SORRY, I
    AIN'T GOT IT, YOU COULD HAVE
    IT, ETC.)
MOON HAS HIS EYES ON YOU, THE

Johnson, Brian

BACK IN BLACK
YOU SHOOK ME ALL NIGHT LONG

Johnson, Bruce

BEACH GIRL

Johnson, Buddy

DID YOU SEE JACKIE ROBINSON HIT
    THAT BALL?
HITTIN' ON ME
I'M JUST YOUR FOOL
SINCE I FELL FOR YOU
WHEN MY MAN COMES HOME

Johnson, Buster

WANG, WANG BLUES, THE

Johnson, Charles

RUBBER BISCUIT

Johnson, Chic

G'BYE NOW
OH GEE, OH GOSH, OH GOLLY, I'M
    IN LOVE

Johnson, Clarence

I'M GOING TO WEAR YOU OFF MY
    MIND
LOVE JONES

Johnson, Claude

WHAT'S YOUR NAME?

Johnson, Earl King

TEASIN' YOU

Johnson, Edward

JERSEY BOUNCE

Johnson, Emanuel

GLORIA

Johnson, Enotris

JENNY, JENNY
JENNY, TAKE A RIDE!
LONG TALL SALLY
MISS ANN

Johnson, Frank

WE'RE GETTING CARELESS WITH
    OUR LOVE
YOU'VE BEEN DOING WRONG FOR
    SO LONG

Johnson, Fred

ALL IN MY MIND

Johnson, General

BRING THE BOYS HOME
ONE MONKEY DON'T STOP NO SHOW
PATCHES (I'M DEPENDING ON YOU)
PAY TO THE PIPER
SOMEBODY'S BEEN SLEEPING (IN
    MY BED)
STICK-UP
WANT ADS

Johnson, George

I'LL BE GOOD TO YOU
STOMP!

Johnson, Harold

YOU'RE A SPECIAL PART OF ME

Johnson, Haven

MY LAST AFFAIR

Johnson, Hazel

IT'S TOO LATE, BABY, TOO LATE

Johnson, Henry Paul

WORLD IS ROUND, THE

Johnson, Herbert

FACE TO FACE

Johnson, Hiram

COULD THIS BE MAGIC

Johnson, Howard E.

AM I WASTING MY TIME ON YOU?
AT THE MOVING PICTURE BALL
BRING BACK MY DADDY TO ME
(WHAT DO WE DO ON A) DEW-DEW-
    DEWY DAY
EVERYTHING'S MADE FOR LOVE
FEATHER YOUR NEST
FRECKLES
GEORGIA
GID-AP GARIBALDI
I'D LIKE TO SEE THE KAISER WITH
    A LILY IN HIS HAND
I DON'T WANT TO GET WELL (I'M IN
    LOVE WITH A BEAUTIFUL NURSE)
IF HE CAN FIGHT LIKE HE CAN
    LOVE, GOOD NIGHT GERMANY
IRELAND MUST BE HEAVEN, FOR
    MY MOTHER CAME FROM THERE
I SCREAM, YOU SCREAM (WE ALL
    SCREAM FOR ICE CREAM)
JUST A LITTLE CLOSER
JUST LIKE WASHINGTON CROSSED
    THE DELAWARE, GENERAL
    PERSHING WILL CROSS THE
    RHINE
M-O-T-H-E-R (A WORD THAT MEANS
    THE WORLD TO ME)
ROCK-A-BYE MOON
ROCKAWAY
SIAM
SINGING A SONG TO THE STARS
SWEET LADY
THERE'S A BROKEN HEART FOR
    EVERY LIGHT ON BROADWAY
WHAT DO YOU WANT TO MAKE
    THOSE EYES AT ME FOR?
WHEN THE MOON COMES OVER THE
    MOUNTAIN
WHERE DO WE GO FROM HERE?

Johnson, Howard E.

YOU'LL NEVER KNOW THAT OLD
    HOME TOWN OF MINE

Johnson, Hoydt

YOU'RE THE NEAREST THING TO
    HEAVEN

Johnson, James, Jr.

BUSTIN' OUT
YOU AND I

Johnson, James

STRANDED IN THE JUNGLE

Johnson, James C.

JOINT IS JUMPIN', THE

Johnson, James P.

CAROLINA SHOUT
CHARLESTON
DON'T CRY, BABY
IF I COULD BE WITH YOU (ONE
    HOUR TONIGHT)
IVY, CLING TO ME
MISTER DEEP BLUE SEA
OLD FASHIONED LOVE
PORTER'S LOVE SONG TO A
    CHAMBERMAID, A
THERE'S NO TWO WAYS ABOUT
    LOVE

Johnson, James Weldon

LIFT EVERY VOICE AND SING
MAIDEN WITH THE DREAMY EYES
MY CASTLE ON THE NILE
OLD FLAG NEVER TOUCHED THE
    GROUND, THE
ROLL THEM COTTON BALES
TELL ME, DUSKY MAIDEN

Johnson, Janice Marie

BOOGIE OOGIE OOGIE

Johnson, Jay

BLUE CHRISTMAS

Johnson, J. C.

BELIEVE IT, BELOVED
DON'T LET YOUR LOVE GO WRONG
DUSKY STEVEDORE
EMPTY BED BLUES
GUESS WHO'S IN TOWN
HAUNTED HOUSE BLUES
HOW YA BABY?
IT'S WEARIN' ME DOWN
LOUISIANA
PATTY CAKE, PATTY CAKE (BAKER
    MAN)
RHYTHM AND ROMANCE
TAKE YOUR TOMORROW (AND GIVE
    ME TODAY)
TRAV'LIN' ALL ALONE
WHEN
YOU STAYED AWAY TOO LONG

Johnson, Jesse

BE YOUR MAN
CRAZAY
EVERYBODY DANCE
JUNGLE LOVE

Johnson, Jimmy

ALABAMA STOMP
I NEED LOVIN'
YOUR LOVE IS ALL THAT I CRAVE

Johnson, J. Rosamond

CONGO LOVE SONG
LAZY MOON
LIFT EVERY VOICE AND SING
MY CASTLE ON THE NILE
OH! DIDN'T HE RAMBLE
OLD FLAG NEVER TOUCHED THE
    GROUND, THE
ROLL THEM COTTON BALES
TELL ME, DUSKY MAIDEN
UNDER THE BAMBOO TREE (IF YOU
    LAK-A ME LIKE I LAK-A YOU)

Johnson, Kevin

ROCK 'N' ROLL (I GAVE YOU THE
    BEST YEARS OF MY LIFE)

Johnson, Louis

I'LL BE GOOD TO YOU
STOMP!

Johnson, Louis A.

SWEET LOVE

Johnson, Lucille

ALL RIGHT LOUIE, DROP THE GUN

Johnson, Marvin

COME TO ME

Johnson, Michael

CRYING SHAME
GIVE ME WINGS

Johnson, Pete

BOOGIE WOOGIE PRAYER
CHERRY RED
PINEY BROWN BLUES
ROLL 'EM PETE
WEE BABY BLUES

Johnson, Philander

SOMEWHERE IN FRANCE IS THE
    LILY

Johnson, Richard

WILL YOUR LAWYER TALK TO GOD?

Johnson, Robert

CROSSROADS

Johnson, Robert Earl

I'LL LOVE YOU FOREVER

Johnson, Syl

IS IT BECAUSE I'M BLACK?

Johnson, Ted

JUST A PAIR OF BLUE EYES

Johnson, Terry

BABY, BABY, DON'T CRY
HERE I GO AGAIN
MALINDA

Johnson, Valerie

STOMP!

Johnson, Walter

YOUR LOVE

Johnson, William

DOLIMITE
PRETTY EYED BABY
RELAX
TUXEDO JUNCTION
TWO TRIBES
WELCOME TO THE PLEASUREDOME

Johnson, William D.

WOUND TIME CAN'T ERASE, A

Johnston, Arthur

ALL YOU WANT TO DO IS DANCE
BETWEEN A KISS AND A SIGH
BLACK MOONLIGHT
COCKTAILS FOR TWO
DAY YOU CAME ALONG, THE
DOWN THE OLD OX ROAD
EBONY RHAPSODY
IF I ONLY HAD A MATCH
I GUESS IT HAD TO BE THAT WAY
I'M A LITTLE BLACKBIRD LOOKING
    FOR A BLUEBIRD
I'M SITTING HIGH ON A HILLTOP
IT'S THE NATURAL THING TO DO
I'VE GOT A POCKETFUL OF
    SUNSHINE
I WAS SAYING TO THE MOON
JUST ONE MORE CHANCE
LEARN TO CROON
LET'S CALL A HEART A HEART
LIVE AND LOVE TONIGHT

MANDY, MAKE UP YOUR MIND
MOON GOT IN MY EYES, THE
MOON SONG
MOONSTRUCK
MY OLD FLAME
NEW ORLEANS
ONE, TWO, BUTTON YOUR SHOE
PENNIES FROM HEAVEN
SO DO I
SONG OF THE SOUTH
SUGAR PLUM
THANKS
THANKS A MILLION
TWO TOGETHER

Johnston, Bob

LOOK WHAT YOU'VE DONE

Johnston, Bruce

I WRITE THE SONGS
RENDEZVOUS

Johnston, Diane

MILES AND MILES OF TEXAS

Johnston, Patricia

I'LL REMEMBER APRIL

Johnston, Tom

CHINA GROVE
LISTEN TO THE MUSIC
LONG TRAIN RUNNIN'

Johnstone, Dave

WRAP HER UP

Johnstone, David

GROW SOME FUNK OF YOUR OWN

Joiner, James

FALLEN STAR, A
LOVELY WORK OF ART, A

Jolicoeur, David

ME, MYSELF, AND I

Jolivette, B.

THIS SHOULD GO ON FOREVER

Jolley, Steve

CRUEL SUMMER

Jolson, Al

ANNIVERSARY SONG
AVALON
BACK IN YOUR OWN BACK YARD
BAGDAD
CALIFORNIA, HERE I COME
EGG AND I, THE
EVANGELINE
FOUR WALLS
GOLDEN GATE
I'LL SAY SHE DOES
I'M IN SEVENTH HEAVEN
KEEP SMILING AT TROUBLE
LITTLE PAL
ME AND MY SHADOW
MIAMI
MOTHER OF MINE, I STILL HAVE
    YOU
'N' EVERYTHING
ON THE ROAD TO CALAIS
SONNY BOY
STELLA
THERE'S A RAINBOW 'ROUND MY
    SHOULDER
USED TO YOU
WHY CAN'T YOU?
YOO-HOO
YOU AIN'T HEARD NOTHING YET

Jones, Ada

LET'S TAKE AN OLD-FASHIONED
    WALK

Jones, Alan Rankin

EASY STREET

Jones, Andrew

WHEN YOU DANCE

Jones, Biff

SUDDENLY THERE'S A VALLEY

Jones, Booker T.

GREEN ONIONS
HIP HUG-HER
HOLE IN THE WALL
I FORGOT TO BE YOUR LOVER
I'VE NEVER FOUND A GIRL (TO LOVE ME LIKE YOU DO)
SOUL-LIMBO
TIME IS TIGHT
TO BE A LOVER

Jones, Brian

PLAY WITH FIRE

Jones, Bucky

DO YOU WANNA GO TO HEAVEN
ONLY ONE YOU
WAR IS HELL (ON THE HOMEFRONT TOO)

Jones, Charles

I LOVE YOU MADLY

Jones, Curt

ARE YOU SINGLE?

Jones, David

WE'VE COME TOO FAR TO END IT NOW

Jones, David, Jr.

LOVE ME FOR A REASON

Jones, David Lynn

BONNIE JEAN (LITTLE SISTER)
LIVING IN THE PROMISELAND

Jones, Dory

RUBBERNECKIN'

Jones, Earle C.

EVERYBODY TWO-STEP
HARBOR OF LOVE, THE
I WONDER WHERE MY LOVIN' MAN HAS GONE
ON MOBILE BAY
THAT OLD GIRL OF MINE

Jones, Eddie

I ONLY WANT A BUDDY, NOT A SWEETHEART

Jones, Eddie "Guitar Slim"

THINGS THAT I USED TO DO, THE

Jones, Floyd

ON THE ROAD AGAIN

Jones, Frederick

COULDN'T GET IT RIGHT

Jones, George

FOUR-O-THIRTY-THREE
JUST ONE MORE
LIFE TO GO
MAKE UP YOUR MIND
SEASONS OF MY HEART
TAKE ME
WHAT AM I WORTH
WHO SHOT SAM?
WHY, BABY, WHY?
WINDOW UP ABOVE, THE
YOU GOTTA BE MY BABY

Jones, Glenn

WE'VE ONLY JUST BEGUN (THE ROMANCE IS NOT OVER)

Jones, Gloria

IF I WERE YOUR WOMAN
MY MISTAKE (WAS TO LOVE YOU)

Jones, Howard

LIFE IN ONE DAY
NO ONE IS TO BLAME
THINGS CAN ONLY GET BETTER
YOU KNOW I LOVE YOU . . . DON'T YOU?

Jones, Isham

BROKEN HEARTED MELODY
DOWN WHERE THE SUN GOES DOWN
GIVE A BROKEN HEART A BREAK
I CAN'T BELIEVE IT'S TRUE
IF YOU WERE ONLY MINE
I'LL NEVER HAVE TO DREAM AGAIN
I'LL SEE YOU IN MY DREAMS
I'M TIRED OF EVERYTHING BUT YOU
INDIANA MOON
IT HAD TO BE YOU
IT'S FUNNY TO EVERYONE BUT ME
IVY, CLING TO ME
I WOULDN'T CHANGE YOU FOR THE WORLD
LAWD, YOU MADE THE NIGHT TOO LONG
LET THAT BE A LESSON TO YOU
MEET ME IN BUBBLE LAND
MY CASTLE IN SPAIN
ONE I LOVE, THE (BELONGS TO SOMEBODY ELSE)
ON THE ALAMO
SPAIN
SWINGIN' DOWN THE LANE
THERE IS NO GREATER LOVE
WHAT'S THE USE?
WHERE IS THAT OLD GIRL OF MINE?
WHY CAN'T THIS NIGHT GO ON FOREVER?
WHY COULDN'T IT BE POOR LITTLE ME?
WOODEN SOLDIER AND THE CHINA DOLL, THE
YOU'RE JUST A DREAM COME TRUE
YOU'VE GOT ME CRYING AGAIN

Jones, James

RE-ENLISTMENT BLUES

Jones, Jill

GET ME TO THE WORLD ON TIME

Jones, Jimmie

IS IT BECAUSE I'M BLACK?

Jones, Jimmy

HANDY MAN

Jones, Joe

IKO IKO
YOU TALK TOO MUCH

Jones, John Paul

BLACK DOG
FOOL IN THE RAIN
GOOD TIMES, BAD TIMES
HEARTBREAKER
WHOLE LOTTA LOVE

Jones, L.

GYPSY MAN

Jones, Lee

I AIN'T GOT TO LOVE NOBODY ELSE

Jones, Marilyn

IKO IKO

Jones, Marshall

FIRE
FUNKY WORM
SKIN TIGHT
SWEET STICKY THING
WHO'D SHE COO

Jones, Maryhall

LOVE ROLLERCOASTER

Jones, Mick

BLUE MORNING, BLUE DAY
DIRTY WHITE BOY
DOUBLE VISION
DOWN ON LOVE
FEELS LIKE THE FIRST TIME
HEAD GAMES
I DON'T WANT TO LIVE WITHOUT
    YOU
I WANT TO KNOW WHAT LOVE IS
JUKE BOX HERO
LONG, LONG WAY FROM HOME
ROCK THE CASBAH
SAY YOU WILL
THAT WAS YESTERDAY
TRAIN IN VAIN (STAND BY ME)
URGENT
WAITING FOR A GIRL LIKE YOU

Jones, Mike

COLD AS ICE

Jones, Nat

AIN'T THAT A GROOVE
BRING IT UP
DON'T BE A DROP-OUT

Jones, Ollie

LOVE MAKES THE WORLD GO
    'ROUND
SEND FOR ME
STEP BY STEP
TIGER

Jones, Paul H.

I WOULDN'T CHANGE YOU IF I
    COULD

Jones, Paul Lawrence

LOVE'S COMIN' AT YA

Jones, Phalon

SOUL FINGER

Jones, Quincy

COME BACK, CHARLESTON BLUE
DO IT TO IT
EYES OF LOVE, THE (CAROL'S
    THEME)
FOR LOVE OF IVY
IN THE HEAT OF THE NIGHT
LOVE IS IN CONTROL (FINGER ON
    THE TRIGGER)
MISS CELIE'S BLUES
MONEY IS
P.Y.T. (PRETTY YOUNG THING)
STUFF LIKE THAT
YAH MO B THERE

Jones, Ralph

PLEASE DON'T LET ME LOVE YOU

Jones, Raymond

STAY WITH ME TONIGHT

Jones, Richard M.

TROUBLE IN MIND
YOUR RED WAGON

Jones, Rick

I CAN TAKE OR LEAVE YOUR
    LOVING
CHUCK E.'S IN LOVE
REAL END, THE
YOUNG BLOOD

Jones, Rose Ella

QUIET STORM
VIRGIN MAN

Jones, Sharon

IKO IKO

Jones, Shirley

YOU DONE ME WRONG

Jones, Sidney

AMOROUS GOLDFISH, THE
CHIN-CHIN-CHINAMAN
CHON KINA
SIX LITTLE WIVES

Jones, Stan

CHEYENNE
RIDERS IN THE SKY (A COWBOY
    LEGEND) (A.K.A. GHOST RIDERS
    IN THE SKY)
WHIRLWIND
WRINGLE WRANGLE

Jones, Stephen

WHAT DO YOU DO SUNDAY, MARY?

Jones, Steve

TAKE IT EASY

Jones, Tom

EVERYTHING BEAUTIFUL HAPPENS
    AT NIGHT
HONEYMOON IS OVER, THE
I CAN SEE IT
IS IT REALLY ME?
LOVE, DON'T TURN AWAY
MUCH MORE
MY CUP RUNNETH OVER
SIMPLE LITTLE THINGS
SOON IT'S GONNA RAIN
THEY WERE YOU
TRY TO REMEMBER

Jones, Tom, III

OLD TIME ROCK AND ROLL

Jones, Walter

I DON'T WANT TO DO WRONG

Jones, Willie

EVEN THO'

Jonzun, Michael

CANDY GIRL

Joplin, Janis

DOWN ON ME
KOZMIC BLUES

Joplin, Scott

ENTERTAINER, THE
MAPLE LEAF RAG

Jordan, Archie

DRIFTER
HAPPY BIRTHDAY, DEAR
    HEARTACHE
IT WAS ALMOST LIKE A SONG
LET'S TAKE THE LONG WAY AROUND
    THE WORLD
WHAT A DIFFERENCE YOU'VE MADE
    IN MY LIFE

Jordan, Cathy

JOSÉ CUERVO

Jordan, Fred

BELLE

Jordan, Joe

ORIGINAL DIXIELAND ONE-STEP

Jordan, Lonnie

CISCO KID, THE
L.A. SUNSHINE
LOW RIDER
ME AND BABY BROTHER
SLIPPIN' INTO DARKNESS
SPILL THE WINE
SUMMER
WHY CAN'T WE BE FRIENDS?
WORLD IS A GHETTO, THE

Jordan, Louis

BLUE LIGHT BOOGIE
DON'T BURN THE CANDLE AT BOTH
    ENDS
IS YOU IS OR IS YOU AIN'T MY
    BABY?
RATION BLUES
RUN JOE
SATURDAY NIGHT FISH FRY
YOU CAN'T GET THAT NO MORE

Jordan, Robert

(MY HEART GOES) KA-DING-DONG

Jordan, Roy

BOOGLIE WOOGLIE PIGGY
I'LL NEVER KNOW
MY LOVE'S A GENTLE MAN

Josea, Joe

CHERRY PIE
OOP SHOOP
PEACE OF MIND
SWEET SIXTEEN
YOU UPSET ME, BABY

Joseph, Daniel

MURPHY'S LAW

Josie, Lou

MIDNIGHT CONFESSIONS

Jouannest, Gerard

MARIEKE
SONS OF . . .

Jourdan, M.

FREE AGAIN

Jovan, Nick

CITY OF ANGELS

Joy, Benny

TAKE MY RING OFF YOUR FINGER

Joy, Homer

STREETS OF BAKERSFIELD

Joy, Leonard

DON'T LET ME DREAM

Joyce, Dorothea

JEREMY
LOVE'S LINES, ANGLES AND
RHYMES

Joyce, Jack

I WANNA GO HOME

Joyce, Roger

IT FEELS SO GOOD TO BE LOVED SO
BAD

Joyner, Carole

YOUNG LOVE

Judge, Jack

IT'S A LONG WAY TO TIPPERARY

Judson, J. G.

WON'T YOU BE MY SWEETHEART?

Judson, Lester

I WANT TO BE EVIL

Julia, Al

I CRIED A TEAR

Julian, Don

JERK, THE

Julien, Michael

LET'S LIVE FOR TODAY

Junior, Marvin

OH, WHAT A NIGHT

Jurgens, Dick

CARELESS
DAY DREAMS COME TRUE AT NIGHT
ELMER'S TUNE

IF I KNEW THEN (WHAT I KNOW
NOW)
IT'S A HUNDRED TO ONE
MILLION DREAMS AGO, A
ONE DOZEN ROSES

Jurmann, Walter

ALL GOD'S CHILLUN GOT RHYTHM
BLUE VENETIAN WATERS
COSI COSA
MY HEART IS SINGING
SAN FRANCISCO
SOMEONE TO CARE FOR ME
WHEN I LOOK AT YOU
YOU'RE ALL I NEED

Justis, Bill

DROWNIN' MY SORROWS
RAUNCHY
WAYS OF A WOMAN IN LOVE, THE

Justman, Seth

ANGEL IN BLUE
CENTERFOLD
COME BACK
FREEZE-FRAME
GIVE IT TO ME
LOVE STINKS
MUST OF GOT LOST
ONE LAST KISS
YOU'RE THE ONLY ONE

Kabak, Milton

OH, BABE!

Kaempfert, Bert

AFRIKAAN BEAT
DANKE SCHOEN
LADY
LONELY IS THE NAME
L-O-V-E
MY WAY OF LIFE
NOW AND FOREVER
SPANISH EYES
STRANGERS IN THE NIGHT
SWINGIN' SAFARI, A
WIEDERSEH'N
WOODEN HEART

WORLD WE KNEW, THE (OVER AND
OVER)
YOU TURNED MY WORLD AROUND

Kagna, Eric

STRAIGHT FROM THE HEART

Kahal, Irving

AH, THE MOON IS HERE
BY A WATERFALL
CORN SILK
DON'T HANG YOUR DREAMS ON A
RAINBOW
EV'RY DAY
HOW CAN YOU SAY "NO" (WHEN
ALL THE WORLD IS SAYING
"YES")?
HOW DO I KNOW IT'S SUNDAY?
I CAN DREAM, CAN'T I?
I LEFT MY SUGAR STANDING IN THE
RAIN
I'LL BE SEEING YOU
IT WAS ONLY A SUN SHOWER
LET A SMILE BE YOUR UMBRELLA
LONELY LANE
MOONLIGHT SAVING TIME
NIGHT IS YOUNG AND YOU'RE SO
BEAUTIFUL, THE
NOW I'M A LADY
SATAN'S HOLIDAY
SIMPLE AND SWEET
SITTIN' ON A BACKYARD FENCE
THERE'S SOMETHING ABOUT A ROSE
(THAT REMINDS ME OF YOU)
THINGS THAT WERE MADE FOR
LOVE, THE (YOU CAN'T TAKE
AWAY)
THREE'S A CROWD
WEDDING BELLS ARE BREAKING UP
THAT OLD GANG OF MINE
WHEN I TAKE MY SUGAR TO TEA
WHEN TOMORROW COMES
YOU BROUGHT A NEW KIND OF
LOVE TO ME

Kahan, Stanley

GIRL WITH THE GOLDEN BRAIDS,
THE
TALK TO ME

Kahaneck, Elroy

TRYIN' TO BEAT THE MORNING
   HOME

Kahn, Art

YOU DON'T LIKE IT—NOT MUCH

Kahn, Donald

END OF A BEAUTIFUL FRIENDSHIP

Kahn, Grace LeBoy

DREAM A LITTLE LONGER
LAZY DAY

Kahn, Gus

AIN'T WE GOT FUN?
ALL GOD'S CHILLUN GOT RHYTHM
ALONE AT LAST
AROUND THE CORNER
BABY
BARCELONA
BELOVED
BESIDE A BABBLING BROOK
BIMINI BAY
BLUE LOVEBIRD
BLUE VENETIAN WATERS
BROKEN HEARTED MELODY
BUILDING A HOME FOR YOU
BUT I DO, YOU KNOW I DO
CARIOCA
CAROLINA IN THE MORNING
CHARLEY, MY BOY
CHLO-E
CLOUDS
COQUETTE
DANCING IN THE MOONLIGHT
DAY DREAMING
DIXIE HIGHWAY
DIXIE VAGABOND
DO WHAT YOU DO
DREAM A LITTLE DREAM OF ME
EARFUL OF MUSIC, AN
EVERYBODY RAG WITH ME
FAREWELL TO DREAMS
FLYING DOWN TO RIO
FOOTLOOSE AND FANCY FREE
FOR MY SWEETHEART
GOOFUS

GOT NO TIME
GUILTY
HA-CHA-CHA
HANGIN' ON THE GARDEN GATE
HERE WE ARE
HE'S THE LAST WORD
HONOLULU
HOUR OF PARTING, THE
HOW STRANGE
IF YOU SEE SALLY
I'LL NEVER BE THE SAME
I'LL SAY SHE DOES
I'LL SEE YOU IN MY DREAMS
I'M BRINGING A RED, RED ROSE
I'M SITTING HIGH ON A HILLTOP
I'M SORRY, SALLY
I'M THROUGH WITH LOVE
I NEVER KNEW (THAT ROSES GREW)
ISN'T SHE THE SWEETEST THING?
   (OH MAW, OH PAW)
IT HAD TO BE YOU
I'VE GOT A POCKETFUL OF
   SUNSHINE
I'VE HAD MY MOMENTS
I WISH I HAD A GIRL
I WONDER WHERE MY BABY IS
   TONIGHT
JOSEPHINE
JUST A BIRD'S EYE VIEW OF MY
   OLD KENTUCKY HOME
KENTUCKY'S WAY OF SAYING GOOD
   MORNIN'
LAST NIGHT I DREAMED YOU
   KISSED ME
LAZY DAY
LET'S SING AGAIN
LET'S TALK ABOUT MY SWEETIE
LITTLE OLD CLOCK ON THE
   MANTEL, THE
LITTLE STREET WHERE OLD
   FRIENDS MEET, A
LIZA (ALL THE CLOUDS'LL ROLL
   AWAY)
LOVABLE
LOVE ME FOREVER
LOVE ME OR LEAVE ME
LOVE SONG FROM LONG AGO, A
MAKIN' WHOOPEE
MEMORIES
MILLION DREAMS, A
MINDIN' MY BUSINESS
MUSIC MAKES ME
MY BABY JUST CARES FOR ME

MY BUDDY
MY DREAMY CHINA LADY
MY HEART IS SINGING
MY ISLE OF GOLDEN DREAMS
MY OHIO HOME
MY SWEETIE TURNED ME DOWN
'N' EVERYTHING
NEW ORLEANS
NO, NO, NORA
NOBODY'S SWEETHEART
NOW THAT YOU'RE GONE
OKAY TOOTS
OLD PLAYMATE
ONE I LOVE, THE (BELONGS TO
   SOMEBODY ELSE)
ONE NIGHT OF LOVE
ON THE ALAMO
ON THE GOOD SHIP MARY ANN
ON THE ROAD TO HOME SWEET
   HOME
ORCHIDS IN THE MOONLIGHT
PERSIAN RUG
PRETTY BABY
READY FOR THE RIVER
RIPTIDE
SAILIN' AWAY ON THE HENRY CLAY
SAN FRANCISCO
SING ME A BABY SONG
SITTIN' IN A CORNER
SLEEPY HEAD
SO AT LAST IT'S COME TO THIS
SOMEONE TO CARE FOR ME
SOME SUNDAY MORNING
SOMETIME
SPAIN
SUGAR PLUM
SUNSHINE AND ROSES
SWEETHEART DARLIN'
SWEETHEART OF MY STUDENT
   DAYS
SWINGIN' DOWN THE LANE
TEN LITTLE MILES FROM TOWN
THANKS A MILLION
THAT CERTAIN PARTY
THERE AIN'T NO MAYBE IN MY
   BABY'S EYES
THIS NIGHT WILL BE MY SOUVENIR
TONIGHT IS MINE
TOOT, TOOT, TOOTSIE, GOODBYE
TWO TOGETHER
UKULELE LADY
VOICE IN THE OLD VILLAGE CHOIR,
   THE

WAITIN' AT THE GATE FOR KATY
WALTZING IN THE CLOUDS
WALTZ YOU SAVED FOR ME, THE
WAS I TO BLAME FOR FALLING IN
　LOVE WITH YOU?
WHAT HAVE WE GOT TO LOSE?
WHEN LIGHTS ARE LOW
WHEN MY SHIP COMES IN
WHEN YOU AND I WERE
　SEVENTEEN
WHERE IS THAT OLD GIRL OF
　MINE?
WHERE THE MORNING GLORIES
　GROW
WHERE THE SHY LITTLE VIOLETS
　GROW
WHY COULDN'T IT BE POOR LITTLE
　ME?
WITH ALL MY HEART
YES SIR! THAT'S MY BABY
YOU AIN'T HEARD NOTHING YET
YOU'RE ALL I NEED
YOUR EYES HAVE TOLD ME SO
YOU STEPPED OUT OF A DREAM
YOU'VE GOT EVERYTHING

Kahn, Murl

PETTICOATS OF PORTUGAL

Kahn, Roger Wolfe

CRAZY RHYTHM
IMAGINATION

Kahne, David

GIRL IN TROUBLE, A (IS A
　TEMPORARY THING)

Kaihan, Maewa

NOW IS THE HOUR (MAORI
　FAREWELL SONG)

Kailimai, Henry

ON THE BEACH AT WAIKIKI

Kaiserman, Mauricio

FEELINGS

Kallman, Emmerich

DEAR EYES THAT HAUNT ME
LOVE HAS WINGS
LOVE'S OWN SWEET SONG
PLAY GYPSIES, DANCE GYPSIES
SOFTLY THRO' THE SUMMER NIGHT
THROW ME A ROSE
WE TWO SHALL MEET AGAIN

Kalmanoff, Martin

AT A SIDEWALK PENNY ARCADE
FIRST NAME INITIAL
JUST SAY I LOVE HER
UTOPIA

Kalmar, Bert

ALL ALONE MONDAY
ALL THE QUAKERS ARE SHOULDER
　SHAKERS DOWN IN QUAKER
　TOWN
BEAUTIFUL GIRLS
DANCING THE DEVIL AWAY
EGG AND I, THE
EVERYONE SAYS "I LOVE YOU"
GHOST OF THE VIOLIN, THE
HAPPY ENDING
HELLO, HAWAII, HOW ARE YOU?
HOORAY FOR CAPTAIN SPAULDING
I GAVE YOU UP JUST BEFORE YOU
　THREW ME DOWN
I LOVE YOU SO MUCH
I'M A VAMP FROM EAST BROADWAY
I'M SO AFRAID OF YOU
IN THE LAND OF HARMONY
IT WAS MEANT TO BE
I'VE BEEN FLOATING DOWN THE
　OLD GREEN RIVER
I WANNA BE LOVED BY YOU
KEEP ON DOIN' WHAT YOU'RE DOIN'
KEEP ROMANCE ALIVE
KEEP YOUR UNDERSHIRT ON
KISS TO BUILD A DREAM ON, A
LOOK WHAT YOU'VE DONE
MANDY 'N' ME
MY SUNNY TENNESSEE
NEVERTHELESS (I'M IN LOVE WITH
　YOU)
OH, WHAT A PAL WAS MARY
ONLY WHEN YOU'RE IN MY ARMS
SAME OLD MOON, THE

SHEIK OF AVENUE B, THE
SHE'S MINE, ALL MINE
SNOOPS, THE LAWYER
SO LONG, OO LONG
TAKE YOUR GIRLIE TO THE MOVIES
　(IF YOU CAN'T MAKE LOVE AT
　HOME)
THINKING OF YOU
THREE LITTLE WORDS
TIMBUCTOO
TIRED OF IT ALL
UP IN THE CLOUDS
WATCHING THE CLOUDS ROLL BY
WHAT A PERFECT COMBINATION
WHAT WOULD I CARE?
WHEN YOU DREAM ABOUT HAWAII
WHERE DID YOU GET THAT GIRL?
WHERE DO THEY GO WHEN THEY
　ROW, ROW, ROW?
WHO'S SORRY NOW?
YOU SAID IT

Kamano, John N.

I'M A LONELY LITTLE PETUNIA (IN
　AN ONION PATCH)

Kamen, Michael

I DO THE ROCK

Kander, John

AFTER ALL THESE YEARS
ALL THAT JAZZ
ALL THE CHILDREN IN A ROW
APPLE DOESN'T FALL, THE
BEAUTIFUL
BOBO'S
CABARET
COLORED LIGHTS
GRASS IS ALWAYS GREENER, THE
HARMONY
HOW LUCKY CAN YOU GET
I DON'T CARE MUCH
IF YOU COULD SEE HER (THE
　GORILLA SONG)
I TOLD YOU SO
IT'S THE STRANGEST THING
LIFE OF THE PARTY, THE
LUCKY LADY
MARRIED (HEIRATEN)
MAYBE THIS TIME

Kander, John

MEESKITE
MONEY, MONEY (MAKES THE
    WORLD GO ROUND)
MONEY SONG, THE (SITTING
    PRETTY)
MY COLORING BOOK
MY OWN BEST FRIEND
MY OWN SPACE
ONE OF THE BOYS
RAZZLE DAZZLE
SHINE IT ON
THEME FROM "NEW YORK, NEW
    YORK"
TOMORROW BELONGS TO ME
WE CAN MAKE IT
WILLKOMMEN

Kane, Artie

DON'T ASK TO STAY UNTIL
    TOMORROW

Kane, John

CUZZ YOU'RE SO SWEET

Kane, Kieran

CAN'T STOP MY HEART FROM
    LOVING YOU
DON'T WORRY 'BOUT ME BABY
JUST LOVIN' YOU

Kann, Kal

DON'T HANG UP

Kanner, Hal

I GUESS I'LL GET THE PAPERS (AND
    GO HOME)

Kanter, Hillary

LOVIN' ONLY ME

Kantner, Paul

BALLAD OF YOU AND ME AND
    POONEIL
JANE
VOLUNTEERS
WATCH HER RIDE

Kaper, Bronislaw

ALL GOD'S CHILLUN GOT RHYTHM
BLUE LOVEBIRD
BLUE VENETIAN WATERS
COSI COSA
FOREVER DARLING
GLORIA'S THEME
HI-LILLI, HI-LO
INVITATION
LOVE SONG FROM "MUTINY ON THE
    BOUNTY"
MY HEART IS SINGING
ON GREEN DOLPHIN STREET
SAN FRANCISCO
SOMEBODY UP THERE LIKES ME
SOMEONE TO CARE FOR ME
YOU'RE ALL I NEED

Kapp, David

160 ACRES
DANCE WITH A DOLLY (WITH A
    HOLE IN HER STOCKING)
EVEN NOW
FOR THE FIRST TIME (I'VE FALLEN
    IN LOVE)
JUST A PRAYER AWAY
WELL, ALL RIGHT!

Karak, George

RUNAWAY

Karas, Anton

THIRD MAN THEME

Karen, Kenny

DARKEST STREET IN TOWN

Karen, Tommy

MORE AND MORE

Karger, Fred

FROM HERE TO ETERNITY
GIDGET
RE-ENLISTMENT BLUES

Karl, Raymond

MAMBO JAMBO

Karlin, Fred

COME FOLLOW, FOLLOW ME
EARLY IN THE MORNING
FOR ALL WE KNOW

Karlin, Meg

EARLY IN THE MORNING

Karliski, Steve

MOLLY
NO ONE'S GONNA HURT YOU
    ANYMORE
YELLOW BANDANA, THE
YES, MR. PETERS

Karp, Craig

IF IT DON'T COME EASY

Kasenetz, Jerry

GOODY GOODY GUMDROPS

Kasha, Al

CANDLE ON THE WATER
DON'T WAKE ME UP IN THE
    MORNING, MICHAEL
LET'S START ALL OVER AGAIN
LOVE NEVER GOES AWAY
MORNING AFTER, THE
MY EMPTY ARMS
ONE MORE MOUNTAIN TO CLIMB
SWITCH-A-ROO, THE
WE MAY NEVER LOVE LIKE THIS
    AGAIN
WILL YOU BE STAYING AFTER
    SUNDAY?

Kashif

I'M IN LOVE
INSIDE LOVE (SO PERSONAL)
LOVE COME DOWN

Kassel, Art

AROUND THE CORNER
DON'T LET JULIA FOOL YA
DOODLE DOO DOO
ECHO SAID "NO," THE
HELL'S BELLS
SOBBIN' BLUES

Katscher, Robert

ELIZABETH
GOOD EVENING, FRIENDS
WHEN DAY IS DONE

Katz, Jeff

GOODY GOODY GUMDROPS

Katz, William

MR. TOUCHDOWN, U.S.A.

Kaufman, Al

AND THEN IT'S HEAVEN
ASK ANYONE WHO KNOWS
HOW MANY HEARTS HAVE YOU
    BROKEN?
MOMENTS IN THE MOONLIGHT
ME, MYSELF AND I (ARE ALL IN
    LOVE WITH YOU)

Kaufman, George S.

JUNE MOON

Kaufman, Paul

MY TOWN, MY GUY, AND ME
POETRY IN MOTION
THERE'S NO LIVIN' WITHOUT YOUR
    LOVIN'

Kaukonen, Jorma

PRETTY AS YOU FEEL

Kavelin, Al

I GIVE YOU MY WORD

Kawohl, Dietmar

GIRL I'M GONNA MISS YOU

Kay, Dean

THAT'S LIFE

Kay, John

IT'S NEVER TOO LATE
MAGIC CARPET RIDE
MONSTER
MOVE OVER
ROCK ME

Kay, Julian

DUM-DOT SONG

Kay, Mack

GOODBYE DEAR, I'LL BE BACK IN A
    YEAR

Kaye, Buddy

"A"—YOU'RE ADORABLE (THE
    ALPHABET SONG)
ALL CRIED OUT
BANJO BOY
DON'T BE A BABY, BABY
FULL MOON AND EMPTY ARMS
GIVE US THIS DAY
I'LL CLOSE MY EYES
ITALIAN THEME, THE
NOT AS A STRANGER
OLD SONGS, THE
OPEN DOOR, OPEN ARMS
PENNY A KISS, PENNY A HUG, A
RHYTHM 'N' BLUES (MAMA'S GOT
    THE RHYTHM, PAPA'S GOT THE
    BLUES)
SPEEDY GONZALES
SWEET WILLIAM
THIS IS NO LAUGHING MATTER
THOUGHTLESS
TILL THE END OF TIME
TREASURE OF SIERRA MADRE, THE

Kaye, Florence

ASK ME

THAT'S OLD FASHIONED (THAT'S THE
    WAY LOVE SHOULD BE)
YOU'RE THE DEVIL IN DISGUISE

Kaye, Helen

MISSING IN ACTION

Kaye, Norman

LET'S LOVE
SAY IT WITH YOUR HEART

Kaye, Sammy

TELL ME YOU LOVE ME
UNTIL TOMORROW

Kaye, Tommy

ONE MAN BAND

Kaylan, Howard

ELENORE
LADY BLUE

Kaz, Eric

DEEP INSIDE MY HEART
HEARTBEAT
HEARTS ON FIRE
HI, MOM!
LOVE HAS NO PRIDE
THAT'S WHAT LOVE IS ALL ABOUT

Keagy, Kelly

SISTER CHRISTIAN

Keane, Tom

SECRET OF MY SUCCESS, THE
WILL YOU STILL LOVE ME?

Kearney, Ramsey

EMOTIONS

Keddington, Ruth

THEME FROM "THE PROUD ONES"

Keefer, Arnett

DOGGONE IT, BABY, I'M IN LOVE

Keefer, Arrett "Rusty"

SKINNY MINNIE

Keefer, George

DREAM DADDY

Keene, John

SOMETHING IN THE AIR

Keene, Kahn

CHARMING LITTLE FAKER
SCATTERBRAIN

Keene, Tom

THROUGH THE FIRE

Kehner, Clarence

BOBBY SOX TO STOCKINGS

Keidel, Hal

HI-DIDDLE-DIDDLE

Keith, Barbara

FREE THE PEOPLE

Keith, E. Austin

WHEN I'M GONE YOU'LL SOON
FORGET

Keith, Larry

BETTER LOVE NEXT TIME
I KEEP COMING BACK
THIS TIME I'M IN IT FOR LOVE

Keith, Marilyn

YELLOW BIRD

Keith, Vivian

BEFORE THE NEXT TEARDROP
FALLS

Kellem, Milton

GONNA GET ALONG WITHOUT YA
NOW

Keller, Jack

ALMOST THERE
BREAKIN' IN A BRAND NEW
BROKEN HEART
DON'T ASK ME TO BE FRIENDS
DON'T READ THE LETTER
DON'T TRY TO FIGHT IT, BABY
EASY COME, EASY GO
EVERYBODY'S SOMEBODY'S FOOL
HOW CAN I MEET HER?
IT STARTED ALL OVER AGAIN
I WISH I'D NEVER BEEN BORN
JUST BETWEEN YOU AND ME
JUST FOR OLD TIME'S SAKE
LET'S TURKEY TROT
MY HEART HAS A MIND OF ITS OWN
PLEASE DON'T ASK ABOUT
BARBARA
POOR LITTLE PUPPET
RUN TO HIM
SEATTLE
VENUS IN BLUE JEANS
YOUR USED TO BE

Keller, Jerry

HERE COMES SUMMER
MAN AND A WOMAN, A

Keller, Jim

867-5309/JENNY

Keller, Leonard

ALEXANDER THE SWOOSE (HALF
SWAN—HALF GOOSE)

Kellette, John W.

I'M FOREVER BLOWING BUBBLES

Kelley, Chet

GIRL IN LOVE
TIME WON'T LET ME

Kellum, Murry

IF YOU'RE GONNA PLAY IN TEXAS
(YOU GOTTA HAVE A FIDDLE IN
THE BAND)

Kelly, Casey

ANYONE WHO ISN'T ME TONIGHT
COWBOY RIDES AWAY, THE
SOMEWHERE DOWN THE LINE

Kelly, Eban

YOU AND ME TONIGHT

Kelly, Jerry

TURN-DOWN DAY

Kelly, John M.

THROW HIM DOWN MCCLOSKEY

Kelly, John T.

I LONG TO SEE THE GIRL I LEFT
BEHIND

Kelly, John W.

SLIDE, KELLY, SLIDE

Kelly, Paul

PERSONALLY
STEALING IN THE NAME OF THE
LORD

Kelly, Rich

MAKE IT REAL

Kelly, Rick

I DO YOU

Kelly, Sherman

DANCING IN THE MOONLIGHT

Kelly, Thomas

TAKE CARE OF YOUR HOMEWORK

Kelly, Tom

ALONE
ETERNAL FLAME
FIRE AND ICE
IN MY DREAMS
LIKE A VIRGIN
SO EMOTIONAL
TRUE COLORS

Kelso, M.

BOB WILLS BOOGIE

Kemp, Gary

TRUE

Kemp, Hal

WHEN SUMMER IS GONE (OH, HOW
I'LL MISS YOU)

Kemp, Johnny

JUST GOT PAID

Kemp, Wayne

DARLING, YOU KNOW I WOULDN'T
LIE
I JUST CAME TO GET MY BABY
I'LL LEAVE THIS WORLD LOVING
YOU
I'M THE ONLY HELL (MAMA EVER
RAISED)
NEXT IN LINE
ONE PIECE AT A TIME
THAT'S WHEN SHE STARTED TO
STOP LOVING YOU

Kemper, Ronnie

IT'S A HUNDRED TO ONE

Kempf, Rolf

HELLO—HORAY

Kempner, Nicholas

YOU'VE MADE ME HAPPY TODAY

Kenbrovin, Jean

I'M FOREVER BLOWING BUBBLES

Kendall, Dolly

OVER THREE HILLS

Kendis, James

ANGEL EYES
BILLY (FOR WHEN I WALK)
COME OUT OF THE KITCHEN, MARY
ANN
FEATHER YOUR NEST
GYPSY DREAM ROSE
HAVANA
IF I HAD MY WAY
I'M LIKE A SHIP WITHOUT A SAIL
NAT'AN, FOR WHAT ARE YOU
WAITIN', NAT'AN
UNDERNEATH THE RUSSIAN MOON
WHEN IT'S NIGHT TIME IN ITALY,
IT'S WEDNESDAY OVER HERE

Kendricks, Kevin

BACK AND FORTH

Kennedy, Harry

SAY "AU REVOIR" BUT NOT
"GOODBYE"

Kennedy, James B.

TEDDY BEARS' PICNIC, THE

Kennedy, Jerry

TO MAKE LOVE SWEETER FOR YOU

Kennedy, Jimmy

AND MIMI

APPLE BLOSSOM WEDDING, AN
APRIL IN PORTUGAL
CINDERELLA, STAY IN MY ARMS
DID YOUR MOTHER COME FROM
IRELAND?
DOWN THE TRAIL OF ACHIN'
HEARTS
HARBOR LIGHTS
HOME TOWN
HOUR NEVER PASSES, AN
ISLE OF CAPRI
ISTANBUL (NOT CONSTANTINOPLE)
MAGIC TANGO, THE
MILLER'S DAUGHTER MARIANNE,
THE
MY BOLERO
MY PRAYER
ON THE OLD SPANISH TRAIL
PLAY TO ME, GYPSY
RED SAILS IN THE SUNSET
ROLL ALONG, COVERED WAGON
SERENADE IN THE NIGHT
SOUTH OF THE BORDER (DOWN
MEXICO WAY)
SWEET HEARTACHES
TWO BOUQUETS

Kennedy, Joseph Hamilton

OLE FAITHFUL

Kennedy, Mary Ann

I'LL STILL BE LOVING YOU
RING ON HER FINGER, TIME ON
HER HANDS

Kennedy, Michael

HEARTBEAT—IT'S A LOVEBEAT

Kennedy, Ray

EVERY TIME I THINK OF YOU
ISN'T IT TIME
SAIL ON SAILOR

Kennedy, Steve

WHEN I DIE

Kenner, Bill

PARADISE TONIGHT

Kenner, Chris

I LIKE IT LIKE THAT
LAND OF 1000 DANCES
SOMETHING YOU GOT

Kenner, Roy

RUN RUN RUN

Kennerly, Paul

BORN TO RUN
CRY MYSELF TO SLEEP
GIVE A LITTLE LOVE
HAVE MERCY
YOUNG LOVE (STRONG LOVE)

Kennett, Karl

JUST ONE GIRL
STAY IN YOUR OWN BACK YARD
ZIZZY, ZE ZYM, ZYM!

Kenny, Charles

CARELESSLY
CATHEDRAL IN THE PINES
DREAM VALLEY
EVERY MINUTE OF THE HOUR
GONE FISHIN'
LAST NIGHT
LEANIN' ON THE OLE TOP RAIL
LOVE LETTERS IN THE SAND
MAKE-BELIEVE ISLAND
MY CABIN OF DREAMS
RUNNING THROUGH MY MIND
SCATTERED TOYS
THERE'S A GOLD MINE IN THE SKY
WHILE A CIGARETTE WAS BURNING
WHITE SAILS

Kenny, Gerald

I MADE IT THROUGH THE RAIN

Kenny, Nick

AND SO LITTLE TIME

CARELESSLY
CATHEDRAL IN THE PINES
DREAM VALLEY
DROP ME OFF IN HARLEM
EVERY MINUTE OF THE HOUR
GONE FISHIN'
LAST NIGHT
LEANIN' ON THE OLE TOP RAIL
LOVE LETTERS IN THE SAND
MAKE-BELIEVE ISLAND
MUST WE SAY GOODNIGHT SO
   SOON?
MY CABIN OF DREAMS
ORANGE BLOSSOM LANE
RUNNING THROUGH MY MIND
SCATTERED TOYS
THERE'S A GOLD MINE IN THE SKY
WHILE A CIGARETTE WAS BURNING
WHITE SAILS

Kent, Al

WHOLE WORLD IS A STAGE, THE
YOU'VE GOT TO PAY THE PRICE

Kent, Arthur

DON'T GO TO STRANGERS
END OF THE WORLD, THE
RING-A-LING-A-LARIO
TAKE GOOD CARE OF HER
WE GO WELL TOGETHER
WONDER WHEN MY BABY'S COMING
   HOME
YOU NEVER MISS THE WATER TILL
   THE WELL RUNS DRY

Kent, Charlotte

OVERNIGHT
WHAT A LIFE!
WHAT HAVE WE GOT TO LOSE?

Kent, George

(HOW CAN I WRITE ON PAPER)
   WHAT I FEEL IN MY HEART

Kent, Jeff

ROCK OF AGES

Kent, Leonard

HOLD TIGHT—HOLD TIGHT (WANT
   SOME SEA FOOD, MAMA)

Kent, Sandra

I NEVER HAD A WORRY IN THE
   WORLD

Kent, Walter

AH, BUT IT HAPPENS
APPLE BLOSSOMS AND CHAPEL
   BELLS
ENDLESSLY
GERTIE FROM BIZERTE
I CROSS MY FINGERS
I'LL BE HOME FOR CHRISTMAS
I'M GONNA LIVE TILL I DIE
I NEVER MENTION YOUR NAME
LAST MILE HOME, THE
LOVE IS LIKE A CIGARETTE
PU-LEEZE, MR. HEMINGWAY
TOO MUCH IN LOVE
WHEN THE ROSES BLOOM AGAIN
WHITE CLIFFS OF DOVER, THE
   (THERE'LL BE BLUEBIRDS OVER)

Kenton, Stan

AND HER TEARS FLOWED LIKE
   WINE
ARTISTRY IN RHYTHM

Kerker, Gustav

LITTLE BIRDIES LEARNING HOW TO
   FLY
SHE IS THE BELLE OF NEW YORK

Kern, James V.

LITTLE RED FOX, THE (N'YA, N'YA,
   YA CAN'T CATCH ME)

Kern, Jerome

AH STILL SUITS ME
ALLEGHENY AL
ALL IN FUN
ALL THE THINGS YOU ARE
ALL THROUGH THE DAY

AND LOVE WAS BORN
ANY MOMENT NOW
BABES IN THE WOOD
BILL
BLUE DANUBE BLUES
BOJANGLES OF HARLEM
CALIFORN-I-AY
CAN I FORGET YOU?
CAN'T HELP LOVIN' DAT MAN
CAN'T HELP SINGING
CLEOPATTERER
DANCING TIME
DAY DREAMING
DEARLY BELOVED
DON'T EVER LEAVE ME
D'YE LOVE ME?
FINE ROMANCE
FOLKS WHO LIVE ON THE HILL, THE
GOOD MORNING, DEARIE
HAVE A HEART
HEAVEN IN MY ARMS
HERE AM I
HIGH, WIDE AND HANDSOME
HOW'D YOU LIKE TO SPOON WITH ME?
I DREAM TOO MUCH
I GOT LOVE
I'LL BE HARD TO HANDLE
I MIGHT FALL BACK ON YOU
I'M OLD FASHIONED
I'M THE ECHO (YOU'RE THE SONG)
IN ARCADY
IN EGERN ON THE TEGERN SEE
IN LOVE IN VAIN
IN LOVE WITH LOVE
ISN'T IT GREAT TO BE MARRIED?
I'VE TOLD EV'RY LITTLE STAR
I WON'T DANCE
JOCKEY ON THE CAROUSEL, THE
JUST LET ME LOOK AT YOU
KA-LU-A
LAND WHERE THE GOOD SONGS GO, THE
LAST TIME I SAW PARIS, THE
LEAVE IT TO JANE
LEFT ALL ALONE AGAIN BLUES
LET'S BEGIN
LET'S SAY GOODNIGHT 'TIL IT'S MORNING
LIFE UPON THE WICKED STAGE
LONG AGO AND FAR AWAY
LOOK FOR THE SILVER LINING

LOVELY TO LOOK AT
MAGIC MELODY, THE
MAKE BELIEVE
MAKE WAY FOR TOMORROW
MISTER CHAMBERLAIN
MORE AND MORE
NEVER GONNA DANCE
NIGHT WAS MADE FOR LOVE, THE
NOBODY ELSE BUT ME
NODDING ROSES
OH, LADY! LADY!!
OL' MAN RIVER
ONCE IN A BLUE MOON
ONE MOMENT ALONE
OUR SONG
PARIS IS A PARADISE FOR COONS
PICK YOURSELF UP
POOR PIERROT
PUT ME TO THE TEST
RAGGEDY ANN
RECKLESS
REMIND ME
SALLY
SAME SORT OF GIRL
SHE DIDN'T SAY "YES"
SIREN'S SONG, THE
SMOKE GETS IN YOUR EYES
SOME SORT OF SOMEBODY
SOMETHING HAD TO HAPPEN
SONG IS YOU, THE
SUNNY
SURE THING
THAT LUCKY FELLOW
THEY DIDN'T BELIEVE ME
TILL THE CLOUDS ROLL BY
TOUCH OF YOUR HAND, THE
TRY TO FORGET
'TWAS NOT SO LONG AGO
TWO LITTLE BLUEBIRDS
UP WITH THE LARK
WALTZ IN SPRINGTIME
WAY YOU LOOK TONIGHT, THE
WHIP-POOR-WILL
WHISTLING BOY, THE
WHO?
WHOSE BABY ARE YOU?
WHY DO I LOVE YOU?
WHY WAS I BORN?
WILD ROSE
WINDMILL UNDER THE STARS
YESTERDAY
YOU ARE LOVE
YOU COULDN'T BE CUTER

YOU KNOW AND I KNOW
YOU'RE DEVASTATING
YOU'RE HERE AND I'M HERE
YOU WERE NEVER LOVELIER
YOU WILL, WON'T YOU?

Kerr, Harry D.

DO YOU EVER THINK OF ME?
HOODOO MAN, THE
NEAPOLITAN NIGHTS (OH, NIGHTS OF SPLENDOR)

Kerr, Jean

PUSSYFOOT, THE

Kerr, Jim

ALIVE AND KICKING
SANCTIFY YOURSELF

Kerr, Peter

FIRE!

Kerr, Richard

I'LL NEVER LOVE THIS WAY AGAIN
I'M DREAMING
LOOKS LIKE WE MADE IT
MANDY (A.K.A. BRANDY)
NO NIGHT SO LONG
SOMEWHERE IN THE NIGHT

Kerr, Walter

PUSSYFOOT, THE

Kerry, Joe

SHE BLINDED ME WITH SCIENCE

Kersey, Ron

DISCO INFERNO

Kershaw, Doug

CAJUN STRIPPER, THE
LOUISIANA MAN

Kershaw, Rusty

CAJUN STRIPPER, THE

Kesler, Stanley A.

I FORGOT TO REMEMBER TO
    FORGET

Kessel, Barney

SWEDISH PASTRY

Kesslair, Bernard

LOVE IN EVERY ROOM

Kessler, Mary

BABY LOVE

Kester, Max

LOVE LOCKED OUT

Ketelbey, Albert W.

IN A MONASTERY GARDEN
IN A PERSIAN MARKET

Kettner, Alfons

WHAT YOU WON'T DO FOR LOVE

Key, Jimmy

LAST DAY IN THE MINES

Keyes, Bert

ANGEL SMILE
LOVE ON A TWO-WAY STREET

Keyes, John

TOO WEAK TO FIGHT

Keys, James

SH-BOOM (LIFE COULD BE A
    DREAM)

Khan, Chaka

SWEET THING
YOU GOT THE LOVE

Khatchaturian, Aram

SABRE DANCE
SABRE DANCE BOOGIE

Khent, Allison R.

16 CANDLES
TROUBLE IN PARADISE

Khoury, George

SEA OF LOVE

Kibble, Perry

BOOGIE OOGIE OOGIE

Kidd, Johnny

SHAKIN' ALL OVER

Kiefer, Tom

NOBODY'S FOOL

Kihn, Greg

BREAKUP SONG, THE (THEY DON'T
    WRITE 'EM)
HAPPY MAN
JEOPARDY

Kilburn, Duncan

PRETTY IN PINK

Kilgore, Merle

AIN'T NOTHING BUT A MAN
HAPPY TO BE WITH YOU
(I'M THE GIRL ON) WOLVERTON
    MOUNTAIN
LOVE HAS MADE YOU BEAUTIFUL
MORE AND MORE
OLD RECORDS
RING OF FIRE

SHE UNDERSTANDS ME (A.K.A.
    DUM-DE-DA)
SHE WENT A LITTLE BIT FARTHER
TIGER WOMAN
WHY CAN'T YOU FEEL SORRY FOR
    ME?
WOLVERTON MOUNTAIN
YOU'LL DRIVE ME BACK (INTO HER
    ARMS AGAIN)

Killen, Buddy

BALLAD OF TWO BROTHERS
FOREVER
I MAY NEVER GET TO HEAVEN
LOSING YOUR LOVE
SUGAR LIPS

Killen, William

AIN'T GONNA BUMP NO MORE
    (WITH NO BIG FAT WOMAN)

Killion, Leo V.

BY-U, BY-O (THE LOU'SIANA
    LULLABY)
HUT-SUT SONG, THE

Kilmer, Joyce

TREES

Kim, Andy

HOW'D WE EVER GET THIS WAY?
JINGLE JANGLE
RAINBOW RIDE
ROCK ME GENTLY
SHOOT 'EM UP, BABY
SO GOOD TOGETHER
SUGAR, SUGAR
SUNSHINE

Kimball, Jennifer

BOP
I WILL BE THERE

Kincaid, Jesse Lee

BABY, YOU COME ROLLIN 'CROSS
    MY MIND

King, Ben E.

I'LL BE THERE
STAND BY ME

King, Bob

TIGHTER, TIGHTER

King, Carole

AT THE CLUB
BEEN TO CANAAN
BELIEVE IN HUMANITY
CHAINS
CHICKEN SOUP WITH RICE
CORAZON
CRYING IN THE RAIN
DON'T BRING ME DOWN
DON'T SAY NOTHIN' BAD (ABOUT MY
    BABY)
EVERY BREATH I TAKE
GO AWAY LITTLE GIRL
GOIN' BACK
HALFWAY TO PARADISE
HAPPY TIMES (ARE HERE TO
    STAY)
HER ROYAL MAJESTY
HE'S A BAD BOY
HEY GIRL
HI-DE-HO
HOW MANY TEARS
HUNG ON YOU
I CAN'T HEAR YOU NO MORE
I CAN'T STAY MAD AT YOU
I FEEL THE EARTH MOVE
I'M INTO SOMETHING GOOD
IT MIGHT AS WELL RAIN UNTIL
    SEPTEMBER
IT'S GOING TO TAKE SOME TIME
IT'S TOO LATE
I'VE GOT BONNIE
I WANT TO STAY HERE
I WASN'T BORN TO FOLLOW
JAZZMAN
JUST ONCE IN MY LIFE
KEEP YOUR HANDS OFF MY BABY
LOCO-MOTION, THE
MURPHY'S ROMANCE
NATURAL WOMAN, A (YOU MAKE
    ME FEEL LIKE)
NIGHTINGALE
OH NO, NOT MY BABY

OLD SMOKEY LOCOMOTION
ONE FINE DAY
ONLY LOVE IS REAL
ON THIS SIDE OF GOODBYE
PLEASANT VALLEY SUNDAY
POINT OF NO RETURN
POOR LITTLE RICH GIRL
SMACKWATER JACK
SO FAR AWAY
SOME KIND-A WONDERFUL (A.K.A.
    SOME KIND OF WONDERFUL)
SWEET SEASONS
TAKE GOOD CARE OF MY BABY
TAPESTRY
THIS LITTLE GIRL
UP ON THE ROOF
WALKING PROUD
WHAT A SWEET THING THAT WAS
WHEN MY LITTLE GIRL IS SMILING
WILL YOU LOVE ME TOMORROW?
YOU'VE GOT A FRIEND

King, Charles E.

HAWAIIAN WEDDING SONG, THE
SONG OF THE ISLANDS

King, Claude

(I'M THE GIRL ON) WOLVERTON
    MOUNTAIN
TIGER WOMAN
WOLVERTON MOUNTAIN

King, Edward

SATURDAY NIGHT SPECIAL
SWEET HOME ALABAMA

King, Edward C.

TOMORROW

King, Freddy

HIDE AWAY
SAN-HO-ZAY

King, Harry

GENERAL HOSPI-TALE

King, Jack

EVERYTHING'S BEEN DONE BEFORE
HOW AM I TO KNOW?

King, Jay

WHY YOU TREAT ME SO BAD

King, Jimmy

SOUL FINGER

King, Kenneth

EVERYONE'S GONE TO THE MOON
IT'S GOOD NEWS WEEK

King, Mark

RUNNING IN THE FAMILY
SOMETHING ABOUT YOU

King, Nelson

THERE'LL BE NO TEARDROPS
    TONIGHT

King, Pearl

I HEAR YOU KNOCKING
ONE NIGHT
WITCHCRAFT

King, Pee Wee

BONAPARTE'S RETREAT
I'LL FORGIVE YOU, BUT I CAN'T
    FORGET
SLOW POKE
TENNESSEE POLKA
TENNESSEE TANGO
TENNESSEE TEARS
TENNESSEE WALTZ
YOU BELONG TO ME

King, Ray

TRUCK DRIVIN' SON-OF-A-GUN

King, Riley "B. B."

ASK ME NO QUESTIONS

King, Riley "B. B."

GHETTO WOMAN
PARTIN' TIME
PAYING THE COST TO BE BOSS
PEACE OF MIND
PLEASE LOVE ME
SO EXCITED
SWEET SIXTEEN
THREE O'CLOCK BLUES
WHEN I'M WRONG
WHY I SING THE BLUES
WOKE UP THIS MORNING
YOU KNOW I LOVE YOU

King, Robert A.

BEAUTIFUL OHIO
I AIN'T NOBODY'S DARLING
I SCREAM, YOU SCREAM (WE ALL
    SCREAM FOR ICE CREAM)
I'VE GOT THE YES WE HAVE NO
    BANANAS BLUES
KEEP YOUR SKIRTS DOWN, MARY
    ANN
MOONLIGHT ON THE COLORADO
TOOT, TOOT, TOOTSIE, GOODBYE
WHY DID I KISS THAT GIRL?

King, Robert L.

DRAGGIN' THE LINE

King, Roy

I'LL PRAY FOR YOU

King, S.

LADY (YOU BRING ME UP)

King, Stoddard

THERE'S A LONG, LONG TRAIL

King, Tom

BEATNIK FLY
CROSSFIRE
GIRL IN LOVE
RED RIVER ROCK
REVEILLE ROCK
TIME WON'T LET ME

King, Wally

LESSONS IN LOVE

King, Wayne

BEAUTIFUL LOVE
BLUE HOURS
CORN SILK
GOOFUS
JOSEPHINE
WALTZ YOU SAVED FOR ME, THE

King, William

BRICK HOUSE
LADY (YOU BRING ME UP)
SLIPPERY WHEN WET
SWEET LOVE
TOO HOT TA TROT

Kingsbery, Peter

WHEN YOUR HEART IS WEAK

Kingsley, Gershon

POPCORN

Kingston, Larry

LOVIN' MACHINE, THE
WOMEN DO FUNNY THINGS TO ME

Kipling, Rudyard

DANNY DEEVER
ON THE ROAD TO MANDALAY
RECESSIONAL

Kipner, Nat

TOO MUCH, TOO LITTLE, TOO LATE

Kipner, Steven

HARD HABIT TO BREAK
IF SHE WOULD HAVE BEEN
    FAITHFUL
PHYSICAL
TWIST OF FATE

Kipps, Charles

WALK AWAY FROM LOVE

Kirby, Dave

IS ANYBODY GOIN' TO SAN
    ANTONE?

Kirk, Curtis

I WOULDN'T TRADE YOU FOR THE
    WORLD

Kirk, Eddie

SO ROUND, SO FIRM, SO FULLY
    PACKED

Kirk, Reece

OUR LOVE IS ON THE FAULTLINE

Kirkeby, Ed

ALL THAT MEAT AND NO POTATOES

Kirkland, Leroy

ALL IN MY MIND
GOOD LOVIN'
SOMETHING'S GOT A HOLD ON ME
WHEN YOU DANCE

Kirkman, Terry

CHERISH
EVERYTHING THAT TOUCHES YOU
SIX MAN BAND

Kirkpatrick, Jess

'LEVEN-THIRTY SATURDAY NIGHT

Kisco, Charles

IT'S A LONESOME OLD TOWN (WHEN
    YOU'RE NOT AROUND)

Kitchings, Irene

SOME OTHER SPRING

Kitson, Ron

HAPPY BIRTHDAY, MERRY
    CHRISTMAS

Klages, Raymond

BLUE SHADOWS
CHEER UP
CLIMBING UP THE LADDER OF LOVE
DOIN' THE RACCOON
HUGS AND KISSES
IT MIGHT HAVE BEEN A DIFF'RENT
    STORY
I WONDER WHY
JUST YOU, JUST ME
LOW DOWN RHYTHM
ONCE IN A LIFETIME
ONE STEP TO HEAVEN
PARDON ME, PRETTY BABY
ROLL UP THE CARPET
TIME WILL TELL
TWENTY-ONE DOLLARS A DAY—
    ONCE A MONTH

Klauber, Marcy

I GET THE BLUES WHEN IT RAINS

Kleban, Edward

AT THE BALLET
DANCE: TEN; LOOKS: THREE
HELLO TWELVE, HELLO THIRTEEN,
    HELLO LOVE
I CAN DO THAT
MUSIC AND THE MIRROR, THE
ONE
WHAT I DID FOR LOVE

Klein, Gary

BOBBY'S GIRL

Klein, Lou

GAY CABALLERO, A
IF I HAD MY WAY
POPCORN MAN

Klein, Manuel

IT'S A LONG LANE THAT HAS NO
    TURNING

Klein, Paul

LITTLE BLUE MAN, THE
THAT DO MAKE IT NICE

Kleinhauf, Henry

JOHNSON RAG

Klender, R.

DEAR MR. JESUS

Klenner, John

CRYING MYSELF TO SLEEP
DOWN THE RIVER OF GOLDEN
    DREAMS
HEARTACHES
I'M STILL CARING
JAPANSY
JUST FRIENDS
LONELY TROUBADOUR
ON THE STREET OF REGRET
SMOKE DREAMS
WHEN THE MIGHTY ORGAN PLAYS
    THE SONG OF SONGS FOR ME
WHISPER THAT YOU LOVE ME

Klickmann, F. Henri

FLOATIN' DOWN TO COTTON TOWN
SWEET HAWAIIAN MOONLIGHT
WATERS OF THE PERKIOMEN

Kling, Reno

NOWHERE ROAD

Klingman, Mark

FRIENDS

Klohr, John N.

BILLBOARD, THE

Klose, Othmar

HEAR MY SONG, VIOLETTA

Knape, Skip

GOD, LOVE, AND ROCK AND ROLL

Knight, Baker

ANYTIME AT ALL
COWBOY BOOTS
DON'T THE GIRLS ALL GET
    PRETTIER AT CLOSING TIME?
I GOT A FEELING
LONESOME TOWN
NEVER BE ANYONE ELSE BUT YOU
NOBODY'S BABY AGAIN
NOT ENOUGH INDIANS
SOMEWHERE THERE'S A SOMEONE
SWEETER THAN YOU
WEEK IN THE COUNTRY, A
WONDER OF YOU, THE

Knight, Frederick

RING MY BELL

Knight, Gary

RIVER IS WIDE, THE

Knight, Gladys

DADDY COULD SWEAR, I DECLARE
I DON'T WANT TO DO WRONG
SAVE THE OVERTIME FOR ME

Knight, Holly

INVINCIBLE
IT DIDN'T TAKE LONG
LOVE IS A BATTLEFIELD
LOVE TOUCH (THEME FROM "LEGAL
    EAGLES")
NEVER
OBSESSION
ONE OF THE LIVING
THERE'S THE GIRL
WARRIOR, THE

Knight, Jerry

BREAKIN' . . . THERE'S NO
   STOPPING US
CRUSH ON YOU

Knight, Meradi, Jr.

I DON'T WANT TO DO WRONG

Knight, Merrald (Bubba)

DADDY COULD SWEAR, I DECLARE
SAVE THE OVERTIME FOR ME

Knight, Vick

MELANCHOLY MOOD

Knipper, Lev

MEADOWLAND (A.K.A.
   MEADOWLANDS)

Kniss, Richard L.

SUNSHINE ON MY SHOULDERS

Knobloch, Fred

AMERICAN ME
USED TO BLUE
WHY NOT ME

Knopf, Edwin H.

EVERYTHING'S BEEN DONE BEFORE

Knopfler, Mark

LADY WRITER
MONEY FOR NOTHING
PRIVATE DANCER
SKATEAWAY
SO FAR AWAY
SULTANS OF SWING
WALK OF LIFE

Knott, Joe

ADD SOME MUSIC TO YOUR DAY

Knox, Buddy

HULA LOVE
I'M STICKIN' WITH YOU
PARTY DOLL
ROCK YOUR LITTLE BABY TO SLEEP

Koch, John

I WANT YOU ALL TO MYSELF (JUST
   YOU)

Koda, Cub

SMOKIN' IN THE BOYS' ROOM

Koehler, Charles

LEAVE ME WITH A SMILE

Koehler, Ted

AND THERE YOU ARE
ANIMAL CRACKERS IN MY SOUP
AS LONG AS I LIVE
BEST WISHES
BETWEEN THE DEVIL AND THE
   DEEP BLUE SEA
BREAKFAST BALL
COTTON
CURLY TOP
DON'T WORRY 'BOUT ME
DREAMY MELODY
EV'RY NIGHT ABOUT THIS TIME
FEELIN' HIGH AND HAPPY
GET HAPPY
HAPPY AS THE DAY IS LONG
HERE GOES
HEY, WHAT DID THE BLUEBIRD
   SAY?
HITTIN' THE BOTTLE
I CAN'T FACE THE MUSIC (WITHOUT
   SINGING THE BLUES)
IF I WERE SURE OF YOU
I GOTTA RIGHT TO SING THE BLUES
ILL WIND
I LOVE A PARADE
I'M SHOOTING HIGH
IT'S GREAT TO BE IN LOVE AGAIN
I'VE GOT MY FINGERS CROSSED
I'VE GOT THE WORLD ON A STRING
KICKING THE GONG AROUND
LET'S FALL IN LOVE

LINDA
LOVE FOR LOVE
LOVE IS LOVE ANYWHERE
LOVELY LADY
MARCH OF TIME, THE
ME AND THE BLUES
MINNIE THE MOOCHER'S WEDDING
   DAY
MUSIC, MUSIC, EVERYWHERE
NOW I KNOW
OUT IN THE COLD AGAIN
PICTURE ME WITHOUT YOU
RAISIN' THE RENT
SAY WHEN
SIMPLE THINGS IN LIFE, THE
SING, MY HEART
SOME SUNDAY MORNING
SPREADIN' RHYTHM AROUND
STAY ON THE RIGHT SIDE, SISTER
STOP! YOU'RE BREAKIN' MY HEART
STORMY WEATHER
SWEET DREAMS, SWEETHEART
TELL ME WITH A LOVE SONG
TESS'S TORCH SONG
THERE'S NO TWO WAYS ABOUT
   LOVE
TRUCKIN'
WE'VE COME A LONG WAY
   TOGETHER
WHAT GOES UP MUST COME DOWN
WHEN LIGHTS ARE LOW
WHEN LOVE COMES SWINGING
   ALONG
WHEN THE SUN COMES OUT
WHOSE BIG BABY ARE YOU?
WRAP YOUR TROUBLES IN DREAMS

Koffman, Moe

SWINGIN' SHEPHERD BLUES, THE

Koger, George

VIENI, VIENI

Kohan, Buzz

ONE MORE TIME

Kohler, Donna Jeane

HULA HOOP SONG, THE

Kohler, Fred

GOIN' GONE

Kohlman, Churchill

CRY

Kolber, Larry

FORGET ME NOT
I LOVE HOW YOU LOVE ME
PATCHES
SWEET LITTLE YOU
YELLOW BANDANA, THE
YES, MR. PETERS

Koller, Fred

LONE STAR STATE OF MIND

Kong, Leslie

ISRAELITES

Koninsky, Sadie

ELI GREEN'S CAKEWALK

Kool & The Gang

BIG FUN
CELEBRATION
CHERISH
EMERGENCY
FRESH
GET DOWN ON IT
HOLIDAY
JOANNA
JUNGLE BOOGIE
SPIRIT OF THE BOOGIE
STONE LOVE
TONIGHT

Kooper, Al

I CAN'T QUIT HER
I MUST BE SEEING THINGS
THIS DIAMOND RING

Kooymans, George

RADAR LOVE

TWILIGHT ZONE

Koplow, Don Howard

OH, HAPPY DAY

Koppelman, Charles

YOGI

Korb, Arthur

GO ON WITH THE WEDDING
IT TAKES TIME

Kornfeld, Artie

DEAD MAN'S CURVE
I ADORE HIM
PIED PIPER, THE
RAIN, THE PARK, AND OTHER
    THINGS, THE
WE CAN FLY

Korngold, Erich Wolfgang

LOVE FOR LOVE
MUSIC IN THE NIGHT

Kortchmar, Danny

ALL SHE WANTS TO DO IS DANCE
DIRTY LAUNDRY
HONEY, DON'T LEAVE L.A.
NOT ENOUGH LOVE IN THE WORLD
SUNSET GRILL
TENDER IS THE NIGHT

Kortlander, Max

TELL ME (WHY NIGHTS ARE
    LONELY)

Kosloff, Ira

I WANT YOU, I NEED YOU, I LOVE
    YOU

Kosma, Joseph

AUTUMN LEAVES

Kostalanetz, Andre

MOON LOVE
ON THE ISLE OF MAY

Kotchmar, Danny

SOMEBODY'S BABY

Kotscher, Edmund

LIECHTENSTEINER POLKA

Kraemer, Peter

HELLO, HELLO

Krakeur, Jacques

WHEN A LADY MEETS A
    GENTLEMAN DOWN SOUTH

Kramer, Alex

AIN'T NOBODY HERE BUT US
    CHICKENS
CANDY
COMME ÇI, COMME ÇA
FAR AWAY PLACES
HIGH ON A WINDY HILL
IT ALL COMES BACK TO ME NOW
IT'S LOVE, LOVE, LOVE
LOVE SOMEBODY
MONEY IS THE ROOT OF ALL EVIL
MY SISTER AND I
NO MAN IS AN ISLAND
NO OTHER ARMS, NO OTHER LIPS
THAT'S THE BEGINNING OF THE
    END
YOU'LL NEVER GET AWAY

Krampf, Craig

OH, SHERRIE

Kreigsmann, James

HAPPY ORGAN, THE

Kreisler, Fritz

CAPRICE VIENNOIS
I'M IN LOVE

Kreisler, Fritz

LIEBESFREUD
LIEBESLIED
OLD REFRAIN, THE
SCHON ROSMARIN (FAIR ROSMARIN)
STARS IN MY EYES
TAMBOURIN CHINOIS
WHO CAN TELL

Kresa, Helmy

THAT'S MY DESIRE

Kretschmer, R.

CRAZY

Kretzmer, Herbert

DRINK WITH ME TO DAYS GONE BY
I DREAMED A DREAM
IN THE SUMMER OF HIS YEARS
YESTERDAY, WHEN I WAS YOUNG

Krieger, Henry

AND I AM TELLING YOU I'M NOT
   GOING
CADILLAC CAR
ONE NIGHT ONLY

Krieger, Robert

HELLO, I LOVE YOU
LIGHT MY FIRE
LOVE HER MADLY
LOVE ME TWO TIMES
PEOPLE ARE STRANGE
RIDERS ON THE STORM
ROADHOUSE BLUES
TELL ALL THE PEOPLE
TOUCH ME
UNKNOWN SOLDIER
WISHFUL, SINFUL

Kriegsmann, James J.

JOEY

Krippene, Roe, and Broad

EVERYBODY'S MAKING MONEY BUT
   TSCHAIKOVSKY

Krise, Ray

JOHN SILVER

Kristofferson, Kris

FOR THE GOOD TIMES
HELP ME MAKE IT THROUGH THE
   NIGHT
I'D RATHER BE SORRY
LOVING HER WAS EASIER (THAN
   ANYTHING I'LL EVER DO AGAIN)
ME AND BOBBY MCGEE
ONE DAY AT A TIME
PLEASE DON'T TELL ME HOW THE
   STORY ENDS
SUNDAY MORNIN' COMIN' DOWN
TAKER, THE
VIET NAM BLUES
WHY ME

Krondes, Jimmy

END, THE (A.K.A. AT THE END OF
   THE RAINBOW)
SUMMER SOUVENIRS
WARM

Krueger, Bennie

SUNDAY

Krueger, Jim

WE JUST DISAGREE

Kruetzmann, Billy

TRUCKIN'

Kruger, Jerrie

I HEARD YOU CRIED LAST NIGHT

Krupa, Gene

APURKSODY
BOLERO AT THE SAVOY
BOOGIE BLUES
DRUMBOOGIE
DRUMMIN' MAN

Kuhn, Lee

ALL THAT GLITTERS IS NOT GOLD

Kuller, Sid

I WISH I WUZ

Kummel, Leslie

I WILL ALWAYS THINK ABOUT YOU
THINGS I'D LIKE TO SAY

Kummer, Clare

DEARIE

Kunkel, Russ

TENDER IS THE NIGHT

Kupka, Stephen

SO VERY HARD TO GO
WHAT IS HIP?
YOU'RE STILL A YOUNG MAN

Kupps, Marty

TWO DIVIDED BY LOVE

Kurhajetz, Jon

GONNA TAKE A LOT OF RIVER

Kurtz, Manny

BLUE INTERLUDE
IN A SENTIMENTAL MOOD
ROMANCE RUNS IN THE FAMILY
WHEN A PRINCE OF A FELLA
   MEETS A CINDERELLA

Kusik, Larry

AS IF I DIDN'T KNOW
GAMES THAT LOVERS PLAY
HAPPY SUMMER DAYS
LADY
LOVE THEME FROM "ROMEO AND
   JULIET" (A TIME FOR US)

LOVE THEME FROM "THE
GODFATHER" (A.K.A. SPEAK
SOFTLY LOVE)
MAKING MEMORIES
PEOPLE LIKE YOU
WHEN THE SNOW IS ON THE ROSES

Kuykendall, Jeannie

SWEET DESIRE

Kynard, Ben

RED TOP

La Bostrie, D.

TUTTI FRUTTI

LaBounty, Bill

HOT ROD HEARTS
I GOT DREAMS
LYNDA
THIS NIGHT WON'T LAST FOREVER
USED TO BLUE
WEEKEND, THE
WHERE DID I GO WRONG

Lacalle, Joseph M.

AMAPOLA (PRETTY LITTLE POPPY)

Lada, Anton

ARKANSAS BLUES

LaFarge, Guy

RIVER SEINE, THE (A.K.A. LA
SEINE)

LaFarge, Peter

BALLAD OF IRA HAYES, THE

Laflamme, David

WHITE BIRD

Laflamme, Linda

WHITE BIRD

Lago, Mario

AURORA

Lai, Francis

LIVE FOR LIFE
MAN AND A WOMAN, A
THEME FROM "LOVE STORY"

Laine, Denny

GIRLS' SCHOOL
LONDON TOWN
MULL OF KINTYRE

Laine, Frankie

IT ONLY HAPPENS ONCE
WE'LL BE TOGETHER AGAIN

Laing, L.

FOR YASGUR'S FARM

Lair, John

MAN WHO COMES AROUND, THE

Laird, Elmer

POISON LOVE

Laird-Clowes, Nick

LIFE IN A NORTHERN TOWN

Lake, Bonnie

MAN WITH A HORN
SANDMAN

Lake, Frank

BLESS 'EM ALL

Lake, Greg

LUCKY MAN

Lake, Sol

LONELY BULL, THE

MEXICAN SHUFFLE

Lakeside

FANTASTIC VOYAGE

La La

SECRET LADY

Lamagna, Carl

FLOWER OF DAWN

Lamarque, Avril

LITTLE SHOEMAKER, THE

LaMarre, Rene

LOVE ME! LOVE ME! LOVE ME!

Lamb, Arthur J.

ANY OLD PORT IN A STORM
ASLEEP IN THE DEEP
BIRD IN A GILDED CAGE, A
BIRD ON NELLIE'S HAT, THE
BIRD THAT NEVER SINGS, THE
GOODBYE, SWEETHEART, GOODBYE
JENNIE LEE
LINGER LONGER GIRL, THE
MANSION OF ACHING HEARTS, THE
PICNIC FOR TWO, A
WHEN THE BELL IN THE
LIGHTHOUSE RINGS DING DONG
WHEN THE BIRDS IN GEORGIA SING
OF TENNESSEE
WHEN THE MOCKING BIRDS ARE
SINGING IN THE WILDWOOD
WHEN YOU'VE HAD A LITTLE LOVE
YOU WANT A LITTLE MORE
YOU SPLASH ME AND I'LL SPLASH
YOU

Lamb, Henry

VOLUNTEER ORGANIST, THE

Lambert, Dave

WHAT'S THIS?

Lambert, Dennis

AIN'T NO WOMAN LIKE THE ONE I
GOT
ARE YOU MAN ENOUGH?
COUNTRY BOY (YOU GOT YOUR FEET
IN L.A.)
DON'T LOOK ANY FURTHER
DON'T PULL YOUR LOVE
DO THE FREDDIE
DREAM ON
FINE MESS, A
GIVE IT TO THE PEOPLE
GOIN' TO THE BANK
IT ONLY TAKES A MINUTE
KEEPER OF THE CASTLE
LOOK IN MY EYES PRETTY WOMAN
NIGHTSHIFT
ONE CHAIN DON'T MAKE NO PRISON
ONE TIN SOLDIER (THE LEGEND OF
BILLY JACK)
REMEMBER WHAT I TOLD YOU TO
FORGET
TWO DIVIDED BY LOVE
UP AND DOWN
WE BUILT THIS CITY

Lamm, Robert

25 OR 6 TO 4
BEGINNINGS
DOES ANYBODY REALLY KNOW
WHAT TIME IT IS?
FREE
HARRY TRUMAN
QUESTIONS 67 AND 68
SATURDAY IN THE PARK

Lamont, J.

FRIGHT NIGHT

Lampe, J. Bodewalt

CREOLE BELLE
VISION OF SALOME, A

Lampert, Diane

BREAK IT TO ME GENTLY
SILENT RUNNING
TOUCH OF PINK, A
YOUR NAME IS BEAUTIFUL

Lampl, Carl

CLOSE TO YOU
THOUGHTLESS

Lance, Bobby

HOUSE THAT JACK BUILT, THE

Lance, Major

MATADOR, THE

Land, Harry

MASHED POTATO TIME

Land, Leon

LAY DOWN YOUR ARMS

Landau, Mike

SECRET OF MY SUCCESS. THE

Landau, William

SACRED

Landesman, Fran

BALLAD OF THE SAD YOUNG MEN,
THE
LAUGH, I THOUGHT I'D DIE
SPRING CAN REALLY HANG YOU UP
THE MOST

Landsberg, Phyllis G.

"A" TEAM, THE

Lane, Boyd

FOOTPRINTS IN THE SNOW

Lane, Burton

BEGAT, THE
CHIN UP, CHEERIO, CARRY ON!
COME BACK TO ME
DANCING ON A DIME
EVERYTHING I HAVE IS YOURS
FEUDIN' AND FIGHTIN'

GUESS WHO
HAVE A HEART
HEIGH HO, THE GANG'S ALL HERE
HOW ABOUT YOU?
HOW ARE THINGS IN GLOCCA
MORRA?
HOW COULD YOU BELIEVE ME
WHEN I SAID I LOVE YOU WHEN
YOU KNOW I'VE BEEN A LIAR
ALL MY LIFE
HOW'DJA LIKE TO LOVE ME?
HURRY, IT'S LOVELY UP HERE
I DUG A DITCH (IN WICHITA)
IF THIS ISN'T LOVE
I HEAR MUSIC
I LEFT MY HAT IN HAITI
I'LL REMEMBER
I'LL TAKE TALLULAH
I WANT TO BE A MINSTREL MAN
I WISH I WAS THE WILLOW
LADY'S IN LOVE WITH YOU, THE
LAST CALL FOR LOVE
LET'S GO BAVARIAN
LIKE ME A LITTLE BIT LESS (LOVE
ME A LITTLE BIT MORE)
LISTEN MY CHILDREN AND YOU
SHALL HEAR
LOOK TO THE RAINBOW
LOOK WHO'S HERE
MELINDA
MOMENTS LIKE THIS
NECESSITY
NO MORE TEARS
OLD DEVIL MOON
ON A CLEAR DAY YOU CAN SEE
FOREVER
ONE MORE WALK AROUND THE
GARDEN
POOR YOU
SAYS MY HEART
SHE WASN'T YOU
SMARTY
SOMETHING SORT OF GRANDISH
STOP! YOU'RE BREAKIN' MY HEART
SWING HIGH, SWING LOW
'TAINT NO USE
THAT GREAT COME-AND-GET-IT DAY
THERE'S A GREAT DAY COMING
MAÑANA
TONY'S WIFE
TOO LATE NOW
WHAT DID I HAVE THAT I DON'T
HAVE

WHEN I'M NOT NEAR THE GIRL I
   LOVE
WHEN THE IDLE POOR BECOME
   THE IDLE RICH
WHY HIM?
WORLD IS IN MY ARMS, THE
YOU'RE ALL THE WORLD TO ME
YOU'RE MY THRILL
YOUR HEAD ON MY SHOULDER
YOU TOOK THE WORDS RIGHT OUT
   OF MY MOUTH

Lane, Eddie

BLESS YOU

Lane, Grace

CLINGING VINE

Lane, Herb

DISCO NIGHTS (ROCK-FREAK)

Lane, Ken

EVERYBODY LOVES SOMEBODY

Lane, Red

DARLING, YOU KNOW I WOULDN'T
   LIE
MY FRIEND ON THE RIGHT
'TILL I GET IT RIGHT
WALK ON OUT OF MY MIND

Lane, Ronnie

ITCHYCOO PARK

Lane, William

TIMES OF YOUR LIFE

Laney, King

WHY DON'T YOU BELIEVE ME

Lang, Eddie

IN THE BOTTLE BLUES
KICKIN' THE CAT

Lang, John

BROKEN WINGS
KYRIE

Langdon, Chris

ROSE, ROSE, I LOVE YOU

Lange, Arthur

AMERICA, HERE'S MY BOY
WE'RE GOING OVER

Lange, Henry

HOT LIPS

Lange, Johnny

BLUE SHADOWS ON THE TRAIL
DEACON JONES
I LOST MY SUGAR IN SALT LAKE
   CITY
LITTLE RED FOX, THE (N'YA, N'YA,
   YA CAN'T CATCH ME)
MEXICO JOE
MULE TRAIN
PECOS BILL
SOMEBODY BIGGER THAN YOU AND
   I
UNCLE REMUS SAID
WITHOUT YOUR LOVE

Lange, Lee

CARA MIA

Lange, Mutt

ANIMAL

Lange, Robert John

DO YOU BELIEVE IN LOVE
FOOLIN'
GET OUTTA MY DREAMS, GET INTO
   MY CAR
HYSTERIA
LOVE BITES
LOVIN' EVERY MINUTE OF IT
   (CYCLONE RIDGE)
POUR SOME SUGAR ON ME

ROCK OF AGES
WHEN THE GOING GETS TOUGH,
   THE TOUGH GET GOING

Langhorne, Bruce

APPLE DUMPLING GAME, THE

Langston, Joe

COTTON MILL MAN

Lanier, Donnie H.

HERE WE GO AGAIN

Lanier, Verdell

IT'S YOU THAT I NEED

Lanjean, Marc

THE TOUCH (LE GRISBI)

LaPallo, Joseph

I'M HAPPY THAT LOVE HAS FOUND
   YOU

LaPread, Ronald

BRICK HOUSE
SLIPPERY WHEN WET
SWEET LOVE
TOO HOT TA TROT

Lara, Agustin

LAMP ON THE CORNER, THE
TONIGHT WILL LIVE
YOU BELONG TO MY HEART

Lara, Maria Teresa

BE MINE TONIGHT

Laracuente, David

HAPPY MUSIC

Larden, Dennis

PUT YOUR MIND AT EASE

Larden, Lorry

PUT YOUR MIND AT EASE

Lardner, Ring

JUNE MOON
PROHIBITION BLUES

Larimer, Robert

WHO'S PERFECT?

Larkin, Nelson

I'LL PIN A NOTE ON YOUR PILLOW
LOVE HAS NO RIGHT

Larkin, Richard

HURRY, HURRY

LaRocca, Nick

AT THE JAZZ BAND BALL
BARNYARD BLUE
CLARINET MARMALADE
FIDGETY FEET
ORIGINAL DIXIELAND ONE-STEP
OSTRICH WALK
TIGER RAG

LaRosa, Julius

EH, CUMPARI!

Larson, Glen

BIG MAN
EARLY IN THE MORNING (DOWN BY
    THE STATION)
TWENTY-SIX MILES (SANTA
    CATALINA)

Larson, Mel

I AM LOVE

Larue, Jacques

CHERRY PINK AND APPLE BLOSSOM
    WHITE

LaRusso, Andrea

DRESS YOU UP

LaSalle, Denise

MARRIED BUT NOT TO EACH OTHER
NOW RUN AND TELL THAT
TRAPPED BY A THING CALLED
    LOVE

Lascalles, Martin

LOVE IS A HOUSE

Lasco, Morry

BEWARE (BROTHER, BEWARE)

Lashley, Lou S.

OH, YOU MILLION DOLLAR BABY

Laska, Edward

ALCOHOLIC BLUES, THE
HOW'D YOU LIKE TO SPOON WITH
    ME?

Lasky, Jesse L.

DEAR OLD BROADWAY

Lasley, David

LEAD ME ON
LOVE ME AGAIN

Last, James

GAMES THAT LOVERS PLAY
HAPPY HEART
NOW I KNOW
WHEN THE SNOW IS ON THE ROSES

Laswell, Bill

ROCKIT

Latham, Dwight

I'M MY OWN GRANDPAW
    (GRANDMAW)

Latouche, John

BALLAD FOR AMERICANS
CABIN IN THE SKY
CAE CAE
HONEY IN THE HONEYCOMB
IT'S THE GOING HOME TOGETHER
I'VE GOT ME
LAZY AFTERNOON
STRANGE
SUMMER IS A-COMIN' IN
TAKING A CHANCE ON LOVE
TOMORROW MOUNTAIN

Lauder, Harry

FOU THE NOO (OR, SOMETHING IN
    THE BOTTLE FOR THE MORNING)
I LOVE A LASSIE (OR, MA SCOTCH
    BLUEBELL)
ROAMIN' IN THE GLOAMIN'
SHE IS MY DAISY
STOP YER TICKLING, JOCK!
TOBERMORY
WEE DEOCH-AN-DORIS
WHEN I GET BACK AGAIN TO
    BONNIE SCOTLAND

Lauper, Cyndi

CHANGE OF HEART
GOONIES 'R' GOOD ENOUGH, THE
SHE BOP
STEADY
TIME AFTER TIME

Laurence, Paul

(YOU'RE PUTTIN') A RUSH ON ME
I'M IN LOVE
JAM TONIGHT
ROCK ME TONIGHT (FOR OLD TIMES
    SAKE)
STRUNG OUT
TASTY LOVE

Laurie, Linda

LEAVE ME ALONE (RUBY RED
    DRESS)

Lava, William

CHEYENNE

Lavere, Frank

ALMOST ALWAYS

Lavoie, Kent

DON'T EXPECT ME TO BE YOUR
  FRIEND
DON'T TELL ME GOODNIGHT
I'D LOVE YOU TO WANT ME
ME AND YOU AND A DOG NAMED
  BOO

Law, Simon

BACK TO LIFE

Lawlor, Charles B.

SIDEWALKS OF NEW YORK, THE

Lawnhurst, Vee

ACCENT ON YOUTH
ALIBI BABY
AND THEN SOME
CROSS PATCH
DAY I LET YOU GET AWAY, THE
I COULDN'T TELL THEM WHAT TO
  DO
I'M KEEPING COMPANY
JOHNNY ZERO
MUTINY IN THE PARLOR
NO OTHER LOVE
PLEASE KEEP ME IN YOUR DREAMS
US ON A BUS
WHAT'S THE NAME OF THAT SONG?

Lawrence, Alfred J.

COME ALONG, MY MANDY

Lawrence, Bernie

LET HER DANCE

Lawrence, Charles

AND HER TEARS FLOWED LIKE
  WINE
IT MUST HAVE BEEN A DREAM

Lawrence, Elliot

STRANGE THINGS ARE HAPPENING
  (HO HO, HEE HEE, HA HA)

Lawrence, Jack

ALL OR NOTHING AT ALL
BEYOND THE SEA
BIG BOY BLUE
CHOO CHOO TRAIN (CH-CH-FOO)
CONCERTO FOR TWO
DELICADO
FAITH
FOOLIN' MYSELF
HANDFUL OF STARS, A
HAND IN HAND
HOLD MY HAND
HUCKLEBERRY DUCK
IF I DIDN'T CARE
I GOT EVERYTHING I WANT
I HAD A BALL
I'LL HATE MYSELF IN THE MORNING
IN THE MOON MIST
LINDA
MOONLIGHT MASQUERADE
MUSIC FROM BEYOND THE MOON
MY HEART ISN'T IN IT
NO ONE BUT YOU
OTHER HALF OF ME, THE
OUTSIDE OF PARADISE
PASSING BY
PLAY, FIDDLE, PLAY
POOR PEOPLE OF PARIS, THE
SLEEPY LAGOON
SO FAR, SO GOOD
SUNRISE SERENADE
SYMPHONY
TENDERLY
TO YOU, MY LOVE
VAGABOND DREAMS
VALENTINO TANGO, THE (NOCHE DE
  AMOUR)
WHAT'S YOUR STORY, MORNING
  GLORY?
WHAT WILL I TELL MY HEART?

WITH THE WIND AND THE RAIN IN
  YOUR HAIR
YES, MY DARLING DAUGHTER

Lawrence, Karen

LOVE THEME FROM "EYES OF
  LAURA MARS" (A.K.A. PRISONER)

Lawrence, Neil

SWEETER THAN THE SWEETEST

Lawrence, Stephen

YOU TAKE MY BREATH AWAY

Lawrence, Steve

CAN'T GET OVER (THE BOSSA NOVA)

Lawrence, Trevor

I'M SO EXCITED

Lawson, Herbert Happy

ANY TIME (A.K.A. ANYTIME)

Lay, Deoin

IT DON'T HURT ME HALF AS BAD

Layton, Turner

AFTER YOU'VE GONE
DEAR OLD SOUTHLAND
DOWN BY THE RIVER
EVERYBODY'S GONE CRAZY 'BOUT
  THE DOGGONE BLUES
STRUT MISS LIZZIE
SWEET EMALINA, MY GAL
WAY DOWN YONDER IN NEW
  ORLEANS

Lazar, David

GOTTA TRAVEL ON

Lazaros, Thomas

BIG CITY MISS RUTH ANN

Lazarus, Emma

GIVE ME YOUR TIRED, YOUR POOR

Lea, Jim

CUM ON FEEL THE NOIZE
MY OH MY
RUN, RUNAWAY

Leach, Curtis

GOLDEN GUITAR

Leakes, Melvin

MAN AND A HALF, A

Leander, Mike

ANOTHER TIME, ANOTHER PLACE
DO YOU WANNA TOUCH ME (OH
    YEAH)
EARLY IN THE MORNING
KNIGHT IN RUSTY ARMOUR
LADY GODIVA
ROCK AND ROLL PART 2

Leavitt, William G.

MY BABY'S COMING HOME

LeBaron, William

DEEP IN YOUR EYES
I'M IN LOVE
LETTER SONG
LITTLE GIRLS, GOODBYE
ON MIAMI SHORE
WHO CAN TELL
YOU ARE FREE

Lebieg, Earl

SLEEP

Lebish, Louis

DANCE WITH ME

LeBlanc, Emmanuel

DISCO NIGHTS (ROCK-FREAK)

LeBlanc, Lenny

FALLING

Leblond, A. G.

TITINA

LeBon, Simon

ELECTION DAY
NOTORIOUS

Lebowsky, Stan

T.L.C. TENDER LOVE AND CARE
WAYWARD WIND, THE

LeBoy, Grace

EVERYBODY RAG WITH ME
I WISH I HAD A GIRL
ON THE GOOD SHIP MARY ANN

LeBrunn, George

OH! ISN'T IT SINGULAR!

Lebsock, Jack

BLESS YOUR HEART

Lecuona, Ernesto

ALWAYS IN MY HEART
ANDALUCIA
ANGELS CAME THRU, THE
ANOTHER NIGHT LIKE THIS
AT THE CROSSROADS
BREEZE AND I, THE
FROM ONE LOVE TO ANOTHER
JUNGLE DRUMS
MALAGUEÑA
MARIA, MY OWN
ONE MORE TOMORROW
SAY "SI SI"
SIBONEY
TWO HEARTS THAT PASS IN THE
    NIGHT

Lecuona, Margarita

BABALU

TABOO

Ledbetter, Huddie "Leadbelly"

GOODNIGHT, IRENE

Ledesma, Ishmael

GET OFF
HOT NUMBER

Ledo, Les

IT'S JUST A LITTLE BIT TOO LATE

Lee, Albert

COUNTRY BOY

Lee, Allyn

DOIN' OUR THING

Lee, Arthur

7 AND 7 IS

Lee, Byron

JAMAICA SKA

Lee, Craig

DREAMSVILLE, OHIO

Lee, Curtis

PRETTY LITTLE ANGEL EYES

Lee, David

AND THE CRADLE WILL ROCK
IN THE SUMMER OF HIS YEARS

Lee, Dickey

DODO, THE
DOOR'S ALWAYS OPEN, THE
I'LL BE LEAVING ALONE
I SAW LINDA YESTERDAY
I'VE BEEN AROUND LONG ENOUGH
    TO KNOW

LET'S FALL TO PIECES TOGETHER
SHE THINKS I STILL CARE

Lee, Ernie

TENNESSEE TEARS

Lee, Ethel

SPEEDY GONZALES

Lee, Geddy

LIMELIGHT
NEW WORLD MAN
SPIRIT OF RADIO, THE
TOM SAWYER

Lee, James, Jr.

IN A MOMENT

Lee, Jay

YELLOW BALLOON, THE

Lee, Jimmy

BRUSH THOSE TEARS FROM YOUR
   EYES
IF YOU DON'T, SOMEBODY ELSE
   WILL

Lee, Julia

GOTTA GIMME WHATCHA GOT

Lee, Larry

FOURTEEN CARAT MIND
JACKIE BLUE

Lee, Laura

DIRTY MAN

Lee, Leonard

FEEL SO FINE
FEEL SO GOOD
LET THE GOOD TIMES ROLL

Lee, Lester

CHRISTMAS DREAMING
DREAMER WITH A PENNY
HOW DO I KNOW IT'S REAL?
I'M GONE
INFLATION
LADY LOVE
MAN FROM LARAMIE, THE
NAUGHTY ANGELINE
PENNSYLVANIA POLKA
SADIE THOMPSON'S SONG

Lee, Martin

SAVE YOUR KISSES FOR ME

Lee, Marvin

LIVERY STABLE BLUES

Lee, Nancy

STROLL, THE

Lee, Orrie

WALTZING MATILDA

Lee, Peggy

DON'T BE SO MEAN TO BABY
   ('CAUSE BABY'S SO GOOD TO
   YOU)
HE'S A TRAMP
I DON'T KNOW ENOUGH ABOUT YOU
I'M GONNA GO FISHIN'
IT'S A GOOD DAY
JOHNNY GUITAR
MAÑANA (IS SOON ENOUGH FOR ME)
SIAMESE CAT SONG, THE
TOM THUMB'S TUNE
WHAT MORE CAN A WOMAN DO?
WHERE CAN I GO WITHOUT YOU?

Lee, Stella

QUEEN OF THE SENIOR PROM
USKA DARA (A TURKISH TALE)

Lee, Sydney

MY LOVE, FORGIVE ME (AMORE,
   SCUSAMI)

Lee, Tommy

GIRLS, GIRLS, GIRLS

Leeds, Milton

BELLS OF SAN RAQUEL, THE
MISIRLOU
PERFIDIA
WHO SHOT THE HOLE IN MY
   SOMBRERO?
YOU, YOU, YOU ARE THE ONE

Lees, Gene

QUIET NIGHTS OF QUIET STARS
   (CORCOVADO)
WALTZ FOR DEBBY

Leeson, M.

FOR YOUR EYES ONLY

Leeson, Mike

TAKE ME HOME TONIGHT

Leeway, Joe

DOCTOR! DOCTOR!
HOLD ME NOW
KING FOR A DAY
LAY YOUR HANDS ON ME
LOVE ON YOUR SIDE

Leffler, John

ANOTHER WORLD

Leftenant, Nathan

BACK AND FORTH
SHE'S STRANGE

Legassick, S.

ONE HEARTBEAT

Legrand, Michel

BRIAN'S SONG
HAPPY (LOVE THEME FROM "LADY
   SINGS THE BLUES")
HIS EYES—HER EYES
HOW DO YOU KEEP THE MUSIC
   PLAYING?
I WILL WAIT FOR YOU
ONCE UPON A SUMMERTIME
PAPA, CAN YOU HEAR ME?
PIECES OF DREAMS
SUMMER ME, WINTER ME
THEME FROM "SUMMER OF '42"
WATCH WHAT HAPPENS
WAY HE MAKES ME FEEL, THE
WHAT ARE YOU DOING THE REST
   OF YOUR LIFE?
WINDMILLS OF YOUR MIND, THE

Lehac, Ned

YOU FORGOT YOUR GLOVES

Lehar, Franz

GIGOLETTE
GOLD AND SILVER
I LOVE YOU SO (THE MERRY WIDOW
   WALTZ)
MAXIM'S
MY LITTLE NEST OF HEAVENLY
   BLUE
PRETTY EDELWEISS
SAY NOT LOVE IS A DREAM
VILIA
WHITE DOVE, THE
YOURS IS MY HEART ALONE

Lehman, John

FIRST BORN
NIGHT

Lehman, Kenny

DANCE, DANCE, DANCE (YOWSAH,
   YOWSAH, YOWSAH)

Lehmann, Johnny

ALONE AT LAST
T.L.C. TENDER LOVE AND CARE

WHY DOES IT GET SO LATE SO
   EARLY?

Leib, Bell

BLOND SAILOR, THE

Leiber, Jerry

ALONG CAME JONES
(YOU'RE SO SQUARE) BABY, I DON'T
   CARE
BERNIE'S TUNE
BLACK DENIM TROUSERS AND
   MOTORCYCLE BOOTS
BOSSA NOVA BABY
CHARLIE BROWN
DON'T
DOWN IN MEXICO
DRIP DROP
D. W. WASHBURN
GIRLS I NEVER KISSED, THE
HOUND DOG
I (WHO HAVE NOTHING)
I KEEP FORGETTIN' (EVERY TIME
   YOU'RE NEAR)
I'LL BE THERE
I'M A WOMAN
I NEED YOUR LOVIN' (BAZOOM)
IS THAT ALL THERE IS?
I WANNA DO MORE
JAILHOUSE ROCK
JUST TELL HER JIM SAID HELLO
LOVE ME
LOVE POTION NUMBER NINE
LOVING YOU
LUCKY LIPS
MAN WHO ROBBED THE BANK AT
   SANTA FE, THE
ON BROADWAY
ONLY IN AMERICA
POISON IVY
RUBY BABY
SEARCHIN'
(WHEN SHE NEEDS GOOD LOVIN')
   SHE COMES TO ME
SHE'S NOT YOU
SPANISH HARLEM
STAND BY ME
THERE GOES MY BABY
TREAT ME NICE
YAKETY YAK
YOUNG BLOOD

Leiber, O.

FOREVER YOUR GIRL

Leigh, Carolyn

BE A PERFORMER
BEST IS YET TO COME, THE
DEEP DOWN INSIDE
FIREFLY
GIVE A LITTLE WHISTLE
HERE'S TO US
HEY, LOOK ME OVER!
HIBISCUS
HOW LITTLE WE KNOW (HOW
   LITTLE IT MATTERS)
I'M FLYING
I'M WAITING JUST FOR YOU
IT AMAZES ME
I'VE GOTTA CROW
I'VE GOT YOUR NUMBER
I WON'T GROW UP
JUST BECAUSE YOU'RE YOU
KANSAS CITY
LITTLE ME
OTHER SIDE OF THE TRACKS, THE
PASS ME BY
PLAYBOY THEME
POOR LITTLE HOLLYWOOD STAR
REAL LIVE GIRL
RULES OF THE ROAD, THE
SPRING IN MAINE
STAY WITH ME
STEP TO THE REAR
TALL HOPE
TEMPO OF THE TIMES, THE
TENDER SHEPHERD
WHAT TAKES MY FANCY
WHEN IN ROME (I DO AS THE
   ROMANS DO)
WITCHCRAFT
YOU FASCINATE ME SO
YOUNG AT HEART
YOU'VE COME HOME

Leigh, Fred W.

POOR JOHN
WAITING AT THE CHURCH

Leigh, Mitch

DIS-ADVANTAGES OF YOU, THE

IMPOSSIBLE DREAM, THE (THE QUEST)

Leigh, R.

COME FROM THE HEART

Leigh, Richard

DON'T IT MAKE MY BROWN EYES BLUE
I'LL GET OVER YOU
LIFE'S HIGHWAY
THAT'S THE THING ABOUT LOVE

Leighton, Bert

STEAMBOAT BILL

Leighton, Frank

STEAMBOAT BILL

Leiken, Molly Ann

EIGHT IS ENOUGH
MOMENT BY MOMENT

Leikin, Mary Ann

OTHER SIDE OF THE MOUNTAIN, PART 2

Leip, Hans

LILI MARLENE

Leitch, Donovan

ATLANTIS
BROTHER SUN, SISTER MOON
CATCH THE WIND
EPISTLE TO DIPPY
GOO GOO BARABAJAGAL (LOVE IS HOT)
HURDY GURDY MAN
JENNIFER JUNIPER
LALENA
MELLOW YELLOW
MUSEUM
SUNSHINE SUPERMAN
THERE IS A MOUNTAIN

TO SUSAN ON THE WEST COAST WAITING
WEAR YOUR LOVE LIKE HEAVEN

Leka, Paul

GREEN TAMBOURINE
JELLY JUNGLE (OF ORANGE MARMALADE)
NA NA HEY HEY (KISS HIM GOODBYE)
RICE IS NICE

Leleiohaku, Prince

HAWAIIAN WAR CHANT

Lemaire, Sonny

GIVE ME ONE MORE CHANCE
I CAN'T GET CLOSE ENOUGH
I DON'T WANT TO BE A MEMORY
IT'LL BE ME
JUST IN CASE
SHE'S A MIRACLE
SHE'S TOO GOOD TO BE TRUE

Lemare, Jules

I'M GONNA GET YOU
SWEET AND LOVELY

Lemonnier, H. A.

TITINA

Lendell, Mike

MARY IN THE MORNING

Lenghurst, Pearl

BE-BOP BABY

Lengsfelder, Hans

HAYFOOT, STRAWFOOT
PERDIDO

Lennon, John

#9 DREAM
ALL MY LOVING

ALL TOGETHER NOW
ALL YOU NEED IS LOVE
AND I LOVE HER
AND I LOVE HIM
ANOTHER GIRL
BABY, YOU'RE A RICH MAN
BACK IN THE U.S.S.R.
BAD TO ME
BALLAD OF JOHN AND YOKO, THE
BIRTHDAY
CAN'T BUY ME LOVE
COLD TURKEY
COME TOGETHER
DAY TRIPPER
DEAR PRUDENCE
DON'T LET ME DOWN
DO YOU WANT TO KNOW A SECRET?
DRIVE MY CAR
EIGHT DAYS A WEEK
ELEANOR RIGBY
FAME
FOOL ON THE HILL, THE
FROM A WINDOW
FROM ME TO YOU
GET BACK
GIVE PEACE A CHANCE
GOODBYE
GOOD DAY SUNSHINE
GOT TO GET YOU INTO MY LIFE
HARD DAY'S NIGHT, A
HELLO, GOODBYE
HELP!
HELTER SKELTER
HERE, THERE AND EVERYWHERE
HEY JUDE
I AM THE WALRUS
I DON'T WANT TO SEE YOU AGAIN
I DON'T WANT TO SPOIL THE PARTY
I FEEL FINE
IF I FELL
I'LL CRY INSTEAD
I'LL KEEP YOU SATISFIED
(P.S.) I LOVE YOU
IMAGINE
I'M HAPPY JUST TO DANCE WITH YOU
IN MY LIFE
INSTANT KARMA (WE ALL SHINE ON)
I SAW HER STANDING THERE
I SHOULD HAVE KNOWN BETTER
IT'S ALL DOWN TO GOODNIGHT VIENNA

Lennon, John

IT'S FOR YOU
IT'S ONLY LOVE
I WANT TO HOLD YOUR HAND
JULIA
JUST LIKE STARTING OVER
LADY MADONNA
LET IT BE
LONG AND WINDING ROAD, THE
LOVELY RITA (METER MAID)
LOVE ME DO
LUCY IN THE SKY WITH DIAMONDS
MAGICAL MYSTERY TOUR, THE
MICHELLE
MIND GAMES
MOTHER
NOBODY I KNOW
NOBODY TOLD ME
NORWEGIAN WOOD
NOWHERE MAN
OB-LA-DI, OB-LA-DA
OH! DARLING
PAPERBACK WRITER
PENNY LANE
PLEASE PLEASE ME
POWER TO THE PEOPLE
RAIN
REVOLUTION
RINGO'S THEME (THIS BOY)
ROCKY RACCOON
SGT. PEPPER'S LONELY HEARTS
    CLUB BAND
SHE CAME IN THROUGH THE
    BATHROOM WINDOW
SHE LOVES YOU
SHE SAID SHE SAID
SHE'S A WOMAN
STRAWBERRY FIELDS FOREVER
TELL ME WHY
THANK YOU GIRL
THERE'S A PLACE
TICKET TO RIDE
WATCHING THE WHEELS
WE CAN WORK IT OUT
WHATEVER GETS YOU THROUGH
    THE NIGHT
WHAT GOES ON
WHEN I'M 64
WITH A LITTLE HELP FROM MY
    FRIENDS
WOMAN
WORKING CLASS HERO
WORLD WITHOUT LOVE, A
YELLOW SUBMARINE

YES IT IS
YESTERDAY
YOU CAN'T DO THAT
YOU'VE GOT TO HIDE YOUR LOVE
    AWAY
YOU WON'T SEE ME

Lennon, Julian

TOO LATE FOR GOODBYES
VALOTTE

Lennox, Annie

HERE COMES THE RAIN AGAIN
LOVE IS A STRANGER
MISSIONARY MAN
SISTERS ARE DOIN' IT FOR
    THEMSELVES
SWEET DREAMS (ARE MADE OF
    THIS)
WHO'S THAT GIRL?
WOULD I LIE TO YOU?

Lenoir, Jean

SPEAK TO ME OF LOVE

Lenox, Jean

I DON'T CARE

Leo, Josh

BABY'S GOT A HOLD ON ME

Leon, David

RIDE!

Leonard, Anita

SUNDAY KIND OF LOVE, A

Leonard, Eddie

IDA! SWEET AS APPLE CIDER
OH, DIDN'T IT RAIN?
ROLL DEM ROLY BOLY EYES

Leonard, G.

I'M ON FIRE

Leonard, Harlan

SOUTHERN FRIED

Leonard, Mark

MISSING YOU

Leonard, Michael

I'M ALL SMILES

Leonard, Pat

LA ISLA BONITA
LIKE A PRAYER
LIVE TO TELL
ONE GOOD WOMAN
WHO'S THAT GIRL

Leonetti, Tommy

KUM BA YAH

Leopolo, Glenn

BACK WHEN MY HAIR WAS SHORT

Lerios, Cory

COOL LOVE
DON'T WANT TO LIVE WITHOUT IT
I WANT YOU TONIGHT
LOVE WILL FIND A WAY
WHATCHA GONNA DO?

Lerner, Alan Jay

ALMOST LIKE BEING IN LOVE
ANOTHER AUTUMN
BRIGADOON
CAMELOT
COCO
COME BACK TO ME
COME TO ME, BEND TO ME
DAY BEFORE SPRING, THE
FOLLOW ME
GABRIELLE
GET ME TO THE CHURCH ON TIME
GIGI
GREEN-UP TIME
GUENEVERE
HEATHER ON THE HILL, THE

HERE I'LL STAY

HOW COULD YOU BELIEVE ME
    WHEN I SAID I LOVE YOU WHEN
    YOU KNOW I'VE BEEN A LIAR
    ALL MY LIFE

HOW TO HANDLE A WOMAN

HURRY, IT'S LOVELY UP HERE

I COULD HAVE DANCED ALL NIGHT

IF EVER I WOULD LEAVE YOU

I LEFT MY HAT IN HAITI

I'LL GO HOME WITH BONNIE JEAN

I LOVED YOU ONCE IN SILENCE

I LOVE YOU THIS MORNING

I'M AN ORDINARY MAN

I'M GLAD I'M NOT YOUNG ANYMORE

I'M ON MY WAY

I REMEMBER IT WELL

I STILL SEE ELISA

I TALK TO THE TREES

IT'S A BORE

I'VE GROWN ACCUSTOMED TO HER
    FACE

I WONDER WHAT THE KING IS
    DOING TONIGHT

JUG OF WINE, A

JUST YOU WAIT

LITTLE PRINCE, THE (FROM WHO
    KNOWS WHERE)

LUSTY MONTH OF MAY, THE

MELINDA

MY LAST LOVE

NIGHT THEY INVENTED
    CHAMPAGNE, THE

ON A CLEAR DAY YOU CAN SEE
    FOREVER

ONE MORE WALK AROUND THE
    GARDEN

ON THE STREET WHERE YOU LIVE

RAIN IN SPAIN, THE

SAY A PRAYER FOR ME TONIGHT

SEVEN DEADLY VIRTUES, THE

SHE WASN'T YOU

SHOW ME

SIMPLE JOYS OF MAIDENHOOD, THE

THANK HEAVEN FOR LITTLE GIRLS

THEN YOU MAY TAKE ME TO THE
    FAIR

THERE BUT FOR YOU GO I

THEY CALL THE WIND MARIA

TOO LATE NOW

WALTZ AT MAXIM'S (A.K.A. SHE IS
    NOT THINKING OF ME)

WAND'RIN STAR

WHAT DID I HAVE THAT I DON'T
    HAVE

WHAT DO THE SIMPLE FOLKS DO?

WHY CAN'T THE ENGLISH?

WHY HIM?

WITH A LITTLE BIT OF LUCK

WOULDN'T IT BE LOVERLY?

YOU HAVEN'T CHANGED AT ALL

YOU'RE ALL THE WORLD TO ME

Lerner, Sammy

DUST OFF THAT OLD PIANNA (OH,
    SUZANNA)

FALLING IN LOVE AGAIN (CAN'T
    HELP IT)

I'M POPEYE THE SAILOR MAN

IS IT TRUE WHAT THEY SAY ABOUT
    DIXIE?

JUDY

POPEYE THE SAILOR MAN

SASKATCHEWAN

Lesh, Philip

TRUCKIN'

Leslie, Edgar

ALL THE QUAKERS ARE SHOULDER
    SHAKERS DOWN IN QUAKER
    TOWN

AMERICA, I LOVE YOU

AMONG MY SOUVENIRS

AND I STILL DO

AT A PERFUME COUNTER

BLUE (AND BROKEN HEARTED)

BY THE RIVER SAINTE MARIE

CALIFORNIA AND YOU

CLING TO ME

COME ON, PAPA

CRAZY PEOPLE

DIRTY HANDS, DIRTY FACE

FOR ME AND MY GAL

GETTING SOME FUN OUT OF LIFE

HE'D HAVE TO GET UNDER—GET
    OUT AND GET UNDER

HELLO, HAWAII, HOW ARE YOU?

IN A LITTLE GYPSY TEA ROOM

IN THE GOLD FIELDS OF NEVADA

IT LOOKS LIKE RAIN IN CHERRY
    BLOSSOM LANE

I WAKE UP SMILING

JUST A LITTLE HOME FOR THE OLD
    FOLKS

KANSAS CITY KITTY

LITTLE BIT INDEPENDENT, A

LONESOME

LOST IN A DREAM

LOVELY

ME AND THE MAN IN THE MOON

MIDNIGHT BLUE

MISTAKES

MOON OVER MIAMI

MOON WAS YELLOW, THE

MY TROUBLES ARE OVER

OH, WHAT A PAL WAS MARY

OH, YOU MILLION DOLLAR DOLL

ON THE 'GIN, 'GIN, 'GINNY SHORE

ON TREASURE ISLAND

RAINBOW VALLEY

REACHING FOR SOMEONE (AND NOT
    FINDING ANYONE THERE)

REMINISCING

ROBINS AND ROSES

ROLLING STONES

ROMANCE

ROSE OF THE RIO GRANDE

SADIE SALOME, GO HOME!

TAIN'T NO SIN (TO TAKE OFF YOUR
    SKIN AND DANCE AROUND IN
    YOUR BONES)

TAKE YOUR GIRLIE TO THE MOVIES
    (IF YOU CAN'T MAKE LOVE AT
    HOME)

WAIT TILL SHE SEES YOU IN YOUR
    UNIFORM

WE MUST BE VIGILANT

WERE YOU FOOLIN'?

WHEN ALEXANDER TAKES HIS
    RAGTIME BAND TO FRANCE

WHEN KENTUCKY BIDS THE WORLD
    "GOOD MORNING"

WHEN THE GROWN-UP LADIES ACT
    LIKE BABIES (I'VE GOT TO LOVE
    'EM, THAT'S ALL)

WHEN THE SHEPHERD LEADS THE
    SHEEP BACK HOME

YOU'VE GOT ME IN THE PALM OF
    YOUR HAND

Leslie, Henry

I'D LIKE TO SEE THE KAISER WITH
    A LILY IN HIS HAND

Leslie, Thomas

SHE'S JUST MY STYLE

Leslie, Tom

SUKIYAKI

Lessing, Edith Maida

OH! YOU CIRCUS DAY

Lester, Chester

SHE LEFT LOVE ALL OVER ME

Letters, Will

HAS ANYBODY HERE SEEN KELLY?

Levant, Oscar

AFTERGLOW
BLAME IT ON MY YOUTH
DON'T MENTION LOVE TO ME
IF YOU WANT THE RAINBOW (YOU
    MUST HAVE THE RAIN)
KEEP SWEEPING THE COBWEBS OFF
    THE MOON
LADY, PLAY YOUR MANDOLIN
LOVABLE AND SWEET
PARDON MY LOVE
THERE'S NOTHING WRONG WITH A
    KISS
UNTIL TODAY
WACKY DUST

Levay, Silvester

FLY, ROBIN, FLY
GET UP AND BOOGIE (THAT'S
    RIGHT)

Leveen, Raymond

I WONDER
TI-PI-TIN

Levenson, Neil

DENISE

Levenson, Robert

MY BELGIAN ROSE

Lever, Timothy

BRAND NEW LOVER
YOU SPIN ME ROUND LIKE A
    RECORD

Levere, Frank

HAVE YOU HEARD?
PRETEND

Levert, Gerald

MAMACITA
MY FOREVER LOVE
PULL OVER

Leverton, Buck

SWISS BOY, THE

Levi, Maurice

AIRY, FAIRY LILLIAN

Levin, Ira

SHE TOUCHED ME

Levine, Gene

LONE STAR STATE OF MIND

Levine, Irving

CANDIDA

Levine, Irwin

BLACK PEARL
I CAN'T QUIT HER
I MUST BE SEEING THINGS
I WOKE UP IN LOVE THIS MORNING
KNOCK THREE TIMES
LITTLE LONELY ONE
SAY, HAS ANYBODY SEEN MY
    SWEET GYPSY ROSE
STEPPIN' OUT (GONNA BOOGIE
    TONIGHT)

THIS DIAMOND RING
TIE A YELLOW RIBBON ROUND THE
    OLE OAK TREE
YOUR HUSBAND—MY WIFE

Levine, Joey

CHEWY CHEWY
DOWN AT LULU'S
GIMME, GIMME GOOD LOVIN'
MAKE BELIEVE
MERCY
QUICK JOEY SMALL (RUN, JOEY,
    RUN)
SHAKE
YUMMY, YUMMY, YUMMY

Levinson, Lou

HERE IN MY HEART

Levitin, L. O.

SPILL THE WINE

Levitt, Estelle

DON'T SAY YOU DON'T REMEMBER
I CAN'T GROW PEACHES ON A
    CHERRY TREE
IN THE NAME OF LOVE
ISN'T IT LONELY TOGETHER
THIS DOOR SWINGS BOTH WAYS

Levy, Eunice

KO KO MO (I LOVE YOU SO)

Levy, Gail

MERCY, MERCY, MERCY

Levy, Jacques

HURRICANE
MOZAMBIQUE

Levy, Marc

LAY DOWN SALLY

Levy, Morris

CALIFORNIA SUN
MY BOY LOLLIPOP
WHY DO FOOLS FALL IN LOVE?

Levy, Sol P.

THAT NAUGHTY WALTZ

Levy, Vincent

MERCY, MERCY, MERCY

Lewine, Richard

I FELL IN LOVE WITH YOU

Lewis, Al

ALL-AMERICAN GIRL
BLUEBERRY HILL
BREEZE, THE (THAT'S BRINGIN' MY
   HONEY BACK TO ME)
CINCINNATI DANCING PIG
CROSS-EYED KELLY (FROM PENN-
   SYL-VAN-EYE-AY)
EVERY NOW AND THEN
FINGER OF SUSPICION POINTS AT
   YOU, THE
GONNA GET A GIRL
GOT THE BENCH, GOT THE PARK
   (BUT I HAVEN'T GOT YOU)
HE'S SO UNUSUAL
I'M READY
INVITATION TO A BROKEN HEART
ISN'T IT A SHAME?
LANE IN SPAIN, A
LIVIN' IN THE SUNLIGHT, LOVIN' IN
   THE MOONLIGHT
MEANEST THING YOU EVER DID
   WAS KISS ME, THE
NINE LITTLE MILES FROM TEN-TEN-
   TENNESSEE
NINETY-NINE OUT OF A HUNDRED
   (WANT TO BE LOVED)
NO! NO! A THOUSAND TIMES NO!
   (YOU SHALL NOT BUY MY
   CARESS)
NOW'S THE TIME TO FALL IN LOVE
   (POTATOES ARE CHEAPER—
   TOMATOES ARE CHEAPER)
ONE NIGHT IN MONTE CARLO

ON THE BUMPY ROAD TO LOVE
OVER SOMEBODY ELSE'S SHOULDER
ROSE O'DAY (THE FILLA-FA-DUSHA
   SONG)
START THE DAY RIGHT
TEARS ON MY PILLOW
UNDER A STRAWBERRY MOON
WAY BACK HOME
WHAT'S THE MATTER WITH ME?
WHEN I'M THE PRESIDENT
(AS LONG AS YOU'RE NOT IN LOVE
   WITH ANYONE ELSE) WHY DON'T
   YOU FALL IN LOVE WITH ME?
YOU GOTTA BE A FOOTBALL HERO

Lewis, Barbara

HELLO STRANGER
PUPPY LOVE

Lewis, B. G.

MILORD

Lewis, Bobby

ONE TRACK MIND

Lewis, Brian

SHAPE OF THINGS TO COME, THE

Lewis, Calvin H.

WHEN A MAN (WOMAN) LOVES A
   WOMAN (MAN)

Lewis, Clarence

YA YA

Lewis, Curtis R.

TODAY I SING THE BLUES

Lewis, David

ALWAYS
CIRCLES
SECRET LOVERS
TOUCH A FOUR LEAF CLOVER

Lewis, Dorothy

THIS WHITE CIRCLE ON MY FINGER

Lewis, Edna

I WISH THAT WE WERE MARRIED
JUDY'S TURN TO CRY
LIPSTICK ON YOUR COLLAR

Lewis, Gary

EVERYBODY LOVES A CLOWN
SHE'S JUST MY STYLE

Lewis, Happy

MY LITTLE COUSIN

Lewis, Harold

NIGHTFALL
THIS LITTLE PIGGIE WENT TO
   MARKET

Lewis, Henry

WILD, WILD WOMEN ARE MAKING A
   WILD MAN OF ME, THE

Lewis, Huey

HEART OF ROCK AND ROLL, THE
HIP TO BE SQUARE
IF THIS IS IT
I KNOW WHAT I LIKE
I WANT A NEW DRUG
POWER OF LOVE, THE
STUCK WITH YOU

Lewis, Hugh X.

B. J. THE D. J.
TAKE MY RING OFF YOUR FINGER
WHAT I NEED MOST

Lewis, Jack

TEEN AGE IDOL

Lewis, J. C., Jr.

MILLION DREAMS, A

Lewis, Jerry Lee

HIGH SCHOOL CONFIDENTIAL

Lewis, Jimmy

IF YOU WERE MINE

Lewis, Jonathan

ALWAYS

Lewis, Kenneth

I FOOLED YOU THIS TIME

Lewis, Margaret

BUFFALO SOLDIER
GIRL MOST LIKELY, THE
RECONSIDER ME
SOUL SHAKE
THERE NEVER WAS A TIME

Lewis, Meade Lux

BOOGIE WOOGIE PRAYER
HONKY TONK TRAIN (A.K.A. HONKY
   TONK TRAIN BLUES)
YANCEY SPECIAL

Lewis, Mike

AIN'T IT TRUE?

Lewis, Miriam

PORT-AU-PRINCE
TEARS AND LAUGHTER

Lewis, Morgan

HOW HIGH THE MOON
OLD SOFT SHOE, THE
TEETER TOTTER TESSIE

Lewis, Richard A.

GET A JOB

Lewis, Roger

DOWN BY THE WINEGAR WOIKS

LOVE IS THE DRUG
OCEANA ROLL, THE
ONE DOZEN ROSES

Lewis, Ronnie

SHE BLEW A GOOD THING

Lewis, Russell R.

GROOVY SITUATION

Lewis, Sam M.

ABSENCE MAKES THE HEART GROW
   FONDER (FOR SOMEBODY ELSE)
ARRAH GO ON, I'M GONNA GO
   BACK TO OREGON
BEAUTIFUL LADY IN BLUE, A
CLOSE TO ME
COVER ME UP WITH THE SUNSHINE
   OF VIRGINIA
'CROSS THE GREAT DIVIDE (I'LL
   WAIT FOR YOU)
CRYIN' FOR THE CAROLINES
DADDY LONG LEGS
DINAH
DON'T CRY, FRENCHY, DON'T CRY
DON'T WAKE UP MY HEART
FIVE FOOT TWO, EYES OF BLUE
   (HAS ANYBODY SEEN MY GIRL)
FOR ALL WE KNOW
GLOOMY SUNDAY
GOT HER OFF MY HANDS BUT
   CAN'T GET HER OFF MY MIND
HAPPY GO LUCKY LANE
HAVE A LITTLE FAITH IN ME
HELLO, CENTRAL, GIVE ME NO
   MAN'S LAND
HIGH, HIGH, HIGH UP IN THE HILLS
HOW YA GONNA KEEP 'EM DOWN
   ON THE FARM (AFTER THEY'VE
   SEEN PAREE)?
HUCKLEBERRY FINN
I BELIEVE IN MIRACLES
I'D LOVE TO FALL ASLEEP AND
   WAKE UP IN MY MAMMY'S ARMS
IF I KNOCK THE "L" OUT OF KELLY
I KISS YOUR HAND, MADAME
I'LL BE HAPPY WHEN THE
   PREACHER MAKES YOU MINE

I'M A FOOL FOR LOVING YOU
I'M ALL BOUND 'ROUND WITH THE
   MASON DIXON LINE
I'M GONNA MAKE HAY WHILE THE
   SUN SHINES IN VIRGINIA
I'M SITTING ON TOP OF THE WORLD
IN A LITTLE SPANISH TOWN
IN SHADOWLAND
JUST A BABY'S PRAYER AT
   TWILIGHT
JUST FRIENDS
KEEP SWEEPING THE COBWEBS OFF
   THE MOON
KING FOR A DAY
LAST TWO WEEKS IN JULY, THE
LAUGH, CLOWN, LAUGH
LAWD, YOU MADE THE NIGHT TOO
   LONG
LOVEY CAME BACK
MEET ME AT THE STATION, DEAR
MY LITTLE GIRL
MY MAMMY
MY MOTHER'S ROSARY (OR, TEN
   BABY FINGERS AND TEN BABY
   TOES)
NOW OR NEVER
OH, HOW I WISH I COULD SLEEP
   UNTIL MY DADDY COMES HOME
OLD PAL, WHY DON'T YOU ANSWER
   ME
ONE MINUTE TO ONE
PUT AWAY A LITTLE RAY OF
   GOLDEN SUNSHINE (FOR A
   RAINY DAY)
REVENGE
ROCK-A-BYE YOUR BABY WITH A
   DIXIE MELODY
SINGIN' THE BLUES (TILL MY
   DADDY COMES HOME)
SONG OF THE FOOL
STREET OF DREAMS
TAKE IN THE SUN, HANG OUT THE
   MOON
THAT MELLOW MELODY
THEN YOU'VE NEVER BEEN BLUE
THERE'S A CRADLE IN CAROLINE
THERE'S A LITTLE LANE WITHOUT
   A TURNING ON THE WAY TO
   HOME, SWEET HOME
THINGS MIGHT HAVE BEEN SO
   DIFFERENT
THIS TIME IT'S LOVE
TOO LATE

TUCK ME TO SLEEP IN MY OLD
'TUCKY HOME
WE WERE THE BEST OF FRIENDS
WHEN YOU'RE A LONG, LONG WAY
FROM HOME
WHERE DID ROBINSON CRUSOE GO
WITH FRIDAY ON SATURDAY
NIGHT?
WHY DO THEY ALL TAKE THE
NIGHT BOAT TO ALBANY?
YOU'RE A MILLION MILES FROM
NOWHERE (WHEN YOU'RE ONE
LITTLE MILE FROM HOME)

Lewis, Stanley

I'LL BE HOME
SUSIE-Q

Lewis, Steve

SUD BUSTIN' BLUES

Lewis, Ted

BEE'S KNEES
IS EVERYBODY HAPPY NOW?
WHEN MY BABY SMILES AT ME

Lewis, Terry

CAN YOU STAND THE RAIN
CONTROL
DIAMONDS
ENCORE
EVERYTHING I MISS AT HOME
FAKE
FINEST, THE
FISHNET
HUMAN
I DIDN'T MEAN TO TURN YOU ON
IF IT ISN'T LOVE
JUST BE GOOD TO ME
JUST THE FACTS
JUST THE WAY YOU LIKE IT
KEEP YOUR EYE ON ME
LET'S WAIT AWHILE
MAKING LOVE IN THE RAIN
MISS YOU MUCH
NASTY
NEVER KNEW LOVE LIKE THIS
SATURDAY LOVE
TENDER LOVE

WHAT HAVE YOU DONE FOR ME
LATELY
WHEN I THINK OF YOU

Lewis, Wayne

ALWAYS
CIRCLES
SECRET LOVERS
TOUCH A FOUR LEAF CLOVER

Libbey, Dee

MANGOS

Liberace

SINCERELY YOURS

Lichty, Kathleen

ALMOST ALWAYS

Lickley, Mark

LOOK OF LOVE (PART ONE)

Lieberman, Clyde

SPACEBALLS

Liebert, Richard

COME DANCE WITH ME

Liebling, Howard

CALIFORNIA NIGHTS
SUNSHINE, LOLLIPOPS, AND
RAINBOWS

Liebman, Joseph

WHEN THE FOG ROLLS IN TO SAN
FRANCISCO

Liebowitz, Joseph

WEDDING SAMBA, THE

Lief, Max

HOW LONG WILL IT LAST?

SHE'S SUCH A COMFORT TO ME

Lief, Nathaniel

SHE'S SUCH A COMFORT TO ME

Lieurance, Thurlow

BY THE WATERS OF MINNETONKA

Lifeson, Alex

LIMELIGHT
NEW WORLD MAN
SPIRIT OF RADIO, THE
TOM SAWYER

Liggins, Jimmy

DON'T PUT ME DOWN

Liggins, Joe

HONEYDRIPPER, THE
PINK CHAMPAGNE

Lightfoot, Gordon

CAREFREE HIGHWAY
COTTON JENNY
EARLY MORNIN' RAIN
FOR LOVIN' ME
IF YOU COULD READ MY MIND
RAINY DAY PEOPLE
RIBBON OF DARKNESS
STEEL RAIL BLUES
SUNDOWN
WRECK OF THE EDMUND
FITZGERALD, THE

Liles, Kevin

GIRL, YOU KNOW IT'S TRUE

Liliuokalani, Queen

ALOHA OE (FAREWELL TO THEE)

Lilley, Joseph J.

JINGLE, JANGLE, JINGLE

Lillington, Marcus

HANDS TO HEAVEN
HOW CAN I FALL

Lilly, R. P.

PLANT A WATERMELON ON MY
    GRAVE AND LET THE JUICE SOAK
    THROUGH

Limahl

TOO SHY

Limbo, Sonny

KEY LARGO

Lincke, Paul

CHIMES OF SPRING
GLOW-WORM, THE
SPRING, BEAUTIFUL SPRING

Lincoln, Harry J.

MIDNIGHT FIRE ALARM

Lincoln, Philamore

TEMMA HARBOUR

Lincoln, Shedrick

RUBBER BISCUIT

Lind, Bob

ELUSIVE BUTTERFLY

Lind, Jon

BOOGIE WONDERLAND
CRAZY FOR YOU

Lind, W. Murdock

WHISTLING RUFUS

Linde, Dennis

BURNING LOVE

I'M GONNA GET YOU
MORNIN' MORNIN'
THEN IT'S LOVE
WALKIN' A BROKEN HEART

Lindeman, Edith

LITTLE THINGS MEAN A LOT

Linden, Dave

LOVE IS A HURTIN' THING

Linden, Kathy

BILLY

Lindgren, Alan

HELLO AGAIN

Lindsay, John

ASIA

Lindsay, Mark

DON'T TAKE IT SO HARD
GOOD THING
GREAT AIRPLANE STRIKE, THE
HIM OR ME, WHAT'S IT GONNA BE?
I HAD A DREAM
LET ME
MR. SUN, MR. MOON
PEACE OF MIND
STEPPIN' OUT
TOO MUCH TALK
UPS AND DOWNS

Lindsay, Ted

TOO MANY LOVERS

Lindsey, Bucky

IT DON'T HURT ME HALF AS BAD

Lindsey, David

TWO STORY HOUSE

Lindt, R.

LIECHTENSTEINER POLKA

Lindup, Mark

SOMETHING ABOUT YOU

Ling, Sam

BAD LUCK
EDDIE, MY LOVE

Linhart, Buzzy

FRIENDS

Link, Harry

BY MY SIDE
I'M JUST WILD ABOUT ANIMAL
    CRACKERS
I'VE GOT A FEELING I'M FALLING
THESE FOOLISH THINGS (REMIND
    ME OF YOU)
YOU'RE THE ONE I CARE FOR

Link, Peter

TOMORROW IS THE FIRST DAY OF
    THE REST OF MY LIFE
(IF YOU LET ME MAKE LOVE TO YOU
    THEN) WHY CAN'T I TOUCH YOU?

Linn, Roger

PROMISES

Linton, William

EASIER SAID THAN DONE

Linzer, Sandy

ATTACK
BABY, MAKE YOUR OWN SWEET
    MUSIC
BON BON VIE (GIMME THE GOOD
    LIFE)
DAWN (GO AWAY)
KEEP THE BALL ROLLIN'
LET'S HANG ON
LOVER'S CONCERTO, A

MORNIN' BEAUTIFUL
NATIVE NEW YORKER
OPUS 17 (DON'T YOU WORRY 'BOUT
    ME)

Lippman, Sid

"A"—YOU'RE ADORABLE (THE
    ALPHABET SONG)
AFTER GRADUATION DAY
CHICKERY CHICK
FOOL IN LOVE, A
HOUSE WITH LOVE IN IT, A
I'M THRILLED
IT COULDN'T BE TRUE (OR COULD
    IT?)
LAROO, LAROO LILLI BOLERO
MY SUGAR IS SO REFINED
THAT'S THE CHANCE YOU TAKE
THESE THINGS YOU LEFT ME
THROUGH THE EYES OF LOVE
TOO YOUNG

Lipscomb, Belinda

OPERATOR

Lipsius, Fred

GO DOWN GAMBLIN'

Lipton, Leonard

PUFF THE MAGIC DRAGON

Lisbona, Edward

ANGELINA

Lissauer, John

CAME SO FAR FOR BEAUTY

Lissauer, Robert

HELLO AND GOODBYE
I FEEL SO LOW WHEN I'M HIGH
LIE DETECTOR
MAKE ME THRILL
TOO TRUE

Little, Eric

MY TIME IS YOUR TIME

Little, George A.

FUNNY, DEAR, WHAT LOVE CAN DO
HAWAIIAN BUTTERFLY
SO TIRED
THEY NEEDED A SONG BIRD IN
    HEAVEN (SO GOD TOOK CARUSO
    AWAY)

Little, Jack

EV'RYBODY LOVES YOU
HOLD ME
HONESTLY
I MAY BE DANCING WITH
    SOMEBODY ELSE
IN A SHANTY IN OLD SHANTY TOWN
JEALOUS
THERE'S OCEANS OF LOVE BY THE
    BEAUTIFUL SEA
TING-A-LING (THE WALTZ OF THE
    BELLS)
WHEN YOU'RE OVER SIXTY, AND
    YOU FEEL LIKE SWEET SIXTEEN
YOU BROKE THE ONLY HEART THAT
    EVER LOVED YOU
YOU'RE A HEAVENLY THING

Littlefield, Willie

FAREWELL
IT'S MIDNIGHT

Littlejohn, Jimmy

WALKING THE STREETS

Little Milton

GRITS AIN'T GROCERIES (ALL
    AROUND THE WORLD)

Littman, J.

STRUT

Livgren, Kerry

CARRY ON, WAYWARD SUE

DUST IN THE WIND
PEOPLE OF THE SOUTH WIND
PLAY THE GAME TONIGHT

Livingston, Alan

I TAUT I SAW A PUDDY TAT

Livingston, Bill

GET RHYTHM IN YOUR FEET
POPCORN MAN

Livingston, Fud

AU REET
I'M THROUGH WITH LOVE

Livingston, Jay

ALL THE TIME
ALMOST IN YOUR ARMS (A.K.A.
    LOVE SONG FROM "HOUSEBOAT")
ANGEL
ANOTHER TIME, ANOTHER PLACE
BESIDE YOU
BING! BANG! BONG!
BONANZA!
BONNE NUIT—GOODNIGHT
BUTTONS AND BOWS
CAT AND THE CANARY, THE
COPPER CANYON
DEAR HEART
ERES TU (TOUCH THE WIND)
EVERYTHING BEAUTIFUL
FEMININITY
G'BYE NOW
GIVE IT ALL YOU'VE GOT
GOLDEN EARRINGS
HAVIN' A WONDERFUL WISH
HERE'S TO LOVE
HOME COOKIN'
I'LL ALWAYS LOVE YOU
IN THE ARMS OF LOVE
LIFE IS A BEAUTIFUL THING
MARSHMALLOW MOON
MISTO CRISTOFO COLUMBO
MONA LISA
MY BELOVED
MY LOVE LOVES ME
QUE SERA SERA (WHATEVER WILL
    BE, WILL BE)
RUBY AND THE PEARL, THE

SILVER BELLS
SONG OF DELILAH
SONG OF SURRENDER
SQUARE IN THE SOCIAL CIRCLE, A
STREETS OF LAREDO, THE
STUFF LIKE THAT THERE
TAMMY
THIS HAPPY FEELING
THOUSAND VIOLINS, A
TO EACH HIS OWN
YOU DON'T KNOW HIM

Livingston, Jerry

77 SUNSET STRIP
ADIOS AMIGO
ASHBY DE LA ZOOCH
BABY, BABY, BABY
BALLAD OF CAT BALLOU, THE
BIBBIDI-BOBBIDI-BOO
BLUE AND SENTIMENTAL
BLUEBELL
CHI-BABA, CHI-BABA (MY BAMBINA
    GO TO SLEEP)
CLOSE TO YOU
(WHEN IT'S) DARKNESS ON THE
    DELTA
DON'T YOU LOVE ME ANYMORE?
DREAM IS A WISH YOUR HEART
    MAKES, A
FUZZY WUZZY
HANGING TREE, THE
I'M A BIG GIRL NOW
IN A BLUE AND PENSIVE MOOD
IT'S THE TALK OF THE TOWN
I'VE GOT AN INVITATION TO A
    DANCE
JUST A KID NAMED JOE
LEARNING
MAIRZY DOATS
MOONRISE ON THE LOWLANDS
OL' PAPPY
SHE BROKE MY HEART IN THREE
    PLACES
SIXTY SECONDS GOT TOGETHER
STAR GAZING
STORY OF A STARRY NIGHT, THE
SWEET STRANGER
TWELFTH OF NEVER, THE
UNDER A BLANKET OF BLUE
WAKE THE TOWN AND TELL THE
    PEOPLE
WISH ME A RAINBOW

YOU AND YOUR BEAUTIFUL EYES
YOUNG EMOTIONS

Livraghi, R.

MAN WITHOUT LOVE, A

Lloyd, Bill

CRAZY OVER YOU

Lloyd, Harold

TASTE OF YOUR LOVE

Lloyd, Harry

I BELIEVE I'M GONNA LOVE YOU
I JUST FALL IN LOVE AGAIN

Lloyd, Michael

I WAS MADE FOR DANCIN'

Lloyd, Robert

GOOD MORNING, MR. ZIP-ZIP-ZIP!
    (WITH YOUR HAIR CUT JUST AS
    SHORT AS MINE)

Lockhart, Eugene

WORLD IS WAITING FOR THE
    SUNRISE, THE

Locklin, Hank

SEND ME THE PILLOW YOU DREAM
    ON

Loden, James

FOR RENT

Lodge, David

MAJOR TOM (COMING HOME)

Lodge, John

I'M JUST A SINGER (IN A ROCK AND
    ROLL BAND)
ISN'T LIFE STRANGE?

STEPPIN' IN A SLIDE ZONE

Loeb, John Jacob

BOO-HOO
GET OUT THOSE OLD RECORDS
GOT THE JITTERS
HEREAFTER
IT'S NEVER TOO LATE (TO SAY
    YOU'RE SORRY)
MA! I MISS YOUR APPLE PIE
MAHARAJAH OF MAGADOR, THE
MASQUERADE
REFLECTIONS IN THE WATER
ROSEMARY
ROSIE THE RIVETER
SAILBOAT IN THE MOONLIGHT, A
SEEMS LIKE OLD TIMES
SERENADE TO A MAID
SWEETIE PIE
TWO LITTLE BLUE LITTLE EYES
WAIT TILL SHE SEES YOU IN YOUR
    UNIFORM

Loehr, Herman

WHERE MY CARAVAN HAS RESTED

Loesser, Frank

ADELAIDE
ADELAIDE'S LAMENT
ANYWHERE I WANDER
BABY, IT'S COLD OUTSIDE
BIG D
BLOOP, BLEEP!
BOYS IN THE BACK ROOM, THE
BROTHERHOOD OF MAN
BUSHEL AND A PECK, A
CAN'T GET OUT OF THIS MOOD
COLLEGE SWING
COMPANY WAY, THE
DANCING ON A DIME
DOLORES
DON'T CRY
DREAMER, THE
FIDGETY JOE
FIRST CLASS PRIVATE MARY BROWN
FOLLOW THE FOLD
FUDDY DUDDY WATCHMAKER, THE
FUGUE FOR TINHORNS
GRAND OLD IVY
GUYS AND DOLLS

HAPPY GO LUCKY

HAPPY TO MAKE YOUR ACQUAINTANCE

HAVE I STAYED AWAY TOO LONG?

HEART AND SOUL

HOOP-DE-DOO

HOW'DJA LIKE TO LOVE ME?

HOW SWEET YOU ARE

HOW TO

I BELIEVE IN YOU

I DON'T WANT TO WALK WITHOUT YOU

I FALL IN LOVE WITH YOU EVERY DAY

IF I WERE A BELL

I GET THE NECK OF THE CHICKEN

I GO FOR THAT

I HEAR MUSIC

I'LL KNOW

I'LL NEVER LET A DAY PASS BY

I'M HANS CHRISTIAN ANDERSEN

I'M RIDIN' FOR A FALL

INCH WORM

IN MY ARMS

I SAID NO

I'VE NEVER BEEN IN LOVE BEFORE

I WISH I DIDN'T LOVE YOU SO

I WISH I WAS THE WILLOW

I WISH I WERE TWINS

JINGLE, JANGLE, JINGLE

JOEY, JOEY, JOEY

JUNK MAN

JUST ANOTHER POLKA

KISS THE BOYS GOODBYE

LADY'S IN LOVE WITH YOU, THE

LAST THING I WANT IS YOUR PITY, THE

LEAVE US FACE IT

LET'S GET LOST

LOVE FROM A HEART OF GOLD

LOVELIER THAN EVER

LOVELY ONE

LUCK BE A LADY

MAKE A MIRACLE

MOMENTS LIKE THIS

MOON OF MANAKOORA, THE

MOON OVER BURMA

MORE I CANNOT WISH YOU

MOST HAPPY FELLA, THE

MURDER, HE SAYS

MUSIC OF HOME, THE

MY! MY!

MY DARLING, MY DARLING

MY HEART IS SO FULL OF YOU

MY TIME OF DAY

NEVER WILL I MARRY

NEW ASHMOLEAN MARCHING SOCIETY AND STUDENTS' CONSERVATORY BAND

NO TWO PEOPLE

NOW THAT I NEED YOU (WHERE ARE YOU)

ON A SLOW BOAT TO CHINA

ONCE IN LOVE WITH AMY

PARIS ORIGINAL

PET ME, POPPA

POPPA DON'T PREACH TO ME

PRAISE THE LORD AND PASS THE AMMUNITION

RODGER YOUNG

RUMBLE, RUMBLE, RUMBLE

SAND IN MY SHOES

SAY IT (OVER AND OVER AGAIN)

SAYS MY HEART

SEWING MACHINE, THE

SING A TROPICAL SONG

SIT DOWN, YOU'RE ROCKING THE BOAT

SMALL FRY

SNUG AS A BUG IN A RUG

SOMEBODY SOMEWHERE

SPRING WILL BE A LITTLE LATE THIS YEAR

STANDING ON THE CORNER

STRANGE ENCHANTMENT

SUE ME

SUMMERTIME LOVE

TAKE BACK YOUR MINK

TALLAHASSEE

THANK YOUR LUCKY STARS

THAT SENTIMENTAL SANDWICH

THEY'RE EITHER TOO YOUNG OR TOO OLD

THUMBELINA

TOUCH OF TEXAS, A

TUNE FOR HUMMING, A

TUNNEL OF LOVE, THE

TWO SLEEPY PEOPLE

UGLY DUCKLING, THE

WARM ALL OVER

WAVE TO ME MY LADY

WE'RE THE COUPLE IN THE CASTLE

WHAT ARE YOU DOING NEW YEAR'S EVE?

WHAT DO YOU DO IN THE INFANTRY?

WHY FIGHT THE FEELING?

WOMAN IN LOVE, A

WONDERFUL COPENHAGEN

Loewe, Bernie

SWINGIN' SCHOOL

Loewe, Frederick

ALMOST LIKE BEING IN LOVE

ANOTHER AUTUMN

BRIGADOON

CAMELOT

COME TO ME, BEND TO ME

DAY BEFORE SPRING, THE

FOLLOW ME

GET ME TO THE CHURCH ON TIME

GIGI

GUENEVERE

HEATHER ON THE HILL, THE

HOW TO HANDLE A WOMAN

I COULD HAVE DANCED ALL NIGHT

IF EVER I WOULD LEAVE YOU

I'LL GO HOME WITH BONNIE JEAN

I LOVED YOU ONCE IN SILENCE

I LOVE YOU THIS MORNING

I'M AN ORDINARY MAN

I'M GLAD I'M NOT YOUNG ANYMORE

I'M ON MY WAY

I REMEMBER IT WELL

I STILL SEE ELISA

I TALK TO THE TREES

IT'S A BORE

I'VE GROWN ACCUSTOMED TO HER FACE

I WONDER WHAT THE KING IS DOING TONIGHT

JUG OF WINE, A

JUST YOU WAIT

LITTLE PRINCE, THE (FROM WHO KNOWS WHERE)

LUSTY MONTH OF MAY, THE

MY LAST LOVE

NIGHT THEY INVENTED CHAMPAGNE, THE

ON THE STREET WHERE YOU LIVE

RAIN IN SPAIN, THE

SAY A PRAYER FOR ME TONIGHT

SEVEN DEADLY VIRTUES, THE

SHOW ME

SIMPLE JOYS OF MAIDENHOOD, THE

THANK HEAVEN FOR LITTLE GIRLS

THEN YOU MAY TAKE ME TO THE
   FAIR
THERE BUT FOR YOU GO I
THEY CALL THE WIND MARIA
WALTZ AT MAXIM'S (A.K.A. SHE IS
   NOT THINKING OF ME)
WALTZ WAS BORN IN VIENNA, A
WAND'RIN STAR
WHAT DO THE SIMPLE FOLKS DO?
WHY CAN'T THE ENGLISH?
WITH A LITTLE BIT OF LUCK
WOULDN'T IT BE LOVERLY?
YOU HAVEN'T CHANGED AT ALL

Logan, Frederick Knight

MISSOURI WALTZ
PALE MOON

Logan, Harold

COME INTO MY HEART
I'M GONNA GET MARRIED
LADY LUCK
PERSONALITY (YOU'VE GOT)
QUESTION
STAGGER LEE
WHERE WERE YOU (ON OUR
   WEDDING DAY)?

Loggins, Danny

VAHEVELA

Loggins, Dave

40 HOUR WEEK (FOR A LIVIN')
DON'T UNDERESTIMATE MY LOVE
   FOR YOU
HEARTBEAT IN THE DARKNESS
I'LL NEVER STOP LOVING YOU
LOVE WILL FIND ITS WAY TO YOU
MAKIN' UP FOR LOST TIME (THE
   "DALLAS" LOVERS' SONG)
MORNING DESIRE
ONE PROMISE TOO LATE
PIECES OF APRIL
PLEASE COME TO BOSTON
WE'VE GOT A GOOD FIRE GOIN'
WHEELS
YOU MAKE ME WANT TO MAKE YOU
   MINE

Loggins, Kenny

DANNY'S SONG
DON'T FIGHT IT
FOOTLOOSE
HEART TO HEART
HOUSE AT POOH CORNER
I BELIEVE IN LOVE
I'M ALRIGHT
LOVE SONG, A
MY MUSIC
NOBODY'S FOOL
THIS IS IT
WATCHING THE RIVER RUN
WHAT A FOOL BELIEVES
WHENEVER I CALL YOU "FRIEND"
YOUR MAMA DON'T DANCE

Lohr, Herman

LITTLE GREY HOME IN THE WEST

Loman, Jules

GOODBYE SUE
HEAVENLY HIDEAWAY
RHYTHM 'N' BLUES (MAMA'S GOT
   THE RHYTHM, PAPA'S GOT THE
   BLUES)

Lomas

EXPRESS

Lomax, Alan

GOODNIGHT, IRENE
INSIDE—LOOKING OUT

Lomax, John

GOODNIGHT, IRENE

Lombardo, Carmen

ADDRESS UNKNOWN
BOO-HOO
CONFUCIUS SAY
COQUETTE
FOOTLOOSE AND FANCY FREE
GET OUT THOSE OLD RECORDS
GIVE ME YOUR AFFECTION, HONEY

IT'S NEVER TOO LATE (TO SAY
   YOU'RE SORRY)
JUNGLE DRUMS
LANE IN SPAIN, A
LAST NIGHT I DREAMED YOU
   KISSED ME
LIGHTS ARE LOW, THE MUSIC IS
   SWEET, THE
MA! I MISS YOUR APPLE PIE
NIGHT ON THE WATER
OH! MOYTLE
OOOH! LOOK-A THERE, AIN'T SHE
   PRETTY?
POWDER YOUR FACE WITH
   SUNSHINE (SMILE! SMILE! SMILE!)
RETURN TO ME (RITORNA A ME)
RIDIN' AROUND IN THE RAIN
SAILBOAT IN THE MOONLIGHT, A
SEEMS LIKE OLD TIMES
SNUGGLED ON YOUR SHOULDER
SWEETEST MUSIC THIS SIDE OF
   HEAVEN, THE
SWEETHEARTS ON PARADE
THRILL OF A LIFETIME
WAKE UP AND SING

London, Eve

ENVY

London, Mark

BEST OF BOTH WORLDS
TO SIR WITH LOVE

Lones, James L.

PHILLY FREEZE, THE

Long, Andy Iona

SOUTH SEA ISLAND MAGIC

Long, Burt

CINDY, OH CINDY

Long, Frances

ROOM IN YOUR HEART

Long, Frederick "Shorty"

DEVIL WITH THE BLUE DRESS ON
HERE COMES THE JUDGE

Long, Jimmy

THAT SILVER HAIRED DADDY OF
    MINE

Long, Kenn

ALPHAGENESIS
DECLARATION

Lopez, Gilbert

HAPPY, HAPPY BIRTHDAY BABY

Lopez, Joan Calderon

ERES TU (TOUCH THE WIND)

Lopez, Ray

BEE'S KNEES

Lopez, Trini

I'M COMIN' HOME, CINDY
SINNER MAN

Lopez, Vincent

KNOCK, KNOCK, WHO'S THERE?

Loraine, William

SALOME

Lorber, John

WHERE WERE YOU WHEN I WAS
    FALLING IN LOVE

Lorber, Sam

DARE ME

Lord, Jon

SMOKE ON THE WATER

WOMAN FROM TOKYO

Lordan, Jerry

APACHE
APACHE '65
SCARLETT O'HARA

Loren, Bryan

BABY TELL ME, CAN YOU DANCE

Lorenzo, Ange

SLEEPY TIME GAL

Loring, Jet

LOVIN' THINGS, THE

Loring, Richard

DEACON JONES
DON'T LET ME DREAM
SUMMERTIME LIES
TOUCH OF PINK, A

Lorraine, Sam

SADIE'S SHAWL

Lorraine, William

DECEMBER AND MAY (OR, MOLLIE
    NEWELL DON'T BE CRUEL)

Lottermoser, Daniel

VAHEVELA

Loucheim, Stuart F.

MIXED EMOTIONS

Loudermilk, John D.

ABILENE
AMIGO'S GUITAR
BAD NEWS
BREAK MY MIND
(HE'S MY) DREAMBOAT
EBONY EYES
GRIN AND BEAR IT

HOLLYWOOD
INDIAN RESERVATION (THE LAMENT
    OF THE CHEROKEE RESERVATION
    INDIAN)
I WANNA LIVE
JAMES (HOLD THE LADDER STEADY)
NORMAN
PAPER TIGER
ROSE AND A BABY RUTH, A
SAD MOVIES (MAKE ME CRY)
SITTIN' IN THE BALCONY
TALK BACK TREMBLING LIPS
THEN YOU CAN TELL ME GOODBYE
THIS LITTLE BIRD
THOU SHALT NOT STEAL
TOBACCO ROAD
TORTURE
WATERLOO
WHAT A WOMAN IN LOVE WON'T DO

Loughnane, Lee

CALL ON ME
NO TELL LOVER

Louiguy

CHERRY PINK AND APPLE BLOSSOM
    WHITE
LA VIE EN ROSE

Louis, Guy

DON'T FORGET I STILL LOVE YOU
I CAN'T STOP THINKING OF YOU

Louis, Jimmy

BRIDGE WASHED OUT, THE
I NEVER HAD THE ONE I WANTED
SITTIN' ON A ROCK (CRYIN' IN A
    CREEK)

Louvin, Charles

ARE YOU TEASING ME?
IF I COULD ONLY WIN YOUR LOVE
IS ZAT YOU, MYRTLE?
I TAKE THE CHANCE

Louvin, Ira

ARE YOU TEASING ME?
IF I COULD ONLY WIN YOUR LOVE
IS ZAT YOU, MYRTLE?
I TAKE THE CHANCE

Love, Geoff

HE'S GOT THE WHOLE WORLD IN
   HIS HANDS

Love, Mike

ADD SOME MUSIC TO YOUR DAY
ALMOST SUMMER
CALIFORNIA SAGA (ON MY WAY TO
   SUNNY CALIFORN-I-A)
DARLIN'
DO IT AGAIN
GETCHA BACK
GOOD VIBRATIONS
KOKOMO
PLEASE LET ME WONDER
SURFIN' SAFARI
WILD HONEY

Loveday, Carroll

SHRINE OF SAINT CECILIA, THE
THAT'S MY DESIRE

Lovell, Royal

ANCHORS AWEIGH

Lovett, Leroy

AFTER THE LIGHTS GO DOWN
CAN'T I?

Lovett, Lyle

GOD WILL
SHE'S NO LADY

Lovett, Winfred "Blue"

KISS AND SAY GOODBYE

Lowe, Bernie

BUTTERFLY

CHERIE
DING-A-LING
FISH, THE
GOOD TIME BABY
REMEMBER YOU'RE MINE
(LET ME BE YOUR) TEDDY BEAR
TEEN AGE PRAYER
TWENTY MILES
WE GOT LOVE
WILD ONE

Lowe, Bert

SWEETHEART OF ALL MY DREAMS
   (I LOVE YOU, I LOVE YOU, I LOVE
   YOU)

Lowe, Chris

IT'S A SIN
OPPORTUNITIES (LET'S MAKE LOTS
   OF MONEY)
WEST END GIRLS
WHAT HAVE I DONE TO DESERVE
   THIS?

Lowe, Jim

GAMBLER'S GUITAR
LIGHTHOUSE

Lowe, Nick

CRUEL TO BE KIND

Lowe, Ruth

I'LL NEVER SMILE AGAIN
PUT YOUR DREAMS AWAY (FOR
   ANOTHER DAY)

Lowe, Sammy

BEAR MASH BLUES

Lowen, David

WE BELONG

Lowery, Donny

OLD FLAME

WHY DOES IT HAVE TO BE (WRONG
   OR RIGHT)

Lown, Bert

BYE BYE BLUES
BY MY SIDE
YOU'RE THE ONE I CARE FOR

Lubahn, Doug

TREAT ME RIGHT

Luban, Francia

GAY RANCHERO, A (LAS ALTENITAS)
SAY "SI SI"

Lubbock, Jeremy

BEST OF ME, THE

Lubin, Joe

CHA-HUA-HUA
MIDNIGHT LACE
PLEASE DON'T EAT THE DAISIES
SECRET, THE
TEACHER'S PET
TUTTI FRUTTI

Luboff, Norman

YELLOW BIRD

Lucas, Ann

LOOSE TALK

Lucas, Buddy

STEAMBOAT

Lucas, Carroll

HOW SOON (WILL I BE SEEING
   YOU)?

Lucas, Clarence

PERFECT SONG, THE
SONG OF SONGS, THE

Lucas, Reginald

BORDERLINE
CLOSER I GET TO YOU, THE
NEVER KNEW LOVE LIKE THIS
    BEFORE
SWEET SENSATION
WHAT CHA GONNA DO WITH MY
    LOVIN'

Lucchesi, Roger

PORTUGUESE WASHERWOMEN, THE

Luccisano, Joseph

THERE'S A MOON OUT TONIGHT

Lucia, Peter

CRIMSON AND CLOVER

Lucian, Marc Boon

SAUSALITO SUMMERNIGHT

Luckesch, Rudolf

HEAR MY SONG, VIOLETTA

Luders, Gustav

HEIDELBERG STEIN SONG
MESSAGE OF THE VIOLET, THE
TALE OF A BUMBLE BEE, THE
TALE OF THE KANGAROO, THE
TALE OF THE SEASHELL
TALE OF THE TURTLE DOVE, THE

Lugo, F.

I NEED SOMEBODY

Lukather, Steve

I'LL BE OVER YOU
I WON'T HOLD YOU BACK
SHE'S A BEAUTY
TURN YOUR LOVE AROUND

Luke, Robin

SUSIE DARLIN'

Lunceford, Jimmie

DREAM OF YOU
RHYTHM IN MY NURSERY RHYMES
RHYTHM IS OUR BUSINESS

Lunsford, Orville

ALL-AMERICAN BOY, THE

Lunt, Stephen

GOONIES 'R' GOOD ENOUGH, THE
SHE BOP

Lurie, Elliot

BRANDY (YOU'RE A FINE GIRL)

Lusini, Mauro

SON OF A TRAVELIN' MAN

Lutcher, Nellie

HE'S A REAL GONE GUY
HURRY ON DOWN

Luther, Frank

BARNACLE BILL THE SAILOR

Luttazzi, L.

SOUVENIR D'ITALIE

Lutz, Michael

SMOKIN' IN THE BOYS' ROOM

Lyall, Bill

MAGIC

Lyle, Graham

BREAK AWAY
HEART IN NEW YORK, A
JOE KNOWS HOW TO LIVE
MAYBE YOUR BABY'S GOT THE
    BLUES
TYPICAL MALE

WE DON'T NEED ANOTHER HERO
    (THUNDERDOME)
WHAT'S LOVE GOT TO DO WITH IT
WHAT YOU GET IS WHAT YOU SEE

Lyle, Lessie

FOREVER AND ALWAYS

Lyman, Abe

AFTER I SAY I'M SORRY (WHAT CAN
    I SAY?)
DID YOU MEAN IT?
I CRIED FOR YOU
MANDALAY
MARY LOU

Lymon, Frank

WHY DO FOOLS FALL IN LOVE?

Lyn, Merril

I GIVE YOU MY WORD

Lyn, Shirley

I OVERLOOKED AN ORCHID
MISTER MOON

Lynch, George

DREAM WARRIORS

Lynes, Gary

LOVE ME FOREVER

Lynn, Cheryl

GOT TO BE REAL

Lynn, E. E.

UNDER THE MOON

Lynn, Loretta

COAL MINER'S DAUGHTER
DEAR UNCLE SAM
DON'T COME HOME A-DRINKIN'
    (WITH LOVIN' ON YOUR MIND)

FIST CITY
I WANNA BE FREE
RATED X
TO MAKE A MAN (FEEL LIKE A
   MAN)
YOU AIN'T WOMAN ENOUGH
YOU'RE LOOKIN' AT COUNTRY
YOU WANNA GIVE ME A LIFT

Lynne, Jeff

ALL OVER THE WORLD
CALLING AMERICA
CAN'T GET IT OUT OF MY HEAD
DON'T BRING ME DOWN
DO YA
EVIL WOMAN
HOLD ON TIGHT
LIVIN' THING
ROCK 'N' ROLL IS KING
SHINE A LITTLE LOVE
STRANGE MAGIC
SWEET TALKIN' WOMAN
TELEPHONE LINE
TURN TO STONE
XANADU

Lynott, Phil

BOYS ARE BACK IN TOWN, THE

Lynton, Everett

I NEVER SEE MAGGIE ALONE

Lyon, Del

ONE ROSE, THE (THAT'S LEFT IN MY
   HEART)

Lyon, James

BABY, HOLD ON

Lyons, Joe

WHEN IT'S LAMP LIGHTIN' TIME IN
   THE VALLEY

Lytell, Jimmy

BLUES SERENADE, A

Mabon, Willie

I DON'T KNOW
I'M MAD

Macaulay, Tony

BABY, NOW THAT I'VE FOUND YOU
BABY, TAKE ME IN YOUR ARMS
DON'T GIVE UP ON US
LAST NIGHT I DIDN'T GET TO SLEEP
   AT ALL
LOVE GROWS (WHERE MY
   ROSEMARY GOES)
MY MARIE
SMILE A LITTLE SMILE FOR ME

MacBoyle, Darl

BRING BACK THOSE WONDERFUL
   DAYS
"FOREVER" IS A LONG, LONG TIME
TO HAVE, TO HOLD, TO LOVE

MacColl, Ewan

FIRST TIME EVER I SAW YOUR
   FACE, THE

MacColl, Kirsty

THEY DON'T KNOW

MacDermot, Galt

AFRICAN WALTZ
AIN'T GOT NO
AIR
AQUARIUS
DON'T PUT IT DOWN
EASY TO BE HARD
FRANK MILLS
GOOD MORNING STARSHINE
HARE KISHNA (A.K.A. BE-IN)
I GOT LIFE
LET THE SUNSHINE IN (A.K.A. THE
   FLESH FAILURES)
LOVE HAS DRIVEN ME SANE
WALKING IN SPACE
WHAT A PIECE OF WORK IS MAN
WHERE DO I GO?

MacDonald, Ballard

AT THE END OF THE ROAD
BEAUTIFUL OHIO
BEND DOWN, SISTER
BREEZE (BLOW MY BABY BACK TO
   ME)
BRING BACK THOSE MINSTREL
   DAYS
CLAP HANDS! HERE COMES
   CHARLEY!
DOWN IN BOM-BOMBAY
HOT HEELS
I'M FOLLOWING YOU
(BACK HOME AGAIN IN) INDIANA
IT TAKES A LITTLE RAIN WITH THE
   SUNSHINE TO MAKE THE WORLD
   GO 'ROUND
I'VE GOT THE TIME, I'VE GOT THE
   PLACE, BUT IT'S HARD TO FIND
   THE GIRL
I WISH I HAD MY OLD GIRL BACK
   AGAIN
LAND OF MY BEST GIRL, THE
LITTLE HOUSE UPON THE HILL, THE
MIMI
ON THE MISSISSIPPI
PARADE OF THE WOODEN SOLDIERS
PINEY RIDGE
PLAY THAT BARBER SHOP CHORD
ROSE OF WASHINGTON SQUARE
SHE IS THE SUNSHINE OF VIRGINIA
SOMEBODY LOVES ME
TEN LITTLE BOTTLES
THERE'S A GIRL IN THE HEART OF
   MARYLAND (WITH A HEART THAT
   BELONGS TO ME)
THREE WONDERFUL LETTERS FROM
   HOME
TIP-TOP TIPPERARY MARY
TRAIL OF THE LONESOME PINE,
   THE
WINGS

MacDonald, Jimmy

AT A SIDEWALK PENNY ARCADE
I LOVE THE SUNSHINE OF YOUR
   SMILE

MacDonald, M.

STUFF LIKE THAT

MacDonald, Pat

FUTURE'S SO BRIGHT, I GOTTA
  WEAR SHADES

MacDonald, Ralph

JUST THE TWO OF US
WHERE IS THE LOVE

MacDonough, Glen

ABSINTHE FRAPPE
AL FRESCO
ASK HER WHILE THE BAND IS
  PLAYING
BANDANNA LAND
KNOT OF BLUE, A
LOVE IS LIKE A CIGARETTE
MARCH OF THE TOYS, THE
ROSE OF THE WORLD
THOSE WERE THE HAPPY DAYS
TOYLAND

MacGimsey, Robert

SHADRACH (MESHACH, ABENIGO)
THAT'S WHAT I LIKE ABOUT THE
  WEST

MacGregor, J. Chalmers "Chummy"

IT MUST BE JELLY ('CAUSE JAM
  DON'T SHAKE LIKE THAT)

Mack, Andrew

HEART OF MY HEART, I LOVE YOU
  (THE STORY OF THE ROSE)
MY PEARL'S A BOWERY GIRL

Mack, Cecil

ALL IN DOWN AND OUT (SORRY, I
  AIN'T GOT IT, YOU COULD HAVE
  IT, ETC.)
CHARLESTON
GOOD MORNING, CARRIE
HE'S A COUSIN OF MINE
IF HE COMES IN, I'M GOING OUT
JOSEPHINE, MY JO
LITTLE GYPSY MAID, THE

OLD FASHIONED LOVE
SHINE
TEASING
THAT MINOR STRAIN
YOU'RE IN THE RIGHT CHURCH,
  BUT THE WRONG PEW

Mack, Geoffrey

I'VE BEEN EVERYWHERE

Mack, Ira

BEATNIK FLY
RED RIVER ROCK
REVEILLE ROCK

Mack, Keith

BEAT OF A HEART

Mack, Ronnie

HE'S SO FINE

MacKenzie, Leonard

CHIQUITA BANANA

MacKenzie, Red

GEORGIANNA

Mackenzie, Scott

KOKOMO

Mackintosh, Bill

GODS WERE ANGRY WITH ME, THE

Mackintosh, Rona

GODS WERE ANGRY WITH ME, THE

MacLean, Ross

TOO FAT POLKA

MacLellan, Gene

PUT YOUR HAND IN THE HAND
SNOWBIRD

Macleod, Jack

BABY, TAKE ME IN YOUR ARMS

Macleod, John

BABY, NOW THAT I'VE FOUND YOU

MacLeod, Murray

SUNSHINE GIRL

MacMurrough, Dermot

MACUSHLA

MacNeil, Michael

SANCTIFY YOURSELF

MacNeil, Terry

HELLO, HELLO

Macrae, Fred

WHERE DOES A LITTLE TEAR COME
  FROM?

MacRae, Johnny

I'D LOVE TO LAY YOU DOWN
I STILL BELIEVE IN WALTZES
LIVING PROOF
MANY HAPPY HANGOVERS TO YOU
WHISKEY, IF YOU WERE A WOMAN

Macy, J. C.

GOOD NIGHT, LITTLE GIRL, GOOD
  NIGHT

Macy, Marvin

MY EVERYTHING

Madaglia, Neal

BEAUTIFUL EYES

Madara, John

DAWN OF CORRECTION

FLY, THE
LIKE A BABY
ONE, TWO, THREE (1-2-3)

Madden, Edward

BLUE BELL
BY THE LIGHT OF THE SILVERY
MOON
CHANTICLEER RAG, THE
COME ON AND PLAY BALL WITH ME
CONSOLATION
DADDY'S LITTLE GIRL
DOWN IN JUNGLE TOWN
I'D RATHER BE A LOBSTER THAN A
WISE GUY
I'VE GOT A FEELING FOR YOU (OR,
WAY DOWN IN MY HEART)
I'VE TAKEN QUITE A FANCY TO YOU
JIMMY VALENTINE
LANKY YANKEE BOYS IN BLUE, THE
LEADER OF THE GERMAN BAND,
THE
LITTLE BOY CALLED "TAPS"
MOONLIGHT BAY (A.K.A. ON
MOONLIGHT BAY)
MY COUSIN CARUS'
PARIS IS A PARADISE FOR COONS
PLEASE COME AND PLAY IN MY
YARD
SHE WAITS BY THE DEEP BLUE SEA
SILVER BELL
STARLIGHT
TWO BLUE EYES, TWO LITTLE BABY
SHOES
UP, UP, UP IN MY AEROPLANE
WHEN YOU WORE A PINAFORE

Madden, Frank

MAYBE

Maddox, Pee Wee

WISHING RING

Maddux, Murphy

I'VE BEEN SEARCHING

Maddux, Pee Wee

WORLD OF MAKE BELIEVE

Madera, John

YOU DON'T OWN ME

Madison, Nat

MY CABIN OF DREAMS

Madison, Paul

MOONRAY

Madonna

ANGEL
CAUSING A COMMOTION
LA ISLA BONITA
OPEN YOUR HEART
PAPA DON'T PREACH
SIDEWALK TALK
TRUE BLUE
WHO'S THAT GIRL

Madriguera, Enric

ADIOS

Maduri, Carl A., Jr.

HULA HOOP SONG, THE

Mael, Ron

COOL PLACES

Mael, Russell

COOL PLACES

Maffit, Rocky

TRY AGAIN

Magidson, Herb

ACCORDING TO THE MOONLIGHT
BARRELHOUSE BESSIE FROM BASIN
STREET
BEAU NIGHT IN HOTCHKISS
CORNERS
BLACK EYED SUSAN BROWN
BLUE SKY AVENUE

CONCHITA, MARQUITA, LOLITA,
PEPITA, ROSITA, JUANITA LOPEZ
CONTINENTAL, THE
ENJOY YOURSELF (IT'S LATER THAN
YOU THINK)
GONE WITH THE WIND
GOODNIGHT ANGEL
HERE'S TO ROMANCE
HUMMIN' TO MYSELF (I'VE GOT THE
WORDS—I'VE GOT THE TUNE)
I CAN'T LOVE YOU ANYMORE (ANY
MORE THAN I DO)
I KNEW YOU WHEN
I'LL BUY THAT DREAM
I'LL DANCE AT YOUR WEDDING
I'M STEPPING OUT WITH A MEMORY
TONIGHT
LET'S HAVE ANOTHER CIGARETTE
LINGER IN MY ARMS A LITTLE
LONGER, BABY
MASQUERADE IS OVER, THE
MIDNIGHT IN PARIS
MUSIC, MAESTRO, PLEASE!
NEEDLE IN A HAY STACK, A
OLD, OLD CASTLE IN SCOTLAND, AN
PINK COCKTAIL FOR A BLUE LADY,
A
SAY A PRAYER FOR THE BOYS OVER
THERE
SINGIN' IN THE BATHTUB
SOMETHING I DREAMED LAST
NIGHT
'TAINT NO USE
TALKIN' TO MYSELF
TWINKLE, TWINKLE, LITTLE STAR
VIOLINS FROM NOWHERE
YOU'RE NOT SO EASY TO FORGET

Magill, Jacqueline

MARY LOU

Magine, Frank

DREAMY MELODY
SAVE THE LAST DANCE FOR ME

Magness, Cliff

ALL I NEED

Maguire, Sylvester

IF I HAD A THOUSAND LIVES TO
LIVE

Maher, Brent

GIRL'S NIGHT OUT, A
I KNOW WHERE I'M GOING
LESSON IN LEAVIN', A
ROCKIN' WITH THE RHYTHM OF
THE RAIN
TURN IT LOOSE
WEEKEND, THE

Mahoney, Jack

KENTUCKY DAYS
RING ON THE FINGER IS WORTH
TWO ON THE PHONE, A
WHEN YOU WORE A TULIP AND I
WORE A BIG RED ROSE

Maiden, Tony

AT MIDNIGHT (MY LOVE WILL LIFT
YOU UP)
SWEET THING

Mainegra, Richard

HERE'S SOME LOVE
SEPARATE WAYS

Mainieri, Mike

JESSE

Makeba, Miriam

PATA PATA

Makowitz, Donald

(I'VE HAD) THE TIME OF MY LIFE

Malavasi, Mauro

PARADISE

Malie, Tommy

HIGHWAYS ARE HAPPY WAYS

JEALOUS
LOOKING AT THE WORLD THROUGH
ROSE COLORED GLASSES

Malkin, Norman

HEY, MR. BANJO

Mallah, Linda

I DO YOU
MAKE IT REAL

Mallette, Wanda

LOOKIN' FOR LOVE

Mallfried, Lea

YOU COULD HAVE BEEN WITH ME

Malloy, David

DRIVIN' MY LIFE AWAY
GONE TOO FAR
I JUST WANT TO LOVE YOU
I LOVE A RAINY NIGHT
LOVE WILL TURN YOU AROUND
SOMEONE COULD LOSE A HEART
TONIGHT
STEP BY STEP
SUSPICIONS

Malneck, Matty

AND THEN YOUR LIPS MET MINE
EENY, MEENY, MEINY, MO
FIDGETY JOE
GOODY GOODY
IF I HAD A MILLION DOLLARS
IF YOU WERE MINE
I GO FOR THAT
I'LL NEVER BE THE SAME
I'M THROUGH WITH LOVE
I SAW HER AT EIGHT O'CLOCK
MARY HAD A LITTLE LAMB
OLD PLAYMATE
PARDON MY SOUTHERN ACCENT
SHANGRI-LA
SNUG AS A BUG IN A RUG
SO AT LAST IT'S COME TO THIS
STAIRWAY TO THE STARS

Malone, Deadric

AIN'T NOTHING YOU CAN DO
AIN'T THAT LOVING YOU
ANNIE GET YOUR YO-YO
BLIND MAN
CALL ON ME
DON'T CRY NO MORE
EIGHT MEN, FOUR WOMEN
I PITY THE FOOL
SHARE YOUR LOVE WITH ME
THAT'S THE WAY LOVE IS
TURN ON YOUR LOVELIGHT
YOU'RE GONNA MAKE ME CRY

Malone, George

BOOK OF LOVE

Malone, Johnny

PLEASE LOVE ME FOREVER

Maloo, Kurt

CAPTAIN OF HER HEART, THE

Malotte, Albert Hay

FERDINAND THE BULL
SONG OF THE OPEN ROAD

Malsby, Lynn

I MISS YOU

Maltby, Richard

SIX FLATS UNFURNISHED

Maltby, Richard, Jr.

EASIER TO LOVE
FATHERHOOD BLUES
HANDFUL OF KEYS
HAVING MYSELF A FINE TIME
I WANT IT ALL
JITTERBUG WALTZ, THE
LOUNGING AT THE WALDORF
NO MORE SONGS FOR ME
STORY GOES ON, THE

Maltin, Bernard

BECAUSE OF ONCE UPON A TIME

ManaZucca

I LOVE LIFE

Manchester, Melissa

BETTER DAYS
COME IN FROM THE RAIN
JUST TOO MANY PEOPLE
MIDNIGHT BLUE
WHENEVER I CALL YOU "FRIEND"

Mancini, Henry

ALL HIS CHILDREN
BABY ELEPHANT WALK (A.K.A.
   THEME FROM "HATARI")
BACHELOR IN PARADISE
CHARADE
CHICAGO, ILLINOIS
COME TO ME
CRAZY WORLD
DAYS OF WINE AND ROSES
DEAR HEART
DON'T YOU FORGET IT
FINE MESS, A
IN THE ARMS OF LOVE
IT'S EASY TO SAY (A.K.A. SONG
   FROM "10")
LIFE IN A LOOKING GLASS
MOON RIVER
MOVE 'EM OUT
MR. LUCKY
PETER GUNN
PINK PANTHER THEME, THE
SEND A LITTLE LOVE MY WAY
SIMPLY MEANT TO BE
SWEETHEART TREE, THE
TIME TO CARE, A
WHISTLING AWAY THE DARK

Mandel, Johnny

EMILY
SHADOW OF YOUR SMILE, THE
SONG FROM M*A*S*H (SUICIDE IS
   PAINLESS)
TIME FOR LOVE, A

Mangione, Chuck

FEELS SO GOOD
GIVE IT ALL YOU GOT
HILL WHERE THE LORD HIDES

Mangold, Mark

I FOUND SOMEONE

Manigault, Bobby

TROGLODYTE (CAVE MAN)

Manilow, Barry

COPACABANA (AT THE COPA)
COULD IT BE MAGIC
DAYBREAK
EVEN NOW
I MADE IT THROUGH THE RAIN
IT'S A MIRACLE
SOME KIND OF FRIEND
THIS ONE'S FOR YOU

Manker, Sidney

RAUNCHY

Mann, Aimee

VOICES CARRY

Mann, Barry

ALL I NEED TO KNOW
AMY
BLAME IT ON THE BOSSA NOVA
BLESS YOU
BROWN EYED WOMAN
COME ON OVER TO MY PLACE
CONSCIENCE
DON'T BE AFRAID, LITTLE DARLIN'
DON'T MAKE MY BABY BLUE
FOOTSTEPS
GRASS IS GREENER, THE
HEART (I HEAR YOU BEATING)
HERE YOU COME AGAIN
HE'S SURE THE BOY I LOVE
HOME OF THE BRAVE
HOW CAN I TELL HER IT'S OVER?
HOW MUCH LOVE
HUNGRY
IF A WOMAN ANSWERS (HANG UP
   THE PHONE)
I JUST CAN'T HELP BELIEVING
I'LL NEVER DANCE AGAIN
I'LL TAKE YOU HOME
I LOVE HOW YOU LOVE ME
I'M GONNA BE STRONG
IT'S GETTING BETTER
I WANT YOU TO MEET MY BABY
JOHNNY LOVES ME
KICKS
LOVE LIVES ON
MAGIC TOWN
MAKE YOUR OWN KIND OF MUSIC
MARY'S LITTLE LAMB
MY DAD
NEVER GONNA LET YOU GO
NEW WORLD COMING
ON BROADWAY
ONLY IN AMERICA
PATCHES
PEACE, BROTHER, PEACE
PROUD
ROCK AND ROLL LULLABY
SATURDAY NIGHT AT THE MOVIES
SHAPE OF THINGS TO COME
SHE SAY (OOM DOOBY DOOM)
SO LONG DIXIE
SOMETIMES WHEN WE TOUCH
SOMEWHERE OUT THERE
(YOU'RE MY) SOUL AND INSPIRATION
SWEET LITTLE YOU
UPTOWN
WALKING IN THE RAIN
WAY OF A CLOWN, THE
WE GOTTA GET OUT OF THIS PLACE
WE'RE GOING ALL THE WAY
WHO PUT THE BOMP (IN THE BOMP,
   BOMP, BOMP)
YOU'VE LOST THAT LOVIN' FEELIN'

Mann, David

BOUTONNIERE
DEARIE
DON'T GO TO STRANGERS
DOWNHEARTED
IN THE WEE SMALL HOURS OF THE
   MORNING
I'VE ONLY MYSELF TO BLAME
NO MOON AT ALL
PASSING FANCY

SOMEBODY BAD STOLE DE WEDDING BELL (WHO'S GOT DE DING DONG?)
THERE, I'VE SAID IT AGAIN
THESE WILL BE THE BEST YEARS OF OUR LIVES

Mann, Herbie

MEMPHIS UNDERGROUND

Mann, Jack

MIDNIGHT MASQUERADE

Mann, Kal

BRISTOL STOMP
BUTTERFLY
CHA CHA CHA, THE
CHERIE
DANCIN' PARTY
DING-A-LING
DO THE BIRD
FISH, THE
GOOD TIME BABY
GRAVY (FOR MY MASHED POTATOES)
HEY BOBBA NEEDLE
LET'S TWIST AGAIN
LODDY LO
POPEYE THE HITCHHIKER
REMEMBER YOU'RE MINE
SLOW TWISTIN'
SOUTH STREET
I QUIT MY PRETTY MAMA
SWINGIN' SCHOOL
(LET ME BE YOUR) TEDDY BEAR
TWENTY MILES
TWISTIN' U.S.A.
WAH WATUSI, THE
WE GOT LOVE
WILD ONE
WILDWOOD DAYS
YOU CAN'T SIT DOWN

Mann, Lois

ANNIE HAD A BABY
I'LL SAIL MY SHIP ALONE
I QUIT MY PRETTY MAMA
SIGNED, SEALED AND DELIVERED
SITTIN' ON IT ALL THE TIME
SWEETER THAN THE FLOWERS

WELL, OH WELL

Mann, Lorene

DON'T GO NEAR THE INDIANS
IT KEEPS RIGHT ON A-HURTIN' (SINCE I LEFT)
LEFT TO RIGHT

Mann, Paul

AND SO DO I
ANGEL IN DISGUISE
FINGER OF SUSPICION POINTS AT YOU, THE
INVITATION TO A BROKEN HEART
MAKE LOVE TO ME
PUT YOUR DREAMS AWAY (FOR ANOTHER DAY)
THEY SAY

Mann, Rita

PASSING STRANGERS

Manne, Joe

MEET ME IN BUBBLE LAND

Manner, Henry

WE COULD MAKE SUCH BEAUTIFUL MUSIC

Manners, Gerry

MAN UPSTAIRS, THE

Manners, Henry

DELILAH

Manners, Zeke

INFLATION
PENNSYLVANIA POLKA

Manning, Dick

ALLEGHENY MOON
ARE YOU REALLY MINE?
DENNIS THE MENACE
DON'T STAY AWAY TOO LONG

FASCINATION
GILLY, GILLY, OSSENFEFFER, KATSENELLEN BOGEN BY THE SEA
HAWAIIAN WEDDING SONG, THE
HOT DIGGITY (DOG ZIGGITY BOOM)
I CAN'T TELL A WALTZ FROM A TANGO
I STILL FEEL THE SAME ABOUT YOU
IVY ROSE
JILTED
LA PLUME DE MA TANTE
MAMA, TEACH ME TO DANCE
MAMA WILL BARK
MI CASA, SU CASA (MY HOUSE IS YOUR HOUSE)
MOON TALK
MORNINGSIDE OF THE MOUNTAIN, THE
O DIO MIO
OH-OH, I'M FALLING IN LOVE AGAIN
PAPA LOVES MAMBO
PUSSY CAT SONG, THE (NYOW! NYOT NYOW!)
ROSANNE
SECRETLY
TAKES TWO TO TANGO
TORERO
TREASURE OF SIERRA MADRE, THE

Manone, Wingy

TAR PAPER STOMP

Manson, Eddy

JOEY'S THEME

Mantz, Nancie

GREEN LIGHT
I HAD TOO MUCH TO DREAM (LAST NIGHT)

Manuel, Richard

TEARS OF RAGE

Manus, Jack

AM I WASTING MY TIME?
MY COUSIN LOUELLA
VANITY

Manzanero, Armando

IT'S IMPOSSIBLE

Manzarek, Ray

HELLO, I LOVE YOU
LIGHT MY FIRE
LOVE HER MADLY
LOVE ME TWO TIMES
PEOPLE ARE STRANGE
RIDERS ON THE STORM
ROADHOUSE BLUES
TOUCH ME
UNKNOWN SOLDIER
WISHFUL, SINFUL

Mara, Ta

EVERYBODY DANCE

Marais, Dee

POOR MAN'S RICHES

Marais, Josef

A-ROUND THE CORNER (BENEATH
   THE BERRY TREE)
MA SAYS, PA SAYS
SUGARBUSH

Marascalco, John

BE MY GUEST
GOOD GOLLY MISS MOLLY
GOODNIGHT MY LOVE (PLEASANT
   DREAMS)
READY TEDDY
RIP IT UP
SEND ME SOME LOVIN'

Marbet, Rolf

CALL ME DARLING

Marcellino, Gerald

I AM LOVE
SAD TOMORROWS

Marchetti, F. D.

FASCINATION

Marco, Sano

MAY I NEVER LOVE AGAIN

Marcotte, Don

DORMI, DORMI
I THINK OF YOU
IT'S ALL OVER NOW
YOU'RE ALWAYS THERE

Marcucci, Bob

DEDE DINAH
I'LL WAIT FOR YOU
SWINGIN' ON A RAINBOW
WHY
WITH ALL MY HEART

Marcus, Bob

PATRICIA
PLEASE PLAY OUR SONG (MISTER
   RECORD MAN)

Marcus, Sol

AND THEN IT'S HEAVEN
ASK ANYONE WHO KNOWS
CANCEL THE FLOWERS
DON'T LET ME BE MISUNDERSTOOD
FISHIN' FOR THE MOON
I DON'T WANT TO SET THE WORLD
   ON FIRE
STRICTLY INSTRUMENTAL
TILL THEN
WHEN THE LIGHTS GO ON AGAIN
   (ALL OVER THE WORLD)

Marden, Pauline

PACK UP YOUR SORROWS

Mardones, Benny

INTO THE NIGHT

Mareno, Ricci

I BELIEVE YOU
I GOT YOU

Mares, Paul

FAREWELL BLUES
MAKE LOVE TO ME
MILENBERG JOYS
TIN ROOF BLUES

Maresca, Ernest

CHILD OF CLAY
DONNA THE PRIMA DONNA
LOVERS WHO WANDER
NO ONE KNOWS
RUNAROUND SUE
SHOUT! SHOUT! (KNOCK YOURSELF
   OUT)
WANDERER, THE
WHENEVER A TEENAGER CRIES

Margetson, E. J.

TOMMY, LAD!

Margo, Mitchell

I HEAR TRUMPETS BLOW

Margo, Philip

I HEAR TRUMPETS BLOW

Margolin, Stuart

DAY AFTER DAY (IT'S SLIPPIN'
   AWAY)

Maria, Antonio

SAMBA DE ORFEO

Mariash, Jane

LAST ONE TO KNOW, THE

Marie, Teena

LOVERGIRL
OOO LA LA LA

Marin, Richard "Cheech"

BASKETBALL JONES FEATURING
  TYRONE SHOELACES
EARACHE MY EYE FEATURING
  ALICE BOWIE

Marinell, Leroy

WEREWOLVES OF LONDON

Marinos, Jimmy

TALKING IN YOUR SLEEP

Marion, Dave

HER EYES DON'T SHINE LIKE
  DIAMONDS
ONLY ONE GIRL IN THE WORLD FOR
  ME

Marion, George, Jr.

ADORABLE
IT SEEMS TO BE SPRING
MY FUTURE JUST PASSED
MY SWEETER THAN SWEET
RASTUS ON PARADE
SLIGHTLY LESS THAN WONDERFUL

Marion, Will

WHO DAY SAY CHICKEN IN DIS
  CROWD

Mariz, Antonio

DAY IN THE LIFE OF A FOOL, A
MANHA DE CARNAVAL

Markantonatos, David

MASTER JACK

Markes, Larry

ALONG THE NAVAJO TRAIL
IT TAKES A LONG, LONG TRAIN
  WITH A RED CABOOSE (TO
  CARRY MY BLUES AWAY)

I TIPPED MY HAT (AND SLOWLY
  RODE AWAY)
MAD ABOUT HIM, SAD ABOUT HIM,
  HOW CAN I BE GLAD ABOUT HIM
  BLUES
MAY YOU ALWAYS

Markham, Dewey "Pigmeat"

HERE COMES THE JUDGE

Marks, Charley

WHERE DO YOU WORK-A, JOHN?
  (ON THE DELAWARE LACKAWAN')

Marks, Edward B.

DECEMBER AND MAY (OR, MOLLIE
  NEWELL DON'T BE CRUEL)
HIS LAST THOUGHTS WERE OF YOU
LITTLE LOST CHILD, THE
MOTHER WAS A LADY (OR, IF JACK
  WERE ONLY HERE)
NO ONE EVER LOVED YOU MORE
  THAN I

Marks, Gerald

ALL OF ME
BABY, WHAT ELSE CAN I DO?
DUST OFF THAT OLD PIANNA (OH,
  SUZANNA)
I'LL CRY TOMORROW
IS IT TRUE WHAT THEY SAY ABOUT
  DIXIE?
SASKATCHEWAN
THAT'S WHAT I WANT FOR
  CHRISTMAS
YOU'RE THE ONE (YOU BEAUTIFUL
  SON-OF-A-GUN)

Marks, Johnny

ADDRESS UNKNOWN
DON'T CROSS YOUR FINGERS, CROSS
  YOUR HEART
HOLLY, JOLLY CHRISTMAS, A
RUDOLPH THE RED-NOSED
  REINDEER
SHE'LL ALWAYS REMEMBER

Marks, Rose

DO SOMETHING FOR ME
SIXTY MINUTE MAN
THAT'S WHAT YOU'RE DOING TO ME

Marks, Walter

I CAN
I'VE GOTTA BE ME
WE GOT US

Markush, Fred

TAKE ME IN YOUR ARMS

Markwell, Mark

ARE YOU REALLY MINE?
OH-OH, I'M FALLING IN LOVE AGAIN
SECRETLY

Marley, Bob

I SHOT THE SHERIFF
STIR IT UP

Marley, David Nesta

TUMBLIN' DOWN

Marlin, Marsha

COME FOLLOW, FOLLOW ME

Marlow, Ric

TASTE OF HONEY, A

Marlowe, Jerry

LET'S BE SWEETHEARTS AGAIN

Marrero, Marta

TOY SOLDIERS

Marriott, Steve

HOT 'N' NASTY
ITCHYCOO PARK

Mars, Mick

GIRLS, GIRLS, GIRLS

Mars, Richard

BEST OF ME, THE

Marsala, Joe

AND SO TO SLEEP AGAIN
DON'T CRY, JOE (LET HER GO, LET
    HER GO, LET HER GO)

Marsden, Bernie

HERE I GO AGAIN

Marsden, Gerry

DON'T LET THE SUN CATCH YOU
    CRYING
FERRY ACROSS THE MERSEY
IT'S GONNA BE ALL RIGHT

Marsh, Doyle

DAYS OF SAND AND SHOVELS, THE

Marsh, Nick

I GO CRAZY

Marsh, Roy

I NEVER KNEW I COULD LOVE
    ANYBODY (LIKE I'M LOVING YOU)

Marshall, Charles

I HEAR YOU CALLING ME

Marshall, Ed

VENUS

Marshall, Henry I.

BE MY LITTLE BABY BUMBLE BEE
MALINDA
MARY, YOU'RE A LITTLE BIT OLD
    FASHIONED
ON THE 5:15

Marshall, James

DEVIL WENT DOWN TO GEORGIA,
    THE
IN AMERICA

Marshall, Michael

RUMORS

Marshall, Sherman

I'M DOIN' FINE NOW
LADY LOVE
THEN CAME YOU

Marti, José

GUANTANAMERA

Martin, Angela

L. DAVID SLOANE

Martin, Bill

MY BOY
SATURDAY NIGHT
TILL WE TWO ARE ONE

Martin, Bobbi

FOR THE LOVE OF HIM

Martin, Cedric

BABY, I'M HOOKED (RIGHT INTO
    YOUR LOVE)

Martin, D.

GOIN' DOWN

Martin, David

BREAKFAST WITH THE BLUES
CAN'T SMILE WITHOUT YOU

Martin, Dude

JUST A PAIR OF BLUE EYES

Martin, Earl

LAZY DAY

Martin, Easthope

COME TO THE FAIR

Martin, Freddy

TONIGHT WE LOVE

Martin, Glenn

IF WE'RE NOT BACK IN LOVE BY
    MONDAY
I'M JUST ME
IS ANYBODY GOIN' TO SAN
    ANTONE?
IT'S NOT LOVE (BUT IT'S NOT BAD)

Martin, Grady

SNAP YOUR FINGERS

Martin, Herbert

I'M ALL SMILES

Martin, Hugh

BIRMIN'HAM
BOY NEXT DOOR, THE
BUCKLE DOWN, WINSOCKI
CONNECTICUT
EV'RY TIME
FOREVER AND A DAY
HAVE YOURSELF A MERRY LITTLE
    CHRISTMAS
IF I GAVE YOU
I KNOW YOUR HEART
I'M THE FIRST GIRL IN THE SECOND
    ROW (IN THE THIRD SCENE OF
    THE FOURTH NUMBER)
JOINT IS REALLY JUMPIN' AT
    CARNEGIE HALL
JUST A LITTLE JOINT WITH A JUKE
    BOX
LOVE
OCCASIONAL MAN, AN
PASS THAT PEACE PIPE
SHADY LADY BIRD
SOMETHING TELLS ME

THREE B'S, THE
TROLLEY SONG, THE
WAS SHE PRETTIER THAN I?
WHAT DO YOU THINK I AM?
YOU'D BETTER LOVE ME

Martin, J. D.

DON'T GO TO STRANGERS
I'LL NEVER STOP LOVING YOU
LONELY ALONE
LOVE WILL FIND ITS WAY TO YOU

Martin, John

BAD CASE OF LOVING YOU
  (DOCTOR, DOCTOR)

Martin, Larry

FORGET ME NOT
TILL WE TWO ARE ONE

Martin, Laura

MOUNTAIN OF LOVE

Martin, Lennie

SINCE I DON'T HAVE YOU

Martin, Linda

CHICK-A-BOOM (DON'T YA JES' LOVE
  IT)

Martin, Moon

NO CHANCE
ROLENE

Martin, Naomi

LET'S TAKE THE LONG WAY AROUND
  THE WORLD
MY EYES CAN ONLY SEE AS FAR AS
  YOU

Martin, Ray

BLUE VIOLINS
GYPSY FIDDLER

Martin, Richard

LET IT RAIN

Martin, Sam

YOU CALL EVERYBODY DARLING

Martin, Steve

CRUEL SHOES
GRANDMOTHER'S SONG
KING TUT

Martin, Tony

BABY'S GOTTEN GOOD AT GOODBYE

Martin, Trade

TAKE ME FOR A LITTLE WHILE

Martin, Troy

BABY'S GOTTEN GOOD AT GOODBYE

Martina, Roberto

CAE CAE

Martine, Layng

RUB IT IN
SHOULD I DO IT
WAY DOWN

Martine, Lewis

COME GO WITH ME
LET ME BE THE ONE
POINT OF NO RETURN
SEASONS

Martinez, Nigel

NIGHT (FEEL LIKE GETTING DOWN)

Martinez, R.

I NEED SOMEBODY

Martinez, Rudy

96 TEARS

Martins, David

STEEL MEN

Martita (Margery S. Wolpin)

MY JEALOUS EYES (THAT TURNED
  FROM BLUE TO GREEN)

Marvin, Frankie

HONEY, DO YOU THINK IT'S
  WRONG?

Marvin, Hank

SAM

Marvin, Johnny

AT THE CLOSE OF A LONG, LONG
  DAY
DUST
GOODBYE, LITTLE DARLIN',
  GOODBYE

Marx, Richard

CRAZY
DON'T MEAN NOTHING
ENDLESS SUMMER NIGHTS
HOLD ON TO THE NIGHTS
RIGHT HERE WAITING
SHOULD'VE KNOWN BETTER

Marzano, Norman

DO SOMETHING TO ME

Mas, Carolyne

STILLSANE

Masakela, Hugh

SARAFINA

Mascari, Eddie

I GOT A WIFE

Maschwitz, Eric

AT THE BALALAIKA
HE WEARS A PAIR OF SILVER
WINGS
NIGHTINGALE SANG IN BERKELEY
SQUARE, A
RAINY DAY REFRAIN, A
THESE FOOLISH THINGS (REMIND
ME OF YOU)
WORLD IS MINE, THE

Maser, Mort

SOMEHOW

Mason, Barbara

OH, HOW IT HURTS
SAD, SAD GIRL
YES, I'M READY

Mason, Barry

DELILAH
HERE IT COMES AGAIN
I NEVER SAID GOODBYE
KISS ME GOODBYE
LAST WALTZ, THE
LES BICYCLETTES DE BELSIZE
LOVE GROWS (WHERE MY
ROSEMARY GOES)
LOVE ME TONIGHT
MAN WITHOUT LOVE, A
MY MARIE
SAY YOU'LL STAY UNTIL TOMORROW
WINTER WORLD OF LOVE

Mason, David

FEELIN' ALRIGHT
LET IT GO, LET IT FLOW
ONLY YOU KNOW AND I KNOW

Mason, James

I DIG ROCK AND ROLL MUSIC

Mason, John

OPEN THE DOOR, RICHARD

Mason, Marilyn

LOVE TAKES TIME

Mason, Melvin

I DO

Mason, Vincent

ME, MYSELF, AND I

Masser, Michael

DIDN'T WE ALMOST HAVE IT ALL
GREATEST LOVE OF ALL, THE
IF EVER YOU'RE IN MY ARMS
AGAIN
IT'S MY TURN
LAST TIME I SAW HIM
NOBODY WANTS TO BE ALONE
NOTHING'S GONNA CHANGE MY
LOVE FOR YOU
SAVING ALL MY LOVE FOR YOU
SOMEONE THAT I USED TO LOVE
SO SAD THE SONG
THEME FROM "MAHOGANY" (DO
YOU KNOW WHERE YOU'RE
GOING TO?)
TONIGHT I CELEBRATE MY LOVE
TOUCH ME IN THE MORNING

Massey, Curt

PETTICOAT JUNCTION

Massey, Guy

PRISONER'S SONG, THE (A.K.A. IF I
HAD THE WINGS OF AN ANGEL)

Massey, Louise

MY ADOBE HACIENDA

Mastelotto

IS IT LOVE

Masters, Frankie

CHARMING LITTLE FAKER
SCATTERBRAIN

Masters, Johnnie

HONEYMOON ON A ROCKET SHIP

Matassa, Cosimo

JUST A DREAM

Mather, Robert

SEXY EYES

Mathews, Johnnie

GONNA SEND YOU BACK TO
GEORGIA (A.K.A. GONNA SEND
YOU BACK TO WALKER)

Mathieson, Gregory

TELEFONE (LONG DISTANCE LOVE
AFFAIR)

Mathis, "Country" Johnny

PLEASE TALK TO MY HEART

Mathis, Johnny

IF YOU DON'T, SOMEBODY ELSE
WILL

Matkosky, Dennis

MANIAC
MIRROR, MIRROR

Matson, Vera

LOVE ME TENDER
POOR BOY

Matthewman, Stuart

NEVER AS GOOD AS THE FIRST
TIME
PARADISE

Matthews, Charles

MICHAEL
WHITE SILVER SANDS

Matthews, Jason

GIVE ME THE MOON OVER
  BROOKLYN

Matthews, J. Sherrie

HEY, RUBE!

Matthias, Jack

JUMP TOWN
TRUMPET BLUES

Mattis, David J.

CLOCK, THE

Matz, Peter

GOTTA MOVE

Maubon, L.

TITINA

Maudley, Frank

I RAN (SO FAR AWAY)

Maugeri, Rudi

CRAZY 'BOUT YA, BABY

Maxted, Billy

MANHATTAN SPIRITUAL

Maxwell, Eddie

LET'S BE SWEETHEARTS AGAIN

Maxwell, Robert

EBB TIDE
LITTLE DIPPER
SHANGRI-LA

May, Billy

I TAUT I SAW A PUDDY TAT
LEAN BABY
SOMEWHERE IN THE NIGHT

May, Winifred

DREAM OF OLWEN, THE

Mayer, Henry

MY MELODY OF LOVE
SUMMER WIND

Mayer, Jon

IN MY LONELINESS

Mayer, Ray

NOW WE KNOW

Mayer, Tim

COME AS YOU ARE

Mayfield, Curtis

CHOICE OF COLORS
COME SEE
FIND ANOTHER GIRL
FOOL FOR YOU
FREDDIE'S DEAD
GYPSY WOMAN
HE DON'T LOVE YOU (LIKE I LOVE
  YOU)
HE WILL BREAK YOUR HEART
  (A.K.A. HE DON'T LOVE YOU—
  LIKE I LOVE YOU)
HEY LITTLE GIRL
HOOKED ON YOUR LOVE
I CAN'T WORK NO LONGER
I'M SO PROUD
IT'S ALL OVER
IT'S ALL RIGHT
JUMBO
KEEP ON PUSHING
LET'S DO IT AGAIN
LOOK INTO YOUR HEART
MAMA DIDN'T LIE
MEETING OVER YONDER
MONKEY TIME, THE

NOTHING CAN STOP ME
ON AND ON
PEOPLE, GET READY
PIECE OF THE ACTION, A
RHYTHM
ROCK WITH ME
SOMETHING HE CAN FEEL
SUPERFLY
THINK NOTHING ABOUT IT
THIS IS MY COUNTRY
UM, UM, UM, UM, UM, UM
WE'RE A WINNER
WOMAN'S GOT SOUL
YOU'VE BEEN CHEATIN'

Mayfield, Percy

HIT THE ROAD, JACK
LOST LOVE
PLEASE SEND ME SOMEONE TO
  LOVE

Mayhew, Aubrey

TOUCH MY HEART

Mayhew, Billy

IT'S A SIN TO TELL A LIE

Mayne, Martin

I REMEMBER THE CORNFIELDS

Mayo, Harry A.

SINGER IN THE BALCONY, THE

Mays, Lyle

THIS IS NOT AMERICA

McAleese, Thomas

REFLECTIONS OF MY LIFE

McAlpin, Vernice

ALL ALONE IN THIS WORLD
  WITHOUT YOU
TO MY SORROW
WHAT IS LIFE WITHOUT LOVE?

McAlpin, Vic

ALMOST
ANOTHER
ANYMORE
BEFORE THIS DAY ENDS
BREAKFAST WITH THE BLUES
HOME OF THE BLUES
I'D RATHER LOAN YOU OUT
I'M IN LOVE
I WENT OUT OF MY WAY (TO MAKE
   YOU HAPPY)
LET'S LIVE A LITTLE
LOVER'S QUARREL, A

McAnally, Mac

MINIMUM LOVE
OLD FLAME
ONE OWNER HEART
YOU'RE MY FIRST LADY

McAuliffe, Leon

PANHANDLE RAG
STEEL GUITAR RAG

McAvoy, Dan

BEER THAT MADE MILWAUKEE
   FAMOUS, THE

McAvoy, J. P.

DREAMING

McBride, Jim

ROSE IN PARADISE

McBride, Patrick

I COULD NEVER LIE TO YOU

McBrien, Rod

ISN'T IT LONELY TOGETHER

McBroom, Amanda

ROSE, THE

McCaffrey, James

ROLL ON, MISSISSIPPI, ROLL ON

McCain, Larry

HIM OR ME

McCall, Deborah

FINS

McCall, Dorrell

ELEVEN ROSES

McCall, Toussaint

NOTHING TAKES THE PLACE OF YOU

McCann, Peter

DO YOU WANNA MAKE LOVE
NOBODY FALLS LIKE A FOOL
RIGHT TIME OF THE NIGHT
SHE'S SINGLE AGAIN

McCants, Clemmie

DOIN' OUR THING

McCarey, Leo

AFFAIR TO REMEMBER, AN
SATAN NEVER SLEEPS

McCarron, Charles

AT THE LEVEE ON REVIVAL DAY
BLUES MY NAUGHTY SWEETY GIVES
   TO ME, THE
DOWN IN HONKY TONKY TOWN
DOWN WHERE THE SWANEE RIVER
   FLOWS
FIDO IS A HOT DOG NOW
OH! HOW SHE COULD YACKI,
   HACKI, WICKI, WACKI, WOO
POOR PAULINE
WHEN OLD BILL BAILEY PLAYS THE
   UKULELE

McCarthy, Charles

AT LEAST YOU COULD SAY HELLO

McCarthy, Joseph

ADORING YOU
ALICE BLUE GOWN
BEATRICE FAIRFAX, TELL ME WHAT
   TO DO!
CASTLE OF DREAMS
FOLLOWING THE SUN AROUND.
HIGH SOCIETY BLUES
I FOUND THE END OF THE
   RAINBOW
IF WE CAN'T BE THE SAME OLD
   SWEETHEARTS (WE'LL JUST BE
   THE SAME OLD FRIENDS)
IF YOU'RE IN LOVE, YOU'LL WALTZ
IF YOUR HEART'S IN THE GAME
I'M ALWAYS CHASING RAINBOWS
I'M CRYING JUST FOR YOU
I'M IN THE MARKET FOR YOU
I MISS YOU MOST OF ALL
IRELAND MUST BE HEAVEN, FOR
   MY MOTHER CAME FROM THERE
IRENE
JOURNEY'S END
KEEP YOUR EYE ON THE BALL
KINKAJOU, THE
LADY LUCK, SMILE ON ME
LET'S KISS AND MAKE UP
LOVE, HONOR AND OBEY
MY BABY'S ARMS
NATURALLY
NORWAY
OUI, OUI, MARIE
RANGERS' SONG, THE
RIO RITA
SING SONG GIRL
SOMEONE LOVES YOU AFTER ALL
SWEETHEART, WE NEED EACH
   OTHER
TEN PINS IN THE SKY
THAT'S HOW I NEED YOU
THERE'S A LITTLE SPARK OF LOVE
   STILL BURNING
THEY GO WILD, SIMPLY WILD,
   OVER ME
THROUGH (HOW CAN YOU SAY
   WE'RE THROUGH?)
WHAT DO YOU WANT TO MAKE
   THOSE EYES AT ME FOR?

WHEN I GET YOU ALONE TONIGHT
WHY DON'T YOU?
YOU MADE ME LOVE YOU (I DIDN'T
    WANT TO DO IT)
YOU'RE ALWAYS IN MY ARMS
YOU THINK OF EV'RYTHING
YOU'VE GOT ME OUT ON A LIMB

McCarthy, Joseph Allan

BOY FROM TEXAS, A GIRL FROM
    TENNESSEE, A
EARLY MORNING BLUES
I'M GONNA LAUGH YOU RIGHT OUT
    OF MY LIFE
ISN'T HE ADORABLE?
MEADOWS OF HEAVEN, THE
RAMBLING ROSE
RIVIERA, THE
WHY TRY TO CHANGE ME NOW?

McCarthy, Pat

DREAMS ARE A DIME A DOZEN

McCartney, Linda

ANOTHER DAY
BAND ON THE RUN
GIVE IRELAND BACK TO THE IRISH
HELEN WHEELS
HI, HI, HI
JET
JUNIOR'S FARM
LET 'EM IN
LISTEN TO WHAT THE MAN SAID
LIVE AND LET DIE
MARY HAD A LITTLE LAMB
MY LOVE
SALLY G
SILLY LOVE SONGS
UNCLE ALBERT/ADMIRAL HALSEY

McCartney, Paul

ALL MY LOVING
ALL TOGETHER NOW
ALL YOU NEED IS LOVE
AND I LOVE HER
AND I LOVE HIM
ANOTHER DAY
ANOTHER GIRL

ARROW THROUGH ME
BABY, YOU'RE A RICH MAN
BACK IN THE U.S.S.R.
BAD TO ME
BALLAD OF JOHN AND YOKO, THE
BAND ON THE RUN
BIRTHDAY
CAN'T BUY ME LOVE
COME AND GET IT
COME TOGETHER
COMING UP (LIVE AT GLASGOW)
DAY TRIPPER
DEAR PRUDENCE
DON'T LET ME DOWN
DO YOU WANT TO KNOW A SECRET?
DRIVE MY CAR
EBONY AND IVORY
EIGHT DAYS A WEEK
ELEANOR RIGBY
FOOL ON THE HILL, THE
FROM A WINDOW
FROM ME TO YOU
GET BACK
GETTING CLOSER
GIRLS' SCHOOL
GIVE IRELAND BACK TO THE IRISH
GIVE PEACE A CHANCE
GOODBYE
GOOD DAY SUNSHINE
GOODNIGHT TONIGHT
GOT TO GET YOU INTO MY LIFE
HARD DAY'S NIGHT, A
HELEN WHEELS
HELLO, GOODBYE
HELP!
HELTER SKELTER
HERE, THERE AND EVERYWHERE
HEY JUDE
HI, HI, HI
I AM THE WALRUS
I DON'T WANT TO SEE YOU AGAIN
I DON'T WANT TO SPOIL THE
    PARTY
I FEEL FINE
IF I FELL
I'LL CRY INSTEAD
I'LL KEEP YOU SATISFIED
(P.S.) I LOVE YOU
I'M HAPPY JUST TO DANCE WITH
    YOU
IN MY LIFE
I SAW HER STANDING THERE
I SHOULD HAVE KNOWN BETTER

IT'S FOR YOU
IT'S ONLY LOVE
I'VE HAD ENOUGH
I WANT TO HOLD YOUR HAND
JET
JULIA
JUNIOR'S FARM
LADY MADONNA
LET 'EM IN
LET IT BE
LISTEN TO WHAT THE MAN SAID
LIVE AND LET DIE
LONDON TOWN
LONG AND WINDING ROAD, THE
LOVELY RITA (METER MAID)
LOVE ME DO
LUCY IN THE SKY WITH DIAMONDS
MAGICAL MYSTERY TOUR, THE
MARY HAD A LITTLE LAMB
MAYBE I'M AMAZED
MICHELLE
MINE FOR ME
MULL OF KINTYRE
MY LOVE
NOBODY I KNOW
NO MORE LONELY NIGHTS
NORWEGIAN WOOD
NOWHERE MAN
OB-LA-DI, OB-LA-DA
OH! DARLING
ON THE WINGS OF A NIGHTINGALE
PAPERBACK WRITER
PENNY LANE
PLEASE PLEASE ME
RAIN
REVOLUTION
RINGO'S THEME (THIS BOY)
ROCKY RACCOON
SALLY G
SAY SAY SAY
SGT. PEPPER'S LONELY HEARTS
    CLUB BAND
SHE CAME IN THROUGH THE
    BATHROOM WINDOW
SHE LOVES YOU
SHE SAID SHE SAID
SHE'S A WOMAN
SILLY LOVE SONGS
SO BAD
SPIES LIKE US
STRAWBERRY FIELDS FOREVER
TAKE IT AWAY
TELL ME WHY

McCullough, James

RETURN OF THE RED BARON, THE

McCullough, John

RETURN OF THE RED BARON, THE

McDaniel, Ellas (Bo Diddley)

BO DIDDLEY
I'M A MAN
OH YEAH!
SAY, MAN

McDaniels, D.

MEN ALL PAUSE, THE

McDaniels, Eugene

ROAD RUNNER

McDaniels, Gene

COMPARED TO WHAT
FEEL LIKE MAKIN' LOVE

McDermott, John, Jr.

(MY HEART GOES) KA-DING-DONG

McDiarmid, Don

LITTLE BROWN GAL

McDill, Bob

AMANDA
BABY'S GOT HER BLUE JEANS ON
BIG WHEELS IN THE MOONLIGHT
DON'T CLOSE YOUR EYES
DOOR'S ALWAYS OPEN, THE
EVERYTHING THAT GLITTERS (IS
    NOT GOLD)
FALLING AGAIN
GOOD OLE BOYS LIKE ME
IF HOLLYWOOD DON'T NEED YOU
IT MUST BE LOVE
I'VE BEEN AROUND LONG ENOUGH
    TO KNOW
NOBODY LIKES SAD SONGS

REDNECKS, WHITE SOCKS, AND
    BLUE RIBBON BEER
SAY IT AGAIN
TURN OUT THE LIGHT AND LOVE
    ME TONIGHT
WE BELIEVE IN HAPPY ENDINGS
WHAT SHE IS (IS A WOMAN IN
    LOVE)
WHY DON'T YOU SPEND THE NIGHT
YOU NEVER MISS A REAL GOOD
    THING

McDonald, Ian

COURT OF THE CRIMSON KING
LONG, LONG WAY FROM HOME

McDonald, Joe

BREAKFAST FOR TWO
I FEEL-LIKE-I'M-FIXIN'-TO-DIE RAG
NOT SO SWEET MARTHA LORRAINE

McDonald, Michael

DEPENDIN' ON YOU
HEART TO HEART
IT KEEPS YOU RUNNING
MINUTE BY MINUTE
NO WAY OUT
REAL LOVE
TAKIN' IT TO THE STREETS
THIS IS IT
WHAT A FOOL BELIEVES
YAH MO B THERE
YOU BELONG TO ME

McDonald, M. H.

I'LL WAIT

McDonald, Skeets

YOU TOOK HER OFF MY HANDS
    (NOW PLEASE TAKE HER OFF MY
    MIND)

McDonough, Glen

I CAN'T DO THIS SUM

McDowell, Mitch "General Kane"

CRACK KILLED APPLEJACK

McDowell, Ronnie

KING IS GONE, THE

McDuff, Eddie

HELLO TROUBLE

McDuffie, Kenneth

BETWEEN BLUE EYES AND JEANS
GOOD WOMAN BLUES

McElhone, John

HONEYTHIEF, THE

McElroy, Thomas

LITTLE WALTER
WHY YOU TREAT ME SO BAD

McEntire, Reba

LET THE MUSIC LIFT YOU UP

McFadden, Gene

AIN'T NO STOPPIN' US NOW
BACK STABBERS
BAD LUCK
FALLING
I DON'T WANT TO LOSE YOUR LOVE
LITTLE BIT MORE, A
WAKE UP EVERYBODY

McFadden, Tony

FORGET ME NOTS

McFaddin, Theresa

ONE LOVE IN MY LIFETIME

McFarland, J. Leslie

LITTLE CHILDREN
STUCK ON YOU

McFerrin, Bobby

DON'T WORRY, BE HAPPY

McGarrigle, Anna

HEART LIKE A WHEEL

McGavisk, James

GEE, BUT IT'S GREAT TO MEET A
FRIEND FROM YOUR HOME TOWN

McGee, Parker

AMERICAN MUSIC
I'D REALLY LOVE TO SEE YOU
TONIGHT
IF YOU EVER CHANGE YOUR MIND
NIGHTS ARE FOREVER WITHOUT
YOU

McGhee, Granville "Stick"

DRINKIN' THING

McGhee, John

HOLDING ON (WHEN LOVE IS GONE)

McGinty, Bennie Lee

AIN'T GONNA BUMP NO MORE
(WITH NO BIG FAT WOMAN)

McGlennon, Felix

ACTIONS SPEAK LOUDER THAN
WORDS
AND HER GOLDEN HAIR WAS
HANGING DOWN HER BACK
COMRADES
I FORGET, I FORGET
MR. CAPTAIN, STOP THE SHIP (I
WANT TO GET OFF AND WALK)

McGlohon, Loonis Reeves

LONG NIGHT, A

McGrane, Paul

HAYFOOT, STRAWFOOT
JUKE BOX SATURDAY NIGHT

McGrath, Fulton

MANDY IS TWO

McGraw, George Donald

WOO-HOO

McGrier, Allen

SQUARE BIZ
OOO LA LA LA

McGriff, Edna

HEAVENLY FATHER

McGuinn, James

5 D (FIFTH DIMENSION)
EIGHT MILES HIGH
IT WON'T BE WRONG
MR. SPACEMAN
SO YOU WANT TO BE A ROCK 'N'
ROLL STAR
YOU SHOWED ME

McGuinn, Roger

BALLAD OF EASY RIDER
CHILD OF THE UNIVERSE

McGuire, Barry

GREEN, GREEN

McGuire, Bud

SHINE, SHINE, SHINE

McHan, Don

PILL, THE

McHugh, Jimmy

AS THE GIRLS GO

BABY!
BAD HUMOR MAN, THE
BLAME IT ON THE RHUMBA
BLUE AGAIN
BUTTON UP YOUR HEART
CAN'T GET OUT OF THIS MOOD
CAROLINA, I'M COMING BACK TO
YOU
CLEAR OUT OF THIS WORLD
COLLEGIANA
COMIN' IN ON A WING AND A
PRAYER
CUBAN LOVE SONG
DIGA DIGA DOO
DIG YOU LATER (A HUBBA-HUBBA-
HUBBA)
DINNER AT EIGHT
DOIN' THE NEW LOW-DOWN
DON'T BELIEVE EVERYTHING YOU
DREAM
DON'T BLAME ME
DREAM, DREAM, DREAM
EVERYTHING IS HOTSY TOTSY NOW
EXACTLY LIKE YOU
FIRST LADY WALTZ
FUDDY DUDDY WATCHMAKER, THE
FUTURISTIC RHYTHM
GO HOME AND TELL YOUR MOTHER
GOODBYE BLUES
HAPPY GO LUCKY
HERE COMES HEAVEN AGAIN
HEY, WHAT DID THE BLUEBIRD
SAY?
HEY, YOUNG FELLA
HOORAY FOR LOVE
HOW BLUE THE NIGHT
HOW MANY TIMES DO I HAVE TO
TELL YOU?
I CAN'T BELIEVE THAT YOU'RE IN
LOVE WITH ME
I CAN'T GIVE YOU ANYTHING BUT
LOVE
I COULD KISS YOU FOR THAT
I COULDN'T SLEEP A WINK LAST
NIGHT
I'D KNOW YOU ANYWHERE
I DON'T CARE WHO KNOWS IT
I FEEL A SONG COMIN' ON
I GET THE NECK OF THE CHICKEN
I GOT LUCKY IN THE RAIN
I HIT A NEW HIGH
I'M IN THE MOOD FOR LOVE
I'M LIVIN' IN A GREAT BIG WAY

I'M SHOOTING HIGH
I MUST HAVE THAT MAN
IN A GREAT BIG WAY
IN A MOMENT OF MADNESS
IN THE MIDDLE OF NOWHERE
IS IT POSSIBLE?
IT'S A MOST UNUSUAL DAY
IT'S GREAT TO BE IN LOVE AGAIN
IT'S THE DARNDEST THING
I'VE GOT A ONE TRACK MIND
I'VE GOT MY FINGERS CROSSED
I WALKED IN
I WON'T DANCE
JAMBOREE
JUST HOT !
LATIN TUNE, A MANHATTAN MOON,
   AND YOU, A
LET'S GET LOST
LET'S GIVE LOVE ANOTHER CHANCE
LET'S SING AGAIN
LET'S SIT AND TALK ABOUT YOU
LIFE CAN BE BEAUTIFUL
LONESOMEST GIRL IN TOWN, THE
LOST IN A FOG
LOVELY LADY
LOVELY TO LOOK AT
LOVELY WAY TO SPEND AN
   EVENING, A
LUCKY FELLA
MURDER, HE SAYS
MUSIC STOPPED, THE
MY, HOW THE TIME GOES BY
MY! MY!
MY DANCING LADY
MY DREAM OF THE BIG PARADE
MY FINE FEATHERED FRIEND
MY OWN
ON THE SUNNY SIDE OF THE
   STREET
OUT WHERE THE BLUES BEGIN
PICTURE ME WITHOUT YOU
PORGY
RENDEZVOUS TIME IN PAREE
SAY A PRAYER FOR THE BOYS OVER
   THERE
SAY IT (OVER AND OVER AGAIN)
SERENADE TO THE STARS, A
SING A TROPICAL SONG
SINGIN' THE BLUES
SOUTH AMERICAN WAY
SPEAKING CONFIDENTIALLY
SPREADIN' RHYTHM AROUND
TAKE IT EASY

THANK YOU FOR A LOVELY
   EVENING
THAT FOOLISH FEELING
THERE'S A NEW STAR IN HEAVEN
   TONIGHT—RUDOLPH VALENTINO
THERE'S SOMETHING IN THE AIR
THIS NEVER HAPPENED BEFORE
TOO YOUNG TO GO STEADY
TOP OF THE TOWN
TOUCH OF TEXAS, A
TRAMPS AT SEA
WHAT HAS BECOME OF HINKY
   DINKY PARLAY VOO?
WHEN MY SUGAR WALKS DOWN
   THE STREET
WHEN YOU AND I WERE YOUNG,
   MAGGIE, BLUES
WHERE ARE YOU?
WHERE THE LAZY RIVER GOES BY
WITH A BANJO ON MY KNEE
WITH ALL MY HEART
YOU'RE AN ANGEL
YOU'RE AS PRETTY AS A PICTURE
YOU'RE A SWEETHEART
YOU'RE MY DISH
YOU'RE THE ONE
YOU SAY THE NICEST THINGS, BABY
YOU SEND ME
YOU'VE GOT ME THIS WAY (WHATTA
   YA GONNA DO ABOUT IT?)

McIntosh, Carl

HANGIN' ON A STRING
   (CONTEMPLATING)

McIntosh, Robbie

CUT THE CAKE

McIntyre, Lani

ONE ROSE, THE (THAT'S LEFT IN MY
   HEART)

McIntyre, Mark

MONEY TREE, THE
TROUBLE WITH HARRY, THE

McIntyre, Onnie

CUT THE CAKE

McKay, Albert

BEST OF MY LOVE
SATURDAY NITE
SEPTEMBER
SING A SONG

McKee, Maria

SWEET, SWEET BABY (I'M FALLING)

McKenna, William J.

EVERYBODY LOVES AN IRISH SONG
HAS ANYBODY HERE SEEN KELLY?

McKenney, Stanley

HOMELY GIRL

McKenzie, Marion

LITTLE TOWN FLIRT

McKenzie, Scott

WHAT ABOUT ME

McKinley, Ray

HOODLE ADDLE
MY GUY'S COME BACK

McKinney, Jimmy

I DON'T WANT TO LOSE YOUR LOVE
LITTLE BIT MORE, A

McKinney, Sami

JUST BECAUSE

McKinney, Sylvia

IT'S GONNA WORK OUT FINE

McKuen, Rod

ALLY ALLY OXEN FREE
IF YOU GO AWAY
JEAN
SEASONS IN THE SUN
SING BOY SING

McKuen, Rod

WORLD I USED TO KNOW, THE

McLaughlin, Pat

LYNDA

McLean, Don

AMERICAN PIE
AND I LOVE YOU SO
CASTLES IN THE AIR
DREIDEL
IF WE TRY
VINCENT
WONDERFUL BABY

McLellan, C. M. S.

BY THE SASKATCHEWAN
KISS WALTZ
MY BEAUTIFUL LADY (KISS WALTZ)
OH! OH! DELPHINE
VENUS WALTZ

McLemore, William

I'LL BE TRUE

McLeod, Bill

HONEYTHIEF, THE

McLeod, Brian

MY GIRL (GONE, GONE, GONE)

McLeod, Marilyn

LET ME TICKLE YOUR FANCY
LOVE HANGOVER
POPS, WE LOVE YOU (A TRIBUTE TO
FATHER)
YOU CAN'T TURN ME OFF (IN THE
MIDDLE OF TURNING ME ON)

McLeod, Odell

THAT GLORY BOUND TRAIN

McMahan, Sharon

SOMEDAY WE'RE GONNA LOVE
AGAIN

McManus, Pat

AMERICAN MADE
LITTLE ROCK

McMichael, Ted

BY-U, BY-O (THE LOU'SIANA
LULLABY)
HUT-SUT SONG, THE

McMichen, C. "Pappy"

PEACH PICKING TIME DOWN IN
GEORGIA

McMurray, Clay

IF I WERE YOUR WOMAN
MAKE ME THE WOMAN THAT YOU
GO HOME TO

McNamara, Ted

SOONER OR LATER

McNaughton, F.

RIVERS OF BABYLON

McNeely, Cecil J.

DEACON'S HOP

McNeely, Jay

THERE'S SOMETHING ON YOUR
MIND

McNeil, Landy

IF I COULD REACH YOU

McNeil, Michael

ALIVE AND KICKING

McNicol, Steve

YOU, I

McPhail, Lindsay

SAN

McPhatter, Clyde

HONEY LOVE
TA TA

McPherson, Harry

ROLL ALONG, PRAIRIE MOON

McPherson, Jim

JANE

McPherson, Tim

BACKFIELD IN MOTION

McPherson, Warner

HOW LONG WILL IT TAKE
I'M GONNA MOVE ON
IS IT WRONG (FOR LOVING YOU)
LEAVE MY DREAM ALONE
TALKIN' TO THE WALL
THEN A TEAR FELL

McQueen, George

FOOL IN LOVE, A

McRae, Floyd F.

SH-BOOM (LIFE COULD BE A
DREAM)

McRae, Johnny

DON'T CALL HIM A COWBOY

McRae, Teddy

ALL SHE WANTS TO DO IS ROCK
A-SLEEPIN' AT THE FOOT OF THE
BED
BACK BAY SHUFFLE
LOVE, LOVE, LOVE
TRAFFIC JAM
YOU SHOWED ME THE WAY

McRee, Bob

LOVER'S HOLIDAY
PICKIN' WILD MOUNTAIN BERRIES

McShann, Jay

CONFESSIN' THE BLUES
HANDS OFF
HOOTIE BLUES

McShear, Tony

TOO MANY TIMES

McVea, Jack

OH, THAT'LL BE JOYFUL
OPEN THE DOOR, RICHARD

McVey, Cameron

BUFFALO STANCE

McVie, Christine

DON'T STOP
EVERYWHERE
GOT A HOLD ON ME
HOLD ME
LITTLE LIES
OVER MY HEAD
SAY YOU LOVE ME
THINK ABOUT ME
YOU MAKE LOVING FUN

Meacham, E. H.

AMERICAN PATROL
WE MUST BE VIGILANT

Meade, Norman

CRY BABY

Meadows, Fred

YOU WERE ONLY FOOLING (WHILE I
WAS FALLING IN LOVE)

Meadows, J.

CUTIE PIE

Mears, John

ALWAYS HAVE ALWAYS WILL
I FOUND THE END OF THE
RAINBOW

Meassager, Andre

LONG AGO IN ALCALA

Meaux, Huey P.

RAINS CAME, THE

Mecum, Dudley

ANGRY

Medeira, Paul

I'M GLAD THERE IS YOU

Medici, L.

NEW ORLEANS LADIES

Medina, Mamie

THAT DA DA STRAIN

Medley, Bill

GO AHEAD AND CRY
LITTLE LATIN LUPE LU

Medley, Phil

IF I DIDN'T HAVE A DIME (TO PLAY
THE JUKEBOX)
MILLION TO ONE, A
TWIST AND SHOUT

Medonça, Newton

DESIFINADO
MEDITATION (MEDITACAO)
ONE NOTE SAMBA

Medora, John

AT THE HOP

Medress, Henry

I HEAR TRUMPETS BLOW

Meehan, Danny

WHERE ARE YOU GOING

Meek, Joe

TELSTAR

Meher, T.

CENTURY'S END

Mehlinger, Artie

HIAWATHA'S MELODY OF LOVE

Meier, Dieter

OH YEAH

Meinard, Helen

APRIL IN MY HEART

Meine, Klaus

ROCK YOU LIKE A HURRICANE

Meinken, Fred

WABASH BLUES

Meisner, Randy

DEEP INSIDE MY HEART
HEARTS ON FIRE
TAKE IT TO THE LIMIT

Mekler, Gabriel

KOZMIC BLUES
MOVE OVER

Melcher, Terry

BEACH GIRL
GETCHA BACK
GOOD THING
GREAT AIRPLANE STRIKE, THE

HIM OR ME, WHAT'S IT GONNA BE?
I HAD A DREAM
KOKOMO
PEACE OF MIND
UPS AND DOWNS

Melfi, Johnny

KID AGAIN, A

Mellencamp, John Cougar

AIN'T EVEN DONE WITH THE NIGHT
AUTHORITY SONG, THE
CHECK IT OUT
CHERRY BOMB
CRUMBLIN' DOWN
HAND TO HOLD ON TO
HURT SO GOOD
I NEED A LOVER
JACK AND DIANE
LONELY OL' NIGHT
PAPER IN FIRE
PINK HOUSES
SMALL PARADISE
SMALL TOWN

Mellin, Robert

BLUEBIRD ON YOUR WINDOWSILL
    (THERE'S A)
I'M ALWAYS HEARING WEDDING
    BELLS
I'M YOURS
IT ISN'T RIGHT
MAN WITH THE BANJO, THE
MY ONE AND ONLY LOVE
STRANGER ON THE SHORE
YOU, YOU, YOU

Mellor, Tom

COME ALONG, MY MANDY
WHEN IT'S APPLE BLOSSOM TIME IN
    NORMANDY

Melody, Lord

MAMA LOOK A BOOBOO

Melrose, Walter

COPENHAGEN
DOCTOR JAZZ
MAKE LOVE TO ME
SUGAR FOOT STOMP
TIN ROOF BLUES

Melshee, Mart

BRIDGE WASHED OUT, THE
SITTIN' ON A ROCK (CRYIN' IN A
    CREEK)

Melsher, Irving

CRY BABY CRY
SO LONG
THERE'S NO WINGS ON MY ANGEL

Melson, Joe

BLUE ANGEL
BLUE BAYOU
CROWD, THE
CRYING
I'M HURTIN'
ONLY THE LONELY (KNOW THE WAY
    I FEEL)
RUN, BABY, RUN (BACK INTO MY
    ARMS)
RUNNING SCARED

Meltzer, Richard

BURNIN' FOR YOU

Members, Jackie

THIN LINE BETWEEN LOVE AND
    HATE

Mencher, Murray

ALICE IN WONDERLAND
DON'T BREAK THE HEART THAT
    LOVES YOU
FLOWERS FOR MADAME
FOLLOW THE BOYS
IT'S NO FUN
I WANT A LITTLE GIRL
MEANEST THING YOU EVER DID
    WAS KISS ME, THE

OLD WATER MILL, AN
ON THE BUMPY ROAD TO LOVE
RO-RO-ROLLIN' ALONG
SING A LITTLE LOW DOWN TUNE
TAKE ANOTHER GUESS
THROW ANOTHER LOG ON THE FIRE
WHOSE HEART ARE YOU BREAKING
    TONIGHT?
YOU CAN'T PULL THE WOOL OVER
    MY EYES

Mende, Gunther

POWER OF LOVE, THE

Mendelsohn, Fred

DON'T BE ANGRY
RED RIVER ROCK

Mendez, Ricardo Lopez

AMOR
STARS IN YOUR EYES (A.K.A. MARS)

Menendez, Nilo

GREEN EYES

Menken, Alan

FEED ME: GIT IT
KISS THE GIRL
MEAN GREEN MOTHER FROM
    OUTER SPACE
MEEK SHALL INHERIT, THE
SOMEWHERE THAT'S GREEN
UNDER THE SEA

Mercer, Johnny

AC-CENT-TCHU-ATE THE POSITIVE
AFTERBEAT, THE
AFTER TWELVE O'CLOCK
AND THE ANGELS SING
ANY PLACE I HANG MY HAT IS
    HOME
ARTHUR MURRAY TAUGHT ME
    DANCING IN A HURRY
AUTUMN LEAVES
BAD HUMOR MAN, THE
BERNADINE

BIG MOVIE SHOW IN THE SKY
BILBAO SONG, THE
BLESS YORE BEAUTIFUL HIDE
BLUE RAIN
BLUES IN THE NIGHT
BOB WHITE (WHATCHA GONNA SWING TONIGHT?)
CAKEWALK YOUR LADY
CAPTAINS OF THE CLOUDS
CHARADE
COME RAIN OR COME SHINE
CONFIDENTIALLY
COULD BE
COWBOY FROM BROOKLYN
CUCKOO IN THE CLOCK
DAY DREAMING ALL NIGHT LONG
DAY IN—DAY OUT
DAYS OF WINE AND ROSES
DEARLY BELOVED
DIXIELAND BAND
DOWN T'UNCLE BILL'S
DREAM
EARLY AUTUMN
EENY, MEENY, MEINY, MO
EMILY
EMPTY TABLES
EVERY SO OFTEN
FACTS OF LIFE, THE
FARE-THEE-WELL TO HARLEM
FLEET'S IN, THE
FOOLS RUSH IN
FOREVER AMBER
GARDEN OF THE MOON
G.I. JIVE
GIRL FRIEND OF THE WHIRLING DERVISH, THE
GLOW-WORM, THE
GOODY GOODY
GOTTA GET SOME SHUT-EYE
HAVE YOU GOT ANY CASTLES, BABY?
HE LOVED ME TILL THE ALL-CLEAR CAME
HERE COME THE BRITISH
HERE'S TO MY LADY
HIT THE ROAD TO DREAMLAND
HOORAY FOR HOLLYWOOD
HOW LITTLE WE KNOW
I COULD KISS YOU FOR THAT
I'D KNOW YOU ANYWHERE
I'D RATHER BE ME
IF I HAD A MILLION DOLLARS
IF I HAD MY DRUTHERS

IF YOU BUILD A BETTER MOUSETRAP
IF YOU WANT TO BE A TOP BANANA
IF YOU WERE MINE
I HAD MYSELF A TRUE LOVE
I'LL CRY TOMORROW
I'LL DREAM TONIGHT
I'M AN OLD COW HAND (FROM THE RIO GRANDE)
I'M BUILDING UP TO AN AWFUL LETDOWN
I'M OLD FASHIONED
I NEVER SAW A BETTER NIGHT
IN THE COOL, COOL, COOL OF THE EVENING
I PROMISE YOU
I REMEMBER YOU
I SAW HER AT EIGHT O'CLOCK
IT'S ABOUT TIME
IT'S A GREAT BIG WORLD
IT'S GREAT TO BE ALIVE
I'VE GOT A ONE TRACK MIND
I'VE HITCHED MY WAGON TO A STAR
I WALK WITH MUSIC
I WANNA BE AROUND
I WONDER WHAT BECAME OF ME
JAMBOREE JONES
JEEPERS CREEPERS
JEZEBEL
JUBILATION T. CORNPONE
JUNE COMES AROUND EVERY YEAR
JUST A QUIET EVENING
LAURA
LAZYBONES
LAZY MOOD
LEGALIZE MY NAME
LET'S TAKE THE LONG WAY HOME
LET THAT BE A LESSON TO YOU
LIFE IS WHAT YOU MAKE IT
LONESOME POLECAT
LOST
LOT IN COMMON, A
LOVE IN A HOME
LOVE IS A MERRY-GO-ROUND
LOVE IS ON THE AIR TONIGHT
LOVE IS WHERE YOU FIND IT
LOVE OF MY LIFE, THE
LOVE WITH THE PROPER STRANGER
MAKE WITH THE KISSES
MANDY IS TWO
MIDNIGHT SUN
MISTER MEADOWLARK

MOON COUNTRY
MOONLIGHT ON THE CAMPUS
MOON RIVER
MUTINY IN THE NURSERY
MY SHINING HOUR
NAMELY YOU
NOT MINE
OLD MUSIC MASTER, THE
ON BEHALF OF THE VISITING FIREMEN
ONCE UPON A SUMMERTIME
ONE FOR MY BABY (AND ONE MORE FOR THE ROAD)
ON THE ATCHISON, TOPEKA, AND THE SANTA FE
OOH, WHAT YOU SAID!
OUT OF BREATH (AND SCARED TO DEATH OF YOU)
OUT OF THIS WORLD
PARDON MY SOUTHERN ACCENT
PETER PIPER
PINK PANTHER THEME, THE
P.S. I LOVE YOU
RIDE, TENDERFOOT, RIDE
SATAN'S LITTLE LAMB
SATIN DOLL
SAY IT WITH A KISS
SAYS WHO? SAYS YOU, SAYS I!
SENTIMENTAL AND MELANCHOLY
SILHOUETTED IN THE MOONLIGHT
SKYLARK
SLUEFOOT
SOBBIN' WOMEN
SOMETHING'S GOTTA GIVE
SOMETHING TELLS ME
SPRING, SPRING, SPRING
STRIP POLKA, THE
SUMMER WIND
SWEETHEART TREE, THE
TALK TO ME, BABY
TANGERINE
THANKSGIVIN'
THAT OLD BLACK MAGIC
THIS TIME THE DREAM'S ON ME
TOO MARVELOUS FOR WORDS
TRAV'LIN' LIGHT
TWO OF A KIND
WAIT AND SEE
WAITER AND THE PORTER AND THE UPSTAIRS MAID, THE
WEEKEND OF A PRIVATE SECRETARY, THE

WHEN A WOMAN LOVES A MAN
WHEN THE WORLD WAS YOUNG
   (AH, THE APPLE TREES)
WHEN YOU HEAR THE TIME SIGNAL
WHEN YOU'RE IN LOVE
WHISTLING AWAY THE DARK
WILD, WILD WEST, THE
WINDMILL UNDER THE STARS
WOMAN'S PREROGATIVE, A
WONDERFUL, WONDERFUL DAY
WOULD'JA FOR A BIG RED APPLE?
YOU AND YOUR LOVE
YOU CAN'T RUN AWAY FROM IT
YOU GROW SWEETER AS THE
   YEARS GO BY
YOU HAVE TAKEN MY HEART
YOU MUST HAVE BEEN A
   BEAUTIFUL BABY
YOU'RE THE ONE
YOU'VE GOT ME THIS WAY (WHATTA
   YA GONNA DO ABOUT IT?)
YOU'VE GOT SOMETHING THERE
YOU WERE NEVER LOVELIER

Mercer, Kelvin

ME, MYSELF, AND I

Merchant, Michael Dee

TIME

Mercury, Freddie

BICYCLE RACE
BODY LANGUAGE
BOHEMIAN RHAPSODY
CRAZY LITTLE THING CALLED LOVE
KILLER QUEEN
SOMEBODY TO LOVE
WE ARE THE CHAMPIONS

Merl, Maurice

I'M A LONELY LITTLE PETUNIA (IN
   AN ONION PATCH)

Meroff, Benny

LONELY MELODY

Merrell, Wanda

PEPINO'S FRIEND PASQUAL (THE
   ITALIAN PUSSY-CAT)
PEPINO THE ITALIAN MOUSE

Merrill, Alan

I LOVE ROCK 'N' ROLL

Merrill, Blanche

I'M AN INDIAN

Merrill, Bob

ABOVE THE STARS
ABSENT MINDED ME
BEAUTIFUL CANDY
BELLE, BELLE, MY LIBERTY BELLE
BUTTERFLIES
CANDY AND CAKE
CAUSE I LOVE YOU, THAT'S A-WHY
CHICKEN SONG, THE (I AIN'T
   GONNA TAKE IT SETTIN' DOWN)
CORNET MAN
DID YOU CLOSE YOUR EYES? (WHEN
   WE KISSED)
DOGGIE IN THE WINDOW, THE
DON'T RAIN ON MY PARADE
FEET UP (PAT HIM ON THE PO-PO)
FLINGS
FOOL'S PARADISE
FUNNY (NOT MUCH)
FUNNY GIRL
HER FACE
HONEYCOMB
IF I KNEW YOU WERE COMIN' I'D'VE
   BAKED A CAKE
I'M THE GREATEST STAR
IT'S ALWAYS LOVE
IT'S GOOD TO BE ALIVE
LET ME IN
LOOK AT 'ER
LOVE MAKES THE WORLD GO
   'ROUND
LOVER'S GOLD
MAKE YOURSELF COMFORTABLE
MAMBO ITALIANO
MIRA (CAN YOU IMAGINE THAT?)
MIRACLE OF LOVE
MUSIC THAT MAKES ME DANCE,
   THE

MY TRULY, TRULY FAIR
PEOPLE
PITTSBURGH, PENNSYLVANIA
SADIE, SADIE
SHE'S MY LOVE
SO LONG, SALLY
SPARROW IN THE TREE TOP
STAYING YOUNG
SUNSHINE GIRL (HAS RAINDROPS IN
   HER EYES)
SWEET OLD FASHIONED GIRL, A
TAKE ME ALONG
THAT HOUND DOG IN THE WINDOW
TINA MARIE
TOYS
WALKIN' TO MISSOURI
WE COULD BE CLOSE
WHEN THE BOYS TALK ABOUT THE
   GIRLS
WHO ARE YOU NOW?
WHY DOES IT HAVE TO RAIN ON
   SUNDAY?
YES, MY HEART
YOU ARE WOMAN, I AM MAN
YOU DON'T HAVE TO BE A BABY TO
   CRY

Merrill, George

HOW WILL I KNOW
I WANNA DANCE WITH SOMEBODY
   (WHO LOVES ME)
SIMPLY MEANT TO BE
WAITING FOR A STAR TO FALL

Merritt, Leon

MAMA, COME GET YOUR BABY BOY

Merritt, Neal

MAY THE BIRD OF PARADISE FLY
   UP YOUR NOSE

Merritt, O. O.

BON VOYAGE
THAT'S WHY I WAS BORN

Merson, Billy

SPANIARD THAT BLIGHTED MY LIFE,
   THE

Mescoli, Gino

MY LOVE, FORGIVE ME (AMORE, SCUSAMI)

Meshel, Wilbur

L. DAVID SLOANE

Meskill, Jack

AU REVOIR, PLEASANT DREAMS
HERE COMES EMILY BROWN
IT MIGHT HAVE BEEN A DIFF'RENT STORY
I WAS LUCKY
ONE LITTLE RAINDROP
ON THE BEACH AT BALI-BALI
PARDON ME, PRETTY BABY
RHYTHM OF THE RAIN
SANTA CLAUS IS RIDING THE TRAIL
SMILE, DARN YA, SMILE
THERE'S DANGER IN YOUR EYES, CHERIE
WERE YOU SINCERE?
WONDERFUL YOU

Messenheimer, Sam

SINGING A VAGABOND SONG

Messina, Jim

MY MUSIC
THINKING OF YOU
WATCHING THE RIVER RUN
YOU BETTER THINK TWICE
YOUR MAMA DON'T DANCE

Metcalf, John W.

ABSENT

Metcalfe, Clive

SUMMER SONG, A

Metcalfe, Gerald

PRISONER OF HOPE

Metheny, Pat

THIS IS NOT AMERICA

Methuen, Florence

WHEN YOU LOOK IN THE HEART OF A ROSE

Metis, Frank

ENCHANTED SEA, THE

Metis, John, Jr.

NEED YOUR LOVE SO BAD

Metz, Theodore H.

HOT TIME IN THE OLD TOWN TONIGHT

Metzger, Ros

ONE CIGARETTE FOR TWO

Mevis, Alan R.

FOOL HEARTED MEMORY

Mevis, Blake

IF YOU'RE THINKING YOU WANT A STRANGER (THERE'S ONE COMING HOME)

Meyer, Chuck

SUDDENLY THERE'S A VALLEY

Meyer, Don

FOR HEAVEN'S SAKE

Meyer, George W.

BRING BACK MY DADDY TO ME
BRING BACK MY GOLDEN DREAMS
BROWN EYES, WHY ARE YOU BLUE?
COVER ME UP WITH THE SUNSHINE OF VIRGINIA
'CROSS THE GREAT DIVIDE (I'LL WAIT FOR YOU)
DEAR OLD ROSE
DON'T WAKE UP MY HEART
EVERYTHING IS PEACHES DOWN IN GEORGIA
FOR ME AND MY GAL
GIRLIE WAS JUST MADE TO LOVE, A
HIAWATHA'S MELODY OF LOVE
HONEY-LOVE
I BELIEVE IN MIRACLES
IF HE CAN FIGHT LIKE HE CAN LOVE, GOOD NIGHT GERMANY
IF I CAN'T HAVE YOU
IF I ONLY HAD A MATCH
I'M A LITTLE BLACKBIRD LOOKING FOR A BLUEBIRD
I'M AWFULLY GLAD I MET YOU
I'M GROWING FONDER OF YOU
I'M SURE OF EVERYTHING BUT YOU
IN A LITTLE BOOKSHOP
IN THE LAND OF BEGINNING AGAIN
JUST LIKE WASHINGTON CROSSED THE DELAWARE, GENERAL PERSHING WILL CROSS THE RHINE
LONESOME
MANDY, MAKE UP YOUR MIND
MY MOTHER'S ROSARY (OR, TEN BABY FINGERS AND TEN BABY TOES)
MY SONG OF THE NILE
RING ON THE FINGER IS WORTH TWO ON THE PHONE, A
SITTIN' IN A CORNER
SOMEBODY ELSE, IT'S ALWAYS SOMEBODY ELSE
THAT MELLOW MELODY
THAT WAS BEFORE I MET YOU
THERE ARE SUCH THINGS
THERE'S A DIXIE GIRL WHO'S LONGING FOR A YANKEE DOODLE BOY
THERE'S A LITTLE LANE WITHOUT A TURNING ON THE WAY TO HOME, SWEET HOME
TO WHOM IT MAY CONCERN
TUCK ME TO SLEEP IN MY OLD 'TUCKY HOME
WE WERE THE BEST OF FRIENDS
WHEN YOU'RE A LONG, LONG WAY FROM HOME
WHERE DID ROBINSON CRUSOE GO WITH FRIDAY ON SATURDAY NIGHT?

Meyer, George W.

YOU TAUGHT ME HOW TO LOVE
  YOU, NOW TEACH ME TO FORGET

Meyer, Joseph

ACCORDING TO THE MOONLIGHT
BLUE RIVER
BUT I DID
CALIFORNIA, HERE I COME
CHERRY BLOSSOMS ON CAPITOL
  HILL
CLAP HANDS! HERE COMES
  CHARLEY!
CRAZY RHYTHM
CUP OF COFFEE, A SANDWICH AND
  YOU, A
FANCY OUR MEETING
GOLDEN GATE
HAPPY GO LUCKY LANE
HEADIN' FOR LOUISVILLE
HELLO 'TUCKY
HOW LONG WILL IT LAST?
HUNKADOLA
HURRY HOME
IF YOU KNEW SUSIE (LIKE I KNOW
  SUSIE)
IMAGINATION
ISN'T IT HEAVENLY?
IT'S AN OLD SOUTHERN CUSTOM
I WISH I WERE TWINS
JUNK MAN
JUST A LITTLE CLOSER
LOVE LIES
MEADOWS OF HEAVEN, THE
MY HONEY'S LOVIN' ARMS
PASSÉ
SINGING A SONG TO THE STARS
SOMETHING TO LIVE FOR
YOU'RE SIMPLY DELISH

Meyer, Richard

SUPER BOWL SHUFFLE

Meyer, Stanley

ONE EARLY MORNING

Meyers, Billy

BUGLE CALL RAG
NOBODY'S SWEETHEART
ORIENTAL

Michael, George

CARELESS WHISPER
EDGE OF HEAVEN, THE
EVERYTHING SHE WANTS
FAITH
FATHER FIGURE
FREEDOM
I'M YOUR MAN
I WANT YOUR SEX
KISSING A FOOL
MONKEY
ONE MORE TRY
WAKE ME UP BEFORE YOU GO-GO

Michael, M.

CARRIE

Michael, Steven

SOMEONE YOU LOVE

Michael, William

MISSION BELL

Michaels, Bret

I WON'T FORGET YOU
NOTHIN' BUT A GOOD TIME
TALK DIRTY TO ME

Michaels, Lee

DO YOU KNOW WHAT I MEAN

Michaels, Tony

HAPPY

Michalski, J.

PSYCHOTIC REACTION

Michels, Walter

SAN

Mickens, Robert

HOLLYWOOD SWINGING

Middlebrook, Ralph

FIRE
FUNKY WORM
LOVE ROLLERCOASTER
SKIN TIGHT
SWEET STICKY THING
WHO'D SHE COO

Middlebrooks, Harry

SPOOKY

Midler, Bette

YOU'RE MOVIN' OUT TODAY

Midnight, Charlie

LIVING IN AMERICA

Midnight Star

HEADLINES

Mierisch, Fred E.

AT THE LEVEE ON REVIVAL DAY

Migliacci, Francesco

SON OF A TRAVELIN' MAN

Mikaljohn

I LOVE THE WAY YOU LOVE

Miketta, Bob

ROBIN HOOD

Mikolas, Joe

MEXICAN PEARLS

Milburn, Ken

STOP THE START (OF TEARS IN MY
  HEART)

Miles, Alfred H.

ANCHORS AWEIGH

Miles, C. Austin

IN THE GARDEN (HE WALKS WITH
ME AND HE TALKS WITH ME)

Miles, Dick

COFFEE SONG, THE (THEY'VE GOT
AN AWFUL LOT OF COFFEE IN
BRAZIL)
I'LL REMEMBER SUZANNE

Miles, Nat

YOU'RE ALWAYS THERE

Miles, Richard

JACK, YOU'RE DEAD

Miley, Bubber

DOWN IN THE MOUTH BLUES
EAST ST. LOUIS TOODLE-OO
GOIN' TO TOWN
LENOX AVENUE SHUFFLE

Millas, Larry

YOU WOULDN'T LISTEN

Miller, Bernard

I CAN'T STAND THE RAIN

Miller, Bernie

BERNIE'S TUNE

Miller, Bob

CHIME BELLS
SEVEN YEARS WITH THE WRONG
WOMAN
THINGS THAT MIGHT HAVE BEEN
TWENTY-ONE YEARS

Miller, Bobby

ALWAYS TOGETHER
DOES ANYBODY KNOW I'M HERE?
STAY IN MY CORNER
THERE IS

WEAR IT ON OUR FACE

Miller, C.

GYPSY MAN

Miller, Charles

CISCO KID, THE
L.A. SUNSHINE
LOW RIDER
ME AND BABY BROTHER
SUMMER
WHEN YOUR LOVE GROWS COLD
WHY CAN'T WE BE FRIENDS?
WORLD IS A GHETTO, THE
YOU REMIND ME OF THE GIRL THAT
USED TO GO TO SCHOOL WITH
ME!

Miller, Eddie

AFTER LOVING YOU
I'D RATHER DRINK MUDDY WATER
LAZY MOOD
RELEASE ME
THANKS A LOT
THERE SHE GOES

Miller, Ed E.

DON'T LET THE RAIN COME DOWN
(CROOKED LITTLE MAN)

Miller, Ellen

DON'T SAY YOU DON'T REMEMBER

Miller, Everett

OUT OF BREATH (AND SCARED TO
DEATH OF YOU)

Miller, Francis

MARRIED BUT NOT TO EACH OTHER

Miller, Frank

GREENFIELDS
LOVE IS A GOLDEN RING
MARIANNE
MEMORIES ARE MADE OF THIS

MISTER TAP TOE

Miller, Frankie

BLACKLAND FARMER
LIE TO YOU FOR YOUR LOVE
WHEN I'M AWAY FROM YOU

Miller, Glenn

MOONLIGHT SERENADE

Miller, Helen

CHARMS
FOOLISH LITTLE GIRL
IT HURTS TO BE IN LOVE
MAKE ME YOUR BABY
PRINCESS IN RAGS

Miller, Henry S.

CAT CAME BACK, THE

Miller, Herb

NIGHT

Miller, J.

PLANET ROCK
THIS SHOULD GO ON FOREVER

Miller, J. D.

CRY, CRY, DARLING
IT WASN'T GOD WHO MADE HONKY
TONK ANGELS
THAT'S ME WITHOUT YOU
WITHOUT YOU

Miller, Jimmy

I'M A MAN

Miller, Joseph Taps

WHAM

Miller, Julian H.

MORE BEER

Miller, Kim

I GOT MY MIND MADE UP (YOU CAN
    GET IT GIRL)

Miller, Lost John

ANSWER TO RAINBOW AT MIDNIGHT
RAINBOW AT MIDNIGHT

Miller, M.

OASIS

Miller, Marcus

ANY LOVE
DA'BUTT
GET IT RIGHT
JUMP TO IT
'TILL MY BABY COMES HOME

Miller, Mark

STEP THAT STEP

Miller, Melvin

BURNING BRIDGES

Miller, Ned

BEHIND THE TEARS
DARK MOON
DON'T MIND THE RAIN
DO WHAT YOU DO, DO WELL
FROM A JACK TO A KING
INVISIBLE TEARS
LITTLE JOE
MY SUPPRESSED DESIRE
SNOW FLAKE
SUNDAY
WHO'S BEEN CHEATIN' WHO?
WHY SHOULD I CRY OVER YOU?
YOU DON'T LIKE IT—NOT MUCH

Miller, Roger

BILLY BAYOU
CHUG-A-LUG
DANG ME
DERN YA
DON'T WE ALL HAVE THE RIGHT

DO-WACKA-DO
ENGINE, ENGINE NUMBER NINE
ENGLAND SWINGS
HALF A MIND
HEARTACHE FOR A KEEPSAKE
HOME
HUSBANDS AND WIVES
IT HAPPENED JUST THAT WAY
KANSAS CITY STAR
KING OF THE ROAD
LAST WORD IN LONESOME IS ME,
    THE
LESS AND LESS
LOCK, STOCK, AND TEARDROPS
MEADOWGREEN
MUDDY WATER
MY EARS SHOULD BURN (WHEN
    FOOLS ARE TALKED ABOUT)
MY UNCLE USED TO LOVE ME BUT
    SHE DIED
ONE DYIN' AND A BURYIN'
PRIVATE JOHN Q.
QUEEN OF THE HOUSE
RIVER IN THE RAIN
WALKIN', TALKIN', CRYIN', BARELY
    BEATIN', BROKEN HEART
WALKING IN THE SUNSHINE
WHEN TWO WORLDS COLLIDE
WORLD SO FULL OF LOVE, A
YOU CAN'T ROLLER SKATE IN A
    BUFFALO HERD
YOU DON'T WANT MY LOVE

Miller, Ronald

FOR ONCE IN MY LIFE
HEAVEN HELP US ALL
I'VE NEVER BEEN TO ME
MERCY, MERCY
PLACE IN THE SUN, A
STEAL ON HOME
TOUCH ME IN THE MORNING
TRAVLIN' MAN
YESTER-ME, YESTER-YOU,
    YESTERDAY

Miller, Scott

I GOT MY MIND MADE UP (YOU CAN
    GET IT GIRL)

Miller, Seymour

SOMEBODY NOBODY LOVES

Miller, Sidney

COME TO BABY, DO
I WAITED A LITTLE TOO LONG
WHAT DO I HAVE TO DO TO MAKE
    YOU LOVE ME?

Miller, Sonny

GOT A DATE WITH AN ANGEL
SILVER WINGS IN THE MOONLIGHT

Miller, Steve

ABRACADABRA
FLY LIKE AN EAGLE
I WANT TO MAKE THE WORLD TURN
    AROUND
JOKER, THE
LIVING IN THE U.S.A.
ROCK'N ME
SWINGTOWN
TAKE THE MONEY AND RUN

Miller, Sue

BEHIND THE TEARS
DO WHAT YOU DO, DO WELL
INVISIBLE TEARS
WHO'S BEEN CHEATIN' WHO?

Miller, William

DADDY'S HOME

Miller, William H.

THOUSAND MILES AWAY, A

Millinder, Lucius "Lucky"

APOLLO JUMP
I'M WAITING JUST FOR YOU
LITTLE GIRL, DON'T CRY
SNEAKY PETE
SWEET SLUMBER
WHO THREW THE WHISKEY IN THE
    WELL?

Millington, Jean

CHARITY BALL

Millington, June

CHARITY BALL

Millrose, Vic

I'LL TRY ANYTHING
LAST CHANCE TO TURN AROUND
THIS GIRL IS A WOMAN NOW

Mills, A. J.

SHIP AHOY!—ALL THE NICE GIRLS
LOVE A SAILOR

Mills, Annette

BOOMPS-A-DAISY

Mills, Carley

IF I CARED A LITTLE BIT LESS

Mills, Charles

KNIGHT IN RUSTY ARMOUR
LADY GODIVA

Mills, Frank

MUSIC BOX DANCER

Mills, Gordon

I'M THE LONELY ONE
IT'S NOT UNUSUAL
LITTLE YOU
NOT RESPONSIBLE

Mills, Hank

GIRL ON THE BILLBOARD
KAY
LITTLE OLE WINEDRINKER ME

Mills, Irving

AZURE
BLACK BUTTERFLY

BLAME IT ON MY LAST AFFAIR
BLUE INTERLUDE
BLUE LOU
BLUES IN MY HEART
BONEYARD SHUFFLE
CARAVAN
DOUBLE CHECK STOMP
DOWN SOUTH CAMP MEETIN'
DUSK ON THE DESERT
EVERYTHING IS HOTSY TOTSY
    NOW
HARMONY IN HARLEM
IF DREAMS COME TRUE
IF YOU WERE IN MY PLACE
I LET A SONG GO OUT OF MY
    HEART
I'LL NEVER TELL YOU I LOVE YOU
I'M A HUNDRED PERCENT FOR YOU
IN A SENTIMENTAL MOOD
IT DON'T MEAN A THING (IF IT
    AIN'T GOT THAT SWING)
JITTER BUG
LIKE A BOLT FROM THE BLUE
LONESOME NIGHTS
LONESOMEST GIRL IN TOWN, THE
LONG ABOUT MIDNIGHT
LOST IN MEDITATION
LOVESICK BLUES
MINNIE THE MOOCHER (THE HO DE
    HO SONG)
MOOD INDIGO
MOONGLOW
MOON IS GRINNING AT ME, THE
MR. GHOST GOES TO TOWN
ORGAN GRINDER'S SWING
PRELUDE TO A KISS
PYRAMID
RING DEM BELLS
RIVERBOAT SHUFFLE
ROCKIN' IN RHYTHM
SCATTIN' AT THE KIT KAT
SIDEWALKS OF CUBA
SKRONTCH
SLOW FREIGHT
SOLITUDE
SOMEONE STOLE GABRIEL'S HORN
SOPHISTICATED LADY
STEPPIN' INTO SWING SOCIETY
STRAIGHTEN UP AND FLY RIGHT
SYMPHONY IN RIFFS
THAT AIN'T RIGHT
THERE'S A NEW STAR IN HEAVEN
    TONIGHT—RUDOLPH VALENTINO

THERE'S NO TWO WAYS ABOUT
    LOVE
THERE'S SOMETHING ABOUT AN
    OLD LOVE
WASHBOARD BLUES
WHAT HAS BECOME OF HINKY
    DINKY PARLAY VOO?
WHEN MY SUGAR WALKS DOWN
    THE STREET
YEARNING FOR LOVE
YOU'RE NOT THE KIND

Mills, Jay

EV'RY DAY AWAY FROM YOU

Mills, Kerry

ANY OLD PORT IN A STORM
AT A GEORGIA CAMP MEETING
HAPPY DAYS IN DIXIE
LET BYGONES BE BYGONES
LONGEST WAY 'ROUND IS THE
    SHORTEST WAY HOME, THE
MEET ME IN ST. LOUIS, LOUIS
RASTUS ON PARADE
RED WING (AN INDIAN FABLE)
TAKE ME AROUND AGAIN
WHEN THE BEES ARE IN THE HIVE
WHISTLING RUFUS

Mills, Kevin

I GO CRAZY

Mills, Mike

FALL ON ME
IT'S THE END OF THE WORLD AS
    WE KNOW IT (AND I FEEL FINE)
ONE I LOVE, THE
RADIO FREE EUROPE
ROMANCE
SOUTH CENTRAL RAIN (I'M SORRY)

Milman, Henry Hart

RIDE ON, RIDE ON

Milsap, Ronnie

SHOW HER

Milton, Jay

DON'T FORGET TONIGHT,
   TOMORROW
MINKA

Milton, Roy

BEST WISHES
INFORMATION BLUES

Mims, Joe

GET ON THE GOOD FOOT

Miner, Raynard

(YOUR LOVE KEEPS LIFTING ME)
   HIGHER AND HIGHER
RECOVERY
RESCUE ME
THERE IS
WE'RE GONNA MAKE IT
WHO'S CHEATING WHO?

Minkoff, Fran

BORNING DAY, THE
COME AWAY MELINDA

Minnifield, E.

HOLD ME

Minnigerode, Meade

WHIFFENPOOF SONG, THE

Minshall, Paul

IT'S ONLY MAKE BELIEVE

Minucci, Ulpio

DOMANI (TOMORROW)
I'LL NEVER KNOW
MY LOVE'S A GENTLE MAN

Miranda, Bob

GIRL ON A SWING

Miro, José

HIJACK

Miron, Issachar

TZENA, TZENA, TZENA

Misraki, Paul

MARIA FROM BAHIA
PASSING BY

Mitchell, Charles

YOU ARE MY SUNSHINE

Mitchell, Dan

IF YOU'RE GONNA PLAY IN TEXAS
   (YOU GOTTA HAVE A FIDDLE IN
   THE BAND)

Mitchell, George D.

ACE IN THE HOLE

Mitchell, James

FLOAT ON
I GO CRAZY

Mitchell, John

TWO OF HEARTS

Mitchell, Johnny

I BELIEVE IN YOU
WE BELONG TOGETHER

Mitchell, Joni

BIG YELLOW TAXI
BOTH SIDES NOW (A.K.A. FROM
   BOTH SIDES NOW)
CAREY
CHELSEA MORNING
CIRCLE GAME, THE
FOR THE ROSES
FREE MAN IN PARIS
GOOD FRIENDS
HELP ME

IN FRANCE THEY KISS ON MAIN
   STREET
LAST TIME I SAW RICHARD, THE
MICHAEL FROM THE MOUNTAINS
RAISED ON ROBBERY
URGE FOR GOING
WOODSTOCK
YOU TURN ME ON, I'M A RADIO

Mitchell, Mel

PASSING STRANGERS
PETTICOATS OF PORTUGAL
POOR BOY

Mitchell, Paul

TRYIN' TO LOVE TWO

Mitchell, Phillip

AS LONG AS HE TAKES CARE OF
   HOME
STARTING ALL OVER AGAIN

Mitchell, Robert

FLAME, THE

Mitchell, Sidney D.

AIN'T YOU ASHAMED?
ALL MY LIFE
AT THE CODFISH BALL
BALBOA
BIG CITY BLUES
BREAKAWAY, THE
EARLY BIRD
FOLLOW YOUR HEART
HITTIN' THE CEILING
IT'S LOVE I'M AFTER
LAUGHING IRISH EYES
MAMMY'S CHOCOLATE SOLDIER
MELODY FROM THE SKY, A
MOONSHINE OVER KENTUCKY
ONE IN A MILLION
SATURDAY
SEVENTH HEAVEN
SING A LITTLE LOVE SONG
SUGAR
TEXAS TORNADO
THAT'S YOU, BABY
TO WHOM IT MAY CONCERN

TOY TRUMPET, THE
TWILIGHT ON THE TRAIL
WALKING WITH SUSIE
WHO'S AFRAID OF LOVE?
WHY TALK ABOUT LOVE?
WOULD YOU RATHER BE A COLONEL
  WITH AN EAGLE ON YOUR
  SHOULDER OR A PRIVATE WITH
  A CHICKEN ON YOUR KNEE?
YOU DO THE DARNDEST THINGS,
  BABY
YOU KEEP SENDING 'EM OVER AND
  WE'LL KEEP KNOCKING 'EM
  DOWN
YOU'RE SLIGHTLY TERRIFIC
YOU TURNED THE TABLES ON ME

Mitchell, Steve

JUMP (FOR MY LOVE)

Mitchell, Willie

CALL ME (COME BACK HOME)
ECHOES OF LOVE
I'M STILL IN LOVE WITH YOU
LET'S STAY TOGETHER
LIVIN' FOR YOU
LOOK WHAT YOU DONE FOR ME
L-O-V-E (LOVE)
YOU OUGHT TO BE WITH ME

Mitchum, Robert

HEY! MISTER COTTON-PICKER

Mitoo, Jackie

PASS THE DUTCHIE

Mittenthal, Joseph

WHAT'S THE USE OF LOVING IF YOU
  CAN'T LOVE ALL THE TIME?

Mize, Billy

MY BABY WALKS ALL OVER ME

Mize, Buddy R.

SHOE GOES ON THE OTHER FOOT
  TONIGHT, THE

Mize, Vernon

I'VE RUN OUT OF TOMORROWS

Mizell, Fonce

ABC
I WANT YOU ALL TO MYSELF (JUST
  YOU)
LOVE YOU SAVE, THE
MAMA'S PEARL
SUGAR DADDY

Mizzy, Vic

CHOO'N GUM
DIDJA EVER?
I HAD A LITTLE TALK WITH THE
  LORD
I LIKE IT, I LIKE IT
I'LL NEVER FAIL YOU
JONES BOY, THE
KILLE KILLE (INDIAN LOVE TALK)
MY DREAMS ARE GETTING BETTER
  ALL THE TIME
PRETTY KITTY BLUE EYES
TAKE IT EASY
THERE'S A FAR AWAY LOOK IN
  YOUR EYE
THREE LITTLE SISTERS
WHOLE WORLD IS SINGING MY
  SONG, THE
WITH A HEY AND A HI AND A HO-
  HO-HO

Moarli, Jacques

IN THE NAVY

Mockridge, Cyril

IT'S A WOMAN'S WORLD

Modeliste, Joseph

CISSY STRUT
LOOK-KA PY PY
SOPHISTICATED CISSY

Modugno, Domenico

ASK ME
CIAO, CIAO, BAMBINA

STAY HERE WITH ME
VOLARE (A.K.A. NEL BLU, DIPINTO
  DI BLU)

Moeller, Tommy

CONCRETE AND CLAY

Moffatt, Hugh

OLD FLAMES (CAN'T HOLD A
  CANDLE TO YOU)

Moffett, Pamela

BABY COME CLOSE

Moffitt, Kenneth R.

OH JULIE

Mogo

AL DI LA
BELLA LINDA

Mohawk, Essra

CHANGE OF HEART

Mohr, Halsey K.

LIBERTY BELL, IT'S TIME TO RING
  AGAIN
PINEY RIDGE
THEY'RE WEARING 'EM HIGHER IN
  HAWAII

Moir, Monte

PLEASURE PRINCIPLE, THE

Molinare, Nicanor

CHIU, CHIU

Moll, Billy

AT THE CLOSE OF A LONG, LONG
  DAY
GID-AP GARIBALDI
HANG OUT THE STARS IN INDIANA

I SCREAM, YOU SCREAM (WE ALL
    SCREAM FOR ICE CREAM)
I WANT A LITTLE GIRL
MOONLIGHT ON THE COLORADO
RO-RO-ROLLIN' ALONG
SO THE BLUEBIRDS AND THE
    BLACKBIRDS GOT TOGETHER
WRAP YOUR TROUBLES IN DREAMS

Möller, Friedrich Wilhelm

HAPPY WANDERER, THE (VAL-DE-
    RI, VAL-DE-RA)

Mollica, James, III

ATOMIC

Moman, Chips

ANOTHER SOMEBODY DONE
    SOMEBODY WRONG SONG
LAST NIGHT
LUCKENBACH, TEXAS (BACK TO THE
    BASICS OF LOVE)
PARTNERS AFTER ALL
THIS TIME
WURLITZER PRIZE, THE (I DON'T
    WANT TO GET OVER YOU)

Monaco, James V.

ALL THAT I WANT IS YOU
APPLE FOR THE TEACHER, AN
APRIL PLAYED THE FIDDLE
BEATRICE FAIRFAX, TELL ME WHAT
    TO DO!
CARESSES
CRAZY PEOPLE
CRYING FOR JOY
DIRTY HANDS, DIRTY FACE
DON'T LET THAT MOON GET AWAY
EAST SIDE OF HEAVEN
EV'RY NIGHT ABOUT THIS TIME
GO FLY A KITE
HANG YOUR HEART ON A HICKORY
    LIMB
I CAN'T BEGIN TO TELL YOU
IF WE CAN'T BE THE SAME OLD
    SWEETHEARTS (WE'LL JUST BE
    THE SAME OLD FRIENDS)

I HAVEN'T TIME TO BE A
    MILLIONAIRE
I'LL TAKE CARE OF YOUR CARES
I'M CRYING JUST FOR YOU
I MISS YOU MOST OF ALL
I'M MAKING BELIEVE
IT MIGHT HAVE BEEN A DIFF'RENT
    STORY
I'VE GOT A POCKETFUL OF
    DREAMS
LAUGH AND CALL IT LOVE
LONESOME LOVER
MAN AND HIS DREAM, A
ME AND THE BOY FRIEND
ME AND THE MAN IN THE MOON
MEET THE SUN HALF WAY
MY HEART IS TAKING LESSONS
MY TROUBLES ARE OVER
OH, MR. DREAM MAN (PLEASE LET
    ME DREAM SOME MORE)
OH! YOU CIRCUS DAY
ONCE TOO OFTEN
ONLY, ONLY ONE FOR ME, THE
ONLY FOREVER
ON THE SENTIMENTAL SIDE
PESSIMISTIC CHARACTER, THE
    (WITH THE CRAB APPLE FACE)
PIGEON WALK
RED LIPS KISS MY BLUES AWAY
RHYTHM OF THE RIVER
ROW, ROW, ROW
SING A SONG OF SUNBEAMS
SIX LESSONS FROM MADAME LA
    ZONGA
STILL THE BLUEBIRD SINGS
SWEET POTATO PIPER
TEN LITTLE BOTTLES
THAT'S FOR ME
THAT SLY OLD GENTLEMAN (FROM
    FEATHERBED LANE)
THIS IS MY NIGHT TO DREAM
THROUGH (HOW CAN YOU SAY
    WE'RE THROUGH?)
TIME ALONE WILL TELL
TOO ROMANTIC
WE MUSN'T SAY GOODBYE
WHAT DO YOU WANT TO MAKE
    THOSE EYES AT ME FOR?
WHEN THE MOON COMES OVER
    MADISON SQUARE
YOU KNOW YOU BELONG TO
    SOMEBODY ELSE (SO WHY DON'T
    YOU LEAVE ME ALONE)

YOU MADE ME LOVE YOU (I DIDN'T
    WANT TO DO IT)
YOU'RE GONNA LOSE YOUR GAL
YOU'VE GOT ME IN THE PALM OF
    YOUR HAND

Monckton, Lionel

BOY GUESSED RIGHT, THE
BRING ME A ROSE
GIRL WITH A BROGUE, THE
SOCIETY (OH! I LOVE SOCIETY)
SOLDIERS IN THE PARK, THE
TOY MONKEY, THE

Monde, Alan

PRIDE IS BACK, THE

Money, Eddie

BABY, HOLD ON
MAYBE I'M A FOOL
THINK I'M IN LOVE
TWO TICKETS TO PARADISE

Monk, Thelonious

BEMSHA SWING
BLUE MONK
CRISS-CROSS
EPISTROPHY
IN WALKED BUD
MISTERIOSO
'ROUND ABOUT MIDNIGHT
RUBY, MY DEAR
STRAIGHT, NO CHASER
WELL, YOU NEEDN'T!

Monnot, Marguerite

DIS-DONC, DIS-DONC
IF YOU LOVE ME (REALLY LOVE ME)
IRMA LA DOUCE
IT IS BETTER TO LOVE
JESSICA
JUST COME HOME
MILORD
POOR PEOPLE OF PARIS, THE
WILL YOU REMEMBER

Monroe, Bill

BLUE MOON OF KENTUCKY
KENTUCKY WALTZ
ROCKY ROAD BLUES
UNCLE PEN

Monroe, Vaughn

RACING WITH THE MOON

Montague, Nathaniel

UP ON THE MOUNTAIN

Montana, Patsy

I WANT TO BE A COWBOY'S
SWEETHEART

Montana, Vincent, Jr.

NICE 'N NAASTY

Monte, C.

I CAN'T GROW PEACHES ON A
CHERRY TREE

Monte, Lou

LAZY MARY

Montenegro, Hugo

SEATTLE

Montez, Chris

LET'S DANCE

Montgomery, Bob

BACK IN BABY'S ARMS
LOVE'S MADE A FOOL OF YOU
MISTY BLUE

Montgomery, Carl

SIX DAYS ON THE ROAD

Montgomery, Earl

FOUR-O-THIRTY-THREE
WHAT'S YOUR MAMA'S NAME,
CHILD?

Montgomery, Garth

CHIQUITA BANANA

Montgomery, L.

DREAMIN'

Montgomery, Marshall

PAL OF MY CRADLE DAYS

Montgomery, Melba

WE MUST HAVE BEEN OUT OF OUR
MINDS

Moody, Russell

WEAR MY RING AROUND YOUR
NECK

Moon, Christopher

SOFT AND WET

Moon, Tony

SORROW ON THE ROCKS

Mooney, Harold

RIGAMAROLE
SWAMP FIRE

Mooney, Ralph

CRAZY ARMS

Moore, B.

LOOKING FOR MORE IN '64
ONE FOR THE MONEY

Moore, Barry

WHAT'S HE DOIN' IN MY WORLD?

Moore, Billy

PATIENCE AND FORTITUDE

Moore, Charlie

I AIN'T GOT TO LOVE NOBODY ELSE

Moore, Connie

SLOW WALK

Moore, Daniel

MY MARIA
SHAMBALA

Moore, Debra Mae

HEAVEN IN YOUR EYES

Moore, Elizabeth

LAROO, LAROO, LILLI BOLERO

Moore, Fleecie

AIN'T THAT JUST LIKE A WOMAN
BEANS AND CORN BREAD
BEWARE (BROTHER, BEWARE)
BUZZ ME
CALDONIA (A.K.A. CALDONIA
BOOGIE)
LET THE GOOD TIMES ROLL

Moore, Glen

VERDICT, THE
YOU'RE ALL I WANT FOR
CHRISTMAS

Moore, Hayward E.

AMERICA IS MY HOME

Moore, James

BABY, SCRATCH MY BACK
BREAKS, THE

Moore, J. B.

GOT TO GET YOU OFF MY MIND

Moore, John C.

AT MY FRONT DOOR (CRAZY LITTLE
  MAMA SONG)

Moore, Johnny

MERRY CHRISTMAS BABY

Moore, Julian

DIS-DONC, DIS-DONC

Moore, K.

YOU AND ME TONIGHT

Moore, Marvin

FOUR WALLS
GREEN DOOR, THE
I DREAMED
WHERE WERE YOU WHEN I
  NEEDED YOU?

Moore, Merle

HEART STRINGS

Moore, Monette

GRAVEYARD BOUND BLUES

Moore, Pete

LOVE MACHINE

Moore, Phil

BLOW OUT THE CANDLE
I FEEL SO SMOOCHIE
I'M GONNA SEE MY BABY
SHOO-SHOO BABY

Moore, Raymond

I'D RATHER BE AN OLD MAN'S
  SWEETHEART (THAN A YOUNG
  MAN'S FOOL)
MAN AND A HALF, A
SWEET MARIE
WHEN SWEET MARIE WAS SWEET
  SIXTEEN

Moore, Ren

I HAVE LEARNED TO RESPECT THE
  POWER OF LOVE
YOU DON'T HAVE TO CRY
YOUR SMILE

Moore, Robert

SEARCHING FOR MY LOVE

Moore, Robin

BALLAD OF THE GREEN BERETS,
  THE

Moore, Tim

CHARMER
SECOND AVENUE

Moore, W.

ONE MORE HEARTACHE

Moore, Warren

AIN'T THAT PECULIAR?
COME ON, DO THE JERK
GOING TO A GO-GO
HERE I GO AGAIN
I'LL BE DOGGONE
IT'S GROWING
MY BABY
MY GIRL HAS GONE
OOH BABY BABY
SINCE I LOST MY BABY
TAKE THIS HEART OF MINE
TRACKS OF MY TEARS, THE

Moorer, Gilbert

AND GET AWAY
GET ON UP
LEARNING TO FLY

Mora, Helene

KATHLEEN

Moraine, Lyle L.

CHRISTMAS ISLAND

Morakis, Takis

BOY ON A DOLPHIN

Morales, Carlton

VALOTTE

Morales, Esy

JUNGLE FANTASY

Morales, Noro

WALTER WINCHELL RHUMBA

Morali, Jacques

BEST DISCO IN TOWN, THE
MACHO MAN
Y.M.C.A.

Moran, Ed

MORNING AFTER THE NIGHT
  BEFORE, THE

Moran, Edward P.

DREAM OF YOU
NO WEDDING BELLS FOR ME

Moran, Jack

NONE OF MY BUSINESS
SKIP A ROPE

Moranis, Rick

TAKE OFF

Morbelli, R.

BOTCH-A-ME (BA-BA-BACIAMI
  PICCINA)

More, Julian

IRMA LA DOUCE

Morehead, James T.

SENTIMENTAL ME

Morehead, Jim

I NEVER HAD A WORRY IN THE
　　WORLD

Morehouse, Chauncey

KRAZY KAT

Moreland, Marc

MEXICAN RADIO

Moret, Neil (Charles N. Daniels)

CHLO-E
HIAWATHA
MICKEY
MOONLIGHT
MOONLIGHT AND ROSES
PEGGY
PERSIAN RUG
SHE'S FUNNY THAT WAY (I GOT A
　　WOMAN, CRAZY FOR ME)
SONG OF THE WANDERER
YOU TELL ME YOUR DREAM

Moretti, Raoul

SOUS LES TOITS DE PARIS (UNDER A
　　ROOF IN PAREE)

Moreu, G.

IF SHE SHOULD COME TO YOU (LA
　　MONTANA)

Moreve, Rushton

MAGIC CARPET RIDE

Morey, Larry

FERDINAND THE BULL
HEIGH-HO
I'M WISHING
LAVENDAR BLUE (DILLY DILLY)
LOVE IS A SONG
MY HEART GOES A-GADDING
ONE SONG
SOMEDAY MY PRINCE WILL COME
WHISTLE WHILE YOU WORK

WITH A SMILE AND A SONG
WORLD OWES ME A LIVING, THE

Morgan, Al

HALF A HEART IS ALL YOU LEFT
　　ME (WHEN YOU BROKE MY
　　HEART IN TWO)

Morgan, Carey

BLUES MY NAUGHTY SWEETY GIVES
　　TO ME, THE
BUGLE CALL RAG
MY HAWAIIAN SUNRISE
RAIN
SIPPING CIDER THRU A STRAW

Morgan, Dennis

I KNEW YOU WERE WAITING FOR
　　ME
I WAS COUNTRY WHEN COUNTRY
　　WASN'T COOL
I WOULDN'T HAVE MISSED IT FOR
　　THE WORLD
MY HEART CAN'T TELL YOU NO
NOBODY
ONLY A LONELY HEART KNOWS
SHE KEEPS THE HOME FIRES
　　BURNING
SLEEPING SINGLE IN A DOUBLE BED
SMOKEY MOUNTAIN RAIN
YEARS

Morgan, Dorinda

MAN UPSTAIRS, THE

Morgan, Freddy

HEY, MR. BANJO

Morgan, George

CANDY KISSES
I'M IN LOVE
RAINBOW IN MY HEART

Morgan, James

DON'T BITE THE HAND THAT'S
　　FEEDING YOU

Morgan, Jamie

BUFFALO STANCE

Morgan, Lee

KING IS GONE, THE

Morgan, May H.

BLESS THIS HOUSE

Morgan, Melissa

IF YOU CAN DO IT: I CAN TOO!!

Morgan, Russ

DOES YOUR HEART BEAT FOR ME?
FLOWER OF DAWN
IT'S EIGHT O'CLOCK
SO LONG
SOMEBODY ELSE IS TAKING MY
　　PLACE
SO TIRED
SWEET ELOISE
YOU'RE NOBODY TILL SOMEBODY
　　LOVES YOU

Morgan, T.

CUTIE PIE

Morganfield, McKinley

GOT MY MOJO WORKING

Morier, John

MAKING EVERY MINUTE COUNT

Moroder, Giorgio

BREAKDANCE
CALL ME
CAT PEOPLE (PUTTING OUT FIRE)
CHASE, THE
DANGER ZONE
FLASHDANCE . . . WHAT A FEELING
HEAVEN KNOWS
I FEEL LOVE
IT'S ALL WRONG, BUT IT'S ALL
　　RIGHT

LOVE TO LOVE YOU, BABY
NEVER ENDING STORY
ON THE RADIO
OVER THE TOP
SEDUCTION, THE (LOVE THEME
   FROM "AMERICAN GIGOLO")
TAKE MY BREATH AWAY (LOVE
   THEME FROM "PETER GUNN")
WANDERER, THE
WINNER TAKES IT ALL

Morosco, Oliver

MY WONDERFUL DREAM GIRL

Moross, Jerome

IT'S THE GOING HOME TOGETHER
LAZY AFTERNOON
STAY WITH ME

Morricone, Ennio

GOOD, THE BAD AND THE UGLY,
   THE

Morris, Bob

BUCKAROO
IT TAKES A LOT OF MONEY
MADE IN JAPAN

Morris, Doug

RESPECTABLE
SWEET TALKIN' GUY

Morris, Faye

MADE IN JAPAN

Morris, Gary

BABY BYE BYE
LEAVE ME LONELY
MAKIN' UP FOR LOST TIME (THE
   "DALLAS" LOVERS' SONG)
PLAIN BROWN WRAPPER

Morris, Harry B.

ALGY, THE PICCADILLY JOHNNY
   WITH THE LITTLE GLASS EYE

Morris, Joe

SHAKE A HAND

Morris, John

ANY TIME, ANY PLACE, ANYWHERE
BLAZING SADDLES
KNOCK, KNOCK, WHO'S THERE?
PARADIDDLE JOE

Morris, Lamar

ELEVEN ROSES
THESE LONELY HANDS OF MINE

Morris, Lee

BLUE VELVET
IF I ONLY HAD A MATCH

Morris, Margie

YOU WANTED SOMEONE TO PLAY
   WITH (I WANTED SOMEONE TO
   LOVE)

Morris, Richard

HONEY CHILE
(WE'VE GOT) HONEY LOVE
LOVE BUG LEAVE MY HEART ALONE
STOP HER ON SIGHT (S.O.S.)

Morris, Rod

BIMBO
NORTH WIND

Morris, Roger

PRETTY IN PINK

Morrison, Bob

I STILL BELIEVE IN WALTZES
LOOKIN' FOR LOVE
LOVE THE WORLD AWAY
WHISKEY, IF YOU WERE A WOMAN

Morrison, Brian

DON'T CALL HIM A COWBOY

Morrison, Dan

FRIENDS
LOVING UP A STORM

Morrison, Eddie

MADISON TIME

Morrison, Jim

HELLO, I LOVE YOU
LIGHT MY FIRE
LOVE ME TWO TIMES
PEOPLE ARE STRANGE
RIDERS ON THE STORM
ROADHOUSE BLUES
TOUCH ME
UNKNOWN SOLDIER
WISHFUL, SINFUL
YOU MAKE ME REAL

Morrison, Robert

ARE YOU ON THE ROAD TO LOVIN'
   ME AGAIN?
YOU DECORATED MY LIFE

Morrison, Van

BLUE MONEY
BROWN EYED GIRL
CALL ME UP IN DREAMLAND
COME RUNNING
CRAZY LOVE
GLORIA
INTO THE MYSTIC
I SHALL SING
MOONDANCE
MYSTIC EYES
TUPELO HONEY
WAVELENGTH
WILD NIGHT

Morrison, Vonie

ACT NATURALLY

Morrison, W.

FUNKY WORM

Morrison, Walter

ONE NATION UNDER A GROOVE

Morrow, Geoff

CAN'T SMILE WITHOUT YOU

Morrow, Jack

FOR RENT
YOU'RE THE REASON (I'M IN LOVE)

Morse, Steve

ALL I WANTED

Morse, Theodora (Dolly)

BLUE BELL
SIBONEY

Morse, Theodore F.

ANOTHER RAG
ARRAH WANNA
BLUE BELL
BOBBIN' UP AND DOWN
CONSOLATION
DADDY'S LITTLE GIRL
DEAR OLD GIRL
DOWN IN JUNGLE TOWN
GOOD OLD U.S.A., THE
HAIL, HAIL, THE GANG'S ALL HERE
HURRAH FOR BAFFIN'S BAY!
I'D RATHER BE A LOBSTER THAN A WISE GUY
IT'S GREAT TO BE A SOLDIER MAN
I'VE GOT A FEELING FOR YOU (OR, WAY DOWN IN MY HEART)
I'VE TAKEN QUITE A FANCY TO YOU
JUST A LITTLE ROCKING CHAIR AND YOU
KEEP A LITTLE COZY CORNER IN YOUR HEART FOR ME
KEEP ON THE SUNNY SIDE
LAND OF THE HEART'S DESIRE, THE
LANKY YANKEE BOYS IN BLUE, THE
LEADER OF THE GERMAN BAND, THE
LITTLE BOY CALLED "TAPS"
LONGING FOR YOU

MAKE BELIEVE
M-O-T-H-E-R (A WORD THAT MEANS THE WORLD TO ME)
NOBODY'S LITTLE GIRL
ONE CALLED "MOTHER" AND THE OTHER "HOME SWEET HOME"
PLEASE COME AND PLAY IN MY YARD
SHE'S THE FAIREST LITTLE FLOWER DEAR OLD DIXIE EVER GREW
SHE WAITS BY THE DEEP BLUE SEA
STARLIGHT
TWO BLUE EYES, TWO LITTLE BABY SHOES
WHEN UNCLE JOE PLAYS A RAG ON HIS OLD BANJO
WHEN YOU WORE A PINAFORE
WHERE THE SOUTHERN ROSES GROW
WON'T YOU BE MY HONEY?

Morse, Woolson

ASK THE MAN IN THE MOON
PRETTY GIRL, A

Mortimer, Al

FOR THE LOVE OF HIM

Morton, Ferdinand "Jelly Roll"

BIG FOOT HAM
BLACK BOTTOM STOMP
GRANDPA'S SPELLS
JELLY ROLL BLUES
KANSAS CITY STOMP(S)
KING PORTER STOMP
MILENBERG JOYS
MR. JELLY LORD
NEW ORLEANS BUMP
WILD MAN BLUES
WOLVERINE BLUES

Morton, George

GIVE HIM A GREAT BIG KISS
I CAN NEVER GO HOME ANYMORE
LEADER OF THE PACK
REMEMBER (WALKIN' IN THE SAND)

Morton, Hugh

LITTLE BIRDIES LEARNING HOW TO FLY
SHE IS THE BELLE OF NEW YORK

Mosely, Bob

AU REET

Mosely, Leo

PRETTY EYED BABY

Mosely, Robert

BIG COLD WIND
MIDNIGHT FLYER
SINCE I MADE YOU CRY

Mosley, Robert

GOODBYE, MY LOVER, GOODBYE
SHA-LA-LA

Moss, Jeffrey

RUBBER DUCKIE
THIS WAY TO SESAME STREET

Moss, John

CHURCH OF THE POISON MIND
DO YOU REALLY WANT TO HURT ME
I'LL TUMBLE 4 YA
IT'S A MIRACLE
KARMA CHAMELEON
MISS ME BLIND
MOVE AWAY

Moss, Marie

UNTIL SUNRISE

Moss, Neil

HOLDING BACK THE YEARS

Moss, Tyrone

EVERYBODY'S EVERYTHING

Mosser, Peter

Mosser, Peter

MORGEN (A.K.A. ONE MORE
  SUNRISE)

Mossman, Ted

FULL MOON AND EMPTY ARMS
TILL THE END OF TIME

Moten, Bennie

IT'S HARD TO LAUGH OR SMILE
KANSAS CITY SHUFFLE
MOTEN STOMP
MOTEN SWING
SOUTH

Moten, Buster

MOTEN SWING

Moten, Mae

MERCY, MR. PERCY

Mothersbaugh, Mark

THEME FROM "DOCTOR DETROIT"
WHIP IT

Motola, George

GOODNIGHT MY LOVE (PLEASANT
  DREAMS)

Motzan, Otto

BRIGHT EYES

Moulton, Herb

MAKIN' LOVE, MOUNTAIN STYLE

Moy, Melvin

HOME COOKIN'

Moy, Sylvia

HONEY CHILE
(WE'VE GOT) HONEY LOVE
I'M WONDERING

IT TAKES TWO
I WAS MADE TO LOVE HER
LOVE BUG LEAVE MY HEART ALONE
MY BABY LOVES ME
MY CHERIE AMOUR
NOTHING'S TOO GOOD FOR MY
  BABY
SHOO-BE-DOO-BE-DOO-DA-DAY
UPTIGHT (EVERYTHING'S ALRIGHT)
WHAT AM I GOING TO DO WITHOUT
  YOUR LOVE?

Moyers, Helen

SET HIM FREE

Mozian, Roger King

ASIA MINOR

Msarurgwa

SKOKIAAN

Mtume, James

CLOSER I GET TO YOU, THE
JUICY FRUIT
NEVER KNEW LOVE LIKE THIS
  BEFORE
SWEET SENSATION
WHAT CHA GONNA DO WITH MY
  LOVIN'
YOU, ME AND HE

Mueller, Gus

WANG, WANG BLUES, THE

Mueller, Mark

NOTHIN' AT ALL

Muhammad, M.

LADIES NIGHT

Muir, Lewis F.

HERE COMES MY DADDY (OH POP-
  OH POP-OH POP)
HITCHY-KOO
MAMMY JINNY'S JUBILEE

PLAY THAT BARBER SHOP CHORD
RAGTIME COWBOY JOE
WAITING FOR THE ROBERT E. LEE

Muldrow, Cornell

YOU CAN'T SIT DOWN

Mullaly, W. S.

MOTTOES FRAMED UPON THE WALL

Mullan, Jack

HE

Mullen, J. B.

DOWN ON THE BRANDYWINE

Mullen, Larry, Jr.

I WILL FOLLOW
NEW YEAR'S DAY
PRIDE (IN THE NAME OF LOVE)

Mullen, R. A.

BABY'S PRAYER

Muller, Randy

CALL ME
MOVIN'

Mullican, Moon

CHEROKEE BOOGIE (EH-OH-
  ALEENA)
NEW PRETTY BLONDE (A.K.A. JOLE
  BLON)

Mulligan, Gerry

JERU

Mullins, Cam

I WON'T MENTION IT AGAIN

Mullins, Johnny

BLUE KENTUCKY GIRL

1534

SUCCESS

Mullis, Woody

DARLENE
THIS MISSIN' YOU HEART OF MINE

Mundy, James

AIR MAIL SPECIAL
BLACK VELVET
BOLERO AT THE SAVOY
CAVERNISM
DON'CHA GO 'WAY MAD
LOVER IS BLUE, A
SO FAR, SO GOOD
SOLO FLIGHT
SWINGTIME IN THE ROCKIES
TRAV'LIN' LIGHT

Munnings, Ralph

FUNKY NASSAU

Munro, Bill

WHEN MY BABY SMILES AT ME

Munson, Eddie

IDA! SWEET AS APPLE CIDER

Murden, Orlando

FOR ONCE IN MY LIFE

Murph, Randolph

LOVE JONES

Murphey, Michael

CAROLINA IN THE PINES
GERONIMO'S CADILLAC
STILL TAKING CHANCES
WILDFIRE

Murphy, Audie

SHUTTERS AND BOARDS

Murphy, Barry

WE CAN'T HIDE IT ANYMORE

Murphy, C. W.

HAS ANYBODY HERE SEEN KELLY?

Murphy, Jesse

OUR ANNIVERSARY

Murphy, Mic

DON'T DISTURB THIS GROOVE

Murphy, Mike

AIRPLANE SONG (MY AIRPLANE)

Murphy, Owen

BY SPECIAL PERMISSION OF THE
    COPYRIGHT OWNERS, I LOVE
    YOU
OH, BABY

Murphy, Ralph

HALF THE WAY

Murphy, Stanley

BE MY LITTLE BABY BUMBLE BEE
MALINDA
OH! HOW SHE COULD YACKI,
    HACKI, WICKI, WACKI, WOO
ON THE 5:15
PUT ON YOUR OLD GREY BONNET
SHE TOOK MOTHER'S ADVICE
SUGAR MOON

Murphy, Walter

FIFTH OF BEETHOVEN, A

Murrah, Roger

HEARTS AREN'T MADE TO BREAK
    (THEY'RE MADE TO LOVE)
HIGH COTTON
IT TAKES A LITTLE RAIN (TO MAKE
    LOVE GROW)

LIFE'S HIGHWAY
MY ROUGH AND ROWDY DAYS
SOUTHERN RAINS
THIS CRAZY LOVE
WE'RE IN THIS LOVE TOGETHER

Murray, Billy

LET'S TAKE AN OLD-FASHIONED
    WALK

Murray, Fred

I'M HENRY VIII, I AM

Murray, Henry, Jr.

SHE BLEW A GOOD THING

Murray, Jean

SPLISH SPLASH

Murray, John (Jack)

DO THE NEW YORK
HAPPY-GO-LUCKY YOU (AND
    BROKEN HEARTED ME)
HAVE A LITTLE DREAM ON ME
IF I LOVE AGAIN
OH, WHAT A THRILL
TWO LOVES HAVE I

Murray, Lyn

I WISH I WUZ

Murray, Maurice

CRAZY HEART

Murray, Mitch

BALLAD OF BONNIE AND CLYDE,
    THE
BILLY, DON'T BE A HERO
EVEN THE BAD TIMES ARE GOOD
HITCHIN' A RIDE
HOW DO YOU DO IT
I KNEW IT ALL THE TIME
I'M TELLING YOU NOW
NIGHT CHICAGO DIED, THE
YOU WERE MADE FOR ME

Murray, Tom

GOD BLESS US ALL

Murrells, Norman

HOUSE OF BAMBOO

Muse, Clarence

WHEN IT'S SLEEPY TIME DOWN
   SOUTH

Musel, Bob

BAND OF GOLD
EARTHBOUND

Musker, Frank

EVERY WOMAN IN THE WORLD
HEAVEN ON THE SEVENTH FLOOR
MARRIED MEN
MODERN GIRL

Mustacchi, Joseph

MILORD

Mustaine, Dave

IN MY DARKEST HOUR

Myers, Benedict

GOMEN NASAI (FORGIVE ME)

Myers, Dwight

JUST COOLIN'

Myers, Frank

SOMETIMES A LADY
YOU AND I
YOU'RE NEVER TOO OLD FOR
   YOUNG LOVE
YOU SHOULD HAVE BEEN GONE BY
   NOW

Myers, Frank J.

I GOT MEXICO

Myers, Henry

IN CHI CHI CASTENANGO
SLOW RIVER

Myers, Randy

BRIGHTON HILL
LOVE WILL FIND A WAY
PUT A LITTLE LOVE IN YOUR HEART

Myers, Richard

HOLD MY HAND
JERICHO
MY DARLING

Myers, Sherman

MOONLIGHT ON THE GANGES

Myles, Billy

JOKER, THE (THAT'S WHAT THEY
   CALL ME)
NO LOVE (BUT YOUR LOVE)
YOU WERE MADE FOR (ALL MY
   LOVE)

Myrow, Josef

AUTUMN NOCTURNE
BABY, WON'T YOU SAY YOU LOVE
   ME?
BY THE WAY
COMMENT ALLEZ-VOUS? (HOW ARE
   THINGS WITH YOU?)
FIVE O'CLOCK WHISTLE, THE
HAUNTING ME
IF AND WHEN
IF I'M LUCKY
I NEVER FELT THIS WAY BEFORE
IT HAPPENS EVERY SPRING
KOKOMO, INDIANA
LADY LOVES, A
LULLABY IN BLUE
ONE MORE TOMORROW
ON THE BOARDWALK IN ATLANTIC
   CITY
SOMEWHERE IN THE NIGHT
VELVET MOON
WALKING ALONG WITH BILLY
WHAT DID I DO?

WILHELMINA
YOU DO
YOU MAKE ME FEEL SO YOUNG

Mysels, George

HEAVEN DROPS HER CURTAIN
   DOWN
I WANT YOU, I NEED YOU, I LOVE
   YOU
ONE LITTLE CANDLE

Mysels, Sammy

AT LEAST YOU COULD SAY HELLO
BIM BAM BABY
DREAMS ARE A DIME A DOZEN
HEAVEN DROPS HER CURTAIN
   DOWN
HIS FEET TOO BIG FOR DE BED
IS THERE SOMEBODY ELSE?
MENTION MY NAME IN SHEBOYGAN
RED SILK STOCKINGS AND GREEN
   PERFUME
SINGING HILLS, THE
STRANGE LONELINESS, A
THERE'S A CHILL ON THE HILL
   TONIGHT
THROWIN' STONES AT THE SUN
WALKIN' DOWN TO WASHINGTON
WE THREE (MY ECHO, MY SHADOW,
   AND ME)
YESTERDAY'S GARDENIAS
YOU FORGOT ABOUT ME

Myx, James, Jr.

INNER CITY BLUES (MAKE ME
   WANNA HOLLER)

Nabbie, Jimmie

YOU ARE MY LOVE

Nadel, Warren

AFTER SCHOOL

Nader, Neval

FLY BY NIGHT
MECCA

Nagle, Ron

DON'T TOUCH ME THERE

Nahan, Irv

DANCE WITH ME

Nakamura, Hachidai

SUKIYAKI

Nance, Dolores

ENDLESS SLEEP

Nance, Jack

IT'S ONLY MAKE BELIEVE
STORY OF MY LOVE, THE

Nanini, Oliver

MEXICAN RADIO

Napier-Bell, Simon

YOU DON'T HAVE TO SAY YOU LOVE
ME

Napoleon, Phil

JUST HOT!

Napton, Johnny

MY DEVOTION

Nascime, Alfred Ricardo de

BANDIT, THE

Naset, C.

DREAMY MELODY

Nash, Brian

WELCOME TO THE PLEASUREDOME

Nash, Graham

CARRIE-ANNE
CHICAGO
DEAR ELOISE
JENNIFER ECCLES
JUST A SONG BEFORE I GO
MARRAKESH EXPRESS
ON A CAROUSEL
OUR HOUSE
PAY YOU BACK WITH INTEREST
STOP, STOP, STOP
TEACH YOUR CHILDREN
TELL ME TO MY FACE
WASTED ON THE WAY

Nash, Johnny

HOLD ME TIGHT
I CAN SEE CLEARLY NOW
WHAT KIND OF LOVE IS THIS?

Nash, Ogden

FOOLISH HEART
I'M A STRANGER HERE MYSELF
JUST LIKE A MAN
MADLY IN LOVE
ROUNDABOUT
SPEAK LOW
THAT'S HIM
WESTWIND

Natel, J. M.

I DREAMED A DREAM

Nathan, Casper

MEET ME IN BUBBLE LAND

Nathan, Charles

SAY YOU'RE MINE AGAIN
SOMEWHERE THERE IS SOMEONE

Nathan, N.

HOLE IN THE WALL

Nauman, Paul

BALL OF FIRE

DO SOMETHING TO ME

Navarro, Daniel

WE BELONG

Navarro, Esther

SPEEDOO

Naylor, Charles

SHAKE ME I RATTLE (SQUEEZE ME I
CRY)

Nazareth, Ernesto

BLAME IT ON THE SAMBA

Nazelles, Rene

SOUS LES TOITS DE PARIS (UNDER A
ROOF IN PAREE)

Nebb, Jimmy

NO ARMS CAN EVER HOLD YOU

Neese, Chuck

REDNECKS, WHITE SOCKS, AND
BLUE RIBBON BEER

Negulesco, Dusty

IT IS BETTER TO LOVE
JESSICA
WILL YOU REMEMBER

Neiburg, Al J.

(WHEN IT'S) DARKNESS ON THE
DELTA
I'M CONFESSIN' THAT I LOVE YOU
IN A BLUE AND PENSIVE MOOD
IT'S A HAP-HAP-HAPPY DAY
IT'S THE TALK OF THE TOWN
I'VE GOT AN INVITATION TO A
DANCE
LEARNING
MOONRISE ON THE LOWLANDS
OL' PAPPY
STAR GAZING

Neiburg, Al J.

SWEET SLUMBER
UNDER A BLANKET OF BLUE

Neil, Christopher

ALL I NEED
TAKEN IN

Neil, Fred

CANDY MAN
EVERYBODY'S TALKING

Neil, Marcia

FUNNY (NOT MUCH)

Neilsen-Chapman, Beth

STRONG ENOUGH TO BEND

Nelson, Benjamin

THERE GOES MY BABY

Nelson, Betty

DON'T PLAY THAT SONG (YOU LIED)

Nelson, D. C.

TOO LATE

Nelson, Dennis

HYPERACTIVE

Nelson, Earl

DUCK, THE
HARLEM SHUFFLE

Nelson, Ed, Jr.

I'M THROWING RICE (AT THE GIRL I
    LOVE)
ONE KISS TOO MANY
SEND TEN PRETTY FLOWERS (TO MY
    GIRL IN TENNESSEE)
SHOW ME THE WAY BACK TO YOUR
    HEART
WILL SANTY COME TO SHANTY
    TOWN?

Nelson, Ed G.

AUF WIEDERSEHEN, MY DEAR
HANG YOUR HEAD IN SHAME
    (DON'T YOUR CONSCIENCE EVER
    BOTHER YOU)
I APOLOGIZE
LOVE CAME OUT OF THE NIGHT
PAL THAT I LOVED, THE (STOLE THE
    GAL THAT I LOVED)
PEGGY O'NEIL
PRETTY KITTY KELLY
SETTIN' THE WOODS ON FIRE
TEN LITTLE FINGERS AND TEN
    LITTLE TOES (DOWN IN
    TENNESSEE)
WHEN YANKEE DOODLE LEARNS TO
    PARLEZ-VOUS FRANCAIS

Nelson, Gene

BURNIN' OLD MEMORIES
EIGHTEEN WHEELS AND A DOZEN
    ROSES

Nelson, Gerald H.

TRAGEDY

Nelson, Harrison

I GOT LOADED

Nelson, Jimmy

"T" 99 BLUES

Nelson, Oliver

HOBO FLATS

Nelson, Ozzie

AND THEN YOUR LIPS MET MINE
I'M LOOKING FOR A GUY WHO
    PLAYS ALTO AND BARITONE AND
    DOUBLES ON A CLARINET AND
    WEARS A SIZE 37 SUIT

Nelson, Paul

BURNIN' OLD MEMORIES

EIGHTEEN WHEELS AND A DOZEN
    ROSES

Nelson, Portia

SUNDAY IN NEW YORK

Nelson, Prince Rogers

1999
ALPHABET STREET
BATDANCE
CONTROVERSY
COOL
DELIRIOUS
DO ME BABY
GLAMOROUS LIFE, THE
HOUSEQUAKE
I COULD NEVER TAKE THE PLACE
    OF YOUR MAN
I FEEL FOR YOU
IT'S GONNA BE A BEAUTIFUL NIGHT
I WANNA BE YOUR LOVER
I WOULD DIE 4 U
JUNGLE LOVE
LET'S GO CRAZY
LITTLE RED CORVETTE
LOVE BIZARRE, A
MANIC MONDAY
POP LIFE
PURPLE RAIN
RASPBERRY BERET
SIGN O' THE TIMES
SOFT AND WET
STAND BACK
STILL WAITING
SUGAR WALLS
U GIT THE LOOK
WHEN DOVES CRY
WHEN YOU WERE MINE

Nelson, Richard

PUT ANOTHER CHAIR AT THE TABLE

Nelson, Rick

GARDEN PARTY

Nelson, Sander

TEEN BEAT

Nelson, Sandy

LET THERE BE DRUMS

Nelson, Stephen

SONGBIRD

Nelson, Steve

BOUQUET OF ROSES
FROSTY THE SNOWMAN
HANG YOUR HEAD IN SHAME
(DON'T YOUR CONSCIENCE EVER
BOTHER YOU)
HEART FULL OF LOVE, A (FOR A
HANDFUL OF KISSES)
I'M THROWING RICE (AT THE GIRL I
LOVE)
ONE KISS TOO MANY
PETER COTTONTAIL
SAY IT WITH YOUR HEART
SEND TEN PRETTY FLOWERS (TO MY
GIRL IN TENNESSEE)
SHOW ME THE WAY BACK TO YOUR
HEART
SMOKEY THE BEAR
WILL SANTY COME TO SHANTY
TOWN?

Nelson, Willie

ANGEL FLYING TOO CLOSE TO THE
GROUND
CRAZY
FORGIVING YOU WAS EASY
FUNNY HOW TIME SLIPS AWAY
(A.K.A. FUNNY)
GOOD-HEARTED WOMAN, A
HELLO FOOL
HELLO WALLS
I'M STILL NOT OVER YOU
ON THE ROAD AGAIN
PLACE TO FALL APART, A
THREE DAYS
TOUCH ME

Nemo, Henry

BLAME IT ON MY LAST AFFAIR
DON'T TAKE YOUR LOVE FROM ME
HIP, HIP, HOORAY
IF YOU WERE IN MY PLACE

I LET A SONG GO OUT OF MY
HEART
SKRONTCH
STEPPIN' INTO SWING SOCIETY
THERE'LL SOON BE A RAINBOW
'TIS AUTUMN

Nero, Paul

HOT CANARY, THE

Nesbitt, Harry

MADEMOISELLE
WITHOUT THAT CERTAIN THING

Nesbitt, Max

MADEMOISELLE
WITHOUT THAT CERTAIN THING

Nesmith, Michael

DIFFERENT DRUM
GIRL I KNEW SOMEWHERE, THE
JOANNE
SILVER MOON
SOME OF SHELLY'S BLUES
TAPIOCA TUNDRA

Neuman, Klauss-Gunter

WONDERLAND BY NIGHT

Nevil, Robbie

C'EST LA VIE
DOMINOES
IT'S NOT OVER ('TIL IT'S OVER)
WOT'S IT TO YA

Neville, Arthur

CISSY STRUT
LOOK-KA PY PY
SOPHISTICATED CISSY

Neville, Naomi

CERTAIN GIRL, A
LIPSTICK TRACES (ON A CIGARETTE)
RIDE YOUR PONY

WHIPPED CREAM

Nevin, Ethelbert

LITTLE BOY BLUE
MIGHTY LAK' A ROSE
ROSARY, THE

Nevins, Morty

LOVER'S GOLD
THESE THINGS I OFFER YOU (FOR A
LIFETIME)
TWILIGHT TIME

Newbury, Mickey

AMERICAN TRILOGY, AN
FUNNY, FAMILIAR, FORGOTTEN
FEELINGS
HERE COMES THE RAIN, BABY
JUST DROPPED IN (TO SEE WHAT
CONDITION MY CONDITION WAS
IN)
SHE EVEN WOKE ME UP TO SAY
GOODBYE
SWEET MEMORIES

Newell, Norman

FORGET DOMANI
MELBA WALTZ, THE
MORE (THEME FROM "MONDO
CANE")
OUR LOVE STORY
SAY WONDERFUL THINGS
TO THE DOOR OF THE SUN (ALLE
PORTE DEL SOLE)
WHITE ROSE OF ATHENS, THE

Newley, Anthony

CANDY MAN, THE
FEELING GOOD
GOLDFINGER
GONNA BUILD A MOUNTAIN
JOKER, THE
LOOK AT THAT FACE
MY FIRST LOVE SONG
ONCE IN A LIFETIME
SOMEONE NICE LIKE YOU
SWEET BEGINNING
TYPICALLY ENGLISH

WHAT KIND OF FOOL AM I?
WHO CAN I TURN TO (WHEN
 NOBODY NEEDS ME)
WONDERFUL DAY LIKE TODAY, A

Newman, Alfred

"AIRPORT" LOVE THEME
ANASTASIA
BEST OF EVERYTHING, THE
MOON OF MANAKOORA, THE
STREET SCENE
THROUGH A LONG AND SLEEPLESS
 NIGHT

Newman, Charles

BOY IN KHAKI, A GIRL IN LACE, A
DREAM TRAIN
FLOWERS FOR MADAME
GRASS IS GETTING GREENER ALL
 THE TIME, THE
HE'S MY UNCLE
I CAN'T BELIEVE IT'S TRUE
IF YOU WERE ONLY MINE
I'LL NEVER HAVE TO DREAM AGAIN
I MET HER ON MONDAY
I'M PAINTING THE TOWN RED
IN YOUR OWN LITTLE WAY
IT'S NO FUN
I WOULDN'T CHANGE YOU FOR THE
 WORLD
MEANEST THING YOU EVER DID
 WAS KISS ME, THE
SILVER SHADOWS AND BROKEN
 DREAMS
SIX LESSONS FROM MADAME LA
 ZONGA
SLOW BUT SURE
SWEETHEARTS ON PARADE
TAKE ANOTHER GUESS
TINY LITTLE FINGERPRINTS
WAS I TO BLAME FOR FALLING IN
 LOVE WITH YOU?
WHAT'S THE USE?
WHY CAN'T THIS NIGHT GO ON
 FOREVER?
WHY DON'T WE DO THIS MORE
 OFTEN?
WOODEN SOLDIER AND THE CHINA
 DOLL, THE
YOU CAN'T PULL THE WOOL OVER
 MY EYES

YOU'RE JUST A DREAM COME TRUE
YOU'VE GOT ME CRYING AGAIN

Newman, Emil

LOST APRIL

Newman, Floyd

LAST NIGHT

Newman, Herbert

BIRDS AND THE BEES, THE
SO THIS IS LOVE
WAYWARD WIND, THE

Newman, Jimmy

CRY, CRY, DARLING

Newman, Joel

KISSES SWEETER THAN WINE

Newman, Lionel

AGAIN
COWBOY AND THE LADY, THE
NEVER
RIVER OF NO RETURN
THEME FROM "ADVENTURES IN
 PARADISE"

Newman, Randy

BLUES, THE
HE GIVES US ALL HIS LOVE
I LOVE TO SEE YOU SMILE
I THINK IT'S GOING TO RAIN TODAY
MAMA TOLD ME (NOT TO COME)
MY LITTLE BUTTERCUP
NATURAL, THE
ONE MORE HOUR
SHORT PEOPLE

Newsome, Betty Jean

IT'S A MAN'S, MAN'S, MAN'S WORLD

Newton, Eddie

CASEY JONES

Newton, Eileen

SOMEWHERE A VOICE IS CALLING

Newton, Rev. John

AMAZING GRACE

Newton, Wood

BOBBIE SUE
TWENTY YEARS AGO
WHAT I DIDN'T DO

Nichol, Al

ELENORE

Nichol, Steve

HANGIN' ON A STRING
 (CONTEMPLATING)

Nicholas, James Hayden

BETTER MAN

Nicholl, Don

THREE'S COMPANY

Nicholls, Billy

WITHOUT YOUR LOVE

Nicholls, Horatio

AMONG MY SOUVENIRS
MISTAKES
SAY A LITTLE PRAYER FOR ME

Nichols, Alberta

I JUST COULDN'T TAKE IT, BABY
LOVE LIKE OURS, A
PADAM, PADAM
UNTIL THE REAL THING COMES
 ALONG (IT WILL HAVE TO DO)
YOU CAN'T STOP ME FROM LOVING
 YOU
YOUR MOTHER'S SON-IN-LAW

Nichols, Billy

DO IT ('TILL YOU'RE SATISFIED)

Nichols, George A.

I'VE WAITED, HONEY, WAITED LONG
   FOR YOU

Nichols, Roger

I WON'T LAST A DAY WITHOUT YOU
OUT IN THE COUNTRY
RAINY DAYS AND MONDAYS
TALK IT OVER IN THE MORNING
TIMES OF YOUR LIFE
WE'VE ONLY JUST BEGUN

Nichols, Sam

THAT WILD AND WICKED LOOK IN
   YOUR EYE
YELLOW ROSES

Nicholson, Gary

THAT'S THE THING ABOUT LOVE

Nicholson, M.

MARIE FROM SUNNY ITALY

Nichtern, David

MIDNIGHT AT THE OASIS

Nicks, Stevie

DREAMS
EDGE OF SEVENTEEN (JUST LIKE
   THE WHITE WINGED DOVE)
I CAN'T WAIT
IF ANYONE FAILS
LEATHER AND LACE
RHIANNON (WILL YOU EVER WIN)
SARA
SEVEN WONDERS
STAND BACK

Nielsen, Rick

EVERYTHING WORKS IF YOU LET IT
I WANT YOU TO WANT ME

SURRENDER

Niessen, Carl

ASK ME

Niessen, Charly

BANJO BOY

Nightingale, Fred

SUGAR AND SPICE

Nilsson, Harry

COCONUT
I GUESS THE LORD MUST BE IN
   NEW YORK CITY
JUMP INTO THE FIRE
ME AND MY ARROW
ONE
REMEMBER (CHRISTMAS)
SPACEMAN
STORY OF ROCK AND ROLL, THE
WITHOUT HER

Nims, Walter

PRECIOUS AND FEW

Nini, Diane

GLORY OF LOVE

Niquet, F. J.

TITINA

Nisa

TORERO

Nitzsche, Jack

NEEDLES AND PINS
UP WHERE WE BELONG

Nivert, Taffy

FRIENDS WITH YOU
TAKE ME HOME, COUNTRY ROADS

Nix, Don

LOSER (WITH A BROKEN HEART),
   THE

Nix, Robert

CHAMPAGNE JAM
CHERRY HILL PARK
IMAGINARY LOVER
I'M NOT GONNA LET IT BOTHER ME
   TONIGHT
SO IN TO YOU

Nix, Sally

ALL MY LOVE BELONGS TO YOU
I CAN'T GO ON WITHOUT YOU
I LOVE YOU, YES I DO
I WANT A BOWLEGGED WOMAN
SNEAKY PETE

Nixon, Tom

DO THE FUNKY PENGUIN

Noack, Eddie

THESE HANDS

Noah, Peter

SAN ANTONIO STROLL

Nobel, Gib

LOVE T.K.O.

Noble, Harry

HOLD ME, THRILL ME, KISS ME

Noble, James

BLUE FLAME

Noble, Johnny

HAWAIIAN WAR CHANT
LITTLE BROWN GAL
MY LITTLE GRASS SHACK (IN
   KEALAKAKUA, HAWAII)

Noble, Keith

SUMMER SONG, A

Noble, Michael

TWENTY YEARS AGO
WHAT I DIDN'T DO

Noble, Ray

BY THE FIRESIDE (IN THE
    GLOAMING)
CHANGE YOUR MIND
CHEROKEE
GOODNIGHT SWEETHEART
IF YOU LOVE ME
I HADN'T ANYONE TILL YOU
IT'S ALL FORGOTTEN NOW
LOVE IS THE SWEETEST THING
LOVE LOCKED OUT
TOUCH OF YOUR LIPS, THE
VERY THOUGHT OF YOU, THE
WHAT MORE CAN I ASK?
WHY STARS COME OUT AT NIGHT
YOU'RE SO DESIRABLE

Nocentelli, Leo

CISSY STRUT
LOOK-KA PY PY
SOPHISTICATED CISSY

Noe, Dale

MISSING YOU

Nolan, Bob

BLUE PRAIRIE
COOL WATER
TOUCH OF GOD'S HAND, THE
TUMBLING TUMBLEWEEDS

Nolan, Kenny

GET DANCIN'
I LIKE DREAMIN'
LADY MARMALADE
LOVE'S GROWN DEEP
MY EYES ADORED YOU

Nolan, Michael

LITTLE ANNIE ROONEY

Noland, A.

FUNKY WORM

Noll, Albert W.

DOAN YE CRY, MAH HONEY

Noonan, Steve

BUY ME FOR THE RAIN

Norlind, Lloyd B.

OUT OF THE SILENCE

Norman, Monty

DIS-DONC, DIS-DONC
IRMA LA DOUCE
JAMES BOND THEME, THE

Norman, Pierre

YOU BROUGHT A NEW KIND OF
    LOVE TO ME

Norrell, Charles E.

THESE LONELY HANDS OF MINE

North, Alex

I'LL CRY TOMORROW
LONG HOT SUMMER, THE
THEME FROM "THE MISFITS"
UNCHAINED MELODY

North, Chris

NICE, NICE, VERY NICE

Northern, Johnny

MY ANGEL BABY

Northington, Gene

PASS THE BOOZE

Norton, Daniel

GEE!

Norton, Frederic

ANY TIME'S KISSING TIME
COBBLER'S SONG, THE
ROBBERS' MARCH, THE

Norton, George A.

ALL THAT GLITTERS IS NOT GOLD
MEMPHIS BLUES
MY MELANCHOLY BABY
SHE WORE A YELLOW RIBBON

Norvas, Bill

MAKE LOVE TO ME
YOU GOTTA LOVE EVERYBODY

Norwood, Denise Haas

GARDEN OF EDEN, THE

Norworth, Jack

BACK TO MY OLD HOME TOWN
COME ALONG, MY MANDY
GOOD EVENING, CAROLINE
HONEY BOY
SHINE ON, HARVEST MOON
SMARTY
TAKE ME OUT TO THE BALLGAME
TURN OFF YOUR LIGHT, MR. MOON
    MAN

Nova, Aldo

FANTASY

Novarro, Ramon

LONELY

Novello, Ivor

AND HER MOTHER CAME TOO
KEEP THE HOME FIRES BURNING
WE'LL GATHER LILACS (NOW THAT
    YOU'RE HOME ONCE MORE)

Nowa, Charles

HAPPY JOURNEY

Nowels, Rick

HEAVEN IS A PLACE ON EARTH
I CAN'T WAIT

Nugent, Maude

SWEET ROSIE O'GRADY

Nugent, Ted

CAT SCRATCH FEVER
JOURNEY TO THE CENTER OF THE
  MIND
WANGO TANGO
YANK ME, CRANK ME

Null, Cecil A.

I FORGOT MORE THAN YOU'LL EVER
  KNOW

Numan, Gary

CARS

Nunn, Bobby

ROCKET 2 U

Nunn, Earl

I'LL NEVER LET YOU WORRY MY
  MIND
SMOKE ON THE WATER

Nunn, Terri

SEX (I'M A . . .)

Nunn, Trevor

MEMORY

Nutter, Carl

SOLITAIRE

Nyro, Laura

AND WHEN I DIE
BLOWING AWAY
ELI'S COMING
FLIM FLAM MAN
SAVE THE COUNTRY
STONED SOUL PICNIC
STONEY END
SWEET BLINDNESS
TIME AND LOVE
WEDDING BELL BLUES

Oakey, Phil

DON'T YOU WANT ME
KEEP FEELING (FASCINATION)

Oakland, Ben

BEAU NIGHT IN HOTCHKISS
  CORNERS
CHAMPAGNE WALTZ, THE
DO THE NEW YORK
IF I LOVE AGAIN
IF IT'S YOU
I'LL DANCE AT YOUR WEDDING
I'LL TAKE ROMANCE
I'M A HUNDRED PERCENT FOR YOU
I'M COUNTING ON YOU
JAVA JIVE
LIKE A BOLT FROM THE BLUE
MIST IS OVER THE MOON, A
OLD, OLD CASTLE IN SCOTLAND, AN
PINK COCKTAIL FOR A BLUE LADY,
  A
ROSES IN DECEMBER
SIDEWALKS OF CUBA
TWINKLE, TWINKLE, LITTLE STAR
YOU'RE NOT SO EASY TO FORGET

Oates, John

ADULT EDUCATION
ELECTRIC BLUE
I CAN'T GO FOR THAT (NO CAN DO)
MANEATER
OUT OF TOUCH
SARA SMILE
SHE'S GONE
YOU MAKE MY DREAMS

O'Brien, Bob

ZOOT SUIT (FOR MY SUNDAY GIRL)

O'Brien, Jack

MY GREATEST MISTAKE

O'Brien, Richard

WHATEVER HAPPENED TO
  SATURDAY NIGHT

Obstoj, Jeanette

SECRET SEPARATION

Ocasek, Ric

DRIVE
EMOTION IN MOTION
GOOD TIMES ROLL
IT'S ALL I CAN DO
JUST WHAT I NEEDED
LET'S GO
MAGIC
MY BEST FRIEND'S GIRL
SHAKE IT UP
SINCE YOU'RE GONE
SOMETHING TO GRAB FOR
TONIGHT SHE COMES
YOU ARE THE GIRL
YOU MIGHT THINK

Ocean, Billy

CARIBBEAN QUEEN (NO MORE LOVE
  ON THE RUN)
COLOUR OF LOVE, THE
GET OUTTA MY DREAMS, GET INTO
  MY CAR
LOVE IS FOREVER
LOVE ZONE
MYSTERY LADY
NIGHT (FEEL LIKE GETTING DOWN)
SUDDENLY
THERE'LL BE SAD SONGS (TO MAKE
  YOU CRY)
WHEN THE GOING GETS TOUGH,
  THE TOUGH GET GOING

Ochs, Phil

THERE BUT FOR FORTUNE

O'Connor, C. W.

DOWN THE FIELD

O'Connor, Desmond

BE MINE!
HOW LUCKY YOU ARE
LET'S DO IT AGAIN

O'Connor, Donald

I WAITED A LITTLE TOO LONG

O'Connor, Gary

BACK WHERE YOU BELONG

O'Connor, Robert

MOVE IN A LITTLE CLOSER, BABY

O'Connor, Shamus

MACNAMARA'S BAND

Oda, Randy

THINK I'M IN LOVE

O'Day, Alan

ANGIE BABY
ROCK AND ROLL HEAVEN
UNDERCOVER ANGEL

O'Dea, James

HIAWATHA
MOONLIGHT
SAMMY

O'Dell, Brooks

(1-2-3-4-5-6-7) COUNT THE DAYS

O'Dell, Doye

DEAR OKIE

O'Dell, Kenny

BEAUTIFUL PEOPLE
BEHIND CLOSED DOORS
I TAKE IT ON HOME
LIZZIE AND THE RAINMAN
MAMA, HE'S CRAZY

Odette, Marcelene

FULL MOON (NOCHE DE LUNA)

O'Donnell, Charles

MY PONY BOY

O'Dowd, George "Boy George"

CHURCH OF THE POISON MIND
DO YOU REALLY WANT TO HURT ME
I'LL TUMBLE 4 YA
IT'S A MIRACLE
KARMA CHAMELEON
MISS ME BLIND
MOVE AWAY

O'Flynn, Charles

I'M SURE OF EVERYTHING BUT YOU
I'M TICKLED PINK WITH A BLUE-
    EYED BABY
JUNGLE DRUMS
NEIGHBORS
ON A BLUE AND MOONLESS NIGHT
ROSES ARE FORGET-ME-NOTS
SMILE, DARN YA, SMILE
STRANGERS
SWINGING IN A HAMMOCK

Ogdon, Ina Duley

BRIGHTEN THE CORNER WHERE
  YOU ARE

Ogerman, Claus

YOUR OTHER LOVE

O'Hara, Fiske

IRELAND IS IRELAND TO ME

O'Hara, Geoffrey

GIVE A MAN A HORSE HE CAN
  RIDE
K-K-K-KATY

O'Hara, James

CAN'T STOP MY HEART FROM
    LOVING YOU
GRANDPA (TELL ME 'BOUT THE
    GOOD OLD DAYS)
JUST LOVIN' YOU
OLDER WOMEN

O'Hara, Michael

JUST BECAUSE

Ohman, Phil

LOST

O'Kanes, The

DADDIES NEED TO GROW UP TOO

O'Keefe, Danny

GOOD TIME CHARLIE'S GOT THE
  BLUES

O'Keefe, Walter

HENRY'S MADE A LADY OUT OF
  LIZZIE
LITTLE BY LITTLE
MAN ON THE FLYING TRAPEZE, THE

Oland, Pamela Philips

SOMETHING IN YOUR EYES

Olcott, Chauncey

I LOVE THE NAME OF MARY
ISLE O'DREAMS, THE
MOTHER MACHREE
MY WILD IRISH ROSE
WHEN IRISH EYES ARE SMILING

Oldfield, Mike

FAMILY MAN
TUBULAR BELLS

Oldham, Dewey Lindon

CRY LIKE A BABY
I MET HER IN CHURCH
I'M YOUR PUPPET
IT TEARS ME UP
SWEET INSPIRATION
TAKE ME (JUST AS I AM)
WISH YOU DIDN'T HAVE TO GO

Olias, Lotar

BLUE MIRAGE (DON'T GO)

Oliphant, Newt

SAME OLD STORY, THE

Oliver, James

ITCHY TWITCHY FEELING

Oliver, Jimmy

TA TA

Oliver, Joe "King"

CANAL STREET BLUES
CHIMES BLUES
DOCTOR JAZZ
IN THE BOTTLE BLUES
SNAG IT
SUGAR FOOT STOMP
TOO LATE

Oliver, Sean

WISHING WELL

Oliver, Sy

DREAM OF YOU
EASY DOES IT
FOR DANCERS ONLY
NEIANI
OPUS NO. 1
RUMBLE

'TAINT WHAT YOU DO (IT'S THE WAY
  THAT 'CHA DO IT)
WELL, GIT IN!
YES, INDEED!

Oliver, Victor

PARADE OF THE WOODEN SOLDIERS

Oliviera, Aloysio

TICO-TICO

Olivieri, Dino

I'LL BE YOURS (J'ATTENDRAI)

Oliviero, Nino

ALL
MORE (THEME FROM "MONDO
  CANE")

Olman, Abe

DOWN AMONG THE SHELTERING
  PALMS
DOWN BY THE O-HI-O
I'M WAITING FOR SHIPS THAT
  NEVER COME IN
OH JOHNNY, OH JOHNNY, OH!
RED ONION RAG
WINTER GARDEN RAG

Olsen, Estella

THINK OF ME (WHEN YOU'RE
  LONELY)

Olsen, George

GONNA BUILD A BIG FENCE
  AROUND TEXAS

Olsen, Ole

G'BYE NOW
OH GEE, OH GOSH, OH GOLLY, I'M
  IN LOVE

Olshey, Alex

I LOVE YOU MUCH TOO MUCH

Omartian, Michael

GET USED TO IT
HOLLYWOOD
INFATUATION
I THINK IT'S LOVE
I WOULDN'T TREAT A DOG (THE
  WAY YOU TREATED ME)
(CLOSEST THING TO) PERFECT
SHE WORKS HARD FOR THE MONEY

OMD

SO IN LOVE

Onerati, Henry

LITTLE DRUMMER BOY, THE

Ono, Yoko

WALKING ON THIN ICE

Openshaw, John

JUNE BROUGHT THE ROSES
LOVE SENDS A LITTLE GIFT OF
  ROSES

Oppenheim, Dave

HOLD ME
I MAY BE DANCING WITH
  SOMEBODY ELSE
IT'S THE GIRL
WHEN A LADY MEETS A
  GENTLEMAN DOWN SOUTH
WHEN YOU'RE OVER SIXTY, AND
  YOU FEEL LIKE SWEET SIXTEEN

Oppenheimer, George

I FEEL A SONG COMIN' ON

Orange, Walter

BRICK HOUSE
NIGHTSHIFT
SLIPPERY WHEN WET
SWEET LOVE
TOO HOT TA TROT

Orbe

SONG OF JOY

Orbison, Roy

BLUE ANGEL
BLUE BAYOU
COMMUNICATION BREAKDOWN
CROWD, THE
CRYING
FALLING
GOODNIGHT
I'M HURTIN'
IN DREAMS
IT'S OVER
OH, PRETTY WOMAN
ONLY THE LONELY (KNOW THE WAY
    I FEEL)
RIDE AWAY
RUNNING SCARED
SEE RUBY FALL
TWINKLE TOES
WORKIN' FOR THE MAN
(SAY) YOU'RE MY GIRL

O'Reilly, P. J.

FOR YOU ALONE

Orent, Milton

IN THE LAND OF OO-BLA-DEE

Organ, Jerry

CRYING MY HEART OUT OVER YOU

Orlob, Harold

ASK THE STARS
I'LL REMEMBER YOU
I WONDER WHO'S KISSING HER
    NOW
WAITING

Orlowski, Anne

RUBBER BALL

Ormont, David

MY KINGDOM FOR A KISS

Ornadel, Cyril

IF I RULED THE WORLD
PORTRAIT OF MY LOVE

Ornelas, René

ANGELITO
LO MUCHO TE QUIERO (THE MORE I
    LOVE YOU)

O'Rourke, Dennis

HONKY TONK MOON

Orr, Charles

GAL WHO INVENTED KISSIN', THE

Ortolani, Riz

FORGET DOMANI
MORE (THEME FROM "MONDO
    CANE")
SEVENTH DAWN, THE
TILL LOVE TOUCHES YOUR LIFE

Ory, Edward "Kid"

MUSKRAT (OR MUSKAT) RAMBLE

Orzabal, Roy

EVERYBODY WANTS TO RULE THE
    WORLD

Orzabel, Roland

SHOUT

Osborn, Joe

CATCH A LITTLE RAINDROP

Osborn, Victor

DANCE (DISCO HEAT)

Osborne, Gary

BLUE EYES
I'M DREAMING
LITTLE JEANNIE

PART-TIME LOVE

Osborne, Jeffrey

DON'T YOU GET SO MAD
HOLDING ON (WHEN LOVE IS GONE)
I REALLY DON'T NEED NO LIGHT
ON THE WINGS OF LOVE

Osborne, Jimmy

DEATH OF LITTLE KATHY FISCUS,
    THE

Osborne, Nat

AS LONG AS THE SHAMROCK
    GROWS GREEN
TAKE ME BACK TO THE GARDEN OF
    LOVE
YOU WANTED SOMEONE TO PLAY
    WITH (I WANTED SOMEONE TO
    LOVE)

Osborne, Will

BESIDE AN OPEN FIREPLACE
BETWEEN 18TH AND 19TH ON
    CHESTNUT STREET
ON A BLUE AND MOONLESS NIGHT
POMPTON TURNPIKE
ROSES ARE FORGET-ME-NOTS
SWEET, SWEET LOVE

Oskar, Lee

GYPSY MAN
L. A. SUNSHINE
LOW RIDER
ME AND BABY BROTHER
SLIPPIN' INTO DARKNESS
SUMMER
WHY CAN'T WE BE FRIENDS?
WORLD IS A GHETTO, THE

Oslin, K. T.

80'S LADIES
DO YA'
HEY BOBBY
HOLD ME
I'LL ALWAYS COME BACK

Osmond, Alan

CRAZY HORSES
DOWN BY THE LAZY RIVER
HOLD HER TIGHT

Osmond, Merrill

CRAZY HORSES
DOWN BY THE LAZY RIVER
HOLD HER TIGHT

Osmond, Wayne

CRAZY HORSES
HOLD HER TIGHT

Osser, Edna

I DREAM OF YOU
LAST TIME I SAW YOU, THE
ROSANNE
THERE'S GOOD BLUES TONIGHT

Osser, Glenn (Abe)

ROSANNE
THERE'S GOOD BLUES TONIGHT

Osterman, Jack

CAN'T YOU UNDERSTAND?
IS EVERYBODY HAPPY NOW?

O'Sullivan, Raymond (Gilbert)

ALONE AGAIN (NATURALLY)
CLAIR
GET DOWN
OUT OF THE QUESTION

Oswald, John

HEAVEN

Otis, Clyde

BABY (YOU'VE GOT WHAT IT TAKES)
BOLL WEEVIL SONG, THE
CALL ME
DONCHA' THINK IT'S TIME
ENDLESSLY

FOR MY BABY
I'M TOO FAR GONE (TO TURN
    AROUND)
IT'S JUST A MATTER OF TIME
KIDDIO
LOOKING BACK
MOTHER NATURE, FATHER TIME
NO OTHER ONE
OUT OF SIGHT, OUT OF MIND
ROCKIN' GOOD WAY (TO MESS
    AROUND AND FALL IN LOVE), A
SO CLOSE
STROLL, THE
THANK YOU PRETTY BABY
THAT'S ALL THERE IS TO THAT
THINK TWICE
THIS BITTER EARTH

Otis, Johnny

ALL NIGHT LONG
CUPID'S BOOGIE
DANCE WITH ME HENRY
DECEIVIN' BLUES
DOUBLE CROSSING BLUES
EVERY BEAT OF MY HEART
GEE, BABY
MISTRUSTIN' BLUES
ROCKIN' BLUES
SO FINE
WILLIE AND THE HAND JIVE

Otis, Shuggie

STRAWBERRY LETTER 23

O'Toole, Mark

RELAX
TWO TRIBES
WELCOME TO THE PLEASUREDOME

Ott, Vi

WHY DOES IT HAVE TO RAIN ON
    SUNDAY?

Ousley, "King" Curtis

JEALOUS LOVE
MEMPHIS SOUL STEW
SOUL SERENADE
SOUL TWIST

Overbea, Danny

FORTY CUPS OF COFFEE

Overstreet, Benton

GEORGE BLUES
THERE'LL BE SOME CHANGES MADE

Overstreet, Paul

AMERICAN ME
DIGGIN' UP BONES
FOREVER AND EVER, AMEN
HOUSTON SOLUTION
I WON'T TAKE LESS THAN YOUR
    LOVE
LONG LINE OF LOVE, A
LOVE HELPS THOSE
NO PLACE LIKE HOME
ONE LOVE AT A TIME
ON THE OTHER HAND
SAME OLE ME
WHEN YOU SAY NOTHING AT ALL
YOU AGAIN

Owen, Anita

DAISIES WON'T TELL
SWEET BUNCH OF DAISIES

Owen, Cray

CRACK KILLED APPLEJACK

Owen, Fuzzy

DEAR JOHN LETTER, A
ONE YOU SLIP AROUND WITH, THE
SAME OLD ME, THE

Owen, Randy

FALLIN' AGAIN
FEELS SO RIGHT
LADY DOWN ON LOVE
MOUNTAIN MUSIC
TENNESSEE RIVER
WHY LADY WHY

Owens, A. E., Jr.

YOU'RE FOR ME

Owens, A. L. "Doodle"

ALL I HAVE TO OFFER YOU IS ME
I CAN'T BELIEVE THAT YOU'VE
   STOPPED LOVING ME
JOHNNY ONE TIME
WHERE DID THEY GO, LORD

Owens, B. E.

PUT IT OFF UNTIL TOMORROW

Owens, Bill

COMPANY YOU KEEP, THE

Owens, Bonnie

LEGEND OF BONNIE AND CLYDE,
   THE

Owens, Buck

BEFORE YOU GO
CRYING TIME
EXCUSE ME (I THINK I'VE GOT A
   HEARTACHE)
FOOLIN' AROUND
HOW LONG WILL MY BABY BE
   GONE?
I DON'T CARE (JUST AS LONG AS
   YOU LOVE ME)
I'VE GOT A TIGER BY THE TAIL
KANSAS CITY SONG
LET THE WORLD KEEP ON A
   TURNIN'
LOVE'S GONNA LIVE HERE
MOMMY FOR A DAY
MY HEART SKIPS A BEAT
NOBODY'S FOOL BUT YOURS
ONLY YOU (CAN BREAK MY HEART)
OPEN UP YOUR HEART
ROLLIN' IN MY SWEET BABY'S ARMS
SAM'S PLACE
SWEET ROSIE JONES
TALL, DARK STRANGER
TOGETHER AGAIN
UNDER THE INFLUENCE OF LOVE
UNDER YOUR SPELL AGAIN
WAITIN' IN YOUR WELFARE LINE
WE'RE THE TALK OF THE TOWN
WHERE DOES THE GOOD TIMES GO?
WHO'S GONNA MOW YOUR GRASS?

YOUR TENDER LOVING CARE

Owens, Cliff

ANY WAY YOU WANT ME (THAT'S
   HOW I WILL BE)

Owens, Don

COLD DARK WATERS

Owens, Harry

COCOANUT GROVE
DANCING UNDER THE STARS
DOWN WHERE THE TRADE WINDS
   BLOW
DREAMY HAWAIIAN MOON
LINGER AWHILE
SING ME A SONG OF THE ISLANDS
SWEET LEILANI
TO YOU, SWEETHEART, ALOHA

Owens, Jack

BY-U, BY-O (THE LOU'SIANA
   LULLABY)
CYNTHIA'S IN LOVE
HI, NEIGHBOR!
HOW SOON (WILL I BE SEEING
   YOU)?
HUT-SUT SONG, THE

Owens, Kelly

I BEG OF YOU
THAT'S ALL THERE IS TO THAT

Owens, Melvin

SUPER BOWL SHUFFLE

Owens, Tex

CATTLE CALL, THE

Ozen, Barbara Lynn

YOU'LL LOSE A GOOD THING

Pace, D.

LOVE ME TONIGHT

MAN WITHOUT LOVE, A
SUDDENLY YOU LOVE ME

Pack, David

ALL I NEED
BIGGEST PART OF ME
HOLDIN' ON TO YESTERDAY
HOW MUCH I FEEL
NICE, NICE, VERY NICE
YOU'RE THE ONLY WOMAN (YOU
   AND I)

Pack, Marshall T.

BALLAD OF WILD RIVER, THE

Paden, Frank

I DO

Padgett, Jack

COW TOWN

Padilla, Jose

PAREE!
VALENCIA
WHO'LL BUY MY VIOLETS?

Page, Jimmy

BLACK DOG
FOOL IN THE RAIN
GOOD TIMES, BAD TIMES
HAPPENINGS TEN YEARS TIME AGO
HEARTBREAKER
IMMIGRANT SONG
LIVING LOVING MAID (SHE'S JUST A
   WOMAN)
WHOLE LOTTA LOVE

Page, Martin

THESE DREAMS
WE BUILT THIS CITY

Page, Richard

BROKEN WINGS
IS IT LOVE
KYRIE

Page, Scott

TOO MANY TIMES

Paice, Ian

SMOKE ON THE WATER
WOMAN FROM TOKYO

Paich, David

99
AFRICA
GOT TO BE REAL
HOLD THE LINE
HOUSTON (I'M COMIN' TO SEE YOU)
IT'S OVER
LIDO SHUFFLE
LOWDOWN
MISS SUN
ROSANNA

Paiva, Jararaca

I WANT MY MAMA (A.K.A. MAMA YO
    QUIERO)

Paiva, Vincente

I WANT MY MAMA (A.K.A. MAMA YO
    QUIERO)

Palas, Lisa

"YOU'VE GOT" THE TOUCH

Paley, Herman

ANGEL EYES
BILLY (FOR WHEN I WALK)
COME BACK TO ARIZONA
HAVANA
SWEET LITTLE BUTTERCUP
WHEN IT'S NIGHTTIME DOWN IN
    BURGUNDY

Paley, Lou

COME TO THE MOON
SOMETHING ABOUT LOVE

Palitz, Morty

WHILE WE'RE YOUNG

Pallavicini, Vito

MY LOVE, FORGIVE ME (AMORE,
    SCUSAMI)

Pallini, Bruno

ROCKIN' SOUL

Palmar, Wally

TALKING IN YOUR SLEEP

Palmer, David

LOOK OF LOVE (PART ONE)
NIGHTINGALE
SPANISH EDDIE

Palmer, Donald

JAZZMAN

Palmer, Florrie

MORNING TRAIN (NINE TO FIVE)

Palmer, Jack

BOOG-IT
EVERYBODY LOVES MY BABY (BUT
    MY BABY DON'T LOVE NOBODY
    BUT ME)
I FOUND A NEW BABY
JUMPIN' JIVE, THE

Palmer, John E.

BAND PLAYED ON, THE

Palmer, P.

I'M NO ANGEL

Palmer, Robert

ADDICTED TO LOVE
HYPERACTIVE
SIMPLY IRRESISTIBLE

SOME LIKE IT HOT
YOU'RE GONNA GET WHAT'S
    COMING

Palmer, Winfred

11TH HOUR MELODY

Panella, Frank

OLD GREY MARE, THE (SHE AIN'T
    WHAT SHE USED TO BE)

Pankow, James

ALIVE AGAIN
FEELIN' STRONGER EVERY DAY
JUST YOU 'N' ME
MAKE ME SMILE
OLD DAYS
(I'VE BEEN) SEARCHIN' SO LONG

Panzer, Marty

EVEN NOW
IT'S A MIRACLE
THIS ONE'S FOR YOU
THROUGH THE YEARS

Panzeri, Mario

COME PRIMA (FOR THE FIRST TIME)
FERRYBOAT SERENADE, THE
LOVE ME TONIGHT
MAN WITHOUT LOVE, A
SUDDENLY YOU LOVE ME
TO THE DOOR OF THE SUN (ALLE
    PORTE DEL SOLE)

Paoli, Gino

PHOENIX LOVE THEME, THE
YOU'RE MY WORLD

Paparelli, Frank

NIGHT IN TUNISIA, A

Pappalardi, F.

FOR YASGUR'S FARM

Pardini, Lou

I WONDER WHO SHE'S SEEING NOW
JUST TO SEE HER

Parham, Pylia

I WANT TO KNOW

Parham, Tiny

DRUMMIN' MAN

Paris, Adenaye

SOONER OR LATER

Paris, Ekundayo

IT'S ECSTASY WHEN YOU LAY DOWN
    NEXT TO ME
SOONER OR LATER

Paris, James B.

CALICO RAG
GUITAR POLKA
I'M LOSING MY MIND OVER YOU
IT'S UP TO YOU

Parish, Mitchell

ALL I NEED IS YOU
ALL MY LOVE
ANGEL
BABY, WHEN YOU AIN'T THERE
BELLE OF THE BALL
BLOND SAILOR, THE
BLUE SKIRT WALTZ, THE
BLUES SERENADE, A
CABIN IN THE COTTON
CAROLINA ROLLING STONE
CHRISTMAS NIGHT IN HARLEM
CIAO, CIAO, BAMBINA
CORRINE, CORRINA (CORINNA,
    CORINNA)
DEEP PURPLE
DOES YOUR HEART BEAT FOR ME?
DON'T BE THAT WAY
DOWN A CAROLINA LANE
DREAM, DREAM, DREAM
EMALINE
EVENIN'

HANDS ACROSS THE TABLE
I'M A HUNDRED PERCENT FOR YOU
I'M SATISFIED
IS THAT RELIGION?
IT HAPPENS TO THE BEST OF
    FRIENDS
IT'S WONDERFUL
LAMP IS LOW, THE
LAZY RHAPSODY
LET ME LOVE YOU TONIGHT
LIKE A BOLT FROM THE BLUE
LILACS IN THE RAIN
LOUISIANA FAIRY TALE
MADEMOISELLE DE PAREE
MOON FELL IN THE RIVER, THE
MOON IS A SILVER DOLLAR, THE
MOONLIGHT LOVE
MOONLIGHT SERENADE
MR. GHOST GOES TO TOWN
ONE MORNING IN MAY
ORANGE BLOSSOM LANE
ORCHIDS FOR REMEMBRANCE
ORGAN GRINDER'S SWING
RUBY
SCAT SONG, THE
SENTIMENTAL GENTLEMAN FROM
    GEORGIA
SERENATA
SIDEWALKS OF CUBA
SLEIGH RIDE
SOPHISTICATED LADY
SOPHISTICATED SWING
STAIRWAY TO THE STARS
STAR DUST
STARLIT HOUR, THE
STARS FELL ON ALABAMA
SWEET LORRAINE
TAKE ME IN YOUR ARMS
TZENA, TZENA, TZENA
VOLARE (A.K.A. NEL BLU, DIPINTO
    DI BLU)
YEARNING FOR LOVE

Parissi, Robert

PLAY THAT FUNKY MUSIC

Parker, Albert R.

WE'LL MEET AGAIN

Parker, Barry

SAND AND THE SEA, THE

Parker, Brian

CONCRETE AND CLAY

Parker, Charlie

BILLIE'S BOUNCE
CONFIRMATION
DONNA LEE
HOOTIE BLUES
NOW'S THE TIME
ORNITHOLOGY
YARDBIRD SUITE

Parker, Dale

AS FAR AS I'M CONCERNED
LITTLE ANGEL WITH A DIRTY FACE

Parker, Dorothy

HOW AM I TO KNOW?
I WISHED ON THE MOON

Parker, Eula

VILLAGE OF ST. BERNADETTE, THE

Parker, Graham

HOLD BACK THE NIGHT
LIFE GETS BETTER
WAKE UP (NEXT TO YOU)

Parker, Herman, Jr.

MYSTERY TRAIN

Parker, John

HARD HABIT TO BREAK
TRA LA LA

Parker, Jonathan

BABY SITTIN' BOOGIE

Parker, Judy

DECEMBER 1963 (OH, WHAT A
  NIGHT)
WHO LOVES YOU

Parker, Ray, Jr.

GHOSTBUSTERS
I DON'T THINK THAT MAN SHOULD
  SLEEP ALONE
I STILL CAN'T GET OVER LOVING
  YOU
JACK AND JILL
JAMIE
LET ME GO
MR. TELEPHONE MAN
OTHER WOMAN, THE
OVER YOU
WOMAN NEEDS LOVE, A (JUST LIKE
  YOU DO)
YOU CAN'T CHANGE THAT
YOU GOT THE LOVE

Parker, Richard

COMIN' IN AND OUT OF YOUR LIFE
OO WEE BABY, I LOVE YOU

Parker, Robert

BAREFOOTIN'

Parker, Rod

DONDE ESTA SANTA CLAUS?
  (WHERE IS SANTA CLAUS?)

Parker, Ross

I WON'T TELL A SOUL
SONG OF JOY
THERE'LL ALWAYS BE AN ENGLAND

Parker, Sol

DANSERO
THIS LOVE OF MINE

Parker, Wayne

SOMEDAY

Parks, Carson

CAB DRIVER
SOMETHIN' STUPID

Parks, Larry

BREAD AND BUTTER

Parks, Van Dyke

COME TO THE SUNSHINE
HEROES AND VILLAINS

Parks, Weldon

DANCING MACHINE

Parman, Cliff

PRETEND
SANDS OF GOLD

Parnes, Paul

HAPPINESS IS
NEXT STEP IS LOVE, THE

Parr, Harry

BLUEBIRD OF HAPPINESS

Parr, John

ST. ELMO'S FIRE (MAN IN MOTION)

Parries, Fred

PARADIDDLE JOE

Parris, Fred

IN THE STILL OF THE NITE (A.K.A.
  I'LL REMEMBER)
LOST IN THE FIFTIES TONIGHT (IN
  THE STILL OF THE NIGHT)

Parrish, Avery

AFTER HOURS

Parsons, Alan

EYE IN THE SKY
GAMES PEOPLE PLAY
TIME

Parsons, Bill

ALL-AMERICAN BOY, THE

Parsons, Donovan

SHE'S SUCH A COMFORT TO ME

Parsons, Geoffrey

CHEE CHEE-OO CHEE (SANG THE
  LITTLE BIRD)
ETERNALLY (A.K.A. LIMELIGHT OR
  THE TERRY THEME)
IF YOU GO
IF YOU LOVE ME (REALLY LOVE ME)
LITTLE SHOEMAKER, THE
OH, MY PAPA
SMILE

Parton, Candy

I WANT TO KNOW YOU BEFORE WE
  MAKE LOVE

Parton, Des

DAS SWEET DREAMER

Parton, Dolly

9 TO 5
ALL I CAN DO
BABY I'M BURNIN'
BARGAIN STORE, THE
COAT OF MANY COLORS
COMPANY YOU KEEP, THE
DADDY WAS AN OLD TIME
  PREACHER MAN
I WILL ALWAYS LOVE YOU
JOLENE
JOSHUA
LIGHT OF A CLEAR BLUE MORNING
LOVE IS LIKE A BUTTERFLY
MAKING PLANS
PUT IT OFF UNTIL TOMORROW
SEEKER, THE

Payne, Kim

MIDNIGHT RIDER

Payne, Leo

BLUE SIDE OF LONESOME
CRY-BABY HEART
I HEARD A HEART BREAK LAST
    NIGHT
I LOVE YOU BECAUSE
TAKE ME
THINGS HAVE GONE TO PIECES
YOU CAN'T PICK A ROSE IN
    DECEMBER
YOU'VE STILL GOT A PLACE IN MY
    HEART

Payne, Scherrie

CRUMBS OFF THE TABLE

Payton, Dennis

NINETEEN DAYS
SATISFIED WITH YOU

Peacock, Trevor

MRS. BROWN, YOU'VE GOT A
    LOVELY DAUGHTER

Pearcy, Stephen

ROUND AND ROUND

Pearl, Leslie

YOU NEVER GAVE UP ON ME

Pearson, Derrick

HAVE YOU HAD YOUR LOVE TODAY

Pearson, Eugene

THOUSAND STARS, A

Peart, Neil

LIMELIGHT
NEW WORLD MAN
SPIRIT OF RADIO, THE

TOM SAWYER

Pease, Harry

I DON'T WANT TO GET WELL (I'M IN
    LOVE WITH A BEAUTIFUL NURSE)
PAL THAT I LOVED, THE (STOLE THE
    GAL THAT I LOVED)
PEGGY O'NEIL
PRETTY KITTY KELLY
TEN LITTLE FINGERS AND TEN
    LITTLE TOES (DOWN IN
    TENNESSEE)

Pease, Sharon

SNATCH AND GRAB IT

Pebbles

MERCEDES BOY

Peck, Raymond

BABY
LANTERN OF LOVE

Peddy, A. R.

HONKY TONK SONG
I'M TIRED
WHY, WHY

Pedrick, Bob

IF YOU DON'T WANT MY LOVE

Pedroski, Lefty

BROOKLYN

Peebles, Ann

I CAN'T STAND THE RAIN

Peebles, Melvin Van

AIN'T LOVE GRAND

Peek, Dan

TODAY'S THE DAY

Peeples, Curt

EVEN THO'

Pegues, Louis

UP AND DOWN

Pelletieri, Vito

UNLOVED AND UNCLAIMED

Pelosi, Don

BELLA BELLA MARIE
LITTLE OLD MILL, THE (WENT
    ROUND AND ROUND)

Peltier, Allen N.

DAY FOR DECISION

Pena, Paul

JET AIRLINER

Penn, Arthur A.

CARISSIMA
IT'S A LONG LANE THAT HAS NO
    TURNING
LAMPLIT HOUR, THE
MAGIC OF YOUR EYES, THE
SMILIN' THROUGH
SUNRISE AND YOU

Penney, Ed

QUEEN OF THE SENIOR PROM
SOMEBODY'S KNOCKIN'

Penniman, Richard

GIRL CAN'T HELP IT, THE
GREAT GOSH A'MIGHTY! (IT'S A
    MATTER OF TIME)
JENNY, JENNY
JENNY, TAKE A RIDE!
KEEP A KNOCKIN'
LONG TALL SALLY
LUCILLE
MISS ANN
SHE'S GOT IT

SLIPPIN' AND SLIDIN' (PEEPIN' AND
   HIDIN')
TUTTI FRUTTI

Pennington, Dan

CRY LIKE A BABY
I MET HER IN CHURCH
I'M YOUR PUPPET
IT TEARS ME UP
SWEET INSPIRATION
TAKE ME (JUST AS I AM)
WISH YOU DIDN'T HAVE TO GO

Pennington, James P.

GIVE ME ONE MORE CHANCE
I CAN'T GET CLOSE ENOUGH
I DON'T WANT TO BE A MEMORY
IT'LL BE ME
JUST IN CASE
SHE'S A MIRACLE
SHE'S TOO GOOD TO BE TRUE
TAKE ME DOWN

Pennington, Ray

I'M A RAMBLIN' MAN
STAY AWAY FROM MY BABY
THREE HEARTS IN A TANGLE
WALKING ON NEW GRASS

Penny, Hank

BLOODSHOT EYES
MISSOURI

Penny, Joe

ANGEL BABY

Penny, Lee

MY ADOBE HACIENDA

Penrose, Jule

IF IT'S TRUE

Penzabene, Roger

END OF OUR ROAD, THE

I COULD NEVER LOVE ANOTHER
   (AFTER LOVING YOU)
I WISH IT WOULD RAIN
YOU'RE MY EVERYTHING

Peoples, Alisa

DON'T STOP THE MUSIC

Pepper, Buddy

DON'T TELL ME
PILLOW TALK
SORRY
VAYA CON DIOS (MAY GOD BE WITH
   YOU)

Peppers, Bill

I WAS THE ONE
MY LIPS ARE SEALED

Peppers, Jimmy

LOVE TAKES CARE OF ME

Peppiatt, Frank

BALLAD OF IRVING, THE

Percy, Michael

BRAND NEW LOVER
YOU SPIN ME ROUND LIKE A
   RECORD

Peretti, Hugo

BIMBOMBEY
CAN'T HELP FALLING IN LOVE
CRAZY OTTO RAG, THE
EXPERIENCE UNNECESSARY
HELLO HEARTACHE, GOODBYE
   LOVE
LET'S PUT IT ALL TOGETHER
LION SLEEPS TONIGHT, THE
WILD IN THE COUNTRY

Perez, Louie

WILL THE WOLF SURVIVE?

Perkins, Barney

WANT ADS

Perkins, Carl Lee

BLUE SUEDE SHOES
BOPPIN' THE BLUES
DADDY SANG BASS
MATCHBOX
YOUR TRUE LOVE

Perkins, Frank

CABIN IN THE COTTON
DOWN A CAROLINA LANE
EMALINE
FANDANGO
SCAT SONG, THE
SENTIMENTAL GENTLEMAN FROM
   GEORGIA
STARS FELL ON ALABAMA

Perkins, Ray

DOWN THE OLD CHURCH AISLE
LADY LUCK
ONLY SONG I KNOW, THE
SMILING IRISH EYES
UNDER A TEXAS MOON

Perkins, William H.

AT THE END OF A BEAUTIFUL DAY

Perne, Nils Johan

SHRINE OF SAINT CECILIA, THE

Perren, Chris

LITTLE BIT OF LOVE (IS ALL IT
   TAKES), A

Perren, Freddie

ABC
BOOGIE FEVER
DO IT BABY
HEAVEN MUST BE MISSING AN
   ANGEL
HOT LINE
I PLEDGE MY LOVE

I WANT YOU ALL TO MYSELF (JUST
    YOU)
I WILL SURVIVE
LOVE YOU SAVE, THE
MAKIN' IT
MAMA'S PEARL
REUNITED
SHAKE YOUR GROOVE THING
SUGAR DADDY
THAT ONCE IN A LIFETIME
WHODUNIT

Perricone, Jack

RUN JOEY RUN

Perrin

MAMMY'S LITTLE PUMPKIN
    COLORED COON

Perry, Barney

WALKING IN RHYTHM

Perry, Betty Sue

BEFORE I'M OVER YOU
HOME YOU'RE TEARING DOWN, THE
ROLL MUDDY RIVER
WINE, WOMEN AND SONG

Perry, Greg S.

BRING THE BOYS HOME
ONE MONKEY DON'T STOP NO SHOW
PAY TO THE PIPER
SOMEBODY'S BEEN SLEEPING (IN
    MY BED)
STICK-UP
WANT ADS

Perry, Herb

I'M NEVER SATISFIED

Perry, Joe

DUDE (LOOKS LIKE A LADY)
WALK THIS WAY

Perry, Leonard

ONE LOVE IN MY LIFETIME

Perry, Phil

UNITED TOGETHER

Perry, Roger

KID AGAIN, A

Perry, Steve

AFTER THE FALL
ANY WAY YOU WANT IT
BE GOOD TO YOURSELF
DON'T FIGHT IT
DON'T STOP BELIEVIN'
FOOLISH HEART
I'LL BE ALRIGHT WITHOUT YOU
LOVIN', TOUCHIN', SQEEZIN'
OH, SHERRIE
ONLY THE YOUNG
OPEN ARMS
SEND HER MY LOVE
SEPARATE WAYS
STILL THEY RIDE
SUZANNE
WHO'S CRYING NOW

Perryman, Willie

RED'S BOOGIE

Persson, Mats

LISTEN TO YOUR HEART

Pert, M.

FAMILY MAN

Pesce, Joey

VOICES CARRY

Pescetto, Jeff

LOVIN' ON NEXT TO NOTHIN'
SPACEBALLS

Pessis, Andre

WALKING ON A THIN LINE

Pestalozza, A.

CIRIBIRIBIN

Peterik, Jim

AMERICAN HEARTBEAT
BURNING HEART
CAUGHT UP IN YOU
EYE OF THE TIGER
HIGH ON YOU
I CAN'T HOLD BACK
IS THIS LOVE
VEHICLE
YOU WOULDN'T LISTEN

Peters, Ben

BEFORE THE NEXT TEARDROP
    FALLS
DAYTIME FRIENDS
IT'S GONNA TAKE A LITTLE BIT
    LONGER
KISS AN ANGEL GOOD MORNIN'
LOVE PUT A SONG IN MY HEART
MORE TO ME
TELL ME WHAT IT'S LIKE
THAT'S A NO NO
TURN THE WORLD AROUND THE
    OTHER WAY

Peters, Jerry

GOING IN CIRCLES

Peters, Lisa

VERY SPECIAL

Petersburski, J.

OH, DONNA CLARA

Peterson, Al

BORN TO WANDER

Peterson, Betty

MY HAPPINESS

Peterson, Ernie

I WANT TO BE THE ONLY ONE

Pether, Henry E.

MOLLY DEAR, IT'S YOU I'M AFTER
POOR JOHN
WAITING AT THE CHURCH

Petkere, Bernice

BY A RIPPLING STREAM
CLOSE YOUR EYES
LADY I LOVE, THE
LULLABY OF THE LEAVES
STARLIGHT

Petrie, H. W.

AS DEEP AS THE DEEP BLUE SEA
ASLEEP IN THE DEEP
DAVEY JONES' LOCKER
I DON'T WANT TO PLAY IN YOUR
    YARD
WHERE THE SUNSET TURNS THE
    OCEAN'S BLUE TO GOLD

Petrik, Jim

SEARCH IS OVER, THE

Petrillo, Caesar

JIM

Petrillo, Mike

TELL IT TO THE RAIN

Petrunka, Myrna

ARE YOU MINE?

Pettaway, William

GIRL, YOU KNOW IT'S TRUE

Pettis, Jack

BUGLE CALL RAG

Petty, Norman

ALMOST PARADISE
NOT FADE AWAY
PEGGY SUE
RAVE ON
THAT'LL BE THE DAY
TRUE LOVE WAYS

Petty, Tom

BREAKDOWN
DON'T COME AROUND HERE NO
    MORE
DON'T DO ME LIKE THAT
HERE COMES MY GIRL
I NEED TO KNOW
JAMMIN' ME
LET ME UP (I'VE HAD ENOUGH)
LISTEN TO HER HEART
NEVER BE YOU
REFUGEE
STOP DRAGGIN' MY HEART AROUND
WAITING, THE
WAY TO BE WICKED
YOU GOT LUCKY

Peverett, Dave

SLOW RIDE
THIRD TIME LUCKY (FIRST TIME I
    WAS A FOOL)

Peyton, Dave

I AIN'T GOT NOBODY

Pfeil, Jacob

BLOND SAILOR, THE

Pfrimmer, Don

BY NOW
DRIFTER
MY HEART
SHE KEEPS THE HOMES FIRES
    BURNING

YOU'RE THE LAST THING I NEEDED
    TONIGHT
YOU SHOULD HAVE BEEN GONE BY
    NOW

Pharis, Hod

I HEARD THE BLUEBIRDS SONG

Philipp, Adolph

ALMA, WHERE DO YOU LIVE?

Philippe-Gerard, Angela

WHEN THE WORLD WAS YOUNG
    (AH, THE APPLE TREES)

Philippe-Gerard, M.

MYSTERY STREET

Philips, Gary

BREAKUP SONG, THE (THEY DON'T
    WRITE 'EM)

Philleo, Estelle

OUT WHERE THE WEST BEGINS

Phillinganes, Greg

LOVE WILL CONQUER ALL
SE LA

Phillips, Billy

FALLING BACK TO YOU

Phillips, Charlie

SUGARTIME

Phillips, Dolores

COME TOMORROW

Phillips, Fred

GOODBYE, LITTLE GIRL OF MY
    DREAMS

GOT HER OFF MY HANDS BUT
    CAN'T GET HER OFF MY MIND
GOT THE BENCH, GOT THE PARK
    (BUT I HAVEN'T GOT YOU)

Phillips, Herman

PASSWORD

Phillips, J. C.

GREEN-EYED LADY

Phillips, John

CALIFORNIA DREAMIN'
CREEQUE ALLEY
DANCING BEAR
GO WHERE YOU WANNA GO
I SAW HER AGAIN
KOKOMO
LIKE AN OLD TIME MOVIE
LOOK THROUGH MY WINDOW
MISSISSIPPI
MONDAY, MONDAY
SAFE IN MY GARDEN
SAN FRANCISCO (BE SURE TO WEAR
    SOME FLOWERS IN YOUR HAIR)
TWELVE THIRTY (YOUNG GIRLS ARE
    COMING TO THE CANYON)
WORDS OF LOVE

Phillips, Katherine

GONNA BUILD A BIG FENCE
    AROUND TEXAS

Phillips, Marvin

CHERRY PIE
DREAM GIRL

Phillips, Michelle G.

CALIFORNIA DREAMIN'
CREEQUE ALLEY

Phillips, Mike

BIG RIVER, BIG MAN
NORTH TO ALASKA

Phillips, Mildred

MAMBO ROCK

Phillips, Sam C.

MYSTERY TRAIN

Phillips, Stu

BEYOND THE VALLEY OF THE
    DOLLS

Philp, James

JEWEL OF ASIA, THE

Photoglo, Jim

FISHIN' IN THE DARK

Piaf, Edith

IF YOU LOVE ME (REALLY LOVE ME)
I'LL REMEMBER TODAY
JUST COME HOME
LA VIE EN ROSE
WHAT CAN I DO?

Piano, Tony

STORY OF OUR LOVE, THE

Piantadosi, Al

BABY SHOES
CURSE OF AN ACHING HEART, THE
    (OR, YOU MADE ME WHAT I AM
    TODAY)
I DIDN'T RAISE MY BOY TO BE A
    SOLDIER
MY MARIUCCIA TAKE A STEAMBOAT
PAL OF MY CRADLE DAYS
SEND ME AWAY WITH A SMILE
THAT'S HOW I NEED YOU
WHAT A WONDERFUL MOTHER
    YOU'D BE
WHEN YOU PLAY IN THE GAME OF
    LOVE
WHEN YOU'RE IN LOVE WITH
    SOMEONE (WHO IS NOT IN LOVE
    WITH YOU)

WILD, WILD WOMEN ARE MAKING A
    WILD MAN OF ME, THE

Picariello, Frederick A.

TALLAHASSEE LASSIE

Piccirillo, Mike

TELL ME TOMORROW

Piccolo, Steve

SELF CONTROL

Pickett, Bobby

MONSTER MASH

Pickett, Phil

IT'S A MIRACLE
KARMA CHAMELEON
MOVE AWAY

Pickett, Wilson

DON'T KNOCK MY LOVE
I FOUND A LOVE
IF YOU NEED ME
I'M A MIDNIGHT MOVER
IN THE MIDNIGHT HOUR
IT'S TOO LATE

Picone, Vito

LITTLE STAR

Pierce, D.

I NEED LOVE

Pierce, Don

TIMBROOK

Pierce, John

COOL LOVE

Pierce, Marvin

FIRE

LOVE ROLLERCOASTER
SKIN TIGHT
SWEET STICKY THING
WHO'D SHE COO

Pierce, Tony

CROSS MY BROKEN HEART

Pierce, Webb

CRAZY WILD DESIRE
EVEN THO'
FALLEN ANGEL
FALLING BACK TO YOU
HOLIDAY FOR LOVE
HOW DO YOU TALK TO A BABY?
I AIN'T NEVER
I DON'T CARE
LAST WALTZ, THE
LEAVIN' ON YOUR MIND
LET FORGIVENESS IN
LITTLE ROSA
MORE AND MORE
SLOWLY
SWEET LIPS
THAT HEART BELONGS TO ME
THOSE WONDERFUL YEARS
THOUSAND MILES AGO, A
TUPELO COUNTY JAIL
YES, I KNOW WHY
YOU'RE NOT MINE ANYMORE

Piercy, Andrew

DER KOMMISSAR

Pierson, Cather

LOVE SHACK

Pierson, Kate

PRIVATE IDAHO

Pigford, Nelson

IT'S ECSTASY WHEN YOU LAY DOWN
NEXT TO ME

Piggot, S.

LIVING IN A BOX

Pike, Victoria

IT FEELS SO GOOD TO BE LOVED SO
BAD
RAIN IN MY HEART

Pilat, Lorenzo

LOVE ME TONIGHT
SUDDENLY YOU LOVE ME
TO THE DOOR OF THE SUN (ALLE
PORTE DEL SOLE)

Pilcer, Harry

GABY GLIDE, THE

Piller, Gene

MR. TOUCHDOWN, U.S.A.

Pilson, Jeff

DREAM WARRIORS

Pinchi

SUMMERTIME IN VENICE

Pinkard, James S.

COCA COLA COWBOY

Pinkard, Maceo

CONGRATULATIONS
DON'T BE LIKE THAT
GIMME A LITTLE KISS, WILL YA,
HUH?
HERE COMES THE SHOW BOAT
IS THAT RELIGION?
MAMMY O'MINE
SUGAR
SWEET GEORGIA BROWN
THEM THERE EYES

Pinkard, Sandy

BLESSED ARE THE BELIEVERS
I CAN TELL BY THE WAY YOU
DANCE (YOU'RE GONNA LOVE ME
TONIGHT)

YOU'RE THE REASON GOD MADE
OKLAHOMA

Pinter, Harold

YOU HAVE THE CHOICE

Pinz, Shelley

GREEN TAMBOURINE
JELLY JUNGLE (OF ORANGE
MARMALADE)
RICE IS NICE

Pippa, Salvatore

LONELY TEENAGER

Pippin, Don

HOLD ME IN YOUR ARMS

Pippin, Steve

BETTER LOVE NEXT TIME
THIS TIME I'M IN IT FOR LOVE

Piron, Armand J.

I WISH I COULD SHIMMY LIKE MY
SISTER KATE
MAMA'S GONE, GOODBYE
SUD BUSTIN' BLUES

Pirroni, Marco

GOODY TWO SHOES

Pisano, Gigi

PANSY

Pistilli, Gene

MEDICINE MAN
SUNDAY WILL NEVER BE THE SAME
TOO GONE TOO LONG

Pitchford, Dean

AFTER ALL
ALMOST PARADISE . . . LOVE
THEME FROM "FOOTLOOSE"

DANCING IN THE SHEETS
DON'T CALL IT LOVE
FAME
FOOTLOOSE
HOLDING OUT FOR A HERO
LET'S HEAR IT FOR THE BOY
MAKE ME LOSE CONTROL
ONE SUNNY DAY
YOU SHOULD HEAR HOW SHE TALKS
    ABOUT YOU

Pitchford, Steve

DON'T FIGHT IT

Pitman, Jack

BEYOND THE REEF

Pitney, Gene

HELLO, MARY LOU
HE'S A REBEL
(I WANNA) LOVE MY LIFE AWAY

Pitt, Eugene

MY TRUE STORY

Pitts, Clyde

SWEETHEART OF THE YEAR

Pitts, Tom

I NEVER KNEW I COULD LOVE
    ANYBODY (LIKE I'M LOVING YOU)

Pixley, Frank

HEIDELBERG STEIN SONG
MESSAGE OF THE VIOLET, THE
TALE OF A BUMBLE BEE, THE
TALE OF THE KANGAROO, THE
TALE OF THE SEASHELL
TALE OF THE TURTLE DOVE, THE

Place, Mary Kay

BABY BOY

Plant, Robert

BIG LOG
BLACK DOG
D'YER MAKER
FOOL IN THE RAIN
HEARTBREAKER
IMMIGRANT SONG
LIVING LOVING MAID (SHE'S JUST A
    WOMAN)
WHOLE LOTTA LOVE

Plante, Jacques

DOMINO
MYSTERY STREET

Plater, Bobby

JERSEY BOUNCE

Pleis, Jack

(BUT AS THEY SAY) THAT'S LIFE

Plummer, Howard, Jr.

I CAN'T LOVE YOU ENOUGH
STILL

Pober, Leon

PEARLY SHELLS

Pockriss, Lee

BIG DADDY
CALCUTTA
CATCH A FALLING STAR
DOMMAGE, DOMMAGE (TOO BAD,
    TOO BAD)
HANDBAG IS NOT A PROPER
    MOTHER, A
I KNOW THE FEELING
ITSY BITSY TEENIE WEENIE POLKA
    DOT BIKINI
JIMMY'S GIRL
JOHNNY ANGEL
KOOKIE LITTLE PARADISE, A
LEADER OF THE LAUNDROMAT
MY HEART IS AN OPEN BOOK
MY LITTLE CORNER OF THE WORLD
ONLY ONE, THE

PLAYGROUND IN MY MIND
SEVEN LITTLE GIRLS SITTING IN
    THE BACK SEAT
STARBRIGHT
TAR AND CEMENT
TRACY
WHAT IS LOVE?
WHEN JULIE COMES AROUND
WILKES-BARRE, PA.
YOU LOVE ME

Podoler, Richard

LET THERE BE DRUMS

Poe, Coy

DON'T BE AFRAID TO TELL YOUR
    MOTHER
OBJECT OF MY AFFECTION, THE
THAT'S WHAT YOU THINK
WHAT'S THE REASON (I'M NOT
    PLEASIN' YOU)?

Poindexter, Richard

HYPNOTIZED
THIN LINE BETWEEN LOVE AND
    HATE

Poindexter, Robert

THIN LINE BETWEEN LOVE AND
    HATE

Pointer, Anita

FAIRYTALE
HOW LONG (BETCHA' GOT A CHICK
    ON THE SIDE)
I'M SO EXCITED

Pointer, Bonnie

FAIRYTALE
HOW LONG (BETCHA' GOT A CHICK
    ON THE SIDE)

Pointer, June

HOW LONG (BETCHA' GOT A CHICK
    ON THE SIDE)
I'M SO EXCITED

Pointer, Ruth

HOW LONG (BETCHA' GOT A CHICK
   ON THE SIDE)
I'M SO EXCITED

Pola, Edward

CARAMBA! IT'S THE SAMBA!
DOO DE DOO ON AN OLD KAZOO
GENTLEMAN OBVIOUSLY DOESN'T
   BELIEVE, THE
I DIDN'T SLIP, I WASN'T PUSHED, I
   FELL
I LOVE THE WAY YOU SAY
   GOODNIGHT
I RAISED MY HAT
I SAID MY PAJAMAS (AND PUT ON
   MY PRAY'RS)
LONGEST WALK, THE
MARCHING ALONG TOGETHER
QUICKSILVER
SHE'LL ALWAYS REMEMBER
YOU BROKE YOUR PROMISE

Politti, Paul

IT MAY BE WINTER OUTSIDE (BUT
   IN MY HEART IT'S SPRING)
THOSE OLDIES BUT GOODIES
   (REMIND ME OF YOU)

Polk, Herscholt

AIN'T UNDERSTANDING MELLOW

Poll, Ruth

BRING BACK THE THRILL
THOSE THINGS MONEY CAN'T BUY

Polla, W. C.

DANCING TAMBOURINE

Pollack, Ben

MAKE LOVE TO ME
PECKIN'
TIN ROOF BLUES

Pollack, David A.

NIGHT WIND

Pollack, Jeanne

LA PACHANGA

Pollack, Lew

ANGELA MIA (MY ANGEL)
AT THE CODFISH BALL
BALBOA
BUDDHA
CHARMAINE
CHEATIN' ON ME
DIANE (I'M IN HEAVEN WHEN I SEE
   YOU SMILE)
EARLY BIRD
HE'S MY UNCLE
I'M MISSIN' MAMMY'S KISSIN' (AND I
   KNOW SHE'S MISSIN' MINE)
IT'S LOVE I'M AFTER
MISS ANNABELLE LEE
MOONSHINE OVER KENTUCKY
MY YIDDISHE MOMME
ONE IN A MILLION
RIGHT SOMEBODY TO LOVE, THE
SEVENTH HEAVEN
SILVER SHADOWS AND BROKEN
   DREAMS
SING, BABY, SING
SOMEDAY, SOMEWHERE (WE'LL
   MEET AGAIN)
SOME SWEET DAY
TEXAS TORNADO
THAT'S A-PLENTY
TOY TRUMPET, THE
TWO CIGARETTES IN THE DARK
WATER UNDER THE BRIDGE
WHO'S AFRAID OF LOVE?
WHY NOT STRING ALONG WITH ME?
WHY TALK ABOUT LOVE?
YOU DO THE DARNDEST THINGS,
   BABY
YOU'RE SLIGHTLY TERRIFIC

Pollock, Channing

I LOVE LOVE
LAND OF THE HEART'S DESIRE, THE
MY MAN (MON HOMME)

Polnareff, Michel

AME CALINE (A.K.A. SOUL COAXING)

Pomerantz, David

STORYBOOK CHILDREN (DAYBREAK)

Pomeranz, David

OLD SONGS, THE
TRYIN' TO GET THE FEELING AGAIN

Pomeroy, George S.

WHIFFENPOOF SONG, THE

Pomus, Doc

CAN'T GET USED TO LOSING YOU
GO, JIMMY, GO
HIS LATEST FLAME (MARIE'S THE
   NAME)
HOPELESS
HOUND DOG MAN
HUSHABYE
I'M A MAN
KISS ME QUICK
LET'S DO THE FREDDIE
LITTLE SISTER
MESS OF BLUES, A
MORE THAN A MIRACLE
MY HAPPINESS FOREVER
NO ONE
PLAIN JANE
SAVE THE LAST DANCE FOR ME
SEVEN DAY WEEKEND
SHE'S NOT YOU
(YOU MAKE ME FEEL) SO GOOD
SURRENDER
SUSPICION
SWEETS FOR MY SWEET
TEENAGER IN LOVE, A
THIS MAGIC MOMENT
TURN ME LOOSE
VIVA LAS VEGAS
WRONG FOR EACH OTHER
YOUNG BLOOD

Ponce, Manual M.

ESTRELLITA

Poncia, Vini

I WAS MADE FOR LOVIN' YOU
JUST TOO MANY PEOPLE
NEW YORK'S A LONELY TOWN
OH MY MY
YOU MAKE ME FEEL LIKE DANCING

Ponger, Robert

DER KOMMISSAR

Pons, Jim

ELENORE

Pop, Iggy

CHINA GIRL

Pope, Pauline

RACING WITH THE MOON

Popp, André

LOVE IS BLUE
PORTUGUESE WASHERWOMEN, THE

Porcaro, Jeff

AFRICA
HUMAN NATURE

Poree, Anita

BOOGIE DOWN
GOING IN CIRCLES
KEEP ON TRUCKIN'
LOVE OR LET ME BE LONELY

Portal, Otilio

SWEET AND GENTLE

Portela, Raul

LISBON ANTIGUA (IN OLD LISBON)

Porter, Andrew

YOU'RE A SPECIAL PART OF ME

Porter, Cole

ACE IN THE HOLE
AFTER YOU, WHO?
ALLEZ-VOUS-EN (GO AWAY)
ALL OF YOU
ALL THROUGH THE NIGHT
ALWAYS TRUE TO YOU IN MY FASHION
ANOTHER OP'NIN', ANOTHER SHOW
ANYTHING GOES
AT LONG LAST LOVE
BE A CLOWN
BEGIN THE BEGUINE
BIANEA
BLOW, GABRIEL, BLOW
BRUSH UP YOUR SHAKESPEARE
BUT IN THE MORNING, NO!
BY THE MISSISSINEWAH
ÇA C'EST L'AMOUR
CAN-CAN
C'EST MAGNIFIQUE
COULD IT BE YOU
DO I LOVE YOU?
DON'T FENCE ME IN
DON'T LOOK AT ME THAT WAY
DOWN IN THE DEPTHS (ON THE NINETIETH FLOOR)
DREAM DANCING
EASY TO LOVE
EV'RYTHING I LOVE
EV'RYTIME WE SAY GOODBYE
FAREWELL AMANDA
FIND ME A PRIMITIVE MAN
FOR NO RHYME OR REASON
FRIENDSHIP
FROM NOW ON
FROM THIS MOMENT ON
GET OUT OF TOWN
GREAT INDOORS, THE
HEY, BABE, HEY
HEY, GOOD-LOOKIN'
HIGH SOCIETY CALYPSO
HOW COULD WE BE WRONG
HOW'S YOUR ROMANCE?
I ALWAYS KNEW
I AM IN LOVE
I AM LOVED
I CONCENTRATE ON YOU
I GET A KICK OUT OF YOU
I HAPPEN TO LIKE NEW YORK
I HATE MEN
I LOVE PARIS

I LOVE YOU
I LOVE YOU, SAMANTHA
I'M GETTING MYSELF READY FOR YOU
I'M IN LOVE AGAIN
I'M UNLUCKY AT GAMBLING
IN THE STILL OF THE NIGHT
IT'S A CHEMICAL REACTION, THAT'S ALL
IT'S ALL RIGHT WITH ME
IT'S DE-LOVELY
I'VE A SHOOTING BOX IN SCOTLAND
I'VE A STRANGE NEW RHYTHM IN MY HEART
I'VE COME TO WIVE IT WEALTHILY IN PADUA
I'VE GOT MY EYES ON YOU
I'VE GOT YOU ON MY MIND
I'VE GOT YOU UNDER MY SKIN
JOSEPHINE
JUST ONE OF THOSE THINGS
KATIE WENT TO HAWAII
LAZIEST GAL IN TOWN, THE
LET'S BE BUDDIES
LET'S DO IT (LET'S FALL IN LOVE)
LET'S FLY AWAY
LET'S MISBEHAVE
LET'S NOT TALK ABOUT LOVE
LITTLE SKIPPER FROM HEAVEN ABOVE, A
LIVE AND LET LIVE
LOOKING AT YOU
LOVE FOR SALE
LOVE OF MY LIFE
MACK THE BLACK
MAKE IT ANOTHER OLD-FASHIONED PLEASE
ME AND MARIE
MIND IF I MAKE LOVE TO YOU
MISS OTIS REGRETS (SHE'S UNABLE TO LUNCH TODAY)
MOST GENTLEMEN DON'T LIKE LOVE
MY HEART BELONGS TO DADDY
MY MOTHER WOULD LOVE YOU
NEVER GIVE ANYTHING AWAY
NIGHT AND DAY
NINA
NOBODY'S CHASING ME
NOW YOU HAS JAZZ
OLD-FASHIONED GARDEN
ONLY ANOTHER BOY AND GIRL

Porter, Cole

OZARKS ARE CALLIN' ME HOME,
   THE
PAREE, WHAT DID YOU DO TO ME?
PARIS LOVES LOVERS
PICTURE OF YOU WITHOUT ME, A
PIPE DREAMING
RAP TAP ON WOOD
RED, HOT AND BLUE
RIDIN' HIGH
ROSALIE
SATIN AND SILK
SHOULD I TELL YOU I LOVE YOU?
SIBERIA
SILK STOCKINGS
SINCE I KISSED MY BABY GOODBYE
SO IN LOVE
SOMETHING FOR THE BOYS
SOMETHING TO SHOUT ABOUT
SO NEAR AND YET SO FAR
STEREOPHONIC SOUND
SWINGIN' THE JINX AWAY
TAKE ME BACK TO MANHATTAN
TALE OF AN OYSTER, THE
THANK YOU SO MUCH, MRS.
   LOWSBOROUGH-GOODBY
TOO DARN HOT
TRUE LOVE
TWO LITTLE BABES IN THE WOOD
USE YOUR IMAGINATION
WELL, DID YOU EVAH? (WHAT A
   SWELL PARTY THIS IS)
WE OPEN IN VENICE
WERE THINE THAT SPECIAL FACE
WHAT IS THIS THING CALLED
   LOVE?
WHEN I WAS A LITTLE CUCKOO
WHEN LOVE BECKONED
WHERE, OH WHERE?
WHERE HAVE YOU BEEN?
WHERE IS THE LIFE THAT LATE I
   LED?
WHERE WOULD YOU GET YOUR
   COAT?
WHO KNOWS?
WHO WANTS TO BE A MILLIONAIRE?
WHY CAN'T YOU BEHAVE?
WHY SHOULDN'T I?
WITHOUT LOVE
WUNDERBAR
YOU CAN DO NO WRONG
YOU'D BE SO NICE TO COME
   HOME TO
YOU DON'T KNOW PAREE

YOU DON'T REMIND ME
YOU DO SOMETHING TO ME
YOU'RE SENSATIONAL
YOU'RE THE TOP
YOU'VE GOT THAT THING

Porter, David

B-A-B-Y
BORN AGAIN
HOLD ON! I'M COMIN'
I TAKE WHAT I WANT
I THANK YOU
LET ME BE GOOD TO YOU
SOUL MAN
SOUL SISTER, BROWN SUGAR
SWEETER HE IS, THE
WHEN SOMETHING IS WRONG WITH
   MY BABY
WRAP IT UP
YOU DON'T KNOW LIKE I KNOW
YOUR GOOD THING IS ABOUT TO
   END

Porter, Del

YA WANNA BUY A BUNNY?

Porter, George, Jr.

CISSY STRUT
LOOK-KA PY PY
SOPHISTICATED CISSY

Porter, Jake

KO KO MO (I LOVE YOU SO)
OH, THAT'LL BE JOYFUL

Porter, Lew

LITTLE RED FOX, THE (N'YA, N'YA,
   YA CAN'T CATCH ME)
NEED YOU
YOU TOLD A LIE (I BELIEVED YOU)

Porter, Robbie

IT AIN'T COOL TO BE CRAZY ABOUT
   YOU

Porter, Royce

OCEAN FRONT PROPERTY
WHAT'S GOING ON IN YOUR WORLD?

Portnoy, Gary

WHERE EVERYBODY KNOWS YOUR
   NAME

Posford, George

AT THE BALALAIKA
LAZY DAY
LET ME GIVE MY HAPPINESS TO
   YOU
THREE WISHES
WORLD IS MINE, THE

Post, Bill

SIXTEEN REASONS

Post, Doree

SIXTEEN REASONS

Post, Jim

REACH OUT OF THE DARKNESS

Post, Mike

ROCKFORD FILES, THE
THEME FROM "HILL STREET BLUES"
THEME FROM "MAGNUM P. I."
THEME FROM "THE GREATEST
   AMERICAN HERO" (BELIEVE IT
   OR NOT)

Poterat, Louis

I'LL BE YOURS (J'ATTENDRAI)

Potter, Brian

AIN'T NO WOMAN LIKE THE ONE I
   GOT
ARE YOU MAN ENOUGH?
COUNTRY BOY (YOU GOT YOUR FEET
   IN L.A.)
DON'T PULL YOUR LOVE
DREAM ON

GIVE IT TO THE PEOPLE
IT ONLY TAKES A MINUTE
KEEPER OF THE CASTLE
LOOK IN MY EYES PRETTY WOMAN
ONE CHAIN DON'T MAKE NO PRISON
ONE TIN SOLDIER (THE LEGEND OF
    BILLY JACK)
REMEMBER WHAT I TOLD YOU TO
    FORGET
TWO DIVIDED BY LOVE

Potts, Junior

SHOW ME THE WAY

Potts, Sylvester

BOO-GA-LOO

Pought, Emma R.

MR. LEE

Pought, Jannie

MR. LEE

Poulton, Curt

WHEN IT'S LAMP LIGHTIN' TIME IN
    THE VALLEY

Pounds, Mrs. Jessie Brown

BEAUTIFUL ISLE OF SOMEWHERE

Powell, Archie

5-10-15-20 (25-30 YEARS OF LOVE)

Powell, Dan

MAKE IT REAL

Powell, Felix

PACK UP YOUR TROUBLES IN YOUR
    OLD KIT BAG (AND SMILE, SMILE,
    SMILE)

Powell, Max

FOOL, FOOL, FOOL
MEMORY NO. 1

Powell, Mel

MISSION TO MOSCOW
MY GUY'S COME BACK

Powell, Roger

SET ME FREE

Powell, Teddy

AM I PROUD?
BEWILDERED
HEAVEN HELP THIS HEART OF MINE
I COULDN'T BELIEVE MY EYES
IF MY HEART COULD ONLY TALK
ROLLIN' PLAINS
SNAKE CHARMER, THE
TAKE ME BACK TO MY BOOTS AND
    SADDLE
YOU BROKE THE ONLY HEART THAT
    EVER LOVED YOU
YOU WON'T BE SATISFIED (UNTIL
    YOU BREAK MY HEART)

Powers, Chester

GET TOGETHER (A.K.A. LET'S GET
    TOGETHER)

Powers, Freddy

I ALWAYS GET LUCKY WITH YOU
NATURAL HIGH
PLACE TO FALL APART, A

Powers, Quentin

WHOEVER'S IN NEW ENGLAND

Powers, Tony

98.6
AIN'T GONNA LIE
LAZY DAY
WHY DO LOVERS BREAK EACH
    OTHER'S HEARTS?

Prado, Miguel

TIME WAS

Prado, Perez

MAMBO JAMBO
PARIS
PATRICIA

Prager, Stephen

FLY, ROBIN, FLY
GET UP AND BOOGIE (THAT'S
    RIGHT)

Pratt, Andy

AVENGING ANNIE

Pratt, Charles E.

DON'T GO OUT TONIGHT, BOY

Pratt, Harry

SEE SAW

Pratt, Paul

HOT HOUSE RAG

Preis, Rex

I'LL BE BACK

Presley, Elvis

ALL SHOOK UP
DON'T BE CRUEL
HEARTBREAK HOTEL
LOVE ME TENDER
POOR BOY

Presley, Reg

I CAN'T CONTROL MYSELF
LOVE IS ALL AROUND
WITH A GIRL LIKE YOU

Pressly, Eric

I CAN'T WAIT

Preston, Billy

GREAT GOSH A'MIGHTY! (IT'S A
    MATTER OF TIME)
NOTHING FROM NOTHING
OUTA-SPACE
SPACE RACE
STRUTTIN'
WILL IT GO ROUND IN CIRCLES
YOU ARE SO BEAUTIFUL

Preston, Leroy

LETTER THAT JOHNNY WALKER
    READ, THE

Prestopino, Greg

BREAK MY STRIDE

Prestwood, Hugh

HARD TIMES FOR LOVERS
MOON IS STILL OVER HER
    SHOULDER, THE
SOUND OF GOODBYE, THE

Prevert, Jacques

AUTUMN LEAVES

Previn, André

COCO
FARAWAY PART OF TOWN, THE
GABRIELLE
I LIKE MYSELF
I'LL PLANT MY OWN TREE
LIKE LOVE
LIKE YOUNG
SECOND CHANCE, A
THAT'S HOW IT WENT ALL RIGHT
THEME FROM "VALLEY OF THE
    DOLLS"
YOU'RE GONNA HEAR FROM ME

Previn, Dory Langdon

BAD AND THE BEAUTIFUL, THE
    (A.K.A. LOVE IS FOR THE VERY
    YOUNG)
COME SATURDAY MORNING
DADDY'S GONE A-HUNTING

FARAWAY PART OF TOWN, THE
I'LL PLANT MY OWN TREE
LAST TANGO IN PARIS
LIKE LOVE
MORNING AFTER
PEPE
SECOND CHANCE, A
SO LONG, BIG TIME!
THAT'S HOW IT WENT ALL RIGHT
THEME FROM "VALLEY OF THE
    DOLLS"
YOU'RE GONNA HEAR FROM ME

Previte, Franke

HUNGRY EYES
SWEETHEART
(I'VE HAD) THE TIME OF MY LIFE

Price, Alan

HOUSE OF THE RISING SUN
I'M CRYING
O LUCKY MAN!

Price, Chilton

SLOW POKE
YOU BELONG TO ME

Price, Dock, Jr.

YOUR TIME TO CRY

Price, Georgie

ANGEL CHILD
NORMANDY

Price, Harvey

HEAVEN KNOWS
TEMPTATION EYES

Price, Leo

SEND ME SOME LOVIN'

Price, Lloyd

COME INTO MY HEART
I'M GONNA GET MARRIED
JUST BECAUSE

LADY LUCK
LAWDY MISS CLAWDY
OOOH, OOOH, OOOH
PERSONALITY (YOU'VE GOT)
QUESTION
STAGGER LEE
WHERE WERE YOU (ON OUR
    WEDDING DAY)?

Price, Michael

HEARTBREAK KID, THE
I WOULDN'T TREAT A DOG (THE
    WAY YOU TREATED ME)

Price, Ray

GIVE ME MORE, MORE, MORE OF
    YOUR KISSES
I'LL BE THERE IF YOU EVER WANT
    ME
I'M TIRED
SOFT RAIN
YOU DONE ME WRONG

Price, Webb

SANDS OF GOLD

Prichard, Henry

SILVER AND GOLD

Priest, Steve

ACTION
FOX ON THE RUN

Prieto, Joaquin

WEDDING, THE (LA NOVIA)

Prim, Gary

CONGRATULATIONS
RESERVATIONS FOR TWO

Prima, Louis

OH, BABE!
PLEASE NO SQUEEZA DA BANANA
ROBIN HOOD
SING, SING, SING

SUNDAY KIND OF LOVE, A

Primrose, Joe

ST. JAMES INFIRMARY

Prince, Graham

'TAINT NOBODY'S BIZNESS IF I DO

Prince, Hughie

BEAT ME DADDY, EIGHT TO THE
  BAR
BOOGIE WOOGIE BUGLE BOY (OF
  COMPANY B)
BOUNCE ME BROTHER WITH A
  SOLID FOUR
FUNNY (NOT MUCH)
I GUESS I'LL GET THE PAPERS (AND
  GO HOME)
RHUMBOOGIE
SHE HAD TO GO AND LOSE IT AT
  THE ASTOR

Prince, William Rodney

HOT SMOKE AND SASSAFRAS

Prince & The Revolution

KISS

Prine, John

LOVE IS ON A ROLL

Pritchard, Henry

I DON'T WANT TO LOVE YOU (LIKE I
  DO)
KENTUCKY
TAKE CARE (WHEN YOU SAY "TE
  QUIERO")

Pritchard, John, Jr.

CAN'T STOP DANCIN'

Pritchett, Travis

TELL HIM NO

Prober, Leon

TINY BUBBLES

Proffer, Spencer

STORYBOOK CHILDREN (DAYBREAK)

Profit, Clarence

LULLABY IN RHYTHM

Prokop, Skip

ONE FINE MORNING

Prosen, Sidney

TILL I WALTZ AGAIN WITH YOU

Protheroe, Brian

PINBALL

Provost, Heinz

INTERMEZZO

Pruitt, Johnnie

BERTHA BUTT BOOGIE, THE
HEY, LEROY, YOUR MAMA'S CALLIN'
  YOU

Pryor, Arthur

RAZZAZZA MAZZAZZA
WHISTLER AND HIS DOG, THE

Puck, Harry

CALIFORNIA AND YOU
LITTLE HOUSE UPON THE HILL, THE
WHERE DID YOU GET THAT GIRL?

Puente, Tito

OYE COMO VA

Puerta, Joseph

HOLDIN' ON TO YESTERDAY
NICE, NICE, VERY NICE

Pugh, Phil

THEN CAME YOU

Pugsley, Jerry

PARADIDDLE JOE

Pullins, Leroy

I'M A NUT
KNEE DEEP

Purdy, W. T.

ON WISCONSIN

Puree, Ernest

APOLLO JUMP

Purvis, Charlie

GO ON WITH THE WEDDING

Putman, Curly

BALLAD OF TWO BROTHERS
BLOOD RED AND GOIN' DOWN
D-I-V-O-R-C-E
DO YOU WANNA GO TO HEAVEN
GREEN, GREEN GRASS OF HOME
HE STOPPED LOVING HER TODAY
I'LL BE COMING BACK FOR MORE
I THINK I KNOW
I WISH THAT I COULD HURT THAT
  WAY AGAIN
JUST FOR YOU
MY ELUSIVE DREAMS
WAR IS HELL (ON THE HOMEFRONT
  TOO)

Pyle, Harry

MEET ME AT NO SPECIAL PLACE
  (AND I'LL BE THERE AT NO
  PARTICULAR TIME)

Quadling, Lew

CARELESS
DO YOU CARE?
MILLION DREAMS AGO, A

Quadling, Lew

SAM'S SONG

Quander, Diane

CAUGHT UP IN THE RAPTURE

Quarto, Charles

GERONIMO'S CADILLAC

Quasha, Sol

CHAIN GANG

Queen

ONE VISION
UNDER PRESSURE

Queen, John

AIN'T DAT A SHAME?
JUST BECAUSE SHE MADE THEM
GOO-GOO EYES

Quenzer, Arthur

COWBOY AND THE LADY, THE
MOONRAY

Quick, Clarence E.

COME GO WITH ME
WHISPERING BELLS

Quicksell, Howard

WAY I FEEL TODAY, THE

Quillen, Charles

BY NOW
I WOULDN'T HAVE MISSED IT FOR
THE WORLD
MY HEART
WHAT'S A MEMORY LIKE YOU
(DOING IN A LOVE LIKE THIS)

Quinn, Dan W.

SAME SWEET GIRL TO-DAY, THE

Quinn, Peter

CURLY SHUFFLE, THE

Quintela, Eddy

LITTLE LIES

Quin-Tones, The

DOWN THE AISLE OF LOVE

Quittenton, Martin

MAGGIE MAY
YOU WEAR IT WELL

Qunta, A.

CRAZY

Rabbitt, Eddie

DRIVIN' MY LIFE AWAY
GONE TOO FAR
I JUST WANT TO LOVE YOU
I LOVE A RAINY NIGHT
I WANNA DANCE WITH YOU
KENTUCKY RAIN
PURE LOVE
SOMEONE COULD LOSE A HEART
TONIGHT
STEP BY STEP
SUSPICIONS
WARNING SIGN

Rabin, Trevor

OWNER OF A LONELY HEART

Rabon, Mike

I SEE THE LIGHT
SOUND OF LOVE
WESTERN UNION
ZIP CODE

Rachek, Andrew

NAVY BLUE

Radcliffe, Peter

YOU'RE THE FIRST, THE LAST, MY
EVERYTHING

Radford, Dave

IT'S TULIP TIME IN HOLLAND
SONG OF PERSIA
WHERE THE BLACK-EYED SUSANS
GROW

Radner, Gilda

GIMME MICK

Rado, James

AIN'T GOT NO
AIR
AQUARIUS
DON'T PUT IT DOWN
EASY TO BE HARD
FRANK MILLS
GOOD MORNING STARSHINE
HARE KRISHNA (A.K.A. BE-IN)
I GOT LIFE
LET THE SUNSHINE IN (A.K.A. THE
FLESH FAILURES)
WALKING IN SPACE
WHERE DO I GO?

Rae, Jackie

HAPPY HEART

Raeburn, Boyd

SLIDER

Rafelson, Peter

OPEN YOUR HEART

Rafferty, Gerry

BAKER STREET
DAYS GONE DOWN (STILL GOT THE
LIGHT IN YOUR EYES)
GET IT RIGHT NEXT TIME
RIGHT DOWN THE LINE
STUCK IN THE MIDDLE WITH YOU

Raggi, Lorenzo

ROCKIN' SOUL

Ragin, Melvin

MAGIC MAN

Ragni, Gerome

AIN'T GOT NO
AIR
AQUARIUS
DON'T PUT IT DOWN
EASY TO BE HARD
FRANK MILLS
GOOD MORNING STARSHINE
HARE KRISHNA (A.K.A. BE-IN)
I GOT LIFE
LET THE SUNSHINE IN (A.K.A. THE
    FLESH FAILURES)
WALKING IN SPACE
WHERE DO I GO?

Ragovoy, Jerry

AIN'T NOBODY HOME
GET IT WHILE YOU CAN
I'LL TAKE GOOD CARE OF YOU
MORE THAN A MIRACLE
PATA PATA
PIECE OF MY HEART
TIME IS ON MY SIDE
WHAT'S IT GONNA BE?

Rainey, Gertrude "Ma"

BO-WEAVIL BLUES
COUNTING THE BLUES
MOONSHINE BLUES
SEE SEE RIDER BLUES (A.K.A. C. C.
    RIDER)

Rainger, Ralph

BLOSSOMS ON BROADWAY
BLUEBIRDS IN THE MOONLIGHT
BLUE HAWAII
DOUBLE TROUBLE
EASY LIVING
EBB TIDE
FAITHFUL FOREVER
FUNNY OLD HILLS, THE
GIVE ME LIBERTY OR GIVE ME
    LOVE
GUY WHAT TAKES HIS TIME, A
HAVIN' MYSELF A TIME
HERE IS MY HEART
HERE LIES LOVE
HERE'S LOVE IN YOUR EYE
HERE YOU ARE
HILLS OF OLD WYOMIN', THE
I DON'T WANT TO MAKE HISTORY (I
    JUST WANT TO MAKE LOVE)
IF I SHOULD LOSE YOU
I HAVE EYES
I'LL TAKE AN OPTION ON YOU
I'M A BLACK SHEEP WHO'S BLUE
IN A LITTLE HULA HEAVEN
IN THE PARK IN PAREE
I WISHED ON THE MOON
JOOBALAI
JUNE IN JANUARY
LITTLE KISS AT TWILIGHT, A
LITTLE ROSE OF THE RANCHO
LONG AGO AND FAR AWAY
LOOK WHAT I'VE GOT
LOVE IN BLOOM
LOW-DOWN LULLABY
MAMA, THAT MOON IS HERE AGAIN
MISS BROWN TO YOU
MOANIN' LOW
PLEASE
RENDEZVOUS WITH A DREAM
SILVER ON THE STAGE
SWEET IS THE WORD FOR YOU
TAKE A LESSON FROM THE LARK
THANKS FOR THE MEMORY
(IF IT ISN'T PAIN) THEN IT ISN'T
    LOVE
THIS IS THE NIGHT
THUNDER OVER PARADISE
WHAT GOES ON HERE IN MY
    HEART?
WHAT HAVE YOU GOT THAT GETS
    ME?
WHEN A WOMAN LOVES A MAN
WHY DREAM?
WITH EVERY BREATH I TAKE
YOU CAME TO MY RESCUE
YOU'RE A SWEET LITTLE
    HEADACHE
YOU STARTED SOMETHING
YOU TOOK THE WORDS RIGHT OUT
    OF MY HEART

Rains, Chick

DOWN TO MY LAST BROKEN HEART
HEADACHE TOMORROW, A (OR, A
    HEARTACHE TONIGHT)
SOMEBODY SHOULD LEAVE

Rainwater, Marvin

GONNA FIND ME A BLUEBIRD
I GOTTA GO GET MY BABY
I MISS YOU ALREADY
WHY CAN'T YOU FEEL SORRY FOR
    ME?

Raksin, David

BAD AND THE BEAUTIFUL, THE
    (A.K.A. LOVE IS FOR THE VERY
    YOUNG)
FOREVER AMBER
LAURA
SLOWLY
SYLVIA
THEME FROM "BEN CASEY"

Raleigh, Ben

BLUE WINTER
DEAD END STREET
DUNGAREE DOLL
EL RANCHO ROCK
FAITH CAN MOVE MOUNTAINS
I DON'T WANNA BE A LOSER
LAUGHING ON THE OUTSIDE
    (CRYING ON THE INSIDE)
LOVE IS A HURTIN' THING
LOVE IS ALL WE NEED
MIDNIGHT MARY
SHE'S A FOOL
TELL LAURA I LOVE HER
WASN'T IT YOU?
WONDERFUL! WONDERFUL!
YOU'RE SO UNDERSTANDING
YOUR OTHER LOVE
YOU WALK BY

Ralphs, Mick

CAN'T GET ENOUGH
FEEL LIKE MAKIN' LOVE
MOVIN' ON

Ralston, Everett

PINCH ME

Ralton, Harry

I REMEMBER THE CORNFIELDS

Ram, Buck

AFTERGLOW
AT YOUR BECK AND CALL
BOOG-IT
CHEW, CHEW, CHEW, CHEW YOUR
   BUBBLE GUM
COME PRIMA (FOR THE FIRST TIME)
ENCHANTED
GREAT PRETENDER, THE
HAVE MERCY
I'LL BE HOME FOR CHRISTMAS
MAGIC TOUCH, THE (YOU'VE GOT)
ONLY YOU
SLOW FREIGHT
TWILIGHT TIME

Rambeau, Eddie

KISS ME, SAILOR

Ramikin, Phil

BUFFALO STANCE

Ramin, Sid

MUSIC TO WATCH GIRLS BY

Ramirez, Roger "Ram"

LOVER MAN (OH, WHERE CAN YOU
   BE?)
MAD ABOUT YOU

Ramos, Silvano R.

EL RANCHO GRANDE
EL RANCHO ROCK

Ramsden, Nico

I WANNA BE A COWBOY

Ramsey, Ken

GREENBACK DOLLAR

Ramsey, Willis Alan

MUSKRAT LOVE

Rancifer, Roderick

I AM LOVE

Rand, Ande

ONLY YOU

Rand, Lionel

LET THERE BE LOVE

Randall, Denny

ATTACK
NATIVE NEW YORKER

Randazzo, Teddy

BIG WIDE WORLD
GOIN' OUT OF MY HEAD
HAVE YOU LOOKED INTO YOUR
   HEART?
HURT SO BAD
I'M ON THE OUTSIDE (LOOKING IN)
IT FEELS SO GOOD TO BE LOVED SO
   BAD
IT'S GONNA TAKE A MIRACLE
PRETTY BLUE EYES
RAIN IN MY HEART
SINNER MAN
TAKE ME BACK

Randell, Buddy

LIES

Randell, Denny

BABY, MAKE YOUR OWN SWEET
   MUSIC
I WANNA DANCE WIT' CHOO (DOO
   DAT DANCE)
KEEP THE BALL ROLLIN'
LET'S HANG ON

LOVER'S CONCERTO, A
OPUS 17 (DON'T YOU WORRY 'BOUT
   ME)
SWEARIN' TO GOD

Randi, Don

MEXICAN PEARLS

Randle, Earl

ECHOES OF LOVE
I'LL BE AROUND
I'M GONNA TEAR YOUR PLAYHOUSE
   DOWN

Randolph, Boots

YAKETY SAX

Randolph, Eugene

TEAR FELL, A

Randolph, Jimi

YOU AND ME TONIGHT

Randolph, Zilner T.

OL' MAN MOSE

Raney, Wayne

BLUES, STAY AWAY FROM ME
WHY DON'T YOU HAUL OFF AND
   LOVE ME?

Rankin, Kenny

IN THE NAME OF LOVE
PEACEFUL

Rans, Robert

DANCE WITH ME
DO YA WANNA GET FUNKY WITH
   ME
MATERIAL GIRL

Ransom, Ray

DAZZ

DUSIC

Ranucci, Renato

ARRIVEDERCI, ROMA (GOODBYE TO
  ROME)

Rapee, Erno

ANGELA MIA (MY ANGEL)
CHARMAINE
DIANE (I'M IN HEAVEN WHEN I SEE
  YOU SMILE)
SOMEDAY, SOMEWHERE (WE'LL
  MEET AGAIN)

Raposo, Joe

AMERICA IS
BEIN' GREEN
FIRST TIME IT HAPPENS, THE
SING (SING A SONG)
THIS WAY TO SESAME STREET
THREE'S COMPANY

Rappaport, Robert

MARTIAN HOP

Rappaport, Steve

MARTIAN HOP

Rappolo, Leon

MAKE LOVE TO ME
MILENBERG JOYS
TIN ROOF BLUES

Rarebell, Herman

ROCK YOU LIKE A HURRICANE

Rasbach, Otto

TREES

Raskin, Gene

THOSE WERE THE DAYS

Raskin, Milton

SOMEWHERE IN THE NIGHT

Raskin, Willie

FIFTY MILLION FRENCHMEN (CAN'T
  BE WRONG)
I FOUND A ROSE IN THE DEVIL'S
  GARDEN
THEY CUT DOWN THE OLD PINE
  TREE
WEDDING BELLS ARE BREAKING UP
  THAT OLD GANG OF MINE

Rath, Fred

JUST A GIRL THAT MEN FORGET

Rauch, Fred

ANSWER ME, MY LOVE
I'M ALWAYS HEARING WEDDING
  BELLS

Raven, Carol

LA CUMPARSITA

Raven, Eddy

I GOT MEXICO
IN A LETTER TO YOU
SOMETIMES A LADY
YOU SHOULD HAVE BEEN GONE BY
  NOW

Ray, Alan

YOU DON'T LOVE ME ANYMORE

Ray, Arthur

DOWN IN THE MOUTH BLUES
GRAVEYARD BOUND BLUES
LENOX AVENUE SHUFFLE

Ray, B.

ONE HEARTBEAT

Ray, Eddy

HEARTS OF STONE

Ray, Elmer

ON MY MIND AGAIN

Ray, Harry

LOOK AT ME (I'M IN LOVE)
SEXY MAMA
SPECIAL LADY

Ray, Johnnie

LITTLE WHITE CLOUD THAT CRIED,
  THE

Ray, Lillian

SUNSHINE OF YOUR SMILE, THE

Rayburn, Gene

HOP-SCOTCH POLKA (SCOTCH HOT)

Raye, Don

AIN'T THAT JUST LIKE A MAN?
BEAT ME DADDY, EIGHT TO THE
  BAR
BOOGIE WOOGIE BUGLE BOY (OF
  COMPANY B)
BOUNCE ME BROTHER WITH A
  SOLID FOUR
COW-COW BOOGIE
DADDY-O (I'M GONNA TEACH YOU
  SOME BLUES)
DOMINO
DOWN THE ROAD A PIECE
DO YOU CALL THAT A BUDDY?
FOR DANCERS ONLY
HE'S MY GUY
HEY, MR. POSTMAN
HOUSE OF BLUE LIGHTS
I'LL REMEMBER APRIL
I LOVE YOU MUCH TOO MUCH
I'M LOOKING OUT THE WINDOW
IRRESISTIBLE YOU
IT'S WHATCHA DO WITH WHATCHA
  GOT
JUDALINE

JUST FOR A THRILL
LOVE THEME FROM "LA STRADA"
MILKMAN, KEEP THOSE BOTTLES
    QUIET
MISTER FIVE BY FIVE
MUSIC MAKERS
PIG FOOT PETE
RHUMBOOGIE
RHYTHM IN MY NURSERY RHYMES
SHE HAD TO GO AND LOSE IT AT
    THE ASTOR
SONG WAS BORN, A
STAR EYES
THEY WERE DOIN' THE MAMBO
THIS IS MY COUNTRY
WELL, ALL RIGHT!
WHY BEGIN AGAIN? (A.K.A. PASTEL
    BLUE)
YET . . . I KNOW
YOU DON'T KNOW WHAT LOVE IS
YOUR RED WAGON

Raymond, Jeffrey

YOU DON'T LOVE ME ANYMORE

Raymond, Lewis

SWING, BROTHER, SWING

Raymond, Tony

AIRY, FAIRY LILLIAN

Raymonde, Ivor

I ONLY WANT TO BE WITH YOU
STAY AWHILE

Razaf, Andy

AIN'TCHA GLAD?
AIN'T MISBEHAVIN'
ALLIGATOR CRAWL
BLACK AND BLUE
BLUE, TURNING GREY OVER YOU
CHRISTOPHER COLUMBUS
CONCENTRATIN' (ON YOU)
DEEP FOREST
DUSKY STEVEDORE
GEE BABY, AIN'T I GOOD TO YOU?
GUESS WHO'S IN TOWN
HONEYSUCKLE ROSE

HOW CAN YOU FACE ME?
IF IT AIN'T LOVE
I'M GONNA MOVE TO THE
    OUTSKIRTS OF TOWN
IN THE MOOD
JOINT IS JUMPIN', THE
KEEPIN' OUT OF MISCHIEF NOW
LONESOME ME
LOUISIANA
LOVER'S LULLABY, A
MAKE BELIEVE BALLROOM
MASSACHUSETTS
MEMORIES OF YOU
MILKMAN'S MATINEE, THE
MISSISSIPPI BASIN
MY FATE IS IN YOUR HANDS
ON REVIVAL DAY
PATTY CAKE, PATTY CAKE (BAKER
    MAN)
PORTER'S LOVE SONG TO A
    CHAMBERMAID, A
REEFER MAN
S'POSIN'
STEALIN' APPLES
STOMPIN' AT THE SAVOY
STRANGE AS IT SEEMS
SWEET SAVANNAH SUE
TAKE YOUR TOMORROW (AND GIVE
    ME TODAY)
THAT'S WHAT I LIKE 'BOUT THE
    SOUTH
WAY I FEEL TODAY, THE
WHEN
YANCEY SPECIAL
YOU'RE LUCKY TO ME
ZONKY

Rea, Chris

FOOL (IF YOU THINK IT'S OVER)

Rea, D.

FOR YASGUR'S FARM

Read, John Dawson

FRIEND OF MINE IS GOING BLIND, A

Reagan, Russ

DEDICATION SONG, THE

Reardon, Frank

SAME OLD SATURDAY NIGHT

Reardon, Jack

GOOD LIFE, THE
WHEN
WORRIED GUY

Rebennack, Mac

RIGHT PLACE, WRONG TIME
SUCH A NIGHT

Record, Eugene

HAVE YOU SEEN HER?
HOMELY GIRL
LOVE MAKES A WOMAN
OH GIRL
SOULFUL STRUT (A.K.A. AM I THE
    SAME GIRL?)
THERE'LL COME A TIME
TWO LITTLE KIDS

Rector, Johnny

MARRIED BY THE BIBLE, DIVORCED
    BY THE LAW

Rector, Ricky

DARLENE

Redbird, William Chief

CHEROKEE BOOGIE (EH-OH-
    ALEENA)

Redd, Gene

PLEASE COME HOME FOR
    CHRISTMAS

Redd, Henry J.

FREE

Redd, Ramona

(OPEN UP THE DOOR) LET THE
    GOOD TIMES IN

Reddick, James

TRYING TO HOLD ON TO MY
 WOMAN

Redding, Edward C.

END OF A LOVE AFFAIR, THE

Redding, Otis

AMEN
FA-FA-FA-FA-FA (SAD SONG)
HAPPY SONG (DUM, DUM), THE
I CAN'T TURN YOU LOOSE
I'VE BEEN LOVING YOU TOO LONG
 (TO STOP NOW)
I'VE GOT DREAMS TO REMEMBER
MR. PITIFUL
RESPECT
SECURITY
SWEET SOUL MUSIC
(SITTIN' ON) THE DOCK OF THE BAY

Redding, Van Ross

BABY, I'M HOOKED (RIGHT INTO
 YOUR LOVE)

Redding, Velma

I'VE GOT DREAMS TO REMEMBER

Reddy, Helen

I AM WOMAN

Redi, P. G.

NON DIMENTICAR (DON'T FORGET)

Redman, Don

CHANT OF THE WEED
CHERRY
GEE BABY, AIN'T I GOOD TO YOU?
HOW'M I DOIN'? (HEY, HEY!)
IF IT AIN'T LOVE
IF IT'S TRUE
I HEARD
NO ONE ELSE BUT YOU
SAVE IT, PRETTY MAMA
AY I FEEL TODAY, THE

Redmond, Dick

JUST FOR NOW

Redmond, John

CHRISTMAS IN KILLARNEY
CROSSTOWN
DREAM, DREAM, DREAM
GAUCHO SERENADE, THE
I CAME, I SAW, I CONGA'D
I LET A SONG GO OUT OF MY
 HEART
MAN WITH THE MANDOLIN, THE

Reed, David

ALL FOR LOVE OF YOU
ELI GREEN'S CAKEWALK
HANDICAP, THE
LOVE ME AND THE WORLD IS MINE
MISTER JOHNSON, DON'T GET GAY
MY HEART HAS LEARNED TO LOVE
 YOU, NOW DO NOT SAY GOODBYE

Reed, Jackie

WHEN THERE'S NO YOU

Reed, Jerry

AMOS MOSES
BALLAD OF GATOR MCCLUSKY
CRUDE OIL BLUES, THE
EAST BOUND AND DOWN
GUITAR MAN
LEGEND, THE
MISERY LOVES COMPANY
THAT'S ALL YOU GOTTA DO
U.S. MALE
WHEN YOU'RE HOT, YOU'RE HOT

Reed, Jimmy

AIN'T THAT LOVIN' YOU, BABY
BRIGHT LIGHTS, BIG CITY
HONEST I DO
YOU GOT ME DIZZY

Reed, Leonard

IT'S OVER BECAUSE WE'RE
 THROUGH

Reed, Les

DAUGHTER OF DARKNESS
DELILAH
EVERYBODY KNOWS
HERE IT COMES AGAIN
I NEVER SAID GOODBYE
IT'S NOT UNUSUAL
KISS ME GOODBYE
LAST WALTZ, THE
LES BICYCLETTES DE BELSIZE
THERE'S A KIND OF HUSH (ALL
 OVER THE WORLD)
WHEN THERE'S NO YOU
WINTER WORLD OF LOVE

Reed, Lou

WALK ON THE WILD SIDE
WORLD WITHOUT HEROES, A

Reed, Matcher James

YOU DON'T HAVE TO GO

Reed, Mike

FALLIN' FOR YOU FOR YEARS

Reed, Nancy Binns

OH, HAPPY DAY

Reed, Robert

GOOD TO GO

Reed, T., Jr.

GOOD TO GO

Reede, Jon

JUST ONE OF THE GUYS

Reese, Claude

ALL DRESSED UP WITH A BROKEN
 HEART

Reeve, Ivan

DON'T BLAME THE CHILDREN

Reeves, Del

SING A LITTLE SONG OF
   HEARTACHE

Reeves, Eddie

ALL I EVER NEED IS YOU
DON'T CHANGE ON ME
RINGS

Reeves, Ellen

SING A LITTLE SONG OF
   HEARTACHE

Reeves, Jim

AM I LOSING YOU?
I'M GETTIN' BETTER
IS IT REALLY OVER?
THEN I'LL STOP LOVING YOU
(HOW CAN I WRITE ON PAPER)
   WHAT I FEEL IN MY HEART
YONDER COMES A SUCKER

Regan, Russ

CINNAMON CINDER, THE (IT'S A
   VERY NICE DANCE)

Regney, Noel

DOMINIQUE
DO YOU HEAR WHAT I HEAR?
RAIN, RAIN GO AWAY

Rehak, Bud

KISS ME, SAILOR

Rehbein, Herbert

LADY
LONELY IS THE NAME
MY WAY OF LIFE
WIEDERSEH'N
WORLD WE KNEW, THE (OVER AND
   OVER)
YOU TURNED MY WORLD AROUND

Reichel, Fritz Schulz

MAN WITH THE BANJO, THE

Reichner, Bickley "Bix"

I NEED YOUR LOVE TONIGHT
MAMBO ROCK
PAPA LOVES MAMBO
STOP! IT'S WONDERFUL
STOP BEATIN' ROUND THE
   MULBERRY BUSH
TEEN AGE PRAYER
THERE'S NO PLACE LIKE YOUR
   ARMS
WHEN I GO A-DREAMIN'
YA GOT ME
YOU BETTER GO NOW

Reid, Antonio

DIAL MY HEART
EVERY LITTLE STEP
IT'S NO CRIME
LOVER IN ME, THE
LOVE SAW IT
ON OUR OWN
SUPERWOMAN

Reid, Billy

GYPSY, THE
I'LL CLOSE MY EYES
I'M WALKING BEHIND YOU
IT'S A PITY TO SAY GOODNIGHT
TREE IN THE MEADOW, A

Reid, Clarence

CLEAN UP WOMAN
GIRLS CAN'T DO WHAT THE GUYS
   DO
NOBODY BUT YOU, BABE
ROCKIN' CHAIR

Reid, Dick

I STILL FEEL THE SAME ABOUT YOU

Reid, Don

DON'T WAIT ON ME

DO YOU KNOW YOU ARE MY
   SUNSHINE
GREEN YEARS
I'LL GO TO MY GRAVE LOVING YOU

Reid, Harold

BED OF ROSE'S
DON'T WAIT ON ME
DO YOU KNOW YOU ARE MY
   SUNSHINE

Reid, Ivan

WHEN I'M GONE I WON'T FORGET

Reid, Keith

CONQUISTADOR
HOMBURG
WHITER SHADE OF PALE, A

Reid, L. A.

DON'T BE CRUEL
GIRLFRIEND
I LOVE YOU BABE
ROCK STEADY

Reid, Mike

IN LOVE
LOST IN THE FIFTIES TONIGHT (IN
   THE STILL OF THE NIGHT)
OLD FOLKS
ONE GOOD WELL
SHE KEEPS THE HOME FIRES
   BURNING
STILL LOSING YOU
STRANGER IN MY HOUSE
TO ME
WHERE DO THE NIGHTS GO

Reid, Roscoe

MAKING BELIEVE

Reid, Sam

SOMEDAY

Reid, Tom

HOW DO I TURN YOU ON

Reilly, M.

FAMILY MAN

Reine, Johnny

RED RIVER ROSE
WEDDING OF LILI MARLENE, THE

Reinfeld, John

VIOLET AND A ROSE, THE

Reinhardt, Gladys

WHITE SILVER SANDS

Reinhardt, Heinrich

DAY DREAMS
FOUNTAIN FAY
TWO LITTLE LOVE BEES

Reisch, Walter

TELL ME WHY YOU SMILE, MONA
  LISA
TWO HEARTS IN THREE-QUARTER
  TIME

Reisfeld, Bert

CALL ME DARLING
THREE BELLS, THE (A.K.A. JIMMY
  BROWN SONG, THE)

Reisman, Joe

JOEY'S SONG
RING-A-LING-A-LARIO

Reisner, C. Francis

GOODBYE BROADWAY, HELLO
  FRANCE

Reitz, William J.

FAIRY TALES

Reizner, June

BARRY'S BOYS

Relf, Bob

HARLEM SHUFFLE

Relf, Keith

HAPPENINGS TEN YEARS TIME AGO
OVER UNDER SIDEWAYS DOWN
SHAPES OF THINGS

Remigi, M.

CAN I TRUST YOU?

Ren, Malou

ONE TRACK MIND
TOSSIN' AND TURNIN'

Renard, Jean

LOSING YOU

Rendine, Furio

PANSY

Rene, Henri

WAGON TRAIN

René, Leon

DUSTY ROAD
GLORIA
I LOST MY SUGAR IN SALT LAKE
  CITY
I SOLD MY HEART TO THE JUNK
  MAN
MEXICO JOE
SOMEONE'S ROCKING MY
  DREAMBOAT
WHEN IT'S SLEEPY TIME DOWN
  SOUTH
WHEN THE SWALLOWS COMES BACK
  TO CAPISTRANO

René, Otis

DUSTY ROAD
I'M LOST
I SOLD MY HEART TO THE JUNK
  MAN
SOMEONE'S ROCKING MY
  DREAMBOAT
WHEN IT'S SLEEPY TIME DOWN
  SOUTH

Reneau, Bud

GOT MY HEART SET ON YOU

Reneau, George

DAYS OF SAND AND SHOVELS, THE

Renis, Tony

ALL OF YOU
TONIGHT I'LL SAY A PRAYER

Reno, Mike

HEAVEN IN YOUR EYES
THIS COULD BE THE NIGHT
WORKING FOR THE WEEKEND

Reser, Harry

GOONA GOO, THE

Resnick, Arthur

CHIP CHIP
GOOD LOVIN'
I'VE GOT SAND IN MY SHOES
LITTLE BIT OF HEAVEN, A
ONE KISS FOR OLD TIMES' SAKE
QUICK JOEY SMALL (RUN, JOEY,
  RUN)
UNDER THE BOARDWALK
YUMMY, YUMMY, YUMMY

Resnick, Kris

CHEWY CHEWY
DOWN AT LULU'S
SHAKE

Reswick, Pam

I LIVE FOR YOUR LOVE

Reuss, Alan

MORE AND MORE

Revaux, Jacques

MY WAY

Revel, Harry

AFRAID TO DREAM
AND SO TO BED
ARE YOU IN THE MOOD FOR
  MISCHIEF?
ARE YOU WITH IT?
BOY AND A GIRL WERE DANCING, A
BUT DEFINITELY
COLLEGE RHYTHM
DANGER—LOVE AT WORK
DID YOU EVER SEE A DREAM
  WALKING?
DOIN' THE UPTOWN LOWDOWN
DON'T LET IT BOTHER YOU
FROM THE TOP OF YOUR HEAD TO
  THE TIP OF YOUR TOES
GOOD MORNING GLORY
GOOD NIGHT, LOVELY LITTLE LADY
GOODNIGHT, MY LOVE
GOT ME DOIN' THINGS
GOT MY MIND ON MUSIC
HEAD OVER HEELS IN LOVE
HELP YOURSELF TO HAPPINESS
I FEEL LIKE A FEATHER IN THE
  BREEZE
IF I HAD A DOZEN HEARTS
I'M HUMMIN'—I'M WHISTLIN'—I'M
  SINGIN'
I'M LIKE A FISH OUT OF WATER
I NEVER KNEW HEAVEN COULD
  SPEAK
IN OLD CHICAGO
I PLAYED FIDDLE FOR THE CZAR
IT'S SWELL OF YOU
IT'S THE ANIMAL IN ME
IT'S WITHIN YOUR POWER
IT WAS A NIGHT IN JUNE
I'VE GOT A DATE WITH A DREAM
I'VE GOT MY HEART SET ON YOU

I WANNA BE IN WINCHELL'S
  COLUMN
I WANNA GO TO THE ZOO
I WISH I WERE ALADDIN
JET
JUST BEYOND THE RAINBOW
LET'S GIVE THREE CHEERS FOR
  LOVE
LET'S K-NOCK K-NEES
LISTEN TO THE GERMAN BAND
LOVELINESS OF YOU, THE
LOVE THY NEIGHBOR
MAY I?
MAY I HAVE THE NEXT ROMANCE
  WITH YOU?
MEET THE BEAT OF MY HEART
NEVER IN A MILLION YEARS
OH, MY GOODNESS
OLD STRAW HAT, AN
ONCE IN A BLUE MOON
ONE NEVER KNOWS, DOES ONE?
ORCHID TO YOU, AN
PARIS IN THE SPRING
PLEASE PARDON US, WE'RE IN
  LOVE
REMEMBER ME TO CAROLINA
SHE REMINDS ME OF YOU
SLAP POLKA, THE
STAR FELL OUT OF HEAVEN, A
STAY AS SWEET AS YOU ARE
STRAIGHT FROM THE SHOULDER
  (RIGHT FROM THE HEART)
SWEET AS A SONG
SWEET SOMEONE
SWING IS HERE TO STAY
TAKE A NUMBER FROM ONE TO TEN
TAKES TWO TO MAKE A BARGAIN
THANKS FOR EV'RYTHING
THERE'S A BLUEBIRD AT MY
  WINDOW
TREE WAS A TREE, A
TWO FOR TONIGHT
UNDERNEATH THE HARLEM MOON
WAKE UP AND LIVE
WERE YOUR EARS BURNING?
WHEN I'M WITH YOU
WHEN THERE'S A BREEZE ON LAKE
  LOUISE
WILL I EVER KNOW?
WITH MY EYES WIDE OPEN I'M
  DREAMING
WITHOUT A WORD OF WARNING
WOULD THERE BE LOVE?

YOU CAN'T HAVE EVERYTHING
YOU GOTTA S-M-I-L-E TO BE H-A-
  DOUBLE P-Y
YOU GO YOUR WAY (AND I'LL GO
  CRAZY)
YOU HIT THE SPOT
YOU'RE MY PAST, PRESENT AND
  FUTURE
YOU'RE SUCH A COMFORT TO ME

Revere, Paul

GOOD THING
GREAT AIRPLANE STRIKE, THE
STEPPIN' OUT

Revil, Rupi

LITTLE SHOEMAKER, THE

Rew, Kimberly

WALKING ON SUNSHINE

Reyam, G.

RIVERS OF BABYLON

Reynolds, Allen

DODO, THE
FIVE O'CLOCK WORLD
I SAW LINDA YESTERDAY
READY FOR THE TIMES TO GET
  BETTER

Reynolds, Arthur

JESUS IS JUST ALRIGHT

Reynolds, Dick

IF I EVER LOVE AGAIN
SILVER THREADS AND GOLDEN
  NEEDLES

Reynolds, Ellis

I'M CONFESSIN' THAT I LOVE YOU

Reynolds, Herbert

AUF WIEDERSEHEN

NODDING ROSES
THROW ME A ROSE
VALENTINE

Reynolds, Isaac G.

WON'T YOU BE MY LITTLE GIRL?

Reynolds, J. J.

BATTLE OF KOOKAMONGA, THE

Reynolds, Jody

ENDLESS SLEEP

Reynolds, Lawrence

JESUS IS A SOUL MAN

Reynolds, Malvina

LITTLE BOXES
MORNINGTOWN RIDE
TURN AROUND
WHAT HAVE THEY DONE TO THE
    RAIN?

Reynolds, Paul

I RAN (SO FAR AWAY)

Reynolds, Thomas

DAY AFTER DAY (IT'S SLIPPIN'
    AWAY)

Rhodes, David

MY GUITAR IS MY SWEETHEART

Rhodes, Dusty

UNDER YOUR SPELL AGAIN

Rhodes, Emmitt

FRESH AS A DAISY

Rhodes, Jack

BEAUTIFUL LIES
CONSCIENCE, I'M GUILTY

SATISFIED MIND, A
SILVER THREADS AND GOLDEN
    NEEDLES

Rhodes, Nick

ELECTION DAY
NOTORIOUS

Rhodes, Sandra

CLOWN, THE
HOW MUCH CAN A LONELY HEART
    STAND?

Rhodes, Stan

SUNDAY KIND OF LOVE, A

Rhody, Alan

I'LL BE TRUE TO YOU

Ricardel, Joe

FRIM FRAM SAUCE, THE
WISE OLD OWL, THE

Ricca, Lou

DREAM, DREAM, DREAM
GOODBYE SUE
HEAVENLY HIDEAWAY

Ricci, Joe

JUST ASK YOUR HEART

Rice, Andy

DUST
GIRL TROUBLE

Rice, Bill

AIN'T SHE SOMETHIN' ELSE
DAY THE WORLD STOOD STILL, THE
EASY PART'S OVER, THE
GIVING UP EASY
I'M NOT THAT LONELY YET
WONDER COULD I LIVE THERE
    ANYMORE

Rice, Bonny

MUSTANG SALLY

Rice, Denzil

THERE'S A HONKY TONK ANGEL
    (WHO'LL TAKE ME BACK IN)

Rice, Howie

LOVIN' ON NEXT TO NOTHIN'

Rice, Lt. Gitz

DEAR OLD PAL OF MINE

Rice, Mack

CHEAPER TO KEEP HER
DO THE FUNKY PENGUIN
RESPECT YOURSELF

Rice, Mary S.

I'M NOT THAT LONELY YET

Rice, Ronald

I COULD NEVER LIE TO YOU
I WILL ALWAYS THINK ABOUT YOU
THINGS I'D LIKE TO SAY

Rice, Seymour A.

YOU TELL ME YOUR DREAM

Rice, Tim

ALL TIME HIGH
BUENOS AIRES
CHRISTMAS DREAM
DON'T CRY FOR ME, ARGENTINA
EVERYTHING'S ALRIGHT
I DON'T KNOW HOW TO LOVE HIM
I KNEW HIM SO WELL
ONE NIGHT IN BANGKOK
SUPERSTAR

Rice, Verlie

SHAKE A TAIL FEATHER
TWINE TIME

Rice, Wilburn

SHE'S PULLING ME BACK AGAIN

Rich, Alan

I LIVE FOR YOUR LOVE
LOVIN' ON NEXT TO NOTHIN'

Rich, Charlie

EVERY TIME YOU TOUCH ME (I GET
    HIGH)
LONELY WEEKENDS
ON MY KNEES
THERE WON'T BE ANYMORE
WAYS OF A WOMAN IN LOVE, THE

Rich, Don

BEFORE YOU GO
THINK OF ME (WHEN YOU'RE
    LONELY)
WAITIN' IN YOUR WELFARE LINE

Rich, Fred

I'M JUST WILD ABOUT ANIMAL
    CRACKERS

Rich, James

YAKETY SAX

Rich, Max

AIN'TCHA?
I DON'T MIND WALKING IN THE
    RAIN
MAKIN' FACES AT THE MAN IN THE
    MOON
SMILE, DARN YA, SMILE
WONDERFUL YOU

Richard, Cliff

BACHELOR BOY

Richard, Renald

GREENBACKS

Richards, Deke

ABC
I CAN'T DANCE TO THAT MUSIC
    YOU'RE PLAYIN'
I WANT YOU ALL TO MYSELF (JUST
    YOU)
LOVE CHILD
LOVE YOU SAVE, THE
MAMA'S PEARL
SUGAR DADDY

Richards, Dick

DOWN ON THE FARM IN HARVEST
    TIME

Richards, Jack

HE
QUEEN OF THE SENIOR PROM

Richards, Johnny

YOUNG AT HEART

Richards, Keith

19TH NERVOUS BREAKDOWN
ANGIE
AS TEARS GO BY
BEAST OF BURDEN
BROWN SUGAR
CRAZY MAMA
DANDELION
DOO DOO DOO DOO DOO
    (HEARTBREAKER)
EMOTIONAL RESCUE
FOOL TO CRY
GET OFF MY CLOUD
GIMME SHELTER
HANG FIRE
HAPPY
HAVE YOU SEEN YOUR MOTHER,
    BABY, STANDING IN THE
    SHADOW?
HEART OF STONE
HONKY TONK WOMEN
HOT STUFF
I CAN'T GET NO SATISFACTION
IT'S ONLY ROCK 'N' ROLL (BUT I
    LIKE IT)
JUMPIN' JACK FLASH

LADY JANE
LAST TIME, THE
LET'S SPEND THE NIGHT TOGETHER
MEMO FROM TURNER
MISS YOU
MOTHER'S LITTLE HELPER
OUT OF TIME
PAINT IT BLACK
PLAY WITH FIRE
RUBY TUESDAY
SHATTERED
SHE'S A RAINBOW
SHE'S SO COLD
SHE WAS HOT
START ME UP
STREET FIGHTING MAN
TELL ME (YOU'RE COMING BACK)
TUMBLING DICE
UNDERCOVER OF THE NIGHT
WAITING ON A FRIEND
WE LOVE YOU
WILD HORSES
YOU CAN'T ALWAYS GET WHAT YOU
    WANT

Richards, Nick

I WANNA BE A COWBOY

Richards, Regina

BABY LOVE

Richardson, Arthur

TOO FAT POLKA

Richardson, Clive

EARTHBOUND

Richardson, David

WILDFLOWER

Richardson, J. P.

BEGGAR TO A KING
CHANTILLY LACE
RUNNING BEAR
WHITE LIGHTNING

Richardson, Newt

LOVER'S QUARREL, A

Richey, George

I'M STILL LOVING YOU
KEEP ME IN MIND
'TILL I CAN MAKE IT ON MY OWN
WOMAN LIVES FOR LOVE, A
YOU AND ME

Richie, Brenda

YOU ARE

Richie, Lionel

ALL NIGHT LONG (ALL NIGHT)
BALLERINA GIRL
BRICK HOUSE
DANCING ON THE CEILING
EASY
ENDLESS LOVE
HAPPY PEOPLE
HELLO
JUST TO BE CLOSE TO YOU
LADY
LOVE WILL CONQUER ALL
MISS CELIE'S BLUES
MISSING YOU
MY LOVE
OH NO
PENNY LOVER
RUNNING WITH THE NIGHT
SAIL ON
SAY YOU, SAY ME (UNDER TITLE
    SONG OF "WHITE NIGHTS")
SE LA
SLIPPERY WHEN WET
STILL
STUCK ON YOU
SWEET LOVE
THREE TIMES A LADY
TOO HOT TA TROT
TRULY
WE ARE THE WORLD
YOU ARE

Richman, Daniel

ALONE AT A TABLE FOR TWO

Richman, Harry

C'EST VOUS (IT'S YOU)
HELP YOURSELF TO HAPPINESS
LIFE BEGINS WHEN YOU'RE IN LOVE
MISS ANNABELLE LEE
MOONLIGHT SAVING TIME
MUDDY WATER
ONE LITTLE RAINDROP
RO-RO-ROLLIN' ALONG
SINGING A VAGABOND SONG
THERE'S DANGER IN YOUR EYES,
    CHERIE

Richmond, Frank J.

TAKE ME BACK TO YOUR HEART
    AGAIN

Richmond, Paul

SHINING STAR

Richrath, Gary

IN YOUR LETTER
TAKE IT ON THE RUN

Ricketts, Bob

CHARLESTON CRAZY

Ricketts, David

WELCOME TO THE BOOMTOWN

Ricks, Jimmy

ROCK ME ALL NIGHT LONG

Ricks, Lee

CEMENT MIXER (PUT-TI, PUT-TI)
DOWN BY THE STATION

Riddle, Hank

UNTIL I MET YOU

Riddle, Nelson

JOHNNY CONCHO THEME (WAIT FOR
    ME)

LOLITA YA-YA
NAKED CITY THEME
ROUTE 66 THEME
UNTOUCHABLES, THE

Ridge, Antonia

HAPPY WANDERER, THE (VAL-DE-
    RI, VAL-DE-RA)

Ridgeley, Andrew

CARELESS WHISPER

Ridgway, Stanard

MEXICAN RADIO

Ridley, Greg

HOT 'N' NASTY

Riefoli, Raffaele

SELF CONTROL

Rieley, Jack

SAIL ON SAILOR

Riggs, Thomas Lawrason

I'VE A SHOOTING BOX IN SCOTLAND

Rigual, Carlos

LOVE ME WITH ALL YOUR HEART
    (CUANDO CALIENTE EL SOL)

Rigual, Mario

LOVE ME WITH ALL YOUR HEART
    (CUANDO CALIENTE EL SOL)

Riley, Edward

JUST COOLIN'
THEY WANT MONEY

Riley, Melvin

LOVE YOU DOWN

Riley, Melvin

OH, SHEILA
READY FOR THE WORLD

Riley, Michael

I'M GONNA CLAP MY HANDS
MUSIC GOES 'ROUND AND 'ROUND,
THE

Riley, Robert S.

JUST WALKING IN THE RAIN
ROLLIN' STONE

Riley, Teddy

I LIKE
I WANT HER
MAKE IT LAST FOREVER
SOMETHING JUST AIN'T RIGHT

Rimsky-Korsakoff, Nicholas

SONG OF INDIA

Ringle, Dave

ROLL ON, MISSISSIPPI, ROLL ON
WABASH BLUES

Rinker, Al

DREAMSVILLE, OHIO
READY, WILLING AND ABLE
YOU STARTED SOMETHING

Rio, Chuck

TEQUILA

Riopelle, Jerry

ALL STRUNG OUT
DAY AFTER DAY (IT'S SLIPPIN'
AWAY)
SUNSHINE GIRL

Riordan, David

GREEN-EYED LADY

Rios, Carlos

DANCING ON THE CEILING

Riperton, Minnie

ADVENTURES IN PARADISE
LOVIN' YOU

Risbrook

EXPRESS

Riser, Paul

I DON'T KNOW WHY
WHAT BECOMES OF THE
BROKENHEARTED?

Ritchie, Ian

SHE'S HAVING A BABY

Ritenour, Lee

IS IT YOU

Ritter, Tex

DEAR JOHN
I'M WASTIN' MY TEARS ON YOU
LONG TIME GONE
ROCK AND RYE POLKA
YOU WILL HAVE TO PAY (FOR YOUR
YESTERDAY)

Rivera, E.

GREEN EYES

Rivers, Johnny

POOR SIDE OF TOWN

Rives, Ada

BATTLESHIP KATE

Rives, Tubby

HALF A HEART IS ALL YOU LEFT
ME (WHEN YOU BROKE MY
HEART IN TWO)

Roach, Jimmy

MY WHOLE WORLD ENDED (THE
MOMENT YOU LEFT ME)

Roach, Joseph Maloy

ONE LITTLE CANDLE

Robb, Paul

WHAT'S ON YOUR MIND (PURE
ENERGY)

Robbins, Ayn

GONNA FLY NOW (THEME FROM
"ROCKY")
SOMEONE'S WAITING FOR YOU

Robbins, C. A.

WASHINGTON AND LEE SWING

Robbins, Corky

WHISPERING WINDS

Robbins, Dave

BLUEST EYES IN TEXAS

Robbins, Dennis

CHURCH ON CUMBERLAND ROAD,
THE
(DO YOU LOVE ME) JUST SAY YES

Robbins, Fran

HOUSE THAT JACK BUILT, THE

Robbins, Kent

I DON'T THINK SHE'S IN LOVE
ANYMORE
I'LL COME BACK AS ANOTHER
WOMAN
I'M A STAND BY MY WOMAN MAN
LOVE IS ALIVE
ONE GOOD WELL
YOUNG LOVE (STRONG LOVE)
YOU'RE MY JAMAICA

Robbins, Marty

BEGGING TO YOU
BIG IRON
COWBOY IN THE CONTINENTAL SUIT,
    THE
DEVIL WOMAN
DON'T WORRY
EL PASO
EL PASO CITY
GIRL FROM SPANISH TOWN, THE
I COULDN'T KEEP FROM CRYING
I'LL GO ON ALONE
IT'S YOUR WORLD
LOVE IS IN THE AIR
MY WOMAN, MY WOMAN, MY WIFE
NOT SO LONG AGO
ONE OF THESE DAYS
PLEASE DON'T BLAME ME
SHE WAS ONLY SEVENTEEN (HE
    WAS ONE YEAR MORE)
TONIGHT CARMEN
WHITE SPORT COAT, A (AND A PINK
    CARNATION)
YOU DON'T OWE ME A THING
YOU GAVE ME A MOUNTAIN

Robe, Harold

DEAR OLD PAL OF MINE

Roberds, Fred "Smokey"

SUNSHINE GIRL

Robert, Camille

MADELON

Roberti, Roberto

AURORA

Roberts, Allan

ANGELINA (THE WAITRESS AT THE
    PIZZERIA)
DREAMER WITH A PENNY
EITHER IT'S LOVE OR IT ISN'T
GOOD, GOOD, GOOD (THAT'S YOU—
    THAT'S YOU)

INTO EACH LIFE SOME RAIN MUST
    FALL
INVITATION TO THE BLUES
I WISH
KISSIN' BUG BOOGIE
ME, MYSELF AND I (ARE ALL IN
    LOVE WITH YOU)
NAUGHTY ANGELINE
NOODLIN' RAG
PUT THE BLAME ON MAME
RAINBOW RHAPSODY
RIVER SEINE, THE (A.K.A. LA
    SEINE)
TAMPICO
THAT OLE DEVIL CALLED LOVE
THEY CAN'T CONVINCE ME
TIRED
TO KNOW YOU IS TO LOVE YOU
YOU ALWAYS HURT THE ONE YOU
    LOVE
YOU CAN'T SEE THE SUN WHEN
    YOU'RE CRYIN'

Roberts, Austin

100% CHANCE OF RAIN
I.O.U.
OVER YOU
STRONG HEART

Roberts, Bob

KING OF THE WHOLE WIDE WORLD
TALL PAUL
WHERE DO YOU COME FROM?

Roberts, Bruce

DYNAMITE
FIGHT
FLAMES OF PARADISE
MAIN EVENT, THE
MAKING LOVE
NO MORE TEARS (ENOUGH IS
    ENOUGH)
TOO CLOSE TO PARADISE
YOU'RE MOVIN' OUT TODAY
YOU'RE THE ONLY ONE
YOU SHOULD BE MINE (THE WOO
    WOO SONG)

Roberts, C. Luckeyth "Luckey"

MASSACHUSETTS
MOONLIGHT COCKTAIL
ROCKAWAY

Roberts, Don

PRACTICE MAKES PERFECT

Roberts, Jack

HERE'S SOME LOVE

Roberts, Jay

OOP BOP SH' BAM

Roberts, Johnny

MY BOY LOLLIPOP

Roberts, Lee G.

SMILES

Roberts, Lya

JUST YOUNG

Roberts, Marty

YOU CAN'T HAVE MY LOVE

Roberts, Paddy

JOHNNY (IS THE BOY FOR ME)
LAY DOWN YOUR ARMS

Roberts, Paul

DRIVER'S SEAT
THERE'S A STAR SPANGLED BANNER
    WAVING SOMEWHERE

Roberts, Rhoda

PUT A LIGHT IN THE WINDOW
SWINGIN' SHEPHERD BLUES, THE

Roberts, Rick

COLORADO
JUST REMEMBER I LOVE YOU
STRANGE WAY
YOU ARE THE WOMAN

Roberts, Ruth

FIRST THING EVERY MORNING (AND
   THE LAST THING EVERY NIGHT),
   THE
MR. TOUCHDOWN, U.S.A.

Robertson, Brian

LIVING YEARS, THE
SILENT RUNNING (ON DANGEROUS
   GROUND)

Robertson, D.

CUTIE PIE

Robertson, Dick

AT LEAST YOU COULD SAY HELLO
GOODNIGHT, WHEREVER YOU ARE
IS THERE SOMEBODY ELSE?
LITTLE ON THE LONELY SIDE, A
THERE'S A CHILL ON THE HILL
   TONIGHT
WE THREE (MY ECHO, MY SHADOW,
   AND ME)
YESTERDAY'S GARDENIAS
YOU FORGOT ABOUT ME

Robertson, Don

ANYTHING THAT'S PART OF YOU
BORN TO BE WITH YOU
DOES HE MEAN THAT MUCH TO
   YOU?
DOES MY RING HURT YOUR
   FINGER?
GO BACK YOU FOOL
HAPPY WHISTLER
HUMMINGBIRD
I DON'T HURT ANYMORE
I LOVE YOU MORE AND MORE
   EVERY DAY
I'M YOURS

I REALLY DON'T WANT TO KNOW
NINETY MILES AN HOUR ON A
   DEAD-END STREET
PLEASE HELP ME, I'M FALLING
   (A.K.A. I CAN'T HELP YOU, I'M
   FALLING)
RINGO
YOU'RE FREE TO GO

Robertson, Robbie

BETWEEN TRAINS
IT'S IN THE WAY YOU USE IT
LIFE IS A CARNIVAL
NIGHT THEY DROVE OLD DIXIE
   DOWN, THE
OPHELIA
RAG, MAMA, RAG
SWEET FIRE OF LOVE
UP ON CRIPPLE CREEK
WEIGHT, THE

Robey, Don

FARTHER UP THE ROAD
I'M GONNA PLAY THE HONKY
   TONKS
PLEDGING MY LOVE

Robie, J.

PLANET ROCK

Robin, Leo

ALWAYS IN ALL WAYS
AWAKE IN A DREAM
BEYOND THE BLUE HORIZON
BLOSSOMS ON BROADWAY
BLUEBIRDS IN THE MOONLIGHT
BLUE HAWAII
BYE BYE BABY
DIAMONDS ARE A GIRL'S BEST
   FRIEND
DOUBLE TROUBLE
EASY LIVING
EBB TIDE
FAITHFUL FOREVER
FOR EVERY MAN THERE'S A
   WOMAN
FUNNY OLD HILLS, THE
GAL IN CALICO, A

GATHER LIP ROUGE WHILE YOU
   MAY
GIVE ME A BAND AND MY BABY
GIVE ME A MOMENT PLEASE
GIVE ME LIBERTY OR GIVE ME
   LOVE
HALLELUJAH!
HAVE YOU FORGOTTEN (THE
   THRILL)?
HAVIN' MYSELF A TIME
HERE IS MY HEART
HERE LIES LOVE
HERE'S LOVE IN YOUR EYE
HERE YOU ARE
HILLS OF OLD WYOMIN', THE
HOORAY FOR LOVE
I CAN'T ESCAPE FROM YOU
I'D LOVE TO SPEND (ONE HOUR
   WITH YOU)
I DON'T WANT TO MAKE HISTORY (I
   JUST WANT TO MAKE LOVE)
IF I SHOULD LOSE YOU
IF I WERE KING
I HAVE EYES
I HAVE TO HAVE YOU
I'LL TAKE AN OPTION ON YOU
I'M A BLACK SHEEP WHO'S BLUE
IN A LITTLE HULA HEAVEN
IN LOVE IN VAIN
IN PARIS AND IN LOVE
IN THE PARK IN PAREE
IT'S A GREAT LIFE (IF YOU DON'T
   WEAKEN)
IT'S BIGGER THAN YOU AND ME
IT'S DELIGHTFUL DOWN IN CHILE
IT WAS WRITTEN IN THE STARS
JERICHO
JOOBALAI
JOURNEY TO A STAR, A
JUNE IN JANUARY
KINDA LONESOME
LATER TONIGHT
LITTLE GIRL FROM LITTLE ROCK, A
LITTLE KISS AT TWILIGHT, A
LITTLE ROSE OF THE RANCHO
LONG AGO AND FAR AWAY
LOOK WHAT I'VE GOT
LOST IN LOVELINESS
LOUISE
LOVE IN BLOOM
LOVE IS JUST AROUND THE CORNER
LOW-DOWN LULLABY
MAMA, THAT MOON IS HERE AGAIN

MISS BROWN TO YOU
MOONLIGHT AND SHADOWS
MY CUTIE'S DUE AT TWO TO TWO
 TODAY
MY FLAMING HEART
MY HEART AND I
MY HEART WON'T SAY GOODBYE
MY IDEAL
NO LOVE, NO NOTHIN'
OH, BUT I DO
(I'D LOVE TO SPEND) ONE HOUR
 WITH YOU
ONE LOVE
PAREE!
PLEASE
PRISONER OF LOVE
RAINY NIGHT IN RIO, A
RENDEZVOUS WITH A DREAM
SAILOR BEWARE
SILVER ON THE STAGE
SOMETHING IN THE WIND
SO-O-O-O-O IN LOVE
SWEET IS THE WORD FOR YOU
TAKE A LESSON FROM THE LARK
THANKS FOR THE MEMORY
(IF IT ISN'T PAIN) THEN IT ISN'T
 LOVE
THIS IS THE MOMENT
THROUGH A THOUSAND DREAMS
THUNDER OVER PARADISE
TRUE BLUE LOU
TURNTABLE SONG, THE
UP WITH THE LARK
WAIT 'TIL YOU SEE MA CHERIE
WE WILL ALWAYS BE SWEETHEARTS
WHAT GOES ON HERE IN MY
 HEART?
WHAT HAVE YOU GOT THAT GETS
 ME?
WHAT'S GOOD ABOUT GOODBYE?
WHAT WOULD YOU DO?
WHEN HE COMES HOME TO ME
WHISPERS IN THE DARK
WHY, OH WHY?
WHY DREAM?
WITH EVERY BREATH I TAKE
YOU CAME TO MY RESCUE
YOU'RE A SWEET LITTLE
 HEADACHE
YOU STARTED SOMETHING
YOU TOOK THE WORDS RIGHT OUT
 OF MY HEART
ZING A LITTLE ZONG

Robin, Sid

CONGRATULATIONS
FLYIN' HOME
I MISS YOU SO
MY BABY SAID YES
NO ONE TO CRY TO
UNDECIDED
WE GO WELL TOGETHER
WHAT TO DO

Robinson, A.

TWO HEARTS IN THREE-QUARTER
 TIME

Robinson, Betty

BABY'S BACK AGAIN
WHAT'S HE DOIN' IN MY WORLD?

Robinson, Bobby

WARM AND TENDER LOVE

Robinson, Carson

LIFE GETS TEE-JUS, DON'T IT

Robinson, Earl

BALLAD FOR AMERICANS
BLACK AND WHITE
HOUSE I LIVE IN, THE (THAT'S
 AMERICA TO ME)
JOE HILL
SAID I TO MY HEART, SAID I

Robinson, Eddie

SHAKE IT WELL

Robinson, Edward

HOLD TIGHT—HOLD TIGHT (WANT
 SOME SEA FOOD, MAMA)

Robinson, Eric

DANCE (DISCO HEAT)

Robinson, Floyd

MAKIN' LOVE

Robinson, Frank K.

I'VE FOUND SOMEONE OF MY OWN

Robinson, Jessie Mae

BLACK NIGHT
BLUE LIGHT BOOGIE
I WENT TO YOUR WEDDING
KEEP IT A SECRET
OLD MAID BOOGIE
OTHER WOMAN, THE
SEVEN LONG DAYS

Robinson, J. Russel

AGGRAVATIN' PAPA (DON'T YOU TRY
 TO TWO-TIME ME)
BEALE STREET MAMA
GET RHYTHM IN YOUR FEET
HALF-WAY TO HEAVEN
IS I IN LOVE? I IS
I WON'T BELIEVE IT
MARGIE
MARY LOU
MEET ME AT NO SPECIAL PLACE
 (AND I'LL BE THERE AT NO
 PARTICULAR TIME)
MEMORIES OF FRANCE
ORIGINAL DIXIELAND ONE-STEP
PALESTEENA
PORTRAIT OF JENNIE
REEFER MAN
RHYTHM KING
SINGIN' THE BLUES (TILL MY
 DADDY COMES HOME)

Robinson, Morgan

YA YA

Robinson, Nadine

I CAN'T SEE FOR LOOKIN'

Robinson, Patrick

NOTHING TAKES THE PLACE OF YOU

Robinson, Prince

APOLLO JUMP

Robinson, Rainey

MORE AND MORE

Robinson, Sharon

NEW ATTITUDE

Robinson, Sylvia

LOVE IS STRANGE
LOVE ON A TWO-WAY STREET
MESSAGE, THE
PILLOW TALK
SEXY MAMA
SHAME, SHAME, SHAME

Robinson, Will

"YOU'VE GOT" THE TOUCH

Robinson, William "Smokey"

AIN'T THAT PECULIAR?
AS LONG AS I KNOW HE'S MINE
BABY, BABY, DON'T CRY
BABY COME CLOSE
BABY THAT'S BACKATCHA
BEING WITH YOU
COME ON, DO THE JERK
COMPOSER, THE
CRUISIN'
DOGGONE RIGHT
DON'T LET HIM SHOP AROUND
DON'T MESS WITH BILL
FIRST I LOOK AT THE PURSE
FLOY JOY
GET READY
GOING TO A GO-GO
HAPPY (LOVE THEME FROM "LADY
  SINGS THE BLUES")
HERE I AM BABY
HERE I GO AGAIN
HE'S A GOOD GUY (YES HE IS)
HUNTER GETS CAPTURED BY THE
  GAME, THE
I DON'T BLAME YOU AT ALL
IF YOU CAN WANT

I KNOW HOW HE FEELS
I'LL BE DOGGONE
I'LL TRY SOMETHING NEW
I SECOND THAT EMOTION
IT'S GROWING
LAUGHING BOY
LET ME BE THE CLOCK
LOVE I SAW IN YOU WAS JUST A
  MIRAGE, THE
LOVE SHE CAN COUNT ON, A
MALINDA
MORE LOVE
MY BABY
MY BABY MUST BE A MAGICIAN
MY GIRL
MY GIRL HAS GONE
MY GUY
ONE MORE HEARTACHE
ONE WHO REALLY LOVES YOU, THE
OOH BABY BABY
POINT IT OUT
QUIET STORM
SHOP AROUND
SINCE I LOST MY BABY
SPECIAL OCCASION
STILL WATER (LOVE)
SWEET HARMONY
TAKE THIS HEART OF MINE
TEARS OF A CLOWN, THE
TRACKS OF MY TEARS, THE
TWO LOVERS
VIRGIN MAN
WAY YOU DO THE THINGS YOU DO,
  THE
WHAT'S EASY FOR TWO IS SO HARD
  FOR ONE
WHEN I'M GONE
YESTER LOVE
YOU BEAT ME TO THE PUNCH
YOU'RE THE ONE (I NEED)
YOUR OLD STANDBY
YOU'VE REALLY GOT A HOLD ON
  ME

Robison, Carson

BARNACLE BILL THE SAILOR
CARRY ME BACK TO THE LONE
  PRAIRIE
MY BLUE RIDGE MOUNTAIN HOME
THERE'S A BRIDLE HANGIN' ON THE
  WALL
WRECK OF THE SHENANDOAH, THE

Robison, Willard

BARRELHOUSE MUSIC
COTTAGE FOR SALE, A
DON'T SMOKE IN BED
MISSOURI WALKING PREACHER,
  THE
NOW WE KNOW
OLD FOLKS
PEACEFUL VALLEY
ROUND THE OLD DESERTED FARM
'TAIN'T SO, HONEY, 'TAIN'T SO

Robledo, Julian

THREE O'CLOCK IN THE MORNING

Robles, Daniel

EL CONDOR PASA

Robyn, Alfred George

MY SAN DOMINGO MAID

Rocco, Tommy

LET'S FALL TO PIECES TOGETHER
LITTLE GOOD NEWS, A
SLOW BURN
STRONG HEART

Rochinski, Stanley

POWDER YOUR FACE WITH
  SUNSHINE (SMILE! SMILE! SMILE!)

Rock, Joseph

I'VE GOT DREAMS TO REMEMBER
SINCE I DON'T HAVE YOU
THIS I SWEAR

Rocket, Rikki

I WON'T FORGET YOU
NOTHIN' BUT A GOOD TIME
TALK DIRTY TO ME

Rockwell

SOMEBODY'S WATCHING ME

Rodde, Roy

HAVE YOU HEARD?
IS IT ANY WONDER?
WHY DON'T YOU BELIEVE ME

Roddie, Vin

BON VOYAGE
THAT'S WHY I WAS BORN

Rodemich, Gene

SHANGHAI SHUFFLE

Roden, Robert F.

AIN'T YOU COMING BACK TO OLD
NEW HAMPSHIRE, MOLLY?
DOWN BY THE SILVERY RIO
GRANDE
THERE'S A DIXIE GIRL WHO'S
LONGING FOR A YANKEE
DOODLE BOY
WHEN IT'S MOONLIGHT ON THE
PRAIRIE

Rodgers, Dick

BETWEEN 18TH AND 19TH ON
CHESTNUT STREET

Rodgers, Gaby

JACKSON

Rodgers, Jimmie

ANY OLD TIME
BLUE YODEL
BLUE YODEL #8 (A.K.A. NEW MULE
SKINNER BLUES)
GAMBLIN' POLKA DOT BLUES
IN THE JAILHOUSE NOW
IT'S OVER
MOTHER, THE QUEEN OF MY
HEART
MY LITTLE LADY
PEACH PICKING TIME DOWN IN
GEORGIA
T FOR TEXAS (A.K.A. BLUE YODEL
NO. 1)
TRAIN WHISTLE BLUES

TRAVELIN' BLUES

Rodgers, Nile

COMING TO AMERICA
DANCE, DANCE, DANCE (YOWSAH,
YOWSAH, YOWSAH)
GOOD TIMES
HE'S THE GREATEST DANCER
I'M COMING OUT
I WANT YOUR LOVE
LE FREAK
SOUP FOR ONE
UPSIDE DOWN
WE ARE FAMILY

Rodgers, Paul

ALL RIGHT NOW
FEEL LIKE MAKIN' LOVE
ROCK 'N' ROLL FANTASY

Rodgers, Richard

ALL AT ONCE YOU LOVE HER
ALL ER NOTHIN'
ANY OLD PLACE WITH YOU
AWAY FROM YOU
BABES IN ARMS
BABY'S AWAKE NOW
BABY'S BEST FRIEND, A
BAD IN EVERYMAN, THE
BALI HA'I
BEWITCHED, BOTHERED, AND
BEWILDERED
BLOODY MARY
BLUE MOON
BLUE ROOM, THE
BYE AND BYE
CAN'T YOU DO A FRIEND A FAVOR
CAROUSEL WALTZ, THE
CIRCUS IS ON PARADE, THE
CLIMB EV'RY MOUNTAIN
COCK-EYED OPTIMIST, A
DANCING ON THE CEILING
DEN OF INIQUITY
DITES-MOI
DO I HEAR A WALTZ?
DO I HEAR YOU SAYING, "I LOVE
YOU"?
DO I LOVE YOU BECAUSE YOU'RE
BEAUTIFUL?
DO-RE-MI

DOWN BY THE RIVER
EVERYBODY'S GOT A HOME BUT ME
EVERYTHING'S UP TO DATE IN
(KANSAS CITY)
EV'RY SUNDAY AFTERNOON
EV'RYTHING I'VE GOT
FALLING IN LOVE WITH LOVE
FELLOW NEEDS A GIRL, A
FROM ANOTHER WORLD
GENTLEMAN IS A DOPE, THE
GETTING TO KNOW YOU
GIRL FRIEND, THE
GIVE IT BACK TO THE INDIANS
GLAD TO BE UNHAPPY
GRAND AVENUE
HALLELUJAH, I'M A BUM
HAPPY HUNTING HORN
HAPPY TALK
HAVE YOU MET MISS JONES?
HEART IS QUICKER THAN THE EYE,
THE
HELLO, YOUNG LOVERS
HERE IN MY ARMS (IT'S ADORABLE)
HONEY BUN
HOW CAN YOU FORGET?
HOW TO WIN FRIENDS AND
INFLUENCE PEOPLE
HUNDRED MILLION MIRACLES, A
I CAIN'T SAY NO
I COULD WRITE A BOOK
I DIDN'T KNOW WHAT TIME IT WAS
I DO NOT KNOW A DAY I DID NOT
LOVE YOU
I'D RATHER BE RIGHT
I ENJOY BEING A GIRL
I FEEL AT HOME WITH YOU
IF I LOVED YOU
I HAVE DREAMED
I HAVEN'T GOT A WORRY IN THE
WORLD
I LIKE TO RECOGNIZE THE TUNE
I MARRIED AN ANGEL
I'M GONNA WASH THAT MAN RIGHT
OUTA MY HAIR
I MUST LOVE YOU
I'M YOUR GIRL
IN MY OWN LITTLE CORNER
ISN'T IT KINDA FUN?
ISN'T IT ROMANTIC?
IT MIGHT AS WELL BE SPRING
IT NEVER ENTERED MY MIND
IT'S A GRAND NIGHT FOR SINGING
IT'S EASY TO REMEMBER

IT'S GOT TO BE LOVE
IT'S THE LITTLE THINGS IN TEXAS
I'VE GOT FIVE DOLLARS
I WHISTLE A HAPPY TUNE
I WISH I WERE IN LOVE AGAIN
JOHNNY ONE NOTE
JUNE IS BUSTIN' OUT ALL OVER
KANSAS CITY (EVERYTHING'S UP TO DATE IN)
KEEP IT GAY
LADY IS A TRAMP, THE
LA LA LA
LIKE ORDINARY PEOPLE DO
LITTLE BIRDIE TOLD ME SO, A
LITTLE GIRL BLUE
LOADS OF LOVE
LONELINESS OF EVENING
LONELY GOATHERD, THE
LOOK NO FURTHER
LOVE, LOOK AWAY
LOVELY NIGHT, A
LOVE ME TONIGHT
LOVE NEVER WENT TO COLLEGE
LOVER
MAINE
MANHATTAN
MANY A NEW DAY
MARCH OF THE SIAMESE CHILDREN
MARIA
MARRIAGE TYPE LOVE
MISTER SNOW
MIMI
MORE THAN JUST A FRIEND
MOST BEAUTIFUL GIRL IN THE WORLD, THE
MOUNTAIN GREENERY
MY FAVORITE THINGS
MY FUNNY VALENTINE
MY HEART STOOD STILL
MY MAN IS ON THE MAKE
MY ROMANCE
NEVER SAY NO TO A MAN
NEXT TIME IT HAPPENS, THE
NOBODY'S HEART (BELONGS TO ME)
NOBODY TOLD ME
NO OTHER LOVE
NO STRINGS
OH, WHAT A BEAUTIFUL MORNIN'
OKLAHOMA
ON YOUR TOES
OUT OF MY DREAMS
PEOPLE WILL SAY WE'RE IN LOVE
PORE JUD IS DAID

PUZZLEMENT, A
QUIET NIGHT
REAL NICE CLAMBAKE, A
SEND FOR ME
SENTIMENTAL ME
SHALL WE DANCE?
SHIP WITHOUT A SAIL, A
SING FOR YOUR SUPPER
SIXTEEN GOING ON SEVENTEEN
SLAUGHTER ON TENTH AVENUE
SO FAR
SOLILOQUY
SOME ENCHANTED EVENING
SOMETHING WONDERFUL
SOON
SOUND OF MUSIC, THE
SPRING IS HERE
SUNDAY
SURREY WITH THE FRINGE ON TOP, THE
SWEETEST SOUNDS, THE
SWEET THURSDAY
TAKE THE MOMENT
TEN CENTS A DANCE
THAT'S FOR ME
THAT'S LOVE
THAT'S THE RHYTHM OF THE DAY
THERE IS NOTHIN' LIKE A DAME
THERE'S A BOY IN HARLEM
THERE'S A SMALL HOTEL
THIS CAN'T BE LOVE
THIS FUNNY WORLD
THIS ISN'T HEAVEN
THIS NEARLY WAS MINE
THOU SWELL
TO KEEP MY LOVE ALIVE
TOO GOOD FOR THE AVERAGE MAN
TREE IN THE PARK, A
TWO BY TWO
VERY SPECIAL DAY, A
WAIT TILL YOU SEE HER
WAY OUT WEST (ON WEST END AVENUE)
WE KISS IN A SHADOW
WE'LL BE THE SAME
WHAT IS A MAN?
WHAT'S THE USE OF WOND'RIN'?
WHEN I GO ON THE STAGE
WHERE OR WHEN
WHERE'S THAT RAINBOW?
WHY CAN'T I?
WHY DO YOU SUPPOSE?
WILLING AND EAGER

WITH A SONG IN MY HEART
WONDERFUL GUY, A
YOU ARE BEAUTIFUL
YOU ARE NEVER AWAY
YOU ARE TOO BEAUTIFUL
YOU'LL NEVER WALK ALONE
YOU MUSN'T KICK IT AROUND
YOUNGER THAN SPRINGTIME
YOU'RE A QUEER ONE, JULIE JORDAN
YOU'RE NEARER
YOU'RE THE CATS
YOURS SINCERELY
YOU TOOK ADVANTAGE OF ME
YOU'VE GOT TO BE CAREFULLY TAUGHT
ZIP

Rodin, Gil

BIG NOISE FROM WINNETKA
BOOGIE WOOGIE MAXIXE

Rodney, Don

FOUR WINDS AND THE SEVEN SEAS

Rodor, J.

UNDER THE BRIDGES OF PARIS

Rodriguez, Augustin

YOURS

Rodriguez, F.

I NEED SOMEBODY

Rodriguez, G. H. Matos

LA CUMPARSITA

Rodriguez, Johnny

RIDIN' MY THUMB TO MEXICO
YOU ALWAYS COME BACK (TO HURTING ME)

Roe, Tommy

DIZZY

EVERYBODY
HEATHER HONEY
HOORAY FOR HAZEL
IT'S NOW WINTER'S DAY
JAM UP JELLY TIGHT
SHEILA
SWEET PEA

Roemheld, Heinz

RUBY
VALENTINO TANGO, THE (NOCHE DE
   AMOUR)

Roeser, Donald

BURNIN' FOR YOU
DON'T FEAR THE REAPER

Rogan, Jimmy

STARDUST ON THE MOON
WHEN A GYPSY MAKES HIS VIOLIN
   CRY

Rogers, Alex

BON BON BUDDY
I MAY BE CRAZY BUT I AIN'T NO
   FOOL
IVY, CLING TO ME
LET IT ALONE
NOBODY
ROCKAWAY

Rogers, Bobby

WAY YOU DO THE THINGS YOU DO,
   THE

Rogers, Dick

POMPTON TURNPIKE

Rogers, E. W.

MY FRIEND, THE MAJOR
WHEN A FELLAH HAS TURNED
   SIXTEEN

Rogers, Kay

HUNDRED POUNDS OF CLAY, A

RUNNIN' OUT OF FOOLS

Rogers, Kenny

CRAZY
LOVE OR SOMETHING LIKE IT
LOVE WILL TURN YOU AROUND

Rogers, Robert

AIN'T THAT PECULIAR?
COME ON, DO THE JERK
FIRST I LOOK AT THE PURSE
GOING TO A GO-GO
MY BABY
ONE MORE HEARTACHE

**Rogers, Robert
Cameron**

ROSARY, THE

Rogers, Ronnie

DIXIELAND DELIGHT
HEART AND SOUL

Rogers, Smokey

GONE
THO' I TRIED (I CAN'T FORGET YOU)

Rogers, Stanley

DEVIL'S GUN

Roig, Gonzalo

YOURS

Rolfe, Sam

BALLAD OF PALADIN, THE

Rollins, Don

I'M NOT CRAZY YET
OTHER WOMAN, THE
RACE IS ON, THE

Rollins, Jack

DOES HE MEAN THAT MUCH TO
   YOU?
FROSTY THE SNOWMAN
I DON'T HURT ANYMORE
PETER COTTONTAIL
SMOKEY THE BEAR

Rollins, Sonny

AIREGIN
ST. THOMAS

Roma, Caro

CAN'T YOU HEAR ME CALLIN',
   CAROLINE?
IN THE GARDEN OF MY HEART

Roma, Del

I WILL FOLLOW HIM

Roman, Arnie

PROVE YOUR LOVE

Romani, David

PARADISE

Romans, Alain C.

PADRE

Romberg, Sigmund

AUF WIEDERSEHEN
CLOSE AS PAGES IN A BOOK
DANCE, MY DARLINGS
DEEP IN MY HEART, DEAR
DESERT SONG, THE
DRINKING SONG (DRINK! DRINK!
   DRINK!)
FAREWELL TO DREAMS
FASCINATION
FRENCH MILITARY MARCHING SONG
GOLDEN DAYS
I BUILT A DREAM ONE DAY
IN PARIS AND IN LOVE
JUST ONCE AROUND THE CLOCK
JUST WE TWO

LITTLE CHURCH AROUND THE
    CORNER, THE
LITTLE PEACH
LOST IN LOVELINESS
LOVER, COME BACK TO ME
LOVE SONG FROM LONG AGO, A
MARIANNE
MOTHER
MY HEART WON'T SAY GOODBYE
NIGHT IS YOUNG, THE
NINA ROSA
ONE ALONE
ONE KISS
RIFF SONG, THE (HO!)
ROAD TO PARADISE, THE
ROMANCE
SERENADE
SILVER MOON
SOFTLY, AS IN A MORNING SUNRISE
SONG OF LOVE
STOUTHEARTED MEN
WANTING YOU
WHEN HEARTS ARE YOUNG
WHEN I GROW TOO OLD TO DREAM
WILL YOU REMEMBER?
YOUR LAND AND MY LAND
YOUR SMILES, YOUR TEARS
YOU WILL REMEMBER VIENNA
ZING ZING—ZOOM ZOOM

Rome, Harold

ALL OF A SUDDEN MY HEART SINGS
ALONG WITH ME
ANYONE WOULD LOVE YOU
BE KIND TO YOUR PARENTS
CALL ME MISTER
FAIR WARNING
FANNY
GIFT TODAY, A (THE BAR MITZVAH
    SONG)
GOING HOME TRAIN
HAVE I TOLD YOU LATELY?
I HAVE TO TELL YOU
I LIKE YOU
I SAY HELLO
LOVE IS A VERY LIGHT THING
MISS MARMELSTEIN
MOMMA, MOMMA
MONEY SONG, THE
NOBODY MAKES A PASS AT ME
ONCE KNEW A FELLA
RED BALL EXPRESS, THE

RESTLESS HEART
SING ME A SONG WITH SOCIAL
    SIGNIFICANCE
SOUTH AMERICA, TAKE IT AWAY
SUNDAY IN THE PARK
UNITED NATIONS ON THE MARCH
WELCOME HOME
WHAT CAN I DO?
WHERE DID THE NIGHT GO?
WISH YOU WERE HERE

Rome, Ritchie

BEST DISCO IN TOWN, THE

Romeo, Beresford

BACK TO LIFE
KEEP ON MOVIN'

Romeo, Tony

BLESSED IS THE RAIN
I'M GONNA MAKE YOU MINE
INDIAN LAKE
I THINK I LOVE YOU
POOR BABY
WELCOME ME, LOVE

Romero, Charles

HIPPY HIPPY SHAKE

Ronell, Ann

BABY'S BIRTHDAY PARTY
LINDA
MY HEART IS SHOWING (DON'T
    LOOK NOW, BUT)
RAIN ON THE ROOF
WHO'S AFRAID OF THE BIG BAD
    WOLF?
WILLOW WEEP FOR ME

Ronklyn, George

MY MARIUCCIA TAKE A STEAMBOAT

Ronstadt, Linda

IT'S SO EASY

Rosa, Malia

FOREVER AND EVER

Rosas, Cesar

SET ME FREE (ROSA LEE)

Rose, Billy

BACK IN YOUR OWN BACK YARD
BARBARA
BARNEY GOOGLE
BUILDING A NEST FOR MARY
CHEERFUL LITTLE EARFUL
CLAP HANDS! HERE COMES
    CHARLEY!
COME ON, SPARK PLUG!
COOKING BREAKFAST FOR THE ONE
    I LOVE
CRYING FOR JOY
CUP OF COFFEE, A SANDWICH AND
    YOU, A
DOES THE SPEARMINT LOSE ITS
    FLAVOR ON THE BEDPOST OVER
    NIGHT?
DON'T BRING LULU
EVANGELINE
FIFTY MILLION FRENCHMEN (CAN'T
    BE WRONG)
FOLLOW THE SWALLOW
FOUR WALLS
GOLDEN GATE
GOT THE JITTERS
GREAT DAY!
HAPPY DAYS AND LONELY NIGHTS
HAVE A LITTLE DREAM ON ME
HELLO, MONTREAL
HERE COMES THE SHOW BOAT
HOT HEELS
HOUSE IS HAUNTED, THE (BY THE
    ECHO OF YOUR LAST GOODBYE)
I CAN'T GET THE ONE I WANT
I'D RATHER BE BLUE OVER YOU
    (THAN BE HAPPY WITH
    SOMEBODY ELSE)
IF I HAD A GIRL LIKE YOU
I FOUND A MILLION DOLLAR BABY
    (IN A FIVE AND TEN CENT
    STORE)
IF YOU WANT THE RAINBOW (YOU
    MUST HAVE THE RAIN)
I GOT A CODE IN MY DOSE

I'M FOR YOU ONE HUNDRED
    PERCENT
IN THE MERRY MONTH OF MAYBE
IN THE MIDDLE OF THE NIGHT
IT HAPPENED IN MONTEREY
IT'S ONLY A PAPER MOON
I'VE GOT A FEELING I'M FALLING
I WANNA BE LOVED
I WONDER WHO'S DANCING WITH
    YOU TONIGHT
MAH JONG
ME AND MY SHADOW
MORE THAN YOU KNOW
NIGHT IS YOUNG AND YOU'RE SO
    BEAUTIFUL, THE
OVERNIGHT
POOR PAPA (HE'S GOT NUTHIN' AT
    ALL)
SHE'S EVERYBODY'S SWEETHEART
    (BUT NOBODY'S GAL)
SWANEE BUTTERFLY
THAT OLD GANG OF MINE
THERE'S A RAINBOW
    'ROUND MY SHOULDER
TONIGHT YOU BELONG TO ME
TWELVE O'CLOCK AT NIGHT
WHEN A WOMAN LOVES A MAN
WHEN THE MORNING GLORIES
    WAKE UP IN THE MORNING
WITHOUT A SONG
WOULD YOU LIKE TO TAKE A
    WALK?
YOURS FOR A SONG
YOU TELL HER, I S-T-U-T-T-E-R
YOU THINK OF EV'RYTHING
YOU'VE GOT TO SEE MAMMA EV'RY
    NIGHT (OR YOU CAN'T SEE
    MAMMA AT ALL)

Rose, C. E.

MY FILIPINO ROSE

Rose, Dan

STOP THE START (OF TEARS IN MY
    HEART)

Rose, David

CALIFORNIA MELODIES
DANCE OF THE SPANISH ONION
HOLIDAY FOR STRINGS

ONE LOVE
OUR WALTZ
SO-O-O-O-O IN LOVE
STRIPPER, THE

Rose, Ed

BABY SHOES
BUDDHA
HE WALKED RIGHT IN, TURNED
    AROUND, AND WALKED RIGHT
    OUT AGAIN
IF YOU CARED FOR ME
OH JOHNNY, OH JOHNNY, OH!
TAKE ME AROUND AGAIN

Rose, Fred

AT MAIL CALL TODAY
BEFORE YOU CALL
BE HONEST WITH ME
BLUE EYES CRYING IN THE RAIN
BLUES IN MY MIND
CRAZY HEART
'DEED I DO
END OF THE WORLD, THE
FLAMIN' MAMIE
FOGGY RIVER
HANG YOUR HEAD IN SHAME
    (DON'T YOUR CONSCIENCE EVER
    BOTHER YOU)
HONEST AND TRULY
I'D NEVER STAND IN YOUR WAY
I HANG MY HEAD AND CRY
I'LL NEVER GET OUT OF THIS
    WORLD ALIVE
I'M TRUSTING IN YOU
IT'S A SIN
JIMTOWN BLUES
KAW-LIGA
LONELY RIVER
LOVE CAME OUT OF THE NIGHT
MANSION ON THE HILL, A
PAIR OF BROKEN HEARTS, A
PINS AND NEEDLES (IN MY HEART)
PRODIGAL SON, THE
RED HOT MAMA
ROLY POLY
SETTIN' THE WOODS ON FIRE
TAKE THESE CHAINS FROM MY
    HEART
TEARS ON MY PILLOW
TEXARKANA BABY

TWEEDLE-O-TWILL
WALTZ OF THE WIND
WE LIVE IN TWO DIFFERENT
    WORLDS
YESTERDAY'S ROSES
YOU DON'T CARE WHAT HAPPENS
    TO ME
YOU'LL BE SORRY WHEN I'M GONE

Rose, L. Arthur

LAMBETH WALK

Rose, Pam

I'LL STILL BE LOVING YOU
RING ON HER FINGER, TIME ON
    HER HANDS

Rose, Tim

MORNING DEW

Rose, Vincent

AVALON
BLUEBERRY HILL
LINGER AWHILE
PARDON ME, PRETTY BABY
SONG OF THE MOONBEAMS
UMBRELLA MAN, THE
WERE YOU SINCERE?
WHISPERING

Roseland, Don

HIT AND RUN AFFAIR

Rosen, Leonard

BEAUTIFUL EYES

Rosen, Robert F.

MY LITTLE GEORGIA ROSE

Rosenberg, Marvin

IMAGE OF A GIRL

Rosenfeld, Monroe H.

AND HER GOLDEN HAIR WAS
   HANGING DOWN HER BACK
BIRD THAT NEVER SINGS, THE
DOWN AT THE HUSKIN' BEE
DOWN WHERE THE SILV'RY
   MOHAWK FLOWS
GOLD WILL BUY MOST ANYTHING
   BUT A TRUE GIRL'S HEART
JUST FOR THE SAKE OF OUR
   DAUGHTER
SHE WAS HAPPY TILL SHE MET YOU
TAKE BACK YOUR GOLD
WITH ALL HER FAULTS I LOVE HER
   STILL

Rosenman, Leonard

THEME FROM "EAST OF EDEN"

Rosenthal, Harry

GEORGIA ROSE

Rosey, George (George M. Rosenberg)

HANDICAP, THE
HONEYMOON, THE

Rosner, George

NIGHTINGALE

Rosoff, Charles

WHEN YOU AND I WERE
   SEVENTEEN

Ross, Adam

SACRED

Ross, Adrian

I LOVE YOU SO (THE MERRY WIDOW
   WALTZ)
LITTLE LOVE, A LITTLE KISS, A
LONG AGO IN ALCALA
LOVE, HERE IS MY HEART!
MAXIM'S
SIX LITTLE WIVES

VILIA

Ross, Annie

TWISTED

Ross, Arthur

I WANNA BE WHERE YOU ARE
I WANT YOU

Ross, Bernice

DON'T JUST STAND THERE
I'LL MAKE ALL YOUR DREAMS
   COME TRUE
SAY SOMETHING FUNNY
WHITE ON WHITE

Ross, Beverly

CANDY MAN
DIM, DIM, THE LIGHTS (I WANT
   SOME ATMOSPHERE)
JUDY'S TURN TO CRY
LOLLIPOP

Ross, Davey

SHAPE OF THINGS TO COME, THE

Ross, Edward

JIM

Ross, James

SOUTHERN FRIED

Ross, Jerry

ACORN IN THE MEADOW
EVEN NOW
FINI
HEART
HERNANDO'S HIDEAWAY
HEY THERE
I'M GONNA MAKE YOU LOVE ME
I'M NOT AT ALL IN LOVE
MR. DREAM MERCHANT
RAGS TO RICHES
SHOELESS JOE FROM HANNIBAL,
   MO

SMALL TALK
STEAM HEAT
STRANGE LITTLE GIRL
THERE ONCE WAS A MAN
TRUE LOVE GOES ON AND ON
TWO LOST SOULS
WHATEVER LOLA WANTS (LOLA
   GETS)
WHAT WOULD YOU DO?
WHO'S GOT THE PAIN?
YOU'RE SO MUCH A PART OF ME

Ross, Lee

CURTAIN IN THE WINDOW
HEART TO HEART TALK
LONELY TEARDROPS
MY SHOES KEEP WALKING BACK TO
   YOU

Ross, Lewis

KEEP ON SMILIN'

Ross, M.

BUST A MOVE

Ross, Marv

FIND ANOTHER FOOL
HARDEN MY HEART
TAKE ME TO HEART

Ross, Merria

LOVE IS IN CONTROL (FINGER ON
   THE TRIGGER)

Rossi, Francis Michael

PICTURES OF MATCHSTICK MEN

Rossington, Gary

SWEET HOME ALABAMA
WHAT'S YOUR NAME

Rossini, G.

NOW THAT I'M IN LOVE

Rostill, John

IF YOU LOVE ME (LET ME KNOW)
LET ME BE THERE
PLEASE MR. PLEASE

Rota, Nino

CLOWNS, THE
LA DOLCE VITA (THE SWEET LIFE)
LOVE THEME FROM "LA STRADA"
LOVE THEME FROM "ROMEO AND
    JULIET" (A TIME FOR US)
LOVE THEME FROM "THE
    GODFATHER" (A.K.A. SPEAK
    SOFTLY LOVE)
WAR AND PEACE

Rotella, Johnny

LOOKIN' FOR LOVE

Roth, Bernie

FORTY DAYS AND FORTY NIGHTS

Roth, David Lee

DANCE THE NIGHT AWAY
I'LL WAIT
JUMP
JUST LIKE PARADISE
PANAMA

Roth, I. J.

CHA-HUA-HUA
SECRET, THE

Roth, Lillian

I'LL CRY TOMORROW

Roth, Murray

I'M A LONESOME LITTLE RAINDROP
    (LOOKING FOR A PLACE TO FALL)
WHEN YOU WANT 'EM, YOU CAN'T
    GET 'EM (WHEN YOU GOT 'EM,
    YOU DON'T WANT 'EM)

Rotha, M.

THAT'S ALL I WANT FROM YOU

Rothberg, Bob

NIGHT WIND
YOU OR NO ONE

Rothrock, Claire

OLD CAPE COD

Roubanis, N.

MISIRLOU

Rourke, Michael E.

LEMON IN THE GARDEN OF LOVE, A
THEY DIDN'T BELIEVE ME

Rouse, Ervin T.

ORANGE BLOSSOM SPECIAL
SWEETER THAN THE FLOWERS

Rouzoud, Rene

POOR PEOPLE OF PARIS, THE

Rowe

EXPRESS

Rowe, Josephine V.

MACUSHLA

Rowe, Red

CUDDLE BUGGIN' BABY

Rowland, Kevin

COME ON EILEEN

Rox, John

IT'S A BIG, WIDE, WONDERFUL
    WORLD

Royal, Dale

TEDDY BEAR

Royal, Fred

SOFT WINDS

Royster, Joseph

IF YOU WANNA BE HAPPY
NEW ORLEANS
QUARTER TO THREE
TWIST, TWIST SENORA

Rozier, Dessie

HOT PASTRAMI

Rozsa, Miklos

LOVE THEME FROM "EL CID" (THE
    FALCON AND THE DOVE)
SPELLBOUND (A.K.A. SPELLBOUND
    CONCERTO)
STRANGE LOVE

Rubens, Maurice

IS EVERYBODY HAPPY NOW?

Rubens, Paul

I CAN'T TAKE MY EYES OFF YOU

Rubicam, Shannon

HOW WILL I KNOW
I WANNA DANCE WITH SOMEBODY
    (WHO LOVES ME)
SIMPLY MEANT TO BE
WAITING FOR A STAR TO FALL

Rubin, Rick

(YOU GOTTA) FIGHT FOR YOUR
    RIGHT (TO PARTY)
GOING BACK TO CALI

Ruby, Harry

ALL ALONE MONDAY

AND HE'D SAY "OO-LA-LA! WEE-
   WEE"
ANOTHER NIGHT LIKE THIS
BEAUTIFUL GIRLS
COME ON, PAPA
DADDY LONG LEGS
DANCING THE DEVIL AWAY
DO YOU LOVE ME?
EVERYONE SAYS "I LOVE YOU"
GIVE ME THE SIMPLE LIFE
HAPPY ENDING
HOORAY FOR CAPTAIN SPAULDING
I GAVE YOU UP JUST BEFORE YOU
   THREW ME DOWN
I LOVE YOU SO MUCH
I'M A VAMP FROM EAST BROADWAY
I'M SO AFRAID OF YOU
IT WAS MEANT TO BE
I WANNA BE LOVED BY YOU
I WISH I COULD TELL YOU
KEEP ON DOIN' WHAT YOU'RE DOIN'
KEEP ROMANCE ALIVE
KEEP YOUR UNDERSHIRT ON
KISS TO BUILD A DREAM ON, A
LOOK WHAT YOU'VE DONE
MAYBE IT'S BECAUSE
MY SUNNY TENNESSEE
NEVERTHELESS (I'M IN LOVE WITH
   YOU)
ONLY WHEN YOU'RE IN MY ARMS
SAME OLD MOON, THE
SHEIK OF AVENUE B, THE
SHE'S MINE, ALL MINE
SNOOPS, THE LAWYER
SO LONG, OO LONG
THINKING OF YOU
THREE LITTLE WORDS
TIMBUCTOO
TIRED OF IT ALL
UP IN THE CLOUDS
WATCHING THE CLOUDS ROLL BY
WHAT A PERFECT COMBINATION
WHAT'LL WE DO ON A SATURDAY
   NIGHT WHEN THE TOWN GOES
   DRY?
WHAT WOULD I CARE?
WHEN YOU DREAM ABOUT HAWAII
WHERE DO THEY GO WHEN THEY
   ROW, ROW, ROW?
WHO'S SORRY NOW?
YOU KEEP SENDING 'EM OVER AND
   WE'LL KEEP KNOCKING 'EM
   DOWN

Ruby, Herman

CECILIA
EGG AND I, THE
I CAN'T GET THE ONE I WANT
IF I COULD LEARN TO LOVE (AS
   WELL AS I FIGHT)
I'LL ALWAYS BE IN LOVE WITH YOU
MY HONEY'S LOVIN' ARMS
MY SUNNY TENNESSEE
SMILING IRISH EYES
TWELVE O'CLOCK AT NIGHT

Ruddy, Charles Louis

MY MOTHER'S LULLABY

Rudolph, Richard

ADVENTURES IN PARADISE
LOVIN' YOU

Rugolo, Pete

BRING BACK THE THRILL
THREE STARS WILL SHINE TONIGHT
   (THEME FROM "DR. KILDARE")

Ruiz, Gabriel

AMOR
CUANTO LE GUSTA (LA PARRANDA)
STARS IN YOUR EYES (A.K.A. MARS)

Ruiz, Pablo Beltran

SWAY (A.K.A. QUIEN SERA)

Rule, James

ALL OVER NOTHING AT ALL
GOODBYE SUE

Rundgren, Todd

BE NICE TO ME
CAN WE STILL BE FRIENDS
HELLO, IT'S ME
I SAW THE LIGHT
LOVE IS THE ANSWER
REAL MAN
SET ME FREE
WE GOTTA GET YOU A WOMAN

Rush, Alan

WALKIN' A BROKEN HEART

Rush, Jennifer

POWER OF LOVE, THE

Rush, William

I'M SO ANXIOUS

Rushen, Patrice

FEELS SO REAL (WON'T LET GO)
FORGET ME NOTS
HAVEN'T YOU HEARD

Rushing, James

BABY, DON'T TELL ON ME
CAJUN MOON
DON'T YOU MISS YOUR BABY?
GOIN' TO CHICAGO BLUES
GOOD MORNING BLUES
HOPE YOU'RE FEELIN' ME LIKE I'M
   FEELIN' YOU
SENT FOR YOU YESTERDAY, AND
   HERE YOU COME TODAY

Ruskin, Harry

I MAY BE WRONG (BUT I THINK
   YOU'RE WONDERFUL)
I'M ONE OF GOD'S CHILDREN (WHO
   HASN'T GOT WINGS)

Russell, Al

CABARET
IT'S LIKE TAKING CANDY FROM A
   BABY

Russell, Arthur

AU REET

Russell, Benee

I'LL LOVE YOU IN MY DREAMS
KATINKA
LONESOME IN THE MOONLIGHT

LOVE IS LIKE THAT (WHAT CAN YOU DO?)

YOU DIDN'T WANT ME WHEN YOU HAD ME (SO WHY DO YOU WANT ME NOW?)

Russell, Bert

CRY BABY

CRY TO ME

HANG ON SLOOPY

IF I DIDN'T HAVE A DIME (TO PLAY THE JUKEBOX)

LITTLE BIT OF SOAP, A

TELL HIM

TWIST AND SHOUT

Russell, Bob

A BANDA (PARADE)

AT THE CROSSROADS

BABALU

BALLERINA

BI-I-BI

BRAZIL

CIRCUS

CRAZY, HE CALLS ME

DO NOTHIN' TILL YOU HEAR FROM ME

DON'T GET AROUND MUCH ANYMORE

EYES OF LOVE, THE (CAROL'S THEME)

FOR LOVE OF IVY

FRENESI

FULL MOON (NOCHE DE LUNA)

HALF A PHOTOGRAPH

HE AIN'T HEAVY . . . HE'S MY BROTHER

I DIDN'T KNOW ABOUT YOU

IT'S LIKE TAKING CANDY FROM A BABY

JUST WHEN WE'RE FALLING IN LOVE

LADY LOVE

MARIA ELENA

MATINEE

MISIRLOU

NO OTHER LOVE

ONCE

TABOO

TIME WAS

WAGON TRAIN

WOULD I LOVE YOU (LOVE YOU, LOVE YOU)

YOU CAME A LONG WAY FROM ST. LOUIS

Russell, Bobby

1432 FRANKLIN PIKE CIRCLE HERO

HONEY

JOKER WENT WILD, THE

LITTLE GREEN APPLES

NIGHT THE LIGHTS WENT OUT IN GEORGIA, THE

POPSICLE

SURE GONNA MISS HER

Russell, Brenda

DINNER WITH GERSHWIN

PIANO IN THE DARK

Russell, Graham

ALL OUT OF LOVE

LOST IN LOVE

ONE THAT YOU LOVE, THE

SWEET DREAMS

Russell, Harry

WE DON'T WANT THE BACON, WHAT WE WANT IS A PIECE OF THE RHINE

Russell, James J.

WHERE THE RIVER SHANNON FLOWS

Russell, Johnny

ACT NATURALLY

HURT HER ONCE FOR ME

LET'S FALL TO PIECES TOGETHER

YOU'LL BE BACK (EVERY NIGHT IN MY DREAMS)

Russell, Larry

VAYA CON DIOS (MAY GOD BE WITH YOU)

Russell, Leon

BACK TO THE ISLAND

BLUEBIRD

BLUES POWER

DELTA LADY

EVERYBODY LOVES A CLOWN

LOSER (WITH A BROKEN HEART), THE

RAINBOW IN YOUR EYES

SHE'S JUST MY STYLE

SUPERSTAR

THIS MASQUERADE

TIGHT ROPE

YOU DON'T HAVE TO PAINT ME A PICTURE

Russell, Luis

BACK O' TOWN BLUES

Russin, Babe

TERESA

Rutherford, Mike

ALL I NEED

FOLLOW YOU FOLLOW ME

IN TOO DEEP

INVISIBLE TOUCH

LAND OF CONFUSION

LIVING YEARS, THE

NO REPLY AT ALL

SILENT RUNNING (ON DANGEROUS GROUND)

TAKEN IN

THAT'S ALL

THROWING IT ALL AWAY

TONIGHT, TONIGHT, TONIGHT

YOUR OWN SPECIAL WAY

Ryan, Ben

GANG THAT SANG HEART OF MY HEART, THE (A.K.A. HEART OF MY HEART)

INKA DINKA DOO

M-I-S-S-I-S-S-I-P-P-I

ONE CIGARETTE FOR TWO

WHEN FRANCIS DANCES WITH ME

Ryan, Charles

HOT ROD LINCOLN

Ryan, Jim

DON'T LET THE RAIN FALL DOWN ON ME

Ryan, Patti

LOOKIN' FOR LOVE

Ryan, Randy

PUT THAT RING ON MY FINGER

Ryder, Mitch

JOY

Ryerson, Frank

BLUE CHAMPAGNE

Ryskind, Morrie

NOBODY WANTS ME
WHY DO YA ROLL THOSE EYES?

Sacco, Lou

TWO FACES HAVE I

Sacco, Tony

BREEZE, THE (THAT'S BRINGIN' MY HONEY BACK TO ME)

Sadler, Barry

"A" TEAM, THE
BALLAD OF THE GREEN BERETS, THE

Safka, Melanie

BITTER BAD
BRAND NEW KEY
LAY DOWN (CANDLES IN THE WIND)
LOOK WHAT THEY'VE DONE TO MY SONG, MA
NICKEL SONG

PEACE WILL COME (ACCORDING TO PLAN)
RING THE LIVING BELL

Sager, Carole Bayer

ARTHUR'S THEME (THE BEST THAT YOU CAN DO)
BETTER DAYS
BETTER THAN EVER
BREAK IT TO ME GENTLY
COME IN FROM THE RAIN
DON'T CRY OUT LOUD
EVERCHANGING TIMES
GROOVY KIND OF LOVE, A
HEARTBREAKER
I'D RATHER LEAVE WHILE I'M IN LOVE
IF HE REALLY KNEW ME
IF YOU REMEMBER ME
I STILL BELIEVE IN LOVE
IT'S MY TURN
JENNIFER
JUST FOR TONIGHT
LOOKING THROUGH THE EYES OF LOVE
LOVE POWER
MAKING LOVE
MIDNIGHT BLUE
NOBODY DOES IT BETTER
ON MY OWN
OVER YOU
THAT'S WHAT FRIENDS ARE FOR
THEY DON'T MAKE THEM LIKE THEY USED TO
THEY'RE PLAYING OUR SONG
TOO CLOSE TO PARADISE
WHEN I NEED YOU
YOU'RE MOVIN' OUT TODAY
YOU'RE THE ONLY ONE

Sagle, Charles

WHERE THE BLUE AND LONELY GO

Sahm, Douglas

MENDOCINO
SHE'S ABOUT A MOVER

Sain, Oliver

DON'T MESS UP A GOOD THING

Sainte-Marie, Buffy

I'M GONNA BE A COUNTRY GIRL AGAIN
UNIVERSAL SOLDIER, THE
UNTIL IT'S TIME FOR YOU TO GO
UP WHERE WE BELONG

Sallis, Sadie Nordin

ENCLOSED, ONE BROKEN HEART

Sallitt, Norman

HERE I AM (JUST WHEN I THOUGHT I WAS OVER YOU)

Salmirs-Bernstein

JOEY

Salmon, Arthur L.

HOMING

Salter, William

JUST THE TWO OF US
WHERE IS THE LOVE

Salvador, Henri

I WILL LIVE MY LIFE FOR YOU
MELODIE D'AMOUR

Sam, Senora

I'LL BE GOOD TO YOU

Sambora, Richie

BAD MEDICINE
BORN TO BE MY BABY
I'LL BE THERE FOR YOU
LIVIN' ON A PRAYER
WANTED DEAD OR ALIVE
YOU GIVE LOVE A BAD NAME

Samoht, Yennik

STONED LOVE

Sample, Joe

ADVENTURES IN PARADISE
I'M SO GLAD I'M STANDING HERE
    TODAY

Sampson, Edgar

BLUE LOU
DON'T BE THAT WAY
IF DREAMS COME TRUE
LULLABY IN RHYTHM
STOMPIN' AT THE SAVOY

Sampson, Phil

I LOVED 'EM EVERY ONE

Samudio, Domingo "Sam"

JU JU HAND
WOOLY BULLY

Samuels, Arthur

ALIBI BABY

Samuels, Eddie

CALLA CALLA

Samuels, Frank

GYPSY DREAM ROSE
UNDERNEATH THE RUSSIAN MOON

Samuels, Jerry

AS IF I DIDN'T KNOW
SHELTER OF YOUR ARMS, THE
THEY'RE COMING TO TAKE ME
    AWAY, HA-HAAA!

Samuels, Walter G.

FIESTA
HEAVEN HELP THIS HEART OF MINE
I COULDN'T BELIEVE MY EYES
IF MY HEART COULD ONLY TALK
MARCH WINDS AND APRIL
    SHOWERS
ROLLIN' PLAINS

TAKE ME BACK TO MY BOOTS AND
    SADDLE
TRUE

Samuels, Zelda

LOOKIN' FOR A LOVE

Samwell-Smith, Paul

OVER UNDER SIDEWAYS DOWN
SHAPES OF THINGS

Sanchez, Al

COME WHAT MAY

Sanders, Alma M.

LITTLE TOWN IN THE OULD
    COUNTRY DOWN
THAT TUMBLE-DOWN SHACK IN
    ATHLONE

Sanders, Joe

BELOVED
NIGHT HAWK BLUES

Sanders, Lenny

I GET IDEAS (WHEN I DANCE WITH
    YOU)
I'M BITIN' MY FINGERNAILS AND
    THINKING OF YOU
OVER THREE HILLS

Sanders, Sonny

IF YOU NEED ME

Sanders, William

LOVE MAKES A WOMAN
SOULFUL STRUT (A.K.A. AM I THE
    SAME GIRL?)

Sanders, Zell

LONELY NIGHTS
SALLY, GO ROUND THE ROSES

Sanderson, David R.

POOR BOY

Sanderson, Wilfred

UNTIL

Sandford, Chas

FIRE WITH FIRE
MISSING YOU
TALK TO ME

Sandler, George

PA-PAYA MAMA

Sands, Tommy

SING BOY SING

Sanford, Bill

ROCK ME ALL NIGHT LONG

Sanford, Dick

HIS FEET TOO BIG FOR DE BED
MENTION MY NAME IN SHEBOYGAN
RED SILK STOCKINGS AND GREEN
    PERFUME
SINGING HILLS, THE
WALKIN' DOWN TO WASHINGTON

Sanford, Ed

SMOKE FROM A DISTANT FIRE

Sanicola, Henry

THIS LOVE OF MINE

Sanson, Veronique Marie

EMOTION (AMOREUSE)

Sansone, Tony

WALK AWAY RENEE

Santana, Carlos

EVERYBODY'S EVERYTHING

Santly, Henry

I'M SITTING PRETTY IN A PRETTY
    LITTLE CITY
YOU SAID IT

Santly, Joseph H.

AT THE MOVING PICTURE BALL
BIG BUTTER AND EGG MAN, THE
BUILDING A HOME FOR YOU
HAWAIIAN BUTTERFLY
TAMIAMI TRAIL
THERE'S YES! YES! IN YOUR EYES

Santly, Lester

I'M NOBODY'S BABY

Santos, Larry

CANDY GIRL

Sapaugh, Thomas

TRY A LITTLE KINDNESS

Sargent, Eva

COLUMBUS STOCKADE BLUES

Saroyan, William

COME ON-A MY HOUSE

Satchell, Clarence

FIRE
LOVE ROLLERCOASTER
SKIN TIGHT
SWEET STICKY THING
WHO'D SHE COO

Sauer, Robert

WHEN IT'S SPRINGTIME IN THE
    ROCKIES

Saunders, Red

HAMBONE

Saussy, Tupper

MORNING GIRL

Sauter, Joe

AIN'T IT TRUE?

Savage, John

PHOTOGRAPH

Savage, Kay Jeanne

WALK THROUGH THIS WORLD WITH
    ME

Savage, Rick

ANIMAL
HYSTERIA
LOVE BITES
POUR SOME SUGAR ON ME

Savigar, Kevin

PASSION
TONIGHT I'M YOURS (DON'T HURT
    ME)
YOUNG TURKS

Savino, Domenico

MOONLIGHT LOVE

Savitt, Jan

720 IN THE BOOKS
IT'S A WONDERFUL WORLD
QUAKER CITY JAZZ

Savoy, Ronnie

WHOLE WORLD IS A STAGE, THE

Sawyer, Jean

PAINTED, TAINTED ROSE

Sawyer, Pam

BABY, LET'S WAIT
GOTTA HOLD ON TO THIS FEELING
IF I DIDN'T LOVE YOU
IF I EVER LOSE THIS HEAVEN
IF I WERE YOUR WOMAN
I'M LIVIN' IN SHAME
LAST TIME I SAW HIM
LET ME TICKLE YOUR FANCY
LOVE CHILD
LOVE HANGOVER
MY MISTAKE (WAS TO LOVE YOU)
MY WHOLE WORLD ENDED (THE
    MOMENT YOU LEFT ME)
POPS, WE LOVE YOU (A TRIBUTE TO
    FATHER)
YESTERDAY'S DREAMS
YOU CAN'T TURN ME OFF (IN THE
    MIDDLE OF TURNING ME ON)

Saxon, David

ARE THESE REALLY MINE?
FREE
THERE'LL SOON BE A RAINBOW
THERE MUST BE A WAY
VAGABOND SHOES

Saxon, Sky

CAN'T SEEM TO MAKE YOU MINE
PUSHIN' TOO HARD

Sayer, Leo

DREAMING
GIVING IT ALL AWAY
HOW MUCH LOVE
LONG TALL GLASSES (I CAN DANCE)
SHOW MUST GO ON, THE
YOU MAKE ME FEEL LIKE DANCING

Sayers, Henry J.

TA-RA-RA-BOOM-DE-RE

Scaggs, Boz

BREAKDOWN DEAD AHEAD
HOLLYWOOD
IT'S OVER
LIDO SHUFFLE

LOOK WHAT YOU'VE DONE TO ME
LOWDOWN
MISS SUN
WE'RE ALL ALONE

Scaife, Ronny

THEME FROM "THE MEN"

Scala, Ralph

(WE AIN'T GOT) NOTHIN' YET

Scales, Harvey

DISCO LADY
LOVE IS BETTER IN THE A.M.

Scanlan, William J.

MOLLY O!

Scarborough, Skip

GIVING YOU THE BEST THAT I GOT
LOVE BALLAD
LOVE CHANGES
LOVE OR LET ME BE LONELY

Scarlett, Leroi

I DON'T WANT ANOTHER SISTER

Scelsa, Gary

I'D STILL SAY YES

Scelsa, Gregory Paul

LUCKY CHARM

Schachter, Julius

LET'S MAKE UP BEFORE WE SAY
    GOODNIGHT

Schack, Marilyn

JAVA

Schafer, Bob

LOUISIANA

WHEN

Schafer, Jack

WONDERING

Schafer, Milton

AFTER LOVING YOU
ONE LITTLE WORLD APART
SHE TOUCHED ME

Scharf, Stuart

GIVE A DAMN
LIKE TO GET TO KNOW YOU

Scharf, Walter

BEN
LOOK AT ME
WALKING TALL

Scharfenberger, Werner

SAILOR (YOUR HOME IS THE SEA)

Scheck, George

DONDE ESTA SANTA CLAUS?
    (WHERE IS SANTA CLAUS?)

Schenck, Joe

ALL SHE'D SAY WAS "UMH HUM"
BABY'S PRAYER WILL SOON BE
    ANSWERED
OH! HOW SHE CAN SING

Schenker, Rudolf

ROCK YOU LIKE A HURRICANE

Schertzinger, Victor

ARTHUR MURRAY TAUGHT ME
    DANCING IN A HURRY
DREAM LOVER
FLEET'S IN, THE
FOLLOW YOUR HEART
IF YOU BUILD A BETTER
    MOUSETRAP
I'LL NEVER LET A DAY PASS BY

I REMEMBER YOU
KISS THE BOYS GOODBYE
LIFE BEGINS WHEN YOU'RE IN LOVE
LOVE ME FOREVER
LOVE PASSES BY
MAGNOLIAS IN THE MOONLIGHT
MARCHETA
MARCH OF THE GRENADIERS
MOON AND THE WILLOW TREE, THE
MY LOVE PARADE
MY WONDERFUL DREAM GIRL
NOT MINE
ONE NIGHT OF LOVE
PARIS, STAY THE SAME
SAND IN MY SHOES
TANGERINE
WHEN YOU HEAR THE TIME SIGNAL

Schickele, Peter

SILENT RUNNING

Schiff, Abe

TIME OUT FOR TEARS

Schiff, Steve

DON'T YOU (FORGET ABOUT ME)

Schifrin, Lalo

ALL FOR THE LOVE OF SUNSHINE
CAT, THE
CINCINNATI KID, THE
"MISSION: IMPOSSIBLE" THEME

Schiller, Allen

COME WHAT MAY

Schilling, Peter

MAJOR TOM (COMING HOME)

Schless, Peter

ON THE WINGS OF LOVE

Schlitz, Don

40 HOUR WEEK (FOR A LIVIN')
CRAZY FROM THE HEART

FOREVER AND EVER, AMEN
GAMBLER, THE
HOUSTON SOLUTION
I KNOW WHERE I'M GOING
I WON'T TAKE LESS THAN YOUR
    LOVE
ONE PROMISE TOO LATE
ON THE OTHER HAND
ROCKIN' WITH THE RHYTHM OF
    THE RAIN
STRONG ENOUGH TO BEND
TURN IT LOOSE
WHEN YOU SAY NOTHING AT ALL
YOU AGAIN

Schmid, Johann C.

GARDEN OF ROSES, THE

Schmidt, Erwin R.

CAROLINA SUNSHINE
DRIFTING AND DREAMING

Schmidt, Harvey

EVERYTHING BEAUTIFUL HAPPENS
    AT NIGHT
HONEYMOON IS OVER, THE
I CAN SEE IT
IS IT REALLY ME?
LOVE, DON'T TURN AWAY
MUCH MORE
MY CUP RUNNETH OVER
SIMPLE LITTLE THINGS
THEY WERE YOU
TRY TO REMEMBER
SOON IT'S GONNA RAIN

Schmit, Timothy

BOYS NIGHT OUT
I CAN'T TELL YOU WHY

Schneider, Florian

AUTOBAHN

Schneider, Fred

LOVE SHACK
PRIVATE IDAHO
ROCK LOBSTER

Schneider, Michael Cary

MORE THAN JUST THE TWO OF US

Schnug, Edward

QUESTION OF TEMPERATURE, A

Schock, Harriet

AIN'T NO WAY TO TREAT A LADY

Schoebel, Elmer

BUGLE CALL RAG
FAREWELL BLUES
NOBODY'S SWEETHEART
ORIENTAL
PRINCE OF WAILS
TEN LITTLE MILES FROM TOWN

Schoen, Vic

AMEN (YEA-MAN)
FOR DANCERS ONLY

Schofield, Willie

I FOUND A LOVE
YOU'RE SO FINE

Scholl, Jack

ALICE IN WONDERLAND
ISN'T LOVE THE GRANDEST THING?
LOVE PASSES BY
MAKIN' LOVE, MOUNTAIN STYLE
MY LITTLE BUCKAROO
OLD WATER MILL, AN
SING A LITTLE LOW DOWN TUNE
THROW ANOTHER LOG ON THE FIRE
THRU THE COURTESY OF LOVE
WHO CARES WHAT PEOPLE SAY?
WISH THAT I WISH TONIGHT, THE
YOU, YOU DARLIN'

Scholz, Tom

AMANDA
CAN'TCHA SAY (YOU BELIEVE IN
    ME)
DON'T LOOK BACK

LONG TIME
MORE THAN A FEELING
WE'RE READY

Schon, Neal

ANY WAY YOU WANT IT
BE GOOD TO YOURSELF
DON'T STOP BELIEVIN'
I'LL BE ALRIGHT WITHOUT YOU
ONLY THE YOUNG
STILL THEY RIDE
WHEEL IN THE SKY

Schönberg, Claude-Michel

DRINK WITH ME TO DAYS GONE BY
I DREAMED A DREAM

Schonberger, John

WHISPERING

Schraubstader, Carl

LAST NIGHT ON THE BACK PORCH (I
    LOVED HER BEST OF ALL)

Schroeder, Aaron

ANY WAY YOU WANT ME (THAT'S
    HOW I WILL BE)
AT A SIDEWALK PENNY ARCADE
BECAUSE THEY'RE YOUNG
BIG HUNK O' LOVE, A
DON'T LET HER GO
FIRST ANNIVERSARY
FIRST NAME INITIAL
FOOLS' HALL OF FAME
FRENCH FOREIGN LEGION
GOOD LUCK CHARM
HEY, LITTLE LUCY! (DON'TCHA PUT
    NO LIPSTICK ON)
I GOT STUNG
I'M GONNA KNOCK ON YOUR DOOR
IT'S NOW OR NEVER
IT'S ONLY THE BEGINNING
I WAS THE ONE
MANDOLINS IN THE MOONLIGHT
RUBBER BALL
SEEIN' THE RIGHT LOVE GO WRONG
STUCK ON YOU

TIME AND THE RIVER
TWIXT TWELVE AND TWENTY
UTOPIA

Schroeder, Don

THOSE WONDERFUL YEARS

Schroeder, John

WALKIN' BACK TO HAPPINESS

Schroek, Arthur

LOVIN' THINGS, THE

Schuckett, Ralph

ANOTHER WORLD

Schulberg, Budd

MAMA GUITAR

Schultz, Jimmy

QUAKER CITY JAZZ

Schultze, Norbert

LILI MARLENE

Schumann, Walter

DRAGNET
IT'S DREAMTIME
ST. GEORGE AND THE DRAGONET

Schurz, Mary Jean

THERE STANDS THE GLASS

Schuster, Ira

DANCE OF THE PAPER DOLLS
DID YOU EVER GET THAT FEELING
  IN THE MOONLIGHT?
HOLD ME
I AM AN AMERICAN
I'M ALONE BECAUSE I LOVE YOU
I MAY BE DANCING WITH
  SOMEBODY ELSE
IN A SHANTY IN OLD SHANTY TOWN

TEN LITTLE FINGERS AND TEN
  LITTLE TOES (DOWN IN
  TENNESSEE)
WHEN YOU'RE OVER SIXTY, AND
  YOU FEEL LIKE SWEET SIXTEEN

Schuster, Joe

DANCE OF THE PAPER DOLLS

Schutt, Arthur

GEORGIA JUBILEE

Schuyler, Thom

AMERICAN ME
HURRICANE
I DON'T KNOW WHERE TO START
LONG LINE OF LOVE, A
LOVE OUT LOUD
LOVE WILL TURN YOU AROUND

Schwab, Charles M.

SLOW RIVER

Schwabach, Kurt

DANKE SCHOEN

Schwandt, Wilbur

DREAM A LITTLE DREAM OF ME

Schwartz, Arthur

AFTER ALL, YOU'RE ALL I'M AFTER
ALONE TOGETHER
ALONE TOO LONG
BEFORE I KISS THE WORLD
  GOODBYE
BY MYSELF
DANCING IN THE DARK
DON'T BE A WOMAN IF YOU CAN
DREAMER, THE
FAREWELL, MY LOVELY
GAL IN CALICO, A
GOOD-BYE JONAH
GOT A BRAN' NEW SUIT
HANG UP
HAPPY HABIT
HAUNTED HEART

HIGH AND LOW
HOTTENTOT POTENTATE, THE
HOW CAN I EVER BE ALONE?
HOW SWEET YOU ARE
IF THERE IS SOMEONE LOVELIER
  THAN YOU
I GUESS I'LL HAVE TO CHANGE MY
  PLAN (THE BLUE PAJAMA SONG)
I'LL BUY YOU A STAR
I LOVE LOUISA
I'M LIKE A NEW BROOM
I'M RIDIN' FOR A FALL
I SEE YOUR FACE BEFORE ME
I STILL LOOK AT YOU THAT WAY
IT'S ALL YOURS
LOOK WHO'S DANCING
LOUISIANA HAYRIDE
LOVE AND LEARN
LOVE IS A DANCING THING
LOVE IS THE REASON
LUCKY SEVEN
MAGIC MOMENT
MAKE THE MAN LOVE ME
MORE LOVE THAN YOUR LOVE
NEW SUN IN THE SKY
OH, BUT I DO
OLD FLAME NEVER DIES, AN
ON THE OLD PARK BENCH
RAINY DAY, A
RAINY NIGHT IN RIO, A
RELAX-AY-VOO
RHODE ISLAND IS FAMOUS FOR YOU
SHE'S SUCH A COMFORT TO ME
SHINE ON YOUR SHOES, A
SOMETHING TO REMEMBER YOU BY
SOMETHING YOU NEVER HAD
  BEFORE
TENNESSEE FISH FRY
THANK YOUR LUCKY STARS
THAT'S ENTERTAINMENT
THEN I'LL BE TIRED OF YOU
THERE'S NO HOLDING ME
THEY'RE EITHER TOO YOUNG OR
  TOO OLD
THIEF IN THE NIGHT
THIS IS IT
THROUGH A THOUSAND DREAMS
TRIPLETS
TROUBLE IN PARADISE
UNDER YOUR SPELL
WAITIN' FOR THE EVENING TRAIN
WHAT A WONDERFUL WORLD
YOU AND I KNOW

YOU AND THE NIGHT AND THE
MUSIC

Schwartz, Eddie

DON'T SHED A TEAR
HIT ME WITH YOUR BEST SHOT

Schwartz, Jean

ANY OLD PLACE I HANG MY HAT IS
HOME SWEET HOME TO ME
AU REVOIR, PLEASANT DREAMS
BACK TO THE CAROLINA YOU LOVE
BEDELIA
CHINATOWN, MY CHINATOWN
DON'T PUT ME OFF AT BUFFALO
ANY MORE
GHOST THAT NEVER WALKED, THE
GOODBYE, MR. RAGTIME
GOODNIGHT, MY OWN TRUE LOVE
HAT MY FATHER WORE ON ST.
PATRICK'S DAY, THE
HELLO, CENTRAL, GIVE ME NO
MAN'S LAND
HELLO, HAWAII, HOW ARE YOU?
I'LL MAKE A RING AROUND ROSIE
I LOVE THE LADIES
I'M ALL BOUND 'ROUND WITH THE
MASON DIXON LINE
I'M TIRED
I'M UNLUCKY
IN A LITTLE RED BARN (ON A FARM
DOWN IN INDIANA)
KISS YOUR MINSTREL BOY
GOODBYE
LOVE DAYS
MEET ME IN ROSE-TIME, ROSIE
MISTER DOOLEY
MY GUIDING STAR
MY IRISH MOLLY O
OH, MARIE
ONE LITTLE RAINDROP
OVER THE HILLS AND FAR AWAY
ROCK-A-BYE YOUR BABY WITH A
DIXIE MELODY
SINCE SISTER NELL HEARD
PADEREWSKI PLAY
SIT DOWN, YOU'RE ROCKING THE
BOAT!
TRUST IN ME
WHEN MR. SHAKESPEARE COMES
TO TOWN

WHY DO THEY ALL TAKE THE
NIGHT BOAT TO ALBANY?

Schwartz, Melvin H.

BABY TALK

Schwartz, Nat

BELIEVE IT, BELOVED
DON'T LET YOUR LOVE GO WRONG
YOU STAYED AWAY TOO LONG

Schwartz, Robert

RESPECTABLE
SWEET TALKIN' GUY

Schwartz, Stephen

BRAND NEW WORLD
CORNER OF THE SKY
DAY BY DAY
NO TIME AT ALL
SPREAD A LITTLE SUNSHINE

Schweers, John

AMAZING LOVE
DON'T FIGHT THE FEELINGS OF
LOVE
WHAT GOES ON WHEN THE SUN
GOES DOWN

Scoggins, C. H.

WHERE THE SILV'RY COLORADO
WENDS ITS WAY

Scollard, Clinton

SYLVIA

Scooter, Rudy

DEAR OKIE

Score, Ali

I RAN (SO FAR AWAY)

Score, Mike

I RAN (SO FAR AWAY)

Scott, Andy

ACTION
FOX ON THE RUN
LOVE IS LIKE OXYGEN

Scott, Bennett

SHIP AHOY!—ALL THE NICE GIRLS
LOVE A SAILOR

Scott, Bertha

I MISS YOU SO

Scott, Bobby

HE AIN'T HEAVY . . . HE'S MY
BROTHER
TASTE OF HONEY, A
WHERE ARE YOU GOING

Scott, Bon

HIGHWAY TO HELL

Scott, C. K.

WHO DO YOU THINK YOU ARE?

Scott, Clement

NOW IS THE HOUR (MAORI
FAREWELL SONG)
OH, PROMISE ME

Scott, Clifford

HONKY TONK

Scott, Clive

SKY HIGH

Scott, David

WHISPERS (GETTIN' LOUDER)

Scott, Emerson

SOMEONE'S ROCKING MY
   DREAMBOAT

Scott, Howard

CISCO KID, THE
GYPSY MAN
L. A. SUNSHINE
LOW RIDER
ME AND BABY BROTHER
SLIPPIN' INTO DARKNESS
SPILL THE WINE
SUMMER
WHY CAN'T WE BE FRIENDS?
WORLD IS A GHETTO, THE

Scott, Jack

GOODBYE BABY
MY TRUE LOVE
WHAT IN THE WORLD'S COME OVER
   YOU?

Scott, Johnnie

I'M SORRY DEAR
MAYBE IT'S BECAUSE

Scott, John Prindle

RIDE ON, RIDE ON

Scott, Joseph

AIN'T NOTHING YOU CAN DO
ANNIE GET YOUR YO-YO
BLIND MAN
TURN ON YOUR LOVELIGHT

Scott, Linda

DON'T BET MONEY, HONEY

Scott, Maurice

I'VE GOT RINGS ON MY FINGERS
   (OR, MUMBO JUMBO JIJIBOO J.
   O'SHEA)

Scott, Oliver

YEARNING FOR YOUR LOVE

Scott, Raymond

CHRISTMAS NIGHT IN HARLEM
DINNER MUSIC FOR A PACK OF
   HUNGRY CANNIBALS
HUCKLEBERRY DUCK
IN AN EIGHTEENTH CENTURY
   DRAWING ROOM
MOUNTAIN HIGH, VALLEY LOW
POWERHOUSE
TOY TRUMPET, THE
TWILIGHT IN TURKEY
WAR DANCE FOR WOODEN INDIANS

Scott, Robin

CHURCH ON CUMBERLAND ROAD,
   THE
POP MUZIK

Scott, Ronnie

ABERGAVENNY
IT'S A HEARTACHE

Scott, Tom

UPTOWN SATURDAY NIGHT

Scott, Winfield

BOP-TING-A-LING
BURN THAT CANDLE
(SUCH AN) EASY QUESTION
MANY TEARS AGO
ONE BROKEN HEART FOR SALE
RETURN TO SENDER
TWEEDLE DEE
YES TONIGHT, JOSEPHINE

Scotti, William

MY MOONLIGHT MADONNA

Scotto, Vincent

IT'S DELIGHTFUL TO BE MARRIED
TWO LOVES HAVE I
UNDER THE BRIDGES OF PARIS

VIENI, VIENI

Scruggs, Earl

FOGGY MOUNTAIN BREAKDOWN

Scruggs, Gary

RIGHT HAND MAN

Scruggs, Randy

DON'T MAKE IT EASY FOR ME
LOVE HAS NO RIGHT
YOUR LOVE'S ON THE LINE

Seago, Eddie

ANOTHER TIME, ANOTHER PLACE
EARLY IN THE MORNING

Seals, Chuck

CRAZY ARMS

Seals, Dan

EVERYTHING THAT GLITTERS (IS
   NOT GOLD)
ONE FRIEND
THREE TIME LOSER
YOU STILL MOVE ME

Seals, James

DIAMOND GIRL
GET CLOSER
HUMMINGBIRD
I'LL PLAY FOR YOU
SUMMER BREEZE
UNBORN CHILD
WE MAY NEVER PASS THIS WAY
   (AGAIN)

Seals, Troy

BAYOU BOYS
COUNTRY GIRLS
DON'T TAKE IT AWAY
DOWN ON THE FARM
FALLIN' FOR YOU FOR YEARS
FEELIN'S
I'VE GOT A ROCK AND ROLL HEART

I WON'T NEED YOU ANYMORE
(ALWAYS AND FOREVER)
JOE KNOWS HOW TO LIVE
LOST IN THE FIFTIES TONIGHT (IN
THE STILL OF THE NIGHT)
MAYBE YOUR BABY'S GOT THE
BLUES
SEVEN SPANISH ANGELS
THERE'S A HONKY TONK ANGEL
(WHO'LL TAKE ME BACK IN)
WHEN WE MAKE LOVE

Seamons, Sandra

WALK THROUGH THIS WORLD WITH
ME

Sears, Al

CASTLE ROCK

Sears, Pete

PLAY ON LOVE

Sears, Zelda

DEEP IN MY HEART
HONEY-BUN
TAKE A LITTLE ONE-STEP
TIE A STRING AROUND YOUR
FINGER

Sebastian, John

DARLING BE HOME SOON
DAYDREAM
DID YOU EVER HAVE TO MAKE UP
YOUR MIND?
DO YOU BELIEVE IN MAGIC?
LOVIN' YOU
MONEY
NASHVILLE CATS
RAIN ON THE ROOF
SHE IS STILL A MYSTERY
SHE'S A LADY
SIX O'CLOCK
SUMMER IN THE CITY
WELCOME BACK
YOU DIDN'T HAVE TO BE SO NICE
YOUNGER GIRL

Sebastian, Mark

SUMMER IN THE CITY

Sebert, Rosemary

OLD FLAMES (CAN'T HOLD A
CANDLE TO YOU)

Seckler, Bill

WHO'S YEHOODI?

Secon, Paul

YOU NEVER MISS THE WATER TILL
THE WELL RUNS DRY

Secunda, Sholem

BEI MIR BIST DU SCHOEN (MEANS
THAT YOU'RE GRAND)

Sedaka, Neil

ALICE IN WONDERLAND
ANOTHER SLEEPLESS NIGHT
BAD BLOOD
BAD GIRL
BREAKING UP IS HARD TO DO
CALENDAR GIRL
CLOSEST THING TO HEAVEN, THE
DIARY, THE
FALLIN'
FRANKIE
HAPPY BIRTHDAY, SWEET SIXTEEN
HUNGRY YEARS, THE
I GO APE
IMMIGRANT, THE
I WAITED TOO LONG
KING OF CLOWNS
LAUGHTER IN THE RAIN
LET'S GO STEADY AGAIN
LITTLE DEVIL
LONELY NIGHT (ANGEL FACE)
LOVE IN THE SHADOWS
LOVE WILL KEEP US TOGETHER
NEXT DOOR TO AN ANGEL
OH! CAROL
ONE DAY OF YOUR LIFE
PUPPET MAN
RUN SAMSON RUN
SHOULD'VE NEVER LET YOU GO

SOLITAIRE
STAIRWAY TO HEAVEN
STUPID CUPID
THAT'S WHEN THE MUSIC TAKES ME
TURN ON THE SUNSHINE
WHERE THE BOYS ARE
WORKIN' ON A GROOVY THING
YOU MEAN EVERYTHING TO ME
YOU NEVER DONE IT LIKE THAT

Seeger, Pete

GUANTANAMERA
IF I HAD A HAMMER
MY DIRTY STREAM (THE HUDSON
RIVER SONG)
OLD DEVIL TIME
ON TOP OF OLD SMOKY
TURN! TURN! TURN!
WHERE HAVE ALL THE FLOWERS
GONE?

Seelen, Jerry

C'EST SI BON
HOW DO I KNOW IT'S REAL?

Seeley, Blossom

MY SWEET SUZANNE

Segal, Jack

BOY FROM TEXAS, A GIRL FROM
TENNESSEE, A
FOR ONCE IN YOUR LIFE
HARD TO GET
I'LL REMEMBER SUZANNE
LAUGHING BOY
NOTHING EVER CHANGES MY LOVE
FOR YOU
SCARLET RIBBONS
WHEN SUNNY GETS BLUE

Segar, Charles

KEY TO THE HIGHWAY

Seger, Bob

AGAINST THE WIND
AMERICAN STORM
EVEN NOW

FIRE LAKE
GET OUT OF DENVER
HEARTACHE TONIGHT
HOLLYWOOD NIGHTS
KATMANDU
LIKE A ROCK
LUCIFER
MAINSTREET
NIGHT MOVES
RAMBLIN' GAMBLIN' MAN
ROCK AND ROLL NEVER FORGETS
SHAKEDOWN
STILL THE SAME
UNDERSTANDING
WE'VE GOT TONIGHT
YOU'LL ACCOMP'NY ME

Segure, Roger

AMEN (YEA-MAN)

Seibert, T. Lawrence

CASEY JONES

Seiler, Eddie

AND THEN IT'S HEAVEN
ASK ANYONE WHO KNOWS
CANCEL THE FLOWERS
FISHIN' FOR THE MOON
I DON'T WANT TO SET THE WORLD
    ON FIRE
STRICTLY INSTRUMENTAL
TILL THEN
WHEN THE LIGHTS GO ON AGAIN
    (ALL OVER THE WORLD)

Seitz, Ernest

WORLD IS WAITING FOR THE
    SUNRISE, THE

Selden, Albert

WHEN I FALL IN LOVE

Selden, Edgar

ALL THAT I ASK OF YOU IS LOVE

Self, Ronnie

ANYBODY BUT ME
CIRCUMSTANCES
EVENTUALLY
EVERYBODY LOVES ME BUT YOU
I'M SORRY
SWEET NOTHIN'S

Selsman, Victor

DO YOU WANNA JUMP, CHILDREN?
I WON'T BELIEVE IT

Sembello, Danny

LIVE MY LIFE

Sembello, David

NEUTRON DANCE

Sembello, Michael

DON'T YOU GET SO MAD
MANIAC
MIRROR, MIRROR
STIR IT UP

Sendak, Maurice

CHICKEN SOUP WITH RICE

Seneca, Joe

BREAK IT TO ME GENTLY
TALK TO ME, TALK TO ME

Senn, Tony

WORLD IS ROUND, THE

Sepe, Tony

YOU'RE THE FIRST, THE LAST, MY
    EVERYTHING

September, Anthony

NINETY-NINE WAYS

Seracini, Severio

CHEE CHEE-OO CHEE (SANG THE
    LITTLE BIRD)

Seraphine, Danny

NO TELL LOVER

Seress, Rezso

GLOOMY SUNDAY

Sergio, Paulo

SUMMER SAMBA (SO NICE)

Serota, Rick

THREE TIMES IN LOVE

Serrato, E.

I NEED SOMEBODY

Service, Paul

DISCO NIGHTS (ROCK-FREAK)

Sessions, Don

THANKS A LOT

Setser, Eddie

COUNTRY GIRLS
DOWN ON THE FARM
I'VE GOT A ROCK AND ROLL HEART
SEVEN SPANISH ANGELS

Settle, Mike

BUT YOU KNOW I LOVE YOU

Setzer, Brian

ROCK THIS TOWN
(SHE'S) SEXY + 17
STRAY CAT STRUT

Severinsen, Doc

STOP AND SMELL THE ROSES

Sexter, Ruth

BOY WITHOUT A GIRL, A

Sexton, Charlie

BEAT'S SO LONELY

Sexton, John

AUF WIEDERSEH'N, SWEETHEART

Seymour, Tot

ACCENT ON YOUTH
ALIBI BABY
AND THEN SOME
CROSS PATCH
DAY I LET YOU GET AWAY, THE
I MISS A LITTLE MISS
NO OTHER LOVE
ON THE BEACH WITH YOU
PLEASE KEEP ME IN YOUR DREAMS
SWINGING IN A HAMMOCK
US ON A BUS
WHAT'S THE NAME OF THAT SONG?

Shabalala, Joseph

DIAMONDS ON THE SOLES OF HER
    SHOES

Shackford, Charles

LET BYGONES BE BYGONES

Shad, Ellen

JUNCO PARTNER

Shaddick, Terry

PHYSICAL

Shafer, Lyndia J.

ALL MY EX'S LIVE IN TEXAS

Shafer, Sanger

ALL MY EX'S LIVE IN TEXAS
I WONDER DO YOU THINK OF ME

Shafer, Whitey

THAT'S THE WAY LOVE GOES

Shaffer, Lloyd

SMOKE DREAMS

Shaffer, Paul

GIMME MICK
IT'S RAINING MEN
YOU LOOK MARVELOUS

Shaffer, Randy

SHE'S NOT REALLY CHEATIN' (SHE'S
    JUST GETTIN' EVEN)

Shaffner, Catherine

I DON'T WANT TO DO WRONG

Shaftel, Arthur

ATLANTA, G.A.
JUST A LITTLE BIT SOUTH OF
    NORTH CAROLINA
LOVE IS SO TERRIFIC

Shakespeare, Gil

BEACH BABY

Shakespeare, William

WHAT A PIECE OF WORK IS MAN

Shand, Terry

CHICKEN SONG, THE (I AIN'T
    GONNA TAKE IT SETTIN' DOWN)
CRY BABY CRY
DANCE WITH A DOLLY (WITH A
    HOLE IN HER STOCKING)
GIVE ME THE MOON OVER
    BROOKLYN
I DOUBLE DARE YOU
IF YOU'RE EVER DOWN IN TEXAS,
    LOOK ME UP
I'M GONNA LOCK MY HEART (AND
    THROW AWAY THE KEY)

I'M SO RIGHT TONIGHT (BUT I'VE
    BEEN SO WRONG FOR SO LONG)
I WANNA WRAP YOU UP
LOW DOWN RHYTHM IN A TOP HAT
MY EXTRAORDINARY GAL
WHAT'S THE MATTER WITH ME?
WHY DOESN'T SOMEBODY TELL ME
    THESE THINGS?
YOU DON'T HAVE TO BE A BABY TO
    CRY

Shank, Joe

UNSUSPECTING HEART

Shanklin, Wayne

BIG HURT, THE
CHANSON D'AMOUR (SONG OF LOVE)
JEZEBEL
LITTLE CHILD
PRIMROSE LANE

Shannon, Del

HATS OFF TO LARRY
I GO TO PIECES
KEEP SEARCHIN' (WE'LL FOLLOW
    THE SUN)
LITTLE TOWN FLIRT
RUNAWAY
STRANGER IN TOWN

Shannon, James Royce

MISSOURI WALTZ
TOO-RA-LOO-RA-LOO-RAL (THAT'S
    AN IRISH LULLABY)

Shannon, Ronnie

BABY I LOVE YOU
I CAN'T SEE MYSELF LEAVING YOU
I NEVER LOVED A MAN (THE WAY I
    LOVE YOU)

Shannon, Tom

WILD WEEKEND

Shaper, Harold

SOFTLY, AS I LEAVE YOU

Shapiro, Brad

DON'T KNOCK MY LOVE

Shapiro, D.

LET'S LIVE FOR TODAY

Shapiro, Dan

HOW DO I KNOW IT'S REAL?
I WANNA GET MARRIED

Shapiro, Joe

ROUND AND ROUND
THINK TWICE
TREASURE OF LOVE

Shapiro, Maurice

WHY

Shapiro, Mogol

LET'S LIVE FOR TODAY

Shapiro, Susan

ASK ANYONE IN LOVE

Shapiro, Ted

ASK ANYONE IN LOVE
HANDFUL OF STARS, A
IF I HAD YOU
THIS IS NO DREAM
TO YOU
WINTER WEATHER

Shapiro, Tom

ARE YOU EVER GONNA LOVE ME
IN A NEW YORK MINUTE

Sharbutt, Del

ROMANTIC GUY, I, A
SILVER AND GOLD

Sharp, Martha

BORN A WOMAN

COME BACK WHEN YOU GROW UP
MAYBE JUST TODAY
SINGLE GIRL

Sharp, Randy

TENDER LIE, A
WHY DOES IT HAVE TO BE (WRONG
OR RIGHT)

Sharp, Todd

GOT A HOLD ON ME

Sharpe, Jack

SO RARE

Sharpe, Mike

SPOOKY

Sharples, Winston

IT'S A HAP-HAP-HAPPY DAY

Sharpley, Bill

AGENT DOUBLE-O-SOUL

Sharron, Marti

COME ON (SHOUT)
JUMP (FOR MY LOVE)

Shaver, Billy Jo

I'M JUST AN OLD CHUNK OF COAL
(BUT I'M GONNA BE A DIAMOND
SOME DAY)

Shavers, Charlie

UNDECIDED
WHY BEGIN AGAIN? (A.K.A. PASTEL
BLUE)

Shaw, Artie

ANY OLD TIME
BACK BAY SHUFFLE
CONCERTO FOR CLARINET
IF IT'S YOU

LOVE OF MY LIFE, THE
MOONRAY
NIGHTMARE
NON-STOP FLIGHT
SUMMIT RIDGE DRIVE
TRAFFIC JAM
WHY BEGIN AGAIN? (A.K.A. PASTEL
BLUE)

Shaw, Barnett

NIGHT MUST FALL

Shaw, Cha Cha

LOVE WILL FIND A WAY

Shaw, Milton

EMANON

Shaw, Sydney

DREAMY

Shaw, Tommy

BLUE COLLAR MAN (LONG NIGHTS)
REMO'S THEME (WHAT IF)
RENEGADE
SING FOR THE DAY
TOO MUCH TIME ON MY HANDS

Shawn, Nelson

JIM

Shay, Larry

BEAUTIFUL
DON'T CROSS YOUR FINGERS, CROSS
YOUR HEART
EVERYWHERE YOU GO
GET OUT AND GET UNDER THE
MOON
HIGHWAYS ARE HAPPY WAYS
I'M KNEE DEEP IN DAISIES (AND
HEAD OVER HEELS IN LOVE)
TIE ME TO YOUR APRON STRINGS
AGAIN
WHEN YOU'RE SMILING (THE
WHOLE WORLD SMILES WITH
YOU)

WHO WOULDN'T BE JEALOUS OF
   YOU?

Shayne, Gloria

ALMOST THERE
DO YOU HEAR WHAT I HEAR?
GOODBYE CRUEL WORLD
MEN IN MY LITTLE GIRL'S LIFE, THE
RAIN, RAIN GO AWAY

Shayne, J. H. "Freddie"

MR. FREDDIE BLUES

Shayne, Larry

KATHY O'
SINNER KISSED AN ANGEL, A

Sheafe, M. W.

WASHINGTON AND LEE SWING

Shean, Al

MISTER GALLAGHER AND MISTER
   SHEAN

Shear, Jules

ALL THROUGH THE NIGHT
STEADY

Shearer, Jimmy

IN MY DREAMS

Shearing, George

LULLABY OF BIRDLAND

Sheehy, Eleanore

BEAT ME DADDY, EIGHT TO THE
   BAR

Sheeley, Shari

DUM DUM
HEART IN HAND
HE'S SO HEAVENLY

POOR LITTLE FOOL

Sheets, Scott

FIRE AND ICE

Shefter, Bert

LAMP IS LOW, THE

Shelby, William

AND THE BEAT GOES ON
IT'S A LOVE THING
MAKE THAT MOVE
SECOND TIME AROUND, THE

Sheldon, Ernie

BABY, THE RAIN MUST FALL
SEATTLE
SONS OF KATIE ELDER, THE

Sheldon, Jon

LIMBO ROCK
MASHED POTATO TIME
RIDE!

Shelley, Gladys

EXPERIENCE UNNECESSARY
HOW DID HE LOOK?
THERE SHALL BE NO NIGHT

Shelton, James

LAMPLIGHT
LILAC WINE

Shelton, Louie

YOU'RE THE LOVE

Shelton, Maria

BLACK LACE

Shelton, Marla

IF I HAD A WISHING RING

Shephard, Shep

HONKY TONK

Sheppard, James

DADDY'S HOME
I WON'T BE THE FOOL ANYMORE
THOUSAND MILES AWAY, A

Sheppard, T. G.

TRYIN' TO BEAT THE MORNING
   HOME

Sheppard, William E.

AND GET AWAY
GET ON UP

Shepperd, Drey

I MADE IT THROUGH THE RAIN

Sher, Jack

KATHY O'

Sheridan, Lee

SAVE YOUR KISSES FOR ME

Sheridan, Tony

WHY

Sherin, Ukie

DON'T FORGET TONIGHT,
   TOMORROW

Sherman, Al

COMES A-LONG A-LOVE
CROSS-EYED KELLY (FROM PENN-
   SYL-VAN-EYE-AY)
DARLING, NOT WITHOUT YOU
(WHAT DO WE DO ON A) DEW-DEW-
   DEWY DAY
EVERY NOW AND THEN
EVERYTHING'S MADE FOR LOVE
GOT THE BENCH, GOT THE PARK
   (BUT I HAVEN'T GOT YOU)

HELLO MUDDAH, HELLO FADDUH!
(A LETTER FROM CAMP)
HE'S SO UNUSUAL
I MUST BE DREAMING
ISN'T IT A SHAME?
LIVIN' IN THE SUNLIGHT, LOVIN' IN
THE MOONLIGHT
ME TOO (HO, HO, HA, HA)
MOOD THAT I'M IN, THE
NINE LITTLE MILES FROM TEN-TEN-
TENNESSEE
NINETY-NINE OUT OF A HUNDRED
(WANT TO BE LOVED)
NO! NO! A THOUSAND TIMES NO!
(YOU SHALL NOT BUY MY
CARESS)
NOW'S THE TIME TO FALL IN LOVE
(POTATOES ARE CHEAPER—
TOMATOES ARE CHEAPER)
ON A LITTLE BAMBOO BRIDGE
ONE NIGHT IN MONTE CARLO
ON THE BEACH AT BALI-BALI
OVER SOMEBODY ELSE'S SHOULDER
PRETENDING
SAVE YOUR SORROW (FOR
TOMORROW)
TAKE ANOTHER GUESS
WHEN I'M THE PRESIDENT
YOU GOTTA BE A FOOTBALL HERO

Sherman, Jimmy

LOVER MAN (OH, WHERE CAN YOU
BE?)

Sherman, Joe

ANYTHING CAN HAPPEN MAMBO
ESO BESO (THAT KISS)
GRADUATION DAY
JUKE BOX BABY
POR FAVOR (PLEASE)
RAMBLIN' ROSE
STOLEN MOMENTS
THAT SUNDAY, THAT SUMMER
TOYS IN THE ATTIC

Sherman, Noel

ESO BESO (THAT KISS)
GRADUATION DAY
JUKE BOX BABY

MORGEN (A.K.A. ONE MORE
SUNRISE)
POR FAVOR (PLEASE)
RAMBLIN' ROSE
TOPKAPI

Sherman, Richard M.

AGE OF NOT BELIEVING
CHIM CHIM CHEREE
CHING-CHING AND A DING DING
DING
CHITTY CHITTY BANG BANG
FEED THE BIRDS
FREEBOOTIN'
HUSHABYE MOUNTAIN
I LOVE TO LAUGH
JOLLY HOLIDAY
LET'S GET TOGETHER
LET'S GO FLY A KITE
LIFE I LEAD, THE
MON AMOUR PERDU (MY LOST
LOVE)
MOTHER EARTH AND FATHER TIME
PINEAPPLE PRINCESS
RIVER SONG
SLIPPER AND THE ROSE WALTZ,
THE
SPOONFUL OF SUGAR, A
STEP IN TIME
SUPERCALIFRAGILISTICEXPIALIDO-
CIOUS
TALL PAUL
TOM SAWYER
WHERE DID THE GOOD TIMES GO?
YOU'RE SIXTEEN

Sherman, Robert B.

AGE OF NOT BELIEVING
CHIM CHIM CHEREE
CHING-CHING AND A DING DING
DING
CHITTY CHITTY BANG BANG
FEED THE BIRDS
FREEBOOTIN'
HUSHABYE MOUNTAIN
I LOVE TO LAUGH
JOLLY HOLIDAY
LET'S GET TOGETHER
LET'S GO FLY A KITE
LIFE I LEAD, THE

MON AMOUR PERDU (MY LOST
LOVE)
MOTHER EARTH AND FATHER TIME
PINEAPPLE PRINCESS
RIVER SONG
SLIPPER AND THE ROSE WALTZ,
THE
SPOONFUL OF SUGAR, A
STEP IN TIME
SUPERCALIFRAGILISTICEXPIALIDO-
CIOUS
TALL PAUL
TOM SAWYER
WHERE DID THE GOOD TIMES GO?
YOU'RE SIXTEEN

Sherr, Jack

YOURS

Sherrell, John

CHURCH ON CUMBERLAND ROAD,
THE

Sherrick

JUST CALL

Sherrill, Billy

ALMOST PERSUADED
ALREADY IT'S HEAVEN
ANOTHER LONELY SONG
EVERY TIME YOU TOUCH ME (I GET
HIGH)
GOOD LOVIN' (MAKES IT RIGHT)
HAVE A LITTLE FAITH
HE LOVES ME ALL THE WAY
I DON'T WANNA PLAY HOUSE
I'LL SEE HIM THROUGH
I LOVE MY FRIEND
I'M A STAND BY MY WOMAN MAN
I'M DOWN TO MY LAST "I LOVE
YOU"
KIDS SAY THE DARNDEST THINGS
KISS AWAY
LOSER'S CATHEDRAL
LULLABY OF LOVE
MOST BEAUTIFUL GIRL, THE
MY ELUSIVE DREAMS
MY MAN, A SWEET MAN
MY WOMAN'S GOOD TO ME

SINGING MY SONG
SOUTHTOWN, U.S.A.
STAND BY YOUR MAN
SUGAR LIPS
SWEET AND INNOCENT
TAKE ME TO YOUR WORLD
TAKIN' IT EASY
'TILL I CAN MAKE IT ON MY OWN
VERY SPECIAL LOVE SONG, A
WAYS TO LOVE A MAN, THE
WE SURE CAN LOVE EACH OTHER
WITH ONE EXCEPTION
WOMAN ALWAYS KNOWS, A
YOU AND ME
YOU MEAN THE WORLD TO ME
YOUR GOOD GIRL'S GONNA GO BAD

Sherrill, John Scott

CRY, CRY, CRY
(DO YOU LOVE ME) JUST SAY YES
THAT ROCK WON'T ROLL

Sherrill, Mark

TAKIN' IT EASY

Sherry, George

KISSES DON'T LIE

Sherwin, Manning

I FALL IN LOVE WITH YOU EVERY
    DAY
LOVELY ONE
NIGHTINGALE SANG IN BERKELEY
    SQUARE, A

Shider, Gary

ONE NATION UNDER A GROOVE

Shields, Harvey

WAY I FEEL TONIGHT, THE

Shields, Larry

AT THE JAZZ BAND BALL
BARNYARD BLUE
CLARINET MARMALADE
FIDGETY FEET

OSTRICH WALK
TIGER RAG

Shields, Ren

COME, TAKE A TRIP IN MY AIRSHIP
COME TO THE LAND OF BOHEMIA
IN THE GOOD OLD SUMMERTIME
IN THE MERRY MONTH OF MAY
IT'S MOONLIGHT ALL THE TIME ON
    BROADWAY
LONGEST WAY 'ROUND IS THE
    SHORTEST WAY HOME, THE
STEAMBOAT BILL
UP IN A BALLOON
WALTZ ME AROUND AGAIN, WILLIE
    ('ROUND, 'ROUND, 'ROUND)

Shifrin, Lalo

PEOPLE ALONE

Shifrin, Sue

SO GOOD

Shilkret, Jack

MAKE BELIEVE

Shilkret, Nathaniel

DOWN THE RIVER OF GOLDEN
    DREAMS
FIRST TIME I SAW YOU, THE
JEANNINE, I DREAM OF LILAC TIME
LONESOME ROAD, THE
SOME SWEET DAY

Ship, G.

FOR YASGUR'S FARM

Shipley, Ellen

HEAVEN IS A PLACE ON EARTH

Shipley, Thomas

ONE TOKE OVER THE LINE
TARKIO ROAD

Shire, David

EASIER TO LOVE
FATHERHOOD BLUES
HAVING MYSELF A FINE TIME
I'LL NEVER SAY GOODBYE
IT GOES LIKE IT GOES
I WANT IT ALL
NO MORE SONGS FOR ME
STORY GOES ON, THE
WASHINGTON SQUARE
WITH YOU I'M BORN AGAIN

Shirl, Jimmy

BELOVED, BE FAITHFUL
CASTLE ROCK
COME TO THE MARTI GRAS
DELILAH
I BELIEVE
MY FRIEND
SONATA

Shirley, Jerry

HOT 'N' NASTY

Shockley, Stephen

AND THE BEAT GOES ON

Shook, Jerry

LOVE LOOKS GOOD ON YOU

Shorrock, Glenn

COOL CHANGE
HELP IS ON ITS WAY
MAN ON YOUR MIND

Shoss, Herman

TANGLED MIND

Shostakovich, Dmitri

UNITED NATIONS ON THE MARCH

Shreeve, M.

TOUCH ME (I WANT YOUR BODY)

Shull, Chester R.

SIN

Shuman, Alden

BANJO'S BACK IN TOWN, THE
SEVEN LONELY DAYS

Shuman, Earl

ANOTHER CUP OF COFFEE
BANJO'S BACK IN TOWN, THE
CATERINA
CLINGING VINE
CLOSE TO CATHY
DONDI
HEY THERE LONELY BOY (A.K.A. HEY THERE LONELY GIRL)
HOTEL HAPPINESS
I'VE BEEN HERE!
LEFT RIGHT OUT OF YOUR HEART
MOST PEOPLE GET MARRIED
MY SHY VIOLET
OUR EVERLASTING LOVE
SEVEN LONELY DAYS
STARRY EYED
YOUNG NEW MEXICAN PUPPETEER, THE

Shuman, Frank

CARIBBEAN COCKTAIL
PENGUIN AT THE WALDORF

Shuman, Mort

AMSTERDAM
CAN'T GET USED TO LOSING YOU
CAROUSEL
GET IT WHILE YOU CAN
GO, JIMMY, GO
HIS LATEST FLAME (MARIE'S THE NAME)
HOUND DOG MAN
HUSHABYE
IF WE ONLY HAVE LOVE
I'M A MAN
KISS ME QUICK
LITTLE CHILDREN
LITTLE SISTER
MADELEINE
MESS OF BLUES, A

NO ONE
PLAIN JANE
SAVE THE LAST DANCE FOR ME
SEVEN DAY WEEKEND
(YOU MAKE ME FEEL) SO GOOD
SONS OF . . .
SURRENDER
SUSPICION
SWEETS FOR MY SWEET
TEENAGER IN LOVE, A
THIS MAGIC MOMENT
TURN ME LOOSE
VIVA LAS VEGAS
WHAT'S IT GONNA BE?
WRONG FOR EACH OTHER

Shurtz, Mary Jean

DAD GAVE MY DOG AWAY

Shury, Gerald

UP IN A PUFF OF SMOKE

Siders, Irving

SLOW WALK

Sidmos, John

DO YOU FEEL LIKE WE DO

Sidney, George

CREOLE BELLE
TO LOVE AGAIN

Sieczynski, Rudolf

VIENNA DREAMS

Siegel, Al

AFTER YOU
PANAMANIA

Siegel, Arthur

LOVE IS A SIMPLE THING
MONOTONOUS
PENNY CANDY

Siegel, Jay

I HEAR TRUMPETS BLOW

Siegel, Monty

HUMMIN' TO MYSELF (I'VE GOT THE WORDS—I'VE GOT THE TUNE)

Sievier, Bruce R.

HEART OF STONE, A
SPEAK TO ME OF LOVE
YOU'RE BLASE

Sigidi

TAKE YOUR TIME (DO IT RIGHT)

Sigler, Bunny

DO YOU GET ENOUGH LOVE
SAY IT AGAIN

Sigler, Jack

LOVE (CAN MAKE YOU HAPPY)

Sigler, Maurice

CRAZY WITH LOVE
EVERYTHING'S IN RHYTHM WITH MY HEART
HERE IT IS MONDAY AND I'VE STILL GOT A DOLLAR
IF YOU EVER CHANGE YOUR MIND
I'M IN A DANCING MOOD
I SAW STARS
JIMMY HAD A NICKEL
LITTLE MAN, YOU'VE HAD A BUSY DAY
SHE SHALL HAVE MUSIC
TELL ME A STORY
THERE ISN'T ANY LIMIT TO MY LOVE
THIS'LL MAKE YOU WHISTLE
WHY DON'T YOU PRACTICE WHAT YOU PREACH?

Sigman, Carl

11TH HOUR MELODY

ALL TOO SOON
ANSWER ME, MY LOVE
ARRIVEDERCI, ROMA (GOODBYE TO
   ROME)
BALLERINA
BIG BRASS BAND FROM BRAZIL,
   THE
BLOSSOMS ON THE BOUGH, THE
CARELESS HANDS
CHERRY BLOSSOMS ON CAPITOL
   HILL
CIVILIZATION (BONGO, BONGO,
   BONGO)
CRAZY, HE CALLS ME
CREEP, THE
DAY IN THE LIFE OF A FOOL, A
DAY THE RAINS CAME, THE
DREAM ALONG WITH ME (I'M ON
   MY WAY TO A STAR)
EBB TIDE
ENJOY YOURSELF (IT'S LATER THAN
   YOU THINK)
FUNNY THING
HOP-SCOTCH POLKA (SCOTCH HOT)
I COULD HAVE TOLD YOU
IF YOU COULD SEE ME NOW
IF YOU TURN ME DOWN
IT'S ALL IN THE GAME
JUST COME HOME
LONELY IS THE NAME
LOSING YOU
LOVE LIES
MARSHMALLOW WORLD, A
MATINEE
MY FAIR LADY
MY HEART CRIES FOR YOU
MY WAY OF LIFE
ONCE AROUND THE MOON
PASSÉ
PENNSYLVANIA 6-5000
SHANGRI-LA
SIX BOYS AND SEVEN GIRLS
SOUVENIR D'ITALIE
SUMMERTIME IN VENICE
THEME FROM "LOVE STORY"
THOUSAND ISLANDS SONG, THE (I
   LEFT MY LOVE ON ONE OF THE
   THOUSAND ISLANDS)
TILL
TWENTY-FOUR HOURS OF SUNSHINE
WALTER WINCHELL RHUMBA
WHAT NOW MY LOVE
WORLD OUTSIDE, THE

WORLD WE KNEW, THE (OVER AND
   OVER)
YOU'RE MY WORLD

Signorelli, Frank

AND THEN YOUR LIPS MET MINE
BLUES SERENADE, A
I'LL NEVER BE THE SAME
JUST HOT!
SO AT LAST IT'S COME TO THIS
STAIRWAY TO THE STARS

Silbar, Jeff

HE'S A HEARTACHE (LOOKING FOR
   A PLACE TO HAPPEN)
WHERE WERE YOU WHEN I WAS
   FALLING IN LOVE
WIND BENEATH MY WINGS (A.K.A.
   HERO)

Silbert, Sharon

HEY, LITTLE LUCY! (DON'TCHA PUT
   NO LIPSTICK ON)

Silesu, Lao

LITTLE LOVE, A LITTLE KISS, A
LOVE, HERE IS MY HEART!

Sills, Stephen

BLUEBIRD
SIT DOWN, I THINK I LOVE YOU

Silva, William

WHERE THE BLUE AND LONELY GO

Silver, Abner

AND SO LITTLE TIME
ANGEL CHILD
BARBARA
BEBE
C'EST VOUS (IT'S YOU)
CHASING SHADOWS
CROSS-EYED KELLY (FROM PENN-
   SYL-VAN-EYE-AY)
DARLING, NOT WITHOUT YOU
DON'T LET HER GO

EVERY NOW AND THEN
FAREWELL TO ARMS
HAVE YOU FORGOTTEN SO SOON?
HE'S SO UNUSUAL
HOW DID HE LOOK?
I LAUGHED AT LOVE
I'M GOIN' SOUTH
ISN'T IT A SHAME?
MARY ANN
MOOD THAT I'M IN, THE
MY HOME TOWN IS A ONE HORSE
   TOWN (BUT IT'S BIG ENOUGH FOR
   ME)
MY LOVE FOR YOU
NEW MOON AND AN OLD
   SERENADE, A
NO! NO! A THOUSAND TIMES NO!
   (YOU SHALL NOT BUY MY
   CARESS)
NORMANDY
OLD CURIOSITY SHOP, AN
ONE NIGHT IN MONTE CARLO
ON THE BEACH AT BALI-BALI
PU-LEEZE, MR. HEMINGWAY
SAY IT WHILE DANCING
THERE GOES MY HEART
THERE SHALL BE NO NIGHT
WITH THESE HANDS

Silver, Frank

YES! WE HAVE NO BANANAS

Silver, Horace

PREACHER, THE

Silver, Lisa

40 HOUR WEEK (FOR A LIVIN')
ONE PROMISE TOO LATE

Silver, Maxwell

HE WALKED RIGHT IN, TURNED
   AROUND, AND WALKED RIGHT
   OUT AGAIN

Silverman, Charles

LOOK THROUGH ANY WINDOW

Silvers, Dolores Vicki

LEARNIN' THE BLUES

Silvers, Louis

APRIL SHOWERS
MOTHER OF MINE, I STILL HAVE
   YOU
WEARY RIVER

Silvers, Phil

NANCY (WITH THE LAUGHING FACE)

Silvers, Sid

DID YOU MEAN IT?
LOVE AND KISSES
WHEN YOU DREAM ABOUT HAWAII

Silverstein, David

BEND DOWN, SISTER

Silverstein, Shel

BOA CONSTRICTOR
BOY NAMED SUE, A
COVER OF "ROLLING STONE," THE
DADDY, WHAT IF
FREE AS A BIRD
HERE I AM AGAIN
HEY, LORETTA
I GOT STONED AND I MISSED IT
LOVIN' YOU MORE
MARIE LAVEAU
ONE'S ON THE WAY
SUNNY SIDE OF LIFE
SYLVIA'S MOTHER
TAKER, THE
UNICORN, THE

Simay, Joey

PINCH ME

Simeone, Harry

LITTLE DRUMMER BOY, THE

Simington, Lamar

GOODBYE, MY LOVER, GOODBYE

Simkins, Lewis

LONG GONE

Simmons, Billy

M-I-S-S-I-S-S-I-P-P-I

Simmons, Charles

LOVE DON'T LOVE NOBODY
MIGHTY LOVE, A
THEY JUST CAN'T STOP IT (THE
   GAMES PEOPLE PLAY)

Simmons, Daryl

DIAL MY HEART
DON'T BE CRUEL
IT'S NO CRIME
LOVE SAW IT
LUCKY CHARM
ON OUR OWN
SUPERWOMAN

Simmons, Gene

CALLING DR. LOVE
CHRISTINE SIXTEEN
ROCK AND ROLL ALL NITE
WORLD WITHOUT HEROES, A

Simmons, Joyce

MEN ALL PAUSE, THE

Simmons, Lonnie

BURN RUBBER (WHY YOU WANNA
   HURT ME)
DON'T STOP THE MUSIC
EARLY IN THE MORNING

Simmons, Pat

BLACK WATER
DEPENDIN' ON YOU
ECHOES OF LOVE

Simmons, Rousseau

PLEASURE MAD

Simmons, Russell

BREAKS, THE

Simmons, William

FREAK-A-ZOID

Simms, Alice D.

ENCORE, CHERIE

Simms, Earl

FUNKY STREET

Simms, Joseph

AIN'T IT A SHAME

Simon, Bob

WHAT AM I GONNA DO ABOUT YOU

Simon, Carly

ANTICIPATION
ATTITUDE DANCING
COMING AROUND AGAIN
HAVEN'T GOT TIME FOR THE PAIN
JESSE
LET THE RIVER RUN
RIGHT THING TO DO, THE
STUFF THAT DREAMS ARE MADE OF
THAT'S THE WAY I'VE ALWAYS
   HEARD IT SHOULD BE
VENGEANCE
YOU BELONG TO ME
YOU'RE SO VAIN

Simon, D.

I NEED LOVE

Simon, Howard

GONNA GET A GIRL

Simon, Joe

GET DOWN, GET DOWN (GET ON
    THE FLOOR)
POWER OF LOVE
THEME FROM "CLEOPATRA JONES"
YOUR TIME TO CRY

Simon, Nat

AND MIMI
APPLE BLOSSOM WEDDING, AN
BAMBOO
COAX ME A LITTLE BIT
CROSSTOWN
DOWN THE TRAIL OF ACHIN'
    HEARTS
GAUCHO SERENADE, THE
GOODY GOODBYE
HER BATHING SUIT NEVER GOT
    WET
IN MY LITTLE RED BOOK
ISTANBUL (NOT CONSTANTINOPLE)
IS THAT THE WAY TO TREAT A
    SWEETHEART?
I WISH THAT I COULD HIDE INSIDE
    THIS LETTER
LITTLE CURLY HAIR IN A HIGH
    CHAIR
LITTLE LADY MAKE BELIEVE
MAMA DOLL SONG, THE
MY BOLERO
NO CAN DO
OLD LAMP-LIGHTER, THE
POINCIANA (SONG OF THE TREE)
ROSEWOOD SPINET, A
SWEET HEARTACHES
THROWIN' STONES AT THE SUN
WAIT FOR ME, MARY
YOU'RE IN MY POWER (HA, HA, HA)

Simon, Paul

50 WAYS TO LEAVE YOUR LOVER
59TH STREET BRIDGE SONG, THE
    (A.K.A. FEELIN' GROOVY)
ALLERGIES
AMERICA
AMERICAN TUNE
AT THE ZOO
BIG, BRIGHT GREEN PLEASURE
    MACHINE, THE
BOXER, THE

BRIDGE OVER TROUBLED WATER
CECILIA
DANGLING CONVERSATION, THE
DIAMONDS ON THE SOLES OF HER
    SHOES
DUNCAN
EL CONDOR PASA
FAKIN' IT
FOR EMILY, WHENEVER I MAY FIND
    HER
GONE AT LAST
GRACELAND
HAZY SHADE OF WINTER, A
HEY, SCHOOLGIRL
HOMEWARD BOUND
I AM A ROCK
KODACHROME
LATE IN THE EVENING
LOVES ME LIKE A ROCK
ME AND JULIO DOWN BY THE
    SCHOOLYARD
MOTHER AND CHILD REUNION
MRS. ROBINSON
MY LITTLE TOWN
ONE TRICK PONY
RED RUBBER BALL
ROCK THE CASBAH
SCARBOROUGH FAIR—CANTICLE
SLIP SLIDIN' AWAY
SOUNDS OF SILENCE, THE
STILL CRAZY AFTER ALL THESE
    YEARS
YOU CAN CALL ME AL

Simon, Robert A.

BY SPECIAL PERMISSION OF THE
    COPYRIGHT OWNERS, I LOVE
    YOU

Simon, Scott

SANDY

Simone, Nina

MISSISSIPPI GODDAM
TO BE YOUNG, GIFTED AND BLACK

Simons, Moises

MARTA

Simons, Peter

UNITED WE STAND

Simons, Seymour

AIN'T YOU ASHAMED?
ALL OF ME
BREEZIN' ALONG WITH THE BREEZE
HONEY
IT'S THE LITTLE THINGS THAT
    COUNT
JUST LIKE A GYPSY
NOW THAT SUMMER IS GONE
SWEETHEART OF MY STUDENT
    DAYS
WHY WORRY?

Simpkins, Lewis C.

NIGHT TRAIN

Simpson, Fitzroy

PASS THE DUTCHIE

Simpson, Red

KANSAS CITY SONG
SAM'S PLACE

Simpson, Valerie

AIN'T NO MOUNTAIN HIGH ENOUGH
AIN'T NOTHING LIKE THE REAL
    THING
BOSS, THE
CALIFORNIA SOUL
COUNT YOUR BLESSINGS
GOOD LOVIN' AIN'T EASY TO COME
    BY
I DON'T NEED NO DOCTOR
I'M EVERY WOMAN
KEEP ON LOVIN' ME HONEY
LANDLORD
LET'S GO GET STONED
REACH OUT AND TOUCH
    (SOMEBODY'S HAND)
REMEMBER ME
SOLID
SOME THINGS YOU NEVER GET
    USED TO
STREET CORNER

STUFF LIKE THAT
WHAT YOU GAVE ME
YOU'RE ALL I NEED TO GET BY
YOUR PRECIOUS LOVE

Sims, Gerald

DEAR LOVER
SINCE YOU SHOWED ME HOW TO BE
    HAPPY

Sinatra, Frank

I'M A FOOL TO WANT YOU
THIS LOVE OF MINE

Sinfield, Peter

COURT OF THE CRIMSON KING

Singer, Artie

AT THE HOP

Singer, Bob

UNSUSPECTING HEART

Singer, Dolph

JUST AROUND THE CORNER

Singer, Guy

WITHER THOU GOEST

Singer, Lou

GYPSY WITHOUT A SOUL, A
LOST IN MEDITATION
ONE MEAT BALL
SLEEPY SERENADE
YOUNG AND WARM AND
    WONDERFUL

Singletary, Larry

HIM OR ME

Singleton, Charles

APPLE GREEN
DON'T FORBID ME

HE TREATS YOUR DAUGHTER MEAN
    (MAMA)
HURTS ME TO MY HEART
IF I MAY
JUST AS MUCH AS EVER
JUST BE YOURSELF
LADY
LIGHT OF LOVE
MAMBO BABY
MY PERSONAL POSSESSION
(MY HEART GOES) PIDDILY PATTER
    PATTER
SHE'S STRANGE
SPANISH EYES
STRANGERS IN THE NIGHT
THIS TIME
WHEEL OF HURT, THE

Singleton, Don

FOOL FOR YOUR LOVE

Singleton, Margie

FLOWER OF LOVE
LAURA (WHAT'S HE GOT THAT I
    AIN'T GOT?)
LIE TO ME
SHE UNDERSTANDS ME (A.K.A.
    DUM-DE-DA)

Singleton, Shelby

AM I THAT EASY TO FORGET?

Singleton, Stephen

LOOK OF LOVE (PART ONE)

Sissle, Noble

AIN'T YOU COMIN' BACK, MARY
    ANN, TO MARYLAND?
BANDANA DAYS
I'M JUST WILD ABOUT HARRY
LOVE WILL FIND A WAY
SHUFFLE ALONG

Six, Tom

GOTTA TRAVEL ON

Sixx, Nikki

GIRLS, GIRLS, GIRLS

Sizemore, Arthur

SO TIRED

Skardina, Gary

COME ON (SHOUT)
JUMP (FOR MY LOVE)

Skidmore, Will

IT'S NOBODY'S BUSINESS BUT MY
    OWN

Skill, Mile

TALKING IN YOUR SLEEP

Skinner, Albert

AWAY ALL BOATS

Skinner, Frank

AWAY ALL BOATS

Skinner, Graham

HONEYTHIEF, THE

Skinner, Jimmie

I FOUND MY GIRL IN THE U.S.A.
LET'S SAY GOODBYE LIKE WE SAID
    HELLO

Skinner, Jolyon

COLOUR OF LOVE, THE

Skinner, Terry

EVEN THE NIGHTS ARE BETTER
HAVE YOU EVER LOVED SOMEBODY
MAMA'S NEVER SEEN THOSE EYES
TOUCH ME WHEN WE'RE DANCING

Sklerov, Gloria

I BELIEVE I'M GONNA LOVE YOU
I JUST FALL IN LOVE AGAIN

Skye, John

I'M SO IN LOVE WITH YOU

Skylar, Sunny

AMOR
AND SO TO SLEEP AGAIN
ARE THESE REALLY MINE?
ASK ME
ATLANTA, G.A.
BE MINE TONIGHT
BESAME MUCHO
DON'T WAIT TOO LONG
FIFTEEN MINUTE INTERMISSION
GOTTA BE THIS OR THAT
HAIR OF GOLD, EYES OF BLUE
I'D BE LOST WITHOUT YOU
IT MUST BE JELLY ('CAUSE JAM
    DON'T SHAKE LIKE THAT)
IT'S ALL OVER NOW
JUST A LITTLE BIT SOUTH OF
    NORTH CAROLINA
LOVE IS SO TERRIFIC
MOVE IT OVER
PUSSY CAT
PUT THAT RING ON MY FINGER
RUBY DUBY DU
SONG OF NEW ORLEANS
WAITIN' FOR THE TRAIN TO COME
    IN
YOU'RE BREAKING MY HEART

Skylark

SYSTEM OF SURVIVAL

Skyliners, The

SINCE I DON'T HAVE YOU
THIS I SWEAR

Slack, Freddie

HOUSE OF BLUE LIGHTS
KISS GOODNIGHT, A

Slate, Johnny

BETTER LOVE NEXT TIME
FRIENDS
I KEEP COMING BACK
LOVING UP A STORM

Slater, Terry

BOWLING GREEN

Slay, Frank C. Jr.

BUZZ BUZZ A-DIDDLE IT
JUMP OVER
LA DEE DAH
LUCKY LADYBUG
SILHOUETTES
TALLAHASSEE LASSIE
TRANSISTOR SISTER

Sledge, Joni

ALL AMERICAN GIRLS

Slick, Darby

SOMEBODY TO LOVE

Slick, Grace

PLAY ON LOVE
SEASONS
WHITE RABBIT

Sloan, Phil

ANOTHER DAY, ANOTHER
    HEARTACHE
EVE OF DESTRUCTION
(HERE THEY COME) FROM ALL
    OVER THE WORLD
I FOUND A GIRL
LET ME BE
MUST TO AVOID, A
SECRET AGENT MAN
THINGS I SHOULD HAVE SAID
UNLESS YOU CARE
YOU BABY

Sloane, A. Baldwin

ALEXANDER'S BAG-PIPE BAND

HEAVEN WILL PROTECT THE
    WORKING GIRL
LIFE IS ONLY WHAT YOU MAKE IT,
    AFTER ALL
THOSE WERE THE HAPPY DAYS
WHEN YOU AIN'T GOT NO MORE
    MONEY, WELL, YOU NEEDN'T
    COME ROUND

Sloane, Mae A.

MY PAJAMA BEAUTY

Small, Allan

WEDDING SAMBA, THE

Small, Danny

WITHOUT LOVE (THERE IS NOTHING)

Smalley, Victor H.

THAT LOVIN' RAG

Smalls, Charlie

EASE ON DOWN THE ROAD

Smiley, Arthur

CRUEL LOVE

Smith, Adolph

I DIDN'T WANT TO DO IT

Smith, Al

BIG BOSS MAN

Smith, Alfred

BABY, YOU'VE GOT IT
GIMME LITTLE SIGN
OOGUM BOOGUM SONG, THE

Smith, Anthony

WILD THING

Smith, Arthur

DUELING BANJOS
GUITAR-BOOGIE

Smith, Arthur Q.

I WOULDN'T CHANGE YOU IF I
   COULD
MISSING IN ACTION

Smith, Beasley

BEG YOUR PARDON
GOD'S COUNTRY
I'D RATHER DIE YOUNG
NIGHT TRAIN TO MEMPHIS
OLD MASTER PAINTER, THE
SUNDAY DOWN IN TENNESSEE
THAT LUCKY OLD SUN (JUST ROLLS
   AROUND HEAVEN ALL DAY)

Smith, Ben

I DREAMT I DWELT IN HARLEM

Smith, Bessie

JAIL HOUSE BLUES

Smith, Bill

I WOULDN'T TRADE YOU FOR THE
   WORLD
TWENTY FEET OF MUDDY WATER

Smith, Billy Dawn

ANGELS LISTENED IN, THE
JUST BORN (TO BE YOUR BABY)
LOVE HAS JOINED US TOGETHER
STEP BY STEP
TO THE AISLE
TROUBLE IN PARADISE

Smith, Bob

SHIMMY, SHIMMY, KO-KO-BOP

Smith, Bobby

TIPPIN' IN

Smith, Carl

(YOUR LOVE KEEPS LIFTING ME)
   HIGHER AND HIGHER
I OVERLOOKED AN ORCHID
MISTER MOON
TEN THOUSAND DRUMS
WHO'S CHEATING WHO?

Smith, Carl William

RECOVERY
RESCUE ME
WE'RE GONNA MAKE IT

Smith, Carole

DON'T KEEP ME HANGING ON
TRUE LOVE'S A BLESSING

Smith, Charles

HOLLYWOOD SWINGING
LADIES NIGHT
MISLED
OPEN SESAME
STONE LOVE
TAKE MY HEART (YOU CAN HAVE IT
   IF YOU WANT IT)

Smith, Chris

AFTER ALL THAT I'VE BEEN TO YOU
ALL IN DOWN AND OUT (SORRY, I
   AIN'T GOT IT, YOU COULD HAVE
   IT, ETC.)
AT THE LEVEE ON REVIVAL DAY
BALLIN' THE JACK
BEANS! BEANS!! BEANS!!!
CAKE WALKING BABIES FROM
   HOME
COME AFTER BREAKFAST, BRING
   'LONG YOUR LUNCH AND LEAVE
   'FORE SUPPER TIME
CONSTANTLY
DOWN IN HONKY TONKY TOWN
FIFTEEN CENTS
HE'S A COUSIN OF MINE
IF HE COMES IN, I'M GOING OUT
LONG GONE
LOVE, HONOR AND OBEY
YOU'RE IN THE RIGHT CHURCH,
   BUT THE WRONG PEW

Smith, Clarence "Pinetop"

BOOGIE WOOGIE
PINE TOP'S BOOGIE WOOGIE

Smith, Connie

I'LL COME RUNNING

Smith, Dick

WHEN A GYPSY MAKES HIS VIOLIN
   CRY

Smith, Don M.

DOUBLE SHOT (OF MY BABY'S LOVE)

Smith, E. B.

OH, BABE, WHAT WOULD YOU SAY?

Smith, Edgar

COME BACK, MY HONEY BOY, TO
   ME
HEAVEN WILL PROTECT THE
   WORKING GIRL
KISS ME, HONEY, DO
LIFE IS ONLY WHAT YOU MAKE IT,
   AFTER ALL
MA BLUSHIN' ROSIE

Smith, Ernestine

STRANDED IN THE JUNGLE

Smith, Ethel

LOVE IS STRANGE

Smith, Floyd

SINCE YOU SHOWED ME HOW TO BE
   HAPPY
THERE'LL COME A TIME

Smith, Frankie

DOUBLE DUTCH BUS

Smith, Fred Sledge

AIN'T THAT LOVE
DUCK, THE
PEANUT BUTTER
WESTERN MOVIES

Smith, George Totten

LAUGHING WATER

Smith, Rev. Guy

GREAT SPECKLE(D) BIRD, THE

Smith, Harry B.

BRIGHT EYES
BROWN OCTOBER ALE
CUPID AND I
DANCING FOOL
DEAR EYES THAT HAUNT ME
GYPSY LOVE SONG (SLUMBER ON,
    MY LITTLE GYPSY SWEETHEART)
IF ONLY YOU WERE MINE
I WONDER IF YOU STILL CARE FOR
    ME
LITTLE GYPSY MAID, THE
MY ANGELINE
PLAY GYPSIES, DANCE GYPSIES
QUILLER HAS THE BRAINS
SAME SORT OF GIRL
SHEIK OF ARABY, THE
THERE ONCE WAS AN OWL
TO THE LAND OF MY OWN
    ROMANCE
WE TWO SHALL MEET AGAIN
WHEN YOU'RE WEARING THE BALL
    AND CHAIN
WOMAN IS ONLY A WOMAN, BUT A
    GOOD CIGAR IS A SMOKE, A
YOU BELONG TO ME
YOU'RE HERE AND I'M HERE
YOURS IS MY HEART ALONE

Smith, H. E.

WORLD OF MAKE BELIEVE

Smith, Huey

ROCKIN' PNEUMONIA AND THE
    BOOGIE WOOGIE FLU

Smith, J.

CRYIN', PRAYIN', WISHIN', WAITIN'

Smith, Jack

GIMME A LITTLE KISS, WILL YA,
    HUH?

Smith, James

SLIPPIN' AND SLIDIN' (PEEPIN' AND
    HIDIN')

Smith, James Todd

I'M BAD

Smith, Jerry Dean

(DOWN AT) PAPA JOE'S
TRUCK STOP

Smith, Jerry Lee

LAST NIGHT

Smith, Jesse

I DO

Smith, Jimmy

I PROMISE TO REMEMBER

Smith, Joe

WALK A MILE IN MY SHOES

Smith, John

I CAN'T WAIT

Smith, Johnny

WALK, DON'T RUN

Smith, J. T.

GOING BACK TO CALL
I NEED LOVE

Smith, Kate

MAKIN' FACES AT THE MAN IN THE
    MOON
WHEN THE MOON COMES OVER THE
    MOUNTAIN

Smith, Kenneth Leslie

ON THE OLD SPANISH TRAIL

Smith, Laura R.

LITTLE SIR ECHO

Smith, Lawrence

BREAKS, THE

Smith, Lloyd

I'M GOING TO WEAR YOU OFF MY
    MIND
SAD GIRL

Smith, Marion

TEARDROPS WILL FALL

Smith, Mike

BITS AND PIECES
CAN'T YOU SEE THAT SHE'S MINE?
COME HOME
GLAD ALL OVER
PLEASE TELL ME WHY
TRY TOO HARD

Smith, Mira

BUFFALO SOLDIER
GIRL MOST LIKELY, THE
RECONSIDER ME
SOUL SHAKE
THERE NEVER WAS A TIME

Smith, Neal

EIGHTEEN

Smith, Patti

BECAUSE THE NIGHT

FREDERICK

Smith, Ray

COUNTRY BOY
FIFTEEN YEARS AGO
SHE NEEDS SOMEONE TO HOLD
 HER (WHEN SHE CRIES)

Smith, Richard B.

BREEZE, THE (THAT'S BRINGIN' MY
 HONEY BACK TO ME)
I'M KEEPING THOSE KEEPSAKES
 FOR YOU
WINTER WONDERLAND

Smith, Rickey

SAVE THE OVERTIME FOR ME

Smith, Ricky

MAKE THAT MOVE

Smith, Robert B.

ALL THE WORLD LOVES A LOVER
ANGEL FACE
ANGELUS, THE
COME DOWN MA' EVENIN' STAR
CRICKET ON THE HEARTH, THE
DAY DREAMS
FOUNTAIN FAY
I MIGHT BE YOUR ONCE-IN-A-WHILE
IT'S A CUTE LITTLE WAY OF MY
 OWN
SOMEONE LIKE YOU
SPRINGTIME OF LIFE, THE
SWEETHEARTS
TWO LITTLE LOVE BEES

Smith, Russell

BIG OLE BREW
DON'T GO TO STRANGERS
HEARTBEAT IN THE DARKNESS
THIRD RATE ROMANCE

Smith, Sandra

BRIDGE WASHED OUT, THE

Smith, Stuff

I'SE A MUGGIN'
IT'S WONDERFUL

Smith, Tab

HARVARD BLUES

Smith, Victor

WITH YOUR LOVE

Smith, Warren

I'M GOING TO WEAR YOU OFF MY
 MIND

Smith, Whispering

MEAN WOMAN BLUES

Smith, Will

PARENTS JUST DON'T UNDERSTAND

Smith, William

PROMISES, PROMISES
WHEN I DIE

Smith, William H.

ECHO OF SPRING

Smith, Willie

KEEP YOUR TEMPER

Smith, Willie "The Lion"

SWEETER THAN THE SWEETEST

Smith, Zack

BEAT OF A HEART
GOODBYE TO YOU
LOVE'S GOT A LINE ON YOU

Smotherman, Michael

TOMB OF THE UNKNOWN LOVE

TOO MANY TIMES

Smyth, Charles

OUR HOUSE

Smyth, Patty

BEAT OF A HEART

Snider, Charles

KID'S A DREAMER, THE

Snider, Martin

KID'S A DREAMER, THE

Snow, Hank

BLUEBIRD ISLAND
GOLDEN ROCKET
I'M MOVIN' ON
MUSIC MAKIN' MAMA FROM
 MEMPHIS
RHUMBA BOOGIE
UNWANTED SIGN UPON YOUR
 HEART

Snow, Leida

IN MY LONELINESS

Snow, Phoebe

POETRY MAN

Snow, Tom

AFTER ALL
ALL I NEED TO KNOW
ALL THE RIGHT MOVES
DEEPER THAN THE NIGHT
DON'T CALL IT LOVE
HE'S SO SHY
IF EVER YOU'RE IN MY ARMS
 AGAIN
I WILL BE THERE
LET'S HEAR IT FOR THE BOY
MAKE A MOVE ON ME
SO FAR SO GOOD
SOMEWHERE DOWN THE ROAD

YOU SHOULD HEAR HOW SHE TALKS ABOUT YOU

Snyder, David

HOW LONG HAS IT BEEN?

Snyder, Eddie

CAN I TRUST YOU?
GAMES THAT LOVERS PLAY
GIRL WITH THE GOLDEN BRAIDS, THE
LOVE THEME FROM "ROMEO AND JULIET" (A TIME FOR US)
MAKING MEMORIES
PEOPLE LIKE YOU
RUSTY BELLS
SPANISH EYES
STRANGERS IN THE NIGHT
TALK TO ME
WHAT WILL MY MARY SAY?
WHEEL OF HURT, THE
WHEN THE SNOW IS ON THE ROSES

Snyder, Ted

ALEXANDER AND HIS CLARINET
BEAUTIFUL EYES
DANCING FOOL
GHOST OF THE VIOLIN, THE
IF YOU CARED FOR ME
IN THE LAND OF HARMONY
IT WAS ONLY A SUN SHOWER
KISS ME, MY HONEY, KISS ME
MEET ME AT THE STATION, DEAR
MY WIFE'S GONE TO THE COUNTRY, HURRAH! HURRAH!
NEXT TO YOUR MOTHER, WHO DO YOU LOVE?
OH, HOW THAT GERMAN COULD LOVE
OH, THAT BEAUTIFUL RAG
PIANO MAN
SHEIK OF ARABY, THE
SHE WAS A DEAR LITTLE GIRL
SPANISH LOVE
THAT MYSTERIOUS RAG
THERE'S A GIRL IN HAVANA
THERE'S A GIRL IN THIS WORLD FOR EVERY BOY, AND A BOY FOR EVERY GIRL
UNDER THE MOON

WHO'S SORRY NOW?

Sobotka, Joe

LET LOVE COME BETWEEN US

Soehnel, Ray

HEART FULL OF LOVE, A (FOR A HANDFUL OF KISSES)

Soehnel, Zel

SHOW ME THE WAY BACK TO YOUR HEART

Sokole, Lucy Bender

I'M KEEPING COMPANY

Solley, Pete

TALKING IN YOUR SLEEP

Solman, Alfred

BIRD ON NELLIE'S HAT, THE
IF I HAD A THOUSAND LIVES TO LIVE
LINGER LONGER GIRL, THE
THERE'S A QUAKER DOWN IN QUAKER TOWN
WHEN THE BELL IN THE LIGHTHOUSE RINGS DING DONG
YOU'RE MORE THAN THE WORLD TO ME
YOU SPLASH ME AND I'LL SPLASH YOU

Soloway, Sy

LIPS OF WINE

Somerville, Jimmy

SMALLTOWN BOY

Sommer, Bert

AND SUDDENLY
WE'RE ALL PLAYING IN THE SAME BAND

Sommers, John Martin

THANK GOD I'M A COUNTRY BOY

Sondheim, Stephen

AGONY
ALL I NEED IS THE GIRL
AMERICA
ANOTHER HUNDRED PEOPLE
ANYONE CAN WHISTLE
BARCELONA
BEAUTIFUL
BEING ALIVE
BROADWAY BABY
CHILDREN AND ART
CHRYSANTHEMUM TEA
COMEDY TONIGHT
COOL
DO I HEAR A WALTZ?
EVER AFTER
EVERYBODY OUGHT TO HAVE A MAID
EVERYBODY SAYS DON'T
EVERYTHING'S COMING UP ROSES
GEE, OFFICER KRUPKE
GIRLS OF SUMMER, THE
GOOD THING GOING
GREEN FINCH AND LINNET BIRD
HILLS OF TOMORROW, THE
I FEEL PRETTY
I'M STILL HERE
IN BUDDY'S EYES
IT WOULD HAVE BEEN WONDERFUL
I'VE GOT YOU TO LEAN ON
JOHANNA
LADIES WHO LUNCH, THE
LET ME ENTERTAIN YOU
LITTLE LAMB
LOSING MY MIND
LOVE, I HEAR
LOVELY
MARIA
MARRY ME A LITTLE
MOVE ON
NO ONE IS ALONE
NOT A DAY GOES BY
NOT WHILE I'M AROUND
ONE HAND, ONE HEART
OUR TIME
PARADE IN TOWN, A
PRETTY WOMEN
PUTTING IT TOGETHER

RIGHT GIRL, THE
ROAD YOU DIDN'T TAKE, THE
SEE WHAT IT GETS YOU
SEND-IN THE CLOWNS
SIDE BY SIDE BY SIDE
SILLY PEOPLE
SMALL WORLD
SOME PEOPLE
SOMETHING'S COMING
SOMEWHERE
SUNDAY
TAKE THE MOMENT
THAT'LL SHOW HIM
THERE WON'T BE TRUMPETS
TOGETHER WHEREVER WE GO
TONIGHT
TOO MANY MORNINGS
WEEKEND IN THE COUNTRY, A
WITH SO LITTLE TO BE SURE OF
YOU COULD DRIVE A PERSON
   CRAZY
YOU'LL NEVER GET AWAY FROM ME

Sosenko, Anna

DARLING, JE VOUS AIME, BEAUCOUP
I'LL BE YOURS (J'ATTENDRAI)

Sosnik, Harry

LAZY RHAPSODY

Sothern, Hal

I DREAMED OF A HILLBILLY
   HEAVEN

Sour, Robert

BODY AND SOUL
I SEE A MILLION PEOPLE (BUT ALL I
   CAN SEE IS YOU)
WE COULD MAKE SUCH BEAUTIFUL
   MUSIC

Sourire, Soeur, O. P.

DOMINIQUE

Sousa, John Philip

EL CAPITAN
HANDS ACROSS THE SEA

KING COTTON
STARS AND STRIPES FOREVER
WASHINGTON POST MARCH

Souter, Joe

LET ME TELL YOU ABOUT LOVE

South, Jo

DON'T IT MAKE YOU WANT TO GO
   HOME?
DOWN IN THE BOONDOCKS
GAMES PEOPLE PLAY
HOW CAN I UNLOVE YOU
I KNEW YOU WHEN
I'VE GOT TO BE SOMEBODY
(I NEVER PROMISED YOU A) ROSE
   GARDEN
THESE ARE NOT MY PEOPLE
YO-YO

Souther, J. D.

BEST OF MY LOVE
FAITHLESS LOVE
HEARTACHE TONIGHT
HER TOWN TOO
JAMES DEAN
NEW KID IN TOWN
YOU'RE ONLY LONELY

Southerland, Loys

DON'T STAY AWAY
LET OLD MOTHER NATURE HAVE
   HER WAY
THROW YOUR LOVE MY WAY

Souvaine, Henry

DREAMING
NOBODY WANTS ME
WOULD'JA FOR A BIG RED APPLE?

Sovine, Red

GIDDYUP GO
LITTLE ROSA
MISSING YOU
TEDDY BEAR

Sowder, Kenny

LONELY STREET

Spaeth, Sigmund

CHANSONETTE
MY LITTLE NEST OF HEAVENLY
   BLUE

Spain, Irene

DEATH OF FLOYD COLLINS, THE

Span, Norman

MAN SMART, WOMAN SMARTER
TWISTING MATILDA

Spargo, Tony

AT THE JAZZ BAND BALL
BARNYARD BLUE
CLARINET MARMALADE
FIDGETY FEET
OSTRICH WALK
TIGER RAG

Sparks, Randy

GREEN, GREEN
SATURDAY NIGHT
TODAY

Speaks, Oley

MORNING
ON THE ROAD TO MANDALAY
SYLVIA
WHEN THE BOYS COME HOME

Spear, Eric

MEET MISTER CALLAGHAN

Spector, Abner

SMOKEY PLACES

Spector, Lona

SALLY, GO ROUND THE ROSES

Spector, Phil

BABY, I LOVE YOU
BE MY BABY
BLACK PEARL
CHAPEL OF LOVE
DA DOO RON RON (WHEN HE
    WALKED ME HOME)
FINE, FINE BOY, A
HUNG ON YOU
I CAN HEAR MUSIC
JUST ONCE IN MY LIFE
LITTLE BOY
RIVER DEEP—MOUNTAIN HIGH
SECOND HAND LOVE
SPANISH HARLEM
TAKE ME HOME TONIGHT
THEN HE KISSED ME
THERE'S NO OTHER (LIKE MY BABY)
TO KNOW HIM IS TO LOVE HIM
WAIT 'TIL MY BOBBY GETS HOME
WALKING IN THE RAIN
WHY DO LOVERS BREAK EACH
    OTHER'S HEARTS?
YOU'VE LOST THAT LOVIN' FEELIN'

Spence, Lew

MARRIAGE-GO-ROUND, THE
NICE 'N' EASY
THAT FACE

Spence, Tim

CIGARETTES, WHUSKY AND WILD,
    WILD WOMEN

Spencer, Carl

LET HER DANCE

Spencer, Casey

I'M A HAPPY MAN

Spencer, Glenn

ROSES

Spencer, Herbert

LOST APRIL
UNDERNEATH THE STARS

Spencer, Judy

SOFT SUMMER BREEZE

Spencer, Otis

BROADWAY ROSE

Spencer, Richard

COLOR HIM FATHER

Spencer, Robert

MY BOY LOLLIPOP

Spencer, Sean

GIRL, YOU KNOW IT'S TRUE

Spencer, Tim

BLUE PRAIRIE
CARELESS KISSES
ROOM FULL OF ROSES
ROSES
TIMBER TRAIL, THE

Spice, Ian

HOW CAN I FALL

Spickard, Bob

PIPELINE

Spiedel, Charles

DOWN BY THE SILVERY RIO
    GRANDE

Spielman, Fred

GO TO SLEEP, GO TO SLEEP, GO TO
    SLEEP
IT ONLY HURTS FOR A LITTLE
    WHILE
LONGEST WALK, THE
ONE FINGER MELODY
PAPER ROSES
SHEPHERD SERENADE
YAWNING SONG, THE

Spier, Larry

MEMORY LANE
PUT YOUR LITTLE FOOT RIGHT OUT
WAS IT A DREAM?

Spikes, Benjamin F.

SOMEDAY SWEETHEART
WOLVERINE BLUES

Spikes, John C.

SOMEDAY SWEETHEART
WOLVERINE BLUES

Spilton, Alan

LOVER COME BACK

Spina, Harold

ANNIE DOESN'T LIVE HERE
    ANYMORE
BEAT OF MY HEART, THE
BE MINE
GRASS IS GETTING GREENER ALL
    THE TIME, THE
I COULD USE A DREAM
IRRESISTIBLE
I STILL LOVE TO KISS YOU
    GOODNIGHT
IT'S DARK ON OBSERVATORY HILL
IT'S SO NICE TO HAVE A MAN
    AROUND THE HOUSE
I'VE GOT A WARM SPOT IN MY
    HEART FOR YOU
LAZY SUMMER NIGHT
LOVE DROPPED IN FOR TEA
MY VERY GOOD FRIEND, THE
    MILKMAN
NOW YOU'VE GOT ME DOING IT
ONCE
SHADOWS ON THE SWANEE
VELVET GLOVE, THE
WOULD I LOVE YOU (LOVE YOU,
    LOVE YOU)
YOU'RE NOT THE ONLY OYSTER IN
    THE STEW
YOU'RE SO DARN CHARMING

Spinks, John

ALL THE LOVE IN THE WORLD
YOUR LOVE

Spiro, Harold

LITTLE GAMES

Spirt, John

MARTIAN HOP

Spitalny, Maurice

ANGELS WITH DIRTY FACES
START THE DAY RIGHT

Spitalny, Phil

SAVE THE LAST DANCE FOR ME

Spivey, William

OPERATOR

Spolan, Gloria

HYPNOTIZED

Spoliansky, Mischa

HOUR OF PARTING, THE
MELBA WALTZ, THE

Sporn, Murray

JAVA

Spotswood, Willie

HOLD TIGHT—HOLD TIGHT (WANT
    SOME SEA FOOD, MAMA)

Spotti, Pino

I WANT TO BE WANTED

Sprague, A. W.

STEIN SONG (UNIVERSITY OF
    MAINE)

Sprigato, Sylvester

IT ISN'T FAIR

Spriggs, Michael

TWENTY YEARS AGO

Springer, George E.

LIES

Springer, Joan

LOVIN' SPREE

Springer, Phil

ALL CRIED OUT
HOW LITTLE WE KNOW (HOW
    LITTLE IT MATTERS)
LOVIN' SPREE
MOONLIGHT GAMBLER
SANTA BABY
SWEET WILLIAM

Springer, Tony

SANTA BABY

Springfield, Rick

AFFAIR OF THE HEART
BOP 'TIL YOU DROP
BRUCE
DON'T TALK TO STRANGERS
DON'T WALK AWAY
HUMAN TOUCH
JESSIE'S GIRL
LOVE IS ALRIGHT TONITE
LOVE SOMEBODY
SOULS
SPEAK TO THE SKY

Springfield, Tom

GEORGY GIRL
I'LL NEVER FIND ANOTHER YOU
WORLD OF OUR OWN, A

Springsteen, Bruce

BADLANDS

BECAUSE THE NIGHT
BLINDED BY THE LIGHT
BORN IN THE U.S.A.
BORN TO RUN
BRILLIANT DISGUISE
COVER ME
DANCING IN THE DARK
FADE AWAY
FIRE
GLORY DAYS
GROWIN' UP
HUNGRY HEART
I'M GOIN' DOWN
I'M ON FIRE
LIGHT OF DAY
MY HOMETOWN
ONE STEP UP
OUT OF WORK
PINK CADILLAC
PROVE IT ALL NIGHT
RIVER, THE
SPARE PARTS
SPIRIT IN THE NIGHT
TENTH AVENUE FREEZE-OUT
THIS LITTLE GIRL
TUNNEL OF LOVE

Squier, Billy

EVERYBODY WANTS YOU
IN THE DARK
ROCK ME TONITE
STROKE, THE

Squire, Chris

AND YOU AND I
OWNER OF A LONELY HEART

Squire, W. H.

THREE FOR JACK

Squires, Harry D.

CAROLINA ROLLING STONE

Stacey, Gladys

CRYING MY HEART OUT OVER YOU

Staedtler, Darrell

FIRE I CAN'T PUT OUT, A

Stafford, Jim

MY GIRL BILL
SPIDERS AND SNAKES
TURN LOOSE OF MY LEG
WILDWOOD WEED
YOUR BULLDOG DRINKS
   CHAMPAGNE

Stafford, Joseph, Jr.

MY PLEDGE OF LOVE

Stahl, Felix

MANY TIMES

Stahl, Tim

WHITE HORSE

Stallman, Lou

DON'T PITY ME
EVERYBODY'S GOT THE RIGHT TO
   LOVE
IT'S GONNA TAKE A MIRACLE
I'VE COME OF AGE
ROUND AND ROUND
TREASURE OF LOVE
YOGI

Stallone, Frank

FAR FROM OVER

Stallworth, Lloyd

LOST SOMEONE

Stamford, John J.

MACNAMARA'S BAND

Stammers, Frank

ASK THE STARS
I'LL REMEMBER YOU

Stamper, Dave

DADDY HAS A SWEETHEART (AND
   MOTHER IS HER NAME)
DANCE AWAY THE NIGHT
GARDEN OF MY DREAMS
LONELY LITTLE MELODY
MY RAMBLER ROSE
'NEATH THE SOUTH SEA MOON
NIJINSKY
SALLY, WON'T YOU COME BACK
SWEET SIXTEEN
THROW ME A KISS
TULIP TIME

Standley, Johnny

IT'S IN THE BOOK

Stanford, Arnold

I CAN'T SEE FOR LOOKIN'

Stanford, Dick

JOHNNY CONCHO THEME (WAIT FOR
   ME)

Stanford, Dok

HEY! MISTER COTTON-PICKER

Stange, Stanislaus

LETTER SONG, THE
MY HERO
MY OWN UNITED STATES
SWEET THOUGHTS OF HOME

Stanley, Eddie Y.

BOTCH-A-ME (BA-BA-BACIAMI
   PICCINA)

Stanley, Edwin

THAT NAUGHTY WALTZ

Stanley, Hal

HALF A PHOTOGRAPH
MAN UPSTAIRS, THE

Stanley, Ian

EVERYBODY WANTS TO RULE THE
   WORLD
SHOUT

Stanley, Jack

THEY NEEDED A SONG BIRD IN
   HEAVEN (SO GOD TOOK CARUSO
   AWAY)

Stanley, Paul

BETH
DETROIT ROCK CITY
HARD LUCK WOMAN
I WAS MADE FOR LOVIN' YOU
LICK IT UP
WORLD WITHOUT HEROES, A

Stanley, Ralph

JUNE BROUGHT THE ROSES

Stanley, Ray

GLENDORA

Stanshall, Vivian

ARC OF A DIVER

Stanton, Albert

ABILENE
LION SLEEPS TONIGHT, THE

Stanton, Arnold

ROVING KIND, THE

Stanton, Frank

JUST A-WEARYIN' FOR YOU
MIGHTY LAK' A ROSE

Stanton, Frank H.

ROMANTIC GUY, I, A

Stanton, Frank L.

MORNING

Stanton, Irene

PRIDE
UNLOVED, UNWANTED

Stanziale, Peggy

DRESS YOU UP

Stapp, Jack

CHATTANOOGIE SHOE SHINE BOY

Starcher, Buddy

HISTORY REPEATS ITSELF

Starkey, Richard

BACK OFF BOOGALOO
IT DON'T COME EASY

Starks, John

PAYBACK, THE

Starling, Jade

CATCH ME (I'M FALLING)

Starns, Neva

MARRIED BY THE BIBLE, DIVORCED
  BY THE LAW

Starr, Edwin

TWENTY-FIVE MILES

Starr, Hattie

LITTLE ALABAMA COON

Starr, Maurice

CANDY GIRL
HANGIN' TOUGH
I'LL BE LOVING YOU (FOREVER)

Starr, Randy

ADAM AND EVIL
ALMOST IN LOVE
CARNY TOWN
COULD I FALL IN LOVE?
DATIN'
ENCHANTED SEA, THE
FATE
GIRL I NEVER LOVED, THE
I KNOW WHERE I'M GOIN'
I'VE GOT NEWS FOR YOU
KISSIN' COUSINS
LOOK OUT, BROADWAY
OLD MACDONALD
TELL ANOTHER LIE
WHO NEEDS MONEY?

Starr, Ringo

OH MY MY
PHOTOGRAPH

Statler, Darrell

IT'S ANOTHER WORLD

Stead, Arthur

GOONIES 'R' GOOD ENOUGH, THE

Steagall, Russell Don

HERE WE GO AGAIN

Steals, Melvin

COULD IT BE I'M FALLING IN LOVE?

Steals, Mervin

COULD IT BE I'M FALLING IN LOVE?

Steele, David

GOOD THING
SHE DRIVES ME CRAZY

Steele, Larry

IF I'D BEEN THE ONE

Steele, Lois

IVORY TOWER
WANTED

Steele, Porter

HIGH SOCIETY

Steele, Ted

SMOKE DREAMS

Stegall, Keith

HURRICANE
LONELY NIGHTS
SEXY EYES
WE'RE IN THIS LOVE TOGETHER

Stegmeyer, Bill

SYMPHONY FOR SUSAN, A

Stein, Chris

DREAMING
HARDEST PART, THE
HEART OF GLASS
RAPTURE

Stein, Lou

SOFT SANDS

Stein, Murray

BABY (YOU'VE GOT WHAT IT TAKES)

Stein, William

ORANGE COLORED SKY
WAVE TO ME MY LADY

Steinbachek, Larry

SMALLTOWN BOY

Steinberg, Billy

ALONE
ETERNAL FLAME
HOW DO I MAKE YOU

LIKE A VIRGIN
SO EMOTIONAL
TRUE COLORS

Steinberg, Lewis

GREEN ONIONS

Steinberg, Samuel

JOSEPH! JOSEPH!

Steiner, Howard

DON'T BE A BABY, BABY

Steiner, Jacqueline

M.T.A., THE

Steiner, Max

ANGEL
COME NEXT SPRING
HONEY-BABE
IT CAN'T BE WRONG
MY OWN TRUE LOVE (TARA'S
    THEME)
SOMEDAY I'LL MEET YOU AGAIN
TARA'S THEME
THEME FROM "A SUMMER PLACE"
THEME FROM "THE DARK AT THE
    TOP OF THE STAIRS"
TOMORROW IS FOREVER

Steininger, Franz

I RAISED MY HAT
MARCHING ALONG TOGETHER

Steinman, Jim

HOLDING OUT FOR A HERO
I'M GONNA LOVE HER FOR THE
    BOTH OF US
LEFT IN THE DARK
MAKING LOVE OUT OF NOTHING AT
    ALL
PARADISE BY THE DASHBOARD
    LIGHT
READ 'EM AND WEEP
TONIGHT IS WHAT IT MEANS TO BE
    YOUNG

TOTAL ECLIPSE OF THE HEART
TWO OUT OF THREE AIN'T BAD
YOU TOOK THE WORDS RIGHT OUT
    OF MY MOUTH

Stellman, Marcel

I WILL LIVE MY LIFE FOR YOU
JOHNNY (IS THE BOY FOR ME)

Stephen, S.

NEW FOOL AT AN OLD GAME

Stephens, Geoff

DADDY, DON'T YOU WALK SO FAST
DAUGHTER OF DARKNESS
DOCTOR'S ORDERS
IT'S LIKE WE NEVER SAID
    GOODBYE
SMILE A LITTLE SMILE FOR ME
WINCHESTER CATHEDRAL

Stephens, Richard

WHEELS

Stephenson, Vern

BLUEST EYES IN TEXAS
WHEN I DREAM

Stephenson, Willie

I DO

Stept, Sam H.

ALL MY LIFE
BREAKIN' IN A PAIR OF SHOES
COMES LOVE
CONGRATULATIONS
DON'T SIT UNDER THE APPLE TREE
    (WITH ANYONE ELSE BUT ME)
DO SOMETHING
GOOD LITTLE, BAD LITTLE YOU
I CAME HERE TO TALK FOR JOE
I CAN'T AFFORD TO DREAM
I FALL IN LOVE WITH YOU EV'RY
    DAY
I'LL ALWAYS BE IN LOVE WITH YOU
I'M PAINTING THE TOWN RED

IT SEEMS LIKE OLD TIMES
I'VE HAD THIS FEELING BEFORE
I WANT YOU FOR CHRISTMAS
LAUGHING IRISH EYES
LET'S MAKE MEMORIES TONIGHT
MY FIRST IMPRESSION OF YOU
PLEASE DON'T TALK ABOUT ME
    WHEN I'M GONE
SWEET HEARTACHE
SWINGY LITTLE THING
THAT'S MY WEAKNESS NOW
THIS IS WORTH FIGHTING FOR
TINY LITTLE FINGERPRINTS
WE'VE COME A LONG WAY
    TOGETHER
WHEN THEY ASK ABOUT YOU

Sterling, Andrew B.

ALEXANDER, DON'T YOU LOVE
    YOUR BABY NO MORE?
ALL ABOARD FOR BLANKET BAY
ALL ABOARD FOR DREAMLAND
AMERICA, HERE'S MY BOY
BYE BYE DEARIE
CAN YOU TAME WILD WIMMEN?
CLOSE TO MY HEART
DARLING SUE
DOWN WHERE THE COTTON
    BLOSSOMS GROW
EYES OF BLUES, EYES OF BROWN
GOODBYE, BOYS
GOOD-BYE, ELIZA JANE
HANNAH, WON'T YOU OPEN THAT
    DOOR?
IN THE EVENING BY THE
    MOONLIGHT
I WONDER IF SHE'S WAITING
JUST A LITTLE LOVIN'
KEEP YOUR SKIRTS DOWN, MARY
    ANN
KNOCK WOOD
LAST NIGHT WAS THE END OF THE
    WORLD
LITTLE BUNCH OF SHAMROCKS, A
MEET ME IN ST. LOUIS, LOUIS
MY OLD NEW HAMPSHIRE HOME
ON A SUNDAY AFTERNOON
ON THE OLD FALL RIVER LINE
STRIKE UP THE BAND, HERE COMES
    A SAILOR
TAKE ME BACK TO NEW YORK
    TOWN

THEY'RE ALL SWEETIES
UNDER THE ANHEUSER BUSH
UNDER THE YUM-YUM TREE
WAIT TILL THE SUN SHINES, NELLIE
WE'RE GOING OVER
WHAT YOU GOIN' TO DO WHEN THE
    RENT COMES ROUND? (OR,
    RUFUS RASTUS JOHNSON BROWN)
WHEN KATE AND I WERE COMIN'
    THRO' THE RYE
WHEN MY BABY SMILES AT ME
WHERE THE MORNING GLORIES
    TWINE AROUND THE DOOR
WHERE THE SWEET MAGNOLIAS
    GROW
YOU'LL ALWAYS BE THE SAME
    SWEET GIRL

Sterling, Costen

EYES OF BLUE, EYES OF BROWN

Stern, Henry R.

DOWN AT THE HUSKIN' BEE

Stern, Jack

I WAS LUCKY
RHYTHM OF THE RAIN
TOO BEAUTIFUL FOR WORDS

Stern, Joseph W.

HIS LAST THOUGHTS WERE OF YOU
LITTLE LOST CHILD, THE
MOTHER WAS A LADY (OR, IF JACK
    WERE ONLY HERE)
NO ONE EVER LOVED YOU MORE
    THAN I

Stern, Toni

IT'S GOING TO TAKE SOME TIME
IT'S TOO LATE
SWEET SEASONS

Sternberg, Liam

WALK LIKE AN EGYPTIAN

Stevens, Cat

FIRST CUT IS THE DEEPEST, THE
HERE COMES MY BABY
MOON SHADOW
MORNING HAS BROKEN
OH VERY YOUNG
PEACE TRAIN
READY
SITTING
WILD WORLD

Stevens, Even

DRIVIN' MY LIFE AWAY
GONE TOO FAR
I JUST WANT TO LOVE YOU
I LOVE A RAINY NIGHT
LOVIN' ONLY ME
LOVE WILL TURN YOU AROUND
SOMEONE COULD LOSE A HEART
    TONIGHT
STEP BY STEP
SUSPICIONS
WARNING SIGN
WHEN YOU'RE IN LOVE WITH A
    BEAUTIFUL WOMAN

Stevens, Geoff

THERE'S A KIND OF HUSH (ALL
    OVER THE WORLD)

Stevens, Hunt

LASTING LOVE

Stevens, Jay

ROCKY

Stevens, Leith

JULIE

Stevens, Leonard

I FAW DOWN AN' GO BOOM!

Stevens, M.

OASIS

Stevens, Mark

DA'BUTT

Stevens, Mort

HAWAII FIVE-O

Stevens, Ray

AHAB THE ARAB
CAN'T STOP DANCIN'
EVERYTHING IS BEAUTIFUL
GITARZAN
JEREMIAH PEABODY'S
    POLYUNSATURATED QUICK
    DISSOLVING FAST ACTING
    PLEASANT TASTING GREEN AND
    PURPLE PILLS
MR. BUSINESSMAN
SANTA CLAUS IS WATCHING YOU
STREAK, THE

Stevens, Steve

EYES WITHOUT A FACE
REBEL YELL

Stevenson, Bobby

FOR MY GOOD FORTUNE
HEY, LITTLE GIRL
PLEASE SAY YOU'RE FOOLIN'
SO MANY WAYS
START MOVIN' (IN MY DIRECTION)

Stevenson, B. W.

MY MARIA

Stevenson, John

ROCK AND ROLL HEAVEN

Stevenson, William

ASK THE LONELY
BEECHWOOD 4-5789
CAN YOU JERK LIKE ME
DANCING IN THE STREET
DANGER HEARTBREAK DEAD
    AHEAD
DEVIL WITH THE BLUE DRESS ON

I'LL ALWAYS LOVE YOU
I'LL KEEP HOLDING ON
IT SHOULD HAVE BEEN ME
IT TAKES TWO
JAMIE
MY BABY LOVES ME
NEEDLE IN A HAYSTACK
NOTHING'S TOO GOOD FOR MY
    BABY
PLAYBOY
PRIDE AND JOY
STUBBORN KIND OF FELLOW
WHAT AM I GOING TO DO WITHOUT
    YOUR LOVE?
WILD ONE
YOU'VE BEEN IN LOVE TOO LONG

Stevenson, W. S.

AM I THAT EASY TO FORGET?
HOT ROD LINCOLN
LET ME BE THE ONE
LONELY STREET
RELEASE ME
STOP THE WORLD (AND LET ME OFF)
THAT'S WHEN I SEE THE BLUES (IN
    YOUR PRETTY BROWN EYES)
THERE SHE GOES
WHAT'S HE DOIN' IN MY WORLD?

Stewart, Al

COME CLOSER TO ME
DON'T TELEPHONE, DON'T
    TELEGRAPH, TELL A WOMAN
ON THE BORDER
SONG ON THE RADIO
TIME PASSAGES
YEAR OF THE CAT

Stewart, Billy

I DO LOVE YOU
SITTING IN THE PARK

Stewart, C.

CRYIN', PRAYIN', WISHIN', WAITIN'

Stewart, Dave

DON'T COME AROUND HERE NO
    MORE

HERE COMES THE RAIN AGAIN
LET'S WORK
LOVE IS A STRANGER
MISSIONARY MAN
SISTERS ARE DOIN' IT FOR
    THEMSELVES
SWEET DREAMS (ARE MADE OF
    THIS)
WHO'S THAT GIRL?
WOULD I LIE TO YOU?

Stewart, Dorothy

GIVE ME YOUR HAND
NOW IS THE HOUR (MAORI
    FAREWELL SONG)

Stewart, Eric

ART FOR ART'S SAKE
DREADLOCK HOLIDAY
I'M MANDY, FLY ME
I'M NOT IN LOVE
PEOPLE IN LOVE
THINGS WE DO FOR LOVE, THE

Stewart, Harris

LONELY NIGHTS

Stewart, Harry

I YUST GO NUTS AT CHRISTMAS

Stewart, Henry

SOLDIER'S LAST LETTER

Stewart, John

DAYDREAM BELIEVER
GOLD
RUNAWAY TRAIN

Stewart, Larry

PLEASE PLAY OUR SONG (MISTER
    RECORD MAN)

Stewart, Michael

COLORS OF MY LIFE, THE
HEY THERE, GOOD TIMES

I LOVE MY WIFE
LOVE MAKES SUCH FOOLS OF US
    ALL

Stewart, Redd

SLOW POKE
TENNESSEE TANGO
TENNESSEE WALTZ
WHICH ONE IS TO BLAME?
YOU BELONG TO ME

Stewart, Rex

BOY MEETS HORN

Stewart, Rod

AIN'T LOVE A BITCH
BABY JANE
DO YA THINK I'M SEXY?
DO YOU THINK I'M DISCO?
HOT LEGS
I WAS ONLY JOKING
INFATUATION
KILLING OF GEORGIE, THE
MAGGIE MAY
PASSION
STAY WITH ME
TONIGHT I'M YOURS (DON'T HURT
    ME)
TONIGHT'S THE NIGHT (GONNA BE
    ALRIGHT)
YOUNG TURKS
YOU'RE IN LOVE WITH SOMEONE
YOU WEAR IT WELL

Stewart, Sandy

IF ANYONE FAILS
SEVEN WONDERS

Stewart, Slam

FLAT FOOT FLOOGIE, THE

Stewart, Sly

C'MON AND SWIM

Stewart, Steven

SMOKE FROM A DISTANT FIRE

Stewart, Sylvester

DANCE TO THE MUSIC
EVERYBODY IS A STAR
EVERYDAY PEOPLE
FAMILY AFFAIR
HOT FUN IN THE SUMMERTIME
IF YOU WANT ME TO STAY
I WANT TO TAKE YOU HIGHER
M'LADY
RUNNIN' AWAY
SMILIN'
STAND!
THANK YOU (FALETTINME BE MICE
  ELF AGIN)
TIME FOR LIVIN' (TIME FOR GIVIN')

Stewart, Wynn

SING A SAD SONG
WISHFUL THINKING
YOU TOOK HER OFF MY HANDS
  (NOW PLEASE TAKE HER OFF MY
  MIND)

St. Helier, Ivy

COAL BLACK MAMMY

Stidham, Arbee

MY HEART BELONGS TO YOU

Stieger, Jimmy

LOOKING AT THE WORLD THROUGH
  ROSE COLORED GLASSES

Stilgoe, Richard

ALL I ASK OF YOU
LIGHT AT THE END OF THE TUNNEL
MUSIC OF THE NIGHT, THE
PHANTOM OF THE OPERA, THE
STARLIGHT EXPRESS

Stillman, Al

AFTERGLOW
AND THAT REMINDS ME (A.K.A. MY
  HEART REMINDS ME)
BLESS 'EM ALL
BREEZE AND I, THE

CAN YOU FIND IT IN YOUR HEART
CHANCES ARE
COCKEYED MAYOR OF KAUNAKAKAI
DON'CHA GO 'WAY MAD
DON'T YOU FORGET IT
ENCHANTED ISLAND
EVERY STEP OF THE WAY
GOOD-BYE JONAH
HAPPY ANNIVERSARY
HOME FOR THE HOLIDAYS
I BELIEVE
IF DREAMS COME TRUE
IN MY LITTLE RED BOOK
IN THE MIDDLE OF MAY
IT MUST HAVE BEEN A DREAM
IT'S NOT FOR ME TO SAY
I WANT MY MAMA (A.K.A. MAMA YO
  QUIERO)
JUKE BOX SATURDAY NIGHT
KING OF SWING
LAMP OF MEMORY, THE
LITTLE BOY, THE
LITTLE JACK FROST GET LOST
MANY DREAMS AGO
MOMENTS TO REMEMBER
MY ONE AND ONLY HEART
NO, NOT MUCH
OLD FLAME NEVER DIES, AN
ONE, TWO, THREE, KICK
ROOM WITH A VIEW, A
SAY "SI SI"
TEACHER, TEACHER
TELL ME THAT YOU LOVE ME
THERE'S ONLY ONE OF YOU
WAY OF LOVE, THE
WHO DO YOU KNOW IN HEAVEN
  (THAT MADE YOU THE ANGEL
  YOU ARE)?
WHO NEEDS YOU?
WITH THEE I SWING
YOU ALONE (SOLO TU)
YOU AND I KNOW

Stills, Stephen

CHANGE PARTNERS
FOR WHAT IT'S WORTH (STOP, HEY
  WHAT'S THAT SOUND)
LOVE THE ONE YOU'RE WITH
ROCK 'N' ROLL WOMAN
SIT YOURSELF DOWN
SOUTHERN CROSS

Sting

BE STILL MY BEATING HEART
DON'T STAND SO CLOSE TO ME
EVERY BREATH YOU TAKE
EVERY LITTLE THING SHE DOES IS
  MAGIC
FORTRESS AROUND YOUR HEART
IF YOU LOVE SOMEBODY SET THEM
  FREE
LOVE IS THE SEVENTH WAVE
MONEY FOR NOTHING
RUSSIANS
SPIRITS IN THE MATERIAL
  WORLD
SYNCHRONICITY II
WE'LL BE TOGETHER
WRAPPED AROUND YOUR FINGER

Stipe, Michael

FALL ON ME
IT'S THE END OF THE WORLD AS
  WE KNOW IT (AND I FEEL FINE)
ONE I LOVE, THE
RADIO FREE EUROPE
ROMANCE
SOUTH CENTRAL RAIN (I'M SORRY)

Stites, Gary

LONELY FOR YOU

Stitzel, Mel

DOODLE DOO DOO
MAKE LOVE TO ME
TIN ROOF BLUES

St. John

SMOOTH OPERATOR

St. John, Dick

YELLOW BALLOON, THE
YOUNG AND IN LOVE

St. Lewis, Kenny

BOOGIE FEVER
HEAVEN MUST BE MISSING AN
  ANGEL

St. Lewis, Kenny

HOT LINE
WHODUNIT

St. Louis, Louis

SANDY

St. Nicholas, Nick

IT'S NEVER TOO LATE

Stock, Larry

BLUEBERRY HILL
DID YOU EVER GET THAT FEELING
  IN THE MOONLIGHT?
IN A LITTLE DUTCH KINDERGARTEN
MORNINGSIDE OF THE MOUNTAIN,
  THE
TELL ME A STORY
UMBRELLA MAN, THE
YOU'RE NOBODY TILL SOMEBODY
  LOVES YOU
YOU WON'T BE SATISFIED (UNTIL
  YOU BREAK MY HEART)

Stock, Mike

I HEARD A RUMOR
I SHOULD BE SO LUCKY
NEVER GONNA GIVE YOU UP
TOGETHER FOREVER

Stoddard, George E.

WAITING

Stoddard, Harry

I GET THE BLUES WHEN IT RAINS

Stokes, Byron D.

SWEETHEART OF SIGMA CHI, THE

Stokes, Michael

GLORIA
IT'S YOU THAT I NEED
MAGIC MAN

Stole, J. W.

I WILL FOLLOW HIM

Stoll, George

LOVE ON A GREYHOUND BUS
YOUNG MAN WITH A HORN, THE

Stoller, Mike

ALONG CAME JONES
(YOU'RE SO SQUARE) BABY, I DON'T
  CARE
BERNIE'S TUNE
BLACK DENIM TROUSERS AND
  MOTORCYCLE BOOTS
BOSSA NOVA BABY
CHARLIE BROWN
DON'T
DOWN IN MEXICO
DRIP DROP
D. W. WASHBURN
GIRLS I NEVER KISSED, THE
HOUND DOG
I (WHO HAVE NOTHING)
I KEEP FORGETTIN' (EVERY TIME
  YOU'RE NEAR)
I'LL BE THERE
I'M A WOMAN
I NEED YOUR LOVIN' (BAZOOM)
IS THAT ALL THERE IS?
I WANNA DO MORE
JAILHOUSE ROCK
JUST TELL HER JIM SAID HELLO
KANSAS CITY
LOVE ME
LOVE POTION NUMBER NINE
LOVING YOU
LUCKY LIPS
MAN WHO ROBBED THE BANK AT
  SANTA FE, THE
ON BROADWAY
ONLY IN AMERICA
POISON IVY
RUBY BABY
SEARCHIN'
(WHEN SHE NEEDS GOOD LOVIN')
  SHE COMES TO ME
SHE'S NOT YOU
STAND BY ME
THERE GOES MY BABY
TREAT ME NICE

YAKETY YAK
YOUNG BLOOD

Stoloff, Morris

TO LOVE AGAIN

Stolz, Robert

DAWN
TELL ME WHY YOU SMILE, MONA
  LISA
TWO HEARTS IN THREE-QUARTER
  TIME
WALTZING IN THE CLOUDS

Stone, Bob

ARE YOU HAPPY, BABY
BEYOND THE VALLEY OF THE
  DOLLS

Stone, Cliffie

ANTICIPATION BLUES
DIVORCE ME C.O.D.
NO VACANCY
SMOKEY MOUNTAIN BOOGIE
SO ROUND, SO FIRM, SO FULLY
  PACKED
STEEL GUITAR RAG
SWEET TEMPTATION
THREE TIMES SEVEN

Stone, Gregory

LET'S DANCE

Stone, Harry

CHATTANOOGIE SHOE SHINE BOY

Stone, Helen

MEXICALI ROSE

Stone, Henry

TWO HEARTS

Stone, Jesse

COLE SLAW

DON'T LET GO
GOOD LOVIN'
IDAHO
MONEY HONEY
SORGHUM SWITCH

Stone, Joseph

I JUST DON'T KNOW

Stone, Robert

GYPSYS

Stone, Wilson

WAR AND PEACE

Stoner, Mickey

I GUESS I'LL HAVE TO DREAM THE
REST
IT'S MAKE BELIEVE BALLROOM
TIME

Stookey, Paul

I DIG ROCK AND ROLL MUSIC
MAN OF CONSTANT SORROW
WEDDING SONG (THERE IS LOVE)

Storball, Donald

COOL JERK

Storch, Eberhard

AUF WIEDERSEH'N, SWEETHEART

Stordahl, Axel

DAY BY DAY
I SHOULD CARE
NEIANI

Storie, Carl

DANCIN' SHOES

Story, Carl

I OVERLOOKED AN ORCHID

Stothart, Herbert

BAMBALINA
CHARMING
COSSACK LOVE SONG (DON'T
FORGET ME)
CUBAN LOVE SONG
DAWN
DONKEY SERENADE
FLANNEL PETTICOAT GAL
HEADIN' HOME
HOW STRANGE?
IF HE CARED
I WANNA BE LOVED BY YOU
LONELY
MOUNTIES, THE (A.K.A. SONG OF
THE MOUNTIES)
RIDE, COSSACK, RIDE
ROGUE SONG, THE
SHEPHERD'S SERENADE, THE
SONG OF THE FLAME
SONG OF THE SHIRT, THE
SWEETHEART DARLIN'
TOODLE-OO
TRAMPS AT SEA
VODKA
WHEN I'M LOOKING AT YOU
WILDFLOWER

Stott, Harold

CHIRPY CHIRPY CHEEP CHEEP

Stough, Tommy

WORLD IS ROUND, THE

Stovall, Mary

FIRST DATE, FIRST KISS, FIRST
LOVE

Stover, Elgie

BELLS, THE

Stover, G. H.

ON THE BEACH AT WAIKIKI

Strachey, Jack

NO ORCHIDS FOR MY LADY

THESE FOOLISH THINGS (REMIND
ME OF YOU)

Straight, Charlie

FUNNY, DEAR, WHAT LOVE CAN DO
PRETTY LIPS

Straigis, Roy

SO MUCH IN LOVE

Strain, Samuel

RUBBER BISCUIT

Strait, George

IF YOU AIN'T LOVIN' (YOU AIN'T
LIVIN')

Strandlund, Bob

ALREADY GONE

Strandlund, Robb

I CAN TELL BY THE WAY YOU
DANCE (YOU'RE GONNA LOVE ME
TONIGHT)

Strange, Billy

CLEAN UP YOUR OWN BACK YARD
MEMORIES

Strange, William E.

LIMBO ROCK

Stranks, Alan

NO ORCHIDS FOR MY LADY

Strasser, Eugene

I'M SO MISERABLE WITHOUT YOU

Straus, Oscar

LETTER SONG, THE
LOVE'S ROUNDELAY
MY HERO

ONE MORE HOUR OF LOVE
SWEETEST MAID OF ALL
WE WILL ALWAYS BE SWEETHEARTS
WHILE HEARTS ARE SINGING

Strauss, Arthur

ST. THERESE OF THE ROSES

Strayhorn, Billy

CHELSEA BRIDGE
EIGHTH VEIL, THE
I'M CHECKING OUT—GO'OM BYE
JUST A-SITTIN' AND A-ROCKIN'
LUSH LIFE
SATIN DOLL
TAKE THE "A" TRAIN

Street, R.

I'M ON FIRE

Streisand, Barbra

EVERGREEN (LOVE THEME FROM "A
    STAR IS BORN")

Striano, Alfred

THERE'S A MOON OUT TONIGHT

Strickland, Eric

CAN U READ MY LIPS

Strickland, J. K.

LOVE SHACK
PRIVATE IDAHO

Strickland, Lily

MAH LINDY LOU

Stride, Harry

BECAUSE OF ONCE UPON A TIME
BLESS YOUR HEART
HAPPIEST MOMENTS OF LIFE, THE
PLEASE HANDLE WITH CARE

Strike, Liza

SUMMER NIGHTS

Stroll, Jon

SWEET CREAM LADIES, FORWARD
    MARCH

Stromberg, John

COME BACK, MY HONEY BOY, TO
    ME
COME DOWN MA' EVENIN' STAR
KISS ME, HONEY, DO
MA BLUSHIN' ROSIE
MY BEST GIRL'S A NEW YORKER
    (CORKER)

Strong, Barrett

BALL OF CONFUSION (THAT'S WHAT
    THE WORLD IS TODAY)
CLOUD NINE
DON'T LET HIM TAKE YOUR LOVE
    FROM ME
DON'T LET THE JONESES GET YOU
    DOWN
END OF OUR ROAD, THE
FRIENDSHIP TRAIN
GONNA GIVE HER ALL THE LOVE
    I'VE GOT
I CAN'T GET NEXT TO YOU
I COULD NEVER LOVE ANOTHER
    (AFTER LOVING YOU)
I HEARD IT THROUGH THE
    GRAPEVINE
I WISH IT WOULD RAIN
JAMIE
JUST MY IMAGINATION (RUNNING
    AWAY WITH ME)
PAPA WAS A ROLLIN' STONE
PLEASE RETURN YOUR LOVE TO ME
PSYCHEDELIC SHACK
RUN AWAY CHILD, RUNNING WILD
STAY IN MY CORNER
SUPERSTAR (REMEMBER HOW YOU
    GOT WHERE YOU ARE)
THAT'S THE WAY LOVE IS
TOO BUSY THINKING ABOUT MY
    BABY
UNDISPUTED TRUTH, THE
USE YOUR HEAD

WAR

Strother, Cynthia

BERMUDA

Strother, Eugene R.

BERMUDA

Strouse, Charles

BABY, TALK TO ME
BEFORE THE PARADE PASSES BY
BORN TOO LATE
BRAND NEW WORLD
BYE BYE BIRDIE
CAN'T YOU SEE IT?
DON'T FORGET 127TH STREET
EASY STREET
GOLDEN BOY
HONESTLY SINCERE
HOW LOVELY TO BE A WOMAN
HOW'M I DOIN'
HYMN FOR A SUNDAY EVENING
I DON'T NEED ANYTHING BUT YOU
I'M FASCINATING
IT'S THE HARD KNOCK LIFE
I'VE JUST SEEN HER (AS NOBODY
    ELSE HAS SEEN HER)
I WANT TO BE WITH YOU
KIDS
LORNA'S HERE
LOT OF LIVIN' TO DO, A
MATING GAME, THE
MAYBE
NIGHTLIFE
NIGHT SONG
ONCE UPON A TIME
ONE BOY
ONE LAST KISS
PUT ON A HAPPY FACE
ROSIE
SPANISH ROSE
TELEPHONE HOUR, THE
THERE WAS A CROOKED MAN
THIS IS THE LIFE
THOSE WERE THE DAYS
TOMORROW
WELCOME TO THE THEATRE
WE LOVE YOU BEATLES
WHAT DID I EVER SEE IN HIM?
WHILE THE CITY SLEEPS

YOU'VE GOT POSSIBILITIES

Strozier, Gordon

OH, SHEILA

Strummer, Joe

ROCK THE CASBAH
TRAIN IN VAIN (STAND BY ME)

Strunk, Jud

DAISY A DAY

Struzick, Edward

FALLING
SHARING THE NIGHT TOGETHER

Stryker, Fred

BROKEN DOWN MERRY-GO-ROUND
WITHOUT YOUR LOVE

Strykert, Roy

DOWN UNDER

Stuart, Allan

LA ROSITA

Stuart, Chad

WHAT DO YOU WANT WITH ME?

Stuart, David

SUMMER SONG, A

Stuart, Eddie

HIS NAME WAS DEAN

Stuart, Hamish

CUT THE CAKE
PICK UP THE PIECES

Stuart, Jack

SO TIRED

Stuart, James

WHAT CHA' GONNA DO FOR ME

Stuart, Leslie

SHADE OF THE PALM, THE
TELL ME PRETTY MAIDEN (ARE THERE ANY MORE AT HOME LIKE YOU?)

Stubbs, Terry

HAVE YOU HAD YOUR LOVE TODAY

Stuckey, Nathan

POP A TOP
SWEET THANG
WAITIN' IN YOUR WELFARE LINE

Stutz, Carl

DANGER! HEARTBREAK AHEAD
LITTLE THINGS MEAN A LOT

Styne, Jule

ABSENT MINDED ME
ALL I NEED IS THE GIRL
ALL YOU NEED IS A QUARTER
AND THEN YOU KISSED ME
ANYWHERE
ASKING FOR YOU
AS LONG AS THERE'S MUSIC
AT THE CAFE RENDEVOUS
BARRELHOUSE BESSIE FROM BASIN STREET
BLAME MY ABSENT-MINDED HEART
BROOKLYN BRIDGE
BYE BYE BABY
CAN'T YOU READ BETWEEN THE LINES?
CHANGE OF HEART, A
CHARM OF YOU, THE
CLOSE HARMONY
COME OUT, COME OUT, WHEREVER YOU ARE
COMES ONCE IN A LIFETIME
CONCHITA, MARQUITA, LOLITA, PEPITA, ROSITA, JUANITA LOPEZ
CORNET MAN

CRY LIKE THE WIND
DIAMONDS ARE A GIRL'S BEST FRIEND
DISTANT MELODY
DON'T RAIN ON MY PARADE
EVERYTHING'S COMING UP ROSES
EV'RY DAY I LOVE YOU (JUST A LITTLE BIT MORE)
EV'RY STREET'S A BOULEVARD IN OLD NEW YORK
FADE OUT—FADE IN
FIDDLE DEE DEE
FIREWORKS
FIVE MINUTES MORE
FUNNY GIRL
GIVE ME A BAND AND MY BABY
GUESS I'LL HANG MY TEARS OUT TO DRY
HOLD ME—HOLD ME—HOLD ME
HOW CAN YOU DESCRIBE A FACE?
HOW DO YOU SPEAK TO AN ANGEL?
I BEGGED HER
I BELIEVE
I DON'T CARE IF IT RAINS ALL NIGHT
I DON'T WANT TO WALK WITHOUT YOU
I FALL IN LOVE TOO EASILY
I FEEL LIKE I'M GONNA LIVE FOREVER
I GOTTA GAL I LOVE (IN NORTH AND SOUTH DAKOTA)
I KNOW ABOUT LOVE
I'LL WALK ALONE
I LOVE AN OLD FASHIONED SONG
I'M GLAD I WAITED FOR YOU
I'M IN LOVE
I'M THE GREATEST STAR
I'M WITH YOU
INDEPENDENT (ON MY OWN)
IN THE COOL OF THE EVENING
I SAID NO
I STILL GET JEALOUS
IT'S A GREAT FEELING
IT'S ALWAYS LOVE
IT'S BEEN A LONG, LONG TIME
IT'S BIGGER THAN YOU AND ME
IT'S DELIGHTFUL DOWN IN CHILE
IT'S MAGIC
IT'S THE SAME OLD DREAM
IT'S YOU OR NO ONE
I'VE HEARD THAT SONG BEFORE
I'VE NEVER FORGOTTEN

JUST IN TIME
LET IT SNOW! LET IT SNOW! LET IT SNOW!
LET ME ENTERTAIN YOU
LITTLE GIRL FROM LITTLE ROCK, A
LITTLE JOE
LITTLE LAMB
LONG BEFORE I KNEW YOU
LOOKING BACK
LOVE ME
MAKE SOMEONE HAPPY
MONEY BURNS A HOLE IN MY POCKET
MU-CHA-CHA
MUSIC THAT MAKES ME DANCE, THE
NEVER NEVER LAND
NOW
ON A SUNDAY BY THE SEA
PAPA, WON'T YOU DANCE WITH ME?
PARTY'S OVER, THE
PEOPLE
POOR LITTLE RHODE ISLAND
PUT 'EM IN A BOX, TIE 'EM WITH A RIBBON, AND THROW 'EM IN THE DEEP BLUE SEA
SADIE, SADIE
SATURDAY NIGHT (IS THE LONELIEST NIGHT IN THE WEEK)
SAY, DARLING
SMALL WORLD
SOME OTHER TIME
SOME PEOPLE
SONG'S GOTTA COME FROM THE HEART, THE
STAY WITH THE HAPPY PEOPLE
SUNDAY
THAT'S WHAT I LIKE
THERE GOES THAT SONG AGAIN
THERE'S NOTHING LIKE A MODEL "T"
THINGS WE DID LAST SUMMER, THE
THREE COINS IN THE FOUNTAIN
TIME AFTER TIME
TOGETHER WHEREVER WE GO
VICT'RY POLKA
WE COULD BE CLOSE
WHAT AM I GONNA DO ABOUT YOU?
WHAT MAKES THE SUNSET?
WHAT'S NEW AT THE ZOO?
WHERE DID YOU LEARN TO LOVE?
WHO AM I?
WHO DID? I DID

WHO KNOWS WHAT MIGHT HAVE BEEN?
YOU ARE WOMAN, I AM MAN
YOU'LL NEVER GET AWAY FROM ME
YOU MUSN'T BE DISCOURAGED
YOU'RE THE CAUSE OF IT ALL

Suber, Virginia

KNOTHOLE

Sudano, Bruce

BAD GIRLS
BALL OF FIRE
(CLOSEST THING TO) PERFECT
STARTING OVER AGAIN

Suddoth, J. Guy

BOOZE AND BLUES

Suessdorf, Karl

MOONLIGHT IN VERMONT

Suesse, Dana

HAVE YOU FORGOTTEN (THE THRILL)?
HO-HUM
JAZZ NOCTURNE
MOON ABOUT TOWN
MY SILENT LOVE
NIGHT IS YOUNG AND YOU'RE SO BEAUTIFUL, THE
TABLE IN THE CORNER, A
THIS CHANGING WORLD
WHISTLING IN THE DARK
YOU OUGHTA BE IN PICTURES
YOURS FOR A SONG

Sullivan, Alex

GEORGIA ROSE

Sullivan, Arthur

HAIL, HAIL, THE GANG'S ALL HERE

Sullivan, Dan J.

YOU'RE AS WELCOME AS THE FLOWERS IN MAY

Sullivan, Frankie

AMERICAN HEARTBEAT
BURNING HEART
CAUGHT UP IN YOU
EYE OF THE TIGER
HIGH ON YOU
I CAN'T HOLD BACK
IS THIS LOVE
SEARCH IS OVER, THE

Sullivan, Gene

WHEN MY BLUE MOON TURNS TO GOLD AGAIN

Sullivan, Henry

I MAY BE WRONG (BUT I THINK YOU'RE WONDERFUL)

Sullivan, Jeri

RUM AND COCA-COLA

Sullivan, Joe

GIN MILL BLUES
LITTLE ROCK GETAWAY

Sullivan, Joseph J.

WHERE DID YOU GET THAT HAT?

Sullivan, Larry

CINCO ROBLES (A.K.A. FIVE OAKS)

Sullivan, Terry

SHE SELLS SEA SHELLS

Sulton, Kasim

SET ME FREE

Summer, Donna

BAD GIRLS
DIM ALL THE LIGHTS
HEAVEN KNOWS
I FEEL LOVE
LOVE TO LOVE YOU, BABY
ON THE RADIO
SHE WORKS HARD FOR THE MONEY
STARTING OVER AGAIN
WANDERER, THE

Summers, Amiel

BIG JOHN

Summons, Daryl

LOVER IN ME, THE

Sumner, Gordon "Sting"

DE DO DO DO DE DA DA DA
MESSAGE IN A BOTTLE
ROXANNE

Sundelof, Fritz G.

OPEN DOOR, OPEN ARMS

Sundgaard, Arnold

LONG JOHN

Sunshine, Marion

MARY, YOU'RE A LITTLE BIT OLD
    FASHIONED
PEANUT VENDOR, THE

Sure, Al B.

NITE AND DAY
OFF ON YOUR OWN (GIRL)

Surgal, Alan

CHIU, CHIU

Surrey, Jean

TEEN ANGEL

Surrey, Red

TEEN ANGEL

Sussman, Bruce

COPACABANA (AT THE COPA)
I MADE IT THROUGH THE RAIN

Sutherland, Gavin

SAILING

Sutherland, Iain

ARMS OF MARY

Sutton, Brenda

SHAKE IT UP TONIGHT
THERE WILL COME A DAY (I'M
    GONNA HAPPEN TO YOU)

Sutton, Charles

SEE SAW

Sutton, Glenn

ALMOST PERSUADED
ALREADY IT'S HEAVEN
HAVE A LITTLE FAITH
I DON'T WANNA PLAY HOUSE
I'M DOWN TO MY LAST "I LOVE
    YOU"
I'M STILL LOVING YOU
KEEP ME IN MIND
KIDS SAY THE DARNDEST THINGS
KISS AWAY
LOSER'S CATHEDRAL
MY WOMAN'S GOOD TO ME
SINGING MY SONG
TAKE ME TO YOUR WORLD
TO MAKE LOVE SWEETER FOR YOU
WAYS TO LOVE A MAN, THE
WHAT'S MADE MILWAUKEE FAMOUS
    (HAS MADE A LOSER OUT OF ME)
WITH ONE EXCEPTION
WOMAN LIVES FOR LOVE, A
YOU MEAN THE WORLD TO ME
YOU'RE MY MAN
YOUR GOOD GIRL'S GONNA GO BAD

Sutton, Harry O.

I DON'T CARE

Sutton, Michael

SHAKE IT UP TONIGHT
THERE WILL COME A DAY (I'M
    GONNA HAPPEN TO YOU)

Sutton, Tommy

I WISH I HAD A NICKEL

Swados, Elizabeth

I CAN HAVE IT ALL

Swain, Royce

TWICE AS MUCH

Swain, Tony

CRUEL SUMMER

Swan, Billy

I CAN HELP
LOVER, PLEASE

Swan, E. A.

ROOM WITH A VIEW, A
WHEN YOUR LOVER HAS GONE

Swander, Don

DEEP IN THE HEART OF TEXAS

Swanstrom, Arthur

BLUES MY NAUGHTY SWEETIE
    GIVES TO ME, THE
COME UP AND SEE ME SOMETIME
CROSS YOUR FINGERS
MORNING, NOON AND NIGHT
RAIN
TWENTY-FOUR HOURS A DAY
WHY?

Swayze, Patrick

SHE'S LIKE THE WIND

Swearingen, Leroy

GOODBYE, MY LOVER, GOODBYE

Sweat, Keith

I WANT HER
MAKE IT LAST FOREVER
SOMETHING JUST AIN'T RIGHT

Sweatman, Wilbur

BATTLESHIP KATE

Sweeney, Chuck

YOUNG IDEAS

Sweesy, Henry

YOU CAN'T BREAK MY HEART
('CAUSE IT'S ALREADY BROKEN)

Sweet, Philip

I DON'T WANT TO HAVE TO MARRY
YOU

Sweet, Rachel

HAIRSPRAY

Swern, Philip

UP IN A PUFF OF SMOKE

Swift, Kay

CAN THIS BE LOVE?
CAN'T WE BE FRIENDS?
FINE AND DANDY

Swirsky, Seth

PROVE YOUR LOVE
TELL IT TO MY HEART

Switch

I CALL YOUR NAME

Sybil

DON'T MAKE ME OVER

Sykes, John

IS THIS LOVE
STILL OF THE NIGHT

Sykes, Keith

VOLCANO

Sykes, Roosevelt

DRIVING WHEEL

Sylvers, Edmund

HIGH SCHOOL DANCE

Sylvers, James

HIGH SCHOOL DANCE

Sylvers, Joseph

HIGH SCHOOL DANCE

Sylvers, Leon

AND THE BEAT GOES ON
DEAD GIVEAWAY
HIGH SCHOOL DANCE
SECOND TIME AROUND, THE

Sylvia, Margo

HAPPY, HAPPY BIRTHDAY BABY

Symes, Marty

BY THE RIVER OF THE ROSES
(WHEN IT'S) DARKNESS ON THE
DELTA
HOW MANY HEARTS HAVE YOU
BROKEN?
I HAVE BUT ONE HEART
IN A BLUE AND PENSIVE MOOD

IT'S THE TALK OF THE TOWN
I'VE GOT AN INVITATION TO A
DANCE
LEARNING
MARY HAD A LITTLE LAMB
OL' PAPPY
PRETENDING
STAR GAZING
TARA TALARA TALA
THERE IS NO GREATER LOVE
TIPPIN' IN
UNDER A BLANKET OF BLUE
YOU CAN TELL SHE COMES FROM
DIXIE

Szinnyey, Stephen Ivor

WHEN THE CHERRY BLOSSOMS
FALL

Tabet, Andre

THERE IS NO BREEZE

Tableporter, Mitchell

NEED YOU
YOU TOLD A LIE (I BELIEVED YOU)

Tabrar, Joseph

DADDY WOULDN'T BUY ME A BOW-
WOW

Taccani, S.

COME PRIMA (FOR THE FIRST TIME)
ON AN EVENING IN ROMA

Tagg, Eric

IS IT YOU

Taggart, George

MOTH AND THE FLAME, THE

Taggert, Milton

WHEN IT'S SPRINGTIME IN THE
ROCKIES

Talbert, Homer

AIN'T UNDERSTANDING MELLOW

Talbot, Howard

MY MOTTER

Tallarico, Steve

DREAM ON

Talley, Lewis

DEAR JOHN LETTER, A

Tanega, Norma

WALKIN' MY CAT NAMED DOG

Tanner, Marc

JUST ONE OF THE GUYS

Tarney, Alan

DREAMING
LITTLE IN LOVE, A
WE DON'T TALK ANYMORE

Tarplin, Marvin

AIN'T THAT PECULIAR?
BABY COME CLOSE
CRUISIN'
DOGGONE RIGHT
GOING TO A GO-GO
I'LL BE DOGGONE
LOVE I SAW IN YOU WAS JUST A
    MIRAGE, THE
MY GIRL HAS GONE
ONE MORE HEARTACHE
POINT IT OUT
TAKE THIS HEART OF MINE
TRACKS OF MY TEARS, THE

Tarver, Ben

ANY OTHER WAY
COME TO THE MASQUERADE
HULLA-BALOO-BALAY
MAN WITH A LOAD OF MISCHIEF
ONCE YOU'VE HAD A LITTLE TASTE

Tate, Arthur F.

SOMEWHERE A VOICE IS CALLING

Tate, Danny

AFFAIR OF THE HEART

Tate, Laurie

ANY TIME, ANY PLACE, ANYWHERE

Taub, Jules

BAD LUCK
I'M IN THE MOOD
IT'S MIDNIGHT
PLEASE LOVE ME
"T" 99 BLUES
THREE O'CLOCK BLUES
WOKE UP THIS MORNING
YOU KNOW I LOVE YOU

Tauber, Doris

FOOLED
THEM THERE EYES

Taubert, Robert

TRIANGLE

Taupin, Bernie

BENNIE AND THE JETS
BITCH IS BACK, THE
BORDER SONG
CANDLE IN THE WIND
CROCODILE ROCK
DANIEL
DON'T GO BREAKING MY HEART
DON'T LET THE SUN GO DOWN ON
    ME
EMPTY GARDEN (HEY HEY JOHNNY)
FRIENDS
GOODBYE YELLOW BRICK ROAD
GROW SOME FUNK OF YOUR OWN
HONKY CAT
HOW YOU GONNA SEE ME NOW
I DON'T WANNA GO ON WITH YOU
    LIKE THAT
I FEEL LIKE A BULLET (IN THE GUN
    OF ROBERT FORD)
I GUESS THAT'S WHY THEY CALL IT
    THE BLUES
I'M STILL STANDING
ISLAND GIRL
KISS THE BRIDE
LEVON
NIKITA
PHILADELPHIA FREEDOM
ROCKET MAN
SAD SONGS (SAY SO MUCH)
SATURDAY NIGHT'S ALRIGHT FOR
    FIGHTING
SNOOKEROO
SOMEONE SAVED MY LIFE TONIGHT
SORRY SEEMS TO BE THE HARDEST
    WORD
THESE DREAMS
TINY DANCER
WE BUILT THIS CITY
WHO WEARS THESE SHOES?
WRAP HER UP
YOUR SONG

Taylor, Andy

SOME LIKE IT HOT
TAKE IT EASY

Taylor, Baxter, III

MARIE LAVEAU

Taylor, Beloyd

GETAWAY

Taylor, Bill

I WOULDN'T TRADE YOU FOR THE
    WORLD

Taylor, Carmen

LITTLE MAMA
SEVEN DAYS

Taylor, Carmol

HE LOVES ME ALL THE WAY
MY MAN, A SWEET MAN
WILD AS A WILD CAT

Taylor, Chip

ANGEL OF THE MORNING
COUNTRY GIRL—CITY MAN
I CAN MAKE IT WITH YOU
I CAN'T LET GO
I'LL HOLD OUT MY HAND
MAKE ME BELONG TO YOU
STEP OUT OF YOUR MIND
WILD THING

Taylor, Chuck

BURNING OF ATLANTA, THE

Taylor, Danny

GOOD LOVIN'

Taylor, Deron

I WANNA TESTIFY

Taylor, Earl

MY SOUTHERN ROSE

Taylor, Helen

BLESS THIS HOUSE
COME TO THE FAIR

Taylor, Herbert H.

IN THE WILDWOOD WHERE THE
    BLUEBELLS GROW

Taylor, Irving

CARAMBA! IT'S THE SAMBA!
DOO DE DOO ON AN OLD KAZOO
EVERYBODY LOVES SOMEBODY
I'LL NEVER FAIL YOU
KILLE KILLE (INDIAN LOVE TALK)
KOOKIE, KOOKIE (LEND ME YOUR
    COMB)
LILY BELLE
ONE-ZY TWO-ZY (I LOVE YOU-ZY)
QUICKSILVER
TAKE IT EASY
THERE'S A FAR AWAY LOOK IN
    YOUR EYE
THREE LITTLE SISTERS

YOU BROKE YOUR PROMISE

Taylor, Jack

BAND OF GOLD
EARTHBOUND

Taylor, Jake

DAD GAVE MY DOG AWAY

Taylor, James

BROTHER TRUCKER
COUNTRY ROAD
DON'T LET ME BE LONELY TONIGHT
FIRE AND RAIN
HARD TIMES
HER TOWN TOO
MEXICO
MILLWORK
ONE MAN PARADE
SHOWER THE PEOPLE
STEAMROLLER BLUES
STONE LOVE
TAKE MY HEART (YOU CAN HAVE IT
    IF YOU WANT IT)
VICTORY
YOUR SMILING FACE

Taylor, James "J. T."

LADIES NIGHT
MISLED

Taylor, John

BOY FROM NEW YORK CITY, THE
GET ON UP
I DO WHAT I DO
NOTORIOUS
SOME LIKE IT HOT

Taylor, Livingston

CAROLINA DAY

Taylor, Mary

QUEEN OF THE HOUSE

Taylor, Michael

ROCKY MOUNTAIN HIGH
SUNSHINE ON MY SHOULDERS

Taylor, Raymond

I WANT TO BE EVIL

Taylor, R. Dean

ALL I NEED
I'M LIVIN' IN SHAME
INDIANA WANTS ME
LOVE CHILD

Taylor, Robert

MAYBE I'M A FOOL
SHA-LA-LA
TWO SHADOWS ON YOUR WINDOW

Taylor, Roger

ELECTION DAY
RADIO GA-GA

Taylor, Ron

TOO MUCH IS NOT ENOUGH

Taylor, Rudolph

BURN RUBBER (WHY YOU WANNA
    HURT ME)
EARLY IN THE MORNING

Taylor, Tell

CIRIBIRIBIN
DOWN BY THE OLD MILL STREAM

Taylor, William E.

THERE MUST BE MORE TO LOVE
    THAN THIS

Tchaikowsky, Peter I.

CONCERTO FOR TWO
PIANO CONCERTO IN B FLAT

Teat, Elson

LONESOME WHISTLE BLUES

Tebelak, John-Michael

DAY BY DAY

Tedesco, L.

GENERAL HOSPI-TALE

Tee, R.

STUFF LIKE THAT

Teegarden, David

GOD, LOVE, AND ROCK AND ROLL

Teetor, Macy O.

LOST

Teifer, Gerry

FULL TIME JOB

Tellez, Pablo

SUAVECITO

Telson, Bob

CALLING YOU

Temklin, Harold

VACATION

Tempchin, Jack

ALREADY GONE
ONE YOU LOVE, THE
PEACEFUL EASY FEELING
SEXY GIRL
SMUGGLER'S BLUES
SWAYIN' TO THE MUSIC (A.K.A.
    SLOW DANCING)

Temperton, Rod

ALWAYS AND FOREVER

BABY, COME TO ME
BOOGIE NIGHTS
GIVE ME THE NIGHT
GROOVE LINE, THE
LOVE IS IN CONTROL (FINGER ON
    THE TRIGGER)
MAN SIZE LOVE
MISS CELIE'S BLUES
OFF THE WALL
ROCK WITH YOU
STOMP!
SWEET FREEDOM
THRILLER
YAH MO B THERE

Tempest, Joey

CARRIE
FINAL COUNTDOWN, THE

Temple, George

SLIDER

Templeton, Alec

BACH GOES TO TOWN

Tempo, Nino

ALL STRUNG OUT

Tench, Ben

NEVER BE YOU
NOT ENOUGH LOVE IN THE WORLD
SUNSET GRILL
SWEET, SWEET BABY (I'M FALLING)

Tennant, Neil

WEST END GIRLS
WHAT HAVE I DONE TO DESERVE
    THIS?

Tennant, Nick

IT'S A SIN
OPPORTUNITIES (LET'S MAKE LOTS
    OF MONEY)

Tenney, Jack B.

MEXICALI ROSE

Tennille, Toni

DO THAT TO ME ONE MORE TIME
WAY I WANT TO TOUCH YOU, THE

Tepper, Robert

INTO THE NIGHT

Tepper, Sid

ALL THAT I AM
DON'T COME RUNNING BACK TO ME
IF I HAD A GIRL
KEWPIE DOLL
MY BONNIE LASSIE
NAUGHTY LADY OF SHADY LANE,
    THE
NUTTIN' FOR CHRISTMAS
ON LONDON BRIDGE
PUPPET ON A STRING
RED ROSES FOR A BLUE LADY
SAY SOMETHING SWEET TO YOUR
    SWEETHEART
STAIRWAY OF LOVE
STAY
STOP! AND THINK IT OVER
SUMMER SOUNDS
THANKS, MISTER FLORIST
WHEN THE BOY IN YOUR ARMS (IS
    THE BOY IN YOUR HEART)
WONDERFUL WORLD OF THE
    YOUNG, THE

Terker, Arthur

MEET ME AT NO SPECIAL PLACE
    (AND I'LL BE THERE AT NO
    PARTICULAR TIME)
THERE'S EVERYTHING NICE ABOUT
    YOU (THERE'S SOMETHING NICE
    ABOUT EVERYONE)

Terrell, Wilbur

SLIP AWAY
TELL MAMA

Terris, Dorothy

THREE O'CLOCK IN THE MORNING
WONDERFUL ONE (MY)

Terry, Dewey, Jr.

JOLLY GREEN GIANT

Terry, Dewey

I'M LEAVING IT (ALL) UP TO YOU

Terry, George

LAY DOWN SALLY

Terry, Johnny

PLEASE, PLEASE, PLEASE

Teschemacher, Edward

BECAUSE
GARDEN OF YOUR HEART, THE
TOMMY, LAD!
UNTIL
WHERE MY CARAVAN HAS RESTED

Testa, Alberto

CAN I TRUST YOU?
I WANT TO BE WANTED
QUANDO, QUANDO, QUANDO (TELL
   ME WHEN)
TONIGHT I'LL SAY A PRAYER

Tetteroo, Peter

MA BELLE AMIE

Tex, Joe

BABY, YOU'RE RIGHT
BUYING A BOOK
HOLD WHAT YOU'VE GOT
I GOTCHA
I WANT TO (DO EVERYTHING FOR
   YOU)
KEEP THE ONE YOU GOT
LOVE YOU SAVE (MAY BE YOUR
   OWN), THE
MEN ARE GETTIN' SCARCE

PAPA WAS TOO
SHOW ME
SKINNY LEGS AND ALL
SWEET WOMAN LIKE YOU, A
S.Y.S.L.J.F.M. (THE LETTER SONG)
YOU BETTER GET IT
YOU SAID A BAD WORD

Thaler, Rudolf

CIRIBIRIBIN

Tharp, Winston

OUT OF SPACE
PANIC IS ON, THE

Tharpe, Sister Rosetta

UP ABOVE MY HEAD, I HEAR MUSIC
   IN THE AIR

Theard, Sammy

LET THE GOOD TIMES ROLL
YOU CAN'T GET THAT NO MORE
(I'LL BE GLAD WHEN YOU'RE DEAD)
   YOU RASCAL YOU

Theodorakis, Mikis

ZORBA THE GREEK

Thiele, Robert

WHAT A WONDERFUL WORLD

Thielemans, Jean

BLUESETTE

Thielhelm, Emil

(WE AIN'T GOT) NOTHIN' YET

Thomas, Arthur

OLD RECORDS
SIGNS

Thomas, Carla

GEE WHIZ! (LOOK AT HIS EYES)

Thomas, Clifton

LOVER'S HOLIDAY
PICKIN' WILD MOUNTAIN BERRIES

Thomas, Dave

TAKE OFF

Thomas, David Clayton

GO DOWN GAMBLIN'

Thomas, Dennis

HOLLYWOOD SWINGING
OPEN SESAME

Thomas, Dick

I LOST THE BEST PAL THAT I HAD
SIOUX CITY SUE

Thomas, Don

THIS DOOR SWINGS BOTH WAYS

Thomas, Edward

HIGH STEEL

Thomas, Edward, Jr.

LOVER'S HOLIDAY
PICKIN' WILD MOUNTAIN BERRIES

Thomas, Gene

PLAYBOY

Thomas, Gerry

TROGLODYTE (CAVE MAN)

Thomas, Harry

HOLD 'EM JOE
MATILDA, MATILDA!

Thomas, Harvey

FLIRTIN' WITH DISASTER

Thomas, Hersal

SUITCASE BLUES

Thomas, Ian

HOLD ON
RUNNER, THE

Thomas, Jeff

DON'T TRY TO LAY NO BOOGIE
    WOOGIE ON THE KING OF ROCK
    AND ROLL

Thomas, Jessie

IKO IKO

Thomas, Jimmie

ROCKIN' ROBIN

Thomas, Joe

GOT YOU ON MY MIND
I WON'T BE THE FOOL ANYMORE
MELANCHOLY ME

Thomas, John

HEARTBREAK (IT'S HURTING ME)

Thomas, LaVerne

THERE MUST BE MORE TO LOVE
    THAN THIS

Thomas, Leslie

EVERYBODY LOVES A CLOWN

Thomas, Lester

BY THE SAD SEA WAVES

Thomas, Michael

HAWAII TATTOO

Thomas, Millard

SUZANNE (EV'RY NIGHT WHEN THE
    SUN GOES DOWN)

Thomas, R.

WHY'D YOU COME HERE LOOKIN'
    LIKE THAT

Thomas, Ronald

GIRL OF MY DREAMS

Thomas, Rufus

DO THE FUNKY PENGUIN
WALKING THE DOG

Thomas, Timmy

WHY CAN'T WE LIVE TOGETHER

Thomas, Wilfred

ROSE, ROSE, I LOVE YOU

Thomasson, Gene Edward

RINGS OF GOLD

Thompson

EXPRESS

Thompson, Alfonso "Sonny"

LONG GONE

Thompson, Ali

TAKE A LITTLE RHYTHM

Thompson, Bonnie

TURN BACK THE HANDS OF TIME

Thompson, Sir Charles

JUST WHEN WE'RE FALLING IN
    LOVE

ROBBINS NEST

Thompson, Denny

TIJUANA JAIL, THE

Thompson, Hank

BLACKBOARD OF MY HEART
BREAKIN' THE RULES
DON'T TAKE IT OUT ON ME
GREEN LIGHT
I'LL NEVER GET OUT OF THIS
    WORLD ALIVE
I'VE RUN OUT OF TOMORROWS
ON TAP, IN THE CAN, OR IN THE
    BOTTLE
RUB-A-DUB-DUB
SHE'S JUST A WHOLE LOT LIKE YOU
WAITING IN THE LOBBY OF YOUR
    HEART
WE'VE GONE TOO FAR
WHOA! SAILOR!
WILDWOOD FLOWER
YESTERDAY'S GIRL
YOU CAN'T HAVE MY LOVE

Thompson, Harlan

DANCE AWAY THE NIGHT
ENDING WITH A KISS
FATAL FASCINATION
FROM BROADWAY TO MAIN STREET
I'D RATHER BE THE GIRL IN YOUR
    ARMS
I LOVE YOU
IT MUST BE LOVE
MELODY IN SPRING
YOU AND I

Thompson, Kay

ELOISE
LOVE ON A GREYHOUND BUS
PROMISE ME LOVE
YOU GOTTA LOVE EVERYBODY

Thompson, Linda

TELLING ME LIES

Thompson, Marcus

RUMORS

Thompson, Sonny

HIDE AWAY
SAN-HO-ZAY
THREE HEARTS IN A TANGLE

Thompson, Wayne Carson

ALWAYS ON MY MIND
DO IT AGAIN, A LITTLE BIT SLOWER
I SEE THE WANT IN YOUR EYES
LETTER, THE
NEON RAINBOW
NO LOVE AT ALL
SHE'S ACTIN' SINGLE (I'M DRINKIN' DOUBLES)
SOUL DEEP
WHO'S JULIE?

Thomson, Ali

REALLY WANNA KNOW YOU

Thomson, James

GIVE A MAN A HORSE HE CAN RIDE

Thorn, George

STORY OF LOVE, THE
SWEET AND GENTLE

Thornhill, Claude

SNOWFALL

Thornton, James

BRIDGE OF SIGHS
DON'T GIVE UP THE OLD LOVE FOR NEW
GOING FOR A PARDON
IT DON'T SEEM LIKE THE SAME OLD SMILE
MY SWEETHEART'S THE MAN IN THE MOON
ON THE BENCHES IN THE PARK

REMEMBER POOR MOTHER AT HOME
SHE MAY HAVE SEEN BETTER DAYS
STREETS OF CAIRO (SHE NEVER SAW THE)
THERE'S A LITTLE STAR SHINING FOR YOU
UPPER TEN, LOWER FIVE
WHEN YOU WERE SWEET SIXTEEN

Thornton, Willie May

BALL AND CHAIN

Thorpe, Eddie

YOU'RE STILL MINE

Thorsen, Art

IT'S IN THE BOOK

Throckmorton, James

TRYING TO LOVE TWO WOMEN

Throckmorton, Jim

HOW LONG HAS IT BEEN?

Throckmorton, Sonny

COWBOY RIDES AWAY, THE
FRIDAY NIGHT BLUES
I FEEL LIKE LOVING YOU AGAIN
IF WE'RE NOT BACK IN LOVE BY MONDAY
I WISH I WAS EIGHTEEN AGAIN
LAST CHEATER'S WALTZ
MIDDLE-AGE CRAZY
THINKING OF A RENDEZVOUS
WAY I AM, THE

Thurston, Henry

I'LL SAIL MY SHIP ALONE

Tibbles, George

SOMETHING OLD, SOMETHING NEW
WOODY WOODPECKER
WORRY, WORRY, WORRY

Tierney, Harry

ADORING YOU
ALICE BLUE GOWN
CASTLE OF DREAMS
FOLLOWING THE SUN AROUND
I FOUND THE END OF THE RAINBOW
IF YOU'RE IN LOVE, YOU'LL WALTZ
IF YOUR HEART'S IN THE GAME
IRENE
IT'S A CUTE LITTLE WAY OF MY OWN
JOURNEY'S END
KEEP YOUR EYE ON THE BALL
KINKAJOU, THE
LADY LUCK, SMILE ON ME
LET'S KISS AND MAKE UP
M-I-S-S-I-S-S-I-P-P-I
MY BABY'S ARMS
RANGERS' SONG, THE
RIO RITA
SOMEONE LOVES YOU AFTER ALL
SWEETHEART, WE NEED EACH OTHER
WHY DON'T YOU?
YOU'RE ALWAYS IN MY ARMS
YOU'VE GOT ME OUT ON A LIMB

Tilbrook, Glenn

TEMPTED
HOURGLASS

Tilghman, Bill

RAVE ON

Tillis, Mel

ALL THE TIME
BURNING MEMORIES
CRAZY WILD DESIRE
DETROIT CITY
EMOTIONS
HEART OVER MIND
HOLIDAY FOR LOVE
HONEY (OPEN THAT DOOR)
HONKY TONK SONG
I AIN'T NEVER
I'M TIRED
LITTLE OLE YOU
LOCO WEED

OLD FAITHFUL
ONE MORE TIME
RUBY, DON'T TAKE YOUR LOVE TO
    TOWN
SAWMILL
TAKE TIME
TEN THOUSAND DRUMS
THOUSAND MILES AGO, A
TUPELO COUNTY JAIL
UNMITIGATED GALL
VIOLET AND A ROSE, THE
WALK ON, BOY

Tillison, Carroll

YOU DON'T HAVE TO PAINT ME A
    PICTURE

Tillman, Abrim

BABY LET ME TAKE YOU IN MY
    ARMS

Tillman, Floyd

EACH NIGHT AT NINE
G.I. BLUES
I GOTTA HAVE MY BABY BACK
I'LL KEEP ON LOVING YOU
I'LL NEVER SLIP AROUND AGAIN
I LOVE YOU SO MUCH IT HURTS
IT MAKES NO DIFFERENCE NOW
SLIPPING AROUND
THEY TOOK THE STARS OUT OF
    HEAVEN

Tillotson, Johnny

IT KEEPS RIGHT ON A-HURTIN'
    (SINCE I LEFT)
WITHOUT YOU

Tilsley, Henry B.

I NEVER SEE MAGGIE ALONE
LADY OF SPAIN
LET'S ALL SING LIKE THE BIRDIES
    SING
UNLESS

Timas, Rick

COOL IT NOW

COUNT ME OUT

Timberg, Sammy

IT'S A HAP-HAP-HAPPY DAY

Timbur, Dalton

TIMBER, I'M FALLING IN LOVE

Timien, Sidney

MY TOOT TOOT

Tinturin, Peter

BIG BOY BLUE
FOOLIN' MYSELF
IT'S ABOUT TIME
OUTSIDE OF PARADISE
WHAT WILL I TELL MY HEART?
YOU OR NO ONE

Tiomkin, Dimitri

BALLAD OF THE ALAMO
BLOWING WILD (A.K.A. BALLAD OF
    BLACK GOLD, THE)
DUEL IN THE SUN
FRIENDLY PERSUASION (A.K.A.
    THEE I LOVE)
GIANT
GREEN LEAVES OF SUMMER, THE
GUNS OF NAVARONE, THE
HAJJI BABA (PERSIAN LAMENT)
HIGH AND THE MIGHTY, THE
HIGH NOON (A.K.A. DO NOT
    FORSAKE ME)
PEKING THEME, THE (SO LITTLE
    TIME)
RAWHIDE
RETURN TO PARADISE
RIO BRAVO
STRANGE ARE THE WAYS OF LOVE
STRANGE LADY IN TOWN
THEME FROM "THE SUNDOWNERS"
THEME FROM "THE UNFORGIVEN"
    (THE NEED FOR LOVE)
TOWN WITHOUT PITY
WILD IS THE WIND

Tipton, Bill

KNOCK, KNOCK, WHO'S THERE?

Tipton, Glenn

YOU'VE GOT ANOTHER THING
    COMIN'

Titelman, Russ

SAILOR BOY

Titheradge, Peter Dion

AND HER MOTHER CAME TOO

Titsworth, Paul

I'M IN LOVE WITH YOU

Titus, Libby

LOVE HAS NO PRIDE

Tizol, Juan

CARAVAN
GYPSY WITHOUT A SOUL, A
LOST IN MEDITATION
PERDIDO

Tobani, Theodore Moses

HEARTS AND FLOWERS

Tobias, Charles

AFTER MY LAUGHTER CAME TEARS
ALICE IN WONDERLAND
ALL OVER THE WORLD
AM I GONNA HAVE TROUBLE WITH
    YOU?
BROKEN RECORD, THE
COAX ME A LITTLE BIT
COMES LOVE
(WHAT DO WE DO ON A) DEW-DEW-
    DEWY DAY
DON'T BE LIKE THAT
DON'T SIT UNDER THE APPLE TREE
    (WITH ANYONE ELSE BUT ME)

DON'T SWEETHEART ME
EVERYTHING'S MADE FOR LOVE
EV'RY DAY AWAY FROM YOU
FLOWERS FOR MADAME
FOR THE FIRST TIME (I'VE FALLEN
  IN LOVE)
GEE, BUT YOU'RE SWELL
GET OUT AND GET UNDER THE
  MOON
GOODNIGHT LITTLE GIRL OF MY
  DREAMS
HER BATHING SUIT NEVER GOT
  WET
I CAME HERE TO TALK FOR JOE
I CAN GET IT FOR YOU WHOLESALE
I CAN'T AFFORD TO DREAM
I'M PAINTING THE TOWN RED
IN THE VALLEY OF THE MOON
IS THAT THE WAY TO TREAT A
  SWEETHEART?
IT SEEMS LIKE OLD TIMES
I WANT YOU FOR CHRISTMAS
I WISH THAT I COULD HIDE INSIDE
  THIS LETTER
JUST ANOTHER DAY WASTED AWAY
  (WAITING FOR YOU)
JUST A PRAYER AWAY
KATHY O'
LET'S MAKE MEMORIES TONIGHT
LITTLE CURLY HAIR IN A HIGH
  CHAIR
LITTLE LADY MAKE BELIEVE
LOVE YA
MAMA DOLL SONG, THE
ME TOO (HO, HO, HA, HA)
MISS YOU
MY FIRST IMPRESSION OF YOU
NO CAN DO
OH! MOYTLE
OLD LAMP-LIGHTER, THE
OLD WATER MILL, AN
ROSE O'DAY (THE FILLA-FA-DUSHA
  SONG)
ROSEWOOD SPINET, A
SING A LITTLE LOW DOWN TUNE
SOMEBODY LOVES YOU
SOMEWHERE IN OLD WYOMING
SPRING HAS SPRUNG
START THE DAY RIGHT
THAT'S WHERE I CAME IN
THINGS THAT WERE MADE FOR
  LOVE, THE (YOU CAN'T TAKE
  AWAY)

THOSE LAZY-HAZY-CRAZY DAYS OF
  SUMMER
THROW ANOTHER LOG ON THE FIRE
TIME WAITS FOR NO ONE
TINY LITTLE FINGERPRINTS
TOMORROW IS FOREVER
TRADE WINDS
TWO TICKETS TO GEORGIA
WAIT FOR ME, MARY
WAKE UP AND SING
WHEN YOUR HAIR HAS TURNED TO
  SILVER (I WILL LOVE YOU JUST
  THE SAME)
WOULD YOU BELIEVE ME?
ZING ZING—ZOOM ZOOM

Tobias, Fred

BORN TOO LATE
FOLLOWED CLOSELY BY TEARDROPS
GOOD TIMIN'
LITTLE BITTY GIRL
ONE OF US (WILL WEEP TONIGHT)

Tobias, Harry

AT YOUR COMMAND
GO TO SLEEPY, BABY
HERE YOU COME WITH LOVE
IF IT WASN'T FOR THE MOON
I'M GONNA GET YOU
I'M SORRY DEAR
IT'S A LONESOME OLD TOWN (WHEN
  YOU'RE NOT AROUND)
LOST AND FOUND
LOVE IS ALL
MISS YOU
NO REGRETS
OO-OO ERNEST, ARE YOU EARNEST
  WITH ME?
SAIL ALONG, SILV'RY MOON
SONG OF THE MOONBEAMS
SWEET AND LOVELY
WAIT FOR ME, MARY
WHAT IS IT?
WILD HONEY

Tobias, Henry

COOKING BREAKFAST FOR THE ONE
  I LOVE
GO TO SLEEPY, BABY
IF I HAD MY LIFE TO LIVE OVER

KATINKA
MISS YOU

Tobias, Ken

STAY AWHILE

Tobin, George

CINNAMON

Todaro, Phil

WILD WEEKEND

Todd, Clarence

OOOH! LOOK-A THERE, AIN'T SHE
  PRETTY?

Todd, Jerry

THREE A.M.

Tolhurst, Kerryn

MAN ON YOUR MIND

Tollerton, Nell

CRUISING DOWN THE RIVER (ON A
  SUNDAY AFTERNOON)

Tomlin, Pinky

DON'T BE AFRAID TO TELL YOUR
  MOTHER
IF IT WASN'T FOR THE MOON
LOST AND FOUND
LOVE BUG WILL BITE YOU, THE (IF
  YOU DON'T WATCH OUT)
LOVE IS ALL
OBJECT OF MY AFFECTION, THE
THAT'S WHAT YOU THINK
WHAT'S THE REASON (I'M NOT
  PLEASIN' YOU)?

Tomsco, Barbara

SAY I AM (WHAT I AM)

Tomsco, George

SAY I AM (WHAT I AM)

Tom Tom Club

GENIUS OF LOVE

Toni C.

LOVE WILL SAVE THE DAY

Tony! Toni! Tone!

LITTLE WALTER

Toombs, Jack

ALMOST

Toombs, Rudolph

24 HOURS A DAY (365 DAYS A
   YEAR)
5-10-15 HOURS
CRAWLIN'
DADDY, DADDY
EASY, EASY BABY
GUM DROP
IT HURTS TO BE IN LOVE
LONESOME WHISTLE BLUES
ONE MINT JULEP
ONE SCOTCH, ONE BOURBON, ONE
   BEER
TEARDROPS FROM MY EYES

Toon, E.

LADIES NIGHT

Tormé, Mel

BORN TO BE BLUE
CHRISTMAS SONG, THE
COUNTRY FAIR
LAMENT TO LOVE
STRANGER IN TOWN, A

Torok, Mitchell

CARIBBEAN
(OPEN UP THE DOOR) LET THE
   GOOD TIMES IN

MEXICAN JOE
YOU ARE THE ONE

Torre, Janice

PAPER ROSES

Torrence, Dean

BUCKET "T"

Torres, Jimmy

WHEELS

Tosti, Blaise

AFFAIR OF THE HEART
SWEET SUMMER LOVIN'

Tourjee, Homer

WON'T YOU BE MY LITTLE GIRL?

Toussaint, Allan

ALL THESE THINGS
GET OUT OF MY LIFE, WOMAN
HOLY COW
I LIKE IT LIKE THAT
JAVA
MOTHER-IN-LAW
SOUTHERN NIGHTS
WORKING IN THE COAL MINE
YES WE CAN CAN

Touzet, Rene

LET ME LOVE YOU TONIGHT

Towber, Chaim

I LOVE YOU MUCH TOO MUCH

Towers, Leo

BELLA BELLA MARIE
LITTLE OLD MILL, THE (WENT
   ROUND AND ROUND)
SILVER WINGS IN THE MOONLIGHT

Towers, Michael

NOBODY'S FOOL

Towne, Billy

NEVER ON SUNDAY

Towne, Charlie

MAMBO JAMBO

Townes, Jeff

PARENTS JUST DON'T UNDERSTAND

Townsend, David

HAPPY
LATELY

Townsend, Ed

CLOSER THAN FRIENDS
FOR YOUR LOVE
LOVE OF MY MAN, THE
SOONER OR LATER

Townsend, John

SMOKE FROM A DISTANT FIRE

Townshend, Edward

FINALLY GOT MYSELF TOGETHER
   (I'M A CHANGED MAN)
LET'S GET IT ON

Townshend, Peter

5:15
AFTER THE FIRE
ATHENA
BEHIND BLUE EYES
CALL ME LIGHTNING
CHAMPAGNE
DON'T LET GO THE COAT
HAPPY JACK
I CAN SEE FOR MILES
I CAN'T EXPLAIN
I'M FREE
JOIN TOGETHER
LET MY LOVE OPEN THE DOOR

Townshend, Peter

LITTLE IS ENOUGH, A
LONG LIVE ROCK
LOVE, REIGN O'ER ME
MAGIC BUS, THE
MY GENERATION
OVERTURE FROM "TOMMY" (A ROCK
   OPERA)
PICTURES OF LILY
PINBALL WIZARD
REAL ME, THE
ROUGH BOYS
SEEKER, THE
SEE ME, FEEL ME
SQUEEZE BOX
SUBSTITUTE
WHO ARE YOU
YOU BETTER YOU BET

Tozzi, Umberto

GLORIA

Trace, Al

BRUSH THOSE TEARS FROM YOUR
   EYES

Trace, Ben

YOU CALL EVERYBODY DARLING

Tracey, William

BRING BACK MY DADDY TO ME
GEE, BUT IT'S GREAT TO MEET A
   FRIEND FROM YOUR HOME TOWN
IN THE TOWN WHERE I WAS BORN
IS MY BABY BLUE TONIGHT?
MAMMY O'MINE
PLAY THAT BARBER SHOP CHORD
THEM THERE EYES
YOU CAN HAVE HIM, I DON'T WANT
   HIM, DIDN'T LOVE HIM ANYHOW
   BLUES!

Trader, Bill

FOOL SUCH AS I, A (NOW AND THEN
   THERE'S)

Traditional

BEAUTIFUL BROWN EYES

COTTONFIELDS
FRANKIE AND JOHNNY
LOCH LOMOND
MIDNIGHT SPECIAL
TOM DOOLEY
TOUCH A HAND, MAKE A FRIEND
WADE IN THE WATER
WANDERIN'
WEARY BLUES
WRECK OF THE JOHN B (A.K.A.
   SLOOP JOHN B)

Trail, Buck

GIRL WATCHER

Tramp, Mike

WAIT

Tran, Jay D.

ONLY A LONELY HEART SEES

Trapani, Tulio

CARA MIA

Travers, Harry

HONEYTHIEF, THE

Travis, Merle

CINCINNATI LOU
DARK AS A DUNGEON
DIVORCE ME C.O.D.
FAT GAL
I WANT TO BE SURE
NINE POUND HAMMER
NO VACANCY
SIXTEEN TONS
SMOKE! SMOKE! SMOKE! (THAT
   CIGARETTE)
SO ROUND, SO FIRM, SO FULLY
   PACKED
STEEL GUITAR RAG
SWEET TEMPTATION
THAT'S ALL
THREE TIMES SEVEN

Travis, Randy

I TOLD YOU SO

Treadwell, George

DANCE WITH ME
THERE GOES MY BABY

Trebandt, Terry

TURN TO STONE

Trenet, Charles

BEYOND THE SEA
I WISH YOU LOVE

Trent, Jackie

COLOR MY WORLD
DON'T GIVE UP
DON'T SLEEP IN THE SUBWAY
I COULDN'T LIVE WITHOUT YOUR
   LOVE
OTHER MAN'S GRASS IS ALWAYS
   GREENER, THE
WHO AM I?

Trent, Jo

GOTTA FEELIN' FOR YOU
HERE YOU COME WITH LOVE
I JUST ROLL ALONG
JIG WALK
LAZY WEATHER
MUDDY WATER
MY KINDA LOVE
RHYTHM KING

Trevelyan, Arthur

DOWN IN POVERTY ROW

Trevor, Huntley

WHEN IT'S APPLE BLOSSOM TIME IN
   NORMANDY

Trevor, Van

BORN TO BE IN LOVE WITH YOU

Trim, Paul

MAMMY BLUE

Trimachi, Bobbi

1, 2, 3, RED LIGHT

Trimachi, Sal

1, 2, 3, RED LIGHT

Trivers, Barry

DO THE NEW YORK
EVERY DAY'S A HOLIDAY
OH, WHAT A THRILL
TWO LOVES HAVE I

Troiano, Domenic

RUN RUN RUN

Trotter, Don

LOVE LAND

Troup, Bobby

BABY, BABY, ALL THE TIME
DADDY
MEANING OF THE BLUES, THE
(GET YOUR KICKS ON) ROUTE 66

Troutman, Larry

DANCE FLOOR
I WANT TO BE YOUR MAN

Troutman, Roger "Zapp"

DANCE FLOOR
MORE BOUNCE TO THE OUNCE

Trowbridge, Don

YOU'VE JUST STEPPED IN (FROM
STEPPING OUT ON ME)

Troxel, Gary

COME SOFTLY TO ME

Troy, Henry

CAKE WALKING BABIES FROM
HOME
GIN HOUSE BLUES, THE

Trudeau, Garry

I CAN HAVE IT ALL

True, Christopher

WHY HAVE YOU LEFT THE ONE YOU
LEFT ME FOR

True, Mark

TOO MANY LOVERS

Truehitt, Pee Wee

MARRIED BY THE BIBLE, DIVORCED
BY THE LAW

Trumbauer, Frank

KRAZY KAT

Tubb, Ernest

DON'T JUST STAND THERE (WHEN
YOU FEEL LIKE YOU'RE IN LOVE)
DON'T LOOK NOW (BUT YOUR
BROKEN HEART IS SHOWIN')
FOREVER IS ENDING TODAY
I'LL ALWAYS BE GLAD TO TAKE YOU
BACK
I'M BITIN' MY FINGERNAILS AND
THINKING OF YOU
IT'S BEEN SO LONG, DARLIN'
I WONDER WHY YOU SAID
"GOODBYE"
KEEP MY MEM'RY IN YOUR HEART
LET'S SAY GOODBYE LIKE WE SAID
HELLO
LETTERS HAVE NO ARMS
SEAMAN'S BLUES
SOLDIER'S LAST LETTER
THERE'S A LITTLE BIT OF
EVERYTHING IN TEXAS
THROW YOUR LOVE MY WAY
TOMORROW NEVER COMES
TRY ME ONE MORE TIME

WALKING THE FLOOR OVER YOU
YESTERDAY'S TEARS
YOU NEARLY LOSE YOUR MIND

Tubb, Glenn

REPEAT AFTER ME
SKIP A ROPE
SWEET LIPS
TELL HER SO
TWO STORY HOUSE

Tubb, Justin

BE GLAD
DERN YA
IMAGINE THAT
LONESOME 7-7203
LOVE IS NO EXCUSE
TAKE A LETTER, MISS GRAY
WALKIN', TALKIN', CRYIN', BARELY
BEATIN', BROKEN HEART

Tubb, Talmadge "Billy"

SEAMAN'S BLUES

Tubbs, Pierre

BUT IT'S ALRIGHT
RIGHT BACK WHERE WE STARTED
FROM

Tubert, Bob

GOING THROUGH THE MOTIONS (OF
LIVING)
HERE COMES HEAVEN
I'LL KEEP HOLDING ON (JUST TO
YOUR LOVE)
OUR WINTER LOVE
RING DANG DOO
SATIN PILLOWS
YOU'RE THE ONLY WORLD I KNOW

Tucker, Alonzo

BABY WORKOUT
SWITCH-A-ROO, THE

Tucker, Annette

GET ME TO THE WORLD ON TIME

GREEN LIGHT
I HAD TOO MUCH TO DREAM (LAST NIGHT)

Tucker, Ben

COMIN' HOME BABY

Tucker, Johnny

DANCE OF THE PAPER DOLLS

Tucker, Mike

FOX ON THE RUN

Tucker, Orrin

ESPECIALLY FOR YOU
MY RESISTANCE IS LOW
PINCH ME

Tucker, Tanya

IT'S ONLY FOR YOU

Tucker, Tommy

MAN WHO COMES AROUND, THE

Tuggle, Brent

JUST LIKE PARADISE

Tuller, Grant Colfax

FACE TO FACE

Tuminello, Phil

CAN I STEAL A LITTLE LOVE?

Turgeon, Bruce

MIDNIGHT BLUE

Turk, Roy

AFTER MY LAUGHTER CAME TEARS
AGGRAVATIN' PAPA (DON'T YOU TRY TO TWO-TIME ME)
ARE YOU LONESOME TONIGHT?
BEALE STREET MAMA

BLUE HOURS
CAN'T YOU SEE?
CONTENTED
EVENING STAR
FREE AND EASY, THE
GIMME A LITTLE KISS, WILL YA, HUH?
HOW CAN YOU SAY YOU LOVE ME?
I COULDN'T TELL THEM WHAT TO DO
I DON'T KNOW WHY
I'LL FOLLOW YOU
I'LL GET BY
I'LL NEVER ASK FOR MORE
I'M A LITTLE BLACKBIRD LOOKING FOR A BLUEBIRD
I'M GONNA CHARLESTON BACK TO CHARLESTON
INTO MY HEART
JUST ANOTHER DAY WASTED AWAY (WAITING FOR YOU)
LOVE, YOU FUNNY THING
MANDY, MAKE UP YOUR MIND
MEAN TO ME
MY SWEETIE WENT AWAY (SHE DIDN'T SAY WHERE, WHEN, OR WHY)
OH HOW I LAUGH WHEN I THINK HOW I CRIED ABOUT YOU
TO BE IN LOVE
WALKIN' MY BABY BACK HOME
WE'RE FRIENDS AGAIN
WHERE THE BLUE OF THE NIGHT MEETS THE GOLD OF THE DAY
WHY DANCE?
YES, I'M LONESOME TONIGHT
YOU'LL GET BY
YOU OUGHTA SEE MY BABY

Turnbow, Jay

BREAD AND BUTTER

Turnbridge, Joseph

GOT A DATE WITH AN ANGEL

Turner, C. Fred

LET IT RIDE

Turner, Charles

ROLL ON DOWN THE HIGHWAY

Turner, Eric

HEAVEN

Turner, Houston

BEST DRESSED BEGGAR (IN TOWN), THE

Turner, Ike

FOOL IN LOVE, A
GOODBYE, SO LONG
I'M BLUE (THE GONG-GONG SONG)
POOR FOOL

Turner, Jesse Lee

LITTLE SPACE GIRL

Turner, Joe

CHERRY RED
PINEY BROWN BLUES
ROLL 'EM PETE
WEE BABY BLUES

Turner, Joe Lynn

STONE COLD

Turner, John

AUF WIEDERSEH'N, SWEETHEART
BANDIT, THE
CHEE CHEE-OO CHEE (SANG THE LITTLE BIRD)
LITTLE SHOEMAKER, THE
OH, MY PAPA
SMILE

Turner, Leonard

JUNGLE LOVE

Turner, Lou Willie

FLIP FLOP AND FLY
HONEY HUSH

Turner, Mick

ACTION

Turner, Raye

WATCHING YOU

Turner, Reginald

DON'T LET THE GREEN GRASS FOOL
YOU

Turner, Scott

HICKTOWN
MEXICAN DRUMMER MAN
SHUTTERS AND BOARDS

Turner, Tina

NUTBUSH CITY LIMITS

Turner, Titus

HEY, DOLL BABY
STICKS AND STONES
TELL ME WHY

Turner, Zeb

IT'S A SIN

Tuttle, Jerry

IT'S ALRIGHT

Tuvim, Abe

GAY RANCHERO, A (LAS ALTENITAS)

Tweel, Jeff

EVERYTIME TWO FOOLS COLLIDE
MORNIN' RIDE

Twilley, Dwight

GIRLS
I'M ON FIRE

Twitty, Conway

AFTER ALL THE GOOD IS GONE
CLOWN, THE
GAMES THAT DADDIES PLAY, THE
HELLO DARLIN'
I CAN'T BELIEVE SHE GIVES IT ALL
    TO ME
IT'S ONLY MAKE BELIEVE
I'VE ALREADY LOVED YOU IN MY
    MIND
LINDA ON MY MIND
LOST HER LOVE ON OUR LAST DATE
PLAY, GUITAR PLAY
STORY OF MY LOVE, THE
TO SEE MY ANGEL CRY
WALK ME TO THE DOOR
YOU'VE NEVER BEEN THIS FAR
    BEFORE

Twomey, Kay

HEY! JEALOUS LOVER
IN A LITTLE BOOKSHOP
JOHNNY DOUGHBOY FOUND A ROSE
    IN IRELAND
MELANCHOLY MINSTREL, THE
NEVER LET HER GO
OO! WHAT YOU DO TO ME
SATISFACTION GUARANTEED
SERENADE OF THE BELLS
STRANGE SENSATION
WOODEN HEART

Tyler, Adele

BOBBIE SUE

Tyler, Alvin

JAVA

Tyler, Daniel

BOBBIE SUE
TWENTY YEARS AGO

Tyler, Johnny

OAKIE BOOGIE

Tyler, Steve

ANGEL
DUDE (LOOKS LIKE A LADY)
LAST CHILD
WALK THIS WAY

Tyler, Toby

BLUES ON PARADE

Tyler, T. Texas

COURTIN' IN THE RAIN
DAD GAVE MY DOG AWAY
DECK OF CARDS, THE

Tyme, January

ONE MAN BAND

Tyrell, Steve

IT'S ONLY LOVE

Tyson, Ian

FOUR STRONG WINDS
SOMEDAY SOON

U2

DESIRE
IN GOD'S COUNTRY
I STILL HAVEN'T FOUND WHAT I'M
    LOOKING FOR
SWEET FIRE OF LOVE
WHERE THE STREETS HAVE NO
    NAME
WITH OR WITHOUT YOU

Udall, Lyn

JUST AS THE SUN WENT DOWN
JUST ONE GIRL
STAY IN YOUR OWN BACK YARD
ZIZZY, ZE ZUM, ZUM!

Udell, Peter

BIG DADDY
GINNY COME LATELY
HE SAYS THE SAME THINGS TO ME

Udell, Peter

HURTING EACH OTHER
I GOT LOVE
LET ME BELONG TO YOU
NEXT TO LOVIN' (I LIKE FIGHTIN')
PURLIE
SAVE YOUR HEART FOR ME
WALK HIM UP THE STAIRS

Uhl, Richard

ROMANTIC GUY, I, A

Uhry, Alfred

SLEEPY MAN

Ulvaeus, Bjorn

CHIQUITITA
DANCING QUEEN
FERNANDO
I DO, I DO, I DO, I DO, I DO
I KNEW HIM SO WELL
KNOWING ME, KNOWING YOU
NAME OF THE GAME, THE
ONE NIGHT IN BANGKOK
S.O.S.
TAKE A CHANCE ON ME
WATERLOO
WINNER TAKES IT ALL, THE

Umiliani, Piero

MAH-NA-MAH-NA

Unger, Stella

C'EST LA VIE
DON'T CRY, BABY
MAN WITH A DREAM, A
WHERE IS THAT SOMEONE FOR ME?

Uniman, Mimi

LONG LONELY NIGHTS

Upoon, Dean

WHEN IT'S LAMP LIGHTIN' TIME IN
   THE VALLEY

Upton, Pat

MORE TODAY THAN YESTERDAY

Urbano, Al

SERENADE OF THE BELLS

Ure, Midge

DO THEY KNOW IT'S CHRISTMAS?

Usher, Gary

DON'T GIVE IN TO HIM
IN MY ROOM

UTFO

ROXANNE, ROXANNE

Vacek, Karel

PLAY TO ME, GYPSY

Valaquen, Kurt

WHAT'S ON YOUR MIND (PURE
   ENERGY)

Val, Jack

ALL DRESSED UP WITH A BROKEN
   HEART
JUST SAY I LOVE HER

Vale, Mike

BALL OF FIRE
CRYSTAL BLUE PERSUASION
SUGAR ON SUNDAY

Vale, Peter

SO GOOD
TAKE ME HOME TONIGHT

Valens, Ritchie

COME ON, LET'S GO
DONNA

Valenti, Dino

HEY JOE

Valentine, Gerald

OH, SHEILA

Valentine, Kathy

HEAD OVER HEELS
VACATION

Valier, Alton J.

NEIGHBOR, NEIGHBOR

Vallance, Jim

BACK TO PARADISE
HEARTS ON FIRE
HEAT OF THE NIGHT
HEAVEN
IT'S ONLY LOVE
LET ME DOWN EASY
LIKE NO OTHER NIGHT
NOW AND FOREVER (YOU AND ME)
RUN TO YOU
SOMEBODY
SOMEDAY
SUMMER OF '69
TEACHER TEACHER
THIS TIME
WHAT ABOUT LOVE?

Valle, Marcos

SUMMER SAMBA (SO NICE)

Vallee, Rudy

BETTY CO-ED
DEEP NIGHT
I'M JUST A VAGABOND LOVER
I'M STILL CARING
OH! MA-MA (THE BUTCHER BOY)
OLD MAN HARLEM
TWO LITTLE BLUE LITTLE EYES
VIENI, VIENI

Vallins, John

TOO MUCH, TOO LITTLE, TOO LATE

Valory, Diane

WHEEL IN THE SKY

Valvano, Michael

IF THIS IS LOVE (I'D RATHER BE LONELY)

Van, Gus

ALL SHE'D SAY WAS "UMH HUM"
BABY'S PRAYER WILL SOON BE ANSWERED
OH! HOW SHE CAN SING

Van, Mel

HIT AND RUN AFFAIR

Vanadore, Lester

ALONE WITH YOU
I'D RATHER LOAN YOU OUT
TOO MUCH TO LOSE

Van Alstyne, Egbert

BABY
BACK, BACK, BACK TO BALTIMORE
BEAUTIFUL LOVE
CHEYENNE (SHY ANN)
DRIFTING AND DREAMING
GOODNIGHT, LADIES
I'M AFRAID TO COME HOME IN THE DARK
IN DEAR OLD GEORGIA
IN THE SHADE OF THE OLD APPLE TREE
IT LOOKS TO ME LIKE A BIG NIGHT TONIGHT
KENTUCKY'S WAY OF SAYING GOOD MORNIN'
MEMORIES
MY DREAMY CHINA LADY
NAUGHTY, NAUGHTY, NAUGHTY
NAVAJO
ON THE ROAD TO HOME SWEET HOME
PRETTY BABY
SAILIN' AWAY ON THE HENRY CLAY
SAN ANTONIO
SUNSHINE AND ROSES

THAT OLD GIRL OF MINE
THERE NEVER WAS A GIRL LIKE YOU
WHAT'S THE MATTER WITH FATHER
WHEN I WAS TWENTY-ONE AND YOU WERE SWEET SIXTEEN
WHO ARE YOU WITH TONIGHT?
WON'T YOU COME OVER TO MY HOUSE?
YOUR EYES HAVE TOLD ME SO

Vance, L.

DISCO LADY

Vance, Paul

CALCUTTA
CAN I TRUST YOU?
CATCH A FALLING STAR
DOMMAGE, DOMMAGE (TOO BAD, TOO BAD)
GINA
ITSY BITSY TEENIE WEENIE POLKA DOT BIKINI
JIMMY'S GIRL
KING SIZE PAPA
LEADER OF THE LAUNDROMAT
PLAYGROUND IN MY MIND
RUN JOEY RUN
STARBRIGHT
TAR AND CEMENT
TRACY
WHAT IS LOVE?
WHAT WILL MY MARY SAY?
WHEN JULIE COMES AROUND

Vanda, Harry

GOOD TIMES
LOVE IS IN THE AIR
YESTERDAY'S HERO

Vandross, Luther

ANY LOVE
GET IT RIGHT
GIVE ME THE REASON
I REALLY DIDN'T MEAN IT
JUMP TO IT
STOP TO LOVE
THERE'S NOTHING BETTER THAN LOVE

'TILL MY BABY COMES HOME

van Eijck, Hans

MA BELLE AMIE

Vangelis

CHARIOTS OF FIRE (RACE TO THE END)
HYMNE

Van Halen, Alex

AND THE CRADLE WILL ROCK
DANCE THE NIGHT AWAY
DREAMS
I'LL WAIT
JUMP
LOVE WALKS IN
PANAMA
WHEN IT'S LOVE
WHY CAN'T THIS BE LOVE

Van Halen, Eddie

AND THE CRADLE WILL ROCK
DANCE THE NIGHT AWAY
DREAMS
I'LL WAIT
JUMP
LOVE WALKS IN
PANAMA
WHEN IT'S LOVE
WHY CAN'T THIS BE LOVE

Van Hemert, Hans Christian

HOW DO YOU DO?

Van Heusen, James

ACCIDENTS WILL HAPPEN
AIN'T GOT A DIME TO MY NAME
ALL I REMEMBER IS YOU
ALL MY TOMORROWS
ALL THE WAY
ALL THIS AND HEAVEN TOO
AND YOU'LL BE HOME
APALACHICOLA, FLA.
AREN'T YOU GLAD YOU'RE YOU?
AS LONG AS I'M DREAMING

Van Heusen, James

BLUEBIRDS IN MY BELFRY
BLUE RAIN
BOYS' NIGHT OUT, THE
BUSY DOING NOTHING
BUT BEAUTIFUL
CALL ME IRRESPONSIBLE
CAN I HELP IT?
CHICAGO STYLE
CONSTANTLY
COUNTRY STYLE
DARN THAT DREAM
DAY AFTER FOREVER, THE
DEAREST, DAREST I?
DEEP IN A DREAM
DO YOU KNOW WHY?
DO YOU WANNA JUMP, CHILDREN?
EMPTY TABLES
EVERYTHING MAKES MUSIC WHEN
    YOU'RE IN LOVE
EXPERIENCE
FOR THE FIRST HUNDRED YEARS
FRIEND OF YOURS, A
GOING MY WAY
GOOD FOR NOTHIN' BUT LOVE
GOOD-TIME CHARLEY
GOT THE MOON IN MY POCKET
HARD WAY, THE
HARMONY
HEAVEN CAN WAIT
HERE'S THAT RAINY DAY
HIGH HOPES
HIGH ON THE LIST
HIS ROCKING HORSE RAN AWAY
HORSE TOLD ME, THE
HOW D'YA TALK TO A GIRL
HOW LONG DID I DREAM?
HUMPTY DUMPTY HEART
I COULD HAVE TOLD YOU
I DON'T THINK I'M IN LOVE
IF YOU PLEASE
IF YOU STUB YOUR TOE ON THE
    MOON
I LIKE TO LEAD WHEN I DANCE
IMAGINATION
IMPATIENT YEARS, THE
ISN'T THAT JUST LIKE LOVE
IT COULD HAPPEN TO YOU
I THOUGHT ABOUT YOU
IT'S ALWAYS YOU
IT'S ANYBODY'S SPRING
IT'S BETTER IN THE DARK
IT'S THE DREAMER IN ME
JUST MY LUCK

JUST PLAIN LONESOME
LET'S NOT BE SENSIBLE
LIFE IS SO PECULIAR
LIKE SOMEONE IN LOVE
LOVE AND MARRIAGE
LOVE IS THE DARNDEST THING
MAKE WITH THE KISSES
MAN WITH THE GOLDEN ARM, THE
MOONLIGHT BECOMES YOU
MR. BOOZE
MY DREAM SONATA
MY HEART GOES CRAZY
MY HEART IS A HOBO
MY KIND OF TOWN (CHICAGO IS)
NANCY (WITH THE LAUGHING FACE)
NOT AS A STRANGER
OH, YOU CRAZY MOON
ONCE AND FOR ALWAYS
ONLY THE LONELY
PEACE, BROTHER
PERSONALITY
POCKETFUL OF MIRACLES
POLKA DOTS AND MOONBEAMS
PUT IT THERE, PAL
ROAD TO HONG KONG, THE
ROAD TO MOROCCO
ROMEO SMITH AND JULIET JONES
SECOND TIME AROUND, THE
SECRET OF CHRISTMAS, THE
SEPTEMBER OF MY YEARS
SHAKE DOWN THE STARS
SLEIGHRIDE IN JULY
SMILE RIGHT BACK AT THE SUN
SO HELP ME (IF I DON'T LOVE YOU)
SONG FROM "SOME CAME RUNNING"
    (A.K.A. TO LOVE AND BE LOVED)
SO WOULD I
SPEAKING OF HEAVEN
STAR!
STYLE
SUDDENLY IT'S SPRING
SUNDAY, MONDAY, OR ALWAYS
SUNSHINE CAKE
(WE'VE GOT A) SURE THING
SWINGIN' A DREAM
SWINGING ON A STAR
TEAMWORK
TENDER TRAP, THE
THAT LITTLE DREAM GOT NOWHERE
THEY CAME TO CORDURA
THOROUGHLY MODERN MILLIE
UNDER THE YUM-   YUM TREE
USE YOUR NOGGIN'

WAKE ME WHEN IT'S OVER
WALKING HAPPY
WARMER THAN A WHISPER
WELCOME TO MY DREAM
WHEN A PRINCE OF A FELLA
    MEETS A CINDERELLA
WHEN IS SOMETIME?
WHERE LOVE HAS GONE
WHO WAS THAT LADY?
WOULD YOU
YAH-TA-TA, YAH-TA-TA (TALK, TALK,
    TALK)
YOU DON'T HAVE TO KNOW THE
    LANGUAGE
YOU LUCKY PEOPLE, YOU
YOU'RE DANGEROUS
YOU THINK OF EV'RYTHING

Van Hoy, Rafe

BABY I LIED
FRIDAY NIGHT BLUES
GOLDEN RING
I WISH THAT I COULD HURT THAT
    WAY AGAIN
LADY LAY DOWN
LET'S STOP TALKIN' ABOUT IT
SOMEBODY'S GONNA LOVE YOU
WHAT'S FOREVER FOR

Van Leer, Thijs

HOCUS POCUS

Van Leeuwen, Robbie

VENUS

Vann, Al

MUST WE SAY GOODNIGHT SO
    SOON?

Vann, Teddy

LOOP DE LOOP
LOVE POWER

Vannelli, Gino

LIVING INSIDE MYSELF
PEOPLE GOTTA MOVE

Vannelli, Ross

I JUST WANNA STOP

Vannier, Angela

WHEN THE WORLD WAS YOUNG
(AH, THE APPLE TREES)

Van Peebles, Melvin

LILLY DONE THE ZAMPOUGHI
EVERY TIME I PULLED HER
COATTAIL

Van Steeden, Peter

HOME

Van Torgeron, John

IT'S NOT OVER ('TIL IT'S OVER)

Van Warner, Randy

I GUESS IT NEVER HURTS TO HURT
SOMETIMES
JUST WHEN I NEEDED YOU THE
MOST

Van Winkle, Joseph

MISTER CUSTER

Van Zandt, Townes

PANCHO AND LEFTY

Van Zant, Donnie

IF I'D BEEN THE ONE

Van Zant, Ronnie

BABY, I LOVE YOUR WAY
FREE BIRD
SATURDAY NIGHT SPECIAL
SWEET HOME ALABAMA
WHAT'S YOUR NAME

Van Zant, Steve

SUN CITY

SWEET, SWEET BABY (I'M FALLING)
TRAIL OF BROKEN TREATIES

Varga, Carolyn

WHEN HE TOUCHES ME (NOTHING
ELSE MATTERS)

Varna, Henri

VIENI, VIENI

Varnick, Ted

AM I IN LOVE?
GHOST TOWN
IN THE MIDDLE OF AN ISLAND

Vasin, D.

TELL ME YOU'RE MINE

Vasoir, Claude Andre

LET ME TRY AGAIN

Vastano, John

DEEPER THAN THE NIGHT

Vatro, R.

ANNA

Vaucaire, Michel

I'VE BEEN HERE!
NO REGRETS (NON, JE NE
REGRETTE RIEN)

Vaughan, Sharon

MY HEROES HAVE ALWAYS BEEN
COWBOYS

Vaughn, Billy

I'D RATHER DIE YOUNG
TRYING

Vaughn, D.

FALL IN LOVE WITH ME

Vaughn, George

BLUE YODEL #8 (A.K.A. NEW MULE
SKINNER BLUES)
SUGARFOOT RAG

Vaughn, Jack

GOODBYE JIMMY, GOODBYE

Vaughn, Michael

LOVE ME WITH ALL YOUR HEART
(CUANDO CALIENTE EL SOL)

Vaughn, Wayne

FALL IN LOVE WITH ME
LET'S GROOVE

Veale, Cal

PILLOW THAT WHISPERS, THE

Veasey, J.

FARTHER UP THE ROAD

Vega, Suzanne

LUKA

Vegas, Lolly

COME AND GET YOUR LOVE
NIKI HOEKY
WITCH QUEEN OF NEW ORLEANS,
THE

Vegas, Pat

NIKI HOEKY
WITCH QUEEN OF NEW ORLEANS,
THE

Veitch, Trevor

GLORIA
TELEFONE (LONG DISTANCE LOVE
AFFAIR)

Vejvoda, Jaromir

BEER BARREL POLKA

Velazquez, Consuelo

BESAME MUCHO

Velona, Tony

DOMANI (TOMORROW)
LOLLIPOPS AND ROSES
MUSIC TO WATCH GIRLS BY

Venet, Steve

ACTION
PEACHES 'N CREAM

Venosa, Arthur

LITTLE STAR

Venuti, Joe

KICKIN' THE CAT

Vera, Billy

AT THIS MOMENT
MAKE ME BELONG TO YOU

Veran, Florence

GIGI

Vere, Marcus

LIVING IN A BOX

Verissimo, Alvaro

WHERE THE BLUE AND LONELY GO

Verner, H. C.

WON'T YOU BE MY SWEETHEART?

Vernor, F. Dudleigh

SWEETHEART OF SIGMA CHI, THE

Vetter, Cyril E.

DOUBLE SHOT (OF MY BABY'S LOVE)

Vicars, Harold

SONG OF SONGS, THE

Vickery, Mack

I'M THE ONLY HELL (MAMA EVER
    RAISED)
SHE WENT A LITTLE BIT FARTHER

Victor, Floyd

KISS GOODNIGHT, A

Vidalin, Maurice

IT MUST BE HIM

Vigil, Rafael

BAD BOY

Villard, Jean

THREE BELLS, THE (A.K.A. JIMMY
    BROWN SONG, THE)

Villoldo, A. G.

EL CHOCLO

Vimmerstedt, Sadie

I WANNA BE AROUND

Vincent, Gene

BE-BOP-A-LULA

Vincent, Hunter

DROWNIN' MY SORROWS

Vincent, John

ROCKIN' PNEUMONIA AND THE
    BOOGIE WOOGIE FLU

Vincent, Larry

IF I HAD MY LIFE TO LIVE OVER

Vincent, Nat

BRING BACK THOSE WONDERFUL
    DAYS
LA VEEDA
RAILROAD JIM
THAT RAILROAD RAG
WHEN OLD BILL BAILEY PLAYS THE
    UKULELE
WHEN THE BLOOM IS ON THE SAGE

Vincent, Ronnie

TELL ME YOU'RE MINE

Vincent, Stan

LOOKING FOR LOVE
O-O-H CHILD

Vincent, Vinnie

LICK IT UP

Vinton, Bobby

COMIN' HOME SOLDIER
L-O-N-E-L-Y
MR. LONELY
MY MELODY OF LOVE

Violinsky, Sol

WHEN FRANCIS DANCES WITH ME

Vipperman, Carl

1982

Viscione, Antonio

LUNA ROSSA (A.K.A. BLUSHING
    MOON)

Vitale, Joey

ROCKY MOUNTAIN WAY

Vitali, Linda

I DON'T WANT TO LOSE YOUR LOVE
LITTLE BIT MORE, A

Volman, Mark

ELENORE

Von Hoof, Herricas

HOW DO YOU DO?

Vonnegut, Kurt, Jr.

NICE, NICE, VERY NICE

Von Tilzer, Albert

ALCOHOLIC BLUES, THE
AS LONG AS I HAVE YOU
AU REVOIR, BUT NOT GOODBYE,
    SOLDIER BOY
CARRIE (MARRY HARRY)
CHILI BEAN
DAPPER DAN (THE SHEIK OF
    ALABAM')
"FOREVER" IS A LONG, LONG TIME
GIVE ME THE MOONLIGHT, GIVE ME
    THE GIRL
GOOD EVENING, CAROLINE
GOOD MORNING, CARRIE
HONEY BOY
I'LL BE WITH YOU IN APPLE
    BLOSSOM TIME
I MAY BE GONE FOR A LONG, LONG
    TIME
I'M THE LONESOMEST GAL IN TOWN
IT'S THE IRISH IN YOUR EYES, IT'S
    THE IRISH IN YOUR SMILE
I USED TO LOVE YOU (BUT IT'S ALL
    OVER NOW)
KENTUCKY SUE
MOON HAS HIS EYES ON YOU, THE
MY CUTIE'S DUE AT TWO TO TWO
    TODAY
MY LITTLE GIRL
NORA MALONE (CALL ME BY
    PHONE)
OH, BY JINGO! OH, BY GEE!
    (YOU'RE THE ONLY GIRL FOR ME)
OH! HOW SHE COULD YACKI,
    HACKI, WICKI, WACKI, WOO

PICNIC FOR TWO, A
PLEASE DON'T TAKE MY LOVIN'
    MAN AWAY
PUCKER UP YOUR LIPS, MISS LINDY
PUT YOUR ARMS AROUND ME,
    HONEY
ROLL ALONG, PRAIRIE MOON
SMARTY
TAKE ME OUT TO THE BALLGAME
TAKE ME UP WITH YOU, DEARIE
TEASING
THAT'S WHAT THE DAISY SAID
WATERS OF VENICE (OR, FLOATING
    DOWN THE SLEEPY LAGOON)

Von Tilzer, Andrew

GOODBYE, BOYS

Von Tilzer, Harry

ALEXANDER, DON'T YOU LOVE
    YOUR BABY NO MORE?
ALL ABOARD FOR BLANKET BAY
ALL ABOARD FOR DREAMLAND
ALL ALONE
AND THE GREEN GRASS GREW ALL
    AROUND
BIRD IN A GILDED CAGE, A
BYE BYE DEARIE
CAN YOU TAME WILD WIMMEN?
CLOSE TO MY HEART
CUBANOLA GLIDE, THE
DARLING SUE
DON'T TAKE ME HOME
DOWN ON THE FARM (THEY ALL
    ASK FOR YOU)
DOWN WHERE THE COTTON
    BLOSSOMS GROW
DOWN WHERE THE WURZBURGER
    FLOWS
GOOD-BYE, ELIZA JANE
GOODBYE, SWEETHEART, GOODBYE
HANNAH, WON'T YOU OPEN THAT
    DOOR?
I'D LEAVE MY HAPPY HOME FOR
    YOU
I'LL LEND YOU EVERYTHING I'VE
    GOT EXCEPT MY WIFE
I LOVE IT
IN THE EVENING BY THE
    MOONLIGHT
IN THE SWEET BYE AND BYE

I WANT A GIRL (JUST LIKE THE
    GIRL THAT MARRIED DEAR OLD
    DAD)
I WONDER IF SHE'S WAITING
JENNIE LEE
JUST A LITTLE LOVIN'
JUST AROUND THE CORNER
KNOCK WOOD
LAST NIGHT WAS THE END OF THE
    WORLD
LITTLE BUNCH OF SHAMROCKS, A
MAKING EYES
MANSION OF ACHING HEARTS, THE
MY OLD NEW HAMPSHIRE HOME
ON A SUNDAY AFTERNOON
ON THE OLD FALL RIVER LINE
PARDON ME, MY DEAR ALPHONSE,
    AFTER YOU, MY DEAR GASTON
PLEASE GO 'WAY AND LET ME
    SLEEP
SNAP YOUR FINGERS AND AWAY
    YOU GO
TAKE ME BACK TO NEW YORK
    TOWN
THAT OLD IRISH MOTHER OF MINE
THEY'RE ALL SWEETIES
UNDER THE ANHEUSER BUSH
UNDER THE YUM-TUM TREE
WAIT TILL THE SUN SHINES, NELLIE
WAIT TILL YOU GET THEM UP IN
    THE AIR, BOYS
WHAT YOU GOIN' TO DO WHEN THE
    RENT COMES ROUND? (OR,
    RUFUS RASTUS JOHNSON BROWN)
WHEN KATE AND I WERE COMIN'
    THRO' THE RYE
WHEN THE HARVEST DAYS ARE
    OVER, JESSIE DEAR
WHERE THE MORNING GLORIES
    TWINE AROUND THE DOOR
WHERE THE SWEET MAGNOLIAS
    GROW
YOU'LL ALWAYS BE THE SAME
    SWEET GIRL

Voorhees, Donald

MUSIC OF LOVE (A.K.A. THE BELL
    WALTZ)

Voss, Faye

SUGAR SHACK

Voudouris, Roger

GET USED TO IT

Vundernik, Robert

SAUSALITO SUMMERNIGHT

Waaktaar, Pal

LIVING DAYLIGHTS, THE
SUN ALWAYS SHINES IN T.V., THE
TAKE ON ME

Wachendorf, Myron

PETER RABBIT

Wachtel, Robert

WEREWOLVES OF LONDON

Wachtel, Waddy

HER TOWN TOO

Waddington, Tony

CAN'T STOP LOVING YOU
NOTHING BUT A HEARTACHE

Wade, Betty

ALL ALONE IN THIS WORLD
    WITHOUT YOU

Wade, Cliff

HEARTBREAKER

Wade, Herman Avery

I'VE GOT A PAIN IN MY SAWDUST

Wadey, Steve

BLACK IS BLACK

Wadhams, William

LET HIM GO

Waggner, George

MARY LOU

Waggoner, David

EVIL WOMAN (A.K.A. EVIL MAN)

Wagner, Dick

HOW YOU GONNA SEE ME NOW
I NEVER CRY
JUST AS I AM
ONLY WOMEN
YOU AND ME

Wagner, Larry

CARIBBEAN COCKTAIL
LOVER'S LULLABY, A
NO NAME JIVE
PENGUIN AT THE WALDORF
RHYTHM OF RAINDROPS, THE
    (A.K.A. OVER THE RHYTHM OF
    RAINDROPS)
TURN BACK THE HANDS OF TIME

Wagner, Walter Lewis

SLIDE

Wagoner, Porter

TRADE MARK

Wainman, Phil

LITTLE GAMES

Wainwright, Loudon, III

DEAD SKUNK

Waite, John

MISSING YOU
RESTLESS HEART

Waits, Tom

DOWNTOWN TRAIN
ON THE NICKEL

Wakefield, Frank

UP TO MY NECK IN HIGH MUDDY
    WATER

Wakefield, Kathy

NATHAN JONES
ONE HUNDRED WAYS
THERE WILL COME A DAY (I'M
    GONNA HAPPEN TO YOU)

Wakelin, Johnny

BLACK SUPERMAN—"MUHAMMAD
    ALI"

Wakeling, Dave

SHE'S HAVING A BABY

Wakely, Jimmy

IF YOU KNEW WHAT IT MEANT TO
    BE LONESOME
TOO LATE

Walden, Dana

HOW 'BOUT US
TRY AGAIN

Walden, Lisa

ALL AMERICAN GIRLS

Walden, Narada Michael

ALL AMERICAN GIRLS
BABY COME TO ME
DON'T MAKE ME WAIT FOR LOVE
FREEWAY OF LOVE
HOW WILL I KNOW
JIMMY LEE
LET ME BE YOUR ANGEL
PUT YOUR MOUTH ON ME
WE DON'T HAVE TO TAKE OUR
    CLOTHES OFF
WHO'S ZOOMIN' WHO
YOU'RE A FRIEND OF MINE

Waldman, Robert

SLEEPY MAN

Waldman, Wendy

FISHIN' IN THE DARK
HEARTBEAT
LONG HOT SUMMER NIGHTS

Walker, Allan

STRANGE THINGS ARE HAPPENING
(HO HO, HEE HEE, HA HA)

Walker, Barclay

GOODBYE, MA! GOODBYE, PA!
GOODBYE, MULE!

Walker, Bee

HEY! JEALOUS LOVER

Walker, Billy

ANYTHING YOUR HEART DESIRES
HEART BE CAREFUL
WILLIE THE WEEPER

Walker, B. J., Jr.

I WANNA DANCE WITH YOU

Walker, Cindy

ANNA MARIE
BUBBLES IN MY BEER
CHEROKEE MAIDEN
CHINA DOLL
DIME A DOZEN
DISTANT DRUMS
DREAM BABY (HOW LONG MUST I
DREAM)
GIVE ME LOVE
GOLD RUSH IS OVER, THE
HEAVEN SAYS HELLO
I DON'T CARE
IN THE MISTY MOONLIGHT
LEONA
NIGHT WATCH, THE
SUGAR MOON

TAKE ME IN YOUR ARMS AND HOLD
ME
THANK YOU FOR CALLING
THIS IS IT
TRIFLIN' GAL
WARM RED WINE
YOU ARE MY TREASURE
YOU DON'T KNOW ME

Walker, Dennis

RIGHT NEXT DOOR (BECAUSE OF
ME)

Walker, Don

WACK WACK

Walker, Gary

ACCORDING TO MY HEART
REPENTING
TRADE MARK

Walker, George

VOODOO MAN, THE
WHEN IT'S ALL GOIN' OUT, AND
NOTHIN' COMIN' IN

Walker, Ira

I WANNA GO BACK

Walker, James J.

WILL YOU LOVE ME IN DECEMBER
AS YOU DO IN MAY?

Walker, Jerry Jeff

MR. BOJANGLES

Walker, Kurt

BREAKS, THE

Walker, Marshall

IT'S NOBODY'S BUSINESS BUT MY
OWN

Walker, Raymond

FIDO IS A HOT DOG NOW
POOR PAULINE

Walker, W. Raymond

GOODNIGHT, NURSE

Walker, Wayne P.

ALL THE TIME
ARE YOU SINCERE?
BIG WIND
BURNING MEMORIES
CAJUN QUEEN, THE
FALLEN ANGEL
FOOL, FOOL, FOOL
HELLO OUT THERE
HOLIDAY FOR LOVE
HOW DO YOU TALK TO A BABY?
IF IT PLEASES YOU
I THANK MY LUCKY STARS
I'VE GOT A NEW HEARTACHE
LEAVIN' ON YOUR MIND
LITTLE BOY SAD
LITTLE HEARTACHE, A
LITTLE OLE YOU
MEMORY NO. 1
PRIDE
SWEET LIPS
UNLOVED, UNWANTED
WALK ON, BOY
WHY, WHY

Walker, Wiley

WHEN MY BLUE MOON TURNS TO
GOLD AGAIN

Walker, William S.

HALF A HEART IS ALL YOU LEFT
ME (WHEN YOU BROKE MY
HEART IN TWO)

Wallace, Bill

BACK STREET AFFAIR
CLAP FOR THE WOLFMAN

Wallace, Chester

MOONLIGHT ON THE GANGES

Wallace, J. H.

HE TREATS YOUR DAUGHTER MEAN
(MAMA)

Wallace, J. L.

EVEN THE NIGHTS ARE BETTER
MAMA'S NEVER SEEN THOSE EYES
TOUCH ME WHEN WE'RE DANCING

Wallace, Oliver

DER FUEHRER'S FACE
HINDUSTAN
WHEN I SEE AN ELEPHANT FLY

Wallace, Paul

I WISH I HAD MY OLD GIRL BACK
AGAIN

Wallace, Raymond

WHEN THE ORGAN PLAYED AT
TWILIGHT

Waller, Jack

GOT A DATE WITH AN ANGEL

Waller, Thomas "Fats"

AIN'TCHA GLAD?
AIN'T MISBEHAVIN'
ALLIGATOR CRAWL
ALL THAT MEAT AND NO POTATOES
BLACK AND BLUE
BLUE, TURNING GREY OVER YOU
CONCENTRATIN' (ON YOU)
HANDFUL OF KEYS
HONEYSUCKLE ROSE
HOW CAN YOU FACE ME?
HOW YA BABY?
IF IT AIN'T LOVE
I'M CRAZY 'BOUT MY BABY
I'VE GOT A FEELING I'M FALLING
JITTERBUG WALTZ, THE
JOINT IS JUMPIN', THE

KEEPIN' OUT OF MISCHIEF NOW
LONESOME ME
LOUNGING AT THE WALDORF
MY FATE IS IN YOUR HANDS
PANIC IS ON, THE
PATTY CAKE, PATTY CAKE (BAKER
MAN)
ROLLIN' DOWN THE RIVER
SLIGHTLY LESS THAN WONDERFUL
SQUEEZE ME
STEALIN' APPLES
STRANGE AS IT SEEMS
SWEET SAVANNAH SUE
TAKE IT FROM ME
VIPER'S DRAG
ZONKY

Wallinger, Karl

SHIP OF FOOLS (SAVE ME FROM
TOMORROW)

Wallington, George

GODCHILD
LEMON DROP

Wallis, Jay

ALL BY YOURSELF IN THE
MOONLIGHT

Walls, Van

CHAINS OF LOVE

Walsh, Brock

AUTOMATIC
WOT'S IT TO YA

Walsh, Dan

HEARTBREAK KID, THE
HEAVEN KNOWS
I WOULDN'T TREAT A DOG (THE
WAY YOU TREATED ME)
TEMPTATION EYES

Walsh, Ellis

SATURDAY NIGHT FISH FRY

Walsh, J. Brandon

TEASIN'

Walsh, Joe

ALL NIGHT LONG
LIFE IN THE FAST LANE
LIFE'S BEEN GOOD
ROCKY MOUNTAIN WAY
TURN TO STONE

Walsh, Steve

ALL I WANTED

Walters, Rocky

SHOW, THE

Waltzer, Oscar

MY TRUE STORY

Wand, Hart A.

DALLAS BLUES

Wanda, Harry

FRIDAY ON MY MIND

Wann, Jim

SISTER

Wansel, Dexter

IF ONLY YOU KNEW

Ward

EXPRESS

Ward, Billy

BELLS, THE
HAVE MERCY, BABY
SIXTY MINUTE MAN
THAT'S WHAT YOU'RE DOING TO ME

Ward, Charles B.

BAND PLAYED ON, THE
ONLY A BOWERY BOY
STRIKE UP THE BAND, HERE COMES
A SAILOR

Ward, Edward

ALWAYS AND ALWAYS
JUST AN HOUR OF LOVE
MISS WONDERFUL

Ward, Gil

TELL HER YOU LOVE HER EVERY
DAY

Ward, Sam

JUST SAY I LOVE HER

Ward, William E.

DO SOMETHING FOR ME

Ware, Leon

HOLD TIGHT—HOLD TIGHT (WANT
SOME SEA FOOD, MAMA)
I DREAMT I DWELT IN HARLEM
IF I EVER LOSE THIS HEAVEN
I WANNA BE WHERE YOU ARE
I WANT YOU

Warfield, Charles

BABY, WON'T YOU PLEASE COME
HOME

Wariner, Steve

BABY I'M YOURS
I GOT DREAMS
I SHOULD BE WITH YOU
WHERE DID I GO WRONG
YOU CAN DREAM OF ME

Waring, Tom

SO BEATS MY HEART FOR YOU
WAY BACK HOME

Warman, Cy

SWEET MARIE

Warner, Henry Edward

I'VE GOT A PAIN IN MY SAWDUST

Warren, Blackie

PATIENCE AND FORTITUDE

Warren, Bob

CITY CALLED HEAVEN
NUMBER 10 LULLABY LANE

Warren, Bobby

GROOVY GRUBWORM

Warren, Bunny

RUBBERNECKIN'

Warren, Diane

ALL I WANT IS FOREVER
BLAME IT ON THE RAIN
DEEPER LOVE
I DON'T WANNA LIVE WITHOUT
YOUR LOVE
IF I COULD TURN BACK TIME
I GET WEAK
LOOK AWAY
NOTHING'S GONNA STOP US NOW
RHYTHM OF THE NIGHT
SOLITAIRE
WHEN I SEE YOU SMILE
WHO WILL YOU RUN TO?

Warren, Edward C.

TAKE GOOD CARE OF HER

Warren, Guy

THAT HAPPY FEELING

Warren, Harry

ABOUT A QUARTER TO NINE

ABSENCE MAKES THE HEART GROW
FONDER (FOR SOMEBODY ELSE)
AFFAIR TO REMEMBER, AN
ALL'S FAIR IN LOVE AND WAR
AM I IN LOVE?
ANGEL
AT LAST
AWAY DOWN SOUTH IN HEAVEN
BOULEVARD OF BROKEN DREAMS,
THE
BUILD A LITTLE HOME
BY THE RIVER SAINTE MARIE
CAUSE MY BABY SAYS IT'S SO
CHATTANOOGA CHOO CHOO
CHEERFUL LITTLE EARFUL
CHICA CHICA BOOM CHIC
COFFEE IN THE MORNING, KISSES
IN THE NIGHT
COFFEE TIME
CONFIDENTIALLY
COWBOY FROM BROOKLYN
CRYIN' FOR THE CAROLINES
DAMES
DAY DREAMING ALL NIGHT
LONG
DEVIL MAY CARE
DON'T GIVE UP THE SHIP
(SHIPMATES ALL FOREVER)
DON'T SAY GOODNIGHT
DORMI, DORMI, DORMI
DOWN ARGENTINA WAY
EVERY SO OFTEN
FAIR AND WARMER
FORTY-SECOND STREET
FRIENDLY STAR
GARDEN OF THE MOON
GID-AP GARIBALDI
GIRL AT THE IRONING BOARD, THE
GIRL FRIEND OF THE WHIRLING
DERVISH, THE
GOIN' TO HEAVEN ON A MULE
GO INTO YOUR DANCE
GOOD OLD FASHIONED COCKTAIL, A
(WITH A GOOD OLD FASHIONED
GIRL)
HAVE A LITTLE FAITH IN ME
HELLO, MONTREAL
HERE WE ARE
HONEYMOON HOTEL
HONOLULU
HOW COULD YOU?
I, YI, YI, YI, YI (I LIKE YOU VERY
MUCH)

I'D LOVE TO TAKE ORDERS FROM YOU

I'D RATHER LISTEN TO YOUR EYES

I FOUND A MILLION DOLLAR BABY (IN A FIVE AND TEN CENT STORE)

IF YOU FEEL LIKE SINGING, SING

I HAD THE CRAZIEST DREAM

I KNOW NOW

I KNOW WHY (AND SO DO YOU)

I'LL SING YOU A THOUSAND LOVE SONGS

I'LL STRING ALONG WITH YOU

I LOVE MY BABY (MY BABY LOVES ME)

I'M GOIN' SHOPPIN' WITH YOU

I'M YOUNG AND HEALTHY

IN ACAPULCO

INNAMORATA (SWEETHEART)

IN THE MERRY MONTH OF MAYBE

I ONLY HAVE EYES FOR YOU

IT HAPPENED IN SUN VALLEY

IT'S A GREAT BIG WORLD

I'VE GOT A GAL IN KALAMAZOO

I'VE GOT TO SING A TORCH SONG

I WANNA GO BACK TO BALI

I WISH I KNEW

I WOULDN'T TAKE A MILLION

JEEPERS CREEPERS

JEZEBEL

JOURNEY TO A STAR, A

KEEP YOUNG AND BEAUTIFUL

KISS POLKA, THE

LEGEND OF WYATT EARP, THE

LITTLE HOUSE THAT LOVE BUILT, THE

LITTLE THINGS YOU USED TO DO, THE

LOVE IS WHERE YOU FIND IT

LULLABLY OF BROADWAY

LULU'S BACK IN TOWN

MARTY

ME AND THE BLUES

MELODY FOR TWO

MORE I SEE YOU, THE

MY DREAM IS YOURS

MY HEART TELLS ME

MY KINGDOM FOR A KISS

MY ONE AND ONLY HIGHLAND FLING

NAGASAKI

NO LOVE, NO NOTHIN'

NO MORE LOVE

OCTOROON

OLD MAN SUNSHINE, LITTLE BOY BLUEBIRD

ONE SWEET LETTER FROM YOU

ONLY, ONLY ONE FOR ME, THE

ON THE ATCHISON, TOPEKA, AND THE SANTA FE

OOH! THAT KISS

OUTSIDE OF YOU

PAGE MISS GLORY

PEOPLE LIKE YOU AND ME

PETTIN' IN THE PARK

PLAY ME AN OLD FASHIONED MELODY

POEM SET TO MUSIC, A

REMEMBER ME?

REMEMBER MY FORGOTTEN MAN

REMINISCING

RIVER AND ME, THE

ROSE IN HER HAIR, THE

ROSE OF THE RIO GRANDE

ROSE TATTOO, THE

SATAN NEVER SLEEPS

SAY IT WITH A KISS

SEA OF THE MOON, THE

SEPTEMBER IN THE RAIN

SERENADE IN BLUE

SHADOW WALTZ

SHANGHAI LIL

SHE'S A LATIN FROM MANHATTAN

SHOES WITH WINGS ON

SHUFFLE OFF TO BUFFALO

SING A LITTLE JINGLE

SOMEBODY

SOMEONE LIKE YOU

SOMETHING TELLS ME

SONG OF SURRENDER

SONG OF THE MARINES, THE

STANLEY STEAMER, THE

SUMMER NIGHT

SWEET MUSIC

TEARS FROM MY INKWELL

TELLING IT TO THE DAISIES

THAT'S AMORE

THAT'S SABOTAGE

THERE'S A LULL IN MY LIFE

THERE WILL NEVER BE ANOTHER YOU

THEY MET IN RIO

THIS HEART OF MINE

THIS IS ALWAYS

THIS NIGHT WILL BE MY SOUVENIR

THREE'S A CROWD

TOO MANY TEARS

TORCH SONG, THE

TRA-LA-LA-LA

TROPICAL MAGIC

TWO DREAMS MET

WAIL OF THE WINDS

WAIT AND SEE

WEEK-END IN HAVANA, A

WEEKEND IN THE COUNTRY, A

WE'RE IN THE MONEY (A.K.A. THE GOLD DIGGERS' SONG)

WHEN THE SHEPHERD LEADS THE SHEEP BACK HOME

WHERE AM I?

WHERE DO YOU WORK-A, JOHN? (ON THE DELAWARE LACKAWAN')

WHERE THE SHY LITTLE VIOLETS GROW

WHERE THE SWEET FORGET-ME-NOTS REMEMBER

WHY DO I DREAM THOSE DREAMS?

WILD, WILD WEST, THE

WITH PLENTY OF MONEY AND YOU

WONDER BAR

WORDS ARE IN MY HEART, THE

WOULD YOU LIKE TO TAKE A WALK?

YA GOTTA KNOW HOW TO LOVE

YOLANDA

YOU CAN'T SAY NO TO A SOLDIER

YOU LET ME DOWN

YOU'LL NEVER KNOW

YOU MUST HAVE BEEN A BEAUTIFUL BABY

YOUNG AND HEALTHY

YOU'RE GETTING TO BE A HABIT WITH ME

YOU'RE MY EVERYTHING

YOU SAY THE SWEETEST THINGS, BABY

YOU WONDERFUL YOU

ZING A LITTLE ZONG

Warren, James

EVERYBODY'S GOT TO LEARN SOMETIME

WHERE THE BLUE AND LONELY GO

Warren, William

WILD SIDE OF LIFE, THE

Warshauer, Frank

IT ISN'T FAIR

Washburn, Lalomie

AT MIDNIGHT (MY LOVE WILL LIFT YOU UP)

Washburne, Joe "Country"

OH, MONAH
ONE DOZEN ROSES

Washington, Carol

MR. BIG STUFF

Washington, Ferdinand

I'LL BE HOME
PLEDGING MY LOVE

Washington, Fred

FEELS SO REAL (WON'T LET GO)
FORGET ME NOTS

Washington, Leon

HAMBONE

Washington, Ned

3:10 TO YUMA
BABY MINE
BOY TEN FEET TALL, A
BREAKIN' IN A PAIR OF SHOES
CAN'T WE TALK IT OVER?
COSI COSA
DON'T CALL IT LOVE
DON'T LET ME DREAM
FIRST LADY WALTZ
GIVE A LITTLE WHISTLE
GIVE ME A HEART TO SING TO
GOT THE SOUTH IN MY SOUL
GREATEST SHOW ON EARTH, THE
HAJJI BABA (PERSIAN LAMENT)
HEADIN' HOME
HIGH AND THE MIGHTY, THE
HIGH NOON (A.K.A. DO NOT
   FORSAKE ME)

HUNDRED YEARS FROM TODAY, A
I DON'T STAND A GHOST OF A
   CHANCE WITH YOU
I'LL BE FAITHFUL
I'M GETTIN' SENTIMENTAL OVER
   YOU
I WANT YOU FOR CHRISTMAS
LAMP ON THE CORNER, THE
LAZY RHAPSODY
LOVE IS THE THING
LOVE LIKE THIS, A
LOVE ME
LOVE ME TONIGHT
MAKIN' FACES AT THE MAN IN THE
   MOON
MAN FROM LARAMIE, THE
MY FOOLISH HEART
MY LOVE
NEARNESS OF YOU, THE
ONE LOOK AT YOU
ON GREEN DOLPHIN STREET
RAWHIDE
RETURN TO PARADISE
RIO DE JANEIRO
SADIE THOMPSON'S SONG
SINGIN' IN THE BATHTUB
SMOKE RINGS
SOMEDAY I'LL MEET YOU AGAIN
SOMEONE STOLE GABRIEL'S HORN
STELLA BY STARLIGHT
STRANGE ARE THE WAYS OF
   LOVE
STRANGE LADY IN TOWN
SWEET HEARTACHE
SWEET MADNESS
THEME FROM "THE UNFORGIVEN"
   (THE NEED FOR LOVE)
TO LOVE AGAIN
TONIGHT WILL LIVE
TOWN WITHOUT PITY
TURN ON THE OLD MUSIC BOX
WALTZING IN A DREAM
WHEN I SEE AN ELEPHANT FLY
WHEN YOU WISH UPON A STAR
WILD IS THE WIND
YOU'RE MY THRILL
YOUR LOVE

Washington, Oscar

NIGHT TRAIN

Washington, Patti

GIDGET

Washington, Steve

ARE YOU SINGLE?
MAKE THAT MOVE
MAKE UP YOUR MIND
WATCHING YOU

Wasson, Craig

HERE I AM

Waterman, Pete

I HEARD A RUMOR
I SHOULD BE SO LUCKY
NEVER GONNA GIVE YOU UP
TOGETHER FOREVER

Waters, Chris

ARE YOU EVER GONNA LOVE ME
IN A NEW YORK MINUTE

Waters, Roger

ANOTHER BRICK IN THE WALL
MONEY
RADIO WAVES

Waters, Safford

BELLE OF AVENOO A, THE

Waters, Stephen

SO GOOD

Watkins, Charles

TELL HER YOU LOVE HER EVERY
   DAY

Watkins, Viola

GEE!

Watley, Jody

DON'T YOU WANT ME

WHEN KENTUCKY BIDS THE WORLD
"GOOD MORNING"
(AS LONG AS YOU'RE NOT IN LOVE
WITH ANYONE ELSE) WHY DON'T
YOU FALL IN LOVE WITH ME?

Wayne, Sid

ANYTHING CAN HAPPEN MAMBO
DO THE CLAM
FIRST ANNIVERSARY
I'M GONNA KNOCK ON YOUR DOOR
I NEED YOUR LOVE TONIGHT
IT'S IMPOSSIBLE
IT'S ONLY THE BEGINNING
MANGOS
MY LOVE FOR YOU
NINETY-NINE YEARS (DEAD OR
ALIVE)
SEE YOU IN SEPTEMBER
SPINOUT
STOLEN MOMENTS
TWO DIFFERENT WORLDS

Weatherley, Frederick E.

DANNY BOY
LONG AGO IN ALCALA
ROSES OF PICARDY
THREE FOR JACK

Weatherly, James

WHERE DO I PUT HER MEMORY?
YOU ARE A SONG

Weatherly, Jim

BEST THING THAT EVER HAPPENED
TO ME, THE
MIDNIGHT TRAIN TO GEORGIA
NEED TO BE, THE
NEITHER ONE OF US (WANTS TO BE
THE FIRST TO SAY GOODBYE)
WHERE PEACEFUL WATERS FLOW

Weatherspoon, William

WHAT BECOMES OF THE
BROKENHEARTED?
WOMEN'S LOVE RIGHTS

Weaver, Blue

(OUR LOVE) DON'T THROW IT ALL
AWAY
HOLD ON TO MY LOVE

Webb, Chick

HAVE MERCY
LET'S GET TOGETHER
STOMPIN' AT THE SAVOY
YOU SHOWED ME THE WAY

Webb, Danny

ONE SUMMER NIGHT

Webb, Jim

ALL I KNOW
BY THE TIME I GET TO PHOENIX
CARPET MAN
DIDN'T WE
GALVESTON
HIGHWAYMAN
HONEY COME BACK
IT'S A SIN WHEN YOU LOVE
SOMEBODY
MACARTHUR PARK
PAPER CUP
UP—UP AND AWAY
WHERE'S THE PLAYGROUND SUSIE
WICHITA LINEMAN
WORST THAT COULD HAPPEN, THE
YARD WENT ON FOREVER, THE

Webb, Laura

MR. LEE

Webb, Mark

THIS ORCHID MEANS GOODBYE

Webber, Andrew Lloyd

ALL I ASK OF YOU
BUENOS AIRES
CHRISTMAS DREAM
COME BACK WITH THE SAME LOOK
IN YOUR EYES
DON'T CRY FOR ME, ARGENTINA

EVERYTHING'S ALRIGHT
GUS THE THEATRE CAT
I DON'T KNOW HOW TO LOVE HIM
MEMORY
MUSIC OF THE NIGHT, THE
PHANTOM OF THE OPERA, THE
STARLIGHT EXPRESS
SUPERSTAR
TELL ME ON A SUNDAY
UNEXPECTED SONG

Weber, Rollie

WE'RE THE TALK OF THE TOWN

Webster, Dan

WATCHING YOU

Webster, Paul Francis

ANASTASIA
APRIL LOVE
BALLAD OF THE ALAMO
BALTIMORE ORIOLE
BELOVED
BLACK COFFEE
BLOWING WILD (A.K.A. BALLAD OF
BLACK GOLD, THE)
BLUEBELL
BOY ON A DOLPHIN
BUBBLE LOO, BUBBLE LOO
CERTAIN SMILE, A
CHOCOLATE SHAKE
FRIENDLY PERSUASION (A.K.A.
THEE I LOVE)
GIANT
GOT THE JITTERS
GREEN LEAVES OF SUMMER, THE
GUNS OF NAVARONE, THE
HONEY-BABE
HOW IT LIES, HOW IT LIES, HOW IT
LIES!
IF I HAD A DOZEN HEARTS
I GOT IT BAD AND THAT AIN'T
GOOD
I'LL WALK WITH GOD
I'M LIKE A FISH OUT OF WATER
INVITATION
I SPEAK TO THE STARS
JUMP FOR JOY

LAMPLIGHTER'S SERENADE, THE
LILY OF LAGUNA
LITTLE LOVE CAN GO A LONG,
   LONG WAY, A
LOVE IS A MANY-SPLENDORED
   THING
LOVELIEST NIGHT IN THE YEAR,
   THE
LOVE SONG FROM "MUTINY ON THE
   BOUNTY"
LOVE THEME FROM "EL CID" (THE
   FALCON AND THE DOVE)
MASQUERADE
MAVERICK
MEMPHIS IN JUNE
MERRY CHRISTMAS POLKA, THE
MY MOONLIGHT MADONNA
ONE IS A LONELY NUMBER
PADRE
PEKING THEME, THE (SO LITTLE
   TIME)
PUT YOUR HEART IN A SONG
RAINBOW ON THE RIVER
REFLECTIONS IN THE WATER
REMEMBER ME TO CAROLINA
RIO BRAVO
SECRET LOVE
SEVENTH DAWN, THE
SHADOW OF YOUR SMILE, THE
SINCERELY YOURS
SLAP POLKA, THE
SOMEWHERE MY LOVE (LARA'S
   THEME)
SONG ANGELS SING, THE
SONG OF RAINTREE COUNTY, THE
STRANGE ARE THE WAYS OF LOVE
SUNNY SIDE OF THINGS, THE
SYLVIA
TENDER IS THE NIGHT
THREE RIVERS, THE (THE
   ALLEGHENY, SUSQUEHANNA,
   AND THE OLD MONONGAHELA)
TIME FOR LOVE, A
TWELFTH OF NEVER, THE
TWO CIGARETTES IN THE DARK
TWO LITTLE BLUE LITTLE EYES
VERY PRECIOUS LOVE, A
WATERMELON WEATHER
WATER UNDER THE BRIDGE
WHAT'S YOUR STORY, MORNING
   GLORY?
WHEN I LOOK AT YOU
YOU WAS

Webster, R. A.

LAST FAREWELL, THE

Webster, Warner

SHIRLEY

Webster, Warwick

MAN IN THE RAINCOAT, THE

Wechter, Julius

SPANISH FLEA

Weeden, Howard

BANJO SONG, A

Weeks, Anson

I'M SORRY DEAR

Weeks, Harold

HINDUSTAN

Weeks, Ricardo

I WONDER WHY

Weems, Hermon

YOU'VE GOT TO PAY THE PRICE

Weems, Ted

OH, MONAH

Weersma, Melle

PENNY SERENADE

Weide, Johnny

MONTEREY

Weider, John

SAN FRANCISCAN NIGHTS
SKY PILOT
WHEN I WAS YOUNG

Weil, Cynthia

ALL I NEED TO KNOW
ALL OF YOU
AMY
BLAME IT ON THE BOSSA NOVA
BLESS YOU
BROWN EYED WOMAN
COME ON OVER TO MY PLACE
CONSCIENCE
DON'T BE AFRAID, LITTLE DARLIN'
DON'T MAKE MY BABY BLUE
HAPPY TIMES (ARE HERE TO STAY)
HEART (I HEAR YOU BEATING)
HERE YOU COME AGAIN
HE'S SO SHY
HE'S SURE THE BOY I LOVE
HOME OF THE BRAVE
HOW CAN I TELL HER IT'S OVER?
HUNGRY
IF A WOMAN ANSWERS (HANG UP
   THE PHONE)
IF EVER YOU'RE IN MY ARMS
   AGAIN
I JUST CAN'T HELP BELIEVING
I'LL TAKE YOU HOME
I'M GONNA BE STRONG
IT'S GETTING BETTER
I WANT YOU TO MEET MY BABY
JOHNNY LOVES ME
KICKS
LOVE LIVES ON
LOVE WILL CONQUER ALL
MAGIC TOWN
MAKE YOUR OWN KIND OF MUSIC
MARY'S LITTLE LAMB
MY DAD
NEVER GONNA LET YOU GO
NEW WORLD COMING
ON BROADWAY
ONLY IN AMERICA
PEACE, BROTHER, PEACE
PROUD
ROCK AND ROLL LULLABY
RUNNING WITH THE NIGHT
SATURDAY NIGHT AT THE MOVIES
SHAPE OF THINGS TO COME
SO FAR SO GOOD
SO LONG DIXIE
SOMEWHERE DOWN THE ROAD
SOMEWHERE OUT THERE
(YOU'RE MY) SOUL AND INSPIRATION
THROUGH THE FIRE

UPTOWN
WALKING IN THE RAIN
WE GOTTA GET OUT OF THIS PLACE
WE'RE GOING ALL THE WAY
YOU'VE LOST THAT LOVIN' FEELIN'

Weill, Harry

DON'T LEAVE ME DOLLY

Weill, Irving

TRIPOLI (THE SHORES OF)

Weill, Kurt

ALABAMA SONG
ALL AT ONCE
BILBAO SONG, THE
FOOLISH HEART
GREEN-UP TIME
HERE I'LL STAY
I'M A STRANGER HERE MYSELF
IT NEVER WAS YOU
JENNY (THE SAGA OF)
LITTLE GRAY HOUSE, THE
LOST IN THE STARS
MACK THE KNIFE (A.K.A. MORITAT)
MILE AFTER MILE
MOON-FACED, STARRY-EYED
MY HEART IS SHOWING (DON'T
   LOOK NOW, BUT)
MY SHIP
ONE LIFE TO LIVE
ON THE RIO GRANDE
PIRATE JENNY
PRINCESS OF PURE DELIGHT
SEPTEMBER SONG
SPEAK LOW
STAY WELL
TCHAIKOWSKY (AND OTHER
   RUSSIANS)
THAT'S HIM
THIS IS NEW
TO LOVE YOU AND TO LOSE YOU
WESTWIND
WHAT GOOD WOULD THE MOON BE?

Weinberg, Mortimer

WHERE DO YOU WORK-A, JOHN?
   (ON THE DELAWARE LACKAWAN')

Weinman, Bernard

TOO MUCH

Weinstein, Bobby

BIG WIDE WORLD
GOIN' OUT OF MY HEAD
HAVE YOU LOOKED INTO YOUR
   HEART?
I'M ON THE OUTSIDE (LOOKING IN)
IT'S GONNA TAKE A MIRACLE
PRETTY BLUE EYES
SINNER MAN
SWEET CREAM LADIES, FORWARD
   MARCH

Weir, Bob

MUSIC NEVER STOPPED, THE
SUGAR MAGNOLIA
TRUCKIN'

Weis, Danny

APRICOT BRANDY

Weisberg, Dave

DOWN BY THE SILVERY RIO
   GRANDE

Weiser, Irving

THERE I GO

Weisman, Ben

ALL I SEE IS YOU
DON'T ASK ME WHY
DO THE CLAM
FAME AND FORTUNE
LONELY BLUE BOY
MOONLIGHT SWIM
MY LIPS ARE SEALED
NEVER LET HER GO
NIGHT HAS A THOUSAND EYES, THE
OO! WHAT YOU DO TO ME
ROCK-A-HULA BABY
SATISFACTION GUARANTEED
SPINOUT
STRANGE SENSATION
WOODEN HEART

Weiss, David

WHERE DID YOUR HEART GO?

Weiss, Donna

BETTE DAVIS EYES

Weiss, George David

CAN ANYONE EXPLAIN? (NO! NO!
   NO!)
CAN'T HELP FALLING IN LOVE
CONFESS
CROSS OVER THE BRIDGE
DANCIN' WITH SOMEONE (LONGIN'
   FOR YOU)
DON'T CALL MY NAME
ECHOES
FUN AND FANCY FREE
GIRL!, A GIRL!, A (ZOOM-BA DI ALLI
   NELLA)
HELLO HEARTACHE, GOODBYE
   LOVE
HEY, LITTLE LUCY! (DON'TCHA PUT
   NO LIPSTICK ON)
HOW IMPORTANT CAN IT BE?
I DON'T SEE ME IN YOUR EYES
   ANYMORE
I'LL NEVER BE FREE
I'M AVAILABLE
I RAN ALL THE WAY HOME
I WANT TO THANK YOUR FOLKS
JET
LET'S PUT IT ALL TOGETHER
LION SLEEPS TONIGHT, THE
LULLABY OF BIRDLAND
MANDOLINS IN THE MOONLIGHT
MELODY TIME
MR. WONDERFUL
OH! WHAT IT SEEMED TO BE
PIANISSIMO
RUMORS ARE FLYING
SUMMER LOVE
SURRENDER
THAT SUNDAY, THAT SUMMER
THESE THINGS I OFFER YOU (FOR A
   LIFETIME)
TOO CLOSE FOR COMFORT
TO THINK YOU'VE CHOSEN ME
TOYS IN THE ATTIC
WHAT A WONDERFUL WORLD
WHEEL OF FORTUNE

Weiss, George David

WILD IN THE COUNTRY

Weiss, Larry

MORE THAN THE EYE CAN SEE
MR. DREAM MERCHANT
RHINESTONE COWBOY

Weiss, Laurence

BEND ME, SHAPE ME
HELP ME, GIRL
MR. WISHING WELL

Weiss, Marion

I WISH THAT WE WERE MARRIED

Weiss, Sam

I BELIEVE IN YOU
WE BELONG TOGETHER

Weiss, Stephan

AND SO DO I
ANGEL IN DISGUISE
MAKE LOVE TO ME
MUSIC! MUSIC! MUSIC!
PUT YOUR DREAMS AWAY (FOR
    ANOTHER DAY)
THEY SAY
WHILE YOU DANCED, DANCED,
    DANCED (I WALKED IN WITH A
    SMILE)

Weitz, Mark

TOMORROW

Welch, Bob

EBONY EYES
SENTIMENTAL LADY

Welch, Bruce

BACHELOR BOY
PLEASE MR. PLEASE

Welch, Dan

FIRST DATE, FIRST KISS, FIRST
    LOVE
GO AWAY WITH ME
SPANISH FIRE BALL

Welch, Kevin

PLAIN BROWN WRAPPER

Welch, Robert

PRECIOUS LOVE

Weldon, Frank

CHRISTMAS IN KILLARNEY
GOODNIGHT, WHEREVER YOU ARE
I CAME, I SAW, I CONGA'D
I LIKE MOUNTAIN MUSIC
LITTLE ON THE LONELY SIDE, A
MAN WITH THE MANDOLIN, THE
NEIGHBORS

Weldon, William

I'M GONNA MOVE TO THE
    OUTSKIRTS OF TOWN
SOMEBODY DONE CHANGE THE
    LOCK

Weller, Freddy

DIZZY
JAM UP JELLY TIGHT

Weller, Paul

MY EVER CHANGING MOODS

Wells, Bryan

PLACE IN THE SUN, A
TRAVLIN' MAN
YESTER-ME, YESTER-YOU,
    YESTERDAY

Wells, Carl

LET ME BE GOOD TO YOU

Wells, Ed

CASUAL LOOK, A

Wells, Gilbert

RED HOT MAMA

Wells, Henry

LITTLE JOE FROM CHICAGO

Wells, Jack

JOAN OF ARC, THEY ARE CALLING
    YOU

Wells, James Thomas

WKRP IN CINCINNATI

Wells, Kevin

WALKING ON A THIN LINE

Wells, Peggy Sue

DON'T COME HOME A-DRINKIN'
    (WITH LOVIN' ON YOUR MIND)

Wells, Robert

BAD IS FOR OTHER PEOPLE
BORN TO BE BLUE
CHRISTMAS SONG, THE
COMMENT ALLEZ-VOUS? (HOW ARE
    THINGS WITH YOU?)
COUNTRY FAIR
ELOISE
FROM HERE TO ETERNITY
IT'S EASY TO SAY (A.K.A. SONG
    FROM "10")
RE-ENLISTMENT BLUES
WHAT EVERY GIRL SHOULD KNOW

Wells, Roy

LONELY WINE

Wendling, Pete

ALL THE QUAKERS ARE SHOULDER
SHAKERS DOWN IN QUAKER
TOWN
BY THE SYCAMORE TREE
CRYING MYSELF TO SLEEP
DON'T WAKE UP MY HEART
GIVE ME YOUR AFFECTION, HONEY
I BELIEVE IN MIRACLES
I'LL BE BLUE, JUST THINKING OF
YOU
I'M A FOOL FOR LOVING YOU
I'M GROWING FONDER OF YOU
I'M SURE OF EVERYTHING BUT YOU
I'M TICKLED PINK WITH A BLUE-
EYED BABY
OH, HOW I WISH I COULD SLEEP
UNTIL MY DADDY COMES HOME
OH, WHAT A PAL WAS MARY
ON THE STREET OF REGRET
RED LIPS KISS MY BLUES AWAY
SWINGING IN A HAMMOCK
TAKE YOUR GIRLIE TO THE MOVIES
(IF YOU CAN'T MAKE LOVE AT
HOME)
THANKS TO YOU
THERE'S DANGER IN YOUR EYES,
CHERIE
THERE'S EVERYTHING NICE ABOUT
YOU (THERE'S SOMETHING NICE
ABOUT EVERYONE)
WE WERE THE BEST OF FRIENDS
WONDERFUL YOU
YAAKA HULA HICKEY DULA

Wenrich, Percy

BABY
IT'S MOONLIGHT ALL THE TIME ON
BROADWAY
KENTUCKY DAYS
LANTERN OF LOVE
MOONLIGHT BAY (A.K.A. ON
MOONLIGHT BAY)
PUT ON YOUR OLD GREY BONNET
SAIL ALONG, SILV'RY MOON
SHE TOOK MOTHER'S ADVICE
SILVER BELL
SUGAR MOON
UP IN A BALLOON
WAY OUT YONDER IN THE GOLDEN
WEST

WHEN YOU WORE A TULIP AND I
WORE A BIG RED ROSE
WHERE DO WE GO FROM HERE?

Wenzlaff, Erwin

I GOT A WIFE

Werber, Carl

CAST YOUR FATE TO THE WIND

Werfel, Steve

I LIVE FOR YOUR LOVE

Werner, Joe

WONDERING

Werner, Kay

ROCK IT FOR ME

Werner, Sue

ROCK IT FOR ME

Wesley, Fred

GET ON THE GOOD FOOT
HOT PANTS (SHE GOT TO USE WHAT
SHE GOT TO GET WHAT SHE
WANTS)
PAYBACK, THE

Weslyn, Louis

BABY ROSE
SEND ME AWAY WITH A SMILE

West, Arthur

SEE, SAW, MARGERY DAW

West, Bill

HERE COMES MY BABY BACK
AGAIN
IS THIS ME?
WOULD YOU HOLD IT AGAINST ME?

West, Bob

I'LL BE THERE
YOU'RE SO FINE

West, Bobby

IF YOU TALK IN YOUR SLEEP
I'M A FOOL
SEPARATE WAYS

West, David

PORTRAIT OF MY LOVE

West, Dottie

COUNTRY SUNSHINE
HERE COMES MY BABY BACK
AGAIN
IS THIS ME?
WOULD YOU HOLD IT AGAINST ME?

West, Eugene

BROADWAY ROSE
ROLL ON, MISSISSIPPI, ROLL ON
YOU KNOW YOU BELONG TO
SOMEBODY ELSE (SO WHY DON'T
YOU LEAVE ME ALONE)

West, Hedy

FIVE HUNDRED MILES AWAY FROM
HOME

West, Jerry

MEAN WOMAN BLUES

West, Kyle

NITE AND DAY
OFF ON YOUR OWN (GIRL)

West, Norman

HEARSAY

West, Pat

YOU MIGHT HAVE BELONGED TO
ANOTHER

West, Paul

I'M ON THE WATER WAGON NOW
YOU'LL ALWAYS BE JUST SWEET
   SIXTEEN TO ME

West, Rick

HOLLYWOOD SWINGING
TROUBLE IN THE FIELDS

West, Robert

I FOUND A LOVE

West, Roy

I'M BITIN' MY FINGERNAILS AND
   THINKING OF YOU
OVER THREE HILLS

West, Sonny

RAVE ON

West, Tommy

AMERICAN CITY SUITE
MEDICINE MAN

Westberry, Kent

AIR MAIL TO HEAVEN
BE GLAD
HELLO OUT THERE
I JUST DON'T UNDERSTAND

Western, Johnny

BALLAD OF PALADIN, THE

Westlake, Clive

ALL I SEE IS YOU
MINUTE OF YOUR TIME, A

Westmoreland, Paul

DETOUR

Weston, Paul

CONGRATULATIONS

DAY BY DAY
GANDY DANCERS' BALL, THE
HEY, MR. POSTMAN
INDISCRETION
I SHOULD CARE
NO OTHER LOVE
SHRIMP BOATS

Weston, R. P.

I'M HENRY VIII, I AM
I'VE GOT RINGS ON MY FINGERS
   (OR, MUMBO JUMBO JIJIBOO J.
   O'SHEA)

Weston, Willie

JOAN OF ARC, THEY ARE CALLING
   YOU

West-Oram, Jamie

ARE WE OURSELVES?
ONE THING LEADS TO ANOTHER
SECRET SEPARATION
STAND OR FALL

Wetron, R. P.

SISTER SUSIE'S SEWING SHIRTS FOR
   SOLDIERS

Wetton, John

DON'T CRY
HEAT OF THE MOMENT
ONLY TIME WILL TELL

Wetzel, Ray

INTERMISSION RIFF

Wever, Ned

I CAN'T RESIST YOU
SING A NEW SONG
SWEET STRANGER
TROUBLE IN PARADISE
TRUST IN ME

Wexler, Jerry

EVERYBODY NEEDS SOMEBODY TO
   LOVE
LITTLE MAMA
MINIMUM LOVE
NATURAL WOMAN, A (YOU MAKE
   ME FEEL LIKE)
TWENTY-FIVE MILES

Weymouth, Tina

AND SHE WAS
BURNING DOWN THE HOUSE
ONCE IN A LIFETIME
PSYCHO KILLER

Wheatley, Horace

SAWMILL

Wheeler, Billy Edd

BLISTERED
COWARD OF THE COUNTY
JACKSON
MAN WHO ROBBED THE BANK AT
   SANTA FE, THE
ODE TO THE LITTLE BROWN SHACK
   OUT BACK
REVEREND MR. BLACK

Wheeler, Cheryl

ADDICTED

Wheeler, Francis

DANCING FOOL
IT WAS ONLY A SUN SHOWER
I WONDER IF YOU STILL CARE FOR
   ME
LET A SMILE BE YOUR UMBRELLA
SHEIK OF ARABY, THE
THERE'S SOMETHING ABOUT A ROSE
   (THAT REMINDS ME OF YOU)
UNDER THE MOON

Wheeler, Onie

GO HOME
LET'S INVITE THEM OVER

Whelan, Ekko

THERE'S A NEW MOON OVER MY
  SHOULDER

Whelan, James

MAD ABOUT YOU

Whidden, Jay

DOWN IN DEAR OLD NEW ORLEANS

Whipple, Sterling

I'LL BE COMING BACK FOR MORE
LAST GAME OF THE SEASON, THE
  (A BLIND MAN IN THE
  BLEACHERS)
PRISONER OF HOPE

Whitcomb, Ian

YOU TURN ME ON (THE TURN ON
  SONG)

Whitcup, Leonard

AM I PROUD?
"A" TEAM, THE
BEWILDERED
FIESTA
FROM THE VINE CAME THE GRAPE
HEAVEN HELP THIS HEART OF MINE
I AM AN AMERICAN
I COULDN'T BELIEVE MY EYES
IF MY HEART COULD ONLY TALK
KISSIN' ON THE PHONE
MARCH WINDS AND APRIL
  SHOWERS
ROLLIN' PLAINS
SNAKE CHARMER, THE
TAKE ME BACK TO MY BOOTS AND
  SADDLE
TRUE

White, Alan

AFTER THE LIGHTS GO DOWN

White, Barry

CAN'T GET ENOUGH OF YOUR LOVE,
  BABE
I BELONG TO YOU
I'M GONNA LOVE YOU JUST A
  LITTLE BIT MORE, BABY
IT MAY BE WINTER OUTSIDE (BUT
  IN MY HEART IT'S SPRING)
LOVE'S THEME
NEVER, NEVER GONNA GIVE YA UP
OH WHAT A NIGHT FOR DANCING
SATIN SOUL
WALKIN' IN THE RAIN WITH THE
  ONE I LOVE
WHAT AM I GONNA DO WITH YOU
YOU'RE THE FIRST, THE LAST, MY
  EVERYTHING

White, Bert

CANADIAN CAPERS

White, Calvin

FEEL SO GOOD

White, Carl

BIRD'S THE WORD, THE
PAPA-OOM-MOW-MOW
SURFIN' BIRD

White, Chris

HOLD YOUR HEAD UP
I LOVE YOU

White, David

AT THE HOP
DAWN OF CORRECTION
FLY, THE
LIKE A BABY
ROCK AND ROLL IS HERE TO STAY
YOU DON'T OWN ME

White, Earl

CYNTHIA'S IN LOVE

White, Eddie

AT A SIDEWALK PENNY ARCADE
SO FAR, SO GOOD

White, Edward R.

C'EST LA VIE
CRAZY OTTO RAG, THE
FLOWERS MEAN FORGIVENESS
HAPPINESS STREET (CORNER
  SUNSHINE SQUARE)

White, Gary

LONG LONG TIME

White, Harry

EVENIN'

White, Johnny

TEN LITTLE FINGERS AND TEN
  LITTLE TOES (DOWN IN
  TENNESSEE)

White, L. E.

AFTER THE FIRE IS GONE
I LOVE YOU MORE TODAY
TO SEE MY ANGEL CRY

White, Lee "Lasses"

IF YOU KNEW WHAT IT MEANT TO
  BE LONESOME
MINE, ALL MINE

White, Mark

BE NEAR ME
(HOW TO BE A) MILLIONAIRE
WHEN SMOKEY SINGS

White, Maurice

BEST OF MY LOVE
FALL IN LOVE WITH ME
FANTASY
I AM LOVE
SATURDAY NITE
SEPTEMBER

SERPENTINE FIRE
SHINING STAR
SING A SONG
THAT'S THE WAY OF THE WORLD

White, Pat

IT'S THE SAME OLD SHILLELAGH

White, Peter

TIME PASSAGES

White, Ronald

MY GIRL
MY GIRL HAS GONE
ONE MORE HEARTACHE
YOU BEAT ME TO THE PUNCH

White, Ted

(SWEET, SWEET BABY) SINCE
    YOU'VE BEEN GONE
THINK

White, Tony Joe

POLK SALAD ANNIE
RAINY NIGHT IN GEORGIA, A
ROOSEVELT AND IRA LEE (NIGHT
    OF THE MOCCASIN)

White, Verdine

FANTASY
SERPENTINE FIRE

White, Willie

I'D LOVE TO BE A MONKEY IN THE
    ZOO
OH HOW I LAUGH WHEN I THINK
    HOW I CRIED ABOUT YOU

Whited, Donald

COME ON, DO THE JERK

Whitehead, John

AIN'T NO STOPPIN' US NOW
BACK STABBERS

BAD LUCK
I DON'T WANT TO LOSE YOUR LOVE
WAKE UP EVERYBODY

Whitehead, Peter

MACHO MAN

Whitelaw, Reid

GOODY GOODY GUMDROPS

Whiteman, Paul

FLAMIN' MAMIE
WHEN THE ONE YOU LOVE LOVES
    YOU
WONDERFUL ONE (MY)

Whiteshide, Bobby

COMIN' IN AND OUT OF YOUR LIFE

Whitfield, Norman

AIN'T TOO PROUD TO BEG
BALL OF CONFUSION (THAT'S WHAT
    THE WORLD IS TODAY)
BEAUTY IS ONLY SKIN DEEP
CAR WASH
CLOUD NINE
DON'T LET HIM TAKE YOUR LOVE
    FROM ME
DON'T LET THE JONESES GET YOU
    DOWN
END OF OUR ROAD, THE
EVERYBODY NEEDS LOVE
FRIENDSHIP TRAIN
GONNA GIVE HER ALL THE LOVE
    I'VE GOT
HEY GIRL (I LIKE YOUR STYLE)
I CAN'T GET NEXT TO YOU
I COULD NEVER LOVE ANOTHER
    (AFTER LOVING YOU)
I HEARD IT THROUGH THE
    GRAPEVINE
I KNOW I'M LOSING YOU
IT SHOULD HAVE BEEN ME
I WANT TO GET NEXT TO YOU
I WISH IT WOULD RAIN
JUST MY IMAGINATION (RUNNING
    AWAY WITH ME)

LONELINESS MADE ME REALIZE
    (IT'S YOU I NEED)
NEEDLE IN A HAYSTACK
OOH BOY
PAPA WAS A ROLLIN' STONE
PLEASE RETURN YOUR LOVE TO ME
PRIDE AND JOY
PSYCHEDELIC SHACK
RUN AWAY CHILD, RUNNING WILD
SUPERSTAR (REMEMBER HOW YOU
    GOT WHERE YOU ARE)
THAT'S THE WAY LOVE IS
THEME SONG FROM "WHICH WAY IS
    UP?"
TOO BUSY THINKING ABOUT MY
    BABY
TOO MANY FISH IN THE SEA
UNDISPUTED TRUTH, THE
WAR
YOU'RE MY EVERYTHING

Whitford, Brad

LAST CHILD

Whiting, George

BEAUTIFUL EYES
BELIEVE IT, BELOVED
DON'T LET YOUR LOVE GO WRONG
EV'RY LITTLE BIT HELPS
HIGH UP ON A HILL TOP
I'LL BE BLUE, JUST THINKING OF
    YOU
MY BLUE HEAVEN
MY WIFE'S GONE TO THE COUNTRY,
    HURRAH! HURRAH!
RHYTHM AND ROMANCE
WEST OF THE GREAT DIVIDE
YOU STAYED AWAY TOO LONG

Whiting, Richard A.

ADORABLE
AIN'T WE GOT FUN?
ALWAYS IN ALL WAYS
AND THEY CALLED IT DIXIELAND
    (THEY MADE IT TWICE AS NICE
    AS PARADISE)
BEYOND THE BLUE HORIZON
BIMINI BAY
BREEZIN' ALONG WITH THE BREEZE
DOUBLE TROUBLE

EADIE WAS A LADY
GATHER LIP ROUGE WHILE YOU
  MAY
GIVE ME A MOMENT PLEASE
GOT NO TIME
GUILTY
HAVE YOU GOT ANY CASTLES,
  BABY?
HONEY
HOORAY FOR HOLLYWOOD
HORSES
I CAN'T ESCAPE FROM YOU
I HAVE TO HAVE YOU
I'LL DREAM TONIGHT
IT'S A GREAT LIFE (IF YOU DON'T
  WEAKEN)
IT SEEMS TO BE SPRING
IT'S TULIP TIME IN HOLLAND
IT WAS SWEET OF YOU
I'VE HITCHED MY WAGON TO A
  STAR
I WONDER WHERE MY LOVIN' MAN
  HAS GONE
JAPANESE SANDMAN, THE
JUST A QUIET EVENING
LET THAT BE A LESSON TO YOU
LOUISE
LOVE IS ON THE AIR TONIGHT
MAMMY'S LITTLE COAL BLACK ROSE
MISS BROWN TO YOU
MOONLIGHT ON THE CAMPUS
MY FUTURE JUST PASSED
MY FUTURE STAR
MY IDEAL
MY SWEETER THAN SWEET
(I'D LOVE TO SPEND) ONE HOUR
  WITH YOU
ON THE GOOD SHIP LOLLIPOP
PETER PIPER
RIDE, TENDERFOOT, RIDE
ROCK AND ROLL
SAILOR BEWARE
SENTIMENTAL AND MELANCHOLY
SHE'S FUNNY THAT WAY (I GOT A
  WOMAN, CRAZY FOR ME)
SILHOUETTED IN THE MOONLIGHT
SLEEPY TIME GAL
SOME SUNDAY MORNING
SONG OF PERSIA
SORRY
TEA LEAVES
TILL WE MEET AGAIN
TOO MARVELOUS FOR WORDS

TRUE BLUE LOU
UKULELE LADY
WAITIN' AT THE GATE FOR KATY
WAIT 'TIL YOU SEE MA CHERIE
WHAT WOULD YOU DO?
WHEN DID YOU LEAVE HEAVEN?
WHEN SHALL WE MEET AGAIN?
WHERE THE BLACK-EYED SUSANS
  GROW
WHERE THE MORNING GLORIES
  GROW
WHY DREAM?
YES TO YOU
YOU'RE AN OLD SMOOTHIE
YOU'VE GOT SOMETHING THERE

Whitley, Ray

BACK IN THE SADDLE AGAIN
I HANG MY HEAD AND CRY
I'VE BEEN HURT
RUN, RUN, LOOK AND SEE
WHAT KIND OF FOOL (DO YOU
  THINK I AM)?

Whitlock, Tom

DANGER ZONE
OVER THE TOP
TAKE MY BREATH AWAY (LOVE
  THEME FROM "PETER GUNN")
WINNER TAKES IT ALL

Whitlock, William "Billy"

HOP-SCOTCH POLKA (SCOTCH HOT)

Whitney, Howard

MOSQUITO'S PARADE, THE

Whitney, Joan

AIN'T NOBODY HERE BUT US
  CHICKENS
CANDY
COMME ÇI, COMME ÇA
FAR AWAY PLACES
HIGH ON A WINDY HILL
IT ALL COMES BACK TO ME NOW
IT'S LOVE, LOVE, LOVE
LOVE SOMEBODY

MONEY IS THE ROOT OF ALL EVIL
MY SISTER AND I
NO MAN IS AN ISLAND
NO OTHER ARMS, NO OTHER LIPS
THAT'S THE BEGINNING OF THE
  END
YOU'LL NEVER GET AWAY

Whitsett, Carson

WHY NOT ME

Whitson, Beth Slater

DON'T WAKE ME UP, I'M DREAMING
LET ME CALL YOU SWEETHEART
MEET ME TONIGHT IN DREAMLAND

Whitson, Tex

I ALWAYS GET LUCKY WITH YOU

Whittaker, Roger

LAST FAREWELL, THE
YOU ARE MY MIRACLE

Whitten, Danny

I DON'T WANT TO TALK ABOUT IT

Wickham, Vicki

YOU DON'T HAVE TO SAY YOU LOVE
  ME

Widelitz, Stacey

SHE'S LIKE THE WIND

Wiedlin, Jane

OUR LIPS ARE SEALED
VACATION

Wiegand, Larry

EVIL WOMAN (A.K.A. EVIL MAN)

Wiegand, Richard

EVIL WOMAN (A.K.A. EVIL MAN)

Wiener, Herb

IT'S MY PARTY
JOEY

Wiener, Jean

THE TOUCH (LE GRISBI)

Wiener, Stuart

TO THE AISLE

Wier, Rusty

DON'T IT MAKE YOU WANNA
DANCE?

Wiggins, Jay

SAD GIRL

Wilburn, Doyle

SOMEBODY'S BACK IN TOWN
YOU'RE NOT MINE ANYMORE

Wilburn, Teddy

DOWN BY THE RIVER
SOMEBODY'S BACK IN TOWN
YOU'RE NOT MINE ANYMORE

Wilcox, Ella Wheeler

LAUGH AND THE WORLD LAUGHS
WITH YOU

Wilcox, Harlow

GROOVY GRUBWORM

Wilcox, John

SET ME FREE

Wilde, Marty

ABERGAVENNY
KIDS IN AMERICA

Wilde, Ricky

KIDS IN AMERICA

Wilder, Alec

ALL THE KING'S HORSES
GOODBYE, JOHN
IF SHE SHOULD COME TO YOU (LA
   MONTANA)
I'LL BE AROUND
I'LL WAIT
IT'S SO PEACEFUL IN THE COUNTRY
LONELY NIGHT
LONG NIGHT, A
LOVE AMONG THE YOUNG
PHOENIX LOVE THEME, THE
SOFT AS SPRING
TROUBLE IS A MAN
WHERE IS THE ONE?
WHILE WE'RE YOUNG
WHO CAN I TURN TO?

Wilder, John

YELLOW ROSE, THE

Wilder, Matthew

BREAK MY STRIDE

Wildes, Bill

ONE STEP FORWARD

Wildhorn, Frank

WHERE DO BROKEN HEARTS GO

Wilding, Bobby

HURT SO BAD

Wiley, Lee

GOT THE SOUTH IN MY SOUL

Wilhite, Monte

WHEN SUMMER IS GONE

Wilke, Nicola

HAPPY JOURNEY

Wilkin, John

G.T.O.

Wilkin, Marijohn

FALLEN ANGEL
GREENER PASTURES
GRIN AND BEAR IT
I JUST DON'T UNDERSTAND
LONG BLACK VEIL
OLD SHOWBOAT
ONE DAY AT A TIME
P.T. 109
TAKE TIME
WATERLOO

Wilkins, A. E.

WHAT MORE CAN I ASK?

Wilkins, David

COMING ON STRONG

Wilkins, Ronnie

LAND OF MILK AND HONEY, THE
SON-OF-A-PREACHER MAN
SPREAD IT ON THICK

Wilkinson, Dudley

BECAUSE OF YOU

Willemetz, Albert

VALENTINE

Willensky, Elliot

GOT TO BE THERE

Willet, Chappie

BLUE RHYTHM FANTASY

Willet, Slim

DON'T LET THE STARS GET IN YOUR
    EYES
I LET THE STARS GET IN MY EYES
LET ME KNOW
ON MY MIND AGAIN

Williams, Alvin

RANG TANG DING DONG (I AM THE
    JAPANESE SANDMAN)

Williams, André

FUNKY JUDGE
SHAKE A TAIL FEATHER
TWINE TIME

Williams, Arthur

FUNNY THING

Williams, Aston "Deacon"

WHERE THE MOUNTAINS MEET THE
    SKY

Williams, Barney

BABY, IT'S YOU

Williams, Bernie

DUKE OF EARL

Williams, Bert

CONSTANTLY
LET IT ALONE
NOBODY
THAT'S A-PLENTY
VOODOO MAN, THE
WHEN IT'S ALL GOIN' OUT, AND
    NOTHIN' COMIN' IN

Williams, Bob

(I WOULD DO) ANYTHING FOR YOU

Williams, Charles

DREAM OF OLWEN, THE
JEALOUS LOVER (A.K.A. THEME
    FROM "THE APARTMENT")
THEME FROM "THE APARTMENT"

Williams, Charlie

FIVE HUNDRED MILES AWAY FROM
    HOME
HICKTOWN
I GOT STRIPES
MILLION YEARS OR SO, A
SOMETHING PRETTY

Williams, Clarence

BABY, WON'T YOU PLEASE COME
    HOME
CAKE WALKING BABIES FROM
    HOME
ECHO OF SPRING
GRAVIER STREET BLUES
GULF COAST BLUES
I AIN'T GONNA GIVE NOBODY NONE
    O' THIS JELLY ROLL
IN THE BOTTLE BLUES
JAIL HOUSE BLUES
ROYAL GARDEN BLUES
SHOUT, SISTER, SHOUT
SQUEEZE ME
SUGAR BLUES
SWING, BROTHER, SWING
'TAINT NOBODY'S BIZNESS IF I DO
UGLY CHILE (A.K.A. YOU'RE SOME
    PRETTY DOLL)
WHAT'S THE MATTER NOW?

Williams, Cootie

EPISTROPHY

Williams, Curley

M-I-S-S-I-S-S-I-P-P-I

Williams, Curtis

MISLED

Williams, Dave

WHOLE LOT-TA SHAKIN' GOIN' ON

Williams, David

DON'T HOLD BACK

Williams, Dick

BALLAD OF IRVING, THE

Williams, Don

I'LL NEVER BE IN LOVE AGAIN
I WOULDN'T BE A MAN
LOVE ME OVER AGAIN
TILL THE RIVERS ALL RUN DRY

Williams, E.

PLANET ROCK

Williams, Edna

I DON'T WANT ANOTHER SISTER

Williams, Frank

I'M LIVIN' IN SHAME

Williams, Fred

FREIGHT TRAIN

Williams, George

IT MUST BE JELLY ('CAUSE JAM
    DON'T SHAKE LIKE THAT)
SO MUCH IN LOVE

Williams, Hank

BABY, WE'RE REALLY IN LOVE
CAJUN BABY
COLD, COLD HEART
HALF AS MUCH
HEY, GOOD LOOKIN
HONKY TONK BLUES
HONKY TONKIN'
HOWLIN' AT THE MOON
I CAN'T HELP IT (IF I'M STILL IN
    LOVE WITH YOU)

I JUST DON'T LIKE THIS KIND OF
   LIVIN'
I'M A LONG GONE DADDY
I'M SO LONESOME I COULD CRY
I SAW THE LIGHT
I WON'T BE HOME NO MORE
JAMBALAYA (ON THE BAYOU)
KAW-LIGA
LONG GONE LONESOME BLUES
LOST HIGHWAY
LOVESICK BLUES
MANSION ON THE HILL, A
MIND YOUR OWN BUSINESS
MOANIN' THE BLUES
MOVE IT ON OVER
PAN AMERICAN
RAMBLIN' MAN
THERE'LL BE NO TEARDROPS
   TONIGHT
WEARY BLUES FROM WAITIN'
WHY DON'T YOU LOVE ME?
WHY SHOULD WE TRY ANYMORE?
YOU'RE GONNA CHANGE (OR I'M
   GONNA LEAVE)
YOUR CHEATIN' HEART
YOU WIN AGAIN

Williams, Hank, Jr.

ALL MY ROWDY FRIENDS (HAVE
   SETTLED DOWN)
ALL MY ROWDY FRIENDS ARE
   COMING OVER TONIGHT
BORN TO BOOGIE
CAJUN BABY
COUNTRY BOY CAN SURVIVE, A
FAMILY TRADITION
I'M FOR LOVE
IT'S ALL OVER (BUT THE CRYING)
LAST LOVE SONG, THE
STANDING IN THE SHADOWS
WHISKEY BENT AND HELL BOUND
WOMEN I'VE NEVER HAD
YOUNG COUNTRY

Williams, Harry

BACK, BACK, BACK TO BALTIMORE
CHEYENNE (SHY ANN)
DON'T BLAME IT ALL ON BROADWAY
GOODNIGHT, LADIES
I'M AFRAID TO COME HOME IN THE
   DARK

IN DEAR OLD GEORGIA
IN THE SHADE OF THE OLD APPLE
   TREE
IT LOOKS TO ME LIKE A BIG NIGHT
   TONIGHT
IT'S A LONG WAY TO TIPPERARY
MICKEY
NAUGHTY, NAUGHTY, NAUGHTY
NAVAJO
OH, YOU CUTIE
PEGGY
ROSE ROOM
SAN ANTONIO
THERE NEVER WAS A GIRL LIKE
   YOU
WHAT'S THE MATTER WITH FATHER
WHEN I WAS TWENTY-ONE AND YOU
   WERE SWEET SIXTEEN
WHO ARE YOU WITH TONIGHT?
WON'T YOU COME OVER TO MY
   HOUSE?

Williams, Hugh

HARBOR LIGHTS

Williams, James

SOMETHING'S ON YOUR MIND

Williams, Jerry

GIVING IT UP FOR YOUR LOVE
I'M GONNA MAKE YOU LOVE ME
SHE'S A HEARTBREAKER

Williams, Jerry, Jr.

SHE'S ALL I GOT

Williams, Jerry Lynn

FOREVER MAN

Williams, Jimmy

FIRE
(YOU DON'T KNOW) HOW GLAD I AM
LOVE ROLLERCOASTER
LOVER'S QUESTION, A
SKIN TIGHT
SWEET STICKY THING
THINK TWICE

WHO'D SHE COO

Williams, J. Mayo

CORRINE, CORRINA (CORINNA,
   CORINNA)
DRINKIN' THING
FARE THEE HONEY, FARE THEE
   WELL
FINE BROWN FRAME
RUSTY DUSTY BLUES
WHEN MY MAN COMES HOME

Williams, John

CAN YOU READ MY MIND (LOVE
   THEME FROM "SUPERMAN")
DADDY'S GONE A-HUNTING
EMPIRE STRIKES BACK, THE
FROGGY BOTTOM
IF WE WERE IN LOVE
NICE TO BE AROUND
"STAR WARS" TITLE THEME
THEME FROM "CLOSE ENCOUNTERS
   OF THE THIRD KIND"
THEME FROM "JAWS"

Williams, Joseph F.

START OF A ROMANCE

Williams, Kenneth

EVERYBODY PLAYS THE FOOL

Williams, Larry

BONY MORONIE
LET YOUR LOVE FLOW
SHORT FAT FANNIE

Williams, Lawrence E.

SLOW DOWN

Williams, Lawton

FRAULEIN
GEISHA GIRL
SHAME ON ME

Williams, Leona

SOMEDAY WHEN THINGS ARE GOOD
YOU TAKE ME FOR GRANTED

Williams, M.

ONE FOR THE MONEY

Williams, Mary Lou

CAMEL HOP
IN THE LAND OF OO-BLA-DEE
LITTLE JOE FROM CHICAGO
MARY'S IDEA
PRETTY EYED BABY
ROLL 'EM
WHAT'S YOUR STORY, MORNING
GLORY?

Williams, Mason

CLASSICAL GAS

Williams, Matt

I GOTTA KNOW

Williams, Maurice

LITTLE DARLIN'
MAY I
STAY

Williams, Mentor

DRIFT AWAY
WHEN WE MAKE LOVE

Williams, Milan

BRICK HOUSE
MACHINE GUN
OLD-FASHION LOVE
SLIPPERY WHEN WET
SWEET LOVE
TOO HOT TA TROT
WONDERLAND

Williams, O.

I'M ON FIRE

Williams, Otis

TWO HEARTS

Williams, Patrick

ONE AND ONLY, THE

Williams, Paul

CRIED LIKE A BABY
EVERGREEN (LOVE THEME FROM "A
STAR IS BORN")
FAMILY OF MAN, THE
I'M FEELING FINE
I WON'T LAST A DAY WITHOUT YOU
JOHN WAYNE
"LOVE BOAT" THEME
MY FAIR SHARE
NICE TO BE AROUND
OLD FASHIONED LOVE SONG, AN
OUT IN THE COUNTRY
RAINBOW CONNECTION
RAINY DAYS AND MONDAYS
TALK IT OVER IN THE MORNING
WATCH CLOSELY NOW
WE'VE ONLY JUST BEGUN
WOMAN IN THE MOON, THE
YOU AND ME AGAINST THE WORLD

Williams, Ralph

MR. BIG STUFF

Williams, Red

TRYIN' TO BEAT THE MORNING
HOME

Williams, Rich

PLAY THE GAME TONIGHT

Williams, Spencer

ARKANSAS BLUES
BASIN STREET BLUES
EVERYBODY LOVES MY BABY (BUT
MY BABY DON'T LOVE NOBODY
BUT ME)
GEORGIA GRIND
I AIN'T GONNA GIVE NOBODY NONE
O' THIS JELLY ROLL

I AIN'T GOT NOBODY
I FOUND A NEW BABY
JUST A MOOD
ROYAL GARDEN BLUES
SHIM-ME-SHA-WABBLE
TICKET AGENT, EASE YOUR
WINDOW DOWN
TISHOMINGO BLUES
WHAT'S THE MATTER NOW?
WHEN LIGHTS ARE LOW

Williams, Tennessee

NOT A SOUL

Williams, Tex

DON'T TELEPHONE, DON'T
TELEGRAPH, TELL A WOMAN
SMOKE! SMOKE! SMOKE! (THAT
CIGARETTE)

Williams, Thomas

PRETTY GIRLS EVERYWHERE

Williams, W. R.

I'D LOVE TO LIVE IN LOVELAND

Williams, Yvonne

(1-2-3-4-5-6-7) COUNT THE DAYS

Williamson, Catherine

SKINNY MINNIE

Williamston, Wade

MOVIN'

Williams-White, Mary Vesta

CONGRATULATIONS
SWEET, SWEET LOVE

Willing, Foy

NO ONE TO CRY TO
TEXAS BLUES

Willis, Alec

BOOGIE WONDERLAND

Willis, Alice

I AM LOVE

Willis, Allee

ALL AMERICAN GIRLS
BE THERE
I WANT YOU TONIGHT
LEAD ME ON
LIVE MY LIFE
NEUTRON DANCE
SEPTEMBER
STIR IT UP
WHAT HAVE I DONE TO DESERVE
   THIS?

Willis, Chuck

CLOSE YOUR EYES
DON'T DECEIVE ME
DOOR IS STILL OPEN TO MY HEART,
   THE
HANG UP MY ROCK AND ROLL
   SHOES
I FEEL SO BAD
IT'S TOO LATE
OH, WHAT A DREAM
WHATCHA' GONNA DO WHEN YOUR
   BABY LEAVES YOU
YOU'RE STILL MY BABY
YOU'RE THE LAST THING I NEEDED
   TONIGHT

Willis, David

IF YOU'RE THINKING YOU WANT A
   STRANGER (THERE'S ONE
   COMING HOME)

Willis, Eddie

HOME COOKIN'

Willis, Ginger

LUMBERJACK, THE

Willis, Hal

LUMBERJACK, THE

Willis, Marvin

FLOAT ON

Willis, Pete

BRINGIN' ON THE HEARTBREAK
PHOTOGRAPH

Willis, Victor

IN THE NAVY
MACHO MAN
Y.M.C.A.

Willoughby, Joe

RUN JOE

Willoughby, Tanyayette

PARADISE

Willows, The

CHURCH BELLS MAY RING

Wills, Alice

LOVE ME AGAIN

Wills, Bob

BOB WILLS BOOGIE
BUBBLES IN MY BEER
FADED LOVE
KEEPER OF MY HEART
MY SHOES KEEP WALKING BACK TO
   YOU
SAN ANTONIO ROSE (A.K.A. NEW
   SAN ANTONIO ROSE)
STARS AND STRIPES ON IWO JIMA
STAY A LITTLE LONGER
SUGAR MOON

Wills, John

FADED LOVE
RAG MOP

Wills, Rick

DO YOU FEEL LIKE WE DO

Willson, Meredith

ARM IN ARM
BEING IN LOVE
BELLY UP TO THE BAR, BOYS
DOLCE FAR NIENTE
GOODNIGHT MY SOMEONE
HERE'S LOVE
HE'S MY FRIEND
I AIN'T DOWN YET
IF I KNEW
I'LL NEVER SAY NO
I SEE THE MOON
IT'S BEGINNING TO LOOK A LOT
   LIKE CHRISTMAS
IT'S YOU
LIDA ROSE
MARIAN THE LIBRARIAN
MAY THE GOOD LORD BLESS AND
   KEEP YOU
MY STATE, MY KANSAS, MY HOME
PEONY BUSH, THE
PINE CONES AND HOLLY BERRIES
SEVENTY-SIX TROMBONES
TILL THERE WAS YOU
TWO IN LOVE
YOU AND I
YOU DON'T KNOW

Wilson, Al

GOING UP THE COUNTRY
IN THE LITTLE RED SCHOOL HOUSE
ON THE ROAD AGAIN
WILD, WILD WOMEN ARE MAKING A
   WILD MAN OF ME, THE

Wilson, Ann

BARRACUDA
BEST MAN IN THE WORLD, THE
CRAZY ON YOU
DREAMBOAT ANNIE
EVEN IT UP
HEARTLESS
MAGIC MAN
NEVER
STRAIGHT ON

Wilson, Anthony

BROTHER LOUIE
DISCO QUEEN
YOU SEXY THING

Wilson, Belinda

IF IT AIN'T ONE THING . . . IT'S
ANOTHER

Wilson, Ben

I'LL SHARE MY WORLD WITH YOU

Wilson, Brian

ADD SOME MUSIC TO YOUR DAY
ALMOST SUMMER
BE TRUE TO YOUR SCHOOL
CALIFORNIA GIRLS
CAROLINE, NO
DANCE, DANCE, DANCE
DARLIN'
DEAD MAN'S CURVE
DO IT AGAIN
DON'T WORRY BABY
DRAG CITY
FRIENDS
FUN, FUN, FUN
GOD ONLY KNOWS
GOOD VIBRATIONS
HELP ME, RHONDA
HEROES AND VILLAINS
I GET AROUND
IN MY ROOM
LITTLE GIRL I ONCE KNEW, THE
LITTLE HONDA
PLEASE LET ME WONDER
SAIL ON SAILOR
SHUT DOWN
SURF CITY
SURFER GIRL
SURFIN' SAFARI
WHEN I GROW UP (TO BE A MAN)
WILD HONEY
WOULDN'T IT BE NICE?

Wilson, Carl

DANCE, DANCE, DANCE
FRIENDS

Wilson, Charles

BURN RUBBER (WHY YOU WANNA
HURT ME)
EARLY IN THE MORNING

Wilson, Clyde

SHE'S NOT JUST ANOTHER WOMAN

Wilson, Cynthia

LOVE SHACK
PRIVATE IDAHO

Wilson, Dan

WAR IS HELL (ON THE HOMEFRONT
TOO)

Wilson, Dennis

FRIENDS

Wilson, Earl

KISSIN' ON THE PHONE

Wilson, Floyd F.

GO, BOY, GO

Wilson, Forest

KO KO MO (I LOVE YOU SO)

Wilson, Frank

ALL I NEED
BOOGIE DOWN
CHAINED
KEEP ON TRUCKIN'
LOVE CHILD
STILL WATER (LOVE)
STONED LOVE
UP THE LADDER TO THE ROOF
WHOLE LOT OF SHAKIN' IN MY
HEART (SINCE I MET YOU)
YOU'VE MADE ME SO VERY HAPPY

Wilson, George

HOT ROD RACE

Wilson, Gerald

VIVA TIRADO

Wilson, Herbert

I WALK ALONE

Wilson, Hugh

WKRP IN CINCINNATI

Wilson, Irving M.

KID DAYS

Wilson, Jackie

BABY WORKOUT
YOU BETTER KNOW IT
YOU WERE MADE FOR (ALL MY
LOVE)

Wilson, Jeff

LET ME LOVE YOU TONIGHT

Wilson, Jim

MY EVERYTHING

Wilson, Johnny

LOVE THE WORLD AWAY

Wilson, Kim

TUFF ENUFF

Wilson, Marie

ANYMORE
BEFORE THIS DAY ENDS
SET HIM FREE

Wilson, Marty

STORY UNTOLD, A

Wilson, Melvin

IT'S BEEN A LONG TIME

Wilson, Meri

TELEPHONE MAN

Wilson, Nancy

BARRACUDA
BEST MAN IN THE WORLD, THE
CRAZY ON YOU
DREAMBOAT ANNIE
EVEN IT UP
HEARTLESS
MAGIC MAN
STRAIGHT ON
THERE'S THE GIRL

Wilson, Neil

CIELITO LINDO (AY, AY, AY, AY)

Wilson, Norro

ANOTHER LONELY SONG
BABY, BABY (I KNOW YOU'RE A
    LADY)
HE LOVES ME ALL THE WAY
I'LL SEE HIM THROUGH
I LOVE MY FRIEND
MOST BEAUTIFUL GIRL, THE
MY MAN, A SWEET MAN
SURROUND ME WITH LOVE
VERY SPECIAL LOVE SONG, A
WOMAN LIVES FOR LOVE, A

Wilson, Ricky

PRIVATE IDAHO
ROCK LOBSTER

Wilson, Robb

FOR ALL WE KNOW

Wilson, Ron

SURFER JOE
WIPE OUT
YEARNING FOR YOUR LOVE

Wilson, Sandy

I COULD BE HAPPY WITH YOU

Wilson, Tony

EMMA

Wilson, Turner

BIRD'S THE WORD, THE
PAPA-OOM-MOW-MOW
SURFIN' BIRD

Wilson, Vance

OH WHAT A NIGHT FOR DANCING

Wilson, Wally

POWERFUL STUFF

Wilson, Walter

AIN'T DAT A SHAME?

Wilson, Wesley

DO YOU CALL THAT A BUDDY?
DO YOUR DUTY
GIMME A PIGFOOT
I'M DOWN IN THE DUMPS
TAKE ME FOR A BUGGY RIDE

Wilson, Woody

BALL OF FIRE

Wimperis, Arthur

BRING ME A ROSE
GIRL WITH A BROGUE, THE
LITTLE PEACH
MY MOTTER

Winbush, Angela

ANGEL
I HAVE LEARNED TO RESPECT THE
    POWER OF LOVE
SHOW ME THE WAY
SMOOTH SAILIN' TONIGHT
SPEND THE NIGHT (CE SOIR)
YOU DON'T HAVE TO CRY
YOUR SMILE

Winchester, Jesse

I'M GONNA MISS YOU, GIRL
RHUMBA GIRL

Windom, H. H.

FATAL WEDDING, THE

Windsor, Peter

YOU ARE NOT MY FIRST LOVE

Wine, Toni

BLACK PEARL
CANDIDA
GROOVY KIND OF LOVE, A
YOUR HUSBAND—MY WIFE

Winegar, Frank

WHEN A GYPSY MAKES HIS VIOLIN
    CRY

Winfree, Dick

CHINA BOY

Wingate, Eddie

WHOLE WORLD IS A STAGE, THE

Wingate, Philip

I DON'T WANT TO PLAY IN YOUR
    YARD

Wingfield, Pete

EIGHTEEN WITH A BULLET

Winkler, Franz

FOREVER AND EVER

Winkler, Gerhard

ANSWER ME, MY LOVE
BELLA BELLA MARIE

Winkler, Ray

WELCOME TO MY WORLD

Winley, Paul

I'VE GOT MY EYES ON YOU
RINKY DINK

Winn, Hal

CINDY'S BIRTHDAY
THREE STARS WILL SHINE TONIGHT
(THEME FROM "DR. KILDARE")

Winn, Jerry

BABY, YOU'VE GOT IT
GIMME LITTLE SIGN

Winner, Septimus

WHISPERING HOPE

Winter, Edgar

FRANKENSTEIN

Winter, Kurt

CLAP FOR THE WOLFMAN
HAND ME DOWN WORLD
RAIN DANCE

Winters, Don

TOO MANY TIMES
YOU'RE RUNNING WILD

Winters, George

I'M SO MISERABLE WITHOUT YOU

Winwood, Muff

GIMME SOME LOVIN'

Winwood, Steve

ARC OF A DIVER
BACK IN THE HIGH LIFE AGAIN
DON'T YOU KNOW WHAT THE NIGHT
CAN DO?

EMPTY PAGES
FINER THINGS, THE
FREEDOM OVERSPILL
GIMME SOME LOVIN'
HIGHER LOVE
I'M A MAN
PAPER SUN
ROLL WITH IT
VALERIE
WHILE YOU SEE A CHANCE

Wirges, William

CHIQUITA BANANA

Wise, Fred

"A"—YOU'RE ADORABLE (THE
ALPHABET SONG)
ADAM AND EVIL
BELLS OF SAN RAQUEL, THE
BEST MAN, THE
CARNY TOWN
DATIN'
DON'T ASK ME WHY
FAME AND FORTUNE
I'VE GOT NEWS FOR YOU
I WON'T CRY ANYMORE
KISSIN' COUSINS
LONELY BLUE BOY
LOOK OUT, BROADWAY
MELANCHOLY MINSTREL, THE
MISIRLOU
NEVER LET HER GO
NIGHTINGALE
OO! WHAT YOU DO TO ME
ROCK-A-HULA BABY
ROSES IN THE RAIN
SATISFACTION GUARANTEED
SLIDER
STRANGE SENSATION
TELL ANOTHER LIE
WOODEN HEART
YOU, YOU, YOU ARE THE ONE

Wiseman, Scott

HAVE I TOLD YOU LATELY THAT I
LOVE YOU?
REMEMBER ME (WHEN THE CANDLE
LIGHTS ARE GLEANING)

Wisner, Jimmy

DON'T THROW YOUR LOVE AWAY

Withers, Bill

AIN'T NO SUNSHINE
GRANDMA'S HANDS
JUST THE TWO OF US
LEAN ON ME
USE ME

Witherspoon, William

I'VE PASSED THIS WAY BEFORE

Witmark, Frank M.

ZENDA WALTZES

Witt, Max S.

MOTH AND THE FLAME, THE
MY LITTLE GEORGIA ROSE

Wittstatt, Hans

PEPE

Wodehouse, P. G.

BILL
CLEOPATTERER
HAVE A HEART
LAND WHERE THE GOOD SONGS GO,
THE
LEAVE IT TO JANE
MARCH OF THE MUSKETEERS
MISTER CHAMBERLAIN
OH, LADY! LADY!!
OH GEE! OH JOY!
SIREN'S SONG, THE
THERE'S A LIGHT IN YOUR EYES
THERE'S LIFE IN THE OLD DOG YET
THROW ME A ROSE
TILL THE CLOUDS ROLL BY

Wolcott, Charles

RUBY DUBY DU
SOONER OR LATER
TWO SILHOUETTES

Woldin, Judd

ALAIYO
SWEET TIME

Wolf, Dick

AFTER SCHOOL
FATE
I KNOW WHERE I'M GOIN'

Wolf, Don

LOVE IS ALL WE NEED

Wolf, Ina

NO WAY OUT
SARA
WHO'S JOHNNY

Wolf, Jack

HO HO SONG, THE
I'M A FOOL TO WANT YOU

Wolf, Peter

COME AS YOU ARE
COME BACK
EVERYBODY HAVE FUN TONIGHT
FREEZE-FRAME
GIVE IT TO ME
LIGHTS OUT
LOVE STINKS
MUST OF GOT LOST
NO WAY OUT
ONE LAST KISS
SARA
WE BUILT THIS CITY
WHO'S JOHNNY
YOU'RE THE ONLY ONE

Wolf, Rennold

I LOVE LOVE
YOU CANNOT MAKE YOUR SHIMMY
SHAKE ON TEA

Wolf, Tommy

BALLAD OF THE SAD YOUNG MEN,
THE

LAUGH, I THOUGHT I'D DIE
SPRING CAN REALLY HANG YOU UP
THE MOST

Wolfe, Danny

SUGAR MOON

Wolfe, Jacques

GLORY ROAD, DE
SHORT'NIN' BREAD

Wolfe, Shirley

LIPS OF WINE

Wolfe, Steve

IT'S A HEARTACHE

Wolfer, Bill

DANCING IN THE SHEETS
ONE SUNNY DAY

Wolfert, David

HEARTBREAKER
SONGBIRD

Wolff, Elliott

COLD HEARTED
STRAIGHT UP

Wolfolk, Carl

CAN I CHANGE MY MIND?
IS IT SOMETHING YOU'VE GOT?

Wolfson, Mack

C'EST LA VIE
CRAZY OTTO RAG, THE
FLOWERS MEAN FORGIVENESS
HAPPINESS STREET (CORNER
SUNSHINE SQUARE)

Wolinski, David

AIN'T NOBODY
DO YOU LOVE WHAT YOU FEEL?

I REALLY DON'T NEED NO LIGHT

Woloschuk, John

CALLING OCCUPANTS OF
INTERPLANETARY CRAFT

Womack, Bobby

ACROSS 110TH STREET
BREEZIN'
I FOUND A TRUE LOVE
I'M A MIDNIGHT MOVER
I'M IN LOVE
JEALOUS LOVE
LOVE HAS FINALLY COME AT LAST
WOMAN'S GOTTA HAVE IT

Womack, Cecil

LOVE T.K.O.

Wonder, Stevie

ALL IN LOVE IS FAIR
BOOGIE ON REGGAE WOMAN
DO I DO
DON'T YOU WORRY 'BOUT A THING
GO HOME
HIGHER GROUND
I AIN'T GONNA STAND FOR IT
I DON'T KNOW WHY
IF YOU REALLY LOVE ME
I JUST CALLED TO SAY I LOVE YOU
I'M WONDERING
I THINK IT'S LOVE
IT'S A SHAME
I WAS MADE TO LOVE HER
I WISH
LET'S GET SERIOUS
LIVING FOR THE CITY
LOVE LIGHT IN FLIGHT
LOVING YOU IS SWEETER THAN
EVER
MASTER BLASTER (JAMMIN')
MY CHERIE AMOUR
PART-TIME LOVER
SEND ONE YOUR LOVE
SHOO-BE-DOO-BE-DOO-DA-DAY
SIGNED, SEALED, DELIVERED I'M
YOURS
SIR DUKE
SKELETONS

SUPERSTITION
SUPERWOMAN (WHERE WERE YOU
WHEN I NEEDED YOU)
TEARS OF A CLOWN, THE
TELL ME SOMETHING GOOD
THAT GIRL
UNTIL YOU COME BACK TO ME
(THAT'S WHAT I'M GONNA DO)
UPTIGHT (EVERYTHING'S ALRIGHT)
YOU ARE THE SUNSHINE OF MY
LIFE
YOU HAVEN'T DONE NOTHIN'
YOU MET YOUR MATCH
YOU WILL KNOW

Wood, Bobby

BETTER LOVE NEXT TIME, A
HALF THE WAY
TALKING IN YOUR SLEEP

Wood, Clement

GLORY ROAD, DE

Wood, Cyrus

LADY IN ERMINE, THE
WHEN HEARTS ARE YOUNG

Wood, Frank

MOLLY DEAR, IT'S YOU I'M AFTER

Wood, Guy

AFTER ALL
CINCINNATI DANCING PIG
FAITH CAN MOVE MOUNTAINS
FISHIN' FOR THE MOON
FRENCH FOREIGN LEGION
GIRL WITH THE HEATHER GREEN
EYES
LITTLE BOY, THE
MUSIC FROM BEYOND THE MOON
MUSIC OF LOVE (A.K.A. THE BELL
WALTZ)
MY ONE AND ONLY LOVE
OLD CURIOSITY SHOP, AN
RHYTHM OF RAINDROPS, THE
(A.K.A. OVER THE RHYTHM OF
RAINDROPS)
ROCK-A-BYE BABY

SHOO-FLY PIE AND APPLE PAN
DOWDY
TILL THEN
VANITY
WEDDING, THE

Wood, Haydn

BROWN BIRD SINGING, A
ROSES OF PICARDY

Wood, Ken

HAPPY ORGAN, THE

Wood, Lauren

PLEASE DON'T LEAVE

Wood, Lee

LITTLE BROWN GAL

Wood, Leo

BEE'S KNEES
CHERIE
HONEST AND TRULY
RUNNIN' WILD!
SOMEBODY STOLE MY GAL
WANG, WANG BLUES, THE

Wood, Peter

YEAR OF THE CAT

Wood, Randy

I'D RATHER DIE YOUNG

Wood, Ron

STAY WITH ME

Wood, Stuart

MONEY HONEY

Woodall, Booth

DOGHOUSE BOOGIE

Woodard, Steve

LET ME LOVE YOU TONIGHT

Woode, Henri

ROSETTA
SWEET SLUMBER
YOU TAUGHT ME TO LOVE AGAIN

Woodeforde-Finden, Amy

KASHMIRI, SONG

Woodford, Terry

ANGEL IN YOUR ARMS
YOU'VE BEEN DOING WRONG FOR
SO LONG

Woodley, Bruce

RED RUBBER BALL

Woodley, James

MYSTERY LADY

Woodruffe, Jezz

BIG LOG

Woods

EXPRESS

Woods, Adam

STAND OR FALL

Woods, Eddie

ADIOS
GREEN EYES

Woods, Harry

ALL OF A SUDDEN
CLOUDS WILL SOON ROLL BY, THE
DANCING WITH MY SHADOW

HANG OUT THE STARS IN INDIANA
HEIGH-HO, EVERYBODY, HEIGH-HO
HUSTLIN' AND BUSTLIN' FOR
    BABY
I'LL NEVER SAY "NEVER AGAIN"
    AGAIN
I'M GOIN' SOUTH
I'M LOOKING OVER A FOUR LEAF
    CLOVER
I NEARLY LET LOVE GO SLIPPING
    THROUGH MY FINGERS
IS IT POSSIBLE?
JUST AN ECHO IN THE VALLEY
JUST LIKE A BUTTERFLY (THAT'S
    CAUGHT IN THE RAIN)
LITTLE KISS EACH MORNING, A
    LITTLE KISS EACH NIGHT, A
LITTLE STREET WHERE OLD
    FRIENDS MEET, A
LOVABLE
MAN FROM THE SOUTH, THE (WITH
    A BIG CIGAR IN HIS MOUTH)
ME TOO (HO, HO, HA, HA)
MOONBEAM, KISS HER FOR ME
MOONBEAMS
MY HAT'S ON THE SIDE OF MY
    HEAD
OVER MY SHOULDER
PADDLIN' MADELIN' HOME
PINK ELEPHANTS
POOR PAPA (HE'S GOT NUTHIN' AT
    ALL)
RIVER, STAY 'WAY FROM MY DOOR
SHE'S A GREAT, GREAT GIRL
SIDE BY SIDE
TAKE IN THE SUN, HANG OUT THE
    MOON
TRY A LITTLE TENDERNESS
VOICE IN THE OLD VILLAGE CHOIR,
    THE
WE JUST COULDN'T SAY GOODBYE
WHAT A DAY!
WHAT A LITTLE MOONLIGHT CAN
    DO
WHAT DO I CARE WHAT SOMEBODY
    SAID?
WHEN THE MOON COMES OVER THE
    MOUNTAIN
WHEN THE RED, RED ROBIN COMES
    BOB, BOB, BOBBIN' ALONG
WHEN YOU'VE GOT A LITTLE
    SPRINGTIME IN YOUR HEART
YOU DARLIN'

Woods, Hosie

WALK RIGHT IN

Woods, Pearl

SOMETHING'S GOT A HOLD ON ME

Woods, Peter

GIRL IN TROUBLE, A (IS A
    TEMPORARY THING)

Woods, Sonny

I NEED YOUR LOVIN'

Woods, William

CLEO'S BACK
CLEO'S MOOD

Woods, Willie

DO THE BOOMERANG
SHAKE AND FINGERPOP

Woodward, Dan

ROSE AND A PRAYER, A

Woodward, Keren

I HEARD A RUMOR

Woodward, Matthew

PRETTY EDELWEISS

Woody, Michael

HE'S BACK AND I'M BLUE

Woolery, Chuck

NATURALLY STONED

Wooley, Bruce

VIDEO KILLED THE RADIO STAR

Wooley, Sheb

ARE YOU SATISFIED?
I NEVER HAD THE ONE I WANTED
PURPLE PEOPLE EATER, THE
THAT'S MY PA
WHEN MEXICAN JOE MET JOLE
    BLON

Woolfson, Eric

DAMNED IF I DO
EYE IN THE SKY
GAMES PEOPLE PLAY
TIME

Woolsey, Mary Hale

WHEN IT'S SPRINGTIME IN THE
    ROCKIES

Work, Henry C.

WRECK OF THE OLD '97

Work, Jimmy

MAKING BELIEVE
TENNESSEE BORDER
TENNESSEE BORDER NO. 2

Workman, Lyle

I DON'T MIND AT ALL

Worrell, Bernie

AQUA BOOGIE (A PSYCHOALPHADIS-
    COBETABIOAQUADOLOOP)
FLASH LIGHT

Worth, Billy

EACH MOMENT (SPENT WITH YOU)

Worth, Bobby

DO I WORRY?
DON'T YOU KNOW
FELLOW ON A FURLOUGH, A
LAZY COUNTRYSIDE
TIL REVEILLE (LIGHTS OUT—)
TONIGHT WE LOVE

Worth, Leah

CORNS FOR MY COUNTRY
MEANING OF THE BLUES, THE

Worth, Marion

ARE YOU WILLING, WILLIE?
THAT'S MY KIND OF LOVE

Wray, Bill

THIS COULD BE THE NIGHT

Wray, Link

RAW-HIDE

Wright, Andrew

WHEN A MAN (WOMAN) LOVES A
    WOMAN (MAN)

Wright, B., Jr.

I'M ON FIRE

Wright, Benjamin

ONE HUNDRED WAYS

Wright, Charles

DO YOUR THING
EXPRESS YOURSELF
LOVE LAND

Wright, Dorothy

CINCO ROBLES (A.K.A. FIVE OAKS)

Wright, Ellen

VIOLETS

Wright, Fred Howard

WHEN THE BLOOM IS ON THE SAGE

Wright, Gary

DREAM WEAVER
LOVE IS ALIVE

REALLY WANNA KNOW YOU

Wright, Gavin

ONCE YOU GET STARTED

Wright, Gregory

YOU'RE A SPECIAL PART OF ME

Wright, Johnnie

ONE BY ONE
YOU AND ME

Wright, M.

I PREFER THE MOONLIGHT
NOBODY FALLS LIKE A FOOL

Wright, Mark

PARADISE TONIGHT

Wright, Maurice

LET'S GROOVE

Wright, Muriel D.

AMIGO'S GUITAR

Wright, Philip Adrian

DON'T YOU WANT ME

Wright, Richard

KING JOE

Wright, Robert

ALWAYS AND ALWAYS
AND THIS IS MY BELOVED
AT THE BALALAIKA
BAUBLES, BANGLES AND BEADS
DONKEY SERENADE
ELENA
FATE
FROG AND THE GROG, THE
HORSE WITH THE DREAMY EYES,
    THE
IF THIS IS GOODBYE

I LOVE YOU
IT'S A BLUE WORLD
NIGHT OF MY NIGHTS
NOT SINCE NINEVEH
RHYMES HAVE I
RIDE, COSSACK, RIDE
SANDS OF TIME, THE
STRANGE MUSIC
STRANGER IN PARADISE
SWEET DANGER
TO LOOK UPON MY LOVE

Wright, Robert B.

I DREAMT I DWELT IN HARLEM
JERSEY BOUNCE

Wright, Steve

BREAKUP SONG, THE (THEY DON'T
    WRITE 'EM)
HAPPY MAN
JEOPARDY

Wright, Syreeta

IF YOU REALLY LOVE ME
IT'S A SHAME
SIGNED, SEALED, DELIVERED I'M
    YOURS

Wrightsill, Robert

I AIN'T GOT TO LOVE NOBODY ELSE

Wrubel, Allie

AND SO GOODBYE
AS YOU DESIRE ME
AT THE FLYING "W"
BOY IN KHAKI, A GIRL IN LACE, A
DON'T CALL IT LOVE
EMPEROR JONES
EVERYBODY HAS A LAUGHING
    PLACE
FARE THEE WELL, ANNABELLE
FAREWELL TO ARMS
FIRST TIME I SAW YOU, THE
FLIRTATION WALK
FORSAKING ALL OTHERS
GONE WITH THE WIND
GOODNIGHT ANGEL
GOTTA GET ME SOMEBODY TO LOVE

Wrubel, Allie

HAPPINESS AHEAD
I CAN'T LOVE YOU ANYMORE (ANY
    MORE THAN I DO)
I LIVE FOR LOVE
I'LL BE FAITHFUL
I'LL BUY THAT DREAM
I MET HER ON MONDAY
I'M STEPPING OUT WITH A MEMORY
    TONIGHT
I SEE TWO LOVERS
JOHNNY FEDORA AND ALICE BLUE
    BONNET
LADY FROM 29 PALMS, THE
LADY IN RED, THE
LET'S HAVE ANOTHER CIGARETTE
LITTLE TOOT
MASQUERADE IS OVER, THE
MINE ALONE
MR. AND MRS. IS THE NAME
MUSIC, MAESTRO, PLEASE!
NOW YOU'RE IN MY ARMS
POP! GOES YOUR HEART
SO NICE SEEING YOU AGAIN
TO ME
TRY TO SEE IT MY WAY
WHERE DO I GO FROM YOU?
WHY DOES IT GET SO LATE SO
    EARLY?
WHY DON'T WE DO THIS MORE
    OFTEN?
YOU AND ME THAT USED TO BE,
    THE
ZIP-A-DEE-DOO-DAH

Wulschner, Flora

FORGOTTEN

Wyatt, Bennett

THAT'S ME WITHOUT YOU

Wyatt, Ric, Jr.

LITTLE BIT OF LOVE (IS ALL IT
    TAKES), A

Wyche, Sid

ALRIGHT, OKAY, YOU WIN
BIG HUNK O' LOVE, A
LOVE, LOVE, LOVE
TALK THAT TALK

WOMAN, A LOVER, A FRIEND, A

Wyker, John

LET LOVE COME BETWEEN US
MOTORCYCLE MAMA

Wyle, George

CARAMBA! IT'S THE SAMBA!
DOO DE DOO ON AN OLD KAZOO
I DIDN'T SLIP, I WASN'T PUSHED, I
    FELL
I LOVE THE WAY YOU SAY
    GOODNIGHT
I SAID MY PAJAMAS (AND PUT ON
    MY PRAY'RS)
QUICKSILVER
YOU BROKE YOUR PROMISE

Wylie, Richard

WITH THIS RING

Wyman, Bill

PLAY WITH FIRE

Wynette, Tammy

ANOTHER LONELY SONG
I'M A STAND BY MY WOMAN MAN
SINGING MY SONG
STAND BY YOUR MAN
'TILL I CAN MAKE IT ON MY OWN
TWO STORY HOUSE
WAYS TO LOVE A MAN, THE
WE SURE CAN LOVE EACH OTHER

Wynn, Larry

FIVE GUYS NAMED MOE

Wynn, Phil

KNEE DEEP (NOT JUST)
ME, MYSELF, AND I

Wyrick, Barbara

IN MY EYES
TELL ME A LIE

Yakus, Herb

CHAIN GANG

Yakus, Milton

GO ON WITH THE WEDDING
OLD CAPE COD

Yancy, Marvin

HERE I AM (COME AND TAKE ME)
INSEPARABLE
I'VE GOT LOVE ON MY MIND
MORE YOU DO IT, THE (THE MORE I
    LIKE IT DONE)
OUR LOVE
SOPHISTICATED LADY (SHE'S A
    DIFFERENT LADY)
THIS WILL BE (AN EVERLASTING
    LOVE)

Yandell, Paul

I'LL REPOSSESS MY HEART

Yankovic, Al

EAT IT

Yarian, Christine

DO IT BABY

Yarrow, Peter

DAY IS DONE
MAN OF CONSTANT SORROW
PUFF THE MAGIC DRAGON
TORN BETWEEN TWO LOVERS

Yates, Carolyn Jean

I WON'T MENTION IT AGAIN

Yates, Steven

ALLY ALLY OXEN FREE

Yauch, Adam

(YOU GOTTA) FIGHT FOR YOUR
    RIGHT (TO PARTY)

Yellen, Jack

ACCORDING TO THE MOONLIGHT
AIN'T SHE SWEET?
AIN'T THAT A GRAND AND
    GLORIOUS FEELING?
ALABAMA JUBILEE
ALL ABOARD FOR DIXIELAND
ARE YOU FROM DIXIE? ('CAUSE I'M
    FROM DIXIE TOO)
ARE YOU HAVIN' ANY FUN?
BAGDAD
BENCH IN THE PARK, A
CHEATIN' ON ME
CRAZY WORDS, CRAZY TUNE (VO-
    DO-DE-O-DO)
DOWN BY THE O-HI-O
FORGIVE ME
GLAD RAG DOLL
GOODNIGHT, MY BEAUTIFUL
HAPPY DAYS ARE HERE AGAIN
HAPPY FEET
HAPPY IN LOVE
HARD HEARTED HANNAH (THE
    VAMP OF SAVANNAH)
HE'S A GOOD MAN TO HAVE
    AROUND
HOLD MY HAND
HOW'S EVERY LITTLE THING IN
    DIXIE?
HUNKADOLA
I LIKE TO DO THINGS FOR YOU
I'M THE LAST OF THE RED HOT
    MAMMAS
I'M WAITING FOR SHIPS THAT
    NEVER COME IN
IS SHE MY GIRL FRIEND?
I STILL LOVE YOU
IT'S AN OLD SOUTHERN CUSTOM
I'VE GOT TO GET HOT
I WONDER WHAT'S BECOME OF
    SALLY
LIFE BEGINS AT SWEET SIXTEEN
LOUISVILLE LOU
LOVIN' SAM, THE SHEIK OF
    ALABAM'
LUCKY ME, LOVABLE YOU
MAMA GOES WHERE PAPA GOES (OR
    PAPA DON'T GO OUT TONIGHT)
MY PET
MY YIDDISHE MOMME
NASTY MAN
OH! HOW SHE CAN SING

PLAYMATES
RIGHT SOMEBODY TO LOVE, THE
SING, BABY, SING
SOMETHING I DREAMED LAST
    NIGHT
SONG OF THE DAWN
SWEET AND HOT
THERE'S A LUMP OF SUGAR DOWN
    IN DIXIE
VO-DO-DO-DE-O BLUES
WHO CARES?
WILDEST GAL IN TOWN, THE
YOUNG MAN'S FANCY, A
YOU SAID IT

Yellin, Robert

UP TO MY NECK IN HIGH MUDDY
    WATER

Yester, James

GOODBYE, COLUMBUS

Yeston, Maury

BE ITALIAN (TI VOGLIO BENE)
FOLIES BERGERE
ONLY WITH YOU
SIMPLE

Yoakam, Dwight

GUITARS, CADILLACS, ETC., ETC.
I SANG DIXIE

Yoell, Larry

I'M JUST AN ORDINARY HUMAN

Youmans, Vincent

BAMBALINA
CARIOCA
COUNTRY COUSIN, THE
DEEP IN MY HEART
DOLLY
DRUMS IN MY HEART
FLANNEL PETTICOAT GAL
FLYING DOWN TO RIO
GREAT DAY!
HALLELUJAH!
HAY, STRAW

HONEY-BUN
I KNOW THAT YOU KNOW
I WANT A MAN
I WANT TO BE HAPPY
I WANT TO BE WITH YOU
KEEPIN' MYSELF FOR YOU
KINDA LIKE YOU
LIKE HE LOVES ME
MORE THAN YOU KNOW
MUSIC MAKES ME
NO, NO, NANETTE
OH, HOW I LONG TO BELONG TO
    YOU
OH ME! OH MY!
ONE GIRL, THE
ORCHIDS IN THE MOONLIGHT
RISE 'N' SHINE
SHOULD I BE SWEET?
SO DO I
SOMETIMES I'M HAPPY
TAKE A LITTLE ONE-STEP
TEA FOR TWO
THROUGH THE YEARS
TIE A STRING AROUND YOUR
    FINGER
TIME ON MY HANDS
TOODLE-OO
TOO MANY RINGS AROUND ROSIE
WEST WIND
"WHERE HAS MY HUBBY GONE?"
    BLUES
WHY, OH WHY?
WILDFLOWER
WITHOUT A SONG
YOU CAN DANCE WITH ANY GIRL
    AT ALL
YOU'RE EVERYWHERE

Young, Alvin E.

GOIN' HOME

Young, Angus

BACK IN BLACK
HIGHWAY TO HELL
YOU SHOOK ME ALL NIGHT LONG

Young, Donny

TOUCH MY HEART

Young, Eldee

WACK WACK

Young, Faron

ALL RIGHT
BACKTRACK
FACE TO THE WALL
GOIN' STEADY
I MISS YOU ALREADY
IT'S A GREAT LIFE
MY FRIEND ON THE RIGHT
THREE DAYS
WINE ME UP
WORLD SO FULL OF LOVE, A
YOU'RE STILL MINE
YOUR OLD USED TO BE

Young, George

FRIDAY ON MY MIND
GOOD TIMES
LOVE IS IN THE AIR

Young, Hilda M.

YOUR OLD USED TO BE

Young, James Oliver "Trummy"

EASY DOES IT
LOVER IS BLUE, A
'TAINT WHAT YOU DO (IT'S THE WAY
  THAT 'CHA DO IT)
TRAV'LIN' LIGHT
WHATCHA KNOW, JOE?

Young, Jesse Colin

DARKNESS, DARKNESS

Young, Joe

ABSENCE MAKES THE HEART GROW
  FONDER (FOR SOMEBODY ELSE)
ALONG THE ROCKY ROCK TO
  DUBLIN
ANNIE DOESN'T LIVE HERE
  ANYMORE
ARRAH GO ON, I'M GONNA GO
  BACK TO OREGON

BECAUSE OF ONCE UPON A TIME
COVER ME UP WITH THE SUNSHINE
  OF VIRGINIA
CRYIN' FOR THE CAROLINES
DADDY LONG LEGS
DINAH
DON'T BLAME IT ALL ON
  BROADWAY
DON'T CRY, FRENCHY, DON'T CRY
DOWN IN DEAR OLD NEW ORLEANS
FIVE FOOT TWO, EYES OF BLUE
  (HAS ANYBODY SEEN MY GIRL)
GOONA GOO, THE
GOT HER OFF MY HANDS BUT
  CAN'T GET HER OFF MY MIND
HAPPY GO LUCKY LANE
HAVE A LITTLE FAITH IN ME
HELLO, CENTRAL, GIVE ME NO
  MAN'S LAND
HIGH, HIGH, HIGH UP IN THE HILLS
HOW YA GONNA KEEP 'EM DOWN
  ON THE FARM (AFTER THEY'VE
  SEEN PAREE)?
HUCKLEBERRY FINN
HUNDRED YEARS FROM TODAY, A
I CAN'T GET MISSISSIPPI OFF MY
  MIND
I'D LOVE TO FALL ASLEEP AND
  WAKE UP IN MY MAMMY'S ARMS
IF I KNOCK THE "L" OUT OF KELLY
I HATE MYSELF (FOR BEING SO
  MEAN TO YOU)
I KISS YOUR HAND, MADAME
I'LL BE HAPPY WHEN THE
  PREACHER MAKES YOU MINE
IMAGE OF YOU, THE
I'M ALL BOUND 'ROUND WITH THE
  MASON DIXON LINE
I'M ALONE BECAUSE I LOVE YOU
I'M GONNA MAKE HAY WHILE THE
  SUN SHINES IN VIRGINIA
I'M GONNA SIT RIGHT DOWN AND
  WRITE MYSELF A LETTER
I'M GROWING FONDER OF YOU
I'M SITTING ON TOP OF THE WORLD
IN A LITTLE RED BARN (ON A FARM
  DOWN IN INDIANA)
IN A LITTLE SPANISH TOWN
IN A SHANTY IN OLD SHANTY TOWN
IN SHADOWLAND
I'VE GOT A NEW LEASE ON LOVE
JUST A BABY'S PRAYER AT
  TWILIGHT

KEEP SWEEPING THE COBWEBS OFF
  THE MOON
KING FOR A DAY
LADY I LOVE, THE
LAUGH, CLOWN, LAUGH
LIFE IS A SONG (LET'S SING IT
  TOGETHER)
LOVEY CAME BACK
LULLABY OF THE LEAVES
MEET ME AT THE STATION, DEAR
MY MAMMY
OH, HOW I WISH I COULD SLEEP
  UNTIL MY DADDY COMES HOME
OLD PAL, WHY DON'T YOU ANSWER
  ME
OOH! THAT KISS
PUT AWAY A LITTLE RAY OF
  GOLDEN SUNSHINE (FOR A
  RAINY DAY)
REVENGE
ROCK-A-BYE YOUR BABY WITH A
  DIXIE MELODY
SHADOWS ON THE SWANEE
SING AN OLD FASHIONED SONG (TO
  A YOUNG SOPHISTICATED LADY)
SINGIN' THE BLUES (TILL MY
  DADDY COMES HOME)
SLEEP, COME ON AND TAKE ME
SNUGGLED ON YOUR SHOULDER
STARLIGHT
TAKE IN THE SUN, HANG OUT THE
  MOON
TAKE MY HEART (AND DO WITH IT
  WHAT YOU PLEASE)
TELLING IT TO THE DAISIES
THEN YOU'VE NEVER BEEN BLUE
THERE'S A CRADLE IN
  CAROLINE
THERE'S FROST ON THE MOON
TO A SWEET PRETTY THING
TORCH SONG, THE
TUCK ME TO SLEEP IN MY OLD
  'TUCKY HOME
TWO HEARTS IN THREE-QUARTER
  TIME
TWO TICKETS TO GEORGIA
WAS THAT THE HUMAN THING TO
  DO?
WHEN THE ANGELUS IS RINGING
WHEN THE GROWN-UP LADIES ACT
  LIKE BABIES (I'VE GOT TO LOVE
  'EM, THAT'S ALL)
WHEN YOU'RE AWAY

WHERE DID ROBINSON CRUSOE GO
 WITH FRIDAY ON SATURDAY
 NIGHT?
WHY DO THEY ALL TAKE THE
 NIGHT BOAT TO ALBANY?
YAAKA HULA HICKEY DULA
YOU DROPPED ME LIKE A RED HOT
 PENNY
YOU'RE A HEAVENLY THING
YOU'RE A MILLION MILES FROM
 NOWHERE (WHEN YOU'RE ONE
 LITTLE MILE FROM HOME)
YOU'RE GONNA LOSE YOUR GAL
YOU'RE MY EVERYTHING

Young, John, Jr.

MY BOY—FLAT TOP
SEVENTEEN

Young, John Paul

YESTERDAY'S HERO

Young, Kenny

AI NO CORRIDA
ARIZONA
DON'T GO OUT INTO THE RAIN
 (YOU'RE GONNA MELT)
I'VE GOT SAND IN MY SHOES
JUST A LITTLE BIT BETTER
LITTLE BIT OF HEAVEN, A
ONE KISS FOR OLD TIMES' SAKE
UNDER THE BOARDWALK
WHEN LIKING TURNS TO LOVING

Young, Lester

BABY, DON'T TELL ON ME
TICKLE TOE

Young, Linda

I DON'T MIND THE THORNS (IF
 YOU'RE THE ROSE)

Young, M.

BUST A MOVE
WILD THING

Young, Malcolm

BACK IN BLACK
HIGHWAY TO HELL
YOU SHOOK ME ALL NIGHT LONG

Young, Neil

AFTER THE GOLDRUSH
AMERICAN DREAM
ARE YOU READY FOR THE
 COUNTRY?
CINNAMON GIRL
DOWN BY THE RIVER
HEART OF GOLD
LET IT SHINE
LOTTA LOVE
LOVE IS A ROSE
OHIO
OLD MAN
ONLY LOVE CAN BREAK YOUR
 HEART
WALK ON
WAR SONG

Young, Otha

SWEETEST THING (I'VE EVER
 KNOWN), THE

Young, Reggie

I FOUND A TRUE LOVE

Young, Rida Johnson

AH! SWEET MYSTERY OF LIFE
I CAN'T TAKE MY EYES OFF YOU
I'M FALLING IN LOVE WITH
 SOMEONE
ITALIAN STREET SONG
JUMP JIM CROW
MOTHER
MOTHER MACHREE
MY DREAM GIRL
'NEATH THE SOUTHERN MOON
ROAD TO PARADISE, THE
SOMETIME
TRAMP! TRAMP! TRAMP!
WHEN LOVE IS YOUNG IN
 SPRINGTIME
WILL YOU REMEMBER?

Young, Rusty

CRAZY LOVE

Young, Sheila

I LOVE YOU FOR ALL SEASONS

Young, Starleana

ARE YOU SINGLE?
MAKE UP YOUR MIND

Young, Steve

PUMP UP THE VOLUME

Young, Victor

ALONE AT LAST
AROUND THE WORLD
BEAUTIFUL LOVE
BLUE STAR (THE MEDIC THEME)
CAN'T WE TALK IT OVER?
CAN'T YOU UNDERSTAND?
C'EST LA VIE
GIVE ME A HEART TO SING TO
GOLDEN EARRINGS
GOT THE SOUTH IN MY SOUL
GREATEST SHOW ON EARTH, THE
HUNDRED YEARS FROM TODAY, A
I DON'T STAND A GHOST OF A
 CHANCE WITH YOU
JOHNNY GUITAR
LOVE IS THE THING
LOVE LETTERS
LOVE LIKE THIS, A
LOVE ME
LOVE ME TONIGHT
MAN WITH A DREAM, A
MY FOOLISH HEART
MY LOVE
OLD MAN OF THE MOUNTAIN
ONE LOOK AT YOU
OUR VERY OWN
SEARCHING WIND, THE
SHANE
SONG OF DELILAH
SONG OF SURRENDER
STELLA BY STARLIGHT
STREET OF DREAMS
SWEET MADNESS
SWEET SUE (JUST YOU)

Young, Victor

TOO LATE
WALTZING IN A DREAM
WAS I TO BLAME FOR FALLING IN
   LOVE WITH YOU?
WEAVER OF DREAMS, A
WHEN I FALL IN LOVE
WHERE CAN I GO WITHOUT YOU?
WHERE IS THAT SOMEONE FOR ME?
WRITTEN ON THE WIND

Young, Willie David

KEEP ON DANCING

Yradier, S.

CIELITO LINDO (AY, AY, AY, AY)

Yrain, Maurice

MY MAN (MON HOMME)

Zamecnik, J. S.

NEAPOLITAN NIGHTS (OH, NIGHTS
   OF SPLENDOR)
WINGS

Zamora, Arthur

CAN U READ MY LIPS

Zanetis, Alex

AS LONG AS I LIVE
AS USUAL
BACKTRACK
BIG WIND
GUILTY
I'M GONNA CHANGE EVERYTHING
I'M SAVING MY LOVE
ME
SNAP YOUR FINGERS

Zanin, Laura

SOLE SOLE SOLE

Zany, King

ALL SHE'D SAY WAS "UMH HUM"

Zappa, Frank

DANCIN' FOOL
DON'T EAT THE YELLOW SNOW
VALLEY GIRL

Zappa, Moon Unit

VALLEY GIRL

Zarate, Abel

SUAVECITO

Zaret, Hy

DEDICATED TO YOU
IT ALL COMES BACK TO ME NOW
MY SISTER AND I
NO OTHER ARMS, NO OTHER LIPS
ONE MEAT BALL
THERE I GO
UNCHAINED MELODY
YOU CAN'T HOLD A MEMORY IN
   YOUR ARMS
YOU'LL NEVER GET AWAY
YOUNG AND WARM AND
   WONDERFUL

Zawinul, Joseph

MERCY, MERCY, MERCY

Zekley, Alan

SOONER OR LATER

Zekley, Gary

I'D WAIT A MILLION YEARS
YELLOW BALLOON, THE

Zeller, Phil

I CAN'T BELIEVE I'M LOSING YOU
I'M COMIN' HOME, CINDY
ON THE SOUTH SIDE OF CHICAGO

Zerato, Lou

BEG, BORROW, AND STEAL

Zero, Jack

PLEASE NO SQUEEZA DA BANANA

Zesses, Nick

HEY BIG BROTHER

Zevon, Warren

POOR, POOR, PITIFUL ME
WEREWOLVES OF LONDON

Zigman, Aaron

CRUSH ON YOU

Zimbalist, Efrem

BELIEVE ME, BELOVED
OH, HOW I LONG FOR SOMEONE

Zimmerman, Charles

ANCHORS AWEIGH

Zimmerman, Leon

I'M JUST A VAGABOND LOVER

Zincavage, Frank

GIRL IN TROUBLE, A (IS A
   TEMPORARY THING)

Zippel, David

IT'S BETTER WITH A BAND

Zucker, Otto

KUM BA YAH

Zwirn, Artie

SORRY, I RAN ALL THE WAY HOME

Selected Bibliography

Author's note: While the investigation and reading for this project involved many more volumes than listed below, the following works were used most often in my research and are those that I found to be the most authoritative and reliable.

ASCAP, *ASCAP Biographical Dictionary*, New York: R. R. Bowker, 1980.

_____. *ASCAP Index of Performed Compositions 1914–1981*, New York: ASCAP, 1981.

Atkinson, Brooks, *Broadway*, New York: Macmillan, 1970.

Barlow, Harold, and Sam Morgenstern, *A Dictionary of Musical Themes*, New York: Crown, 1948.

_____. *A Dictionary of Vocal Themes*, New York: Crown, 1950.

Berry, Peter E. "*. . . And the Hits Just Keep On Comin'*," Syracuse, NY: Syracuse University Press, 1977.

BMI, *BMI Pop Hits*, New York: Broadcast Music, Inc., 1940–1977.

_____. *BMI Country Hits*, New York: Broadcast Music, Inc. 1940–1977.

Boni, Margaret Bradford, and Norman Lloyd, *Songs of the Gilded Age*, New York: Golden Press, 1960.

Bordman, Gerald, *American Musical Theatre*, New York: Oxford University Press, 1986.

_____. *Days to Be Happy, Years to Be Sad, The Life and Music of Vincent Youmans*, New York: Oxford University Press, 1982.

Bronson, Fred, *The Billboard Book of Number One Hits*, New York: Billboard Publications, Inc., 1988.

Cahn, Sammy, *I Should Care*, New York: Arbor House, 1974.

Edwards, Joe, *Top 10's and Trivia of Rock & Roll and Rhythm & Blues, 1950–1973*, St. Louis, MO: Blueberry Hill, 1974.

Fordin, Hugh, *Getting to Know Him, A Biography of Oscar Hammerstein II*, New York: Random House, 1977.

Gilbert, Douglas, *Lost Chords*, Garden City, NY: Doubleday Doran, 1942.

Goldberg, Isaac, *Tin Pan Alley*, New York: John Day Company, 1930.

Green, Abel, and Joe Laurie, Jr. *Show Biz: From Vaude to Video*, New York: Henry Holt, 1951.

Green, Stanley, *Broadway Musicals Show by Show*, Milwaukee, WI: Hal Leonard Books, 1985.

_____. *Encyclopedia of the Musical Theatre*, New York: Da Capo, 1984.

_____. *Encyclopedia of the Musical Film*, New York: Oxford University Press, 1981.

_____. *Rodgers and Hammerstein Fact Book*, New York: Lynn Farnol, 1980.

————. *The World of Musical Comedy*, San Diego, CA: A. S. Barnes, 1980.

————. *Ring Bells! Sing Songs! Broadway Musicals of the 1930's*, New York: Galahad Books, 1971.

Halliwell, Leslie, *Halliwell's Filmgoer's Companion*, New York: Charles Scribner's Sons, 1985.

Hamm, Charles, *Yesterdays*, New York: W. W. Norton, 1983.

Harrison, Max, Charles Fox, and Eric Thacker, *The Essential Jazz Records, Volume 1, Ragtime to Swing*, New York: Da Capo, 1984.

Helander, Brock, *The Rock Who's Who*, New York: Schirmer Books, 1982.

Hirschhorn, Clive, *The Hollywood Musical*, New York: Crown, 1981.

Jablonski, Edward, *Harold Arlen: Happy with the Blues*, New York: Da Capo, 1986.

Jasen, David A. *Recorded Ragtime, 1897–1958*, Hamden, CT: Archon, 1973.

————. *Tin Pan Alley*, New York: Donald I. Fine, 1988.

Katz, Ephraim, *The Film Encyclopedia*, New York: Thomas Y. Crowell, 1979.

Kimball, Robert, and Brendan Gill, *Cole*, New York: Holt, Rinehart and Winston, 1971.

Kimball, Robert, and Alfred Simon, *The Gershwins*, New York: Atheneum, 1973.

Kinkle, Roger D. *The Complete Encyclopedia of Popular Music and Jazz 1900–1950* (Vols. I–IV), New Rochelle, NY: Arlington House, 1974.

Lewine, Richard, and Alfred Simon, *Songs of the Theater*, New York: H. W. Wilson, 1984.

Lomax, Alan, *The Folk Songs of North America*, Garden City, NY: Doubleday, 1960.

Lynch, Richard Chigley, *Broadway on Record*, Westport, CT: Greenwood Press, 1987.

Maltin, Leonard, *TV Movies and Video Guide*, New York: Plume, 1988.

Mattfield, Julius, *Variety Music Cavalcade*, Englewood Cliffs, NJ: Prentice-Hall, 1962.

Meeker, David, *Jazz in the Movies*, New York: Da Capo, 1981.

Mordden, Ethan, *The Hollywood Musical*, New York: St. Martin's Press, 1981.

Pareles, Jon, and Patricia Romanowski, *The Rolling Stone Encyclopedia of Rock and Roll*, New York: Rolling Stone Press, 1983.

Ragan, David, *Who's Who in Hollywood (1900–1976)*, New Rochelle, NY: Arlington House, 1976.

Rodgers, Richard, *Musical Stages*, New York: Random House, 1975.

Rust, Brian, *Jazz Records 1897–1942* (Vols. 1–2), New Rochelle, NY: Arlington House, 1978.

Sanjek, Russell, *American Popular Music and Its Business* (Vols. I–III), New York: Oxford University Press, 1988.

Shapiro, Nat, *Popular Music, An Annotated Index of American Popular Songs (1920–1969)* (6 Vols.), New York: Adrian Press, 1973.

Simon, George T., *The Big Bands*, New York: Macmillan, 1967.

Slonimsky, Nicolas, *Baker's Biographical Dictionary of Musicians*, New York: G. Schirmer, 1958.

Smith, Joe, *Off the Record*, New York: Warner Books, 1988.

Suskin, Steven, *Show Tunes (1905–1985)*, New York: Dodd, Mead, 1986.

Taylor, John Russell, and Arthur Jackson, *The Hollywood Musical*, New York: McGraw-Hill, 1971.

Theroux, Gary, and Bob Gilbert, *The Top Ten*, New York: Simon and Schuster, 1982.

Terkel, Studs, *Giants of Jazz*, New York: Thomas Y. Crowell, 1975.

Uslan, Michael, and Bruce Solomon, *Dick Clark's The First 25 Years of Rock & Roll*, New York: Dell, 1981.

Whitburn, Joel, The following books are compiled by Whitburn from charts published in Billboard and published by Record Research Inc., Menomonee Falls, Wisconsin:

Pop Memories 1890–1954, 1986.

Top Pop Singles 1955–1986, 1987.

Top Country Singles 1944–1988, 1989.

Top R&B Singles 1942–1988, 1988.

The Billboard Book of Top 40 Hits, 1987.

Top Pop Albums 1955–1985, 1985.

Billboard's Music & Video Yearbook, 1987 & 1988.

Wilder, Alec, and James T. Maher, *American Popular Song, The Great Innovators, 1900–1950*, New York: Oxford University Press, 1972.

Wilk, Max, *They're Playing Our Song*, New York: Atheneum, 1973.

Williams, John R. *This Was Your Hit Parade*, Camden, Maine: John R. Williams, 1973.

Zadan, Craig, *Sondheim & Co.*, New York: Avon Books, 1974.

About the Author

ROBERT LISSAUER has spent his life in music and theater. He has functioned as a composer, teacher, music publisher, record producer, and theatrical producer. In his nearly four years of World War II military service, he was the NCO in charge of the music division of Irving Berlin's *This Is the Army* and headed another all-soldier show, *Yanksapoppin'*, formed in Alabama and which toured the Pacific islands from New Caledonia to the Philippines. He has been on the faculties of one university (NYU) and two conservatories (Eastern and Newark). His credits in music publishing and record production number over one thousand songs. He served as Vice-President and General Manager of The Vincent Youmans Company for twenty-one years, at times in conjunction with his own companies. He has been involved also in the production of numerous Broadway and off-Broadway musical productions and was co-producer of three children, Geoffrey, John, and Lianne.